THE READER'S ENCYCLOPEDIA

The READER'S ENCYCLOPEDIA

THIRD EDITION

William Rose Benét

A & C Black • London

Third edition published in Great Britain 1988 by A & C Black (Publishers) Limited, 35 Bedford Row, London WC1R 4JH

ISBN 0-7136-2972-X

Third edition published in the United States of America under the title *Benét's Reader's Encyclopedia* by Harper & Row, Publishers, Inc., 10 East 53rd Street, New York, N.Y. 10022. Published simultaneously in Canada by Fitzhenry & Whiteside Limited, Toronto.

Designed by C. Linda Dingler.

British Library Cataloguing in Publication Data

Benét, William Rose
   The Reader's encyclopedia.—3rd ed.
   1. Literature, modern—20th century—Dictionaries
   I. Title
   803'.21 PN41
ISBN 0-7136-2972-X

Printed in the United States of America

Notes About the Third Edition

Since William Rose Benét's death in 1950, many editors have played a part in keeping this book up-to-date and many have contributed or reviewed entries. Their names are listed below with grateful acknowledgment.

The revision work for this third edition began more than ten years ago. In addition to reviewing every entry in the second edition for possible revision and addition of new material, editors and contributors created entries on new works as well as on writers who had not previously been included with an eye to expanding the book's international scope.

The book was completely redesigned and adjustments were made so that information is easier to find, but, by and large, it follows the format readers have become familiar with:

- Authors with pen names appear under the name by which they are best known.
- Titles of works beginning with frequently used phrases such as *The History of . . .* , *The Adventures of . . .* , etc., are found under the first significant word (e.g., **Tom Sawyer, The Adventures of**).
- Cross-referenced terms, those that are themselves entries in the book, are set in SMALL CAPITAL LETTERS.
- Entries on non-English-language works appear under the form of the title more familiar to English-speaking readers. A cross-reference is provided under the other form of the title if that is also frequently encountered.
- In the text of an entry, foreign-language titles are generally given in the original form followed by a translation of the title. If the work has been published in a notable English translation, the title and date of publication of the translation follow the abbreviation "tr."

- Dates cited for nondramatic literary works are those of first publication, unless otherwise indicated. Dates of plays are those of first performance, when known, unless production was long delayed; otherwise, the date of the first known printing is given.
- The following abbreviations are used:

abbr	abbreviation, abbreviated	IE	Indo-European
abr	abridgment, abridged	Ir	Ireland, Irish
AF	Anglo-French	Isr	Israel
Afrik	Afrikaans	Ital	Italy, Italian
Arab	Arabic	Jap	Japan, Japanese
Aram	Aramaic	Lat	Latin
Austral	Australia	lit	literally
b	born	ME	Middle English
Belg	Belgium	MF	Middle French
Brit	British	MHG	Middle High German
Bulg	Bulgaria, Bulgarian	Norw	Norwegian
c	circa	OE	Old English
Celt	Celtic	OF	Old French
Chin	China, Chinese	OI	Old Irish
Colom	Colombia	ON	Old Norse
Czech	Czechoslovakia	Per	Persian
d	died	perf	performed
Dan	Danish	Pol	Poland, Polish
Den	Denmark	Port	Portugal, Portuguese
Du	Dutch	PR	Puerto Rico
ed	editor, edited by	prod	produced
Eng	England, English	pub	published
Fin	Finland, Finnish	r	reigned
fl	flourished	repr	reprinted
Fr	France, French	rev	revision, revised
Gael	Gaelic	Russ	Russia, Russian
Ger	Germany, German	Sans	Sanskrit
Gr	Greece, Greek	Scot	Scottish
Guat	Guatemala	Sp	Spain, Spanish
Heb	Hebrew	suppl	supplement
Icel	Iceland	Sw	Sweden, Swedish

Switz	Switzerland	vol, vols	volume, volumes
tr	translation, translated as	Yugo	Yugoslavia
Turk	Turkey, Turkish		

———————————
━━━━━━━━━━━
———————————

Special acknowledgment is made to Kate Siepmann, who worked for many years to compile, write, and edit the entries in the third edition, with the assistance of the contributors listed in the next paragraph. Special acknowledgment is also made to Perdita Burlingame, who applied her considerable knowledge of literature to the massive manuscript and edited it to the form in which it is now published.

Contributors and consultants to this volume include Steven Bellstrom, Gary Blake, Naftali C. Brandwein, Marilyn Breselor, Sara Castro-Klarén, Robert D. Chambers, Thomas D. Clareson, Martin S. Day, Janet Winecoff Diaz, Lubomir Doležel, George N. Dove, Howard L. Erdman, John H. Ferres, Joseph Fishback, Harry M. Geduld, James Gindin, Holly Hill, Douglas G. Jones, Marilyn Jurich, G. D. Killam, David M. Ketterer, J. R. Krzyzanowski, Steven Ledbetter, A. A. Levin, Elizabeth Massey, Richard D. Mullen, Barbara S. Nolan, Sergio Pacifici, William Phillips, Norma Procopiow, Byron Raizis, Carol Sanger, Kessel Schwartz, Jane Siepmann, Meno Spann, William Spiegelberger, Jr., Michael Tate, Albert Tezla, Wendy Tilghman, Makoto Ueda, Miller Williams, Mark R. Winchell, and T. D. Young.

The publisher also wishes to acknowledge the invaluable contribution of Tamara Glenny, who helped us keep up with the ever-changing information about contemporary authors, and the contributions of Helen Moore, Susan Randol, Eric Wirth, Scott Prentzas, Ann Martin-Leff, Beena Kamlani, Barbara Bergeron, Bitite Vinklers, Roz Barrow, Fred Alexander, and Dan Kirklin.

Carol Cohen

Editorial Director
Trade Reference Division
Harper & Row, Publishers
August 1987

THE READER'S ENCYCLOPEDIA

A

Aakjaer, Jeppe (1866–1930) Danish poet and novelist. As a novelist, Aakjaer was intensely concerned with social misery and the need for reform. *Vredens børn* (*The Children of Wrath*, 1904) described the oppressed existence led by servants on peasant farms. He is best known, however, for his lyric poetry, in which he celebrates the courage of the peasants and the beauties of his native Jutland. A merry simplicity characterizes the poetry of such collections as *Fri felt* (1906), *Rugens sange* (1906; tr *Songs of the Heath*, 1962), and *Den Sommer og den Eng* (1910).

Aaron In the Bible, the brother of Moses, the founder of the priesthood and the first high priest. He helped Moses in calling down the TEN PLAGUES and leading the Children of Israel out of Egypt (c1200 BC). Aaron directed the construction of the golden calf (made of gold earrings and other jewelry), which was idolatrously worshiped by the Israelites as the god of their deliverance, while Moses was receiving the Ten Commandments from Jehovah (Ex. 32). Aaron did not receive an inheritance in Canaan, as a punishment for doubting God's ability to bring water out of a rock.

Aaron's Rod The name given to the rod of the tribe of Levi, used by Aaron during the Ten Plagues and the crossing of the Red Sea. When Aaron left his rod in front of the Ark, in the Tabernacle, it miraculously blossomed and bore almonds. This was interpreted as evidence of Jehovah's choice of Aaron as high priest (Num. 17:8).

Abaddon The angel of the bottomless pit in *The Revelation of St. John the Divine*. Milton uses the name for the bottomless pit itself.

Abbassids The second long dynasty (thirty-seven Caliphs, 750–1258) of the Muslim Empire. They claimed descent from Abbas (566–652), eldest uncle of Muhammed. Their reign was most firmly established and the court at Baghdad most splendid under Haroun-al-Raschid (785–809), the Caliph described in the *Arabian Nights*, and his son Mamun (reigned 813–833).

Abbaye Group A group of French writers and artists. The members bought a house in Créteil near Paris and called it L'Abbaye. They lived there communally for fourteen months (1906–7), supporting themselves in part by printing and selling books. The Abbaye press issued *La Vie unanime* (1908) of Jules ROMAINS, a frequent visitor to the Abbaye. After their separation, members of the group were influential in spreading Romains's ideas of UNANIMISM. Among the group were René Arcos (1881–1948), Georges DUHAMEL, Luc Durtain (1881–1959), Pierre-Jean JOUVE, Charles Vildrac (1882–1971), and the cubist painter Albert Gleizes (1881–1953). The group's experience was the subject of Duhamel's novel *Le Desert de Bièvres* (1937).

Abbey, Edwin Austin (1852–1911) American illustrator and muralist. Abbey's impressionistic pen drawings made him one of the greatest illustrators of the late 19th century. Educated at the Pennsylvania Academy of the Fine Arts, in 1878 he was sent by *Harper's Weekly* to London, where he remained, earning a reputation for his classic illustrations of Herrick, Goldsmith, and Shakespeare. His fine lines and graceful depictions of 17th- and 18th-century England had an important influence on the illustrative techniques of his day. Abbey's best-known mural is *The Quest for the Holy Grail* (completed 1902) in the Boston Public Library.

Abbey Theatre The famous Dublin playhouse, which opened in 1904 with performances of W. B. YEATS's *On Baile's Strand* (1904). The theatre, which was founded for the production of plays by and about the Irish, was an outgrowth of older literary and dramatic groups, the Irish Literary Theatre (1899) and the Irish National Theatre Society (1902), the latter of which was founded by Yeats and Lady Gregory. Thanks to a subsidy from Mrs. A. E. F. Horniman, the Irish National Theatre Society was given use of the theatre; in 1910, with funds from public subscription, the company purchased the theatre. The building burned in 1951 and was reopened in 1966. Among the many dramatists associated with the early days of the theatre were J. M. SYNGE, Sean O'CASEY, A.E. (q.v.), Padraic COLUM, and G. B. SHAW. See IRISH RENAISSANCE.

1

Abbott, George (1887–   )   American playwright, producer, and director. Abbott became a well-
known name on Broadway as the co-author and director of
such popular plays as *The Fall Guy* (1925), *Broadway*
(1926), and *Coquette* (1928). His productions of *Three Men
on a Horse* (1935) and *The Boys from Syracuse* (1938),
based on *A Comedy of Errors*, established him as New
York's high priest of farce. Other Abbott hits, most of
which were collaborations, include *Call Me Madam*
(1950), *The Pajama Game* (1954), *Damn Yankees* (1955),
and *Fiorello!* (1959; with Jerome WEIDMAN), for which he
was awarded the PULITZER PRIZE. He is also the author of a
candid autobiography, *Mister Abbott* (1963), and of a
novel, *Try-Out* (1979). In 1983 there was a revival of the
musical *On Your Toes*.

Abdera   A maritime city of Thrace whose inhabitants were proverbial in ancient times for their stupidity.
Abderitan laughter came to mean scoffing or incessant
laughter. It was so called because Abdera was the birthplace of Democritus, the laughing philosopher, who is
regarded as the greatest among the Greek physical philosophers.

Abderite, The   See DEMOCRITUS.

Abednego   See SHADRACH, MESHACH, AND ABED-
NEGO.

Abe Kōbō (1924–   )   Japanese novelist and playwright. A Tokyo resident for most of his adult life—and
better known in his own country for his successful plays
than his fiction—Abe is concerned with such problems of
modern urban life as alienation, loneliness, and loss of
individual identity. His novels and plays are characterized
by avant-garde techniques and scientific nomenclature.
Among his representative works are *Suna no onna* (1962; tr
The Woman in the Dunes, 1964), *Tanin no kao* (1964; tr
The Face of Another, 1966), and *Moetsukita chizu* (1967; tr
The Ruined Map, 1969). Having studied medicine as a
youth, he also wrote works of science fiction like *Dai yon
kanpyōki* (1959; tr *Inter Ice Age Four*, 1970).

More recently, Abe Kōbō has written *Hakootoko* (1973;
tr *The Box Man*, 1975), a story about a man who attempts
to avoid anxieties and become nobody by placing a cardboard box over himself. The cardboard box is a symbol for
both the ills and the evils of society, as well as a traditional
symbol for the masks employed by Japanese actors. This
was followed by *Mikkar* (1978; tr *Secret Rendezvous*, 1979),
a thriller with both mythological and psychological motifs
interwoven into its main plot. He remains the most eloquent voice in Japanese literature on the theme of alienation as a condition of modern society.

Abel   See CAIN.

Abélard, Pierre (1079–1142)   French scholastic
philosopher and theologian. Abélard studied under Roscel-
linus (b 1050), exponent of extreme NOMINALISM, then
under William of Champeaux (1070–1121), supporter of
realism. In this controversy of medieval theology, Abélard
evolved a middle position called *conceptualism*, holding
that both particular objects and universal concepts are real.
However, he angered the clergy, who emphasized faith
rather than dialectic argument and proof, with his rationalistic approach to Church dogma, especially the dogma of
the Trinity. Thus Saint BERNARD OF CLAIRVAUX persecuted
him as a heretic, and Abélard died on his way to Rome to
appeal to the Pope against a condemnation on this charge.
Nevertheless, Abélard had been extremely popular as a lecturer; when he had to leave Notre Dame, his students followed him to various monasteries. His influence and his
writings, such as SIC ET NON, increased the popularity of
Aristotelian logic over that of Platonic theory.

His popular fame, however, resulted from his tragic love
affair with HÉLOÏSE. Moved by his *Historia calamitatum*
(c1134), Héloïse wrote to him, and they exchanged their
famous letters of love and suffering, including Abélard's
advice on how she should conduct the convent he had
turned over to her in 1129.

Abe Lincoln in Illinois (1938)   A play by Robert
E. SHERWOOD. Awarded a PULITZER PRIZE, it deals with the
life of Lincoln up to his election to the presidency; the dialogue contains selections from a number of Lincoln's own
speeches and writings.

Abercrombie, Lascelles (1881–1938)   English
poet and critic. As a poet associated with the GEORGIANS,
Abercrombie was known mostly for his verse dramas *The
Sale of St. Thomas* (1911) and *The End of the World*
(1915), both included in *Collected Poems* (1930). His intel-
ligently reasoned critical works include *Essay Towards a
Theory of Art* (1922), *Principles of Literary Criticism*
(19??), and *Poetry: Its Music and Meaning* (1932; repr
1970).

Abie's Irish Rose (1922)   A comedy by Anne
Nichols. It had one of the longest records of performance
(2,327) in the history of the theatre. A Jewish boy and an
Irish Catholic girl, fearing to tell their fathers that they are
in love, are married by a Methodist minister. The play
formed the basis for a novel (1927), a radio program (1942),
and a movie (1946).

Abigail   In the Old Testament, the wife of Nabal
and later of David (1 Sam. 25:3). Abigail referred to herself
as the handmaid of David. In Elizabethan usage, the name
came to signify a lady's maid. It is used in works by Marlowe, Beaumont and Fletcher, Swift, and Fielding. The
name was further popularized by Abigail Hill (Mrs.
Masham), the influential waiting-woman to Queen Anne.

abracadabra   A cabalistic charm, supposedly constructed from the initials of the Hebrew words *Ab* (Father),
Ben (Son), and *Ruach Acadasch* (Holy Spirit) and once
used as an antidote against various physical ills. From its
role as charm, it has come to be associated with any meaningless jargon and is a term frequently used by magicians.

The word was originally written on parchment and suspended from the neck by a linen thread, in the following form:

```
A B R A C A D A B R A
 A B R A C A D A B R
  A B R A C A D A B
   A B R A C A D A
    A B R A C A D
     A B R A C A
      A B R A C
       A B R A
        A B R
         A B
          A
```

Abraham   In the OLD TESTAMENT, the founder and first patriarch of the Hebrew people. Chosen by JEHOVAH to establish a new nation, Abraham emigrated with his wife, SARAH, and his nephew, LOT, from Ur, a rich city of Mesopotamia, to CANAAN. There he had two sons: ISHMAEL, by Sarah's servant, HAGAR; and ISAAC, by Sarah. Jehovah and Abraham made a covenant (Gen. 17:6–8), according to which Jehovah promised that He would be God to Abraham and his children and that they would inherit and dwell in the land of Canaan. In return, Abraham promised that every male child of the future generations would be circumcised, as a token of the covenant. Later, Jehovah tested Abraham's loyalty by commanding him to sacrifice Isaac. Abraham obeyed but was stopped at the fatal moment by an angel and commended by Jehovah, who reaffirmed the terms of the covenant (Gen. 22:1–19). See PROMISED LAND.

Abraham ben Meïr ibn Ezra   (c1092–1168) Spanish Jewish scholar. One of the most distinguished scholars of his day, he wrote scientific treatises, biblical commentaries, and outstanding poems. He is the speaker in Browning's famous poem RABBI BEN EZRA.

Abraham Lincoln   A biography by Carl SANDBURG. The first part, entitled *Abraham Lincoln: The Prairie Years*, was published in two volumes in 1926, and the second part, *Abraham Lincoln: The War Years*, was published in four volumes in 1939. For Sandburg, Lincoln was the archetypal figure of American democracy; the preparation of the biography, the second part of which won a PULITZER PRIZE, occupied many years of the poet's life.

Abraham-man   A begging impostor, a pretended lunatic. In Tudor and early Stuart times, inmates of Bedlam who were not dangerously mad were kept in the "Abraham Ward" and allowed out from time to time in distinctive clothes, to supplement their scanty rations by begging. Richard Head, a writer of the latter part of the 17th century, says that many healthy rogues, imitating these TOM O' BEDLAMS, "used to array themselves with party-coloured ribbons, tape in their hats, a fox-tail hanging down, a long stick with streamers, and beg alms; but for all their seeming madness, they had wit enough to steal as they went along."

Abrahams, Peter [Henry]   (1919–   )   South African novelist. Abrahams's early novels *Song of the City* (1945) and *Mine Boy* (1946; U.S. 1955) were the first by a black South African to draw attention to the plight of blacks in his country. *The Path of Thunder* (1948; repr 1975) and *A Night of Their Own* (1965) also realistically convey a sense of the personal and public tragedies of *apartheid*. *A Wreath for Udomo* (1956) was prophetic in suggesting the means by which African colonies would achieve their independence, and it identified many of the dilemmas which these emergent countries would face after independence. His other works include the autobiographical *Tell Freedom: Memories of Africa* (1954) and *This Island Now* (1966), a novel set in Jamaica, to which he moved in 1956. In 1985 he published *The View from Coyaba*, a tough and critical novel about the black struggle for freedom in the West Indies, the American South, and Africa.

Abraham's bosom   A figure of speech from the NEW TESTAMENT (Luke 16:22) to represent heaven as a return to the state of paternal care, specifically the protection of ABRAHAM, father of the Hebrew people. The Christian interpretation is one of heaven as a place where the soul dwells in the immediate presence of God.

abraxas   A cabalistic word. It was used by the Gnostics to denote the Supreme Being, the source of 365 emanations, the sum of the numbers represented by the Greek letters of the word totaling 365. It was frequently engraved on gems (hence known as *abraxas stones*) that were used as amulets or talismans. By some authorities, the name is given as that of one of the horses of AURORA, the dawn goddess.

Absalom   In the Old Testament, the handsome and rebellious third son of David, king of Israel, who "stole the hearts of the men of Israel" and plotted to become king in his father's stead (2 Sam. 15:6). Riding on a mule in the decisive battle at Ephraim, Absalom was caught by his hair in an oak tree; finding him so suspended, one of David's soldiers killed him despite previous commands of the king. David's lament, "O my son Absalom, my son, my son Absalom! would God I had died for thee, O Absalom, my son, my son!" has become a classic expression of paternal grief.

Dryden gave the name Absalom to the duke of Monmouth, Charles II's natural son, in his satire ABSALOM AND ACHITOPHEL.

Absalom, Absalom!   (1936)   A novel by William FAULKNER. The story centers on Thomas SUTPEN, the son of a West Virginia poor white, and his attempts to fulfill his "grand design" to be accepted as a Southern aristocrat and founder of a wealthy family. He establishes himself in Jefferson, Mississippi, and, at the climax of his career, he is elected colonel of Jefferson's regiment in the Civil War. Returning to his estate, Sutpen's Hundred, after the war, he finds the plantation in ruins. His daughter Judith's half brother and part-black lover, Charles Bon, has been killed by Sutpen's son, who has disappeared, and Judith has become a confirmed spinster, raising Charles's son. Sutpen's attempt to have another son by a poor-white girl ends in his murder by her grandfather. When the Sutpen saga comes to an end in 1910, all that is left of Sutpen's dream is an idiot black, Jim Bond, his only living descendant, howling in the ashes of the burned house.

In place of the sustained interior monologue Faulkner used in THE SOUND AND THE FURY, the story is projected by means of three narrators; their personalities and concerns are revealed as each tells the story of Sutpen. Miss Rosa Coldfield, Sutpen's sister-in-law, first tells the story to Quentin COMPSON shortly before his departure for Harvard; her story is supplemented by that of Quentin's father; and Quentin in turn relates the whole story, with his own interpretation, to his Harvard roommate, Shreve McCannon. The title is taken from the story of ABSALOM in the Old Testament.

Absalom and Achitophel (1681) A political satire in verse by John DRYDEN. Written in heroic couplets, the poem attacks Puritan attempts to exclude the duke of York, the legitimate heir, from the throne of England because of his Catholicism. Using Biblical terminology, Dryden describes the efforts of Achitophel (the earl of Shaftesbury) to incite Absalom (the duke of Monmouth, illegitimate son of Charles II) to rebellion against his father. A second part, written by Nahum TATE and revised by Dryden, who added two hundred lines, appeared in 1682. See BATHSHEBA.

Abse, Dannie (1923–   ) Welsh poet, playwright, and novelist. A practicing physician, Abse first received literary recognition with a volume of poetry, *After Every Green Thing* (1949), and a play, *Fire in Heaven* (1948). Selected volumes of poetry, with a striking use of anatomical detail, were published in 1963 and 1970, and *Collected Poems* in 1977. His plays include *The Joker* (1962), *The Dogs of Pavlov* (1969), and *Pythagoras* (1976). His first novel, *Ash on a Young Man's Sleeve* (1954), was an autobiographical account of a Welsh Jew growing up in the 1930s. *Some Corner of an English Field* (1956) uses the military as a metaphor for the illnesses of modern society, and *O. Jones, O. Jones* (1970) is a comic treatment of a medical student as reformer. Abse's focus on social reform is explicit in his noteworthy book of nonfiction, *Medicine on Trial* (1967).

Recent works include a volume of verse, *Way Out in the Centre* (1981), and an autobiography, published in two volumes, *A Poet in the Family* (1974) and *A Strong Dose of Myself* (1983).

Absolute, Sir Anthony A character in Sheridan's comedy THE RIVALS. He is a testy but warmhearted old gentleman who imagines that he possesses a most angelic temper and that, when he quarrels with others, it is they, not he, who are out of sorts.

Absolute, Captain Jack The hero of Sheridan's comedy THE RIVALS. The clever and gallant son of Sir Anthony Absolute, he is a rival of Bob Acres for the hand of Lydia Languish, to whom he is known only as Ensign Beverley.

abstract expressionism One of the most important developments in American art; also called "action painting." The movement, which began in the 1940s, was the result of a variety of influences, including the neo-expressionist works of Wassily KANDINSKY, FUTURISM, SURREALISM, DADA, and LES FAUVES. A group of European painters living in America, including Hans Hofmann, Willem DE KOONING, Mark ROTHKO, and Arshile GORKY (often loosely referred to as "The New York School") had an important catalytic effect on this phase of American painting. Highly individualistic and diverse in style, abstract expressionist paintings are generally large, nonrepresentational canvasses, using bold color, line, or isolated shapes in a free-associative way. The original response to such works was hostile, but by the 1950s, abstract expressionism had firmly established its international importance. Well known among the many painters associated with this style are Jackson POLLOCK, Robert MOTHERWELL, Adolph Gottlieb, and William Baziotes.

absurd A philosophical term for a fundamental lack of reasonableness and coherence in human existence. The philosophical and theological roots of the term can be traced to Tertullian (160?–?230), an early Father of the Church who argued that the surest sign of the truth of Christianity is its absurdity. He posited that the idea of an infinite deity incarnating himself and undergoing suffering for human beings is so irrational that no one would invent such a story; therefore it must be true. Tertullian's summary statement was *Creo quia absurdum est* (I believe because it is absurd). Centuries later, Søren KIERKEGAARD reemphasized the absurdity of Christianity. He suggested that rational "proofs," however convincing, are blocks, not aids, to faith: A faith that requires proofs is no faith at all. One can only choose Christianity, with its manifest absurdities, or choose an alternative way of life, with its latent absurdities. The choice of Christianity is a "leap of faith" for which there are no strictly rational criteria.

With Martin HEIDEGGER, Karl JASPERS, and Jean-Paul SARTRE, the concept of absurdity became almost completely secularized as the basis for EXISTENTIALISM. According to the existentialist concept, man is thrown into an alien, irrational world in which he must create his own identity through a series of choices for which there are no guides or criteria. Because man cannot avoid making choices—to refrain from choosing is a choice—man is condemned to be free. This absurdity is an inescapable part of the human situation. In his novel NAUSEA, Sartre regards it as the irresoluble paradox of human existence.

The concept of the absurd in modern literature originated with the early surrealists, in works such as Alfred Jarry's play UBU ROI. The concept is used by Albert Camus in his essay THE MYTH OF SISYPHUS and in his novel THE STRANGER, where he emphasizes the psychological implications of the absurd.

Writers have also attempted to convey the concept of the absurd through deliberate distortions and violations of conventional forms, to undermine ordinary expectations of continuity and rationality. Among the most notable writers in the literature and THEATRE OF THE ABSURD are Samuel BECKETT, Eugène IONESCO, and Jean GENET.

Abzu   In Sumerian mythology, the river that is supposed to surround the earth. The Abzu seems almost identical with the Greek Oceanus, the "river of ocean." In Babylonian mythology, it is personified as Apsu, the fresh water, who has existed from the beginning of time with his wife Tiamat, the salt water; he plays an important role in the WAR OF THE GODS. The Sumerian ENKI and the Babylonian EA, almost identical gods of water and of wisdom, live in a palace in the Abzu, which was probably the Persian Gulf, the shores of which in early days may have reached northward to the city of Eridu.

Académie française   The French Academy. Originating in secret meetings of literary men in Paris around the year 1630, the Academy was established by order of the king, at Cardinal RICHELIEU's urging, in 1635. Made up of forty members, supposedly the most distinguished living men of French letters, the Academy took as its purpose the protection and perfection of the French language and began compiling an authoritative dictionary in 1639; the task has not yet been completed. The Academy also undertook the composition of definitive treatises on grammar, poetry, and rhetoric. Ordered by Richelieu to censure Corneille's LE CID, the Academy early adopted a policy of advocating old rules and traditions at the expense of innovation and change. In the late 18th century, the PHILOSOPHES gained a majority in the Academy and briefly influenced it with their views. Inactive during the Revolution, the Academy was reestablished in 1803 by NAPOLEON as part of the Institut de France and two years later took up headquarters in the Palais Mazarin, which it still occupies. Inevitably the Academy is a conservative body, reflecting the tastes of its membership—those, by definition, of age and secure reputation. Including many of the most significant names in past and present French literature, criticism, and philosophy, the membership nonetheless reveals several surprising omissions, most regrettably that of MOLIÈRE. In this century, the Academy may be said to have fairly represented the cultural life of France and, in general, to

have exercised a beneficent effect upon the preservation of the language. In 1981 Marguerite YOURCENAR became the first woman to be elected to the Academy.

Academy   The name of PLATO's school near Athens. It was named after a legendary hero, Hecademus or Academus. The school had a long history, continuing until Justinian suppressed the philosophic schools in AD 529.

Acastus   In Greek mythology, a son of PELIAS. He sailed with the ARGONAUTS and, after his father's death, became king of Iolcus. Believing the lie of his wife Cretheis that PELEUS had made advances to her, he tried to kill him. Later Peleus conquered Iolcus and killed Acastus.

acatalexis   A metrically complete line of poetry where every foot is totally filled out, as in the following example from Christopher Marlowe's *Tragical History of Doctor Faustus* (c1588):

Was THIS / the FACE / that LAUNCHED / a THOU/sand SHIPS?

The opposite of acatalexis is catalexis, the omission of part of a foot in a line of verse.

Accademia della Crusca   (Ital, "Academy of the Chaff")   Florentine literary academy founded in 1583 to purify Tuscan, the literary language of the Italian Renaissance. It was opposed to TASSO in the debate over the merits of his GERUSALEMME LIBERATA. The first part of its official dictionary appeared in 1612, and the work is still in progress.

accent meter   (1) Accentual METER, that is, verse based on the alternation of accented and unaccented syllables. English prosody is based on accent meter, as opposed to quantitative meter, or verse based on the alternation of long and short syllables, which is the basis of Greek and Latin prosody.

(2) Meter that depends only upon the number of accented syllables in the line and disregards the unaccented syllables. The feet that make up the line may be of any kind, including the monosyllabic foot. Accent verse has always been prevalent in popular ballads and songs, and it is often used for effect in modern poetry. An example from *Sir Patrick Spens*, an early Scottish ballad of unknown authorship, is:

O LANG, / LANG, / may the LA/dies STAND
　　Wi thair GOLD / KEMS / in thair HAIR,
WAiting / FOR thair / AIN deir / LORDS,
　　For THEY'LL / se THAME / na MAIR.

accismus   A form of IRONY involving an insincere modesty or a feigned refusal of something actually desired. In Shakespeare's JULIUS CAESAR, Caesar's reluctance to accept the crown is an example of accismus.

Account of My Hut, An   (Hōjō ki, 1212)   Japanese miscellany, a brief account of the personal experiences of Kamo no Chōmei (1155–1216). It details the natural disasters that visited Kyoto during the late HEIAN period and describes the life led by the author at his hermitage. Strongly Buddhist in tone, it emphasizes the impermanence of life.

Aceldama (Gr, "field of blood") A field in the Hinnon Valley near Jerusalem that (Matt. 27:6–8) was purchased by the priests with the thirty pieces of silver ("the blood money") thrown down by Judas Iscariot after his betrayal of Jesus. It had been used as a source of clay for pottery and was later used as Jerusalem's burial place for paupers and strangers; hence the term *potter's field* (Matt. 27:7) came to be used for any such graveyard. According to Acts (1:18), Judas bought the field, fell into it, and "burst asunder." The usual version (Matt. 27:5) of Judas's death is that he hanged himself.

Achates In Vergil's AENEID, the constant companion of Aeneas. Thus, a *fidus Achates* is synonymous with a faithful companion and bosom friend.

Achebe, Chinua (1930–   ) Nigerian novelist, poet, short-story writer, and essayist. One of Africa's best-known writers, Achebe gained an international audience with his first novel, THINGS FALL APART, now regarded as a classic. With a vision that is at once ironic, neutral, and tragic, Achebe repeatedly treats the theme of the impact on tribal life of alien colonial rule. The theme is initiated in *Things Fall Apart* and developed in *No Longer at Ease* (1960), *Arrow of God* (1964), and in some of his short stories in *Girls at War* (1972). A *Man of the People* (1966) is a biting satirical farce that provides an exposé of corrupt African politicians. Achebe's style is characterized by a plain English, a clear narrative, and the use of local imagery and folk legend. Among his other books are *Beware Soul-Brother* (1972), a volume of verse; and the children's stories *Chike and the River* (1966), *How the Leopard Got His Claws* (1972), *The Flute* (1977), and *The Drum* (1977). In 1983 he published a collection of essays entitled *The Trouble with Nigeria*. He is the founding editor of *Okike*, a literary journal.

Achebe's works deal with the African problems of traditionalism and ritual as opposed to modernism and the emulation of Western concepts and ideas, and they ultimately transcend their local situations to become universal in concern and theme.

Achelous The largest river in ancient Greece, which separated Aetolia from Acarnania, and the god thereof. Achelous was capable of assuming different bodily forms. In a battle with HERACLES for the hand of the beautiful DEIANIRA, he changed from a man to a serpent and finally to a bull. Heracles wrestled from his head one of his horns, which the NAIADS turned into the CORNUCOPIA. According to one legend, he lay with MELPOMENE and fathered the SIRENS. He was also the father of Callirrhoe, whom he gave in marriage to ALCMAEON.

Acheron (Gr, "river of sorrows") One of the five rivers of the infernal regions into which Phlegethon, a river of liquid fire, and Cocytus, whose name means "river of lamentation," flow; also, the lower world (HADES) itself. Several actual Greek rivers, in addition, were called by this name. See STYX.

Achilles In Greek mythology, the son of PELEUS and the Nereid THETIS, and king of the MYRMIDONS, a Thessalian tribe. Achilles is the hero of Homer's ILIAD and became the prototype of the Greeks' conception of manly valor and beauty. He took part in the Trojan War on the side of the Greeks as their most illustrious warrior, and he slew the Trojan hero Hector. Achilles had been dipped in the STYX by his mother, which rendered him invulnerable except in the heel by which she held him. He was fatally wounded there by an arrow shot by Paris, Hector's younger brother, or, according to another version of the story, by the god Apollo, who had assumed Paris' shape. The phrase *Achilles' heel* is used to describe the vulnerable point in the character of a person or nation.

Achitophel In the Old Testament, David's traitorous counselor. Achitophel deserted to ABSALOM, who was trying to supersede his father, but hanged himself when his advice was disregarded (2 Sam. 17). In his satire ABSALOM AND ACHITOPHEL, Dryden used this name for the earl of Shaftesbury.

Acis In classical legend, a handsome young Sicilian shepherd, son of a NAIAD. The lover of the NEREID Galatea, Acis was crushed beneath a rock by his jealous rival, the Cyclops POLYPHEMUS. The blood flowing from Acis' body was turned into water and formed the river Acis. *Acis and Galatea* (1721) is an opera by HANDEL based on this story.

Acmeism A movement in Russian poetry, active from about 1910 to 1917. The Acmeists, who belonged to a group known as the Poets' Guild, got their name from the high poetic standards they professed. They advocated concision in poetry, clear and concrete imagery, and precise use of words. The movement was a reaction against the mysticism and stylistic vagueness of the symbolist school of poetry, which had held sway in Russian literature from about 1895. The leading Acmeists were Nikolai GUMILYOV, Anna AKHMATOVA, and Osip MANDELSHTAM.

Acquainted with the Night (1928) A sonnet by Robert FROST. Written in *terza rima* and one of Frost's few poems set in the city, it is a mystical poem of loneliness and despair: "the time was neither wrong nor right," it declares.

Acres, Bob A character in Sheridan's comedy THE RIVALS. A country gentleman, Acres is the rival of Captain Jack Absolute for the hand of Lydia Languish. He tries to ape the man of fashion, affects elaborate oaths, and blusters mightily, but, when his courage is put to the test, he proves himself an abject coward.

Acrisius In Greek mythology, king of Argos and the father of Danae. An oracle declared that Danae would give birth to a son who would kill him, so Acrisius kept his daughter shut up in a brazen tower. Here she became the mother of Perseus by Zeus, who appeared in the form of a shower of gold. The king of Argos now ordered his daughter and her infant to be put into a chest and cast adrift on the sea, but they were rescued by Dictys, a fisherman. When grown to manhood, Perseus accidentally struck the foot of Acrisius with a quoit, and the blow caused his death, thus fulfilling the oracle.

acropolis (Gr, "high city") The citadel of a Greek city, generally situated on a hill. The Acropolis at Athens, a rocky plateau about two hundred feet high, was the site of the ancient town. It was surrounded by walls, which were destroyed by the Persians in 480 BC, and later rebuilt by Themistocles. The Acropolis was the center of religious activity; many temples and statues of Athene were located there. The ERECHTHEUM, the PARTHENON, and the Propylaea are among the best known of its monuments. The acropolis of Thebes was the Cadmeia; that of Corinth, the Acrocorinth.

acrostic A composition, often in verse, in which a set or sets of letters (such as the first, middle, or last of each line) spell out a word, a word group, or part of the alphabet. Twelve Psalms of the Old Testament are written acrostically, the 119th being an ingenious alphabetic acrostic. The Latin poets wrote acrostic verse, and the early English poet CYNEWULF signed his name to his works in acrostic runes. The Elizabethan Sir John Davies wrote twenty-six *Hymns of Astraea*, in which the first letters of the lines spell *Elisabetha Regina* twenty-six times. Edgar Allan POE demonstrated skill in devising acrostics on the names of his loved ones. Charles LAMB devised a well-known acrostic conundrum spelling his name (*Lamb*) and pseudonym (*Elia*). Abecedarian hymns, designed to aid the memorizing of the alphabet, may be counted acrostics, and perhaps for this reason men of letters have held the form in low esteem, as being little more than a childish riddle. The word *acrostic* is also applied to any word square which reads the same horizontally as vertically.

act The main division of a play. There were no distinct acts in ancient Greek drama, primarily because there were no costume or scenery changes; different episodes were separated by the CHORUS. The Romans were the first to divide their plays into acts, and HORACE set the number at five. The five-act principle generally held until the late 19th century, when playwrights like IBSEN began to combine the fourth and fifth acts. Shortened forms of one-act plays were also developed by the end of the 19th century. In 20th-century drama, a three-act form, consisting of an introduction, development, and climax, predominated. Musical comedies often use only two acts. In much contemporary drama, the act has been replaced by an episodic format, in which traditional act divisions are altogether ignored.

Actaeon In Greek mythology, the son of Aristaeus and Autonoë. Having accidentally observed Artemis in her bath, while hunting on Mount Cithaeron, Actaeon was changed by the goddess into a stag and torn to pieces by his own hounds.

acte gratuit See GIDE, ANDRÉ.

Action française, L' A political group whose organ was the newspaper *L'Action française*, founded in 1899. An extreme right-wing movement, it advocated monarchist, anti-Semitic, and Roman Catholic principles, serving as a focal point for rightist sympathies. Leon DAUDET and Charles Maurras were the chief editors of *L'Action française*; its last issue was published on August 24, 1944, and spoke out in favor of Marshal Pétain.

Act of Settlement An act passed during the reign of William III (1701) in England, limiting the crown, after Queen Anne's succession, to members of the House of Hanover, provided they were Protestant. As a result of this act, the reign of the House of Stuart ended and that of Hanover began.

Act of Union Specifically, the Act of 1706 declaring that on and after May 1, 1707, England and Scotland should have a united parliament. The two countries had been united under one sovereign since 1603. The term is also applied to the Act of 1536 incorporating Wales with England, and to that of 1800 establishing a legislative union of Great Britain and Ireland on and after January 1, 1801.

Acts of the Apostles A book of the NEW TESTAMENT. It is the earliest history of the Christian Church in existence, beginning with JESUS' ascension to heaven and ending with the imprisonment of St. PAUL. It is thought that the author was St. LUKE, the physician, who also wrote The Gospel According to St. LUKE. The book reports the preachings and events in the lives of the APOSTLES, particularly of St. PETER and St. Paul, who released Christianity from the conservative restrictions of Judaism and preached it as a new, universal religion.

Adam and Eve The first man and woman, according to the Old Testament. The initial chapters of Genesis tell the story of their creation, their sin in eating the FORBIDDEN FRUIT from "the tree of knowledge of good and evil" (Gen. 3:9), and their expulsion from Paradise, or the Garden of Eden, to thereafter "till the ground." Milton retells the story of "man's first disobedience" in *Paradise Lost* (1667). See LILITH.

the old Adam; the offending Adam Adam, as the head of unredeemed man, stands for "original sin," or "man without regenerating grace."

the second Adam; the new Adam Jesus Christ is so called.

Adam's ale Water, because the first man had nothing else to drink; in Scotland, it is sometimes called *Adam's wine*.

Adam's apple The protuberance in the forepart of the throat, the anterior extremity of the thyroid cartilage of the larynx; so called from the legend that a piece of the forbidden fruit stuck in Adam's throat.

Adam's Peak A mountain in Ceylon where, according to Muslim legend, Adam bewailed his expulsion from Paradise, standing on one foot for two hundred years to expiate his crime; Gabriel then took him to Mount Arafat, where he found Eve.

Adam Bede (1859) A novel by George ELIOT. The highly principled Adam Bede loves Hetty Sorrel, a pretty, superficial girl. Although Adam tries to save her, she fancies herself the wife of the young squire Arthur Donnithorne, who seduces her and then leaves her. In her grief, she consents to marry Adam, but before they are wed, she discovers that she is pregnant. She tries in vain to find Arthur, but in the end is found guilty of the murder of her child and is transported for life. Adam finally marries Dinah Morris, a young Methodist preacher.

Adam de la Halle (called Adam le Bossu, d 1288) French poet and composer. Adam wrote a charmingly simple pastourelle with music, *Li Gieus de Robin et Marion* (*The Play of Robin and Marion*), performed before the French court in Naples between 1275 and 1285. Because of this work, he is sometimes (inappropriately) called the father of the OPÉRA COMIQUE. He is also the earliest composer known to have written polyphonic secular songs (earlier TROUBADOUR and TROUVÈRE songs consisted of unaccompanied melodies).

Adams, Abigail [Smith] (1744–1818) Wife of John Adams, noted as a letter writer. The daughter of a Congregational minister, she married Adams in 1764. Her lively, perceptive letters, first published in 1840 in a selected form by her grandson Charles Francis Adams, mirror the affection and respect that existed between the Adamses and give a valuable picture of social and political life in the infant republic; they are included in their entirety in *Family Papers* (2 vols, 1963), the second series of *The Adams Papers* published by Harvard University.

Adams, Parson Abraham The quixotic, vain, staunch friend of the hero of JOSEPH ANDREWS, a novel by Henry Fielding. He is a guileless clergyman, totally ignorant of the ways of the world, always seeking the good in others. The element of paradoxical discussion that he introduces into the novel gives the book its truly comic character. He was drawn from Fielding's friend the Rev. William Young, who edited Robert Ainsworth's *Latin-English Dictionary* (1752).

Adams, Charles Francis, Jr. (1835–1915) American lawyer, railroad expert, and historian. The grandson of John Quincy Adams and the brother of Henry Adams, Charles Francis was a successful businessman who in time became disgusted with the "low instinct" of money-getting, and so turned to writing history. He was chiefly interested in the history of Massachusetts and wrote *Three Episodes of Massachusetts History* (1892) and *Massachu-*

setts: *Its History and Historians* (1893). Earlier he had exposed corruption in railroads in *Chapters of Erie and Other Essays* (1871) and *Railroads: Their Origins and Problems* (1878). He published lives of Richard Henry Dana (1891) and of his father (1900), as well as an *Autobiography* (1916).

Adams, Hannah (1755–1831) American historian. The first professional woman writer in the United States, Adams wrote *Alphabetical Compendium of the Various Sects . . . from the Beginning of the Christian Era* (1784) and *A Summary History of New England* (1799).

Adams, Henry [Brooks] (1838–1918) American historian and man of letters. A member of the famous Adams family of statesmen, Henry Adams felt himself more suited to scholarship than to political action. He worked for a time as a journalist and as editor of the *North American Review*. At the same time (1870–76), he taught medieval, European, and American history at Harvard. Adams's first important book was the nine-volume study *The History of the United States of America During the Administrations of Thomas Jefferson and James Madison* (1889–91), in which he deterministically argued that men cannot change the course of history.

In 1872 Adams married Marian Hooper. Greatly distressed after her suicide in 1885, he traveled to the Orient and renewed an interest in science, certain principles of which he applied to a theory of history. His most important books, MONT-SAINT-MICHEL AND CHARTRES and THE EDUCATION OF HENRY ADAMS, reflect his lifelong quest for order and unity in a world he considered to be in the process of disintegration. His two novels, DEMOCRACY and ESTHER, also reflect his two absorbing concerns: corruption in a capitalistic government and loss of religious faith caused by new scientific discoveries. Adams's letters (2 vols, 1930, 1938) contain some of his most lucid writing and reveal a man of warmth and sensibility.

Adams, John (1735–1826) Second president of the U.S. (1797–1801). A graduate of Harvard, Adams was admitted to the bar in 1758 and was carrying on a successful law practice when the Stamp Act crisis of 1765 drew him into politics. In a series of articles, later collected as *A Dissertation on the Canon and Feudal Law* (1768), he argued that the Stamp Act was contrary to the "inherent rights of mankind." He was a delegate to the first and second Continental Congresses and was an ardent advocate of the Declaration of Independence when it was presented to the congress.

In 1785, after several years' service as minister to France, Britain, and Holland, he began to write his *Defense of the Constitutions of Government of the United States of America* (1787–88), in which he discussed the history of republican government. Elected vice president under Washington, he became president in 1797. He quarreled with Hamilton over a treaty with France in 1800, and the resulting split in the Federalist Party contributed to his loss to JEFFERSON in 1800. After his retirement from the presidency, he returned to his home in Quincy, Massachusetts, and renewed his old friendship with Jefferson. Both men died within a few hours of each other on July 4, 1826.

Adams's essentially conservative political philosophy placed him between the extreme federalism of Hamilton and the agrarianism of Jefferson. His concept of republicanism was based on a "balance" of power that would prevent the power-hungry from gaining control, and his awareness of the weaknesses and vices of mankind led him to put his faith in the "natural aristocracy" of a few men, who, like himself, would use the power vested in them for the good of the people rather than for their private ends. The *Diary and Autobiography of John Adams* (4 vols, 1961) and *Family Papers* (2 vols, 1963) have been published by Harvard University Press, as the opening sections of *The Adams Papers*. See ADAMS, ABIGAIL.

Adams, John Quincy (1767–1848)   Sixth president of the U.S. (1825–29). Adams accompanied his father, John Adams, to France in 1778, studied in European schools, and was graduated from Harvard in 1787. In 1791, in a series of eleven articles signed Publicola, he replied to Thomas Paine's *Rights of Man*, defending the rights of the minority in opposition to Paine's contention that the majority must prevail. After holding several diplomatic posts, Adams became secretary of state in 1817; he secured Florida from Spain in 1819 and was largely responsible for the promulgation of the MONROE DOCTRINE in 1823. In 1824 Adams, Andrew Jackson, Henry Clay, and William H. Crawford were the four candidates for the presidency. Since no candidate received a majority of the electoral votes, the election was given to the House of Representatives. Clay threw his support to Adams, who was elected, and when Adams named Clay secretary of state, Jackson's followers cried "corrupt bargain." This charge, though undoubtedly baseless, hounded Adams during his term of office and contributed to his defeat in 1828. In 1830 he was elected to the House of Representatives, where he served for nearly seventeen years, opposing the annexation of Texas and defending free speech in the face of efforts to stifle debate on the slavery question. Adams's diary, covering more than sixty years, was edited by his son, Charles Francis Adams, and published in twelve volumes as *The Memoirs of John Quincy Adams* (1874–77).

Adams, Nick   The central character in most of the stories of the collection IN OUR TIME, by Ernest HEMINGWAY. He appears also in the famous short story THE KILLERS and in the posthumous collection *Nick Adams Stories* (1972). Adams can be seen as Hemingway's alter-ego; he was the prototype for many subsequent Hemingway heroes.

Adams, Samuel (1722–1803)   American patriot and pamphleteer. Active in arousing public opinion against England before the American Revolution, he was responsible for the creation of the Committee of Correspondence to communicate Boston's grievances to other towns in Massachusetts and "to the World" and prepared for the committee a radical declaration, *State of the Rights of the Colonies* (1772). He was the leading spirit behind the Boston Tea Party and served in the Continental Congress (1774–81), where he advocated immediate independence.

Ada; or Ardor: A Family Chronicle (1969)   A novel by Vladimir NABOKOV. Set in the land of Amerussia, on the planet Antiterra, the novel consists of the memoirs of Dr. Van Veen, with interpolated commentary by his lover and sister Ada. The action of the novel, written in five parts, centers on Van and Ada's long-term incestuous love affair and on Van's effort to write his philosophical treatise *The Texture of Time*. The novel is loose and rambling and contains some of Nabokov's most inventive verbal games and experiments with time. Its allusions and themes draw on the history of European literature, the history of art, science fiction, and lepidopterology, among other things.

Addams, Jane (1860–1935)   American leader in social work and in the pacifist and women's suffrage movements. Addams is famous for her pioneering work as cofounder of Hull House, Chicago, one of the first and most influential settlement houses in America. In 1931 she shared the Nobel Peace Prize with Nicholas Murray Butler. Besides a number of books and articles on social problems, Addams wrote two autobiographical works: *Twenty Years at Hull House* (1910) and *The Second Twenty Years at Hull House* (1931).

Addison, Joseph (1672–1719)   English poet, essayist, and critic. In association with Richard STEELE, Addison perfected the essay as a literary form in his contributions to THE TATLER and THE SPECTATOR. His prose style was the model for pure and elegant English until the end of the 18th century; his comments on manners and morals were widely influential in forming the middle-class ideal of a dispassionate, tolerant, Christian world-citizen. *The Campaign* (1704), celebrating the victory at Blenheim, and his hymn "The Spacious Firmament on High" (1712) are his most famous poems. His musical play *Rosamond* (1705) was an attack on popular Italian operas, and his blank-verse tragedy *Cato* (1713) was enormously popular, combining an appeal to the party-spirit of the Whigs and an avowed intention to purge the stage of immorality. Addison is bitterly attacked by Alexander Pope in the character of Atticus in EPISTLE TO DR. ARBUTHNOT (1735).

Ade, George (1866–1944)   American humorist and playwright. Ade first achieved popularity in the columns of the Chicago *Record*, with the creation of the brash but good-hearted Artie. Stories of a "colored" bootblack and a gentlemanly liar were added, the three becoming the titular heroes of *Artie* (1896), *Pink Marsh* (1897), and *Doc' Horne* (1899). In 1898 he began to write the stories that were collected as FABLES IN SLANG. He commenced his career as a playwright with a successful musical comedy, *The Sultan of Sulu* (1902), later writing *The County Chairman* (1903), a play directed against political corruption; *The College Widow* (1904); and *Father and the Boys* (1908).

Adler, Alfred (1870–1937)   Austrian psychiatrist and psychologist. A disciple of Sigmund FREUD, Adler later rejected Freud's emphasis on the libido and developed a system of "individual psychology." Adler maintained that, because of their dependence, all children begin with a sense of inferiority, which they can successfully overcome by developing a sense of their competence and their secure place in the social order. He coined the term "inferiority complex" to describe the neurotic reaction by which one either succumbs to or overcompensates for feelings of inadequacy. His major work on the subject is *The Practice and Theory of Individual Psychology* (1923). *Cooperation Between the Sexes* (1978) is a collection of his writings on women, love, marriage, and sexuality.

Adler, Felix (1851–1933)   German-born American educator and leader in social welfare. Adler came to America as a youth, graduated from Columbia (1870), and pursued further studies in Germany. He founded the New York Society of Ethical Culture in 1876, from which a worldwide Ethical Culture movement later developed. The society emphasized the need for a stronger morality (apart from any single theological dogma) in all personal, professional, and political relationships and placed great importance on the moral education of children. Adler established the first free kindergarten for New York City's poor, which later grew into the first vocational school that combined manual training and ethical instruction in its curriculum. In 1884 Adler helped to establish the first Tenement House Commission; he arranged for trained nurses to visit the poor, lobbied for parks and playgrounds in depressed urban areas, and served for a time as chairman of the National Child Labor Committee. Adler advanced his views in such books as *The Moral Instruction of Children* (1892), *An Ethical Philosophy of Life* (1918), and *The Reconstruction of the Spiritual Ideal* (1923).

Admetus   See ALCESTIS; ARGONAUTS.

Adolphe (1815)   A novel by Benjamin CONSTANT DE REBECQUE. Adolphe, the novel's young protagonist, has been influenced by his early relationship with a woman of strong intellectual convictions and is unable to adopt the conventional masks of society. Having finished his studies, he sets out upon a period of travel in Germany and Poland. While visiting at a small German court, he establishes a liaison with Ellénore, mistress of Count P—. Adolphe, who began the affair out of pride rather than love, is deeply probed by the author, who points out that his inability to terminate the relationship is a result of his guilt, which leaves him desolate when Ellénore dies. The work, considered to be based in part on Constant's relationship with

Mme de STAËL, is a precursor of the modern psychological novel.

Adonai   See JEHOVAH.

Adonais (1821)   A poem by Percy Bysshe SHELLEY. When Keats died in 1821, Shelley was moved to compose this elegy for his friend. He gave Keats the name of Adonais, probably in allusion to the mourning for Adonis. *Adonais* is considered one of the greatest elegies in the English language.

Adonis   In Greek mythology, a beautiful youth, a parallel character to the Babylonian TAMMUZ. He was the result of an incestuous union between Myrrha and her father, Cinyras. APHRODITE fell in love with Adonis and hid him in a chest, which she gave to PERSEPHONE for safekeeping. When Persephone opened the chest and discovered this most beautiful young man, she too fell in love with Adonis and refused to give him up to Aphrodite. Zeus judged the case and ordered that Adonis spend half the year on earth with Aphrodite and half in the underworld with Persephone. According to a different legend, Adonis was killed by a boar, which some versions identify as Aphrodite's jealous lover ARES in disguise, and it was when he entered the underworld that Persephone fell in love with him.

The myth is one of many in which a young god dies and is resurrected, symbolizing the cycle of growing seasons. Part of the cult of Adonis included the planting of "gardens of Adonis"—seeds sown in shallow soil that withered as quickly as they sprouted. The name of the god is derived from the Phoenician *adon* ("lord"), which appears in the Hebrew *adonai*, used as a substitute for the name *Yahweh* (JEHOVAH).

Adonis (pseudonym of ᶜAlī Ahmad Saᶜīd, 1930–   )   Among the most important of modern Lebanese poets. Adonis's highly intellectual verse shows the influence of French EXISTENTIALISM, although it remains strongly Arabic in character and themes. He edited an important anthology of Arabic poetry, *Dīwān ash-shiᶜr al-ᶜarabi* (1964). Selections of his poetry in English translation appeared in *The Blood of Adonis* (1971). In 1982 this volume was reissued, with the addition of three long, previously untranslated poems, under the title *Transformations of the Lover*. It is illustrated with calligraphic fragments of the text.

Adullam   The cave in which David took refuge when he fled from King Saul. This stronghold attracted "every one that was in debt, and every one that was discontented" (1 Sam. 22:1–2).

Advancement of Learning, The (1605)   A treatise on philosophy by Francis BACON. Considered an excellent example of Renaissance thought, it extols the pursuit of learning and critically surveys the existing state of knowledge. Bacon later wrote a greatly expanded version, *De Dignitate et Augmentis Scientiarum* (1623), to form the first part of his projected INSTAURATIO MAGNA.

Advent (fr Lat, *adventus*, "the coming to") The four weeks immediately preceding Christmas. Advent commemorates the first coming of Christ and anticipates the second: the one to redeem, the other to judge the world. The season begins the Sunday on or nearest St. Andrew's Day (November 30). There is an old tradition of preaching on the "Four Last Things" on the Advent Sundays: death, judgment, heaven, and hell.

Adventists Christian religious sects believing that the second coming of Christ and the end of the world are near at hand.

Adventures For many titles beginning with the words *The Adventures of . . .* , see the following proper names. For example, *The Adventures of Tom Sawyer* is found under *Tom Sawyer, The Adventures of.*

A.E. (pen name of George William Russell, 1867–1935) Irish poet, painter, and journalist. An ardent social idealist, Russell was an active member of the Irish nationalist movement and the agricultural cooperative movement. Together with W. B. YEATS, he was one of the leading lights of the IRISH RENAISSANCE and was associated with the founding of the Dublin Lodge of the Theosophical Society for occult study (see Mme BLAVATSKY). His mystical poetry, in such volumes as *Homeward: Songs by the Way* (1894), *The Earth Breath* (1897), *Divine Vision* (1904), and *House of the Titans* (1934), is based on visions, magic, and Eastern religious ideas. He wrote of these interests in *Candle of Vision* (1918). His verse play, *Deirdre* (1906), was one of the early productions of the Irish National Theatre Society at the ABBEY THEATRE. *The Living Torch* (1937) is a collection of prose writings. His *Letters* were published in 1961.

Aeacus King of Pythia, noted for his piety. A son of Zeus and the nymph Aegina, Aeacus was the father of Telamon and Peleus by Endeis and of Phocus by Psamathe. The elder sons killed Phocus from jealousy and so were banished. When all Greece was ravaged by drought because of PELOPS' murder of Stymphalus, Aeacus' prayers brought rain. At his death, he became either a warder or a judge in Hades.

aedile In ancient Rome, one of four magistrates whose duty it was to maintain order in the city and to take charge of public games and buildings. An aedile corresponded roughly to a modern commissioner of public works. His supervision of public games gave him great opportunities for gaining favor with the populace. Although a small sum was appropriated from the public treasury for these games, an aedile generally expended much more from his own purse to make the show magnificent and thus win votes for the next office in the CURSUS HONORUM, that of praetor.

Aeetes See MEDEA.

Aegeon See BRIAREUS.

Aegeus A legendary king of Athens, father of THESEUS. Aegeus threw himself into the sea, thinking mistakenly that Theseus' expedition to Crete had failed. The Aegean Sea, according to tradition, was so named as a result of this event.

aegis (fr Gr, *aix*, "goat") Variously interpreted as a shield made of goatskin or as the awesome thundercloud of Zeus. HOMER depicts the aegis as an impregnable shield made by the god HEPHAESTUS. On occasion Zeus lent the aegis to other gods, particularly Athene and APOLLO. The aegis symbolized the gods' special powers. Hence the term has come to denote authority and protection.

Aelfric (called Grammaticus, "the Grammarian," c955–c1020) English clergyman and scholar, a prolific writer in both Latin and Old English. Aelfric wrote a series of 120 homilies and saints' lives (990–998), then a treatise on the Old and New Testaments and a *Heptateuch*, a vernacular translation of portions of the first seven books of the Bible. His prose is alliterative and rhythmical, the finest in Old English. Concerned with the revival of learning, he wrote a Latin grammar and Latin-English glossary.

Aeneas The hero of Vergil's AENEID. Aeneas was the son of the mortal ANCHISES and the goddess Aphrodite. According to Homer, he fought against the Greeks in the Trojan War and, after the sack of Troy, reigned in the Troad. Vergil, however, used another legend, according to which Aeneas carried his father, Anchises, on his shoulders out of the burning city and, with a band of followers, set out to establish a new nation; after wandering for many years, he is said to have arrived in Italy, where he founded the colony from which the Romans traced their origin. The epithet often applied to him is *pious*, i.e., devoted to the service of the gods and deeply aware of his obligations to his family and his country. See ASCANIUS.

Aeneid An epic poem by VERGIL, composed of twelve books, in which the legendary Trojan origin of the Roman people is glorified. Vergil traces the lineage of the Julii from Iulus or ASCANIUS, the son of the Trojan hero AENEAS, down to Octavius Caesar (later Augustus), whose newly established principate the poem endorses. The poem was written at the request of the emperor and, though it was left unfinished at the sudden death of the poet (19 BC), it was greeted with enthusiasm by all educated Romans because of its nationalistic purpose.

In Book I, Aeneas and his Trojan followers are driven by a storm to the shores of Carthage and are hospitably entertained by Queen DIDO. In Book II, Aeneas tells the tale of the wooden horse and of the destruction of Troy. He describes his escape from the burning city with his father, ANCHISES, his son Ascanius, and several followers. His wife was lost and died during their flight. The narrative is continued in Book III, in which Aeneas recounts the perils he encountered on the westward voyage from Troy and the death of his father. Book IV tells of Dido's love for Aeneas, his departure from Carthage, and her suicide and cremation on a great funeral pyre. In Book V, Aeneas and his followers reach Sicily and hold funeral games in honor of Anchises. Aeneas visits Anchises in the underworld in Book VI, sees the future generations of Romans, and is told of their exploits. Here appear the much quoted lines of Anchises to Aeneas concerning the task of the Romans: "Roman, remember that you shall rule the nations by your authority, for this is to be your skill, to make peace the custom, to spare the conquered, and to wage war until the haughty are brought low."

In Book VII, LATINUS, king of the Latini, entertains Aeneas and promises his daughter LAVINIA to him in marriage, but Prince Turnus, who has already been betrothed to her by her mother, raises an army to resist Aeneas. Book VIII tells of the preparations for war on both sides and of Aeneas' visit to Latium, the future home of the Romans. In Book IX, Turnus, in the absence of Aeneas, fires the Trojan ships and assaults their camp. The episode of Nisus and Euryalus, in which the two Trojans die heroically trying to infiltrate the enemy camp, occurs here. The war between Turnus and Aeneas is depicted in Book X. Here Mezentius and his son Lausas are slain by Aeneas. In Book XI, the battle continues. Book XII tells of the single combat between Aeneas and Turnus and of the death of Turnus. See ACHATES; PALINURUS.

Aeolus (1) In Greek mythology, the god of the winds, which Aeolus kept imprisoned in the Aeolian islands. He freed them at his own choice or at the wish of other gods. In the *Odyssey*, Book X, he aided Odysseus in his homeward voyage by fastening the unfavorable winds in a leather bag and giving it into Odysseus' keeping, with a warning not to open it. While Odysseus slept, however, his seamen, thinking that he was secreting treasure from them, opened the bag, and the ship was blown back to its starting point. Angrily, Aeolus refused to cooperate further.

(2) The grandson of Deucalion, the Greek Noah, and eponymous ancestor of the Aeolian Greeks.

Aeschylus (525–456 BC) A Greek tragic dramatist. Aeschylus was born of an aristocratic family in Eleusis. In his youth, he fought against the Persians in the great battles of Marathon, Salamis, and Plataea. He seems to have been prouder of these feats than of his immense success as a playwright, which he did not even mention in the epitaph that, according to tradition, he wrote for himself. After sixteen years of writing, he won his first prize for tragedy in 484 BC; he won his last with his masterpiece the ORESTEIA, twenty-five years later. In 476 BC he had paid a successful visit to the court of Hiero I, Tyrant of Syracuse; three years before his death, he again went to Sicily, this time to Gela. According to a popular story, he was killed when an eagle dropped a tortoise on his bald head, mistaking it for a stone. The story is improved with the mention of an oracular prophecy that he would die of a blow from heaven.

Aeschylus wrote ninety plays, but only seven of them have survived: THE SUPPLIANT WOMEN, THE PERSIANS, the SEVEN AGAINST THEBES, PROMETHEUS BOUND, and the *Oresteia*, a trilogy. This last is the only extant example of the trilogies on related themes that were common in Aeschylus' day; it includes *Agamemnon*, the *Libation Bearers*, and the *Eumenides*. Aeschylus is noted for the grandeur of his language and of his subjects, which encompass not only the struggles between historical heroes (*The Persians*) and mythical (*Agamemnon*), but the grim conflict between the old laws and the new (*Eumenides*) and, in a sense, between man and gods (*Prometheus Bound*). Aeschylus' poetry is tense, closely packed, exciting, often somewhat rough, compared with the polished lines of Sophocles. His imagery is strong, startling, and sometimes forced, but always effective. The antithesis of Euripides' relatively colloquial speech, Aeschylus' dialogue is far from natural but is well suited to the tragic immensity of his themes.

Aeschylus was a practical and imaginative man of the theatre, as well as an inspired poet. He was the first to use a second actor in addition to the chorus; this permitted for the first time dialogue between individuals. He also introduced elaborate costumes and the high-soled *cothurnoi* that gave his actors added stature. He seems to have enjoyed colorful effects; *The Persians* is filled with pageantry, and old Oceanus appears in *Prometheus Bound* riding on a sort of four-legged bird, perhaps the original of modern vaudeville's two-man horse. Tradition says that some of his costumes were so splendid that the hierophants at Eleusis copied them for their own vestments. The story is also told that his presentation in *Eumenides* of the chorus of Erinyes, hideous creatures with black skins and red tongues, so terrified the audience that women had miscarriages and children convulsions.

Aesir The collective name of the Norse gods, who lived in heavenly ASGARD. There were said to be twelve gods and some twenty-four to thirty goddesses, but the number seems variable. The following may be mentioned: Odin, the chief of the gods; Thor, Odin's eldest son and god of thunder; Tiu, another son, the god of wisdom; Balder, the Scandinavian Apollo; Bragi, god of poetry; Vidar, god of silence; Hoder the blind, slayer of Balder; Hermoder, Odin's son and messenger; Hoenir, a minor god; Odnir, husband of Freya, the Scandinavian Aphrodite; Loki, the god of mischief; and Vali, Odin's youngest son.

Wives of the Aesir Odin's wife was Frigga; Thor's wife was Sif; Balder's wife was Nanna; Bragi's wife was Iduna; Loki's wife was Siguna.

The important deities mentioned above are more fully treated under their names.

Aesop Greek fabulist. According to tradition, the author of *Aesop's Fables* was a Phrygian slave who probably lived from 620 to 560 BC. It is inferable from Aristotle's mention of Aesop's acting as a public defender that he was freed from slavery, and Plutarch's statement that the Athenians erected a noble statue of him would tend to contradict the tradition that Aesop was deformed. There is little information on Aesop's life, and several scholars have consequently been led to doubt that he ever existed at all. The earliest extant collections of Aesop's stories were made by various Greek versifiers and Latin translators, to whose compilations were added tales from Oriental and ancient sources, to form what we now know as *Aesop's Fables*. The majority of European fables, including those of LA FONTAINE, are largely derived from these succinct tales, in which talking animals illustrate human vices, follies, and virtues. Since some of Aesop's fables have been discovered on Egyptian papyri dating from eight hundred to one thousand years before his time, it cannot be claimed that he was by any means the author of all the fables.

aesthetic distance   A term that describes the ability to objectify experience in art and present it as independent from its maker. For the audience, aesthetic distance means an awareness of the separation of art and reality and an objective response to what is artistically presented. The concept goes back to ARISTOTLE, who believed that art was life reshaped into a pleasing and significant form.

aestheticism   Generally, a term applied to a way of perceiving things that was common among the writers and artists of the 19th century who adhered to the doctrine of ART FOR ART'S SAKE. The movement, or cult, was largely influenced by German romantics, particularly GOETHE. Because of the quest for beauty and the insistence that art should serve no moral or didactic purpose, it was related to and coincident with the work of the PRE-RAPHAELITE BROTHERHOOD and the PARNASSIANS. Major exponents of aestheticism in America were Edgar Allan POE and Ralph Waldo EMERSON.

Aetna   See ETNA.

Afanasyev, Alexandr Nikolayevich (1826-1871) Russian folklorist. *Russian Fairy Tales* (tr 1945) contains selected translations of Afanasyev's collections of Russian folklore. His work represents the first systematic compilation of Russian folk tales.

affective fallacy   A critical term denoting the confusion between what a literary work *is* and what it *does*. That is, a work should be judged solely on its literary components, not by its emotional (or affective) impact on the reader. It was first identified as a critical "error" by Monroe Beardsley and W. K. Wimsatt in *The Verbal Icon* (1954). It is related to intentional fallacy, in which a work is judged according to what the author presumably intended to say or in relation to the author's biography.

Affluent Society, The (1958)   A book on the U.S. economy by John Kenneth GALBRAITH. In it Galbraith contends that, because of technological advances and increased productivity, by the mid-20th century, consumer goods and material comforts were available to Americans in near-overabundance. He suggested that the "quality of life" would improve if spending power were shifted from the private sector to the public sector, in efforts to increase educational facilities and eliminate such problems as pollution and urban decay. The "quality of life" concept provoked considerable debate in government, in business, and among laymen, and the book's title became a catch-phrase to describe Americans at the peak of prosperity.

Afreet (or Afrit)   In Muslim mythology, the second most powerful of the five classes of JINN, or devils. They are of gigantic stature, very malicious, and inspire dread. Legend holds that King Solomon once tamed an Afreet and made it submissive to his will.

African Queen, The (1935)   A novel by C. S. FORESTER. It is the comic-heroic story of a missionary's sister and a timid Cockney engineer who try to blow up a German gunboat from their asthmatic steam launch, the *African Queen*. In 1951 it was made into a popular movie, starring Humphrey Bogart and Katharine Hepburn, with a screenplay by James AGEE.

After Many a Summer Dies the Swan (1939) A novel by Aldous HUXLEY. Centered around Jo Stoyte, a Californian oil magnate afraid of old age and death, it is a satire of some aspects of American life. Jeremy Pordage, working on some old English manuscripts, discovers that an 18th-century earl used the same rejuvenating system Stoyte is experimenting with. They go to England and find the earl, over two hundred years old, a filthy ape. Old Mr. Propter is spokesman for Huxley's spiritual philosophy.

Afternoon of a Faun, The   See APRÈS-MIDI D'UN FAUNE, L'.

Against the Grain (A rebours, 1884; also tr as *Against Nature*)   A novel by Joris Karl HUYSMANS. Its subject is the quest of its DÉCADENT hero, Des Esseintes, for the rare and perverse in sensation. Restless and discontent, Des Esseintes seeks release from the ennui of existence in perfumes, music, painting, the love of circus acrobats, and the study of medieval Latin literature.

Agamemnon   (1) The king of Mycenae, son of ATREUS, and leader of the Greeks at the siege of Troy. Homer makes him ruler over all Argos. He was the brother of Menelaus, the theft of whose wife, Helen, by Paris brought on the Trojan War. Before the expedition against Troy could sail, Agamemnon's daughter IPHIGENIA was sacrificed to Diana to appease that goddess for a sacred stag Agamemnon had killed. At Troy, Agamemnon's quarrel with Achilles cost the Greeks many lives and delayed the end of the war. (See ILIAD.) After the sack of Troy, Agamemnon returned home, only to be murdered by his wife, Clytemnestra, who was living as the paramour of Aegisthus.

(2) A tragedy by Aeschylus, the first in his ORESTEIA trilogy.

Agassiz, Jean Louis Rodolphe (1807–1873) Swiss naturalist, teacher, and author. Agassiz came to the U.S. in 1846 as a lecturer with an established reputation; deciding to remain permanently, he became widely known as a professor at Harvard and curator of the Agassiz Museum at Cambridge. He was the founder of the Marine Biological Laboratory at Woods Hole, Massachusetts. A fluent writer on geology and zoology, Agassiz showed an astonishing command of English. His major work is called *Contributions to the Natural History of the United States of America* (4 vols, 1857–62). An effective teacher of laymen and scientists, he epitomized his method in the directive: "Go to Nature; take the facts in your own hands; look, and see for yourself!" Opposed to the Darwinian theory of evolution, Agassiz did succeed in arousing interest in the natural sciences and establishing methods of study and classification. A member of the famous Saturday Club, he exchanged ideas with leading men of letters.

Agastya In Hindu mythology, the legendary sage and pioneer in the epic age of the Aryanization of south India. Supposed to have been born in a jar, Agastya is also known as Kumbhayoni, or "jar-born." Legend says that he presented to his pupil Rama the invincible bow and inexhaustible quiver of Vishnu. According to another legend, as he was walking one day with Vishnu, the insolent ocean asked the god who the pigmy (the "jar-born" dwarf) was that strutted by his side. When Vishnu replied that it was the patriarch Agastya, who would restore earth to its true balance, the ocean contemptuously spat its spray in Agastya's face. Agastya, in revenge, drank it dry.

Agate, James Evershed (1877–1947) English drama critic. Agate wrote for the Manchester *Guardian*, serving as its theatre critic from 1907 to 1914. For the last twenty-four years of his life, he was drama critic for the London *Sunday Times*. He developed a large and faithful following, inspired largely by the obvious enthusiasm he communicated about the theatre and theatre people. His autobiographical diaries, collectively entitled *Ego*, were published in nine volumes (1935-48).

Agathocles (361–289 BC) Tyrant of Sicily (316–304 BC). The son of a potter, Agathocles raised himself from the ranks to become general of the army. There is a story that he always kept an earthen pot at hand in memory of his origin. When he attacked the Carthaginians, he "carried the war into Africa" and "burned his ships behind him," that his soldiers might know they must either conquer or die. Agathocles died of poison administered by his grandson. He is the hero of an English tragedy by Richard Perrington, a French tragedy by Voltaire, and a German novel by Caroline Pichler, all called by his name.

Agave In classic mythology, a daughter of Cadmus and mother of Pentheus, whom she tore to pieces in a mad fury, under the illusion that he was a wild beast. This episode forms a part of Euripides' drama *Bacchae*. See BACCHANTS.

Agee, James (1909–1955) American writer. Agee was raised in the Cumberland mountain region of Tennessee, which provided the setting for his two autobiographical novels and is the likely basis for his penetrating insights into the American poor. His first novel, *The Morning Watch* (1951), is the story of a young boy's struggle and failure to attain true contrition in church. The extent of Agee's actual religious torment is documented in the posthumously collected *Letters to Father Flye* (1962). Agee's only other novel, his masterwork, *A Death in the Family* (1957), was left unfinished at his death. The novel, which won a PULITZER PRIZE, recounts with extraordinary sensitivity the impact of a man's death on the surviving members of his family. Hounded by financial problems, Agee channeled his creative energies into money-making ventures. His work as a film critic and scriptwriter is collected in the two volumes of *Agee on Film* (1958, 1960). Commissioned to write an article for *Fortune* magazine, Agee spent time with several Alabama sharecropping families. The result was not an article but the powerfully moving book *Let Us Now Praise Famous Men* (1941; with photographs by Walker Evans). *Collected Poems* (1968) and *Collected Short Prose* (1969) are other examples of Agee's writing.

Age of Anxiety, The (1947) A long poem by W. H. AUDEN. It concerns three men and a woman who meet by chance in a New York bar in wartime; all are suffering from the modern malaise and feel guilty, isolated, and rootless. In a common dream, they set out on a quest through a barren wasteland. Hope in Christianity is presented as the solution to their problems. The title has frequently been used as a name to describe the mid-20th century.

The Age of Anxiety is also the name of a ballet, danced to Leonard Bernstein's Second Symphony.

Age of Innocence, The (1920) A novel by Edith WHARTON. A satirical picture of social life in New York during the 1870s, it describes the marriage of Newland Archer to May Welland, who is bound by the tribal code of the elite. Although he is attracted to her unconventional cousin, Ellen Olenska, they are both too obedient to the code to seek happiness together.

Age of Reason An epithet for the 18th century. See ENLIGHTENMENT.

Age of Reason, The A controversial treatise (1794–96) by Thomas PAINE, expounding the deistic view of revealed religion. The work was widely denounced in America as immoral and atheistic.

(2) A novel (1945) by Jean-Paul SARTRE. See ROADS TO FREEDOM, THE.

Agincourt, Battle of (1415) A battle in northern France. The English army defeated the more numerous, better armed French. It is the setting for Shakespeare's

HENRY V and Michael Drayton's "The Ballad of Agincourt" (c1605).

Aglaia (1) One of the three Charites (GRACES) of classical mythology.

(2) In Dostoyevsky's novel THE IDIOT, the fiancée of Prince Myshkin.

Agnès In Molière's comedy L'ECOLE DES FEMMES, the girl on whom Arnolphe tries out his educational experiments, with the aim of turning her into a perfect wife for himself. She has been brought up in a country convent and kept totally in ignorance of the difference between the sexes, conventional proprieties, the mysteries of marriage, and so on. When removed from the convent, she treats men like schoolgirls, playing with them and kissing them. An *Agnès* is therefore any naïve and innocent young girl. The French have the expression *Elle fait l'Agnès*, that is, she is pretending to be wholly unsophisticated and ingenuous.

Agnes Grey (1847) A novel by Anne BRONTË, published with her sister Emily's *Wuthering Heights*. It is a quiet account of the life of an ill-treated, lonely governess who eventually marries Mr. Weston, a curate.

Agni (Sans, "fire; the god of fire") A central deity in HINDUISM. Fire was the central element in Vedic ritual, which focused on the sacrifice. As god of the Vedic priests (through the fire sacrifice) and of the home (residing in the hearth), Agni is the bearer of offerings of men to the gods and the bringer of gods to the sacrificial altar. In one of the *Brahmanas*, Agni is associated with the movement of Aryan tribes eastward into India, clearing the land intended for settlement through purifying fire.

Agnon, Shmuel Yosef (born Samuel Josef Czaczkes, 1888–1970) Hebrew writer. Born in Galicia, Agnon received a traditional Jewish education and made extensive study of Hasidic stories. He immigrated to Palestine in 1907. As other Hebrew writers were influenced by European trends, Agnon reintroduced traditional Hebrew styles and became the undisputed master of modern Hebrew fiction. His work represents a fusion of irony, sophisticated realism, and a dreamlike romanticism. At the center of his creation stands the Jew in his various psychological and sociological manifestations: the man of faith, the nihilist, the victim of pogroms and the Holocaust, the pioneer, and the saint. Noteworthy among those works translated into English are *Ha-khnasat kallah* (1930; tr *The Bridal Canopy*, 1937), *Yamim noraim* (1937; tr *Days of Awe*, 1948), *Oreah natah lalun* (1939; tr *A Guest for the Night*, 1968), and *Ad olam* (1954; tr *Forever More*, 1961). *Twenty-One Stories* appeared in 1970. Agnon was awarded the NOBEL PRIZE in Literature in 1966, the first Hebrew writer to be so honored.

agon See OLD COMEDY.

Agravain, Sir (or Sir Aggravaine) In ARTHURIAN LEGEND, a knight of the Round Table and a son of Margawse. In Malory's MORTE D'ARTHUR, he is the brother of the knights GAWAIN, GARETH, and Gaheris and half-brother of MORDRED.

Agrippina (d AD 59) Daughter of Agrippina and GERMANICUS CAESAR, sister of the emperor Caligula, and mother of the emperor NERO. Agrippina persuaded her husband, the emperor CLAUDIUS, to name Nero, her son by a previous marriage, as his successor over his own son BRITANNICUS; subsequently she had Claudius poisoned. After he became emperor, Nero, after many elaborate and thwarted attempts, finally succeeded in having Agrippina murdered.

Agrippina's mother was the granddaughter of Augustus, wife of Germanicus Caesar, and mother of Caligula. She was banished by Tiberius to the isle of Pandatarra, where she died (AD 33).

Aguecheek, Sir Andrew In Shakespeare's TWELFTH NIGHT, a silly old fop with "3,000 ducats a year." Very fond of the table but with a shrewd understanding that "beef had done harm to his wit," Sir Andrew thinks himself "old in nothing but in understanding" and boasts that he can "cut a caper, dance the coranto, walk a jig, and take delight in masques," like a young man.

Ahab (1) In the Old Testament, a king of Israel whose name has become a byword for wickedness. Ahab is remembered especially for his hostility to the prophet Elijah and for his countenance of profane cults. At the instigation of his wife Jezebel, he executed Naboth on false charges in order to obtain possession of a vineyard which Naboth owned and refused to sell. His story is told in 1 Kings 16–22.

(2) The monomaniacal captain of the *Pequod* in Melville's MOBY-DICK.

Ahasuerus (1) In the Old Testament, king of the Medes and Persians, as related in the book of ESTHER.

(2) In medieval legend, one of the names given THE WANDERING JEW.

Ahi In Vedic myth, the dark cloud dragon or serpent who keeps the waters of fruitfulness from the earth. Ahi is the personification either of drought or of winter, whose death allows the frozen waters to thaw and flow again. INDRA slew Ahi with a thunderbolt, thus releasing the rain and replenishing the earth.

áhimsa (Sans, "noninjury") A doctrine associated with BUDDHISM and JAINISM and later absorbed into HINDUISM, on the nontaking of human or animal life. Mahatma GANDHI incorporated this into his technique of nonviolent civil disobedience, as the nationalist movement developed in 20th-century India.

Ahmed, Prince A character in the *Arabian Nights*, noted for the tent given him by the fairy Paribanou, which would cover a whole army but might be carried in one's pocket. Ahmed is also associated with the apple of Samarkand, which would cure all diseases.

Aholibamah   In the Old Testament, the name of one of Esau's wives (Gen. 36:2) and of a duke, or leader, of Edom (Gen. 36:41). In Byron's poem *Heaven and Earth* (1824), she is a proud, ambitious, queenlike beauty, the daughter of Cain's son and loved by the seraph Samiasa.

Ahura Mazda   See ORMUZD.

Ah, Wilderness! (1933)   A play by Eugene O'NEILL. The only real comedy O'Neill wrote, it is the light-hearted story of a middle-class American adolescent, Tommy Miller, and his first experiences in an adult world, on July 4, 1906. The play is particularly interesting in the context of O'Neill's other work because of its uncharacteristic celebration of "All-American" values. Although O'Neill is a largely autobiographical playwright, he said that *Ah, Wilderness!* is the story of "a boyhood I never had." Perhaps he intended as well to portray an America that never was.

Aichinger, Ilse (1921–   )   Austrian novelist and writer of short stories and radio plays. Although only in peripheral contact with the Nazi terror, she experienced the limbo of fear and hopelessness in which she and other dissenters lived. In the first few years after World War II, she abandoned her study of medicine to complete her first novel, *Die größere Hoffnung* (1948; tr *Herod's Children*, 1963), which deals with the hopes and fears of Jewish children in HITLER's Reich. Her later writing experimented with new narrative forms: dialogues and radio plays, some of which have been translated in *Ilse Aichinger: Selected Short Stories and Dialogue* (1966). The main motif in all her later writing is concern about and exaltation of human values in a world that increasingly disregards them.

Aiglon, L'   See ROSTAND, EDMOND.

Aiken, Conrad [Potter] (1889–1973)   American writer. When Aiken was a small boy, Aiken's father killed his wife and then himself, a tragedy that had an inestimable effect on Aiken's development. Most of his work reflects his intense interest in psychoanalysis and the development of identity. Of the many influences Aiken acknowledged, the writings of FREUD, Havelock ELLIS, William JAMES, Edgar Allan POE, and the French SYMBOLISTS are evident in his work. He graduated from Harvard in 1912, in the same era as T. S. ELIOT, Walter LIPPMANN, Van Wyck BROOKS, and E. E. CUMMINGS. His autobiographical book USHANT affords much insight into these and other literary figures he knew.

The forms and sounds of music pervade all of Aiken's highly introspective poetry, collected in such volumes as *The Jig of Forslin* (1916), *The Charnel Rose* (1918), *Selected Poems* (1929; PULITZER PRIZE, 1930), *Brownstone Eclogues* (1942), *The Kid* (1947), and *Collected Poems 1916–1970* (1970). His fiction—*Collected Novels* (1964), including the psychologically interesting BLUE VOYAGE—is fraught with symbolism and shows him to be a master of interior monologue. It had a shaping influence on the works of many young writers of the day, including his protégé Malcolm LOWRY. Aiken's critical essays are compiled in *A Reviewer's ABC* (1958); his *Collected Short Stories* appeared in 1960. As editor of Emily DICKINSON's *Selected Poems* (1924), Aiken was largely responsible for establishing that poet's posthumous literary reputation. *The Selected Letters of Conrad Aiken* (1978) contains correspondence with such literary colleagues as Wallace STEVENS, Harriet MONROE, and Edmund WILSON.

Airāvata   In Hindu mythology, the holy elephant, ridden by INDRA. Airāvata was supposedly created when BRAHMĀ chanted seven sacred songs over two halves of an eggshell. In Shaivite HINDUISM, Airāvata is associated with GANESA.

Aitmatov, Chingiz (1928–   )   Soviet novelist, short-story writer, and playwright. Born in the Central Asian republic of Kirghizia, Aitmatov inherited a love for Russian literature from his father (who died in 1937, a victim of STALIN's terror) and for traditional Kirghiz folktales and customs from his mother. In 1952 he qualified as a veterinary technician and published his first story. After a period of study in Moscow, Aitmatov returned home to work as a journalist in 1958 and soon gained a national reputation with the publication in the journal *Novy mir* of "Jamilya" (1959), a love story that challenged both traditional Kirghiz custom and the new "socialist" morality. This and other short stories were followed by two thoughtful novels, *Proshchai, Gulsary!* (1966; tr *Farewell, Gulsary*, 1970) and *Bely parakhod* (1970; tr *The White Ship*, 1972). Aitmatov is best known in the West for his play (written with Kaltai Mukhamedzhanov) *Voskhozhdenie na Fudzhiamu* (1973; tr *The Ascent of Mount Fuji*, 1975). A subtle treatment of the suppression of dissidents, it caused a sensation when first produced in Moscow in 1973. One of the few genuinely talented writers to emerge from the government's drive to transform the non-Russian nationalities into parts of the total Soviet state, Aitmatov has begun increasingly to criticize the impact of Russification, collectivization, and a non-nomadic way of life on traditional Kirghiz society. A subsequent work to appear in English is the novel *The Day Is Longer Than a Hundred Years* (1980; tr 1983).

Ajax   The most famous hero of the Trojan War after ACHILLES. Ajax was king of Salamis, a man of giant stature, daring and self-confident, son of Telamon. When the armor of Achilles was awarded to Odysseus instead of to himself, he turned mad from vexation and stabbed himself. His deeds are narrated by HOMER and later poets. SOPHOCLES wrote a tragedy called *Ajax*, in which "the madman" scourges a ram he mistakes for Odysseus. His encounter with a flock of sheep, which he fancied in his madness to be the sons of ATREUS, AGAMEMNON and MENELAUS, has been mentioned at greater or lesser length by several Greek and Roman poets. This Ajax is introduced by SHAKESPEARE in his drama TROILUS AND CRESSIDA.

Ajax the Less   In Greek legend, son of Oileus, king of Locris. The night Troy was taken, Ajax offered violence to Cassandra, the prophetic daughter of PRIAM; in consequence, his ship was driven on a rock, and he perished at sea.

Akbar (1542–1605)   Generally considered the greatest of the Muslim emperors of India, of the MOGUL EMPIRE. Akbar unified vast areas of the subcontinent, introduced a variety of administrative and social reforms, and eventually declared a state religion, the Din Illahi (Divine Faith), which focused on himself personally. He was highly praised in historical literature, even by the Hindus, for the active propagation of communal harmony.

Akhmadulina, Bella [Akhatovna] (1937–   )   Soviet poet. Akhmadulina has generally been regarded as the most brilliant woman poet of the generation of YEV-TUSHENKO and VOZNESENSKY. Her relatively small and sporadic output has made her less of the Soviet equivalent of a media figure than she was during the 1950s and 1960s partly through her enormously successful poetry readings and partly as the wife, successively, of two prominent writers, Yevgeny Yevtushenko and Yuri Nagibin. Akhmadulina's simple, direct, introspective style owes much to the tradition of ACMEISM and to TSVETAYEVNA and PASTERNAK; one of her best-known long poems is *Moya rodoslovnaya* (*My Genealogy*, 1964), whose theme derives from PUSHKIN's poem of the same name. She was a contributor to *Metropol*, the 1979 anthology edited by a number of well-known writers whose suppression by the censors aroused a storm of protest.

Akhmatova, Anna (pen name of Anna Andreyevna Gorenko, 1888–1966)   Russian poet. An outstanding member of the Acmeist school (see ACMEISM), Akhmatova married the poet Nikolai GUMILYOV in 1910 and divorced him in 1918. Between 1912 and 1923, she published half a dozen volumes of poems, the best of which included *Vecher* (*Evening*, 1912) and *Anno Domini* (1922). Her poetry, principally intimate and personal love lyrics, is in the Acmeist tradition of clarity and sharpness of imagery. Akhmatova's abstinence from political themes led to an attack on her in 1946 by the Soviet cultural overseer Andrei Zhdanov and to her expulsion from the Soviet Writers' Union. She had published little since 1923—being completely unpublished at all for one seventeen-year stretch —but after 1958 she began writing again; *Poema bez geroya* (1960; tr *Poem without a Hero*, 1973) and *Rekviem* (tr *Requiem*, 1964), the underground anthem of those who suffered under Stalin, are two of her important works from this later period. Although sections of *Requiem* had been published in the Soviet Union before her death, the entire work was not published in her country until 1987. Near the

end of her life she was recognized officially again and reinstated in the Writers' Union.

Aksakov, Sergei Timofeyevich (1791–1859)   Russian writer. Born in Ufa, in the eastern steppes of Russia, Aksakov attended the University of Kazan and entered government service in Moscow. His early writing consisted mainly of essays and articles on the theatre. The novelist Gogol, who became a close friend of Aksakov in the early 1830s, urged him to write the reminiscences of his early life in the steppe country. Aksakov produced three autobiographical works: *Semeinaya khronika* (*The Family Chronicle*, 1856), *Vospominaniya* (*Reminiscences*, 1856), and *Detskiye gody bagrova vnuka* (*Years of Childhood of Bagrov's Grandson*, 1858). In the *Chronicle* and *Years of Childhood*, Aksakov used fictitious names for his family. All three of these works, which are masterpieces of description and narration, have become classics in Russian literature. Aksakov's prose style is placed on a level with the best Russian prose writers, including PUSHKIN, LERMONTOV, and TURGENEV. The love of the old patriarchal Russian way of life that is revealed in Aksakov's memoirs was passed on to his children. Two of his sons, Konstantin (1817–60) and Ivan (1823–86), became leading members of SLAVOPHILISM.

Aksyonov, Vasily [Pavlovich] (1932–   )   Soviet novelist, short-story writer, and playwright. Aksyonov, considered one of the best novelists of his generation writing in Russian, has had a personal and literary career reflecting much of the course of Soviet history over the past forty years. Both his parents spent years in labor camps, victims of STALIN's purges; his mother, Evgenia Ginzburg, became famous with her memoirs of life in the camps, *Journey into the Whirlwind* and *Within the Whirlwind*. Part of Aksyonov's childhood was spent with his mother in Siberian exile and is recreated in his most ambitious novel, *Ozhog* (1975; tr *The Burn*, 1984), a book whose larger themes are the author's growing disillusion with the writer's fate under a repressive regime and his testimony to the slow destruction of his generation's hopes.

After his graduation from medical school (he practiced for several years before becoming a full-time writer), Aksyonov published his second novel, *Zvezdnyi bilet* (1961; tr *A Ticket to the Stars*, 1963), toward the end of the period of political relaxation known as THE THAW. It dealt in highly colloquial style with the relatively taboo subject of the inner yearnings and sexual adventures of Soviet teenagers, and it shocked and thrilled the public, catapulting the author to immediate notoriety. Aksyonov found it increasingly difficult to publish his work as his interest turned to more avant-garde and grotesque satire. After his effort in 1979 to create an anthology free of censorship, *Metropol*, Aksyonov resigned from the Writers' Union when two of his fellow editors were expelled and was forced in 1980 to emigrate, eventually settling in the U.S. A collection of stories, *The Steel Bird*, was published in 1979, and a satirical fantasy, *The Island of Crimea*, in 1983.

Aladdin   One of the most celebrated characters in the *Arabian Nights*, hero of the story "Aladdin or the Wonderful Lamp." The son of Mustafa, a poor tailor of China, Aladdin is a lazy, obstinate, and mischievous boy when the tale opens. One day an African magician accosts him, pretending to be his uncle, and sends him into a cave to bring up a "wonderful lamp," giving him a "ring of safety." Aladdin secures the lamp but will not hand it to the magician till he is out of the cave, whereupon the magician shuts him up and departs for Africa. Wringing his hands in despair, Aladdin accidentally rubs the lamp and learns of its magic power as two genii appear to do his bidding. He asks to be delivered from the cave and is returned to his home. By means of this lamp, he obtains untold wealth, builds a superb palace, and marries Badroulboudour, the sultan's daughter. After a time, the African magician, offering new lamps for old, obtains the lamp from Aladdin's wife and causes the palace to be transported into Africa. Ultimately, however, Aladdin poisons the magician, regains the lamp, and has his palace restored to its original place in China.

Alain   (pen name of Émile Chartier, 1868–1951) French philosopher, essayist, and teacher. Alain took his pseudonym from the 15th-century poet Alain Chartier. Believing that to be alive is to be aware of the limitations of the mind, Alain imbued a generation of disciples with the will to resist conformity. His writings were most often in the form of *propos*, short aphoristic essays much like fables or parables, which taught a practical lesson through imagistic narrative. Some of the many thousands of these *propos* have been collected in books about politics, his firm pacifism, psychology, philosophy, and literary criticism, including *Les Cent et un propos d'Alain* (5 vols, 1908–29) and *Mars, ou la guerre jugée* (1921).

Alain-Fournier   (pen name of Henri Fournier, 1886–1914)   French novelist. Alain-Fournier grew up in the beautiful countryside of La Chapelle-d'Angillon, in the department of Cher. The son of two schoolteachers, he wandered from the merchant marine, to military service, to a career in journalism. In 1914 Alain-Fournier died in action, leaving one work which alone secured his reputation as a significant French novelist: LE GRAND MEAULNES, a hauntingly nostalgic story about his own idealized love for a girl he scarcely knew.

Alamo   A fortified mission in San Antonio, Texas. In 1836, during the Texas rebellion against Mexico, a force of Texans under William B. Travis was besieged there by a much larger Mexican army, led by General Santa Anna. When the Mexicans succeeded in gaining entrance after a thirteen-day bombardment, every remaining defender was killed in hand-to-hand combat. Among those killed were Davy Crockett and James Bowie. "Remember the Alamo!" became a battle slogan of the Mexican War.

Alarcón, Pedro Antonio de (1833–1891)   Spanish novelist. Alarcón's fame rests on his shorter works, particularly his humorous tale based on popular ballad tradition, "El sombrero de tres picos" ("The Three-Cornered Hat," 1874). His humor again raised him to prominence with the publication of the novelette *El capitán Veneno* (*Captain Venom* or *Captain Poison*, 1881). Also well known are his full-length work, *El escándalo* (1875), which points out the redeeming effects of an innocent girl's love upon a quarrelsome aristocrat, and the novel *El niño de la bola* (1880).

Alarcón y Mendoza, Juan Ruiz de (c1581–1639) Mexican-born Spanish dramatist. Alarcón, who spent most of his life in Spain, studied at Salamanca and was appointed to the Council of the Indies in 1626. His humped back and touchy temperament made him a target for the gibes of rival dramatists, such as Lope de Vega.

A restrained and painstaking artist who paid close attention to style and characterization, he wrote twenty-four plays, most of which were published in 1628 and 1634. The best known of these are the "comedies of ethics," in which the comic element enforces a moral lesson: *Las paredes oyen*, a study of slander; *Mudarse por mejorarse*, which assails inconstancy in love; *La prueba de las promesas*, an attack on ingratitude; and LA VERDAD SOSPECHOSA.

À la recherche du temps perdu   See PROUST, MARCEL; REMEMBRANCE OF THINGS PAST.

Alas y Ureña, Leopoldo [Enrique García] (pseudonym Clarín, 1852–1901)   Spanish novelist, short-story writer, and critic. Alas's fame is due to his two-volume novel *La Regenta* (1884–85), considered the Spanish MADAME BOVARY and certainly one of the major works of 19th-century European fiction. In the novel, Alas applies a mixture of attenuated naturalism and psychological interpretation to Spanish provincial life, portraying his heroine, Ana Ozores, as crushed by the boredom and malice characteristic of her native town. *Su único hijo* (1890), his only other novel, has less to commend it.

Albany, duke of   In Shakespeare's KING LEAR, the gentle, wise, and courageous husband of the ruthless Goneril, eldest daughter of Lear. Albany is horrified at Goneril's behavior toward her father. At the play's end he and EDGAR are left to rule England.

albatross   The largest web-footed bird. It is the subject of many superstitions, especially among sailors. Coleridge's RIME OF THE ANCIENT MARINER is based on the belief that it is fatal to shoot an albatross.

Albee, Edward [Franklin] (1928–   )   American playwright. Albee's experimental one-act plays—*The Zoo Story* (performed first in German, W. Berlin, 1959), *The Death of Bessie Smith* (1960), *The Sandbox* (1960),

Box (1968), and *Quotations from Chairman Mao Tse-Tung* (1968)—earned him a reputation as the leading American exponent of the THEATRE OF THE ABSURD. However, his best-known and most dramatically successful play, WHO'S AFRAID OF VIRGINIA WOOLF?, reveals the more traditional influences of O'NEILL and STRINDBERG. Most of his work, including *Tiny Alice* (1965) and *A Delicate Balance* (1966; PULITZER PRIZE), deals with questions of illusion versus reality, possession versus communion, violence as an aspect of love, and domination versus submission. His characters tend to be desperate players in cruel psychological games: as manipulated as they are manipulating, as destructive as they are destroyed; when female, they are likely to be domineering emotional vampires. Albee made brilliant adaptations for the stage in *The Ballad of the Sad Café* (1963; from the novella by Carson McCULLERS), *Malcolm* (1966; from the novel by James PURDY), and *Everything in the Garden* (1967; from a play by Giles Cooper). He also produced a stage adaptation of NABOKOV's *Lolita* (1981). *All Over* (1971) and *Seascape* (1975; Pulitzer Prize) were Albee originals, the former hailed by critics as a profound masterpiece that developed earlier themes.

Alberich   In Scandinavian and German legend, the dwarf who guards the treasure of the Nibelungs, owners of a magic ring. Alberich plays a prominent part in both the *Völsunga Saga* and the *Nibelungenlied*. In Wagner's musical drama, *Der Ring des Nibelungen* (1876), Loki and Wotan steal the ring and treasure, and Alberich's curse follows the ring wherever it goes.

Albert, Prince (full name Albert Francis Charles Augustus Emmanuel of Saxe-Coburg-Gotha, 1819–1861) German husband of Queen VICTORIA and prince-consort of England, son of the Duke of Saxe-Coburg-Gotha. Through his tact and abiding interest in the arts and science, he overcame the initial distrust of the English people. It was largely through his work that the Great Exhibition of 1851 was successful. His death left the queen and the nation in deep mourning.

Alberti, Leon Battista (1402–1472)   Florentine writer, humanist, and architect. A veritable Renaissance man, Alberti wrote poetry, plays, moral and philosophical essays, and scientific inquiries. In addition, he dabbled in painting and practiced architecture. Among the structures built from his designs are the Rucellai Palace and Loggia, the facades of Santa Maria Novella in Florence and the church of San Francisco in Rimini. His treatise on architecture, *De re aedificatoria* (1452; pub 1485) had a considerable influence on the style of Renaissance architecture. Equally influential was his work on painting, *De pictura* (1435), the first work of its kind to consider both artistic theory and technique. In his discussion of sculpture, *De statua* (1464), he described a system based on human proportions which allows the correct placement of figures within a space. Among his literary works are a play written

in such perfect imitation of the Latin poets that Aldo Manutius thought it an original and his masterpiece, the treatise *Della famiglia* (*On the Family*, 1437–41), which uses the dialogue form to discuss his social philosophy and which presents a valuable portrait of life in his day.

Alberti, Rafael (1902–   )   Spanish poet and playwright. Born in Cádiz, Alberti began his artistic career as a cubist painter. His early volumes of verse, *Marinero en tierra* (1924), *La amante canciones* (1925), *El alba del alhelí* (1927), and *Cal y canto* (1927), exploit folkloric motifs. Thereafter associated with the GENERACIÓN DEL 27, he shifted to SURREALISM in his best-known work, SOBRE LOS ÁNGELES. During the 1930s, Alberti's work became increasingly political. The first major Spanish poet to embrace Communism, he became the poet of the workers and of revolution during the Spanish Civil War, as in *Entre el clavel y la espada* (1938). He immigrated to Argentina and spent three highly productive decades there, refusing to return to Spain while "enemies of the people" retained power. He finally ended his exile in 1977, after the death of Franco. In 1983 Alberti was awarded the Cervantes Prize, the Spanish-speaking world's highest literary accolade, for the body of his work.

Alberti is also known for his popular plays, *El hombre deshabitado* (1930), *El adefesio* (1944), and *Noche de guerra en el Museo del Prado* (1956). In his autobiographical collection of anecdotes and stories *La arboleda perída y otras prosas* (1942; tr *The Lost Grove: Portrait of a Spanish Poet in Exile*, 1976), Alberti gives a vivid picture of the generation of 1927, including García Lorca and Salvador Dali. Fifty poems from his *Poesias completas* are translated in *The Owl's Insomnia* (1973).

Albertine [Simonet]   The mistress of the narrator in Marcel Proust's REMEMBRANCE OF THINGS PAST. Albertine refuses him when they meet at Balbec but later comes to live with him in Paris, although secretly continuing to have affairs with other women. Tormented by his jealousy, she leaves him—only to be killed accidentally by being thrown from a horse.

Albertine disparue   See REMEMBRANCE OF THINGS PAST.

Albertus Magnus (1206?–1280)   German scholastic philosopher and churchman. His works include paraphrases of Aristotle's works, and he was very advanced for his day in his knowledge of experimental science. His teachings had great influence; Thomas AQUINAS was one of his students. He was canonized in 1932.

Albion   An ancient and poetical name for Great Britain. It is thought to have been so called from the white (Lat, *albus*) cliffs that face Gaul, but possibly from the Celtic *alp*, *ailp*, "rock; cliff; mountain." It was Napoleon who called England *Albion Perfide* (Perfidious Albion).

Alcaic verse   A Greek lyrical meter named for and purportedly invented by the lyric poet Alcaeus (fl c600 BC).

Because the syllabic pattern is virtually impossible to reproduce in English, the Alcaic measure is little more than a curiosity in English poetry. The pattern is usually one of a poem of four stanzas of four lines each, the first two lines composed of eleven syllables, the third of nine, and the fourth of ten. Probably the best example in English is from Tennyson's "Milton":

O migh/ty-mouthed / in/ventor of / harmonies,
O skilled / to sing / of / Time or E/ternity.
 God-gift/ed or/gan-voice / of Eng/land,
 Milton, a / name to re/sound for / ages.

alcalde de Zalamea, El (The Mayor of Zalamea, c1640)   A tragic drama by Pedro CALDERÓN DE LA BARCA. This play was originally written by Lope de Vega, but Calderón adapted it, giving to the realism of the former master a more profound and intellectual outlook. Among the characters created by Calderón is the hero, Pedro Crespo, a farmer who is elected *alcalde*, or mayor, of Zalamea.

Don Álvaro, an army captain quartered in Pedro's home, violates his host's daughter and refuses to marry her; he does not believe that he has to answer to commoners for his conduct. After Pedro has Don Álvaro jailed, Don Lope, the captain's superior officer, demands his freedom, and King Philip II, who has arrived in Zalamea, agrees that Pedro has exceeded his authority. However, when Pedro reveals that the captain has been strangled in prison, the king, forced to admit that justice has been done, makes Pedro perpetual mayor of the town. This play, like many of Lope's works, is a protest against the capricious and despotic feudal nobility and upholds the dignity of the middle class.

Alceste   The hero of Molière's comedy LE MISAN- THROPE. Alceste is disgusted with society. Courtesy seems to him the vice of fops, and the customary forms of civilized life no better than hypocrisy. He is in love with Celimène, a coquette who produces caustic "portraits" of her friends behind their backs and who embodies all the qualities with which he is most impatient.

Alcestis (438 BC)   The earliest extant play by EURIPI- DES. It tells the story of Alcestis, a daughter of Pelias and wife of Admetus, king of Pherae. In gratitude for past kindnesses, Apollo had promised that Admetus might escape death if someone would consent to die in his place. When the time came, Admetus' aged parents refused to do so, but Alcestis voluntarily descended to Hades, from which Heracles soon rescued her. The drunken, comic Heracles makes this a tragicomedy; it was originally presented in lieu of a SATYR PLAY. By implication, it called into question the Athenian attitude toward women. In Gluck's opera *Alceste* (1767), the heroine is saved by the intervention of Apollo.

Alchemist, The (1610)   A comedy by Ben JONSON. Subtle, a clever quack, and his whorish colleague, Doll Common, set up shop in the house of Lovewit while the latter is away. With the help of Lovewit's servant, Jeremy

or Face, the "alchemists" succeed in tricking a whole series of gullible scoundrels, such as Abel Drugger, who seeks charms and advice on how to set up his tobacco shop for maximum good fortune; Dapper, a gambler in need of a familiar spirit (whom he is forced to await while bound in a privy with a gingerbread gag in his mouth); two sanctimonious Puritan Brethren, Ananias and Tribulation Wholesome, who hope to extend their philanthropies and their power by means of alchemy; and, most important, Sir Epicure Mammon, a miser and lecher, who dreams of inordinate sensual pleasure. These and others, including Kastril, a young country fellow, who wishes to learn to quarrel like a gallant, are adroitly fleeced by Subtle and his colleagues, until the return of Lovewit, who cleverly routs the quacks and takes advantage of their various accumulated gains.

Alcibiades (c450–404 BC)   An Athenian general and politician. Arrogant and ambitious, Alcibiades called democracy "acknowledged folly." He was brilliant but dissolute and ostentatious, earning both the admiration and the disgust of his fellow citizens. Alcibiades' courage and ambition won him an appointment as general. When Segesta appealed to Athens for aid against Selinus, Alcibiades spoke in favor of the ill-omened expedition. Spurred on by his speech, the Athenians sent him at the head of a huge fleet (415 BC). Just before the sailing, he was implicated in a sacrilegious mockery of the Eleusinian mysteries. After the fleet had sailed, he was recalled for trial but escaped to Sparta. There, in revenge for the Athenians' confiscating his property and sentencing him to death, he traitorously informed the Spartans of Athens' weak defenses. Sparta successfully cut off Athens' control over the farmlands through Decelea. Finally, he was forced to flee Sparta because of the jealousy of their leaders. When the Athenian democracy was overthrown, he was welcomed back to his native city. There, on the eve of a battle with Sparta, he was distrusted again. He fled to Persia, where he was killed on Sparta's orders. Alcibiades' return to Athens is incidentally treated in Shakespeare's TIMON OF ATHENS; he also appears in Plato's dialogues the PHAEDO and the SYMPOSIUM and is caricatured in Aristophanes' THE CLOUDS.

Alcina   The sister of Morgana and a personification of sensual pleasure in the Orlando poems of Boiardo and Ariosto. In the latter's ORLANDO FURIOSO, she reigns, like Circe, over an island of oblivion filled with luring enchantments. She turns her lovers into trees, stones, and wild beasts after tiring of them. RUGGIERO, one of her victims, stays with her until rescued by Melissa, who also restores Astolfo after Alcina had turned him into a myrtle tree.

Alcmaeon   In Greek mythology, a son of Amphiaraus and Eriphyle. As children, Alcmaeon and his brother Amphilochus were enjoined by their father to avenge him on his wife for the treachery that drove him into the fatal war as one of THE SEVEN AGAINST THEBES. When Alcmaeon was grown, Eriphyle, bribed by Thersander, repeated her treachery, by sending Alcmaeon too into war with Thebes. He led the EPIGONI to victory and, on his return, killed his mother. Dying, she laid a curse on any land that would shelter him, and the ERINYES drove him mad.

Alcmaeon wandered through many lands. Phegeus, king of Psophis, married him to his daughter Arsinoe, and Alcmaeon gave her Harmonia's necklace, with which his mother had been bribed. Eriphyle's curse brought famine on the land, and Alcmaeon left Psophis. He wandered to the river Achelous. On its delta, which had not existed when the curse was laid, he was at last free from madness. The river god Achelous gave his daughter Callirrhoe to Alcmaeon.

She bore him two sons, Acarnan and Amphoteros, but soon demanded the necklace for herself. Alcmaeon returned to Psophis and tricked Phegeus into giving him the necklace. As he was leaving, the trick was discovered, and Alcmaeon was killed by Phegeus' sons. Callirrhoe, meanwhile, had been lending her favors to the amorous Zeus. At her request, he caused her sons by Alcmaeon to grow to manhood overnight. They killed Phegeus' sons and finally dedicated the necklace to Apollo at Delphi, where it was still shown in classical times.

Alcman   A celebrated Dorian lyric poet of Sparta. Alcman flourished in the first half of the 7th century BC.

Alcmena   In Greek mythology, the mother of HERACLES by Zeus. Alcmena's cuckolded husband was AMPHITRYON.

Alcofribas   The pseudonym assumed by François RABELAIS in Books I and II of his GARGANTUA AND PANTAGRUEL. Alcofribas Nasier is an anagram of François Rabelais. Books III, IV, and V were all signed "M. Fran. [or Francoys] Rabelais, Docteur en Médecine."

Alcott, [Amos] Bronson (1799–1888)   American philosopher, teacher, and poet. After a period as itinerant peddler, Alcott organized an unorthodox school whose advanced methods and racially mixed enrollment caused public indignation. For a time, he ran a cooperative experimental farm called Fruitlands. He then served as superintendent of schools in Concord, Massachusetts, but it was not until his daughter Louisa May ALCOTT succeeded as a writer that any measure of financial security was assured his family. In Concord he set up a school of philosophy with William T. Harris; together, they disseminated Alcott's benevolent philosophy. He published little but kept extensive journals; his most important published work includes *Tablets* (1868), *Observations on the Principles and Methods of Infant Instruction* (1830), and his contributions of *Orphic Sayings* (1840–44) to *The Dial*.

Alcott, Louisa May (1832–1888)   American novelist. Although Alcott had been determined from a young age to write, the family's circumstances made it necessary for her to work at menial jobs to help support the family.

Her father, Bronson ALCOTT, to whom the family was devoted, kept them poor with a succession of philanthropic and educational schemes. Alcott wrote her first publicly acknowledged book, *Flower Fables* (1848), when she was sixteen, but her first success was not until 1863, with *Hospital Sketches*, a volume based on letters she wrote for soldiers while an untrained nurse during the CIVIL WAR. Unknown to her family and public, Louisa had begun writing "rubbishy novels," sometimes anonymously, sometimes as "A. N. Barnard," to contribute to the family income. With great gusto she wrote, for *Frank Leslie's Illustrated Newspaper* and *Flag of Our Union*, gothic tales with such titles as "Pauline's Passion and Punishment," "The Abbot's Ghost: or Maurice Trahern's Temptations," and "Behind a Mask: or A Woman's Power." Fresh, vigorous, and very good reading, they include one romance, "Perilous Play," in which the hero and heroine are brought together at a hashish party. After the success of LITTLE WOMEN, however, Louisa May Alcott no longer needed "A. N. Barnard" to make money, and perhaps by then she had tired of her secret career. She concentrated on her semiautobiographical novels, which became classics for children. Among these later works is *Little Men* (1871), the sequel to *Little Women*.

Alcuin of York (735–804)   English scholar. Trained at the cathedral school of York, set up by one of the Venerable Bede's students, Alcuin was invited to France by Charlemagne to aid in the revival of learning and ecclesiastical reform. He established a school at the royal court and another at Tours, thus helping to return to the Continent the Christian learning and culture that had been preserved mainly in the English monasteries.

Alden, John   See COURTSHIP OF MILES STANDISH, THE.

Aldington, Richard (1892–1962)   English poet, novelist, biographer, and translator. At one time married to the American poet Hilda DOOLITTLE, Aldington was a member of the group that introduced IMAGISM. He was among those who, after World War I, found England barren and sterile. His collection of poems *Images of War* (1919) expresses his disgust with the war itself; *Soft Answers* (1932) is a collection of savage satires. His chief novels are *Death of a Hero* (1929) and *All Men Are Enemies* (1933). His best-known biographies are *D. H. Lawrence: Portrait of a Genius, But . . .* (1950) and *Lawrence of Arabia* (1955). *Life for Life's Sake* (1941) is an autobiography.

Aldiss, Brian W[ilson] (1925–   )   English author, anthologist, and critic, primarily involved with SCIENCE FICTION. After writing such superior but essentially conventional science fiction as *Non-Stop* (1958; U.S., *Starship*) and *Hothouse* (1962; U.S., *The Long Afternoon of Earth*), Aldiss became a leading member of the British "New Wave," a movement (associated with the magazine *New Worlds*) concerned with combining science fiction and literary experimentation. Thus, *Report on Probability A* (1968) makes use of NOUVEAU ROMAN techniques, while the language of *Barefoot in the Head* (1969) owes much to FINNEGANS WAKE. His bawdy, fictionalized autobiography, the "Horatio Stubbs" series, which includes *The Hand-Reared Boy* (1970) and *A Soldier Erect* (1971), shares with his science fiction a humor combined with a serious concern with change. Aldiss's critical work is best represented by his history of science fiction, *Billion Year Spree* (1973). Among his many other works are *Frankenstein Unbound* (1973), *Enemies of the System* (1978), and *A Rude Awakening* (1979), along with numerous anthologies and story collections. *An Island Called Moreau* (1981) is his own adaptation of H. G. WELLS's *The Island of Dr. Moreau* (1896).

Aldrich, Thomas Bailey (1836–1907) American poet, editor, novelist, and playwright. Aldrich first received widespread attention with the publication of his poem "The Ballad of Babie Bell" in the collection *The Bells* (1855). After a career as a journalist and a war correspondent, he became editor of the *Atlantic Monthly* (1881–1900), in which he first published many of his famous stories, including "Marjorie Daw" (1873). Other popular works include the detective story *The Stillwater Tragedy* (1880) and Aldrich's best-known novel, THE STORY OF A BAD BOY, based on his own childhood in New Hampshire.

Alecto In classic myth, one of the ERINYES (Furies).

Alegría, Ciro (1909–1966) Peruvian novelist. Frequently at odds with the repressive measures of his government, Alegría lived in exile in Chile from the age of twenty-five. All his major works deal with the lives of Peruvian Indians, although, rather than drawing individual heroes, he deals with entire Indian communities, creating a kind of aggregate protagonist. In his first two novels, *La serpente de oro* (1935; tr *The Golden Serpent*, 1963) and *Los perros hambrientos* (1936), set on the river Marañón and in the high Andes, respectively, he describes the hard-fought struggle for survival against the massive forces of nature. In his best-known novel, *El mundo es ancho y ajeno* (1941; tr *Broad and Alien Is the World*, 1941), the white man, not nature, is the adversary, as an entire Indian community in northern Peru is displaced by the scheming of a greedy landowner. His other novels include *Duello de caballeros* (1963) and *Lázaro* (1973). An edition of his *Novelas completas* was published in 1964.

Aleichem, Shalom (pen name of Solomon J. Rabinowitz, 1859–1916) Russian-born Yiddish humorist. For some years a rabbi, Shalom Aleichem escaped the 1905 pogrom in Russia and later immigrated to the U.S. His stories of Jewish life in the Eastern European *shtetl* ("village") and in America, noted for their humor and pathos, reveal a full gallery of Jewish types and helped to establish Yiddish as a literary language. The play *Fiddler on the Roof*, based on his stories about Tevye the milkman,

brought him worldwide recognition. His works that have been translated into English appear in such collections as *Shalom Aleichem Panorama* (1948), *Adventures of Mottel the Cantor's Son* (1953), *Stories and Satires* (1959), *Collected Stories of Shalom Aleichem* (1965), and *The Best of Shalom Aleichem* (1979). Shalom Aleichem often played a comic role in his own stories. His pen name, a familiar Yiddish greeting derived from the Hebrew, means "peace be with you."

Aleixandre [y Merlo], Vicente (1898–1984) Spanish poet, born in Seville. Aleixandre spent his childhood in Málaga, the inspiration of many of his poems, and his youth in Madrid, where he began the study of law and economics. A chance encounter with Dámaso ALONSO stimulated his poetic bent. Early works were written under the influence of DARÍO, Antonio MACHADO, and Juan Ramón JIMÉNEZ. Withdrawn and in delicate health, he wrote secretly until his first poems were published by friends in the *Revista de Occidente* (1926). He won the Premio Nacional de Literatura in 1933 and election to the Royal Academy of the Language in 1950.

Like others of the GENERACIÓN DEL 27 in Spain, Aleixandre went through a surrealist period (in the 1930s), and, during the years after World War II, he drew close to the social poets. An emphasis on the linking of strange metaphors, a preference for FREE VERSE, and great technical skill are the principal characteristics of his collected poems from the "pure poetry" in *Ámbito* (1928), the surrealist *Espadas como labios* (1932), and *Pasión de la tierra* (1935). *La destrucción o el amor* (1935) is one of his most influential works, together with *Sombra del paraíso* (1944), wherein the poet evokes a tropical, childhood world of innocence and love. *En un vasto dominio* (1962) and *Diálogos del concimiento* (1975) reveal his capacity for continued growth and experimentation at an advanced age. Aleixandre, who exerted a profound influence after World War II on lyricists in Spain, was awarded the NOBEL PRIZE in Literature in 1977. After that, several collections of his poetry appeared in English, including *Twenty Poems* (1977) and *A Longing for the Light* (1979).

Alemán, Mateo (1547–after 1613) Spanish novelist. The son of a prison doctor, Alemán studied in Seville, Salamanca, and Alcalá and spent some twenty years as a government accountant. He was twice imprisoned for debt. In 1608 he went to Mexico in the company of Archbishop García Guerra, whose life he published in 1613.

Alemán is remembered chiefly as the author of GUZMÁN DE ALFARACHE, the second great picaresque novel, after *Lazarillo de Tormes* (1554). The first part appeared in 1599, and, after Juan José Martí, a Valencian lawyer, produced a spurious sequel (1602), Alemán himself wrote a continuation (1604), in which he good-naturedly lampooned Martí. Alemán also wrote a biography of Saint

Anthony of Padua (1604) and *Ortografía castellana* (1609), a treatise on spelling.

Alencar, José Martiniano de (1829–1877)   Brazilian novelist. Probably Brazil's finest romantic novelist, Alencar is known for his idealized portraits of Indians and for his deep feeling for the Brazilian landscape. His most popular novels are *O Guarani* (1857) and *Iracema* (1865; tr *Iracema, The Honey Lips: A Legend of Brazil*, 1886), both of which deal with love between Indian and white.

Aleshkovsky, Yuz (1929–   )   Soviet novelist, short-story writer, and songwriter. Aleshkovsky was born in Siberia of working-class parents but spent most of his life in Moscow until he immigrated to the United States in 1978. Largely self-educated, he earned his living at a variety of jobs, including driving a truck, eventually discovering in himself a talent for writing songs and children's stories. Almost none of his work was published legally in the Soviet Union, however; his first novel to be translated into English, *Kangaroo* (tr 1986), a wild, slangy, scatological satire, was written "for the desk drawer" in 1974. He has written several other novels and short stories, of which some have been translated into English and collected under the title *Nikolai Nikolaevich* (1980).

Alexander VI, Pope   See BORGIA.

Alexander the Great (Alexander III of Macedon, 356–323 BC)   The son of Philip of Macedon, and conqueror of the civilized world. Alexander was appointed to his father's position as leader of the Greek confederation. He did away with his rivals to the throne, razing Thebes. He then began the invasion and conquest of Asia and defeated Darius III, king of Persia. He marched through Syria, Egypt, Babylon, Susa, and Persepolis, founding the city of Alexandria in 331 BC. Adopting the oriental customs of his captives, Alexander married a series of eastern princesses. On their way through India, his exhausted troops rebelled, and Alexander was forced to begin the return to Macedon. He fell ill of a fever and died after three days' illness, at the age of thirty-three. Alexander achieved the extension of Greek civilization into the East. His reign ushered in the Hellenistic Age. See BUCEPHALUS.

Admired for his courage and frequent generous and humane acts, Alexander figures in many English and French medieval romances. French heroic verse of six feet became known as the ALEXANDRINE. Alexander's life is the subject of a tragedy by Racine, *Alexandre le Grand* (1665), and of Lyly's *Alexander and Campaspe* (1581).

Alexandrian Library   The most famous library of antiquity. Located in Alexandria, it was the principal center of Hellenistic culture under the Ptolemies, and contained hundreds of thousands of rolls. Among its earliest librarians were Callimachus and Apollonius of Rhodes. In his *Caesar and Cleopatra* (1899), G. B. Shaw treats humorously the burning of the library by Julius Caesar. It was burned and partly consumed in 391; in 642, according

to a dubious legend, the caliph Omar seized the city and used the library's books to "heat the baths of the city for six months." It is said that it contained 700,000 volumes, and the reason given by the Muslim destroyer for the destruction of the library was that the books were unnecessary in any case, for all knowledge that was necessary to man was contained in the Koran, and any knowledge contained in the library that was not in the Koran must be pernicious. Most modern experts, however, agree that the story of the library's destruction by Omar is probably apocryphal. See ARISTARCHUS.

Alexandria Quartet, The   Four novels by Lawrence DURRELL: *Justine* (1957), *Balthazar* (1958), *Mountolive* (1958), and *Clea* (1960). The complex plot is made more complex by Durrell's attempt "to complete a four-decker novel whose form is based on the relativity proposition." Each novel presents a different point of view and different truths about the same characters. Diaries and letters and novels-within-novels give still other views. *Justine* is about the love affair between the narrator, Darley, and the fascinating, enigmatic Justine. In *Balthazar*, Darley learns through Balthazar, a mutual friend, that Justine really loved his successful rival author, Pursewarden. Her apparently serene marriage to Nessim was really a cover for their illegal political activities—gun-running into British-held Palestine. *Mountolive* is a third-person novel (the "time" element in the relativity scheme) about a British diplomat in love with Nessim's mother but obliged to discover who is organizing the gun-running. *Clea*, narrated again by Darley, brings the threads of the story together and ends in an idyllic love between him and the serene painter Clea.

Brilliant exotic and melodramatic episodes and a flamboyant poetical style enrich the works. Among the vivid characters are Melissa, a sad, lost night-club dancer; Narouz, a primitive, silent man who suddenly becomes a religious prophet; and Scobie, a comical old English homosexual. Durrell calls *The Quartet* "a big city poem." It is a wonderful evocation of Alexandria, an exotic and sordid city haunted by figures from its past, from the ancient alchemists to Antony and Cleopatra. *The Quartet* is also an investigation of modern love and a study of the growth of an artist.

Alexandrine   In prosody, a line of six iambic feet (iambic hexameter). The Alexandrine is the standard French heroic line, just as iambic pentameter is the standard line for English heroic verse. The name is thought to derive from *Li Romans d'Alexandre*, a 12th-century French romance written in that measure, relating the deeds of Alexander of Macedon (ALEXANDER THE GREAT). The Alexandrine was introduced in England by Michael Drayton and others in the 16th century but never took root as a dominant measure in English poetry, perhaps because English, being an uninflected language, requires fewer syllables than French to express its meaning. However, the Alexandrine is used singly as the final line of the Spenserian stanza, where it affords a contrast to the predominant iambic pentameter.

Alfieri, Vittorio (1749–1803)   Italian dramatist and poet. Alfieri wrote nineteen tragedies (1775–87) scrupulously observant of the classical unities and typified by a portrayal of the protagonist's struggle against moral and political tyranny. Among his dramas are *Cleopatra*; *Filippo*, whose protagonist is Philip II of Spain; *Antigone*; *Agamennone*; *Oreste*; *Virginia*; *Saul*; *Mirra*; and *Bruto primo*, dedicated to George Washington, "the liberator of America" (1787). He also wrote sonnets and odes, five of which are grouped under the title *L'America libera* (1781–83), to celebrate the newly acquired independence of the U.S. In his lengthy and exciting *Vita* (*Autobiography*, 1804), he analyzed and exalted himself as a poet dedicated to the extirpation of all forms of political and intellectual bondage. His hatred of tyranny and love of freedom helped to revive the national spirit of Italy.

Alfonso X (known as El Sabio, "The Sage" or "The Learned"; 1221–1284)   King of Castile and Leon (1252–84), scholar, and poet. Alfonso is generally regarded as a political failure, his reign being marred by his futile attempts to capture the imperial crown and by a disastrous conflict with his second son, later Sancho IV. His true fame rests on his activities as a patron of art and learning. Scholars flocked to his court, where, under his direction, they translated Arabic and Latin writings, copied manuscripts, and compiled historical, scientific, and legal works. Under his guidance, Castilian laws and customs were codified in *Las siete partidas*, begun about 1256, which presents a minute and accurate picture of 13th-century society. He was also responsible for the compilation of the *Primera crónica general* or *Estoria de España*, a history of Spain from the deluge through the reign of Ferdinand III, Alfonso's father. Begun in 1270 and completed during the reign of Sancho IV, it is drawn from biblical, classical, and Arabic sources, as well as from Spanish chronicles and epics, such as the *Poema de mio Cid*. Many scholarly and literary works are also ascribed to Alfonso's authorship, notably the charming *Cantigas de Santa María*, over four hundred poems in Galician in honor of the Virgin.

Alfred (called Alfred the Great, c849–c900)   King of Wessex in England (871–900). Alfred began fighting against the Danes in 866 under his brother Aethelred, completing his first series of battles the year of his accession to the throne. He repulsed further attacks in 878 and between 893 and 897, when the Danes were defeated and retreated toward the north or into France.

Aside from his military successes, which made possible his successors' reconquest and unification of the rest of England, Alfred is known for the excellence of his domestic rule. He codified the laws and established a court school

with scholars from abroad to promote the education of his people. He began a great translation project, determined to make available in Old English vernacular prose all the books he considered important, which then existed only in Latin. He himself translated Pope Gregory I's *Pastoral Care*, the world history by the 5th-century historian and theologian Paulus Orosius, and THE CONSOLATION OF PHILOSOPHY by Boethius. His *Blostman* ("blossoms," i.e. "anthology") is largely culled from the *Soliloquies* of St. Augustine of Hippo. He had other scholars translate Gregory's *Dialogues* and Bede's *Ecclesiastical History of the English People* and undertake the writing of the ANGLO-SAXON CHRONICLE.

Alger, Horatio, Jr. (1832–1899)   American writer of books for boys. The oldest child of a Unitarian minister, Alger attended Harvard College and Harvard Divinity School but fled to Paris as a rebellious bohemian. He was finally persuaded to return to the U.S. and became a minister. In 1866 he was made chaplain of a Newsboys' Lodging House, to which he devoted his time, money, and affection for the rest of his life.

Although Alger wished to write novels for adults, he actually turned out about 120 books for boys. Among the most popular were the *Ragged Dick Series* (1867), the *Luck and Pluck Series* (1869), and the *Tattered Tom Series* (1871). The heroes were bootblacks or newsboys whose virtue was invariably rewarded with success. Alger also wrote juvenile biographies of famous men. Because of the subject matter of his books, Alger's name became identified with the American ideal of rising from poverty to success through self-reliance and hard work.

Algonquin Round Table   See WOOLLCOTT, ALEXANDER.

Algren, Nelson (1909–1981)   American novelist and short-story writer. Along with James T. FARRELL and Richard WRIGHT, Algren wrote brutally realistic novels about life in the Chicago slums. *Somebody in Boots* (1935), *Never Come Morning* (1942), THE MAN WITH THE GOLDEN ARM, A *Walk on the Wild Side* (1956), and the stories in *The Neon Wilderness* (1947) offer no-frills glimpses of the human casualties of urban poverty. He also wrote accounts of his travels in *Who Lost an American?* (1963), *Notes from a Sea Diary* (1965), and *The Last Carousel* (1973), a collection of short fiction and reminiscences from 1942 to 1972. His well-known affair with Simone de BEAUVOIR was fictionalized by her in *The Mandarins* (1956).

Alhambra (fr Arab, *kal'-at al hamra*, "the red castle")   A citadel and palace at Granada, Spain, built by Moorish kings in the 13th century. The buildings stand on a plateau some thirty-five acres in area and are surrounded by a reddish brick wall. Considered one of the finest examples of Moorish architecture in Spain, the palace consists largely of two rectangular courts, the Court of the Pool or of the Myrtles and the Court of the Lions, and their adjoining chambers. The latter court contains a famous central fountain, consisting of an alabaster basin supported by twelve lions of white marble. While he was an attaché at the American legation in Madrid, Washington Irving spent much time in the Alhambra and wrote a well-known volume of sketches and tales called *Legends of the Alhambra* (1832, 1852).

Ali Baba and the Forty Thieves One of the most popular stories in THE ARABIAN NIGHTS' ENTERTAINMENTS. Hidden in a tree, the poor woodcutter Ali Baba sees a band of robbers enter a secret cave by saying the magic words "Open Sesame." When they leave, he repeats the spell, gains access to the treasure, and becomes rich by carrying off gold from the stolen hoards. His brother, Cassim, also discovers the secret but forgets the word "Sesame" and cries "Open, Wheat! Open, Barley!" to the door; he is killed by the thieves, who find him trapped within the cave. Their captain tries several schemes to catch Ali Baba, but is always outwitted by the woodcutter's female slave, Morgiana, who kills the whole band by pouring boiling oil into the jars where they have hidden themselves.

Alice Adams (1921) A novel by Booth TARKINGTON. It describes the disintegration of the middle-class Adams family in a small Midwestern town. The father, a minor employee in a drug company, has a nagging, ambitious wife and a shiftless son. Alice, his daughter, yearning for wealth and admiration and seeing herself always in a romantic role, almost deceives herself into believing that her fanciful explanations for the crudities of her family are valid. At the end of the book, her hopes doomed, she is seen bravely entering the stairway that leads to Frincke's Business College.

Alice's Adventures in Wonderland (1865) A whimsical story by Lewis CARROLL. The little girl Alice falls down a well into a strange country where everything happens with a fantastic illogicality. She finds that she can become a giantess or a pygmy by nibbling alternate sides of a magic mushroom, and she has a series of remarkable adventures with the WHITE RABBIT, the CHESHIRE CAT, the MOCK TURTLE, the QUEEN OF HEARTS, the HATTER, the MARCH HARE, the DUCHESS, the DORMOUSE, and other strange characters. See FATHER WILLIAM; THROUGH THE LOOKING GLASS.

alienation effect (Ger, V*erfremdungseffekt*) An aspect of Bertolt BRECHT's dramatic theory. Dramatic techniques of contrast and contradiction are used to destroy the illusory nature of theatre and to instill in both actors and audience an awareness of the distinction between fantasy and reality. By causing the spectator to detach himself from the dramatic action rather than identifying with it, Brecht hoped that a play would become a vehicle for enlightening the public to new discoveries about their socio-political surroundings. The concept is central to Brecht's idea of EPIC THEATRE.

Allah (fr Arab, *el illah*, "the god"; or Aram, *Alaha*, "God") The Muslim designation for the one God. MUHAMMED's enunciation of his monotheism in effect raised the word from lower to uppercase, i.e., from "god" to "God." The attributes of Allah are contained in the "ninety-nine beautiful names" by which he is described in the KORAN.

allegory In literature, an extended METAPHOR in which characters, objects, incidents, and descriptions carry one or more sets of fully developed meanings in addition to the apparent and literal ones. John Bunyan's *Pilgrim's Progress* (1678–84), for example, is apparently about a man named Christian who leaves his home and journeys to the Heavenly City. However, it is clear that Christian stands for any Christian man and that the incidents of his journey represent the temptations and trials that beset any Christian man throughout his life on earth.

Allegory has been a favorite form all over the world and was particularly strong in Europe during the Middle Ages. Spenser's *Faerie Queene* (1590–96), though late, is perhaps the best-known example.

In art, especially of the Middle Ages, allegory was also a favorite device; in particular, it was used to depict good and evil engaged in symbolic action. See PERSONIFICATION.

Allegro, L' (1632) A poem by John MILTON, the title of which means literally the cheerful or merry one. It is a pastoral idyll, celebrating a mood of gaiety and contrasting with the author's IL PENSEROSO. The poem, like its companion piece, is written in Milton's early style, characterized by an Elizabethan freshness and vividness and a remarkable command of verbal music.

Allen, Ethan (1738–1789) American Revolutionary soldier and hero of early Vermont. He commanded the Green Mountain Boys, a regiment originally raised by some Vermont settlers to fight a claim on their land by Governor Tryon of New York. With eighty-three of the Green Mountain Boys and aided by Benedict Arnold, Allen seized Fort Ticonderoga in 1775. His own *Narrative of Captain Ethan Allen's Captivity* (1779) tells of his capture by the British after a rash attempt to take Montreal. He is the hero of Daniel Pierce Thompson's novel *Green Mountain Boys* (1839).

Allen, [William] Hervey (1889–1949) American historical novelist. He is best known for his first novel, the long and phenomenally successful *Anthony Adverse* (1933). Allen began his career with several volumes of verse and also wrote *Israfel* (1926), a biography of Edgar Allan Poe.

Allen, Woody (pseudonym of Allen Stewart Konigsberg, 1935–   ) American film director, writer, and actor. Allen began as a comedy writer and stand-up comedian and drew most of his material from events or fantasies in his own life, finding a rich vein of humor in his own insecurities. In his comedy routines and in many of his films, he depicts himself as the prototypical modern man, who lives in a perpetual state of anxiety, haunted by women, the certainty of death, self-loathing, and the guilt-ridden vestiges of inherited religion. His early films—*Take the Money and Run* (1969), *Bananas* (1970), *Everything You Always Wanted to Know about Sex but Were Afraid to Ask* (1972)—which he cowrote, directed, and starred in, were all unabashed attempts at making people laugh. The immensely successful *Annie Hall* (1977), a poignant, directly autobiographical film about a failed love affair that won the 1977 Academy Awards for best director and best original screenplay, the National Society of Film Critics award, and the New York Film Critics Circle award, indicated the more serious paths his filmmaking was to take in the future. *Interiors* (1978) was an unremittingly serious psychological drama in the mold of Ingmar Bergman; this was followed by *Manhattan* (1979), a loving and romantic portrait of his native city; *Stardust Memories* (1980); *A Midsummer Night's Sex Comedy* (1982); *Zelig* (1983); *Broadway Danny Rose* (1984); *The Purple Rose of Cairo* (1985); and *Radio Days* (1987). Perhaps his most successful film is *Hannah and Her Sisters* (1986), at once a contemporary perspective on the family and a poetical evocation of New York City, a city that in the film loses much of its harshness under the softer, kinder light of its beautiful old buildings and graceful architectural forms.

Allen has also written plays: *Don't Drink the Water* (1966), *Play It Again, Sam* (1969; filmed 1972), and *The Floating Lightbulb* (1981), all produced on Broadway. Allen's ironic and colorful stories and short pieces, many of which first appeared in THE NEW YORKER, were collected in *Getting Even* (1971), *Without Feathers* (1976), and *Side Effects* (1980).

All for Love, or The World Well Lost (1678) A tragedy in blank verse by John DRYDEN. In strict observance of the classical unities, Dryden describes the last day on earth of Antony and Cleopatra. Simpler in plot though less stirring than Shakespeare's version of the famous story, Dryden's play focuses on the conflict between Cleopatra, on the one hand, and Antony's wife, Octavia, his general Ventidius, and his friend Dolabella, on the other, as they vie for possession of Antony's soul.

All God's Chillun Got Wings (1924) A play by Eugene O'NEILL. White Ella Downey marries black Jim Harris, who is struggling to become a lawyer. The tragic consequences of her mental inferiority are intensified by the latent racial prejudice she shows in a desperate effort to gain superiority, before lapsing into insanity and a regression to childhood.

All Hallows' Day See ALL SAINTS' DAY.
All Hallows' Eve See HALLOWE'EN.
alliteration In poetry and prose, the repetition of sounds or syllables, especially initial consonants, as in the sentence "Peter Piper picked a peck of pickled peppers."

Like ASSONANCE and CONSONANCE, alliteration tends to unify the passage or poem in which it occurs and in that function may be considered a form of RHYME. See ALLITERATIVE VERSE.

Alliterative Morte d'Arthur, The See ARTHURIAN LEGEND.

alliterative verse A form of versification originating in Old Germanic poetry. In OLD ENGLISH (or Anglo-Saxon) poetry, each long line is divided into two short lines by a pause, or CAESURA. Each short line contains one or two stressed syllables or words. The first stressed word in the second half-line indicates the alliteration. The second stressed word of that line usually does not alliterate, as the following example from BEOWULF illustrates:

Thaer maeg níchta géhwaem   níht wundor séon
fýr on flóde.   No thaes fród léofath
gúmena beárna   that thóne gránd wíte

                                        (lines 1365–67)

or, as translated by Meno Spann:

There each night   awful wonder is seen
Fire on flood   There's no wise one I fear
Born by a woman   that the bottom would know.

There may be three or four alliterating words in the long line. The number of unaccented words is not fixed.

This verse was used in the heroic LAIS recited by minstrels, as well as in proverbs, magic spells, riddles, and the like. The use of this unrhymed alliterative meter continued after the Teutons were converted to Christianity. It was revived in the 14th century, in such works as PIERS PLOWMAN and SIR GAWAIN AND THE GREEN KNIGHT. Among the appearances of this form in the 19th and 20th centuries, the most widely known is Wagner's *Der Ring des Nibelungen* (1876).

All Quiet on the Western Front (Im Westen nichts Neues, 1929) A novel by Erich Maria REMARQUE. It is the best known of the antiwar literature written during the period 1920–39, expressing the horror and futility of war.

All Saints' Day (or All Hallows) A feast in honor of all Christian saints. Between 603 and 610 Pope Boniface IV changed the heathen temple called the Pantheon into a Christian church and dedicated it to the honor of all the martyrs. The feast was first observed on May 1, but in 834 it was changed to November 1, and its use extended to the whole Christian Church. It is a major feast of the Church.

The medieval English name *All Hallows* is derived from *halig*, Old English for "holy" (man), hence, a saint. In France the day is called *Toussaint*. Much folklore and superstition are associated with the eve of the day, called HALLOWE'EN.

All Souls' Day The popular name for the Commemoration of All the Faithful Departed. It is observed by the Roman Catholic Church on November 2. It was instituted by Abbot Odilo of Cluny in 993 and soon spread to the rest of the Western Church. In many parts of Europe, it is the custom to place lighted candles on graves of friends and family the previous evening.

All's Well That Ends Well (c1602)   A comedy by William SHAKESPEARE. After curing the king of France of a malady, Helena, the daughter of a famous physician, is rewarded by the king's giving her in marriage to Bertram, the young count of Rousillon, whom she has long loved. He, however, scorns her and departs for the Florentine war, stating that until Helena obtains the ring on his finger and produces his child, he will not return nor can she call him husband. Disguised as a pilgrim, Helena follows Bertram to Florence, where she discovers that he is enamored of a young Florentine girl. She arranges an assignation and takes the girl's place, obtaining the ring and conceiving the child. Hearing false reports of Helena's death, Bertram returns to France. When she suddenly appears, having fulfilled his terms, she at last wins his love.

The plot, taken from Boccaccio's *Decameron*, was a familiar folk legend reworked by Shakespeare. See PAROL-LES.

All the King's Men (1946)   A novel by Robert Penn WARREN. Jack Burden, a young intellectual, narrates the story of the rise and fall of Willie Stark, a Southern demagogue obviously modeled on the Louisiana politician Huey Long. Burden is forced to confront the problem of good and evil in Stark's career and, at the end of the book, is led to a new self-understanding. The novel won a PULITZER PRIZE in 1947. A film based on the novel was made in 1950; it was adapted for the stage in 1960.

almanac   A book or pamphlet containing an assortment of information. Almanacs originated in the 15th century and initially consisted of astrological or astronomical charts, used primarily to predict weather. By the 18th century, the almanac had become a popular form of reading matter and included humorous sayings, maxims, helpful advice, and even poems and short fiction. Early American almanacs, such as Benjamin Franklin's POOR RICHARD'S ALMANACK, were handbooks of agriculture, meteorology, morality, and humor; an extant example of the form is *The Old Farmer's Almanack*, first published by Robert Bailey Thomas in 1793. Other modern almanacs, such as *The World Almanac*, have dispensed with humor and forecasts and offer exhaustive compendia of statistical and historical information.

Almanach de Gotha   A European social register. A German periodical publication begun in 1763, it gives data on all royal or titled European families.

alpha and omega   The first and last letters of the Greek alphabet; hence, the beginning and the end. In the Bible, Jesus says, "I am Alpha and Omega, the beginning and the end, the first and the last" (Rev. 22:13).

Alsop, Joseph [Wright] (1910–   ) and **Stewart [Johonnot Oliver]** (1914–1974)   American journalists. From 1945 to 1958, the two brothers wrote the informative and opinionated syndicated column "Matter of Fact." In 1958, when Stewart became an editor for the *Saturday Evening Post*, Joseph continued the column alone. Stewart then wrote a bimonthly column for *Newsweek* until his death. His battles with the rare blood disease that eventually took his life are stirringly described in his book *Stay of Execution* (1973). The brothers are the authors, individually and jointly, of several books, chiefly in the field of current history.

Altamirano, Ignacio Manuel (1834–1893)   Mexican novelist and poet. A full-blooded Indian, Altamirano was an adherent of Benito Juárez and fought against the French intervention in Mexico. In 1869 he founded *Renacimiento*, a review to encourage literary activity, almost moribund after fifteen years of turbulence. He became the mentor of the younger generation, to whom he advocated the importance of creating a literature rooted in national life. His poetry consists of a single volume of *Rimas* (1880), written before 1867 and notable for its description of the Mexican landscape. Altamirano's preoccupation with purely Mexican scenes and customs is also evident in the prose works for which he is best known: *Clemencia* (1869), a love story set against the background of the French intervention; *La navidad en las montañas* (1870), a novelette; and *El Zarco* (1901), a novel dealing with bandits in the state of Morelos.

Altolaquirre, Manuel (1905–1959)   Spanish poet. Altolaquirre was peripherally associated with the GENERACIÓN DEL 27, and, like some of the poets in that group, he drew on traditional folk motifs for much of his early poetry: *Las islas invitades* (1926), *Ejemplo* (1927), *Un día* (1931), and *Amor* (1931). After his participation on the Republican side of the Spanish Civil War, he lived as an exile, mostly in Mexico. There he wrote such volumes as *Nube temporal* (1939), *Fin de amor* (1949), and *Poemas en América* (1955), which treated themes of love and isolation. He was killed in a car crash on a visit to Spain in 1959. His *Poesías completas* appeared in 1960.

Aluko, Timothy Mofolorunso (1918–   )   Nigerian novelist. Aluko's novels—*One Man, One Wife* (1959), *One Man, One Matchet* (1964), *Kinsman and Foreman* (1966), *Chief the Honorable Minister* (1970), and *His Worshipful Majesty* (1973)—deal with conflicts of ideals and values in African families, villages, and political situations. He uses folk materials in a documentary fashion to draw affectionate, lightly ironic portraits of his countrymen.

Alvarez, A[lfred] (1929–   )   English critic, poet, and novelist. Alvarez is known for his personal approach to criticism, for a lively, readable style, and for his particular interest in poets who wrote under severe emotional strain, such as Sylvia PLATH, John BERRYMAN, and Robert LOWELL. His works of criticism include *The Shaping Spirit* (1958; U.S., *Stewards of Excellence*), *The School of Donne* (1962), and *Beyond All This Fiddle* (1969). *The New Poetry* (1962; rev 1966) was an influential anthology of post-World War II poetry. *The Savage God* (1971), one of his best-known books, is a subjective study of suicide and its relationship to literature. His own poetry includes *Lost* (1968) and *Apparition* (1971). *Hers* (1975) and *Hunt* (1979) are novels. Recent works include the nonfiction *Life After Marriage* (1982), about divorce, and *The Biggest Game in Town* (1983), about gambling, and *Offshore* (1986), a book about life in the North Sea oilfields.

Amadi, Elechi (1934–   )   Nigerian novelist. Amadi's work is pervaded by a genuine respect for the dignity of individuals. His novels *The Concubine* (1966) and *The Great Ponds* (1969) describe a primitive society little touched by modern pressures and ruled by supernatural forces, where feuds between villages upset the delicate political structures, but where, in the end, good sense and humanity prevail. He also wrote an autobiographical memoir of the Nigerian civil war, *Sunset in Biafra* (1973).

Amadís de Gaula (Amadis of Gaul, 16th century) Spanish romance of chivalry. The first extant version (1508), consisting of four books, was compiled by Garci Rodriquez de Montalvo, also known as Garci Gutiérrez Ordóñez de Montalvo (fl 1500). Montalvo stated that he merely edited and revised the original text; however, it is known that the fourth book is his own addition. The origin of the story remains obscure, though it appeared in both Spain and Portugal as early as the 14th century.

The romance incorporates many details from the BRETON LAIS of ARTHURIAN LEGEND. Amadís, who exemplifies the chivalric ideals of valor, purity, and fidelity, is the illegitimate son of Perión, king of Gaul (Wales), and Elisena, princess of Brittany. Soon after birth, he is abandoned by his mother, who puts his cradle in the sea; for this reason, he is also known as *el Doncel del Mar*, "Child of the Sea." He is rescued by the knight Gandalés and is educated in the court of the king of Scotland, where at the age of twelve he falls in love with Oriana, daughter of Lisuarte, king of England. Amadís then performs a series of incredible exploits, triumphing over sundry giants and monsters, always remaining faithful to his lady-love. Other notable characters include Galaor, Amadís's brother; his cousin, Agrajes; the Fairy Urganda, *la Desconocida*, "the Unknown"; and Archelaüs, a mischievous enchanter.

The work won enormous popularity throughout Europe and inspired numerous imitations and sequels, including Montalvo's own, *Las sergas de Esplandian* (1510), about the son of Amadís. The barber and priest in Cervantes's DON QUIXOTE called it "the best of all the books of its kind," a verdict with which later generations concurred.

Amado, Jorge (1912–   )   Brazilian novelist. Amado is a prolific writer, whose more than twenty novels have been translated into over thirty languages. His early writing, as can be seen in novels like *O paiz do carnaval* (*Carnival Land*, 1932), *Cacau* (1933), *Jubiaba* (1935), *Mar morto* (1936), and *Capitaes de areia* (1937), centers on the lives of the poor and attacks the injustices in Brazilian society. In the novels written in the 1950s and 1960s, such as GABRIELA, CLOVE AND CINNAMON, *Doña Flor e seus dois maridos* (1966; tr *Dona Flor and Her Two Husbands*, 1969), and *Tieta do agreste* (1979), Amado's heroines typically are young women who have transcended the debilitating circumstances of their poverty-stricken backgrounds and grown into self-sufficient and strong adults. *Doña Flor e seus dois maridos* was made into a successful film in 1980. Amado's writing remains unique for its ability to convey both the degrading circumstances of poverty and its perception of the joy and beauty of life. The vibrant sounds, colors, and particular rhythms of his native land are effectively conveyed in his novels.

In 1984 Amado was made a member of France's Legion of Honor.

Amalrik, Andrei [Alekseyvich] (1938–1980) Soviet essayist, historian, and dramatist. Amalrik began a lifelong struggle with the Soviet system as a student at Moscow University, from which he was expelled in 1963 when his diploma dissertation offended the authorities with its conclusion that Norse traders had significantly influenced early Russian civilization. Between 1962 and 1963 Amalrik wrote a number of satirical plays, some of which were translated into English as *Nose! Nose! No-se!* (1973). His works, which in Russia circulated only in SAMIZDAT, were eventually published in the West, beginning with Amalrik's description of his first period of exile, *Involuntary Journey to Siberia* (1966; tr 1970), and a brilliant essay, *Will the Soviet Union Survive Until 1984?* (1970), which challenged the prevailing liberal view that the Soviet system would eventually be weakened by its own inflexibility and bureaucracy. As a result, in 1970 Amalrik was again imprisoned in intolerable conditions, during which he nearly died of meningitis, all of which is described in his last work, *Notes of a Revolutionary* (tr 1982). In 1976 he and his wife were allowed to immigrate to the West, eventually settling in France. In 1980 Amalrik was killed in a car accident on his way to a conference in Madrid on the Helsinki accords.

Amazons   A mythical race of women warriors. Ancient accounts differ as to where the Amazons lived; Herodotus places them in Scythia, north of the Black Sea; Apollonius Rhodius' *Argonautica* has them inhabiting a portion of the south shore. According to the legend, they were a hardy lot, burning off their right breasts in order that they might draw the bow better. They either destroyed or sent away any male children they had as a result of encounters with neighboring tribes. Among the Greek myths, there are many legends of encounters with them. HERACLES fought them in order to acquire the girdle worn by their queen, HIPPOLYTA. He acquired it either by killing Hippolyta or by capturing her general, Melanippe, and holding her for ransom. Theseus also fought the Amazons and made one of them, named either Hippolyta or Antiope, his wife. His son Hippolytus was their offspring. Hippolyta appears as the wife of Theseus, duke of Athens, in Shakespeare's A MIDSUMMER NIGHT'S DREAM.

Ambassadors, The (1903)   A novel by Henry JAMES. The central character and first "ambassador," Lambert Strether, is sent to Paris by Mrs. Newsome, a wealthy widow whom he plans to marry, in order to persuade her son Chad to come home. Chad is deeply involved with a charming French woman, Madame de Vionnet, and the novel deals chiefly with Strether's gradual conversion to the idea that life may hold more real meaning for Chad in Paris than in Woollett, Massachusetts. Strether comes to this conclusion in spite of his discovery that Chad and Mme de Vionnet are, in fact, more than just good friends. After the arrival of a second ambassador, Chad's sister Sarah, Strether decides to return to Woollett, urging Chad to remain in Paris. The essence of the novel is in Strether's remark, "Live all you can; it's a mistake not to."

ambiguity   The intentional or unintentional expression of a word or idea that implies more than one meaning and usually leaves uncertainty in the reader. The term was applied to literary criticism by William EMPSON in *Seven Types of Ambiguity* (1930), a study in which he outlined and defined seven different kinds of verbal nuance. He maintained that language functioning with artistic complexity connotes as much and often more than it denotes.

ambiguous oath   A folklore motif, especially popular in medieval literature. An outstanding example may be found in the legend of TRISTAN AND ISEULT. Setting forth for the trial that is to determine whether she is guilty of a love affair with Tristan, Iseult sends word to Tristan to disguise himself as a poor pilgrim and meet her on the way. At her request, he then carries her across a stream so that she will not get wet. She is then able to swear at the trial that no one but King Mark (her husband) and "that poor pilgrim" who carried her across the stream has ever held her in his arms. She is subsequently absolved.

Ambler, Eric (1909–   )   English novelist and screenwriter. Ambler is best known for his realistic novels of espionage, usually dealing with ordinary Englishmen who find themselves enmeshed in a web of international intrigue. These include *Epitaph for a Spy* (1938), *The Mask of Dimitrios* (1939; U.S., *The Coffin of Dimitrios*), *Journey into Fear* (1940), *Judgment on Deltchev* (1951), *A Passage of Arms* (1959), *The Siege of the Villa Lipp* (1977), and *The Cave of Time* (1981). Two previously published novels, *The Levanter* and *Doctor Frigo*, were republished

in 1982, four years before the publication of his autobiography, *Here Lies: An Autobiography* (1986). Ambler's writing is notable for the deftness of his style and the realistic portrayal of the characters in his works.

ambrosia (fr Gr, *ambrotos*, "immortal")   An elixir of life, the food of the gods that conferred immortality. HOMER portrays the gods using it as food, as an unguent, as perfume, and as fodder for horses. It was the divine food that was brought by doves to ZEUS and is contrasted with NECTAR, the divine drink. The concept of ambrosia may have developed from an idealization of honey. It is more likely that ambrosia was the common and primitive cereal food of early Greece.

Ambrosio, or the Monk   See MONK, THE.

Amelia (1751)   A novel by Henry FIELDING. Amelia, the idealized heroine, is the long-suffering, virtuous wife of Captain Booth, an impoverished army officer who has been unjustly thrown into prison. During his absence, his false friend Captain James makes overtures to Amelia, but her virtue prevails against him. In prison with Captain Booth is Miss Matthews, an adventuress who lures him into an affair, leaving him conscience-stricken. He is released from prison and Amelia forgives him, but soon after, he is thrown into debtor's prison for gambling. The situation is saved when Amelia receives an inheritance, and the two retire to the country to live a peaceful life.

America   Designation for both North and South America. Loose usage applies it chiefly to the U.S. The German cartographer Martin Waldseemüller (1470–1518) called the southern part of the newly discovered continent *America*, after the Italian navigator Amerigo VESPUCCI, one of the discoverers of South America. Waldseemüller published his map of the world in 1507, but the name *America*, which appeared there for the first time, was adopted for the entire continent only toward the end of the 16th century.

American, The (1877)   A novel by Henry JAMES. Christopher Newman, a wealthy, self-made American in France, hopes to marry Claire de Cintré, a widowed daughter of the De Bellegardes, but that aristocratic old French family finally succeeds in circumventing him. Although Newman plans to retaliate by publishing proof that Claire's mother and brother were the virtual murderers of her father, he decides to give up his design because revenge is "really not his game." Both the contrast between the simple, innocent American and the sophisticated, corrupt European and the necessity for renunciation later became common Jamesian themes.

American Academy of Arts and Letters   The inner circle of the National Institute of Arts and Letters. The latter, founded in 1898, created the smaller society in 1904 to honor its more distinguished members. The first seven men elected to its membership were William Dean HOWELLS, Augustus SAINT-GAUDENS, E. C. STEDMAN,

John LaFarge, Mark Twain, John Hay, and Edward Mac-Dowell. The aim of the academy is to give "the stamp of its approval" to the best in American art and literature from the past and present.

American Caravan, The (1927–1936)   An annual publication of American poetry and fiction. Its aim was to exhibit the best of contemporary literature, and its first editor was Van Wyck Brooks. A number of well-known writers, including Ernest Hemingway, were represented in its pages.

American Civil War   See Civil War, American.

American Crisis, The (1776–1783)   A series of sixteen pamphlets written by Thomas Paine, widely distributed in the American colonies, and touching on all of the important issues of the Revolution. The famous first *Crisis* paper, beginning, "These are the times that try men's souls," was ordered by Washington to be read to his troops on the eve of the battle of Trenton. In later *Crisis* papers, Paine called for a strong federal union.

American Dilemma, An   See Myrdal, Gunnar.

American Language, The (1919, 1921, 1923, 1936; Supplement One, 1945; Supplement Two, 1948; 4th ed, abridged with supplements, annotations, and new material by Raven I. McDavid, Jr., 1963)   A philological treatise by H. L. Mencken. Believing at first that the American language and English were diverging, Mencken found that, by 1923, American English had become the more powerful tongue and was leading British English along with it. He set out to examine the two streams of language and their differences in vocabulary, spelling, and pronunciation. His study gave particular attention to American slang, proper names, and the incorporation of non-English dialects in America. Ironically, Mencken's work won him a place among the scholars he had attacked and scorned.

American Mercury, The   An iconoclastic magazine founded in 1924 and edited by H. L. Mencken and George Jean Nathan. Among its contributors were Lewis Mumford, Sinclair Lewis, Carl Sandburg, and Vachel Lindsay. After Mencken's retirement in 1933, it was published as a pocket-size miscellany of conservative tendencies by Lawrence E. Spivak. It eventually became a rightist organ of limited circulation, owned by millionaire J. Russell Maguire.

American Notes (1842)   A volume of travel sketches by Charles Dickens. The book was well received in England, but gave great offense in the U.S. Besides advocating the abolition of slavery, Dickens made many harsh and somewhat patronizing observations about the rawness and narrowness of life and manners in America.

American Revolution   The war for independence (1775–1783) waged by the former British colonies in the present U.S. against the mother country. The conflict stemmed from the political and economic grievances of the colonists, especially after the French and Indian War, when the British decided to end their former policy of "salutary neglect" toward the colonies by enacting such revenue-raising measures as the Stamp Act and the Townshend Acts of 1767. Fanned by the writings of Samuel Adams and others, American resentment increased and erupted in such incidents as the Boston Massacre and the Boston Tea Party. The gathering of the first Continental Congress in 1774 was followed by the clash of British regulars and Minute Men at Lexington and Concord; Congress named George Washington commander-in-chief of its forces in 1775 and promulgated the Declaration of Independence, largely the work of Thomas Jefferson, the following year. Important American leaders in the battles that followed were Ethan Allen, Benedict Arnold, Horatio Gates (1728?–1806), George Rogers Clark, Anthony Wayne (1745–96), Francis Marion, and John Paul Jones. The entry of France into the war against England in 1778 was a major factor in the final American victory; at the siege of Yorktown, a French fleet blockaded the harbor, while Washington was assisted by the forces of the Comte de Rochambeau and the Marquis de Lafayette. The Treaty of Paris, signed after lengthy negotiations by John Adams, Benjamin Franklin, and John Jay, ended the war.

The American struggle for freedom was accompanied by much literary activity, most of it political in nature, as seen in the works of Thomas Paine, John Trumbull, and Francis Hopkinson (1737–91). Philip Freneau is sometimes called "the poet of the American Revolution."

See Bunker Hill, battle of; Hale, Nathan; Hancock, John; Henry, Patrick; Revere, Paul.

American Songbag, The (1927)   A collection of folk songs and ballads made by Carl Sandburg. In tours of the country, Sandburg himself sang many of these songs, accompanying them on his banjo or guitar. He recorded a number of them, perhaps the best known being "The Boll-Weevil."

American Tragedy, An (1925)   A novel by Theodore Dreiser. The author based his realistic and vivid study on the actual case of Chester Gillette, who murdered Grace Brown at Big Moose Lake in the Adirondacks in July 1906. Dreiser, who gave his protagonist the name Clyde Griffiths, at times faithfully follows the original facts; at other moments, he transcends them with his own interpretations. Clyde Griffiths's boyhood, for example, reproduces some of the details of Dreiser's own earlier years.

In revolt against the poverty and piety of his Midwestern family, Clyde becomes a bellboy in a luxurious hotel and, after being involved in an automobile accident for which he is legally responsible, is employed by a distant relative, owner of a collar factory in upper New York State. There Clyde seduces Roberta Alden, an employee at the factory, but falls in love with Sondra Finchley, a girl of the local aristocracy, who symbolizes the wealth and glamor that he has been seeking. Clyde's relationship with Sondra is menaced when Roberta, now pregnant, demands that he marry her, and he carefully devises a plan to murder her. He lacks the courage to carry out his scheme, when he takes Roberta rowing on an isolated lake, but the boat accidentally overturns, and he allows Roberta to drown while he swims away. Clyde is accused of murder, and the remainder of the book is a powerful depiction of his subsequent trial, conviction, and execution. Although Clyde is portrayed as a weakling, Dreiser squarely indicts America's industrial society for dazzling persons like Clyde with the dream of an unattainable and meretricious luxury.

Amerika (1927; tr 1938)   An unfinished novel by Franz KAFKA, written between 1912 and 1914, originally titled *Der Verschollene*, published posthumously by Max Brod. It deals with the adventures and ordeals of a young European in an unreal, expressionistically depicted America. Karl Rossman is a social misfit who has been rejected by his family and has encountered numerous difficulties in his attempts to settle down; just as there is some hope for his finding acceptance, the story stops. The first chapter was completed and published separately in 1913 as "Der Heizer" ("The Stoker").

Amichai, Yehuda (1924–   )   Israeli poet, novelist, and short-story writer. Although much of Amichai's poetry focuses on war, he is able to describe its horrors by maintaining a clear distance between himself and his subject. The result is a finely controlled emotional pitch that allows the poet to convey his sense of pain and outrage without pathos or sentimentality. He writes colloquially, in language that is always commensurate with emotional experience. He was awarded Israel's prestigious prize for poetry in 1982.

His volumes of verse include *Now and in Other Days* (1955), *Two Hopes Away* (1958), *In the Park* (1959), *Collected Poems* (1963), *Poems* (1969), *Songs of Jerusalem and Myself* (1973), *Amen* (1977), *Time* (1979), *Love Poems* (1980), and *Great Tranquillity* (1983). *Selected Poems*, a collection of some of his finest verse, was published in 1986. Among his other writings are a novel, *Not of This Time, Not of This Place* (1963); a play, *Journey to Nineveh* (1962); and a radio play, *Bells and Trains* (1966). *The World Is a Room and Other Stories*, a collection of stories written in the 1950s, was published in 1984, and *Travels*, originally published in Hebrew in 1968, was published in English in 1986.

Amidism (or Pure Land Buddhism)   One of many Buddhist sects in Japan. Amidism emphasizes salvation through the devout repetition of a simple liturgical phrase. It stems from a form of Buddhist salvationism which had its origins in northern India and Central Asia, from where it spread through China, where elements from popular folk religions were incorporated. Its aim is rebirth of the devout

soul in the Western Paradise of the Amida (Sans, *Amitabha*; Chin, *A-mi-t'o*) Buddha.

In Japan, Amida pietism flourished at the Enryakuji Temple at Mt. Hici, center of the TENDAI Sect. Its leading exponents were Genshin (942–1017), Hōnen (1133–1212), founder of the Jōdo Sect, and Shinran (1173–1262), founder of the Shin Sect. Amidism represents a shift in appeal from the elite to the common people. Recitation with faith of the single phrase *Namu Amida Buddha* ("Hail to the Amida Buddha") is the sole requirement for rebirth in Amida's Paradise. It has long been influential in literature and the visual arts.

Aminta   A famous Renaissance pastoral play by TASSO, written and first performed in 1573. The plot begins with the appearance of Venus's son Amor in the guise of a shepherd, determined to aim his arrows at the most obdurate nymph of Diana, Silvia, whose haughtiness has repulsed all lovers. Her friend Dafne (Daphne) tries to persuade her to fall in love with the shepherd Aminta, but she prefers the hunt; at the same time, Aminta spurns Amarilli, who loves him desperately. Aminta tells his friend Tirsi that there is no hope of gaining Silvia, as the wise Mopso has seen the future and confirmed the hopelessness of the pursuit. Now Satiro (the Satyr), also enamored of Silvia, decides to take her by force while she bathes. Aminta rescues her, but she flees from him. Later, believing Silvia dead, Aminta attempts suicide; but he survives to find Silvia convinced of his love and loving him in return. They wed and the play closes with the appearance of Venus, arrived to discover her unruly son and put an end to his mischief by taking him back to the Olympian court from which he had strayed.

Amis, Kingsley (1922–   )   English novelist and poet. Amis's numerous comic novels include LUCKY JIM, *That Uncertain Feeling* (1955), *I Like It Here* (1958), *I Want It Now* (1968), *Ending Up* (1974), and *Jake's Thing* (1978). They usually feature profane and idiosyncratic antiheroes with violent antipathies to sham and hypocrisy. A *Case of Samples* (1956) is a collection of intellectual, light-hearted poems. Amis has also written about SCIENCE FICTION in *New Maps of Hell* (1960) and has produced an admiring study, *Rudyard Kipling and His World* (1976). He edited *The New Oxford Book of English Light Verse* (1978), besides publishing his own *Collected Poems, 1944–1979* (1979). *Russian Hide-and-Seek*, an "alternative world" novel and *Collected Short Stories* were published in 1980. In 1984 his novels *Stanley and the Women* and *How's Your Glass?* were published. His novel *The Old Devils* won the Booker Prize in 1986.

Amish   See MENNONITE.

Ammons, A[rchie] R[andolph] (1926–   )   American poet. Ammons is best known for his poems detailing the observations of a solitary sojourner in the north Atlantic coastal region. His poems are piled-up impressions of nature and reflections on the self. His most famous work is *Tape for the Turn of the Year* (1965), a book-length poem of short lines typed on a roll of adding-machine paper. In this journal-like work, the poet records external events, as well as his own philosophical meditations. Ammons was awarded the 1973 National Book Award for *Collected Poems, 1951–1971* (1972).

Amos In the OLD TESTAMENT, the third book of the Minor Prophets, although it is chronologically the earliest of those books. Amos prophesied in a time of great prosperity in the northern kingdom, but the prosperity was accompanied by widespread corruption, immorality, and social injustice. Amos, a herdsman, received his calling as a prophet and vigorously protested the idolatry of his contemporaries. He foretold the destruction of Israel in five visions, the last of which promised redemption and the rebuilding of Israel after all sinners have died "by the sword" (Amos 9:10–15).

Amphion A son of Zeus and Antiope. Amphion became a famous musician and reigned, with his twin brother, in Thebes. Antiope, a daughter of Nycteus, the ruler of Thebes, lay with Zeus but was driven from the city by her angry father. While fleeing to Sicyon, she gave birth to twins, Amphion and Zethus, on Mount Cithaeron. They were raised by shepherds and, on reaching manhood, learned of their mother's fate. Nycteus having died, his brother Lycus, now king, had brought Antiope back to Thebes, where he and his wife Dirce had long mistreated her. The twins went to Thebes, killed Lycus, and tied Dirce to the horns of a bull; she died at the Theban spring named for her.

Amphion and Zethus now shared the Theban throne and together built the city walls, though Amphion accomplished his part of the task by playing such ravishing music that the stones moved into place of their own accord. Amphion married NIOBE, but her arrogance led to the slaying by Apollo and Artemis of their many children and, according to some accounts, of Amphion himself. Zethus married Thebe, who gave her name to the city.

Amphitryon In Greek mythology, a king of Mycenae cuckolded by Zeus. The god assumed the likeness of Amphitryon for the purpose of visiting his wife, Alcmena, and gave a banquet at his house; but Amphitryon came home and claimed the honor of being the master of the house. As far as the servants and guests were concerned, the dispute was soon decided: "He who gave the feast was to them the host." Alcmena became the mother of HERACLES. This legend is the subject of three famous comedies by Plautus, Molière, and Dryden, all called *Amphitryon*. In 1929 there appeared a play entitled *Amphitryon 38*, meaning that it was the thirty-eighth treatment of the famous theme, by the French dramatist Jean Giraudoux (1882–1944).

amrita (Sans, "without death") In Hindu mythology, the elixir of immortality, analogous to the AMBROSIA in classical mythology. Among early Indo-Aryans, it was probably the juice of a plant from which a sweet nectar was prepared. The source of preservation of youth for the gods, amrita was saved from destruction in a great flood by the god VISHNU in his incarnation as the tortoise (*kurma*).

Amyclaean silence Named for Amyclae, a Laconian town south of Sparta. Amyclae was ruled by the mythical TYNDAREUS. The inhabitants had so often been alarmed by false rumors of the approach of invading Spartans that they made a decree forbidding mention of the subject. When the Spartans actually came no one dared give the warning, and the town was taken. Hence the phrase "more silent than Amyclae."

An The Sumerian god of heaven. Born of Nammu, the primeval sea, An and his sister-wife Ki (Earth) were originally joined as one, but their offspring ENLIL, the god of the air, separated them. An's place as head of the Sumerian pantheon was taken by Enlil. An is the same as the Babylonian god Anu.

Anabaptists A general name for many Protestant sects that appeared in Germany during the 16th and 17th centuries. Although the groups were usually in conflict with one another, most of them believed they were restoring the purity of the primitive Christian church. Most practiced adult baptism, as described in the Bible, and several were involved with social and economic agitation.

Anabasis See XENOPHON.

anachronism A term used to distinguish anything out of its proper time. Shakespeare's references to cannons in *King John*, a play which takes place before cannons came into use, to clocks in JULIUS CAESAR, and to billiards in ANTONY AND CLEOPATRA are examples of anachronisms. In literature, anachronisms are sometimes used deliberately as comic devices or to emphasize universal timelessness.

Anacreontic poetry Verse written by or derived from that of Anacreon (563–478 BC), the Greek lyric poet of Teos, in Ionia. He wrote with singular charm on such themes as the pleasures of love and wine. Contemporary political events and persons also engaged his attention. The following pattern is typically an anacreontic meter:

⏑⏑_⏑_⏑__

Over the next several centuries, his themes and style were imitated, often in anacreontic meter, by Greek poetasters, and a collection of about sixty poems has survived, to which the term Anacreontic poetry applies.

anacrusis In prosody, the addition of an extra unaccented syllable or syllables at the beginning of a verse, before the regular rhythm is established. In the following example from Blake's "The Tyger," the *And* is unaccented:

When the stars threw down their spears
And watered heaven with their tears.

anagoge   An elevation of the mind to things celestial. Specifically, the term is used to refer to exegesis that gives a mystical or spiritual meaning or application to the words of the Bible, as opposed to their literal, moral, or allegorical interpretation. See FOUR SENSES.

anagram   The rearrangement of the letters in a word or phrase to make another word or phrase. Anagrams are a common feature of crossword puzzles and are sometimes used by authors to conceal proper names. *Drab* is an anagram of *bard*; the name of Samuel Butler's *Erewhon* (1872) is an anagram for *nowhere*. See PALINDROME.

Analects   (Lun-yü, compiled 5th to 4th centuries BC) One of the Chinese FOUR BOOKS. It is a collection of the sayings of CONFUCIUS and of anecdotes about him and his disciples. Its brief and unsystematic pronouncements on ethics, government, ritual, literature, and so on were a fundamental part of education in traditional China. It was translated by Arthur WALEY as *The Analects of Confucius* (1938).

The term is also used generally for collected fragments or passages from an author's writings.

anapest   In English prosody, a metrical foot consisting of three syllables, the first two unaccented and the third accented. The word *cig-a-*RETTE is an anapest. The METER made up of such units is called anapestic meter, and the following lines are a good example.

I am MON/arch of ALL / I survey . . .
I am LORD / of the FOWL / and the BRUTE.

Cowper, "Alexander Selkirk"

Anarchiad, The   (1786–1787)   An American satirical epic poem, published anonymously in twelve installments of the New Haven *Gazette*. David Humphries, Lemuel Hopkins, Joel BARLOW, John TRUMBULL, and other HARTFORD WITS collaborated in its composition. It is chiefly an attack on French philosophy, paper money, Shays's Rebellion, and the condescending attitude of Europeans toward Americans.

Anatomy of Melancholy, The   (1621)   A prose work by Robert BURTON. Elaborately organized as a medical treatise, the *Anatomy* not only deals with various morbid mental states, their causes, symptoms, and cures, but is a compendium of notable utterances on the human condition in general, compiled from classical, scholastic, and contemporary sources. Melancholy, for Burton, embraced everything from raving lunacy to philosophical and occasional pessimism; as his quotations illustrate, it is "the character of mortality." The book is witty, pedantic, quaint, imaginative, inexhaustively rich, and, from Milton on, it has been pillaged by numerous authors.

Anaxagoras   (500?–428 BC)   A Greek philosopher, teacher of PERICLES, THUCYDIDES, EURIPIDES, and possibly of SOCRATES. He believed in a dualistic universe, consisting of a chaotic mass of tiny particles or seeds that compose matter, and an ordering force that imparts motion. He called this force *nous*, or mind. Anaxagoras was also an astronomer, and correctly explained eclipses. He studied the size of the sun, the phases of the moon, and the behavior of meteors. Because his views conflicted with the state religion, Anaxagoras was charged with impiety and banished from the Athens he had made the center of philosophic argumentation. He is sometimes referred to as Anaxagoras of Clazomenae, after his birthplace in Asia Minor.

Anchises   In classic legend, a member of the royal house of Troy and the father of AENEAS by APHRODITE, who had fallen in love with him because of his beauty. According to Vergil, when Troy fell, Aeneas carried his aged father out of the burning city on his shoulders. Anchises died during Aeneas' wanderings and was buried in Sicily (AENEID, Book III).

Ancient Mariner   See RIME OF THE ANCIENT MARINER, THE.

Andersen, Hans Christian   (1805–1875)   Danish writer of fairy tales, poet, novelist, and dramatist. A skilled writer in all these genres, Hans Christian Andersen owes his worldwide fame to his fairy stories. Always popular with children, the 168 tales contain a mature wisdom together with gay whimsy. Andersen invested stories of folk and legendary origin with moral and symbolic significance. He could convey a fine perception of life's ironies while describing the fate of a tin soldier or a drab duckling. Among his best-known stories are "The Red Shoes," "The Ugly Duckling," "The Emperor's Clothes," "The Tinder Box," and "The Fir Tree." The tales appeared from 1835 to 1872. Andersen's complete tales have been issued in several English editions.

Anderson, Maxwell   (1888–1959)   American playwright. Anderson is known for his experiments in verse drama, his insistence on the necessity of an inner moral struggle, and his success in the field of historical drama. After an early play, *White Desert* (1923), Anderson began collaborating with Laurence Stallings, the two producing WHAT PRICE GLORY?; *First Flight* (1925), about Andrew JACKSON; and *The Buccaneer* (1925), a play about Sir Henry MORGAN. He wrote *Outside Looking In* (1925), based on Jim Tully's *Beggars of Life*, and *Saturday's Children* (1928), a domestic comedy; he then wrote with Harold Hickerson the first play to deal with the SACCO-VANZETTI case, *Gods of the Lightning* (1928). Anderson was to return later to this theme with his successful WINTERSET.

In the 1930s Anderson returned to historical drama and wrote two plays dealing with 16th-century themes: *Elizabeth the Queen* (1930) and *Mary of Scotland* (1934). *Valley Forge* (1934), a reinterpretation of Washington, followed. It was a prolific time for Anderson: NIGHT OVER TAOS; *Both Your Houses* (1933); *High Tor* (1937), which mingles real people and ghosts, past and present; *Knickerbocker Holiday*

(1938), a musical written with Kurt WEILL; and *Key Largo* (1939), about a man who struggles to redeem himself for an act of cowardice during the Spanish Civil War, were all written in the 1930s.

World War II was reflected in several Anderson plays of the early 1940s: *Candle in the Wind* (1941), an anti-Nazi play set in Paris; *The Eve of St. Mark* (1942); and *Storm Operation* (1944). After World War II, Anderson returned again to historical drama, with *Joan of Lorraine* (1946), one of the most frequently revived of his plays; *Anne of the Thousand Days* (1948), a favorable interpretation of Henry VIII; and *Barefoot in Athens* (1951), a play about Socrates. Also noteworthy among Anderson's late dramas are *Lost in the Stars* (1949), a dramatization of Alan Paton's *Cry, the Beloved Country* (1948); and *The Bad Seed* (1955), the story of a grotesquely evil little girl, based on a novel by William March.

Although his reputation faltered somewhat after his death, Anderson was regarded by many during the 1930s and 1940s as a superior playwright to Eugene O'NEILL. His collection of essays on playwriting, *Off Broadway*, appeared in 1947. *Notes on a Dream*, a collection of his poems, was published in 1972. *Dramatist in America* (1977) contains Anderson's letters from 1912 to 1958.

Anderson, Robert W[oodruff] (1917–   ) American playwright and novelist. *Tea and Sympathy* (1953; screenplay, 1956), Anderson's first and greatest success, was the story of a sensitive boy unjustly suspected of homosexuality, who is helped through his misery by the compassionate wife of his housemaster. *All Summer Long* (1955), adapted from Donald Wetzel's novel *A Wreath and a Curse*, was followed by *Silent Night, Lonely Night* (1960) and his second large-scale success, *You Know I Can't Hear You When the Water's Running* (1967). *I Never Sang for My Father* (1968) was another Broadway hit. Anderson's novel *After* (1973), about a young wife's death and the shattered husband's ultimate finding of a second great love, is semiautobiographical. *Getting Up and Going Home* (1978) is a novel about love and marriage in the 1970s.

Anderson, Sherwood (1876–1941)   American short-story writer and novelist. Born in Ohio, largely self-educated, Anderson worked in various businesses before 1912, when he suffered a breakdown precipitated by the conflicting demands of his family, business, and creative life. He left his wife and job and went to Chicago. There he met Midwestern writers associated with the Chicago literary renaissance, notably Theodore DREISER and Carl SANDBURG, and began his own literary career (see CHICAGO GROUP). His first two novels were *Windy McPherson's Son* (1916) and *Marching Man* (1917). His third was his masterpiece, WINESBURG, OHIO. A picture of life in a typical Midwestern town, as seen through the eyes of its inhabitants, it brought Anderson recognition as a leader in the revolt against established literary traditions. Though his

style was decried by a later generation as artless and sentimental, it was for his time a significant breakthrough to an individual and original expression which had a measurable influence on Ernest HEMINGWAY and William FAULKNER, among others.

Though he wrote other novels, such as *Poor White* (1920) and *Dark Laughter* (1925), a best-seller, Anderson never again equalled his achievement in *Winesburg, Ohio*. Some of his short stories, however, came close, notably the title stories of his two best collections: THE TRIUMPH OF THE EGG and *Horses and Men* (1923). In 1927 Anderson moved to Marion, Virginia, where he purchased and edited two newspapers, one Republican, one Democrat. *The Buck Fever Papers*, not published until 1972, are stories of this time. He had written two autobiographical books in earlier years: *A Story Teller's Story* (1924) and *Tar: A Midwest Childhood* (1926). His *Memoirs* (1942) and *Letters* (1953) were published posthumously, as was the more definitive *The Memoirs of Sherwood Anderson* (1969).

Andō Hiroshige (1787–1858)   Japanese painter and wood-block artist. Andō is famous for his *Tōkaidō Gojūsan-tsugi* (*Fifty-three Stations Along the Tōkaidō Highway*) and as the last great master of the wood-block (*ukiyoe*) print. His work is said to have influenced Western painters, notably Whistler.

And Quiet Flows the Don   See QUIET DON, THE.

Andrade, Mario [Raul] de [Morais] (1893–1945)   Brazilian poet and novelist. Andrade's first book of poetry, *Há uma gôta de sangue em cada poema* (1917), was self-consciously lyrical and elegant. Then, with the sharp images and hard-edged, conversational diction of his second volume, *Paulicéia desvairada* (1922; tr *Hallucinated City*, 1968), he all but launched Brazilian modernism and was thereafter one of its most dedicated proponents. His novel *Macunaima* (1928) was a grandly successful exploration of what Andrade saw as the interwoven native and imported myths of the Brazilian people, which he wrote in an amalgam of arbitrarily combined Brazilian dialects. His *O moviemento modernisto* (1942), a milestone in modern criticism, is essential to an understanding of the literary history of Brazil. Andrade's verse is collected in *Poésias completas* (1955).

Andrew, St.   One of the twelve disciples of Jesus; the brother of St. Peter. St. Andrew is depicted in Christian art as an old man with long white hair and beard, holding the Gospel in his right hand and leaning on a cross like the letter X, termed *St. Andrew's cross*. His day is November 30. It is said that he suffered martyrdom in Patrae (AD 70).

Andrews, Pamela   See PAMELA, OR VIRTUE REWARDED.

Andreyev, Leonid Nikolayevich (1871–1919) Russian writer. Born in the province of Oriol, Andreyev studied law at the universities of St. Petersburg and Moscow, during which time extreme mental depression led to several suicide attempts. He graduated in 1897 but turned to writing instead of law for a living, receiving aid and encouragement from Maksim Gorky. Among the best of Andreyev's earlier works were *V tumanye* (*In the Fog*, 1902) and *Mysl* (*Thought*, 1902), the first dealing with awakened sexuality in a young boy, the second with insanity and murder. Such sensational themes were at this time still treated in a realistic manner by Andreyev, but, from this period on, his work became increasingly complex, often strained in its search for sensational effect and symbolic import. This is especially apparent in a work such as *Krasnyi smekh* (*The Red Laugh*, 1904), a horrific tale of the madness and terror of war. The same tendencies are evident in Andreyev's plays, which include HE WHO GETS SLAPPED, *Chiorniye maski* (*The Black Maskers*, 1908), *Anafema* (*Anathema*, 1909), and *Zhizn cheloveka* (*The Life of Man*, 1906).

Andrić, Ivo (1892–1975)   Yugoslav novelist and short-story writer. Born to a family of poor artisans, Andrić set the scenes of most of his novels and stories in his native Bosnia. He was active in the National Revolutionary Youth Organization before World War I, spent three years as a political prisoner, and later spent years in Yugoslavia's diplomatic service and parliament. Among Andrić's best-known works are his Bosnian trilogy: *Travnicka hronika* (tr *Bosnian Story*, 1958), *Gospodjica* (tr *The Woman from Sarajevo*, 1965), and THE BRIDGE ON THE DRINA, all published in 1945. His writings are dominated by a sense of Kierkegaardian pessimism and personal isolation; his characters emerge as penetrating psychological portraits. Andrić was awarded the NOBEL PRIZE in Literature in 1961. In 1982 Andrić's *Wegzeichen* (*Road Markings*) was published in Munich. A collection of thoughts, personal impressions, and aphorisms, it gives the reader a far clearer picture of the reticent writer than do his other works.

Androcles   According to Aulus Gellius, a Roman slave of the 1st century, who removed a thorn from the paw of a lion. When Androcles was later thrown into the arena, the grateful beast began to caress him, and they were both set free. George Bernard Shaw used this story as the basis of his play *Androcles and the Lion* (1912).

Andromache   In Homer's *Iliad*, the wife of Hector. Andromache appears in Euripides' THE TROJAN WOMEN and is the heroine of his *Andromache* (430–424 BC). In the latter play, she has been carried off to Thessaly by Neoptolemus, Achilles' son, has borne him a child, and has been abandoned in favor of Hermione, the daughter of Menelaus and Helen. Her sufferings at their hands are the substance of the play, which, in portraying the Spartans as cruel and cowardly, served as an effective political indictment of the Athenians' enemies. Racine wrote a tragedy about Andromache, entitled ANDROMAQUE. She also appears as Hector's wife in Shakespeare's TROILUS AND CRESSIDA.

Andromaque (1667)   A tragedy by Jean RACINE. It is based on the Greek legend of ANDROMACHE but differs from it in several details of interrelation between the characters. The play is set in Epirus after the fall of Troy. Andromaque is loved by her captor Pyrrhus, whom she hates, but his action arouses the jealousy of his fiancée Hermione. Pyrrhus threatens to surrender Andromaque's son Astyanax to the Greeks if she will not yield to him. In exchange for his promise to protect her son, she agrees to marry Pyrrhus but secretly intends to remain faithful to her dead husband Hector by killing herself after the wedding. The rejected Hermione persuades Orestes, the Greek ambassador, who has come to demand Andromaque's son, to murder Pyrrhus; in exchange, she agrees to flee with him. But after the murder she reviles him and in her remorse commits suicide upon the funeral pyre of her adored Pyrrhus. Orestes goes mad. *Andromaque* is held by French critics to constitute the first representation in tragedy of the psychology of passion.

Andromeda   (1) In Greek mythology, the daughter of Cepheus and Cassiopeia. Because Andromeda's mother boasted that she was more beautiful than the NEREIDS, they induced Poseidon to send a sea-monster against Ethiopia, and an oracle declared that Andromeda must be sacrificed to it. Chained to a rock near Joppa, she was rescued by PERSEUS, who married her. He also killed Phineus, her former betrothed, and all his companions. She was placed among the stars upon her death.

(2) The title of a long poem (1858) by Charles KINGSLEY.

angel (fr Gr, *angelos*, "messenger")   (1) In theology, a celestial being. In postcanonical and apocalyptic literature, angels are grouped in varying orders, and the hierarchy thus constructed was adapted to church uses by the early Christian Fathers. In his *De hierarchia celesti*, the pseudo-Dionysius (early 5th century) gives the names of the nine orders; they are taken from the New Testament (Eph. 1:21 and Col. 1:16) and are as follows:

(i) SERAPHIM, Cherubim, and Thrones, in the first circle of the heavenly hierarchy.

(ii) Dominions, Virtues, and Powers, in the second circle.

(iii) Principalities, Archangels, and Angels, in the third circle.

The seven holy angels are Michael, Gabriel, Raphael, Uriel, Chamuel, Jophiel, and Zadkiel. Michael and Gabriel are mentioned in the Bible; the others appear in Apocryphal books.

Milton (*Paradise Lost*, Bk. 1, 392) gives a list of the fallen angels.

Muslims say that angels were created from pure, bright gems, the genii from fire, and man from clay.

(2) An obsolete English coin, current from the time of Edward IV to that of Charles I, bearing the figure of the archangel Michael slaying the dragon. Its value varied from 6s. 8d. in 1465 (when first coined) to 10s. under Edward VI. It was the coin presented to persons touched for the King's Evil.

Angelica (1) The bewitching heroine of the Orlando poems of Boiardo and Ariosto (see ORLANDO FURIOSO and ORLANDO INNAMORATO).

(2) A central character in William Congreve's comedy LOVE FOR LOVE.

Angelico, Fra [Giovanni] (pseudonym of Guido di Pietro, 1387–1455) Italian painter. A Dominican friar of Fiesole, near Florence, Fra Angelico worked in Rome, Orvieto, and Florence. It was there that he completed the well-known series of frescoes for the monastery of San Marco, as a result of the patronage of Cosimo de' Medici. In 1447 Fra Angelico was summoned to Rome by Pope Nicholas V for the purpose of painting several scenes from the life of Saint Lawrence, which were to be hung in the Vatican. A religious painter of grace and simplicity coupled with an admirable purity and delicacy of color, he did not share his contemporaries' enthusiasm for the new scientific naturalism of the day.

Angelo (1) In Shakespeare's MEASURE FOR MEASURE, the puritanical lord deputy who governs Vienna in the absence of Duke Vincentio. Although Angelo is widely known as "a man of stricture and firm abstinence," his austerity masks a violent inner nature.

(2) In Shakespeare's THE COMEDY OF ERRORS, a goldsmith who, having fashioned a gold chain for Antipholus of Ephesus, mistakenly gives it to Antipholus of Syracuse.

Angelou, Maya (1928–   ) American writer. Angelou's autobiographical books, *I Know Why the Caged Bird Sings* (1970), *Gather Together in My Name* (1974), *Singin' and Swingin' and Gettin' Merry Like Christmas* (1976), and *The Heart of a Woman* (1981), chronicle her varied, often harsh experiences of growing up in Arkansas, of being raped at seven, of bearing a child at sixteen, and of her work—as an actress, as a school administrator in Africa, and as a poet. She celebrates in the black experience the capacity not merely to survive but to grow and to triumph over adversity as well. The same theme is echoed in her poetry, collected in such volumes as *Just Give Me a Cool Drink of Water 'Fore I Diiie* (1972), *And Still I Rise* (1978), and *Shaker, Why Don't You Sing?* (1983). In 1986 she published *All God's Children Need Traveling Shoes.*

Angel Pavement (1930) A novel by J. B. PRIESTLEY. Set in London, it is the story of small businessmen and a grasping capitalist.

Angelus A prayer in the Western church that commemorates the story of the Annunciation of the Angel GABRIEL to the mother of Jesus. In Latin, the opening words of the prayer are *Angelus Domini* ("the angel of the Lord"), hence its name. In the Roman Catholic church, the prayer is recited three times a day, at 6 A.M., noon, and 6 P.M., at the sound of a bell called the *Angelus.* MILLET gave this title to one of his best-known paintings.

Anglo-Saxon Chronicle, The (also called Old English Annals, c891–924) An Old English history of England, begun under the direction of King ALFRED, still a major historical source. The early material is adapted from BEDE's work and from records kept by the monasteries. After the account of Alfred's wars against the Danes, the *Chronicle* was officially kept up year by year until 924, after which the various extant manuscript copies of it show fragmentary continuations by different authors, one with entries as late as 1154.

Angry Young Men Although now largely obsolete, an epithet that enjoyed great popularity in the 1950s, when it was applied to an unaffiliated group of English writers. Taken from the title of Leslie Allen Paul's autobiography, *Angry Young Man* (1951), the term became widely used in connection with the kind of bitter dissidence expressed in John Osborne's play LOOK BACK IN ANGER. The so-called Angry Young Men of British letters voiced their suspicion and resentment of the static English Establishment—its culture, manners, snobbism, and hypocrisy—chiefly through the novel and drama. Also identified with the group were the novelists Kingsley AMIS, Colin WILSON, John WAIN, and Alan SILLITOE and the playwright Arnold Wesker.

Angstrom, Harry The main character in three novels by John UPDIKE. Nicknamed "Rabbit," Angstrom is a middle-class Everyman in contemporary America. He tries to escape his wife and the tedium of adult life in *Rabbit Run* (1960) by frequently leaving home. In *Rabbit Redux* (1971), Rabbit's attention remains focused on the small joys and crises of his personal life and he fails to notice the tumultuous events of the 1960s surging around him: the moon landing, VIETNAM WAR protests, the drug culture, and radical black activism.

The middle-aged and successful owner of a Toyota automobile dealership, Rabbit continues to fail in his domestic relationships and to feel ill at ease in life in *Rabbit Is Rich* (1981), a novel that in 1982 won the PULITZER PRIZE and an American Book Award. Through Angstrom, Updike chronicles three decades of American life.

Animal Farm (1945) A satirical fable by George ORWELL. Some farm animals get tired of their servitude to man and start a revolution, to run the farm as they want. They are betrayed, however, into a worse servitude by their leaders, the pigs. The pigs' slogan is "All animals are equal, but some animals are more equal than others." The book is a satire on the development of the Russian revolution under Stalin.

animals in heaven The ten animals which, according to Muslim legend, have been allowed to enter paradise. They are (1) Jonah's *whale*; (2) Solomon's *ant*; (3) the *ram* caught by Abraham and sacrificed instead of Isaac; (4) the *lapwing* of Balkis; (5) the *camel* of the prophet Saleh; (6) Balaam's *ass*; (7) the *ox* of Moses; (8) the *dog* Kratim or Katmir of the Seven Sleepers; (9) Al Borak, Muhammed's *ass*; and (10) Noah's *dove*.

An Lu-shan Rebellion (755–763)   A rebellion and civil war in China during the T'ANG dynasty. Led by An Lu-shan, a general of non-Chinese origin and a favorite at the court, the upheaval forced the flight of the emperor and his court to southwest China. The capital and north China were devastated, so much so that this rebellion marks the beginning of the decline of the dynasty and the end of Chinese dominance in Central Asia. The famous poets LI PO and TU FU, among many others, were swept up in the events. The emperor's flight and the tragic death of his favorite concubine are popular themes in later Chinese literature.

Annabel Lee (1849)   A poem by Edgar Allan POE. Its subject, Poe's favorite, is the death of a beautiful woman.

Anna Christie (1922)   A drama by Eugene O'NEILL. Anna is the daughter of Chris Christopherson, a Swedish captain who has come to regard all evil and misfortune as the work of "dat old davil sea." He had sent her away to be brought up in Minnesota, but in the play she turns up in port and falls in love with both the sea and a brawny Irish seaman named Mat Burke. When she confesses to a shameful past in St. Paul, her father and her lover both repudiate her. In the end, however, she is forgiven. The play won a PULITZER PRIZE in 1922. It was made into a film (1930) and a musical comedy, *New Girl in Town* (1957), by George ABBOTT; the original play was revived on Broadway in 1977.

Anna Karenina (1873–1876)   A novel by Count Leo TOLSTOY. The author's second great major novel, it is the story of a tragic, adulterous love. Anna meets and falls in love with Aleksei Vronski, a handsome young officer. She abandons her child and husband in order to be with Vronski. When she thinks Vronski has tired of her, she kills herself by leaping under a train. The idea for the story reputedly came to Tolstoy after he had viewed the body of a young woman who committed a similar suicide. A subplot concerns the contrasting happy marriage of Konstantin Levin and his young wife Kitty. Levin's search for meaning in his life and his love for a natural, simple existence on his estate are reflections of Tolstoy's own moods and thoughts of the time. While working on the novel, Tolstoy began to experience the doubts and torments which he describes in *A Confession* (1879–81).

Annales Cambriae (c955)   A Latin history of Wales, importantly connected with the origins of ARTHURIAN LEGEND. It notes that, at the battle of Mount Badon, a historical Arthur (prototype of King Arthur) wore a cross on his shield and that Arthur and Medraut (a historical MORDRED) fell at the battle of Camlan in the year 537.

Anna Livia Plurabelle   The romantic heroine, both woman and water, of James Joyce's FINNEGANS WAKE. Anna is the wife of H. C. EARWICKER and personifies the river Liffey that runs through Dublin. The initials *A. L. P.* are interwoven throughout the novel, to represent the universal feminine principle.

Anna of the Five Towns (1902)   A novel by Arnold BENNETT. The first of Bennett's novels dealing with the Potteries region, it is a naturalistic account of an ordinary woman's life as well as a study of the repressive effects of Wesleyan religion.

Anne of Green Gables   See MONTGOMERY, L. M.

Anniversaries, The   The general title of two long elegiac poems by John DONNE: *An Anatomy of the World* (1611) and *Of the Progresse of the Soule* (1612). Ostensibly written in memory of Elizabeth, young daughter of his patron, Sir Robert Drury, they are more concerned with the typical Donne themes of intellectual disorder and temporal decay.

anno Domini   Latin for "in the Year of our Lord"; i.e., in the year since the Nativity: generally abbreviated to AD. It was Dionysius Exiguus who fixed the date of the Nativity; he lived in the early 6th century, and his computation is probably late by some three to six years. The custom of determining dates on this basis is said to be the result of the work of the Venerable Bede.

Annunciation, Day of the   March 25, the day of the angel's (traditionally Gabriel's) announcement to the Virgin Mary of the forthcoming birth to her of the Messiah.

Annus Mirabilis (1667)   A poem by John DRYDEN, the title of which is Latin for "year of wonders." The poem describes the London fire and the Dutch war, the chief events of the year 1666. In a preface to the poem, Dryden discusses his conception of the poetic imagination.

Ann Veronica (1909)   A novel by H. G. WELLS. It is the story of the heroine's struggle for independence, sexual freedom, and equality with men.

Anouilh, Jean (1910–   )   French dramatist and screenwriter. *The Ermine* (1932) first presented Anouilh's major recurrent theme, the "great thirst for purity." His plays, ANTIGONE and THE LARK, for example, work through the juxtaposition of opposing qualities or themes, like youth and age, poverty and wealth, or the poetry of fantasy or art contrasted with the sullying demands of practicality in the real world. Anouilh grouped his plays and published them under several descriptive headings: *Pièces roses*, *Pièces noires*, *Pièces brillantes*, and *Pièces grinçantes* (respectively, plays light, dark, sparkling, and grating).

Anouilh's later plays include *La Culotte* (1978) and *Le Nombril* (1981), which was a tremendous success when it played in London in 1984. Some of his best-known films include *Monsieur Vincent* (1969), *Pattes blanches* (1948), and *Une Caprice de Caroline chérie* (1950).

Antaeus   In Greek mythology, a gigantic wrestler, a son of Earth and Sea, Ge and Poseidon. Antaeus' strength was invincible as long as he touched the earth, and, when he was lifted from it, his strength was renewed on touching it again. Heracles succeeded in killing this charmed giant by lifting him from the earth and squeezing him to death.

antagonist   See PROTAGONIST.

Anthony, St.   First Christian monastic. St. Anthony lived in the 3rd or 4th century and founded a fraternity of ascetics who lived in the deserts of Egypt. The story of his temptations by the devil is a well-known subject of literature and art. It is the basis of Flaubert's novel *La Tentation de Saint Antoine* (1874).

Anthony, Susan B[rownell]   (1820–1906) American reformer and leader of the women's suffrage movement. As a seventeen-year-old teacher, Anthony began her feminist activities by agitating for equal pay for women teachers, coeducation, and college education for women. In 1852, after she was prevented from speaking at a temperance meeting because of her sex, she formed the Women's State Temperance Society of New York. She firmly believed that women could effectively contribute to social reform, once they had the same privileges and rights as men, and lectured and campaigned for women's rights throughout her life. With Elizabeth Cady STANTON, she organized the National Woman Suffrage Association (1869), and in 1890 this group merged with another to form the National American Woman Suffrage Association, of which Anthony was president (1892–1900). In 1872 she challenged the federal government on women's franchise under the fourteenth amendment, by leading a group of women to the polls in Rochester, New York. She was arrested and tried and ultimately lost the case. She was also a radical abolitionist even before the CIVIL WAR and supported Negro suffrage for both men and women. With Elizabeth Cady Stanton and Matilda Joslyn Gage, she compiled volumes 1–3 and edited volume 4 of the *History of Woman Suffrage* (6 vols, 1881–1922). In 1978 her image appeared on the face of the silver dollar; Anthony was the first woman in history to be pictured on American currency.

Anthony of Padua, St.   (1195–1231)   Franciscan friar, preacher, and theologian. St. Anthony was born in Portugal but spent his life teaching theology in France and Italy; he died in Padua. There is a legend that St. Anthony preached to a school of fishes that listened attentively until he was finished.

Antic Hay   (1923)   A satirical novel by Aldous HUXLEY. Comical and bitter, it is about a group of London intellectuals and their long, learned, futile conversations, in which everything seems valueless—God, love, art,

learning, social reform, science. The central character is timid Theodore Gumbril, Junior, who gives up his job as a teacher to try to sell a new kind of trousers with built-in air cushion seats. He purchases a thick beard to help him act the part of a confident, aggressive man in business and in love. As in *Crome Yellow* (1921), the general atmosphere of despair is deepened when the hero loses his girl.

Antichrist   A Biblical term referring to a "man of sin" or Satanic figure who denies the Father and Son and disowns the incarnation and messianic role of JESUS. The term was used first in the NEW TESTAMENT, but the figure of an enemy of God, a false messiah, or an incarnation of evil who would lead the faithful astray appeared in ancient Babylonian myth and in early Judaic belief. According to some legends, the presence of the Antichrist would precede the Second Coming of Christ, who would destroy the Antichrist before the Last Judgment. Such stories are founded chiefly in THE REVELATION OF SAINT JOHN THE DIVINE and the Second Epistle to the THESSALONIANS. The blasphemous beast with seven heads and ten horns, associated with the mystic number 666, is identified with the Antichrist (Rev. 13–14). The early Christians associated the Antichrist with CALIGULA and NERO; the name has since been applied to many who have opposed the Church and to many powerful enemies of faith or peace.

anticlimax   A critical term, the first recorded definition of which comes from Dr. Samuel JOHNSON: "a sentence in which the last part expresses something lower than the first." It is often used deliberately for comic effect to create an ironical letdown by descending from a noble tone or image to a trivial or ludicrous one. For example, in Henry FIELDING's burlesque *The Tragedy of Tragedies* (1731), Lord Grizzle addresses Princess Huncamunca: "Oh! Huncamunca, Huncamunca, Oh!/ Thy pouting Breasts, like Kettle-Drums of Brass,/ Beat everlasting loud Alarms of Joy. . . ." BATHOS is an unintentional anticlimax.

Antigone   In Greek mythology, the elder daughter of Oedipus. Antigone is the heroine of Sophocles' tragedy ANTIGONE, and a principal character in his *Oedipus at Colonus* and in Euripides' PHOENICIAN WOMEN. She appears briefly in the interpolated ending of Aeschylus' SEVEN AGAINST THEBES.

Antigone   One of the earliest extant tragedies of SOPHOCLES. After the defeat of the expedition of THE SEVEN AGAINST THEBES, Creon, now king, decrees that the body of Polyneices shall lie unburied, in defiance of the rites due the dead. Antigone, OEDIPUS' daughter, gives her brother a token burial and, though she is affianced to his son Haemon, Creon condemns her to be buried alive. Warned by TIRESIAS, he regrets his act too late; Antigone and Haemon kill themselves, and Creon's wife Eurydice does the same on hearing the news.

Antigone (1942) A play by Jean ANOUILH, first produced despite censorship as an allegory of France under the Vichy government.

anti-hero A protagonist who lacks traditional heroic virtues and noble qualities and is sometimes inept, cowardly, stupid, or dishonest, yet sensitive. The type is best represented in modern fiction and drama, although it appears as early as 1605, in DON QUIXOTE. James Joyce's Leopold Bloom in ULYSSES, Kingsley Amis's Jim Dixon in LUCKY JIM, and Joseph Heller's Yossarian in CATCH-22 are anti-heroes.

Antin, David (1932–   ) American poet, art critic. *Definitions* (1967), *Autobiography* (1967), and *Code of Flag Behavior* (1968) contain Antin's early and more conventionally structured verse. In 1976 he published a volume entitled *talking at the boundaries*, a collection of "talk poems," consisting of improvisations recorded on tape and then transcribed on the typewriter. Antin describes these texts as "scores of oral poems" that recall classical oral poetry. He attempts to restore narrative to contemporary verse by making poetry a series of anecdotes. Although at first sight the text seems like prose, careful reading reveals a highly organized and selective employment of poetic language and imagery. Antin published *Who's Listening Out There?* in 1980 and *Tuning* in 1984.

Antiquary, The (1816) A novel by Sir Walter SCOTT, his own favorite among his works. It deals with the love of William Lovel for the daughter of Sir Arthur Wardour in the time of George III.

Antonio (1) The title character of Shakespeare's MERCHANT OF VENICE.

(2) The treacherous brother of Prospero in Shakespeare's THE TEMPEST. With the help of Alonso, the king of Naples, Antonio has usurped Prospero's dukedom and cast him and his infant daughter adrift on a rotting bark. He is never troubled by conscience but is, at last, forced to restore his brother's rightful position to him.

Antony, Mark (Latin name Marcus Antonius, c82–30 BC) Roman triumvir and general. Antony was one of the tribunes who in 49 BC supported Caesar and joined him before crossing the RUBICON. He was appointed consul in 44 and, after Caesar's death, swung the populace against the assassins to his favor with his eloquent oratory. It was at this time that CICERO delivered his famous Philippics (orations) against Antony. In 43 the Second TRIUMVIRATE of Antony, Octavius (later Augustus), and Lepidus was formed. Caesar's assassins, Brutus and Cassius, were defeated at Philippi in 42. From the year 40 on, Antony lived chiefly at Alexandria with CLEOPATRA, queen of Egypt, abandoning his wife Octavia, sister of Octavius. Open hostilities between Octavius and Antony broke out, and in 31 the combined forces of Antony and Cleopatra were defeated by Octavius at Actium. Antony committed suicide in Egypt after hearing a false report of Cleopatra's death (circulated, some say, by Cleopatra herself in an attempt to win Octavius's favor by causing Antony's death).

In Shakespeare's JULIUS CAESAR, he is portrayed as a devoted friend of Caesar. Though he is fond of revelry and amusements, he is also a shrewd strategist and capable general. After Caesar's death, he skillfully turns public opinion against the assassins by means of his funeral oration, which begins with the famous lines:

> Friends, Romans, countrymen, lend me your ears;
> I come to bury Caesar, not to praise him.
> The evil that men do lives after them,
> The good is oft interred with their bones;
> So let it be with Caesar.

Antony is depicted in Shakespeare's ANTONY AND CLEOPATRA as a declining hero, torn between his love for Cleopatra and his political ambitions. After his death, Agrippa utters a fitting epitaph:

> A rarer spirit never
> Did steer humanity; but you, gods, will give us
> Some faults to make us men.

Antony and Cleopatra (c1607) A tragedy by William SHAKESPEARE. Having given himself over to a life of sensual pleasure with CLEOPATRA in Egypt, Marc ANTONY returns to Rome upon hearing of his wife's death and of an attack on Italy by the forces of Sextus Pompeius. In Rome the differences between Antony and the two other triumvirs, Octavius CAESAR and Lepidus, are patched up by Antony's marriage to OCTAVIA, the sister of Octavius. When Antony, succumbing to Cleopatra's enticements, returns to Egypt, Octavius seizes upon the insult to his sister as a pretext for attacking his erstwhile ally. Octavius wins the naval battle of Actium when Cleopatra's fleet deserts. Antony, after unsuccessfully seeking to make terms with the victor, hurls defiance at him. Defeated in a later land battle and believing Cleopatra dead, the despairing Antony falls on his sword. Hearing that she is still alive, he is taken to her and lives long enough to lay his last kiss upon her lips. When Cleopatra learns that Octavius, now sole master of the empire, plans to lead her in triumph through Rome, the proud and imperious queen applies an asp to her bosom and joins her lover in death.

Shakespeare's source for the play was Sir Thomas North's translation (1579) of Plutarch's *Lives*. Dryden's drama *All for Love* (1678) also describes the last days of Antony and Cleopatra and for many years was more frequently performed than the Shakespearean version. See ENOBARBUS, DOMITIUS.

Apes of God, The (1930) A novel by Wyndham LEWIS. It is an epic satire on the rich Bohemian artistic coteries, which in Lewis's eyes reflected the social decay of the period. Among writers satirized are the Sitwell family, Gertrude Stein, James Joyce, and Virginia Woolf and the Bloomsbury Group.

aphorism   A compact statement, such as a MAXIM or PROVERB, that concisely expresses a principle or common experience. The term was first used by HIPPOCRATES. The beginning sentence of his *Aphorisms* is a well-known example: "Life is short, art is long, opportunity fleeting, experimenting dangerous, reasoning difficult."

Aphrodite   The Greek goddess of erotic love and marriage. Although Homer calls Aphrodite a daughter of Zeus and Dione, the more common story has her born from the foam that gathered about the severed parts of the emasculated Uranus. She is said to have first stepped ashore on the island of Cythera, just off the coast of Laconia, hence her epithet *Cytherea*. Her name was identified by the Greeks with the word *aphros*, "seafoam." As an Olympian deity, she was the wife of Hephaestus but the lover of Ares. A familiar story about her tells how Hephaestus trapped her in bed with Ares, by throwing a delicate golden net over them, and displayed their embarrassment to the other gods. In late Greek myth, Aphrodite was called the mother of EROS.

It is generally agreed that Aphrodite was originally an Asiatic goddess similar to ISHTAR. An ancient center of her worship was the island of Cyprus, for which she was often called *Cypris*. In Rome, she was identified with Venus. See ADONIS.

apocalyptic literature (fr Gr, *apokalupsis*, "uncovering")   A type of prophetic literature common in ancient Hebrew and early Christian writing. It is filled with veiled symbolism (see FOUR HORSEMEN OF THE APOCALYPSE) and inspired by visions of the future triumph of the Messianic kingdom. THE REVELATION OF SAINT JOHN THE DIVINE is often called the *Apocalypse*.

Apocrypha (fr Gr, *apokrupto*, "hidden")   Certain Old Testament books of doubtful authority. These books are included in the Greek (Septuagint) and Latin (Vulgate) versions of the Old Testament but are usually regarded as noncanonical or of secondary value by other Christians and Jews. They are seldom printed in Protestant Bibles, but, in the Authorized Version of 1611, they are given immediately after the Old Testament. The New Testament also has a large number of apocryphal books associated with it, consisting of later gospels, epistles, apocalypses, and such fragments as the *Logia*. ORIGEN was the first to apply the term to books used by the church, to designate writings of a questionable character; it has come to signify false and heretical literature.

Apollinaire, Guillaume (born Wilhelm Apollinaris de Kostrowitski, 1880–1918)   Italian-born French poet and critic. In 1898 he met Alfred JARRY in Paris and was attracted to *l'esprit nouveau*, the new spirit in esthetic theory, which sought an exciting synthesis of the arts. A friend of PICASSO, BRAQUE, and other avant-garde artists, Apollinaire wrote *Antitradition futuriste* and *Les Peintres cubistes* (tr *The Cubist Painters*, 1949) in 1913. The latter

work first established CUBISM as a school of painting. The poems in *Alcools* (1913; tr 1964) combined classical verse forms with modern imagery, involving transcriptions of street conversations overheard by chance and the absence of punctuation. In *Calligrammes* (1918; tr 1980), Apollinaire used words to draw lines in patterns suggestive of various objects: a watch, the rain, the Eiffel Tower. This controversial typography was thought to carry poetry to its extreme limits. He called *Les Mamelles de Tiresias* (1903; pub 1917) a "drame surréaliste," apparently the source of the name of the surrealist movement (see SURREALISM). It was made into an opera (1947) by Francis POULENC. Apollinaire's other works include short stories in *L'Hérésiarque et Cie* (1910) and *Le Poète assassiné* (1916; tr *The Poet Assassinated*, 1968); a verse play, *Couleur du temps* (1918); the posthumously published poems in *Ombre de mon amour* (1948); and letters in *Tendre comme le souvenir* (1952).

Apollo   A Greek god, son of Zeus and Leto. Originally, perhaps, a god of flocks, Apollo also became a god of healing, music, and archery. As Phoebus Apollo, he came to be the god of light but not properly of the sun. He was born, with his sister Artemis, on the island of Delos, where his mother had taken refuge from the jealous Hera. At an early age, he killed the Python, the sacred snake of the DELPHIC ORACLE, and took charge of that oracle, which had previously belonged to a succession of earth goddesses. Though implacable in anger, as the fates of MARSYAS and NIOBE show, he was surprisingly unsuccessful in love, to judge from the number of nymphs and mortals, such as DAPHNE and Marpessa, who rejected his advances. Nevertheless, he has been called "the most Greek of Greek gods," speaking more than once for modern concepts of justice and human relations, as opposed to the more primitive traditions. The most notable example of this tendency is his defense of Orestes on the Areopagus, dramatized in Aeschylus' *Eumenides*.

Apollonian and Dionysiac   Terms used by Friedrich Nietzsche in THE BIRTH OF TRAGEDY to designate the two central principles in Greek culture. The Apollonian, which corresponds to Schopenhauer's *principium individuationis* ("principle of individuation"), is the basis of all analytic distinctions. Everything that is part of the unique individuality of a man or thing is Apollonian in character; all types of *form* or *structure* are Apollonian, since form serves to define or individualize that which is formed; thus, sculpture is the most Apollonian of the arts, since it relies entirely on form for its effect. Rational thought is also Apollonian, since it is structured and makes distinctions.

The Dionysiac, which corresponds roughly to Schopenhauer's conception of "will," is directly opposed to the Apollonian. Drunkenness and madness are Dionysiac because they break down a man's individual character; all forms of enthusiasm and ecstasy are Dionysiac, for in such states a man gives up his individuality and submerges himself in a greater whole; music is the most Dionysiac of the arts, since it appeals directly to man's instinctive, chaotic emotions and not to his formally reasoning mind.

Nietzsche believed that both forces were present in Greek tragedy and that true tragedy could be produced only by the tension between them. He used the names *Apollonian* and *Dionysiac* for the two forces because Apollo, as the sun god, represents light, clarity, and form, whereas Dionysus, as the wine god, represents drunkenness and ecstasy.

Apologie for Poetrie, An   An essay by Sir Philip SIDNEY, written 1580–83 in answer to an attack on poetry by the Puritan Stephen Gosson in *The School of Abuse* (1579). Sidney's essay defines as poetry all imaginative writing. In addition to defending its worth and replying to Puritan accusations against it, Sidney gives his own critical appraisal of the poetry and drama of the time. Two different editions of the essay, one titled *An Apologie for Poetrie*, the other *The Defense of Poesie*, were posthumously published in 1595.

Apology for Raymond Sebond   (Apologie de Raimond Sebond)   The longest of the ESSAYS of Michel de MONTAIGNE. It gives fullest expression to his skeptical philosophy. Montaigne's "defense" of the treatise of Sebond, a 15th-century Spaniard who attempted to demonstrate the existence of God by analogy with the hierarchy of nature in which man occupies the highest rung, was a pretense for demolishing the validity of reasoning altogether. Sebond's proof, asserted Montaigne, was no less credible than any other proof. Man vainly believes himself superior to the rest of creation by virtue of his reason, whereas in fact all his theorizing has not uncovered a single universal truth. Montaigne's skepticism was an affirmation of the relativity of knowledge and was essentially a healthy reaction to the excessive faith in reason of the early Renaissance. It cleared his mind of preconceptions and prepared him for a search for wisdom based not on intellectual speculation but on his own experience.

aposiopesis   Deliberate failure to complete a sentence, for rhetorical effect. As a figure of speech, the form is often used to convey an impression of extreme exasperation or to imply a threat, as, for example, in "If you do that, why, I'll—" in which the rest of the sentence is understood.

apostles   (fr Gr, *apostolos*, "messenger; envoy") Jesus' twelve original disciples: PETER, ANDREW, JAMES THE LESS, JOHN, PHILIP, BARTHOLOMEW, THOMAS, MATTHEW, Simon the Canaanite (also Simon Zelotes), JUDE (also Thaddaeus and Lebbaeus), JAMES THE GREATER, and JUDAS ISCARIOT. Jesus gave His message to the apostles personally and gave them the task of being his witness after His death.

He shared with them the LAST SUPPER, which has become the fundamental sacrament of Christian worship.

To the apostles, Jesus entrusted the work of establishing the Church, with Peter to be the "rock" upon which it was built. Matthias was later chosen to take Judas Iscariot's place. All of the apostles met martyr's deaths except John and, of course, Judas Iscariot, who committed suicide.

Beside Judas Iscariot, two other apostles have not been canonized: Philip and Simon the Canaanite. Paul, though not one of the original twelve, is always classed as an apostle, as is often Barnabas, Paul's companion in his first mission.

Apostolic Fathers   A term used since the late 16th century to describe the early Christian writers whose work dates from the late 1st to the early 2nd century and who were thought to have had contact with the APOSTLES. The five Apostolic Fathers most referred to are Clement of Rome, Hermas, Ignatius, BARNABAS, and Polycarp. Some of their writings were held as sacred texts by early Christian groups and came close to consideration as NEW TESTAMENT canon. They are of particular historical interest since they illuminate early Christian doctrine and practice and show the influence of Judaism on early Christianity.

apostrophe   A figure of speech, the direct address of a person or thing, usually absent, for rhetorical effect. The thing addressed is often personified, as in "Hence, loathed Melancholy!" which begins Milton's "L'Allegro." The object of the apostrophe is frequently a real person, living or dead, as in "Milton, thou shouldst be living at this hour," the beginning of Wordsworth's sonnet on Milton.

Appian Way   (Lat, Via Appia)   The oldest and best preserved of all the Roman roads. It leads from Rome to Brundisium (Brindisi) by way of Capua. This "queen of roads" was commenced by Appius Claudius, the censor, in 312 BC.

apple of discord   In Greek mythology, the initial cause of the Trojan War. All the gods and goddesses except Eris (Discord) were invited to the wedding of Thetis and Peleus. In revenge, Eris threw among the guests a golden apple inscribed "For the fairest." Hera, Athene, and Aphrodite claimed it and were referred to Paris, the handsomest man in the world, for judgment. See JUDGMENT OF PARIS.

Appleseed, Johnny   (nickname of John Chapman, 1774–1845)   American orchardist and folk hero. Born in Massachusetts, Chapman wandered westward to Pennsylvania, Ohio, Illinois, and Indiana. For fifty years, he led a nomadic existence, preaching and distributing apple seeds to all he met. It is said that the orchards of the four states above owe their origin to Chapman's seeds.

Johnny Appleseed has become a favorite American folk hero, celebrated in many stories and poems. Vachel LINDSAY, who frequently referred to him, wrote a long poem called "In Praise of Johnny Appleseed" (1923).

apples of perpetual youth   In Scandinavian mythology, magical golden apples. They were in the keeping of Idhunn, daughter of the dwarf Svald and wife of Bragi. By tasting them, the gods preserve their youth.

apples of Sodom   Fruit which, in classical tradition, grew beside the Dead Sea. They are lovely in appearance but full of ashes within. Josephus, Strabo, Tacitus, and others speak of them, probably referring to the gallnuts produced by the insect *Cynips insana*.

Après-midi d'un faune, L'   (The Afternoon of a Faun, 1876)   A poem by Stephane MALLARMÉ. It presents the wandering thoughts of a faun on a drowsy summer afternoon. The poem inspired Debussy's *Prélude à l'après-midi d'un faune* (1894), which was choreographed and danced by Nijinsky for Diaghilev's Russian Ballet in 1912.

Apsarases   In Hindu mythology, heavenly nymphs who tempted ascetics in their meditation. See URVASĪ.

Apuleius, Lucius   (fl c AD 155)   Latin writer. Apuleius is best known today for his prose romance *Metamorphoses*, or THE GOLDEN ASS, written in eleven volumes and the only Latin novel that survives in its entirety. Here, in a prose style as odd and fanciful as the tale itself, he narrates the story of a man who, transformed into a donkey, wanders from land to land observing the preposterous and brutal foibles of mankind. In one of the episodes, Apuleius recounts the famous story of Cupid and PSYCHE.

Aquinas, St. Thomas   (c1225–1274)   Italian scholastic theologian and philosopher, often called the Angelic Doctor (Lat, *Doctor Angelicus*). Aquinas came from a noble family, who strongly objected when he joined the Dominican Order in 1243 and forcibly detained him for over a year. He finally reached Paris and began his studies under ALBERTUS MAGNUS, whom he followed to Cologne in 1248. He began teaching at Paris in 1252 and thereafter taught alternately in Paris and in Italy. In 1254 he began his commentaries on the *Sentences* of Peter LOMBARD, on Boethius, and on the Bible, revealing Albertus Magnus and St. AUGUSTINE of Hippo as the greatest influences on his thought.

The treatises that followed were later incorporated into his two great *Summae*, or summaries of human knowledge. The *Summa [de Veritate Catholicae Fidei] contra Gentiles* (1259–64) defends "the truth of the Catholic faith against the pagans" by making clear the distinction between the realms of reason and of faith: reason seeks knowledge from experimental and logical evidence, while faith seeks understanding through revelation but uses the knowledge provided by reason. Thus they can never be in conflict, and both come from and reveal God as the source of all truth. The SUMMA THEOLOGICA, his greatest work, continues on this basis to summarize all that is known about God and man from the sources of both reason and faith.

Aquinas's followers were called *Thomists* in later scholastic disputes, especially with the Scotists (see John DUNS

SCOTUS). His synthesis of theology and philosophy, known as Thomism, has since been officially recognized as a cornerstone in the doctrines of the Roman Catholic Church.

Arabian Nights' Entertainments, The   A collection of ancient Persian-Indian-Arabian tales, originally in Arabic, arranged in its present form about 1450, probably in Cairo. The collection is also known as *A Thousand and One Nights*. Although the stories are discrete in plot, they are unified by SCHEHERAZADE, the supposed teller; she postpones her execution by telling her husband, SCHAHRIAH, a story night after night, without revealing the climax until the following session.

The first European translation, into French, was Antoine Galland's twelve-volume (1704–17) free rendering of the oldest known manuscript, that of 1548. In 1840 E. W. Lane published a new scholarly English translation (3 vols); John Payne's translation appeared in nine volumes, 1882–84; and Sir Richard Burton's monumental English version (10 vols) was issued only to subscribers by the Kamashastra Society of Benares in 1885–86. Among the more recent editions is a four-volume edition by Powys Mathers, completed in 1937. See ALI BABA AND THE FORTY THIEVES; CALENDER; CARPET, MAGIC; SINBAD THE SAILOR.

Arab-Israeli conflict   Hostilities that have erupted between Israel and its neighboring states since the proclamation of the republic of Israel in 1948, such as the Six-Day War of 1967 in which the Old City of Jerusalem, the Sinai peninsula, the Gaza Strip, the West Bank, and the Golan Heights fell under Israeli rule, the Yom Kippur War in 1973, and a series of other battles, as well as many attacks by terrorists. The Arab-Israeli conflict is the subject of many books and the background in many novels and poems.

Arachne   In Greek mythology, a Lydian maiden who challenged Athena to compete with her in needle tapestry. Athena metamorphosed Arachne into a spider out of jealousy. *Arachnida* is the scientific name for spiders, scorpions, and mites.

Aragon, house of   A noble family of Spanish origin. Its members ruled in Sicily and later in southern Italy from the 13th through the 15th century. At Naples, the outstanding King Alfonso of Aragon (1385–1458), surnamed the Great, who ruled from 1443, was a celebrated patron of Humanists and poets. Under his inspiration, the men of letters gathered at his court founded the Neapolitan Academy, which included such men as Pontano and Sannazaro.

Aragon, Louis   (1897–1982)   French novelist, poet, and essayist. After brief associations with CUBISM and DADA, Aragon was attracted to the freedom of expression in SURREALISM and under its influence wrote *Le Paysan de Paris* (1926; tr *Nightwalker*, 1970). He soon broke with this movement, however, criticizing the ideal of "pure poetry" in *Traité du style* (1928), and became a Communist in

1930, thereafter to devote his art to the ideal of social revolution. He was prosecuted for his poem *The Red Front* (1931), but responded with more poetry—*Persécuteur persécuté* (1931) and *Hourra l'Oural* (1934)—and with contributions to leftist magazines. His social novels depicting "the real world," as the series is collectively titled, include: *Les Cloches de Bâle* (1934; tr *The Bells of Basel*, 1936), *Les Beaux Quartiers*, (1936; tr *Residential Quarters*, 1938), and *Les Voyageurs de l'impériale* (1941; tr *The Century Was Young*, 1941). *Aurélien* (1944) and *Les Communistes* (1949) are autobiographical. Aragon abandoned current politics, however, in *La Semaine sainte* (1958; tr *Holy Week*, 1961), a panoramic epic of the flight of Louis XVIII at the beginning of Napoleon's one hundred days in 1815.

His other books of poetry include *Le Crève-coeur* (1941), *Les Yeux d'Elsa* (1942), *Brocéliande* (1942), and *Le Nouveau Crève-coeur* (1948). Many of these poems describe his participation in the Resistance and his love for his Russian-born wife, the writer Elsa TRIOLET. *L'Oeuvre poétique* (7 vols) was published in 1974. *Chroniques de la pluie et du beau temps* (1979) is a collection of his critical essays.

Aramis   One of the famous trio in Dumas's THE THREE MUSKETEERS and a prominent character in its sequels *Twenty Years After* (1845) and *The Viscount of Bragelonne* (1848–50). Aramis, always soberly garbed in black, regularly swore that he would soon forego his adventures for a pious life in a monastery.

Araucana, La   (1569–1590)   An epic poem by Alfonso de Ercilla y Zúñiga (1533–94), Spanish soldier and poet who went to Chile after the conquest and fought against the indomitable Araucanian Indians. The stubborn resistance of the Araucanians against Spanish rule is the theme of the poem. Ercilla stresses the nobility and valor of the Indians and of their leaders Lautaro and Caupolicán, who are drawn in Homeric proportions.

Arbuthnot, John   (1667–1735)   Scottish writer and court physician to Queen Anne. Arbuthnot was a close friend of Alexander Pope and Jonathan Swift and formed with them the SCRIBLERUS CLUB. His works include *The History of* JOHN BULL, which typified and fixed John Bull as the personification of England; *The Art of Political Lying* (1712), an essay; *Know Thyself* (1734), a philosophic poem; and *The Memoirs of Martinus Scriblerus* (1741), an attack on pedantry. He is the addressee of Pope's EPISTLE TO DR. ARBUTHNOT.

Arcadia   A district of the Greek Peloponnesus. According to Vergil, it was the home of pastoral simplicity and happiness. This notion was an early example of an illusion that has beset sophisticated intellectuals ever since: namely, that a simple, rustic life is not only idyllic but also somehow nobler than a more complex urban existence. The Arcadians were, as a matter of fact, the most backward of the Greeks, retaining to a relatively late date primitive,

even savage customs that had long since died out elsewhere in Greece. Hence, to less poetically minded authors, the term *Arcadian* came to have a derogatory meaning.

The name *Arcadia* was taken by Sir Philip SIDNEY as the title of his famous pastoral romance (1590) and was soon generally adopted into English with much the old Vergilian significance. A 17th-century painting by Guercino and a more famous one by Poussin of a slightly later date show a shepherd's tomb on which is the inscription *Et in Arcadia ego* ("Also in Arcadia [am] I"), signifying presumably that death is present even in the most ideal earthly life.

archangel   A chief angel. In Judeo-Christian Scriptures and legend, there are four: Michael, the warrior; Raphael, the healer; Gabriel, the herald; and Uriel, the bringer of light. In the Koran, the four are Michael, the champion of the faith; Gabriel, the angel of revelations; Azrael, the angel of death; and Israfel, who sounds the trumpet of the resurrection. In the medieval hierarchy (see ANGEL), the archangels comprise the second order of the third division.

Archer, Isabel   The heroine of Henry James's PORTRAIT OF A LADY. A girl of great vitality, Isabel has an insatiable thirst for experience, which causes her to reject the proposal of Lord Warburton, a wealthy and cultivated Englishman, and to marry the shadowy and sinister Osmond. At all times treated sympathetically by James, she comes to realize the danger of her American expansiveness. Nevertheless, she asserts her inner freedom by refusing to leave the man she married.

archetype   Generally, a prototype or original pattern or a paradigm or abstract idea of a class of things that represents the typical and essential elements shared by all varieties of that class. In literature, myth, folklore, and religion, the term can be applied to images, themes, symbols, ideas, characters, and situations that appeal to our unconscious racial memory. T. S. ELIOT explains this memory as civilized man's "pre-logical mentality." The archetype, or primordial image, touches this "pre-logical mentality." The psychology of Carl JUNG and the comparative anthropology of J. G. FRAZER have given the study of archetypal patterns greater usefulness in literary criticism.

Archetypes can be primitive and universal and consist of general themes like birth, death, coming of age, love, guilt, redemption, conflict between free will and destiny, rivalry between members of the family, fertility rites; of characters like the hero rebel, the wanderer, the devil, the buffoon; and of creatures like the lion, serpent, or eagle.

Archimedes   (c287–212 BC)   Syracusan mathematician, astronomer, and inventor. Several of Archimedes' treatises, including that on the sphere and the cylinder, are still extant. Archimedes discovered the principle of the displacement of water, which, by means of specific gravity, he used to test the amount of base metal in the crown of Hieron, ruler of Syracuse. He is said to have exclaimed

"EUREKA," or "I have found it," when the principle occurred to him as he stepped into his bath.

archy and mehitabel The famous cockroach and cat created by Don MARQUIS in his newspaper column. Their stories were written at night in Marquis's deserted office by the literary archy, who was obliged to write without capitalization because he could not operate the shift key on the typewriter. Archy often related the ribald adventures of the indomitable mehitabel, whose motto was "toujours gai." The volume *the lives and times of archy and mehitabel* (1940) contains the original collection of the columns, *archy and mehitabel* (1927), and its sequels, *archy's life of mehitabel* (1933) and *archy does his part* (1935).

Arden, John (1930–) English playwright. Arden's work exemplifies the rugged individualism associated with his native Yorkshire. Trained as an architect, he writes carefully structured, nonconformist plays, usually based on a central paradox. Characteristic of his plays is a studied ambiguity, a juxtaposition of opposites in character, action, feeling, or social position, and a refusal to assign any moral absolutes—all qualities evident in his best-known work, *Serjeant Musgrave's Dance* (1960). Like much of his work, his first full-scale production, *Live Like Pigs* (1958), is written in a mixture of prose and ballad-like verse. *Armstrong's Last Goodnight* (1965) uses the Scottish border wars of the 1550s as a parable of the recurrent clash between freedom and political order. Several of Arden's subsequent plays were written in collaboration with his actress-wife, Margaretta D'Arcy, including the political plays *Ars Longa Vita Brevis* (1965), *Harold Muggins Is a Martyr* (first performed in 1968), and *The Ballygombeen Bequest* (first performed in Belfast, N. Ireland, in 1972).

Arendt, Hannah (1906–1975) German political philosopher, naturalized U.S. citizen 1950. Arendt received her doctorate at the age of twenty-two from the University of Heidelberg, where she studied with Karl JASPERS. She fled HITLER's Germany in 1933 and eventually settled in the U.S. (1941), where she held numerous teaching posts and became the first woman to be appointed full professor at Princeton University. She ended her career at the New School for Social Research in New York. Her reputation as a profound and independent philosophical analyst of political systems was launched with the publication of *The Origins of Totalitarianism* (1951), in which she documented the belief that Nazism and Communism had their roots in the anti-Semitism and imperialism of the 19th century. She continued to offer challenging and unconventional theories about the decline of values in modern society, in such books as *The Human Condition* (1958), *Between Past and Future* (1961), and *Crises of the Republic* (1972). A storm of controversy surrounded the publication of *Eichmann in Jerusalem: A Report on the Banality of Evil* (1963), in which she suggested that even the Jews could be held partly responsible for Germany's barbarisms in World War II. Her other works include *On Revolution* (1963) and *On Violence* (1970), in which she suggested that violence is a response to powerlessness. Her philosophically most ambitious work, *The Life of the Mind* (1978), a three-volume study of the fundamental mental activities thinking, willing, and judging, though unfinished (only the volumes *Thinking* and *Willing* were completed), is a penetrating analysis of the processes of the mind and of their corresponding effects on action.

Areopagitica (1644) A pamphlet by John MILTON, written as an argument against restriction of freedom of the press. Probably Milton's best-known prose work, because of the greatness of its cause and the eloquence of its rhetoric, it commands more interest than most of his other theological or political writings.

Areopagus The hill of Ares, located in Athens, west of the Acropolis. According to Greek myth, it was so named because it was there that Ares was tried for the murder of Halirrhothios, son of Poseidon. According to another story, the hill was named after an epithet of Athene, who had cast the deciding vote in the second trial of Orestes, supposedly held on this hill.

The name was also applied to a council of former *archons*, who assembled there. Under DRACO, the council had the duty of judging murderers and exercised general administrative powers. Ephialtes and PERICLES reduced the scope of its function.

Ares The Greek god of war, a son of Zeus and Hera. Ares was a lover of APHRODITE, by whom he had several children, but he also had various other mistresses. Probably Thracian in origin, Ares had no characteristics except belligerence and therefore was rather disapproved of by the Greeks.

Argonauts A group of mythological heroes. The Argonauts sailed to Colchis to recover the GOLDEN FLEECE. Jason had demanded the throne of Iolcos from Pelias, who had usurped it from his brother Aeson, Jason's father. Pelias agreed, if Jason would first return the Fleece to Greece. Those who joined Jason in this adventure included HERACLES, ORPHEUS, Castor and Polydeuces, Peleus, Melampus, Mopsus, Meleager, Atalanta, Admetus, Aeolus' winged sons Calais and Zetes, the lynx-eyed Lynceus and his quarrelsome brother Idas, Telamon, Pelias' own son Acastus, and many others. ARGUS built their ship, the *Argo*, under Athene's direction, and Hera aided them throughout the voyage so as to punish Pelias for refusing to worship her.

Their first stop was Lemnos, where the women, lonely after having killed their husbands a year before, vainly entreated them to stay. They were hospitably received by the Doliones but killed their king Cyzicus by mistake. In Mysia, when Heracles' beautiful young favorite Hylas was drowned in a spring by a love-struck naiad, Heracles would not give up the search for Hylas and had to be left behind.

The Argonauts were challenged to box by Amycus, king of the Bebryces, who had killed many strangers in this manner. Polydeuces accepted the challenge and quickly killed Amycus. At Salmydessus they saw blind old King Phineus, whose days were made miserable by the Harpies, which stole or befouled his food before he could eat—a punishment for his having revealed too much, as a seer, of the ways of Zeus. Zetes and Calais saved him by pursuing the Harpies until Iris promised that they would not return. In gratitude, Phineus gave the Argonauts much useful advice.

With the help of this advice and of Athene's aid, the Argonauts passed through the Clashing Rocks, which usually sprang together to crush ships between them. Later, their shouts and the clashing of their shields drove off the birds of Ares, which attacked them with a hail of sharp plumes. By a happy chance, they saved the four sons of Phrixus from shipwreck and were led by them to their home, Colchis, where King Aeetes kept the Fleece. The cruel Aeetes promised to relinquish the Fleece if Jason could pass a test: he must plow a field with two fire-breathing bulls, sow dragon's teeth, and fight the armed men who would spring up (see also SPARTI). Jason succeeded with the secret aid of Aeetes' daughter MEDEA, who had fallen in love with him. Aeetes refused to honor his promise, but Medea lulled to sleep the dragon that guarded the Fleece, and the Argonauts escaped with both Medea and the Fleece.

The Argonauts were pursued but escaped again, when Jason and Medea treacherously slew her half-brother Apsyrtus and (according to some versions) flung pieces of his body from the ship. Zeus ordained that the Argonauts suffer many hardships for this outrage before reaching home. Making their way via the Danube, Rhine, and Rhone to the Mediterranean, they reached the island of Aea, where Circe, Aeetes' sister, purified Jason and Medea of murder. Thetis helped them past the Wandering Rocks; the singing of Orpheus got them safely past the SIRENS. While they were entertained by the Phaeacians, Queen Arete secretly arranged the marriage of Jason and Medea, and King Alcinous protected the Argonauts from pursuing Colchians.

Blown to the coast of Africa, they were marooned with their ship in the desert, but they were helped or encouraged by Libyan nymphs, by the Hesperides, and by the god Triton. As they neared Crete, the bronze giant Talus nearly crushed their ship with rocks but was destroyed by Medea's sorcery. The Argonauts returned to Iolcos, where a trick of Medea's disposed of Pelias, and, Aeson having died, Acastus became king. Jason returned the Fleece to the temple of Laphystian Zeus in Orchomenus.

Next to the Trojan War, the voyage of the *Argo* was the event most often celebrated in Greek epic. It is the subject in particular of the *Argonautica*, the masterpiece of Apollonius of Rhodes, which is notable for the psychological realism with which its characters are treated, its memorable picture of Medea, and its remarkably unheroic portrayal of its hero, Jason.

Arguedas, Alcides (1879–1946) Bolivian novelist, historian, and diplomat. Although Arguedas spent many years in Europe, especially in France, where he was Bolivian consul, his best-known writings reflect his abiding concern with the problems of his homeland. He is remembered primarily for three works, each in a different field. *Pueblo enfermo* (1909) is a pessimistic and controversial analysis of Bolivian society. One of the most famous of the Indianist novels, *Raza de bronce* (1919) describes the exploitation of Bolivian Indians by inhuman landlords. Arguedas's most enduring work may be his five-volume *Historia de Bolivia* (1920–29), which covers that country's history from 1809 to 1872.

Arguedas, José María (1911–1969) Peruvian novelist and poet. Arguedas was among the first Latin American writers to write about the Indian from an inner perspective. He grew up in Indian communities and was trained as an anthropologist, experiences which contributed to his ability to capture in his fiction a full array of the emotion and thought of the disappearing Indian culture of Peru. His work is distinguished by extensive use of Quechua Indian songs, language, and syntax. In *Agua* (1935), *Yawar Fiesta* (1941), and *Los ríos profundos* (1958; tr *Deep Rivers*, 1978), Arguedas creates Indian characters of unprecedented warmth and ample human dimensions, emphasizing that only when Peru accepts the Indian with pride, along with the Mestizo and Criollo cultures, will the country move forward. An unusual and powerful amalgam of lyricism and violence characterizes Arguedas's later short stories and novels: *Todas las sangres* (1964), about Peru's racial mixtures, and *El zorro de arriba y el zorro de abajo* (1971), left unfinished when Arguedas committed suicide.

Argus (or Argos) (1) A fabulous creature. According to Greek mythology, Argus had one hundred eyes, for which he was called *Panoptes*. Hera set him to watch Io, of whom she was jealous. Hermes, however, acting under orders of Zeus, who had his eye on Io, charmed Argus to sleep and slew him. Hera changed Argus into a peacock, whose tail was full of eyes. "Argus-eyed," therefore, means jealously watchful.

(2) The builder of the ship *Argo* for the ARGONAUTS. Argus was assisted by Athene.

(3) Odysseus' faithful dog, who, in the ODYSSEY, recognized his old master on his return to Ithaca.

Ariadne In Greek mythology, daughter of Minos, king of Crete. Ariadne gave Theseus a clew of thread to guide him out of the Cretan LABYRINTH. Theseus married his deliverer but forsook her when he arrived at Naxos. Later she became the wife of Dionysus. It is generally agreed that Ariadne was the name of a Cretan mother-goddess. Richard Strauss wrote an opera called *Ariadne auf Naxos* (1912).

Arians The followers of ARIUS, a presbyter of the church of Alexandria, in the 4th century. He maintained (1) that the Father and Son are distinct beings; (2) that the Son, though divine, is not equal to the Father; (3) that the Son had a state of existence previous to His appearance on earth, but not from eternity; and (4) that the Messiah was not a real man, but a divine being in a case of flesh. The Arian tenets varied from time to time and also among their different sections. The heresy was formally anathematized at the COUNCIL OF NICAEA (325), but the sect was not and never has been wholly extinguished.

Ariel A sprite in Shakespeare's THE TEMPEST. Ariel has been freed by PROSPERO from a pine rift in which he was imprisoned by the evil witch Sycorax. Invisible at will, all light and spirit, he seems to symbolize man's imagination. After serving Prospero faithfully, Ariel is at last freed when his master renounces his magic.

Ariel (1900) An essay by José Enrique RODÓ, which had a tremendous impact on Hispanic American intellectuals. Rodó appealed to the youth of Spanish America to aspire to the spirituality, idealism, and rationality symbolized by Shakespeare's Ariel and to reject the brutishness and sensuality represented by Caliban. Because Rodó censured U.S. materialism and utilitarianism in the essay, many readers erroneously assumed that he was pitting Anglo-Saxon crassness against Latin idealism. The essay is, however, a generalized guide for the future. It was translated into English in 1922 by F. J. Stimson.

Ariel (1965) A collection of poems by Sylvia PLATH. Written in the last few months before Plath's suicide in 1963, *Ariel* charts the pathological aspects of an era, as well as those of the poet herself. The poems tend to dehumanize people by converting them into metaphors of horror: mannequins, figures cut out of paper, victims of Nazism, etc. Hallucinatory imagery provides a nightmare context for the "I" of the poems, who is cut off from herself, her loved ones, her culture. The poems are love songs to Death.

Arion (fl c700 BC) A Greek poet and musician. According to legend, Arion was cast into the sea by mariners but was carried to Taenaros on the back of a dolphin.

Ariosto, Lodovico (1474–1533) Italian poet. Ariosto was born at Reggio, in Modena, and served the Este family of Ferrara for most of his life. His poems, satires, and learned plays were popular and respected in his day, but his masterpiece remains the ORLANDO FURIOSO (*Roland Mad*). A continuation of BOIARDO's epic ORLANDO INNAMORATO (*Roland in Love*), it is a long narrative poem in octave stanzas, dealing with the adventures of ROLAND and other knights of Charlemagne in wars against the Saracens.

Aristarchus (Aristarchus of Samothrace, fl 156 BC) The greatest critic of antiquity and head of the Alexandrian library. Aristarchus' labors were chiefly directed to the ILIAD and ODYSSEY of HOMER. He divided them into twenty-four books each, marking every doubtful line with an obelus and every one he considered especially beautiful with an asterisk. He succeeded his teacher, ARISTOPHANES OF BYZANTIUM, at the library in Alexandria.

Aristides (530–468 BC) An Athenian statesman and general. Aristides is called *The Just* for his impartiality and honesty, which have become proverbial. According to tradition, an illiterate Athenian once came to Aristides, whom he did not recognize, and asked him to write the name of Aristides on a ballot demanding his ostracism from the state. The man explained that he had grown tired of hearing Aristides forever called *The Just*. Without revealing his identity, Aristides wrote his own name.

Aristophanes (445–c380 BC) A Greek comic playwright. Little is known of Aristophanes' life except that his first produced play won a second prize when he was only eighteen, and he continued to write fine comedies at a rate of about one a year for more than twenty years. His last two extant plays, *Ecclesiazusae* (392) and *Plutus* (388), were produced after the fall of Athens in 404 BC. Perhaps because it was no longer possible for him to criticize the state freely, these comedies are considerably inferior to his earlier works.

Aristophanes was a brilliant if somewhat wide-swinging social satirist, who used the traditional freedom of OLD COMEDY to ridicule public figures, institutions, and even the gods. His favorite butts were the demagogue Cleon, whom he attacked in THE KNIGHTS and several other plays, and Euripides, who was lampooned in THE FROGS and THESMOPHORIAZUSAI. Socrates is the victim in THE CLOUDS, in which Aristophanes inaccurately and unfairly makes him a wily sophist who teaches men to cheat others through cunning argumentation. It is apparent that the playwright was conservative in his views, disapproving of Euripides' humanizing of the gods and heroes, of modern trends in music and philosophy, and of the war with Sparta, whose rigid traditionalism he may even have admired. As a practical writer of comedy, however, he also knew that it is easier to draw laughter by ridiculing newfangled fads than by pointing out absurdities in modes of behavior that are generally accepted.

Another indication of the license permitted Old Comedy is the open but never prurient obscenity of the plays, a custom that began with their origin in one aspect of the fertility rites of Dionysus. (Aristophanes' eleven plays are only surviving examples of Old Comedy.) It is all the more striking that Aristophanes does not hesitate to make Dionysus, the patron of the dramatic festivals, an absurd figure in *The Frogs* or to give men the upper hand over the gods in THE BIRDS.

Aristophanes was the most imaginatively original of the Greek playwrights, in that, while the others wrote of (supposedly) historical figures, he invented not only completely new characters and situations but even entire worlds out of whole cloth. He was also a fine poet who wrote delicate and charming lyrics in his choral songs. His masterpiece, *The Birds*, is a remarkable example of both these outstanding qualities. In it he creates a delightfully improbable kingdom of birds and men, Cloudcuckooland, and his characters, both feathered and otherwise, sing one lovely lyric after another all through the play. Unfortunately for modern audiences, some of the qualities that make Aristophanes' comedies successful are difficult or impossible to reproduce in modern English: his poetry, his topical satire, and his knack for puns and garbled literary allusions. In spite of this, his comic genius was so universal that a great deal of the humor of his plays still comes through.

Aristophanes of Byzantium (fl 195 BC)   A leading critic, head of the Alexandrian library. Aristophanes is known for his editing of the works of Homer and for devising, or at least standardizing, the accents since used in the Greek language. These accents were intended for the benefit of foreigners learning Greek, a language that all educated people were expected to know in the days of the Roman empire. He was the predecessor and teacher of ARISTARCHUS.

Aristotle (384–322 BC)   Greek philosopher, born at Stagira. Brought up in a family of moderate wealth and position, Aristotle went at the age of eighteen to Athens to study in Plato's Academy, where he remained for twenty years, until the death of his teacher. He moved to Assos, then to Mytilene, then to Macedon, whence he was invited by King Philip to tutor the young Alexander. Aristotle remained in Macedonia for eight years, until Philip was assassinated (336 BC) and Alexander succeeded to the throne. Much of Aristotle's work in natural history was done during the time he spent in Assos, Mytilene, and Macedon. On his return to Athens, he taught at the LYCEUM. Finally, at Alexander's death in 323 BC, Aristotle left Athens, where there was an upsurge of anti-Macedonian feeling, and retired to Chalcis, where he died a year later.

The works for which he was most widely known among the ancients have been lost, but fragments indicate that they were dialogues written in a highly polished rhetorical style. These are referred to as his exoteric writings, or those designed for the general public outside his school. A second class of writings, the esoteric, or those designed for use by the students of the Lyceum, has survived. These are called the acroamatic writings and are known to us as the treatises of Aristotle. A third class of writings, the hypomnematic, or memoranda, has also been lost.

The treatises include first the logical works (*Categories, Topics, De interpretatione, Prior Analytics, Posterior Ana-*

lytics, Sophistical Refutations) known as the *Organon*, or instrument. For Aristotle, logic was preparation for scientific knowledge, not knowledge itself. He was the first to insist on rigorous scientific procedure, and his method of demonstration by the syllogism and by dialectic, or reasoning from the opinions of others, became standard philosophic method. Aristotle maintained that all human knowledge originates in sensible experiences, out of which the soul perceives the universal.

Aristotle's natural philosophy, contained in the eight books of the *Physics*, examines the physical universe. They include the important distinction between the substance (or essence) of a thing and its accidental properties. Other works in this group include *On the Heavens* (*De caelo*), *On Coming into Being and Passing Away* (*De generatione et corruptione*), and *Meteorology* (*Meteorologic*). *Parva naturalia* and *De anima* are his works on psychology. He wrote an introduction to biology called *Historia animalium*, in which he classified the animals, their methods of reproduction, and their evolution. In his treatises on metaphysics, known as *Metaphysica*, Aristotle discusses theology, or primary philosophy, which he considered the highest type of theoretical science. Unlike his teacher Plato, he does not posit a separate world of perfect Forms or Ideas but always finds form immanent in matter.

There are two Aristotelian ethical treatises, known as the *Nicomachean Ethics* and the *Eudemian Ethics*. According to the former, happiness is the goal of life. Pleasure, fame, and wealth, however, will not bring one the highest happiness, which is achieved only through the contemplation of philosophic truth, because it exercises man's peculiar virtue, the rational principle.

In Aristotle's *Politics* (eight books), the good of the individual is identified with the good of the city-state. The study of human good is thus a political inquiry, as it is in Plato. Aristotle discusses different types of government, finally preferring monarchy, an aristocracy of men of virtue, or constitutional government of the majority. Slavery is considered natural in Aristotle's politics, because some men are adapted by nature to be the physical instruments of others. Aristotle's *Rhetoric* treats methods of persuasion; the *Poetics* is his great contribution to literary criticism.

Called by Dante "the master of those who know," Aristotle mastered every field of learning known to the Greeks. His influence on St. Thomas Aquinas and the medieval world, through the translation of the Arabic scholar Averroes, was profound and enduring.

Arius (c256–336)   Greek ecclesiastic. Arius lived and taught in Alexandria. His teachings on the nature of God constitute what is called the Arian heresy or Arianism. Arius felt that God is separate from the world, alone and unknowable. He taught that Jesus was a mortal, created being, not fully divine, and as such should be worshiped as secondary to God. At the church councils of Nicaea (325) and Constantinople (381), Arius and his followers were condemned as teachers of false doctrine. See ARIANS.

Ark of the Covenant A wooden chest (possibly a model of a temple) overlaid with gold, in which the presence of Jehovah was believed to dwell when communicating with Israel. The Ark was portable and was carried into battle. Its contents are thought to have been the stone tablets recording the law as given to Moses. It was installed in the Holy of Holies of Solomon's temple at Jerusalem. The fate of the original Ark is not known: it disappeared after the fall of Jerusalem in 586 BC.

Arlen, Michael (1895–1956) Armenian-born English author. Arlen wrote well-crafted novels about fashionable society that were popular in the 1920s and 1930s. The best known is THE GREEN HAT.

Armada, Spanish (also known as the Invincible Armada; Sp, *armada*, "fleet") The fleet assembled in 1588 by PHILIP II of Spain for the conquest of England. The armada, which consisted of some 130 ships and carried over thirty thousand troops, set sail from Lisbon on May 29 under the command of the duke of Medina Sidonia. Its destination was the Netherlands, where the fleet was to pick up an army under Alexander Farnese, the duke of Parma, and transport it across the channel for an invasion of England.

After being forced by a storm to put in at Corunna for repairs, the armada was sighted by the English near Plymouth on July 29. Medina Sidonia, who was under orders to sail directly to the Netherlands, retired before the lighter and more maneuverable ships of the English fleet, suffering several losses, until he anchored at Calais on August 6. Farnese's army, hemmed in by the Dutch fleet, was unable to stir. On August 7, the English sent fire ships among the Spanish vessels, forcing them to flee. The following day, the bitterest engagement of the campaign was fought off Gravelines, the Spaniards being bested by the gunnery of the combined English and Dutch fleets. A favorable change of wind enabled the armada to make for the North Sea and return to Spain by sailing around Scotland and Ireland, where severe storms caused further losses. The Spaniards lost over 63 ships and nine thousand men in the campaign, and Spanish prestige suffered a severe blow.

Armageddon The site for the last great battle between the forces of good and the forces of evil before the Day of Judgment (Rev. 16:16). The Hebrew word supposedly refers to *Megiddo*, which, in the history of Israel, was the scene of many battles. The word has come to mean any great final struggle or conflict and is comparable to RAGNAROK in Norse mythology.

Armida In Tasso's GERUSALEMME LIBERATA, a beautiful sorceress and niece of the enchanter Idraot.

Armida's garden A garden of gorgeous sensual delights, from lush flowers and fruits to alluring nymphs bathing in fountains, in a castle where Armida lives. It symbolizes the attractions of the senses and their power over human reason. As such, it links Armida with Circe and Alcina and is the inspiration of Spenser's Bower of Bliss.

Armida's girdle A magical girdle of incomparable beauty and worth worn by Armida. The source of many of her powers, it enables her to know and do whatever she wills.

Armies of the Night (1968) A book by Norman MAILER, subtitled "History as a Novel, the Novel as History." The title is derived from the final line of Matthew Arnold's DOVER BEACH. This first-person account of a massive anti-Vietnam War march on the Pentagon in October 1967 uses the narrative and descriptive techniques of fiction to report Mailer's perceptions of and participation in a moment of history. The blend of fact and fictional style exemplified what Tom WOLFE called the "new journalism." The book won the National Book Award and the PULITZER PRIZE in general nonfiction.

Arminianism A religious heresy, opposed to Calvinism. It began in Holland in the early 17th century and then spread to England and the colonies in America. It denied the leading Calvinistic tenets that only the elect were to benefit by the sacrifice of Christ's death and that the human will was powerless to reject or to forfeit divine grace once it had been received; it also opposed the doctrine of absolute predestination. Jonathan EDWARDS violently attacked Arminianism in America.

Arminius (18 BC–AD 21) Assumed to be the Latin form for Hermann, the heroic chief of the Germanic Cherusci tribe. Although he had served in the Roman army as commander of Germanic contingents, he led the Cherusci against their Roman oppressors. In AD 9 they annihilated three legions (about twenty thousand men) in the Teutoburg forest (Westphalia). The battle is important in world history because it ensured the survival of the Germanic element in Western culture. TACITUS called Arminius "without doubt the liberator of Germania." Arminius was murdered by relatives five years after his defeat by GERMANICUS, but his memory lived on in heroic LAIS among Teutonic tribes. Since the early 16th century, he has been a Germanic hero, celebrated in history and literature but also in chauvinistic propaganda. Dramas about the *Hermannsschlacht* ("Arminius's battle") were written by KLOPSTOCK (1769), Heinrich von KLEIST (1808), and GRABBE (1838).

Armory Show An exhibition of American and European modern art held in the 69th Regiment Armory, New York City, in 1913. Among the organizers and contributors were Arthur Davies and John SLOAN. At this show, Americans got their first look at the revolutionary work of such artists as Matisse, Kandinsky, Brancusi, Maillol, Picasso, and Braque. The painting that most attracted public attention was Marcel Duchamp's *Nude Descending a Staircase*, which one critic renamed "explosion in a shingle factory." In general, the conservative art critics were hostile to the show, especially to the foreign works, which were much more extreme than those from the U.S. The public, however, flocked to the show: over 250,000 people paid to see the wild-looking European painting and sculpture. A few were conscious at once of what the Armory Show implied for art in America: modern art had arrived full-fledged from Europe, and it was in the U.S. to stay.

In the winter of 1963, the fiftieth anniversary of the Armory Show was celebrated in the same building. All of the works hung in the original show that could be traced were reexhibited, most of those jeered at in 1913 being now considered masterpieces—or even outmoded.

Arms and the Man (1894)   A play by George Bernard SHAW. Set in Bulgaria, it satirizes romantic attitudes about war. The title is taken from the first line of Vergil's AENEID: *Arma virumque cano* ("I sing of arms and the man"). The libretto of the comic opera *The Chocolate Soldier* (1909) by Oskar Straus was unofficially based on the play.

Arnim, Ludwig Joachim von (known as Achim von Arnim, 1781–1831)   German novelist, poet, and dramatist. Achim von Arnim was a close friend of Clemens BRENTANO, whose sister Elisabeth ("Bettina," 1785–1859) he married in 1811. With Brentano, he edited the famous folksong collection *Des Knaben Wunderhorn* (*The Boy's Wonderhorn*; vol 1, 1805; vol 2, 1808; vol 3, 1818), which immediately seized the public imagination, kindled an interest in the German past, and ushered in the second great wave of GERMAN ROMANTICISM. Although he wrote several plays, his other most notable contribution was to the romantic historical novel, particularly with *Isabella von Ägypten* (1812; tr *Isabella of Egypt*, 1927) and the unfinished *Die Kronenwächter* (*Guardians of the Crown*, 1817), about Germany during the REFORMATION.

Arnold, Matthew (1822–1888)   English critic and poet. The son of Thomas Arnold (1795–1842), the clergyman who became headmaster of Rugby and made it one of England's most renowned public schools, young Arnold began his literary career as a poet, publishing *The Strayed Reveler and Other Poems* (1849); *Empedocles on Etna and Other Poems* (1852); *Poems* (1853); *Poems, Second Series* (1855); *Merope*, a dramatic poem (1858); and *New Poems* (1867). His poetry tends to be elegiac and brooding, and at its best is among the finest expressions of the plight of the sensitive Victorian caught between "two worlds, one dead,/ The other powerless to be born." His most famous poems are THE SCHOLAR-GIPSY, based on the legend of an Oxford student who, in poverty, joined a band of gypsies; "Stanzas from the Grande Chartreuse" (1855), in which the narrator, visiting a Carthusian monastery, mourns the loss of faith in the modern world; "Thyrsis" (1866), an elegy written on the death of Arnold's friend Arthur Hugh Clough, which Swinburne adjudged, after Milton's *Lycidas* and Shelley's *Adonais*, the finest elegy in the English language;

and DOVER BEACH, perhaps his best-known poem, which uses the image of the sea as a metaphor for the Sea of Faith, ebbing away from the naked shores of the world.

In 1857 Arnold was elected to the professorship of poetry at Oxford. During the ten years that he held this position, he delivered many of the lectures that were to become part of his essays on criticism. The best-known collections of these are *On Translating Homer* (1861), *Essays in Criticism* (1st series, 1865; 2nd series, 1888), CULTURE AND ANARCHY, and *Literature and Dogma* (1873). Seeing literature as both shaper and sustainer of the highest elements of culture, he urged that the great mass of the public—the "Philistine" middle class—be educated to improve its response to literature (and culture). He argued for high standards of literary judgment, using the "lines and expressions of the great masters . . . as a touchstone to other poetry." He believed that the English were too immersed in the spirit of "Hebraism," or strictness of conscience and rightness of conduct, and not sufficiently touched by the symmetry and spontaneity of "Hellenism"; he saw religious fundamentalism as one expression of this Hebraism, and Arnold attempted to interpret the Bible as literature and show that, as in all great poetry, the poetry of the Bible contained the moral and spiritual truths that were the essence of religion. He saw the task of the critic as "a disinterested endeavor to learn and propagate the best that is known and thought in the world." He is of importance as a shaper of both English and American criticism, up to the time of T. S. Eliot.

Arnolphe   In Molière's comedy L'ECOLE DES FEMMES, a man of wealth with stern ideas on the proper training of girls to make good wives. He applies his educational methods to Agnès, whom, in time, he intends to make his wife.

Arnoux, Mme Marie   One of the main characters in the novel L'EDUCATION SENTIMENTALE by Gustave Flaubert. Frédéric Moreau suffers the passion of unrequited love for Mme Arnoux during the years of her marriage. In an ironic conclusion, when she comes to him, a middle-aged widow, Frédéric rejects her offer of love.

Around the World in Eighty Days (Le Tour du monde en quatre-vingt jours, 1873)   A romance by Jules VERNE. The hero, Phileas Fogg, undertakes his hasty world tour as the result of a bet made at his London club. He and his French valet Passepartout meet with some fantastic adventures, but these are overcome by the loyal servant and the endlessly inventive Fogg. The feat they perform is incredible for its day; Fogg wins his bet, having circled the world in only eighty days.

Arp, Jean (or Hans Arp, 1887–1966)   German-born French artist and poet. Arp was associated with such avant-garde groups as the BLAUE REITER in Munich; with Hugo Ball, among others, he founded the DADA Cabaret Voltaire in Zurich (1916). He is known for his subtle use of abstract curved forms in such varied media as sculpture, bas reliefs, collages, and wood blocks. His writings include the poetry in *Worttraüme und schwarze Sterne* (*Word-Dreams and Black Stars*, 1953), and *Arp on Arp* (1972, ed Marcel Jean).

Arrabal, Fernando (1932–   )   Spanish playwright and novelist, born in Spanish Morocco, resident in France since 1955. Arrabal writes in Spanish, though his works, translated by his wife, appear first in French. His plays are written in the tradition of the THEATRE OF THE ABSURD—in a style he has called "panic theatre," an effort to create an all-embracing art that can reconcile and comprehend opposites and contradictions—illustrating the way life attaches political, psychological, theological, and linguistic restrictions to freedom. His plays shock and entertain through surrealistic devices and are filled with ritual, sexual fantasies, anarchy, and blasphemy. His first play, *Pique-nique en campagne* (1959; tr *Picnic on the Battlefield*, 1967), was written at the age of fourteen and is still the most frequently performed of all his plays. Arrabal is probably best known for *L'Architecte et l'empereur d'Assyrie* (*The Architect and the Emperor of Assyria*, 1969), first performed in 1967, in which two buffoons meet on a desert island and play out the master-slave relationship. Another well-known shorter play is *Guernica* (1967; tr 1969), which dramatizes the terrible bombing of the hapless Basque village by German planes during the Spanish Civil War. *Et ils passèrent des menottes aux fleurs* (1969; tr *And They Put Handcuffs on the Flowers*, 1971), inspired by Arrabal's experience as a prisoner in Franco's Spain, is considered the most powerful of his political plays. *The Red Madonna, or a Damsel in Distress* (1986) is based on the true story of a well-born Spanish woman who decides to have a child out of wedlock. Arrabal has also written several novels, one of which, *Baal Babylone* (1959; tr *Baal Babylon*, 1961), he subsequently made into a film, *Viva la muerte* (1971).

Arrivi, Francesco (1915–   )   Puerto Rico's most important dramatist. Arrivi's early plays, such as *El diablo se humaniza* (1940), *Club de solteros* (1940), and *Alumbramiento* (1945), were realistic social documentaries. His later work grew increasingly poetic, with more carefully drawn characters, as in his trilogy about Puerto Rico's history and people, *Máscara puertorrigneña* (1971).

Arrowsmith (1925)   A novel by Sinclair LEWIS. It follows the career of Dr. Martin Arrowsmith from his training through a small-town practice, the health department of a small city, an "institute" sponsored by a rich man and his wife, to an isolated West Indian island and an equally isolated Vermont farm. In his quest for pure science, Arrowsmith encounters meanness, corruption, and misunderstanding; he is often frustrated, and he finally fails when he himself refuses to carry his principles to their logical extreme. Filled with medical lore, the novel is frequently

satiric and caused much controversy when it was first published.

Arsinoé   (1) The false prude of Molière's comedy LE MISANTHROPE.

(2) The scheming stepmother in Pierre Corneille's tragedy *Nicomède* (1651).

Ars Poetica (The Art of Poetry, c13 BC)   A treatise by the Roman poet HORACE, laying down rules for the writing of poetry. English critics of the Renaissance and post-Renaissance periods were greatly influenced by this work.

Artagnan, Charles de Baatz d' (1623–1673)   One of the famous guardsmen whose amazing adventures Alexandre Dumas narrates in THE THREE MUSKETEERS, *Twenty Years After* (1845), and *The Viscount of Bragelonne* (1848–50). The works follow d'Artagnan through his various exploits to his death as Comte d'Artagnan, marshal of France. He is always the soldier—quick-witted, quick-tempered, and extraordinarily brave.

Artaud, Antonin (1896–1948)   French actor, producer, dramatic theorist, and poet. Artaud was briefly associated with André BRETON and the surrealist movement, but he rejected their ideas because of their involvement with politics. In 1926 he founded the Théâtre Alfred-Jarry, but it failed within two years. He was by turns fascinated with Balinese theatre, Mexican religions, and Irish mythology. Tortured throughout most of his life by poverty, drug addiction, and mental and physical illness, he left a legacy that took nearly thirty years to reach fruition in the works of such avant-garde dramatists as Samuel BECKETT, Eugène IONESCO, Jean GENET, and Edward ALBEE.

Artaud rejected psychological and narrative realism in the theatre. He also distrusted words and spoken dialogue, calling instead for a language of gestures, shapes, light, and movement to express the magical, metaphysical aspect of man—his concept of "total theatre." In *Le Théâtre de la cruauté* (1935; tr *The Theater of Cruelty*, 1977) and *Le Théâtre et son double* (1938; tr *The Theater and Its Double*, 1958), he argued that symbolic myths and archetypes should liberate the audience through the ruthless portrayal of the internal conflicts of the human mind. By creating as few barriers as possible between the spectator and the drama on stage, he evolved an improvisational, spontaneous theatre, anticipating the "happenings" of the 1960s. See THEATRE OF CRUELTY; THEATRE OF THE ABSURD.

Artemis   Greek goddess of hunting and childbirth, daughter of Leto and sister of Apollo. Perhaps originally a Cretan goddess of fertility, Artemis came to be regarded as a virgin, who demanded chastity from her female attendants and even from her male devotees, such as HIPPOLYTUS. Her attendants (who were either local goddesses or local versions of Artemis herself) included HECATE, CALLISTO, Opis, Britomartis, and the mortal Iphigenia. She figures importantly in Euripides' plays HIPPOLYTUS and *Iphigenia in Aulis* (see IPHIGENIA).

Artemis of Ephesus, temple of   One of the SEVEN WONDERS OF THE ANCIENT WORLD. It contained a famous statue of the goddess—a cone surmounted by a bust and covered with breasts—which was said to have fallen from Heaven. However, Minucius, in the second century AD, described it as a wooden statue, and Pliny, a contemporary, claimed that it was made of ebony. As Diana of the Ephesians, this goddess, who bears a somewhat doubtful relationship to the Greek ARTEMIS, appears in an episode in Acts 19:24–28.

art for art's sake   English equivalent of the French *l'art pour l'art*, which itself derives from Edgar Allan Poe in *The Poetic Principle*:

There neither exists nor can exist any work more thoroughly dignified . . . than the poem which is a poem and nothing more—the poem written solely for the poem's sake.

The doctrine which this represents, that the aim of art should be creation and the perfection of technical expression rather than the service of a moral, political, or didactic end, had been evolving ever since the romantic period. It was adumbrated by Coleridge and given early expression by Poe in the above treatise, flowered among the French symbolist poets and their English associate Walter Pater, and reached its culmination in surrealism and the aesthetic theory of I. A. Richards. It was the dominant theory of art and especially of poetry until the 1930s, when the proletarian and Marxist movements in literature threatened for a time to revive the 18th-century didactic theories. After the beginning of World War II in 1939, the latter movements began to lose much of their influence.

Artful Dodger   A young thief in Charles Dickens's OLIVER TWIST, pupil of Fagin. The Dodger became perfectly adept in villainy and in pickpocketing especially.

artha (Sans, "thing; object; substance")   One of HINDUISM's four legitimate ENDS OF MAN, normally taken to mean material possessions and including political power. Relevant teaching is termed *Arthashastra* (authoritative instruction in the art of material possession), the most famous and comprehensive treatise being that attributed to Kautilya, the legendary chancellor of the emperor Chandragupta Maurya (end of 4th century BC). Kautilya's *Arthashastra* has been likened to the works of PLATO, ARISTOTLE, and MACHIAVELLI for its systematic exploration of statecraft.

Arthur   The hero of a great cycle of medieval romance (see ARTHURIAN LEGEND). There was a historical Arthur, a Celtic chieftain who lived in Wales during the 6th century. Little is known of him except that he was mortally wounded (according to the ANNALES CAMBRIAE) in the battle of Camlan and was taken to GLASTONBURY, where he died. However, while elements of the historical Arthur have been infused into the medieval romances, evidence indicates that there was an earlier, mythical Arthur, possibly a Celtic deity, whose origins are unknown. In telling and retelling the story of Arthur and in attempting to produce a coherent narrative out of diverse sources, the medieval romancers introduced Christian and other elements, not originally Arthurian, thus further confusing its origin. Despite the strong influence of Christianity in the later versions of Arthur, scholars detect the Celtic myth in which the GRAIL is a thinly disguised caldron of plenty and the opponents of Arthur and his knights the last echoes of earlier, long-displaced deities.

By the time the Arthurian legends were given permanent shape in Malory's *Morte d'Arthur* (c1469), the figure of Arthur as a legendary hero had become fairly distinct. He was the natural son of UTHER PENDRAGON and IGRAINE (see MERLIN) and was raised by Sir Ector. By pulling the sword EXCALIBUR from a block of stone, he proved his right to the throne of England. He subdued twelve rebellious princes, of whom LOT, king of Norway, was chief, and won twelve great battles against the Saxon invaders. About his ROUND TABLE, he gathered a group of knights whose deeds of daring and chivalry won his court high renown. Arthur himself became known far and wide as a mighty warrior and a just and generous ruler. His wife was GUINEVERE, his most valiant knight LAUNCELOT. In the earlier romances, the ruin that finally overtakes Arthur was due entirely to Guinevere and the traitorous MORDRED; the story of her illicit love for Launcelot and its demoralizing effect on the court was added later. In distinct contrast to Malory and the older romancers, who say that Arthur's sons were born out of wedlock, Tennyson in his IDYLLS OF THE KING makes Arthur a man of the highest morals, not only absolutely loyal to Guinevere but requiring that his knights "cleave to one maiden only." The treason that brought an end to Arthur's court was hatched while he was away on conquest. After his return and defeat in a final, terrible battle, the mortally wounded king was borne away to the island of AVALON, where some accounts say that he was buried, while others say that he dwells with his sister MORGAN LE FAY "till he shall come again full twice as fair to rule over his people."

Arthur, Timothy Shay   See TEN NIGHTS IN A BARROOM.

Arthurian legend   A great body of literature that revolves around the partly mythical, partly historical figure of King ARTHUR. It seems to have neither traceable beginning nor foreseeable end, but the earliest extant written references to Arthur are found in Welsh literature of the 6th century. Sources of information include the writings of the historian Gildas (c540), a poem entitled *Gododin* (c600), the work of the historian NENNIUS (c800), the ANNALES CAMBRIAE (c955), THE SPOILS OF ANNWN (10th century), and the very important MABINOGION, a collection of tales that includes *Kulhwch and Olwen*, perhaps the earliest, full-fledged Arthurian romance.

In the 12th century, the fame of Arthur spread to England, where it was noted by William of Malmesbury in his *Gesta Regum Anglorum* (*Chronicle of the Kings of England*, c1120–28). In Geoffrey of Monmouth's Latin HISTORY OF THE KINGS OF BRITAIN, Arthur attained full stature, becoming a great national figure, the hero-king of marvelous deeds, accompanied by such figures as MERLIN, GUINEVERE, GAWAIN, and MORDRED. UTHER PENDRAGON also made his appearance in context with the now traditional story of Arthur's conception, and there is what may be the first mention of Arthur's departure, mortally wounded, for AVALON.

The Norman poet Wace transformed the work of Geoffrey of Monmouth into an elegant verse chronicle, ROMAN DE BRUT. In this adaptation, the chivalric setting was expanded; the Round Table was introduced for the first time; and the death of Arthur was further dramatized by the suggestion that he had gone to Avalon to be healed of his wounds, with the expectation of returning one day to Britain.

The innovations of the French poet CHRÉTIEN DE TROYES involved, essentially, the unification of existing Arthurian materials into new narrative form. He wrote individual tales that highlighted the deeds of individual knights. The best known of these is *Lancelot*, a story that recounts the intensely enacted drama of Launcelot's adventures in the name of his great and undying love for Queen Guinevere, thus introducing into the stream of Arthurian legend that wondrous knight, Launcelot, and the important medieval theme of COURTLY LOVE.

The English priest Layamon (fl 1198–1207) took the chronicle of Wace as his model and wrote THE BRUT—perhaps the first of the legends of Arthur to be composed in the English language. Layamon elaborated on the Round Table motif, effectively mixed native folk tradition with Norman elegance, and drew upon Celtic lore for a description of Arthur's journey to Avalon, where Morgan le Fay waited to heal his wounds.

During the 13th century, the tales of Arthur enjoyed a period of popularity in Germany, which resulted in such works as those of Gottfried von Strassburg (early 13th century) and WOLFRAM VON ESCHENBACH. In the 14th century, Arthurian legend saw an artistic revival that produced two especially important pieces of English literature: *The Alliterative Morte d'Arthur* (c1360) and SIR GAWAIN AND THE GREEN KNIGHT. In the first, an anonymous work, Gawain is the central figure, and it is his death, not Arthur's, that is the dramatic high point of the poem. Even his murderer, Mordred, weeps bitterly that it was his destiny to kill such a knight. The emphasis is on an early English kind of epic treatment, so that this version has an affinity more with *Beowulf* than with the customary form of Arthurian romance. Norman lightness and Celtic magic have no place in this work. When Arthur dies, he is carried to Glastonbury, not Avalon, for a Christian burial.

The second important poem of the 14th-century English revival, *Sir Gawain and the Green Knight*, is one of the most important examples of Arthurian literature; its unknown author ranks with Chaucer as one of the greatest of the Middle English poets.

In the 15th century, the legends of Arthur were gathered together and given ultimate shape in Sir Thomas Malory's great English prose classic, LE MORTE D'ARTHUR. This rendition is, above all else, the work of a master story-teller. It was one of the works chosen for publication in 1485 by William Caxton, the first English printer, who gave it the title *Le Morte d'Arthur* and complained in a famous preface that Arthur was far better known and appreciated in other countries than his own. Caxton's complaint was subsequently more than answered as, one after the other, English poets dipped into Arthurian legend; the legend and the characters, however, changed, and the many versions reflect the changes in ideals, tastes, and preferences wrought by time. The Arthur in Spenser's THE FAERIE QUEENE, for example, is the ideal of manhood and bears little resemblance to earlier portraits of Arthur.

Perhaps the best-known modern retelling of the story of Arthur is Tennyson's IDYLLS OF THE KING. Like all the later romancers, Tennyson leaned heavily on Malory, but his approach is very different. The sin of Launcelot and Guinevere as the evil cause of the failure of the Round Table is strongly emphasized. Tennyson is often criticized for his shadowy, unreal, almost symbolic depiction of Arthur.

The story of Arthur has been told in the 19th and 20th centuries by such men as William Morris, Edwin Arlington Robinson, John Masefield, and Mark Twain, who burlesqued the romance of Arthur in *A Connecticut Yankee in King Arthur's Court* (1889).

The popularity of the story of Arthur continues, being more recently retold, for example, by T. H. White in *The Once and Future King* (1958). This work has served to demonstrate once more the astonishing appeal of the legendary king, once a remote Celtic chieftain, whose name has already figured in literature for at least fourteen hundred years.

Articles of Confederation and Perpetual Union The constitution by which the United States was governed from 1781 until the ratification of the new CONSTITUTION in 1789. The central government created by the Articles lacked strength because each state remained sovereign and independent; there was no effective executive officer, and Congress lacked the power to levy taxes. To remedy these defects, a Constitutional Convention was called in 1787, which resulted in the writing of a new constitution.

art nouveau Primarily a movement in decoration and applied design at the end of the 19th century. Its influence spread through Europe and pervaded painting, architecture, and, ultimately, even music and literature before fading, with the advent of World War I. Occurring in reaction to the eclecticism of the 19th century, *art nouveau* was hailed as totally original and unprecedented, arising from timeless, universal forms. Central to the aesthetic was organic fluidity, evoked by the plantlike or serpentine curves that are its hallmark. In Germany, *art nouveau* was called *Jugendstil* ("youth style"), after the journal *Jugend* (1896); other contemporary reviews reflecting the trend and its shaping influences were *Pan* (1895–1900), Beardsley's *Yellow Book* (1894), and V*er Sacrum* (1898), the organ of the Vienna Secession. In painting, the works of KLIMT and the Belgian Henry van de Velde (1863–1957) are exemplary, but numerous other artists were caught up in the movement. The ornate Spanish buildings of Antonio GAUDÍ and the Paris Métro stations of Hector Guimard (1867–1942) are the most famous architectural manifestations. The posters of Theophile Steinlen (1859–1923), the stage designs of Leon Bakst (1866–1924), the illustrations of Aubrey BEARDSLEY, and the glassware of Louis TIFFANY are all outstanding decorative applications of *art nouveau*. Ultimately, the movement deteriorated to a trite and superficial fashion, but its influence continues to be seen in surviving artifacts and occasional revivals of *art nouveau* decoration.

Aryan language (fr Sans, *arya*, "noble")   The Indo-European family of languages, from the name which the Hindus and Iranians used to distinguish themselves from the nations they conquered. The place of origin of these languages is not definitely known, authorities differing so widely as between a locality enclosed by the river Oxus and the Hindu-Kush Mountains, at one extreme, and the shores of the Baltic Sea at the other. The Aryan family of languages includes the Persian, Indic (Hindi, Sanskrit, etc.), Latin, Greek, and Celtic, with all the European except Basque, Turkish, Hungarian, and Finnic. It is sometimes called the Indo-European, sometimes the Indo-Germanic, and sometimes the Japhetic.

Asbjørnsen, Peter Christian (1812–1885)   Norwegian folklorist and naturalist. Written in collaboration with Jørgen E. Moe (1813–82), Asbjørnsen's four-volume collection *Norwegian Folk Stories* (1841–44) was a major contribution to the study of comparative FOLKLORE. Selections from the folk stories were translated as *Popular Tales from the Norse* (1858), *Fairy Tales from the Far North* (1881), and *East o' Sun and West o' Moon* (1917).

Ascanius (also known as Iulus)   In classic legend, the son of AENEAS. Ascanius escaped with his father from Troy and later ruled over the kingdom in Italy which his father had secured. After Aeneas' death, Ascanius himself built its capital, Alba Longa. The gens Julia (or Iulia), to which Julius Caesar and Octavius Caesar belonged, supposedly derived its name from Ascanius' other name, Iulus,

and accordingly sought to trace its lineage from the earliest ancestors of the Roman people. See AENEID.

Ascent of F6, The (1936)   A drama in verse by W. H. AUDEN and Christopher ISHERWOOD. In a political crisis involving a border dispute, Michael Ransom, a famous mountaineer, is persuaded to lead an expedition up F6, a mountain the natives of "British Sudoland" believe to be haunted in such a way that each man meets his own demon there. One by one, the climbers are killed, each because of some particular obsession or defect of character. Auden's concerns with both social and psychological conditions are manifested through the skillful use of symbolism.

Asch, Sholem (1880–1957)   Polish-born American novelist and dramatist. Asch, who wrote his books chiefly in Yiddish, is best known for his biblical novels: *The Nazarene* (1939), *The Apostle* (1943), and *Mary* (1949). These books reflect his conviction that Christianity should be considered the logical continuation of Judaism. *East River* (1946), a novel set in New York, illustrates the formation of the American character through the merging of diverse races and creeds. He wrote several plays; one, *The God of Vengeance*, was produced by Max Reinhardt in Berlin in 1910. Asch's later works include *Moses* (1951), *A Passage in the Night* (1953), *The Prophet* (1955), and *From Many Countries* (1958).

Ascham, Roger (1515–1568)   English prose writer and teacher, tutor to Elizabeth before her accession to the throne, later connected with her court as Greek preceptor. In his writings, he urged the adoption of sports in an educational curriculum and defended English prose as a literary medium. His best-known works are *Toxophilus* (1545), a treatise on archery, and THE SCHOOLMASTER (1570), which expounds his pedagogical theories.

Asclepius   Greek god of healing, son of Apollo and Coronis. Apollo killed the mother for infidelity but saved the unborn child, giving it into the care of CHIRON. Asclepius became extraordinarily proficient in medicine, but, when he brought Hippolytus back to life, Zeus, thinking he had gone too far in interfering with divine prerogative, destroyed him with a thunderbolt. In revenge, Apollo killed the Cyclopes. Asclepius was the father of Podalirus and Machaon, heroes at Troy, and of various daughters, who were mere personifications of one form or another of healing.

Asgard (fr ON, *as*, "god," *gard*[h], "enclosure; yard")   The celestial dwelling place of the Scandinavian gods, equivalent to the Olympus of Greek mythology. It was said to be situated in the center of the universe and to be accessible only by the rainbow bridge (*Bifrost*). Valhalla was the most famous great hall of its many regions and mansions, which also included Gladsheim, Vingolf, Valaskjalf, and Ydalir.

Ashbery, John [Lawrence] (1927–   ) American poet. A long-time friend of Kenneth KOCH and Frank O'HARA, Ashbery was associated for a time with the NEW YORK SCHOOL of poetry. He writes obscure, demanding verse that thematically resembles the TRANSCENDENTALISM of 19th-century American poetry. Echoing EMERSON, Ashbery envisions the world and human speech as emblems. In his early volume *The Tennis Court Oath* (1962), the transparency of self and its location in all things are themes reminiscent of Emerson and Walt WHITMAN. In *The Double Dream of Spring* (1970), Ashbery's use of ellipsis and allusion converts autobiographical material into fantasy or a dimly recalled dream. SELF-PORTRAIT IN A CONVEX MIRROR, for which Ashbery was awarded the unprecedented sweep of the 1976 PULITZER PRIZE, National Book Award, and National Book Critics Circle Prize, represents a further leap into shadowy reality. Painting is used here as a major structural device, specifically a self-portrait by Parmigianino, which prompts Ashbery to create poetically his own: a contemporary, spiritual portrait of depth and beauty. *Houseboat Days* (1977) represents more experimentation with the limits of art and the ways in which it may objectify reality. *Three Plays*, all "comedies of form," were published in 1978; other volumes of poetry include *As We Know* (1979) and *Shadow Train* (1981). Ashbery's *A Wave* (the title poem in a collection of forty poems) was published in 1984; as in his earlier poetry, words and images are eloquently brought together to illustrate the sense of flux metaphorically represented by the wave. In 1984, Ashbery, together with Fred Chappell, was awarded the Bollingen Prize for Poetry.

Ashcan School (also called The Eight and The New York Realists)   A term applied, loosely and belatedly, to a group of American realist painters. Although they never actually formed a school, eight painters—Robert Henri (1865–1929), John SLOAN, Maurice PRENDERGAST, George Luks (1867–1933), Everett Shinn (1876–1953), William Glackens (1870–1938), Ernest LAWSON, and Arthur B. DAVIES—held an independent exhibition at The Macbeth Gallery in New York in February 1908. Their paintings, which featured prizefights, bars, and city street scenes, rather than the decorative pictures that were fashionable at the turn of the century, were greeted with a storm of critical disapproval. The exhibition and the work of the artists involved, however, exerted an enormous influence on the development of American realistic painting.

Ashenden   The name W. Somerset MAUGHAM used for his own appearances in CAKES AND ALE. It is also the title of his novel *Ashenden, or The British Agent* (1928), based on his experiences with the British Secret Service during World War I.

Ashford, Daisy (1882–1972)   English writer, known as the author of *The Young Visiters* (1919). It is a story about Mr. Salteena, a butcher's son, and his rise to high society. It is noted for its misspellings and its accurate but naive observations of adults, resulting in fine, unconscious satire. The preface to the book was written by J. M. BARRIE, who claimed that the author, then a grown woman, was nine when she wrote it; hence, a "Daisy Ashford" is an imaginative, precocious child.

Ashley, Lady Brett   The principal female character in Ernest Hemingway's novel THE SUN ALSO RISES. An Englishwoman, in Spain while she divorces her husband, Lady Brett seeks to hide the emptiness of her life in friendship with the impotent Jake Barnes and an affair with the bullfighter Pedro Romero. She typifies the aimless pursuit of leisure of "the lost generation."

Ashley, Maurice [Percy] (1907–   )   English historian and biographer. A prolific historian of 17th-century England, Ashley began his career as a research assistant to Sir Winston CHURCHILL. His studies of Oliver Cromwell and the Commonwealth have been widely praised, as have his biographical works on members of the British and French monarchies. Among his many works are *Charles II* (1971), *James II* (1977), and *General Monck* (1977), the latter two being impeccably researched, balanced portraits of their controversial subjects.

ashrama   The Sanskrit name for the four stages of life in HINDUISM: (1) *brahmachārin*, the austere life of a student of sacred lore; (2) *grhasthya*, the life of a householder with wife and family; (3) *vānaprastha*, the life of a hermit, involving increasing separation from worldly affairs after the birth of grandchildren; (4) SANNYĀSIN, the life of a homeless wanderer, with all earthly ties broken. Combined with *varna* ("CASTE") and DHARMA, *ashrama* is integral to the basic Hindu doctrine of *varnashramadharma*, or sacred duty appropriate to one's rank and stage of life.

Ashton-Warner, Sylvia [Constance] (1908–   )   New Zealand novelist and teacher. Ashton-Warner's autobiographical writings—*Teacher* (1963), *Myself* (1967), *Spearpoint* (1972), and *I Passed This Way* (1980)—all reflect her experiences as a teacher in the New Zealand bush, her commitment to racial understanding, and her dedication to creative teaching principles. Her first two novels were praised for the psychological intensity of the main characterizations. *Spinster* (1958) contains a fictional elaboration of Ashton-Warner's "Creative Teaching Scheme," as applied by a lonely, neurotic, but highly gifted teacher. *Incense to Idols* (1960) is an exotic narrative in which a *femme fatale* falls hopelessly in love with a priest. Other novels are *Bell Call* (1965), *Greenstone* (1966), and *Three* (1970).

Ashtoreth   See ISHTAR.

Ash Wednesday   The first day of LENT, so-called from the ancient custom of sprinkling ashes on the heads of the clergy and people. The ashes are prepared from the palms blessed on Palm Sunday the previous year, symbolizing penitence and mourning. As the ashes are placed on the head, the priest says, "Remember, man, that thou art dust, and unto dust thou shalt return."

Ash Wednesday (1930)   A poem by T. S. ELIOT. The first of his poems to celebrate the peace found in orthodox Christianity, it is a poetic liturgy, meditation, and approach to mystical communion with God.

Asia   (1) In classic mythology, one of the Oceanides, usually spoken of as wife of Iapetus and mother of Prometheus. In his PROMETHEUS UNBOUND, Shelley makes Asia play an important part as Prometheus' wife.

(2) According to the Koran, the wife of the Pharaoh who brought up Moses. Asia's husband tortured her for believing in Moses, but she was taken alive into paradise. Muhammed numbers her among the four perfect women.

As I Lay Dying (1930)   A novel by William FAULKNER. It tells the story of the death of Addie Bundren and the ordeals her family undergoes in carrying the body to Jefferson, Mississippi, for burial. Her husband, Anse; her four sons, Cash, Darl, Jewel, and Vardaman; her daughter, Dewey Dell; and several neighbors all reveal their relationships with Addie in the course of the story. A series of mishaps besets the family: in crossing a flooding river, the mules are drowned, Cash's leg is broken, and the coffin is upset and rescued by Jewel. Later, the family rests at a farmhouse, where Darl sets fire to the barn, in an attempt to destroy the now-putrescent corpse; again the coffin is rescued by Jewel. The family finally reaches Jefferson, where Addie is buried; Darl is taken to the insane asylum, and Anse acquires a new wife.

In the course of the narrative, it is revealed that Jewel was born of Addie's affair with Whitfield, a local preacher. Her relationship to Anse had been spiritually and emotionally barren, based on words alone. Significantly, Jewel is a silent man, active and passionate, while Darl is sensitive and perceptive, living in the world of his own mind.

The story unfolds in some sixty short sections, each labeled with the name of the character who narrates his thoughts and perceptions; as in THE SOUND AND THE FURY, Faulkner uses the STREAM OF CONSCIOUSNESS technique. A grim story of the ordeals of fire and water, the novel is often comic, ending with the new wife, who is "duck-shaped" and popeyed.

Asimov, Isaac (1920–   )   Russian-born, American-educated writer and scientist. Asimov became an associate professor of biochemistry at Boston University in 1955, and a full professor in 1979. In 1979 he published *Opus 200*, a selection of favorite pieces from his second hundred books (*Opus 100* [1969] was a comparable volume, marking his first hundred). Asimov's extraordinary output includes textbooks, popular science for young readers, lucid interpretations of science for older readers, *Asimov's Guide to Shakespeare* (2 vols, 1970), *Isaac Asimov's Treasury of Humor* (1971), and an exuberant spate of science fiction novels and fantasies, some of which were written under the pseudonym Paul French. The two volumes *The Far Ends of Time and Earth* and *Prisoners of the Stars* (1979) offer a collection of his fiction. Among his interpretations of science are *Building Blocks of the Universe* (1957); *The Intelligent Man's Guide to Science* (2 vols, 1960; rev 1965); *The Stars in Their Courses* (1971); *Until the Sun Dies* (1977), about black holes; *Life and Time* (1978); and *A Choice of Catastrophes* (1979), about the disasters that threaten the world and the physical laws that keep it from falling apart. *In Memory Yet Green* (1979) and *In Joy Still Felt* (1980) are two volumes of autobiography. Recent works include *In the Beginning* (1981), *Foundation's Edge* (1982), *The Robots of Dawn* (1983), *Asimov's New Guide to Science* (1984), *The History of Physics* (1984), *Opus 300* (1984), and *The Exploding Suns: The Secrets of the Supernovas* (1985).

Ask (or Askr)   In Norse mythology, the first man, created out of an ash tree by Odin, Vili, and Ve. The first woman, created out of an elm, was Embla.

Asmodée   The devil-companion of Don CLÉOFAS, in Alain René LESAGE's picaresque novel *Le Diable boiteux* (1707), sometimes entitled *Asmodeus* or *The Devil on Two Sticks* in English translations. Asmodée is an engaging little lame devil, with a great deal more gaiety than malice. He takes pleasure in showing his companion human ugliness and depravity by lifting the roofs off houses in Madrid.

Asmodeus   The "evil demon" who appears in the Apocryphal book of Tobit. The business of Asmodeus was "to plot against the newly wedded and . . . sever them utterly by many calamities." According to Hebrew mythology, Asmodeus fell in love with Sara, daughter of Raguel, and slew her seven husbands in succession, each on his bridal night. He was exorcised and driven into Egypt by a charm made by TOBIAS (on the advice of the angel Raphael) from the heart and liver of a fish burnt on perfumed ashes (Tobit 6:14; 7:2). In the Talmud, Asmodeus is called "king of the devils." In Milton's PARADISE LOST (IV), Asmodeus is an evil spirit; in Book VI, Asmodai is a rebel angel vanquished by Raphael.

Aspasia   (1) A Milesian woman (fl 440 BC) celebrated for her beauty and talents. Aspasia lived at Athens as mistress of PERICLES, and her house became the center of literary and philosophical society; hence *Aspasia* means a fascinating and cultured courtesan. Walter Savage Landor wrote a series of imaginary letters, *Pericles and Aspasia* (1836).

(2) Titular heroine of Beaumont and Fletcher's drama THE MAID'S TRAGEDY. Aspasia is betrothed to Amintor, but the King, wishing to provide a husband for his mistress Evadne, commands Amintor to marry Evadne instead. Aspasia is a pathetic figure, the very type of ill-fortune and wretchedness, but she bears her fate with patience even when she becomes a jest and byword. Her tragic death gives the drama its name.

Aspects of the Novel (1927)   A literary study by
E. M. FORSTER. Defining the novel as any work of prose
fiction, Forster discusses the components, or "aspects," of a
novel in terms of character, plot, "fantasy," "prophecy" (or
symbolism), "pattern," and "rhythm." Because, he maintains, all art aspires to the depth and effects of music, the
novel should be structured as if it were a symphony. In his
discussion of "character," from which all other aspects of
the novel proceed, he formulates his famous distinction
between flat and round characters.

Aspern Papers, The (1888)   A novella by Henry
JAMES. According to passages in his notebook, James based
The Aspern Papers on a story he had heard concerning the
mistress of Byron, then living, who was in possession of
several unpublished papers and letters of both Byron and
Shelley. The narrator of *The Aspern Papers* learns that the
former mistress of the romantic poet Jeffrey Aspern is still
living in Venice and has in her possession a collection of
the poet's papers, which she will not permit to be published. In hope of gaining access to the papers, the narrator
rents a room from the old lady and her middle-aged niece,
but his plans are frustrated when, at the old lady's death,
the niece demands marriage as the price of the papers.

Assassins   A small Islamic sect. For two hundred
years, it terrified Europe with its secret murders. It was
founded by Hassan-i-Sabbah near the end of the 11th century. From the nearly impregnable mountain stronghold of
Alamut in Persia and later from the Syrian stronghold of
Masyad, the Assassins harried the Crusaders and their rival
Islamic sects, remaining unbroken in power even by the
great Saladin. They were finally destroyed in the 13th century by the Tatar prince Hulagu and, somewhat later, in
Syria, by the Egyptian Sultan Baybars.

The name *Assassins* is derived from *hashish*, a drug
made from hemp, with which, according to tradition, the
victorious Assassins were rewarded upon their return from
successful depradations. The secret of their long reign of
terror was the absolute obedience that the young men of
the sect were required to give to their leaders. The name of
the sect soon came into the languages of Europe as a synonym for murderer.

Assembly   During the FRENCH REVOLUTION, a representative body that had three names: the National, Constituent, and Legislative. In 1789 the *tiers état* (THIRD
ESTATE) declared itself to be the National Assembly and
controlling body and took the so-called OATH OF THE TEN-
NIS COURT. Shortly thereafter, reinforced by a majority of
clergy and a minority of nobles, it called itself the Constituent Assembly; in 1791 it framed and voted the first written
constitution in French history. The Constituent Assembly
was succeeded by the Legislative Assembly (1791), which
voted the war against Austria and the imprisonment of
Louis XVI, thus opposing the constitutional monarchy. In
September 1792, the Legislative Assembly was succeeded

by the National Convention, which immediately decreed
the abolition of the monarchy. With this formality, the
struggle among the various republican factions
—GIRONDISTS, JACOBINS, CORDELIERS, adherents of
ROBESPIERRE—began.

Assommoir, L' (The Dram Shop, 1877)   One of
the novels in the ROUGON-MACQUART series by Emile
ZOLA. Written in the argot of the Paris streets, *L'Assommoir*
is a study of the demoralizing effects of alcohol on the lives
of the working class. Although Zola had great compassion
for these miserable people, his book was attacked as
immoral because of the sordid nature of the subject.

assonance   In poetry and prose, the identity of
vowel sounds, as in the words *scream* and *beech*. Assonance
is one of the many phonetic devices that serve to unify
poetry and prose. In poetry it is frequently substituted for
RHYME and, in this use, is sometimes referred to as *vowel
rhyme*. See ALLITERATION; CONSONANCE.

Assumption, Feast of the   August 15th, so
called in honor of the Virgin Mary. In Catholic tradition,
she was taken to heaven that day (AD 45) in her corporeal
form, being at the time seventy-five years of age. There is a
legend that the Virgin was raised soon after her death and
assumed to glory by a special privilege before the general
resurrection.

Assur (or Ashur)   The principal god of Assyria, which
bears his name. The Baal of the Assyrian capital of Nineveh, Assur took over much of the dominant role that had
been played by the Babylonian MARDUK.

Assur-bani-pal (or Ashurbanipal, d 626? BC)   King
of Assyria. The son of Esar-Haddon, Assur-bani-pal ruled
Assyria, while his twin brother Samus-sum-yukin ruled
Babylonia. Against great odds, Assur-bani-pal maintained
his supremacy over Egypt and put down a Tyrian revolt.
The most powerful of Assyria's rulers, he either subjugated
or dominated the Manna, the Elamites, and the Cilicians.
He also quelled a revolt by his brother in Babylonia and
harassed the northern Arabians. However, Assur-bani-pal
had overreached himself and exhausted the resources of his
own country, to the extent that it collapsed completely not
long after his death. He left behind him, however, a legacy
of enormous importance for modern times: he had caused
to be prepared for his royal library a large number of the
most important literary works of the Near East; preserved
on tablets, these were excavated in the middle of the 19th
century in the ruins of Nineveh, his capital. Some characteristics of Assur-bani-pal are recognizable in the legendary
SARDANAPALUS.

Astarte   See ISHTAR.

Astolfo   In medieval romance, one of the twelve
famous PALADINS of Charlemagne. An English duke,
Astolfo joined the emperor in his struggles against the
Saracens. Known primarily for his great boasting, he was
also generous, courteous, gay, and singularly handsome.

He appears in the *Morgante Maggiore* of Pulci and the Orlando poems of Boiardo and Ariosto. In Ariosto, he rides a whale to the enchanted island of the witch Alcina and is detained by her until she tires of him. Transformed into a myrtle tree, he is rescued by MELISSA. Astolfo then journeys to the moon in search of Orlando's lost wits, which he brings back in a phial.

Astrophel and Stella   A sonnet sequence by Sir Philip SIDNEY, written 1580–84 and posthumously published in 1591. The "Stella" of the sonnets was Penelope Devereux. "Astrophel" ("star-lover") is a Greek pun on Sidney's name. After Sidney's death in 1586, his friend Edmund Spenser wrote an elegy called "Astrophel."

Asturias, Miguel Angel (1899–1974)   Guatemalan novelist, short-story writer, and poet. Asturias spent much of his life in exile because of his public opposition to dictatorial rule. When he was sympathetic to his country's leadership, he served as ambassador to El Salvador and later to France. He took a law degree in 1923 and then went to London to study economics and to Paris to study anthropology, where he encountered French translations of Mayan writings. He proceeded to translate the sacred Mayan text *Popol Vuh* into Spanish in 1925, developing a deep concern for the Mayan culture that was to weave its myth and history through everything he wrote, though never to the exclusion of his social and political statements. His greatest novel is *El señor presidente* (1946; tr *El Señor Presidente*, 1964), a phantasmagoric satire on Latin American military dictators, based largely on the regime of Manuel Estrada Cabrera, president of Guatemala from 1898 to 1920. *Viento fuerte* (1950; tr *Strong Wind*, 1968), *El papa verde* (1954; tr *The Green Pope*, 1971), and *Los ojos de los enterrados* (1960; tr *The Eyes of the Interred*, 1973) comprise a trilogy attacking the exploitation by U.S.-owned fruit companies of the Guatemalan banana plantations. *Week-end en Guatemala* (1956) is a collection of stories about the C.I.A.-directed overthrow of the government of Jacobo Arbenz, whom Asturias had supported. After Arbenz's ouster, Asturias went into exile, returning to Guatemala in 1966. In 1967 he was appointed ambassador to France, the same year in which he was awarded the NOBEL PRIZE in Literature.

As You Like It (c1600)   A pastoral comedy by William Shakespeare. Duke Frederick has banished the rightful duke, who is his brother and Rosalind's father, to the forest of Arden. Rosalind first meets ORLANDO after a contest in which he has felled Duke Frederick's wrestler Charles. Shortly afterwards, Orlando is forced to flee to the forest to escape the plots of his jealous brother Oliver. When Rosalind incurs her uncle's wrath and must also flee, Frederick's daughter Celia and TOUCHSTONE the clown accompany her. In the forest of Arden, Rosalind, who has disguised herself as a youth by the name of Ganymede, meets Orlando and leads him through a series of

episodes in which he unwittingly confides his love for her. Meanwhile, Oliver comes to the forest, and, when Orlando saves him from death, the brothers are reconciled. In subsequent scenes, Touchstone woos the dull-witted Audrey, Oliver woos Celia, the shepherd Silvius woos Phebe, and Phebe woos the disguised Rosalind. At last, Rosalind reveals her identity, and the four pairs of lovers are united in the feast of Hymen before the banished duke and his followers. Rosalind's father is restored to his dukedom when Duke Frederick is converted by a monk and decides to enter a monastery. The story is based on Thomas Lodge's romance *Rosalynde: Euphues' Golden Legacie* (1590). See JAQUES.

Atahualpa (1500?–1533)   Inca emperor of Peru. Becoming ruler of the northern part of the Inca empire upon the death of his father, Huayna Capac, in 1527, Atahualpa wrested the southern portion from his half-brother Huascar. The dissension produced by this fratricidal conflict facilitated the Spanish conquest led by Francisco Pizarro, who captured Atahualpa in 1532. Although Atahualpa was promised his freedom in exchange for a huge ransom of gold and silver, Pizarro accused him of conspiring against the Spaniards and had him executed.

Atala (1801)   A novel by François René de CHATEAUBRIAND. A melancholy tale of violent passion, set in the primeval woods of North America, it is generally cited as signalizing the beginning of the romantic movement in French literature.

Atalanta   In Greek legend, a daughter of Iasus (some authorities say Zeus) and Clymene. Atalanta took part in the Calydonian boar hunt and drew first blood. Being very swift of foot, she refused to marry unless the suitor should first defeat her in a race. Melanion overcame her at last by dropping, one after another, during the race, three golden apples that had been given him for the purpose by Venus. Atalanta was not proof against the temptation to pick them up, and so lost the race and became a wife. In the Boeotian form of the legend, Hippomenes takes the place of Melanion. In some legends, Atalanta was also one of the Argonauts. William Morris made this legend the subject of one of the tales in his *Earthly Paradise* (1868–70), and Swinburne wrote a dramatic poem, ATALANTA IN CALYDON, on the same theme.

Atalanta in Calydon (1865)   A tragedy by Algernon Charles SWINBURNE. It is based on the Greek legend of Atalanta and the Calydonian boar. It is remembered today chiefly for its choruses, particularly the "Hymn to Artemis."

Athaliah   In the Old Testament (2 Kings 11), the daughter of Ahab and Jezebel and the wife of Joram, king of Judah. After the death of her son Ahaziah, Athaliah gained the throne by murdering forty-two princes of the house of David. She reigned six years, but in the seventh, Joash, who had escaped the massacre, was proclaimed the rightful king. Attracted by the shouts of the people at his coronation, Athaliah entered the temple, where she was killed by the mob. Racine's last tragedy, ATHALIE, is based on this story.

Athalie (1691) A tragedy by Jean RACINE. It is based on the Old Testament story of Athaliah and Joash. Because it was written for the schoolgirls of St-Cyr, the play includes songs sung by a chorus of Levite maidens. *Athalie* was Racine's last work for the stage and is considered by many critics the most nearly perfect example of French classical tragedy.

Athene The Greek goddess of war, handicraft, and wisdom. According to the most familiar story, Athene sprang fully armed from the head of Zeus when Hephaestus split it open with an axe. Zeus had previously swallowed his consort Metis, her mother, on learning that she would bear a child who would rule the gods. Another story, perhaps earlier, indicates that her birth was associated with some stream or lake; this may have been told of her as an ancient pre-Hellenic deity. In a dispute with Poseidon as to who should be patron of Athens, she won that distinction by bestowing on the Athenians the boon of the olive tree. The PARTHENON was dedicated to her.

In most myths, Athene was a virgin, though originally she may have been a mother-goddess. She appears in innumerable myths, but none better displays her unique intellectual qualities than her role in the ODYSSEY as the constant friend and adviser of the clever and imaginative Odysseus.

Athos One of the famous friends and adventurers in Dumas's THE THREE MUSKETEERS. Athos also appears in the sequels *Twenty Years After* (1845) and *The Viscount of Bragelonne* (1848–50). He is unfailingly the gallant gentleman, quiet and reserved.

Atlantis A mythic island supposed to have once existed in the western sea. In the *Timaeus* and *Critias*, PLATO described the highly developed civilization that was there, and SOLON was told of it by an Egyptian priest, who said it was destroyed nine thousand years before his time by an earthquake. The legend has persisted, and the name is identified with an ideal, utopian society. Interest in the island continues with groups occasionally searching for its site. See NEW ATLANTIS, THE.

Atlas In Greek mythology, one of the TITANS, son of Iapetus and Clymene. For his share in the war of the Titans, Atlas was condemned by Zeus to uphold the heavens on his shoulders. He was stationed on the Atlas mountains in Africa, and the tale is merely a poetical way of saying that they prop up the heavens, because they are so lofty. The PLEIADES were Atlas' daughters.

The figure of Atlas with the world on his back was employed by the Flemish geographer Mercator (1512–94, real name Gerhard Kremer), on the title page of his collection of maps in the 16th century. The name has since been used to mean a book of maps.

atman (Sans, "vital breath; self; soul") In HINDUISM, the internal essence of the single individual. From the UPANISHADS onward, it is implicitly identified with BRAHMAN, the all-pervasive world spirit. Recognition of the union of *atman* and *brahman* through a variety of behaviors is the central element in achieving *moksha*, the release from the cycle of birth and rebirth.

atonality In music, the absence of tonality. Atonality negates the primacy of a keynote or tonic; the notion of a scale built upon the tonic, to which certain of the twelve notes of the chromatic scale belong and to which others are foreign; the building of harmonic combinations exclusively in thirds; and the distinction between consonant and dissonant combinations, especially the need to resolve dissonances into consonances.

Arnold SCHOENBERG is generally considered to have been the first composer of atonal music and the prime systematizer of its methods. He eventually elaborated a twelve-tone method of composition in which the notes of the chromatic scale were organized into an inviolable order, or "row," so that no note might be emphasized at the expense of any other. While the term *atonal* first implied an experimental rebellion against the single tonal center, it eventually came to designate the systematic negation of tonality through absolute equality of all tones. The organizational methods by which such music has sought to preserve its atonality have proved to be of greater value to contemporary music than the somewhat negative doctrine of atonality itself. Theoreticians, including Schoenberg, have questioned whether it is not a contradiction in terms to speak of "atonal music," and many hold that true atonality is, in practice, impossible.

Atreus, the house of The royal line of Mycenae, whose terrible story was a favorite source for the Athenian tragic dramatists. Atreus and Thyestes, sons of Pelops, became rivals for the throne of Mycenae, left vacant by the death of their brother-in-law Sthenelus and his son Eurystheus. Thyestes suggested that it should go to the possessor of the golden lamb. Atreus, who had previously hidden one in a chest, agreed, not knowing that his wife Aerope had given it to Thyestes, who had seduced her. Thyestes won the throne, but lost it when Atreus, with the aid of Zeus, made the sun move backward, an omen that proved Thyestes a usurper. Learning of the seduction, Atreus invited Thyestes to a banquet, served him his sons in a stew, then banished him, but not before Thyestes had cursed the house of Atreus.

Thyestes learned from the Delphic oracle that he could avenge himself only by begetting a son by his own daughter Pelopia. He ravished her at night, unrecognized. Atreus, having killed Aerope, the mother of Agamemnon and Menelaus, now married Pelopia, thinking her the daughter of King Thesprotus of Sicyon. Bearing Thyestes' child, she exposed it out of shame, but it was rescued by shepherds and named Aegisthus. Atreus learned of the child and believed it to be his own. Later he sent Aegisthus to kill Thyestes, but Thyestes revealed himself as Aegisthus' father. Pelopia killed herself in shame, and Aegisthus killed Atreus. Thyestes, avenged, became ruler of Mycenae again. Later, however, Atreus' son Agamemnon drove out Thyestes and killed his son Tantalus, married the latter's wife, Clytemnestra, and became king of Mycenae.

Clytemnestra bore a son, Orestes, and three daughters, IPHIGENIA, ELECTRA, and Chrysothemis. She never forgave her husband for the sacrifice of Iphigenia, but, taking Aegisthus as a lover, conspired with him to kill Agamemnon. When he returned from the Trojan War, they slew him in his bath. They also slew his captive, CASSANDRA. Electra, however, had smuggled away Orestes for his safety to the Phocian king, Strophius, who brought him up with his own son, Pylades. Grown to manhood, Orestes returned and, with Electra's help, avenged his father by killing both his mother and Aegisthus.

For this crime, which had been approved in advance by the Delphic oracle, he was driven mad by the ERINYES (Furies) of his mother. Later he was tried for his crime on the Areopagus, with Apollo pleading his case. He did not regain his sanity, however, until, on the advice of Apollo, he recovered an image from the temple of Taurian Artemis. There his life was saved by Iphigenia, who had been transported thither by Artemis at the time of the supposed sacrifice. Returning to Mycenae, he killed the new king, Aletes, Aegisthus' son, and ultimately ruled Argos and Sparta, as well. His friend Pylades, who had accompanied him to Tauris, married Electra. With the return of Orestes' sanity, Thyestes' curse on the house of Atreus—or that of Myrtilus on the seed of PELOPS—was finally lifted.

The events from the return of Agamemnon to the trial of Orestes are told in the only extant trilogy of Greek tragedies, the *Oresteia* (458 BC) of Aeschylus: the *Agamemnon* recounts his murder; *The Libation Bearers* (*Choephori*), the vengeance of Orestes; the *Eumenides*, his trial. Various parts of the story are also told in Sophocles' ELECTRA, Euripides' ELECTRA, ORESTES, and his plays on Iphigenia, and in Seneca's *Thyestes* and *Agamemnon*. Eugene O'Neill retold much of the story in modern terms in his MOURNING BECOMES ELECTRA. Jean-Paul Sartre adapted the story for his play THE FLIES. Gerhart HAUPTMANN's *Atriden-Tetralogie* (*Atrides Tetralogy*) is a monumental treatment of the downfall of the house of Atreus.

Atropos   In Greek mythology, that one of the three FATES whose office it was to cut the thread of life with a pair of scissors.

Attucks, Crispus   See BOSTON MASSACRE.

Attila (d 453)   King of the Huns. Attila is notorious for his attacks and inroads upon Europe during the final stages of the Roman Empire. He overran the Balkans (447–50), causing great destruction. In 451 he invaded Gaul but was forced to withdraw after a series of defeats. He and his soldiers were feared for their cruelty and vandalism; Attila himself was called "the scourge of God." Pierre Corneille made him the hero of a tragedy, *Attila* (1667). He appears in the *Nibelungenlied* under the name Etzel and in the *Völsunga Saga* as Atli.

Atwood, Margaret (1939–   )   Canadian poet, novelist, and critic. After the appearance of her second book of poems, *The Circle Game* (1966), Atwood became a dominant figure in Canadian letters. In this and her other volumes of poetry—*The Animals in That Country* (1968), *The Journals of Susanna Moodie* (1970), *Procedures for Underground* (1970), *Power Politics* (1971), *Selected Poems* (1976), *Two-Headed Poems* (1981)—her principal subject is the survival of consciousness in an unstable, manipulative world. Her novels, including *The Edible Woman* (1969), *Surfacing* (1972), *Lady Oracle* (1976), and *Life Before Man* (1980), elaborate the themes of her poetry with ironic wit and subtle variation. Later novels include *Bodily Harm* (1981), *Murder in the Dark* (1983), and *The Handmaid's Tale* (1986). There have been two collections of short stories in recent years, *Dancing Girls* (1977) and *Bluebeard's Egg* (1983). *Second Words: Selected Critical Prose* was published in 1982. *Interlunar*, her tenth collection of poetry, appeared in 1984.

Aub, Max (1903–1972)   Spanish novelist and dramatist. Born in Paris of a German father and a French mother, Aub moved to Spain with his family at the outbreak of World War I. Passionately involved with his adopted country, Aub was early active in liberal political movements and avant-garde literature in association with GARCÍA LORCA, Rafael ALBERTI, Salvador DALÍ, and Luis BUÑUEL. After the end of the Spanish Civil War in 1939, he spent three years in concentration camps in France and North Africa and finally escaped to Mexico, where he continued his literary and intellectual activities for some three decades. He died in Mexico City, having produced a copious number of novels, short stories, plays, and scripts for movies and television. Most of his works are characterized by aggressive sociopolitical protest or by an autobiographical reconstruction of the period immediately prior to and during the Spanish Civil War, the exodus thereafter, and the experience of exile. Representative of his ironic humor are *Las buenas intenciones* (1954) and the several novels of the "Campo" series, including *Campo cerrado* (1943), *Campo de sangre* (1945), and *Campo abierto* (1951). *Campo del moro* (1963), his most ambitious undertaking, is a vast chronicle spanning the time from the end of the Spanish Civil War until shortly before Aub's death.

Aucassin and Nicolette (early 13th century) French *chante-fable* in alternating prose and verse, one of the best medieval love romances. Aucassin, son of the Provençal Count of Beaucaire, falls in love with Nicolette, a slave captured from the Saracens. The count separates them by imprisonment, but Nicolette escapes and Aucassin follows, and they spend three years together until they are captured by Saracens. Aucassin is shipwrecked near home and, his father having died, becomes count. Nicolette is carried to Carthage, where she is recognized as the king's daughter, but she flees an unwelcome marriage and finds her way to Beaucaire, disguised as a minstrel, so that the lovers are happily reunited.

Auchincloss, Louis [Stanton] (1917–   ) American novelist, short-story writer, essayist, and biographer. A member of a prominent old New York family and a successful lawyer, Auchincloss wrote the first of his many novels, *The Indifferent Children* (1947), as "Andrew Lee." Among the best known of his subsequent novels, all of which deal with well-placed establishment figures, are *Portrait in Brownstone* (1962), *The Rector of Justin* (1964), *I Come as a Thief* (1972), *The Winthrop Covenant* (1976), *The Country Cousin* (1978), and *The House of the Prophet* (1980). *The Injustice Collectors* (1950) and *Powers of Attorney* (1963) are collections of thematically related short stories. His works of nonfiction include his autobiography, *A Writer's Capital* (1974; 1979), biographies of Edith Wharton (1971) and Cardinal Richelieu (1972), and an illustrated historical study of Queen Victoria and her circle, *Persons of Consequence* (1979). *The Cat and the King* (1981) is a historical novel based on the court of Louis XIV. He also wrote a critical study of Henry JAMES, *Reflections of a Jacobite* (1961), and a collection of essays, *Life, Law and Letters* (1979). Auchincloss's later novels include *Watch Fires* (1982) and *The Book Class* (1984). In 1984 he published a work of nonfiction entitled *False Dawn: Women in the Age of the Sun King* (1984).

Auden, W[ystan] H[ugh] (1907–1973)   English poet and dramatist. Regarded as one of the major poets of the 20th century, he wrote his most influential work during the 1930s, when he was the best known of the group of British left-wing writers that included the poets C. DAY LEWIS and Stephen SPENDER and the dramatist and novelist Christopher ISHERWOOD. Auden served in the Spanish Civil War, and a number of his most famous lyrics came out of that experience. His early work reveals his belief that society could be cured of its political and economic diseases by socialism, and of its psychological diseases by psychoanalysis. However, during World War II, Christianity became Auden's central preoccupation, and the influence of MARX and FREUD gave way to that of KIERKEGAARD and the modern Protestant theologians. The poem *New Year Letter* (1941; U.S., *The Double Man*) is Auden's own analysis of his development and his changing views. He edited and rewrote subsequent reprints of his poetry in order to omit what no longer suited his poetic, political, and religious ideas.

Auden's work is marked by wit and expert use of elaborate verse forms, but he also wrote in the popular music-hall tradition. His chief early works are *Poems* (1930), *The Orators* (1932), *Look, Stranger!* (1936; U.S., *On This Island*, 1937), and *Another Time* (1940). For the GROUP THEATRE, he wrote several experimental Marxist plays: *The Dance of Death* (1933) and, with Christopher Isherwood, *The Dog beneath the Skin* (1935), THE ASCENT OF F6, and *On the Frontier* (1938). He collaborated with Louis MACNEICE on the verse and prose work *Letters from Iceland* (1937) and with Isherwood on *Journey to a War* (1939), about the war between Japan and China. The work of Auden's later period includes *The Quest* (1941), a sonnet sequence; *For the Time Being* (1944), a "Christmas oratorio"; *The Sea and the Mirror* (1944), a "commentary" on THE TEMPEST; and THE AGE OF ANXIETY. *Nones* (1951), *The Shield of Achilles* (1955), *Homage to Clio* (1960), and *City Without Walls* (1969) are later collections of poems. Auden collaborated with Chester Kallman on the libretto of Stravinsky's opera *The Rake's Progress* (1951). *The Enchafed Flood* (1950) and *The Dyer's Hand* (1962) are collections of critical essays. He edited the *Oxford Book of Light Verse* (1938) and selections from Kierkegaard (1952). Auden immigrated to the U.S. in 1939 and became an American citizen, but returned to Europe near the end of his life. A revised edition of his *Selected Poems* appeared in 1979.

Audubon, John James (1785–1851)   Haitian-born American naturalist and artist. Educated in France, Audubon came to the U.S. in 1803. He traveled widely in the U.S. and Canada in search of material for his study of animals, which he depicted in firm, detailed drawings tinted in watercolor. The dramatic, lifelike setting of his subjects gave his works the vitality that distinguished him among the fine artists and illustrators of the 19th century. *The Birds of America*, published in England between 1827 and 1838, is his best-known work.

Augean stables   The stables of Augeas (Augeias), a mythological king of Elis, in Greece. These stables, in which he kept three thousand oxen, had not been cleaned for thirty years. One of the labors of Heracles was to clean them, which he did by causing two rivers to run through them. Hence, the phrase *to cleanse the Augean stables* means to clear away an accumulated mass of corruption.

Augie March, The Adventures of (1953)   A novel by Saul BELLOW. This modern picaresque novel about a Chicago youth who grows up during the depression years brought its author national recognition. Because he will not accept any defining role in life, Augie finds himself being swept along in a current of alternately hilarious and tragic events. Unlike his brother Simon, who marries the daughter of a wealthy Chicago coaldealer in order to rise from his lower-class Jewish environment, Augie refuses every opportunity for a settled existence. He suffers some hard knocks, but, as he says, there is an *"animal ridens* in me, the laughing creature, forever rising up."

Augustan age The golden age of Roman literature, which covered the reign of AUGUSTUS Caesar (27 BC– AD 14). The Augustan age has also come to describe the apogee of any national literature, as, for example, the age of Swift and Pope in 18th-century England, which is often called the Augustan age of English literature.

The imperial period of Roman history begins with the establishment (27 BC) of the principate (a thinly disguised monarchy) of Augustus after his decisive defeat of Mark Antony at Actium (31 BC). Unlike republican Rome (see CICERONIAN AGE), the long, dictatorial peace of Augustus was not a time of free public debate. Oratory was useless, for there was no one to be swayed by skillful argument: the senate was a rubber-stamp parliament, and the people were voiceless. Augustus alone steered the ship of state. Historians had to be wary of adhering too closely to the facts of recent history. Only LIVY, with his lofty, patriotic aim of reminding his contemporaries of the glories of their republican past, could survive as a practicing historian.

Poetry, however, was not so inhibited. Under the patronage of the emperor and his wealthy supporter MAECENAS, the period was the crowning epoch of Latin poetry. VERGIL, perhaps the greatest of the Roman poets, began his first successful work, the *Bucolics*, in the year of Cicero's death (43 BC). He soon found encouragement and patronage in the retinue of the young Octavius (Augustus). His subsequent works, the *Georgics* (30 BC) and the *Aeneid* (19 BC), were intended, at least in part, to support the large-scale reforms in public morality and public thinking instituted by Augustus.

Another great poet of the period, the satirist and lyricist HORACE, was very different from Vergil in style and subject. His great achievement was to give new life to Roman satire and to naturalize in Rome the metrical forms of the older Greek odes. Other poets of this period include Tibullus and PROPERTIUS, both writers of love elegies.

Although the Augustan age was an age of poetry, the one great poet who was born at its beginning and who was, in certain ways, its popular spokesman died in exile three years after the emperor's death. This was OVID, who wrote love elegies, mock didactics, and the phantasmagorical epic, *The Metamorphoses*. This poet's last, pathetic years on the bleak shores of the Black Sea bring to a close the Augustan age of Roman literature.

Augustine, St. (Latin name Aurelius Augustinus, 354–430) Early Christian church father and philosopher. Born in Roman North Africa of a Christian mother and a pagan father, Augustine received his early training primarily in Latin literature and earned his living as a teacher of rhetoric in Carthage, Rome, and Milan from 374 to 387. He joined the MANICHAEANS for a number of years but was disillusioned and, after a period of skepti-

cism, was converted to Christianity by St. Ambrose and baptized in 387. He returned to Africa and established a monastic community; in 391 he had ordained a priest at Hippo, becoming bishop there in 395. His CONFESSIONS vividly record his spiritual experiences and development during this period.

For the remainder of his life, he preached and wrote prolifically, defining points of Christian doctrine and engaging in theological controversy with the Manichaeans, the Donatists, and the Pelagians. He maintained the importance of a single, unified Church and developed a theory of sin, grace, and predestination that not only became basic to the doctrines of the Roman Catholic Church, but later was also used as the justification for the tenets of Calvin, Luther, and the Jansenists.

Other important writings include *On the Trinity (De Trinitate*, 400–16), THE CITY OF GOD, *On Nature and Grace (De natura et gratia*, 415), and the *Retractions* (*Retractationes*, 426), in which he revised some of the more exaggerated statements he had made earlier.

Augustine of Canterbury, St. (d 604?) First archbishop of Canterbury. Augustine was responsible for the Christianization of England and was called "Apostle of the English." A prior of the Benedictine monastery of St. Andrew in Rome, he was sent by Pope Gregory I (c595) to lead a missionary group of forty monks to England. When he landed at Thanet in 597, King Ethelbert of Kent received him hospitably; Ethelbert's Frankish wife, Bertha, was already a Christian, and the king soon accepted baptism. Augustine went to Arles in France to be consecrated as "bishop of the English," then returned to and, with Ethelbert's support of his mission, baptized ten thousand converts the same year. He was made archbishop of Canterbury in 601, consecrated Christ Church there in 603, and tried in vain to reconcile the Celtic bishops in the rest of England with the Roman Church.

Augustus (original name Caius Octavius, 63 BC–AD 14) First emperor of Rome. After his adoption by his great-uncle Julius Caesar (about 45 BC), he called himself Caius Julius Caesar Octavianus. It was thus, as Caesar's lawful heir, that the nineteen-year-old Octavius, upon Caesar's assassination (44 BC), skillfully lured Caesar's legions over to his side and formed, with Mark ANTONY and Lepidus, the Second TRIUMVIRATE. He pressed the war against Caesar's assassins, Brutus and Cassius, and, after helping to crush the rebels at PHILIPPI (42 BC), he successfully maneuvered Antony into accepting the eastern Mediterranean provinces as his share of empire. Between the years 40 and 31 BC, Octavius consolidated his control over the West, that is, Italy, Gaul, and Spain. His "cold war" with Antony finally broke out into open hostilities at Actium (31 BC), off the northwestern coast of Greece. There the combined naval forces of Antony and of CLEOPA-

TRA, the ambitious queen of Egypt, met Octavius's well-trained armada and were decisively defeated.

After this victory, Octavius celebrated a splendid triumph: Rome greeted him as its savior and showed itself willing to accept his sole sovereignty for forty-four years. In 28 BC he was made *princeps senatus* (first senator); on January 17 of the next year he received the honorary title *Augustus* (by which he was thenceforth known); and, in a series of senatorial bequests, he was made consul, tribune, and proconsul. Despite this gradual assumption of complete dictatorial power, his avowed aim was the restoration of the Roman Republic and the purification of its social and religious life. Whatever reforms he did accomplish, however, he did so on his own, bypassing the Senate and the Comitia.

The accomplishments of Augustus include the construction of public buildings—libraries, temples, monuments—he boasted that he had found Rome in brick and left it in marble, the revival of ancient religious rites, the restoration of the calendar (the month August was named after him), the reorganization of the political structure of the Empire, and the fostering of a native Roman literature. (See AUGUSTAN AGE.) His greatest accomplishment, however—the one that made all these others possible—was the long periods of peace he was able to maintain through his mastery of the art of statesmanship.

Octavius Caesar appears briefly in Shakespeare's JULIUS CAESAR. In Shakespeare's ANTONY AND CLEOPATRA, he is presented as a cold and puritanical man of relentless purpose, the "man of the future," as contrasted with the declining Antony.

auld lang syne (Scot, "old long ago")   In the olden time, in days gone by. "Auld Lang Syne" (1788, pub 1796), usually attributed to Robert BURNS, is really a new version by him of a very much older song; in Watson's Collection (1711), it is attributed to one Francis Sempill (d 1682), but it is probably even earlier. Burns, in a letter to James Thomson, writes that "It is the old song of the olden times, which has never been in print. . . . I took it down from an old man's singing."

Aurora   The Roman name for the goddess of dawn. Aurora was Eos in Greek mythology.

Austen, Jane (1775–1817)   English novelist, often regarded as the greatest of women novelists. The seventh child of a country parson, Jane Austen passed her days, like many an English lady of the time, almost entirely within her family circle. The only dramatic event of her life was an attachment to a clergyman who died before they could become engaged, but this was an obscure and doubtful episode, producing little outward change in her life. She never married, had no contact with London literary life, and spent all her time, when not writing, on ordinary domestic duties, among her numerous nephews and nieces. Out of the materials of such a narrow world, in fact

precisely by sticking scrupulously to that narrow world, she made great literature. Her completed novels, SENSE AND SENSIBILITY, PRIDE AND PREJUDICE, MANSFIELD PARK, EMMA, NORTHANGER ABBEY, and PERSUASION, are distinguished by their satirical wit and brilliant comedy, complex and subtle view of human nature, exquisite moral discrimination, and unobtrusive perfection of style. These qualities elevate her little world of struggling clerical families, husband-hunting mothers and daughters, eligible clergymen and landowners, country fools and snobs, into an enduring microcosm of the great world.

Austerlitz, battle of (also called the battle of the three emperors)   A famous battle on December 2, 1805, in Moravia, now Czechoslovakia, where Napoleon Bonaparte inflicted a heavy defeat upon the armies of Russia and Austria. The emperors of all three states were on the field, being in personal command of their forces.

auteur theory   A theory of film criticism and analysis that derived from the writings of François TRUFFAUT, Jean-Luc GODARD, Eric ROHMER, and others, which appeared in the influential magazine *Cahiers du cinéma* in the early 1950s. In an article printed in *Cahiers* in 1954, Truffaut proposed "la politique des auteurs" in an effort to free directors from traditional script-dominated films. Truffaut and his colleagues, who were to become the vanguard of the NEW WAVE, held that, although films are collaborative efforts, they should ultimately bear the artistic stamp of the director, whose personal vision creates a film as an author (*auteur*) would create a book. The theory was first championed in the U.S. by the critic Andrew Sarris.

Autobiography of Alice B. Toklas, The (1933)   An autobiography by Gertrude STEIN, written as though the author were her secretary and companion, Miss Toklas. Although the book provoked an attack by other Parisian writers and artists in *Testimony against Gertrude Stein* (1935), it remains a fascinating account of the expatriate life in the Paris of that period.

Alice B. Toklas's own account of her life with Gertrude Stein appeared in *What Is Remembered* (1963).

Autobiography of Benjamin Franklin, The   One of the most popular works of Benjamin FRANKLIN, translated into virtually every language. Covering only the period of his life up to his prewar stay in London as representative of the Pennsylvania Assembly, it was written at intervals beginning in 1771; the final segment was completed shortly before the author's death. Parts of the autobiography were published in France between 1791 and 1798, but the complete work did not appear until 1868. Franklin's many interests—philosophy, politics, religion, literature, and practical affairs—and his energetic pursuit of them have made his autobiography an American classic.

Autocrat of the Breakfast-Table, The (1858)   A series of essays by the elder Oliver Wendell HOLMES. A heterogeneous collection of boarders gather around the table, providing an audience for the wit and philosophy of the Autocrat. The essays take the form of conversations that generally develop into monologues. Cleverly and epigrammatically, the Autocrat discourses on social, theological, and scientific topics. The book, seemingly disconnected, is unified by the recurring themes and personalities. Holmes includes several of his poems.

Autolycus   A notorious thief of Greek mythology and son of Hermes. Shakespeare uses his name for the merry balladmonger and peddler in THE WINTER'S TALE, who "having flown over many knavish professions, . . . settled only on rogue." His songs, such as "When daffodils begin to peer," are justly famous.

automatic writing   See SURREALISM.

auto sacramental   A one-act religious drama, expounding on the tenets of Catholicism, that was popular in Spain from the 13th to the 18th century. The genre was perfected by CALDERÓN, who wrote over eighty *autos*. In 1736 Charles III prohibited their performance.

Avalon   In ARTHURIAN LEGEND, the island to which King ARTHUR is taken after he has been mortally wounded in the terrible, final battle. One of the earliest mentions of the island occurs in the 12th-century Latin *History of the Kings of Britain*, by Geoffrey of Monmouth. A short time later, in his *Roman de Brut*, Wace mentions that King Arthur expects to return from Avalon as "the hope of Britain" after his wounds have been healed. Later versions of this dramatic incident elaborate on and expand the whole considerably. In Malory's *Morte d'Arthur* (c1469), for example, the barge that comes to take Arthur to Avalon is signaled to by throwing the sword EXCALIBUR into the lake, and the barge itself is filled with the three mysterious, beautiful other-world queens. See GLASTONBURY.

avant-garde   (Fr, "advance guard")   Art and literature that is ahead of its time, is innovative, and often attacks established conventions.

Avare, L' (The Miser, 1668)   A comedy by MOLIÈRE. It is derived from Plautus's *Aulularia*. HARPAGON, a wealthy miser, wishes to marry his daughter Elise to an old man, Anselme, since Anselme does not require a dowry. The miser himself wants to marry his son Cléante's beloved, Mariane. Cléante arranges the theft of his father's money box and, in order to regain his treasure, Harpagon permits Cléante to marry Mariane. Elise is allowed to marry her beloved, Calère, when her father discovers him to be the son and heir of Anselme. A happy ending balances the grim picture of inhuman greed.

avatar   (fr Sans, *avatara*, "descent; appearance," hence "incarnation")   In Hindu mythology, the advent to earth of a deity in a visible form. The ten avatars of VISHNU are the most celebrated.

Ave Maria   (also Hail Mary or Angelic[al] Salutation) A prayer to the Virgin Mary, originating in the Bible (Luke 1:28, 1:42). The present form of the prayer was fixed by Pope Pius V in the 16th century. The smaller beads of a rosary are often called *Aves* or *Hail Marys*, the longer ones *paternosters* or *Our Fathers*.

Avernus   A lake in Campania in central Italy. Its sulphurous and mephitic vapors gave rise in ancient times to the belief that it was the entrance to the infernal regions. Hence, *Avernus* is used as a synonym for hell or the infernal regions.

Avesta   The sacred book of the Zoroastrians and Parsees, dating in its present form from the 3rd and 4th centuries AD, collected from the ancient writings, sermons, and oral traditions of Zoroaster before 800 BC. The books are sometimes called the *Zend-Avesta*, from a misunderstanding of the term *Avesta-Zend* (*Avesta* means the text, and *zend* its interpretation; hence the latter name has been given to the ancient Iranian language in which the Avistak-va-Zand is written).

It is only a fragment, consisting of five parts: (1) the Yasna, the chief liturgical portion, including Gathas, or hymns; (2) the Vispered, another liturgical work; (3) the Vendidad, which, like the biblical Pentateuch, contains the laws; (4) the Yashts, dealing with stories of the different gods; (5) the Khordah, a book of private devotions.

Avicenna   (Arabic name Abn-Ali al-Husayn ibn-Sina, c980–c1037)   Persian philosopher and physician. A Latin translation of Avicenna's *Canon of Medicine* was used in Europe as the standard medical textbook until the 17th century. His *al-Shifa* (*Book of Recovery*), including sections on logic, physics, and metaphysics, reveals his own adaptation of Aristotle's philosophy.

Awkward Age, The (1899)   A novel by Henry JAMES. It concerns the emergence of an English society girl from "the awkward age" into maturity and understanding. A rival of her mother in love for young Vanderbank, Nanda Brookenham is surrounded by older persons who are scheming and plotting. Vanderbank marries neither her nor her mother, and Nanda, disillusioned by her friends, goes to live in the country home of Mr. Longdon, an older man who had once been in love with her grandmother.

Axel's Castle   See WILSON, EDMUND.

axiom   A self-evident truth. In logic, an axiom is an accepted premise that requires no demonstration.

Ayckbourn, Alan (1939–   )   English playwright. Ayckbourn mines the comic possibilities in, as he puts it, "man's inhumanity to woman and woman's inhumanity to man . . . [and] the whole physical world's inhumanity to us all." Material objects invariably do not work the way they are supposed to, and his characters, more through ineptitude or thick-headed insensitivity than out of calculated malice, make life intolerable for those around them. In *Standing Room Only* (1961), city traffic becomes so impossibly tangled that people take up residence in their cars. His first major success, *Relatively Speaking* (1967), is a comic farce of mistaken identity. The utterly inert hero of

Time and Time Again (1972) manages still to be at the center of mayhem. Ayckbourn is also known for his ingenious use of theatrical sets, staging simultaneous glimpses of different couples in their kitchens, living rooms, and bedrooms in *How the Other Half Loves* (1969), *Absurd Person Singular* (1972), and *Bedroom Farce* (1977). *The Norman Conquests* (1974), a trilogy of full-length plays, is a comic saga of a family's problems. Other comedies that probe the marital, family, job, and social frustrations of his mostly middle-class British subjects include *Absent Friends* (1975), *Just between Ourselves* (1976), and *Sisterly Feelings* (1980). While he is a brilliant manipulator of farcical situations, the strength of his plays lies in his ability to create entirely recognizable, if pathetic, characters.

Later productions include *Season's Greetings* (1982), *Way Upstream* (1982), *Making Tracks* (1983), *Intimate Exchanges* (1984), and *A Chorus of Disapproval* (1985).

Ayer, Sir A[lfred] J[ules] (1910–   )   English philosopher. Ayer was the foremost British exponent of LOGICAL POSITIVISM and a central figure of the so-called Oxford philosophers. His *Language, Truth, and Logic* (1936) was the first statement of logical-positivist theories in English. Ayer's own approach to truth, or meaning, involved a careful analysis of language. Other works by Ayer include *The Problem of Knowledge* (1956), a collection of essays entitled *Logical Positivism* (1959), *Probability and Evidence* (1972), and *The Central Questions of Philosophy* (1973). *Parts of My Life* (1977) is an autobiography of his first thirty-five years. Its sequel, *More of My Life*, appeared in 1984. Two collections of essays have appeared in recent years, *Philosophy in the Twentieth Century* (1982) and *Freedom and Morality and Other Essays* (1984). *Wittgenstein* (1985) is an analysis of Wittgenstein's philosophical procedures and theories. In 1977 Ayer was made a member of France's Legion of Honor.

Aymé, Marcel [André] (1902–1967)   French fiction writer. Aymé's novels are usually sophisticated satire, such as *La Jument verte* (1933; tr *The Green Mare*, 1955), *Le Moulin de la sourdine* (1936; tr *The Secret Stream*, 1953), *La Belle Image* (1942; tr *The Second Face*, 1951), and *Les Tiroirs de l'inconnu* (1960; tr *The Conscience of Love*, 1962). His short stories are known for their wittily realistic development of fantastic or burlesque situations. English translations of his stories include *Across Paris, and Other Stories* (1961) and *The Walker through Walls, and Other Stories* (1972). He also wrote a number of children's books and the plays *Clérambard* (1958) and *Le Minotaure* (1967).

Azazel   A Hebrew name symbolizing an evil spirit living in the wilderness. It is mentioned in connection with services held on the Day of Atonement (Yom Kippur), in which lots were cast on two goats: one for the Lord and the other for Azazel (Lev. 16). The goat for Azazel was referred to as the SCAPEGOAT. Milton uses the name for the standard-bearer of the rebel angels in PARADISE LOST.

Azevedo, Aluízio (1857–1913)   Brazilian novelist. The first exponent of naturalism in Brazil, Azevedo was a shrewd critic of contemporary society. His best-known work, *O Mulato* (1881), deals with the status of the mixed-blood in Brazil. He also wrote *Casa de Pensão* (1884), about the residents of a boarding house in Rio de Janeiro, and *O Cortiço* (1890), translated as *A Brazilian Tenement*.

Azrael   In Muslim theology, the angel of death who watches over the dying and takes the soul from the body. Azrael is one of the four highest angels at the throne of Allah, whom he serves as messenger. He will be the last to die but will do so at the second trump of the archangel.

the wings of Azrael   The approach of death; the signs of death coming on the dying.

Aztecs   A Nahuatl-speaking tribe of Indians who dominated much of Mexico at the time of the Spanish conquest (1519–21) under Hernán CORTEZ. In the 12th century, the Aztecs moved into the valley of Anahuac from the northwest and gradually subdued neighboring tribes, turning them into tribute-paying vassals. The "emperor" of the Aztecs was chosen by a supreme council, which represented the twenty clans that comprised the Aztec tribe. See MONTEZUMA II; TENOCHTITLÁN.

Azuela, Mariano (1873–1952)   Mexican novelist. After serving as a doctor in the Mexican Revolution, Azuela moved to Mexico City in 1916 and devoted the rest of his life to his two professions, medicine and writing. In his forty-one novels, which touch on virtually every aspect of Mexican life during the first half of the 20th century, Azuela revealed an unwavering concern for social justice and human dignity. Among his best-known works are *Mala yerba* (1909; tr *Marcela*, 1932), an indictment of the powerful land-owning class; LOS DE ABAJO, about the revolution and considered by many to be his finest novel; *Los caciques* (1917; tr *The Bosses*, 1957), an attack on the political bosses of a small Mexican city; and *Las moscas* (1918; tr *The Flies*, 1957), an incisive examination of political opportunism.

B

Baal (plural form Baalim)   An epithet for any of a number of ancient Semitic gods. A Semitic word meaning "lord" or "possessor," *Baal* was usually applied to a god as lord of a city or other place. The title thus became applied to a great many local gods; even the Hebrew Yahweh was so referred to in earlier days by the ancient Israelites. Originally a sort of fertility demon, Baal became individualized in various localities, notably as the Babylonian BEL and the Canaanite Baal. As the storm god, he plays the principal role in the Canaanite POEM OF BAAL. Variations of the name also occur in the Greek *Belus* and in such Carthaginian compounds as *Hannibal*. In Tyre, the local Baal was known as Melkarth. The worship of Baalim was firmly established in Canaan at the time of the Israelites' entry. The Israelites adopted many of the Canaanite rites in their own worship of Jehovah. Moses, ELIJAH, and other prophets denounced this form of Baalim worship as heathenism; hence *Baal* came to mean a false god. Baal was also a nature god symbolizing generation, whose appearance, along with that of Ashtoreth (ISHTAR), was considered a necessary prelude to spring.

Babar   The elephant featured in a series of French children's books. *The Story of Babar* (1933), written and illustrated by Jean de Brunhoff (1899–1937), was the first in a series of stories about Babar and his family. The series was continued by the author's son, Laurent de Brunhoff.

Babbitt (1922)   A satirical novel by Sinclair LEWIS. It presents a portrait of George Follansbee Babbitt, a middle-aged realtor, booster, and joiner in Zenith, the Zip City. He is unimaginative, self-important, and hopelessly middle class. Withal, he is vaguely dissatisfied and tries to alter the pattern of his life by flirting with liberalism and by entering a liaison with an attractive widow, only to find that his dread of ostracism is greater than his desire for escape. He does, however, encourage the rebellion of his son, Ted, saying, "Don't be scared of the family. No, nor all of Zenith. Nor of yourself, the way I've been." The name of the book identified an American type and gave a new word to the language.

Babel, Isaak [Emmanuilovich] (1894–?1939)   Russian short-story writer. Babel was born in Odessa of a middle-class Jewish family. He developed an early interest in literature, particularly the works of Flaubert and Maupassant. His first published stories appeared in a journal edited by Maksim Gorky. The older writer recognized Babel's talent but advised him to see more of life before doing more writing. During the civil war following the revolution, Babel was attached to the cavalry detachment of General Budenny, fighting in Poland. He recorded his experiences in the volume of stories entitled RED CAVALRY. The next year he published ODESSA TALES, about his early life in the port city. A memorable character of the Odessa stories is Benya Krik, the Jewish gangster leader.

The success of Babel's work was immense. His vivid descriptions of the brutality rampant during the war in Poland were rendered in short, exquisitely polished stories. A unique feature of his work was his habit of treating his romantic material in a sharply honed classical style, reminiscent of Maupassant at his most concise. Babel's knowledge of the powerful effect of concision in literature is revealed in a line from one of his stories: "There is no iron that can enter the human heart with such stupefying effect as a period placed at just the right moment." The effort it took to achieve his remarkable effects is revealed by Babel's friend, the writer Konstantin Paustovski, in his reminiscences. Babel showed Paustovski a two-hundred-page manuscript, which turned out to be twenty-two versions of one of Babel's short stories.

Babel's popularity waned in the 1930s. The chief reasons for this seem to have been his neglect of political themes in his work and a growing resentment, under Stalin, of the way he depicted the warriors of Budenny's regiment. He disappeared about 1938, apparently a victim of the purges then going on. He is reputed to have been executed or to have died in a concentration camp, but no real facts about his fate have been divulged.

Babel, Tower of   A structure erected after the Flood by the descendents of NOAH when they reached

Babylonia. According to Gen. 11, the plan was to build a tower that would reach to heaven, but Jehovah, displeased by the arrogance and presumption of the builders, "confounded their speech" so they could not understand one another and "scattered them abroad from thence upon the face of all the earth." The story provides a biblical explanation for the diversity of languages in the world. *Tower of Babel* has come to signify an ambitious or visionary scheme; the word *babel* has become associated with a confused uproar in which nothing can be heard but the hubbub.

Baber   See MOGUL EMPIRE.

Babington's conspiracy   A plot against the life of Elizabeth I. Anthony Babington (1561–86), formerly a page to MARY, QUEEN OF SCOTS, was induced by the priest John Ballard to organize a conspiracy in 1586 to assassinate Queen Elizabeth, lead a Catholic uprising, and release Mary from confinement. The plot was detected, and Babington and a dozen others were executed. A few months later, Mary was beheaded, largely on the grounds of evidence of her complicity in the plot, supposedly contained in letters between her and Babington.

Babi-Yar   See YEVTUSHENKO, YEVGENY ALEKSANDROVICH.

Bacchanalia   Festival held in ancient Rome in honor of BACCHUS, the name under which the Greek god Dionysus was better known in Rome. Like the Greek Dionysia, the feast was eventually characterized by drunkenness, debauchery, and licentiousness of all kinds, so that the word *bacchanalian* came to mean wild and drunken.

bacchants   Followers of the Greek god DIONYSUS, or Bacchus. Also known as *maenads*, they engaged in wild ritual dancing on wooded mountains, during which they tore apart and ate fawns and perhaps human victims. They are probably an oriental addition (see CYBELE) to the cult of the Thracian god Dionysus. Their revels on Mount Cithaeron are detailed in Euripides' drama *The Bacchants*.

Bacchants, The   (Bacchae, 408–406 BC)   A tragedy by EURIPIDES. It deals with the tragic punishment of Pentheus, king of Thebes, who imprisons DIONYSUS and is torn to pieces by his own mother, Agave, during a bacchanalian orgy. Gilbert Murray pointed out that this of all plays most closely resembles in form the Dionysian mysteries from which Greek tragedy sprang. (See BACCHANTS.)

Bacchelli, Riccardo   (1891–1985)   Italian critic, novelist, dramatist, and poet. A writer of historical novels, Bacchelli has been compared to Alessandro Manzoni because of the serenity of his outlook on life, his congenial humor, serious scholarship, and preoccupation with language and style.

Bacchelli was an artillery officer in World War I and the editor of *La ronda* (1919–23), an influential literary review published in Rome. The review proposed that contemporary Italian literature reaffirm its classical traditions by drawing inspiration from the Renaissance, Leopardi, and Manzoni.

Bacchelli's best-known work is the two-thousand-page historical novel *Il mulino del Po* (3 vols, 1935–40; pub 1948–50), translated as *The Mill on the Po* (2 vols, 1950) and *Nothing New Under the Sun* (1955). The novel is a saga of Italian life from the Napoleonic Wars to World War I. Other works include the historical novel *Il diavolo al Pontelungo* (1927; tr *The Devil at the Long Bridge*, 1929); *Mal d'Africa* (1934), which recounts the African travels of the 19th-century Italian explorer Gaetano Casati; and *Il figlio di Stalin* (1953; tr *Seed of Steel*, 1963), a novel about the last days of Joseph Stalin. *Rapporto segreto dall'inglese di mille parole*, a novel about space flight set in an unnamed country that is clearly America, was published in 1967, and *L'Afrodite*, another novel, appeared in 1969. *Versi et rime*, a three-volume collection of poetry, was published in 1971–73.

Bacchus   In Roman mythology, the god of wine. He was, in fact, a Greek god (Bakchos was one of the names of the Greek DIONYSUS), the Roman god of wine having been Liber. Bacchus was worshipped in the annual, riotous festival called the BACCHANALIA, similar to the Greek Dionysia. However, the fat and drunken Bacchus, familiar from so many paintings of the Renaissance period, was a later concept, completely out of keeping with the classic view of Bacchus as a handsome young man and a powerful god. In the *Lusiad* (1572) of Camoëns, Bacchus is the guardian power of Islam and an evil demon of Zeus.

Bach, Johann Sebastian   (1685–1750)   Outstanding German composer of the late Baroque. Bach's enormous musical output falls roughly into three categories, which reflect the nature of his employment at various times of his life. First, he began his career as an organist; in this capacity, he wrote a vast number of sonatas, preludes, fugues, toccatas, and chorale preludes for organ, some of which were designed for use in the Lutheran service, some as concert showpieces when he was commissioned to test newly built or reconstructed organs. Then, as court musician to Prince Leopold in Köthen (1717–23), he wrote primarily abstract instrumental music for solo instruments or chamber ensemble; the *Brandenburg Concertos*, the keyboard suites, and the violin concertos were composed during this period, as was the first part of the *Well-Tempered Clavier*, a set of preludes and fugues for harpsichord, exploiting all twenty-four major and minor keys, a feat made possible by the recently adopted method of "tempered" tuning of the scale, in which all semitones are equal.

For the last twenty-seven years of his life, he was cantor of the St. Thomas Church and School in Leipzig. He entered into his duties there with extraordinary energy and produced the bulk of his output of church cantatas (roughly 150 works) in the first five years after his arrival. His church-related compositions at Leipzig also include the *St. John Passion* (1723), the *St. Matthew Passion* (1729), the *Christmas Oratorio* (1734), and the *Mass in B Minor.* By 1738, after repeated attempts to improve conditions for the church music, Bach essentially gave up composing cantatas (although he continued to direct the performance of earlier compositions) and turned to other musical outlets, such as the university students' Collegium Musicum, for which he composed some of his best-known secular cantatas (e.g., the *Coffee Cantata*). In his last fifteen years, he turned increasingly to abstract and technically complex polyphonic genres, especially canon and fugue. It was during these years that he composed the *Goldberg Variations, A Musical Offering,* and the *Art of Fugue.*

In his own lifetime, Bach was most highly regarded as an organist. His reputation as a composer was overshadowed by G. P. Telemann, among others, and very few of his works were published in his lifetime. By the end of his life, Bach's music was discarded as an outdated vestige of the old contrapuntal style. Although his music attracted some attention from MOZART and others in the years after his death, it was not until MENDELSSOHN revived the *St. Matthew Passion* in 1829 that Bach's stature as one of the greatest composers of all time began to be recognized.

Bach's work represents the culmination of the technical and musical ideas of the Baroque era. A devout Lutheran, Bach composed both secular and religious music with a profoundly spiritual force, fortified by an unparalleled attention to architectonic organization. It is interesting that a composer of such stirring and transporting music lived such a limited life. He apparently read very little, had virtually no interest in the other arts, and never traveled outside of Germany.

Bachelard, Gaston (1884–1962)   French philosopher and literary theorist. Trained in the physical sciences, Bachelard ultimately became professor of the philosophy of science at the Sorbonne. In such books as *Le Nouvel Esprit scientifique* (1934) and *La Philosophie du non* (1940; tr *The Philosophy of No,* 1968), he advanced his conception of science as a dynamic and changing field. He maintained that the interaction of reason, imagination, and experience constantly changes the nature of knowledge itself; rather than rejecting previously held notions of scientific fact when they are disproved, he saw the importance of fully understanding accumulated knowledge from the past and synthesizing it or reformulating it in light of new discoveries. His interest in the nature of scientific thought led to his analysis of the poetic imagination, which, as opposed to traditional scientific inquiry, is fully reliant on insight, intuition, and vision. Like C. G. JUNG, he believed in a collective unconscious and saw the recurrence of archetypal elements—earth, air, fire, water (basic also to the natural sciences)—as the basis of poetic endeavor. This phenomenological analysis of the basic substance of a piece of

literature rather than of its content had a profound influence on subsequent literary criticism, most notably in the work of Roland BARTHES. Bachelard's seminal books on the subject include *La Psychanalyse du feu* (1938; tr *The Psychoanalysis of Fire,* 1968), *L'Eau et les rêves* (*Water and Dreams,* 1942), *L'Air et les songes* (*Air and Visions,* 1943), *La Poétique de l'éspace* (1958; tr *The Poetics of Space,* 1964), and *La Poétique de la rêverie* (1960; tr *The Poetics of Reverie,* 1969).

Back to Methuselah (1921)   A five-part play cycle by George Bernard SHAW, which he called the "metabiological pentateuch." The five parts, titled *In the Beginning, The Gospel of the Brothers Barnabas, The Thing Happens, Tragedy of an Elderly Gentleman,* and *As Far as Thought Can Reach,* comprise a satirical fantasy on the prolongation of life and the perfectibility of the human race. The scenes are set in the Garden of Eden, in England in 1920, and in successive stages of the future, ending in AD 31,920, when the span of life has been increased and man has become almost wholly intellect. This progress is accomplished not through science but through the strength of human will engaged in creative evolution.

Bacon, Francis (1561–1626)   English philosopher, statesman, and essayist. Bacon served as solicitor general and attorney general under JAMES I and was appointed lord chancellor in 1618. He was created Baron Verulam (1618) and Viscount St. Albans in 1621, the same year in which he was removed from office for accepting a bribe from a litigant. While performing his legal duties for the Crown, Bacon also published works on the philosophy of science and tried unsuccessfully to persuade the king to finance institutions for scientific inquiry.

Violently opposed to speculative philosophies and the syllogistic quibbling of the Schoolmen (see SCHOLASTICISM), Bacon argued that the only knowledge of importance to man was empirically rooted in the natural world (see EMPIRICISM) and that this knowledge should be amassed and studied in a judicious, systematic fashion. He found merit in the materialist theories of DEMOCRITUS and even more in the discoveries of COPERNICUS and GALILEO. For Bacon, a clear system of scientific inquiry would assure man's mastery over the natural world. He deplored generalizations that might obscure the exceptions to every rule and vigorously sought the negative for every positive, in order to bring both into a unified system of thought. In these respects, his ideas anticipated aspects of UTILITARIANISM, particularly in the work of John Stuart MILL.

Bacon proposed to outline his theory of knowledge in the impossibly ambitious INSTAURATIO MAGNA. Of this, only two of his projected six parts were successfully completed: THE ADVANCEMENT OF LEARNING, which he expanded in the Latin text *De Dignitate et Augmentis Scientiarum* (1623), and NOVUM ORGANUM, in which he outlined his inductive method of investigation of the natural world.

Although philosophers and scientists alike repudiated both his theories and his methodology, Bacon's delineation of the principles of an inductive scientific method constituted a breakthrough in the Renaissance approach to science.

Particularly notable among his other works are THE NEW ATLANTIS, the ideas in which were incorporated in the founding of the Royal Society (1662), and his ESSAYS OR COUNSELS, which included some of his most distinguished writing in English. See BACONIAN CONTROVERSY.

Bacon, Roger (c1214–1294)   English philosopher and scientist. Bacon was called Doctor Mirabilis, or the Admirable Doctor. His encyclopedic *Opus majus* (1267) urged that, in order to make the Roman Catholic Church the leader in the civilization of mankind, Christian studies should be expanded to include all the sciences; he placed great emphasis on the importance of mathematics and experimental science, disciplines practically ignored in the learning of the time. His writings indicate his own interest in optics, chemistry, and astrology, and he is credited with having foreseen the practical possibilities of the telescope, lenses to correct vision, gunpowder, and mechanical navigation and flight. His *Opus minus* (1267–68) is an alchemical treatise; the *Opus tertium* (1267–68) stresses the utility of scientific knowledge, saying that without it philosophy becomes absurd. In 1278 the Franciscans, whom he joined about 1250, declared his works heretical, and he was imprisoned until 1292. He was working on a "compendium of theological studies" when he died.

Because of his advanced thinking on the need for experimental science and its practical possibilities, the popular imagination credited him with all sorts of magical achievements, supposedly the result of a league with the Devil. These legends began gathering at the beginning of the 14th century and appear in such works as Robert Greene's comedy *Friar Bacon and Friar Bungay* (1589). See BRAZEN HEAD.

Baconian controversy   An argument, first advanced in the mid-18th century, that William SHAKESPEARE did not write the plays attributed to him. The idea is based on the notion that Shakespeare, being a nobody from provincial Stratford, lacked the social background, education, and temperament to have written his masterpieces. The first claim for Sir Francis BACON as the true author was put forth by William Henry Smith in 1856; the following year Delia Bacon made an elaborate defense for Bacon's authorship in *The Philosophy of Shakespeare's Plays*. New "proof," in the form of a cryptogram of Bacon's signature in some of the plays, was offered by Ignatius Donnelly in *The Great Cryptogram* (1888) and by Mrs. E. W. Gallup in *The Bi-Lateral Cypher of Francis Bacon* (1900). Other writers, not satisfied that the evidence of authorship pointed to Bacon, attempted to prove the plays were really the work of Edward de Vere, earl of Oxford, or Roger Manners, earl of Rutland, or William Stanley, earl of Derby, or Henry Wriothesley, earl of Southampton, or Christopher Marlowe. There is no evidence that any of these men except Marlowe (who died in 1593 at the age of twenty-nine) ever wrote a line of blank verse. In orthodox Shakespearean scholarship, these controversies are ignored and it is assumed that Shakespeare wrote the plays.

Baedeker, Karl (1801–1859)   German printer who began the publication of a widely known series of guidebooks. *Baedeker* has since become almost synonymous with *guidebook*.

Bagehot, Walter (1826–1877)   English economist and critic. Bagehot was editor of the *Economist* (1860–77) and is known for his lucid, highly readable, idiosyncratic works on political economy, history, and literature. *The English Constitution* (1867) is a classic in its field; other works of note are *Physics and Politics* (1872) and *Literary Studies* (1879).

Bagnold, Enid (maiden name and pen name of Lady Roderick Jones, 1889–1981)   English novelist and playwright. Bagnold is the author of the successful novels *Serena Blandish* (1924), NATIONAL VELVET, and *The Girl's Journey* (1954). In her later years she wrote primarily for the stage, most notably *The Chalk Garden* (1956), *The Chinese Prime Minister* (1961), and *A Matter of Gravity* (1976). Her *Autobiography* appeared in 1969.

Bahaism   The doctrines of the Bahais, emphasizing the spiritual unity of mankind, advocating universal peace, and imbued with mild Oriental mysticism. The Bahais succeeded the Persian religious sect of Babism. Bahaism was founded by Mizra Husayn Ali in 1863.

Bailey, Nathan (or Nathaniel Bailey, d 1742)   English lexicographer. Bailey's *Universal Etymological English Dictionary* (1721) marks the beginning of modern English lexicography, in the sense of objective registration of the complete body of words in the language. It served as the point of departure for the famous dictionary of Samuel Johnson.

Bainbridge, Beryl [Margaret] (1934–   )   English novelist. Bainbridge's novels are distinguished by the uncommon psychological acuity with which she treats ordinary people in working-class environments. Much of her macabre, black-comic fiction draws on her reflections and memories of growing up in Liverpool under the violent shadow of World War II. Like most of her books, her first novel, *A Weekend with Claude* (1967), centers on an act of violence. *Another Part of the Wood* (1968) examines the death of a child which occurred because negligent adults were preoccupied with their own sexual concerns. *Harriet Said* (1972) begins with an accidental killing by a thirteen-year-old girl. Bainbridge's comic irony and macabre sense of the destructive forces lurking beneath the familiar are again evident in *The Bottle Factory Outing* (1974), *Sweet William* (1975), *A Quiet Life* (1976), and *Injury Time* (1976). *Young Adolf* (1978) is an imaginative reconstruction of Adolf HITLER's probable visit to his half-brother in Liverpool in 1912 (to avoid conscription), revealing the violence, paranoia, and posturing of the young man, who craved affection but did nothing to win it. *Winter Garden* (1980) is a thriller about an English artist who disappears in Russia. In 1984 Bainbridge published the diary she kept during the filming of a BBC television series in 1983, entitled *English Journey; or, The Road to Milton Keynes.*

Bairam   The name given to two great Muslim feasts. The *Lesser* begins on the new moon of the month Shawwal, at the termination of the fast of Ramadan, and lasts three days. The *Greater* is celebrated on the tenth day of the twelfth month, Dhul Hijja, lasts for four days, and forms the concluding ceremony of the pilgrimage to Mecca. It comes seventy days after the Lesser Bairam.

Bajazet (1672)   A tragedy by Jean RACINE. The play is purportedly based on actual events that took place in Constantinople in 1638. It depicts the imprisoned Bajazet's pretense of love for the sultana Roxane, who plans to free him in order to marry him and place him on the throne, which is to be seized from her husband. Discovering Bajazet's love for the princess Atalide, Roxane allows him to be executed; discovering her infidelity, the sultan orders Roxane's execution; and, discovering her lover's death, Atalide commits suicide.

Bajazet is also a character (the strongest of Tamburlaine's foes) in Christopher Marlowe's play TAMBURLAINE THE GREAT.

baker, the   A name applied to LOUIS XVI of France. He was called "the baker" (*le boulanger*), his queen MARIE ANTOINETTE, "the baker's wife" (*la boulangère*), and the dauphin, "the shop boy" (*le petit mitron*) by the rabble who, after besieging Versailles on October 6, 1789, escorted them to Paris. When the king learned from them that there was a bread famine in Paris, he ordered supplies of flour sent there. During the return to Paris, chariots loaded with wheat and flour preceded the king's carriage, and National Guards carried loaves of bread or sausages on the end of their bayonets.

Bakunin, Mikhail Aleksandrovich (1814–1876) Russian revolutionary and anarchist leader. Born into a cultured noble family, Bakunin was educated at a military school in St. Petersburg and served for a short time as an army officer. He resigned from the army and moved to Moscow, where he met the radical journalists Vissarion Belinski and Alexander Hertzen and plunged into the study of German philosophy, which was in vogue with the Russian intellectuals of the time. In 1840 Bakunin went to Berlin to continue his studies. He befriended the novelist Ivan Turgenev, who was also studying in Berlin. Turgenev is reputed to have used Bakunin as the model for the idealistic hero of his novel *Rudin*. While in Berlin, Bakunin published one of his most important early articles, *Reaktzyia v Germanii* (*Reaction in Germany*, 1842). In the article is

the phrase that was later adopted as an anarchist slogan: "The passion for destruction is also a creative passion."

Bakunin took part in revolutionary agitation in Germany, Austria, and France during 1848. He was arrested and extradited to Russia the following year. After being in prison for almost ten years, he was exiled to Siberia, from which he escaped in 1861, making his way to Europe via Japan and the U.S. He remained in Europe for the rest of his life, mostly in Geneva and London. By the late 1860s, Bakunin's anarchist views were fully formed, and he expounded them in the periodical *Narodnoe delo* (*The People's Cause*), which he published in Geneva.

Bakunin was a tireless if not always effective revolutionary schemer. An observer of his activities during the Paris revolt of 1848 said of him: "On the first day of a revolution he is a treasure; on the second he ought to be shot." This kind of revolutionary zeal led to Bakunin's expulsion from the First International in 1872 on charges of opposing the leadership, headed by Karl Marx, and of setting up a rival revolutionary organization.

Balaam   In the Old Testament (Num. 22–23), a prophet of Pethor whom Balak, king of Moab, had persuaded to prophesy against the Israelites invading his territory. On the way to utter the curse, Balaam was forced three times to beat the ass upon which he was riding, when it stopped short, blocked by God's angel. "Then Jehovah opened the eyes of Balaam and he saw the angel of the Lord standing in the way" (Num. 22:31). Balaam refused to curse Israel but pronounced his blessing instead.

Balbec   The French seaside resort visited by the narrator in Marcel PROUST's *Remembrance of Things Past* (1913–27). It is based on resorts of the Normandy coast, such as Trouville and Cabourg.

Balboa, Vasco Núñez de (1475–1517)   Spanish explorer. Sailing to America in 1500, Balboa became leader of the small colony of Darien on the isthmus of Panama. In 1513, after an arduous trek across the isthmus with 190 picked companions, Balboa discovered the Pacific Ocean, which he named the South Sea, and took possession of it in the name of Spain. He later incurred the enmity of Pedro Arias de Avila (known as Pedrarias), governor of Panama, who had him beheaded on a trumped-up charge of treason.

Balcony, The (Le Balcon, 1956; tr 1957)   A drama by Jean GENET. Men who come to Madame Irma's brothel to enact their secret ambitions begin to fulfill the roles of the fantasies they have been playing. All, however, find that active responsibility is less satisfying than their dream projections. The Chief of Police discovers that he cannot become the modern hero until a customer comes to enact a heroic image of him; the revolutionary leader finds that the social system he sought to destroy actually represents the kind of tyranny he craves to control himself. A play of mirrors and ritual, sex and power, *The Balcony* is one of the most successful and imaginative pieces in the avant-garde repertoire.

Balder   In Norse mythology, the god of light, summer, innocence, and purity, called "the good." The son of Odin and Frigga, Balder dwelt at Breidhablik, one of the mansions of Asgard. He is said to have been slain by his rival Hoder while fighting for possession of the beautiful Nanna, after Holder had obtained Miming's sword, by which alone Balder could be wounded. Another legend tells that Frigga bound all things by oath not to harm him, but she accidentally omitted the mistletoe. Loki learned this and armed his blind brother Hoder with a mistletoe twig, with which, after all else had been tried, Balder was slain. His huge ship was used for his funeral pyre, where he was joined by his faithful wife Nanna. His death brought general consternation to the gods and formed the prelude to their final overthrow. See VALI.

Among modern poems written around the Balder legend are Matthew Arnold's "Balder Dead," William Morris's "Funeral of Balder," Robert Buchanan's "Balder the Beautiful," and Longfellow's "Tegner's Drapa."

Bald Soprano, The (La Cantatrice chauve, 1950; tr 1956)   An antiplay by Eugène IONESCO. It burlesques the nonsensical stuffiness of a middle-class English home by stringing together the clichés of a foreign-language phrase book. Characters without identity repeat empty gestures and banal commonplaces in a mock-serious, tragi-comic parody of existence.

Baldwin, James (1924–   )   American novelist and essayist. Baldwin's first novel, *Go Tell It on the Mountain* (1953), about the religious awakening of a fourteen-year-old black youth, was based closely on Baldwin's own experiences as a young storefront preacher in Harlem. His subsequent novels, including *Giovanni's Room* (1956), *Another Country* (1962), *Tell Me How Long the Train's Been Gone* (1968), and *If Beale Street Could Talk* (1974), are movingly written accounts of a black man's emotional and sexual torments. Baldwin is a distinguished essayist whose nonfiction works include *Notes of a Native Son* (1955), *Nobody Knows My Name* (1961), and *The Fire Next Time* (1963), all passionately angry indictments of an American society that institutionalizes race discrimination. In his own protest against inhumane conditions, Baldwin left the U.S. at twenty-four to live in France, where most of his work has been written; he returned to America in 1977. He has also written plays, such as *The Amen Corner* (1955), *Blues for Mister Charlie* (1964), and *One Day, When I Was Lost* (1973), a script based on *The Autobiography of Malcolm X*. Baldwin's sixth novel, *Just Above My Head* (1979), is a thirty-year saga of a group of Harlem friends whose individual odysseys through wars, poverty, and the civil-rights struggle bring them to various fates. In 1985 he published *The Price of the Ticket: Collected Non-Fiction, 1948–1985*, and in 1986, *Evidence of Things Not Seen*, an analysis of racism in the light of the Atlanta murders of black children.

Balin, Sir   In Arthurian legend, one of the knights of the Round Table, brother of Sir Balan. In Malory's *Morte d'Arthur* (c1469), the two brothers unwittingly kill each other in single combat, neither recognizing the other until just before death. At their request, they are buried in one grave by Merlin. Tennyson gives a much-altered version of the story in *Idylls of the King* (1859–72).

ballad   A narrative song, originally chiefly of popular origin. Ballads fall into types according to subject and include the domestic tragedy, concerning a murder or family feud; the historical ballad, dealing with historical events; the outlaw ballad, celebrating a popular rebel against established law, such as ROBIN HOOD or Jesse JAMES; the Scottish coronach, or lament ballad; and the folkloric ballad. Among early ballads, coronach and historical ballads and those involving romance elements were usually composed by minstrels attached to noblemen's courts and were written with a sense of literary values and for a definite audience. The other types were popular products transmitted by oral tradition and had much charm but little artistic finish. In the U.S., many folk ballads are survivals or variants of the old English ballads. However, there are a number of indigenous types, dealing with such subjects as occupational pursuits (CASEY JONES), blacks and other national or ethnic groups (JOHN HENRY), various sections of the country, famous battles, and actual or legendary heroes.

English and Scottish ballads dating from the 14th to the 16th century are to be found in Percy's RELIQUES OF ANCIENT ENGLISH POETRY and James Francis CHILD's *English and Scottish Popular Ballads* (1857–58). Many literary ballads have been written by later poets; among them may be mentioned Campbell's LORD ULLIN'S DAUGHTER, Rossetti's SISTER HELEN, and Stephen Vincent BENÉT's *Ballad of William Sycamore* (1923).

ballade   A traditional verse form first appearing in Provençal literature. The ballade was developed in France and reached its height during the 14th century, when it first came into English. François Villon (15th century) probably wrote the best-known ballades in literary history.

The ballade consists of three stanzas and an envoi, and its distinguishing feature is a refrain that appears as the last line of each stanza. The stanza may be of seven, eight, or ten lines. The ballade royal, written in RHYME ROYAL, has a fourth stanza instead of an envoi. Only three or four rhymes are used in all. The refrain adds to the meaning of the poem in every occurrence; the envoi is usually addressed to the poet's patron or to someone concerned with the subject of the poem. CHAUCER's *Ballade of Good Counsel* and SWINBURNE's "Ballad of Dreamland" are good examples in English. See CHANT ROYAL.

Ballad of Dead Ladies, The (1869)   An English translation by Dante Gabriel ROSSETTI of the famous "Ballade des dames du temps jadis" (1461) of the medieval French poet François VILLON.

Ballad of Reading Gaol, The (1898)   A poem by Oscar WILDE. It is the study of a man condemned to die and is drawn from the author's experiences in the prison of the title.

Ballets Russes   See DIAGHILEV, SERGEI.

Baly (or Bali)   One of the great kings in the legends of India. Baly founded the city called by his name, redressed wrongs, upheld justice, and was generous and charitable, so that at death he became one of the judges of hell. One day a dwarf asked the mighty monarch to allow him to measure three of his own paces for a hut to dwell in. Baly smiled and gave him permission. The first pace of the dwarf encompassed the earth, the second the heavens, and the third the infernal regions. Baly realized immediately that the dwarf was an incarnation of Vishnu and worshiped him. Vishnu made Baly king of hell and permitted him to revisit the earth once a year, on the first full moon of November.

Balzac, Honoré de (1799–1850)   French novelist. Born at Tours, Balzac attended the Sorbonne, where he acquired a passionate interest in literature. Unsuccessful experiments in the sensational novel and increasing debts marked his early years. At the age of thirty, Balzac published his first successful novel, LES CHOUANS, and began the literary career that was to be as astoundingly prolific as it was important—he wrote more than ninety novels and tales. As with Stendhal and Flaubert, the romantic and the realistic coexist in both Balzac's character and his writings. Considered to be a founder of the realistic school, Balzac uses vast reams of meticulous detail and faithfully depicts ordinary and undistinguished lives. Carefully documented, his novels are objective in their point of view and wide in their scope. Juxtaposed, however, with these realistic elements are the flagrantly romantic qualities of melodramatic plots, violent passions, and rhetorical passages. Balzac's characters are romantic in their extremism. Like the men and women of Dickens, they are painted in such bold strokes that they move away from human reality. Character traits, in such people as M. Grandet or Père Goriot, become heightened and exaggerated.

LA COMÉDIE HUMAINE is Balzac's tour de force, his masterpiece. The product of twenty years of creative labor, *La Comédie humaine* is an attempt to present a complete social history of France in a thorough and scientific manner. The conception alone testifies to Balzac's almost superhuman energy and his unfailing vitality. Some of the finest novels in the series include EUGÉNIE GRANDET, LE PÈRE GORIOT, *La Recherche de l'absolu* (1834), and *César Birotteau* (1837). In style, Balzac's works are not graceful and polished. A strain of coarseness in the man and the work, a lack of concern with delicacy and subtlety, contributed to the clumsy strength of his prose. Balzac worked in breadth, not depth, and on his enormous canvas an unwieldy but intensely alive panoramic vision of France took shape.

Ban, King   In Arthurian legend (e.g., Malory's *Morte d'Arthur*), the king of Benwick and father of Sir Launcelot.

Bandeira [Filho], Manuel [Carneirode Sousa] (1886–1968)   Brazilian poet and essayist. Tuberculosis cut short Bandeira's studies in architecture. While living in a Swiss sanatorium, he came in contact with several French surrealists, notably Paul ÉLUARD. By 1914, on his return to Brazil, he had already written a book-length manuscript of poems. Although he consistently dissociated himself from any poetic movements, his work in the 1920s —particularly *O ritmo dissoluto* (1924) and *Libertinagem* (1930)—was hailed as the spearhead of MODERNISMO. Distinguished for its irony and tragic wit, Bandeira's poetics advocate "using all the words, especially barbarisms; and all the rhythms, especially those beyond metrics." Apart from his unceasing experimentation with form, Bandeira introduced the Brazilian vernacular and the African folklore of his native Recife into serious poetry. His collected works, *Poesia e prosa* (2 vols, 1958), includes essays, art criticism, and an autobiography, as well as his verse.

Banerjee, Tarashankar (1898–1971)   Indian novelist. One of Bengal's greatest novelists, Banerjee is largely concerned in his writings with the decay of the landlord class, and his sympathies lie with the oppressed peasantry. Most highly esteemed of his many books are *Rai kamal* (1934; tr *The Eternal Locust*, 1945) and *Ganadevata* (tr *Temple Pavilion*, 1969).

Banerji, Bibhuti Bhusan (1894–1950)   Bengali novelist. Banerji was an immensely popular author of over fifty books, including novels, short stories, translations, and books on the occult and astrology. His masterpiece, *Pather Panchali* (1928; tr *The Song of the Road*, 1968), set in a small village north of Calcutta, is essentially an episodic childhood idyll of Apu and his sister Durga. The novel and its sequel, *Aparajita* (1932), became international classics after Satyajit RAY's screen adaptations, *Pather Panchali* (1954), *The Unvanquished* (1956), and *The World of Apu* (1959).

Banquo   In Shakespeare's MACBETH, the thane of Lochaber and a general in the king's army. Banquo is slain by order of Macbeth because the witches had foretold that his descendants would reign over Scotland. His ghost later appears to Macbeth at a banquet, though it is invisible to the others present. Described as having a "royalty of nature," a "dauntless temper of mind," and a "wisdom that doth guide his valor," he serves as a foil to the ambition-driven Macbeth.

The name *Banquo* is given in many old genealogies of the Scottish kings, but Shakespeare's character is not drawn from history. See FLEANCE.

baptism The rite of Christian initiation. Baptism is performed by pouring or sprinkling water on a person or by immersing him briefly in water, accompanied usually with the formula "I baptize thee in the name of the Father, and of the Son, and of the Holy Ghost." The rite is held to wash away the stain of ORIGINAL SIN and to make the recipient a member of the Christian church. Much controversy has surrounded the mode of administration and the age at which baptism should be administered. See ANABAPTISTS; SACRAMENT.

Barabbas The robber and insurrectionary leader whom Pilate released from prison instead of Jesus, according to the custom that, at the feast of Passover, one prisoner, chosen by popular demand, should be freed (Matt. 27).

Baraka, Imamu Amiri (formerly LeRoi Jones, 1934–   ) American poet and playwright. DUTCHMAN, a taut one-act play, part realistic, part ritualistic, crystalizing the conflicts between white and black cultures, established Baraka as an important force in stimulating black playwriting and production. Baraka's other major play, *Slave Ship* (1967), relies on music and action as much as language to unfold its haunting story. Baraka's theatre is aggressive and provocative, yet lyrical in its theatrical effect. His prolific output of essays and poetry includes *Preface to a Twenty Volume Suicide Note* (1961), *The Dead Lecturer* (1964), *Black Magic* (1969), and *Hard Facts* (1976); his work is collected in *Selected Plays and Prose* and *Selected Poetry* (both 1979). Two other works appeared in 1979: a collection of poetry, *AM/TRAK* and *Spring Song*. *Reggae or Not*, prose writings, appeared in 1981. Baraka's later works have become increasingly polemical in tone, and his insistence on black separatism and the importance of eliminating the white race has led to his desertion by the white liberals who lionized him even as he harangued them.

Barbara Frietchie (1863) A poem by John Greenleaf WHITTIER. The central incident in the poem is the fictional encounter between Barbara Frietchie and Stonewall Jackson. He forbade his Confederate troops to harm her, when she prominently displayed a Union flag. Ninety-six years old, she stood at her window in Frederick, Maryland:

> "Shoot, if you must, this old gray head,
> But spare your country's flag," she said.

Barber of Seville, The (1775) The title of a comedy by BEAUMARCHAIS and of two operas, one by Rossini (1816) and the other by Giovanni Paisiello (c1776), both based on the play. FIGARO, a rascal of a barber, aids his former master, Count Almaviva, to gain entrance to the house of Bartholo, so that the count can woo Bartholo's ward, Rosine, a beautiful young girl with whom Almaviva is in love. With Figaro's help, he succeeds in marrying her in spite of old Bartholo's precautions.

Barbizon School The name given to a loosely associated group of French landscape painters. Opposed to the classical teachings of the Academy and inspired by 17th-century Flemish landscapists, they withdrew from the Academy and, from 1830 to 1870, made their center at Barbizon, in the forest of Fontainebleau. COROT and MILLET are often linked to the school, but the principal figures were Theodore Rousseau (1812–67) and Charles François Daubigny (1817–78), who advocated the direct observation of nature and clear depictions of natural scenes. The Barbizon painters anticipated techniques employed by the impressionists and had a considerable influence on American art of the period.

Barchester Towers (1857) One of the best known of the novels of Anthony TROLLOPE in the BARSETSHIRE series. A sequel to *The Warden* (1855), it is a novel of clerical intrigue, showing the struggle between the trenchant Mrs. PROUDIE, the bishop's wife, and the insidious chaplain, Mr. Slope. Each wishes to become the dominant voice in the quiet cathedral town of Barchester. Mrs. Proudie eventually triumphs.

Bardell, Mrs. In Charles Dickens's PICKWICK PAPERS, a widowed landlady of "apartments for single gentlemen" in Goswell Street. Long an admirer of Mr. Pickwick, she misinterprets some innocent remarks of his as a proposal of marriage and is induced by the unprincipled lawyers Dodson and Fogg to sue for breach of promise. A verdict is obtained against Pickwick, but Mrs. Bardell is subsequently arrested for refusing to pay the costs of the trial and is lodged in prison.

Bard of Avon A popular epithet for SHAKESPEARE, who was born and buried at Stratford-upon-Avon.

Bardolph Sir John Falstaff's corporal in Shakespeare's HENRY IV: PART I and PART II and in THE MERRY WIVES OF WINDSOR. In HENRY V, he is promoted to lieutenant. He is a lowbred, drunken swaggerer whose red, pimply nose wins him the nickname "Knight of the Burning Lamp."

Barefoot Boy, The (1855) A poem by John Greenleaf WHITTIER. Its subject is the joy of a country childhood.

Baring, Maurice (1874–1945) English novelist, poet, essayist, and playwright. Until 1912, Baring worked as a journalist in Russia and wrote several studies of Russian culture and literature. His *Collected Poems* were published in 1925. He also wrote such plays as *The Grey Stocking* (1912) and novels and stories, including *Cat's Cradle* (1925) and *Tinker's Leave* (1927). *The Puppet Show of Memory* (1922) is his autobiography.

Barker, George [Granville] (1913–   ) English poet. Like that of his contemporary, Dylan THOMAS, Barker's poetry is at turns ecstatic, romantic, and violent, characterized by extravagant imagery and great technical dexterity in the use of puns, rhythms, and other verbal devices. It is also often didactic and concerned with moral and political issues. Collections of his poetry include *Calamiterror* (1937), inspired by the Spanish Civil War; *Eros in Dogma* (1944); *Collected Poems* (1957); *The View from a Blind I* (1962); *At Thurgarton Church* (1969); and *Villa Stellar* (1978).

Barkis In Charles Dickens's DAVID COPPERFIELD, the carrier who courts Clara PEGGOTTY by asking David to tell her "Barkis is willin'." Peggotty takes the hint and becomes Mrs. Barkis.

Barkley, Catherine The heroine of Ernest Hemingway's novel A FAREWELL TO ARMS. An English nurse in an Italian hospital, Barkley has a brief affair with the American lieutenant Frederic Henry but dies bearing his child.

Barlow, Joel (1754–1812) American poet and diplomat, a leader of the anti-Federalist party, and one of the best known of the HARTFORD WITS. In 1788 he left for Europe as a representative of some American business interests. He stayed abroad for seventeen years and in 1795 was appointed American consul to Algiers. In Europe he shed his conservatism, became an ardent democrat, and befriended Thomas Paine.

Barlow's most popular poem was THE HASTY PUDDING; his most ambitious was *The Vision of Columbus*, first published in 1787 and later revised, lengthened, and reissued in epic form as THE COLUMBIAD. He was one of the authors of THE ANARCHIAD and also wrote *Advice to the Privileged Orders* (1792), a controversial prose tract embodying his democratic ideals.

Barmecide feast An imaginary feast where the dishes are empty; hence, a reference to any appealing illusion. The allusion is to such a banquet given in jest for the poor Schacabac by a rich Barmecide prince in the *Arabian Nights* story "The Barber's Sixth Brother." The starving Schacabac pretends to eat and enjoy the empty dishes set before him, but, when illusory wine is offered him, he feigns drunkenness and knocks the Barmecide down. The latter sees the humor of the situation, forgives Schacabac, and provides him with food to his heart's content.

Barnabas In the New Testament, a companion of Paul and Mark. Barnabas accompanied them both on the first missionary journey. Barnabas was to go with Paul on his second journey and urged Paul to take Mark, Barnabas's nephew, with them. Paul refused, however, since Mark had left them before the first journey was over. As a result, Paul took Silas with him, and neither Mark nor Barnabas went. It is thought that Mark wrote his Gospel at the urging of Barnabas, perhaps under his direction.

Barnaby Rudge (1841) A novel by Charles DICKENS. The book revolves around the anti-Catholic GORDON RIOTS of 1780, in which Barnaby innocently participates for the pleasure of carrying a flag and wearing a blue bow. Barnaby is a half-wit, a fact mysteriously connected with the fact that his father murdered his employer and a fellow

servant on the night of Barnaby's birth. Of conspicuous appearance, Barnaby is pale, with long red hair; he dresses all in green and carries a large raven named Grip in a basket on his back. He is identified as a leading rioter and condemned to death but is reprieved through the influence of Gabriel Varden. He spends the rest of his life with his mother in a cottage near Maypole, happily employed with his poultry and his garden.

Barnaby's father, Mr. Rudge, is mistakenly believed to have been murdered the same night as Mr. Haredale, his employer. After the murder, he is seen by many in the locality but is thought to be a ghost. Years later, he joins the Gordon rioters and is sent to Newgate but makes his escape when it is burned down.

The plot of this book is one of Dickens's weakest, and the novel's chief interest lies in its depiction of the terrible riots. In exploring causes for the riots, Dickens finds the answer in a government that is heedless of the needs of its poor. A similar theme is dealt with in A TALE OF TWO CITIES.

Barnacle The name given by Charles Dickens in LITTLE DORRIT to a "very high family and a very large family" active in governmental circles, nine of whom appear in the novel. They are bungling and incompetent. In all of them—particularly in Mr. Tite Barnacle, a permanent official in the CIRCUMLOCUTION OFFICE—Dickens satirizes governmental red tape.

Barnes, Djuna (1892–1982) American novelist and short-story writer. For many years a resident of Europe, Barnes was the author of three experimental plays produced in 1919–20 by the PROVINCETOWN PLAYERS: *Three from the Earth, An Irish Triangle,* and *Kurzy from the Sea. Ryder* (1928) and *Nightwood* (1936) are her best-known books. The latter, with an introduction by T. S. ELIOT, is an experimental novel dealing with the Parisian artistic underground. After the publication of *Nightwood*, however, Barnes became a recluse. She published only one play and two poems after this, the main reason for her lack of fame today; in her time she was extraordinarily influential. *The Antiphon* (1958) is a surrealistic play in blank verse. Her *Selected Works* appeared in 1962. In 1983, soon after her death, *Smoke and Other Early Stories* was published for the first time. *Interviews* (1985), a collection of newspaper and magazine conversations with celebrities, presents forty portraits of varied people and is illustrated with Barnes's own drawings.

Barnes, Jake The principal male character in Ernest Hemingway's novel THE SUN ALSO RISES. Made impotent by a war wound, Barnes is hopelessly attracted to Lady Brett Ashley. Though in many ways his life is as aimless as those of the other "lost generation" characters, he lives by a code of behavior that gives him considerable stability.

Barnes, William (1801–1886) English poet and philologist. Of Dorsetshire yeoman stock, Barnes educated himself to such purpose that he became acquainted with some sixty languages, in addition to being a capable wood engraver, archaeologist, musician, and mathematician. He spent most of his life as a country schoolmaster and parson, publishing numerous philological works and composing the poems in Dorset dialect on which his fame rests. The poems are distinguished by simplicity and humor, fresh and vivid descriptions of nature, and an unaffected and native pastoral quality. His works include *Poems of Rural Life in the Dorset Dialect* (1844, 1862) and *Poems of Rural Life in Common English* (1868).

Baroja y Nessi, Pío (1872–1956) Spanish novelist and memoirist. A cynical stoic and disillusioned idealist, Baroja was a member of the individualistic GENERACIÓN DEL 98. His best-known and perhaps most characteristic work is the neonaturalistic novel *El árbol de la ciencia* (1911; tr *The Tree of Knowledge*, 1928), a portrait of the restless and disoriented intellectual Andrés Hurtado, who ends his life in suicide. An anarchist (in theory only) much influenced by NIETZSCHE and SCHOPENHAUER, Baroja wrote many trilogies, often dealing with the artist or intellectual's search for identity or with his Basque homeland (as in *Tierra vasca*, 1900–1909). His works are a blend of IMPRESSIONISM and NATURALISM, in the first case, or tend toward the novel of adventure, as in his work on Basque maritime life, *Las inquietudes de Shanti Andía* (1911; tr *The Restlessness of Shanti Andía*, 1959).

baroque A term applied to certain tendencies in European art in the latter 16th, the 17th, and the first half of the 18th centuries. Initially and still primarily, *baroque* referred to a free, exuberant style of architecture that supplanted the restrained and balanced style of the earlier RENAISSANCE, but it was later applied to similar tendencies in painting, music, sculpture, and literature. The baroque style was dramatic, grandiose, ornate, and full of motifs and forms expressive of conflict and energy. Originating in Italy and Spain, it spread throughout Europe, but it is closely identified, especially in architecture, with Catholic Europe and was virtually the official style of the Counter-Reformation. In literature, the baroque spirit reflected the intense religious ideals of the age, often combining sensuous imagery with mysticism, as in the works of John Donne, Richard Crashaw, and other metaphysical poets. Also, such literary movements as Marinism (see Giambattista MARINO) in Italy, GONGORISM in Spain, and EUPHUISM in England were part of the baroque period. The word *baroque* has been used pejoratively, signifying a false, fantastic, overemphatic style, but such a sense is justified, if at all, only when applied to late-baroque style, such as ROCOCO.

Barrack-Room Ballads (1892) A volume of poems by Rudyard KIPLING, celebrating the British soldier and army life throughout the Empire, written in ballad meters and frequently in Cockney diction. Among the poems are FUZZY WUZZY, GUNGA DIN, "Mandalay," and TOMMY.

Barrès, [Augustin-] Maurice (1862–1923) French novelist, journalist, and politician. Barrès's first novel trilogy, *Le Culte du moi* (1888–91), portrayed the inner life of an egoist who, in trying to develop his individual self, discovers his need for others. The trilogy *Le Roman de l'énergie nationale* (1897–1903) is a social and philosophical commentary based on his own public life. Most famous of the nationalistic trilogy *Les Bastions de l'est* (1905–21) is *Colette Baudoche; The Story of a Young Girl of Metz* (1918). Barrès wrote other novels, including *La Colline inspirée* (*The Sacred Hill*, 1913), and many articles about World War I, collected in *L'Ame française et la guerre* (11 vols, 1917–22) and *Chronique de la grande guerre* (14 vols, 1920–24).

Barretts of Wimpole Street, The (1930) A successful play by Rudolf Besier (1878–1942), produced in London and New York. It was based on the romance of Robert and Elizabeth Barrett Browning.

Barrie, Sir J[ames] M[atthew] (1860–1937) Scottish dramatist and novelist, known for the whimsy and sentimental fantasy of his work. Barrie's best-known plays are *Quality Street* (1901), *The Admirable Crichton* (1902), PETER PAN, *Alice Sit-by-the-Fire* (1905), *What Every Woman Knows* (1908), and *Dear Brutus* (1917). His outstanding prose works include *A Window in Thrums* (1889); *The Little Minister* (1891), a novel, dramatized in 1897; *Margaret Ogilvy* (1896), a biography of his mother; and *Sentimental Tommy* (1896), a novel.

Barrios, Eduardo (1884–1963) Chilean novelist and short-story writer. After wandering throughout Latin America and working at a variety of jobs, Barrios settled in Santiago, where he served in the 1920s as minister of education and director of the national library. His mastery of the psychological tale is especially evident in the portrayal of hypersensitive personalities. Such is the ten-year-old protagonist of the novelette *El niño que enloqueció de amor* (1915), who falls in love with one of his mother's friends. The hero of *Un perdido* (1917) is an overwrought weakling who, unable to cope with reality, finds refuge in alcohol. Barrios's best work is probably *El hermano asno* (1922; tr *Brother Ass*, 1942), which deals with the inner conflicts of Brother Lázaro and Brother Rufino, two Franciscan monks. *Gran señor y rajadiablos* (1948) follows José Pedro Valverde, one of literature's most strongly drawn characters, through a life centered mostly about a large *fundo* (ranch). Barrios's last novel, *Los hombres del hombre* (1950), is a lyrical story of sexual jealousy and insecurity in family life.

Barry, Philip (1896–1949) American playwright. His work consists of sophisticated comedies and dramas of life among the wealthier classes, although he experimented with fantasy and mysticism in such plays as *Hotel Universe* (1930) and *Here Come the Clowns* (1938). Notable among his plays are *You and I* (1922), *Paris Bound* (1927), *Holiday* (1929), *The Animal Kingdom* (1932), and THE PHILADELPHIA STORY.

Barrymore   An American theatrical family. Maurice Barrymore (real name Herbert Blythe, 1847–1905), a handsome leading man, and his wife, Georgiana Drew (1856–93), were the first to use the Barrymore name. They had three children: Lionel, Ethel, and John, all three of whom also became successful in the theatre. They wrote prolifically about themselves in many autobiographies, among them *We Barrymores* by Lionel Barrymore (1951) and *Memories* by Ethel Barrymore (1955). John wrote about his life and family in *Confessions of an Actor* (1926); it was followed by John's daughter Diana's autobiography, *Too Much Too Soon* (1958). They were also the subjects of *The Royal Family* (1927), a satirical play by George S. Kaufman and Edna Ferber. Gene Fowler's *Good Night, Sweet Prince* (1943) is mainly about John but includes much about the others as well.

Barsetshire, Chronicles of   A series of novels by Anthony TROLLOPE. Known also as the Cathedral Stories, they comprise *The Warden* (1855), BARCHESTER TOWERS, *Doctor Thorne* (1858), *Framley Parsonage* (1861), *The Small House at Allington* (1864), and *The Last Chronicle of Barset* (1867). In them, Trollope disturbs the placidity of the cathedral town of Barchester with a series of agitations that ripple the clerical pools. The same characters reappear in most of them; among the best-known characters are Bishop and Mrs. PROUDIE, Archdeacon Grantly, Rev. Septimus Harding, Rev. Mr. Crawley, the Thornes, Mr. Slope, Lady Arabella Gresham, and Signora Madeleine Neroni. Descendants of these families appear in the novels of Angela Thirkell.

Barstow, Stan[ley] (1928–   )   English novelist and playwright. One of a number of northern English working-class writers who came into prominence in the late 1950s and early 1960s, Barstow first achieved recognition with *A Kind of Loving* (1960). All his fiction is set in his native Yorkshire, usually in the grubby towns of factory smoke and row houses. *Ask Me Tomorrow* (1962) and *Joby* (1964) confirmed his reputation as a writer of more than regional interest, revealing his interest in how a man defines himself and his character against a frequently hostile environment. Barstow's work for television and theatre includes a 1974 adaptation of his fifth novel, *A Raging Calm* (1968; U.S., *The Hidden Part*), and a stage treatment of Ibsen's *An Enemy of the People* (1974). His later novels include *A Brother's Tale* (1980) and *The Glad Eye* (1984).

Bart, Lily   See HOUSE OF MIRTH, THE.

Barth, John [Simmons] (1930–   )   American novelist and short-story writer. Barth has spent many years in academia and, to the extent that his novels are concerned with the relationship between language and reality, he is considered an "academic" novelist. Although his first two novels—*The Floating Opera* (1956; rev 1967) and *The End of the Road* (1958; rev 1967)—are formally realistic, they are thematically tinged with elements of existential absurdism. His third novel, THE SOT-WEED FACTOR, is a bawdy parody of PICARESQUE historical fiction that further blurs the distinction between reality and illusion. Believing that the novel, as a form, is near the end of its tether, Barth plays intricate word games, manipulates fictional forms, and sets his numb and nihilistic anti-heroes in situations that waver between the real and the surreal. Following his epic, comic allegory of modern despair, *Giles Goat-Boy* (1966), Barth published *Lost in the Funhouse* (1968), a collection of stories "written" for voice and tape recorder. He was awarded the National Book Award in 1973 for the three novellas in *Chimera* (1972). In *Letters* (1979) he reuses characters from his previous fiction in an elaborate burlesque of the EPISTOLARY NOVEL. In 1982 *Sabbatical: A Romance* was published, and in 1984 *The Friday Book: Essays and Other Nonfiction* appeared.

Barthelme, Donald (1931–   )   American novelist and short-story writer. A distinctive and much-imitated writer, Barthelme portrays a comic, absurdist vision of the violence and apathy of the modern world. His collage-like, disjointed prose employs clichés, television ads, and other media jargon. His devices range from the mock essay to stories consisting of numbered sentences or one long sentence. The short pieces of fiction collected in *Come Back, Dr. Caligari* (1964), *Unspeakable Practices, Unnatural Acts* (1968), *City Life* (1970), *Guilty Pleasures* (1974), *Amateurs* (1976), and *Great Days* (1979) have been called "verbal objects," the verbal equivalents of POP ART, reflecting Barthelme's belief that contemporary reality can be rendered only in fragments. His novels include *Snow White* (1967), a deadpan parody of the fairy tale, and *The Dead Father* (1975), one of his few works to follow something of a narrative line. In recent years, he has published other collections of stories, among them *Sixty Stories* (1982) and *Overnight to Many Distant Cities* (1983).

Barthes, Roland (1915–1980)   French literary critic and theorist. Barthes was in the forefront of France's "nouveaux critiques" in the two decades before his death. His theories on literature were drawn from such varied fields as sociology, anthropology, psychoanalysis, linguistics, and, most particularly, semiology (the study of signs) and STRUCTURALISM. Taking off from BACHELARD's phenomenological approach to consciousness, Barthes asserted that language is a system of signs that reflects the society and time in which it is used. For him, the critic's function is to study and decipher the signs used for expression, rather than to analyze the meaning of the work or to assess its value. His best-known and most controversial theoretical work was *Le Degré zero de l'écriture* (1953; tr *Writing Degree Zero*, 1967), which discusses writers from the 17th to 20th centuries and their search for a language of "zero degree," that is, a language free from the associations of the past. Also important was his *Eléments de sémiologie* (1964; tr *Elements of Semiology*, 1964). Among his many other works, in which he also analyzed the nonliterary signs evident in popular culture, are *Mythologies* (1957; tr 1972), *Sur Racine* (1963; tr *On Racine*, 1964), *Critique et vérité* (1966; tr *Image-Music-Text*, 1978), and *Fragments d'un discours amoureux* (1977; tr *A Lover's Discourse: Fragments*, 1978). Recent years have seen *L'Obvie et l'obtus* (1982; tr *The Responsibility of Forms: Critical Essays on Music, Art and Representation*, 1985), *The Grain of the Voice: Interviews 1962–1980* (1985), and *Le Bruissement de la langue* (1984; tr *The Rustle of Language*, 1986).

Bartholomew, St.   One of the twelve disciples of Jesus. The symbol of St. Bartholomew is a knife, in allusion to the one with which he was flayed alive. He is commemorated on August 24.

Bartleby the Scrivener (1853)   A long short story by Herman MELVILLE, originally published in *Putnam's Monthly Magazine* and later in THE PIAZZA TALES. The narrator, who operates a law firm on Wall Street, employs a scrivener, Bartleby, whose job it is to copy and proofread legal documents. Eventually, Bartleby rejects these chores, stares blankly at an empty wall, and answers all entreaties with, "I should prefer not to." Unable to persuade Bartleby either to work or to leave, the narrator moves to a new office, and the scrivener is taken to prison. Refusing all the privileges his former employer's vague sense of responsibility has bought for him, he dies of starvation.

Bartlett, John (1820–1905)   American bookseller, editor, and publisher. Self-taught, Bartlett worked in the University Book Store in Cambridge, Massachusetts, where he impressed his customers with the breadth of his learning. While at that job, he compiled his most famous book, *Familiar Quotations* (1855), which ran through nine editions in his lifetime and numerous subsequent editions after his death. He also published *A New Method of Chess Notation* (1857), *A Shakespeare Phrase Book* (1881), and *A New and Complete Concordance to Shakespeare* (1894). Following his work as a bookseller, he was employed by Little, Brown & Co.; he became a partner in 1865 and a senior partner in 1878.

Bartók, Béla (1881–1945)   Hungarian composer, pianist, and collector of folk songs. Bartók first made his reputation as a pianist; his own compositions were not popularly received until after his death. A deep interest in the folk tunes of Hungary led him on searches (many with Zoltán KODÁLY) for hitherto unheard songs and dances, which he transcribed and published. The influence of folk music is apparent in many of Bartók's pieces, such as *Duke Bluebeard's Castle* (1911), an opera with libretto by Béla Balász (see BLUEBEARD), the piano pieces *Allegro barbaro* (1911) and *Mikrokosmos* (6 vols, 1926–37), as well as much of his chamber music and piano concerti. Following a hostile reaction to his ballet the *Miraculous Mandarin* (1919), Bartók determined never again to appear on stage in his native land. It was not until after his death that he was recognized as one of the foremost composers of the 20th century.

Bartram, William (1739–1823)   American naturalist, explorer, and writer. Bartram's father, John (1699–1777), was the chief botanist of the American colonies and the founder of the Philadelphia Botanical Gardens. In 1773 William undertook the first botanical exploration of the wild terrain of the Carolinas, Georgia, and Florida. He recorded every detail of the hitherto unseen and uncatalogued flora and fauna in *The Travels of William Bartram* (1791). The book was immensely popular in Europe, where people were fascinated by his loving description of wildlife and Indians and by his meticulous, beautiful drawings. Among the writers on whom the book had a clear impact were WORDSWORTH and COLERIDGE in England and CHATEAUBRIAND in France. The book went largely ignored in the U.S. until Mark VAN DOREN revived it in a 1928 edition.

Baruch, Bernard M[annes] (1870–1965)   American businessman and statesman. A graduate of the City College of New York, whose school of business administration is named after him, Baruch became a rich man through his shrewdness in finance while he was still in his twenties. He held several key government posts connected with the war effort during World War I. He was named U.S. representative to the U.N. Atomic Energy Commission in 1946. He is the author of *American Industry in the War* (1941), *A Philosophy of Our Time* (1954), *Baruch: My Own Story* (1957), and *Baruch: The Public Years* (1960). As an elder statesman, he was for many years a valued, if unofficial, adviser to presidents, his "office" a famous park bench in Jackson Square, opposite the White House.

Barzun, Jacques [Martin] (1907–   )   French-born American writer and educator. Barzun began teaching at Columbia University in 1928 and became dean of faculties and provost in 1958. Originally a student of history and law, Barzun brought his scholarly approach to the study of a diverse range of contemporary problems. Among his many works are *Race: A Study in Modern Superstition* (1937), *Darwin, Marx, Wagner* (1941), *The Teacher in America* (1945), *Berlioz and the Romantic Century* (2 vols, 1950), and *The American University* (1968). Barzun's analysis of contemporary arts is contained in *The Use and Abuse of Art* (1974). *Clio and the Doctors* (1974) traces the influence of psychoanalysis on the interpretation of history. Recent works include the highly acclaimed *Simple and Direct: A Rhetoric for Writers* (with Georgia Dunbar, 1975) and *A Stroll with William James* (1983).

Basel, Council of   The last of the great reform councils of the 15th century. Beginning at Basel in 1431 and continuing until 1443 at Ferrara, Florence, and Rome, it brought about a temporary reunion of the Greek and Roman churches and further stimulated the REVIVAL OF LEARNING.

Bashō   See MATSUO BASHŌ.

Basic English   A simple form of English designed by C. K. OGDEN. It has 850 words, with rules for their use and expansions of sense, and 150 more bridge words for specific fields, such as medicine, chemistry, and physics, which have themselves a body of internationally common words or signs. Working with Ogden on its development was I. A. RICHARDS, who took the system to schools and universities in China as a help in the teaching of English at all levels. Its possible use as an international language was the reason Sir Winston CHURCHILL, one of its strong supporters, gave part of his talk at a Harvard commencement in Basic English. Before his death in 1979, Richards was again in China, working on the use of Basic for international purposes. [*Ed. note: This entry is written in Basic English.*]

Bassani, Georgio (1916–   )   Italian poet, screenwriter, and novelist. Bassani made his adopted city of Ferrara and its small but fascinating Jewish community the subject of his poetic world. A careful, polished stylist, he produced a body of work whose major theme is the suffering endured by Italian Jews between the mid-1930s and the end of World War II. Of his books, the best known is *Il giardino dei Finzi-Contini* (1962; tr *The Garden of the Finzi-Continis*, 1965), which was made into a motion picture by Vittorio de Sica. Other works include *Cinque storie ferraresi* (1956; tr *Five Stories of Ferrara*, 1971) and the somber *L'airone* (1968; tr *The Heron*, 1970).

As consultant to the Italian publisher Feltrinelli, Bassani was responsible for the publication of Lampedusa's THE LEOPARD. In 1980 Bassani published a collection of prose, *Il romanzo di Ferrara*, and in 1982 a volume of verse, *In rima e sonza*, poems about Ferrara and the landscapes in the region of the Po.

Bassanio   The impecunious and quick-witted friend of Antonio in Shakespeare's MERCHANT OF VENICE. He borrows three thousand ducats from Antonio in order to woo Portia, a wealthy heiress of Belmont. In accordance with her father's will, Portia can marry only that suitor who successfully chooses from among three caskets the one that contains her portrait. With the help of a hint from Portia, Bassanio rejects the gold and silver caskets and, selecting the leaden one, opens it to find "fair Portia's counterfeit."

Bastille (fr OF, *bastir*, now *bâtir*, "to build")   A famous state prison in Paris. It was commenced by Charles V as a royal chateau in 1370 and was first used as a prison by Louis XI. It was seized and sacked by the mob in the French Revolution, July 14, 1789. Bastille Day is celebrated in France much as the Fourth of July is in the U.S. The prison was finally demolished and the Place de la Bastille laid out on its site. *Bastille* has come to mean a state prison for political offenders.

Bataille, Georges (1897–1962)   French novelist, philosophical theorist, and art critic. Bataille's works reflect his mystical quest for a supreme ideal of anguished eroticism and for a release from oppressive, bourgeois values, particularly those he felt were embodied by organized Christianity. He was profoundly influenced by NIETZSCHE and felt that the full release of instinctual drives and erotic excess was the only means by which one could take control of one's spirit. His novels include *Histoire de l'oeil* (1928; tr *The Story of the Eye*, 1967), *Le Coupable* (1943), *Le Bleu du ciel* (1945; tr *Blue of Noon*, 1978), and *L'Abbé C* (1950). He is well known for his literary and philosophical essays, particularly *L'Expérience intérieure* (1943), *L'Érotisme ou la muse en question de l'être* (1957; tr *Death and Sensuality*, 1962), *La Littérature et le mal* (1957; tr *Literature and Evil*, 1973), and *Les Larmes d'Eros* (1961). He founded (1946) the highly respected journal *Critique*.

Bate, W[alter] Jackson (1918–   )   American literary critic and biographer. Bate's early works, such as *The Stylistic Development of Keats* (1945) and *The Achievement of Samuel Johnson* (1955) were scholarly works of close textual analysis. He first won wide readership with his critical biography *John Keats* (1963; PULITZER PRIZE). This was followed by a short biography of Coleridge (1968). His best-known book is *Samuel Johnson* (1978; Pulitzer Prize), a monumental biography that includes a careful analysis of the moral and intellectual preoccupations that guided Johnson's work.

Bates, H[erbert] E[rnest] (1905–1974)   English writer. Known first as a master of the short story, Bates drew loving but unsentimental sketches of rural England, bringing to life its sturdy, laconic people and the beauty of the land they live on. He is also the author of more than thirty novels, including a best-seller about a British bomber crew in World War II, *Fair Stood the Wind for France* (1944). Among his comic novels centering on the Rabelaisian farming family of Pop and Ma Larkin was the popular *The Darling Buds of May* (1958). *The Vanished World* (1969) was the first of his three volumes of autobiography (1969–71).

Bates, Miss   A character in Jane Austen's EMMA. An old maid, garrulous and a dreadful bore, Miss Bates is nevertheless "a happy woman and a woman no one named without good will. . . . She loved everybody, was interested in everybody's happiness."

Bateson, F[rederick] W[ilse] (1901–1978)   English literary critic, editor, and scholar. Bateson's work is distinguished both by a strong social orientation and by the assertion that a critical interpretation of literature must be accompanied by a historical awareness of the period in which the work was produced. In *English Poetry and the English Language* (1934; rev 1973), he explores the relationship between language patterns and forms of poetry. These concerns are expanded in *English Poetry: A Critical Introduction* (1950; rev 1966), a provocative if unorthodox examination of the correspondence between social and economic factors and the poetry of particular periods of English history. Considered something of a maverick in the literary establishment, Bateson also wrote *Wordsworth: A Reinterpretation* (1954), *A Guide to English Literature* (1965; rev 1976), and *Essays in Critical Dissent* (1972).

bathos   A figure of speech which descends from the sublime to the ridiculous in an attempt to create a grandiose or pathetic effect. The term describes an unintentional ANTICLIMAX.

Bathsheba   In the Old Testament, the beautiful wife of Uriah the Hittite, sinfully loved by David, who gave orders that Uriah, his captain, should be sent into the most dangerous part of the battle, where he was slain. Bathsheba was afterwards the wife of David and mother of Solomon (2 Sam. 11:1–24).

Bathsheba is also a character in John Dryden's ABSALOM AND ACHITOPHEL, intended to represent Louise Kerouatte, Duchess of Portsmouth, a favorite of Charles II of England.

Battle Hymn of the Republic (1862)   An American patriotic tune, with words by Julia Ward HOWE. The song was written during the CIVIL WAR, when Howe was requested to write new words for the popular Union Army song "John Brown's Body."

Battle of Britain   A term applied to bombing raids on Great Britain by German airplanes during World War II, especially during the summer of 1940.

Battle of the Books, The (1704)   A prose mock-heroic satire by Jonathan SWIFT, written in 1697 and published with A TALE OF A TUB. It ridicules a literary squabble of the day as to the comparative merits of ancient and modern authors, touched off by Sir William Temple's essay *Of Ancient and Modern Learning* and continued by Richard BENTLEY, among others. Swift showed his contempt for the entire controversy and, more broadly, for modern scholarship, criticism, and poetry, by giving an account of a battle between modern and ancient books in St. James's Library, the outcome of which remains uncertain. The mock epic similes of the spider, signifying the moderns, and the bee, signifying the ancients, are among the most famous in all of literature.

Battle of the Frogs and Mice (Batrachomyomachia)   A mock-heroic Greek poem of early date. War is caused by a frog's leaving his mouse friend to drown in the middle of a pond. When both sides are arrayed for battle, a band of gnats sounds the attack, and, after a bloody battle, the frogs are defeated, but an army of land-crabs coming up saves the race from extermination, and the vic-torious mice make their way home in terrible disorder. The name of the mouse-king is Troxartes, probably a pun on *Tros*, a Trojan, and the poem is in many ways a burlesque of the *Iliad*. There is a 14th-century German skit on the same theme by G. Rollenhagen, a Meistersinger.

Battle of the Spurs   (1) A battle (1302) near Courtrai, Belgium, between a Flemish army and the French under Philip IV. The battle is so called because the victorious Flemings gathered from the field more than seven hundred gilt spurs worn by French nobles slain in the fight.

(2) A battle (1513) near Guinegate, France, between the English under Henry VIII and the French under Louis XII. The name is said to derive from the flight of the French cavalry.

Battle-Pieces and Aspects of the War (1866)   A collection of poems by Herman MELVILLE. The tone of these seventy-two poems about the CIVIL WAR is elegiac rather than vengeful. Melville does not celebrate martial spirit but rather deplores the human suffering. He is mournful and compassionate, as he sees the early death of young men and the ruin of the country.

Baucis and Philemon   See PHILEMON AND BAUCIS.

Baudelaire, Charles Pierre (1821–1867)   French poet, one of the most important figures among the French SYMBOLISTS. Baudelaire's typically DÉCADENT life was ultimately tragic; his debauched, violent, and eccentric existence brought him to an early and painful death at the age of forty-six. In Paris, he first began to write as a critic and translator, introducing the works of Edgar Allan Poe to Europe through translations that have since become French classics. Baudelaire published only a single volume of poetry, LES FLEURS DU MAL. Stylistically, in its pure and carefully classical form, his verse in some ways resembles that of the Parnassians, but it is far more significant, in that it foreshadows the development of modern poetry. Baudelaire's poems are filled with subtle nuances and with almost painfully delicate suggestiveness. The sensuous matter of a poem is conveyed in beautifully striking images. He is famous for his doctrine of correspondences, an exploration of the relationship of the various senses that lends a startling newness to his work. Not only Baudelaire's technique but his subject matter—the beauty of the perverse or the morbid and the probing analysis of complex emotional states—has been reflected in 20th-century poetry.

Bauhaus (Ger, "house of architecture")   A school of architecture and design, founded in Weimar, Germany, in 1919 by Walter GROPIUS. The school stressed functionalism in art and tried to unite the creative arts and the technology of modern mass production with 20th-century architecture. In addition to more strictly architectural studies, courses in painting, handicrafts, the theater, and typography were given by outstanding artists, including Lyonel Feininger, Vassily Kandinsky, and Paul Klee. Functionalism, or the international style, in architecture and a number of examples of industrial design, such as the tubular lighting and steel furniture of Marcel BREUER, were first developed at the Bauhaus. In 1925 the school moved to the buildings designed for it by Gropius in Dessau; three years later, Mies van der Rohe became its director.

The Bauhaus was attacked by Hitler's regime, and in 1933 it was forced to close. However, its great influence on modern architecture and design continued in Europe and the U.S. through its masters and students.

Baum, L[yman] Frank (1856–1919)   American journalist, playwright, and author of children's books. His most famous book, *The Wonderful Wizard of Oz* (1900), was the story of a young girl carried off by a Kansas tornado to the magical land of Oz. He produced a dramatization of the book in 1902, and in 1939 it was made into an immensely popular film, *The Wizard of Oz*, starring Judy Garland. He wrote a subsequent series of tales for the young about the mythical land of Oz, but they did not match the quality of the perennially beloved first one.

Bayle, Pierre (1647–1706)   French philosopher. Bayle's *Dictionnaire historique et critique* (*Historical and Critical Dictionary*, 1697–1706), his most important work, treats its biographical, theological, and philosophical subjects orthodoxly and reserves dissent for the voluminous footnotes. Its directness pleased the philosophes, and it influenced Diderot in the compiling of the *Encyclopédie*.

Bay Psalm Book (1640)   A metrical translation of the Biblical psalms by Richard MATHER, Thomas Welde, John ELIOT, and twenty-seven other ministers of the Massachusetts Bay Colony. The book—the first bound book printed in the English colonies—was published by Stephen DAY in Cambridge in an edition of seventeen hundred copies. Its full title is *The Whole Booke of Psalms Faithfully Translated into English Metre*.

Bazarov, Evgeni Vasil'yev   The central character of Ivan Turgenev's novel FATHERS AND SONS. A representative of the young democratic generation rising in Russia about the middle of the 19th century, Bazarov is a hardheaded materialist, with nothing but scorn for the old aristocratic order. He is regarded as one of Turgenev's most successful character portrayals.

Beard, Charles A[ustin] (1874–1948)   American historian. Having joined the faculty of Columbia University in 1904, Beard resigned in 1917 to protest the dismissal of two of his colleagues for pacifism. Later he helped to organize the New School for Social Research. Beard was particularly interested in the interrelation of economics and politics. One of his best-known works, *An Economic Interpretation of the Constitution* (1913), advanced the controversial theory that the framers of the Constitution, as property owners, were chiefly interested in constructing a charter to protect their wealth. A strong advocate of the idea that the study of history should include consideration of all cultural forces, Beard stated the case in *A Charter for*

the Social Sciences in the Schools (1932), a book which had an important effect on the teaching of history. He wrote several books with his wife, Mary R[itter] Beard (1876–1958), a historian of feminism and the labor movement. The best known of their collaborations are *The Rise of American Civilization* (2 vols, 1927; rev 1933), *America in Mid-Passage* (1939), and *The American Spirit* (1943). Beard's early liberalism faded toward the end of his life. An isolationist in foreign policy and an outspoken critic of Franklin D. Roosevelt, he advocated very conservative ideas in his last two books, *American Foreign Policy in the Making* (1946) and *President Roosevelt and the Coming of the War* (1948).

Beardsley, Aubrey Vincent (1872–1898)   English artist. Beardsley is known for his black and white drawings on fantastic and erotic subjects, representative of an English aesthetic movement in the 1890s. He died of tuberculosis at the age of twenty-six. In a working life of only eight years, he became one of the most important illustrators of his day, with editions of such works as Oscar Wilde's *Salomé* (1894), Pope's *Rape of the Lock* (1896), and Ben Jonson's *Volpone* (1898). He also wrote fiction, which was collected and published as *Under the Hill* in 1904. See ART NOUVEAU; YELLOW BOOK, THE.

beast epic (or beast fable)   A tale or collection of tales written in MOCK EPIC, allegorical style, in which the central characters are animals and the tone is often satirical. Phaedrus's Latin fable collection inspired many medieval versions, such as Pierre de Saint-Cloud's *Roman de Renart* (1173) and Chaucer's treatment of the Chanticleer story in the NUN'S PRIEST'S TALE. See BESTIARIES.

Beatitudes   The sayings of Jesus in the opening verses of the SERMON ON THE MOUNT (Matt. 5:3–12), beginning "Blessed are the poor in spirit" and naming the virtues that make their possessor blessed.

beat movement   A group of American writers and artists who found a voice during the 1950s and proved to be culturally influential during the turbulent 1960s. Although they never had a stated manifesto or program, the beats' creative efforts and lifestyles bespoke a vehement rejection of middle-class life and values. With a few exceptions, they were not considered respectable by the literary or social establishment until the 1970s. Then the ideas they championed—pacifism; reverence for nature at the expense of sophisticated technological pursuits; and stress on enhancing one's consciousness, whatever the methods employed—became ideas much of the nation championed as well. They came to be venerably regarded as descendants of American TRANSCENDENTALISM, Thoreauvian in their distrust of the machine and Whitmanesque in their faith in America and the individual.

Geographically, the main figures were located on the east and west coasts: Jack KEROUAC, Allen GINSBERG, Gregory CORSO, and William BURROUGHS in New York; Gary

SNYDER, Lawrence FERLINGHETTI, Kenneth REXROTH, and Michael McCLURE in San Francisco. The nomenclature *beat* was coined by Kerouac from *beatific*. City Lights Books, established by Ferlinghetti, became their official publishing organ. The three most sensational volumes to appear were Ginsberg's HOWL, a long incantatory poem, which depicts America as a horrifying wasteland; Kerouac's ON THE ROAD, a novel about a rootless individual who wanders around America in search of an unshaped life; and Burroughs's *Naked Lunch* (1957), a hallucinatory novel about a faceless addict living in a sick, institutional society. At the time of publication, these books were surrounded by such publicity that it took a decade before their literary features and merits were objectively evaluated. Of the group, Ginsberg emerged as the most distinctive writer. His poetry, modeled after the free rhythms of Walt WHITMAN, William Carlos WILLIAMS, and jazz, has been praised as visionary and compelling.

Beatrice (1) The beloved of DANTE. He records the history of his love for her in LA VITA NUOVA, increasingly idealizing her until she becomes his spiritual inspiration. Thus, in the DIVINE COMEDY, she is the symbol of divine revelation through faith and guides him through Paradise. The original Beatrice was probably Beatrice Portinari (1266–90), who married Simone de' Bardi.

(2) The high-spirited niece of Leonato in Shakespeare's MUCH ADO ABOUT NOTHING. Although she has sworn to have no man, she is attracted to Benedick, with whom she engages in a constant battle of wits. She is one of Shakespeare's most famous heroines.

Beau Geste (1924) A best-selling novel by P. C. WREN about life in the French Foreign Legion. Beau Geste is the name the hero assumes.

Beauharnais, Joséphine de (born Marie Joséphine Rose Tascher de la Pagerie, 1763–1814) French empress. Born in Martinique, Joséphine was first married to the vicomte Alexandre Beauharnais, who was executed as a counterrevolutionist in 1794. She had two children by this marriage, Eugène and Hortense, who became queen of Holland and mother of Napoleon III.

Joséphine was a prominent figure in Parisian society when she met NAPOLEON BONAPARTE, then a comparatively obscure army officer whose reputation was on the rise. He fell passionately in love with her, as his letters testify, and they were married on March 9, 1796. At Napoleon's coronation, she was crowned empress of France (December 2, 1804). In 1809 Napoleon divorced her, as she had not provided him with an heir. She spent her last years in retirement at her lovely home in La Malmaison, occasionally receiving a visit from Napoleon.

Beaumarchais (assumed name of Pierre Augustin Caron, 1732–1799) French dramatist, courtier, and watchmaker to Louis XV. Beaumarchais is best known for his two comic masterpieces THE BARBER OF SEVILLE and *The Marriage of Figaro* (1784), both of which deal with the exploits of one of the world's cleverest servants, FIGARO. In addition to his *Mémoires* (1774), he wrote three minor plays: *Eugénie* (1767), *Les Deux Amis* (1770), and *La Mère coupable* (1792). He was also librettist of the opera *Tarare* (1787).

Beaumont and Fletcher Francis Beaumont (c1584–1616) and John Fletcher (1579–1625), English dramatists. Their names are always linked because of the plays on which they collaborated; these include such tragicomedies as PHILASTER, *A King and No King* (1611), and THE MAID'S TRAGEDY. In these and other plays, Beaumont and Fletcher foreshadowed and influenced Restoration drama. Other fruits of the collaboration include *The Nice Valour* (1606?), *Wit at Several Weapons* (1606), *The Captain* (c1611), *Love's Pilgrimage* (1615?), and *The Scornful Lady* (c1614).

In addition, Fletcher wrote a number of plays both alone and in collaboration with other dramatists. He was at his best when he could bring his lyric talents and sophistication to bear on such comedies of manners as THE WILD GOOSE CHASE, *The Scornful Lady* (c1614), *Wit without Money* (1614), and *Rule a Wife and Have a Wife* (1624). He also excelled at tragicomedy, a form he and Beaumont had made their own. His unaided plays in this genre include *A Wife for a Month* (1624) and *The Humorous Lieutenant* (1619). Fletcher is the author of the famous pastoral play THE FAITHFUL SHEPHERDESS. In collaboration with Philip Massinger, he wrote *The Bloody Brother* (1615?), *The Tragedy of Sir John Van Olden Barnavelt* (1619), *The False One* (1620), and *The Double Marriage* (1620). He is said to have collaborated with Shakespeare on HENRY VIII and THE TWO NOBLE KINSMEN.

Beaumont also wrote several plays alone, two of which are noteworthy: THE KNIGHT OF THE BURNING PESTLE and *The Woman Hater* (c1606), a comedy of humors.

Beauty and the Beast A well-known fairy tale first recorded in STRAPAROLA's *Le piacevoli notti* (1550) and popularized by PERRAULT's French version in 1697. Beauty saves the life of her father by consenting to live with the Beast. The Beast, being freed from a spell by Beauty's love, becomes a handsome prince and marries her. The tale was the subject of the opera *Zémire and Azore* (1771) by André Gretry (1741–1813) and a film by Jean COCTEAU, *La Belle et la bête* (1946).

Beauvoir, Simone de (1908–1986) French novelist and essayist. Beauvoir met Jean-Paul SARTRE in 1929, beginning a personal and professional companionship that lasted until Sartre's death in 1980. With Sartre and his circle of leftist intellectuals, Beauvoir became profoundly involved in defining the philosophy of EXISTENTIALISM and thereafter served as one of its most articulate exponents. After the publication of her first novel, *L'Invitée* (1943; tr *She Came to Stay*, 1949), she abandoned the teaching of philosophy and devoted herself to writing. Like her subsequent novels, *Le Sang des autres* (1945; tr *The Blood of Others*, 1948) and *Tous les hommes sont mortels* (1946; tr *All Men Are Mortal*, 1955), it dealt with the existentialist dilemma of human freedom in a world in which God does not exist. Her best-known novel, LES MANDARINS, is a ROMAN À CLEF with perceptive portraits of Sartre, CAMUS, and Nelson ALGREN, among others.

She was also a distinguished writer of essays and nonfiction prose. Her long essay, *Le Deuxième Sexe* (1949; tr *The Second Sex*, 1953), a thorough analysis of women's secondary status in society, became a classic of feminist literature. Equally effective was her book on the social and psychological dynamics of aging, *La Vieillesse* (1970; tr *The Coming of Age*, 1972). Her penetrating intelligence is perhaps most evident in her autobiographical volumes: *Mémoires d'une jeune fille rangée* (1958; tr *Memoirs of a Dutiful Daughter*, 1959); *La Force de l'âge* (1960; tr *The Prime of Life*, 1962); *La Force des choses* (1963; tr *The Force of Circumstance*, 1965); *Une Mort très douce* (1964; tr *A Very Easy Death*, 1966), about the death of her mother; and *Tout compte fait* (1972; tr *All Said and Done*, 1974). Beauvoir's many other works include the essays *Pyrrhus et Cinéas* (1944) and *Pour une morale de l'ambiguité* (1947; tr *The Ethics of Ambiguity*, 1949); *Les Bouches inutiles* (1945), a play; the travel diary *L'Amérique au jour le jour* (1948; tr *America Day by Day*, 1953); *La Longue Marche* (1957; tr *The Long March*, 1958), a sympathetic description of Communist China; and the satirical novel *Les Belles Images* (1966, tr 1968). *When Things of the Spirit Come First*, a collection of five early stories, was published in 1982. She wrote about her fifty-year relationship with Sartre in *Adieux: A Farewell to Sartre* (1984). See TEMPS MODERNES, LES.

Beaux' Stratagem, The (1707)   A comedy by George FARQUHAR. Thomas Aimwell and his friend Archer, the two beaux, having run through all their money, set out fortune-hunting and come to Lichfield as "master and man." Aimwell pretends to be very unwell, and, as Lady Bountiful's hobby is tending the sick, she orders him to be removed to her mansion. Here he and Dorinda, daughter of Lady Bountiful, fall in love and finally marry. Archer falls in love with Mrs. Sullen, wife of Lady Bountiful's son Squire Sullen.

Beckett, Samuel (1906–   )   Irish-born French novelist, dramatist, and poet. A close friend of James JOYCE, Beckett settled in Paris in 1937. The title figure in Beckett's first novel, *Murphy* (1938), in his agonized attempts to escape his body to find the life of the mind, is in many ways a prototype for Beckett's later creations. With the notable exceptions of the novel *Watt* (1944; pub 1953) and the plays KRAPP'S LAST TAPE and *Happy Days* (1961), Beckett wrote most of his works after 1939 in French, then translated them into English. Between 1947 and 1957, he

wrote the works on which his reputation most securely rests: the novel trilogy MOLLOY, MALONE DIES, and THE UNNAMABLE and the plays WAITING FOR GODOT and END-GAME. Considered major works in the literature of the ABSURD, all of these pieces present a comically pessimistic allegory of man's condition. In some, the traditionally farcical gestures of the circus clown and the vaudeville actor are used to portray human weakness, frustration, and helplessness. His characters typically advance through worsening stages of decrepitude and paralysis; such human bonds as they form are the coupling of tyrant and victim or, at best, of two pathetically groping dependencies. In a world where life is both chaotic and meaningless, except in its inevitable degeneration toward death, the only freedom that exists is in the mind. Because they live only in their minds, Beckett's characters are free to invent other characters, whose existence becomes the proof of their own. The freedom to invent is linked to the compulsive need to express; throughout Beckett's work, language is used as the only weapon against chaos, at the same time that he reveals the incapacity of language for any meaningful expression. In much of his later work, Beckett experimented with eliminating the physical world altogether, using disembodied voices or even no voice at all, as in *Breath* (1971), a thirty-second piece in which the only sound is a faint cry. Similarly, in *Company* (1980), in pared-down prose, a man incapable of speech hears a voice reminiscing about the events in his past.

Beckett was awarded the NOBEL PRIZE in Literature in 1969. The following year, his *Collected Works* were published in sixteen volumes. Subsequent selections and collections include *Collected Poems in English and French* (1977; rev 1984), *I Can't Go On, I'll Go On* (1976), and *Ends and Odds* (1976), which contains eight new dramatic pieces: ("Ends") *Not I, That Time, Footfalls,* and *Ghost Trio;* and ("Odds") *Theatre I, Theatre II, Radio I,* and *Radio II.*

Recent works include a collection of five plays, *Catastrophes et autres dramaticulus* (1982). The title play appeared in *The New Yorker* and was originally written for the then imprisoned Czech playwright Vaclav Havel. *Disjecta: Miscellaneous Writings and a Dramatic Fragment* appeared in 1983 and *Worstward Ho* in 1984.

Bede (called the Venerable Bede, c673–735)   English historian and scholar. A monk at the Northumbrian monastery at Jarrow, Bede wrote over thirty works of history, grammar, science, theological commentary, etc. His best-known work is *Historia ecclesiastica gentis Anglorum* (*Ecclesiastical History of the English People*, 731), from the Roman invasion of England to 731, now a major source of historical and legendary information. It was translated into Old English under King ALFRED and also provided the material for the early part of THE ANGLO-SAXON CHRONICLE.

Bedivere, Sir   In Arthurian legend, a dignitary of King Arthur's court. In Malory's *Morte d'Arthur* (c1469), it is Sir Bedivere who, at the request of the dying Arthur, throws the sword Excalibur into the lake, and then bears the king to the barge that waits to carry him to AVALON.

bedlam   A lunatic asylum or madhouse. The word is a contraction of *Bethlehem*, St. Mary of Bethlehem being the name of a religious house in London that was converted into a hospital for lunatics in 1402. See TOM O' BEDLAM.

Bednyi, Demyan (pen name of Efim Alekseyevich Pridvorov, 1883–1945)   Soviet poet. A peasant by origin, Bednyi became the most popular Soviet poet in the early years of the regime, churning out topical verse in profusion. His pen name, Bednyi, means "poor" in Russian. His crude propaganda poetry earned him a prominent place in Soviet letters until 1936, when his opera libretto, *Bogatyri* (*Epic Heroes*), displeased the authorities because it spoofed the Russian epic tradition of folk poetry and the introduction of Christianity to Russia. The old Bolshevik had failed to realize that, at that point in history, the party viewed the epic tradition as a national treasure and the spread of Christianity as a progressive occurrence. Bednyi was reprimanded and never regained his popularity.

Beecher, Henry Ward (1813–1887)   American clergyman, editor, and writer. The son of Lyman Beecher and brother of Harriet Beecher Stowe, he attended a school conducted by his sister Catherine, in which he was the only boy among some forty girls. He was graduated from Amherst College in 1834 and from Lane Theological Seminary in Cincinnati in 1837. An intensely emotional man, Beecher won a huge following with his sermons, in which he extolled the love of God and man; he also attacked slavery and advocated woman's suffrage and free trade. From 1861 to 1864, he was editor of *The Independent* and, from 1870 to 1881, of *The Christian Union*. In 1874 he was sued for damages by Theodore Tilton, who accused him of adultery with Mrs. Tilton. Although the jury could not reach a verdict and a council of Congregational churches found him innocent, Beecher's reputation was permanently damaged.

His *Seven Lectures to Young Men* (1844), a series of addresses on such topics as "Industry and Idleness" and "Gamblers and Gambling," was widely read. He also wrote a book of essays, *Plain and Pleasant Talk about Fruits, Flowers, and Farming* (1859), and *Norwood* (1867), a novel.

Beecher, Lyman (1775–1863)   American preacher and author. Beecher became one of the outstanding preachers of his day; he was the father of a large family, of which four children became famous: Catherine, Edward, Henry Ward, and Harriet Beecher Stowe. Opposed to Catholicism and the use of liquor, Beecher supported traditional Calvinism and instituted drastic domestic discipline

in his home. Even he, however, was accused of heresy, although he was finally acquitted by the synod. In addition to several pastorates in New England and New York, Beecher was president of the Lane Theological Seminary in Cincinnati (1832–52). His sermons and articles were collected in *Works* (1852), and his *Autobiography* appeared in 1864. The Beecher household probably provided the details for Harriet Beecher Stowe's *Oldtown Folks* (1869).

Beelzebub (fr Heb, *Baalzebub*, "lord of flies") Originally a local Philistine god (or BAAL) of Ekron. Beelzebub was thought to have oracular powers and the power to afflict or protect his people from the sickness carried by flies. In the NEW TESTAMENT (Matt. 12:24), the Jews accuse Jesus of driving out devils by the power of Beelzebub, called the Prince of Devils. In PARADISE LOST, Milton makes him one of the chief lords of hell, next to SATAN in power and rank.

Beerbohm, Sir Max (1872–1956)   English essayist and caricaturist. Beerbohm was a brilliant figure among the so-called decadents of turn-of-the-century London. He contributed to THE YELLOW BOOK, an influential literary journal, while he was still at Oxford, writing irreverent parodies (as in *A Christmas Garland*, 1896) and drawing brilliant caricatures under the signature "Max." Some of his caricatures were published in *The Poet's Corner* (1904) and *Rossetti and His Circle* (1922). His later works include a satire of Oxford in the novel ZULEIKA DOBSON and essays, such as those collected in *A Defense of Cosmetics* (1922) and *Around Theatres* (1930). He remained legendary for his wit, brilliance, and powers of satire even after he went to Italy to live out his middle and old age in quiet retirement.

Beer-Hall Putsch   See HITLER, ADOLF.

Beethoven, Ludwig van (1770–1827)   German composer. As a child in Bonn, Beethoven displayed unmistakable musical talent, which his father tried to exploit commercially, but he was never a prodigy on the order of MOZART, whom he met in 1787 when he visited Vienna. Forced to return home by his mother's illness and death, he was unable to move to Vienna until 1792, by which time Mozart, with whom Beethoven had hoped to study, had died, so he worked with HAYDN and J. G. Albrechtsberger (1736–1809). Before long he began to make a mark, first as a pianist, then as a daring and unorthodox composer.

His works achieved great success, though not always at first hearing. Through much of his lifetime, he was universally regarded as the greatest living composer, though one whose works made great demands on listener and performer alike. Even among the more prolific composers, Beethoven's repertory is vast. His own instrument was the piano: for it, he composed thirty-two sonatas and five concertos, as well as many chamber works—trios, violin sonatas, cello sonatas—in which it is employed. In addition, there are sixteen string quartets, acknowledged to be the greatest body of work ever written in that medium, nine symphonies, which continue to be central to the orchestral repertory, and *Fidelio* (1805), an opera, one of Beethoven's own favorite works. His other vocal music includes a *Mass in C, Op. 86,* and the great *Missa Solemnis in D, Op. 123.* These, together with the *Ninth Symphony* and the last string quartets and piano sonatas, are the major compositions of his "last period," after he had become totally deaf. Many of these latter works were widely regarded as incomprehensible until the 20th century.

As a composer, he brought the classical forms (sonata, variation) to the highest degree of coherent and logical organization ever achieved. Yet the underlying emotional content, which later composers were quick to recognize, is purely romantic in its expressiveness. Beethoven was the first composer to live fairly well independently of the traditional patronage of the church or the nobility.

Beggar's Opera, The (1728)   A ballad opera by John GAY, first produced at Lincoln's Inn Fields in London, a theatre managed by John RICH. Very little escapes satiric treatment in this work; barbs are aimed at the elaborate, current Italian operatic style, at the prime minister Walpole, at marriage, at ladies and gentlemen, at lawyers, and at trade. The songs, many of them set to popular English and Scottish tunes, were arranged and scored by John Christopher Pepusch, who composed the overture.

The story concerns Peachum, a receiver of stolen goods. His biggest business is done with Captain Macheath, a highwayman with whom Peachum's daughter Polly has fallen in love. They marry secretly, and Peachum, now unable to use Polly in his business, gets his revenge by informing on Macheath and collecting the reward money. Macheath is taken off to Newgate prison, which is run by the corrupt Lockit, who is in league with Peachum. Lockit's daughter Lucy falls in love with Macheath and helps him to escape. He is captured but saved from hanging by the mock intervention of a beggar and a player, since it would never do to let the fine hero die. This happy ending satirizes the sentimental tragedy of the day. Bertolt Brecht and Kurt Weill used *The Beggar's Opera* as the basis for their THREEPENNY OPERA.

Behan, Brendan (1923–1964)   Irish playwright and wit. Born in Dublin at the time of civil strife in Ireland, Behan reflected in his life and works the zest, vitality, and macabre sense of humor of that tempestuous era. His early life was strongly influenced by the close association of his family with the Irish Republican Army, an association continued by Brendan, who, at the age of sixteen, was arrested by English authorities for the possession of explosives with the intent of blowing up a battleship. He was found guilty and sentenced to three years in an English reform school, an experience he recounts with uninhibited gusto in the autobiographical *Borstal Boy* (1958). Behan subsequently

served two more prison terms, the second of which resulted in his being deported to France. Having spent a good portion of his youth in jail, he utilized this experience as the basis of his two plays, *The Quare Fellow* (1956), a memorable exercise of gallows humor, and *The Hostage* (1958). Despite his considerable reputation as a playwright, he was perhaps better known for his alcoholic exploits, accounts of which were featured prominently in the English and American press. For this reason, he was dismissed by some critics as a buffoon, more interested in publicity than in playwrighting, trading on a stereotyped conception of the wild young Irishman. For Behan, however, drinking was an essential expression of his approach to (and quarrel with) social reality. *Hold Your Hour and Have Another* (1964) is a collection of Behan's humorous pieces. A novel, *The Scarperer* (1964), was published posthumously.

Behn, Mrs. Aphra (1640–1689)   English novelist and dramatist. The first English female professional writer, Behn wrote a number of complicated comedies of intrigue, such as *The Rover, or The Banished Cavaliers: Parts I and II* (1677, 1680), *Sir Patient Fancy* (1678), and *The City Heiress, or Sir Timothy Treat-All* (1682). Her best-known novel is *Oroonoko, or the History of the Royal Slave* (c1678). She served Charles II as a spy in Antwerp.

Behrman, S[amuel] N[athaniel] (1893–1973)   American dramatist and biographer. The first of Behrman's highly civilized comedies of manners to appear in New York was *The Second Man* (1927), in a production by the Theatre Guild. From then until his last play, *But for Whom Charlie* (1964), he turned out a succession of witty dramatic commentaries on life in turbulent times, the success of which was measured both by the box office and by the caliber of the actors who were eager to work in his plays. Among these pieces were *Biography* (1932), about a woman painter and a journalist; *Rain from Heaven* (1934), one of the first plays to recognize the Nazi menace; *End of Summer* (1936); *Wine of Choice* (1938), about the difficulties of liberalism; NO TIME FOR COMEDY; *Fanny* (1954), a musical with Joshua Logan; and *Lord Pengo* (1962), a comedy based on Behrman's own biography of the art dealer Duveen (1952). He was also known for his fine adaptations, particularly *Serena Blandish* (1928) from the novel by Enid BAGNOLD, and *Amphitryon 38* (1937), from the play by the French dramatist Jean GIRAUDOUX. He also wrote numerous screenplays; an autobiography, *The Worcester Account* (1954), dramatized as *The Cold Wind and the Warm* (1958); and a memoir of Max BEERBOHM, *Portrait of Max* (1960). Behrman's memoirs, *People in a Diary,* were published in 1972.

Being and Nothingness (L'Être et le néant, 1943)   A long philosophical treatise by Jean-Paul SARTRE. Subtitled "an essay on phenomenological ontology," it is Sartre's major attempt to systematize his theoretical analysis of the human condition and human consciousness which underlies EXISTENTIALISM. Postulating that for humanity existence precedes essence, he concludes that the very "nothingness" of human essence in a world without God or meaning allows each person infinite potentialities in the shaping of his or her life, limited by the facts of the external world, but not by any *a priori* conditions of so-called human nature.

Bel The supreme Babylonian god of the earth and atmosphere, called the god of lords. Said to have created man and the universe, Bel symbolizes male generative power. *Bel* is the same word as BAAL in Phoenician and Hebrew.

In *Bel and the Dragon*, an Old Testament Apocryphal book appended to the book of Daniel, Daniel exposes the trickery of the priest of Bel in Babylon and convinces the king that Bel is only an image and not an actual living deity.

Belasco, David (1859–1931) American theatrical producer and dramatist. Belasco produced nearly four hundred plays, many of them by American playwrights, and greatly influenced the American theatre by promoting emotional performances and realistic stage properties. He began his own career as a playwright by collaborating with James A. Hearne on *Hearts of Oak* (1879), in which he toured the country as an actor. His best-known plays include *The Heart of Maryland* (1895), a Civil War story inspired by Rose Hartwick Thorpe's poem "Curfew Must Not Ring Tonight" (1867); THE GIRL OF THE GOLDEN WEST; and *The Return of Peter Grimm* (1911).

Belch, Sir Toby In Shakespeare's TWELFTH NIGHT, Olivia's riotous, bibulous uncle. Sir Toby extracts drinking money from the foolish Sir Andrew Aguecheek by pretending to advance the latter's suit for Olivia.

Belial See SATAN.

Belinda The heroine of Alexander Pope's mock-heroic poem THE RAPE OF THE LOCK, who is described as the fairest of mortals:

> If to her share some Female Errors fall,
> Look on her Face and you'll forget 'em all.

Belinda is also the title of a play (1918) by A. A. Milne and a novel (1928) by Hilaire Belloc.

Belinsky, Vissarion Grigoryevich (1811–1848) Russian literary critic and journalist. Belinsky gained prominence in literary circles for his *Literaturnye mechtaniya* (*Literary Reveries*, 1834), dealing with the development of Russian literature since the 17th century. He became the literary critic on the influential journal *Otechestvennye zapiski* (*Fatherland Notes*) and, from 1846 to his death, on the *Sovremennik* (*The Contemporary*). The critical articles he wrote during these years, such as his annual surveys of Russian literature, were to have an overwhelming influence on the future course of Russian literary criticism. Belinsky's ideas formed the theoretical basis for the NATURAL SCHOOL in Russian literature, which

insisted that literature treat its subjects—especially poverty and exploitation of the people—realistically, with the aim of social reform. Although later critics exaggerated the social aspect of Belinsky's literary doctrine, he was not entirely unaware of artistic quality. This fact is particularly evident in parts of the series of articles that he wrote from 1843 to 1846 on the work of Pushkin. But Belinsky's fervent interest in social issues did occasionally blind him in regard to literary facts; he hailed Gogol as a great realist, and this erroneous label stuck to Gogol until the 20th century. Whatever confusion he introduced into Russian critical theory and practice, Belinsky did at least serve Russian literature by insisting on its importance. He also encouraged the early efforts of some of Russia's finest writers, such as Lermontov, Gogol, Turgenev, and Dostoyevsky. Belinsky's social bias has made him one of the ever-quoted oracles of Soviet literary criticism.

Belkin, Tales of (Povesti Belkina, 1830) A cycle of five short stories by Aleksandr PUSHKIN, with an introduction dealing with the life of the fictitious compiler of the tales, Ivan Petrovich Belkin. The tales are "Vystrel" ("The Shot"), "Metel" ("The Snowstorm"), "Grobovshchik" ("The Undertaker"), "Stantzionnyi smotritel" ("The Stationmaster"), and "Baryshnya-Krest'yanka" ("The Lady-Rustic"). The best known of the tales is probably "The Stationmaster," which contains one of the first carefully drawn portraits in Russian literature of a character who is not a member of the nobility. Belkin, whose rather commonplace life is recounted in the introduction, became famous as a literary character in his own right. Pushkin later wrote a prose fragment, *Istoriya sela Goryukhina* (*History of the Village of Goryukhin*, 1830), which purports to be an autobiography of Belkin. The extraordinary description of such an ordinary figure as Belkin is credited with being one of the first steps toward the realism which predominated in later 19th-century Russian literature.

Bell, Acton, Ellis, and **Currer** The pseudonyms adopted by Anne, Emily, and Charlotte BRONTË, respectively. In 1846 the Brontës published a volume entitled *Poems by Currer, Ellis, and Acton Bell*.

Bell, [Arthur] Clive [Howard] (1881–1964) English critic of art and literature. A member of the BLOOMSBURY GROUP, he married Vanessa Stephen, the sister of Virginia WOOLF. His modernist aesthetic, centered on the theory of "significant form," is expressed in *Art* (1914), *Since Cézanne* (1922), *Proust* (1929), and *An Account of French Painting* (1932). His son Julian (1908–37), author of *Work for the Winter* (1936), a collection of poems, was killed while driving an ambulance for the Loyalists during the Spanish Civil War. His grandson Quentin Bell (1910–) became Virginia Woolf's biographer and literary executor.

Bell, Gertrude [Margaret Lowthian] (1868–1926) English writer, archaeologist, and explorer.

Through extensive travels in the Middle East, which she described vividly in such books as *The Desert and the Sown* (1907) and *The Thousand and One Churches* (1909), Bell became one of the foremost authorities on Arabia and its surrounding territories. Along with T. E. LAWRENCE, she was an articulate advocate for Arab independence and was instrumental in helping to establish the Arab kingdom of Iraq. Her *Letters* (1927) offer a fascinating chronicle of her explorations and discoveries.

Bell, The (1958)   A comic, philosophic novel by Iris MURDOCH. Set in a lay religious community attached to a convent, the story is concerned with the complex needs and self-deceptions that bind each member to the group. The bell, which represents the ideals of the community, precipitates the final scandal that forces the group to disband. The members regain their freedom, but not all are able to deal with it.

Bella, Giacomo   See FUTURISM.

bell, book, and candle   A reference to features of the solemn ritual of major excommunication, as performed in the medieval Church of Rome. The decree of anathema, the official curse of excommunication, was read from the book of church ritual; the attendant priests held candles, which were dashed to the ground, symbolizing the extinction of grace and joy in the soul of the accused; and a bell was tolled, perhaps to simulate the tolling for the dead.

The phrase *bell, book, and candle* appears in Shakespeare's KING JOHN (III, 3): "Bell, book, and candle shall not drive me back,/ When gold and silver becks me to come on." Here, as in general usage, it represents the power and authority of Christianity.

Bell, Book, and Candle (1950) is also the title of a play by John Van Druten (1901–57), about a beautiful present-day witch who falls in love with a man and loses her powers as a sorceress.

Belle Dame sans merci, La (1819)   A ballad by John KEATS. Its title and general theme are taken from an early French poem by Alain Chartier that was translated into English by Sir Richard Ros (not by Geoffrey Chaucer, to whom it is often mistakenly attributed). Keats retains much of the medieval imagery of the French original.

Bellerophon   A grandson of Sisyphus. While living at the Argive court of King Proetus, Bellerophon incurred the enmity of the queen, Antaea, by rejecting her advances. She falsely accused him to her husband, who sent him with a letter to Iobates, the king of Lycia, his wife's father, recounting the charge and praying that the bearer might be put to death. Iobates, unwilling to slay Bellerophon himself, gave him many hazardous tasks (including the killing of the CHIMAERA), but as he was successful in all of them, Iobates made him his heir and gave him his daughter for a wife. Later Bellerophon is fabled to have attempted to fly to heaven on the winged horse Pegasus, but Zeus sent a gadfly to sting the horse, and the rider was

overthrown. The revenge of Antaea is a familiar theme in folktale, found also in the stories of PHAEDRA and of Joseph and Potiphar's wife.

Belli, Carlos Germán (1927–   )   Peruvian poet. Belli writes ironically about modern man's sense of himself as a miscast figure in nature. In Belli's verse, peculiar combinations of archaic conceits, hyperbole, and everyday language make man appear as a sad, unintended error, ambulating in the midst of nebulous technology, language, and desire. His sense of this imperfect and nostalgic beast is recorded in ¡O *hada cibernetica!* (1961), the work that established Belli as one of the most significant contemporary Spanish American poets. He also published *El pie sobre el cuelo* (1967) and *Sextinas y otros poemas* (1970).

Belli, Giuseppe Bioacchino (1791–1863)   Italian poet. Belli grew up during the turbulent years of Napoleon's occupation of Rome. Although much of his early work was conventional in form and diction, by 1816 he began a series of over two thousand sonnets, using the free language of the Roman dialect. His vivid, often ribald verse provides a rich picture of the Rome of his day, from compassionate portraits of lower-class figures to unbridled lampoons of corrupt church officials. Because of his outraged reaction to the revolutionary violence of 1848, he asked on his deathbed that his anticlerical poems be destroyed. His confessor saved them, however, and saw that they were published. The first major English translation of his works, *The Sonnets of Giuseppe Belli*, was published in 1981.

Bellini, Giovanni (c1430–1516)   Venetian painter. The son of the artist Iacopo Bellini (c1400–c1470), both he and his brother Gentile Bellini (c1427–1507) were strongly influenced by their father's work and also by their brother-in-law, the painter Andrea MANTEGNA, during their early years at Padua. Within the context of the new medium of oil painting, however, Giovanni moved away from Mantegna's severity, toward a great richness and mellowness of color. His devoutly religious Madonnas and serene altarpieces also reveal a deep appreciation of landscape and of the effect of light and color on atmosphere. His interest in light and color, contrasted with the Florentine emphasis on line and modeling, was to become, in the hands of Giorgione and Titian, his two greatest pupils, the glory of the Venetian school of painting. Among his masterpieces are *Christ Blessing*, the *Pietà*, and the *Agony in the Garden*.

Bello, Andrés (1781–1865)   Venezuelan scholar and poet. As one of the most promising young men in Caracas, Bello studied classical literature, law, and philosophy; his interest in the natural sciences was stimulated by his meeting with Alexander von Humboldt, who greatly influenced him. In 1810 Bello was sent to England to seek support for the revolutionary junta of Caracas, as part of a three-man delegation that also included Simón Bolívar. In

England, where he remained for nearly twenty years, he began his famous edition of the *Poema del Cid*, based on the 12th-century text, and wrote his best-known poems: *Alocución a la poesía* (1823), a declaration of literary independence, in which he exhorts the Muse to abandon Europe for America, and *La agricultura de la zona tórrida* (1826), notable for its description of the plants of America, in which realistic detail is combined with classical allusions. From 1829 until his death, Bello resided in Chile, where he held important government posts, was a founder and first president of the University of Chile, and was the chief architect of the Chilean civil code. During this period, he published *La oración por todos* (1843), an adaptation of Hugo's *La Prière pour tous* (1830) that is sometimes considered better than the original. His most enduring achievement, however, is probably his *Gramática de la lengua castellana* (1847), still the outstanding authority on Spanish grammar. See SARMIENTO, DOMINGO FAUSTINO.

Belloc, Hilaire (pen name of Joseph Hilaire Pierre Belloc, 1870–1953) English writer. Born in France, Belloc was a prolific author of light verse, essays, travel books, history, biography, works of Roman Catholic and conservative polemic, and fiction. Like G. K. Chesterton, with whom he had many attitudes in common, he engaged in a great deal of influential controversy, attacking the ideas of H. G. Wells and Bernard Shaw; Shaw called the pair the Chesterbelloc. He is now best remembered for his light, witty writing and for his verse for children. His humorous, mock-moral books for children include *The Bad Child's Book of Beasts* (1896), CAUTIONARY TALES, and *Cautionary Verses* (1941). His elegant, witty essays appeared in such volumes as *On Nothing* (1908) and *On Everything* (1909). *The Path to Rome* (1902) is a travel book strongly flavored with humor and Catholic feeling; *Places* (1942) is a collection of short travel essays. He also wrote *History of England* (1925–27) and biographies of Robespierre (1901), Wolsey (1930), and others. A collection of his letters was published in 1959.

Bellona In Roman mythology, the goddess of war and either wife or sister of MARS.

Bellow, Saul (1915–) Canadian-born American novelist. Born of Russian-Jewish parents, Bellow was brought up in Montreal and Chicago. His first two novels were *Dangling Man* (1944), a story of a man waiting to go into the army, who is both repelled by the thought and drawn by the idea of escaping into its anonymity, and *The Victim* (1947), a powerful and compassionate portrait of urban alienation. Together, they effectively introduced a new style to American fiction. The "Gentile" era of FITZGERALD, HEMINGWAY, and FAULKNER began, with Bellow, to give way to a new Jewish tradition and a sense of moral and social alarm. Bellow's characters are generally antiheroes caught up in the existential dilemma of trying to define themselves with some measure of dignity despite the constant impediments of objective and subjective circumstances. As in the picaresque comedy *The Adventures of* AUGIE MARCH, for which Bellow received the National Book Award, his beleaguered souls attempt to discover what being human is in a world that is "too much of everything." After the brilliant novella *Seize the Day* (1956), in which the central character is tossed between love and hate for his impossible father, Bellow's sense of moral crisis was exercised in *Henderson the Rain King* (1959), *Herzog* (1964), and *Mr. Sammler's Planet* (1970). Bellow is a writer who deals with weighty philosophical concerns with compassion and humor. *Humboldt's Gift* (1975, PULITZER PRIZE), one of his most important works, was partly inspired by the tragic life and death of Bellow's friend, the poet Delmore SCHWARTZ. In *The Dean's December* (1982), he depicts and contrasts corruption in Chicago and repression in Bucharest. *Him with His Foot in His Mouth* (1984), a collection of five stories, was particularly well received throughout the world. His novel *More Die of Heartbreak* was published in 1987. Bellow was awarded the NOBEL PRIZE in Literature in 1976; he was cited by the Swedish Academy for "the human understanding and subtle analysis of contemporary culture that are combined in his work." He has also written the play *The Last Analysis* (1964). *To Jerusalem and Back* (1976) is an account of a trip to Israel.

beloved disciple St. JOHN the evangelist, one of the twelve APOSTLES.

beloved physician St. LUKE the evangelist. The beloved physician mentioned by St. Paul in Colossians (4:14) is presumed to be this Luke.

Beloved Returns, The (Lotte in Weimar, 1939) A novel by Thomas MANN. It is based on an imaginary incident in the life of Goethe: Charlotte ("Lotte") Buff, who was Goethe's sweetheart when he was young and who is thought to have been the model for the character Lotte in Goethe's THE SORROWS OF YOUNG WERTHER, comes to Weimar many years later and reencounters the now old and established Goethe. Although in real life this incident never occurred, Mann has used it to make many intriguing explorations into Goethe's work and personality.

Beltine (or Beltane) May 1, one of the four great feast days of the ancient Celtic year. SAMAIN and Beltine are the feast days that divide the year into two halves, the hot and the cold seasons. See IMBOLC; LUGNASAD.

Bely, Andrei (pen name of Boris Nikolayevich Bugayev, 1880–1934) Russian poet and novelist. One of the SYMBOLISTS, Bely, like BLOK, was early in his career under the influence of the mystical ideas of the philosopher Vladimir SOLOVYOV. A student of philosophy and mathematics at the University of Moscow, Bely published his first poetry in 1901. He greeted the revolution enthusiastically with a long poem, *Khristos voskrese* (*Christ Is Risen*, 1918). Bely's best work is his prose, which includes the novels *Ser-*

ebryanyi golub' (*The Silver Dove*, 1910), *Peterburg* (*Petersburg*, 1913), and *Kotik Letayev* (1918). Bely's prose style is rich, ornamental, and complex, often reminiscent of that of James Joyce in English. His later ideas had their source mainly in the anthroposophy of Rudolf Steiner, of whom Bely became a disciple. Bely left Russia in 1921 but returned in 1923, when he tried unsuccessfully to acclimate himself to the new society. His last years were spent writing his three volumes of memoirs, which were published between 1929 and 1933: *Na rubezhe dvukh stoletii* (*On the Border of Two Centuries*), *Nachalo veka,* (*The Beginning of a Century*), and *Mezhdu dvukh revolyutsii* (*Between Two Revolutions*). He included in his memoirs his reminiscences of Aleksandr Blok, his friend and fellow poet.

Bembo, Pietro Cardinal (1470–1547)   Italian prelate and man of letters. Famed as a reformer and legislator of language and literature, Bembo imposed classicist norms on the Tuscan tongue through his writings and his editions of such writers as Petrarch and Dante. Made a cardinal in 1539, he was a candidate for the papacy at the time of his death. His most famous works are the *Asolani* (1505), a group of dialogues on the nature of love, which take their title from Asolo, the setting of the work, and the *Prose della volgar lingua* (*Essays on the Vernacular Tongue*, 1525).

Bemelmans, Ludwig (1898–1962)   Austrian-born American writer and painter. Bemelmans's experiences in the hotel and restaurant business furnished material for his many entertaining stories and novels; he is also known for the charm of his books for children, especially *Madeleine* (1939). His work, written in a seemingly naïve though highly sophisticated style, was often illustrated by his own watercolors and drawings. Among his many books are *Hansi* (1934), *My War with the United States* (1937), *Hotel Splendide* (1940), *Now I Lay Me Down to Sleep* (1944), *The One I Love Best* (1954), *The World of Bemelmans* (1955), *My Life in Art* (1958), and *Are You Hungry Are You Cold* (1960).

Benares (or Banaras, now Varanasi)   HINDUISM's most holy city, on the GANGES River in east central India. Famous as a place of pilgrimage for the living, it is also considered a most auspicious place in which to die and be cremated, the ashes being dispersed into the sacred waters of the river. It is known to Hindus as *Kasi* or *Kashi*.

Benassis, Dr.   See COUNTRY DOCTOR, THE.

Benavente [y Martínez], Jacinto (1866–1954) Spanish playwright, associated with the GENERACIÓN DEL 98. An aristocrat and a conservative, Benavente broke with the tradition of melodrama prevalent in Spanish theatre during the last decades of the 19th century and created an understated style based on skillful dialogue and subtle satire. He was a prolific dramatist whose works dominated the Spanish stage during the first third of the 20th century. *Los intereses creados* (1907; tr *Bonds of Interest*, 1917), consid-

ered his masterpiece, incorporates techniques of the Italian COMMEDIA DELL'ARTE. Other well-known plays include *La malquerida* (1913; tr *The Passion Flower*, 1920) and *Señora ama* (1908). In 1922, Benavente was awarded the NOBEL PRIZE in Literature.

Benchley, Robert [Charles] (1889–1945) American drama critic, essayist, humorist, actor, and screenwriter. Highly successful in movies and on the radio, Benchley was admired for his short film *How to Sleep* (1935) and his famous sketch *The Treasurer's Report* (1930). In his essays, Benchley portrayed his life as a series of frustrations and humiliations; his humor is based on the situation of the average American man, faced with the complexities of 20th-century life. Among his works are *20,000 Leagues under the Sea, or, David Copperfield* (1928), *From Bed to Worse* (1934), *My Ten Years in a Quandary* (1936), *Benchley Beside Himself* (1943), and the posthumous *Chips Off the Old Benchley* (1949). His son Nathaniel wrote a biography of him in 1955.

Benedick   In Shakespeare's MUCH ADO ABOUT NOTHING, a self-assured, cynical, and witty young nobleman of Padua. Although Benedick has forsworn women, he constantly engages in repartee with the sharp-tongued Beatrice, with whom he is at last united through the conspiracy of their friends. The name has become a byword for a supposedly confirmed bachelor who finally marries.

Benét, Stephen Vincent (1898–1943)   American poet, short-story writer, and novelist. Benét's work was marked by his interest in fantasy and American themes. His early collections of verse include *Five Men and Pompey* (1915), *Young Adventure* (1918), *Heavens and Earth* (1920), *The Ballad of William Sycamore* (1923), and *Tiger Joy* (1925). *King David* (1923) is a narrative poem about the biblical ruler. Benét's most famous poem, the Civil War narrative JOHN BROWN'S BODY, won a PULITZER PRIZE in 1929. *Litany for Dictatorships* (1935) attacks totalitarian states. *Western Star* (1943), the first part of an American epic left unfinished at his death, was awarded a posthumous Pulitzer Prize (1944). He was the brother of William Rose BENÉT.

Benét, William Rose (1886–1950)   American poet, critic, and editor. Benét was the brother of Stephen Vincent BENÉT and was married for a time to the poet Elinor WYLIE. He was an enthusiastic and prolific poet; his collections include *Merchants from Cathay* (1913), *Starry Harness* (1933), *The Stairway of Surprise* (1947), and *The Spirit of the Scene* (1951). He also wrote a novel in verse, *Rip Tide* (1932), and a PULITZER PRIZE-winning verse autobiography, *The Dust Which Is God* (1941). One of the founders of THE SATURDAY REVIEW *of Literature*, he served on its editorial board and conducted the column of literary miscellany "The Phoenix Nest" for many years. He was the original editor of *The Reader's Encyclopedia* (1948).

Ben-Hur: A Tale of the Christ (1880)   A novel by Lew WALLACE. The book grew out of a railroad-car discussion that the author had with Robert Ingersoll, the free thinker. They discussed the divinity of Christ, and Wallace decided to study the life and times of Jesus. The book centers on Judah Ben-Hur, a young aristocratic Jew, who is falsely accused of seeking to murder the Roman governor of Palestine. Sent to the galleys, he escapes, becomes a Roman officer, engages in a climactic chariot race with his betrayer, the false friend Messala, and is finally converted to Christianity. The highly popular book has been staged and twice made into a motion picture.

benizuri-e   See UKIYOE.

Benjamin   In the OLD TESTAMENT, the youngest son of JACOB and RACHEL and, next to Joseph, Jacob's favorite. *Benjamin* means "son of my right hand." When Jacob sent his sons from CANAAN to buy corn from Egypt during the famine, he refused to let Benjamin go, "lest peradventure mischief befall him" (Gen. 42:4). Unknown to Jacob, Joseph was in charge of the granaries in Egypt. When his brothers came to him, Joseph told them, without revealing his identity, that they must bring their youngest brother back to him to prove they were not spies. When they did so, Joseph feasted them and gave them grain but, after they had gone, sent word after them that his silver cup had been stolen. When a search was made, it was found in Benjamin's sack, where it had been placed by Joseph's orders. Joseph then revealed his identity and arranged for his father's migration to Egypt.

Benjamin's descendants formed the tribe of Benjamin; they were stalwart warriors and defenders of freedom. Israel's first king, SAUL, came from this tribe, as did the Apostle PAUL.

Benjamin, Walter (1892–1940)   German essayist. A brilliant and idiosyncratic philosopher-critic, Benjamin died a suicide when fleeing Nazi Europe for the U.S. After his thesis was rejected by the University of Frankfurt, he abandoned academics to write essays and criticism. A revised version of his thesis was published as *Ursprung des deutschen Trauerspiel* (1928; tr *The Origin of German Tragic Drama*, 1977); it is his longest and most ambitious work. Along with his own form of Marxist social criticism, he also wrote on film, art, and European cities and on the work of PROUST and BAUDELAIRE. His essays on art and literature approached a philosophy of language and history. The first of his collected works was reissued in German in 1972. Among the English translations are *Illuminations* (tr 1968; *Illuminationen*, 1961) and *Reflections* (1978), a selection of essays, aphorisms, and autobiographical writings.

Bennet, Elizabeth   See PRIDE AND PREJUDICE.

Bennett, [Enoch] Arnold (1867–1931)   English novelist, playwright, and journalist. Bennett's finest novels are THE OLD WIVES' TALE and CLAYHANGER. Both are set in the industrial district in the English midlands where he was born, known as Five Towns in his novels. A humble clerk with literary ambitions, Bennett went to London at twenty-one. His autobiographical *A Man from the North* (1898) describes this period. He became a successful journalist, editing a woman's magazine, writing "Pocket Philosophies," such as *How to Live on 24 Hours a Day* (1908), and doing influential reviewing. In 1903 he went to live in Paris for some years and married a Frenchwoman. Influenced by the writings of Zola, Bennett wrote naturalistic novels, studies of how his characters are the creatures of their environment. Among these are his two best novels and *Anna of the Five Towns* (1902), *Whom God Hath Joined* (1906), *Hilda Lessways* (1911), *These Twain* (1915), *Riceyman Steps* (1923), *Lord Raingo* (1926), and *Imperial Palace* (1930). Among his collections of short stories are *Tales of the Five Towns* (1905) and *The Matador of the Five Towns* (1912). His successful comic novels are *A Great Man* (1904), *Buried Alive* (1908), *The Card* (1911; U.S. *Denry the Audacious*); and *Mr. Prohack* (1922). With Edward Knoblock, he wrote *Milestones* (1912), a successful drama about the rise of an industrial family. Bennett also wrote deliberate commercial fiction, such as *Sacred and Profane Love* (1905), for he wanted—and achieved—success, a famous-actress mistress, and a yacht.

Like the naturalistic novelists who were his contemporaries, his friend H. G. WELLS and John GALSWORTHY, Bennett was attacked by the modernist Virginia Woolf, and he is now somewhat neglected. His best work is distinguished by his rendering of the passage of time, his accurate descriptions of ordinary, apparently quite dull and unromantic lives, and his sympathetic portrayals of women.

Bennett, James Gordon (1795–1872)   Scottish-born American newspaper editor. Bennett came to America in 1819 and settled finally in New York City, serving on the staff of *The Enquirer* and *The Courier*. On May 6, 1835, he founded the New York *Herald* and remained its editor until his retirement in 1867. It was an aggressive, widely read paper, notable for its extensive news coverage and lively editorials. According to Gerald W. Johnson, Bennett "filled his paper with vulgarity, vituperation, and scandal, but he got the news." His son, James Gordon Bennett (1841–1918), succeeded him as editor in 1867. The younger Bennett sent Stanley to Africa to find Livingstone and supported other expeditions to Africa and the Arctic. He was the founder of the Paris edition of the *Herald* (1887).

Benson, A[rthur] C[hristopher] (1862–1925)   English scholar, best known as the author of volumes of essays, including *From a College Window* (1906). Benson wrote the words of the song "Land of Hope and Glory." His father was archbishop of Canterbury; his brother, E[dward] F[rederic] Benson (1867–1940), wrote light novels, including *Dodo* (1893), which was supposed to be based on the character of the future Lady Oxford and created a sensation; a third brother, R[obert] H[ugh] Benson (1871–1914), became a Roman Catholic and wrote historical and contemporary novels with a strongly religious tone.

Bentham, Jeremy (1748–1832)   English philosopher of the utilitarian school. Bentham's social and philosophical ideas are to be found in his *Fragment on Government* (1776) and *Introduction to Principles of Morals and Legislation* (1789). He held it to be a "sacred truth" that "the greatest happiness of the greatest number is the foundation of morals and legislation," and he tried to work out scientifically, on a quantitative scale, the values of pleasure and pain in moral motivation. See UTILITARIANISM.

Bentley, E[dmund] C[lerihew] (1875–1956) English writer of detective stories and originator of a form of humorous biographical verse called the CLERIHEW. Bentley's novel TRENT'S LAST CASE is a classic of detective fiction.

Beowulf (early 8th century?)   An Old English (Anglo-Saxon) epic of almost thirty-two hundred lines in ALLITERATIVE VERSE. *Beowulf* is the earliest extant written composition of such length in English and indeed in all Teutonic literature. Its content was based on Norse legends, merged with historical events of the early sixth century in Denmark; this oral tradition was carried to England by Danish invaders of the mid-6th century, fused with the Christianity they absorbed there, and finally written down by a single but unknown poet c700.

Hrothgar, king of the Danes on the island of Zealand, has built the mead hall Heorot for feasting his warriors, but they abandon it because of the murderous ravages of the monster GRENDEL. Beowulf, nephew of King Hygelac of the Geats (on the coast of southern Sweden facing the Danes), comes with fourteen warriors to challenge the monster and is received by Hrothgar at a great feast. The Geats spend the night in the mead hall; Grendel comes, and in a mighty fight Beowulf with his bare hands wrenches the monster's arm from his shoulder and mounts it as a trophy. The next day, Hrothgar gives a triumphant feast in Heorot, but, as they sleep that night, Grendel's mother comes to avenge her son, slaying a Dane and stealing the severed arm. Beowulf plunges into the demon-infested pond where the monsters live and wrestles with Grendel's mother. The sword Hrunting, which Unferth lent him, proves of no use, but he finds a sword crafted by the giants and beheads her. Then he severs the head of Grendel, who has died there of his wound, to bring back as a trophy. He and his Geats receive many gifts from Hrothgar when they leave and from Hygelac when they reach home. Hygelac and his son both die in wars with the Swedes, so that Beowulf eventually becomes king of the Geats, ruling well for fifty years. Then a fire-breathing dragon, angered because a man has stolen a goblet from his

hoarded treasure, begins to ravage the land. Beowulf goes out to slay it, but all his warriors fearfully desert him, except young Wiglaf. Although together they kill the dragon, Beowulf receives his own death-wound. Wiglaf berates his companions for cowardice, and Beowulf is given a stately burial.

The story is not told chronologically, however; events are often anticipated in prophecy or interpolated later in retrospect. Long speeches of celebration or lamentation, long descriptions of the feasts, and digressions into genealogy and history all give a colorful picture of life at that time. Memorable episodes not actually a part of the main action include Unferth's insult to Beowulf at the first feast, Beowulf's answering description of his swimming contest with Breca, and the tale of Finn and Hildeburh, sung by a minstrel at the second feast (see FINNSBURG).

Beppo (1818)   A satirical poem by Lord BYRON. Beppo is the husband of Laura, a Venetian lady. He is taken captive at Troy, becomes a Turk, joins a band of pirates, grows rich, and, after several years' absence, returns to his native land, where he discovers his wife at a carnival ball with her *cavaliero servente*. He makes himself known to her, and they live together again as man and wife.

Berceo, Gonzalo de (c1180–c1246)   Earliest Spanish poet known by name. A secular priest at the Benedictine monastery of San Millán de la Cogolla, Berceo was a prolific writer of pious religious verse in the vernacular. His best-known poems are works dedicated to the Virgin, notably *Milagros de Nuestra Señora*, and lives of saints, such as *Vida de Domingo de Silos*.

Berdyayev, Nikolai Aleksandrovich (1874–1948)   Russian religious philosopher. A Marxist in his youth, Berdyayev turned to religious views and played a large part in the renaissance of religious and philosophical thought in Russian intellectual life early in the 20th century. His writings, mainly aphoristic in form, often deal with the problem of freedom and man's relationship to the world in the light of this problem. His works include *Dukhovnyi krisis intelligentziya* (*The Spiritual Crisis of the Intelligentsia*, 1910), *Filosofiya svobody* (*The Philosophy of Freedom*, 1911), *Smysl tvorchestva* (*The Meaning of Creativity*, 1916), and studies of Dostoyevsky and of Russian religious and philosophical thinkers.

In 1922, with a number of other Russian intellectuals, Berdyayev was expelled from the Soviet Union. He went to Berlin and then in 1925 to Paris, where he continued to write, edited a journal (*The Way*; Russian *Put'*), and worked for the Y.M.C.A. Press, a publisher of religious and philosophical works.

Among his works to be posthumously translated into English are *The Beginning and the End* (1952), *Truth and Revelation* (1953), and *The Origin of Russian Communism* (1960).

Bérénice (1670)   A tragedy by Jean RACINE. The emperor Titus, newly acceded to the throne, learns that the Romans object to his marrying the foreigner Bérénice, queen of Palestine. Despite his love for her, he obeys the mandate of his people, and the lovers separate forever. Literary tradition holds that the duchesse d'Orléans arranged for Racine and Corneille to write plays on this subject, each in ignorance that the other was doing the same. In the resulting contest, Racine's play was judged the better. See TITE ET BÉRÉNICE.

Berenice (1835)   A tale by Edgar Allan POE. Egaeus is in love with his epileptic cousin, Berenice. Fascinated by her teeth, he draws them when she is presumed dead, after a fit. Berenice returns to life in a comic-horror climax.

Berenson, Bernard (1865–1959)   American art critic and connoisseur. A long-time resident of Italy, Berenson was the greatest authority of his generation on Italian art from the 13th to the 17th century. He was responsible for selecting numerous private and museum collections and, through his writings, became one of the most important arbiters of artistic taste. His series of books on Italian Renaissance painters, beginning with *Venetian Painters of the Renaissance* (1894), remain classics in the field. I Tatti, his villa near Florence, with its magnificent library and superb art collection, attracted artists and writers from all over the world. At his death, it became a European outpost of Harvard University. Sections of Berenson's extensive diaries were published in *Rumor and Reflection* (1958), *The Passionate Sightseer* (1960), and *Sunset and Twilight* (1963).

Berg, Alban (1885–1935)   Austrian composer. Berg obtained his musical training almost entirely as the pupil of Arnold SCHOENBERG. Although he employed his teacher's twelve-tone method of composition, he remained closer to the large gestures of late romantic music (especially MAHLER) than did his fellow pupil, Anton WEBERN. Partly for this reason, Berg's music has always seemed more immediately accessible to audiences than that of either Schoenberg or Webern.

Among his major works, his opera *Wozzeck* (performed 1925), based closely on the drama WOYZECK by Georg Büchner, made him famous; it is one of the few 20th-century operas that can be added to the repertory of indubitable masterpieces.

Berger, Thomas [Louis] (1924–   )   American novelist. Berger's black-comic novels deal with the American past and present. His Reinhart trilogy—*Crazy in Berlin* (1958), *Reinhart in Love* (1962), and *Vital Parts* (1970) —depicts the follies and frustrations of Carlo Reinhart from the end of World War II to the beginning of 1970. The ingenuous Reinhart proves no match for the hostile and cynical world he encounters. By the end of *Vital Parts*, he is trapped in a pointless suburban life, from which he seeks escape through a pathetic scheme to freeze and revive his body. In *Little Big Man* (1964), Berger satirizes the western, presenting the West through the eyes of the only white survivor of the Battle of Little Big Horn. *Who Is Teddy Villanova?* (1977) is a parody of HARD-BOILED FICTION. *Arthur Rex* (1978) is an exuberant spoof of the legend of Camelot. *Neighbors* (1980) is a Kafkaesque novel about the bizarre assaults by two young neighbors on a pudgy country landowner. Berger's novel *Nowhere* was published in 1985.

Bergman, Hjalmar [Frederik Elgerus] (1883–1931)   Swedish novelist, dramatist, and short-story writer. An expressionist similar in many ways to STRINDBERG, Bergman found his first major success with the novel *Markurells i Wädköping* (1919; tr *God's Orchid*, 1923), which was followed by *Farmor och vår Herre* (1921; tr *Thy Rod and Thy Staff*, 1937) and *Chefen fru Ingeborg* (1924; tr *The Head of the Firm*, 1936). His early plays were tragedies in the style of MAETERLINCK, although he became best known for such ironic comedies as *Petrasket* (1928; tr *The Baron's Will*, 1968), about a Jewish businessman. Essentially pessimistic about the human condition, he used tragicomedy or comedy as a foil for his evident despair.

Bergman, Ingmar (1918–   )   Swedish film director, scriptwriter, and producer. The son of a clergyman, Bergman began his career in the theatre in 1938. He first won wide acclaim for his screenplay *Torment* (1944). Thereafter, as writer, director, and producer, he had complete creative authority over his films and worked repeatedly with a devoted group of actors and film crew. His early work, filmed strikingly in black and white—*The Seventh Seal* (1956), *Wild Strawberries* (1957), *The Virgin Spring* (1959), *Through a Glass Darkly* (1960)—was characterized by obscurity, heavy symbolism, and an earnest concern with questions of religious faith. From 1963 to 1966, he was director of Stockholm's Royal Dramatic Theatre. Beginning with *Persona* (1966), his work became more directly autobiographical. The characters in such films as *A Passion of Anna* (1969); *The Touch* (1970), his first film in English; and *Cries and Whispers* (1972), his first color film, all confront the inescapable fact of their own aloneness. *Cries and Whispers* also represents another theme common to Bergman's later work: the frank and intimate exploration of family relationships, particularly their psychological torment and the resulting moral paralysis. *Scenes from a Marriage* (1974), filmed for television, and *Autumn Sonata* (1978) continue this theme. In a lighter vein, Bergman also produced *Smiles of a Summer Night* (1955), *Waiting Women* (1952), and *The Magic Flute* (1975), based on Mozart's opera. *Fanny and Alexander* appeared in 1983. Bergman has also published *Four Stories* (1977).

Bergotte   A famous author in Marcel Proust's REMEMBRANCE OF THINGS PAST. Bergotte's work greatly influences the narrator, who admires the delicate, exquisite style of his writing.

Bergson, Henri (1859–1941)   French philosopher. During his lifetime, Bergson enjoyed wide popularity as a professor at the Collège de France; his lectures were always crowded, and his books were eagerly read. His influence upon modern literature and thought has been profound. Bergson's philosophy is complex, but the basic premise of his intellectual system is a faith in direct intuition as a means of attaining knowledge. To the experimental and rationalistic methods of science, he opposed an antirational and mystical approach to understanding. Change or movement, Bergson believed, was the basis of all reality. Time should not be measured scientifically or mechanically, since for the human being time operates as a continuous flow in which past and present are inseparable from the memory and the consciousness. This theory of time in relation to the human self figures prominently in the long work of Marcel Proust, REMEMBRANCE OF THINGS PAST.

Bergson's interest in biological evolution led to the formulation of his theory of *élan vital*, a spirit of energy and life which moves all living things, and to the publication of his famous work *L'Évolution créatrice* (1907; tr *Creative Evolution*, 1913). His chief philosophical works are *Essai sur les données immédiates de la conscience* (1888; tr *Time and Free Will*, 1910), *Matière et mémoire* (1896; tr *Matter and Memory*, 1913), *Le Rire* (1901; tr *Laughter*, 1914), *Revue de métaphysique et de morale* (1903; tr *Introduction to Metaphysics*, 1912), *L'Energie spirituelle* (1919; tr *Mind-Energy*, 1920), *Les Deux Sources de la morale et de la religion* (1932; tr *Two Sources of Morality and Religion*, 1935), and *La Pensée et le mouvant* (1934; tr *The Creative Mind*, 1936). He was awarded the NOBEL PRIZE in Literature in 1927. Of Jewish parentage, Bergson renounced the honors and posts awarded him by the French government in 1940, as a protest against the hostile legislation passed by the Vichy government against the Jews.

Berkeley, George (1685–1753)   Irish-born English bishop and philosopher. Berkeley was one of the earliest and most influential thinkers of the philosophic school of idealism. In what is known as his "immaterialist hypothesis," he denied the existence of matter. Berkeley maintained that to be is to be perceived (*esse est percepi*); that is, nothing exists unless it perceives or is perceived, and, to this extent, his ideas were rooted in EMPIRICISM. He maintained that material objects are ideas in our minds, with no independent existence. Because things do exist, he reasoned, they are "necessarily perceived by an infinite mind; therefore, there is an infinite mind, or God." He felt that scientific theories have no truths of their own but have value only to the extent that they can be used to predict experience.

Berkeley wrote most of his serious philosophical works as a young man. His chief works in that vein are *Essay towards a New Theory of Vision* (1709), *Treatise Concern-*ing the Principles of Human Knowledge (1710), and *Three Dialogues between Hylas and Philonous* (1713).

From 1728 to 1732, he lived in the American colony of Rhode Island, while awaiting funds from Parliament to establish a missionary college in Bermuda. The funds were never forthcoming, but it was during his American sojourn that he wrote *Alciphron, or the Minute Philosopher* (1732). His last work was SIRIS: A CHAIN OF PHILOSOPHICAL REFLEXIONS AND INQUIRIES CONCERNING THE VIRTUES OF TAR-WATER.

Berlin, Irving (real name Israel Baline, 1888–   )   Russian-born American composer. Berlin is known for his popular songs and lyrics, especially those of a sentimental or patriotic nature, such as "Blue Skies" (1927), "God Bless America" (1939), and "White Christmas" (1942). His first hit was "Alexander's Ragtime Band" (1911), which assured his place in the annals of ragtime and jazz. He then wrote songs for Florenz Ziegfeld and for the Music Box Revue (1921–24), and later became famous for the scores of such musical comedies as *As Thousands Cheer* (1933), *Annie Get Your Gun* (1946), and *Call Me Madam* (1950). He has over eight hundred songs to his credit.

Berlin had an extraordinary range of musical styles and was one of the few in the American music business (Cole PORTER was another) who could successfully write both words and music. His accomplishments were all the more impressive in light of the fact that he had no musical training; he played only the black keys on his piano and only in the key of F sharp. He had a mechanism built into his piano that would change keys for him.

Berlin, Sir Isaiah (1909–   )   Latvian-born English philosopher. Berlin's family emigrated from Russia to England when he was eleven. His writings are concerned with the history of ideas and with the role of ideas in political action. Berlin makes a distinction between two visions of reality: that of the monists, who believe in a single, unifying principle, and that of the pluralists, who embrace many, often contradictory, theories of being. Adopting a phrase from Archilochus, "The fox knows many things, the hedgehog knows but one big thing," Berlin's famous essay *The Hedgehog and the Fox* (1953) suggests that Tolstoy's view of history was determined by an unending struggle between the two visions. In *Historical Inevitability* (1955), the same distinction is applied to questions of determinism and free choice. *Four Essays on Liberty* (1968), a landmark in political philosophy, articulates Berlin's belief that man is morally free and is able to affect the events in his life. *Russian Thinkers* (1978) is the first of four volumes of his collected writings. It was followed by *Concepts and Categories* (1979), philosophical writings; *Against the Current* (1980), essays on the history of ideas; and *Personal Impressions* (1981), reflections on important figures Berlin knew whose ideas became the visions that shaped their lives.

Berlin Stories   See ISHERWOOD, CHRISTOPHER.

Berlioz, [Louis] Hector (1803–1869) French romantic composer and conductor. Berlioz's *Treatise on Modern Instrumentation and Orchestration* (1844) established a new concept of the symphony orchestra and remains a basic text. His literary works, which give excellent descriptions of his musical environment, have been collected in ten volumes. His musical works, many with massive orchestras, are conceived almost entirely as musical embodiments of literary ideas. The *Symphonie fantastique* (1830), subtitled *Episode in the Life of an Artist*, is the first piece of sustained narrative music, the forerunner of the tone poems of Franz LISZT and Richard STRAUSS. The "program" of the symphony concerns an unhappy love; the artist's sweetheart is perceived as a melody, the *idée fixe*, which recurs in every movement. Despite the detailed summary that the composer attached to the score, the music is entirely capable of standing on its own.

Harold en Italie (1834) and *Roméo et Juliette* (1839) are two other programmatic symphonies. Other important works are the *Messe des morts* (*Requiem Mass*, 1837), the oratorio *L'Enfance du Christ* (*The Childhood of Christ*, 1854), and the gigantic opera *Les Troyens* (*The Trojans*, 1865–69), based on the tragic love of DIDO and Aeneas.

Berma A character in Marcel Proust's REMEMBRANCE OF THINGS PAST. Partially modeled on Sarah Bernhardt, Berma is a great actress particularly famous for her roles in Racine's plays.

Bermoothes An old name for Bermuda and the name of the island in Shakespeare's THE TEMPEST. The adventures of Sir George Somers, who was shipwrecked there with a group of colonists in 1609, may have furnished some of Shakespeare's material for the play.

Bernabò of Genoa A tale from Boccaccio's DECAMERON (II, 9). Bernabò makes a wager with a fellow merchant, Ambrogiuolo, that Bernabò's wife Ginevra will not succumb to any man in his absence. Ambrogiuolo, stealing into Ginevra's room while she is asleep, removes some of her garments and observes that she has a mole under her breast. He then confronts Bernabò with the items he stole and his knowledge of the mole as proof of his having slept with Ginevra. Convinced he has truly lost his wager and deeply grieved by his wife's supposed infidelity, Bernabò orders her death. But Ginevra persuades her executioner to show Bernabò her blood-stained garments and let her flee into exile. Disguising herself as a youth, Sicurano da Finale, Ginevra goes to sea with a Catalan merchant and reaches Alexandria, where the sultan takes her into his service. One day, she encounters Ambrogiuolo, who has come to sell his goods, including the garments taken from her room in Genoa that fateful night. Recognizing them, she asks to buy them and persuades him to tell how he got them. Knowing the truth at last, she sends for Bernabò and calls upon the sultan to judge Ambrogiuolo. She then startles all three of them by revealing herself as Ginevra. The sultan condemns Ambrogiuolo to death and sends Ginevra and Bernabò home, reconciled and joyous, to Genoa. The plot was borrowed by Shakespeare for *Cymbeline*.

Bernadette of Lourdes, St. (real name Bernadette Soubirous, 1844–1879) French peasant girl canonized as a saint on December 8, 1933. Bernadette was tending her sheep in February 1858, when the Virgin Mary appeared to her several times in a vision and revealed the miraculous healing properties of the waters springing from the grotto in which she was standing. Lourdes, a town of the Gave de Pan in the department of Hautes-Pyrénées, is the site of the famous grotto, which has become one of the principal Roman Catholic shrines and where many miraculous cures have been reported. Emile Zola drew inspiration from this story for his novel *Lourdes* (1894). THE SONG OF BERNADETTE is a similarly inspired historical novel by Franz Werfel.

Bernanos, Georges (1888–1948) French novelist and political writer. Before World War I, Bernanos was a supporter of the ACTION FRANÇAISE, although he later broke with that group. His novels, all dealing with the conflicting forces of God and Satan, reflect his fervent Catholicism and his intense concern with moral and spiritual problems. *Sous le soleil de Satan* (1926; tr *The Star of Satan*, 1940) and THE DIARY OF A COUNTRY PRIEST both stress the heroism of the spiritual struggles of rural clerics. His other novels include *La Joie* (1929; tr *Joy*, 1948), *Un Mauvais Rêve* (1935; pub 1951; tr *Night Is Darkest*, 1953), and MONSIEUR OUINE, thought by many to be his greatest work. In his political essays, Bernanos opposed parliamentary democracy because it did not provide enough protection from the greedy and the power-mad, and he urged a return to monarchy to institute a new moral order. He was a dedicated Royalist until he witnessed firsthand the atrocities of the Spanish Civil War, which inspired his angry polemic against Franco in *Les Grandes Cimetières sous la lune* (1938; tr *A Diary of My Times*, 1938). He lived in self-exile in Brazil from 1938 to 1945. His anti-Vichy writings of World War II are collected in *Lettre aux Anglais* (1942; tr *A Plea for Liberty*, 1944), *La France contre les robots* (1947), and *Le Chemin de la Croix des Ames* (1948). *Dialogues des Carmelites* (1949; tr *The Carmelites*, 1961), a play, was adapted as an opera (1952) by Francis POULENC. Bernanos's *Correspondence* appeared in two volumes in 1971.

Bernardin de Saint-Pierre, Jacques Henri (1737–1814) French author and one-time civil engineer. He traveled extensively in western Europe from 1761 to 1766, with the intention of promoting a scheme to regenerate society. A malcontent like ROUSSEAU, he returned to Paris in 1770, where he became the former's disciple and intimate friend, sharing his love of nature and horror of civilization. In 1784 he published his *Etudes de la nature*, a remarkable series of exotic descriptions of nature. Their object is to show the perfection of nature, the work of a good God solicitous of man's welfare. The precision, charm, and mastery of the language, new to French literature, are marred at times by the infantilism of the author's reasoning and by his sentimentality; his "philosophy" is at times a caricature of Rousseau's. The fourth part of these *Etudes* comprises his most famous work, the short novel PAUL ET VIRGINIE. Stylistically, Bernardin de Saint-Pierre is a precursor of Chateaubriand in his vivid use of pictorial description.

Bernard of Clairvaux, St. (1090–1153) French ecclesiastic. In 1113 Bernard entered the Cistercian abbey of Citeaux; two years later, he became the founder and abbot of a new Cistercian monastery at Clairvaux, a post he held until his death. His fame as a preacher soon spread, bringing crowds of pilgrims to Clairvaux, but Bernard refused all offers of ecclesiastical preferment. Nevertheless, his importance and prestige grew rapidly: through his work, the Cistercians became the greatest order in western Christendom, and he himself the greatest influence, at first in France and later throughout western Europe. He was instrumental in the success of Pope Innocent II's cause over the claims of the antipope, Cardinal Peter of Leon. In 1141 he secured an official condemnation of Pierre Abelard's works at the Council of Sens. In 1146 he summoned the people to join in a crusade, in the name of Pope Eugenius II, and Louis VII of France, with many others, was moved to organize the Second Crusade. He was canonized in 1173.

Bernini, [Giovanni] Lorenzo (1598–1680) Italian sculptor and architect. The dominant influence on European sculpture for over a century, Bernini was a typically baroque artist and did not shy away from whirling movement and illusionistic representation in stone. He is known for his consummate portrait busts and his fountains, particularly the fountain of Trevi and, in Rome, the fountain of the Four Rivers. His religious works include the skillfully carved Saint Theresa group in Rome's Santa Maria della Vittoria, theatrically lit by a hidden overhead window, and the exuberant setting for the chair of Saint Peter. His best-known architectural achievement is the double colonnade of the Piazza of Saint Peter (1656–68).

Berryman, John (1914–1972) American poet. Berryman's poetry, sometimes mannered, elliptical, and convoluted, is distinguished by precise technical control and continued experiments with style. The early volumes —*Poems* (1942), *The Dispossessed* (1948), *Sonnets*, which was written in the 1940s but not published until 1967, and *Short Poems* (1967; also written earlier)—are comparatively rooted in formal tradition. With the publication of HOMAGE TO MISTRESS BRADSTREET, in which he used the double conceit of the 17th-century American poet Anne Bradstreet as his mistress and alter ego, Berryman made bold inroads

into a new poetic style. Contemporary critics hailed it as the most important book of poetry since T. S. Eliot's FOUR QUARTETS.

Following *His Thoughts Made Pockets & the Plane Buckt* (1958), he published *77 Dream Songs* (1964), which won the PULITZER PRIZE, and *His Toy, His Dream, His Rest* (1968). Published together as THE DREAM SONGS, this long poem—sometimes loosely called a verse novel —marked the consolidation of Berryman's unique stylistic technique and his personal voice. His major work, it is characterized by wrenched syntax, rhythmic changes, and an extraordinary combination of the archaic and the colloquial.

Berryman is regarded, along with Robert LOWELL, as one of the CONFESSIONAL POETS. Through the various masks of Henry, Mr. Bones, and an unnamed interlocutor, in *The Dream Songs* he describes agonies and despairs, both his own and those of the poet as artistic exile. *Love and Fame* (1970) contains frankly autobiographical accounts of the poet's lustful adventures, his struggles with madness and alcoholism, and his musings on suicide, and ends with a hint at some sustaining religious inspiration.

In 1972 Berryman, whose father had shot himself when Berryman was twelve, jumped to his death from a bridge over the Mississippi River. He had, at that point, prepared several books for publication, including *Delusions, Etc.* (1972), which picked up where *Love and Fame* left off, with poems about God, as well as some earlier verse, and *The Freedom of the Poet* (1976), a collection of erudite prose pieces and criticism. Among his other posthumous publications are *Selected Poems* (1972); *Recovery* (1973), an unfinished autobiographical novel; and *Henry's Fate* (1977), previously unpublished poems from 1967 to 1972. Berryman also wrote the first important critical biography of Stephen Crane (1950).

berserker In Scandinavian mythology, a wild, ferocious, warlike being who was sometimes possessed of supernatural strength and fury. One account says the name originated from the grandson of the eight-handed Starkader, called *boer-serce* ("bare of mail") because he went into battle unharnessed. Another holds that the name means simply men who have assumed the form of bears. The word is used in English both as an adjective denoting excessive fury and as a noun denoting one possessed of such.

Bertram, Edmund See MANSFIELD PARK.

Bertram, Harry See GUY MANNERING.

Besant, Annie (born Wood, 1847–1933) English author, theosophist, and political radical. Besant separated from her clergyman husband and became associated with Charles Bradlaugh in the free-thought movement. An advocate of socialism and social reform, she was a member of the FABIAN SOCIETY, an organizer of labor unions, and a worker among impoverished and delinquent children.

Later, after meeting Mme Blavatsky, she became a leading theosophist in England. Interest in occult theology took her to India (1889), where she founded the Central Hindu College at Benares. Both in India and later back in England, she agitated for home rule in India. Among her best-known religious works are *Karma* (1895), *Four Great Religions* (1897), and *Wisdom of the Upanishads* (1906). Her other works include *Autobiography* (1893), *How India Wrought for Freedom* (1915), and *India, Bond or Free* (1926). See THEOSOPHY.

Besier, Rudolf See BARRETTS OF WIMPOLE STREET, THE.

Bess, Good Queen ELIZABETH I of England.

Bester, Alfred (1913–) American science-fiction author. Bester, who earned his living writing scripts for comics, radio, and TV, writes science fiction only occasionally, but two of his early works, *The Demolished Man* (1953) and *The Stars My Destination* (1957), became landmarks in the genre, noted for their combination of fast-paced "space opera" plotting (in the tradition of E. E. "Doc" SMITH) with wit and stylistic pyrotechnics. Other works include *Starlight* (1977), a collection of his short fiction, and *Golem 100* (1980), a novel set in the 22nd century.

bestiaries Allegorical poems or books giving descriptions of various animals or stories concerning them, with a Christian application or moral appended to each. Although the characteristics and habits assigned to each animal were largely legendary, bestiaries were often treated during the Middle Ages as treatises on natural history, as well as moral instruction, and were highly popular.

The beast-fable, popular from Aesop to the medieval *Reynard the Fox*, was usually satirical and pragmatic in its moral; a 4th-century work in Greek was probably the first to turn animal descriptions into specifically Christian allegory, and its translations into Latin *Physiologi* were the basis of most English and Continental bestiaries. The best known are the Latin *Physiologus* (11th century) by the abbot Theobaldus, the *Bestiary* by the Anglo-Norman poet Phillippe de Thaün, and an anonymous Middle English *Bestiary* (c1250).

Bethany A town of Palestine on the Mount of Olives. Bethany was the home of Lazarus, brother of Mary and Martha, who was raised from the dead by Jesus.

Bethgelert or The Grave of the Greyhound (1811) A ballad by William Robert Spencer (1769–1834), retelling a story common in Oriental and then in medieval European literature. In this version, Gelert is a hound given by King John to Llewelyn the Great, who returns from the hunt one day to find his dog covered with blood and his infant son missing from an overturned cradle. Believing that Gelert has eaten the child, Llewelyn stabs him, but the hound's dying scream awakens the infant, who cries out from where he is hidden under a pile of coverings, and under the bed is found a huge wolf killed by Gelert.

Bethlehem The ancient town in Judea, Palestine, where Jesus was born. Also the scene of Rachel's death, the home of Ruth and Naomi, and the city of David, Bethlehem is mentioned frequently in both the Old and the New Testaments.

Beti, Mongo (real name Alexandre Biyidi, 1932–) Cameroonian novelist, writing in French. Biyidi used the pen name Eza Boto for his first novel, *Ville cruelle* (1953). Thereafter, as Mongo Beti, he published *Le Pauvre Christ de Bomba* (1956; tr *The Poor Christ of Bomba*, 1971), *Mission terminée* (1957; tr *Mission to Kala*, 1964), and *Le Roi miraculé* (1958; tr *King Lazarus*, 1971). Taken together, his novels present a picture of social life and attitudes during the French colonial period in Africa. On the surface, Biyidi's novels are marked by abundant invention and ribald humor. However, they also reveal, through an insistent satire, a sustained attack on colonialism, the misunderstandings it occasioned, and the tragic waste it produced. Beti's translated novel *Perpetua and the Habit of Unhappiness* was published in 1978.

Betjeman, Sir John (1906–1984) English poet and architectural authority. In satirical light verse, Betjeman's poems celebrate the English countryside and ordinary provincial and suburban life. They nostalgically evoke the Victorian era and a past or passing English culture. Among his many volumes of verse are *Continual Dew* (1937), *New Bats in Old Belfries* (1945), *A Few Late Chrysanthemums* (1955), and *Collected Poems* (1958, rev 1970). *Summoned by Bells* (1960) is a verse autobiography. He also wrote several books on English churches and architecture, including *Ghastly Good Taste* (1933, pub U.S. 1972) and *A Pictorial History of English Architecture* (1972). He was made England's POET LAUREATE in 1972, and remained so until his death.

Bettelheim, Bruno (1903–) Austrian-born American psychologist, educator, and author. Bettelheim came to the U.S. in 1939 as a survivor of the Nazi concentration camps. Drawing from this experience, he wrote the widely read and influential study *Individual and Mass Behavior in Extreme Situations* (1943). He is best known, however, for his psychiatric work with severely disturbed children and its application to the study and education of normal children. *Love Is Not Enough* (1950), addressed to parents and general readership, describes his work in his Orthogenic School for emotionally disturbed children and outlines means for meeting both children's and parents' needs in the modern family situation. Among his many other books are *The Children of the Dream* (1969), about communal childbearing in the kibbutz, *A Home for the Heart* (1974), and *The Uses of Enchantment* (1976), in which he discusses the psycho-social importance of fairy tales. *Surviving and Other Essays* (1979) contains diverse essays on problems in American society, on surviving under extreme duress, and on childhood schizophrenia. *Freud and Man's Soul* was published in 1983.

Betti, Ugo (1892–1953)   Italian poet and playwright. The son of an eminent jurist, Betti too was a high-court judge; by the end of his life, he was recognized as one of the most important modern Italian playwrights. Not surprisingly, many of his twenty-six works for theatre had a courtroom setting. In such plays as *Frana allo scalo nord* (1935) and *Corruziona al Palazzo di Giustizia* (1944), he explored the theme of human corruption and the ways in which justice often finds itself in conflict with human ambition for money and power. Other works include *Delitto all'isola delle capre* (1950; tr *Crime on Goat Island*, 1960) and *Una strana serata* (1948), a collection of short stories.

Between the Acts (1941)   A novel by Virginia WOOLF. It describes a pageant on English history, written and directed by Miss La Trobe, and its effects on the people who watch it. Most of the audience misunderstand it in various ways; a clergyman reduces its vision to a sermon. But, for a moment, Woolf implies, the pageant—or art —has imposed order on the chaos of human life.

Beulah, land of   In Bunyan's PILGRIM'S PROGRESS, that land of heavenly joy where the pilgrims tarry until they are summoned to enter the Celestial City; the paradise before the resurrection. The name Beulah occurs in the Bible (Isa. 62:4).

Beverley, Ensign   See ABSOLUTE, CAPTAIN JACK.

Beverly, Robert (c1673–1722)   American historian of the Virginia colony. Beverly's chief work is *The History and Present State of Virginia*, issued in London in 1705. It is one of the earliest self-consciously American works. "I am an Indian," Beverly wrote, "and don't pretend to be exact in my language."

Beyle, Marie Henri   See STENDHAL.

Beyond Good and Evil (Jenseits von Gut und Böse, 1886)   A philosophical work by Friedrich NIETZSCHE, in the form of a collection of aphorisms. In it, Nietzsche expresses his desire for a "transvaluation of all values." He contends that no human values are absolute; that all value distinctions (such as that between "good" and "evil") are artificial, the result of mere traditional prejudices; and that humanity should discard its old, outmoded values (such as "good" and "evil") in favor of ones more suited to contemporary cultural reality.

Beyond the Horizon (1920)   A play by Eugene O'NEILL. The Mayo brothers love the same woman; Robert, who had wanted to seek adventure "beyond the horizon," stays home to marry the woman, and the prosaic Andrew goes to sea and later to the Argentine. In the end, Robert dies embittered but happy "with the right of release —beyond the horizon." The play was awarded a PULITZER PRIZE.

Bezukhov, Pierre   A central character in Tolstoy's WAR AND PEACE. Like Prince Andrey BOLKONSKY, Pierre has a poor first marriage, but he later falls in love with Natasha ROSTOVA. After an attempt to assassinate Napoleon, Pierre is captured by the French, who bring him on their disastrous retreat from Moscow. Released during a Cossack raid, Pierre learns of the deaths of his wife and of his great friend, Prince Andrey. After much soul-searching, Pierre eventually learns the sheer joy of being alive. He marries Natasha and lives happily. Pierre represents to Tolstoy the triumph of a humanistic way of life.

Bhagavadgītā (Sans, "the song of god")   An eighteen-part discussion between the god KRISHNA, an avatar of Vishnu appearing as a charioteer, and Arjuna, a warrior about to enter battle, on the nature and meaning of life. Sometimes called the New Testament of Hinduism, it is an interpolation in the great Hindu epic the MAHĀBHĀRATA. On the battlefield of Kurukshetra, Arjuna, one of the Pandava brothers, is dejected and confused and hesitates to join battle with his kinsmen, the Kauravas, mainly on the ground that to take another's life is not acceptable. Krishna initially counsels Arjuna that the true self (ATMAN) survives corporeal death and that killing is thus not so final an act as Arjuna believes. Thereafter, the dialogue ranges widely on the subject of human existence and its relationship to the cosmic order, and it dwells extensively on three broad approaches to existence and ultimate release (*moksha*) from corporeal entanglements and unreality (MAYA): (1) KARMA, or the path of prescribed action as defined by DHARMA, or sacred duty; (2) *jnana*, or the path of knowledge; and (3) *bhakti*, or the path of devotion.

The *Gita*, as it is often called, has had a substantial impact on western thought. Unfortunately, many of the readily available renderings are not faithful to the letter and spirit of the Sanskrit text, and many tend to gloss over ambiguities in order to place the text firmly within one or another interpretive tradition. With such caveats in mind, the heavily Christianized translation by Juan Mascaro (1962) and that of Swami Prabhavananda and Christopher Isherwood (1954) may be recommended. The translation and interpretation by Franklin Edgerton (1944) is a faithful if sometimes tedious classic.

Bhartrihari (7th century AD)   Hindu poet. Bhartrihari is considered by many to be the greatest writer of Sanskrit lyric poetry. Some of his verses have been widely translated, under the titles *Good Conduct, Passion of Love, Renunciation*. It is disputed whether or not he is the grammarian of the same name and author of the *Vākyapadīya* (*Treatise on Words and Sentences*), who probably lived in the 6th century AD.

Bhasa (c3rd century AD)   Sanskrit dramatist. Bhasa's works show great skill in narrative, exquisite poetry, the depiction of human sentiment, and excellent stagecraft. *Svapna-Vasavadatta* (*The Dream of Vasavadatta*) is the most popular of the thirteen Bhasa plays discovered in 1912 by Pandit Ganapati Sāstrī.

Bhavabhuti (8th century AD)   Indian playwright. Bhavabhuti is praised for his subtle handling of poignant scenes and his mastery of Sanskrit as a poetic language. Two of his plays, *Mahāvīracarita* (tr *Portrait of a Hero*, 1871) and *Uttararāmacarita* (tr *Rama's Later Story*, 1915), retell the RĀMĀYANA story in a highly dramatic and sometimes sentimentalized form; a third, *Malati-madhava* (Fr tr 1885) deals with a legendary tale.

Bianchi and Neri (Ital, "Whites and Blacks") Rival factions within the Guelph party in Tuscany about 1300 (see GUELPHS AND GHIBELLINES). The Bianchi wanted to maintain Florence as a democratic constitutionality independent of both emperor and pope; the Neri were willing to compromise with the pope to gain power against the emperor. See DANTE.

Bible (fr Gr, *biblos*, "book")   The Christian sacred book. Actually a collection of books, the Holy Bible, as it is often called, is divided into two parts: the OLD TESTAMENT and the NEW TESTAMENT. The former contains thirty-nine books, according to the Protestants, with a supplement of fourteen books known as the APOCRYPHA; other churches include part or all of the Apocrypha in the Old Testament. The New Testament contains twenty-seven books.

The Old Testament was compiled from the 13th to the 1st century BC. No original manuscripts have survived, and present versions are based on two primary sources: the SEPTUAGINT, a Greek translation from the Hebrew, made in Alexandria about 250 BC, and the Massoretic Text, the work of a group of trained Jewish scholars, beginning in the 6th century after Christ, whose purpose was to correct and preserve the Hebrew versions then available. The Massoretic Text was completed by the end of the 10th century. The Septuagint became the accepted Christian version of the Old Testament, while the Massoretic Text has remained the Hebrew canon. Other important versions of the Old Testament are the Samarian Pentateuch, a 4th-century BC text preserved by the Samaritan community, and the VULGATE, a Latin translation by St. Jerome begun in AD 382. The Vulgate is still the authorized Roman Catholic version.

The New Testament was written, probably in Greek, during the 1st century; however, the earliest manuscripts date from the 3rd and 4th centuries. There is no doubt that, in the years between the date of its original composition and those of extant manuscripts, numerous textual changes were made through poor copying and interpretive additions or subtractions. There are five general types of text identifiable in early manuscripts. When the New Testament canon was defined in AD 367, an attempt was made to standardize the texts. Of the 150,000 variants of New Testament text, only 50 are significant, and no essential doctrine is affected by any of them.

The greatest number of New Testament texts are in Greek, but there are early Latin texts, parts of which were incorporated into the Vulgate. The New Testament is by far the best-preserved document from the ancient world; there are about 175 papyri from the 2nd to the 4th centuries and close to 3,000 manuscripts that date from before the invention of printing.

Bible, English versions   The principal versions of the English Bible are:

American Revised Version   A separate version published in 1901, the work of the American Committee on the Revised Version. It differs in a few particulars from the Revised Version.

Authorized or King James Version   The version in general use in England. It was made by a body of scholars working at the command of King James I (hence it is sometimes known as the King James Bible) from 1604 to 1611, and it was published in 1611. The modern Authorized Version is, however, by no means an exact reprint of that originally authorized by King James; a large number of typographical errors which occurred in the first edition have been corrected, the orthography and punctuation have been modernized, and the use of italics, capital letters, etc. altered. The Bishops' Bible was used as the basis of the text, but Tyndale's, Matthew's, Coverdale's, and the Geneva translations were also followed when they agreed better with the original. The King James Version became the Bible of almost all English-speaking Protestant sects, and its influence can be detected in nearly every subsequent version. It is still much in use and remains, in its simplicity and eloquence, the most beautifully written of all Bibles in the language. Its literary influence is inestimable; besides its direct effect on many important writers, it has been regarded as a major force in keeping English relatively unchanged since the 17th century.

Bishops' Bible   A version made at the instigation of Archbishop Parker (hence also called Matthew Parker's Bible), to which most of the Anglican bishops were contributors. It was a revision of the Great Bible; it first appeared in 1568 and by 1602 had reached its eighteenth edition. It is this edition that forms the basis of the Authorized Version. See Treacle Bible.

Coverdale's Bible   The first complete English Bible to be printed. It was published in 1535 by Miles Coverdale. As Coverdale knew neither Hebrew nor Greek, his translation is from Latin and German sources, notably the Vulgate, another Latin version by Sanctes Pegninus (1527–28), Luther's German version (1534), and the Swiss-German version of Zwingli and Juda (Zurich, 1527–29). He used Tyndale's translations of the New Testament and the Pentateuch. The first edition was printed in Antwerp, but the second (Southwark, 1537) was the first Bible printed in England. Matthew's Bible is largely based on Coverdale's. See Bug Bible.

Cranmer's Bible A name given to the Great Bible of 1540. It—and later issues of it—contained a prologue by Archbishop Cranmer, and, on the title page, a woodcut by Holbein shows Henry VIII seated while Cranmer and Thomas Cromwell distribute copies to the people.

Douay Version A translation of the Vulgate made by English Catholic scholars in France. The New Testament was published in Rheims in 1582 and the Old Testament in Douay in 1609. It is sometimes called the Rheims-Douay Version. See Rosin Bible.

Geneva Bible A revision of Tyndale and the Great Bible, undertaken by English exiles in Geneva during the Marian persecutions and first published in 1560. It was the work of William Whittingham (a brother-in-law of Calvin), assisted by Anthony Gilby and Thomas Sampson. Whittingham had previously published a translation of the New Testament (1557). The Genevan version, one of the most important in the history of the English Bible, was the first to be printed in roman type instead of black letter, the first in which the chapters are divided into verses (taken from Robert Stephan's Greek-Latin Testament of 1537), and the first in which italics are used for explanatory and connective words and phrases (taken from Theodore Beza's New Testament of 1556). It was immensely popular: from 1560 to 1616, no year passed without a new edition, and at least two hundred are known. It was the Bible used by Shakespeare. In every edition, the word *breeches* is used in Gen. 3:7; as a result, this is popularly called the Breeches Bible. See Goose Bible; Placemakers' Bible.

Great Bible Coverdale's 1539 revision of his own 1535 edition, collated with Tyndale and Matthew. It was made at the request of Thomas Cromwell. Its name comes from its large size (10 by 15 inches). The printing was begun by Regnault in Paris, halted by the Inquisition, and completed by Richard Graften and Edward Whitchurch in London. A second revision in 1540 is often called Cranmer's Bible.

King James Bible See Authorized Version.

Matthew Parker's Bible The Bishops' Bible.

Matthew's Bible A pronouncedly Protestant version published in 1537 as having been "truly and purely translated in English by Thomas Matthew," which was a pseudonym, adopted for purposes of safety, of John Rogers, an assistant of Tyndale. It was probably printed in Antwerp. The text is made up of the Pentateuch from Tyndale's version, together with his hitherto unprinted translation of Joshua to 2 Chronicles inclusive and his revised edition of the New Testament, with Coverdale's version of the rest of the Old Testament and the Apocrypha. It was quickly superseded by the Great Bible, but it is of importance as it formed the starting-point for the revisions which culminated in the Authorized Version. See Bug Bible.

Revised Standard Version An American version that appeared in 1952; the New Testament was published in 1946. It employs a modern American idiom and has been widely accepted by Protestants.

Revised Version A revision of the Authorized Version begun in 1870 by a body of twenty-five English scholars (assisted and advised by an American Committee). The New Testament was published in 1881, the complete Bible in 1885, and the Apocrypha in 1895.

Rheims-Douay Version See Douay Version.

Taverner's Bible An independent translation by a Greek scholar, Richard Taverner, printed in 1539 (the same year as the Great Bible) by T. Petit for T. Berthelet. It had no influence on the Authorized Version but is remarkable for its vigorous, idiomatic English and for being the first English Bible to include a third book of Maccabees in the Apocrypha.

Tyndale's Bible The first printed English New Testament, translated by William Tyndale (Cologne, Worms, 1525). He followed it with the Pentateuch (Marburg, Hesse, 1530 or 1531), Jonah, Old Testament lessons appointed to be read in place of the Epistles, and a manuscript translation of the Old Testament to the end of Chronicles, which was afterwards used in Matthew's Bible. His revisions of the New Testament were issued in 1534 and 1535. Tyndale's principal authority was Erasmus's edition of the Greek Testament, but he also used Erasmus's Latin translation of the same, the Vulgate, and Luther's German version. Tyndale's version fixed the style and tone of the English Bible: about 90 percent of his translation is retained in the Authorized Version. In 1535 he was arrested and was put to death as a heretic the following year.

Wyclif's Bible The name given to two translations of the Vulgate, one completed in 1380 and the other a few years later. Wyclif was neither the translator nor concerned with the translation of either of these. Nicholas of Hereford made the first version as far as Baruch 3:20; who was responsible for the remainder is not known. The second version has been ascribed to John Purvey, a follower of Wyclif. The Bible of 1380 was the first complete version in English, being a word-for-word translation of the Vulgate into a Midland dialect. The complete Wyclif's Bible remained unprinted until 1850, when the monumental edition of both versions was published by Forshall and Madden. Printings of the New Testament had appeared in the previous century.

Bible, specially named editions

The following Bibles are named either from typographical errors or archaic words that they contain or from some special circumstance connected with them:

Adulterous Bible The Wicked Bible.

Bamberg Bible The Thirty-six Line Bible.

Bear Bible The Spanish Protestant version printed at Basle in 1569, so called because the woodcut device on the title page is a bear.

Bedell's Bible A translation of the Authorized Version into Irish carried out under the direction of Bedell (d 1642), bishop of Kilmore and Ardagh.

Breeches Bible A name given to the Geneva Bible because Gen. 3:7 is translated, "The eyes of them bothe were opened . . . and they sowed figge-tree leaves together and made themselves breeches." This reading occurs in every edition of the Geneva Bible but not in any other version, though it is given in the then unprinted Wyclif manuscript ("þa sewiden þe levis of a fige tre and madin brechis") and also in the translation of the Pentateuch given in Caxton's edition of Voragine's *Golden Legend* (1483).

Brother's Bible The Kralitz Bible.

Bug Bible A name given to Coverdale's Bible of 1535 because Ps. 91:5 is translated, "Thou shalt not nede to be afrayed for eny bugges by night." The same reading occurs in Matthew's Bible and its reprints; the Authorized and Revised Versions both read "terror."

Complutensian Polyglot The great edition, in six folio volumes, containing the Hebrew and Greek texts, the Septuagint, the Vulgate, and the Chaldee paraphrase of the Pentateuch, with a Latin translation. It also includes Greek and Hebrew grammars and a Hebrew dictionary; it was prepared and printed at the expense of Cardinal Ximenes, and it was printed at Alcala (the ancient Complutum) near Madrid, 1513–17.

Discharge Bible An edition printed in 1806 containing *discharge* for *charge* in 1 Tim. 5:21, "I *dis*charge thee before God, . . . that thou observe these things. . . ."

Ears to Ear Bible An edition of 1810, in which Matt. 13:43 reads, "Who hath ears to *ear*, let him hear."

Ferrara Bible The first Spanish edition of the Old Testament, translated from the Hebrew in 1553 for the use of the Spanish Jews. A second edition was published in the same year for Christians.

Forty-two Line Bible The Mazarin Bible.

Goose Bible The editions of the Geneva Bible printed in Dort (or Dordrecht), Holland; the Dort press had a goose as its device.

Gutenberg Bible The Mazarin Bible.

He and She Bibles The two earliest editions of the Authorized Version (both 1611). In the first (now known as the He Bible), Ruth 3:15 reads, "and *he* went into the city"; the other (now known as the She Bible) has the variant *she*. *He* is the correct translation of the Hebrew, but nearly all modern versions—with the exception of the Revised Version—perpetuate the confusion and print *she*.

Idle Bible An edition of 1809 in which "the idole shepherd" (Zech. 11:17) is printed "the idle shepherd." In the Revised Version, the translation is "the worthless shepherd."

Kralitz Bible The Bible printed by the United Brethren of Moravia (hence, known as the Brother's Bible) at Kralitz (1579–93).

Leda Bible The third edition (second folio) of the Bishop's Bible published in 1572, so called because the decoration to the initial in the Epistle to the Hebrews is a startling and incongruous woodcut of Jupiter visiting Leda in the guise of a swan. This and several other decorations in the New Testament of this edition were from an edition of Ovid's *Metamorphoses*; they created such a storm of protest that they were never afterwards used.

Leopolita Bible A Polish translation of the Vulgate by John of Lemberg (ancient Leopolis), published in 1561 at Cracow.

Mazarin Bible The first Bible to be printed (an edition of the Vulgate) and the first large book to be printed from movable metal type. It contains no date but was probably printed in 1455 and was certainly on sale by the middle of 1456. It was printed at Mainz, but there is some question about who the printer was; it is now thought to have been either Johannes GUTENBERG or Fust and Schöffer. It is frequently called the Gutenberg Bible. By bibliographers it is usually known as the Forty-two Line Bible (having forty-two lines to the page), to differentiate it from the Bamberg Bible of thirty-six lines. Its popular name is due to the fact that the copy found in the Mazarin Library, Paris, in 1760, was the first to be known and described.

Murderers' Bible An edition of 1801 in which the misprint *murderers* for *murmurers* makes Jude 16 read, "These are murderers, complainers, walking after their own lusts . . ."

Old Cracow Bible The Leopolita Bible.

Ostrog Bible The first complete Slavonic edition, printed at Ostrog, Volhynia, Russia, in 1581.

Pfister's Bible The Thirty-six Line Bible.

Place-makers' Bible The second edition of the Geneva Bible, 1562, so called from the printer's error in Matt. 5:9, "Blessed are the placemakers [peacemakers], for they shall be called the children of God." It has also been called the Whig Bible.

Printers' Bible An edition of about 1702 which makes David pathetically complain that "printers [princes] have persecuted me without a cause" (Ps. 119:161).

Proof Bible (Probe-Bible) The revised version of the first impression of Luther's German Bible. A final revised edition appeared in 1892.

Rebecca's Camels Bible An edition printed in 1823 in which Gen. 24:61 reads, "Rebecca arose, and her camels," instead of "her damsels."

Rosin Bible A name sometimes given to the Douay Version of 1609, so called because it has in Jer. 8:22, "Is there noe rosin in Galaad." The Authorized Version translates the word by *balm*, but gives *rosin* in the margin as an alternative. See Treacle Bible.

Sacy's Bible A French translation, so called from Louis Isaac le Maistre de Sacy, director of Port Royal, 1650–79.

Schelhorn's Bible A name sometimes given to the Thirty-six Line Bible.

September Bible Luther's German translation of the New Testament, published anonymously at Wittenberg in September 1522.

She Bible See He and She Bibles.

Standing Fishes Bible An edition of 1806 in which Ezek. 47:10 reads, "And it shall come to pass that the fishes [fishers] shall stand on it, ..."

Thirty-six Line Bible A Latin Bible of thirty-six lines to the column, probably printed by A. Pfister at Bamberg in 1460. It is also known as the Bamberg and Pfister's Bible and sometimes as Schelhorn's, as it was first described by the German bibliographer J. G. Schelhorn in 1760.

Thumb Bible An edition printed at Aberdeen in 1670; it measures one inch square by a half inch thick.

To-remain Bible A Bible printed at Cambridge in 1805, in which Gal. 4:29 reads, "he that was born after the flesh persecuted him that was born after the spirit to remain, even so it is now." The words *to remain* were added in error by the compositor, the editor having answered a proofreader's query as to the comma after *spirit* with the penciled reply "to remain" in the margin. The mistake was repeated in the first 8vo edition published by the Bible Society (1805) and in their 12mo edition (1819).

Treacle Bible A popular name for the Bishops' Bible (1568), because in it Jer. 8:22 reads, "Is there no tryacle in Gilead, is there no phisition there?" In the same Bible, *tryacle* is also given for *balm* in Jer. 46:11 and in Ezek. 27:17. Coverdale's Bible (1535) also uses the word *triacle*. See Rosin Bible.

Unrighteous Bible An edition printed at Cambridge in 1653, containing the printer's error, "Know ye not that the unrighteous shall inherit the Kingdom of God?" (1 Cor. 6:9). It should read "shall *not* inherit." The same edition gave Rom. 6:13 as, "Neither yield ye your members as instruments of righteousness unto sin," in place of "*un*righteousness." This edition is sometimes known as the Wicked Bible.

Vinegar Bible An edition printed at the Clarendon Press, Oxford, in 1717, with the heading to Luke 20, "Parable of the Vinegar" instead of "Parable of the Vineyard."

Wicked Bible An edition in which the word *not* is omitted in the seventh commandment, making it "Thou shalt commit adultery." It was printed in 1632 in London by Baker and Lucas, who were fined £300 for their unfortunate error. See Unrighteous Bible.

Wife-hater Bible An edition of 1810 in which the word *life* in Luke 14:26 is printed *wife*. It reads, "If any man come to me, and hate not his father . . . yea, and his own wife also. . . ."

Wuyck's Bible The Polish Bible authorized by the Roman Catholics and printed at Cracow in 1599. The translation was made by the Jesuit Jacob Wuyck.

Zurich Bible A German version (1530) composed of Luther's translation of the New Testament and portions of the Old, with the remainder and the Apocrypha by other translators.

Bible in Spain, The (1843) A travel book by George Borrow (1803–81), considered one of the best in the English language. Supposedly based on Borrow's experiences in Spain as a colporteur for the Bible Society, it probably contains much material of his own invention. However, the book is thought to give a valid picture of Spanish life during the Carlist troubles.

Biblia Pauperum (Lat, "the poor man's Bible") A picture-book, widely used by the illiterate in the Middle Ages in place of the Bible. It was designed to illustrate the leading events in the salvation of man; later manuscripts as a rule had a Latin inscription to each picture. These *Biblia* were probably the earliest books to be printed in Europe, first from blocks and later with movable type.

Bickerstaff, Isaac A fictitious astrologer invented by Jonathan SWIFT to silence John Partridge, an almanac maker who had achieved a reputation as something of a prophet. In his almanac *Predictions for the ensuing year by Isaac Bickerstaff* (1708), Swift predicted Partridge's death on March 29. On March 30, he published a convincing account of the prophecy's fulfillment in *An Elegy of Mr. Partridge* (1708). The hoax was successful despite Partridge's protests that he was still very much alive. The joke was popular, and Richard Steele capitalized on Bickerstaff's fame by making him the supposed editor of THE TATLER.

Bidpai, Fables of (c750) An Arabic version of a collection of Indian fables common to Buddhism and Brahminism, also known as *Kalilah and Dimnah*. They were collected in the Sanskrit *Panchatantra* and translated into Persian about AD 55. *Bidpai* means court scholar, and the allegorical animal stories are told as a wise man's advice to a young Indian prince.

Biedermeier In German literature, a tendency found most strongly in the period 1815–48, during which most parts of Germany were governed by oppressive conservative regimes, such as those of Prussia and Austria. Biedermeier is often thought of as the antithesis of the *Jung Deutschland* ("Young Germany") movement. Whereas the Young Germans stressed social criticism in thought, vigorous realism in style, and heroism in their characters, Biedermeier authors favored social conservatism in thought, didacticism in style, and a capacity for quiet resignation in their characters. The Biedermeier tendency is distinguished from romanticism by its emphasis on a sober, resigned attitude toward the world, as opposed to the romantics' high-flown, fundamentally optimistic striving for the ideal. The late Swabian phase of German romanticism, however, nearly coincides with the Biedermeier. No major authors are purely and simply Biedermeier, but the three most important figures in whom the tendency is clearly marked are GRILLPARZER, MÖRIKE, and STIFTER. The term originated with the fictional character Gottlieb Biedermaier lampooned by Ludwig Eichrodt (1827–92) and others in the periodical *Fliegende Blätter*.

Bierce, Ambrose [Gwinett] (1842–1914?) American journalist, short-story writer, and poet. Emerging from a sternly religious Ohio family, Bierce fought with distinction in the Civil War, then settled in San Francisco, where he turned to journalism. He became writer-editor of the San Francisco *News-Letter* and made his reputation there as a scathing satirist who could make or break a writer with his acid comments. He began publishing stories of his own and, with his friends Joaquin MILLER, Bret HARTE, and Mark TWAIN, formed an important literary circle of the day. Following marriage to a wealthy miner's daughter, Bierce took his bride to England, where they stayed for four years. There Bierce published *Cobwebs from an Empty Skull* (1874). Back in San Francisco with a freshly polished wit, he began to write his famous column "The Prattler" (1887–1906), a mixture of literary gossip, epigrams, and stories. Later, as Washington correspondent for the Hearst newspapers, he wrote also for *Cosmopolitan* and prepared his collected works (12 vols, 1909–12). Divorced in 1904, he broke completely with his family and gradually lost touch with friends. In 1913 he disappeared into Mexico. His fate remains unknown.

Bierce's fame rests on three volumes: IN THE MIDST OF LIFE, *Can Such Things Be?* (1893), and *The Devil's Dictionary* (1911; first published as *The Cynic's Word Book*, 1906). He had a peculiar knack for establishing an atmosphere of horror through suggestive, realistic detail. His wit was sardonic, cruel, and brilliant; his style, crisp and incisive. He was a clever epigrammist and a forerunner of such American realists as Stephen CRANE. His contemporaries felt in him a force of genius that was never fully realized.

Bifrost (fr Icel, *bifa*, "tremble," *rost*, "path") In Scandinavian mythology, the rainbow bridge between Asgard, heaven, and Midgard, earth. The various colors of the rainbow were said to be reflections of its precious stones. Heimdall was keeper of the bridge, which was expected to collapse at Ragnarok under the weight of the onrushing sons of Muspelheim.

Big Bertha See KRUPP.

Big Brother A tyrannical political leader who assumes the role of protective elder brother. The term was invented by George Orwell. See 1984.

Bigelow, John (1817–1911) American writer and diplomat. Bigelow was co-owner and coeditor with William Cullen BRYANT of the New York *Evening Post* (1848–61) before he went to France, first as consul-general, then as minister (1861–66). During his tenure in France, he discovered Benjamin Franklin's *Autobiography* in manuscript, which he edited and published in 1868. His biography *Benjamin Franklin* was published in 1874. In the

same year, Bigelow was appointed secretary of state to the incoming governor of New York, Samuel J. Tilden. In 1888 Bigelow wrote a valuable historical study, *France and the Confederate Navy*. He later wrote biographies of William Cullen Bryant (1893) and Samuel J. Tilden (1895). His own autobiography is *Retrospections of an Active Life* (5 vols, 1909–13).

Big-Endians In Jonathan Swift's GULLIVER'S TRAVELS, a religious faction in the kingdom of LILLIPUT, who make it a matter of conscience to break their eggs at the big end. The Big-Endians are looked on as heretics by the orthodox party, who break theirs at the little end. The Big-Endians typify the Catholics, and the Little-Endians the Protestants.

Biggers, Earl Derr See CHAN, CHARLIE.

Biglow Papers, The (1848) A series of poems and prose sketches by James Russell LOWELL. A second series was issued during the Civil War and collected in 1867.

This work marks Lowell's first appearance as poet, abolitionist, and defender of American democracy. The first series is concerned with the Mexican War; the second treats the Civil War. The poems are written in dialect, while the accompanying prose remains in standard English. There are three central characters: Hosea Biglow, a forthright commentator on current affairs; his friend, Birdofredom Sawin, a scoundrel; and the Reverend Homer Wilbur, used by Lowell as a foil for the first two characters. The series satirizes politicians and their doctrines, the cowardice of editors, and the follies of the wealthy, North and South. More significant than his satire is Lowell's use of language. His treatment of Yankee dialect is an important contribution to the literature of the American language.

Big Money, The (1936) A novel by John DOS PASSOS, the last book in the trilogy *U.S.A.* (q.v.). The novel portrays the extravagance and corruption of the 1920s, culminating in the stock-market crash of 1929 and in the personal tragedy or moral defeat of several of the leading characters. There are short interspersed biographies of such men as Henry FORD, Frank Lloyd WRIGHT, William Randolph HEARST, and Rudolph Valentino.

Bildungsroman (Ger, "novel of education"; also called *Entwicklungsroman*, "novel of development") A type of novel, common in German literature, which treats the personal development of a single individual, usually in youth. The definitive example of the form is Goethe's *Wilhelm Meisters Lehrjahre* (*Wilhelm Meister's Apprenticeship*, 1795–96), which exercised an extremely strong influence on subsequent German novels. The *Bildungsroman* represents the culmination of a long tradition, but strictly speaking the term may not be applied to any work earlier than *Wilhelm Meister*. Both Wolfram's *Parzival* (early 13th century) and Grimmelshausen's *Simplizius Simplizissimus* (1668 et seq), though treating individual development, are primarily concerned with depicting a Christian world order, and Wieland's *Agathon* (1766) concentrates more on philosophical ideas than on personal development as such. Among the greatest 19th-century *Bildungsromane*, all of which were influenced by *Wilhelm Meister*, are Novalis's *Heinrich von Ofterdingen* (1802), Eichendorff's *Ahnung und Gegenwart* (*Presentiment and the Present*, 1815), Stifter's *Der Nachsommer* (*Indian Summer*, 1857), and Keller's GREEN HENRY. A 20th-century example is Mann's *The Magic Mountain* (1924). Among English novels, Dickens's *David Copperfield* (1850) shows the general characteristics of the form. See KÜNSTLERROMAN; WILHELM MEISTER.

Billings, Josh (pen name of Henry Wheeler Shaw, 1818–1885)   American auctioneer, real-estate agent, and humorist. After taking up many occupations, Shaw turned to writing humorous essays; after he studied the techniques of Artemus WARD and adopted cacography, he became famous. He published volumes of *Sayings* (1865, 1866) and a series of *Allminax* (1869–79). Among his other writings are *Josh Billings on Ice and Other Things* (1868), *Josh Billings' Struggling with Things* (1881), and *Josh Billings, His Works Complete* (4 vols, 1888). The Yankee humorist has been both highly praised and ignored; Charles H. Smith called him "Aesop and Ben Franklin, condensed and abridged."

Bill of Rights   The first ten amendments to the CONSTITUTION OF THE UNITED STATES, guaranteeing against infringement of civil liberties by the federal government. Among the rights guaranteed are freedom of speech, freedom of the press, freedom of religion, and right to trial by jury. The Bill of Rights became part of the Constitution on December 15, 1791.

The English Bill of Rights was first enacted in 1689. The spirit of this statute influenced constitutional development in other countries, including the U.S.

Billy Budd, Foretopman (pub 1924)   A novella by Herman MELVILLE. Billy, innocently good, is cruelly antagonized by Claggart, the evil master-at-arms. Unjustly accused before the captain by Claggart, Billy, speechless with rage, strikes the schemer and kills him. Captain Vere, who loves Billy as his son, decides that he must uphold law and hang the boy. Vere's first obligation is the preservation of social welfare; justice, rather than mercy, must be administered to maintain order. Billy, understanding, mounts the yardarm willingly, crying "God bless Captain Vere." The posthumously published book represents the final flowering of Melville the symbolist, his last statement on the collision of good and evil, a theme he contemplated throughout his life.

Binyon, [Robert] Lawrence (1869–1943)   English poet and art historian. Binyon is best known for his highly respected translation of Dante's DIVINE COMEDY (1933, 1943) into TERZA RIMA. His own restrained but deeply felt poetry includes *The North Star* (1941) and *The Burning of the Leaves* (1944), and his verse dramas, *Attila* (1907) and *Brief Candles* (1938). He also wrote several pioneering works on Oriental art and translated poems from the Japanese.

Biographia Literaria (2 vols, 1817)   A prose work by Samuel Taylor COLERIDGE. It contains essays on literary criticism and develops the author's distinction between FANCY AND IMAGINATION. The book also contains a discussion of the distinction between reason and understanding, an explanation of Coleridge's concept of a WILLING SUSPENSION OF DISBELIEF, a trenchant critical analysis of WORDSWORTH's poetry, and detailed discussions of portions of the philosophies of KANT, SCHELLING, and FICHTE.

Birches (1916)   A poem by Robert FROST. One of Frost's best-known poems, "Birches" describes the trees bent to the ground by ice storms; the poet imagines that they had been bent by a boy swinging on them and wishes, when he himself is "weary of considerations," to climb toward heaven in a birch tree "till the tree could bear no more,/ But dipped its top and set me down again."

Birds, The (Ornithes, 414 BC)   A comedy by ARISTOPHANES. Euelpides and Pithetaerus, fugitives from Athenian taxation and litigation, persuade the birds to found a city in the clouds, Nephelococcygia ("Cloud-cuckoo-land"). There they will be strategically placed to prevent the delightful smoke from the sacrifices of mortals from reaching the gods, unless the gods comply with the birds' demands. The plan is successful, the gods capitulate, and the birds and their two Athenian friends presumably live happily ever after. The comedy, filled with delightful fancies and lovely lyrics, is Aristophanes' masterpiece.

Birney, [Alfred] Earle (1904–   )   Canadian poet and novelist. Born in Alberta, Birney was a farm laborer, logger, and sailor before he went into academic life and began writing verse. *David and Other Poems* (1942) and *Now Is Time* (1945) brought him recognition, but his strong influence on contemporary Canadian poets began with his experimental poetry of the 1960s. Due in part to the influence of the BLACK MOUNTAIN POETS, he abandoned his earlier poetry of left-wing polemics for an apolitical poetry of fact, observation, and acceptance. *Rag and Bone Shop* (1971) and *What's So Big about Green?* (1973) established him as a leading Canadian practitioner of "concrete poetry." His *Selected Poems* was published in 1966, *Collected Poems* in 1975. Other volumes include *Ghost in the Wheels* (1977) and *Fall by Fury* (1978). Birney has also written two novels: *Turvey* (1949), a humorous World War II story, and *Down the Long Table* (1955), a satire of leftist opportunism in the 1930s.

Birrell, Augustine (1850–1933)   English essayist and statesman. A lawyer, professor of law, parliamentarian, and one-time chief secretary of Ireland (1907–16), Birrell is known for his essays on English authors and literature, OBITER DICTA, *Res Judicatae* (1892), *Collected Essays and*

Addresses (1922), and *More Obiter Dicta* (1924). These are usually acute, judicious, and trenchantly witty. He also wrote the biographies *Charlotte Brontë* (1885), *Hazlitt* (1902), and *Marvell* (1905).

Birthday Party, The (1958)   A three-act play by Harold PINTER, set in a seedy English boardinghouse by the sea. Stanley Webber, pampered by a maternal landlady, finds his comfortable life interrupted by the arrival of two sinister men, Goldberg and McCann, agents of a person or persons unknown, who ostensibly are looking for rooms. It becomes clear, however, that their mission is to intimidate Stanley. So successfully do they wield their mysterious authority, hurling questions and accusations at Stanley, that in the end they lead him, muted and broken, to a waiting car outside; but they, too, seem to be infected by the same fear and uncertainty they imposed on Stanley.

Birthmark, The (1846)   A story by Nathaniel HAW-THORNE. Aylmer, a scientist, insists on removing a small birthmark from the cheek of his otherwise perfect wife, Georgiana. He succeeds, but Georgiana, no longer human, dies. In his attempt to master nature, Aylmer has "rejected the best the earth could offer."

Birth of Tragedy from the Spirit of Music, The (Die Geburt der Tragödie aus dem Geiste der Musik, 1872)   A long philosophical essay by Friedrich NIETZSCHE. As a work of classical scholarship, it marks the final overthrow of WINCKELMANN's naïve conception of Greek culture as being perfectly static and blissful. Nietzsche sees in ancient Greece the tension and interaction of two opposed forces: the Apollonian, on the one hand, which corresponds to Winckelmann's ideas, and the dark, mysterious Dionysiac, on the other. In particular, he attempts to trace the development of Greek tragedy from the original Dionysiac chorus and to show its decline as a result of Euripides' and Socrates' excessive Apollonian rationalism. The book ends with the hope that modern German music, specifically that of Richard Wagner, might give birth to a new tragic age. Nietzsche's early idolization of Wagner is still strong here, but in 1876 he broke with the composer and later polemicized frequently against him. See APOL-LONIAN AND DIONYSIAC.

Bishop, Elizabeth (1911–1979)   American poet. Bishop's first book of poems was *North and South* (1946). In 1955 she reissued that book with *A Cold Spring*; the double volume was awarded the 1956 PULITZER PRIZE for poetry. She was an avid traveler, living in many parts of the world and finally settling in Brazil. She wrote a number of travel books, including *Questions of Travel* (1965) and *Brazil* (1967). Her poems are largely descriptive, written in a modern idiom with great stylistic subtlety. *Complete Poems*, published in 1969, won the National Book Award in 1970. *Geography III* (1977), a ten-poem picture of her life, seen through places she remembers, is meditative but vivid, spare almost to the point of austerity. Bishop was

considered by many a "poet's poet," but her deceptively simple style carries with it an undercurrent of tenderness that also touches less sophisticated readers. She edited *An Anthology of 20th Century Brazilian Poetry* (1972) with Emanuel Brasil.

Bitov, Andrei Georgiyevich (1937–   )   Soviet writer. Educated in Leningrad at the Institute of Mining Engineering, Bitov first gained widespread recognition in 1963, with the publication of *Bolshoy shar* (*The Big Balloon*), a collection of stories reflecting, through highly subtle and psychological insights, the growing awareness in children of life's mystery and beauty. Bitov continued his focus on youth in his short novel *Takoye dolgoye detstvo* (*Such a Long Childhood*, 1965), but he turned to broader, more philosophical themes in his novel *Pushkinsky dom* (*Pushkin's House*, 1978), which resounds with echoes of Russia's cultural and literary history yet has never been published in the Soviet Union. Bitov is now recognized as a major writer of his generation in the U.S.S.R.

Biyidi, Alexandre   See BETI, MONGO.

Bizet, Alexandre César Léopold (called Georges Bizet, 1838–1875)   French composer. Bizet's talent manifested itself at the age of seventeen, in a brilliant *Symphony in C*, which, however, was unknown and unperformed until 1935. His best work is for the stage, including the operas *Les Pêcheurs de perles* (*The Pearl Fishers*, 1863) and *La Jolie Fille de Perth* (*The Fair Maid of Perth*, 1867, after Walter SCOTT). His masterpiece and the finest work in the genre of OPÉRA COMIQUE is *Carmen* (1875; based on a story by MERIMÉE), which has remained one of the most popular of all operas.

Björnson, Björnstjerne (1832–1910)   Norwegian poet, novelist, and playwright. Björnson's interest in his people was first reflected in his "peasant novels" *Synnöve solbakken* (1857; tr *Trust and Trial*, 1881), *Arne* (1858; tr 1890), and *En glad gut* (1860; tr *A Happy Boy*, 1896). He carried his interest in Norwegian history and legend into his early plays, notably the trilogy of *Sigurd slembe* (1862; tr *Sigurd the Bastard*, 1888). A friend and rival of Henrik IBSEN, he also wrote plays of social realism which, though inferior to Ibsen's work, had greater popular success; the best of these are *Redaktøren* (1874; tr *The Editor*, 1914), *En fallit* (1875; tr *The Bankrupt*, 1914), and *Over ævne i* (1883; tr *Beyond Our Power*, 1913). Björnson also published two volumes of poetry: *Digte og sange* (1870; tr *Poems and Songs*, 1915) and *Arnljot Gelline* (1870), an epic. Among his later novels are *Det flager i byen og paa havnen* (1884; tr *Flags Are Flying in Town and Port*, 1892) and *Paa Guds veje* (1889; tr *In God's Way*, 1890), both of which are concerned with the problems of heredity and education. He was awarded the NOBEL PRIZE in Literature in 1903.

Black Beauty, The Autobiography of a Horse (1877)   An imaginary autobiography of the horse Black

Beauty, by Anna Sewell (1820–78). In describing the ill treatment the horse receives from a series of owners, the author pleads for humane treatment of animals.

Black Book, The (1936; pub Paris 1938, U.S. 1960) The first serious novel by Lawrence DURRELL. Showing the strong influence of Henry MILLER, it is the chaotically unstructured diary of Lawrence Lucifer, a school teacher living in a seedy London hotel. Its publication in the U.S. and England was delayed largely because of its crude and violent language. Though T. S. ELIOT, then an editor for Faber & Faber, admired the book greatly, he rejected it as too much ahead of its time. The book contains Durrell's reflections on sex and love and the horrible indignities that both can bring about, themes he developed more fully in later works, particularly the ALEXANDRIA QUARTET.

Blackburn, Paul (1926–1971)   American poet and translator. Blackburn's career as a poet was cut short by his untimely death at the age of forty-five. His brief years of productivity showed continued growth and excellence, marked by increasing attempts at new verse forms. As a practitioner of PROJECTIVE VERSE, he was often linked to the BLACK MOUNTAIN POETS. He spent a considerable part of his adult years in France and Spain, where he studied and translated the medieval Provençal poets. His own style was a fusion of his experiments with what he termed "the floating period" and a modern adaptation of the limpid sensuality of the Provençal poets. His volumes *Brooklyn-Manhattan Transit: A Bouquet for Flatbush* (1960) and *The Cities* (1967) are lyrical etchings of city life, ranging from pieces on religious processions in Spain to scenes in the New York City subway. His reputation was established with *In, On, Or About the Premises* (1968), in which he demonstrates a witty, satirical, and compassionate sense of humor and a mastery of verse rhythms. His *Collected Poems 1949–1966* was published in 1977.

Blackburn, Thomas (1916–1977)   English poet and critic. Among Blackburn's collections of mystical and visionary verse are *A Smell of Burning* (1961) and *The Fourth Man* (1971). *The Price of an Eye* (1961) contains essays on poetry.

Blackfriars   The name of two successive London theatres, both housed in the same building of an old Black Friars' monastery between Ludgate Hill and the Thames. The building was first leased as a theatre (1576) by Sir William More to the Master of The Children of Windsor Chapel, for the public performance of their plays before production at Court, and was used by them until 1584.

The second Blackfriars Theatre was housed in the same building after James Burbage's purchase (1596) of the property from More. After Burbage's death (1597), the property belonged to his son Richard, who leased it (1600) to Henry Evans and Nathaniel Giles for performances by the Children of the Chapel. Evans gave up his lease in 1608, and Burbage formed a company of owners consisting of him-

self, his brother Cuthbert, four of the King's Men (Shakespeare, Heminge, Condell, and Sly), and Thomas Evans. In 1609 the King's Men moved into their new theatre, which became the center of the WAR OF THE THEATRES. Beaumont and Fletcher's plays and Shakespeare's last plays date from this time.

Blackfriars remained in operation as a theatre until 1642, when all the theatres were closed. The building was dismantled in 1655. Until very recently, the site was occupied by the offices of the *Times* of London.

black humor   A substantial aspect of the THEATRE OF THE ABSURD and of much modern fiction. The term describes sardonically humorous effects derived from mordant wit and morbid or grotesque situations that deal with anxiety, suffering, or death. The tone is often one of resignation, anger, or bitterness.

Black Mass   See SATANISM.

Black Mischief (1932)   A novel by Evelyn WAUGH. It is a farcical satire on various attempts to "civilize" a primitive country. The emperor himself introduces boots and contraceptives, which his subjects eat. The English and French try to take over the country; in the course of their efforts, the hero, at a native banquet, is given some of his girlfriend to eat.

Blackmore, Richard Doddridge (1825–1900) English novelist. Blackmore wrote a number of novels of romance and adventure, of which LORNA DOONE is best known. His books are particularly notable for their secondary characters and for descriptions of England's West Country, in which many of them are set. Among his other works are *Craddock Nowell* (1866), *Clara Vaughan* (1864), and *Christowell* (1882).

Black Mountain Poets, The   A group of poets affiliated with the experimental Black Mountain College in North Carolina during the early 1950s. Consolidated by a mutual ideology, they developed a poetic form known as PROJECTIVE VERSE. Charles OLSON, the central figure of the group, outlined the poetic theory in his essay "Projective Verse" (1950). He advocated a verse form that restores the oral or bardic aspect to poetry. The individual poet's breath rhythm was the factor dictating the poem's form; this produced varied spatial and typographical formulations for the compositions. Olson described this technique as "composition by field."

The cluster of poets associated with Olson were Robert CREELEY, Robert DUNCAN, Ed DORN, Paul BLACKBURN, and Denise LEVERTOV. Although there are vast variations in their styles, they all, for a time, adhered to Olson's prosodic doctrines. Olson's use of anthropological, geographical, and historical material to construct a "mythos of place" was also adapted by the others in varying degrees. Two magazines, *Black Mountain Review* and *Origin*, served as outlets for their work. By the mid-1960s, the group had realized their objectives. They dispersed and entered the larger poetic mainstream, in which political, antiwar, and ecological concerns outweighed factional artistic movements.

Blackmur, R[ichard] P[almer] (1904–1965) American critic and poet. An astute student of 20th-century British and American poetry, Blackmur is known for his penetrating analyses of the nature of poetry and the function of the literary critic. Although he had no formal schooling after high school, Blackmur was an influential theorist of the NEW CRITICISM in his capacity as professor of English at Princeton. In *The Double Agent* (1935), he argued that form *and* content comprise the meaning of modern poetry. In the title essay of *Language As Gesture* (1952), he described linguistic gesture as "the outward dramatic play of inward and imaged meaning." Among his works are *The Expense of Greatness* (1940), *The Lion and the Honeycomb* (1955), *New Criticism in the United States* (1959), and the posthumously published *A Primer of Ignorance* (1967) and *Poems by R. P. Blackmur* (1978).

Black Riders and Other Lines, The (1895)   A book of poems by Stephen Crane. Partly inspired by the work of Emily DICKINSON, the "other lines" of this collection are often epigrammatic parables written in terse, economically phrased free verse. The title poem comes from a boyhood experience in which Crane, after watching the waves beat against the shore, dreamed of black riders on black horses galloping up out of the water. In *Stephen Crane: A Critical Biography* (1950), John BERRYMAN pointed out that the dream held great significance for Crane throughout his life.

Blackstone, Sir William (1723–1780)   English jurist. The famous *Commentaries* (1765–69) bearing Blackstone's name were for more than a century fundamental in any study of English law. Hence *Blackstone* is synonymous with the law.

Black Tulip, The (La Tulipe noire, 1895)   A historical romance by Alexandre DUMAS. Set in Holland in the 17th century, the tale revolves about the struggle between two political factions.

Blackwood, Algernon (1869–1951)   English novelist and short-story writer. Blackwood's first published book, *The Empty House* (1906), was a collection of ghost stories. His early interest in psychic phenomena is reflected in his novels, *Jimbo* (1909), *The Centaur* (1911), and *A Prisoner in Fairyland* (1913). His many other collections of stories include *Pan's Garden* (1912), *The Dance of Death* (1927), and *Tales of the Uncanny and Supernatural* (1949).

Blackwood's Magazine   A Scottish literary magazine, founded in 1817. *Blackwood's* was strongly Tory in its political sympathies and violently opposed in its literary outlook to the so-called COCKNEY SCHOOL of poets. John Gibson Lockhart and James Hogg were well-known and influential members of the *Blackwood's* staff.

Blair, Eric   See ORWELL, GEORGE.

Blais, Marie-Claire (1939–   )   Quebec novelist and poet. Blais's first two novels, *La Belle Bête* (1959; tr *Mad Shadows*, 1960) and *Tête blanche* (1960; tr 1961) earned her critical acclaim for the lyric beauty with which she wrote of the fate of children in a bleak, bigoted, claustrophobic Quebec. In these early novels and in the highly esteemed *Une Saison dans la vie d'Emmanuel* (1965; tr *A Season in the Life of Emmanuel*, 1966) and *L'Insoumise* (1966; tr *The Fugitive*, 1978), a monstrous world of brutal parents and perverted priests corrupts the young, whose only escape is into mysticism, dreams, or death. *Les Manuscrits de Pauline Archange* (1968), *Vivre! Vivre!* (1969; tr together with the preceding as *The Manuscripts of Pauline Archange*, 1970), and *Les Apparences* (1970) present revolt and freedom as a possible alternative for its young heroine. Marking a further affirmative trend, *Un Joualonais sa joualonie* (1973; tr *St. Lawrence Blues*, 1974) is a comic invention celebrating the liberation of Quebec from its past. Blais's two volumes of poetry, *Pays voilés* (1963) and *Existences* (1964), date from her years in France and the U.S., before the new cultural and political climate in Quebec drew her back to her homeland.

Blake, Nicholas   The pen name under which C. DAY LEWIS wrote detective stories.

Blake, William (1757–1827)   English poet, engraver, painter, and mystic. Apprenticed in 1771 to an engraver, Blake later illustrated his own work with copperplate engravings and watercolors. He also illustrated Young's *Night Thoughts*, Gray's *Poems*, the book of Job, and Dante's *Divine Comedy*. As a poet, he is known for his mysticism and complex, sometimes obscure symbolism. His visionary world is extremely important to his work. An antinomian, he bypasses the Church and experiences God directly; from boyhood on, he had visions and from them created his personal mythology, of which URIZEN is a part. As his devoted wife remarked, "I have very little of Mr. Blake's company; he is always in Paradise." His works, in some of which both text and illustrations were engraved, include *Poetical Sketches* (1783); SONGS OF INNOCENCE and SONGS OF EXPERIENCE; and the so-called prophetic books, including THE BOOK OF THEL, THE MARRIAGE OF HEAVEN AND HELL, *The Gates of Paradise* (1793), *The Visions of the Daughters of Albion* (1793), *The Song of Los*, and *The Book of Los* (both 1795). He also wrote JERUSALEM, *The Emanation of the Giant Albion* (1804), and MILTON.

Blanchefleur   See FLORES AND BLANCHEFLEUR.

Blanchot, Maurice (1907–   )   French critic and fiction writer. Sharing affinities with MALLARMÉ and KAFKA, Blanchot displays highly abstruse, metaphysical thinking about language, the solitude of the artist, the absurdity of existence, and death. In his critical writings, such as *L'Espace littéraire* (1955; tr *The Space of Literature*, 1982), *Le Livre à venir* (1959), *L'Amitié* (1971), and

Le Pas au-delà (1973), he develops approaches to the origins and contradictions of artistic creation. Blanchot's works of fiction, including *Thomas l'obscur* (1941; rev 1950, 1971; tr *Thomas the Obscure*, 1973), *Aminadab* (1942), *Le Très-Haut* (1948), and *L'Arrêt de mort* (1948; tr *Death Sentence*, 1978), are austere meditations on the interpenetrations within language of the self, the other, and nothingness. In a simple yet hauntingly elliptical prose, Blanchot's work elaborates the striving for a Nietzschean "willed moment" that can overcome while embracing the paradoxes central to writing and consciousness.

Blanco Fombona, Rufino (1874–1944)   Venezuelan novelist, short-story writer, poet, and essayist. Blanco Fombona was an exile during the long dictatorship of Juan Vicente Gómez, returning to Venezuela after the latter's death in 1935. His writing reflects his angry dismay at the stupidity, iniquity, and sordidness that he seemed to find everywhere. Accordingly his novels are weakened by bits of heavy-handed social satire and political propaganda. They include *El hombre de hierro* (1907), which depicts the triumph of evil over virtue; *El hombre de oro* (*The Man of Gold*, 1916), which exposes the venality and incompetence of Venezuelan politicians; and *La mitra en la mano* (1927), the story of an ambitious priest, a character that has been called a Venezuelan Elmer Gantry. *Cuentos americanos* (1904) and *Dramas mínimos* (1920) are his best-known collections of short stories. His poetry, which includes the collections *Pequeña ópera lírica* (1904) and *Cantos de la prisión y del destierro* (1911), shows the influence of MODERNISMO. Among his other works are *Letras y letrados de Hispano-América* (1908) and *Grandes escritores de América* (1917), literary criticism; *La lámpara de Aladino* (1915), autobiographical sketches; and *El conquistador español en el siglo XVI* (1922), a study of the Spanish conquerors. Blanco Fombona also edited the letters of Simon Bolívar, and he edited and published several series of great American books.

blank verse   In prosody, unrhymed verse. In English, the term usually means unrhymed iambic pentameter. In classical prosody, rhyme was not used at all; with the introduction of rhyme in the Middle Ages, blank verse disappeared. It was reintroduced in the 16th century and in England became the standard medium of dramatic poetry and frequently of epic poetry. Shakespeare's plays, for example, are written mostly in blank verse.

Blasco Ibañez, Vicente (1867–1928)   Spanish novelist. Blasco Ibañez's early, naturalistic novels, dealing with life in his native Valencia, are generally considered his best; these include *La barraca* (*The Cabin*, 1898) and *Cañas y barro* (*Reeds and Mud*, 1902). Later he wrote the novels that won him great popularity and financial rewards, perhaps at the expense of his literary reputation. Among these are *Los cuatro jinetes del Apocalipsis* (*The Four Horsemen of the Apocalypse*, 1916), a World War I story, and *Sangre y arena* (*Blood and Sand*, 1909).

Blast   A two-issue magazine (1914–15) edited by Wyndham LEWIS in association with Ezra POUND. In unconventional typography, it advocated VORTICISM in art and literature. See LITTLE MAGAZINES.

Blaue Reiter, Der (Ger, "The Blue Rider")   An association of artists formed in Munich around Wassily KANDINSKY and Franz Marc (1880–1916). In 1911 Kandinsky and Marc prepared a compendium of artistic studies, entitled *Der blaue Reiter*, in which they announced their aim of demonstrating how the "inner desire of the artist expresses itself in different ways." In the same year, they mounted an exhibition of their work, along with such other artists as Henri ROUSSEAU and the composer Harold SCHOENBERG. In 1912 the group was enlarged to include the BRÜCKE artists, Georges BRAQUE, PICASSO, Casimir MALEVICH, and Paul KLEE, among others. The group's yearbook of 1912 reveals its iconoclastic spirit, and many avant-garde movements of the time, such as CUBISM, are introduced in its pages.

The group dispersed in 1914, at the outbreak of World War I, but continued to be known as the most fruitful association of artists in prewar Germany.

Blavatsky, Helena Petrovna (called Mme Blavatsky, 1831–1891)   Russian-born spiritualist medium, magician, and occultist. Blavatsky founded the Theosophical Society. She wrote *Isis Unveiled* (1877) and *The Secret Doctrine* (1888), influential books of occult lore. She toured India, Europe, and the U.S., developing and preaching her doctrines. The poet William Butler Yeats was profoundly influenced by her work. See THEOSOPHY.

Bleak House (1852)   A novel by Charles DICKENS. The heroine is Esther Summerson, or rather Esther Hawdon, illegitimate daughter of Lady Dedlock and Captain Hawdon; Esther herself does not know her origins, and Lady Dedlock believes Esther to be dead. A ward of Mr. Jarndyce, Esther lives with him at Bleak House. Sir Leicester Dedlock's lawyer, Mr. Tulkinghorn, begins to suspect Lady Dedlock's secret past and unravels it; when Tulkinghorn is found dead, Lady Dedlock is suspected; she disappears and is later found dead. Tulkinghorn was actually killed by Lady Dedlock's maid, a fact uncovered by the wily detective, Mr. Bucket. Esther ultimately marries Dr. Woodcourt.

In the background of the novel is the interminable suit of *Jarndyce* vs. *Jarndyce*. Beginning as a dispute as to how the trusts under a Jarndyce will were to be administered, the suit drags on from year to year, from generation to generation. Two of the heirs are Richard Carstone and Ada Clare, his pretty cousin, who marry and live at Bleak House with John Jarndyce and Esther. When the case is finally settled, it is in Carstone's favor, but all the funds have been dissipated by the litigation. Carstone dies and Ada lives on at Bleak House with their son.

In this novel, Dickens attacks the delays and archaic absurdities of the courts, which he knew about firsthand from his frustrating and unprofitable experience of trying to sue the pirate publishers of "A Christmas Carol." See JEL-LYBY, MRS.; SKIMPOLE, HAROLD.

Blefescu   In Jonathan Swift's GULLIVER'S TRAVELS, an island, northeast of LILLIPUT, inhabited by pygmies. It is supposed to represent France.

Blenheim, battle of   During the War of the Spanish Succession, the battle (1704) in which John Churchill, duke of MARLBOROUGH, defeated Marshal Tallard at Blenheim on the upper Danube. It was the most resounding and decisive victory enjoyed by the British on the Continent since Agincourt. Louis XIV's schemes for pushing his frontiers up to the Rhine were thus thwarted, and French prestige was badly shaken. The poem "The Battle of Blenheim" (1798) was written by Robert Southey.

Blenheim Steps   The site of an anatomical school on Bond Street in London, over which Sir Astley Cooper presided. Here "resurrectionists" were sure to find a ready mart for their gruesome wares, for which they received sums of money varying from £3 to £10, and sometimes more. Hence, *going to Blenheim Steps* means going to be dissected or being unearthed from one's grave.

Blessed Damozel, The (1850)   A poem by Dante Gabriel ROSSETTI, giving expression to the longing of the "blessed damozel" in heaven for her lover on earth.

Blest Gana, Alberto (1830–1920)   Chilean novelist. One of the outstanding realists of Latin-American fiction, Blest Gana, who spent many years in France, sought to be the Balzac of Chile. His best-known novel is *Martín Rivas* (1862). Dealing with the experiences of an impoverished provincial youth who falls in love with a girl of the aristocracy, the work gives an incisive, satirical view of Chilean society in the 1850s. Other works by Blest Gana include *Durante la reconquista* (1897), an epic of Chile's struggle for independence, and *Los transplantados* (1904), which depicts decadent Chilean émigrés in Paris.

Bligh, William (1754–1817)   English admiral and master of H.M.S. *Bounty*. Having sailed with Captain Cook on his second expedition, when the breadfruit tree was discovered, Bligh was sent in 1787 on the *Bounty* to acquire specimens of the tropical tree for transplantation in the West Indies. His extreme severity led to mutiny, and Bligh, with eighteen others, was set adrift. He succeeded in navigating nearly four thousand miles of open sea and lived to carry out his original mission. His adventure is known from Byron's poem "The Island" and from a trilogy of novels by Charles Nordhoff and James Norman Hall, beginning with MUTINY ON THE BOUNTY. Bligh published his own account of the events in A *Narrative of the Mutiny* (1790).

Blind Bard (or Blind Poet)   An epithet frequently applied to Homer. The tradition of Homer's blindness may possibly be related to that of Demodocus, the blind rhapsode at the court of Alcinous, in the *Odyssey*.

Blish, James [Benjamin] (1921–1975)   American science-fiction author. Blish was the author of numerous short stories, including "Surface Tension" (1952), which is about life in the microcosm; his best work appears in two tetralogies: the Spenglerian *Cities in Flight* (1955–62), in which Earth's cities roam the universe looking for work, and the somewhat miscellaneous *After Such Knowledge*, which is concerned with the relationship between religious and scientific knowledge. The latter series includes the much admired A *Case of Conscience* (1958) and the fine historical novel about Roger Bacon, *Doctor Mirabilis* (1964). Blish also wrote a number of children's books and novelizations of the television series *Star Trek*. Under the name William Atheling, Jr., he produced two important early works of science-fiction criticism: *The Issue at Hand* (1964) and *More Issues at Hand* (1970). *The Best of James Blish* was published in 1979.

Bliss (1920)   The title story in a collection by Katherine MANSFIELD. It describes a blissful afternoon and evening in the life of Bertha Young, who loves her husband, her baby, and her home. In an ironic ending typical of Mansfield's work, Bertha discovers that her husband is being unfaithful to her.

Blithedale Romance, The (1852)   A novel by Nathaniel HAWTHORNE. Blithedale, a Utopian community, is modeled on BROOK FARM, the Transcendentalist experiment at West Roxbury, Massachusetts, in which Hawthorne had participated ten years before he wrote the novel. Miles Coverdale, the narrator, is a coldly inquisitive observer; in revealing his knowledge of the other members of the community, he reveals himself. Zenobia, a dark, queenly woman, is in love with Hollingsworth, an egoistic reformer who plans to convert Blithedale into an experiment in prison reform.

Priscilla, a pale innocent girl, fallen under the evil influence of the mesmerist Westervelt, has performed as the Veiled Lady of Zenobia's story. Taking refuge at Blithedale, she is revealed to be the half-sister of Zenobia. When Hollingsworth admits his love for Priscilla, Zenobia drowns herself. Hollingsworth, shocked by the experience, abandons his schemes, depending on Priscilla for strength. Coverdale, in the final chapter, admits that he, too, had always loved Priscilla. See FULLER, MARGARET.

Blixen, Baroness Karen   See DINESEN, ISAK.

Bloch, Ernest (1880–1959)   Swiss-born American composer. Many of Bloch's works have a Hebraic flavor derived from traditional Jewish melodies and modes, as in his cello rhapsody, *Schelomo* (1916). His *Concerto Grosso No. 1* (1925) is a typical example of the return to old forms, engendered by neoclassicism.

Blok, Aleksandr Aleksandrovich (1880–1921)
Russian poet. The greatest of the Russian SYMBOLISTS, Blok
is generally ranked as one of the half-dozen major poets in
Russian literature. Blok's early poems *Stikhi o prekrasnoi
damye* (*Songs of the Beautiful Lady*, 1904) are hymns to a
mystical vision of Sophia, a tendency originating with the
philosopher Vladimir SOLOVYOV that played a large role in
Russian symbolist poetry. Blok's loss of faith in his mystical
experience of the eternal feminine was reflected in later
poetry and plays, which grew increasingly bitter, gloomy,
and ironic. In his lyrical drama *Balaganchik* (*The Puppet
Show*, 1905), he ridiculed his former beliefs. Another play,
Neznakomka (*The Stranger*, 1906), depicts the former
Beautiful Lady as a common prostitute. A poem of this
title, written at the same time, expresses Blok's wish to
escape the pain of his disappointment in drink. He also
attempted to find solace in love affairs, although toward the
end of his life he claimed that he had had only two loves in
his life: his wife Lyubov (a daughter of the scientist Mende-
leyev) "and all the others."

Bloc's masterpiece is his long poem THE TWELVE, an
impressionistic picture of St. Petersburg during the early
days of the revolution. Another well-known work is *Skify*
(*The Scythians*, 1918), an address of both challenge and
proffered friendship to the West from the new revolutionary Russia. Blok worked on a long autobiographical poem,
Vozmezdiye (*Retribution*), from 1910 until his death, completing one chapter and parts of two others.

Blok's standing as one of the greatest Russian poets is
based on a large body of lyrics, several excellent verse dramas, and his long poem *The Twelve*. His importance as an
innovator in Russian prosody is also great. He created the
new accentual verse in Russian known as *dolniki*, which is
based only on the number of stresses per line, allowing any
number of unstressed syllables between the stresses. This
break with the classic prosody of syllabic-accentual verse,
which took into account both stressed and unstressed syllables, introduced a new freedom into modern Russian
poetry, which was used to good account by later poets such
as MAYAKOVSKY, ESENIN, and Anna AKHMATOVA.

Blood Wedding   See GARCÍA LORCA, FEDERICO.

Bloody Assizes   The popular name for the trials
conducted in England in 1685 by Lord Chief Justice
George Jeffreys after the collapse of Monmouth's Rebellion. Hundreds of both actual and presumed supporters of
the duke of MONMOUTH were executed or sold into West-
Indian slavery. The trials, which were brief, brutal, and
flagrantly unjust, became a byword for relentless cruelty.

Bloody Mary   See MARY I.

Bloom, Leopold   The central character in James
Joyce's novel ULYSSES. Bloom is an advertising canvasser of
Jewish origin, living in Dublin. He is an unheroic but
affirmative character, whose wanderings about Dublin are
ironically contrasted with the epic voyage of Ulysses.

Bloom is humane and generous, self-conscious and guilt-
ridden; throughout the book his quest for love is frustrated
and his best instincts are stifled. Only through his
daydreams does Bloom find fulfillment as a social, political, and ethical human being. His rejection by Ireland may
thus be seen as Joyce's indictment of a culture that is only
artificially civilized. Symbolically, Bloom is linked to a
variety of literary and historical figures, among them, Elijah, Moses, and Jesus.

Bloom, Molly   One of the three chief characters in
James Joyce's novel ULYSSES. Molly is the wife of Leopold
BLOOM, to whom she is unfaithful. A sardonic counterpart
of Penelope in the *Odyssey*, she is a sensual, intuitive
woman, for Joyce a symbol of the universal feminine principle. The final section of the novel consists of her famous
STREAM OF CONSCIOUSNESS monologue, a single uninterrupted sentence, ending in an affirmation of life: "Yes."

Bloomsbury Group, The   A group of English
writers and artists who gathered regularly in the Bloomsbury section of London before, during, and after World
War I. Their unconventional life-style, socialist views, and
aesthetic sensibility combined to give "Bloomsbury" a connotation outside the circle of somewhat precious snobbery.
Central to the group were artists Vanessa and Clive BELL,
Roger FRY, and Duncan Grant; writers Leonard and Virginia WOOLF, Lytton STRACHEY, and E. M. FORSTER; and
the economist John Maynard KEYNES. Cambridge educated and the artistic and intellectual pace-setters of their
generation, they were devoted adherents of the philosopher
G. E. MOORE and were frequently joined at their "Thursday evenings" by such Cambridge luminaries as Bertrand
RUSSELL and Rupert BROOKE.

Bloudy Tenent, The (1644)   A tract pleading for
religious toleration, written by Roger WILLIAMS during a
controversy with John COTTON. Its full title is *The Bloudy
Tenent of Persecution, for Cause of Conscience, Discussed
in a Conference between Truth and Peace*. It urges freedom
of belief for Catholics, Jews, and pagans, as well as for
Protestants. An advocate of democracy in government,
Williams also declared that the "foundation of civill power
lies in the people." Cotton wrote a reply entitled *The
Bloudy Tenent, Washed, and Made White in the Bloud of
the Lamb* (1647). Williams rejoined with *The Bloudy
Tenent Yet More Bloudy by Mr. Cotton's Endeavour to
Wash it White in the Bloud of the Lamb* (1652), in which
he reaffirmed that each man must believe what his conscience tells him. Both writings are considered to be among
the most forceful and eloquent prose written in the American colonies in the 17th century.

Bluebeard   The villain of the tale "Barbe-bleue"
(1697) by Charles PERRAULT in his CONTES DE MA MÈRE
L'OYE. Bluebeard entrusts the keys of his castle to each of
his new brides in turn, with the warning not to open a door
behind which, unknown to them, bodies are strewn. None

can restrain her curiosity, and Bluebeard murders six wives for their disobedience before the seventh bride has the good fortune to escape him. Based on the crimes of the murderer Gilles de RETZ, the Bluebeard story has been the basis for numerous burlesques and dramatizations. Maurice Maeterlinck made it the subject of his *Ariane et Barbe-bleue* (1901).

Béla BARTÓK's opera *Duke Bluebeard's Castle* (1911) was composed to a libretto by Béla Balász, in which the horrific elements of the tale were minimized and Bluebeard became a discontented, searching philosopher. Jacques OFFENBACH's operetta *Barbe-Bleue* (1866) was a rollicking burlesque, based only loosely on the Bluebeard theme.

Blue Hotel, The (1899)   A short story by Stephen CRANE. First published in *The Monster and Other Stories*, it is one of Crane's finest. A Swede comes to a Nebraska hotel, his mind filled with the romantic violence of Western DIME NOVELS. Expecting violence, he finally provokes it, leaves the hotel, and is eventually killed in another fight in a bar. The question of who was responsible for the Swede's death gives rise to a heated argument among the characters, one of whom remarks, "Every sin is the result of a collaboration." The point of the story, however, may not be the moral complicity of the characters, but rather the inexplicable mystery of a universe which, like the blizzard that rages outside throughout the story, cares nothing for man's fate.

Blue Rider   See BLAUE REITER, DER.

Blues and Grays   In the American Civil War, the Union and Confederate forces, respectively, from the color of their uniforms. "The Blue and the Gray" (1867), a sentimental poem by Francis Miles Finch, which was often recited at Memorial Day ceremonies, was inspired by women in Columbus, Mississippi, who strewed flowers over the graves of both Union and Confederate dead.

bluestocking   A female pedant; a woman of pretentious intellectual interests. The term derives from meetings (c1750) that took place at the home of Elizabeth Montagu (1720–1800), where literary discussions replaced card games and gossip. Evidently one of the guests, a Mr. Benjamin Stillingfleet, always wore blue stockings (rather than the customary white for formal wear); hence the derisive reference to the group as the "Bluestocking Club."

Blunden, Edmund (1896–1974)   English poet and critic. Associated with the GEORGIAN poets, Blunden wrote mainly nature poetry inspired by the English countryside. He received the Military Cross in World War I; his *Undertones of War* (1928) is one of the major works of wartime poetic and prose reminiscence. His volumes of poetry include *The Shepherd* (1922), *Shells by a Stream* (1944), *Poems of Many Years* (1957), and *A Hong Kong House* (1962). The last is a reflection of the many years he spent as a lecturer in Hong Kong.

Blunt, Wilfrid Scawen (1840–1922)   English poet, author, diplomat, and explorer. Blunt traveled in a diplomatic and private capacity throughout Europe, the Near East, and India. He was bitterly opposed to 19th-century British policies of imperialism and exploitation and once served a prison term for an inflammatory speech in Ireland. His best poems, a few lyrics from *Love Sonnets of Proteus* (1880) and *A New Pilgrimage* (1889), survive through their genuine force, pathos, and subtlety. Blunt also wrote long political poems, such as *The Wind and the Whirlwind* (1883) and *Satan Absolved* (1899). Of his numerous prose works—mostly dealing with injustices of the British Empire—the most interesting are the famous *My Diaries, 1888–1914* (1920–21), which were withdrawn by their publisher because of their revelations of British secret diplomacy. *The Poetical Works* (2 vols) appeared in 1914.

Bly, Nelly   See SEAMAN, ELIZABETH COCHRANE.

Bly, Robert [Elwood] (1926–   )   American poet, editor, and translator. Born in Minnesota, Bly writes poetry characterized by vivid regional description and a generally antirationalist philosophy, which he ascribes to the influence of C. G. JUNG. His most distinguished volumes of poetry include *Silence in the Snowy Fields* (1962), *The Light Around the Body* (1967), for which he won the National Book Award in 1968, and *Sleepers Joining Hands* (1973). In these volumes, Bly employs the "deep image," a stylistic device whereby the unconscious is manifested in a surrealistic mode. Bly's dominant images —darkness, water, and death—are thematically functional. He writes of the death of rational or material man, in order that the true inner man may live. In the late 1960s, he wrote fiercely polemical poems against the Vietnam war. As founder-editor of the magazine *The Seventies* (formerly *The Fifties* and *The Sixties*), he publicized and translated poets whose philosophic and aesthetic leanings were congenial to his own. Recent works published include *This Tree Will Be Here for a Thousand Years* (1979), considered to be a late sequel to *Silence in the Snowy Fields*, and *Waking from Newton's Sleep: Selected Essays of Literary Imagination* (1986).

Boadicea (d AD 62)   Celtic queen of the Iceni, Britons of Norfolk and Suffolk. Also known as the Warrior Queen, Boadicea rebelled against Roman rule, taking poison after being defeated in battle when the revolt was quelled.

Boanerges (Gr, "sons of thunder")   Jesus' name (Mark 3:17) for his disciples James and John, because they wanted to call "fire to come down from heaven" to consume the Samaritans for not "receiving" Jesus (Luke 9:54).

Boar's Head Tavern   A London tavern. The Boar's Head was made immortal by Shakespeare in HENRY IV, as the favorite haunt of Prince Hal and Sir John Falstaff. The tavern was located in Eastcheap, on the site of the present statue of William IV, and was in existence until 1831.

Boas, Franz (1858–1942)   German-born American anthropologist. The most influential figure in the development of American anthropology, Boas came to North America in 1883 on an expedition to study the Eskimo culture on Baffin Island. From 1886 to 1889, while at Clark University, he studied the Indians of British Columbia. By 1899 Boas was professor of anthropology, a new department at Columbia University. During his thirty-seven years of teaching there and consulting at the American Museum of Natural History, he shaped American anthropology, emphasizing linguistic analysis and rigorous scientific method. Among his many works are *The Mind of Primitive Man* (1911; rev 1938), *Anthropology and Modern Life* (1928; rev 1932), and several volumes of collected papers, including *Race and Democratic Society* (1945). His student and eminent colleague Ruth Benedict was the teacher of Margaret MEAD.

Bobadil, Captain   A character in Ben Jonson's comedy EVERY MAN IN HIS HUMOUR. A military braggart, Bobadil is an ignorant, clever bully, completely cowardly, but is thought by his dupes to be an amazing hero.

Boccaccio, Giovanni (1313–1375)   Italian prose writer and poet. Boccaccio was born at Certaldo (or possibly, as he hinted in one of his works, at Paris) and spent part of his youth at Naples (1327–41). He enjoyed fashionable Neapolitan society, but not his father's merchant trade and the study of the law. From 1341 to his death, he was mainly at Florence, where he pursued his chosen career as a man of letters. His prolific output, including many works of prose and poetry that were the first of their kind in Italian or European literature, entitle him to a place beside Petrarch as a founder of the Italian Renaissance. His scholarly works in Latin were written mainly toward the end of his life, when a spiritual crisis persuaded him to reject all vernacular writing as sinful. While not enjoying the popularity of his earlier efforts, these Latin works, with their interest in classical antiquity, were seminal in the growth of Humanism. Of the same order are his attempts to have Homer translated and made more accessible at a time when few knew Greek. On the recommendation of his close friend Petrarch, he supported an incompetent Greek scholar in his own home until a bad translation was completed. Still loyal to the vernacular tradition, he also lectured on Dante and wrote a eulogy of him during that final period.

In chronological order, his Italian works are as follows: *Caccia di Diana* (*Diana's Hunt*), the first Italian hunting poem in *terza rima*, written 1334–36; the prose romance FILOCOLO, including the THIRTEEN QUESTIONS OF LOVE; the FILOSTRATO, a romance in *ottava rima* and the first of its kind written by a man of letters; the TESEIDA, in octaves, the first Tuscan epic; the *Ameto* (1341–42), a prose

romance with pastoral setting and characters; the *Amoroso visione* (1342–43), an allegorical poem in *terzine*; FIAMMETTA, a psychological romance whose heroine may be a real woman or the poetic equivalent of Beatrice and Laura; the *Ninfale Fiesolano* (1346), the first Italian idyll, done in octaves; the DECAMERON, his most famous work; the *Corbaccio* (1366), a satire against women; the eulogy of Dante; and a commentary on the *Divine Comedy*. The Latin works of the final period were *De casibus virorum illustrium* (*The Fate of Illustrious Men*), *De claris mulieribus* (*On Famous Women*), and *De genealogiis deorum gentilium* (*Genealogies of the Pagan Gods*), whose thirteenth book contains a defense of poetry.

Bodas de sangre   See GARCÍA LORCA, FEDERICO.

Bodenheim, Maxwell (1893–1954)   American poet and novelist. One of the most notorious of the Bohemians who came to Greenwich Village during the 1920s, Bodenheim was influenced in his early work by the romanticists and imagists, but later, for example in his novel *Lights in the Valley* (1942), he espoused various proletarian causes. Among his volumes of poetry are *Introducing Irony* (1922), *Bringing Jazz* (1930), and *Selected Poems, 1914–1944* (1946). *Crazy Man* (1924), *Sixty Seconds* (1929), and *Naked on Roller Skates* (1929) are novels. Bodenheim carried on several feuds with his literary contemporaries, the most famous one being with Ben HECHT. In 1954 he and his third wife were found murdered in a dingy, heatless room.

bodhisattva (Sans, "being of wisdom")   In Buddhism, one who has attained the status of a Buddha but who postpones his entry to Buddhahood in order to assist others in their quest for the Truth.

Bodin, Jean (1530–1596)   French lawyer and political philosopher. Bodin is noted for his *Six Books of a Republic* (1576) and his *Method for the Easy Comprehension of History* (1566). Almost alone among 16th-century thinkers, Bodin attempted to devise a comprehensive theory of political society that would reconcile liberty and subjection, yet satisfy conscience and reason, without regard to divine or supernatural sanction.

Two principles are evident in his political philosophy. Political sovereignty is defined in terms of power: the state consists of a relation between political inferiors and a political superior, and law is a command from the latter to the former. For Bodin, it was necessary to see this relation as consonant with conscience. Therefore, he affirmed that both the sovereign, or political superior, and the subject, or political inferior, were bound by natural law: the sovereign, to command in accordance with justice; the subject, to obey in accordance with justice. These two principles were further developed by illustrious political philosophers later. Bodin's theory of sovereignty found favor with HOBBES, and his conception of natural law as an ethical foundation for the state was greatly expanded on by GROTIUS and LOCKE.

Bodleian Library   A celebrated library at Oxford University. Projected by Sir Thomas Bodley in 1598, it was opened in 1602. It is famous for its collection of rare books and valuable manuscripts.

Body of Liberties, The (1641)   A code of laws for the government of the Massachusetts colony, combining the common law of England with the Mosaic law. Prepared by a committee led by Nathaniel WARD, it is ranked by some critics with the Magna Charta and the Bill of Rights in its recognition of fundamental human rights. In 1648 an enlarged code was published under the title of *The Laws and Liberties of Massachusetts*.

Boeotian   A rude, unlettered person; a dull blockhead. The ancient Boeotians loved agricultural and pastoral pursuits, so the Athenians used to say they were as dull and thick as their own atmosphere. However, HESIOD, PINDAR, and PLUTARCH were all Boeotians.

Boer War   The usual name for the war (1899–1902) between Great Britain and the joint forces of the Transvaal Republic and the Orange Free State. The war was the culmination of a long-standing conflict between the British and the Boers (South Africans of Dutch descent), both of whom had interests in South Africa. The immediate cause of the war was Great Britain's refusal to withdraw troops stationed in Transvaal. The Boers had considerable success in the beginning of the war but soon gave way to Britain's superior force. The war ended with the fall of Pretoria (1900), and organized Boer resistance disappeared. Peace was not formally arrived at until 1902.

Boethius (full name Anicius Manlius Severinus Boethius, c480–c524)   Roman philosopher. Appointed consul in 510, Boethius served under Theodoric the Great, until he was accused of treason and executed. Boethius is best known for THE CONSOLATION OF PHILOSOPHY, written while he was imprisoned, awaiting final sentence. He also translated works by Aristotle and the neo-Platonist Porphyry and wrote a number of philosophical treatises, especially on logic, which became textbooks for the Schoolmen of the Middle Ages and were their major source of knowledge about the thinkers of antiquity.

Bogan, Louise (1897–1970)   American poet and critic. Bogan's subtle and intellectual poetry shows the influence of the English METAPHYSICAL POETS. Her work appeared in *Body of This Death* (1923), *Dark Summer* (1929), *Collected Poems* (1954; co-winner of the BOLLINGEN PRIZE), *The Blue Estuaries 1923–68* (1968), and *Poet's Alphabet* (1970). A poetry reviewer for many years at THE NEW YORKER, Bogan also wrote the well-received *Achievement in American Poetry, 1900–1950* (1951) and *Selected Criticism: Poetry and Prose* (1955). Her selected letters appeared as *What the Woman Lived* (1973), edited by her literary executor, Ruth Limmer. *Journey Around My Room* (1980) is an autobiographical "mosaic," also compiled by Ruth Limmer.

Böhme, Jakob (1575–1624)   German mystic. Böhme's thought is often termed nature mysticism, because of his belief in the unity of nature as a vehicle for immediate contemplation of God and because of his concept of natural language (*lingua adamica*) as the language of the Holy Ghost. Böhme, who was a cobbler by trade, thought of his ideas as a development of Protestantism but found himself under attack by both the Protestant and Catholic clergy. He subsequently became known as the father of modern THEOSOPHY. His most famous works are *Aurora oder die Morgenröte im Aufgang* (*Aurora, or the Rising Dawn*, 1612), *Beschreibung der drei Prinzipien göttlichen Wesens* (*Description of the Three Principles of Divine Essence*, 1619), and *Mysterium Magnum* (1623). His work was of great influence on later German thought, particularly on the philosophers associated with GERMAN ROMANTICISM.

Boiardo, Matteo Maria (count of Scandiano, 1441–1494)   Italian poet at the ducal court of Ferrara. While serving the Este family as their regent for Modena and Reggio, Boiardo composed love poems and his famous romantic epic, ORLANDO INNAMORATO (*Roland in Love*). Left unfinished at his death, it was taken up and continued by ARIOSTO in his ORLANDO FURIOSO (*Roland Mad*).

Boïto, Arrigo (pseudonym Tobia Goria, 1842–1918)   Italian poet, librettist, and composer. Strongly influenced by the Romantic cult of the Middle Ages, Boïto wrote verse that linked an antiquarian's interest in medieval lore with a moralist's preoccupation with the Faust-like struggle of good and evil in the individual. A member of the SCAPIGLIATURA group of writers, he published his collected verse in *Il libro dei versi* (1877) and a legend in verse, *Re orso* (1902).

Boïto wrote the music and libretto for *Mefistofele* (1868), a fantastic and excessively romantic opera that first ran for over six hours and caused riots in the audience. Among his other compositions are the libretti for VERDI's *Otello* (1887) and *Falstaff* (1893).

Bojer, Johan (1872–1959)   Norwegian novelist. A popular writer outside his own country, Bojer enjoyed a prolific literary career. His best-known work in the English-speaking world is *Den store hunger* (1916; tr *The Great Hunger*, 1919). More valuable for their artistic merit are his sensitive and powerful novels of peasant life—*Den siste viking* (1921; tr *The Last of the Vikings*, 1923), *Vor egen stamira* (1924; tr *The Emigrants*, 1926), and *Folk ved sjøen* (1929; tr *Folks by the Sea*, 1931).

Bok, Edward W[illiam] (1863–1930)   Dutch-born American editor. Bok founded the *Brooklyn Magazine* (later *Cosmopolitan*) in 1893. Under his thirty-year stewardship (1889–1919), *The Ladies' Home Journal* exerted great influence both on the American home and on other women's magazines. He added the short fiction of serious writers and included articles of public interest, using the

Journal as a vehicle for his campaign on behalf of world peace and for his private war against billboards and the common drinking cup. His autobiography, *The Americanization of Edward Bok* (1920), won a PULITZER PRIZE.

Boleyn, Anne (c1507–1536)   Queen consort of HENRY VIII, mother of ELIZABETH I. A lady of honor to Henry's first queen, Catherine of Aragon, Anne soon attracted the attention of the king, to whom she was secretly married in January 1533. Some months later, Henry's first marriage was declared invalid, and Anne was crowned queen. After the disappointing birth of a daughter (the future Queen Elizabeth), a miscarriage, and a stillborn son, Anne lost favor with Henry. In 1536 she was made to stand trial for adultery, was condemned, along with five men accused of being her lovers, and executed.

Bolingbroke, Viscount   See ST. JOHN, HENRY.

Bolívar, Simón (known as El Libertador, 1783–1830) Venezuelan revolutionary leader and statesman. The scion of a wealthy Creole family, Bolívar was educated largely in Europe, where he absorbed the ideas of the Enlightenment and fell under the spell of Napoleon's reputation. During a visit to Rome, it is said, he vowed on the Aventine hill to free America from Spanish domination. Upon his return to Venezuela in 1810, he plunged into the separatist movement and emerged as its leader by 1813. Undismayed by numerous setbacks, he declared a war to extinction and won the independence of Colombia at the battle of Boyacá and that of Venezuela at the battle of Carabobo. The two regions, together with Ecuador, were incorporated in the republic of Gran Colombia, with Bolívar as president.

After his famous meeting with SAN MARTÍN at Guayaquil, Bolívar proceeded to Peru, most of which was still controlled by Spain. Bolívar's victory at Junín and that of his chief lieutenant, Antonio José de Sucre, at Ayacucho virtually ended Spanish resistance to the independence movement. He approved the creation of an independent republic, which was named Bolivia in his honor, in the region of Upper Peru, and wrote a constitution for it, embodying his republican, though authoritarian, principles. One of the first advocates of hemispheric solidarity, Bolívar sponsored a congress of American states in Panama (1826). Although unsuccessful, the congress is regarded as the forerunner of the contemporary Pan-American movement. Bolívar's last years were embittered by disputes with his former associates and by the disintegration of Gran Colombia; in 1828 he barely escaped assassination in Bogotá.

Because of the vigor and lucidity of his prose, Bolívar is considered an important figure in Latin-American literature. One of his best-known works is his letter from Jamaica (1815), an analysis of conditions in South America and a political program for the future. Another is his address to the congress of Angostura (now Ciudad Bolívar,

Venezuela; 1818), in which he outlined a constitution for Gran Colombia that would provide order with freedom.

Bolkonsky, Prince Andrey   One of the central characters of Tolstoy's WAR AND PEACE. In his unhappy first marriage, Prince Andrei was arrogant and cynical. The loss of Natasha, whom he loves, causes him to take on a new fierceness in the war with Napoleon. He and Natasha fall in love again after she nurses the wounds he received at Borodino, but he dies as a result of these wounds.

Böll, Heinrich (1917–1985)   German novelist and short-story writer. Böll developed a hatred for Fascism, belligerent nationalism, and war when, as a young man, he served in HITLER's National Labor Service and later fought in World War II. His second volume of stories, *Wanderer, kommst du nach Spa . . .* (1950; tr *Traveller, If You Come to Spa . . .*, 1956), and first novel *Wo warst du, Adam?* (1951; tr *Adam, Where Art Thou?*, 1955) both contain bitterly realistic accounts of the horrors of war. Böll's subsequent writing dealt with the emptiness and disillusionment of the post-World War II period and, as in THE CLOWN, indicted the materialism that followed in its wake. His works became increasingly polemical: *Und sagte kein einziges Wort* (1953; tr *And Never Said a Word*, 1978) reflects the postwar shortages and also contains satirical jabs at the Catholic Church. *Entfernung von der Truppe* (1964; tr *Absent Without Leave and Other Stories*, 1965) and *Das Ende einer Dienstfahrt* (1966; tr *End of a Mission*, 1968) continued his sharp attacks on militaristic values. Much of Böll's work repeatedly reexamines a shameful past and reminds the reader that many of the same evils persist in the present. This is particularly evident in perhaps his best-known work, *Billiard um halb zehn* (1959; tr *Billiards at Half-Past Nine*, 1961), in which three generations of a family of architects come to terms with their pasts, and in *Gruppenbild mit Dame* (1971; tr *Group Portrait with Lady*, 1973), which traces the decline of a war-widow from the prewar years, through the Nazi era, and into the post-war prosperity. In 1979 Böll wrote a satirical novel, *Safety Net*, which was well received on both sides of the Atlantic, and in 1981 published *What's to Become of the Boy? or: Something to Do with Books*, a memoir. *Ein- und Zusprüche: Schriften, Reden und Prosa 1981–1983*, a collection of reviews, speeches at literary occasions, and other prose, was published in 1984. In 1986 *The Stories of Heinrich Böll* was published posthumously.

Böll's outspoken attacks on false cultural values earned him harsh criticism from conservative circles. In 1972, he was awarded the NOBEL PRIZE in Literature. Unusually, Böll was a best-selling author in both East and West Germany.

Bollingen Prize   An annual award in poetry. First presented in 1949 under the auspices of the Library of Congress, the award was sponsored by the Bollingen Foundation, a philanthropic trust created by Paul Mellon. A distinguished board of writers gave the first award to Ezra POUND for his PISAN CANTOS, causing a lengthy and bitter controversy. The debate centered on the degree to which a poet's political and social views might damage the quality of his work. The result of the controversy was that the Bollingen Foundation canceled future prizes. In 1950, however, it was announced that the Bollingen Prize in Poetry would be awarded by the Yale University Library. Since then, distinguished living poets have been given the prestigious prize annually. In 1960 a Bollingen Prize for Poetry Translation was established to honor distinguished translations of poetry into English.

Bolshevik (or Bolshevist) A member of the Russian revolutionary party headed by LENIN that seized power in October 1917. The term originated at the congress of the Russian Social Democratic Party in London in 1903, when Lenin's radical wing of the party prevailed in a dispute, and the name *Bolshevik* was adopted by the group. The word comes from the Russian *bolshe*, "larger"; the name *Menshevik*, adopted by the contending faction, comes from *mensheu* "smaller."

Bolt, Robert [Oxton] (1924–) English playwright. Bolt's reputation rests on his historical dramas, all of which involve confrontations of differing values that have altered history. The best known of these, *A Man for All Seasons* (1960), deals with Sir Thomas More's struggle to keep his conscience inviolate while serving King Henry VIII, creating a dramatic clash between principle and power. In *Vivat! Vivat! Regina* (1971), Bolt returns to the 16th century, this time examining the confrontation between Elizabeth I and the vividly defiant Mary, Queen of Scots. *State of Revolution* (1977) depicts the struggle among Lenin, Trotsky, Stalin, and others to define and implement the Russian Revolution, showing the corrosive effects of dictatorial power on both people and leaders. Apart from other theatre pieces, Bolt also has written radio scripts and screenplays, notably *Lawrence of Arabia* (1962), *Doctor Zhivago* (1966), and *Ryan's Daughter* (1970).

Bombal, María Luisa (1910–) Chilean novelist. In Bombal's *La última niebla* (1935; tr *The House of Mist*, 1947) and *La amortajada* (1938; tr *The Shrouded Woman*, 1948) an irrational world breaks into the otherwise traditional realism of the Chilean novel. Bombal's characters, especially the women, inhabit an emotional zone closer to dream, fantasy, and death than to everyday life, although they are grounded in particular historical settings. In *La amortajada* a dead woman relives, in a series of impressionistic takes, the hopelessness of her family relations and the futility of romantic love.

Bonaparte, Napoleon See NAPOLEON BONAPARTE.

Bonaventure, St. (originally Giovanni di Fidanza, c1221–1274) Italian theologian, mystic, and scholastic philosopher, called the Seraphic Doctor. A Franciscan, Bonaventure placed more emphasis on faith and less on reason than St. Thomas Aquinas, and he is best known for *Itinerarium mentis ad Deum* (tr *The Mind's Road to God*, 1953). This, like his other works, explains that the direct contemplation of God is the goal of all the arts and sciences; philosophy's task is to discern intimations of God first in the external world, then in the soul itself, which is the image of God, and thus to prepare the mind for its ultimate mystic union with God. Bonaventure furthered the cult of the Virgin Mary and wrote lives of Christ and St. Francis of Assisi, as well as the treatises *Breviloquium*, *Soliloquium*, and *De reductione artium ad theologiam*.

Bond, Edward (1934–) English playwright. Bond's plays deal with the brutality of people who have lost hope for better social conditions and know no other way to express their resentment. Two of his works, *Saved* (1965) and *Early Morning* (1968), were banned in England, the former because of a scene in which a baby is stoned to death in a carriage. The bans caused a public furor, which led to the end of censorship for the English stage. In *Narrow Road to the Deep North* (1968), violence begets violence as two rivals destroy each other in an attempt to conquer a city. Bond uses visual images as adeptly as dialogue to express his disgust with the cruelty of society. His attack on human indifference to inhumanity is nowhere more cogent than in *Bingo* (1974), where he uses Shakespeare as an example of a man who, although he was fully aware of the evils in his own society, failed to rise up against it. He has also published *The Women* (1978), *The Restoration* (1981), *Human Cannon* (1985), and *War Plays* (1985).

Bond, James Secret agent 007, the tough, suave hero of the popular novels of international espionage by Ian FLEMING.

Bondarev, Yury Vasilyevich (1924–) Soviet prose writer. After serving in the army during World War II, Bondarev began writing short stories as a student at the Gorky Literary Institute in Moscow. His short novels *Batalyony prosyat ognya* (*Battalions Ask for Fire*, 1957) and *Posledniye zalpy* (1959; tr *The Last Shots*, 1961) best convey Bondarev's focus on morality in wartime. Using colloquial language and a singular, personal perspective, Bondarev, like KAZAKEVICH, poses the dilemma facing the Soviet soldier, the choice between almost certain death at the front and just as certain court-martial and execution for cowardice at home. Bondarev's later novels *Tishina* (1962; tr *Silence*, 1965) and *Dvoye* (*Two People*, 1964) concern the post-World War II purges. Nonetheless, Bondarev's ideological stance remains acceptable, by Soviet standards, and his works are widely published.

Bonhomme Richard The French form of Benjamin Franklin's pseudonym, Richard SAUNDERS. It is also the name of John Paul JONES's famous man-of-war, a refitted French vessel, which was rechristened in Franklin's honor.

Bonjour Tristesse (1954)   A short novel by Françoise SAGAN about teenage Cécile's jealous and tragic plot to prevent her father's remarriage by scheming with his mistress and her own lover.

Bonnefoy, Yves (1923–   )   French poet and critic. Bonnefoy's early writing career and reputation were based on his translations of SHAKESPEARE and his literary criticism, which he published in the form of scholarly monographs. Bonnefoy studied philosophy under Gaston BACHELARD and Jean Wahl, and his concern with the mystical role of words reflects their influence on his thought. His poetry is imagistic and is often set against a natural, elemental landscape—air, fire, water, trees, stone—and aims at recreating a reality lost to the modern world. His works include *Du Mouvement et de l'immobilité de Douve* (1953; tr *On the Motion and Immobility of Douve*, 1968), *Pierre écrite* (1965; tr *Words on Stone*, 1976), and *Dans le leurre du seuil* (*In the Lure of the Threshold*, 1975), all of which are included in *Poèmes* (1978). *Un Rêve fait à Mantoue* (1967), *L'Arrière-pays* (1972), *L'Ordalie* (1975), and *Rue traversière* (1977) are collections of essays.

Bonnie Prince Charlie   See PRETENDER.

Book of Changes (I ching)   One of the Chinese FIVE CLASSICS, also known as *Changes of Chou*. The *I ching* is a book of divinations to which, according to legend, CONFUCIUS, as editor, appended some commentaries. It consists of sixty-four hexagrams made of broken and unbroken lines, with accompanying text. By throwing coins or manipulating yarrow stalks the petitioner chooses any one or, usually, two of these hexagrams by lot. The corresponding text reveals the questioner's prospects or provides guidance in what to do. The message is couched in a generalized language derived from the YIN AND YANG philosophy, whose principles are believed to operate in all of nature. The sixty-four hexagrams are made by combining any two of the following trigrams, each named for a different natural phenomenon:

Heaven	Thunder	Water	Mountain
☰	☳	☵	☶

Earth	Wind	Fire	Lake
☷	☴	☲	☱

The *I ching* escaped destruction in the book-burning by the Ch'in monarchs in 213 BC. It has always enjoyed wide appeal in China, later in Japan, and most recently in the West, both as a fortune-telling manual and as a metaphysical account of the processes of nature.

Book of Documents (Shu ching)   One of the Chinese FIVE CLASSICS. The first Chinese work of history, the *Shu ching* contains speeches, pronouncements, and treatises dating to the first half of the CHOU dynasty (1027–256 BC). The language is obscure, and much of the text is of doubtful authenticity. See CHINESE LITERATURE.

Book of Martyrs, The   The popular title given to John FOXE's *Actes and Monuments of These Latter Perilous Days* (1563).

Book of Odes (Shih ching)   One of the Chinese FIVE CLASSICS. The oldest collection of Chinese poetry, the *Shih ching* was probably compiled during the CHOU dynasty; tradition attributes the arrangement to CONFUCIUS. The collection consists of 305 songs—folk songs, odes concerned with political life, and ritual hymns for formal occasions. The four-character, alternately rhyming lines, rich in nature symbolism, provided a pattern for much Chinese verse. See CHINESE LITERATURE.

Book of Rites (Li chi)   One of the Chinese FIVE CLASSICS. A compilation of the early first century BC, the *Li chi* is composed of various older texts dealing with music, court etiquette, ritual practice, education, and other subjects. It underlines the importance Confucian philosophy gives to ritual and correct behavior.

Book of the Dead, The   (1) A collection of magic incantations, prayers, and exorcisms, used in the religion of ancient Egypt as a guidebook for the dead on their journey through the underworld. Though not exactly such, it has been described by some as the Egyptian Bible.

(2) A Tibetan account of the preparation of a dying soul for the forty-nine days to be spent in an intermediate state. It embodies a view of life after death that the psychologist C. G. JUNG saw as a reflection of the racial unconscious. It gained some notoriety because its descriptions of the intermediate state compare closely with visions induced by hallucinogenic drugs.

Book of the Duchess, The (1369)   A poem by Geoffrey CHAUCER, of 1,335 lines in octosyllabic couplets. Based largely on French sources, particularly the *Roman de la Rose* and several works of Guillaume de Machaut, it was almost certainly written as an elegy on the occasion of the death of Blanche of Lancaster, first wife of Chaucer's patron, John of Gaunt. The poet reads the classical story of Halcyon and Ceyx until he falls asleep. Then he dreams of joining a hunt and meeting a knight in black, who laments the way Fortune has beaten him at the game of life by introducing him to a most perfect lady, letting him marry her and live with her in bliss, then snatching her away in death.

Book of Thel, The (1789)   The first of William BLAKE's mystical writings, known collectively as his prophetic books. Its theme is death, redemption, and eternity. It is written in free verse.

Boone, Daniel (1734–1820)   American frontiersman. Boone is known for his exploration and settlement of Kentucky and has been celebrated by a number of American and English writers, including Cooper and Byron, in *Don Juan* (1823). His adventures were popularized in the supposedly autobiographical account included in *Discovery, Settlement and Present State of Kentucky* (1784), written by John Filson, and have passed into American folk-lore.

Booth, John Wilkes (1838–1865)   American actor and assassin. The son of Junius Brutus Booth and brother of Edwin Booth, he was known for playing Shakespearean roles. During a performance of *Our American Cousin* at Ford's Theater in Washington on April 14, 1865, he shot President Lincoln and escaped, shouting *"Sic semper tyrannis! The South is avenged!"* Two weeks later, he was trapped in a barn near Bowling Green, Virginia; the barn was fired after he refused to surrender, and he probably shot himself.

Booth, William (1829–1912)   English preacher, founder of the SALVATION ARMY (1865). Booth is noted for his work among the urban poor. He is the subject of a poem by Vachel Lindsay, GENERAL WILLIAM BOOTH ENTERS INTO HEAVEN.

Borden, Lizzie (1860–1927)   American woman indicted in a celebrated murder case. On August 4, 1892, she was charged with having murdered her father and step-mother with an axe in their home in Fall River, Massachusetts, and her trial was followed with eager interest all over the country. She was acquitted, but the murder became the subject of numerous ballads and songs that failed to accept the verdict. The most famous is the anonymous quatrain:

> Lizzie Borden took an axe
> And gave her mother forty whacks;
> When she saw what she had done,
> She gave her father forty-one.

The crime was never solved. Edmund Pearson argued Lizzie's guilt in *The Trial of Lizzie Borden* (1937), but she was ardently defended by Edward Radin in *Lizzie Borden: The Untold Story* (1961).

The case has been the subject of numerous literary works, notably the dramas *Nine Pine Street* (1933) by John Colton and *The Legend of Lizzie* (1959) by Reginald Lawrence; a one-act play, *Goodbye, Miss Lizzie Borden* (1947) by Lillian de la Torre; and such novels as *The Long Arm* (1895) by Mary E. Wilkins Freeman and *Lizzie Borden* (1939) by Marie Belloc Lowndes. Agnes de Mille's *Fall River Legend* (1948) is a ballet based on the case. The case continues to hold interest. As late as 1985, a biography, *Lizzie*, by Frank Spiering attempted to establish that Lizzie's older sister Emma committed the murders and covers a hitherto-neglected area—the lives of the two sisters after the court case and the acquittal in the tiny Massachusetts town.

Boreas   In Greek mythology, the god of the north wind, and the north wind itself. Boreas was the son of Astraeus, a Titan, and Eos, the morning, and lived in a cave of Mount Haemus in Thrace. He loved the nymph Orithyia and tried to be gentle with her. Since he could not speak soothingly or sing softly, he carried her off, true to

his real character. He was by her the father of Zetes and Calais, who both took part in the ARGONAUTS' expedition.

Borges, Jorge Luis (1899–1986)   Argentinian short-story writer, essayist, poet, and man of letters. Borges was one of the first Latin American writers to achieve international as well as national fame. His reputation rests equally on his poetry, fiction, and critical/philosophical works. Borges's writing is unmistakably local in the realities it perceives but is universal in its conceptions, manifesting the ultimate metaphysical preoccupations of man—time, destiny, and the absurdity of human existence. One of Borges's most famous images is that of life as a labyrinth through which one passes, vainly seeking to understand the many facets of human existence. Only art can triumph over the chaos of existence, crystallizing and unifying experience and providing a sense of structure, validity, and form. His writing, which is a blend of myth, fantasy, symbolism, and erudition, has had a considerable influence on the attitudes and styles of a number of writers. Borges's eyesight, affected by a congenital disease, deteriorated radically in the 1950s; by 1970 he was almost totally blind and had to rely entirely on dictation for his writing.

Among his many acclaimed prose works are *Ficciones* (1944; tr *Ficciones*, 1962), *El Aleph* (1949; tr *The Aleph and Other Stories*, 1970), *El infirme de Brodie* (1970; tr *Dr. Brodie's Report*, 1972), *El Libro de arena* (1975; tr *The Book of Sand*, 1977), *Antologia personal* (1961; tr *A Personal Anthology*, 1967), *Nuevo essayos dantescos* (*Nine Dantesque Essays*, 1982), *Sietas noches* (1980; tr *Seven Nights*, 1984), and *Los conjurados* (*The Conspirators*, 1985), the last written shortly before his death. His verse has been collected in a translation, *Selected Poems: 1923–1967* (1972).

The recipient of many literary awards and prizes, in 1983 Borges was awarded the Legion of Honor and was decorated by France's President Mitterand for the body of his work.

Borgese, Giuseppe Antonio (1882–1952)   Italian playwright, novelist, critic, teacher, and advocate of world unity. An outspoken opponent of Fascism, Borgese immigrated to the U.S. in 1931, became a citizen in 1938, and taught in various American universities.

He wrote several volumes of criticism, including *Storia della critica romantica in Italia* (1905, 1920) and *La vita e il libro* (1910–13). He also wrote *Rubé* (1921; tr 1923), a fictionalized account of a young intellectual caught in the confusing ideological struggles between the right and the left in post-World War I Italy. In 1937 he published *Goliath*, a compelling study (written in English, his second language) of Fascism and the history of authoritarian rule in Italy.

Other works include the novel *I vivi e la morte* (1923) and several volumes of short stories, *La città sconosciuta* (1924), *Le belle* (1927), and *Il sole non è tramontato*

(1929). Among his works written for the theatre are *L'arciduca* (1924) and *Lazzaro* (1924).

Borgia (or de Borja)   A Spanish family that rose to prominence in Italy during the Renaissance. It has since become a symbol of unbridled power, lust, and greed. Its chief figures are:

Alonso Borgia (1385–1458)   Became Pope Calixtus III in 1455 and laid the foundation of his family's power and influence in Italy.

Rodrigo Borgia (1431–1503)   Reigned as Pope Alexander VI from 1492. A nephew of Calixtus III and father of Cesare and Lucrezia, Rodrigo exerted tremendous efforts in order to secure wealth and high station for his children.

Cesare Borgia (1476–1507)   Son of Rodrigo, brother of Lucrezia, and, for many, the very embodiment of Renaissance individualism in its sinister form. The favorite of his father, Cesare was made archbishop of Valencia in 1492 and a cardinal the following year. In 1498, released from ecclesiastical duties, he traveled to France as papal legate and was made duc de Valentinois by a grateful Louis XII (thereafter he was known as Valentino, or *il duca Valentino*). After a marriage to the sister of the king of Navarre, Cesare returned to Italy and became standard bearer of the Church, as well as its captain general. Using his military skill and cunning, he proceeded to consolidate the states of the church and to carve out a principality for himself among the conquered territories, incidentally winning the admiration of Machiavelli, who found his swift cruelty and treachery appropriate to the goal envisioned. The death of his father and the accession to the throne of Peter by the hostile Julius II brought his brief but meteoric career to a halt, for he was unable to rally his forces in the midst of a serious illness and soon found himself compelled to leave Italy under guard. In Spain, where he managed to free himself from prison, he finally met his end in a skirmish at the age of thirty-one. Like the other Borgias, he left behind a legend filled with murders, including those of his own brothers, incest with his sister, insatiable greed, and unbridled cruelty. Modern scholars doubt the incest and many of the murders but cannot find evidence that the other ingredients of his reputation are mere fiction.

Lucrezia Borgia (1480–1519)   Daughter of Rodrigo, sister of Cesare, and one of the most famous (and infamous) women of history. A pawn in the designs of her father and brother, Lucrezia was married three times. The first marriage was annulled; the second ended when her husband was murdered; the third, to Alfonso I of Este, duke of Ferrara, was a purely political match forced down the reluctant throats of the Estensi. Despite Lucrezia's exemplary life at Ferrara, gossip, scandal, rumors, and legends swirled about her and her family, so that she came down to posterity burdened with imputations of poisonings, incestuous relations with brother and father, illegitimate children, and generally whorish behavior. Thus Victor Hugo's play

Lucrèce Borgia (1833) and Donizetti's opera *Lucrezia Borgia* (1833) tell the story of her natural son Gennaro, who turned against his mother before a final recognition and reconciliation, but there is no basis for the tale in fact. Modern scholars discount much—but not all—of her evil reputation on the grounds that, as a Borgia and a Spaniard, as well as an illegitimate daughter of a pope, she became the target for the hatred stirred by her family's power and political activity in Italy. The praise heaped upon her by the poets Bembo and Ariosto is now regarded as more than mere flattery.

Borglum, [John] Gutzon [de la Mothe] (1867–1941)   American sculptor. Borglum's most famous undertaking was the carving of the faces of Washington, Jefferson, Lincoln, and Theodore Roosevelt in gigantic scale on Mount Rushmore, South Dakota (1930–41), for which the U.S. Congress paid just over one and a half million dollars. He also sculpted the massive marble head of Lincoln in the Capitol building in Washington, D.C.

Boris Godunov (1825)   A historical drama by Aleksandr Pushkin. It is based on the career of Boris Fyodorovich Godunov, when he was czar of Russia (1598–1605). In the play, Boris is haunted by his guilt over the murder of the tsarevich Dmitry. A pretender to the throne, who claims to be Dmitry but is actually an ambitious young monk, invades Russia. Boris tightens his rule and prepares to defend his throne, but he falls ill and dies, tortured by visions of the murdered prince. The composer Mussorgsky used this play as the basis of his opera (1869–74) of the same name.

Borodin, Aleksandr Porfyryevich (1833–1887)   Russian composer, also a chemist. Borodin made use of Russian folk themes in much of his music and is considered to have influenced Debussy, Ravel, Stravinsky, and Sibelius. He wrote operas, symphonies, chamber music, and numerous songs. His best-known works are *In the Steppes of Central Asia* (1880), a tone poem, and the *Polovtsian Dances* from *Prince Igor*, an unfinished opera later completed by Rimsky-Korsakov and Aleksandr Glazunov.

Borodino   The site of a decisive battle between Napoleon's forces and the Russian armies in September 1812. The battle, which opened the way for Napoleon's entry into Moscow, is described in War and Peace.

Bors, Sir   In Arthurian legend, one of the knights of the Round Table and uncle of Launcelot. In Malory's *Morte d'Arthur* (c1469), Sir Bors is one of the three knights to be granted sight of the Holy Grail, the others being Percival and Galahad, who wins the quest.

Borstal Boy   See Behan, Brendan.

Boscán Almogáver, Juan (c1498–1542)   Spanish poet. A native of Barcelona, Boscán served as a soldier in Italy and as a tutor to the duke of Alba. In 1526 he met Andrea Navagiero, the Venetian ambassador, who persuaded him to write Castilian poetry employing Italian forms and meters. Because of his efforts, he is remembered for having popularized Italianate verse in Spain. In 1543, the year after his death, his widow published his collected poetry. Included in this work are ninety-two sonnets and eleven *Canciones*; a long *Historia de Leandro y Hero* in unrhymed hendecasyllables; two *Epístolas*, one of which is addressed to Diego Hurtado de Mendoza; and *Octava rima*, an allegory based on Bembo's *Stanze*. He also wrote an excellent prose translation (1534) of Castiglione's *Il cortegiano* (1528). See GARCILASO DE LA VEGA.

Bosch, Hieronymus (or Jerome Bosch; real name Hieronymus van Aken, 1450?–1516)   Flemish painter. Bosch, who was so named from his birthplace, 's Hertogenbosch, Netherlands, painted religious pictures, scenes of heaven and hell, and allegories in which exquisite panoramas serve as background to the action of fantastic creatures and demons. His personal symbolism of sin and evil, dependent on contemporary literature, astrology, and popular beliefs, has led to contradictory interpretations, but the extreme delicacy, the refinement, and the richness of imagination displayed by his work is incontrovertible. After Bosch's death, a large portion of his work, including the famous *Garden of Earthly Delight*, was brought to Spain by Philip II.

Bosco, Henri [Ferdinand Joseph Marius] (1888–1976)   French novelist of the Provence region. Bosco's stories, characterized by poetic fantasy, evocation of the Provençal landscape, and subtly menacing, mysterious atmospheres, are filled with sensual human warmth, as well as mystical Catholicism. The theme of violence lurking beneath quiet exteriors is treated in *Le Mas Théotime* (1945; tr *Farm in Provence*, 1947), his best-known novel. Also highly regarded are his fantasy involving two children, *L'Âne culotte* (1937; tr *Culotte the Donkey*, 1980), and its sequels, *Hyacintine* (1940), *Le Jardin d'Hyacinthe* (1946), and the novel *Malicroix* (1948). His other novels include *Monsieur Carre-Benoît à la campagne* (1947; tr *Monsieur Carre-Benoît in the Country*, 1956), *Un Rameau de la nuit* (1950; tr *Dark Bough*, 1955), and *Barboche* (1957; tr 1959). Bosco's memoirs were published in three volumes as *Souvenirs* (1961–66).

Boston Hymn (1863)   A poem by Ralph Waldo EMERSON. The poet celebrates freedom, denouncing kings and aristocrats. "Boston Hymn" is one of Emerson's most fervent expressions.

Bostonians, The (1886)   A novel by Henry JAMES. *The Bostonians* satirically portrays a strong-minded Boston feminist, Olive Chancellor, representing a new generation of "do-gooders," who thinks she has found a kindred soul in a beautiful and impressionable girl, Verena Tarrant. The plot turns on the domination of one woman by another and on the struggle between Olive and Basil Ransom for Verena. The theme was suggested by Alphonse

Daudet's *Evangeliste* (1883), but James intended it to be at the same time "a tale very characteristic of our social conditions." Bostonians attacked the novel angrily as a false portrayal of their city, and many American critics censured James for his lack of local feeling. It was one of the first American novels to deal more or less explicitly with lesbianism.

Boston Massacre   A clash between the townspeople of Boston and British troops on March 5, 1770. Sent to Boston to protect the customs commissioners, the soldiers fired on a mob of men and boys, killing five civilians. Further violence was averted by the withdrawal of the troops to some islands in the harbor. The slain leader of the mob was the black hero Crispus Attucks (1723?–70).

Boston News-Letter   The first newspaper published in the American colonies to have a permanent life. John Campbell, postmaster at Boston, published the first issue on April 24, 1704. The paper ran until 1776.

Boston Public Occurrences   The first newspaper to be published in the American colonies, appearing in 1690. It lasted only one day, because its publisher failed to get a government license.

Boston Tea Party   The destruction in Boston Harbor of 342 chests of tea by citizens disguised as Indians, led by Samuel Adams, on December 16, 1773. The colonists were protesting an act of Parliament designed to save the East India Company from bankruptcy, at the expense of the colonists.

Boswell, James (1740–1795)   Scottish biographer and man of letters. Boswell is best known as a diarist and as the biographer of Dr. Samuel JOHNSON. He was called to the Scottish bar in 1766 and practiced law for twenty years. He met Dr. Johnson in 1763 and visited him yearly on vacations to London until he moved there. In 1786 he settled permanently in London, entered the English bar, but met with little success there. His literary fame and success began with *An Account of Corsica* (1768), a defense of Corsica's abortive struggle for freedom against the republic of Genoa. In 1773 he accompanied Dr. Johnson on a journey to Scotland; his account of the trip, *The Journal of a Tour to the Hebrides with Samuel Johnson, L L.D.*, appeared in 1785, by which time he was already working on THE LIFE OF SAMUEL JOHNSON, LL.D. Boswell was a man of great wit and charm; his personality was marked with extreme turns of hypochondria and gaiety. He noted with amusement the fact that, while he defended Corsican liberty abroad, he was opposed to further extensions of liberty at home. His papers are full of detailed plans for reform and admonitory addresses to himself, such as: "Desperate. This day, *Easter* rouse. Be Johnson. You've done no harm. Be *retenu* [restrained], &c. *What am I?*" Occasionally he even took his own advice. See BOSWELL PAPERS.

Boswell Papers   The papers of James BOSWELL. Long believed to have been lost or destroyed, they constitute one of the most important literary finds of the 20th century. The discoveries include letters and manuscripts of Dr. Samuel JOHNSON and Sir Joshua REYNOLDS, as well as the manuscripts of THE LIFE OF SAMUEL JOHNSON, LL.D., *The Journal of a Tour to the Hebrides with Samuel Johnson, LL.D.*, and Boswell's private journals. The bulk of the material was acquired by Yale University in 1949 and is in the process of being published in two series. The annotated "research edition" will run to at least thirty volumes. A shorter "trade edition" is being published under the editorship of Frederick A. Pottle and others: *Boswell's London Journal, 1762–1763* (1950), *Boswell in Holland, 1763–1764* (1952), *Boswell on the Grand Tour: Germany and Switzerland, 1764* (1953), *Boswell on the Grand Tour: Italy, Corsica, and France, 1765–1766* (1955), *Boswell in Search of a Wife, 1766–1769* (1956), *Boswell for the Defense, 1769–1774* (1959), *Boswell's Journal of a Tour to the Hebrides with Samuel Johnson, 1773* (1962), which was originally published in 1785, *Boswell: The Ominous Years, 1774–1776* (1963), and *Boswell in Extremes, 1776–1778* (1971). The Reynolds manuscript, *Portraits by Sir Joshua Reynolds*, was published by Yale in 1952.

Bosworth, battle of   The concluding battle, on August 22, 1485, of the WARS OF THE ROSES. In the struggle, RICHARD III, the last Yorkist king, was slain, and the victor, Henry Tudor, became HENRY VII of England.

Botticelli, Sandro (real name Alessandro di Mariano dei Filipepi, 1444–1510)   Florentine painter. A pupil of Fra Lippo LIPPI, Botticelli depicted both religious and mythological subjects in a style dependent on the decorative patterns of flowing draperies and exquisite detail, on the graceful elongation of idealized figures, and on the swaying beauty of linear design. The *Primavera* (c1477) and *The Birth of Venus* (c1485), painted for the Medici and now in the Uffizi Gallery in Florence, are his masterpieces in this style. Botticelli also painted portraits of the Medici family and did some illustrations of Dante's *Divine Comedy*. At Rome he was commissioned to plan and execute with other artists the frescoes for the walls of the Sistine Chapel. His own contribution was the *Punishment of Korah, Dathan, and Abiram* (1481). He became a follower of the religious reformer Savonarola during the last years of the 15th century and turned toward the illustration of allegories in a harsher, barer style.

Bottom   A weaver and the leader of the bumbling tradesmen-players who perform the tragedy of Pyramus and Thisbe for Duke Theseus in Shakespeare's MIDSUMMER NIGHT'S DREAM. Bottom is a blustering, pompous, but lovable character who constantly misuses words and wants to enact every part in the play.

Bottom is finally persuaded to settle for the part of Pyramus in one of Shakespeare's funniest burlesques. Flute the bellows mender is chosen to play the heroine Thisbe, though he has "a beard coming." Snug the joiner, who is

"slow of study," has the sole task of roaring like a lion. Snout the tinker, who is also given to bombast, takes the part of a most garrulous Wall. Robin Starveling plays the Moon but "wanes" early. Peter Quince, in bewildered fashion, essays the direction of the whole affair and speaks the prologue. Their combined efforts provide one of Shakespeare's greatest low-comedy scenes.

Boucher, François (1703–1770)   French painter. Boucher's works include scenes, pastorals, portraits, and tapestry cartoons in the rococo style. He was very successful as a decorative artist, in spite of a tendency toward the florid and sensual. His fashionable elegance made him a favorite of Madame de Pompadour and won him the title of court painter in 1765.

Boulanger, Nadia (1887–1979)   French composer, conductor, and teacher. Boulanger is most famous as a teacher of composers, especially two generations of Americans, including Virgil THOMSON, Aaron COPLAND, Roy HARRIS, Walter PISTON, and Elliott CARTER. She also revived much old music, including the works of MONTEVERDI. She herself was a pupil of Gabriel FAURÉ.

Boulez, Pierre (1925–   )   French composer of extremely complex, pointillistic music. Boulez was a pioneer in experiments with electronic music. He is best known for *Le Marteau sans maitre* (1955; for alto and six instruments, with a text by René CHAR), three piano sonatas (1946, 1948, 1957), and *Pli selon pli* (1962; for soprano and orchestra). He is also highly regarded as a pianist and conductor of avant-garde music. After serving as music director of the New York Philharmonic (1971–78), he returned to Paris to direct an institute for research in experimental music. Recent compositions include *Messagesquisse* (1977), *Notations*, Part I (1980), and *Répons* (1981). He has written several papers on musical theory and analysis, including *Penser la musique d'aujourd'hui*.

Bounderby, Josiah   In Charles Dickens's HARD TIMES, a vulgar banker and mill owner described as a "bully of humility." Bounderby is always boasting of his old ignorance and poverty, of an infancy passed in an "eggbox" under the care of his drunken grandmother. Actually, his parents doted on him and educated him at considerable sacrifice, and he now pays them a monthly stipend to keep out of sight. Bounderby marries Louisa Gradgrind, but later she separates from him.

Bourbon   A French royal family whose line also formed ruling dynasties in Spain and Naples. The Bourbon kings of France were Henry IV, Louis XIII, XIV, XV, and XVI (1589–1793). It was said that the family "learned nothing and forgot nothing." Hence a *Bourbon* is anyone who fails to learn by experience. In the U.S., the name was given to the Democratic Party by its opponents.

Bourchier, John (2nd Baron Berners, 1467–1533) English translator and high court official under Henry III. Bourchier's translation (2 vols, 1523, 1525) of FROISSART's

Chronicles is a classic of Tudor English prose. At the king's request, he also translated the early-13th-century French romance *Huon de Bordeaux*, which was published (c1540) posthumously, as were *The Golden Boke of Marcus Aurelius* (1535) and *The Castell of Love* (1540?), his translations from French versions of Spanish works by Antonio de Guevara (c1480–1545) and Diego de San Pedro.

bourgeois drama (Fr, *drame bourgeois*) A type of French play, developed from the COMÉDIE LARMOYANTE, which deals seriously with middle-class family relationships, problems, and duties. Representative plays of this type were often sentimental, morally edifying, melodramatic, mediocre, and humorless. The most famous of these plays are DIDEROT's *Le Fils naturel* (1771) and *Le Père de famille* (1761), SEDAINE's *Le Philosophe sans le savoir* (1765), and Beaumarchais's *La Mère coupable* (1792). Diderot's theories about this type of drama were to have an influence on the social theatre of Emile Augier and Dumas *fils*.

Bourgeois Gentilhomme, Le (The Would-be Gentleman, 1670) A COMÉDIE-BALLET by MOLIÈRE. M. JOURDAIN, a bourgeois and a boor, is determined to make a gentleman of himself and, to that end, studies dancing, fencing, and philosophy, allows himself to be fleeced by the unscrupulous nobleman Dorante, and forbids his daughter's marriage to her beloved Cléonte or to any other commoner. The resourceful Cléonte disguises himself as the son of the Grand Turk and, babbling pseudo-Turkish, dupes M. Jourdain into granting him the girl's hand. A delightful comedy in its own right, the play has survived in the repertory for over three centuries and has often served as a pretext for lavish ballets and *divertissements*.

Bourget, Paul Charles Joseph (1852–1935) French novelist and critic. Bourget's work occupies an important place in the development of the psychological novel, probing with new care and accuracy the state of the inner man. Among his finest novels are *Cruelle enigme* (1885), *Le Disciple* (1889), *Cosmopolis* (1893), and *L'Etape* (1903). His critical works, such as *Etudes de portraits* (1888) and *Pages de doctrine et de critique* (1912), use a similar analytical method. The tone of his later work, however, changed, becoming increasingly moralistic and didactic in such novels as *L'Emigré* (1907) and *Le Démon de midi* (1914).

Bourgh, Lady Catherine de An overbearing "great lady" in Jane Austen's PRIDE AND PREJUDICE. An inveterate snob, Lady Catherine tries to prevent the marriage of Elizabeth and Darcy.

Bourjaily, Vance [Nye] (1922–   ) American writer. Bourjaily's first novel, *The End of My Life* (1947), was the story of a young man's mental and moral disintegration during World War II. During the 1950s, Bourjaily was one of the editors of *Discovery*, a paperback periodical devoted to new authors. His subsequent novels include *The*

Violated (1958), *Confessions of a Spent Youth* (1960), *Now Playing at Canterbury* (1976), and *A Game Men Play* (1980). He also wrote *The Unnatural Enemy* (1963), a collection of his essays and reviews.

Bourke-White, Margaret (1904–1971) American photographer. As staff photographer for *Fortune, Time*, and *Life*, Bourke-White worked all over the world and covered both World War II and the Korean War as correspondent. She is known for her photographic studies of industry and social and economic conditions during the Depression, as well as her portraits of public figures. She was married for a time to Erskine CALDWELL, with whom she collaborated on several works, including *You Have Seen Their Faces* (1937). She described her long struggle against Parkinson's disease in her autobiography, *Portrait of Myself* (1963).

Bourne, Randolph [Silliman] (1886–1918) American critic and essayist. Bourne's progressive ideas on education were given voice in his books *The Gary Schools* (1916) and *Education and Living* (1917). An outspoken pacifist during World War I, he wrote for such publications as THE DIAL, *The New Republic*, and THE MASSES. His pacifist articles were collected in the posthumous volume *Untimely Papers* (1919). After Bourne's death, Van Wyck BROOKS edited *The History of a Literary Radical* (1920; repr 1956). Selected writings from 1911 to 1918 in *The Radical Will* (1978; ed Olaf Hanson) support the central imperative of his social criticism, that "everyone resist the impulses to acquiesce."

Bousoño, Carlos (1923–   ) Spanish poet and literary critic. Bousoño deals, throughout his poetic *œuvre*, with themes of religious doubt, existential anguish, and the fleeting nature of time. His poetry, in the volumes *Subida al amor* (Ascent to Love, 1945), *Primavera de la muerte* (Spring of Death, 1946), *Oda en la ceniza* (Ode in the Ash, 1967), and *Las monedas contra la losa* (Coins against the Stone, 1973) reveals his central preoccupation with life and death, hope and despair, but eventually it is an affirmation of existence in its belief that life, however transitory, is a gift to be cherished. He is also the author of well-known works on literary and poetic theory, most notably *Teoría de la expresión poética* (1952; rev 1966), and is the leading interpreter of the works of Vicente ALEIXANDRE.

Bovary, Emma See MADAME BOVARY.

bowdlerize To expurgate a book. In 1818 an English physician, Thomas Bowdler (1754–1825), gave to the world a ten-volume edition of Shakespeare's works "in which nothing is added to the original text; but those words and expressions are omitted which cannot with propriety be read aloud in a family." Bowdler later treated Gibbon's *Decline and Fall* in the same way. Hence, we have the words *bowdlerist, bowdlerizer, bowdlerism, bowdlerization*, etc.

Bowen, Elizabeth [Dorothea Cole] (1899–1973) Anglo-Irish novelist and short-story writer. Bowen knew members of the BLOOMSBURY GROUP and wrote in the tradition of sensibility, following Henry JAMES and E. M. FORSTER. With satire, irony, and occasional melodrama, she explored the relationships, emotional crises, and failures of feeling of her upper-middle-class characters. Her best-known novels are *The Hotel* (1927), THE HOUSE IN PARIS, THE DEATH OF THE HEART, and THE HEAT OF THE DAY. Among her other books are *The Last September* (1929), *A World of Love* (1955), *A Time in Rome* (1959), *The Little Girls* (1963), and *Eva Trout* (1968). *Bowen's Court* (1942; rev 1964) is a history of ten generations of her family in their house in County Cork, Ireland. Among her collections of short stories are *The Cat Jumps* (1934), *Look at All Those Roses* (1941), and *The Demon Lover* (1945; U.S. *Ivy Gripped The Steps and Other Stories*, 1946). *After-thought: Pieces About Writing* (1962) consists of an autobiographical fragment and literary essays. Another autobiographical piece, along with miscellany left unfinished at her death, was published in *Pictures and Conversations* (1975). *The Collected Stories of Elizabeth Bowen* was issued in 1981.

Bowering, George (1935–   ) Canadian poet and fiction writer. Bowering's editing in the 1960s of the avant-garde newsletter *Tish* set off a "new wave" of Canadian poetry, ultimately inspired, like Bowering's own, by the work of William Carlos WILLIAMS and the BLACK MOUNTAIN POETS. In his verse, including the volumes *Points on the Grid* (1964), *The Man in Yellow Boots* (1965), *Sitting in Mexico* (1970), and *Curious* (1973), he aims at precision and integrity in rendering felt experience, employing the language and cadence of common speech. Among his numerous publications are several novels, including *Mirror on the Floor* (1967) and *A Short Sad Book* (1977), and *A Place to Die* (1973), *Flycatcher* (1974), and *Protective Footwear* (1978), all collections of short stories.

Bowers, Claude [Gernade] (1878–1958) American historian and diplomat. Originally a journalist, Bowers served as ambassador to Spain (1933–39) and to Chile (1939–53), which he describes in the books *My Mission to Spain* (1954), *Embassy Windows* (1958), and *My Life* (1962). Bowers was a highly partisan Democrat; his historical works include a number of books on Thomas JEFFERSON, such as *Jefferson and Hamilton* (1925), *Jefferson in Power* (1936), and *The Young Jefferson* (1945; repr 1969).

Bowles, Jane [Sydney Auer] (1917–1973) American novelist and playwright. In 1952 Bowles moved to Tangier with her husband, Paul Bowles (1910–   ), and remained an expatriate for the rest of her life. Her works include the novel TWO SERIOUS LADIES, the short-story collection *Plain Pleasures* (1966), and the play *In the Summer House* (1954). Although never a popular writer, Bowles held the respect of a small following, including many writers, who responded to her innovative rejection of conventional plot and her lucid, almost nihilistic sense of humor. Her books frequently involve conflicts between repression and rampant sensuality, featuring, on the one hand, women in search of independence and autonomy and, on the other, weak, ineffectual men. Following a belated "rediscovery" of her merit as a writer, her *Collected Works* (1966) was expanded and published as *My Sister's Hand in Mine* (1978).

Bowra, Sir C[ecil] M[aurice] (1898–1971) English classical scholar and professor of poetry at Oxford. Most notable among Bowra's works are his writings on classical literature, including *Tradition and Design in the Iliad* (1930), *Greek Lyric Poetry* (1936; rev 1961), *Heroic Poetry* (1952), *Pindar* (1964), and *Homer* (1972). *In General and in Particular* (1964) is a collection of essays. His interest in modern European poetry was reflected in *Poetry and Politics, 1900–1960* (1966).

Box and Cox (1847) A farce by John Maddison Morton (1811–91). It has been called "the best farce for three characters in the English language." The principal characters are Box and Cox; the third is the thrifty landlady, who rents the same rooms to Box and Cox (one of whom is employed by night, the other by day), in the vain hope that her two tenants will remain ignorant of each other's existence. Hence, there developed the term *Box and Cox arrangement.*

Boxer A member of a secret society in China. The Boxer Uprising in Peking and north China in 1900 was directed against foreigners and was spearheaded by the society, with the encouragement of the failing CH'ING Manchu regime. The Chinese name was *i ho ch'üan,* translated roughly as "righteous and harmonious fists." The Boxers were one of a number of groups in China that believed that martial training ("fists") and magical practices would make their followers invulnerable to attack.

Boyd, Martin à Beckett (1893–1972) Australian novelist. Boyd's novels depict the decline of traditional society and a vanishing aristocracy. In his most successful novel, *Lucinda Brayford* (1946), and in the ambitious "Langton" tetralogy: *Cardboard Crown* (1952), *A Difficult Young Man* (1955), *Outbreak of Love* (1957), and *When Blackbirds Sing* (1962), Boyd emulates Henry JAMES in contrasting the mores of Australia and England.

Boyle, Kay (1903–   ) American short-story writer, novelist, and poet. An early contributor to LITTLE MAGAZINES, Boyle is known for the polish of her highly metaphorical prose and her psychological interest in character. Her novels are set mainly in Europe, where she lived for over thirty years. The stories in *Wedding Day* (1930) were followed by the semiautobiographical novel *Plagued by the Nightingale* (1931). Throughout her work, Boyle exhibits a rare capacity for exploring the subtle nuances of relationships between Europeans and Americans against the background of the human need for love. Her *Collected*

Poems was published in 1962. In 1963 she returned to America to teach at San Francisco State College. Among her subsequent writings are *Testament for My Students* (1970) and *The Underground Woman* (1974). *Fifty Stories* (1980) is Boyle's own anthology of her work.

Boz   The pen name of Charles DICKENS. His *Sketches by Boz* (two series) appeared in 1836. "Boz, my signature in the Morning Chronicle," he tells us, "was the nickname of a pet child, a younger brother, whom I had dubbed Moses, in honor of [Goldsmith's] *The Vicar of Wakefield*, which, being pronounced Bozes, got shortened into Boz."

Brabantio   In Shakespeare's OTHELLO, a Venetian senator and father of Desdemona. When Brabantio learns of Desdemona's secret marriage to Othello, he accuses the Moor of having won his daughter by witchcraft. Since Desdemona insists on remaining with her husband, he is forced to accept the situation, but warns Othello:

> Look to her, Moor, if thou hast eyes to see:
> She has deceiv'd her father, and may thee.

Bracebridge Hall, or The Humorists (1822) A collection of tales and sketches by Washington IRVING. The book is a less successful sequel to *The Sketch Book of Geoffrey Crayon, Gent.* (1819–20).

Brackenridge, Hugh Henry   (1748–1816) American novelist and poet. One of the first writers to consider the native American scene valid material for literature, Brackenridge collaborated with Philip Freneau on *The Rising Glory of America* (1772), a commencement ode at Princeton, and also wrote *The Battle of Bunker Hill* (1776) and *The Death of General Montgomery* (1777), blank-verse dramas in the 18th-century style. His most important work is MODERN CHIVALRY, OR THE ADVENTURES OF CAPTAIN JOHN FARRAGO AND TEAGUE O'REGAN HIS SERVANT.

Bradamante   The warrior maiden of Carolingian legend, prominent in the Orlando poems of BOIARDO and ARIOSTO as the sister of Rinaldo and the beloved of Ruggiero. Known as the Virgin Knight, Bradamante wears white armor and a white plume; her spear magically unhorses any knight it touches. Her marriage to the Moor Ruggiero after his conversion and her subsequent defeat of Rodomonte in single combat form the subject of the last book of Ariosto's poem. The marriage of Bradamante and Ruggiero also enables Ariosto to flatter his noble patrons, the Este family, since the union is said to be the forerunner of the future house of Este. She is also the title character of a play by Robert Garnier. See ORLANDO FURIOSO.

Bradamante (1582)   A play by Robert GARNIER. It is derived from the Carolingian legend of BRADAMANTE and from Ariosto's *Orlando Furioso*. Centering on a combat between the knight Roger and the warrior-maiden Bradamante, with emphasis upon Roger's dilemma in choosing between the claims of love and duty, the play was the first of the French tragicomedies—an enormously popular

genre, in which romance and adventure led to a happy ending, the classical unities being freely disregarded.

Bradbrook, Muriel [Clara] (1909–   ) English literary critic. A renowned scholar, Bradbrook served from 1968 to 1976 as mistress of her alma mater, Girton College, Cambridge. She is best known for her numerous works on Shakespeare and English theatrical history, among them, *Themes and Conventions of Elizabethan Tragedy* (1934; rev 1980), *The Growth and Structure of Elizabethan Comedy* (1955), *Shakespeare, The Poet in His World* (1978), and *John Webster, Citizen and Dramatist* (1980). She has also published works on Andrew Marvell (1940), Joseph Conrad (1941), T. S. Eliot (1950; rev 1972), and Malcolm Lowry (1974). In 1982 she published her *Collected Papers* in two volumes.

Bradbury, Malcolm [Stanley] (1932–   ) English novelist and critic. Bradbury first attracted attention with his extraordinarily funny academic novel, *Eating People Is Wrong* (1959). In this and such subsequent novels as *Stepping Westward* (1965), *The History Man* (1975), and *Rates of Exchange* (1983), he employs farce and sometimes outrageous comedy to deal with basically serious issues, his irony calling attention to values that concern him. He has also written poetry, several plays, a book on Evelyn Waugh (1964), and thoughtful criticisms of the novel form in *What Is a Novel?* (1969), *The Social Context of Modern English Literature* (1971), and *Possibilities: Essays on the State of the Novel* (1973).

Bradbury, Ray [Douglas] (1920–   ) American science-fiction writer. Bradbury's unearthly, fantastic tales combine acute social criticism with fanciful science fiction. He is best known for such short-story collections as *The Martian Chronicles* (1950), *Dandelion Wine* (1957), and *I Sing the Body Electric!* (1969). He also wrote screenplays and plays, as well as the novels *Fahrenheit 451* (1953) and *Something Wicked This Way Comes* (1962). *When Elephants Last in the Dooryard Bloomed* (1972) and *Where Robot Mice & Robot Men Run Around in Robot Towns* (1977) are volumes of verse. *The Stories of Ray Bradbury* (1980) contains one hundred varied stories, demonstrating that Bradbury's interests are by no means confined to science fiction. In 1981 Bradbury published two volumes of verse: *The Haunted Computer and the Android Pope* and *The Ghosts of Forever*.

Bradford, Andrew (1686–1742)   American printer and publisher. On December 22, 1719, Bradford brought out the first number of the *American Weekly Mercury*, the earliest newspaper in Pennsylvania. It continued for more than twenty-six years. From 1713 to 1723, Bradford was the only printer in Pennsylvania.

Bradford, Gamaliel (1863–1932)   American biographer. Bradford is best known for his "psychographs," interpretive portraits depicting the subjective life of his historical and literary subjects. Perhaps the best of these are contained in *American Portraits* (1922), with discussions of Mark Twain, Henry Adams, and Henry James, among others, and *Bare Souls* (1924), portraying Keats, Lamb, Voltaire, and others. One of his most popular volumes is *Damaged Souls* (1923), with analyses of P. T. Barnum and Aaron Burr. His autobiography is *Life and I* (1928). Van Wyck BROOKS edited Bradford's journals (1933) and letters (1934).

Bradford, William (1590?–1657)   English-born American statesman. A leader in the founding of Plymouth, Bradford was governor of the colony from 1621 to his death, except for five years during which he refused election. He was one of the authors of an account of the settlement of Plymouth known as MOURT'S RELATION and is best known for his *History of Plimouth Plantation*, a chronicle of events in the colony from 1620 to 1646, which was not discovered and published until 1856.

Bradley, A[ndrew] C[ecil] (1851–1935)   English scholar. Noted principally as a teacher and critic of poetry, Bradley had a distinguished academic career. His major publication is *Shakespearean Tragedy* (1904), a work that became the starting point of modern criticism on the subject. In this brilliant study, Bradley formulates his definition of Shakespearean tragedy and lays the groundwork for later post-Freudian analyses of the tragic heroes. He is also noted for his *Commentary on Tennyson's "In Memoriam"* (1901) and for *Oxford Lectures on Poetry* (1909). He is the brother of F. H. BRADLEY, the idealist philosopher.

Bradley, F[rancis] H[erbert] (1846–1924)   English idealist philosopher. Bradley's ideas followed from HEGEL's, that mind is more fundamental than matter. In his first major work, *Ethical Studies* (1876), he disputed John Stuart Mill's UTILITARIANISM, which proposed that human happiness is the goal of human behavior. In *The Principles of Logic* (1883), he attacked the empiricists. His best-known and most ambitious work is *Appearance and Reality* (1893), in which he maintains that reality is spiritual. T. S. ELIOT wrote his doctoral dissertation on Bradley; the impersonal nature of Eliot's poetry reflects many of the concepts central to Bradley's philosophy, namely, that reality is a condition of the mind and that it is possible to arrive at truth through the intellect.

Bradstreet, Anne (1612?–1672)   English-born poet of the Massachusetts Bay Colony. By birth an aristocrat, Bradstreet was the daughter of one governor of the colony and wife of another. Although her verse in general alternates between scenes of domestic affection and conventional professions of piety, it shows a sensitivity to beauty not usually associated with the Puritans. THE TENTH MUSE LATELY SPRUNG UP IN AMERICA is the only edition of her poems published in her lifetime and the first volume of original verse to be written in America. She also wrote *Religious Experiences*, an autobiographical sketch, and *Meditations, Divine and Moral*, a collection of aphorisms for the instruction of her son. John Berryman wrote a remarkable poem, *Homage to Mistress Bradstreet* (1956), in which the sexual tenderness of Anne Bradstreet is set against the sternly chaste background of Puritan New England.

Brady, Mathew B. (1823?–1896)   American photographer. The first significant representative of his profession in the U.S., Brady is best known for his photographic record of the Civil War and for portraits of Abraham Lincoln and other outstanding personalities of the time.

Bragg, Melvyn (1939–   )   English novelist. Bragg's characteristic theme has been the impact of class and regional distinctions and conflict on English life. *Without a City Wall* (1968) established Bragg as a novelist of distinction. Its rural setting and theme of the sexual power struggle also define *The Hired Man* (1969) and its sequel, *A Place in England* (1970). *The Nerve* (1971), set mainly in London, is a first-person account of a nervous breakdown. *Speak for England* (1977), *Autumn Manoeuvres* (1978), and *Kingdom Come* (1980) inspired critical comparisons of Bragg with HARDY and D. H. LAWRENCE.

braggadocio   A braggart; one valiant with his tongue but a great coward at heart. The character is from Spenser's THE FAERIE QUEENE, in which Braggadochio appears as a kind of "Intemperance of the Tongue."

Bragi   In Scandinavian mythology, the son of Odin and Frigga, husband of Iduna, and god of poetry, eloquence, and song. Bragi was represented as an old man with a long white beard. With Hermod, he received and welcomed to Valhalla all heroes who fell in battle.

Bragi's apples   An instant cure for weariness, decay of power, ill temper, and failing health. The supply was inexhaustible; after one was eaten, another took its place immediately.

Bragi's cup   A cup which each new king had to drain and pledge by before he ascended the high seat of his fathers.

Bragi's story   A lengthy but interesting tale.

Brahmā   In HINDUISM, one of the TRIMURTI, or trinity of gods, with VISHNU, the preserver, and SHIVA, the destroyer. Brahmā was the creator of the Universe. Brahmā is linked historically to the Vedic god Prajapati, the lord of beings. Unlike Vishnu and Shiva, Brahmā did not become the focal point of a major sect or cult within Hinduism.

brahman   In HINDUISM, the ultimate, undefinable power of the universe, often rendered as "world spirit." Particularly in the UPANISHADS and after, brahman is held to be identical with ATMAN, the internal essence (or soul) of the individual. It is not to be confused with BRAHMIN (brāhman) or BRAHMĀ.

brahmin   A member of the priestly stratum (*varna*) in the four-fold division of the Hindu social hierarchy. The term is not to be confused with BRAHMAN, the undefinable, ultimate power of the universe, or BRAHMĀ, the creator god in the Hindu TRIMURTI. In order to minimize this confusion, many writers intentionally use the secondary transliteration, *brahmin*, as is the case in this volume. See CASTE.

Brahms, Johannes (1833–1897)   German romantic composer. Brahms's works include four symphonies, concertos, chamber music, songs, and choral works, including the popular *Ein deutsches Requiem* (*A German Requiem*, 1867). He was the most successful of the romantic composers in reconciling the conflicting claims of lyricism and classical form, partly because of his study and editing of 16th-, 17th-, and 18th-century music. Brahms's music was the culmination of the tradition of GERMAN ROMANTICISM he inherited from his close and influential friend Robert SCHUMANN. A critical battle was waged during his lifetime between the opposing pro-Brahms and pro-WAGNER forces; Brahms himself was not actively involved in the controversy.

Braine, John [Gerard] (1922–1986)   English novelist. Braine was one of the writers frequently identified with the ANGRY YOUNG MEN. He is the author of the bestselling ROOM AT THE TOP and its sequel, *Life at the Top* (1962). His other novels include *The Jealous God* (1965), *The Queen of a Distant Country* (1972), and *The Pious Agent* (1976), a thriller about British intelligence. *Stay with Me Till Morning*, a novel about industrial Yorkshire, appeared in 1981, and *The Two of Us* in 1984. In 1976 he published a biography of the writer J. B. Priestley.

Bramah, Ernest   See SMITH, ERNEST BRAMAH.

Bramble, Matthew   The chief character in Tobias Smollett's novel HUMPHREY CLINKER. An irascible, eccentric, somewhat valetudinarian bachelor, Bramble initiates the family expedition partly because of ill health and partly to distract the mind of his young niece Lydia Melford, who has fallen in love with a supposedly itinerant actor.

Tabitha Bramble   In the same book, the sister of Matthew Bramble, noted for her bad spelling. She is vain, prim, uncharitable, and in violent search for a husband. She contrives to marry Captain Lismahago, who is content to take her for the sake of her £4,000.

Brancati, Vitaliano (1907–1954)   Italian novelist, essayist, and playwright. Brancati is noted for his comic novels about contemporary social manners and his ironic appraisals of Fascist culture. A trilogy of sexual and political satires, set against the backdrop of rising Italian Fascism in the 1930s and 1940s, includes *Don Giovanni in Sicilia* (1941), *Il bell'Antonio* (1949; tr *Antonio the Great Lover*, 1952; tr *Bell'Antonio*, 1978), and *Paolo il caldo* (1955), left unfinished when he died. One of his best works is a long short story, "Il vecchio con gli stivali" (1945), a particularly ironic tale of a Sicilian clerk during the last months of Fascism in Italy. Other works include *Gli anni perduti* (1941), *I piaceri* (1943), and the play *La governante* (1952).

Brancusi, Constantin (1876–1957)   Rumanian sculptor, settled in France in 1904. Brancusi is known for his radically simplified, abstracted forms, executed in wood, steel, stone, or bronze and finished to a meticulous smoothness. His attempts at finding the most elemental, almost archetypal forms are manifest in such works as the bust *Mademoiselle Pogany* (1923) and *Bird in Space* (1919), a vertical, swelling shaft of highly polished metal.

Brandan, St. (or St. Brendan)   A semilegendary Irish saint. Brandan is said to have been buried (at the age of about ninety-four), in 577, at Clonfert, where he was abbot over three thousand monks. He is best known because of the very popular medieval story of his voyage in search of the EARTHLY PARADISE, which was supposed to be situated on an island in mid-Atlantic. The voyage lasted for seven years, and the story is crowded with marvelous incidents, the very birds and beasts the voyagers encountered being Christians and observing the fasts and festivals of the Church. As late as 1755, St. Brandon's Island, or the Island of San Borandan, was set down in geographical charts as west of the Canary group.

Brandeis, Louis D[embitz] (1856–1941)   American jurist and Zionist leader. Born in Kentucky, Brandeis practiced law in Boston and argued important cases in Illinois, Ohio, California, and Oregon, where the famous "Brandeis brief" convinced the U.S. Supreme Court of the constitutionality of minimum working hours for women. His effective opposition to vested interests and monopolies in every form was formulated as the economic basis of the "New Freedom" used by Woodrow WILSON in his 1912 presidential campaign. His appointment by Wilson to the Supreme Court in 1916 created bitter controversy. Known as the "people's attorney," Brandeis sustained a position of judicial liberalism until he retired from the Court in 1939, often joining Justices HOLMES and, later, CARDOZO in minority dissents. He wrote several books, including *Other People's Money* (1914), *Business, A Profession* (1914), and *The Curse of Bigness* (1934). Brandeis University, founded in 1948, is named after him.

Brandes, Georg Morris Cohen (1842–1927)   Danish literary critic and scholar. Brandes exercised great influence upon Scandinavian thought and literature, serving as leader of *Det moderne gennembruch* ("the modern breaking-through"). In 1871 he began to formulate the principles of a new realism and naturalism, condemning abstract idealism and fantasy in literature. Brandes was the author of several critical biographies, including a study of Henrik Ibsen, who shared his literary goals, in his volume *Critical Studies* (1899). His other studies include *Søren Kierkegaard* (1877), *Esaias Tegnér* (1878), *Wolfgang Goethe* (1914–15), and *François de Voltaire* (1916–17). After spending several years in Germany, Brandes came under the influence of NIETZSCHE's philosophy and disavowed democracy for an aristocratic radicalism.

Brangwen, Ursula   The heroine of two novels by D. H. Lawrence. In THE RAINBOW, her experience as a teacher and rebel from her environment reflects Lawrence's own; in the sequel, WOMEN IN LOVE, she is based more on Lawrence's wife, Frieda LAWRENCE.

Branner, Hans Christian (1903–1966)   Danish novelist, short-story writer, and dramatist. Beginning with his first novel, *Legetøj* (*Toys*, 1936), Branner developed as one of the most important Danish novelists of his generation. Known for subtle psychological insights into his characters, particularly children, he wrote some of his best short fiction in *Om lidt er vi borte* (*In a Little While We Are Gone*, 1939) and *To minutters stilhed* (1944; tr *Two Minutes of Silence*, 1966). His concern with the theme of power is evident in his work. Branner perceived the driving forces behind a thirst for power as loneliness, insecurity, and sexual frustration. Novels such as *Rytteren* (1949; tr *The Riding Master*, 1951) and *Ingen kender natten* (1955; tr *No Man Knows the Night*, 1958) clearly reveal this preoccupation and also manifest the influence of FREUD. He also wrote radio plays and *Søskende* (1951; tr *The Judge*, 1955) and *Thermopylae* (1958) for the stage.

Brant, Joseph (original name Thayendanegea, 1742–1807)   Mohawk chief. During the American Revolution, Brant commanded the Indian forces cooperating with the British and ravaged the Mohawk Valley of New York. An earnest Christian, he also translated the Book of Common Prayer into the Mohawk language.

Brant, Sebastian (1458–1521)   German didactic poet and satirist. Brant was born in Strassburg and spent most of his life as its town clerk. He was educated by the humanists and, for that reason, is often associated with HUMANISM. His highly conservative thinking and his opposition to change in any form, however, make such an identification inappropriate. He is most famous for his didactic satire *Das Narrenschiff* (1494; see SHIP OF FOOLS), which, while exposing all manner of human folly in his day, did a great deal to articulate the moral uncertainty that led to the Protestant REFORMATION.

Braque, Georges (1882–1963)   French painter. Influenced by CÉZANNE and associated for a time with LES FAUVES, Braque collaborated with PICASSO on the development of CUBISM. The severe, analytical angularity of his cubist work, however, gave way to a long series of more representational nudes and still lifes. In another innovation, Braque's use of typesetters' letters in his paintings paved the way for extensive use of collage in both his own and others' art. His *Birds* series (1952–63) brought to a culmination of simplicity his elegant use of line and color.

Brasch, Charles [Orwell] (1909–1973)   New Zealand poet and editor. Educated at Oxford, Brasch did not return to New Zealand until after World War II. Beginning with *The Land and the People* (1939), his abstract, intellectual poetry revealed an ambivalence about the lush and beautiful land of New Zealand, with its shallow human history and parochial culture. In *The Estate*

(1957), however, the poet's sense of alienation and isolation is markedly less pronounced. Brasch also founded and edited (1947–66) the influential literary journal *Landfall*. In 1981 a memoir, *Indirections* (ed James Betram), was published posthumously.

Brathwaite, Edward [Kaman] (1930–   )   Barbadian poet. Brathwaite's most important poetic work is a trilogy—of which *Rights of Passage* (1967) is the first and best-known volume—that seeks to offer a unified historical survey of the involuntary migration of Africans to the Caribbean as slaves and to trace the effects of this dislocation both in historical and psychological terms. The two other volumes of the trilogy, *Masks* (1968) and *Islands* (1969), were published together with *Rights of Passage* in *The Arrivants: A New World Trilogy* (1973). Brathwaite's verse is distinguished by its skillful incorporation of West Indian musical rhythms. In *Mother Poem* (1977) and *Sun Poem* (1982), language is made to serve experience to create the perfect fusion between them.

Braudel, Fernand (1902–1985)   French historian and man of letters. Braudel's two major works, *The Mediterranean and the Mediterranean World in the Age of Philip II* (2 vols, 1949; tr 1972–74) and the grand *Civilization and Capitalism, 15th–18th Century* (3 vols, 1967, rev 1979; rev tr 3 vols: *The Structures of Everyday Life*, 1982; *The Wheels of Commerce*, 1983; *The Perspective of the World*, 1984), firmly established him as one of the greatest historians of the 20th century. He was highly influential as the leader of the school of historical thought associated with the French history journal *Annales*, which emphasized a multidisciplinary approach to historical study.

The chief difference in Braudel's method of historical research and writings lies in its basic principle: that history can be understood only through the daily working lives of people, what they ate, what they wore, how they worked, how they were taxed, how they organized their finances, etc., rather than who they fought and what these battles were. The luminaries of an era are not particularly important from this point of view, since they are usually distinguished from the majority rather than representative of it.

What emerges, among other important data, is what Braudel calls "world-time": a time-scale that is created by different parts of the world that have kept pace with each other and are at comparable levels of social, economic, and cultural development. "World-time" does not, however, aim at presenting the sum total of the achievements of all people but discerns, rather, certain patterns in the way human development has taken place.

Brautigan, Richard (1933–1984)   American novelist and poet. On the basis of the verse collected in *The Pill Versus the Springhill Mine Disaster* (1968) and *Rommel Drives On Deep into Egypt* (1970), Brautigan earned a reputation as an interesting but minor poet. It is in prose fiction that he did his most extensive and original work.

Such books as *A Confederate General from Big Sur* (1965), *Trout Fishing in America* (1967), and *In Watermelon Sugar* (1968) combine elements of the novel, the prose essay, and the dream vision. Short on such conventional narrative elements as plot and character development, these fictions are sustained by Brautigan's bizarre sense of humor and his sure feel for language. Subsequent works include the stories in *Revenge of the Lawn* (1971), the poems in *June 30th, June 30th* (1975), and the novels *Willard & His Bowling Trophies* (1975) and *The Tokyo-Montana Express* (1980).

Brave New World (1932)   A satirical novel by Aldous HUXLEY. Set in the year 632 AF (After Ford), it is a grim picture of the world which Huxley thinks our scientific and social developments have already begun to create. Human embryos are developed in bottles and conditioned to collectivism and passivity. A "savage" is found in New Mexico and imported as an experiment. He has educated himself by reading Shakespeare and believes in spirituality and moral choice; in the new world, he soon goes berserk and kills himself. The title, which is highly ironic, is from Shakespeare's *The Tempest*.

brazen head   A theme of many legends. The legend of the wonderful head of brass that could speak is common in early romances and is of Eastern origin. In *Valentine and Orson*, a gigantic head kept in the castle of the giant Ferragus of Portugal tells those who consult it whatever they require to know, past, present, or to come. The most famous brazen head in English legend is that fabled to have been made by Roger Bacon. It was said that, if Bacon heard it speak, he would succeed in his projects; if not, he would fail. His familiar, Miles, was set to watch, and, while Bacon slept, the head spoke thrice: "Time is"; half an hour later, it said, "Time was." In another half-hour, it said, "Time past," fell down, and was broken to atoms. References to Bacon's brazen head are frequent in literature.

Bread and Wine (Pane e vino, 1937; rev 1962)   A novel by Ignazio SILONE. The hero, Pietro Spina, returns to his native Abruzzi after fifteen years of exile to continue his antifascist agitation. As he travels through the country, disguised as a priest, he sees the inroads made upon the Italian character by Mussolini's rule. Finding that the underground movement is in chaos and doubting the validity of his old revolutionary slogans, he eventually flees to avoid certain arrest. Other important characters include the devout Cristina and Don Benedetto, a priest who is an uncompromising opponent of the regime and who is poisoned by the sacramental wine he drinks as he celebrates mass. In the 1962 version of the novel, the Italian title was changed to *Vino e pane*.

Break, Break, Break (1842)   A poem by Alfred TENNYSON, one of those inspired by the death of his friend Arthur HALLAM.

Brecht, Bertolt (1898–1956)   German poet and dramatist. Despite his explicit commitment to Marxist dogma, Brecht's plays have been immensely popular in the West. His early plays, such as *Trommeln in der Nacht* (1922; tr *Drums in the Night*, 1970), *Im Dickicht der Städte* (1924; tr *In the Jungle of Cities*, 1961), and *Mann ist Mann* (1926; tr *A Man Is a Man*, 1961), show the influence of EXPRESSIONISM. Though they are permeated by a critical irony toward modern society, they do not yet systematically advocate any political doctrine. The early plays do contain, however, evidence of the radical staging techniques that Brecht was to develop in the EPIC THEATRE, which dominated his subsequent productions. The first successful integration of epic-theatre techniques was the result of his collaboration with Kurt WEILL on THE THREEPENNY OPERA, a scathing satire on the modern bourgeoisie. This production, along with RISE AND FALL OF THE CITY MAHOGANNY, marks Brecht's turn to Marxism. In 1933 he was driven from Germany by the rise of Nazism and began a fourteen-year exile in Denmark, Sweden, Finland, and, from 1941 to 1947, the U.S. The plays written during this period include direct attacks on Nazism, as in THE PRIVATE LIFE OF THE MASTER RACE and *Schweyk im Zweiten Weltkrieg* (1943; tr *Schweyk in the Second World War*, 1970); plays with historical settings, such as THE LIFE OF GALILEO and MOTHER COURAGE AND HER CHILDREN; and two Chinese parables, THE GOOD WOMAN OF SETZUAN and THE CAUCASIAN CHALK CIRCLE.

In 1947 Brecht moved to Zurich and went from there to East Berlin in 1949, where he founded the state-supported Berliner Ensemble, to which he devoted the rest of his life. The works from this last period consist almost entirely of adaptations. His plays were performed in many countries and added some prestige to the East German regime. Although he was lavishly endowed by the government, his tenure in East Germany was not without its difficulties. While he was personally an ardent Communist, many of his plays were criticized for lacking the true Communist spirit. He had to change, for example, *Das Verhör des Lukullus* (1939; tr *The Trial of Lucullus*, 1970) because it was too pacifistic in spirit for his employer, an ironic turn of fate for the man who had severely criticized his hero in *The Life of Galileo* for having recanted under the Inquisition's threat of torture. In any case, Brecht's innovative theatrical techniques had a profound effect on the development of modern theatre, as much for the opposition he inspired as for the disciples he collected.

A collection, *Bertolt Brecht Poems 1913–1956*, was published in 1979, bringing together many poems that had not been published during his lifetime.

Brennan, Christopher John (1870–1932)   Australian poet. Strongly influenced by BAUDELAIRE and MALLARMÉ, Brennan ranks among the most notable symbolist poets in English. *Collected Verse* (1960) demonstrates

Brennan's stylistic skill and his lifelong philosophy: mankind lacks its primal, unconscious, harmonious unity and therefore must strive consciously toward the ultimate synthesis of mind, body, and soul.

Brentano, Clemens Maria (1778–1842)   German romantic poet. Brentano was the brother of Bettina von Arnim. In his lyrics, he had a genius for capturing the folk spirit, and it was he who invented the so-called folk legend of the LORELEI, in a poem that appeared in his novel *Godwi* (1800–1801). However, he was also capable of highly sophisticated poems, especially on religious subjects, as in his unfinished *Romanzen vom Rosenkranz* (*Romances of the Rosary*, written 1810 et seq). With his friend and later brother-in-law Achim von Arnim, he edited *Des Knaben Wunderhorn* (*The Boy's Wonderhorn*; vol 1, 1805; vol 2, 1808; vol 3, 1818), a collection of folk songs, and his private collection of folk books provided the material for Görres's treatise on the subject. Brentano's short narrative works include the novella *Geschichte vom braven Kasperl und dem schönen Annerl* (tr *Story of Upright Casper and Lovely Annie*, 1816, pub 1838) and numerous MÄRCHEN. See GERMAN ROMANTICISM; VOLKS-BUCH.

Bresson, Robert (1907–   )   French film director and scriptwriter. Bresson's stark and pared-down films probe the life of the human spirit. For him, the purity of the soul can be achieved only by experiencing evil; grace comes only through suffering. The best known of his highly individualistic films are *Les Dames du Bois de Boulogne* (1945) and *Le Journal d'une curé de campagne* (1951), based on THE DIARY OF A COUNTRY PRIEST by Georges Bernanos. Most of his work is characterized by intentionally slow pacing, rigidly framed closeups, and the use of nonprofessional actors. Among his other films are *Un Condamné à mort s'est échapé* (1956), *Mouchette* (1967), also adapted from a Bernanos novel, *Lancelot du lac* (1974), and *Le Diable probablement* (1977). Bresson's writings about film and film technique were published in *Notes sur le cinématographe* (1975; tr *Notes on Cinematography*, 1977).

Breton, André (1896–1966)   French artist, poet, novelist, and essayist. Breton was greatly influenced by his reading of Arthur Rimbaud's poetry, his studies of Freudian theory, and his own work in psychiatry. His friendship (1916–19) with Jacques Vaché (1895–1919), who committed suicide as a deliberate mark of his contempt for modern society, also made a deep impression. In 1919 Breton met Tristan TZARA and led a group of friends into the DADA movement. By 1921, however, he had rejected Tzara's nihilistic use of the irrational as a mockery of reason in favor of a serious research into the subconscious as the autonomous source of truth and beauty. The results of his experiments in automatic writing were published as *Les Champs magnétiques* (1921), written with Philippe Soupault.

In 1924 he founded SURREALISM; his three manifestoes (1924, 1930, 1942) are the most important theoretical statements of the movement. Other critical essays in its defense include *Les Pas perdus* (1924), *Légitime défense* (1926), *Le Surréalisme et la peinture* (1928; tr *Surrealism and Painting*, 1972), and *Qu'est-que le surréalisme?* (1934; tr *What Is Surrealism?*, 1936).

A growing interest in the study of dreams and psychic states led to the novel NADJA and to *Les Vases communicants* (1932), a study of dreams. Breton joined the Communist Party in 1927 but left it in 1935 after trying unsuccessfully to identify surrealism as the artistic representative of social revolution.

His poems exalting love include those in *Le Revolver à cheveux blancs* (1932), *L'Amour fou* (1937), *Fata Morgana* (1942; tr 1969), and *Arcane 17* (1945).

Bréton de los Herreros, Manuel (1796–1873) Spanish playwright. The clarity of the work of this prominent social satirist makes up for the lack of bitter irony in his comedies about middle-class life. His classic *Marcela, o ¿cual de los tres?* (1831) deals with the problems of a widow beset by three equally unattractive suitors: one arrogant, the second loud, and the third melancholy. He was distinctly opposed to the trends of romanticism, as is evident in his essays, *Elena* (1834), and his antiromantic play, *¡Muérote y verás!* (1837). Other well-known dramas include *El pelo de la dehesa* (1840) and *La escuela de matrimonio* (1852).

Breton lai (or Breton lay)   A rhymed story popular in England in the 14th century, based on earlier French LAIS. Breton lais usually deal with Celtic themes and often draw on material from ARTHURIAN LEGEND. The origin of this literary form is unknown, but it was perfected in the 12th century by MARIE DE FRANCE, who wrote, among others, the lai SIR LAUNFAL. Among the best-known surviving Breton lais in English are *Sir Orfeo* and Chaucer's THE FRANKLIN'S TALE, which speaks of the old Bretons, who rhymed their tales and sang them to musical accompaniment.

Breuer, Marcel (1902–1981)   Hungarian-born American architect. Originally intending to be an artist, Breuer became instead one of the most celebrated architect-designers to emerge from the BAUHAUS. As chief furniture designer there, he was the first to use tubular steel in furniture, and he also pioneered the use of molded plywood. The "Breuer chair," with its cantilevered seat, became a classic of industrial and domestic furniture design. Fleeing the Nazi regime, he moved to England and then to Cambridge, Massachusetts, where he formed a partnership with Walter GROPIUS, his colleague from the Bauhaus. Together they designed many houses, but their greatest impact was as teachers at Harvard, where their students included Philip JOHNSON and Paul Rudolph. In 1946

Breuer moved to New York City to practice independently. He was one of three architects chosen to design the UNESCO building in Paris (1952), and in 1956 he designed the Whitney Museum of American Art in New York. He published *Sun and Shadow: The Philosophy of an Architect* in 1955 and *Adventure in Architecture* in 1958.

Brew, [Osborne Henry] Kwesi (1928–   ) Ghanaian poet. Brew's poetry, published widely in journals and anthologies, as well as in his own volume, *The Shadows of Laughter* (1968), reveals a lyric poet writing in conventional forms. His concern is with love and matters of faith, as well as with individual responsibility and the place of the individual in the community.

Brian Boru, Boroimhe (926–1014) Irish king (after 1002) and national hero. Brian Boru's victory over the Danes at Clontarf (1014) put a permanent end to their sovereignty over Ireland, but he was murdered in his tent after the battle.

Briareus In classic legend, a huge monster with one hundred arms and fifty heads. With his brothers, Cottus and Gyges, Briareus conquered the Titans by hurling three hundred rocks at them at once. Thetis called him to the aid of ZEUS when HERA, ATHENE, and POSEIDON rebelled against him. Briareus was also called Aegeon.

Bricklayer, the A nickname for Ben JONSON, from his stepfather's trade.

Bride Comes to Yellow Sky, The (1898) A short story by Stephen CRANE. Published in the collection *The Open Boat and Other Tales of Adventure*, it deals with the conflict between Sheriff Jack Potter and Scratchy Wilson, one of the old frontier gunfighters. Potter brings his new wife to Yellow Sky and encounters Scratchy, who is looking for a fight. When Scratchy grasps the fact that Potter has no gun, he realizes that the old days are gone forever.

Bride of Lammermoor, The (1819) A historical novel by Sir Walter SCOTT, set in the reign of William III. The titular heroine is Lucy Ashton, daughter of Sir William Ashton, an unscrupulous man who has made great gains in fortune and position by bringing the estate of Lord Ravenswood to ruin through legal trickery. Though he has sworn vengeance, Ravenswood's son Edgar falls in love with Lucy; the lovers plight their troth at the Mermaid's Fountain, but, while Edgar is away, Lucy is forced by her parents to marry the unpleasant, dissolute Frank Hayston, laird of Bucklaw. Deranged with grief, Lucy stabs and critically wounds her bridegroom; she dies in convulsions the following day. Edgar, hearing of the marriage and taking it as Lucy's rejection of him, is on his way to a duel with her brother when he is lost in the quicksand of Kelpies Flow, fulfilling an ancient prophecy. The novel is based on historical incident.

In Donizetti's opera *Lucia di Lammermoor* (1835), which is based on the novel, Bucklaw dies of the wound inflicted by his bride, and Edgar, heartbroken at Lucy's death, stabs himself.

Bride of the Sea Venice. The city was so called from the ancient ceremony of the wedding of the sea and the city by the doge, who threw a ring into the Adriatic, saying, "We wed thee, O sea, in token of perpetual domination." This took place each year on Ascension Day and was enjoined upon the Venetians in 1177 by Pope Alexander III, who gave the doge a gold ring from his own finger in token of the victory achieved by the Venetian fleet at Istria over Frederick Barbarossa, in defense of the pope's quarrel.

Brideshead Revisited (1945) A novel by Evelyn WAUGH, subtitled *The Sacred and Profane Memories of Captain Charles Ryder*. As an undergraduate, Ryder met Sebastian Marchmain and later visited him and his family at Brideshead, their home. Billeted there during World War II, Ryder recalls the members of this family and their individual responses to their Catholic faith.

The novel was made into a multipart film for television by the BBC, shown in 1980 in England and in 1982 in the U.S.

Bridge, The (1930) A long poem by Hart CRANE. In this, his most important work, Crane attempted to synthesize a picture of modern America by the use of symbols from its past and present, centered about the Brooklyn Bridge as a chief symbol of man's aspiration and achievement. Written in several sections, the poem makes use of such figures from the American past as Columbus, Whitman, Poe, and Emily Dickinson; they themselves function as bridges, connecting and fusing the disparate elements of American life into an organic whole. Not only past and present but time and eternity are fused, the latter bridge being furnished by the Mississippi River.

Bridge of San Luis Rey, The (1927) A novel by Thornton WILDER. The winner of a PULITZER PRIZE, it tells of the collapse of a bridge in Peru in 1714. Five travelers on the bridge are killed, and the accident is witnessed by Brother Juniper, a Franciscan friar. The priest wonders whether it really was an accident or a deliberate plan of the Almighty, and his subsequent investigation into the lives of the five people forms the core of the book.

Bridge on the Drina, The (Na Drini ćuprija, 1945; tr 1959) A chronicle by Ivo ANDRIĆ. This long narrative relates in a series of episodes the history of a bridge near the Bosnian town of Višegrad. That history covers three and a half centuries, through much of which the Bosnians lived under Turkish overlords. This is probably the most important of Andrić's several novels about his native Bosnia; it is part of a trilogy that includes *Travnicka hronika* (1945; tr *Bosnian Story*, 1958) and *Gospodjica* (1945; tr *The Woman from Sarajevo*, 1965).

Bridges, Robert (1844–1930) English poet, appointed British POET LAUREATE in 1913. Bridges's poetry is classical in spirit and in diction; he advocated a return to the diction of the 18th century and was a cofounder of the Society for Pure English. His prosody is mildly experimental. He did important work in metrics, including the study *Milton's Prosody* (1893). His *Poetical Works* was published in 1912, and *The Testament of Beauty* in 1929. "A Passerby" is his finest lyric. Bridges also wrote plays, chiefly on classical subjects, and critical essays. Bridges was a friend of Gerard Manley HOPKINS and published his poetry in 1918.

Brigge, Malte Laurids   See NOTEBOOKS OF MALTE LAURIDS BRIGGE, THE.

Brinvilliers, Marquise de (born Marie Madeleine d'Aubray, 1630–1676)   Notorious French poisoner and a favorite subject for writers. Mme de SÉVIGNÉ describes Brinvilliers's execution in her letters.

Briscoe, Lily   A painter, a leading character in Virginia Woolf's novel To THE LIGHTHOUSE.

Briseis   The daughter of Briseus. Briseis was the subject of the quarrel in the ILIAD between Agamemnon and Achilles; when the former robbed Achilles of her, Achilles refused any longer to go to battle, and the Greeks lost ground daily.

Britannia   A personification of the British Empire. The first known representation of Britannia as a female figure sitting on a globe, leaning with one arm on a shield and grasping a spear in the other hand, is on a Roman coin of Antoninus Pius, who died AD 161. The figure reappeared on the English copper coin in 1665, in the reign of Charles II.

Britannicus (original name Claudius Tiberius Germanicus, c AD 41–55)   Son of Messalina and the emperor Claudius, heir apparent to the throne. Through the scheming of his stepmother, AGRIPPINA, he was denied succession to the throne. It is believed that Nero, his half brother, poisoned Britannicus at a banquet. The name Britannicus was given to him by the senate because the conquest of Britain took place at about the time of his birth. He is the subject of a tragedy (1669) by Racine.

Britannicus (1669)   A tragedy by RACINE. The material of the play is derived from Tacitus. Smitten with Junia, the beloved of his half brother Britannicus, the emperor Nero attempts to win her; unsuccessful, he causes Britannicus to be arrested and poisons him. Junia escapes from the palace and becomes a vestal virgin. The play abounds in political subplot and marks Racine's first challenge of CORNEILLE on the older playwright's home ground: political drama.

Brittain, Vera (pen name of Mrs. George Edward Gordon Catlin, 1896–1970)   English essayist and novelist. Brittain's nonfiction includes the autobiographical volumes *Testament of Youth* (1933)—a highly intelligent and very moving account of her struggle to enter university and her work as a nurse in France during World War I —*Testament of Friendship* (1940), and *Testament of Expe-*

rience (1957), as well as *Lady into Woman: A History of Women from Victoria to Elizabeth II* (1953). Among her novels are *The Dark Tide* (1923) and *Account Rendered* (1945).

Britten, [Edward] Benjamin (1913–1976)   English composer. Britten was predominantly a vocal composer, highly adept at setting the English language to music in an effective and appropriate way, first demonstrated in his *Serenade* for tenor solo, horn, and strings (1944), with its settings of selections from TENNYSON, BLAKE, Ben JONSON, KEATS, and others. He was the most successful opera composer of the middle 20th century. Many of his operas express his antiwar sentiments and his deep sympathy with the outcasts of society. The principal works include the operas *Peter Grimes* (1945), *The Rape of Lucretia* (1946), *Albert Herring* (1947; after a story by Maupassant), *Billy Budd* (1951), *The Turn of the Screw* (1954), *A Midsummer Night's Dream* (1960), and *Death in Venice* (1973). His choral works include A *Ceremony of Carols* (1942; settings of 15th-century English texts) and the *War Requiem* (1961), which combines the Latin text of the *Requiem Mass* with English antiwar poems by Wilfred OWEN. Britten was considered by many to be England's greatest composer since Henry Purcell, in the 17th century. In 1976 he was granted a life peerage by Queen Elizabeth II.

Broad, C[harlie] D[unbar] (1887–1971)   English philosopher. Broad's work is distinguished by a thoroughness and clarity of presentation. In such books as *Perception, Physics, and Reality* (1914) and *Scientific Thought* (1923), he takes an analytic approach to the philosophy of sense perception. *The Mind and Its Place in Nature* (1925), which seriously analyzes evidence for life after death, and *Lectures on Psychical Research* (1962) were seminal discussions of psychic phenomena. He was Knightsbridge Professor of Moral Philosophy at Trinity College, Cambridge, until his retirement in 1953. His *Critical Essays in Moral Philosophy* (ed D. R. Cheney) appeared in 1971.

broadside ballads   Popular songs and poems, written in doggerel. They were printed in black letter on a single sheet of paper, decorated with woodcuts, with the name of the tune to which the ballads in question were to be sung, and sold for a penny or two on the street corners of England in the late 16th and early 17th centuries. Their subject matter was taken from political events, battles or wars, murders, strange happenings, executions, freakish births, domestic quarrels, and the like, and they often also included moral exhortations and religious propaganda.

Brobdingnag   The country of giants twelve times the size of man in Jonathan Swift's satire GULLIVER'S TRAVELS. Told by Gulliver of European customs and institutions, the king observes, "I cannot but conclude the bulk of your natives to be the most pernicious race of little vermin that nature ever suffered to crawl upon the earth." The inhuman nobility of this view contrasts with the meanness and pettiness of the people of LILLIPUT. See GLUMDAL-CLITCH.

Broch, Hermann (1886–1951)   Austrian novelist. Broch is best known for *Der Tod des Vergil* (1945; tr *The Death of Vergil*, 1946), in which mythical and penetrating psychological elements are blended in an original and powerful manner that excited comparisons with such writers as JOYCE and MANN. His most famous earlier work, more directly concerned with social and historical problems, is *Die Schlafwandler* (1930–32; tr *The Sleepwalkers*, 1932), a trilogy of novels. Broch had a widely varied background that influenced his writing. He studied philosophy and mathematics, was active in the textile industry, wrote numerous sociological and literary essays in addition to his novels, and died while engaged in research on mass psychology at Yale University. Through the help of Joyce, among others, he was allowed to emigrate from Austria after he was arrested by the Nazis.

Brocken   The highest peak of the Harz range, in Saxony. On the eve of May Day, i.e., the feast of Walburga, or Walpurgis Night, the Brocken was the scene of a famous witches' Sabbath. It is also known for the specter of the Brocken, an optical illusion, first observed on the Brocken, in which shadows of the spectators, greatly magnified, are projected on the mists about the summit of the mountain opposite. In one of De Quincey's opium dreams, there is a powerful description of the Brocken specter.

Brodsky, Joseph (1940–   )   Soviet poet and critic. Born Iosif Alexandrovich in Leningrad, Brodsky began writing poetry in 1958. He also demonstrated considerable talent in rendering Russian translations of Donne and Marvell, and he was exposed to such Western authors as Kafka, Proust, and Faulkner through Polish translations. In 1964 he was tried as a "social parasite" and sentenced to five years at hard labor in Siberia. Within twenty months, however, Brodsky was released, and he returned to Leningrad in 1965. While he was in Siberia, his first book of poems, *Stikhotvoreniya i poemy* (*Short and Long Poems*, 1965), appeared in America. In 1972 Brodsky emigrated from the Soviet Union, becoming an American citizen in 1977. His second book of verse, *Ostanovka v pustyne* (*A Halt in the Wilderness*, 1970), and his third, *Konets prekrasnoy epokhi* (*The End of a Lovely Era*, 1977), contain poems written before and after his exile in Siberia. In style, Brodsky is largely traditional and classical; his poetry focuses on the moral and historical aspects of life, using mythological and religious allusions. His work displays the various influences of MANDELSTAM and PASTERNAK, on the one hand, and of T. S. ELIOT and W. H. AUDEN, on the other. English translations of his work are *Joseph Brodsky: Selected Poems* (1973), *A Part of Speech* (1979), and *Less Than One* (1986), a collection of essays.

Brome, Richard (d 1652)   English dramatist, known for his realistic and satirical comedies of life in London. Brome's best plays are *The City Wit, or The Woman Wears the Breeches* (c1628), *The Weeding of Covent Garden* (1632), *The Sparagus Garden* (1635), and *A Jovial Crew* (1641). He was the last of the comic dramatists of the Tudor-Stuart period.

Bromfield, Louis (1896–1956)   American writer. Bromfield established his reputation with his early novels, the four books of a tetralogy called *Escape*: THE GREEN BAY TREE, *Possession* (1925), *Early Autumn* (1926), and *A Good Woman* (1927). He also received praise for his factual and descriptive accounts of the one-thousand acre Ohio farm he purchased and turned into a productive showcase: *Pleasant Valley* (1945), *Malabar Farm* (1948), *Out of the Earth* (1950), and *From My Experience* (1955). One of his numerous other novels, *The Rains Came* (1937), is set in Malabar, the coastal region of India after which his farm was named.

bromide and sulphite   Words coined by Gelett Burgess in his humorous essay *Are You a Bromide, or The Sulphitic Theory* (1907). In it he explains the terms *bromide* and *sulphite* as applied to psychological rather than chemical analysis. The bromide, according to Burgess, "does his thinking by syndicate. He follows the main-traveled roads, he goes with the crowd." The sulphite, on the other hand, is unconventional, original, everything that the bromide is not.

Bronowski, Jacob (1908–1974)   English scientist and philosopher. As a poet, literary critic, dramatist, physicist, and mathematician, Bronowski was the embodiment of his belief that science, the arts, and the humanities are not distinct entities but different facets of man's capacity for imagination. Throughout his career, he articulated a philosophy for understanding the human condition within the greater laws of nature. In such books as *The Common Sense of Science* (1951) and *Science and Human Values* (1956, rev 1965), he effectively communicated the ideas of science to laymen. He reached his widest audience with his BBC television series *The Ascent of Man* and his book of the same title (1974), tracing mankind's attempt to control the environment. Posthumous collections of his writings include *A Sense of the Future* (1977), essays from 1948 to 1974 on science and creativity and the role of each in a civilized society, and *The Origins of Knowledge and Imagination* (1978), observations on the relationship between human biology, perception, and knowledge.

Bronstein, Lev Davidovich   See TROTSKY, LEON.

Brontë   An English family, originally of Irish descent, that produced three 19th-century novelists: Charlotte, Emily, and Anne. On the death of his wife in 1821, the Reverend Patrick Brontë, a curate, sent for his sister-in-law to help him bring up his six children. A few years later, all the girls except Anne were sent to board at the Clergy Daughters' School at Cowan Bridge; conditions at the school were dreadful, worsened by the administration's belief that physical discomfort was spiritually edifying. The two eldest girls died at the school in 1825, and Charlotte and Emily were returned home. Lowood School in JANE EYRE was based on Charlotte's unhappy memories of Cowan Bridge. During much of their childhood, the four remaining Brontë children were free to roam and play in the Yorkshire moors, giving free reign to their imaginations. Charlotte, with the help of her brother Branwell, created Angria, a vast, imaginary African empire, and wrote of the lives and adventures of its inhabitants. At the same time, Emily kept a journal, the *Gondal Chronicle*, on the wars and intrigues of the Royalists and Republicans in a mysterious North country.

In 1831 Charlotte (1816–55) was sent to Roe Head School, where she returned to teach (1835–38). She worked for a time as a governess and then in 1842 went with Emily to Brussels to study at the school of Constantine Héger, where she taught the following year. Many of the scenes of VILLETTE are based on Charlotte's experiences at the school and on her deep but frustrated emotional attachment to Héger. In 1845 Charlotte made the accidental discovery that Emily and Anne had been writing verse. She herself had composed many poems, and she collected them all into a volume (1846) of poetry signed by Currer (Charlotte), Ellis (Emily), and Acton (Anne) Bell, pseudonyms that they retained throughout their later work. The book, published at their expense, was unsuccessful, selling only two copies. Charlotte soon submitted her first novel, *The Professor*, to a number of publishers, and it was rejected so many times that she finally withdrew it. She nevertheless set to work to complete *Jane Eyre*, which was published and achieved spectacular success.

On the strength of her one novel, WUTHERING HEIGHTS, and the best of her poems, Emily (1818–48) is generally considered to be of greater genius than her sisters. Her mysticism is reflected in her work, especially in her extraordinary novel and in such poems as "The Prisoner," "Remembrance," "The Old Stoic," and "The Visionary." Some skeptics maintained that *Wuthering Heights* was actually the work of her dissipated brother, Patrick Branwell (1817–48), on the grounds that no woman, let alone one who led such a circumscribed life, could have written such a turbulent and passionate book. But Branwell, who was tubercular and addicted to alcohol and possibly to opium, had no literary talent. Emily, who caught cold at his funeral, died a few months after him.

Anne (1820–49), the least talented of the sisters, wrote two novels, AGNES GREY and THE TENANT OF WILDFELL HALL. It is possible that neither of these books would be remembered today if she were not the sister of Charlotte and Emily.

After her sisters' death, Charlotte devoted herself to the care of her father, who was going blind. She completed SHIRLEY, which was well received, as was *Villette*, her last novel. These were years of social lionization, and in London and elsewhere she met Thackeray, Matthew Arnold, Mrs. Gaskell, Harriet Martineau, and others. She married Arthur Bell Nichols, her father's curate, in 1854 and died the following year. *The Professor* was published posthumously in 1857, and *Emma*, a fragment, appeared in 1860.

Bronze Horseman, The (Medny vsadnik, 1833) A long poem by Aleksandr PUSHKIN. Its theme is the conflict between the desires of an ordinary individual, represented by the poor clerk Yevgeny, and the demands of the powerful state, represented by PETER THE GREAT. A flood inundates St. Petersburg, the capital city built on the Neva River at Peter's orders, and drowns Yevgeny's fiancée. Demented by grief, Yevgeny stands before the imposing statue of the emperor and curses Peter's inhuman willfulness, which he blames for his fiancée's death. In a hallucination, he imagines that Peter is chasing him through the streets of the city. After this, Yevgeny is cured of his rebelliousness. Whenever he passes the statue of the emperor, his manner once again shows respect and fear.

Brooke, Dorothea   The idealistic heroine of George Eliot's MIDDLEMARCH. Dorothea's sister Celia and their uncle, Squire Brooke, with whom they live, are also prominent characters.

Brooke, Frances [Moore] (1724–1789)   English-born Canadian novelist. The wife of a clergyman, Brooke followed her husband to Canada, where he was chaplain to the garrison at Quebec. Her four-volume *History of Emily Montague* (1769) had a Canadian setting and is often considered the first Canadian novel. However, Mrs. Brooke's work was based on English models and had no perceptible effect on Canadian literature, though it does give a vivid picture of social life in 18th-century Quebec.

Brooke, Rupert [Chawner] (1887–1915)   English poet. Brooke's striking good looks, personal charm, and obvious intelligence made him the darling of English literati before World War I. His collection of sonnets in *1914 and Other Poems* (1915) expressed the extraordinary idealism of the early war rather than the horrors of actual combat reflected in the works of Wilfred OWEN and Siegfried SASSOON. His death from septicaemia on his way to war service crystallized his legendary status as the epitome of England's idealistic youth. As a poet, Brooke was identified with the GEORGIANS. "Grantchester" and "The Great Lover" are representative of his early, traditional verse. Later, like T. S. ELIOT, he was influenced by his study of 17th-century poetry (he published a study of John WEBSTER in 1911), and he began to write witty and original verse, such as "Heaven" and "Dust."

Brook Farm   A utopian community established in
1841 at West Roxbury, Massachusetts. The members of
the Brook Farm Institute of Agriculture and Education, led
by George RIPLEY, shared equally in work, benefits, and
remuneration; among those associated with the community
were Theodore Parker, William Henry Channing, Nathaniel HAWTHORNE, Margaret FULLER, Charles A. Dana, G.
W. Curtis, and Albert Brisbane. The group, later influenced by FOURIERISM, changed its name to the Brook Farm
Phalanx; in 1846, when the "Central Phalanstery" burned
down, it disbanded. Emerson viewed this experiment made
by his fellow Transcendentalists with skepticism; he called
Brook Farm "the Age of Reason in a patty-pan." Hawthorne, who came to West Roxbury in the hope of finding
an economical way to live and write, soon found communal living unattractive. He modeled the community in THE
BLITHEDALE ROMANCE on Brook Farm.

Brook Kerith, The (1916)   A novel by George
MOORE. A presentation of the life of Jesus, it follows the
customary account as far as the Crucifixion, but Joseph of
Arimathea later finds Jesus still alive. For thirty years afterward Jesus lives as a shepherd by the Brook Kerith. He has
rejected his early belief in himself, which he considers
blasphemy, and, when he finally meets Paul the Apostle
and hears his version of the story, he is horrified and plans
to go to Jerusalem and reveal the truth. Paul, however,
forces him to realize that his story would not be believed.

The ravens fed Elijah by this brook of Palestine, called
Cherith in the Bible.

Brooks, Cleanth (1906–   )   American literary
critic and educator. Brooks became associated with the
NEW CRITICISM, when he coedited (1935–42) THE SOUTH-
ERN REVIEW with Robert Penn WARREN. He and Warren
collaborated on a number of books that became classic
texts: *Understanding Poetry* (1938; rev 1975), *Understanding Fiction* (1943; rev 1959), and *Modern Rhetoric* (1949;
rev 1958). He also wrote *Understanding Drama* (1945)
with Robert Heilman and, with W. K. Wimsatt, the highly
regarded *Literary Criticism: A Short History* (1957). In
these texts and in his own volumes, *Modern Poetry and the
Tradition* (1939) and *The Well Wrought Urn* (1947),
Brooks introduced the tenets of the New Criticism to the
teaching of literature. Brooks's approach to literature
emphasizes close structural analysis, stressing the central
qualities of paradox, irony, symbolism, and dramatic structure. Ranking as major critical works are his two studies
William Faulkner: The Yoknapatawpha Country (1963)
and *William Faulkner: Toward Yoknapatawpha and
Beyond* (1978). See FUGITIVES, THE.

Brooks, Gwendolyn (1917–   )   American poet
and novelist. Brooks is one of the foremost of the black
American poets of the mid-20th century who used their
racial identity to create an art form of universal distinction.
She received the PULITZER PRIZE for Poetry in 1950, for

Annie Allen (1949), when her more highly reputed
volumes were yet to be published: *In the Mecca* in 1968
and *Family Pictures* in 1970, for instance. Taken as a
whole, Brooks's poetry is immersed in the language, the
struggles, and the dreams of American blacks, especially
those of her native Chicago. With a disarming candor, the
poems depict the wounds and inequities which are dealt to
her brethren. However, unlike the works of the more angry
writers of the 1960s, such as James BALDWIN and Imamu
Amiri BARAKA, Brooks's writing delivers its blow quietly.
Hers is a poetry without bathos or self-pity; the rhythms are
simple and joyous, the humor is infectious, and life is generally embraced with *élan*. Recent writings include *Aloneness* (1971), *Report from Part One: An Autobiography*
(1972), *Beckonings* (1975), *Primer for Blacks* (1980), and *To
Disembark* (1981).

Brooks, Van Wyck (1886–1963)   American critic
and biographer. Brooks, with Frank Waldo and James
OPPENHEIM, was for a time associated with the financially
doomed magazine THE SEVEN ARTS. His early writings
—*The Wine of the Puritans* (1908), *America's Coming of
Age* (1915), *The Ordeal of Mark Twain* (1920), and *The
Pilgrimage of Henry James* (1925)—were critical of the
insularity and materialism of America's Puritan heritage.
The Flowering of New England: 1815–1865 (1936; PULIT-
ZER PRIZE) was the first of a series called "Makers and Find-
ers" that included *New England: Indian Summer 1865–
1915* (1940), *The World of Washington Irving* (1944), and
The Times of Melville and Whitman (1947). The series presented the first composite picture of American cultural and
literary development. Among Brooks's many other works
are literary biographies and the autobiographical volumes
Days of Phoenix (1957), *From a Writer's Notebook* (1958),
and *An Autobiography* (1965). His correspondence with
Lewis MUMFORD was published in 1970.

Brophy, [Antonia] Brigid (1929–   )   Anglo-
Irish novelist, critic, and dramatist. Strongly influenced by
both FREUD and G. B. SHAW, Brophy tends to portray life
as a conflict between the life force and the opposing death
instinct. Her early works, such as *The Crown Princess*
(1953), a collection of stories, and *Hackenfeller's Ape*
(1953), have a strong didactic element. An acerbic Swiftian
satire characterizes *Flesh* (1962), *The Snow Ball* (1964),
and *In Transit* (1969). *Prancing Novelist* (1972) is a distinguished study of Ronald FIRBANK, whose influence on
Brophy is most evident in *Palace Without Chairs* (1978), a
whimsical political fable. Her other works include two
books on Aubrey BEARDSLEY: *Black and White* (1968) and
Beardsley and His World (1976).

Brother Jonathan   The generic name for a New
Englander, hence for Americans and America. One
account of its origin tells how, when Washington was in
want of ammunition, he called a council of officers, but no
practical suggestion could be offered. "We must consult

Brother Jonathan," said the general, meaning His Excellency Jonathan Trumbull, governor of the state of Connecticut. This was done, and the difficulty was remedied. *To consult Brother Jonathan* then became a set phrase, and *Brother Jonathan* became a name for the typical shrewd Yankee. He appears as a character in *The Contrast* (1787), a play by Royall Tyler.

Brothers Karamazov, The (Bratya Karamazovy, 1879–1880)   A novel by Dostoyevsky. Considered his best work, it is one of the outstanding novels in world literature. The main plot involves Fyodor Pavlovich Kara-mazov and his four sons: Dmitry, Ivan, Alyosha, and the bastard Smerdyakov. Fyodor Pavlovich, a depraved buffoon, is Dmitry's rival for the affections of the local siren, Grushenka. Violent quarrels over her and over Dmitry's disputed inheritance ensue, until Fyodor Pavlovich is murdered. Dmitry is arrested and brought to trial for the crime. This basic line of action is complicated throughout the novel by a host of other factors masterfully linked to the main plot. The second son, Ivan, a tortured intellectual, gradually realizes that he has secretly wished for his father's death and may have transmitted this wish to Smerdyakov, a grotesque caricature of the brilliant Ivan. Dmitry's relations with his ex-fiancée, Katerina Ivanovna, also prove to have a bearing on his involvement in the crime and his unwillingness to defend himself against the charges. The youngest son, Alyosha, plays no direct part in the crime but acts throughout the book as a religious foil to the depraved Fyodor Pavlovich, the passionate Dmitry, and the rationalistic Ivan. By means of Alyosha, the elder Zosima, who expresses the author's religious views, is introduced into the novel.

Balancing or perhaps outweighing Zosima's religious message is the expression of disbelief enunciated by Ivan. His attitude is forcefully conveyed in the famous "Legend of the Grand Inquisitor," a parable of his own invention, which he relates to Alyosha. Essentially a pessimistic look at man's religious possibilities, the legend has been regarded as evidence of Dostoyevsky's own religious doubts.

Besides being a story of crime and a novel of religious and ethical ideas, the book is in part a social document. The intellectual and political ideas current in 19th-century Russia are introduced by Ivan and the careerist Rakitin, while the legend may be read as a critique of the socialist utopia as well as of religious orthodoxy. The judicial reforms of the later 19th century and the effects they had are revealed during the trial of Dmitry.

The literal, religious, social, and ethical levels of the novel are buttressed by the psychological probings for which Dostoyevsky is well known. The book abounds in instances of the author's mastery in this area, from the portrayal of the corrupt yet shame-filled Fyodor Pavlovich, to the mental disintegration of the brilliant Ivan, to the painful adolescence of Kolya Krasotkin.

Broun, Heywood [Campbell] (1888–1939) American journalist and novelist. Known for his liberal sympathies and opposition to social injustice, Broun wrote for several New York newspapers and magazines. He was equally well known and loved as a kindly, unpunctual fellow whose huge bulk and untidy appearance led him to be called a "one-man slum." The Newspaper Guild, which Broun helped found, has established an annual award for reporting done "in the spirit of Heywood Broun." A *Collected Edition* of his writings appeared in 1941.

Brown, Charles Brockden (1771–1810)   American novelist and editor. Regarded as the first American professional author, Brown introduced the Indian into U.S. fiction and was among the first Americans to win a hearing abroad. Brown anticipated the later deep interest in psychotic characters, foreshadowing Poe's interest in the horrifying. His fame rests on six Gothic romances: *Wieland* (1798), *Ormond* (1799), *Arthur Mervyn* (part 1, 1799; part 2, 1800), *Edgar Huntly* (1799), *Clara Howard* (1801), and *Jane Talbot* (1801).

Brown, Claude (1937–   )   American writer. Brown's reputation rests primarily on his best-selling autobiography, *Manchild in the Promised Land* (1965). The book is a vivid, chillingly authentic depiction of growing up in Harlem's black ghetto. Brown portrays the brutal code of street life, delinquency, his experiences in a succession of correctional institutions, and his eventual escape from Harlem to college. *The Children of Ham* (1976) is a collection of sketches of a group of Harlem adolescents and their attempts to survive in a living hell dominated by heroin.

Brown, John (1800–1859)   American abolitionist. In the 1850s, Brown, an abolitionist since his youth, became obsessed with the idea of freeing the slaves by force. In 1855 he and five sons went to Kansas, then a battleground between pro- and antislavery forces. The following year, with his approval, a small band, including four of his sons, murdered five settlers near Potawatomi Creek during an antislavery raid. Later he and forty men resisted an attack on Osawatomie by proslavery men.

Now nationally known as "Old Brown of Osawatomie," he made plans to foment a slave insurrection in the South. On October 16, 1859, with twenty-one men, he attacked Harper's Ferry, Virginia (now West Virginia) and seized the U.S. arsenal and armory there. A detachment of marines under Col. Robert E. Lee defeated and captured Brown. During his trial for treason, he conducted himself with dignity, maintaining that he had been an instrument in the hands of God. He was convicted and hanged on December 2, a martyr in the eyes of abolitionists.

His career inspired the Civil War marching song "John Brown's Body" and numerous literary works, notably Stephen Vincent Benét's narrative poem *John Brown's Body* (1928).

Brown, Thomas   See FELL, JOHN.

Brown, William Hill (1765–1793)   American novelist, poet, and dramatist, probably the author of THE POWER OF SYMPATHY. Born in Boston, Brown also wrote a series of verse fables, a tragedy, a comedy, and a short novel of incest and seduction, *Ira and Isabella* (1807).

Browne, Charles Farrar   See WARD, ARTEMUS.

Browne, Sir Thomas (1605–1682)   English writer and scholar. Browne was a successful physician who, except for his years of schooling at Oxford and in Europe, spent his life in the town of Norwich. He was knighted in 1671 by Charles II, as a steadfast Royalist famous for his antiquarian scholarship. As Browne himself knew, he had a curiously mixed nature: by temperament melancholy, mystical, and credulous, he was by training a scientist and philosophical skeptic. He was also a lover of language and classical learning, and his sonorous, stirringly cadenced prose style, rich in exotic coinages and striking images, is one of the most remarkable accomplishments in English literature. He is most brilliant when he treats themes that allow the full display of his personality, such as religion in RELIGIO MEDICI and mortality and oblivion in HYDRIOTAPHIA, OR URN BURIAL. His other works are *Pseudodoxia Epidemica*, also called VULGAR ERRORS, *The Garden of Cyrus* (1658), and *Christian Morals*, edited in 1756 by Samuel Johnson.

Brown Girl, Brownstones (1959)   A novel by Paule MARSHALL. The title is derived from the rows of Victorian brownstone houses that abound in the Fulton Park area in Brooklyn, in which Selina Boyce, the main character, lives. Selina is the daughter of Barbadian immigrants who moved to the United States twenty years earlier. After twenty years of labor, mostly as domestics and factory workers, they, along with other Barbadians, have moved out of a cockroach-infested neighborhood to better environs, with dreams of owning their own house. The story involves the Boyce family's attempts to acquire one of the brownstones and rise in the eyes of the other middle-class Barbadians in the area. However, Selina's father, Deighton, has a vision of a perfect house, the only kind of house he would consider living in, since it is the kind of house a white man would want to live in. This vision is at great odds with reality. The money to acquire one of the brownstones is obtained through inheritance. But since the house he wants is not available, Deighton decides to spend every bit of the money on a shopping spree on Fifth Avenue. The money is quickly gone, the dream of the house temporarily abandoned, and, by the end of the novel, the house is wholly abandoned, as the area is picked by inner-city developers for a major project.

In the meantime, Selina has spiritually grown away from home and the ways of her parents. She goes to college and copes with racism, temporarily transcending it through the medium of dance, for which she has a considerable talent

and, when at last on stage, through which she finds release. However, the effects of this are short-lived: at a party following the stage performance, hosted by a rich white family on the Upper East Side, she begins to feel the effects of racism again, through the unconsciously racist comments that are passed socially. The episode helps Selina deal with her experiences more effectively. She emerges, at the end of the novel, a much stronger person, having discovered herself through art.

brownie   The house spirit in Scottish superstition. At night, the brownie is supposed to busy himself in doing little jobs for the family over which he presides. Farms are his favorite abode. Brownies are brown or tawny spirits, in opposition to fairies, which are fair ones. In the U.S., the adventures of the brownies were popularized by a series of *Brownie Books* by Palmer Cox.

Browning, Elizabeth Barrett (1806–1861)   English poet, wife of Robert BROWNING. In childhood she suffered a spinal injury and, until her meeting with Browning, seemed to be doomed to invalidism and seclusion from the world. Barrett and Browning's courtship under the eyes of her jealous, tyrannical father, their elopement, and subsequent happy married life in Italy form one of the most celebrated of literary romances. Hawthorne described Mrs. Browning as "a pale, small person scarcely embodied at all," and this ethereality of her physical appearance is reflected by the palpitating fervor and the unworldly tenderness and purity of her work. Often, however, these qualities decline into stridency, diffuseness, and confusion. Her themes were dictated by her broad humanitarian interests; a deep if unorthodox religious feeling; her affection for her adopted country, Italy; and her love for Browning. Her greatest work, SONNETS FROM THE PORTUGUESE, a sequence of love sonnets addressed to her husband, remains an extraordinary and living achievement. Her other works include *Essay on Mind, with Other Poems* (1826), a translation of Aeschylus' *Prometheus Bound* (1833), *The Seraphim and Other Poems* (1838), *Poems* (1844), *Casa Guidi Windows* (1851), *Aurora Leigh* (1856), *Poems before Congress* (1860), and *Last Poems* (1862). See CRY OF THE CHILDREN, THE; LADY GERALDINE'S COURTSHIP.

Browning, Robert (1812–1889)   English poet. The son of a bank clerk, Browning was long unsuccessful as a poet and was financially dependent upon his family until he was well into adulthood. In his teens, he discovered Shelley and adopted Shelleyan liberalism in opinion and confessionalism in poetry. Accordingly, his first poems —*Pauline* (1833), *Paracelsus* (1835), SORDELLO—were long, personal, and self-consciously poetic, though the latter two supposedly had as their subject actual historic personages. All three works were considered failures, and, from 1837 to 1846, Browning attempted to write verse drama for the stage, again unsuccessfully. In 1845 he met Elizabeth Barrett, then considered one of the outstanding poets of the day, and married her the following year. Partially because of her ill health and partially because of her father's opposition to the marriage, Browning took his wife to Italy and remained there until her death in 1861. The story of their love has been dramatized by Rudolf Besier in THE BARRETTS OF WIMPOLE STREET.

PIPPA PASSES, a dramatic poem included in the collection *Bells and Pomegranates* (1841–46), was among Browning's first significant works; Pippa, a little Italian girl, passes by singing and unwittingly influences the lives of four groups of people. During the next twenty-five years, Browning published many volumes of poetry, all of which sold badly: *Dramatic Lyrics* (1842), which contained "Porphyria's Lover," MY LAST DUCHESS, "Soliloquy in a Spanish Cloister," and "The Pied Piper of Hamelin"; *Dramatic Romances and Lyrics* (1845), which included HOW THEY BROUGHT THE GOOD NEWS FROM GHENT TO AIX and "The Bishop Orders His Tomb at St. Praxed's Church"; *Christmas Eve and Easter Day* (1850), a long poem; and *Men and Women* (1855), which contained many of his best-known poems: FRA LIPPO LIPPI, "Andrea del Sarto," "Bishop Blougram's Apology," "Two in the Campagna," and "A Grammarian's Funeral." In the collection *Dramatis Personae* (1864) were included RABBI BEN EZRA and PROSPICE.

After forty years of poetic obscurity, Browning abruptly came into his own with the publication of the massive THE RING AND THE BOOK. The story, which Browning found in an old manuscript, deals with a 17th-century murder case. In the poem, each of twelve characters presents his view of the action in a long dramatic monologue.

Though his philosophy is now considered less profound than it was at the height of his success, Browning is notable for his psychological insight into character and motivations; his sometimes abrupt but forceful colloquial English; his perfection of the form of the dramatic monologue, in which a speaker tells something of himself and reveals more than he intends or realizes; his learning; and his predilection for Italian Renaissance subjects. See BROWNING, ELIZABETH BARRETT.

Bruce, Robert (called the Bruce, 1274–1329) Scottish national hero, king of Scotland from 1306. Though at first he swore fealty to Edward I of England as king of Scotland (1296), Robert Bruce soon followed the popular leader Sir William WALLACE and raised arms against Edward in a struggle to gain Scottish independence. In July 1297, however, he signed the capitulation of Irvine, whereby Scottish lords were pardoned in return for their allegiance. Bruce took no part in Wallace's continued struggle and final downfall but remained, to all outward appearances, loyal to the English. He was appointed coregent of Scotland, together with William Lamberton and John Comyn; he entered into a secret agreement with Lamberton, binding him to uphold the patriotic cause.

After the execution of Wallace, Bruce murdered (1306) Comyn, an enemy of long standing, and was thenceforth openly committed to the Scottish cause. He was crowned Robert I of Scotland at Scone in 1306; he then set about to win his kingdom. He suffered defeat at Methven, took refuge on the coast of Ireland, was outlawed, and was excommunicated by the pope. After the death of Edward I and Edward II's accession to the throne, Bruce faced an easier opponent. He returned to Scotland and, in a series of engagements, wrested most of Scotland from the English; his crusade finally culminated in the treaty (1327) by which Edward III recognized Scotland as independent and Bruce as its sovereign. Bruce died in 1329 of leprosy, barely enjoying the fruits of his own achievement. See BRUCE, THE; BRUCE AND THE SPIDER.

Bruce, The (c1375) An epic poem by John Barbour (1316?–95). The poem, a mixture of anecdote and accurate history, concerns the deeds of Robert BRUCE, James DOUGLAS, and the struggle for Scottish independence.

Bruce and the spider When Robert BRUCE was forced by the English to retreat to Ireland, he is said one day to have watched a spider try six times to fix its web on a beam in the ceiling. "Now shall this spider," said Bruce, "teach me what I am to do, for I also have failed six times." The spider's seventh effort was successful. Bruce left Ireland, collected three hundred followers, landed at Carrick, and at midnight surprised the English garrison at Turnberry Castle. In *Tales of a Grandfather* (1828–30), Sir Walter Scott tells us that, in remembrance of this incident, it has always been deemed a foul crime in Scotland for any of the name of Bruce to harm a spider.

Brücke, Die (Ger, "The Bridge") A group of German painters, formed in 1905 in Dresden. In rebellion against impressionism, they aimed to found a truly expressive school of German painting. Ernst Ludwig Kirchner and Eric Heckel were among the leaders of the group, whose members were influenced by the art of Africa and the South Seas and by primitive German religious art. Using color in an expressionistic manner, these artists painted dramatic landscapes and nudes, mystical and visionary compositions, and depicted the anguish and loneliness of the street, the circus, and the *café dansant. Die Brücke* was incorporated into the BLAUE REITER movement in 1912.

Bruckner, Anton (1824–1896) Austrian organist and composer of church and symphonic music. A disciple of Richard WAGNER, Bruckner taught theory and organ at the Vienna Conservatorium from 1868 to 1891. Because of his Wagnerian leanings, his music was greeted with hostility by the pro-BRAHMS forces in Vienna. His works include nine symphonies, three masses, and numerous shorter pieces of church music.

Bruckner, Ferdinand (pseudonym of Theodor Tagger, 1891–1958) Austrian poet and dramatist. Bruckner was a poet in his early years in Vienna, where he started the expressionist magazine *Marsyas*. His focus shifted to drama in 1923, when he moved to Berlin and founded the Renaissance Theatre. His early plays, including *Krankheit der Jugend* (*Illness of Youth*, 1926) and *Die Verbrecher* (*The Criminals*, 1928), were strong expressionist dramas dealing with social ills. Here he also wrote his first and best-known historical play, *Elisabeth von England* (*Elizabeth of England*, 1930). Forced to flee the Nazis, Bruckner spent from 1933 to 1948 in America. Beginning with *Die Rassen* (*The Races*, 1933), an early indictment of National Socialism, most of his writing during this period was concerned with dictatorship in one guise or another, including a play in two parts, *Simón Bolívar* (1943–45). Back in Austria, then in West Berlin, after the war, he began to use classical structures or motifs, as in *Pyrrhus und Andromache* (1952), as a framework for his criticism of the failures of the present. Bruckner's central concern was to dramatize the individual's difficulty in maintaining his integrity in the face of social and political pressures.

Bruegel, Pieter (1525?–1569) Flemish painter. Bruegel painted scenes from peasant life, fantastic recreations of biblical subjects, such as the Tower of Babel, and landscapes composed of closely observed details combined to form an immense panorama in which small figures enact religious dramas and perform common tasks. His splendidly composed and brightly colored, realistic paintings are noted for their keen and often humorous observation of nature and mankind. Bruegel had two sons, Pieter the Younger (1564?–1637?), who often copied his father, and Jan (1568–1625), called Velvet Bruegel, who painted landscapes, allegorical pictures, and still lifes.

Brunelleschi, Filippo (1377–1446) Florentine architect and goldsmith. Brunelleschi used his knowledge of Gothic and Romanesque architecture in spanning the immense space covered by his dome for the cathedral of Florence, while, in such buildings as the Pazzi Chapel, the Church of San Lorenzo, the Pitti Palace (1446), the Hospital of the Innocenti (1419), and the Church of the Santo Spirito (1435), he introduced the classical elements—columns, arches, ornamental details—that are an integral part of Renaissance architecture. His classicism was spurred by a trip to Rome in 1433 with his friend DONATELLO for the purpose of studying the Roman ruins. Along with Donatello and other Florentine artists, he shared the patronage of Cosimo de' Medici. He also invented linear perspective: the mathematical device for the construction of a rational space, with depth and interval, as seen from a single point of view.

Brunhild See NIBELUNGENLIED, THE; VÖLSUNGA SAGA.

Brunhoff, Jean de See BABAR.

Brut, The (c1205) A Middle English verse rendition by the English priest Layamon (fl 1198–1207) of Wace's Norman French ROMAN DE BRUT. A mixture of alliteration and rhyme, it is the first long poem in Middle English with any claim to literary quality, marking the first appearance of the story of King Arthur in English. It relates the mythical history of Britain from its founding by BRUTE, a descendant of Aeneas, to the year 689. It contains versions of the stories of King LEIR (Lear), CYMBELINE, and other legendary kings of Britain. See ARTHURIAN LEGEND.

Brute (or Brutus) In Geoffrey of Monmouth's HISTORY OF THE KINGS OF BRITAIN, a mythical ancestor of the British. According to Geoffrey, Brute is the great-grandson of the Trojan Aeneas. After an adventurous life, he lands in England, which—says the writer—he calls Britain after his own name. His three sons are Albanact, Camber, and Locrine.

Brutus, Dennis (1924–   ) South African poet, born in Rhodesia. Brutus's outspoken protests against South Africa's participation in the Olympic Games and the injustices of the apartheid state led to his official banishment from the teaching profession. Detained as a political prisoner, he was severely wounded, allegedly while attempting to escape. A year after his release from prison in 1965, he left South Africa to live and teach in England and the U.S. Among his several volumes of poetry are *Sirens, Knuckles, Boots* (1963), *Letters to Martha* (1968), *A Simple Lust* (1973), *China Poems* (1975), *Stubborn Hope* (1978), and *Salutes and Censures* (1982). Although the poems are inspired by and written against the backdrop of violence engendered by the apartheid state, many of them are essentially love poems. His political sentiments, as they emerge in his poetry, are leavened with humor, compassion, and tenderness.

Brutus, Lucius Junius Roman CONSUL (509 BC). One of the first two consuls in Rome's history, Brutus is known as the founder of the Roman Republic. According to legend, he feigned idiocy in order to escape the fate of his father and brother, who were killed by his uncle Tarquinius Superbus, king of Rome. When Sextus, son of Tarquinius Superbus, ravished LUCRETIA, Brutus cast off his feigned simple-mindedness and swore vengeance; he led the insurrection which expelled the Tarquins from Rome and changed the magistracy of kings to that of consuls. Brutus and Tarquinius Collatinus, husband of Lucretia, were chosen consuls.

Brutus, Marcus Junius (c85–42 BC) Roman politician and general. Brutus was known for his devotion to the ideals of the republic, and, in the civil struggle between CAESAR and Pompey, he supported the latter, who had legality on his side. After the battle at Pharsalus (48 BC), which ended in the defeat of Pompey, Caesar pardoned Brutus and made him one of his companions. Caesar appointed him governor of Cisalpine Gaul (46) and praetor (44). His love for Caesar notwithstanding, Brutus was persuaded by CASSIUS to join the plot to murder Caesar; he was deluded into thinking that this act would recall the ideals of the republic, which had disintegrated under Caesar's dictatorship. Accordingly, Caesar was murdered on the IDES of March in 44 by a group of conspirators under Brutus and Cassius. Mark ANTONY turned public opinion against the conspirators in his oration at Caesar's funeral, and Brutus and Cassius fled Rome. Both raised armies, and Antony and Octavius, Caesar's lawful heir (later Augustus), temporarily suspended their struggle for power and marched against them. In the first engagement at Philippi (42) Brutus was victorious over Octavius, while Cassius, overwhelmed by Antony's forces, committed suicide. In the second engagement, Brutus's forces were surrounded by those of Octavius, and Brutus committed suicide. According to Plutarch, when Antony found Brutus's body, he wrapped it up in his own robe for burial and had the ashes sent to Servilia, Brutus's mother. Another story, however, says that Antony had Brutus's head cut off and flung it at the feet of a statue of Caesar. See ET TU, BRUTE.

In Shakespeare's JULIUS CAESAR, Brutus is depicted as an idealist, "high in all the people's hearts," who joins the conspiracy out of love of country. Antony's eulogy is famous:

> This was the noblest Roman of them all;
> All the conspirators save only he
> Did that they did in envy of great Caesar;
> He only, in a general honest thought,
> And common good to all, made one of them.

Bryan, William Jennings (known as the Great Commoner and the Boy Orator of the Platte; 1860–1925) American political leader and orator. Having been twice elected to Congress (1890, 1892), Bryan became editor of the Omaha *World-Herald* after an unsuccessful Senate bid in 1894. In 1896 he won the Democratic presidential nomination, when, as an advocate of the free coinage of silver, he electrified the convention with the famous "Cross of Gold" speech, which ended: "You shall not press down upon the brow of labor this crown of thorns, you shall not crucify mankind upon a cross of gold." After a strenuous campaign, in which he won the support of Southern and Western agrarians, he lost to William McKinley by fewer than 600,000 votes. In 1901 he founded a weekly newspaper, the *Commoner*, which he edited until 1913. Again an unsuccessful presidential candidate in 1900 and 1908, he was named secretary of state by President Wilson, but he resigned in 1915, when he felt that the president's policies might involve the U.S. in World War I. After the war, his fundamentalist religious beliefs led him to take part in a movement to prevent the teaching of evolution in American schools; in 1925 he served as prosecutor in the celebrated SCOPES TRIAL.

Bryan was one of the most popular lecturers on the Chautauqua circuit; best loved of all his talks was one on "The Prince of Peace," which he repeated innumerable times until 1924. Vachel Lindsay paid tribute to Bryan in his poem "Bryan, Bryan, Bryan: The Campaign of 1896, as Viewed at the Time by a 16-Year-Old" (1919), but he was pilloried in H. L. Mencken's *In Memoriam: W. J. B.* (*Prejudices*, 5th Series, 1926).

Bryant, William Cullen (1794–1878) American poet, critic, and editor. Bryant's early beliefs were Calvinist, his politics Federalist, and his tastes classical. During his life, he moved from these attitudes to almost opposite ones, finally achieving a balanced view.

After beginning at the law, he achieved early fame when his poems were published in 1817. In 1825 he went to New York from his native Massachusetts to work on the New York *Evening Post*. Later he became its editor and a leading Democrat; he supported Lincoln, encouraged liberal causes, and espoused a less severe religion. Throughout his life, he continued to write poetry but rarely achieved the quality of his earliest work, THANATOPSIS, TO A WATERFOWL, and INSCRIPTION FOR THE ENTRANCE TO A WOOD. Bryant's important works include early political satire in *The Embargo* (1808), collected *Poems* (1832), *The Fountain* (1842), and *The Flood of Years* (1876). He translated the *Iliad* (1870) and the *Odyssey* (1871).

Bryher (pen name of Annie Winifred Ellerman Macpherson, 1894–1983) English historical novelist. A highly accomplished writer of historical fiction, Bryher was distinguished for her ability to impart the atmosphere and feeling of the time about which she wrote. *The Fourteenth of October* (1951) and *The January Tale* (1966) deal with the effects of the Norman invasions on the Saxons. Episodes in the history of the Greek and Roman empires are the focus in *Roman Wall* (1954), *Gate to the Sea* (1958), and *The Coin of Carthage* (1963), set during the Punic Wars. *The Heart to Artemis* (1962), her autobiography, is a vivid chronicle of her own time.

Bryusov, Valery Yaklovich (1873–1924) Russian poet. One of the founders of the SYMBOLIST movement, Bryusov established in 1904 the journal *Vesy* (*The Scales*), which became an important showcase for the symbolist work of the next five years. Bryusov was heavily influenced by the French Symbolists and transmitted this influence into the Russian movement. His major collections of verse are *Urbi et Orbi* (1903) and *Stephanos* (1905). Bryusov accepted the BOLSHEVIK regime, and, as a consequence, his work, while not as politically oriented as the Soviets would like, is at least accepted and reprinted in the Soviet Union.

Buber, Martin (1878–1965) Philosopher, theologian, and Zionist thinker. Born in Vienna, Buber studied at universities in Vienna, Leipzig, Zurich, and Berlin; he immigrated to Palestine in 1938. Buber saw in Israel an ideal place for the fulfillment of both nationalist and humanist aspirations. His deeply religious world view, rooted in HASIDISM, emphasized the relationship between man and man and between man and God, rather than that between man and State. His philosophical and religious treatises, particularly *Ich und Du* (1923; tr *I and Thou*, 1937), had a considerable influence on Christian as well as Jewish thinkers. His other literary endeavors include a cotranslation, with Franz Rosenzweig, of the Bible into German (1925–61), *Die Geschichten des Rabbi Nachman* (1906; tr *Tales of Rabbi Nachman*, 1956), and *Königtum Gottes* (1932; tr *Kingship of God*, 1967).

Bucephalus (fr Gr, *boukephalos*, "bull-headed") The favorite horse of Alexander the Great. Philip II had determined to destroy the high-spirited horse, which no one could mount, but allowed his son to try his skill first. Observing that the horse was terrified by its own shadow, Alexander turned its eyes into the sun and was able to mount. By taming him, Alexander fulfilled an oracle concerning the succession to the throne of Macedon.

Buchan, Sir John (1st Baron Tweedsmuir, 1875–1940) Scottish writer and governor general of Canada. Buchan wrote many romantic adventure stories with idyllic natural settings. His first successful book was *Prester John* (1910), a romance of South Africa. THE THIRTY-NINE STEPS, *Greenmantle* (1916), and *The Three Hostages* (1924) are adventure and spy novels, whose hero is Richard HANNAY. Other stories, such as *Huntingtower* (1922), are about a group of Scottish slum boys called the Gorbals Die-Hards. *John Macnab* (1925) is about poaching, hunting, and fishing in Scotland. Buchan's biographies include a life of Cromwell (1934) and a life of Cromwell's Scottish contemporary, *Montrose* (1928). *Memory-Hold-the-Door* (1940) is an autobiography.

Büchner, Georg (1813–1837) German dramatist. Büchner is known especially for the brilliant imagination and theatrical skill with which he treats social, human, and metaphysical problems in the plays DANTONS TOD and WOYZECK. Inspired in his student days by the ideals of the French Revolution of 1789, he became a political radical and in 1834 publicized a militant socialist program in his tract *Der hessische Landbote* (*The Hessian Messenger*), which violently attacked the oppressive archduchy of Hesse. As a dramatist, he reinforced his socialist sympathies with a brutally stark, realistic style that caused him to be regarded as a forerunner of naturalism. But he was also a master of metaphysical symbolism, and his works contain passages of the highest poetic beauty. Other products of his short career are the comedy *Leonce und Lena* (written 1836) and the fragmentary novella *Lenz* (1879), about the life of the poet Reinhold Lenz.

Buck, Pearl S[ydenstricker] (1892–1973) American novelist. The daughter of American missionaries, Buck was raised in China and is best known for her books about Chinese life. Part of her purpose was to make the East understandable to the West. She was awarded the PULITZER PRIZE in 1932 for her most famous work, THE GOOD EARTH, the first novel of a trilogy which included *Sons* (1932) and *A House Divided* (1935). She received the NOBEL PRIZE in Literature in 1938.

During her marriage to the missionary John Lossing Buck, she taught at Chinese universities. In 1932 she returned to America and in 1935 married her publisher, Richard F. Walsh. Buck's work tended to enjoy more popular than critical acclaim, although *The Spirit and The Flesh* (1944), which contains her biographies of her missionary parents, was highly regarded. Among her books —more than eighty-five in all—are plays, books for children, biographies, translations, and such novels as *Dragon Seed* (1942), *Imperial Woman* (1956), *The Living Reed* (1963), and *Mandala* (1970). Her two autobiographical works are *My Several Worlds: A Personal Record* (1954) and *A Bridge for Passing* (1962). She translated the Chinese classic SHUI HU CHUAN, under the title *All Men Are Brothers* (1933). She also wrote five novels with an American setting under the pseudonym John Sedges.

Buckingham, George Villiers, 1st duke of (1592–1628) English nobleman, whose erratic political and military policies caused continual friction with Parliament and foreign powers. The profligate favorite of James I, Buckingham was known for his good looks, and his face at death was described as "the face of an angel." He was assassinated by John Felton (1595?–1628). He was used as a character by Scott in *The Fortunes of Nigel* (1822) and by Dumas in *The Three Musketeers* (1844).

Buckingham, George Villiers, 2nd duke of (1628–1687) English nobleman and writer. The son of the 1st duke of Buckingham and a favorite of Charles II, he was a member of the court clique known as the CABAL, his name furnishing the third letter of the famous acronym. With Samuel Butler, Thomas Sprat, and others, he wrote *The Rehearsal* (1671), a burlesque tragedy satirizing Dryden. He is a character in Scott's *Peveril of the Peak* (1822) and *Woodstock* (1826) and in Dryden's *Absalom and Achitophel* (1681).

Buckingham, Henry Stafford, 2nd duke of (1454–1483) English nobleman, a staunch supporter of Richard III in the early part of his reign. He later rebelled against Richard and was captured and executed. In Shakespeare's RICHARD III, he is depicted as the crafty "second self" of the king, but he balks at Richard's demand that he kill the two sons of Edward IV.

Bucolics (Bucolica, written 43–37 BC) Ten pastoral poems by VERGIL, also known as the *Eclogues* (Lat, *Eclogae*). Though based on the idyls of Theocritus, the *Bucolics* are sophisticated tours de force and subtle allegories of contemporary events and persons. As Vergil's first notable achievement, they mark the beginning of his writing career and his entry into the literary circle of Augustus and Maecenas.

The first bucolic portrays the anguish of a shepherd forced to leave his ancestral lands. This is a reference to the threatened confiscation of Vergil's lands by Mark Antony in 43. The second is the love song of CORYDON for the boy Alexis. An amoebaean contest, i.e., a singing contest in which one shepherd sings an impromptu couplet, to which the other must reply with a variation of tone and subject matter, composes the third poem. Interwoven into this rustic game of wits are references to Vergil's patrons and to the farm, which, through his patrons' influence, was restored to the poet.

The fourth poem is perhaps the most famous bucolic of all. In it, Vergil predicts a new age of peace for the world, which will be ushered in by the birth of a child. Often called the *Messianic Eclogue*, this poem has been variously interpreted as a natal poem for an expected child (either that of Mark Antony and Octavia or of Octavius Caesar and Scribonia) and as an inspired prophecy of the birth of Christ. It was because of this poem that medieval Christians revered Vergil as a pagan prophet whom God had chosen to prepare the world for the coming of the Prince of Peace.

The fifth poem is an elegant exchange of songs by two shepherds; its subject is elegaic—the death of a young shepherd, Damon—but it actually refers to the death of Julius Caesar. The sixth is the *Song of Silenus*, a capsule cosmogony which seems to show Vergil's acquaintance with Lucretius's *De rerum natura*. The seventh poem is another amoebaean singing contest.

The eighth bucolic contains two love elegies, in both of which the singers use magical refrains. The poem is sometimes called *Pharmaceutria* ("sorcery"). The ninth is a gracious exchange of songs between a young man and an old man, in which there are many oblique references to the death of Caesar, the Roman civil wars, and the confiscations.

The final bucolic is dedicated to Gallus, a leading patrician and writer of elegies who was an early protector of Vergil. This poem is in the form of a consolation sent to Gallus, who is brokenhearted over the infidelity of his mistress. Many authorities now claim that this artificial piece is a clever pastiche of Gallus's own love lyrics.

Vergil's *Bucolics* were the principal influence on pastoral tradition after the Renaissance, and their calm elegance became the dominant tone of pastoral verse. The refrain "Sweete Themmes, runne softly, till I end my song" in Spenser's *Prothalamion* is an echo of the recurrent refrain in the eighth bucolic: *Incipe Maenalios mecum, mea tibia, versus;* and the opening of Milton's *Lycidas*, "Yet once more, O ye laurels, and once more,/ Ye myrtles brown . . . / I come to pluck" is an adaption of *Et vos, o lauri, carpam te, proxima myrte*, in the second.

Budd, Lanny   See SINCLAIR, UPTON.

Buddenbrooks (1901; tr 1924)   The first novel by Thomas MANN, considered an outstanding achievement in German fiction. The novel is a chronicle of the material and spiritual decline of a prosperous patrician family. Drawing from autobiographical material, as well as from the clear influences of SCHOPENHAUER and WAGNER, Mann provides penetrating psychological insights into individual characters and German society in general. As the novel opens, both Johann Buddenbrook, Sr., the patriarch, and his son Johann, Jr. (Consul Buddenbrook) are exemplary bearers of the family's solid and rational tradition. However, symptoms of decadence begin to appear in the consul's children: the daughter, Toni, is aimless and fickle; Christian is an outright ne'er-do-well; and Thomas, who takes over the family business, has a repressed potential for decadence, manifested by his occasional attraction to art and philosophy and his inability to keep the family fortune from declining. In Thomas's son, Hanno, the symbolic connection between art and decadence and the symbolic antithesis between art and life culminate. Hanno is frail and sickly, fond of music and filled with creative longings. He dies at the age of fifteen, a victim of typhoid fever, bringing the family line to an end.

Buddha (Sans, "the enlightened one")   Title given to Siddhārtha Gautama (563–483 BC), also known as Shākyamuni, the founder of BUDDHISM. Traditionally, Buddha is said to have been born into the royal family of the warrior (KSHATRIYA) caste. Hindu priests, interpreting a dream his mother had before he was born, predicted that he would be a great leader or teacher. He was raised in luxurious comfort and, at sixteen, married his cousin, Yasodharā. The first crucial stage of his spiritual and philosophical development occurred when he was twenty-nine. After a series of excursions beyond the palace walls, he became aware of the inescapability of aging, disease, and death. On another excursion, he saw a priest and determined to discover the reason for the priest's apparent serenity in the midst of universal suffering. Not long after the birth of his son, Rāhula, he renounced his princely life, left his wife and child, and set off as a wandering ascetic in search of enlightenment. After six years of study, meditation, and fasting, he finally sat beneath a pipal tree at Bodh Gaya, determined not to rise again until he reached true enlightenment. He withstood the attacks of the evil tempter Mara and finally, at the age of thirty-six, came to see the eternal truths he had been seeking. In his first sermon, to five ascetics who had accompanied him, he outlined the Four Noble Truths and the Eightfold Path (see BUDDHISM) that were to become the foundations of Buddhist teaching. He taught for forty-five years and died at the age of eighty.

Buddhism (fr Sans, *bodhi*, "enlightenment")   The system of religion inaugurated in the 6th century BC by Siddhārtha Gautama, called the BUDDHA. Buddhism's earliest doctrines were based on the Four Noble Truths:

1) Life is suffering.

2) The cause of suffering is "birth sin," or craving and desire.

3) Suffering can be ended only by NIRVANA, the extinguishment of desire.

4) This can be accomplished by the Eightfold Path to righteousness: right views, right intentions, right speech, right conduct, right livelihood, right effort, right mindfulness, and right meditation.

The abstract nature of the Buddhist system of thought, together with the overgrowth of its monastic system and the superior vitality and energy of HINDUISM, caused it to decline in India itself, but it spread rapidly to surrounding countries and took permanent hold in Ceylon, Tibet, China, and Japan.

Early Indian Buddhism (Theravāda or Hīnayāna) emphasized personal salvation; later Mahāyāna Buddhism developed, promising salvation for all. Mahāyāna Buddhism is the principal form of Buddhism in Central Asia, China, and Japan. Hīnayāna is still practiced in Sri Lanka. Numerous sects and variant teachings exist, ranging from highly academic and abstruse doctrines to simple salvation. See DHARMA; KARMA; SAMSĀRA.

Buffalo Bill   See CODY, WILLIAM F.

Buffon, Comte Georges Louis Leclerc de (1707–1788)   French naturalist, curator of the Jardin du Roi from 1739. Buffon is best known for his *Histoire naturelle* (36 vols, 1749–88), continued in eight volumes by his assistants and published in 1804; his *Epoques de la nature* (1779); and his *Théorie de la terre* (1749). His works deal with the earth, minerals, animals, and man. He helped lay the foundations for 19th-century work in natural science, especially in zoology and comparative anatomy, and was the first to write a history of the earth in terms of a series of successive geologic stages. Buffon's theories (e.g., his development of geographic zoology) anticipated those of Lamarck and Darwin. The *Discours sur le style*, his inaugural address to the French ACADEMY in 1753, reflects his concern with literary style: "Style is the man himself" is a famous quotation from it. His writing is vivid, eloquent, and majestic.

Bugayev, Boris Nikolayevich   See BELY, ANDREI.

Building of the Ship, The (1849)   A poem by Henry Wadsworth LONGFELLOW. Often considered his best ode, the poem describes the building of a ship, interweaving the details with those of the approaching marriage of the builder's daughter and the owner's son. The ship is used as a symbol for life itself and, at the end, for the Union.

Bukharin, Nikolay Ivanovich (1888–1939) Russian Communist leader and editor. Bukharin joined the BOLSHEVIKS in 1906 and was a leader in the movement by 1912, when he coedited with LENIN the party organ,

Pravda. In 1916 he was editor of the revolutionary paper *Novy mir* (*The New World*) in New York. The head of the Third International (1926–29), he was expelled from the party, only to be later reinstated. Suspected of being a supporter of TROTSKY, he was arrested and executed in the purges of 1938.

Bulfinch, Thomas (1796–1867)   American teacher and writer. Bulfinch held a business post throughout his life, devoting his leisure to writing. His *Age of Fable* (1855) is still used in American schools as an introduction to Greek, Roman, Scandinavian, and Celtic mythology. *The Age of Chivalry* (1858), another straightforward, expurgated popularization of mythology, has pleased many young readers.

Bulgakov, Mikhail Afanasyevich (1891–1940) Russian novelist, playwright, and short-story writer. Best known during his lifetime for his play *Dni Turbinykh* (1926; tr *Days of the Turbins*, 1934), Bulgakov became internationally famous with the posthumous appearance of his novel *Master i Margarita* (1966; tr *The Master and Margarita*, 1967). This work first appeared in censored form in the Soviet journal *Moskva*. In 1973 a Soviet volume of his works, entitled *Romany* (*Novels*), was published, which included *Belaya gvardiya* (tr *The White Guard*, 1969) and *Teatralny roman* (tr *Black Snow*, 1967).

Bullins, Ed (1935–   )   American playwright, novelist, and poet. Bullins moved into prominence in the New York theatre in 1968 with his first production of one-act plays, including *Clara's Old Man*, *The Electronic Nigger*, and *A Son Come Home*. Of the fifty or more plays that followed, most are part of a cycle depicting the changing lives of blacks in the 20th century, beginning with *In the Wine Time* (1968). The plays are often angry in tone, dealing with urban blacks in northern ghettoes, wholly divorced from their southern past, and using street language to express the harshness of everyday living. *The Taking of Miss Janie* (1975) received the New York Drama Critics' Circle best-play award. Bullins has also written a volume of verse, *To Raise the Dead and Foretell the Future* (1971); a collection of short fiction, *The Hungered One* (1971); and a novel, *The Reluctant Rapist* (1973).

Bullitt, William C[hristian] (1891–1967)   American diplomat. An early advocate of official recognition of the Communist government in Russia, Bullitt became the first U.S. ambassador to the U.S.S.R. (1933–36). He later served as ambassador to France (1936–41) and ambassador-at-large in the Mideast (1941–42). He wrote one novel, *It's Not Done* (1926), in addition to such nonfiction as *Report to the American People* (1940) and *The Great Globe Itself* (1946). His diplomatic letters to Franklin D. ROOSEVELT are collected in *For the President* (1972; ed O. H. Bullitt).

Bull Run   A brook in Virginia and the site of two battles during the U.S. Civil War. In the first battle of Bull Run (July 21, 1861), Union forces, confident of an easy victory that would enable them to push on to Richmond, were initially successful, but the stand of the Confederate brigade led by Thomas Jackson, which won him the nickname "Stonewall," and the arrival of reinforcements turned the apparent Union victory into rout. The second battle of Bull Run (August 30, 1862) also ended in defeat for the Union. These battles are sometimes known as the battles of Manassas, from nearby Manassas Junction.

Bulwer-Lytton, Edward George Earle Lytton (1st Baron Lytton, 1803–1873)   English novelist and dramatist. A member of Parliament for fifteen years, Bulwer-Lytton served as colonial secretary from 1858 to 1859 and was created a peer in 1866. Among his notable historical novels are *Eugene Aram* (1832), THE LAST DAYS OF POMPEII, *Rienzi* (1835), *Leila* (1838), *The Last of the Barons* (1843), and *Harold* (1848). Scholarly in their historical detail and often heavy, but just as often thrilling in their narrative, these books held the interest of several generations of readers. In addition, Bulwer-Lytton wrote the supernatural tales *Zanoni* (1842) and *A Strange Story* (1862), the long poem *King Arthur* (1849), and numerous dramas, including *Richelieu* (1839) and *Money* (1840)—the latter reflecting his occasional attraction to social themes.

Bumble, Mr.   In Charles Dickens's OLIVER TWIST, a minor official in the workhouse where Oliver is brought up. Bumble is a cruel, fussy man with mighty ideas of his own importance. He has given to the language the word *bumbledom*, for the officious arrogance and conceit of the petty dignitary. After marriage to Mrs. Corney, the high and mighty Bumble is sadly henpecked.

Bumppo, Natty   The central figure in THE LEATHERSTOCKING TALES, a series of novels by James Fenimore COOPER. Called by many names in the novels, among them Leatherstocking, Hawkeye, Deerslayer, Pathfinder, and *La Longue Carabine*, Natty remains the uncorrupted natural man. Companioned by Chingachgook, a Mohican chief, Natty prefers the moral code of the Indians to the selfish exploitation of nature by white settlers. Superior to the Indians in woodcraft, he is loyal and courageous, a voluntary outcast who follows the wilderness westward.

Bunch, Mother   A noted London alewife of the late Elizabethan period, nominal source of many jests and anecdotes, and often mentioned in Elizabethan drama. The "Epistle to the Merrie Reader" in *Pasquil's Jests, mixed with Mother Bunches Merriments* (1604) gives the following description of her:

She spent most of her time in telling tales, and when she laughed, she was heard from Aldgate to the Monuments at Westminster, and all Southwarke stood in Amazement. . . . She dwelt in Cornhill, neere the Exchange, and sold strong Ale . . . and lived an hundreth, seventy and five years, two days and a quarter, and halfe a minute.

Other books were named after her, such as *Mother Bunch's Closet newly Broke Open* (1609), "containing rare

secrets of art and nature, tried and experienced by learned philosophers, and recommended to all ingenious young men and maids, teaching them how to get good wives and husbands."

Bundren, Addie   The principal character in William Faulkner's novel AS I LAY DYING. Although she dies near the beginning of the story, much of the action of the characters is determined by their relationships with the dead woman.

Bungay, Thomas (called Friar Bungay, fl 1280) An English Franciscan who lectured at Oxford and Cambridge. Bungay's story is much overlaid with legend; he was popularly known as a magician and is represented in this guise in later literature. In the old prose romance *The Famous History of Friar Bacon* and in Robert GREENE's *Friar Bacon and Friar Bungay* (1589), he appears as the assistant to Roger BACON in his diabolical scientific experiments. He also appears in Bulwer-Lytton's novel THE LAST OF THE BARONS.

Bunin, Ivan Alekseyevich (1870–1953)   Russian novelist, short-story writer, and poet. Bunin was the first Russian to win the NOBEL PRIZE in Literature (1933). Bunin emigrated from Russia in 1918 and lived in France until his death. He is famous chiefly for his prose works, which have a closer kinship with the prose of the 19th-century masters than with the modernist experiments of his own period. His novels *Derevnya* (1910; tr *The Village*, 1923) and *Sukhodol* (1911; tr *Dry Valley*, 1935), written in the restrained "classical" style of TURGENEV, GONCHAROV, or CHEKHOV, depict the stagnation of life in provincial Russia. His short story "Gospodin iz San Frantsisko" (1914; tr "The Gentleman from San Francisco," 1922) is world famous. Bunin's poetry is less highly esteemed than his prose, but he did a number of successful translations into Russian, notably of the works of LONGFELLOW and BYRON.

Bunker Hill, battle of   The first great battle of the American Revolution, which occurred on June 17, 1775. To control the high ground overlooking Boston, American troops built a redoubt on nearby Breed's Hill. Under General Howe, twenty-four hundred British troops assaulted the hill but were repulsed twice with heavy losses. After the third assault, the Americans, their powder exhausted, retreated to Bunker Hill, where nearly a fourth of them were slain or wounded.

bunraku   Japanese puppet theater. Developed during the TOKUGAWA period, the most important bunraku plays were written by CHIKAMATSU Monzaemon. The dolls, about three feet in size, are remarkably lifelike; they are operated by puppet masters who sit on the stage and move about with their puppets. The musical narrative (JŌRURI) is chanted by a reciter (*gidayu*) to the accompaniment of instruments. Many of the same plays have been adapted to the KABUKI drama.

Bunting, Basil (1900–1985)   English poet. A friend and admirer of Ezra POUND, Bunting was strongly influenced by the Pound-ELIOT-imagist era, with its emphasis on concentration and the concrete image and with its broad range of classical, oriental, and modern allusions. (See IMAGISM.) Although Pound admired his work and included it in *Active Anthology* (1933), Bunting remained relatively unknown for many years. *Briggflatts* (1966), a long, semiautobiographical poem, firmly established his reputation as a poet. It is musical in tone, and its wealth of allusions ranges from the landscape of Northumbria, where the poet was born, to music, history, myth, and folklore. The result is a work that makes tremendous demands on its reader, but it is also the finest example of the lyrical intensity of Bunting's poetry. His *Collected Poems* was published in 1968 and again in 1978.

Buntline, Ned   See JUDSON, E. Z. C.

Buñuel, Luis (1900–1983)   Spanish-born film director and screenwriter, who worked in Mexico and France, as well as in Spain. Buñuel began his career as a surrealist with such films as *Un Chien andalou* (codirected with Salvador DALI, 1928) and *L'Age d'or* (1930), both cowritten with Dali. The latter, his most seminal work, established his reputation as cinema's greatest anarchist and iconoclast, exposing the hypocrisies and insanities of modern civilization in general and established religion in particular. In his Mexican films of the 1940s and 1950s, the surrealism was somewhat muted; nevertheless, such pictures as *Los olvidados* (1950) and *El* (1953) offered disturbing visions of the brutalization of children and the workings of sadistic violence within an apparently ideal marriage. With his later Spanish and French films —*Viridiana* (1961), *Belle de Jour* (1966), *Tristana* (1970), *The Discreet Charm of the Bourgeoisie* (1972), and *That Obscure Object of Desire* (1977)—Buñuel sharpened his dissecting techniques to concentrate on increasingly subtle exposés of modern bourgeois society. In 1983 the translation of his autobiography, *My Last Sign*, appeared shortly after his death.

Bunyan, John (1628–1688)   English writer and preacher. The son of a Bedfordshire tinker, Bunyan adopted his father's trade and served in the Parliamentary army from 1644 to 1646. In 1648 or 1649, he married a woman whose dowry included two devotional books which, he later said, first turned his thoughts to religion. After a period of intense spiritual struggle, he joined the Baptist church at Bedford and later became a lay preacher. His refusal to obey royal edicts banning nonconformist preaching led to his imprisonment from 1660 to 1672. During these twelve years, he devoted himself to study of the Bible and Foxe's *Book of Martyrs* and wrote many of his books, including his autobiography, GRACE ABOUNDING TO THE CHIEF OF SINNERS. Upon his release, he became minister of the nonconformist church at Bedford, a posi-

tion which he held for the rest of his life. In 1675 he was again imprisoned for a few months, during which time he wrote his most celebrated work, PILGRIM'S PROGRESS.

His other writings, all religious in character, most of them allegorical, include *The Holy City, or the New Jerusalem* (1665), *A Confession of My Faith, and a Reason of My Practice* (1672), *The Life and Death of Mr. Badman* (1680), and *The Holy War* (1682). An outstanding narrative genius, he wrote in a style that has been highly praised for its simplicity, vigor, and concreteness.

Bunyan, Paul   A legendary lumberjack of the American northwestern forests. A comic folk hero, Paul Bunyan is frequently the subject of tall tales, in which each storyteller strives to surpass the others in exaggeration. It is said that the dragging of Bunyan's pick cut out the Grand Canyon. When he builds a hotel, he has the "last seven stories put on hinges so's they could be swung back for to let the moon go by."

The legend of Paul Bunyan may have first appeared in Quebec or in northern Ontario; James Stevens traced him to a French-Canadian logger named Paul Bunyon, who won a reputation as a prodigious fighter in the Papineau Rebellion against England in 1837 and later became famous as the boss of a logging camp. Paul Bunyan's first appearance in print seems to be in an advertising pamphlet, *Paul Bunyan and His Big Blue Ox* (1914), published by the Red River Lumber Company. Written and illustrated by W. B. Laughead, it immediately became popular and was reissued many times. Among those who have retold the Bunyan stories are Virginia Tunvey, Esther Shepard, James Stevens, Glen Rounds, Dell J. McCormick, and Acel Garland. Daniel Hoffman studied the legend in his book *Paul Bunyan: Last of the Frontier Demigods* (1952).

Burbage, James (d 1597)   English actor and theatre-builder. In 1576 Burbage leased land in Shoreditch and built on it the first theatre in England specifically intended for stage performances. It was known simply as The Theatre. In 1596 he acquired a house in Blackfriars which, being roofed over, was used for plays during the winter months. After Burbage's death, his sons dismantled The Theatre and reerected it in Bankside, where it became the GLOBE theatre. See BURBAGE, RICHARD.

Burbage, Richard (1567?–1619)   English actor, son of James BURBAGE. Richard and his brother Cuthbert Burbage inherited a share in their father's two playhouses, The Theatre and the BLACKFRIARS. Because of difficulties about the lease of the site of The Theatre, they transported the building to a location in Bankside, where it was reassembled as the GLOBE theatre. Richard, one of the chief actors of his day, acted every major part in the plays of Shakespeare, as well as in those of Ben Jonson and Beaumont and Fletcher, and was particularly celebrated for his roles in tragedy. He was also a painter of some note, and the Felton portrait of Shakespeare is sometimes ascribed to him.

Burckhardt, Jakob Christoph (1818–1897) Swiss historian of art and culture. Burckhardt's best-known work is *Die Kultur der Renaissance in Italien* (1860; tr *The Civilization of the Renaissance in Italy*, many editions), for many years the classic analysis of the Renaissance. According to Burckhardt, Italy's unique political organization, based on the city-state rather than feudalism, had fostered the individualism upon which the Renaissance spirit rested. Thus Italy was the cradle of the Renaissance and of modern man.

Burgess, Anthony (born John Anthony Burgess Wilson, 1917–   ) English novelist and critic. A prolific, versatile, and comic writer, Burgess has an extraordinary facility with language. His novels are generally episodic in structure, written with extravagant use of puns, riddles, and allusions; his major characters are usually comic victims. His first three novels, the so-called Malayan trilogy, were written when he was an education officer for the Colonial Office in Malaya and were later published as *The Long Day Wanes* (1964). In *A Clockwork Orange* (1962), he envisions a future state terrorized by teenage gangs who speak Nadsat, a language created by Burgess from British and American slang and Russian. Among his many other novels are *The Right to an Answer* (1960), *The Wanting Seed* (1962), *Beard's Roman Women* (1976), and *1985* (1978). He has also written novels about Shakespeare (*Nothing Like the Sun*, 1964), Keats (*Abba Abba*, 1976), and Jesus (*Man of Nazareth*, 1979). *Earthly Powers* (1980) is a long novel that amounts to a personal, social, and intellectual history of the 20th century, as seen through the eyes of an eighty-one-year-old homosexual novelist. Burgess's literary studies include *The Novel Now* (1967), *Shakespeare* (1970), and *Joysprick: An Introduction to the Language of James Joyce* (1973). He also translated, adapted for modern stage, and wrote the music for *Cyrano de Bergerac* (1971). *The End of the World News: An Entertainment* (1983) is an innovatory novel. *Enderby's Dark Lady, or No End to Enderby* (1984) is set in Indiana.

Burke, Edmund (1729–1797)   Irish-born English statesman and author, known for his orations in the House of Commons. Burke was sympathetic toward the American colonies and the Irish Catholics and was a strong enemy of the French Revolution. Among his most famous speeches are ON AMERICAN TAXATION, ON CONCILIATION WITH THE COLONIES, and *On the Nabob of Arcot's Private Debts* (1785), in which Burke discusses the great prosecution of Warren HASTINGS and tries to make him the scapegoat for all the abuses connected with the regime of the East India Company. His published works include *A Vindication of Natural Society* (1756), an ironic attack on deism; *A Philosophical Inquiry into the Origin of Our Ideas of the Sublime and Beautiful* (1756), a pioneer study in the psychological basis of aesthetic enjoyment; *Observations on the Present State of the Nation* (1769); *Thoughts on the Cause of the Present Discontents* (1770), in which Burke declares that politics deals with men and nations in actuality, never in bloodless abstractions; *Letter to the Sheriffs of Bristol* (1777); REFLECTIONS ON THE FRENCH REVOLUTION; and *Letters on the Proposals for Peace with the Regicide Directory of France* (1796–97). He was associated with Samuel Johnson and Sir Joshua Reynolds in 1764 in forming the Literary Club. His influence on early-19th-century German national economists is particularly pronounced.

Burke, Kenneth [Duva] (1897–   )   American critic, philosopher, and translator. Although Burke began his career as a music critic, his contribution to modern literary criticism, particularly the NEW CRITICISM, was significant. His approach to literature is based on the psychological aspects of the written word and its effect as *symbolic action*—language as symbol. Among his important works are *Counter-Statement* (1931; rev 1968), *The Philosophy of Literary Form: Studies in Symbolic Action* (1941; rev 1957, 1974), *A Grammar of Motives* (1945), and *Language as Symbolic Action* (1966). He also wrote *Toward a Better Life* (1932; rev 1966); *The Complete White Oxen* (1968), his collected short fiction; and *Collected Poems 1915–1967* (1968). Burke's translations of the German authors Thomas MANN, Oswald SPENGLER, and Hugo von HOFMANNSTHAL contributed greatly to making these writers known in America. Burke was awarded the National Medal for Literature in 1981.

burlador de Sevilla y el convidado de piedra, El (The Libertine of Seville and the Stone Guest, pub 1630)   A play by TIRSO DE MOLINA. It gave to world literature one of its most enduring character types, Don Juan. Based on a 14th-century Sevillan chronicle, Tirso's play relates how Don Juan Tenorio, a dissolute young rake, kills Don Gonzalo Ulloa, father of one of his lady loves, in a duel. Later Don Juan pulls the beard of a stone effigy of Don Gonzalo and invites the figure to dinner. The statue accepts and returns the hospitality by inviting Don Juan to an entertainment at Don Gonzalo's tomb, where Don Juan is strangled by the stone figure and his soul is carried off to hell.

Tirso's Don Juan, the first in a long line of successors, ignores the conventions of honor; he seeks only to secure his pleasure. At the same time, he is profoundly religious and noble, exemplifying the conflict between the morality inherited from the Middle Ages and the libertinism fostered by the Renaissance. Among the most notable of later works in which Tirso's character appears are Byron's DON JUAN, Mozart's *Don Giovanni* (1787), Zorrilla's DON JUAN TENORIO, and Shaw's MAN AND SUPERMAN.

burlesque   A form of comedy, generally associated with stage performances, that achieves its effects through distortion, exaggeration, and imitation. Characteristically involving a paradoxical relationship between the subject matter and the manner of presentation, its humor often comes from a ridiculous treatment of a serious subject, or vice versa. A famous example of the genre is John Gay's burlesque of Italian opera, THE BEGGAR'S OPERA.

Burne-Jones, Sir Edward Coley (1833–1898) English painter. A member of the PRE-RAPHAELITE BROTHERHOOD, Burne-Jones was accorded wide public acclaim. Largely influenced by Dante Gabriel ROSSETTI, he painted, in such works as *Merciful Knight* (1863), classical, religious, medieval, literary, and symbolic scenes in a mystical though technically mannered style. His stained-glass designs are in many English churches; he also produced the woodcut illustrations for the Kelmscott Press edition of CHAUCER'S works. He was a close friend of William MORRIS and an uncle of Rudyard KIPLING.

Burnett, Frances [Eliza] Hodgson (1849–1924) English-born American author of popular romances for children, the most famous of which is LITTLE LORD FAUNTLEROY. Other works include *Sara Crewe* (1888), *The Secret Garden* (1911), and *The One I Knew Best of All* (1893), an autobiography.

Burney, Fanny (Madame d'Arblay, 1752–1840) English author. The daughter of a prominent musician and keeper of robes in the queen's household, Burney is chiefly known for her *Diaries and Letters, 1778–1840* (1842–48), *Early Diary, 1768–1778* (1889), and her novels EVELINA, OR THE HISTORY OF A YOUNG LADY'S ENTRANCE INTO THE WORLD; CECILIA, OR MEMOIRS OF AN HEIRESS; *Camilla* (1796); and *The Wanderer, or, Female Difficulties* (1814). She was one of the first novelists to deal with the experiences of a young girl coming in contact with the social world, and she may be regarded as a link between Samuel RICHARDSON and Jane AUSTEN in the history of the novel.

Burning Babe, The (written c1593, pub 1595) A mystical religious poem by Robert SOUTHWELL, in which the poet has a vision of the suffering infant Christ on Christmas day.

burning bush In the Old Testament, a bush burning with fire and not consumed (Ex. 3:2). It was out of this bush that the voice of God spoke to Moses on Mount Horeb, telling him that the Children of Israel were to be delivered from the oppression of the Egyptians and brought, under the leadership of Moses, into the land of Canaan. Because of its scriptural connotation and in commemoration of the church's early history of persecution, the burning bush became an emblem of the Presbyterian Church.

Burning Bush, The See UNDSET, SIGRID.

Burns, Robert (1759–1796) Scottish poet, generally considered the greatest of his nation. Self-educated, the son of a humble cotter and a farm laborer himself, Burns became a social as well as a literary sensation with the publication of his early poems in 1786. He is best known for his lyrics, written in the Scottish vernacular, on nature, love, patriotism, and peasant life. Among the most famous of these last are those addressed to a clergyman with whose theology he disagreed and against whom he had a personal grudge: THE HOLY FAIR, "Holy Willie's Prayer," "Address to the Unco Guid," and "Address to the Deil." He also wrote "To a Mouse," "To a Mountain Daisy," "Sweet Afton," "Ye Flowery Banks," "A Red, Red Rose," SCOTS, WHA HAE, "John Anderson My Jo," AULD LANG SYNE, and "A Man's a Man for a' That," which expresses Burns's democratic opinions. His longer poems include THE COTTER'S SATURDAY NIGHT, TAM O'SHANTER, and *The Jolly Beggars* (1785).

Like CHAUCER and BYRON, Burns was a master of the technique of using conversational rhythms in poetry. He almost always wrote to an old tune for which he sought appropriate words: "These old Scottish airs are so nobly sentimental that when one would compose for them, to *south* the tune, as our Scotch phrase is, over and over, is the readiest way to catch the inspiration, and raise the bard into that glorious enthusiasm so strongly characteristic of our old Scotch poetry." See HIGHLAND MARY.

Burnt Njal The hero of one of the best known of the early Icelandic sagas, *The Story of Burnt Njal*. The plot concerns the grim blood feud between the families of two well-to-do landowners, Njal and Gunnar, who are personal friends. Hallgerda, the spiteful and selfish wife of Gunnar, is the instigator of the feud, which progresses with a regular alternation of murders between the two sides until it culminates in the burning of Njal's home and his death within.

Burnt Norton See FOUR QUARTETS.

Burnt-Out Case, A (1960) A novel by Graham GREENE. Set in a leper colony in the Congo, it is the story of a famous architect who is a spiritual leper and "burnt-out case."

Burr, Aaron (1756–1836) American politician. After distinguishing himself in the American Revolution, Burr served in the U.S. Senate (1791–97) and organized a strong Democratic machine in New York through the previously nonpolitical Tammany Society. He was vice president (1801–05) under Jefferson, whom he had tied in electoral votes in the election of 1800. Burr's long-standing enmity with Alexander Hamilton culminated in a duel (1804), in which Hamilton was killed and which ruined Burr personally and politically. In 1806 he became involved in a conspiracy in the Old Southwest, the nature of which has never been fully clarified, and was tried for and acquitted of treason. Burr appears as a character in several novels, including H. B. Stowe's *The Minister Wooing* (1859), Gertrude Atherton's *The Conqueror* (1902), Kenneth Roberts's *Arundel* (1930), Anya SETON's *My Theodosia* (1941), and Gore Vidal's *Burr* (1973).

He has been the subject of many biographies, notably James Parton's *The Life and Times of Aaron Burr* (1858), S. H. Wandell and Meade Minnegerode's *Aaron Burr* (1925), W. F. McCaleb's *The Aaron Burr Conspiracy* (1936), Milton Lomask's two-volume *Aaron Burr* (1979, 1982), and Nathan Schachner's *Aaron Burr: A Biography* (1983).

Burroughs, Edgar Rice See TARZAN.

Burroughs, John (1837–1921) American naturalist, essayist, and poet. After a number of jobs, including work as a treasury clerk in Washington, D.C., and as a bank examiner (1873–84), Burroughs settled at Riverby on the Hudson River and pursued his first love: observation of nature. A close friend of many of the most prominent men of his day, Walt WHITMAN, Thomas EDISON, and Theodore ROOSEVELT among them, Burroughs was widely known for his natural history collections and for his many essays on nature, written in a vivid, concrete, and pleasantly readable style. Among the best known of his nature writings are *Wake-Robin* (1871), *Riverby* (1894), *Ways of Nature* (1905), and *Leaf and Tendril* (1908). He also wrote the first biographical study of Walt Whitman, *Notes on Walt Whitman as Poet and Person* (1867), a considerable portion of which was purportedly written by Whitman himself. The book was later expanded to *Walt Whitman: A Study* (1896). Burroughs himself published one volume of poetry, *Bird and Bough* (1906). His later books include *The Summit of the Years* (1913), *The Breath of Life* (1915), and *Accepting the Universe* (1922).

Burroughs, William S[eward] (1914–   ) American novelist. Burroughs's writing has been simultaneously dismissed as self-indulgent drivel and hailed as a major force in American literature. Burroughs was a drug addict for some fifteen years; his first two novels, *Junk* (1953; written under the name William Lee; reissued as *Junkie*, 1964) and the controversial *Naked Lunch* (1959), deal graphically with the gruesome and surreal world of the addict. His other works, including *The Soft Machine* (1961; rev 1966), *The Ticket That Exploded* (1962), *Nova Express* (1964), and *Exterminator!* (1973), are characterized by a rapid-fire, disjointed prose.

In his acid satires of contemporary society, Burroughs deals repeatedly with the themes of the death of God, homosexuality, and the evils of technology. In 1978 he published *The Third Mind*, with Brion Gysin, explaining his writing techniques. A major figure in the BEAT MOVEMENT, he had an important influence on Allen GINSBERG and other beat writers. *City of the Red Night* (1980) is a bizarre fantasy, in which time is telescoped as the world suffers the effects of a mysterious plague. In 1985 Burroughs published two novels, *Queer* and *Mind Wars*.

Burton, Sir Richard Francis (1821–1890) English explorer and writer of travel books. Burton's *First Footsteps in Eastern Africa* (1856) is an account of his travels with John Speke (1827–64). In 1858 the two went to East Africa again, where Burton discovered Lake Tanganyika and Speke discovered Lake Victoria. As British consul, Burton traveled in West Africa, Brazil, Damascus, and Trieste. He published more than thirty narratives on his travels. He also made a literal translation of the *Arabian Nights*.

Burton, Robert (1577–1640) English churchman and prose writer. Burton entered Oxford as a student in 1593, later becoming vicar of St. Thomas, Oxford, and keeper of his college library. Thereafter he never left the little university town. He was a passionate scholar with a consuming curiosity about every phase of learning: medicine, history, literature, science, and theology. He possessed, moreover, an extraordinary memory, a great power of systematizing facts, and the gifts of eloquence, sympathy, and dry wit. Except for a few minor Latin pieces, he left only one work, THE ANATOMY OF MELANCHOLY, into which he poured a lifetime's hoard of classical and curious learning.

Busch, Wilhelm (1832–1908) German caricaturist and poet. Beginning with *Max und Moritz* (1865; tr *Max and Maurice*, 1870), Busch became Germany's most renowned artist-poet. In a series of picture stories (*Bildergeschichte*), combining satirical verse and forceful line drawings, he took potshots not only at 19th-century philistinism and hypocrisy but also at the tragicomical aspects of human life in general. Early American comic strips, such as the "Katzenjammer Kids," were direct imitations of Busch's picture stories.

bush balladeers 19th-century Australian popular poets. The British ballad tradition, combined with rugged Australian country life, early produced anonymous bush (i.e., rural) ballads. Such poets as Henry LAWSON and "Banjo" PATTERSON encouraged a tradition of frontier poetry by writing robust pieces on Australia's heroic age of sheepherding and cattleherding.

bushidō (Jap, "way of the warrior") At first an unwritten code of ethics, devised for the moral and spiritual guidance of the entire military class by military leaders during the KAMAKURA period, bushidō was codified during the TOKUGAWA regime. Emphasis was always placed upon personal and reciprocal loyalty and duty, both among samurai and between samurai and lord. By the Tokugawa period, the code had evolved to incorporate both the aesthetic and the ascetic elements that are contained in ZEN discipline.

Bussy D'Ambois (c1604) A tragedy by George CHAPMAN. Bussy, a poor countryman who has gained the patronage of Monsieur, the king's brother, finds favor at the court of Henri III, despite the enmity of the duke of Guise, whose wife Bussy has been courting. Soon, however, his attentions turn to Tamyra, countess of Montsurry, and he becomes Monsieur's rival for the lady's affections. Where Monsieur fails, Bussy succeeds and becomes

Tamyra's lover. Eventually, Count Montsurry forces Tamyra, his wife, to write a letter to Bussy, imploring him to come to her. Bussy falls into the trap and is killed by Montsurry.

Butler, Samuel (1612–1680)   English poet, most famous for HUDIBRAS, a mock-epic satirizing the Puritans. Butler's work is distinguished by its relentless exposure of cant, hypocrisy, and human absurdity and by its arresting figures of speech, odd rhymes, and witty parade of learning. His *Genuine Remains in Verse and Prose* (1759) contains a set of *Characters* in the manner of THEOPHRASTUS and *The Elephant in the Moon*, a verse satire on the Royal Society. *The Rehearsal* (1671) was a burlesque satire of DRYDEN, written with Thomas Sprat (1635–1713) and the 2nd duke of BUCKINGHAM (George Villiers), among others.

Butler, Samuel (1835–1902)   English satirist, novelist, Homeric scholar, and translator. Son of a clergyman and grandson of Bishop Samuel Butler, whose biography (1902) he wrote, Butler too was destined for the church; upon graduation from Cambridge, however, religious doubts caused him to abandon his plans, and he immigrated to New Zealand (1859–64), where he accumulated a small fortune in sheep farming.

A brilliant amateur biologist, Butler was immediately attracted to Darwin's theory of evolution, but, believing Darwin had excluded mind from the life process, he subsequently took exception to certain aspects of Darwinism, in a series of criticisms which he elaborated throughout his life. His essay "The Deadlock in Darwinism" and his books on evolution—*Life and Habit* (1877), *Evolution, Old and New* (1879), *Unconscious Memory* (1880), and *Luck or Cunning?* (1887)—are still very readable.

His satiric masterpiece, EREWHON, attacked contemporary attitudes in social morals, religion, and science. *The Fair Heaven* (1873) is a subtle, ironic attack on revealed religion, presented in the guise of a convincing defense of the gospels, yet in fact undermining them. *Erewhon Revisited* (1901) is a continuation of his attack on revealed religions.

Butler also wrote *The Authoress of the Odyssey* (1897), in which he seriously defends his conviction that the *Odyssey* was written by a woman; *Shakespeare's Sonnets Reconsidered* (1899); and THE WAY OF ALL FLESH, a novel, perhaps his best-known work. He was an extremely versatile, original, and brilliant writer, one of the most searching critics of his age.

Butor, Michel (1926–   )   French novelist and essayist, a leading writer of the NOUVEAU ROMAN. Butor's first novel, *Passage de Milan* (1954), is a structural study of a Parisian apartment building and its inhabitants. *L'Emploi du temps* (1956; tr *Passing Time*, 1960) and *La Modification* (1957; tr *A Change of Heart*, 1959) are experiments showing the effects of the passing of time and its alterations of reality on human perceptions and relationships. *Degrés*

(1960; tr *Degrees*, 1961) is a study of an hour in a French lycée, and *Mobile* (1962; tr 1963) is a patchwork of impressions of the U.S. Butor is a highly sophisticated, intelligent writer, whose main themes—changes in space and time, the artist's dilemma in recreating reality—allow the development of a subtle, complex style and a technique of mystification. His other works include autobiographical essays, *Le Génie du lieu* (1958; tr *Boomerang*, 1978); literary criticism, *Répertoire* (1960), *Répertoire II* (1964), and *Les Compagnons de Pantagruel* (1976); and the novel *Description de San Marco* (1963). His poetic journals were published in three volumes entitled *Illustrations* (1964, 1969, 1973). *Répertoire V*, the fifth and final volume in the *Répertoire* volumes of criticism, was published in 1982. In 1984, Butor published *Improvisation sur Flaubert suivi de Michel Butor or Mayence*.

Butterfly Dream of Chuang Tzu, The   A well-known story from the second chapter of the CHUANG TZU. It is a characteristically poetic illustration of the Taoist philosopher's concept of the relativity of reality and illusion. Chuang Tzu awakens from a dream in which he was a butterfly. For a moment, he does not know if he is Chuang Tzu dreaming that he is a butterfly or a butterfly dreaming that he is Chuang Tzu.

Buzfuz, Serjeant   In Charles Dickens's PICKWICK PAPERS, the pleader retained by the unprincipled lawyers Dodson and Fogg for the plaintiff in the celebrated case of *Bardell* versus *Pickwick*. Serjeant Buzfuz is an able orator, who proves that Mr. Pickwick's innocent note about "chops and tomato sauce" is a declaration of love and that his reminder "not to forget the warming-pan" is only a flimsy cover to express the ardor of his affection.

Bykov, Vasily Vladimirovich (1924–   )   Soviet novelist, born in the Belorussian Soviet Republic. His first popular work, *Myortvym ne bolno* (*The Dead Feel No Pain*, 1966), established Bykov as an eminent war writer but aroused considerable criticism by its forthright vision of warfare. In his later works, Bykov softened his tone but retained his forthrightness: his abhorrence of cruelty and allusion to the frightful cost of victory on the eastern front represent a revised Soviet perception of the war. *Kruglyansky most* (*The Kruglyansky Bridge*, 1969), *Sotnikov* (1970; tr *The Ordeal*, 1972), *Obelisk* (1973), and *Volchya staya* (*The Wolf Pack*, 1975) all appeared in the Soviet literary magazine *Novy mir*.

byliny   The epic poems of the Russian peasantry, in song form. A number of specific heroes reappear throughout these songs. Their feats are fantastic and are often engagingly ingenuous. Many of the *byliny* are divided into cycles, such as the cycle of Kiev, the cycle of Novgorod, the cycle of IVAN THE TERRIBLE, and others. They range in time from the earliest mythological periods to the 18th century.

Byrd, William (1543?–1623)   English composer. Byrd wrote music for every genre and medium known in England in his day, and he excelled at all of them. His secular songs were sometimes based on texts by Sir Philip SIDNEY, OVID, ARIOSTO, and other poets. He retained the older English style of abstract polyphony in the face of a passion for the Italianate madrigal in the late 16th century, although he showed in one or two pieces that he could also compose in the madrigal style as well as anyone. He was one of the first composers to write songs for solo voice with an instrumental accompaniment (he used the consort of viols for that purpose, rather than lute or virginals). Byrd pioneered in the field of independent instrumental music, both for consort of viols and for virginal or harpsichord. However, the greatest part of his output consists of liturgical works for both the Catholic and Anglican church (he himself remained a lifelong Roman Catholic), where his brilliant technique achieved its finest results.

Byrd, William (1674–1744)   American historian of the Virginia colony, scholar, explorer, and member of the Royal Society of London, one of the most cultivated men in colonial America. Byrd's best-known works are *The History of the Dividing Line*, concerning the dispute over the boundary between Virginia and North Carolina, *A Journey to the Land of Eden*, and *A Progress to the Mines*. They are included in a collection of his papers, known as *The Westover Manuscripts*, first published in 1841. Diaries which Byrd kept in shorthand as a hobby for several years were discovered nearly two hundred years after his death and published as *The Secret Diary of William Byrd of Westover* (1941) and *Another Secret Diary* (1942).

Byron, George Gordon [Noel] (6th baron Byron of Rochdale, called Lord Byron; 1788–1824)   English poet. In both his works and his life, he created the "Byronic hero"—a defiant, melancholy young man, brooding on some mysterious, unforgivable sin in his past. Whatever Byron's sin was, he never told, but neither did he deny the legends of wildness, evil, and debauchery that grew up about his name. The heroes of Byron's poems are generally swashbuckling brigands who perform heroic feats. Byron himself, however, was short, somewhat stout, and limped from a club foot.

His profligate father died when Byron was three years old, and he was raised in Scotland by his mother. He was educated at Harrow and at Trinity College, Cambridge, receiving an M.A. from the latter in 1808. In 1809 he took his seat in the House of Lords, having come into the family title and estates through the death of his great-uncle in 1798. His first published work, *Hours of Idleness* (1807), a collection of poems, was given a devastating—and accurate —review by the *Edinburgh Review*. This review was answered by Byron in the virulent satire, ENGLISH BARDS AND SCOTCH REVIEWERS. After a very short time in Parliament, Byron and his friend J. C. Hobhouse left England

for a tour of the Mediterranean that took them from Spain to the Near East. The trip fired Byron's romantic nature with tantalizing views of the Orient and supplied material for many of his later works.

Following his return to England (1811), Byron published the first two cantos of CHILDE HAROLD'S PILGRIMAGE, a fictionalized account of his trip. *Childe Harold* was an immediate success; as Byron put it, he woke up one morning to find himself famous. In the next two years, he published *The Giaour* (1813), *The Bride of Abydos* (1813), THE CORSAIR, and *Lara* (1814).

Byron was much admired by women and had been involved in several intrigues before he married Anne Isabella MILBANKE in 1815. However, his promiscuous behavior after the marriage completely destroyed his reputation. Shortly after the birth of their daughter (1815), Lady Byron separated from her husband. Byron later spoke bitterly of the marriage, referring to their honeymoon as a "treaclemoon," and, once a deed of separation had been signed, he left England, never to return.

He traveled to Switzerland, where he lived with the Shelleys at Lake Geneva. Byron began a liaison with Clara Clairmont but moved restlessly on, arriving in Venice in November 1816 in the company of his friend Hobhouse. He spent the next six years in Italy, always championing and often taking part in the Italian nationalist movement. In 1819 Byron met and fell in love with the seventeen-year-old countess Theresa GUICCIOLI, and critics have attributed much of the poet's enthusiasm for Italy to her influence. With Leigh Hunt, Byron edited *The Liberal* (1822), but after the collapse of the *Carbonari* movement, they were left without a cause. The next year, following the death of Shelley, Byron outfitted a ship and sailed to Greece to take part in the battle for Greek independence. He died, feverstricken, at Missolonghi in January 1824. After being given full military honors in Greece, his body was shipped back to England for burial at Newstead Abbey, his baronial seat.

Byron's poetic output was never slowed down by his political and personal adventures. While in Italy, he finished *Childe Harold* (1816, 1817) and wrote *The Siege of Corinth* (1816), *Parisina* (1816), and THE PRISONER OF CHILLON, all poetic narratives. In 1817 he wrote his first poetic drama, MANFRED, which was followed by *Marino Faliero* (1820), *Cain, a Mystery* (1821), *Heaven and Earth* (1822), *Werner or The Inheritance* (1822), and *The Deformed Transformed* (1824). Among Byron's most accomplished works are his satires, such as BEPPO, *The Vision of Judgement* (1822), in which he answers the attack on him by the poet Robert SOUTHEY; *The Age of Bronze* (1823); and his masterpiece, DON JUAN. *Don Juan*, begun in 1819, was still unfinished when Byron died. This sixteen-thousand-line poem in sixteen cantos was continually added to by the poet, and as such it can be read as a contemporaneous account of the author's moods and feelings.

Byron used *Don Juan* as a platform to express many of his sardonic opinions of people and events. The protagonist is, of course, Byron himself, only thinly disguised as the famous Spanish rake.

As a poet and especially as one of the English romantics, Byron has found less favor than Keats or Shelley; he is looked on as the embodiment of romanticism rather than its spokesman. The bizarre aspects of Byron's life have somewhat overshadowed his technical virtuosity as a poet: the man has been more closely examined than his work. However, at its best, Byron's poetry shows an extraordinary rhyming ability combined with a free-flowing, dynamic style. His work rarely has the profundity found in that of Shelley or Keats, but his oeuvre as a whole is a forceful expression of the majesty and desolation of history, the vanity of pomp, and the fleeting quality of fame. His work has always been more popular in Europe, especially Germany, than in England and the U.S. See DESTRUCTION OF SENNACHERIB, THE.

Byronic hero   See BYRON, GEORGE GORDON.

Byrsa   The citadel of Carthage. Byrsa was built, according to legend, by DIDO, who was told by the local ruler that she might purchase as much land as could be enclosed within a bull's hide. By cutting the hide into narrow strips, she obtained a sizable piece of land. The hide (Gr, *byrsa*) supposedly gave the place its name; in fact, the name comes from a Phoenician word meaning "citadel."

Byzantine Empire   The eastern or Greek division of the Roman Empire, sometimes called the Later or Eastern Roman Empire. For the purposes of administration, DIOCLETIAN (ruled 284–305) divided the rule of the empire among four emperors, an experiment that led to twenty years of civil strife after his abdication. The empire was reunited in 324, when CONSTANTINE THE GREAT, defeating all his rivals, became sole ruler of the whole empire.

The Byzantine Empire may be dated from Constantine's creation of a second capital, modeled on Rome, at BYZANTIUM, which he renamed Constantinople (now Istanbul).

From the establishment of this city as a second Rome, the division of east from west was formalized, and the east soon emerged as the dominant half. More important, unlike Rome, with its pagan history, Constantinople was from the very first Christian, and it was Greek, thus dividing east from west still further. As Rome declined and finally fell (476), the Byzantine Empire flourished: it was a major if not the most important single power in Europe up to the mid-11th century. Politically, it played the highly significant role of protecting Europe, through the Middle Ages, against invasions from western Asia. The absolute monarchy, with the monarch elected by God, instituted by Constantine the Great remained largely unchanged throughout the long life of the empire, which fell at the hands of the Turks in 1453. See JUSTINIAN.

The iconography of the Byzantine Empire developed out of Christian symbolism. Its chief features are the circle, dome, and round arch; its chief symbols are the lily, cross, vesica, and nimbus. Saint Sophia at Constantinople and Saint Mark's at Venice are fine exemplars of Byzantine architecture and decoration.

Byzantium   A city on the European shore at the mouth of the Thracian Bosporus. It was first established by Megarian colonists (c657 BC). In the 6th century BC, it came under Persian rule and then alternately under Spartan and Athenian rule in the 5th and 4th centuries. After its revolt from the second Athenian League (357), it was independent and became an ally of Rome at the time of the Third Macedonian War. It subsequently came under Roman rule and was chosen by Constantine the Great for his new capital; he renamed it CONSTANTINOPLE; now called Istanbul, it is a major city in Turkey.

Byzantium appears as a central symbol in the poetry of William Butler YEATS. It occurs in "Sailing to Byzantium" and in "Byzantium," where it represents the richness of an artistic civilization and the triumph of art over time and death.

C

Cabal In English history, an influential clique of ministers at the court of Charles II from 1667 to 1674. The group derived its name from the initials of its members (Clifford, Ashley, Buckingham, Arlington, and Lauderdale), who were notorious for their intrigues and corruption. The word *cabal*, which is now used to signify a body of political intriguers, was probably popularized by the activities of the English Cabal, but it had long been associated with secrecy and magic. See CABALA.

cabala (or kabbalah; fr Heb, *qabbalah*, "tradition") The oral traditions of the Jews, said to have been delivered by Moses to the rabbis and handed down through the centuries by word of mouth. In the Middle Ages, the word was a popular term for the Jewish theosophy describing the World of Souls. The rabbis, or cabalists, who were the guardians of the cabala were feared as possessing secrets of magical powers.

Cabell, James Branch (1879–1958) American novelist and essayist. Cabell's first novel was *The Eagle's Shadow* (1904). It was in his second, *Gallantry* (1907), that he invented his own domain, the mythical Poictesme, a medieval French province which was to be the setting for a long series of symbolic and satirical novels. Cabell traced the history and families of his imagined land from 1234 to 1750, describing in detail the kingdom's laws, customs, and easy sexual morality; a central character in many of the novels was the jaded idealist Dom Manuel. An attempt to legally suppress one of the novels, *Jurgen* (1919), as obscene propelled the series onto best-seller lists. In addition to novels, Cabell wrote several works of nonfiction and poetry.

Cable, George Washington (1844–1925) American short-story writer and novelist. Cable is known for his tales dealing with the Creoles of New Orleans; he was part of the local color movement of the late 19th century and a master of the various dialects of his native city. His first literary success was *Old Creole Days* (1879), a collection of stories, to which *Madame Delphine* (1881) was added in later editions. THE GRANDISSIMES, a complex novel of social forces and his most widely read work today, showed Cable to be an important writer, whose treatment of race relations and violence was to foreshadow such later Southern writers as William Faulkner and Robert Penn Warren. *Dr. Sevier* (1884) attacked the corruption of New Orleans in the period before the Civil War.

A reformer and an enemy of slavery, Cable published *The Silent South* in 1885. This argument for better treatment of blacks and for prison reform increased the animosity of the Creoles toward Cable, forcing him to move to Massachusetts, where he continued to write on social problems, in *The Negro Question* (1888) and *The Southern Struggle for Pure Government* (1890).

Cabot, John (1450–1498) and **Sebastian** (c1476–1557) Outstanding Italian navigators and explorers. The senior Cabot traveled to the Orient in 1480 in hope of improving the spice trade. While there, he became impressed with the need for a northwest passage to Cathay: this was to become the ruling passion of his career and that of his son. Cabot traveled to England, settling in Bristol, where he received a patent of discovery from Henry VII. He set sail in 1497, accompanied by his son, on a voyage of discovery. He reached Baffin Land and cruised along the Newfoundland coast, which he thought to be Asia; a second voyage in 1498 carried him to the Delaware Capes and Hatteras. He is generally credited with the discovery of the North American continent.

John Cabot's son Sebastian, an expert cartographer as well as explorer, made an unsuccessful attempt to locate the northwest passage in 1509. He was then commissioned by the Spanish to explore the possibility of a southwest passage to the Pacific; from 1526 to 1529, he was in South America, following the River Plate. In 1533 he became the governor of a joint stock Company of Merchant Adventurers, whose aim was to find a northeast passage to China; their expedition reached Russia and opened trade possibilities instead. Sebastian died wealthy and famous, but he never realized his elusive goal.

Cabrera Infante, Guillermo (1929–   ) Cuban novelist and short-story writer. Cabrera Infante played an important role in Cuban literary affairs under Castro and was sent to Brussels as cultural attaché. The relationship ended, however, in 1965, when he severed his connections with the Castro government and with Cuba. His most famous work is *Tres tristes tigres* (1965; tr *Three Trapped Tigers*, 1971), a funny, dark novel of disoriented characters who continually seek for some significance they never find. Written with a verbal extravagance reminiscent of James JOYCE, the story is set against the backdrop of nightlife in the last days of Batista's Havana. His other books include *Vista del amanecer en el tropics* (1974; tr *View of Dawn in the Tropics*, 1978), consisting of vignettes of violence and deception throughout Cuba's history; *Exorcismos de estilo* (1976); and *La Habana para un infante difunto* (1979). *Holy Smoke* (1986), a novel, was written originally in English.

caccia (Ital, "hunt; chase") An Italian poem in FREE VERSE using short lines. Popular during the Italian Renaissance, *caccia* generally portrayed the hunt or any outdoor recreation, with appropriate exclamations and conversational figures of speech. Some were set to music, but few survive.

cacophony Harsh or dissonant combinations of sound. Although cacophony is sometimes used, particularly by poets, for intentional effect, the word is most often a critical term for a flawed or poorly conceived phonic presentation. It is the opposite of EUPHONY.

Cadenus One of SWIFT's many pseudonyms, an anagram of *decanus* (Lat, "dean"). It appears in *Cadenus and Vanessa* (1713, pub 1726), one of Swift's best poems, which gives an account of his relationship with Esther Vanhomrigh and was written to dispel her passion for him. The poem also reflects Swift's zeal for improving the minds of young ladies, which had begun with his tutorship of ESTHER JOHNSON. At the request of Esther Vanhomrigh, *Cadenus and Vanessa* was published after her death.

Cadignan, Diane de The Duchess of Maufrigneuse, afterwards Princess of Cadignan. One of Balzac's most heartless and brilliant women, the Princess is the mistress of many of the men who appear in the novels of LA COMÉDIE HUMAINE. She is the heroine of *Les Secrets de la Princesse de Cadignan* (1839).

Cadmus In Greek mythology, a son of Agenor and Telephassa. Sent from their Phoenician home to seek their sister Europe, Cadmus and his brothers were told not to return without her. The Delphic oracle advised him to give up the search and to found a city where a cow with a moon-shaped mark lay down to rest. This he did at Thebes in Boeotia. Killing a dragon sacred to Ares, he sowed its teeth, and armed men sprang up from the ground (see also SPARTI). When he flung a stone among them, they killed each other, except for five, who became his allies.

At a wedding attended by the gods, Cadmus married Harmonia, daughter of Ares and Aphrodite; she bore him a son, Polydorus, and four daughters, Autonoë, Ino, Agave, and SEMELE. He fortified the Theban acropolis, the Cadmeia. In his old age, he resigned the throne to his grandson Pentheus, after whose early death Cadmus and Harmonia migrated to Illyria and ultimately became serpents. Through Polydorus, Cadmus fathered the ill-fated dynasty that ended with Oedipus' grandsons. He appears in Euripides' tragedy *The Bacchae* as a follower of Semele's son Dionysus. See BACCHANTS, THE.

Caedmon (d 680?) Old English religious poet. According to Bede, Caedmon was an illiterate herdsman who received divine inspiration in a dream to write religious poetry. He entered a monastery and made narrative poetry in ALLITERATIVE VERSE of the scriptural histories told to him. Actually, there is only one hymn which he certainly composed; the rest of the "Caedmonian manuscript" is the work of several different authors. The first "book" has adaptations of Genesis, Exodus, and Daniel. The second, called *Christ and Satan*, is of much later date, perhaps even 9th century. See CYNEWULF.

Caesar, [Caius] Julius (100–44 BC) Roman general and statesman. After a brilliant early career in politics, where he distinguished himself in oratory, and in generalship, which he displayed in Spain (61–60 BC), Caesar was elected consul in 59. In 60 BC he joined with Pompey and Crassus in the First Triumvirate. After his consulate, as was customary, he was allotted the governorship of a province: his choice was GAUL. From 58 to 49, he pushed back the boundaries of Roman Gaul, until he had conquered all of central Europe from the Rhine to the Pyrenees. In 49 Pompey and the leaders of the Senate, fearing the prestige of Caesar and the strength of his fanatically loyal legions, ordered him to resign his command and return to Rome without his army. This he refused to do: "The die is cast," he is reported to have said as he led his army across the RUBICON into Italy. Pompey fled, together with many members of the senatorial party, including Cicero and Cato the Younger. Following his opponents to Thessaly, in northern Greece, Caesar defeated them in the battle of Pharsalus (48). In subsequent campaigns, he secured his firm hold on the empire in several ways: he placed CLEOPATRA on the throne of Egypt (48); he defeated the king of Pontus at the Battle of Zela (47); he crushed the remainder of the senatorial army at Thapsus, in North Africa (46). His return to Rome in the spring of 46 was marked by lavish public festivals. He was hailed as a demigod; the name of the fifth month (*Quintilis*) in the Roman calendar was changed to *Julius* (July) in his honor. During the year that followed, Caesar made many reforms in the senatorial system and in the general management of the empire. His most durable reform, however, was his revision of the calendar. With the help of an Alexandrian astronomer, he established the Julian calendar, which, with minor changes, is the one we use today. It went into effect on January 1, 45 BC.

Opposition to Caesar on the part of the aristocratic party was still seething beneath the surface of Roman politics. On March 15, 44 (the IDES of March), a group led by CASSIUS Longinus and Marcus Junius BRUTUS assassinated Caesar, thus bringing to a sudden end uncompleted plans for the reorganization of Rome and the empire.

Caesar was one of the foremost orators of his age; only Cicero was esteemed the more persuasive of the two speakers. He also found time to record some of the history that he himself helped to make. His COMMENTARIES ON THE GALLIC WAR and his *Commentaries on the Civil War* (45), which latter was unfinished, show him as a clear and vigorous prose stylist.

Even in his lifetime, the name *Caesar* represented the Roman *Imperium*. By the time of Jesus—75 years later—it was used to connote civil government. When Diocletian, at the end of the 3rd century, split the empire into East and West, he appointed two Caesars as vice-regents. Through the Middle Ages to the present day, Caesar's name has survived as *Kaiser* and *Tsar* or *Czar*.

Caesar appears in many historical dramas, notably in Shakespeare's JULIUS CAESAR and George Bernard Shaw's CAESAR AND CLEOPATRA. In *Julius Caesar*, Brutus is actually the main interest of the play, while Caesar is drawn as a weakling and a braggart. This characterization has often been criticized as untrue to history.

With the famous words *Veni, vidi, vici* ("I came, I saw, I conquered") Caesar announced his overthrow of Pharnaces, king of Pontus.

The expression "Caesar's wife must be above suspicion" has its origin in the incident when Caesar divorced his wife Pompeia after her name became linked with Clodius's, not because he believed her to be guilty, but because the wife of Caesar must not even be suspected of crime. See CALPURNIA.

Caesar, Octavius   See AUGUSTUS.

Caesar and Cleopatra (1899)   A play by George Bernard SHAW. A wise, unsentimental Caesar is the center of a loose plot about political intrigue in ancient Egypt. Shaw gives unfamiliar personalities to both Caesar and Cleopatra. Not Shakespeare's "serpent of the old Nile," this Cleopatra is a giddy teenager, convinced the Romans are monsters. Under Caesar's tutelage, she loses her charm and becomes a precocious adult. Caesar, balding and practical, is amused by Cleopatra, history, and himself. Shaw's plot is taken directly from Plutarch's *Parallel Lives*.

caesura   In prosody, a break or pause in the flow of a line of poetry for rhetorical effect. The caesura is as related to meaning as to verse technique, since it must be occasioned by a sense pause, such as the end of one sentence and the beginning of another. Formerly subject to the strict rules of classical prosody, the caesura is now used freely and naturally to vary the music of the line and thus of the entire poem.

Cahiers de la quinzaine   See PÉGUY, CHARLES.

Caiaphas   In the New Testament, a high priest before whom Jesus was brought to trial. Caiaphas was a member of the Sanhedrin.

Cain   In the Old Testament, the son of Adam and Eve and the murderer of his brother Abel. Cain killed his brother out of jealousy when Abel's sacrifice of the firstlings of his flock proved more acceptable to Jehovah than his own sacrifice of the fruit of the ground. Then Jehovah, to signify his disapproval, cast his curse upon him and made Cain "a fugitive and a vagabond in the earth." The rivalry of a shepherd for the approval of a deity is as old as Sumerian literature. See DUMUZI.

According to Muslim tradition, Cain refused to follow his father's desire that he marry Abel's twin sister, Jumella, and instead married his own twin sister, Aclima. God rejected Cain's sacrifice to signify his disapproval of this marriage.

Byron wrote a dramatic poem *Cain, a Mystery* (1821) based on the Bible narrative. Coleridge's prose poem *The Wanderings of Cain* (1798) is on the same subject.

Cain, James M[allahan] (1892–1977)   American novelist. Cain established a reputation as a writer of HARD-BOILED FICTION with his first novel, *The Postman Always Rings Twice* (1934; staged 1936; filmed 1946 and 1981), the story of a young hobo who has an affair with the wife of a roadside stand owner and plots with her to murder her husband and collect his insurance. Other novels are *Mildred Pierce* (1941), *Double Indemnity* (1943), *Past All Dishonor* (1946), *The Magician's Wife* (1965), and *Rainbow's End* (1975).

Cakes and Ale (1930)   A novel by W. Somerset MAUGHAM. It is a satire of English literary life, in which ASHENDEN and Kear (a popular novelist based on Hugh Walpole) reexamine the life of the great Victorian writer Driffield. Driffield was said to be based on Thomas Hardy, but Maugham vigorously denied it. The central character is Rosie, Driffield's first wife, an exuberant, promiscuous barmaid.

Calandrino and the Heliotrope   A tale from Boccaccio's THE DECAMERON. It tells of the simpleton Calandrino and his belief that there is a stone called the heliotrope that can make him invisible. Imagining he has found it, he eludes his friends Bruno and Buffalmacco and returns home. When his wife scolds him for bringing home so many stones, he beats her, convinced that she has destroyed the virtues of his find. Only when his friends confess the jest is he persuaded not to beat her again. Calandrino appears in several of the *Decameron* stories.

Calder, Alexander (1898–1976)   American sculptor and painter, known for his airily exuberant *mobiles*, the name Marcel DUCHAMP gave to the sculpture form Calder evolved with wire and brightly painted metal cutouts. Early training as an engineer in his native Philadelphia no doubt helped him understand how to estimate the effect of moving air on the shapes he made and balanced on a core. Later he went on to *stabiles*, large abstract, immobile sculptures for public buildings, parks, and gardens. At the opposite extreme were portraits done in wire and his miniature circus (1932). MIRÓ and MONDRIAN, with whom Calder worked early in his career in Paris, remained a visible influence on his buoyant art.

Calderón de la Barca [y Henao], Pedro (1600–1681)   Spanish dramatist, one of his country's great literary figures. Born in Madrid of a prosperous family of the lower aristocracy, Calderón was educated at the Jesuit college there and attended the university at Salamanca. Beginning his literary career about 1620, he was a soldier as well as a successful playwright. In 1651 he became a priest. After his ordination, he wrote only AUTOS SACRAMENTALES and command plays for the court theatre.

Calderón brought to the theatre a fine power of reasoning, an intellectual outlook, a keen dramatic instinct, and a delicate imagination. He was a typical writer of the Baroque period, frequently given to metaphors and artificially imposed symbols. His philosophy was influenced by such stoics as Epictetus and Seneca and by St. Augustine and St. Thomas Aquinas. His pessimism can be traced to a biblical origin in Job and Ecclesiastes. Most of the *comedias* and *autos* written at the end of his life proclaim the vanity of life and the emptiness of human existence.

Calderón wrote more than 120 plays and some seventy *autos*: there are, in addition, about twenty short pieces, such as *entremeses* and *zarzuelas*. Among the best-known works of Calderón's early period, in which he gave vent to his rebellious and restless personality, are EL ALCALDE DE ZALAMEA, considered one of his finest plays; *La devoción de la cruz* (*Devotion to the Cross*), which shows how devotion to the cross can negate even the most heinous crimes; *El cisma de Inglaterra*, dealing with Henry VIII and Anne Boleyn; *La niña de Gómez Arias*; and *Luis Pérez el Gallego*.

Like other dramatists of Spain's Golden Age, Calderón wrote several dramas based on *pundonor*, or the point of honor, a theme with which he is often associated. The concept in this case is limited to conjugal honor. According to the code, apparently condoned by Calderón, the barest rumor of a wife's infidelity gave her husband the right to take her life. Plays in this vein include EL MÉDICO DE SU HONRA; *A secreto agravio, secreta venganza*; and *El pintor de su deshonra*.

Calderón also wrote intricate, ingenious *comedias de capa y espada*, or cloak-and-sword comedies, filled with duels, secret hiding places, and veiled women. Among the best of these are *Hombre pobre todo es trazas*, *El astrólogo*

fingido, and *La dama duende*. In the more philosophical epoch of Calderón's career, the following plays are noteworthy: LA VIDA ES SUEÑO, often considered his masterpiece; EL MÁGICO PRODIGIOSO; *En esta vida todo es verdad y todo es mentira*; and *Saber del bien y del mal*.

Calderón is regarded as the outstanding writer of *autos sacramentales*, a genre which he perfected. His *autos* include EL GRAN TEATRO DEL MUNDO, *La cena de Baltazar*, and *El divino Orfeo*.

Caldwell, Erskine [Preston] (1903–1987) American novelist and short-story writer. The best of Caldwell's many books deal in an earthy and starkly tragic way with life among sharecroppers and blacks in his native Georgia. After working as a menial laborer, cotton picker, and professional football player, Caldwell began his writing career with some powerful short stories, notably "Country Full of Swedes" (1933). TOBACCO ROAD is his best-known novel, along with GOD'S LITTLE ACRE, which, when it emerged from an obscenity trial, became a worldwide bestseller. Although many of his books were less successful, Caldwell retained his direct style and an impeccable ear for dialect. He collaborated on a number of books with Margaret BOURKE-WHITE, his wife for five years, including *You Have Seen Their Faces* (1937). *Call It Experience* (1951) is a literary autobiography. Among his other works of fiction are *Trouble in July* (1940), *Complete Short Stories* (1953), *Close to Home* (1962), the comical *Miss Mama Aimee* (1968), and *Annette* (1973). *Afternoons in Mid-America* (1976) is a book of Caldwellian impressions of ordinary people.

Caldwell, [Janet Miriam] Taylor [Holland] (1900–1985)   English-born American novelist. Caldwell's career, during which she produced a long succession of massive best-sellers, began with *Dynasty of Death* (1938), about two families who control a huge munitions trust. This story was continued in *The Eagles Gather* (1940) and *The Final Hour* (1944). She dealt again with families of wealth and power in *This Side of Innocence* (1946). Among her many other popular novels are *Dear and Glorious Physician* (1959), about St. LUKE; *Great Lion of God* (1970), about St. PAUL; *Ceremony of the Innocent* (1976); and *Answer as a Man* (1981).

Caleb   In the Old Testament, a Hebrew leader at the time of the conquest of Canaan. Caleb was one of the twelve spies sent by Moses to appraise the strength of Canaan and to judge whether the Israelites were strong enough to invade it. Because he and Joshua were the only ones who reported favorably, they were the only ones of their generation permitted to enter the Promised Land.

Caleb Williams, The Adventures of, or Things as They Are (1794)   A novel by William GODWIN. Highly suspenseful, it anticipates detective fiction, in some respects, and is a social commentary on the relative positions of the privileged and lower classes. Caleb

Williams is a young man in the service of Falkland, an aristocrat who values his good name above everything else. Quite accidentally, Caleb discovers that Falkland has committed a murder for which an innocent person has been executed. Although Caleb would never reveal his master's crime, Falkland has him imprisoned on false charges. Caleb then escapes from prison but is relentlessly tracked down by the suspicious Falkland. As a last resort, Caleb tells the truth and Falkland is forced to confess. Caleb suffers terrible self-reproach at having caused his master's ruin. This novel was dramatized by George Colman, the younger (1762–1836), under the title of *The Iron Chest*.

Caledonia   The ancient Roman name for Scotland, now used only in poetry and in a few special connections.

calender (fr Per, *galandar*)   A member of a begging order of dervishes, founded in the 13th century by Qalandar Yusuf al-Andalusi, a native of Spain, who obliged its members to be perpetual wanderers. This feature has made the calenders prominent in Eastern romance. The story of the Three Calenders in the *Arabian Nights* is well known; they are three royal princes, disguised as begging dervishes, each of whom has lost his right eye.

Tale of the First Calender   No names are given. This calender was the son of a king and nephew of another king. While on a visit to his uncle, his father died and the vizier usurped the throne. When the prince returned, he was seized and his right eye pulled out. The uncle died and the usurping vizier made himself master of this kingdom also. The hapless young prince assumed the garb of a calender, wandered to Baghdad, and being received into the house of the three sisters, tells his tale in the hearing of the Caliph Haroun-al-Raschid.

Tale of the Second Calender   No names are given. This calender, like the first, was the son of a king. On his way to India, he was attacked by robbers and, though he contrived to escape, lost all his possessions. In his flight, he came to a large city where he encountered a tailor who gave him food and lodging. In order to earn a living, he became a woodsman, and he accidentally discovered an underground palace in which a beautiful lady was kept confined by an evil genius. Intent on liberating her, he kicked down the talisman; the genius killed the lady and turned the prince into an ape. As an ape he was taken on board ship and transported to a large commercial city, where he was made vizier to the sultan. The sultan's daughter undertook to disenchant him; to accomplish this, she had to fight with the malignant genius. She succeeded in killing the genius and restoring the enchanted prince, but she received such severe injuries in the struggle that she died, and a spark of fire that flew into the right eye of the prince destroyed it. The sultan was so heartbroken at the death of his only child that he insisted on the prince's quitting the kingdom without delay. He assumed the garb of a calender and, being

received into the hospitable house of the three sisters, tells his tale before Caliph Haroun-al-Raschid.

Tale of the Third Calender   This calender, King Agib, was wrecked on the loadstone mountain, which had drawn all the nails and iron bolts from his ship, but he overthrew the bronze statue on the mountaintop, the cause of the mischief. Agib then visited ten young men, each of whom had lost his right eye, and was carried by a roc to the palace of forty princesses, with whom he stayed a year. The princesses were then obliged to leave for forty days, but they entrusted him with the keys of the palace, with free permission to enter every room but one. On the fortieth day, curiosity finally induced him to open this room, where he saw a horse which carried him through the air to Baghdad. The horse then deposited him, and knocked out his right eye with a whisk of its tail, as it had done to the ten young men whom it had previously met.

calends   The first day of the Roman month. See IDES; NONES.

Caliban   In Shakespeare's THE TEMPEST, the deformed, half-human slave of Prospero. The son of the witch Sycorax and a devil, Caliban symbolizes mankind's primitive urges.

Robert BROWNING's poem "Caliban upon Setebos, or Natural Theology in the Island" is an attempt to express for such a creature as Caliban his crude philosophy of God and the universe. Percy MacKaye wrote a poetic drama, *Caliban* (1916), showing the regeneration of Caliban through love for Miranda.

Caligula (original name Caius Caesar, AD 12–41) Roman emperor (37–41). Son of Agrippina and GERMANICUS CAESAR, Caligula was brought up among the legions in Germany, where the soldiers gave him his nickname, Caligula, because he wore the soldier's boot (*caliga*). He was held high in the emperor Tiberius's favor; on Tiberius's death, which was either caused or helped along by Caligula, he succeeded to the throne. Caligula was at first revered by the people as the son of Germanicus, but, after a serious illness, he appeared very much changed and behaved like a madman. His wild extravagance led him to extortion and plunder. He was finally murdered, and his uncle Claudius was chosen to succeed him. He is the main character in the play CALIGULA by Albert Camus.

Caligula (1944)   A play by Albert CAMUS. The author makes the Roman emperor a sensitive man horrified by what Camus calls elsewhere the absurd condition of human life. Caligula adds to the senselessness by arbitrary acts of violence, obeying the mistaken logic that he can escape the condition of man by severing all his ties with humanity and thus, by asserting his own freedom, achieve the impossible. His seemingly mad complicity in his own assassination symbolizes his failure.

Calisher, Hortense (1911–   )   American novelist and short-story writer. Calisher's first, partly autobiographical, stories appeared in THE NEW YORKER. Many of her early stories featured Hester Elkin and her large Jewish family living in New York City. Her most frequently anthologized story, "In Greenwich There Are Many Gravelled Walks" (1951), focuses on a man, his loneliness, and a final promise of companionship. The full range of her short fiction is contained in *Collected Stories* (1975). Apart from the facts that she is an acknowledged master of style and that her work offers intricately drawn insights into her characters, Calisher's writing defies easy classification. Characters in her first novel, *False Entry* (1961), reappear in an entirely different context in *The New Yorkers* (1969). Both *Journal from Ellipsia* (1965) and *Queenie* (1971) contain spoofs of American sexual mores, the former by presenting alternatives of another planet, the latter through the eyes of an "old-fashioned girl." Other novels include *Texture of Life* (1963), an intimate portrait of a marriage, and *On Keeping Women* (1977).

Callaghan, Morley [Edward] (1903–) Canadian novelist and short-story writer. After meeting Ernest HEMINGWAY in Toronto in the 1920s, Callaghan went to Paris, where he became acquainted with the American expatriates and contributed to *This Quarter*, TRANSITION, and other little magazines. This period is recalled in his memoir *That Summer in Paris* (1963). His novels, which are noted for their "hard-boiled" realism, include *Strange Fugitive* (1928), *The Loved and the Lost* (1951), *The Many Colored Coat* (1960), and *A Fine and Private Place* (1975). His stories are collected in *Now That April's Here* (1936) and *Stories* (1959, 1967).

Calligrammes   See APOLLINAIRE, GUILLAUME.

Calliope   The Muse of epic poetry, generally held to be the chief of the nine MUSES. Calliope was the mother of ORPHEUS, by either APOLLO or King Oeagrus.

Callisto   An Arcadian nymph metamorphosed into a she-bear by ARTEMIS for not remaining a virgin like her other attendants. Her son Arcas, having met her in the chase, would have killed her, but Zeus converted him into a he-bear and placed them both in the heavens, where they are recognized as the Great and Little Bear. Arcas was the eponymous ancestor of the Arcadians.

Call It Sleep (written 1934)   The only novel of the Austro-Hungarian-born American novelist and short-story writer Henry Roth (1906–   ). Few critics recognized the book's merits when it first appeared. It was reissued in 1960, in paperback in 1964, and was hailed, belatedly, as one of the finest works of PROLETARIAN LITERATURE. The novel records six years in the life of a Jewish immigrant boy, David Schearl, in a New York ghetto just prior to World War I. His paranoid father is unable to hold a job and becomes increasingly menacing to the young son who is shielded by the doting mother. The story becomes a nightmarish vision—rendered in a STREAM OF CONSCIOUSNESS style from the boy's vantage point—of David's oedipal

conflicts and his fears of the streets, the dark, and inhabitants of the ghetto.

Call of the Wild, The (1903)   A novel by Jack LONDON. Buck, half-St. Bernard, half-Scottish sheepdog, is stolen from his comfortable home in California and pressed into service as a sledge dog in the Klondike. At first he is abused by both man and dog, but he learns to fight ruthlessly. He becomes lead dog on a sledge team, after bettering Spitz, the vicious old leader, in a brutal fight to the death. In John Thornton, he finally finds a master whom he can respect and love. When Thornton is killed by Indians, Buck breaks away to the wilds and becomes the leader of a wolf pack, returning each year to the site of Thornton's death. The book, illustrating London's recurrent Darwinian theme of the need for adaptation to survive, was an immediate success and thrust London into a position of unaccustomed wealth. See WHITE FANG.

Calpurnia   Third wife of Julius Caesar. They were married in 59 BC. On the night before he was assassinated, Calpurnia dreamed that a templelike gable, dedicated in his honor, smashed to the ground and that Caesar lay dying in her arms. She is a character in Shakespeare's JULIUS CAESAR; she begs Caesar not to attend the Senate. Caesar's first two wives were Cornelia and Pompeia.

Calvary (or Golgotha)   Site of the crucifixion of JESUS. Though Calvary is assumed to be in the city of JERUSALEM or its environs, its exact location is still disputed by biblical scholars. *Calvary* and *Golgotha* are both translations of words meaning "skull," and the site derives its name either from the configuration of the land or from the legend that Adam's skull is buried there. Both terms are now synonymous with any scene of martyrdom and are often used to mean an experience of acute mental anguish.

Calvin, John (adapted form of Jean Cauvin, 1509–1564)   French Protestant reformer. Calvin's theological doctrines had tremendous influence, particularly in the Puritan religion of England, Scotland, and America.

Calvin had an early background of humanism; as a student of Latin and Greek, he was familiar with the writings of PLATO, SENECA, and St. AUGUSTINE. Because of the radical Protestant views expressed in a public speech he wrote in 1533, to be delivered at an inaugural ceremony at the University of Paris, Calvin was forced to flee the capital and soon France as well. He established himself in Geneva, strictly enforcing his theological doctrines and rules of conduct. His greatest work is INSTITUTES OF THE CHRISTIAN RELIGION.

Calvinism as a religious system is the theological foundation of the Reformed, or Presbyterian, churches, which is to say, of non-Lutheran, non-Anglican Protestantism. It recognized only the BIBLE as a source of knowledge and of authority in questions of belief. Its chief principles were (1) the total depravity of man, as a result of Adam's fall; (2) the absolute power of the will of God; (3) the superiority of faith to good works, since man has no will of his own; (4) salvation by grace from God rather than by any act of the will of man; and (5) the divine predestination of those to be saved, or the Elect, although, since no one can tell whether he is a member of the Elect, all must lead holy and pious lives, acknowledging God's supreme power and obeying his commands.

Calvin's pessimistic interpretation of Christian doctrine was coupled with a repressive attitude toward pleasure and frivolity. The zeal with which his followers taught and imposed his views assured his position as one of the most influential theologians in the West. See PROTESTANT ETHIC.

Calvino, Italo (1923–1985)   Italian novelist and short-story writer. Calvino's first novel, *Il sentiero dei nidi di ragno* (1947; tr *The Path to the Nest of Spiders*, 1956), written when he was only twenty-four, was based on his wartime experiences in the Italian Resistance. Basically a realistic work, it also revealed his inclination toward fantasy, more fully realized in a trilogy inspired by ORLANDO FURIOSO: *I nostri antenati* (*Our Forefathers*, 1960; tr in 2 vols, *Baron in the Trees*, 1959, and *The NonExistent Knight and The Cloven Viscount*, 1962). The fantastic elements of these fables are presented in sharply realistic prose that is lyrical, ironic, and precisely descriptive. His other fantasies include *Le cosmicomiche* (1965; tr *Cosmicomics*, 1968), a series of tales on the evolution of the universe, narrated by the timeless Qfwfq; *Le città invisibili* (1972; tr *Invisible Cities*, 1974), poetic prose discourses by Marco Polo to Kublai Khan; and *Il castello dei destini incrociati* (1973; tr *The Castle of Crossed Destinies*, 1977), written originally to accompany a collection of tarot cards. *Fiabe italiane* (1956; tr *Italian Fables*, 1959), Calvino's renderings of folk tales he collected from all over Italy, reveals his preoccupation with the act of storytelling. *Se una notte d'inverno un viaggatore* (1979; tr *If on a Winter's Night a Traveller*, 1981) is an intricate fancy involving the reader as its central character, consisting of a series of novels as they begin but never end.

Calvino's work remains truly contemporary yet classic in tone and theme. *Difficult Loves* (1984), a collection of short stories, conveyed the light, airy quality of Calvino's finest prose. *Mr. Palomar* (1985), in press at the time of Calvino's death, is a triumphant work, enormously funny and a fine example of the author's inventiveness and stylistic originality.

Calydonian boar   A creature of Greek legend. Oeneus, king of Calydon, in Aetolia, having neglected to sacrifice to ARTEMIS, was punished by the goddess's sending a ferocious boar to ravage his lands. A band of heroes collected to hunt the boar, which was eventually slain by MELEAGER after it had been first wounded by ATALANTA. A dispute over the boar's head led to a war between the neighboring tribe of Curetes and the Calydonians. This was one of the most famous sagas of Greece but is not recorded in any outstanding single work.

Calypso   (1) In Homer's ODYSSEY, the nymph of the island of Ogygia. Calypso detains the shipwrecked ODYSSEUS there seven years. Loyal to PENELOPE, he refuses her offer of immortality if he stays, and at last, at ZEUS's command, she helps him to continue on his way toward Ithaca.

(2) West Indian music with syncopated African rhythms, usually sung in satiric, balladlike verses which are spontaneously improvised by the performers. It has no apparent connection with HOMER's nymph.

Cambridge Critics   A group of 20th-century English critics, originating at Cambridge University. They rejected the traditional method of studying a work of literature in the light of historical, biographical, or other external factors, in favor of close scrutiny of the text itself. This analytic approach was particularly fruitful when applied to complex modern poetry. I. A. RICHARDS was the early center of the group. He and his pupil and associate William EMPSON, both poets themselves, were pioneers in the study of ambiguity in poetry. F. R. LEAVIS, one of the founders of the literary magazine *Scrutiny* and also originally associated with Richards, later became the major force in Cambridge criticism. The fact that this school of criticism originated at Cambridge was integrally connected with the presence there of the great linguistic philosophers G. E. MOORE, Ludwig WITTGENSTEIN, and Bertrand RUSSELL. See LOGICAL POSITIVISM; NEW CRITICISM.

Cambridge Platonists   A group of English liberal philosophic-religious thinkers of the latter half of the 17th century, whose general aim was to effect a reconciliation between reason and mystical religiosity. Their mode of thought and terminology were taken chiefly from Plato and the Neoplatonists. They were vehemently opposed to Hobbes's materialism, their most important doctrine being the absolute existence of right and wrong. The outstanding members of the group were Ralph Cudworth (1617–88), Nathaniel Culverwel (1618–51), Joseph Glanvill (1636–80), Henry More (1614–87), Benjamin Whichcote (1609–83), and John Smith (1616–52). Their thought may be summarized in Smith's words: "To follow reason is to follow God."

Camelot   A place name prominent in Arthurian literature, one of the spots where King ARTHUR held court. In many of the legends, we find both Camelot and Caerleon as court capitals, each being appropriate, apparently, to certain times of the year. For example, Caerleon is sometimes found to be the place where King Arthur and his court celebrated Pentecost, and Camelot the place where the court went for the celebration of Christmas.

Camille   (1) In Pierre Corneille's tragedy HORACE, the sister of Horace and the fiancée of Curiace, Horace's opponent in combat. When Horace kills Curiace, Camille curses Rome, and her infuriated brother slays her.

(2) See DAME AUX CAMÉLIAS, LA.

Camino Real See WILLIAMS, TENNESSEE.

Camões, Luis Vaz de (or Luis Vaz de Camoëns; 1524?–1580) Portuguese poet. After being banished from court because of his romance with Caterina de Ataíde (the Natercia of his poems), a lady-in-waiting to the queen, Camões served in North Africa, where he lost his right eye in an engagement with the Moors. In 1552 he was imprisoned for wounding a court official in a street brawl. Sailing to India in 1553 as a common soldier, he was later named official trustee for the property of the dead and absent in Macao and was briefly imprisoned for allegedly embezzling government funds. After numerous hardships, he managed to return to Lisbon in 1570.

Camões's best-known work is his epic poem, OS LUSIADAS, notable for its synthesis of national, religious, and humanistic themes. He is also regarded as one of Portugal's greatest lyric poets, largely because of his sonnets and *canções*. His other works include three plays: *Os anfitriões*, which was inspired by Plautus's *Amphitruo*; *El-Rei Seleuco*, based on an episode in Plutarch; and *Philodemo*.

Campbell, Roy (1902–1957) South African poet. A neofascist and disciple of Wyndham LEWIS, Campbell wrote satires and poems of colorful nature description. He was converted to Catholicism in about 1935. He fought on the Fascist side in the Spanish Civil War; *Flowering Rifle* (1939) is a long satiric poem celebrating Franco's victory. Among his collections of poems are *The Flaming Terrapin* (1924), *Adamastor* (1930), and *Talking Bronco* (1946). He translated the poems of St. John of the Cross and wrote two autobiographies: *Broken Record* (1934) and *Light on a Dark Horse* (1952).

Campbell, Thomas (1777–1844) Scottish poet, best known for his literary ballad LORD ULLIN'S DAUGHTER. Campbell also produced some notable martial lyrics, including *Ye Mariners of England* (1800), *Hohenlinden* (1802), and *The Battle of the Baltic* (1809). Of his longer narrative works, only *Gertrude of Wyoming* (1809) retains interest. Campbell was an editor (*The New Monthly Magazine*) and anthologist of some influence in his day.

Campion, Thomas (1567–1620) English poet and musician. Campion is famous for his songs written to music of his own composition, collected in such volumes as *A Book of Airs* (1601), *Two Books of Airs* (c1613), and *The Third and Fourth Books of Airs* (c1617). His lyrics possess rare charm and freshness, as well as a melodiousness and metrical variety that reflect their musical origin. He was also the author of *Observation in the Art of English Poesy* (1602), an argument for the use of classical, quantitative meters in English verse, which prompted Samuel Daniel's *Defence of Ryme* (1602).

Campos de Castilla (1912; rev and augmented, 1917) Perhaps the most characteristic and definitive book of poems by Antonio MACHADO. Published the year of his wife's death but written almost entirely before then, it offers a resumé of his years in Soria, the northern provincial town where he taught, married, and lived for a time. Typical of the GENERACIÓN DEL 98 in its awareness of Spain's decadence and yet almost mystical in its portrayal of Castilian landscape, *Campos de Castilla* breaks with Machado's early modernism and symbolism for a sober, restrained, and masterful portrayal of the poet's soul in response to the geography about him.

Camus, Albert (1913–1960) Algerian-born French philosopher, novelist, dramatist, and journalist. After studying philosophy at the University of Algiers, Camus organized (1935) the *Théâtre de l'equipe*, a young avant-garde dramatic group, and worked with it until 1938. Then, until the beginning of World War II, he worked both in North Africa and in Paris as a journalist. It was between 1937 and 1941 that he wrote the works that made him famous: the novel THE STRANGER, the essay THE MYTH OF SISYPHUS, and the play CALIGULA. He also sketched LE MALENTENDU, which he finished in 1943. All four works present aspects of the ABSURD, the plight of man and his need for clarity and rationality in confrontation with the unreasonable silence of the universe. These works form the basis of Camus's artistic and philosophical vision: the tragedy of man's failure to apprehend his condition or, if he does, to find the human values by which he can transcend it.

After the occupation of France by the Germans in 1941, Camus became one of the intellectual leaders of the Resistance movement. He helped found the underground newspaper *Combat* in 1943, was its chief editor during the war, and continued to write for it until 1946, when it began open publication after the liberation of France. Camus was a close associate of Jean-Paul SARTRE and his circle; although they cooperated on their Resistance activities, the differences between their philosophical positions became more and more apparent. Camus has sometimes been classified among the existentialists, but he himself refuted their position in many of his writings. See EXISTENTIALISM.

His commitment to the humanistic attitude, which affirms values such as individual freedom and love between men, is reflected in the novel THE PLAGUE, about men doing their futile best in the face of disaster. The short novel THE FALL is a bitter comment on the difficulty of finding a mode of active life compatible with total consciousness both of the *absurd* and of one's inescapable solidarity with other human beings.

During the late 1950s, Camus renewed his active interest in the theatre, writing and directing stage adaptations of William FAULKNER's REQUIEM FOR A NUN and Dostoyevsky's THE POSSESSED. He was awarded the NOBEL PRIZE in Literature in 1957.

THE REBEL is a book-length statement of Camus's philosophical views. In *Actuelles I–III* (1950, 1953, 1958) are essays on political, social, and literary questions collected from *Combat* and elsewhere; *Resistance, Rebellion, and Death* (1961) is an English selection from these. Other works include the early essays *L'Envers et l'endroit* (1937) and *Noces* (1939), mostly sympathetic sketches of North Africa; *Lettres à un ami allemand* (*Letters to a German Friend*, 1945), written during the war; the plays *État de siège* (1948; tr *State of Siege*, 1958) and *Les Justes* (1950; tr *The Just Assassins*, 1958); and the six short stories in *L'Exil et le royaume* (1957; tr *The Exile and the Kingdom*, 1958).

On January 4, 1960, Camus was killed in an automobile crash while returning to Paris from the South of France.

Canaan   An ancient region of vague boundaries. Canaan lay roughly between the Jordan River and the Mediterranean Sea. This Promised Land of the Israelites was actually rather infertile. A mixture of Semites and Indo-Europeans lived there until the Israelites conquered much of the area. The Semites, worshippers of *baalim* (see BAAL), had a fairly rich culture, many evidences of which have been uncovered in the 20th century at Ugarit and elsewhere. Most of them were under the domination of Egypt or, for a time, of the Hittites. The civilization of Phoenicia was to a considerable extent a continuation of that of Canaan.

The rabbinical tradition that Canaan, a son of HAM, was the first of the seven sinners who made idols for the heathens reflects the regrettable history of Israelitish backsliding into the baal-worship of their Canaanite neighbors. For Canaanite literature, see THE POEM OF BAAL and THE POEM OF AQHAT.

Canaletto, Antonio (or Antonio Canale, 1697–1768)   Venetian painter, known for his broad views of Venice. Canaletto rendered architectural detail with great precision and flawless perspective and bathed his scenes in a clear light of sharp contrasts. Bernardo Bellotto (1724–80), his nephew and pupil, is also sometimes called Canaletto.

Cancer Ward (Rakovy korpus, 1968; tr 1968)   A novel by Aleksandr Solzhenitsyn. Set mostly in a provincial cancer ward, the novel traces the ways in which a number of moribund patients come to terms with their death, centering on an investigation of the moral and psychological development of the exiled hero, Kostoglotov. This novel, in which the cancer ward has been widely interpreted as symbolizing the Soviet state, was typeset for publication in the Soviet Union but never published there.

Candida (1903)   A play by George Bernard SHAW. This is one of Shaw's theatrically most successful works; its subject is marriage. Candida Morell's husband is a hearty, popular Christian Socialist clergyman. Eugene Marchbanks is an eighteen-year-old rhapsodic, visionary poet who is in love with Candida. Forced to choose between them, she remains with her husband when she realizes that he needs her, being the weaker of the two men. The plot of *Candida* shows the influence of Ibsen's A DOLL'S HOUSE. Shaw, however, has reversed the roles of puppet and master: Morell's seeming strength wholly rests on Candida's dignity and character.

Candide, ou L'Optimisme (1759)   VOLTAIRE'S most popular philosophical novel. It satirizes the optimistic creed of LEIBNITZ: "All is for the best in this best of all possible worlds." Dr. PANGLOSS, tutor to the hero, Candide, is the embodiment of this theory, maintaining it through thick and thin, despite the most blatant evidence to the contrary. Misadventures begin when young Candide is kicked out of the castle of Thunder-ten-tronckh for making love to the baron's daughter, Cunégonde. Thereafter, he, Cunégonde, and Pangloss embark—sometimes singly, sometimes together—on a long series of disastrous adventures. After being impressed into the Bulgarian army, Candide is beaten nearly to death; he deserts and flees to Holland, where he learns that Cunégonde and her family have been massacred. He and Pangloss go to Lisbon, arriving in time for the historic earthquake (1755); there they are condemned by the Inquisition, and Pangloss is hanged. But Cunégonde—alive, after all—saves Candide, who later finds it necessary to kill a Jew and an Inquisitor to discourage them from pursuing Cunégonde. Still hunted by the Inquisition, Candide leaves Cunégonde and, with his valet Cacambo, flees to safety among the Jesuits, who are warring on Spain and Portugal. Candide kills their general, a Jesuit who is none other than Cunégonde's brother. He flees to El Dorado but, because he misses Cunégonde, leaves, loaded with riches. He returns to France, where he is threatened with imprisonment and cheated out of his fortune by swindlers. He travels to Portsmouth and then to Venice, where he learns that Cunégonde has been captured by pirates and is washing towels in Constantinople. On the ship to Turkey, Candide discovers that two of the galley slaves are none other than Cunégonde's brother, whom he did not kill, and Pangloss, who had not been properly hanged. He finally finds Cunégonde, now very ugly, and marries her against his will. All of them finally settle down on a little farm. Pangloss insists that all these calamities happened for the best. Candide replies, "Il faut cultiver notre jardin" ("We must cultivate our garden"). All the disasters in the novel have historical precedents, and we may conclude from Candide's last remark either that work is far more profitable than vain speculation or that work is the antidote to man's unhappy lot.

Candlemas Day   The popular name for the Feast of the Purification of the Virgin Mary, February 2. On this day, Jesus was presented by her in the Temple. The feast is so called from the custom of blessing on this day all the candles which will be used in a church throughout the year. They symbolize Christ as "the light of the world" and "a light to lighten the Gentiles," phrases spoken of Jesus at the time of his Presentation by the aged Simeon. There is also a weather legend associated with the day.

Canetti, Elias (1905–   )   Bulgarian-born writer. Canetti and his works defy national categorization. He was born in Bulgaria to a family of Sephardic Jews; his father was Turkish, his mother of Spanish descent. When Canetti was six, his family immigrated to England, but he moved again with his mother to Vienna in 1912, after his father's death. Canetti then lived and studied in Switzerland, Germany, and Austria, earning his doctorate in chemistry from the University of Vienna in 1929. In 1938 he moved to France; a year later, he settled and remained in England. Much of this early life is described in two autobiographical volumes, *Die gerette Zunge* (1977; tr *The Tongue Set Free*, 1979) and *Die Fackel im Ohr* (1980; tr *The Torch in The Ear*, 1982). Throughout his polyglot upbringing, Canetti's intellectual and cultural identification was with Germany, and all his books are written in German.

His first and only novel was *Die Blendung* (1935; tr *Tower of Babel*, 1947; *Auto-da-fé*, 1966). It depicts the madness of a reclusive sinologist, Professor Kien. Lured away from his library by his housekeeper, whom he marries, he is exposed to the horrors of the world, rendered by Canetti in grotesque and excruciating detail. Ruined and in despair, Kien finally returns to his literary sanctuary and sets fire to himself and his books. *Die Blendung* was intended to be the first of eight novels, each charting the obsessions of monomaniacs in a fragmented world. Instead, Canetti turned his own insatiable appetite for knowledge to a period of twenty-five years' study, which culminated in his nonfiction masterwork, *Masse und Macht* (1960; tr *Crowds and Power*, 1962, 1978). Drawn from a lifetime's preoccupation with the relationship of the individual to society and with the nature of communication, *Masse und Macht* applies virtually all intellectual disciplines to the psychopathology of crowds and to man's fear of freedom and of death. Canetti's profound insights are guided by his own contempt for power and those who would make power a religion.

Thereafter, he published a characteristically detailed and unsettling account of a visit to Morocco in *Die Stimmen von Marrakesch* (1967; tr *The Voices of Marrakesh*, 1978); a brilliant study of Kafka, *Der andere Prozeß* (1969; tr *Kafka's Other Trial*, 1974); and *Der Ohrenzeuge* (1974; tr *The Earwitness*, 1979), fifty sketches of monomania. Canetti's work is original, highly literal, and minutely attentive to the sounds and meanings of language. In 1981 Canetti was awarded the NOBEL PRIZE in Literature, the first Bulgarian to be so honored.

Canfield, Dorothy   See FISHER, DOROTHY CANFIELD.

Cannery Row (1945)   A novel by John STEINBECK. In this episodic work, Steinbeck returns to the style of *Tortilla Flat* (1935) to produce a rambling account of the adventures and misadventures of workers in a California cannery and their friends. One character, Doc, was reportedly modeled on the marine biologist Edward F. Ricketts (1896–1948), with whom Steinbeck collaborated on *The Sea of Cortez* (1941). The character reappears in the sequel, *Sweet Thursday* (1954).

Canonization, The (1633)   A poem by John DONNE, in which he claims that the reciprocal love between him and his mistress is so deep and unworldly as to make them saints of love. It is a fine example of the vehemently colloquial and ingeniously conceited style typical of Donne.

Canon's Yeoman's Tale, The   One of THE CANTERBURY TALES of Geoffrey CHAUCER. In the *Prologue*, a Canon and his Yeoman overtake the pilgrims. The Host asks if the Canon can tell a story, and the Yeoman begins to reveal his master's craftiness as a fraudulent alchemist. The Canon bids him be silent, but he has decided to leave the alchemist's service, so he continues his vituperative report, and the Canon rides off to avoid shame. The Yeoman bitterly describes the apparatus and processes of the "cursed craft" of alchemy and all the money and labor lost in searching for the elixir to turn base metals into gold. Then he tells a tale about a canon, not his ex-master, who pretends to take a priest into his confidence and let him help in the conversion of quicksilver and copper to silver. The canon effects the exchange by sleight of hand, but the duped priest believes in the actual transmutation of the metal and asks to buy the formula. The canon accepts forty pounds, making him think it a bargain price, and can never be found by the priest again.

Cantatrice chauve, La   See BALD SOPRANO, THE.

Canterbury Tales, The (c1387–1400)   A poetic work by Geoffrey CHAUCER. Although unfinished, it is his longest and his finest work, written in decasyllabic couplets, except as noted in the entries in *Benét's Reader's Encyclopedia* for the individual tales. The *General Prologue* establishes the framework for the stories: the poet has joined with thirty others (although the *Prologue* says twenty-nine) to make the usual April pilgrimage to Becket's shrine at Canterbury; he describes each of his companions, who are of widely varying classes and occupations. Their host at the Tabard Inn, Harry Bailly, proposes to come with them and serve as judge in a story-telling contest to occupy the long hours of the journey; each pilgrim is to tell two stories on the way to Canterbury and two on the way back, and the teller of the best tale will get a free dinner at the Tabard upon their return. Chaucer wrote only twenty-four tales, however: twenty-one are told by characters described in the *Prologue*, one is told by the Canon's Yeoman, who joins the group after they have already started, and Chaucer himself begins one tale, and when interrupted tells a second. In addition to the characters who do narrate tales (see below), Chaucer describes the Knight's

Yeoman, two Priests accompanying the Prioress, a Haberdasher, a Carpenter, a Weaver, a Dyer, a Tapicer (weaver of tapestry), and a Plowman.

Although such frame stories were common in Chaucer's day, Chaucer was an innovator in his choice of such a diverse assembly of narrators, in the concomitant diversity of style of their tales (from chivalric romance to bawdy FABLIAUX, from folk tale to sermon), and in the way he develops the drama of the interaction of his characters' personalities. With a few exceptions, where Chaucer obviously had not thoroughly worked out his scheme, the tales and the manner of their telling (except for the convention of their being in verse) are completely suited to the nature of their tellers. Between the actual narratives are interludes in which the characters talk—often argue—with each other and with the host, revealing much about themselves. These episodes usually occur in the "prologues" to the tales, and each is described in connection with the tale it accompanies. See:

CANON'S YEOMAN'S TALE (the fraudulent alchemist)
CLERK'S TALE (patient Griselda)
COOK'S TALE (Perkin)
FRANKLIN'S TALE (Dorigen, Arveragus, and Aurelius)
FRIAR'S TALE (the summoner and the Devil)
KNIGHT'S TALE (Palamon and Arcite)
MANCIPLE'S TALE (the tell-tale crow)
MAN OF LAW'S TALE (Constance)
MELIBEE (told by Chaucer)
MERCHANT'S TALE (January and May)
MILLER'S TALE (Nicholas, Alison, and Absolon)
MONK'S TALE (the falls of illustrious men)
NUN'S PRIEST'S TALE (Chauntecleer and Pertelote)
PARDONER'S TALE (the revellers who seek Death)
PARSON'S TALE (sermon on Penitence)
PHYSICIAN'S TALE (Virginia)
PRIORESS'S TALE (the murdered boy who sings)
REEVE'S TALE (the miller's family and the students)
SECOND NUN'S TALE (Life of St. Cecilia)
SHIPMAN'S TALE (the miserly merchant, his wife, and the monk)
SQUIRE'S TALE (Cambuscan and Canacee)
SUMMONER'S TALE (Thomas and the friar)
THOPAS, SIR (told by Chaucer)
WIFE OF BATH'S TALE (the knight and the hag)

canto (Ital, "song")   A term for the subdivisions of an epic or narrative poem, which are the equivalent of chapters in a book.

Cantos   An incomplete epic poem by Ezra POUND, published in several sections: *Cantos I–XVI* (1925), *A Draft of XXX Cantos* (1930), *Eleven New Cantos XXXI–XLI* (1934), *Fifth Decad of Cantos* (1937), *Cantos LII–LXXI* (1940), *Cantos* (1948), THE PISAN CANTOS, SECTION: ROCK DRILL 85–95 DE LOS CANTARES, *Thrones: 96–109 de*

los Cantares (1959), *Drafts and Fragments of Cantos CX–CXVI* (1968). The first sections of the *Cantos* were published in magazine form as early as 1917. Pound's conception of his epic changed several times during different phases of his life. Originally intended as a didactic treatise for "philistine" Americans, it combined elements from classical myth, ancient Oriental poetry, Provençal ballads, and modern economic theory, to create a vast, disjointed panorama of the growth of civilization. A monumental work of poetic enterprise, *The Cantos'* loose metrical structure and violent juxtapositions were once described by Pound himself as a "rag bag." Central to their conception is the use of ODYSSEUS as a man in search of a culture and of Ovid's METAMORPHOSES as a touchstone of individual and cultural transformation. Pound quotes liberally from the literary and historical documents of the ancient Greeks, the medieval Provençal poets, writers of the Italian Renaissance, and American statesmen of the Jeffersonian period. His economic beliefs, particularly regarding usury, play an important part throughout the work, most notably in large sections devoted to American politics and to the Chinese. The entire collection of *Cantos* was published in one volume in 1971.

Canute (or Knut, 994–1035)   Danish king who finally became King of England (after 1016) as well, taking an English wife and maintaining peace and security. A 12th-century legend describes how he rebuked his flatterers by commanding the waves to stand still—in vain, of course —to show the limits of his power. *The Song of Canute* is an early 12th-century lyric in Middle English, supposedly composed by Canute while rowing past the abbey of Ely and hearing the music of the services.

canzone   Italian lyric form of verse, popular during the Middle Ages and the Renaissance. Derived from the Provençal *canso*, it normally consisted of from five to seven stanzas, each echoing the first in number of lines and in rhyme scheme. A final short stanza (the *congedo*, or *commiato*) follows the pattern of the Provençal *tornada* or the French *envoi* in addressing the poem itself or in directing it on a mission to some personage. The subject matter is usually amatory but might also be political, satiric, or humorous. *Canzoni* were written at the Sicilian court of Emperor Frederick II in the 13th century and later by Dante, Petrarch, Boccaccio, and the leading poets of the Renaissance. In English, an example of the canzone form is Spenser's marriage hymn the *Epithalamion*.

Čapek, Karel (1890–1938)   Czech dramatist, novelist, and journalist. Čapek was the most popular writer of the "first" Czech republic (1918–38). In his writings, he defended the democratic and humanistic ideals of its founder, President T. G. Masaryk. Čapek's *Hovory's T. G. Masarykem* (1928; tr *President Masaryk Tells His Story*, 1934) offers intimate insights into Masaryk's life, political struggles, and philosophical opinions. Čapek's early stories and plays, most notably *Ze života hmyzu* (1922; tr *The Life of Insects*, 1923), were written with his brother Josef, a prominent avant-garde painter and writer. He gained an international reputation with his science fiction drama, *R.U.R. = Rossum's Universal Robots* (1921; tr 1923), which introduced the word *robot* to the language. *Věc Makropulos* (1922; tr *The Macropulous Secret*, 1927) deals with the scientific prolongation of life. *Krakatit* (1924; tr 1925) is a thrilling science fiction novel involving international intrigue and the invention of an atomic bomb. In his late drama *Bílá nemoc* (1937; tr *Power and Glory*, 1938) and in the satirical novel *Válka s mloky* (1936; tr *The War with the Newts*, 1937), Čapek blends science fiction themes with his firmly held antitotalitarian beliefs.

Although most widely known for his science fiction, Čapek is perhaps at his best in the trilogy consisting of *Hordubal* (1933; tr 1934), *Povětroň* (1934; tr *Meteor*, 1935), and *Obyčejný život* (1934; tr *An Ordinary Life*, 1936). These novels, conducted in the form of a multiperspective narrative, are psychologically penetrating explorations of the quest for the true self. The same narrative technique is used in the unfinished novel *Život a dílo skladatele Foltyna* (1939; tr *The Cheat*, 1941). His last complete novel, *První parta* (1937; tr *The First Rescue Party*, 1939), deals with the theme of masculine heroism in a mine disaster. Čapek settled on the mystery genre for his stories collected in *Povídky z jedne kapsy, Povídky z druhe kapsy* (1929; tr *Tales from Two Pockets*, 1932). Also extremely popular were his occasional writings, notably *Anglické listy* (1924; tr *Letters from England*, 1925).

Capetians The third dynasty of the kings of France (987–1328). Their feudal domain was Ile de France; its central location facilitated their consolidation of power and administration. The succeeding Valois and Bourbon dynasties were branches of the Capet family.

Capital See KAPITAL, DAS.

Capitoline geese Sacred geese kept on the Capitoline Hill of Rome. According to tradition, when the Gauls invaded Rome, a detachment in single file clambered up the hill of the capitol so silently that the foremost man reached the top without being challenged. When he was striding over the rampart, some geese, disturbed by the noise, began to cackle and awoke the garrison. Marcus Manlius rushed to the wall and hurled the fellow over the precipice. To commemorate this event (390 BC), the Romans carried a golden goose to the capitol every year.

Capote, Truman (1924–1984) American writer. Born in New Orleans, Capote made an impressive literary debut at twenty-four, with his novel OTHER VOICES, OTHER ROOMS. Like his other early fiction, *The Grass Harp* (1951) and the stories in *A Tree of Night* (1949) and *Breakfast at Tiffany's* (1958), *Other Voices, Other Rooms* created a subtly surreal world, slightly sinister and grotesque, in which the fine line between dream and reality was blurred.

Capote's fictional characters tend to be alienated, both from others and from a view of what is "normal"; they struggle with the intricacy and pain of establishing an identity in a brutal and unwelcoming world. Capote also wrote profiles and travel sketches, many of which first appeared in THE NEW YORKER, which were published in *Local Color* (1950) and *The Muses Are Heard* (1956), an account of a *Porgy and Bess* troupe's tour of Moscow. His reportorial talents and his fascination with the psychopathology of an individual were given full rein in his most successful book, *In Cold Blood* (1966), a breathtaking account of a grotesque series of murders by two men in Kansas, which Capote called a "nonfiction novel." After a period of soul-searching, mental collapse, and bouts with drugs and alcoholism, Capote produced *Music for Chameleons* (1983), a miscellany of stories, reportage, autobiographical pieces, and one long nonfiction account of a crime. In this book, Capote attempted to develop a new, experimental style that employed elements from all forms of writing—poetry, novels, film scripts, reporting, plays, and the like. A projected novel, *Unanswered Prayers*, remained unfinished at his death.

Captain Hook See PETER PAN.

Captive, The See REMEMBRANCE OF THINGS PAST.

Capuana, Luigi (1839–1915) Italian novelist, critic, and journalist, self-appointed champion of Zola's NATURALISM. Capuana's own fiction reveals the influence of the psychological and introspective fictional methods then in vogue in France, England, and Russia. But, true to Zola's techniques, this is tempered by realistic descriptions and a simplicity and precision in style. His theorization of Zolaesque realism laid the foundation for *verismo*, which was to find in Giovanni VERGA its best practitioner.

Capuana's first novel, *Giacinta* (1879), is the best example of his techniques and demonstrates his theoretical preoccupations. Later novels include *Il Marchese di Roccaverdina* (1901), about the guilt and emotional suicide of a marquis who murders his mistress's husband, and *Profuma* (1890), a novel about a woman whose nervous condition causes her body to emit a strange odor.

Capulet and Montague The English names of the Capelletti and the Montecchi, two noble families of 14th-century Verona. The feud between the two houses has been immortalized by Shakespeare's ROMEO AND JULIET.

Old Capulet, Juliet's father, is an irascible, unimaginative man who loves his daughter but is incensed when she refuses to marry Paris, the husband he has chosen for her. Upon hearing of the death of the two lovers, he is reconciled with Lord Montague, Romeo's father, who vows to erect a golden statue to the "true and faithful Juliet."

Caracalla (full Latin name Marcus Aurelius Antonius, AD 188–217) Roman emperor (211–217). Caracalla was nicknamed Caracalla after the long, hooded tunic worn by the Gauls, which he wore after he became emperor. He and his brother Geta succeeded to the throne after their father's death, but Caracalla had his brother assassinated, along with several of the most distinguished statesmen in the country. His reign was marked by cruelty and treachery. He was murdered by the praetorian prefect.

Caravaggio, Michelangelo Merisi da (also known as Amerigi da Caravaggio, 1573–1610) Italian painter. Reacting against MANNERISM and idealism, Caravaggio introduced a powerful realism and revolutionary uses of light in his paintings of biblical scenes. His naturalistic method of employing crude peasant types in religious scenes scandalized many, but his influence was widely felt among such later painters as VELÁZQUEZ and RUBENS. His paintings are striking for their dramatic use of unnaturally lit figures against a dark, or even black, background, with neither ornamentation nor landscape included. Among his masterpieces are the *Deposition of Christ* (1604) and the *Beheading of John the Baptist* (1608).

Carbonari (Ital, "charcoal burners") The name given to a secret political association that flourished in Italy and France early in the 19th century. The group first came into being during the reign (1808–15) of Joachim Murat in Naples. The movement originally sought to free Italy from foreign domination, but democratic and republican sentiments later arose as well. After the failure of several uprisings, the Carbonari were absorbed by MAZZINI's Young Italy society. The movement gained prominence in France after 1820.

Cardozo, Benjamin Nathan (1870–1938) American jurist. Cardozo was appointed by Herbert HOOVER to the U.S. Supreme Court in 1932, to succeed Oliver Wendell HOLMES. A liberal who believed that the law should reflect social change, Cardozo wrote five important books: *The Nature of the Judicial Process* (1921), *The Growth of the Law* (1924), *The Paradoxes of Legal Science* (1928), *Law and Literature* (1931), and *Law Is Justice* (1938). For both style and content, his legal opinions are regarded as classics.

Carducci, Giosuè (1835–1907) Italian poet and literary critic. Self-proclaimed antiromantic classicist, patriot, liberal, and freemason, Carducci was professor of Italian literature at the University of Bologna from 1860 to 1904. The aims and struggles of the *Risorgimento* are reflected in such works as *Juvenilia* (1860), *Levia gravia* (1868), *Giambi ed epodi* (1879), and *Rime nuove* (1887), while *Odi barbare* (1877–89) and *Rime e ritmi* (1898) reveal his predilection for classical motifs and meters and archaic language; throughout, there is a positive endorsement of liberal ideology. *L'inno a Satana* (*The Hymn to Satan*, 1863; pub 1870) is a vigorous manifesto of rebellion, in which the obscurantism and asceticism of traditional religion are denounced while human achievement in material progress is praised. Awarded the NOBEL PRIZE in

Literature (1906), he is considered the national poet of modern Italy.

Caretaker, The (1960) A three-act play by Harold PINTER. Mick, a flippant conniver, has entrusted a house to his brain-damaged brother, Aston. When Aston takes an interest in an old tramp named Davies, Mick sees that the situation can be used to bring him once again in contact with his brother, and he schemes to use Davies accordingly. Ensconced in the house as a caretaker, Davies goes from servile slavery to greedy aggression and, arousing Mick's jealousy and anger, is finally thrown back on the streets. The subtle struggle for territory, the ambiguous dialogue, and the sense of menace provide the context for this play's central concern: how to sustain identity in a world that demands conformity as the price of survival.

Carew, Jan [Rynveld] (1925–   ) Guyanan novelist. Educated in Guyana, the U.S., and Prague, Carew has also lived in London, where he was variously actor, journalist, editor, and radio playwright. For all his travels, Guyana is usually the setting of his novels, which contrast the simplicity and beauty of village life with the destructive effects of civilization. He often employs the parable form, as in *Black Midas* (1958), and acknowledges the influence of the modern primitive painters, GAUGUIN and ROUSSEAU. Among his other works are *The Last Barbarian* (1960), *Moscow Is Not My Mecca* (1964), and a volume of poetry, *Sea Drums in My Blood* (1981).

Carew, Thomas (c1595–c1639) English poet. One of the SONS OF BEN, Carew was the first and probably best of the CAVALIER POETS. A courtier of Charles I, Carew was a sensualist and libertine who, it is said, repented on his deathbed. His work shows the influence of DONNE as well as of JONSON: not only are there phrases, cadences, and themes reminiscent of Donne, but Carew's poetry has a richness of conceit and a play of intellect rare in Cavalier verse. In their essential spirit, however—their melody, grace, and polish—his poems reflect the art of Jonson. Carew wrote numerous songs and light love lyrics, such as "Ask Me No More Where Jove Bestows" and "Mediocrity in Love Rejected," and a number of more serious pieces, distinguished by their perspicacity, tact, and feeling, such as the lovely epitaph on Maria Wentworth. His collected poetry appeared in the posthumous volume *Poems* (1640), and he was also the author of a masque, *Coelum Britannicum* (1633).

Carlos, Don (1545–1568) Spanish prince. The son of Philip II by his first wife, Mary of Portugal, Don Carlos was mentally and physically unsound and was subject to fits of maniacal rage. He was betrothed to Elizabeth of Valois, but Philip married her himself. Later Don Carlos conceived a bitter hatred for his father, hindering his policies whenever possible. When he laid plans to leave Spain secretly, he was imprisoned at Philip's orders and died a few months later. Although he probably died of natural causes, it was widely rumored that he had been murdered at his father's instigation. The unlucky prince was the subject of Schiller's tragedy DON CARLOS and of dramas by Thomas Otway and Vittorio Alfieri. Verdi based one of his finest operas, *Don Carlo* or *Don Carlos* (1867), on Schiller's play.

Carlyle, Thomas (1795–1881)   Scottish-born English prose writer. Carlyle is remembered for his explosive attacks on sham, hypocrisy, and excessive materialism; his distrust of democracy and the mob; and his highly romantic belief in the power of the individual, especially the strong, heroic leader. During much of his life, he struggled courageously—though hardly quietly—with poverty and "dyspepsia" (probably painful gastric ulcers). He was influenced in his early career by German literature, which he helped to popularize in England, being a particular admirer of Schiller and Goethe.

Carlyle's best-known book is THE FRENCH REVOLUTION. Of his public lectures, the famous *On Heroes, Hero-worship, and the Heroic in History* (1841) best expresses his cult of the leader. His hatred of *laissez-faire* policies, his fears of the destruction of personality by the machines of industrialism, and his distrust of social legislators are to be found in the essays *Chartism* (1839), *Past and Present* (1843), and *Latter Day Pamphlets* (1850). Among his biographies are *Life of Schiller* (1823–24), *Cromwell* (1845), *The Life of Sterling* (1851), and *History of Frederick II of Prussia, Called Frederick the Great* (1858–65). SARTOR RESARTUS, called a spiritual biography, is one of his most characteristic works; it aroused violent protest when published. Carlyle's style is savage and apocalyptic; it is marked by unusual words and figures of speech, agitated and mounting rhythms, and expressions influenced by the German language. See WELSH, JANE.

carmagnole   Costume of French Revolutionists: wide-collared jacket, wide, black pantaloons, red cap, and scarlet or tricolored waistcoat. The jacket was adopted from that worn in the south of France by the Piedmontese workmen of Carmagnola.

Carmagnole   A Red Republican song and dance of the time of the French Revolution, with the refrain:

Dansons la Carmagnole,—Vive le son, vive le son—
Dansons la Carmagnole,—Vive le son du canon!

Carman, [William] Bliss (1861–1929)   Canadian poet, essayist, and lecturer. Carman is best known for his collaboration with Richard Hovey (1864–1900) on *Songs from Vagabondia* (1894) and its sequels. Among his other volumes of poetry are the allegorical *Behind the Arras* (1895), *Sappho* (1905), and *Sanctuary* (1929), sonnets of New England. Carman wrote frequently about his theories of poetry and art in such works as *The Friendship of Art* (1904) and *The Poetry of Life* (1905). He was made poet laureate of Canada in 1928.

Carmelites   An order of mendicant friars. The order was founded at Mt. Carmel by the Crusader Berthold in the 12th century. Expelled from the Holy Land by the Saracens in the 13th century, they came to Europe. The order of Carmelite nuns dates from the 15th century, the greatest being the Spanish mystic St. Teresa of Avila, who organized the austere branch of the discalced (shoeless) Carmelites, in contrast to the traditional Carmelites of the mitigated rule.

Carnegie, Andrew (1835–1919)   Scottish-born American industrialist and philanthropist. Starting as a bobbin boy in Pennsylvania at $1.20 a week, Carnegie achieved a commanding position in the steel industry through his organizing ability and his acumen as a judge of men. After selling his steel interests to U.S. Steel for $250 million in 1901, Carnegie, a life-long pacifist, devoted himself to philanthropy, providing funds for numerous public libraries and for such institutions as the Carnegie Endowment for International Peace. His philanthropy was inspired by his conviction that men who amassed great wealth were morally obligated to use it for the public good. He first expressed this doctrine, known as "the gospel of wealth," in the article *Wealth* in 1889. His other writings include *Triumphant Democracy* (1886), *The Gospel of Wealth and Other Timely Essays* (1889), and an *Autobiography* (1920).

Carnegie, Dale   See HOW TO WIN FRIENDS AND INFLUENCE PEOPLE.

Carolingians   Second dynasty of Frankish kings. The Carolingians held the office of "mayor of the palace" under the weak later Merovingian kings, but they were the virtual rulers, particularly Charles Martel (689?–741) and his son Pepin the Short (c714–68), who finally deposed the nominal ruler in 751 and was anointed king of the Franks by the Pope in 754. His two sons jointly inherited the crown, but when Carloman (751–71) died, CHARLEMAGNE became sole king. His battles greatly enlarged his territory to include most of France, Germany, and northern Italy, and in 800 Pope Leo III crowned Charlemagne Emperor of the West, thus identifying his temporal power with the interests of Christianity. An effective administrator, he was especially known for his attempt to revive learning and culture, sometimes known as the *Carolingian Renaissance*. To reeducate the clergy, he established schools and imported scholars from abroad, including ALCUIN of York. After his death, however, internal divisions weakened the empire, and the reign of his successors ended in Germany in 911 and in France in 987.

The *Carolingian legends* are the romances of medieval and Renaissance Europe dealing with the supposed adventures of Charlemagne's PALADINS. See especially those associated with ROLAND.

Caron, Pierre Augustin   See BEAUMARCHAIS.

carpe diem (Lat, "seize the day") A phrase originally used by HORACE in his *Odes*. An exhortation to enjoy life's present pleasures, because the future is uncertain, it became a favorite motif of the CAVALIER POETS. Robert HERRICK's "To the Virgins" elaborates the theme in love poetry:

> Gather ye rosebuds while ye may,
> Old Time is still a-flying;
> And this same flower that smiles today,
> Tomorrow will be dying.

Carpentier [y Valmont], Alejo (1904–1980) Cuban novelist, essayist, and musicologist. Carpentier's early studies in music and architecture, along with his exposure to SURREALISM in Paris in the 1920s and 1930s, had considerable influence on his constant experimentation with spatial and temporal narrative structures. By integrating surrealistic techniques with the African folk legacy of the Caribbean, he sought to establish a basis by which the extraordinary history of humanity in the New World could be expressed. In his preface to his novel *El reino de este mundo* (1949; tr *The Kingdom of This World*, 1957), which is a strange, brilliant depiction of Haitian history, he introduced the concept of MAGIC REALISM, which blurs the frontiers between dream and reality and juxtaposes all stages of history without regard to conventional chronology. In his novels *Los pasos perdidos* (1953; tr *The Lost Steps*, 1956), considered Carpentier's best work, and *El siglo de las luces* (1962; tr *Explosion in a Cathedral*, 1963), and especially in the stories in *Guerra del tiempo* (1958; tr *The War of Time*, 1970), he broke with established narrative forms and pursued the meaning of personal and historical time. *El recurso del metodo* (1974; tr *Reasons of State*, 1976) is a bitterly satirical treatment of a Latin American dictator. His *Cuentos completos* appeared in 1979.

carpet, magic In Eastern wonder tales and romances, a stock device for transporting a character to any place he wished to go. It is sometimes termed *Prince Housain's carpet* because of the role it plays in the well-known story of Prince Ahmed in the *Arabian Nights*. The most popular magic carpet, however, was that of King Solomon, which, according to the Islamic legend related in the Koran, was of green silk. When he traveled, his throne was placed on it, and it was large enough for all his forces to stand upon; in order to screen his party from the sun, the birds formed a canopy over them with their wings.

carpetbagger In U.S. history, a derisive epithet applied to Northerners who went south to take part in Reconstruction governments. To disgruntled Southerners, the carpetbags these men carried were indicative of their transience and lack of property interests in the South.

Carrera Andrade, Jorge (1903–1978) Ecuadorian poet and essayist. A well-traveled diplomat and anthropologist, Carrera Andrade reveals in his poetry an intense identification with his native Indian forebears. His first selected edition of verse was *Registro del mundo* (1940), which was followed by *Lugar de origen* (1945) and *Edades poéticas* (1958). In all his work, he employs somewhat impressionistic techniques to evoke very clear images of his native land. Along with other writers of his generation, he pioneered the adaptation of the HAIKU to the Spanish language. An English translation of his *Selected Poems* (tr H. R. Hays) appeared in 1972; his complete poems in Spanish are published in *Obra poética completa* (1976).

Carroll, Lewis (pen name of Charles Lutwidge Dodgson, 1832–1898) English author, mathematician, and photographer. A lecturer in mathematics at Christ Church, Oxford, Carroll was shy and stammering and reputedly a boring lecturer, whose mathematical writings include *An Elementary Treatise on Determinants* (1867), *Euclid and His Modern Rivals* (1879), *Curiosa Mathematica* (1888), and *Symbolic Logic* (1896). He was ordained as a deacon but never preached, and he was a talented portrait photographer. His principal enthusiasm, however, was for little girls, for whom he created many amusing games and puzzles and for one of whom, Alice Liddell, he wrote his famous ALICE'S ADVENTURES IN WONDERLAND and THROUGH THE LOOKING GLASS. These became highly popular among adult readers; theorists of surrealism in the 20th century seriously interpreted Carroll's works as early embodiments of their own principles; and Freudians have made much of the symbolism of the Alice books. Carroll's other works of fantasy and nonsense include *The Hunting of the Snark, An Agony in Eight Fits* (verses, 1876), *Sylvie and Bruno* (1889), and *Sylvie and Bruno Concluded* (1893). Through these works run veins of satire, parody, masterfully inverted logic, and extremely suggestive symbolism. See TENNIEL, SIR JOHN.

Carson, Kit (real name Christopher Carson, 1809–1868). American trapper, guide, and folk hero. Born in Kentucky, Carson moved with his family to Missouri, and he then went alone to Taos, New Mexico. He worked at different frontier jobs and became a guide for exploring parties, leading J. C. FRÉMONT's three western expeditions (1842, 1843, 1845). Frémont's widely read report on the expedition contained flattering accounts of Carson's cunning and bravery, which gave him semilegendary status. He later played an important part in the conquest of California during the Mexican War and fought in New Mexico during the Civil War, rising to the rank of brigadier general. Tales of his exploits spread and soon caught the imagination of writers and raconteurs. Joaquin MILLER's poem *Kit Carson's Ride* (1871) recounts Carson's rescue of his Indian bride from a prairie fire on his wedding day. Carson figures as a friend of the bishop in Willa Cather's DEATH COMES TO THE ARCHBISHOP. He also appears as the hero of DIME NOVELS, songs, and folk legends. *Kit Carson's Autobiography*, edited by Blanche C. Grant, appeared in 1926.

Carson, Rachel L[ouise] (1907–1964)   American writer and marine biologist. Carson's *The Sea Around Us* (1951) and *The Edge of the Sea* (1955) are known as works of literary as well as scientific merit. She maintained her impeccable style, while arousing far more discussion and controversy, with *The Silent Spring* (1962), in which she contended that the indiscriminate use of weed killers and insecticides constituted a hazard to wildlife and to human beings. Her provocative work inspired many subsequent environmental studies.

Carter, Jimmy (full name James Earl Carter, Jr., 1924–   )   Thirty-ninth president of the U.S. (1977–81). A graduate of Annapolis Naval Academy, Carter spent several years on battleships and submarines and studied nuclear physics and engineering at Union College in Schenectady, New York. When his father died in 1953, Carter returned to Plains, Georgia, to take over the foundering family business, rebuilding and expanding various enterprises. He became active in civic and church affairs and was elected governor of Georgia in 1970. His inaugural address, which proclaimed an end to racial discrimination, made national headlines.

Carter won the presidential election against the incumbent, Gerald R. FORD, in November 1976. He caused a stir by walking the mile and a half from the Capitol building to the White House following his inaugural address, revealing his determination to remain close to ordinary people. While president, he taught a Bible class at The First Baptist Church in Washington, D.C.

Soon after taking office, Carter issued a full pardon to VIETNAM WAR draft resisters. He supported liberal issues such as human rights, the Equal Rights Amendment, consumer rights, abortion rights, and raising the minimum wage. He created the Department of Energy and worked to pass energy-conservation measures. Carter initiated the Middle East summit at Camp David, Maryland, which concluded on September 17, 1978, with Israeli premier Menachem Begin and Egyptian president Anwar Sadat agreeing to a framework for a peace treaty between their two countries. Peace treaties were signed in Israel and Egypt in 1979. The Camp David summit and the signing of the 1979 Middle East peace treaties constituted major victories for Carter. His other successes included his energy program and the Panama Canal treaties (1978). His failures included his plans for tax and welfare changes and the reorganization of the Federal government. Carter also had to confront double-digit inflation, a serious recession, the Soviet invasion of Afghanistan (1979), and the seizure of American hostages in Teheran, Iran (1979). Carter won his party's renomination in 1980, in a surprising victory over the popular senator Edward Kennedy, but lost the 1980 presidential election to Republican Ronald REAGAN. He is the author of *Keeping Faith: Memoirs of a President* (1982), *Negotiations: The Alternative to Hostility* (1984), and *The*

Blood of Abraham: Insights into the Middle East (1985). *Everything to Gain: Making the Most of the Rest of Your Life* (1987) is a first-person reminiscence of the former president and his wife, Rosalynn, after leaving the White House in 1980, as well as a self-help book for retired people. His wife is the author of *First Lady from Plains* (1984).

Carter, Nick   A fictional American detective, who has appeared in over a thousand stories. Nick Carter was apparently invented by John R. Coryell (1848–1924), who worked in a writing team with Thomas Chalmers Harbaugh (1849–1924) and Frederick Van Rensselaer Dey (1861?–1922). Nick made his first appearance in *The Old Detective's Pupil* (1886). The Nick Carter DIME NOVELS were extremely popular, and other writers continued the series in stories, movies, and radio plays.

Carthage   Ancient city and state in North Africa. Founded in the 9th century BC by Phoenicians from the kingdom of Tyre, Carthage was located on a peninsula near the site of modern Tunis. According to Roman legend, it was founded by DIDO. It became dominant among Phoenician cities in North Africa, founded several colonies in Africa, and held sway over the native agricultural population of a large region. Carthage carried on considerable trading activities along the coasts of the Mediterranean and founded colonies in Spain, Sardinia, and Sicily. There existed between Rome and Carthage a number of treaties restricting Rome from interfering with Carthaginian trade. These treaties governed the relations between Rome and Carthage until the PUNIC WARS. Carthage was ultimately burned to the ground by the Romans in the Third Punic War (149–146 BC).

Carthago delenda est (Lat, "Carthage must be destroyed") is the phrase with which CATO THE ELDER ended all his speeches in the senate.

Carthusians (fr *Chartreuse*, near Grenoble, France)   An order of monks. The Carthusian Order was founded in 1084 by St. Bruno. The monks were sworn to perpetual silence, continuous wearing of hair shirts, and eating of only one meal a day. A principal source of revenue for the order is from the sale of Chartreuse, the liqueur made by the monks from a secret formula.

Cartier, Jacques (1491–1557)   French navigator. During the second of his three voyages to America, Cartier sailed up the St. Lawrence River, which he discovered, to an Indian village called Hochelaga, which he renamed Montréal, "Mount Royal."

Cartier-Bresson, Henri (1908–   )   French photographer. Originally a painter, Cartier-Bresson became one of the world's leading photojournalists. Influenced by Man RAY and the popular filmmakers of his time, he is known for his lyrical yet straightforward photographs of people engaged in ordinary activities. He was instrumental in founding Magnum Photos, a large and vastly influential agency of documentary photographers, cooperatively owned and operated by its members.

As a cinematographer, Cartier-Bresson assisted Jean RENOIR on two films, *A Day in the Country* (1937) and *The Rules of the Game* (1939). His own *The Return* (1945), a film about homecoming French prisoners of war of World War II, typifies his sensitive, poignant approach to documentary subjects. His photographs are collected in many books, including *The Europeans* (1955), *Man and Machine* (1969), and *About Russia* (1974).

Carton, Sydney   The hero of Charles Dickens's *A TALE OF TWO CITIES*. Carton is a dissipated young man whose temperament is contrasted with that of Charles Darnay; the great physical resemblance of the two is an important factor in the plot. Carton loves Lucie Manette, but, knowing of her attachment to Darnay, never attempts to win her. His love for her, however, brings out his nobler qualities and ultimately brings him to die on the guillotine in place of Darnay. His last thoughts are the famous lines, "It is a far, far better thing that I do, than I have ever done; it is a far, far better rest, that I go to, than I have ever known."

cartoon   In art, a picture on cardboard or heavy paper, especially a full-size preliminary sketch, often in color, for a fresco, tapestry, mosaic, oil painting, or stained glass. In modern usage, a cartoon is also a satiric or humorous drawing or a type of motion picture in which the frames are drawings rather than photographs. Although pictorial satire has existed in Europe from the time of the REFORMATION, the first satirical drawings to be called cartoons were those of John Leech (1817–64) in the British magazine PUNCH. The political cartoon, making an editorial point by means of such devices as caricature and pictorial symbols, antedates the purely humorous cartoon, in which the drawing often serves merely as an illustration for a comical caption.

Cary, [Arthur] Joyce [Lunel]   (1888–1957) Anglo-Irish novelist. From 1913 to 1920, Cary worked for the Nigerian political service. All of his early novels —including *Aissa Saved* (1932), *An American Visitor* (1933), *The African Witch* (1936), and *Mister Johnson* (1939)—are set in Africa and are about Africans, interracial problems, and the responsibilities of government and law. His semiautobiographical *A House of Children* (1941) gives an impression of his Irish childhood. Trained as an artist, he brought his understanding of a painter's problems to his best-known novel, THE HORSE'S MOUTH, the third novel in a trilogy that also included *Herself Surprised* (1941) and *To Be a Pilgrim* (1942). In these and his later books, Cary treats aspects of English social history with a Dickensian humor and a celebration of the power of the creative imagination. After such novels as *Charlie Is My Darling* (1940), *The Moonlight* (1946), and *A Fearful Joy* (1949), Cary wrote another trilogy about politics, consisting of PRISONER OF GRACE, *Except the Lord* (1953), and *Not Honour More* (1955). *The Captive and the Free* (1959), dealing with religious questions, was left unfinished at his death.

Casanova [de Seingalt], Giovanni Jacopo (1725–1798)   Italian adventurer. After his expulsion from a Venetian seminary for scandalous misconduct, Casanova commenced a lively career as charlatan, gambler, and lover that took him to all the capitals of Europe. His fortunes fluctuated widely: in 1755, for example, he was imprisoned in Venice for impiety and magic, but after making a daring escape, he turned up in Paris, where he enjoyed temporary affluence as director of the state lottery and came in contact with such luminaries as Louis XV, ROUSSEAU, and Mme de POMPADOUR. In 1785 he was made librarian at Count Waldstein's castle of Dux in Bohemia, where he remained until his death. His famous *Mémoires* (12 vols, 1826–38) are no doubt unreliable as to his own career but are of great interest historically. The first full edition of his autobiography was translated into English by W. R. Trask in six volumes (1966–71).

casa verde, La   See VARGAS LLOSA, MARIO.

Case of the Sergeant Grischa, The (Der Streit um den Sergeanten Grischa, 1927; tr 1927)   A novel by Arnold ZWEIG. Longing for home, the Russian sergeant Grischa Paprotkin escapes from the camp where he is being held prisoner of war. When he is recaptured by the Germans, he takes on the identity of a Russian deserter, not knowing that deserters are shot as possible spies. Condemned to death, he confesses the truth, and the officers agree to revoke the death sentence; but the vicious general Schlieffenzahn, who has heard about the case, orders that the innocent Grischa be shot.

Casey Jones   American ballad about a train wreck. It is probably based on the wreck in 1900 of the Cannonball Express, whose driver, John Luther Jones (1864–1900), was born in Cayce, Kentucky, hence the nickname Casey. Two railroad men, T. Lawrence Seibert and Eddie Newton, who published the song in 1909, may have been the authors.

casket letters   Eight letters and a series of poems supposedly written by MARY, QUEEN OF SCOTS, to James, Earl of Bothwell. At least one of these was held to prove her complicity with Bothwell in the murder of her husband, Henry, Lord Darnley. The letters were found in a casket that fell into the hands of the Earl of Morton in 1567, four months after Darnley's death and a few days after Mary's surrender to the rebelling Scottish lords. The following year, the letters were used as evidence in the investigation of the charges brought against Mary by the rebels. All trace of the original letters disappeared after 1584, and their authenticity is still a matter of dispute.

Caspar   See GASPAR.
Casperl   See GASPAR.

Cassandra In Greek mythology, a daughter of PRIAM and HECUBA. Cassandra was gifted by Apollo with the power of prophecy. However, when she refused the god's advances, he ordained that no one would believe her predictions, although they were invariably correct. She was carried off to Argos by AGAMEMNON and was killed with him by CLYTEMNESTRA and Aegisthus. She appears prominently in Euripides' THE TROJAN WOMEN and Aeschylus' *Agamemnon*, as well as in Shakespeare's TROILUS AND CRESSIDA. Her name has come to be used to mean any prophet of doom.

Cassatt, Mary (1845–1926) American painter and printmaker. Cassatt resided most of her life in France, where she was associated with Edgar DEGAS and the impressionists, and it was primarily her work that introduced IMPRESSIONISM to America. She treated the theme of maternity with objectivity and an interest in simple, everyday gestures, often deriving her style from Japanese prints.

Cassio, Michael In Shakespeare's OTHELLO, the handsome young Florentine whom Othello appoints as his lieutenant. Iago, jealous of the preference shown to Cassio, encourages his weakness for drink and involves him in a brawl, causing his dismissal. Iago then convinces Othello that Cassio is Desdemona's lover. When Iago's plot is uncovered, after the murder of Desdemona, Othello reinstates Cassio and asks his pardon before committing suicide.

Cassiopeia In Greek mythology, the wife of Cepheus, king of Ethiopia, and mother of ANDROMEDA. In consequence of her boasting of the beauty of her daughter, she was sent to the heavens as the constellation Cassiopeia, the chief stars of which form the outline of a lady seated in a chair and holding up both arms in supplication.

Cassius (full name Caius Cassius Longinus, d 42 BC) Roman general and politician. During the civil war between CAESAR and POMPEY, Cassius allied himself with Pompey. After Pompey's defeat at Pharsalus (48 BC), Caesar pardoned Cassius and made him praetor (44). Unlike BRUTUS, however, Cassius never ceased to be Caesar's enemy, in spite of the favor shown him. It was Cassius who conceived the plot against the dictator's life and who persuaded Brutus to join the conspiracy. After Caesar's murder, public opinion turned against the conspirators, and they fled from Rome. Cassius and Brutus met the forces of Octavius and ANTONY at Philippi (42); during the first engagement, Cassius, overwhelmed by Antony's forces, precipitately committed suicide, not knowing that Brutus had driven Octavius from the field. Brutus's forces were defeated some days later.

In Shakespeare's JULIUS CAESAR, Cassius is depicted as the instigator of the plot to assassinate Caesar. Grasping and ambitious, he urges the reluctant Brutus to join the conspiracy, pointing out, in a famous speech, that each man controls his own destiny:

> The fault, dear Brutus, is not in our stars,
> But in ourselves, that we are underlings.

Caesar says of him:

> Yon Cassius has a lean and hungry look;
> He thinks too much: such men are dangerous.

At Philippi, rashly assuming that Brutus has been defeated, Cassius commits suicide and thus helps turn Brutus's initial victory into overwhelming defeat.

Cassola, Carlo (1917–) Italian novelist. Cassola's early literary production is tied to the prosa d'arte school, with its emphasis on stylistic refinement. Most of the novels written between the early 1950s and 1960 derive their inspiration from the war and the Italian Resistance. *Fausto e Anna* (1952, rev 1964; tr *Fausto and Anna*, 1960) and *La ragazza di Bube* (1960; tr *Bèbo's Girl*, 1962) are the best narratives of this phase. His fiction has become increasingly existentialist in tone, with an emphasis on the daily struggle of existence in a world of mediocrity and curbed passions. *Un cuore arido* (1961; tr *An Arid Heart*, 1964) illustrates this preoccupation. In general, his fiction is set in Tuscany, more specifically in the Cecina-Volterra-Pomerance triangle. His characters are farmhands, hunters, lumberjacks, and miners, resigned to common tasks yet striving to achieve a measure of happiness. Especially noteworthy among his numerous books are *Il taglio del bosco* (1955), *Storia di Ada* (1967), and *Una relazione* (1969).

Castalia A fountain of Parnassus sacred to the MUSES. Its waters had the power of inspiring with the gift of poetry those who drank of them.

caste (fr Port, *casta*, "race; breed") A Western term used to refer to the system of social stratification in Hindu India. There are two major categories in the Hindu system to which the term is applied:

(1) V*arna* (Sans, "color"), the fourfold division of Hindu society, which includes the BRAHMIN (priest), KSHATRIYA (warrior), VAISHYA (producer), and SUDRA (menial). The so-called UNTOUCHABLES later came to comprise a fifth category, below the sudra; they are associated with the most defiling tasks, as defined by orthodox HINDUISM.

(2) *Jati*, referring to the social status determined by birth and lineage.

Castiglione, Baldassare (1478–1529) Italian diplomat, writer, and courtier. One of the most important and influential authors in Europe during the Renaissance, Castiglione was born at Mantua, where he served the Gonzaga family, then moved to Urbino and the service of its duke, Guidobaldo da Montefeltro. In 1506 he was in England to receive the Order of the Garter for his master from Henry VII. In 1524 he went to Spain as papal envoy; he died there in 1529, universally mourned. Although he wrote poetry in various genres, his chief work is *Il libro del cortegiano* (*The Book of the Courtier*), better known simply as *Il cortegiano* (THE COURTIER). Finished in 1518, the book sets forth in a series of dialogues the author's conception of the ideal courtier and the norms of courtesy in a cultured society. Castiglione's portrait, done by his friend Raphael, is one of the masterpieces of the Louvre museum.

Castle, The (Das Schloß, 1922, pub posthumously, 1926; tr 1930) An unfinished novel by Franz KAFKA, prepared for publication by Max BROD. In its bare essentials, it is the story of a man against a bureaucracy. The hero, known only as K., is constantly frustrated in his efforts to gain entrance into a mysterious castle to which he believes he has been summoned to work as a land surveyor. The castle is administered by an extraordinarily complicated and incompetent bureaucratic hierarchy that refuses to either recognize or reject K.'s claim. He is put to work instead as a school janitor and is denied his right to practice his craft. According to Brod, Kafka intended K., an ailing man throughout the novel, to die of exhaustion at the end of the novel.

In his epilogue to the first edition, Brod added his allegorical interpretation of the work, equating K.'s struggle with the human quest for an understanding of the ways of an incomprehensible God and identifying K.'s frustration as a symbol of the human condition. Other interpretations view the novel as a grotesque satire of life in the West.

Castle of Indolence (1748) A poem in Spenserian stanzas by James THOMSON. The castle is situated in the land of Drowsiness, where every sense is steeped in enervating delights. The owner is an enchanter who deprives all who enter his domains of their energy and free will. In Canto II, Selvaggio, the Knight of Arts and Industry, breaks the spell cast by the wizard Indolence. It is considered Thomson's best work by many critics.

Castle of Otranto, The (1764) A GOTHIC NOVEL, the first of that genre in English, by Horace WALPOLE. The villain, Manfred, prince of Otranto, inhabits the castle of Otranto and rules the realm unlawfully; his grandfather had poisoned Alfonso, the rightful ruler, and it had been cryptically prophesied that the usurpers would prevail so long as the castle was big enough to hold the rightful ruler. Manfred plans to marry his son Conrad to Isabella, daughter of the marquis of Vicenza, but, in one of many supernatural events, Conrad is crushed to death in the courtyard by a gigantic helmet. Manfred then determines to marry Isabella himself, in the hope that she will present him with another heir, whom he needs in order to maintain control of the realm. Isabella, terrified of Manfred, is aided in her escape by the handsome young peasant Theodore. In fulfillment of the prophesy, Alfonso's ghost, grown too large for the castle, tears it down and rises from the ruin, proclaiming Theodore, the future husband of Isabella, the true heir to Otranto.

Castle Rackrent (1800) A novel by Maria EDGEWORTH, depicting the dissolute life of Irish landlords of the 18th century. Watched by their ineffectual tenantry, a succession of irresponsible members of the Rackrent family dissipate their fortunes until they reach the verge of destitution.

Castor and Polydeuces In Greek mythology, twins sons of LEDA and TYNDAREUS or ZEUS, called the Dioscuri. Beginning with their births, their lives and adventures are told in many versions. Both may have been the mortal sons of Tyndareus or both immortal sons of Zeus, but the commonest tale makes Castor mortal. They sailed with the ARGONAUTS, and it was Polydeuces, a great boxer, who killed Amycus, the brutal Bebrycian king, in a boxing match. Later they quarreled with another pair of twins, Lynceus and Idas; in the ensuing fight, all but Polydeuces were killed. Polydeuces begged his father Zeus to let him share his immortality with his brother. This wish being granted, they either spend one day together in heaven, the next in HADES, or they alternate in separately spending a day in each.

Castor and Polydeuces became patron gods of mariners, appearing in St. Elmo's fire. In late myth, they were identified as the constellation Gemini. Their cult became highly popular in Rome, where Polydeuces was known as Pollux.

Castorp, Hans The central figure in Thomas Mann's novel THE MAGIC MOUNTAIN. Castorp is a young marine engineer of middling talents, the son of a Hamburg merchant family. He is described early in the book as an "unwritten sheet of paper," by which Mann means that his personality has yet to take shape. He is essentially passive and reflects the characters and events about him more than he acts upon them.

Castro, Inés de (c1310–1355) Spanish noblewoman. Castro was the mistress of Dom Pedro, eldest son and heir of King Alfonso IV of Portugal. Pedro married her after the death of his first wife, and Alfonso, fearful that she and her powerful family constituted a threat to the dynasty, had her put to death. Upon his accession to the throne in 1357, Pedro had her body exhumed and placed upon a throne, forcing his courtiers to render her the homage denied her in life. Her remains were later taken to Alcobaça, where a magnificent mausoleum was built for them. Many writers have retold her tragic story, notably Camões in OS LUSIADAS and Luis VÉLEZ DE GUEVARA in *Reinar después de morir* (1652).

cat A domesticated feline to which many curious beliefs have adhered. In Egypt, the cat was sacred to Isis, or the moon. It was held in great veneration and was worshiped with great ceremony as a symbol of the moon, not only because it is more active after sunset but from the dilation and contraction of its pupils, symbolical of waxing and waning. The goddess Bast (Bubastis), representative of the life-giving solar heat, was portrayed as having the head of a cat, probably because that animal likes to bask in the sun. Diodorus tells us that whoever killed a cat, even by accident, was by the Egyptians punished by death; according to Egyptian tradition, Artemis assumed the form of a cat and thus excited the fury of the giants.

In ancient Rome, because the cat was a symbol of liberty, no animal is more an enemy to all constraint than a cat. The goddess Liberty was represented holding a cup in one hand, a broken scepter in the other, with a cat lying at her feet.

Medieval superstition held that Satan's favorite form was a black cat. Hence witches were said to have cats as their familiars.

catachresis (1) The wrong use of one word for another, as in "his action was most affective" instead of "effective."

(2) The use of an especially farfetched figure of speech, such as one involving literal impossibility or paradox, as in a mixed metaphor.

catalogue verse A poetic device that lists persons, places, things, or ideas to establish a common theme. An ancient device, its purpose was originally informative and didactic. Modern examples can be found in the poetry of Walt WHITMAN, Vachel LINDSAY, and Allen GINSBERG, among others.

catastasis (1) In rhetoric, the narrative introduction to a speech.

(2) In classical drama, the third of four stages of dramatic production, in which the action is heightened or intensified. See CATASTROPHE; EPITASIS; PROTASIS.

catastrophe (Gr, "overturning") In classical dramatic structure, a term for the final unwinding of the plot, in which dramatic conflict comes to an end. The ancients divided dramatic action into four parts: PROTASIS (introduction), EPITASIS (continuance), CATASTASIS (heightening), and CATASTROPHE (outcome). The term corresponds to the modern and more frequently used DÉNOUEMENT.

Catcher in the Rye, The (1951) A novel by J. D. SALINGER. It deals with two days in the life of Holden Caulfield, who has run away from his prep school just before the start of the Christmas vacation; unwilling to go home, Holden drifts about in New York, getting himself into a series of wryly humorous adventures. The sophistication and amazing but credible articulateness of this slightly unbalanced adolescent uniquely convey contemporary youth's dissatisfaction with adult society.

Catch-22 (1961) A novel by Joseph HELLER. Set on the imaginary island of Pianosa during World War II, the novel centers on the ANTI-HERO Captain Yossarian and his attempts to survive the fanatical lunacy of his bomber squadron's commanders long enough to get home. With the death toll rising, the quota of bombing missions required for home-leave is repeatedly increased. By pleading insanity, Yossarian hopes to find a way out until the doctor quotes the notorious Catch-22: a man "would be crazy to fly more missions and sane if he didn't, but if he was sane, he had to fly them. If he flew them he was crazy and didn't have to; but if he didn't, he was sane and had to." The phrase has become a part of the American lexicon, indicating any dilemma.

categorical imperative See CRITIQUE OF PRACTICAL REASON.

Cather, Willa [Sibert] (1876–1947) American novelist. As a child, Cather, who was born in Virginia, was taken to Nebraska, which later provided her with the setting for much of her finest work. After working as a newspaperwoman in Pittsburgh and as a teacher in Allegheny, Pennsylvania, she joined the staff of *McClure's Magazine* in New York City.

Cather's first novel was *Alexander's Bridge* (1912), the story of an engineer, Bartley Alexander, torn between love for his wife and an actress he had known in his youth. She then wrote three novels dealing with the life of the immigrant settlers in the Middle West: O PIONEERS!, THE SONG OF THE LARK, and MY ÁNTONIA. Two later novels, ONE OF OURS and A LOST LADY, are concerned with the Midwest and their characters' relation to its pioneer past. With *The Professor's House* (1925) and DEATH COMES FOR THE ARCHBISHOP, Cather turned to the Southwest. Her interest in Roman Catholicism, shown in the latter book, was continued in *Shadows on the Rock* (1931), a novel about 18th-century Quebec. Other novels are *My Mortal Enemy* (1926), *Lucy Gayheart* (1935), and *Sapphira and the Slave Girl* (1940). Her short stories and novelettes were collected in *The Troll Garden* (1905), YOUTH AND THE BRIGHT MEDUSA, *Obscure Destinies* (1932), and *The Old Beauty and Others* (1948).

Cather's high regard for the courage and industry of the pioneers seemed in time to become a deep hatred for the modern world. She was, according to Maxwell Geismar, "an aristocrat in an equalitarian order, an agrarian writer in an industrial order, a defender of the spiritual graces in the midst of an increasingly materialistic culture."

Catherine de Médicis (1519–1589) Italian-born queen of France. The great-granddaughter of Lorenzo the Magnificent, Catherine married the future Henry II of France in 1533 and was the mother of Francis II, Charles IX, and Henry III. As regent during the minority of Charles, she intrigued with both the Huguenots and the Roman Catholic party and in 1572 persuaded Charles to order the MASSACRE OF ST. BARTHOLOMEW.

Catherine the Great (Catherine II; Russian name Ekaterina Alekseyevna, 1729–1796) Empress of Russia (1762–96). Catherine's reign was marked by increased contact with the West. At that time, French culture was predominant in Europe, and the empress herself took part in the intellectual life of the continent, corresponding regularly with VOLTAIRE, Baron von GRIMM, and DIDEROT. The beginning of Catherine's reign promised liberalization of the regime in Russia. She intended to reform the legal code of the country, for this purpose composing a *Nakaz* (*Instruction*) on which the reforms were to be based. Much of the material in the *Nakaz* came from such liberal thinkers as MONTESQUIEU and Beccaria. Catherine's liberal attitude changed as a result of the peasant uprising (1773–74) led by Yemelyan Pugachev (1743–75) and also as a result of the FRENCH REVOLUTION in 1789. The change in attitude led to a banning of satirical journals in Russia, which the empress had encouraged for a time. The primary target of the ban was Nikolay Ivanovich NOVIKOV, whose criticism of Russian society was becoming too sharp for Catherine's taste. Novikov was imprisoned in 1791 and was freed after her death. Another notable victim of the empress's conservatism was Aleksandr RADISHCHEV, who published his now-famous *Puteshestviye iz Peterburga v Moskvu* (1790; tr A *Journey from Petersburg to Moscow*, 1858). Radishchev's criticisms of Russian life incensed Catherine, and their author was exiled to Siberia.

Catherine's chief political achievements were the acquisition of land in the Ukraine that had long been held by Poland and the establishment of Russia's frontier on the coast of the Black Sea. Her unfulfilled dream of conquering CONSTANTINOPLE from the Turks was later taken up by other nationalist political thinkers.

Catiline (full Latin name Lucius Sergius Catilina, d 62 BC)   Roman conspirator. An able but unscrupulous patrician, Catiline organized a conspiracy of similarly desperate men to overthrow the Roman government by force. The plot was discovered by CICERO, who exposed it in his four eloquent orations *In Catilinam*. Driven from Rome by Cicero's first speech, Catiline later fell in battle against the Roman army. He is the subject of a tragedy (1611) by Ben Jonson.

Catlin, George (1796–1872)   American artist. A self-taught artist, Catlin traveled in the American Midwest, painting the Indians in an effort to document their nobility before they were dispersed by the rapid advance of settlers from the East and from Europe. A collection of his work, organized by Catlin himself as a touring exhibit, was placed in the Smithsonian Institution in Washington, D.C. He was the author of several books, including *Life amongst the Indians* (1861).

Cato, Marcus Porcius (known as Cato the Elder, 234–149 BC)   Roman statesman. Cato's long public career was a constant struggle against enemies of the state abroad and against moral laxity at home. As censor, Cato became the stern arbiter of Roman manners and did his utmost to suppress all innovations in thought and behavior. All that did not fit his severe code of moral rectitude he labeled un-Roman. Despite the decisive defeat of CARTHAGE in 202 BC, he still regarded it as Rome's persistent enemy, and he ended each of his speeches in the Senate with the phrase *Carthago delenda est* ("Carthage must be destroyed"). In 146, three years after the death of Cato, Carthage was at last evacuated and burnt, and its rubble was leveled with ploughs and oxen.

Except for his treatise *De re rustica* (also known as *De agri cultura*), Cato's writings, including *Origines*, his great work on Roman history, are now lost. His prose style was admired for its vigor and terseness.

Cato, Marcus Porcius (known as Cato the Younger, 95–46 BC)   Roman statesman. The great-grandson of Cato the Elder, he is often considered the last of the Romans of the old school. Unwilling to win by bribing the populace, he lost an election but gained the admiration of the Roman nobility. In Caesar's conflict with POMPEY, Cato backed the latter and, after Pompey's defeat at Pharsalus, went with him into exile. When Caesar's legions defeated the army of the nobility in North Africa, Cato —then at Utica—took his own life. The conservative Senatorial Party went on to revere him as a saint and renamed him *Cato Uticensis* ("Cato of Utica") for his last stoic act of defiance. Of him, Lucan wrote: *Victrix causa diis placuit, sed victa Catoni!* ("The gods were pleased with the cause that won—Cato with the cause that lost!"). His death is described in Addison's tragedy *Cato* (1713).

Cat on a Hot Tin Roof (1955)   A play by Tennessee WILLIAMS. It deals with the neurotic Pollitt family, living in the Mississippi Delta. "Big Daddy" Pollitt is dying of cancer; Gooper, the older son, and his wife plot to gain Big Daddy's property. Brick, the younger son, an alcoholic ex-football star, and his wife, Maggie ("the cat"), are driven apart when Brick accuses Maggie of being responsible for his friend's death. In a confrontation with his father, Brick admits his failings and Maggie untruthfully announces that she is pregnant, in an attempt to help her husband gain his inheritance. At the end of the play, the audience is left with a hope of reconciliation between Brick and Maggie. The play was awarded a PULITZER PRIZE in 1955.

Cattle-Raid of Cooley, The   In Gaelic literature, an 8th-century epic tale from the ULSTER CYCLE. It is perhaps the most important of the early Irish sagas. Queen Medb, queen of Cruachain, brings war against the Ulstermen, and CÚ CHULAINN alone defends the territory against her army for a long period. The most poignant moment in the tale is the combat between Cú Chulainn and his own foster brother, Ferdiad, whom he ultimately kills. This tale had considerable influence on the writers involved in the 19th-century IRISH RENAISSANCE.

Catton, [Charles] Bruce (1899–1978)   American historian and journalist. After working for various newspapers, Catton entered government service in 1942 and later served as director of information for the War Production Board. From this experience came his book *War Lords of Washington* (1948). He became deeply interested in the CIVIL WAR, but it was not until 1952, when he retired from public service, that he devoted full time to writing Civil War history. His works in this field include *Mr. Lincoln's Army* (1951), dealing with the early years of the war; *Glory Road* (1952), concerning the campaigns of 1862–63; *A Stillness at Appomattox* (1953), which won the PULITZER PRIZE and the National Book Award; and *Grant Moves South* (1960). *The Coming Fury* (1961), *Terrible Swift Sword* (1963), and *Never Call Retreat* (1965) are the three volumes of Catton's centennial history of the war. *Grant Takes Command* (1969) and *Gettysburg: The Final Fury* (1974) are further Civil War history. *Waiting for the Morning Train* (1972) is a memoir of Catton's boyhood in Michigan.

Catullus, Gaius Valerius (87?–?54 BC) Roman lyric poet. Born in Verona, Catullus went to Rome as a young man. Through his charm and precocious brilliance, he gained easy admittance to the refined and prodigal society of the day; through his ardent susceptibility, he fell disastrously in love with a young Roman matron. She was the beautiful, gifted, and unscrupulous Clodia, sister of the notorious Clodius Pulcher (see CICERO). She became his dark muse, the "Lesbia" of his poetry, and her life and personality are closely intertwined with the life and lyrics of Catullus.

At thirty, Catullus found himself bankrupt, emotionally as well as financially, and in 57 BC, after his final break with Clodia, he traveled to Asia with his friend Gaius Memmius, who was taking the post of propraetor of Bithynia. On his way back to Rome, a year later, he passed his brother's grave near Troy. Here he probably wrote the famous ode that ends *Frater, ave atque vale* ("Brother, hail and farewell"). He died himself not long afterwards, at the age of thirty-three at the most.

Of his poems, composed in a number of lyric meters, 116 are extant. Among them are such celebrated love lyrics as *Vivamus, mea Lesbia, atque amemus* and *Odi et amo*; the mock threnody on the death of Lesbia's parrot; the *Lament of Atthis*; the miniature epic on the marriage of Peleus and Thetis; and a host of stinging epigrammatic attacks on his personal enemies.

Catullus brought many Greek rhythms into Latin literature and was the first Roman poet to exploit fully the classical lyric meters. He exerted wide influence on subsequent poets, such as Tibullus (54?–18 BC), PROPERTIUS, OVID, HORACE, and MARTIAL. In English literature, his influence can be traced in the Elizabethan wedding odes and in the Caroline lyrics.

Caucasian Chalk Circle, The (Der kaukasische Kreidekreis, 1944–45; first performed in English, 1948; in German, 1954; pub 1954) A play by Bertolt BRECHT, based on KLABUND's version of a 13th-century Chinese play, THE CIRCLE OF CHALK. The play consists of six scenes, two of which use the parable as a play within a play. The play opens in Russia after World War II. The ownership of a valley in the Caucasus is disputed between two communes, one of which inhabited the valley before the war, the other of which came to the valley during the war and developed an irrigation system that turned it into prosperous growing land. When it is decided that the latter commune has the more valid claim, a storyteller recounts an ancient parable that is performed by actors. The story concerns the servant girl, Grusche, who saves the life of the governor's child during a feudal upheaval. She raises the child until the governor is restored to power, at which point his wife demands the return of her son. When Grusche refuses to oblige, the case is judged by Azdak, who places the child inside a chalked circle, instructing the two women to pull him out. The governor's wife pulls with great force, while Grusche, afraid of hurting the child, yields. Azdak then awards the child to Grusche, recognizing that she has shown greater love. This episode illustrates the common theme in Brechtian drama that social ties are more important than blood ties.

Cautionary Tales (1907) Verses for children by Hilaire BELLOC. They are mock-moral anecdotes about the fearful fates of children who chew string, tell lies, or bang doors.

Cavafy, Constantine P[eter] (1863–1933) Greek poet. Alexandria, where Cavafy was born and lived as a civil servant, acted as an inspiration and focal point for much of his historical, contemplative, and autobiographically erotic verse. Influenced by classical, Hellenistic, and later 19th-century French and British poetry, Cavafy wrote fewer than three hundred lyrics, plus a few articles. His pamphlet *Poems* appeared in 1904 (rev 1910). Most of his poems were printed on separate sheets for distribution to individual friends. Admired by E. M. FORSTER, who read his poems in 1914, his work began to attract the attention of T. S. ELIOT (1923), T. E. LAWRENCE, and later of W. H. AUDEN and Lawrence DURRELL. The latter two freely acknowledged Cavafy's impact on their work. The best English translations of his poetry are the bilingual *Collected Poems* (tr E. Keeley, P. Sherrard, and G. Savidis, 1975), and *The Complete Poems of Cavafy* (tr R. Dalven, 1976).

In all Cavafy lyrics, the style is direct and dramatic; the language is an unadorned mixture of formal and colloquial with a studied use of classic or Hellenistic expressions. Cavafy found inspiration in major and minor historical characters and events, and he wrote of his own homosexual experiences with remarkable originality and candor. A master of irony, unmoved by lofty ideals or superficial patriotism, in his celebrated "Ithaca," "Waiting for the Barbarians," "Nero's Term," and "Thermopylae," Cavafy expressed an almost existential attitude vis-à-vis the vicissitudes of the human condition.

Cavalcanti, Guido (1250–1300) Italian poet. Cavalcanti was one of the STILNOVISTI group and a close friend of DANTE. Most of his love songs, the *Canzone* *d'amore*, were addressed to a French lady named Mandetta. They were translated by Dante Gabriel ROS-SETTI (1861) and by Ezra POUND (1911).

Cavalier poets   English lyric poets associated with the court of Charles I, chief of whom were Robert HER-RICK, Thomas CAREW, John SUCKLING, and Richard LOVE-LACE. They are best known as writers of frank, high-spirited, gracefully fanciful love poems and songs. See SONS OF BEN.

Cavendish, Margaret (duchess of Newcastle, 1624?–1674)   English noblewoman, one of the outstanding writers of her sex in the 17th century, known for her eccentricity of dress and behavior. Cavendish wrote prolifically, producing thirteen printed books. Her best-known work is her *Sociable Letters* (1664), presenting a vivid picture of her times. She also wrote *The Life of William Cavendish* (1667), a biography of her husband, the duke of Newcastle, who had been a devoted follower of both Charles I and Charles II.

Caves du Vatican, Les   See LAFCADIO'S ADVEN-TURES.

Caxton, William (c1422–1491)   The first English printer, also an important translator. Caxton moved to Bruges, where he established himself as a dealer in textiles, remaining active in commerce until about 1470, even serving as governor (1465–69) of the English Association of Merchant Adventurers in the Low Countries. Between 1469 and 1471, he translated a French romance about the Trojan War, then, to meet the great demand for the book, set about learning the new art of printing, probably with Colard Mansion at a press in Bruges. In 1474 or 1475, his *Recuyell of the Historyes of Troye* became the first book ever printed in English. The second was *The Game and Playe of the Chesse* (1475), which he had also translated from French.

Caxton established a printing press in Westminster when he moved to England in 1476, and thereafter printed nearly eighty books, including the *Mirrour of the World* (1481), *The Golden Legend* (1483), Malory's *Morte d'Arthur* (1485), and the works of Boethius, Chaucer, and John Gower. Many of the books were his own translations from the French, including a great many of the Carolingian and Arthurian romances. What Caxton chose to print naturally became the staple reading matter for the English reading public of his time. His assistant Wynkyn de Worde became his successor after his death, reprinting many of Caxton's most popular titles.

Čech, Svatopluk (1846–1908)   Czech epic poet and satirist. Čech celebrated Slavic traits and democratic ideals in his epic poems *Evropa* (1878) and *Slavie* (1884). One of his best-known pieces of lyrical political satire is *Hanuman* (1884; tr W. W. Strickland, 1894).

Cecil, Lord [Edward Christian] David [Gascoyne] (1902–1986)   English literary critic and biographer. Among his urbane studies are *Early Victorian Novelists* (1934); *The Young Melbourne* (1939); *Lord M.* (1954), the second part of his biography of Melbourne; *The Fine Art of Reading* (1957); *Visionary and Dreamer* (1969), a discussion of the painters Samuel Palmer and Edward Burne-Jones; *Library Looking Glass* (1975); and *A Portrait of Jane Austen* (1978).

Cecilia, St.   A Roman lady who underwent martyrdom in the 3d century. St. Cecilia is the patron saint of the blind, being herself blind; she is also held to be the patroness of musicians and the inventor of the organ. According to tradition, an angel fell in love with her for her musical skill and used to visit her nightly. Her husband saw the heavenly visitant, who thereupon gave to both a crown of martyrdom, which he brought from Paradise. DRYDEN and POPE wrote odes in her honor, and both speak of her charming an angel by her musical powers. See SECOND NUN'S TALE, THE.

Cecilia, or Memoirs of an Heiress (1782)   A novel by Fanny BURNEY. In order to keep her fortune, Cecilia Beverly, an heiress of somewhat inferior birth, must marry a man who will adopt her name. Mortimer Delvile loves her, but his family is proud of its antiquity, and only he can perpetuate its name. Their love is thwarted by this and other obstacles, particularly the schemes and prejudices of those who wish to make use of Cecilia for their own ends. The two finally marry secretly, but further misunderstanding separates them until Delvile locates her by placing an advertisement in the agony column of the daily newspaper.

Cecrops   The traditional founder of Athens and first king of Attica. Supposed to have sprung from the ground, Cecrops was represented as half man, half serpent.

Cela [Trulock], Camilo José (1916–   )   Spanish novelist, essayist, and publisher. *La familia de Pascual Duarte* (1942; tr *The Family of Pascal Duarte*, 1964), Cela's extraordinarily successful first novel, initiated the technique called *tremendismo* (cumulative violence and despair). Written in the bitter aftermath of the Spanish Civil War, in which Cela had fought on Franco's side, this novel, the purported autobiography of a murderer awaiting execution, had enormous influence during the decade after its publication. *La colmena* (1951; tr *The Hive*, 1953), a neorealist and objectivist social satire, and *San Camilo, 36* (1969) are among his best novels. A member of the Royal Spanish Academy, he was designated a senator by the monarchy in 1977. Among his other works are *Rol de cornudas* (1976), *Vuelta de hoja* (1981), and *Mazurca para dos muertos* (1983).

Celebrated Jumping Frog of Calaveras County, The (1865)   A story by Mark TWAIN. It is based on an actual event reported in the California newspapers. Jim Smiley, a miner, bets that his frog, Dan'l Webster, can outjump any other. A stranger accepts the dare;

while Jim is distracted, the stranger pours quail shot into Dan'l. The story, reprinted many times, appeared in Twain's first book, a collection of tales called *The Celebrated Jumping Frog* (1867).

Celeus In Greek legend, a king of Eleusis, husband of Metaneira. Celeus sheltered DEMETER when she was wandering in search of her daughter. In return, Demeter wished to give his son Demophon immortality. When Metaneira objected to her placing the infant in the fire to immortalize him, Demeter angrily revealed herself as a goddess. She instituted the famous ELEUSINIAN MYSTERIES and bestowed on Celeus' other son, Triptolemus, the honor of being mankind's teacher in the use of the plough.

Célimène In Molière's comedy LE MISANTHROPE, a coquette courted by ALCESTE, the misanthropist. Hence, the name has become a synonym for any flagrant coquette.

Céline, Louis-Ferdinand (pen name of Dr. Louis-Ferdinand Destouches, 1894–1961) French novelist. Céline is best known for the misanthropic invective of JOURNEY TO THE END OF THE NIGHT and *Mort à credit* (1936; tr *Death on the Installment Plan*, 1938), which depict everything as evil, decaying, or insane. He looked to Communism but, after a trip to Russia, renounced it in *Mea culpa* (1937). He then turned to Fascism with the violently anti-Semitic diatribe *Bagatelles pour un massacre* (1937) and a bitter attack on the "degenerate" French in *École des cadavres* (1938). Rejected from military service during World War II, he practiced medicine in Paris and vacillated between support and denunciation of Hitler. After *La Bande de Guignol* (1944; tr *Guignol's Band*, 1954), which describes his experiences in the London underworld during World War I, Céline followed the Vichy government to Germany, then fled to Denmark and was imprisoned. Not until 1951, when he was cleared of charges of collaboration, was he allowed to return to Paris, where he continued writing and practicing medicine until his death. *D'un château l'autre* (1957; tr *Castle to Castle*, 1968) and *Nord* (1960; tr *North*, 1972), both dealing with the grotesque Nazi nightmare world, are his last major works.

Cellini, Benvenuto (1500–1571) Florentine goldsmith, sculptor, and author of one of the world's great autobiographies. First published in 1730, the *Autobiography* (1558–62) was begun when Cellini started dictating his memoirs to an apprentice. It tells of his adventures in Italy and France, his relations with popes and kings and with fellow artists, and his production of such works as the Perseus statue. A fairly complete picture of the times emerges from the work, though distorted by the author's exaggeration of his own role in events. Its realism, vivid descriptions, racy style, and, above all, its portrait of a genuine personality have exerted a strong influence on historians of the Renaissance, such as BURCKHARDT, who see it as confirming the view that the key to the period is the emergence of modern individualism. Goethe's translation and Berlioz's musical interpretation are examples of its continuing impact on other artists.

Cement (Tzement, 1925) A novel by Feodor Vasilyevich GLADKOV. The book was one of the first to deal with the problems of reconstruction and industrialization in the Soviet Union after the civil war. It is now ranked as one of the early Soviet classics.

Cénacle In 19th-century France, the name of a literary and political group meeting in the salon of Charles Nodier and, later, the name of a similar group led by Victor HUGO. Honoré de BALZAC made use of this designation in some of the novels of LA COMÉDIE HUMAINE; among the most active members of this fictional cénacle were Daniel d'Arthez, Henri de Marsay, and Horace Bianchon.

Cenci, Beatrice (1577–1599) A historical personage. Cenci is known as the Beautiful Parricide, from a famous portrait in Rome's Barberini palace, attributed to Guido Reni. She was the daughter of Francesco Cenci (1549–98), a choleric, cruel, and vice-laden Roman nobleman. With her mother and two brothers, Beatrice successfully plotted the death of her father at the hands of hired bravos. It is possible, however, that the immediate provocation of the murder was Francesco's discovery of his daughter's intimacy with one of the family's stewards.

The plot was revealed by one of the bravos, and the conspirators were brought to trial. Great sympathy was aroused by the plight of the young, beautiful Beatrice, and her attorney attempted to play upon this by falsely claiming that Francesco had tried to commit incest with her. However, Pope Clement VIII refused the sought-for pardon, and, on September 11, 1599, Beatrice was beheaded. Her story has been a favorite theme of poetry and art, the most famous use being Shelley's tragedy *The Cenci* (1819), in which she is treated sympathetically.

Cendrars, Blaise (born Frédéric-Louis Sauser, 1887–1961) Swiss-born French poet and novelist. A great traveler, reader, and natural storyteller, Cendrars has been called "one of the greatest liars of all time" because of the deliberate fantasy and mystery in which he cloaked his life. His innovative poetic techniques, which influenced APOLLINAIRE, are characterized by rapidly evoked "snapshot" imagery of the modern world, as in *Prose du Transsibérien* (1913), *Panama ou les aventures de mes sept oncles* (1918), and *Dix-neuf Poèmes élastiques* (1919). His novels combine reportage, science fiction, historical fact, and autobiography, but they have in common the themes of mystical adventure and the celebration of life. They include *L'Or* (1925; tr *Sutter's Gold*, 1926), *Moravagine* (1926; tr 1970), *Dan Yack* (1929), *Rhum* (1930), *L'Homme foudroyé* (1945; tr *The Astonished Man*, 1970), *La Main coupée* (1946), *Bourlinguer* (1948; abr tr *Planus*, 1972), and *Le Lotissement du ciel* (1949).

censor In ancient Rome, a magistrate of high rank. His duty was to take the census, see that Senate vacancies were filled, take inventory on government finances, allot government contracts for public works, and investigate and, if necessary, correct the state of public morality. Originally, two censors were elected for a five-year period, called a *lustrum*; in 433 BC, the term of office was shortened to eighteen months. As a distinct office, the censorship disappeared in the reign of Domitian (AD 84).

Centaurs In classic mythology, beings who were half horse and half man. The Centaurs fought with the LAPITHS at the marriage feast of PIRITHOUS, were expelled from their country, and took refuge on Mount Pindus. CHIRON was the most famous of the centaurs. Both Lapiths and Centaurs are thought originally to have been actual Thessalian tribes.

cento (Lat, "patchwork") A literary composition, especially a poem, of lines or parts from the writings of established authors, and with a meaning and message different from the original. Centos were freely produced during the decadent period of Greece and Rome; Ausonius (c310–95), who put together the scandalous *Cento Nuptialis*, with lines taken from VERGIL, enunciated rules concerning their composition. Among well-known examples are the *Homerocentones*, taken by Byzantine compilers from HOMER, the *Cento Vergilianus* by Proba Falconia (4th century), which used Vergil to relate biblical history, and the Christian hymns devised by the monk Metellus (12th century) from the works of Vergil and HORACE.

Cephalus and Procris A famous couple in classic legend. Cephalus was Procris' husband. She deserted him out of jealousy. Searching for her, he rested a while under a tree. Procris, knowing of his whereabouts, crept through some bushes to ascertain if a rival was with him, and hearing the noise and thinking it to be made by some wild beast, he hurled his javelin into the bushes and slew her. When the unhappy man discovered what he had done, he slew himself with the same javelin.

Cerberus In Greek mythology, the three-headed dog, keeper of the entrance of the infernal regions. HERACLES dragged the monster to earth, to show him to Eurystheus, the King of Mycenae who imposed Heracles' twelve famous labors, and then took him back. The Sibyl who conducted AENEAS through the lower world threw the dog into a profound sleep with a cake seasoned with poppies and honey (*Aeneid* vi, 417–25). The phrase *give a sop to Cerberus* therefore means to give a bribe, to quiet a troublesome person.

Ceres An Italian goddess of fertility, later identified with the Greek DEMETER.

Cervantes [Saavedra], Miguel de (1547–1616) Spanish novelist, dramatist, and poet. Born in Alcalá de Henares, Cervantes came from a good though impecunious family. Little is known of his education except that in 1568 he was a student of the Madrid humanist Juan López de Hoyos, who edited an elegaic volume on the death of Queen Isabel de Valois, to which Cervantes contributed some verses. In 1569 he went to Italy, became a soldier, and fought in the battle of Lepanto (1571), in which he acquitted himself with distinction and lost the use of his left hand; he was extremely proud of his role in the famous victory and of the nickname he had earned, *el manco de Lepanto*. As Cervantes was returning to Spain with his brother on the galley *El Sol* in 1575, the ship was captured by Barbary pirates, and the two brothers were taken to Algiers as slaves. Miguel remained in captivity for five years, during which he made several romantic if futile efforts to escape. His ransom of five hundred ducats was finally paid by the Trinitarian friars.

Having returned to Spain, Cervantes married Catalina de Salazar y Palacios in 1584, fathered an illegitimate daughter, and in 1587 secured employment as a purchasing agent for the navy. In this capacity, he traveled throughout the country, often becoming involved in disputes with communities reluctant to part with their crops; on one occasion, he was excommunicated for seizing grain that belonged to the church. Twice he was imprisoned for debt.

In 1605 Cervantes and his family, who were then living in Valladolid, were accused of complicity in the death of a young nobleman. They were later absolved, but the records of the case give evidence of the poverty and wretchedness of Cervantes's mode of existence at the time. His position improved considerably, however, after the publication of the first part of DON QUIXOTE in the same year. Although Cervantes's previous literary efforts had met with little success, *Don Quixote* immediately caught the fancy of the reading public. Moving to Madrid, he devoted his last years to writing.

Cervantes's reputation as one of the greatest writers in history rests almost entirely on *Don Quixote* and on the twelve short stories known as the NOVELAS EJEMPLARES. His literary production, however, was considerable. *La Galatea* (1585), a pastoral romance, was his first long work; similar in form and content to other novels of this type, it received little contemporary notice and is remembered largely because of its authorship. Cervantes repeatedly promised to write a continuation, but it never appeared.

He next turned his attention to the stage and wrote between twenty and thirty plays in the years immediately following 1585. Two extant dramas of this period are *El trato de Argel* and *La Numancia*, both of which were first printed in 1784. The former, dealing with the life of Christian slaves in Algiers, is of interest only because of its autobiographical details. The latter, which recounts the siege and capture of Numantia by the Romans under Scipio Africanus, has won wider approbation, partly because of some powerful scenes and partly because of its expressions of patriotism. In 1615 Cervantes published his *Ocho comedias, y ocho entremeses nuevos*. Only one of the full-length plays, *Pedro de Urdemalas*, has met with critical favor, but the *entremeses*, or interludes, are highly regarded for their sprightly and realistic pictures of Bohemian life.

Cervantes himself realized that he was deficient in poetic gifts, a judgment confirmed by later generations. Aside from his plays, his most ambitious work in verse is the *Viaje del Parnaso* (1614), an allegory which consists largely of a rather tedious though good-natured review of contemporary poets. *Los trabajos de Persiles y Sigismunda* (1617) is a verse romance in the manner of Heliodorus, which Cervantes thought would be either the worst or the best book in the Spanish language. Though some critics have boggled at the fantastic geography of its early scenes and the incredible adventures of its characters, others have praised its polished style.

Regardless of its merits, the *Persiles* will be remembered, if only for its dedication and prologue. Addressed to the conde de Lemos, the dedication was signed on April 19, 1616, just four days before Cervantes's death. Quoting an old ballad, *Puesto ya el pié en el estribo* ("one foot already in the stirrup"), Cervantes takes leave of his patron and of the world with the same gallantry and grace that characterized both his life and his work.

Césaire, Aimé (1913–   )   Martinique-born poet, essayist, and playwright, writing in French. Former Martiniquan deputy to the French Chamber of Deputies and mayor of the capital city of Fort-de-France, Césaire has had a career in public service as well as a broad European education. His poetry is vividly colorful and rhythmical yet also has a clear didactic purpose: to break down colonialist traditions and assert the proud heritage of black people. To that end, Césaire developed, along with Léon DAMAS and Léopold SENGHOR, the concept of NÉGRITUDE as a literary and social movement to resist assimilation and celebrate the qualities and accomplishments of blacks. His works of poetry include *Cahier d'un retour au pays natal* (1947; tr *Return to My Native Land*, 1969), *Les Armes miraculeuses* (1946), *Ferrements* (1960), and *Cadastre* (1961; tr 1972). In 1984 these and other poems were translated in *Aimé Césaire: The Collected Poetry*. He also wrote such plays as *Une saison au Congo* (1966; tr *A Season in the Congo*, 1969), based on the death of Patrice Lumumba, and numerous essays, including *Discours sur le colonialisme* (1951; tr *Discourse on Colonialism*, 1972) and *Moi, Laminaire* (1982).

cestus   (1) The girdle of APHRODITE, made by her husband, HEPHAESTUS. It was reputed to possess magical power to move to ardent love. By a poetical fiction, all women of irresistible attraction are supposed to be wearers of Aphrodite's girdle, or the *cestus*. It is introduced by Spenser in THE FAERIE QUEENE as the girdle of Florimel. It gave to those who could wear it "the virtue of chaste love

and wifehood true," but if any woman not chaste and faithful put it on, it "loosed or tore asunder."

(2) The *cestus* in Roman games was a covering for the hands of boxers, made of leather bands and often loaded with lead or iron.

Cézanne, Paul (1839–1906)   French painter. The great master of postimpressionism and perhaps the greatest figure in modern French painting, Cézanne was born in Aix-en-Provence, the son of a banker. His early works were low in key and heavy in medium, but after 1870 he began to paint out of doors and allied himself with the impressionists. By 1876 he had already begun to accentuate mass, rather than light, in an effort to achieve a better illusion of volume. Cézanne's statement that "Nature must be treated through the cylinder, the sphere, the cone" summarizes his desire "to make of impressionism something as solid and durable as the painting in the museums." This search led him to displace visual planes, to raise the horizon, to construct his paintings in such a way that each departure from nature would increase the impression of form and depth. He retained the pure colors of impressionism, but used them to build up volume through the contrast of tones. He spent much of his life as a recluse in Provence, painting the famous still lifes, landscapes, and portraits, which were then unknown except to a few of his contemporaries. It was not until the last decade of the century that his reputation began to grow. Cézanne is said to have been in the mind of Emile ZOLA, his former schoolmate and friend, during the composition of *L'Œuvre* (1886); Zola represents his hero as a restless painter and failure.

Chaadayev, Pyotr Yakovlevich (1794–1856) Russian philosophical thinker. Chaadayev is famous for his *Philosophical Letters*, which compare Russia's past and present condition unfavorably to that of the Western nations. The publication of the first letter in 1836 brought down a storm of abuse and police persecution on Chaadayev, who was officially declared insane and put under house arrest for a time.

Chadwick, George W[hitefield] (1854–1931) American composer. Chadwick was deeply indebted to German musical thinking. He studied in Leipzig and Munich, where his overture *Rip Van Winkle* made a strong impression. He returned to Boston in 1880; there he was a member of the artistic circles frequented by members of the American realist school, including William Dean HOWELLS. He taught at the New England Conservatory from 1882; as director of that institution (1897–1930), he was responsible for its development as a full conservatory of national importance. His music is romantic in conception, with an imaginative and colorful treatment of the orchestra. Of all the academic American composers of his generation, he is the one most likely to display a Yankee sense of humor and realism, particularly in the *Second Symphony* (1886), the *String Quartet No. 4 in E minor* (1896), the

Symphonic Sketches (1895–1904), and the symphonic poem *Tam O'Shanter* (1915; after Robert BURNS).

Chagall, Marc (1889–1985)   Russian-born French painter. From his earliest expressionistic paintings (scenes of village life among Russian Jews), Chagall developed an individual style of great poetry and brightness. Following his arrival in Paris in 1910, he adapted cubist principles to his highly imaginative works of fantasy, which depicted such things as a pair of lovers floating over or nesting in large bouquets of flowers. In the early 1920s he produced some of his famous illustrations, notably for Gogol's *Dead Souls* (1948) and the *Fables of La Fontaine* (1952). As he survived two world wars and the Russian Revolution, Chagall increasingly introduced social and religious elements into his art, painting numerous crucifixions and such monumental works as the twelve stained-glass panels installed in the synagogue of Jerusalem's Hadassa Medical Center in 1962. He also painted a ceiling in the Paris Opera in 1964 and an enormous mural for the Metropolitan Opera at Lincoln Center in New York City in 1966.

He wrote *Ma Vie* (1931; tr *My Life*, 1957), and illustrated many books, including *The Arabian Nights, Stories from Boccaccio*, and the Bible.

Chain of Being   See GREAT CHAIN OF BEING.

Chairs, The (Les Chaises, 1951; tr 1958)   A tragic farce by Eugène IONESCO. It presents a Kafkaesque image of modern man. An old lighthouse keeper, preparing to die, invites a group of guests to a gathering, where his final words of wisdom will be delivered. In a scene that is both a dramatic and a symbolic *tour de force*, he and his wife rush desperately about to seat an enormous crowd of imaginary guests. The bare, empty stage juxtaposed with the frenzied human effort offer an absurd image of modern man, isolated, frustrated, and unable to order the chaos of life. A final irony, ludicrous and bitter, is the audience's discovery that the orator can neither read nor write.

Chambered Nautilus, The (1858)   A poem by Oliver Wendell HOLMES. The sea creature that enlarges its shell as it grows is an example to the human being:

Build thee more stately mansions, O my soul,

. . . .

Leaving thine outgrown shell by life's unresting sea!

Chamberlain, Neville (1869–1940)   Conservative prime minister of England from 1937 to 1940. Chamberlain is remembered chiefly for his role in the Munich meeting with Hitler in September 1938, in which he pursued a policy of appeasement. For a time, his name became synonymous with betrayal in the writing of Marxists and liberals, who considered that he had delivered Czechoslovakia into the hands of the Nazis. He was succeeded in office by Winston CHURCHILL.

Chamber Music (1907)   A volume of poems, mainly love lyrics, by James JOYCE. They show the influ-

ence of the Elizabethan poets and of the early William Butler YEATS and his circle.

Chamisso, Adalbert von (1781–1838)   German poet and botanist. Chamisso is famous for his ballads and the story PETER SCHLEMIHLS WUNDERSAME GESCHICHTE. He was one of the first poets to turn away from the unswerving idealism of earlier GERMAN ROMANTICISM and to write with a genuine love for the common people; for example, he wrote poems about beggars and washerwomen. Chamisso was appointed botanist to a Russian ship and published a diary of his expedition around the world. He was custodian of the botanical gardens in Berlin.

Champlain, Samuel de (1567–1635)   French explorer. He discovered and explored Lake Champlain and in 1608 founded the colony of Quebec.

Champollion, Jean François (1790–1832)   Famous French Egyptologist. As a result of Champollion's study of the Rosetta Stone, he obtained a clue for deciphering Egyptian hieroglyphics.

Chan, Charlie   A shrewd Chinese detective, living in Hawaii, who appears in several stories by Earl Derr Biggers (1884–1933). Given to wise, philosophical reflections, Chan acts on the assumption that, if he can understand a man's character, he can predict his actions in any given circumstance. He first appeared in *The House without a Key* (1925). Later Chan stories include *The Chinese Parrot* (1926); *Behind That Curtain* (1929); *Charlie Chan Carries On* (1930); *Keeper of the Keys* (1932).

Ch'an Buddhism   A meditative sect of BUDDHISM in China, the equivalent of ZEN BUDDHISM in Japan. Meditation was widely used in all forms of Buddhism in India and China, but Ch'an was the first to put almost exclusive emphasis on it. Traditionally Bodhidharma (5th century) is given as the founder in China, and the sixth patriarch, Hui-neng (d 713), is honored as the developer of the sect as a religion. The actual history is unclear, but by the T'ANG dynasty (618–906), Ch'an had gained great popularity, and there were numerous teachers throughout China. Ch'an advocates "direct seeing into one's own mind" and realizing Buddhahood in oneself. It emphasizes the teacher-disciple relationship, transmission "from mind to mind" rather than through written words, and "sudden enlightenment" (Chinese *wu*, Japanese SATORI), or an instantaneous apprehension of one's Buddha nature. After the Buddhist persecutions of 845, it became the dominant school in China. By the SUNG period (960–1279), it had split into various sects and an organized church had been developed. It was the Ch'an of this time that was transmitted to Japan, together with the elaborate KŌAN system. The two principal branches are *Lin-chi* (Japanese *Rinzai*) and *Ts'ao-tung* (Japanese *Sōtō*), both of which flourish in Japan today. By the MING period (1368–1644), it had lost its vitality and had become mixed with the Pure Land School, or AMIDISM.

Chance Acquaintance, A (1873)   A novel by William Dean HOWELLS. Kitty Ellison falls in love with Miles Arbuton, a young Bostonian, while they travel on the St. Lawrence River. They become engaged, but Miles, meeting some fashionable and snobbish friends, ignores Kitty. She breaks the engagement, knowing she cannot be happy with a Boston Brahmin.

Chancellorsville, battle of   In U.S. history, a Civil War battle that occurred on May 2–4, 1863, near Fredericksburg, Virginia. The Union army under Gen. Joseph Hooker was defeated by Confederate forces under Gen. Robert E. Lee. Thomas ("Stonewall") Jackson, the Confederate general, was accidentally shot by his own men during the battle and died of pneumonia on May 10. This battle is said to have furnished the background for Stephen Crane's *Red Badge of Courage* (1895).

Chandler, Raymond [Thornton] (1888–1959) American detective story writer. Educated in England, Chandler had the highest respect for "civilized culture," and yet it was in the seamier side of California low life that he flourished as a writer. A master of HARD-BOILED FICTION, he wrote detective stories distinguished for their literate presentation and acutely critical eye. Chandler created the brash but honorable private detective Philip Marlowe, whose exploits began in Chandler's first novel, *The Big Sleep* (1939). The success of his first book was matched by *Farewell, My Lovely* (1940), *The High Window* (1942), *The Lady in the Lake* (1943), and *The Long Goodbye* (1954), his last novel. *The Simple Art of Murder* (1950), a collection of shorter pieces, contains an excellent and well-known essay on writing crime fiction.

Changeling, The (c1623)   A tragedy by Thomas MIDDLETON and William ROWLEY. Beatrice Joanna, a young noblewoman betrothed to Alonzo De Piracquo, falls in love with Alsemero, a Venetian gentleman. After postponing the wedding, she calls in Deflores, her father's ugly servant, whom she has always despised, and enlists his aid in killing Alonzo. After Deflores, who adores Beatrice Joanna, has dispatched Alonzo, he claims her person as his reward. Horrified, she refuses, but Deflores, a desperate man, swears to tell all unless she becomes his mistress. Trapped, she agrees. She marries Alsemero but, fearful of exposure, substitutes her virginal servant Diaphanta in the bridal bed. When Diaphanta lingers too long, Deflores sets fire to the house and kills the girl in her burning chamber. But by this time, Beatrice Joanna and Deflores have been found out. Confronted by Alsemero, they confess, and Deflores kills both Beatrice and himself.

Channing, William Ellery (1780–1842)   American clergyman. An ordained Congregational minister, Channing came to reject Calvinism, especially its emphasis on the depravity of mankind. At the ordination of Jared Sparks in 1819, he delivered a sermon that led to the formal emergence of Unitarianism, and he became the apos-

tle of the movement. An advocate of abolition and other social reforms, he was one of the leading propagandists of the era. His ideas contributed to the formulation of Transcendentalism and influenced that movement's leaders, particularly Emerson, who published some of Channing's writings in THE DIAL. See BROOK FARM.

Chanson de Roland   See ROLAND.

chansons de geste (Fr, "songs of deeds")   The medieval French metrical romances celebrating the heroic deeds of historical and legendary knights. The epics of the 11th and early 12th centuries were divided into lays or stanzas of irregular length, usually with ten-syllable lines united by assonance or a single rhyme. They glorified the code of chivalric honor in battle and gave little place to women. By the 13th and 14th centuries, the role of women and romantic love became more important, regular rhyme schemes were introduced, and the ALEXANDRINE (twelve-syllable line), which later became the standard for French classical verse, became popular.

Most of the *chansons de geste*, sung by JONGLEURS and court minstrels, were composed by TROUVÈRES about Charlemagne's PALADINS and their families or the knights who were his enemies. They were arranged in cycles around the principal hero of a family. The *chanson de geste* commanded the widest audience of any medieval genre.

One of the earliest and best was the *Chanson de* ROLAND. Other groups center on Charlemagne's childhood, his wars in Spain, his pilgrimage to Jerusalem. There is an important cycle about *Garin de Monglane* and his descendants, including the chanson *Girard de Viane*, which describes Roland's meeting with OLIVIER. Another is the *Geste de* DOON DE MAYANCE, grouping the traitors and the families at war with Charlemagne. See LAI.

chant royal   An elaboration of the BALLADE form. The chant royal was developed in medieval France and used for serious and stately themes. It was not introduced in England until the latter part of the 19th century, during the revival of interest in French forms. It is a sixty-line poem having five stanzas of eleven lines and an ENVOI of five lines, each ending with the refrain, as in the ballade. The rhyme scheme of the stanza is a-b-a-b-c-c-d-d-e-d-e, and of the *envoi*, d-d-e-d-e.

Chanukah   See HANUKKAH.

Chaos   In Greek mythology, the original void. Out of Chaos, according to HESIOD, came GE (Earth), TARTARUS (Infernal Regions), EROS (Love), EREBUS (Darkness), and NYX (Night). The Orphics (see ORPHISM) claimed that Chaos, Night, and Darkness coexisted and that Love came from an egg laid by Night; Eros parthenogenetically produced the first generation of gods.

chapbook   Originally one of the books carried about for sale by *chapmen* (tradesmen; *chap* "purchase; bargain"). Hence, any book of a similar nature, a tract, small

collection of ballads, or the like. See CHILDREN'S LITERA-
TURE.

Chaplin, Charlie (full name Sir Charles Spencer
Chaplin, 1889–1977)   English-born motion-picture
actor, director, writer, producer, and composer. Chaplin,
one of the greatest tragicomic mimes, is internationally
famous as the creator of the Tramp, the heartbreakingly
goodwilled character with baggy pants, oversized shoes, a
derby hat, and an awkward walk. The Tramp's naïve
approach to life invariably involves him in dangerous situations or ludicrous predicaments that are resolved as if by
divine grace. Chaplin made his screen debut with Mack
SENNETT's Keystone Films in 1914. In the next few years,
he appeared in such short silent films as *The Count, Easy
Street,* and *The Cure.* In 1919, with D. W. GRIFFITH and
others, he founded United Artists. Among his most memorable films are *The Kid* (1921), *The Gold Rush* (1925), *City
Lights* (1931), *Modern Times* (1936), *The Great Dictator*
(1940; his first "talkie"), *Monsieur Verdoux* (1947), and
Limelight (1952). In all of them, Chaplin himself was producer, director, scenarist, and star. In 1952, after a long
period of political difficulties and disaffection with the
American public, Chaplin moved to Switzerland, where
he died twenty-five years later. He was knighted by the
Queen of England in 1975.

Chapman, George (1559?–1634)   English poet,
scholar, and playwright. Chapman is best remembered
today for the first English translation of the works of
HOMER, which began with his *Seven Books of the Iliad* in
1598. In 1611 he published the entire *Iliad,* in 1615 the
Odyssey, and in 1616 *The Whole Works of Homer.* The
translation, in rhymed couplets, often departs from and
expands upon the original, but it is a notable poetic
achievement in its own right. It was praised by LAMB and
COLERIDGE, and most memorably by KEATS in his sonnet
"On First Looking into Chapman's Homer." Among
Chapman's poems are *The Shadow of Night* (1594) and
Ovid's Banquet of Sense (1595). He completed Christopher
MARLOWE's unfinished *Hero and Leander* (1598), and
wrote a number of plays, of which the best known are the
tragedies BUSSY D'AMBOIS (c1604) and its sequel, *The
Revenge of Bussy D'Ambois* (c1610). However, some schol-
ars feel his best plays were his romantic comedies, such as
All Fools (c1599) and *May Day* (c1602). His other plays
include *The Blind Beggar of Alexandria* (1596), *An Humor-
ous Day's Mirth* (1597), *The Gentleman Usher* (c1602),
Monsieur D'Olive (1604), and *Charles, Duke of Byron,* I &
II (1607-8).

Chapman, John   See APPLESEED, JOHNNY.

Chapygin, Aleksey Pavlovich (1870–1937)
Russian novelist. Drawing heavily from folklore and his
own peasant heritage, Chapygin wrote two historical
novels, *Razin Stepan* (1926–27; tr *Stepan Razin,* 1946)
and *Gulyashchiye lyudi* (*Itinerant Folk,* 1934–37), the lat-

ter of which established Chapygin as a major figure in the
Russian historical novel and has itself become a classic in
that genre.

Char, René (1907–   )   French poet of the Midi
region. Char was a close friend of Paul ÉLUARD, and his
early poetry, particularly *Le Marteau sans maître* (1934),
bears the distinct stamp of SURREALISM. He was active in the
French Resistance during World War II, a fact that is
reflected in such volumes as *Seuls demeurent* (1945) and
Feuillets d'Hypnos (1946; tr *Leaves of Hypnos,* 1973). For
Char, the function of poetry is primarily revelatory; he
seeks to invest words with new associations that will shed
light on the meaning of existence. Char's later hermetic
poetry tends more toward prose and reveals a close communion with nature and with the landscape of his native
Vaucluse and expresses a humanistic exaltation of man.
Among his works are *À la santé du serpent* (1954), *Aro-
mates chasseurs* (1975), and *Fenêtres dormantes et porte sur
le toit* (1979). *The Poems of René Char* (1976) is a selection
of his work in English translation.

character writers   A school of English prose writers in the first half of the 17th century. They wrote sketches
of men and women—either as individuals or types—in
descriptive, analytical, or satirical form, as observed in the
life of their time. Many of them were influenced by the
work of THEOPHRASTUS, the Athenian Peripatetic philosopher, who wrote studies of thirty types of personality, such
as the Flatterer and the Grumbler, under the title of *Characters.* The best-known English character writers are
Joseph HALL, Owen Felltham (1602?–1668), Sir Thomas
OVERBURY, and John Earle (1601?–1665).

Charge of the Light Brigade, The (written 1854)
A poem by Alfred TENNYSON celebrating the famous "death
charge of the six hundred" at Balaclava in the Crimea,
October 25, 1854. A British brigade, knowing the folly of
their orders, charged the Russian line and was decimated:

> Theirs not to make reply,
> Theirs not to reason why,
> Theirs but to do and die.
> Into the valley of Death
>   Rode the six hundred.

Charis   According to HOMER, one of the GRACES and
wife of HEPHAESTUS. In later times, the name was applied
to any of the three Graces (Charites).

Charlemagne (Charles the Great, 742–814)
Frankish king, crowned Emperor of the West in 800 (see
CAROLINGIANS). Charlemagne and the knights said to be his
PALADINS became the center of a number of CHANSONS DE
GESTE, or medieval epic romances, most having very little
basis in fact, except for the defeat of the rear guard at RON-
CESVALLES. Famous versions of these legends include the
French *Chanson de* ROLAND and, in Italian, Pulci's MOR-
GANTE MAGGIORE, Boiardo's ORLANDO INNAMORATO, and
Ariosto's ORLANDO FURIOSO.

Charles   In Shakespeare's As You Like It, a wrestler in Duke Frederick's court, whom Orlando challenges and defeats.

Charles V (also known as Charles I of Spain, 1500–1558)   Holy Roman Emperor. The son of Philip the Fair of Flanders and Joanna the Mad of Spain, Charles inherited Burgundy and Flanders upon his father's death (1506) and, because of his mother's insanity, acceded to the throne of Spain after the demise of his grandfather, Ferdinand II, in 1516. Spanish resentment against the Flemishborn youth was heightened when he secured election as Holy Roman Emperor in 1519 at great expense and without consulting the *cortes*, or parliament, of Spain. During Charles's absence in Germany, this resentment erupted in the revolt of the *comuneros*, or townsmen, in which nobles and commoners were at first arrayed against the monarchy but which later turned into a class struggle. Other rebellions broke out in Valencia and among the *Moriscos*, or converted Moors, of Spain.

After the suppression of these revolts, Spain enjoyed internal peace and prosperity while Charles devoted himself to foreign affairs. There were several wars with France, whose ruler, Francis I, feared Hapsburg domination of Europe. Challenging Turkish designs in the Mediterranean and in central Europe, Charles captured Tunis in 1535 but failed to take Algiers in 1541. He also attempted to suppress Lutheranism in Germany.

Disillusioned by the frustration of his hopes for religious and political peace in Europe and burdened by debt, Charles decided to give up his many crowns, assigning the imperial title to his brother Ferdinand and his hereditary possessions to his son Philip. In 1556 he retired to the Hieronymite convent of Yuste in Estremadura, where he lived in seclusion until his death.

Charles I (1600–1649)   Stuart king of England (1625–49) and second son of James I. The first years of Charles's reign were marked by disputes with Parliament over matters of finance, religion, and foreign policy. In 1629 he dissolved Parliament and ruled alone for eleven years, but in 1640 he was compelled to recall Parliament to deal with the problems of the Scottish rebellion and a growing lack of money. From this point on, the conflict between King and Commons became more intense; the former's stubbornness and duplicity and the latter's insistence on its rights and its generally anti-Anglican (Puritan) character led to the Civil War and to Charles's beheading in 1649. In his private personality, Charles was a virtuous, deeply pious, and courageous man, as his deportment at his trial and execution revealed; but his public character was marred by double-dealing, obstinacy, ingratitude to friends, and a lack of political intelligence. Charles is a prominent character in Dumas's *Twenty Years After* (1845).

Charles II (1630–1685)   Stuart king of England (1660–85). Charles was proclaimed king in Scotland after the death of his father, Charles I, but it was only after eleven years of exile, struggle, and disappointment that he assumed the throne of England. This restoration was brought about by compromise and by Parliament's invitation, not by force of arms, and throughout Charles's reign, he was obliged to intrigue and maneuver for parliamentary support. A brother of the openly Catholic James, he was eager to obtain a wider measure of religious tolerance in England, to strengthen the monarchy, and to ensure the succession of James. He failed in his first goal and attained only a very partial and transient success with the others. His reign was disturbed by shifting alliances, several wars, numerous actual and fictitious conspiracies, the Great Plague (1665), and the Fire of London (1666), but it was greatly productive in literature, science, and architecture. Charles II was an easygoing, intelligent, pleasure-loving, witty man, notorious for the number of his amours and illegitimate offspring. He is an important character in Scott's Peveril of the Peak and *Woodstock* (1826). See Gwyn, Nell.

Charles VII (of France)   See Dauphin.

Charles, Duc d'Orléans (1391–1465)   French poet, son of Louis d'Orléans (brother of King Charles VI), and father of King Louis XII. In 1415 Charles was taken captive to England, where he wrote most of his graceful *ballades* and *rondeaux*. After his ransom in 1460, he established a miniature court at Blois as a patron of the arts, entertaining François Villon and others.

Charles, Nick   A detective created by Dashiell Hammett. Nick Charles first appeared in *The Thin Man* (1932). A witty and debonair man, he was a striking contrast to Hammett's other famous detective, Sam Spade.

Charlotte Temple (pub England, 1791; U.S., 1794)   An early American novel by Susannah Haswell Rowson (1762–1824). Originally entitled *Charlotte, a Tale of Truth*, it has run through more than a hundred editions and is still occasionally read. The heroine is lured from her English home and deserted in New York by a British officer named Montraville, who later repents. Rowson wrote a sequel, *Charlotte's Daughter*, better known as *Lucy Temple*, published posthumously in 1828.

Charlus, Baron Palamède [Mémé] de   An important aristocrat in Marcel Proust's Remembrance of Things Past. One of the Guermantes, he cultivates his reputation as a virile woman-chaser but is secretly a homosexual.

Charon   In classical mythology, the ferryman of the Styx. Charon's toll was a coin, about equal in value to a penny, which was placed in the mouth or the hand of the dead by the ancient Greeks to pay him for ferrying the spirit across the river Styx to Elysium.

Charterhouse of Parma, The (La Chartreuse de Parme, 1839)   A historical novel by STENDHAL. In essence the tale is a chronicle of the adventures of its young hero, Fabrizio del Dongo. Set in the post-Napoleonic era, this remarkable analysis of ROMANTICISM leads us through the battle of Waterloo, life and intrigue in a small Italian court, romantic love, imprisonment, and the priesthood, finally terminating in a Carthusian monastery.

Chartism   The political movement and program of the group of English reformers known as Chartists (1838–49). Their main target of criticism was the Reform Bill of 1832, which had failed to extend the vote to the working-man. Their principal demands, published in "the People's Charter," were for universal manhood suffrage and for the annual election of parliament, abolition of property qualifications and payment to members of parliament, vote by ballot, and equal representation in electoral districts. Members of the group were mostly industrial workers led by radical intellectuals. Chartism disappeared from the political scene after 1849, but all the Chartists' aims, with the exception of annual parliaments, were ultimately realized.

The Chartist Clergyman   Charles KINGSLEY, so called because of his sympathy with Chartism and other working-class movements.

Charybdis   See SCYLLA AND CHARYBDIS.

Chase, Mary Ellen (1887–1973)   American writer and teacher. Chase is known best for her regional novels, dealing with her native Maine sea coast. Of these, *Mary Peters* (1934) and *Silas Crockett* (1935) are perhaps her best. The latter, chronicling the history of a Yankee family through four generations, has as its theme the hardships inflicted on old clipper sailors by the introduction of steamships.

Chateaubriand, François René de (1768–1848) French writer, forerunner of ROMANTICISM. The work of Chateaubriand is characterized by egotistical melancholy, impassioned emotion, and a love of untamed nature. His interest in Roman Catholicism and the Middle Ages, in exotic countries and primitive tribes, foreshadows typically romantic concerns. Chateaubriand's novels ATALA and RENÉ deal with North America and the North American Indians. *Les Martyrs* (1809) and *L'Itinéraire de Paris à Jérusalem et de Jérusalem à Paris* (1811) are concerned with Greece, the Holy Land, and the Near East. Other works include LE GÉNIE DU CHRISTIANISME and MÉMOIRES D'OUTRE-TOMBE. Chateaubriand's political career was a stormy one. He favored the Bourbon monarchy and served it as ambassador to England, Italy, and Germany and as minister of foreign affairs.

Châtelet, Gabrielle Emilie Le Tonnelier de Breteuil, Marquise du (1706–1749)   French mathematician and physicist. Mistress of VOLTAIRE, Châtelet lived with him at Montjeu and at her château at Cirey (in Lorraine). The liaison lasted fourteen years, until her death. The marquise had an intense interest in the theories of LEIBNITZ and NEWTON and propagated the latter's ideas in France. She wrote *Traité sur le bonheur* (1749) and *Traduction des principes de Newton* (1756). See EMILIE.

Chatterton, Thomas (1752–1770)   English poet. Chatterton's literary fabrications are distinguished by their poetic genius. While still a boy, living in Bristol, he wrote a number of poems couched in elaborately archaic spelling that he declared to be the work of one Thomas Rowley, a nonexistent monk, poet, and antiquarian of the 15th century. In this way, Chatterton evolved a romance of Bristol centering on William Canynges, a merchant who became lord mayor. Notable poems in this series are *Bristowe Tragedie: or, the Dethe of Syr Charles Bawdin* (1772) and *An Excelente Balade of Charitie* (1777). His deception was successful for a while, although it was exposed in 1777–78 by Thomas Tyrwhitt and Thomas Warton. Chatterton also wrote *Apostate Will* (1764), a satire, and *The Revenge* (1770), a successful burlesque opera. In despair at his poverty, after moving to London, he killed himself at the age of seventeen by taking poison. A volume of his collected works was published in 1803. Chatterton was a favorite figure of the English Romantic poets, becoming for them the prototype of the neglected genius.

Chaucer, Geoffrey (c1343–1400)   English poet and public servant, by far the most important writer of Middle English and considered one of the finest poets in literature. Chaucer's family had been in the royal service, and in 1357 he is known to have been already in the service of the wife of Prince Lionel and to have met John of Gaunt, another of the King's sons, who became one of his most important patrons. He joined the English army's invasion of France in 1359, was captured, and was ransomed by King Edward III in 1360. His activities for the next six years remain unknown: he may have been with Lionel in Ireland, he may have attended law school, he may already have entered the King's service. About 1366 he married Philippa, one of the Queen's attendants and the sister of Katherine Swynford, later John of Gaunt's mistress, then wife. Philippa apparently gave him two sons, "little Lewis," to whom Chaucer addressed A *Treatise on the Astrolabe* (1391), and Thomas, highly successful in public service in the 15th century. There may have been one daughter, or perhaps two, but the evidence is uncertain.

In 1367 Chaucer was given a life pension by the King, and he apparently remained in the royal service thereafter, going abroad on a number of more or less secret diplomatic missions between 1368 and 1378, mostly to France. The two trips into Italy (1372–73 and 1378) proved extremely important in his literary development because of his discovery of the works of DANTE, BOCCACCIO, and PETRARCH, which greatly influenced his own; it is probable that he read all their major works except Boccaccio's DECAMERON, and he knew many of those tales through Petrarch and French translations.

In 1374 he was given a house of his own and was made Controller of Customs on wools, skins, and hides; in 1382 he was also given control of Petty Custom on wines and other goods. About 1385 he established his residence in Kent, where he was elected justice of the peace and briefly (1386) a member of Parliament. After his wife died, in 1387, his financial fortunes worsened, possibly through political retaliation for his opposition to the Gloucester cause in the years of Richard II's minority, following Edward's death in 1377. At any rate, soon after Richard came of age, he appointed Chaucer Clerk of the King's Works (1389), in charge of the maintenance and repair of public buildings, parks, bridges, etc. Chaucer resigned this position in 1391 and was appointed deputy forester of a royal forest in Somerset. He retained his residence at Kent and continued his activities in London, however. In 1394 Richard awarded him another life pension, Chaucer having resigned the first one in 1388. He seems to have been in attendance (1395–96) on Henry Bolingbroke, John of Gaunt's son, who deposed Richard in 1399 and who, as Henry IV, increased Chaucer's annuity.

Chaucer's early work is heavily influenced by the French tradition of the poetry of love. It includes the BOOK OF THE DUCHESS and the *Romaunt of the Rose* (probably c1370; a translation, of which only the beginning is now extant, of the French ROMANCE OF THE ROSE), both in octosyllabic couplets. *Saint Cecilia*, later used as the SECOND NUN'S TALE, was probably written about 1373; most of the trage-dies incorporated into the MONK'S TALE were written about 1374.

The HOUSE OF FAME and *Anelida and Arcite*, written about six years later, are considered transitional works, for they begin to show the influence of Italian literature, although they are still essentially in the French tradition. Soon afterward Chaucer translated as *Boece* the CONSOLA-TION OF PHILOSOPHY by Boethius. About the same period, he wrote the PARLIAMENT OF FOWLS and, within a few years, *Palamon and Arcite*, later adapted as the KNIGHT'S TALE, as well as TROILUS AND CRISEYDE and the LEGEND OF GOOD WOMEN. This is called his period of Italian influ-ence.

His period of maturity is considered to begin in 1387, with the writing of the *General Prologue* to the unfinished CANTERBURY TALES. He certainly worked on them through 1394 and probably until his death. In addition, he revised some of his earlier work and wrote the *Treatise on the Astrolabe*. There are also sixteen short poems, written at various periods in his career, in different stanzaic forms, and five poems of doubtful authorship.

In the early 1370s Chaucer began to abandon the octo-syllabic couplets of his early works—although he used the

form once more in the *House of Fame*—largely in favor of RHYME ROYAL, although he also tried eight- and nine-line stanza forms. In the mid-1380s he first began to use the decasyllabic couplet, probably in *Palamon and Arcite* (although it was possibly first written in stanzaic form and then adapted for *The Knight's Tale*) and certainly in the *Legend of Good Women*. This is the first known English use of the decasyllabic couplet, which Chaucer then used for most of the *Canterbury Tales* and which evolved into the heroic couplet.

Chaucerian roundel A variation of the French RONDEL form, first written by CHAUCER. The Chaucerian roundel is characterized by the repetition of the first line as a refrain at the end of the second and third stanzas. It has ten lines, and its rhyme scheme, A being the refrain, is A-b-b, a-b-A, a-b-b-A.

chauvinism Blind and pugnacious patriotism of an exaggerated kind; unreasoning jingoism. The term comes from the name of Nicholas Chauvin, a soldier of the French Republic and Empire, who was madly devoted to NAPOLEON I and his cause. He became a familiar type in a number of 19th-century plays, and his name became synonymous with bellicose patriotism. In the 1960s, the term *male chauvinism*, describing an attitude that insists on the notion of masculine superiority, was given currency by the women's liberation movement.

Chayefsky, Paddy [Sidney] (1923–1981) Amer-ican playwright and screenwriter. An extraordinary ear for dialogue and a concern with the dehumanization of con-temporary society mark all of Chayefsky's work. *Marty* (1953), a TV play about a romance between two lonely people in the Bronx, brought Chayefsky to public atten-tion. His first Broadway play, *Middle of the Night* (1956), about a middle-class Jewish love affair, also began as a tele-vision script. His next three plays were *The Tenth Man* (1959), *Gideon* (1961), and *The Passion of Josef D.* (1964), a grimly satirical burlesque-revue about STALIN. Chayefsky also wrote the screenplays for *The Americanization of Emily* (1964), *The Hospital* (1971), and *Network* (1976), a satire of contemporary America as reflected in the infight-ing at a major TV network. His novel *Altered States* (1978), a science fiction thriller in which a scientist's quest for truth leads him through drug-induced states to mystical probings of consciousness, was filmed in 1980.

Cheeryble brothers In Charles Dickens's novel NICHOLAS NICKLEBY, two brothers, Ned and Charles. Wealthy, self-made London merchants, they are ever ready to help those struggling against the buffets of fortune.

Cheever, John (1912–1982) American short-story writer and novelist. Much of Cheever's writing is character-ized by subtle, ironic attacks on the immorality of affluent suburbia. His stories, many of which originally appeared in THE NEW YORKER, have been collected in such books as *The Enormous Radio* (1953), *The Housebreaker of Shady*

Hill (1958), *The Brigadier and the Golf Widow* (1964), and *The World of Apples* (1973). Many of the best known are assembled chronologically in *The Stories of John Cheever* (1978). Cheever's best-selling novel *The Wapshot Chronicle* (1957) was followed by *The Wapshot Scandal* (1964) and *Bullet Park* (1969).

Although his novels were often considered less successful than his stories, the appearance of *Falconer* (1977) firmly established Cheever as a novelist of the first rank. In *Falconer*, Cheever brings his hero out of the swimming pools and the well-kept lawns of suburbia and sets him in jail, as an apparent fratricide. In a strikingly different style, he confronts his well-used metaphor of confinement and isolation. In 1985 his daughter Susan Cheever published *Home Before Dark: A Personal Memoir of John Cheever.*

Cheka   The secret police body established in 1917 in Russia to guard against counterrevolutionary activity. The name is an abbreviation for "Extraordinary Commission for the Combat of Counterrevolution, Sabotage, and Breech of Duty by Officials." In 1922 it was replaced by the GPU, or State Political Administration, which shortly thereafter became the OGPU (United State Political Administration). In 1934 secret police duties were taken over by the NKVD (People's Commissariat of Internal Affairs). In 1946 this body was changed to the MVD (Ministry of Internal Affairs). After 1946, the Soviet security service was placed in the hands of the KGB (Committee of State Security).

Chekhov, Anton Pavlovich (1860–1904)   Russian playwright and short-story writer, noted for his masterful short stories and lyrical dramas. Chekhov was born in Taganrog, in the south of Russia, the third of six children. He was the son of a merchant and the grandson of an ex-serf who had purchased his freedom. Chekhov attended secondary school in Taganrog and in 1879 enrolled in the School of Medicine at the University of Moscow. He graduated in 1884. While at the university, Chekhov had to earn money to help support his large family. Following the example of his older brother Aleksandr, he began contributing stories, short sketches, and jokes to journals and papers. Many of these early stories were published under pen names, such as Antosha Chekhonte Ch. and The Doctor Without Patients. *Skazki Melpomeny (Tales of Melpomene*, 1884) was the first published volume of Chekhov's stories. Other early collections of tales are *Pyotrye rasskazy (Motley Tales*, 1886) and *V sumerkakh (In the Twilight*, 1887).

Chekhov's work attracted the attention of the writer Dmitry GRIGOROVICH, who encouraged the young author to continue writing and introduced him to Aleksey Suvorin, publisher of *Novoye vremya*, a leading St. Petersburg daily. The more secure financial position offered by this connection enabled Chekhov to pay more attention to improving the quality of his stories. The number of stories written each year fell steadily, but the artistic quality of the work improved, and Chekhov's reputation grew.

In 1890 Chekhov made a trip to the prison island of Sakhalin, in the Far East. His observations and experiences are related in *Ostrovo Sakhalina (Sakhalin Island*, 1893). He made the trip despite his weakened condition from the tuberculosis that had appeared while he was still a student at the university. The whole of Chekhov's short life was a constant struggle against the steady advance of the disease. After his return to Russia, Chekhov took part in relief work during the 1892 famine. He then bought a small estate at Melikhovo, not far from Moscow, and moved there with his family. While living at Melikhovo, Chekhov created some of his best-known works, including the tales WARD No. 6, "Uchitel slovestnosti" ("The Teacher of Literature," 1894), MY LIFE, and PEASANTS. During this period, he also produced two of his major plays, THE SEAGULL and UNCLE VANYA. *The Seagull* was first performed in St. Petersburg in 1896. It was so badly received that Chekhov vowed to give up playwriting. Two years later, however, the drama was put on with great success by the newly formed Moscow Art Theatre. Chekhov's play was so important in establishing the reputation of the new repertory theatre that the directors made a gull the emblem of the company.

In 1898 his failing health forced Chekhov to move to the milder southern climate of Yalta, in the Crimea. Here he often met with the writers Maksim GORKY and Count Leo TOLSTOY. From this time until the end of his life, Chekhov's creative activity was centered mainly in drama. The few major stories of these later years were "Dama s sobachkoi" ("The Lady with the Dog," 1898), IN THE RAVINE, "Arkhiverei" ("The Bishop," 1902), and "Nevesta" ("Bethrothed," 1903).

In 1901 Chekhov married Olga Knipper, a Moscow Art Theatre actress. The couple lived apart much of the time, because Chekhov's ill health forced him to remain in the warmer climate at Yalta. During this period, Chekhov wrote for the Art Theatre his two famous plays THE CHERRY ORCHARD and THE THREE SISTERS.

Chekhov's failing health induced doctors to send him to the health resort at Badenweiler, Germany, in 1904. He died there in July.

The main theme of Chekhov's prose fiction is the pathos of life caused by the inability of human beings to respond to or even communicate with one another and the pervading mood of sadness and hopelessness arising from this situation. This characteristic theme is clearly seen in A DREARY STORY, which is usually regarded as the first work of Chekhov's mature period, that is, after his comic and satirical stories. Chekhov was equally adept at creating a lyrical atmosphere, engendered by man's response to nature and untouched by the pain of relations as they exist between people. His most successful story of this type is

"Step" ("The Steppe," 1888), describing a long trip across the plains, as experienced by a young boy on his way to school in a distant town.

Chekhov is famed as a master of the short story. Although some of his best prose pieces are almost novel-length, the stories, as well as his better-known short works, achieve their effect with a minimum of artistic means. All of Chekhov's best work is an illustration of his dictum: "Conciseness is the sister of talent."

Chekhov's plays deal with the passing of the vitality of the Russian landed gentry. His characters, helpless before the changes taking place in 19th-century Russia, take refuge in elaborate, improbable dreams of renewed prosperity. His plots are simple, mere outlines for the creation of atmosphere and delineation of character. The result is a group of plays combining comedy, pathos, anticlimax, and digression in a wholly natural effect that seems to belie the careful workmanship of the dramatist. *Ivanov* (1887) and the four major plays already mentioned are among the finest in the modern repertory. His shorter plays include *Medved* (*The Bear*, 1888), *Tragik ponevole* (*A Tragedian in Spite of Himself*, 1889), *Svadba* (*The Wedding*, 1889), *Na bolshoi doroge* (*On the High Road*, 1884), *Yubilei* (*The Jubilee*, 1891), *Predlozheniye* (*The Proposal*, 1888), and *Lebedinaya pesnya* (1887).

Chemins de la liberté, Les   See ROADS TO FREEDOM, THE.

Chénier, André Marie de (1762–1794)   French poet, often considered the greatest of 18th-century France. Chénier's *Bucoliques* and, to a lesser extent, his *Elégies* reflect his early love and remarkable understanding of Greek antiquity. At first sympathetic with the French Revolution, he was later horrified at the excesses of the Jacobins and wrote pamphlets denouncing them. He was arrested and guillotined by order of ROBESPIERRE, whom he had attacked. During his imprisonment, he wrote, on bits of smuggled paper, his satiric and bitter *Iambes* against his persecutors, and his last, most famous ode, *La Jeune Captive*, inspired by a fellow victim. His philosophical poetry (e.g., *L'Invention*) gives poetic expression to the scientific ideas of his age. Most of his works were published posthumously in 1819. His life inspired Giordano's opera *Andrea Chénier* (1896).

Chernyshevsky, Nikolay Gavrilovich (1828–1889)   Russian critic and editor. For three years after graduation from the university at St. Petersburg, Chernyshevsky was a schoolteacher in his native Saratov. In 1853 he returned to St. Petersburg and began his journalistic career on *Sovremennik* (*The Contemporary*), which he turned into the period's leading radical publication. Chernyshevsky became the chief spokesman for the radical wing in literature; in their critical writings, he and his younger colleague DOBROLYUBOV gave further emphasis to the social aspect of literature, which the renowned critic

BELINSKY had brought to light. Chernyshevsky supplied an example of the literature he praised in his didactic novel *Chto delat?* (*What Is To Be Done?*, 1863), in which he expounded his ideas of how the true revolutionary should think and behave. Though the work is more of an ideological tract than a novel, it suited the mood of the times and attained wide popularity. In the Soviet Union, it is now regarded as a revolutionary classic. Chernyshevsky was arrested in 1862 for revolutionary activities; he was sentenced to seven years at hard labor with twenty years of exile in Siberia. In 1883 he was permitted to leave Siberia because of his health. He returned to Russia and lived out his life in Saratov.

Cherry Orchard, The (Vishnovy sad, 1904)   A play by Anton CHEKHOV. Its four acts portray the declining fortunes of the Ranevskys, a landowning family, who are about to lose their estate and their beloved cherry orchard. Poor management, neglect, and impracticality have brought the family to the point of bankruptcy, but no one is able to act to head off the disaster. The suggestion of the practical businessman Lopakhin that the family chop down the orchard and build houses on the land is met with horror. For the Ranevskys, the orchard represents the pleasant past, before the mysterious forces of the changing times threatened their idyllic existence. The estate is finally sold from under the hapless family. Lopakhin buys the land and proceeds to carry out his plan to destroy the orchard and erect houses. As the family sadly prepares to depart, the sound of an axe chopping down a tree is heard from offstage.

The play, regarded as one of Chekhov's finest dramatic works, is both a penetrating study of the changing way of life in Russia at the end of the 19th century and a vivid depiction of what the change means to the people involved. The stage portraits of the Ranevskys, with their inability to do anything to save themselves, and of Lopakhin, the representative of a new rising class in society, are masterpieces of dramatic creation.

Cheshire cat   In Lewis Carroll's ALICE'S ADVENTURES IN WONDERLAND, a creature that has the ability to vanish at will, its grin being the last thing to go.

Chesnutt, Charles W[addell] (1858–1932)   American novelist. Chesnutt, sometimes called "the first Negro novelist," was a teacher, newspaperman and lawyer. His first story, "The Goophered Grapevine," appeared in *The Atlantic* in 1887. His first book, *The Conjure Woman* (1899), centered on Uncle Julius McAdoo, a character not unlike Joel Chandler HARRIS's Uncle Remus. His later books dealt with race prejudice, the best known being *The Wife of His Youth and Other Stories of the Color Line* (1899). In 1928 Chesnutt received the Spingarn gold medal for his pioneer work in depicting the struggles of black Americans.

Chester Cycle   See MYSTERY PLAYS.

Chesterfield, Philip Dormer Stanhope, 4th earl of (1694–1773)   Statesman and man of letters. A friend of Alexander POPE and an important patron of letters, Lord Chesterfield was unsuccessful in his belated attempt to patronize Samuel Johnson's DICTIONARY OF THE ENGLISH LANGUAGE after it had been completed. Johnson's rebuke is famous:

Is not a patron, My Lord, one who looks with unconcern on a Man struggling in the water and when he has reached ground encumbers him with help?

Johnson's comment on Chesterfield's *Letters* to his natural son Philip Stanhope is equally well known: "They teach the morals of a whore, and the manners of a dancing master." The judgment is too severe. Written between 1737 and 1768, Lord Chesterfield's *Letters to His Son* (1774) form one of the classic portraits of an ideal 18th-century gentleman.

Chesterton, G[ilbert] K[eith] (1874–1936) English journalist, essayist, novelist, and poet; author of biography, history, literary criticism, and polemical works. Like his friend Hilaire BELLOC, Chesterton was a propagandist of his Catholicism and his conservative political views (the two were referred to as Chesterbelloc). Chesterton became a Catholic in 1922, but he had always been a traditionalist, admiring the Victorians, romanticizing the Middle Ages, and attacking H. G. Wells and Bernard Shaw. He is best remembered for his essays, such as "On Running after One's Hat" (1908), which are merry and witty, and for such poems as "Lepanto" (1911), which are full of gusto. Sometimes he conveyed his serious ideas in fantastic novels, as in *The Napoleon of Notting Hill* (1904), *The Man Who Was Thursday* (1908), and a series of detective novels, beginning with *The Innocence of Father Brown* (1911), in which the priest Father Brown is sleuth. Chesterton wrote the fine study *The Victorian Age in Literature* (1913). Among his polemical works are *Heretics* (1905), *Orthodoxy* (1908), *What's Wrong with the World?* (1910), and *The Everlasting Man* (1925), an outline of history.

Chevy Chase   One of the oldest ballads in English. There is some evidence that it may have grown out of the Battle of Otterborne, and a Scottish version exists earlier than 1549. It is included in Percy's RELIQUES OF ANCIENT ENGLISH POETRY.

Chicago Group (or Chicago Renaissance)   A group of American writers. From about 1912 to about 1925, Chicago seemed well on its way to becoming the literary capital of the U.S. Although many of the writers dealt with Middle Western subjects, the literary activity also had a cosmopolitan scope, especially through such literary magazines as Harriet Monroe's POETRY and Margaret Anderson's *Little Review*. The term is variously used to include such writers as H. B. FULLER, Theodore DREISER, Ben HECHT, Sherwood ANDERSON, Edgar Lee MASTERS, and Carl SANDBURG.

Chichikov, Pavel Ivanovich   The central character of Nikolay GOGOL's novel DEAD SOULS. Plump and prosperous-looking, appearing as respectable as he claims to be, Chichikov is actually an unctuous swindler. A totally mediocre man, whose only abilities are a knowledge of social form and a talent for flattery, he almost succeeds in his dishonest scheme because he allows the people he swindles to believe they are swindling him.

Chikamatsu Monzaemon (1653–1725)   Japanese dramatist. Early in his career, Chikamatsu wrote for the KABUKI stage, but later he turned to writing of puppet plays (BUNRAKU), producing such masterpieces as *sonezaki shinjū* (1703; tr *Love Suicides at Sonezaki*, 1955), *Kokusenya kassen* (1715; tr *Battles of Coxinga*, 1951), and *Shinjū ten no Amijima* (1720; tr *Love Suicide at Amijima*, 1953). He was especially skilled in creating tense dramatic situations in which two conflicting emotions, like love and honor, clash head-on within the play's character. Chikamatsu was also largely responsible for developing the *sewamono* (contemporary drama on contemporary themes) in the JŌRURI repertoire.

Child, Francis James (1825–1896)   American philologist. Professor of Middle English at Harvard, Child was an authority on Chaucer and his contemporaries. For many years Child occupied himself with the collection in eight volumes of *English and Scottish Popular Ballads* (1857–58). It was revised from 1883 to 1898, and issued in ten volumes under the title *The English and Scottish Popular Ballads*. This most authoritative work in its field printed 305 distinct English and Scottish ballads, as many as possible from manuscript sources, with varying versions and exhaustive critical comment and notes.

childe   A medieval title of honor. In times of chivalry, noble youths who were on probation as candidates for knighthood were called *infants, valets, damoysels, bacheliers,* and *childe.*

Childe Harold's Pilgrimage (Cantos I and II published 1812; Canto III, 1816; Canto IV, 1818)   A long narrative poem in SPENSERIAN STANZAS by Lord BYRON. The romantically melancholy hero, Childe Harold, disillusioned with a life devoted to the pursuit of pleasure, embarks on a solitary pilgrimage through Portugal, Spain, the Ionian Islands, Albania, Greece, Belgium, the Rhine valley, the Alps, and the Jura. The poet evokes the events and people associated with each place: Rousseau and Julie, Napoleon, the battles of Waterloo and Spain, the bondage of Greece. In the fourth canto, Byron drops the device of the hero to speak directly to the reader, describing the great men and historical associations of the Italian cities. The poem satisfied the popular craving for descriptive travel literature of Byron's day and did much to establish the poet's fame.

Childerness, The   See HUMAN AGE, THE.

Childe Rowland   Younger brother of "the fair Burd Ellen" in the old Scottish ballad. Guided by the enchanter Merlin, Rowland undertakes to bring back his sister from Elfland, whither the fairies have carried her, and succeeds in his perilous exploit.

Childhood (Detstvo, 1913–1914)   The first volume of an autobiographical trilogy by Maksim GORKY. The other two volumes are V lyudakh (My Apprenticeship, 1916) and Moi universitety (My Universities, 1923). Of the three volumes, published together in English translation as Autobiography (1953), Childhood is the richest in insight and incident, chiefly because of the memorable portrait in it of Gorky's grandmother, Akulina Ivanovna Kashirina.

Childhood, Boyhood, and **Youth** (Detstvo, Otrochestvo, Yunost'; 1852, 1854, 1857)   An autobiographical trilogy by Count Leo TOLSTOY. Childhood was the first of Tolstoy's works to receive wide attention. The descriptions of life on a provincial estate are among the best depictions of nature in Russian literature.

Children of Adam (1860–1867)   A group of poems in Walt Whitman's LEAVES OF GRASS. The poems praise physical love and procreation; Whitman claims that Adam's children have lost the Garden of Eden through the degradation of their senses. Body and soul are not separate, but one. "Lusty, phallic," Whitman is the unashamed "chanter of Adamic songs."

Children of Heracles, The (Heracleidae, 427? BC)   A tragedy by EURIPIDES. Eurystheus, the cruel king of Argos who had forced HERACLES to perform the twelve labors, has continued to persecute the hero's children after his death. Led by old Iolaus, Heracles' trusted friend, they win the protection of Demophon, king of Athens. Iolaus, made young again for one day, fights with the Athenians against the Argives. Eurystheus is captured and put to death.

Written at the height of the Peloponnesian War, the play praises Athens as a champion of freedom and points out that Sparta, now her enemy, should be grateful to the city that had defended the children of Heracles, from whom the Spartans claimed descent.

Children's Hour, The (1860)   A poem by Henry Wadsworth LONGFELLOW. It is devoted to the poet's three daughters by his first wife, Mary Potter.

Children's Hour, The (1936)   A play by Lillian HELLMAN, detailing the psychologically devastating effects when two boarding-school teachers are accused of lesbianism by a malicious and unbalanced student. It was Hellman's first Broadway success and was filmed in 1962.

children's literature   Generally, a category of literature written and designed specifically for the entertainment, enrichment, and/or education of young people. The field embraces all literary genres and all manner of subject matter. Works are frequently shorter and are simpler in vocabulary and syntax than in adult literature; they can include experiences familiar to young people or

deal purely in the realm of fantasy. Illustration is often considered to be either coequal with or an essential supplement to the text, particularly in books intended to be read to the very young. Before the advent of printing, both children and adults enjoyed an oral tradition of ballads, tales, legends, epics, and fables. Apart from Malory's MORTE D'ARTHUR, which was widely popular among young and old alike, children of the Middle Ages partook of little more than the instructive Latin texts inscribed by the great monastic teachers. Still primarily for didactic purposes, there appeared various "courtesy books" during the Renaissance and the somber Puritan primers of the 17th century. Orbis sensualium pictus (1658; tr The Visible World, 1659) by Jan Comenius is considered to be the first picture book for children. Numerous imitations followed. With the 18th century came widely read CHAPBOOKS, which often included such popular folk tales as TOM THUMB, "Jack the Giant Killer," and "Dick Whittington and His Cat." At the same time, the classics ROBINSON CRUSOE and GULLIVER'S TRAVELS, originally intended for adults, were eagerly devoured by young readers.

The modern concept of children's literature, however, really began in the mid-18th century when John NEWBERY (who was later to open the first children's bookshop in London) published A Pretty Little Pocket Book (1744). Newbery's inexpensive and well-illustrated publications —including Mother Goose Rhymes (1765) and The Renowned History of Little GOODY TWO-SHOES—advanced the notion that literature could be written for the sheer enjoyment and amusement of juvenile readers. Newbery's recognition of the special needs and delights of children was not embraced by all 18th-century writers. Such books as The History of Sanford and Merton (1783–89) and stories by Maria EDGEWORTH were solemn and still didactic in tone.

Children's books of the 19th century tended to present models of good behavior, as with the Rollo books by Jacob Abbott (1803–79), the Peter Parley series by Samuel Goodrich (1793–1860), and Martha Farquharson's ELSIE DINSMORE books. Nonetheless, there did emerge such notably different books as Thomas Bailey Aldrich's THE STORY OF A BAD BOY and Twain's The Adventures of TOM SAWYER. Alcott's LITTLE WOMEN presented realistic, even rollicking views of childhood, as did HANS BRINKER OR THE SILVER SKATES and HEIDI. The 19th century also marked the emergence of the popular folk-tale collections of Hans Christian ANDERSEN and the brothers GRIMM, among others. The latter half of the century saw the publication of such classic fantasies as Lewis Carroll's ALICE'S ADVENTURES IN WONDERLAND, George MACDONALD's At the Back of the North Wind (1871), and Lorenzini's PINOCCHIO.

Children's magazines also began to flourish at the end of the 19th century. In England, the first real children's magazine, The Charm (1852), emphasized the imaginative over the didactic, but it lasted only two years. The successful *Aunt Judy's Magazine* (1868), edited by "Mrs. Gatty," and featuring stories by "Mrs. Emery," emphasized home and family life. In America, *The Youth's Companion* (1827–29) merged with *The American Boy* and ran until 1941. Horace Scudder (1838–1902) brought out *The Riverside Magazine* in 1867. Although the magazine ran only three years, Scudder broke new ground by seeking the best in writing and illustration and by launching the *Riverside Literature Series for Young People*. The best and most influential of the children's magazines was ST. NICHOLAS, edited by Mary Mapes Dodge from 1873 until her death in 1905.

By the 20th century, the proliferation of literature for children extended to every genre. Beatrix POTTER's animal stories became classics, as did Kenneth Grahame's WIND IN THE WILLOWS, P. L. TRAVERS's *Mary Poppins* (1934), and E. B. WHITE's *Charlotte's Web* (1952). The tradition of verse written specifically for children in the 19th century by Edward LEAR and Robert Louis Stevenson in A CHILD'S GARDEN OF VERSES was continued in the 20th century by Walter DE LA MARE. Folk tales from all over the world were superbly retold in such books as *The King's Drum and Other African Tales* (1962) by Harold Courlander and in *The Fools of Chelm and Their History* (1973) by Isaac Bashevis SINGER. Along with these appeared innumerable books of biography, SCIENCE FICTION, adventure, history, and drama. The latter half of the 20th century saw an increased number of books for children dealing realistically and directly with such contemporary social and political problems as divorce, racism, drug and alcohol abuse, and environmental deterioration.

Child's Garden of Verses, A (1885)   A small collection of verses by Robert Louis STEVENSON. Written expressly for children and from a child's point of view, they have nevertheless delighted adults as much as children since they were written. Among the favorite titles are "My Shadow" and "The Lamplighter."

Chillingworth, Roger   The vengeful husband of Hester Prynne in Hawthorne's THE SCARLET LETTER.

Chimaera   One of the monstrous offspring of TYPHON and Echidna. The chimaera is generally represented as having the head of a lion, the body of a goat, and the tail of a serpent. It was killed by BELLEROPHON, mounted (in most versions) on the winged horse Pegasus.

Ch'in   The first Chinese empire (221–206 BC), it succeeded the CHOU dynasty. Ch'in Shih-huang, the first emperor of the Ch'in, unified the country administratively, standardized weights and measures and the writing system, and completed the Great Wall. The thought of the Legalist School prevailed during this brief but important dynasty. It was followed by the HAN dynasty.

Chinese literature   The earliest examples of Chinese writing are found etched on bone or cast in bronze and are over three thousand years old. These short inscrip-

tions, used in divination or in commemoration of important events, demonstrate the unique qualities of the Chinese language and writing system even at this early date. The ancient symbols, which grew out of pictures and visual metaphors, are independent of the sound of the word they represent and are in most cases the same as in modern Chinese, once allowances are made for certain changes in their shape. These old inscriptions, however, are of more interest as examples of paleography than as literature.

The first anthology of Chinese poetry, the BOOK OF ODES (*Shih ching*, 8th to 6th centuries BC), appeared during the CHOU dynasty (1027 BC–256 BC). Another anthology, the ELEGIES OF CH'U (*Ch'u tz'u*, 4th to 3rd century BC), originated on the southern edges of the Chinese cultural area; its impassioned tone contrasts sharply with the restraint of the earlier *Odes* and has had an abiding influence on later writing. Two features of this and all Chinese verse are the use of rhyme and a metrical system based on syllable count. The latter half of the Chou dynasty was a period of social change and military conflict, an uncertain environment that seems to have stimulated a great outpouring of philosophical thought. CONFUCIUS and Mencius (372–289 BC) stressed a conservative political and moral theory whose ethical and didactic views dominated literary thinking until modern times. The Taoists LAO TZU and CHUANG TZU, with their skepticism about government and their concept of the relativism of moral values, seem to contradict the Confucian vision. In the manner of Chinese eclecticism, though, these views came to be seen as complementary aspects of a whole philosophy of living. The CH'IN dynasty (221 BC–206 BC) unified China and attempted to suppress all philosophies except that of the Legalist School, but the brief rule of the dynasty allowed many destroyed texts to be reconstructed. During the HAN dynasty (206 BC–AD 220) the writing of history became one of the principal responsibilities of government. Ssu-ma Ch'ien's (145? BC–90? BC) monumental history, the *Shih chi*, not only set the pattern for subsequent official histories but also established many of the conventions used by later writers of fiction. After the Han dynasty, the period of interregnum known as the SIX DYNASTIES (222–589) was another time of constant warfare and great historical changes, of the spread and domestication of BUDDHISM and of literary theorizing and criticism, which began to show some independence from Confucian ideas.

By the time of the T'ANG dynasty (618–907) the new surge of cultural and political accomplishments had been well prepared by the previous age. The T'ang was the golden age of poetry, with such figures as WANG WEI, LI PO, TU FU, and PO CHÜ-I. It is also the era in which the writing of fiction became well established. Ch'an Buddhism, a native Chinese sect with many concepts similar to those of the Taoists, had great influence among literary men. After the persecutions of 845, however, the Buddhist faith never again played an important role in politics. Lyric poetry (*shih*) reached its peak during the T'ang, and, although poets continued to write in the old forms, creative energy flowed mostly to the new musical genres of the SUNG (960–1279) and YUAN dynasties (1279–1368). There are some examples of fiction and dramatic entertainment which date to the T'ang, but the real growth of these forms followed the establishment of large urban centers and the spread of literacy to the merchant classes of the Sung and Yuan periods. The purely written literary language of the scholar-official class was not suitable for these new types of writing. Instead, the spoken colloquial language of the times became the medium for stories, novels, and plays. This literature was read by all levels of society but never had the sanction of Confucian orthodoxy. Colloquial fiction was thus not a completely respectable field of activity or study until the 20th century. Still, many great novels were written, among the most famous being ROMANCE OF THE THREE KINGDOMS, JOURNEY TO THE WEST, THE GOLDEN LOTUS, and THE DREAM OF THE RED CHAMBER. Most of these works show deficiencies in plotting and characterization when compared to European novels, but their unofficial status and the fact that they were often banned partly explain this. *The Dream of the Red Chamber*, however, in its profound and moving psychological depiction of its characters, is fully the equal of fictional art anywhere. The Ch'ing also saw great activity in literary and philological scholarship and in the making of encyclopedias and compendia of all sorts. Since the literary revolution of the early 1920s, in which HU SHIH played such an important role, there has been considerable ferment and controversy in literature. Writers turned their backs on tradition and set out to create a new literature based on Western models and on the use of the spoken vernacular. The short story and essay are of particularly high quality. The names of LU HSUN, PA CHIN, and LAO SHE acquired some renown in the Western world.

Ch'ing (or Manchu)   A series of rulers of China (1644–1911), established by the Manchus, a non-Chinese but strongly sinicized people who conquered the native MING dynasty and founded the Ch'ing. In its early years, the Ch'ing was one of China's most powerful and glorious periods, but, under the weight of internal corruption and encroachment by Western colonial powers, it collapsed and was replaced by the Chinese Republic on January 1, 1912.

Chirico, Giorgio de (1888–1978)   Greek-born Italian painter. Chirico's most well-known work was done in the years 1911 to 1920 and exerted a strong influence on SURREALISM. He is known for his enigmatic landscapes, in which solitary, mannequinlike figures and elements of classical architecture create a feeling of foreboding by means of exaggerated perspective, lengthened shadows, and barren space. His later paintings, often featuring classical

subject matter, had been dismissed as academic but received increased attention following his death.

Chiron   A learned centaur. Chiron taught music, medicine, and hunting to ACHILLES, HERACLES, Asklepios, JASON, and many other heroes. A son of Cronos and Philyra, he is often spoken of as a king or leader of the Thessalian centaurs. Accidentally wounded by one of Heracles' poisoned arrows, Chiron gave up his immortality to PROMETHEUS in order to find relief from the unbearable pain in death.

chivalry   The system of customs and conventions connected with knighthood in the Middle Ages. Derived from the French word *chevalier*, meaning "horseman" or "knight," chivalry was originally associated with the business of recruiting knights for the purpose of making war. It came to include the curriculum of training the young knight to fight, to hunt, to serve his lord, to govern his own vassals, and ultimately it evolved into that courtly ideal in which the true knight was not only courageous and skillful in war but also generous, pious, and courteous. When the championing of the weak began to be emphasized as part of the ideal, chivalry became as important in peace as in war, and, among other things, the tournament flourished. Another component of the chivalric code was the ideal of COURTLY LOVE, an element that further refined the knight by requiring that he be poet and musician and that he be dedicated to some lady of his choice.

Chloe   The shepherdess beloved by Daphnis in the pastoral romance of Longus, entitled DAPHNIS AND CHLOE. Hence Chloe has become a generic name among romance writers and pastoral poets for a rustic maiden, not always of the artless variety.

Chopin, Frédéric [François] (1810–1849) Composer and pianist. Born near Warsaw of a French father and Polish mother, Chopin spent much of his career in France, where he became the outstanding pianist and composer for piano of the romantic era. His divided heritage was apparent both in his residence and his music. Nearly all his compositions are for piano; he elevated such dances as mazurkas and polonaises to the level of serious music. Chopin circulated among a lively group of artists and aristocrats in Paris and eventually became involved in a ten-year liaison with the writer George SAND. His music was admired greatly by Robert SCHUMANN, who was helpful in establishing his success. Chopin died, at thirty-nine, of tuberculosis, after a long period of weakness and suffering.

Chopin, Kate [O'Flaherty] (1851–1904)   American short-story writer and novelist. Chopin is known for her portrayal of Creole life in Louisiana. Her best short fiction was included in two collections of stories: *Bayou Folk* (1894) and *A Night in Acadie* (1897). Her last novel, *The Awakening* (1899), a tale of extramarital love and miscegenation, created a storm of criticism when it was first published. Ignored for over fifty years, the book was rediscovered in the 1960s and celebrated for its open treatment of a woman's search for self-understanding.

Choquette, Robert (1905–   )   U.S.-born Canadian poet. Although Choquette wrote a long radio series, *Métropole*, and some rural novels, his greatest achievement is his poetry. In his first book of poems, *A travers les vents* (1925), he showed a passionate feeling for the north country, more lyrical and less morbid than much Canadian writing about that region. The poems in his second book, *Metropolitan Museum* (1931), contrast the serene art in the museum with the frantic life of the city around it. His other works include *Poésies nouvelles* (1933) and *Suite marine* (1953).

choragos   In early Greek classical drama, the leader of the chorus. See CORYPHAEUS.

chorus   A group of singers and dancers who performed in ancient Greek religious festivals and dramatic performances. The chorus later became an essential part of Greek tragedy. Used differently by different dramatists, it generally represented the voice of tradition and served as a commentator on the action. The role of the chorus became more subordinate, and, in Elizabethan drama, it was often taken by a single actor. T. S. Eliot used it effectively in MURDER IN THE CATHEDRAL. The term is also applied to a refrain repeated after a stanza of a poem or song.

Chou   The second Chinese dynasty (c1027–256 BC). Following the SHANG dynasty, the Chou was the classic age of Chinese civilization. The BOOK OF ODES, in literature, and the thought of CONFUCIUS, LAO TZU, CHUANG TZU, and Mencius (372–289 BC) all emerged in this period of great philosophical activity. The royal house of Chou was destroyed by the feudal state of CH'IN, which later united all China in 221 BC.

Chouans, Les (1829)   A historical novel by Honoré de BALZAC. His first literary success, it now forms part of LA COMÉDIE HUMAINE. The heroine is the beautiful spy Marie de Verneuil, and the hero is the marquis de Montauran, a Royalist leader. The Chouans themselves were French peasant insurgents, supporters of the royalist cause at the time of the Revolution. Jean Cottereau, their first leader, was nicknamed *Chouan*—a corruption of the French *chatuant*, "screech owl"—because of his secret call in times of danger.

Chrétien de Troyes (fl 1160–1190)   French poet at the court of Marie de Champagne and Philip of Flanders. Chrétien wrote some of the earliest Arthurian romances, including EREC ET ENIDE, *Cligés*, and *Yvain, ou le chevalier au Lion*. Two of his most important works are *Lancelot, ou le chevalier de la charrette* (*Launcelot, or the Knight of the Cart*) and *Perceval, ou le conte du Graal* (*Perceval, or the Story of the Grail*), which were left incomplete at his death. *Lancelot* deals with the adventures of the Arthurian LAUNCELOT, and *Perceval* (see PERCIVAL) is the earliest literary version of the Grail legend. *Guillaume*

d'Angleterre, a version of the life of St. Eustace, has been attributed to him by some scholars.

Christian   (1) A follower of Jesus. The first use of the word occurred at Antioch (Acts 11:26).

(2) The pilgrim hero of Bunyan's PILGRIM'S PROGRESS. Christian's journey from the City of Destruction to the Celestial City forms the substance of Part I.

Christian Science   See EDDY, MARY BAKER.

Christie, Agatha (born Agatha Mary Clarissa Miller, 1890–1976)   English detective-story writer, the most widely translated author in English. Author of over eighty novels, Christie also wrote romantic fiction under the pseudonym Mary Westmacott. Her stock-in-trade, however, was the detective novel, usually featuring her idiosyncratic sleuths Hercule POIROT, a vain but clever Belgian, or Miss Jane Marple, a shrewd and elderly spinster with an endless fascination for murder. Public interest in Christie was stirred up when as a young woman she vanished; the disappearance and reemergence were never fully explained. Christie had a particular interest in abnormal psychology, although her characters are generally caricatures of the provincial leisure class, tended by a variety of servants, gardeners, and nurses. The perennial favorites among her works are *The Mysterious Affair at Styles* (1920); *The Murder of Roger Ackroyd* (1926), thought by many to be her most ingenious work; *Murder on the Orient Express* (1934); *And Then There Were None* (1940); and *The Pale Horse* (1961). Several of her stories were adapted to the stage, the most successful being *Mousetrap* (1952), the longest-running play in theatre history, and *Witness for the Prosecution* (1953). *Come, Tell Me How You Live* (1946) and *An Autobiography* (1977) are about her own life.

Christina de Pisan (c1364–c1430)   Italian-born French poet and scholar. Christina de Pisan turned to writing at twenty-five, when she was left a widow with three children, and was probably the first woman since antiquity to earn her livelihood as an author. Her poetry includes love lyrics, a patriotic glorification of JOAN OF ARC, and three longer philosophical poems. Her prose works include *La Cité des dames* (*The City of Ladies*, 1405), largely adapted from BOCCACCIO'S *De claris mulieribus*; treatises on education and history; and two defenses of women (1399, 1400) against the satirical accusations in Jean de Meung's *Roman de la Rose* (see ROMANCE OF THE ROSE).

Christmas, Joe   The protagonist of William Faulkner's LIGHT IN AUGUST. The illegitimate child of Milly Hines and a man supposedly Mexican, Joe is placed in an orphanage by his fanatically religious grandfather, who believes him to be part black. He is adopted by a strict Calvinist couple, who know nothing of his origins. After wandering through the Southwest for several years, Joe arrives in Jefferson, Mississippi, where he has an affair with a white woman, kills her, and becomes the object of a manhunt. At home in neither the world of the whites nor that of the blacks, Joe continually alienates himself from both worlds and rushes to castration and death at the hands of a mob.

Christmas Carol, A (1843)   A Christmas story by Charles DICKENS. The subject is the conversion of Scrooge, "a grasping old sinner," by a series of visions of Christmases past, present, and to come. Scrooge has glimpses of his life as a schoolboy, apprentice, and young lover; of the joyous home of Bob CRATCHIT, his underpaid clerk; and of what his lot would be if he were to die now, heartless and despised. These visions wholly change his nature, and he becomes benevolent and cheerful, loving all and by all beloved. Although Dickens wrote the story partly for the income it would bring, he said afterwards that he laughed and cried over it as he did over no other story.

Christmas Day   The popular English name for the Feast of the Nativity of Jesus Christ, December 25. This date was first set in 336, by the Roman Church, the Eastern Churches having earlier settled on the date of January 6 as the Feast of the EPIPHANY. December 25 was observed in pagan Rome as the festival *Natalis Invicti Solis* ("Birth of the Unconquered Sun"), sacred to the god MITHRAS. Christmas became a great popular festival in the Middle Ages, which led to objections by some of the Reformers. The observance was forbidden in England under the Commonwealth (1644–60) and in Calvinist New England.

Christo   (real name Christo Javacheff, 1935–   ) Hungarian-born American artist. Christo is the creator of environmental artworks on an enormous scale. Early projects involved wrapping and packaging of monuments and buildings, such as *Packed Museum of Contemporary Art* (1969), and even entire geographical sites, such as his *Wrapped Coast, Little Bay, Australia* (1969). He gained international prominence with his *Valley Curtain* (1971), a translucent orange curtain over a quarter of a mile long. His California *Running Fence* (1976) was eighteen feet high and twenty-four miles long, crossing natural and man-made obstructions to create mammoth patterns of light and line.

Christo de espaldas, El (1952)   A novel by Eduardo Caballero Calderón (1910–   ). Written in a realistic, documentary style, this is the story of a young man suspected of political parricide during Colombia's civil wars (1948–58). In a parallel development, a young priest, who has remained neutral in the war, learns the identity of the real murderer in confession. His vow of silence renders him an outcast of the town and of the church. The bishop deprives him of his parish in the belief that "Christ has turned his back" on the priest, but it is the priest who understands that it is men who have turned on Christ.

Christophe, Henri (1767–1820)   King of Haiti. Christophe served as lieutenant to TOUSSAINT L'OUVERTURE in the revolution against the French (1791).

He succeeded Dessalines as head of the government, under the title Henri I. In 1820 a rebellion of his subjects caused him to commit suicide, with a legendary silver bullet.

Christopher, St.   Once a saint and martyr of the Greek and Latin churches, dropped from the liturgical calendar in 1969. *Christopher* means "Christ-bearer." According to legend, he carried a child across a river, and, although a large and strong man, he staggered and nearly fell under a huge weight. The child revealed he was Christ, who bore the weight of the world in his hands. From then on, Christopher devoted his life to serving Christ. He was the patron saint of travelers and the protecting saint against floods, fire, and earthquake. His image was often placed opposite church doors, because it was believed that to see his image kept one free from harm.

Christopher Robin   The son of A. A. MILNE, for whom the POOH books were written. As the only human figure in an idyllic animal world, the child Christopher Robin presides over events as a responsible, benevolent adult. Christopher Milne's book *The Enchanted Places* (1975) is a memoir of the real Christopher Robin and Winnie-the-Pooh.

Christ Stopped at Eboli (Cristo si è fermato a Eboli, 1945; tr 1948)   An autobiographical essay by the writer and painter Carlo Levi (1902–75). The book narrates in an eloquent, moving way the experience and the life the author shared with the peasants of two hamlets in southern Italy, where he had been sent for his "subversive" political activities during the Fascist régime. The book did much to force the world to understand the tragic plight of the regions south of Rome and alleviate the misery of a section of Italy long neglected and exploited for economic or political reasons.

chronicle play   A play employing—sometimes very loosely—historical events as the basis for its action. One of the earliest examples in English is John Bale's *Kynge Johan* (c1548). Among the finest examples are Shakespeare's RICHARD II and HENRY IV and Christopher MARLOWE's *Edward II* (1592).

Chronicles of England, Scotland, and Ireland (1577)   A history by Raphael HOLINSHED. The *Chronicles* was the source of much of the material used in Shakespeare's MACBETH, KING LEAR, and CYMBELINE. The section concerning the history of Scotland is said to be chiefly a translation of *Scotorum Historiae* (1527) by Hector Boece. In 1587 a second and expanded edition was published, but parts of it did not please Queen Elizabeth, and she tried to have it suppressed.

Chronicles I and II   Two OLD TESTAMENT books, originally one book in the Hebrew canon. The Chronicles provide an account of the history of Israel under DAVID and SOLOMON and parallel the material covered in SAMUEL and KINGS. The First Chronicle contains elaborate genealogies that trace the Jewish ancestry back to Adam and tells of the history of David's reign and the honor he brought to the Hebrew people. It ends with David's death and the succession of his son Solomon. The Second Chronicle describes the building of the temple in Jerusalem and praises the wisdom of Solomon, and then follows the history from the reign of REHOBOAM to the destruction of Jerusalem and the Babylonian captivity. The book ends, as the book of EZRA begins, with the charge of CYRUS THE GREAT to restore worship in Jerusalem.

Chrononhotonthologos (1734)   A burlesque of contemporary drama by Henry Carey, subtitled "the Most Tragical Tragedy that was ever Tragedized by any company of Tragedians." The title is the name of the King of Queerumania, the pompous main character, and is used for any bombastic person who delivers inflated address. The play is noted for its frank criticism of the theatre of its day.

Chryseis   In Homer's ILIAD, daughter of Chryses, a priest of APOLLO. Chryseis was famed for her beauty. During the TROJAN WAR, she was taken captive and allotted to AGAMEMNON, king of Argos. When he refused to accept ransom, Chryses evoked a plague, and Agamemnon was forced to let her go.

Chuang Tzu (Chin, "Master Chuang")   A Chinese Taoist text, attributed to and named after Chuang Chou (traditional dates 369–286 BC). Its themes are the primacy of nature over the world of man and his government and the relativity of such concepts as good and evil. It is a work of great poetic and imaginative power. See BUTTERFLY DREAM OF CHUANG TZU, THE; TAOISM.

Chu Hsi (1130–1200)   Chinese Confucian scholar, largely responsible for the Confucian revival (Neo-Confucianism) in the SUNG dynasty. Chu Hsi synthesized, reorganized, and reinterpreted the teachings, adopting elements from BUDDHISM and TAOISM, to form a new Confucian system that became the orthodox philosophy until the establishment of the Republic in 1912. His teachings were of considerable importance in Japan, particularly during the TOKUGAWA period, when they were adopted as the official state philosophy. See CONFUCIANISM.

Chukovskaya, Lidia Korneyevna (1907–   )   Soviet novelist and literary critic. Chukovskaya was born in Helsinki, Finland. Whereas her critical works, including studies of HERZEN and the Decembrists, were published in the Soviet Union, her novels *Opustelyidom* (1966; tr *The Deserted House*, 1967) and *Spusk pod vodu* (1972; tr *Going Under*, 1972) have appeared only abroad. Each novel explores, with great subtlety and incisiveness, the moral and psychological aspects of Stalin's terror campaigns against the intelligentsia.

Ch'un-ch'iu   See SPRING AND AUTUMN ANNALS.

Chung-yung   See MEAN, THE.

Church, Frederic [Edvan] (1826–1900)   American painter. For some twenty years, Church was the lead-ing painter of the HUDSON RIVER SCHOOL. Church's early works exhibit the melodramatic style of his teacher, Thomas COLE. Later works reveal a scientific attention to detail, as well as the dramatic portrayal of the effects of natural light in storms; *Heart of the Andes* (1859) is an important example.

Church, Richard Thomas (1893–1972)   English poet, novelist, and literary critic. Church's books of poetry, in the pastoral tradition, include *Collected Poems* (1948), *The Inheritors* (1957), and *North of Rome* (1960). His prose works include the novels *The Porch* (1937) and *Little Miss Moffatt* (1969) and the autobiographical *Over the Bridge* (1955), *The Golden Sovereign* (1957), and *The Voyage Home* (1964).

Churchill, Charles (1731–1764)   English poet and clergyman, known for his biting satiric verse. Churchill's major works are *The Rosciad* (1761), an attack on London actors and acting, which is often ranked with Pope's *Dunciad*; *The Ghost* (1762), an account of the notorious COCK LANE GHOST episode, ridiculing Samuel Johnson for his interest in it; *The Prophecy of Famine, a Scots Pastoral* (1763), a verse satire voicing English distrust of Scotland; *The Duellist* (1764), a poem defending the political position of John Wilkes and attacking all his detractors, particularly Smollett; *Gotham* (1764), a verse epistle setting forth the "idea of a patriot king" (see Henry ST. JOHN); and *The Candidate* (1764), a poetic attack on the conservative political policies of Cambridge University.

Churchill, Winston (1871–1947)   American novelist, noted for his enormously successful historical romances. Churchill's second novel, RICHARD CARVEL, sold over one million copies. THE CRISIS, *The Crossing* (1904), *Coniston* (1906), and *Mr. Crewe's Career* (1908), about the control of state politics by railroad interests, followed. Churchill's interest in religion and social questions was reflected in his later books: *Inside the Cup* (1913), *A Far Country* (1915), *The Dwelling Place of Light* (1917), and *The Uncharted Way: The Psychology of the Gospel Doctrine* (1940).

Churchill, Sir Winston [Leonard Spencer] (1874–1965)   English statesman and author. A political conservative, though often a maverick confounding party labels, Churchill held many important posts in British government between 1910 and 1955. He is regarded as one of the greatest statesmen of the 20th century. As England's prime minister during World War II, Churchill braced his allies all over the world with his vitality and boldness and his confidence in the capacity of Britain to survive against any odds. He is well known as an orator, particularly for his ability to create memorable phrases that aroused both courage and hope. In a speech in Fulton, Missouri, in 1946, he coined the term *Iron Curtain*, warning of the Soviet Union's expansionist tendencies. From his earliest days, he was a prolific writer of history, politics, and biography.

Prominent among these works are a history of World War II in six volumes (1948–54), and *A History of the English-Speaking Peoples* (4 vols, 1956–58). In 1953 he was awarded the NOBEL PRIZE in Literature.

Chūsingura   The title of various dramas popular in both the BUNRAKU and KABUKI repertoires. Based on actual historical events, the story concerns the revenge taken by forty-seven loyal samurai of Edo who avenge the humiliation and forced suicide of their lord. After attaining their objectives, the forty-seven likewise committed suicide, thus honoring the code of BUSHIDŌ. Purportedly the most accurate and certainly the best-known rendering of the story is the puppet play *Kanadehon Chūsingura* (1748), written by Takeda Izumo (1691–1756), Miyoshi Shoraku (1696–1775?), and Namiki Senryo (1695–1751). The story is known in English as *The Treasury of the Loyal Retainers* or as *The League of the Loyal Ronin*.

Chute, La   See FALL, THE.

Ch'ü tz'u   See ELEGIES OF CH'Ü.

Ch'ü Yuan   See ELEGIES OF CH'Ü.

Ciardi, John (1916–1985)   American poet, teacher, and critic. Poetry editor of the SATURDAY REVIEW for many years, Ciardi wrote numerous essays on the art of reading and enjoying poetry, notable for their lively wit, perception, and common sense. Among his critical works are *How Does a Poem Mean?* (1960) and *Dialogue with an Audience* (1963), a collection of his articles and readers' responses from his first seven years on the *Saturday Review*. Ciardi's poetry tends to be ironic, but it is not without its muted depths and power. Beginning with *Homeward to America* (1940), he wrote numerous volumes, including *Other Skies* (1947), *I Marry You* (1958), *Person to Person* (1964), and *For Instance* (1979). He also translated Dante's *Inferno* (1954) in TERZA RIMA and into idiomatic English to recall Dante's use of the vernacular. His translations of the *Purgatorio* and *Paradiso* appeared in 1961 and 1970 respectively. *A Browser's Dictionary* (1980) and *A Second Browser's Dictionary* (1983) provide a full exploration of the origins of selected words and phrases. He also wrote several books for children, including *I Met a Man* (1961) and *Fast and Slow* (1974).

Cibber, Colley (1671–1757)   English dramatist, poet, and actor. Cibber is best known for the sentimental comedy *The Careless Husband* (1704) and such others as *Love's Last Shift* (1696), *She Would and She Would Not* (1702), and *The Provoked Husband* (1728), an adaptation of Molière's *Tartuffe*. He also wrote a famous description of the Restoration and early 18th-century theatre, *Apology for the Life of Mr. Colley Cibber, Comedian* (1740). Cibber was POET LAUREATE for twenty-seven years from 1730, was generally considered one of the worst poets to hold the office, and even admitted that he was granted the post for being a good Whig. POPE's biting comments on him in THE DUNCIAD are revealing.

Cicero, Marcus Tullius (106–43 BC)   Roman orator, statesman, and man of letters. After carefully preparing himself for a career in law, Cicero made his oratorical debut under the dictatorship of Sulla, his first public success occurring in 80 BC. The next two years he spent in Greece and Rhodes, where he continued his study of philosophy and rhetoric. After his return to Rome, he was elected quaestor (76) and aedile (70). In the year of his aedileship, he was asked by the Sicilians to be their attorney against their former governor Verres. Even though his opponent was Hortensius, the most famous orator of the day, Cicero was able to amass such a convincing array of evidence of the dishonesty and cruelty of Verres that the defendant took the first chance to slip into voluntary exile. In 67 Cicero was overwhelmingly elected praetor and as such came out in favor of the Manilian Law, the proposal that would confer on POMPEY complete command in his war with MITHRIDATES. Thus, in his first purely political oration, Cicero registered himself on the side of Pompey and the aristocratic party.

Cicero himself, however, was of equestrian rank; he was a parvenu, or *novus homo*, whose family had never been distinguished by holding public office. Although he was a member of the aristocratic party, he was looked down upon by many members of his own faction. Nevertheless, in 64 BC he succeeded in being elected consul of Rome. It was this year of his consulate (63) that marked his greatest success: the almost singlehanded foiling of the conspiracy of CATILINE. His four brilliant orations against Catiline (*In Catilinam*) show that Cicero was not only a master of the Roman art of pleading but also a master of the equally Roman art of politics; he emerges as a beleaguered patriot protecting himself from paid assassins, a shrewd chief of state gathering the means to overcome a civil criminal, and a clever propagandist presenting himself to the people as one greater than Romulus, for Romulus merely founded Rome, while Cicero was its savior. Catiline and his army were defeated, and the principal conspirators were summarily executed.

Soon afterward, however, Cicero's influence waned. His enemies became more outspoken. Finally, in 58 BC, CLODIUS PULCHER had a bill passed that declared anyone who had executed a Roman citizen without trial an outlaw. In the face of growing popular indignation, Cicero voluntarily retired to Greece. The sentence of banishment was pronounced *in absentia*, his properties destroyed or confiscated, and his wife and daughter harassed.

Through the influence of his friends, he was recalled from exile within a year and a half, and entirely restored to his former rank within the commonwealth, but he found himself obliged to spend the next six years defending these same friends from their political enemies. His orations in defense of Sestius, Plancius, and Milo date from this period. In the 50s he also found time for study and for writing. He returned to the two great enthusiasms of his youth: philosophy and the art of rhetoric. Between the years 54 and 51, he wrote *De re publica*, a six-book work on political philosophy, of which about one third is extant. In 55 he wrote his great treatise on oratory, *De oratore*. Written in the form of a dialogue, this treatise deals with the proper training for an orator, the style and treatment appropriate to particular themes, and the manner of delivery most apt to sway an audience.

But there was no longer a place for oratory in the Roman world. The senate was dwarfed by the figures of Julius CAESAR and Pompey, and these two giants called for war. In 49 BC, after long hesitation, Cicero left Italy and pledged his life and fortune to the cause of Pompey. In the next year, when Caesar crushed Pompey in the battle of Pharsalus, Cicero realized that the cherished traditions of republican Rome were crumbling. Even though the victorious Caesar pardoned him and welcomed him back to Rome, Cicero, shaken and disillusioned, remained aloof from politics. He retired to his villa in the mountains of Tuscany and sought out what he called *otium cum dignitate* ("leisure with dignity"). Between the years 47 and 44, he wrote the five books of the *Tusculanae disputationes*, on the subject of happiness; his works on theology and augury, *De natura Deorum* and *De divinatione*; his two dialogues on old age and friendship, DE SENECTUTE and DE AMICITIA; and his handbook on Stoic morality, *De officiis*.

In 44 BC, with the death of Caesar, Cicero, then in his sixty-third year, saw his chance to reenter politics and to save Rome from demagoguery and chaos. He hoped to play the role of the elder statesman and to serve as guardian to the young Octavius. Accordingly, he attacked Mark ANTONY in fourteen orations known as Philippics. But Octavius turned against his would-be ally and, joining Antony and Lepidus in the Second TRIUMVIRATE, declared Cicero an outlaw. Cicero tried to escape to Greece but was overtaken by a mob of bounty hunters; his head and right hand were presented to his enemy Antony, who had them placed on the rostrum in the Forum, where the orator had first won his glory.

Cicero was not only Rome's greatest orator; he was perhaps its most articulate philosopher. Through his philosophical treatises, he helped to make Latin a strong, yet surprisingly flexible, vehicle for logical speculation. Through his mastery of Latin prose, he transformed Latin from a blunt utilitarian language—one most fit for merchants, generals, and lawyers—to a rich chromatic language that rivaled Greek in its capacity to convey at the same time the gamut of feelings and the fine distinction of ideas.

Cicero's prose style is rhetorical, in the best sense of the word; it is intended to persuade. It has always been contrasted with the style of TACITUS and SALLUST, who both preferred a tight, tersely emphatic prose to the symphonic sonorities of Cicero. These two stylistic schools continued in conflict into the 16th and 17th centuries, when in England the Tacitean style of Francis BACON was contrasted with the Ciceronian style of Jeremy TAYLOR. See ATTICUS; CICERONIAN AGE.

Ciceronian age   In its intellectual aspects, the last years of republican Rome. The Ciceronian age, or the age of CICERO, dates from the emergence of Cicero (80 BC) to the empire under AUGUSTUS (27 BC). The prose—as well as the politics—of the late republic was dominated by Marcus Tullius Cicero. Like CATO the Elder, Cicero was a versatile writer-statesman, but, where Cato was representative of the sharp, straightforward, vernacular Latin style, Cicero was the creator and preeminent representative of the smooth and rhetorically powerful Hellenized style. A master of oratory, Cicero was also a thoughtful and thorough student of literary criticism, a foremost authority on Stoic philosophy, and a brilliant letter writer. Other prose writers of the period include the historians Julius CAESAR and SALLUST, both of whom set a high standard of excellence for all subsequent Roman historians, and Terentius Varro (116–27 BC), reputedly the most learned and productive scholar of his time.

Although the Ciceronian age is conspicuously an age of prose, it also embraces LUCRETIUS and CATULLUS, two of the most significant poets in Latin literature. Lucretius wielded the dactylic hexameter of Ennius in his long and passionate poem on Epicurean science, *De rerum natura*. Catullus was the first truly successful writer of Latin lyric poems. These he modeled on the literary forms of the Alexandrine school of Hellenistic Greek literature.

With the murder of Cicero (43 BC), the last great voice of Roman republicanism was stilled. The transition to the imperial period had begun, and its dominant figure was to be the young Octavius Caesar, later Augustus. In his struggle with Mark ANTONY, from the death of Julius CAESAR (44) to its culmination at Actium (31), Rome leaves behind her old republican ideals to become an empire, and the Ciceronian age gives way to the AUGUSTAN AGE.

Cid, Le   (The Cid, 1637)   A tragedy by Pierre CORNEILLE. One of Corneille's most powerful tragedies, *Le Cid* is considered by many critics to mark the beginning of modern French drama. The playwright borrowed from Guillén de Castro y Bellvís's treatment of the subject but compressed the material into a swiftly moving play.

Cid, Poema del   An epic poem in Spanish, also known as *Cantar de mio Cid* and written about 1140 by an unknown Castilian bard. The poem has survived only in a single manuscript copy, from which several pages are missing, made in 1307 by one Per Abbat. It was first published in 1779 by Tomás Antonio Sánchez.

The poem is based on the exploits of Rodrigo or Ruy Díaz de Bivar (c1043–1099), who was known as *el Cid* (fr Arab, *Sidi*, "lord"). Born near Burgos, he was named chief marshal, or *alférez*, of the royal army by Sancho II of Castile and later served under Sancho's brother and successor, Alfonso VI, who banished him because of personal differences. The Cid fought both for and against the Moorish rulers, who at that time controlled much of the Iberian peninsula. A highlight of his career was his conquest of Valencia (1094), which halted Almoravid expansion in Spain. In 1074 he married Doña Jimena Díaz, a niece of Alfonso. He was also known as *el Campeador* ("the Champion").

Consisting of 3,735 lines, the poem is divided into three parts, or *cantares*. The first deals with the Cid's exile and concludes with his defeat of the count of Barcelona. A famous episode describes his entry into Burgos, where no one will speak to him until a little girl explains that King Alfonso has warned the people to refuse him lodging. In the second part, the Cid captures Valencia and is reconciled with the king, and he marries his two daughters, Doña Elvira and Doña Sol, to two nobles, the *infantes*, or heirs, of Carrión. The third part recounts the outrageous conduct of Rodrigo's sons-in-law, who beat and abandon their wives. The Cid avenges himself by defeating them in a trial by combat and then arranges the marriage of his daughters to the princes of Navarre and Aragon.

Similar in form to the *Chanson de* ROLAND, the poem is notable for its simplicity and directness and for its exact, picturesque detail. Despite the inclusion of much legendary material, the figure of the Cid, who is depicted as the model Castilian warrior, is not idealized to an extravagant degree.

The Cid appeared in many other medieval poems, among them the epic *Cantar de Rodrigo*, which was written about 1400 and is based almost entirely on legend. Later authors also made use of this theme, notably Juan de la Cueva, Lope de VEGA, Guillén de Castro y Bellvís, and Juan Eugenio HARTZENBUSCH. Castro y Bellvís's *Mocedades del Cid* was the direct source of Corneille's LE CID. Present knowledge about the historical character and the *Poema de mio Cid* is derived largely from the exhaustive investigations of Ramón MENÉNDEZ PIDAL, who published a three-volume critical edition (1908–11).

Cimabue, Giovanni (real name Cenni di Pepo, c1240–c1302)   Florentine painter. Tradition celebrates Cimabue as the father of Italian painting and the teacher of GIOTTO. He was himself taught by Byzantine artists, so that several iconlike Madonnas and Crucifixions have been attributed to him, but there are no extant works that can be positively established as his. His renown among his contemporaries is attested to by Dante, who describes him in the *Purgatorio*, as having "held the field" until surpassed by Giotto.

Cimetière marin, Le (The Graveyard by the Sea, 1932)   A poem by Paul VALÉRY. Written in decasyllabic six-line stanzas, it describes the dazzling noon of the Medi-

terranean coast, where Valéry spent his boyhood. The narrator ironically contrasts the attractive clarity of timeless intellectuality with the inevitable decay of all that lives in reality. He concludes, however, that for a mortal being "It is necessary to try to live."

Cimmerians   A legendary tribe. HOMER placed the Cimmerians beyond OCEANUS, in a land of never-ending gloom. Immediately beyond was HADES. PLINY placed Cimmeria near the Lake AVERNUS, in Italy, where "the sun never penetrates." The phrase *Cimmerian darkness* signifies intense darkness.

Historically, the name is given to a nomad tribe from the Crimean region who, under pressure from the Sarmatians and Scythians, overran Asia Minor in 635 BC.

Cinderella (Fr, *Cendrillon*; Ger, *Aschenbrötel*; "the little cinder girl")   The heroine of an ancient fairy tale. The story, probably of Eastern origin, was mentioned in 16th-century German literature and was popularized in Perrault's CONTES DE MA MÈRE L' OYE. Cinderella is the drudge of the household, while her elder sisters go to balls. At length, a fairy godmother enables Cinderella to go to the Prince's ball. The Prince, of course, falls in love with her, and she is later rediscovered by him by means of a glass slipper that she has dropped and that will fit no foot but her own. (Perrault is believed to have confounded *vair*, "ermine," with *verre*, "glass," thus first giving Cinderella this unlikely footwear.) The details of the complete story, not found in most children's books, are somewhat gruesome. Rossini's delightful opera *La Cenerentola* (1817) is based on a considerably modified version of the story.

cinéma-vérité (Fr, "film truth")   A style of documentary filmmaking that emphasizes the power of the camera to record impromptu events directly. The term and the technique derive from the Russian director Dziga Vertov (1896–1954), who, in 1924, used the term *Kino-Pravda* ("film truth") to describe his films, which were made outside the studio, without actors, set, or script. For Vertov, the only authentic cinema was that which provided a truthful record of events and actions by direct filming. Vertov's principal counterpart in the U.S. was Robert FLAHERTY, whose documentary depiction of Alaskan Eskimos in *Nanook of the North* (1922) was based on similar aims.

Changes in film technology from cumbersome equipment to portable cameras and tape recorders resulted in widespread interest in *cinéma-vérité* techniques in the U.S. and Europe in the 1950s and 1960s. Although specific elements of the genre vary with individual filmmakers, they have in common the minimization of the role of director and the emphasis of the role of the cameraman as the one who can capture aspects of reality that might have meaning to others.

Cinna (1640)   A tragedy by Pierre CORNEILLE. It is based on an episode in Roman history recounted in Seneca's *De clementia*. Though trusted by the emperor Augustus, Cinna leads a conspiracy to overthrow him, encouraged by his beloved Amélie, who desires to avenge the death of her father. Maxime, a fellow conspirator also in love with Amélie, betrays the plot, hoping to cause Cinna's arrest. The last act focuses on Augustus's struggle to choose between mercy and revenge. Ultimately, he pardons the lovers as well as the treacherous Maxime. The play reflects Corneille's interest in political subjects.

cinquain   In prosody, a quintet or five-line stanza. The term is also used to designate the five-line poem of two, four, six, eight, and two syllables respectively; this form was invented by Adelaide Crapsey (1878–1914), who was greatly influenced by the Japanese HAIKU and TANKA.

Just now,
Out of the strange
Still dusk—as strange, as still—
A white moth flew. Why am I grown
So cold?

Adelaide Crapsey, "The Warning"

cinquecento   (Ital, "the five hundreds")   Italian designation of the 16th century. This is the age of the high RENAISSANCE—of ARIOSTO and CASTIGLIONE, MACHIAVELLI and ARETINO; in art history, the age of RAPHAEL, LEONARDO DA VINCI, and MICHAELANGELO and of the advent of MANNERISM and the proto-Baroque.

Circe   A sorceress of Greek mythology. Circe lived on the island of Aeaea. When Odysseus landed there, Circe turned his companions into swine, but he resisted this metamorphosis by virtue of a herb called *moly*, given him by Hermes.

Circe was Aetes' sister and the aunt of Medea. She purified Jason and Medea for the murder of Absyrtus and gave them advice on their homeward journey.

Circle of Chalk, The   A Chinese classical play of the Yuan dynasty (1259–1368), sometimes attributed to Li Hsing-Tao. The lovely Chang-hi-tang is sold to a teahouse by her destitute family and is bought by Mr. Ma, the tax collector, to whom she bears a son. Jealous for her position as head wife and heir, Mrs. Ma poisons her husband's tea and bribes witnesses to testify that Chang-hi-tang has murdered him and that the concubine's child is really her own. The new emperor, who has ordered all cases involving the death penalty retried before him, listens to the evidence; he then places the child in a chalk circle and directs Mrs. Ma and Chang-hi-tang each to take hold of one of the baby's arms and thus gain the child by pulling him out of the circle. When Mrs. Ma wins this contest, for Chang-hi-tang is unwilling to hurt the child by pulling at all, the emperor decides that the concubine is the rightful mother and Mrs. Ma the murderess, and he leaves it to Chang-hi-tang to pronounce justice. She orders Mrs. Ma to make herself a cup of tea and to let her conscience decide what sort of tea it ought to be. In later adaptations additional symbolic chalk circles and a love affair between the emperor and

Chang-hi-tang were added. Bertolt Brecht used the play as the basis of his CAUCASIAN CHALK CIRCLE, in which the stagecraft is purportedly modeled on the classical Chinese convention and moralistic and socio-economic didacticisms replace the subtlety and beautifully lyric verse that distinguish the original.

A very similar story is told in the Bible of a wise judgment of SOLOMON.

Circumlocution Office   A term applied in ridicule by Charles Dickens in LITTLE DORRIT to public offices in England, because each person tries to shuffle off every task onto someone else. Hence, routine formality and the red tape of bureaucracy.

Cities of the Plain   See REMEMBRANCE OF THINGS PAST.

Citizen of the World, The   (1762)   An epistolary novel by Oliver GOLDSMITH. In almost colloquial prose, it is supposedly written by a Chinese philosopher, Lien Chi Altangi, who visits England and reports on it to his friends in the East. The letters were published with the subtitle *Letters from a Chinese Philosopher Residing in London to his Friends in the East.* In these "Chinese Letters," Goldsmith is typical of his day in his praise of simplicity. Here the main catchword is Nature's "simple plan." The philosopher's observations are supplemented by those of his friend, the Man in Black, by Beau Tibbs, and by Lady Betty Tempest. The letters are linked by a subplot, in which the philosopher's son rescues the Man in Black's daughter from captivity in Persia, brings her to England, and marries her. The novel first appeared as a series of essays in Newbury's *Public Ledger* (1760–61) under the title *The Chinese Letters.* This device of the Oriental traveler was perfected in MONTESQUIEU's *Lettres persanes* (1721).

City in the Sea, The   (1831)   A poem by Edgar Allan POE. The poet evokes a grim landscape in melodic lines. His description of the shrine includes the well-known lines:

Whose wreathèd friezes intertwine
The viol, the violet and the vine.

City Lights Press   See FERLINGHETTI, LAWRENCE.

City of Dreadful Night, The   (1874)   A long poem by the Victorian poet James THOMSON, first published serially in the *National Reformer*, published in book form in *The City of Dreadful Night, And Other Poems* (1880). It describes an imaginary city of misery and horror created out of the author's own sense of despair as, afflicted with insomnia, he walked at night through the streets of London.

City of God, The   (De civitate Dei; 22 vols, 413–426) A long treatise by St. AUGUSTINE. It is an apology for Christianity against the accusation that the Church was responsible for the decline of the Roman Empire. It interprets human history as a conflict between the City of God (*Civitas Dei*), which includes the body of Christians belonging to the Church, and the Earthly City (*Civitas Terrena*), composed of pagans and heretical Christians. Augustine foresees that, through the will of God, the people of the City of God will eventually win immortality, those in the Earthly City destruction.

city of refuge   A sacred area. MOSES, at the command of God, set apart three cities on the east of Jordan, and Joshua added three others on the west, whither any person who had killed someone inadvertently might flee for refuge. The three on the east of Jordan were Bezer, Ramoth, and Golan; the three on the west were Hebron, Shechem, and Kedesh (Deut. 4:43; Josh. 20:1–8).

MEDINA, in Arabia, where MUHAMMED took refuge when driven by conspirators from Mecca, is also known as the *city of refuge*. He received a warm welcome when he entered Medina in AD 622.

Civil Disobedience (1849)   An essay by Henry David THOREAU. Its major premise is "that government is best which governs least." Thoreau asserts that a man's first loyalty is to his own nature; true to himself, he may then be true to a government. The essay influenced GANDHI's doctrine of passive resistance.

Civil War, American   A war (1861–65) between the U.S. and eleven Southern states that seceded from the Union and formed the Confederate States of America. It is also known as the War of Secession, the War of Rebellion, and the War Between the States. The war was the result of long-standing social and economic differences between North and South that gradually became apparent after the WAR OF 1812. Sectional conflict over such issues as tariff regulations and the extension of slavery was temporarily abated by the activities of Henry CLAY and Daniel WEBSTER, among others, but, by the 1850s, the opposing positions of each side had become firmly entrenched. The principal objective of the North was to keep the Union together, although emancipation of the slaves became a secondary aim after 1862. Historians continue to debate whether or not the war could have been averted.

Upon receiving news of Abraham LINCOLN's election to the presidency in 1860, South Carolina seceded, followed by ten other states, which then organized the Confederate government and elected Jefferson DAVIS president in 1861. On April 12, 1861, the Confederate attack on Fort SUMTER began the actual fighting.

Although Union hopes for a quick victory were dashed by their rout by the Confederates at BULL RUN, it gradually became evident that, despite the brilliant leadership of the Confederate generals Robert E. LEE and Thomas ("Stonewall") JACKSON, the superior forces of the North would ultimately prevail. This was especially true when Confederate expectations of securing foreign recognition and aid were disappointed by the Union victory at GETTYSBURG and Gen. GRANT's successful siege of Vicksburg (1863). In 1864 Grant, now supreme commander of the Union forces,

turned to the conquest of Richmond, the Confederate capital, while Gen. W. T. SHERMAN undertook his famous march to the sea. After a gallant defense, Lee was forced to evacuate Richmond (April 2, 1865) and surrendered to Grant at Appomattox Courthouse, Virginia, on April 9.

With the possible exception of the Napoleonic Wars, no other conflict has produced more books. Among the most famous novels inspired by the war are Stephen Crane's THE RED BADGE OF COURAGE, Winston Churchill's THE CRISIS, and Margaret Mitchell's GONE WITH THE WIND. Among the many other novelists who wrote about the war are Nelson PAGE, Mary JOHNSTON, Ellen Glasgow (1874–1945), and MacKinlay KANTOR. Verse dealing with the famous conflict was written by such poets as John Greenleaf WHITTIER, Henry TIMROD, Paul Hamilton HAYNE, Walt WHITMAN, and Stephen Vincent BENÉT. Edmund WILSON's *Patriotic Gore* (1962) consists of essays on 19th-century Civil War literature.

Civil War, English (or The Great Rebellion)   A civil war brought on by conflict between CHARLES I and the LONG PARLIAMENT over economic, political, and religious issues. The war had two phases. The first (1642–46) was fought between the Royalist party, which included most of the nobles and gentry and adherents of the Church of England, and the Parliamentary party, which was supported by Presbyterians and other dissenters and the middle classes in general. In 1643 the Scottish COVENANTERS joined the Parliamentary cause. After initial Royalist successes, this phase ended with Parliamentary victories at Marston Moor (1644) and Naseby (1645).

The second phase, which lasted from about 1648 to 1652, followed the acquisition of power by the Parliamentary army and more radical dissenters, or Independents, led by Oliver CROMWELL. The struggle was now between this group, on the one hand, and the king, who was executed in 1649, conservative members of Parliament, Irish Royalists, and the Scots, now allied with Charles II, on the other. In the Preston campaign (1648), the Irish War (1649–50), and the battles of Dunbar (1650) and Worcester (1651), Cromwell emerged victorious. See HAMPDEN, JOHN.

Clair, René (real name René-Lucien Chomette, 1898–1981)   French film director, producer, and writer. From his first effort in *Paris qui dort* (1924), Clair revealed a unique sense of the absurd, especially as embodied in the French bourgeois. His films are known for their satiric bent, tinged by an ironic pessimism. *Italian Straw Hat* (1927) was the culmination of his work in silent films. With the advent of sound, Clair continued to experiment, producing his famous trilogy *Sous les toits de Paris* (1929), *Le Million* (1931), and *À nous la liberté* (1931). In these films, he combined an ingenious mingling of music and dialogue with silent-film techniques. He spent several unsuccessful years in Hollywood during World War II, but he returned to France and regained his stride with *Le Silence est d'or* (1947), *Les Grandes Manoeuvres* (1955), and *Porte des lilas* (1954). In 1960 he became the first film director ever elected to the ACADÉMIE FRANÇAISE.

Clare, John (1793–1864) English poet. Clare was born into a barely literate, impoverished Northamptonshire peasant family, had little formal education, and long supported himself as a farm laborer. After the appearance of his first book, *Poems Descriptive of Rural Life and Scenery* (1820), he became famous as a peasant poet, the curiosity of one London Season. Thereafter, however, he was plagued by ill health, neglect, poverty, and finally madness. In 1837 he was committed to a mental asylum, and he died in confinement. Much of Clare's voluminous verse lacks distinction, but his best poems possess a startling originality and directness of vision, ranking high among English nature poetry. Aside from his first volume, his works include *The Village Minstrel* (1821), *The Shepherd's Calendar* (1827), and *The Rural Muse* (1835). The edition *Selected Poems and Prose of John Clare* (1967; ed Robinson and Summerfield) includes many poems written in madness.

Clarel; A Poem and a Pilgrimage in the Holy Land (1876) A long poem by Herman MELVILLE. Clarel, a young theological student, oscillates between faith and doubt. In love with Ruth, a Jewish girl, he leaves her to join a group of pilgrims traveling from Jerusalem to Gethsemane, the Dead Sea, and Bethlehem. The pilgrims, conversing with Clarel, represent almost every persuasion. They are Nehemiah, a saintly old man who knows the time of the Second Coming; Vine, a seclusive aesthete resembling Melville's friend Nathaniel Hawthorne; Derwent, an Emersonian optimist; Mortmain and Ungar, cynical pessimists; Margoth, a materialist; a Dominican friar; and many others. When Clarel returns, he finds that Ruth has died; he is left alone to face reality, the possessor of new wisdom. Melville asks if civilization can survive, after science has caused a loss of faith. His poem, though technically weak, has considerable intellectual strength.

Clarence, George, third duke of (1449–1478) English noble, son of Richard Plantagenet, duke of York. Clarence originally took up arms against his brothers Edward (IV) and Richard (III) but was later reconciled with them. Convinced that Clarence was plotting against him, Edward had him imprisoned, and it is said that he was drowned in a butt of malmsey wine. In Shakespeare's RICHARD III, he is depicted as the victim of Richard's machinations and is arrested when Richard revives an old prophecy that "G of Edward's heirs the murderer shall be." He also appears in Shakespeare's HENRY VI: PART III.

Clarendon, Edward Hyde, first earl of (1609–1674) English historian and statesman. An influential adviser to Charles I and lord chancellor under Charles II, Clarendon was falsely accused of treason and banished in

1667. In France he wrote his *Life* (1759) and completed his chief work, *The History of the Rebellion and Civil Wars in England* (1702–4). The *History* is best known for Clarendon's perceptive and tolerant character sketches of the leading personages of the time. His daughter Anne married the duke of York, later James II, and bore two daughters, who became Queen Mary and Queen Anne.

Clarendon Press A printing establishment connected with Oxford University, England. It was founded partly with the profits from the first earl of Clarendon, Edward Hyde's *History of the Rebellion*.

Clarin See ALAS Y UREÑA, LEOPOLDO.

Clarissa Harlowe (1747–1748) An epistolary novel by Samuel RICHARDSON, generally considered to be his masterpiece. Its original title is *Clarissa, or, The History of a Young Lady*. It is the longest novel in the English language, totaling about one million words. It is noted for its subtle and penetrating psychological treatment of character. Clarissa has been coldly commanded by her tyrannical family to marry Mr. Solmes, a man she despises. She refuses, even though it pains her to defy her parents. Locked in her room, isolated from family and friends, Clarissa corresponds secretly with Robert LOVELACE, a suitor disapproved of by her family; she finally throws herself upon his protection and flees with him. It soon becomes clear to her, however, that Lovelace's sole aim is to seduce her. Her virtue is so great that Lovelace becomes obsessively absorbed in breaking it down; convinced finally that she will never yield to him, he becomes desperate, drugs and rapes her. He then proposes marriage, but Clarissa refuses, retires to a solitary dwelling, and dies of grief and shame. Lovelace, whose heart the reader never really knows, is killed in a duel with Colonel Morden, Clarissa's cousin. Rousseau was greatly influenced by *Clarissa Harlowe* in his novel, *Julie, ou La* NOUVELLE HÉLOÏSE.

Clark, Kenneth [Mackenzie], Lord Clark of Saltwood (1903–1983) English art historian. Early in his life, Clark followed the advice of Arnold Bennett: "If an Englishman feels equally drawn to painting and writing, he should write." He worked in Italy with Bernard BERENSON and established himself as a leading scholar of the Italian Renaissance. His monumental *Catalogue of Drawings of Leonardo da Vinci in the Collection of His Majesty the King at Windsor Castle* (1935; rev as . . . *of Her Majesty the Queen* . . ., 1968) was the first chronological record of Leonardo's work. Clark subsequently wrote and lectured on a wide range of subjects, from 19th-century poetry to English landscape painting to Chinese and modern art. Endowed with a rare capacity to communicate his delight in art, he became widely known with his popular *Civilisation*, a BBC television series and book (1969) on the artistic development of the European mind. His other works include *The Nude: A Study in Ideal Form* (1956); *An Introduction to Rembrandt* (1978); two works of autobiography,

Another Part of the Wood (1974) and *The Other Half* (1977).

Clarke, Arthur C[harles] (1917–   )   English author of SCIENCE FICTION and nonfiction on such topics as space flight and underwater research. With training in physics and mathematics, Clarke, like Isaac ASIMOV, has a solid scientific background, exemplified in such nonfiction works as *The Exploration of Space* (1951) and *Voices from the Sky* (1965). His article "Extra-Terrestrial Relays" (1945) pointed, for the first time in print, to the possibility of a global TV satellite. Clarke was twice chairman of the British Interplanetary Society (1946–47, 1950–53) before moving to Sri Lanka, where he pursued his interest in deep-sea diving. His science fiction—including such stories as "The Nine Billion Names of God" and "The Star" (1955) and such novels as *Childhood's End* (1953), *The City and the Stars* (1956), *2001: A Space Odyssey* (1968; written simultaneously with the screenplay, on which he collaborated with Stanley KUBRICK), and *The Fountains of Paradise* (1979)—reveals the influence of Olaf STAPLEDON in its blend of science and evolutionary mysticism.

classical   (1) Usually, a term referring to the CLASSICS, or to the 5th and 4th centuries BC in Greece and the 1st centuries BC and AD in Rome, when each culture had reached its artistic culmination.

(2) In literature and art in general, a term used to express, with reference either to a single work or to an entire age, dominance of form over content; technical precision over emotional expressiveness; clarity, restraint, and rationality over ambiguity, extravagance, and free play of the imagination. Classicism is opposed to ROMANTICISM. See NEOCLASSICISM.

(3) In music, the term is applied to a work that accepts certain basic conventions of form and structure as the natural framework for the expression of ideas, as distinguished from music that is more concerned with the expression of individual emotions than with the achievement of formal unity. The term is usually restricted to music from 1730 to 1830, the period marked by the rise of the symphony and the composers HAYDN and MOZART. It is often used loosely to mean serious art music as opposed to popular, folk, or ethnic music.

classics   Any work or body of work of the first or highest order. The term comes from the Roman division of society into five classes. Any citizen who belonged to the highest class was called *classicus*; the rest were said to be *infra classem*, that is, beneath the class. Accordingly writers of the best or first class were called *classici auctores*, "classic authors." The term can also refer simply to the literary or artistic works of ancient Greece and Rome.

Claudel, Paul [Louis Charles Marie] (1868–1955)   French dramatist, poet, and diplomat. After spending his boyhood in a small village, Claudel went with his family to Paris. He believed he had lost the conventional Catholic faith of his parents, but at eighteen he rediscovered the revelation of the supernatural in Arthur RIMBAUD's *Les Illuminations* and *Une Saison en enfer*. That Christmas Eve, during a service at Notre Dame Cathedral, he suddenly felt himself permanently converted to fervent faith. He spent four years attending MALLARMÉ's symbolist salons and discovering the literature that was to influence him most—the Bible, Aeschylus, Vergil, and Dante.

In 1889 he published *Tête d'or* and wrote *La Cité*, both poetic dramas showing the influence of the SYMBOLISTS. In 1893 he began his career as a foreign diplomat and went as a consul to New York and Boston; during that year he wrote *L'Échange* (1893), a play set on the East Coast of the U.S., and translated the *Agamemnon* of Aeschylus into French. In 1895 he went to China, which he describes in the prose poems of *Connaissance de l'est* (1900). The collection of his plays, *L'Arbre* (1901), published the following year, contained *La Jeune Fille Violaine*, which Claudel later adapted as the well-known THE TIDINGS BROUGHT TO MARY. He published the poetic drama *Break of Noon* in 1905 and THE HOSTAGE in 1909. In 1916 he completed the translation of the last two plays of Aeschylus' *Oresteia* trilogy. Between 1919 and 1924, he wrote the long play THE SATIN SLIPPER, greatly influenced by the NŌ theatre of Japan. Of his later works, the best known are the dramatic oratorios *Le Livre de Christophe Colomb* (1927; tr *The Book of Christopher Columbus*, 1930), with music by Darius MILHAUD, and *Jeanne d'Arc au bûcher* (1938), with music by Arthur HONEGER. Throughout this time, Claudel traveled widely, serving as ambassador to Japan (1921–27), to the U.S. (1927–33), and to Belgium (1933–35), after which he lived in retirement, primarily in a country home in France.

Claudine   Heroine of four semiautobiographical novels by COLETTE: *Claudine à l'école* (1900; tr *Claudine at School*, 1956), *Claudine à Paris* (*Claudine in Paris*, 1901), *Claudine en ménage* (*Claudine Married*, 1902), and *Claudine s'en va* (1903; tr *The Innocent Wife*, 1934).

Claudio   (1) The brother of the virtuous Isabella in Shakespeare's MEASURE FOR MEASURE. Claudio is the pivotal character in the play, embodying humanity's weakness and standing between the strict purity of Isabella and the cruel austerity of Angelo.

(2) In Shakespeare's MUCH ADO ABOUT NOTHING, a handsome young Florentine lord, who has served with distinction in the army of Don Pedro. Claudio falls in love at first sight with Hero.

Claudius   In Shakespeare's HAMLET, the uncle of Hamlet. Before the play opens, Claudius has poisoned his brother, the king of Denmark, married his widow, and ascended the throne. Shakespeare depicts him as a sensual though able ruler whose lust for power fails to be tempered by the gnawing of his conscience.

Claudius I (full Latin name Tiberius Claudius Drusus Nero Germanicus, 10 BC–AD 54)   Roman emperor (AD 41–54). Claudius was excluded from public affairs by Caligula, his predecessor and nephew. When Caligula was murdered in AD 41, Claudius was proclaimed emperor by the praetorian guard. He was persuaded by AGRIPPINA, his second wife, to set aside his own son BRITANNICUS and adopt her son by a former marriage, Lucius Domitius (later NERO), as his successor. When Claudius, too late, repented this move, he was poisoned by Agrippina. Claudius was noted for his writing, but none of his work is extant. He is the principal character in two historical novels, *I, Claudius* (1934) and *Claudius the God* (1934), by Robert Graves.

Claus, Santa   See SANTA CLAUS.

Clavell, James [duMaresq] (1924–   ) English-born American novelist and scriptwriter. Clavell immigrated to the U.S. in 1953 and was naturalized ten years later. His first novel, *King Rat* (1962), was based on his experience as a prisoner of war in Japanese prison camps during World War II. His name subsequently became solidly identified with Japan and the Orient by virtue of his massively successful historical novels *Tai-Pan* (1966), *Shōgun* (1975), and *Noble House* (1981). He has also written numerous film scripts, including *The Great Escape* (1963) and *To Sir With Love* (1969). His other works include *The Children's Story* (1982) and *Whirlwind* (1986).

Clavileño   In Cervantes's DON QUIXOTE, the wooden horse on which the knight and his squire make a fantastic journey through the air. It is governed by a wooden pin in its forehead. Such a flying horse is a well-known figure in European and Near Eastern folklore.

Clay   A short story in James Joyce's DUBLINERS. It is about a very ordinary, ineffectual, pitiful spinster called Maria, who goes to the family party of a man to whom she was nurse when he was a child. The story, which has little action, is largely a character study of Maria. During a blindfold party game, the children play a trick on her, making her put her fingers in a dish of wet clay. The clay is a symbol of her character; she herself is a symbol of Ireland.

Clay, Henry (1777–1852)   American statesman, often called *The Great Pacificator*. As a member of Congress from Kentucky, Clay was Speaker of the House (1811–20, 1823–25) and a leader of the "war hawks," who urged war with Great Britain before 1812. After running unsuccessfully for the presidency in 1824, he was named secretary of state by John Quincy ADAMS. He later served in the U.S. Senate (1831–42, 1849–52), where he espoused an "American System" of internal improvements and protective tariffs to strengthen the national economy. In 1832 and 1844, he was the unsuccessful Whig candidate for president; he is credited with saying, "I would rather be right than be President." Devoted to the preservation of the

Union, he was largely responsible for the enactment of the COMPROMISE OF 1850.

Clayhanger (1910)   The first novel in a series by Arnold BENNETT. It deals with the conflict between Edwin Clayhanger and his dominating, puritanical father over Edwin's work and his love for Hilda Lessways. The bigamy of Hilda's husband complicates the plot. The novel has notable descriptions of Five Towns life. In *Hilda Lessways* (1911), the same events are narrated from Hilda's point of view; *These Twain* (1916) is a study of the couple in married life; and *The Roll Call* (1918) is about Hilda's son, George.

Clea   See ALEXANDRIA QUARTET, THE.

Cléante   The name given by Molière to three of his characters. (1) In LE MALADE IMAGINAIRE, the lover of Angélique, the daughter of Argan. (2) In L'AVARE, the son of Harpagon. (3) In LE TARTUFFE, the brother-in-law of Orgon.

Cleisthenes (fl 507 BC)   Athenian statesman, considered the second founder of the democracy. Cleisthenes saw that the divisiveness of the clans would forever keep SOLON's government from working well. Cleisthenes' organization aimed to do away with local political influence. Taking the natural divisions of the *demes* as the basis for the Athenian state, he divided the country into three regions: the city, the coast, and the inland area. Each of the regions was divided into ten *trittyes*, a total of thirty. From the thirty *trittyes*, Cleisthenes formed ten groups of three, so that none of the ten groups had two *trittyes* from the same region. Each group, though it was based on artificial geography, was known as a tribe. Local political action was ended, and all citizens worked for the general good. Cleisthenes replaced Solon's Council of Four Hundred (based on the four clans) with a Council of Five Hundred, fifty from each tribe. The operation of the Council shows that the Athenians understood representative government. Cleisthenes is also supposed to have initiated the practice of ostracism.

Clélie, Histoire Romaine (1654–1660)   A novel in ten volumes by Madeleine de SCUDÉRY. Derived and enormously elaborated from the Roman legend of Cloelia, the novel recounts the tribulations endured by Clélie as hostage of Sextus Tarquinus and climaxes with her swimming of the Tiber and her long-sought reunion with her lover Aronce. Rich in digressions, the novel includes the *carte de tendre*, an imaginative map of the amorous sentiments, drawn up by Madeleine de Scudéry with the aid of her salon.

Clemenceau, Georges [Eugène Benjamin] (1841–1929)   French statesman and writer. Clemenceau is best known for his career as a statesman, first as a senator (1902–20) and as Minister of the Interior (1906), and then for two terms as premier of the Third Republic (1906–9 and 1917–20). He was the French representative at the

Versailles peace conference in 1919, about which he wrote in *Grandeurs et misères d'une victoire* (1930; tr *The Grandeur and Misery of Victory*, 1930). Earlier in his life, Clemenceau had worked as a journalist, including a job as correspondent with Grant's army in the American Civil War. He was an ardent supporter of Dreyfus and agitated for a new verdict in the case. He wrote the novel *Les plus forts* (1898) and the play *Le Voile de bonheur* (1901).

Clemens, Samuel Langhorne   See TWAIN, MARK.

Clement VII, Pope   See MEDICI.

Cleopatra (Cleopatra VII, 69–30 BC)   Last Macedonian queen of Egypt. From 51 to 49 BC, Cleopatra was joint ruler with and wife of her brother Ptolemy XIII, in accordance with Egyptian tradition. She was driven from the throne by her brother but reinstated by Julius CAESAR in 48; this gave rise to a war between Caesar and Ptolemy XIII, in which the latter was killed, and his younger brother, Ptolemy XIV, ascended the throne and married Cleopatra. Cleopatra lived with Caesar in Rome from 46 to 44 and had by him a son, Ptolemy XV, who was later put to death by Augustus. Returning to Egypt after Caesar's assassination, Cleopatra gave her support to the Second Triumvirate of ANTONY, Octavius (later Augustus), and Lepidus, against the republicans Brutus and Cassius. Mark Antony, who had been appointed to rule over Asia and the East, succumbed completely to her charms and abandoned his wife Octavia, to live with Cleopatra. They had three children. After the defeat of Antony and Cleopatra at Actium, Antony killed himself on hearing a false report of her death; some say she spread the report herself to gain favor with Octavius by causing Antony's death. When she heard that Octavius planned to exhibit her triumphantly in Rome, she committed suicide by applying a poison asp to her bosom. Famed for her extraordinary charm and beauty, she was also highly cultivated.

The capricious and imperious queen is one of the most complex and fully developed of Shakespeare's female characters. In his ANTONY AND CLEOPATRA, she is a wildly erratic, jealous, and avaricious woman, but withal sincerely in love with Antony. The famous speech of Enobarbus aptly describes her:

> Age cannot wither her, nor custom stale
> Her infinite variety; other women cloy
> The appetites they feed, but she makes hungry
> Where most she satisfies; for vilest things
> Become themselves in her, that the holy priests
> Bless her when she is riggish.

She also appears in Dryden's ALL FOR LOVE OR THE WORLD WELL LOST and Shaw's CAESAR AND CLEOPATRA.

clerihew   A comic, four-line verse made up of two couplets, invented by Edmund Clerihew BENTLEY. They are often satiric or ridiculous biographies of famous people,

the lines being a succession of non sequiturs. Bentley wrote the following example at the age of sixteen:

> Sir Humphrey Davy
> Detested gravy.
> He lived in the odium
> Of having discovered sodium.

Clerk's Tale, The   One of THE CANTERBURY TALES of Geoffrey CHAUCER, written in RHYME ROYAL and based on a Latin adaptation by Petrarch of the one hundredth tale in Boccaccio's DECAMERON (see GRISELDA). The people of Saluzzo urge their Marquis Walter to marry and provide a successor. He chooses Griselda, the virtuous, lovely, and hard-working daughter of the poorest man in town. She promises that she will always willingly obey him, proves well gifted for helping him rule, and is much beloved by the people, but he insists on trying her steadfast devotion to the extreme. He takes both of their children away from her shortly after birth, telling her that he must kill them because the people feel that his heirs must not share her lowly ancestry. Finally he divorces her, sending her home, then recalling her to supervise the preparation of the palace and the reception of a new bride. She does everything willingly, until finally Walter reveals that the supposed bride and her brother are Griselda's own children, secretly raised by Walter's sister, and all live in affectionate happiness thereafter. Chaucer implies humorously that the story cannot literally mean that Griselda's behavior, any more than Walter's, is worthy of emulation, but rather that the story is an allegory of the constancy all should show in unavoidable adversity.

Cleveland, [Stephen] Grover (1837–1908) Twenty-second and twenty-fourth president of the U.S. (1884–88, 1892–96). Having served as mayor of Buffalo, New York, and as governor of New York, Cleveland was elected to the presidency on the Democratic ticket in 1884, defeating James G. Blaine. In 1886 he married Frances Folsom, in the first presidential wedding held in the White House. He ran for a second term in 1888 and was defeated by Benjamin Harrison, whom he in turn defeated in 1892. During the Panic of 1893, he secured the repeal of the Sherman Silver Purchase Act to end a drain in U.S. gold reserves. In 1894 he alienated labor by sending troops to Illinois to prevent interference with the mails during the Pullman Strike. He also invoked the Monroe Doctrine to help settle a boundary dispute between Venezuela and British Guiana. The hero of Paul Leicester Ford's *The Honorable Peter Stirling* (1894) is supposedly modeled on Cleveland.

Cleveland, John (or John Clieveland, 1613–1658) English METAPHYSICAL POET. A reader in rhetoric at Cambridge and a Royalist during the English Civil War, Cleveland wrote satire in both verse and prose against the Puritans. In his poetry, the metaphysical CONCEIT was carried to its point of greatest extravagance, degenerating often to a kind of witty ornamentation. He was very popular in his day and was imitated by numerous lesser poets. The most complete and authentic volume of his work was *Clievelandi Vindiciae, or Clieveland's Genuine Remains* (1677).

cliché (Fr, "stereotype plate for printing") A phrase or expression that has become trite and dull from overuse. "Sadder but wiser," "looming on the horizon," "fit as a fiddle," "green with envy," and "white as snow" are examples of clichés.

Clinker, Humphrey See HUMPHREY CLINKER, THE EXPEDITION OF.

Clio In classical mythology, one of the nine MUSES, the Muse of history and heroic poetry.

The English writer Joseph ADDISON adopted the name as a pseudonym, perhaps because many of his papers in *The Spectator* are signed with one of the four letters in this word, probably from the initial letters of Chelsea, London, Islington, Office.

Clive, Robert (baron Clive of Plassey, 1725–1774) Founder of the empire of British India and governor of Bengal (1764), who obtained for the East India Company sovereignty over the whole province. On his return to England in 1767, Clive met a storm of obloquy and inquiries into his actions, and although he was acquitted, he later committed suicide.

Clodius Pulcher, Publius (d 52 BC) Roman patrician and tribune. Clodius was known as a profligate and as a bitter enemy of CICERO. Cicero had disproved Clodius's alibi when the latter was accused of profaning the rites of the Bona Dea by attending them in disguise, and, though through bribery Clodius was acquitted, he hated Cicero and harassed him from then on. It was Clodius who passed a bill exiling anyone who put a Roman to death without right of appeal—a measure directed against Cicero, who had had members of the Cataline conspiracy executed—and thus sent Cicero into exile (58). Clodius was the brother of the notorious Clodia, the Lesbia of Catullus's poetry.

Cloelia In the legendary history of Rome, a Roman maiden, one of the hostages given to Lars Porsena. Cloelia made her escape from the Etruscan camp by swimming across the Tiber. She was sent back by the honorable Romans; Porsena, however, in recognition of her courage, not only set her at liberty but also released her fellow hostages. Mlle. de Scudéry took this story as the framework for her celebrated romance *Clélie*, published in ten volumes (1654–60).

Cloete, [Edward Fairly] Stuart [Graham] (1897–1976) South African novelist, born in Paris, educated in England. Cloete's best-known novel, *The Turning Wheels* (1937), was the first in a series of novels tracing the history of a family from the Boer settlement in South Africa to 1930. Because of its treatment of interracial love affairs, *The Turning Wheels* and four of his subsequent novels were banned in South Africa from 1937 to 1974. Other novels dealing with the Boer period include *The Curve and the Tusk* (1952) and *The Fiercest Heart* (1960). He also wrote such travel books as *The African Giant* (1955) and *West with the Sun* (1962), and two volumes of autobiography, *A Victorian Son* (1972) and *The Gambler* (1973).

Cloister and the Hearth, The (1861) A historical novel by Charles READE. The action takes place on the Continent in the latter years of the 15th century. Among the historical characters of note whom Reade introduces into the narrative are Froissart, Gringoire, Deschamps, Luther, Villon, and—as a child—Erasmus. The story centers around the tragically thwarted love of Erasmus's parents: Gerard, a talented calligrapher, and the red-haired Margaret, daughter of Peter Brandt. A forged letter convinces Gerard of Margaret's death, and, after a period of despair and wild living, he becomes a monk of the Dominican order, unaware that Margaret has given birth to Erasmus, his son. When, after many adventures and misadventures, the pair meet again, Gerard is unable, because of his vows, to live with his family. He manages, however, to settle nearby. Margaret soon dies of the plague, and the heartbroken Gerard dies shortly thereafter.

Clorinda In the GERUSALEMME LIBERATA of Tasso, a pagan warrior maid from Persia. Clorinda is the daughter of King Senapo (Senapus) of Ethiopia, but, when she is born, her mother the queen, fearful that the child's white complexion would arouse the suspicions of the king, substitutes a black child for her and gives her up to the care of the eunuch Arsete. At one point, Arsete loses her and she is suckled by a tiger. Later, he finds her again and takes her to the East, where she grows up skilled in arms. At the battle of Antioch, to which she comes to fight the knights of the First Crusade, she meets briefly and falls deeply in love with TANCREDI (Tancred), one of the leading Crusaders. When she offers her arms to the king of Jerusalem, Aladino, in exchange for the lives of Sofronia and Olindo, she finds herself once again in combat with her beloved. Unwittingly, Tancred wounds her in a night attack. Before she dies in his arms, she seeks baptism, having learned from Arsete of her Christian parentage. Tancred, in desperate grief, grants her wish and receives her forgiveness. Later, he has a vision of her in heaven.

Cloud, The (1820) A poem by Percy Bysshe SHELLEY. A lyrical description by a cloud of its cyclical journey from the sky to the earth and back once more to the sky, it expresses the poet's pantheism and his idea of nature's eternal alternation, rebirth, and recurrence.

Cloudcuckooland (Nephelococcygia) A Utopian city built in the sky by the birds in Aristophanes' comedy *The Birds*. It has come to refer to visionary schemes in general.

Clouds, The (Nephelai, 423 BC) A comedy by Aristophanes. This clever satire unfairly equates Socrates with the Sophists, noted for their capacity to use argument cunningly to prove whatever point they wished to make, whereas the actual Socrates seriously criticized them, believing that argument was useful only if it arrived at truth. A dishonest farmer, Strepsiades, encourages his son Phidippides to enroll in Socrates' school, the Thinkery, where he can learn to evade his numerous creditors through shrewd argument. Strepsiades is delighted with his son's immense success, until the young man turns his new talent against his father. At this point, the old man regrets turning away from the old virtues and ends by setting fire to the Thinkery.

Clown, The (Ansichten eines Clowns, 1963; tr 1965) A novel by Heinrich BÖLL. Disturbed by the ease with which German society and his middle-class parents forget their Nazi past and enjoy the post-World War II prosperity, Hans Schnier leaves home to make his living as a mimic. He moves from place to place, accompanied by his lover, Marie, showing amused audiences the follies of their lives in clever pantomimes. After five years, Marie leaves him, exhausted and disgusted because he refuses to marry her and assure her that their children will be educated in the Catholic faith. Her departure marks the beginning of Hans's professional and personal decline; he ends up a common beggar in the Bonn railway station. The novel is one of Böll's most eloquent attacks on German materialistic values and on the complacency and hypocrisy of the Catholic Church.

Clytemnestra In Greek legend, the daughter of Tyndareus and Leda. Clytemnestra became the wife of Agamemnon, whom she and her paramour Aegisthus later murdered after his return from Troy. She was slain by her son Orestes. See ATREUS, THE HOUSE OF.

Clytie In classical mythology, an ocean nymph, in love with the sun god. Clytie's love passed unnoticed, and she was changed into the heliotrope, or sunflower, which traditionally still turns to the sun, following him through his daily course.

Cobb, Irvin S[hrewsbury] (1876–1944) American writer and newspaperman. A well-known humorist and columnist for newspapers, *The Saturday Evening Post*, and *Cosmopolitan*, Cobb is best known for his amusing Judge PRIEST stories. He wrote over sixty books, including humorous skits and travel books, such as *Europe Revised* (1914), and an autobiography, *Exit Laughing* (1941). Cobb was an important figure in American humor, in the tradition of Artemus WARD and Mark TWAIN.

Coburn, Alvin Langdon (1882–1966) British photographer. Born in Boston, Coburn became a naturalized British subject in 1932. In 1902, with Alfred STIEGLITZ, he was a founder of Photo-Secession, a group working to establish photography as a fine art. His "vortographs," exhibited in 1917, were the first truly abstract photographs, reflecting the influence of the cubist and vorticist painters,

whom he met through Stieglitz; *Vortograph of Ezra Pound* is an often-reproduced example. He worked with many of the literary figures of his day, illustrating H. G. WELLS's *Door in the Wall and Other Stories* (1905), *Novels and Tales of Henry James* (1908), and SHELLEY's *The Cloud* (1912). His illustrated autobiography was published in 1966.

cockatrice A fabulous and heraldic monster with the wings of a fowl, tail of a dragon, and head of a cock. The cockatrice was so called because it was said to be produced from a cock's egg hatched by a serpent. According to legend, the very look of this monster would cause instant death. In consequence of the crest with which the head is crowned, the creature is also called a basilisk. Isaiah (King James version) says, "The weaned child shall put his hand on the cockatrice' den" (Is. 11:8), to signify that the most obnoxious animal should not hurt the most feeble of God's creatures.

Cock Lane Ghost The ghost of one Mrs. Kent, who appeared as a "luminous lady" and was supposedly responsible for mysterious noises. This fraud, perpetrated in Cock Lane, Smithfield, London, by a man and his eleven-year-old daughter, was exposed in 1762. Samuel Johnson took an interest in the ghost and was satirized for believing in it by Charles CHURCHILL in his poem "The Ghost"; Johnson's interest, of course, did not stem from credulity but from a determination to expose the fraud.

Cockney School An epithet applied by John Gibson LOCKHART to the group of writers that included Leigh HUNT, HAZLITT, SHELLEY, and KEATS. The group was largely composed of Londoners, and Lockhart, who was a devoted partisan of the LAKE POETS and a fierce enemy of writers whose aims or principles varied from his own, sneeringly referred to Hunt as "the Cockney Homer" and to Hazlitt as "the Cockney Aristotle."

Cocktail Party, The (1949) A verse play by T. S. ELIOT. On one level, the play is a contemporary drawing-room comedy dealing with the marriage of Edward and Lavinia and Edward's affair with Celia; on another, it is a profound religious work dealing with redemption. The verse is written in the rhythms of conversation, with passages of incantation and repetition.

Cocteau, Jean (1889–1963) French poet, novelist, dramatist, essayist, film writer, and director. In the vanguard of almost every experimental artistic movement in the first half of the 20th century, particularly CUBISM and SURREALISM, Cocteau produced work in virtually every genre of artistic expression, from ceramics and mural decoration to musical composition. He is best known, however, as a writer and for his lively association with the most creative innovators of his day, including PICASSO, STRAVINSKY, Blaise CENDRARS, and the composers of Les SIX. Through all his works runs the theme of the poet-angel, defier of destiny and guardian of the divine in man. The poet can be glimpsed in children and legendary heroes, but he risks being lost in the disorder of the modern world.

Cocteau's work in the theatre was largely presaged by his ballet productions for Diaghilev's Ballets Russes. The most famous of his modernistic ballets are *Parade* (1917), with music by Eric Satie and scenery by Picasso; *Le Boeuf sur le toit* (1920), with music by Darius Milhaud and decor by Raoul Dufy; and *Les Mariés de la tour Eiffel* (1921), with music by Les Six. His theatrical productions included both adaptations of myths and legends and pieces of his own creation. Well known among those of the first category were *Antigone* (1922; tr 1962); *Orphée* (1926; tr *Orpheus*, 1962); *Oedipe-Roi* (1928; tr *Oedipus Rex*, 1962); *La Machine infernale* (1934; tr *The Infernal Machine*, 1936), also on the Oedipal theme; *Les Chevaliers de la Table Ronde* (1937), drawn from Arthurian legend; and *Bacchus* (1951). Original plots include *La Voix humaine* (1930; tr *The Human Voice*, 1951), *Les Parents terribles* (1938), *La Machine à écrire* (1941; tr *The Typewriter*, 1947); and *L'Aigle a deux têtes* (1946; tr *The Eagle Has Two Heads*, 1947).

Cocteau's poetic novels are *Thomas l'imposteur* (1923; tr *The Imposter*, 1957), set in World War I; *Le Grande Ecart* (1923; tr *The Grand Ecart*, 1925); and Les Enfants terribles. He also wrote and directed films, many of which were based on his own plays or novels. His most famous films include the surrealistic *Le Sang d'un poète* (*The Blood of a Poet*, 1932), *L'Éternel Retour* (*The Eternal Return*, 1944), *La Belle et la bête* (*Beauty and the Beast*, 1945), *Les Parents terribles* (1948), *Les Enfants terribles* (1950), *Orphée* (1950), and *Le Testament d'Orphée* (1960).

In addition to a number of volumes of poetry, his works include the drawings, verse, and prose of *Le Potomak* (1913, pub 1919); the critical essays in *Le Rappel à l'ordre* (1926; tr *A Call to Order*, 1926); and the autobiographical books *Opium* (1930; tr 1932), *Portraits—Souvenir* (1935; tr *Paris Album*, 1956), and *Cahiers* (1956; tr *Journals*, 1969). *Cocteau's World* (1973; ed and tr M. Crosland) is an anthology of his writings.

Cody, William F[rederick] (known as Buffalo Bill, 1846–1917)   American scout, showman, and folk hero. An expert horseman and marksman, Cody was a rider for the pony express, a frontier scout, and a hunter of buffalo. After 1883 he toured the U.S. and Europe in his Wild West Show. Cody's career was popularized by the dime novels of E.Z.C. Judson (Ned Buntline), who claimed that he had given Cody his sobriquet.

Coehlo Neto, Enrique [Maximiano] (1864–1934)   Brazilian novelist and short-story writer. Coehlo Neto wrote numerous novels and stories of psychological realism in a sensual, Parnassian prose. *Inverno em flor* (1897) is an in-depth probe into the psychopathology of his central character's moral and erotic degeneration. *A conquista* (1899) together with *Fogo fatuo* (1929) provides an excellent fictionalized documentary of his life and the intellectual climate of his generation. *O turbilhão* (1906), perhaps the highest point of his uneven career, portrays with great insight and compassion the corporal and spiritual decay of a "decent" family.

cogito ergo sum   (Lat, "I think, therefore I exist") The axiom of Descartes. It was formulated as the starting place of his system of philosophy. Descartes, at the beginning, provisionally doubted everything, but he could not doubt the existence of himself, for the mere fact that *I* doubt presupposes the existence of the *I*: in other words, the doubt could not exist without the doubter.

Cohan, George M[ichael] (1878–1942)   American actor, song writer, playwright, and producer. As a child, Cohan acted in vaudeville in a family theatrical group, The Four Cohans. The first play that he wrote, produced, and acted in was *The Governor's Son* (1901). He followed this with *Little Johnny Jones* (1904), in which he played a role always thereafter associated with him, "the Yankee Doodle Boy." Among his musicals and dramas were *Forty-Five Minutes from Broadway* (1906); *Get-Rich-Quick Wallingford* (1908); *Broadway Jones* (1912), a play and musical about a young spendthrift; and *Seven Keys to Baldpate* (1913), based on a novel by Earl Derr Biggers. In the course of his career, Cohan wrote many songs that have remained American favorites: "Over There," "I'm a Yankee Doodle Dandy," "Grand Old Flag," "Give My Regards to Broadway," and "Mary Is a Grand Old Name."

Coignard, Jérôme   A character created by Anatole France. Coignard is an irreverent, licentious abbé who also manages to be a wise and witty philosopher. The chief personage in *La Rôtisserie de la reine Pédauque* and *Les Opinions de Jérôme Coignard* (both 1893), Coignard is one of France's most popular characters. Many of the author's own beliefs and opinions are voiced by him.

Colbert, Jean Baptiste (1619–1683)   French statesman. After hastening the downfall of Fouquet, Colbert was made controller general of finance by Louis XIV in 1665. Although Colbert initiated many wise reforms, the costs of the king's wars and courtly extravagances defeated his plans to increase national prosperity. Colbert founded several academies and was a patron of men of letters.

Colchis   In Greek mythology, a city at the eastern end of the Black Sea on the River Phasis. Colchis was ruled by Aeetes, from whom the Argonauts stole the Golden Fleece.

Cold Comfort Farm (1932)   A novel by Stella Gibbons (1902–   ). A brilliant parody of the novel of rustic pessimism, such as those written by Mary Webb (see Precious Bane) and other writers in the Hardy tradition, it virtually put an end to a widely popular genre.

Cole, King   Legendary English king, best known as the Old King Cole of the nursery rhyme. He is sometimes identified with the Coel who, according to Geoffrey of Monmouth, made himself king of the Britons in the 3rd century, was the father of St. Helena and thus the grandfather of the Emperor Constantine the Great. He appears often in literature, as in John Masefield's poem "King Cole" (1921).

Cole, Thomas (1801–1848)   British-born American painter. For a time after his family's arrival in Ohio in 1818, Cole worked as an itinerant portrait painter, but it was as a landscape painter that he achieved his greatest fame. He moved to Philadelphia, where he studied at the Pennsylvania Academy of Design, and in 1826 to New York, where he founded the National Academy of Design and became a leading member of the HUDSON RIVER SCHOOL of landscape painters. His paintings, such as *The Oxbow* (1836), executed in his studio after sketches from nature, came increasingly to reflect the conflict between the popular taste for realistic rendition of the natural landscape and Cole's own penchant for moralistic and romantic themes. The series *The Voyage of Life* (1840) reveals this later didacticism.

Coleridge, Samuel Taylor (1772–1834)   English poet, essayist, and critic. The son of a Devonshire clergyman, Coleridge was a precocious, dreamy boy; he attended Christ's Hospital school, where he met Charles Lamb and formed a friendship that was to last a lifetime. He attended Cambridge (1791–93, 1794) but did not receive a degree. In 1794 he met Robert Southey at Oxford, and the two developed their plan, called *pantisocracy*, to establish a small, ideal community in the U.S. Unable to finance their project, they had to abandon it. In the meantime, because marriage was an essential factor in the pantisocratic scheme, Coleridge became engaged to Sarah Fricker, sister of Southey's fiancée, only to discover, too late, that his love for Mary Evans was reciprocated. His unfortunate marriage (1795) to Miss Fricker ended in separation some seven years later.

In 1796 Coleridge published his first volume of poetry and in the same year began the publication of *The Watchman*, a liberal political periodical, which lasted only ten issues. He was by now in great financial difficulty and was considering entering the Unitarian ministry, when the brothers Josiah and Thomas Wedgwood granted him an annuity of 150 pounds, thus enabling him to pursue his literary career.

In 1797 Coleridge formed a friendship with Wordsworth, a friendship that stimulated Coleridge's finest achievements in poetry, including THE RIME OF THE ANCIENT MARINER, KUBLA KHAN, and the first part of "Christabel." Wordsworth and Coleridge together published LYRICAL BALLADS and subsequently traveled to Germany, where Coleridge studied philosophy at Göttingen University and mastered the German language. On their return to England (1799), Coleridge translated Schiller's *Wallenstein*. Afflicted by the damp climate of the Lake District, where he had settled in order to be near Wordsworth, Coleridge took up opium as a remedy and swiftly became addicted. After the second part of "Christabel" and "Dejection: An Ode" (1802), Coleridge wrote very little poetry. Hoping to improve his health, he sailed to Malta in 1804 but returned to England in 1806 without improvement. From 1808 to 1819, he gave seven series of lectures on Shakespeare and other literary subjects, which were brilliant if disorganized. During the years 1809 and 1810 he published a politico-philosophical review, *The Friend*, and a revised version of his tragedy *Osorio* (written 1797) was successfully produced in 1813. Three years later, Coleridge took up residence with a doctor, in order to control his opium addiction. In 1817 he republished his earlier poems and BIOGRAPHIA LITERARIA, which contains a good deal of information on Wordsworth as well as much of Coleridge's finest literary criticism. Although his poetic achievement was small in quantity, Coleridge was without a doubt the most perceptive English critic of his time and was virtually the intellectual spokesman for the English romantic movement.

Colette (pen name of Sidonie Gabrielle Colette, 1873–1954)   French novelist. The CLAUDINE books, written with Colette's husband, were published under his pseudonym, Willy. After their collaboration ended in 1904 and until 1916, she used the name Colette Willy, then Colette. She became a music-hall dancer and mime, and she wrote *La Vagabonde* (1910; tr 1912), *L'Envers du music-hall* (1913), and *Mitsou* (1919). Remarried twice, she continued to write wry, penetrating novels of the demimonde and the feminine heart, often the aging one, as in *Chéri* (1920; tr 1929) and *La Fin de Chéri* (1926). Her best-known works include *Gigi* (1945; tr 1952), her childhood reminiscences in *La Maison de Claudine* (1922; tr *My Mother's House*, 1953) and *Sido* (1929; tr 1953), her description of the German occupation in *Paris de ma fenêtre* (1944), and her late memoirs, published in *L'Étoile Vesper* (1946; tr *The Evening Star*, 1973) and *Le Fanal bleu* (1949; tr *The Blue Lantern*, 1953). *The Collected Stories of Colette* appeared in 1983.

Colin Clouts Come Home Againe (1595)   A long allegorical pastoral poem by Edmund SPENSER. The shepherd Colin Clout describes to his fellow-shepherds his journey with the Shepherd of the Ocean (Sir Walter Raleigh) to the land of the beautiful shepherdess Cynthia (Queen Elizabeth). Colin Clout also appears in THE SHEPHEARDES CALENDER.

Collar, The (1633)   A poem by George HERBERT, in which the author, after rebelling against his profitless service of God, is abruptly and totally reconciled. The poem makes use of irregular line lengths and rhymes to achieve a remarkable dramatic effect. The collar is the clerical collar, emblem of servitude to God.

Collection, The (1962)   A one-act play by Harold
PINTER. It is about a homosexual man who is accused of
making love to another man's wife. The husband enters
into a strange, aggressive relationship with the accused,
perhaps in an attempt to enrage the homosexual's partner
as he himself feels outrage and injury. *The Collection* was
first produced on BBC television (1961).

Collège de France   An institution of higher learning in Paris. Founded by Francis I in 1530 at the instigation of Guillaume Budé (1468–1540), it represented an
attempt to place humanistic studies on an equal footing
with the theological studies provided at the Sorbonne.
Hebrew and Greek were taught for the first time, thus earning the Collège the plaudits of enthusiastic humanists such
as Rabelais and Ronsard. First known as the Collège des
Lecteurs royaux, it has been called the Collège de France
since the Revolution.

Collier, John (1901–1980)   English-born American
short-story writer and novelist. Collier's first novel, *His
Monkey Wife: Or, Married to a Chimp* (1931), was written
in the sardonic and fantastic vein that characterized his
later work. His other novels include *Full Circle* (1933) and
Defy the Foul Fiend (1934). He is best known for his
numerous short stories, which are witty, satiric, grotesque,
often macabre, and graced with a delicate style. Many of
his best stories are collected in *Fancies and Goodnights*
(1951).

Collin, Jacques   The consummate villain of
Honoré de Balzac's LA COMÉDIE HUMAINE. Collin plays a
part in many of the novels. In LE PÈRE GORIOT, under the
name and disguise of Vautrin, he makes love to the landlady and eats her cheap scanty food, until the spiteful Mlle
Michonneau gives him up to the police. Collin also
appears in *Les Splendeurs et misères des courtisanes* (1843)
and *La Dernière Incarnation de Vautrin* (1847), as a Spanish priest and philosopher.

Collins, Mr.   In Jane Austen's PRIDE AND PREJU-
DICE, a self-important clergyman, very much the toady and
prig. Elizabeth Bennet refuses Mr. Collins's proposal of
marriage, and he marries Charlotte Lucas instead.

Collins, [William] Wilkie (1824–1889)   English
novelist, best known as the author of THE WOMAN IN
WHITE and THE MOONSTONE. Collins is considered by
some to have been the first English author of bona fide
detective and mystery novels. Collins was a good friend of
Charles Dickens, a contributor to Dickens's magazines and
occasional collaborator. The two men admired and influenced each other, and, though their talents are in other
respects unequal, Collins occasionally rivaled Dickens in
the creation of character and mood and excelled him in
handling plot. Among Collins's other books are *The New
Magdalen* (1873), *The Haunted Hotel* (1879), and *Heart
and Science* (1883).

Collins, William (1721–1759)   English poet. One
of the preromantics of the 18th century, Collins wrote only
a small quantity of poetry, consisting chiefly of odes on
nature subjects in a quiet, melancholy vein, distinguished
by their smoothness and their skillful use of sound effects.
Such work, centering on a personified abstraction, came to
be called the descriptive or allegorical ode. His best-known
poems, many of which were published in *Odes on Several
Descriptive and Allegorical Subjects* (1746), are "Ode to
Evening" (1746); "How Sleep the Brave" (1746); "Dirge in
Cymbeline" (1744); and "Ode Occasioned by the Death of
Mr. Thomson" (1749), commemorating his significant literary relationship with the poet James Thomson. Collins's
view of poetry, as set forth in his "Ode on the Poetical
Character" (1746), is that it is essentially imaginative,
divine in origin, and wild and impassioned in method and
insight. All his life, Collins suffered from poverty and illness, and he became insane before his death.

Collodi   See PINOCCHIO, THE ADVENTURES OF.

Colonna, Francesco (1432?–?1527)   Italian
author and Dominican monk. Colonna created one of the
most beautiful and mystifying books of the Italian Renaissance, the *Hypnerotomachia Poliphili* (*The Strife of Love in
a Dream with the Lover of Polia*). Written in 1467, it was
published by Aldus in 1499, with nearly twenty woodcuts.
In two books and in a Latinized Italian prose, the author
tells of the dream journey of Poliphilus and of his love for
Polia. Beneath the surface of its allegorical and romantic
plot lie various esoteric meanings and devices, such as the
fact that the initial letters of its chapters spell out the
author's name and address. An anonymous Elizabethan
translation spread its influence, and its appeal extended to
modern times, as in Charles Reade's CLOISTER AND THE
HEARTH.

Colonna, Vittoria (1492–1547)   Italian poet.
Colonna was a friend of MICHELANGELO, who addressed
several of his poems to her. Her own poems include sonnets on her dead husband, Ferrante d'Avalos, and upon
religious themes. They were published in her *Canzoniere*
(*Song Book*, 1538).

coloquio de los perros, El   One of the stories in
Cervantes's NOVELAS EJEMPLARES. In this PICARESQUE tale,
the dog Berganza is given the power of speech for one night
and describes to another dog his experiences under various
masters, satirizing human behavior in the process.

**Colossians, The Epistle of Paul the Apostle
to the**   A book of the New Testament. Colossians is a
letter written by Paul, while he was in prison, to the early
Christians of Colossae, the ancient city of Phrygia in Asia
Minor. He urges them to ignore the syncretic ideas then
common in the Near East.

Colossus of Maroussi, The   See MILLER,
HENRY.

Colossus of Rhodes A gigantic statue of HELIOS on the island of Rhodes. Completed about 280 BC, this famous statue commemorated the successful defense of Rhodes against Demetrius Poliorcetes in 304 BC. One of the SEVEN WONDERS OF THE WORLD, it stood 105 feet high and is said to have been made from the warlike engines abandoned by DEMETRIUS. It was designed and built by the sculptor Chares, a pupil of Lycippus. The story that it fell and destroyed the harbor arose only in the 16th century.

Colum, Padraic (1881–1972) Irish poet and dramatist, resident in the U.S. after 1914. Colum was associated with the IRISH RENAISSANCE and the Irish National Theatre (later the ABBEY THEATRE) with William Butler YEATS, A.E. (q.v.), Lady GREGORY, and J. M. SYNGE. That theatre saw the production of his two naturalistic dramas, *Broken Soul* (1903; rev as *The Fiddler's House*, 1907) and *Thomas Muskerry* (1910). His plays, however, showed less promise than his poetry, which was appreciated for its lyricism and rich celebration of the language of rural Ireland. Colum's volumes of verse include the early poems in *Wild Earth* (1907), about Irish country life, *Poems* (1932; rev as *Collected Poems*, 1953), and *Images of Departure* (1968). Many of his poems, notably "She Passed Through the Fair," have been set to music and are familiar as songs. He also wrote books on folklore, travel books, and novels, including *Castle Conquer* (1923) and *The Flying Swans* (1957). With his wife, Mary, he wrote *Our Friend James Joyce* (1958).

Columba, St. (Irish name Colum, 521–597) An Irish saint. After establishing several churches and monasteries in Ireland, the nobly born Columba converted the Picts in northern Scotland, where he founded more monasteries.

Columban, St. (543–615) An Irish saint. Most of Columban's life was devoted to the founding of monasteries in France, Switzerland, and Italy. Several of his erudite writings are extant.

Columbiad, The (1807) An epic poem by Joel BARLOW, first published in briefer form as *The Vision of Columbus* (1787). Columbus is taken by Hesper, the spirit of the Western World, to the Mount of Visiton and there foresees the future of the North American continent.

Columbine (fr Ital, *columbina*, "little dove") A stock character from COMMEDIA DELL'ARTE, representing a shrewd, vivacious, and coquettish maidservant. Columbine is the daughter of PANTALOON and the sweetheart of HARLEQUIN. She was transplanted to English pantomime, and, in the mid-18th century, she was given new vitality, under a variety of names. See PIERROT.

Columbus, Christopher (Spanish name Cristóbal Colón; Italian name Cristoforo Colombo; 1451–1506) Discoverer of America. The son of a Genoese wool weaver, Columbus went to sea as a youth, becoming a skilled navigator. He conceived a plan to reach Asia by sailing westward, but was rebuffed at the English, French, and Portuguese courts; in 1492 FERDINAND and ISABELLA of Spain finally agreed to sponsor the voyage, naming him Admiral of the Ocean Sea, Viceroy, and governor of the lands he might discover.

Columbus set sail from Palos, Spain, on August 3, 1492, with a fleet of three ships: the *Niña*, the *Pinta*, and the flagship *Santa María*—and some ninety officers and men. On October 12, he made his first landfall, at an island in the Bahamas, probably Guanahuani, which he called San Salvador. Ignorant of the fact that he had discovered a new world, Columbus then reached Cuba and Hispaniola (Santo Domingo), where he established a settlement called Navidad, and sailed for Spain.

During his second voyage (1493–96), Columbus discovered Puerto Rico and Jamaica. However, he began to have difficulties with the Spaniards on Hispaniola, who chafed at his iron discipline. Returning to America in 1498, he touched Trinidad and sailed along the coast of Venezuela. Meanwhile the trouble on Hispaniola continued, and Francisco Bobadilla, who had been sent as royal commissioner to investigate complaints against Columbus, ordered him back to Spain in chains. Though none of his political powers were restored, Columbus was permitted to undertake a fourth voyage (1502–4), during which he explored the coast of Central America. After being marooned on Jamaica for over a year, he returned to Spain, where he died in poverty and neglect. Both Seville and Santo Domingo claim to possess his remains.

The best known of Columbus's writings is the journal of his first voyage. Washington Irving wrote a biography, *History of the Life and Voyages of Columbus* (1828), based on material he gathered while serving as an attaché at the American legation in Madrid. Poems about the great discoverer include James Russell LOWELL's "Columbus" (1847), Walt WHITMAN's "The Prayer of Columbus" (1874), and Joaquin Miller's "Columbus" (1896). Paul CLAUDEL wrote a dramatic oratorio, *The Book of Christopher Columbus* (1927), with music by Darius Milhaud.

Combray A French village in REMEMBRANCE OF THINGS PAST, by Marcel PROUST. The narrator's family visit relatives there, and it is the scene of many of his childhood memories, including the walks along the MÉSÉGLISE WAY and the Guermantes Way. Based on the village of Illiers, southwest of Chartres on the Loire River, it includes some details from Proust's birthplace in the Parisian suburb of Auteuil.

comedia de capa y espada (Sp, "cloak-and-sword play") A form of Spanish drama, dealing with the upper middle classes and deriving its name from the typical street costume of these groups. Stressing incident rather than characterization, these plays have complex and romantic plots that employ such devices as mistaken identities, disguises, and mutual misunderstandings. Lope de VEGA and CALDERÓN wrote excellent examples of this type of play.

comédie-ballet   A theatrical form, originally devised by MOLIÈRE for the entertainment of Louis XIV, consisting of comedy with ballet inserted between the acts. The *comédie-ballet* was one of the most popular entertainments of 17th-century France.

Comédie française (also known as Le Théâtre français or La Maison de Molière)   French national theatre. Formed officially in 1680 by decree of Louis XIV, the Comédie française had previously been closely associated with MOLIÈRE and his company. For nearly a century (1689–1770), it performed in a converted tennis court; then it moved to the Salle des Machines at the Tuileries; and in 1789 it obtained a new theatre, which later became the Odéon, near the Luxembourg gardens. The French Revolution caused a split in the company; the conservative group stayed at the Odéon, which was shortly later destroyed by fire, while the liberal members moved to a theatre on the rue de Richelieu, where, after the company was reunited in 1799, the Comédie française has continued to operate to the present day.

Comédie humaine, La (Fr, "The Human Comedy")   The title given by Honoré de BALZAC in 1841 to the whole body of his work, including both completed and projected novels. The vast canvas of the work is France itself, seen from a variety of perspectives and peopled by more than two thousand characters. Individuals of all social classes are depicted with accuracy and massive detail. A forerunner of such naturalistic works as those of ZOLA and the GONCOURT brothers, *La Comédie humaine* is divided into three main areas of study: manners, philosophy, and marriage. The first group is subdivided into scenes of private, provincial, Parisian, country, political, and military life. Among the best known of these novels are LES CHOUANS, EUGÉNIE GRANDET, LE PÈRE GORIOT, *La Recherche de l'absolu* (1834), *César Birotteau* (1837), *Le Curé de village* (1839), LA COUSINE BETTE, THE COUNTRY DOCTOR, and COUSIN PONS.

comédie larmoyante (Fr, "tearful comedy")   A popular French 18th-century type of sentimental comedy, in which the exaggeratedly pathetic situations of the characters made the audience weep. Concern with the triumph of virtue afforded playwrights the opportunity of moralizing to excess. Examples of this type of play are to be found in *La Fausse Antipathie* (1733), *Le Préjugé à la mode* (1735), and *Mélanide* (1741) by La Chausée (1692–1754); in VOLTAIRE's *L'Enfant prodigue* (1736) and *Nanine* (1749); and in *Le Glorieux* (1732) by Destouches (1680–1754). The *comédie larmoyante* was to develop into the BOURGEOIS DRAMA.

comedy (fr Gr, *komos*, "revel")   A form of literature designed to amuse by use of wit, humor, criticism, or ridicule. It is often distinguished from TRAGEDY, which tries to evoke profound emotions from the audience. In the POETICS, Aristotle makes a distinction between the two, noting that, in comedy, characters are figures from daily life in everyday situations. Comedy is usually identified as a dramatic form, but the term can also be applied to nondramatic works, such as Dante's DIVINE COMEDY. As a dramatic genre, the form grew out of the raucous village processions associated with fertility rites in the worship of the Greek god DIONYSUS.

The first recognized dramatic form was Attic OLD COMEDY, in which a series of scenes of farce, SATIRE, BURLESQUE, or political invective were linked by a CHORUS. The scathing social satires of ARISTOPHANES were the best examples of Old Comedy, which declined after the defeat of Athens into Middle Comedy, of which there are no extant examples. By the 4th century BC, comedy, in the form of New Comedy, had taken a more literary and romantic turn. The plays of MENANDER, the best known of the period, influenced the Roman playwrights PLAUTUS and TERENCE.

Roman comedy in turn influenced comic drama of the Middle Ages, which, although discouraged by the Church, was kept alive in folk plays and festivals and in farcical scenes in MIRACLE PLAYS.

The INTERLUDES of the late 15th and early 16th centuries form a link between miracle plays and ELIZABETHAN comedy. These brief entertainments, presented between courses at a feast, with their realistic characters and traces of classic Roman comedy, contributed to the secularization of comedy.

John LYLY and Nicholas Udall (1504–56) are considered the first English comic dramatists, and English comic drama can be said to begin with Udall's RALPH ROISTER DOISTER. The COMMEDIA DELL'ARTE developed in Italy at the same time. This improvisational theatre, using stock characters speaking local dialects in often farcical situations, had a great influence on European comedy.

During the RENAISSANCE, English comedy attained a fine level of sophistication in the works of SHAKESPEARE and Ben JONSON. Influenced by classical drama, Jonson demonstrated his mastery of biting satire, whereas Shakespeare perfected the romantic comedy, although his work encompassed a wider range, from the farcical to the tragicomic. During the 17th century, French comedy flourished in the works of MOLIÈRE, who combined classical influences and COMMEDIA DELL'ARTE in his satires and comedies.

The sobering effect of the 16th and 17th centuries, in which theorists and moralists maintained that the purpose of comedy was not only to amuse and entertain but also to instruct, led to the total suppression of the form in England during the revolution. With the RESTORATION, the theatre was revived, and the witty and licentious COMEDY OF MANNERS, with its satirical tone and artificial forms, was staged by such playwrights as CONGREVE and WYCHERLEY.

The sentimental comedy in England and its French counterpart, the COMÉDIE LARMOYANTE, succeeded Restoration drama. These exaggerated, sentimental plays, designed to make the audience weep more than laugh, continued in vogue until the return of the witty and satirical comedies of manners of GOLDSMITH and SHERIDAN.

No new comic form emerged after the popularity of sentimental comedies until the late 20th century; however, many playwrights worked within and perfected established comic conventions. In France, SCRIBE wrote a large number of comedies, known as WELL-MADE PLAYS. CHEKHOV produced his subtle character comedies about Russian aristocracy. G. B. SHAW wrote philosophical comedies, intended more for a reading than a stage audience, and used plays such as MAN AND SUPERMAN as vehicles for his unorthodox and iconoclastic ideas.

The most significant contribution to comic drama in the 20th century has been the THEATRE OF THE ABSURD, a form of drama characterized by BLACK HUMOR and unconventional forms and subject matter. See BECKETT, SAMUEL; IONESCO, EUGÈNE.

Comedy of Errors, The (c1594) A comedy by
William SHAKESPEARE. Aemilia, wife of Aegeon, has twin sons, both named Antipholus, who, shipwrecked in infancy, have been carried one to Syracuse, the other to Ephesus. The play represents Antipholus of Syracuse going in search of his brother; to make the confusion of identities more absurd, the brothers each have a slave named DROMIO, and the Dromios are also indistinguishable twins. Adriana, the wife of the Ephesian, mistakes the Syracusan for her husband and later has her real husband arrested as a madman. Great confusion results, but ultimately the matter is brought into court. Not only do the brothers recognize each other at last, but their mother, Aemilia, now an abbess, in whose priory the Syracusan had taken refuge during the excitement, and their father, Aegeon, who had come to Ephesus to search for his son, appear in court, and the entire family is reunited. The sources of the plot are the *Menaechmi* and the *Amphitruo* of PLAUTUS, both written in the 2nd century BC.

comedy of humours A form of drama based on
the medieval and Renaissance theory of HUMOURS, the physiological interpretation of character and personality. Different characters represented various types who were ruled by a particular trait, passion, or humour. Although common to medieval allegories, the form was popularized by Ben Jonson with EVERY MAN IN HIS HUMOUR and *Every Man Out of His Humour* (1599). He explains the formula for humorous characters:

Some one peculiar quality
Doth so possess a man, that it doth draw
All his affects, his spirits, and his powers,
In their confluctions, all to run one way.

comedy of manners A form of drama written
during the RESTORATION period, usually satirical and concerned with conventions and manners of a sophisticated and artificial society. Often the satire is directed against aberrant social behavior, the dialogue is witty and polished, and the plot frequently involves illicit lovers. Characters are more often types than individuals. Congreve's THE WAY OF THE WORLD typified the English Restoration comedy of manners. The form was revived by Goldsmith in SHE STOOPS TO CONQUER and by Sheridan in THE RIVALS. Noël COWARD made the form popular in modern theatre.

comedy of morals A form of dramatic satire that
uses ridicule to correct vices and pretension. Molière's TARTUFFE is an example of this form.

comic relief The relaxation of the audience's tension by means of an interpolated comic episode in a serious play. Its function is to permit a stronger renewal of the emotional surge. Some critics hold that the function of such scenes is not relief but increased tension through senseless and ironical juxtaposition of opposites. A good example is the grave-diggers' scene in HAMLET.

Commager, Henry Steele (1902–   ) American historian. A native of Pittsburgh, Pennsylvania, Commager was educated at the University of Chicago. From 1939 to 1956, he taught history at Columbia University; in 1956 he joined the faculty of Amherst College. His books on American history are highly regarded among both scholars and the general public. Among his many works, including some of his frequent collaborations, are *The Growth of the American Republic* (1930), written with S. E. MORISON and subsequently revised and expanded; *Theodore Parker* (1936); *America: The Story of a Free People* (1942), with Allan NEVINS; *Majority Rule and Minority Rights* (1943); *The American Mind* (1950); and *The Search for a Usable Past* (1967). He also edited, again with Nevins, *The Documents of American History* (1934) and the fifty-volume *Rise of the American Nation* series. Commager's contribution to America's bicentennial was *The Empire of Reason* (1977), in which he asserts that post-Revolutionary America was the most enlightened period in world history.

commedia dell'arte (Ital, "comedy of the profession; comedy of skill") Italian dramatic genre dating from the mid-16th century, when professional theatrical companies, especially the famous Gelosi ("The Jealous Ones") began to include in their repertoire a new form of comedy, characterized by improvisation upon a bare outline of plot (*scenario*) and the use of stock characters, some wearing masks, that combined features of the learned as well as the popular drama. It is this testing of the actor's virtuosity and skill, not an association with a professional craft or guild, that gave the genre its name. Among the famous and enduring stock characters were "the beautiful young lady,"

an ingenue with a name such as Julia or Lucinda; her "lover," handsome but impecunious, sometimes called Octavio; Pantalone, a Venetian merchant, as foolish as he is wealthy; the Doctor, sometimes called Graziano, who is a hopeless pedant; a braggart captain, later called Scaramuccia; and a collection of servants who provide anything from sparkling wit to acrobatics as they move in and out of the story, sometimes helping, at other times hindering the affairs of their masters and mistresses. The oldest of the wily or blundering manservants is Zanni (a dialect version of *Gianni* or *Giovanni*); later the word was used to designate a whole troupe of comedians. Later variations of the type included Arlecchino or Harlequin, famous for his particolored costume (derived from the original patched garments he wore); he is sometimes called Truffaldino or Mezzetino; Tartaglia, noted for his eyeglasses and his comic stuttering; Brighella, the usual companion of Arlecchino; and Pulcinella, who speaks in Neapolitan dialect, has a tremendous nose, and is always hungry—he survives in the Punch and Judy shows of the puppet theatre. The *commedia dell'arte* was popular in Italy and, thanks to traveling companies, throughout Europe for several hundred years; it strongly influenced the development of European comedy and of individual writers such as Molière, Goldoni, and Gozzi.

Commemoration Ode (1865)   A poem by James Russell Lowell, more accurately entitled "Ode Recited at the Harvard Commemoration." It was written on request in honor of the Harvard students who had died in the Civil War. In its published form, Lowell added sixty-six lines, beginning with the famous "Such was he, our Martyr-Chief."

Commentaries on the Gallic War (c58–44 bc) A historical work in seven books by Julius Caesar. Written in a brisk, straightforward third person, each book covering one year, it narrates the campaigns, starting in 58 bc, by which Caesar made Gaul a permanent part of the empire. Though not intended as polished literature, the work is valued as a masterpiece of clear, concise Latin and historical accuracy. Caesar, who had never lost a campaign or left the field before the enemy, had no reason to exaggerate or misrepresent; perhaps the only subjective note in the *Commentaries* is introduced in his justification of the war.

Committee of Public Safety (Comité de salut public)   A committee that assumed direction of the French government from 1793 to 1795. Formed on April 6, 1793, and theoretically subordinate to the Constitutional Convention, this committee soon concentrated all power in its hands and instituted the Reign of Terror. Its most famous members were Robespierre, Antoine Saint-Just, Georges Couthon, Lazare Carnot, and Bertrand Barrère.

commonplace book   A notebook of quotations, ideas, words, and phrases, collected and often classified according to subject matter. Commonplace books are used for reference, as a storage place for thoughts, or as a collected miscellany of arguments on any given theme.

Common Sense (1776)   A political treatise by Thomas Paine, urging immediate separation from England. In a few months, more than a hundred thousand copies were published in America. The work was influential in bringing about the Declaration of Independence.

Commune of Paris   (1) The revolutionary government established in Paris during 1792 by the representatives of the communes, the smallest administrative districts of France. It led to the period known as the Reign of Terror.

(2) The insurrectionary government that took possession of Paris (March 18–May 28, 1871), after the withdrawal of the Prussian troops.

Communist Manifesto, The (Das Kommunistische Manifest, 1848)   A pamphlet by Karl Marx and Friedrich Engels, the classic document of communist theory. It analyzes history in terms of class conflict, predicts the imminent overthrow of the ruling bourgeoisie by the oppressed proletariat, and envisions a resulting classless society in which personal property would be abolished. The *Manifesto* calls upon the proletariat of the world to unite and strengthen itself for this final revolution.

Compensation (1841)   An essay by Ralph Waldo Emerson. The writer claims that evil is balanced by good, that "every sweet hath its sour; every evil its good." The doctrine of compensation, precluding the necessity for an afterlife, caused Emerson to be criticized by the religiously orthodox, as well as by liberals who considered his view too naïve.

Complaint of Deor   See Deor's Lament.

Compleat Angler, The, or the Contemplative Man's Recreation   (1653)   A treatise on fishing by Izaak Walton. It takes the form of a dialogue, in which Piscator (an angler) tries to convince Venator (a hunter) that fishing is the superior sport. Their friend Auceps, a fowler, is silenced early in the work. Charles Cotton wrote a continuation, which appeared in the fifth edition (1676).

Compromise of 1850   In U.S. history, a collective name for five acts of Congress that attempted to settle the controversy over the extension of slavery into the territory recently acquired from Mexico. In the Senate, Henry Clay and Daniel Webster supported compromise measures, John C. Calhoun pleaded for equal rights for the South, and William Seward argued that "a higher law" forbade constitutional safeguards for slavery. The compromise bills provided for the admission of California as a free state and for the establishment of territorial governments in New Mexico and Utah without restrictions regarding slavery; in addition, the Fugitive Slave Law was strengthened, and the slave trade was abolished in the District of Columbia.

Compson A family in THE SOUND AND THE FURY and other works by William FAULKNER. One of the old, aristocratic families of YOKNAPATAWPHA COUNTY, the Compsons trace their American ancestry back to the early 18th century, but, by the early 20th century, the family is decaying. In the 1930s, the family property is sold and the last male Compson is a childless bachelor. The family includes Benjamin, the idiot of *The Sound and the Fury*; Candace (Caddy), a girl whose checkered career includes a seduction, a marriage to a banker and another to a motion-picture executive, and who is last seen in Paris during the German occupation; Jason Lycurgus Compson I, the first of the family to settle in Mississippi; Jason II, a brigadier general in the Civil War, to whom Thomas Sutpen of ABSALOM, ABSALOM! tells part of his story; Jason III, an intelligent but ineffectual lawyer, who first sells some of the family property; Jason IV, a shrewd and selfish storekeeper, who sells the remaining property; Quentin Compson, the illegitimate daughter of Caddy; Quentin MacLachan Compson, an introspective young man, who commits suicide at Harvard in 1910.

In addition to *The Sound and the Fury*, the Compson family appears in the short story "That Evening Sun," and Quentin MacLachan Compson is one of the three narrators in *Absalom, Absalom!* (1936).

Compton-Burnett, Ivy (1892–1969) English novelist. A pitiless observer of human nature, Compton-Burnett wrote witty and terrifying social comedies of family life—all in dialogue. Her novels are set in large country houses, between 1885 and 1901, and are characterized by mannered, aphoristic dialogue between members of an in-grown household. The story that emerges almost invariably involves a power struggle between an exploitive tyrant and his victims (often servants or precocious children), which precipitates some violent crime. Among her many novels are *Pastors and Masters* (1925), *Brothers and Sisters* (1929), *A House and Its Head* (1935), *Manservant and Maidservant* (1947; U.S. *Bullivant and the Lambs*, 1948), *Two Worlds and Their Ways* (1949), *Mother and Son* (1956), and *The Mighty and Their Fall* (1962).

Comte, [Isidore] Auguste [Marie François] (1798–1857) French philosopher. Known as the founder of positivism, Comte sought to apply the methods of observation and experimentation used in the sciences to philosophy, social science, and even religion. He hoped that, through the use of such methods, rather than through idealistic appeal to absolute principles, social reform might be achieved. The philosophy of positivism admits only knowledge gained by the scientific method as real or positive. *Cours de philosophie positive* (6 vols, 1830–42) is Comte's basic formulation of the doctrine. Comte had a significant influence on the thought of his time. Both TAINE and John Stuart MILL show the effect of his ideas in their own philosophical writings.

Comus (1634) A MASQUE by John MILTON. In late Roman mythology, Comus was the god of sensual pleasure, son of Bacchus and Circe. The name is from the Greek *komos*, "revel." In the masque, a young lady is left in the woods by her two brothers, who have gone to find food for her. She falls into the hands of Comus, who tries to persuade her to become his consort, queen of his band of riotous monsters. She resists and is almost rescued by her brothers, aided by an attendant spirit, but a spell has been cast upon her, which is broken by the power of Sabrina, nymph of the river Severn.

The masque was first performed in the Ludlow castle of the earl of Bridgewater, whose three children played the parts of the brothers and sister. Its theme is the struggle between chaste temperance and sensual pleasure; both causes are eloquently represented, and its richness of language and fancy make it one of the greatest works of its kind.

conceit A whimsical, ingenious, extended METAPHOR, in which an object, scene, person, situation, or emotion is presented in terms of a simpler analogue, usually chosen from nature or a context familiar to author and reader alike. First developed by PETRARCH, the conceit became a standard stylistic device in poetry and spread to England in the 16th century.

The METAPHYSICAL POETS, by extending the range of poetic analogy into the realms of science, religion, learning, and practical life, produced a distinct and arresting kind of conceit. Their aim was to startle the reader by showing a very exact correspondence between a thought or emotion and some particular aspect of a seemingly alien and inappropriate object. A famous example is found in these lines from DONNE's "A Valediction: Forbidding Mourning," in which, parting from his mistress, he uses the figure of a drawing compass to describe the bond between their souls:

> If they be two, they are two so
>   As stiffe twin compasses are two,
> Thy soule the fixt foot, makes no show
>   To move, but doth, if th'other doe.
>
> And though it in the center sit,
>   Yet when the other far doth rome,
> It leanes, and hearkens after it,
>   And growes erect, as that comes home.

Here the conceit is adapted as the best means of expressing a complicated thought; its exactitude and naturalness give it force. With the later metaphysical poets, such as John CLEVELAND and Abraham COWLEY, the conceit becomes more fanciful, less exact, at best a kind of witty ornament, at worst absurdity, as when Cleveland speaks of his mistress's hand:

> So soft, 'tis air but once removed,
> Tender as 'twere a jelly gloved.
>
> Cleveland, "Fuscara"

conceptism (or conceptismo; fr Sp, *concepto*, "a conceit") A 17th-century Spanish stylistic form which sought to express clever and penetrating ideas by means of verbal devices such as puns, antitheses, and epigrams. Often, however, originality and wit were achieved at the expense of thought and common sense. Conceptism is best exemplified in the works of Baltasar GRACIÁN, whose *Agudeza y arte de ingenio* (1648) exhaustively describes every type of literary conceit. See GONGORISM.

Concord Hymn (1836) A poem by Ralph Waldo EMERSON. Written at the completion of the Concord Monument, the poem includes the famous lines:

Here once the embattled farmers stood
And fired the shot heard round the world.

condottiere A professional soldier of fortune who leads or conducts a band of mercenaries. During the Italian Renaissance, these captains were commissioned to fight wars in support of the city states and petty duchies. Some of them, such as the SFORZA, eventually became nobles themselves; others (the Gonzaga and Montefeltro families) sold their armed services even though they were already nobles in possession of states and petty principalities. Foreigners, such as the famous Sir John Hawkwood, an English captain, numbered among their ranks. Their legendary cruelty is captured by Verrocchio in his statue of Bartolommeo Colleoni, which still frightens tourists in Venice.

Confession, A (Ispoved, 1879–1881) An account by Count Leo TOLSTOY of the spiritual crisis leading to the formation of the religious and philosophical ideas he preached in his later years. The work records Tolstoy's growing discontent with life as he experienced it in civilized society and his gradual conclusion that living close to nature was requisite for the ideal life. *A Confession* is regarded as one of Tolstoy's most powerful nonfiction works because of its effective depiction of the intense spiritual struggles of one of the world's great geniuses.

Confessional Poets, The A group of American poets who developed a lyric mode that, by virtue of its explicit themes and personal outpourings, became known as "confessional." The popularity of this mode, which gained impetus in the early 1950s and lasted nearly two decades, was so widespread that it is difficult to consign to it a central geographical location, a common technical approach, or even a common theme. In a broad sense, the movement's origins reach as far back as CATULLUS or SAPPHO, but its more recent predecessors are the Romantic poets, WORDSWORTH in particular. It is also indebted to the French SYMBOLISTS, notably BAUDELAIRE and RIMBAUD, for the use of the subjective and frequently nightmarish landscape as a reflection of objective reality. The tonal source for confessional poetry was the post-World War II legacy of disenchantment and angst. The confessional poets tended to project this tone through self-effacing, sometimes guilt-ridden visions of themselves. Indeed, since several of the more distinguished practitioners (John BERRYMAN, Sylvia PLATH, Anne SEXTON) committed suicide, the mode was often referred to as the "murderous art."

Confessional poetry came into prominence when two widely hailed volumes appeared in 1959: Robert Lowell's LIFE STUDIES and *Heart's Needle* by W. D. Snodgrass (1926–   ). Each dramatizes the poet's personal life: in *Life Studies*, Lowell explores his experiences in a mental hospital, his marital discord, and other problems; in *Heart's Needle*, Snodgrass examines his relationship with his daughter following his divorce. Both volumes represented a thematic breakthrough and encouraged talented younger poets, especially Plath and Sexton, to explore their personal experiences in verse. The early representatives of the mode had technical mastery over their material, which conferred formality and universality upon the poetry. In lesser hands, the "enterprise in going naked" resulted in cliché-ridden, self-indulgent compositions that heralded the decline of the mode.

confessions A form of autobiography or simulated autobiography. Intimate and possibly guilty matters not usually disclosed are confessed, presumably to serve some didactic purpose. Confessions constitute a literary genre which began with the *Confessions of St. Augustine*. They reached the height of their development in the era of romanticism, when they already began to show symptoms of narcissistic decadence. Among the most famous confessions in literature are ROUSSEAU's *Confessions* and DE QUINCEY's *Confessions of an English Opium Eater*.

Confessions An autobiography by Jean-Jacques ROUSSEAU. The twelve volumes, written between 1766 and 1770, were published posthumously (I–VI, 1781; VII–XII, 1788). In this work, Rousseau "frankly and sincerely" reveals the details of his erratic and rebellious life. Scholars find, however, that his unconscious motivation was to justify himself in the eyes of his supposedly numerous persecutors. The autobiographical account given in *Confessions* is supplemented by the three dialogues written in 1775–76: *Rousseau juge de Jean-Jacques*, *Rêveries du promeneur solitaire*, and *Correspondance*. They inaugurated a fashion in literature for confessions, but Rousseau's successors, such as Chateaubriand, Lamartine, George Sand, and Renan, lack his openness.

Confessions of an English Opium Eater (1822) A largely autobiographical work by Thomas DE QUINCEY. It gives an account of the poet's early life and describes the growth and effects of his habit of taking opium.

Confessions of Felix Krull: Confidence Man (Bekenntnisse des Hochstaplers Felix Krull, 1954; tr 1955) An unfinished novel by Thomas MANN. In its adventurous and episodic quality, it is his closest approach to the PICARESQUE novel. Krull, a charming young man with absolutely no moral awareness, avoids military service and takes a job in a hotel. This begins a series of erotic and criminal escapades that eventually lead the young man to prison, from where he purportedly writes his confessions. Like many of Mann's characters, Krull represents the artist, and his profession indicates the symbolic connection in Mann's mind between the artist and the actor, or charlatan.

Confessions of Saint Augustine, The (397–401)   A spiritual autobiography by St. AUGUSTINE. He describes his devoutly Christian mother, Monica, his life with the concubine who gave him his son, Adeodatus (371–89), his exploration of Manichaeanism and neo-Platonism, and his conversion to Christianity. Designed to show the details of the soul's progress, from enjoyment of the beauties outside itself to a study of its own nature and finally to joy in the knowledge of God, the work was the first in literature to be concerned entirely with an introspective analysis of the author's own spiritual and emotional experiences.

Confidence-Man, The: His Masquerade (1857)   A novel by Herman MELVILLE. The scene is a Mississippi River boat, ironically named the *Fidele*. A plotless satire taking place on April Fool's Day, the book is filled with characters difficult to distinguish from one another; most of them are different manifestations of the confidence man. A sign hanging on the door of the *Fidele*'s barbershop expresses the theme: "No Trust." The confidence man, king of a world without principle, succeeds in gulling men by capitalizing on false hopes and offering false pity. At the end of the book, the flickering light hanging above the table where an old man reads the Bible goes out completely.

Confucianism   Chinese political and moral philosophy, based on the teachings of CONFUCIUS. Originally one of several rival teachings during the CHOU dynasty (1027–256 BC), it found little favor at first but, by the 2nd century BC, had become the official creed of China. Essentially it was a guide for statecraft and moral instruction that stressed management of society through a carefully defined system of social and familial relationships. It was enlarged upon and developed by Mencius (372–289 BC), often regarded, after Confucius, as the second Chinese sage. In the 3rd century BC the HSÜN TZU, the first Confucian text in expository form, further elaborated and organized the teachings, and, by the HAN dynasty, it had become the orthodox doctrine, which dominated Chinese political and ethical thought until the early 20th century. During the Han dynasty, many extraneous elements, such as the YIN AND YANG theory, were introduced. Attempts were also made to deify Confucius and to use Confucian doctrines as justification for the absolute right of emperors. Throughout its history, Confucianism came into frequent conflict with BUDDHISM and TAOISM, but it retained its position as the official state philosophy largely because of the Imperial

University and the examination system for government employees that perpetuated its power. The SUNG dynasty witnessed a great Confucian revival under the leadership of CHU HSI and his school. The teachings were reorganized, using Buddhist and Taoist ideas and adding a metaphysical system, and came to be known as neo-Confucianism.

A minute examination of the precepts of Confucian sages as well as all external phenomena was called for, and the FOUR BOOKS became the basis for all education. Neo-Confucianism had great influence in Japan, where it became the basis on which the TOKUGAWA government was organized. See FIVE CLASSICS.

Confucius (Chinese name Kung Fu-tse, 551?–479 BC)   Chinese political and ethical philosopher and would-be reformer. Failing to achieve personal ambitions and success, Confucius taught a large number of disciples who carried on, developed, and greatly altered his teachings, so that, by the second century BC, they formed the dominant philosophy in China. Confucius advocated a this-worldly, rational philosophy, which emphasizes humanity (*jen*), reverence for the ancient sages, and government by personal virtue.

Congo, The: A Study of the Negro Race (1914)   A poem by Vachel LINDSAY. He attempted to represent black ragtime rhythms in verse by means of various verbal effects. It falls into three sections: "Their Basic Savagery," "Their Irrepressible High Spirits," and "The Hope of Their Religion."

Congreve, William (1670–1729)   English dramatist, usually considered the greatest master of the Restoration comedy of manners. The son of an English army officer stationed in Ireland, Congreve was educated at the Kilkenny School, where Swift was a schoolmate, and at Trinity College, Dublin. His first play, *The Old Bachelor* (1693), which was produced under Dryden's auspices, was widely acclaimed. It was followed by three other comedies: *The Double Dealer* (1693), LOVE FOR LOVE, and his masterpiece, THE WAY OF THE WORLD. In these plays, Congreve revealed a genius for urbane, scintillating wit that rivaled Molière's. He also wrote a tragedy, *The Mourning Bride* (1697), remembered chiefly as the source of such oft-quoted phrases as "Music hath charms to soothe a savage breast." The same year, he engaged in controversy with the Reverend Jeremy Collier (1650–1726), who attacked the lewdness of the English stage, and Congreve was prosecuted as a result of the exchange. After 1700 Congreve gave up writing for the theatre and spent the rest of his life in the company of such friends as Swift, Steele, and Pope, who dedicated his translation of the *Iliad* to him; the visiting Voltaire, however, regretted that the "writer" had turned into a "gentleman."

Coningsby, or the New Generation (1844)   A novel by Benjamin DISRAELI. It contains many of his political opinions on the social issues of his day. Several prominent contemporary figures appear, thinly disguised, in the book, and much of its popularity may be credited to the interest in identifying them. Gladstone is said to be depicted as Millbank, the Marquis of Hertford as the Marquis of Monmouth, and Coningsby may represent either Lord Littleton or Lord Lincoln. A notable character is the Jew Sidonia, said to be drawn partly from Baron Alfred de Rothschild, partly from the author himself.

Connecticut Yankee in King Arthur's Court, A (1889)

A novel by Mark TWAIN. A blow on the head conveys the superintendent of a Hartford arms factory back to the days of King ARTHUR. As the Yankee's ingenuity and know-how encounter the world of medieval superstition, Twain takes the opportunity to satirize the Old World, chivalry, kings, and the church. Many of the Arthurian knights are depicted, as seen through the unimpressed eyes of the Yankee. He marries and has a child, but another blow restores him to his own time.

Connelly, Marc[us Cook] (1890–1980)

American playwright. Best known for his biblical fantasy THE GREEN PASTURES, Connelly also wrote *The Farmer Takes a Wife* (1934) and *Story for Strangers* (1948), a parable about a talking horse. Connelly and George S. KAUFMAN collaborated on a number of successful productions, notably *Dulcy* (1921); *To the Ladies* (1922), a study in illusions; *Merton of the Movies* (1922), a dramatization of H. L. Wilson's satiric novel about Hollywood; and *Beggar on Horseback* (1924). Connelly, a founding member, along with Robert BENCHLEY, Dorothy PARKER, and others, of the literary group known as the ALGONQUIN ROUND TABLE, was well along in years before he published his first novel, *A Souvenir from Quam* (1965), in which he lampooned spy thrillers. His memoirs, *Voices Off-Stage*, were published in 1968.

Connolly, Cyril (1903–1974)

English essayist, critic, and novelist. Connolly founded and edited the magazine *Horizon* (1939–50). His best-known book, after *Enemies of Promise*, is *The Unquiet Grave* (1944), a collection of melancholy PENSÉES, APHORISMS, and quotations, published under the pen name PALINURUS. His literary criticism includes *The Condemned Playground* (1944), *Previous Convictions* (1963), and *The Evening Colonnade* (1973). His other works include the partly autobiographical *Enemies of Promise* (1938), a brilliant collection of literary essays, and the novel *The Rock Pool* (1935).

Conquest, [George] Robert [Ackworth] (1917–)

English poet, novelist, and Sovietologist. An admirer of science, Conquest has asserted that his main theme is the poet's relationship to the phenomenal universe. He attempts to portray the whole of reality, combining the intellectual and the emotive. His anthology *New Lines* (1956) made him a recognized leader of a group of poets, including Philip LARKIN, Thom GUNN, and Kingsley AMIS, who reacted against romanticism and believed in returning to the central tradition of well-crafted English poetry. His major poetry appears in *Poems* (1955), *Between Mars and Venus* (1962), and *Arias from a Love Opera* (1969). A lucid writer with a wide range of interests, he has also written a science fiction novel, *A World of Difference* (1955), and several works on the Soviet Union: *The Great Terror* (1968), about the Stalinist purges; *Where Marx Went Wrong* (1971), a study of the deviations from Marxism during and after the Russian Revolution; and *Kolyma: The Arctic Death Camps* (1978), about the most inhuman of Stalin's many strategies against dissenters. *The Abomination of Moab* (1979) is a collection of miscellaneous pieces.

Conquistador (1932)

A narrative poem by Archibald MACLEISH. Awarded the 1933 PULITZER PRIZE in poetry, it is based on an eye-witness account of the Spanish expedition led by Hernando CORTEZ to Mexico in the 16th century, written by Bernal DÍAZ DEL CASTILLO. Heroic and realistic, it emphasizes the love of individual men for adventure, rather than official plans for expansion, as the real motive for the expedition.

Conrad, Joseph (born Teodor Jósef Konrad Korzeniowski, 1857–1924)

Polish-born English novelist. Known primarily as a writer of sea stories in his own time, he is now highly regarded as a novelist whose writings display a deep moral consciousness and masterful narrative technique. He was influenced in the latter by Henry JAMES. NOSTROMO, HEART OF DARKNESS, and LORD JIM are regarded as his greatest works. His early novels, including *Almayer's Folly* (1895), AN OUTCAST OF THE ISLANDS, and THE NIGGER OF THE NARCISSUS, are full of romantic description in an atmosphere of mystery and brooding. YOUTH, TYPHOON, THE SHADOW-LINE, and, in some respects, most of his tales describe the testing of men's characters in conditions of extreme danger and difficulty. Conrad is always concerned with moral dilemmas, isolation, and the psychology of inner urges. Among his other novels are THE SECRET AGENT, UNDER WESTERN EYES, *Chance* (1914), VICTORY, *The Arrow of Gold* (1919), and *The Rescue* (1920). THE SECRET SHARER is a remarkable short story. Conrad collaborated with Ford Madox FORD on two novels: *The Inheritors* (1901) and *Romance* (1903). He also wrote, in a personal vein, *The Mirror of the Sea* (1906), *Some Reminiscences* (1912; U.S., *A Personal Record*), and *Notes on Life and Letters* (1921).

The son of a Polish nobleman, writer, and militant nationalist, Conrad had an adventurous youth. He read widely in Polish and French but knew no English until 1878, when he went to sea on a British merchant ship, rising eventually to the rank of captain. In 1886 he became a naturalized British subject. In 1895 he left the sea, published his first novel, *Almayer's Folly*, married, and settled down near London to write. He became not only a major novelist of the 20th century but also a highly distinguished stylist in his adopted language.

Conscience, Hendrik (1812–1883) Flemish novelist. The most important and influential figure in the Flemish literary renaissance of the late 19th century, Conscience gave up the custom of writing in French and published the first modern novel written in Flemish: *In't wonderjaer 1566* (*In the Year of Marvels, 1566,* 1837). Of his over eighty novels and stories, his historical romance, *De leeuw van Vlaanderen* (*The Lion of Flanders,* 1838), is considered his masterwork. Conscience wrote simply and directly to ordinary people, glorifying the Flemish past and painting romantic pictures of contemporary village life. A writer of stature throughout Europe, he did more than any other writer to engender a spirit of pride in the Flemish people and language.

Consolation of Philosophy, The (De consolatione philosophiae, c524) A philosophical work by BOETHIUS. Written while Boethius was in prison awaiting execution, it consists of a dialogue in alternating prose and verse between the author, lamenting his own sorrows, and a majestic woman, who is the incarnation of his guardian Philosophy. She develops a modified form of Neoplatonism and Stoicism, demonstrating the unreality of earthly fortunes, then proving that the highest good and the highest happiness are in God, and reconciling the apparent contradictions concerning the existence of evil, if God is all-good and all-powerful, and the existence of man's free will, if God has foreknowledge of everything. The work became very popular; it inspired many translations, including English ones by King Alfred, Chaucer, and Queen Elizabeth.

consonance In poetry and prose, the identity of consonants, as in the words *leaves* and *lives.* Like ASSONANCE and ALLITERATION, consonance is related to RHYME, in that it involves degrees of identity of sound and serves to unify a poem.

Constable, John (1776–1837) English landscape painter. Mostly self-taught, Constable repeatedly sketched the same scenes, notably Salisbury cathedral, under varying conditions. In order to impart to his naturalistic landscapes the impression of moving clouds and changing light, he used looser, less blended brushstrokes than were usual at his time. Constable painted more finished exhibition pieces, yet he gained little recognition in England. In France, however, Eugène DELACROIX learned much from his brighter colors, the BARBIZON SCHOOL was influenced by the directness of his observation, and later the Impressionists admired his temporary effects of light.

Constant de Rebecque, Henri Benjamin (known as Benjamin Constant, 1767–1830) Swiss-born French politician, journalist, and novelist, best remembered for his short novel ADOLPHE. His famous liaison with Mme de STAËL began in 1794 and lasted for seventeen years. From 1816 he devoted himself to his brilliant political career, writing political and religious treatises, including a pamphlet attacking Napoleon. His journals are of great interest.

Constantine I (called Constantine the Great, AD 272–337) Roman emperor (306–37). On the death of his father, Constantine laid claim to part of the empire and was acknowledged as master of the countries beyond the Alps. He defeated Maxentius, who had possession of Italy, in the battle of the Milvian Bridge (312), where, according to legend, a cross appeared to him in the sky, bearing the words *in hoc signo vinces* ("by this sign you will conquer"). He was converted to Christianity in 313. He defeated Licinius (323), who had gained possession of the East, and Constantine thus became sole emperor of the whole empire. He called the great COUNCIL OF NICAEA (325) where the NICENE CREED was adopted. Constantine chose Byzantium as his capital and renamed it CONSTANTINOPLE, after himself. See BYZANTINE EMPIRE.

Constantinople The Christian capital of the Roman empire, founded by CONSTANTINE THE GREAT and dedicated in AD 330, on the site of ancient Byzantium. It remained the center of the BYZANTINE EMPIRE, the successor to the Eastern Roman Empire, until 1453, when it fell to the Turks. Constantinople is now the Turkish city of Istanbul.

Constant Nymph, The (1924) A consistently popular novel by Margaret KENNEDY. It concerns the family and friends of Albert Sanger, an eccentric musician who is the father of numerous children. His children, both legitimate and illegitimate and all talented, are known collectively as Sanger's circus. The nymph is fifteen-year-old Teresa Sanger, who has to deal with adult problems of love and fidelity.

Constitution of the United States of America The fundamental law of the U.S., framed in 1787 and in effect since March 1789, supplanting the ARTICLES OF CONFEDERATION signed in 1781. The Constitution established a republican form of government for the U.S., with separate executive, legislative, and judicial branches. Twenty-six amendments to the original instrument have been adopted. See BILL OF RIGHTS.

constructivism An art movement initiated in Russia c1913 by Vladimir Tatlin (1885–1953). Constructivism was primarily a philosophy of art and architecture, but it also found application, particularly in Russia, in literature and the theatre. It had its origin in the machine-aesthetic of FUTURISM and in many respects represented a sculptural interpretation of CUBISM. The brothers Naum [Pevsner] Gabo (1890–1977) and Antoine Pevsner (1886–1962) developed Tatlin's ideas of abstract constructions into sculptural experiments with form, space, and motion, making use of contrasting scales and planes, and set forth the movement's principles in the *Realist Manifesto* (1920).

By the early 1920s constructivism's radical abstraction fell into official disfavor in Russia, resulting in two distinct factions. Tatlin remained in the U.S.S.R., applying toned-down constructivist ideas to less controversial problems of industrial design, film, and posters. Gabo and Pevsner left Russia and continued their work in France and in Germany at the BAUHAUS, whence constructivism's influence was extended to the U.S. Thus constructivism spanned three decades and three continents. It effectively shaped de STIJL painting and the international style of architecture, through which its impact continued to be felt in the 1950s.

Constructivist poetry flourished in the 1920s but never really spread outside Russia. Known pejoratively as the "smithy poets," its proponents sought to fuse the energy and efficiency of the technological revolution with Russia's revolutionary ideology, in epic paeans to proletarian industry.

Constructivist ideas took a firmer hold in the theatre, primarily through the work of Vsevolod MEYERHOLD. Meyerhold developed "biomechanics," whereby acting was seen as a mechanical process, the actors functioning as harmonious components of an efficient machine. Staging consisted of bare scaffolding and machine parts, requiring unusual physical discipline and agility on the part of performers.

Consuelo (1842)   A novel by George SAND. The title character, a gypsy girl raised in the streets of Venice, is discovered by the maestro Porporo and becomes a successful opera singer. She eventually marries a Bohemian count and travels with Joseph HAYDN to Vienna. Her adventures end in Berlin, where she is feted and admired by Frederick the Great. *La Comtesse de Rudolstadt* (1843–45) is a sequel.

consul   One of the two chief magistrates of the ancient Roman republic, chosen annually in the Campus Martius ("Field of Mars," a grassy plain along the Tiber River used for elections, martial exercises, games, etc.). In the early ages of Rome, the consuls were chosen by noble families, but in 367 BC the people were extended the privilege of electing one from among themselves. The consuls were the highest civil authority; they commanded the army and presided over the senate. At the expiration of one year of office, the consul was sent to govern a province and was then called a proconsul. The office continued under the empire and, although almost entirely stripped of its power, was a coveted position until AD 534. The original consulate was established in 509 BC, when the people chose Tarquinius Collatinus and Lucius Junius BRUTUS as consuls, after Brutus had driven Tarquinius Superbus, seventh and last of the Roman kings, out of Rome.

Contes de ma mère l'Oye (Mother Goose Tales, 1697)   A book of fairy tales by Charles PERRAULT. Drawing upon popular folk stories, Perrault collected the tales into a single volume and gave them the simple and graceful form in which they are known today. The *Contes* included "La Belle au bois dormant" ("The Sleeping Beauty"), "Le Petit Chaperon rouge" (LITTLE RED RIDING-HOOD), "La Barbe-Bleue" (BLUEBEARD), "Le Maître-chat ou le chat botté" ("Puss-in-Boots"), "Les Fées" ("The Fairies"), "Cendrillon ou la petite pantoufle de verre" ("CINDERELLA, or The Little Glass Slipper"), "Riquet à la houppe," and "Le Petit Poucet" (TOM THUMB).

Continental Congress   The congress of representatives from the British colonies of North America. The First Continental Congress was convened in Philadelphia in 1774 to consider grievances against the mother country. The Second Continental Congress adopted the Declaration of Independence, organized the Revolutionary Army, and conducted diplomatic negotiations with foreign nations. After the ratification of the Articles of Confederation (1781), it functioned as the central governing body of the new republic under the title The United States in Congress Assembled.

Cook's Tale, The   An unfinished fragment in THE CANTERBURY TALES of Geoffrey CHAUCER. Roger the Cook laughs at *The Reeve's Tale* and offers to tell a similarly bawdy jest. He begins a story about the apprentice Perkin, a reveler too fond of dice and women for his master's taste. A metrical romance sometimes called *The Cook's Tale of Gamelyn* has been erroneously attributed to Chaucer, who probably at one time intended to adapt it. See GAMELYN.

Coolidge, [John] Calvin (1872–1933)   Thirtieth president of the U.S. (1923–29). Coolidge first won national attention when, as governor of Massachusetts, he broke the Boston police strike of 1919, declaring that there was "no right to strike against the public safety by anybody, anywhere, any time." In 1920 he became the Republican vice presidential nominee and, succeeding to the presidency on the death of Warren G. HARDING, was elected in his own right in 1924. In 1927 he announced that he did not "choose to run" for the presidency again. An uncompromising Republican, noted for his taciturnity and frugality, Coolidge wrote an *Autobiography* (1929). He was the subject of a well-known biography by William Allen White, *A Puritan in Babylon* (1938).

Cooper, James Fenimore (1789–1851)   American novelist. James Fenimore Cooper, a son of the wealthy landowner Judge William Cooper, who founded Cooperstown, New York, was born in Burlington, New Jersey. After his expulsion from Yale, he became a sailor; in 1811 he married Susan DeLancey and occupied himself as a gentleman farmer. At the age of thirty-one, he wrote his first novel. Although *Precaution* (1820) was a failure, Cooper continued to write. In 1823 he wrote THE PIONEERS and *The Pilot*, both works of signal importance in American literature. *The Pilot* is the first American novel of the sea, and *The Pioneers* introduces the character of Natty BUMPPO, the natural man uncorrupted by civilization. Natty has taken on mythic significance in the history of the American imagination. Cooper's audience demanded that

Natty be revived in THE LAST OF THE MOHICANS, THE PRAIRIE, THE PATHFINDER, and THE DEERSLAYER.

From 1826 to 1833, the Coopers lived abroad. Turning out novels at a prolific rate, Cooper returned to Jacksonian America dismayed to discover that the democracy he had defended abroad had turned to mobocracy. He was outspoken in his criticism and was denounced in the American press. In the 1840s, while involved in numerous lawsuits, he wrote an antirent trilogy, THE LITTLEPAGE MANUSCRIPTS, in which he defended the existence of a landed gentry as a stabilizing force in democracy. *Satanstoe* (1845), with its lively portraits of contrasting Yankee, Middle Colony, and Dutch manners in colonial New York, is one of Cooper's most successful books.

Although Cooper's literary craftsmanship can rarely be admired, his fifty-odd volumes, in their use of the American landscape and their unique creation of Leatherstocking, constitute the foundation of American literature. See LEATHERSTOCKING TALES, THE.

Copernicus, Nicolaus (Polish name Niklas Koppernigk, 1473–1543) Polish astronomer. Copernicus laid the foundations for modern astronomy by upsetting the Ptolemaic system of astronomy, which had prevailed since the 2nd century. PTOLEMY had placed the earth at the center of the universe; Copernicus advanced the theory that the earth and all the other planets revolved around the sun in individual orbits while spinning on their axes. He finished his treatise on this subject, *De revolutionibus orbium coelestium* (*On the Revolutions of Heavenly Bodies*), in 1530, but it was not published until 1543, when its author lay dying. Opposition to his theories was theological as well as scientific: not only had Copernicus questioned and rejected the wisdom of the ancients, he had displaced man from the center of the universe.

Cophetua A mythical king of Africa. Of great wealth, Cophetua fell in love with a beggar girl, Penelophon (Zenelophon in Shakespeare's *Love's Labour's Lost*, IV, i), and married her. He is the hero of a ballad in Percy's *Reliques*, and Tennyson versified the tale in "The Beggar-Maid."

Copland, Aaron (1900–) American composer. Copland is probably the best-known representative of American nationalism in music. His most popular works employ American subjects and styles, often modeled on jazz or folk music, as, for example, in *Music for the Theatre* (1925), *El Salon México* (1937), and the PULITZER PRIZE–winning ballet *Appalachian Spring* (1944). He has been concerned with improving general understanding of modern music by organizing concerts, conducting, and writing such books as *What to Listen for in Music* (1939), *Our New Music* (1941), *Music and the Imagination* (1952), and *Copland on Music* (1960).

Copley, John Singleton (1738–1815) American painter. Copley began his career as a portrait painter in

Boston and carried it on in Philadelphia and New York, painting most of the prominent early Americans with a masterly clarity and brilliance of line and characterization. Benjamin WEST, who had gone to England to live, persuaded Copley to move there in 1775. He continued to paint portraits, but his fame in England was based chiefly on vast historical dramas, such as *The Death of Lord Chatham* (Tate Gallery, London), for which he was made a member of the Royal Academy.

Copt (fr Arab, *cubt*; ultimately fr Gk, *Aigyptios*, "Egyptian") A Christian native of the United Arab Republic, presumably a descendant from the ancient Egyptians whose ancestors neither converted to ISLAM nor intermarried with the Moslems. The term, more restrictedly, designates a member of the Coptic Church. The head of the Coptic Church, the patriarch of Alexandria, is the direct successor of the 5th-century patriarchs of the Eastern Church, who precipitated a schism from the dominant Christian church. The Coptic language, now found only in the liturgy of the Coptic Church, is the variety of ancient Egyptian spoken in early Christian times; it is written in Greek capital letters. St. ANTHONY, the first Christian monastic, was a Copt.

copyright The exclusive right by statute to reproduce, publish, and sell works of literature, music, art, drama, choreographic work, motion pictures, and other audiovisual works and sound recordings. The first copyright act in England was that of 1709, subsequently subjected to various modifications and additions. In 1842 a new act was passed, granting copyright for forty-two years after publication or until seven years after the author's death, whichever should be the longer period. This act was superseded by the Copyright Act of 1911, under which the period of protection was extended to fifty years after the death of the author, irrespective of date of publication. This act deals also with copyright in photographs, engravings, architectural designs, musical compositions, and phonograph records.

The first copyright act in the U.S. was enacted by the states of Connecticut and Massachusetts in 1783, following vigorous agitation by Noah WEBSTER. The first national statute, passed in 1790, was modeled upon the then-existing British law. Additional acts were passed in 1846, 1856, 1859, 1865, and 1909. U.S. copyrights may be secured under a copyright Act effective January 1, 1978, for a period of seventy-five years from publication or one hundred years from creation, whichever is shorter. The term for works created on or after January 1, 1978, lasts for the author's life plus an additional fifty years. Under the new law, all visually perceptible copies of a work must bear the symbol ©, the word *copyright*, or its abbreviation, the name of the owner of the copyright, and the date of publication. Copyright protection has been extended to original works of authorship fixed in any tangible means of expression, known now or later developed.

Influenced by lobbyists for book manufacturers reluctant to extend U.S. copyright to books manufactured abroad, the U.S. did not sign the Berne International Copyright Convention (1886), and thus, until the formulating of the Universal Copyright Convention, under the auspices of UNESCO, a certain confusion existed in the field of U.S. international copyright. The U.S., most other western countries, including the U.S.S.R., which signed in 1973, and many Asian countries have signed the Universal Copyright Convention, but a worldwide international copyright does not yet exist.

Corbière, Edouard Joachim (known as Tristan Corbière, 1845–1875)   French poet. Associated with the symbolist school, in his *Gens de mers* (published in *Les Amours jaunes*, 1873), Corbière treated the world of those who live upon the sea in a realistic and forceful manner. See SYMBOLISTS.

Corbusier, Le   See LE CORBUSIER.

Corday, Charlotte (1768–1793)   French patriot who stabbed Jean Paul MARAT to death in his bath. Corday was an adherent of the Revolution and sympathized with the GIRONDISTS, but she was repelled by the excesses of the REIGN OF TERROR. She was guillotined on July 17, 1793.

Cordelia   In Shakespeare's KING LEAR, the youngest daughter of Lear. Cordelia is disinherited by Lear because she lacks the "glib and oily art" of flattery. Her simplicity and sincerity move the king of France to marry her despite her disinheritance. It is of her that Lear speaks the famous lines: "Her voice was ever soft, gentle and low, an excellent thing in woman."

Cordelier (Fr, "cord-wearer")   A Franciscan friar of the strict rule. In the Middle Ages, the Cordeliers distinguished themselves in philosophy and theology. DUNS SCOTUS was one of their most distinguished members. The traditional origin of the name is that, in the reign of St. Louis, they repulsed an army of infidels, and the king asked who those *gens de cordelics* ("corded people") were.

Cordeliers   French Revolutionary club of 1790, known officially as *La Société des Amis des Droits de l'Homme et du Citoyen*. MARAT, DANTON, and ROBESPIERRE were among the speakers at its meetings. The club played an active part in overthrowing both the monarchy and the GIRONDISTS. It ceased to function in 1794, when its leading members were guillotined. The name *Cordeliers* comes from the old (Franciscan) Cordelier monastery, where the club held its meetings.

Corelli, Marie (pen name of Mary Mackay, 1855–1924)   English romantic novelist. At first hoping to become a musician, Mackay turned to writing after a "psychical experience" and became sensationally popular at the end of the 19th century. Her first novel, *A Romance of Two Worlds* (1886), like most of her other books, was

about "spirit power and universal love." She also wrote *The Soul of Lilith* (1892), *The Sorrows of Satan* (1895), *Barabbas* (1900), and many others. By the latter part of the 20th century, a number of her books had been brought out in new editions.

Corinna's Going A-Maying (1648)   A poem by Robert HERRICK, in which the poet implores his late-sleeping mistress to rise and join the May Day festivities. Against a background of spring freshness and picturesque country rite, he sings of life's shortness, urging love and "the harmless folly of the time."

Corinne, or Italy (1807)   A romantic novel by Mme. de STAËL. Oswald Nevil, an English lord, recuperating in Rome, meets the famous poetess Corinne, who, half-English and half-Italian, has exiled herself from her native England. They fall in love, and Nevil wishes to marry Corinne, but she hesitates, fearing the rigidity of the English life she once knew; her present unconventional life is too dear to her. Oswald, forced to return to England, later gives in to the pressures of his social milieu and marries the wholly English Lucile, half sister of Corinne. When she learns of the marriage, Corinne dies of grief. Idealistic and passionate, *Corinne* is a psychological study of two tormented souls and is a celebrated description of Italian civilization and mores.

Corinthians, The Epistles of Paul the Apostle to the   Two books of the New Testament. They are letters written by Paul to the troubled Christian church in the cosmopolitan Greek city of Corinth. The two canonical letters incorporate parts of two other letters. The Christians in Corinth were exposed to the very worldly, licentious atmosphere of that city. Paul tells them to ignore these influences; he also deals with a crisis over internal dissension and local authority. These two books are of particular historical interest because of the insight they offer into 1st-century Christians' problems with the pagan world. 1 Cor. 13 contains Paul's beautiful discourse on Christian love, one of the most noteworthy chapters in the Bible.

Coriolanus, The Tragedy of (c1608)   A tragedy by SHAKESPEARE. Caius Martius, an honorable but haughty patrician, defeats the Volscians under Tullus Aufidius at Corioli and is given the name Coriolanus. He is then persuaded to seek election to the consulship, though the thought of currying favor with the masses repels him. When Brutus and Sicinius, two unscrupulous tribunes, incite the populace against him, Coriolanus angrily denounces the plebeians for their fickleness and ingratitude and is driven from the city. Enraged by the treatment he has received, he joins the forces of Aufidius, who is preparing another attack on Rome. As the Volscian army menaces Rome, Menenius and Cominius, two old friends, unsuccessfully plead with Coriolanus to spare the city, but he remains obdurate until VOLUMNIA, his mother, and Virgilia, his wife, add their appeals to the others. Coriolanus raises the siege and tries to explain his conduct to the Volscians. Aufidius, envious of the Roman's prestige, accuses him of treachery, and, as the Volscians hurl abuse at him, Coriolanus is murdered by agents of Aufidius.

The direct source of the play is Thomas North's translation (1579) of Plutarch's *Lives*, which records the career of the legendary patrician.

Corneille, Pierre (1606–1684)   French dramatist. Son of a lawyer, Corneille abandoned a career at the bar in order to write for the theatre, initially under the patronage of Richelieu, one of the cardinal's *cinq auteurs*. *Mélite* (1629), his first play and a comedy of manners, was successfully produced in Paris. There followed the tragicomedy *Clitandre* (1632), seven comedies of only moderate interest, and his first tragedy, MÉDÉE. Although LE CID won an enormous popular success, Richelieu persuaded the Académie française to censure the play's violation of the dramatic unities as well as its emotional style. Madame de Rambouillet's salon also expressed doubt concerning the play's merit. For three years, chastened and disturbed, Corneille wrote nothing for the theatre. He finally broke his silence with the tragedies HORACE, CINNA, POLYEUCTE, *La Mort de Pompée* (1642), *Rodogune* (1644), *Héraclius* (1647), *Andromède* (1650), *Nicomède* (1651), and a comedy, *Le Menteur* (1643). With *Le Cid*, these tragedies marked Corneille's brief leadership of the French stage. After the failure of *Pertharite* (1651), Corneille withdrew to Rouen. In 1659 he returned to the theatre with *Oedipe* (1659), only to find that, during his absence, the public had come to prefer the directness and simplicity of Racine to the complexity of his own late style. The plays of Corneille's decline include the tragedies *La Toison d'or* (*The Golden Fleece*, 1660), *Sertorius* (1662), *Sophonisbe* (1663), *Othon* (1664), *Agésilas* (1666), *Attila* (1667), *Suréna* (1674), and the comedies TITE ET BÉRÉNICE and *Pulchérie* (1672). Corneille eventually retired from the theatre and translated *The Imitation of Christ* into French verse.

Corneille can be considered the prime shaper of the French classic theatre. While earlier writers had attempted a tragedy of actions, Corneille sought tragedy in the depiction of the human soul, thus substituting an interior drama for the exterior drama of his predecessors. Borrowing the greater part of his subjects from classical mythology and history, Corneille excelled in the creation of tragic protagonists: men and women of heroic dimension caught in the conflict of reason, will, or duty with an all-powerful love or hatred. Propelled by the highest sentiments and gifted with an enormous will to triumph over the obstacles of destiny, his characters are drawn in large, bold strokes and sometimes, in the magnificence of their deeds and language, exceed the bounds of humanity and rise to the superhuman.

Corneille, Thomas (1625–1709)   French playwright and brother of Pierre Corneille. A skilled technician and an accomplished imitator, he kept the French theatre stocked with workmanlike though not highly original plays during the interval between Pierre Corneille's great tragedies and those of RACINE. Notable among his works are the romantic tragedy *Timocrate* (1656), based on an episode in La Calprenède's *Cléopâtre*, and the heroic tragedy *Ariane* (1672), based on the ARIADNE legend.

Cornhuskers (1918)   A collection of poems by Carl SANDBURG. It includes such well-known poems as "Cool Tombs," "Prairie," "Caboose Thoughts," "Wilderness," "Chicago Poet," "Testament," and "Haunts."

Cornucopia   The horn of plenty, an ancient symbol of the bounty of growing things. In Greek mythology, it is identified as the horn of Amaltheia, the goat that had suckled the infant ZEUS; it provided an endless supply of whatever food its possessor desired. In another legend, it is said to be the horn of ACHELOUS.

Cornwall, duke of   In Shakespeare's KING LEAR, the grasping, ruthless husband of Lear's daughter Regan. When Gloucester shelters Lear, Cornwall plucks Gloucester's eyes out in revenge. A servant, horrified at the cruel deed, kills Cornwall and is in turn killed by Regan.

Cornwallis, Charles, 1st marquis (1738–1805)   English major general in the American Revolution. Cornwallis defeated General Greene at Guilford Courthouse, North Carolina, but was forced to surrender at Yorktown shortly thereafter. He later served as viceroy of Ireland and governor-general of India.

Coronación (1957; tr Coronation, 1965)   A novel by JOSÉ DONOSO. *Coronación* portrays the decline and ruin of an aristocratic Chilean family in the person of a half-mad old lady and her senile grandson. The old lady's bizarre desires—to have a crowning ceremony at her birthday celebration—are anticipated and indulged by her host of physically strong and vividly aware maids, who eventually claim her possessions and perhaps even her place in life.

Coronado, Francisco Vásquez de (1510–1554) Spanish explorer. In 1540 Coronado left Mexico, as commander of an expedition to conquer the Seven Cities of Cibola, in present New Mexico, which earlier explorers had described in glowing terms. After undergoing extreme hardships and traversing what is now Arizona, New Mexico, Texas, Oklahoma, and Kansas, Coronado returned to Mexico empty-handed and disillusioned. One of his men, García López de CALDERÓN, discovered the Grand Canyon on a side expedition.

Corot, Jean Baptiste Camille (1796–1875) French landscape painter. The least realistic of the BARBIZON SCHOOL, Corot had a style that evolved from the influence of contemporary classicism to the poetic rendition of landscapes, in which a silver-grey haze envelops and harmonizes perfectly balanced figures and trees. Corot's work also includes historical subjects and figure paintings, the latter only being less prized than his landscapes today.

Correggio, Antonio Allegri da (c1489–1534) Italian painter. Correggio is known for his use of chiaroscuro (the interplay of light and dark) and blurred outlines in mythological paintings. These have a sensuous, almost seductive, sweetness and reveal his use of light and trompe l'oeil to create the illusion of church ceilings opening up into the heavens. His mythological paintings—*Antiope, Jupiter and Io, Ganymede*—strongly influenced French painting during the 18th century. His frescos on the octagonal cupola of the cathedral at Parma were a leading source of later baroque ceiling decoration in Italy and throughout Europe.

Corsair, The (1814)   A narrative poem by Lord BYRON. The pirate chief CONRAD disguises himself as a dervish, in order to enter the palace of Sultan Seyd. He is discovered and imprisoned, but Gulnare, queen of the harem, releases him, and he returns to the pirates' isle, only to find that Medora, his true love, has died in his absence. He therefore returns to his native Greece, where he heads a rebellion and is shot. Upon his death, his page Kaled is discovered to be Gulnare in disguise. *Lara* (1814), another narrative poem, deals with Conrad's last adventures in Spain, where he has returned as Lara. He lives a strange and secluded life until he is recognized and killed. Conrad and Lara are prototypes of the Byronic hero, extravagant, romantic, and mysterious.

Corso, [Nunzio] Gregory (1930–   )   American poet. A child of immigrant parents, Corso was raised in New York City, largely by foster parents, and in reform schools and prison. His childhood memory of the Depression years is present in much of his writing. In the early 1950s he met Allen GINSBERG and Jack KEROUAC, and in 1956 he settled in San Francisco, where he became a pivotal member of the BEAT MOVEMENT. His early reputation was established with the publication of *Gasoline* (1958) and *Happy Birthday of Death* (1960), which are, like his other works, uninhibited in subject matter and open in form and reverberate with a Whitmanesque belief in the holiness of the common man. The titles of several of his volumes attest to Corso's particular brand of idealism: *Long Live Man* (1962), *There Is Time Yet to Run Back through Life and Expiate All That's Been Sadly Done* (1965), and *Elegiac Feelings American* (1970). Later works include *Earth Egg* (1974) and *Herald of the Autochthonic Spirit* (1981). Corso's writing is a deeply felt plea for America to restore the democratic ardor of its early founders.

Cortázar, Julio (1914–1984)   Argentine writer, born in Brussels, Belgium. In 1920 Cortázar's family moved back to Argentina. In 1951, in opposition to Juan Perón's regime, he left for France, where he worked as a translator for UNESCO. In 1981 he accepted French citizenship.

Cortázar's writing has been compared to the work of the Argentinian writer Jorge Luis BORGES. As with Borges, Cortázar's preoccupations are with metaphysical themes: life, death, reincarnation, the power of the imagination, and the quest for identity. His writing style is distinctive for its inventiveness, originality, and use of vivid imagery. Cortázar's first novel was *Los premios* (1960; tr *The Winners*, 1965). It was followed by his widely acclaimed novel RAYUELA, Cortázor's first experiment with "reader participation," and by 62: *Modelo para armar* (1968; tr *62: A Model Kit*, 1972) and *Libro de Manuel* (1973; tr *A Manual for Manuel*, 1979). *Un tal Lucas* (1979; tr *A Certain Lucas*, 1984) is an intricately plotted novel about Lucas, an iconoclastic Argentinian jazz aficionado, who delights in breaking codes of social behavior and whose intellectual life and emotions are conveyed to the reader through both retrospection and descriptive accounts of events that actually take place.

Cortázar also wrote many short stories: his collections include *A Change of Light* (1980) and *We Love Glenda So Much* (1983). Three months after his death, *Salvo el crepusculo* (1984), a collection of verse illustrated with Picasso's erotic drawings, was published.

cortegiano, Il   See COURTIER, THE.

Cortez, Hernando (Spanish name Hernán Cortés, 1485–1547)   Spanish conqueror of Mexico. Cortez arrived in the New World in 1504 and was mayor of Santiago, Cuba, when he was ordered by Governor Velázquez to lead an expedition to Mexico. Velázquez later tried to halt the voyage, but Cortez had already set sail (1519). Reaching the mainland, he was fortunate in acquiring the services of two interpreters, one of whom was the famed Malinche or Doña Marina, daughter of an Aztec chieftain, whom the Maya had enslaved; she became Cortez's mistress as well as his confidante.

After founding the city of Vera Cruz, Cortez moved against the Aztec capital at Tenochtitlán, forming alliances with other Indian tribes, such as the Tlaxcalans, who hated the Aztecs. When some of the more faint-hearted Spaniards spoke of returning to Cuba, Cortez ordered their ships to be destroyed.

Although MONTEZUMA, the Aztec chief at Tenochtitlán, was outwardly friendly, Cortez captured him and held him as a hostage. Upon hearing that Velázquez, in an attempt to reassert his authority over Mexico, had dispatched another expedition under Pánfilo de Narváez, Cortez returned to the seacoast and persuaded Narváez's men to desert their commander and join him. Back in Tenochtitlán, he found that the actions of Pedro de Alvarado, his deputy, had incited the Indians to revolt and that Montezuma had been killed. During the disastrous *noche triste*, or "sad night" (June 30, 1520), the Spaniards were forced to flee, with the loss of many men. Cortez immediately began to plan another campaign against Tenochtitlán, which was captured the following year. Though he was granted many honors and was created marquis of the Valley of Oaxaca, Cortez gradually lost his political power in Mexico and was supplanted in 1535 by the first viceroy, Antonio de Mendoza.

Cortez himself gave a vivid description of the conquest of Mexico in five letters he wrote to Charles V of Spain. The best-known account, however, is the history of Bernal DÍAZ DEL CASTILLO, which Archibald MacLeish used as the basis of his poem *Conquistador* (1932). Novels laid in this period include Lew Wallace's *The Fair God* (1873) and Samuel Shellabarger's *Captain from Castile* (1945).

Corvino (Ital, "raven") A greedy merchant in Jonson's comedy VOLPONE, OR THE FOX. Though very jealous of his innocent young wife, Celia, Corvino willingly offers her to the lecherous Volpone in the hope of inheriting some of his money.

Corvo, Baron See ROLFE, FREDERICK.

Cory, William Johnson (1823–1892) English poet and classicist. Cory published a single volume of verse, *Ionica* (1858), in which is found the famous translation from Callimachus, "Heraclitus," beginning "They told me, Heraclitus, they told me you were dead."

Corydon A conventional name for a rustic or shepherd; a brainless, love-sick youth derived from the shepherd in Vergil's *Bucolic* II.

coryphaeus The leader of the chorus in Greek classical drama. An earlier term for the same office was *choragos*. Both words have been used figuratively to apply to the leader of any group or, more especially, its most active member.

Cossacks, The (Kazaki, 1863) A novel by Count Leo TOLSTOY. The central character, Olenin, tired of life in civilized society, attempts to find happiness among the wild, free-living Cossacks of the Caucasus. The portraits of the old Cossack Eroshka and the native girl Maryana are especially successful. Critics generally cite this short work as the finest book written by Tolstoy before WAR AND PEACE.

Cotter's Saturday Night, The (1786) A sentimental poem in Spenserian stanzas by Robert BURNS, famous for its description of Scottish peasant life and for the story of Jenny.

Cotton, Charles (1630–1687) English poet and translator. Cotton is best known for his translation (1685) of Montaigne's *Essays*, a clear, faithful, and vigorous version that is often preferred to the earlier Florio translation. An intimate friend of Izaak WALTON, he wrote a treatise on fly-fishing, which was included in the fifth edition (1676) of THE COMPLEAT ANGLER. Cotton was also the author of several other translations from the French, some rather scurrilous burlesques of VERGIL and LUCIAN, and a number of poems on fishing, country life, and related subjects. These last, which have a certain homely charm and fidelity to the

rural scene, collected in *Poems on Several Occasions* (1689), were admired by WORDSWORTH, COLERIDGE, and LAMB.

Cotton, John (1584–1652) English-born Puritan clergyman and writer. Dissatisfied with conditions in England, Cotton, who was already a famous clergyman, immigrated to Boston in 1633 and became one of the colony's most influential leaders. Known for his tireless scholarship and aristocratic political views, he wrote numerous works, including *The Keys of the Kingdom of Heaven* (1644); *Milk for Babes* (1646), a children's catechism; and *The Bloudy Tenent Washed* (1647), part of a celebrated controversy with Roger Williams. Cotton MATHER was his grandson.

Cotton, Sir Robert Bruce (1571–1631) English antiquary, collector of books, manuscripts, coins, medals, etc. He was the founder of the famous Cottonian Library, now part of the British Library, which contained many otherwise unobtainable manuscripts saved from destroyed monasteries, including those of BEOWULF, THE PEARL, and SIR GAWAIN AND THE GREEN KNIGHT. The identifying titles of the manuscripts were derived from the busts of Roman emperors that adorned the bookcases holding these collections; thus, the *Beowulf* manuscript is called Cotton Vitellius A XV from the Emperor Vitellius, and the manuscript of *The Pearl* is known as Cotton Nero A X from the Emperor Nero.

Cotton allowed the free use of his library to leading scholars of his time and presented manuscripts from his collection to the BODLEIAN LIBRARY when it was founded. His library was bequeathed to the English nation on the death of his grandson in 1701.

Cotytto The Thracian goddess of fertility, worshiped at Athens with licentious rites.

Council of Nicaea (325) The first ecumenical council of the Christian Church. Called by CONSTANTINE THE GREAT, it was held in Nicaea, a small town in Bithynia, Asia Minor. The major undertaking of the council was a discussion of the views of ARIUS, who held that Jesus was the most exalted human of all time but had not been created out of nothing nor was eternally existent and that he was capable of right and wrong in his own free will. The council's decision was against Arius, ascribing a purely divine nature to Jesus (see TRINITY).

The council published a confession of faith called the Nicene Creed. It was based on an older creed that had been used in Caesarea, but it carefully defined the orthodox doctrine of the Trinity. The Nicene Creed is used (with minor changes) in the liturgies of the Roman, Greek, and Anglican churches, and its doctrinal teachings have been accepted by most Protestants.

Counterfeiters, The (Les Faux-Monnayeurs, 1926) A novel by André GIDE. The novelist Edouard keeps a journal of events in order to write a novel about the nature of reality. The intrigues of a gang of counterfeiters symbolize the counterfeit personalities with which people disguise themselves to conform hypocritically to convention or to deceive themselves. The adolescent boys Bernard Profitendieu and Olivier Molinier, having left home in order to be free to find and develop their true selves, encounter many varieties of hypocrisy and self-deception in human relationships and barely escape falling into such poses themselves. Both begin by seeking a close emotional tie with Edouard. Each, however, comes to recognize that Edouard is inadequate as an ideal for emulation, particularly when the novelist cannot recognize the psychological reality of the schoolboy Boris's useless suicide, which is an indirect result of the counterfeiters' machinations.

Counter-Reformation The Roman Catholic reaction to the Protestant Reformation of the 16th century. Beginning with the Council of Trent and later through the efforts of the INQUISITION and the JESUITS, the Roman church sought to consolidate its position and win back its former adherents. Literature and the other arts became involved as vehicles for the renewal of faith and the propagandizing of Roman Catholic dogma. Artists were bound by conscience and external pressure to help or at least not hinder the cause. The so-called Counter-Reformation style in literature, sometimes identified with or considered a part of the baroque style, flourished during the latter half of the 16th century and the first half of the 17th century. It was characterized by the use of rhetoric, a straining after the ironic, the paradoxical, and the witty, attempts to render reality as well as the world of the spirit in concrete and highly sensuous imagery, especially in religious verse. Though its leading practitioners in Italy, Spain, France, and England, poets such as TASSO, Marino, Ceppède, Góngora, Lope de VEGA, Southwell, and CRASHAW, were Catholics, the style left its mark on such Protestant poets as D'Aubigné and DONNE in their use of the metaphysical conceit.

Countess Cathleen, The (1891) A poetic drama by William Butler YEATS. It describes how the countess Cathleen sells her soul to the devil in exchange for the souls of the starving Irish peasants. In her wanderings through Ireland, the Countess Cathleen is accompanied by Oona, an old nurse, and Aleel, a poet who loves her in vain. The part of the countess was written for Maud GONNE. The play was one of the first produced by the company that was later to become the ABBEY THEATRE company. At its first production, it provoked a riot by Catholics offended at what they considered Yeats's theological irregularity in having God save the heroine's soul at the end.

Count Julian (Reivindicación del Conde Don Julián, 1970; tr 1974) A novel by Juan GOYTISOLO. Combining dreams, temporal juxtapositions and dislocations, literary criticism, and free association, this work presents Count Julian, the narrator's alter ego, as a psychological reincarnation of the governor who betrayed Spain to the Arabs in

711. Both victim and executioner, the narrator attacks every aspect of traditional Spanish orthodoxy, the Franco government, bourgeois pretensions, and the Catholic Church in attempts at finding revenge for the Spanish Inquisition and the expulsion of the Moors and Jews from Spain.

Count of Monte Cristo, The (Le Comte de Monte Cristo, 1844) A romance by Alexandre DUMAS. The hero, Edmond Dantès, is about to begin a blissful existence as captain of his vessel and husband of his sweetheart, when a false political charge condemns him to life imprisonment. He escapes, in a highly dramatic manner, and flees to the island of Monte Cristo. With the aid of a treasure he unearths, Dantès becomes a powerful and darkly mysterious figure. Eventually, all who wronged him suffer his revenge.

Country Doctor, The (Le Médecin de campagne, 1833) A novel, part of LA COMÉDIE HUMAINE, by Honoré de BALZAC. The title character is Dr. Benassis, whose kindly spirit and indefatigable efforts on behalf of the people of his village make him universally beloved.

Country of the Pointed Firs, The (1896) A book of tales and sketches by Sarah Orne JEWETT. Thinly bound together by a faint thread of plot, the entire series describes a Maine seaport town from the point of view of a summer resident. The portraits of the townspeople are sympathetically drawn. Willa Cather thought so well of the book that she placed it beside HUCKLEBERRY FINN and THE SCARLET LETTER.

Country Wife, The (1675) A comedy by William WYCHERLEY. Pinchwife, an overly jealous husband, brings his simple country wife, Margery, to London for the marriage of his sister Alithea to the credulous Sparkish. Despite Pinchwife's efforts, Margery soon becomes familiar with the fashionable ways of the city and ends by cuckolding him with the libertine Horner, who has spread the rumor that he himself is a eunuch to facilitate his access to willing wives. Thus Pinchwife's jealousy leads his wife to infidelity, while Sparkish eventually loses Alithea because of excessive confidence in her loyalty.

In 1766 Garrick rewrote the play as *The Country Girl*, modifying some of its bawdiness.

Coup, The See UPDIKE, JOHN.

Couperus, Louis Marie Anne (1863–1923) Dutch novelist. Couperus spent much of his childhood in the Dutch East Indies, where his father was a colonial official, and he lived for many years in Italy. He was a cosmopolitan writer and, influenced strongly by ZOLA, was the leading figure of the Dutch realist school of fiction. In over thirty novels, his recurrent preoccupation was with the role that fate plays in people's lives. This is particularly evident in his most outstanding single novel, *Van oude menschen, de dingen die voorbijaan* (1906; tr *Old People and the Things That Pass*, 1963), in which a murder committed in the past deeply affects an elderly couple and their grown children. His masterwork, for which he is best known, was the tetralogy beginning with *The Book of the* SMALL SOULS, a richly detailed chronicle of Dutch middle-class life written on the scale of Galsworthy's FORSYTE SAGA.

couplet In prosody, a pair of lines forming a unit, usually either because they are set off as a separate stanza or because they rhyme. The best-known couplet is the so-called HEROIC COUPLET.

Courbet, Gustave (1819–1877) French painter. Spokesman of realism, Courbet painted straightforward, unembellished, oversized scenes of everyday life and autobiographical events. Although he was decried by his conservative contemporaries, he rejected harmonious composition and color in his desire to express truth and achieved a forceful expression, especially in his landscapes.

Courtier, The (Il cortegiano, 1528) A Renaissance courtesy book by Baldassare CASTIGLIONE. Written in 1518, its four books of dialogues describe the conversations held at the court of Urbino on four successive evenings in 1507. The main interlocutors are Federico Fregoso, Lodovico Di Canossa, Bernardo Bibbiena, Giuliano de' Medici, Pietro Bembo, Ottaviano Fregoso, and Emilia Pia, who, along with the hostess, Elisabetta Gonzaga, acts as moderator. In the first book, the ideal courtier is said to require noble birth, skill in arms, courage, a handsome appearance, and dexterity in swimming, hunting, dancing, and the arts. He must be able to write and speak well, but above all without affectation. The manner of doing these things must be nonchalant and natural (*sprezzatura*).

The second book is devoted to language, the kind and the occasion of speech, as well as the manner of addressing oneself to princes and friends. Bibbiena dominates the discussion with a long treatment of jests and witticisms. The third book features Giuliano de' Medici's discourse on the *donna di palazzo*, the court lady, who is required to maintain her femininity while displaying a knowledge of letters, the arts, and how to entertain the court. She must be morally superior, an injunction that produces a lengthy debate on the chastity of women and the problems of amatory relationships at court.

The fourth book deals with the final and true role of the ideal courtier: to guide his prince in matters of government and state. After further discussion of the education of the prince and the best forms of political organization, Bembo concludes the book with a rhapsodic explanation of platonic love, the union of beauty and goodness in the ascent to God.

Not long after its publication, the book was translated into French, German, Spanish, and Russian. The English version of Sir Thomas Hoby (1561) insured its popularity in England, where it influenced the writings of Spenser and Sidney, the plays of Shakespeare, and the educational and social theory and practice of the English Renaissance.

With the courtesy books of Guazzo and Della Casa, it formed a trio of crucial landmarks in the development of English attitudes toward the requirements of being a gentleman.

courtly love (Fr, *amour courtois*) A medieval code of attitudes toward love and of the highly conventionalized conduct considered suitable for noble lords and ladies. It postulates the adoration and respect of a gallant and courageous knight or courtier for a beautiful, intelligent, lofty-minded noblewoman, who usually remains chaste and unattainable. He performs noble deeds for her sake but suffers terribly because she remains indifferent or, even if she favors his devotion, because her purity and his respect for it prevent the consummation of their love. Often he must keep secret the name of his beloved, although he carries her scarf or glove into battle or celebrates her beauty in song, for the lady is usually married to someone else; a basic tenet of the code is the incompatibility of love with marriage. Nevertheless, the lover welcomes the suffering of his passion, for it ennobles him and inspires him to great achievements.

The tradition of courtly love seems to have first been popularized by the Provençal TROUBADOURS of southern France in the 11th century. Through ELEANOR OF AQUITAINE's patronage of the troubadours, the convention spread to the royal courts of northern France, of England, and then of Germany (see MINNESINGERS). Eleanor's daughter Marie de Champagne urged her chaplain Andreas Capellanus to write a treatise on the art of love; and the "court of love," in which a group of court gentlefolk gather to debate specific theoretical problems of conduct in the interpretation of the code, became popular as a social pastime and a literary convention. The principles of courtly love were embodied in the first part of the allegorical ROMANCE OF THE ROSE and in medieval romances such as the cycles concerning King Arthur, Tristan and Iseult, and Troilus and Cressida, most notably in the version of the Launcelot legend by Chrétien de Troyes.

In Italy, the STILNOVISTI of the late 13th century adapted the tradition in a "sweet new style," which further idealized the role of woman in the spiritual elevation of the man who adores her. This worship of the beloved thus became fused with the cult of the Virgin Mary and with the concept of the ideal in Platonism. By the 16th century, courtly love had become only one aspect of the code governing the entire bearing and conduct of the courtier and his lady. The most famous handbook of courtly behavior was Castiglione's THE COURTIER, translated into English by Sir Thomas Hoby in 1561. This and the Stilnovistic works of Dante and Petrarch, all identifying physical beauty and social decorum with moral and ultimately with spiritual worth and the approach to a platonic ideal, greatly influenced much Elizabethan writing, such as that of Sir Philip Sidney and Edmund Spenser. The exaltation of a worthy woman because of the elevating aspect of courtly love is especially prominent in Spenser's *Four Hymns*.

Courtship of Miles Standish, The (1858)   A long narrative poem by Henry Wadsworth LONGFELLOW. The captain of the Plymouth settlement, Miles STANDISH, sends his friend John Alden to woo Priscilla Mullins for him. Despite his honest pleas for the older man, Priscilla prefers John as a husband. When Miles is reported killed, the lovers plan their marriage. On the eve of the wedding, Standish returns to give his blessings to the young couple.

Cousine Bette, La (1846)   A novel, part of LA COMÉDIE HUMAINE, by Honoré de BALZAC. The title character, Lisbeth Fischer, is a harsh old spinster who masks frustration and bitterness behind a facade of good will. Driven by fierce jealousy, she deliberately destroys a romance between her young niece and a Polish sculptor.

Cousin Pons, Le (1847)   A novel, part of LA COMÉDIE HUMAINE, by Honoré de BALZAC. The hero, Silvain Pons, is a musical composer who squanders most of his income on works of art. Ugly and lonely, he becomes a glutton and social parasite as he grows older.

Cousins, Norman (1915–   )   American journalist and editor. As editor of the SATURDAY REVIEW from 1942 to 1971, Cousins was responsible for dropping the words *of Literature* from the title and expanding the scope of the magazine to include the other arts and world affairs. After his departure from the *Saturday Review*, Cousins founded (1972) and edited *World* magazine. He has written several books on world federalism and foreign policy. In a more reflective vein, *The Celebration of Life* (1974) is a dialogue on immortality and infinity. *Anatomy of an Illness* (1979), written from the point of view of a patient, contains Cousins's reflections on the factors (including laughter) involved in the will to live. *Human Options* (1981) is an autobiography.

Covenanters   A term applied, during the 16th and 17th centuries, to the Scottish Presbyterians who banded together in a series of agreements, or covenants, to defend their religion against royal encroachments. In 1643 the English Parliament and the Scots drew up a Solemn League and Covenant that provided for changes in the English church in conformity with Presbyterian principles; in return, the Covenanters agreed to join the Parliamentary struggle against Charles I.

Coventry Cycle   See MYSTERY PLAYS.

Coverdale, Miles   (1) An English priest, (1488–1568) converted to Lutheranism and translator of the first complete Bible in English (1535). See BIBLE, ENGLISH VERSIONS.

(2) The narrator and a leading character of Hawthorne's BLITHEDALE ROMANCE.

Coverley, Sir Roger de   The simple, good, and altogether delightful country squire created by Richard STEELE as a chief character in the imaginary club that supposedly wrote THE SPECTATOR. Roger de Coverley was further developed by Joseph ADDISON, and it is to Addison that we are indebted for this portrait of a perfect English gentleman in the reign of Queen Anne. *Roger de Coverley* is the name of a country dance similar to the Virginia Reel, and it was Addison's fiction that Sir Roger's great-grandfather invented the dance.

Coward, Noël [Pierce] (1899–1973)   English playwright, composer, and actor. Coward is best known for his witty, brittle, and sophisticated comedies about the British leisure class. He began as a child actor at twelve and attracted considerable attention a dozen years later as the lead in his own play *The Vortex* (1924). His heyday was in the 1920s and 1930s, with such plays and musical revues as *Hay Fever* (1925), *Bitter Sweet* (1929), *Private Lives* (1930), and *Blithe Spirit* (1941). He also wrote several spirited patriotic pieces, including *Cavalcade* (1931) and *This Happy Breed* (1943), and the film *In Which We Serve* (1942). Subsequent successes were *Quadrille* (1952), a costume piece, and *Song at Twilight* (1966), a partly autobiographical play about a homosexual writer at the end of his career. *Present Indicative* (1937) and *Future Indefinite* (1954) are two volumes of his autobiography, the first being a buoyant account of his love affair with the theatre, the second, about his experience as an entertainer during the war. *Pomp and Circumstance* (1960) is a novel. He also wrote poetry and nearly three hundred songs, including the well-known "Don't Put Your Daughter on the Stage, Mrs. Worthington" and "Mad Dogs and Englishmen."

Cowards, The   See ŠKVORECKÝ, JOSEF.

Cowley, Abraham (1618–1667)   English METAPHYSICAL POET and essayist. Cowley's conceits were fantastic and extreme, popular in his own day, but regarded with disfavor by the time of Dryden. He was also famous as the originator of the English Pindaric ode. Cowley published his first volume, *Poetical Blossoms* (1633), at the age of fifteen; later works include "Davideis" (1656), his best-known poem.

Cowley, Hannah (1743–1809)   English dramatist. One of the earliest English female playwrights, Cowley wrote a number of comedies of manners touched with sentimentality. Among the best are *The Belle's Stratagem* (1780) and *A Bold Stroke for a Husband* (1783).

Cowley, Malcolm (1898–   )   American critic and poet. A member of the American colony in France in the 1920s, Cowley wrote about expatriate members of the LOST GENERATION in *Exile's Return* (1934; rev 1951) and again in *A Second Flowering* (1973). He also wrote an influential study of William FAULKNER's works in the introduction to *The Portable Faulkner* (1946), to be followed later by *The Faulkner-Cowley File: Letters and Memoirs 1944–1962* (1966). Among his other books on literary trends and personalities are *The Literary Situation* (1954), an analysis of the writer's place in American society; *Fitz-*

gerald and the Jazz Age (1966); *A Many-Windowed House* (1970), collected essays; *And I Worked At the Writer's Trade* (1978), covering sixty years of American literary history; and *The Dream of the Golden Mountains* (1980), reminiscences of writers in the 1930s. Cowley has written two volumes of poetry, *Blue Juniata* (1929) and *The Dry Season* (1941). *The View from Eighty* (1980) contains his reflections on aging.

Cowper, William (1731–1800)   English preromantic poet. From the time he was twenty-four, Cowper suffered from a religious mania and was subject to fits of despair—he was convinced that he was excluded from salvation—and intermittent attacks of insanity. After his first breakdown, he went to Huntingdon to board with Morley Unwin, until Unwin's death (1767). He then moved, with the widowed Mary Unwin, to OLNEY and continued to live with her until her death (1796). His poetic career began late in life, with the production of hymns, didactic verse, nature lyrics, and religious poetry. His best-known poem is THE TASK. Others, also well known, include "Truth," "The Progress of Error," "Expostulation," "Hope," "Charity," "Conversation," and "Retirement," all published in 1782, *The Diverting History of* JOHN GILPIN, a humorous ballad published with *The Task*, and the *Olney Hymns* (1779). He also translated Homer (1791) and, on his death, left many letters and introspective autobiographical writings. Cowper was interested in freeing English verse from the facility of the followers of Pope. "Give me a manly rough line," writes Cowper, "with a deal of meaning in it, rather than a whole poem full of musical periods, that have nothing but their oily smoothness to recommend them." His last work was the tragic poem "The Castaway" (pub 1803).

Cowperwood, Frank Algernon   The central character in a trilogy of novels by Theodore DREISER. Patterned after Charles T. Yerkes (1837–1905), the transportation magnate and financier, Cowperwood is a man with an overweening desire for power, which drives him in ruthless pursuit of financial dominance but fails to bring him happiness. The novels in the trilogy are THE FINANCIER, THE TITAN, and *The Stoic* (1947).

Cozzens, James Gould (1903–1978)   American novelist. Cozzens was known as something of a literary maverick, by virtue of his social and stylistic conservatism. His novels, which generally deal with the moral dilemmas and compromises of upper-middle-class people, have been both praised and attacked by critics. *S.S. San Pedro* (1931), based on the sinking of the *Vestris* in 1928, was the first of his works to attract wide attention. *Guard of Honor* (1948), which won a PULITZER PRIZE, is the story of a colonel's efforts to hold a Florida air force base together in World War II. *By Love Possessed* (1957) became such a best-seller that it inspired a famous attack by critic Dwight MACDONALD in *Commentary*, called "By Cozzens Possessed." Other

writings include the novels *The Last Adam* (1933) and *Morning Noon and Night* (1968) and the collection of stories *Children and Others* (1964). *Just Representations* (1978) is a Cozzens anthology, with an autobiographical comment by the author.

Crabbe, George (1754–1832)   English poet. Crabbe escaped extreme poverty through the financial assistance of Edmund Burke. Considered a transitional figure between neoclassicism and romanticism, Crabbe wrote in the heroic couplet; his sympathies were humanitarian but opposed to sentimentality. His best-known poem is THE VILLAGE, a realistic answer to Oliver Goldsmith's *The Deserted Village*. Other poems by Crabbe, similar in theme to *The Village*, include *The Newspaper* (1785), *The Parish Register* (1807), and *The Borough* (1810). "Peter Grimes," one of the most powerful tales in *The Borough*, is the subject of a tragic opera, first produced in 1945, by Benjamin Britten.

Crabbed Age and Youth (1599)   An anonymous Elizabethan lyric, presenting a series of antitheses between youth and age.

cracker-barrel humor   A genre of American folk humor that originated in New England general stores, where the cracker barrel provided a convenient seat for rustic wits. Cracker-barrel humorists were known as cracker-barrel philosophers. Originally storytelling and gossip, cracker-barrel humor grew to mean shrewd, homely, Yankee wit, and finally American folk humor in general. Many American humorists—among them James Russell LOWELL, Artemus WARD, Josh BILLINGS, and Mark TWAIN—made use of the characteristic malapropisms (see MALAPROP, MRS.), epigrammatic forms, and homespun metaphors of cracker-barrel humor. See also TALL TALE; YANKEE.

Craig's Wife (1925)   A play by George KELLY. It is a study of a selfish, narrow woman, more interested in her house than in her husband; by the end of the play, everyone has left her, and she is alone with the house. It was awarded a PULITZER PRIZE.

Cranach, Lucas, the Elder (1472–1553)   German painter and engraver. Although not a master draughtsman, Cranach's vivid and original portraits earned him the position of court painter to three successive electors of Saxony. As a friend and supporter of Martin LUTHER, Cranach produced a number of mythological and biblical paintings, including *Crucifixion* (1502), in which both Luther and Cranach are pictured. His son, Lucas Cranach the Younger (1515–86), enjoyed much of his father's popularity and produced work that was surprisingly similar.

Crane, [Harold] Hart (1899–1932)   American poet. One of the first to attempt to express the spirit of a mechanized 20th century in valid and appropriate poetic terms, Crane is known for his unique, imaginative, and powerful creative talent. Strongly influenced by such poets as Arthur RIMBAUD and T. S. ELIOT, he nevertheless created his own distinctive style of dramatic rhetoric and extremely complex, compact imagery. In constant revolt from a father who had little appreciation for his poetic gifts, Crane often used elements from his own life for the stuff of his poetry. As a young man, he came to New York from Ohio, worked at various jobs, and wrote poetry, which was finally published in *Poetry*, the *Little Review*, and other little magazines. In 1926 he published his first collection of verse, *White Buildings*, containing an inscription from Rimbaud, whose influence is clear.

Crane reacted strongly to the poetry of T. S. Eliot, recognizing the power of the verse at the same time that he rejected the negative view of modern culture found especially in THE WASTE LAND. Crane's THE BRIDGE was in part an answer to Eliot, an attempt to evoke the "myth of America," to write a poem that would fuse American culture, past, present, and future, into one ecstatic whole. (This rejection of cultural pessimism was not new to Crane; it infused several of the poems in *White Buildings*, notably "For the Marriage of Faustus and Helen.") The poem remains one of the major achievements of 20th-century poetry.

Always torn by personal difficulties, in the throes of despair over what he considered his failing literary powers, Crane committed suicide by jumping overboard from the ship bringing him back from Mexico, where he had gone on a Guggenheim fellowship to write a poem on the Spanish Conquest.

After his death, a volume of poems collected for publication, *Key West: An Island Sheaf*, was found. This group, together with other unpublished poems, was included in *Collected Verse* (1933).

Crane, Ichabod   A character in Washington IRVING's tale THE LEGEND OF SLEEPY HOLLOW. Crane is a gawky schoolmaster, described as resembling "some scarecrow eloped from a field."

Crane, Stephen [Townley] (1871–1900)   American novelist, short-story writer, and poet. In his short life, Crane managed to produce work that assured him a permanent place in American literature. Often called the first modern American writer, he has been variously described as a realist, an impressionist, a naturalist, and a symbolist.

His first novel, MAGGIE: A GIRL OF THE STREETS, was published at his own expense. Although it was ignored by reviewers, this starkly realistic study of New York slum life earned Crane the respect of Hamlin GARLAND and William Dean HOWELLS. In 1895 Crane published both THE RED BADGE OF COURAGE, which brought him immense international prestige, and his first volume of poems, THE BLACK RIDERS, which anticipated the FREE VERSE styles of much of 20th-century poetry. *George's Mother* (1896) appeared the following year. Sent on a journalistic errand to Cuba, Crane was on board the *Commodore* when it sank on New

Year's Day 1897. The story THE OPEN BOAT is based on this experience.

Crane married (probably in 1897) Cora Taylor, owner of a Florida brothel. The marriage, combined with his unorthodox reputation, provoked such scandalous speculation about his private life that Crane took his bride abroad. They went to Greece as war correspondents, an experience that produced the novel *Active Service* (1899). At the end of the war, they established themselves in England. During the Spanish-American War, Crane went to Cuba as a foreign correspondent. Plagued by ill health and financial difficulties, he returned to his friends in England (among them, Joseph CONRAD) and died of tuberculosis at the age of twenty-eight. From his last years, the stories THE BRIDE COMES TO YELLOW SKY and THE BLUE HOTEL may be singled out for special note; the latter is included in *The Monster and Other Stories* (1899), whose title story is also much praised. Other works include WAR IS KIND, a book of poems; WHILOMVILLE STORIES; *Last Words* (1902); and *Sullivan County Sketches* (compiled by Melvin Shoberlin; 1949).

Cranford (1853)   A story by E. C. GASKELL, dealing with the life of the peaceful little English village of Cranford, inhabited chiefly by old ladies who practice elegant economy and a quaint social decorum under the leadership of the Honorable Mrs. Jamieson. The chief characters are the two Miss Jenkyns: Miss Deborah and Miss Mattie.

Cranmer, Thomas (1489–1556)   Archbishop of Canterbury. Cranmer first came to the attention of HENRY VIII through his suggestions regarding Henry's divorce from Catherine of Aragon. He was made Archbishop in 1533 and contributed substantially to the progress of the English Reformation by encouraging the circulation of the Bible in English, in the preparation of the First and Second Prayer Books of Edward VI, and in the formulation of the forty-two (now thirty-nine) Articles of Religion. In 1553 he was persuaded to sign the dying request of Edward VI to give the crown to Lady Jane GREY. After Lady Jane's brief reign and the accession of the Catholic Mary, Cranmer was sent to the Tower. He was burned at the stake for heresy in 1556.

Crashaw, Richard (1612–1649)   English METAPHYSICAL POET. Although Crashaw's father was a Puritan preacher, the poet became a convert to Catholicism in his early thirties. From the beginning of the English Civil War until his death, he lived in exile on the continent, first in Paris and later attached to the household of Cardinal Palotto and to the shrine of Loreto in Italy.

Crashaw is best known for his religious verse, though he wrote a good deal of secular verse and much Latin poetry. Even before his conversion, his religious poems reflected a straining, passionate mysticism and a love of lush, sensuous imagery and ornate conceits, in the manner of the

Marinist Italian poetry of the 16th and early 17th centuries. Although he was partly inspired to write religious verse by his reading of George Herbert's *The Temple* (1633), Crashaw's work is distinguished by a luxuriance and high-keyed emotiveness alien to Herbert. His style is highly individual and uneven: he is capable of an ardor and brilliance hardly surpassed in literature, but he can also be overwrought and tasteless.

In 1646 Crashaw published *Steps to the Temple*, a collection that contains his well-known secular poems "Musics Duel" (1646) and WISHES TO HIS SUPPOSED MISTRESS, and his religious poems to SS. Theresa and Mary Magdalene. "The Flaming Heart," a hymn to St. Theresa, which deals with her precocious piety and mystic transports, shows Crashaw at his strongest; but "St. Mary Magdalene, or The Weeper," in which he describes her penitential tears in a series of extended and extravagant images, contains overelaborate conceits and bathetic passages. Other works by Crashaw are *Epigrammatum Sacrorum Liber* (1634) and *Carmen Deo Nostro* (1652).

Cratchit, Bob   In Charles Dickens's A CHRISTMAS CAROL, the clerk of Ebenezer Scrooge. Though Cratchit has to maintain nine dependents on meager wages, his home, unlike his employer's, is filled with happiness and love.

Tiny Tim Cratchit   The little lame son of Bob Cratchit, a winsome and beloved child. In the ordinary course of events, he was doomed to an early death, but Scrooge, after his change of character, makes Tiny Tim his special care.

Crazy Jane   A beggar, the spokesman and heroine of a series of poems by William Butler YEATS. Advocating the natural joys of life, she flouts conventional morality, especially in "Crazy Jane and the Bishop."

Creakle   In Charles Dickens's DAVID COPPERFIELD, a hard, vulgar schoolmaster to whose charge David is entrusted and in whose school he first makes the acquaintance of STEERFORTH. The portrait of Creakle is Dickens's protest against the harsh treatment meted out to children by schoolmasters.

creation myths   Traditional stories that attempt to explain the origin of the world. The earliest known myth of the creation is from Sumer of the third millennium BC. First was the goddess Nammu, the primeval sea; she gave birth to An, the sky god, and Ki, the earth god—earth and sky, both solid elements, being joined together. Their offspring Enlil, the god of air, separated them. He lighted his realm by begetting Nanna, the moon god, who in turn fathered Utu, the sun god. Enlil next impregnated Ki, who gave birth to Enki, the god of water and of wisdom. Enki ordered the universe but was unable to create man—a task that the goddess Nintu accomplished by molding him of clay.

In the Babylonian creation myth of the WAR OF THE GODS (*Enuma elish*), Marduk forms man out of the blood and bones of Kingu, a henchman of the defeated Tiamat. An Egyptian belief was that the original sun god, Atum, standing on a mound in the midst of the slowly receding primeval waters, gave birth parthenogenetically to the other gods and to those parts of the universe that they embodied. According to the familiar biblical story, in the first chapter of Genesis, the universe and man were created by Yahweh in seven days, beginning with light and ending with man and woman. In the second chapter appears a variation on the creation of man, which is older and closer to folk tale; woman is created of a rib detached from Adam while he sleeps. Christian theology added that the Son and the Holy Ghost existed with Yahweh from before the creation. The Eastern branch of the Church, however, denied that Jesus had existed from the beginning and the resulting "*filioque* controversy" was the ostensible cause of the split between Eastern and Western churches in 1054.

The first Greek description of creation, in the *Theogony*, attributed to Hesiod, seems to have been a theological elaboration of genuine myth. First to exist was Chaos, from which came Earth, Tartarus, Love, Darkness, and Night. Night and Darkness gave birth to Day and the upper air (Aether). Earth parthenogenetically produced Heaven, Mountains, and Sea. After this prelude, the Hesiodic version proceeds with nearly universal mythic elements, which are probably far older. Uniting with Heaven (Uranus), Earth (Ge) gave birth to Oceanus and the Titans. The last of these was Cronus, who overthrew and emasculated his father, only to be supplanted in turn by his son Zeus (see KUMARBI). A highly artificial myth current in the doctrines of Orphism claimed that Chaos, Night, and Darkness existed at the beginning; Love (Eros) sprang from an egg laid by Night and himself gave birth to the other gods. The creation of human beings seems not to have interested the Greeks very deeply; of various versions, the most prominent made Prometheus their creator—he having molded them of clay.

In Vedic mythology, creation began with Aditi, celestial space. Sky and Earth were sometimes regarded as the first goddesses, sometimes as the original male and female elements, which are known to so many other mythologies; later the sky was personified as Varuna. The first man was Manu; his daughter-mate Ida was born of the food that he offered as a sacrifice to Vishnu in gratitude for being saved from the flood.

credo (Lat, "I believe")   A creed or confession of faith. The most important historical Christian creeds are the *Apostles'* and the *Nicene* (both 4th century) and the *Athanasian* (5th century). Later credal statements of importance are found in the *Decrees of the Council of Trent* (1563), the *Augsburg Confession* (1530), and the *Westminster Confession of Faith* (1647).

Creeley, Robert [White] (1926–   )   American poet, novelist, essayist, and short-story writer. Creeley began to achieve recognition as a poet when, in the early 1950s, he became affiliated with the BLACK MOUNTAIN POETS. He helped found and edited, for seven years, this group's journal, *Black Mountain Review*. A disciple and defender of Charles OLSON, Creeley composes PROJECTIVE VERSE in a style that is notably spare and laconic; his primary subject is love and the infinite incongruities that characterize love relationships. There is a distinct dearth of imagery in his poetry; the themes are rendered in a cerebral rather than sensual manner. For Creeley, the intent of the poem is definition, not description. Among his many volumes of poetry are *For Love: Poems, 1950–1960* (1962), *Divisions and Other Early Poems* (1968), *A Day Book* (1972), *Thirty Things* (1974), *Hello: A Journal* (1978), and *Later* (1979). He has also written a novel, *The Island* (1963). With the publication of his *Selected Poems* (1976), he was hailed as a master of verse technique, relentlessly pursuing a purity of form and idea. In 1984 *The Complete Prose* appeared.

Creon   (1) In Greek mythology, a king of Thebes. The brother of Jocasta, Creon served as regent after the death of her husband Laius and became king after the death of Eteocles in the War of THE SEVEN AGAINST THEBES. He condemned Oedipus' daughter ANTIGONE to death and, repenting too late, lost his own son Haemon as a consequence.

(2) A king of Corinth, whose daughter Glauce married Jason and met her horrible fate through the jealousy of MEDEA. Creon appears in Euripides' tragedy MEDEA.

Crepuscolari, I (Ital, "the twilight poets," a name coined by the critic G. A. Borgese)   A group of Italian poets of the early 20th century whose work is notable for its use of musical and mood-conveying language and its general tone of despondency. Their attitude represents a reaction to the content-poetry and rhetorical style of CARDUCCI and D'ANNUNZIO, favoring instead the unadorned language and homely themes typical of PASCOLI. An affinity existed with the French SYMBOLISTS (Valéry, Rimbaud, and Mallarmé). Guido Gozzano (1883–1916) was the most competent exponent of the movement.

Crèvecœur, Michel Guillaume Jean de (pen name J. Hector St. John, 1735–1813)   French author, agronomist, traveler, and settler in America from 1754 to 1780. After having traveled through Canada, the Great Lakes region, and Pennsylvania, Crèvecœur settled on a farm in the colony of New York. Here, between 1770 and 1781, he wrote LETTERS FROM AN AMERICAN FARMER, an extremely popular series of essay-letters. On his return to the U.S. to serve as French consul in 1783, he did much to improve Franco-American relations. More letters, found in 1922 and published as *Sketches of Eighteenth Century America* (1925), give informative and accurate descriptions of colonial American rural life. He also wrote *Voyage dans la haute Pennsylvanie et dans l'état de New York, par un*

membre adoptif de la nation Onéida (1801), an account of his early travels and of the American Indians, which he pretended to have translated from an original manuscript. Selections from *Voyage* were translated and published under the title *Crèvecœur's Eighteenth-Century Travels in Pennsylvania and New York* (1961) by Percy G. Adams.

Crews, Harry [Eugene] (1935–   )   American novelist and journalist. Crews, a Southerner, writes with a biting, sardonic humor about obsessed, decadent, or grotesque characters in bizarre situations. He first gained recognition with *The Gospel Singer* (1968), which was followed by such novels as *The Hawk Is Dying* (1973), *The Gypsy's Curse* (1974), *A Feast of Snakes* (1976) and *All We Need of Hell* (1987). *A Childhood: A Biography of a Place* (1978) is a vivid evocation of the Georgia of his youth. Selections from his column in *Esquire* magazine were published in *Blood and Grits* (1979).

Cricket on the Hearth (1845)   A Christmas tale by Charles DICKENS. In the happy home of John Peerybingle and his wife Dot, the cricket on the hearth chirps when all is well and is silent when unhappiness pervades. They take in an elderly boarder whom John soon discovers is a young man in disguise. His suspicions are aroused when he sees this man with his arm around Dot. The cricket takes things in hand, counseling John not to find fault. Soon the young man, who turns out to be Edward Plummer, bursts in with his young bride May Fielding. He explains all: after his long absence, he had come back disguised so that he could ascertain whether May truly loved Tackleton, the man she was to marry. Happiness returns to the house and Edward is reunited with his father Caleb and his blind sister Bertha.

Crime and Punishment (Prestupleniye i nakazaniye, 1866)   A novel by Fyodor DOSTOYEVSKY. The poor student Raskolnikov, after a long period of brooding over his poverty and the helpless position of his mother and young sister, plans and carries out the murder of an old woman pawnbroker. Surprised in the act, he kills the old woman's demented sister too. His motives for the murder are then reexamined. Raskolnikov, whose name is derived from the Russian word for *schismatic*, has claimed that he needed the money to help his family, that with the money he could raise himself up and become a benefactor to mankind, and finally that, by transgressing the law, he could show a boldness that would put him in the same category as NAPOLEON. One by one, Raskolnikov's motives are proven false as his conscience works on him. He instinctively feels disgust for his act and is unable to bring himself to use the stolen money. The torments of conscience he endures prove to him that he lacks the qualities of an amoral superman. He turns for sympathy to SONYA Marmeladovna, a young girl forced into prostitution to support her drunken father, his wife, and three small children. Sonya urges Raskolnikov to confess his crime. The police inspector Porfiry Petrovich, an astute psychologist, already strongly suspects Raskolnikov and simply waits for the confession that he is sure is forthcoming. Raskolnikov finally does break down, although he stubbornly refuses to admit sorrow for having killed the old pawnbroker. He is sentenced to Siberia, where Sonya devotedly follows him, and there he gradually begins to achieve the peace and humility necessary for his sincere repentance.

The novel, the first of Dostoyevsky's five large works, reveals the mastery of psychological observation and analysis for which the author is hailed. Besides the depiction of Raskolnikov's anguished mind before, during, and after the crime, there are vivid studies of the profligate SVIDRI-GAILOV, the saintly Sonya, and her drunken father, MARME-LADOV.

Crimean War A war (1854–56) fought by Turkey, with its allies England, France, and Sardinia, against Russia. It succeeded for the time being in shattering Russia's ambitions of leadership in southeastern Europe. The chief battles were at Alma, Balaklava, Inkerman, and the famous siege of Sevastopol. The result was the Treaty and Declaration of Paris (1856), in which the integrity of Turkey was guaranteed, the Black Sea neutralized, and Danubian navigation declared free. An event in this war was celebrated by Tennyson in his poem "The Charge of the Light Brigade" (written in 1854). It was also the scene of Florence Nightingale's heroic activities as a nurse.

Crime of Sylvestre Bonnard, The (Le Crime de Sylvestre Bonnard, 1881) A novel by Anatole FRANCE. Bonnard is a kind-hearted, absent-minded old archeologist. The aged scholar's crime is the kidnapping of Jeanne Alexandre, the orphaned daughter of his former love, from a school in which she is abused and unhappy. Threatening complications result, but when it is discovered that Jeanne's guardian is an embezzler, she is made the legal ward of Bonnard.

Criseida The heroine of Giovanni BOCCACCIO's romance Il Filostrato and the prototype of Chaucer's heroine in his TROILUS AND CRISEYDE.

Criseyde The beloved of Troilus in Geoffrey Chaucer's TROILUS AND CRISEYDE. Criseyde is more complicated than her prototype in Boccaccio's Il Filostrato; although a practical opportunist, she is genuinely affectionate, not the heartlessly fickle girl she becomes in Shakespeare's Troilus and Cressida.

Crisis, The (1901) A historical novel by Winston CHURCHILL. The action occurs mainly in St. Louis during the controversy over slavery. The hero, Stephen Brice, is a Yankee; the heroine, Virginia Carvel, a Southerner. The novel shows the inevitability of the Civil War, yet it stresses the fact that neither side wanted it. The book includes a notable portrait of Lincoln.

Criterion, The A quarterly literary review (1922–39), edited in London by T. S. ELIOT. Its first issue carried Eliot's THE WASTE LAND into print for the first time. It also introduced the British public to the works of numerous modern European writers, including Paul VALÉRY and Marcel PROUST. See LITTLE MAGAZINES.

Critique of Judgment (Kritik der Urteilskraft, 1790) A philosophical work by Immanuel KANT, containing his aesthetic philosophy. Kant believed that the representation of a thing in art constitutes a partial understanding of the "thing in itself" (Ding an sich).

Critique of Practical Reason (Kritik der praktischen Vernunft, 1788) A philosophical work by Immanuel KANT, in which he constructed a philosophy of ethics based on practical reason, or the free will of man. Since the moral law itself is unconditional and universal, it is called the categorical imperative; its basic formulation is "Act only on that maxim whereby you can at the same time will that it should become a universal law." Our knowledge of God is obtained through our moral feelings, not through pure reason.

Critique of Pure Reason (Kritik der reinen Vernunft, 1781) A philosophical work by Immanuel KANT, in which he maintained that all sense experience must be inherently rational and therefore that rational knowledge about experience is possible. However, although reason can understand a thing considered as an object of experience, reason cannot understand the "thing in itself" (Ding an sich).

Croce, Benedetto (1866–1952) Italian philosopher, literary critic, and historian. A prolific writer, of encyclopedic range, Croce set forth his philosophical system, in which the influence of German idealism is discernible, in the four volumes of his Filosofia dello spirito: Estetica come scienza dell'espressione e linguistica generale (1902), Logica come scienza del concetto puro (1905), Filosofia della pratica, economica, ed etica (1908), and Teoria e storia della storiografia (1916). He was perhaps most influential as an aesthetician, emphasizing the intuitive nature of art.

He also wrote numerous works of literary criticism, including La poesia di Dante (1920) and the six-volume Letteratura della nuova Italia (1914–40). Among his other works are Materialismo storico ed economia marxista (1900), Breviario di estetica (1913), and Storia d'Italia dal 1871 al 1915 (1927). For twenty-seven years he edited La critica, a bimonthly magazine.

A staunch liberal during the Fascist regime, he was a member of the post-World War II Committee of Liberation, a delegate to the constitution-making Italian Parliament (1945–47), and president of the Italian Liberal Party until 1947.

Crockett, David (known as Davy Crockett, 1786–1836) American frontiersman, public official, and folk hero. After serving as a scout under Andrew Jackson in the Creek War of 1813–14, Crockett became a justice of the peace in Tennessee; he later boasted that none of his decisions, which were based on "natural-born sense instead of law learning," was ever reversed. He was also a prodigious hunter of bears and claimed to have killed over a hundred in eight or nine months. A humorous suggestion that he run for Congress led him to undertake the race, and he was elected for three terms (1827–31, 1833–35), becoming known as the "coonskin Congressman." His opposition to the policies of President Jackson endeared him to the Whigs but cost him his seat, and he decided to go to Texas, where he died fighting heroically at the ALAMO. He was speedily made into an American folk hero, who could talk the language of animals, ride the lightning, lie with extravagant grandeur, and whip his weight in wildcats.

Several books have been attributed to Crockett, notably *A Narrative of the Life of David Crockett* (1834). He may also have had a hand in some of the *Crockett Almanacs*, which appeared from 1835 to 1856. They contained the usual meteorological and astronomical data, as well as tall tales involving such figures as Crockett, Daniel Boone, and Kit Carson.

crocodile   A symbol of deity among the ancient Egyptians. According to Plutarch, it is the only aquatic animal that has its eyes covered with a thin transparent membrane, by reason of which it sees and is not seen, as God sees all, Himself not being seen. To this, he adds: "The Egyptians worship God symbolically in the crocodile, that being the only animal without a tongue, like the Divine Logos, which standeth not in need of speech" (*De Iside et Osiride*). Achilles Tatius says, "The number of its teeth equals the number of days in a year." Another tradition is that, during the seven days held sacred to Apis, the crocodile will harm no one.

"Crocodile tears" are hypocritical tears. The tale is that crocodiles moan and sigh like a person in deep distress to lure travelers to the spot and even shed tears over their prey while in the act of devouring it. Shakespeare refers to this in the second part of *Henry VI* (1592).

Croesus (fl 550 BC)   A king of Lydia famous for his wealth. According to a story recounted by Herodotus, Croesus was once visited by SOLON, who, instead of calling Croesus the happiest of mortals, as the vain ruler had expected, said, "Account no man happy before his death." Croesus indignantly dismissed Solon, but the Greek proved to be right. Later, misinterpreting an oracle from Delphi that war with Persia would cause the fall of a great empire, Croesus attacked Cyrus, king of Persia, in 546 BC. The kingdom to fall turned out to be his own. Sentenced to death by fire, Croesus called the name of Solon, recalling too late his wisdom. Cyrus, upon inquiry, learned the story of the interview, and countermanded the death sentence. Instead he made Croesus one of his trusted advisers.

Unfortunately for the story, it is chronologically impossible, since the dates of Croesus and Solon did not coincide.

The remark attributed to Solon was a popular proverb; it appears as the final lines of Sophocles' *Oedipus Tyrannos*, among other places.

Crofts, Freeman Wills (1879–1957)   Anglo-Irish writer of detective stories. Beginning with *The Cask* (1920), one of his cleverest novels, Crofts wrote nearly forty books, many of which featured the tireless and fastidious detective Inspector French.

Crome Yellow (1921)   A satirical novel by Aldous HUXLEY. It is concerned with the odd, learned conversations and comic adventures of a group of people gathered at a country house party: Mrs. Wimbush, who believes in spiritualism; Mr. Wimbush, who reads aloud portions of his absurd history of his house, Crome; Mr. Scogan, who is planning a "Rational State" much like the one Huxley describes in BRAVE NEW WORLD; and other eccentrics. The central character is Denis Stone, an ineffectual young poet whose banal verse is included in the novel. His one decisive action takes him away from the woman he shyly and secretly loves.

Cromwell, Oliver (1599–1658)   English Puritan leader and Lord Protector of the Realm (1653–58). As commander of the famous cavalry regiment called Ironsides, Cromwell contributed to the Parliamentary victories at Edgehill and Marston Moor and, as joint commander of the New Model Army, defeated the Royalists at Naseby. After the execution of Charles I, he led an army against the rebellious Roman Catholics of Ireland, whom he persecuted so relentlessly that his name is still regarded there with odium. Although he refused the title of king, his powers as Lord Protector were such that he was able to rule as virtual dictator. An efficient administrator, he permitted religious toleration and pursued a vigorous foreign policy. His son Richard, trained to be his successor, alienated both the army and Parliament and was dismissed in 1659.

Cromwell, Thomas, Earl of Essex (1485?–1540)   English statesman. In 1524 Cromwell was employed by Cardinal Wolsey to survey some of the smaller monasteries, with a view to their suppression. He was attached to Wolsey until the latter's fall from royal favor in 1529, after which time Cromwell himself rose steadily in power. According to Cardinal Pole, Cromwell urged HENRY VIII to proclaim himself head of the church and thereby make unnecessary a papal dispensation for his divorce from Catherine of Aragon. When the Act of Supremacy established the king as head of the Church in 1534, Cromwell's policy was made law, and he became Henry's chief adviser in ecclesiastical matters. He became Lord Chamberlain in 1539, but the following year incurred Henry's disfavor over the king's marriage to Anne of Cleves, which Cromwell had fostered in the hope of gaining the support of German Protestants. He was accused of treason by his enemies and was executed in 1540.

Cronin, A[rchibald] J[oseph] (1896–1981) Scottish novelist and physician. Many of Cronin's best-selling novels are about the medical profession. Among his best-known books are *Hatter's Castle* (1931), *Three Loves* (1932), *The Citadel* (1937), *The Keys of the Kingdom* (1941), *The Judas Tree* (1961), and *A Pocketful of Rye* (1969). *Dr. Finlay's Casebook*, a popular and long-running television series in Britain, was based on several of his books.

Cronos One of the *Titans* of Greek mythology, the father of ZEUS. Born of URANUS (sky) and GE (earth), he married his sister RHEA. Learning from Ge that one of his sons would dethrone him, he swallowed his children, HESTIA, DEMETER, HERA, HADES, and POSEIDON, but Rhea rescued Zeus, who did indeed overthrow Cronos, as had been predicted, but only after tricking Cronos into regurgitating the children he had swallowed.

Cronos is believed to have been an ancient pre-Hellenic god of fertility. The sickle with which he is depicted in art probably was his attribute as a god of crops, though the Greeks explained that this was the sickle with which he had castrated his father, Uranus. The Romans identified Cronos with their deity SATURN.

cross An ancient symbol of many uses. Long before the birth of Christ, it was used in Carthage for ornamental purposes. Runic crosses were set up by the Scandinavians as boundary marks and were erected over the graves of kings and heroes. According to Cicero, the staff with which the Roman augur marked out the heavens was in the shape of a cross. The Egyptians employed it as a sacred symbol, and two buns marked with crosses were discovered at Herculaneum. It was a sacred symbol among the Aztecs long before the landing of Cortez. It was worshiped in Cozumel and Palenque; in Tabasco, it symbolized the god of rain. It was also the emblem of Quetzalcoatl as lord of the four cardinal points and their respective winds.

There are many legends about the cross of the Crucifixion. It is said to have been made of four kinds of wood: palm, cedar, olive, and cypress, signifying the four quarters of the globe. Another legend says that Solomon cut down a cedar and buried it on the spot where the pool of Bethesda later stood. Shortly before the Crucifixion, the cedar floated to the surface of the pool and was used as the upright of the cross. During the Middle Ages, enough fragments of the "true cross" were sold as relics to account for an entire forest of crosses. According to legend, the Emperor Constantine, on his march to Rome, saw a luminous cross in the sky, with the motto *In hoc signo vinces* ("by this sign conquer"). The night before the battle of Saxarubra (312), a dream instructed the emperor to inscribe the cross and the motto on the shields of his soldiers. He obeyed the voice and the vision and won the battle. A very similar legend has been applied to various other conquerors, however. The cross generally associated with the Cru-

cifixion in art is a Latin cross, or *crux immissa*. St. Andrew's cross, the *crux decussata*, is shaped like an X; the tau cross, or *crux commissa*, is very ancient, a T shape, thought to have been originally a phallic emblem.

The tau cross with a circle at the top, the *crux ansata*, was common to various Egyptian deities, including Isis and Osiris. The circle signifies the eternal preserver of the world. The tau is the monogram of Thoth, the Egyptian Hermes, the god of wisdom.

Crossing Brooklyn Ferry (1856) A poem by Walt WHITMAN. The poet feels himself to be one with all those who cross from shore to shore. Regardless of time and space, he shares the experience of life itself.

Crossing the Bar (1889) A famous poem by Alfred TENNYSON, which uses, as a metaphor for death, a description of putting out to sea on a calm evening. Before his death, the author instructed his publishers to insert it at the end of each section of his works.

Cross Purposes See MALENTENDU, LE.

Crotchet Castle (1831) A novel by Thomas Love PEACOCK. A delightful satire on romantic themes, the book is a humorously erudite discussion of various curious topics. The central one is an argument to determine the most desirable period of history, with the Rev. Folliott contending for Athenian Greece, Mr. MacQuedy for contemporary Scotland, and Mr. Chainmail for the Middle Ages.

Crowley, [Edward] Aleister (1875–1947) English poet and author of books on magic and occult lore. Crowley was a legendary figure, notorious for his celebrations of Black Magic rites. He wrote such books as *Songs of the Spirit* (1898) and *The Diary of a Drug Fiend* (1922). He is the subject of Somerset MAUGHAM's novel *The Magician*.

Crucible, The (1953) A play by Arthur MILLER, about the Salem, Massachusetts, witchcraft trials of 1692. Raising the question of freedom of conscience, it provided a parallel to McCarthyism in America during the early 1950s.

Crusades (fr MF, *croisade*; Sp, *cruzada*; Lat, *crux*; "cross") Christian holy wars fought during the Middle Ages at the behest of various popes. The term derives from the cross worn by the Crusaders to signify their pledge to fight for God. Politically the Crusades were undertaken for the purpose of establishing a European protectorate over Palestine; they also came to be viewed as an offensive against the threat of a Muslim invasion of Europe. Spiritually the Crusades were viewed as a material "pilgrim's progress" toward Christ's sepulcher, a means of acting out in this world what one hoped to attain in the next. With the exception of the Seventh Crusade (1248–49), led by St. Louis, king of France, the Crusades of the 13th century emphasized the political rather than the religious aspects of the "holy" war.

Historically and militarily, the Crusades were not, on balance, successful, yet they stimulated exploration and trade with the East. Art and literature brought the exoticism of the Eastern lands to even the simplest peasants. The CHANSONS DE GESTE developed a whole cycle devoted to the legendary deeds of the leaders of the First Crusade. Semiliturgical plays, using Crusade motifs, and Latin and vernacular chronicles, telling of the various campaigns, all made the feats and legends of the Crusaders a part of the everyday reality of Europe.

Cruz, Sor Juana Inés de la (1651?–1695)   Mexican poet, the first to write purely Mexican poems and not simply Spanish poems written in the New World. Cruz was born, probably out of wedlock, to a Spanish father and a Creole mother and was recognized very early in her life as a person of astounding abilities. At three she was slipping away from her home to eavesdrop on her older sister's classes at school, where she learned to read and write. At six she asked her mother to dress her as a boy so that she could attend the university. She was in her teens and had read all the books in her father's library when word of her remarkable beauty and great learning caused the viceroy, for the sake of show, to order her examined by forty university professors from all fields of study. She overwhelmed them at every point and became lady-in-waiting to the viceroy's wife. It was during her three years at court that she began writing poems.

Quite suddenly, at nineteen, she entered a convent. She filled her cell not only with books but also with scientific paraphernalia, musical instruments, and maps, until her superiors ordered her to devote herself wholly to pious duties. When she resisted the order and wrote treatises attacking the theological reasoning behind the principle that women should submit without question to the decisions of men, she was called a heretic. She responded with such rigorous penance that her fellow nuns had to restrain her for her own physical health.

She never again took up her studies or her writing; during an outbreak of plague in 1695, when she was forty-three, she worked without rest ministering to other nuns, contracted the disease, and died.

Her early poetry was the courtly verse of the time, imitative and constricted. Her later work was clearly Mexican in tone and often attacked the exploitative male attitude toward women.

Cry of the Children, The (1843)   A poem by Elizabeth Barrett BROWNING, expressing intense sympathy for the victims of child labor in the English mines and factories of her day and indicting those who were responsible for their exploitation.

Crystal Palace   See VICTORIAN.

cubism   An artistic movement begun in 1907 in Paris. It was influenced by the structural simplifications of African sculpture and by CÉZANNE's concepts of geometry in the visual representation of objects. Cubism is characterized by a reduction of objects, figures, and occasionally of landscapes to their basic geometric forms. This effect is achieved by flattening and superimposing planes, without the use of perspective or light. Analytical cubism (1910–12) increased the breakdown of forms and simultaneously represented various aspects of the same object. Monochromatic and austere, this phase led to the inclusion on the canvas of such materials as sand, glass, newspaper, and cloth. With synthetic cubism (1913–14), the planes grew larger and more varied, form and color reappeared, and reality was represented in its most general terms. Pablo PICASSO and Georges BRAQUE, the founders of cubism in the visual arts, were its most outstanding representatives.

In literature, the poets Guillaume APOLLINAIRE, Max JACOB, Pierre REVERDY, and André Salmon (1881–1969) helped to form cubist doctrines and collaborated on the cubist bulletins, although they preferred the term *l'esprit nouveau* ("the new spirit") to *cubism*. They experimented with cubistic poetry, arranging apparently imagistic lines in clear-cut blocks. The results were the immediate precursors of surrealistic poetry: Apollinaire's *Alcools* (1913) and *Calligrammes* (1918); Jean Cocteau's *Ode à Picasso* (1917); Jacob's *Le Laboratoire central* (1921); Reverdy's *Les Ardoises du toit* (1918) and *Cravates de chanvre* (1922); and Salmon's *Prikaz* (1919).

Cú Chulainn (original name Setanta)   In Gaelic literature, chiefly the ULSTER CYCLE, an Irish warrior of pagan times, a great hero of legendary feats. Cú Chulainn is sometimes described as "the Achilles of the Gael." Ostensibly of mortal parentage, Cú Chulainn is represented to be in fact the son of the sun god Lugh. When, as a mere child, he is attacked by a ferocious hound, he kills it; when he sees the grief of its owner, Culain, he takes on the role of watchdog until a hound can be found to replace the one he killed. He is thereafter known as "the hound of Culain," or Cú Chulainn. As a young man, he receives training at arms from the woman warrior Scathach on the isle of Scathach, now Skye. When Scathach is attacked by Aoife, another female warrior, Cú Chulainn subdues Aoife and makes love to her; when leaving the island, he instructs her to send their son Conlaoch to Ireland when he comes of age, under a vow to let no man stop him or force him to reveal his name. Conlaoch arrives in Ireland years later and kills so many warriors that he becomes embattled with Cú Chulainn, who kills him, learning his identity too late. In one version, they kill each other; in another, Cú Chulainn, in his grief, does battle with the sea and finally sinks, exhausted, into it.

In the most widely known version of the Cú Chulainn story, Cú Chulainn singlehandedly deters the invading army of Queen Maeve until the Red Branch warriors of Ulster awaken from an enchantment. In this version, Cú Chulainn duels with his foster brother, Ferdiad. (See CATTLE-RAID OF COOLEY.) Some years later, Medb, queen of Cruachain, gathers an army for the express purpose of killing Cú Chulainn and succeeds by creating, with the help of magic, an imaginary host with whom he fights to exhaustion. Fatally wounded, Cú Chulainn binds himself to a pillar and dies standing and facing the enemy. Emer, his widow, to whom he had returned after being seduced by Fand, the wife of the sea god Mananaan, throws herself into his grave and dies. During the Irish Renaissance, Cú Chulainn became a favorite subject for poets, notably W. B. YEATS, who describes his central exploit in the play *On Baile's Strand* (1904).

cuckold　　The husband of an adulterous wife. The name derives from *cuckoo*, the chief characteristic of this bird being to deposit its eggs in other birds' nests. Dr. Johnson explained that "it was usual to alarm a husband at the approach of an adulterer by calling out Cuckoo, which by mistake was applied in time to the person warned." The cuckold was traditionally supposed to wear horns as the attribute of his condition. The usage is ancient; the Romans used to call an adulterer a cuckoo.

Cullen, Countee (1903–1946)　　American poet. Cullen's early books of verse—*Color* (1926) and *Copper Sun* (1927)—established him as a leading member of the HARLEM RENAISSANCE. His poetry followed traditional verse forms, based in part on the works of John KEATS, and dealt with racial themes. In addition to a novel, *One Way to Heaven* (1931), he published several other verse collections, including *The Ballad of the Brown Girl* (1927), *The Black Christ and Other Poems* (1929), and *The Medea and Some Poems* (1929). *The Lost Zoo* (1940) and *My Lives and How I Lost Them* (1942) are children's books.

Culloden (or Drummossie Moor)　　A heath in Scotland where the duke of Cumberland defeated Prince Charles Edward Stuart (the Young PRETENDER) on April 27, 1746. The old Scottish ballad of Culloden begins "Drummossie Moor, Drummossie Day!" See MACDONALD, FLORA.

Culture and Anarchy (1869)　　A collection of essays on political and social conditions by Matthew ARNOLD. In these are found some of his most famous arguments for the role of literary culture in the spiritual life of England. The collection includes the famous essay *Hebraism and Hellenism.*

Cummings, E[dward] E[stlin] (1894–1962) American poet, critic, novelist, and painter. One of the most gifted and independent poets of his era, Cummings was born in Cambridge, Massachusetts, and educated at Harvard. Although he is best known for his poetry, such prose pieces as the novel THE ENORMOUS ROOM; *Him* (1927), an expressionist drama; and *Eimi* (1933), his impressions of Russia, are considered his most substantial works.

His verse is known for its eccentric use of typography and punctuation to indicate rhythmic pattern and interwoven meaning of his poems. He is known as well for his exten-

sive use of slang, dialect, and the rhythms of jazz. Cummings's poetry includes lyrical love poems, joyful celebrations of sex, humorous character sketches, and bitter satires on the foibles and institutions of his time. His first volume, sixty-six poems, called *Tulips and Chimneys* (1923), was followed by fifteen others, including: *XLI Poems* (1925), *ViVa* (1931), *50 Poems* (1940), *1 × 1* (1944), *Ninety-five Poems* (1958), and *73 Poems* (1962). *The Complete Poems 1913–1962* (2 vols) was published in 1972. He also wrote *Santa Claus* (1946), a play; a satirical ballet, *Tom* (1935); and *i, six nonlectures* (1953), a book of autobiographical essays. Until the 1930s, he preferred the lowercase e. e. cummings. In 1976 the complete original manuscript of *Tulips and Chimneys*, containing 152 poems, was published for the first time.

Cunctator (Lat, "the delayer")　　Epithet for Quintus Fabius Maximus (d 203 BC), the Roman general who harassed Hannibal by avoiding direct engagements and who wore him out by marches, countermarches, and skirmishes from a distance. The English FABIAN SOCIETY was so named in honor of this policy.

Cunningham, J[ames] V[incent] (1911–1985) American poet, scholar, and critic. From Jesuit schools, Cunningham went to Stanford University, where he became one of the most prominent of the group of poets surrounding Yvor WINTERS. His laconic, highly compressed verse soon won admiration in its own right. His volumes of verse range from *The Helmsman* (1942), *The Judge Is Fury* (1947), and *Doctor Drink* (1950) to *The Exclusions of a Rhyme* (1960), *To What Strangers, What Welcome* (1964), *Some Salt* (1967), and *Collected Poems and Epigrams* (1971). His theory of verse as "metrical speech" is clarified in two prose commentaries on the "poetic experience": *The Quest of the Opal* (1950) and *The Journal of John Cardan* (1964). Cunningham wrote two distinguished works of literary criticism—*Woe or Wonder* (1951), his doctoral dissertation, on Shakespeare, and *Tradition and Poetic Structure* (1960). He also edited two literary studies, *The Renaissance in England* (1966) and *Problem of Style* (1966). His *Collected Essays* appeared in 1977.

Cunninghame-Graham, Robert Bontine (1856–1936)　　Scottish travel and short-story writer and historian. Cunninghame-Graham's many stories and sketches, Latin American histories, and travel books all reflect the extraordinary life of action he led before he turned to writing. He left Britain at seventeen to work on an Argentinian cattle ranch. For the next fifteen years, he rode horses and riverboats all over South America, Mexico, and the southwestern U.S., living the rugged life of a gaucho and absorbing the stories of the roustabouts, ranchers, and Indians he encountered. He returned to his ancestral estate in Scotland at the death of his father in 1884 and turned his energies, still vigorous, to politics. He espoused many radical programs, became the only Socialist member of Parliament, opposing every aspect of British imperialism and actively supporting Irish and Scottish nationalist causes, until he failed to be reelected by his own Scottish Labor Party in 1892. He then began a successful writing career, with such books as *Mogreb-el-Acksa, or Journey in Morocco* (1898), which inspired his friend G. B. Shaw's play, *Captain Brassbound's Conversion* (1900). He was also a close friend of Joseph CONRAD, who used him as a model for Charles Gould in NOSTROMO. The "best stories" of Cunninghame-Graham were reissued in 1980 under the title *Reincarnation.*

Cupid   In Roman mythology, the god of love, son of Venus and Mercury, and counterpart of the Greek EROS. Cupid is usually represented as an exquisite boy with wings, bearing a bow and quiver of arrows, and is often described as blind or blindfolded. The bow is used to shoot the arrows, which are invisible and which cause the one shot to fall irrevocably in love. Originally depicted as a young man, as in the myth of Cupid and PSYCHE, Cupid later developed into the familiar cherubic but mischievous little boy.

Curetes   In Greek mythology, sons of RHEA. The Curetes protected the infant Zeus from Cronos by covering his cries with the clashing of their shields as he grew up in a cave on Mount Dicte in Crete. They were regularly associated with the rites of Zeus' mother Rhea and were identified by the Greeks with the Corybantes, who performed a similar function in the rites of CYBELE. Jane Harrison, in her *Themis*, suggests that both were minor divinities who had originally been the young men (*kouroi*) who took children from their mothers at puberty and initiated them in noisy rites into manhood and full membership in the tribe. (The Curetes were also a tribe who were neighbors of the Calydonians.)

Curiatii   In legendary Roman history, the three brothers who engaged in combat against the three HORATII.

Curie, Marie Sklodowska (1867–1934)   Polish scientist. Curie is best known for her discovery, with her husband, Pierre Curie, of radium. With A. H. Becquerel, they were awarded the NOBEL PRIZE in Physics (1903) for this discovery. She again won the Nobel Prize in 1911, this time in chemistry. *Madame Curie* (1937) is a biography written by her daughter Eve Curie. Her other daughter, Irène Curie-Joliot, with her husband, Frédéric Joliot, also won the NOBEL PRIZE in Chemistry (1935).

Curnow, [Thomas] Allen [Munro] (1911–   )   New Zealand poet, critic, and editor. Ranked among New Zealand's foremost poets, Curnow's technically intricate verse draws on the land, the history, and the people of New Zealand for both subject matter and imagery. His major collections are *A Small Room with Large Windows* (1962) and *Collected Poems* (1974). His critical introductions to three anthologies of New Zealand verse (1945, 1951, 1960)

attempt to identify an indigenous tradition in New Zealand poetry.

Curry, John Steuart (1897–1946)   American painter. One of the leading American regionalist painters in the 1930s, Curry is known for his portrayals of life in the American Midwest, particularly in his native Kansas. Among his best-known works are a series of paintings of the Ringling Brothers Circus (1932), *Wisconsin Landscape* (1940), and the murals he painted in the Kansas State Capitol as part of the American Scene project of the W.P.A.

cursus honorum (Lat, "course of honors")   In ancient Rome, the steps up the ladder of political success. In order of influence, the magistrates whose offices were generally included in the *cursus honorum* were the TRIBUNE, the QUAESTOR, the AEDILE, the PRAETOR, and the CONSUL. By the time he reached the consulate, the Roman politician had usually made his fortune and was ready to be assigned the comfortable governorship of a conquered province.

Curtis, G[eorge] W[illiam] (1824–1892)   American editor and essayist. While still a young man, Curtis lived at BROOK FARM, where he was profoundly influenced by transcendental thought. He served as coeditor of *Putnam's Monthly* and later as editor of HARPER'S MAGAZINE, where he began the influential column "The Easy Chair." He was an advocate of abolition, women's suffrage, and labor relations. Among his published works are the satirical *Potiphar Papers* (1853) and *Prue and I* (1857), a collection of essays on the theme that wealth is not a requisite to happiness. Other essays were collected in *Literary and Social Essays* (1894).

Cusa, Nicholas of (also known as Nicholas Cusanus, 1401–1464)   German cardinal and early forerunner of Copernicus. Born at Cusa (Kues), near Trier in Germany, he became an ecclesiastical statesman and a theologian but was also an outstanding humanist, philosopher, and mathematician. Cusa was famous in his day as a brilliant student at Padua, a papal legate at the age of twenty-five, and an influential figure at the Council of Basel (1433). His trip to Constantinople a few years later brought about the Council of Ferrara (1438), which led to the temporary union of the Eastern and Western churches and brought many Greek scholars to Italy (see HUMANISM; REVIVAL OF LEARNING). As deputy to his friend Pope Pius II, he was able to write philosophical works in peace and deal in them with esoteric and subtle ideas. He intuited notions later explored by COPERNICUS and Bruno (1548–1600)—the infinity of the universe, the cosmological relevance of mathematics, the coincidence of opposites. His most famous work, *De docta ignorantia* (*On Learned Ignorance*, 1440), insists on the simplicity of truth against the Aristotelian weaving of abstractions and verbal webs.

Custer, George Armstrong (1839–1876)   American general. Custer is best known for his "last stand"

(1876) at the Little Big Horn River in Dakota Territory, when he and his troops were overwhelmed and annihilated by Sioux warriors under Crazy Horse. Custer's wife, Elizabeth Bacon Custer (1843–1933), described their life together in *Boots and Saddles* (1885). See SITTING BULL.

Custom of the Country, The (1913)   A novel by Edith WHARTON. The heroine is Undine Spragg, a ruthless social climber who, through several marriages and divorces, samples the pleasures of money and aristocratic titles before finding her own level and marrying the youth from her home town who has become a millionaire.

Cutty Sark (fr Scot, *cutty*, "short," *sark* "shirt")   A witch in Robert BURNS's poem TAM O'SHANTER. Burns uses the term jocularly to describe the witch that catches Tam's eye. *Cutty* is also used to describe a short, plump woman and, by extension, is used playfully to describe a hussy.

Cybele   An ancient Asian goddess identified by the Greeks with RHEA. Originally a bisexual earth goddess, Cybele was made a female by the gods. Jealously in love with the beautiful youth Attis, who was preparing to marry a nymph, she drove him to madness, in which he castrated himself and died. She mourned for him thereafter. Cybele was celebrated in orgiastic rites by eunuch priests.

In her rites, she was always associated with the corybantes, a group of young men who dance and play musical instruments. Because these rites were similar to those of Rhea and her attendant CURETES, which were also widely practiced in Phrygia, the two became identified. Cybele, one of whose names was the Great Mother, became an important goddess in Rome, where she was known as *Magna Deum Mater*.

Cyclic poets   Epic poets. For some centuries after Homer, the Cyclics continued to write narratives filling out the story of the Trojan War and a cycle of poems about Thebes. In spite of various traditions, little is known about either the poems or their authors. It is probable, however, that they supplied later mythographers with a great deal of their material.

cyclopean masonry   The gigantic old Pelasgic ruins of Greece, Asia Minor, and Italy, such as the Gallery of Tiryns, the Gate of Lions at Mycenae, the Treasury of Athens, and the Tombs of Phoroneus and Danaos. They are composed of huge blocks fitted together without mortar, with marvelous nicety, and are fabled to be the work of the CYCLOPS. The term is also applied to similar structures in many parts of the world.

Cyclops (fr Gr, *kyklops*, "circular eye")   Any of a group of giants, offspring of Ge and Uranus. Hesiod listed three Cyclopes, named Brontes, Steropes, and Arges, who forged Zeus' thunderbolts. Each had only one eye, which was set in the middle of his forehead.

The most famous of the Cyclopes was Polyphemus, whose cannibal welcome to Odysseus and his sailors is related both in the *Odyssey* and in Euripides' satyr play *Cyclops*.

Cygne, Le (The Swan, 1885)   A poem by Stéphane MALLARMÉ. A swan is trapped in a frozen lake. Its beautiful flight is impossible, held in the more pure and mysterious state of unrealized possibility, of "useless exile." (*Le cygne* is pronounced the same as *le signe*, the poetic "sign.") Images of whiteness, ice, and snow and ASSONANCE of the French sound *i* are used to create the poem's atmosphere.

Cymbeline   One of the kings in the 12th-century HISTORY OF THE KINGS OF BRITAIN, by Geoffrey of Monmouth. When Caesar invaded Britain he forced the Britons to pay tribute and took Cymbeline with him as a hostage. Cymbeline was brought up in Rome as a Roman. When he became king of Britain, he lived peacefully with the Romans. After his death, his sons Guiderius and Arviragus refused to pay tribute, and a new Roman invasion ensued. Some five centuries after Geoffrey, he became the titular central figure of Shakespeare's play *Cymbeline*.

Cymbeline (c1610)   A play by William SHAKESPEARE. Cymbeline, king of Britain, upon hearing of the secret marriage between his daughter IMOGEN and Posthumus Leonatus, a gentleman of his court, banishes Posthumus, who goes to Rome. There he meets the cynical IACHIMO, who makes a wager that, going to Britain, he will cause Imogen to be unfaithful. When Imogen scorns his advances, Iachimo resorts to subterfuge. He gains access to her bedroom in the dead of night, steals her bracelet, and convinces Posthumus that he has won the wager. The outraged husband orders his servant Pisanio to murder Imogen, but the kindly fellow allows her to escape dressed as a boy. In the wilds of Wales, she comes upon the banished lord Belarius, who is living with Cymbeline's two sons, Guiderius and Arviragus, whom he had abducted as infants. Eventually Iachimo's villainy is exposed, Imogen and Posthumus are reconciled, and Cymbeline is reunited with his sons.

The historical source of the play is Holinshed's *Chronicles* (1577), but the theme of the wager is taken from Boccaccio's *Decameron*. Although the highly complicated plot often seems to be a parody of the extravagance of Elizabethan drama, the play itself contains much beautiful and moving poetry, "Hark! hark! the lark" and "Fear no more the heat o' the sun" being famous examples.

Cynara   The lady to whom the best-known poem of Ernest Dowson (1867–1900) is addressed. Each stanza closes: "I have been faithful to thee, Cynara, in my fashion." The poem has a Latin title: *Non sum qualis eram bonae sub regno Cynarae*.

Cynewulf (early 9th century)   Old English religious poet. Cynewulf's identity is known because he wove RUNES spelling his name into the ends of four poems in ALLITERATIVE VERSE: *The Fates of the Apostles*; the *Ascension*; *Juliana*; and *Elene*, the story of St. Helena and her son Constantine. In the *Exeter Book* (c975), the *Ascension* is preceded by the *Incarnation* and followed by the *Last Judgment*, also attributed to Cynewulf, the three poems being commonly known as *Christ*. The more than eighty "riddles" in the *Exeter Book* were long attributed to Cynewulf, but he probably wrote very few of them. His work probably influenced the unknown authors of *Christ and Satan* (see CAEDMON), of *Andreas*, and of the remaining "riddles," which are short poems of description, some simple, some very obscure.

Cynics   A Greek school of philosophy. It was founded at Athens by Antisthenes (c455–c360 BC), a pupil of Socrates. Antisthenes held that happiness is to be attained only by freedom from desires. The principles of the Cynics were illustrated in the life of DIOGENES. The school may have been named after Antisthenes' school in the gymnasium at Cynosarges, or it may have been derived from *kyon* (dog), Diogenes' nickname. The views of the Cynics were later adopted and modified by the Stoics under Zeno.

Cynthia   The moon; a surname of ARTEMIS or Diana. The Roman Diana, who personified the moon, was so called from Mount Cynthus in Delos, where she was born.

Cyprian, St. (full name Thascius Caecilius Cyprianus, c200–258)   The first Christian bishop to suffer martyrdom. The son of a wealthy patrician family, Cyprian was converted to Christianity (246), made bishop of Carthage (248), and there beheaded as a martyr (258). His *Let-*ters are an important source of information about the early Christian church.

Cyrano de Bergerac, Savinien (1619–1655) French author and playwright. In his fantasies *Histoire comique des états et empires de la lune* (*Comical History of the States and Empires of the Moon*, 1656) and *Histoire comique des états et empires du soleil* (*Comical History of the States and Empires of the Sun*, 1661), Cyrano recounts his imaginary visits to the moon and sun; his descriptions of their people and institutions are broadly satirical of the society and politics of his own day. He also composed the comedy *Le Pédant joué* (*The Pedant Tricked*, 1654) and the tragedy *La Mort d'Agrippine* (*The Death of Agrippina*, 1653), both still recognized as poetic and remarkable works. A freethinker and a soldier, famed for his skill in duels as well as for his inordinately long nose, Cyrano served as inspiration for the central character in Edmond ROSTAND's play *Cyrano de Bergerac* (1897).

Cyrus the Great (d 529 BC)   The founder of the Persian Empire. Cyrus dethroned his grandfather Astyages and conquered Lydia and Babylonia. He permitted the exiled Jews to rebuild Jerusalem, as recorded in the Old Testament, and treated generously the conquered Lydian king CROESUS. Legends surrounding his birth are related by HERODOTUS.

Cytherea   An epithet of APHRODITE, from her first setting foot on the island of Cythera after her birth from seafoam.

D

dactyl   In English prosody, a metrical foot consisting of three syllables, the first accented and the second and third unaccented. The word WON-*der-ful* is a dactyl. The METER made up of such units is called dactylic meter. The six-foot dactylic line was the epic verse of Latin and Greek poetry and was used by HOMER and VERGIL. An example in English is "THIS is the / FORest pri/MEval, the / MURmuring / PINES and the / HEMlocks . . ." from Longfellow's *Evangeline*.

dada (or dadaism; fr Fr, *dada*, "hobby horse")   A literary and artistic movement founded in 1916 in Zurich by Tristan Tzara, with the artist Hans ARP, the poet Hugo Ball, and the medical student Richard Huelsenbeck. The name was chosen by random selection from a dictionary. The movement was devoted to the negation of all traditional values in philosophy and the arts. Its form was a protest against what its leaders felt was the insane destruction of civilized life and thought during World War I. The *Dada* review proclaimed its intention to replace logic and reason with deliberate madness and to substitute intentionally discordant chaos for established notions of beauty or harmony in the arts. Dadaists mocked conventional behavior through an antirational type of exhibition that was to be the precursor of the HAPPENINGS nearly half a century later. Dada meetings turned into riots; art exhibits were mocking hoaxes. The former cubist painter Francis Picabia, who had been leading a similar movement in New York with Marcel DUCHAMP, joined Tzara's group in 1918. The following year they joined in Paris with André BRETON, who, with Louis ARAGON, Paul ÉLUARD, and Philippe SOUPAULT, founded the ironically titled review *Littérature*. While Tzara continued his sensational efforts at pure negation, the Germans in the group adapted the revolt to the service of communism. Breton and his group became interested in the subconscious, breaking with Tzara in 1921 and officially founding SURREALISM in 1924. Dadaism was revived in the 1930s in parts of England and America, and certain aspects of it survive in the THEATRE OF THE ABSURD.

Daedalus   In Greek mythology, a fabulously cunning artisan. An Athenian, the son of Metion and descendant of HEPHAESTUS, Daedalus was exiled from Athens for murdering his apprentice TALUS or Perdix. Fleeing to Crete, he earned a questionable distinction by constructing the wooden cow in which MINOS' queen PASIPHAË was able to satisfy her passion for a bull. He was then faced with the necessity of providing a place to keep their offspring, the MINOTAUR; for this purpose, he built the famous LABYRINTH.

Having made himself so useful to Minos, he was imprisoned in his own Labyrinth so that he could not leave the king's service. Making wings of wax and feathers for himself and his son ICARUS, he flew away to Sicily. Icarus, however, disobeying his father's instructions, flew too close to the sun; the wings melted and he fell to his death in the sea.

daemon   A minor divinity in ancient Greece. Originally beneficent spirits of the dead who insured fertility and often had animal as well as human forms, certain daemones became more individualized in function and ultimately developed into heroes or gods. DIONYSUS retained most clearly the character of a fertility daemon.

daemonic (Ger, *das Dämonische*)   In a special sense, a quality of certain characters in Goethe's works, such as the heroes of GÖTZ VON BERLICHINGEN and EGMONT. The daemonic figure is endowed with a powerful, uncannily attractive, individual force that sweeps other people along in its violent destiny. In FAUST, it is Mephistopheles rather than Faust himself who exemplifies this quality. In his famous poem "Urworte, Orphisch" ("Primal Orphic Words," 1817), Goethe defines the basic elements in human destiny as Daemon, Chance, Love, Necessity, and Hope; Daemon refers to each man's unique, inborn, developmental force, the unalterable law of his own individual growth.

Daffodils, The (1807)   A famous nature poem by William WORDSWORTH. The poem is characteristic of English romanticism in its appreciation of an object of nature for its own sake.

Dagon   A god of the PHILISTINES. Dagon was supposed (from very uncertain etymological and mythological indications) to have been symbolized as half man and half fish. He is mentioned by Milton in PARADISE LOST and SAMSON AGONISTES. See SATAN.

Daguerre, Louis Jacques Mandé (1787–1851) French artist and inventor. As an apprentice designer at the Paris Opéra, Daguerre painted panoramas, which led to his invention in 1822 of the *diorama*. A two-sided painting whose appearance changes according to the direction of the light fixed upon it, the diorama facilitated the realistic imitation on the stage of natural and atmospheric phenomena. Daguerre was the inventor of the *daguerreotype*, the forerunner of the modern photograph. Based on the photographic experimentation of J. N. Niépce (1765–1833), the daguerreotype was the first permanent impression of the *camera-obscura* image. Daguerre's process, though revolutionary, produced only individual positive prints and was soon replaced by processes that made possible multiple prints from a single negative.

Dahl, Roald (1916–   ) Welsh-born short-story writer living in England. During World War II, in which he served in the RAF, Dahl worked in Washington, D.C., for a time and began publishing stories in the *Saturday Evening Post* and soon became known for his mastery of the macabre. *Over to You* (1946), *Kiss Kiss* (1960), and *Switch Bitch* (1974) are among his books of short fiction. *My Uncle Oswald* (1979), Dahl's first full-length novel, is a characteristically bizarre story of a scheme for procuring and selling the sperm of the world's most powerful and brilliant men. He also wrote such screenplays as *You Only Live Twice* (1965) and *Chitty Chitty Bang Bang* (1967), as well as a number of very popular books for children, including *James and the Giant Peach* (1961) and *Charlie and the Chocolate Factory* (1964). Other works include *Dirty Beasts* (1982), *Revolting Rhymes* (1982), *The BFG* (1982), and *The Witches* (1983).

Dahlberg, Edward (1900–1977) American critic, novelist, essayist, and poet. Dahlberg, the illegitimate son of an itinerant woman-barber, spent years in and out of orphanages and, at seventeen, traveled the U.S. as a hobo. The bitter experiences of his early life provided the basis for his first two novels, *Bottom Dogs* (1929) and *From Flushing to Calvary* (1932), and for his autobiography, *Because I Was Flesh* (1964). Although his early novels were hailed as prime examples of PROLETARIAN LITERATURE, he later renounced naturalistic writing in favor of a highly allusive, epigrammatic, often archaic prose style, particularly in his essays and criticism. His critical works, which include *Do These Bones Live?* (1941; rev as *Can These Bones Live*, 1960), *The Flea of Sodom* (1950), and *The Sorrows of Priapus* (1957), attacked contemporary culture and dissented

from prevailing literary assessments of such idols of American fiction as FAULKNER, HEMINGWAY, and FITZGERALD. Among the few writers whom he praised were THOREAU, Sherwood ANDERSON, and Theodore DREISER. Other works include *The Truth Is More Sacred* (1961), *The Carnal Myth* (1968), and *The Confessions of Edward Dahlberg* (1971).

Dahn, Felix (1834–1912) German author. Dahn wrote poetry and several plays. He was one of the foremost practitioners of the PROFESSORENROMAN ("professorial novels"). The best known of his detailed historical works in the genre is *Ein Kampf um Rom* (A Struggle for Rome, 1876), a four-volume account of the Ostrogoth empire.

Daiches, David (1912–   ) Scottish literary critic. Daiches's interest in the extent to which contemporary cultural values are reflected in a writer's work informs his criticism. *The Novel and the Modern World* (1939) deals with the problems faced by writers of fiction in the 20th century. Among his other works are *Literature and Society* (1938); an important critical introduction, *Virginia Woolf* (1942); *A Critical History of English Literature* (1960); and critical biographies of Robert Louis Stevenson (1947) and Robert Burns (1950), among others. *A Third World* (1971) is his autobiography, containing an account of his many years of teaching in America. *Literary Landscapes of the British Isles* (1979) discusses the effects of specific locales on the creative imagination of certain English writers.

These were followed by *A Companion to Scottish Culture* (1981), *Literature and Gentility in Scotland* (1982), *Robert Fergusson* (1982), *Milton's Paradise Lost* (1983), and *God and the Poets* (1984).

Daisy Miller (1878) A novelette by Henry JAMES. It deals with an unsophisticated, "strikingly, admirably pretty" girl from Schenectady traveling in Europe who runs athwart the conventions of a group of Europeanized Americans who enforce the rules of the older European community with unthinking severity. The book aroused controversy when it first appeared, some reviewers taking it as a libel on American manners, but it later became one of the most popular of James's writings.

Dalai Lama   See LAMA.

Dali, Salvador (1904–   ) Spanish painter and etcher. Dali's paintings of irrational subjects were done in a meticulously realistic style. Long a disciple of SURREALISM, he also experimented with pointillism, scientific CUBISM, FUTURISM, CONSTRUCTIVISM, and bulletism, which involves shooting a 16th-century blunderbuss filled with graphite at a blank etching plate and printing the resulting pattern. Many critics dismiss Dali as merely an artistic prankster; however, his work has been purchased and displayed by New York's Museum of Modern Art and Metropolitan Museum of Art, among many other institutions. Perhaps his most famous painting is *The Persistence of Memory*

(1931), a desolate landscape with limp, melting watches sagging over cliffs and leafless trees. He has written numerous autobiographical works and collaborated on film scripts with Luis BUÑUEL.

Dalloway, Mrs.   See MRS. DALLOWAY.

Damas, Léon [Gontran] (1912–1978)   Guianan poet, short-story writer, critic, scholar, and statesman. Damas was born in French Guiana and educated there and in Paris, where he met Leopold SENGHOR and Aimé CÉSAIRE. Together they organized the magazine *L'Étudiant noir* (1934), which became the first voice of NÉGRITUDE, the movement of pride in African culture that was to have a profound, revitalizing effect on black thinking and writing. Damas's poetry, published in such volumes as *Pigments* (1937), *Graffiti* (1952), and *African Songs of Love, War, Grief, and Abuse* (1961), exemplifies African and Antilles motifs and evokes African sounds and rhythms.

Damascus   A city in Syria on the edge of the desert. Famous for its silks and steel, Damascus is generally considered the oldest continuously inhabited city in the world. It is frequently referred to in the OLD TESTAMENT (Gen. 14:15; 15:2). Its role in the history of PAUL's sudden and complete conversion (ACTS 9) is alluded to in references to "the road to Damascus."

Damayantī   A legendary Hindu princess in the epic MAHĀBHĀRATA. Damayantī chooses as her husband NALA, despite the fact that four gods, knowing her intention, have taken his appearance. Damayantī provides an example of *svayamvara*, or selection of a marriage partner by choice of the bride, as contrasted with the more common practice of arranged marriages.

Dame aux camélias, La (Camille, 1852)   A play by Alexandre DUMAS, *fils*. The work was first published as a novel (1848). The heroine, Marguerite Gauthier, known in America as Camille, is a beautiful courtesan who has become part of the fashionable world of Paris. Scorning the wealthy Count de Varville, who has offered to relieve her debts should she once more become his mistress, she escapes to the country with her penniless lover Armand Duval. Here Camille makes her great sacrifice. Giving Armand, whom she truly loves, the impression that she has tired of their life together, but actually at the request of his family, she returns to Paris and her life of frivolity. The tale concludes with the ultimate tragic reunion of Armand and the dying Camille. This sentimental story, dealing with a real moral and social problem, is also the basis of Verdi's opera *La Traviata*.

Damien de Veuster, Joseph (known as Father Damien, 1840–1889) A Belgian Roman Catholic missionary. Damien worked with the lepers in a government hospital on Molokai Island in the Hawaiian group, where he contracted leprosy and died. Robert Louis Stevenson wrote a famous essay, *Father Damien: An Open Letter to the Rev. Dr. Hyde* (1890).

Damocles' sword   A symbol of impending peril. Damocles, a sycophant of Dionysius the Elder, of Syracuse, was invited by the tyrant to try the felicity he so much envied. Accepting, he was set down to a sumptuous banquet, but overhead was a sword suspended by a hair. Damocles was afraid to stir, and the banquet was a tantalizing torment to him. The story is alluded to by CICERO and HORACE, among others.

Damon and Pythias   Two inseparable friends of Greek legend. They were Syracusans of the first half of the fourth century BC. Pythias, condemned to death by the tyrant Dionysius, obtained leave to go home to arrange his affairs on condition that Damon agree to take his place and be executed should Pythias not return. Pythias was delayed, Damon was led to execution, but his friend arrived just in time to save him. Dionysius was so struck with this honorable friendship that he pardoned both of them.

Dana, Richard Henry, Jr. (1815–1882)   American lawyer and writer. During his student days, Dana had serious difficulty with his eyes; he shipped out as a common sailor to improve his health. He might have traveled as a passenger but chose the more strenuous course of working on the *Pilgrim* on a voyage around Cape Horn in 1834. He returned home in 1836, his health much improved. From the journal he had kept, he wrote the American sea classic TWO YEARS BEFORE THE MAST. The same year, he finished law school and was admitted to the bar; his experiences at sea led him to become a sailor's lawyer. He wrote a manual for sailors, *The Seaman's Friend* (1841), which became an authority on naval law.

Danaë   The daughter of King ACRISIUS of Argos. Because the Delphic oracle predicted that his death would come at the hands of his daughter's son, Acrisius built a tower of brass and shut Danaë in it. But ZEUS visited her as a shower of gold and made her the mother of PERSEUS. Acrisius then set mother and son adrift in a chest, but they were saved by Zeus.

Danaides   The fifty daughters of Danaus. Danaides were punished in HADES for having murdered their husbands on their wedding night by having to draw water everlastingly in sieves from a deep well. The reason for their gory deed was told in a trilogy of plays by Aeschylus, of which only THE SUPPLIANT WOMEN remains.

Dance of Death   An allegorical representation of the triumph of Death over people of every age and class, reminding men of their mortality and the need for repentance. It is believed to have originated in 13th-century France and developed into two general forms. One consisted of a solemn dialogue between Death and his subjects, ending with Death leading a procession of victims off-stage to the grave. The other was the wilder *danse macabre*, in which the dead themselves lead the dance, rather than an abstract personification of Death. The latter possibly derived its name from the Dance of the Maccabees (*chorae Machaebarum*), reenacting the slaughter of the MACCABEES. The dance was a popular subject of morality plays of the late Middle Ages and appeared frequently in the work of artists, notably the woodcuts of Hans HOLBEIN. Versions of the dance may be found in many MYSTERY PLAYS devoted to the ANTICHRIST and in the EVERYMAN imagery, in which friends of the deceased link arms and follow the corpse to the grave.

Dance of Death, The (Dödsdansen, 1901) A double play by August STRINDBERG. One of Strindberg's most powerful plays, *The Dance of Death* is characterized by intense psychological realism in its presentation of a love-hate relationship between husband and wife. Alice has been virtually imprisoned by Edgar, her tyrannical husband, for twenty-five years; now he is gravely ill. The conflict focuses on his attempts to maintain his domination of his wife and her attempts at retaliatory torture.

Dance to the Music of Time, A (1951–1975) A sequence of twelve novels by Anthony POWELL. The novels, spanning a period of over fifty years, from the early 1920s, describe the school days, youth, and maturity of the narrator-hero, Nicholas Jenkins, and his upper-class cohorts, especially the egregious Widmerpool. Though primarily satiric in tone, they express an underlying melancholy about life and time reminiscent of Marcel PROUST. The novels in the series are A *Question of Upbringing* (1951), A *Buyer's Market* (1952), *The Acceptance World* (1955), *At Lady Molly's* (1957), *Casanova's Chinese Restaurant* (1960), *The Kindly Ones* (1962), *The Valley of Bones* (1964), *The Soldier's Art* (1966), *The Military Philosophers* (1968), *Books Do Furnish a Room* (1971), *Temporary Kings* (1973), and *Hearing Secret Harmonies* (1975).

Dancourt, Florent Carton (known as Sieur d'Ancourt, 1661–1725) French comic playwright. Jesuit-educated and intended for the law, Dancourt married an actress and devoted himself to acting and playwriting instead. His prose comedies are informal in style and often reveal their hasty composition, but rollicking satire and topical subject matter redeem such works as *Le Chevalier à la mode* (1687), *La Loterie* (*The Lottery*, 1697), and *Le Notaire obligeant* (*The Obliging Notary*, 1685), in which Dancourt lampooned decadent aristocracy, social climbers, financial fraud, speculation, judicial inefficiency, and other vices and foibles of his day.

Dangerfield, Sebastian See DONLEAVY, J. P.

Dangling Man See BELLOW, SAUL.

Daniel A biblical hero whose deeds and prophecies are recorded in the OLD TESTAMENT book of his name. For continuing to pray to his own God during the Babylonian captivity, which followed the conquest of Jerusalem by the Babylonians (586 BC), he was cast into a den of lions but was divinely delivered. Especially gifted with "understanding in all visions and dreams" (Dan. 2:17), he successfully exercised this gift by interpreting NEBUCHADNEZZAR's disquieting dreams, as well as the mysterious HANDWRITING ON THE WALL that disturbed the revelry of Belshazzar (Dan. 5:5).

Nothing is known of Daniel except what appears in his book. The first half of the book tells the story of the Hebrew prophet living in Babylon during the exile; the second half is his prophetic vision.

It is now thought that the book was written c164 BC instead of in the 6th century BC and that Daniel's "predictions" were history by the time of writing.

Daniel, Samuel (c1562–1619) English poet and dramatist. Daniel is known for the purity of his diction, the smoothness and grace of his verse: he was called "well-languaged Daniel" by contemporaries. His works include the famous SONNET SEQUENCE *Delia* (1592, with numerous later "augmented" editions); *The Complaint of Rosamund* (1592), a first-person narrative of the sort found in the MIRROR FOR MAGISTRATES; *The Civil Wars* (1595–1609), a verse history of the WARS OF THE ROSES; A *Defense of Rime* (1603), an essay answering Thomas CAMPION's attack on English rhymed and accentual verse; and *The Vision of the Twelve Goddesses* (1604), the first MASQUE to be written for the new court of JAMES I. He wrote two tragedies in the style of SENECA, *Cleopatra* (c1593) and *Philotas* (1604).

Daniel, Yuly Markovich (pen name Nikolay Arzhak, 1925–) Soviet short-story writer. In the early 1960s, Daniel wrote some satirical short stories that were published in Paris under his pseudonym. They were collected in a volume entitled *Govorit Moskva* (*This Is Moscow Speaking*) and appeared in a Polish translation in 1966. That same year, the Soviet authorities, having traced the authorship of the stories to Daniel, brought him to trial with Andrey SINYAVSKY, who had also published abroad under a pseudonym. In court, Daniel's satirizing and his rejection of realism for the fantastic and absurd were deemed anti-Soviet. One story, "Chelovek iz Minapa" ("The Man from Minap," 1963), particularly irked the officials; in it a young Communist claims that he can determine the sex of a fetus by thinking of either Karl Marx or Klara Zetkin during coitus. For his writings, Daniel received five years' hard labor. He was unexpectedly released in 1970, although forbidden to live in Moscow or to publish under his real name. His trial marked the end of THE THAW in Soviet literature.

Daniel Deronda (1874–1876) The last novel of George ELIOT. The heroine, Gwendolyn Harleth, marries Henleigh Grandcourt in order to avoid impending destitution of herself and her mother; this she does in spite of a promise made to the mother of his illegitimate children. Grandcourt turns out to be a tyrannical, selfish man, bent on breaking Gwendolyn's high-spiritedness. When Grandcourt drowns in a moment of delay before

Gwendolyn throws him a rope, she blames herself. In her distress she turns to Daniel Deronda, a man of fine character whom she has long admired. His sympathetic advice and her suffering, caused by the realization that he will never marry her, serve to develop her finer qualities. Deronda, a man of the highest ideals, has been brought up by his rich guardian as a Christian but learns that he is a Jew. He marries Mirah Cohen, whom he had saved from suicide. In Mordecai, who turns out to be Mirah's lost brother, he finds a friend who inspires him with the cause of Jewish nationalism. After Mordecai's death, he and Mirah go to Palestine to live.

Daniels, Jonathan [Worth] (1902–1981) American journalist and writer. The son of Josephus DANIELS, he succeeded his father as editor of the Raleigh, North Carolina, *News and Observer* from 1948 to 1970. *Frontier on the Potomac* (1946) describes the Washington, D.C., scene from 1943 to 1945, when he was an administrative assistant to President Franklin ROOSEVELT. Daniels's books include: *Tar Heels: A Portrait of North Carolina* (1941), *The End of Innocence* (1954), *Robert E. Lee* (1960), *Ordeal of Ambition: Jefferson, Hamilton, Burr* (1970), *The Randolphs of Virginia* (1972), and *The Gentlemanly Serpent* (1974).

Daniels, Josephus (1862–1948) American journalist and statesman. Born in Washington, North Carolina, Daniels was editor of the Raleigh, North Carolina, *News and Observer* from 1884 until his death. He served as Secretary of the Navy (1913–21) under both terms of Woodrow WILSON's presidency. Among his books are *The Life of Woodrow Wilson* (1924; repr 1971) and *The Wilson Era* (2 vols, 1944–45). As ambassador to Mexico (1933–41), he did a great deal to stabilize relations between the two countries. His autobiographical volumes are of great historical interest: *Tar Heel Editor* (1939), *Editor in Politics* (1941), and *Shirt Sleeve Diplomat* (1947).

Dannay, Frederic See QUEEN, ELLERY.

D'Annunzio, Gabriele (1836–1938) Italian poet, novelist, dramatist, and soldier. D'Annunzio was an exceptionally prolific writer whose principal artistic aim seems to have been the detailed and verbally precise analysis of passion. His heroes, very much like D'Annunzio himself, typify *fin de siècle* decadence, unfettered by the bourgeois ethic. Their refined ability to enjoy sensual pleasure and to experience "perfect passion" makes them a law unto themselves, suggestive of Nietzsche's ÜBERMENSCH. There is a notable absence of any concern for morality, conscience, or thought in his work, so that the well-exercised pleasures of the senses alone give meaning to life.

The D'Annunzian hero first appeared in the novel *Il piacere* (1889; tr *The Child of Pleasure*, 1898), in the person of the amoral sybarite Andrea Sperelli. His other novels include *L'innocente* (1892; tr *The Intruder*, 1898), *Il trionfo della morte* (1894; tr *The Triumph of Death*, 1898; repr 1975), and THE FLAME OF LIFE, based on his celebrated

liaison with the actress Eleonora Duse (1859–1924). Among his best-known dramas are *La citta morta* (1898; tr *The Dead City*, 1902), LA GIOCONDA, *Francesca da Rimini* (1901; see PAOLO AND FRANCESCA), and *La figlia di Jorio* (1904; tr *The Daughter of Jorio*, 1907). Many of his poems are included in *Le laudi* (1903–12), particularly in the third book, *Alcione*. He also wrote short stories describing peasant life in his native Abruzzi: "Terra vergine" (1882), "Libro delle vergine" (1884), and "San Pantaleone" (1886).

An ardent nationalist, he led a band of soldiers into the city of Fiume, now in Yugoslavia, in 1919 and held it for fifteen months in defiance of Italy's obligations under the Treaty of VERSAILLES. He later supported the Fascist Party.

danse macabre See DANCE OF DEATH.

Dante (full name Dante Alighieri, 1265–1321) Italian poet. The first important author to write in Italian and one of the greatest poets in all literature, Dante was born in Florence, where he became thoroughly educated in both classical and Christian literature. As a young man, he joined actively in both the politics and the actual fighting in the wars between the GUELPHS AND GHIBELLINES. He belonged to the Bianchi, one of the rival factions within the Guelph party, and when their opponents, the Neri, finally achieved power late in 1301, Dante and many others were sentenced to perpetual banishment (1302), condemned to death by burning should they be caught again in Florence. The Bianchi soon made an alliance with the Ghibelline party and attempted several unsuccessful attacks on Florence. Their hopes ended with the death (1313) of the emperor Henry VII, who they had hoped would reunite Germany and Italy. Thereafter, Dante spent most of his time writing his *Commedia* (see THE DIVINE COMEDY) under the patronage of Ghibelline leaders, one in Verona, then one in Ravenna. The exact period of the composition of the *Commedia* is unknown. Dante may have begun it as early as 1300, more probably 1307, but the major part of the writing was almost certainly done after 1315, and the last section completed shortly before his death.

Dante had first met BEATRICE in 1274 when he was nine; their second meeting was nine years later. After her death in 1290, he wrote LA VITA NUOVA, which reveals the significance of his idealized love for her as the inspiration for most of his works. He finally married Gemma Donati (1292?), by whom he had two sons and one or two daughters; she did not, however, accompany him into exile in 1302.

Dante's early works include a number of amatory lyrics in the form of the CANZONE and the SONNET, many of which appear in *La vita nuova* and in the unfinished *Il convivio* or *Convito* (*The Banquet*, 1304–7), which consists of three long commentaries, encyclopedic in scope, each on one of his own *canzoni* (see STILNOVISTI).

De vulgari eloquentia (1304–6) is a Latin treatise "on the vernacular tongue." In opposition to the general assumption of his day that Latin must be used for all important writing, Dante urges that the courtly Italian used for amatory lyrics be enriched with the best from every spoken dialect and established as a serious literary language, thus unifying the separated Italian territories by the creation of a national culture. He also analyzes several Italian dialects, anticipating the much later science of linguistics, and considers various problems of literary style and specific poetic forms, especially the *canzone*. In fact, Dante used his native Tuscan for the *Commedia* and *La vita nuova* and thereby established that dialect as the ancestor of modern Italian.

In the Latin treatise *De monarchia* ("on monarchy," usually translated as *On World Government*, c1313) Dante presents the political perspective that also becomes a major theme in the *Commedia*. He believes that a unified temporal authority, the Holy Roman Empire, is necessary, but deplores the rivalry for supreme political power currently raging between the emperors and the papacy. He prophesies that peace will be achieved only when the universal monarchy of the empire is established and recognized as being dependent only on God, although reverent toward the spiritual authority of the Church. Then Church and State will be allies with separate responsibilities in guiding mankind to peaceful happiness on earth and bliss in heaven.

Other works include two *Eclogues* (c1319) in Latin verse; the *Quaestio de aqua et terra* (1320), a scholastic treatise on physics; and thirteen Latin *Epistles*, including both personal and political letters.

Danton, Georges Jacques (1759–1794)   French lawyer, orator, and leader of the FRENCH REVOLUTION. Danton became a leader of the CORDELIERS early in the Revolution, became a member of the Legislative ASSEMBLY in 1792, and was a major figure in the storming of the Tuilleries. In the new republic, he was the minister of justice. He instituted the Revolutionary Tribunal (March 10, 1793). Now a partisan of peace, he came into increasing conflict with ROBESPIERRE, who later charged him and his followers with a conspiracy to overthrow the government. His trial was a mockery, and he was guillotined. His death is the subject of a dramatic poem, *Dantons Tod* (*Danton's Death*, 1835) by Georg Büchner. In a speech (September 2, 1792) inspired by the dangers of the European alliance against revolutionary France, Danton uttered the famous words: *Il nous faut de l'audace, encore de l'audace, et toujours de l'audace, et la France est sauvée.* ("We must dare and dare, and dare again, and France is saved.")

Dantons Tod (*Danton's Death*, 1835)   A drama by Georg BÜCHNER, depicting with convincing psychological perception and frequent ironic humor the steps leading up to the execution of Georges Jacques DANTON. The play is starkly realistic; Danton first appears in it as a tired, apathetic, somewhat licentious, and rather unrevolutionary character. But this, by contrast, only increases the effectiveness of his idealistic commitment when he finally defies Robespierre.

Daphne   In Greek mythology, the daughter of a river-god, loved by APOLLO. Daphne fled from the amorous god and escaped by being changed into a laurel, thenceforth the favorite tree of Apollo.

Daphnis   In Greek mythology, the Sicilian shepherd who invented pastoral poetry. Though Daphnis was the son of HERMES and of a nymph and a half-brother of PAN, he was unfortunate in love, being blinded by a nymph for a not very clear reason. He made up sad but lovely songs on the subject and was eventually taken up to heaven by Hermes. On the other hand, THEOCRITUS, the human inventor of the PASTORAL, claims in his first idyl that Daphnis died of unrequited love, a punishment from Aphrodite for having refused the love of women.

Daphnis and Chloë   A Greek PASTORAL poem, generally ascribed to the sophist Longus (4th or 5th century AD). It tells the story of the tender love of Daphnis and Chloë, the children of a goatherd and a shepherd. It owes its fame in modern times to the French version by Amyot (1559).

Da Ponte, Lorenzo (1749–1838)   Italian poet and librettist. Appointed poet to the Italian Theatre in Vienna, Da Ponte was commissioned by Mozart to write libretti for *The Marriage of Figaro* (1786), *Don Giovanni* (1787), and *Così fan tutte* (1790). In 1805 he immigrated to the U.S., where he worked as a grocer in New Jersey and a medicine salesman before he became the first professor of Italian literature at Columbia University, in 1830. His colorful *Memoirs* were published in four volumes (1823–27).

Darby and Joan   A designation for a loving, old-fashioned, virtuous married couple. The names appear in a ballad called "The Happy Old Couple," probably written by Henry Woodfall, and the original characters are said to have been John Darby of Bartholomew Close, who died in 1730, and his wife. Woodfall served his apprenticeship as a printer to John Darby. Some authorities attribute the ballad to Matthew Prior. It was originally distributed as a broadside ballad in 1748.

D'Arcy, Margaretta   See ARDEN, JOHN.

Dardanelles   The ancient HELLESPONT, a strait between Europe and Asiatic Turkey. During World War I the Allies attacked the Turks here and suffered defeat. In 1941 it was the gateway to Russia from the Mediterranean, but Turkey, as neutral, refused passage. Its fortifications were so strong that no attempt on it was made by sea.

Dare, Virginia (1587–?)   The first child of English parents born in America. She and her parents were among the settlers who disappeared from the "lost colony" at Roanoke Island.

Darío, Rubén (pen name of Félix Rubén García Sarmiento, 1867–1916)   Nicaraguan poet and essayist, famed as the high priest of MODERNISMO. Raised by relatives, Darío wrote verse as a child and was known in Central America as "the boy poet." In 1886 he went to Chile, where he published his first major work, *Azul* (1888), a collection of verse and prose sketches that bore the imprint of the French PARNASSIANS and revealed the fondness for lush, exotic imagery that was to characterize his work. In 1890 he returned to Central America and the first of his two unhappy marriages. After a short visit to Spain in 1892, he moved to Buenos Aires. The appearance of *Prosas profanas* (1896; tr 1922), in which the influence of the French SYMBOLISTS is fused with that of the Parnassians, marked the highpoint of the modernist movement. In 1898 Darío went again to Spain, now as a correspondent for *La nación*, a Buenos Aires newspaper. He was acclaimed by the intellectuals of Spain's GENERACIÓN DEL 98, who, like Darío, were profoundly affected by the outcome of the Spanish-American War. *Cantos de vida y esperanza*, generally regarded as his best work, appeared in 1905. It shows the technical excellence and lyric beauty of his earlier poetry, but there is greater freedom and a new feeling for the native themes, which he had previously rejected. Darío's concern for "our America" is also evident in "A Roosevelt," a poetic diatribe against the U.S., motivated by the seizure of Panama in 1903, and in *Canto a la Argentina* (1910). Darío's later work reveals a growing disillusionment and despair. Although he was named Nicaraguan minister to Spain in 1908, his last years were marred by financial difficulties and poor health, due in part to his heavy drinking. In 1915, after an unsuccessful lecture tour of the U.S., he was stricken by pneumonia in New York and died soon after his return to Nicaragua. Darío's influence on Spanish poetry can be measured by the statement of Pedro Henríquez Ureña that "of any poem written in Spanish, it can be told with certainty whether it was written before or after him." *The Selected Poems of Rubén Darío* appeared in English translation in 1965.

Darius I (known as Darius the Great, c550–486 BC) King of Persia. A member of a younger branch of the royal family, Darius assumed the throne in 521 after quelling a rebellion led by the magician Gautama, who claimed to be Bardiya, brother of the dead king Cambyses. Darius was an excellent administrator, extended the boundaries of the Persian Empire, and built an imposing capital at Persepolis. His exploits are recorded on the famous monument at Behistun in Iran.

According to legend, Darius was one of seven Persian princes who agreed that he should be king whose horse neighed first; his was the first to do so when he tethered a mare near it.

Darius III (surnamed Codomannus, c380–330 BC) Last king of Persia. Defeated by ALEXANDER THE GREAT at the Granicus river, at Issus, and at Arbela, Darius was killed by one of his own satraps.

Legend relates that when Alexander succeeded to the Macedonian throne, Darius sent to him for the traditional tribute of golden eggs, but Alexander answered, "The bird which laid them is flown to the other world, where Darius must seek them." The Persian king then sent him a bat and ball, in ridicule of his youth, but Alexander told the messengers that with the bat he would beat the ball of power from their master's hand. Lastly, Darius sent him a bitter melon as emblem of the grief in store for him; but the Macedonian declared that he would make the shah eat his own fruit.

Darkness at Noon (1941)   A satirical and powerful novel by Arthur KOESTLER about the abuses and brutalities of the totalitarian prison state. Nicholas Rubashov, ex-Commissar of the People and once a powerful man in the party, is held on false charges. Through the psychologically destructive events that precipitate Rubashov's demoralized state and his eventual execution, Koestler graphically portrays the psyche of the prison state.

Although it is implied that the state Koestler describes is Russia during the Moscow trials, the novel is an indictment of totalitarian systems everywhere. It is both far-reaching and frightening in its implications and eloquently conveys human helplessness in the face of the invasion of the mind by the police state, a force one cannot hope to understand. The inevitable result of such a system is the concomitant loss of human freedom, which is symbolized by the prison, and the eventual execution of men, not because they are threats—Rubashov, by the time he is executed, is no longer a threat—but because the state can thus perpetuate an atmosphere of fear. By doing so, it maintains a complete, Godlike hold over the people and ensures its own survival. The novel has few equals in its depiction of the horrors of the totalitarian state.

Darnay, Charles   In Charles Dickens's A TALE OF TWO CITIES, a teacher of languages who loves Lucie Manette and marries her. Darnay is a French aristocrat, nephew of the Marquis de St. Evrémonde, and has changed his name, immigrating to England in rebellion against his family, who have committed grave injustices against peasants. Because of his family, he is considered an enemy of the revolution, and, when he returns to Paris to help an old servant unjustly imprisoned, he himself is arrested and sentenced to the guillotine; he is saved by the self-sacrificing intervention of Sydney Carton.

Darnley, Henry Stuart, Lord (1545–1567) Great-grandson of Henry VII, and the second husband of MARY, QUEEN OF SCOTS. Displeased at not receiving the crown matrimonial from Mary, Darnley became jealous of David Rizzio, one of her favorite counselors, and was an accomplice in his murder. Shortly thereafter, Darnley himself was murdered, possibly with Mary's knowledge, at

Kirk o' Field, a solitary house near Edinburgh; the house was blown up with gunpowder, and Darnley's body, apparently strangled, was found nearby.

Darrow, Clarence [Seward] (1857–1938) American lawyer, lecturer, and writer. As a well-paid railroad lawyer, Darrow viewed the causes he defended unsympathetically. In the wake of the famous Pullman strike (1894), he resigned his position with the railroads and won national recognition for his unsuccessful defense of Eugene DEBS. Categorically opposed to capital punishment, he saved numerous alleged murderers from execution, including the notorious Nathan Leopold and Richard Loeb, who murdered a young boy (1924). In 1925 he served as chief defense counsel in the SCOPES TRIAL. Although he lost the case, he destroyed the reputation of the prosecuting attorney, William Jennings BRYAN, when the latter took the stand to defend a fundamentalist interpretation of the Bible.

Darrow wrote two novels, *Farmington* (1904) and *An Eye for an Eye* (1905). Among his other writings are *Crime: Its Cause and Its Treatment* (1922); *Infidels and Heretics* (with Wallace Rice, 1929), an anthology; and *The Story of My Life* (1932). A collection of his brilliant defense summations, *Attorney for the Damned* (ed A. Weinberg), appeared in 1957. Darrow appears in *Inherit the Wind* (1955), a play based on the Scopes trial, by Robert E. Lee and Jerome Lawrence, and in Meyer Levin's *Compulsion* (1956), based on the Loeb–Leopold case.

darshana (Sans, "viewing") In HINDUISM, the six orthodox schools of Hindu philosophy, all of which accept the Vedic scriptures as divine law and outline approaches to *moksha*, or salvation, the release from the cycle of birth, death, and rebirth. They are: (1) *Mīmāmsā*, which relies on the ritual practices in the VEDAS as the way to salvation; (2) *Vedānta*, teachings based on the UPANISHADS; (3) *Sankhya*, a nontheistic school that instills principles relating to a strict dualism of soul and matter; (4) and (5) *Nyāya* and *Vaisheshika*, both of which teach that the Vedas are divinely revealed and which attempt logical-scientific explanations for existence and reality; and (6) *Yoga*, which teaches the path to moksha through various mental and physical exercises and meditation.

Darwin, Charles Robert (1809–1882) English naturalist; grandson of Erasmus DARWIN. An original expounder of the theory of evolution by natural selection, since known as Darwinism, he was to have a profound influence on human concepts of life and the universe. Although he studied medicine at Edinburgh and prepared for the ministry at Cambridge, his abiding interest was natural history. And it was as naturalist that he sailed on the *Beagle* (1831–36) on an expedition to southern islands, South American coasts, and Australia. On his return to England, he published *Zoology of the Voyage of the Beagle* (1840). As secretary of the Geological Society (1838–41),

he came into contact with the noted geologist Sir Charles Lyell (1797–1875), who urged him to write on his experiments in inbreeding and his theory of evolution by natural selection. He received (1858) from Alfred Russel Wallace (1823–1913) an abstract outlining an identical theory of natural selection, arrived at independently. He published Wallace's essay along with his own, written in 1844, in 1858. In 1859 he published his ORIGIN OF SPECIES; it is said that the first edition sold out in one day, and immediately a raging controversy arose. Within one year, the book's importance as the leading work in natural philosophy in the history of mankind was recognized. Darwin's later important works include *The Movements and Habits of Climbing Plants* (1865), *The Variation of Animals and Plants under Domestication* (1868), *The Descent of Man* (1871), and *Selection in Relation to Sex* (1871). See SCOPES TRIAL.

Darwin, Erasmus (1731–1802) English physician, botanist, and poet. Darwin is the author of *The Botanic Garden* (1789, 1791), a didactic poem in heroic couplets, discoursing on plants and flowers according to the theories of Linnaeus. Darwin's *Zoönomia* (1794–96) is a treatise on evolutionary development, not, however, in the sense that his grandson Charles Robert DARWIN was to assign to that term.

Dasharatha In the Rāmāyana, the king of Ayodhya, father of Rāma. Dasharatha had three chief queens, all of whom were childless. After he performed the horse sacrifice ritual *ashvamedha*, Rāma was born to Kaushalya; Lakshmana and Shatrughana to Sumitra; and Bharata to KAIKEYĪ. After he ordered Rāma into fourteen years' exile, keeping a promise to the evil-minded Kaikeyī, he died of a broken heart.

Daudet, Alphonse (1840–1897) French novelist of the naturalist school. Daudet is noted for his keen observation, his sympathetic portrayal of character, and his vivid presentation of incident. His novels deal with life in Provence, his birthplace, and with the various social classes of Paris. The Provençal stories (see TARTARIN), vigorous and good-humored, include LETTRES DE MON MOULIN, *Tartarin de Tarascon* (1872), *Tartarin sur les Alpes* (1885), and *Port-Tarascon* (1890). Daudet's novels of Parisian manners include *Le Nabab* (1877), *Numa Roumestan* (1881), *Les Rois en exil* (1879), and *Sapho* (1884).

Daudet, Léon (1868–1942) French journalist and writer. The son of Alphonse DAUDET, he gave up medicine to devote himself to political journalism. His intemperate, antidemocratic articles, polemical essays, and diatribes at first appeared in *Le Gaulois*, *Le Figaro*, and the fanatically anti-Semitic *La Libre Parole*. In 1908, Daudet became coeditor with Charles Maurras of the ultraroyalist Catholic journal L'ACTION FRANÇAISE. For twenty years, the force of his invective was feared, and he wielded a political influence that enabled him to be elected to the Chamber of

Deputies, where he served from 1919 to 1924. His influence was, however, insufficient to sustain a murder charge which he had brought against the chauffeur in whose cab his son had committed suicide. The chauffeur prosecuted him, and, following a noisy trial, he was sentenced to prison for defamation. With royalist help, he escaped and fled to Belgium in 1927. Besides his journalism, Daudet wrote several novels, including *Les Morticoles* (1894) and *Sylla et son destin* (1922). His nonfiction books include *L'Avant-guerre* (1913), *Souvenirs* (1914), *L'Hérédo* (1916), *Le Monde des images* (1919), and *Le Stupide XIXe Siècle* (1922).

Daumier, Honoré (1808–1879)   French painter, lithographer, and caricaturist. Early in his career, while on the staff of *La Caricature*, Daumier's grotesque depictions of Emperor Louis-Philippe brought him a six-month prison sentence. After *La Caricature* was suppressed in 1835, he joined the staff of *Charivari* and continued to produce an enormous number of powerful lithographs, commenting with bitter satire on the faults of the bourgeoisie, the corruption of the law, and the injustices of his age. Among his best-known and most scathing lithographs, both published in 1834, are *Le Ventre legislatif* and *Rue Transonian, 14 Avril*. He also sculpted small clay busts, which served as models for many of his drawings. The direct, economically stated paintings done near the end of his life are noted for their superb handling of light and shade but were largely unappreciated until after his death. Nearly blind, he died in Valmondois in a house presented to him by Jean Baptiste Camille COROT.

Dauphin   The heir to the French crown under the Valois and Bourbon dynasties. Guy VIII, count of Vienne, was the first so styled, apparently because he wore as his emblem a dolphin. The title descended in the family until 1349, when Humbert III ceded his *seigneurie*, the Dauphiné, to Philippe VI (du Valois), one condition being that the heir of France assume the title of *le Dauphin*. The first French prince so called was Jean, who succeeded Philippe; the last was a Duc d'Angoulême, son of Charles X, who renounced the title in 1830. The Dauphin remembered in connection with JOAN OF ARC was Charles VII (1403–61), the son of the feeble-minded Charles VI. The early part of his reign was wasted in internal dissensions within the court, which the weak Dauphin was unable to put down. Thanks to the efforts of Joan, he was crowned in 1429, but it was not till some years later that a group of more vigorous councilors was able to make the new king take a firm policy. Eventually, partly due to the influence of his remarkable mistress Agnes Sorel, Charles became a fairly strong monarch. Apparently embarrassed over his lack of support for Joan during her lifetime, he arranged for her rehabilitation about twenty-five years later.

The so-called Lost Dauphin was Charles, son of Louis XVI and Marie Antoinette, called, after his father's death,

Louis XVII by French loyalists. According to official accounts, he died in prison two years later. But the secrecy surrounding his death inevitably led sympathizers to believe that he had actually escaped. In later years, innumerable pretenders appeared who claimed to be the Lost Dauphin.

Davenant, Sir William (1606–1668)   English dramatist and poet, thought by some to be an illegitimate son of Shakespeare. Davenant's *Siege of Rhodes* (1656), a heroic tragedy with "musical recitative," is considered the first English opera. Though his writing was very popular in his time, his only outstanding work is *Gondibert* (1651), a heroic poem formed on the aesthetic theories of Hobbes and anticipating Dryden's style.

David   The shepherd-king of the OLD TESTAMENT and the reputed author of many of the PSALMS. The youngest son of JESSE, David was secretly anointed king by the prophet SAMUEL while SAUL was still on the throne. Stories of his early life are concerned with his immortal friendship for Saul's son Jonathan and with Saul's growing jealousy. Though he charmed away the black moods of Saul with his harp (1 Sam. 16:23), he was, for many years, forced to flee from Saul's anger. When no one else would venture to respond to the giant's challenge, he killed Goliath, the huge champion of the PHILISTINES, with only his slingshot and some stones (1 Sam. 17).

After the deaths of Saul and Jonathan, David became the second king of Israel (c1000–c960 BC). Events of his latter years include his guilty love for BATHSHEBA and his grief over the revolt of his son ABSALOM.

David, St. (fl 6th century AD)   The patron saint of Wales. Legend relates that David was son of Xantus, Prince of Cereticu, now called Cardiganshire. He was brought up a priest, became an ascetic in the Isle of Wight, preached to the Britons, confuted Pelagius, and was preferred to the see of Caerleon or Menevia (i.e., *main aw*, "narrow water or firth"). Here the saint had received his early education, and when Dyvrig, the archbishop, resigned his see to him, St. David removed the archiepiscopal residence to Menevia, which was henceforth called St. David's. The waters of Bath "owe their warmth and salutary qualities to the benediction of this saint." The leek worn by Welshmen on St. David's Day is in memory of a complete victory obtained by them over the Saxons (March 1, 640). This victory is ascribed to the prayers of St. David and his judicious adoption of a leek in the cap, that the Britons might readily recognize each other. The Saxons, having no badge, not unfrequently turned their swords against their own supporters.

David, [Jacques] Louis (1748–1825)   French painter. An accomplished realist, David lent the precision of his drawing to a measured and heroic art, inspired by that of republican Rome, and became the undisputed leader of French classicism. He was passionately committed to the ideals of the French Revolution, and he produced one of his masterpieces, the *Death of Marat* (1793), during that time. In most of his paintings, he set his figures in static, theatrical poses, emphasizing his belief that emotion should be subordinated to moral duty. He became court painter on the accession of NAPOLEON I and produced such well-known works as *Bonaparte Crossing the Alps* (1801) and the *Coronation of Josephine* (1805–7). The figures in his historical canvasses are sharply lit and sculptural in quality but often harshly colored. His exactitude was more suited to the art of portraiture, of which outstanding examples include *Madame Récamier* (1800), *Pope Pius VII* (1805), and *Bernard* (1820). David's enormous influence declined when the Bourbons returned to power, forcing him into exile in Belgium.

David Copperfield (1849–1850)   A novel by Charles DICKENS, admittedly autobiographical. As a small boy David is sent by his cruel stepfather Mr. Murdstone to Mr. CREAKLE's school, where he is mistreated but meets an older boy, STEERFORTH, whom he idolizes. After his mother's death, he is dispatched to London to make his living; here he pastes labels on bottles in a warehouse by day and is the single lodger of the poverty-stricken, though optimistic, Mr. MICAWBER and his family. David finally runs away to his great-aunt Betsey TROTWOOD, who becomes his guardian. During a further period of school life, he settles down to board with Mr. Wickfield, a lawyer, and finds a warm friend in Wickfield's daughter Agnes. Unaware of Agnes's deep devotion to him, David goes to work for a law firm in London and marries Dora Spenlow, a frivolous, childlike woman, who dies soon after. Neither his literary success nor his marriage has brought him the peace and happiness he yearns for, and David turns to Agnes with the realization that he has always loved her. She is involved in extricating her father from the deceits of the unctuous Uriah HEEP, who has gained a financial hold over them. With the help of Mr. Micawber, Uriah Heep is foiled; David marries Agnes and together they find happiness.

David Copperfield is a devastating exposé of the inhuman treatment of children in 19th-century England. Among the well-known secondary characters in the book are BARKIS and the PEGGOTTY family.

Davie, Donald [Alfred] (1922–   )   English poet and critic. Davie's early antiromantic poetry, beginning with *Brides of Reason* (1955), was characterized by wit and a concern for verse technique. Other collections of verse include *The Forests of Lithuania* (1960), *Events and Wisdoms* (1964), *Orpheus* (1974), and *Collected Poems: 1970–1983* (1984). The influence of William EMPSON is evident in both Davie's poetic and his critical works. Among his works of criticism are *Purity of Diction in English Verse* (1952); *Articulate Energy* (1955), about syntax in English poetry; and *Thomas Hardy and British Poetry*

(1972). *The Poet in the Imaginary Museum* (1978) is a collection of occasional pieces. Davie's concern with literature and Christianity is evident in such works as *A Gathered Church: The Literature of the English Dissenting Interest 1700–1930* (1978), his edition of *The New Oxford Book of Christian Verse* (1981), and *Dissenting Voice: Enlightenment and Christian Dissent* (1982). *Journals: Early Fifties Early Sixties* (1977) was followed by another autobiographical retrospective in 1982. *Selected Poems* was published in 1985.

Davies, W[illiam] H[enry] (1871–1940)   Welsh-born English poet. Davies wrote simple, Wordsworthian poems on nature and was associated with the GEORGIANS. Until he was over thirty, he was a hobo and peddler by choice. His best-known book is his prose *Autobiography of a Super-tramp* (1908).

Daviot, Gordon   See TEY, JOSEPHINE.

Davis, Elmer [Holmes] (1890–1958)   American journalist and radio commentator. Born in Indiana, Davis was a Rhodes scholar and then worked for ten years for the *New York Times* (1914–24), writing a history of that newspaper in 1921. He joined the staff of CBS in 1939, left radio work to head the Office of War Information (1942–45), and then returned to broadcasting (1945–53), this time for ABC, on which he broadcast his famous, uniquely informative, five-minute nightly news analysis. Known for his fearless interpretation of events, he attacked Senator Joseph McCARTHY in a collection of essays entitled *But We Were Born Free* (1954). Davis also wrote several works of fiction, notably *Giant Killer* (1928), a novel telling the story of King David from a rationalist viewpoint.

Davis, Jefferson (1808–1889)   American statesman. A graduate of West Point, Davis was wounded at the battle of Buena Vista in the Mexican War. In 1847, he became U.S. Senator from Mississippi and later served as secretary of war under Franklin Pierce. Again elected to the Senate in 1857, he resigned when Mississippi seceded, and he was chosen president of the Confederacy in 1861. His policies, however, aroused much controversy within Confederate ranks. After the Civil War, he was captured and imprisoned. In 1866 he was indicted for treason but was never tried.

Davis, Rebecca [Blaine] Harding (1831–1910)   American author. Mother of Richard Harding DAVIS, she was one of the earliest American realists, known for her attempts to deal in fiction with the life of industrial workers, the problems of blacks, and political corruption. Her first success was the muckraking *Life in the Iron Mills*, published in the *Atlantic Monthly* in April 1861. This was followed by *Margaret Howth* (1862), a novel set in an Indiana milltown. *Waiting for the Verdict* (1868) was a story about racial bias; *John Andross* (1874) was a tale of political corruption. She also raised a large family and, from 1869 to the mid-1870s, was an associate editor of the New York *Tribune*.

Davis, Richard Harding (1864–1916) American journalist and novelist. The son of novelist Rebecca Harding DAVIS, he covered wars all over the world, and his vivid, dramatic dispatches made him the leading reporter of his day. Aided by his good looks and sartorial elegance, he became equally famous as a personality, the embodiment of "the mauve decade" of the 1890s. Although his fiction is considered somewhat slick and superficial, he was a skillful storyteller and created several memorable characters, notably Gallegher, the enterprising office boy, and Cortland Van Bibber, the Robin Hood of the social set.

Davy Jones A sailor's name for the evil spirit of the sea. The term seems to be a corruption of *Duffy* or *Duppy Jonah*, the word *duffy* or *duppy* standing, among the blacks of the West Indies, for "a haunting spirit or ghost." *Jones* is a corruption of *Jonah*, the prophet who was thrown into the sea. "He's gone to Davy Jones's locker" is the nautical way of saying that a messmate has been buried at sea.

Day, Clarence [Shepard], Jr. (1874–1935) American writer. Day is best known for his unique collections of humorous sketches based on reminiscences of his parents: *God and My Father* (1932), LIFE WITH FATHER, and *Life with Mother* (1937). The long-running Broadway play *Life with Father* (1939), by Russel Crouse and Howard LINDSAY, was based on these volumes. Day also wrote *This Simian World* (1920) and *Scenes from the Mesozoic* (1935), light verse with illustrations by the author.

Day, Stephen (or Stephen Daye, 1594?–1668) The first printer in New England. Day brought out the *Bay Psalm Book* (1640), the first book printed in the English colonies. The town of Cambridge, Massachusetts, granted him three hundred acres of land for "being the first that sett upon printing."

Day Lewis, C[ecil] (1904–1972) Irish-born English poet, critic, and author of detective stories under the pen name Nicholas Blake. Associated during the 1930s with the then-Marxist poets W. H. Auden and Stephen Spender, he, like them, wrote much didactic verse and used the imagery of industrial society; his poems of the time were frequently parodies. His later poetry is more personal and reflective. Among his collections of poetry are *From Feathers to Iron* (1931), *The Magnetic Mountain* (1933), *Poems, 1943–1947* (1948), *The Gate* (1962), and *Selections from His Poetry* (1967). *A Hope for Poetry* (1934) and *Revolution in Writing* (1935) are critical essays on the aims of the Marxist poets. He made good verse translations of Vergil's *Georgics* (1941) and *Aeneid* (1952) and also wrote a novel for children, *The Otterbury Incident*. Among his detective novels is *The Worm of Death* (1961). He was named POET LAUREATE in 1968.

Day of Atonement (Heb, *Yom Kippur*) The most solemn Jewish fast. It culminates the ten days of penitence at the beginning of the Jewish New Year, falling on the tenth day of the seventh month (Tishri). In ancient times, a priest made atonement for the whole community; a bullock was sacrificed, its blood sprinkled on the Ark of the Covenant, and a SCAPEGOAT selected to carry the people's sins "into a solitary land." It involved abstinence from all labor, food, and drink and the recitation of penitent prayers for forgiveness.

Day of Doom, The (1662) A celebrated poem by Michael WIGGLESWORTH. It describes the Day of Judgment and the sentencing to punishment in Hell of sinners and of infants who died before baptism. So popular was the poem that no first or second edition of it exists; the copies were apparently thumbed to shreds. It is estimated that one out of every twenty persons in the Bay colony bought a copy, making it the first American best-seller.

Day of Remembrance (or Day of Awe) See ROSH HASHANAH.

Day of the Locust, The (1939) A novel by Nathanael WEST. Set in Hollywood, where the author wrote screenplays for the last years of his life, the book deals with Homer Simpson, who arrives in southern California to find a group of appalling misfits living lives of monotony and boredom. The book culminates in a surrealistic riot at a movie premiere.

Days (1852) One of the best poems by Ralph Waldo EMERSON. It expresses this thought from his essay *Works and Days:* "He only is rich who owns the day."

Days of the Turbins (Dni Turbinikh, 1926) A drama by Mikhail BULGAKOV. It gives a well-balanced account of the conflict during the Russian Revolution between the Czarist White Guard and the forces of the Red Army.

Deacon's Masterpiece, The, or, The Wonderful "One-Hoss Shay" (1858) A poem by Oliver Wendell HOLMES. The deacon built his shay so sturdily that it would never break down; based on logic, it lasted a hundred years. The shay never did break down; it simply fell apart all at once: "Just as bubbles do when they burst." Clearly Holmes was satirizing Calvinist dogma or any inflexible though highly logical system designed for permanence.

Dead, The The last and most famous of the short stories in James Joyce's DUBLINERS (1914). It concerns Gabriel Conroy, an Irish college teacher. Gabriel and his wife Gretta spend the evening at his elderly aunts' Christmas dance, a rather moribund affair; one incident after another makes Gabriel feel more and more a social failure. Seeing his wife look radiant after hearing an old song, he takes her home in a romantic mood. She tells him the song reminded her of a boy called Michael Furey, who was once in love with her, but who died when he was seventeen. In a famous last paragraph, Joyce describes Gabriel looking at the snow and thinking of his aunts who will soon be dead, of himself who is spiritually almost dead, and of his wife's dead lover.

Dead Queen   See CASTRO, INES DE.

Dead Sea Scrolls (also called Qumram manuscripts) The fragmentary remains of a large library of the ancient Jewish sect of Essenes. They were discovered in 1947 in a cave around the Qumram Valley of the Dead Sea. Thousands of fragments of manuscripts comprise the archaeological discovery; over a hundred scrolls of Old Testament books—all except the book of Esther—have appeared. The oldest texts date from 200 BC, a thousand years older than any previously existing documents.

Dead Souls (Myortvye dushi, 1842)   A novel by Nikolay GOGOL. It relates the adventures of the archswindler Pavel CHICHIKOV. This hero, who has already been in trouble for shady deals when he appears on the scene, has conceived a weird scheme for making his fortune anew. He intends to buy from landowners all their serfs who have died since the last census was taken. These serfs are still alive, according to government records, and the landowner has to pay taxes on them until the next census strikes them off the list. Chichikov's plan is to pay the owner a small sum, assume the burden of the taxes on these "dead souls" himself, and become the rightful owner of them. Then he intends to mortgage them and to acquire real estate of his own in eastern Russia. The novel follows Chichikov as he makes friends with the right people in town and visits the local landowners, to each of whom he gently puts his strange proposition. He neglects to tell them, however, what he plans to do with the dead souls once he has them. The description of the landowners he visits, their reactions to his proposal, and Chichikov's reactions to their reactions make up some of the finest scenes in the novel. Eventually rumors spread through the town about Chichikov's deals with the landowners MANILOV, SOBAKEVICH, KOROBOCHKA, and PLYUSHKIN. The obnoxious Nozdryov adds lies of his own invention to the rumors, and Chichikov finally wings his way from the town in his troika.

Gogol was working on a second part to the novel, in which Chichikov was to be reformed into a genuinely respectable citizen. The author destroyed most of the manuscript shortly before his death, and only fragments of it have survived.

Dead Souls has been unanimously acclaimed as one of the greatest novels in the Russian language for its characterizations, humor, and style. The perpetual question of whether Gogol was a realist or a fantasist has created differences of opinion, however, about just what kind of novel Gogol wrote. The influential critic Vissarion Belinsky accepted Gogol's fiction as being truthful to Russian life. This view, retained by later radical critics, is the official Soviet doctrine on Gogol. Other critics have stressed the many fantastic elements in Gogol's work: the grotesque caricatures of real people that compose his characters, the

extravagance of his imagery, and the use of hyperbolic language.

De amicitia (44 BC)   A dialogue on the subject of friendship by CICERO. The chief interlocutor is Gaius Laelius Sapiens. Hence the essay is also known as the *Laelius*.

Dear Judas, and Other Poems (1929)   A collection by Robinson JEFFERS. The title poem is an attempt to rehabilitate the reputation of Judas. He is presented as a man who loves Jesus but finds him grown too fond of power. Judas therefore betrays him in the belief that he will be jailed for a few days and then released, escaping later execution as a rebel.

Death Comes for the Archbishop (1927)   A novel by Willa CATHER. It describes the missionary efforts of the French bishop Jean Latour and his vicar, Father Joseph Vaillant, to establish a diocese in the territory of New Mexico. The novel is based on the lives of the two eminent French clerics Bishop Jean Baptiste Lamy (1814–88) and Father Joseph Machebeuf. They prevail over all adversities to build a cathedral in the wilderness.

Death in Venice (Der Tod in Venedig, 1912; tr 1925)   A novella by Thomas MANN. Gustav von Aschenbach, the hero, is a successful author, proud of the self-discipline with which he has ordered his life and work. On a trip to Venice, however, he becomes aware of mysterious decadent potentialities in himself, and he finally succumbs to a consuming love for a frail but beautiful Polish boy named Tadzio. Though he learns that there is danger of a cholera epidemic in Venice, he finds he cannot leave the city, and eventually he dies of the disease. The story is permeated by a rich and varied symbolism, with frequent overtones from Greek literature and mythology.

Death Notebooks, The (1974)   A collection of poems by Anne SEXTON. These confessional poems explore the psyche of a contemporary woman in frank and ribald language. The persona is obsessed with death, with her role as mother, and with her role as a sexual woman. In a sometimes coy, sometimes self-effacing manner, Sexton brings significance and color to the trivial details and events of everyday life. Underlying all the poems, however, is a religious tone that suggests the poet's longing for some kind of affirmation or belief. Many of the poems parody religious literature; "O Ye Tongues" is a group of psalms that attempt to incorporate biblical themes into contemporary life. The poems achieve intensity through the use of refrains, repetition, bouncing rhythms, and startling juxtapositions of imagery.

Death of Artemio Cruz, The (La muerte de Artemio Cruz, 1962; tr 1964)   A novel by Carlos FUENTES. Fuentes takes a deep plunge into the dying body and the sharply aware conscience of Artemio Cruz, a political boss of contemporary Mexico. As Cruz's entire life passes before him, his personality unfolds into an adversary I/Thou relationship. A third voice sets the events recalled by the accusatory "Thou" and the defensive "I" into objective historical frames. The story of the agonizing Cruz amounts to a tale of survival by betrayal of friends, ideals, and country. When the accusatory voice forces Cruz into shame for his cynicism and immorality, his ego protests that at least he survived, while all the idealists are dead. The power of the story itself is heightened by the brilliant use of STREAM OF CONSCIOUSNESS technique, which provides a multileveled depiction of life in Mexico during and after the revolution of 1910.

Death of a Salesman (1949)   A play by Arthur MILLER. A bitter indictment of American values, it is the story of Willy Loman, a traveling salesman, who experiences a profound sense of failure as he discovers signs of aging in himself and takes stock of his accomplishments. The play ends in his suicide.

Death of Ivan Ilyich, The (Smert Ivana Ilyicha, 1886)   A story by TOLSTOY. It concerns the thoughts on life and death of a dying man. An ordinary man who had never particularly bothered himself about large questions, Ivan Ilyich is forced into his contemplation by the discovery that he will soon die of cancer. The problems he ponders are similar to those that acutely occupied Tolstoy himself when he went through the spiritual crisis described in A CONFESSION. Ivan Ilyich's acceptance of death as part of the natural order of things recalls a similar conclusion reached by Prince Andrey BOLKONSKY in WAR AND PEACE.

Death of the Heart, The (1938)   A novel by Elizabeth BOWEN. It is the story of Portia Quayne, an illegitimate sixteen-year-old girl who comes to live with her half-brother when her mother dies. To escape from the arid, artificial, unfeeling social world of her London relatives, she falls in love with ordinary, insensitive Eddie—who is soon found holding hands with someone else. Innocence and idealism die in Portia's heart, but she also grows up into an acceptance of the world as it is.

Death of the Hired Man, The (1914)   A poem by Robert FROST. It narrates the argument between a farmer and his wife over whether or not to keep a defeated old hired hand, who, in his last hours, has returned to them. When the farmer seeks out the man, he finds him dead. The poem contains the kind of folk wisdom that made Frost popular, but it also has an almost mystical undercurrent giving layers of meaning beyond the obvious debate.

Deborah   In the OLD TESTAMENT, a Hebrew prophet and judge of Israel (Judg. 4:4). Deborah summoned Barak to fight against the tyranny of Jabin, prophesied success, and accompanied him in battle against Sisera, captain of Jabin's army. After their victory over the Canaanites, she sang a famous song of triumph (Judg. 5), considered by scholars to be one of the oldest pieces of writing in the Old Testament.

Debrett, John (1752–1822)   English publisher and original compiler of the *Peerage of England, Scotland, and Ireland* (1802) and the *Baronetage of England* (1808).

Debs, Eugene V[ictor] (1855–1926)   American socialist leader. Founder of the Social Democratic Party and its leader during the period of its greatest influence (1897–1916), Debs was a candidate for the presidency five times and was renowned for his campaign oratory. He came to prominence as a leader of the famous Pullman strike in Chicago (1894) and was imprisoned for his participation. (See Clarence DARROW.) A powerful figure in American politics, he always insisted on the primacy of democratic procedures. His *Writings and Speeches* were collected in 1948 by Arthur M. Schlesinger, Jr.

Debussy, Claude [Achille] (1862–1918)   French composer. Debussy is identified with musical impressionism, although he preferred to call himself simply *musicien français*. Certain revolutionary characteristics of his work, such as unresolved discords, exotic scales, and free forms, prepared the way for many developments of modern music. His best-known pieces include *Suite Bergamasque* (1890–1905), a piano suite containing the famous *Clair de lune*; *Prélude à l'après-midi d'un faune* (1894), a tone poem inspired by Mallarmé's eclogue L'APRÈS-MIDI D'UN FAUNE; *Pelléas et Mélisande* (1902), his only opera, composed to Maeterlinck's play; *La Mer* (*The Sea*, 1905), a tone poem; *Children's Corner Suite* (1908), a piano suite; and *Jeux* (*Games*, 1913), a ballet.

decadence   A term used in literary or art history for the decline that marks the end of a great artistic period. The term is relative to the particular period it identifies, and the general characteristics of decadence are often self-consciousness, artificiality, overrefinement, and perversity. See DÉCADENTS.

décadents   A term applied narrowly to the group of French poets whose leaders were Rimbaud, Verlaine, and Mallarmé (see SYMBOLISTS). Broadly and more popularly, the term *décadents* is applied to the poets and prose writers, chiefly French, of the postromantic period. Morbid and perverse tastes, unconventional and often sensational social behavior, and hyperaesthetic temperaments characterize the *décadents*. In their writings, they placed emphasis upon creative self-expression, advancing the ideal of pure art. In his novel AGAINST THE GRAIN, J. K. Huysmans creates a hero who is the epitome of the *décadent*. Oscar WILDE is the leading figure in the English counterpart of this French phenomenon.

Decameron, The (fr Gr, *deca*, "ten," *hēmera*, "day")   A collection of tales by Giovanni BOCCACCIO, written 1351–53. The title refers to the frame story: in the year of the Black Death, 1348, seven young ladies and three young gallants meet in a Florentine church and decide to escape from the city to the hills of Fiesole. There they spend the time in telling stories on ten days. The hundred novelle, ranging from anecdotes and fabliaux to folk tales and fairy tales of ancient lineage, include many that became famous and influential in European literature: *Ser Ciappelletto*, BERNABÒ OF GENOA, *Gillette of Narbonne*, *The Revenge of Tancred*, ISABELLA, OR THE POT OF BASIL, *The Eaten Heart*, *Brother Cipolla*, *A Garden in January*, CALANDRINO AND THE HELIOTROPE, TITUS AND GISIPPUS, and GRISELDA. It is unlikely that CHAUCER knew the book, though he used similar stories, but the tales have appeared in the works of other English and European writers in a steady stream up to modern times. They have also been used for plays, operas, and paintings.

Decembrist revolt   A short-lived, unsuccessful uprising in Russia in December 1825. Led by young nobles of some of Russia's oldest families, the Decembrists wanted to institute a constitutional form of government and deny the throne to Nicholas I, following his accession on the death of Alexander I. The insurgents were arrested; five were executed, and over a hundred exiled to Siberia. The revolt was the first such uprising led by members of the aristocracy. The event has been a constant point of reference for Russian revolutionaries and writers as an example of a courageous bid for freedom. The Decembrists included many friends of the poet PUSHKIN, but he was never proved to have been involved in the affair.

Declaration of Independence   The public act by which the Second Continental Congress, on July 4, 1776, declared the thirteen North American colonies to be free and independent of Great Britain. New York alone did not ratify the act until July 9. It was signed on August 2, 1776, by the representatives of all thirteen colonies. Nominally it was the work of a drafting committee, but actually Thomas JEFFERSON wrote the declaration practically in its entirety.

Declaration of the Rights of Man (La Déclaration des droits de l'homme et du citoyen)   In French history, a document setting forth the principles of the FRENCH REVOLUTION. Consisting of a preamble and seventeen articles, it was modeled on the American Declaration of Independence and was voted by the Constituent ASSEMBLY on August 27, 1789.

Decline and Fall (1928)   A bitter, farcical, satiric novel by Evelyn WAUGH. Paul Pennyfeather, the unfortunate hero, is unjustly expelled from Oxford and turns to teaching at an appalling boys' school. He falls in love with the mother of one of his pupils and is arrested and imprisoned for unknowingly working in her white-slave-trade business. Finally he returns to Oxford to study theology.

Decline and Fall of the Roman Empire, The History of the (1776–1788)   A history by Edward GIBBON. Although later scholarship has superseded much of the information in this work, it has taken its place among the classical works of historical literature in the English language. The work is divided into three periods and covers a total of thirteen centuries: from the rule of Trajan and the Antonines to the decay of the Western Empire; from the era of Justinian in the Eastern Empire to the founding of the Holy Roman Empire in the west under Charlemagne; and from the restoration of the Western Empire to the capture of Constantinople by the Turks in 1453. Gibbon's point of view is best expressed in his observation that history is a record of "little more than the crimes, follies, and misfortunes of mankind."

Decline of the West, The   See SPENGLER, OSWALD.

decorum   The ideal of propriety, or appropriateness. Stemming from CLASSICAL authors, it was defined and put into practice as a literary principle by the neoclassicists of the latter part of the 17th and the 18th centuries. In accordance with this principle, literature, especially poetry, was required to be polished, dignified, clear, rational, moderate, conventional, and "elevated"; in order to achieve elegance, Latinized diction and generality and abstraction in figurative language were preferred elements of style. Wide use of the EPITHET was one result of the latter tendency. Leading exponents of the principle of decorum were Nicholas Boileau (1636–1711), POPE, and Samuel JOHNSON. See NEOCLASSICISM.

Dee, John (1527–1608)   English mathematician and astrologer. A magician who had practiced at various European courts, Dee was imprisoned in England soon after the accession of Mary Tudor, on the charge of having practiced sorcery against her life. He was released in 1555 and later enjoyed the favor of Elizabeth, whom he instructed in astrology. He wrote numerous works on astrology and mathematics.

Deer Park, The   See MAILER, NORMAN.

Deerslayer, The (1841)   A novel by James Fenimore COOPER. Although it was the last of THE LEATHERSTOCKING TALES to be written, *The Deerslayer* is the novel of Natty BUMPPO's youth. The scene is Lake Otsego, New York, called Glimmerglass in the story. Young hunters Natty and his friend Hurry Harry March live with the Delaware Indians. They fight the Hurons with the aid of the British. Part of the story deals with the fruitless attempts of Judith Hutter to interest Natty romantically. Chingachgook, the Delaware chief who becomes Natty's companion in other volumes, enters the hero's life in this book.

Defarge, M.   In Charles Dickens's A TALE OF TWO CITIES, a revolutionist, keeper of a wine shop in the Faubourg St. Antoine, in Paris. Defarge is a rough, bull-necked, implacable-looking man.

Mme Defarge   M. Defarge's wife, a harsh, remorseless woman and a revolutionary fanatic. It is her sister whom St. Evrémonde attacks, and in her revenge she is instrumental in having Charles Darnay sentenced to the guillotine because he is related to the marquis. She has compiled a list of aristocrats and enemies of the Revolution, encoded in the stitches of her knitting. Knitting incessantly while watching the daily executions at the guillotine, she is a perfect example of the TRICOTEUSES.

Defender of the Faith (Lat, *Fidei Defensor*) Henry VIII of England. A title given to him by Pope Leo X in 1521, for a Latin treatise, *On the Seven Sacraments*. Ironically, it was Henry who later took England out of the Roman church. Later monarchs of Great Britain have retained this title, up to the present day.

Défense et illustration de la langue française (1549)   A treatise on poetry by Joachim DU BELLAY, which served as the doctrine of the French poets of the PLÉIADE. It contained two main propositions: (1) that the French language be "defended" as a mode of poetic expression against those who were trying to rival the classic poets by writing in Latin; (2) that, in order to attain its full potential of expression, French must be "illustrated" or embellished by borrowing from Greek and Latin and by the use of archaic, dialectal, and technical words. "Illustration" also included the imitation of literary formulas discovered by the ancients and the adoption of poetic forms such as the classical ode and the Italian sonnet. None of these ideas was new with Du Bellay, who sought to raise poetry to the eminence it had enjoyed in ancient times, but, by fitting them into a coherent system, he gave form to the revolutionary aims of the Renaissance poets.

Defense of Poesie, The   Alternate title of AN APOLOGIE FOR POETRIE, by Sir Philip Sidney.

Deffand, Marie de Vichy-Chamrond, Marquise du (1697–1780)   Witty and cynical French noblewoman, leader in Parisian social life and literary and philosophical circles. Deffand's salon was frequented by Turgot, d'Alembert, Marivaux, Baron de Grimm, and others. When she lost her sight in 1754, she engaged Julie LESPINASSE as a companion; a violent quarrel between the two broke up the salon. Her correspondence with Voltaire, Montesquieu, Horace Walpole, and others documents 18th-century society.

Déficit, Madame   Contemptuous name given to MARIE ANTOINETTE because she was always demanding money of her ministers and never had any. See BAKER, THE.

Definition of Love, The (1681)   A poem by Andrew MARVELL, dealing with exalted passion and the impossibility of its fulfillment.

Defoe, Daniel (1660–1731)   English novelist, pamphleteer, journalist, and political agent. Defoe is celebrated for his frank and dramatic realism in fiction and for the accuracy, vigor, and lucidity of his journalism. Defoe was born Daniel Foe, son of a London tallow-chandler (he added the genteel *De* when over forty years of age). He is best known for his novels ROBINSON CRUSOE and MOLL FLANDERS, and for his JOURNAL OF THE PLAGUE YEAR, a his-

torical reconstruction. Others of his works include *The True-Born Englishman* (1701), a rugged, satirical poem on English hatred of foreigners, pointing out that, in fact, there is no true-born Englishman; *The Shortest Way with the Dissenters* (1702), satirizing ecclesiastical intolerance in the extreme right of the Church of England by ironically proposing that all Non-Conformist preachers be hanged —for which he was imprisoned and pilloried; *A Tour Thro' the Whole Island of Great Britain* (1724–27), in three volumes, an important source for early English economic life; and several novels other than his most famous. Defoe edited, from 1704 to 1713, *The Review*, a newspaper that anticipated *The Tatler* and *The Spectator*, though it laid much greater stress on discussions of commerce and the news than did the others. He supported King William III and was later a secret agent in the pay of the moderate Tories under Robert Harley (1705). Defoe was also the first author of ghost stories in modern English literature, an example of which is "A True Relation of the Apparition of One Mrs. Veal" (1706).

De Forest, John William (1826–1906)   American novelist and memoirist. At the outbreak of the Civil War, De Forest joined the Union army; after Lee's surrender, he served as the head of the Freedman's Bureau in South Carolina. His best-known novel, *Miss Ravenel's Conversion from Secession to Loyalty* (1867), while satirizing puritanical New England, supports the Unionist cause and includes realistic battle scenes. His posthumously published memoirs are included in *A Volunteer's Adventures* (1946) and *A Union Officer in the Reconstruction* (1948). An early American realist, De Forest was admired by William Dean HOWELLS and is considered a forerunner of Stephen CRANE.

Degas, [Hilaire Germain] Edgar (1834–1917) French painter. Associated with the impressionists, although he was not interested in landscape, Degas is noted for his mastery of motion, his superb line and color, and the veracity of his observation. He painted, drew, made lithographs and etchings, and modeled clay figures, but his favorite medium was pastels. He portrayed ballet dancers at work or in the glare of spotlights, milliners, laundresses, and women at their toilette, with scientific attention to the strained, even ungraceful, momentary positions of unobserved movement—and transfigured his subjects. It was from the Japanese, whose prints became known in France about 1860, that Degas derived much of the intimacy of presentation, originality of composition, and heightened decorative quality that mark his painting.

de Gaulle, Charles [André Joseph Marie] (1890–1970)   French general and statesman. After the surrender of France to German forces in 1940, de Gaulle rallied his countrymen to the cause of a Free France, refusing to accept the terms of the armistice with Germany. Court-martialed in absentia and condemned to death

(August 1940), he appointed himself leader of the Free French and established his headquarters in England. At the Casablanca Conference with Winston Churchill and Franklin D. Roosevelt, he represented France. After the war, de Gaulle served as head of a provisional government, from November 1944 to January 1946. During twelve years of retirement from political life, he wrote and published his three-volume memoirs, *Mémoires de guerre* (1954–59). In English the books are titled *The Call to Honour (1940–1942)*, *Unity (1942–1944)*, and *Salvation (1944–1946)*. In June 1958, at the height of the Algerian crisis, de Gaulle became the last premier of the Fourth Republic. A new constitution, providing for a much strengthened executive branch, was drafted, and de Gaulle was elected the first President of the French Fifth Republic in December 1958.

degree   In the medieval and Elizabethan concept of order, the principle by which all things are ranked according to their importance in the universal scheme. Heavenly beings, men, and forms of matter were all assigned precise places in the GREAT CHAIN OF BEING, in which, for example, God was above the angels, a king above his subjects, and gold above other metals. Several of SHAKESPEARE's plays are concerned with the chaos that inevitably ensues on earth and even among heavenly bodies when a monarch—for example, KING LEAR—fails to maintain *degree* within his realm. Ulysses eloquently expresses some aspects of the idea in TROILUS AND CRESSIDA (I, iii, 82–129).

Dehmel, Richard (1863–1920)   German lyric poet, influenced by NIETZSCHE. Dehmel's early work, like that of his friend LILIENCRON, shows characteristics of NATURALISM but he quickly developed an ecstatic subjective style similar to that of EXPRESSIONISM. His best-known volumes include *Erlösungen* (*Salvations*, 1891), *Weib und Welt* (*Woman and the World*, 1896), and *Schöne wilde Welt* (*Beautiful Wild World*, 1913).

Deianira   See NESSUS.

Dei plenus (Lat, "full of the god")   Inspired, or possessed by frenzy, as the MAENADS in Greco-Roman mythology, who celebrated the orgiastic rites of Dionysus, or the Corybantes in their dancing to Cybele.

Deirdre   The heroine of the greatest love story in Irish legend, found in the ULSTER CYCLE. Like the elopement tale THE PURSUIT OF DIARMUID AND GRÁINNE, the story of Deirdre is an early parallel to episodes in the Tristan and Iseult legend. The story has many versions, but, in general, Deirdre is the daughter of Felim, storyteller to Conchobar, king of Ulster. When she is born, it is prophesied that she will be the most beautiful woman of Ireland and that she will bring bloodshed and death. To avert the prophecy, Conchobar determines to marry her when she comes of age. She is raised by the nurse Lavarcham in a secluded house in the woods, where she sees no one but a few servants. Lavarcham's stories about Naisi, nephew of Conchobar and son of Usnech, fire her

young imagination, and her constant pleas finally persuade Lavarcham to bring him to the house. Deirdre falls in love with him, and, with Naisi's two brothers, the two flee to Alba, or Scotland, to avoid the wrath of Conchobar. Ultimately they are persuaded to return, and, betrayed, the sons of Usnech are killed. In some versions, Deirdre kills herself at the grave of Naisi; in others, finding herself a captive of Conchobar, she dashes her brains against a rock. Synge's play *Deirdre of the Sorrows* (1910) is based on this legend, as is Yeats's *Deirdre* (1907). It was beautifully retold in James Stephens's *Deirdre* (1923).

deism   A belief in the existence of a personal God who is manifested neither supernaturally in history nor immanently in nature. Deism has been called "natural religion"; it is based on reason, as opposed to revelation. It sprang up with the spread of scientific knowledge during the Renaissance and reached its height in the 18th century. Notable adherents of deism included Edward HERBERT of Cherbury, the third earl of Shaftesbury, and Henry ST. JOHN in England, and VOLTAIRE and the Encyclopedists in France. Their views affected literature—for example, Pope's AN ESSAY ON MAN—and the views of nature entertained by WORDSWORTH, COLERIDGE, and others.

déjà vu (Fr, "already seen; previously seen")   An experience involving a feeling of familiarity in a place where one has never been before or in a situation one has never before experienced. Sensations of this sort have been cited by PLATO and many others since as evidence of reincarnation, on the assumption that the feelings of familiarity are based on partly revived memories of a previous life.

Dekker, Thomas (1572?–?1632)   English dramatist. Dekker was one of the Henslowe group who worked long and hard to produce the quantities of plays needed by that company. Consequently his plays are often hastily constructed but brightened by charming verse and Dekker's warm, easy feeling for people. Among his best are *The Shoemaker's Holiday* (1600), THE HONEST WHORE: PARTS I AND II, and the allegorical OLD FORTUNATUS. Most of his plays, however, were written in collaboration: THE ROARING GIRL, with Thomas Middleton; *The Virgin Martyr* (c1620), with Philip Massinger; *The Witch of Edmonton* (1621), with John Ford and William Rowley; and *The Sun's Darling* (1624), with Ford.

He was also a pamphleteer. His best-known pamphlet, *The Gull's Hornbook* (1609), is a satirical account of the life of London gallants.

de Kooning, Willem (1904–   )   Dutch-born American artist. Variously preoccupied with figurative and nonfigurative approaches to painting, de Kooning had a strong influence on American ABSTRACT EXPRESSIONISM. In the 1950s, his series of paintings entitled *Woman I* made a dramatic impact on the art world, with its unrestrained color and emotional, often violent, portrayal of the female form.

In 1979 de Kooning was awarded the Andrew W. Mellon Prize, and in 1983 the Whitney Museum of American Art mounted a retrospective of his work.

Delacroix, [Ferdinand-Victor] Eugène (1798–1863)   French painter. Delacroix was one of the great colorists of the romantic movement. He used both literary and historical subjects for his paintings, but he was also involved in contemporary struggles, as evidenced by two of his most famous works, *The Massacre of Chios* (1824) and *Liberty Leading the People* (1831). Following a visit to North Africa in 1832, he produced richer, more exotically imaginative paintings, as in *Algerian Women in Their Harem* (1834). Delacroix stressed movement and color for emotive and dramatic purposes. His vibrant palette, heightened by the juxtaposition of complementary colors, and his observation that shadows have colors, anticipated the development of IMPRESSIONISM. His famous *Journals*, written from 1823 to 1824 (tr 1937; repr 1972), offer an extraordinary record of an artist's life and works.

Delafield, E. M. (pen name of Elizabeth Monica Dashwood, 1890–1943)   English novelist. Delafield wrote ironic comedies of manners, among them DIARY OF A PROVINCIAL LADY and *The Provincial Lady in America* (1934).

De la Mare, Walter (1873–1956)   English poet, novelist, and anthologist. De la Mare was a romantic writer whose work expressed his interest in childhood, nature, dreams, and the uncanny. Much of his writing is nominally for children. Among his collections of poetry are *The Listeners* (1912), the title poem of which is his most famous and successful lyric; *Peacock Pie* (1913); and *Collected Poems* (1942). His prose writings include novels, notably *Memoirs of a Midget* (1921); *Early One Morning* (1935), a book about children; and short stories. Among De la Mare's fine anthologies are *Come Hither* (1923) and *Behold, This Dreamer!* (1939).

Delaney, Shelagh (1930–   )   English playwright. Delaney writes with wit and bawdy humor about the English working class, into which she was born. Her first play, *A Taste of Honey* (1958), was written when she was eighteen. The heroine is pregnant with the illegitimate child of a black sailor. She is helped by the companionship of her friend, a homosexual artist. Delaney's second play, *The Lion in Love* (1960), is the story of an impecunious street peddler and his extravagant wife. As with her first play, this work is filled with an extraordinary collection of vivid, unique characters. It was followed by *Sweetly Sings the Donkey* in 1963.

She wrote some filmscripts, *Charlie Bubbles* (1968) and *Dance with a Stranger* (1984), and did several plays for BBC TV, including *The House That Jack Built* (1977).

Deledda, Grazia (1871–1936)   Italian novelist. Deledda is noted for her numerous novels and short stories depicting the life and sensual passions of the peasants of her native Sardinia. An incidental rather than a deliberate realist, she transformed Sardinia, as she confessed, into a country of "myths and legends." Unlike Giovanni VERGA, the master of *verismo* whose work she admired, she concentrated on the inner experiences and the repressed libido of her characters. Among her best-known works are *Elias Portulu* (1903), *Cenere* (1904; tr *Ashes*, 1908); *L'edera* (1908), and *La madre* (1920; tr *The Mother*, 1922). She was awarded the NOBEL PRIZE in Literature in 1926, the second Italian, after CARDUCCI, to be so honored. Her autobiographical novel *Cosima* (1937) appeared posthumously.

Delia   The name of many ladies addressed in poetry. Delia was a shepherdess in Vergil's BUCOLICS and the lady love of Roman elegiac poet Albius Tibullus (54?–18 BC). The Delia of POPE's satires is the second Lady Delorraine of Ledwell Park.

Delias   The Delian ship (i.e., the ship of Delos) that, according to legend, THESEUS made; it carried him to Crete when he slew the MINOTAUR. In memory of this, it was sent every fourth year with a solemn deputation to the Delian APOLLO. During the festival, which lasted thirty days, no Athenian could be put to death. SOCRATES was condemned during this period; his death was deferred till the return of the sacred vessel. The ship had been so often repaired that not a stick of the original vessel remained at that time.

Delibes [Setién], Miguel (1920–   )   Spanish novelist, essayist, and short-story writer. Delibes's early realistic novels, beginning with *La sombra del ciprés es alagada* (*The Cypress's Shadow Is Long*, 1948), eschew such experimental forms as interior monologue (see STREAM OF CONSCIOUSNESS) and temporal fragmentation that occur in some of his later fiction. Much of his work is concerned with the decline of rural Castile. In *El camino* (1950; tr *The Path*, 1961) he evokes, in a tender and sensitive vein, an innocent childhood world in conflict with civilization. In *La hoja roja* (*The Red Leaf*, 1959) and *Las ratas* (*The Rats*, 1961) he analyzes old age and the process of dying. *Diario de un cazador* (*Hunter's Diary*, 1955) is a neorealist novel exploring man's relationship to nature. His two most experimental novels, *Cinco horas con Mario* (*Five Hours with Mario*, 1966) and *Parábola del náufrago* (*Parable of a Shipwrecked Man*, 1969), employ a recurring theme of his work: the plight of the individual engaged in a losing battle against the dehumanizing forces of a technological world. Delibes has developed an extremely personal, sardonic style, rich in its use of irony, colloquial language, and psychological insight.

Delight in Disorder (1648)   A poem by Robert HERRICK. He pleads for "a sweet disorder in the dress" on the grounds that the little imperfections in a lady's dress are particularly beguiling.

Delilah   A PHILISTINE woman in the OLD TESTAMENT who was mistress of SAMSON and betrayed him. When she discovered that Samson's strength lay in his hair, she allowed it to be shaved off so that he could be captured by the Philistines (Judg. 16). Her name has come to be associated with any fascinating and deceitful woman.

De Lisser, Herbert G[eorge] (1878–1944) Jamaican novelist. Of mixed Portuguese, Jewish, and African ancestry, De Lisser worked as a journalist, serving as editor of *The Gleaner*. A central figure in the development of modern West Indian writing, De Lisser introduced the first black West Indian heroine, in *Jane's Career* (1913). His other novels, which have elements of the metaphysical as well as social realism, include *Susan Proudleigh* (1915); *The White Witch of Rosehall* (1929), his best-known work; and *Arawak Girl*, published posthumously in 1958.

Dell, Ethel M. (pen name of Ethel Mary Savage, 1881–1939)   English novelist. Dell is the author of such best-selling romantic novels as *The Way of an Eagle* (1912) and *Rocks of Valpré* (1914).

Dell, Floyd (1887–1969)   American journalist, novelist, and playwright. Early associated with the CHICAGO GROUP of writers, Dell moved to New York and became one of the forefront of "rebels" in Greenwich Village from 1914 through the 1920s. While in New York, he was associate editor of the leftist periodicals *The Masses* and *The Liberator*. He later became known for a number of novels dealing with disillusion and bohemian life after World War I. Because he was one of the first of his generation to write openly of sexual matters, his novels were considered daring —even dangerous—at the time. His most popular novels were *Moon Calf* (1920) and its sequel, *The Briary Bush* (1921), partly autobiographical novels of growing up in small-town Illinois. Dell's early plays were produced by the Liberal Club in New York and by the PROVINCETOWN PLAYERS. *Little Accident* (1928), a comedy based on his novel *The Unmarried Father* (1927), was his most successful play. *Love in the Machine Age* (1930) is a reasoned statement of his attitudes toward sex. *Homecoming* (1933) is an autobiography. He also edited, with Paul Jordan Smith, an edition (1927) of Burton's THE ANATOMY OF MELANCHOLY.

Della Casa, Giovanni (1503–1556)   Florentine cleric and author. Della Casa wrote the popular courtesy book *Il galateo* (1551–55). Unlike *The Courtier* of Castiglione, it is realistically concerned with minor problems of good manners in polite, rather than courtly, society. It was translated by Peterson in 1576, in time to influence Elizabethan concepts of courtesy. *Sapere il galateo* ("to know the *Galateo*") is a popular Italian phrase signifying that one is polite.

Della-Cruscans   A clique of English poets who met originally in Florence in the latter part of the 18th century. Their sentimental, affected work, which appeared in the periodical magazines the *World* and the *Oracle*, created for a time quite a furor but was gibbeted in *The Baviad* (1794) and *The Maeviad* (1795) of William Gifford. The clique took its name from the Accademia della Crusca (literally, "academy of chaff"), which was founded in Florence in 1582 with the object of purifying the Italian language—sifting away its "chaff"—and which published an important dictionary in 1611. Members of the clique included Robert Merry, who signed himself "Della Crusca," Hannah Cowley, who signed herself Anna Matilda, James Cobb, a writer of farces, James Boswell, Thomas Morton, George Colman, and Elizabeth Robinson.

Della Rovere   Italian family prominent during the Renaissance. In 1506, the Della Rovere became dukes of Urbino, when Guidobaldo of Montefeltro died leaving no heir.

Francesco della Rovere (1414–1484)   Became Pope Sixtus IV in 1471. The famous Sistine Chapel of the Vatican bears his name.

Giuliano della Rovere (1443–1513)   Nephew of Francesco, became Pope Julius II in 1503, at the age of sixty; still he led the papal forces in the field. Before his death he had founded the Vatican Museum, begun the construction of St. Peter's, and employed Raphael, Bramante, and Michelangelo in various projects.

Delos   A small island in the Cyclades where APOLLO and ARTEMIS were born. Having been the only place to accept LETO when she was ready to give birth to these gods, it was honored by becoming sacred to Apollo. This story is told in the *Homeric Hymn to Delian Apollo*. Delos was said to have been a floating island, which POSEIDON finally made fast to the bottom of the sea.

Delphic oracle   An ancient oracle at Delphi, on the southern slope of Mount Parnassus. It was of extremely ancient origin, having originally belonged to a chthonic deity. AESCHYLUS' claim in the *Eumenides* that it belonged successively to GE, THEMIS, and Phoebe—two of whom, at least, were earth goddesses—may not be far from wrong. In later times, the oracle was taken over by APOLLO, who, according to the *Homeric Hymn to Pythian Apollo*, killed the python, a sacred snake associated with the oracle. The oracular utterances were made by the Pythia, a priestess who sat on a tripod over a cleft in the rock. Her incomprehensible mouthings were interpreted by a priest.

Although there were many oracles in the Greek world, the Delphic oracle was regarded as a final authority in religious matters. A great many of the most famous Greek myths involve the working out of oracles that issued from Delphi.

Associated with the shrine was the *omphalos*, a sacred stone that was regarded as the navel of the world, though various other centers made the same claim. Some authorities believe that the *omphalos* was the phallic cap of a tomb, possibly that of the python, since many oracles were associated with the tombs of heroes. In the first part of the

Eumenides, ORESTES clings to the *omphalos* in seeking sanctuary from the ERINYES, or Furies.

Delphine (1802)   Epistolary romantic novel by Mme de STAËL. It is the story of unfulfilled love between Delphine and Léonce, a character inspired by Benjamin CONSTANT DE REBECQUE. In the end, he is shot as a traitor, and she poisons herself. See VERNON, MME DE.

Demeter   The Greek goddess of corn. Demeter's principal myth concerned the abduction of her daughter PERSEPHONE by HADES, which took place in Sicily. When the young goddess, called also simply Kore (daughter), plucked a certain flower, the earth opened, and Hades snatched her away to the underworld in his chariot. Demeter, bearing torches, sought her all over the world until HELIOS told her what had happened. She left Olympus, in anger that the gods had permitted the abduction, and the earth grew desolate. Appearing as an old woman in the village of Eleusis, she was hospitably received by King CELEUS and his wife Metaneira. She tended their son Demophoon and would have immortalized him in the fire had not Metaneira seen her doing so and screamed. The goddess thereupon revealed her true identity and commanded that her rites should be celebrated at Eleusis.

Disturbed at the blight on the earth, ZEUS approached Hades to bring about a reconciliation. Because Persephone had eaten pomegranate seeds in the underworld, she was not allowed to leave permanently, but it was arranged that she should spend two thirds of every year with her mother. In gratitude for Eleusinian hospitality, Demeter gave a bag of seeds to Celeus' son Triptolemus and sent him in a chariot by winged dragons throughout the world to plant grain and teach its culture.

Demeter was very widely worshiped, but her most important cult center remained Eleusis, her major festival the ELEUSINIAN MYSTERIES. For other legends of Demeter, see PELOPS.

Demetrius   In Shakespeare's MIDSUMMER NIGHT'S DREAM, a young man betrothed to Hermia by her father's decree. When she escapes to the forest with her lover Lysander, Demetrius pursues them and is pursued in turn by Helena, his jilted sweetheart.

Demian (1919; tr 1923)   A novel by Herman HESSE. Demian is a BILDUNGSROMAN featuring young Emil Sinclair. Largely through the crude aggression of a school bully, Sinclair becomes troubled by the realization that life consists of conflicting, opposite forces. His confusion is both cleared and compounded by the appearance of a mysterious older boy named Max Demian. Both Demian and his mother become central influences in Sinclair's life, although their encounters are sporadic. In a letter, Demian tells Sinclair of the devil-god Abraxas, who is the embodiment of a fusion of all good and evil, of destruction and creation. When he is wounded in the war, Sinclair has a vision of Demian, in which his death is implied. From that time on, Sinclair feels himself to be the possessor of the wisdom and understanding he had attributed to Demian. The novel is one of Hesse's most poignant statements of the terrors and torments of adolescence.

De Mille, Cecil B[lount] (1881–1959)   American motion-picture producer and director. De Mille began his long association with Hollywood when he went there in 1913 and directed *The Squaw Man* (1914), one of the first feature-length movies ever made. In 1921 he became president of Cecil B. De Mille Productions, and, with a remarkable ability to anticipate the public taste, he began to produce the monumental motion-picture extravaganzas identified with his name. Among the best known of these are *The Ten Commandments* (1923; remake, 1956), *The King of Kings* (1927), *The Sign of the Cross* (1932), *The Plainsman* (1936), *Union Pacific* (1939), and *The Greatest Show on Earth* (1952). De Mille's flamboyant style and autocratic manner became the stereotype of the Hollywood director. His extravagant productions established the pattern for feature-length Hollywood studio films for years to come. His *Autobiography* (ed D. Hayne) appeared in 1959.

demiurge (fr Gr, *demiourgos*, "worker of the people") Any power or personality creating a world, real or imaginary. The modern meaning goes back to PLATO's use of the word for the inferior god who created the world.

Democracy (1880)   A novel by Henry ADAMS, first published anonymously. A social and political satire based on the corruption of the second Grant administration, the book includes characters modeled on President Hayes and James G. Blaine. A charming and intelligent young widow, Madeleine Lee, moves to Washington "to touch with her own hands the massive machinery of society." She finally rejects an offer of marriage from a senator who has compromised his moral integrity for political advantage.

Democratic Vistas (1871)   An essay by Walt WHITMAN. The poet, alarmed by the "hollowness of heart" in post-Civil War America, sees a decline in vigor and moral consciousness. Although the U.S. has enjoyed "unprecedented materialistic advancement," it has become increasingly superficial in social, moral, and intellectual spheres. "We live," says Whitman, "in an atmosphere of hypocrisy throughout." Turning to the future, he envisions, in an America disburdened of foreign imitation, the rise of a group of artists. These men and women are needed, for "the work of the New World is not ended, but only fairly begun."

Democritus (c460–c370 BC)   A philosopher, also called the Abderite and, from his cheerful disposition, the Laughing Philosopher. Democritus was born in ABDERA and traveled widely. He adopted the atomistic theory of LEUCIPPUS, holding that the universe is composed of atoms that move about in space and form themselves into bodies. Atoms are eternal, while bodies perish; the soul is a form of fire, which animates the human body. Democritus also held that pleasure, along with self-control, was the goal of life. He is supposed to have put out his eyes in order that he might think without outside disturbances.

Demogorgon   A terrible deity capable of producing the most horrible effects. He is first mentioned by the 4th-century Christian writer Lactantius, who, in so doing, is believed to have broken the spell of a mystery. *Demogorgon* is supposed to be identical with the infernal Power of the ancients, the very mention of whose name brought death and disaster, to whom reference is made by Lucan and others. Hence, Milton speaks of "the dreaded name of Demogorgon" in *Paradise Lost*. According to Ariosto, Demogorgon was a king of the elves and fays who lived on the Himalayas, and once in five years summoned all his subjects before him to give an account of their stewardship. Spenser, in *The Faerie Queene*, says that he dwells in the deep abyss with the three fatal sisters. Shelley so calls eternity in *Prometheus Unbound*.

Demosthenes (383–322 BC)   The most famous of Greek orators. Opposed to the encroachment of Philip II of Macedon, Demosthenes delivered the first *Philippic* in 351 BC. Five years later, he was sent as an ambassador, with nine others, to conclude a peace with Philip. Dissatisfied with the agreement, Demosthenes refused to honor its terms. When Philip broke the treaty shortly afterward, the Greek patriotic party chose Demosthenes as its leader. After Philip's assassination in 336 BC, Demosthenes was one of the leaders of the anti-Macedon uprising. Alexander demanded his arrest, but he was spared. When Harpalus, the Macedonian treasurer, fled to Athens, the seven hundred talents he had stolen from Alexander were placed in a vault to be returned; later, Demosthenes was accused of having accepted part of the money as a bribe. He was forced into exile, though the patriotic party recalled him at the death of Alexander. In 322 BC, the joint rulers of Macedon, Antipater, and Craterus captured Athens, and Demosthenes took poison to escape arrest. His major orations are the three *Philippics* (351, 344, 341 BC), three *Olynthiacs* (349 BC), *On the Peace* (346 BC), *On the Embassy* (344 BC), *On the Affairs of the Chersonese* (341 BC), and *On the Crown* (330 BC).

Demosthenes is supposed to have overcome speech defects by speaking over the roar of the sea with pebbles in his mouth. He rigorously applied himself to the development of a fine style, combining great rhetorical skill with simplicity and directness of language. His arguments were designed to appeal to a popular audience. Sixty-one speeches have come down to us under his name, although some are not considered genuine. He influenced, among others, Cicero, Quintilian, Burke, Fox, and Pitt.

demotic writing   An Egyptian hieroglyphic script, developed in the 5th century BC. A simplified form of HIERATIC writing, running from left to right in horizontal lines, it was first used mainly for social and business purposes but later for religious and literary purposes as well. It continued to be employed by the priests of Isis as late as AD 452.

Denikin, Anton Ivanovich (1872–1947)   Russian general. In 1917 Denikin supported the attempt of Kornilov (1870–1918) to overthrow the BOLSHEVIK regime. After Kornilov's death in the civil war, Denikin succeeded him as the supreme commander of the White armies and led the anti-Bolshevik forces in the south of Russia until General Wrangel took over the command in 1920. Denikin then fled to CONSTANTINOPLE and in 1926 immigrated to France.

dénouement (Fr, "untying")   In drama and fiction, the final unwinding of the tangled elements of the plot, which ends the suspense; it follows the climax. The word is also applied to the resolution of complicated sets of actions in life. See CATASTROPHE.

Deor's Lament (9th century?)   Old English poem of forty-two lines in ALLITERATIVE VERSE, also called "The Complaint of Deor." The poet describes the misfortunes of Germanic heroes, which overshadow his own sad luck in being ousted by his lord in favor of another minstrel. There are seven unequal stanzas with the recurring refrain that as "that has passed, this will too."

de profundis (Lat, "out of the deep"; hence, an extremely bitter cry of wretchedness)   A name for Ps. 130 from the first two words in the Latin version. It forms part of the Roman Catholic burial service. Oscar Wilde's letter to Lord Alfred Douglas, a personal essay of confession and reminiscence written in prison, bore the title *De Profundis* (1905).

Deputy, The   See HOCHHUTH, ROLF.

De Quincey, Thomas (1785–1859)   English essayist and critic. De Quincey is famous for CONFESSIONS OF AN ENGLISH OPIUM EATER, a fascinating memoir distinguished by great imaginative power and prose that is splendid and elaborate without stiffness. These qualities are also present in his personal and fugitive essays such as *Suspiria de Profundis* (1845), *The English Mail Coach* (1849), and *Murder Considered as One of the Fine Arts* (1827, 1839). One of the major critics of the romantic movement, he had clear, judicious taste and remarkable insight, and was learned and original though sometimes prolix and vague. He was closely associated with Wordsworth and Coleridge, residing for a time in the Lake Country, and was also acquainted with Lamb, Hazlitt, Hood, and other literary figures. Much of his work appeared in such journals as *Blackwood's Magazine* and was collected by himself in the twenty-four-volume *Writings* (1851–59).

Derain, André (1880–1954)   French painter. Derain was an original member of LES FAUVES, and his work was characterized by spontaneous brushstrokes and vibrant color, particularly in the landscapes he painted between 1905 and 1907. After this period, his work showed the successive influences of CÉZANNE and CUBISM and, later, of Italian primitives and African sculpture. Always an eclectic painter, Derain experimented with sculpture and woodblocks and designed sets for DIAGHILEV's Ballets Russes.

Derleth, August [William] (1909–1971)   American novelist and poet. Derleth is best known for his *Sac Prairie Saga*, a group of regional novels depicting life in a Wisconsin community (modeled on Sauk City) from 1830 to the mid-20th century, including *Still Is the Summer Night* (1937), *Wind over Wisconsin* (1938), and *Restless Is the River* (1939). He was deeply interested in science fiction and fantasy writing and was largely responsible for the popularization of H. P. LOVECRAFT's horror fiction after Lovecraft's death through the founding of Arkham House, the publisher that kept the work of Lovecraft and many of his followers in print.

De Roberto, Federico (1866–1927)   Italian novelist and critic. De Roberto began his writing career as a literary and art critic for the Milanese newspaper *Corriere della sera*. He became a member of the circle of naturalistic writers in Milan that included G. ROVETTA and G. VERGA, whose biography De Roberto began but never completed. By virtue of his objective and scholarly historical novels, *I vicere* (1894; tr *The Viceroys*, 1962) and *L'imperio* (pub posthumously, 1929), he was considered a leading exponent of *verismo* (see Luigi CAPUANA).

Derzhavin, Gavril Romanovich (1743–1816)   Russian poet. Though Derzhavin's verse is less polished than that of Pushkin and Tyutchev, his work can bear comparison with any Russian poetry for power and vividness. His best works are *Bog* (*Ode to God*, 1784), *Na smert knyazya Meshcherskogo* (*On the Death of Prince Meshchersky*, 1779), and *Felitsa* (1782). This last work is an ode to Catherine the Great, whom Derzhavin served as a court poet and administrator.

Desai, Anita (1937–   )   Indian novelist, writing in English. Although many of her books are set in modernized, urban India, her novels tend to focus more on the psychological and spiritual malaise of her characters than on contemporary social issues. Her work includes the novels *Cry, The Peacock* (1963), *Voices in the City* (1965), *Bye-Bye, Blackbird* (1968), *Where Shall We Go This Summer?* (1975), *Fire on the Mountain* (1977), *Clear Light of Day* (1980), and *In Custody* (1984), which was nominated for the Booker Prize. She has also written numerous short stories.

Descartes, René (1596–1650)   French mathematician and philosopher. As a mathematician, Descartes devised new systems of algebraic notation, and he is regarded as the originator of analytic geometry and the modern scientific method. His philosophical theories provided the basis for 17th-century RATIONALISM, in that he accepted certain *a priori* truths (truths not derived from experience) and sought to devise a system of philosophic thought based above all on methods of deduction and what he called "methodical doubt." While he accepted that some ideas could develop from experience, Descartes was steadfast in his belief that other ideas are "innate." He formulated his famous axiom *Cogito ergo sum* ("I think, therefore I exist"), which he took to be irrefutable evidence of the existence of the mind. From this, he postulated the existence of God and the existence of matter. Because none of these "facts" could be discerned from sensory experience, they must be "innate ideas." He conceived a dualistic system, in which he divided the universe into mutually exclusive but interacting spirit (or mind) and matter; the spirit is subject to reason, and matter is subject to mechanical laws. The principles of his philosophy were outlined in *Discours de la methode* (*Discourse on Method*, 1637) and *Principia philosophiae* (*Principles of Philosophy*, 1644), both of which challenged the metaphysical view of the universe that was associated with SCHOLASTICISM. See MALEBRANCHE, NICHOLAS.

descent to the underworld   The motif of numerous stories in the mythology and folklore of all peoples. The descent is usually made to rescue someone either abducted or rightfully dead, to find the answer to a question or discover a secret from the ruler of the underworld, or to seize some treasure. To partake of the food of the dead (or of fairyland in later folklore) prevents the visitor from ever returning. Among the most famous descent stories are the Greek myths of ORPHEUS and Eurydice, DEMETER and Persephone, and HERACLES' bringing of CERBERUS up from Hades and his rescue of ALCESTIS. Also well known are the Babylonian story of ISHTAR's descent to rescue TAMMUZ and the Norse myth of Hermod's journey to Hel to bring back BALDER. There are similar tales in Hindu, Chinese, and Japanese writings, and among the Ainus, Melanesians, North American Indians, and Eskimos. Descents to Hell are common also in early Christian literature.

Desdemona   The innocent, artless, and lovely heroine of Shakespeare's OTHELLO. Desdemona is the daughter of BRABANTIO.

De senectute (44 BC)   An essay on old age by CICERO, written in the form of a dialogue. Its main speaker, Cato the Elder, discourses to his younger friends on the advantages of a serene old age. From his name, it is often called the *Cato Major*.

Deserted Village, The (1770)   A poem by Oliver GOLDSMITH, portraying the rural depopulation of the latter half of the 18th century. He attributes it to the increase in luxury, foreign trade, the enclosure of open pastures by absentee landowners, and the cancerous growth of London. The poem is dedicated to Sir Joshua REYNOLDS.

De Sica, Vittorio (1901?–1974)   Italian film director and actor. De Sica began as a leading man in movies popular in Italy but little-seen elsewhere. He made his directing debut with *Red Roses* (1939). His most powerful films, *Shoeshine* (1946), *The Bicycle Thief* (1948), and the reflective, somewhat abstract *Umberto D* (1952), all produced in post-World War II Italy, are prime examples of NEOREALIST CINEMA. His later works, some of which are lighter and more romantic in tone, include *Two Women* (1962), *Yesterday, Today, and Tomorrow* (1963), *Marriage Italian Style* (1964), and *The Garden of the Finzi-Continis* (1971).

Desire Under the Elms (1924)   A tragedy by Eugene O'NEILL. Set in New England, it deals with Ephraim Cabot and his new young wife, Abbie. Abbie seduces Eben, the youngest son of Ephraim, hoping to bear a son she can claim is Ephraim's. When it appears to Eben that Abbie has used him only for her own ends, he threatens to expose her infidelity; to prove her love for him, she smothers the child. Based, in terms of plot, on the Phaedra-Hippolytus story, the play exemplifies O'Neill's interest in Freudian psychology and in the conflict between a repressive Calvinism and Dionysian surrender.

de Soto, Hernando (or Fernando de Soto, 1500?–1542)   Spanish explorer. Having served with Pizarro in Peru, de Soto won permission from Charles V to conquer Florida, where he landed in 1539 with some six hundred men. For the next three years, he wandered through present Georgia, the Carolinas, Alabama, Mississippi, Arkansas, and Louisiana; though he found no gold, he is credited with discovering the Mississippi River in 1541. He died on the banks of the Mississippi, and his body was sunk in the river by his men.

destruccion o el amor, La   See ALEIXANDRE, VICENTE.

Destruction of Sennacherib, The (1815)   A well-known poem by Lord BYRON. It vividly portrays the annihilating plague that struck down the invading army of the Assyrian king SENNACHERIB in Palestine during the 7th century BC.

Deucalion's flood   The deluge of Greek legend. Deucalion, son of PROMETHEUS and Clymene, was king of Phthia, in Thessaly. When ZEUS sent the deluge, Deucalion built a ship, and he and his wife, Pyrrha, were the only mortals saved. The ship at last rested on Mount Parnassus, and Deucalion was told by the oracle of THEMIS that, to restore the human race, he must cast the bones of his mother behind him. The two cast the stones of their mother Earth as directed. Those thrown by Deucalion became men; those thrown by his wife became women.

deus ex machina (Lat, "god from the machine") A theatrical device used in Greek tragedy. In several plays of EURIPIDES, a god appears at the last moment to provide the solution to the tangled problems of the main characters. The god is let down from the sky on a sort of crane. The phrase has come to refer to a playwright's use of external means to solve the problems of his characters—a practice generally frowned upon.

Deuteronomy   A book of the OLD TESTAMENT, the last book of the PENTATEUCH. It reiterates the Mosaic law and, ending with the death of MOSES, contains the final episodes in his life. It was probably written during the reign of Manasseh (c698–643 BC). Either suppressed or forgotten for a generation, the book was discovered in 621 BC hidden in the temple. It has been expanded by later writers. The original parts (most of chapters 5–26 and 28) are thought to be the first book ever canonized as divine law.

Deutsch, Babette (1895–1982)   American poet and critic. Deutsch's poems, known for their technical skill and social implications, have been collected in many volumes, including *Animal, Vegetable, Mineral* (1954), *Coming of Age* (1959), and *Collected Poems* (1963, 1969). *Potable Gold* (1929) and *Poetry in Our Time* (1952, 1963) are among her works of criticism. As well as writing four novels and several children's books, Deutsch also translated German and Russian verse, usually in collaboration with her husband, Avraam Yarmolinsky, the critic and scholar.

devil (fr Gr, *diabolos*, "slanderer")   In Jewish and Christian theology, an apostate spirit. The name is also given to the chief of devils, known as *the Devil*, who is the supreme spirit of evil, the adversary of God, the enemy and tempter of man, and the ruler of Hell. In the BIBLE and APOCRYPHA, the Devil is variously referred to as SATAN, ASMODEUS, BEELZEBUB, SAMAEL, and, according to the Church Fathers, as LUCIFER. His name in Islam is EBLIS, which, like *devil*, is derived from the Greek. Devils' names in literature and popular usage include MEPHISTOPHELES, Auld Nick, Auld Hornie, Auld Ane, Clootie, and Hangie.

The Devil and devils are frequently represented with a cloven foot, since rabbinical writers refer to them as *seirizzim* ("goats"). As the goat is the prototype of uncleanliness, the prince of unclean spirits is aptly represented under this emblem.

Devil and Daniel Webster, The (1937)   A popular short story by Stephen Vincent BENÉT. First published in the *Saturday Evening Post* and then in the collection *Thirteen O'Clock*, it was adapted as an opera (1938) with music by Douglas S. Moore, and later as a play (1939) and a film (1941, under the title *All That Money Can Buy*). The story concerns Jabez Stone, a New England farmer, who sells his soul to the Devil for material prosperity. He is saved from paying his debt by the oratorical eloquence of Daniel Webster, who argues his case before a demonic jury.

Devil's advocate (Lat, *advocatus diaboli*)   A person appointed to test the claims of a candidate for canonization before a papal court. He advances all arguments he can against the candidate, who is defended by the *advocatus dei* ("God's advocate"), who says all he can in support of the proposed canonization. By extension, the term is used of a destructive critic, one who deliberately searches for flaws in order to bring out the whole truth.

It is also the title of a novel (1959) by Morris L. WEST that was dramatized (1961) by Dore Schary (1905–1980).

Devil's Disciple, The (1897)   A melodrama by George Bernard SHAW. It is set in America during the Revolution. Dick Dudgeon, a reprobate, allows himself, to his own surprise, to be arrested by the English and sentenced to death in place of Parson Anderson. The parson, too, finds a new side to his personality, when he leads an armed band to fight the British and rescue Dick. Shaw's thesis is that convention and circumstance fix a person's life, but under crisis people make startling discoveries about themselves. An exciting and brilliant play, *The Devil's Disciple* makes particular fun of the military.

Devil's General, The (Des Teufels General, 1946; tr 1950)   A play by Carl ZUCKMAYER. It depicts the inner struggle of a *Luftwaffe* general who, though in principle opposed to Nazism, manages to rationalize his position as a servant of the regime. But when he is confronted by a saboteur, a man true to his principles, who is doing his best to hamper the German war effort, the general recognizes the untenability of his own compromise and deliberately flies off to his death in a sabotaged plane.

Devotions upon Emergent Occasions (1624) A series of meditations on the "Variable, and therefore miserable condition of Man" by John DONNE. The work was ostensibly written during a long, grave illness. Its style is highly metaphorical and complex. It contains the famous passage from which Ernest Hemingway drew the title of FOR WHOM THE BELL TOLLS:

No man is an Iland, intire of it selfe; every man is a peece of the Continent, a part of the maine; if a Clod bee washed away by the Sea, Europe is the lesse, as well as if a Promontorie were . . . ; any mans death diminishes me, because I am involved in Mankinde; And therefore never send to know for whom the bell tolls; It tolls for thee.

DeVoto, Bernard A[ugustine] (1897–1955) American historian and critic. DeVoto first gained public attention for his *Mark Twain's America* (1932), a rebuttal of Van Wyck BROOKS's *The Ordeal of Mark Twain* (1920). He taught at Northwestern University (1922–27) and at Harvard (1929–36), filled "The Easy Chair" of HARPER's MAGAZINE (1935–55), and wrote several novels. His most respected work, however, was his historical writing, notably the three-volume study of the American West, *The Year of Decision: 1846* (1943), *Across the Wide Missouri* (1947, PULITZER PRIZE), and *The Course of Empire* (1952).

DeVries, Peter (1910–   )   American novelist. From 1938 to 1944, DeVries worked as an editor of POETRY magazine; he then began his long association with THE NEW YORKER, in which much of his short fiction was published. In over twenty novels—including *The Tunnel of Love* (1954), *Through the Fields of Clover* (1961), *Into Your Tent I'll Creep* (1971), *Madder Music* (1977), *Consenting Adults* (1980), *Sauce for the Goose* (1981), and *Slouching*

towards Kalamazoo (1983)—DeVries has applied his antic humor to the foibles and excesses of affluent middle-class exurbanites. His vision is informed by the ethical attitudes of his Dutch Calvinist upbringing, although he has strenuously rejected its theology. Through his various fictional personae, DeVries manages consistently to amuse without losing sight of the moral dimensions of his art.

Devushkin, Makar Alekseyevich   The hero of Fyodor DOSTOYEVSKY's short novel POOR FOLK. Devushkin is a timid clerk, desperately in love with Varvara Alekseyevna Dobroselova and acutely conscious of the impossibility of his love because of his greater age and extreme poverty. His condition is sharply brought home to him when he reads Nikolay GOGOL's short story THE OVERCOAT, which portrays a downtrodden clerk too much like Devushkin himself. He complains about writers dealing with such subjects in one of his letters to Varvara.

Dewey, John (1859–1952)   American teacher, philosopher, and educational reformer. A believer in William James's PRAGMATISM, Dewey employed the principles of that philosophy in his progressive movement in education. He advocated "learning by doing," rejecting traditional autocratic methods of teaching by rote. Although his principles were adapted by many, not all of Dewey's disciples were restrained by his common sense. Among his many books are *The School and Society* (1899; rev 1908, 1915, 1932), *Interest and Effort in Education* (1913), *Democracy and Education* (1916), *The Quest for Certainty* (1929), *Art as Experience* (1934), and *The Problems of Men* (1946).

Dewey decimal system   A system of book classification for library cataloguing. Devised by Melvil Dewey in 1876, it divides books into ten main groups that classify the general fields of knowledge. Each main group is further broken down into smaller groups, and so on, so that categories are represented by figures from 000 to 999. For example, literature, including novels, plays, poetry, and criticism, is covered by 800–899. More specific subdivisions within each group are designated by the use of decimal points; hence the name. Many university libraries have abandoned the Dewey system for that used by the Library of Congress, but the system is still used by many public libraries.

Dexter, Timothy (1747–1806)   American merchant and eccentric. Becoming enormously wealthy as the result of a series of transactions that ordinarily would have proved disastrous, he named himself Lord Timothy Dexter and built a great mansion in Newburyport, Massachusetts. He wrote an admiring and amusing account of his own exploits in *A Pickle for the Knowing Ones, or Plain Truths in a Homespun Dress* (1802). The book had no punctuation, but in a second edition, Dexter satisfied his critics by including a page full of various punctuation marks, inviting his readers to "peper and solt it as they plese." John P. MARQUAND, who grew up in Newburyport, wrote a biography, *Lord Timothy Dexter* (1925), which he revised as *Timothy Dexter Revisited* (1960).

dharma (Sans, "that which binds, supports, sustains") A concept with different meanings in HINDUISM and BUDDHISM. In Hinduism, *dharma* is a sacred law of society denoting moral order, the performance of duty, and the forms of conduct becoming to different classes or persons. It is also one of the four legitimate ENDS OF MAN, with ARTHA, material gain; KARMA, physical pleasure; and *moksha*, spiritual release, salvation. In Buddhism, dharma is the law of BUDDHA, the basic doctrine of the Four Noble Truths; it is one of the Three Jewels of the faith, the other two being the person of Buddha and the *sangha*, or Buddhist monastic community.

dhoti In India, a loin cloth of varying length and material, usually cotton. Wrapped and tied differently according to region and, in some cases, caste, it was associated with GANDHI's dress, symbolizing the poverty of India's suffering millions.

Diaghilev, Sergey Pavlovich (1872–1929) Russian ballet impresario and art critic. Diaghilev constantly encouraged new ideas and techniques, first as an art critic and as founder (1898) of the influential journal *Mir iskusstva* (*The World of Art*). In 1909 he founded and directed the Ballets Russes in Paris, which had an enormous impact on the direction modern ballet would take. Diaghilev set his dancers in constant motion; he conceived of music, set design, and costume as integral, coequal aspects of the dance. To such ends, he attracted the composing talents of Claude DEBUSSY, Maurice RAVEL, Igor STRAVINSKY, and members of Les SIX, among others. PICASSO, BRAQUE, CHAGALL, and DERAIN were among the many artists to design his sets. In addition, the Ballets Russes presented some of the greatest dancers in the world, choreographed by the likes of Léonide Massine, George Balanchine, and Serge Lifar. Diaghilev's inestimable influence has been the subject of many studies and biographies.

Dial, The A magazine founded in New England in 1840. The organ of the Transcendentalist movement, its founders were Theodore PARKER, Bronson ALCOTT, Orestes Brownson, Margaret FULLER, and Ralph Waldo EMERSON. Fuller served as editor from 1840 to 1842, and Emerson, with THOREAU's help, took over until 1844, when the magazine ceased publication. During its short history, it wielded a great deal of influence in literary, philosophic, and religious thought. In addition to publishing the work of its founders, *The Dial* published the poetry of Jones VERY and William Ellery CHANNING.

Since 1844, other magazines have taken the same name. Moncure Conway founded the second *Dial* in 1860, in Cincinnati. In 1880, a conservative group founded the third *Dial* in Chicago. When it moved to New York in 1918, it became the outstanding literary review of its time. Until 1920, with the aid of Conrad AIKEN, Randolph

BOURNE, and Van Wyck BROOKS, it published articles by leading radical thinkers, including John DEWEY and Thorstein VEBLEN. After 1920, it was devoted to the encouragement of avant-garde authors. Marianne MOORE became editor in 1925. The magazine ceased publication four years later.

A fourth *Dial*, first a literary quarterly edited by James Silberman, then an annual, ran from 1959 to 1962.

dialectical materialism The natural philosophy of Marxism (see Karl MARX), formulated chiefly by Friedrich ENGELS. Dialectical materialism is MATERIALISM in opposition to idealism, particularly the idealism of HEGEL. In this view, matter is primary; mind cannot exist without a material basis. Mind is not, however, identical with matter or reducible to it. The "dialectical" aspect of this view is found in its claim that there are contradictions in nature and that, through the conflict of opposites, change takes place. The dialectical pattern of conflict and resolution is largely based on Hegel's philosophy. The pattern is usually described as moving from a "thesis" to its opposite, an "antithesis," then to a "synthesis" on a new level.

diamond necklace affair A famous scandal in French history (1783–85). The jewelers Böhmer and Bassenge had originally made the necklace, containing five hundred diamonds, for Mme Du Barry; but, after the death of Louis XV, they were unable to dispose of it. To recoup their investment, they repeatedly but unsuccessfully pressed MARIE ANTOINETTE to buy it. The scheming, so-called Comtesse, Jeanne de La Motte, a high-class courtesan, knowing that Cardinal de Rohan, a rich, profligate churchman, wished to ingratiate himself with the queen —partly because he fatuously believed he could become her lover and partly to regain royal favor—fraudulently persuaded him that Marie Antoinette secretly wished to buy the necklace, convincing him that the queen had chosen him to negotiate with the jewelers on her behalf. He agreed to act as intermediary and to deliver the necklace to Mme de La Motte, who in turn would deliver it to Marie Antoinette. To lend credibility to her ruse, Mme de La Motte arranged for a young modiste and woman of the streets to impersonate the queen at a short garden meeting with Rohan; she also forged several letters which fanned the cardinal's infatuation and confirmed his role as go-between. He made a down payment on the necklace and delivered it to Mme de La Motte, who, with her young accomplice and lover Rétaux de Villette, took it apart, sold the individual diamonds in England and Paris, and kept the money. Böhmer tried to collect the balance from the Queen, insisting that she had authorized Rohan to purchase it. The Queen, indignant at being accused of dishonesty, reported the affair to her husband, Louis XVI, who caused a sensation by having the cardinal arrested publicly. At the ensuing trial, Rohan was exonerated but exiled to the country by the king, who still believed him guilty; Marie Antoinette was cleared of any duplicity; Mme de La Motte was publicly branded, whipped, and sentenced to life imprisonment. She later escaped to England, where she wrote her memoirs, accusing the queen.

Diana An ancient Italian and Roman divinity. Diana was later identified with the Olympian goddess ARTEMIS.

Diane de Poitiers (1499–1566) Mistress of Henry II of France. Diane wielded immense power over Henry, who was ten years her junior, until his death in 1559. She spent her last years at her château at Anet, which had been designed for her by Philibert Delorme, a celebrated architect.

Diary of a Country Priest, The (Journal d'un curé de campagne, 1936; tr 1937) A novel by Georges BERNANOS. It movingly depicts the saintly struggles of a young priest with his failing health and his greedy and ungrateful parish. Tormented by his search for true service to God, the priest sees his parish projects fail, and he dies, defeated but absolved.

Diary of Anne Frank See FRANK, ANNE.

Diary of a Provincial Lady (1930) A novel, in diary form, by E. M. DELAFIELD. A phlegmatic husband, disconcerting children, temperamental servants, and dreadful neighbors are the problems of ordinary upper-middle-class domestic life of the period.

Diary of a Writer, A (Dnevnik pisatelya, 1873, 1876–77, 1880–81) A series of collected articles and short sketches, published in the form of a journal, by DOSTOYEVSKY. He began the project as a section in *Grazhdanin* (*The Citizen*), a weekly newspaper he edited (1873–74). The so-called diary was concerned mostly with political and social questions, although Dostoyevsky did publish in it a few of his short stories, including "Krotkaya" ("The Meek One," 1876) and "Son smeshnogo cheloveka" ("The Dream of a Ridiculous Man," 1877). In 1880 the diary contained Dostoyevsky's famous speech at the Pushkin celebration in Moscow.

Diaspora Exile or dispersion, used almost invariably with reference to the exile of the Jewish people from the land of Israel. *Diaspora* may be used to refer not only to the state of being in exile, but also to the place of exile—any place outside of Israel where Jews are living—to the communities in exile, and to a state of mind that results from living in exile. The Hebrew term *galut* (also *golus*, *galuth*) expresses the Jew's feeling of living as a member of a relatively defenseless minority, subject to injustice if not to outright persecution, of an unfulfilled life and destiny as a Jew, and of living in an unredeemed—though not unredeemable—world.

Díaz, Porfirio (1830–1915) Mexican dictator. An erstwhile supporter of JUÁREZ, Díaz seized power in 1876 and ruled Mexico for thirty-five years. Although his regime brought political and fiscal stability, only a handful of politicians, landowners, and foreign capitalists prospered, while the rural masses lived in virtual servitude. Díaz was ousted in 1911 and died in exile in Paris.

Díaz del Castillo, Bernal (1496–1584) Spanish soldier and historian. Díaz was one of the four hundred soldiers who took part in the Spanish conquest of Mexico; he later settled down on an estate in Guatemala. Piqued by an official history of the conquest, which he felt unduly glorified the achievements of Cortez, Díaz, then an octogenarian, attempted to tell what really happened in his *Historia verdadera de la conquista de la Nueva España* (*True History of the Conquest of New Spain*, 1632), perhaps the best popular history in the Spanish language. With a plethora of minute yet vivid detail, Díaz celebrates the exploits of the common soldiers who accompanied Cortez, in a style remarkable for its homely vigor. An intensely personal document, in which Díaz does not minimize his own achievements and depicts Cortez as a very fallible human being, the work gives an excellent picture of the individuality and tenacity that characterized the 16th-century conquistadors. The book was the source for Archibald MacLeish's CONQUISTADOR.

dibrach See PYRRHIC.

Dichtung und Wahrheit (Poetry and Truth, 1811–33) An autobiography by GOETHE. It is not so much a simple recounting of the events of his life as an attempt to explain the major strains of his inner development and set forth the essential principles on which his poetic activity was based.

Dickens, Charles (1812–1870) English novelist, the most popular and considered by many the greatest of his country. Like that of the children in many of his novels, Dickens's childhood was a difficult and unhappy one; his father, a navy clerk, was constantly in debt and was thrown into debtors' prison, and Dickens was sent to work in a blacking factory at the age of twelve. Most bitter for him was his parents' failure to educate him. He reacted to this indifference by working hard, a lifelong characteristic. He became an office boy in a law firm, then a county reporter, and finally a reporter of debates in Parliament for the *Morning Chronicle* in 1835. His *Sketches by Boz*, satires on daily life, were serialized in the *Old Monthly Magazine* (1833–35). Immediately asked to do another series, he wrote *The Posthumous Papers of the Pickwick Club*, better known simply as the PICKWICK PAPERS; these were illustrated by Phiz (H. K. Browne) and made Dickens successful at twenty-four. With OLIVER TWIST, Dickens began his indictment of the society of his place and time, a society that grossly mistreated and abused the poor, especially children, driving them to crime. While he was working on *Twist*, his wife Catherine's sister died; his deep grief and lifelong utterances of love for this sister-in-law underline his less profound relationship with his wife, from whom he was separated in 1858. They had ten children.

NICHOLAS NICKLEBY, like *Oliver Twist*, was serialized in *Bentley's Miscellany*. The next two, BARNABY RUDGE and THE OLD CURIOSITY SHOP, were serialized in Dickens's own new weekly periodical, *Master Humphrey's Clock*; they were his least successful novels. In 1842 Dickens made a trip to the U.S., where he trod on native sensibilities by urging the abolition of slavery and the establishment of an international copyright. Back in England, he published his insulting AMERICAN NOTES and MARTIN CHUZZLEWIT, a powerfully satiric novel of selfishness, hypocrisy, and financial speculation as it bloomed in insular England and in the open spaces but narrow minds of the U.S. Dickens met with sensational success with the publication of A CHRISTMAS CAROL and he followed it in consecutive years with other Christmas books, including CRICKET ON THE HEARTH. His next novel, DOMBEY AND SON, was written in Switzerland.

In 1850 Dickens founded the weekly *Household Words* and in 1859 another weekly, *All the Year Round*, both of which he kept until his death; most of his later works were published in these periodicals.

With DAVID COPPERFIELD, his more mature works begin. Autobiographical, it was Dickens's own favorite. In BLEAK HOUSE, an exposé of political corruption and court delay, Dickens displays a gloomy lack of faith in the ability of governmental institutions, held together with red tape and filled with archaic practices, to benefit the people. HARD TIMES is a protest against utilitarian lack of feeling and imagination and is perhaps Dickens's most single-minded social novel. Further disillusionment came in LITTLE DORRIT, which included memories of Dickens's father in debtors' prison. Next came his dramatic novel A TALE OF TWO CITIES. This was soon followed by GREAT EXPECTATIONS, considered by many as his finest work. OUR MUTUAL FRIEND is highly regarded by some critics, but others find it humorless, diffuse, and contrived. In 1858 Dickens began to give public readings, which he continued on his second visit to the U.S., in 1867–68. He died in England while working on his novel *The Mystery of* EDWIN DROOD. He was buried in Westminster Abbey.

No other English writer has created a world of characters so distinctively cruel or suffering, comic or repugnant as Dickens has; no other writer has written so convincingly of the wrongs inflicted on children by adults in the 19th century. Attacks on Dickens's sentimentality and tendency to caricature have detracted little from his stature as a great humorist and creator of characters; these he brought to life with a wealth of meaningful detail, a myriad of odd gestures, expressions, speech patterns, and physiognomies. As a social critic, he focused sharply on the iniquities and inequities of his environment. See BOZ.

Dickey, James [Lafayette] (1923–   ) American poet and novelist. As a writer, guitar player, hunter, woodsman, and war hero, Dickey emulates the Renaissance man in both his life and his letters. He is a native Georgian, aware of both the virtues and the guilt of the Southern agrarian past. In his most famous volumes of verse, *Helmets* (1964) and *Buckdancer's Choice* (1965), Dickey writes of the suburban man striving to retain a primitive and tribal authenticity in his values and behavior. Indeed, the theme of a primal, preconscious communion with the forces of the natural world pervades his work. He writes an open verse in which rhythm takes precedence over rhyme. His earlier poetry moved toward a longer narrative form, which was realized in *The Zodiac* (1976), a poem in twelve parts, about an alcoholic who goes to Amsterdam to write and to die. Here Dickey writes with a long and flexible line in eloquent, powerful language. His best-selling novel *Deliverance* (1970) also deals with modern men in the primal wilderness, exposing readers (as in much of his poetry) to scenes of violence and nightmarish horror. Subsequent volumes of verse include *The Strength of Fields* (1979), *Puella* (1982), *False Youth: Four Seasons* (1983), and *The Central Motion* (1983). *Alnilam*, a novel, was published in 1987.

Dickinson, Emily (1830–1886)   American poet. One of the three children of Edward Dickinson, lawyer and treasurer of Amherst College, Dickinson shared a cultivated family life. After attending Amherst Institute and Mount Holyoke Female Seminary, she retired to her home; later, dressing only in white, she rarely came down from her room to meet her guests.

Her father, a stern Calvinist who served a term in Congress, dominated his daughter's life. Among the other men who influenced her were the Reverend Charles Wadsworth, whose trip to California is cryptically referred to in the poetry; Samuel Bowles, editor of the Springfield *Daily Republican*, where one of her poems appeared; Benjamin F. Newton, a short-lived scholar and lawyer, who introduced her to the works of Emerson; T. W. Higginson, soldier and critic; and Judge Otis P. Lord, a family friend.

Throughout her adult life, Dickinson wrote poetry; only two of the almost two thousand poems she wrote were published in her lifetime. Uniformly short, consisting usually of four-line stanzas, the poems are written in a terse, aphoristic style. Although she personally rejected Calvinist theology, Dickinson was influenced by the philosophy of Jonathan Edwards; like Emerson, she found that spirit manifested itself in nature. Physically isolated, she belongs in the tradition of American poetry that includes Whitman and Robert Frost.

dictator   In ancient Rome, the temporary supreme commander. In times of great national danger, the senate would call upon the consuls to appoint a dictator, who would hold office for no longer than six months.

Dicte   A Cretan mountain where, in a cave, ZEUS was born and where he was protected by nymphs and CURETES and suckled by the goat Amaltheia. An actual cave in this mountain has been proved by excavation to have been a center of a Minoan cult that centered on a young child. Some legends hold that Zeus was born on Mount IDA.

diction   Word choice, in verbal expression, with all that such choice implies in questions of correctness, clarity, and style. The *mot juste*, or exactly right word, is the ideal of good diction. Popularly, it is often confused with enunciation.

Dictionary of the English Language (1755)   A monumental work by Samuel JOHNSON, which made his reputation and was the standard dictionary until Noah WEBSTER'S. In 1747 Johnson applied to Lord CHESTERFIELD for patronage and was refused; upon completion of the work, Chesterfield made a belated offer, which Johnson then refused in a famous letter. In his preface to the *Dictionary*, addressing critics, Johnson wrote, ". . . and it may repress the triumph of malignant criticism to observe, that if our language is not here fully displayed, I have only failed in an attempt which no human powers have hitherto completed."

didactic poetry   Poetry to teach factual information or moral lessons. Didactic verse has since time immemorial combined the mnemonic virtues of rhyme and rhythm with information to be memorized, as in the nursery rhyme "Thirty Days Hath September." In the view of some philosophers, the underlying aim of all literature is at least in part didactic; but, aside from such an underlying aim, purely didactic poetry is no longer written. Some examples of didactic poetry in literary history are LUCRETIUS's *De rerum natura*, Vergil's GEORGICS, Erasmus DARWIN's *Botanic Garden*, and Pope's AN ESSAY ON MAN.

Diderot, Denis (nicknamed Pantophile Diderot, 1713–1784)   French encyclopedist, materialistic philosopher, novelist, satirist, dramatist, and art critic. Until recently, Diderot was famous mainly for having compiled and edited, with d'ALEMBERT and others, the ENCYCLOPÉDIE OU DICTIONNAIRE RAISONNÉ DES SCIENCES, DES ARTS ET DES MÉTIERS (28 vols, 5 suppls, 2 index vols). Among his philosophic works are *Pensées philosophiques* (1746), which is deistic in thought and a defense of human passions; *Lettre sur les aveugles . . .* (1749), a study of how the blind learn, containing his view on materialism (he was imprisoned for three months because of this work); *Lettre sur les sourds et les muets* (1749), one of the first studies on the deaf and dumb, as well as an inquiry into aesthetics; and *Pensées sur l'interprétation de la nature* (1753), containing ideas which foreshadow discoveries in biology, the theory of transformism, and natural selection. Diderot's audacity and profundity in scientific thought are strikingly illustrated in his *Le Rêve de d'Alembert* (1769, pub 1830), one of his three dramatic dialogues, in which he presents surprising insights into the physical, moral, and social universe; in it is found the first modern conception of the cellular structure of

matter. His novels include *Les Bijoux indiscrets* (1748); *La Religieuse* (written 1760, pub 1796), an attack on life in convents; LE NEVEU DE RAMEAU (1762), a dialectical satire on contemporary society and conventional morality; and the satirico-philosophical JACQUES LE FATALISTE, in which Diderot poses the problem of freedom versus predeterminism and at the same time experiments with the form of the novel. Among Diderot's plays, the most famous are *Le Père de famille* (1758) and *Le Fils naturel* (1757). Moral in tone and rather mediocre, they illustrate his theories on the drama and became prototypes for the BOURGEOIS DRAMA. Diderot's theories on the drama, which he developed in several essays, e.g., *Paradoxe sur le comédien* (1773–78, pub 1830), were put into practice by Émile Augier and Dumas fils, in their moralistic, social-minded plays. In the *Salons* (1759–81), written for Baron de Grimm's *Correspondance littéraire, philosophique et critique*, Diderot inaugurated art criticism as a literary genre. His *Lettres à Sophie Volland* attest to his genius as a letter-writer.

Didion, Joan (1934–   )   American novelist and essayist. In her two collections of essays, *Slouching towards Bethlehem* (1968) and *The White Album* (1979), Didion's insights into the culture of the 1960s focus on her native California as a metaphor for the lost American Dream. Her novels also depict the disorder, loss, anxiety, and human and cultural disintegration of modern life. The heroines in *Run River* (1963), *Play It As It Lays* (1970), and *A Book of Common Prayer* (1977) seem to drift numbly through the painful, often melodramatic events of their lives. Emotion is implied or suggested by startling dialogue and vivid details. *Salvador* (1983), reportage on the plight of El Salvador, and *Democracy*, a novel (1984), are both successful recent works. In Didion's books, the pioneering American spirit is replaced by a lack of belief, a creed of "me-ism," and eternal motion without direction. Didion, with her controlled, laconic style, is noted for her careful delineation of character, her manipulation of time, and her ability to suggest significance through detail.

Dido   The name given by Vergil in his AENEID to the founder and queen of Carthage. According to Roman legend, Dido fled from Phoenicia to North Africa after her brother PYGMALION, king of Tyre, had murdered her husband, Sychaeus, for his wealth. (See BYRSA.) The name *Dido* was also an epithet of the Phoenician goddess Astarte.

In Vergil's poem, she hospitably receives AENEAS and the Trojans when they are shipwrecked on her shores. Through the plotting of the goddess VENUS, she falls in love with Aeneas and tries to persuade him to settle in North Africa and share Carthage with her. But when the will of the gods is announced to him by their messenger MERCURY, Aeneas yields, half against his will: he must abandon Dido and found his own nation in Italy. After his departure, Dido, in grief, takes her life by the sword and is cremated on a great funeral pyre, which Aeneas, now far out to sea, beholds burning on the shore.

OVID's *Heroides* contains a letter, supposedly written by Dido to Aeneas, in which she reminds him of all she has done for him and begs him to remain. Other works dealing with the unfortunate queen include the tragedy *Dido, Queen of Carthage* (c1593), possibly written by NASHE and MARLOWE; PURCELL's opera *Dido and Aeneas* (1689); and the opera *Didon* (1783) by Piccinni (1728–1800).

Dies Irae (Lat, "day of wrath")   A famous medieval hymn on the Last Judgment, probably composed by Thomas of Celano (d 1255), a native of Abruzzi. It is derived from the Vulgate version of Joel 2:31 and is used in the Mass for the Dead and on ALL SOULS' DAY. The plain-song melody associated with the text has been employed by many composers since the romantic era (Berlioz, Liszt, Mussorgsky, Rachmaninoff, and others) to connote death.

dilettante (Ital, "one who takes delight in a thing") Like *amateur*, "one who likes a thing," *dilettante* is especially applied with reference to the fine arts. Since mere fondness of an art guarantees neither knowledge nor ability, both *amateur* and *dilettante* have come to mean one who dabbles in a given subject. The Spanish word *aficionado* carries the sense of the knowledgeable enthusiast that the other two words have nearly lost.

Dill Pickle, A (1920)   A short story by Katherine MANSFIELD. A pair of lovers meet by chance in a restaurant after they have been separated for six years. In the half hour they spend together, she rediscovers his charm and regrets ever leaving him, then rediscovers his faults and leaves him sitting in the restaurant. A sour dill pickle in an anecdote he tells functions as a symbol for the whole experience.

dime novel   A cheaply made, often sensational and melodramatic paperback novel of history, crime, or adventure, printed in America in the latter half of the 19th century and priced at ten cents. The firm of Beadle and Adams was the best-known publisher of dime novels. Their most popular series was E. L. Wheeler's frontier tales of Deadwood Dick. The WESTERN originated with the dime novel.

dimeter   In prosody, a line of verse containing two metrical feet. It may be in any meter, usually identified together with the name of the meter, as iambic dimeter, trochaic dimeter, etc.

Dimmesdale, Arthur   The guilty minister in Hawthorne's THE SCARLET LETTER.

Dinesen, Isak (pseudonym of Baroness Karen Dinesen Blixen, 1885–1962)   Danish short-story writer. Married to her cousin, Baron Blixen, Isak Dinesen lived from 1914 to 1931 on a coffee plantation in British East Africa, now Kenya. *Out of Africa* (1937), published simultaneously in English and Danish, is a sensitive account of her experiences there. It was made into a film in 1985. Her first book, *Seven Gothic Tales* (1934), was published in English and received immediate critical acclaim; *Winter's*

Tales (1942) is another well-known collection. During the German occupation of Denmark, Dinesen published a symbolic critique of the conquerors, *Gengoedelsens Veje* (1944; tr *The Angelic Avengers*, 1947), under the name Pierre Andrézel. A delicate subtlety of both mood and expression characterizes her acutely perceptive, often mysterious stories. A posthumous collection of stories, *Carnival* (1977), contains all the elements of her major works: an ironic juxtaposition of past and present, skillful use of the masquerade, and a remarkable blend of romance and wit. *Daguerreotypes and Other Essays* (1979) is a collection of her nonfiction writing.

Dingdong   An anglicism for Dindenault, the sea-going sheep trader in Rabelais's GARGANTUA AND PANTAGRUEL who sells PANURGE a ram for an exorbitant price. Panurge punishes Dingdong by heaving the ram overboard, thus causing the whole herd to stampede into the sea, dragging the trader with them. Panurge declares that such good sport was well worth the price he had paid for the ram.

Dinggedicht (Ger, "thing poem")   A lyric poem about an objective entity, which, though it is most often a material thing, may also be a person or situation. The poet seeks not so much to describe from his own point of view as to recreate the intrinsic essence of the object in question, to get inside the object, as it were. Ideally, the reader should react to the poem as though he were reacting, on a deeper and more perceptive level than usual, to the thing itself. In many poems of this type, those by Eduard MÖRIKE and Conrad Ferdinand MEYER, for example, the subject is a work of art, but Rainer Maria RILKE, with whom the term *Dinggedicht* is most often associated, expanded the technique to include such subjects as living animals, human situations, and common household objects. The *Dinggedicht* is recognized in German literary criticism as a distinct poetic form.

Dinmont, Dandie   An eccentric and humorous farmer in Scott's GUY MANNERING. Dinmont owns two terriers, Mustard and Pepper, reputedly the progenitors of the Dandie Dinmont breed.

Diocletian[us, Gaius Aurelius Valerius] (AD 245–313)   Roman emperor (284–305). Diocletian inaugurated the period of the partnership of emperors. He ruled with Maximian from 285 and divided the empire again (293) to include Constantius Chlorus and Galerius as rulers. Diocletian governed the eastern portion. At the instigation of his colleague Galerius, he began a terrible ten-year persecution of the Christians in 303. Diocletian abdicated (305) and retired to his native Dalmatia, where he spent the last years of his life.

Diogenes (c412–323 BC)   The Greek CYNIC philosopher, pupil of Antisthenes. According to SENECA, Diogenes lived in a tub. The ascetic Diogenes is said to have searched with a lantern in daylight for an honest man. He exposed the vanity and selfishness of men. Diogenes' contempt for worldly goods is indicated by his reply to ALEX-ANDER THE GREAT, when the latter asked if he could do the philosopher any favor. Diogenes answered, "Yes, move out of my sunshine." Diogenes' nickname was *kyon*, or dog, a comment on his mode of living.

Diomedean swap   An exchange in which all the benefit is on one side. The expression is based on an incident related by Homer in the ILIAD. During the prescribed exchange of credentials before a fight to the death, the Greek hero DIOMEDES and the Trojan hero GLAUCUS discover that their families had been allied. Forgetting their quarrel, they exchange armor, but Glaucus' armor is pure gold, while Diomedes' is only brass. Homer remarks that ZEUS must have addled Glaucus' wits.

Dionysiac   See APOLLONIAN AND DIONYSIAC.

Dionysus (also known as Bacchus in Roman mythology)   The Greek god of wine and fertile crops, the son of ZEUS and SEMELE. Saved from his dead mother, the unborn child was sewed into Zeus' thigh. After his birth, Dionysus was torn to pieces by the TITANS at the jealous HERA's instigation. Revived by RHEA, he was transformed into a kid and raised by nymphs. As a young man, he invented wine and introduced the vine to many lands, accompanied everywhere by a troop of maenads and suitors. Those who opposed his orgiastic rites were driven mad or otherwise destroyed. He married ARIADNE, whom THESEUS had deserted in the island of Naxos. Later he took the place of HESTIA as one of the twelve Olympians and raised his mother from Hades under the name of Thyone.

The important festivals, among them the ELEUSINIAN MYSTERIES and the Athenian Antestheria, celebrated the cult of Dionysus as the DAEMON of reviving vegetation in the spring. An influential development of this cult was ORPHISM, which in turn influenced the philosophies of PYTHAGORAS and PLATO. Euripides' play THE BACCHANTS tells the story of Dionysus' gory triumph over PENTHEUS, king of Thebes. It is generally acknowledged that drama, especially tragedy, developed out of the traditional ceremonies performed at Dionysian festivals to celebrate the death and resurrection of the god.

Directory   The name of the executive body of government in France created by the Constitution of 1795 during the FRENCH REVOLUTION; it lasted from October 1795 to November 1799. The Directory consisted of five men elected by the Council of Five Hundred and the Council of the Elders (or *Anciens*). Ineffective because of internal dissensions, corruption, and bankruptcy, it was overthrown by NAPOLEON.

dirge   A lamentation sung or recited at a funeral or composed in commemoration of a death.

Dirty Hands (Les Mains sales, 1948; tr 1949)   A drama by Jean-Paul SARTRE. The play was produced on Broadway under the title *Red Gloves*. Louis's faction of the Proletarian Party consider Hoederer's policies inexpedient.

To kill him, the young intellectual Hugo is sent to Hoederer's house as a secretary, accompanied by his wife Jessica. Hugo delays his murder, however, increasingly impressed by Hoederer. He finally shoots him when he finds Hoederer kissing Jessica, but he does it with no definable motive, neither jealousy nor political conviction. The Party eventually switches to Hoederer's policies, and, after his prison term, Hugo is examined to see if he is "salvageable" for further Party work; if not, he will be shot. In despair because Hoederer's death now has no public meaning, as the act of killing has no private meaning for him, Hugo tries to claim the significance of both by refusing to be "salvageable." The play dramatizes the dilemma that, in order to accomplish anything, a man must be willing to have "dirty hands"—that is, apparently, to accept the argument that the end justifies the means. Hoederer, who does so, seems most "real" as a person to Hugo and Jessica; idealistic Hugo suffers when he discovers that he cannot.

Dis   A name for HADES and hence the lower world.

Dismas   The usual name in the APOCRYPHA for the penitent thief. Dismas was crucified with JESUS. He became the patron saint of thieves. The impenitent thief is commonly known as *Gesmas* or *Gestas*. Longfellow, in his GOLDEN LEGEND, calls the penitent Titus and his fellow thief Dumachus.

Disney, Walt[er Ellis] (1901–1966)   American motion-picture producer and pioneer in animated films. Disney began as a commercial artist; in 1923 he went to Hollywood and created the first of his animated cartoons. His series of films featuring Oswald the Rabbit won wide favor. After Oswald came the universally famous Mickey Mouse and Donald Duck. He produced *The Three Little Pigs* in 1933 and thereafter turned his attention to full-length animated pictures; *Snow White and the Seven Dwarfs* (1936), *Fantasia* (1940), and *Dumbo* (1942) are among the best known of these. *The Living Desert* (1953) was the first in a long line of distinguished and original documentary films on wildlife and nature. Disney created a multimillion-dollar film and amusement empire, which continued to produce films under his auspices, although he himself became less intimately involved in the production process.

Disraeli, Benjamin (first earl of Beaconsfield, 1804–1881)   English statesman and novelist. A member of Parliament, leader of the opposition in Commons, thrice chancellor of the exchequer, and twice prime minister, Disraeli was created a peer in 1876. It was by his initiative that Britain acquired the Suez canal in 1875, and he was responsible for having Queen Victoria proclaimed Empress of India and for negotiating "peace with honor" at the Congress of Berlin. As a young man, Disraeli had hesitated in deciding between a political and a literary career; his best novels, written at this time, are marked by acute wit, sharp realism, and a totally individual and often fantastic style.

His novels include *Vivian Grey* (1826) and *The Young Duke* (1831), his two earliest works; *Contarini Fleming*, a psychological romance (1832), and *The Wondrous Tale of Alroy*, a historical novel (1833), both of which reveal the pride which Disraeli, a baptized Anglican, felt in his Jewish ancestry, a pride which he was to retain throughout his life; *Henrietta Temple*, a love story (1836); *Venetia* (1837), which presented in fictionalized form episodes from the lives of Byron and Shelley; CONINGSBY, OR THE NEW GENERATION, first in a projected political trilogy; SYBIL, the second in the series, a depiction of the Chartist movement with such a frank portrayal of labor conditions that it was instrumental in provoking factory reform; TANCRED, OR THE NEW CRUSADE, the last novel in the trilogy, an implicit proposal that English politics and church seek a revitalizing inspiration from Semitic sources; and two political novels dating from late in his political career, *Lothair* (1870) and *Endymion* (1880). Disraeli's nonfictional works are now chiefly of historical interest, but, like his novels, they exemplify his conservative convictions, his disdain for the theories of abstract rights and the a priori systems of the utilitarians, his trust in democratic Toryism, his acceptance of the duty of social reform, and his pride in empire and crown.

Dissertation on Roast Pig, A   One of the most famous of Charles LAMB's *Essays of Elia*. It is a humorous account of the "accidental discovery" of the process of cooking pork.

Dissertation upon Parties (1735)   A well-known political pamphlet by Henry ST. JOHN, Viscount Bolingbroke, which rejects the notion of divine right of kings and sets forth the idea of a king, free from the restrictions of party factionalism, who would assume leadership and preserve both a balanced government and traditional civil liberties.

dissociation of sensibility   A phrase coined by T. S. ELIOT in *The Metaphysical Poets* (1921). According to Eliot, the 17th-century poets could "feel their thought as immediately as the odour of a rose." In the poetry of John DONNE, for example, he saw a fusion of thought and feeling. But on into the latter part of the century, with the poetry of MILTON and DRYDEN, a dissociation of sensibility set in. Thought and feeling became disjointed, and poets became either intellectual or emotional, but not both. Like the French SYMBOLISTS, Eliot was trying to recapture a union of emotion and intellect.

dissonance   Harsh and inharmonious sounds that are discordant with the words and rhythms surrounding them in a line or sentence. Poets like Robert BROWNING used dissonance intentionally to create particular effects.

distich   The classical designation of a unit of two lines in a strophic poem for choral recitation. The term is used in English only in relation to or in translations of poetry from other languages. The elegaic distich of classical times consists of a hexameter followed by a pentameter, a form also used by Goethe and Schiller in poetic aphorisms. An example by Schiller, which is a characterization of the distich, reads, in Coleridge's translation:

> In the hexameter rises the fountain's silvery column,
> In the pentameter aye falling in melody back.

dithyramb (fr Gr, *dithyrambos*, "a choric hymn") A kind of lyric poetry sung in strophic verse by a chorus and leader in honor of the god DIONYSUS. Dithyrambic poetry flourished for several centuries. The subject matter was extended to stories of heroes and their exploits, but there remained a close association with Dionysus. In the 5th century, the music of the dithyramb became highly excited and more important than the words, giving rise to the modern connotation of frenzied, impassioned poetry. It was traditionally ascribed to Arion of Lesbos (about 620 BC), who was thereafter called the father of dithyrambic poetry. It was also said to be the origin of drama.

Dives (fr Lat, *dives*, "rich man")   The traditional name for the man of wealth in JESUS' parable of the beggar, LAZARUS (Luke 16:19). As the parable goes, Dives enjoys a sumptuous feast in his mansion, while Lazarus lies starving and ill at his gateway. In the hereafter, Lazarus is found safely in ABRAHAM'S BOSOM, while Dives suffers anguish in HELL.

Divine Comedy, The (Commedia, completed 1321; called *Divina commedia* after the 16th century)   An epic poem by DANTE, his major work. It has one hundred cantos in TERZA RIMA, divided equally (after an introductory canto in the first section) into three sections of thirty-three cantos each. The poet finds himself lost in the wood of Error on Good Friday, 1300. He is met by the spirit of Vergil, the great classical poet whom Dante considers the incarnation of the highest knowledge attainable by the human mind. Vergil conducts him through Hell to free him of the temptation to sin; then on Easter morning they begin the ascent of the mountain of Purgatory to purify Dante's soul of even the capacity for error. Vergil must leave Dante at the top of the mountain, for man alone, without grace, can go no further; but in the Earthly Paradise there Dante meets BEATRICE, who represents divine revelation, and she conducts him through Paradise to God. For details of each section, see INFERNO; PURGATORIO; PARADISO.

The cosmology, angelology, and theology of the work are based firmly on the system of St. Thomas AQUINAS, but Dante considered the Church of his time a "harlot" no longer serving God—he meets seven popes in the Inferno, for instance—and was therefore frequently considered a heretic. The characters whom Dante meets on his journey are drawn largely from ancient Roman history and from recent and contemporary Italian history, including Dante's personal friends and enemies; their vivid portraiture and the constant allusions to human affairs make the work, although in structure a description of the Beyond, actually a realistic picture and intensely involved analysis of every aspect of earthly human life. Dante's literal journey is also an allegory of the progress of the individual soul toward God and the progress of political and social mankind toward peace on earth; it is a compassionate, although moral, evaluation of human nature and a mystic vision of the Absolute toward which it strives. Thus the universality of the drama and the lyric vigor of the poetry are far more important than the specific doctrinal content.

Diving into the Wreck (1973)   A collection of poems by Adrienne RICH. As the title suggests, the speaker in these poems dives into the wreckage of life and tries to find meaning. Rich uses water imagery, a metaphor for the origin of life, to explore the "wreck" of civilization and to relate her experiences as a "survivor." Patriarchy and male-dominated culture are viewed as crippling elements. The poet's thesis is that the nurturing proclivity of women should form the basis for a new kind of human community, a society unscarred by sexual distinctions. The general tone of the book is political. Much of the argument is embedded in metaphor and matriarchal myths. The poems are written mostly in first person and follow the unrhymed, open form of random thoughts being recorded. The volume received the National Book Award in 1974.

Divinity School Address, The (1838)   An address by Ralph Waldo EMERSON. Delivered before the graduates of the Harvard Divinity School, the address shocked Boston's conservative clergymen. Emerson stressed the divinity of man and the humanity of Christ. He denied miracles and did not quote scripture. Evil was represented as possessing a negative character; instead of a positive force, it became a vacuum into which good would easily flow. Further, he upheld intuition, rather than ritual, as a means of knowing God.

Dix, Otto (1891–1961)   German painter. Prior to 1920, Dix painted in a variety of styles, experimenting with IMPRESSIONISM, CUBISM, and DADA; afterwards he became, along with George GROSZ, a leader of the *Neue Sachlichkeit* ("new objectivity") movement, with which he is generally associated. His work is painstakingly detailed, but features are grossly distorted and intensely expressive of his revulsion at war and all forms of human degradation. His portraits, like that of the dancer Anita Berber (1925), are gentler but just as fastidious and incisive. At the end of his career, after World War II, he painted large, expressionistic religious and allegorical scenes.

Dixie   A nostalgically regarded American paradise in the South. It is also the popular name of a song, originally entitled "I Wish I Was in Dixie's Land," composed by Daniel Decatur Emmett in 1859. A great favorite in the South, the song was taken up by the soldiers in the Confederate army. Fanny Crosby wrote a Union version of the text in 1861, known as "Dixie for the Union."

The origin of the word *Dixie* is obscure. It has been suggested that it is related to the Mason and Dixon line; others believe that a Louisiana bank, printing its pre-Civil War bills in French with a big *DIX* ("ten") in the middle of the ten-dollar notes, made the South the land of "dixies." A further, ironic derivation is from the name of a slaveholder on Manhattan Island in the late 18th century; so benevolent was he that when his slaves were moved down south, they pined for "Dixie's land" up north.

Dixon, Jim   In Kingsley Amis's novel LUCKY JIM, a young university teacher beset by comic misfortunes.

djinn   See JINN.

Döblin, Alfred (1878–1957)   German novelist, essayist, and physician. A Jew and a Socialist, Döblin fled Germany in 1933, living for a time in France and later in the U.S. He returned to Germany in 1945 as a convert to Catholicism but went back to France in 1951, where he remained for the rest of his life. Döblin was one of the leading narrative writers associated with EXPRESSIONISM, and his novels reflect an interest in the political and social forces that affect individuals. His major novel, *Berlin Alexanderplatz* (1929; tr 1931), is a masterpiece of realistic description and probing insights into the psychological torment of an ex-convict attempting to reintegrate his life with "normal" society. Stylistically, the novel reveals the influence of DOS PASSOS and James JOYCE.

Dobrolyubov, Nikolay Aleksandrovich (1836–1861)   Russian journalist and literary critic. After graduating from the St. Petersburg Pedagogical Institute in 1857, Dobrolyubov began his brief career on the journal *Sovremennik* (*The Contemporary*). Like his colleague CHERNYSHEVSKY, Dobrolyubov emphasized the social usefulness of literature. The best known of his critical essays are *Tyomnoye Tsarstvo* (*The Kingdom of Darkness*, 1859), a study of Ostrovsky's drama *The Storm*; *Chto takoye Oblomovshchina?* (*What Is Oblomovshchina?*, 1859), on Goncharov's novel *Oblomov*; and *Kogda zhe pridyot nastoyashchy den?* (*When Will the Real Day Come?*, 1860), on Turgenev's novel *On the Eve*. BELINSKY, CHERNYSHEVSKY, and Dobrolyubov formed the triumvirate of 19th-century critics most often cited in Soviet literary criticism.

doctor   A scholastic or honorary title conferred by a university. Today in English the word is commonly synonymous with physician, from the degree M.D., Doctor of Medicine. In the medieval universities, doctors were advanced students who were usually also teachers. The Schoolmen, or theologians who lectured in the cloisters and cathedral schools, were also called doctors.

Dr. Faustus, The Tragical History of (first performed 1588; first pub 1604)   A play by Christopher MARLOWE. The yearning for the infinite that characterizes Marlowe's heroes is embodied in Dr. Faustus, the seeker after power through knowledge. The legend of the scholar who sells his soul to the Devil becomes a powerful portrait of a man torn by conflicting desires. In a scene that borrows from earlier morality drama, a good and bad angel, external representations of inner conflict, battle over the soul of Faustus. Despite the moral at the end, which advises the wise to heed the awful fate of Faustus, Marlowe's attitude throughout is one of sympathy and understanding for the boundless longings of his hero.

Doctor in Spite of Himself, The   See MÉDECIN MALGRÉ LUI, LE.

Dr. Jekyll   See STRANGE CASE OF DR. JEKYLL AND MR. HYDE, THE.

Doctorow, E[dgar] L[awrence] (1931–   ) American novelist. Doctorow was educated at Kenyon College and, after service in the army, worked as an editor. His first two novels were attempts at combining serious thematic ideas with popular literary genres. *Welcome to Hard Times* (1960), using the format of the western, examines the power of evil over goodness and idealism. *Big as Life* (1966) employed devices from SCIENCE FICTION to expose the conflict and malaise of modern man. A serious political novel, *The Book of Daniel* (1971), was inspired by the execution of Julius and Ethel Rosenberg. Although all of his books received critical acclaim, it was not until the publication of RAGTIME that Doctorow became well known to the general public. In his next novel, *Loon Lake* (1980), he employed shifting perspectives, moving backward and forward in history; *Lives of the Poets* (1984) is a collection of short stories unified by its concluding novella. Doctorow's novel *World's Fair* won the American Book Award in 1986.

Doctors of the Church   Certain early Christian Fathers, noted for their exceptional learning and holiness, especially four in the Greek (or Eastern) Church and four in the Latin (or Western) Church.

Eastern Church   St. Athanasius of Alexandria (d 373), who defended the divinity of Christ against the Arians; St. Basil the Great of Caesarea (d ?379) and his co-worker St. Gregory of Nazianzus (d ?389); and the eloquent St. John Chrysostom (d 407), Archbishop of Constantinople.

Western Church   St. Jerome (d 420), translator of the Vulgate; St. Ambrose (d 397), bishop of Milan; St. Augustine (d 430), bishop of Hippo; and St. Gregory the Great (d 604), the pope who sent St. Augustine, the Apostle of the Anglo-Saxons, to England.

Doctor Zhivago (Doktor Zhivago, 1957)   A novel by Boris PASTERNAK. This famous book centers on the experiences of a member of the intelligentsia during the Russian Revolution. The hero of the story, Yury Zhivago, is a young doctor with a mild interest in the coming revolution and a great interest in literature. He composes poems, mostly with religious overtones; twenty-five of his verses form the last part of the novel. Zhivago's discussions with his uncle Kolya and his friends contain most of the explicit anti-Marxist passages that offended Soviet censors. The novel was refused publication in the Soviet Union but was published abroad, bringing down on Pasternak's head the wrath of Soviet officialdom. Soviet authorities were as much bothered by the religious spirit pervading the novel as they were by the outspoken opposition to Marxism, which is implied throughout the book in the frequent contrast between the revolution's attempt to order men's lives rationally and the free, living spirit Zhivago finds in nature and in such characters as his mistress, Lara. Zhivago's and the author's sympathies are always obviously with life, as opposed to the ideas about life held by the Marxists. The poetic spirit of the book is enhanced by the language in which it is written. In the original Russian, the lines often fall into cadences of verse and strike the reader with the intense force usually associated with well-written poetry.

Dodona   A famous oracle in the village of Dodona in Epirus and the most ancient of Greece. It was dedicated to ZEUS, and the oracles were delivered from the tops of oak and other trees, the rustling of the wind in the branches being interpreted by the priests. Also, brazen vessels and plates were suspended from the branches, and these, being struck together when the wind blew, gave various sounds from which responses were concocted. Hence the Greek phrase *kalkos Dodones* ("brass of Dodona"), a babbler, or one who talks an infinite deal of nothing.

According to tradition, two black pigeons took their flight from Thebes, in Egypt; one flew to Libya, and the other to Dodona. On the spot where the former alighted, the temple of Zeus Ammon was erected; in the place where the other settled, the oracle of Zeus was established, and there the responses were made by the black pigeons that inhabited the surrounding groves. This fable is probably based on a pun upon the word *peleiai*, which usually meant "old women" but, in the dialect of the Epirots, "pigeons or doves."

dog   An animal that in medieval art symbolizes fidelity. A dog is represented as lying at the feet of St. Bernard, St. Benignus, and St. Wendelin; as licking the wounds of St. Roch; as carrying a lighted torch in representations of St. Dominic. In monuments, the dog is placed at the feet of women to symbolize affection and fidelity, as a lion is placed at the feet of men to signify courage and magnanimity. Many of the Crusaders are represented with their feet on a dog, to show that they followed the standard of the Lord as faithfully as a dog follows the footsteps of his master.

Dogberry   A pompous but comical constable in Shakespeare's MUCH ADO ABOUT NOTHING. Dogberry has a habit of confusing his words, sagely remarking, for example, that "comparisons are odorous." He and his crony Verges take Borachio into custody as a suspicious character and ask Leonato to question him. Leonato fails to comprehend their garbled story, however, and Don John's plot against Hero and CLAUDIO nearly succeeds.

doggerel Originally, loose and irregular verse, often comic or burlesque. It gave the impression of having been quickly and casually composed, as in HUDIBRAS, Butler's satirical epic. A pejorative meaning has now become attached to the word, connoting triviality of subject matter and inexpertness of technique, as in "mere doggerel."

Dog Star Sirius, the brightest star in the firmament. Its influence was supposed in ancient times to cause great heat, pestilence, etc. It was called Dog Star (*Caniculus*) because it belongs to the constellation *Canis Major* (larger dog).

Doktor Faustus (1947; tr 1948) A novel by Thomas MANN. In it the intense and tragic career of the hero, Adrian LEVERKÜHN, a composer, is made to parallel the collapse of Germany in World War II. To achieve this end, Mann employs the device of having another character, Serenus ZEITBLOM, narrate Leverkühn's story from memory, while the war is going on, and intersperse his narrative with remarks about the present situation. In this way, it is implied that it is the same demonic and always potentially destructive energy inherent in Leverkühn's music that is also, on a larger scale, behind the outburst of Nazism. Mann thus suggests that the violent FAUSTIAN drive, when it is not diverted into art or when there is no single artistic genius to harness it into creative process, will be perverted and result in grossly subhuman degradation. Thus, Mann is concerned here with his favorite theme, the artist's isolation in the world, but, whereas earlier treatments such as TONIO KRÖGER had shown the artist attempting to get along with the world's values, here the world is seen attempting to cope with a force that is proper only to art.

Dolgoruki, Arkadi Makarovich The hero of Dostoyevsky's novel THE RAW YOUTH. Arkadi is the illegitimate son of Versilov.

Makar Ivanovich Dolgoruki The nominal father of Arkadi, Makar is an old former serf who has become a religious pilgrim. He preaches humility and love and a striving for seemliness in relations among men. He has often been compared to a similar peasant philosopher, Platon Karatayev in Tolstoy's WAR AND PEACE.

Dolliver Romance, The (1876) An unfinished novel by Nathaniel HAWTHORNE. It was supposed to have been published serially in *The Atlantic Monthly*, but the author died before his plans were realized.

Dr. Dolliver attempts to prepare an elixir of life so that he might live to care for his granddaughter, Pansie. In contrast to the selfless Dolliver, Colonel Dabney demands the elixir for purely selfish reasons. Dabney finally dies, ironically, of an overdose of the elixir.

Doll's House, A (1879) A play by Henrik IBSEN. Sheltered, petted, and expected to behave like an amiable nitwit by first her father and then her husband, Nora Helmer has committed forgery in order to get money to save her husband's life. Though she has repaid the money, her husband finally finds out about her act. His behavior makes Nora realize that, in their eight years of marriage, he has never looked on her as a human being but only as a doll, and she leaves him in order to learn to become a person in her own right.

Dombey and Son (1848) A novel by Charles DICKENS. The proud, unfeeling Mr. Dombey has but one ambition in life: to have a son so that his firm might be called Dombey and Son. When his son Paul is born, he promises to fulfill this ambition, which overrides even grief at the death of Mrs. Dombey. Young Paul, a delicate, sensitive boy, is quite unequal to the great things expected of him; he is sent to Mr. Blimber's school and gives way under the strain of the discipline. In his short life, he wins the love of all who know him. Mr. Dombey is embittered by Paul's death. Florence, his daughter, lives on with him, trying desperately to win his love, but she has succeeded only in incurring his hatred because she lives while her brother died. Dombey marries again, but his second wife, Edith Granger, runs off with Mr. Carker, his business manager. Florence marries the kind young Walter Gay. Dombey's firm fails, and, alone and miserable, he finds himself longing for the sweet and kind daughter whom he treated so coldly. The two are reconciled, and Dombey tries to expiate his past through his grandchildren.

The novel is noted for its complex structure. The symbolism of death as the sea and of life as the flow of the river into the sea, seen often in Dickens's later novels, is first used here.

Dombrovsky, Yuri Osipovich (1909–1978) Soviet novelist. Arrested in 1937, Dombrovsky spent the next twenty years of his life in a Siberian labor camp, returning to Moscow in 1957. He produced one of the very few investigations of the purge years of 1938–39 to be published in the Soviet Union, *Khranitel drevnostei* (1964; tr *The Keeper of Antiquities*, 1969), in which the setting of a museum headed by a rather ignorant but ideologically correct military man serves as microcosm of the general madness and paranoia in Soviet society under Stalin. His other notable works include *Obezyana prikhodit za svoim cherepom* (*The Monkey Is Coming to Get His Skull*, 1959) and *Fakultet nenuzhnykh veshchey* (*The Faculty of Useless Things*, 1978), a personal memoir of his prison experience, published in Paris.

Dom Casmurro (1900) A novel by Joachim Maria MACHADO DE ASSIS. The narrator, a middle-aged lawyer nicknamed Dom Casmurro (roughly "Mr. Peevish") because of his difficult disposition, reflects on his adolescence and on his youthful romance with Capitú, whom he later married. An aura of uncertainty and ambiguity hovers over the book—not even the question of Capitú's adulterous relationship with Escobar, her husband's best friend, is fully settled. Written in a limpid, wryly humorous style, the novel is largely plotless and is frequently interrupted by the narrator's asides. The book was translated into English in 1953 (repr 1966) by H. Caldwell.

Domdaniel (fr Lat, *domus*, "house; home," *Danielis*, "of Daniel") A fabled abode of evil spirits, gnomes, and enchanters, "under the roots of the ocean" off Tunis, or elsewhere. It first appears in Chaves and Cazotte's *Continuation of the Arabian Nights* (1788–93), was introduced by Southey into his *Thalaba the Destroyer* (1801), and was used by CARLYLE as synonymous with a den of iniquity.

It was the alma mater of the infamous Madame Mim in T. H. WHITE's *The Sword in the Stone* (1939).

Domenichino (real name Domenico Zampieri, 1581–1641) Italian painter. A product of the eclectic academy of the Carracci at Bologna, Domenichino is noted for his religious and mythological works, including the *Last Communion of St. Jerome* (1614) and several fresco and easel treatments of the life of St. Cecilia, patroness of music.

Domesday Book (or Doomsday Book; ME, *domesday*, "day of judgment"; 1086) Latin record of a census and survey of most of England. It was compiled at the order of William the Conqueror. All property is described and evaluated in detail, along with a census of its inhabitants and its domestic animals, as of (1) the time of Edward the Confessor, (2) the time of William's bestowal of the estates on their new owners, and (3) the time of the survey and future potential. The records were probably so named because they were the final authority for property litigation; they served as the basis for tax assessments until 1522. Other similar records were often called the *Domesday Book* of a given locality; E. L. Masters used the title for a collection of verse (1920).

Dominic, St. (1170–1221) Spanish-born Roman Catholic priest and founder of the Dominican order. An important church official in his native Spain, St. Dominic went to Languedoc in 1205 to preach orthodox doctrine to the Albigenses, but, contrary to the tradition, he was not an "inquisitor," nor did he take a personal part in the bloody massacre of the Albigenses, who held to the Manichaean heresy. In 1215 he organized his band of followers into the Dominican order, or Preaching Friars, devoted to missionary work.

Dominicans The popular name for the Order of Preachers founded by St. Dominic in 1215. The most famous member of the Order was a theologian, St. Thomas AQUINAS. The Dominicans early acquired the punning sobriquet *Domini canes* (Lat, "dogs of the Lord") because of their swift and vigorous penetration into the life of the Church over all of Europe. In England, they were formerly called Black Friars, from their black dress; in France, Jacobins, because their mother establishment in Paris was in the rue St. Jacques.

Dom Juan ou le festin de pierre (Don Juan or the Stone Guest, 1665) A prose comedy by MOLIÈRE. It is derived from the play EL BURLADOR DE SEVILLA Y EL CONVIDADO DE PIEDRA of Tirso de Molina. The rake DON JUAN abducts Elvire, marries her, and abandons her—not the first time he has so mistreated a woman. He then ironically invites the statue of a man he has murdered to dinner; the statue accepts and returns the invitation, and, as it takes Don Juan by the hand, a fiery chasm opens and swallows him. Molière added the character Elvire as well as many characteristic touches to this grim tale. There are scenes of sparkling comedy; the valet Sganarelle is timidity incarnate, and Don Juan assumes the traits common to the libertine nobility of Molière's day. Perhaps for this reason the play, though enormously popular, was suppressed. It was later put into verse by Thomas CORNEILLE.

Doña Bárbara (1929) A novel by Rómulo GALLEGOS. The central character, Doña Bárbara, as her name implies, symbolizes barbarism. Believing herself possessed of supernatural powers, she rules a vast domain on the Venezuelan *llanos* and bends men to her will through bribery, intimidation, and murder. Some saw in Doña Bárbara's rapacity and ruthlessness a resemblance to the practices of Juan Vicente Gómez, Venezuelan dictator when the book was published. As the dictator was among those who saw the resemblance, Gallegos went into exile. The novel was translated into English in 1931 (repr 1948) by Robert Malloy.

Donalbain In Shakespeare's MACBETH, the younger son of DUNCAN, the murdered king, and the brother of Malcolm. Donalbain flees to Ireland after his father's death.

Don Alvaro o la fuerza del sino (1835) A romantic tragedy in prose and verse by Ángel Saavedra, duque de RIVAS. Don Alvaro, in love with Doña Leonor, accidentally kills the girl's father, then slays her two brothers in a duel. Before he dies, the younger brother kills Doña Leonor in the mistaken belief that she is the paramour of his father's murderer. Stricken with grief, Don Alvaro leaps to his death. This play was the basis of VERDI's opera *La forza del destino* (1862).

Donatello (real name Donato di Niccolò di Betto Bardi, 1386–1466) Florentine sculptor. An associate of Filippo BRUNELLESCHI and Lorenzo GHIBERTI, Donatello studied antique sculpture but rejected the serenity of its idealized beauty in favor of a more vigorous style. In stone and bronze, in reliefs and in free-standing statues admirably integrated with their architectural setting, he stressed power of expression and dramatic action. His masterpieces include *The Boy David*, the first large bronze free-standing nude since classical times, and the bronze equestrian statue of Gattamelata, also the first of its kind since antiquity.

Donatus (4th century) The most famous Latin grammar, the full title of which is *Donatus de octibus partibus orationis*. It was named after its author, Aelius

Donatus, a Roman grammarian (fl 333), who was one of the instructors of St. Jerome.

Don Carlos (1787)   A play by Friedrich SCHILLER, loosely based on the life of the son of the Spanish king Philip II. Don CARLOS's libertarian idealism is shared by the older and more experienced Marquis Posa, and the two plot against the tyrannical king. The prince, however, is suspected; in order to save him, Posa contrives to draw all suspicion upon himself and is murdered by the king. Carlos is then offered his freedom, but, in a last, unconsidered burst of idealism, he defies the king and is turned over to the Inquisition for execution. The play is the basis of VERDI's opera *Don Carlos* (1867).

Donizetti, Gaetano (1797–1848)   Prolific Italian composer of opera. Drawing on the conventions established by ROSSINI, Donizetti wrote some seventy works in the typical patterns of 19th-century Italian opera. His works show lyric grace but little refinement. They were composed at great speed for opera houses in which novelty was an important factor. He wrote both comic and tragic operas; neglected for a time, many of them are now back in performance. His most famous tragic operas are *Lucrezia Borgia* (1833), *Maria Stuarda* (1834), *Lucia di Lammermoor* (1835), *Roberto Devereux* (1837), and *La favorite* (1840). Of his comic operas, the most frequently performed are *L'elisir d'amore* (1832), *La fille du régiment* (1840), and *Don Pasquale* (1843).

Don Juan   A legendary profligate. The origin of the central theme of his widespread legend—that of a statue of a dead man who accepts a libertine's invitation to dinner —is not known. Its first appearance in any literary form was in Tirso de Molina's EL BURLADOR DE SEVILLA, which gave the hero the identity that he has retained ever since: Don Juan, a young nobleman of Seville. It also suggested the internal complications of his nature that have endlessly fascinated writers and composers. The name of Tirso's hero quickly became a synonym for an obsessive and unscrupulous pursuer of women.

The basic plot of this play soon reached France, by way of Italy, and was used in several plays, most notably Molière's DOM JUAN OU LE FESTIN DE PIERRE, which introduced the figure of Elvire, Don Juan's wife. The attempts of English writers to treat Don Juan, such as SHADWELL's *The Libertine* (1676), were unimpressive until G. B. Shaw included his "Don Juan in Hell" scene in MAN AND SUPERMAN. The only significant one of several Spanish versions of the legend after *El burlador de Sevilla* was DON JUAN TENORIO (1844), by José Zorrilla y Moral. Among the French versions after Molière's day were stories and plays by Prosper MERIMÉE, DUMAS PÈRE, Alfred de MUSSET, BALZAC, and FLAUBERT. PUSHKIN wrote a short verse drama that closely followed the Don Juan legend, *The Stone Guest* (see LITTLE TRAGEDIES).

The most famous of all forms of the story is undoubtedly Mozart's great opera *Don Giovanni* (1787), written to a libretto by Lorenzo DA PONTE, although there were several slightly earlier operatic versions. Another outstanding musical work inspired by the Don Juan legend is Richard STRAUSS's tone poem *Don Juan* (1888).

Don Juan (1819–1824)   An unfinished epic satire by Lord BYRON. Byron's DON JUAN only slightly resembles the legendary Spanish rake. He begins his adventures in Spain, but is sent abroad at the age of sixteen by his mother, Donna INEZ. His ship is wrecked, and he is cast up on a Greek island, where he is nursed back to health by the beautiful Haidée. Lambro, the girl's father, discovers the lovers together, captures Juan, and sells him as a slave to GULBEYAS, the sultana of Constantinople. However, Juan then falls in love with Dudu, a beautiful girl in the harem, and so arouses the jealousy of Gulbeyas that he barely escapes with his life. His next adventure takes him to Russia, where as a soldier he attracts the favor of the Empress Catherine. She sends Juan to England as a courier. The poem breaks off with Juan in England.

Don Juan is sprinkled with long digressions in which Byron, through his hero, gives his views on wealth, power, society, chastity, poets, diplomats, and England. It is written in *ottava rima* and, even in its incomplete state, contains sixteen thousand lines in its sixteen cantos.

Don Juan Tenorio (1844)   A drama in verse by José ZORRILLA Y MORAL. In Zorrilla's version of the DON JUAN legend, the hero falls in love with the virtuous Doña Inés, repents of his sins, and is saved by her prayers on his behalf. Though Zorrilla himself deprecated his work, it is one of Spain's most popular plays and is regularly performed during the first week in November.

Donleavy, J[ames] P[atrick] (1926–   )   Irish novelist, dramatist, and short-story writer. American-born, Irish-educated, Donleavy became an Irish citizen in 1967. His first novel, *The Ginger Man*, was published in Paris in 1955. It was not until 1965 that it appeared in an unexpurgated edition in the U.S. The central character, Sebastian Dangerfield, an American expatriate law student at Dublin's Trinity College, is the brawling outsider who lives in a world of fantasy to escape despair and loneliness. Donleavy uses the third person to describe what Dangerfield does, the first person to reveal his thoughts, enabling him to be both objective and subjective. Donleavy claims that his themes emerge from an emotional autobiography and acknowledges KAFKA as a principal influence. His other novels include *A Singular Man* (1963), *The Onion Eaters* (1971), *The Destinies of Darcy Dancer, Gentleman* (1977), *Schultz* (1979), and *Leila* (1983). He has also written the tongue-in-cheek yet satirical *De Alfonce Tennis, the Superlative Game of Creative Champions* (1984).

Donne, John (1572?–1631)   English poet, first and greatest of the METAPHYSICAL POETS. Donne was of good family, bred as a Roman Catholic, well educated in theology and law, and in his youth a lover of company and elegant women. In 1614, after a long period of hardship following his secret marriage to Anne More, and as his hopes of secular preferment waned, he was converted to Anglicanism. Ordained in 1615, six years later he became dean of St. Paul's Cathedral and possibly the most influential preacher in England.

Donne's best-known poetry falls into two classes, the early ironic and erotic verse and the later religious poems. In his verse satires and in such lyrics as Go and Catch a Falling Star (often entitled "Song") and "Woman's Constancy," Donne makes a witty display of worldliness, skepticism, and fickleness. Other poems, such as "The Extasie," The Anniversaries, The Canonization, and Twicknam Garden, are moving expressions of passion or grief. Donne's love poetry is remarkable for its close analysis of the nature and psychology of love; in its emotional sophistication and highly personal tone, it differs markedly from the conventional courtly love poetry of Donne's day. The later religious poems powerfully express the yearning for union with God of a man obsessed with death, oppressed by his sense of human limitation and sin, by an almost invincible doubt of salvation. Among the most famous of these poems are the sonnets "Death Be Not Proud" and "Batter My Heart, Three Person'd God" and the "Hymne to God the Father."

Donne also wrote numerous elegies, epigrams, and verse letters; many sermons; and the Devotions upon Emergent Occasions, an extraordinary series of meditations on the theme of sickness and mortality. This last prose work, together with The Anniversaries, reveals his preoccupation with the themes of mutability and death, and of the paradoxical human union of spirit and matter, themes which are crucial even in the love poems.

Donne's poetry is marked by intellectual power, deep learning, and intense emotion. His imagery, to which the adjective *metaphysical* was chiefly applied, is powerful and striking; it was drawn from Scholastic philosophy, the science of the day, trades and professions, and the simple, commonplace things of everyday life. His meter is irregular and dramatic, preserving the cadence and immediacy of ordinary speech.

Donne's poems were published in 1633 and were very popular and widely imitated during the next generation. He was almost unknown, however, during the 18th century and was disapproved of by Samuel Johnson. A few of the Romantics appreciated his works, but it was only in the 20th century that interest in him was revived to any considerable extent. See CONCEIT.

Donnybrook Fair   A fair held near Dublin in August from the time of King John till 1855. It was noted for its bacchanalian orgies and light-hearted rioting. The name has become proverbial for a disorderly gathering.

Donoso, José (1924–   )   Chilean novelist and short-story writer. His sometimes dreamlike novels, while not an interconnected series in the strict sense, constitute a continuing exploration of the Chilean culture. Coronación examines the decadence of the wealthy class in Chile. It was followed by *Este domingo* (1966; tr *This Sunday*, 1967), *El lugar sin limites* (1966; tr *Hell Has No Limits*, 1972), and *El obsceno pajaro de las noches* (1970; tr *The Obscene Bird of Night*, 1973), all of which delve into aspects of the decay and corruption of Chilean society. Other works of fiction include *Cuentos* (1971; tr *Charleston and Other Stories*, 1977); the three novellas in *Tres novelitas burguesas* (1973; tr *Sacred Families*, 1977); and the novels *La misteriosa desparación de la marquesita de Loria* (1980) and *A House in the Country* (1984). *Historia personal del "boom"* (1972; tr *The Boom in Spanish-American Literature*, 1977) is a work of personal history and literary criticism.

Don Quixote (1605, 1615)   A novel by Miguel de Cervantes, the full title of which is *Don Quixote de la Mancha, El ingenioso hidalgo*. Alonso Quijano is a gaunt country gentleman, kindly and dignified, who lives in the province of La Mancha. His mind is so crazed by reading romances of chivalry that he believes himself called upon to redress the wrongs of the whole world. Changing his name to Don Quixote de la Mancha, he is knighted by an innkeeper whose miserable hostelry he mistakes for a castle. As his lady love, he chooses a peasant girl named Aldonza Lorenzo, whom he transforms into Dulcinea del Toboso. Don Quixote now sallies forth into the world, but after several mishaps, including a beating administered by some merchants whom he challenges to a passage at arms, he returns to his home. Undaunted, he asks Sancho Panza, an ignorant rustic, to be his squire and promises to reward him with the governorship of the first lands they conquer. Riding Rocinante, a nag as bony as himself, Don Quixote sets out a second time, accompanied by Sancho on his ass Dapple.

During his travels, Don Quixote's overexcited imagination blinds him to reality: he thinks windmills to be giants, flocks of sheep to be armies, and galley-slaves to be oppressed gentlemen. Toward the end of the novel, Sancho is named governor of the isle of Barataria, a mock title given to him by some noblemen whose only aim is to make sport of the squire and his master. After being bested in a duel with the Knight of the White Moon, in reality a student of his acquaintance in disguise, Don Quixote, tired and disillusioned, returns to La Mancha and, shortly before his death, renounces books of knight-errantry.

The first part of *Don Quixote*, which may have been conceived while Cervantes was in prison, was first printed in 1605 in Madrid by Juan de la Cuesta. In 1614 a second part was published by an unknown author who used the pseudonym Alonso Fernández de Avellaneda. This bit of plagiarism, though not an unusual practice at the time, spurred Cervantes to complete his own sequel, which appeared the following year and is usually considered superior to the first part.

Although it is generally agreed that Cervantes meant his novel to be a satire on the exaggerated chivalric romances of his time, some critics have interpreted it as an ironic story of an idealist frustrated and mocked in a materialistic world. Others have seen it as a veiled attack on the Catholic church or on contemporary Spanish politics. To many, the contrasting figures of Don Quixote and Sancho Panza, the visionary idealist and the practical realist, symbolize the duality of the Spanish character. With its variegated assortment of minor characters, shepherds, innkeepers, students, priests, and nobles, the novel also gives a panoramic view of 17th-century Spanish society. At the same time, its essential humanity has made it a universal favorite. See CLAVILEÑO.

Don Segundo Sombra (1926; tr Shadows in the Pampas, 1935)   A novel by Ricardo GÜIRALDES. Güiraldes was a wealthy cosmopolite who traveled widely, but, in this novel, he draws on his childhood experiences at La Porteña, his family's ranch in Buenos Aires province. The narrator of the novel is a boy who runs away from the aunts who have raised him and attaches himself to Don Segundo Sombra, an itinerant ranch worker. During their five-year odyssey, the boy learns from his teacher not only how to be an expert cowboy and horseman but also how to live with courage and honor, according to the gaucho code. After discovering that he is the illegitimate son of a wealthy rancher, who has left him his estate, the young man accepts his legacy and acquires a measure of formal culture. Don Segundo, feeling that there is no longer need for his tutelage, goes on his lonely way. Considered the outstanding prose fictional example of GAUCHO LITERATURE, the novel captures the essence of the gaucho myth in the scenes of life on the pampas and, above all, in the idealized figure of Don Segundo.

Dooley, Mr.   See DUNNE, FINLEY PETER.

Doolittle, Dr.   The animal-loving doctor hero of a series of children's books by Hugh Lofting (1886–1947), the English-born American writer and illustrator. The kindly and resourceful Doctor, the first man to learn the languages of the animals, with an entourage that includes Dab-Dab the duck, Jip the dog, and Gub-Gub the pig, takes part in many delightful and fantastic adventures, including *The Adventures of Dr. Doolittle*, *Dr. Doolittle's Circus*, and *The Voyages of Dr. Doolittle*.

Doolittle, Hilda (pen name H.D., 1886–1961) American poet. Doolittle met and fell in love with Ezra POUND in 1905, when she was an undergraduate at Bryn Mawr, he a graduate student at the University of Pennsylvania. Her father put a stop to the romance, but not before Pound had given her a hand-bound sheaf of poems

called *Hilda's Book*, the full story of what, for H.D., was a rapturous affair from which she never fully recovered; Pound's poems to her did not come to light until the publication of *End to Torment: A Memoir of Ezra Pound by H.D.* (1979; ed N. H. Pearson and M. King). The memoir was begun in 1958, when H.D. was undergoing psychoanalysis in Switzerland and while Pound was still incarcerated in St. Elizabeths mental hospital in Washington, D.C.

Doolittle, perhaps following Pound, went to Europe in 1911. Her poetry, noted for its precise visualizations of scenes, images, and objects, became almost immediately and forever identified with IMAGISM. In 1913 she married the English poet Richard ALDINGTON and thereafter lived abroad. She had numerous love relationships, the most enduring of which was with the English historical novelist Winifred BRYHER. *Sea Garden* (1916), her first book of poetry, was followed by *Hymen* (1921); *Heliodora and Other Poems* (1924); *Collected Poems* (1925; 1940); *Hippolytus Temporizes* (1927), a verse tragedy; *The Flowering of the Rod* (1946); and *Bid Me to Live* (1960). *Helen in Egypt* (1961), a book-length poem, was published posthumously. She also wrote fiction, usually dealing with classical themes, as in *Palimpsest* (1926) and *Hedylus* (1928).

Doon   A river in Ayrshire, Scotland, celebrated in the poems of Robert BURNS.

Doon de Mayence   A medieval cycle of CHANSONS DE GESTE about the heroes opposed, at least part of the time, to Charlemagne. They include the histories of GANELON, Ogier the Dane, and the four sons of Aymon.

Doppelgänger (Ger, *doppel*, "double," *gänger*, "walker")   An apparition that generally represents another side of a character's personality. The Doppelgänger can personify one's demonic counterpart (as in E.T.A. HOFFMANN's *The Devil's Elixirs*, 1816), or an alter ego, as in Poe's "William Wilson" (1839). Frequently the appearance of the apparition presages imminent death. It has been used by many writers, including DOSTOYEVSKY and CONRAD, for its psychological and philosophical fascination. Heinrich HEINE's poem "Der Doppelgänger" was set to music in one of Franz SCHUBERT's best-known lieder.

Doré, [Paul] Gustave (1832–1882)   French illustrator and graphic artist. Doré is famous for his imaginative and masterfully executed drawings and book illustrations, particularly his editions of Balzac's *Contes drolatiques* (1855), Cervantes's DON QUIXOTE (1863), and the Bible (1866). The paintings and sculptures he produced in his later years are less admired than his drawings and lithographs.

Doria, Andrea (c1468–1560)   Genoese admiral; called Father of Peace and Liberator of Genoa. In 1951 his name was given to a luxury liner of the Italian Line, which sank (July 25, 1956) during a transatlantic crossing after having been rammed by the S.S. *Stockholm*. The name is also that given to one of the main characters in SCHILLER's *Fiesko*.

Dorian (or Doric)   Pertaining to the Dorians, traditionally the last of the groups of tribes who invaded Greece in preclassical times. The so-called Dorian invasion, probably from the North, early in the 12th century BC, put an end to the Mycenaean era and was long thought to have caused a protracted Dark Age, although the process is now considered to have been much less clear-cut and complete than was formerly supposed.

In classical times, Doric attitudes were identified with solidity and simplicity, as in the Doric order of architecture, characterized by plain, chaste forms. The Dorian mode in music, a scale that may be reproduced by playing all the white notes from one D to the next on a piano, was regarded by Plato as being conducive to sobriety and other virtues needed by the citizen of an ideal state.

Dormouse (fr Fr, *dormir*, "to sleep")   The mouse in ALICE'S ADVENTURES IN WONDERLAND. The dormouse is thrust into a teapot by the Hatter and the March Hare.

Dorn, Ed[ward Merton] (1929–   )   American poet and novelist. Much of Dorn's poetry is clearly aligned with the work of the BLACK MOUNTAIN POETS. In *From Gloucester Out* (1964), he employs the techniques of PROJECTIVE VERSE and makes clear reference to the influence of Charles OLSON. Thematically, his poetry is concerned with human relationships and the natural and social forces that shape them. Dorn is also known for his keen sense of the American landscape, particularly the Northwest, especially in *Geography* (1965), *The North Atlantic Turbine* (1967), and *The Cosmology of Finding Your Spot* (1969). Dorn's best-known work is *Slinger* (1970–75), a book-length poem in four parts. It is a raucous, farcical epic, in which the hero embarks on a journey, in search ostensibly of millionaire Howard Hughes but really of the vitality of American frontier life or its contemporary equivalent. Dorn's *Collected Poems* was published in 1975.

Dorotea, La (1632)   A prose romance in dialogue by Lope de VEGA. He called it "the most beloved of my works." The novel is partly autobiographical, and the Dorotea of the title is the actress Elena Osorio, with whom Lope had an affair and whom he called Filis in other works. He wrote the book at an early age but revised it years later, including details of his liaison with Marta de Nevares. *La Dorotea* was influenced by *La Celestina* (1499), whose main character is reincarnated in Lope's work by Gerarda.

Dorothea, St.   A martyr under DIOCLETIAN about 303. St. Dorothea is represented with a rose branch in her hand, a wreath of roses on her head, and roses with fruit by her side; sometimes with also an angel carrying a basket with three apples and three roses. The legend is that Theophilus, the judge's secretary, scoffingly said to her, as she was going to execution, "Send me some fruit and roses,

Dorothea, when you get to Paradise." Immediately after her execution, while Theophilus was at dinner with a party of companions, a young angel brought to him a basket of apples and roses, saying, "From Dorothea in Paradise," and vanished. Theophilus, of course, was a convert from that moment. The story forms the basis of MASSINGER's tragedy *The Virgin Martyr* (1622).

Dos Passos, John [Roderigo] (1896–1970)   American writer. Dos Passos was one of a group of Harvard writers who graduated shortly before World War I. With E. E. CUMMINGS and Ernest HEMINGWAY, Dos Passos joined the Norton-Harjes Ambulance Service during the war. From this experience came his first book, *One Man's Initiation—1917* (1919) and, two years later, his first successful novel, THREE SOLDIERS. A newspaperman and freelance writer after the war, he published his next important novel, MANHATTAN TRANSFER, in 1925, a book that was significant both for his firm assumption of the role of the artist as social critic and for his first experiments with interior monologue, STREAM OF CONSCIOUSNESS, "newsreel," and cinematic techniques in fiction. In the late 1920s, he used "movie" techniques in two plays, *The Garbage Man* (1926) and *Airways, Inc.* (1928). In 1930 Dos Passos published THE 42ND PARALLEL, followed by *1919* (q.v.), and THE BIG MONEY, the three of which were published together as *U.S.A.* (q.v.) in 1937. The trilogy is noted for its technical innovations and mastery of language. Such devices as incisive biographies, "camera eye" (revealing the author's perspective), newsreel sequences, and free association are woven into the narrative proper to produce a formidable portrait of an alienated society. A massive achievement, *U.S.A.* is a vast portrait of American life, with the nation itself as protagonist. His second trilogy, eventually published under the title *District of Columbia* (1952), began with *Adventures of a Young Man* (1939). This saga of the Spottswood family also included *Number One* (1943) and *The Grand Design* (1949); together they mark the progression of Dos Passos's bitter disillusionment with his earlier left-wing views. In *The Ground We Stand On* (1941), with sketches of great Americans, he reaffirmed his concern for the freedom of the individual but in an increasingly conservative vein, strongly colored with pessimism.

As his own faith in the future waned, so did the broad appeal of Dos Passos's books, particularly since the stylistic innovations of his earlier work no longer had the same freshness and impact twenty or more years later. In the 1950s, Dos Passos ordered his subsequent novels into a series he called "Contemporary Chronicles." The first, *Chosen Country* (1951), is a romance, with autobiographical overtones, of the Pignatelli family, beginning before the Civil War. *Midcentury* (1961), the twelfth of the series, shows Dos Passos as still an acute critic of modern society. After its publication, he worked on various nonfiction pieces, including *The Best Times* (1966), a memoir, but returned in 1968 to his "forlorn Chronicles of Despair." The result was *Century's Ebb* (1975), which was completed shortly before his death and which contains a clear self-portrait, in the character of Jay Pignatelli. *The Fourteenth Chronicle* (1973) is a posthumously edited collection of his letters and diaries.

Dostoyevsky, Fyodor Mikhailovich (1821–1881)   Russian novelist. One of the most outstanding and influential writers of modern literature, Dostoyevsky was born in Moscow, the son of a doctor and the second of eight children. When he was sixteen years old, Dostoyevsky's mother died. A year later, he was enrolled in the Military Engineering School in St. Petersburg. His elder brother Mikhail had also applied but was turned down by medical examiners. Young Dostoyevsky was left alone, in an atmosphere uncongenial to his nature, without Mikhail, his closest friend, and with what he considered an insufficient allowance. His letters to his father begin to sound a note that is often to be heard in his later correspondence: his desperate need for money. Another problem was his work at the school: drawing plans for military fortifications interested him far less than reading literature. Before his graduation, in 1843, Dostoyevsky had already decided that his career would not be in military engineering. He remained in the army's service just a little over a year after graduation. He then resigned and took up his lifelong occupation as a writer.

Dostoyevsky's first publication (1844) was a translation of BALZAC's novel EUGÉNIE GRANDET. Meanwhile, he was working on a novel of his own, a work in epistolary form, entitled POOR FOLK. The manuscript reached the leading critic of the day, Vissarion BELINSKY, probably by way of Dostoyevsky's friend Dmitry Grigorovich and the poet Nikolay NEKRASOV. Belinsky read the work and launched into ecstatic praise for it. *Poor Folk* perfectly fulfilled his idea of what literature should be—it showed compassion for the poor and downtrodden and succeeded in stirring the humanitarian feelings of the reader. Belinsky's approval was enough to ensure Dostoyevsky's reputation as a talented new writer. The novel was published in 1846 in the *Petersburg Miscellany*, edited by Nekrasov. A few weeks later, THE DOUBLE, Dostoyevsky's second work, appeared. This short novel is a study of a poor clerk's mental disintegration. It was less pleasing to the critics and public. In 1840 Dostoyevsky also published a short story, "Gospodin Prokharchin" ("Mr. Prokharchin"). The critical acclaim at first given Dostoyevsky's work was now absent: *The Double*, "Mr. Prokharchin," and "Khozyayka" ("The Landlady," 1847) were all failures in Belinsky's estimation. The adverse criticism strained Dostoyevsky's relations with Belinsky and the circle of young writers surrounding him, including Nekrasov and Ivan TURGENEV—the feud with Turgenev becoming a lifetime preoccupation of Dostoyevsky's.

A more serious problem than bad reviews or literary feuds began about this time for the young author: the onset of the epileptic attacks that were to plague him throughout his life. Some writers, including FREUD, have speculated that these attacks actually began earlier, about the time Dostoyevsky's father was murdered by his serfs in 1839. This theory holds that the attacks were a form of self-punishment for Dostoyevsky's suppressed wish for his father's death and that his later mania for gambling was similarly caused. The preoccupation with the theme of parricide in Dostoyevsky's last novel, THE BROTHERS KARAMAZOV, is also evidence of his feeling of guilt, according to this view.

In 1848 Dostoyevsky published three short stories: "Slaboye serdtse" ("A Faint Heart"), "Chestny vor" ("The Honest Thief"), and "Belye nochi" ("White Nights"). In the last of these stories, the emphasis on the unreal and miragelike quality of St. Petersburg foreshadows a theme that was developed further in some of his later works. At this time, Dostoyevsky was also working on a novel, *Netochka Nezvanova*, which he never completed. It was during this year that he became involved with a group of young intellectuals headed by Mikhail Vasilyevich Petrashevsky. The Petrashevsky circle, as the group was known, met to read and discuss the works of the French Utopian socialists and other political and social topics forbidden open discussion by the tsarist regime. In 1849 the members of the group were arrested. They were charged, among other things, with having read the banned letter of Belinsky to Nikolay GOGOL and of having conspired to set up a secret printing press. After eight months in prison, during which time he wrote another short story, "Malenky geroy" ("The Little Hero"), Dostoyevsky was taken, with his alleged fellow conspirators, to the site of their execution. At the last moment, they were informed that their sentence was actually to be exile and imprisonment in Siberia. The shattering experience of the near-execution never left Dostoyevsky. He used the episode in his novel THE IDIOT and mentioned it in his journalistic writings.

Dostoyevsky was sentenced to four years in the labor camp at Omsk, after which he was obliged to enlist for a four-year term in the army, most of which time he served at Semipalatinsk. These years have been described by Dostoyevsky as vitally important ones for his development as a writer. His enforced contact with the convicts at Omsk gave him a knowledge of the Russian lower classes possessed by no other Russian author. During his prison term the only book allowed him was the New Testament, which he read constantly and which directed his thoughts toward the religious view of life so prominent in his novels. The fruits of his observations and thought in the Omsk prison are contained in THE HOUSE OF THE DEAD.

While serving his army term, Dostoyevsky met and, after a hectic courtship, married the widow Marya Dmitryevna Isayeva in 1857. In 1859 he was allowed to resign from the army and to return to European Russia, settling first in Tver and then returning to St. Petersburg. In Siberia, he began to write again, and he arrived in the capital with two short novels: *Dyadushkin son* (*Uncle's Dream*) and THE FRIEND OF THE FAMILY, both published in 1859. In 1861 his brother Mikhail began to publish the journal *Vremya* (*Time*). In this periodical, Dostoyevsky published the novel THE INSULTED AND INJURED, in which one of his major ideas, the beneficial effects of suffering, was first enunciated. He also serialized his *House of the Dead* in the journal.

In the summer of 1862, Dostoyevsky made his first trip to Europe, visiting Paris, London, and Geneva. His impressions of what he saw are contained in *Zimnye zametki o letnykh vpechatleniyakh* (*Winter Notes on Summer Impressions*, 1863).

The journal *Vremya* was suppressed by the government in 1863 because of an unfortunate article on the Polish rebellion of that year. Dostoyevsky, who had been editing the publication, made his second trip abroad at this time. This time, however, he had a companion, Apollinariya (Polina) Suslova, a young woman who had contributed a short piece to *Vremya* in 1861. Dostoyevsky's relations with his wife had been strained for some time. Whether Polina was a cause or a result of this situation is unclear. It is certain, however, that Polina was a torment to him. She was reputedly Dostoyevsky's model for the "infernal woman" whom he depicted in his later novels. On the trip through Europe, Dostoyevsky visited the gambling houses at Wiesbaden, Germany, where he gave in to the mania that, for some years, was to continue to trouble him.

Returning to Russia in 1864, Dostoyevsky became editor of the new journal published by his brother. In this periodical, *Epokha* (*Epoch*), appeared NOTES FROM UNDERGROUND, the work that is generally cited, because of its artistic excellence and psychological acuteness, as the first of Dostoyevsky's mature writings. Dostoyevsky wrote the work while tending his dying wife, who was at last succumbing to the consumption that had long afflicted her. Shortly after her death, Dostoyevsky had another blow: the death of his brother Mikhail. Left with the care of Mikhail's family as well as with that of his own stepson, he labored desperately to make *Epokha* a successful publication. The conservative political slant he gave the journal lessened its popularity, however, and in 1865 the venture had to be abandoned. Dostoyevsky made another trip to Europe, where he again met Polina, did some gambling, and worked on a novel he hoped would pull him out of his financial predicament. This work, CRIME AND PUNISHMENT, was published in 1866. In the same year, Dostoyevsky published a short novel, THE GAMBLER. The deadline for this work was fast approaching, and the novelist had to hire a stenographer to take down the work in shorthand and transcribe it. The woman he hired for the job, Anna

Grigoryevna Snitkina, became Dostoyevsky's second wife, in 1867. The couple went abroad to escape creditors the following year. They lived in Dresden, Baden-Baden, and Geneva, always in financial straits made worse by Dostoyevsky's intermittent gambling sprees. On the trip to Geneva, they stopped off in Basel, where Dostoyevsky saw HOLBEIN's painting *Dead Christ* in the museum. The strong impression of the work prompted Dostoyevsky to include a discussion of it in the novel he was then writing. This work, published in serial form in 1868, was *The Idiot*. The effort involved in attempting to portray the saintly Myshkin in the novel was made more agonizing by the death of his infant daughter Sonya, at the age of three months.

During 1869 Dostoyevsky and Anna moved restlessly about Europe, from Switzerland, to Italy, to Austria, and finally to Dresden again. There a second daughter, Lyubov, was born. Dostoyevsky was at work during this period on one of his best short novels, THE ETERNAL HUSBAND. At the same time, he was making preliminary notes for a massive work, to be contained in several novels, that would deal with the religious problems that had been the center of his thought for some years. The work was to be "the life of a great sinner," tracing his early growth, his falling away from faith, and his ultimate redemption. The broad scope of ideas contained in the plan was to include all of Dostoyevsky's late novels. STAVROGIN, the sinister hero of THE POSSESSED, could be taken as a depiction of the great sinner who had lost his faith, as could Ivan KARAMAZOV. Arkady, the young hero of THE RAW YOUTH, in some respects resembles the nascent sinner who has not yet set out on the journey through the "furnace of doubt" that leads to religious faith. The idea of a movement into the world and back to faith is also present in THE BROTHERS KARAMAZOV.

After his return to Russia in 1871, Dostoyevsky again entered journalistic work, editing the weekly *Grazhdanin* (*The Citizen*) in 1873–74. In 1876 he published the first part of his A DIARY OF A WRITER. This publication, which was also issued in 1877 and in 1880–81, contained articles on political, social, and literary topics, as well as some original short stories, including "Krotkaya" ("A Gentle Spirit," 1876) and "Son smeshnogo cheloveka" ("The Dream of a Ridiculous Man," 1877). These last years of Dostoyevsky's life were financially the best ones he had known. Professionally he was also at his peak, especially after the publication of THE BROTHERS KARAMAZOV. The climax of his long career came with his speech at the PUSHKIN celebration in Moscow in 1880, in which he cited the poet as a model of his own ideas about the unique, all-embracing universality of the Russian character. In January 1881, Dostoyevsky died in St. Petersburg.

Since his death, Dostoyevsky's reputation as one of the greatest writers in literary history has steadily grown. The acuteness of his psychological perceptions and analyses has amazed later experts in psychology, including Freud. Dostoyevsky's philosophical profundity has provided a rich field of investigation and imitation for writers and philosophers. His range of philosophical ideas and approaches has led to his being acclaimed as a forerunner by such diverse groups as Russian Orthodox thinkers and atheistic existentialist writers. With TOLSTOY, Dostoyevsky ranks as a supreme master of the realistic novel—Russia's major contribution to literature. Dostoyevsky's artistic methods have until recently received less attention than his psychological and philosophical ideas. That he was above all a master artist has been attested by readers the world over and, perhaps more convincingly, by other great novelists who have an intimate knowledge of the craft of fiction.

In the Soviet Union, Dostoyevsky has enjoyed less public recognition than he has in other countries. His well-known animus toward socialism and his emphasis on religion and the innate irrationalism of the psychological processes of the individual mind have made him unattractive to the guardians of Soviet literary policy.

Double, The (Dvoinik, 1846)   A short novel by DOSTOYEVSKY. The Double is a fantastic tale, similar in style and conception to some of GOGOL's work, particularly to Diary of a Madman (1835), which also depicts the mental disintegration of the hero. Yakov Petrovich GOLYADKIN, the hero of The Double, is a lowly civil servant who awkwardly and unsuccessfully pursues the daughter of his employer. After some cruel rebuffs, a strangeness enters Golyadkin's world, and another Golyadkin, his absolute double, appears on the scene. Where the old Golyadkin had fumbled, the young Golyadkin is adroit. This double is soon a favorite in exactly the way the first Golyadkin yearned to be. The nightmare ends when Golyadkin is taken away from his phantoms to a madhouse.

Doughty, Charles Montagu (1843–1926)   English traveler and writer. Doughty is best known for his Travels in Arabia Deserta (1888), an account of two years of tribulation and wandering in Arabia, notable for its vivid picture of Bedouin life and its curious, intriguing style, which combines English words and phrases with many Arabic expressions. Doughty also wrote a number of poems —which share some of the peculiarities of his prose—of which the best known is the lengthy The Dawn in Britain (1906).

Douglas   A family in Scottish history, legend, and romance. There were two branches: the Black Douglases, or senior branch, and the Red Douglases, who came to the fore later. They are prominent in Sir Walter SCOTT's novels, notably:

Sir James   The first of the Black Douglases. See James DOUGLAS.

Archibald the Grim   Natural son of "the Good Sir James." He is prominent in The Fair Maid of Perth (1828).

James Douglas   Earl of Morton, one of the Red Douglases. He figures prominently in The Monastery (1820) and The Abbot (1820).

Ellen Douglas   Heroine of Scott's narrative poem, THE LADY OF THE LAKE.

Douglas, Lord Alfred (1870–1945)   English poet, noted as a sonnet writer. His relationship with Oscar Wilde provoked his father, Lord Queensberry, to action that led to Wilde's conviction for homosexual practices. See DE PROFUNDIS.

Douglas, James (called Black Douglas, 1286–1330) Scottish chieftain. In the days of Robert BRUCE and Edward II, Douglas invaded England and plundered many towns and villages in the North. In his History of Scotland, Sir Walter Scott writes: "It was said that the name of this indefatigable and successful chief had become so formidable that women in the northern countries, used to still their froward children by threatening them with the Black Douglas." Douglas destroyed an English garrison three times, and it is on one of these incidents that Scott based his novel Castle Dangerous (1832).

Douglas, [George] Norman (1868–1952)   English novelist and travel writer. Best known for the novel SOUTH WIND, Douglas lived for many years on the island of Capri and in Italy and other Mediterranean countries, and he made these the settings for his books. An art lover and a scholar (biologist, geologist, archaeologist, and classicist), he was also a hedonist and a skeptic. His interests are uniquely blended in his books. In Siren Land (1911), his first book, he established his style. It is a traveler's lively description of Sorrento and Capri, interspersed with learned, fantastic, and lightly satirical essays. Fountains in the Sand (1912) is about Tunisia, and Old Calabria (1915), considered his best travel book, is about southern Italy.

Douglas, Stephen A[rnold] (1813–1861) American statesman, known as the Little Giant. After holding several state offices in Illinois, Douglas was elected to Congress in 1843 and to the U.S. Senate in 1847. He introduced the Kansas-Nebraska Act, which incorporated the principle of popular sovereignty, but lost the support of Southern Democrats when he opposed the proslavery Lecompton constitution for Kansas, which he claimed violated popular sovereignty. During his famous debates (1858) with Abraham LINCOLN, when both were candidates for the Senate, Douglas formulated his "Freeport doctrine," maintaining that the people of a territory might admit or exclude slavery, because slavery could not exist unless it was supported by local police regulations. Although Douglas won the Senate seat, the Freeport doctrine further alienated Southerners and probably cost him their backing for the 1860 Democratic nomination. In 1860 Douglas was the presidential candidate of Northern Democrats and lost to Lincoln.

Douglas, William O[rville] (1898–1980) American jurist and writer. After receiving his law degree from Columbia, Douglas taught law at Yale and entered government service in 1929. He served as chairman of the Securities and Exchange Commission until his appointment to the U.S. Supreme Court by Franklin D. ROOSEVELT in 1939. A vigorous proponent of New Deal policies, Douglas was known as one of the most liberal members of the Court. His retirement in 1975 ended the longest term of service for any justice in Supreme Court history. In 1953 Douglas granted a stay of execution to Julius and Ethel Rosenberg, who had been convicted of spying for the Soviet Union. The Rosenbergs were subsequently executed, and Douglas's stand provoked an unsuccessful attempt by the House of Representatives to impeach him. Among his more than thirty books are many concerned with the American legal system and civil liberties, including *We the Judges* (1956), *A Living Bill of Rights* (1961), *The Anatomy of Liberty* (1963), and *Points of Rebellion* (1970); others deal with the outdoors, such as *My Wilderness: The Pacific West* (1960) and *The Three Hundred Year War: A Chronicle of Ecological Disaster* (1972). His travel writings, including *Strange Lands and Friendly People* (1951), *North from Malaya* (1953), and *Russian Journey* (1956), give usually expert and always lively reports on political conditions and foreign scenes. *Of Men and Mountains* (1950) and *Go East, Young Man* (1975) are autobiographical, as is *The Court Years 1939–1975* (1980).

Douglass, Frederick (1817?–1895) American abolitionist, orator, and journalist. The son of a slave and a white father, Douglass escaped to the North in 1838. A speech he delivered at an antislavery convention in Nantucket in 1841 made such an impression that he was soon in great demand as a speaker. Mobbed and beaten because of his views, he described his experiences in an outspoken *Narrative of the Life of Frederick Douglass* (1845). After a two-year stay in Great Britain, where he earned enough money to buy his freedom, he founded *The North Star*, a newspaper he published for seventeen years, advocating the use of black troops during the Civil War and civil rights for freedmen. He held various public offices after the war.

Dove Cottage The house where Dorothy and William WORDSWORTH made their home, from 1799 to 1807, at Grasmere in the English Lake District. See LAKE POETS.

Dover Beach (1867) A poem by Matthew ARNOLD, expressing his pessimism with regard to the future of the modern world and advocating personal fidelity and love as the rather desperate substitute for the ebbing "sea of faith":

Ah, love, let us be true
To one another! for the world, which seems
To lie before us like a land of dreams,
So various, so beautiful, so new,
Hath really neither joy, nor love, nor light,
Nor certitude, nor peace, nor help for pain;

And we are here as on a darkling plain
Swept with confused alarms of struggle and flight,
Where ignorant armies clash by night.

Dowsabell (fr Fr, *douce et belle*, "sweet and beautiful") A common name for a sweetheart, especially an unsophisticated country girl, in poems of Elizabethan times. Michael DRAYTON wrote a poem called "The Ballad of Dowsabell" (1606).

Dowson, Ernest See CYNARA.

Doyle, Sir Arthur Conan (1859–1930) English novelist, known chiefly for his series of tales concerning Sherlock HOLMES. Also noteworthy are his historical novels, *The White Company* (1891), dealing with the adventures of a company of Saxon bowmen in the French/English wars of the 14th century, and the series of Napoleonic tales centering on Brigadier Gerard, and his imaginative fantasy *The Lost World* (1912). The Holmes stories, conceived to augment Doyle's income from an unsuccessful medical practice, quickly made their author famous. At one point, tiring of the detective, Doyle attempted to exterminate him, in *The Memoirs of Sherlock Holmes* (1894), but the clamor of his admirers forced him to resurrect Holmes for several further volumes, and his popularity has waned little since. Doyle was much interested in the occult and wrote a *History of Spiritualism* (1926).

Drabble, Margaret (1939–   ) English novelist. Drabble's novels are traditional in form. Her central characters are often perceptive and intelligent women; in addition, most are married, with children. Drabble thus combines the career woman and the mother in one complex character torn between her need for emotional freedom and her maternal instincts. This conflict is treated directly in *The Garrick Year* (1964) and *The Millstone* (1965; U.S., *Thank You All Very Much*). Drabble's heroines also wrestle with their consciences, as in *The Waterfall* (1969) and *The Needle's Eye* (1972). In *The Realms of Gold* (1975) and *The Ice Age* (1977), Drabble's concerns were opened up to a more general analysis of the state of modern British society and its relationship to the past. Her other novels include *A Summer Bird-Cage* (1963), *Jerusalem the Golden* (1967), and *The Middle Ground* (1980). She has also written a biography of Arnold Bennett (1974) and a history of Britain in the Victorian era, *For Queen and Country* (1979). In 1985 the fifth edition of *The Oxford Companion to English Literature*, which she edited, was published.

Draco (fl 650 BC) An Athenian legislator. In 621 BC Draco was given extraordinary power to codify the laws of Athens for the first time. His work was designed to replace individual revenge with public justice. His code was known for its severity; the 4th-century orator Demades commented that the code was written in blood rather than ink. The death penalty was prescribed for several crimes, and cases of murder were to be tried by the AREOPAGUS. Under

Draco's Code, debtors could be claimed as slaves. SOLON abolished the Code except for the law relating to murder.

The name has given rise to the word *draconian*.

dragon (fr Gr, *drakon*, "snake") A mythical beast. Found in the mythology and folklore of innumerable peoples, it was commonly conceived of as a kind of large serpent of hostile disposition. In its earliest forms, it was a monster sea serpent, perhaps suggested to the primitive mind by the undulating surface and unruly habits of rivers and seas. The first known example is the Sumerian Kur, though its precise appearance is not clear from the three extant myths in which he or she appears. Kur, like all dragons, seems to have existed mainly to be killed by a hero; the Sumerian champions who accomplished this feat were ENKI, NINURTA, and the goddess INANNA.

The basic theme of the sea dragons slain by a hero was developed further by the Babylonian conquerors of Sumeria in the story of the WAR OF THE GODS, in which the primeval sea, TIAMAT, the mother of the gods, is regarded as a dragon; she is killed by the hero MARDUK. Among the Canaanites, it is BAAL, the storm god, who subdues YAM, the dragon of the sea. The Hebrew Yahweh is similarly credited with the destruction of the leviathan, of RAHAB, and of simply "the dragon." Several Greek heroes slay dragons that are also associated with water and with the Near East. PERSEUS rescued ANDROMEDA from a sea monster in Canaan; the Canaanite CADMUS killed a dragon that guarded a spring at Thebes. The HYDRA, as the name implies, was also a water creature, and HERACLES had many Near Eastern connections. Even the famous feat attributed to St. GEORGE is an echo of the Perseus myth, for St. George killed his dragon at Lydda very near to Joppa, where Perseus' dragon ravaged the land.

Another common class of dragons guarded sacred places. This notion may have sprung from the widespread belief that the dead returned as serpents (Cadmus himself became one) and were often venerated as such. Sacred snakes were associated with many oracles, including that at Delphi, and for such religious festivals as the Thesmophoria at Athens. Dragons guarded the apples of the HESPERIDES and the GOLDEN FLEECE. The less benevolent dragons of northern Europe guarded hoards of treasure, which were wrested from them by such heroes as BEOWULF and Sigurd (SIEGFRIED).

The dragons of Chinese and Japanese mythology are totally different from the hostile varieties. Powerful spirits of air, sea, and earth, they are generally benevolent and are responsible to a considerable degree for the orderly functioning of natural phenomena.

Among the ancient Britons and Welsh, the dragon was the national symbol on the war standard; hence the term PENDRAGON for the *dux bellorum*, or leader in war (Welsh, *pen*, "head; chief"). See GRENDEL.

Drake, Sir Francis (1540?–1596) First English circumnavigator of the globe. After sailing as a privateer against Spanish vessels in the West Indies, Drake set off on his round-the-world voyage in December 1577. He passed through the Straits of Magellan, up the coast of South America, and as far as 48° north latitude along the North American coast, which he named New Albion and claimed in the name of Elizabeth. He then sailed to Celebes, around the Cape of Good Hope, and back to England, returning in October 1580. He fought against the Spanish Armada in 1588 and died in the course of an expedition to the West Indies.

Drake, Temple A character in William Faulkner's SANCTUARY and REQUIEM FOR A NUN. A seventeen-year-old college student in *Sanctuary*, Temple is a provocative and irresponsible girl who invites by her actions the rape she half fears and half desires. Playing the part of the victim, she subsequently allows herself to be kept at a brothel by POPEYE and perjures herself at the murder trial of an innocent man, less out of malice toward the accused than out of indifference. In *Requiem for a Nun*, she persists in her former attitudes by refusing, until the very end, to see herself as anything but a respectable woman wronged by circumstance.

dramatic irony A theatrical device, consisting in the conscious production by the author of an ironical situation, i.e., a marked incongruity between a character's words and the action, as for instance in Schiller's WALLENSTEIN when the hero (not aware of the plot on his life, of which the audience has been informed) says before going to bed: "I intend to take a long rest." The understanding of the unintentional play on words imparts to the audience for a moment the role of "an omniscient god of the drama."

Dram Shop, The See ASSOMMOIR, L'.

Draupadi In Hindu legend, daughter of king Drupada and wife of the five Pandava brothers (in the MAHĀBHĀRATA). In the epic, she is a strong-willed, proud character, whose outrage at being disrobed in the palace hall by Duryodhana is one of the major factors in leading up to the battle of Kurukshetra, when the Pandavas take revenge on Duryodhana.

Draupnir See ODIN.

Drayman Henschel (*Fuhrmann Henschel*, 1899) A drama by Gerhart HAUPTMANN. A man has promised his late wife to be faithful to her memory. However, he is trapped into marriage by the machinations of his ambitious housekeeper. Oppressed and bullied by her, he finally commits suicide.

Drayton, Michael (1563–1631) English poet. Born in the same county (Warwickshire) as SHAKESPEARE, Drayton matched the master in the range, if not the quality, of his poetic achievement. Always experimenting and continually revising, Drayton wrote SONNETS, dramas, ODES, mythological poems, satires, PASTORALS, and historical verse narratives. His works include *Idea, the Shepherd's Garland* (1593); *Idea's Mirror* (1594), a SONNET SEQUENCE; *England's Heroical Epistles* (1597); *Polyolbion* (1612–22), a poetical survey of the topography of England; *Nimphidia* (1627), a charming minor epic set in a fairy atmosphere; *Idea*, a completely revised version of his earlier sonnet sequence; and *The Muses Elyzium* (1630). Drayton also wrote a number of plays that have not survived. According to one tradition, it was as a result of a "merry meeting" with Drayton and Ben JONSON that Shakespeare contracted the illness that resulted in his death.

Dream Children: A Reverie (1822) One of the best-known essays of Charles LAMB, prompted by the death of the author's brother James. In it, Lamb describes an imaginary conversation with the children he has never had.

Dream of Gerontius, A (1866) A poem by John Henry NEWMAN, in which Gerontius makes his last journey to God, carried by his guardian angel through a world of good and evil spirits. *A Dream of Gerontius* has been set to music in the form of an oratorio by Sir Edward ELGAR (1900).

Dream of the Red Chamber, The (Hung lou meng) A Chinese autobiographical novel by Ts'ao Hsueh-ch'in (1715?–63). The novel depicts the decline in the fortunes of the large, aristocratic Chia family. It is written with great psychological insight and is unique among Chinese novels for the depth and subtlety of its characterization. It is also known as *Shih-t'ou chi* (*The Story of the Stone*). See CHINESE LITERATURE.

Dream of the Rood, The Old English religious poem, one of the finest, of 156 lines in ALLITERATIVE VERSE. A fragment of it is inscribed (early 8th century) on a stone cross in Scotland, and the Vercelli Book, a collection of Old English manuscripts discovered in 1822, has a complete version (late 9th century). The poet lyrically describes dreaming that the Rood, or True Cross, speaks to him about its own history and urges him to promote its cult. Then he tells how the dream has changed his life, alluding to Christ's life in his own prayer for heavenly reward.

dreams, the gates of Two gates in HADES, one of ivory and one of horn. Dreams that delude pass through the ivory gate, those that come true pass through the gate of horn. This fancy depends upon two puns: "ivory" in Greek is *elephas*, and the verb *eliphairo* means "to cheat with empty hopes"; the Greek for "horn" is *keras*, and the verb *karanoo* means "to accomplish." ANCHISES dismissed AENEAS through the ivory gate, on quitting the infernal regions, to indicate the unreality of his vision.

Dream Songs, The (1969) A collection of poems by John BERRYMAN. The *Songs* initially appeared in two volumes: *47 Dream Songs* (1964) and *His Toy, His Dream, His Rest* (1968). After Berryman's death in 1972, editor John Haffenden published *Henry's Fate and Other Poems 1967–1972* (1977). This volume contained forty-five *Songs*

that had not been incorporated into the 1969 edition. The posthumous additions are not artistically equal to the earlier *Songs* and, in subject matter, are grimly prophetic of Berryman's eventual suicide.

The Dream Songs are monologues spoken by a persona, Mr. Henry, who is at once Berryman and contemporary man. That the poems are both dreams and songs attests to their subjectivity and unconscious allusions, as well as to their musical format. Each *Song* has a regular pattern of three six-line stanzas. The syntax, however, is irregular and is intended to reflect the tense, dissociated speaker. Mr. Henry, a volatile, lustful, self-centered persona, leads the reader through a volley of intense reactions to death, love, fame, and creative activity. The total effect of the *Songs* is of desperation continuously opposed by determination to celebrate life's "unforbidding Majesty."

Dreary Story, A (Skuchnaya istoriya, 1889) A story by Anton Chekhov, subtitled *From the Notebook of an Old Man*. The story is usually regarded as the starting point for Chekhov's mature writings. In it he introduces the theme of the difficulty of real communication between people, which he was to take up in so many of his later works. The old man of the tale, Professor Nikolay Stepanovich, realizes, as his life draws to a close, that he has lived without a unifying ideal to make a whole of his personal, professional, and social relationships. As he reviews his life, it seems fragmented, aimless, and worthless. The same kind of despair is experienced by his young ward Katya. Because neither can really communicate with the other, both the professor and Katya are left to endure their agonies alone.

Dred Scott decision A U.S. Supreme Court decision in 1857 in the case of Dred Scott (1795?–1858), a slave who had been taken by his master from Missouri to Illinois and Wisconsin, where slavery was prohibited. After his return to Missouri, Scott sued for his liberty, on the basis of his residence in free territory. Deciding against Scott, the court held that he was not a citizen of the U.S. and therefore could not bring suit in a federal court and that the MISSOURI COMPROMISE, which forbade slavery in Wisconsin, was unconstitutional because it deprived persons of their property (i.e., their slaves) without due process of law. The decision was bitterly attacked by Northern abolitionists because it declared in effect that slavery could not be barred from the territories.

Dreigroschenoper, Die See THREEPENNY OPERA, THE.

Dreiser, Theodore [Herman Albert] (1871–1945) American novelist. A leading light of the CHICAGO GROUP, Dreiser is known as one of the principal exponents of American NATURALISM. Although many critics have inveighed against the crudeness of his style, the power and importance of his work cannot be denied.

The twelfth of thirteen children in a strict Catholic family, Dreiser grew up in poverty and received only a sketchy education. He was, however, a voracious and intelligent reader, and the impact of such writers as HAWTHORNE, POE, BALZAC, Herbert SPENSER, and FREUD is clear not only in his writing but also in his strenuous reaction against organized religion. After a year at Indiana University and a peripatetic career as a newspaperman, Dreiser completed his first novel, SISTER CARRIE, in 1900. Because of its frankness and unconventional moral viewpoint, the book was suppressed by his publisher, Doubleday, Page & Co., for more than a decade, during which its despondent author gave up writing fiction. He suffered a nervous breakdown, separated from his wife, and finally secured an extremely lucrative position with Butterick Publications, publishers of women's magazines. He began to write again in 1910 and, the following year, published JENNIE GERHARDT, like *Sister Carrie*, the story of a "fallen woman," partly modeled on his own sister. Its success, resulting in a 1919 edition of his first novel, freed Dreiser to write about life as he saw it. With THE FINANCIER, he began his "trilogy of desire," the story of a captain of high finance, Frank Cowperwood. Influenced by the evolutionary ideas of Herbert Spenser and by Nietzsche's concept of the ÜBERMENSCH, Dreiser managed to combine with these ideas a poetic sense of the mystery and beauty of the universe, which begins to emerge in THE TITAN and flowers finally in the third work in the trilogy, *The Stoic* (written pre-1920, pub 1947). THE "GENIUS" and its sequel, *The Bulwark* (1946), written during the same period, were about the weaknesses and troubles of an American artist. Both *The Bulwark* and *The Stoic* show evidence of a mystic strain that became more pronounced in his later years. If these novels were partly based on himself, Dreiser was also then writing straight autobiography in *A Traveller at Forty* (1913), *A Hoosier Holiday* (1916), and *A Book about Myself* (1922; repub as *Newspaper Days*, 1931). *Hey Rub-a-Dub Dub: A Book of the Mystery and Terror and Wonder of Life* was published in 1920.

In 1925 came AN AMERICAN TRAGEDY, a novel based on the famous case of Chester Gillette's murder of Grace Brown, generally considered Dreiser's finest achievement. In 1927 he visited Russia, publishing afterwards the two books that marked his acceptance of socialism and his rejection of his former despairing emphasis on fate: *Dreiser Looks at Russia* (1928) and *Tragic America* (1931). From this point on, he concerned himself more and more with left-wing politics. Although his novels were initially held to be amoral, his principal concern had always been with the conflict between human needs and the demands of society for material success; his view of the determinants of human life remained generally mechanistic and tragic. Other works include *Plays of the Natural and Supernatural* (1916), *Free and Other Stories* (1918), *The Hand of the Potter* (1919), *Twelve Men* (1919), *The Color of a Great City* (1923), *Moods* (1926), *A Gallery of Women* (1929), *Fine Furniture* (1930), and *Epitaph* (1930). *The Letters of Theodore Dreiser* (3 vols, ed R. Elias) appeared in 1959; *Theodore Dreiser: A Selection of Uncollected Prose* (ed D. Pizer) was published in 1977.

Drew, Nancy   See STRATEMEYER, EDWARD L.

Dreyer, Carl Theodor (1889–1968)   Danish film director, whose work spanned the silent and sound periods. Dreyer's masterwork, one of the pinnacles of silent film, is *La Passion de Jeanne d'Arc* (1928), in which enormous closeups are made to reveal Joan's emotional conflicts and ultimate spiritual ecstasy. Among his finest later films were the great horror movie V*ampyr* (1932), based on a story by LE FANU, and his final masterpiece, *Gertrud* (1964), which again deals with the expression of feeling from "the depths of the soul."

Dreyfus, Alfred (1859–1935)   Central figure in the famous Dreyfus case, which divided France for almost four years. An officer of Jewish descent in the French artillery, Captain Dreyfus was accused and convicted of having betrayed military secrets. In 1894 he was sent to Devil's Island to serve a sentence of life imprisonment. Evidence attesting to the innocence of Dreyfus and to the guilt of a Major Esterhazy was uncovered but suppressed by the military. Dreyfus was finally pardoned in 1906 by the *Cour de Cassation*. He became a symbol of injustice for liberal intellectuals who vigorously opposed such right-wing reactionary forces as the military and the church. Emile Zola wrote the letter J'ACCUSE, and many other men of letters were ardent Dreyfus supporters. In REMEMBRANCE OF THINGS PAST, Marcel Proust gives an excellent picture of the alignment of French opinion on the controversial case, which is also dealt with in Anatole France's satirical series *Histoire contemporaine* (1896–1901).

Drinkwater, John (1882–1937)   English poet, dramatist, and biographer. Drinkwater's poetry belongs to the GEORGIAN school. He wrote historical and biographical plays, such as *Abraham Lincoln* (1918) and *Mary Stuart* (1921). *Inheritance* (1931) and *Discovery* (1932) are autobiographical volumes.

Dromio of Ephesus and Dromio of Syracuse In Shakespeare's THE COMEDY OF ERRORS, the merry identical twins who are the servants of the identical twins Antipholus of Ephesus and Antipholus of Syracuse. The twin Dromios are roundly beaten and sent hither and yon in the confusion that results when they and their masters, unbeknownst to each other, end up in the same city.

Dropping the Pilot   The title of a political cartoon in the English magazine PUNCH by Sir John TENNIEL. It dramatized the resignation of Bismarck after his disagreement with Kaiser Wilhelm II in 1890. Bismarck, as the old pilot, solemnly leaves his ship while the youthful emperor, now in sole command, watches.

Droste-Hülshoff, Annette von   (1797–1848) German poet. Droste-Hülshoff is remembered especially for ballads in which she combines vivid renderings of natural scenes from her Westphalian homeland with a swift, subtle narrative gift and a compact use of language. Another side of her nature, deeply religious, is seen in the collection *Das geistliche Jahr* (*The Spiritual Year*, 1851). Her famous novella *Die Judenbuche* (*The Jews' Beech Tree*, 1842), though set in a simple rustic atmosphere, is psychologically deep and succeeds in evoking a powerful sense of mystery about the workings of fate.

Drugger, Abel   A character in Ben Jonson's comedy THE ALCHEMIST. A seller of tobacco, Drugger is artless and gullible in the extreme. He is building a new house and comes to Subtle the "alchemist" to find out on which side to set the shop-door, how to dispose the shelves so as to ensure most luck, on what days he may trust his customers, and when it will be unlucky for him to do so.

Druid (Lat, *druides* or *druidae*; fr OI, *drui*, or Gael, *draoi*, "knowledge of the oak; great knowledge")   Member of the pre-Christian Celtic class of priests, religious teachers, and sorcerers. Practically our only literary sources of knowledge of the druidic cult are Pliny and the *Commentaries* of Caesar, which say that the rites of the Druids were conducted in oak groves and that they regarded the oak and the mistletoe with particular veneration, that they studied the stars and nature generally, that they believed in the transmigration of souls, and that they dealt in magic. Their distinguishing badge was a serpent's egg (see DRUID'S EGG), to which powerful properties were credited. The order seems to have been highly organized, and, according to Strabo, every chief had his druid, and every chief druid was allowed a guard of thirty men. Because of the significance of religion in Celtic culture, the Druids were the most important class among the Celts. They helped identify the king's successor, they advised the king, and they were arbitrators in all kinds of disputes.

Druid's egg   A fabled egg hatched by the joint labor of several serpents and buoyed into the air by their hissing. The person who caught it had to ride off at full speed, to avoid being stung to death, but was sure to prevail in every contest and to be courted by those in power. Pliny says he had seen one of them and that it was about as large as a moderate-sized apple.

Drummond of Hawthornden, William (1585–1649)   Scottish poet. Owner of an extensive library and ardently Royalist in politics, Drummond translated French and Italian lyric poetry, especially the works of Ronsard, Passerat, and Desportes. His own verse, which includes *Flowers of Zion* (1623), is known for its grace and smoothness. He also left interesting notes on Ben JONSON's conversation during the latter's visit to Hawthornden in 1618.

Drums Along the Mohawk (1936)   A historical novel by Walter D. EDMONDS. The bitter struggle in the Mohawk Valley between the supporters of the American Revolution and their British foes is vividly portrayed. Stress is laid on the destructiveness of the Tories and their Indian allies. The novel is based on the kind of careful research that Edmonds described in "How You Begin a Novel" (*Atlantic Monthly*, August 1936).

Druon, Maurice (pen name of Maurice Kessel, 1918–   )   French novelist. Druon first gained recognition with his three-novel cycle, *La Fin des hommes* (1948–51; tr *The Curtain Falls*, 1952–59), a detailed chronicle of the moral and commercial corruption of two bourgeois families between the two world wars. The trilogy includes *Les Grandes Familles* (1948, PRIX GONCOURT; tr *The Rise of Simon Lachaume*, 1952), *La Chute des corps* (1950; tr *Feet of Clay*, 1959), and *Rendezvous aux enfers* (1951; tr *Rendezvous in Hell*, 1959). His most ambitious subsequent project was *Les Rois maudits* (7 vols, 1955–77), a series of historical novels about the French monarchy in the 14th century. Among his other works are *Alexandre le Grand* (1958; tr *Alexander the Great*, 1960), a biography, and *The Glass Coffin* (tr 1963), a collection of stories.

Drury, Allen [Stuart] (1918–   )   American novelist and journalist. A prolific writer, Drury is best known for his first novel, *Advise and Consent* (1959), a PULITZER PRIZE-winning fictionalization of the inner workings of the U.S. Senate. Drawn largely from his experiences as a political correspondent in Washington, D.C., many of Drury's subsequent novels, written from a point of view both antiliberal and anticommunist, have so closely mirrored actual events that they could almost be considered ROMANS À CLEF.

Drury Lane   A street in London named after Drury House, which was built by Sir William Drury in the time of Henry VIII. The street has been the site of several theatres of the same name, the first of which was built by Thomas Killigrew in 1663 as the Theatre Royal and was described by Samuel PEPYS. After it was destroyed by fire in 1672, a new theatre, designed by Christopher WREN, was erected on the site of the present Drury Lane Theatre and was opened in 1674.

Druses   A people and sect living in the hills of Syria, Lebanon, Israel, and Jordan. Their unitarian faith combines Moslem, Christian, Jewish, and Sufist ideas. They offer devotions in both mosques and churches, worship the images of saints, and observe the fast of Ramadan. Their name is probably derived from that of their first apostle, Ismail Darazi or Durzi (11th century AD).

Browning wrote a tragedy, *Return of the Druses* (1841).

dryad (fr Gr, *drys*, "oak")   In Greek mythology, a tree nymph. Originally the dryads were specifically oak nymphs, but the name came to be applied to all tree nymphs. Nature spirits who died with the trees they inhabited, they were also called *hamadryads*. The most famous of them perhaps was Eurydice, the wife of ORPHEUS.

Dryden, John (1631–1700)   English poet, dramatist, and critic. Dryden was the outstanding figure in letters during the RESTORATION and was literary dictator of his age.

Dryden came from a good but impecunious country family with a Parliamentarian and Church of England background. In his middle twenties, he went to London, where his gifts were quickly recognized in intellectual circles, though he had to struggle for years to earn a respectable living by means of his plays and translations. Dryden made several radical shifts in his religion and politics: in 1659 he eulogized Cromwell in the *Heroick Stanzas*; a year later, he celebrated Charles II in *Astraea Redux*; in 1682 he published RELIGIO LAICI, a defense of Anglicanism; five years later, THE HIND AND THE PANTHER revealed him as an ardent partisan of Catholicism and Catholic James II. In 1688, however, he refused to take an oath of allegiance to William and Mary, remaining loyal to James II at the cost of important offices, including the laureateship of England.

Dryden's earliest work, such as his elegy "Upon the Death of Lord Hastings" (1650), is in the extravagant late metaphysical vein of COWLEY. Soon he developed a more restrained and natural style, close to normal cultivated speech and employing the heroic couplet to emphasize its finish and point. This was to be the dominant poetic style for a century, though perhaps never more forceful and various than it was in Dryden's hands. It was a vehicle particularly well adapted to satirical and didactic works, such as ABSALOM AND ACHITOPHEL, THE MEDAL, MACFLECKNOE, *Religio Laici*, and *The Hind and the Panther*. Dryden also used it in his translations of Vergil and other Latin poets and in a number of his plays, although his greatest play, ALL FOR LOVE, is written in blank verse. His prose writings are also of great importance: the orderly, lucid, and masculine style that distinguishes his prefaces and critical essays, such as the ESSAY OF DRAMATIC POESY, became one of the chief models for modern prose. These works reveal Dryden as an acute and extraordinarily sensible critic.

In addition to those referred to above, the following poems deserve mention: the lyrics "To Mrs. Killegrew" (1686), "A Song for St. Cecilia's Day" (1687), and "Alexander's Feast" (1697); a number of longer poems, such as ANNUS MIRABILIS; and his paraphrases and translations of Chaucer, Boccaccio, Ovid, Juvenal, Lucretius, and Homer. Other memorable plays by Dryden are *The Indian Emperor* (1665), *Almanzor and Almahide, or The Conquest of Granada* (1670), *Aurengzebe* (1675), and *Don Sebastian* (1690).

Du Barry, Marie Jeanne Bécu, Comtesse (1743–1793)   Adventuress and mistress of Louis XV from 1768 to his death (1774). Mme Du Barry ruled both king and court and was famous for her prodigality as a patron of artists and men of letters. She was guillotined on December 7, 1793.

Du Bellay, Joachim (1522–1560)   French poet. A companion of RONSARD at the Collège de Coqueret in Paris, Du Bellay was one of the founders of the PLÉIADE and author of its poetic program: DÉFENSE ET ILLUSTRATION DE LA LANGUE FRANÇAISE. His melancholy nature easily lent itself to the Petrarchan type of idealized love then in vogue, a tendency reflected in his first work, *L'Olive* (1549), the first French collection of sonnets; yet, the following year, he produced *A une dame*, a biting satire of this very convention. In 1553, ailing and downcast at his failure to win royal favor, he accompanied his cousin Cardinal Du Bellay to Rome as his secretary. He approached Rome with the reverence of a confirmed Latinist and left it four years later greatly disillusioned. Upon his return to France in 1558, he published four volumes: the *Poemata*, written in Latin in the style of the Italian humanists; *Les Antiquités de Rome*, in which he exalted ancient Rome; *Les Regrets*, in which he bitterly satirized the mediocrity of contemporary Rome and expressed his regrets over his self-imposed exile; and the *Divers jeux rustiques*, in which he freed himself from his cares and relaxed into pastoral pieces and sensual love poems. The *Poète courtisan* (1559) was a last embittered satire on the court poets.

Second only to Ronsard in the eyes of his contemporaries and posterity, Du Bellay could not reconcile himself to this position and harbored a jealousy which he did not always attempt to hide.

Dubliners (1914)   A collection of short stories by James JOYCE. By dealing successively with incidents in the childhood, adolescence, maturity, and public life of Dubliners, Joyce provides a picture of the paralyzing world from which he fled. Most of the characters and scenes are mean and petty, sometimes tragic; they are drawn from ordinary Catholic middle-class life. The style is simple and moving, more in the manner of Anton Chekhov than in that of the author's more famous works. In all the stories, Joyce uses a device he named the EPIPHANY, a sudden remark, symbol, or moment that epitomizes and clarifies the meaning of a complex experience. Among the best known of the stories are THE SISTERS, "Counterparts," CLAY, "Ivy Day in the Committee Room," and THE DEAD. Several of the characters introduced in *Dubliners* reappear in ULYSSES.

Joyce had difficulty in finding a publisher for his book, and it did not appear until many years after it had been written. It was severely attacked because the names of actual persons and places in Dublin are mentioned in it.

DuBois, Guy Pène (1884–1958)   American painter and critic. A student of Robert Henri (1865–1929) and W. M. CHASE, DuBois showed some work in the ARMORY SHOW. His simple, mannequinlike figures, frozen against plain theatre, café, or gallery backgrounds, have become classics of American art.

Du Bois, W[illiam] E[dward] B[urghardt]
(1868–1963)   American civil rights leader and writer.
The descendant of a French Huguenot and an African
slave, Du Bois received his B.A., M.A., and Ph.D. degrees
from Harvard. Among the first important leaders to advocate complete economic, political, and social equality for
blacks, Du Bois cofounded (1909) the National Negro
Committee, which later became the N.A.A.C.P. He
taught history and economics at Atlanta University from
1897 to 1910 and from 1932 to 1944. In the intervening
years, he served as editor of the N.A.A.C.P. magazine,
Crisis. He lived the last two years of his life in Ghana,
joined the Communist Party, and edited an *African Encyclopedia for Africans*. Among his many influential writings
are *The Souls of Black Folk* (1903), *John Brown* (1909), and
The Black Flame (1957–61). His *Autobiography* appeared
posthumously, in 1968.

Dubuffet, Jean (1901–   )   French painter.
Dubuffet did not start painting in earnest until he was forty,
having engaged in various enterprises to support his family
until then. He was a champion of *art brut*, the naïve but
powerful artwork of prisoners, psychotics, and other unusual amateurs. His own work reflects his admiration of
force and spontaneity over culture and discipline. His
paintings, such as *The Lost Traveller* (1950), often consist
of sand, ashes, or glass bound in paste or varnish. Later
works in more conventional media suggest jigsaw puzzles,
with black lines surrounding convoluted, interlocking
forms and figures.

Duchamp, Marcel (1887–1968)   French painter of
the DADA movement. Duchamp's futuristic *Nude Descending a Staircase* (1912), an experiment in depicting motion
on canvas, caused a sensation at the ARMORY SHOW.
Always associated in one way or another with surrealist
techniques, Duchamp anticipated many elements of POP
ART by displaying commonplace objects as art, such as
Fountain, an ordinary urinal. His brother, Raymond
Duchamp-Villon (1876–1918), was a cubist sculptor, and
his half-brother, Jacques Villon (1875–1963), was a cubist
painter of note.

Duchess, the   A character in Lewis Carroll's
ALICE'S ADVENTURES IN WONDERLAND. The duchess wal-
lops her baby till it howls and sings this lullaby to it:

Speak roughly to your little boy,
And beat him when he sneezes;
He only does it to annoy,
Because he knows it teases.

Duchess of Malfi, The (c1613)   A tragedy by
John WEBSTER. The last of the great Elizabethan dramas, it
deals movingly with the disastrous marriage of a noblewoman and a commoner. The duchess, the widowed sister of
Ferdinand, duke of Calabria, and of the cardinal, offends
them by marrying her steward, Antonio. The lovers are
forced to separate: Antonio flees, and the duchess is kept

prisoner in her house, where she is subjected to mental torture. Bosola, the cardinal's henchman, strangles the duchess and her children and later murders Antonio. The play
is based on William PAINTER's *The Palace of Pleasure*
(1566–67).

Du côté de chez Swann   See REMEMBRANCE OF
THINGS PAST.

Dudintsev, Vladimir Dmitrievich (1918–   )
Soviet novelist. His novel *Ne khlebom yedinym* (1956; tr
NOT BY BREAD ALONE, 1957) created a sensation with its
criticism of Soviet bureaucracy. Dudintsev was attacked by
Soviet critics in violent terms until Khrushchev, in May
1959, finally put an end to the prolonged controversy by
declaring that Dudintsev was not an enemy of the regime
but had merely erred in his efforts to criticize some aspects
of Soviet society.

Dudley, Robert, earl of Leicester (1531–1558)
Favorite of ELIZABETH I. The brother of Guildford Dudley
(the husband of Lady Jane GREY), Robert Dudley was condemned to death after the attempt to place Lady Jane on
the throne had failed. He was pardoned by Elizabeth I and
became Master of Ordnance and one of her chief favorites
at court. She made him a Knight of the Garter, created
him earl of Leicester, and gave him a castle at Kenilworth.
His wife, Amy Robsart, died under somewhat suspicious
circumstances, but there is no proof that her death—which
freed Leicester to marry Elizabeth if she would have him
—was anything but accidental. He is a main character in
Sir Walter Scott's novel KENILWORTH.

Duessa   An evil enchantress in Spenser's THE
FAERIE QUEENE (Books I, II, and V), representing variously
the Roman Catholic Church, Mary Tudor, and Mary,
Queen of Scots.

Dufay, Guillaume (c1400–1474)   Flemish (Belgian) composer, who lived and worked in Italy, Savoy,
Burgundy, and Flanders. At the end of his life, Dufay was
the most highly regarded composer in Europe. His finest
music was written for the church, but he composed lively
secular pieces as well. It was he who first established the
practice of having polyphonic music sung by a chorus;
hitherto each part had been performed by a single voice or
instrument. He is regarded as the first great composer of the
Renaissance; his Mass compositions, in particular, created
the musical language adopted by most later 15th-century
composers.

Dufy, Raoul (1877–1953)   French painter and illustrator. Dufy's early works were much in the style of IMPRES-
SIONISM. Later, influenced by MATISSE and LES FAUVES, his
work showed a more spontaneous use of color. After a
period as a fabric designer and book illustrator, he developed a distinct style of briefly drawn brushstrokes and fresh
colors. His landscapes, sea scenes, and ironic views of
street life and race tracks are among the most characteristic
of his mature paintings.

Duhamel, Georges (pen name of Denis Thévenin, 1884–1966)   French dramatist, novelist, essayist, and poet. A leading member of the ABBAYE GROUP, Duhamel wrote several plays early in his career: *La Lumière* (1911; tr *The Light*, 1914), *Le Combat* (1913; tr 1915), and *L'Œuvre des athlètes* (1920). His *Vie des martyrs* (1917; tr *New Book of Martyrs*, 1918) and *Civilisation* (1918, PRIX GONCOURT; tr *Civilization*, 1919) describe his experiences as a doctor on the front lines and in hospitals during World War I. But the best known of Duhamel's writings are the ROMANS-FLEUVES, *Vie et aventures de Salavin* (5 vols, 1920–32), the story of a mediocre yet idealistic man who tries to become a saint but fails, and *La Chronique des Pasquiers* (10 vols, 1933–45), a semiautobiographical portrait of a family under the Third Republic. His essay *La Possession du monde* (1919) urges, as do his novels, the cultivation of the inner life on which is based the fraternity of mankind.

Duino Elegies (Duineser Elegien, 1923; tr 1930)   A series of poems by Rainer Maria RILKE. They are elegiac in mood though not, strictly speaking, in form and meter. In them, Rilke develops his own highly personal solutions to existential problems and to those posed by the industrial age. Duino is a castle near Trieste, where Rilke in 1911–12 was a guest of the Princess Marie von Thurn und Taxis, to whom he presented the poems.

Dujardin, Edouard (1861–1949)   French writer. A poet and a distinguished editor, Dujardin allied himself with the symbolists. He is known for his influential novel LES LAURIERS SONT COUPÉS, the first example of STREAM OF CONSCIOUSNESS.

Dukhobors (fr Russ, *Dukhobortsi*, "spirit wrestlers") A religious sect that arose among Kharkov peasants in the mid-18th century. Guided by "inner light," they rejected the authority of Church and State and led communal lives under "inspired" leaders. Their beliefs have been compared to those of Quakers. Internal dissensions and resistance to military service subjected them to a series of forced migrations and dispersals.

Thousands removed to western Canada in 1898, where they founded prosperous if turbulent settlements as the Christian Community of Universal Brotherhood. Their sporadic protests against taxes and compulsory education (especially those led by the violent Sons of Freedom) have taken the form of fires, bombings, and marches in the nude, which abated in the late 1950s, after a new threat of expulsion.

Dulce et Decorum Est (1920)   A poem by Wilfred OWEN, bitterly denouncing war. The title is ironic, being a quotation from Horace: *Dulce et decorum est pro patria mori* ("It is sweet and fitting to die for one's country").

Dulcinea del Toboso   The lady love of DON QUIXOTE in Cervantes's novel. Her real name is Aldonza Lorenzo, but the knight dubs her Dulcinea del Toboso.

"Her flowing hair," says the knight, "is of gold, her forehead the Elysian fields, her eyebrows two celestial arches, her eyes a pair of glorious suns, her cheeks two beds of roses, her lips two coral portals that guard her teeth of Oriental pearl, her neck is alabaster, her hands are polished ivory, and her bosom whiter than the new-fallen snow." According to Sancho PANZA, she is "a stout-built sturdy wench, who could pitch the bar as well as any young fellow in the parish."

Duma   Russian parliamentary body created in 1905. Its function was to advise Czar Nicolas II in matters of legislation. It was overthrown by the RUSSIAN REVOLUTION.

Dumas, Alexandre (known as Dumas *père*, 1802–1870)   French novelist and dramatist. Alexandre Dumas has become almost legendary for his prolific literary output (almost three hundred volumes) and the rollicking gusto with which he lived and wrote. Dumas maintained a corps of collaborators—whom he termed his factory—who were engaged in searching through earlier memoir writers for suitably exciting plots. Accused of altering historical fact to suit his fictional purposes and of pilfering unscrupulously from other writers, Dumas remained supremely indifferent to such charges. His historical romances, all of the swashbuckling variety, include such favorites as THE COUNT OF MONTE CRISTO, THE THREE MUSKETEERS, THE BLACK TULIP, *Twenty Years After* (1845), and *The Viscount of Bragelonne* (1848–50). Critics point quickly—and rightly—to the excessive melodrama of Dumas's work, to his lack of psychological perception, and to his careless style, but the color and drama of his novels continue to ensure their popularity. In France, Dumas is noted for his plays: *Henri III et sa cour* (1829), *Napoléon Bonaparte* (1831), *Antony* (1831), and *La Tour de Nesle* (1832).

Dumas, Alexandre (known as Dumas *fils*, or Dumas the younger; 1824–1895)   French dramatist. The bastard son of the novelist Alexandre Dumas, the younger Dumas became an extremely popular playwright during the Second Empire. In technique, his plays were realistic; for subjects, he chose moral and social problems, depicting the adulterous intrigues and financial scandals of the upper social classes. Among Dumas's most successful works were LA DAME AUX CAMÉLIAS, *Le Demi-Monde* (1855), *La Question d'argent* (1857), *Un Père prodigue* (1859), *L'Ami des femmes* (1864), and *Les Idées de Mme Aubray* (1867). Heavy-handed didacticism characterized his later dramas.

du Maurier, Daphne (1907–   )   English novelist and short-story writer. Du Maurier's popular novels, including the famous *Rebecca* (1938), are compounded of melodrama, romance, Cornish scenery, and some history. They include *Jamaica Inn* (1936), *Frenchman's Creek* (1941), and *The King's General* (1946). She wrote several plays, notably *The Years Between* (1944). She has also published three books about her family: *Gerald: A Portrait* (1934), about her actor father; *The du Mauriers* (1937); and

The Young George du Maurier (1951), a collection of her famous grandfather's letters. Since 1980 she has published *The Rendez-vous and Other Stories* (1980) and *The Rebecca Notebook and Other Memories* (1981). In 1977 her autobiography, *Myself When Young*, appeared.

du Maurier, George [Louis Palmella Busson] (1834–1896)   English novelist and illustrator. Du Maurier illustrated the work of THACKERAY, HARDY, JAMES, and MEREDITH, and was famous for his caricatures in *Punch*. His novels, *Peter Ibbetson* (1891), the highly successful TRILBY, and *The Martian* (1896), are tinged with social satire and colored with the memories of the author's days as an art student in Paris. He also wrote light verse in English and French, which was popular in its day. A selection of his letters, *The Young George du Maurier* (1951), was edited by his granddaughter, Daphne DU MAURIER.

dumb show   A pantomime performance used as part of a play. It was often a part of Elizabethan drama, used as a prologue to foreshadow action or presented between acts or within the play itself. The pantomimed murder of the King that begins HAMLET is a dumb show that foreshadows the play within the play presented before Claudius.

Dumb Waiter, The (1960)   A one-act play by Harold PINTER. The two characters are assassins waiting in a hotel room for their victim to arrive. When an order for a Chinese meal is sent to them on the dumbwaiter, they assume that their room was once a restaurant. They fill the order as best they can with candy and biscuit. They are deluged with orders for food from an unknown person, who they feel is testing them. As the time approaches for the killing, one of the assassins, a questioning, childish person, starts to feel remorse for their other victims. He leaves the room; when he returns, his partner kills him.

Dumuzi   A Sumerian shepherd-god, known elsewhere as TAMMUZ. Dumuzi was loved by Inanna (Ishtar). Although he does not appear in the extant Sumerian myth of her descent into the underworld, the close parallel with Ishtar's search for Tammuz makes it highly likely that that was the purpose of Inanna's descent.

Dumuzi also is a central figure in a myth in which he, a shepherd, disputes with the farmer-god Enkimdu for the favor of Inanna. Although Dumuzi is elsewhere her lover, she here prefers the farmer. This is one of several Sumerian myths with an obvious parallel to the story of CAIN and Abel.

Dunbar, Paul Laurence (1872–1906)   American poet. Dunbar is noted for his highly skilled use of black themes and dialect. Writing at a time when literary regionalism was in vogue, he was undoubtedly influenced by Thomas Nelson PAGE. Although he was the son of a slave, his poetry is sentimental and lacks the bitterness of the work of later black writers. *Lyrics of Lowly Life* (1896) is his most famous collection. It was followed by *Lyrics of the Hearth-*side (1899), *Lyrics of Love and Laughter* (1903), and *Lyrics of Sunshine and Shadow* (1905). He also wrote novels, including *The Uncalled* (1898) and *The Sport of the Gods* (1902).

Dunbar, William (1465?–?1530)   Scottish poet. For a time Dunbar was a Franciscan friar and later a diplomatic agent for James IV of Scotland. His works include *The Thrissel and the Rois* (*The Thistle and the Rose*, 1503), a political allegory; *The Dance of the Sevin Deidly Sinnis* (1503–8), a religious dream vision; *The Goldyn Targe* (c1508), an allegory in the tradition of *The Romance of the Rose*; *Lament of the Makaris* (i.e., "poets"; c1508), an elegy on the death of great poets of the past that has been compared to the poetry of François VILLON; and *The Two Marryit Women and the Wedo* (c1508), a satire on women.

Duncan   In Shakespeare's MACBETH, the generous and gracious king of Scotland whom Macbeth murders to attain the crown. When prodded by his wife to do the deed, even Macbeth protests against it, extolling Duncan's virtues:

> Besides, this Duncan
> Hath borne his faculties so meek, hath been
> So clear in his great office, that his virtues
> Will plead like angels trumpet-tongued against
> The deep damnation of his taking-off.

Duncan, Isadora (1878–1927)   American dancer. A major innovator of dance, Duncan was not well received in America until after she had been acclaimed all over Europe, establishing a school in Berlin in 1904 and one later in Moscow. Duncan's free movement, her Greek tunic, long scarves, and bare feet, symbolizing revolt against traditional "school" steps in ballet, led to improvisational modern dance. As flamboyant and extravagant in her private life as she was celebrated on the stage, Duncan had an ill-fated affair with the stage designer Gordon Craig, and was married for one year (1922–23) to the Russian poet Sergei ESENIN. She had been performing in France in 1927, when she was strangled by her scarf, which caught in the wheel of her automobile.

Duncan, Robert [Edward] (1919–   )   American poet. At one time an editor of the *Experimental Review* and *Phoenix*, Duncan became one of the leading San Francisco poets of the late 1940s. He taught at Black Mountain College in 1956 and was influential among younger poets both as an artist and as a theorist. His distinctive work, written in the free forms of PROJECTIVE VERSE, is characterized by lyricism, irony, and intensity. He frequently employs syntactical jumps and eccentric spellings. Collections of his poetry include *Selected Poems* (1959), *The First Decade: Selected Poems 1940–50* (1968), *Derivations: Selected Poems 1950–56* (1968), and *The February Plan* (1978).

Dunciad, The (1728; rev 1729, 1742, 1743)   The "dunce-epic," a satire in heroic couplets by Alexander

POPE. The first version, in three books, was written under the influence of SWIFT; it attacked all critics of Pope's works, as poetasters, publishers, and pedants. In 1729 this version, with changes, was republished as *The Dunciad Variorum*. A fourth book, *The New Dunciad*, appeared in 1742, and the final version, *The Dunciad in Four Books*, was published a year later. In the first book, the leading role was initially given to playwright and critic Lewis Theobald (1688–1744), who had attacked Pope's edition of Shakespeare; in the final version, it is Colley CIBBER who is named king of the Dunces, his rule extending over the empires of Emptiness and Dullness. The second book, a burlesque of the account of funeral games for Anchises in Vergil's AENEID, depicts Cibber's coronation; it is celebrated with games and contests and, as everyone drowses off to sleep, poetry-reading. In the third book, Cibber falls asleep and sees, in his dreams, the past, present, and future; in all three, Dullness prevails. In the fourth book, Dullness reigns supreme over scholarship, art, and science. The goddess of Dullness, thus firmly entrenched, gives directions to her several agents to encourage foolish and trifling pursuits and to discourage thought, and night and chaos are finally restored. *The Dunciad* is considered among Pope's crowning achievements, and, in spite of its topicality, its satire is still fresh and biting.

Dunne, Finley Peter (1867–1936)   American journalist and humorist. Dunne worked for several newspapers in his native Chicago, writing his first "Mr. Dooley" essays for the *Evening Post*. Later he became part owner of the *American Magazine*, to which he contributed a pungent department entitled "In the Interpreter's House," and was editor of *Collier's* (1918–19). However, his fame rests entirely and solidly on his creation of Martin Dooley, an imaginary Irishman who presided over a small saloon on Chicago's West Side. From the days of the Spanish American War to World War I, Mr. Dooley reviewed public men and affairs with a wit and wisdom that made him a national institution. Many of the more than seven hundred essays featuring Mr. Dooley were collected in such books as *Mr. Dooley in Peace and War* (1898) and *Mr. Dooley in the Hearts of His Countrymen* (1899). *Mr. Dooley Remembers: The Informal Memoirs of Finley Peter Dunne* (1963) was edited by his son Philip Dunne.

Dunne, John William (1875–1949)   English author of *An Experiment with Time* (1927) and *The New Immortality* (1938). These books of popular philosophy purported to demonstrate, through mathematics, the immortality of the soul and the principle of serialism (that the individual passes through a single sequence of time as he lives, but that all other times and places exist simultaneously always). Dunne's books influenced J. B. PRIESTLEY and others.

Dunsany, Lord (Edward John Moreton Drax Plunkett, 1878–1957)   Irish dramatist and poet. A member of the Anglo-Irish gentry, Dunsany was educated at Eton. After service in the Boer War (1899–1902), he became active in the newly founded ABBEY THEATRE. In 1909 his play *The Glittering Gates*, produced at the Abbey by William Butler YEATS, won quick acclaim. This was followed by a number of other successes, many of them one-act plays, the best known of which are *A Night at an Inn* (1916), his finest play; *The Laughter of the Gods* (1916); and *If* (1922). Superficially his work appears to be merely the naïve expression of Celtic whimsy with the usual assortment of fairies and other supernatural creatures. Dunsany, however, employed this background to satirize human behavior with a disarmingly simple, seemingly unconscious, wit.

Duns Scotus, John (c1265–c1308)   Scottish scholastic theologian, known as the "Doctor Subtilis." Duns Scotus joined the Franciscans and was a teacher at Oxford, Paris, and Cologne, becoming famous for his defense of the dogma of the Immaculate Conception and for his description of man's free will as a horse capable of throwing off grace, its rider. Declaring that the existence of God or the immortality of the human soul cannot be proved by human reason, he thus challenged the harmony of faith and reason, of theology and philosophy, so important in the system of St. Thomas AQUINAS. For centuries, his followers, called *Scotists*, disputed with the Thomists over this and other doctrinal questions. Eventually Scotism was modified until it resembled Thomism on most issues.

Duns Scotus's theories are formulated in his metaphysical treatises *De rerum principio*, *Questiones*, *Opus Oxoniense* and in the commentaries on the *Sentences* of Peter LOMBARD. Although he had tried to urge philosophy's greater dependence on divine revelation, by showing the limitations of human reason, the controversy had the opposite effect of lessening philosophy's concern with theology. His opposition to classical studies led in the Renaissance to the use of his name (Duns, Dunse, or Dunce) for a pedantic sophist incapable of real learning, and thence to the current meaning of *dunce* as a stupid, dull-witted person.

Dunstable, John (c1390–1453)   One of the most important English composers of the 15th century; also a mathematician and astronomer. Dunstable spent much of his life in France, where he introduced the English predilection for full triadic harmony into the genres practiced on the Continent, thus strongly influencing the development of the characteristic "sweetness" of Renaissance music.

Dupes, Day of (Journée des Dupes)   November 11, 1630, when Marie de Médicis and Gaston, Duc d'Orléans extracted from Louis XIII the promise that he would dismiss his minister Cardinal RICHELIEU. The cardinal went immediately to Versailles, the king repented, and Richelieu became more powerful than ever. Marie de Médicis and Gaston, the dupes, paid dearly for their short triumph.

Dupin, C. Auguste   An amateur detective created by Edgar Allan POE. Appearing in the three stories Poe called his ratiocinative tales—"The Mystery of Marie Rôget," THE MURDERS IN THE RUE MORGUE, and THE PURLOINED LETTER—Dupin works solely by deductive method. His unofficial status, bewildered friend and narrator, and cold logic have become familiar characteristics of the literary detectives modeled on him.

Durant, Will[iam James] (1885–1981)   American historian, philosopher, and teacher. Perhaps the greatest popularizer of philosophic ideas in American publishing history, Durant originally wrote *The Story of Philosophy* (1926) as a lecture series. The book was so popular that it was translated into a dozen languages and soon sold over one million copies. Durant then embarked on his life's project, *The Story of Civilization* (10 vols, 1935–67). The series began with *Our Oriental Heritage* (1935) and ended with *Rousseau and the Revolution* (1967), which won the PULITZER PRIZE, and *The Age of Napoleon* (1975). The last three volumes of the monumental history were written in collaboration with his wife, Ariel Durant.

Duras, Marguerite (pen name of Marguerite Donnadieu, 1914–   )   French novelist and filmmaker. Duras, born in Indochina, left for France at the age of seventeen to study law at the Sorbonne. Duras's early reputation was based on her role as film director and screenwriter. Since 1959, she has directed over a dozen films and written many filmscripts, among them *Hiroshima, mon amour* (1960). A spare but lucid style characterizes her over fifteen novels, two of which are autobiographical and recount her childhood years in Indochina: *Un Barrage contre le Pacifique* (1950; tr *The Sea Wall*, 1952) and *L'Amant* (1984; tr *The Lover*, 1985). The former is about a Frenchwoman who attempts to give her children a better life by investing in a tract of land to grow rice; her constant battle to preserve the land from devastation by the swelling floods from the Pacific forms the crux of the story. The latter novel has recurrent themes and images from *The Sea Wall*, but the main story explores the awakening sexual consciousness of a sixteen-year-old French girl in relation to her older, Chinese lover.

Other well-known works include *Abahn Sabana David* (1970), an anticommunist, antipolitical novel set in the Stalin era that stems from Duras's own commitment to and eventual expulsion from the Communist Party; *Le Marin de Gibraltar* (1952; tr *The Sailor from Gibraltar*, 1966), and *Le Vice Consul* (1965; tr *The Vice-Consul*, 1968). *Savannah Bay*, an enigmatic play that makes its impact through the clever reversal of roles and the simple, unadorned language that Duras is famous for, was published in 1982. In 1986 Duras published *The Malady of Death*, a novella about death and dying.

Durendal   The magic sword of ROLAND (Orlando). Once used by Hector, Durendal was given to Roland by

CHARLEMAGNE in some stories, by Malagigi the magician in others.

Dürer, Albrecht (1471–1528)   German painter and engraver. Travels in Italy in 1494 and 1505 familiarized Dürer with that country's search for clarity in art. At first he followed the German Gothic tradition of linear unrest and vehemence, but this style gradually gave way to greater breadth and simplicity, until he achieved a classical art of great expressiveness. Acutely aware of his own importance as an artist and increasingly interested in the teachings of Martin Luther, he sought to reconcile the strictness of the Reformation with the humanistic aspects of the Renaissance and its classical concern with ideal beauty. In the process, he created the greatest expression of German Renaissance art. He painted a number of famous religious works and self-portraits, but he is particularly renowned for his numerous woodcuts and engravings depicting Apocalyptic visions, allegories, the Passion of Christ, and the life of the Virgin. The delicacy and strength of his hand is also demonstrated by portrait and landscape drawings and by minute studies of animals and details of nature. During his last years, he wrote theoretical works on geometry and perspective and on anatomy and human proportion.

Durga   In HINDUISM, a consort of SHIVA, representing the feminine strength or creative force (see SHAKTI). In the RĀMĀYANA, Durga is depicted as a great warrior invoked by Rāma so that he would have the power to conquer the evil RAVANA. *Durga puja*, a festival worshiping Durga, held usually from September through October, is one of Bengal's greatest religious festivals. The last day of the *Durga puja* coincides with a comparable festival in northern India, DUSSERAH, which commemorates Rāma's victory over Ravana. She is a benign aspect of KALI.

Durrell, Gerald [Malcolm] (1925–   )   English zoologist and writer. Brother of Lawrence DURRELL, in *The Bafut Beagles* (1953), *My Family and Other Animals* (1956), *A Zoo in My Luggage* (1960), *Birds, Beasts, and Relatives* (1969), and *Golden Bats and Pink Pigeons* (1977), among other books, Durrell brings both animals and people hilariously to life.

Durrell, Lawrence [George] (1912–   )   Anglo-Irish novelist, poet, and playwright. Durrell's first novel, THE BLACK BOOK, was published in Paris with the help of Henry MILLER, but his reputation as a novelist was not established until *Justine* (1957) signaled the beginning of THE ALEXANDRIA QUARTET. The tetralogy is an intricate study of love in many forms and of the exotic international society of Alexandria. Durrell's many books, both fiction and nonfiction, are about the Mediterranean and Aegean islands where he lived and worked for some years for the British Foreign Office. Notable among these is *Bitter Lemons* (1957), a vivid, many-faceted account of Cyprus during the British-Turkish-Greek struggles there. Durrell's verse, romantic, taut, and often humorous, began appearing in

1938; it includes *Collected Poems* (1956), *Red Limbo Lingo* (1971), and *Vega and Other Poems* (1973). He also wrote the poetic dramas *Sappho* (1950) and *Acte* (1961). His later fiction includes *The Revolt of Aphrodite* (1974) and two novels, *Monsieur* (1974) and *Livia, or Buried Alive* (1979), which are part of a projected series set in the south of France.

Dürrenmatt, Friedrich (1921–   )   Swiss playwright, writing in German. Dürrenmatt is known for his mastery of the bizarre and for the penetrating irony with which he comments on both the contemporary world and the helplessness of man in general. His two most important works are tragicomedies: *Die Ehe des Herrn Mississippi* (1952; prod New York as *Fools Are Passing Through*, 1958; tr *The Marriage of Mr. Mississippi*, 1964), a grotesque, surrealistic skit about the breakdown of moral and social values, and THE VISIT, an ironic modern counterpart to the old theme of the man who sacrifices himself for the sake of the community. Like his compatriot Max FRISCH, Dürrenmatt followed BRECHT's lead by frequently disrupting the stage-illusion in order to make the audience think in a more detached way about the ideas being presented (see ALIENATION EFFECT). Dürrenmatt has also written several serious detective novels, as well as his well-known essay on modern drama, *Theaterprobleme* (1955; tr *Problems of the Theatre*, 1966).

Duse, Eleonora   See D'ANNUNZIO, GABRIELE.

Dusserah   One of HINDUISM's most popular festivals, falling in October and lasting ten days. It celebrates the triumph of good over evil, symbolized by a reenactment of the battle between Rāma and RAVANA, as told in the RĀMĀYANA.

Dutch Courtezan, The (1604)   A drama by John MARSTON. Freevil, in love with the gentle Beatrice, wishes to break off his old relationship with Franceschina, the Dutch courtesan. To twit his upright friend Malheureux, he takes him to Franceschina's house, where the young man falls under the courtesan's spell. Discovering the facts about Freevil's forthcoming marriage, Franceschina turns to Malheureux and promises to give herself to him when he brings her Freevil's ring as a token that the latter is dead. Malheureux informs Freevil of her offer, and the two stage a mock quarrel. Malheureux hurries to Franceschina with the ring and then finds that she has betrayed him to the authorities. As Malheureux is about to be executed, Freevil appears and reveals the subterfuge.

Dutchman (1964)   A play in one act by Imamu Amiri BARAKA. *Dutchman* is set in a subway car on a hot summer evening. Lulu, a striking white woman, sits next to a young black man named Clay and talks to him. While her seductive banter captures his interest, her escalating jibes at his white man's values, clothing, and speech bewilder and finally goad him into a burst of anguished hatred, belying his courteous manner. Black people, he tells her,

must mask their true feelings, which are murderously antiwhite, in order to survive and keep their sanity. Lulu reacts by stabbing Clay, forcing the other passengers to throw his body off the train, and ordering them to get off when the train stops. There another young black man gets on. Like the legendary Flying Dutchman, condemned to sail until Judgment Day, the subway will continue its journey, and Lulu will continue her lethal confrontations. This play has been called Baraka's metaphor for all white-black relationships in the United States.

Dutch Wars   Three wars fought between England and the United Provinces (Holland) in 1652–54, 1664–67, and 1672–74. The first two were inspired by commercial rivalry and consisted largely of naval engagements and raids upon shipping and colonies. Among these was the British raid on New Amsterdam in 1664, which brought about the cession of that colony. The third war, very unpopular in England, was brought about by the desire of Charles II's ally, Louis XIV of France, to seize the Spanish Netherlands. Overall the wars were to England's advantage, but the Dutch were able to preserve the integrity of their home territory and government.

Dutourd, Jean (1920–   )   French novelist and essayist. Dutourd is best known for the satirical humor of *Une Tête de chien* (1950; tr *A Dog's Head*, 1951), *Au bon beurre* (1952; tr *The Best Butter*, 1955), *Doucin, confession* (1955; tr *Five A.M.*, 1956), and *2024* (1975).

Duun, Olav [Julius] (1876–1939)   Norwegian novelist. Although many of his novels are set in his native Namdalen and are infused with his own Trøndelag dialect, Duun deals with the universal theme of man's struggle with the natural, social, and psychological forces that surround him. His greatest achievements are the novel series *Juvikfolke* (6 vols, 1918–23; tr *The People of Juvik*, 1930–35) and *Menneske og maktene* (1938; tr *Floodtide of Fate*, 1960). He wrote in *landsmaal*, or Nynorsk ("New Norwegian"), the spoken language of Norway, rather than the traditional literary Dano-Norwegian, *riksmaal*.

Duval, Claude (1643–1670)   A highwayman, famed in legend and ballad. Duval was hanged at Tyburn and provided with an epitaph beginning: "Here lies Du Vall: Reader, if male thou art look to thy purse, if female, to thy heart."

Duveneck, Frank (1848–1919)   American painter. Originally a restrained painter of Kentucky churches, Duveneck traveled in 1870 to Munich, where he learned to paint vigorous presentations with bold brushstrokes. He imported the style to the U.S., where it greatly influenced the course of 20th-century painting, particularly the members of the ASHCAN SCHOOL. His most famous work, *Whistling Boy* (1872), details only the face of the sitter; all the rest is vaguely sketched.

Dvořák, Antonin (1841–1904)   Czech composer. Among the most versatile of the 19th-century composers,

Dvořák wrote energetic, optimistic music largely drawn from the themes of Czech folk music. He was a friend of BRAHMS and was greatly influenced by SCHUBERT, BEETHOVEN, and WAGNER. Aside from a prodigious output of chamber music, vocal and orchestral works, and operas, Dvořák wrote nine symphonies, the best known of which is the *Symphony from the New World* (1893), written when he was director of the National Conservatory of Music in New York City.

dwarf   A tiny, often misshapen person. Dwarfs have figured in the legends and mythology of nearly every race, and PLINY gives particulars of whole races of them, possibly following travelers' reports of African Pygmies. Among the Teutonic and Scandinavian peoples, dwarfs held an important place in mythology. They generally were believed to dwell in rocks, caves, and recesses of the earth, to be the guardians of its mineral wealth and precious stones, and to be very skillful in the working of these. They had their own king and as a rule were not inimical to man but could, on occasion, be intensely vindictive and mischievous. They play an important role in Wagner's opera cycle *Ring des Nibelungen* (1876).

Dwight, Timothy (1752–1817)   American poet and educator, a grandson of Jonathan EDWARDS, and leader of the HARTFORD WITS. A Calvinist in religion and Federalist in politics, Dwight was president of Yale (1795–1817), whose staff and curricula he brilliantly developed. His most popular poems were *The Conquest of Canaan* (1785), *The Triumph of Infidelity* (1788), and *Greenfield Hill* (1794). A clergyman, Dwight served as a chaplain in the Revolutionary army and wrote many sermons, 173 of which were collected as *Theology, Explained and Defended* (1818–19).

dybbuk (Heb, "a clinging thing")   In Jewish folklore, the migrating soul of a dead person that enters the body of a living person in the form of a malevolent spirit and renders him mad or corrupt. The dybbuk could be exorcised but only at great peril to the body it inhabited. *The Dybbuk*, by S. Ansky, is a classic of the Yiddish theatre. *The Tenth Man*, by Paddy CHAYEFSKY, is about a dybbuk.

dynastic histories   Chinese historical works detailing the history of the various ruling houses. They begin with the HAN dynasty (206 BC–AD 220) and continue until the CH'ING, or Manchu, dynasty (1644–1911). There are altogether twenty-four such histories, each composed by writers of the dynasty following one which had fallen.

Dzhugashvili, Iosef Visarionovich   See STALIN, JOSEPH.

E

Ea The Babylonian god of water and of wisdom. Developed from the Sumerian ENKI, Ea was one of the most important gods in the pantheon. It was he who, to a considerable extent, established the orderly functions of earth, sky, and sea, especially as they affect man, though specific functions such as irrigation or the growth of grain were in the hands of lesser gods. It was Ea whose wisdom or cunning often saved the universe and the other gods from disaster. He disposed of the stone monster of KUMARBI when it threatened heaven; he alone of the gods found the means to save ISHTAR from the underworld; and he saved mankind from the flood by warning UTNAPISHTIM to build his ark, as explained in the *Epic of* GILGAMESH.

Each and All (1839) A poem by Ralph Waldo EMERSON. Written on the occasion of a seashore walk, it is an expression of faith in the oneness of the universe. The poet praises the "perfect whole" in which all parts are interdependent. "Each and All" was later collected in Emerson's *Poems* (1847).

eagle A large, powerful predatory bird. The eagle is used in many lands and ages as an emblem symbolizing strength and swiftness. The Romans used it from the time of Marius as the ensign of a legion. The French under the Empire assumed the same device. The golden eagle and the spread eagle, devices of the emperors of the East, adapted from the ensigns of the ancient kings of Babylon and Persia, of the Ptolemies and the Seleucides, came to commemorate the Crusades. In Christian art, the eagle is emblematic of St. John the Evangelist, because, like that bird, he looked on "the sun of glory." St. Augustine, St. Gregory the Great, and St. Prisca are also often shown with an eagle.

When Charlemagne was made leader of the Holy Roman Empire, he joined the German eagle, which faces right, to the Roman eagle, which faces left. The resulting double-headed eagle thus became the emblem of the Holy Roman Empire and of the Austrian Empire, which regarded itself as its successor. In Russia the same emblem symbolized the Eastern or Byzantine Empire and the Western or Roman Empire, supposedly combined under the Russian Ivan Vasilyevich when, in 1472, he married Sophia, the niece of Constantine XIV, the last emperor of Byzantium. The phrase in Psalm 103, "Thy youth is renewed like the eagle's," refers to an ancient superstition that every ten years the eagle soars into the fiery region and plunges thence into the sea, where, molting its feathers, it acquires new life.

The American white, or bald, eagle, found in all parts of North America, became the national emblem of the United States by an act of Congress in 1782. See PHOENIX.

Eakins, Thomas (1844–1916) American painter. Eakins was a leading figure in the Philadelphia art scene, as a professor of anatomy and later director of the Pennsylvania Academy of Fine Arts, where his advocacy of painting from the nude provoked considerable scandal, leading to his resignation in 1886 and to the formation of the Philadelphia Art Students' League. Eakins made photographs to aid in preparing his paintings and worked with Eadweard MUYBRIDGE on photographic studies of human and animal locomotion. He is known for his rowing scenes and for the Rembrandtesque lighting and uncompromising objectivity in such works as the controversial *Clinic of Dr. Gross* (1875).

Earhart, Amelia (1898–1937) American aviator. The first woman pilot to cross the Atlantic Ocean in an airplane (1928), Earhart was also the first woman to make the same crossing alone (1932) and the first woman to make a solo flight from Hawaii to California (1935). She was married to the publisher G. P. Putnam (1887–1950) and was herself the author of several books, notably *Last Flight* (1938), edited by her husband. Earhart and a copilot were lost in the Pacific (July 1937) in an attempt to fly around the world.

Earthly Paradise A place of perfect beauty, peace, and immortality, widely believed in the Middle Ages to exist on earth in some undiscovered land. It was sometimes identified with the Garden of EDEN, located in the Near East, and given biblical authority by the Book of GENESIS.

In Genesis, it was made clear that the garden was not destroyed after the FALL OF MAN but only barred to him by an angel with a flaming sword. Sometimes it was situated in the Far East, as in a legendary letter from PRESTER JOHN, which locates it within three days' journey of his kingdom. Other maps and reports place it variously in the Atlantic, Pacific, and Indian Oceans. See ST. BRANDAN.

Earthly Paradise (4 vols, 1868–70)   A collection of narrative poems by William MORRIS. The prologue recounts the flight of a band of Norse sailors from the Black Death and their search for the Earthly Paradise. They finally come to rest in "a nameless city in a distant sea." Then follows a series of banquets at which twenty-four tales are told; each month, one of the Norsemen tells a medieval saga of romance, and one of the hosts relates a classical myth. In between is a lyric poem for each month, describing the changing landscape.

Earwicker, Humphrey Chimpden   The protagonist of James Joyce's novel FINNEGANS WAKE. Literally a middle-aged Irish tavern keeper with a guilty conscience, Earwicker represents all sinful mankind. His initials, HCE, are interwoven throughout the book.

East Coker   See FOUR QUARTETS.

Easter   The festival commemorating the resurrection of Christ. For most non-English-speaking Christians, the feast is called by some modification of the root word *pasch*, derived from *Pesach*, the Hebrew word for PASSOVER. The word Easter is derived from the Anglo-Saxon *eastre*, a festival held at the vernal equinox in honor of the Teutonic goddess of dawn, Eostre. Because the two celebrations fell at roughly the same time, the name of the pre-Christian festival was assumed by the Christians.

Easter Day is the first Sunday after the fourteenth day of the Paschal moon. The Paschal moon is the first moon whose fourteenth day comes on or after the vernal equinox (March 21). Consequently, Easter Sunday cannot be earlier than March 22 nor later than April 25. This was fixed by the council of Nicaea, AD 325.

Easter's importance is emphasized liturgically by the preparatory period of penitence, called LENT, lasting forty weekdays and ending in the ceremonies of Holy Week, which immediately precedes Easter. Holy Week begins with Palm Sunday, on which palms are blessed and a procession is held, symbolizing JESUS' entry into Jerusalem. MAUNDY THURSDAY celebrates the sacrament of the Eucharist, which Jesus instituted at THE LAST SUPPER (Matt. 26). The next day, GOOD FRIDAY, commemorates the crucifixion of Jesus, and Holy Saturday, the resting of his body in the tomb. The Easter Vigil mass, held at midnight as Easter Day begins, signals the joy of Christ's resurrection: the paschal candle, symbolizing Christ as the light of the world, is lit; bells are rung; the statues, crucifixes, and pictures in the church, which had been covered during Passiontide (the last two weeks of Lent), are uncovered, and the Alleluia is sung. White, symbolic of joy, light, and

purity, is the liturgical color for Easter. It was formerly a common belief that the sun danced on Easter Day.

Easter Rebellion   An abortive revolution staged on Easter Monday, 1916, in Dublin by the Irish Republican Brotherhood (see FENIANS) in an attempt to secure independence from England. Frustrated by English delay in granting home rule, the Brotherhood—under the leadership of Patrick PEARSE and James Connolly (1870–1916) —seized the general post office and a number of other locations in Dublin, proclaiming an Irish republic. The rebels, about two thousand in number, held their positions for six days before succumbing to the overwhelming superiority of the English forces. The ruthless behavior of the British soldiers, coupled with the execution of all the rebel leaders, led to a wave of violent anti-British sentiment, and the rebellion became a rallying point for all Irishmen. Among those executed along with Pearse were Thomas MacDonagh (1878–1916) and Joseph Plunkett (1887–1916). The events were celebrated in a number of literary works, notably W. B. YEATS's "Easter, 1916" and Sean O'CASEY's *The Plough and the Stars*.

East Lynne (1861)   A novel by Mrs. Henry WOOD, which was immensely popular, particularly in a dramatic version. Its heroine, Lady Isabel Vane, after running off with another man, returns to her remarried husband disguised as a nurse to care for her own children. After keeping up this pretense for a considerable time, she is at last reconciled to her husband.

East of Eden (1952)   A novel by John STEINBECK. Based on the biblical story of Cain and Abel, the book centers on the lives of Adam Trask and his two sons, Cal and Aron. Adam settles in the Salinas Valley in California with his wife, Cathy, who bears the two boys, leaves her husband, and becomes a prostitute. Adam, who favors Aron, is at first unable to forgive Cal when he drives Aron to his death by telling him that their mother is a prostitute.

Eberhart, Richard (1904–   )   American poet and teacher. Eberhart's lyric poetry is characterized by short lines, few rhymes, and the use of abstract symbols from which the poet draws parallels to philosophical or metaphysical ideas. His recent works include the acclaimed *Ways of Light* (1980) and *The Long Reach* (1984). Noted for its direct simplicity, Eberhart's verse has also been collected in *Collected Poems 1930–1960* (1960) and *Selected Poems 1930–1976* (1976). In 1982, he earned the accolade of a Richard Eberhart day in Rhode Island, by the proclamation of the governor.

Eblis   In Muslim legend, the Devil, called AZAZEL before the fall, who rules over the evil genii, or JINN. When Adam was created, Allah commanded all the angels to worship him, but Azazel replied, "Me thou hast created of smokeless fire, and shall I reverence a creature made of dust?" Allah was angry at this insolent answer, turned the disobedient angel into a Sheytan (devil), and he became the father of devils. Another Muslim tradition has it that before life was breathed into Adam, all the angels came to look at the shape of clay, among them Azazel, who, knowing that Allah intended man to be his superior, vowed never to acknowledge him as such and kicked the figure until it rang.

Eblis had five sons: *Tir*, author of fatal accidents; *Awar*, the demon of lubricity; *Dasim*, author of discord; *Sut*, father of lies; and *Zalambur*, author of mercantile dishonesty.

Eça de Queiroz, José Maria (1845–1900) Portuguese novelist and short-story writer. Considered Portugal's greatest novelist, Eça de Queiroz is best known for *O crime do Padre Amaro* (*The Sin of Father Amaro*, 1876), a naturalistic satire directed against clerical corruption, which was based on his observations as a municipal official in the province of Leiria. His gift for ironic social criticism was further revealed in *O primo Basílio* (*Cousin Basilio*, 1878), a study of a middle-class Lisbon family, and *Os Maias* (1880), about upper-class life.

Ecclesiastes A book of the OLD TESTAMENT. Its authorship was formerly ascribed to SOLOMON because of the opening textual reference to "the words of the Preacher, the son of David, king in Jerusalem," but it is now generally assigned to an unnamed author of the 3rd century BC. The book appears to be the work of an older man who repeatedly searches for wisdom and meaning in life and finds instead that "all is vanity" (Eccles. 1:2). In a world of despotism and oppression, the one good reserved for man is to "rejoice in his labor; this is the gift of God" (Eccles. 5:19). The book has a somewhat despairing tone, with its emphasis on the evil in man and the universality of death. It contains the well-known passage that begins "To every thing there is a season, and a time to every purpose under heaven . . ." (Eccles. 3:1–8).

Echegaray [y Eizaguirre], José (1832–1916) Spanish dramatist. Trained as a mathematician, Echegaray then turned to economics; he was appointed minister of finance and founded the Bank of Spain. It was not until a period of brief exile in 1874 that he began to write plays. In the next thirty years, he wrote nearly seventy plays and became the most popular dramatist in Spain. His works, which enlarge upon the romantic theme of melancholic passion, are noted for their high degree of technical skill and their ability to keep audiences engaged despite relatively simple plots. The best known of his fustian compositions are *O locura o santidad* (1877), in which a Quixotic hero is accused of folly for attempting to pass along his fortune to its rightful owners, and EL GRAN GALEOTO, in which society is blamed for the tragic developments that befall its three characters. In 1904 Echegaray shared the NOBEL PRIZE in Literature with Frédéric MISTRAL.

Echeverría, Esteban (1805–1851) Argentine poet. During a five-year stay in Paris, Echeverría absorbed the tenets of French romanticism, which permeate his works of poetry, especially *Elvira, o la novia del Plata* (1832), *Con-*

suelos (1834), and *La cautiva* (1837), notable for its depiction of the Argentine pampa and its inhabitants. Echeverría's opposition to dictator Juan Manuel de ROSAS led him and other idealistic youths to form the *Asociación de Mayo*, a secret revolutionary group dedicated to liberal, democratic principles. His hatred for Rosas also inspired him to write EL MATADERO, the work for which he is probably best known today.

Echo A nymph of Greek mythology. There are several stories of why Echo seemed to be merely a disembodied voice. Perhaps the commonest is that she pined away from unrequited love for NARCISSUS until only her voice remained. According to another story, HERA, annoyed at Echo's babbling while she was trying to spy on ZEUS, took away the nymph's speech, allowing her only to echo others. Yet a third version explains that PAN, furious that she could not love him, maddened some shepherds until they tore her into such tiny pieces that nothing was left but her voice.

eclectic (fr Gr, *ek-legein*, "to choose; to select") Selectiveness as a way of living. The name given to those who do not attach themselves to any special school (especially philosophers and painters) but pick and choose from various systems, selecting and harmonizing those doctrines and methods that suit them.

eclogue A formal pastoral poem in the form of a dialogue or soliloquy (see MONOLOGUE). There are a variety of conventional types, such as a singing contest between two shepherds, a dialogue between two shepherds or between a shepherd and his mistress, a lament for a dead shepherd, a love song, or a eulogy. Loosely the term means any short poem with pastoral elements. See BUCOLICS.

Eco, Umberto (1932–   ) Italian writer and semiotician. Eco's early work in semiotics, recognized as ground-breaking and original, was developed in his later studies, such as *La struttura assente* (1968). The basic assumptions of his work are rooted in the theories of Ferdinand de Saussure, CLAUDE LÉVI-STRAUSS, and Roland BARTHES, but Eco's own contribution is in the area of meaning or significance. Perhaps his most influential works are *A Theory of Semiotics* (1976), a truly semiotic work in that it is Eco's own translation into English and rewriting of his earlier book *La struttura assente*, and *The Role of the Reader: Explorations in the Semiotics of Texts* (1979).

In 1980 Eco published his first novel, *Il nome della rose* (tr *The Name of the Rose*, 1983). Despite the intellectual demands it makes on the reader—it contains large chunks of mostly untranslated Latin, for instance—it was an instant success in Europe and in the U.S. The novel, a suspenseful tale of murder in a Benedictine monastery in 1327, brings together Eco's formidable erudition about the Middle Ages and his intellectual concerns and theoretical assumptions in the field of semiotics. Since then, Eco has published *Postille a Il nome della rose* (1983; tr *Postscript to*

"The Name of the Rose," 1984) and *Travels in Hyperreality* (1986), a collection of essays on art and society.

Ecole des femmes, L' (The School for Wives, 1662)   A verse comedy by MOLIÈRE. ARNOLPHE has arranged for his beloved AGNÈS to be raised in total innocence, in order that she may never prove unfaithful when he marries her. Because of her unsophistication, Horace is able to win her affections and persuades her to run away with him. Unaware of Arnolphe's relation to the girl, Horace asks him to hide her. Arnolphe is about to spirit her away to a convent when it is revealed that Agnès's father, the rich Enrique, has arranged with Horace's father for their children to be married. The play was criticized for supposed moral as well as literary flaws, and Molière replied to his critics in two works: *La Critique de l'Ecole des femmes* (1663) and *L'Impromptu de Versailles* (1663).

Ecole des femmes, L'   A novel trilogy by André GIDE about the position of women in the modern world. It includes *The School for Wives* (1929), *Robert* (1929), and *Geneviève* (1936).

Ector, Sir   In Malory's MORTE D'ARTHUR, the foster father of King ARTHUR and father of Sir KAY.

Edda   The name given to two Icelandic collections of early Scandinavian mythology. The manuscripts comprising the *Elder* or *Poetic Edda* (written 9th to 12th century) were discovered about 1643 by the Icelandic Bishop Brynjolf Sveinsson (1605–75), who erroneously attributed them to Saemund Sigfusson (1056–1133) and called the work *The Edda of Saemund*. The thirty-four lays, or poems, tell the mythological stories of the Old Norse gods and heroes.

The *Younger* or *Prose Edda*, also called the *Snorra Edda* (early 13th century), was written by SNORRI STURLUSON. In five parts, it includes a prefatory account of the creation of the world and of pagan poetry; the stories of early Scandinavian mythology; further legends of the gods, given as the "sayings of BRAGI," god of poetry; the *Skalda*, a detailed account of the rules of ancient prosody; and the *Hattatal*, a technical analysis of meters. Other linguistic treatises and a list of poets were added after Sturluson's death.

Eddy, Mary Baker (1821–1910)   American religious leader, editor, and author. The founder of the religious movement Christian Science, Eddy published *Science and Health* (1875) as an exposition of her ideas and as the official statement of the organization she headed. In this book and others of her *Miscellaneous Writings* (1896), she taught that pain, disease, old age, and death were "errors." She founded the Church of Christ, Scientist, in Boston (1879) and the newspaper *The Christian Science Monitor* (1908). Eddy was influenced by TRANSCENDENTALISM and, particularly, by the work of Ralph Waldo EMERSON. The doctrines of Christian Science are summarized in the first sentence of Eddy's *Science and Health*: "The Prayer that reforms the sinner and heals the sick is an absolute faith that all things are possible to God."

Edel, Leon (1907–   )   Canadian-born American biographer and critic. Edel is known as the definitive scholar of Henry JAMES. His five-volume biography of James (1953–71) includes *Henry James: The Conquest of London, 1870–1881* and *Henry James: The Middle Years, 1882–1895* (both pub 1962), for which he was awarded the PULITZER PRIZE and the National Book Award. He has edited James's plays, stories, and letters and the Bodley Head edition of James's complete works. Among Edel's other biographical works are *James Joyce: The Last Journey* (1947), *Willa Cather: A Critical Biography* (1953; with E. K. Brown), and *Henry David Thoreau* (1970). His critical writings include *The Psychological Novel* (1955; rev as *The Modern Psychological Novel*, 1964), and *Bloomsbury: A House of Lions* (1979), a study of the BLOOMSBURY GROUP. Edel is also the editor of Edmund WILSON's journals, published by decades beginning with *The Twenties* (1975) and *The Thirties* (1980). Edel's analysis of his craft, published in *Telling Lives* (1979), argues that biography is a legitimate literary form in its own right.

Edel's one-volume revised edition of the multivolume biography of Henry James won the 1985 American Book Award for biography.

Eden   The garden in which ADAM AND EVE lived before the FALL OF MAN (Gen. 2:5). In Eden the first couple led a life free from cares until, in disobedience to the command of JEHOVAH, they ate the forbidden fruit of the tree of knowledge. They were thereupon expelled, and ever since man has lived "by the sweat of his brow." Eden is frequently used to describe an idyllically beautiful spot. See EARTHLY PARADISE.

Edgar   In Shakespeare's KING LEAR, the legitimate son of the earl of Gloucester. Edgar is disinherited because of his bastard brother EDMUND's lies. After Gloucester has been blinded and ousted from his castle by REGAN and CORNWALL, Edgar finds him and saves him from suicide. He then kills the treacherous Edmund.

Edgeworth, Maria (1767–1849)   Irish novelist, best known for her novel CASTLE RACKRENT. Many of Edgeworth's other works have their setting in Irish life, among them *Belinda* (1801), *The Absentee* (1812), *Vivian* (1812), and *Ormond* (1817). She wrote in the tradition of the novel of manners in which Jane AUSTEN excelled but was also very sensitive to local atmosphere and portrayed national character with great sympathy. In this respect she influenced her friend Sir Walter SCOTT. Her letters as well as her novels are still highly readable.

Edison, Thomas Alva (1847–1931)   American inventor. Educated by his mother, with only three months of formal schooling, Edison began work as a newsboy on the railroad at the age of twelve. He later worked as a telegraph operator and began inventing a receiver and transmitter for the automatic telegraph. During his lifetime he patented over thirteen hundred inventions, including the phonograph, the microphone, and the incandescent electric lamp. His Pearl Street plant in New York City was the first centralized electric-light power plant in the world. He invented the Kinetoscope (peep-show machine) and later developed talking motion pictures. Edison is credited with the definition of genius as 2 percent inspiration and 98 percent perspiration.

Editions de Minuit, Les   See VERCORS.

Edmonds, Walter D[umaux] (1903–   ) American novelist. Edmonds's popular historical novels are nearly all set in his native upstate New York and are noted for their careful research and lively narrative style. His novel *Rome Haul* (1929) was dramatized by Marc CONNELLY and Frank Elser as *The Farmer Takes a Wife* (1934). Among the best known of his subsequent novels are *Erie Water* (1933), DRUMS ALONG THE MOHAWK, *Chad Hanna* (1940), *In the Hands of the Senecas* (1947), *The Boyds of Black River* (1953), *They Had a Horse* (1962), and *Wolf Hunt* (1972). Edmonds has also written straight history and several books for children, notably *Bert Breen's Barn* (1975), which won the National Book Award in 1976.

Edmund   In Shakespeare's KING LEAR, the bastard son of the earl of Gloucester. He instigates the disinheritance of his half-brother EDGAR, betrays his father, and schemes with Lear's daughter GONERIL to poison her husband, ALBANY. Mortally wounded by Edgar, the repentant Edmund tries unsuccessfully to save CORDELIA, Lear's youngest daughter, from execution.

Edo   The old name for Tokyo, capital of the shogunate during the TOKUGAWA period in Japan.

Education of Henry Adams, The (privately printed in 1907; pub posthumously, 1918)   An autobiographical work by Henry ADAMS, subtitled *A Study of 20th Century Multiplicity*. Adams uses himself as a model of modern man, searching for coherence in a fragmented universe. In the chapter "The Virgin and the Dynamo," Adams compares the 13th century and its concept of an ordered universe, symbolized by the Virgin, to the 20th-century "multiverse" in which man is secondary to the dynamo, symbol of mechanistic force. This comparison is central to his discussion in MONT-SAINT-MICHEL AND CHARTRES. He concludes that his "education" was inadequate to prepare him for the conflicts of the modern world. Not a complete autobiography, the book omits any mention of the thirteen years of Adams's marriage and the seven years following his wife's suicide. It does, however, present a vivid picture of the people and places the author knew.

Education sentimentale, L' (Sentimental Education, 1869)   A novel by Gustave FLAUBERT. Flaubert presents a picture of life among French dilettantes, intellectuals, and revolutionaries at the time of the decline and fall of Louis Philippe's monarchy and the Revolution of 1848. The events of the Revolution and the establishment of the Second Empire, carefully documented, provide a further background for the main action. The novel's protagonist, Frédéric Moreau, is an egotistical and ambitious young man who comes to Paris from the provinces determined to pattern his life upon literature's romantic hero. He undergoes the romantic passion of unrequited love for Mme Arnoux, but does not forego involvement in several less ideal and ultimately disillusioning affairs. Like the desires of Emma Bovary (see MADAME BOVARY), his dreams are pathetic and sometimes contemptible. Like Emma, too, Moreau is a wholly real person, whom Flaubert draws with truly objective detachment and complete artistic mastery.

Edward   A medieval English ballad which has many versions. In most of these, a young man named Edward explains to his mother that he has killed his father. In some variations, there is the suggestion that the mother encouraged the murder. A modern version of this "domestic tragedy" ballad may be found in a poem by Robinson JEFFERS: "Such Counsels You Gave to Me" (1937).

Edward II (1284–1327)   King of England (after 1307). A weak and dissipated king, governed by a series of unpopular advisors and favorites, Edward was overthrown in a rebellion headed by his wife and son (subsequently Edward III) and gruesomely murdered at Berkley Castle. He is the subject of a play by Christopher MARLOWE.

Edward VI (Edward Tudor, 1537–1553)   King of England (1547–53). The son of Henry VIII and his third wife, Jane SEYMOUR, Edward became king when he was only nine years old. He was under the Protectorate first of his uncle, Edward Seymour, lord Somerset, and then of John Dudley, duke of Northumberland. Largely through Northumberland's machinations, Edward signed a deposition willing the crown to his second cousin, Lady Jane GREY, who was also Northumberland's daughter-in-law.

Edward VIII   See WINDSOR, DUKE OF.

Edwardian   Pertaining to English life and letters in the early years of the 20th century, a period corresponding roughly to the reign (1901–10) of Edward VII. In general, the era witnessed a relaxation of Victorian conservatism and complacency, together with a questioning and criticism of authority and accepted social values. G. B. SHAW, Arnold BENNETT, and H. G. WELLS were among the writers who reflected these tendencies. The term is also used to refer to the opulence and elegance of the period. Victoria SACKVILLE-WEST described the era in her novel *The Edwardians* (1930).

Edwards, Jonathan (1703–1758)   American theologian and philosopher. In his early youth Edwards was a precociously brilliant scholar, showing a keen interest in scientific observation. His early philosophical thought tended toward Idealism under the influence of LOCKE, and many of his ideas resembled those of George BERKELEY, whose work at that time he did not know.

Edwards's theology was more basically Calvinistic than that of earlier Puritan divines, who emphasized the covenantal relation between God and man, rather than the absolute supremacy of a God bound by no contract. He believed "that the essence of all religion lies in holy love" and that sin was a "property of the species," which both justified God's punishment of man and made possible mercy and redemption. His sermon on *Sinners in the Hands of an Angry God* (1741), so horrifying to later readers, was in fact an exhortation on the necessity of salvation, as well as a reminder of the torments that awaited the unregenerate. His beliefs on the place of the emotions in religious experience led him to champion the "GREAT AWAKENING," in which he saw dramatic conversions as evidence of the "peculiar and immediate" manifestation of God. Among his works are *A Faithful Narrative of the Surprising Work of God in the Conversion of Many Hundred Souls* (1737) and *A Careful and Strict Enquiry into Freedom of the Will* (1754).

Edwin Drood, The Mystery of (1870) An unfinished novel by Charles DICKENS. The orphans Edwin Drood and Rosa Bud have been betrothed by their fathers, and are to marry when Edwin is twenty-one, though the obligatory nature of the agreement has in fact made love between them impossible. Rosa arouses the admiration of two men: Edwin's ostensibly devoted Uncle Jasper, a disagreeable hypocrite who loves her passionately, and Neville Landless, a youth who detests Edwin for his mistreatment of the young girl. At their last meeting before they are to be wed, Edwin and Rosa acknowledge that they can never be happy together and break their engagement. The same night Edwin mysteriously disappears, and Jasper, who has done all he can to aggravate the enmity between Edwin and Neville, accuses the latter of murdering his nephew. Rosa's guardian notices Jasper's displeasure on learning that the engagement had been broken before the disappearance. Neville is arrested, but, since no body can be found, he is released untried. Jasper, however, continues to connive against Neville and to pursue the terrified Rosa, while a mysterious Mr. Datchery appears on the scene to frustrate Jasper's intrigues. At this point the novel breaks off. In the absence of any solution left by Dickens, it has been a favorite puzzle of literary detectives to attempt to solve the mystery. The most convincing proposed solutions generally hinge on two questions: whether or not Edwin is actually dead, and what Mr. Datchery's true identity is. Some have held that Datchery is actually Rosa.

Effi Briest (1894) A novel by Theodor FONTANE. Effi Briest, a young woman from a well-established family in Hohen-crommen, is married off by her parents to her mother's old sweetheart, Baron von Instetten, a highly eligible member of the Prussian nobility, and an embodiment of the discipline and values of the Prussian military establishment. It is a suitable match, but the two are ill-suited to each other. Effi, an impetuous, spontaneous, open young woman is totally at odds with her cold, calculating, utterly rational though affectionate husband. In his many absences from Kessin, the tiny Baltic seaport which is their home, Effi develops an intimate relationship, and is even-

tually seduced by Major Crampas, a stock character in such situations: mustachioed, a gambler, and a ladies'-man to boot. By the time Instetten becomes aware of the fact, the family has moved to Berlin, where Instetten, on his steady rise up the ladder in Prussian government circles, has been posted. Instetten does the "proper" thing, according to the Prussian military and social code; he challenges Crampas to a duel in which Crampas is the loser. Effi is made to move out of the house and into an apartment on her own, separated from her dear daughter Annie, who is now in Instetten's care. Burdened by grief and a terrible sense of guilt, Effi falls ill and is sent home to her parents in Hohen-crommen, where she eventually dies.

The novel is considered a masterpiece of German realism, not only for the way in which it mirrors the rather ordinary lives and concerns of the average inhabitants of the town Instetten lives in but also for the highly skillful way in which the characters are developed. It is also notable for the pertinent philosophical issues it raises and the subtlety of its solution to perhaps the greatest problem that has preoccupied man: namely, what is happiness and wherein is it to be found? The simple answer: in little things, in the simple pleasures of everyday life, in the peace and quiet that Effi discovered in the days before her death. It continues to be highly regarded today and has been put on a par with other European realist novels like MADAME BOVARY and ANNA KARENINA, which are similar in content and theme. A film of *Effi Briest* was produced in 1974 by Rainer Werner FASSBINDER.

Egeria In Roman legend, the nymph who instructed Numa Pompilius (715–672 BC), second king of Rome, in his wise legislation. Hence, a woman counselor, especially a woman who advises and influences a statesman.

Egmont (pub 1788) A tragedy by Johann Wolfgang von GOETHE. It is based on the downfall of a historical Count Egmont (1522–68) who was executed in connection with the Netherlandic revolt against Spain. Like Goethe's earlier GÖTZ VON BERLICHINGEN, Egmont is upright and straightforward in his striving for freedom but unable to survive in an atmosphere of subtle political machinations. Though Goethe was already working on the play in 1776, in his STURM UND DRANG period, he did not finish it until his second year in Italy, when his ideas had already taken a strong turn toward the classical. This change is reflected in the play's relative polish of form and language as compared with *Götz*. Beethoven wrote his famous *Egmont* music for Goethe's play. See DAEMONIC.

ego See FREUD, SIGMUND.

Egoist, The (1879) A novel by George MEREDITH. The "egoist" is Sir Willoughby Patterne of Patterne Hall, possessed of good looks, wealth, and all the virtues except humility and a sense of humor. He invites his fiancée, Clara Middleton, and her father, a clergyman who loves good food and wine, to spend a month at the Hall, where he is the idol of his two old aunts. Clara—"a rogue in porcelain" as Mrs. Mountstuart Jenkinson, the clever widow who regulates the social life of the countryside, pronounces her—is soon longing to extricate herself from the attentions of her self-centered lover. She is thankful for the diversion of Patterne's merry Irish guest, De Craye, who makes violent love to her, but gives her confidence to Vernon Whitford, Patterne's cousin and secretary. Patterne, who has had a sad experience previously, is in mortal dread of being jilted by Clara, and to preserve his dignity he proposes to his former worshiper Laetitia Dale, whom he had made use of for this same purpose before. Many complications arise, but Vernon and Clara finally confess their love, and Patterne is forced to plead with the now thoroughly disillusioned Laetitia to become the mistress of Patterne Hall.

Egoist, The   A LITTLE MAGAZINE published in England between 1911 and 1919. Originally founded as a feminist publication, it became the chief organ of imagist poetry (see IMAGISM), introducing the work of such writers as Hilda DOOLITTLE, Richard ALDINGTON, Rebecca WEST, T. S. ELIOT, and Ezra POUND to English readers.

Eguren, José María (1882–1942)   Peruvian poet. Originally identified with MODERNISMO and particularly the symbolist influence associated with that movement, Eguren's work represents a thorough renovation of technique. His major volumes, *Simbólicas* (1911), *La canción de las figuras* (1916), and *Poesías* (1929), evoke a personal, dreamlike, quizzical, often mysteriously wounded vision of the world. Before César VALLEJO, he was the greatest Peruvian poet. His *Poesías completas* first appeared in 1955 and were reprinted and supplemented in 1961 and 1970.

Egyptian Book of the Dead   See BOOK OF THE DEAD.

Eichendorff, Joseph, Freiherr von (1788–1857) German romantic poet. Eichendorff is most famous for his many poems that treat idyllically the unspoiled woods of his Silesian homeland and for the long story *Aus dem Leben eines Taugenichts* (*From the Life of a Ne'er-Do-Well*, 1826). His novel *Ahnung und Gegenwart* (*Presentiment and the Present*, 1815), a BILDUNGSROMAN, reflects Eichendorff's Catholicism in that the hero ends by renouncing this world and entering a monastery. During his career, Eichendorff was a friend of many of the German romantics (see GERMAN ROMANTICISM), including F. SCHLEGEL, ARNIM, and BRENTANO, and later in life he wrote a number of works on literary history: for example, *Über die ethische und religiöse Bedeutung der neueren romantischen Poesie in Deutschland* (*On the Ethical and Religious Importance of Recent Romantic Poetry in Germany*, 1847).

Eight, The   See ASHCAN SCHOOL.

Einstein, Albert (1879–1955)   German-born, Swiss-educated American physicist. In 1905, while Einstein was getting his doctorate in Zurich, he first enunciated "the special theory of relativity." In 1913 he was made director of theoretical physics at the Kaiser Wilhelm Institute in Berlin. Three years later he formulated the "general theory of relativity" and was writing his landmark work, *Relativity: The Special and the General Theory* (1918; 1947). In 1921 he was awarded the Nobel Prize in Physics for his studies in the motion of the atom, the photoelectric effect, gravitation-and-inertia, and the space-time continuum, the inter-relatedness of which he demonstrated in *The Meaning of Relativity* (1921). In 1950, he achieved the clear mathematical formula for relativity, which he published in an appendix to a new edition of the 1921 book. One of the great original thinkers in history, Einstein was also instrumental in developing quantum theory, but it was to his own quest for a unified field theory embracing all these phenomena that he was devoted in the years that followed.

Einstein was a Jew, outspokenly opposed to HITLER. When his German property was confiscated and his citizenship revoked in 1934, he went to the Institute for Advanced Study in Princeton, to which he had been invited the previous year. In 1940 he became an American citizen. Convinced pacifist though he was, he was one of the group of scientists to suggest that the energy of split atoms could be used in bombs. After he retired in 1945, he wrote about his own philosophy in, for example, *The World As I See It* (1950) and *Ideas and Opinions* (1954). *Einstein on Peace* (1960) was edited by Otto Nathan and Heinz Norden after his death.

Eisenhower, Dwight D[avid] (1890–1969) American general and thirty-fourth president of the U.S. (1953–61). Born in Denison, Texas, Eisenhower graduated in 1915 from the U.S. Military Academy at West Point. In 1942 he was made commander of the Allied forces landing in North Africa. He became a full general in February 1943, was appointed Supreme Commander of the Allied Expeditionary Forces in Europe, led the Normandy invasion, and directed the final overthrow of the Nazis (1944–45). He later became chief of staff in Washington and told his own story of the European war in *Crusade in Europe* (1948). He was president of Columbia University from 1948 to 1952, taking a leave of absence to serve as Supreme Allied Commander in Europe and to set up NATO.

Eisenhower defeated Adlai E. Stevenson in the 1952 presidential election. As president he generally took a middle road in his policies, continuing foreign aid and advocating a balanced budget, while he opposed government control in private enterprise. He was reelected in 1956, again defeating Stevenson. *Mandate for Change, 1953–1956*, the first volume of Eisenhower's account of his administrations, *The White House Years*, appeared in 1963, followed by the second volume, *Waging Peace*, in 1965.

Eisenstein, Sergey Mikhailovich (1898–1948) Russian motion-picture director. Eisenstein has been acclaimed as one of the greatest of all film directors; his methods of cutting and mounting film to gain the effects of montage and dynamic progression have been widely imitated. He was trained as a civil engineer and architect, then served in the Bolshevik army as a volunteer (1918–20). His first film, *Strike* (1924), is notable for its skillful handling of crowd movement. Several remarkable scenes in *Potemkin* (1926) are even more significant as milestones in the development of cinematic technique. Among his other famous films are *Ten Days That Shook the World* (1928), the never-completed epic *Que Viva Mexico* (1931–32), *Alexander Nevsky* (1928), and *Ivan the Terrible* (Part I, 1941; Part II, 1946), which was planned as a trilogy.

Eisteddfod   The Welsh national congress of bards. It had its origin in an extremely old Welsh assembly called the Gorsedd; in its present form it probably began in the 12th century. Eisteddfod literally means "a session." Minstrelsy has been an important part of Welsh culture from the earliest days, and the present purpose of the Eisteddfod is to maintain an interest in the ancient traditions.

Ekelöf, [Bengt] Gunnar (1907–1968)   Swedish poet. Ekelöf's verse, some of the greatest ever written in Swedish, represents his attempt to pare away all illusion to get at the barest nature of experience which, for him, lies in reflection and feeling. Although much of his work is obscure and esoteric, it is consistently powerful and profoundly influential. Among the translations in English are *Selected Poems* (tr 1967), *I Do Best Alone at Night* (tr 1968), and *Selected Poems* (tr 1972), co-translated by W. H. AUDEN.

Ekwensi, Cyprian (1921–   )   Nigerian novelist and short-story writer. Ekwensi's fiction effectively chronicles the disastrous implications of rapid modernization in a society still deeply rooted within village traditions and tribal hierarchies. His characters are engulfed by the modern, urban environment of the city: its slums and its night clubs, its cold, hard glitter, and its lack of humanity sharply highlight the historical mistrust between the colonials/whites and the colonized/blacks, as well as tribal hostilities and political corruption. His novels include *People of the City* (1954), *Jagua Nana* (1961), *Burning Grass* (1962), *Beautiful Feathers* (1963), and *Iska* (1966). *Motherless Baby*, a novella, and *Divided We Stand*, a novel, were published in 1980.

El   The supreme god of many ancient Semitic races in the Near East. El was represented in the form of a bull. The golden calf of the OLD TESTAMENT probably was sacred to one of his offspring. See POEM OF AQHAT, THE; POEM OF BAAL, THE.

Elaine   In Arthurian romance, the name given to two ladies, both of whom love LAUNCELOT. In Malory's MORTE D'ARTHUR, the first Elaine is the daughter of King Pelles. Falling in love with Sir Launcelot, she takes on for a night the likeness of Queen GUINEVERE, in order to deceive him. As a result, a son is born to them, and he is given the name of GALAHAD.

The second Elaine, known as the "lily maid of Astolat," is the Elaine of Tennyson's "Lancelot and Elaine" in his IDYLLS OF THE KING, in which he recasts Malory's version of the story. This Elaine loved Launcelot "with that love which was her doom." Her love is so great that she dies of it. According to her request, her dead body is then placed on a barge, a lily in her right hand and a letter, avowing her love and showing the innocence of Launcelot, in her left. The barge, steered by an old servitor, moves down the river, and, when it stops at the palace entrance, Arthur orders the body borne in. The letter is read, and Arthur directs that the maiden shall be buried like a queen, with her sad story blazoned on her tomb. Tennyson has also told her story in his "The Lady of Shalott."

El Dorado (Sp, "the gilded")   A legendary king. El Dorado was the supposed King of Manoa, a fabulous city of immense wealth localized by early explorers on the Amazon. He was said to be covered with oil and then powdered with gold dust. This operation had been performed so many times that he was permanently, and literally, gilded. Many expeditions, from both Spain and England (two of which were led by Sir Walter RALEIGH), tried to discover El Dorado, and the name was later transferred to his supposed territory. Hence, the term refers to any place or realm of fabulous richness.

Eleanor of Aquitaine (c1122–1204)   Queen of Louis VII of France (1137–51), then of Henry II of England (1152–1204), mother of four sons, including Richard I and King John. Because she was heiress of Aquitaine, about half of southern France, England claimed possession of the region, thus adding fresh fuel to the ongoing wars with France, which continued for much of the next four hundred years. She backed the rebellion of her sons against Henry II (1173), for which she was imprisoned (1174–89). Richard released her after his accession to the throne, and when he went on his crusade, she protected his interests against John. Later she reconciled the brothers and continued to be politically important during John's reign. An ardent patron of the Provençal TROUBADOURS, she was influential in bringing them and their works to her courts.

Electra   (1) In Greek mythology, a daughter of AGAMEMNON and CLYTEMNESTRA, and sister of Orestes. Her tragic story (see House of ATREUS) was told by each of the three great Athenian dramatists, AESCHYLUS in his *Oresteia* trilogy, Sophocles and Euripides in their plays called ELECTRA. Richard Strauss wrote an opera of a version of Sophocles' play by Hugo von HOFMANNSTHAL (1903). MOURNING BECOMES ELECTRA, a trilogy of plays by Eugene O'Neill, is a retelling of the *Oresteia* story set in 19th-century New England. Jean GIRAUDOUX also adapted the story for his play *Électre* (1937).

(2) One of the PLEIADES, daughter of ATLAS, mother of Dardanus. She is known as "the lost Pleiad," for it is said that she disappeared a little before the TROJAN WAR, that she might be saved the mortification of seeing the ruin of

her beloved city. She showed herself occasionally to mortals but always in the guise of a comet.

Electra (413 BC)   A drama by EURIPIDES. Aegisthus has forced Electra to marry a kindly old farmer so that she cannot enter into a dangerous marriage with some great prince. Electra has no power to avenge her father as the wife of a peasant; her only hope is Orestes. The play opens in the peasant's small hut in the mountains. The peasant speaks the prologue, after which Orestes and Pylades enter furtively. Various devices lead gradually to the recognition of brother and sister, which comes about through the summoning of the old servant of Agamemnon who rescued Orestes as a baby. In this play the murder of Aegisthus precedes that of Clytemnestra. Aegisthus is portrayed as the real force behind the usurpation; Clytemnestra is represented as being to some degree the victim of circumstances. In this way the play leads up to the murder of Clytemnestra, who is summoned to the peasant's hut on the pretext that Electra has just had a child. Clytemnestra goes inside, to be met by Orestes and Electra. Euripides' presentation is designed to inspire the utmost horror at the act and great pity for the victim. The play ends with the beginning of the madness of Orestes, brought on by the Erinyes.

Electra (414? BC)   A tragedy by SOPHOCLES. *Electra* deals with the return of Orestes to Argos and the murder of Clytemnestra. Electra is the heroine; as in the *Philoctetes* and the *Oedipus at Colonus*, Sophocles isolates his tragic hero in order to emphasize the qualities of heroism and tragic endurance. As a consequence, the murder of Clytemnestra and Aegisthus is left to the very end; the climax of the play is the long recognition scene between Orestes and Electra. Also, in order to develop the character of Electra to the fullest extent, Sophocles leaves Orestes almost blank; he is the avenger, a paragon of virtue, and nothing more. Thus the recognition scene is the fitting climax, since Electra's trials are now over. Clytemnestra is the real enemy, and Aegisthus is no threat. Euripides reverses this emphasis in order to make Clytemnestra's death more unnecessary and more horrible; Sophocles' determination to represent the murder as an example of "natural recoil" necessitates a strong character for the queen.

Elegies of Ch'ü (Ch'u tz'u)   An anthology of poetry compiled in the 2nd century AD. Many of the poems are traditionally ascribed to Ch'ü Yuan (4th century BC), who sings of his misfortunes at the court of the southern Chinese state of Ch'u. Much of the poetry is lush and ecstatic in its imagery and emotionalism and was clearly influenced by shamanistic religious practices. See CHINESE LITERATURE.

elegy (fr Gr, *elegeia*)   In classical prosody a poem in elegiac DISTICHS, in modern prosody a lyrical poem of plaintive content and mood, especially a poem of lament for someone or something departed. Thought to be among the greatest elegies in English are Milton's LYCIDAS, Shel-

ley's ADONAIS, Tennyson's IN MEMORIAM, and Matthew ARNOLD's "Thyrsis," all poems of mourning, and Gray's ELEGY WRITTEN IN A COUNTRY CHURCHYARD in a more general plaintive vein.

Elegy Written in a Country Churchyard (1742?–50, pub 1751)   A poem by Thomas GRAY, probably the most popular—and often considered the greatest—poem written in the 18th century. Its familiar theme deals with rural life combined with the tragic dignity inherent in man. This pastoral idealization and meditation on death is made even more subjective at the end by the introduction of "The Epitaph."

Eleusinian Mysteries   Ancient Greek religious rites. They were performed in honor of DEMETER and her daughter PERSEPHONE (Kore) at Eleusis in Attica. Begun probably in late Mycenaean times, with the introduction of the worship of Demeter to Eleusis, these rites became the most famous mysteries in the Greek or Roman world, and continued to be celebrated well into the Christian era. The secret of the rites was so successfully guarded that, in spite of their tremendous importance, no one can say precisely what they were. It is known, however, that they centered about the abduction of Persephone by HADES, her return, and the subsequent reconciliation of Demeter and Hades. In short, they celebrated the revival of corn in the springtime. Also connected with the rite in some way was a youthful godling Iacchus, about whom almost nothing is known, except that he was later identified with DIONYSUS.

Elgar, Sir Edward [William] (1857–1934)   One of the great English orchestral composers. Although from a musical family, Elgar received no formal training. He is probably best known for a musical portrait of his friends, *The Enigma Variations* (1899), and the oratorios *The Dream of Gerontius* (1900), *The Apostles* (1903), and *The Kingdom* (1906). He also wrote the well-known march "Pomp and Circumstance" (1902).

Elgin marbles   A collection of Greek sculptures, mainly of the Phidian school (see PHIDIAS). It includes the bulk of the surviving sculptural decoration of the Parthenon. The works were removed from Athens (1803–12) by Lord Elgin and were purchased by the British government in 1816. The collection now resides in the British Museum in London.

Elia   See LAMB, CHARLES.

Eliade, Mircea (1907–1986)   Rumanian-born religious historian, philosopher, and novelist. In 1956, when Eliade came to the U.S. to lecture on the history of religion, he was already well known in Europe both for his novels and his studies in yoga, Indian philosophy, and the structure of religion. *Le Mythe de l'éternel retour* (1949; tr *The Myth of the Eternal Return*, 1955), an interpretation of religious symbols and imagery, earned him an international reputation as a pioneer in the systematic study of religious history. Eliade was a Christian and a Jungian; his works, such as *Mythes, rêves, et mystères* (1957; tr *Myths,*

Dreams and Mysteries, 1960) and *Aspects du mythe* (1963; tr *Myth and Reality*, 1964), stress the relevance of ancient religions for contemporary man. In 1978, *Forbidden Forest* (*Forêt interdite*, 1955) was published, the English version of a novel that Eliade considered his masterpiece. That same year, he also published the first volume of his monumental *History of Religious Ideas*. *The Old Man and the Bureaucrats* (1979) is an allusive and symbolic novella in which a schoolteacher detained for questioning by Communist authorities beguiles his captors with stories.

Elihu   A name given to several OLD TESTAMENT characters, the most notable being found in the book of JOB. Here, Elihu attempts to reason with Job about his troubles, after the three false comforters have spoken (Job 32).

Elijah   In the OLD TESTAMENT, a Hebrew prophet who lived during the 9th century BC in the reign of AHAB. During the great drought which he foretold, he was fed miraculously by ravens near the stream Cherith and by Zarephath's widow, whose dead son he restored to life. He opposed the prophets of BAAL and challenged them to a dramatic contest on Mount Carmel, where two altars were built, one to Baal and one to JEHOVAH. Baal was deaf to the repeated cries of his prophets, but Jehovah answered Elijah by sending fire from heaven. The story of Elijah's discouragement under the juniper tree is well known (see 1 Kings 19:4). He did not die but was carried up to heaven in a whirlwind (2 Kings 2:11). He cast his mantle on ELISHA, whom he had anointed prophet in his stead; hence, the phrase *Elijah's mantle* signifies succession to any office.

Eliot, George   (pen name of Mary Ann, or Marian, Evans, 1819–1880)   English novelist. Of the first rank among Victorian novelists, Eliot was the daughter of a Warwickshire land agent, a man of strong Evangelical Protestant feeling. Her severance from her father's religion was a great source of conflict for her and distress for him. Early in the 1840s she became acquainted with the new and "advanced" biblical and theological scholarship of Germany and translated D. F. Strauss's *Leben Jesu* (*Life of Jesus*, 1846). After her father's death, she began to associate with a group of rationalists in London; one of them, John Chapman, took her on as assistant editor for the *Westminster Review*, a post she held from 1851 to 1854. She became a friend of Herbert Spencer and through him met George Henry Lewes (1817–78). Although Lewes was separated from his wife, he could not obtain a divorce, and, in 1854, Eliot entered into an irregular union with him that lasted until his death (1878); they lived as man and wife and were accepted as such by their friends.

Eliot was on the verge of middle age before she wrote her first fiction. In 1857 (when she assumed her pen name) her first works of fiction—three short stories—appeared in *Blackwood's* and were published later as the volume *Scenes of Clerical Life* (1858). ADAM BEDE, her first full-length novel, followed soon after, and in 1860 came THE MILL ON THE FLOSS, followed by SILAS MARNER in 1861. Inspired by

a trip to Florence, she did a great deal of painstaking research in the Italian Renaissance and produced her only historical novel, ROMOLA, in 1863. Turning again to the contemporary scene in England, she wrote FELIX HOLT, THE RADICAL and MIDDLEMARCH, considered not only Eliot's finest work but one of the greatest novels to come out of 19th-century England. Her last novel, DANIEL DERONDA, is peopled with characters who illustrate her moral philosophy. In 1880, two years after Lewes's death, she married J. W. Cross, a clergyman twenty years her junior. She died later in the same year.

Eliot's fiction was regarded for many years as didactic and wholly Victorian in moral and social attitude. This view was advanced by her young husband's selected editing of her papers, *George Eliot's Life As Related in Her Letters and Journals* (3 vols, 1885–86). Subsequent studies, however, based on other sources and the internal evidence provided in her *Letters* (ed G. S. Haight; 7 vols, 1954–55) and *Essays* (ed T. Pinney, 1963) significantly enlarge this view. Eliot's fiction is certainly a vehicle for serious discussion of the social and moral problems of her time, but the greatest preoccupation of this complex and unconventional woman was not moral improvement but insight into the internal reasons for the choices made by her characters in their struggles to arrive at an individual and mature view of life.

Eliot, T[homas] S[tearns]   (1888–1965)   American-born English poet, critic, and dramatist. Eliot lived in England from 1914 and became a British subject in 1927. Eliot is universally recognized as one of the major poets of the 20th century, and his reputation grew to almost mythic proportions during his own lifetime. Because of its radical innovations in poetic technique and subject matter, his poetry revolutionized the literary conventions bequeathed by the Romantics and Victorians and gave expression to the spirit of the world after World War I.

Eliot was born in St. Louis, Missouri. He was educated at Harvard, where his flair for eclectic scholarship and his keen sensitivity to the social-psychological currents of the day were already marked characteristics, according to the reminiscences of his fellow students. Feeling that the poetry of his own country and day could be of little use to him as a literary model he turned to the poetry of other nations and epochs. The English JACOBEANS and the French SYMBOLISTS were revelations to him; his indebtedness to LAFORGUE and BAUDELAIRE is already apparent in his undergraduate poems. After graduate work at Harvard, the Sorbonne, and Oxford, Eliot settled in London in 1915. There he came under the influence of Ezra POUND, who recognized Eliot's genius at once, and criticized and encouraged his work. Pound was also largely responsible for getting the early poems into print; he saw to the publication of THE LOVE SONG OF J. ALFRED PRUFROCK in *Poetry* in 1915 and introduced Eliot to Harriet Weaver, who published his first volume of verse, *Prufrock and Other Observations*, in 1917. With his early work in print, Eliot's reputation quickly grew. By the time THE WASTE LAND appeared in 1922, his position was firmly established among the avant garde, and he had become the recognized leader of younger poets.

In technique, as in subject matter, Eliot's poetry broke with the literary conventions of his day, conventions that he felt were inadequate to express the experience of the modern world. In order to capture the spirit of a new age, he believed it was necessary to create new poetic forms and a new poetic language, which, in turn, might break up current modes of perception and change contemporary attitudes. Perhaps his most important technical innovations were twofold: instead of "poetic diction" Eliot used the idiom and natural rhythms of speech, and instead of relying on abstractions he expressed himself solely through sense impressions (see DISSOCIATION OF SENSIBILITY). The subject matter of his early poems also reflected the world about him. For material, he drew on his own social background as well as the surrounding squalor of an industrial age. In such poems as "Prufrock," PORTRAIT OF A LADY, GERONTION, the SWEENEY poems, *The Waste Land,* and THE HOLLOW MEN, he depicts the emotional impoverishment, boredom, and spiritual emptiness common both to the dying genteel world of devitalized social rituals and to the new urban materialistic world. Eliot's later poetry reflects his conversion to Anglicanism in the late 1920s. In poems such as ASH WEDNESDAY, "Journey of the Magi," and "Marina," he portrays alternating states of despair, skepticism, hope, and joy in the soul's struggle for renewal. FOUR QUARTETS is generally acknowledged to be the major work of this latter period. It is a series of four long meditative poems in which Eliot weaves together his complex thoughts on the irreconcilable tension between man's position in the space-time world and his desire to escape its dimensions. He also wrote poems in a lighter vein, such as "The Hippopotamus" (1920) and OLD POSSUM's *Book of Practical Cats* (1939).

In an early essay, TRADITION AND THE INDIVIDUAL TALENT, Eliot propounded the doctrine that poetry should be impersonal, transmuting private feelings into general truths. This view is closely connected with his belief in the indebtedness of the poet to the tradition of the past and the necessity for incorporating the experience of the past into the poetry of the present. His early critical essays were collected in *The Sacred Wood* (1920), a volume that established his reputation as a critic and had an enormous impact on contemporary literary taste. By exalting the Elizabethan dramatists, METAPHYSICAL POETS, DANTE, and the French poets of the 19th century, and attacking MILTON and the Victorian and Romantic poets, he effected a general change in literary values. Among his critical works are *The Use of Poetry and the Use of Criticism* (1933) and *The Classics and the Man of Letters* (1942). After joining the church, Eliot devoted much of his prose writing to cultural problems, particularly the place of religion in society. *After*

Strange Gods: A Primer of Modern Heresy (1934), *The Idea of a Christian Society* (1939), and *Notes Towards the Definition of Culture* (1940) are books of social criticism. In *For Lancelot Andrewes,* a collection of essays published in 1928, Eliot declared himself "an Anglo-Catholic in religion, a classicist in literature, and a royalist in politics," and the labels stuck, despite his changing opinions. From his earlier exploratory essays in literary values to his later essays, in which he frequently reversed or modified his previous positions, Eliot's judgments have often been taken to be dogmatic, though in fact he always viewed them as tentative.

In *Poetry and Drama* (1951) Eliot discussed the problems he faced in attempting to revive poetic drama for the modern stage. His first play, MURDER IN THE CATHEDRAL, is generally considered to be his best. It was followed by THE FAMILY REUNION, THE COCKTAIL PARTY, *The Confidential Clerk* (1953), and *The Elder Statesman* (1958).

Eliot was long associated with Faber & Faber, the British publishers, and was a director of the firm at his death. He received the NOBEL PRIZE in 1948. His *Collected Poems* and *Collected Plays* both appeared in 1962.

Elisha In the OLD TESTAMENT, a Hebrew prophet. Elisha was selected by ELIJAH to be his successor. In contrast to his predecessor, Elisha was urbane and sophisticated. His ministry lasted for fifty years, during which time he was counselor to four kings of Israel (c850–790 BC). His work (which included many civic projects) and his prophecies are recorded in 2 Kings.

elixir of life The potion of the alchemists to prolong life indefinitely. It was imagined sometimes as a dry drug, sometimes as a fluid. *Elixir* (Arab, "a powder for sprinkling on wounds") also meant among alchemists the philosopher's stone, the tincture for transmuting metals, and the name is now given to any sovereign remedy for disease, especially one of a quack character.

Eliza (1) A character in Harriet Beecher Stowe's UNCLE TOM's CABIN. Her flight with her baby over the ice floes of the Ohio river provides one of the most dramatic moments in both the novel and the plays based on the book.

(2) Eliza Draper, wife of an official of the East India Company, to whom Laurence Sterne addressed *The Bramine's Journal* which he kept from April to August 1767, after her departure from London to India, and the *Letters of Yorick to Eliza* (1775). The letters are a sentimental account of their passionate but platonic love affair in 1766. *The Letters of Eliza to Yorick* (1775) and *Letters Supposed to Have Been Written by Yorick and Eliza* (1779) are forgeries.

Elizabeth See JOHN THE BAPTIST.

Elizabeth I [Elizabeth Tudor] (1533–1603) Queen of England (1558–1603), daughter of HENRY VIII and Anne BOLEYN. Elizabeth was proclaimed queen by Parliament on the death of her elder half-sister, MARY I.

She reestablished Protestantism and the supremacy of ruler over Pope in England, ended foreign religious and political domination, and helped, with her claim of being "mere English" and her refusal to take a foreign consort, to strengthen England's growing sense of nationality and unity. Among the major political events of her reign was the execution of MARY, QUEEN OF SCOTS, for complicity in a Catholic plot against the life of Elizabeth. The death of the Catholic queen may have been the final stroke that moved Philip of Spain to action; the following year, in 1588, he sent the "invincible Armada" against England and was soundly defeated.

Elizabeth's long reign was marked by domestic peace and prosperity, by the growth of England as a naval power, by the beginnings of what was to become a great colonial empire, and by a general spirit of expansion that was reflected in both geographical and literary exploration; it was an age that produced perhaps more "firsts" and more "greats" in English literature than any other. Elizabeth's Court was the source of much of the lyric poetry of the time, and she numbered among her courtiers such men as Sir Philip SIDNEY. Edmund SPENSER honored her as Gloriana, Queen of Fairyland, in his allegory THE FAERIE QUEENE. She was fond of plays and pageants, and many of Shakespeare's plays were presented at her Court. See ELIZABETHAN.

Elizabeth is a central character in Sir Walter Scott's KENILWORTH. She is the subject of Lytton Strachey's biography *Elizabeth and Essex* (1928) and Maxwell Anderson's drama *Elizabeth the Queen* (1930).

Elizabeth II (1926–   ) Queen of Great Britain and Northern Ireland (1952–   ). She is married to Philip, duke of Edinburgh.

Elizabethan Pertaining to the forty-five-year period (1558–1603) of the reign of ELIZABETH I of England, sometimes considered the English renaissance. In both literary and political history Elizabeth's reign divides itself into two distinct phases: an early, seemingly undistinguished period in which her tenuous hold on royal authority and the Elizabethan writer's experimental probing of his language (which had hitherto been regarded as an inferior, even barbaric tongue) were gradually becoming consolidated; and a later, dazzlingly brilliant and enormously successful era. This began, in the political realm, with the execution of Mary Stuart (MARY, QUEEN OF SCOTS) in 1587, and in literature with the publication of Edmund Spenser's THE SHEPHEARDES CALENDER (1579). It is this latter quarter of a century that is generally identified as Elizabethan. (In drama the term is often used to embrace all activity relative to the stage until the closing of the theatres in 1642.) Nevertheless, it was in the early period that the groundwork was laid for the later, great achievements.

The first two years of Elizabeth's reign were marked by two events in literature, insignificant in themselves but representative of interests, attitudes, and linguistic developments that were to bear fruit near the close of the century. These were the publication of the first full translation of Vergil's AENEID into English and of the first extant edition of THE MIRROR FOR MAGISTRATES. These two works, both of which were extremely popular throughout the reign, reflected the two chief sources of the Elizabethan inheritance: classical humanism, with its grand and noble conception of the dignity of man, and in the case of *The Mirror for Magistrates*, the medieval tragic sense of life, with its intense concentration on the fact of death. From these diverse sources, the later Elizabethans managed to fuse a picture of man and the universe that was sweeping and heroic, and at the same time circumscribed by the overwhelming sense of human mortality. One of the most comprehensive portrayals of this conception is Christopher Marlowe's DR. FAUSTUS. Surely the finest expression of this vision is Hamlet's apostrophe on man:

What a piece of work is a man! how noble in reason! how infinite in faculty! in form and moving how express and admirable! in action how like an angel! in apprehension how like a god! the beauty of the world! the paragon of animals! And yet, to me, what is this quintessence of dust?

Although the greatest literary achievement of the Elizabethans lies in drama, their accomplishments in the other genres are only slightly less substantial. To the development of English the Elizabethans contributed, on one level, the ornate, rhetorical, expansive prose derived from CICERO and culminating in the massive dignity of Richard HOOKER's *Laws of Ecclesiastical Polity*. On another level, the Elizabethans enriched the language through the racy colloquialism that characterizes the prose pamphlets of the period, written by such men as Robert GREENE, Thomas NASHE, and the pseudonymous "Martin Marprelate." (See MARPRELATE CONTROVERSY.) Probably the finest prose achievement in this latter category is the magnificent translation by John Florio (1553–1625) of the *Essays of Montaigne*.

In poetry the great monument of the Elizabethan era (as well as being in tone and style a very representative poem) is Edmund Spenser's THE FAERIE QUEENE. In the six elaborately constructed, enormously detailed allegorical books comprising the poem, he attempted to write a great moral epic that would glorify Elizabeth and England as VERGIL had glorified Augustus Caesar and Rome. Spenser also contributed to another significant Elizabethan poetic development: the sonnet sequence. But here both Spenser, in his *Amoretti* (1595), and Sir Philip Sidney, in his pioneering sequence ASTROPHEL AND STELLA, were overshadowed by the mysterious, unorthodox, untitled collection we know as THE SONNETS OF SHAKESPEARE. Other well-known sequences were Samuel DANIEL's *Delia* (1592) and Michael DRAYTON's *Idea* (1593).

It is in the drama of the period, however, that the vitality, splendor, and diversity we identify as Elizabethan is

exuberantly displayed. Emerging from the primitive MORAL-
ITY PLAYS and INTERLUDES of the earlier part of the century,
Elizabethan drama, possibly as a result of the upsurge of
national identity and patriotic fervor that followed the victory over the Spanish ARMADA, began to attract a new
school of playwrights. Chief of these was the titanic figure
of Christopher MARLOWE, defying all moral and metrical
conventions as he attempted to capture the spirit of the age
in his portraits of the "overreachers" in such plays as TAM-
BURLAINE THE GREAT, THE JEW OF MALTA, and *Dr. Faustus*. The instrument of Marlowe's expression was BLANK
VERSE, a new and staid meter that he transformed into a
thundering drum roll, later characterized by Ben JONSON as
"Marlowe's mighty line." At the same time the drama was
developing in lesser keys. George PEELE and John LYLY
experimented to combine light fantasy and romantic comedy in such plays as *The Arraignment of Paris* (1581) and
Endymion (1591) to the delight of the Court, the agency
which stood as a buffer between the acting companies and
the growing militance of the Puritan opposition to the
stage. This opposition forced the players to set up their
theatres outside London proper in a suburb on the south
side of the Thames. Playgoing became increasingly popular
among the non-Puritan population. Plays such as Thomas
Kyd's THE SPANISH TRAGEDY enjoyed an unparalleled success and the Theatre (the first public theatre, built in 1576
by James BURBAGE) became so popular that by 1585 a second playhouse, the Curtain, was being used to accommodate the overflow.

Into this heady atmosphere stepped the man whom
many regard as the supreme literary artist of all time. In
1588 SHAKESPEARE was twenty-four and, like the nation
itself, newly conscious of his powers and of the capacity of
the English language as a fit vehicle to serve those powers.
He capitalized on the revolutionary treatment that Marlowe had given blank verse, achieving a greater range and
flexibility than his predecessors had been capable of, and
he responded to the newly developing national mood with
a series of CHRONICLE PLAYS (the Histories). These plays
helped to articulate a sense of national self-identity best
epitomized by John of Gaunt's speech in RICHARD II:

> This royal throne of kings, this sceptred isle,
> This earth of majesty, this seat of Mars,
> This other Eden, demi-paradise,
> This fortress built by Nature for herself
> Against infection and the hand of war,
> This happy breed of men, this little world,
> This precious stone set in the silver sea, . . .

This glorification of the nation proved, however, to be
the least of his contributions. He managed to run the
gamut of comic potential, ranging from the slapstick farce
of THE MERRY WIVES OF WINDSOR through the romantic
fantasy of A MIDSUMMER NIGHT'S DREAM to the dark satire
of MEASURE FOR MEASURE. Finally he produced in his trag-

edies those explorations of the human condition that are
familiar to everyone.

By 1600, three years before the death of Elizabeth, the
Elizabethan vision had begun to fade, and the literature
that mirrored the life of its time underwent a change (see
JACOBEAN). The literature of the 1590s, a literature rich in
harmony, profuse and expansive in detail, and essentially
affirmative in its vision of life, had lost its vitality and
splendor and had already begun to be parodied. The old
queen, now almost seventy, and childless, had not designated an heir. The earl of Essex, whose brilliance and daring epitomized the era, had suffered a humiliating defeat in
the Irish campaign, and insurrection was in the air. The
Renaissance in England was over and the "counter-Renais-
sance" had begun.

Elizabeth of Hungary, St. (1207–1231)   Patron
saint of queens, being herself a queen. Her day is November 19. She gave so bountifully to the poor that she starved
her own household. One day her husband met her going
out with her apron filled with something heavy and
demanded of her what she was carrying. "Only flowers, my
lord," said Elizabeth, and to save the lie God converted the
loaves of bread into flowers. She is the heroine of KINGS-
LEY's dramatic poem *The Saint's Tragedy* (1846).

Elkin, Stanley [Lawrence] (1930–   )   American novelist. Elkin is a black-humorist whose novels
employ a mixture of commonplace and outrageous situations to articulate an absurdist vision of the excess and
waste of American life. His plots tend to take second place
to his dazzling language. Many of his novels, including
Boswell (1964), *A Bad Man* (1967), *The Dick Gibson Show*
(1971), and *The Franchiser* (1976), revolve around a single
central character who either manipulates others or is
manipulated by them. Secondary characters provide much
of the rich, anecdotal material and graphic imagery for
which Elkin is noted. Elkin's shorter fiction is collected in
Kibitzers and Criers, Criers and Kibitzers (1966) and
Searches and Seizures (1973). *The Living End* (1979) is a
comic fantasy on life and afterlife.

Elle et lui (He and She, 1859)   A novel by George
SAND. The author describes in retrospect her version of the
love affair with Alfred de MUSSET. Musset had died two
years earlier, but his brother Paul published *Lui et elle* as a
protest against Sand's interpretation of the affair and its
complexities.

Elliott, George P[aul] (1918–1980)   American
novelist, short-story writer, essayist, and critic. Elliott's
writing in a variety of genres is unified by an affirmation of
Christian morality, humanism, and the fundamental mysteries of existence. His fiction includes the story collections
Among the Dangs (1962) and *An Hour of Last Things*
(1968), and the novels *Parktilden Village* (1958), *David
Knudsen* (1962), *In the World* (1965), and *Muriel* (1972).
His poetry is collected in *Fever and Chills* (1961) and *From
the Berkeley Hills* (1969). *A Piece of Lettuce* (1964) and

Conversions: Literature and the Modernist Deviation (1971) are volumes of critical essays and personal reminiscences.

ellipsis   A figure of speech in which a word or number of words, which have little importance to the logical construction of the sentence, are left out and are supplied by the reader.

Ellis, [Henry] Havelock (1859–1939)   English psychologist, essayist, and art critic. Ellis is best known for his pioneering and at that time scandalous studies in sexual psychology, including *Man and Woman* (1894), *Studies in the Psychology of Sex* (6 vols, 1897–1910), and *The Erotic Rights of Women* (1918). *The Dance of Life* (1923), in which the dance is made to symbolize the vital rhythm of the universe, was his most popular book. He also wrote essays on art and literature, *Little Essays of Love and Virtue* (1922, 1931), and *My Life* (1939), a revealing autobiography.

Ellison, Ralph [Waldo] (1914–   )   American writer. Ellison's substantial literary reputation rests entirely on his extraordinary first novel, INVISIBLE MAN, which won the National Book Award in 1953. Apart from its probing analysis of alienation and the problems of identity, it was hailed as an outstanding naturalistic depiction of the plight of the black man in America. Ellison, who has taught at several colleges and universities and was Albert Schweitzer Professor of the Humanities at New York University (1970–79), has also written *Shadow and Act* (1964), a collection of essays on race, the artist, and society.

Elmer Gantry (1927)   A novel by Sinclair LEWIS. It deals with a brazen ex-football player who enters the ministry and, through his half-plagiarized sermons, his physical attractiveness, and his unerring instinct for promotion, becomes a successful evangelist and later the leader of a large Middle Western church. Carefully researched, the novel was realistic enough to shock both the faithful and unfaithful.

Elmire   In Molière's comedy LE TARTUFFE, the wily wife of ORGON. By a clever ruse Elmire unmasks the hypocrite Tartuffe and finally convinces her husband of his duplicity.

Elohistic and Jehovistic Scriptures   Elohim and JEHOVAH (Yahwe) are the most common of the many names given by the ancient Hebrews to the Deity. The fact that they are both used with interchangeable senses in the PENTATEUCH gave rise to the widely held theory that this group of five books was written in two different periods. The Elohistic paragraphs, being more simple, more primitive, more narrative, and more pastoral, are held to be the older. The later Jehovistic paragraphs, which indicate a knowledge of geography and history and seem to exalt the priestly office, are of a more elaborate character and were subsequently woven into the Elohistic narrative.

This theory was originally stated by Jean Astruc, the French scholar, in his *Conjectures sur les mémoires*

originaux, dont il paroit que Moyse s'est servi pour composer le livre de la Genèse (1753), a book that formed the starting point for all modern criticism of the Pentateuch.

Elsie Dinsmore   Title of one of the twenty-six "Elsie Books" by the American author Martha Finley (real name Martha Farquharson, 1828–1909). The books deal with the trials and adventures of Elsie Dinsmore, a pious little prig who remains a paragon of virtue, although she is persecuted by associates and relatives. Her story proved so popular with 19th-century girl readers that the series was continued until long after Elsie had become a grandmother.

Elsie Venner: A Romance of Destiny (1861)   A novel by Oliver Wendell HOLMES. Elsie, whose mother was bitten by a snake while carrying her, has distinctly serpentine qualities. Isolated from other human beings, she never removes the heavy gold necklace that presumably hides an unsightly and revealing mark. Although she falls in love with Bernard Langdon, the young schoolteacher, her strange and repellent nature forbids the return of affection. Only her black mammy understands Elsie's mystery. In the attempt to humanize herself, the girl dies. Through Elsie Venner, Holmes opposes the Calvinist belief that a human being may be held morally responsible for an inherited flaw. He considered the doctrine of Original Sin a barbarism. For Holmes, the physician or psychologist, not the preacher, should treat the morally diseased.

Elsinore   The English name of Helsingör, a city in Denmark on the island of Zealand. Elsinore is the site of Kronberg Castle, the traditional scene of Shakespeare's HAMLET.

Éluard, Paul (pen name of Eugène Grindel, 1895–1952)   French poet. After his interest in DADA, Éluard became, with André BRETON, one of the founders of SURREALISM. *Les Nécessités d'une vie et les conséquences des rêves* (1921) gave flashes of the "living reality" of dreams; *Mourir de ne pas mourir* (1924) built a bridge of pure and passionate poetry between dream and reality. Then Éluard became the poet of the couple, of loving communion with the other as well as with the universe of nature: *Capitale de la douleur* (1926; tr *Capital of Pain*, 1973), *L'Amour la poésie* (1929), *La Vie immédiate* (1932), *La Rose publique* (1934), and *Les Yeux fertiles* (1936). Deeply moved by the Spanish Civil War and World War II, Éluard extended this communion to the fraternity of mankind in *Livre ouvert* (1940), *Poésie et vérité* (1942), *Au rendezvous allemand* (1944), *Poèmes politiques* (1948), and *Le Dur Désir de durer* (1950). *Poésie ininterrompue* (1946) is his most extensive and eloquent expression of love, both for his wife and for his fellow man. His *Dernières Poèmes d'amour* (1963) and *Oeuvres complètes* (2 vols, 1968) were published posthumously.

Elvire   In Molière's DOM JUAN OU LE FESTIN DE PIERRE, the woman whom Juan abducts and marries, only to abandon.

Elyot, Sir Thomas (or Sir Thomas Eliot, 1499?–1546) English humanist, diplomat, and prose writer. Elyot is best known for *The Book Named the Governor* (1531). The first treatise on education published in English, it is regarded as one of the important 16th-century contributions to the development of English prose. He also wrote *Of the Knowledge Which Maketh a Wise Man* (1533); *The Castel of Helth* (1534), a popular treatise on medicine; and the first complete Latin-English dictionary (1538). His many translations from Latin and Greek helped to spread the reading of the classics throughout the educated classes of England. Elyot is said to be an ancestor of the 20th-century American-born poet T. S. ELIOT, in whose poem "East Coker" (1940) are quotations from the work of Sir Thomas.

Elysium The abode of the blessed in Greek mythology. Hence the Elysian Fields, the Paradise or Happy Land of the Greek poets. *Elysian* means "happy; delightful."

Elytis, Odysseus (1911–   ) Greek poet. Elytis originally enrolled to study law but gave up his studies to pursue his writing ambitions. It was the body of verse written in the 1950s, specifically *To axion esti* (1959; tr *The Axion Esti of Odysseus Elytis*, 1974) and *Hexe kai mia typheis ghia ton ouran* (*Six and One Regrets for the Sky*, 1960), that established Elytis's reputation internationally. His verse, atmospheric in quality and evocative of the local landscape and climate of Elytis's Aegean island environment, is a fusion of Greek myth, history, and nature with the modern 20th-century consciousness. His is considered one of the most powerful contemporary lyrical voices to emerge from Greece.

In 1979, Elytis was awarded the NOBEL PRIZE in Literature. Two further collections of poetry, *Anihtá hartia*, second ed (1982) and *Imeroloyio atheatou Apriliou* (1984), have enhanced his reputation for lyrical gracefulness.

Emancipation Proclamation A proclamation issued by President Abraham LINCOLN on January 1, 1863, declaring that all slaves in areas still in rebellion against the U.S. were henceforth to be free. The proclamation did not affect slaves in the border states nor in territory under U.S. military occupation. A preliminary proclamation had been issued on September 22, 1862, after the Union success at Antietam had bolstered the likelihood of ultimate victory over the Confederacy. Slavery was not completely abolished until the adoption of the thirteenth amendment to the Constitution in 1865.

Embla See ASK.

emblem books Pictures and sayings collected in books during the RENAISSANCE and BAROQUE periods. An emblem was originally a symbolic picture illustrating a moral idea, but during these periods, when emblems were immensely popular, the picture was always accompanied by a motto or pungent phrase and a short poem expanding upon the moral significance of the scene depicted. The illustration is commonly called the *cor* ("heart"), and the accompanying poetry the *anima* ("soul") of the emblem. An example would be a depiction of Hercules standing between a bearded sage representing wisdom and a satanic figure representing vice. The motto above says, "When Vice and Vertue Youth shall wooe,/ Tis hard to say, which way 'twill go." Below the picture is a stanza in which the idea is treated at greater length (from George Wither's *A Collection of Emblemes*, 1635). A famous European emblem book was that of the Italian Andrea Alciati (1492–1550); in England, Francis QUARLES's *Emblems, Divine and Moral* (1635) was immensely popular. Emblems and emblem books, the latter's appeal boosted by the development of engraving, influenced many poets in their choice and treatment of subject matter and descriptive detail.

Emerson, Ralph Waldo (1803–1882) American poet, essayist, and philosopher. After a studious but undistinguished career at Harvard, and a brief period of teaching, Emerson entered the ministry. He was appointed to the Old Second Church in Boston, his native city, but soon became an unwilling preacher. Unable in conscience to administer the sacrament of the Lord's Supper, he resigned his pastorate at the death of his young wife, Ellen Tucker. The following year, 1832, he sailed for Europe. Visiting LANDOR, CARLYLE, and COLERIDGE, he began to formulate his own philosophy. Emerson's friendship with Carlyle was both lasting and significant. The insights of the British thinker helped him to reconcile some of his own confusions. Two other trips to England followed, in 1847 and 1872, but neither was as vital as the first.

On his return to New England, Emerson became known for the challenges to traditional thought in his essays and lectures. His first book, NATURE, summarized his major ideas. In 1835, he married Lydia Jackson and settled in Concord, Massachusetts. The center of a literary circle, "the sage of Concord" became the chief spokesman for TRANSCENDENTALISM. Other members of his group included Margaret FULLER, Bronson ALCOTT, Henry THOREAU, and W. E. CHANNING.

Among Emerson's best work are ESSAYS, FIRST AND SECOND SERIES; *Poems* (1847); REPRESENTATIVE MEN; *The Conduct of Life* (1860) and *English Traits* (1865). His best-known addresses are *The American Scholar* (1837) and THE DIVINITY SCHOOL ADDRESS. For two years, 1842–44, Emerson edited the Transcendentalist journal, THE DIAL.

Emerson's philosophy is characterized by its reliance on intuition as the only way to comprehend reality. His conception of life as "spiritual vision" owes much to the work of PLOTINUS. He was influenced, too, by SWEDENBORG and BÖHME. Like THOREAU and WHITMAN, he was attracted to mystical Indian literature and philosophy.

Emerson's unit of thought is the epigrammatic sentence. His prose style is not clearly organized or easy to follow but has moments of great brilliance. Emerson wrote a poetic prose; intuitive rather than logical in form, the essays are ordered by recurring themes and images. His poetry, on the other hand, is often called harsh and didactic; he knew himself to be a "husky singer."

A believer in the "divine sufficiency of the individual," Emerson was a steady optimist. His refusal to grant the positive existence of evil caused MELVILLE, HAWTHORNE, and Henry James, Sr., among others, to doubt his judgment. In spite of skepticism, Emerson's beliefs—that each man shares in the Over-Soul, or God; that Nature is a manifestation of Spirit; and that man possesses, within himself, the means to all knowledge—expressed in his memorable sentences, are of central importance in the history of American culture. See BOSTON HYMN; BRAHMA; CONCORD HYMN; DAYS; EACH AND ALL; MERLIN; VERY, JONES.

Emile, ou l'Education (1762)   An educational romance by Jean Jacques ROUSSEAU. It describes, in loose, story form, the bringing up of the boy Émile according to what Rousseau calls the principles of nature. He emphasizes character formation, learning by experience and observation, physical exercise, the mastery of useful trades, judgment, and hard work. One of the dominant principles of Rousseau's theory is that the child is not an adult and should not be treated as such until he is ready. Hitherto education was usually inconsiderate of the various psychic stages of a child's development; Rousseau deserves credit for showing that the object and the methods of education should change with these stages. In Book IV, Émile's moral and religious education is summarized in the "Profession de foi du vicaire Savoyard." The natural religion that Rousseau advocates in this section led to his persecution by the church authorities. Book V deals with the education of Sophie, a young woman intended for Émile's wife. Her unique purpose is to please men, and to be charming, modest, virtuous, and submissive. (Curiously enough, in his sequel *Émile et Sophie*, Rousseau relates the infidelity of Sophie and the breakup of their marriage.) The work had a notable influence on pedagogical theory in France, Germany, and England. It was immediately translated into English. The thinking of educators of the 19th century, Friedrich Wilhelm August Froebel, Johann Heinrich Pestalozzi, and Johann Friedrich Herbart, is derived directly from Rousseau.

Emilia   (1) In Shakespeare's OTHELLO, IAGO's sharp-tongued wife and faithful waiting-woman to Desdemona. When she publicly denounces Iago's villainy, he stabs her, and she dies at her mistress's feet.

(2) Heroine of Boccaccio's TESEIDA.

Emilia Galotti (1772)   A tragedy by Gotthold Ephraim LESSING in which Emilia, a young middle-class woman, unwittingly arouses the passion of a prince, who has her bridegroom murdered and hopes to make her his mistress. In the end, to preserve her honor, her father stabs her to death.

Emilie   The "divine Emilie," to whom VOLTAIRE wrote verses, was Marquise du CHÂTELET, with whom he lived at Cirey from 1734 to her death in 1749.

Emma (1816)   A novel by Jane AUSTEN. Charming, willful Emma Woodhouse has no responsibilities other than the care of an indulgent father. To amuse herself she plays with other people's affairs, planning their lives the way she sees fit. Her first project is pretty, vapid Harriet Smith, a parlor-boarder at a nearby school and the natural daughter of an unknown person. Encouraging her to aspire to the hand of Mr. Elton, a young clergyman, Emma prevents Harriet's accepting the offer of the far more appropriate Robert Martin, a young farmer. Emma's plans go awry: the snobbish, ambitious Elton first aspires to Emma's hand, and, haughtily rejected, chooses instead the crass, pretentious daughter of a wealthy family for his bride. Other moves, notably Emma's interference in the courtship of Jane Fairfax and Frank Churchill, are not any more successful. When Harriet shows signs of attachment to Knightly, a somewhat dictatorial but frank and generous gentleman, Emma appreciates the folly and thoughtlessness of her meddling; she discovers that her long friendship with Knightly has grown into love. Propriety and common sense prevail: Emma marries Knightly; Harriet marries her first love, Robert Martin. The book is much concerned with the themes of self-delusion and notions of class and decorum fundamental to English society. See BATES, MISS.

Emmet, Robert (1778–1803)   Irish patriot. The son of a liberal-minded, well-to-do physician, Emmet became involved, while still in college, in the cause of the UNITED IRISHMEN; the latter fought, sometimes with violence, for the rights of Irish Catholics who had been deprived of their land under Cromwell. In 1803, Emmet was part of an insurrection that was put down by the British. Although he could have escaped, he remained in Dublin to protect his followers and the woman he loved, Sarah Curran. He was tried for treason and executed at the age of twenty-five by hanging and decapitation.

Empedocles (fl 444 BC)   A Greek philosopher, interested in biology, medicine, and physics. In his work called *On Nature*, an epic poem in hexameters, Empedocles identifies four immutable elements in the universe: earth, air, fire, and water. The things of this world are produced by the association and dissociation of these elements. Empedocles called the two opposing forces love and strife. In another poem, called *Purifications*, Empedocles approves of the doctrine of transmigration. According to Greek tradition, Empedocles threw himself into the crater of Mt. Etna. In his poem "Empedocles on Etna" (1852), Matthew ARNOLD found the philosopher a figure expressive of his own pessimism.

Emperor Jones, The (1920)   A play by Eugene O'NEILL. Set on an island in the West Indies, the play deals with a former Pullman porter, Brutus Jones, who has set himself up as emperor. When the play begins the natives are beginning to revolt, and Jones is forced to flee. As he rushes through the jungle the tom-toms beat steadily, and he becomes more and more the victim of his own terror. Jones retrogresses on the evolutionary ladder, becoming a participant in a slave auction and finally the victim of his—and mankind's—aboriginal fears. In the end he is killed by the natives who use the silver bullets Jones had said were necessary. A sensation as a play, *Emperor Jones* was also successful as an opera (1933) by Louis Gruenberg, with a libretto by Kathleen de Jaffa.

empiricism A theory of philosophy that maintains that all knowledge is necessarily derived from experience and the utilization of the five senses. Basically, as contrasted with RATIONALISM, empiricism denies the existence of *a priori* ideas, that is, ideas that are arrived at independently of experience. Beginning in the 17th century, empiricism was a dominant tradition, particularly in British philosophy. LOCKE, BERKELEY, HUME, and MILL are the most prominent of the British empiricists, although their specific applications and interpretations vary. Locke exemplified the empiricist view in his attack on the rationalist doctrine of "innate ideas." He maintained that the newborn mind is devoid of all knowledge and that ideas develop as a result of sensation and reflection on sensations. Berkeley concluded that all objects were simply collections of perceived ideas, that nothing could exist without perception. His position eventually led to the theory of phenomenology. Hume carried Berkeley's hypotheses to the extreme position that there is no knowledge other than that which can be observed directly. Mill stated that all real knowledge is inductive and empirical and saw even the laws of logic and mathematics as generalizations from experience.

Empson, William (1906–1984) English poet and critic. Empson was a mathematician before he became a poet, and his verse is characterized by frequent scientific reference and its wit, ingenuity, and obscurity. His complicated notes on his verse add to the crossword-puzzle effect. His poems, appearing in *Poems* (1935), *The Gathering Storm* (1940), and *Collected Poems* (1949), are metaphysical in substance, lyrical in tone, and restrained in technique, often written in such traditional forms as the VILLANELLE and TERZA RIMA. Although his poetic output was small, his work had a great effect on young English poets of the 1950s, such as Kingsley AMIS, Donald DAVIE, Thom GUNN, and John WAIN. Even more influential were his seminal books of critical analysis: *Seven Types of Ambiguity* (1930), *Some Versions of Pastoral* (1935), *The Structure of Complex Words* (1951), and *Using Biography* (1985). Stimulated in the first instance by the theories of his teacher, I. A. RICHARDS, these original works established Empson as one of the leading CAMBRIDGE CRITICS.

empyrean In Ptolemaic philosophy, the last of the five heavens. It was made of pure elemental fire and was the seat of the deity. Called the empyrean from the Greek *empyros*, "fiery," it was employed in Christian angelology —for instance, by Dante in his DIVINE COMEDY—as the abode of God and the angels.

Encina, Juan del (1468?–?1529) Spanish dramatist and poet. Encina took minor orders as a youth, was in the service of the duke of Alba, and later lived in Rome. In 1519 he visited the Holy Land, where he was ordained and said his first mass. Often called "the father of Spanish drama," he is best known for his dramatic pieces, usually called *églogas* or "eclogues," which were published in various editions of his *Cancionero* (1496). Most of these plays have religious themes and were performed before aristocratic audiences; the characters, however, are usually Spanish peasants, realistically and humorously portrayed, who speak a rustic dialect, *sayagués*, that became a stock theatrical device. Among his most famous works in this genre are the two eclogues in which Pascuala, Mingo, and the squire Gil appear; the Carnival *Egloga de Antruejo*; and the farcical *Auto del repelón*, dealing with a brawl between peasants and Salamanca students. After his stay in Rome, Encina wrote three plays which reveal the influence of Italian pastoral poetry and represent an attempt to elevate the drama; these are *Egloga de Plácida y Victoriano*, *Egloga de tres pastores*, and *Egloga de Cristino y Febea*. He also wrote numerous *villancicos*, or Christmas carols, which were used at the end of most of his plays.

encomium A Greek poem or speech in praise of a hero, originally sung after the triumphal procession celebrating the victor in games. The form was imitated by Latin poets, and today means any writing of praise.

Encyclopédie, ou Dictionnaire raisonné des sciences, des arts et des métiers (Methodical Dictionary of the Sciences, Arts, and Trades, 1751–1780) A French encyclopedia. Based originally on an idea to translate the English *Cyclopaedia* of Ephraim Chambers, the work's whole scope was greatly expanded by DIDEROT, and his coeditors d'ALEMBERT and Louis de Jaucourt. The contributions of such famous *encyclopédistes* (also called PHILOSOPHES) as Condillac, HELVÉTIUS, MONTESQUIEU, ROUSSEAU, Quesnay, Turgot, and Diderot himself helped make it the great literary monument of the 18th century, even though many of the articles were written by hack writers under the direction of Jaucourt. The work mirrors that French brand of 18th-century philosophical skepticism and scientific determinism which was derived from BACON, LOCKE, and DESCARTES among others. Its spirit of inquiry led it to combat superstition; the supernatural; religious authority, intolerance, and persecution; unequal distribution of wealth; fiscal privileges; and abuses of justice. Attention was paid to the latest scientific discoveries, particularly in the natural sciences. Reforms in government, education, and commerce were prudently advocated. One new feature of the encyclopedia was the inclusion of articles and plates on the mechanical trades (weaving, paper-making, printing, etc.). An ingenious system of cross-references often led the reader to another article that ridiculed the contradictions accepted in the theological discussion of the first article; hence, the Jesuits opposed it, causing the encyclopedia to be temporarily suppressed in 1752 and 1759 by the government, and condemned by the pope in 1759. Though the history of the suppression of this work is generally recounted as one of energetic and efficacious persecution by the government and the church, in fact this is not so. The relatively few attempts at suppression were half-hearted on the part of the government and had little or no effect on its final publication. Mme de POMPADOUR along with several government officials, among whom was Chrétien-Guillaume de Malesherbes (1721–94), an enlightened administrator and director of *la librairie* (the governmental censoring body), did everything in their power to encourage its publication for the public good. Diderot, with the help of Jaucourt, worked tirelessly to bring out the "clandestine" edition in Paris, which appeared in seventeen volumes (plus eleven volumes of plates) between 1751 and 1772. Diderot had no hand in the five-volume supplement (1776–77), or in the two analytical index volumes (1780). Other editions followed. In spite of its imbalance (for example, six lines devoted to *Alpes* and one column to artichoke recipes), errors, and unacknowledged plagiarism, it was a highly successful business venture. At one point there were four thousand subscribers, and the profit is said to have been 300 percent.

Endgame (Fin de partie, 1957; tr 1958)   A play by Samuel BECKETT. The blind chair-bound autocrat Hamm, whose parents Nagg and Nell are confined to ashcans, learns from his servant Clov of the disappearance of objects and the deaths of people in a disintegrating world.

Endicott, John (or John Endecott, 1589?–1665) English-born governor of the Massachusetts Bay Colony. Endicott served as the first governor of the colony (1628–30) until the arrival of John WINTHROP. A zealous Puritan, he persecuted Quakers and the followers of Thomas MORTON. He is the title character of "Endicott and the Red Cross" (1837), a short story by HAWTHORNE, and of one of LONGFELLOW's *New England Tragedies* (1868).

Endō, Shūsaku (1923–   )   Japanese novelist and playwright. A Catholic writer who studied in France for three years, Endō is preoccupied with issues relating to Japanese-Western cultural conflict. His principal works, such as *Umi to dokuyaku* (1958; tr *The Sea and Poison*, 1971); *Chinmoku* (1966; tr *Silence*, 1969), and *Ōgon no kuni* (1966; tr *The Golden Country*, 1970), probe into the non-Christian nature of traditional Japanese morality. He has also written many popular novels, including *Obakasan* (1959; tr *Wonderful Fool*, 1974).

Endor, witch of   See WITCH.

ends of man   The four legitimate goals in HINDUISM. They are: (1) DHARMA, sacred duty; (2) ARTHA, material gain; (3) KAMA, physical pleasure, including, but not only sexual; (4) *moksha*, spiritual release, salvation. The pursuit of these vary according to one's social rank and stage of life. See ASHRAMA.

Endymion   In Greek mythology, a beautiful youth, sometimes a shepherd. As he slept on Mount Latmus, he so moved the cold heart of SELENE, the moon goddess, that she came down and kissed him and lay at his side. He woke to find her gone, but the dreams that she gave him were so strong and enthralling that he begged ZEUS to give him immortality and allow him to sleep perpetually on Mount Latmus. Other accounts say that Selene herself bound him by an enchantment so that she might come and kiss him whenever she liked. There are, in fact, innumerable explanations in myth of Endymion's sleep. KEATS used the story as the framework of his long allegory *Endymion* (1818), and it forms the basis of LYLY's comedy *Endimion, the Man in the Moone* (1585) and Benjamin DISRAELI's novel *Endymion* (1880).

Enemy of the People, An   See IBSEN, HENRIK.

Enfants terribles, Les (1929; tr *Children of the Game*, 1955, and *The Holy Terrors*, 1957)   A novel by Jean COCTEAU about the fantasy-world rituals and fierce amoral passions of a young brother and sister. Cocteau adapted it for a film which he directed in 1950.

Engels, Friedrich (1820–1895)   German socialist and collaborator of Karl MARX, whom he met in Paris in 1844. Together they wrote THE COMMUNIST MANIFESTO, although Engels gave Marx the credit for its theoretical formulation. Engels completed DAS KAPITAL after Marx's death.

England, rulers of   Egbert, originally king of the West Saxons, conquered the other English realms, making himself master of all England.

SAXONS

Egbert	829– 839
Ethelwulf	839– 858
Ethelbald	858– 860
Ethelbert	860– 866
Ethelred I	866– 871
Alfred the Great	871– 899
Edward the Elder	899– 924
Athelstan	924– 940
Edmund I	940– 946
Edred	946– 955
Edwy	955– 959
Edgar	959– 975
Edward the Martyr	975– 978
Ethelred II	978–1016
Edmund II	1016

DANES

Canute	1016–1035
Harold I	1035–1040
Hardecanute	1040–1042

SAXONS	
Edward the Confessor	1042–1066
Harold II	1066

HOUSE OF NORMANDY	
William I	1066–1087
William II	1087–1100
Henry I	1100–1135
Stephen	1135–1154

HOUSE OF PLANTAGENET	
Henry II	1154–1189
Richard I	1189–1199
John	1199–1216
Henry III	1216–1272
Edward I	1272–1307
Edward II	1307–1327
Edward III	1327–1377
Richard II	1377–1399

HOUSE OF LANCASTER	
Henry IV	1399–1413
Henry V	1413–1422
Henry VI	1422–1461

HOUSE OF YORK	
Edward IV	1461–1470

HOUSE OF LANCASTER	
Henry VI	1470–1471

HOUSE OF YORK	
Edward IV	1471–1483
Edward V	1483
Richard III	1483–1485

HOUSE OF TUDOR	
Henry VII	1485–1509
Henry VIII	1509–1547
Edward VI	1547–1553
Lady Jane Grey	1553
Mary I	1553–1558
Elizabeth I	1558–1603

HOUSE OF STUART	
James I	1603–1625
Charles I	1625–1649

COMMONWEALTH	
Council of State	1649–1653
Oliver Cromwell (Lord Protector)	1653–1658
Richard Cromwell (Lord Protector)	1658–1659

HOUSE OF STUART	
Charles II	1660–1685
James II	1685–1688
William III and Mary II (d 1694)	1689–1702
Anne	1702–1714

HOUSE OF HANOVER	
George I	1714–1727
George II	1727–1760
George III	1760–1820
George IV	1820–1830
William IV	1830–1837
Victoria	1837–1901

HOUSE OF SAXE-COBURG	
Edward VII	1901–1910

HOUSE OF WINDSOR	
George V	1910–1936
Edward VIII	1936
George VI	1936–1952
Elizabeth II	1952–

England's Helicon (1600)   One of the miscellanies (see TOTTEL'S MISCELLANY), or collections of poetry, published in the ELIZABETHAN period. It is distinguished by the good taste shown in the selection of its contents, and unique in that the editors deliberately limited the book to PASTORAL poetry. It contains work by SHAKESPEARE, SIDNEY, SPENSER, DRAYTON, LODGE, among others.

English and Scottish Popular Ballads   See CHILD, FRANCIS JAMES.

English Bards and Scotch Reviewers (1809) A long verse satire by Lord BYRON. Neoclassical in flavor and written in heroic couplets, it was occasioned by the harsh reception given to Byron's first book of poems, *Hours of Idleness* (1807), by the *Edinburgh Review*. In the poem, Byron not only attacks his critics but the older generation of English romantic poets as well, including WORDSWORTH, COLERIDGE, SCOTT, and SOUTHEY.

Enki   The Sumerian god of water and of wisdom. Enki lived near the ancient city of Eridu in his watery palace in the ABZU—probably the Persian Gulf. This god, like his later Babylonian counterpart EA, was principally responsible for ordering the functions of the elements that affect life on earth. Cleverest of the gods, he provided the land with sweet water, fathered Uttu, the goddess of plants, found a way to rescue INANNA from the underworld, and saved mankind from extermination in the great flood. He was not, however, infallible. While in his cups, he let the seductive goddess slip away with his "divine decrees," which would give supremacy to her favored city of Erech instead of to Eridu. His attempt to create man was a pathetic failure, and it was left to the goddess NINTU to mold of clay a satisfactory human being.

Enkidu   A friend of Gilgamesh in the *Epic of* GIL-GAMESH. Molded of clay, and at first a wild man who lives with the beasts, Enkidu becomes a hero who first defeats Gilgamesh in wrestling, then becomes his fast friend. They share various adventures together, but Enkidu is condemned to death by the gods for his part in slaying the storm bull of heaven. Gilgamesh's search for the secret of eternal life is the result of his grief over Enkidu's death. He appears also in Sumerian mythology.

Enlightenment   The 18th century. This period is variously called the Age of Reason and, in France, *Le Siècle des Lumières*, because its writers as a whole applied reason to religion, politics, morality, and social life. Aside from purely historical events, the 18th century does not lend itself to a chronological view; its unity lay not in a coherent development or progression of ideas, but rather in the intellectual energy and enthusiasm which characterized its writers. Intensely aware of their heritage and dependency upon the ancients, these men clarified, sifted, and developed this heritage.

The rule of Louis XIV had been an oppressive one, and the somber religious tone which it took before the Sun King's death caused the reaction to it to be all the greater. The government, continued by the monarchies of Louis XV (1715–74) and Louis XVI (1774–93), fell ever deeper into discredit. The failure of John Law's Mississippi Bubble (a trade scheme of June, 1720), the increasing national debt due to royal prodigality, and the repeated hiring and dismissal of incapable finance ministers—and even of capable ones like Cardinal Fleury, Turgot, and NECKER —all contributed to the economic instability of France. The necessity for reform became clear. The century culminated in the FRENCH REVOLUTION, a crisis that reflected these economic and social ills; the application of reason to the human situation, so typical of the 18th century, perhaps made it clear to the middle class that the old order did not have to prevail. In most aspects of French culture, the influence of the increasingly economically independent bourgeoisie was to replace that of the aristocracy.

The Enlightenment began by breaking down the older forms of metaphysical and philosophical knowledge; Cartesianism, with its spirit of systems (*esprit de système*), was replaced by a systematic spirit (*esprit systèmatique*)—the a

priori by the a posteriori. In contrast to the 17th century, in which reason represented tradition, authority, stability, the 18th century saw reason as a tool, a means to authority. Questions were no longer envisaged under the aspect of pure thought, but were examined from a social and practical point of view. This preoccupation with the useful caused men to turn to the physical world; writers like VOLTAIRE, DIDEROT, d'ALEMBERT, and MONTESQUIEU made literature out of the natural sciences, astronomy, law, travel, philosophy, politics, and education. The investigation into natural and social phenomena, what we would today broadly designate as science, was called philosophy in the 18th century. The *philosophe* (see PHILOSOPHES) represented an ideal, as did the *honnête homme* in the 17th century, or as the universal man characterized the Renaissance. The philosophers of this age were in search of a concrete anthropology, a knowledge of man in general. This common goal by no means implied a homogeneous point of view: one has only to compare the differences between Voltaire and ROUSSEAU, BUFFON and Condillac, Diderot and HELVÉTIUS.

It is perhaps Condorcet who, in his *Esquisse d'un tableau historique des progrès de l'esprit humain* (*Sketch for a historical picture of the progress of the human mind*, written in 1793–94), best summarizes the optimism and faith in human reason so characteristic of the age. In tracing man from the dawn of history, Condorcet first emphasized the liberation of mankind from ignorance, tyranny, and superstition by means of his science and his reason; he then sketched a hopeful future in which mankind would be free, equal in wealth, in education, and with sexual equality; he finally envisaged the moral, intellectual, and physical improvement, indeed perfection, of humanity that would arise through better instruction, laws, and institutions.

Enlil   The Sumerian storm god of the air. Enlil was born of the union of AN (heaven) and KI (earth), who were regarded as joined together. Enlil separated them—the element air may have been thought to separate the vault of heaven from earth by its own expansion. Enlil married NINLIL, who bore him three gods of the underworld (Nergal, Ninazu, and an unknown god) and Nanna, the moon, who in turn became the father of Utu, the sun. Next Enlil impregnated his mother Ki and produced NINTU, another earth goddess. Enlil became more important in the pantheon than his father An, and in turn he was himself to a degree supplanted from his place as principal god by ENKI. Enlil was the chief god of the Sumerian city of Nippur. In the Babylonian period, MARDUK took on many of his attributes, and Adad became the storm god.

Enobarbus, Domitius   In Shakespeare's ANTONY AND CLEOPATRA, a trusted officer of Antony. He deserts Antony after the defeat at Actium, but when the latter magnanimously sends him his treasure, he is so remorseful that he commits suicide. His astute and witty observations on the behavior of Antony and Cleopatra make him one of Shakespeare's most engaging secondary characters.

Enoch Arden (1864)   A narrative poem by Alfred TENNYSON. Arden is a seaman who has been wrecked on a desert island and, returning home after a long absence, finds his wife married to another. Seeing her happy and prosperous, he resolves not to make himself known, so he leaves the place and dies of a broken heart. Hence, any story that involves a long-lost mate returning to discover his spouse remarried is often described as having an Enoch Arden plot.

Enormous Room, The (1922)   An autobiographical novel by E. E. CUMMINGS. It describes a period of imprisonment in a French military concentration camp near Paris (1917–18), where the author was incarcerated on a false charge of treason. Cummings's own experiences and the personalities of the various other prisoners are presented with their individual psychological reactions to the injustices of their treatment. Ironically structured on John Bunyan's *Pilgrim's Progress*, the book is highly vivid, often even lyrical, in its bitter attack on man's inhumanity to man.

Enquiry Concerning Political Justice, An (1793)   A political and philosophical treatise by William GODWIN with the subtitle "its influence on General Virtue and Happiness." The author examines the systems of government, law, and religion of his day, and concludes that monarchy is corrupt and all government, in fact, an obstacle to the development of mankind. It urges the abolition of all social and political institutions created by man, including government, law, wealth, and marriage, and places total confidence in the fundamental perfectibility of man. This treatise was regarded with horror by the conservative elements of the day, and had a great influence on the English Romantic poets, particularly SHELLEY.

Entertainer, The   See OSBORNE, JOHN.

envoi   The final stanza of a poem, usually shorter than preceding ones, that repeats the refrain. It is often used in the BALLADE, and in this form usually employs a four-line b-c-b-c rhyme scheme.

Envy (Zavist, 1927)   A novel by Yury OLESHA. A notable work of fiction, it portrays the struggle of the individual against the encroachments of the growing collectivist society in Soviet Russia. This hackneyed theme is rendered fresh by Olesha's imaginative use of images and language and by his creation of the memorable characters Ivan Babichev and Nikolay Kavalerov. Both are disaffected, though for different reasons: Babichev because he sees the danger of human feelings being destroyed, and Kavalerov because he yearns for personal glory and envies the less talented people who can make their way in the new system. Babichev's brother, Andrey, is a representative of the adjusted man. He is the director of a Soviet food combine, briskly going about his business, which consists of planning new, cheap cafeterias to feed the masses. Whether Andrey

actually does triumph over his good-for-nothing brother Ivan is, at the end of the book, a moot point. This fact apparently worried Soviet critics, who praised the novel at first and then criticized it severely.

Eos   In Greek mythology the goddess of the dawn. Eos is the daughter of Hyperion and Thea and drives across the sky in a chariot drawn by two horses. It was Eos who asked ZEUS to give TITHONUS immortality; however, she forgot to have him made eternally youthful.

Ephesians, The Epistle of Paul the Apostle to the   A NEW TESTAMENT book. Traditionally ascribed to PAUL, this letter was probably written by someone who used his name and borrowed freely from his epistle to the COLOSSIANS for its content. Consisting of two parts, it first explains God's plan to unite all humanity in Jesus and then shows the role of the Church in the working of this plan.

epic   A very long narrative poem presenting adventures on a grand, heroic scale organically united through a central figure of heroic proportions. The adventures are made up of episodes which contribute to the formation of a race or nation. The earliest epics were formed from various works of unknown poets. Among the best known of these folk epics are the ILIAD and ODYSSEY (attributed to Homer), the Anglo-Saxon BEOWULF, the East Indian MAHĀBHĀRATA, the Spanish CID, the Finnish KALEVALA, the French *Song of* ROLAND, and the German NIBELUNGENLIED.

The so-called classical, or art, epic is distinctly the work of a single author. Influenced largely by VERGIL, it developed certain almost universal characteristics. These include beginning *in medias res*, the invocation of the muse, and the statement of the epic purpose. Other conventions usually observed by writers of epic are descriptions of warfare and the use of the supernatural. Familiar classical epics include Vergil's AENEID, Dante's DIVINE COMEDY, Tasso's GERUSALEMME LIBERATA, Spenser's THE FAERIE QUEENE, and Milton's PARADISE LOST.

Epic Cycle   Anonymous epic poems written in the 7th and 6th centuries BC, all of which are lost but are recounted in later synopses. The term refers generally to poems about events of the TROJAN WAR not included in the ILIAD or the ODYSSEY. Poems of the Epic Cycle include the *Theogonia* and *Titanomachia*, on the creation and early history of the world; *Cypria*, on the theft of Helen; *Aethiopis*, *Ilias Parva*, *Iliu Persis*, and *Nostoi*, continuations of the *Iliad*; and *Telegonia*, on the death of Odysseus. There are other cyclic poems, such as those on Thebes and on heroes such as Heracles, Theseus, and the Argonauts; strictly speaking, however, the term Epic Cycle refers to the Trojan stories alone.

Epicene, or The Silent Woman (1609)   A comedy by Ben JONSON. A gentleman named Morose has resolved to disinherit his nephew, Sir Dauphine, by marrying and producing an heir. A man who can bear no noise, he has discovered a perfect mate, a woman who "spends but six words a day." But just after the wedding,

Epicene, the silent woman, turns into a shrill harpy who belabors her husband mercilessly. Alarmed, Morose tries mightily to break the match, even going so far as to offer Sir Dauphine a generous allowance and his inheritance if he will take the lady off his hands. Sir Dauphine complies immediately by plucking off Epicene's wig, revealing that "she" is a boy whom Dauphine has carefully trained and employed.

Epictetus (fl AD 100)   A Greek Stoic philosopher. An emancipated slave, Epictetus taught in Rome until AD 94, when Emperor Domitian banished all philosophers from the city. He moved to Nicopolis, where he established a school. No written works survive, but his pupil Arrian preserved his essential doctrines in a manual. Epictetus counseled men to wish for nothing that is not under their control. He advocated a serene life, free from unfulfilled desires, and calm in the face of death. He said that a man should behave in life as he would at a banquet, taking only a polite portion of what is offered. See STOICISM.

epic theatre   A type of drama developed in Germany in the 1920s by Bertolt BRECHT and the director Erwin Piscator (1893–1966), who saw theatre as a means to agitate for political change. The epic theatre borrowed some techniques from classical theatre (hence the use of "epic"), such as the CHORUS, and employed, variously, slides, music, film, and placards to alienate the audience and actors alike from traditional theatrical illusions. The dramas were usually not held together by a narrative line, but instead consisted of a series of contrasting episodes, not necessarily connected in time. Brecht felt that by confounding its normal expectations, he could compel the audience to use its critical faculties and, as a result, learn something from the theatrical experience. See ALIENATION EFFECT.

Epicurus (c340–c270 BC)   Greek philosopher, founder of the Epicurean School. The school is often referred to as the Garden, after the place in which Epicurus taught in Athens. Only fragments remain of his work, but his biographer Diogenes Laertius gives the texts of three epistles and forty maxims, which indicate that Epicurus advocated reliance on the senses. In order to reduce man's anxiety, he posited a materialistic physics, in which the universe consisted of Democritean atoms and void. He tried to eliminate superstition and the dread of death. Pleasure, by which Epicurus meant freedom from pain, is the highest good. Serenity, the harmony of mind and body, is best achieved, he said, through virtue and simple living. The current usage of the term *epicure*, to describe one devoted to sensual pleasures, reflects a misunderstanding of the philosophy of Epicurus.

Epigoni   In Greek mythology, the sons of THE SEVEN AGAINST THEBES. They were led by ALCMAEON, a son of Amphiaraus, who had demanded that his sons avenge his death at Thebes. Alcmaeon might have forgotten this vow, but Thersander, the son of POLYNICES, bribed his mother, Epiphyle, to urge him on, as she had earlier urged Amphiaraus. TIRESIAS had warned the Thebans that the city would fall when the last of the Seven died. The only one to survive the earlier siege had been Adrastus, king of Argos. On learning that his son, Aegialeus, one of the Epigoni, had been killed in the new siege, Adrastus died of grief.

Tiresias then advised the Thebans to flee the city at once, which they did, under cover of night. Tiresias, who had lived through seven generations of Theban rulers, at last died. The escaping Thebans continued as far as Hestiaea, where they founded the city. The Epigoni razed Thebes.

epigram   A brief, pithy, pointed, and witty piece of poetry or prose. The epigram was especially popular as a literary form in classic Latin literature and in European and English literature of the RENAISSANCE and neoclassical periods. Coleridge wrote of it:

> What is an epigram? A dwarfish whole,
> Its body brevity, and wit its soul.

epilogue   (1) The final part of a work of literature (except a play), completing and rounding it off; the opposite of preface. (2) After a play, the speech (frequently in verse) addressed by an actor or group of actors to the audience; the opposite of prologue, the speech that precedes a play. (3) In rhetoric, the last of the five divisions of a model oration. (4) In music, the final section of a composition, the coda.

epinicion   An ODE, usually consisting of groups of three STANZAS each, written to celebrate a victory in the Greek Olympic, Pythian, Delphic, Nemean, and Isthmian games. SIMONIDES was one of the foremost practitioners of the genre. Of PINDAR's surviving works, there are forty-four epinicia.

epiphany   A term coined by James JOYCE for the sudden revelation of the essential nature of a thing, person, or situation. Epiphany is the moment in which "the soul of the commonest object . . . seems to us radiant," and may be manifested through any chance word or gesture. Among Joyce's earliest works were little sketches or prose poems, which attempted to record such moments; he called them epiphanies. The clearest explanation of what he meant by epiphany is contained in his autobiographical novel, *Stephen Hero* (written c1914; pub 1944), his first draft of A PORTRAIT OF THE ARTIST AS A YOUNG MAN.

Epiphany (fr Gr, *epiphaneia*, "appearance; manifestation")   The feast on January 6, commemorating the showing of Jesus to the nations, at the time of the visit of the MAGI. One of the oldest of Christian festivals, it originally was the feast of the birth of Jesus, as it still is in the Eastern Churches. In England it was called Twelfth Day, from which comes TWELFTH NIGHT.

Epipsychidion (1821)   A poem by SHELLEY. The title, a word coined by Shelley from Greek, means "this soul out of my soul." Of over seven hundred lines, the poem is addressed to Emilia VIVIANI, whom Shelley regarded as an embodiment of the ideal love and beauty that he constantly sought. Along with an allegorical history of the poet's soul, the poem includes rapturous praise of Emilia Viviani, a famous justification of free love, and a glowing vision of an Edenic isle in the Aegean.

Epistles of John   See JOHN, THE EPISTLES OF.

Epistles of Paul   See PAULINE EPISTLES.

Epistles of Peter   See PETER, THE GENERAL EPISTLES OF.

Epistle to Dr. Arbuthnot (1735)   A satiric poem by Alexander POPE in the form of a dialogue between the poet and Dr. John ARBUTHNOT, a physician and man of letters who was a friend of Pope. The poem gives Pope's judgment on his own work and pitilessly attacks his contemporaries, especially Joseph ADDISON, who is characterized as "the jealous Atticus," and Lord John HERVEY, who is satirized as the effeminate "Sporus."

Epistolae obscurorum virorum (Letters of Unknown Men, 1515, 1517)   A satire on SCHOLASTICISM. It is directed specifically at the reactionary University of Cologne, in the form of letters supposedly written by various church figures to a Cardinal Ortwinus. The book parodies a collection of letters that Ortwinus himself had published under the title of *Epistolae clarorum virorum* (*Letters of Famous Men*). The *Epistolae obscurorum virorum* are a central document of German humanism, and implicitly support Johann REUCHLIN in his struggles with the renegade Jew Pfefferkorn. The authors are not known, but it is quite likely that Ulrich von Hutten (1488–1523) wrote part of the book.

epistolary novel   A novel whose narrative is presented in the form of letters written by one or more characters. The form was made popular in the 18th century with Samuel Richardson's PAMELA and CLARISSA HARLOWE. Although letters are commonly included in novels, the epistolary form has been used infrequently since the 18th century. A notable exception to this is John BARTH's *Letters* (1979), an elaborate novel in epistolary form.

epitasis (Gr, "stretching; increase in intensity")   A technical term applied by grammarians of late antiquity to that part of a drama in which the plot action begins its rise to the climax. It is linked to PROTASIS, the beginning of a drama, CATASTASIS, and CATASTROPHE.

Epithalamion (1595)   Lyric poem by Edmund SPENSER. Written to celebrate his marriage, it has been called his highest poetic achievement.

epithalamium   A song or poem to be sung outside the bridal chamber on a wedding night; generally a bridal hymn or poem. SAPPHO was first to use the form and subsequently it became popular among classical writers. The form was revived in the Renaissance, where various elements became conventionalized: the structure is organized around the events of the wedding day, the character of husband and wife and the role of the poet are established, and muses or gods are invoked. Spenser's EPITHALAMION, in celebration of his own marriage, is the finest example in English.

epithet   An adjective or adjectival phrase that expresses a characteristic of a person or thing; or an apt phrase that is connotative or figurative. "Pure-eyed Faith," "Richard the Lionhearted," and "Age of Reason" are examples of epithets. An epithet can also be a noun or noun phrase used for the same purpose, such as Shakespeare's description of the cock as the "trumpet of the dawn."

Homeric epithets are generally compounded adjectives used repeatedly in the ILIAD and the ODYSSEY to describe people or things, as with "rosy-fingered dawn" and "swift-footed Achilles."

E Pluribus Unum (Lat, "one from many")   The motto for the seal of the U.S. First proposed on August 10, 1776, by a committee composed of John ADAMS, Benjamin FRANKLIN, and Thomas JEFFERSON, it was not officially adopted until 1782. Its first official appearance was on a New Jersey coin in 1786.

Epstein, Sir Jacob (1880–1959)   American-born British sculptor. Epstein settled in England after studying in Paris with RODIN. He is known both for his colossal, bold sculptures in bronze or stone—*Rima* (1925), *Genesis* (1931), *Ecce Homo* (1935), *Madonna and Child* (1950–52) —and for his perceptive portrait busts of prominent statesmen and artists. His larger works were frequently criticized as crude or grotesque, but he developed a distinctive, powerful style with great attention to texture, light, and shadow. His autobiography, *Let There Be Sculpture*, appeared in 1940 (2nd ed, 1962).

Equiano, Olaudah (1745?–1801)   Nigerian autobiographer. Captured by slave traders when he was ten years old, Equiano was taken to the southern states of America. He was then sold to a planter from the West Indies and worked there and aboard slave ships sailing between the Caribbean and England until he was nineteen. By this time he had saved enough money to buy his freedom. He continued a life as a merchant seaman and quartermaster for many years. He was an active member of the antislavery movement in England and personally petitioned Parliament for the abolition of slavery. While in England he married an English woman. He was appointed Commissary of Stores for the freed slaves who were returning to Sierra Leone. He published *The Interesting Narrative of the Life of Olaudah Equiano or Gustavus Vassa, the African* (1789; repr 1966), a remarkable document of detailed recollections of his extraordinary experiences.

Erasmus, Desiderius (1466–1536)   Dutch scholar and philosopher, noted for his satire *Moriae encomium* (*The Praise of Folly*, 1509). Erasmus called his religious outlook "the philosophy of Christ," yet his thought was influenced by varied tendencies, some Christian, some secular. He was affected by the German religious tradition, which stressed personal piety in religion, as well as by the work of Italian humanists such as PICO DELLA MIRANDOLA. He adhered to the view of German pietism that religion was less a matter of ceremony and doctrine than of morality and rational piety, and his classical education and the influence of Pico and other humanists tended to stimulate in him a skeptical, critical attitude toward superstition, clericalism, and excessive religious zeal. He tried to combine the critical, rational, and secular attitude of classical antiquity and Italian humanism with the religious piety of the German Middle Ages. Aware of ecclesiastical corruption, and hostile to the intolerant dogmatism of the Church of his time, he was at first sympathetic to the Reformation and the attempts of LUTHER to reform the Church. Yet, humane and moderate at a time when the Reformation was fanning religious conflict, war, and hatred, he was forced finally to oppose the extremism of Luther and become an enemy of the Reformation.

Erato In classical mythology, the MUSE of lyric and erotic poetry. She is usually represented holding or playing a lyre.

Erdman, Nikolay Robertovich (1902–1970) Soviet playwright and film-script writer. Erdman's first successful comedy, *Mandat* (1925; tr *The Mandate*, 1975), is a farcical satire of the New Economic Policy and the conservative reaction to it; his second work, *Samoubiytsa* (1931; tr *The Suicide*, 1975), which satirizes the early Soviet system and Joseph Stalin himself, was rehearsed but never permitted to open. As Stalin's control of the arts further congealed, Erdman devoted himself exclusively to film scripts and adaptations of existing plays, producing nothing original himself.

Erebus In Greek mythology, the son of CHAOS, brother of Night (NYX); hence darkness personified. His name was given to the gloomy cavern underground through which the Shades had to walk in the course of their passage to HADES.

Erec et Enide The earliest Arthurian romance in French, written in the 12th century by CHRÉTIEN DE TROYES. It tells of Erec, a knight at the court of King ARTHUR, who goes out in search of adventure and stays overnight at a run-down castle; here he meets Enide, the beautiful daughter of the baron who is master of the castle. Erec asks for her hand, marries her, and then retires from the active life of a knight in order to enjoy the pleasures of domestic life. His reputation soon begins to suffer from this, however, and one day he overhears his wife bemoaning the situation. The knight thereupon blames her for the state of affairs in which they find themselves and sets out once more in search of adventure, forcing Enide to accompany him. They have amazing adventures in which Erec proves himself to be of prodigious strength and valor, although he is harsh in his treatment of his wife. Eventu-

ally she is kidnapped by a robber baron while the knight lies in an apparent state of death. He revives in time to rescue her, and at length they are reconciled.

Erechtheum A temple of the tutelary deities of Athens in the ACROPOLIS of Athens. It derived its name from King Erechtheus.

Erenburg, Ilya Grigorievich (1891–1967) Soviet novelist, poet, and journalist. Erenburg spent much of his early life in Paris, where he published his first book of poems (1911). He covered the Spanish Civil War for Soviet newspapers in 1936–37. His first important novel, *Neobychainye pokhozhdeniya Khulio Khurenito* (1922; tr *The Extraordinary Adventures of Julio Jurento*, 1930), is a satire on modern European civilization. His other novels include *Padeniye Parizha* (1941–42; tr *The Fall of Paris*, 1942), dealing with the war in Western Europe before the U.S.S.R.'s involvement; *Burya* (1947; tr *The Storm*, 1949), a war novel; and *Ottepel* (1954; tr *The Thaw*, 1955), an outspoken work about Stalin's regime which gave its name to the period of relaxation of censorship after Stalin's death (See THE THAW).

Erenburg also published his memoirs in the years between 1961 and 1963. Entitled *Lyudy, gody, zhizn* (1960–65; tr *People and Life, First Years of Revolution, Truce, Eve of War,* and *Post-War Years*, 1961–66), they contain interesting revelations about the maneuverings of Soviet intellectual life. Erenburg himself had often been accused of being an opportunist who knew too well how to avoid purges in the literary world. He was, however, a fairly persistent advocate of greater intellectual freedom in Soviet letters and served as a rallying point for Soviet admirers of Western culture.

Erewhon (1872) A satirical novel by Samuel BUTLER about a UTOPIA. In the institutions of Erewhon (an anagram of "Nowhere"), Butler satirizes contemporary English attitudes toward religion, science, crime, etc. *Erewhon* is probably the most brilliant specimen of 19th-century Utopian novels. A sequel, *Erewhon Revisited*, was published in 1901.

Ericson, Leif (fl 1000) Norse explorer, son of ERIC THE RED. According to legend Ericson was returning from Norway to Greenland (c1000) when a storm drove his ship to a shore he called *Vinland* (also *Vineland, Wineland*), variously said to have been Labrador, Newfoundland, or New England. Thus it is asserted that he, not COLUMBUS, was the first European to discover North America.

Eric the Red (c950–c1000) Norwegian explorer, father of Leif ERICSON. Eric the Red fled Norway, then Iceland, to escape murder charges. He named Greenland, which had been discovered one hundred years before, and founded its first colony about 985.

Erikson, Erik (1902–) German-born American psychoanalyst and author. Erikson, who trained as an analyst in Vienna with Sigmund and Anna Freud, is known for his interpretation and adaptation of FREUD's stages of psychosexual development. In *Childhood and Society* (1950), he asserted that there are personal crises that are central to each of eight stages of what he termed "psychosocial" development and considered the effects of culture and society on the ability to resolve these crises and progress healthily to succeeding stages. In this context, he coined the phrase "identity crisis" to describe a conflict widely experienced among young adults. A later book, *Identity: Youth and Crisis* (1968), amplified these theories.

Erikson also wrote "psychohistories," in which he used the psychosocial stages to study the lives of such diverse historical figures as Gandhi and George Bernard Shaw. The most famous of his psychohistories is *Young Man Luther* (1958).

Erinyes   The Furies of Greek mythology. Snaky-haired and hideous women who sprang from the blood of URANUS when he was castrated by his son CRONOS, they lived in the underworld, from which they issued to pursue and drive mad those who had committed such heinous crimes as patricide. They appeared prominently in AESCHYLUS' *Eumenides*, where, after relentlessly harassing ORESTES for the murder of his mother (see the House of ATREUS), they give up vengeful insistence on the ancient law of blood for blood and are thenceforward worshiped in Athens as the Eumenides ("Kindly Ones"). In some accounts there were three, named Tisiphone, Alecto, and Megaera.

Eriphyle   In Greek mythology, the sister of Adrastus and wife of Amphiaraus. In a quarrel, the two men agreed henceforth to let Eriphyle decide their differences. Later, POLYNICES persuaded Adrastus to help him attack Thebes, but Amphiaraus, a seer, opposed the expedition of THE SEVEN AGAINST THEBES, foreseeing that only Adrastus would survive it. Polynices won the support of the vain and greedy Eriphyle by bribing her with Harmonia's necklace. Amphiaraus, bowing to his wife's will because of his vow, joined the expedition, but enjoined his young sons, ALCMAEON and Amphilochus, to avenge his death on his mother and on the Thebans.

On growing to manhood, Alcmaeon might have forgotten his mother's crime had she not repeated it at his own expense. Bribed by Thersander, Polynices' son, she urged Alcmaeon to lead the EPIGONI against Thebes. Alcmaeon returned from the war victorious and, learning of his mother's double treachery, killed her. Like ORESTES, he was pursued by the ERINYES through many tragic events.

Eris   The goddess of discord, sister of ARES. Eris flung the APPLE OF DISCORD. See JUDGMENT OF PARIS.

Erlking (or Ger, *Erlkönig*, "king of the alders"; a mistranslation of the Danish *eller-konge*, "king of the elves") A malevolent goblin of the Black Forest who lures people, especially children, to destruction. Never actually a part of medieval German folk tradition, Erlking was first popularized by GOETHE in his famous ballad "Der Erlkönig." One

of Franz SCHUBERT's most famous songs is a setting of Goethe's poem.

Erminia   In the GERUSALEMME LIBERATA of Tasso, a Syrian maiden whose life was spared by the Crusader Tancredi (TANCRED) at the battle of Antioch. Though Erminia loves him, he is enamored of CLORINDA, the warrior maid from Persia. At one point Erminia, learning that Tancredi lies wounded, goes to him in Clorinda's armor; but both he and the other Christian knights pursue her in the belief that she is Clorinda. Taking pleasant refuge in a beautiful wood, she is cared for by an old shepherd, who extolls the virtues of the pastoral life. Later, in the camp of the Egyptian armies, she informs Vafrino, the shield-bearer of Tancredi sent as a spy, of a plan to disguise a group of infidel warriors in Crusaders' dress so that they can close with and kill GOFFREDO, the Christian general. On the way to Jerusalem with Vafrino, she encounters the wounded Tancredi and nurses him tenderly back to health. After she takes him back to the camp outside the holy city, she disappears from the plot, and Ariosto says nothing further of her fate.

Ernst, Max (1891–1976)   German-born French artist. Originally a student of philosophy with no formal art training, Ernst became an early member of the DADA group in Cologne and one of the founding figures of SURREALISM. A master of collage, a medium he employed in three "collage-novels," *La Femme 100 Têtes* (1929), *Rêve d'une petite fille qui voulut entrer au carmel* (1930), and *Une Semaine de bonté* (1934), he also developed the technique of *frottage* (pencil or chalk rubbings), producing a series of bizarre, often allegorical landscapes. Much of his later life was devoted to painting mystical, highly textured canvases.

Eros   The Greek god of love. According to the accounts in HESIOD, Eros was one of the earliest gods, born of CHAOS at the same time as Mother Earth. He came to be the patron god of beautiful young men. Only in late myth did he become a child, the naughty son of APHRODITE, as he appears in the *Argonautica* and elsewhere. It was in this form that he was identified with the Latin CUPID.

erotic literature   Any form of literature dealing with the sexual aspects of love. The range of eroticism can extend from subtle sexual intimations to explicit descriptions of sexual activity. Distinctions between erotic literature and pornography change according to contemporary mores; there is, however, a general consensus that in erotic literature sexual descriptions constitute only a *part* of the overall effect of a work. Erotic literature has appeared in all cultures at all times. The Indians and Arabs left early works of erotic poetry. Classic examples of literary erotica include OVID's *Ars amatoria*, the KAMA-SUTRA, and the Chinese novel *Chin P'ing Mei*. Erotic poetry flourished in the Renaissance, with SHAKESPEARE's *Venus and Adonis* (1593), MARLOWE's *Hero and Leander* (1598), and much of the poetry of John DONNE. Erotic elements played a strong part in many Restoration dramas. The French have long been able practitioners of erotic writing, as in the case of the

SYMBOLISTS and such works as *Histoire d'O* and *Emmanuel* (1960). D. H. Lawrence's LADY CHATTERLEY'S LOVER is a well-known example of erotic literature that was initially suppressed because its contents were thought to be pornographic.

Erymanthian boar   In Greek mythology, a devastating boar. It had its haunt on the mountain range of Erymanthus between Arcadia and Achaia. It was finally captured by HERACLES.

Esau   In the OLD TESTAMENT, the eldest son of ISAAC and REBEKAH. The name itself means in Hebrew "rough" or "covered with hair." In return for a mess of pottage, it was Esau who sold his birthright to his twin brother JACOB (Gen. 25:33–34). In another story, Jacob put on a hairy animal skin and secured the blessing that his blind father had intended for Esau (Gen. 27).

Escorial, El   A royal palace some twenty-five miles northwest of Madrid, built (1563–84) by PHILIP II. Dedicated to St. Lawrence, on whose feast day the battle of St. Quentin was fought in 1557, the building is in the shape of a gridiron, in commemoration of the gridiron on which St. Lawrence was martyred, and is famed for its artistic and bibliographic treasures. It also contains a monastery with a celebrated art collection and library, a church, and a mausoleum where the kings of Spain lie buried.

Esenin, Sergei Aleksandrovich (1895–1925)   Russian poet. Born of peasant parents, Esenin used the theme of the passing of rural Russia in his poetry. One of the finest lyric poets of the early Soviet period, he was for a time connected with a literary group called the Imaginists, founded in 1919, which, like the English and American Imagists, stressed the importance of the image in poetry. His growing popularity went hand in hand with an increasingly wild life. For a chaotic year (1922–23), he was married to the dancer Isadora Duncan. His drinking bouts grew in length, and he died by hanging himself, having slashed his wrist in a hotel room in Leningrad and written a farewell poem with his blood. His suicide was attributed by the Soviet regime to his mental instability, and Esenin's works have not been suppressed as have those of other disaffected literary figures. His four volumes of lyrics, with their glowing pictures of the Russian countryside, are still popular in Russia.

Esmeralda   See HUNCHBACK OF NOTRE DAME, THE.

Esmond, Henry (or Harry Esmond)   See HENRY ESMOND.

esoteric   Those within, as opposed to *exoteric*, those without. The term originated with PYTHAGORAS, who stood behind a curtain when he gave his lectures. Those who were allowed to attend the lectures, but not to see his face, he called his exoteric disciples; but those who were allowed to enter the veil, his esoterics.

ARISTOTLE adopted the same terms; those who attended his evening lectures, which were of a popular character, he

called his exoterics; and those who attended his more abstruse morning lectures, his esoterics.

esperpentos   See VALLE-INCLÁN, RAMÓN DEL.

Espronceda y Delgado, José (1808–1842)   Spanish poet. Espronceda was a romantic in word and in deed. An early conspiracy left him with no choice but to flee Spain; later he was an ardent supporter of liberalism in Holland, while in 1830 he joined the revolutionary cause in Paris. His work stresses patriotic and Byronic themes. His most famous short poems, which appeared in his *Poesías* (1840), include "A Jarifa en una orgía," "El verdugo," "El mendigo," and "A la patria." However, his reputation rests upon two longer works: *El estudiante de Salamanca* (1839), which deals with the adventures of Félix de Montemar, a typical romantic hero who witnesses his own funeral, and the long dramatic poem *El diablo mundo* (1840–41), considered his masterpiece, which resembles Byron's DON JUAN and contains the famous "Canto a Teresa," dealing with the poet's lost love.

Essay Concerning Human Understanding, An (1690)   A philosophical treatise by John LOCKE dealing with the nature and scope of human knowledge. Its basic premise is the empirical origin of ideas, which can be described as the raw material with which the mind works. The mind of man at birth, Locke claimed, is like a blank sheet of paper, or *tabula rasa*, and possesses no "innate ideas." Man acquires knowledge through experience, which is made up of sensation, impressions of the external world derived through the senses, and reflection, the internal operation of the mind. Knowledge stems from the perception of relationships among ideas. Locke's essay contributed greatly to the growth of 18th-century EMPIRICISM, and, through its influence on the work of HUME, KANT, and others, influenced modern theories of knowledge.

Essay for the Recording of Illustrious Providences, An (1684)   A pseudoscientific treatise by Increase MATHER. The work is a collection of reports involving supernatural incidents in New England, which Mather examines in an attempt to prove and illustrate the intervention of God in human affairs. The book was republished twice in the 19th century as *Remarkable Providences*.

Essay of Dramatic Poesy (1668)   A famous critical essay by John DRYDEN. It is in the form of a conversation among four Englishmen who have ventured out on the Thames in a barge in hope of witnessing an engagement between the Dutch and English fleets. They discuss Greek, French, and English drama, the merits of several dramatists, and the use of blank and rhymed verse in plays.

Essay on Criticism, An (1711)   A didactic poem in HEROIC COUPLETS by Alexander POPE, written when he was twenty-one or younger. It is a discussion, based on neoclassical doctrines, of literary taste and style, principles of verse structure and of criticism, and gives a brief history of criticism. Standards of taste are to be derived from the order found in nature:

Those rules of old discovered, not devised,
Are nature still, but nature methodized.

The poem is sprinkled with well-known couplets:

A little learning is a dangerous thing;
Drink deep, or taste not the Pierian spring.

True wit is nature to advantage dressed,
What oft was thought, but ne'er so well expressed.

Good nature and good sense must ever join;
To err is human, to forgive divine.

Essay on Man, An (1733–1734)   The best-known poem of Alexander POPE. Written in HEROIC COUPLETS, it is divided into four Epistles dealing respectively with man's relation to the universe, to himself, to society, and to happiness. The poem is addressed to, and was inspired by, Henry St. John, Lord Bolingbroke; it expresses a deistic philosophy (see DEISM) loosely derived from LEIBNITZ, being intended to set forth a coherent scheme of the universe, to "vindicate the ways of God to man" and to declare that "whatever is, is right." It is optimistic and shows the characteristic neoclassical faith in reason and respect for tradition and authority. See GREAT CHAIN OF BEING.

Essays (Essais, 1580, 1588)   The masterpiece of the French moralist Michel de MONTAIGNE, creator of the personal discursive essay. Loosely constructed, they ramble at will over any number of subjects like a spirited conversation. The order in which the chapters appear and the division into three books had no logical significance. However, the order in which Montaigne actually wrote has been established and reveals a certain progression in his thought from a classic stoic attitude to one of skepticism (see APOLOGY FOR RAYMOND SEBOND) to a final affirmation of the possibilities in human nature. He found that the knowledge he sought resided in man alone, of which he was a representative. To extract knowledge, therefore, he must learn to know himself, as his great model Socrates had taught. In the *Essays*, he delved into his own experience, gleaned the lessons it held for him, and gradually filled out his "self-portrait." The ideas he expressed on such topics as death, friendship, virtue, suffering, education, politics, freedom, nature, and man are peculiarly his own. At the same time they are universal, since the truth Montaigne found is rooted in human nature itself. Montaigne was highly original in turning attention from academic learning and intellectual theorizing to man himself. Freed from the prejudices of his time, he cleared the way for the consideration of morality, politics, and justice as separate disciplines, independent of religious dogma, whose successful practice was closely related to an understanding of human nature. He has endured because every reader has found not only the portrait of Montaigne in the *Essays*, but glimpses of his own image.

Essays, First and Second Series (1841, 1844)   Two collections of essays by Ralph Waldo EMERSON. The First Series includes the essays called *History*, SELF-RELIANCE, COMPENSATION, *Spiritual Laws, Love, Friendship, Prudence, Heroism*, THE OVER-SOUL, *Circles, Intellect*, and *Art*. The Second Series includes *The Poet, Experience, Character, Manners, Gifts, Nature, Politics*, and *Nominalist and Realist*.

Essays in Idleness (Tsurezure gusa)   Japanese miscellany of the Muromachi period by Yoshida Kenkō (1283–1350), a court official and Buddhist monk. The 243 passages consist of sketches, comments, and anecdotes reflecting both a cynical worldliness and a mildly Buddhistic outlook.

Essays or Counsels, Civil and Moral, The   A collection of brief essays by Francis BACON, published in three editions during his lifetime: a first edition of ten essays (1597); a second of thirty-eight (1612); and a third of fifty-eight (1625). Generally, they deal with questions of personal or public conduct and philosophical or religious matters. They are written in a witty, pithy, widely metaphorical, and highly original style.

Establishment   Popular name originally for those who wield power in Britain and are sometimes humorously and sometimes resentfully considered to form an exclusive society. The Establishment was conceived of as an arm of the British upper class, dedicated to preserving the values, rights, and powers of that class, generally at the expense of the rest of the population. By extension it is also applied to the wealthy and powerful in America and elsewhere.

Este   Italian noble family, lords of the province of Ferrara from the 13th through the 16th century, who took their name from the city of Este (hence also *Estensi*). Their influence on literature and the other arts was especially great during the Renaissance, when their court was a center of activity in the drama and devoted to the romanzo, or romantic epic. The most famous recipients of their patronage were the poets BOIARDO, ARIOSTO, and TASSO. Among the outstanding Estensi were:

Leonello d'Este (1407–1450)   Marquis of Ferrara, man of letters, patron of such artists as ALBERTI, and himself a minor poet of some ability.

Ercole I d'Este (1431–1505)   Duke of Ferrara (1471–1505). Patron of Boiardo, father of two celebrated Renaissance women: Beatrice d'Este (1475–97), wife of Lodovico SFORZA of Milan; and Isabella d'Este (1474–1539), wife of Francesco GONZAGA of Mantua and one of the most learned and cultivated women of her time.

Ippolito d'Este (1479–1520)   Cardinal (1479–1520). Friend of LEONARDO DA VINCI and patron of the poet Ariosto.

Alfonso II d'Este (1533–1597)   Duke of Ferrara (1559–97). Patron of Tasso, who was forced to confine the poet in an asylum after a mental breakdown. Alfonso's sister Eleonora d'Este (1537–81) was once thought to have been the object of Tasso's love, and the reason for his confinement, but this is now considered a fiction.

Luigi d'Este (1538–1586) A cardinal and patron of the poet Tasso until 1572, when the latter entered the service of Duke Alfonso.

Estébanez Calderón, Serafín (1799–1867) Spanish statesman and author. His most famous work is the colorful *Escenas andaluzas* (1847), which deals with the picturesque life, customs, and dress of the inhabitants of the province of Andalusia.

Esther (Hebrew name Hadassah) An OLD TESTAMENT heroine whose story is told in the book bearing her name. An orphan, Esther was adopted by her relative, MORDECAI, a Jew who had saved the Persian king from assassins. When Queen VASHTI defied an order of King AHASUERUS, the beautiful Esther was chosen as his wife. On the advice of Mordecai, she kept her religion a secret until it transpired that a court favorite and rival of Mordecai, named Haman, had secured a decree to kill all the Jews in the Kingdom and to have Mordecai hanged. At a banquet Esther exposed Haman's plot, revealed herself to her king, and made a courageous and eloquent plea for the safety of her people. The king ordered the death of Haman on the gallows he had built for Mordecai and revoked the decree. Orthodox Jews still celebrate the feast of *Purim* to commemorate this deliverance.

Esther (1689) A tragedy in three acts by Jean RACINE. Based on the Book of ESTHER and relating the story of Esther and Ahasuerus, the play was written for the schoolgirls of St.-Cyr at the request of the Marquise de MAINTENON; the nature of the commission explains the unorthodox interpolation of songs by a chorus of Israelite maidens.

Esther (1884) A novel by Henry ADAMS. Esther Dudley, a free-thinking young painter, falls in love with the clergyman Stephen Hazard, but, hostile to his church and alienated by his orthodox views, she breaks their engagement. The character of Esther is thought to be modeled after that of Adams's wife Marian. The artist Wharton, a character in a romantic subplot, may have been drawn from the sculptor Augustus SAINT GAUDENS, who created the impressive memorial to Mrs. Adams in the Rock Creek Cemetery in Washington.

Estrées, Gabrielle d' (1573–1599) Mistress of Henry IV of France. The daughter of the marquis of Cœuvres, she won the affection of Henry when he visited the castle of Cœuvres and became his mistress in 1592, bearing him several children, who were legitimized. Henry's plans to marry Gabrielle after his divorce from Margaret of Valois were cut short by her death.

Eternal City Rome. The epithet occurs in Ovid, Tibullus, and other writers, and in many official documents of the Empire. In Vergil's AENEID, Jupiter tells Venus that he would give to the Romans *imperium sine fine* ("eternal empire").

eternal feminine A phrase from the last lines of Goethe's FAUST, "Das Ewig-Weibliche/Zieht uns hinan" ("The eternal feminine/Draws us onward"). Goethe symbolizes this idea in the Virgin Mary at the end of *Faust*, and both GRETCHEN and HELEN are manifestations of it, but its full meaning is more general. Whereas Mephistopheles represents nihilism, the complete lack of upward striving, the eternal feminine is the goal of all upward striving, of all man's attempts, however futile or misguided, to improve himself or his world.

Eternal Husband, The (Vechny muzh, 1870) A short novel by DOSTOYEVSKY. It is a brilliant psychological study of the relations between a cuckolded husband and his wife's ex-lover. The husband, Pavel Pavlovich Trusotsky, torments himself as well as the lover, Aleksey Ivanovich Velchaninov. He hints to Velchaninov that the daughter his wife bore before she died was actually Velchaninov's. Trusotsky horribly mistreats the girl, who loves him. When she is separated from him, she dies. Velchaninov hopes he has seen the last of Trusotsky, but the half-mad little man turns up again, urging Velchaninov to come and meet his prospective second wife, as if inviting cuckoldry all over again.

Ethan Frome (1911) A short novel by Edith WHARTON. In a typical New England village, the title character barely makes a living out of his stony farm and exists at odds with his wife Zeena, a whining hypochondriac. When Mattie, Zeena's cousin, comes to live with them, love develops between her and Ethan. They try to end their hapless romance by steering a bobsled into a tree; but both end up cripples, tied to a long life of despair with Zeena. Zeena, however, is transformed into a devoted nurse while Mattie becomes the nagging invalid.

Ethical Culture movement See ADLER, FELIX.

Ethiopians (Gr, "burnt-faces") A legendary race of people in Greek mythology. The country of the Ethiopians lay south of Egypt, close to the stream of Ocean. Cepheus, husband of CASSIOPEIA and father of ANDROMEDA, was one of their kings. Memnon, the son of EOS and TITHONUS, who fell in the TROJAN WAR, was another. In Greek drama, mention is often made of various gods being off in Ethiopia, meaning they were a great distance removed from the action of the play.

Ethiopica The story of the loves between Theagenes and Chariclea, by Heliodoros, Greek romance writer and later bishop of Tricca, in Thessaly, in the 4th century. The book, considered the earliest of extant Greek romances, was formed by ten volumes, largely borrowed from by subsequent novelists, and especially by Madeleine de SCUDÉRY, TASSO, GUARINI, and D'Urfé.

Etna (or Aetna) The famous Sicilian volcano. In the AENEID, Vergil ascribes its eruption to the restlessness of Enceladus, a giant who lies buried under the mountain, where the Greek and Latin poets also placed the forges of VULCAN and the smithy of the CYCLOPS.

Étranger, L'   See STRANGER, THE.

Être et le néant, L'   See BEING AND NOTHINGNESS.

Etruscans   An ancient non-Italic race which established itself in northern Italy some time before the 7th century BC. Modern Tuscany is roughly the center of what was their kingdom, Etruria. The Tusci, as they were called by the Romans, gained great power in Italy and the western Mediterranean, and held sway over Rome until 509 BC, when the last Etruscan king was expelled from that city. The Romans feared and hated them for many years thereafter, although they were finally absorbed both politically and culturally into the Roman state. Their art shows influences from Greece, Egypt, Syria, Cyprus, and Mesopotamia, and it, in turn, influenced Roman art. Their language remains undeciphered and their origin a mystery, although the Greek historian Herodotus asserts that they came from Lydia in Asia Minor.

Et tu, Brute   According to SUETONIUS in his *Lives of the Caesars*, Julius CAESAR on being stabbed by Marcus Junius BRUTUS, whom he had counted among his trusted friends, exclaimed: *Et tu, Brute fili* ("You also, O Brutus, my son"). Shakespeare, in his play JULIUS CAESAR, immeasurably heightened the effect of the passage by adding to it an expression of utter despair at such betrayal: "Et tu, Brute! Then fall, Caesar!" The phrase is currently used as an expression of amazement at a sudden revelation of treachery or ingratitude.

Eucharist   (Gr, "thanksgiving"), also known as the Lord's Supper   A Christian SACRAMENT that repeats the actions of Jesus at the LAST SUPPER. It is reported in all of the SYNOPTIC GOSPELS that Jesus took bread and blessed it saying, "Take ye: this is my body" (Mark 14:22), and after drinking wine and giving thanks he said, "This is my blood of the covenant, which is shed for many" (Mark 14:24). Partaking of the Eucharist is called Holy Communion.

Euclid   (fl 300 BC)   A Greek mathematician. Euclid lived and taught at Alexandria. His *Elements* (of geometry) in thirteen books became the basis of future geometry. He is celebrated in Edna St. Vincent MILLAY's well-known line, "Euclid alone has looked on beauty bare."

Eugene Onegin   (Yevgeny Onegin, 1831)   A novel in verse by Aleksandr PUSHKIN. For the influence it had on later Russian literature and in its own right, *Eugene Onegin* is probably Pushkin's most important work. The novel relates the experiences of its Byronic hero, Eugene. Bored with the social life in St. Petersburg, he visits his country estate and meets Tatyana, a young woman who falls in love with him and naively offers herself to him. The bored Eugene is not interested and rather bluntly tells her so. For lack of any other amusement, he then provokes a duel with Lensky, a young romantic poet who has become his friend. Lensky is killed, and Onegin goes back to the world of society. After his departure, Tatyana visits Eugene's country manor, browses through his library, and begins to realize how hollow and artificial he is. A few years later, when Eugene meets Tatyana, who is now the wife of a prince and a prominent member of St. Petersburg society, her beauty and charm, and perhaps her eminence in society, turn his head. He announces his love to her in a letter, as Tatyana had to him years before. Tatyana admits she still loves him but refuses him because of her duty to her husband.

Pushkin's novel has been a rich source of character types for Russian writers. His use of an ironic narrator to tell the story has perhaps been equally influential. This narrative device was especially well developed by DOSTOYEVSKY. The libretto for TCHAIKOVSKY's opera *Eugene Onegin* (1879) was faithfully adapted from Pushkin's novel by the composer's brother Modeste.

Eugénie, Empress   (full name Eugénie Marie de Montijo de Guzmán, Comtesse de Téba, 1826–1920) Wife of NAPOLEON III, and empress of the French (1853–71). She was a leader of fashion, and her feminine charm added brilliance to the French court. Her influence upon her husband reveals her lack of interest in liberal and democratic ideas. After the downfall of the empire, she fled to England, where she was befriended by Queen Victoria.

Eugénie Grandet   (1833)   A novel, part of LA COMÉDIE HUMAINE, by Honoré de BALZAC. Félix Grandet, the embodiment of greed and domestic tyranny, destroys the romance of his daughter Eugénie with her cousin Charles, condemning her to a futile, joyless existence.

Eulenspiegel, Till   (or Tyll Ulenspiegel; called in English Tyll Howleglas or Owlglass)   A German peasant popular in legend as a player of pranks. Tradition makes him a native of Brunswick who died in 1350. The stories associated with his name tell of the often brutal tricks and practical jokes he played, mostly on innkeepers and other tradespeople, but sometimes on priests or noblemen. The first written account was probably a Low German one of about 1483, the next a High German text of 1515. The satire of these seems to emphasize the tricks as the revenge of the peasant upon the townsmen who scorn him as inferior. The rogue's adventures, highly popular and adapted in translations all over Europe, had been printed in England by 1560. Charles de Coster wrote a modernized version in 1867, and Richard STRAUSS used the theme musically in his tone poem *Till Eulenspiegel's Merry Pranks* (1894).

eulogy   A formal piece of writing or an oration in praise of a person or thing; by extension, it has come to mean any general expression of praise.

Eumaeus   The faithful slave and swineherd of Odysseus in the ODYSSEY.

euphony   A term that denotes sounds pleasing to the ear, usually produced by a combination of vowels and liquid consonants. It is the opposite of CACOPHONY.

Euphrosyne   (Gr, "joy")   In classic mythology, one of the three Charites, or GRACES.

Euphues   The chief character of John LYLY's *Euphues, The Anatomy of Wit* (1579) and *Euphues and*

His England (1580). Euphues is a witty, pleasure-loving young Athenian who, sojourning in Naples, attempts to win Lucilla, fiancée of his friend Philautus. This procedure estranges him from Philautus, but when Lucilla chooses a third lover, the unworthy Curio, the two friends are united in disillusionment. There is little plot in either romance; the interest lies chiefly in long philosophic discussions and in the elaborate and affected style that gave rise to the terms EUPHUISM and *euphuist*. This style, marked by ingenious antitheses, alliteration, exempla, complicated figures, and skillfully balanced sentences, was for a while in great vogue. It was frequently parodied, however, and by 1590 a reaction in favor of a more masculine, pithy style had set in.

euphuism   An artificial style of English speech and writing popular in the late ELIZABETHAN and JACOBEAN periods. It derived its name from *Euphues: The Anatomy of Wit* (1579) by John LYLY, who either invented the style or derived it from translations of certain works of a Spanish writer, Antonio de Guevara (c1480–1545). It was characterized by exaggerated BAROQUE refinement and artificiality of style, with plentiful references to mythical birds and beasts, constant alliteration, and the frequent use of unduly neat antitheses. The intent of this elaborate elegance was to woo feminine readers by seeming to edify them, while avoiding scholarly solemnity. Although excessively ornate and artificial, the style helped free English prose from the heavy latinized style and added FANCY AND IMAGINATION to prose writing. The fashion lasted for half a century, and Lyly had many imitators, notably Robert GREENE and Thomas LODGE. See EUPHUES.

eureka (fr Gr, *heureka*, "I have found it")   An exclamation of delight at having made a discovery, said to have originated with ARCHIMEDES, the Syracusan philosopher, when he discovered how to test the purity of Hiero's crown. The tale is that Hiero, a famous tyrant of Syracuse, delivered a certain weight of gold to a smith to be made into a votive crown, but, suspecting that the gold had been alloyed with an inferior metal, asked Archimedes to test it. The philosopher did not know how to proceed, but in stepping into his bath, which was quite full, observed that some of the water ran over. It immediately struck him that a body must remove its own bulk of water when it is immersed; silver is lighter than gold, therefore a pound weight of silver will be more bulky than a pound weight of gold, and would consequently remove more water. In this way he found that the crown was deficient in gold. Vitruvius says: "When the idea flashed across his mind, the philosopher jumped out of the bath exclaiming, '*Heureka! heureka!*' and, without waiting to dress himself, ran home to try the experiment."

Eureka (1848)   An essay on the material and spiritual universe by Edgar Allan POE. Under the influence of Marquis Pierre Simon de Laplace (1749–1827) and NEWTON, Poe presented his view of the universe as a mystic and material unity. An interesting contribution to scientific and philosophic thought, the piece indicates that Poe saw the possibility of non-Euclidean geometry. Many of his notions are surprisingly in agreement with the latest theories of cosmic origin.

Euripides (480?–405 BC)   A Greek tragic playwright. A slightly younger contemporary of AESCHYLUS and SOPHOCLES, and less honored in his time, Euripides is now admired for his remarkably modern attitudes and his profound insights into psychology. In spite of ARISTOPHANES' taunt that his mother had sold vegetables, he was actually high born and well educated. He was twice married, both times unhappily. Although he wrote between eighty and ninety plays, Euripides won prizes only four times. In 409 BC, he left Athens and died at the court of King Archelaus of Macedonia.

According to tradition, Euripides was withdrawn and bookish, and his plays reveal a sharply inquiring mind that must have made him many enemies in Athens. He was cruelly lampooned by Aristophanes in two comedies, THE CLOUDS and the THESMOPHORIAZUSAI. The slanders against him and the relative unpopularity of his plays may account for his leaving Athens when he was still at the height of his powers; yet Sophocles dressed his chorus in mourning when news of Euripides' death reached Athens.

Seventeen tragedies by Euripides remain, beginning with the ALCESTIS in 438 BC, and ending with THE BACCHANTS in about 405 BC. He also wrote the fragmentary SATYR PLAY CYCLOPS about 424–423 BC, and may have written another existing tragedy, *Rhesus*, of which the date is unknown. Although called a tragedy, the *Alcestis* has a strong comic element that relates it more closely to the satyr plays.

Three qualities in Euripides' plays have especially attracted modern readers: his biting social criticism, his subtle psychological analyses of his characters, and their humanity, as compared to the larger-than-life remoteness of the heroes and heroines of Aeschylus and Sophocles. Euripides attacked, at least by implication, many attitudes accepted by the Athenians: the subordinate position of women (*Alcestis*), and foreign women in particular (MEDEA); the unjust treatment of illegitimate children (HIPPOLYTUS); above all, the glory of war (THE TROJAN WOMEN). His own attitude toward his home city of Athens seems to have changed strikingly in the decade between his ANDROMACHE and *The Trojan Women*. The earlier play bitterly attacks the Spartans as cruel and cowardly and seems to imply that the Athenians would never behave in such a manner. In *The Trojan Women*, however, they behave in much the same way to the defeated Trojans, killing the child Astyanax out of fear that the line of Hector will be perpetuated. This play reflected Euripides' disillusionment and outrage over the massacre by Athenians of the inhabitants of Melos, because they had remained neutral in the PELOPONNESIAN WAR. This disgust with war is evident also in the IPHIGENIA IN AULIS, one of his last plays. Even as early as the *Andromache*, however, it was clear that Euripides found no glory in war, but only needless suffering and inhumanity.

Some of the irony of the *Alcestis*, in which Admetus gallantly allows his wife to die for him, may have been lost on the Athenians, who considered men's lives more valuable than those of women. But in the *Medea* the sharp-tongued heroine makes his criticism of the treatment of women abundantly clear. Medea, like Electra and Phaedra (in the *Hippolytus*), is drawn with extraordinarily acute insights into her emotions. They are queens, yet they are extremely human women, rather than heroic personages of tragedy. It was in this reduction of tragic figures to human proportions that Euripides laid the groundwork for the New Comedy that was to come. Euripides' characters speak a much more colloquial language than that of the other tragedians, but it is still poetry of a high order, especially in the choral odes.

Euripides' other plays include ION, IPHIGENIA IN TAURIS, HELEN, ELECTRA, ORESTES, HECUBA, and THE SUPPLIANT WOMEN.

Europa In classical mythology, a daughter of Agenor, or, according to the ILIAD, daughter of Phoenix. She was famed for her beauty. ZEUS, in the form of a white bull, carried her off and swam with her to the island of Crete. She was the mother of MINOS, RHADAMANTHUS, and Evandros or SARPEDON, and, according to some forms of the legend, of the MINOTAUR.

Europeans, The (1878) A novel by Henry JAMES. The plot centers on the visit of "the Europeans," Felix Young, an artist, and his sister, the Baroness Münster, to their New England relatives, the Wentworths. The Europeans hope to gain much from their American cousins. The baroness tries, but fails, to make a wealthy marriage. Felix paints portraits of the Bostonians he meets, eventually marrying one of his kinswomen, who is eager to escape her bleak environment. James tends to treat his themes here comically, and although he portrays the Wentworths' moral solidity with respect, he nevertheless calls attention to their timid provincialism.

Eurydice See ORPHEUS.

Euterpe One of the nine MUSES in classical mythology. She was the Muse of music, patroness of joy and pleasure, and of flute players.

Evangeline, A Tale of Acadie (1847) A narrative poem by Henry Wadsworth LONGFELLOW. The lovers, Gabriel Lajeunesse and Evangeline Bellefontaine, are separated when the British expel the Acadians from Nova Scotia. He is carried to Louisiana, and she to New England. The two spend years searching for one another. Nursing the sick in an epidemic in Philadelphia, she recognizes him as the dying man in her care. Now an old woman, Evangeline also dies, and the two are buried together.

Evans, Walker (1903–1975) American photographer. Born in Chicago, Evans is known for his direct and poignant depictions of rural poverty in America in the 1930s. Equally famous are his photographs of buildings, signs, and billboards, which are remarkable for their straightforward yet mysterious beauty. The picture-within-a-picture, seen in his *Studio Portraits* (1936), is an Evans trademark. He illustrated several books, among them James AGEE's *Let Us Now Praise Famous Men* (1941) and Hart CRANE's *The Bridge* (1930). His photographs were collected and published in several volumes, including *American Photographs* (1938) and *Message from the Interior* (1966).

Evans, William (d 1632) An English giant, nearly eight feet tall. A porter of Charles I, he carried Sir Jeffrey Hudson, the queen's dwarf, in his pocket. Sir Walter Scott wrote of him in PEVERIL OF THE PEAK.

Eve (fr Heb, *hawwāh*, "life") The first woman, the wife of Adam, and "the mother of all living" (Gen. 3:20). Because Eve persuaded Adam to eat the forbidden fruit in the Garden of Eden, her name is often used as a synonym for a temptress. See ADAM AND EVE.

Evelina, or The History of a Young Lady's Entrance into the World (1778) A novel by Fanny BURNEY. After having been brought up in the country by Reverend Arthur Villars, a friend of her grandfather, Evelina Anville is sent to live in London with Villars's friend Lady Howard. Here Evelina is introduced to the ways of society. Though courted by Sir Clement Willoughby, whom she recognizes for the rake that he is, she prefers the gentlemanly Lord Orville. However, they are kept apart by numerous misunderstandings and by the mystery and stigma surrounding Evelina's birth; she turns out to be the daughter of Sir John Belmont and all ends happily.

Evelyn, John (1620–1706) English diarist and miscellaneous writer. A man whose interests ranged from gardening to numismatics, Evelyn held a number of offices under Charles II and was a prominent member of the Royal Society. His varied background and participation in the political events of his day lend interest and importance to his *Diary* (1818), which covers the years from 1631 to 1706.

Eve of St. Agnes, The (1819) A poem by John KEATS. It is based on the legend that on the Eve of St. Agnes, young maidens are allowed a glimpse of their future husbands. Porphyro thus comes to Madeline on St. Agnes's Eve and soon they depart into the timeless world of love. Some of Keats's most striking sensuous imagery is found in this poem.

Everyman (c1500) Most famous of the MORALITY PLAYS, probably translated into English from the Dutch *Elckerlijk* (1495). When Everyman receives a summons from Death, he tries vainly to persuade his friends Fellowship, Kindred, Worldly Goods, Beauty, and others to journey with him; but only Good Deeds remains faithful, although so weak because of Everyman's neglect that Knowledge and Confession must renew his strength so that he can accompany Everyman to the grave. The subtitle reads "A Treatise how the hye Fader of Heven sendeth Dethe to somon every creature to come and gyve a counte of theyr lyves in this Worlde."

Hugo von HOFMANNSTHAL's *Jedermann* (1911) is a reworking of the play into German verse.

Every Man in His Humour (1598) A comedy by Ben JONSON. A familiar classic plot is used as a vehicle for the study of a series of characters, each of whom is possessed by a particular HUMOUR, or dominating characteristic. The plot, which is rife with incident and misunderstanding, concerns the efforts of Young Kno'well and Wellbred to escape or contain the displeasure of their father and brother-in-law respectively. The characters to whom the title applies are: Captain Bobadil, whose humour is bragging of his brave deeds and military courage, and who is thrashed as a coward by Downright; Kitely, whose humour is jealousy of his wife and who is befooled and cured by a trick played on him by Brainworm; Stephen, whose humour is verdant stupidity and who is played on by everyone; Kno'well, whose humour is suspicion of his son; Dame Kitely, whose humour is jealousy of her husband, but she, like him, is cured by a trick devised by Brainworm.

The play exists in two versions, the first of which uses Italian names and places. A sequel, *Every Man Out of His Humour* (1599), has even less coherency of plot but presents a rich collection of the foibles of the time.

Excalibur (OF, *Escalibor*) The sword of King ARTHUR in Arthurian romance. It is called *Caliburn* by GEOFFREY OF MONMOUTH, and *Caledvwlch* in the MABINOGION. There is in Irish legend a famous sword called *Caladbolg*, a name that is thought to mean "hard belly," i.e., capable of consuming anything; this and the name Excalibur are probably connected.

The way that Arthur gains the sword is variously told in ARTHURIAN LEGEND. In some versions, Excalibur is the sword, magically fixed in a stone, that can be withdrawn only by one who is the rightful king of England, and Arthur proves to be the only knight that can pull the sword from the stone. In Malory's MORTE D'ARTHUR, Excalibur is a gift to Arthur from the LADY OF THE LAKE. After the last battle, when Arthur lies mortally wounded, he commands Sir Bedivere to return Excalibur to the lake. Sir Bedivere throws it into the water, and an arm, clothed in white samite, appears to receive it.

Excursion, The A long didactic poem by William WORDSWORTH, forming part of "The Recluse" (1814). It includes discussions of virtue, religious faith, the industrial revolution and its social effects, and the education of children.

Executioner's Song, The See MAILER, NORMAN.

Exiles (1918) A play by James JOYCE. The central character is Richard Rowan, who, like Joyce himself, is an Irish writer who has spent much of his life abroad and feels estranged from Irish society on his return to Dublin. The action concerns various love entanglements between Richard, his common-law wife, Bertha, and his friends. It is a naturalistic play, indebted to the work of IBSEN, whom Joyce greatly admired. Only moderately successful on the stage, *Exiles* is chiefly important for the light it throws on the development of Joyce's ideas about the artist's alienation from society.

existentialism A 20th-century movement in philosophy. Although it grew out of the development of the philosophical tradition all over Europe, it was highly popularized in France in the 1940s and is usually associated with the theories expressed by Jean-Paul SARTRE. The beginnings of existentialism are found in the writings of the Danish Søren KIERKEGAARD, the German Friedrich NIETZSCHE, and the Russian Fyodor DOSTOYEVSKY, although none of them formulated a logical system. The works of the Germans Martin HEIDEGGER and Karl JASPERS were the most immediate influence on Sartre's thinking, along with the method of approach of the phenomenologist Edmund HUSSERL.

All existentialists are concerned with ontology, the study of being. The point of departure is human consciousness and mental processes. In contrast to most previous philosophical systems, which maintain that an *a priori* essence precedes or transcends the individual existence of people or of objects, the existentialists conclude that existence precedes essence. The significance of this for human beings is that the concept that a man has an essential self is shown to be an illusion. A man's self is nothing except what he has become; at any given moment, it is the sum of the life he has shaped until then. The "nothing" he begins with is thus the source of man's freedom, for at each moment it is man's will that can choose how to act or not to act. However, each such decision affects the future doubly: a man is or should be responsible for the consequences of his actions; and each action necessarily excludes the other potential actions for that moment, and their consequences, and thus at least partially limits the potentialities for future actions.

By what standards, then, should man make his decisions? Man's mind cannot discern any meaning for this existence in the universe; when he abandons his illusions, he finds himself horrified by the absurdity of the human condition. The question of the existence of God (or some cosmic purpose) is irrelevant, according to Sartre and the atheistic existentialists, because even if He does exist (which they usually deny), He does not reveal to men the meaning of their lives. Thus man must create a human morality in the absence of any known predetermined absolute values. Honesty with oneself is perhaps the major value common to existentialist thinking; all their writings describe the emotional anguish of trying to achieve it. Sartre calls the "man of good faith" one who understands the human condition described above and fully accepts the responsibility of the freedom it entails. The "man of bad faith" accepts illusion, is deliberately hypocritical, or tries to use the excuse of "good intentions" to escape responsibility for the consequences of his actions, the ramifications of which always involve other people. The man of good faith judges a potential action by estimating the result if everyone, not just himself, were to perform it. Yet despite the difficulty of choice, he does not withdraw from life, but is *engagé*, actively engaged in the business of living with himself and with other men.

The Christian existentialists agree that man can never know God's purpose, but they affirm that it exists and that through a "leap of faith" man can establish his values in accordance with it. However, they too describe the anguish and the responsibility of honest action, for a man can never be certain that his decision is actually based on an intuition of the divine and not on the disguised temptation of evil.

Other writers in the existentialist tradition are Gabriel MARCEL, leader of Christian existentialism in France, the Spaniards Miguel de UNAMUNO and José ORTEGA Y GASSET, and the Jewish mystic Martin BUBER.

Albert CAMUS is often classified with the movement, but he considers many of Sartre's postulates as much an unjustifiable "leap of faith" as that of the religious existentialists. His "man of the ABSURD" resembles Sartre's "man of good faith" in that both acknowledge man's lonely condition in the face of the silence of the universe; both reject despair and commit themselves to the anguish and responsibility of living as best one can; and both consider the exercise of one's own freedom inseparable from the opportunity for all men to exercise theirs, which is contingent on their freedom from poverty, political oppression, and other avoidable external limitations. However, Camus's writings do not attempt to constitute an organized philosophical system of ontology, as do Sartre's.

exodos In classical Greek drama, the last choral passage in a tragedy or comedy, recited or sung as the chorus left the orchestra. See PARODOS.

Exodus (Gr, "a going out") The escape by the Jews from their bondage in Egypt (c1200 BC). Led by MOSES, they crossed the Red Sea and wandered for forty years in the Sinai wilderness, finally reaching Canaan. During this time God revealed His name, His laws, and the destiny of Israel. The covenant between God and Israel promised Israel a "land flowing with milk and honey" in return for homage and reverence.

The book of Exodus is the second volume of the PENTATEUCH. It gives the account of Moses's birth, the Israelites' departure from Egypt, and the beginning of their long journey to Palestine. The twentieth chapter of Exodus contains the TEN COMMANDMENTS.

Exodus is the title of a novel (1958) by Leon URIS about the establishment of the modern state of Israel.

ex pede Herculem An expression meaning "from this sample we may judge of the whole." Literally (Lat), "Hercules [may be drawn] from his foot." PLUTARCH says that PYTHAGORAS calculated the height of HERACLES (Gr for the Lat Hercules) by comparing the lengths of various stadia in Greece. A stadium was six hundred feet in length, but Heracles's stadium at Olympia was much longer; therefore, said the philosopher, the foot of Heracles was proportionately longer than an ordinary foot; and as the foot bears a certain ratio to the height, so the height of Heracles can be easily ascertained. *Ex ungue leonem* ("a lion [may be drawn] from its claw") is a similar phrase.

expressionism Primarily a German movement from about 1900 to the mid-1920s that revolutionized the pictorial arts, literature, drama, dance, cinema, and related fields. To the expressionists, the artist's subjective feelings were all-important; they sought to portray active inner emotion rather than to depict objective reality. The movement was, in virtually all respects, the antithesis of IMPRESSIONISM. It sought to replace passive observation with active expression; aesthetic appreciation with ethical engagement and revolutionary fervor; a refined realism, harmony, and beauty with exaggeration, distortion, dissonance, and ugliness; subtle feelings with intense emotionalism, terror, fury, agony; and aristocratic reserve with brotherly appeals to mankind.

The movement began in art, developed by such groups as DER BLAUE REITER and DIE BRÜCKE. Major expressionist artists include Edvard MUNCH, Ernst BARLACH, Oskar KOKOSCHKA, and Paul KLEE. Forerunners of expressionistic style may be found in earlier European art; for example, in the turbulent lines and violent colors used by VAN GOGH, the fantastic caricatures in GOYA's graphic work, and in the contorted forms of such Gothic artists as GRÜNEWALD.

In reference to literature, expressionism denotes a movement from about 1910 to 1925, closely akin to the corresponding movement in art. It made its first breakthrough in the field of lyric poetry with such figures as George TRAKL, Georg HEYM, Franz WERFEL, and Ernst Stadler (1883–1914), whose verses are fired with an ecstatic hymnic quality and written in a condensed, expressive language. Expressionist drama likewise takes condensation as one of its goals: everything not immediately necessary for expressing the play's central idea is omitted; the external world is merely sketched in; the *dramatis personae* are not characters but types, without fully developed personalities and often without individual names; the successive scenes are sometimes connected only by ideas, not by any continuity of action; and the dialogue is compressed into a "telegram-style." Major playwrights include: Georg KAISER, Ernst TOLLER, Fritz von UNRUH, Ernst Barlach, and Bertolt BRECHT in his earlier work. Narrative prose, finally, did not come into its own as an expressionist medium until after the movement had passed its peak. Major figures are Leonhard FRANK, Alfred DÖBLIN, and again Franz Werfel. In regard to history and politics, expressionism continued the satirical rejection of complacent bourgeois values begun by such writers as Carl Sternheim (1878–1943) and

WEDEKIND. With the coming of World War I, most of the expressionists took a strong pacifist stand. After the war, several of the most powerful figures, including Kaiser, Toller, and Brecht, came out for social revolution; but by the mid-1920s, revolutionary fervor had for the most part given way to a resigned skepticism or outright cynicism. See EXPRESSIONIST CINEMA.

expressionist cinema   A movement in film, particularly in Germany, that reflected and complemented EXPRESSIONISM in painting and theatre. Robert Wiene's silent film *The Cabinet of Dr. Caligari* (1919) is universally recognized as an early classic of expressionist cinema. Among the other expressionist filmmakers were F. W. MURNAU and Fritz LANG. Their aim was to convey inner, subjective experience through external, objective means. Their films were characterized by highly stylized sets and acting; the films were shot in studios where they could employ deliberately exaggerated and dramatic lighting and camera angles to emphasize some particular affect—fear, horror, pain. Aspects of expressionist techniques were later adapted by such directors as Alfred HITCHCOCK and Orson WELLES and were incorporated into many American gangster and horror films.

Eyck, Hubert van (1366?–1420) and **Jan van** (1390?–1441)   The founders of the Flemish school of painting. The brothers van Eyck are reputed to have originated the modern process of oil painting. The only known authentic work by Hubert's hand is the celebrated altarpiece the *Adoration of the Lamb* at Ghent, which was completed by Jan. A polyptich containing over twenty panels, it is generally considered one of the great masterpieces of Western art, in its magnificence of color, skillful handling of light and atmosphere, and deeply religious tone. Both men were artists of keen observation, rendering with vigorous realism and infinite detail the world they saw around them, whether the beauty of flowers, trees, and common objects or the richness of materials and jewels. Through the artistic genius of their religious paintings and portraits and their technical innovations, the brothers van Eyck exerted an enormous influence, revolutionizing painting in northern Europe by breaking with the Gothic tradition and instituting a new realistic vigor.

Ezekiel (6th century BC)   A Hebrew prophet during the Babylonian Exile. Ezekiel's sermons to Israel are found in the OLD TESTAMENT book bearing his name. He stresses the moral responsibility of the Jews for their captivity and calls for a return to godliness and faith.

Ezra   A Jewish priest who led a band of fifteen hundred Jews back to Jerusalem after the Babylonian captivity. The OLD TESTAMENT book of Ezra, coupled with NEHEMIAH in early Hebrew canon, tells of the journey and Ezra's attempts to reestablish the temple and to morally purify the Jewish community.

F

Fabian Society   An association of socialists founded in 1883 by a small group of middle-class intellectuals, including George Bernard SHAW and Beatrice and Sidney Webb. The name is derived from Quintus Fabius (275–203 BC), a Roman general who won his way against Hannibal by wariness and caution rather than violence and defiance. See CUNCTATOR.

fable   A short tale, usually epigrammatic, with animals, men, gods, and even inanimate objects as characters. The action of a fable illustrates a moral which is usually (but not always) explicitly stated at the end. This moral often attains the force of a proverb. The fable form appears early in man's cultural development, being a common part of the oral folk literature of primitive tribes. It appeared in Egyptian papyri of c1500 BC, and in Greece a recognizable fable was included in the works of HESIOD in the 8th century BC. By far the most famous fables are those attributed to AESOP, a Greek slave who lived about 600 BC. In India the fable also appeared early, the great Indian collection, the PANCHATANTRA, having been composed in the 3rd century. Modern fables have been dominated by the genius and style of LA FONTAINE, the great French fabulist of the 17th century, who wrote fables in polished and witty poetry that have been widely translated and imitated.

Fable, A (1954)   A novel by William FAULKNER. Set in France during World War I, A Fable is both an allegory of the passion of Jesus and a study of a world that has renounced individualism and chosen submission to authority and the secular values of power and chauvinism. The novel centers on a young corporal, born in a cow-shed, who enlists in the French army, incites a mutiny, and is eventually executed for cowardice. When the gravesite is struck by an enemy shell, his body disappears. The characters of the novel tend to be either personifications of abstractions or modern versions of biblical figures.

Fable for Critics, A (1848)   A long verse satire by James Russell LOWELL. The fable of Apollo and his dealings with an American critic is of little interest; the poem's value is in the witty profiles in verse of leading writers.

Among the writers satirized in pungent and accurate sketches are EMERSON, LONGFELLOW, HAWTHORNE, POE, COOPER, WHITTIER, HOLMES, and LOWELL himself. The poet makes the important assertion that American literature has come of age.

Fables choisies, mises en vers (Selected Fables, Set in Verse, 1668, 1678–1679, 1694)   A collection of verse fables by Jean de LA FONTAINE. Though freely derived from ancient and modern sources, the fables are stamped with La Fontaine's own gently ironic view of life and society. In colorful and ingenious free verse, by means of animal symbols and spirited dialogues, the author propounds a philosophy of sense and moderation, drawing practical lessons from the tribulations of crows, mice, ants, and the like and holding his fellow men up to affectionate ridicule. The fables, however, are not primarily moralistic in intent, but graceful and worldly stories told for the pleasure of telling.

Fables in Slang (1899)   A collection of sketches by George ADE that first appeared in the Chicago Record. Humorous tales illustrating the common sense of ordinary people, the Fables won attention for their rendering of contemporary American speech. Ade's "slang," however, is not slang, but a picturesque prose with numerous racy colloquialisms and many luxuriant figures of speech.

fabliaux (12th–14th centuries)   Short humorous tales, often ribald or scurrilous. Highly popular in the Middle Ages, they are situation comedies burlesquing the weaknesses of human nature; women, priests, and gullible fools are often the butts of the buffoonery, which sometimes becomes savagely bitter. The material derives from the oral folk tradition of bawdy anecdotes, practical jokes, and clever tricks of revenge, but the term fabliau was first specifically applied to a medieval French literary form, a narrative of three hundred to four hundred lines in octosyllabic couplets. About 150 of these are still extant. Similar prose tales became popular all over Europe, as in Boccaccio's DECAMERON. Apparently only a few narratives in the style of the fabliau were written in England; the most notable are the ones Chaucer included in his CANTERBURY TALES, such as the tales told by the Miller, the Reeve, the Friar, the Summoner, and the Shipman.

Façade (1922)   A long poem by Edith SITWELL. Depending more on striking patterns of sound and imagery than on meaning, the poem caused a sensation when the author gave a reading of it in London. It was set to music by William WALTON.

factotum (fr Lat, *facere totum*, "to do everything") One doing for his employer all sorts of services, sometimes called a *Johannes Factotum*. Formerly the term means a busybody, or much the same as our Jack-of-all-trades, and it is in this sense that Robert GREENE used it in his famous reference to Shakespeare:

There is an upstart Crow beautified with our feathers, that with his *Tygers hart wrapt in a Players hyde*, supposes he is as well able to bumbast out a blanke verse as the best of you: but being an absolute *Johannes fac totum*, is in his owne conceit the onely Shake-scene in a countrie.—*Groatsworth of Wit*, 1592

Facundo (1845)   The popular title of a book by Domingo Faustino SARMIENTO. Its full title is *Civilización y barbarie, Vida de Juan Facundo Quiroga*. One of the classics of Hispanic-American literature, the book is partly an attack on the dictatorship of Juan Manuel de ROSAS, partly a somewhat fanciful biography of Facundo, an Argentine political boss, and partly a sociological analysis of Argentine society. Argentina's troubles, Sarmiento believed, stemmed from the conflict between the civilization of the Europeanized urban classes and the barbarism of the ignorant, untamed gauchos, as exemplified by Rosas and Facundo. Written in a vigorous, spontaneous style, the work is also famous for its description of the Argentine pampas and of gaucho types, such as the outlaw and the tracker. *Facundo* was first translated into English by Mary Tyler Mann, wife of Horace Mann, who was a good friend of Sarmiento.

Fadayev, Aleksandr Aleksandrovich (1901–1956)   Soviet novelist. His early novel *Razgrom* (1927; tr *The Nineteen*, 1929, also tr as *The Rout*) reintroduced the psychological realism of the 19th-century novel into Soviet literature. His story of a band of Red partisans fighting in the Far East contains both excitement and psychological portraits of the characters that make them vivid to the reader. Fadayev's next work, *Posledniy iz Udege* (*The Last of the Udege*, 1930–40), was not as successful. His third work, *Molodaya gvardiya* (1945; tr *The Young Guard*, 1958), depicted underground resistance of young Communists living under the German occupation. The book was criticized for not stressing the leading role of the Communist Party in the resistance. Fadayev dutifully revised it. From 1939 to 1953, he was secretary of the Union of Soviet Writers, a post from which he was removed after Stalin's death. Fadayev shot himself to death in 1956.

Faerie Queene, The (Books I–III, 1590; IV–VI, 1596)   An allegorical epic poem by Edmund SPENSER. *The Faerie Queene* was conceived as a work of twelve books, each of which was to have portrayed, in the person of its leading knight, one of the twelve private moral virtues; the work as a whole was to be unified by the figure of Prince Arthur, the "image of a brave knight," in whom all these virtues were perfected. In the prefatory letter to Sir Walter Raleigh, Spenser indicated that, if the first twelve books were well received, he would go on to "frame the other part of politic virtues" in Arthur after he became king. However, only six books of twelve cantos each and two additional cantos on Mutability (pub 1609) were published, the other books, if they existed, possibly having been burned in the fire that destroyed Spenser's castle at Kilcoman in 1598.

Gloriana, the Faerie Queene, signifies both the abstract concept of Glory and Queen Elizabeth in particular. Drawing heavily from the chivalric romances, Spenser has Prince Arthur see her in a vision and determine to "seek her out in Faeryland." Gloriana is holding her annual twelve-day feast, on each day of which one of the twelve adventures which were to form the twelve proposed books was to begin. Following the traditional epic form, *The Faerie Queene* begins not with the scene of the feast and the begging of the first knight for a boon, but *in medias res*, with the knight already setting out on his adventure.

As a religio-political allegory of the times, *The Faerie Queene* presents aspects of Roman Catholicism in the evil figures of the false Duessa and the wicked enchanter Archimago (Bks. I and II), and attacks the Catholic emperor Philip of Spain, England's greatest enemy, as the tyrant Grantorto (Bk. V); Duessa, executed by Queen Mercilla (Elizabeth) in Book V, here figures as the Catholic Mary, Queen of Scots. The moral allegory is explored in the trials and temptations undergone by the knights representing the virtues. The spiritual allegory of man's quest for salvation is carried on throughout by the structure of the chivalric quest-motif. In each book, the leading knight is associated with a particular virtue.

Book I: The Legend of the Red Cross Knight, or of Holiness   The RED CROSS KNIGHT (Holiness), having put on the Christian armor mentioned by St. Paul, is sent by Gloriana to rescue the parents of the virgin UNA (Truth), who have been imprisoned and their kingdom laid waste by a Dragon. With Una the Knight comes to the den of Error, a monster half woman and half serpent; after a dreadful battle Error is vanquished. They then meet with Archimago (Hypocrisy), a seemingly pious, aged man, and spend the night in his hut. There the Red Cross Knight is subjected to dreams that make him believe Una false, and he abandons her. He comes upon the Saracen knight Sansfoy, accompanied by his lady, Fidessa (DUESSA, Falsehood). The Red Cross Knight slays the Saracen and is beguiled by the lies of Fidessa. Thinking to make a garland for her head, he plucks a branch from a tree, which bleeds, and which reveals itself to be Fradubio (the Doubter), who had been transformed into a tree by Duessa. Meanwhile Una, following her Knight, meets a Lion, who afterward attends her. She spends the night in the hut of Abessa (Superstition), daughter of Corceca (Blind devotion). Kirkrapine (Churchrobber) comes to bring his plunder to his mistress Abessa, but is slain by the Lion. Una travels on, followed by Archimago in disguise as the Red Cross Knight. He overtakes her and they meet Sansloy, who attacks the disguised Archimago and exposes him, and takes Una off to a wild forest. The real Red Cross Knight, by this time, has come with Duessa to the House of Pride, magnificent in appearance but built on a foundation of sand, and ruled by Queen Lucifera (Pride, and chief of the Seven Deadly Sins). Sansjoy arrives and does battle with the Red Cross Knight, who would have killed him but for the magic intervention of Duessa, who causes Sansjoy to disappear and carries him in the car of Night to the Infernal regions, where he is healed of his wounds by Aesculapius. Meanwhile Una, being attacked by Sansloy, is rescued by a troop of fauns and satyrs. Sir Satyrane (Natural chivalry) finds her and accompanies her on her journey. They meet Archimago disguised as a pilgrim, who tells them that the Red Cross Knight is dead.

Duessa, having returned from her journey to the Underworld, persuades the Red Cross Knight to drink from an enchanted pool, which robs him of his strength. He is taken captive by the giant Orgoglio (Arrogant pride), who also makes Duessa his mistress. Una learns of her hero's plight, and meeting by chance Prince Arthur, persuades him to go to the Knight's rescue. Arthur slays the giant, strips Duessa of her rich robes, and reveals her as a loathsome hag. The Red Cross Knight and Una travel on and soon meet Despair, who tempts the Knight to end his life. He is rescued by Una, who brings him to the house of Holiness to be healed. After this he and Una journey to Eden, the land of her captive parents, and after a three-day battle the Knight slays the Dragon. He and Una are betrothed, but before the marriage can take place Archimago, disguised as a messenger, brings a letter from Duessa, who claims that the Knight is betrothed to her. Their falseness is revealed, Archimago is captured and bound in prison, and Una and her Knight are married.

Book II: The Legend of Sir Guyon, or of Temperance
Archimago, having escaped from his confinement, meets Sir Guyon (Temperance) and a Palmer (Sobriety or Prudence), and tells them that the Red Cross Knight has shamefully attacked a virgin; to insure the desired effect, he has disguised Duessa as a weeping virgin and placed her beside the road, and she complains of her dreadful treatment at the hands of the Knight. They travel on and soon they meet the Red Cross Knight, with whom Sir Guyon almost comes to blows before each recognizes the Christian emblem on the other's shield.

Sir Guyon and the Palmer discover the dying Amavia, who tells them how her dead husband, Sir Mordant, had succumbed to the wiles of the enchantress Acrasia (Intemperance), who lives in the Bower of Bliss on the Wandering Island. Amavia dies, and Guyon swears vengeance. They come to a castle in which live three half-sisters, Medina (Golden Mean), Perissa (Excess), and Elissa (Deficiency). Sir Guyon entrusts to Medina Amavia's infant, which he has named Ruddymane because its hands are stained with its mother's blood. He then meets raging Furor and his mother, the hag Occasion; he silences Occasion, whose constant ranting spurs Furor to anger, by putting a lock on her tongue, and binds Furor with a hundred iron chains. Phaon (or Phedon), the young squire whom Furor had been tormenting, tells how through jealousy and rage he had slain his innocent sweetheart, Claribell, and poisoned Philemon, the friend who deceived him. Pyrocles (Fiery anger) arrives, and he and Sir Guyon fight. Brought to his knees, Pyrocles begs for mercy, and is spared. He unbinds Occasion and Furor, but soon falls a victim to them himself.

Cymocles (Loose living), hearing that his brother Pyrocles is dead, leaves the Bower of Bliss and his mistress Acrasia and travels to find Sir Guyon. He is ferried into the Idle Lake by Phaedria (Wantonness), whose dalliance with him soon makes him forget about revenge. Taking him to the Floating Island, she lulls him to sleep, and returns to the strand, where she encounters Sir Guyon seeking a ferry. They meet the awakened and enraged Cymocles, who attacks Guyon, but Phaedria stops their battle. Meanwhile Pyrocles, inflamed by Furor, tries to end his torments by drowning himself in the Idle Lake, but is saved and healed of his fiery wounds by Archimago.

Sir Guyon comes to the den of Mammon, who takes him to the house of Riches, which adjoins Hell. He tries to tempt Guyon to covet his treasure, but the knight refuses all temptations, and asks to be taken back to earth. He is found in a trance by the Palmer just before Pyrocles and Cymocles arrive, bent on vengeance. Thinking him dead, they are about to strip him of his armor when Prince Arthur appears. After a dreadful battle in which both Pyrocles and Cymocles are killed, Guyon revives from his trance and he and Arthur travel to the castle of Alma (the Soul), besieged by the enemies of Temperance. The leader of this rabble is Maleger, the incarnation of evil passions; his twelve troops typify the seven deadly sins and the lusts of the five senses. Arthur gives him terrific battle, but each time Maleger is cast to the ground he rises up even more powerful. Finally Arthur remembers that Earth is Maleger's mother, and restores him each time he falls; so Arthur squeezes the life out of him and throws him in a lake.

After a perilous sea journey Sir Guyon and the Palmer arrive at the Bower of Bliss, where they capture Acrasia in a net, destroy the Bower, and restore to their normal shape the lovers whom Acrasia had transformed into beasts.

Book III: The Legend of Britomart, or of Chastity Sir Guyon sends the captive Acrasia to the Faery Court, and he and Arthur travel on in search of adventure. Meeting an unknown knight, Guyon charges, but is unhorsed, for the strange knight is the lady Britomart (Chastity), who wields an enchanted lance. When Arthur and Guyon go off to rescue the fair Florimell, pursued by a lustful forester, Britomart remains behind, and soon comes to the Castle Joyous, where she finds six knights attacking one. She learns that the lady of the castle demands the love of every knight who comes that way, and if he loves another he is forced to do battle with the six knights. She subdues them and enters the castle, where Queen Malecasta (Lust), thinking her a man, tries to seduce her.

Meanwhile Arthur's squire, Timias, separated from his master, is ambushed by the lustful forester and his brothers, whom he kills in a bloody battle. Badly injured himself, he is discovered by the virgin huntress Belphoebe. She cures his wounds with herbs, but he pines away from love of her. Florimell, fleeing the forester, comes to the cottage of a wicked witch, whose churlish son lusts after the fair virgin. Again she flees, pursued by a monster sent by the witch, and, reaching the sea, escapes in a boat in which a fisherman is sleeping. The witch, however, then creates a counterfeit Florimell, who is borne away one day by Braggadocchio, only to have her taken from him by another knight. The true Florimell, out on the sea, resists the advances of the lustful fisherman; her cries bring the help of Proteus, who takes her to his bower at the bottom of the sea.

Meanwhile Sir Satyrane meets the libertine Sir Paridell, and they come to the castle of Malbecco (Jealousy), an aged miser, and his beautiful young wife, Hellenore. A cunning seducer, Paridell soon persuades Hellenore to run away with him, but before leaving her husband she steals part of his money and sets fire to the rest. Malbecco, torn between pursuing his wife and rescuing his burning money, knows not what to do. Finally he sets off in search of Hellenore, whom Paridell has by now abandoned and who has gone to live with the satyrs. After watching the satyrs with Hellenore, Malbecco is consumed with jealousy and tries to persuade her to return to him, but she refuses. He returns to his buried treasure, only to find that it has been stolen by the servant of Braggadocchio. Mad with jealousy and fury, he casts himself from a cliff—but he is so consumed by wrath that there is nothing left of him but an airy sprite. He crawls into a cave, where he dwells forever in misery.

Britomart comes upon Scudamore (Shield of Love), who is prostrated with grief that his beloved Amoret is a captive of the enchanter Busirane, who torments her because she will not renounce her love for Scudamore. Britomart promises to rescue Amoret, and she and Scudamore ride to Busirane's enchanted castle, which is guarded by a fire through which only Britomart is able to pass. Having found, in the empty but lavishly decorated castle, an iron door that will not open, she waits; and at midnight the door flies open and a strange Masque of Cupid passes through it. When the door opens at midnight the next night, she rushes in, finding the room empty save for Amoret, bound to a pillar, and Busirane. The enchanter and Britomart fight, and Busirane is subdued. He is forced to undo his enchantments and restore Amoret to health, and is himself bound in chains.

Book IV: The Legend of Cambel and Triamond, or of Friendship Amoret and Britomart, in search of Scudamore, meet the knights Blandamour and Paridell, accompanied by Duessa and Ate (Dissension), a foul old hag. Later, Blandamour and Paridell come upon Scudamore, and Paridell attacks him but is badly beaten. Ate lyingly tells Scudamore that she has seen Amoret false to him with Britomart. At this point arrives Sir Ferraugh with the false Florimell he had taken from Braggadocchio. Blandamour, desiring the lovely false Florimell, rides against her knight and captures her. Paridell, egged on by envy and the querulous counsel of Ate, demands that Blandamour share Florimell with him, and the two erstwhile friends come to blows. Later, they come upon the knights Cambel and Triamond and their ladies, Cambina and Canace. Canace, a fair and modest lady loved by many, had refused to love any of her suitors; in order to end the strife among her would-be lovers, her brother Cambel agreed to do battle with the stoutest three, the victor to have his sister. The three bravest and boldest were the triplets Priamond, Diamond, and Triamond, sons of Agape. Cambel, protected by a magic ring, was able to slay both Priamond and Diamond; however, their fairy mother had been granted by the Fates that the spirits of the first of her two sons to die would enter the body of the third, so that when Cambel gave the death-stroke to Triamond it failed to kill him. Neither knight could kill the other, and finally their battle was ended by the appearance of the triplets' sister Cambina, who brought peace. Canace was married to Triamond, and Cambina to Cambel.

Together, all agree to go on to the Tournament held by Sir Satyrane in honor of the lost Florimell, whose golden girdle he had found and now offers as a prize to the lady judged the loveliest. The false Florimell is acclaimed the fairest, but the magic cestus, which will girdle only the waists of the virtuous, will not stay fastened.

Meanwhile Scudamore meets Artegal disguised, and both swear vengeance on Britomart, whom they believe has wronged them. They meet her but are both quickly unhorsed. Artegal, fighting her on foot, strikes off her helmet, and seeing her face falls into a rapture of love. Britomart recognizes Artegal's face as the image of her true love she had seen in her magic mirror, and they become betrothed.

The true Florimell, imprisoned in a dungeon by Proteus, still rejects his advances and is true to her beloved Marinell—who has no use for women, and is still suffering from a wound given him by Britomart. Finally his wound is cured by Tryphon, and he and his mother, Cymodoce, go to the house of Proteus for a great banquet. Marinell chances to overhear Florimell's complaint of her love of him from her dungeon, suddenly falls in love with her, and ultimately has her released.

Book V: The Legend of Artegal, or of Justice Irena (Ireland) goes to the court of the Faerie Queene to complain of the tyrant Grantorto (Great wrong), who withholds her inheritance. Gloriana sends Artegal (Justice) and with him her own groom Talus (Iron man). On their journey Artegal kills Pollente, a Saracen who stations himself on the Bridge Perilous and kills and robs travelers, bestowing the spoils on his daughter Munera. Talus then forces his way into the castle stronghold, casts Munera over the wall and into the river, burns the spoils, and destroys the castle utterly. On their way to the wedding of Florimell and Marinell, Artegal and his groom meet Braggadocchio and the false Florimell. Artegal changes armor with Braggadocchio and wins the tournament thus clad. Later, wearing his own armor as victor of the tournament, Braggadocchio presents the false Florimell; Artegal then proclaims Braggadocchio a fraud and confronts the false Florimell with her true image. The false Florimell promptly melts away and vanishes.

Artegal and Talus rescue Terpine from a band of Amazons about to hang him, and besiege the Amazon city. Radigund, the Queen, offers to meet Artegal in single combat, the winner to become the servant of the loser. Artegal, struck with pity at the sight of Radigund's beautiful face, surrenders to her, and is made her thrall. Talus, however, escapes and brings news of Artegal's plight to Britomart, who kills Radigund and frees Artegal. Traveling on, Artegal meets Prince Arthur rescuing Samient, handmaiden to Queen Mercilla (Mercy). On their way to the Queen they encounter the robber Malengin (Guile), who tries to escape by turning himself into various animals, but is captured and killed by Talus. Arriving at the palace, the knights find Queen Mercilla about to dispense justice; Duessa is brought to the bar and charged with having tried to usurp Mercilla's crown, judged guilty, and executed. At this time appear at the palace two sons of Belge, whose land is held by the tyrant Geryoneo, asking Mercilla for aid. Prince Arthur goes off to rescue Belge, slays the monster, and restores her to her rightful kingdom. Artegal completes his original quest, and frees Irena and conquers Grantorto.

Book VI: The Legend of Calidore, or of Courtesy Sir Calidore (Courtesy), in pursuit of the Blatant Beast (Slander), finds the fair Pastorella, the foster-daughter of a shepherd, and falls in love with her. Finally he rescues her from brigands and takes her to castle Belgard, ruled by Sir

Bellamoure and his wife, the fair Claribell. Calidore leaves Pastorella there and continues on his quest for the Beast. Through a distinctive birthmark Pastorella is revealed to be the long-lost daughter of Bellamoure and Claribell. Calidore conquers the Blatant Beast and binds it in chains.

Fagin In Charles Dickens's OLIVER TWIST, a villainous old Jew who leads a gang of thieves, mostly boys. These he trains to pick pockets and pilfer. Fagin assumes a suave and fawning manner but is grasping and full of cruelty. He is ultimately arrested, tried, and condemned to death. Fagin is one of Dickens's most famous characters.

fairy tales See FOLKLORE.

Faithful Shepherdess, The (1609) A pastoral play by John Fletcher (see BEAUMONT AND FLETCHER). Clorin, the faithful shepherdess, tends the grave of her dead lover and gathers medicinal herbs to benefit mankind. To her is drawn Thenot, who adores her for her loyalty and pines for her so long as she remains indifferent to his pleas. At the opposite pole of behavior are the lusty Amarillis and Cloe, for whom no lover is too forward, and the conniving lechery of the Sullen Shepherd. After many complications in which all the shepherds' and shepherdesses' reactions are tested in various situations, virtue and chastity triumph; lust and lechery are repudiated.

fakir In Arabic-speaking Muslim lands, a religious beggar or mendicant. Many are wanderers who attract attention and alms by performing such acts of austerity as lying on beds of nails; others perform menial offices connected, for example, with burials and the cleaning of mosques.

Falkberget, Johan Petter (1879–1967) Norwegian novelist. The novel cycle *Christianus Sextus* (6 vols, 1927–35), Falkberget's most important work, is set in the mining town of Röros. Although his own early experiences in the mines gave Falkberget an understanding of hardship and suffering, his work is marked by Christian faith and a firm optimism.

Fall, The (La Chute, 1956; tr 1957) A short novel by Albert CAMUS. A former Parisian lawyer explains to a stranger in an Amsterdam bar his current profession of judge-penitent. His bitter honesty prevented him first from winning his own self-esteem through good deeds, then from exhausting his own self-condemnation through debauchery. Knowing that no man is ever innocent, he is still trying to forestall personal judgment by confession, by judging others, and by avoiding any situation demanding action.

Falla [y Matheu], Manuel [Maria] de (1876–1946) Spain's first major composer of instrumental music since the 17th century. Falla studied in Paris, was influenced by the impressionistic technique of DEBUSSY, and developed a brilliant and individual style of orchestration. Aside from *Noches en los jardines de España* (*Nights in the Gardens of Spain*, 1915) and the *Concerto for Harpsichord* (1926), his best-known music, all of it Andalusian in coloring, was written for the stage. His operas include *La vida breve* (1905) and *El retablo de Maese Pedro* (*Master Peter's Puppet Show*, 1923), a puppet opera based on DON QUIXOTE. His ballets include *El amor brujo* (*Wedded by Witchcraft*, 1915) and *El sombrero de tres picos* (*The Three-Cornered Hat*, 1917), the latter based on a comedy of ALARCÓN.

fall of man   The sin of ADAM AND EVE, who, in defiance of God's single command, ate of the FORBIDDEN FRUIT of the tree of knowledge. Thus they (and, according to traditional doctrine, all of their offspring) fell from God's grace. The fall is said to have been the cause of all evil, including death and pain, in the world. In Christian doctrine, the inherence of this evil in mankind is expressed in the concept of ORIGINAL SIN.

Fall of the House of Usher, The (1839)   A tale by Edgar Allan POE. A friend visits Roderick Usher in his old family mansion. The two read together, the friend attempting to dispel Roderick's gloom. Usher plays strange music of his own composition and shows his friend one of his paintings. Although his twin sister, Madeline, has been placed in the family vault dead, Usher is convinced she lives. When she suddenly appears in her blood-stained shroud, brother and sister fall dead together. The visitor, hurriedly departing, turns to see the house split asunder and sink into the tarn.

Falstaff, Sir John   The most famous comic character created by Shakespeare. He appears in HENRY IV: PARTS I and II, and THE MERRY WIVES OF WINDSOR, and his death is given some attention in *Henry V*. Falstaff is a monumentally self-indulgent braggart, the culmination of a line that can be traced back to Plautus's *Miles Gloriosus* and the *capitano* of the COMMEDIA DELL'ARTE. Falstaff is totally unapologetic: he revels in his lechery and chicanery, lies without scruple and, when caught in a lie, unabashedly seeks to turn everything to his own advantage. But his knavery is so engaging and his lust for life so keen that he has become one of the favorite characters of dramatic literature. He holds forth at the Boar's Head Tavern with a rascally crew that includes Bardolph, Nym, Peto, Pistol, and Prince Hal's companion Poins. Later, commissioned by the king to recruit for the army, he assembles the following company: Ralph Mouldy, Simon Shadow, Thomas Wart, Francis Feeble, and Peter Bull-calf.

familiar   A spirit bound to its master's service by a supernatural tie. It is usually represented in the form of a small animal such as a cat, mouse, or poodle.

Family Reunion, The (1939)   A drama in verse by T. S. ELIOT. Combining elements of social comedy and Greek tragedy, it deals with the return of Harry, Lord Monchensey, to his English family home for the birthday of his old mother, Amy. The family think Harry is behaving oddly. Only his wise aunt, Agatha, understands that he has murdered his wife and is seeing the Eumenides, or avenging furies. She tells him that when he was born his father wanted to kill his mother and would have done so if Agatha had not dissuaded him. Harry is bound to suffer from the family curse, especially in the decaying old family house. Agatha presides over Harry's flight; over the disintegration of the rest of the family; and over Amy's death. Like Sir Henry Harcourt-Reilly and Julia in THE COCKTAIL PARTY, she serves as Eliot's mouthpiece.

fancy and imagination   Terms originally used synonymously to designate the power of conceiving and representing mental images of things not present to the senses. Since the early 19th century the terms have been differentiated in aesthetic theory. The Romantic poets William WORDSWORTH and, more especially, Samuel Taylor COLERIDGE in his BIOGRAPHIA LITERARIA distinguished between fancy (a contraction of "fantasy") and imagination, regarding fancy as merely the ability to use the contents of memory in a decorative or illustrative way; it is the playful faculty of mind. Coleridge considered imagination "the prime agent of all human perception," the human equivalent of the creative power of the universe. Imagination is thus creative, unifying, and essentially vital, a function that is capable of shaping a new form or perception of reality. Fancy, on the other hand, may invent novel unrealities by recombining different elements of real things. Thus the character HAMLET, in whom man is ideally represented in both his outward and inward life, is a product of the creative imagination, whereas the Lilliputians of GULLIVER'S TRAVELS, in whom various elements of outward reality are combined, are a product of fancy.

Fangen, Ronald August (1895–1946)   Norwegian novelist, playwright, and critic. In all of his work Fangen speaks eloquently and soberly of a Christian solution to the world's problems; he rejected the communist and materialist doctrines popular between the two world wars. Among his plays are *Synde fald* (1920), *Den forjoettede dag* (1926), and *Som det kunde ha gatt* (1935). His novels include *Nogen unge mennesker* (1929), *Duel* (1932; tr 1934), *Pa bar bunn* (1936), and *En lysets engel* (1945; tr *Both Are My Cousins*, 1949).

Fanon, Frantz (1925–1961)   Martiniquan philosopher. Fanon was educated in Martinique and in France, where he qualified in both medicine and psychiatry. While in France he became associated with Jean-Paul SARTRE and Aimé CÉSAIRE and the cultural and political review *Présence africaine*. He was appointed to the psychiatric department of a hospital in Algeria in 1953, one year before armed rebellion broke out. His experiences in the Algerian war led him to change the psychological analysis of racism which he had put forth in *Peau noire, masques blancs* (1952; tr *Black Skin, White Masks*, 1967). He began to concentrate on the socioeconomic factors, seeing racism as the consequence of political oppression rather than as a psychological aberration. His conclusions about oppression and violence are contained in *Les Damnés de la terre* (1961; tr *The Wretched of the Earth*, 1964), which became a keystone in the revolutionary philosophy of the Third World. Fanon ultimately joined the FLN (the Algerian liberation movement). He served them in many capacities and survived numerous attempts on his life before he succumbed to leukemia in 1961.

Fanshawe (1828)   A novel by Nathaniel HAWTHORNE, published anonymously. Fanshawe, a pale, serious student, falls in love with Ellen Langdon, the ward of Dr. Melmoth, president of Harley College. Rescuing her from an attempted seduction, Fanshawe gives Ellen up to the man he knows she loves and soon dies. The college and its environs are modeled on Hawthorne's *alma mater*, Bowdoin College, in Maine. Influenced by SCOTT and the GOTHIC NOVEL, *Fanshawe* illustrates Hawthorne's developing technique.

farce   An exaggerated type of comedy, full of ludicrous incidents and expressions. The word is the OF *farce*, "stuffing" (from Lat *farcire*, "to stuff"), originally meaning a passage in the vernacular inserted in a Latin text or liturgy. The farce in medieval France came to resemble the earlier FABLIAUX, but specifically for dramatic presentation. Like *La Farce de maistre Pierre* PATHELIN, the most famous, most farces were written in octosyllabic couplets, and burlesqued the foibles and vices of ordinary life, setting the pattern for future French comedy.

Farewell Address   The address prepared by George WASHINGTON on September 17, 1796, just before his retirement from the presidency. Probably written with the aid of HAMILTON and MADISON, it was never delivered publicly. In it Washington explained his reasons for refusing to run for a third term and warned against the dangers of the party system. He advised the U.S. to avoid permanent alliances with foreign nations and to trust to "temporary alliances for extraordinary emergencies." It did not contain the phrase "entangling alliances," with which it is often associated and which appeared in JEFFERSON's first inaugural address.

Farewell to Arms, A (1929)   A novel by Ernest HEMINGWAY. It deals with the romance of Frederic HENRY, an American lieutenant in the Italian ambulance service during World War I, and Catherine Barkley, an English nurse. She becomes pregnant, and after the disastrous Italian retreat from Caporetto (superbly described by Hemingway), Henry deserts, joins Catherine, and escapes with her to Switzerland, where she dies in childbirth. This is one of the best-known novels depicting the tragedy and destruction of World War I.

Far from the Madding Crowd (1874)   A novel by Thomas HARDY. Bathsheba Everdene is loved by Gabriel Oak, a young farmer who becomes bailiff of the farm she inherits; by William Boldwood, who owns a neighboring farm; and by Sergeant Troy, a handsome, inconsiderate young adventurer. She marries Troy, who mistreats her and squanders her money. When he leaves her and is presumed drowned at sea, Bathsheba becomes engaged to Boldwood. Troy, however, reappears, and is murdered by Boldwood, who goes mad as a result of his action and is sent to an institution instead of being sentenced. Bathsheba then marries Gabriel, the steadiest and most faithful of her three suitors.

Farmer George   King George III of England (1738–1820), who reigned from 1760 to his death; so called from his farmerlike manners, taste, dress, and amusements.

> A better farmer ne'er brushed dew from lawn.
>
> Byron, *Vision of Judgment*

Farquhar, George (1678–1707)   English comic dramatist of the early 18th century. Farquhar's plays reveal the growing taste for sentiment, which was beginning to replace the brilliance and wit of the Restoration. His best-known plays are THE BEAUX' STRATAGEM, *The Recruiting Officer* (1706), and *The Constant Couple* (1699).

Farrell, James T[homas] (1904–1979)   American novelist. Known for his many novels depicting lower-middle-class Irish-Catholic life, Farrell was born in the South Side slum section of Chicago, which forms the background for his works. His stories dealing with tough street life began to appear in 1932; they aroused heated controversy, for Farrell wrote in a frankly naturalistic style that echoed the crudities of his chosen milieu. The characters of his novels, in which he sometimes used a STREAM OF CONSCIOUSNESS technique, are presented with almost a sociologist's objectivity. The emphasis is on poverty, religious bigotry, economic inequality, individual frustration, vice, and the destructive influence of environment. Some critics assert that Farrell's turgid style defeated the author's aim; but others praise the powerful, cumulative effect of personal tragedy that distinguishes his most famous work, the STUDS LONIGAN trilogy. Five other novels published between 1936 and 1953 concern Danny O'NEILL, a sensitive refugee from the Lonigan world. Farrell began what was to be a new trilogy with his fiftieth book, *The Dunne Family* (1976), based on the life of his grandmother, but he did not live to complete it. One of his last books was *Olive and Mary Anne* (1978), a collection of stories about unhappy people living apart from reality. Of Farrell's nonfiction, *Note on Literary Criticism* (1936) is one of the most important literary statements of the "proletarian" point of view of the 1930s.

fasces   In ancient Rome, a symbol of authority. Fasces were bundles of birch or elm rods fastened together by a red strap with the blade of an axe projecting from the bundle. The fasces were carried by the left hand, on the left shoulder by the LICTORS who accompanied magistrates. The rods and the axe represented the ruler's authority to punish or execute criminals. Within the city of Rome, the axe was removed in recognition of the accused's right to appeal to the people in the matter of life and death.

Benito MUSSOLINI's Fascist Party, which controlled Italy from 1922 to 1944, used the fasces as its emblem. Fasces have appeared on U.S. coins and adorn many government buildings.

fascism (Ital, *facismo*; fr *fascio*, "bundle; political group") A political system of the extreme right characterized by a dictatorial leadership, a one-party system, totalitarian control of economic and social activity, and exercise of absolute power by the government at the expense of individual liberty. Its principles were put into practice by Benito MUSSOLINI in Italy after 1922. Unlike communism, fascism retains private ownership of land and capital, but most economic activity is controlled by the government. "Fascist" is often used as a term of opprobrium for a person who seems to be against personal liberty or who wishes to use the power of government oppressively.

Fassbinder, Rainer Werner (1946–1982) German film and theatre director and scriptwriter. Fassbinder began as an actor, and started his own theatre company, Antitheatre, in 1967. As director, actor, and writer, he produced both original plays and radical adaptations of classical dramas set in a contemporary context. He also wrote and directed films at a phenomenally prolific rate with more than thirty films to his credit by his early thirties. Fassbinder's numerous films, generally made with his own company of actors, introduced a new strain of social realism into modern German cinema, particularly in their preoccupation with the idleness and alienation created by Germany's prosperity after World War II. Among the best known of his many films are *Warnung vor einer heiligen Nutte* (U.S. *Beware of a Holy Whore*, 1971), which depicts his own process of filmmaking; *Die bitteren Tränen von Petra von Kant* (U.S. *The Bitter Tears of Petra von Kant*, 1972), which explores another of his recurrent themes, homosexuality; *Ali/Fear Eats the Soul* (1974), a romance between an elderly charwoman and a young Moroccan worker; *Despair* (1977), based on NABOKOV's novel, Fassbinder's first English production; and *The Third Generation* (1979), about terrorists. He died at the age of thirty-seven, after directing forty-three films.

Fast, Howard (1914–) American novelist. A prolific writer, Fast has written in practically every genre —short stories, plays, critical essays, poems, thrillers, and science fiction—as well as the historical romances for which he is best known. Many of his novels, including *Citizen Tom Paine* (1943) and *Freedom Road* (1944), espouse radical political causes. He joined the Communist Party in 1943 and broke from it thirteen years later, but not before he was blacklisted and imprisoned (1950) for failing to "name names" for the House Committee on Un-American Activities. Unable to find a publisher, he published several books himself, including the very successful *Spartacus* (1951). Fast's disillusionment with communism is described in *The Naked God* (1957). Among his many other books are *The Crossing* (1971) and a best-selling tril-

ogy about an Italian immigrant family's rise to the heights of San Francisco society: *The Immigrants* (1977), *The Second Generation* (1978), and *The Establishment* (1979). These were followed by *The Legacy* (1981), *Max* (1982), and *The Dinner Party* (1987).

Fastnachtsspiel (Ger, "Shrovetide play") A form of simple, often slapstick, comedy with a clear moral message, current in Germany in the 15th and 16th centuries. The earliest example, however, comes from the 13th century, and the origins of the form are thought to go back to spring fertility rites among the Germanic tribes. Hans SACHS is considered to have perfected the form.

fata (Ital, "fairy") A female supernatural being introduced in Italian medieval romance, usually under the sway of DEMOGORGON. In ORLANDO INNAMORATO we meet with the "Fata Morgana" (see MORGAN LE FAY); in BOIARDO, with the "Fata Silvanella" and others.

A sort of mirage in which objects are reflected in the sea and sometimes on a kind of aerial screen high above it is also called *fata morgana*. It is occasionally seen in the neighborhood of the Straits of Messina, and named from Morgan le Fay, who was fabled by the Norman settlers in England to dwell in Calabria.

fatal raven The emblem on the Danish standard, *Landeyda*, which was consecrated to the war god ODIN. It was said to have been woven and embroidered in one noontide by the daughters of Regner Lodbrok, son of Sigurd. If the Danish arms were destined to defeat, the raven hung his wings; if victory was to attend them, he stood erect and soaring, as if inviting the warriors to follow.

Fates, the (Gr, *moirai*; Lat, *parcae* or *fata*) In Greek mythology, three daughters of Nyx (Night). They controlled the destinies of men. Originally birth goddesses, the Fates came to be represented as three old women who spun the thread of life. They were identified by Hesiod as Clotho (or Kloto), who spun the thread; Lachesis, who measured it out; and Atropos, who cut it. Generally, even ZEUS himself is subject to their decisions.

Father, The (1887) A play by August STRINDBERG. Dealing with the psychological antagonism between men and women, *The Father* centers on the Captain and his inability to prevent the female members of his family from subjugating him. His wife, Laura, torments him by leading him to suspect that Bertha is not his daughter, spreads rumors that he is insane, and finally succeeds in driving him mad and to his death.

Father Brown A Catholic priest and detective, hero of a series of stories by G. K. CHESTERTON.

Fathers and Sons (*Ottsy i deti*, 1862; also tr as *Fathers and Children*) A novel by Ivan TURGENEV. It portrays the conflicts between the older aristocratic generation and the new democratic intelligentsia in Russia during the 1860s. The chief character is the nihilist BAZAROV, who espouses a strictly materialistic attitude toward life. His chief adversary is Pavel Petrovich Kirsanov, an uncle of

Bazarov's friend Arkady, who upholds the aristocratic traditions in the face of Bazarov's ridicule. The novel, which is considered one of Turgenev's finest works, originally aroused widespread controversy in Russia, with both radicals and conservatives denying the accuracy of the portrayal of Bazarov. One side considered it slandered the younger generation; the other accused Turgenev of presenting too favorable a picture of the nihilist. Only Dmitry Pisarev among the radicals accepted the portrayal of Bazarov as accurate.

Father William A humorous ballad by Lewis CARROLL appearing in ALICE'S ADVENTURES IN WONDERLAND; it is a parody of "The Old Man's Comforts" (1799), a poem by Robert SOUTHEY.

Fatima (1) According to the KORAN, the daughter of MUHAMMED, and one of the four perfect women. The other three are Khadijah, the prophet's first wife; Mary, daughter of Imran; and Asia, wife of the pharaoh drowned in the Red Sea.

(2) The name usually given to the last wife of BLUEBEARD.

(3) A female hermit in the ARABIAN NIGHTS who was murdered by the African magician as a part of his schemes against Aladdin.

Faulconbridge, Philip In Shakespeare's KING JOHN, the natural son of Richard I (Coeur de Lion). Leader of John's forces, he is a blunt, fiercely patriotic Englishman who sums up his philosophy in his final speech:

> This England never did, nor never shall,
> Lie at the proud foot of a conqueror,
> But when it first did help to wound itself.
> . . . Nought shall make us rue,
> If England to itself do rest but true.

Faulkner, William (1897–1962) American novelist and short-story writer. Faulkner, who was awarded the NOBEL PRIZE in Literature in 1949, is recognized as one of the greatest of American writers. In his novels, most of them set in the imaginary YOKNAPATAWPHA COUNTY, Mississippi, he created a complex social structure within which he explored the burden of the southern past, the inability of southern aristocracy to meet the demands of modern life, the relations between black and white, and the alienation and loneliness that so beset 20th-century man. In so doing, he drew an immense gallery of vivid and unforgettable characters.

Elements of Faulkner's old Mississippi family's past appear in his books. His great-grandfather Col. William C. Falkner (Faulkner changed the spelling with the publication of his first book) wrote a popular romance, *The White Rose of Memphis* (1880). His violent death in 1889 furnished his great-grandson with material for SARTORIS and THE UNVANQUISHED, in which he was the model for Col. John Sartoris. In 1918 Faulkner enlisted in the Canadian Air Force but did not see active service. After World War I

he briefly attended the University of Mississippi and worked at numerous odd jobs. He published a book of verse, *The Marble Faun*, in 1924 and, with the help of Sherwood ANDERSON, secured the publication of his first novel, *Soldier's Pay*, in 1926.

It was in *Sartoris*, his third book, that Faulkner created Yoknapatawpha County. In the same year (1929) he produced THE SOUND AND THE FURY, by common consent one of his half-dozen masterpieces. Although the styles of the two books are radically different—*The Sound and the Fury* owes much to James JOYCE and the STREAM OF CONSCIOUSNESS technique—both deal with the breakup of old aristocratic southern families. In AS I LAY DYING Faulkner relates a terrifyingly comic story of a ritualized burial journey. But it was not until the publication of SANCTUARY in 1931 that Faulkner achieved any appreciable popular success. He himself did much to mislead the reaction to this novel by suggesting that it was hastily written as a potboiler. In fact, he wrote two versions of it. Grotesquely shocking though it often is, it remains an extraordinary examination of a criminal personality, a book of great craft, allegorical in intent.

THESE THIRTEEN, a volume of short stories, was followed by LIGHT IN AUGUST, the agonizing story of Joe CHRISTMAS. In 1933 Faulkner published another volume of verse, *The Green Bough*. Three years later came the brilliant ABSALOM, ABSALOM! which was critically regarded as a high point in Faulkner's development. Still to come, however, were *The Unvanquished*, a collection of interlocking stories; *The Wild Palms* (1939), also stories; THE HAMLET, the first of a trilogy that would include *The Town* (1957) and *The Mansion* (1959); GO DOWN, MOSES, containing the famous story "The Bear"; INTRUDER IN THE DUST; KNIGHT'S GAMBIT, more stories; REQUIEM FOR A NUN, related to *Sanctuary*; and A FABLE, in which Faulkner left Yoknapatawpha County for the French Army in World War I. This last-mentioned novel won a PULITZER PRIZE, as did *The Reivers* (1962). *The Uncollected Stories of William Faulkner* (ed J. Blotner) was published in 1979.

In the 1930s, many readers saw only the melodramatic violence in Faulkner's writing. It was not until Malcolm COWLEY's introduction to *The Portable Faulkner* (1946), later supplemented by publication of the Faulkner-Cowley correspondence (1967), that the continuity and consistency of his work, as well as his concern with "the tragic fable of southern history," began to be fully understood.

Faunus In Roman mythology, a rural deity, grandson of Saturn and father of LAVINIA's father, LATINUS. Faunus, as well as Silvanus, came to be more and more identified with the Greek PAN, with whom he had many traits in common. His priests were the Luperci, his main festival the LUPERCALIA. When not viewed as an individual, he appeared in the multiformity of the fauns, possibly under the influence of the Greek pans, satyrs, and sileni in their relation with Pan. The fauns were satyrlike beings with tails, horns, goat's legs and feet, and furry, pointed ears. Two festivals called Faunalia were held on February 13 and December 5.

Hawthorne wrote a novel, *The Marble Faun* (1860), in which it is hinted that the hero is a faun. It was suggested by the statue of a youthful faun by Praxiteles, now in the Capitoline Museum in Rome. The same title was used by William FAULKNER for a collection of verse (1924).

One of the best-known poems of Stéphane MALLARMÉ is his *L'Après-midi d'un faune* (*Afternoon of a Faun*). DEBUSSY's orchestral tone poem *Prélude à l'après-midi d'un faune* (*Prelude to Afternoon of a Faun*, 1892) became the firm foundation of the composer's fame.

Fauré, Gabriel [Urbain] (1845–1924)   French composer, organist, and teacher. Fauré is most famous for the supple melodies of his songs, which include settings of poems by VERLAINE, RIMBAUD, BAUDELAIRE, and SULLY PRUDHOMME. Except for the beautiful *Requiem Mass* (1887), his attempts at larger musical forms were less successful. He was the director of the Paris Conservatoire from 1905 to 1920, where Maurice RAVEL and Nadia BOULANGER were among his pupils.

Faust   A legendary figure, the subject of many literary works. The historical personage behind all the various Faust legends seems to have been a German necromancer named Georg Faust (1480?–?1538). Bits of his life are known from contemporary testimony, including that of Philipp MELANCHTHON, but it is impossible to make a complete biography of him. His career was not without success, for he sometimes gained influence in powerful ecclesiastical and worldly courts. The power he enjoyed, combined with the boasting for which he was famous, captured the imagination of many after his death, and various altered and exaggerated versions of his exploits soon began to appear in print (see FAUSTBUCH). The name Johann, given him in the folk books and by Marlowe in DR. FAUSTUS, probably results from confusion with a different magician.

GOETHE was first attracted to the Faust legend by the Faustbuch and a Faust puppet-show he saw in his youth. But it was not until 1808 that the completed play, *Faust, Der Tragödie erster Teil* (*Faust, The First Part of the Tragedy*), first appeared. It is in this Part I that Goethe develops the character of Faust as the old scholar who yearns to comprehend not so much all knowledge as all experience, but finds that in order to do so he must promise his immortal soul to the destructive tempting spirit, MEPHISTOPHELES. The latter helps rejuvenate Faust, who then falls in love with and seduces a young girl named GRETCHEN. She bears him a child, but panics and drowns it, and the last scene of Part I is set in the dungeon where, awaiting execution for her crime, she refuses to flee with Faust and puts her trust in God.

In Part I, Mephistopheles promises to show Faust both "the small world" of personal feeling and experience, and "the great world" of history, politics, and culture. This dis-

tinction neatly parallels the difference between the two parts. In Part II (1832), which is much longer and more allegorical than Part I, Goethe took the opportunity to develop many of his ideas on mythology, cultural development, art, statesmanship, war, courtly life, economics, natural science, and religion, to the extent that the plot is sometimes lost from view. Toward the end, Faust attempts to justify his existence by reclaiming land from the sea in order to found an ideal society, but the plan fails. Faust's soul is finally rescued by a choir of angels who speak the motto *Wer immer strebend sich bemüht,/Den können wir erlösen* ("He who exerts himself in constant striving,/Him we can save"). See ETERNAL FEMININE; HELEN; HOMUNCULUS; WALPURGIS NIGHT.

Thomas Mann, in his DOKTOR FAUSTUS, does not directly treat the Faust legend, but uses it as a parallel to the fall of his own hero, Adrian Leverkühn.

The Faust legend has inspired several operas, including BOÏTO's *Mefistofele* (1866), BERLIOZ's *La Damnation de Faust* (1893), and Busoni's *Doktor Faust* (1925). The most famous of these is Charles GOUNOD's *Faust* (1859), which is based on Goethe's play.

Faustbuch, Das (Ger, "Faust-book")   A term referring to any of the several German folk books (VOLKSBUCH) that relate the career of Dr. Johann FAUST. The first such book was printed by Johann Spies in 1587, and many variations appeared shortly afterward. GOETHE's main sources, however, seem to have been a much later version, by Nikolaus Pfitzer (1674), and an abridgment of Pfitzer's book that appeared in 1725.

Faustian   Of or pertaining to either the historical FAUST or any of his fictional counterparts. From this basic meaning the term has broadened until, in modern usage, it is often used when characterizing any unswerving and unquenchable will to possess all human knowledge or experience.

Fauves, Les   A number of French artists who grouped around MATISSE and exhibited together from 1905 to 1907. Among the artists associated with fauvism are ROUAULT, DERAIN, DUFY, VLAMINCK, and BRAQUE. The outraged critical reaction to their free use of color and distortion of form led to their being called *Les Fauves* ("the wild beasts"). Although Matisse was the only member of the group to continue with the fauvist style, the movement had a revolutionary impact on the development of modern art. Many of its adherents moved on to experiments with CUBISM.

Faux-Monnayeurs, Les   See COUNTERFEITERS, THE.

Feast of Fools   A kind of religious Saturnalia, popular in the Middle Ages. Its chief object was to honor the ass on which Jesus made his triumphant entry into Jerusalem. This liturgical burlesque was held on the Feast of the Circumcision (January 1). The office of the day was chanted in travesty, then a procession was formed, and all sorts of foolery were indulged in, such as playing dice on the altar and priests dressing as women and choirboys. An ass was an essential feature, and from time to time the whole procession imitated braying, especially in the place of "Amen."

Feast of Lanterns   A popular Chinese festival. It is celebrated at the first full moon of each year. Tradition says that the daughter of a famous mandarin fell into a lake one evening. The father and his neighbors went with lanterns to look for her, and happily she was rescued. In commemoration thereof, a festival was ordained, and it grew in time to be the celebrated Feast of Lanterns.

Federalist, The (1787–1788)   A series of eighty-five essays written to urge New York voters to approve the U.S. Constitution. About fifty of the series are said to have been written by Alexander HAMILTON, the others by James MADISON and John JAY. The essays were intended to show how the proposed constitution would create an effective national government in conformity with republican principles. They are now considered outstanding studies in the practical application of political theory.

Fedin, Konstantin Aleksandrovich (1892–1977) Soviet novelist. After serving in the Red Army during the civil war, Fedin published his first story, "Sad" (tr "The Orchard," 1962), in 1920. The theme of the story, which recurs in several of his later works, is the conflict between the old and new in changing Soviet society. His first novel, *Goroda i gody* (1924; tr *Cities and Years*, 1962), also uses this theme, contrasting the vacillating Andrey Startsov, a type of SUPERFLUOUS MAN, with the devoted Communist Kurt Wahn, who eventually kills Startsov as a traitor to the cause. In this work Fedin used the calm, objective description and sober psychological probing typical of the 19th-century Russian novel.

His second novel, *Bratya* (*The Brothers*, 1928), treats the same theme of an individual's acclimation to the revolution in a manner even closer to the classical Russian novel's realism. His next large work, *Pokhishcheniye Yevropy* (*The Rape of Europe*, 1934–35), concerns relations between the West and the new Soviet society.

After World War II Fedin published three more novels, which are considered his best works: *Pervye radosti* (1946; tr *Early Joys*, 1948), *Neobyknovennoye leto* (1948; tr *No Ordinary Summer*, 1950) and *Kostyor* (1961; tr in part as *The Bonfire*, 1962). All portray life in the Volga region of Saratov shortly before World War I and the revolution.

Feiffer, Jules (1929–   )   American cartoonist and writer. Starting in the *Village Voice* in 1956, Feiffer's cartoon strips were soon nationally syndicated. As verbal as they are visual, they satirize the uncertain, alienated middle-class intellectual in thrall to the tenets of psychoanalysis, unable to communicate with his fellows. Feiffer next turned his eye for neuroses and ear for the vernacular to writing plays, the best known of which is the black comedy *Little Murders* (1967).

Felix Holt the Radical (1866)   A novel by George ELIOT. Felix Holt is an ardent young man of strong social convictions who attempts, by living as a watchmaker among the lower classes in his area, to encourage the people to better themselves. Against him is set Harold Transome, who is running for Parliament as a radical, yet possesses none of the social sense of Felix. Felix finds himself in love with Esther, imagined to be the daughter of the local curate, Rufus Lyon. Eventually, Esther has to choose between Felix and Transome. As a complication, Felix, in his efforts to prevent the workers from rioting on Election Day, has accidentally killed a man and is on trial. His trouble brings Esther to the realization that she loves him, and when he is pardoned she becomes his wife. Running through the novel are the legal problems concerning the inheritance of the Transome property and the mystery surrounding Esther's birth.

Fell, John (1625–1686)   English scholar and prelate, subject of the well-known quatrain by Thomas Brown (1663–1704):

I do not love thee, Dr. Fell,
The reason why I cannot tell;
But this I know, and know full well,
I do not love thee, Dr. Fell.

Brown is said to have composed these lines when Fell, who was dean of Christ Church, Oxford, promised to remit a sentence of expulsion if the youth could make an impromptu translation of Martial's thirty-third epigram:

Non amo te, Sabidi, nec possum dicere quare;
Hoc tantum possum dicere non amo te.

Fellini, Federico (1920–   )   Italian film director. Initially, Fellini worked as an actor and scriptwriter in NEOREALIST CINEMA. His first film as director was *The White Sheikh* (1952). He achieved international recognition almost immediately, directing his own screenplays over a long career in such films as *La strada* (1954) and *Le notti di Cabiria* (1956), both of which were awarded Oscars, and *La dolce vita* (1959), *8½* (1963), *Satyricon* (1969), *Amarcord* (1973), and *Casanova* (1976). His films are characterized by obscure, intensely personal fantasies. Like Ingmar BERGMAN, Fellini has gathered his own crew of actors, technicians, and writers, which lends consistency and coherence to his work.

Femmes savantes, Les (The Learned Ladies, 1672) A comedy by MOLIÈRE. It satirizes women who devote themselves to women's rights, science, and philosophy to the neglect of domestic duties and wifely amenities. Philaminte, who is capable of discharging a servant for employing bad grammar, wants to marry Henriette, her daughter, to Trissotin, a man whose tastes and opinions match her own. Her daughter Armande advocates platonic love and science, and her sister Bélise is a self-styled philosopher who imagines that everyone is in love with her. Henriette, who has no sympathy with the lofty flights of her female relatives, is in love with Clitandre, but is prevented from marrying him until her father loses his property through the "*savant*" proclivities of his wife and Trissotin withdraws his suit. Clitandre and Henriette are thereupon united, Clitandre declaring his beloved the "perfect," or thorough, woman—in distinction, Molière implies, from the rest of her family.

Fénelon, François de Salignac de la Mothe- (1651–1715)   French prelate and writer. Fénelon's success in tutoring the duc de Bourgogne, grandson of Louis XIV, won him an appointment to the ACADÉMIE FRANÇAISE, the title of archbishop, and a favored position at court. He lost favor embracing the unorthodox doctrines of QUIETISM, and upon publication of his epic TÉLÉMAQUE, which in offering political advice to the dauphin indirectly reproved the policies of the king, Fénelon was exiled to his diocese. Liberal in his political and educational theories, Fénelon expressed his convictions in *De l'education des filles* (*Concerning the Education of Girls*, 1687) and *Table de Chaulnes* (1711).

Fenian cycle   In GAELIC LITERATURE, a group of tales revolving around the deeds of FIONN MAC CUMHAIL, whose name is the origin of the term Fenian, and his son Oisín, or OSSIAN. The chief Fenian text is the *Colloquy of Old Men*, a discussion between St. Patrick and Ossian; also important is THE PURSUIT OF DIARMUID AND GRÁINNE. Paganism is somewhat modified in the Fenian cycle, Christianity reaching Ireland in the old age of Ossian.

Fenians (or Fenian Brotherhood)   An association of Irish nationalists, founded in New York in 1857 with a view to securing the independence of Ireland. The movement spread over the U.S. and through Ireland (where it absorbed the preexisting Phoenix Society); several attempts at insurrection in Ireland were made as well as an invasion of Canada from the U.S. Eleven "national congresses" were held by the Fenian Brotherhood in the U.S. between 1863 and 1872, after which it continued as a secret society. It was a forerunner to the Irish Republican Brotherhood. The name Fenian is derived from FIONN MAC CUMHAIL, the name of the great, semimythological hero of Ireland. See EASTER REBELLION; YOUNG IRELAND.

Fenris-wolf   In Scandinavian mythology, the wolf of LOKI and brother of HEL, typifying the goading of a guilty conscience. It was said that when he gaped, one jaw touched earth and the other heaven. ODIN sought vainly to chain him but the wolf was expected to swallow Odin at the day of doom. Percy MACKAYE wrote a dramatic poem entitled *Fenris the Wolf* (1905).

Ferber, Edna (1887–1968)   American novelist and short-story writer. Edna Ferber started her long career as a highly successful writer of popular fiction with several collections of short stories. Her best-selling novels include *The Girls* (1921); *So Big* (1924), which was awarded a PULITZER PRIZE and which deals with the struggles of the widowed

Selina DeJong to support herself and her son Dirk; SHOW BOAT; and *Cimarron* (1930), a story of the spectacular land rush of 1889 in Oklahoma. In collaboration with George S. KAUFMAN, Miss Ferber wrote several popular plays: *The Royal Family* (1927), which exhibited the BARRYMORES in a humorous vein; *Dinner at Eight* (1932), about a fashionable dinner party; and *Stage Door* (1936). Among her many later novels are *Giant* (1952), set in Texas, and *Ice Palace* (1958), in Alaska. Her autobiography is *A Peculiar Treasure* (1939; rev 1960); its sequel is *A Kind of Magic* (1963).

Ferdinand   (1) The young king of Navarre who takes an oath with three friends to make his court "a little Academe, still and contemplative in living art" in Shakespeare's LOVE'S LABOUR'S LOST.

(2) The son of Alonso, king of Naples, in Shakespeare's THE TEMPEST. Untouched by worldly corruption, he falls in love at first sight with Prospero's daughter, Miranda, and willingly undergoes the labors Prospero imposes to test his love for her.

Ferdinand II of Aragon (or Ferdinand V of Castile, 1452–1516)   King of Spain. In 1469 Ferdinand married ISABELLA of Castile and, upon her accession to the throne in 1474, the two great kingdoms of Spain were permanently united. During their reign Ferdinand and Isabella sought to consolidate royal power and to assure the racial and religious purity of Spain. The first aim they accomplished by destroying the privileges of the unruly Castilian nobility and by limiting the once-considerable independence of the towns. The second aim was achieved by the establishment of the Spanish INQUISITION (1478) and by the conquest (1492) of Granada, the last Moorish kingdom in Spain. In the same year the Jews of Spain were ordered to become Christians or face expulsion; the same alternatives were offered to the Moors of Castile in 1502. Perhaps the most important event of their reign was the discovery of America in 1492 by Christopher Columbus, whose voyage was made possible by Isabella. Ferdinand expanded Spanish power in Europe, acquiring Naples in 1503 and the kingdom of Navarre in 1512. Upon the death of Isabella in 1504, he ruled Castile as regent for their demented daughter, Joanna the Mad. In 1506 he took a second wife, Germaine de Foix.

Fergus   A famous warrior in the ULSTER CYCLE of Gaelic literature. Fergus also appears in James Joyce's ULYSSES.

Ferlinghetti, Lawrence (1919–   )   American poet, editor, and publisher. A native New Yorker, Ferlinghetti moved to San Francisco in the early 1950s where, in 1953, he founded the City Lights Bookshop. The first publishing venture of the City Lights Press was Ferlinghetti's own book of poems, *Pictures of the Gone World* (1955), which was followed a year later by Allen Ginsberg's HOWL. Ferlinghetti also launched the Pocket Poet Series and edited *The City Lights Journal*, both of which published the work of many members of the BEAT MOVEMENT. His poetry is written in a declamatory style, imbued with political messages, and reflects the raw, uninhibited style common to beat writers. His best-known volume, *A Coney Island of the Mind* (1958), is his most lyrical, least polemical work. Other collections of his poetry include *An Eye on the World* (1967), *Open Eye, Open Heart* (1973), and *Landscapes of Living and Dying* (1979).

Fernández de Lizardi, José Joaquín (1776–1827)   Mexican satirist, frequently writing under the pen name El Pensador Mexicano. Lizardi turned to fiction when his anticlerical and antigovernment poems, pamphlets, and newspaper articles were censored by colonial authorities. A reformist, an outspoken critic of abuses, but not a revolutionary, he is best remembered for *El periquillo sarniento* (1816; tr *The Itching Parrot*, 1942), the first novel written in Latin America. Combining elements of the Spanish PICARESQUE tradition and the 18th-century sentimental novel, Lizardi disguised his criticism of middle-class Mexican life as an adventure novel. He followed this with two more novels, *Noches tristes y día alegre* (1818) and *La quijotita y su prima* (1819), the latter about the education of women. The censors prevented the publication of another novel, *Don Catrín de la Fachenda* (1832), which was published posthumously. His complete works, *Obras*, were published in two volumes in 1963 and 1969.

Ferney, the patriarch of (or the philosopher of Ferney)   Epithet for VOLTAIRE. Ferney is the name for the estate that Voltaire bought near Geneva in 1758 and where he spent the last twenty years of his life. He is known as the patriarch of Ferney because of his fatherly interest in the management of the estate and in his staff of servants. For them and for the local inhabitants, Voltaire built a pottery factory and a church. His grand manner of entertaining his numerous famous visitors also explains this epithet. Secure from political and religious interference at Ferney, because of its geographical location, Voltaire poured forth innumerable vitriolic pamphlets attacking just about everyone who disagreed with him.

Feste   Olivia's clown in Shakespeare's TWELFTH NIGHT. Feste takes part in the pranks against MALVOLIO, and he also sings the well-known song "O mistress mine!"

Fet, Afanasy Afanasyevich (1820–1892)   Russian lyric poet. Fet was the illegitimate son of Afanasy Shenshin, a landowner, and a German woman named Foeth (Fet in Russian). His first volume of poems (1840) received little notice. With the publication of two more books of verse in 1850 and 1856, however, Fet's reputation was established as a lyric poet whose work was unequaled in its melodic quality, his chief themes being love and nature. The quality and concerns of Fet's works were not palatable to the utilitarian critics of the 1860s. They cited his poetry as an example of the sterility of "art for art's sake." One of their favorite targets for ridicule was a short poem by Fet, "Shopot, robkoye dykhaniye" ("Whispering,

Timid, Breathing"). An impressionistic description of the break of dawn, the poem contains no verbs. The unfriendly critical reception of the work induced Fet to stop publishing poetry for more than twenty years. He lived quietly on his estate near the home of his friend Leo TOLSTOY. In the 1880s several more volumes of Fet's poems were published.

Feuchtwanger, Lion (1884–1958)   German novelist. Feuchtwanger was noted for his choice of historical and political themes and for his use of psychoanalytic ideas in the development of characters. The better known of his novels are *Die hässliche Herzogin Margarete Maultasch* (1923; tr *The Ugly Duchess*, 1927), *Jud Süss* (1925; tr *Power*, 1926), *Der jüdische Krieg* (1932; tr *Josephus*, 1932), and *Der Wartesaal* (*The Waiting-Room*), a trilogy including *Erfolg* (1930; tr *Success*, 1930), *Die Geschwister Oppenheim* (1933; tr *The Oppermanns*, 1934), *Exil* (1939; tr *Paris Gazette*, 1940), and *Sunone* (1944; tr 1944). Feuchtwanger was active as a pacifist and a socialist and was forced into exile by the rise of Nazism. He was a friend of Bertolt BRECHT and collaborated with him on several plays, including *Leben Eduards II von England* (*Life of Edward II of England*, 1923), an adaptation of *Edward II* by MARLOWE. See ZWEIG, ARNOLD.

feudalism (or feudal system)   The system of distribution of land and political allegiance prevalent throughout Europe during the Middle Ages. According to its purest form, the king owns all the land over which he rules, but gives portions of it as inheritable fiefs to his vassals, in exchange for loyalty and a specified amount of military service. These feudal lords similarly divide their land among their followers, and the subdivision continues, forming a pyramidal hierarchy in which each nobleman has an obligation to the lord above him and authority over those below him. At the base of the pyramid are the serfs, the farmers who belong to the land they work, owing most of its produce to its lord and changing masters when the land changes hands through gift or marriage alliances or wars.

The feudal system was dominant from the 9th to the 14th centuries, when the rise of the merchant class and the growing importance of the towns began to change the social structure. Some feudal elements, however, such as the hierarchy of the propertied class of nobles, continued through the 19th century.

Feuerbach, Ludwig (1804–1872)   German philosopher. Feuerbach analyzed religion from a psychological and anthropological viewpoint in *Das Wesen des Christentums* (*The Essence of Christianity*, 1841) and *Das Wesen der Religion* (*The Essence of Religion*, 1845). Denying the traditional antithesis of the divine and the human, he maintained that divinity is man's projection of his own human nature. Love and morality, the basis of human relations, are the essence of religion. This tendency toward secularization of religion in the mid-19th century is also found in the work of David Friedrich STRAUSS and Ernest RENAN.

feuilleton The section of a French newspaper devoted to tales, serials, light literature, and criticism. The title of this early-19th-century phenomenon is derived from the French *feuille* ("leaf"), since the first feuilletons were printed on the detachable, lower portion of the page. The word is now applied to pamphlets, generally of a political nature, that are distributed on the street.

Few Figs from Thistles, A (1920) A collection of poems by Edna St. Vincent MILLAY. The second of her collections, this volume differs from the earlier *Renascence and Other Poems* (1917) in its greater tone of sophisticated flippancy. Seeming to epitomize youthful Bohemianism, the poems were widely quoted in Greenwich Village, among the best known of them being "First Fig," "Recuerdo," and "The Philosopher."

Feydeau, Georges (1862–1921) French dramatist. Primarily a writer of farces, Feydeau is known for the hilarious situations and characters in such plays as *L'Hôtel du Libre Exchange* (1894; tr *Hotel Paradiso*, 1956), *Un Fil à la patte* (1899; tr *Not by Bed Alone* in *Four Plays*, 1970), and *Occupe-toi d'Amélie* (1911; adapted by Noël COWARD as *Look After Lulu*, 1959). His *Théâtre complet* appeared in nine volumes (1948–56). Even more than half a century after his death his plays continue to delight audiences.

Fiammetta The lady celebrated by Giovanni BOCCACCIO in his verse and prose works. The literal meaning of her name, flickering or darting fire, suggests his passion for her. *Fiammetta* is also the title of a psychological romance written by Boccaccio in 1344–46, in which she is the heroine describing her abandonment by Panfilo and her subsequent grief. Since she is also called Maria, it was once assumed that Fiammetta was really Maria d'Aquino, the supposed natural daughter of King Robert of Naples. Modern scholars now hold that she was purely fictional, a Boccaccian equivalent of LAURA and other ladies of the lyric tradition.

Fichte, Johann Gottlieb (1762–1814) German philosopher and political thinker. An important force in the development of GERMAN ROMANTICISM, in his *Grundlage der gesammten Wissenschaftslehre* (*Foundation of the Complete Theory of Knowledge*, 1794), he developed the distinction made earlier by KANT between phenomenal reality and the thing-in-itself (see CRITIQUE OF PURE REASON). He maintained that the essence of the universe is ego —mind, that is, or spirit—and that the ego itself posits the material world by a process called productive imagination. Man's ideas do not come from experience of the material world, for his mind is part of the universal creative ego and finds fulfillment in self-conscious unity with it.

Ficino, Marsilio (1433–1499) Italian philosopher and scholar. The first and most influential Platonist of the Renaissance, as a child he was taken into the Florentine household of Cosimo de' MEDICI for the express purpose of learning the philosophy of PLATO and his followers, the Neoplatonists. He soon became the center of a group of intellectuals, including Angelo Poliziano and PICO DELLA MIRANDOLA, loosely called the Florentine Academy. He translated Greek works into Latin, wrote such commentaries as the famous one on Plato's SYMPOSIUM (in Latin and Italian), and composed original treatises. His main impulse seems to have been the desire to reconcile Platonism (actually NEOPLATONISM) with the tradition of Christian thought, as in his *Theologia platonica de immortalitate animorum* (*The Platonic Theology of the Immortality of Souls*, 1482). Among the many European and English writers influenced by his writings are Benvieni, Pico della Mirandola, BEMBO, CASTIGLIONE, SPENSER, and CHAPMAN. Among the poets who read and used him, it was frequently the Platonic theory of spiritual or philosophic love that appealed rather than theological or cosmological theory.

Fiddler's Green The Elysium of sailors; a land flowing with rum and lime juice; a land of perpetual music, mirth, dancing, drinking, and tobacco; a sort of Dixie Land or land of the leal.

Fiedler, Leslie A[aron] (1917–   ) American critic and novelist. Fiedler is best known for his original and provocative works of criticism. He first applied his psychological and sociopolitical insights to American writing in *An End to Innocence* (1955), a collection of magazine pieces. Three major volumes plot the course Fiedler described as his "venture in literary anthropology": LOVE AND DEATH IN THE AMERICAN NOVEL, *Waiting for the End* (1964), and *The Return of the Vanishing American* (1968). His interest in tracing mythic and archetypal elements in literature led him to jettison traditional distinctions between "high art" and "pop" culture. He was centrally concerned with social and racial distinctions in American literature, as between the established white male norm and the "outsiders"—blacks, Jews, Indians, women. His reflections on "difference" culminated in *Freaks* (1977), a survey of attitudes to physically misshapen people in folklore, art, literature, and society from ancient Egypt to the 1970s. *The Inadvertent Epic*, an essay collection, was published in 1979.

In 1971, his *Collected Essays* were published in two volumes. The best known and most controversial of these is "Come Back to the Raft Ag'in, Huck Honey!" (1948), a study of the recurring American motif of love between white and dark-skinned men.

Fielding, Henry (1707–1754) English novelist and playwright, an important figure in the development of the English novel. Fielding's career as a dramatist has been eclipsed by his career as a novelist, and all that is remembered today of his plays is TOM THUMB, a brilliant satirical burlesque of heroic drama, and *Pasquin* (1736) and *The Historical Register for 1736* (1737), two social and political satires. Robert Walpole's Licensing Act of 1737, which was specifically aimed at Fielding, ended the use of the stage for political satire, and so terminated this phase of Fielding's career. Turning to the study of law, he was admitted to the bar; in 1749 he became one of London's first police magistrates, the first to be paid a government salary rather than supporting himself by fines and bribery and a pioneer in the detection of crime with the organization of the "Bow Street runners," as the early police were called after the street that held the principal police court.

In the meantime his literary career continued. From 1739 to 1741 he edited the periodical *Champion.* When Richardson's PAMELA was published, Fielding was moved to parody it, first in APOLOGY FOR THE LIFE OF MRS. SHAMELA ANDREWS, and once again, more brilliantly, in JOSEPH ANDREWS. In 1743 he published three volumes of *Miscellanies,* which included his ironic satire JONATHAN WILD. TOM JONES, his greatest novel, and AMELIA, an early example of social realism, appeared soon after. In 1754, in an attempt to restore his failing health, he made a trip to Portugal and wrote an account of it in A *Journal of a Voyage to Lisbon.* He died in Lisbon.

Field of the Cloth of Gold   A plain near Guines, France. There Henry VIII (of England) had his interview with Francis I (of France) in 1520; so called from the splendor and magnificence displayed on that occasion.

Fierabras (or Ferumbras)   One of Charlemagne's PALADINS in medieval French and English romances. A Saracen giant, son of Balan of Babylon, he has conquered Rome and taken the holy relics. But Olivier defeats him in a duel, and he becomes a Christian knight. His sister, Floripas, is also baptized and marries Guy of Burgundy.

fifteen, the   The JACOBITE rebellion of 1715, when James Edward Stuart, "the Old PRETENDER," with the Earl of Mar, made a half-hearted and unsuccessful attempt to gain the throne of England. The reference is to the year of the attempt, to distinguish it from THE FORTY-FIVE (1745) revolt of "the Young Pretender," Charles Edward Stuart.

fifth column   Enemy sympathizers engaged in sabotage. The term was first used during the Spanish Civil War (1936–39) by General Mola, who stated in a broadcast that he had four columns of soldiers advancing on Madrid and a fifth column of sympathizers within the city who would arise to attack the defenders from the rear. It was made the title of a play (1938) by Ernest HEMINGWAY. The term came into wide use with the German invasion of western Europe when fifth columnists were active.

Figaro   The rascally hero of two comedies by BEAUMARCHAIS: THE BARBER OF SEVILLE and its sequel, *Le Mariage de Figaro, ou la folle journée* (1784). The complicated plot of the latter play concerns Count Almaviva, who is tired of his wife, Rosine, and tries to find solace elsewhere. Figaro, now the count's doorkeeper, loves Suzanne, Rosine's maid. Almaviva, himself taken with Suzanne, is in favor of the marriage between her and Figaro, provided he can exercise his feudal rights over Suzanne. His attempts to achieve his ends are constantly thwarted by various conspiracies, rendering him constantly ridiculous. His infidelity to Rosine is exposed, and Figaro,

having outwitted his master, finally marries Suzanne. Beaumarchais's bitter criticisms of the ruling classes caused the play to be suppressed for three years; he was even imprisoned five days for his audacity; but the public demanded its performance, and its success was possibly the greatest any play has ever had in the history of French theatre. In Figaro's famous, daring monologue (act V, scene 3), he says: "What have you [the nobility] done to deserve such wealth? You took the trouble to be born, and nothing else." MOZART composed an opera based on this play: *Le nozze di Figaro (The Marriage of Figaro,* 1786), in which the political implications are absent.

fili (plural form filid)   A member of the privileged class of early professional poets in Ireland. The filid were responsible for preserving pre-Christian Celtic learnings in the form of oral histories and legends. Their status, determined on the basis of how many such narratives they could recite, was ensured by legal decree and by the magical powers they were reputed to possess.

Filippovna, Natasha   In Dostoyevsky's novel THE IDIOT, the beautiful, tormented woman whose proud nature is continually exacerbated by the memory of a shameful seduction in her youth. Prince Myshkin tries to help her but is able to offer her only his pity. She finally runs away with the passionately jealous ROGOZHIN, who kills her.

Filocolo, Il   A lengthy prose romance by Giovanni BOCCACCIO. Its title, a Greek coinage meaning "Love's Labor," refers to the travails of its leading characters, Florio and Biancofiore. Derived from the French tale FLORES AND BLANCHEFLEUR, it was filled with many episodes and digressions by Boccaccio that later were used by English and other European writers. The most famous of these digressions is the THIRTEEN QUESTIONS OF LOVE.

Filostrato, Il   A romance in octaves by Giovanni BOCCACCIO, whose title means "a man overwhelmed by love." The man is the Trojan Troiolo (Troilus), who loves and wins Criseida with the help of her cousin and his friend Pandaro (Pandarus). But when she leaves the Trojan camp to return to her father on the Greek side, she quickly betrays Troiolo's trust, leaving him stunned by grief. Boccaccio drew the plot from the *Roman de Troie* of Benoît de Sainte-Maure, and supplied Chaucer with the story of his TROILUS AND CRISEYDE.

Filumena, St. (or St. Philomena)   A saint unknown until 1802. A grave was discovered in that year in the catacomb of St. Priscilla on the Salarian Way (leading from Rome to Ancona), with this inscription on the tiles: *lumena paxte cymfi,* which, rearranged, makes *Pax tecum Filumena.* Filumena was at once popularly accepted as a saint, though never canonized, and so many wonders were worked by her that she has been called *La Thaumaturge du Dix-neuvième Siècle.* In 1961, the Vatican officially prohibited her further veneration.

Financier, The (1912)   A novel by Theodore DREI-
SER. It is the first volume in the trilogy that includes THE
TITAN and *The Stoic* (1947). All three deal with a typical
industrial and financial magnate of the late 19th century.
Dreiser admitted that he based his central character, Frank
Algernon Cowperwood, on the figure of Charles T. Yerkes
(1837–1905), who gained control of the Chicago street-rail-
way system. The book begins with a famous scene in which
Cowperwood as a young boy in Philadelphia watches a lobster devour a squid, this act becoming for him a symbol of
what life really is. Working his way upward, the hero is
caught in a stock-market crash and receives a prison sentence for illegal dealings. At the end of the book, when he
is released, he marries and goes to Chicago to begin his
climb again.

Fin de partie   See ENDGAME.

Fingal, An Ancient Epic (1761)   See MACPHER-
SON, JAMES.

Finnabair   In Gaelic literature, the Irish GUINE-
VERE, daughter of Medb and Ailill. One of the figures in
the ULSTER CYCLE, she appears in such tales as the "Cattle-
Raid of Cooley" and "Fled Bricrenn."

Finnegans Wake (1939)   The last and most revolutionary experimental novel by James JOYCE. It is almost
inaccessible to readers who have not done some special
study; a great many volumes of explication have been published since the novel's first, controversial appearance. The
main difficulty is in the language. Joyce uses an elaborate
language of his own devising, made up of puns, PORTMAN-
TEAU WORDS, and words from foreign languages, with endless philological variations. He incorporates literary, historical, and philosophical allusions; names of people and
places in Dublin; Irish references; slang; phrases from
newspapers, popular songs, art, and the world of sport; and
words and syllables from every other imaginable source. By
means of this complex language and its rich connotations,
Joyce is able to relate his slight, rather obscure central story
to the whole historic, psychological, religious, and artistic
experience of mankind. Critics relate Joyce's difficult linguistic method to the scholasticism he encountered during
his strict Catholic education, and his presentation of different levels of meaning simultaneously to the influence of
medieval allegory.

Most literally, the novel presents the dreams and nightmares of H. C. Earwicker and his family as they lie asleep
at night. Their anxieties, secret thoughts, unexpressed
desires, and the events of the past day recur in their minds.
Humphrey Chimpden Earwicker, a Protestant Irishman of
Scandinavian descent (and thus, like Bloom of ULYSSES, an
outsider) is the middle-aged keeper of a tavern in Dublin.
He has a wife, Anna, and three children: Isobel, a daughter
now in her teens, and twin sons, Kevin and Jerry. At some
time in the past Earwicker has accosted someone in PHOE-
NIX PARK, but it is never made clear whether this was a
young girl or a man; he still feels guilty and fears investiga-

tion by the authorities. In his dream Earwicker's personal
guilt is related to various religious taboos and legends, and
he is associated with Lucifer, Adam, Humpty Dumpty,
and other figures. Another sexual taboo and guilt complex
in Earwicker's dream concerns his daughter, Isobel, whom
he substitutes as a love object for his wife; however, to
avoid incest he transforms her into Iseult the Fair and himself into Tristram. He also imagines himself as Jonathan
SWIFT, the Irish writer who loved two women. Because of
the similarity in names, Earwicker is also associated with
earwigs (see Persse O'REILLY). Earwicker represents Everyman and general maleness. His initials, HCE, are interwoven throughout the book, particularly in the recurrent
phrases Here Comes Everybody and Haveth Childer
Everywhere. Anna, his wife, like Molly BLOOM of *Ulysses*,
represents the universal feminine principle, and becomes
identified with the River Liffey, personified in the novel as
Anna Livia Plurabelle. The ANNA LIVIA PLURABELLE sections are among the most remarkable in the novel, being
triumphs of Joyce's poetic prose. Eventually all the women
in the novel merge into this figure as the river merges into
the sea. Earwicker's two sons are complementary opposites.
Jerry, who appears as Shem the Penman, is a rebellious,
introverted artist of the type of Stephen Dedalus, and
Kevin, or Shaun the Postman, is a man of action and an
average, extroverted citizen.

In structure the novel is entirely circular, ending in an
unfinished sentence that is completed by a half sentence at
the beginning. The history of mankind and the river-to-sea
progression of time and individual life are also seen as circular. In Christian thought the fall of man is followed by
the resurrection; Earwicker's mysterious misdeed took place
in Phoenix Park, and the title of the novel refers both to the
Irish hero Finn MacCool (see FIONN MAC CUMHAIL), who
was supposed to return to life someday to be the savior of
Ireland, and to Tim Finnegan, the hero of a music hall
ballad about a man who jumped up indignantly in the
middle of his own wake. Joyce used the ideas of cyclical
repetition of Giambattista Vico; Freud's dream psychology;
Jung's theory of a collective unconscious; and Giordano
Bruno's theory of the complementary but conflicting
nature of opposites (Shem and Shaun).

Joyce began writing *Finnegans Wake* in 1922. During
the seventeen years of its composition the novel was known
as *Work in Progress*, and several parts of it were published
separately as they were completed; the whole work was
revised before publication.

Finnsburg, The Fight at (8th century?)   Old English (Anglo-Saxon) poem, of which only a fifty-line fragment is extant, also called *The Fight at Finnesburh.* In the
version of the story incorporated in BEOWULF, King Finn of
the Frisians has married Hildeburh of the Danes, but
treacherously attacks her brother Hnaef and his followers
while they are his guests. The following spring the Danes

under Hengest kill Finn and carry Hildeburh back to Denmark.

Fionn mac Cumhail (also known as Finn mac Cumhail and Finn MacCool) Legendary Irish hero, hero of the FENIAN CYCLE, and leader of the FENIANS, a band of warriors. He is now believed to have a historical basis, dating back to the 3rd century BC. The Fenians and Fionn himself were famous for their remarkable strength and stature, their fearlessness, and their extraordinary feats. As a child, Fionn was educated in the forest by a poet. His profound wisdom came from his having tasted the salmon of knowledge, which fed on the hazelnuts of wisdom. His life is one of countless adventures with giants and hags; in the service of the high king at Tara, he performs many deeds, and it is for the king that he organizes the Fenians, or Fianna. His life knows two great loves: his first wife, Sedb, mother of his son Oísin, or OSSIAN, and his second wife, Gráinne, who betrays him with his kinsman Diarmuid. THE PURSUIT OF DIARMUID AND GRÁINNE is the best known of the stories of Fionn. Fionn is the hero of James Macpherson's poem *Fingal, an Ancient Epic* (1762), a spurious translation from the Gaelic.

Firbank, [Arthur Annesley] Ronald (1886–1926) English novelist. Heir of the DÉCADENTS of the 1890s, an aesthete and a Catholic, Firbank created fantastic, elegant, wish-fulfillment myths featuring such diverse characters as society ladies, ecclesiastics, lesbians, kings, and nuns. He was a master of dialogue with a merrily vicious wit that carried his characters through a series of bizarre encounters in V*ainglory* (1915), VALMOUTH, *The Flower Beneath the Foot* (1923), *Prancing Nigger* (1924), and *The Eccentricities of Cardinal Pirelli* (1926), which describes, among other things, the Cardinal's death while chasing an appealing choirboy around the altar. Firbank's unconventional approach to the novel and his sharp-edged humor had a clear influence on such writers as Ivy COMPTON-BURNETT and Evelyn WAUGH. His complete works were published in 1961.

Fir Bolg In Gaelic literature, the third race to invade and inhabit Ireland. They were defeated by the fourth race of invaders, the TUATHA DÉ DANANN.

Firdousī (born Abul Qāsim Mansur or Hasan, 941?–1020) Persian epic poet. His major work is the epic SHAH-NAMA. It was written at the request of the Sultan Mahmud ibn Sabuktagin, who wanted a history of Persia. Its completion required thirty-five years. When it was finished in 1010, the sultan did not send the promised reward of a thousand gold pieces for every thousand couplets (sixty thousand in all), but substituted silver instead. In anger Firdousī gave the silver away, wrote a bitterly scurrilous satire that he sent to the sultan, and fled to exile. In Baghdad he wrote a long poem, *Yusuf and Zuleikha*, on the Koranic version of the loves of JOSEPH and POTIPHAR'S WIFE, a popular theme in Persian literature. After nine years he returned

to his birthplace of Tūs, Persia, where he died shortly thereafter.

Fire of London, Great A fire that broke out in a baker's shop in Pudding Lane in 1666 and burned for three days and three nights. Much of the city was destroyed, including the old Gothic cathedral of St. Paul's. In his *Diary*, Samuel PEPYS described how the fire spread "in corners and upon steeples, and between churches and houses as far as we could see . . . in a most horrid malicious bloody flame."

First Circle, The (V kruge pervom, 1968; tr 1968) A novel by Aleksandr SOLZHENITSYN. It depicts life in a *sharashka*, i.e., a prison for educated people who carry on scientific research while serving long terms. Encompassing a span of only three days, this long novel both traces the ineluctable apprehension of Innokenty Artemyevich Vologin, a state counselor in the Ministry of Foreign Affairs, and re-creates, in an integrated web of short chapters, the daily routine and moral condition of the highly educated inmates of the *sharashka*. The experiences of the hero, Nerzhin, parallel those of the author, while the character of Lev Rubin, the longtime Party member who maintains his faith in the Communist ideal despite the injustices done to him and his fellows, is modeled on Lev Kopelev, a central figure in the civil rights movement of the 1960s and 1970s.

First Folio The first collection of the plays of SHAKESPEARE. It was compiled by his fellow actors John Heminges and Henry Condell, and published in 1623, seven years after his death. It contained thirty-six plays (omitting PERICLES, but otherwise including all the plays now considered to be authentic), arranged under the headings of comedies, histories, and tragedies. It was dedicated to two literary patrons, the earl of Pembroke and the earl of Montgomery, and for many years was considered to be a more authoritative text than the earlier quarto editions of individual plays. Several editions appeared, the third of which (second issue, 1664) included seven additional plays, of which only one, the sometimes-disputed *Pericles*, is considered to be the work of Shakespeare. A facsimile edition of the First Folio was published by the Oxford University Press in 1902, and by Yale University Press in 1954.

Fischer, Louis (1896–1970) American writer and journalist. Fischer is known for his keen interest in political developments in Russia and India. Among his many books on these subjects are *Gandhi and Stalin* (1947), *Russia, America and the World* (1961), and *Russia's Road from Peace to War 1917–1941* (1969). A personal disciple of Mahatma GANDHI, Fischer edited the great Indian leader's autobiography (1950). *The Road to Yalta*, a study of Soviet foreign relations between 1941 and 1945, was published in 1972.

fish As a symbol for Jesus, it was used by the early Christians. The letters of the Greek word for fish, ICHTHYS, formed an acrostic of the words Jesus Christ, Son of God, Savior.

Fisher King   One of the chief characters in medieval legends dealing with the quest for the Holy GRAIL. The Fisher King was the keeper of the Grail relics, including the spear of LONGINUS, used to wound Jesus as he hung on the cross. The Fisher King suffered from a wound inflicted by the same spear. The wound destroyed the Fisher King's virility and, by a sympathetic transference, turned his realm into a wasteland. A new and purer guardian of the relics, in the form of the Grail hero, must intervene (see GALAHAD). The task of the hero is not simply to find the relics themselves, which had been stolen, but also to free the king so he may die a peaceful death and bring life and fertility back to the king's realm. See WASTE LAND, THE.

Fisherman's ring   The Pope's signet ring for attesting papal briefs. It bears his name encircling a figure of Peter, a fisherman and first bishop of the Roman Church. A new ring is made for each Pope and is destroyed at his death, to avoid forged documents.

FitzGerald, Edward (1809–1883)   English translator and man of letters. During his lifetime, FitzGerald was known mainly (and by few) for his wit and personal charm; he was "dear old Fitz" to the likes of THACKERAY and TENNYSON. His *Six Dramas of Calderón* (1853) was poorly received when first published, though it was later acclaimed as a great translation. His most famous work, the translation of the RUBÁIYÁT OF OMAR KHAYYÁM, was first published anonymously in 1859. Members of the PRE-RAPHAELITE BROTHERHOOD, particularly Dante Gabriel ROSSETTI, discovered the work and hailed it as a masterpiece. Revised editions appeared in 1868, 1872, and 1879, but it wasn't until the early 1870s that FitzGerald was known to have been the translator. While retaining the spirit and philosophy expressed in the original quatrains, FitzGerald's translation was so free in its rendition as to be virtually an original work, masterful in its concentration, music, and command of tone. FitzGerald's *Letters and Literary Remains* (ed W. A. Wright, 1899) are also of much interest.

Fitzgerald, F[rancis] Scott [Key] (1896–1940) American novelist and short-story writer. One of the most gifted serious writers of his generation, Fitzgerald became known for his novels and stories of the 1920s; he called it the "Jazz Age" and described it as "a new generation grown up to find all Gods dead, all wars fought, all faiths in man shaken." As a spokesman for the JAZZ AGE, Fitzgerald created glittering characters, cynical and irresponsible, trying to turn life into an endless party; as the moralist he felt himself to be, he infused his stories with the sense that something was desperately wrong.

Fitzgerald was born in St. Paul, Minnesota, where his mother's well-to-do family had its roots; he was named after the author of THE STAR-SPANGLED BANNER, an ancestor of his father. He attended Princeton, but did not receive his degree; it was there that he began his lifelong friendship with Edmund WILSON, who became his literary executor. He served in the army, but never saw action, and in fact spent most of his time working on his first novel, THIS SIDE OF PARADISE. Published in 1920, it was a spectacular success. In the same year he married the beautiful Zelda Sayre, daughter of a Montgomery, Alabama, judge, and together they embarked on a life that reads like one of his novels, commuting between the plush hotels and speakeasies of the U.S. and the fashionable resorts of Europe. They lived on the Riviera, in Paris, New York, Long Island, and Washington, D.C. It was a rich, glamorous, intoxicating life that was to end tragically with Zelda's incurable mental illness and Fitzgerald's breakdown.

Fitzgerald followed his first success with a collection of short stories, *Flappers and Philosophers* (1920), and a second novel, *The Beautiful and Damned* (1922), in which he describes the pervading goal of his day as "the final polish of the shoe, the ultimate dab of the clothes brush, and a sort of intellectual There!" *Tales of the Jazz Age* (1922) and *The Vegetable* (a play; 1923) were followed by THE GREAT GATSBY, often considered his finest work. As was his custom, he immediately followed the novel with another collection of short stories, *All the Sad Young Men* (1926).

From this point on, enormous financial and emotional pressures beset Fitzgerald. His next novel, TENDER IS THE NIGHT, was not published until 1934, its progress inhibited by his constant need to sell magazine stories for cash. How the strain of Zelda's illness contributed to his own personal crisis is described in *The Crack-Up* (serial pub, 1936; book, 1945, ed Edmund Wilson). His determined and, to some extent, successful efforts to put the pieces of his life back together and to devote himself entirely to writing ended with his early death. His final novel, *The Last Tycoon* (1941), though unfinished, is considered by many critics to be his best.

Fitzgerald was equally a master of the short-story form; among the finest of these are "The Rich Boy," "A Diamond as Big as the Ritz," and "Babylon Revisited."

Fitzgerald has been the subject of a great many biographical and critical works, notably Arthur Mizener's *The Far Side of Paradise* (1951), Andrew Turnbull's *Scott Fitzgerald* (1962), and *F. Scott Fitzgerald* (1967), by H. D. Piper. Nancy Milford's *Zelda* (1970) sheds interesting light on both Fitzgeralds. Fitzgerald is also the model for the central character in Budd Schulberg's novel *The Disenchanted* (1950).

Fitzgerald's *Letters* (ed A. Turnbull) appeared in 1963. *The Notebooks of F. Scott Fitzgerald* (1978) was the first complete edition of his voluminous notes. Seven collections of his magazine stories were published after his death, the final volume being *The Price Was High: The Last Uncollected Stories of F. Scott Fitzgerald* (1979; ed Matthew J. Brucolli).

Five Classics   Works in the Confucian canon established during the HAN dynasty. They are: BOOK OF ODES, BOOK OF CHANGES, BOOK OF RITES, BOOK OF DOCUMENTS, and the SPRING AND AUTUMN ANNALS. Together with the FOUR BOOKS, they served as the basis of Chinese education until recent times.

Five Nations   (1) A confederation of five related tribes of the Huron-Iroquois linguistic stock: the Mohawks, Oneidas, Onondagas, Cayugas, and Senecas.

(2) The Five Civilized Nations, or Tribes, were the Cherokee, Chickasaw, Choctaw, Creek, and Seminole, so called because they had gone far in absorbing the civilization of the white settlers.

Flagellants   Members of religious associations who hold that the wrath of God can be appeased only by self-scourging. The first wave of this movement spread over Europe, starting from Italy, about the year 1260. Scenes of public processions with the exhibition of bloody self-castigation were repeated on a larger scale at the time of the plague called the black death (about 1348). A group with similar tenets is the PENITENTES, and SHIITE Muslims engage in self-flagellation in the Muharram processions commemorating their martyrs Hasan and Husein.

Flaherty, Robert [Joseph] (1884–1951)   American documentary filmmaker. Born in Michigan, Flaherty spent much of his youth in Canada and, in 1910–16, led several expeditions into the Hudson Bay area. His first film, *Nanook of the North* (1920–22), was the result of two years spent living with an Eskimo family. The careful detail and intimate quality of this film, along with his essentially romantic vision, characterized all of his later work, despite continual struggles with commercial pressures. Among his other important films are *Moana* (1926), *Man of Aran* (1934), *Elephant Boy* (1937), and *Louisiana Story* (1948). Flaherty was the first major film director to make feature-length documentary films; he also pioneered the use of panchromatic film stock.

Flame of Life, The (Il fuoco, 1900; tr 1900)   A novel by Gabriele D'ANNUNZIO. Based largely on the author's liaison with the actress Eleonora Duse (1859–1924), the novel deals with the love affair of La Foscarina, a great tragic actress in her prime, and the young poet Stellio Effrena. The flame of the title is a metaphor for Stellio's passion, which consumes and ultimately destroys both lovers. Partly because of its vividly realistic portrayal of the lovers' alliance, it caused a scandal upon publication.

Flanner, Janet (1892–1978)   American journalist and novelist. A native of the Midwest, Flanner settled in Paris in 1922, where she wrote her only novel, *The Cubical City* (1926), about a young Ohio woman's move to New York. In 1925 she began publishing the Paris letter in THE NEW YORKER under the name "Genêt," a pseudonym given her by Harold ROSS. In a cool and intensely analytical style, she conveyed subtleties of character and nuances of atmosphere providing a vast record of half a century of

French social, political, and cultural events. Along with her book-length profile *Pétain* (1944), her articles were collected in *Men and Monuments* (1957), *Paris Journal: 1944–1965* (1965), *Paris Journal: 1965–1971* (1971), *Paris Was Yesterday: 1925–1939* (1972), and *Janet Flanner's Uncollected Writings* (1979).

Flaubert, Gustave (1821–1880)   French novelist. Born at Rouen in Normandy, Flaubert is one of the great literary artists of the 19th century. Although his name is associated with NATURALISM, his artistic beliefs and ideals may not be so neatly summarized. Victor HUGO, CHATEAUBRIAND, and GAUTIER were the writers whom Flaubert most admired. A deep strain of romanticism in his own nature, which found expression in lyricism and vivid imaginings, was resolutely curbed in the service of his theories of art. Like Gautier, Flaubert believed in perfection of form and in the absolute value of art: *l'art pour l'art* (ART FOR ART'S SAKE). In technique, his work is marked by exactness and accuracy of observation, extreme impersonality and objectivity, and extraordinary balance and precision of style. But his precise, careful portrayal of object and event, although naturalistic in method, was not naturalistic in aim. Flaubert's concern was to create reality through the art of exact selection and the chiseled perfection of his style. Beset by ill health and by personal misfortune, he led a solitary life of rigid discipline. His obsession with the writer's craft is legendary. Hour after hour, he would labor over the rhythm or the music of a particular sentence, seeking *le mot juste*. He wrote MADAME BOVARY, SALAMMBÔ, L'EDUCATION SENTIMENTALE, *La Tentation de Saint-Antoine* (*The Temptation of Saint Anthony*, 1874), and the unfinished *Bouvard et Pécuchet* (1881). The short stories "Un Coeur simple" (A SIMPLE HEART), "La Légende de Saint-Julien-l'Hospitalier," and "Hérodias" appeared in the single volume *Trois Contes* (1877); these masterful tales revealed Flaubert's great command of this genre.

Fleance   In Shakespeare's MACBETH, the son of BANQUO. After the assassination of his father, he escapes to Wales. From him, according to legend, proceeded in a direct line the Stuart line of Scotland, thus fulfilling the witches' prophecy that Banquo's descendants would be kings.

Flecker, James Elroy (1884–1915)   English poet and dramatist. Flecker is known for his iconoclastic manner, his interest in the Mid-East and the Orient (where he served in the Foreign Service), and for the pictorial richness of his writing. His poetic works include *The Golden Journey to Samarkand* (1913), *The Burial in England* (1915), and *Collected Poems* (1916). He also wrote two verse plays, *Don Juan* (pub 1925; prod 1946) and *Hassan* (pub 1922), which was spectacularly produced in London in 1923, with choreography by Fokine and music by Delius. He wrote one novel, *King of Alsander* (1914).

Fleet Street   A street in London now synonymous with English journalism and newspaperdom. It was a famous thoroughfare centuries before the first newspaper was published there at the close of the 18th century. The name derives from the old stream, the Fleet, now subterranean, which flowed nearby.

Fleming, Ian [Lancaster] (1908–1964)   English novelist. Fleming worked as a journalist and, during World War II, in naval intelligence, before he began writing his enormously successful spy thrillers featuring James BOND, the dashing and dangerous British Intelligence agent whose number is 007 and whose career has continued in a series of extremely popular films, most of which are based loosely, if at all, on Fleming's books.

Fletcher, Giles, the younger (1588?–1623) English poet. Fletcher is best known for *Christ's Victorie and Triumph in Heaven and Earth* (1610), a religious poem modeled on the work of SPENSER, which is thought to have had a great influence on MILTON's *Paradise Regained* (1671). He was the son of Giles Fletcher, the elder (1549?–1611), who wrote *Licia* (1593), an early book of SONNET SEQUENCES.

Fletcher, John Gould (1886–1950)   American poet and critic. First associated with IMAGISM and later with the FUGITIVES, Fletcher felt that modern poetry needed new patterns and new subject matter. His *Selected Poems* (1938) won a PULITZER PRIZE. *Irradiations: Sands and Spray* (1915), his first volume of poetry, was followed by such other collections as *Goblins and Pagodas* (1916), *Breakers and Granite* (1921), *The Black Rock* (1928), and *XXIV Elegies* (1935). His prose works include a book on Gauguin (1921), *John Smith—Also Pocahontas* (1928), *The Two Frontiers: A Study in Historical Psychology* (1930), and the autobiography *Life Is My Song* (1937).

Fletcher, Phineas (1582–1650)   English poet. The brother of Giles FLETCHER, the younger, he was a follower and imitator of SPENSER. Fletcher is best known for *The Purple Island* (1633), an allegorical poem on man in terms of the topography and settlement of an island. Among his other works are *Locustae* (1627), an anti-Jesuit poem in Latin, its paraphrased English title being *The Apollyonists*; *Britain's Ida* (1627), a mythological poem in the manner of Spenser and first published as the work of Spenser; and *Piscatory Eclogues and Other Poetical Miscellanies* (1633). MILTON's Satan is believed to have been suggested by the Lucifer of *The Apollyonists*.

Fleurs du mal, Les (The Flowers of Evil, 1857)   A volume of poetry by Charles BAUDELAIRE. Faced with the conflict of good and evil, Baudelaire discards the conventional distinctions and seeks beauty or good in the perverse, the grotesque, and the morbid. His sensibility, painfully alive to all emotions and sensations, lends unity to the various poems.

Flies, The (Les Mouches, 1943; tr 1946)   A play by Jean-Paul SARTRE. The plot is an adaptation of AESCHYLUS' story of ORESTES. ZEUS shares with Aegistheus "the bitterness of knowing men are free," although the townsfolk are content to let their king shoulder their decision-making along with their responsibility for guilt. Orestes is the dangerous man who knows that he is free, and that "human life begins on the far side of despair." To teach his people to be free and responsible, Orestes kills Aegistheus and takes with him the crowd of repulsive flies, the Furies of the Greek drama, who symbolize conscious acceptance of the consequences of one's acts. When it was first produced during the Occupation, the play had overtones of a call to resistance to the Vichy government's collaboration with the Nazis.

Flodden Field, Battle of   A battle in Northumberland on September 9, 1513. James IV of Scotland was defeated and killed by the forces of the earl of Surrey, who was in charge of the action in the absence of Henry VIII. The battle, in which there were up to ten thousand Scottish dead, among them all Scotland's leaders, was made the subject of poems by John SKELTON, Thomas Deloney (1543?–?1600), and others. The battle is described in the sixth canto of Sir Walter Scott's MARMION, A TALE OF FLODDEN FIELD.

flood myths   A very widespread theme in mythology is the destruction of the world by a flood and the survival of one human being, often with his family, thanks to the goodwill of a god. The most famous flood narrative, that of NOAH, is based closely on the far older Babylonian story of UTNAPISHTIM, told in the *Epic of* GILGAMESH. This in turn was based on the Sumerian legend of ZIUSUDRA. In Hindu mythology, VISHNU appears to Manu, the first man, as a fish and warns him of the coming flood; the god himself leads Manu's ship to a safe mooring in the mountains of the North. In the Greek myth, Deucalion (see DEUCALION'S FLOOD), the son of PROMETHEUS, is the hero who, with his wife, Pyrrha, is saved and repopulates the earth. The Hittite Noah was Ullush. Stories of a great flood are also found in many parts of Asia, in Australia, and in North and South America, though they are uncommon in Europe. It has been suggested that these myths arose either from traditions of local floods or from attempts to explain striking configurations of the landscape.

Flora   In Roman mythology, goddess of flowers. Hence, in natural history all the flowers and vegetable productions of a country or locality are called its *flora*.

Flores and Blanchefleur (Floire et Blanchefleur) A medieval metrical romance in French and English. Flores and Blanchefleur are a Christian prince and princess who are brought up together and fall in love. Before Blanchefleur is carried off as a slave by the Saracens, she gives Flores a ring that will tarnish when she is in danger. It warns him, and he pursues her through many adventures to an Oriental emir's harem, which he enters concealed in a basket of roses. When he is discovered, the lovers are sentenced to death, but are pardoned by the emir because of the beauty of their love for each other. Boccaccio adapts this tale in his IL FILOCOLO.

Florit, Eugenio (1903–   )   Cuban poet and literary critic. In the late 1920s the Cuban literary world saw
the emergence of two distinct groups of young poets: on the
one hand was the socially engagé poetry of Nicolás GUIL-
LÉN; on the other was the pure, meditative poetry of Florit.
An elegiac and serene writer, Florit conveys in his verse a
mystical fascination with his native landscape and his own
highly personal musings. *Hábito de esperanza, 1936–1964*
(1965) is the most complete collection of his poems. Florit
has lived in the U.S. since the fall of the Batista regime.

Florizel   The son of Polixenes, king of Bohemia, in
Shakespeare's WINTER'S TALE. During a hunting expedition, Florizel sees PERDITA, supposedly the daughter of a
shepherd, falls in love with her, and courts her under the
assumed name of Doricles. When Polixenes objects to the
match, Florizel flees with her to Sicilia, where it is
revealed that she is the long-lost daughter of that country's
king, LEONTES.

King George IV of England, while Prince of Wales,
adopted the name as a pseudonym during his romance
with "Perdita" Robinson.

Flounder, The (Der Butt, 1977; tr 1978)   Novel by
Günter GRASS based on a loose adaptation of the GRIMM
fairy tale "The Fisherman and His Wife." Grass's modern
version is a Rabelaisian tale of the treatment and position of
women throughout history. The novel spans four thousand
years, with the narrator appearing throughout the millen-
nia in various incarnations, always married to Ilsebill, a
cook, and always maintaining power through the aid of the
magical talking flounder. Grass's fable is, in part, an earthy
culinary history sprinkled with recipes, folklore, and
anthropology. Finally, in the 1970s, the flounder abandons
the masculine cause in disgust at the sorry state that male
dominance has brought to the modern world, and he offers
his services to some radical feminists. They put him on
trial for furthering the destructive male principle and eventually he is thrown back into the sea.

Flying Dutchman   A legendary spectral ship. Supposedly, it can be seen in stormy weather off the Cape of
Good Hope; it is considered an omen of ill luck. Sir Walter
SCOTT, in his note to *Rokeby* (1813), says that the ship was
originally a vessel laden with precious metal, on which a
horrible murder was committed; then plague broke out
among the crew, and no port would allow the vessel to
enter. The ill-fated ship still wanders about like a ghost,
doomed to be sea-tossed, never more to enjoy rest. WAG-
NER's opera *Der Fliegende Holländer* (*The Flying Dutchman*, 1843) embodies the legend in a different form. An
old Dutch captain, in the midst of a struggle with the elements, has sworn an impious oath to round the Cape even
if it takes an eternity to do it. The curse, which is laid on
him for centuries, will be lifted only if he finds a wife willing to sacrifice everything for his sake. The opera deals with
the lifting of the curse by the Norwegian maiden Senta.

Fogazzaro, Antonio (1842–1911)   Italian novelist
and poet. A representative of liberal Catholicism, Fogazzaro attempted to reconcile traditional dogma with the revolutionary advances of modern science, particularly Darwinism. The question was directly addressed in his finest
novel, *Piccolo mondo antico* (1896; tr *The Patriot*, 1906;
The Little World of the Past, 1962), which dramatizes the
antithetical attitudes toward religion held by Franco
Maironi, a rigid Catholic, and his wife, Lucia, an agnostic
rationalist. Only a shared tragedy succeeds in reconciling
their mutual antagonisms in favor of a trusting Christian
faith. This novel began a loosely connected cycle that
includes *Piccolo mondo moderno* (1901; tr *The Sinner*,
1907), *Il santo* (1905; tr *The Saint*, 1906), and *Leila* (1910;
tr 1911), the last two of which were considered heretical
and were placed on the Vatican Index of forbidden books.
In the aggregate, the novels describe a curious symbiosis of
exalted mysticism and impassioned sensuality, suggestive of
SYMBOLIST influence. Other novels include *Malombra*
(1881; tr *The Woman*, 1907) and *Daniele Cortis* (1885; tr
1890).

Fogg, Phileas   Hero of AROUND THE WORLD IN
EIGHTY DAYS by Jules Verne.

Fogo Morto (1943; tr 1944)   A novel by José LINS
DO RÊGO. In this, the last of Lins do Rêgo's six-novel cycle
about plantation life in northeastern Brazil, he portrays the
decadence of a dying aristocracy, intertwining the lives of
characters from the previous five novels. A central figure is
Vittorino, whose fancies of quixotic honor and respect are
treated with irony and compassion. There is a disturbing
tension established between the individual characters and
reality as they watch a new society unravel before their
eyes. The language of this masterwork is steeped in the
consciousness of passing time.

folklore   A term coined by William John Thoms
(1803–85) to apply to rituals, customs, traditions, and
beliefs of unknown origin, accumulated primarily through
oral transmission and basically expressing the concerns of
ordinary people (as opposed to scholars and thinkers). In
the aggregate, folklore includes not only such verbal lore as
tales, EPICS, chants, BALLADS, and riddles but also the
diverse traditions of folk art, folk music, folk dance, and
folk medicine. Central to the study of folklore, and of
much literature, is the folktale. Perrault's LES CONTES DE
MA MÈRE L'OYE were among the first folktales to be published (1697), although Perrault's stylization of the stories
obscured their oral derivations. The first serious collection
of authentically recorded tales was *Kinder- und Hausmärchen* (*Children's and Household Tales*, 1812, 1815,
1822), assembled by Jacob and Wilhelm GRIMM, in which
the brothers stressed the importance of field work in tracing
origins. In Scandinavia, P. C. ASBJØNSEN and J. E. MOE
(1813–82) collected *Norwegian Folk Stories* (1841–44),
while A. N. AFANASYEV began the first systematic collec-

tion of Russian folktales. Joseph Jacobs did the same in England with *Celtic Fairy Tales* (1892).

Beginning with the collections of Henry Rowe SCHOOLCRAFT in the 1820s, folktales of American Indians began to be seen as important to an understanding of native Americans. Black folklore was the focus of Joel Chandler Harris's collection of UNCLE REMUS stories. Appalachian tales were published by Richard Chase in *The Jack Tales* (1943) and in many collections of Ozark stories compiled by Vance Randolph (1892–   ).

Numerous distinctions among types of folktales have been made. Animal tales, common to almost every culture, generally anthropomorphize animal characters in moral stories like AESOP's fables or in BEAST EPICS. Fairy tales, having no basis in fact, emphasize miraculous happenings and fantastic transformations, as in CINDERELLA. Legends, generally set in a particular time or place, deal with a local tradition or relate adventures ascribed to a local figure. Mythical tales abound; set in the distant past, gods and/or the creation motif are prominent. TALL TALES are particularly identified with the U.S. in their accounts of pioneering super-heroes like Paul BUNYAN, taming the wilderness with preposterous feats of strength and bravery. Perhaps the most prevalent type is the MÄRCHEN, usually involving the theme of the quest or heroic journey, with final rewards for goodness and the defeat of evil.

The scholarly study of folklore began after the founding of the first folklore society in London in 1878. From that time, folktales have been systematically collected, classified, and catalogued according to type and motif. Differences commonly arise regarding the origins of tales. Some experts believe tales to have evolved independently in separate cultures (polygenesis), while others theorize that particular tales originated in a single region and were then spread to other parts of the world (diffusion). Similarly, there are numerous explanations of subject matter.

Folktales are variously seen as deteriorations of ancient myths, as survivals of primitive beliefs, as expressions of subconscious fears and desires, or as symbolic explanations for natural phenomena. In any and all of its aspects, the study of folklore offers insights into the practical and spiritual history of man.

folktale See FOLKLORE.

Fomorians In Gaelic literature, a race of giants who periodically came from the sea to raid prehistoric Ireland and inevitably tangled with whoever happened to be inhabiting the island at the time.

Fontane, Theodor (1819–1898) German novelist and poet. In his youth, Fontane was known primarily as a writer of ballads and nonfiction. It wasn't until he was fifty-nine that he turned to fiction, after which he wrote fifteen novels in twenty years. He became his country's greatest master of the social novel and a renowned writer of dialogue. Most of his novels treat the decline of the Prussian nobility and the rise of the bourgeoisie; his characters tend to be people who either live in the past or try unsuccessfully to transcend traditional values. The best known of his novels are: *Irrungen, Wirrungen* (1888; tr *Trials and Tribulations*, 1917); *Frau Jenny Treibel* (1892; tr 1976), and EFFI BRIEST. Fontane's greatness as a novelist was that he developed the novel of realism in Germany to the level it had achieved in France and Russia, yet brought to it the intensity, in characterization and imagery, and the technique, in his personal style, that we associate with the finest art.

Fontenelle, Bernard le Bovier de (1657–1757) French man of letters. *Entretiens sur la pluralité des mondes* (*Conversations on the Plurality of Worlds*, 1686), the best known of Fontenelle's writings, discusses the solar system in terms easily grasped by the general reader. In *Dialogues des morts* (*Dialogues of the Dead*, 1683), historical figures conduct imaginary and witty dialogues on a variety of philosophical subjects. Ostensibly opposing the pagan belief in oracles and upholding the scientific method, the *Histoire des oracles* (*History of Oracles*, 1686) levels a subtle attack at religious orthodoxy and blind obedience to authority. In *Digressions sur les anciens et les modernes* (*Digressions upon the Ancients and the Moderns*, 1688) Fontenelle sides with the moderns, predicting unlimited progress in the arts and sciences.

Fonvizin, Denis Ivanovich (1745–1792) Russian playwright. He is best known for two classic comedies: *Brigadir* (*The Brigadier*, 1769) and *Nedorosl* (*The Minor*, 1782). The second play, considered his masterpiece, satirizes the barbaric habits of the semieducated gentry of the time.

Fool, Lear's In Shakespeare's KING LEAR, the strangely wise companion in motley who travels in the storm with Lear, commenting on the behavior of mankind and peppering his words with song. The character is enigmatic in intent, "a pestilent gall" to Lear because of his bitter, mocking wit. He disappears at that point in the play at which CORDELIA returns to help Lear, and he is believed in some way to represent truth, a trait also reflected in Cordelia, sometimes referred to by Lear as his "fool."

fools Attendants at court. From medieval times until the 17th century, licensed fools, or jesters, were commonly kept at court, and frequently in the retinue of wealthy nobles. Thus we are told that the regent Morton had a fool, Patrick Bonny; HOLBEIN painted Sir Thomas MORE's jester, Patison, in his picture of the chancellor; and as late as 1728 SWIFT wrote an epitaph on Dickie Pearce, the fool of the earl of Suffolk, who died at the age of sixty-three and is buried in Berkeley Churchyard, Gloucestershire. Dagonet, the fool of King Arthur (see LE MORTE D'ARTHUR), is also remembered.

The guild fools of medieval times played an important part in the spread of literature and education. They formed a branch of the Troubadour organization, a force that permeated Europe.

foot See METER.

forbidden fruit Figuratively, unlawful indulgence, from the fruit of the tree of the knowledge of good and evil eaten by ADAM AND EVE in disobedience of God's command. According to Muslim tradition, the forbidden fruit was the banana or Indian fig, because fig leaves were employed to cover the disobedient pair when they felt shame as the result of sin.

Ford, Ford Madox (original name Ford Madox Hueffer, 1873–1939) English novelist and editor. Ford's mother was the daughter of Ford Madox Brown, the Pre-Raphaelite painter, and sister-in-law of William ROSSETTI. Violet HUNT was Ford's mistress for some time. His best novels, THE GOOD SOLDIER and the tetralogy PARADE'S END, are studies of the emotional relationships in marriage and adultery. The early novels *The Inheritors* (1901) and *Romance* (1903) were written in collaboration with Joseph CONRAD, whose oblique narrative method Ford admired and imitated. He wrote critical studies of Conrad (1924) and of Henry James (1913). An important literary editor, Ford founded the *English Review* in 1908 and edited the *Transatlantic Review*, from Paris, from about 1924. He "discovered" D. H. LAWRENCE (see MIRIAM) and was a friend of James JOYCE and Ezra POUND. Among his volumes of autobiography and memoirs are *No Enemy* (1929), *Return to Yesterday* (1931), and *It Was the Nightingale* (1933). During the 1950s, Ford began to be increasingly recognized as a major 20th-century writer.

Ford, Gerald R[udolph, Jr.] (1913–   ) Thirty-eighth president of the U.S. (1974–77) and the only vice president to assume the nation's highest office upon the resignation—rather than the death—of a president (Richard M. NIXON). He earned his law degree at Yale University and served in the Navy during World War II, earning ten battle stars. He won his first election in 1948, becoming a conservative Republican member of the House of Representatives. He served on the Warren Commission, which investigated the November 22, 1963, assassination of President John F. KENNEDY, and cowrote *Portrait of the Assassin* (1965), which publicized the commission's conclusion that Lee Harvey Oswald was not part of a conspiracy. He served as House Minority Leader. A loyal supporter of Richard M. Nixon, he became Nixon's vice president in 1973 when Spiro T. Agnew, facing charges of extortion and bribery, resigned from that office.

As a result of the WATERGATE scandal, President Nixon resigned from office on August 9, 1974, and Gerald R. Ford was immediately sworn in as president. He emphasized an "open presidency" to counteract the negative impact of the Watergate cover-up, but he shocked the country when he proclaimed a full pardon of former president Nixon on September 8, 1974. Ford faced problems of economic recession and inflation, rising unemployment, and an energy shortage. He acted to bolster U.S. ties to Japan and West Germany and followed Nixon's policy of détente with the Soviet Union. Ford's firm reaction to the Cambodian seizure of the American ship *Mayaguez* in May 1975 increased his popularity. He was defeated in 1976 in his bid for election by the Democratic presidential candidate, Jimmy CARTER. Ford is the author of *A Time to Heal: The Autobiography of Gerald R. Ford* (1979). His wife, Betty Ford, is the author of *The Times of My Life* (1978) and *Betty: A Glad Awakening* (1987).

Ford, John (1586–c1640) English dramatist. Ford is known for his portrayal of passion and for his concentration on incest and other sexual abnormalities, as revealed in such works as 'TIS PITY SHE'S A WHORE and *The Broken Heart* (c1629). These characteristics are less apparent in *Perkin Warbeck* (c1633). His other plays include *The Lovers' Melancholy* (1628), *The Lady's Trial* (1638), *The Fancies, Chaste and Noble* (c1635), *Love's Sacrifice* (1630), *The Sun's Darling* (1624), and *The Witch of Edmonton* (c1623), the latter written with William ROWLEY and Thomas DEKKER.

Ford, John (real name Sean Aloysius O'Fienne, 1895–1973) American film director, a master of the Western movie. Ford's vast output of over 125 films falls into three periods. From 1917 until the end of the silent period he specialized in Westerns, reaching his peak with *The Iron Horse* (1924), an epic about building America's first transcontinental railroad. With the exception of *Stagecoach* (1939), his best films during the 1930s and early 1940s were not Westerns but human dramas in a variety of settings, like *The Lost Patrol* (1934), *The Informer* (1935), *Young Mr. Lincoln* (1939), *The Grapes of Wrath* (1940), and *How Green Was My Valley* (1941). A third period, encompassing such pictures as *My Darling Clementine* (1946), *She Wore a Yellow Ribbon* (1949), *The Quiet Man* (1952), and *The Man Who Shot Liberty Valance* (1962), was characterized by rough good humor, a focus on rugged individualism and elemental action played against a background of magnificent Western or Irish landscapes. Ford's reiterated subject is a group of characters confronted by common dangers, revealing their strengths and weaknesses as the situation unfolds.

Forester, C[ecil] S[cott] (1899–1966) English novelist. Forester is best known as the creator of Horatio HORNBLOWER in a series of novels about the British navy during the Napoleonic Wars. His many other successful books include *Payment Deferred* (1926), a crime novel; *The Gun* (1933); THE AFRICAN QUEEN; *The Story of the Naval War of 1812* (1956); *The Last Nine Days of the Bismarck* (1959); and his autobiography, *Long Before Forty* (1967).

formalism A movement in Russian literary theory and criticism during the 1920s. It was characterized by its members' interest in aesthetic as opposed to social aspects of art. Although they lost the dominant place in Soviet literature to the advocates of proletarian and socialist art, the movement did inject into Russian literary criticism a healthy interest in the nature of literature and the problems of literary craft.

Forsh, Olga Dmitriyevna (1873–1961)   Soviet novelist. Forsh's first major novel, *Odety kamnem* (1924–25; tr *Palace and Prison*, 1958), relates the incarceration and subsequent decline into insanity of the revolutionary Mikhail Beyedeman. Acknowledged as a classic historical novel, *Palace and Prison* established Forsh as a founder of the genre in Russia. Her other translated novel, *Perventsy svobody* (1950–53; tr *Pioneers of Freedom*, 1958), focuses on the Decembrist Uprising of 1825. Forsh's first published work appeared under the pseudonym A. Terek.

Forster, E[dward] M[organ] (1879–1970)   English novelist, short-story writer, and essayist. Born into a middle-class family, Forster was raised by his mother (widowed before he was two years old), who remained his devoted companion until her death in 1945. Following an unhappy time at English public schools, he went to King's College, Cambridge, where he first came to know future fellow members of the BLOOMSBURY GROUP. In an early burst of creative activity he published four novels between 1905 and 1910. Of the four, WHERE ANGELS FEAR TO TREAD and A ROOM WITH A VIEW are set in Italy, where he had traveled with his mother. THE LONGEST JOURNEY and HOWARDS END, both set in England, share with the two other novels a gentle irony that reveals the moral and emotional deficiencies of the English upper classes. Forster's central concern was that individuals should "connect the prose with the passion" within themselves. He felt that middle- and upper-class Englishmen lacked a spontaneous capacity for passion and intuition; he believed that pure pragmatism should be tempered by the imagination, mysticism, and sensitivity to nature that he had observed not only in southern Europe, but in the English lower classes.

By the time *Howards End* appeared, Forster had a substantial literary following. Then, aside from a collection of stories (*The Celestial Omnibus*, 1911) and journalistic pieces, he was silent for fourteen years. In 1924 he produced his last and greatest novel, A PASSAGE TO INDIA, a subtle and affecting work depicting the prejudices and injustices of British rule in India that gave full expression to his liberal humanism. After 1924 he published only collections of literary and sociological essays, two biographies, and books of literary criticism, notably ASPECTS OF THE NOVEL, which amplifies the symbolic and structural devices he employed in his own work. His abrupt halt in writing fiction has been the subject of considerable speculation. It has been suggested that Forster feared "literary sterility" after his early successes, that he was unable to deal with subjects and times beyond his sheltered Edwardian youth, or that he was frustrated by his inability to write frankly about his own homosexuality. His one novel dealing with this was *Maurice* (1971), written in 1913 but published only after his death.

Although his reputation has undergone shifts in critical enthusiasm, he is commonly regarded as one of the most important and richly observant novelists of the 20th century. A volume of his *Selected Letters* was published in 1985.

Forsyte Saga, The   A series of novels by John GALSWORTHY. Galsworthy continued to write novels about the Forsyte family throughout his life, but strictly the *Saga* consists of *The Man of Property* (1906), *In Chancery* (1920), and *To Let* (1921). The whole work was published with two additional "interludes," *Indian Summer of a Forsyte* and *Awakening*, in 1922. The Forsytes are a large upper-middle-class London family of conventional, materialistic businessmen. When the *Saga* opens, ten members of the oldest generation are still alive. Most of the novels are concerned with two members of the second generation, Soames Forsyte and Young Jolyon, and their children.

The "man of property" of the first and best-known novel is Soames Forsyte, a typical member of the Forsyte family. His wife, Irene, whom he regards as just another piece of property, falls in love with Philip Bosinney, a young architect. Soames devotes all his money and power to punishing them, and Philip is killed in an accident. *In Chancery* tells of the Forsytes' divorce. Irene marries Young Jolyon, the only sensitive member of the Forsyte family, and Soames marries a French woman, Annette. In *To Let*, Soames's daughter, Fleur, falls in love with Jon, the son of Young Jolyon and Irene; when the young couple learn the truth about their parents, Jon draws back in order to remain loyal to his mother.

A Modern Comedy (1929) is a second series of novels about the Forsytes; it consists of *The White Monkey*, *The Silver Spoon*, *Swan Song*, and two "interludes." This series carries the story up to Galsworthy's own day and is full of descriptions of the contemporary scene—toward which the aging author was unsympathetic. Most of the novels are about Fleur, her husband, Michael Mont, and their friends. *End of the Chapter* (1933) is a little-read trilogy that is also concerned with Fleur and her friends. The Forsytes recur in many of Galsworthy's short stories and even in novels centered on other families.

In *The Forsyte Saga* itself Galsworthy satirizes Soames Forsyte and his materialistic values and champions the artist, the rebel, and the underdog. But in later novels he praises Soames's solid traditionalism, preferring him to the members of the modern young generation.

Fortinbras   In Shakespeare's HAMLET, the prince of Norway. A man of action unlike the introspective Hamlet, Fortinbras has planned to invade Denmark but, deterred by his uncle and Claudio, marches on Poland instead. When Hamlet dies, Fortinbras arrives to claim the Danish throne and to restore order to the kingdom.

Fortuna   In Roman mythology, the goddess of fortune or chance. Fortuna was identified with the Greek TYCHE, and she was often depicted with a rudder, as the pilot of destiny, with wings, or with a wheel. The wheel of fortune was a widely used symbol in medieval art and literature, forming the concept on which John Lydgate's *Falls* of *Princes* (a very long poem written between 1430 and 1438 and first printed in 1494) and Chaucer's *The Monk's Tale* from THE CANTERBURY TALES were based.

Fortunate Life, A (1985)   An autobiographical account by A. B. Facey (1894–1985) of a life devoted, since he was six, to hard labor amid great difficulties and setbacks, with various groups of settlers in the Australian outback. Told with an endearing humility, the story provides an authentic and unique perspective on the sense of adventure and the extreme loneliness that accompanied the settler's efforts to build a life for himself in uncharted and often hostile terrain. Detailed descriptions of the bush animals, trees, and shrubs and the folklore of the outback add to the book's appeal. Its popularity has been attributed to the author's brilliant flair for storytelling and to its portrayal of the quintessential Australian spirit.

Fortunes of Richard Mahony   A trilogy of novels by Henry Handel RICHARDSON. The novels are: *Australia Felix* (1917), *The Way Home* (1925), and *Ultima Thule* (1929). The author's physician father was the model for this undeviatingly realistic portrait of a 19th-century misfit. Always the outsider, Mahony is a Protestant in Catholic Dublin, an alien Briton in Australia, an intellectual amid rough-and-ready pragmatists. While Australia is establishing its nationality and Australians are forging their identity, Mahony fits in nowhere and dies insane.

forty   A number of frequent occurrence in Scripture. Hence it was formerly treated as, in a manner, sacrosanct. MOSES was forty days on the mount; ELIJAH was forty days fed by ravens; the rain of the flood fell forty days, and another forty days expired before NOAH opened the window of the ark; forty days was the period of embalming; Nineveh had forty days to repent; JESUS fasted forty days; He was seen forty days after His resurrection.

St. Swithin betokens forty days' rain or dry weather; a quarantine extends to forty days; forty days, in the Old English law, was the limit for the payment of the fine for manslaughter; the privilege of sanctuary was for forty days; the widow was allowed to remain in her husband's house for forty days after his decease; a knight enjoined forty days' service of his tenant; a stranger, at the expiration of forty days, was compelled to be enrolled in some tithing; Members of Parliament were protected from arrest forty days after the prorogation of the House, and forty days before the House was convened; a new-made burgess had to forfeit forty pence unless he built a house within forty days.

The ancient physicians ascribe many strange changes to the period of forty; the alchemists looked on forty days as the charmed period when the philosopher's stone and elixir of life were to appear.

forty-five, the (sometimes 45)   The second rebellion of the JACOBITES, which occurred in 1745 and failed. Prince Charles, "the Young PRETENDER," had to escape to France with the aid of Flora MACDONALD. See FIFTEEN, THE.

42nd Parallel, The (1930)   A novel by John Dos Passos, the first book in the trilogy later called *U.S.A.* (q.v.). Set in the period immediately before World War I, the novel interweaves episodes from the lives of several characters with the "newsreel" and "camera eye" devices and with biographies of Eugene Debs, Luther Burbank, William Jennings Bryan, Andrew Carnegie, Edison, and others.

The characters, some of whom appear in other parts of the trilogy, include Fainy McCreary ("Mac"), who eventually joins the Mexican Revolution; the ruthless J. Ward Moorehouse; Eleanor Stoddard, with whom he has an affair; and Charley Anderson, who later becomes a war hero and airplane manufacturer. These various interlocking strands are designed to show the U.S. on the eve of the First World War, rather than the development of particular individuals. Although the book is sometimes confusing, it is, nevertheless, a powerful presentation of a vast canvas of human nature and history.

For Whom the Bell Tolls (1940)   A novel by HEMINGWAY. Set against the background of the Spanish Civil War (1936–39), it tells the story of Robert Jordan, an idealistic American college professor, who has come to Spain to fight with the Republican army. He has been assigned to a band of guerrillas led by Pablo and his wife, Pilar, a powerful peasant woman. Jordan's task is to blow up a bridge of strategic importance. He falls in love with Maria, a young Spanish girl who has been raped by the Fascists, and, during the three days they are together, they try to forget the impending event in their passion for each other. There is jealousy and distrust among the peasant members of the guerrilla company, several are killed, and the inefficiency and jealousies of the Communist leaders are revealed, but Jordan carries out his mission. He blows up the bridge successfully but is wounded and left on the hillside to die. The title of the novel is taken from one of the best-known passages in the DEVOTIONS of John Donne.

Foscolo, Ugo (1778–1827)   Italian novelist, poet, and patriot. Foscolo was the author of *Le ultime lettere di Jacopo Ortis* (1802), the first Italian novel in the modern sense of the word. Influenced by Goethe's THE SORROWS OF YOUNG WERTHER, and told in the form of exchanged letters, it relates the story of the futile love of the young student Ortis for a married woman; Ortis's sufferings, compounded of fruitless passion and frustrated patriotism, eventually drive him to suicide. Foscolo's best-known poem, "I sepolcri" (1807), reveals his dual poetic personality in its romantic spirit and neoclassical style.

Foster, Stephen Collins (1826–1864)   American songwriter and popular composer. Among his best-known songs are "My Old Kentucky Home," "Old Folks at Home," "Old Black Joe," and "Jeanie with the Light Brown Hair." His "Oh! Susanna" appeared in 1847 and, becoming extremely popular with the gold-rush "forty-niners," established his success. Many of his songs were used by the black minstrel troupes popular at the time and have become genuine American folk songs. Foster died, almost destitute, in the charity ward of Bellevue Hospital in New York.

Foucault, Michel (1926–1984)   French essayist, philosopher, and historian of ideas. Foucault's complex works probe various aspects of the meaning of culture. He is particularly concerned with identifying the basic principles that underlie the creation of social institutions and the extent to which these principles or concepts are shaped by social and economic forces. His analysis of the ways in which insanity has been defined by Western culture and the ways in which societies deal with its mentally deficient members was the subject of *Histoire de la folie à l'âge classique* (1961; tr *Madness and Civilization*, 1965), and the historical roots of the treatment of criminals are traced in *Surveiller et punir* (1975; tr *Discipline and Punish*, 1977). His affinities with the structuralist approach are most evident in *Les Mots et les choses* (1966; tr *The Order of Things*, 1970) and *L'Archéologie du savoir* (1969; tr *The Archaeology of Knowledge*, 1972). His death came shortly after the publication of the third volume in a projected six-volume *History of Sexuality*, an investigation of the way in which views of sexuality are manipulated by economic forces. See STRUCTURALISM.

Fouché, Joseph (Duke of Otranto, 1759–1820) French minister of police. A master of political intrigue, Fouché was renowned for his espionage system. He served in turn as minister of police, senator, minister of the interior, and again as minister of police. In 1816 Fouché was exiled from France. Stefan Zweig has written a biographical study entitled *Joseph Fouché* (1929).

Fountainhead, The (1943)   A novel by Ayn RAND. The hero of this widely sold book, who is supposedly modeled on Frank Lloyd WRIGHT, is an architect of enormous conceit who nevertheless succeeds in justifying his faith in the permanent values of honest design.

Fouquet, Nicolas (or Nicolas Foucquet, 1615–1680)   French superintendent of finance under Cardinal MAZARIN. At best a haphazard financier, Fouquet bestowed generous favors upon men of letters and incurred the disfavor of King Louis XIV. Arrested by royal order in 1661, he was tried for speculation and sentenced to life imprisonment. He died after nineteen years in prison.

Four Books   The four principal works in the Confucian canon. They are the ANALECTS, the GREAT LEARNING, the MEAN, and the MENCIUS. Except for the *Analects*, these were relatively unimportant works until raised to an exalted status by CHU HSI during the SUNG dynasty (960–1279). From this time they were used as the primary textbooks in the Chinese educational system and served as the basis for civil service examinations until 1905. See FIVE CLASSICS.

Four Horsemen of the Apocalypse   The personifications of the evils of war who appear in the Revela-

tion of St. John the Divine (Rev. 6). They are Conquest, Slaughter, Famine, and Death, and are seen on white, red, black, and pale horses, respectively. The Spanish novelist Vicente BLASCO IBAÑEZ entitled his widely read novel of World War I *Los cuatro jinetes del apocalipsis* (*Four Horsemen of the Apocalypse*, 1916); it has twice been produced as a motion picture.

Four Hundred   The inner circle of New York society, the elite. The term was coined by Ward McAllister (1827–95) in 1892. Because the ballroom of Mrs. William Astor held only four hundred people, McAllister's guest list of that number contained only those he considered to be the most socially respectable. See FOUR MILLION, THE.

Fourierism   The social system advanced by François Marie Charles Fourier (1772–1837), French reformer and economist. In order that men might live in the harmony to which they were naturally predisposed and which could be developed under proper conditions, Fourier envisioned a society in which economic activities would be carried on by phalanxes, groups consisting of some sixteen hundred persons, who would live in common buildings called phalansteries. Products would be divided among the members of each phalanx, with labor receiving the largest share; private property, however, would not be abolished. A republican form of government, with elective officials, would be established. Fourier outlined his ideas in several works, including *Théorie des quatre mouvements* (1808), *Traité de l'association domestique agricole* (1822), and *Le Nouveau Monde industriel* (1829–30). A number of Fourieristic communities and periodicals were founded in France, and several novels by George SAND show the influence of Fourier's ideas. Introduced into the U.S. in 1842 by Albert Brisbane, Fourierism was adopted by the members of BROOK FARM.

Four Million, The (1906)   A collection of twenty-five short stories by O. HENRY. The title, referring to the actual population of New York City at the time, was selected as a rebuttal to the famous remark of Ward McAllister (1827–95) that "there are only about four hundred people in New York society." The book contains O. Henry's famous story THE GIFT OF THE MAGI, although perhaps its best piece is "An Unfinished Story." O. Henry's favorite characters—shop girls, tramps, the humble and lowly in general—people these tales and give utterance to the author's unique brand of gently ironic sentimentality.

Four Noble Truths   See BUDDHISM.

Four P's, The (perf c1520; pub 1544)   An INTERLUDE by John HEYWOOD. It is a debate among a Palmer, a Pardoner, and a Potecary, with a Pedlar acting as judge, as to who can tell the biggest lie. The Palmer, who asserts that he never saw a woman out of temper, wins the prize.

Four Quartets (1943)   A long poem by T. S. ELIOT. Considered by many critics to be Eliot's major poetic achievement, it is an elaborate, allusive meditation on time and eternity, consisting of four poems named for four different places. The first (published in 1936), "Burnt Norton," is set in a house with a rose garden in which children are playing. The second, "East Coker" (1940), is named for the village in England from which Eliot's 17th-century ancestor set out for the New World. "The Dry Salvages" (1941) is named for a group of rocks off the coast of Massachusetts, where Eliot lived as a boy; the poem also has descriptions of the Mississippi, St. Louis having been his childhood home. The last poem, LITTLE GIDDING, is inspired by the religious community of that name and its chapel. It is a wartime poem; there are references to the bombing in London alongside references to the English Civil War. The whole work is as elaborately constructed as a piece of music, with its recurrent imagery, series of symbols (the separate poems are concerned, respectively, with air, earth, water, and fire), and literary, historical, and Christian references. Each poem ends with some words about the poet's craft and the problems of creating a work of art.

Four Saints in Three Acts (1927)   An opera by Virgil THOMSON to a libretto by Gertrude STEIN, first produced in 1934 with an all-black cast. The text exemplifies Stein's unique style: repetitive, sonorous, contradictory, and obscure. The opera is actually divided into four acts, with about a dozen saints, some historical and others fictitious. One famous line is "Pigeons on the grass alas."

four senses   The four varieties of interpretation of scriptural and allegorical writing, also called "the four levels of meaning." They are: (1) historical or literal, (2) allegorical, (3) moral, (4) anagogical. "Jerusalem is *literally* a city in Palestine, *allegorically* the Church, *morally* the believing soul, *anagogically* the heavenly Jerusalem."

Fourteen Points   A statement of American peace aims during World War I. It was made by President Woodrow WILSON in an address to Congress on January 8, 1918. The treaty of VERSAILLES, which ended the war, incorporated several of Wilson's points, including the covenant of the LEAGUE OF NATIONS.

fourth estate   An informal term for members of the press. Edmund BURKE, the English statesman, is credited with originating the term, reputedly having said, "Yonder [the Reporters' Gallery] sits the fourth estate, more important than them all." The three original estates, or groups of the community represented in government, are the Lords Spiritual (the clergy), the Lords Temporal (barons and knights), and the Commons.

Fowler, Henry Watson (1858–1933)   English lexicographer. With his brother F. G. Fowler (1870–1918), he wrote *The King's English* (1906). Fowler compiled a number of dictionaries based on the great *Oxford English Dictionary*. His most famous work is *A Dictionary of Modern English Usage* (1926), a remarkable compilation of learning, wit, humor, and good taste.

Fowles, John (1926–   )   English novelist and essayist. Fowles is a master of style who is known for his

narrative gifts, intelligence, and the textural density of his work. While at Oxford he was much influenced by the French existentialists. He went on to teach at the University of Poitiers for several years and then at a boys' school on the Greek island Spetsai. He is strongly influenced by French and Greek cultures, seeing in both an emphasis on simplicity of form and respect for nature and individual freedom. His first published novel, *The Collector* (1958), about a psychopathic butterfly collector and the girl he kidnaps, is both a brilliant tale of suspense and an allegory of a sick society. This was followed by *The Aristos* (1964), in which can be discerned the philosophical basis for much of his work, and then *The Magus* (1966), a complex philosophical novel set on a Greek island. *The French Lieutenant's Woman* (1969), a brilliant re-creation of a Victorian romance with contemporary twists, secured Fowles's international reputation. In 1977 he published *Daniel Martin*, the story of an English screenwriter's search for himself in his past. All of Fowles's fiction reveals the need for independent self-realization and a recognition of the role hazard plays in even the best-planned lives. Two of his subsequent novels are *Mantissa* (1982) and *A Maggot* (1985).

Fox, Charles James (1749–1806)   Celebrated English statesman and orator. Fox was a Tory member of Parliament at the age of twenty, and two years later became lord of the admiralty under Lord North. Removed from his post at the insistence of King George III, who disliked him both for his personal independence and for the dissoluteness of his life, Fox led the opposition to North's coercive measures against the American colonies. He was foreign secretary (1782–83), first under Rockingham and then in Portland's coalition ministry, the latter being turned out of office by the king's intervention against Fox's India reform bill. He was kept out of office by the king until 1806, when William Pitt the younger died and he again held the portfolio of foreign secretary in the so-called All-The-Talents ministry during the last year before his death. Fox once gave a toast: "Our Sovereign, the people." He urged abolition of slavery, favored the French Revolution, and objected to English participation in Continental wars. He loved literature and made one venture into authorship with *History of the Early Part of the Reign of James II*, which, unfinished, was published two years after his death.

Fox, George (1624–1691)   The founder of the Society of Friends, or QUAKERS. The son of a weaver, and an apprentice to a cobbler, he became an itinerant lay preacher. He was an unusual combination of a mystic and a highly practical man, a fact that led him to denounce social evils in forthright terms that nine times landed him in prison. Nevertheless, he was very widely respected and loved for his remarkable personal qualities. He traveled as a missionary to the West Indies and America, and to Holland and Germany. Beginning about 1650, many persons had been so attracted to his teachings that they were organized in the Society of Friends, who were nicknamed

Quakers. Because of his limited education, his writings were inelegantly though often effectively expressed.

Foxe, John (1516–1587)   English martyrologist. Educated at Oxford, Foxe was made a Deacon in 1550. He was exiled between 1554 and 1559, the years of the reign of the Catholic Mary I, during which time he wrote a first Latin draft of his great work on martyrs. A revised and longer version was published in English in 1563 as *Actes and Monuments of These Latter Perilous Days* (commonly known as *The Book of Martyrs*). Two volumes, enlarged further, appeared in 1570. The *Actes and Monuments* was tremendously influential, being used practically as a companion volume to the Bible in English churches and households for many years. The work is of interest historically for its many accounts of the deaths of contemporary Protestant martyrs.

Fragonard, Jean Honoré (1732–1806)   French painter. A versatile imitator of Antoine WATTEAU and Giambattista TIEPOLO, Fragonard painted and drew landscapes, mythological love scenes, and fashionable outdoor gatherings. With verve and charm, he extended the popularity of ROCOCO up to the time of the FRENCH REVOLUTION.

Fra Lippo Lippi (1855)   A poem in the form of a dramatic MONOLOGUE by Robert BROWNING. The painter, speaking to street guards of Florence who have come upon him in the midst of a night adventure, gives his biography and his views on life and art. See LIPPI, FRA LIPPO.

Frame [Clutha], Janet [Paterson] (1924–   ) New Zealand novelist, short-story writer, and poet. Frame is an idiosyncratic and original writer whose novels explore the tensions between the safe normalcy of daily life and the dangerous realms of madness, nightmare, and death. Her first novel, *Owls Do Cry* (1957), was highly praised for its originality, intricacy of form, and re-creation of New Zealand village life. In the subsequent novels *The Edge of the Alphabet* (1962), *Scented Gardens for the Blind* (1963), *The Rainbirds* (1968; U.S. *Yellow Flowers in the Antipodean Room*), and *Living in the Maniototo* (1979), Frame explores the possibilities of language while creating a world precariously balanced between illusion and reality. Frame's poems are published in *The Pocket Mirror* (1967).

France, Anatole (pen name of Jacques Anatole François Thibault, 1844–1924)   French novelist, poet, and critic. An eminently civilized man of letters, France occupied the chief position in the French literary world for many years. In the 1870s France published poetry. His career as a critic began in 1888, when he was appointed literary editor of *Le Temps*, a popular daily. His criticism is avowedly impressionistic and subjective, the imaginative play of a finely developed mind and cultivated sensibility responding to and revealing his world and age. Elected to the French Academy in 1896, he reached the peak of his fame at the turn of the century. By the time of his election he had published his famous novels THE CRIME OF SYLVES-TER BONNARD; *Thaïs* (1890), made into an opera by Massenet (1894); *La Rôtisserie de la reine Pédauque* (*At the Sign of the Reine Pédauque*, 1893), whose chief character is Jérôme COIGNARD; *Le Lys rouge* (*The Red Lily*, 1894); and a volume of short stories, *L'Etui de nacre* (*The Mother-of-Pearl Box*, 1892). Highly allusive in nature, France's subtle and ironic work displays an urbane cynicism and tolerant mockery. His style, like the tone of his writing, is sophisticated, delicate, and graceful. His later novels include PENGUIN ISLAND, *Les Dieux ont soif* (*The Gods Are Athirst*, 1912), and *La Révolte des anges* (*Revolt of the Angels*, 1914). *Histoire contemporaine* (1896–1901) is a collection of four satirical novels. France's autobiographical works include *Le Livre de mon ami* (*My Friend's Book*, 1885). The relaxed detachment of many of France's writings may be juxtaposed with his passionate interest in the Dreyfus case. France's character, like his career, is interesting for its many facets. He was awarded the NOBEL PRIZE in Literature in 1921.

France, rulers of   Like earlier members of his house, Pepin the Short ruled the domain of the Franks as mayor of the palace on behalf of the ineffectual MEROVINGIANS; the CAROLINGIAN dynasty began when Pepin set aside the last of the "do-nothing kings" and had himself crowned in 751. The monarchy was destroyed by the FRENCH REVOLUTION, and the first Republic established in 1792. NAPOLEON became Emperor in 1804. He was eventually defeated, and the monarchy was briefly restored, to be followed by the Second Republic in 1848, and a Second Empire in 1852. The Third Republic, established in 1852, continued until World War II. In 1940, France fell to Germany. The Vichy government of unoccupied France was a tool of the Germans. The Germans were finally expelled from France, and, after a provisional government, the Fourth Republic was officially proclaimed in 1946. It was undermined by the unpopular colonial war in Algeria, and in 1958 Charles de GAULLE proclaimed the Fifth Republic.

THE CAROLINGIANS

Pepin III (the Short)	751– 768
Charlemagne	768– 814
Louis I (the Pious)	814– 840
Charles II (the Bald)	840– 877
Louis II	877– 879
Louis III	879– 882
Carloman	882– 884
Charles III (the Fat)	884– 887
Eudes (Odo)	888– 898
Charles IV (the Simple)	898– 922
Robert I	922– 923
Rudolf	923– 936
Louis IV	936– 954
Lothair	954– 986
Louis V	986– 987

THE CAPETS

Hugh Capet	987– 996
Robert II	996–1031
Henry I	1031–1060
Philip I	1060–1108
Louis VI	1108–1137
Louis VII	1137–1180
Philip II (Augustus)	1180–1223
Louis VIII	1223–1226
Louis IX (St. Louis)	1226–1270
Philip III	1270–1285
Philip IV (the Fair)	1285–1314
Louis X (the Quarrelsome)	1314–1316
John I	1316
Philip V (the Tall)	1316–1322
Charles IV (the Fair)	1322–1328

HOUSE OF VALOIS

Philip VI	1328–1350
John II (the Good)	1350–1364
Charles V	1364–1380
Charles VI	1380–1422
Charles VII	1422–1461
Louis XI	1461–1483
Charles VIII	1483–1498
Louis XII	1498–1515
Francis I	1515–1547
Henry II	1547–1559
Francis II	1559–1560
Charles IX	1560–1574
Henry III	1574–1589

HOUSE OF BOURBON

Henry IV	1589–1610
Louis XIII	1610–1643
Louis XIV	1643–1715
Louis XV	1715–1774
Louis XVI	1774–1792

FIRST REPUBLIC

National Convention	1792–1795
Directory	1795–1799
Napoleon (Consul)	1799–1804

FIRST EMPIRE

Napoleon I	1804–1814

HOUSE OF BOURBON

Louis XVIII	1814–1824
Charles X	1824–1830

HOUSE OF ORLÉANS

Louis Philippe	1830–1848

SECOND REPUBLIC

Louis Napoleon	1848–1852

SECOND EMPIRE

Napoleon III	1852–1870

From the deposition of Napoleon III, France has been ruled by a succession of political presidents. Those worthy of note will be found listed under their own names.

Francesca, Piero della (real name Piero dei Franceschi, 1420?–1492)   Italian Renaissance painter and mathematician. Francesca came in contact with the monumental tradition of MASACCIO and the scientific studies of BRUNELLESCHI and ALBERTI during a stay in Florence. His own work, in which an almost abstract simplification of forms is fused with a sensitive observation of light effects, creates a world of great solidity, simplicity, and calm. He wrote two mathematical treatises, on perspective and on the five regular solids, and was the first to treat optics and perspective with a purely scientific method. Among his masterpieces are *The Legend of the Holy Cross*, a series of frescoes in the sanctuary of the church of St. Francis at Arezzo; the *Portrait of Federigo da Montefeltro*; *The Resurrection*; and the *Brera Madonna*, his last work.

Francis, Dick (1920–   )   English detective novelist. Francis began his career as a jockey and was the champion steeplechase rider of the 1953–54 season. Retiring in 1957, he turned first to racing journalism, then to mystery-thrillers with a racing background. Tough, knowledgeable, and well written, with a dash of violence and strong moral underpinnings, Francis's more than twenty books have long been best-sellers in England and have become so in the U.S. after the showing in 1980 of a television series based on his 1965 novel, *Odds Against*.

Francis I (1494–1547)   King of France (1515–47). After conquering Milan by his victory at Marignano (1515), Francis tried unsuccessfully to be elected Holy Roman Emperor and waged four wars against his victorious rival, Charles V, who advanced claims to the French duchy of Burgundy and also to Milan. The first war (1521–25) came to an end when Francis was defeated and taken prisoner at Pavia. In the second war (1527–29), he lost his hold on Italy by the treaty of peace signed at Cambrai for him by his mother, Louise of Savoy, and known as the *Paix des Dames*. The third war (1536–38) led to a truce. The fourth war (1542–44) was terminated with the peace of Crespy, which left Francis in possession of Burgundy while Charles retained Milan. Francis's reign is marked by the

Renaissance in France. He himself was a patron of the arts. His sister was the celebrated MARGARET OF NAVARRE.

Franciscans (also called Friars Minor, Minorites, and Grey Friars)   A Catholic religious order. It was founded by Saint FRANCIS OF ASSISI (1209) simply as a confraternity and approved informally by Pope Innocent III (1210). The members made vows of obedience, chastity, and a strict poverty permitting no possessions and dependent solely on the offerings of the faithful. Honorius III confirmed (1223) a new set of rules (including the requirement of a novitiate, etc.) for the now numerous order; but administrative struggles over the conviction of some that the order should be permitted to own the buildings it used and other necessaries eventually split the order (1415) into the Conventuals, following the modified rules, and the more traditional Observants. About 1528 even stricter reforms were instituted by a third branch, the Capuchins. About 1214 Francis had instituted a second order for nuns, called Poor Clares from their leader St. Clara; and about 1221 he organized the Brothers and Sisters of Penance as a third order of laymen, hence called Tertiaries. This important innovation was soon imitated by other religious orders.

Francis Ferdinand (1863–1914)   Archduke of Austria, nephew of FRANCIS JOSEPH I and heir to the imperial throne of Austria. His assassination at Sarajevo, Bosnia, by Gavrilo Princip, a member of a Serbian secret society, was the external cause of the outbreak of World War I.

Francis Joseph I (or Franz Josef, 1830–1916) Emperor of Austria (1848–1916). He succeeded to the throne upon the abdication of his uncle, Ferdinand I, during the revolution of 1848 in Vienna. Throughout his reign he opposed the forces of liberalism and maintained a traditional imperial court. There was much tragedy in his personal life: he was the brother of the ill-fated MAXIMILIAN of Mexico; his wife, Elizabeth, was assassinated in 1898; his only son, Rudolf, committed suicide; and the assassination of his nephew and heir, Archduke FRANCIS FERDINAND, precipitated World War I.

Francis of Assisi, St. (originally Giovanni Francesco Bernardone, 1181 or 1182–1226)   Italian monk, founder of the Order of FRANCISCANS. The son of a prosperous merchant, he turned at about twenty-six to a life of asceticism and mysticism, devoting himself to the care of the poor, the sick, and the leprous, as well as to prayer. Feeling a divine call to imitate Jesus' life and to preach, he gathered about him a small group of followers and drew up (1209) the rules of life for the monastic order called the Friars Minor, later known as the Franciscans. They journeyed to Rome in 1210 and received verbal confirmation from the Pope. Francis joined a pilgrimage to Palestine (1219–20), then resigned his leadership of the now numerous Friars Minor because of internal disputes about administration.

Francis's approach to religion was characterized by its joyousness and its love of nature; he called both animate

and inanimate creations his brothers and sisters, and his preaching to the birds has become a popular subject for artists, as has the episode when two years before his death he is said to have received on his body the *stigmata*, resembling Jesus' wounds, after forty days of fasting on Mount Alverno. He was canonized a saint in 1228, two years after his death; and about a century later the legends and anecdotes about his life, along with his sermons and sayings, were collected as the *Fioretti di S. Francesco d'Assisi* (*Little Flowers of St. Francis*).

Franck, César Auguste (1822–1890)   Belgian-French organist and composer. Franck lived in Paris at a time when audiences almost exclusively patronized opera; consequently his work was largely ignored during his lifetime. Franck's style is romantic and expansive, full of chromatic harmony and modulation. His reputation rests on relatively few pieces, most of which were written after he was fifty years old, such as the *Symphonic Variations* for piano and orchestra (1885), the violin sonata (1886), and *Symphony in D Minor* (1889). He exerted great influence as a teacher.

Franco-Prussian War (also known as the Franco-German War)   A war (1870–71) between France, then ruled by NAPOLEON III, and Prussia, whose prime minister at the time was Otto von Bismarck. Relations between the two powers deteriorated when Bismarck supported the candidacy of Prince Leopold Hohenzollern-Sigmaringen, a relative of King William of Prussia, to the vacant throne of Spain. Prince Leopold eventually withdrew, but Bismarck, who wanted war, edited the famous Ems Telegram describing an interview between William and the French ambassador in such a way as to make it seem that the king had insulted France, which retaliated by declaring war on July 19, 1870. The French were overwhelmed by the well-trained, well-organized Prussian forces, and a large part of the French army and Napoleon himself were forced to surrender at Sedan. A republic was then proclaimed in Paris, which was besieged by the Prussians and capitulated on January 28, 1871. By the treaty of Frankfurt, France lost the provinces of Alsace and Lorraine and agreed to pay an indemnity of five billion francs; an army of occupation would remain in France until the indemnity was paid. Bismarck used the victory to complete German unification, and after the states of Bavaria, Baden, and Württemberg had joined the German Confederation, King William was proclaimed German emperor on January 18, 1871, in the Hall of Mirrors at Versailles.

Frank, Anne (1929–1944)   German-Jewish girl who hid from the Nazis with her parents, their friends, and some other fugitives in an Amsterdam warehouse from 1942 to 1944. Her diary, covering the years of hiding, was found by friends and published as *Het achterhus* (1947); it was later published in English as *The Diary of a Young Girl* (1952). Against the background of the mass murder of European Jewry, the book presents an impressive picture of a group of hunted people forced to live together in almost intolerable proximity. Written with humor as well as insight, it shows a growing girl with all the preoccupations of adolescence and first love. The diary ends three days before the Franks and their group were discovered by the Nazis. Anne died in the extermination camp at Bergen-Belsen in 1944. A dramatization of the book, *The Diary of Anne Frank*, was shown the world over on the stage and as a motion picture.

Frankenstein, or the Modern Prometheus

(1818)   A romance by Mary Wollstonecraft SHELLEY. Frankenstein, a young student, animates a soulless monster made out of corpses from churchyards and dissecting rooms by means of galvanism. Longing for sympathy and shunned by everyone, the creature ultimately turns to evil and brings dreadful retribution on the student for usurping the Creator's prerogative, finally destroying him. Several movies have been based on the novel. Shelley gave no name to the monster, but he is commonly called Frankenstein after his creator, the student. This, of course, is an error.

Frankfurter, Felix (1882–1965)   Austrian-born American jurist and teacher. After a brief career practicing law, Frankfurter taught at Harvard Law School (1914–39) and engaged in various governmental pursuits until his appointment to the U.S. Supreme Court (1939–62). He wrote many legal textbooks as well as *The Case of Sacco and Vanzetti* (1927), *The Public and Its Government* (1930), *Mr. Justice Holmes and the Supreme Court* (1939), and *Law and Men* (1956). *Felix Frankfurter Reminisces*, edited by Harlan B. Phillips, appeared in 1960.

Franklin, Benjamin (1706–1790)   American statesman, author, inventor, printer, and scientist, sometimes called "the wisest American." The son of a Boston tallow chandler, Franklin was apprenticed at twelve to his brother James, a local printer, to whose newspaper he contributed a series of Addisonian essays, the *Dogood Papers* (1722). In 1723 he ran away to Philadelphia, where he set up his own newspaper, published POOR RICHARD'S ALMANACK, and with intense energy established a subscription library, a philosophical society, a fire company, a hospital, a militia, became postmaster of Philadelphia, proposed the University of Pennsylvania, devised bifocal spectacles, a stove, and a water-harmonica. He later performed electrical experiments, leading in 1752 to his invention of the lightning rod, which earned him election to the Royal Society in London, the compliments of Louis XV of France, and several honorary degrees. Active for the colonies throughout the Revolution, he helped draft and was a signer of the Declaration of Independence. He concluded an alliance with France (1778) and was one of the diplomats to negotiate the treaty of peace with Great Britain (1783). In 1787 he attended the Federal Constitutional Convention. His AUTOBIOGRAPHY is considered one of the classics of the genre.

Franklin, [Stella Maria] Miles (1879–1954) Australian novelist. Franklin's ancestry goes back to the first settling of Australia, in 1788. She won early celebrity with her first novel, *My Brilliant Career*, written when she was sixteen, and published, with the help of Henry LAWSON, in 1901. She later came to detest the book, and it was withheld from print for sixty-five years, republished in Australia twelve years after her death and again in 1980. She is best known for novels that epitomize the pastoral age of her country, particularly *All That Swagger* (1936), which chronicles the struggles of an Irish family in Australia from the early settlement to World War I. Many of her first novels on Australian pioneering were published under the pseudonym Brent of Bin Bin. In her will she established an annual prize for the best Australian novel, known as the Miles Franklin Award.

Franklin's Tale, The   One of THE CANTERBURY TALES of Chaucer. Apparently it is based on a tale in Boccaccio's IL FILOCOLO and similar to his tale *Garden in January* in the DECAMERON, although Chaucer attributes it to a Breton LAI. The Franklin opposes the views in THE WIFE OF BATH'S TALE, saying that love flies when constrained by sovereignty. In his tale, Dorigen accepts her husband, Arveragus (or Arviragus), as her servant in love but her lord in marriage. When Arveragus goes off to war, she refuses the advances of the squire Aurelius, playfully promising that she will be his when he removes all the rocks from the coast of Brittany. Arveragus returns, and Aurelius pines until a magician succeeds in making it appear that the rocks have disappeared. Aurelius reminds Dorigen of her promise. She decides she should rather kill herself than dishonor her marriage; but when Arveragus learns the story, he says she must keep her promise, and sends her to meet Aurelius. The squire meets this display of nobility by releasing her from her promise, and the magician, not to be outdone, releases the squire from his one-thousand-pound debt, since the magic did not achieve its purpose.

Fraser, Lady Antonia (1932–   )   English biographer. Her sweeping historical biographies include *Mary, Queen of Scots* (1969), *Oliver Cromwell* (1973), *King James I of England* (1974), and *Charles II* (1979). Based on painstaking research, her books are subtle studies of human beings caught in the crosscurrents of history. *The Weaker Vessel: Women's Lot in Seventeenth Century England* (1984) was enthusiastically received and won several awards. She also writes contemporary mystery novels. Lady Antonia married the playwright Harold PINTER in 1980.

Fraser, G[eorge] S[utherland] (1915–1980) Scottish poet and critic. A kingpin in the short-lived NEW APOCALYPSE movement of the 1940s, Fraser wrote carefully wrought lyrical poetry on personal themes. He is as well known for his critical writings, notably *The Modern Writer and His World* (1951; rev 1964) and *Vision and Rhetoric* (1968), and his studies of Ezra Pound (1960) and Lawrence Durrell (1970).

Frayn, Michael (1933–   )   English journalist, novelist, and playwright. In his novels Frayn has turned his offbeat satirical humor on computers in *The Tin Men* (1965), on espionage in *The Russian Interpreter* (1966), and on journalism in *Towards the End of the Morning* (1967; U.S. *Against Entropy*). A *Very Private Life* (1968) and *Sweet Dreams* (1974) are both fantasies, each fable making its moral point with a light, sardonic touch. Frayn's plays, typically compounded of fast dialogue and absurd situations in spare settings, include *Alphabetical Order* (1973), *Clouds* (1976), *Make and Break* (1980), *Noises Off* (1982), and *Benefactors* (1985). Several of his translations, including *The Cherry Orchard* (1978), *The Fruits of Enlightenment* (1979), and *Wild Honey* (1984), have been produced by the National Theatre of Great Britain.

Frazer, Sir James George (1854–1941)   Scottish scholar and anthropologist. He is best known for his famous work THE GOLDEN BOUGH, which is noted for its important contributions to the study of early religion and anthropology. Other works include *Totemism* (1887), *Folklore in the Old Testament* (1918), and numerous translations of such classical writers as Ovid, Pausanias, and Apollodorus.

Frechette, Louis [Honoré] (1839–1908)   Canadian poet and journalist. Generally regarded as the greatest French Canadian poet of the 19th century, Frechette is best known for *La Légende d'un peuple* (1887), a series of epic poems inspired by the leading events and personages in French Canadian history. In 1880 he became the first Canadian to be honored by the ACADÉMIE FRANÇAISE for his poetic works *Les Fleurs boréales* (1879) and *Les Oiseaux de neige* (1880). He was also Canada's first poet laureate.

Frederick II (known as Frederick the Great, 1712–1786)   King of Prussia (1740–86). He was an enlightened despot who built up the Prussian state through vast territorial acquisitions and domestic reforms. An enthusiastic amateur of music, he composed and played chamber music. He was a patron of the arts and a friend of VOLTAIRE. He wrote voluminously, almost always in French. He built the palace of Sans Souci (1747) near Potsdam. During his later years he was known as *der alte Fritz* ("Old Fritz").

Freeling, Nicolas (1927–   )   English mystery writer. Freeling's books are distinguished by detailed characterizations and subtle perceptions of human nature. He created his best-known character, the Dutch police inspector Piet Van der Valk, in *Love in Amsterdam* (1961), featured him in subsequent novels, then killed him off in *A Long Silence* (1971; U.S. *Auprès de Ma Blonde*) and concentrated on novels which attempt to combine serious fiction with elements of mystery and suspense.

Freeman, Richard Austin (1862–1943)   English surgeon and detective-story writer. Freeman's detective hero is the physician Dr. John Thorndyke, and he is noted for his precisely detailed plots.

Freemasons   The largest secret fraternal organization in the world. It claims, without basis, to trace its origins to Hiram of Tyre and the Temple of Solomon. The modern fraternity had its origin in England in the 18th century, and its connection with masons, the workers in stone, arises from the fact that the founders adopted many of the practices of the old masonic guilds as being suitable to their purpose. These medieval guilds consisted of workmen who, by the nature of their calling, had to move from place to place, and their secret passwords and other rituals were adopted so that when on their travels they could prove without difficulty that they were actually Free and Accepted Masons, and so secure the comradeship of their brother masons as well as get employment. In each district where cathedrals and churches were being built, lodges were created, much as a branch of a trade union would be today, and these had their masters, wardens, and other officials.

free verse (Fr, *vers libre*)   Poetry that uses natural rhythmic cadences, recurrent image patterns, and stressed and unstressed syllables rather than any set metrical scheme. It may be rhymed or unrhymed. Free verse is used in the PSALMS and THE SONG OF SOLOMON in the King James BIBLE. Milton experimented with the form in LYCIDAS and in SAMSON AGONISTES. The French SYMBOLISTS did a great deal to popularize free verse in France, as did Arno HOLZ in Germany and Walt WHITMAN in America. These lines from SONG OF MYSELF are typical of modern free verse:

> I celebrate myself, and sing myself,
> And what I assume you shall assume;
> For every atom belonging to me, as good belongs to you.
>
> I loafe and invite my Soul;
> I lean and loafe at my ease, observing a spear of summer grass.

Freiligrath, Ferdinand (1810–1876)   German liberal political poet, a revolutionary during the 1840s and later a strong admirer of Bismarck. Freiligrath's most famous volume is his *Glaubensbekenntnis* (*Declaration of Faith*, 1842), which led to his break with the Prussian government.

Freischutz (Ger, "free-shooter")   Legendary marksman popular in German folklore of the 14th to 16th centuries. The Devil gives Freischutz seven bullets, six of which will infallibly hit what the marksman aims at, but the last will be directed by the Devil. The account in Apel's *Gespensterbuch* (*Book of Ghosts*, 1810–15) suggested WEBER's opera *Der Freischutz* (1821), libretto by Friedrich Kind (1768–1843). The woodsman Max must win a sharpshooting contest to win the hand of Agathe. Because his marksmanship is not perfect, he allows his colleague Caspar, already a servant of the Devil, to arrange for him to make a pact with the Black Huntsman for the magic bullets. The seventh shot, aimed at a dove, would have killed Agathe, but her bridal wreath deflects it, and Caspar dies instead.

Freki   See ODIN.

Frémont, John C[harles] (1813–1890)   American explorer, soldier, and politician. Frémont, an officer in the U.S. Topographical Corps, made three important expeditions to the Far West, and his *Report of the Exploring Expedition to the Rocky Mountains* (1843), which he wrote with the help of his wife, Jessie, was widely read. During the Mexican War, he played a controversial role in the conquest of California; he was later found guilty of mutiny and disobedience by a court-martial, and although President Polk remitted his sentence, he resigned from the army. In 1856 he ran for the presidency on the antislavery platform of the newly formed Republican Party. After the outbreak of the Civil War, Frémont was given a command in the Department of the West, but was removed because of his radical antislavery policies. From 1878 to 1883 he was territorial governor of Arizona. Irving STONE's *Immortal Wife* (1944) is a biographical novel about the Frémonts.

French and Indian War   The last, most decisive conflict in the 150 years' struggle between France and England for possession of the North American continent. It was the American phase of the SEVEN YEARS' WAR. It began in 1754 and ended with the cession of Canada to Great Britain in the Treaty of Paris (1763).

French Renaissance   The French Renaissance roughly encompasses the 16th century.

Fervor for the Italian Renaissance took hold of the French court following the military campaigns of Charles VIII, Louis XII, and FRANCIS I in Italy. As traffic between Italy and France increased, French art, architecture, and most particularly literature felt the effects. Clément MAROT introduced the Italian sonnet into French poetry. Queen MARGARET OF NAVARRE wrote the first collection of French tales modeled on the DECAMERON of Boccaccio. However, the Italian influence in this period was more intellectual than artistic. French writers developed a new critical spirit and moral sense from reading Greek and Latin literature, which had been rediscovered in Italy. They were humanists, interested in the full development and enjoyment of man's capacities, and they cultivated a taste for the refinements of Italian Renaissance society.

The influence from the south affected particularly the scholars. It was characterized by a philosophical questioning of the long-entrenched dogmas of the Church. French scholars became avid for knowledge as the old taboos fell and the flood of printed matter opened up formerly neglected fields of learning. Francis I engaged Guillaume Budé as his librarian and, at Budé's instigation, founded the COLLÈGE DE FRANCE, where Greek and Hebrew were taught for the first time. The Collège soon became a rallying point for the "Evangelists," those who sought the basis

for faith in the Scriptures themselves, rather than in papal bulls and church decrees.

The two currents of new ideas from the north and from the south merged in the short-lived marriage between humanism and Evangelism which marks the first flowering of the French Renaissance around 1530. The writers of this period shared in differing degrees the general excitement, and all participated in the burst of intense optimism, feverish activity, and exaltation. François RABELAIS emerges as the most important literary figure of the period. Although his GARGANTUA AND PANTAGRUEL is largely a continuation of the medieval fabliaux in form, it fairly breathes the new spirit in its rich multilingual vocabulary and its sheer amassing of detail in every field of knowledge.

The second half of the century saw a distinct change in the tenor of the French Renaissance. The glorious reign of Francis I was followed by the rule of four ineffective kings (Henry II, Francis II, Charles IX, and Henry III), the last three more or less subservient to their mother, CATHERINE DE MÉDICIS. After the publication of John CALVIN's *Institutes* in French in 1541, the happy alliance between humanism and Evangelism was irrevocably ruptured. The early Evangelists were succeeded by militant Protestant reformers who not only challenged Roman Catholicism, but menaced the very basis of French royal authority as well, thereby losing its protection. Henceforth, the Protestant Reformation and humanism went their separate ways. The universal exuberance of the first humanism gave way to a notion of a distinctly French art nourished by Italian and classical example but proudly asserting French genius in the French language. Joachim DU BELLAY gave the clarion call of this new artistic consciousness with his DÉFENSE ET ILLUSTRATION DE LA LANGUE FRANÇAISE in 1549. The *Défense* signaled the formation of the PLÉIADE, a group of poets led by Pierre de RONSARD, whose mission was to raise French poetry to the eminence of Italian and ancient poetry. A parallel group of poets at Lyons, headed by Maurice SCÈVE and Louise LABÉ, had no declared mission, but its poetry was so personal in tone that it too contributed to the liberation of the French literary idiom.

Meanwhile, the rise of Protestantism led to civil war. The country became a bloody battleground of the contending Protestant and Catholic ideologies. Eventually these wars produced their own poets, notably the impassioned Agrippa d'Aubigné (1552–1630). His narrative poem *Les Tragiques* (1616), recounting the horrors suffered by the Protestant martyrs and the divine retribution to come, introduced into French literature the visions of a soul possessed.

The end of the century saw the birth of a new spirit, which was to develop into the classicism of the 17th century. Primitive attempts at a new drama distinct from the popular mystery plays and passion plays of the Middle Ages produced the tragi-comedies of Robert GARNIER, from which Corneille would later draw inspiration. The political chaos resulting from the religious wars brought the realization that national stability depended upon a strong central government free from religious ideology. King HENRY IV established absolute rule, which LOUIS XIV was later to consolidate. The great literary figure of the period was Michel de MONTAIGNE, friend and unofficial counselor to Henry IV. In his ESSAYS, a genre which he invented, Montaigne reflected the general disillusionment over the first period of humanistic optimism and over the ensuing bloody conflicts of the religious wars. He called for a rejection of ideologies in the interest of the first priority, man himself. His greatest concern was the requirements imposed by human nature for its proper development. To learn these requirements nothing less was needed than a rigorous search for the lessons of individual experience. In turning inward to study human psychology as the source of knowledge, Montaigne gave a new and modern meaning to the term "humanism," which extended beyond France to affect all of Europe. He was the great precursor of the ideal *honnête homme* of the 17th century.

French Revolution   The world-famous revolution in France of the THIRD ESTATE against the clergy and nobility, which formally began in May 1789, and ended in December 1799, with NAPOLEON's dictatorship. Until this time, France had been a monarchy with two privileged classes: the nobility and the clergy. Under this old order there was no place for either the new class of economically independent bourgeois or the new class of industrial workers. They, as well as the peasants, bore the brunt of excessive spending on the part of the nobility. Heavy taxes, *corvées* (obligatory services to the king), military service, backward agricultural methods, and internal tariff barriers —all medieval feudal institutions still existing in 18th-century France—were also contributory causes to the revolution; they had been systematically attacked by the major writers of this Age of Reason, particularly by the PHYSIOCRATS. The badly needed economic reform which these latter advocated failed because of the unwillingness of the ruling classes to relinquish any of their privileges. France's national debt was also increased by her participation (which she could ill afford) in the AMERICAN REVOLUTION. On May 5, 1789, the States-General (the assembly of the three Estates of the Realm) was convoked by LOUIS XVI and NECKER in an effort to obtain a general fiscal reform. The third estate, constituting a majority against the ruling classes, defiantly proclaimed itself the National Assembly on June 17, and later, when Louis XVI closed their meeting place, adjourned to an indoor tennis court and took the OATH OF THE TENNIS COURT. The king, on June 27, yielded and legalized this assembly, but at the same time dismissed Necker, at MARIE ANTOINETTE's insistence, and surrounded Versailles with his troops. On July 14 a Paris mob, led by pamphleteer Camille Desmoulins, stormed the Bastille. Louis then recalled Necker and recognized the legal existence of the Constituent Assembly (as the new

National Assembly was called). The Assembly adopted the DECLARATION OF THE RIGHTS OF MAN, proclaiming the fundamental principles of the revolution, and drafted a new constitution creating a limited monarchy. In addition, church lands were nationalized and religious orders suppressed. Meanwhile, radical political clubs, especially the JACOBINS, were gaining power in Paris.

Louis XVI finally accepted the constitution and on October 1, 1791, a new Legislative Assembly was convened. In the same year Louis tried to flee France, as many nobles had already done, but was brought back a prisoner to Paris. The Legislative Assembly consisted of members of various political clubs, more or less radical, like the Feuillants and the CORDELIERS. During this era some of the leaders of the revolution wore the *Bonnet Rouge* ("red cap") of liberty, and "Liberty, Equality, and Fraternity" was their motto. At first, foreign governments were sympathetic to the revolution, but because both the king and French émigrés were inciting European monarchs to intervene on behalf of French royalty, they began to be frightened by the progress of the lower classes. Austria and Prussia issued threats, and on April 20, 1792, war was declared on Austria; three months later Prussia declared war on France. This war began the succession of foreign wars which in turn led to the Napoleonic Wars. The repeated defeats of the Revolutionary armies were attributed to Royalist treason, and on September 2 and 3, 1792, the people invaded the prisons and massacred twelve hundred prisoners (the September Massacres). In Paris, the National Convention, headed by MARAT and DANTON, succeeded the Legislative Assembly, and its first act was to abolish the monarchy; the king was tried for treason and beheaded on January 21, 1793. The Convention tried to continue the war, which by now included England, Spain, and most of the other European countries, but it was torn by internal dissension among the GIRONDISTS, the Montagnards, and the Cordeliers. The Convention established the COMMITTEE OF PUBLIC SAFETY, which ruled France. ROBESPIERRE, now in control of the Jacobins, joined the Committee at the insistence of SAINT-JUST and, as its leader, established a virtual dictatorship. The period following is known as the REIGN OF TERROR, which, because of its excesses, was eliminated by the Convention's coup of 9 THERMIDOR. Once Robespierre was executed, a period of reaction set in, and a new constitution (1795) set up the DIRECTORY. The incompetence, corruption, and intrigues of the Directory and the military reverses of the army brought France to the brink of disaster. Napoleon Bonaparte, hero of the Italian Campaign, returned from Egypt and, with the help of the army and his supporters, overthrew the Directory on 18 Brumaire, and established the Consulate. He was the ruler of France until 1814, when the Bourbon kings were restored to power.

French Revolution, The (1837)   A history in three parts by Thomas CARLYLE. Critics have preferred to call it a drama or a prose epic rather than a history. The central motif is the nemesis that follows upon the oppression of the poor. The work established Carlyle's reputation as a historian and remains widely read to this day.

Freneau, Philip [Morin] (1752–1832) American poet. One of the first American poets to achieve renown for his verse in the U.S., Freneau is best known for his political poems, most of them written at the time of the American Revolution: *A Poem on the Rising Glory of America* (1772), written in collaboration with Hugh Henry BRACK-ENRIDGE on their graduation from Princeton; *American Liberty* (1775); *General Gage's Confession* (1775); and *The British Prison-Ship* (1781), an account of his experiences as a prisoner of war after capture at sea near the West Indies. His poems on nature and on the Indian, considered precursors of the romantic movement in America, include: "The Wild Honey Suckle" (1786), "The Indian Burying Ground" (1788), and "On a Honey-Bee Drinking from a Glass of Wine" (1809).

Freneau was anti-Federalist in his politics and a deist in religion. Admired by JEFFERSON, he edited the *National Gazette* from 1791 to 1793, in which he attacked Alexander HAMILTON.

Freud, Sigmund (1856–1939) Austrian psychiatrist, the originator of psychoanalysis. Freud was trained as a medical doctor at the University of Vienna. He graduated in 1881 but never practiced internal medicine. He soon became interested in neuropathology and studied hypnotism and cerebral anatomy.

He became dissatisfied with hypnotism as a treatment for hysterical patients. However, he had noticed that some patients had fallen into reveries in which they had talked about their problems and afterwards had felt better. From these observations he began to formulate his theory of "free association," which is the kernel of psychoanalysis. In Freudian practice, patients under the guidance of an analyst attempt to recall emotional episodes that aggravated conflicts, and thus recognize and release frustrated emotions. Freud used dream interpretation as one of his basic tools in analysis. The patient's dreams were analyzed for their symbolic content and were used as a guide to the patient's internal life. Freud viewed dreams as a person's means of expressing repressed emotions, and repression was seen as the source of neurotic behavior.

Freud postulated the existence of three internal forces that govern a person's psychic life: (1) the *id*, the instinctual force of life—unconscious, uncontrollable, and isolated; (2) the *ego*, the executive force that has contact with the real world; (3) the *super-ego*, the governing force, or moral conscience, that seeks to control and direct the ego into socially acceptable patterns of behavior.

As his theories began to take concrete form, Freud started to publish his findings. *The Interpretation of Dreams* (1900) was one of the first reports on his independent studies of the subconscious. By this time his work had begun to attract attention outside his native Vienna, and

others took up his cause. In 1908 the first International Congress of Psychoanalysis met in Vienna. Many young doctors, some of them now famous in their own right, attended this meeting; among them were Alfred ADLER, A. A. Brill, Ernest Jones, and Carl JUNG.

From the beginning the very nature of his work made Freud the center of controversy. His theories about sex have been, in general, misunderstood by the public and in varying degrees rejected by many of his followers. Freud maintained that the primary motivating factor in human psychology and human behavior is sexual, but he did not limit this to its purely erotic connotations. The sexual instinct, or libido, as Freud saw it, has many of the aspects ordinarily referred to as "social." He found elements of strong sexuality among children and ascribed most neuroses to the repressive influence of social and individual inhibitions on sex.

Although many of Freud's ideas have been superseded, he is still considered the great innovator in the field of psychiatry. The work of only one other man in this century, Albert EINSTEIN, has had as great an impact on man's way of thinking and acting. Freud's influence has been especially strong on artistic expression, both the fine arts and literature. Such authors as Thomas MANN and James JOYCE embodied much of his thought in their works.

Among Freud's important works are *Three Contributions to the Theory of Sex* (1910), *Wit and Its Relation to the Unconscious* (1916), *Leonardo da Vinci: A Psychosexual Study of an Infantile Reminiscence* (1916), *Totem and Taboo* (1918), *The Ego and the Id* (1927), and *Moses and Monotheism* (1939).

Freud, a Jew, was forced to flee from the Nazis in 1938. He and his family moved to England, where he died, an honored and respected man.

Frey (or Freyr) The Scandinavian god of peace and fertility, the dispenser of rain, and the patron god of Sweden and Iceland. The son of NIÖRD and husband of Gerda, Frey was originally one of the VANIR but was received among the AESIR after the war between the two. Among his treasures was a magic ship, *Skithbathnir*, which could be folded up like a tent; a golden helmet with the crest of a wild boar, *Gullinbursti*; and his horse, *Blodighofi* ("Bloody Hoof").

Freya The Norse goddess of love, fecundity, and death. Freya was the wife of ODIN, but he deserted her for FRIGGA because Freya loved finery more than her husband. One account says that she flies through the air with the wings of a falcon, another that she rides in a chariot drawn by two cats. The chief legends concerning Freya relate the efforts of the giants to carry her off. In one instance THOR, dressed as a veiled bride, impersonates Freya in order to recover his hammer from the giant Thrym.

Freya is also known as *Frea, Frija, Frigg, Frige*, and the like, and it is from her that Friday is named. In Teutonic mythology, Freya and Frigga are the same.

Freyre, Gilberto [De Mello] (1900–) Brazilian sociologist, anthropologist, and social historian. Freyre is best known for *Casa grande e senzala* (1933; tr *The Masters and the Slaves: A Study in the Development of Brazilian Civilization*, 1946) and *Sobrados e mucambos* (1936; tr *The Mansions and the Shanties*, 1963), brilliant studies of Brazilian patriarchal society from the 16th to the 19th centuries. In these and later books, notably *Brazil: An Interpretation* (1945), he defends the position that the fusion of diverse ethnic and cultural elements—Portuguese, Amerindian, and African—has resulted in a distinctively Brazilian civilization. A sampling of his best work is available in English in *A Gilberto Freyre Reader* (1974).

Freytag, Gustav (1816–1895) German novelist and playwright, known for his detailed realism in both style and choice of subject matter. Freytag was a political liberal and was strongly interested in the problems of his day, as is seen in his comedy *Die Journalisten* (*The Journalists*, 1854), which deals with international politics, and his novel *Soll und Haben* (*Should and Have*, 1855) about commercialism. But he always attempted to see his own time in the light of the past, as in *Die Ahnen* (*The Ancestors*, 1873–80), a series of six novels covering most of German history, and *Bilder aus deutscher Vergangenheit* (*Scenes from the German Past*, 1859 et seq), a historical study.

friar (fr Lat, *frater*, "brother") A monk, especially one belonging to one of the four great mendicant orders: FRANCISCANS, DOMINICANS, Augustinians, and CARMELITES.

Friar John An anglicism for Frère Jean des Entommeures (Fr, *entamer*, "to carve the first slice," hence Friar John of the Hearty Eaters or Trenchermen), a major character in Rabelais's GARGANTUA AND PANTAGRUEL. As Gargantua's comrade in arms in Book I, he is the hero of the war against PICROCHOLE. At the end of the war Gargantua gives him the abbey of THÉLÈME as a reward for his bravery. Friar John has all the faults of monks but none of their vices. Ignorant, unclean, and gluttonous, he is also frank, lusty, and courageous. Rabelais clearly had great affection for Friar John and created in him one of his most picturesque characters.

Friar's Tale, The One of THE CANTERBURY TALES of Chaucer. The Friar and the Summoner reveal their enmity, and the Summoner promises to retaliate after the Friar tells his tale. The Friar describes an extremely lewd and dishonest summoner who meets the Devil disguised as a bailiff. The two swear friendship and gossip about their respective techniques of extortion. They pass a carter cursing his horse and cart and hay for being stuck in the mud, his words consigning them to the Devil. But the Devil explains to the Summoner that he cannot take them because the carter does not really mean the curse. Then the Summoner decides to extort money from an innocent woman by threatening her with a summons to the archdea-con for adultery. He ignores her words that send him to the Devil, but the Devil ascertains that she really means them, and gleefully carries the Summoner off to Hell.

Friar Tuck A fat, jovial vagabond friar in the ROBIN HOOD ballads and a character in the May-day plays. His costume consists of a russet habit of the Franciscan order, a red corded girdle with gold tassel, red stockings, and a wallet. He appears in Sir Walter Scott's novel IVANHOE as the "holy clerk of Copmanhurst."

Friday The sixth day of the week. It is named for the goddess FREYA. In the Romance languages it is named for the corresponding Roman goddess VENUS. Friday is traditionally the day when Adam was created, when he was expelled from Paradise, when he repented, when he died, when Jesus was crucified, when the dead will rise for the last judgment. In many Christian churches Friday is a fast day. To spill salt on Friday is a bad omen. It used to be the day for the execution of capital punishment and is often called hangman's day.

Friedman, Bruce Jay (1930–) American novelist, playwright, and short-story writer. Friedman's fiction and plays revolve around themes of ethnic paranoia, sexual neurosis, and strained family relations treated with wry and ribald humor. His first novel, *Stern* (1962), features a caricature of a bungling suburban Jew filled with paranoid delusions about anti-Semitic neighbors. From the son of the domineering mother in *A Mother's Kisses* (1964) to the screenwriter hero of *About Harry Towns* (1975), Friedman's characters are lonely, guilt-ridden victims in a hostile society.

Friend of the Family, The (*Selo Stepanchikovo*, 1859; also tr as *The Village of Stepanchikovo*) A short novel by DOSTOYEVSKY. It portrays the horrible spectacle of a petty and talentless ex-toady, Foma Fomich Opsikin, who rules a household by playing on the guilt feelings he induces in the master of the house. Foma, with his immense aptitude for hypocritical self-righteousness, is a sort of Russian TARTUFFE.

Frigga (or Frigg) The supreme Norse goddess of ASGARD, and wife of ODIN. Frigga presided over marriages and may be identified with the Roman JUNO. In Teutonic mythology, she is identified with FREYA.

Frisch, Max (1911–) Swiss playwright, novelist, and dramatist. Frisch was the youngest son of an architect. His university education in German philology was interrupted by the death of his father. When he took up his studies again he switched to architecture, and has since divided his time between architecture and writing.

Frisch's first major play on war and its destructive aspects was *Nun singen sie wieder* (*Now They're Singing Again*, 1945). This was followed by more sophisticated and complex variations on the same theme: *Santa Cruz* (1944), *Die chinesische Mauer* (1946; tr *The Great Wall of China*, 1969), *Als der Krieg zu Ende war* (1949; tr *When the War Was Over*, 1967), *Graf Öderland* (1951; tr *Count Oeder-*

land, 1962), and *Don Juan oder die Liebe zur Geometrie* (1953; tr *Don Juan or the Love of Geometry*, 1967). Later plays, notably *Biedermann und die Brandstifter* (1958; tr *The Firebugs*, 1963), *Andorra* (1960; tr 1964), and *Triptychon* (1978), take up issues such as corruption, fear, the decay of moral standards, and race prejudice, specifically anti-Semitism.

More recently, Frisch has increasingly concentrated on narrative prose, beginning with *Stiller* (1954; tr *I'm Not Stiller*, 1958); *Homo Faber* (1957; tr 1959), a short novel that plays on the Oedipus theme; and *Mein Name sei Gantenbein* (1964; tr *A Wilderness of Mirrors*, 1965), a novel in which the author attempts to capture what he calls the "purely fictional" by relinquishing the author's traditional omniscient stance and thereby indicating latent possibilities for every situation rather than actual happenings. Frisch's works continue to reflect his preoccupation with the individual's struggle to retain control over his own life and to find a measure of happiness in his private world.

Frobisher, Sir Martin (1535?–1594)   English navigator. Frobisher led three expeditions in search of the Northwest Passage from 1576 to 1578 and discovered Frobisher Bay. He commanded the *Triumph* against the Spanish Armada, was vice-admiral under Sir Francis DRAKE in his expedition to the West Indies (1586), and vice-admiral in Sir John Hawkins's expedition to the Portuguese coast in 1590.

Fröding, Gustaf (1860–1911)   Swedish poet, writer of lyric and religious verse. Fröding's first collection of poems, *Guitarr och dragharmonika* (1891), revealed his unique poetic blend of irony, melancholy, and humor. Other early collections were *Nya dikter* (1894) and *Stänk och flikar* (1896). The poem "En morgondrom" in the latter volume was called pornographic and led to a court case. Acquitted, but shaken and deeply disturbed, Fröding suffered a mental breakdown and was confined to an asylum in 1898. Although he later left the asylum, the remaining years of his life were marked by ill health. *Gralstänk* (1898) contains a series of religious poems that express a faith in the divinity of all things.

Frogs, The (Batrachoi, 405 BC)   A comedy by ARISTOPHANES. In it, DIONYSUS, the patron· of the drama, having grown weary of the lack of inspiring dramatists in Athens, decides to go down to HADES to bring back EURIPIDES. Knowing that HERACLES has already been there, he borrows his famous lion skin as a disguise and sets off with his slave Xanthias. When he arrives in Hades, he discovers that Heracles, who had once stolen the guardian dog CERBERUS, is not popular there, and hastily changes costume with Xanthias. After further confusion over which of the two is actually Dionysus, the god finds Euripides. However, having listened to an argument between him and his rival playwright AESCHYLUS, he decides to return to earth with Aeschylus instead, because he is the weightier playwright. Besides being a charming comedy, the play is a striking

example of the freedom of speech allowed the writer of OLD COMEDY. Dionysus is made an absurd figure, though he was the patron of the festivals at which the comedy was performed.

Froissart, Jean (1337?–?1410)   French poet and historian. Froissart enjoyed the patronage of Queen Philippa of England from 1361 until her death in 1369, and then the protection of two French noblemen. He traveled widely throughout Western Europe seeking firsthand accounts of the events of the HUNDRED YEARS' WAR. His *Chronicles* (1369–c1400) give a vivid picture of Europe from 1325 to 1400, although dates and geography are often inaccurate, and the history is often distorted by perspective, the first volume sympathizing with the English, the last three espousing the French cause. The description of events until 1356 is largely a revision of the chronicle by Jean le Bel (c1290–c1370).

Froissart also wrote a number of graceful lyrics and a long verse romance, *Méliador*.

From Here to Eternity (1951)   A novel by James JONES. It is a story of life in the regular U.S. army before the Japanese attack on Pearl Harbor in 1941. A sprawling (861 pages), powerful, occasionally vulgar book, it caused a sensation at its publication. Jones's writing is vigorous, vivid, and fluent. The title is taken from the well-known phrase "damned from here to eternity," a quotation from "Gentlemen Rankers," Kipling's poem of British army life. It is the first volume in a trilogy about World War II that includes *The Thin Red Line* (1962) and *Whistle* (1978).

Fromm, Erich (1900–1980)   German-born psychoanalyst and philosopher. Fromm came to the U.S. in 1934 to practice psychoanalysis and to lecture at the International Institute for Social Research (1934–39). He subsequently spent many years teaching at numerous American colleges and universities. Fromm parted company with FREUD by accepting social and environmental conditions as forces affecting human behavior. He developed a "humanist psychology," drawing on many disciplines, and sought to identify the sources of what he saw as man's estrangement from himself in an industrialized society. Among his many works, which did much to illuminate for laymen a variety of psychoanalytical and philosophical ideas, are *Escape from Freedom* (1941); its sequel, *Man for Himself* (1947); *The Art of Loving* (1956); *The Crisis of Psychoanalysis* (1970); *The Anatomy of Human Destructiveness* (1973); and *The Greatness and Limitations of Freud's Thought* (1980).

From Morn Till Midnight (Von Morgens bis Mitternachts, 1916; tr 1920)   An expressionist play by Georg KAISER. The hero, a bank teller, attempts to break out of his pitifully circumscribed existence by embezzling a large sum of money. In the space of one day, he leaves his drab family, spends money by the fistful, and frantically pursues Dionysian experiences that turn out to be miserable disappointments. A girl from the Salvation Army, whom he trusted, betrays him to the police. In a state of bitter disillusionment, he shoots himself; his rattling noises at death sound like "ecce . . . homo."

Fronde   An insurrectionary French political party during the minority of Louis XIV and the ministry of Cardinal MAZARIN. The Fronde revolted against the crown (1648–52) but, though successful in temporarily holding the capital, was unable to achieve its aim of curbing royal power and cutting taxes. Members were called *frondeurs* (from the French for "slingshot") by the Court Party, who likened them to boys slinging stones in the street and scampering away at the approach of authority.

Frost, Robert   (1874–1963)   American poet. Although Frost was born in San Francisco, he is best known for his verse dealing with New England life and character. Frost moved east in 1885, attended Dartmouth and Harvard for brief intervals, and held various odd jobs. From 1900 to 1905 he farmed in New Hampshire. But poetry was his real vocation and, in 1912, after his failure to be published in the U.S., he went to England, where for three years he wrote poetry, talked with poets, and published two collections, *A Boy's Will* (1913) and *North of Boston* (1914). The latter book contains several of Frost's best-known poems, including MENDING WALL, THE DEATH OF THE HIRED MAN, "Home Burial," and "A Servant to Servants."

Back in America in 1915, Frost began to gather a reputation, after the American publication of *North of Boston*. Maintaining his creative independence, aloof from the poetic movements of the day, he next published *Mountain Interval* (1916), a volume containing THE ROAD NOT TAKEN, "An Old Man's Winter Night," and BIRCHES. With *New Hampshire* (1923), there is the first indication of Frost's awareness of himself as poet; as he says in the title poem, he is "a creature of literature." There is also present a tone of irony that had earlier been muted. "The Axe-Helve," STOPPING BY WOODS ON A SNOWY EVENING, and "Two Witches" appear in this volume.

A FURTHER RANGE saw the introduction of contemporary concerns in Frost's poetry and the beginning of his later tendency toward abstract philosophizing, which was to result in the two verse dramas *A Masque of Reason* (1945) and *A Masque of Mercy* (1947). Frost's other collections include *West-Running Brook* (1928), *A Witness Tree* (1942), *Steeple Bush* (1947), *Complete Poems* (1949), and *In the Clearing* (1962).

Frost is often seen as opposed to the main tendencies of modern poetry. He is the clear, simple, moral poet who sings of rural, democratic joys and who is, above all, the lover of nature. But although Frost is perhaps most closely akin to Emerson and Emily Dickinson, he clearly learned much from modern poetic movements. If he is the positive poet of rural America, he is also the chronicler of the dark night of the human soul, the sophisticated poet, full of irony and ambiguity. He wrote in traditional verse forms,

but within the poems he created a tension of thought and feeling, reinforced by tension between colloquial speech and traditional metrics, that is unmatched in American poetry. The poem, as he said in the essay "The Figure a Poem Makes," is "a momentary stay against confusion." As an American equivalent of the POET LAUREATE, Frost participated in the inauguration of President John F. KENNEDY in 1961, reading his poem "The Gift Outright" at the ceremony. Frost received numerous public honors and awards, including four PULITZER PRIZES; only the Nobel Prize, which he openly coveted, eluded him.

Frost's *Complete Poems* appeared in 1967. *Selected Letters* (1964), edited by Lawrance Thompson, was followed by a complete edition, *Letters* (ed Arnold Grade), in 1972. Thompson, as Frost's chosen biographer, completed two volumes on the poet's life (1966, 1970); the final volume (1976) was finished by R. H. Winnick after Thompson's death.

Froude, James Anthony   (1818–1894)   English historian. Froude wrote *History of England from the Fall of Wolsey to the Defeat of the Spanish Armada* (1856–70), noted for its graceful style and Protestant bias. As executor of Thomas CARLYLE he wrote *Reminiscences of Carlyle* (1881) and *Life of Thomas Carlyle* (1884).

Fruits of the Earth, The   (Les Nourritures terrestres, 1897; tr 1933)   A poetic work by André GIDE. It is a hymn in prose and poetry to the beauty of all experience, exhorting youth to prepare itself for receiving all the joy of life by casting off all that is artificial or merely conventional. In the 1920s a generation of restless youth adopted the work as a popular handbook of self-liberation.

Fry, Christopher   (born Christopher Harris, 1907–   )   English dramatist. Educated at a Quaker school, the son of an Anglican lay reader, Fry had an actively religious upbringing that strongly influenced his work. His reputation as a playwright of individual style and wit dates from the production of *A Phoenix Too Frequent* (1946), a one-act verse comedy. With *The Lady's Not for Burning* (1948), an immediate success, the Fry trademark of comedy with serious undertones was internationally established, and continued in *Venus Observed* (1950) and *The Dark Is Light Enough* (1954). Fry also wrote notable religious plays, including *A Sleep of Prisoners* (1951) and *Curtmantle* (1961), a major historical drama of the conflict between Henry II and THOMAS À BECKET. Although Fry was enthusiastically received as a revitalizing force in modern verse drama, his popularity dwindled as theatrical fashions tended toward realism. He also translated plays and wrote television and filmscripts. His autobiography, *Can You Find Me: A Family History*, was published in 1978. *Selected Plays* appeared in 1985.

Fry, Elizabeth   (1780–1845)   English Quaker philanthropist, noted as promoter of wide-ranging prison reforms, particularly in the treatment of female prisoners. Her *Memoirs* were published in 1847.

Fry, Roger (1866–1934) English art critic and painter. A member of the BLOOMSBURY GROUP, he was a pioneer in introducing the work of CÉZANNE and other postimpressionist painters (see POSTIMPRESSIONISM) to England. He was at one time curator of paintings at the New York Metropolitan Museum of Art. Among his books are *Vision and Design* (1920), *Transformations* (1926), *Cézanne: A Study of His Development* (1927), and *Reflections on British Painting* (1934). He also edited *Sir Joshua Reynolds' Discourses* (1905). Virginia WOOLF wrote his biography (1940).

Frye, [Herman] Northrop (1912–   ) Canadian literary critic. Frye's writings contributed significantly to literary study after World War II. An early study of William BLAKE, *Fearful Symmetry* (1947), was followed by the influential *Anatomy of Criticism* (1957), which provides a systematic classification of literary modes. Among later critical studies are: *A Natural Perspective* (1965) and *Fools of Time* (1967), on SHAKESPEARE's comedies and tragedies, respectively; *The Return of Eden* (1965) on MILTON; and *T. S. Eliot* (1963). Practical criticism of modern Canadian poetry is collected in *The Bush Garden* (1971). Frye is concerned with the relationship of literature to society, the proper role of the literary critic, and the interaction between individual reader and literary artifact; these themes are pursued in *The Educated Imagination* (1964), *The Well-Tempered Critic* (1963), *The Modern Century* (1967), and *The Critical Path* (1971). *The Secular Scripture* (1976) reflects Frye's preoccupation with "archetypal criticism," or a theory of myths.

Fuenteovejuna (The Sheep Well, c1619) A drama by Lope de VEGA. Based on actual historical records, the story takes place during the reign of Ferdinand and Isabella. Commander Fernán Gómez, the lascivious lord of Fuenteovejuna, violates Laurencia, a peasant girl of the community. She tells her misfortune to the townspeople, who, enraged by her words, storm the commander's castle and put him to death. The king sends a judge to discover the identity of the murderer, but all the villagers, even under torture, will say only that Fuenteovejuna killed him. Impressed by the heroic behavior of the people, the king pardons them and puts the village under the crown's protection.

Fuentes, Carlos (1928–   ) Mexican novelist and short-story writer. A lawyer and a diplomat, Fuentes was born to a wealthy family, received a cosmopolitan education in private schools, and traveled extensively with his diplomat father. Whether in spite of or because of his privileged background, Fuentes's fiction, more than that of any other Mexican novelist of note, represents the frustrated ideals of the Mexican revolution. Particularly in his earlier work, he delves repeatedly into the nation's past and its combined Christian and Indian cultures for insights into the Mexican mind and the society it creates. His ironically titled first novel, *La region mas transparente* (1958; tr

Where the Air Is Clear, 1960), is in effect a panoramic picture of Mexico in the first half-century after the revolution, depicting the class struggles and the greed and purposelessness of a people who suffocated their own revolutionary spirit. This was followed by *Las buenas consciencias* (1959; tr *The Good Conscience*, 1961), about a rebellious boy from a well-to-do family who retreats into the security of his class. Fuentes first gained international critical attention with THE DEATH OF ARTEMIO CRUZ, another metaphorical exposé of modern Mexico. *Cambio de piel* (1967; tr *A Change of Skin*, 1968) again explores the myths and symbols of the past—in this case both European and American —through the personae of four contemporary characters. *Terra nostra* (1975; tr 1976) is a monumental novel revolving around Philip II's construction of the Escorial in the 16th century, wherein the monastic palace and mausoleum represents the "honor and mortification" of Spain. Fuentes's subsequent work includes *Burnt Water* (1980), a collection of stories, and *Una familia lejana* (1981; tr *Distant Relations*, 1981), a novel. *El gringo viejo* (1985; tr *The Old Gringo*, 1985) is a fictionalized, highly acclaimed account of Ambrose Bierce's last days in Mexico.

Fugard, Athol (1932–   ) South African playwright, director, and actor. Fugard's plays are about the survival of the blacks, coloreds, and poor-whites in his troubled country, but their relevance is universal. These social outcasts are victims of oppression and their confrontation with this and the triumph of their spirit create the drama of his work. Fugard's empathy with his characters and insight into their dilemmas are often expressed through humor. *Blood Knot* (1961), the first play ever performed in South Africa with a mixed cast, *Hello and Goodbye* (1965), and *Boesman and Lena* (1969) form a trilogy dealing with family relationships in and around Port Elizabeth, Fugard's home and the setting for most of his plays. Two of the most successful of his later plays, *Sizwe Banzi Is Dead* (1966) and *The Island* (1972), were developed in collaboration with the actors who played the leading roles, John Kani and Winston Ntshona. Another highly successful play was *"Master Harold" . . . and the Boys* (1982). His novel *Tsotsi* (written 1961, pub 1981) is the moral odyssey of a murderous leader of a gang of black hoodlums. *Notebooks 1960– 1977* appeared in 1983.

Fugitives, The (also known as The Agrarians) A group of southern poets and critics, most of whom were associated with Vanderbilt University in the 1920s. As contributors to the poetry magazine *The Fugitive* (1922–25), they developed into one of the most cohesive and widely influential groups in modern American literature. Members of the group included John Crowe RANSOM, Allen TATE, Robert Penn WARREN, Merrill MOORE, and Laura RIDING. They were joined later by Andrew Lytle and Cleanth BROOKS. The group espoused a political conservatism, reaffirming the southern agrarian ideal. They expressed their views in the symposium *I'll Take My Stand: The*

South and the Agrarian Tradition by Twelve Southerners (1930). Their poetry spurned such freer movements as IMAGISM and endorsed the formal classicism of T. S. ELIOT, depicting a relatively grim view of human nature in a complex, structured verse. Critically, they saw a work of literature as an autonomous verbal structure, not to be viewed in the light of social, philosophical, or ethical considerations. Their critical works formed the springboard for the NEW CRITICISM. Although many of the writers concerned subsequently repudiated their initial positions, The Fugitives marked a literary renaissance in the South whose effect was felt by an entire generation of American writers.

Fujiwara   See HEIAN.

Fuller, [Sarah] Margaret (1810–1850)   American editor, essayist, poet, and teacher. Rigorously educated by her father, a Harvard lawyer, Fuller learned Latin and Greek by the age of six, and by age eight was reading Shakespeare. She was raised among Harvard intellectuals and remained a voracious reader and brilliant conversationalist, holding weekly "Conversations for Women" on literary and philosophical subjects. In the 1830s she became associated with EMERSON, THOREAU, William E. CHANNING, and others who were identified with TRANSCENDENTALISM and translated *Eckermann's Conversations with Goethe* in 1839. She edited the Transcendentalist journal THE DIAL for its first two years of publication (1840–42) and became the first woman journalist for the New York *Tribune*. As a woman, an outspoken feminist, and formidable intellectual force, Fuller was regarded as something of an anomaly by her contemporaries. *Woman in the Nineteenth Century* (1845) was a remarkable feminist tract in which she envisioned America as the one place where women might rise above men's tyranny. In 1846, the same year her *Papers on Literature and Art* appeared, she went to Europe and met leading intellectuals and writers, including CARLYLE, George SAND, and the Italian political leader Giuseppe MAZZINI. The following year she went to Italy and became involved in the revolutionary movement there. There she also met Giovanni Angelo, Marquis Ossoli, ten years her junior, and became his mistress. They had a son, and were later married. In May 1850, reluctant to leave Italy but badly in need of money, Fuller, her husband, and infant son set sail for New York. Their boat was shipwrecked near the coast of Fire Island; the body of the boy was washed ashore, but the others were never recovered.

A dynamic and paradoxical figure, Fuller led a difficult and lonely struggle for complete self-realization, both as a woman and an artist. She was caricatured by James Russell Lowell in A FABLE FOR CRITICS and is said to be the model for Zenobia in Hawthorne's THE BLITHEDALE ROMANCE. See BROOK FARM.

Fuller, R[ichard] Buckminster (1895–1983) American architect, engineer, and theoretician. Throughout his inventive and unconventional career, Fuller was preoccupied with finding solutions to the problems of global living, primarily through gaining the maximum benefits from the minimum expenditure of energy and materials. In the 1930s he developed his well-known Dymaxion house (a contraction of *dynamic, maximum,* and *ion*), a futuristic combination of efficient living space and time-saving machines, and his three-wheeled Dymaxion car. His most famous creation is the geodesic dome, a structure based on the idea that the triangle, not the square, is the basic unit of natural structures and that in man-made structures it could be employed for the greatest strength and economy. Among Fuller's many books are *Nine Chains to the Moon* (1938), *Education Automation* (1963), *Operating Manual for Spaceship Earth* (1969), *Utopia or Oblivion* (1969), *Synergetics: Explorations in the Geometry of Thinking* (1975; with E. J. Applewhite), and several volumes of poetry. In *Critical Path* (1981), as in previous works, he warns of the potential for the rise of a power elite that misdirects the development of technology without regard to social needs, leading to the eventual destruction of the planet.

Fuller, Roy [Broadbent] (1912–   )   English poet and novelist. Influenced by W. H. AUDEN and Stephen SPENDER, Fuller's early poems deal with social issues and the Second World War; his later poems are more experimental, dealing frequently with psychological themes. His collections include *Epitaphs and Occasions* (1949), *Counterparts* (1954), *Collected Poems* (1962), and *An Ill-Governed Coast* (1976). Among his novels are *Image of a Society* (1956), *The Ruined Boys* (1959), *The Perfect Fool* (1963), and *My Child, My Sister* (1965).

Furphy, Joseph (pen name Tom Collins, 1843–1912)   Australian novelist. Furphy's only novel, *Such Is Life* (1903), appeared when he was sixty. The novel got little attention initially but proved to be the start of a vigorously realistic trend in Australian writing. A self-educated man, Furphy flouted all the rules and wrote a novel of complete originality. *Such Is Life* came to be recognized as one of the best frontier novels in English.

Further Range, A (1936)   A collection of poems by Robert FROST. It contains several humorous and satirical pieces and a group of epigrams called "Ten Mills." The longest poem in the book, "Build Soil," reflects the poet's concern with contemporary political developments. Also included in the collection are "Desert Places," "Neither Out Far Nor In Deep," "Design," and "Provide, Provide."

Fuseli, John Henry (also known as Johann Heinrich Füssli, 1741–1825)   Swiss-born British painter. Fuseli, an ordained but nonpracticing priest, was a leading figure in the birth of English romantic painting. During the 1770s he studied antique sculpture and the art of MICHELANGELO in Italy; Michelangelo's art became his ideal. Literature provided the other major source for his work; his themes came from SHAKESPEARE, HOMER, DANTE, MILTON, and others. In 1799 he started a Milton gallery, exhibiting his own works based on PARADISE LOST. Fuseli was an influential friend of William BLAKE, a fact that prompted frequent comparison of their work. He was also a poet and translated many scholarly works, including a translation (1765) of WINCKELMANN's *Reflections on the Painting and Sculpture of the Greeks.*

Futabatei Shimei (pen name of Hasegawa Tatsunosuke, 1864–1909)   Japanese novelist and translator. An expert in Russian, Futabatei learned of European realism through Russian novels and helped to introduce it to Japan. His *Ukigumo* (1889; tr 1967) is generally considered Japan's first modern novel, because not only is it written in modern colloquial Japanese, but it was also among the first to portray the effect of Japan's modernization on her people.

futurism   A radical movement in literature and art initiated in 1909 by the Italian poet and novelist Filippo Tommaso Marinetti (1876–1944). His *Manifeste du Futurisme* (1909) called for a revolutionary attitude toward life and art in general, exalting such aspects of contemporary life as speed, machinery, and war. The special manifesto on literature (1912) insisted on courage, audacity, and rebellion as the essential elements of poetry; it advocated freedom for the word (*parole in libertà*), the abolition of syntax, and similar anarchic, "liberating" tendencies. In the field of art, futurism produced its most interesting works before World War I. In their effort to portray dynamic movement and force, futurist painters often presented a moving object in successive stages of motion. Among the representatives of futurist art were the painters Giacomo Bella and Gino Severini and the sculptor Umberto Boccioni. The movement won for a time the endorsement of the Italian fascists.

Futurism influenced modern European literature and art and was also a forerunner of CUBISM, DADA, EXPRESSIONISM, and SURREALISM. Its most immediate effect was felt in Russia, where futurists attempted to do away with what they regarded as stale and hackneyed in Russian poetry, especially the kind of work written by the SYMBOLIST poets. The chief members of the Russian futurists were Velemir KHLEBNIKOV and Vladimir MAYAKOVSKY. The iconoclastic attitude of the futurists was revealed in their manifesto, *Poshchiochina obshchestvennomu vkusu* (A *Slap in the Face of Public Taste*, 1912), which voiced their demand: "Throw Pushkin, Dostoyevsky, Tolstoy . . . overboard from the steamship of modernity." The search for new poetic techniques led Khlebnikov to experiment with "trans-sense language" (Russ, *zaumnayi yazik* or *zaum*), in which words are shorn of their meanings and used only for their sound values. One of Khlebnikov's experiments consisted of a poem, written in 1910, made up of neologisms derived from the word *smekh* ("laughter"). Mayakovsky, the greatest poet of the group, was more successful in developing a new kind of poetry. Its chief features were a rhetorical style, original rhymes, powerful rhythms, and an emphasis on the individual word, rather than the line, as the basis of poetic organization.

Although revolutionary in temper and tone, the work of the futurists was too literary for the Soviet cultural overseers. To propagate their views, the futurists formed the organization known as LEF (Left Front of the Arts) in 1923 and published a journal under that name. The journal failed in 1925, and was revived briefly in 1927–28 as *Novyi LEF* (*New LEF*), but eventually the project died. By this time the proletarian trend in literature, advocated by RAPP (q.v.), was dominant.

Fuzzy Wuzzy (1892)   Title of one of Rudyard Kipling's BARRACK-ROOM BALLADS celebrating the bushy-haired warriors of the Sudan who fought Gordon and Kitchener.

So 'ere's to you, Fuzzy Wuzzy, at your 'ome in the Soudan;
You're a pore benighted 'eathen but a first-class fightin' man.

G

Gaboriau, Emile   See LECOQ, MONSIEUR.

Gabriel   One of the ARCHANGELS who appear in the Jewish, Christian, and Muslim systems of belief. In Hebrew mythology, Gabriel is sometimes regarded as the angel of death, the prince of fire and thunder, but more frequently as one of the Deity's chief messengers and the only angel who can speak Syrian and Chaldee. In the TAL-MUD, he appears as the destroyer of SENNACHERIB's armies, as the man who showed JOSEPH the way, and as one of the angels who buried MOSES.

Christians hold that Gabriel was the angel of the ANNUN-CIATION who appeared to the Virgin MARY; he also announced to Zacharias the future birth of JOHN THE BAP-TIST. It is he who is to blow the trumpet on Judgment Day.

The Muslims call Gabriel the chief of the four favored angels and the spirit of truth. He was the angel who, according to the KORAN, revealed the sacred laws to MUHAMMED.

Milton, in his PARADISE LOST, makes Gabriel chief of the angelic guards placed over Paradise.

Gabriel's hounds are wild geese who, according to legend, are unbaptized souls doomed to wander until Judgment Day.

Gabriela, Clove and Cinnamon (Gabriela, cravo e canela, 1958; tr 1962)   A highly successful novel by Jorge AMADO that focuses on Brazil's internal problems in the 1920s through a Marxist perspective. The Brazilian provinces during this time were still dominated by a feudal system, a system by which the "colonels," through their possessions of vast tracts of land and therefore in key strategic positions in government and society, perpetuated their power by granting favors and meting punishment as they chose to demonstrate their strength. It was a time in which the need for change, for a revaluation of values, was beginning to make itself felt. A central character, Mundinho Falcão, a rich, privileged "colonel" from Rio who has cut himself off from his own family, and come to Ilhéus, a seaport town in Bahia, to make his own fortune, is different. He is motivated by a clear sense of reform and an awareness of the injustices in the prevailing system, and begins to work on vitiating these traditional power systems. In the meantime, Nacib Saad, a restaurant owner who has just lost his talented cook and, therefore, a large portion of his business, comes upon a beautiful homeless migrant in search of work. Gabriela, whose racial composition defies classification, is hired by Nacib Saad as his cook and soon displays a wonderful talent not only for cooking but for lovemaking as well. She soon becomes his mistress and later his wife, although their marriage founders when he realizes that she has been mistress not only to him but also to every handsome young man in town. In the meantime, Falcão's efforts have been successful, and at election time the colonels discover that their power has dwindled so greatly that it is insignificant. Falcão is swept into power. Through Gabriela, Amado has captured a vision of Brazil as it is quintessentially, not hampered by class or by caste and a blend of many different races that live harmoniously; Gabriela is a perfect symbol for a democratic ideal. The novel ends on an optimistic note: Ilhéus faces the future with hope, and a new government is in command. Gabriela is reunited with Nacib Saad and restored to her former position as cook, not wife, in his establishment; and Falcão's partially achieved goals point the way for future total reforms within the system. It is an eminently humane tale, told by a master storyteller.

Gadda, Carlo Emilio (1893–1973)   Italian essayist and novelist. Gadda is considered one of Italy's most daring experimental writers, who used such devices as dialects, deliberate misspellings, and obscure constructions to give his work an unusual degree of realism and depth. His two major novels are *La cognizione del dolore* (1946, rev 1963; tr *Acquainted with Grief*, 1969), set in the imaginary South American land of Maradagàl—which is nevertheless recognizable as Italy—and *Quer pasticciaccio brutto de via Merulana* (1946, rev 1957; tr *That Awful Mess on Via Merulana*, 1965). Set in Fascist Rome, the story revolves around a mysterious murder.

Gaddis, William (1922–   )   American novelist. Gaddis's first novel, *The Recognitions* (1955), was greeted with hostile criticism, but was subsequently hailed as an original work of black-comic fiction. The novel's central character is a dedicated art forger who finds his aesthetic fulfillment in duplication rather than in creation. As he struggles to maintain his eccentric sense of artistic integrity, others seek to exploit his talent for profit. In a broader sense, the novel is a scathing and erudite indictment of religious, moral, and aesthetic hypocrisy. After twenty years, Gaddis published his second and even more experimental novel, *JR* (1975). The title character is a precociously avaricious eleven-year-old, J. R. Vansant, who presides over a vast business empire. Rather than a conventional narrative, the book is a barrage of virtually uninterrupted conversation and monologue of corporate and computer jargon. *Carpenter's Gothic*, his next novel, was published in 1985 and won high praise. By accentuating the perversity and meaninglessness of the language his characters speak, Gaddis projects a world emptied of value.

gadfly   A fly that bites or annoys cattle. In Greek mythology, HERA sent a gadfly to torment the white-horned cow in whose shape ZEUS tried to protect his beloved IO from his wife's jealousy. A gadfly also bit Pegasus and caused him to send BELLEROPHON plunging to the earth.

Gaelic League   An organization founded in Dublin in 1863. Its purpose is to preserve and extend the vernacular use of the Gaelic language, the native tongue of Ireland.

Gaelic literature   The literature of Gaelic-speaking Ireland and Scotland. Irish literature is usually divided as follows: Old Irish (up to 900); Middle Irish (up to 1350); Late Middle, or Early Modern, Irish (up to 1650); and Modern Irish (from 1650). Until the 12th century, Gaelic literature was entirely oral; it was committed to memory by bards (see FILI) and transmitted orally from generation to generation. In the middle period, a few monks began to set it down lest it be entirely forgotten.

Old Irish literature survives in medieval manuscripts, which are copies of older manuscripts; among the most important of these are *Lebor na Huidre* (*The Book of the Dun Cow*), *The Book of Leinster*, *The Yellow Book of Lecan*, *The Book of Ballymote*, and *The Speckled Book*. The romances and sagas contained in these books have been grouped according to characters and subject matter. The major groupings of these hero sagas are three: the MYTHOLOGICAL CYCLE, the ULSTER CYCLE, and the FENIAN CYCLE. The mythological cycle relates various traditions about the early settlement and conquest of Ireland. The Ulster cycle deals with Irish heroes, the greatest of whom is CÚ CHULAINN. The Fenian cycle deals with a much later period and extends into the Christian era, which comes in the extreme old age of Oisin, or Ossian, poet of the Fenians. The cycles are prose narratives interspersed with poetic dialogue.

The later Middle Irish literature written in Gaelic is generally less significant than that of the older periods; unlike the earlier literature, the bulk of which is anonymous, the later medieval literature was written by known poets, several of whom are worthy of mention. The chief bards of the 13th through 15th centuries are Gilbride Albanach McNamee (13th century), the religious poet Donough Mor O'Daly (13th century), and Teig Og O'Higgins (15th century). To this late medieval period also belongs the celebrated Gaelic narrative collection *The Three Sorrows of Story Telling*. The 16th and 17th centuries saw a great poetic revival and the rise of Modern Irish prose. As England conquered Ireland and as Protestantism became firmly established in England, Gaelic literature evinced fiercer patriotism and affirmed Catholicism. The decline of bardic poetry, however, was already under way before CROMWELL's arrival (1649) in Ireland. The prose of the 16th and 17th centuries is transitional; the religious writings and monumental history of Ireland of Geoffrey Keating (1570–c1650) are the very foundation of Modern Irish literature. The number of Gaelic-speaking Irish declined somewhat after the arrival of Cromwell and the settling of English in Ireland; however, the potato famine of 1847 dealt the most severe blow, for, in the consequent depopulation of the country, the Gaelic west was hardest hit and the proportion of Gaelic speakers in Ireland dropped in three short years from three fourths to one quarter.

In the later 19th century, through the efforts of Irish scholars, there came the great Gaelic literary revival that continued into the 20th century. See GAELIC LEAGUE; IRISH RENAISSANCE.

Gaines, Ernest J. (1933–   )   American novelist and short-story writer. Although he has spent little of his adult life in the South, Gaines is concerned in his writing with the landscape, culture, and people of his native southern Louisiana. In his novels *Of Love and Dust* (1967) and *The Autobiography of Miss Jane Pittman* (1971), as in the stories collected in *Bloodline* (1968), his heroes and heroines are poor, uneducated black people who struggle with dignity against the violence and deprivation of a segregated society. *Catherine Carmier* (1964) centers on the intricate relationships among Louisiana's black, white, Cajun, and Creole populations and on the conflict between militant or ambitious young blacks and their more tradition-bound elders. *In My Father's House* (1978) tells the story of a black minister who sells out his followers and is left with a broken dream.

Gainsborough, Thomas (1727–1788)   English painter. Gainsborough rivaled Sir Joshua REYNOLDS as a fashionable portraitist, but his work shows greater simplicity and a lighter, rapid, and vibrant touch. One of the first painters to depict English scenery, he painted landscapes for his own pleasure and liked to portray his sitters in the open, but he allowed his art to be limited by the fashion of the day, which considered landscape a minor genre. Among his delightful portraits is the well-known *Blue Boy*.

Galahad, Sir In the later legends of King Arthur, the purest and noblest knight of the ROUND TABLE. Best known from Malory's MORTE D'ARTHUR, he is the illegitimate son of Sir Lancelot and the princess ELAINE and the last descendant of JOSEPH OF ARIMATHEA. He alone is qualified to fill the SIEGE PERILOUS at the Round Table, and he alone achieves the quest for the Holy GRAIL, heals the FISHER KING, and brings back fertility to his land. His career ends in Sarras, where he finally sees the uncovered chalice and renounces the world, asking God to release him from his material existence.

Later writers, particularly of the romantic period, wrote newer versions of Sir Galahad into the Arthurian legend. Among these are TENNYSON and Mark TWAIN. The name of Sir Galahad has become synonymous with the perfect knight.

Galatea (1) A Nereid; see ACIS.

(2) See PYGMALION.

Galatians, The Epistle of Paul the Apostle to the A NEW TESTAMENT book; an epistle by St. PAUL to various Christian churches in Galatia. The Epistle contains Paul's defense of his authority, declaring that he received his gospel directly from God, not from the original twelve APOSTLES. He argues for the universality of the Christian faith and against sectarian Judaic influences.

Galbraith, John Kenneth (1908–) Canadian-born American economist and writer. Starting as an agricultural economist and a follower of John Maynard KEYNES, Galbraith repeated his conviction that more national wealth should be used for public welfare in many books, all noted for their lucid exegesis and occasionally sharp wit. His concern with the implications of mass poverty throughout the world is reflected in such books as *American Capitalism: The Concept of Countervailing Power* (1952), THE AFFLUENT SOCIETY, *The New Industrial State* (1967; rev 1979), *Economics and the Public Purpose* (1973), and *The Nature of Mass Poverty* (1979), which examines the vicious cycle of poverty in the Third World and the problems inherent in this for wealthy nations. Galbraith has also written numerous essays and memoirs, including *The Scotch* (1964), *Ambassador's Journal* (1969), an account of his years as ambassador to India in the Kennedy administration, and *A Life in Our Times* (1981).

Gale, Zona (1874–1938) American novelist and short-story writer. A native of Wisconsin, Gale is known for her books dealing with small-town life in the Midwest. The most famous of these are *Birth* (1918) and *Miss Lulu Bett* (1920), novels whose stark realism won immediate success.

Galen (Klaudios Galenos, 2d century) A famous Greek physician and philosopher. For centuries Galen was the supreme authority in medicine; hence, any physician.

Galeoto The Italian name of Gallehault, one of the forms of GALAHAD, which has attached to itself a quite divergent meaning. Its modern connotations come from a passage in Dante's INFERNO telling how PAOLO AND FRANCESCA read of a guilty kiss between LAUNCELOT and GUINEVERE and yielded to the suggestion. Gallehault was the knight who had brought Launcelot and the queen together, and he performed the same office for Paolo and Francesca, for "Galeoto was the book and he who wrote it. That day we read no more." Hence, though far from the character of Galahad, Galeoto has become a term for a panderer in Italy and Spain. In José Echegaray's tragedy EL GRAN GALEOTO, gossip is the "Galeoto."

Galilei, Galileo (known as Galileo, 1564–1642) Italian astronomer, physicist, and philosopher. Galileo's achievements led to a new physical and mathematical concept of nature. He discovered the isochronism of the pendulum (1583), hydrostatic balance (1586), Jupiter's satellites (1610), sun spots (1610), and the moon's libration (1637), among other accomplishments. A staunch advocate of COPERNICUS, he found himself in difficulties with the Church, but was not unduly harassed until the publication of his *Dialogo dei due massimi sistemi* (*Dialogue on the Great World Systems*, 1632). The following year he was tried before the INQUISITION on charges of proclaiming and defending the Copernican system, which had been denounced as heretical. Unwilling to sacrifice his remaining years and his work to a fruitless heroism, he recanted his views. Legend has it that after doing so, he muttered *Eppur si muove!* ("And yet it moves!"), in quiet insistence on the earth's motion. During his remaining years he was under close watch, under virtual house arrest, but he was widely acclaimed and revered. The *Dialogue* was the first scientific treatise written in Italian, the layman's language, rather than in the customary Latin. He is the subject of Brecht's play THE LIFE OF GALILEO.

gall Bile; the very bitter fluid secreted by the liver. The word is used figuratively as a symbol of anything of extreme bitterness. The phrase "gall and wormwood" compounds the bitterness.

The gall of bitterness means the bitterest grief; extreme affliction. The ancients taught that grief and joy were subject to the gall as affection was to the heart, knowledge to the kidneys, and the gall of bitterness means the bitter center of bitterness, as the heart of hearts means the innermost recesses of the heart or affections. In the ACTS OF THE APOSTLES it is used to signify the sinfulness of sin, which leads to the bitterest grief. According to tradition, pigeons have no gall, because the dove sent from the ark by NOAH burst its gall out of grief, and none of the pigeon family has had a gall ever since.

Gallant, Mavis (1922–) Canadian short-story writer and novelist. Born and educated in Montreal, Gallant went to Europe in 1950, where she remained, living chiefly in Paris. In her stories, many of which were initially published in THE NEW YORKER, she looks at life with a cool eye, seeing the human experience as both comic and terrifying. Her characters tend to be exiles or survivors trying to cope with alienation or expatriation, their worlds rendered in painstaking detail. Her major collections include *The Other Paris* (1956), *My Heart Is Broken* (1964), *The Pegnitz Junction* (1973), *The End of the World* (1974), and *From the Fifteenth District* (1979). She has also published two novels: *Green Water, Green Sky* (1959) and *A Fairly Good Time* (1970).

Gallegos [Freire], Rómulo (1884–1969)   Venezuelan novelist, educator, and political leader. When lack of funds forced Gallegos to abandon his legal studies, he turned to teaching and served as director of various educational institutions from 1912 to 1930. The publication of DOÑA BÁRBARA, Gallegos's best-known novel, aroused the hostility of Juan Vicente Gómez, Venezuela's dictator, who tried to silence the author by offering him a seat in the senate. Gallegos chose voluntary exile instead, returning to Venezuela after the death of Gómez in 1935. After a liberal coup in 1945, he was elected president of Venezuela for the term 1948–52. Late in 1948, however, Gallegos was deposed by a military junta and remained in exile until the overthrow of Marcos Pérez Jiménez in 1958.

As a novelist, Gallegos is famous for his interpretation of the people and customs of the Venezuelan *llanos*, or tropical prairies, in a realistic style touched by impressionism. Besides *Doña Bárbara*, his best-known novels are *Cantaclaro* (1934) and *Canaima* (1935).

Galsworthy, John (1867–1933)   English novelist and playwright, known for his portrayal of the British upper middle class and for his social satire. Galsworthy's most famous work is his novel series THE FORSYTE SAGA. His plays are remarkable realistic and satirical studies based on different social problems and influenced by the drama of Henrik IBSEN.

Born into an upper-middle-class family like the ones he usually wrote about, Galsworthy was trained as a lawyer, and his legal knowledge colors many of his novels and plays. He turned to literature after he had met Joseph CONRAD on a voyage. A passionate romance with Ada Galsworthy, his cousin's wife, who encouraged his writing, led to their marriage some ten years later, in 1905. Galsworthy's earliest works were written under the pseudonym John Sinjohn. He came to artistic maturity in 1906, with the publication of his novel *The Man of Property* (the first installment of *The Forsyte Saga*) and the production of his play *The Silver Box*. In the work of this early period, Galsworthy attacked the smug conventionality and self-righteous hypocrisy of the middle classes and championed the artist, the rebel, and the underdog. He became less satirical and more sentimental and traditional in his subsequent novels. He refused knighthood in 1918 but accepted the Order of Merit in 1929 and the Nobel Prize in Literature in 1932.

Gálvez, Manuel (1882–1962)   Argentine novelist. Gálvez is best known for his naturalistic novels, in which he mercilessly exposed Argentina's social ills. The novels are reminiscent of DICKENS in their sympathetic treatment of the downtrodden. *La maestra normal* (1914), often considered his best work, is a tale of seduction set in the desperate and monotonous life of the provincial city La Riója.

Gama, Vasco da (c1460–1524)   Portuguese explorer. The first European to discover a sea route to the East, da Gama rounded the Cape of Good Hope on November 22, 1497, sailed along the coast of Africa, and crossed the Indian Ocean to reach Calicut on May 20, 1498. He made a second trip to the East in 1502–3 and was named viceroy of India in 1524. He is the hero of Camões's OS LUSÍADAS and MEYERBEER's opera *L'Africaine*.

Gambler, The (Igrok, 1866)   A short novel by DOSTOYEVSKY. The gambling mania of the tale's hero, Aleksey Ivanovich, is a reflection of the author's own weakness. The heroine of the story, Polina, is based on Polina Suslova, Dostoyevsky's lover in 1862–63.

Gamelyn, The Tale of   A metrical romance in Middle English. Often called *The Cook's Tale of Gamelyn*, it has been erroneously attributed to Chaucer (see THE COOK'S TALE). Gamelyn is the youngest of three brothers. The eldest robs him of his share of their father's property, and after a series of successes and reverses in reclaiming it, Gamelyn takes to the forest and eventually becomes chief of a band of outlaws. The second brother tries to help him and winds up in chains, but Gamelyn returns to overthrow their wicked brother, now sheriff, as well as the dishonest judge and jury. Thomas LODGE adapted the story in his romance *Rosalynde* (1590), a major source for Shakespeare's AS YOU LIKE IT.

gamesmanship   A term popularized by Stephen POTTER through his humorous book *Theory and Practice of Gamesmanship, or the Art of Winning Games without Actually Cheating* (1947).

Gammer Gurton's Needle (1566)   The second-oldest English comedy. It was first performed at Cambridge in 1566, and published in 1575. It was formerly ascribed to John Still (1543?–1607), Bishop of Bath and Winchester, but the claim of William Stevenson (d 1575?) is now generally favored. A coarse and vigorous comedy, it deals with the housewife Gammer Gurton's loss of her needle as she is mending her servant Hodge's breeches; it closes with the painful but farcical discovery of the missing needle in the seat of Hodge's pants.

Gamp, Sarah (usually called Sairey)   A disreputable nurse in Charles Dickens's MARTIN CHUZZLEWIT, famous for her bulky umbrella and perpetual reference to Mrs. Harris, a purely imaginary person whose opinions always confirm her own. She is fond of strong tea and more potent stimulants.

Hence, a regular Gamp came to signify a low-class, drink-sodden, uncertificated maternity nurse, and an umbrella, especially a large, badly rolled cotton one, came to be called a gamp.

Ganapati   See GANESH.

Gance, Abel (1889–1981)   French film director. One of the great innovators of the cinema, Gance directed the antiwar epic *J'accuse!* (1919), the heavily symbolic tragedy *La Roue* (1923), and the monumental *Napoléon* (1927), a magnificent portrayal of the early career of Bonaparte. *Napoléon* is particularly notable for its wide spectrum of cinematic and narrative techniques: elaborate visual metaphors, complex superimpositions, accelerated cross-cutting to heighten the emotional tempo, and the use of the Polyvision process (projecting simultaneous images on a triptych screen) to create the rich counterpoint of a "visual symphony."

Gandhi, Mohandas Karamchand (called Mahatma ["great-souled"] Gandhi, 1869–1948)   Hindu nationalist leader. Gandhi is considered the architect of Indian independence and self-rule. He studied law in England, was admitted to the English bar, and practiced in India. In 1893 he went to South Africa, where he practiced law and became involved in the struggle of Indian settlers there against racial discrimination and for political rights. It was there that Gandhi adopted the dress and life-style of a Hindu ascetic and where he first used the technique of passive resistance (SATYAGRAHA) that later became his most effective weapon against the British in India. After returning to India in 1915, he supported the British in World War I, but in 1919 he formed a politico-religious movement of noncooperation with the British that resulted in his imprisonment for "civil disobedience." In 1924 he became president of the Indian National Congress, a position he held until 1934. During World War II he was again arrested by the British and imprisoned from 1942 to 1944. Upon his release he was a major force in the negotiations after World War II that ultimately led to a free India and the partition of Pakistan as a separate Muslim state. He was shot and killed on January 30, 1948, by a fanatic Hindu nationalist who opposed Gandhi's willingness to negotiate with the Muslims. His tremendous popularity and effectiveness in India were due in part to his devotion to Hindu ideals, his asceticism, and his unique capacity to stir feelings of nationalist fervor. He advocated a unified and free India, a revitalization of cottage industries, particularly clothmaking, and, most important, an end to the social and economic distress of the Indian peasants, specifically, the UNTOUCHABLES. See HARIJAN.

Ganelon (also Gan of Mayence or Gano of Maganza)   The traitor among Charlemagne's PALADINS. In the *Chanson de* ROLAND his betrayal is responsible for the defeat at RONCESVALLES, and he figures prominently as the instigator of discord among the knights in Pulci's MORGANTE MAGGIORE, Boiardo's ORLANDO INNAMORATO, and Ariosto's ORLANDO FURIOSO. He is cited as one of history's notorious traitors in Dante's INFERNO and Chaucer's THE NUN'S PRIEST'S TALE.

Ganesa (also Ganesh or Ganapati)   The god of wisdom or prudence in Hindu mythology. Ganesa is the son of SHIVA and Parvati, and is usually represented with a man's body and an elephant's head; sometimes he is represented as riding on a rat. He is propitiated at the beginning of literary and sacred writings to ensure that the writer will encounter no obstacles. In some versions of the myth, he is the scribe of the Hindu epic the MAHĀBHĀRATA, which was dictated to him by the sage Vyāsa. His worship is confined largely to west India, but he is one of the most popular of the Hindu deities.

Ganges (or Ganga)   The most sacred river of India. Its source is in the western Himalayas and it flows east-southeast across northern India, emptying into the Bay of Bengal by many mouths. In Hindu legend it flows from the feet of BRAHMĀ and down to the earth through the matted locks of SHIVA, the king of yogis and ascetics; hence the ritual necessity for orthodox Hindus to bathe in the holy river on certain days to be rid of their imperfections. Two of HINDUISM's most sacred places, BENARES (Varanasi) and Allahabad (Prayag), are located on the Ganges.

Gant, Eugene   The central character in Thomas Wolfe's autobiographical novels LOOK HOMEWARD, ANGEL and OF TIME AND THE RIVER. Gant is a young man of robust energies and intense emotion; he feels "different" from others, and has vast, romantic yearnings toward love, adventure, personal achievement, and a semimystical, unknown goal that carries him on a virtual pilgrimage through the U.S. and Europe. Other characters with the same family name are likewise drawn from life: Oliver Gant, Eugene's father; Eliza Gant, his mother; and Ben Gant, his older brother.

Ganymede   In Greek mythology, the cup-bearer of ZEUS, successor to HEBE, and a type of youthful male beauty. The son of Tros, an early king of Troy, he was carried off by Zeus on the back of an eagle because of his unusual beauty.

Garbourg, Arne (1851–1924)   Norwegian novelist, poet, playwright, and essayist. Garbourg was the first important novelist to write almost exclusively in *landsmaal* or *Nynorsk*, the spoken language of the country. His highly naturalistic writing is at its best in such early novels as *Bondestudentar* (*Peasant Students*, 1882) and *Mannfolk* (*Menfolk*, 1886). In his later novels, among them *Fred* (1892; tr *Peace*, 1930) and *Den burtkomme faderen* (1899; tr *The Lost Father*, 1920), his concerns deepened and the influence of TOLSTOY is clear. His long verse cycle of peasant life, *Haugtussa* (1895), was set to music by GRIEG.

García Gutiérrez, Antonio (1813–1884)   Spanish dramatist. The most popular of Gutiérrez's many plays is *El trovador* (1836), a romantic historical tragedy that was the basis of VERDI's opera *Il trovatore* (1853). He also wrote

Venganza catalana (1864) and *Juan Lorenzo* (1865), sometimes considered his masterpiece.

García Lorca, Federico (1898–1936)   Spanish poet and playwright. Spain's best-known modern poet, Lorca was born near Granada. He began the study of law but soon abandoned it for the literary life in Madrid, where he associated with intellectuals and artists, including many of the GENERACIÓN DEL 27 as well as Salvador DALI and Luis BUÑUEL, who were chiefly responsible for his exposure to SURREALISM. After a period of great creative activity, which revealed even greater promise, he was brutally shot by Falangist soldiers in the opening days of the Spanish Civil War.

Lorca's first poetic venture, *Libro de poemas* (1921), influenced by JIMÉNEZ and MACHADO, mirrors his childhood and adolescence. His next work, ROMANCERO GITANO, breathed new life into the old tradition of the Spanish ballad and catapulted Lorca to fame. A collection of ballads, evocative of the Andalusian countryside and its gypsy people, the work is a compelling fusion of naïve and primitive folk motifs and a deeply personal, thoroughly modern voice. After an emotional crisis in 1928, Lorca traveled to the U.S., where he wrote his most surrealist collection, *Poeta en Nueva York* (written 1929, pub 1940; tr *Poet in New York*, 1955). It is a tortured work, full of forebodings of death; as with *Romancero*, these poems reflect his haunted vision of common people being inhumanly crushed beneath the great clubfoot of civilization. In *Llanto por Ignacio Sánchez Mejías* (1935; tr *Lament for the Death of a Bullfighter*, 1937), the figure of one man facing death in the bullring brought to full expressive power Lorca's tragic sense of violent death. Considered the greatest elegy in modern Spanish poetry, the work is a moving premonition of Lorca's own death and that of Republican Spain in the Civil War.

Lorca has an equally well-merited reputation as a dramatist. An accomplished musician, amateur painter, and theatrical director, Lorca wrote antirealist puppet plays for a combination of marionettes and live actors; farces; and comedies, notably *La zapatera prodigiosa* (*The Shoemaker's Marvelous Wife*, 1930). His most famous plays, repeatedly revived, are his three tragedies, all dealing with the passions of thwarted womanhood: *Bodas de sangre* (1933; tr *Blood Wedding*, 1939), the story of a bride who runs away with a previous lover, who is subsequently murdered by her husband; *Yerma* (1934; tr 1941), portraying the deadly conflict between a wife's maternal yearnings and her husband's sterility; and *La casa de Bernarda Alba* (1936; tr *The House of Bernarda Alba*, 1936), in which the matriarchal domination and sexual repression Lorca saw as characteristic of Spain lead to suicide, anguish, and despair.

García Márquez, Gabriel (1928–   )   Colombian novelist and short-story writer. García Márquez left Colombia in 1950 on assignment to Europe as a newspaper reporter, and thereafter spent much of his life outside his country. These absences apparently sharpened his feeling for the myths of his people and the lives of those in the backwater villages of Colombia. In his first, short novel, *La hojarasca* (1955; tr *Leaf Storm*, 1972), he introduced the imaginary town Macondo that serves as the setting for many of his later works. His next book, a short novel and a collection of stories, *El coronel no tiene quien le escriba* (1958; tr *No One Writes to the Colonel*, 1968), was widely translated and attracted favorable attention throughout the world. In *Los funerales de la mamà grande* (1962; tr *Big Mama's Funeral*, 1971) a note of the bizarre and the grotesque began to appear in García Márquez's Faulknerian vision, but it was in *La mala hora* (1962; tr *In Evil Hour*, 1979), about a Macondo-like village overcome by chaos, that García Márquez's overwhelmingly rich imagination became more clearly evident. That imagination came to full fruition in his novel ONE HUNDRED YEARS OF SOLITUDE, an epic portrayal of seven generations of a Macondo family; it established him as the master of MAGIC REALISM and assured his worldwide reputation as a major modern novelist. His fifth novel, *El otoño del patriarca* (1975; tr *The Autumn of the Patriarch*, 1976), is a less structured experiment in magic realism, made up of the musings of a dictator who ruled his country for two hundred years. *La increíble y triste historia de la cándida Eréndira y de su abuela desalmada: Siete cuentos* (1972; tr *Innocent Erendira and Other Stories*, 1978) is a collection of representative short fiction. Other works include *Cronica de una muerte anunciada* (1981; tr *Chronicle of a Death Foretold*, 1982); *The Story of a Shipwrecked Sailor* (1955, pub 1986); and *Collected Stories*, stories written between 1967 and 1972. In 1982 García Márquez was awarded the NOBEL PRIZE in Literature.

Garcilaso de la Vega (1501?–1536)   Spanish poet and soldier. Garcilaso spent much of his brief life in Italy, where he lived, as he himself wrote, "Now using the sword, now the pen" (*Tomando, ora la espada, ora la pluma*). Often called "the Spanish Petrarch" because of his successful imitation of Italian poetry, he was a close friend of Juan BOSCÁN, whose widow published his works with those of her husband in 1543. Garcilaso wrote thirty-eight sonnets, five *canciones*, five odes, two elegies, and one *epístola*, or "epistle," which are notable for their technical excellence and delicacy of sentiment. His first eclogue, dealing with the unhappy loves of the shepherds Salicio and Nemoroso, is generally considered his masterpiece.

Garcilaso de la Vega (known as El Inca, 1539–1616)   Peruvian historian. The son of a Spanish knight and an Inca princess, Garcilaso is often regarded as the first spokesman for the South American mestizo. After fighting in European wars for thirty years, he settled in Spain, was ordained a priest, and devoted himself to history. His masterpiece is the *Comentarios reales* (*Royal Commentaries*, 1609), in which he described the Inca Empire and its conquest by Spain. Although some critics have claimed that it gives too fanciful and idealized a picture of Inca civilization, it is still considered a major source of information about pre-Columbian America. Garcilaso also wrote *Florida del Inca* (1605), an account of De Soto's explorations in what is now the southern U.S.

Garden, The (1681)   A poem by Andrew MARVELL. It was written while he was a tutor at the country estate of the Cromwellian general Thomas Fairfax. The poet dwells on the contrast between the innocence, peace, and beauty of the garden and the stress and trouble of the outside world. At the height of his contemplation of the garden, his mind performs a typically Marvellian transformation:

> Annihilating all that's made
> To a green thought in a green shade.

Garden of Eden   See EDEN.

Garden Party, The (1922)   A short story by Katherine MANSFIELD. While a wealthy woman and her daughters are preparing for their garden party, a poor laborer is killed in an accident. Young Laura is sent to take to the widow and orphans the cakes left over from the party; the experience makes her see her own life in a new light for a moment. The reality of the outer world has intruded suddenly and violently upon the delicate artifice she has known as life.

Gardner, Erle Stanley (1889–1970)   American detective story writer. A practicing lawyer for many years, Gardner became one of the most successful writers of crime detection in the history of American publishing. He wrote over one hundred books, most of which employed either Perry Mason, the ingenious lawyer-hero of a long series that began with *The Case of the Velvet Claws* (1933), or the district attorney Douglas Selby, who first appeared in *The D.A. Calls It Murder* (1937). He also wrote many other novels under a variety of pseudonyms.

Gardner, John [Champlin, Jr.] (1933–1982) American novelist and medievalist. Gardner did much to make medieval literature accessible to the general reader, both through his translations of such Middle English classics as *The Complete Works of the Gawain-Poet* (1965) and *Morte d'Arthur* (1971), and through his popular studies of CHAUCER. He is best known, however, as the author of such novels as *The Sunlight Dialogues* (1972), and as an outspoken critic of contemporary novelists. His book *On Moral Fiction* (1978) sets forth his position that literature exists to promote moral values, to be life-affirming, and to tell a story, not to assault narrative forms or to articulate despair. Among his other works are *Grendel* (1971), the BEOWULF story told from the monster's point of view, and *Jason and Medeia* (1973), a novel in verse told from the viewpoint of a modern professor of literature. *The Art of Living* (1981) is a collection of stories.

Gareth, Sir   In ARTHURIAN LEGEND, one of the knights of the ROUND TABLE. In Malory's MORTE D'ARTHUR he is the youngest son of King Lot and MARGAWSE. His

mother, to deter him from entering Arthur's court, says jestingly that she will consent to his doing so only if he conceals his name and goes as a scullion for twelve months. He agrees to this, and Sir Kay, the king's steward, nicknames him Beaumains, because his hands are unusually fine and large. At the end of the year he is knighted, and obtains his first quest when Linet begs the aid of some knight to liberate her sister Liones held prisoner by Sir Ironside in Castle Perilous. Linet treats Sir Gareth with great contempt, calling him a washer of dishes and a kitchen knave, but he overthrows five knights and frees Liones, whom he marries. Tennyson retells the story in "Gareth and Lynette" in his IDYLLS OF THE KING.

While rescuing Queen GUINEVERE from death at the stake, Sir LAUNCELOT unwittingly kills Sir Gareth, who is standing guard, and thus evokes the vow of revenge from Gareth's brothers that ultimately effects the downfall of King Arthur's court and the end of the Round Table. See GAWAIN, SIR.

Gargamelle   In Rabelais's GARGANTUA AND PANTAGRUEL, the daughter of the king of the Parpaillos (Fr, "butterflies"), wife of Grandgousier, and mother of GARGANTUA. In the eleventh month of her pregnancy she goes into labor as a result of eating too much tripe and, after taking an astringent, gives birth to Gargantua through her left ear.

Gargantua (Sp, "gullet")   The name of a giant-hero in medieval folk literature, whom Rabelais made the father of Pantagruel in his satire GARGANTUA AND PANTAGRUEL. He figures in four of the five books, but as a major character only in *La Vie inestimable du grant Gargantua, père de Pantagruel* (1534), which is now known as Book I.

Son of GRANDGOUSIER and GARGAMELLE, Gargantua miraculously enters the world through Gargamelle's left ear, shouting "Drink, drink, drink!" The narrative continues in a similar vein, recounting his extraordinary childhood and adolescence; his trip to Paris on his famous mare, whose tail switches so violently that she fells the entire forest of Orléans; his lawsuit over stealing the bells of Notre Dame Cathedral to hang around his mare's neck; his encyclopedic course of studies in Paris; his defense of his father's lands against the assaults of PICROCHOLE; and his founding of the abbey of THÉLÈME at the war's end. Apart from the buffoonery, the work also provides a biting and realistic satire on various aspects of contemporary society—monasticism, scholastic education, the legalistic pedantry of the theologians at the Sorbonne—and on the causes and effects of tyrannical power. It vividly describes student life in the Latin Quarter of Paris, and provincial life and manners in Rabelais's native Chinon. It contrasts antiquated educational programs with the humanistic studies that were just coming into prominence; despotism with intelligent, humane government; and oppressive monasticism with healthy living.

Gargantua and Pantagruel (1532–1564)   The English title for a five-part satirical work by François RABE-

LAIS. Derived in part fom the medieval FABLIAUX, it was published as follows:

Les Horribles et Espovantables Faictz et prouesses du très renommé Pantagruel, Roy des Dipsodes, fils du grant géant Gargantua (1532), later known as Book II, recounts the life of PANTAGRUEL up to the war against the Dipsodes in UTOPIA.

La Vie inestimable du grant Gargantua, père de Pantagruel (1534), which is now known as Book I, describes the life of GARGANTUA through the founding of the abbey of THÉLÈME.

Le Tiers Livre des faictz et dictz heroiques du noble Pantagruel (Book III, 1546) presents a discussion of the problem faced by Pantagruel's companion PANURGE, who cannot decide whether or not to marry. Pantagruel accompanies Panurge as the latter consults a sibyl, a mute, a poet, an astrologer, a theologian, a physician, a philosopher, and a madman, none of whom can provide a solution. Panurge then persuades Pantagruel and his friends to embark on a voyage to the ORACLE OF THE HOLY BOTTLE for the answer. The book is rich in humanistic learning in the fields of divination, botany, and moral philosophy; at the same time it satirizes poets, judges, fortune-tellers, etc.

Le Quart Livre (Book IV, 1552), which relates the departure for the Holy Bottle in Cathay, reflects the keen interests of the period in the great voyages of discovery. Although in Book II Pantagruel had reached Utopia by sailing around the Cape of Good Hope, this time the voyagers follow the North Atlantic route taken by the French explorer Jacques Cartier. Pantagruel and his companions visit several islands, where they meet the Papimaniacs, the Pope-Figs, and other peoples who serve as targets for Rabelais's satirical thrusts against contemporary society. Like its predecessors, this book was condemned by the Sorbonne for its attacks on the Church.

The posthumous *Cinquième et Dernier Livre* (Book V, 1564), of which sixteen chapters had appeared in 1562 as L'ILE SONNANTE *par maître François Rabelais*, is probably not entirely of Rabelais's authorship. Most modern scholars believe it was published by an imitator who developed sketches and drafts left by Rabelais. As the voyage to Cathay continues, Rabelais launches into a violent satire on religious and legal institutions. At last Pantagruel and his friends arrive at the temple of the Holy Bottle, where the oracle answers Panurge's question by a single word, "Drink!" This reply has been taken to mean that each man must eventually solve his own problems and that life's aim is a never-ending quest for knowledge, from which comes wisdom.

Rabelais was a man of his time who delighted in satirizing the religious, political, legal, and social institutions and practices of 16th-century France. He displayed a characteristically Renaissance thirst for erudition, but he also exalted the development of all human faculties, in accordance with his basic belief that human nature is funda-

mentally good. His universal genius reached far beyond his own century and has influenced numerous later writers, including LA FONTAINE, MOLIÈRE, VOLTAIRE, SWIFT, BALZAC, HUGO, and GAUTIER. See MESSER GASTER.

Garibaldi, Giuseppe (1807–1882)   Italian patriot. An ardent republican and associate of Mazzini, Garibaldi was forced to flee from Italy because of his political activities and lived in South America (1834–48). On his return he served in the army of the short-lived Roman Republic and upon its defeat made a dramatic retreat through central Italy. He escaped to the U.S. (1850–54), where he became a naturalized citizen and worked for a while as a candlemaker on Staten Island. Returning to his native land, in order to secure the unification of Italy, he swore allegiance to King Victor Emmanuel of Sardinia. After taking part in the war against Austria, he invaded the so-called Kingdom of the Two Sicilies with his famous band of one thousand men known as the Red Shirts. After the conquest of Sicily, he crossed to the mainland and drove Francis II from Naples. When the Sicilian king capitulated and Victor Emmanuel was proclaimed king of Italy (1861), Garibaldi withdrew to his farm in Caprera. He later led two unsuccessful expeditions of liberation against Rome and fought on behalf of the French republic in the Franco-Prussian War. On his statue on the Janiculum overlooking Rome is engraved his famous cry, *Roma o Morte* ("Rome or Death").

Garland, [Hannibal] Hamlin (1860–1940) American short-story writer and novelist. Garland is known for his realistic studies of the frustrations of farm life in his native Midwest. In his early twenties, he went to Boston and became a friend of William Dean HOWELLS and others in the Boston literary circle. Influenced by Howells's realism and the single-tax theories of Henry George, he began to write the stories and sketches published in MAIN-TRAVELLED ROADS. Other stories were collected in *Prairie Folks* (1893) and *Wayside Courtships* (1897), later published under a single title as *Other Main-Travelled Roads* (1910). Garland wrote a number of novels espousing populist ideology, such as *Jason Edwards* (1892) and *A Spoil of Office* (1892). *A Little Norsk* (1892) and *Rose Dutcher's Cooly* (1895) both deal with the realities of prairie life. *Crumbling Idols* (1894), Garland's literary manifesto, describes his brand of realism as "veritism," a concern for truth that emphasizes "local color," an art with a "sociologic" basis. This approach had a marked influence on other American writers, notably Stephen CRANE.

Garland's later novels deal with the far West. He is best remembered for two of his eight autobiographical narratives, A SON OF THE MIDDLE BORDER and *A Daughter of the Middle Border* (1921, PULITZER PRIZE).

Garneau, François-Xavier (1809–1866)   Quebec historian and poet. Garneau's classic, three-volume *Histoire du Canada* (1845–48; 4th vol added, 1852) depicted the rich pioneering history of the Canadian settlers and served as an inspiration for writers of several generations. It was the first major literary achievement by a French-Canadian author. Two of his descendants, Hector de SAINT-DENYS-GARNEAU and Anne Hébert, also became important figures in Canadian literature.

Garnett, David (1892–1981)   English novelist. The son of Constance and Edward GARNETT, he first attracted attention with his highly imaginative fantasies, LADY INTO FOX and *A Man in the Zoo* (1924). Among his many novels are *Aspects of Love* (1955), a delicate, odd love story; *A Shot in the Dark* (1958); *Ulterior Motives* (1966); *Plough over the Bones* (1973); and *Up She Rises* (1977). He also edited the papers of other writers, notably T. E. Lawrence (1951), and wrote autobiographical works as well as *Great Friends* (1979), portraits of seventeen writers, many of whom were associated with the BLOOMSBURY GROUP.

Garnett, Edward (1868–1937)   English critic, biographer, and essayist, a well-known man of letters, and father of David GARNETT. The best-esteemed publisher's reader in London, he encouraged and helped to publicize such writers as Joseph CONRAD, John GALSWORTHY, and D. H. LAWRENCE. His wife, Constance Garnett (1862–1946), was renowned for her translations of DOSTOYEVSKY and other Russian authors, much of whose work she made available to English-speaking readers for the first time.

Garnier, Robert (1544–1590)   French dramatist. A fervent Catholic, Garnier was concerned with restoring morality and faith during the religious wars. His own conviction expressed itself in the most lyrical and successful tragic verse dramas written in France before the great period of 17th-century French tragedy. His tragi-comedy BRADAMANTE and tragedy *Les Juives* (1583) are the high points of French Renaissance theatre.

Garrett, George [Palmer, Jr.] (1929–   )   American poet, novelist, short-story writer, and critic. Garrett is a prolific writer who has produced work in several genres. His poetry is written in FREE VERSE, with themes and language from everyday life; his *Collected Poems* was published in 1984. His short stories, including those in the collections *In the Briar Patch* (1961) and *Cold Ground Was My Bed Last Night* (1964), are noted for their vivid depiction of the rural South. His novels draw on diverse subjects: Florida politics in *The Finished Man* (1960); the American occupation of Italy in *Which Ones Are the Enemy?* (1961); evangelical religion in *Do, Lord, Remember Me* (1965); and the life of Sir Walter Raleigh in *Death of the Fox* (1971), the novel that most solidly established Garrett's literary reputation.

Garrick, David (1717–1779)   English actor and theatre manager. He was educated in Lichfield and went to London with Samuel JOHNSON, his teacher and friend. He and his brother started a wine business but were unsuccessful. Garrick turned to acting, and his quick success enabled him to buy part of the patent for Drury Lane; his career as manager began in 1747. He did much to revive SHAKE-SPEARE's popularity and wrote many theatre pieces himself —largely farces and light comedies.

Garrigue, Jean (1914–1972)   American poet and novelist. Garrigue's first collection of poems, *Thirty-Six Poems and a Few Songs*, which appeared in *Five Young American Poets* (1944), focuses on her bitter awareness of individual sacrifice in times dominated by war and ideology, which also constitutes the thematic core of *The Ego and the Centaur* (1947). Her later volumes, *The Monument Rose* (1953) and *Country Without Maps* (1964), show less preoccupation with individual autonomy. At her best, Garrigue displayed a rare musicality.

Garrison, William Lloyd (1805–1879)   American abolitionist. In 1831 Garrison founded *The Liberator*, a weekly newspaper in which he denounced slavery and slaveholders with such vehemence that he was nearly killed by a Boston mob in 1835. He sought complete and immediate freedom for the slaves and demanded that the North repudiate its ties with the South, condemning the Constitution as "a covenant with death and an agreement with hell." *The Liberator* ceased publication in 1865 after the passage of the thirteenth amendment to the Constitution, which abolished slavery.

Gary, Romain (original name Romain Kacew, 1914–1980)   Russian-born French novelist and diplomat. Gary is best known for *L'Education européenne* (1944; tr *A European Education*, 1960), about the Polish resistance during World War II, and for his passionate plea for the protection of wildlife, THE ROOTS OF HEAVEN. Almost all of his novels satirize men's weaknesses and particular types of modern affectation, yet point hopefully to the potential dignity of man. They are generally PICARESQUE tales of adventure and action, written by a man with a gift for storytelling and a wealth of personal experience. Gary's imaginative autobiography, *La Promesse de l'aube* (1960; tr *Promise at Dawn*, 1961), was in effect a tribute to his mother, an indomitable woman who devoted her life to advancing her son's education and career. In 1979 Gary's former wife, the actress Jean Seberg, committed suicide; the following year Gary shot himself.

Gas   The general title of a loose trilogy of expressionistic plays by Georg KAISER: *Die Koralle* (1917; tr *The Coral*, 1929), *Gas I* (1918; tr 1924) and *Gas II* (1920; tr 1931). Taken together, they constitute a monumental indictment of the overmechanization of modern society.

The hero of *The Coral*, who is called the Billionaire, has risen to the highest possible position in industry but is nonetheless constantly tormented by memories of his unhappy childhood. In an attempt to escape himself, he murders the Secretary, who is his double, and acquires the little piece of coral that symbolizes the latter's identity. Though he is to be executed for the crime, he feels exhilarated at having left his rut. In *Gas I*, the Billionaire's son has taken over the plant, which is now producing the gas that drives all other industry. The machinery fails, however, and there is a huge explosion that brings the son to his senses and prompts him to offer the workers land instead of a new gas plant, to offer them mastery over themselves rather than new enslavement to the machine. But his antagonist, the Engineer, persuades the workers to rebuild the plant, and the Billionaire's son is killed in an ensuing riot. In *Gas II*, the last play, the state has taken over the gas plant and is using it to fight a war. The workers attempt to make peace with the enemy, but fail; and the Great Engineer then persuades them to produce and use his new superweapon, a gas bomb. The device is detonated, and the play ends in a vision of total annihilation.

Gaskell, Elizabeth Cleghorn (born Elizabeth Stevenson, 1810–1865) English novelist. Gaskell is known for her depictions of English country life and for her pioneering studies of conflicts between capital and labor in Victorian industrialism. In the former class are the novels CRANFORD and *Wives and Daughters* (1864–66), which show a fine degree of observation and characterization. Her social novels, chiefly MARY BARTON and *North and South* (1855), are notable for their sympathetic portrayal of the oppressed laboring classes in mid-19th-century England. She herself lived mainly in Manchester, a center of the manufacturing regions. Gaskell was the friend of many literary figures in England, including Charlotte BRONTË, whose biography she wrote in 1857, and George ELIOT, whose work she influenced.

Gaspar (also Caspar or the white one) One of the three MAGI. His offering to the infant JESUS was *frankincense*, in token of divinity. At some point in medieval dramatic presentations of the nativity, he became a comic figure. He soon degenerated in Germany into Casperl, a popular comic servant who appeared in puppet shows, notably the FAUST play, in which he is Faust's servant.

Gaspé, Philippe Aubert de (1786–1871) Canadian novelist. Gaspé was high sheriff of the district of Quebec for many years until forced to withdraw from public life because of business difficulties and debts. At the age of seventy-six he published *Les Anciens Canadiens* (*The Canadians of Old*, 1863), a historical romance considered a classic of French-Canadian literature. His *Mémoires* (1866) is a collection of notes and hints for historians.

Gass, William H[oward] (1924–   ) American novelist, philosopher, and short-story writer. All Gass's writing is marked by a subtle treatment of philosophical issues and a careful, almost sensuous attention to words. His fictional characters are defined by their words rather than by conventional description, particularly in the "essay-novella" *Willie Masters' Lonesome Wife* (1968). His novel *Omensetter's Luck* (1966) and the stories in *In the Heart of the Heart of the Country* (1968) use this method to convey a rich sense of the ordinary life of the Midwest. The literary and philosophical essays contained in *Fiction and the Figures of Life* (1970) and *The World Within the Word* (1978) expound the theory that art should be considered as

an entity not replaced by its own interpretation. *Habitations of the Word*, a collection of essays, was published in 1985. It won the National Book Critics Circle Award for criticism, 1985–86.

gate of horn and ivory gate In Greek mythology, the two gates of the abode of Sleep. Through them dreams come forth. Those passing through the gate of horn are true.

Gattopardo, Il See LEOPARD, THE.

gaucho literature A term used to describe literary works dealing with the gaucho, or outlaw cattle hunter, of the Rio de la Plata region of South America. In many works of this type he is treated realistically, and some writers, notably Sarmiento in his FACUNDO, decried his influence on the national life of Argentina and Uruguay. Elsewhere, however, he emerges as a romantic symbol of a pure and uncomplicated past.

The literary manifestations of gaucho folklore sprang from the extemporaneous songs of the gaucho minstrels known as *payadores*. One of the first writers to compose a literary work on the gaucho theme was Hilario Ascasubi (1807–75), author of *Santos Vega* (1851; 1872), a poem narrated by the *payador* Santos Vega, a familiar figure in gaucho legend. The work is notable for the author's careful description of rural life and setting and for his use of authentic gaucho terminology. *Fausto* (1866) by Estanislao del Campo (1834–80) is a mock-epic in which a gaucho who has witnessed a performance of *Faust* describes the action in his own crude language. The outstanding example of gaucho poetry is probably MARTÍN FIERRO, whose title character is drawn in heroic proportions.

Among the first prose writers to concentrate on the gaucho was Eduardo Gutiérrez (1853–90), whose "thrillers," especially *Juan Moreira* (1880), demonstrated the vitality of the genre. Gutiérrez's dramatization (1884) of his work was extremely successful, and the gaucho soon became a familiar theatrical character, notably in the plays of Florencio SÁNCHEZ.

Soledad (1894) by Eduardo Acevedo Díaz is generally considered the prototype of later gaucho novels. Other novelists concerned with the subject were the Uruguayans Javier de Viana (1872–1926), author of the naturalistic *Gaucha* (1899), and Justino Zavala Muniz (1897–   ) and the Argentine Benito Lynch (1885?–1951), whose *Romance de un gaucho* (1930) is written entirely in gaucho idiom. Güiraldes's DON SEGUNDO SOMBRA, an able synthesis of American material and European technique, is widely regarded as the finest gaucho novel.

Gaudí, Antonio (real name Antoni Gaudí i Cornet, 1852–1926) Spanish architect. Gaudí was the architect of highly original, often fantastic buildings in Barcelona. His inspiration ranged from Gothic exaggeration to the ornate richness of ART NOUVEAU. His most spectacular work, the unfinished church of the Sagrada Familia, on which he worked for forty years until his death, is an ornate, dreamlike interpretation of a Gothic cathedral. Other works, such as his apartment house Casa Milá (1905–10), with its undulating and dripping façades, suggest caves and grottoes. Gaudí was uniquely successful in his effort to merge art and architecture, effectively creating enormous, habitable sculpture.

Gauguin, [Eugène Henri] Paul (1848–1903) French painter. One of the most remarkable figures in early modern art, Gauguin didn't begin painting until he was twenty-six. From 1879 to 1886 his work was exhibited with the impressionists. In 1883 he abandoned his job as a brokerage clerk and, two years later, separated from his wife and five children to devote himself completely to his art. Poor and in ill health, he traveled, mostly in France, stayed briefly with Vincent VAN GOGH in Arles, and finally in 1891 set out for Tahiti. He returned to France only once (1893–95) and spent the rest of his life in the South Pacific. There he developed a decorative, highly original and personal style consisting of simplified natural forms on generally flat planes. His use of brilliant, pure, unmixed color and his strong, mysterious figures had an enormous influence on later artists, notably Henri MATISSE and the expressionists. The last years of Gauguin's life were lived in poverty, despair, and great physical discomfort caused by his long-time syphilis. He made an unsuccessful attempt at suicide in 1897, but survived unhappily for another five years. He left an autobiographical account of his life in Tahiti in *Noa Noa* (1897; tr 1947). W. Somerset Maugham's THE MOON AND SIXPENCE is a fictional reconstruction of Gauguin's life.

Gaul (Lat, *Gallia*; hence the English adjective "Gallic") In classical geography the territory that comprises modern France and Belgium and part of northern Italy. Cisalpine Gaul, that is, Gaul on *this* (the Italian) side of the Alps, extended almost as far south as Florence. Transalpine Gaul, that is, Gaul beyond the Alps, included all the Gallic, German, and Celtic tribes from the Rhine to the Pyrenees. Gaul has been used as a literary name for modern France.

gauntlet, to run the To be attacked on all sides, to be severely criticized. The word came into English at the time of the THIRTY YEARS' WAR as *gantlope*, meaning the passage between two files of soldiers, and is the Swedish *gata*, "way; passage" plus *lopp* (connected with English *leap*), "course." The reference is to a punishment formerly common among soldiers and sailors; the company or crew, provided with rope ends, were drawn up in two rows facing each other, and the delinquent had to run between them, while every man dealt him as severe a chastisement as he could.

To throw down the gauntlet means to challenge. The custom in the Middle Ages, when one knight challenged another, was for the challenger to throw his gauntlet on the ground, and if the challenge was accepted the person to whom it was thrown picked it up.

Gautama (or Gotama) The family name of the BUDDHA; his given name was Siddhārtha (Sans, "one whose aim is accomplished"). His father, a ruler of the warrior class, was named Suddhodana; his mother was Maya. See BUDDHISM.

Gautier, Théophile (1811–1872) French poet and novelist. The early poems and prose tales of Gautier move in the realm of the fantastic and the macabre. In his later poetry, however, Gautier stresses perfection of form and achieves a carefully polished beauty. His emphasis on form and his doctrine of *l'art pour l'art* (ART FOR ART'S SAKE) make him a forerunner of the Parnassian school. Gautier's poetry includes *Poésies* (1830); *Albertus* (1832), a fantastic narrative poem; *La Comédie de la mort* (1833), another long poem, dealing with the sensual and the ideal; and *Emaux et camées* (1852), considered the best example of his pure, minutely chiseled style (see PARNASSIANS). Among Gautier's novels and tales are *Les Jeune-France* (1833), *Mlle de Maupin* (1835), *La Jettatura* (1856), and *Le Captaine Fracasse* (1861–63).

Gawain, Sir In ARTHURIAN LEGEND, one of the knights of the ROUND TABLE, nephew (in some versions, cousin) of King ARTHUR, and probably the original hero of the GRAIL quest. One of the earliest figures in the legends of Arthur, he appears in the Welsh *Triads* and the MABINOGION as Gwalchmei. He is the central figure in two major 14th-century English works: *The Alliterative Morte d'Arthur* and SIR GAWAIN AND THE GREEN KNIGHT. He is known as "the Courteous" and is first represented as the flower of chivalrous knighthood, but later writers (including Malory) downgraded him. In Malory's MORTE D'ARTHUR he is the son of King Lot and Queen MARGAWSE. He is King Arthur's favorite cousin and one of the most outstanding of the Round Table knights. He avenges the death of his father by killing King Pellinore, kills Sir Lamerok, who is the lover of his mother, and kills his cousin Sir Uwayne, who is the son of MORGAN LE FAY. Then, when Sir LAUNCELOT unwittingly kills his youngest brother, Sir GARETH, Sir Gawain swears revenge. Twice he challenges Sir Launcelot to single combat at the siege of Benwick, and the second time is fatally wounded by the great knight who so unwillingly fought him. Returning to Britain, Sir Gawain dies, but not before repenting and writing a letter of reconciliation to Sir Launcelot.

Gawain and the Green Knight See SIR GAWAIN AND THE GREEN KNIGHT.

Gay, John (1685–1732) English poet and playwright. A friend of Alexander POPE and member of the SCRIBLERUS CLUB, he is known for his pungent satire and contemporary realism. THE BEGGAR'S OPERA, a satire of Sir Robert WALPOLE and the court of George II, won him enduring fame. Among his other works are *Rural Sports* (1713), a poem dedicated to Pope; *The Shepherd's Week* (1714), six pastorals written partly to parody the pastorals of Ambrose Philips; *Trivia, or the Art of Walking the Streets of*

London (1716), a humorous but realistic depiction of the grotesque aspects of 18th-century London; *Polly*, a sequel to *The Beggar's Opera*, which was suppressed until 1777 because of the virulence of its political satire; and *Fables* (1727–38), a collection of sixty-six tales, the last sixteen of which were published posthumously. In the 18th century, *Fables* rivaled *The Beggar's Opera* in popularity. See RICH, JOHN.

Ge   In Greek mythology the personification of the Earth. Ge is the offspring of CHAOS, or at least comes into being after it. URANUS is both her child and husband. Their children, besides such things as seas and mountains, are the TITANS and Cyclopes. After her separation from Uranus she bore the ERINYES and GIANTS, being fertilized by the blood from his castration. Later she gave birth to TYPHON, whose father was TARTARUS.

Gehenna   The NEW TESTAMENT name for the Valley of Hinnom surrounding Jerusalem. It is the place of eternal torment, the "valley of slaughter" (Jer. 19:6), where sacrifices to BAAL and MOLOCH were offered. See TOPHET.

Geisel, Theodor Seuss   See SEUSS, DR.

geisha   From the TOKUGAWA period, a woman specially trained in the arts of gracious entertaining, including song, dance, flower arranging, and story telling. The institution of the geisha has played a prominent role in Japan's history, particularly since business entertaining has always been done outside the home. Geisha, although usually bound to a geisha house, are selective in choosing their patrons. They are not to be confused with licensed prostitutes.

Gelber, Jack (1932–   )   American playwright. Gelber's first play, *The Connection* (1959), drew considerable attention in the Living Theatre's off-Broadway production. The play, with its minutely realistic depiction of drug addiction, its improvised structure, use of jazz, and interaction with the audience, was held by some critics to herald the birth of the "New American Theatre." Gelber's subsequent plays continued his attack on conventional dramaturgy but none have achieved the success of the first.

Generación del 98   A group of Spanish writers of the early 20th century. Profoundly affected by the outcome of the Spanish-American War (1898), they probed deeply into Spanish life and institutions to find the reasons for their country's disastrous defeat. Their goal was the regeneration of the lost values of Spanish life through education and through opposition to all forms of parochialism. Seeing Spain's insularity as a major factor in her demise they sought to incorporate international influences into Spanish literature, at the same time celebrating the countryside and solid virtues of the Spanish people. The leading poet of the group was Antonio Machado, whose CAMPOS DE CASTILLA epitomized their aims. Other writers associated with the movement were Ramon PÉREZ DE AYALA, Jacinto BENAVENTE, Ramon VALLE-INCLÁN, Pió BAROJA, and Miguel de UNAMUNO. José Martínez RUIZ, one of the

group's most influential essayists, gave the name currency in his essays later published in *Clásicos y modernos* (1913).

Generación del 27   A group of Spanish writers, primarily poets, sometimes called the *Generation of the Dictatorship*, the *Generation of the Republic*, or the *Guillén-Lorca Generation*. The movement involved poets as varied as the intuitive Pedro SALINAS and the precise Jorge GUILLÉN. In their earliest manifestation, the poets showed the influence of SURREALISM, Freudian symbolism, and associative imagery of an intellectual or irrational nature. Picking up on ORTEGA Y GASSET's ideas on the dehumanization of art, the poets, especially Guillén, also experimented with pure poetry. Nonetheless, this dehumanization gave way to a passionate concern with the passage of time and the mysteries of life, love, and death. Along with Guillén and Salinas, other poets in the group—Rafael Alberti, Luis Cernuda, Federico GARCÍA LORCA, Vicente ALEIXANDRE, Gerardo Diego—worked toward a revival of interest in the work of Luis de GÓNGORA, on the three-hundredth anniversary of his death in 1927. The only true surrealist of the group was Cernuda, although García Lorca, Alberti, and Aleixandre flirted with surrealist techniques. Each poet defined poetry in his own way, but whatever their unusual imagery, metaphorical ambiguities, exuberant happiness, or destroyed illusions, this generation, as a group, produced a flurry of creative activity unparalleled in modern Spanish literary history.

Generación del 36   Sometimes called the *Generación del 35* or *Generación de la Guerra*. This group of writers, composed of Luis ROSALES, Dionisio Ridruejo (1912–75), and Leopoldo Panero (1909–62), among others, suffered two traumatic events: the proclamation of the Spanish Republic and the Spanish Civil War. For many critics they represent a lost generation, since their creative activities of the early 1930s were interrupted by the tragic war. 1935 is important because in that year Rosales and Ridruejo produced key poetic works, the first, *Abril* (*April*), and the second, *Plural*. Starting off as disciples of the GENERACIÓN DEL 27, they shared their mentors' interest in Luis de GÓNGORA. Soon they substituted the stylized and graceful poetry of GARCILASO DE LA VEGA, who had died exactly four hundred years earlier, in 1536. They rejected intellectual emphasis for more simple, intimate, and human poetry and returned for their inspiration not only to the Renaissance but also to the poets, especially Antonio MACHADO, of the GENERACIÓN DEL 98. In addition to their early light and joyful poetry, they became interested in social and then existential problems. In highly personal, often nostalgic poetry, they emphasized formal beauty, contemplation of nature, tranquility, harmony, and religious faith.

General's Dog, The   See KIPPHARDT, HEINAR.

General William Booth Enters into Heaven (1913)   A poem by Vachel LINDSAY. Written after the death of the leader of the Salvation Army, it was first published in *Poetry*. It is written in the rhythmic drumbeats of a Salvation Army band, and is intended to be sung to the music of "Washed in the Blood of the Lamb."

Genesis   The first book of the OLD TESTAMENT. In Hebrew it is called *Bereshith*, "in the beginning," from the initial words of the text. The first eleven chapters deal with the creation of the world, the FALL OF MAN and expulsion from the Garden of EDEN, the Flood, and the Dispersion of the Jews. The remaining chapters (12–50) are accounts of the lives of the patriarchs of Israel: ABRAHAM, ISAAC, JACOB, and JOSEPH.

Genet, Jean (1910–1986)   French dramatist and novelist. An admitted homosexual, pimp, and professional thief who had been in and out of jails from the age of ten, Genet was released from a sentence of life imprisonment in 1947 through the intervention of Jean-Paul SARTRE, Jean COCTEAU, and some of France's other leading artists and writers. Genet's novels—*Notre-Dame-des-Fleurs* (1943; tr *Our Lady of the Flowers*, 1949), *Querelle de Brest* (1947; tr *Querelle of Brest*, 1966), *Journal du voleur* (1949, with a preface by Sartre; tr *The Thief's Journal*, 1954), and *Miracle de la rose* (1946; tr *Miracle of the Rose*, 1965)—are thinly veiled autobiographical accounts of underworld life. Their lurid subjects are handled with a graceful, elegant prose style that sanctifies the crimes and purifies the obscenities.

Genet is best known for his plays, which have been both artistic and popular successes: THE MAIDS, *Haute Surveillance* (1949; tr *Deathwatch*, 1954), THE BALCONY, *Les Nègres* (1959; tr *The Blacks*, 1960), and *Les Paravents* (1961; tr *The Screens*, 1962). The plays reveal a concern with the illusory nature of reality, particularly with the ambiguous definitions of good and evil in a society characterized by repression and hypocrisy. Characters struggle against the image imposed on them by others but inevitably fail in their attempts to win freedom. Of all the dramatists of the ABSURD, Genet probes most deeply into the dreams, illusions, and bitterly frustrated longings of the inner self. See THEATRE OF THE ABSURD.

Genghis Khan (1162–1227)   A Mongol emperor. Named Temujin by his father, who died when the boy was thirteen years old, he took the title by which he is commonly remembered, and which means "perfect warrior." Genghis, with the aid of his mother, quickly regained the supremacy of the allied tribes who had defected after his father's death and then proceeded to extensive conquests. He took vast territories in north China, then moved westward through Iran and Iraq, subduing nations wherever he passed. He pillaged much of India as well. Genghis's generals ravaged considerable parts of Russia before returning to their homeland.

Barbarously cruel, Genghis was one of the most brilliant generals of history. His successors, however, could not hold his vast empire together, and it lasted a fairly short period. (See TAMERLANE.) His conquests, nevertheless, had far-reaching effects on history, for they set in motion a chain of events that led to the westward invasions of the Turks and helped to establish the Ottoman Empire. See GOLDEN HORDE; KUBLAI KHAN.

Génie du Christianisme, Le (The Genius of Christianity, 1802)   A treatise on Christianity by François René de CHATEAUBRIAND. The author extols Christianity, describing it as the great force that develops the soul of man, and citing it as the chief source of progress in the modern world. This work not only won great popular approval for Chateaubriand but also earned him the goodwill of NAPOLEON.

Genius (plural form Genii)   In Roman mythology the spirit that presides over the birth of every man and attends him throughout his life. (Women had no individual Genii, but were under the general protection of JUNO.) The Genius, as the individual life-principle, was especially honored on a man's birthday; considered as one's higher self, it was also called to witness a man's oath. There were also corporate Genii: Genii of the family, the tribe, and the nation. Under the empire, the Genius of the emperor was worshiped throughout the Roman world. Moral philosophers, seeking to explain moral conflict within human nature, posited an opposing, evil Genius. In Christian times these two Genii became the guardian angel and his diabolical counterpart.

"Genius," The (1915)   A novel by Theodore DREISER. The hero of this semiautobiographical work is Eugene Witla, a Midwestern artist, who becomes the art director of a large magazine corporation, has numerous love affairs, attains financial and social success, and marries Angela, who dies in childbirth. Witla suffers a breakdown but recovers his health and devotes himself thereafter to painting and to the care of his daughter. According to Helen Dreiser, in her book *My Life with Dreiser* (1951), Witla is a composite of three real persons: the artist Everett Shinn, an art editor whom Dreiser knew, and Dreiser himself.

Genroku   Japanese era (1688–1703) under the reign of the Higashiyama emperor. These years saw the greatest flowering of Japanese literature and culture during the TOKUGAWA period. Today, mention of the Genroku era evokes an image of cultural vitality and creativity. CHIKAMATSU Monzaemon, MATSUO Bashō, and IHARA Saikaku were among the writers active at the time.

Gentlemen Prefer Blondes (1925)   A humorous novel by Anita Loos. Subtitled "The Illuminating Diary of a Professional Lady," it tells the story of Lorelei Lee, a good-looking but not very intelligent girl, who manages to do very well for herself with Mr. Gus Eisman, the Button King. A satire on "the gold-diggers" of Hollywood, the book had an enormous vogue, though rumor has it that some fraction of its popularity may be ascribed to the fact that it was taken seriously by women who thought it a useful handbook on how to get rich.

Geoffrey of Monmouth (c1100–c1155)   Medieval English historian. A canon at Oxford, he wrote the important Latin prose HISTORY OF THE KINGS OF BRITAIN (*Historia regum Britanniae*), one of the sources of the ARTHURIAN LEGEND and of considerable literary influence. He is considered to be the creator of the heroic image of King ARTHUR.

George, St. The patron saint of England since about the time of the institution of the Order of the Garter (1349). St. George was "adopted" by Edward III. He is commemorated on April 23. St. George had been popular in England from the time of the early Crusades, for he was said to have come to the assistance of the Crusaders at Antioch (1098), and many of the Normans (under Robert, son of William the Conqueror) then took him as their patron.

The existence of historical St. George is in doubt, but his legend has been a powerful one. There are various versions of his *Acta*, one saying that he was a tribune and that he was asked to come and subdue a dragon that infested a pond at Silene, Libya, and fed on the dwellers in the neighborhood. St. George came, rescued a princess (Sabra) whom the dragon was about to make its prey, and slew the monster after he had wounded it and the princess had led it home in triumph by her girdle.

The legend of St. George and the dragon is in part a universal folk theme (see ANDROMEDA), in part an allegorical expression of the triumph of the Christian hero over evil, which St. John the Divine beheld under the image of a dragon. Similarly, St. Michael, St. Margaret, St. Sylvester, and St. Martha are all depicted as slaying dragons; the Saviour and the Virgin as treading them under their feet. A snake or a dragon biting its tail was sometimes an attribute of Father Time in Renaissance art.

The legend forms the subject of an old ballad given in Percy's RELIQUES OF ANCIENT ENGLISH POETRY. Spenser introduces St. George into THE FAERIE QUEENE as the Red Cross Knight.

George, Stefan (1868–1933) German poet. Strongly influenced by NIETZSCHE in his youth, George adopted an aristocratic doctrine of the poet as a chosen being, from which he never entirely departed, though later, under the impact of World War I, he became more concerned with political reality and developed a conception of the poet as priest, with a duty not only to himself and his art, but also to his people. George was a prolific translator (e.g., of BAUDELAIRE, DANTE, SHAKESPEARE, the English PRE-RAPHAELITE BROTHERHOOD) and came into personal contact with the French symbolist poets VERLAINE and MALLARMÉ, by whom he was strongly influenced. His most famous collections of poems include: *Das Jahr der Seele* (*The Year of the Soul*, 1897), *Der Stern des Bundes* (*The Star of the Covenant*, 1914), and *Das neue Reich* (*The New Kingdom*, 1928). They were translated in *The Works of Stefan George* (1949). His austere classical style abounds with esoteric mythical allusions and archaic linguistic forms, and his works are rendered still less accessible by

innovations in punctuation and typography. The "George circle," a small group of literary apostles whom he collected about himself, is credited with a major role in the critical "rediscovery" of such important German writers as Friedrich HÖLDERLIN and Jean Paul RICHTER, whose works had fallen into neglect around the turn of the century. See HOFMANNSTHAL, HUGO VON.

Georgians A group of English poets, whose style dominated the early years of the 20th century, and who wrote poetry of nature and rustic life in the traditional manner of WORDSWORTH. The trend was inaugurated by the long narrative poem "The Everlasting Mercy" (1911) by John MASEFIELD and A. E. HOUSMAN's Shropshire ballads; it was turned into a movement by Edward Marsh, who published the biennial anthology *Georgian Poetry* (1912–22). The name reflects the accession of King George V in 1910. The chief Georgian poets were Lascelles ABERCROMBIE, Edmund BLUNDEN, Rupert BROOKE, W. H. DAVIES, John DRINKWATER, Ralph HODGSON, J. C. SQUIRE, and Edward THOMAS.

georgic A poem intended to give instructions on a particular skill, usually associated with the practical aspects of farming or rural life. Although georgics are primarily didactic in purpose, they frequently digress into descriptions of natural beauty and extol the virtues of work and country living. The most famous example is Vergil's GEORGICS.

Georgics A didactic poem in four books on the subject of agriculture, composed in 37–30 BC by VERGIL. As Vergil's BUCOLICS were based on THEOCRITUS' *Idyls*, so his *Georgics* also had a classical Greek precedent: HESIOD's *Works and Days*. Although the work was conceived and executed within the classical genre of the simple didactic, it is more than an agricultural handbook: it is the subtle and profound work of a philosopher-poet. Like the *De rerum natura* of LUCRETIUS, to which it is in many ways a reply, Vergil's *Georgics* is built upon a solid didactic foundation from which it rises naturally to peaks of impassioned eloquence.

Book I contains advice on farming in general. After giving an account of the ills that followed the assassination of Julius CAESAR, the poet prays that the Roman blood spilled at Pharsalus and PHILIPPI may be sufficient to expiate the nation's ancestral guilt and that the young Octavius Caesar (see AUGUSTUS) will save the Roman world from civil war.

In Book II Vergil concerns himself with grapevines and fruit trees, though he again rises above mere instruction. This book also contains a famous paean to the crops and heroes of Italy.

At the beginning of Book III the poet rededicates himself to his work. He takes up the care and propagation of livestock, and at the end of the book describes the effect of a plague that killed all living things.

Unlike Lucretius, who ends his poem with a scene of a plague in Athens, Vergil passes directly into the sunny

Book IV of his *Georgics* and tells a tale of miraculous regeneration. The book is formally concerned with the raising of honey bees, but its most important sections deal with two myths of death and resurrection, one within the other. The bees of Aristaeus, god of beekeeping, have suddenly died. His mother, the sea divinity Cyrene, advises him to consult Proteus, who tells Aristaeus that his bees have been killed by the dryads. The nymphs were avenging the death of Eurydice who, while being pursued by Aristaeus, stepped on a snake and died of its bite. Proteus then relates the pathetic tale of Orpheus and Eurydice. At his mother's suggestion, Aristaeus sacrifices four bulls and four heifers to the shades of Orpheus and Eurydice. After he has let their carcasses rot for nine days, he beholds a swarm of living bees issuing forth from the decaying bellies of the cattle.

Geri   See ODIN.

Géricault, [Jean Louis André] Théodore
(1791–1824)   French painter. The exhibition in 1819 of Géricault's masterpiece, *The Raft of Medusa*, caused a storm of controversy, both because it depicted a shipwreck that had scandalous political implications, and because its free, realistic style marked a turning point in the struggle between classical and romantic schools of painting. A powerful draughtsman and superb colorist, Géricault is equally known for his paintings of animal life, particularly horses, and for vivid historical scenes.

Germanicus Caesar (15 BC–AD 19)   Roman general. Germanicus was adopted by his uncle, the emperor Tiberius, and received command of the legions in Germany. He scored a huge success in his campaign against the Germans (AD 11–16), but just when he was about to conquer the whole area between the Rhine and the Elbe, Tiberius, alarmed at his strength, recalled him to Rome. It was believed by many that Germanicus was poisoned, possibly at Tiberius's bidding. Germanicus had nine children by Agrippina, among whom were the notorious CALIGULA and AGRIPPINA, mother of Nero.

German romanticism   Romanticism in Germany was not one movement but a series of separate ones. The first of these, called Jena romanticism after the small university town where most of the writers met, flourished around 1798–1802 and centered on the brothers F. and A. W. SCHLEGEL. The Schlegels, however, did not regard themselves as the founders of a romantic movement for, in their definition, romantic meant simply modern (from the Middle Ages on), as opposed to classical (Greek and Latin). As romantic authors, they wished to go beyond the classics, but *not* to deny them; in fact, they were very much a part of the philhellenic tradition that also produced WEIMAR CLASSICISM.

But they did set out in new directions. F. Schlegel urged writers to strive for a progressive universal poetry, by which he meant that romantic poetry must constantly develop, that it must not cease to be progressive, and that its ultimate goal must be universal, a synthesized comprehension

of the entire world; these ideals of dynamism and universality were opposed to the Weimar classical ideals of balance and limitation. NOVALIS and WACKENRODER strove for a new synthesis of art and religion. And TIECK and Novalis made new advances in the characteristically romantic form of the MÄRCHEN, which was later developed by BRENTANO and E. T. A. HOFFMANN.

The second of Germany's romantic movements, which flourished in Heidelberg around 1804–8, was less urbane than Jena romanticism and tended more to stress the beauties of unspoiled nature. It was also in Heidelberg romanticism that the romantic interest in German history and folklore, which had begun with Wackenroder and Tieck, first really took root. Major figures in this phase were Achim von ARNIM, Brentano, Joseph von Görres (1776–1848), EICHENDORFF, and the brothers GRIMM.

But in the atmosphere of the growing nationalism that culminated in the wars of liberation against Napoleon (1813–15), German literature took a turn toward REALISM, and it is mainly this which characterizes the work of the Berlin group of about 1808–13, although in their idealism and their frequent use of the *Märchen* form they are still recognizably romantic. Major figures were E. T. A. Hoffmann, Friedrich von Fouqué (1777–1843), CHAMISSO, Heinrich von KLEIST, and again, Arnim and Brentano.

Finally, after the wars of liberation, under the conservative Prussian and Austrian regimes of 1815–48, German romanticism again followed the tenor of the times. The Swabian School, which HEINE attacked vigorously in his *Die romantische Schule* (*The Romantic School*, 1833) and which included UHLAND, Justinus Kerner (1786–1862), LENAU, Wilhelm Hauff (1802–27), and Gustav Schwab (1792–1850), was a primarily conservative group, interested in the preservation of tradition, and was already very like the postromantic BIEDERMEIER movement.

Disparate though it was, there is a unifying principle inherent in German romanticism. In the 18th century, some voices had already been heard against the prevailing rationalism of the age: Johann Georg Hamann (1730–88), HERDER, JACOBI, KLOPSTOCK, the poets of the STURM UND DRANG and of WEIMAR CLASSICISM. In very general terms, German romanticism may be seen as the culmination of all these movements, the final overthrow of the ENLIGHTENMENT, and the definitive redirection of 19th-century literature into nonrationalistic areas of experience. The philosophers most closely associated with German romanticism were FICHTE and SCHELLING. The theologian SCHLEIERMACHER had the greatest influence on German religious thought. See ROMANTIC IRONY.

Germinal (1885)   A novel by Emile ZOLA, one of the ROUGON-MACQUART novels. *Germinal* is a study of the bitter sufferings of workers in the French mines. Zola's intense sympathy for the lower classes and his pleas for social reform find powerful expression in this careful portrait of life in the mines.

Gernsback, Hugo (1884–1967) American publisher, editor, author, and a "father of science fiction." Gernsback immigrated to the United States from Luxembourg, founded the first radio magazine, *Modern Electrics*, and in 1926 the first magazine devoted to what he called "scientifiction," *Amazing Stories*. His own effort in that genre, an ill-written story full of technological predictions entitled *Ralph 124C 41+: A Romance of the Year 2660*, was serialized earlier (1911) in *Modern Electrics*. As a tribute to Gernsback's overall contribution to the field, the awards presented annually at the World Science Fiction Convention since 1953 are called Hugos.

Geronimo (Indian name Goyathlay, 1829?–1909) Indian medicine man and leader of the southernmost band of Chiricahua Apaches. A renowned warrior, Geronimo was distinguished as the last American Indian to surrender formally to the United States. He led a band into Mexico when the Chiricahua reservation was abolished but he was captured and returned to another reservation. In 1881 he escaped again, leading a series of raids throughout the southwest. In 1883 he was captured by General George Crook (1829–90); he escaped again in 1885 and waged war on the Army until 1886, when General Nelson A. Miles (1839–1925) persuaded Geronimo to surrender. He was imprisoned in Florida and then confined to Fort Sill, Oklahoma, where he took up farming, converted to Christianity, and made money selling pictures of himself. He eventually became a celebrity, appearing at public affairs like the Pan-American Exposition at Buffalo in 1901, the St. Louis World's Fair in 1904, and in Theodore Roosevelt's inaugural procession. He dictated his life story to Stephen M. Barrett and it was published as *Geronimo's Story of His Life* (1906, repr 1970).

Géronte The name of the old man who is a stock figure in early French comedy. By Molière's time the character had taken on the unpleasant traits exemplified by the Géronte of LE MÉDECIN MALGRÉ LUI.

Gerontion (1920) A poem by T. S. ELIOT. Spoken by "an old man in a dry month," it is a despairing poem about old age, aridity, the spiritual decay of the world, and the need for and unlikelihood of salvation.

Gershwin, George (1897–1937) American composer. Gershwin began his career by composing popular songs, soon combining them into musical comedies, such as *Of Thee I Sing* (1931; the first musical to win a PULITZER PRIZE). However, his chief importance results from his ability to bring jazz and popular styles into the realm of classical music, especially with the internationally famous works *Rhapsody in Blue* for piano and orchestra (1924) and the opera *Porgy and Bess* (1935; see PORGY). His songs have been collected in *George Gershwin's Song Book* (1932). His brother, Ira Gershwin (1896–1983), was a popular Broadway lyricist who wrote lyrics for many of George's shows; he also worked with Kurt WEILL and Harold ARLEN, among others.

Gertrude In Shakespeare's HAMLET, the queen and mother of Hamlet. A weak-willed woman, who has married her husband's brother and murderer, she draws from Hamlet the cry: "Frailty, thy name is woman!"

Gerusalemme liberata (Jerusalem Delivered) The celebrated romantic epic by Torquato TASSO. Written during the Italian Renaissance, sometime between 1559 and 1575, it was published in a definitive version of twenty cantos in 1581. The whole work had been translated into English by 1600, the accomplishment of Edward Fairfax. Unlike other Renaissance romances, it was based on the historic events of the First Crusade (1096–99) and it utilized several historical characters. The plot begins with a fictional war in its sixth year and the election of GOFFREDO (Godfrey) as the chief of the Christian armies encamped on the plains of Tortosa. As they prepare to attack Jerusalem, its king, Aladino, learns from the enchanter Ismeno that the city will not fall if a statue of the Virgin is removed from a Christian church and placed in a mosque. Finding the statue stolen, Aladino plans revenge on the Christian community of the city, but a young Christian maiden, Sofronia, offers to take the blame, as does her beloved, Olindo, who hopes thereby to save her. Aladino promptly orders both put to death, and they are saved only by the timely appearance of the warrior maiden CLORINDA, who offers her sword in return for their lives. Now the pagan warrior Argante (Argantes), having failed to dissuade Goffredo from the attack, declares war upon the Crusaders. When the Christians attack the holy city, Argante kills their champion Dudone, and the Christians withdraw to do him honors. Heeding the infernal decree of Plutone (Pluto), the enchanter Idraote sends his beautiful niece ARMIDA to confound the Christian camp. She tells Goffredo of her need for ten knights to retake the city of Damascus; he is unwilling, but many more than ten Crusaders follow her away, among them the most puissant in the Christian army. Rinaldo also departs in anger because Goffredo has denounced him for the murder of Gernando, his rival for the command vacated because of the death of Dudone. Argante now challenges the Christian knights and kills Ottone, but his ferocious duel with Tancredi (TANCRED) is interrupted when Erminia, who loves the latter, lures him away by disguising herself as his beloved Clorinda. Goffredo's depleted forces now face the challenge of Solimano (the Soldan, or Solyman), leader of the Arabs, but the archangel Gabriel intervenes to save them. Solimano soon joins forces with Aladino. In the renewed assault by the Crusaders, Tancredi unknowingly wounds Clorinda, who forgives him and is baptized before dying. Goffredo, learning from a vision that only Rinaldo can break the enchantments of Ismeno and free the armies to continue their assault upon the city, sends Guelfo and Ubaldo to bring him back. Dallying with Armida, Rinaldo is finally disenchanted and persuaded to return. With his return, the Crusaders are soon victorious. The unyielding

Argante is killed by Tancredi, but the Egyptian forces, spurred by Armida, try to renew the battle. Rinaldo administers the final defeat to the infidels by killing Solimano and subduing Armida. With Aladino dead and the Egyptian king killed by Goffredo, the Crusaders can enter the great city at will. There, at dawn, led by Goffredo, they worship at the sepulcher of Jesus.

Gervaise   One of the principal characters in the novels of Emile Zola's ROUGON-MACQUART series. Gervaise first appears in L'ASSOMMOIR.

Geryon   In Greek mythology a monster with three bodies and three heads. Geryon's oxen ate human flesh and were guarded by Orthrus, a two-headed dog. HERACLES slew both Geryon and the dog.

Gesta Romanorum (Deeds of the Romans)   Latin collection of tales, many of them of Oriental origin, very popular in the Middle Ages. It may have been compiled in England in the late 13th century; it was printed in 1473 and frequently thereafter, different versions including about one hundred to two hundred tales. The episodes are usually arbitrarily assigned to the reign of a Roman emperor, but there is little real history; a "moral" or "application" follows each tale, purportedly for the use of preachers, but it is not a religious work. CHAUCER, SHAKESPEARE, and later English writers have drawn frequently on the tales for plot material.

Gethsemane   An olive grove or garden on the western slope of the Mount of Olives. It was here that JESUS went to pray after the LAST SUPPER, and that JUDAS ISCARIOT betrayed him (Mark 14:32–43; Matt. 26:36–49). Centuries-old olive trees growing on the site are today tended by monks of the Greek, Armenian, Russian, and Roman Churches.

Gettysburg   A town in southern Pennsylvania and the site of a major battle (July 1–3, 1863), often considered the turning point of the American CIVIL WAR. The Confederates under General LEE were defeated by numerically superior Union troops under Gen. George Meade. Casualties are estimated at about twenty-three thousand for the Union Army, about twenty-eight thousand for the Confederates. Though Lee's retreat into Virginia was temporarily blocked by the flooding of the Potomac, Meade's failure to attack permitted the Confederates to escape on July 13 after the river fell.

Gettysburg Address   An address prepared by President Abraham LINCOLN and delivered on November 19, 1863, at the dedication of the national cemetery at GETTYSBURG battlefield. Lincoln's brief address, which followed a two-hour oration by Edward Everett, the principal speaker of the day, is perhaps the most moving and eloquent statement of the American creed.

Gezelle, Guido (1830–1899)   Flemish poet, priest, and teacher. Acclaimed as Flanders's greatest poet, Gezelle was to Flemish poetry what CONSCIENCE was to the novel. Combining Flemish with the dialect of Western Flanders,

he wrote poems of nature and religion in a lyrical and unaffected style. Although his works—including *Dichtoefeningen* (*Poetic Exercises*, 1858), *Tijdkrans* (*Crown of Time*, 1893), *Rijmnsoer* (*Necklace of Rhymes*, 1897), and *Laatste verzen* (*Last Verses*, 1901)—were often attacked during his life, he was a major impetus in reviving Flemish as a literary language.

Ghelderode, Michel de (1898–1962)   Belgian playwright. Author of over fifty plays, Ghelderode lived in relative obscurity until *Fastes d'enfer* (*Chronicles of Hell*, 1929) was produced in Paris in 1947. Essentially an expressionist, he was influenced by Fernand Crommelynck (1885?–1970), with whom he shared a fascination with medieval Flanders, and by the fantastic paintings of BRUEGHEL and BOSCH. He used the traditions of Belgian puppet theatre to achieve strange and striking effects in such plays as *Pantagleize* (1929), *La Balade du grand macabre* (1934), and *Hop Signor!* (1935). His dramas, close in spirit to Elizabethan farce, feature grotesque caricatures of lonely, psychically damaged people in a perpetual struggle between good and evil. Certainly the most original drama in modern Belgian theatre, Ghelderode's many plays have been collected in the five-volume *Théâtre complet* (1950–57). *Barabbas* (1928), a moving modern version of the Crucifixion, is still performed in Flanders during Holy Week.

Ghiberti, Il (real name Lorenzo di Cione di Ser Buonaccorso, 1378–1455)   Florentine sculptor. Ghiberti's style combines tradition and innovation: the grace of medieval sculpture and a vivid pictorial quality, unparalleled elsewhere, caused by the use of perspective and the manipulation of planes in relief. He executed the famous north and east doors of the baptistry of Florence (1402–22 and 1427–52, respectively), which are elaborately decorated with panels in gilt bronze relief. Toward the end of his life he wrote three *Commentaries* (*I commentarii*) on art, which survive in very imperfect form and include his autobiography and the first account of the lives of the artists of the 14th century.

Ghirlandaio, Il (real name Domenico di Tommaso Bigordi, 1449–1495)   Florentine painter. Ghirlandaio was noted for his religious easel pictures and his narrative frescoes. Influenced by Fra Lippo LIPPI, he in turn influenced the young MICHELANGELO, who worked in his studio. Among his best-known works are the frescoes behind the high altar of Santa Maria Novella in Florence, especially *The Birth of the Virgin*; portraits of Florentine humanists of the Medici circle; the touching *Portrait of an Old Man and a Boy*; the *Adoration of the Shepherds* in the Uffizi; and the wall frescoes of the Sistine Chapel, done with BOTTICELLI.

Ghosts (1881)   A play by Henrik IBSEN. Ten years after her husband's death, Mrs. Alving is about to open an orphanage dedicated to his memory. Her son, Oswald, has just come home from abroad. She reveals to the moralistic Pastor Manders, who many years before had advised her against leaving her husband, that the late Captain Alving had lived and died drunken and profligate, and that Regina, the serving-girl, is actually his daughter. Oswald is beginning to go insane from hereditary syphilis, a legacy from his father; and Mrs. Alving realizes that, in basing her actions on duty rather than love, she has been indirectly responsible both for her husband's dissoluteness and her son's incipient insanity. The "ghosts" in the title refer not only to the disease passed on by her husband, but to the dead conventions and beliefs that led Mrs. Alving to conceal the truth and that kept her from living "for the joy of life."

Giacometti, Alberto (1901–1966) Swiss painter and sculptor, the son of the impressionist painter Giovanni Giacometti (1868–1933). He began his career as a painter but, from 1915 on, concentrated primarily on sculpture. In 1922 Giacometti moved to Paris and became an important exponent of SURREALISM, producing narrow, elongated human figures and semi-abstract symbolic forms. Giacometti's haunting and anguished work, which was viewed by many as an expression of existential despair, exerted a considerable influence on modern sculpture.

Giacosa, Giuseppe (1847–1906) Italian dramatist and librettist. The leading Italian playwright of the late 19th century, Giacosa wrote plays that mirrored the changing popular tastes of his day. Initially (c1870–90), he composed graceful, charming verse plays reflecting the romantic cult of the Middle Ages and the naturalistic interest in precise descriptions of character and setting. *Una partita a scacchi* (1873; tr *The Wager*, 1914), *Il trionfo d'amore* (1875; tr *The Triumph of Love*, 1887), and *La Signora di Challant* (written for Sarah Bernhardt, 1891) are among the plays that belong to this period. Subsequently, influenced both by the problem plays of IBSEN and the European psychological novels then in vogue, he wrote *Tristi amori* (1888; tr *Unhappy Love*, 1916), *Come le foglie* (1900; tr *As the Leaves Fall*, 1911), and *Il piu forte* (1905; tr *The Stranger*, 1916). In collaboration with Luigi Illica (1857–1919), he wrote the libretti to PUCCINI's *La Bohème* (1896), *Tosca* (1899), and *Madama Butterfly* (1904).

Giants (or Gigantes; also Gk, *Gegeneis*, "Earth-born") In Greek mythology, offspring of GE (earth), impregnated by blood from the castrated URANUS (sky). They were in most accounts of human form, but with serpents' tails instead of feet. They warred on the gods, hurling whole trees and giant rocks. They were finally defeated only with the aid of HERACLES. Immortal, they were buried alive under mountains—generally volcanoes. Possibly Oriental in origin, they are thought to have been personifications of the violent forces in nature. They should not be confused with OTUS AND EPHIALTES.

Giants in the Earth: A Saga of the Prairie (1924–1925 in Norwegian; 1927 in English) A novel by Ole E. RÖLVAAG. The first volume of a trilogy that includes *Peder Victorious* (1929) and *Their Father's God* (1931), it is

a stark and realistic work describing the hardships, both mental and physical, of a small group of Norwegian farmers who set out from Minnesota with their families in 1873 to settle in the then unopened Dakota Territory. The novel centers on Per Hansa, his devotion to the land, the growing religious fanaticism of his wife, Beret, and his disappearance in a blizzard.

The hero of the two succeeding novels is Peder Victorious Holm, Per Hansa's youngest son, who marries a devout Irish Catholic, Susie Doheny, and later quarrels with her over the raising of their son, Petie.

Giants in the Earth was successfully dramatized (1928) by Thomas Job and made into an opera (1951) by Douglas Moore.

giaour Among the Muslims, a term used contemptuously for one, especially a Christian, who does not adhere to their faith.

In BYRON's poem "The Giaour" (1813), Leilah, the beautiful concubine of the caliph Hassan, flees with a giaour to her destruction; the giaour later becomes a monk and tells his story while on his deathbed.

Gibbon, Edward (1737–1794) English historian, noted for his masterpiece, *The History of the* DECLINE AND FALL OF THE ROMAN EMPIRE. Gibbon formed the plan for this great work during a tour of Italy (1764) while "musing amidst the ruins of the Capitol." He entered Parliament in 1774 and was made commissioner of trade and plantations. The first volume of his *History*, which appeared in 1776, was very well received, though his chapters on Christianity provoked severe criticism from some quarters. Succeeding volumes were not as warmly received as the first. Gibbon's *Memoirs*, put together by Lord Sheffield, were published in 1796.

Gibran, [Gibran] Kahlil (1883–1931) Syrian-American writer and artist. Born in Lebanon, Gibran with his family immigrated to the U.S. in 1895. He returned to Beirut to enter college at the age of fourteen and later studied art with RODIN in Paris. His earlier works, consisting of prose poems and plays, were written in Arabic and were widely known in the Arab world. Gibran's novels tend to be heavily sentimental, but he was a master of the prose poem, which was the most effective vehicle for his humane, slightly mystical treatment of universal human problems. His best-known work, *The Prophet* (1923), carrying his message of redemption through love, has been translated into thirteen languages and is repeatedly reprinted.

Gibson, Charles Dana (1867–1944) American illustrator. The creator of the "Gibson Girl," Gibson modeled his drawings on his wife, Irene Langhorne, who thus became the gay 90s' ideal of looks and manners. He did satirical illustrations for *Harper's* and *Scribner's* magazines, served as editor of *Life*, and illustrated many books.

Gide, André (1869–1951) French writer and editor. Brought up in an austere Protestant household, Gide reacted passionately against the prohibitions of revealed religion. Yet his search for self—the underlying theme of his more than eighty published works—remained essentially a religious search, and Gide is as well known for his influence as a moralist and a thinker as for his contributions to literature.

At eighteen he met Pierre LOUŸS and other aspiring writers and artists and attended the literary salons of José Maria de HEREDIA and Stéphane MALLARMÉ. In 1891 he published *Les Cahiers d'André Walter*, reflecting his spiritual love for his cousin Madeleine and his conviction that physical desire must be suppressed. He published his first poems the next year, but by 1900 he had practically abandoned this form of writing. Gide shared Paul VALÉRY's fascination with the myth of Narcissus as a symbol of man's hopeless and misdirected yearning for perfection. His friends read the essay *Le Traité du Narcisse* (1891) as a definition of symbolism, but its theories were actually quite differently intended, and Gide soon separated from the group.

With his first trip to North Africa in 1893, Gide broke with his entire past. He rejected mortification of the flesh, believing that harmony of body and soul was possible only if both were satisfied, and deliberately sought sensual experience. His discovery of his homosexual leanings troubled him, but the tolerance of the North Africans and the open encouragement of Oscar WILDE in 1895 freed him of embarrassment. THE FRUITS OF THE EARTH is a hymn to the joy of the search for experience.

Gide considered himself a disturber of youth, ever urging individual self-cultivation, while paradoxically warning against a narcissistic concern with self. His fiction is autobiographical only to the extent that each major figure is an exaggerated personification of one aspect of his own character. Thus, THE IMMORALIST and STRAIT IS THE GATE were conceived as companion pieces to show the unhappy consequences of amoral hedonism in the first and of equally selfish self-abnegation and asceticism in the second.

Always concerned with motivation and the function of man's will, Gide was influenced by DOSTOYEVSKY (his translations and analyses did much to make the Russian novelist popular in France) and agreed that there are both good and evil impulses, not traceable to common motives such as love, hate, or self-interest. He was fascinated by examples of the apparently disinterested *acte gratuit*, or gratuitous act, and concluded that it is motivated solely by a personal need to assert one's individuality and is thus the only human act that reveals one's essential character; LAFCADIO's ADVENTURES presents a murder as such an act.

Gide was twice tempted to find self-development in commitment to something outside himself. His correspondence with his friends Francis JAMMES (pub 1948) and Paul CLAUDEL (pub 1949) reveals their unsuccessful attempt to convert him to Catholicism. Then, on a trip to French Equatorial Africa in 1925, he was horrified by the French treatment of the natives. He expressed his views on the subject in *Voyage au Congo* (1927; tr *Travels in the Congo*, 1930) and *Le Retour du Tchad* (1928), and began to advocate the reform of social institutions, becoming an admirer of the ideal of Communism and its practical experiment in the Soviet Union. But he could not accept the party's orthodox dogma without the right to question, and in 1936 was disillusioned by a visit to the Soviet Union.

The novel THE COUNTERFEITERS exposes the hypocrisy and self-deception with which people try to avoid sincerity. Gide's own obsessive concern with personal and public honesty often led him to face public scandal—especially with his insistence that the bounds of the natural include homosexuality. When *Corydon* (1924), an essay that maintains that the homosexual is harmful neither to himself nor to society, drew violent criticism, Gide answered with IF IT DIE . . . He pursued this ideal of perfect frankness in his comprehensive private, literary, and philosophical *Journals* (1939–50), omitting only the details of his marriage with his cousin Madeleine. After her death (1938), he wrote the painful account of their mutual love and unhappiness, published posthumously as *Et nunc manet in te* (1951; tr *Madeleine*, 1952).

Gide was one of the most influential editors of LA NOUVELLE REVUE FRANÇAISE. In 1947 he was awarded the NOBEL PRIZE for his varied contributions to literature.

Other important works by Gide, available in English, include the satires *Paludes* (1895) and *Le Prométhée mal enchaîné* (1899), collected as *Marshlands and Prometheus Misbound* (1953); the plays *Philoctète* (1899), *Le Roi Candaule* (1901), *Saül* (1903), *Bethsabé* (1912), and *Perséphone* (1934), collected as *My Theatre* (1951); the play *Oedipe* (1931) and the tale *Thésée* (1946), collected as *Two Legends: Theseus and Oedipus* (1950); and the tales *Isabelle* (1911) and THE PASTORAL SYMPHONY, included in *Two Symphonies* (1931). See ECOLE DES FEMMES.

Gideon   In the OLD TESTAMENT, a Hebrew liberator, reformer, and one of the judges of Israel for forty years. With a company of three hundred men, Gideon delivered his people from the Midianites. The army was purposely reduced to three hundred by eliminating all who were afraid and all who drank from a stream instead of lapping the water from their hands. To give the impression of being a huge army, they made a great noise by breaking pitchers and blowing trumpets (Judg. 7:16–20).

Gift of the Magi, The (1906)   A short story by O. HENRY. Containing perhaps the most famous of O. Henry's trick endings, this Yuletide narrative tells how a nearly penniless young husband and wife are each determined to buy the other a suitable Christmas present. He sells his watch to buy her a set of combs; she has her beautiful hair cut off and sells the tresses to buy him a watch fob. The tale was included in THE FOUR MILLION.

Giguère, Roland (1929–   )   Canadian poet, painter, and typographer. SURREALISM in Quebec made its initial impact on Giguère through the painter Borduas and his group, Les Automatistes. It was confirmed by his meeting with André BRETON between 1957 and 1963, when Giguère was working in France. In poems that have both a universal and a local reference, Giguère uses the intuitive and spontaneous, the elemental and erotic to remake the political, moral, and imaginative landscape. Among his books are *Age de la parole* (1965) and *Le Main au feu* (1973).

Gilbert, Sir Humphrey (1539?–1583)   English navigator. The half-brother of Sir Walter RALEIGH, Gilbert made a voyage with him in 1578. He wrote a *Discourse of a Discoverie for a new passage to Cataia* (pub 1576, written and circulated earlier), in which he urged exploration for the discovery of a northwest passage. His arguments probably influenced Sir Martin FROBISHER'S voyages in search of such a passage in 1576–78. He established the first British colony in North America at St. John's, Newfoundland (August 5, 1583), but went down with his ship on the return voyage to England.

Gilbert, Michael [Francis] (1912–   )   English mystery novelist and short-story writer. Gilbert is best known for his books featuring Inspector Hazlerigg, who appeared in his first novel, *Close Quarters* (1947), and again in *Death Has Deep Roots* (1951), among others. Among his later novels are *The Final Throw* (1982), *The Black Seraphim* (1983), and *The Long Journey Home* (1985). A successful lawyer, Gilbert with his legal acumen lends plausibility to his novels.

Gilbert, Sir William S[chwenck] (1836–1911) English dramatist and writer of humorous verse. Gilbert is best remembered as librettist of the Gilbert and Sullivan comic operas. Several of these owe their origin to Gilbert's collection of humorous ballads, *Bab Ballads* (1866–71), which show his great facility in versifying. He had a penchant for whimsicality, nonsense, and topical satire.

Gilbert and Sullivan operas (also called the Savoy Operas)   A series of comic operas, text by William Schwenck GILBERT and music by Arthur Seymour SULLIVAN, originally produced (1881 et seq) at the Savoy Theatre in London by Richard D'Oyly Carte. An outstanding achievement in music collaboration, the titles are *Thespis or The Gods Grown Old* (1871), *Trial by Jury* (1875), *The Sorcerer* (1877), *H. M. S. Pinafore, or The Lass That Loved a Sailor* (1878), *The Pirates of Penzance or The Slave of Duty* (1879), *Patience or Bunthorne's Bride* (1881), *Iolanthe or The Peer and the Peri* (1882), *Princess Ida or Castle Adamant* (1884), *The Mikado or The Town of Titipu* (1885), *Ruddigore* (1887), *The Yeomen of the Guard* (1888), *The Gondoliers* (1889), *Utopia, Limited* (1893), and *The Grand Duke* (1896). The first of these operas, and the last two, written after a serious quarrel between Gilbert and Sullivan, are almost never performed. Highly satiric, the operas poke fun at contemporary Victorian life. The Gilbert and Sullivan following, called Savoyards after the name of the theatre, is still considerable.

Gil Blas de Santillane, Histoire de (1715, 1724, 1735)   A PICARESQUE novel in four volumes by Alain René LESAGE. The extraordinary number of episodes in this novel render any coherent plot summary impossible. The setting is Spanish, but the society depicted is really French. The hero, Gil Blas, leaves home at seventeen to try his fortune at Salamanca; in his journeys he meets a large number of people—adventurers, thieves, valets, actors, authors, doctors, clergymen, and noblemen. Lesage has very little good to say about any of them. Gil Blas himself, though full of good intentions, is a singularly weak character. One critic (Lester G. Crocker) says that Gil Blas goes through the three stages of innocence, corruption, and the triumph of virtue. Among the more famous portraits in the novel are the Archbishop of Granada, Don Alvaro, and Dr. Sangrado. From the literary historical view, Lesage continues the traditions of the realistic novels written in the 17th century by Charles Sorel, Antoine Furetière, and Paul Scarron. This novel also affords a good example of the evolution of the French language between the 17th and 18th centuries, in that an increase in the concision of narrative style is apparent.

Giles, St.   Patron saint of cripples. The tradition is that Childeric, king of France, accidentally wounded a hermit in the knee when hunting; and the hermit, that he might better mortify the flesh, refused to be cured, remaining a cripple for life. His day is September 1, and his symbol a hind, in allusion to the "heaven-directed hind" that went daily to his cave near the mouth of the Rhone to give him milk. He is sometimes represented as an old man with an arrow in his knee and a hind by his side. Churches dedicated to St. Giles were usually situated in the outskirts of a city, and originally outside the city walls, because some cripples and beggars were not permitted to pass the city gates.

Gilgamesh   A mythical hero of Sumer and Babylonia. Though he is best known from the famous Babylonian *Epic of Gilgamesh*, he was originally a Sumerian hero, the king of the ancient city of Erech. In a Sumerian myth, Gilgamesh comes to the aid of the goddess INANNA, who is distressed because she is unable to cut down the *Huluppu* tree in the garden, in order to have furniture made of it: a snake, a dangerous bird, and Lilith have all taken up residence in it. When Gilgamesh chases them away and chops down the tree, Inanna gives him (untranslatable) gifts, but he accidentally drops them into the underworld. His companion ENKIDU undertakes to go after them, but fails to observe the precautions essential in such ventures and cannot return. His ghost, however, is permitted to come back long enough to carry on a lengthy conversation with Gilgamesh. The ending of the myth is unknown from the fragmentary tablets on which it was found.

Gilgamesh, Epic of (c2000 BC)   A Babylonian poem. One of the oldest and most important major epics in literature, it was first discovered on clay tablets in the library of ASSUR-BANI-PAL (668–626 BC). Like the ILIAD and the ODYSSEY, it is composed of far earlier elements of myth and folklore that have been joined into a single poem through a process of gradual accretion. Also, like Homer's epics, it enjoyed immense popularity for centuries; passages from it were frequently quoted in later literature. The epic includes stories, originally separate, of GILGAMESH, a legendary king of Sumerian origin; ENKIDU, a sort of primeval man; Utnapishtim, the Babylonian NOAH; and several other tales.

Gilgamesh was a mighty, part-immortal king of Erech whose subjects eventually prayed for relief from his tyranny. Taking pity on them, the lord of heaven ordered the goddess Aruru to mold out of clay a hairy wild man named Enkidu. This monstrous creature lived with and ate like the beasts, whom he saved from the snares of hunters. Learning of his existence, Gilgamesh sent a young woman to seduce him, after which the animals would have no more to do with him. The woman told him of Gilgamesh's tyranny, and Enkidu resolved to challenge his power. This he did at the New Year's festival, but when he had defeated Gilgamesh in wrestling, the two became fast friends.

The first exploit that they undertook together was to cut down a cedar in the sacred wood guarded by the monster Humbaba, who breathed fire and plague and had one eye that could turn men to stone. They felled the cedar and Humbaba came roaring to the attack, but the sun-god (at the plea of the goddess Ninsun, Gilgamesh's mother) saved them by blinding the monster with hot winds. After the friends defeated and beheaded Humbaba, the goddess ISHTAR endeavored to seduce Gilgamesh, but he reminded her bluntly how she had treated TAMMUZ and other lovers, turning many of them into beasts. Furious, she belabored the lord of heaven with threats until he sent the storm bull of heaven against them, but the two youths promptly killed it and offered its heart to the sun-god. Enkidu now had a series of dreams, which revealed to him that the gods, outraged at this act, had decreed his death. Lying on his bed, he gradually grew weaker until he died.

Grief-stricken, Gilgamesh determined to learn the secret of eternal life by seeking out the sage Utnapishtim, the only mortal ever to have escaped death. In spite of many trials and warnings, Gilgamesh reached the ocean of death and was rowed across it by the ferryman Urshanabi into the presence of Utnapishtim. The old man told him how, in the early days of the earth, a great flood had destroyed his fellow men. He, warned by EA, the god of wisdom, had saved himself and his family by building an ark in which they had floated for seven days and nights until the ark grounded on a mountain. Utnapishtim had then sent out a dove, a swallow, and a raven; and, when the last of these, having found dry land, did not return, he and his family

had offered thanks to the gods for their safety. Utnapishtim and his wife, thereafter, had been sent to the island at the end of the earth, where they now lived and where they had become immortal.

Gilgamesh now understood that this immortality was a special gift of the gods, and that neither Utnapishtim nor any other mortal would ever learn the secret of eternal life. The sage told him, however, of an herb growing at the bottom of the sea that would restore his youth. Taking leave of the old man, Gilgamesh tied stones to his feet, dived into the sea, and found the plant. After he had gone a long way on his journey home to Erech, he stopped to rest and bathe in a spring, laying the plant on the ground. A snake quickly appeared and made off with it; tasting the plant, it cast off its old skin and was made young again. Gilgamesh wept. Now he understood that no human being can escape old age and death. Resigned to the fate that he shared with all men, he returned to his homeland, where he died.

Gill, Brendan (1914–   )   American journalist, short-story writer, and novelist. In 1936 Gill began a long association with THE NEW YORKER, contributing stories and profiles, and serving as its film and theatre critic over a period of more than four decades. An account of his work and his colleagues appeared in *Here at The New Yorker* (1975).

Ginger Man, The   See DONLEAVY, J. P.

Ginsberg, Allen (1926–   )   American poet. Ginsberg is probably the most prominent figure to emerge from the BEAT MOVEMENT. His loosely structured verse is characterized by a spontaneous dictation of experience, with graphic, often crude and unsettling imagery. While much of his work is rhythmically and structurally reminiscent of William Carlos WILLIAMS, his "bardic improvisations" are largely drawn from experiences with hallucinogenic drugs, visions (notably inspired by William BLAKE), and the teachings of ZEN BUDDHISM. With the publication of HOWL AND OTHER POEMS, Ginsberg became a literary and cultural sensation when his publisher, Lawrence FERLINGHETTI, was arrested (later acquitted) for printing obscene material. The *Howl* trial provided the counter culture of the 1950s with a *cause célèbre* and launched Ginsberg on his dual career as a "cultural guru" and a major poet.

The earlier verse published in *Empty Mirror* (1961) reveals his deep debt to Williams's attempts to create a new, uniquely American poetic idiom. KADDISH AND OTHER POEMS, which is regarded by many as Ginsberg's finest work, was published in the same year. As with most of his other verse, *Kaddish* is at once an intensely personal expression and an indictment of the "madness" of society at large. In the writings from 1953 to 1960 that appear in *Reality Sandwiches* (1963), Ginsberg pays homage to his two mentor-friends, Jack KEROUAC and William S. BURROUGHS.

TV Baby Poems (1967), *Planet News 1961–1967* (1968), and *Ankor Wat* (1968) began a series of poems involving specific social and political concerns. Although Ginsberg's status as the "spiritual godfather of the counterculture" during the 1960s and early 1970s sometimes eclipsed his stature as a writer, he continued to produce poetry, notably *Iron Horse* (1972) and *The Fall of America: Poems of These States 1965–1971* (1973). In his later work he is less concerned with presenting the poem as a means of communicating urgency of feeling and more with it as an event in itself. *Mind Breaths* (1978) and *Poems All Over the Place: Mostly Seventies* (1978) contain elements of his earlier work as well as experiments with traditional verse forms.

Ginsberg's published prose includes *Indian Journals* (1970); *Allen Verbatim* (1975), a collection of lectures and essays; and *Journals: Early Fifties, Early Sixties* (1977). *As Ever* (1977) is the collected correspondence of Ginsberg and Neal Cassady. (Cassady was the model for the character Dean Moriarty in Kerouac's ON THE ROAD.) *Collected Poems, 1947–1980* was published in 1985, and *White Shroud: Poems, 1980-1985* appeared in 1986.

Ginzburg, Natalia (1916–   )   Italian novelist, essayist, and playwright. Ginzburg's work is distinguished by a simple, unassuming, and conversational style; her stories generally focus on the unhappiness endured by women, as in her novel *E stato cosi* (1947; tr *The Dry Heart*, 1949). She wrote with great feeling and compassion about life under fascism and the Resistance movement in World War II in *Tutti i nostri ieri* (1952; tr *A Light for Fools*, 1956) and *Le voci della sera* (1961; tr *Voices in the Evening*, 1963). *Lessico famigliare* (1963; tr *Family Sayings*, 1967) is largely autobiographical. *Caro Michele* (1973; tr *No Way*, 1974) is another novel.

Gioconda, La   A portrait by LEONARDO DA VINCI. One of the most famous of paintings, *La Gioconda* is better known as the *Mona Lisa*. Its subject was a Neapolitan noblewoman, Madonna (Mona) Lisa del Giocondo. The portrait, which hangs in the Louvre, is especially noted for the lady's smile, which inspired "The Gioconda Smile," one of Aldous HUXLEY's best-known short stories. It has been pointed out, however, that similar enigmatic smiles were a popular feature of portraits in this period.

Gioconda, La (1898)   A drama by Gabriele D'ANNUNZIO. The title character is a model for a brilliant young sculptor, Lucio Settala. Out of loyalty to his devoted wife, Silvia, he tries to resist the fascination that Gioconda exercises over him. Eventually, however, he leaves Silvia for Gioconda, who he feels is the real inspiration for his art. The play is dedicated to Eleonora Duse (1859–1924), who scored a great success in the title role. Her famous romantic liaison with D'Annunzio served also as the basis for his novel THE FLAME OF LIFE.

Giorgione, Il (also known as Giorgio Barbarelli da Castelfranco, c1478–1510)   Little is known of Giorgione's life and scarcely a half dozen paintings can be safely ascribed to him, yet this young and influential student of Giovanni BELLINI is known as the chief master of the Venetian school of his day. He is celebrated for the sensuous and poetic grace of his work and for his introduction of a new range of subject matter: idyllic scenes of pastoral love that depend for their effect on the golden color harmony that unifies the whole. Among his authenticated works are the enigmatic *Tempest* (1506), the *Fête Champêtre*, the *Castelfranco Madonna* (1504), and *Sleeping Venus*.

Giotto [di Bondone] (1266?–1337)   Florentine fresco painter. The greatest Italian painter of the pre-Renaissance, Giotto was, according to tradition, a pupil of CIMABUE and a friend of DANTE. VASARI acclaimed him for breaking with the rigid Byzantine tradition of his time by introducing the direct observation of nature. His monumental work brought a new strength and force to painting, and he was the first to focus on the human drama in the Christian scenes he painted. He created architectural and landscape backgrounds for his massive, sensitively drawn figures, using subdued color and masterful composition to contribute to the expressive power of each scene. The quality of his genius is best seen in the thirty-eight frescoes in the Scrovegni (Arena) Chapel in Padua, depicting the life of Jesus and other biblical subjects (1305–10); the extent of his actual contribution to the earlier frescoes in the Church of St. Francis at Assisi is a subject of debate among modern art historians, although these frescoes were attributed to him until the 19th century. He also painted frescoes for the Bardi and Peruzzi chapels of the Church of Santa Croce in Florence.

Giovanni, Nikki (1943–   )   American poet. A native of Tennessee, Giovanni explores her consciousness as a black woman in her poetry. She is impatient for social reform, and her poems are flavored with incendiary rhetoric. Images of violence are couched in jarring rhythms, many of which derive from black folk music, jazz, and spirituals. The more successful individual poems deal with her own artistic conflicts: the inclination to dwell purely in the realm of art as opposed to speaking polemically for her black brethren. Her most important books are *Black Feeling, Black Talk* (1968), *Black Judgement* (1969), *Re:Creation* (1970), and *The Women and the Men* (1975). *Cotton Candy on a Rainy Day* (1978) introduced a more introspective, less political note to her poetry.

Giraudoux, [Hippolyte] Jean (1882–1944)   French dramatist, novelist, essayist, and diplomat. Giraudoux combined thirty years of service in the French diplomatic corps (1910–40) with a highly successful and productive writing career. All his works are characterized by a verbal extravagance, elegance, and a virtuosity of imagery and style that verges on poetic fantasy; even in a serious play like TIGER AT THE GATES his delicate touch masks the horror of the apparent inevitability of tragedy.

The early novels *Suzanne et le Pacifique* (1921; tr *Suzanne and the Pacific*, 1923) and *Juliette au pays des hommes* (1924) show Giraudoux's predilection for young female characters who represent the candid innocence of divinity, of nature, and of ideal truth. To grow up or to fall in love is to enter the "terrible convent of human beings" with its heartache, disillusion, and even tragedy; his treatment of the UNDINE tale in the play *Ondine* (1939; tr 1954) has the same theme. Giraudoux has a humanistic and compassionate view of the adult world; nevertheless, he delights in escaping from it in extravagant comedies like THE MADWOMAN OF CHAILLOT.

Many of his plays are based, with varying degrees of fidelity, on Greek myths or biblical stories. Apart from *Tiger at the Gates,* his other plays drawn from these sources include *Amphitryon 38* (1929; tr 1938), *Judith* (1931; tr 1963), *Électre* (1937; tr *Electra,* 1955), and *Sodome et Gomorre* (1943).

Girl of the Golden West, The (1905)   A play by David BELASCO. The heroine is a courageous saloonkeeper in a Western mining camp who falls in love with an outlaw. The play was the basis of Puccini's *La fanciulla del west* (1910), the first grand opera written on an American theme.

Girondists (also called the Gironde or the Girondins) A middle-class political party during the FRENCH REVOLUTION (1791–93). The Girondists were so named because many of their members were from the department of the Gironde. Their point of view was republican: they advocated overthrow of the monarchy, an aggressive foreign policy, and were anticlerical. Although the most powerful party for a time, they were overthrown in June 1793 because of their attempt to soften the ever-rising spirit of fanaticism among the more extreme revolutionists.

Gironella, José María (1917–1976)   Spanish novelist. Gironella achieved considerable popular success, both at home and abroad, with a series of novels about the Spanish Civil War. *Los cipreses creen en Dios* (1953; tr *The Cypresses Believe in God,* 1955), detailing the events leading up to the war, was followed by *Un million de muertos* (1961; tr *One Million Dead,* 1963), *Ha estallado la paz* (1966; tr *Peace After War,* 1969), and *Condenados a vivir* (1971).

Girty, Simon (1741–1818)   American soldier, known as "the Great Renegade." Girty deserted from the Revolutionary Army (1778) and later led British and Indian raiding expeditions. Although he is said to have saved the life of the American soldier and Indian fighter Simon Kenton, Girty was widely known for his brutality. He is the title character of Elinor WYLIE's poem "Simon Girty" and also appears in Stephen Vincent Benét's THE DEVIL AND DANIEL WEBSTER.

Gissing, George [Robert] (1857–1903)   English novelist, critic, and essayist. Gissing's brilliant academic career was cut short when, attempting to reform and support a young prostitute, he was caught stealing money from classmates. He was expelled and imprisoned; soon after he

spent a year of privation and wandering in the U.S., then returned to England. He married the prostitute, entering a life of misery and poverty, and when she died, he remarried, again unhappily.

Gissing's love of the classics, the hardships of his life, and his mixed idealism and pessimism are reflected in his best-known novels, *The Nether World* (1881) and NEW GRUB STREET. These books are characterized by their realism and psychological acuteness, and by the subtlety, grace, and subdued passion of their style. Other aspects of his temperament and talent are exhibited in THE PRIVATE PAPERS OF HENRY RYECROFT and his fine *Charles Dickens: A Critical Study* (1898).

Gjellerup, Karl (1859–1919)   Danish writer long resident in Germany. Gjellerup's interest in German art and music found expression in *Richard Wagner i hans Hovedwaerk* (*Richard Wagner in His Chief Work, the Ring of Nibelung,* 1890). His novels include *En Idealist* (1878), *Germanernes Laerling* (1882), and *Der Pilger Kamanoto* (*The Pilgrim Kamanoto,* 1906), a novel set in India and the only novel by Gjellerup to be translated into English. In 1917 he shared the NOBEL PRIZE in Literature with another Danish writer, Henrik Pontoppidan.

Gladkov, Fyodor Vasilyevich (1883–1958) Soviet novelist. Gladkov is famous as the author of *Tsement* (1926; tr *Cement,* 1929), one of the first proletarian novels of Soviet literature, which had an immense success with Soviet critics. In 1932–38 Gladkov published *Energiya* (*Energy*), describing the building of the Dneprostroy dam. One of his best works is his autobiography, *Povest o detstve* (*Story of My Childhood,* 1949), reminiscent of Gorky's autobiography in style and quality (see CHILDHOOD).

Gladstone, William Ewart (called the Grand Old Man, 1809–1898)   English statesman, financier, and orator. Gladstone's high abilities were early recognized by his party (Whig), and during the short-lived administration of Sir Robert Peel (December 1834–April 1835), he was first made junior lord of the treasury and then undersecretary for the colonies. During his brilliant career he was chancellor of the exchequer (1852–55), leader of the Liberal Party (1867), and Prime Minister four times (1868–74; 1880–85; 1886; 1892–94). Milestones in his career are the disestablishment of the Irish Church, two Home Rule bills for Ireland (1886, 1893), both defeated, and the denunciation of Turkish atrocities in Bulgaria. The most prominent man in politics of his time, he was rivaled only by his Tory opponent, Benjamin DISRAELI. In spite of his full career, he found time for considerable writing on political and literary topics.

glasnost (Russ, "openness")   Term used for the policy of greater permissiveness initiated by Mikhail GORBACHEV that allowed the publication within the Soviet Union of previously suppressed works and new work by hitherto silenced authors. Some of these works include the poem *Requiem* (1935–40) by Anna AKHMATOVA and Boris PASTERNAK's *Doctor Zhivago* (1957). Liberalization in the arts coincided with the release of a number of political prisoners.

Glaspell, Susan (1882–1948)   American novelist and dramatist. With her husband, George Cram Cook, Glaspell organized the PROVINCETOWN PLAYERS, an experimental theatre designed to combat the commercialism of Broadway. For its opening, she and her husband wrote the satiric one-act play *Suppressed Desires* (1915). Glaspell wrote short stories, novels, and plays, including *Alison's House* (1930), which was based on the life of Emily DICKINSON and was awarded a PULITZER PRIZE.

Glasperlenspiel, Das   See MAGISTER LUDI.

Glassco, John (1909–1981)   Canadian poet, novelist, and translator. Born and educated in Montreal, Glassco left McGill University before graduating and went to Paris in 1928, an experience he described in *Memoirs of Montparnasse* (1970). He returned to Quebec in 1935, choosing a rural life, which provided the tone and imagery for much of his elegiac poetry in *A Point of Sky* (1964) and *Selected Poems* (1971). Using various pseudonyms, he also wrote fiction, notably as Miles Underwood, among whose works was *The English Governess* (1960; repr *Harriet Marwood, Governess*, 1976), an attempt to re-create the Victorian novel of masochistic "education."

Glass Menagerie, The (1944)   A play by Tennessee WILLIAMS. With Tom Wingfield narrating both the introduction and the conclusion, the play is set in memory. It takes place shortly before Tom left home for the merchant marine and focuses on his mother, who constantly imagines scenes of the "gentlemen callers" of her girlhood, and on his sister, Laura, a partial cripple who has withdrawn from the real world into the private universe of her glass animals. The mother insists that Tom bring home a gentleman caller for Laura. While he is there, the horn on Laura's glass unicorn is broken, making the animal less of a freak and allowing her momentarily to break out of the world of her menagerie. However, after kissing Laura, the friend admits that he is already engaged; Laura's emergence from her fragile world is left in doubt. The mother and daughter are admittedly based on the author's own mother and his mentally troubled and eventually lobotomized sister.

Glastonbury   An ancient town in Somerset, England, dating from Roman times. It is traditionally associated with ARTHURIAN LEGEND and with the Holy GRAIL. It is at Glastonbury that JOSEPH OF ARIMATHEA is said to have established the first Christian Church in England and, earlier, to have planted his staff, which took root and became the Glastonbury thorn that burst into blossom every Christmas Eve. Local legend has it that Arthur and GUINEVERE are buried there, and it has been recorded of the historical Arthur that he was buried there. Most of the Arthurian

romances, however, place Arthur in AVALON after his death.

Glaucus (1) Once a fisherman of Boeotia. He became a sea-god endowed with the gift of prophecy and instructed APOLLO in the art of soothsaying.

(2) In ancient Greek myth, a son of SISYPHUS and father of BELLEROPHON. Because he would not allow his horses to breed, APHRODITE maddened them until they killed him.

(3) A mythical leader of Lycian troops in the TROJAN WAR. For the story of his meeting with Diomedes, see DIOMEDEAN SWAP.

(4) In ancient Greek myth, a son of MINOS. He drowned in a vat of honey. Minos ordered the seer Polydus, once he had found the child, to revive him. The CURETES told Polydus to find the most pat simile for a cow of three colors. When Polydus mentioned the fruit of the dog rose, he saw a snake and killed it. The snake's mate restored the first snake with an herb, which Polydus promptly used on Glaucus with success. Later, however, Polydus was angry with Minos for confining him to the palace. He had taught the art of divination to Glaucus, but on finally leaving Crete, he made Glaucus spit into his mouth and the boy forgot everything he had learned.

Glinka, Mikhail Ivanovich (1804–1857)   The first important Russian composer. Glinka wrote *Ivan Susanin*, retitled *A Life for the Tsar*, the first Russian national opera, in 1836; *Ruslan and Ludmilla*, after a poem by PUSHKIN, in 1842; and overtures, symphonies, and orchestral suites.

Globe, The   Elizabethan playhouse built in 1599 by Richard and Cuthbert BURBAGE on the Bankside south of the Thames. It became the permanent home of the Lord Chamberlain's (later King's) Men, SHAKESPEARE's company, and it was here that his greatest plays, including *Hamlet*, *Macbeth*, *King Lear*, and *Othello*, were first presented. The Globe was unquestionably the most popular theatre in London and its design—about which there is considerable controversy among scholars—became the model for the numerous theatres that sprang up in the early years of the 17th century. In June 1613 The Globe was consumed by fire during a presentation of Shakespeare's *Henry VIII*. The theatre was rebuilt in 1614 and remained standing until 1644, when it was pulled down to make room for residences.

Gloriana   The Queen of Faeryland in Spenser's FAERIE QUEENE. The name was used as a nickname for ELIZABETH I.

Glorious Revolution   The name given by English Whigs to the movement (1688–89) in which JAMES II was driven from the throne and the crown was offered to William of Orange and his wife, Mary, eldest daughter of James. Carried out by those who opposed James's attempts to impose Catholicism on the country and to restore absolute monarchy, the revolution established the supremacy of Parliament. Although there was little opposition to the revolution in England, James had many supporters in Scotland and Ireland. James's Scottish adherents won the battle of Killiecrankie (1689), but James himself was defeated at the battle of the Boyne in Ireland (1690). See RIGHT, DECLARATION OF.

gloss   (1) An explanation or interpretation, the rendering of an obscure expression. The term is especially used to denote a marginal or interlinear note, of the kind abounding in medieval literature where Latin, Greek, or Hebrew words had to be rendered in the vernacular Teutonic, Romanic, and Celtic tongues. These special glosses are philologically very important and represent the oldest rudiments of bilingual dictionaries.

(2) A running commentary amplifying and explaining a difficult text.

(3) In prosody, a poetic composition that is a variation on a theme. A "texte" is chosen from some poetic work, and succeeding stanzas use a line or a couplet of the texte as the last line or lines until it has all appeared in the composition.

Gloucester, earl of   In Shakespeare's KING LEAR, the faithful old lord who shelters Lear from the storm. His aid to Lear is betrayed by his bastard son, EDMUND, and his eyes are plucked out by Lear's daughter REGAN and her husband, CORNWALL. Evicted from his castle and bent on suicide, Gloucester is saved by his loyal son, EDGAR, whom he had previously disinherited.

Glover, Denis [James Matthews]   (1912–1980) New Zealand poet, typographer, and editor. In the 1930s Glover founded the Caxton Press, which provided an outlet for the finest New Zealand poets of the time and established a tradition of fine printing. Glover's early verse conveys the exuberance of breaking new ground. He rejected derivative colonial verse and took an irreverent view of local life and custom in the satirical poems collected in *Six Easy Ways of Dodging Debt Collectors* (1936) and *The Arraignment of Paris* (1937). In the 1950s he found his most successful poetic voice in the personae of Harry (*Sings Harry and Other Poems*, 1951) and the prospector Arawata Bill (*Arawata Bill: A Sequence of Poems*, 1953). Both figures are solitary observers, at home in the open natural world. The poems are often simple, lyrical descriptions of the New Zealand landscape. Two of his subsequent collections are *Enter without Knocking* (1971) and *Wellington Harbour* (1976).

Gluck, Christoph Willibald [Ritter von]   (1714–1787)   Austrian composer of operas. Gluck began his career with considerable success composing in the standard operatic style of his day, which greatly emphasized vocal display. In *Orfeo* (1762; see ORPHEUS) he created a new style of Italian opera. Conventional virtuosity was abandoned in favor of dramatic truth and a moving simplicity of expression, while the use of a chorus and ballet was adopted from French opera. His choice of this style was largely due to his librettist, Raniero de'Calzabigi. Later "reform" operas were *Alceste* (1767), *Paride e Elena* (1770), *Iphigénie en Aulide* (1774), *Armide* (1777), and *Iphigénie en Tauride* (1779). There was a famous feud in Paris between the "Gluckists" and the followers of Niccolò Piccini (1728–1800).

Glück, Louise [Elisabeth]   (1943–   )   American poet. Glück studied with THE CONFESSIONAL POETS but remained distinctly independent. After a tentative first book, *Firstborn* (1968), she demonstrated a mastery and surety of voice in *The House on Marshland* (1975), *The Garden* (1976), and *Descending Figure* (1980). These poems are mainly about birth, family life, sexual love, and motherhood, yet they have a remote and eerie quality. Glück's dominant themes are separation and man's sense of helplessness in a strange, dreamlike world. In 1985 she published *The Triumph of Achilles*.

Glumdalclitch   In Jonathan Swift's GULLIVER'S TRAVELS, a girl, nine years old, forty feet high, who is Gulliver's nurse in BROBDINGNAG.

Glyn, Elinor   (1864–1943)   English novelist. Replete with tiger skins and violent passion, Glyn's best-selling romantic novels were once considered daring and slightly scandalous. *Three Weeks* (1907), *It* (1927), and *Romantic Adventure: The Autobiography of Elinor Glyn* (1936) are among her best-known works.

gnome   (1) According to the Rosicrucian system, a misshapen elemental spirit. It dwells in the bowels of the earth and guards the mines and quarries. The word seems to have been first used (perhaps invented) by Paracelsus, and to be derived from Gr, *ge-nomos*, "earth-dweller."

(2) A short statement, such as a proverb, maxim, or epigram, intended to express a general truth.

gnomic poetry   A term that applies to verse that makes frequent use of gnomes (see GNOME, def. 2). The 6th-century BC Greek poets THEOGNIS, SOLON, and SIMONIDES, among others, were known as the Gnomic Poets for their pithy, sententious statements on moral or ethical matters. The book of PROVERBS in the Bible is a well-known example of gnomic writing.

Gnostics   (fr Gr, *gnosticos*)   *Knowers*, as opposed to *believers*; various sects in the first six centuries of the Christian era. They tried to accommodate Christianity to the speculations of PYTHAGORAS, PLATO, and other Greek and Oriental philosophers. They taught that knowledge, rather than mere faith, is the true key to salvation. In the Gnostic creed Jesus is esteemed merely as an eon or divine attribute personified, like Mind, Truth, Logos, Church, etc., the whole of which eons made up this divine pleroma, or fullness. St. PAUL, in several of his epistles, speaks of this "fullness [pleroma] of God."

Go and Catch a Falling Star   (1633)   The first line of a famous lyric by John DONNE, often entitled "Song." A series of impossible feats are declared to be less difficult than the task of finding a woman "true and faire."

goat An animal associated from very early times with the idea of sin (see SCAPEGOAT) and with DEVIL lore. It is an old superstition in England and Scotland that a goat is never seen during the whole of a twenty-four-hour period, for once a day it pays a visit to the devil to have its beard combed. Formerly the devil himself was frequently depicted as a goat, and the animal also typifies lust and lechery.

Goat Song (Bocksgesang, 1921; tr 1926) A play by Franz WERFEL. It deals with the elemental frenzy of a group of peasants in revolt who worship a monster, half man and half ram, that has appeared out of the woods. The revolt is suppressed, and the monster killed; but one of the peasant women bears its child, which symbolizes the continued existence of a chaotic potential in man.

Gobbo, Old In Shakespeare's MERCHANT OF VENICE, the "sand-blind, high-gravel blind" father of Launcelot Gobbo. He encounters his son after an absence in an amusing scene of reconciliation.

Launcelot Gobbo A clownish servant, the son of Old Gobbo. He leaves SHYLOCK's service for shorter hours, more pay, and more sleep in the service of BASSANIO.

Go-Between, The (1953) A novel by L. P. HARTLEY. A tragic love triangle is observed by an uncomprehending thirteen-year-old schoolboy, who carries messages between the adult characters.

goblin A familiar demon. It lived, according to popular belief, in private houses and chinks of trees; in many parts miners attribute those strange noises heard in mines to them. The word is the Fr *gobelin*, probably a diminutive of the surname *Gobel*, but perhaps connected with Gr *kobalos*, "impudent rogue; mischievous sprite," or with the Ger KOBOLD. As a specimen of forced etymology, it may be mentioned that Samuel JOHNSON, in his *Dictionary*, records that some derive this word from the name of the *Gibellines*, a faction in Italy; so that *elfe* and *goblin* are *Guelph* and *Gibelline* because the children of either party were terrified by their nurses with the name of the other.

Godard, Jean-Luc (1930–) French filmmaker. A leading director of the NEW WAVE, Godard started out as a critic, then made five short films before directing his first feature, À *bout de souffle* (*Breathless*, 1959), in which the collage of styles and unconventional fusion of the cynical, the poignant, and the tragic immediately revealed its director as an original talent and the cinema's most effective exponent of the existentialist attitudes of the late 1950s. In his many subsequent films—usually made on a low budget and freely improvised while shooting—Godard increasingly used film as a medium for an evolving personal vision of contemporary life. With such films as *Masculin-féminin* (1966), *La Chinoise* (1967), *Weekend* (1967), *Vent d'est* (1969), *Tout va bien* (1972), and *Ici et ailleurs* (1977), he became antinarrative, and even anticinematic, as his original apolitical stance evolved

through anarchism into a committed political radicalism strongly tinged with nihilism.

Godden, Rumer (pen and maiden name of Mrs. Rumer Haynes Dixon, 1907–) English novelist. A prolific and popular novelist who also wrote many books for children, Godden had her first success with *Black Narcissus* (1939), which, like many of her books, is set in India, where she grew up. So is *Breakfast with the Nikolides* (1942), which introduces the first of her many child protagonists, also featured in *An Episode of Sparrows* (1955) and *The Greengage Summer* (1958). Another prominent theme, the nature of time, is central to *Take Three Tenses* (1945) and *China Court: The Hours of a Country House* (1961). *In This House of Brede* (1969) is a subtle, complex novel set in an English Benedictine convent. In collaboration with her sister, Jon Godden, she wrote the charming memoirs *Two under the Indian Sun* (1966) and *Shiva's Pigeons* (1972). In 1980, she turned to India again and wrote the biography *Gulbadan Begum: Portrait of a Rose Princess at the Mughal Court*.

Godfather, The See PUZO, MARIO.

Godfrey, Thomas (1736–1763) American poet and dramatist. The son of a Philadelphia glazier, Godfrey was apprenticed to a local watchmaker at thirteen. Wholly self-educated, he wrote songs and Chaucerian adaptations that were promoted by the clergyman and educator William Smith and the young poets at the College of Philadelphia. He died while on military duty in North Carolina. Two years later his friend Nathaniel Evans collected and published his poems as *Juvenile Poems on Various Subjects*. The volume included Godfrey's PRINCE OF PARTHIA, often called the first American play.

Godiva, Lady (11th century) English benefactress, wife of Earl Leofric of Mercia. According to tradition, she asked her husband to relieve Coventry of certain burdensome taxes (c1040), but he jested that he would do so only if she would ride naked through the marketplace at midday. She did, covered only by her long hair, and Leofric kept his promise. In some versions, she had previously requested all the townspeople to stay indoors at the appointed hour, and not to look at her; one tailor, since known as "Peeping Tom of Coventry," looked through his window, for which a miracle struck him blind. The legend appears in one of Walter Savage LANDOR's *Imaginary Conversations* (1829), Alfred TENNYSON's poem "Godiva, A Tale of Coventry" (1842), and a number of other literary works.

Go Down, Moses (1942) A collection of short stories by William FAULKNER. Set in Faulkner's mythical YOKNAPATAWPHA COUNTY, the stories are unified by a common theme, the ritual of the hunt—whether it be a hunt for Old Ben in "The Bear," for the lovesick black in "Was," for buried gold in "The Fire and the Hearth," or for the black killer in "Pantaloon in Black." All but the last deal with the members, black and white, of the complicated MCCASLIN family, beginning with the second generation in "Was" and ending with the sixth in "Delta Autumn." There is, in addition, an underlying theme of initiation into manhood and the responsibility of carrying out the social traditions.

"The Bear," the most famous of the stories and possibly Faulkner's best, deals mainly with the hunt for Big Ben, an enormous and elusive bear. A shorter but equally important section tells how Isaac McCaslin, through the discovery of his grandfather's black offspring, rejects his claim to the McCaslin plantation and the guilt of slavery with which it is stained.

God's Determinations Touching His Elect

A long poem on the Puritan theory of Grace by Edward TAYLOR, begun around 1685 but unpublished until 1939. It combines elements of the cycle of lyric poems and of the medieval morality play. The imagery is alternately regal and homely, with eleven different verse forms. Although not a play, the poem is cast as a drama. The first act traces man's predicament since the Fall; the second shows Jesus and Satan battling for man's soul; the third describes the difficulties of the Christian life and the soul's fear of unworthiness; the last shows the soul entering the royal coach of Grace and flying to the feast of love in heaven.

God's Little Acre (1933)

A novel by Erskine CALDWELL, dealing with shiftless and amoral Georgia mountaineers. The protagonist has set aside one acre of his land, the income of which is to go to the church, but he constantly shifts the acre's location according to his own momentary plans and needs.

gods of classical mythology

The deities of the Greeks and Romans. The Romans identified many of their own deities with those of the Greeks. Since Greek mythology was far richer and more imaginative, the characteristics of the Greek gods tended to dominate those of the Roman deities. However, in later ages, knowledge of Greek mythology was generally gained through Roman sources, and the Roman names of the gods—and even the Latinized spelling of the Greek names—were more widely known. Those Greek and Roman deities who, in later times, were regarded as equivalent are as follows:

GREEK	ROMAN
Zeus	Jupiter
Apollo	Apollo
Ares	Mars
Hermes	Mercury
Poseidon	Neptune
Hephaestus	Vulcan
Hera	Juno
Demeter	Ceres
Artemis	Diana
Athene	Minerva
Aphrodite	Venus
Hestia	Vesta

These were the twelve chief gods (see individual entries), the Olympians of Greek mythology. Other well-known gods were:

Dionysus (Bakchos)	Bacchus
Eros	Cupid
Hades (Plouton)	Pluto
Cronus	Saturn
Persephone	Proserpina

A Greek hero equally popular with the Romans was HERACLES, whose Latin name is Hercules.

For the chief deities of Scandinavian mythology, see AESIR and VANIR.

God That Failed, The (1950)

A collection of essays edited by R.H.S. Crossman. Written by persons who were attracted to communism in the 1930s and were later disillusioned, it is an important document on a phase of modern history and thought. The contributors are Arthur KOESTLER, Ignazio SILONE, Richard WRIGHT, André GIDE, Louis FISCHER, and Stephen SPENDER.

Godunov, Boris Fyodorovich (1552–1605)

Russian tsar (1598–1605). After the death of Ivan IV (Ivan the Terrible) in 1584, Godunov became regent for the imbecile Fyodor I. He was elected to the throne on the death of Fyodor. The mysterious death of the tsarevich Dmitry (1591) is presumed to have been caused by Boris to clear the path to the throne. As regent he brought new vitality to the Russian nation, regaining land in Sweden and colonizing Siberia. After he became tsar he lost the support of the nobility; his prestige was weakened by the appearance of a pretender claiming to be the murdered Dmitry. Boris died shortly after the false Dmitry invaded from Poland, but before the two men had confronted each other.

The poet PUSHKIN wrote a play called *Boris Godunov*, which was the basis of MUSSORGSKY's opera of the same name.

Godwin, Gail (1937–   )

American novelist and short-story writer. Godwin lived for several years in London and returned to the U.S. for graduate studies in English at the University of Iowa. While still a graduate student, she wrote her first published novel, *The Perfectionists* (1970), the autobiographical story of the rapid collapse of the "perfect" 1960s marriage of an English psychotherapist and his American wife. This and several of Godwin's subsequent novels, particularly *The Odd Woman* (1974) and *A Mother and Two Daughters* (1972), which enjoyed both critical and popular success, examine with sympathy and insight the struggles of intelligent women to come to terms with independence and to achieve a greater degree of self-realization. Godwin has also written *The Finishing School* (1985) and several volumes of short stories, including *Mr. Bedford and the Muses* (1983).

Godwin, William (1756–1836)

English novelist and political theorist. A leading radical of the 18th century,

Godwin believed that it is impossible to be rationally persuaded and not act accordingly, and that therefore, man could live in harmony without law and institutions; he believed in the perfectibility of man. He was influenced by the ideas of ROUSSEAU and the French Encyclopedists, and in turn had a great influence on the English romantics, particularly WORDSWORTH, COLERIDGE, SHELLEY, and BYRON; Shelley's preface to his *Revolt of Islam* (1818) is an excellent exposition of Godwin's ideas. Among Godwin's works are AN ENQUIRY CONCERNING POLITICAL JUSTICE; *The Adventures of* CALEB WILLIAMS, OR THINGS AS THEY ARE, a novel; *St. Leon* (1799), a supernatural tale; and *History of the Commonwealth* (1824–28). Godwin's wife was the feminist Mary WOLLSTONECRAFT, and his daughter, Mary Wollstonecraft SHELLEY, was Shelley's second wife.

Goethe, Johann Wolfgang von (1749–1832) German poet, playwright, and novelist. Besides writing, Goethe held an important cabinet post at the ducal court in Weimar, directed the theatre in that city, and carried on extensive research in science, especially plant biology, on which he wrote *Die Metamorphose der Pflanzen* (*The Metamorphosis of Plants*, 1790), and optics, the subject of his *Zur Farbenlehre* (*On the Theory of Colors*, 1810). In his scientific studies, he always attempted to see the individual phenomenon as part of an organic, developing whole, in opposition to the categorizing science of his time. His poetic works, too, are characterized by this interest in the natural, organic development of things, rather than in any idealistic schemes.

In his early career (1769–76), Goethe was recognized as a leading figure in the STURM UND DRANG. His well-known poem "Prometheus" (written 1774?), with its insistence that man must believe not in gods but in himself alone, might be seen as a motto for the whole movement. HERDER's strong influence upon his thinking during these years is reflected, for example, in his essay V*on deutscher Baukunst* (*On German Architecture*, 1773). The plays GÖTZ VON BERLICHINGEN, *Clavigo* (1774), *Stella* (1774), and EGMONT belong to this initial phase of his development, as do the earliest Faust sketches and the short novel THE SORROWS OF YOUNG WERTHER.

Goethe's youth was emotionally hectic to the point that he sometimes feared for his reason, but in 1775, after a relaxing trip to Switzerland, he made a decisive break with his past and left his native Frankfurt am Main for the small city of Weimar. It was there that he first assumed serious governmental responsibility; and it was there that he met the woman he was to worship for a decade, Charlotte von STEIN. These years, until 1786, were not very productive for Goethe the writer, but they did contribute much to the characteristic personal balance that appears in his later work.

Goethe spent the years 1786–88 in Italy, a trip that he later described in his *Italienische Reise* (*Italian Trip*, 1816) and that significantly influenced his growing commitment to a classical view of art. In Italy, he completed his play IPHIGENIA IN TAURIS, which, along with his *Römische Elegien* (*Roman Elegies*, 1788–90, pub 1795) and the play TORQUATO TASSO, is customarily taken as the beginning of WEIMAR CLASSICISM.

From this point on, Goethe's life was relatively settled and, though he traveled much, his base was always Weimar, where he was, in effect, the court's cultural director. But his poetic development was by no means finished. In 1794 began his close and fruitful friendship with SCHILLER, and the ensuing years saw his work expand into new directions, as in the epic poems REINEKE FUCHS and HERMANN UND DOROTHEA, and the novel WILHELM MEISTER. He was also in contact with the founding figures of GERMAN ROMANTICISM, especially the brothers SCHLEGEL, but marked romantic tendencies do not begin to appear in his work until later: for example, in the novel DIE WAHLVERWANDTSCHAFTEN or in *Der West-ostliche Divan* (*The West-Eastern Divan*, 1819), a lyric cycle that shares the romantics' interest in the Orient; and in Part II of FAUST.

In a sense, Goethe's development came full circle. At the beginning of his so-called classical period (1788–1805), he had repudiated the emotionalism of his own *Werther*; but as time went on, he tended back toward his earlier attitudes. In his lyric *Trilogie der Leidenschaft* (*Trilogy of Passion*, 1824), one poem, addressed to the character Werther, shows the extent of his regained understanding and sympathy for his own youthful works.

At times, Goethe was grossly insensitive to the merits of such great authors as HÖLDERLIN, KLEIST, and HEINE, but with himself he was never less than honest; despite the extraordinary length of time spanned by his career, he never stagnated, but was always learning and expanding, seeking to grasp more of what he regarded as the poet's proper domain, the entire world.

Valuable material about his life and personality may be found in his autobiographical DICHTUNG UND WAHRHEIT and in Johann Eckermann's *Gespräche mit Goethe* (*Conversations with Goethe*, 1836). See DAEMONIC; MÄRCHEN.

Goffredo (Godfrey de Bouillon) The principal character of Tasso's romantic epic GERUSALEMME LIBERATA. When the poem was first translated by Thomas Carew in 1594, and completed by Edward Fairfax in 1600, its English title was *Godfrey of Bullogne*. Godfrey, duke of Lorraine, was the chosen commander of the allied Crusaders who assaulted Jerusalem in the year 1099. He was also for a time king of Jerusalem. In Tasso's poem, though divinely appointed, he must contend with infidel forces, enchantments, infernal spirits, and division in his ranks; but he finally leads the triumphant Christian army into the city. In worship at the sepulcher of Jesus, he hangs his arms in fulfillment of his vow to recover the holy city.

Gog In the BIBLE (Ezek. 38:39), the king of Magog, a northern land whose fierce hordes were to invade Israel. Scholars sometimes identify Gog with Gyges, a ruler of

Lydia in Asia Minor. In Revelation 20:7, Gog and Magog symbolize the enemies of the kingdom of God, in this case Gog being associated with Magog, a son of JAPHETH (Gen. 10:2). Elsewhere (1 Chron. 5:4), Gog is a descendant of Reuben, eldest of the twelve sons of JACOB.

In British legend, Gog and Magog are the sole survivors of a monstrous brood, the offspring of the thirty-three infamous daughters of the Emperor Diocletian, who murdered their husbands and, being set adrift in a ship, reached Albion, where they fell in with a number of demons. Their descendants, a race of giants, were extirpated by BRUTE and his companions, with the exception of Gog and Magog, who were brought in chains to London and were made to do duty as porters at the royal palace, on the site of the London Guildhall, where their effigies have been at least since the reign of Henry V. The old giants were destroyed in the Great Fire of 1666, and the present ones, fourteen feet high, were carved in 1708 by Richard Saunders.

Gogarty, Oliver St. John (1878–1957) Irish physician and writer of memoirs, essays, and poetry. Gogarty was said to be the original Malachi (Buck) Mulligan in James Joyce's ULYSSES. His exuberant memoirs are full of reminiscences of his friends, including JOYCE, W. B. YEATS, and other Irish writers. Among these are *As I Was Going Down Sackville Street* (1937), *I Follow St. Patrick* (1938), and *It Isn't This Time of Year at All!* (1954).

Gogol, Nikolay Vasilyevich (1809–1852) Russian novelist, playwright, and short-story writer. Gogol was born in the province of Poltava in the Ukraine. His father, a member of the petty nobility, had a small estate and was an amateur playwright. Gogol used some lines from his father's plays as epigraphs for his early stories in the collection *Vechera ne khutore bliz Dikanki* (*Evenings on a Farm Near Dikanka*, 1831–32). After attending school in the Ukraine, Gogol went to St. Petersburg, where he worked as a government clerk and as a teacher, for a short while lecturing in history at St. Petersburg University. His first attempt at a literary work, a short poem called "Italia" (1829), was mildly successful. This encouraged Gogol to try a long narrative poem, *Hanz Keuchelgarten* (1829), which turned out to be a disaster. In 1831 Gogol met PUSHKIN and established a friendship that lasted until the great poet's death. Pushkin was impressed with Gogol's Dikanka tales, which were largely based on Ukrainian folklore with an admixture of Gogol's own fantasy. Even these early tales reveal some features characteristic of Gogol's mature style: a rich mixture of vulgarisms and high-flown rhythmical rhetoric with frequent juxtapositions of the two levels.

Gogol's next published work was *Arabeski* (*Arabesques*, 1835), containing a collection of essays and three of his St. Petersburg stories: "Nevsky Prospekt" ("Nevsky Prospect"), "Portret" ("The Portrait"), and "Zapiski sumashedskogo" ("Diary of a Madman"). The last story is a remarkable depiction of the mind of the lunatic Poprishchin, a civil servant who comes to believe that he is the king of Spain. In the same year Gogol published a collection of Ukrainian stories entitled *Mirgorod*, including "Starosvetskiye pomeshchiki" ("Old-World Landowners"), TARAS BULBA, "Vii," and "Povest o tom, kak possorilsya Ivan Ivanovich s Ivanom Nikiforovichem" ("The Story of How Ivan Ivanovich Quarreled with Ivan Nikiforovich." Two more stories, "Kolyaska" ("The Carriage") and "Nos" ("The Nose"), appeared in 1836. "The Nose" is another example of Gogol's predilection for fantasy, a story about a man whose nose abruptly leaves him and gads about town, wearing clothes and riding in a fine carriage. In April 1836, the first performance of Gogol's satiric comedy THE INSPECTOR GENERAL was given. The mixed reaction to the play upset Gogol, who was always extremely sensitive about the attitude of the public toward his work. He left Russia for Europe, and traveled in Italy, Germany, Switzerland, and France, finally settling in Rome. Except for short visits to Russia in 1839–40 and 1841–42, he was abroad for twelve years. Gogol had taken with him from Russia a few chapters of his novel DEAD SOULS, which was completed in Rome and published in 1842 in a four-volume edition of his works. Also in the edition was his famous story THE OVERCOAT and all of his previously published work.

After the publication of the first part of *Dead Souls*, which was well received in Russia, Gogol began to write to friends and to publish requests for material to use in the planned second part of the novel. Whether he felt his creative power failing or he really believed that accounts of daily life from amateur correspondents would be useful is obscure. In ill health and increasingly obsessed with a religious mania, Gogol aimlessly traveled about Europe, took a pilgrimage to Palestine, and eventually returned to Russia in 1848. His reception in his homeland was cool, at least among the radical intelligentsia. Two years before his return, Gogol had published a didactic work entitled *Vybrannye mesta iz perepiski c druzyami* (*Selected Passages from Correspondence with Friends*, 1846), in which he upheld the autocratic tsarist regime and the patriarchal Russian way of life and advised landowners to allow their peasants to read only the Bible lest they pick up dangerous ideas. The book stirred up a storm of protest among the radicals and elicited a violent letter from the critic Vissarion BELINSKY, which became at least as well known in Russia, though it was banned from print, as was the book that caused it to be written. What Belinsky and the other radicals failed to notice was that Gogol himself had never explicitly criticized the social system in Russia. His critics merely assumed that such was the implication of his writings.

From 1848 until his death, Gogol fell more and more into melancholia, aggravated by his fears of damnation. Shortly after burning some of his manuscripts, including the second part of *Dead Souls*, he took to his bed and died.

Gogol is recognized as one of the greatest writers in Russian literature from the point of view of the imaginativeness and stylistic richness of his work. No Russian author has handled the wealth of the Russian language so well. Gogol's choice of everyday life as the basis of much of his work had a profound effect on the future of Russian literature, although the degree and the purposes of his realism, as interpreted by Belinsky and later radical critics, are doubtful. Whether he intended it or not, Gogol's work was held up as a model for later Russian writers, who turned their attention to a sympathetic observation and realistic description of the lower levels of Russian society.

Despite his later evidences of conservatism and religiosity, Gogol is viewed by the Soviet critics, as he was early in his career by Belinsky, as a realist who used his work to point out social evils with the aim of bringing about reform. His development in the last years of his life, including the *Selected Passages*, is regarded officially as the result of mental aberration.

Gold, Herbert (1924–   )   American novelist and short-story writer. In a style combining intricate wordplay with colloquial speech, Gold writes of his characters' struggles in an urban maze of false values. His novels, beginning with *Birth of a Hero* (1951), reveal a sardonic wit and a distinctly Jewish sensibility. His greatest critical successes came with his most personal novels, *Therefore Be Bold* (1960), based on his youth in the 1930s, and *Fathers* (1967), fictionalized memoirs of his Russian-Jewish immigrant family. His own efforts to understand his Jewish heritage are recounted in his autobiography, *My Last Two Thousand Years* (1972).

Gold Bug, The (1843)   A story by Edgar Allan POE. William Le Grand accidentally discovers a cipher giving the location of buried treasure. Unraveling its instructions, he drops the beetle, or gold bug, through one eye of a skull, and unearths a fortune. The story takes place on Sullivan's Island off South Carolina.

Golden Ass, The (2nd century AD)   The common, alternative title of the *Metamorphoses*, a satirical romance, by Lucius APULEIUS. It is narrated in the first person by Lucius, a licentious young man with insatiable curiosity about people and things. While visiting a sorceress in Thessaly, he induces a maid to steal a magic potion that will turn him into an owl. He takes the wrong potion and turns into an ass instead. In this disappointing form he wanders throughout Greece, passing through the hands of a series of owners who mistreat him. Interspersed throughout the narrative are lively stories of intrigue, witchcraft, and love, the most famous of which is Cupid and PSYCHE. Lucius is finally restored to his human form with the help of the goddess Isis.

Ever since its first appearance, *The Golden Ass* has enjoyed an unusually sustained popularity. The book's influence has been considerable and can best be seen in such writers as BOCCACCIO, CERVANTES, and RABELAIS.

Apuleius borrowed his stories and plots from Greek predecessors; he may have based his book on the same work by Lucius of Patrae that inspired LUCIAN's novel *Lucius, or the Ass*.

Golden Bough, The (1890–1915)   A comprehensive work on comparative religion and mythology by Sir James George FRAZER. Beginning with two volumes published in 1890, the study was expanded to thirteen volumes by 1915. Frazer's own single-volume condensation (1923) has become a classic. The title refers to the branch broken from a sacred tree by Aeneas before his descent into the underworld (see KING OF THE WOOD). In a massive cross-cultural analysis, Frazer attempted to discern archetypal or universal elements in religions and magical practices. Although many of his conclusions have been discredited, Frazer's book was a seminal work in its field, and most subsequent scholarship recognizes a great debt to it. Beyond its anthropological applications, Frazer's work influenced approaches to literary analysis and psychoanalysis, particularly in the work of C. G. JUNG. The book played an important part in the conception of Joyce's FINNEGANS WAKE and Eliot's THE WASTE LAND.

Golden Bowl, The (1904)   A novel by Henry JAMES. The heroine, Maggie Verver, the daughter of an American millionaire, marries the impoverished Prince Amerigo. Her old school friend, Charlotte Stant, who has had an affair with the prince, later marries Adam Verver, Maggie's father, and continues her relationship with her lover. The second part of the novel deals with Maggie's discovery of the liaison and with her reaction to it. This is generally considered to be James's most difficult work.

golden calf   An image of worship made of gold earrings and other jewelry by the Hebrews under the direction of AARON, while MOSES was receiving the TEN COMMANDMENTS (Ex. 20) on Mount Sinai. When Moses returned with the two stone tablets on which were written the laws and found his people adoring the image (a form of BAAL-worship), he destroyed the tablets and threw the powdered dust of the calf into the spring of Marah. After he had led his people in repentance, he returned to the mount and received two new tablets.

Golden Dog, The (Le Chien d'or; unauthorized, 1877; authorized, ed. 1896; tr 1877)   A novel by William Kirby (1817–1906), English-born Canadian novelist and editor. This was the first Canadian novel to achieve widespread popularity. The story, set in old French Quebec, served as a model for numerous Canadian historical romances.

Golden Fleece   In Greek mythology, the fleece of pure gold taken from a miraculous winged ram. Athamas, a son of AEOLUS and ruler of Boeotia, married the phantom Nephele (see IXION), who bore him a son, Phrixus, and a daughter, Helle. He also became the father of Learchus and Melicertes by CADMUS' daughter Ino. Jealous of Nephele, Ino persuaded the Boeotian women secretly to parch the seed wheat, then caused a false oracle to be brought from Delphi: only the sacrifice of Phrixus and Helle would save the crops. At the last moment, a winged, golden ram was sent by HERMES, and Phrixus and Helle escaped on its back. As it flew, Helle fell and was drowned in the Hellespont, the straits thereafter named in her honor. Phrixus reached Colchis at the eastern end of the Black Sea; he gave the ram to King Aeetes, who nailed its fleece to an oak in the grove of ARES, and married Aeetes' daughter Chalciope, who bore him four sons. The fleece was later seized by the ARGONAUTS and returned to Iolcus.

Golden Horde   A body of Mongol Tartars of the 13th century. They overran eastern Europe and were so called from the magnificent tent of Batu Khan, grandson of GENGHIS KHAN. The kingdom of the Golden Horde at its height reached from the Dniester to central Asia. It was overthrown by Ivan III of Russia (1480) and broken up into a number of smaller khanates, with that of Astrakhan representing the Golden Horde.

Golden Legend, The (1483)   A compilation of lives of the saints and other ecclesiastical commentaries, one of the most popular books published by William CAXTON. It drew on the material in the Latin *Legenda aurea* of Jacobus de Voragine (1230–98), but was based mostly on French and English versions.

Golden Lotus, The (Chin p'ing mei)   A long Chinese novel written in the late MING dynasty (1368–1644). The story deals with the life and loves of Hsi-men Ch'ing and his six wives, and is celebrated for its extreme naturalism and realistic portrayal of daily life. It was banned during the Ch'ing dynasty because of its explicit eroticism. See CHINESE LITERATURE.

Golding, William [Gerald] (1911–   )   English novelist. Golding's first published novel was LORD OF THE FLIES, which was an immediate success in England and soon became so in the United States, attaining the kind of "contemporary classic" status also enjoyed by Salinger's THE CATCHER IN THE RYE. His subsequent books include *The Inheritors* (1955), PINCHER MARTIN, *Free Fall* (1959), *The Spire* (1964), *The Pyramid* (1967), and *The Scorpion God* (1971). After the publication of *Darkness Visible* (1979) and *Rites of Passage* (1980), popular interest in Golding revived, and his reputation as a highly original writer of moral allegories grew. Golding calls his books fables and uses them to express his grim view of the nature of man. His World War II experiences in the Navy and his years spent teaching small boys have helped to shape his philosophical attitudes. A master of strange situations and ironic twists, Golding enriches his books with literary, mythological, and Christian allusions and symbols. Golding was awarded the NOBEL PRIZE in Literature in 1983. In 1984 he published the novel *The Paper Men*.

Goldoni, Carlo (1707–1793)   Italian dramatist. Born in Venice, Goldoni wrote some 150 comedies through which he became the creator of the modern Italian comedy in the style of MOLIÈRE, superseding the traditional COMMEDIA DELL'ARTE, then vigorously defended by Carlo GOZZI. His comedies, written in Italian and in the Venetian dialect, depict the foibles of the middle and lower classes of Venice and offer a true-to-life portrayal of character and action absent in the older *commedia* technique of improvisation carried out by stock characters. His finest comedies appeared in the years 1748–60. Among them are *La bottega del caffè*, *La locandiera*, *La vedova scaltra*, *La famiglia dell'antiquario*, and the dialect plays *I rusteghi* and *Le barufe chiozote*. In his *Mémoires* (tr 1877), which like his last plays were written in French, he described his verbal warfare with the traditionalists of the theatre and stated: "The secret of the art of a writer of comedies is to cling to nature and never to leave her." A writer for the Italian theatre in Paris and pensioned by Louis XIV, he was impoverished as a result of the FRENCH REVOLUTION.

Goldsmith, Oliver (1731–1774)   Irish-born English poet, playwright, and novelist. Educated in Ireland, Goldsmith left for Edinburgh in 1752 and never returned. He studied medicine for a while at Leyden in 1754, then made the Grand Tour of the Continent, returning to England in 1756, where he became engaged in literary hackwork, and, for a time, was employed by Samuel RICHARDSON, the printer and novelist. His literary fame began with *The Traveller* (1764), a didactic poem surveying national modes of happiness, which was praised by Samuel Johnson and other members of his famous Literary Club. His major works include *An Enquiry into the Present State of Polite Learning in Europe* (1759), a prose essay attributing the decline of polite learning to the inferiority of poets; *The Bee* (1759), a periodical containing perhaps his most famous tales, "Reverie at the Boar's Head Tavern" (1760) and "Asem, An Eastern Tale" (1759); THE CITIZEN OF THE WORLD, a satiric epistolary novel in imitation of MONTESQUIEU's *Lettres Persanes* (1721); THE VICAR OF WAKEFIELD, a novel; THE DESERTED VILLAGE, a poem; and THE GOOD NATUR'D MAN and SHE STOOPS TO CONQUER, comedies. A beloved member of Dr. Johnson's circle, he was noted for his comic verbal *faux-pas*, though it seems that Goldsmith buffooned purposely on occasion without his friends ever suspecting it. At the end of his life he retorted to their raillery in a series of brilliant caricatures, *The Retaliation* (1774). See GOLDY; GOODY TWO-SHOES.

Goldy   The pet name given to Oliver GOLDSMITH by Dr. Samuel JOHNSON. David GARRICK said of Goldsmith, "He wrote like an angel and talked like poor Poll."

golem (Heb, "fetus; unformed mass")   In medieval Jewish folklore, a robot-like servant constructed (usually of clay) to resemble a man and magically endowed with life. According to legend, several of these creatures were created by saintly scholars to help protect oppressed Jews in many parts of Europe. Because of the inability of the monster servants to do anything but follow the instructions of their masters in the most literal way, they frequently caused great destruction. The most famous golem is the Golem of Prague, created by Rabbi Judah Löw in the 16th century.

Goliardic verse   The light Latin verse of 12th- and 13th-century Germany, France, and England by university students and wandering clerics, minstrels, and JONGLEURS. This poetry was of two types: scurrilous satire defying all kinds of civil and ecclesiastical authority, including the Pope; and merry, nonchalant, ribald celebrations of nature, women, and wine, including some drinking songs still popular. The Goliards, as the authors were called, often referred to a mythical Golias as their leader and patron, ironically dignifying him with the titles of "Bishop" (*episcopus*) and "Archpoet" (*archipoeta*). He is sometimes identified with Primus, a 12th-century scholar from Orleans. The *Confession of Golias*, as well as much other Goliardic verse, was once attributed to Walter MAP. A large collection of this poetry, dating from the 13th century and found in a Bavarian monastery, was published in Germany as *Carmina Burana* (1847), some of which J. A. SYMONDS translated in his *Wine, Women, and Song* (1884). Carl Orff set *Carmina Burana* to music in 1935.

Golyadkin, Yakov Petrovich   The hallucination-ridden hero of DOSTOYEVSKY's short novel THE DOUBLE.

Gombrich, Sir E[rnst] H[ans] (1909–   ) Vienna-born British art historian and professor emeritus at the University of London. Throughout his long and distinguished career, Gombrich's commitment to clarity of concept, expression, and visual perception has manifested itself in everything he has written and said on the subject of art. As a scholar and an academic, he brought the Italian Renaissance into sharper focus for many of his readers through articles that were later collected in *Norm and Form* (1966) and *Symbolic Images* (1972). *The Story of Art* (1950), which has run through thirteen editions, is an elegantly presented overview of art through the ages. Gombrich's graceful style, combined with formidable erudition, has endeared him to scholars and general readers alike. Among his works are: *Aby Warburg: An Intellectual Biography* (1970), *In Search of Cultural History* (1972), *Illusion in Nature and Art* (1973), *Means and Ends* (1976), *The Sense of Order* (1979), *Ideals and Idols* (1979), *The Image and the Eye* (1982), and *Tributes* (1984).

Gombrowicz, Witold (1904–1969)   Expatriate Polish novelist and playwright. Gombrowicz, as a young lawyer in Warsaw, published a collection of short stories, *Pamietnik z okresu dojozewania*, in 1933. Four years later he produced a novel, *Ferdydurke* (1937; tr 1961), a surrealist tragicomedy that begins with its thirty-year-old hero turning into an adolescent boy. The theme of older men's preoccupation with immaturity recurs throughout his work. His first play, *Iwona, Ksiezniczka Burgunda* (*Princess Ivona*, 1937), a forerunner of the THEATRE OF THE ABSURD, is a fairy-tale allegory of Poland's tragic history. When the German army marched into Poland a year after the play

was produced, Gombrowicz was in Buenos Aires. It was 1963 before he returned to Europe and settled in the south of France. In the meantime he had written a second play, *Ślub* (*The Marriage*, 1947), and two novels, *TransAtlantyk* (1953) and *Pornografia* (1960; tr 1966), also variations on the youth-age theme. When he was settled in France, he wrote one more novel, *Kosmos* (1965; tr *Cosmos*, 1967). His last play, *Operetka* (1966; prod Paris, 1970; tr *Operetta*, 1971), an absurdist parody of Western civilization, was again ahead of its time, anticipating the avant-garde "total theatre" of the 1970s.

Gómez de la Serna, Ramón (known simply as Ramón, 1888–1963)   Spanish writer. Ramón's massive output includes many well-known biographies as well as novels, plays, essays, and short sketches. He was very much at the center of the Spanish avant-garde in the 1930s; from 1936 until his death he lived in exile in Argentina. His major achievement was his invention of a unique literary form (employed almost exclusively by him) called the *greguería*, which combined humor with a metaphysical conceit to produce a startling or unconventional effect. Short examples are "Bottle, wine's coffin," or "An excess of Fame; defamation." His *greguerías*, present in much of his work, were collected separately in *Flor de greguerías* (1933) and *Total de greguerías* (1955). Also notable among his many books is his lively autobiography, *Automoribundia* (1948).

Gompers, Samuel (1850–1924)   English-born American labor leader. Arriving in the U.S. in 1863, Gompers joined the Cigarmakers' Union and became its president in 1877. He played an important role in the organization of the American Federation of Labor, which he headed from 1886 until his death (except for the year 1895). Devoted to practical ends, such as improvements in wages and hours, he believed that unions should avoid political alliances.

Gonçalves Dias, Antônio (1823–1864)   Brazilian poet and ethnologist. Perhaps Brazil's first truly national poet, Gonçalves Dias was a fervent patriot who wrote verse glorifying the Indian and the tropical landscape. His best-known poem is "Canção do exilio" ("Song of Exile," 1846), whose first lines—"There are palm trees in my homeland, where the sabiá sings"—are familiar to every literate Brazilian.

Goncharov, Ivan Aleksandrovich (1812–1891) Russian novelist. Born in Simbirsk (now Ulyanovsk), Goncharov spent his childhood on the family estate. The richness and comfort of the old patriarchal way of life he experienced there was later immortalized in his major novel, OBLOMOV. Goncharov's idyll in the country ended in 1822, when he was sent to Moscow to complete his education. He was miserable in the city and consoled himself by reading extensively, forming an interest in literature that led him to enroll in the faculty of letters in Moscow University. He graduated in 1834 and entered the civil service.

Goncharov's first important novel, *Obyknovennaya istoriya* (*A Common Story*, 1844), deals with the loss of idealistic dreams when a young provincial encounters life in the city. The theme was later to be touched on in *Oblomov*. The critic Vissarion BELINSKY called *A Common Story* "a terrible blow to romanticism, dreaminess, sentimentality, and provincialism."

In 1849 Goncharov had already completed the first chapters of his masterpiece. He published one of the chapters, "Oblomov's Dream," in that year. Work on the novel was interrupted by a world cruise he took as secretary for a Russian expedition on the ship *Pallada* from 1852 to 1855. He published a description of the journey in *The Frigate "Pallada"* in 1858. The following year, *Oblomov* appeared.

Goncharov retired from government service in 1867 and completed his third novel, *Obryv* (*The Precipice*, 1869), on which he had been working for almost twenty years. The novel contrasts the materialist views of the socialists with those of the old Russian patriarchal world. Goncharov's unmistakable preference for the conservative way of life scandalized the radicals. During the remaining years of his life, Goncharov lived a secluded life in his St. Petersburg apartment, occasionally pulling himself free from his mental depression to take a trip abroad. His writings during this period consist mainly of sketches, articles, and reminiscences. The best known of these works is *Milyon terzani* (*A Million Torments*, 1872), an essay on WOE FROM WIT, the classic Russian comedy by Aleksandr GRIBOYEDOV.

Goncourt, Edmond de (1822–1896) and **Jules de** (1830–1870)   French writers, known as the Brothers Goncourt, who collaborated in their work. Early leaders in the movement of NATURALISM, the Goncourt brothers are forerunners of Emile ZOLA. Such novels as *Germinie Lacerteux* and *Madame Gervaisais* (both 1869) are studies of pathological or degenerate subjects. *La Fille Elisa* (1877), written by Edmond alone, is a realistic description of prostitution. The Brothers Goncourt went to great lengths in order to depict a subject with precision and accuracy. To write *Sœur Philomène* (1861), for example, they went into hospitals, studying the exact conditions. Their work is episodic in form and impersonal in tone. In addition to their naturalistic novels, the Goncourts wrote several studies of 18th-century costumes, art, and furniture. They were also avid collectors of objets d'art and are thought to have been the first to introduce Japanese art into France. See PRIX GONCOURT.

Goneril   In Shakespeare's KING LEAR, the oldest daughter of Lear. The instigator of the cruelties perpetrated on Lear, she refuses to house her father's large entourage. Later she plots with EDMUND to kill her husband, the duke of Albany, poisons her sister REGAN, who also loves Edmund, and finally stabs herself when the plot is discovered.

Gone with the Wind (1936)   A historical novel by Margaret MITCHELL. Mitchell's only book, this Civil War novel was awarded the PULITZER PRIZE in 1937 and sold over twenty million copies in twenty-seven languages. A motion picture version (1939) enjoyed comparable success. The heroine is Scarlett O'Hara, a willful, defiant, and manipulative Southern belle, whose love for Ashley Wilkes is frustrated when he marries the gentle Melanie Hamilton. After being widowed twice, Scarlett marries Rhett Butler, who proves more than a match for her fiery nature. Apart from the ill-fated relationship of Scarlett and Rhett, the novel depicts, from a Southern point of view, the tumult and suffering of the years of war and Reconstruction.

Góngora [y Argote], Luis de (1561–1627) Spanish poet. A native of Córdoba, Góngora studied at Salamanca and though he probably had little vocation for the priesthood, he took minor orders, becoming prebendary of Córdoba's cathedral. In 1617 he was ordained and was named chaplain to King Philip III. After suffering an apoplectic stroke in 1626, he retired to Córdoba, where he died.

Góngora's literary career had two distinct phases. Initially, as a disciple of Fernando de HERRERA, he wrote verse that was relatively simple and remarkable for its exuberance, charm, and wit. These early poems include Italianate sonnets; *romances*, or ballads ("Amarrado al duro banco," "Servía en Orán al rey," "Angélica y Medoro"); and *letrillas*, or songs ("Aprended, flores de mí").

After 1600, however, Góngora deliberately cultivated the abstruse style to which he gave his name, GONGORISM, and for which his enemies dubbed him *Príncipe de las Tinieblas* ("Prince of Darkness"). Written for the intellectual elite, his poems in this manner, particularly the *Fábula de Polifemo y Galatea* (1613?) and the *Soledades* (1613), caused a sensation. Though many, including Cervantes, hailed Góngora's innovations, others, notably Lope de VEGA and QUEVEDO, bitterly attacked him.

Góngora's works were first collected by Juan López de Vicuña in 1627. A more complete collection, including the play *Las firmezas de Isabela* and fragments of two other dramas, was issued in 1633 by Gonzalo de Hozes y Córdoua.

Gongorism (Sp, Gongorismo)   A Spanish literary style, sometimes called *cultismo* or *culteranismo*, used by Luis de GÓNGORA and other 17th-century poets. Designed to appeal to the cultivated (*los cultos*), it is characterized by an emphasis on Latin terms and syntax, by frequent allusions to classical mythology, and lavish use of tropes, metaphors, hyperbole, and antitheses. Gongorism can also be considered as a purely stylistic variant of the contemporaneous literary trend known as CONCEPTISM, which appeared mainly in prose. It had counterparts in the Marinism of Italy (see Giambattista MARINO) and the EUPHUISM of England. Although Góngora used the style to enhance the sonority and richness of his verse, in the hands of lesser poets it became mere affectation, and Gongorism later became synonymous with bad writing.

Gonne, Maud (1866–1953) Irish patriot and philanthropist. In 1903 Gonne married Major MacBride, an Irish patriot who was executed (1916) by the British after the EASTER REBELLION. She was the first diplomatic emissary (1921) of the Irish Free State to Paris. Famous for her beauty and known as an actress, painter, and linguist, she is the heroine of several poems and plays by William Butler YEATS. *A Servant of the Queen*, her autobiography, was published in 1940.

Gonzaga Italian noble family of Mantua. It was famous during the Renaissance for its cultural patronage. Outstanding were:

Lodovico Gonzaga (1414–1478) The marquis who employed the painter MANTEGNA, the architect ALBERTI, and the scholars PICO DELLA MIRANDOLA and Poliziano.

Federico Gonzaga (1440–1484) Son of Ludovico. Federico continued his father's patronage, was skilled in diplomacy, and excelled as a CONDOTTIERE.

Francesco Gonzaga (1466–1519) Son of Federico. Francesco married the famous Isabella D'ESTE and was a military commander during the period.

Elisabetta Gonzaga (1471–1526) Sister of Francesco. Elisabetta married Duke Guidobaldo of Urbino (see MONTEFELTRO) and became the duchess of Castiglione's *Cortegiano* (THE COURTIER).

Federigo Gonzaga (1500–1540) Son of Francesco. Federigo continued the family tradition by employing the painter Giulio Romano and the architect Pietro Aretino. Federigo was the first duke of Mantua, having received the title from Emperor Charles V.

González Prada, Manuel (1848–1918) Peruvian essayist and poet, famous as a polemicist. A member of a distinguished Peruvian family, González Prada fought in the so-called War of the Pacific (1879–83), in which Peru suffered a humiliating defeat at the hands of Chile. In a famous speech (1886), he uttered the phrase "old men to the tomb, young men to work," which became the battle cry of those who sought changes in the established order. Uncompromising and incorruptible, he devoted his life to exposing his country's ills in scathing but highly polished prose, hurling his most impassioned invective at the politicians and at the Roman Catholic Church. He became the intellectual mentor of several generations of Peruvian reformers and revolutionaries. Some of his best-known articles and speeches are collected in *Páginas libres* (1894) and *Horas de lucha* (1908). His best poetry is probably the realistic portrayal of Indian life in *Baladas Peruanas* (1935).

Goodbye, Mr. Chips (1934) A best-selling short novel by James HILTON. It deals sentimentally with the life of an English schoolmaster.

Good Companions, The (1929) A novel by J. B. PRIESTLEY. Good-humored, and filled with comic characters and varied scenes from English life, it is the story of a group of oddly assorted people who run a touring music-hall company called The Good Companions.

Good Earth, The (1931) A novel by Pearl BUCK. It describes the rise of Wang Lung, a Chinese peasant, from poverty to the position of a rich landowner, helped by his patient wife, O-lan. Their vigor, fortitude, persistence, and enduring love of the soil are emphasized throughout. Generally regarded as Pearl Buck's masterpiece, the book won universal acclaim for its sympathetically authentic picture of Chinese life.

Goodfellow, Robin See PUCK.

Good Friday The Friday preceding EASTER Day, the anniversary of JESUS' Crucifixion. "Good" here means *holy*; CHRISTMAS, as well as Shrove Tuesday, used to be called "the good tide." According to old superstition, those born on Christmas Day or Good Friday have the power of seeing and commanding spirits.

Goodman, Paul (1911–1972) American novelist, poet, playwright, philosopher, critic, and psychologist. Despite his enormous output, Goodman was not widely known until he published *Growing Up Absurd* (1960), a popular study of youth and delinquency in an overorganized society. As a political anarchist, he used both fiction and nonfiction to criticize bureaucratic institutions, arguing passionately for a more humane society. His best-known novels include *The Empire City* (1959), a complex narrative of New York life, and the partly autobiographical *Making Do* (1963). An original and discordant thinker in the tradition of THOREAU and WHITMAN, Goodman was forever challenging orthodoxy. The best of his more than fifty works are distilled in *Collected Poems* (1974, 1977) and *The Break-Up of Our Camp* (1978), the first of four volumes of collected stories. His literary, political, and psychological essays were published respectively in *Creator Spirit Come*, *Drawing the Line*, and *Nature Heals* (all 1977).

Good Natur'd Man, The (1768) A comedy by Oliver GOLDSMITH. The story concerns Honeywood, a likeable young man prone to extravagance. His uncle, in order to demonstrate that his friends will abandon him if he has no money, has Honeywood arrested for debt. Honeywood is in love with the beautiful, wealthy Miss Richland. When he is released from prison he assumes that a friend of his in the government is responsible for his freedom, though actually it is Miss Richland. In the end Honeywood's uncle arranges a match with Miss Richland.

Good Queen Bess ELIZABETH I of England.

Good Soldier, The (1915) A novel by Ford Madox FORD. The narrator discovers that for the past nine years his wife has been the mistress of his best friend, Captain Ashburnham, the apparently honorable "Good Soldier" of the title. Conventional appearances and bitter truth are ironically juxtaposed.

Good Soldier Schweik, The See SCHWEIK.

Good Woman of Setzuan, The (Der gute Mensch von Setzuan; written 1939–41; perf and pub 1943) A play by Bertolt BRECHT. Three disillusioned gods come to earth in search of a "good human being." The only person in Setzuan to give them shelter is the prostitute Shen Te. The gods reward her with money, which she uses to open a tobacco shop. Her natural charity, however, leads to bankruptcy. She disguises herself as a "male cousin," Shui Ta, and by ruthless and exploitive business practices gains back the money she had benevolently given away. When Shui Ta finds himself being judged by the gods for the murder of Shen Te, Shen Te removes the mask, remorsefully revealing her true identity and her dilemma. The gods are unable to provide a solution. The play criticizes a social order in which a good person must also be bad in order to survive, and suggests that one cannot rely on the help of the gods. Contemporary critics and translators point out that the correct translation of the title is *The Good Person of Setzuan*.

Goody Two-shoes (1765)   A nursery tale written for the publisher John NEWBERY by Oliver GOLDSMITH. Goody Two-shoes is a very poor child, whose delight at having a pair of shoes is so unbounded that she cannot forbear telling everyone she meets that she has "two shoes"; whence her name. In time, she acquires knowledge and becomes wealthy.

Goose, Mother   A mythical character famous as giving the name to *Mother Goose's Nursery Rhymes*. This name seems to have been first used in English in *Songs for the Nursery, or Mother Goose's Melodies for Children*, published by T. Fleet in Boston, Massachusetts, in 1719. Perrault's CONTES DE MA MÈRE L'OYE had appeared in 1697.

Gorbachev, Mikhail [Sergeyevich] (1931–   ) Soviet leader and General Secretary of the Politburo of the Communist Party of the Soviet Union (1985–   ). Born into a peasant family at Privolnoye, Stravropol territory, Gorbachev worked on a state farm as a youth and earned a law degree from Moscow State University. A member of the Communist Party of the Soviet Union since 1952, he was elected to the Central Committee in 1971 and to full Politburo membership in 1980. He succeeded Konstantin Chernenko as leader of the Soviet Union on March 10, 1985, when Chernenko died after only thirteen months in office. Gorbachev worked to initiate reforms to overcome the stagnation of the economy and the technological backwardness and corruption of traditional Soviet-style central planning. He also initiated crackdowns on alcoholism. Gorbachev's leadership appeared more liberal than that of his predecessors and he introduced a period of GLASNOST ("openness"). In 1986 he released Andrei D. Sakharov, the Soviet dissident physicist, from seventeen years of internal exile, and in early 1987 he ordered the release of many Soviet political prisoners. In the area of arms-control negotiations, Gorbachev and President Ronald REAGAN of the United States found little to agree upon, notably at the Reykjavik, Iceland, summit in October 1986.

Gorboduc, or Ferrex and Porrex (prod 1561, pub 1565)   A play by Thomas SACKVILLE and Thomas NORTON, the first Senecan tragedy in English, the first English play to be written in BLANK VERSE, and one of the first to use English historical material. The story is based on the legendary history of England of GEOFFREY OF MONMOUTH. Gorboduc, a British king, has two sons, Ferrex and Porrex. He divides his kingdom between them, but they quarrel, and Porrex kills his brother. Soon afterward, Porrex himself is murdered in his bed by his mother, who loved Ferrex more. The people, horrified, rebel and kill both the old king and queen. The nobility then kill many of the rebels. Soon, since there are no heirs to the throne, the country falls into civil war and is laid waste.

Gordian knot   An intricate problem. Gordias, a peasant, was chosen king of Phrygia, and dedicated his wagon to ZEUS. The wagon yoke was fastened to a pole so cleverly that it was said that whoever undid the knot would reign over the empire of Asia. Alexander cut the knot with a single stroke of his sword. *Cutting the Gordian knot* became proverbial for the decisive, bold completion of a complicated action.

Gordimer, Nadine (1923–   )   South African novelist and short-story writer. Gordimer was born and educated in South Africa, which, in all its racial and political complexity, is the setting for most of her novels and stories. Her first published works were the story collections *Face to Face* (1949) and *The Soft Voice of the Serpent* (1952). A consummate stylist, Gordimer writes with precision and integrity about a society divided by racist policies. Her firm opposition to the cruelty and injustice of *apartheid* is imparted not through polemic but through psychological insight and careful irony. Among her novels are *The Lying Days* (1953), *Occasion for Loving* (1963), *A Guest of Honour* (1970), *The Conservationist* (1974), and *July's People* (1981). *Burger's Daughter* (1979) is at once her most political and personal novel. Banned for a time in her own country, it deals with the process of the individual self-definition and with the nature of commitment to political and humanitarian ideals. *Something Out There* (1984), a collection of stories, provides, in Gordimer's clear language, a focused, steady vision on a seemingly chaotic society.

Gordon, Adam Lindsay (1833–1870)   Australian BUSH BALLADEER, born in the Azores to Anglo-Indian parents. At twenty, Gordon was shipped from England to Australia by his disgruntled family. There, he pursued a colorful career as a mounted policeman, horse trainer, sheepherder, steeplechase rider, and member of the South Australian Parliament. Gordon's best work is spirited, realistic verse on sporting and rural life. Despondent about financial failures, he committed suicide on the day of publication of *Bush Ballads and Galloping Rhymes* (1870). His collected verses were published in *Poems* (1912).

Gordon, Caroline (1895–1981)   American novelist and short-story writer. Gordon's books are set in the South, many of them in the Kentucky region where she was raised, and deal with themes of personal and social disintegration and the need for salvation. Her best-known novel is the very successful *Penhally* (1931). *The Collected Stories of Caroline Gordon* appeared in 1981. She was married to the poet Allen TATE for thirty years.

Gordon, Charles George (known as Chinese Gordon and Gordon Pasha, 1833–1885)   English soldier. In 1860 Gordon was attached to a British force operating with the French against China, and commanded a Chinese force, called the Ever Victorious Army, against the Taiping rebels (1863–64). He quelled the rebellions after thirty-three engagements and, resigning his command, was presented by the emperor with the yellow jacket and peacock's feather of a mandarin of the first class. He was governor (1874–76) of the equatorial provinces of central Africa in the service of the khedive of Egypt and in 1877 was created pasha by the khedive. As governor-general (1877–79) of the Sudan, Darfur, the equatorial provinces, and the Red Sea littoral, he suppressed slave trade. Sent by the British government in 1884 to the Sudan to assist the khedive in withdrawing the garrisons of the country, which could no longer hold out against the MAHDI, he was besieged by the Mahdi at Khartoum and killed in the storming of the city. There is a fine biographical sketch of Gordon in Lytton STRACHEY's *Eminent Victorians* (1918).

Gordon Riots   The riots that occurred in London in 1780, fomented by Lord George Gordon, to compel the House of Commons to repeal the bill passed in 1778 for the relief of Roman Catholics. Charles Dickens has given a very vivid description of these riots in BARNABY RUDGE.

Gorgias (c483–375 BC)   A Greek philosopher, SOPHIST, and teacher of rhetoric. Gorgias exercised a great influence on the development of classical Greek style: PLATO's dialogue on rhetoric is called *Gorgias*. His lost work, *On Nature or the Non-existent*, is believed to be a refutation of Presocratic argument for a fundamental principle of unity in the universe that underlies all appearances.

Gorgons   Monsters of classical myth. With golden wings and claws of brass, their hair was a mass of live serpents and their aspect was so terrible that all who looked at them were turned to stone. There were three: Stheno, Euryale, and MEDUSA, daughters of Keto and the aged sea-god Phorcys and sisters of the GRAEAE, who guarded them. Medusa, their chief, and the only mortal one, was slain by PERSEUS. The Gorgon's head was a favorite subject in ancient Greek art; because they believed that its power would terrify the enemy, the Greeks carved it on shields and armor and even on city walls. It was also used as an amulet to protect against enchantment.

Gorky, Maksim (pen name of Aleksey Maksimovich Peshkov, 1868–1936)   Russian writer. Gorky was the first great Russian writer to emerge from the ranks of the proletariat. Born in Nizhny Novgorod (now named Gorky), he was orphaned at an early age and lived for a brief time with his grandparents. Financial difficulties forced the boy at the

age of nine to go into the world to make his own way. He was a dishwasher on a Volga steamer, bakery shop worker, fisherman, railroadman, and clerk, as well as a down-and-outer, before he began to write. His hard life drove him to a suicide attempt in 1887. His pen name, Gorky, is the Russian equivalent of "the bitter one."

His first published story, "Makar Chudra" (1892), appeared in a Tiflis newspaper. His stories, sketches, and articles were published in local newspapers in provincial towns, until they finally attracted the notice of the writer and journalist Vladimir KOROLENKO, who helped him get his first stories placed in journals in St. Petersburg. The first story to appear was "Chelkash" (1895). This was followed by a stream of stories, and in 1898 two volumes of Gorky's stories and sketches were issued. By then the one-time tramp was famous all over the country. Gorky's work of this period drew heavily on the kind of life he had himself experienced, which of necessity meant that most of his characters and themes were taken from the lowest level of Russian society. Gorky both depicted the wretched lives of this class of "creatures that once were men" and infused his stories with a heavy dose of protest against the society that allowed such wretchedness to exist. His most successful story of this period was TWENTY-SIX MEN AND A GIRL.

Gorky's popularity and financial success allowed him to embark on a longer work: his first novel, *Foma Gordeyev* (1899), a study of a declining bourgeois merchant family in a Volga town. In the meantime, he had moved to St. Petersburg and founded a publishing house, Znaniye ("knowledge"), that was later to publish such well-known writers as ANDREYEV, KUPRIN, and BUNIN. He also joined the Social Democratic Party and contributed much of his literary earnings to furthering the Marxist revolutionary movement. This activity displeased the government, and, when he was elected an honorary member of the Russian Academy of Science in 1902, the government vetoed the choice. The authors Anton CHEKHOV and Vladimir Korolenko promptly resigned their memberships in protest.

Gorky's formerly romantically tinged realistic pictures of lower-class life became increasingly grim and angry. The most forceful expression of his attitude is the drama THE LOWER DEPTHS, his second play, regarded as his dramatic masterpiece. Gorky's first play was *Meshchanye* (*The Petit-Bourgeois*, 1901; also tr as *Philistines*), an indictment of the philistinism of that class.

For his BOLSHEVIK activities in the revolution of 1905, Gorky was arrested. Public indignation forced his release, and he went abroad, visiting Europe and the U.S., and settling in Capri. In 1907 he issued his didactic novel about the revolutionary movement, MOTHER. Although artistically weak, the book has been a favorite with Soviet literary hucksters. *Skazki ob Itali* (*Tales of Italy*, 1911–12) depicts the lives of the Italian working classes. The next years saw the production of one of Gorky's best works, his autobiographical trilogy. The first part, CHILDHOOD, appeared in

1913–14. The second part, *V lyudakh* (*In the World*), came out in 1916, and the third volume, *Moi universisety* (*My Universities*), in 1923.

Gorky was allowed to return to Russia in 1913. His former sympathy with the Bolsheviks had abated somewhat. He saw unbridled violence as a threat to the existence of what had been worthwhile in the cultural life of the past. When the advocates of Marxism attempted to sweep away the cultural past, Gorky did what he could to save it. He organized the publishing venture Vsemirnaya literatura (World Literature), which helped many writers earn enough to stay alive during the chaotic months following the revolution. He also helped establish a "House of Arts" and a "House of Scholars," which offered writers a place to stay and, more importantly, a place to work. This aspect of Gorky's activity has caused him to be called a bridge between the old classical culture of Russia and the new Soviet culture.

The influence Gorky had with the Bolshevik leaders was often used to good advantage to help writers who were down and out or in trouble with the new regime. He also was active in discovering and encouraging new writers, such as Vsevolod IVANOV and Konstantin FEDIN. Thus, he helped both to preserve the old culture and to foster the new.

In 1921, weakened by his strenuous work, Gorky went abroad for a rest. He remained in Italy until 1928. During this period, in addition to the third volume of his autobiography, he wrote two novels—*Delo Artamonovykh* (*The Artamonov Business*, 1925) and *Zhizn Klima Samgina* (*The Life of Klim Samgin*, 1927–36)—and two plays produced after his return to Russia—*Yegor Bulychov i drugiye* (*Yegor Bulychov and Others*, 1931) and *Dostigayev i drugiye* (*Dostigayev and Others*, 1932). The plays and *The Artamonov Business* all deal with the decay of merchant families. *The Life of Klim Samgin*, a huge work of which four volumes were finished, also treats the decline of a particular class, the intelligentsia.

After his return to the Soviet Union, Gorky helped develop the literary doctrine of SOCIALIST REALISM, which was formed in 1932. His own ideas about what he meant by socialist realism differed somewhat from the official doctrine as it later was interpreted.

Gorky died in 1936 while undergoing medical treatment. In the 1937–38 purge trials, the former chief of the secret police, Yagoda, confessed that Gorky's death was ordered by him as part of the so-called Trotskyite plot. The truth is still unknown.

Gorky's fictional work generally suffers from lack of a controlled style and exhibits a tendency toward excessive philosophical discourse. His place in Russian literature is secure, however, for his autobiographical trilogy and his *Vospominaniya* (*Reminiscences*, 1919) of TOLSTOY, Chekhov, and Andreyev, which are full of sharp insights and interesting anecdotes.

Gospels   See JOHN, THE GOSPEL ACCORDING TO ST.; LUKE, THE GOSPEL ACCORDING TO ST.; MARK, THE GOSPEL ACCORDING TO ST.; MATTHEW, THE GOSPEL ACCORDING TO ST.

Gösta Berlings saga (1891)   A novel of Swedish life by Selma LAGERLÖF. It relates the adventures of the impulsive and temperamental young hero, whose magnetic personality inevitably draws people to him. His turbulent passions just as inevitably involve him, and those attracted to him, in misfortune. Eventually he marries the Countess Elizabeth, whose husband has divorced her. Through Elizabeth's influence and his own efforts, he is able to begin a life that more nearly approximates his ideals.

Gotham, wise men of   Fools, wiseacres. The legend is that King John intended to pass through Gotham, in Nottinghamshire, with his army, and sent heralds to prepare his way. The men of Gotham were resolved, if possible, to prevent this expense and depredation, so they resolved to play the fool. Some raked the moon out of the pond; some made a ring to hedge in a bird; others did equally foolish things. The king then abandoned his intention, and "the wise men" of the village cunningly remarked, "We ween there are more fools pass through Gotham than remain in it."

A collection of popular tales of stupidity was published in the reign of Henry VIII as *Merie Tales of the Mad Men of Gotham, gathered together by A.B. of Phisike, Doctour*. Since that date many other tales have been attached to the inhabitants of Gotham. The old nursery rhyme is well known:

> Three wise men of Gotham
> Went to sea in a bowl;
> If the bowl had been stronger
> My story had been longer.

The name *Gotham* was given to New York City by Washington IRVING in his satirical *Salmagundi Papers* (1807) and has remained in current use.

Gothic novel   A type of novel characterized by horror, violence, supernatural effects, and a taste for the medieval, usually set against a background of Gothic architecture, especially a gloomy and isolated castle. The genre originated in England with Horace Walpole's THE CASTLE OF OTRANTO. In its early forms, and even as late as THE MYSTERIES OF UDOLPHO by Ann Radcliffe, the supernatural is given a naturalistic explanation, the aim being to produce a "correct," i.e., probable, medieval romance. Even so, its excesses produced a satirical reaction, as in Jane Austen's NORTHANGER ABBEY, while conversely, in William Beckford's VATHEK, where Gothic terrors merge with the terrors of an Oriental despotism, the very monstrosities themselves seem to verge on parody. Matthew Lewis's THE MONK marks a new departure: its horrors are frankly supernatural but psychologically symbolic. This development culminates in MELMOTH THE WANDERER by Charles Robert

Maturin, and, in America, in novels by Charles Brockden BROWN, HAWTHORNE, and POE. A similar development took place on the Continent, especially in Germany. In the 20th century, the movement of SURREALISM claimed the Gothic novel as one of its forerunners.

Götterdämmerung The fourth in Richard Wagner's opera series DER RING DES NIBELUNGEN. See RAGNAROK.

Götz von Berlichingen (1773) A play by GOETHE, freely adapted from the life of Götz von Berlichingen (1480–1562), a German knight. In Goethe's treatment, Götz becomes a typical STURM UND DRANG hero, a powerful individual personality, unwaveringly committed to his own straightforward conception of justice, but in the end not able to escape the subtle maneuverings of his political adversaries. Formally, Goethe wished to emulate Shakespeare, in opposition to the prevailing style of neoclassicism, and the play is written in a powerful, rough-and-ready prose, with short pithy scenes and constant changes of setting.

Goudge, Elizabeth (1900–1984) English novelist and writer of children's books. Goudge's popular novels sensitively evoke the English countryside, English history, and the world of children. Among them are *A City of Bells* (1936), *Green Dolphin Street* (1944), and *The Little White Horse* (1946).

Gounod, Charles François (1818–1893) French composer. Gounod began and ended his career writing sacred music, although he spent most of his time writing dramatic pieces. Of these, the operas *Faust* (1859) and *Romeo and Juliet* (1867) are the best known. Among his songs is the famous "Ave Maria," based on the first prelude of BACH's *Well-Tempered Clavier.*

Gower, John (1325?–1408) English poet, a friend of CHAUCER, well known at the courts of Richard II and Henry IV. Gower wrote serious poetry of the allegorical and didactic type common in his day, urging moral and social reforms. His principal works are the French SPECULUM MEDITANTIS, the Latin VOX CLAMANTIS, and the English *Confessio Amantis* (c1386–1390), as well as some lighter short poems in all three languages.

Goya y Lucientes, Francisco José de (1746–1828) Spanish painter and etcher. Goya worked for the Royal Workshop as a designer of cartoons and became Royal Painter in 1786. After the death of Charles III he went on to serve his son, Charles IV, portraying the king, his family, and the nobility in brilliant, often cruelly truthful paintings that rank among the most discerning in the world of art. A severe disease left him deaf at forty-seven, yet the following years mark the peak of his fame. The injustice and inhumanity of the period of the Spanish War of Independence against Napoleon's occupation (1808–14) and of Ferdinand VII's reign (1814–20) elicited a tortured reaction from him. He painted scenes of disasters, madness, and satanism, and executed the series of etchings

entitled *The Disasters of War*, in which he indicted violence and murder with bitter realism and censured the moral dishonesty of those who would not rebel against human misery.

In 1823, Goya left for Bordeaux, in France, where he continued to paint with unshaken confidence and originality. He left an extensive production: portraits, religious paintings, scenes of the Inquisition, of crime, of the people's everyday work, engravings of war, and the bullfight. The paintings were little known outside Spain until 1896, and *The Disasters of War* was not published until 1863, yet Goya exerted a profound influence on modern art. Eugène DELACROIX, Honoré DAUMIER, and Édouard MANET were among the first to be influenced by his visionary representation of the world and by his approach to art, from which he banished all academic conceptions of composition and draftsmanship in order to give color the double role of unifying loosely constructed paintings and of defining the forms.

Goytisolo [Gay], Juan (1931–   ) Spanish novelist and essayist. An expatriate from 1957 until after Franco's death, Goytisolo is one of the best-known novelists of his generation both in and outside Spain. He writes iconoclastic novels burlesquing a Spanish culture that has been victimized by false myths, religiosity, and sexual frustrations. His first novel, *Juegos de manos* (1954; tr *The Young Assassins*, 1959), depicts a lost generation destroyed by the Spanish Civil War, as does *Duelo en el Paraíso* (1955; tr *Children of Chaos*, 1958). In other novels of the 1950s and 1960s, most notably *Señas de identidad* (1966; tr *Marks of Identity*, 1969), he documents the continuing effects of that war and the ensuing dictatorship. In his later masterpieces, COUNT JULIAN and *Juan sin terra* (1975; tr *Juan the Landless*, 1977), he attempts to annihilate traditional language, by using free semantic and phonetic associative chains, humorous stereotypes, puns, and foreign languages. These novels, filled with dream states and interior monologue, produce simultaneous layers of consciousness and combine dialogues from different temporal zones.

Gozzi, Count Carlo (1720–1806) Italian playwright. A member of the Granelleschi Society, whose purpose it was to preserve Tuscan literature from foreign influences, Gozzi ignored theatrical innovation and produced charming and witty plays, many of them dramatized versions of fairy tales. GOETHE and Mme de STAËL, among others, were admirers of his work. His play *Re Turandot* (*King Turandot*, 1762) was translated into German by SCHILLER, and became the basis for operas by WEBER, Busoni, and PUCCINI. *Fiaba dell' amore delle tre melarancie* (*Fable of the Love of Three Oranges*, 1761), which was derived from *Lo cunto de li cunti* of Giambattista Basile (c1575–1632) and presented two rival dramatists, GOLDONI and Chiari, under the satirical guises of a fairy and a magician, revived the stock characters of the Italian comedy of masks and enjoyed a huge popular success. Almost a century and a half later, it was used by PROKOFIEV as the basis for his opera *The Love of Three Oranges.*

Grabbe, Christian Dietrich (1801–1836)   German playwright, known especially for the ironic, often pessimistically cynical and disillusioned attitude that permeates his works. Grabbe's style is an early example of the 19th-century turn toward realism, away from the idealism of such dramatists as SCHILLER. Among his works are *Scherz, Satire, Ironie und tiefere Bedeutung* (*Joke, Satire, Irony and Deeper Significance,* pub 1827) and *Don Juan und Faust* (1829).

Gracchi   A prominent family of republican Rome. Its most famous members were Tiberius Sempronius Gracchus (163?–133 BC) and his brother Gaius Sempronius Gracchus (153–121 BC). As tribune (133), Tiberius secured the enactment, despite much opposition, of an agrarian reform law that would grant public lands to the impoverished Italian peasantry. When, in defiance of custom, he sought a second term as tribune, he and three hundred of his followers were killed in an election riot.

His work was carried on by Gaius, who, as tribune in 123 and 122, sought to regulate the price of grain in Rome and proposed extension of the franchise. Like his brother, he was killed at the instigation of the senate.

The mother of the Gracchi brothers was the famous Cornelia, daughter of SCIPIO AFRICANUS, who was considered the ideal Roman matron. According to tradition, she was once visited by a wealthy woman who displayed her jewels and asked to see Cornelia's. Pointing to her sons, Cornelia replied, "These are my jewels."

Grace Abounding to the Chief of Sinners (1666)   An autobiography by John BUNYAN. Written while Bunyan was in prison, it describes his spiritual struggles and the development of his religious convictions.

Graces   In Roman mythology, the Gratiae, goddesses who embodied beauty and charm. Called by the Greeks the Charites, they were, by some accounts, named Aglaia (Brilliance), Thalia (the Flowering), and Euphrosyne (Joy), though their names and even their number varied. Although they were probably very early spirits of vegetation, they did not in classical times have any cult of importance. They are best known from their many appearances in art.

Gracián, Baltasar (1601–1658)   Spanish prose writer and Jesuit priest. The outstanding exponent of CONCEPTISM, Gracián has been variously regarded as a moral philosopher of considerable depth and as an unoriginal intellectual poseur. His best-known works are *El criticón* (1651, 1653, 1657), an allegorical novel, and *Agudeza y arte de ingenio* (1642, 1648), a manual of conceptism, in which he defined the numerous varieties of literary *agudeza* ("fine distinction; ingenuity"). In *El héroe* (1637), he drew a portrait of the ideal Christian hero. *El discreto* (1646) discusses the twenty-five *realces,* or "adornments,"

which make up the well-bred gentleman, while the *Oráculo manual o arte de prudencia* (1647) is a collection of three hundred maxims that offer a distillation of worldly wisdom.

Graeae   Literally, the gray-haired women. In Greek myth, the sisters and guardians of the GORGONS. They owned only one eye and one tooth among them, which they shared in turn. PERSEUS, robbing them of these, forced them to show him the way to the Gorgons, and to give him their winged sandals, magic wallet, and cap of invisibility. HESIOD mentions only two Graeae, Enyo and Pephredo; later legends add a third, Deino.

Graham, W[illiam] S[ydney] (1918–1986)   Scottish poet. Graham's poetry is musical and emotionally tough, drawing heavily on the lessons to be learned from nature, particularly the sea. Such volumes as *Cage Without Grievance* (1942), *The Seven Journeys* (1944), and *2nd Poems* (1945) suggest Dylan THOMAS in their complexity, obscurity, lyricism, and awareness of mortality. The mature verse of *The White Threshold* (1949) and *The Nightfishing* (1955) is both more intense and more disciplined. After a fifteen-year silence, Graham published *Malcolm Mooney's Land* in 1970. His *Collected Poems: 1942–1977* (1978) was followed by the highly acclaimed volume *Selected Poems* (1980).

Grahame, Kenneth (1859–1932)   English author of essays and children's books. Grahame worked, a bit discontentedly, as Secretary of the Bank of England. He published a collection of essays in *Pagan Papers* (1893) and then gained further recognition with his pieces on an English childhood in *The Golden Age* (1895) and *Dream Days* (1898). His fame as a writer, however, rests securely on THE WIND IN THE WILLOWS, a children's classic dealing with the idyllic river-bank life of a collection of animal characters.

Graham of Claverhouse, John (first Viscount Dundee, known as Bloody Claverse and Bonny Dundee; 1649?–1689)   Scottish soldier. Graham was dubbed "Bloody Claverse" by the Scottish COVENANTERS, whom he persecuted with great severity for twenty years. In 1689 he raised an army of Highlanders to fight for James II and won the battle of Killiecrankie, but was mortally wounded. To JACOBITES he became known as "Bonny Dundee," a semi-legendary hero. He is a character in Scott's novel *Old Mortality* (1816).

Grail (also Holy Grail and Sangreal)   A famous talisman (variously represented as a chalice, dish, stone, and cup into which a lance drips blood), the center around which a huge corpus of medieval legend, romance, and allegory revolves. The precise origin and nature of the Grail are unknown and have been the subject of countless scholarly researches; these have attempted to sort out the features of ancient fertility cults, Celtic myth, and Christianity in the Grail romances. The Grail is best known as the object of a quest on the part of the knights of the ROUND

TABLE in Arthurian legend. It brings healing and food to those who touch it and can be found only by one absolutely pure.

The best-known accounts of the Grail are those that give it a Christian origin and generally run along the following lines: It is the vessel from which Jesus drank at the LAST SUPPER and that afterwards came into the possession of JOSEPH OF ARIMATHEA, who caught in it some of the blood that flowed from the wounds of the crucified Saviour. He carried it with him to England, and it provided him with food, drink, and spiritual sustenance for the rest of his life. It was handed down to his successor and thence from generation to generation, GALAHAD, in Malory's MORTE D'ARTHUR, being Joseph's last descendant. In some accounts it disappears after Joseph brings it to England. In still others, it is the dish out of which Jesus and his disciples ate the paschal lamb at the Last Supper. The theory of a Christian origin of the Grail, however, has been abandoned. Many now hold that the Grail was originally a female sex symbol in ancient fertility rites used with the bleeding lance mentioned in CHRÉTIEN DE TROYES's early account. Jessie L. Weston's discussion of this theory in *From Ritual to Romance* (1920) was the source used by T. S. Eliot for his poem THE WASTE LAND, where the Grail theme occurs in this symbolic form.

The mass of literature concerning the Grail cycle, both ancient and modern, is enormous. The chief sources of the principal groups of legend are the *Peredur* in the *Mabinogion*, which is one of the most archaic forms of the story; the unfinished *Perceval, ou le conte du Graal* by Chrétien de Troyes, in which the Grail is a hollow dish, accompanied by a bleeding lance (see PERCIVAL); Wolfram von Eschenbach's PARZIVAL, the best example of the story as transformed by ecclesiastical influence; a chivalric version by Gottfried von Strassburg; the 13th-century French *Perceval le Gallois* (founded on earlier English and Celtic legends that had no connection with the Grail), showing Percival in his later role as an ascetic hero, translated by Dr. Sebastian Evans (1893) as *The High History of the Holy Grail*; and the *Quête du St. Graal*, which, in its English dress, is found in Malory's *Morte d'Arthur*. It was the French poet Robert de Boron (fl c1215) who, in his *Joseph d'Arimathie ou Le Saint Graal*, first definitely attached the history of the Grail to the Arthurian cycle and first mentioned the Grail as a chalice containing Jesus' blood. The framework of Tennyson's "Holy Grail" in his IDYLLS OF THE KING is taken from Malory.

Grain of Wheat, A (1967)

A novel by NGUGI WA THIONG'O. Set in the days just prior to Kenya's independence, it tells, in flashback sequences, of the experiences of four principal figures in the independence struggle and especially of their relationship to Kihika, a hero of the revolution, hanged by the colonial authorities.

Grandbois, Alain (1900–1975)

Quebec poet. Grandbois's poetry expresses with intensity the conflict between eternity and time. Elegiac and exotic, *Les Iles de la nuit* (1944) profoundly influenced a rising generation of poets. From 1925 until the beginning of World War II, Grandbois lived in France, traveling extensively. His first collection of poems appeared in China in 1934. A collection of short stories, *Avant le chaos*, was published in 1945 when he was again living in Canada. Grandbois the poet is essentially a spiritual traveler, pursuing the absolute through a landscape that echoes both his childhood discovery of Quebec and his wanderings of the globe. Much of his verse is contained in *Poèmes* (1963).

Grandgousier (Fr, "great gullet")

In Rabelais's GARGANTUA AND PANTAGRUEL, the king of Utopia, husband of Gargamelle, and father of Gargantua. Grandgousier, a just and peace-loving patriarch who lives at the Devinière, the house where Rabelais was born, has been identified with the latter's own father.

Grand Guignol

Derived from Guignol, the name of a stock puppet character who originated in Lyon at the end of the 18th century. He was taken to Paris and, perhaps because of his violence and audacity (much like that of Punch in PUNCH AND JUDY), he eventually gave his name to the Théâtre du Grand Guignol, which specialized in stage plays featuring the macabre, including realistic tortures and mutilations. Hence the term Grand Guignol has come to be used for any work that attempts to shock and horrify.

Grand Inquisitor, The Legend of the

In DOSTOYEVSKY's *The Brothers Karamazov*, the parable related by Ivan to Alyosha, expressing the former's religious doubts. The tale relates how Jesus returns to Earth in Seville during the Inquisition and how he is recognized by the people and immediately arrested by the Inquisition leaders. The Grand Inquisitor, a menacing old churchman, visits Jesus' cell and upbraids him for returning, saying that the Church no longer needs him, that he has misapprehended man's nature and has burdened man with too much freedom. The Church, says the Inquisitor, understands that man does not want the burden of free choice but wants to be led. The Church's allegiance has been shifted to the Other, to the Devil, the Inquisitor claims, and Jesus is now only an unwanted distraction. Henceforth, he says, man will be cared for by the new leaders of the Church, who are strong enough to take on themselves the burden of freedom and to guide the weak masses. At the end of his tirade, the Inquisitor throws open the cell door and orders Jesus to leave and never return. Jesus, who has been silent throughout the interview, answers the old man with a kiss on the cheek before leaving, presumably an expression of his love even for the unbeliever.

"The Grand Inquisitor" is the most famous single section of the novel and is often excerpted as an independent piece for anthologies, although its thematic connections with the novel as a whole are strong. The ideas it expresses have been considered formulations of Dostoyevsky's own religious doubts.

Grandissimes, The: A Story of Creole Life (1880)   A novel by George W. CABLE. It is set in New Orleans in the period of the Louisiana Purchase. An outside observer, Frowenfeld, learns of the family feuds, especially those between the De Grapions and the Grandissimes, the race feuds, and the struggle between the new order and the old. The book is filled with vivid characters, notably the Creole mother and daughter Nancanou, and the African king Bras Coupé, who allows himself to be tortured to death rather than be a slave.

Grand Meaulnes, Le (1913; tr *The Wanderer*, 1928, and *The Lost Domain*, 1959)   The novel that won ALAIN-FOURNIER his reputation. Le Grand Meaulnes, the young hero, has a curious adventure at Christmastime. In the middle of the woods he discovers a merry party and a beautiful girl both hidden in an old house. His love for the girl, Yvonne, and his friendship with her brother, Franz, shape his life, bringing him intense joy and intense sorrow. The uniqueness of the novel lies in its delicate combination of fantasy and realism. Actuality and the dream world mingle indistinguishably in the experience of a young boy coming to manhood.

grand opera   A type of opera that is sung throughout. In the more restricted sense, a type of opera performed at the Paris Opéra in the 19th century, in which an attempt was made to overwhelm the spectator with brilliant musical numbers, large crowd scenes, and elaborate spectacle. These operas always had a historical subject (treated very freely), were cast in five acts, and had an important ballet sequence at some point. Examples are ROSSINI's *William Tell*, Auber's *La Muette de Portici*, MEYERBEER's *Les Huguenots*, and VERDI's *Don Carlos*.

Gran Galeoto, El (The Great Galeoto, 1881)   A tragedy by José ECHEGARAY, in which spiteful gossip is the "GALEOTO" of the title. The heroine is suspected by the spying public and finally by her husband, Julian, of improper relations with her young secretary, Ernest. They are innocent, but are powerless to convince Julian, who dies from a wound received in a duel for his wife's honor.

Grani (MHG, "gray-colored")   In the NIBELUNGEN-LIED, SIEGFRIED's horse, of marvelous swiftness.

Granin, Daniil Aleksandrovich (pen name of Daniil German, 1918–   )   Soviet novelist and short-story writer. Trained in electrical engineering, Granin focused on industrial and scientific problems in *Iskateli* (1954; tr *Those Who Seek*, 1956) and in *Idu na grozu* (1962; tr *Into the Storm*, 1965). He first gained recognition with the publication in *Novy mir* of his story "Sobstvennoye mneniye" ("One's Own Opinion," 1956), in which a Soviet scientist realizes that his hope for a courageous career in science is merely self-deception. Granin has also written a number of biographical sketches, including a

screenplay about J. Robert Oppenheimer, and served as secretary of the Leningrad Writers' Union.

Grant, Ulysses S[impson] (1822–1885)   American soldier and eighteenth president of the U.S. (1869–77). A graduate of West Point and a veteran of the Mexican War, Grant later engaged unsuccessfully in farming and business. He entered the Union army in 1861 and, after capturing Forts Henry and Donelson in Tennessee (1862), was promoted to major-general; he led the Union forces at Shiloh (1862) and captured Vicksburg (1863), splitting the Confederacy in half. Appointed commander-in-chief of the Union army in 1864, he moved against Richmond, the Confederate capital, in a slow and costly but ultimately successful campaign and accepted the surrender of General Lee at Appomattox Courthouse. His two presidential terms were marred by extensive graft and corruption that involved such highly placed officials as Secretary of War W. W. Belknap and O. E. Babcock, Grant's private secretary. After his retirement, Grant was left penniless through the failure of a brokerage firm, but his *Personal Memoirs* (1885), which he completed while dying of throat cancer, brought his family nearly $500,000.

gran teatro del mundo, El (The Great Theatre of the World)   An AUTO SACRAMENTAL by Pedro CALDERÓN DE LA BARCA. It deals with the world in terms of a theatrical allegory. The Author (God) presents a performance in which a beggar, a rich man, and other figures, including personifications of vices and virtues, play out their roles. The play demonstrates that the things of this world pass away, and only God is eternal.

Granville-Barker, Harley (1877–1946)   English critic, dramatist, director, and actor. Before World War I, Granville-Barker was noted both as an actor and a dramatist. In 1911–13 his staging of *The Winter's Tale*, *A Midsummer Night's Dream*, and *Twelfth Night* effected a radical change in Shakespeare production. Today Granville-Barker is best known for his critical works, such as his *Prefaces to Shakespeare* (1923–47), which analyze the plays from a director's point of view, and *A Companion to Shakespeare Studies* (1934), which he edited with G. B. Harrison.

Grapes of Wrath, The (1939)   A novel by John STEINBECK. Awarded the PULITZER PRIZE in 1940, this moving and highly successful proletarian novel tells of the hardships of the Joad family. "Okie" farmers, forced out of their home in the Oklahoma dust-bowl region by economic desperation, they drive to California in search of work as migrant fruitpickers. The grandparents die on the way; on their arrival the others are harassed by the police and participate in strike violence, during which Tom, the Joad son, kills a man. At the conclusion of the novel, throughout which descriptive and philosophical passages alternate with narrative portions, the family is defeated but still resolute.

Grass, Günter [Wilhelm] (1927–   )   German novelist, poet, dramatist, essayist, and artist. Grass was born in the Free State of Danzig (now Polish Gdansk) on the Baltic coast, a setting that figures frequently in his fiction. When Grass was eight, Danzig was seized by HITLER; during World War II he was drafted into the German army, was wounded, and was held prisoner until 1946 in the American sector of Germany. Upon his release he worked as a laborer.

In 1949 he began the study of art and sculpture, supporting himself as a drummer in a local jazz band. He moved to Paris in 1955, where he wrote poetry, several unsuccessful plays, and his first novel, THE TIN DRUM, which at once became a world success. As part of what was later called the "Danzig trilogy," this was followed by *Katz und Maus* (1961; tr *Cat and Mouse*, 1963) and *Hundejahre* (1963; tr *Dog Years*, 1965). These works, like his later novels, satirize the periods covered, combining a fierce, sardonic humor, minute realism, and extravagant fantasy.

After the Hitler epoch, the gruesome shadow of which dominates the trilogy, came the *Wirtschaftswunder* ("miraculous economic recovery"), with its increasingly affluent middle class and rebellious, disaffected youth. This clash of the generations created the charged atmosphere of Grass's novel *Örtlich Betäubt* (1969; tr *Local Anaesthetic*, 1970). A committed Socialist, Grass campaigned actively for the election of Chancellor Willy Brandt in 1969. This campaign served as the background for his novel *Aus dem Tagebuch einer Schnecke* (1972; tr *From the Diary of a Snail*, 1973), which interweaves recollections of Danzig with reflections on life and politics in Berlin. His political speeches and essays were published in *Über das Selbstverständliche* (1968; tr *Speak Out*, 1969). Political events of the 1960s and 1970s play a part, though less central, in THE FLOUNDER, which covers four thousand years of history from a culinary and sexual perspective. *The Rat*, a novel in the form of a reminiscence, was published in 1987.

Grass's other works include a number of documentary dramas, notably *Die Plebejer proben den Aufstand* (1966; tr *The Plebeians Rehearse the Uprising*, 1966), which took aim at Brecht's politics, and several volumes of poetry, appearing in English in *Selected Poems* (1965) and *New Poems* (1968). In 1985, he published *On Writing and Politics, 1967–1983*, a collection of speeches and writings that presents a bleaker, darker vision of the world than Grass has so far rendered in his work. He has also written plays, many of which were successfully performed in Germany and elsewhere. In 1986 his play *The Flood* was received enthusiastically in New York.

gratuitous act   See GIDE, ANDRÉ.

Grau [Delgado], Jacinto (1877–1958)   Spanish playwright. In reaction to the synthetic and trite nature of much Spanish theatre, Grau undertook to create an oeuvre of plays that explored serious themes, whether by farce or straight tragedy. Among his best-known plays are *El hijo pródigo* (1918), a thoughtful treatment of the story of the Prodigal Son; two plays dealing with the theme of an aging Don Juan, *Don Juan de Carillana* (1913) and *El burlador que no se burla* (1930); and *El señor de Pigmalión* (1923), a serious "tragi-comic farce" in which life-like puppets reveal the egocentrism and fallibility of human nature.

Graves, Robert [Ranke] (1895–1985)   English poet, novelist, and critic. Graves wrote both lucid, dryly humorous verse and exquisite love poems. Among his many collections of poetry are *Fairies and Fusiliers* (1917) and several volumes of *Collected Poems* (1959, 1965, 1975). Much of his early poetry dealt with the psychological effects of World War I, in which he was badly wounded. His later poetry concerns the importance and impossibility of pure love between a man and a woman. *Good-Bye to All That* (1929) is a striking memoir of his early years, covering his experiences on the front in the war.

Graves's historical novels are at once scholarly and mischievous. He tends to interpret his characters in psychologically unconventional ways, as in *I, Claudius* (1934), *Claudius the God* (1934), *The Golden Fleece* (1944), and *Homer's Daughter* (1955). Among his books of literary criticism are *A Pamphlet Against Anthologies* (1928), written with Laura RIDING, whose personal and literary influence on Graves during their close association between 1926 and 1939 was significant. Other important works of criticism are THE WHITE GODDESS, a study of the mythological sources of poetry, and *Oxford Addresses on Poetry* (1962). *The Long Weekend* (1940), written with Alan Hodge, is a social history of the interwar years in England. *The Nazarene Gospel* (1953; with Joshua Podro) is a bold, scholarly reinterpretation of the origins of Christianity. Notable among his translations and comment is *The Greek Myths* (1955). Graves lived for many years in Majorca, returning to England from 1961 to 1966 to become professor of poetry at Oxford.

Graveyard by the Sea, The   See CIMITIÈRE MARIN, LE.

Gravity's Rainbow (1973)   A novel by Thomas PYNCHON. The novel portrays a nightmarish world after World War II, dominated by a sinister international power group that controls the world through the death-forces of missile technology. Richly layered with diverse thematic threads, shifting literary styles, and masses of scientific and mathematical information, the novel revolves around the search, by Lt. Tyrone Slothrop and more powerful forces, for the mysterious Rocket 00000. On several levels simultaneously the novel is a chart of the modern world's suicidal "progress" toward utter devastation.

Gray, Simon (1936–   )   English playwright and novelist. Gray published three novels before turning to the theatre. His first play, *Wise Child* (1967), established his reputation as a writer of stinging wit and meticulous craftsmanship. *Dutch Uncle* (1969) and *Spoiled* (1971) followed, but it was with *Butley* (1971), a portrait of a dishevelled lecturer whose professional, emotional, and sexual lives are falling apart, that Gray's distinctive blend of humor and pain filled theatres on both sides of the Atlantic. Two later plays, *Close of Play* (1979) and *Quartermaine's Terms* (1981), also have academic settings. *Otherwise Engaged* (1975) is a deft comedy about a publisher who remains resolutely detached from the problems of friends and relatives. *The Common Pursuit* (1984), which centers on the interplay of life and literature as represented by a group of writers and editors, was received enthusiastically in London and New York.

Gray, Thomas (1716–1771)   English poet and noted letter-writer. Gray was one of the forerunners of the romantic movement in England. His most important correspondence was with Horace WALPOLE, Thomas Wharton, and William MASON. His works, largely meditative lyrics and Pindaric odes, are marked by love of nature and melancholy reflection. His poetry includes "Ode to Spring," "Hymn to Adversity," and "Ode on a Distant Prospect of Eton College" (1742), the last of which contains the well-known lines ". . . where ignorance is bliss, / 'Tis folly to be wise"; "Sonnet on the Death of Richard West" (1775); "Ode on the Death of a Favorite Cat, Drowned in a Tub of Gold Fishes" (1748), light verse in the neoclassic manner; ELEGY WRITTEN IN A COUNTRY CHURCHYARD, his most famous work; "The Bard" (1757); "The Progress of Poesy" (1759), on the power of music; "The Fatal Sisters" and "The Descent of Odin" (1761), both in imitation of early Welsh and Norse verse. The biography published by his friend and correspondent William Mason, in 1775, contains many of his famous letters.

Gray expressed his poetic ideal thus: "Extreme conciseness of expression, yet pure, perspicuous, and musical, is one of the grand beauties of lyric poetry. This I have always aimed at, and never could attain."

Gray's Inn   See INNS OF COURT.

Great Awakening   A religious revivalist movement that swept through the American colonies from the 1730s to the 1750s. It was marked by sensational public repentance and conversion and prompted a spate of missionary activity, as well as an interest in such humanitarian causes as the abolition of slavery. It began in Massachusetts with the preaching of Jonathan EDWARDS and was spread through the middle colonies by the Presbyterian preacher William Tennent (1703–64) and the great English evangelist George Whitefield (1714–70). The movement collapsed under the weight of a bitter schism between the forces of Calvinism and the liberals, led by Charles Chauncey, whose views led in time to a form of Universalism or UNITARIANISM. Despite the doctrinal disputes, the Great Awakening had the effect of democratizing American religious practices and crystallizing feeling against the Anglican Church.

Great Bear and Little Bear (Latin names Ursa Major, Ursa Minor)   Constellations. In Greek legend, CALLISTO, a nymph of ARTEMIS, had a son by ZEUS. His wife, HERA (or Zeus himself), changed Callisto into a bear. When she was about to be shot by her son Arcas, Zeus converted mother and son into constellations. The name given to the two constellations, considered as a single group, is Arctos.

The Greek word *arktos*, "bear," is still kept in the names Arcturus ("the bear-ward," from *ouros*, "guardian") and Arctic. The Sanskrit name for the Great Bear is from the verb *rakh*, "to be bright," and it has been suggested that the Greeks named it *arktos* as a result of confusion between the two words. Arcturus was once the name given to the Pole Star.

Encompassed within Great and Little Bear are star formations popularly known as the Big Dipper and the Little Dipper; the latter contains the North Star, which is also known as the Pole Star, Polaris.

Great Chain of Being   An ancient concept of God and the creation that has permeated science, literature, and philosophy since the time of Plato. It was refined in the 18th century by the philosopher G. W. LEIBNITZ. The concept includes three points based on the premise that God's infinite creativity flows into the creation of the fullest possible variety of beings. The following points are consequences of this premise: plenitude—the universe contains every possible form of life; continuity—there is a continuity of species in which each differs from others in only small degrees; and gradation—all creation from God to the lowest form of matter exists in a hierarchical and interconnected system, with man occupying the middle rung between animals and angels. The ideas inherent in the concept are clearly characterized in Pope's AN ESSAY ON MAN.

Great Cham of Literature   A sobriquet for Dr. Samuel JOHNSON first used by Smollett in a letter to Wilkes. *Cham* is an obsolete word, synonymous with *Khan*, applicable to the ruler of the Tartars, the Mongols, and the emperor of China.

Great Expectations (1860–1861)   A novel by Charles DICKENS. The novel traces the growth of Philip Pirrip, called Pip, from a boy of shallow dreams to a man of depth and character. Pip is reared by his sister and her husband, Joe Gargery, a blacksmith. In his youth he is influenced by the eccentric Miss HAVISHAM, who was jilted on her wedding night and who has brought up her adopted niece Estella to hate men. As a young man, Pip is informed that an unknown benefactor has provided money for his education and expects to make him his heir. Forsaking his humbler friends—particularly the faithful Joe—he sets off to London with the firm intention of becoming a gentleman and realizing his "great expectations." He soon learns that his patron is Abel MAGWITCH, a transported convict, whom Pip had helped years earlier; Magwitch also turns out to be Estella's father. With this knowledge Pip's dreams fade; he returns home after Joe saves him from imprisonment for debt, and sets himself to honest work. It is implied that he will marry Estella, whose husband, Bentley Drummle, dies. Among the gallery of characters in the book are Biddy, who becomes Joe's second wife; the Pocket family; Uncle Pumblechook; Dolge Orlick, the murderer of Pip's sister; and Mr. Jaggers.

The novel is regarded by many as Dickens's greatest achievement, although the happy ending, which according to Dickens's biographer John Forster was written on the advice of Bulwer-Lytton and substituted for the less sunny original, detracts from the work somewhat.

Great Gatsby, The (1925)   A novel by F. Scott FITZGERALD. The mysterious Jay Gatsby lives in a luxurious mansion on the Long Island north shore, entertaining hundreds of guests at lavish parties that have become legendary. Nick Carraway, the narrator, lives next door to Gatsby, and Nick's cousin Daisy and her crude but wealthy husband, Tom Buchanan, live directly across the harbor. Gatsby reveals to Nick that he and Daisy had a brief affair before the war and her marriage to Tom. Born James Gatz of a poor midwestern family, he has accumulated enormous wealth through shady transactions solely to make himself the kind of man he thinks Daisy admires: his one dream, and the reason he bought his house and gives his parties, is to get her back. He persuades Nick to bring him and Daisy together again, but he is unable to win her away from Tom. Daisy, driving Gatsby's car, runs over and kills Tom's mistress, Myrtle, unaware of her identity. Myrtle's husband traces the car and shoots Gatsby, who has remained silent in order to protect Daisy. Gatsby's friends and associates have all deserted him, and only Gatsby's father and one former guest attend the funeral. The novel's power derives not from its plot, but from its sharply antagonistic portrayal of wealthy society in America and from the exposure of the "Jazz Age" in all its false glamor, cultural barrenness, moral emptiness, and desperate boredom. Yet for all its bitterness it is probably Fitzgerald's most humane work. It has enjoyed continuous popularity since its first publication and is considered an American classic.

Great God Brown, The (1926)   A play by Eugene O'NEILL. Masks are used to symbolize the varying personalities of the characters as they are and as they appear to other people. The "great god Brown" is a successful businessman, devoid of inner resources; he eventually takes the mask of Dion Anthony (as his name suggests, a Dionysian character), a frustrated artist who dies. With Dion's mask, Brown is accepted by Dion's wife as the real Dion, for she has known and loved only her husband's mask, not his true self.

Great Learning, The   One of the Chinese FOUR BOOKS. Originally one chapter from the BOOK OF RITES, it was elevated to importance in the Confucian educational and philosophical system during the SUNG dynasty (960–1279). It emphasizes self-cultivation.

Great Mother   A nature goddess of ancient Anatolia. Her names and appellations include CYBELE, the mountain mother, the Idaean mother, and still others. In Greek mythology, Cybele is generally associated with Rhea.

Greco, El (sobriquet of Domenikos Theotocopoulos, c1541–1614)   Spanish painter, born in Crete. Having mastered the technique of icon painting in Crete, Greco went to Italy, where he studied the work of TITIAN and TINTORETTO. In 1577 he settled in Toledo, Spain, where, isolated from artistic influences, he developed a highly personal style that retains the movement of BAROQUE drawing while suppressing the very spatial depth that baroque art sought to create. He painted intense portraits, mystic saints, and deeply expressive religious scenes. His use of such effects as discordantly contrasted cool colors, elongated distortions of the human frame, bright illumination, and flashing accents was misunderstood by contemporaries, and the significance of his art was not recognized until the 19th century. His best-known works include *Assumption of the Virgin* (1577), *Burial of the Count of Orgaz* (c1584), *Pentecost* (1604–14), and *View of Toledo* (1600–10).

Greek epic poetry   Greek epic, a development from oral tradition. The earliest extant examples are the ILIAD and the ODYSSEY of HOMER. The functions of the Mycenaean rhapsode (*rhapsodos*), or minstrel, are clearly shown in the character of Demodocus, the blind bard who entertained Odysseus and other guests at the court of the Phaeacian king Alcinous in the *Odyssey*. It was his duty to sing of the great heroes of past and present in order to entertain and please the kings and lords who could afford such a luxury. Unlike Demodocus, most bards probably traveled from court to court. Wherever they stopped, they would find it expedient to recite events that were especially gratifying to the local lord: his own exploits or those of heroes he claimed as forebears, much as VERGIL later made the myths of AENEAS a paean to the glory of Rome and of his personal patron, AUGUSTUS. To this end, the bard would often fabricate a connection between his patron of the moment and some great event or hero, such as the sack of Troy or the deeds of HERACLES. This custom accounts in part for the apparent ubiquity of Heracles and THESEUS and, more important, for the process of gradual accretion, which, over a period of centuries, culminated in such epics as the *Odyssey*, in which a great mass of originally unrelated myths and folk tales adhered to the story of one hero.

An itinerant bard had to be able not only to recall an enormous number of tales, but to recite them in the dactylic hexameters that, by the time of Homer, had already been the traditional language of epic for centuries. Since writing, if it was used at all for literary purposes, must have been only a kind of shorthand, a bard was called upon to perform prodigious feats of memory. At the same time, in adjusting his tales to the requirements of the immediate situation, he had to be able to improvise at length.

The structure of the great Greek epics, even in the relatively literary form in which they have been preserved, shows clearly their oral origins. One of their most striking characteristics is the great number of repeated phrases (for example, epithets such as "wine-dark sea" or "shepherd of the people") that are applied more or less indiscriminately to a variety of places or people. Every bard memorized a vast repertory of these formulae, which he could then apply on the spur of the moment in an appropriate spot in a poem according to the demands of the meter. It was probably this patchwork approach to poetry that earned him the name of rhapsode: "stitcher."

The repetition of stock phrases inevitably tends to monotony, especially when those phrases must, for practical reasons, be kept general enough in tone to be largely interchangeable. It is a measure of the genius of Homer, whoever he may have been, that he was able, within these traditional limitations, to achieve considerable individuality in his characters and to overcome monotony with sheer dramatic and poetic power.

Greek Passion, The (Ho Christos Xanastavronetai, 1951; tr 1954; Brit ed *Christ Recrucified*, 1954)   A novel by Nikos KAZANTZAKIS. Set in Anatolia in 1922, it is a story of the persecution of Greek refugees by the Turkish overlord and, worse, by greedy and cruel fellow-Greeks living in a wealthy village. At the beginning, several villagers are chosen for roles they are to play nine months later in a local passion pageant. By the time Christmas comes, the drama has been forgotten in a succession of violent events, and the cast have played out their assigned roles in real life. A powerful modern morality play, the novel reveals the darker passions in men's lives that deeply concerned Kazantzakis. It was the basis for Jules Dassin's film *He Who Must Die* (1956) and an opera by the composer Bohuslav Martinu.

Greeley, Horace (1811–1872)   American journalist and political leader. As a newspaper printer and editor in New York, Greeley advocated many reform movements, including abolition. He served in Congress (1848–49) and supported the candidacy of LINCOLN for president. Averse to the Republican policy of revenge on the South following the CIVIL WAR, he ran unsuccessfully against GRANT in 1872. Greeley supported the agrarian movement and worked for a liberal policy for settlers; one of his favorite sayings was "Go West, young man." In sympathy with the laboring classes in New York City, he also favored "magnanimity in triumph," a policy of universal amnesty and universal suffrage after the Civil War. His willingness to put up bail for Jefferson DAVIS brought him much abuse, but he never allowed his subscribers' threats to modify his editorial views.

Green, Henry (pen name of Henry Vincent Yorke, 1905–1974)   English novelist. Green's inimitable, unpredictable, frequently enigmatic novels all carry brief titles suggesting inconclusiveness. His work—including *Blindness* (1926), *Living* (1929), *Party Going* (1939), *Caught* (1943), *Back* (1946), and *Concluding* (1948)—is characterized by an unconventional use of language, influenced in part by Gertrude STEIN in its ellipsis and distortion of syntax. He wrote ambiguous comedies of manners, bluntly realistic on the one hand, while carrying mysterious symbolic overtones on the other. A remarkably versatile writer, he presented a wide range of characters, subjects, and styles, with a generally wry view of human inadequacy. In *Loving* (1945), considered his most successful work, his approach is entirely objective, revealing his characters only through their speech; in his last two novels, *Nothing* (1950) and *Doting* (1952), he all but completely eliminates visual description, concentrating on dialogue. In their impressionism and abstraction, his novels have been called the literary counterparts to the works of MONET and PICASSO.

Green, Julien (1900–   )   French novelist of American parentage. Except for the years in which he attended the University of Virginia (1918–22) and a brief period during World War II, Green lived in France and wrote his books in French. He was as much influenced by his Puritan heritage as by the Catholicism to which he converted. His first novel, *Mont-Cinère* (1926; tr *Avarice House*, 1927), is the story of an American family caught between boredom and greed. *Adrienne Mesurat* (1927; tr *The Closed Garden*, 1928) and *Léviathan* (1929; tr *The Dark Journey*, 1929) reflect his obsessive sense of sin, his consciousness of the violence and sadism of which men are capable, and his fascination with and fear of madness and death.

With *Le Visionnaire* (1934; tr *The Dreamer*, 1934) and *Minuit* (1936; tr *Midnight*, 1936), Green entered into a more personal, dreamlike exploration of the constant battle between good and evil, passion and reason. Two of his best novels are *Moïra* (1950) and *Chaque homme dans sa nuit* (1960). Green's *Journal 1926–1972* (9 vols, 1972), which reveals the author's spiritual torment and growth, was partially translated in *Personal Record 1928–1939* (1939) and *Diary 1928–1957* (1962).

Green, Paul E[liot] (1894–1981)   American playwright and teacher. Green is best known for dramas portraying life in the South, often set in his native state of North Carolina. His most important play is *In Abraham's Bosom* (1927), a PULITZER PRIZE-winning drama about a mulatto who tries to establish a school for blacks in a North Carolina town.

Green Bay Tree, The (1924)   A novel by Louis BROMFIELD. It tells the story of Lily Shane, who begins life in a midwestern industrial town and goes to Paris to bear an illegitimate child. Bromfield's first novel, it is also the first novel in the tetralogy entitled *Escape*.

Greene, [Henry] Graham (1904–   )   English novelist, short-story writer, and playwright. Greene is an ardent convert to Catholicism, and his writing reflects his religious views. His novels are unusual combinations of psychological studies, adventure thrillers, and essays on moral and theological dilemmas. Among the best known are *Brighton Rock* (1938), THE POWER AND THE GLORY, THE HEART OF THE MATTER, and A BURNT-OUT CASE. He has also written a number of lighter novels in which the thriller element prevails but which still treat problems of good and evil. Some of these "entertainments," as he calls them, such as THE THIRD MAN, were made into movies.

Greene's settings are varied: Sweden in *England Made Me* (1935); wartime London in *The Ministry of Fear* (1943) and *The End of the Affair* (1951); Haiti in *The Comedians* (1966); South Africa in *The Human Factor* (1978); and Switzerland in *Doctor Fischer of Geneva or the Bomb Party* (1980). The place is usually in a state of seedy decay and the characters in a state of spiritual or psychological purgatory. Greene has a journalist's sense of topicality; many of his novels were set in unusual places just before they became international crisis spots: *The Quiet American* (1955), about a fumbling idealist in cold-war Vietnam; *Our Man in Havana* (1959), a Cuban spy story; *A Burnt-Out Case,* set in the Congo. Greene has also written meditative travel books, such as *Journey Without Maps* (1936); plays, including *The Living Room* (1953) and *The Complaisant Lover* (1959); stories collected in *May We Borrow Your Husband?* (1967) and *Collected Stories* (1973); and his autobiographical works *A Sort of Life* (1971) and *Ways of Escape* (1981).

Greene, Robert (1560?–1592)   English prose writer and dramatist. Greene traveled in Europe, took M.A. degrees from both Oxford and Cambridge, and then appeared in London, where he became known as a UNIVERSITY WIT and a writer of rogue literature. During his brief life he was a remarkably prolific writer, with thirty-eight publications—prose romances, pamphlets, dramas—to his credit at the time of his death. His early prose works show the influence of John LYLY and the Euphuistic style. *Pandosto, the Triumph of Time* (1588) is a prose romance that provided Shakespeare with the plot for THE WINTER'S TALE. *Menaphon* (1589, reprinted as *Greene's Arcadia*) is a pastoral romance modeled after Sir Philip SIDNEY's *Arcadia.*

All Greene's plays were performed posthumously. They include *Friar Bacon and Friar Bungay* (c1589, acted 1594), a comedy that may have been inspired by Marlowe's DR. FAUSTUS, dealing with the legendary alchemical pursuits of Roger BACON and Thomas BUNGAY; *The Scottish History of James IV* (c1591); and, with Thomas LODGE, *A Looking Glass for London and England* (c1590, acted 1592). It is possible that Greene was in part responsible for the original plays dealing with HENRY VI, which Shakespeare allegedly revised and rewrote. In his last pamphlet, *A* GROATSWORTH OF WIT, Greene gives the first contemporary mention of Shakespeare in a warning to his fellow playwrights to beware the upstart actor who, with his "tiger's heart wrapped in a player's hide," is encroaching on their territory and writing plays himself.

As one of the writers hired to reply to the Puritan pamphlets in the Martin MARPRELATE CONTROVERSY, Greene was attacked by Richard Harvey in *Plaine Percevall and the Peace-maker of England* (1590). Greene answered with *A Quip for an Upstart Courtier* (1592), directed against Harvey and his two brothers. By the time Gabriel HARVEY retaliated in *Foure Letters and Certaine Sonnets,* Greene was dead "of a surfeit of pickled herring and Rhenish wine," and his defense was taken up by Thomas NASHE.

Greene's repentance pamphlets, while in part autobiographical, should probably not be taken entirely as documents of personal repentance and confession. They include *Greene's Mourning Garment* (1590); *Never Too Late* (1590); *Farewell to Folly* (1591); and *A Groatsworth of Wit Bought with a Million of Repentance* (1592), which contains the allusion to Shakespeare. His "cony-catching" pamphlets (1591–92) are realistic descriptions of London low-life and underworld activity; they include *A Defense of Cony-Catching; Disputation between a He-Cony-Catcher and a She-Cony-Catcher; The Black Book's Messenger;* and *A Notable Discovery of Cozenage.*

green-eyed monster   IAGO's term for jealousy in Shakespeare's OTHELLO. A greenish complexion was formerly held to be indicative of jealousy; and as cats, lions, tigers, and all the green-eyed tribe "mock the meat they feed on," so jealousy mocks its victim by loving and loathing it at the same time.

Green Hat, The (1924)   A best-selling novel by Michael ARLEN. Its popularity was largely due to the way in which it captured the licentious, disillusioned spirit of the time. With a self-sacrificing heroine and a husband who kills himself on his wedding night because he has syphilis, the novel is a sentimental account of sexual license among the wealthy.

Green Henry (Der grüne Heinrich; first version, 1854; second, 1879–1880)   A largely autobiographical novel by Gottfried KELLER in the tradition of the BILDUNGSROMAN. Heinrich Lee, the hero (called green because all of his boyish clothes were made from his dead father's green uniforms), wishes to become a great painter and expends a great deal of time and energy in this pursuit before he finally discovers that he can never achieve more than moderate competence. In the course of his adventures, however, he neglects his widowed mother, and it is in this aspect of the story that the novel's two versions diverge. In the early version, Heinrich assumes all the blame for his mother's eventual death; his attacks of conscience break both his spirit and body, and he dies. In the later version, however, Heinrich's guilt is not stressed, and he successfully adjusts himself to a life of civic service as a government official.

Green House, The   See VARGAS LLOSA, MARIO.

Green Mansions (1904)   A romance of the South American tropics by William Henry HUDSON. The hero, Mr. Abel, tells the tragic story of his love for the bird girl, Rima, an ethereal maiden whose jungle upbringing has brought her close to the powers and beauty of nature. Abel has just succeeded in awakening the human emotion of love in the half-wild girl when she is killed by a band of savages.

Green Mountain Boys, The (1839)   A novel by Daniel Pierce Thompson (1795–1868), American lawyer, novelist, and historian. The book's central character is the hero Ethan ALLEN. Immensely popular, the novel was the most successful of Thompson's attempts to preserve romantic episodes in early Vermont history and gives a vivid picture of Revolutionary times in Vermont.

Green Pastures, The (1930)   A play by Marc CONNELLY. Based on the sketches in Roark BRADFORD's *Ol' Man Adam an' His Chillun* (1928), it presents reverent though humorous versions of Old Testament stories as they are told by an old southern black preacher in terms of the members of his congregation. The play was awarded the PULITZER PRIZE in 1930.

Greenwich Village (or the Village)   A section of New York City west of Washington Square. Originally a small village of quaint houses, crooked streets, and old barns, Greenwich Village became, by the early 20th century, the home and workplace of bohemian artists, writers, musicians, and radical thinkers. From 1910 to 1930 many of the old buildings were converted to studios, restaurants, cafés, nightclubs, and small theatres where the artists met and showed their work. Several of the novels of Floyd DELL, such as *Janet March* (1923), contain vivid accounts of the Village in its heyday. Among the many other well-known writers who were at one time or another residents are Max Eastman, whose reminiscences of Village life were published in *Enjoyment of Living* (1948), Eugene O'NEILL, Edna St. Vincent MILLAY, E. E. CUMMINGS, Katherine Anne PORTER, and Willa CATHER. Literary and left-wing LITTLE MAGAZINES also flourished, including THE LITTLE REVIEW, THE MASSES, and THE SEVEN ARTS.

As the Village became a more and more fashionable place to live, and as rents increased, many of the artists and writers moved elsewhere, although the bohemian quality of life remained. In the 1950s, with the BEAT MOVEMENT and the emergence of off-Broadway theatres, the Village again became a center of artistic and literary activity, although it was more the artists' auditorium than their home or workplace.

Greg, Sir W[alter] W[ilson] (1875–1959)   English bibliographer and literary scholar. A pioneer in the use of scientific bibliography in literary criticism, he wrote *Pastoral Poetry and Pastoral Drama* (1906), *The Shakespeare First Folio*, and his greatest work, *A Bibliography of the English Printed Drama to the Restoration* (4 vols, 1939–59).

Gregorian chant   The ritual plain song, or *cantus firmus*, a kind of unison music in the eight church modes. A collection of these, edited by Pope Gregory I, has come down to us. It is still used in the services of the Roman Catholic Church and Greek Catholic Church.

Gregorian year   The civil year, according to the correction introduced by Pope Gregory XIII in 1582. The equinox, which occurred on March 25 in the time of Julius CAESAR, fell on March 11 in the year 1582. This was because the Julian calculation of $365\frac{1}{4}$ days to a year was 11 min. 10 sec. too much. Gregory suppressed ten days, so as to make the equinox fall on March 21, as it did at the Council of Nice, and, by some simple arrangements, prevented the recurrence in future of a similar error.

The New Style, as it was called, was adopted in England in 1752, when Wednesday, September 2, was followed by Thursday, September 14.

This gave rise to a double computation: Lady Day, March 25, Old Lady Day, April 6; Midsummer Day, June 24, Old Midsummer Day, July 6; Michaelmas Day, September 29, Old Michaelmas Day, October 11; Christmas Day, December 25, Old Christmas Day, January 6.

Gregory I (called St. Gregory the Great, c540–604)   Benedictine monk elected Pope (590–604). He established the temporal power of the papacy, reformed monastic discipline, and sent AUGUSTINE with forty monks to England. According to tradition it was he who established the liturgical music known as GREGORIAN CHANT.

Gregory VII, St. (original name Hildebrand, c1020–1085)   Italian pope (1073–85). As pope Gregory VII pursued a policy of establishing the papacy as the supreme office in the Church and of protecting the Church from the civil states in Europe. He issued a decree (1075) that prohibited lay investiture of the clergy—that is, clergy could no longer be appointed to office by civil authorities. He called Henry IV of Germany to Rome to answer charges of oppression of the Church and sacrilege. Henry was outraged at Gregory's play for authority and tried to depose him. Gregory responded by excommunicating Henry. Henry did penance in the snow before Gregory's palace at Canossa and gained conditional absolution (1077). In 1078 Gregory renewed the excommunication, and Henry declared war. He appointed Clement III as antipope (1080) and captured Rome in 1084. Gregory was rescued from the castle Sant'Angelo and died in exile at Salerno the next year.

Gregory, Horace [Victor] (1898–1982)   American poet, critic, and translator. Gregory's books of poetry include *Chelsea Rooming House* (1930), *Poems 1930–1940* (1941), *Selected Poems* (1951), *Collected Poems* (1964), and *Another Look* (1976). Much of his verse criticizes middle-class values; some of it presents dramatic vernacular monologues and character studies of the denizens of city slums. A devotee of the classics, he translated the poems of Catullus (1931) and Ovid's *Metamorphoses* (1958). He also wrote

A History of American Poetry, 1900–1940 (1946) with his wife, Marya Zaturenska. Gregory's critical works include an early sympathetic study of D. H. LAWRENCE in *Pilgrim of the Apocalypse* (1933) and *The World of James McNeill Whistler* (1959). His essays are collected in *The Spirit of Time and Place* (1973).

Gregory, Lady Isabella Augusta Perse (1852–1932) Irish dramatist. The first forty years of Lady Gregory's life were from a literary viewpoint extremely uneventful. With the death of her husband, Sir William Gregory, in 1892, however, she developed a strong interest in Irish literature and history, and in 1898, when she met William Butler YEATS, she was ready to lend her talent, wealth, and position to the slowly developing sense of national consciousness that was to burgeon into the Irish literary renaissance. The major focus of her energy was directed to the Irish National Theatre, which later evolved into the ABBEY THEATRE and which she served as a director. In 1914 she wrote a history of the movement, *Our Irish Theatre.*

Her own literary efforts were primarily designed to reawaken the Irish national consciousness through translations and collections of ancient Celtic legend and folklore. She is best known, however, for her one-act plays, which were originally designed as "fillers" for the Abbey program. Among these the best known are *Spreading the News* (1904) and *The Rising of the Moon* (1907). *Seventy Years: Being the Autobiography of Lady Gregory* (ed Colin Smythe, 1976) is a collection of anecdotes, letters, and journal entries that she had thought of as her autobiography. It was first published more than forty years after her death.

Her beautiful estate at Coole in western Ireland is celebrated in Yeats's lovely poem "The Wild Swans at Coole." See IRISH RENAISSANCE.

greguería See GÓMEZ DE LA SERNA, RAMÓN.

Grendel The monster in BEOWULF. He is described as a giant in human shape, a descendant of Cain who lives in a murky pond with his mother among other strange and vicious sea-beasts. For twelve years mother and son come to land occasionally and devour human victims, until Beowulf comes to kill them.

Gretchen (German diminutive for Margarete) In Part I of Goethe's FAUST, the young and simple, lower-class girl whom Faust seduces with the aid of Mephistopheles's magic. She reappears as a penitent spirit at the end of Part II and greets Faust's salvation with joyful song. See ETERNAL FEMININE.

Greuze, Jean Baptiste (1725–1805) French painter. Greuze achieved great success in his lifetime with his narrative genre scenes of morality, such as *The Paralytic Tended by His Children* (1763) and *A Father's Curse: The Ungrateful Son* (1765). Modern viewers tend to dismiss his moralizing paintings as overdramatic, insincere,

and sentimental. He did however paint a series of portraits that remain highly regarded.

Grey, Lady Jane (c1537–1554) The great-granddaughter of Henry VII and for nine days queen of England. At sixteen she was married to Lord Guildford Dudley, whose father, the earl of Northumberland, was Protector of Edward VI. As part of a plan to change the succession of the crown from the Tudors to the Dudleys, Northumberland persuaded the dying Edward to settle the crown on Lady Jane and bypass the claims of Mary and Elizabeth. Lady Jane was proclaimed Queen on July 10, 1553, but by the 19th Mary had gathered powerful supporters, defeated the forces of Northumberland, and was proclaimed Queen by the Lord Mayor. Lady Jane and her husband were imprisoned and finally executed.

Grey, Zane (1875–1939) American writer of Westerns and articles on outdoor life. In 1904 Grey made up his mind that writing rather than dentistry was to be his career. A first-rate storyteller, he won enormous popular success with *Riders of the Purple Sage* (1912) and a long succession of later novels. Possibly his best books are *The Last of the Plainsmen* (1908) and the nonfiction collection *Tales of Fishing* (1925).

Griboyedov, Aleksandr Sergeyevich (1795–1829) Russian playwright. His satirical masterpiece WOE FROM WIT is one of the classics of Russian drama. For most of his career, Griboyedov was a civil servant. His death was spectacular: serving as Russian minister to Persia, he was cut to pieces by a raging mob that sacked the Russian embassy in Tehran. Griboyedov was the subject of an interesting fictionalized biography entitled *Smert Vazir-Mukhtara* (*The Death of Vazir-Mukhtar*, 1929) by the Soviet writer Yury Nikolayevich TYNYANOV.

Grieg, Edvard [Hagerup] (1843–1907) Norwegian composer. The rhythmic and melodic patterns of his work capture the spirit of his homeland. Although Grieg wrote choral works, dances, songs, and sonatas for various instruments, his most characteristic works are for the piano, including ten sets entitled *Lyric Pieces* and the popular *Piano Concerto in A Minor, Op. 16* (1868). His *Peer Gynt Suite*, written as incidental music to IBSEN's play at the author's request, is well known. His songs and chamber music employ subtle and delicate harmonies.

griffin A mythical monster, also called *griffon*, *gryphon*, and similar names. It is fabled to be the offspring of the lion and eagle. Its legs and all from the shoulder to the head are like an eagle; the rest of the body is that of a lion. This creature was sacred to the sun, and kept guard over hidden treasures. The griffins were in perpetual strife with the Arimaspians, a people of Scythia, who rifled the gold mines for the adornment of their hair. The belief apparently grew out of the stylized animal commonly represented in Scythian art, originally perhaps a chicken.

Griffith, D[avid Lewelyn] W[ark] (1875–1948) American motion picture director and producer. One of the pioneers of early filmmaking, Griffith is especially known for his mobile and imaginative use of the camera, and for having invented such techniques as the close-up, the long shot, the flashback, and the fade-out. He was the first to liberate film from the static structure and forced theatrical style that was characteristic of earlier motion pictures. After a period as an actor and script-writer, Griffith became a director (1908) for the Biograph Company. Later he produced films independently and, in 1923, cofounded, with Charlie CHAPLIN and others, the United Artists studio. Among his most famous films are *The Birth of a Nation* (1915), a monumental epic of the Civil War, considered a major landmark in film history; *Hearts of the World* (1918); *Broken Blossoms* (1919); *Way Down East* (1920); and *Orphans of the Storm* (1921), an epic set during the French Revolution.

Grigorovich, Dmitry Vasilyevich (1822–1899) Russian novelist and short-story writer. Grigorovich's father died when he was a child, and he was raised by his French mother and governess. Not until he attended school in Moscow did he learn to read and write Russian. In 1836 he entered the military engineering school in St. Petersburg. One of his fellow students was the future novelist Dostoyevsky. During his four years at the school, Grigorovich developed a strong interest in literature. He made the acquaintance of such leading figures as the critic Vissarion BELINSKY, the poet Nikolay NEKRASOV, and the novelist Ivan TURGENEV. About this time the Natural School in Russian literature, originating in Belinsky's literary doctrines, was in the ascendancy. Grigorovich became one of the leading members of this movement. His first contribution was *Peterburgskiye sharmanshchiki* (*Petersburg Organgrinders*, 1844), a sketch realistically depicting the lives of organ-grinders in the capital. The piece appeared in *Fiziologiya Peterburga* (*Physiology of Petersburg*, 1845), an anthology devoted to an examination of life in St. Petersburg.

Grigorovich's best works were published in the following two years. *Derevnya* (*The Village*, 1846) was one of the first works to deal extensively with peasant life. It was followed by another study of the peasantry: *Anton-Goremyka* (1847). Although they were criticized as presenting a somewhat idealized picture, both these stories did much to make peasant life acceptable material for literature.

Grillparzer, Franz (1791–1872) Austrian dramatist whose work is modeled on the dramas of SHAKESPEARE and CALDERÓN. Though his plays often show a deep, sentimental melancholy about the impossibility of reconciling reality with the ideal, his thought never degenerates into mere romantic lamentation and, like the writers of the BIEDERMEIER movement, he believed that a rewarding life is possible for the man who recognizes and remains within the limits of his nature. His early plays, which are more emotionally extravagant than his later ones, include *Die Ahnfrau* (*The Ancestress*, 1817), a fate-tragedy not unlike

those of Zacharias WERNER, and a tragedy (1818) about the Greek poetess Sappho. But with the trilogy *Das goldene Vliess* (*The Golden Fleece*, 1822), on the story of Jason and Medea, and with the historical tragedy *König Ottokars Glück und Ende* (*King Ottocar's Success and Downfall*, 1825), he hit his dramatic stride, and these plays are among his greatest. His works were not generally well received, however, and after the dismal failure of *Weh dem, der lügt* (*Woe to Him Who Lies*, 1838) he became completely discouraged and never published another play. Still, he continued writing, and among the dramas he left behind at his death are two of his most famous: *Die Jüdin von Toledo* (*The Jewess of Toledo*, completed 1855) and *Ein Bruderzwist in Habsburg* (*A Fraternal Struggle in the House of Hapsburg*, written c1855). His well-known novella *Der arme Spielmann* (*The Poor Minstrel*, written 1831) is a sentimental but carefully constructed masterpiece.

Grimm, Jacob Ludwig Carl (1785–1863) and **Wilhelm Carl** (1786–1859) German scholars. The brothers are considered the founders of Germanic philology as a systematic study. Among the works on which the Grimms collaborated are *Deutsche Sagen* (*German Legends*, 1816) and the famous collection *Kinder- und Hausmärchen* (lit, *Children's and Household Tales*, 1812 et seq), known as *Grimm's Fairy-Tales* (see MÄRCHEN). For the latter, they got most of their material not from written documents but from peasants whom they interviewed; Wilhelm, who tended more toward literary criticism and appreciation than his brother, did most of the transcription. Jacob, more the scholar, wrote a *Deutsche Grammatik* (*German Grammar*, 1819 et seq) in which he formulated "Grimm's Law," the first attempt to explain the consonantal differences between Greek and Latin words and their cognates in the Germanic languages. It was also Jacob who did most of the work on the definitive *Deutsches Wörterbuch* (*German Dictionary*, 1852 et seq), begun by the brothers and still in progress.

Grimmelshausen, Hans Jakob Christoffel von (1610?–1676) German novelist, strongly influenced by the tradition of the PICARESQUE novel in France and Spain. Although contemporary with baroque poets such as Andreas GRYPHIUS, Grimmelshausen used a less ornamented style, which was more accessible to the people. His most famous work is the novel SIMPLICISSIMUS.

Grin, Aleksandr (pen name of Aleksandr Stepanovich Grinevsky, 1880–1932) Russian novelist and short-story writer. Grin's exotic and often fantastic tales became popular when they were first published, but because they departed from the norm of SOCIALIST REALISM were suppressed until THE THAW in 1956, when Grin's popularity was revived with publication of his works. Resembling fairy tales, his best-known stories include "Alye parusa" (1923; tr "Scarlet Sails," 1967), "Blistayushchiy mir" ("The Radiant World," 1923), and "Begushchaya po volnam" ("She Who Runs on the Waves," 1928).

Gris, Juan (real name José Victoriano Gonzales, 1887–1927) Spanish painter. Working in Paris in 1906, Gris was witness to the birth of CUBISM and became one of its leading proponents. He painted still lifes and harlequins, but, whereas other painters began with an object and reduced it to an abstraction, Gris claimed to start with an abstraction, refining it and ultimately representing it as a shape or object. He made collage paintings, often employing the technique, originated by BRAQUE, of intermingling highly abstracted images with carefully painted simulations of wood and other materials, as in *Breakfast* (1915). He earned his living working as a satirical illustrator for such journals as *Le Temoin* and *Le Charivari*; in the 1920s he designed sets and costumes for DIAGHILEV's Ballets Russes.

Griselda (The Patient) The heroine of the final tale of Boccaccio's THE DECAMERON. Her husband, the marquis of Saluzzo, chooses her from among the peasantry, then decides to test her fidelity. First, he pretends their two children are dead by his hand; then he feigns boredom and pretends he has married again, using his own daughter as the supposed new love. Turned out of the house, Griselda endures her sufferings nobly and remains constant until Saluzzo relents; she is then restored to her home and children, having won the love and admiration of her husband and his people.

Basically the JOB story in modern dress, the tale was known to Boccaccio from a French source; it was in turn translated into Latin by PETRARCH. From this Latin version rather than from the Italian source Chaucer drew THE CLERK'S TALE, to which he supplied his own ironic comment on the credibility of the tale:

Grisilde is dead, and eek her pacience,
And both at once buried in Italie.

Groatsworth of Wit Bought with a Million of Repentance, A (1592)

A pamphlet written by Robert GREENE, supposedly while he was dying. It is in part a repentance tract and a warning to his fellow playwrights to eschew evil and thus avoid his own bitter end. It contains the famous reference to SHAKESPEARE as "an upstart crow, beautified with our feathers, that . . . supposes he is as well able to bombast out a blank verse as the best of you; and being an absolute *Johannes fac totum*, is in his own conceit the only Shake-scene in a country."

Gropius, Walter [Adolf] (1883–1969) German architect. Founder and director of the BAUHAUS until 1928, and designer of its second center in Dessau, he worked in the U.S. after 1937. His importance as an educator and theoretician equaled his contributions as an architect.

Grosseteste, Robert (c1175–1253) English prelate and scholar, bishop of Lincoln (after 1235). Grosseteste is known for his determined struggle to protect the English

clergy against both King Henry III and Pope Innocent IV, particularly as to the right of making ecclesiastical appointments. Also important to medieval intellectual life were his voluminous writings on everything from philosophy and theology to husbandry, largely in Latin, but also including *Le Château d'amour* (*The Castle of Love*), a French poem of religious allegory.

Grossman, Vasily Semyonovich (1905–1964) Soviet novelist, short-story writer, and journalist. Grossman studied chemical engineering at the Institute of Physics and Mathematics in Moscow. After gaining notoriety as a war correspondent and writer of the stories "Oborona Leningrada" ("The Defense of Leningrad," 1944) and "Narod bessmerten" ("The People Are Immortal," 1942), Grossman was attacked after the war on charges of "cosmopolitanism" during the anti-Semitic campaign of Andrey Zhdanov. Grossman endured to write the first part of the novel *Za pravoye delo, I* (*For a Just Cause*, 1952), but the vast scope of the novel proved too great for him to master. Shortly before his death Grossman finished his most noted work, *Vsyo techyot* (1970; tr *Forever Flowing*, 1972). This pessimistic novel, which was published abroad posthumously, recalls the purges, famine, and forced collectivization of the thirties, and indicts Leninism as the primary cause for Stalin's abuses. The great pessimism of the novel, however, springs mainly from Grossman's explicit conviction that Leninist fanaticism grows from the same source as the historical Russian fascination for Byzantine Christianity and is, therefore, historically ineluctable. *Life and Fate*, published in France in 1980, enjoyed the same popularity as his earlier work in the West.

Grosz, George (1893–1959) German-American artist. Grosz is known for his venomous satirical caricatures and lithographs in which he attacked militarism, bourgeois vapidity, and narrow-minded capitalists. He was associated with the DADA movement before World War I and was arrested on several occasions for irreverence or blasphemy. With the rise of HITLER, Grosz left Germany, arriving in the U.S. in 1932. Although his art became less aggressively vitriolic, his social conscience was piqued anew by the advent of World War II, as in *Peace, II* (1946). A collection of his drawings, *Ecce Homo* (1965), contains typical works.

Grotius, Hugo (Latinized form of Huig de Groot, 1583–1645) A Dutch jurist and statesman. His *De jure belli et pacis* (1625), written after his escape to France as leader of the Remonstrants, is regarded as the real beginning of the science of international law. His voluminous writings include a number of tragedies.

Group 47 An informal association of German writers founded by Hans Werner Richter and Alfred Andersch, who began meeting in September 1947. Although no literary program was established, the group was united by their common contempt for the bourgeois forces that had helped Hitler's rise to power and in their hope that Germany would recover in the spirit of a liberal socialism. They were concerned with the creation of a new literary language, shunning involved sentence structures and the "lofty" vocabulary that had been used in Nazi propaganda. The interest of leading critics contributed greatly to the prestige of the group, which awarded a highly respected prize each year. Gradually the group's importance declined; it was ridiculed by radical thinkers in the 1960s (including Peter HANDKE) as politically impotent. The group met for the last time in 1967. Writers associated with Group 47 include Heinrich BÖLL, Uwe JOHNSON, Günter GRASS, and Ilse AICHINGER.

Group Theatre, The (1) An American theatre and acting company. The Group Theatre was founded in 1931 by Harold Clurman, Cheryl Crawford, and Lee Strasberg, all of whom had been associated with the PROVINCETOWN PLAYERS. This dedicated troupe, which flourished for a decade, became known for its skillful productions of socially relevant plays, and introduced the work of Clifford ODETS, William SAROYAN, and Robert Ardrey. Among the actors and directors whose careers began with the group are Stella and Luther Adler, Franchot Tone, Morris Carnovsky, and Elia Kazan.

(2) A London theatre and acting company. It flourished during the 1930s, performing Marxist, labor-sympathizing, and experimental plays. W. H. AUDEN and Christopher ISHERWOOD wrote plays for this theatre.

Grove, Frederick Phillip (1871–1948) Canadian novelist and short-story writer. Grove is commonly regarded as the foremost of Canada's prairie writers. His first two books, *Over Prairie Trails* (1922) and *The Turn of the Year* (1923), are partly autobiographical explorations of man's struggle with nature. They show the influence of ZOLA and IBSEN in their view that man is insignificant, lacking in free will, but possessed of an essential dignity nonetheless. Grove's most notable novel is *The Master of the Mill* (1944), which deals with the dehumanizing effects of mechanization on three generations of an Ontario farming family.

Grove, Sir George (1820–1900) English editor and music critic. Grove edited the *Dictionary of Music and Musicians* (4 vols, 1879–89) that bears his name; it has grown through subsequent editions, and has remained the largest music reference work in the English language. In 1882 Grove was appointed the first director of the new Royal College of Music in London.

Grove, Lena A character in William Faulkner's LIGHT IN AUGUST. Although not central to the main action of the story, Lena Grove offers an important and implicit contrast to the violence and death present in the plot. Her confinement symbolically reenacts the confinement of Joe CHRISTMAS's mother, and her placidity and animal unconcern make her a minor kind of Earth Mother, carrying out her natural function of reproduction in a context that seems, but for her, hostile to life and growth.

Growing Up Absurd See GOODMAN, PAUL.

Grub Street The former name of a London street (now Milton Street), famous in the 18th century for literary hacks and struggling writers who lived there. Dr. JOHNSON described it as "much inhabited by writers of small histories, dictionaries, and temporary poems; whence any mean production is called grubstreet." POPE, BYRON, MARVELL, and SWIFT used the term derisively to suggest literary trash. The term is used allusively for needy authors, literary hacks, and their work. George Gissing wrote a novel entitled NEW GRUB STREET.

Grundtvig, Nicolai Frederik Severin (1783–1872) Danish poet, historian, and linguist. Until the death of his father, a clergyman, in 1813, Grundtvig served as a country curate. His prolific writing career began in Copenhagen, where he published poems and articles; he also made several translations into Danish, including *Beowulf* (1820). After a term as vicar (1821–26) that terminated in violent theological controversy, Grundtvig spent two years in England studying Anglo-Saxon manuscripts. He returned to Copenhagen, where he became a bishop in 1861. As a historian, he practiced a romantic approach, treating Scandinavian mythology in *Nordens mythologi* (1808). A religious reformer and educationalist as well, Grundtvig was a figure of great influence in Denmark.

Grundy, Mrs. A fictional figure, the arbiter of taste and morals in a community. "What will Mrs. Grundy say?" is meant as "What will our very proper and strait-laced neighbors say?" Mrs. Grundy is referred to in the first scene of Tom Morton's English comedy *Speed the Plough* (1800). Mrs. Ashfield's jealousy of her neighbor, Mrs. Grundy, provokes this rebuke from farmer Ashfield: "Be quiet, wull ye? Always ding, dinging Dame Grundy into my ears. What will Mrs. Grundy say? What will Mrs. Grundy think? . . ."

Grünewald, Mathias (real name Mathis Gothart Niethart, c1460–1528) German painter. Grünewald is generally regarded as the last and greatest representative of the German gothic school. His work, nearly all of it on religious subjects, has great power and originality, conveying terror and anguish with great expressiveness. Stylistically, his paintings are remarkable for the distortion in drawing, the use of striking silhouettes, heavy *chiaroscuro*, and rich use of color. The complex Isenheim altarpiece (now in the Colmar Museum), on which he worked from about 1512 to 1515, is his masterpiece.

Gruppe 47 See GROUP 47.

Grushenka In Dostoyevsky's THE BROTHERS KARAMAZOV, the beautiful young woman loved by Dmitry KARAMAZOV and pursued by his father, Fyodor Pavlovich. Although her past is checkered and her reputation not the best, Grushenka is as large-hearted in her way as Dmitry himself. Often referred to in the novel as a kitten and a cat, she shows both sets of qualities, being playful and soft at times and crafty and malicious at others. Her love for Dmitry grows, regenerates her, and at the end of the novel she prepares to follow him to his Siberian imprisonment.

Gryphius, Andreas (pen name of Andreas Greif, 1616–1664) German baroque poet and dramatist. Gryphius, like GRIMMELSHAUSEN, was deeply affected by the THIRTY YEARS' WAR. His works frequently deal with the theme of the vanity of human life and of petty human ambitions, and it is characteristic that in his two most famous historical tragedies, *Katharina von Georgien* (*Catherine of Georgia*, 1657) and *Carolus Stuardus* (*Charles Stuart*, 1657), the hero dies a martyr's death. Gryphius's tragic style was strongly influenced by Seneca and by the Dutch drama of his time, but his originality is felt in such works as *Cardenio und Celinde* (1657), which has been called the first "bourgeois tragedy" in Germany, and in his comedies, the most famous of which is *Absurda Comica oder Herr Peter Squentz* (1663). In his lyrics he often combines religious subject matter and classical forms.

Guardi, Francesco (1712–1793) Venetian painter, pupil of Antonio CANALETTO. Using muted tones animated by dabs of bright color and a sketchy touch to suggest details and highlights, he painted intimate, poetic scenes of Venice, its courtyards, canals, and piazzas.

Guarini, Giambattista (1538–1612) Ferrarese poet. Guarini wrote one of the most popular and influential of Renaissance dramas, IL PASTOR FIDO. A pastoral tragicomedy in imitation of TASSO's *Aminta*, it was translated into English by Sir Richard Fanshawe in 1647. In John Fletcher's *The Faithful Shepherdess* (1610), Guarini's faithful shepherd has changed sex, and the plot has been altered, but the English play is based upon the Italian.

Gudrun (1) Sigurd's wife in the VÖLSUNGA SAGA, better known as Kriemhild in the *Nibelungenlied* and Gutrune in Wagner's tetralogy of operas, DER RING DES NIBELUNGEN.

(2) The heroine of the Icelandic LAXDALE SAGA, and daughter of Queen Grimhild. She was a selfish, independent, forceful woman, married successively to Thorwald, Thord, and Bolli, and in love with Kjartan, whose death she caused.

(3) One of the two leading women characters in D. H. LAWRENCE's novel WOMEN IN LOVE. She is believed to have been based on Katherine MANSFIELD.

Gudrun (c1210) A German epic poem written by an unknown Austrian, apparently in imitation of the NIBELUNGENLIED. Its many sea settings are unusual among German tales. Of its three sections, the first concerns Hagen, king of Ireland, and the second describes Hetel's courtship of Hagen's daughter Hilde. In the third part, their daughter Gudrun is engaged to Herwig of Seeland, but is abducted by Hartmut of Normandy. She refuses to marry her captor, so for thirteen years she is forced to do menial servant's work. At last Herwig, accompanied by Gudrun's brother, comes to her rescue, and the lovers are happily married.

Guelphs and Ghibellines Names of the rival political parties in 12th-century Germany, adopted by 13th- and 14th-century Italian parties. The Ghibellines were the supporters of the Holy Roman Emperor, at that time a German; the Guelphs were his opponents, usually supported by the papacy. At the time of DANTE, the Guelphs of Tuscany were bitterly divided into two factions: see BIANCHI AND NERI.

Guermantes, de A large family of the French aristocracy, in Marcel Proust's REMEMBRANCE OF THINGS PAST. Duc Basin, called the Prince de Laume before his father's death, is the elder brother of Baron de CHARLUS and of Mme de Marsantes, the mother of Robert de SAINT-LOUP. Basin's wife, Oriane, the Duchesse de Guermantes, is even more of an aristocrat in her own right, being a descendant of the 8th-century Geneviève de Brabant and a cousin of many of the members of European royalty. She is represented as the most important hostess in French society, and the narrator in his youth goes through a period of worshiping her extravagantly. There are also the Prince and Princesse de Guermantes, and various other relatives by blood and marriage.

Guermantes Way, The See REMEMBRANCE OF THINGS PAST.

Guerre de Troie n'aura pas lieu, La See TIGER AT THE GATES.

Guest, Lady Charlotte Elizabeth See MABINOGION, The.

Guiccioli, Countess Teresa (1801?–1873) Italian noblewoman, known for her long-lasting liaison with Lord BYRON. Guiccioli was still a very young woman, married to a much older man, when in 1819 their relationship began; a year later she left her husband and became Byron's openly acknowledged mistress. The attachment, which lasted the rest of Byron's life, is considered to have had a steadying influence on the poet and to have contributed to his increasing literary skill and facility during his years in Italy. She wrote *My Recollections of Lord Byron* (1868).

Guillaume de Lorris (early 13th century) French poet famous for having written the first part of the ROMANCE OF THE ROSE.

Guillén, Jorge (1893–1984) Spanish poet. In his early association with the GENERACIÓN DEL 27, Guillén contributed to a revival of interest in Luis de GÓNGORA. More than any of his colleagues, he attempted to create a "pure poetry," unaffected by subjective visions but conveying the intense, spontaneous enjoyment of experience and characterized by short, declarative lines punctuated by exclamation marks. His distilled attempts appear primarily in *Cántico*, a work of epic proportion that was augmented in successive editions from 1928 to 1950. Another important work is the trilogy *Clamor*, consisting of *Maremágnum* (1957), *Que van a dar en el mar* (1960), and *A la altura de las circunstancias* (1963). Along with a partial translation of *Cántico* (1963), a selection of his work appears in English translation in *Affirmation: 1919–1966* (1968). Guillén left Spain (1939) after the Spanish Civil War, living and teaching primarily in the U.S. *Y otros poemas* (1973) is a collection of his later works.

Guillén, Nicolás (1902–   )   Cuban poet. A leading figure of the *poesia negra* ("black poetry") movement, Guillén began, with *Motivos de son* (*Sound Themes*, 1930), to build his poems on the myths and music of the Afro-Cuban world. *Sóngaro cosongo* (1931) employs folklore motifs in a further experimental mélange of African rhythms and Guillén's ironic use of Cuban vernacular. In 1934, with the satirical *West Indies, Ltd.*, he turned abruptly to nationalistic, leftist political verse, which he continued in *España* (1937), his poetic defense of the Spanish Loyalists, with whom he fought in the Spanish Civil War. *El son entero* (1947), the title Guillén gave to his collected poems, refers to the unusual beat of Afro-Cuban music, which moves through all his poetry as its most subtle distinguishing quality. His subsequent books include *La paloma de vuelo popular* (1958), *Balada* (1962), *Tengo* (1964), and *Le gran zoo* (1967; tr *The Great Zoo and Other Poems*, 1972).

guillotine   A decapitating machine much used during the French Revolution. A similar device was already in use in the 16th century in the south of France and in Italy, where it was called *mannaia* and was used exclusively for beheading nobles. Joseph Ignace Guillotin (1738–1814), member of the Constitutional Assembly, proposed in 1789 that a uniform method of capital punishment be established and that a machine, surer and swifter than the headsman's hand, be devised to carry it out. Dr. Antoine Louis, then secretary of the French College of Surgeons, was the actual designer of the guillotine, and it was at first called *louison* or *louisette*. It was first used on April 25, 1792. It remained the legal method of execution in France until 1981.

Guinevere   In ARTHURIAN LEGEND, the wife of King ARTHUR. In the many versions in which Guinevere appears, her name is spelled a variety of ways. She is, for example, the Guanhumara of Geoffrey of Monmouth, the early Irish Finnabair, the Welsh Gwenhwyvar. In many of the romances, she is said to be the daughter of King Leodegrance, who, when Arthur and Guinevere are married, gives to Arthur the famous ROUND TABLE.

Like her classical counterparts, HELEN of Troy and PERSEPHONE, Guinevere is one of those legendary heroines who is always being abducted and whose beauty brings betrayal, war, and disaster. In Geoffrey of Monmouth's HISTORY OF THE KINGS OF BRITAIN, she is seduced by Arthur's nephew (or son), MORDRED, thus ultimately bringing about the death of Arthur and an end to many others. In most versions, however, it is Sir LAUNCELOT with whom Guinevere is illicitly involved. In *Lancelot* (c1180) by CHRÉTIEN DE TROYES, it is that ideal knight who must go to

the rescue of Guinevere when she is kidnapped by an unknown knight.

In Malory's MORTE D'ARTHUR, Sir Launcelot is not only often the rescuer of Guinevere, but also her abductor. Here also, however, it is Mordred who, in the absence of Arthur, has usurped the kingdom and wishes to seduce and marry Guinevere. Thus begins the closing tragedy that culminates in the death of Arthur and the end of the order of the Round Table. Arthur hastens back from his expedition against Leo, king of the Romans; Guinevere flees, and a desperate battle is fought in which Mordred is slain and Arthur mortally wounded. Guinevere renounces Launcelot after the death of Arthur and takes the veil at Almesbury, where later she dies. But even at the end, Launcelot must go to carry her away once more. In a vision one night, he is told that Queen Guinevere is dead. Sadly, he goes for her, carries her body to GLASTONBURY, and places it beside the body of King Arthur.

Tennyson, in his IDYLLS OF THE KING, makes Guinevere guilty only in her passion for Launcelot, and not a party to Mordred's treachery.

Güiraldes, Ricardo (1886–1927)   Argentinian novelist and poet. His first four books (one of poetry, three of fiction) had been poorly received when he made his third trip to Paris and discovered the avant-garde of French writers. His prose poem *Xaimaca* (1923), clearly influenced by the SYMBOLISTS, fared better. But it was his masterpiece, DON SEGUNDO SOMBRA, a classic in GAUCHO LITERATURE, that assured his fame. Güiraldes had spent the summers of his childhood on the ranch where he was born and where he learned the lore of the *gaucho* from an older friend and great storyteller, Segundo Ramírez. Güiraldes's attitude toward the *gaucho* is almost one of reverence, but his characters are convincingly of this world. His concern was always with the spiritual condition of the human creature, and he believed that the life-style and mind of the *gaucho* offered a chance to consider that condition at both its best and its most transparent.

Guise   A French ducal house, a branch of the house of Lorraine. The Guise family acquired great political influence upon the accession (1559) of Francis II, who had married MARY, QUEEN OF SCOTS, granddaughter of Claude, first duke of Guise. Henry, third duke of Guise (1550–88), was known, like his father, as *le Balafré* (Fr, "the scarred") because of a battle scar on his face. He became the leader of the Roman Catholic party in French politics and organized the HOLY LEAGUE. The idol of the Parisian mob, Henry probably aspired to the French throne and was murdered at the instigation of Henry III. The league, subsequently under the leadership of the duke of Mayenne, brother of the third duke, was crushed before the end of the 16th century. The direct line of the house of Guise became extinct in 1675. See HENRY IV (of France).

Guitry, Sacha [Alexandre Pierre Georges] (1885–1957)   French writer, actor, and dramatist, son of the actor Lucien Guitry (1860–1925). Extremely popular between the two world wars for his light, sparkling comedies, he wrote over 130 plays, such as *Le Page* (1902), *Nono* (1905), and *Mariette* (1928).

Gulag Archipelago, 1918–1956, The (Arkhipelag Gulag, 3 vols, Paris, 1973–75; tr 3 vols, 1974–78) A "literary investigation" of the network of Soviet prison camps as they existed between 1918 and 1956 by Aleksandr SOLZHENITSYN. A mixture of autobiography, history, and analysis, the relentlessly grim picture of life inside the camps forms the basis for an attack not only on Stalinism and Leninism but also on the whole process of substituting Western rational and secular ideas for Russia's traditional mysticism. The discovery of a manuscript of the book by the KGB led to the author's permitting its Paris publication and eventually to his loss of citizenship and expulsion from the Soviet Union.

Gulbeyas The sultana in Lord Byron's DON JUAN. Having purchased Juan at the slave market and introduced him into the harem in female attire, she is outraged to find that he prefers Dudu, one of the attendant beauties, to herself. She attempts to have them drowned in the Bosphorus, but they escape.

Gulistan (Rose Garden, 1258) A collection of lyrics by the Persian poet SA'DĪ. Polished and accomplished, full of moral reflections, both witty and sweet, it contains sections on kings, dervishes, contentment, love, youth, old age, and social duties, together with many stories and philosophical sayings.

Gulliver's Travels (1726) Best-known title of *Travels into Several Remote Nations of the World, by Lemuel Gulliver*, a satiric masterpiece written in the form of a journal by Jonathan SWIFT. Lemuel Gulliver, a ship's physician, makes four voyages: to LILLIPUT, whose inhabitants are six inches tall; to BROBDINGNAG, a land of giants; to the flying island of LAPUTA, an empire of "wise men"; and to HOUYHNHNMLAND, inhabited by Houyhnhnms and Yahoos. Swift's bitterest work, *Gulliver's Travels* satirizes man's abuse of human reason as reflected in his political, social, and academic institutions; at best, man is foolish; at worst, he is nothing more than an ape. A multifarious book, it is various in its appeal: it is enchantingly playful and fantastic, and is often read by children; it is a witty, allegorical depiction of the political life and values of Swift's time; it is a bitter denunciation of mankind; finally, it is Swift's reflections on man's corruption of his highest attribute, reason.

Gumilyov, Nikolay Stepanovich (1886–1921) Russian poet. Gumilyov was one of the founders of the Acmeist movement. His early travels in Africa were reflected in the exoticism of his poetry. Between 1910 and 1918, he was married to the poet Anna AKHMATOVA, also a member of the Acmeist group. After the revolution, Gumilyov openly expressed his opposition to the Bol-

sheviks, and was executed for conspiracy in 1921. See ACMEISM.

Gunga Din (1892) One of Rudyard Kipling's BARRACK-ROOM BALLADS, in praise of a Hindu water-carrier for a British Indian regiment.

> An' for all 'is dirty 'ide
> 'E was white, clear white, inside. . . .
> . . . You're a better man than I am, Gunga Din.

Gungnir See ODIN.

Gunn, Thom[son William] (1929–   ) English poet. Gunn's poetry, beginning with *Fighting Terms* (1954; rev 1962) and *The Sense of Movement* (1957), reveals a preoccupation with conflicting values: personal and societal, modern and eternal, rational and intuitive. This perpetual dialectic is handled in a disciplined style with spare, powerful poetic language and flexibility of form, from metric to syllabic to FREE VERSE. He has spent a great deal of time in the U.S., and his driving rhythms and often violent imagery align him more closely with many American poets than with his English contemporaries. *My Sad Captains* (1961), in which he experiments with syllabic-metric verse, introduces a new delicacy of tone and feeling. *Touch* (1967) contains two groups of poems, the first about rebirth, the second, *Misanthropos*, seventeen lyrics about the last man on earth after atomic war. *Poems 1950–1966* (1969) was followed by *Moly* (1971), in which the black roots of a moly plant merging with its white flower become a metaphor for those opposites that so concern the poet. His *Selected Poems: 1950–1975* (1979) was followed by *The Passages of Joy* (1982) and *The Occasions of Poetry* (1982).

Gunnarsson, Gunnar (1889–1975) Icelandic novelist, poet, and playwright. Born into a farming family, and largely self-educated, Gunnarsson celebrated in his work the courage and dignity of humble Icelandic people. During an extended stay in Denmark (1910–39), he wrote a series of nostalgic novels about three generations of an Icelandic farm family, *Borgsloegtens historie* (4 vols, 1912–14; one vol tr as *Guest the One-Eyed*, 1920). A longer series of novels, planned as a narrative of Iceland's history, includes *Edbrøre* (1918; tr *The Sworn Brothers*, 1920) and *Salige er de Enfoldige* (1920; tr *Seven Days of Darkness*, 1931).

Gunpowder Plot In English history, a conspiracy of a few Roman Catholics, led by Robert Catesby, to murder JAMES I and the members of both houses of Parliament. The date selected for the attempt was November 5, 1605, when James was to appear in person at the opening of Parliament. The plot was foiled when Guy Fawkes (1570–1606), who had undertaken to fire the gunpowder for the explosion, was arrested in the cellar under the House of Lords on November 4. The failure of the plot is still celebrated in England on November 5 as Guy Fawkes Day.

Gunslinger, The See DORN, ED.

Gunther   Burgundian king who courts Brunhild in the NIBELUNGENLIED and Wagner's opera *Ring des Nibelungen*, known as Gunnar in the VÖLSUNGA SAGA. Gunther is probably partially based on Gundahar, a historical ruler overthrown by the Huns in 436.

Günther, Johann Christian (1695–1723)   German poet admired by GOETHE. Günther's style is halfway between the MANNERISM of the late baroque and the more personal lyric that developed in the 18th century. His works include a tragedy, *Die Eifersucht (Jealousy*, 1715).

Gunther, John (1901–1970)   American journalist and writer. With *Inside Europe* (1936), Gunther established his reputation as a careful researcher and colorful writer, with his own highly readable formula of personal journalism. *Inside Asia* (1939), *Inside Latin America* (1941), *Inside U.S.A.* (1947), *Inside Africa* (1955), and *Inside Russia Today* (1958) followed, and a quarter century later, he came full circle with *Inside Europe Today* (1961). He is also the author of *Death Be Not Proud* (1949), a moving memorial on the death of his son, and *Roosevelt in Retrospect* (1950). Gunther described how and why he wrote the "Inside" books in *A Fragment of Autobiography* (1962).

guru (Sans, "venerable")   In HINDUISM and BUDDHISM, a spiritual teacher and religious guide. Guru was also the title taken by the succession of SIKH spiritual and temporal leaders from 1469 to 1708.

Gustafson, Ralph [Baker] (1909–   )   Canadian poet. Gustafson has edited three important anthologies of Canadian writing: *Anthology of Canadian Poetry* (1942), *Canadian Accent* (1944), and the *Penguin Book of Canadian Verse* (1958; rev 1984). His own verse has evolved from the relatively traditional sonnets in his first volume, *The Golden Chalice* (1935), to the modernist writing in *Rivers Among Rocks* (1960) and *Sift in an Hourglass* (1966). His travels in Europe led to the poems in *Ixion's Wheel* (1969). *Themes and Variations for Sounding Brass* (1972) is a series of laments for those killed by violence in modern political upheavals. His *Selected Poems* was published in 1983.

Gustavus II (Gustavus Adolphus, called the Lion of the North, or the Snow King; 1594–1632)   A king of Sweden. Supporting the Protestant cause in the THIRTY YEARS' WAR, he won the battle of Lützen against Wallenstein, but was mortally wounded. One of the greatest generals of all times, he saved Protestantism in Germany. His death left Sweden under a regency, with his six-year-old daughter, Christina, as nominal queen.

Gutenberg, Johannes (c1400–c1468)   German printer, usually considered the inventor of movable metal type. Documents dating from 1439 indicate that he was involved in various secret operations employing a press and a device presumed to be a type mold. In 1455 at Mainz he entered into a partnership with Johann Fust, a moneylender. The partnership was dissolved five years later when Gutenberg defaulted on the loan and Fust seized

Gutenberg's equipment and stock and continued the operation himself with the help of Peter Schöffer. It is generally accepted that the so-called *Gutenberg Bible*—more properly called the *Mazarin Bible* from its discovery in 1760 in the library of Cardinal MAZARIN in Paris (see BIBLE, SPECIALLY NAMED EDITIONS)—was issued from the press that Gutenberg established and Fust took over. Whether Gutenberg alone was responsible for this edition is uncertain. None of the work ascribed to him bears his name.

After he lost his press to Fust, Gutenberg came under the patronage of Conrad Humery, a syndic of Mainz, and continued to print books. The *Catholicon* of 1460 is a fine example of his later work.

Gutenberg Galaxy, The   See MCLUHAN, MARSHALL.

Guthrie, A[lfred] B[ertram], Jr. (1901–   )   American novelist. Guthrie worked on a newspaper in Kentucky for twenty years before he wrote *The Big Sky* (1947), reshaping into a novel the Western lore of his childhood. *The Way West* (1949), which won the PULITZER PRIZE for fiction in 1950, and *These Thousand Hills* (1956) followed. Together the three novels provide a history of the opening of the West, the Western migration, and frontier life. Carefully researched, they are evocative stories that avoid Western stereotypes. *Arfive* (1970) and *The Last Valley* (1975) continue the Far West series, while *The Genuine Article* (1977) is set in the Southwest. *No Second Wind* (1980) and *Fair Land, Fair Land* (1982) were also successes.

Gutiérrez, Eduardo   See GAUCHO LITERATURE.

Gutiérrez Nájera, Manuel (1859–1895)   Mexican poet, short-story writer, and critic. One of the pioneers of MODERNISMO in Spanish America, Gutiérrez was an aesthetic purist strongly influenced by the French romantics. Through his own poetry, but more through his critical writings and his role as founding editor of Mexico's first modernist journal, *Revista azul*, he did a great deal to encourage an expanded sensuality in the poetic vocabulary. His work is collected in *Poesías completas* (1953) and *Cuentos completas y otras narraciones* (1958).

Gutzkow, Karl (1811–1878)   German novelist and dramatist in the movement of JUNG DEUTSCHLAND ("Young Germany"). Gutzkow's early novel *Wally, die Zweiflerin (Wally, a Doubting Girl*, 1835) aroused a storm of protest because of its extensive treatment of such generally avoided subjects as atheism and free love, and he was jailed for three months as a result. His later social novel, *Die Ritter vom Geiste (The Knights of the Spirit*, 1850–51), though not as sensational as *Wally*, is more competent as a work of art. Among his dramas, the best known is *Uriel Acosta* (1846), which depicts the struggle of a Jew for intellectual freedom.

Guy Mannering (1815)   A novel by Sir Walter SCOTT, set in Scotland at the time of George III. Guy Mannering, a young Englishman traveling in Scotland, stops overnight at the home of the laird of Ellangowan. A son is born to the laird that night and Mannering, a student of astrology, predicts two crises in the boy's life, in his fifth and twenty-first years. He then goes on his way. Some time later, the son, Harry Bertram, disappears at the age of five. His mother dies of shock and the laird lives on only for a few years, leaving his daughter Lucy in the care of Dominie SAMPSON, a friend and schoolteacher, on his death. Mannering, returned from India after years of living there, invites Lucy and Dominie to live with him and his daughter, Julia. He is followed from India by a Captain Brown, whom he erroneously suspects of loving his wife and with whom he has dueled. Brown is actually in love with Julia. In the climax of the book, Brown is recognized by a gypsy; he is Harry Bertram, although he did not know it, and was spirited off by the unscrupulous lawyer Glossin, who got Harry's father's estate for himself since the heir had disappeared. All is restored to Harry and he wins the friendship of Mannering and the hand of Julia. The book is noted not so much for its plot, which brims with coincidences, as for the creation of such notable characters as Meg MERRILIES and Dandie DINMONT.

Guy of Warwick (c1300)   The title of a Middle English romance and the name of its hero. The exploits and adventures of Guy of Warwick are typical of the heroes of non-Arthurian romance, such as Bevis of Hampton, HAVELOK THE DANE, and King HORN. To obtain Phelis (Felice) as his wife, Guy of Warwick undertook many knightly deeds. He rescued the daughter of the emperor of Germany, and went to fight against the Saracens, slaying the doughty Coldran, Elmaye King of Tyre, and the soldan himself. Then he returned and wedded Phelis, but in forty days went back to the Holy Land, where he slew the giant Amarant, and many others. Having achieved all this, he became a hermit near Warwick. Daily he went in disguise to his own castle and begged bread of his wife, Phelis; but on his deathbed he sent her a ring, by which she recognized him, and went to close his dying eyes.

Guzmán, Martín Luis (1887–1976)   Mexican essayist and novelist. During the Mexican Revolution, Guzmán was an adherent first of Venustiano Carranza, then of Pancho VILLA. From 1923 to 1936 he lived in Spain, where he wrote the books that brought him immediate renown. Guzmán's best-known work is *El águila y la serpiente* (1928; tr *The Eagle and the Serpent*, 1928). The title, taken from the Mexican coat of arms, symbolizes for Guzmán the struggle that has characterized Mexico's his-

tory from Aztec times, but especially the violence of the great revolution. Guzmán describes the scenes from that time as an eyewitness, and builds an accurate and moving account of that civil war. The two-volume work, indispensable to any study of the history of modern Mexico, is the base on which Guzmán's fame rests. *La sombra del caudillo* (1929) deals with the cynicism and intrigue of Mexican politics in the 1920s. *Memorias de Pancho Villa* (tr *Memories of Pancho Villa*, 1965) appeared in four volumes from 1938 to 1940. A highly praised collection of brief biographies was published in 1959 under the title *Muertes historicas* (tr *Historical Deaths*, 1959).

Guzmán de Alfarache, Vida del Pícaro (1599, 1604)   A PICARESQUE novel by Mateo ALEMÁN. The book is supposedly the autobiography of a Sevillian rogue who composes it while in forced retirement in the galleys, where he has been sent for defrauding a rich widow. After relating each of his adventures, the narrator adds a long moral; these passages are outstanding for their superb prose and good sense. The book also contains numerous subsidiary tales, such as the famous story of Ozmin and Daraja.

Gwyn, Eleanor (known as Nell Gwyn, 1650–1687) English actress and mistress of Charles II. She is said to have begun her career as an orange-vendor in a London theatre. She became Charles's mistress in 1668 and bore him two sons, one of whom was later made Duke of St. Alban's. According to tradition, the King's dying request to his brother was "Let not poor Nelly starve."

gypsy   A member of a dark-skinned nomadic people. Gypsies first appeared in England about the beginning of the 16th century, and, as they were thought to have come from Egypt, were named *Egyptians*, which soon became corrupted to *Gypcians*, and so to its present form. They call themselves *Romany* (from *rom*, "man; husband"), which is also the name of their language: a debased Hindu dialect with large additions of words from Persian, Armenian, and many European languages. It is thought that early gypsies migrated from northern India.

The name of the largest group of European gypsies is *Atzigan*; this, in Turkey and Greece, became *Tshingian*, in the Balkans and Romania *Tsigan*, in Hungary *Czigany*, in Germany *Zigeuner*, in Italy *Zingari*, in Portugal *Cigano*, and in Spain *Gitano*. The original name is said to mean "dark man."

There is a legend that the gypsies are waifs and strays on the earth because they refused to shelter the Virgin and her child in their flight to Egypt.

H

Habakkuk An OLD TESTAMENT book bearing the name of its author. It is a short, cogitative book written just before the fall of Jerusalem in 586 BC. The author questions the actions of a god who uses a wicked enemy to punish his sinful people. Habakkuk resolves his problems by foreseeing a final triumph over evil by the forces of righteousness and faith.

Hades Lord of the underworld, sometimes known as Pluto or Pluton, the giver of wealth. He was the son of CRONOS and RHEA. With his brothers ZEUS and POSEIDON, he rebelled against his father, and after Cronos' fall the brothers divided the universe among themselves by lot. Hades received the lower regions, where he ruled over the dead, and to which he brought his wife, PERSEPHONE. He is represented as a grim and severe god who seldom left his kingdom.

In later mythology, the underworld itself came to be known as Hades, possibly shortened from the abode of Hades. It is the home of departed spirits, a place of gloom, but not necessarily, like the Christian Hell, a place of punishment and torture. As the state or abode of the dead, it corresponds to the Hebrew *Sheol*, a word which the translators of the Authorized Version frequently replaced with the misleading *Hell*. Hence, Hades is often used as a euphemism for Hell.

Hadith (Arab, "saying; tradition") The traditions about the prophet MUHAMMED's sayings and doings. This compilation, made in the 10th century by the Muslim jurists Moshin and Bokhari, forms a supplement to the KORAN as the TALMUD does to the Jewish Scriptures. The *Hadith* was originally not allowed to be committed to writing, but the danger of the traditions being perverted or forgotten led to their being placed on record.

hadji A pilgrim; specifically, a Muslim who has completed the required pilgrimage, or *hadj*, to MECCA. The word is often prefixed to a name as an epithet of honor. See ISLAM.

Hadrian (full Latin name Publius Aelius Hadrianus, AD 76–138) Roman emperor (117–138). As part of his policy of consolidation and of renouncing conquest, Hadrian established the Euphrates as the eastern boundary of the Roman Empire. He effected the construction in Britain of Hadrian's Wall (120–123) from Solway Firth to the south of Tyne as a protection against the Picts and Scots. He profoundly admired Greek culture and did much to beautify Athens with new buildings. His tomb at Rome and his villa at Tibur are remarkable structures. Hadrian was a learned man, an amateur architect, and a writer of genuine gifts. His reign was one of the finest ages in Roman history, and it continued for many years longer through his foresight in choosing as his successors Antoninus Pius and Marcus Aurelius. Marguerite YOURCENAR wrote a thoughtful fictional biography of Hadrian, which she called a "meditation on history," in *Mémoires d'Hadrien* (*Memoirs of Hadrian*, 1951).

Hadzhi Murad (1911) A novel by TOLSTOY. A short book, written in 1904, it is set during a Cossack uprising in the Caucasus. Replaced as a leader by a rival, Hadzhi deserts to the Russians. He later changes his mind and, pining for his own people, decides to go back to them, even though he knows they will kill him for his desertion. The novel is generally considered one of the most skillful works of Tolstoy's later period.

Hāfiz (pen name of Shams-ud-din Muhammad, c1300–1388) Persian poet. A student of both poetry and theology, Hāfiz became a member of the Sūfi, an Islamic sect, and a professor of Koranic studies; his pen name, Hāfiz, "one who remembers," was the Persian term applied to a scholar who knew the KORAN by heart. The *Dīvān of Hāfiz* is a large collection of odes (*ghazals*) written in five to fifteen couplets (*distichs*) each. The second lines of the couplets rhyme throughout, and the last couplet always introduces the poet's name. An example of a final couplet is: "The laughing wine, the sweet girl's tumbled tresses, / Were more than even Hāfiz could deny!" The odes are arranged alphabetically in the book according to their rhymes. The subjects of the odes include love, wine, birds, flowers, and instability of all things human, and Allah and the prophets. Besides their apparent content, the odes have religious meaning in the mystical terms of the Sūfi.

Best known for his odes, Hāfiz also wrote in other forms, especially the *rubáiyát* (rhymed quatrains).

Hagar   In the OLD TESTAMENT, the Egyptian servant of ABRAHAM's wife, SARAH. When Hagar bore Abraham a son, ISHMAEL, she grew haughty toward her mistress, who remained childless; but after the birth of Sarah's son, ISAAC, Hagar and Ishmael were cast out into the wilderness. On one occasion, when they were perishing of thirst, an angel of the Lord pointed out a spring of water in the desert, thereby saving the lives of Hagar and Ishmael (Gen. 21).

Hagen   Murderer of Siegfried in German legend. A retainer of the Burgundian kings in the NIBELUNGENLIED, he is their half-brother (son of ALBERICH) in Richard Wagner's four-part opera *Ring des Nibelungen.*

Haggadah   The portion of the MIDRASH that contains rabbinical interpretations of the historical and legendary, ethical, parabolic, and speculative parts of the Hebrew Scriptures. The portion devoted to law, practice, and doctrine is called the HALACHAH. They were begun in the 2nd century and completed by the 11th. The term also refers to the ritual recited at the seder feast on the first night of PASSOVER.

Haggai   A biblical prophet and the OLD TESTAMENT book that bears his name. As with his contemporary ZECHARIAH, Haggai prophesied after the Israelites had returned to Jerusalem from the Babylonian captivity. The people are rebuked for their failure to rebuild the temple and are encouraged by Haggai to begin work, with the assurance of God's assistance and mercy. It is promised that the new temple will be greater in glory than the first (Ha. 2:9).

Haggard, Sir [Henry] Rider (1856–1925)   English novelist, whose tense, mysterious stories usually occur in some exotic African setting. His most effective novels are *King Solomon's Mines* (1885), *Allan Quartermain* (1887), SHE, and its sequel, *Ayesha* (1905). Many of his books, notably *She* and *King Solomon's Mines*, have been dramatized and made into motion pictures.

Hagisgrapha   See OLD TESTAMENT.

haiku   A form of Japanese poetry, composed of seventeen syllables (in a 5,7,5 pattern) in three lines. A haiku evokes a complete impression or mood through the juxtaposition of a natural physical element, such as a sound or sight, with a phrase to suggest a season or emotion. Its greatest practitioner was MATSUO BASHŌ, who established the rules for the content of the poems and the allusions permitted. It developed from *haikai*, a form of linked verse popular in the 16th and 17th centuries. *Hokku* is the opening verse in a series of linked verse; haiku is a separate poem of the *haikai* school. The three terms are frequently confused. An example of haiku by Bashō:

Kono michi ya
Yuku hito nashi ni
Aki no kure

This road
No one walks along it
Dusk in autumn.

See TANKA.

Hailey, Arthur (1920–   )   English-born Canadian novelist. Hailey's best-selling novels are fast-paced fictional documentaries, loaded with carefully researched factual detail. The focus is on the airline industry in *Airport* (1968); the auto industry in *Wheels* (1971); banking in *The Moneychangers* (1975); and the pharmaceutical industry in *Strong Medicine* (1984). Hailey's popular success is due in part to his skillful construction of plots and his selection of subjects that affect the well-being, if not the survival, of every reader.

Hail Mary   See AVE MARIA.

Hairy Ape, The (1922)   A play by Eugene O'NEILL. An expressionistic drama, it tells of a crude stoker on a transatlantic liner. Yank, who feels that he "belongs" in the depths of the ship, becomes disillusioned with his life when he and the men are inspected by a society girl. His attempt to climb the evolutionary ladder fails in New York City, where he finally goes to the zoo; realizing that the ape is his nearest kin in spirit, he releases the animal from its cage and is crushed to death by the beast.

Hajar-al-Aswad   In the Muslim faith, a famous black stone, irregularly oval, about seven inches in breadth and surrounded with a circle of gold, which is found in the northeast corner of the KAABA. According to legend, when Abraham wished to build the Kaaba, the stones came to him of their own accord, and he commanded all the faithful to kiss this one. The stone was supposed to have been whiter than milk when it first came from Paradise, but became black through the sins of the millions that had kissed it. On the Day of the Resurrection, it is believed, the stone will have two eyes, by which it will recognize all those who have kissed it, and a tongue with which it will bear witness to ALLAH.

The stone is probably an aerolite, and it was worshiped long before MUHAMMED's day. In the 2nd century AD Maximus Tyrius spoke of the Arabians paying homage to it, and Persian legend states that it was an emblem of Saturn.

Hajji Baba of Ispahan, The Adventures of (1824)   A PICARESQUE romance by James Morier (1780–1849), dealing with life in Persia. The hero is a sort of Persian GIL BLAS whose roguery takes him into all spheres of Persian society. In a satiric sequel, *Hajji Baba in England* (1828), he visits England as a government official, seeing familiar customs with a foreign eye.

Hajji Khalfah (original name Mustata ibn-Abdallah, 1600?–1658)   A Turkish historian and bibliographer. Hajji Khalfah compiled a bibliographical lexicon, with memoirs of the authors, of more than twenty-five thousand books in Arabic, Turkish, and Persian.

Hakīm, Tawfīq al- (1902–   ) Egyptian novelist and playwright. Educated in Paris, al-Hakīm is one of the most sophisticated and prolific writers of the Arab world, and an ardent anti-British nationalist. His plays and novels deal symbolically with social issues and with the problems and virtues of nonconformity. His works, which are widely translated in Europe, particularly in France, include the novels *Awdat ar-rūh* (*The Return of the Spirit*, 1933) and *The Maze of Justice* (tr 1947) and the plays *Scheherezade* (1934), often considered his masterwork, and *Yā tali ᶜal-shajara* (1962; tr *The Tree Climber*, 1966).

Hakluyt, Richard (1553–1616) English scholar and clergyman. As a boy Hakluyt became interested in maps and explorations, and devoted his life to compiling and editing accounts of English voyages of discovery. In 1582 he published his first compilation, *Divers Voyages touching the Discovery of America*. This was followed in 1589 by *Principal Navigations, Traffics, Voyages, and Discoveries of the English Nation*, which was greatly enlarged to three volumes in 1598–1600. Called "the prose epic of the modern English nation," it contains accounts of the voyages of Raleigh, of the Cabots, of Drake's circumnavigation, of Martin Frobisher's search for the Northwest Passage, and the like. His work, which reflects the great exploring spirit of the Elizabethan age, gave additional impetus to English exploration, conquest, and colonization.

Halachah The division of the MIDRASH that deals with civil and religious laws, customs, doctrines, and interpretations handed down by Jewish oral tradition. The folkloric and nonlegal rabbinical literature is contained in the HAGGADAH.

Halbe, Max (1865–1944) German dramatist in the movement of NATURALISM. Although Halbe wrote over two dozen plays, many of them historical dramas, none enjoyed any lasting esteem except *Die Jugend* (1893; tr *When Love Is Young*, 1904). A lovers' tragedy that also treats the conflict between modern personal values and traditional religious ones, it was particularly praised for its psychological insights into adolescence.

halcyon days A time of happiness and prosperity. Halcyon in Greek is the word for a kingfisher, compounded of *hals*, "the sea," and *kyo*, "to brood on." The ancient Sicilians believed that the kingfisher laid its eggs and incubated them on the surface of the sea for fourteen days before the winter solstice. During this time the waves of the sea were always unruffled.

Hale, Nathan (1755–1776) American hero in the Revolutionary War. Hale was sentenced by the British to be hanged as a spy and, according to popular accounts, went to his death with the words "I only regret that I have but one life to lose for my country." This version, however, may be apocryphal. In the diaries of Captain Frederick

Mackenzie, a British officer at the scene, Hale's last words were recorded as "It is the duty of every good officer to obey any orders given him by his commander-in-chief."

Interestingly, the words "What a pity it is that we can die but once to serve our country!" appeared in Joseph ADDISON's *Cato* (1713; act I, scene 4).

Haley, Alex [Palmer] (1921–   ) American writer. Haley began writing while serving in the U.S. Coast Guard. His early adventure stories led to regular assignments for *Playboy* magazine, and eventually to his collaboration on *The Autobiography of Malcolm X* (1965). Nevertheless, he was relatively unknown until the publication of the monumental *Roots* in 1976, which won a special PULITZER PRIZE in 1977. A twelve-year labor of research, *Roots* traces Haley's ancestry back through American slavery to its origins in Africa. The book is a combination of history and fiction; authentic facts are amplified by imaginative detail. Haley has called this genre "faction."

Haliburton, Thomas Chandler (1796–1865) Canadian humorist. In 1856 Haliburton, a lawyer and judge, retired, went to England, and was elected to the House of Commons. A fanatic conservative, he was critical of the U.S., frequently expressed contempt for what he called "the lower orders," and became an avowed enemy of democracy.

In 1835 Haliburton began writing in the newspaper *The Novascotian* humorous sketches about Sam Slick, an itinerant Yankee clockmaker. The first sketches, with others added, were collected in *The Clockmaker, or, The Sayings and Doings of Samuel Slick of Slickville* (1837). This series was followed by several others, including *Sam Slick's Saws and Modern Instances* (1853). The books became very popular, first in Canada, then in the U.S. and England. Sam Slick became the best-known character in the field of Yankee humor and had many imitators.

Hall, Donald (1928–   ) American poet and editor. As poetry editor of the *Paris Review* (1953–61), Hall did much to make younger contemporary poets more widely known by collecting their work in anthologies. *New Poets of England and America* (1957), compiled with Robert Pack and Louis SIMPSON, is an excellent representative collection of poets born between 1917 and 1935. Other anthologies include *New Poets of England and America: Second Selection* (1962; with Robert Pack), *Contemporary American Poetry* (1962, rev 1971), and *American Poetry* (1969). Hall's own poetry is collected in such volumes as *Exiles and Marriages* (1955), *A Roof of Tiger Lilies* (1964), *The Alligator Bride* (1969), and *Kicking the Leaves* (1978). *String Too Short to Be Saved* (1961) is a memoir of his childhood. *Remembering Poets* (1978) contains not only reminiscences, but also Hall's psychological interpretations of such poets as Robert FROST, T. S. ELIOT, Ezra POUND, and Dylan THOMAS. *The Weather for Poetry* (1982) is a perceptive survey of contemporary British, American, and Irish poetry.

Hall, James Norman (1887–1951) American novelist and short-story writer. Hall was coauthor with Charles Bernard NORDHOFF of the remarkably successful trilogy MUTINY ON THE BOUNTY, *Men Against the Sea* (1933), and *Pitcairn's Island* (1934). During the First World War, Hall flew with the Lafayette Escadrille, an experience which provided him with material for subsequent books written both independently and with Nordhoff. Among the books on which they collaborated are *Lafayette Flying Corps* (1920), *Falcons of France* (1929), *The Hurricane* (1936), and *Botany Bay* (1941).

Hall, Radclyffe (1886–1943) English novelist and short-story writer. Her novel *The Well of Loneliness* (1928) caused a sensation because of its sympathetic portrayal of lesbianism. It was banned in England and temporarily suspended in the U.S.

Hallam, Arthur Henry (1811–1833) English poet and essayist whose early death caused Tennyson to write IN MEMORIAM and "Break, Break, Break" (1842). Hallam, who was a close friend of Tennyson and the fiancé of his sister Emily, was touring the Continent when he suddenly died in Vienna. His death was a profound shock to Tennyson and the cause of deep conflict between doubt and faith in the poet's life.

Haller, Harry The hero of Hesse's STEPPENWOLF. Part of the novel's vitality stems from the fact that Haller's experiences, like his initials, are patterned on Hesse's own.

Hallowe'en (or All Hallow's Eve) October 31, in the old Celtic calendar the last day of the year. Its night was the time when all the witches and warlocks were abroad and held their wicked revels. At the introduction of Christianity it was taken over as the eve of ALL SAINTS. It is still devoted to all sorts of games in which the old superstitions can be traced. See SAMAIN.

Hals, Frans (1580?–1666) Dutch portrait and genre painter. Hals's sitters represent every class of society, from officers, burghers, and merchants to fishwives and itinerant entertainers. He represented them in animated and momentary attitudes, capturing a casual glimpse with quick and broad brushstrokes. His work is known for its vitality and, during his later period, for its gray and black tonal harmonies.

Ham In the OLD TESTAMENT, one of the three sons of NOAH, his brothers being SHEM and JAPHETH. According to legend, because Noah and his family alone survived the Flood, their descendants populated the earth. Egypt was called "The Land of Ham" and he was considered to be the eponymous ancestor of the Egyptians and the people of the regions in Africa south of Egypt. Their dark skins were said to be a result of Ham's iniquity in viewing his father drunk and naked, while his brothers walked backward, with averted eyes, to cover Noah (Gen. 9:22–26). When Noah awoke, he knew of his son's transgression and cursed Ham's son, CANAAN.

Hamilton, Alexander (1757–1804) American statesman and chief author of THE FEDERALIST essays. He served as the first secretary of the treasury (1789–95) and recommended fiscal measures, such as the creation of a national bank, that reflected his belief in a strong, centralized government. Distrusting the capacity of the common man, he advocated government by the elite. He was killed in a duel by Aaron BURR, whose political ambitions he had thwarted. He is the subject of Gertrude Atherton's "dramatized biography" *The Conqueror* (1902).

Hamilton, Lady Emma (born Emma Lyon, 1761?–1815) Wife of Sir William Hamilton, mistress of Horatio NELSON. Of humble birth but of great beauty, she became the mistress of Hamilton's nephew, Charles Greville, who sold her to the elderly diplomat in exchange for payment of his debts. She attained great popularity and influence at the court of Naples, where Hamilton was envoy, and there met Nelson, becoming his mistress in 1798. The lovers were extremely open about their relationship, and the birth of Nelson's daughter, Horatia (1801), gave further cause for scandal. After Nelson's death, her extravagance caused her to be imprisoned for debt (1813); she was released a year later and died in poverty in France.

Hamlet, The (1940) A novel by William FAULKNER, the first book of a trilogy that also includes *The Town* (1957) and *The Mansion* (1959). Spanning almost fifty years in time, the trilogy is centered on the innumerable and vicious members of the SNOPES family, the first of whom invades YOKNAPATAWPHA COUNTY early in the 20th century. In the hamlet of Frenchman's Bend, Flem Snopes begins as a clerk in Will Varner's store; through usury, connivance, and thrift, he becomes part owner of the store and husband of Eula VARNER, Will's daughter. In Jefferson, Flem works his way into Colonel Sartoris's bank, finally becoming vice-president. In order to enrich himself still further, he drives the bank president, Manfred De Spain, from town. In *The Mansion*, Flem moves into the now-vacant De Spain mansion, one of the largest and oldest houses in Jefferson. Flem has no human feelings of any kind, caring only for money and for the outward appearance of respectability. He imports a number of cousins —Mink, I.O., Lump, Ike, Eck—whom he installs in various positions in the community, until the local citizens feel that they are overrun with Snopeses.

The novels are loosely episodic, humorous, and ironic. *The Hamlet* is made up of material dealing alternately with horse trading and love—economic life vis-à-vis emotional life. *The Town* continues this contrast on a more sophisticated level, centering on the hopeless and almost comic love of Gavin STEVENS, first for Eula Varner Snopes and then for her daughter Linda, and on the machinations used by Flem to acquire more money. *The Mansion* departs from this scheme, dealing primarily with the attempts of Mink Snopes to return to Jefferson and murder Flem, and with the relationship between Gavin and Linda. Each of the novels is made up of sections narrated mainly by characters who observe the action rather than take part in it, such as V. K. Ratliff, the ubiquitous sewing-machine salesman, and Chick MALLISON, the young nephew of Gavin Stevens.

Hamlet of A. MacLeish, The (1928)   A poem by Archibald MACLEISH. In this dramatic monologue, the poet contrasts Hamlet's situation with that of modern man, symbolized by the poet himself. He attempts to show that the sensitive man today has no knowledge of the evil he tries to fight.

Hamlet, Prince of Denmark (c1601)   A tragedy by SHAKESPEARE. It is his most famous play and one of the most fascinating in world literature.

Hamlet, prince of Denmark, falls into melancholia after the death of his father, the king. CLAUDIUS, his father's brother, has assumed the throne and married Hamlet's mother, GERTRUDE, within two months of the king's death. His father's ghost appears to Hamlet, accuses Claudius of murdering him, and demands revenge. Hamlet then resolves to feign madness in order to disguise his intentions. His rejection of OPHELIA, to whom he has shown attention, leads her father, POLONIUS, to the conclusion that love has driven the prince mad. Unable to bring himself to action and beset by doubts as to the truth of the ghost's words, Hamlet persuades some traveling players to reenact the death of his father. Claudius's violent reaction to the play convinces Hamlet of his uncle's guilt. Later, in his mother's chamber, the prince kills the eavesdropping Polonius, mistaking him for Claudius. Using this murder as a pretext for disposing of the prince, Claudius sends Hamlet to England with ROSENCRANTZ AND GUILDENSTERN, who bear secret letters to the king of England, advising him to put the prince to death. But Hamlet discovers the plot and manages to return to Denmark. Ophelia, driven mad by Hamlet's rejection and the death of her father, commits suicide. Her brother, LAERTES, who has been studying in Paris, returns for her funeral, intent upon revenging himself for the deaths of his father and sister. Inciting him further, Claudius arranges for a duel between Laertes and Hamlet, in which Laertes will be provided with a poisoned sword. To ensure Hamlet's death, Claudius also prepares a cup of poisoned wine. During the duel, Laertes nicks Hamlet with the poisoned sword, while the queen accidentally drinks the poisoned wine and dies. Having unwittingly seized the poisoned rapier in the scuffle, the dying Hamlet kills both Laertes and Claudius. See FORTINBRAS.

Although *Hamlet* is a play of revenge, its greatness lies in the unique and thoughtful nature of the prince, whose temper is philosophical rather than active. He does not so much pursue his revenge as he is swept to it through the events of the play. His preoccupation with the nature and consequences of man's actions has led critics to call him "the first modern man." The complexity and richness of the play have furnished critics and performers with material for hundreds of interpretations.

The earliest source of the play is a story which first appeared in *Historia Danica* (1514) by the Danish chronicler Saxo Grammaticus (c1150–c1220), and was later translated in *Histoires tragiques* (1570) by Pierre de Belleforest. An earlier version of the play (c1589), now lost, is referred to as "Ur-Hamlet," or source Hamlet.

Hammerstein, Oscar, II (1895–1960)   American musical comedy lyricist, librettist, and producer. A talented and prolific theatrical craftsman, Hammerstein wrote in collaboration or singly the book and lyrics for eighteen musicals, including *Show Boat* (1927), *Oklahoma!* (1943), *Carousel* (1945), *South Pacific* (1949), *The King and I* (1951), *Flower Drum Song* (1958), and *The Sound of Music* (1959). Hammerstein collaborated with the best light composers of his day, including Jerome KERN and Richard RODGERS. He also wrote six screenplays, and with Rodgers produced five Broadway hit shows.

Hammett, [Samuel] Dashiell (1894–1961)   American detective story writer. A Pinkerton detective for eight years, Hammett used some of his experiences in the writing of fast-paced and sophisticated crime novels. Acclaimed by many critics for elevating the detective story to the level of literature, he is the acknowledged founder of HARD-BOILED FICTION. In THE MALTESE FALCON he first introduced his famous "private eye," Sam SPADE. *The Thin Man* (1932) offered another immortal sleuth, Nick CHARLES. *Red Harvest* (1929), *The Dain Curse* (1929), and *The Glass Key* (1931) are among his other successful novels. Hammett's life was plagued with ill health, bouts with alcoholism, and a period of imprisonment related to his alleged membership in the Communist Party. His attempt at an autobiographical novel survives in the story "Tulip," which is contained in the posthumous collection *The Big Knockover* (1966), edited by his long-time companion Lillian HELLMAN. Another volume of his stories, *The Continental Op*, edited by Stephen Marcus, appeared in 1974.

Hammurabi   King of Babylon, who reigned 2067–2025 BC. One of the greatest rulers in antiquity, he is chiefly remembered for his remarkable code of laws, which no doubt accounted in part for the success with which he governed much of Mesopotamia.

Hampden, John (1594–1643)   English statesman. He became a popular symbol of resistance to royal tyranny when he fought the attempts of Charles I to collect ship-money from the inland counties without the consent of Parliament. At the outbreak of the CIVIL WAR he raised a regiment for the Parliamentary army and was mortally wounded at Chalgrove Field.

Hamsun, Knut [Pederson] (1859–1952)   Norwegian novelist, poet, and playwright. Born of a farming family, Hamsun spent the years of his young manhood in poverty, wandering from one job to another. Two trips to the U.S. yielded positions as a streetcar conductor, dairy-man, and finally as a fisherman off the coast of Newfoundland. His first novel, *Sult* (1890; tr *Hunger*, 1899), met with considerable critical success and established him as an original and provocative writer. Ignoring the prevailing literary concern with social realism, Hamsun focused on the inner turmoil of the individual. Regarded by many as his greatest achievement, *Mysterier* (1892; tr *Mysteries*, 1971) offered an intense examination of unconscious motivation. Although not so popular as *Pan* (1894; tr 1956), *Victoria* (1898; tr 1929), and *Envandrer spiller med sordin* (1909; tr *With Muted Strings*, 1922), *Mysterier* set an example followed by many younger writers. In many of his later works, Hamsun widened his focus to include the effects of society on an individual, frequently using the wandering hero, August, who appeared in *Landstrykere* (1927; tr *Wayfarers*, 1980), *August* (1930; tr 1932), and *Men livet lever* (1933; tr *The Road Leads On*, 1937). Other novels, like *Segelfloss by* (1915) and *Konere ved vandposten* (1920; tr *The Woman at the Pump*, 1928, 1978), contain angry criticism of modern life. His best-known work is *Markens grode* (1917; tr *The Growth of the Soil*, 1920), in which he describes the elemental existence of two individuals, Inger and Isak, in the rough, open country of Norway. In 1920 Hamsun was awarded the NOBEL PRIZE in Literature. His memoirs, *On Overgrown Paths*, appeared in English in 1967.

Han   Chinese dynasty (206 BC–AD 220), succeeding the CHIN dynasty. The Han dynasty was the Chinese imperial age, which witnessed great developments in science, literature, and the arts. Confucian thought was systematized and established as the dominant ethical and political philosophy. The *Shih chi*, the first historical annal, was composed during this period. The fall of the Han in 220 was followed by the THREE KINGDOMS period.

Hancock, John (1737–1793)   American statesman. Hancock served as president of the Continental Congress (1775–77) and was the first signer of the DECLARATION OF INDEPENDENCE. From the bold legibility with which he signed that document, there developed the expression "John Hancock," meaning a signature.

Handel, George Frideric (1685–1759)   German-born composer; with J. S. BACH, the greatest musical figure of the late Baroque era. While Bach spent his life entirely in Germany, Handel traveled about Europe and, eventually (in 1712), settled permanently in England. Handel's operas played to the largest audiences in Europe, and he enjoyed much greater recognition during his lifetime than did his brilliant contemporary. Whereas Bach's music is intense and focused, Handel's is more expansive. Both Handel and Bach were among the most important composers to BEETHOVEN.

Handel's works are nearly all in two genres: Italian operas and English oratorios and odes. Notable among his forty-six operas are: *Giulio Cesare* (1724), *Rodelinda* (1725), *Sosarmé* (1732), *Orlando* (1733), *Alcina* (1735),

and *Atalanta* (1736). Full of beautiful music, these were rarely performed until a continuing revival began at the turn of the 20th century. His oratorios and odes, usually on biblical subjects, are the most outstanding large choral works in the English language. The best of the oratorios are *Saul* (1739), *Israel in Egypt* (1739), MESSIAH, *Belshazzar* (1744), *Hercules* (1744), *Solomon* (1748), and *Jephtha* (1751). Important secular choral works are: *Acis and Galatea* (1720), *Alexander's Feast* (1736; text by DRYDEN), *Ode for St. Cecilia's Day* (1739; text by Dryden), and *L'Allegro, il Penseroso ed il Moderato* (1744; text of the first two acts by MILTON). Handel also wrote church music, chamber music, and harpsichord suites, but the best known of his other works are the twelve concerti grossi for orchestra (1739), twelve organ concerti (1738–40), the *Water Music* (1715–17), and the *Royal Fireworks Music* (1749), the last two being suites for orchestra.

Handel was a master of vocal arrangements; the oratorio reached its height as a form with him. When he died at seventy-four, he was honored with burial in Westminster Abbey.

Handful of Dust, A (1937)   A novel by Evelyn WAUGH. Satirical in its treatment of upper-class English society, it is a black comedy about Tony Last, owner of a Gothic mansion that he loves. His old-fashioned values cannot support him in the changing modern world. Deserted by his wife, he becomes an explorer in Brazil and is captured and enslaved by a mad old man who forces him to read Dickens aloud every afternoon.

Handke, Peter (1942–   )   Austrian playwright, novelist, and poet. Handke is a radical, versatile, and prolific writer who achieved notoriety with his threefold literary debut in 1966 that included the publication of a novel, *Die Hornissen* (*The Hornets*); a vituperative attack on GROUP 47, read aloud at their convention; and three short plays, in which the actors abandon dramatic roles, discuss the history of the theatre, and then hurl insults at the audience. Subsequent plays in English translation include *Kaspar* (1968; tr 1969), based on the true story of a boy whose first sixteen years were spent hidden in a closet; *Wunschloses Unglück* (1972; tr *A Sorrow Beyond Dreams*, 1975), an objective yet moving memorial to Handke's mother, who committed suicide; *Ritt über den Bodensee* (1970; tr *The Ride Across Lake Constance*, 1976); and *Die Unvernünftigen sterben aus* (1973; tr *They Are Dying Out*, 1979).

The influence of WITTGENSTEIN is evident in Handke's work, as much of it focuses on the way language affects and ultimately restricts consciousness. His characters generally find themselves trapped in "inauthentic existences," alienated from each other and from real existence by hopeless ennui. This is particularly evident in his novels *Die Angst des Tormanns beim Elfmeter* (1970; tr *The Goalie's Anxiety at the Penalty Kick*, 1972), *Die linkshändige Frau* (1976; tr *The Left-Handed Woman*, 1978), *Die Stunde der wahren*

Empfindung (1975; tr *A Moment of True Feeling*, 1977), and *Across* (1987). His poetry includes *Die Innenwelt der Außenwelt der Innenwelt* (1969; tr *The Innerworld of the Outerworld of the Innerworld*, 1974) and *Als das Wunschen noch geholfen hat* (1974; tr *Nonsense and Happiness*, 1976). In 1982 Handke published his journal, *Die Geschichte des Bleistifts*.

handwriting on the wall   An announcement of some coming calamity, or the imminent fulfillment of some doom. The allusion is to the handwriting on BEL-SHAZZAR's palace wall announcing the loss of his kingdom. See DANIEL.

Han Fei Tzu   Chinese philosophical work of the LEGALIST SCHOOL. The author, Han Fei Tzu (c280–233 BC) was a prince of the royal house of the feudal state of HAN and a student of the Confucian philosopher Hsün Tzu. Its harsh, anti-Confucian philosophy of government, which stressed the importance of impartial and impersonal laws, was put into effect during the CH'IN dynasty (221–206 BC) and had a great influence on later Chinese statecraft in spite of the official position of CONFUCIANISM in government.

Hanging Gardens of Babylon   One of the SEVEN WONDERS OF THE ANCIENT WORLD. According to Diodorus Siculus, the garden was four hundred feet square, rising in a series of terraces from the river in the northern part of Babylon. It was provided with earth to a sufficient depth to accommodate trees of a great size. According to tradition, it was built by NEBUCHADNEZZAR to gratify his wife Amytis, who was weary of the flat plains of Babylon and longed for reminders of her native Median hills.

Hanley, James (1901–1985)   Irish-born English novelist. A merchant seaman at thirteen, Hanley educated himself during his ten years at sea and began writing novels, grim, raw, redeemed by courage, about his experience. His second book, the autobiographical *Boy* (1931), was banned. *The Furys Chronicle* (1935–58) is a series of four novels dealing with the despair of urban poverty in the Dublin of his childhood and the rugged vitality of seamen's lives. *Say Nothing* (1962; U.S. 1979) is concerned with loneliness, failure, love, and death in an English boarding-house. *A Dream Journey* (1976), about a failed painter, is characteristic of Hanley's powerful work, with its spare language and relentless insight into character. In addition to other novels, Hanley wrote several volumes of stories, essays, and a number of successful television plays.

Hannah   In the OLD TESTAMENT, the wife of Elkenah and mother of the prophet SAMUEL. She made and kept a vow that if the Lord gave her a child, she would give him to the service of the temple (1 Sam. 1:2).

Hannay, Richard   In John Buchan's THE THIRTY-NINE STEPS and its sequels, a South African mining engineer who becomes a British general and an energetic spy-catcher.

Hannele (Hanneles Himmelfahrt, 1893; tr 1894)   A symbolic drama by Gerhart HAUPTMANN. It combines NAT-URALISM with unusually poetic language and action. A mal-treated village girl tries to drown herself but is rescued and taken to a wretched almshouse, where she lapses into delirium. In her dreams she transforms the place and its dreary inhabitants into a fairy-tale paradise of immense poetic beauty. The heavenly splendor fades away as a doctor, bending over the girl, confirms her death.

Hannibal (247–183 BC)   Carthaginian general, son of Hamilcar Barca. As a child he was taken to Spain by his father and made to swear eternal enmity to Rome, an oath he never forgot. His whole life was a struggle against the Romans. At the outset of the Second Punic War (see PUNIC WARS), he invaded Italy from Spain, crossing the Alps with elephants by way of the Little St. Bernard, and plunged Rome into immediate danger through his victory at Cannae (216). He was ultimately defeated by SCIPIO AFRICANUS and recalled to Africa. Years later, he escaped extradition to Rome by committing suicide.

Hanno   Carthaginian navigator who led a colonizing expedition down the west coast of Africa (5th century BC).

Hanno the Great   Carthaginian politician of the 3rd century BC. He favored peaceful relations with Rome, in opposition to Hamilcar Barca and HANNIBAL.

Hansards   Official reports of Parliamentary proceedings in England, named after Luke Hansard (1752–1828), the printer of the House of Commons journals (from 1774).

Hansberry, Lorraine [Vivian] (1930–1965) American playwright. With her first play, *A Raisin in the Sun* (1959), Hansberry became the youngest American and first black playwright to win the Best Play Award from the New York Drama Critics' Circle. Her work celebrates individuals who stand up for their own and others' dignity. A black family seeking passage out of the Chicago ghetto is the focus of *Raisin*, and the growing realization of real values of its leading character, Walter Lee, is the substance of its action. In *The Sign in Sidney Brustein's Window* (1964), the middle-class Jewish protagonist renews his sense of integrity and social commitment after serious disillusionment. Hansberry's African fantasy, *Les Blancs*, was produced posthumously in 1970. Another posthumous work is *To Be Young, Gifted and Black* (1969), a dramatic self-portrait. Both works were completed by Hansberry's husband and literary executor, Robert Nemiroff, after her death from cancer at thirty-four.

Hans Brinker or The Silver Skates (1865)   A well-known story for children by Mary Mapes Dodge. The hero is a Dutch boy, and the book gives an interesting picture of life in Holland.

Hanseatic League   A confederacy begun in the 13th century among towns of northern Germany for mutual defense, particularly of their trade routes. During the 14th century it expanded to include most German and

Dutch cities, and reached the height of its political and commercial power, making trade agreements with other countries as a unit. The need for the League declined in the 16th century, and the last meeting was held in 1669.

Hanukkah (or Chanukah)   Jewish holiday observed for eight days in December, near the time of the winter solstice. It commemorates the victory of the MACCABEES over the Assyrians and the rededication (165 BC) of their Temple of Jerusalem; for this reason the holiday is also known as the Feast of Dedication. Another name for Hanukkah, the Festival of Lights, refers to the ritual lighting of the eight-branched candelabrum, the *menorah*, during the holiday.

Hanuman   In the RĀMĀYANA, the monkey helpful to RĀMA in constructing a bridge from India to Ceylon. With his followers, he enabled Rama to rescue his wife, SĪTA, from the stronghold of RAVANA, the demon-king of Ceylon. In some parts of India he is worshiped as a deity.

happening   A spontaneous or planned improvised spectacle or performance that developed during the late 1950s. It was frequently an entertainment of a quasi-theatrical nature with little form or logic. Occurring in public places, it often required audience participation and was designed to stimulate or provoke reactions.

Hapsburg   A royal Central European family. Germanic in origin, the family derived its name from the ancient castle of Hapsburg ("hawk's castle") in what is now Switzerland. Counts of Hapsburg were known as early as the 11th century, and it is their descendants who occupied the thrones of Germany, Austria, Hungary, Bohemia, Spain, etc., and for nearly four hundred years were the rulers of the Holy Roman Empire. The still current phrase "a Hapsburg lip" refers to the familial characteristic of a protruding lower lip observable in eighteen generations of Hapsburgs.

Hara   Another name for SHIVA, the destroying aspect of the Hindu TRIMURTI.

harakiri (Jap, *hara*, "abdomen," *kiri*, "cutting")   The vulgar Japanese term for committing suicide by disemboweling oneself with a sharp knife. The more appropriate term is *seppuku*. This form of suicide first came into use in the KAMAKURA period. During the TOKUGAWA period, it came to be employed as a punishment meted out by and to persons of SAMURAI rank; but it also became an accepted form of expressing strenuous protest over some act or policy, or as expiation for some sin against family honor or duty.

hard-boiled fiction   A type of 20th-century American crime story. A sense of realism is generated by laconic, often crude, dialogue; the depiction of cruelty and bloodshed at close range; and the use of sordid environments. The genre was closely associated with the magazine *Black Mask* (founded 1919) and with its editor, Joseph T. Shaw, who later compiled *The Hard-Boiled Omnibus: Early Stories from Black Mask* (1946). Among the earliest

and best writers of hard-boiled novels were Dashiell HAMMETT, Raymond CHANDLER, and W. R. Burnett. Such fiction was originally a serious literary endeavor, not dissimilar in aim to the work of such major writers as Ernest HEMINGWAY and John DOS PASSOS; later it tended to degenerate into the sensationalism and gratuitous violence of writers like Mickey SPILLANE.

Harding, Warren G[amaliel] (1865–1923) Twenty-ninth president of the U.S. (1921–23). Originally the editor and publisher of a newspaper in Marion, Ohio, Harding served as lieutenant governor of the state and was elected to the U.S. Senate in 1915. In 1920 he became the Republican candidate for president after his nomination had been decided upon by a handful of party leaders "in a smoke-filled room." Harding waged a front-porch campaign, promising a "return to normalcy" that appealed to war-weary Americans and won him 404 electoral votes while his Democratic opponent, James M. Cox, received only 127. His administration, one of the least distinguished in American history, is remembered largely for the corruption that flourished as Harding's cronies, especially the notorious "Ohio gang," helped themselves at the federal till. (See TEAPOT DOME.) While returning from a trip to Alaska, Harding became fatally ill in San Francisco. Embolism was listed as the cause of death.

Hard Lot, A (Gorkaya sudbina, 1859)   A drama by Aleksey Pisemsky (1820–81). Dealing with the tragic conflicts caused by a love affair between an estate owner and the wife of one of his serfs, the play is regarded as one of the most powerful realistic tragedies in Russian drama.

Hard Times (1845)   A novel by Charles DICKENS. Thomas Gradgrind, a fanatic of the demonstrable fact, has raised his children, Tom and Louisa, in an atmosphere of grimmest practicality. Louisa marries the banker Josiah BOUNDERBY partly to protect her brother, who is in Bounderby's employ, and partly because her education has resulted in an emotional atrophy that makes her indifferent to her fate. Tom, shallow and unscrupulous, robs Bounderby's bank and contrives to frame Stephen Blackpool, an honest and long-suffering mill hand. Meanwhile, Louisa's dormant emotions begin to awaken, stimulated by disgust for the vulgar Bounderby and the attentions of the charming, amoral James Harthouse. When she runs away to her father and when Tom's guilt is discovered, Gradgrind realizes how his principles have blighted his children's lives. Ultimately Louisa secures a separation from Bounderby and Tom flees the country. The novel is Dickens's harshest indictment of practices and philosophical justifications of mid-19th-century industrialism in England.

Hardy, Alexandre (c1569–1632)   French playwright. A prolific author, Hardy wrote literally hundreds of plays and published thirty-four of them, including the biblical tragedy *Marianne*, in the years 1623–28. An innovator with a sure theatrical flair, Hardy enlivened dramatic movement by omitting the chorus, pruning soliloquies and monologues, introducing confrontations between main characters, and permitting violence on stage. Though poetically and rhetorically inferior to much of his predecessors' work, Hardy's plays achieved an enormous popularity in their time and performed the invaluable service of bridging the gap between the French drama of the Middle Ages and Renaissance and that of the 17th century.

Hardy, Thomas (1840–1928)   English novelist and poet. Hardy was born in Dorsetshire, the region that he later called Wessex in his novels. He trained as an architect and began to practice in 1867, though he soon became disillusioned and sought another medium for expression. He had been writing poems for several years, but he could find no publisher for his verse; he attempted a novel, but his first book, *The Poor Man and the Lady*, was rejected. *Desperate Remedies* (1871) was published anonymously, as was *Under the Greenwood Tree* (1872). In 1873 he published A PAIR OF BLUE EYES under his own name; the book was successful, and he began a full-time literary career. In the next twenty-four years, he produced eleven novels: FAR FROM THE MADDING CROWD, *The Hand of Ethelberta* (1876), THE RETURN OF THE NATIVE, *The Trumpet-Major* (1879), A *Laodicean* (1881), *Two on a Tower* (1882), THE MAYOR OF CASTERBRIDGE, *The Woodlanders* (1887), TESS OF THE D'URBERVILLES, JUDE THE OBSCURE, and *The Well-Beloved* (1897). Hardy's view of life, particularly as shown in his major novels, was one shaped by the prevalent materialistic and deterministic theories of 19th-century science, which saw man as subject to forces he could neither understand nor control; a naturalist, Hardy wrote forceful studies of life in which his characters are continually defeated in their struggle against their physical and social environment, against their own impulses, and against the malevolent caprices of chance. Though his style is often awkward, it has a harsh power that contributes to the almost tragic intensity of his best work.

Hardy's first volume of verses, *Wessex Poems*, appeared in 1898, though it contained poetry he had written since the 1860s. Abandoning the novel, probably because of the shocked public reaction to *Jude the Obscure*, he continued to write poetry, publishing six more volumes of lyrical verse, which were gathered together in the *Collected Poems* of 1931, and one later volume, *Winter Words in Various Moods and Meters* (1928). Sometimes colloquial, uneven, and ragged, Hardy's verse is highly original, and has a wide variety of metrical styles and stanza forms, and a wide scope of tone and attitude, as is apparent from the ironically humorous ballad "The Ruined Maid," the pensive "Darkling Thrush," or the simple but moving "She Hears the Storm." Hardy's most ambitious poetic work, *The Dynasts* (1903, 1906, 1908), is an epic drama on the Napoleonic wars. The first volume of *The Collected Letters of Thomas Hardy* was published in 1978.

Hardy Boys, The   See STRATEMEYER, EDWARD L.

hare   According to tradition, it is unlucky for a hare to cross one's path, because witches transform themselves into hares. In medieval science, the hare was a most melancholy beast, and ate wild succory in the hope of curing itself. Its flesh was supposed to generate melancholy in any who partook of it.

Another superstition was that hares are sexless, or that they change their sex every year. Among the Hindus the hare is sacred to the moon because, as they affirm, the outline of a hare is distinctly visible in the full disk. The idea that a March hare is mad derives from the fact that hares are unusually shy and wild in March, their rutting season. Erasmus, however, says "mad as a marsh hare," and adds, "Hares are wilder in marshes from the absence of hedges and cover."

Hari   Another name for VISHNU, the preserving aspect of the Hindu TRIMURTI.

harijan (Hind, *hari*, "god," *jan*, "people")   Children or people of god. A word used by Mahatma GANDHI to refer to India's UNTOUCHABLES, whose lot he sought to improve and among whom he often lived as he toured the country.

Harington, John (1561–1612)   English satirist and miscellaneous writer. A godson of Queen Elizabeth, Harington translated Ariosto's ORLANDO FURIOSO into English (1591) at her command. He was banished from court because of some of his ribald satires, such as *The Metamorphosis of Ajax* (1596), a Rabelaisian history of privys. He also wrote many pamphlets and epigrams.

Harlem   A section of New York City, inhabited largely by blacks and Latin Americans. It was popular among intellectuals and society people of the 1920s because of its cabarets and speakeasies and its jazz. During the latter 1930s it also became a center of attraction for devotees of swing and boogie-woogie music. Harlem is the scene of *Naked on Roller Skates* (1929), by Maxwell BODENHEIM; ALL GOD'S CHILLUN GOT WINGS, by Eugene O'Neill; and NIGGER HEAVEN, by Carl Van Vechten. The character of its residents is depicted in the works of such black writers as Countee CULLEN, Langston HUGHES, W. E. B. Du BOIS, Ann Petry (1911–   ), and James BALDWIN. See HARLEM RENAISSANCE.

Harlem Renaissance   A literary and artistic movement in the 1920s, centered in HARLEM, New York City. In 1925 Alain Locke (1886–1954), one of the fosterers and founders of the renaissance, published an anthology of current work called *The New Negro: An Interpretation*. In his introduction Locke outlined the new trends in black writing: a discovery by the educated, urbanized blacks of the beauty, vigor, and honesty of life in the Harlem ghetto. They celebrated blackness in repudiation of earlier writers such as Charles W. Chesnutt (1858–1932) and Paul Lawrence DUNBAR, whose work they felt conformed to white literary standards. The leading writers in the movement were: Langston HUGHES, Jean Toomer (1894–1967), Countee CULLEN, Richard WRIGHT, and Zora Neale HUR-

STON. In effect, the Renaissance group consisted of intellectuals in search of an identity: they stood some distance from their own people, yet felt alienated from mainstream American society. They were the forerunners of the revolutionary black writers of the 1960s, James BALDWIN and Imamu Amiri BARAKA.

Harlequin A comedic stage character. Originally *Arlecchino*, a stock figure of *commedia dell'arte* (possibly from the name of a medieval demon or goblin), Harlequin became the buffoon of French and then of English pantomime. He has a shaven head, wears a mask and particolored tights, and carries a wooden sword. Often invisible to all but COLUMBINE, he is a rival of PIERROT or some other clown for her love. His character was adapted to the OPÉRA-COMIQUE and the *comédie bourgeoise* by such writers as Jean-Pierre de Florian (1755–94), Pierre de MARIVAUX, and Alexis Piron (1689–1773).

Harpagon The central character in Molière's comedy L'AVARE. Nothing in life, not even his children, is more important to him than his hoard of money. Both Harpagon and his son Cléante desire to marry Mariane; but when the former, having lost a casket of money, is asked which he prefers—the money or Mariane—he says that he prefers the money, and Cléante marries the lady. Harpagon imagines that everyone is out to rob him, and when his casket is stolen he seizes his own arm in a frenzy. He proposes to give his daughter Elise in marriage to an old man named Anselme, because no dowry will be required. When Elise's lover, Valère, cites reason after reason against the unnatural alliance, the miser makes but one reply: "*sans dot*" ("without dowry"). On another occasion, Harpagon solicits Jacques to tell him what people say about him; when told that he is called a miser and a skinflint, he becomes helplessly enraged and beats poor Jacques in his terrible passion.

Harper's Magazine An American magazine founded in 1850 as *Harper's New Monthly Magazine*. It was called *Harper's Monthly Magazine* after 1900, and after 1925, simply *Harper's Magazine*. During the 19th century it was devoted to literature, and frequently published serials of popular English authors, including DICKENS, TROLLOPE, THACKERAY, and George ELIOT. The department of comment called "The Easy Chair," begun by Donald Grant MITCHELL, was conducted by a series of distinguished editors, among them W. D. HOWELLS and G. W. CURTIS. In a department called the "Editor's Study," begun in 1885, Howells also published important articles on the new realistic fiction. Mark TWAIN, Booth TARKINGTON, Frank R. Stockton, and Woodrow WILSON were regular contributors. After World War I, the magazine began to lose ground, so the editor abandoned illustrations in favor of increased economic, social, and political analysis. Poetry, fiction, and reviews, however, were retained as important features in the magazine.

harpies In Greek mythology, predaceous birds with women's faces. They were daughters of the titaness ELECTRA and sisters of IRIS. They are most familiar from the story that they regularly snatched away the food from the blind king PHINEUS until they were pursued and frightened away by the ARGONAUTS Calais and Zetes, winged sons of BOREAS. They seem to have combined the primitive concepts of wind spirits and predatory ghosts with actual characteristics of carrion birds.

Homer mentions only one harpy. Hesiod gives two, and later writers three. Their names were Ocypeta ("rapid"), Celeno ("blackness"), and Aello ("storm").

Harp-Weaver and Other Poems, The (1923) A collection of poems by Edna St. Vincent MILLAY. This volume, which was awarded a PULITZER PRIZE in poetry, was specially praised for the excellence of the thirty-nine sonnets included, especially for the one beginning "Euclid alone has looked on Beauty bare."

Harrington, [Edward] Michael (1928–   ) American social scientist and author. Harrington is best known for his landmark study *The Other America* (1962; rev 1970), in which he demonstrated how increasing affluence creates a growing subculture of poverty. *The Vast Majority* (1977) discusses the effect of American capitalism on world poverty. In 1984 *The New American Poverty* re-examined the issues first discussed twenty-two years earlier in *The Other America*.

Harris, Frank (1856–1931) Irish-born American journalist, biographer, and novelist. Harris studied law, but finding its practice incompatible with action and adventure, he turned instead to journalism. Through the years he served as editor of some of the leading journals of England and America, including the *Fortnightly Review*, the *Saturday Review*, and *Vanity Fair*. He is remembered primarily for his scandalous quasi-autobiography, entitled *My Life and Loves* (3 vols, 1923–27). The book presents much information about the Victorian literary figures Harris knew, but because of explicit sexual scenes, it was banned in America and England for many years. His other publications include a malicious biography of Oscar Wilde (1916).

Harris, Joel Chandler (1848–1908) American journalist and author. Harris is famous for his humorous adaptations of black folk legends in the Uncle Remus stories. His tales, marked by simple humor and authentic black dialect, are undoubtedly the greatest in the school of black folk literature. He wrote many of his stories first for the Atlanta *Constitution* and later collected them into such works as UNCLE REMUS, HIS SONGS AND HIS SAYINGS, *Nights with Uncle Remus* (1883), and several other collections. They dealt chiefly with animals such as Brer Rabbit, and illustrated such maxims as the ability of intelligence to win out over brute force. Harris also wrote local-color stories of Southern life; these include *Mingo and Other Sketches in Black and White* (1884), which contrasts the aristocracy and the middle class, and the novel *Gabriel Tolliver* (1902), set in the Reconstruction period. *On the Plantation* (1892) is largely autobiographical. See TAR BABY.

Hart, Lorenz [Millon] (1895–1943)   American lyricist. A diminutive man (Hart stood 4 feet 9 inches), troubled throughout his short life by profound unhappiness, Hart nonetheless created the joyous Broadway love songs "With a Song in My Heart," "I Didn't Know What Time It Was," "The Most Beautiful Girl in the World," etc. He collaborated with Richard RODGERS on numerous popular successes, from *The Garrick Gaieties* (1925) and *A Connecticut Yankee* (1927) to *The Boys from Syracuse* (1938), *Pal Joey* (1940), and *By Jupiter* (1942).

Hart, Moss (1904–1961)   American playwright and librettist. Hart began his career with *The Hold-Up Man* (1925), but his first real success came with *Once in a Lifetime* (1930), the first of a long series of plays written in collaboration with George S. KAUFMAN. Together they wrote *Merrily We Roll Along* (1934), the PULITZER PRIZE-winning YOU CAN'T TAKE IT WITH YOU, *I'd Rather Be Right* (1937), *The American Way* (1939), THE MAN WHO CAME TO DINNER, and *George Washington Slept Here* (1940). Hart wrote the libretto for Irving BERLIN's *Face the Music* (1933) and for Kurt WEILL's *Lady in the Dark* (1941). He also wrote the plays *Winged Victory* (1943), *Light Up the Sky* (1948), and *The Climate of Eden* (1952). Hart won the Antoinette Perry Award for his direction of the musical *My Fair Lady* (1956). His autobiography, *Act One* (1959), became a best-seller.

Harte, [Francis] Bret[t] (1836–1902)   American short-story writer, novelist, poet, and humorist. Born in Albany, New York, Harte went to California when he was nineteen. There he mined gold and taught school before he became a journalist and helped found (1868) and edit THE OVERLAND MONTHLY. During the late 1860s, he published a collection of his poetry, *The Lost Galleon and Other Tales* (1867), and his satirical *Condensed Novels* (1867). It was during this period that he wrote his best-remembered pieces: *M'Liss* (1863–64), THE LUCK OF ROARING CAMP, THE OUTCASTS OF POKER FLAT, and PLAIN LANGUAGE FROM TRUTHFUL JAMES. He returned to the East in 1871 and subsequently was unable to continue writing at his previous level. From 1878 to 1885 he served as U.S. consul in Germany and Scotland and was a favorite in European literary circles. He then settled in England.

Harte's work is marked by sentimentality, humor, and a penchant for showing thieves, vagabonds, and miners as more admirable than conventional, law-abiding folk. He is remembered as a pioneer in Western local-color writing.

Hartford Wits   The name given to a group of 18th-century American poets, including Timothy DWIGHT, John TRUMBULL, and Joel BARLOW. The group was also known as the Connecticut Wits and the Yale Poets. Other members of the group, not all of them Yale men, were Lemuel Hopkins (1750–1801), David Humphries (1752–1818), Theodore Dwight, and Richard Alsop. Except for Barlow, the Wits were Federalist in politics and Calvinist in religion. See ANARCHIAD, THE.

Hartley, L[eslie] P[oles] (1895–1972)   English novelist and short-story writer. Frequently compared to Henry JAMES for both his style and his themes, Hartley was a perceptive and ironic observer of the social scene who gave his novels depth through his skillful use of symbolism. Of his many novels, the best known are the *Eustace and Hilda* trilogy (*The Shrimp and the Anemone*, 1944; *The Sixth Heaven*, 1946; and *Eustace and Hilda*, 1947) and THE GO-BETWEEN, both of which reveal an unusual insight into the psyches and viewpoint of children.

Hartzenbusch, Juan Eugenio (1806–1880)   Spanish dramatist. Hartzenbusch's best-known work, *Los amantes de Teruel* (*The Lovers of Teruel*, 1837), is considered one of the major Spanish romantic dramas because of its successful fusion of intense passion, melancholy, and medieval romance.

Harvard, John (1607–1638)   An English clergyman, the son of a butcher, for whom Harvard University is named. Harvard settled at Charlestown, Massachusetts, and became the first benefactor of the college at New Towne, bequeathing to it his library of three hundred volumes and half his estate, valued at £800. The college was renamed Harvard College in his honor in the year of his death, the third year of its existence.

Harvard Classics (1909–1910)   A fifty-volume set of books, containing selections from the literature of the world. It was edited by Charles W. Eliot, president emeritus of Harvard University, and published by P. F. Collier & Son. The original idea for the set can be traced to a chance remark of Eliot: "All the books needed for a real education could be set on a shelf five feet long!" From this remark and its physical makeup, the set is also known as "the Five-Foot Shelf."

Harvey, William (1578–1657)   English physician, physiologist, and anatomist. The discoverer of the theory of the circulation of the blood, Harvey announced his theory to the College of Physicians in 1616, but did not publish his treatise on it until 1628 (*Exercitatio anatomica de motu cordis et sanguinis in animalibus*). He also studied the reproductive functions of animals, and in his *Exercitationes de generatione animalium* (1651) theorized that both parents, not only the male, contribute to the form of the offspring.

Hašek, Jaroslav (1883–1923)   Czech satirist and journalist. His participation in World War I, first as an Austrian soldier, then as a Czech legionnaire in Russia and, finally, as a commissar of the Red Army, was the main source of his literary inspiration. The figure of Švejk appears in prewar satirical short stories; it is developed into a full type in the four-volume unfinished novel *Osudy dobrého vojáka Švejka za světové války* (1921–23; tr *The*

Good Soldier Schweik, 1930, 1974). This gargantuan satire on the decaying military machine of the Austrian-Hungarian empire, and on war in general, chronicles the misadventures of the seemingly idiotic but good-hearted Švejk, which by their very absurdity point up the stupidity of war.

Hasidism   A Jewish religious-social movement which arose in Eastern Europe in the second half of the 18th century. The Hasidic movement was established by Rabbi Israel Baal-Shem-Tov (1700–60), who taught the ways of God through the telling of stories. According to Hasidic teachings, the entire world is blessed with God's presence, and it is the happiness and ecstasy with which one worships God, and the kindness shown toward one's fellow man, that are the important principles guiding man's life.

Hastings, Warren (1732–1818)   English statesman and administrator of India. Hastings went to Calcutta in the East India Company's service in 1750, becoming successively a member of the Calcutta council, governor of Bengal, and governor-general of India. He was impeached in 1788 for corruption and cruelty, chiefly because of his conduct in regard to the zamindar of Benares, whom he deposed, and the begum of Oudh, whose treasures he had allegedly confiscated. Although he was prosecuted by Edmund BURKE, among others, his famous trial resulted in acquittal in 1795. Hastings is the subject of a famous essay by Thomas Babington MACAULAY.

Hastings, Battle of   Battle occurring in 1066 near Senlac in Sussex, England, where Harold II died defending his claim to the English throne against the Norman WILLIAM THE CONQUEROR. William was crowned shortly afterward, thus effecting the "Norman Conquest," which greatly influenced English history, language, and literature.

Hasty Pudding, The (1796)   A mock-heroic poem by Joel BARLOW, describing the making and eating of the celebrated New England mush. It was one of the most popular of Barlow's works.

Hathaway, Anne   The wife of SHAKESPEARE.

Hathor   The Egyptian sky goddess, worshiped under several forms, in whom the sun was supposed to rise and set. As the personification of the sky, Hathor was the female counterpart of OSIRIS and was represented as a cow with a disc and two plumes. Like Isis, she was a goddess of love, mirth, and joy, corresponding to the Greek APHRODITE. Her temple at Denderah still exists.

Hatter, The   A character in Lewis Carroll's ALICE'S ADVENTURES IN WONDERLAND. During the course of a mad tea party he puts a riddle to Alice, "Why is a raven like a writing desk?" to which there is no answer. He has a watch that tells the day but not the time, and his eccentric behavior includes pouring hot tea on the Dormouse in order to wake him. The character is a burlesque of the expression "MAD AS A HATTER."

Hauptmann, Gerhart [Johann Robert] (1862–1946)   German dramatist. Though Hauptmann wanted at first to be a sculptor, he turned early to writing and produced a romantic epic entitled *Promethidenlos* (*The Lot of the Promethides*, 1885). But in accordance with the literary tenor of the times, he soon turned to realism in the story "Bahnwärter Thiel" (1888; tr "Flagman Thiel," 1933), and then, in his first play, *Vor Sonnenaufgang* (1889; tr *Before Dawn*, 1909), he developed a naturalistic style. This play, dedicated to "the consistent realist Bjarne P. Holmsen" (see Arno HOLZ) and influenced by IBSEN, treats the dangers of alcoholism in a starkly down-to-earth manner; it aroused a storm of critical controversy at its first performance and marked the establishment of German NATURALISM as a recognized literary movement. Hauptmann himself wrote several more plays in a similar style, such as *Das Friedensfest* (1890; tr *The Coming of Peace*, 1906) and THE WEAVERS; but in HANNELE, it became clear that his development was taking him away from naturalism. Though there are many naturalistic elements in this play, a large portion of it is taken up by an ecstatic vision of the heaven into which a dying girl is about to enter. Other plays, such as DRAYMAN HENSCHEL, *Rose Bernd* (1903; tr 1913) and *Und Pippa tanzt!* (1906; tr *And Pippa Dances!* 1907), also show this mixture of a basically naturalistic style and subject matter with deeply symbolic overtones or insertions. And finally, in such plays as THE SUNKEN BELL and *Der arme Heinrich* (1902; tr *Poor Henry*, 1913), he does away with naturalistic elements altogether.

After becoming established, Hauptmann was long regarded as the patriarch of modern German literature, but none of his later works had the same immediate appeal or aroused the same stormy controversy as his earlier ones. And yet his later period was by no means barren, and among its notable products are *Der Narr in Christo Emanuel Quint* (1910; tr *The Fool in Christ, Emanuel Quint*, 1912) and *Im Wirbel der Berufung* (*In the Confusion of Vocation*, 1936), both novels; "Der Ketzer von Soana" (1918; tr "The Heretic of Soana," 1923), a story; and the epic *Till Eulenspiegel* (1928). Among his late plays are *Vor Sonnenuntergang* (*Before Sunset*, 1932) and a monumental treatment of the story of the house of ATREUS in his *Atriden-Tetralogie* (*Atrides Tetralogy*), which includes *Iphigenie in Delphi* (1941), *Iphigenie in Aulis* (1943), *Agamemnons Tod* (*Agamemnon's Death*, 1947), and *Elektra* (1948). He was awarded the NOBEL PRIZE in Literature in 1912. See EULENSPIEGEL, TILL.

Havel, Václav (1936–   )   Czech dramatist and poet. Associated with one of the small Prague theatres (Na Zábradlí), Havel was an active participant in the liberalizing movement in Czech culture which led to the "Prague spring" of 1968. After the Soviet-led invasion, he became a spokesman of the Czech civil rights movement (Charter 77), and continues to write despite constant harassment and police surveillance.

Havel's first important play was *Zahradní slavnost* (1963; tr *The Garden Party*, 1969), in which he used the devices of absurdist theatre to satirize the dehumanization of language, human relations, and social institutions. In *Vyrozumění* (1965; tr *The Memorandum*, 1967), the crisis of human communication reaches an extreme point when the bureaucracy introduces an artificial language, Ptydepe, which is too difficult to be mastered. Like ORWELL and ION-ESCO, Havel perceives the crisis of communication as a symptom of deep social malaise. *Ztížená možnost soustředění* (1968; tr *The Increased Difficulty of Concentration*, 1972) was Havel's last play produced in Czechoslovakia; the plays written between 1970 and 1976 were published in Toronto in 1977.

Havelok the Dane   A hero of medieval romance. The orphan son of the Danish king Birkabegn, Havelok is exposed at sea through the treachery of his guardians. When the raft drifts to the coast of Lincolnshire, a fisherman, Grim, finds the young prince and brings him up as his own son. Believed to be a peasant, he is united with a princess who is to be degraded because she stands in the way of certain ambitious nobles. But Havelok, having learned the story of his birth, obtains the aid of an army of Danes to recover his wife's possessions, and in time becomes the king of Denmark.

Havisham, Miss   In Charles Dickens's GREAT EXPECTATIONS, a rich, eccentric old recluse who lives in a decaying mansion. Years before, she was jilted on the eve of her wedding and has since worn a wedding dress, complete with veil, white satin shoes, and bridal flowers in her hair. She has adopted Estella with the design of using her as an instrument of vengeance on the male sex; this she does by educating Estella to hate and torture men. She repents of her schemes just before her death, caused by shock and burns when her ancient gown catches fire.

Estella Havisham   Miss Havisham's ward, later revealed to be the daughter of Abel MAGWITCH. She is a beautiful, self-possessed girl, convinced of her own heartlessness. Pip loves her, but she marries Bentley Drummle, knowing that they will torture each other. After Drummle's death and the misery of her marriage, she is at last ready for Pip's love.

Hawkes, Jacquetta [Hopkins] (1910–   ) English archeologist and writer. Much of Hawkes's early archeological work dealt with the British Isles, notably *Early Britain* (1945) and *A Land* (1951). Her nonarcheological writings include poetry, essays, and *Dragon's Mouth* (1952), a play cowritten with her second husband, J. B. PRIESTLEY. In *The Atlas of Early Man* (1976) she examines human activities at various points in prehistory from a global perspective. *Mortimer Wheeler: Adventurer in Archaeology* was published in 1982.

Hawkes, John [Clendennin Burne, Jr.] (1925–   )   American novelist. A leading experimental novelist, Hawkes sees the modern world as so fragmented and chaotic that it can no longer be described by the ordered conventions of plot, character, and narrative. In such works as *The Blood Oranges* (1971), *Death, Sleep and the Traveler* (1974), and *The Passion Artist* (1979), fantasies, nightmares, and the murky world of the unconscious supersede "reality." Hawkes's vision is a powerful combination of the comic and the unutterably horrible.

Hawkins, Sir John (1532–1595)   English navigator and naval commander. With the expeditions of his nephew Sir Francis DRAKE, Hawkins's privateering voyages to the Spanish-American coast helped bring about the break between England and Spain. As Rear Admiral, Hawkins helped defeat the Spanish Armada in 1588. He died at sea, as second in command under Drake, on an expedition to the West Indies.

Hawks, Howard [Winchester] (1896–1977) American film director. Hawks's films tend to explore either the activities of spirited and sharp-witted heroines (e.g., *His Girl Friday*, 1939) or the camaraderies and tensions that develop within male groups (e.g., *Dawn Patrol*, 1930). The quintessential AUTEUR director, Hawks made successful movies in virtually every one of the standard Hollywood genres and at the same time succeeded in marking his films with his own unique stylistic and thematic characteristics. Among his best films are *Scarface* (1932), *Twentieth Century* (1934), *Bringing Up Baby* (1938), *Only Angels Have Wings* (1939), *To Have and Have Not* (1944), *The Big Sleep* (1946), and *Rio Bravo* (1959).

Hawthorne, Nathaniel (1804–1864)   American novelist and short-story writer. Born into an old New England family, Hawthorne was very much aware of his ancestors. The Hathornes (as they spelled it) participated in the Salem witch trials in the 17th century, and later in the Quaker persecutions. The writer, reflecting on the past, always felt a sense of guilt and made this a theme in his work.

The son of a sea captain, Hawthorne was educated at Bowdoin College, where he knew Franklin Pierce and Henry Wadsworth LONGFELLOW. For twelve years, after his graduation in 1825, he lived in his mother's house in Salem; in virtual retirement, he wrote sketches and stories for annuals and newspapers. In 1828 he anonymously published a novel, FANSHAWE, based on his college life. Suddenly ashamed of his work, he withdrew most of the copies and burned them. Devoting his energies to short fiction, he explored the nature of sin. Hawthorne's first important book was a collection of short tales and sketches called TWICE-TOLD TALES.

In Boston as surveyor of the Customs House, Hawthorne renewed his acquaintance with Longfellow and the literary world. He invested his savings in the Transcendentalist experiment at BROOK FARM in 1841 and married Sophia Peabody the following year. Having found communal living unattractive, Hawthorne brought his bride to the Old Manse in Concord, Massachusetts. The Manse, owned by the Ripleys, had been the home of Ralph Waldo EMERSON. Here the author enjoyed three and a half happy years, during which his first daughter, Una, was born. He published his second collection of stories, MOSSES FROM AN OLD MANSE; this volume was brilliantly reviewed by Herman MELVILLE, establishing an important friendship between the two men.

Later the Hawthornes moved to Salem, where the writer served again as surveyor in a Customs House. Removed from duty in 1849 as a result of political maneuvering, Hawthorne began to write his masterpiece, THE SCARLET LETTER. The book brought him fame and some degree of financial independence. Although collections of early short pieces appeared after 1850, the year marked the end of Hawthorne's dedication to short fiction. He turned to the composition of novels and a few books for children. Living in Lenox, Massachusetts, near Melville, Hawthorne wrote THE HOUSE OF THE SEVEN GABLES and THE BLITHEDALE ROMANCE. He collected the tales and sketches of *The Snow Image and Other Twice-Told Tales* (1815) and wrote a campaign biography for his friend Franklin Pierce. When Pierce was elected president, he appointed Hawthorne consul at Liverpool and Manchester (1853–57). After 1857, Hawthorne traveled through Europe for three years, completing his last published novel, THE MARBLE FAUN, in England.

On his return, Hawthorne collected a series of sketches about England called *Our Old Home* (1863), a delightful record of his literary pilgrimages. During the last decade of his life, he wrote only sporadically. At his death, four unfinished novels were found among his notes. Among these were *Septimus Felton* (1871) and THE DOLLIVER ROMANCE.

Turning to the historical past, Hawthorne found Puritan New England a congenial setting for his work. Claiming the privileges of the romancer, he deplored the lack of material for the artist in contemporary America, a land of shadowless daylight. His precise, almost classic prose style and his use of symbol and allegory made a great impression on his contemporary Herman Melville, and on the later American writers Henry JAMES and William FAULKNER. See TANGLEWOOD TALES.

Hayden, Robert [Earl] (1913–1980)   American poet. Throughout his career, Hayden remained steadfastly independent of poetic schools and movements. His early poetry focused primarily on black history. *Heart-Shape in the Dust* (1940) deals with the sufferings and achievements of an enslaved but undefeated people. *Words in the Mourning Time* (1970) contains elegies for Martin Luther King, Jr., and Robert Kennedy, and antiwar poems. The thematic thrust in Hayden's later work refers to the frustrations of the newly liberated black man. In *Angle of Ascent* (1975) Hayden summons forth figures from the past, such as Nat Turner and Frederick Douglass, transforming them into personal symbols. In *American Journal* (1979) he com-

bines the sounds of street talk with traditional ballad form to evoke the Detroit slums he knew as a youth.

Haydn, Franz Joseph (1732–1809)   Austrian composer. Haydn was *Kapellmeister* of the powerful Esterhazy family in Hungary (1760–90), where he wrote some of his greatest music. In England (1791–92; 1794–95) he wrote and conducted the first performances of his last twelve symphonies, his greatest works in the genre, now known as the "London Symphonies." In Vienna (from 1795), he wrote his last six masses, his finest chamber music, and the two great oratorios *The Creation* and *The Seasons*. His total output includes one hundred four symphonies, concerti, twenty-four operas, fourteen masses and other church music, sixty-eight string quartets, much other chamber music, fifty-two piano sonatas, and songs. Haydn's music shows much development over his long creative life. In the beginning, he was under the influence of a rather superficial group of Viennese composers, but in the long years in the country in Hungary, as Haydn himself says, "There was no one about me to confuse and torment me, and I was compelled to become original." In later years, important influences were the young MOZART and the choral works of HANDEL, which he heard in England; these inspired the writing of the oratorios and left their mark on the late masses. Haydn was a giant force in the development of classical symphonic form and orchestration and a pioneer in string quartets.

Hayne, Paul Hamilton (1830–1886)   American poet. Hayne contributed to the *Southern Literary Messenger* and collected his *Poems* in 1855. Two years later, he founded *Russell's Magazine*. Ardently patriotic, he wrote fervent poems on the CIVIL WAR; one of these is "The Battle of Charleston Harbor." During Sherman's march to the sea, Hayne's mansion was destroyed. He moved to Georgia, where he supported his family entirely from his writings. Among these are *Legends and Lyrics* (1872), *The Mountain of the Lovers* (1875), and *The Broken Battalions* (1885). His work is chiefly distinguished for its landscapes of the South, as in "Aspects of the Pines" and "The Cottage on the Hill." Hayne edited the poems of his friend Henry Timrod (1828–67) in 1873.

Hazard of New Fortunes, A (1890)   A novel by William Dean HOWELLS. A thoughtful commentary on social and economic issues, the novel is about a newly rich Pennsylvania-German, Dryfoos, who moves his family to New York, hoping his son and two daughters may rise in society. To deflect his son, Conrad, from joining the ministry, Dryfoos buys a magazine and makes Conrad its publisher. The plot focuses on the family's difficulties in scaling the New York social ladder and the moral problems of Basil March (also a character in *Their Wedding Journey*, 1871), who is editor of Dryfoos's magazine. When Dryfoos tells him to fire an old socialist on the magazine, March resigns rather than do so. But young Conrad too has turned to radical politics. At a labor riot, Conrad tries to rescue the old socialist from being beaten to death and is himself killed by a stray bullet. Dryfoos sells the magazine to March and takes his daughters to Europe to continue the social climb.

Hazlitt, William (1778–1830) English essayist and literary critic. At first dedicated to a career as a painter, Hazlitt realized his talent was insufficient and turned to writing. Hazlitt became known for his studies and lectures on contemporary authors and the Elizabethan playwrights. His firm political liberalism estranged him from his friends WORDSWORTH, COLERIDGE, and SOUTHEY, because he felt they had betrayed the liberalism of their youth. He went to London in 1808 and became a contributor to newspapers and periodicals, notably the *Edinburgh Review* and the *Examiner*.

After Coleridge, Hazlitt is probably the most penetrating and erudite of the early romantic critics, and is still eminently readable. Among his important works are: *The Characters of Shakespeare's Plays* (1817); *The Round Table* (1817, with Leigh Hunt); *A View of the English Stage* (1818); *Lectures on the English Poets* (1818); *Lectures on the English Comic Writers* (1819); *Lectures on the Dramatic Literature of the Age of Elizabeth* (1820); *Table Talk* (1821–22); *Liber Amoris* (1823), an account of an unhappy love affair; and *The Spirit of the Age* (1825). He is considered one of the greatest masters of English prose.

H.D. See DOOLITTLE, HILDA.

Headlong Hall (1816) A novel by Thomas Love PEACOCK. A brilliantly witty piece, it presents the mildly philosophic opinions on life exchanged by Mrs. Foster, the optimist, Mr. Escot, the pessimist, and Mr. Jenkinson, the status-quo-ite. It is a satire on the idealistic aspirations of romanticism.

Heaney, Seamus [Justin] (1939–   ) Irish poet and writer. Heaney has been cited, notably by Robert LOWELL, as Ireland's best poet since Yeats. Several tensions inherent in Heaney's own situation are reflected in his poetry: his status as a member of the Catholic minority in a predominantly Protestant province; and Northern Ireland's long-drawn-out internal war, where a tenuous and bitter status quo between the warring Catholics and Protestants is frequently punctuated by outbursts of bloody and consuming violence. Although he has been called the "laureate of violence," Heaney's concern is less with the vehicles of violence than with those who are willy-nilly caught up in its upsurge and consequently must suffer it. His concept of violence, moreover, is not based on the current situation alone but stems from his belief that religious violence is inevitably part and parcel of the Irish situation, where, through the centuries, "civilized outrage" has been subdued into muteness by the powerful dynamic of "tribal, intimate revenge." Accordingly, mythological motifs abound in his poetry; there is also concern with rural disintegration, most effectively manifested in his earlier collections of verse, notably *Death of a Naturalist* (1966) and

Door into the Dark (1969), and a theme to which he returned in *Wintering Out* (1972), *North* (1975), and *Field Work* (1979). He has also published a collection of his prose writings, *Preoccupations: Selected Prose 1968–1978* (1980).

Hearn, [Patricio] Lafcadio [Tessima Carlos] (1850–1904) American journalist and author. Of Greek and English-Irish parentage, Hearn was born in the Ionian Islands. He is noted for the poetic prose style of his exotic and fantastic tales; he dedicated himself to "the worship of the Old, the Queer, the Strange, the Exotic, the Monstrous." After some early publication, including translations of stories by Théophile GAUTIER (in *One of Cleopatra's Nights*, 1882), Hearn achieved success in works set in Louisiana and the Caribbean. *Chita* (1887) is a novel about a young girl who survives a tidal wave on a small island; YOUMA is concerned with a slave insurrection.

Hearn's search for the exotic led him to Japan in 1890, where he spent the rest of his life teaching and writing about the Japanese scene. He married a Japanese woman and became a Japanese citizen under the name of Koizumi Yakumo. He published several books on Japan, including *Kokoro* (1896), *In Ghostly Japan* (1899), and *Japan: An Attempt at Interpretation* (1904). But his best work was his first, *Glimpses of Unfamiliar Japan* (1894).

Hearst, William Randolph (1863–1951) American newspaper publisher. Beginning his career on the San Francisco *Daily Examiner* in 1887, Hearst acquired a vast newspaper and magazine empire, which he ruled from his estate, San Simeon, in California. His name early became synonymous with "yellow journalism," and his skill in the methods of mass communication helped magnify a Cuban insurrection into the Spanish-American War. A staunch isolationist, Hearst served in Congress (1903–7) and later ran unsuccessfully for mayor of New York City (1905) and governor of New York (1906). Orson WELLES's *Citizen Kane* (1941) is a fictionalized film portrait of Hearst.

Heartbreak House (written 1913; prod 1920) A play by George Bernard SHAW. It is a complex allegorical work in which Shaw indicts apathy, confusion, and lack of purpose as the causes of the world's problems. The characters—all larger than life and with symbolic names—are gathered at the home of an eccentric sea captain; they each represent an evil in the modern world. Into their midst comes young Ellie Dunn, whose search for a husband Shaw treats as a new generation searching for a way of life. While the play is essentially a pessimistic one, it ends on a note of optimism: The first bombs of a war caused by the old order kill Boss Mangan, the avaricious capitalist, and Ellie selects as her spiritual husband the eccentric old owner of Heartbreak House, Shotover, who represents common sense.

Heart of Darkness (1902) A long short story by Joseph CONRAD. MARLOW tells his friends of an experience in the (then) Belgian Congo, where he once ran a river steamer for a trading company. He describes the cruel colonial exploitation there. Fascinated by reports about the powerful white trader Kurtz, Marlow went into the jungle in search of him, expecting to find in his character a clue to the evil around him. He found Kurtz living with the natives and brought him away, dying; Kurtz's last words were "The horror! The horror!" The "heart of darkness" is the jungle and the primitive, subconscious heart of man.

Heart of Midlothian, The (1818)   A novel by Sir Walter Scott. The title alludes to the old jail at the center of Edinburgh, where the novel opens with scenes of the Porteous riots in 1736, when the commander of the Civic Guard, Captain Porteous, was lynched by a mob of incensed citizens after he had fired on a crowd. The plot concerns Effie Deans, a farmer's daughter, who is seduced by George Staunton, and who is tried and sentenced to death for murdering their child. Her loyal half-sister Jeanie determines to walk to London to seek a pardon from George II and, in spite of all obstacles, actually accomplishes her task. Effie marries Staunton, but shortly afterward he is shot by a gypsy boy, in reality his illegitimate son, who had not died after all. Jeanie marries Reuben Butler, a Presbyterian minister. The novel has a factual basis.

Heart of the Matter, The (1948)   A novel by Graham Greene. Set in West Africa, its hero is Scobie, an English Roman Catholic who is torn between his adulterous love for a young woman and his duty to his wife and his religion.

Heathcliff   The central character of Emily Brontë's novel Wuthering Heights. Spurned by his childhood love, Catherine, he is obsessed with a desire for revenge that not only poisons her life and his but very nearly taints their children. Heathcliff is a romantic, almost demonic figure drawn on a heroic scale.

Heathen Chinee, The   See Plain Language from Truthful James.

Heat of the Day, The (1949)   A novel by Elizabeth Bowen. Set in wartime London, it is a melodramatic but sensitive story of espionage, counter-espionage, and suicide, and of the emotions of the people involved.

heaven (fr OE, *heofon*)   The word properly denotes the abode of the Deity and his angels; also the upper air.

In the Ptolemaic system, the heavens were the successive spheres of space enclosing the central earth at different distances and revolving around it at different speeds. The first seven were those of the so-called planets, the Moon, Mercury, Venus, the Sun, Mars, Jupiter, and Saturn; the eighth was the firmament containing all the fixed stars; the ninth was the crystalline sphere, invented by Hipparchus (2nd century BC) to account for the procession of the equinoxes. These were known as *The Nine Heavens*; the tenth —added much later—was the *primum mobile*.

According to the Muslims, there are seven heavens. *The first heaven* is of pure silver, and here the stars, each with

its angel warder, are hung out like lamps on golden chains; it is the abode of Adam and Eve. *The second heaven* is of pure gold, and is the domain of John the Baptist and Jesus. *The third heaven* is of pearl, and is allotted to Joseph. Here Azrael, the angel of death, is stationed and is forever writing in a large book the names of those just born and blotting out the names of the newly dead. *The fourth heaven* is of white gold, and is Enoch's. Here dwells the Angel of Tears, whose height is "five hundred days' journey," who sheds ceaseless tears for the sins of man. *The fifth heaven* is of silver, and is Aaron's. Here dwells the Avenging Angel, who presides over elemental fire. *The sixth heaven* is composed of ruby and garnet, and is presided over by Moses. Here dwells the Guardian Angel of heaven and earth, half snow and half fire. *The seventh heaven* is formed of divine light beyond the power of tongue to describe, and is ruled by Abraham. Each inhabitant is bigger than the whole earth and has seventy thousand heads, each head seventy thousand mouths, each mouth seventy thousand tongues, and each tongue speaks seventy thousand languages, all forever employed in chanting of the Most High.

To be in the seventh heaven is to be supremely happy. The cabalists maintained that there are seven heavens, each rising in happiness above the other, the seventh being the abode of God and the highest class of angels.

Heaven and Hell (1956)   An essay by Aldous Huxley. It describes the effects the drug mescalin has on the mind, and compares the ecstatic and depressed states it produces with mystics' accounts of heaven and hell. Huxley had described his own experiments with mescalin in *The Doors of Perception* (1954).

Hebbel, [Christian] Friedrich (1813–1863) German dramatist, known especially for the philosophical and historical theories which, though they sometimes enhance his works, often mar the dramatic effect. Almost all Hebbel's plays take place at historical turning points, in accordance with ideas that he formulated in *Mein Wort über das Drama* (*My Word on the Drama*, 1843) and in the preface to his tragedy Maria Magdalena. Among his plays are also the tragedy Judith (1841), about the biblical heroine; *Herodes and Mariamne* (1850); *Agnes Bernaner* (1855), a tragedy of love between a prince and a commoner; *Gyges und sein Ring* (*Gyges and His Ring*, 1856), based on the story of Candaules; and *Die Nibelungen* (1862), a trilogy based on the story of the Nibelungenlied. In style, Hebbel's plays are considered realistic, as opposed to the idealism of the classical and romantic authors of the earlier 19th century.

Hebe   In Greek mythology, the goddess of youth and the daughter of Hera and Zeus. Hebe was the cupbearer of the immortals before Ganymede superseded her. She was the wife of Heracles and had the power of making the aged young again.

Hebrews, The Epistle of Paul the Apostle to the   A New Testament book. Scholars place its date of writing around AD 100, but have been unable to identify its author; it is generally agreed that Hebrews is not an actual PAULINE EPISTLE. One of the most eloquent books in the New Testament, Hebrews stresses the powerful role of JESUS as the highest priest of God, whose personal sacrifice was made for all men.

Hecate   One of the TITANS of Greek mythology. The only one who retained her power under the rule of ZEUS, Hecate became a deity of the lower world after taking part in the search for PERSEPHONE. She taught witchcraft and sorcery and was a goddess of the dead. As she combined the attributes of, and became identified with, SELENE, ARTEMIS, and Persephone, she was represented as a triple goddess and was sometimes described as having three heads: one of a horse, one of a dog, and one of a lion. Her offerings consisted of dogs, honey, and black lambs, which were sacrificed to her at crossroads.

In Shakespeare's MACBETH, she appears as the queen of witches. After berating the three "weird sisters" for having made prophecies to Macbeth without her knowledge, she joins them in completing his destruction.

Hecht, Ben (1893–1964)   American journalist, playwright, and novelist. Born in New York City, Hecht began his career in Chicago, where he worked as a reporter and took part in that city's "literary renaissance" (see CHICAGO GROUP). His first novel, *Erik Dorn* (1921), was based on his experiences as Berlin reporter for the Chicago *News*. A prolific writer, Hecht wrote numerous short stories during his Chicago days, many of them being included in *The Collected Stories of Ben Hecht* (1945).

Hecht collaborated with Charles MACARTHUR on two plays: *The Front Page* (1928), a fast-paced portrayal of newspaper life, and *Twentieth Century* (1932). *A Child of the Century* (1954) is his frank, entertaining, and unconventional autobiography.

Hector   Eldest son of PRIAM, the noblest and most magnanimous of all the Trojan chieftains in Homer's ILIAD. After holding out for ten years, Hector was slain by ACHILLES, who lashed him to his chariot and dragged the dead body in triumph thrice round the walls of Troy. The *Iliad* concludes with the funeral obsequies of Hector and PATROCLUS.

In modern times his name has somewhat deteriorated, for it is used today for a swaggering bully, and "to hector" means to browbeat, bully, bluster.

Hecuba   In Homer's ILIAD, the wife of PRIAM and mother of HECTOR. Hecuba is a tragic figure in Euripides' THE TROJAN WOMEN. In his HECUBA, her grief has made her a kind of Fury. In revenge for the murder of her son POLYDORUS, she blinds the Thracian king Polymestor, after killing his children. According to myth (perhaps through confusion with HECATE), she was transformed into a fiery-eyed hellhound. In Shakespeare's HAMLET, the Player King is deeply moved by his own speech about her, and Hamlet marvels, "What's Hecuba to him, or he to Hecuba?"

Hecuba (?425 BC)   A tragedy by EURIPIDES. Hecuba, queen of Troy, has seen all of her fifty children die except her daughter Polyxena and POLYDORUS, her youngest son, whom she sent to King Polymestor in Thrace at the beginning of the war. As the play begins, she lies exhausted in front of her tent in Chalcidice, where the Greek expedition has taken her. A messenger comes to announce the decision of the Greeks in council: Polyxena must die to assuage the shade of Achilles. Polyxena goes to her death with dignity; soon after, the body of Polydorus is brought onto the stage. When Hecuba learns which of her children this is, she yearns for revenge. She lures Polymestor to her tent, blinds him, and kills his sons. Polymestor is reduced to an animal state as he crawls and gropes his way out of the tent. The closing scene shows Polymestor and Hecuba arguing their cases before Agamemnon. When Agamemnon decides for Hecuba, Polymestor breaks into prophecy and foresees the murder of Agamemnon and the horrible death of Hecuba, who will bark like a dog.

Many critics, approaching *Hecuba* as a drama of character, have found contradictions in the plot, which is divided into two parts: the death of Polyxena and the blinding of Polymestor. Hecuba is involved in both of them, and her character changes through the play, but Euripides' tragic conception concerns more than Hecuba. The theme of the play is the brutality of suffering. Though Hecuba is the principal actor, the climactic speech is the prophecy of Polymestor, which displays Polymestor and Hecuba at the same bestial level. The key to Euripides' purpose is his use of myth; the old tales of Agamemnon's murder and Hecuba's animal metamorphosis become the climax to the long series of brutalities in the play.

Hedda Gabler (1890)   A play by IBSEN. Hedda, a ruthless, neurotic woman, is bored with her dull, scholarly husband, repelled by the idea of her possible pregnancy, and concerned that she may have to forgo certain luxuries if her husband fails to be appointed a professor at the university. She learns that meek Thea Elvsted has helped reform the brilliant but dissipated Eilert Lövberg, who had once been in love with Hedda, and that the success of Lövberg's new book has made him her husband's rival for the professorship. Determined to show her power over Lövberg and thwart Thea's good influence, she lures him back into dissipation. She finds the missing manuscript of a second book, far more important to Lövberg than the first, but lets him believe that it is lost beyond recall. When, in despair, he threatens to end his life, she gives him a pistol and urges him to "die beautifully." He dies quite horribly, and Hedda finds herself in the power of Judge Brack, who knows that Hedda gave Lövberg the pistol and intends to use his knowledge to make her his mistress. Hedda finds this situation unbearable and "dies beautifully" by putting a bullet through her head.

Heep, Uriah   In Charles Dickens's DAVID COPPERFIELD, a clerk of Mr. Wickfield. One of the most famous characters in fiction, he is a detestable sneak, who is everlastingly forcing on one's attention that he is " 'umble." Actually, Uriah is designing and malignant, and he becomes a blackmailing tyrant over Mr. Wickfield. His infamy is brought to light by Mr. Micawber. His name has come to imply ambition and malice cloaked in a false humility.

Hegel, Georg Friedrich Wilhelm (1770–1831) German philosopher. Hegel greatly influenced the study of history and metaphysics, in that he saw reality as a dynamic process rather than as a reflection of static ideals. The process of reality, he maintained, is governed by the dialectical law: every thesis implies its own contradiction, or antithesis, and their conflict ends in a synthesis which again brings forth its antithesis. History, understood in terms of the dialectic, is produced by the conflicting impulses and interests of men, but at the same time shows the progressive self-realization of human reason and freedom. Great men are those whose personal aims coincide with the aim of the historical process; and in the later years of his life, Hegel used this concept of history to justify support of the Prussian state. His concept of the dialectic was developed by many subsequent philosophers, notably Marx and Engels; but the latter discarded Hegelian idealism and applied the dialectic to a materialistic view of history. Hegel's works include *Die Phänomenologie des Geistes* (*The Phenomenology of the Spirit*, 1807) and *Grundlinien der Philosophie des Rechts* (*The Philosophy of Right*, 1821). He was a close friend of both HÖLDERLIN and Friedrich SCHELLING, with whom he held many ideas in common.

hegira (Arab, "the departure") The flight of MUHAMMED from MECCA to MEDINA when he was expelled by the magistrates, July 16, 622. In 639 the caliph Omar decreed that the Muslim calendar would date from this event. By extension, the word has come to mean any exodus undertaken to avoid persecution.

Heian The second Japanese historical period (794–1185), following the NARA period and preceding the KAMAKURA. It saw the development of an exquisitely refined culture under the imperial court at Kyoto. Literature and the arts were marked by an extreme elegance, strongly influenced by Buddhist and Chinese thought. THE TALE OF GENJI and THE PILLOW-BOOK OF SEI SHŌNAGON are products of this age. It was dominated by the Fujiwara family and is also known as the Fujiwara period.

Heiberg, Gunnar Edvard Rode (1857–1929) Norwegian playwright and essayist. A clever satirist, Heiberg mocked the absurd pettiness of Norwegian political life and treated other current concerns in such plays as *Kong Midas* (1890), *Gerts have* (1894), and *Det store lod* (1895). In *Balkonen* (1894; tr *The Balcony*, 1922) and *Kjoerlighedens tragedie* (1904; tr *The Tragedy of Love*, 1921), he turned his lyric powers to an analysis of the primitive force of sexual passion.

Heidegger, Martin (1889–1976) German philosopher, considered a leading figure in modern EXISTENTIALISM. Heidegger has had great influence in German-speaking countries and in France, where SARTRE, in particular, esteemed him, and thereafter in England and America. Heidegger himself was influenced by KIERKEGAARD and NIETZSCHE, and by Edmund HUSSERL, founder of PHENOMENOLOGY.

His complex philosophy is made more difficult by the fact that he spurned some of the conventions of philosophical discourse. He developed a dense, quasipoetic diction by using words according to his interpretation of root meanings reaching back to the pre-Socratic philosophers.

All of Heidegger's work revolves around the essential inquiry: what is the nature of being? In his most important book, *Sein und Zeit* (1927; tr *Being and Time*, 1962), he distinguishes between two types of being: human existence (*Dasein*) and nonhuman presence (*Vorhandensein*). Man, at birth, is "thrown" into existence, not apart from things, but "standing out" from them, as represented in the etymology of *exist*. When the human being becomes absorbed by things, his existence becomes "inauthentic." Man is the only being capable of trying to understand his existence, but he "forfeits" this by allowing himself to be distracted. Authentic existences are lived by those who experience *Angst* ("anxiety; dread") in the face of "nothingness and nowhere." As man confronts nothingness, all the "everydayness" that robs him of his dignity disappears.

In later writings, such as *Gelassenheit* (1959; tr *Discourse on Thinking*, 1966) and *Unterwegs zur Sprache* (1959; tr *On the Way to Language*, 1971), Heidegger became increasingly convinced of the primacy of language in the origin and manifestations of being, and he held poetry to be the privileged form of language. "Language is the house of Being" is one of his characteristic expressions. He urged a meditative "listening" to the world in place of the oppositional posture, as he saw it, of rationalistic thought since Socrates.

Heidelberg romanticism See GERMAN ROMANTICISM.

Heidenstam, [Carl Gustaf] Verner von (1859–1940) Swedish poet and novelist. An aspiring painter, Heidenstam published his first collection of poetry, *Vallfart och vandringsar* (1888), with the encouragement of STRINDBERG. The vigorous modern rhythms and exuberant mood of the poems had a significant effect on young writers who were rebelling against NATURALISM. *Dikter* (1895) and *Nya dikter* (1915) further revealed Heidenstam's lyrical gifts. After 1890 he became chiefly a prose writer; in 1916 he received the NOBEL PRIZE in Literature.

Heidi A children's story of life in the Swiss Alps by Johanna Spyri (1827–1901).

Heike monogatari See TALES OF THE HEIKE, THE.

Heilbroner, Robert [Louis] (1919–   ) American economist and writer. One of Heilbroner's best-known books, *The Worldly Philosophers* (1953, rev 1980), is a lively and engaging analysis of such economic thinkers as Adam SMITH, Karl MARX, and John Maynard KEYNES. Other economic studies which have become popular texts are *The Making of Economic Society* (1962), *The Economic Problem* (1971), and *Beyond Boom and Crash* (1978). Books such as *The Future as History* (1960) and *An Inquiry into the Human Prospect* (1975; rev 1980) earned Heilbroner a reputation as a constructive critic of traditional social values. *Marxism: For and Against* (1980) is a summary of Marxist ideas and the limits of their applicability. *Five Economic Challenges* (1981), written with Lester Thurow, and *Economics Explained* (1982) further elaborate his views.

Heimdall One of the gods of Scandinavian mythology, son of the nine virgin daughters of Aegir and called the White God with the Golden Teeth. As watchman of ASGARD, Heimdall dwelt on the edge of heaven, guarded the rainbow bridge BIFROST, and possessed a mighty horn whose blast could be heard throughout the universe. It was said that he could see for one hundred miles by day or night, that he slept less than a bird, and could hear the grass grow. When RAGNAROK, the twilight of the gods, comes, he will sound his Gjallarhorn to assemble the gods and heroes. See LOKI.

Heimskringla The most important prose collection in Old Norse literature, containing sixteen sagas of Norwegian history through 1177, sketched through the medium of biography, with a compendium of ancient Scandinavian mythology and poetry. Its name comes from its opening words, *Kringla heimsins*, the "circle of the world." The authorship is attributed to SNORRI STURLUSON.

Heine, Heinrich (born Chaim Harry Heine, 1797–1856) German poet, satirist, and journalist of Jewish origin. Heine's ambiguous attitude toward Germany, combining a sincere, sentimental love for the land and the people with biting irony about many German institutions, customs, and literary trends, appears in the early *Reisebilder* (*Travel-Sketches*, 1826 et seq), one of which is *Die Harzreise* (*Trip in the Harz Mountains*, 1826), his first major literary success. Gradually, however, he began to realize that the conflict between his liberal political views and the oppressive conservative regime in Prussia would make it impossible for him to remain in Germany. His attention was specifically drawn to Paris, where both the political ferment of the July Revolution (1830) and the growth of Saint-Simonianism attracted him; in 1831 he went there and remained for the rest of his life. In Paris, he was primarily active as a journalist and critic, writing in both German and French, and much of his work was intended to promote better understanding between his native and adopted lands: for example, *Französische Zustände* (*The Situation in France*, 1833); *Zur Geschichte der Religion und Philosophie in Deutschland* (*On the History of Religion and Philosophy in Germany*, 1834), which was also published in French; and *Die romantische Schule* (*The Romantic School*, 1833). In 1835, a Prussian edict prohibited his writings in Germany, naming him as a leader in the JUNG DEUTSCHLAND ("Young Germany") movement with which he had, however, been only peripherally associated.

In his early poems, notably the *Buch der Lieder* (*Book of Songs*, 1827 et seq), which includes his famous ballad on the LORELEI theme, Heine stands close to GERMAN ROMANTICISM. But though romantic elements remain in his later verse, especially the collection *Romanzero* (1851), there is also a strong tendency toward irony about romanticism, as in the narrative poems *Atta Troll* (1843), about the death of a trained bear, and *Deutschland, ein Wintermärchen* (*Germany, a Winter Tale*, 1844), a political and literary satire. See PLATEN.

Heinlein, Robert A[nson] (1907–   ) American SCIENCE FICTION writer. Heinlein was trained as an engineer at Annapolis and served as a naval officer until 1934. He sold his first stories to *Astounding Science Fiction* in 1939. Many of his early works fit into his "Future History" series, in which a projected sequence of technological, political, and social developments from the years 1950 to 2600 serve as a common background. *The Past Through Tomorrow* (1967) is an omnibus collection of the "Future History" stories. During the same period he wrote books that did not fit into the series, under a variety of pen names. In 1947 he began an immensely successful science fiction series for young people. Such controversial novels as *Starship Troopers* (1959), which struck some readers as having fascist sympathies, and *Stranger in a Strange Land* (1961), with its mixture of sexuality, mysticism, and libertarian-conservative politics, cost him the favor of many science fiction fans but won him a greater general audience.

Heinrich A nobleman in *Der arme Heinrich* (*Poor Heinrich*), an early-13th-century narrative poem by Hartmann von Aue (c1170–c1215) based on German legend. Heinrich is told he will not be cured of his leprosy until a virgin is willing to die for him. As he cannot wish such a sacrifice, he gives away most of his possessions and goes to live with one of his tenant farmers. This man's daughter learns how the cure must be effected and offers herself as the victim. This is enough to cause an instant cure, and Heinrich marries her. Heinrich becomes Prince Henry of Hoheneck in H. W. Longfellow's *The Golden Legend* (1851), and the tale is retold in Gerhart Hauptmann's drama *Der arme Heinrich* (1902).

Heinrich von Ofterdingen Legendary German MINNESINGER, or medieval court poet. NOVALIS uses Heinrich's name for the title and hero of an unfinished symbolic novel (pub 1801), in which the blue flower represents the union of the dream world and the real world for the poet. The novel treats the imaginary development of Heinrich from a completely naïve young man into an accomplished poet. Wagner makes him one of the competing minstrels in TANNHÄUSER. See WARTBURG.

Heinse, Johann Jakob Wilhelm (1749–1803) German novelist. Heinse's justification of immoralism on aesthetic grounds is related to the tendencies of the STURM UND DRANG. His critical works on art, especially Italian painting, are significant, and his interest in this field may also be seen in the novel *Ardinghello oder Die glückseligen Inseln* (*Ardinghello or The Isles of the Blessed*, 1787), which is important in the growth of the BILDUNGSROMAN ("novel of education").

Hel   The daughter of LOKI in Scandinavian mythology, who was queen of the dead and goddess of the lower regions. Here Hel was cast by ODIN to dwell beneath the roots of the sacred ash, YGGDRASILL. The region of Hel was also the home of the spirits of those who had died in their beds, NIFLHEIM, as distinguished from VALHALLA, the abode of heroes slain in battle.

Helen   In Greek mythology, the daughter of ZEUS and LEDA and wife of MENELAUS. Helen's abduction by PARIS led to the TROJAN WAR. In the ILIAD of Homer and THE TROJAN WOMEN of Euripides, she appears as a shallow and self-centered woman, unconcerned with the havoc her infidelity has wrought. Throughout literature from Greek times to the present, she has been a symbol of womanly beauty and sexual attraction. As such she has appeared in many dramas, including Marlowe's DR. FAUSTUS, Goethe's FAUST, and Jean Giraudoux's TIGER AT THE GATES. Euripides' HELEN, however, tells another version of the story. The Helen at Troy was a phantom created by HERA to cause war. Menelaus' faithful wife, kidnapped by HERMES, remained in Egypt throughout the war, but they were finally reunited, despite the attempt of the Egyptian king, Theoclymenus, to marry her by force. This story of the false Helen was attributed to the poet STESICHORUS, who was said by PLATO to have been blinded by Helen (who was also a goddess) for maligning her in verse. He redeemed her reputation, and his own sight, by writing the story of the phantom. GLUCK wrote an opera on the traditional Helen, *Paride ed Elena* (1770). At the imperial court in Part II of Goethe's *Faust*, Faust makes Helen and Paris appear in a magical vision but, forgetting that it is an illusion, falls violently in love with Helen and causes an explosion by his rash attempt to take her from Paris. In the classical WALPURGIS NIGHT, however, he finds the real Helen, and the two of them enjoy a brief idyll that symbolizes the romantic ideal (see the brothers SCHLEGEL) of a synthesis between Nordic and classical cultures. See ETERNAL FEMININE.

Helen (412 BC)   A play by EURIPIDES. Following STESICHORUS' version of the story of HELEN of Troy, the play opens in Egypt. HERMES has brought her there after PARIS has abducted from SPARTA not Helen but a phantom created in her likeness by HERA. She has been kindly treated by King Proteus, but he has died and his son Theoclymenus, who hates the Greeks, wants to marry her. TEUCER arrives and tells of the destruction of Troy seven years before. Thousands have died because of the woman they all believe is Helen; her own mother and brothers have killed themselves in shame at her conduct; MENELAUS and his ships are lost.

Menelaus arrives, however, and, recognizing his wife—the phantom having vanished—bitterly realizes that the TROJAN WAR has been fought for nothing. Pretending that Menelaus is dead, Helen borrows a ship to hold obsequies for him at sea. Together they escape from Theoclymenus and sail for home.

Helen of Kirconnell   A famous Scottish ballad. Helen is the lover of Adam Flemming. One day, while they are standing on the banks of a river, a rival suitor points his gun at Adam. Helen throws herself in front of him and is shot. The two rivals then fight, and the murderer is slain. Wordsworth embodies the same story in his poem "Ellen Irwin."

Helicon   A Boeotian mountain. It was known by the Greeks as the home of the MUSES. Helicon contained the fountains of Aganippe and HIPPOCRENE, connected by "Helicon's harmonious stream." The name is used allusively of poetic inspiration.

Helios   The Greek sun god. Helios rode to his palace in Colchis every night in a golden boat furnished with wings. He appears principally in the myth of PHAËTHON, though his cattle are important in the ODYSSEY. His cult was important on the island of Rhodes; the famous COLOSSUS OF RHODES was a statue of Helios. See HERACLES.

heliotrope (Gr, "turn-to-sun")   The sun god loved the sea nymph CLYTIE, but forsook her for her sister Leucothoe. On discovering this, Clytie pined away; and the god changed her at death to a sunflower, which, always turning toward the sun, is called heliotrope.

The bloodstone, a greenish quartz with veins and spots of red, used to be called heliotrope, the story being that if thrown into a bucket of water, it turned the rays of the sun to blood color. This stone also had the power of rendering its bearer invisible.

Hell   In Christian theology, a place where the souls of men are punished after death; a place of eternal suffering for the damned and for fallen angels. The Christian notion of hell is related to the Judaic concept of *Sheol* (the abode of all dead) and the GEHENNA of the NEW TESTAMENT. It also resembles the Greek HADES. The Christian hell, however, lays more emphasis on sinfulness and suffering than most earlier traditions. The term is occasionally used in a more neutral sense, as with the statement that Jesus descended into hell after the Crucifixion. Here the term is virtually synonymous with *Sheol*. SATAN is frequently referred to as the one who rules over Hell.

Hell has been represented in numerous works of literature, the most famous of which are Dante's DIVINE COMEDY and Milton's PARADISE LOST.

Helle   See GOLDEN FLEECE.

Heller, Joseph (1923–   )   American novelist. Heller's experience as a bombardier in World War II served as the backdrop for his first and best-known novel, CATCH-22. After a long silence, interrupted only by the unsuccessful play *We Bombed in New Haven* (1968), Heller published his second novel, *Something Happened* (1974), a relentlessly pessimistic account of the tedium and *anomie* of middle-class life. *Good as Gold* (1979), a satire on American values and politics, features an ambivalent and self-despising Jewish academic named Bruce Gold. *God Knows* (1984) is a Rabelaisian but ultimately serious retelling of the life of DAVID as found in the OLD TESTAMENT. It was awarded the French Prix Médici Etranger for best foreign novel published in 1985.

Hellespont   The ancient name of the Dardanelles, named for Helle (see GOLDEN FLEECE). In the classical romance, Leander used to swim the Hellespont to visit HERO, a priestess in the city of Sestos. Lord BYRON prided himself upon duplicating this feat.

Hellman, Lillian (1905–1984)   American playwright and memoirist. Hellman's plays are noted for their skillful craftsmanship and their social and psychological concerns. Her first play, *The Children's Hour* (1934), deals with the destructive effects of a young girl's charge that two of her teachers are lesbians. THE LITTLE FOXES and WATCH ON THE RHINE are two of her most successful dramas. Aside from a number of adaptations of European plays and novels, she wrote such plays as *The Searching Wind* (1944), *Another Part of the Forest* (1946), and *Toys in the Attic* (1960). Also distinguished as a writer of prose, Hellman published her memoirs in *An Unfinished Woman* (1969) and *Pentimento* (1973). *Scoundrel Time* (1976) is a personal account of the anticommunist "witch hunts" of the 1950s. These autobiographical books were published together as *Three* (1979). Hellman lived with Dashiell HAMMETT for many years.

Héloïse (1101–1164)   Niece of the Canon Fulbert of Notre Dame Cathedral, famous as the beloved of Pierre ABÉLARD. He was her tutor when he fell in love and seduced Héloïse (1118). They were secretly married after the birth of their son, Astrolabe, although Héloïse tried to dissuade him, fearing the marriage would ruin his career. And in fact, when the marriage became known, Fulbert had Abélard emasculated; Héloïse became a nun and Abélard a monk. Their famous exchange of letters made their story popular as a romantic tragedy, and in 1817 their bodies were reburied in one grave.

helot   A serf of ancient SPARTA. Possibly members of the earlier population of the area enslaved by their Dorian conquerors, they constituted the lowest class in the city-state. According to tradition, Spartan fathers used to ply their helot slaves with liquor on occasion, so that their sons might learn by their disgusting example to detest drunkenness.

Helper, Hinton Rowan (1829–1909)   American writer. Helper, who was born in North Carolina and raised on a plantation, is best known for *The Impending Crisis of the South: How to Meet It* (1857), in which he argued that because of its slave labor the South was economically and culturally far behind the North. On economic, not moral, grounds, he held that slavery should be taxed out of existence and that all blacks, whom he felt to be vastly inferior to whites, should be sent back to Africa. During the election year of 1860, the Republican party distributed 100,000 copies of the book, but in most parts of the South it was illegal to own one.

Helvétius, Claude Adrien (1715–1771)   French materialistic philosopher and encyclopedist. In his most famous work, *De l'esprit* (1758), Helvétius asserts that human minds at birth are uniformly blank and that general progress and well-being therefore depend upon education, institutions, and laws. Utilitarian in his thinking, he states that religion has failed in becoming the framework for morality and that the only real basis for morality and for law is the public interest, i.e., that which is good for the greatest number. For this heretical doctrine the Sorbonne, the Pope, and the *Parlement* had the work condemned and burned. Jeremy BENTHAM and James MILL acknowledge his influence. See PHILOSOPHES.

Hemans, Felicia Dorothea (born Felicia Browne, 1793–1835)   English poet, best known for her lyrics, "The Landing of the Pilgrim Fathers" and "Casabianca."

Hemingway, Ernest [Miller] (1899–1961)   American novelist and short-story writer. Early in his career as a newspaperman and foreign correspondent, Hemingway was already the craftsman whose terse style, with its dramatic understatement and superb dialogue, was to influence several generations of writers. Son of a doctor in rural Illinois, he went to Europe as an ambulance driver in World War I and was seriously wounded when he was eighteen. Later he went to France as a correspondent for the Toronto *Star* and met Ezra POUND and Gertrude STEIN, whose writing had already greatly influenced his own. His first published work was *Three Stories and Ten Poems* (1923), containing the stories "Up in Michigan," "Out of Season," and "My Old Man." IN OUR TIME is a collection of stories, semiautobiographical, about Nick ADAMS, a prototype of later Hemingway heroes.

His first novel, *The Torrents of Spring* (1926), is remembered mainly for the unmannerly burlesque of Sherwood ANDERSON, which was Hemingway's declaration of literary independence. Immediately following it, however, came THE SUN ALSO RISES, a forceful and original novel about the LOST GENERATION after World War I, which established his reputation and is widely considered his finest work. MEN WITHOUT WOMEN, short stories including the famous THE KILLERS and "Fifty Grand," continued his success. For the many critics who find Hemingway at his best in this form, this volume ranks at the top of the list with the later collection, *Winner Take Nothing* (1932). His next novel was A FAREWELL TO ARMS, a vivid and impeccably written love story about a war-time ambulance driver and a nurse. Two pieces of nonfiction followed: *Death in the Afternoon* (1932), with its eulogy of the bullfight ritual, and *Green Hills of Africa* (1935).

In 1937 Hemingway's early dissociation from political matters gave way to involvement, a development marked by the novel TO HAVE AND HAVE NOT, with its dying hero gasping, "One man alone ain't got . . . no chance." That same year, his sympathy with the Loyalist cause in the Civil War took him to Spain as a war correspondent. *The Fifth Column* (1938; adapted for stage by Benjamin Glazer, 1940), celebrating "the nobility and dignity of the Spanish people," was followed by FOR WHOM THE BELL TOLLS, a widely admired novel using the same theme to make a plea for human brotherhood. This was a fertile period for Hemingway, in which he also produced *The First Forty-Nine Hours and Other Stories* (1938), which included the great stories THE SNOWS OF KILIMANJARO and THE SHORT HAPPY LIFE OF FRANCIS MACOMBER.

Occupied during World War II as a war correspondent, Hemingway did not publish another novel until the coolly received *Across the River and into the Trees* (1950), about an aging hero of the First World War revisiting the battleground where he was wounded. Two years later, THE OLD MAN AND THE SEA, a novella, received high critical acclaim and the PULITZER PRIZE. In 1954 Hemingway was awarded the NOBEL PRIZE in Literature. He published nothing more of significance before his suicide in 1961.

The classic Hemingway hero, courting danger to prove himself, obsessed with the fear-courage and tough-tender dialectic, in a sense defined the writer himself. Posthumously published works are *A Moveable Feast* (1964), his memories of Paris in the 1920s; *Islands in the Stream* (1970), a novel; and *The Nick Adams Stories* (1972), concerning the alter-ego who appeared in his early short stories. *Hemingway's Selected Letters 1917–1961* (ed C. Baker) appeared in 1981. In 1985 *The Dangerous Summer*, a novel that had not been published earlier, was issued. It was followed by *The Garden of Eden* (begun in 1946; pub 1986).

Hémon, Louis (1880–1913)   French novelist. Hémon worked as a journalist in England before immigrating to Canada in 1911. The only novel published during his lifetime, *Lizzie Blakeston* (1908), had an English setting. He gained a substantial posthumous reputation, however, with the publication of *Maria Chapdelaine* (1916; tr 1921), a novel about pioneer life in Quebec, which inspired a spate of regional works by French-Canadian writers.

Hengist and Horsa   Two brothers in Geoffrey of Monmouth's HISTORY OF THE KINGS OF BRITAIN. They were Jute invaders of England (c449), whose aid in war against the Picts was enlisted by the ancient British king VOR-

TIGERN. Horsa is said to have been killed in battle in 455, Hengist to have ruled the kingdom of Kent, which they founded, until 488.

Henley, Beth [Becker] (1952–   )   American playwright. Henley, a Southerner who began her theatrical career as an actress and drama teacher, is best known for her PULITZER PRIZE-winning play *Crimes of the Heart* (1978); she also wrote the screenplay for the 1986 film version. This thoughtful, compassionate play about three eccentric sisters and their troubles in a small Mississippi town has been compared with the works of Tennessee WILLIAMS and Flannery O'CONNOR.

Henley, William Ernest (1849–1903)   English poet, dramatist, and editor. As editor of the *National Observer* (1889–94) and the *New Review* (1898–1903), Henley was a revolutionary force in English literature, publishing and defending early works of such writers as BARRIE, HARDY, KIPLING, WELLS, SHAW, and CONRAD. In his own work, he was a pioneer in the use of free verse (*In Hospital*, 1888) and wrote a number of poems of merit and technical accomplishment. Unfortunately, aggressive jingoism mars much of his work, and Henley has had the ill luck to be known, generally, as the author of a single poem, the meretricious INVICTUS.

Henriade, La (1723, repub in 1728 with revisions) An epic poem in ten cantos by VOLTAIRE. It recounts the struggle of Henry of Navarre (later HENRY IV of France) to obtain the throne. Voltaire depicts the assassination of Henry III and the religious wars with the HOLY LEAGUE and by implication condemns civil strife and religious fanaticism.

Henrietta Maria (1609–1669)   Queen consort (1625–49) of Charles I of England and mother of Charles II and James II. The daughter of Henry IV of France, Henrietta was a Roman Catholic. Forced to flee to France (1644), she returned to England after the Restoration.

Henry IV (1050–1106)   Holy Roman emperor. On the death of his father, Henry III, in 1056, he succeeded to the kingdoms of Germany, Italy, and Burgundy. In 1065 Henry was declared of age and assumed the throne. His reign was marked by the great struggle between empire and papacy over the question of lay investiture. Hitherto the emperors had filled the ecclesiastical positions within their dominions at their pleasure. But Pope GREGORY VII decided to claim this power for the papacy, and in 1075 he issued a decree forbidding lay investiture. Almost immediately, Henry responded by filling several sees in Italy with bishops of his own choosing. When Gregory threatened excommunication, Henry called together the German bishops and answered: "I, Henry, king by the grace of God, together with all our bishops, say unto thee, come down, come down from thy throne and be accursed through all the ages." Gregory forthwith deposed the bishops, excommunicated Henry, and declared the thrones of Italy and Germany vacant. Henry was then faced with a revolt in his territories, as his vassals gave him notice that a new emperor would be chosen within the year if he did not relent. Accordingly, the emperor went in 1077 to meet the pope at Canossa. There, outside the castle, Henry garbed as a penitent waited for three days in the snow before Gregory would receive him and grant conditional absolution. When Henry returned to Germany, he found that the princes had elected a new emperor in spite of his penance. Gregory remained neutral for a time, then renewed the excommunication. After Henry had defeated and killed his rival Rudolf, duke of Swabia, he marched on Rome. An attempt at compromise through the convocation of a synod failed, and in 1083 Henry deposed Gregory and installed Clement III, who promptly crowned Henry emperor. Meanwhile, the German princes had chosen a new king, Hermann of Luxemburg, and Henry was compelled to renew the struggle. By 1088 he had restored his authority throughout Germany. He survived conspiracies by his second wife and his eldest son, Conrad, only to be defeated by his second son, Henry, later Henry V, who declared he owed no allegiance to an excommunicated father. In 1105 a diet in Mainz forced Henry IV to abdicate. After escaping to Cologne, he began negotiations with England, France, and Denmark. He was engaged in organizing an army when he died in 1106.

Henry IV (also known as Henry Bolingbroke and Henry of Lancaster, 1367–1413) King of England (1399–1413), the first monarch of the house of Lancaster. The son of John of Gaunt and the grandson of Edward III, Henry IV was banished by RICHARD II in 1398. The following year he invaded England, overthrew Richard, and assumed the crown himself. He is a central character in Shakespeare's HENRY IV: PART I and PART II, and in RICHARD II. The surname Bolingbroke refers to the castle in which he was born.

Henry V (1387–1422) King of England (1413–22). The son of Henry IV, Henry V invaded France in an attempt to reconquer England's former possessions there, winning an important victory at Agincourt (1415). Subsequent military successes and astute diplomacy resulted in the treaty of Troyes (1420), by which Henry was to marry Catherine of Valois, daughter of Charles VI, king of France, and inherit the French crown upon Charles's death. See HENRY V, THE LIFE OF KING.

Henry VII (also known as Henry Tudor, 1457–1509) King of England (1485–1509), the first monarch of the Tudor dynasty. As earl of Richmond and the principal representative of the Lancastrian claim to the throne of England, he defeated Richard III at Bosworth Field in 1485. His subsequent marriage to Elizabeth, daughter of Edward IV, marked the end of the WARS OF THE ROSES. Later he successfully suppressed a rebellion by the Yorkist pretender Perkin Warbeck (c1474–99). He was succeeded by his son Henry VIII.

Henry VIII (Henry Tudor, 1491–1547) Second of the Tudor kings, king of England (1509–47). At the beginning of his reign Henry married Catherine of Aragon, his brother's widow; because of some ecclesiastical protest about the validity of such a union, he was forced to acquire a Papal dispensation. When, nearly twenty years later, Catherine had not borne him a son, personal and political reasons moved him to consider divorce. The Pope was unwilling, doubly so since Rome was in the hands of the Emperor Charles V, Catherine's nephew. Various delays occurred, and finally Henry chose the expedient of overthrowing papal jurisdiction, thus at one fell swoop making possible his divorce, channeling the revenues from monasteries and Church lands away from Rome to the Crown, and, almost incidentally, and for political far more than religious reasons, initiating the English Reformation. Early in 1533, before any kind of divorce had been granted, he secretly married Anne BOLEYN, and a few months later had his first marriage declared void and his second declared valid. This was followed by an Act of Succession, giving the right of succession to the throne to offspring of Anne and denying it to Mary (later MARY I), Catherine's daughter, on the grounds of her illegitimacy. To both this and the Act of Supremacy, by which Henry was made head of the Church, subjects were required to give an oath of acceptance, a thing that no devout Catholic could do, and in default of which Sir Thomas More, formerly Lord Chancellor, was executed for high treason.

Anne, like Catherine before her, bore only one child that lived, and that a daughter, the future ELIZABETH I. In 1536 Anne was dispatched on a charge of adultery, and Henry married Jane Seymour, who died bearing him the much-desired son, destined to become the boy-king Edward VI. In 1540 Henry married the German princess Anne of Cleves, but disliked her and divorced her almost immediately. Catherine Howard, the next of his wives, was soon charged with adultery and beheaded. His last wife was Catherine Parr, a patroness of the arts, who survived him. Before his death Henry fixed the succession in his will, giving it to Edward, Mary, and Elizabeth (though both of his daughters had previously been declared illegitimate), who succeeded him in that order.

Henry IV (also known as Henry of Navarre and Henry the Great, 1553–1610) King of France (1589–1610), the first of the Bourbon dynasty. Raised as a Calvinist, Henry became leader of the French Huguenot party in 1569 after the death of the first prince of Condé. He succeeded to the throne of Navarre as Henry III and married MARGARET OF VALOIS, sister of Charles IX of France, in 1572. When the death of the brother of Henry III, the reigning king of France, made Henry of Navarre heir presumptive, the refusal of the HOLY LEAGUE to recognize his title led to the conflict known as the War of the Three Henrys (Henry III of France, Henry of Navarre, and Henry, duke of GUÍSE). After the assassination of the king of France, Henry's victory over the league at Ivry and his conversion to Catholicism enabled him to secure the crown. One of France's ablest monarchs, Henry initiated a program to hasten recovery from the religious wars. He issued the Edict of NANTES and, in foreign affairs, followed a policy of opposition to the Hapsburgs. He was assassinated by François Ravillac, a Roman Catholic fanatic. See ESTRÉES, GABRIELLE D'; HENRIADE, LA; SULLY, DUC DE.

Henry IV: Part I (c1597–1598)   A historical play by SHAKESPEARE, depicting early years of the reign of England's HENRY IV. After defeating rebellious Scottish barons, Henry PERCY, the famous Hotspur, eldest son of the powerful earl of Northumberland, refuses to yield his prisoners to the king unless his kinsman Edmund Mortimer, captured by the rebellious Welshman Owen Glendower, is ransomed. Since Mortimer is pretender to the throne, Henry refuses his ransom. Angered, the Percy family joins the rebels. Meanwhile, the king's son and heir, Prince Hal, continues to annoy his father by keeping company with the band of revelers led by Sir John FALSTAFF. But, hearing of the uprising, Hal takes command of a part of his father's forces, helping to defeat the rebels at the battle of Shrewsbury (1403). Hal saves his father's life and kills Hotspur.

Henry IV: Part II (c1597–1598)   A historical play by SHAKESPEARE, completing the description of the reign of HENRY IV. Despite the death of Hotspur, the rebellion continues, under the leadership of the earl of Northumberland. Meanwhile, Hal has returned to the riotous company of FALSTAFF. Upon Northumberland's desertion, the rebels negotiate with the king's second son, John of Lancaster, who promises to redress their grievances if they will disband. They accept and are promptly killed by the treacherous prince. News of his enemies' defeat reaches the king on his deathbed. Hal is named king (Henry V) and promptly repudiates his misspent youth by banishing Falstaff from his presence. Shakespeare's source for both plays about Henry IV is Holinshed's *Chronicles* (1577).

Henry V, The Life of King (c1598–1599)   A historical play by SHAKESPEARE. Shortly after his coronation, HENRY V decides to press his claims to the French throne and leads an army into France. He defeats a vastly larger French army at Agincourt (1415), wins the hand of the French princess Catherine of Valois, and is recognized as heir to the French throne. Against this background, Shakespeare reveals Henry's rapport with the doughty English soldiers. The death of FALSTAFF is also reported in the play.

In HENRY IV: PART I and PART II and in *Henry V*, Shakespeare chronicles Henry's life from his days as a profligate youth under the influence of Sir John Falstaff to his victory at Agincourt as king of England. His character is used by Shakespeare as a study in statesmanship. Although Henry steeps himself in the revels and schemes of Falstaff, part of him always remains aloof. For, as he explains:

> I know you all, and will awhile uphold
> The unyok'd humour of your idleness:
> Yet herein will I imitate the sun,
> Who doth permit the base contagious clouds
> To smother up his beauty from the world,
> That when he please again to be himself,
> Being wanted, he may be more wonder'd at.

Henry VI: Part I (c1590–1592)   The first play of a historical trilogy by SHAKESPEARE, depicting the early years of Henry's reign up to his marriage with MARGARET OF ANJOU. After the death of Henry V, the realm of the child king, Henry VI, falls under the control of his uncles, the regents John, duke of Bedford, and Humphrey, duke of Gloucester. War has broken out anew in France; under Joan La Pucelle (see JOAN OF ARC), the French begin to drive the English out. Meanwhile, Richard Plantagenet, having successfully pressed his claims to the title of the duke of York, quarrels with the powerful Beaufort family of the house of Lancaster, setting the stage for the WARS OF THE ROSES. After a temporary reconciliation of Yorkists and Lancastrians, a marriage is arranged between Henry and the daughter of the French earl of Armagnac in order to seal a truce between England and France. However, at the urging of the earl of Suffolk, Henry chooses Margaret of Anjou to be his queen.

Henry VI: Part II (c1590–1592)   The second play of a historical trilogy by SHAKESPEARE, covering the early years of the WARS OF THE ROSES. After his marriage to MARGARET OF ANJOU, Henry is dominated by the queen and the duke of Suffolk, who plot the overthrow of the lord protector, Humphrey, the duke of Gloucester, by convicting Humphrey's wife, the duchess of Gloucester, of sorcery, and thus forcing his shameful retirement. Meanwhile, Richard Plantagenet, having convinced the earl of Salisbury and Richard Neville, earl of Warwick, of his right to the throne, waits for the opportunity to seize it. Before leaving to suppress a revolt in Ireland, he encourages Jack Cade to launch a rebellion in his absence. Subsequently, Richard returns to England and meets and defeats the king's forces at St. Albans (1455).

Henry VI: Part III (c1590–1592)   The third play of a historical trilogy by SHAKESPEARE, covering the downfall of Henry and the victory of the house of York in the person of Edward IV. After the defeat of his forces at St. Albans, Henry begs Richard Plantagenet to allow him to reign during his lifetime. Richard agrees, but MARGARET OF ANJOU, Henry's queen, is set on destroying Richard. At Wakefield, she defeats him and puts him to death. But Richard's sons, Edward (IV) and Richard (III), triumph over Margaret at Towton, and Edward becomes king. Henry, who has fled, returns to England and is imprisoned in the Tower of London. Edward sends Warwick to France to arrange a marriage with Bona, sister of Louis XI. In his absence, Edward marries Lady Elizabeth Grey, and Warwick, annoyed, goes over to Margaret. After several reverses,

Edward defeats Margaret at Tewkesbury (1471), where Henry's son, Edward, prince of Wales, is killed. Shortly thereafter, Richard (III) murders Henry in the Tower. The main sources for the Henry VI trilogy were Holinshed's *Chronicles* (1577) and Edward Hall's *Union of the Noble and Illustrious Families of Lancaster and York* (1547).

Henry VIII, The Famous History of the Life of King (1613) A historical play by SHAKESPEARE. John Fletcher (see BEAUMONT AND FLETCHER) may have written parts of the play.

The drama begins with the return of HENRY VIII from the Field of the Cloth of Gold. Edward Stafford, duke of Buckingham, is about to warn the king of the growing power of Cardinal Wolsey when he is falsely accused of treason and executed. Meanwhile, Henry, who has met Anne Bullen, becomes concerned with the legal aspects of his marriage to Katharine of Aragon. Through Wolsey, he negotiates with the pope for a divorce. But when Wolsey discovers that the king plans to marry Anne, he tries to stop the divorce, is found out, and, while under arrest for treason, dies. Henry's marriage is annulled by Thomas Cranmer, archbishop of Canterbury, and the king marries Anne. Katharine dies, commending her daughter, Mary, to Henry's protection. The nobles, jealous of Cranmer's growing influence, try to discredit him, but Henry protects the archbishop and makes him godfather of the infant Elizabeth. The principal source of the play is Holinshed's *Chronicles* (1577); the portions dealing with Cranmer are derived from Foxe's *Book of Martyrs* (1563).

Henry, Frederic A principal character in Ernest Hemingway's novel A FAREWELL TO ARMS. An American lieutenant in the Italian ambulance service during World War I, he falls in love with an English nurse, Catherine Barkley. He deserts to be with her, but she dies in childbirth.

Henry, John A legendary black hero of American ballads and TALL TALES. Born supposedly in the "Black River country," he was employed in the building of railroads or as a roustabout on river steamboats. John Henry is a man of prodigious strength; in one well-known tale he dies from overexertion, after winning a contest against a steam drill. The tales are apparently based on the exploits of a giant black who worked on the Chesapeake & Ohio Big Bend Tunnel in the early 1870s. In 1931 Guy B. Johnson made a collection of varying ballads in *John Henry: Tracking Down a Negro Legend*. In the same year Roark BRADFORD based a novel, *John Henry*, on several tales. Bradford's novel was later dramatized with music by Jacques Wolfe (1931).

Henry, O. (pen name of William Sydney [earlier spelled Sidney] Porter, 1862–1910) American short-story writer. An extremely popular and prolific writer, O. Henry is noted for his sentimental, semirealistic stories dealing with the lives of modest people and his mastery of the surprise ending. A North Carolinian by birth, Porter moved to Texas, where he became the editor and publisher of the humorous magazine *The Rolling Stone*. When he was charged with embezzling funds from a bank, he fled to Central America, subsequently the scene of *Cabbages and Kings* (1904). He later returned and, although there has been much debate over his actual guilt, served over three years in the federal penitentiary. While in prison, he published the first of his O. Henry stories—"Whistling Dick's Christmas Stocking" (1899)—in *McClure's Magazine*. The pen name is presumed to be an abbreviation of the name of a French pharmacist, Etienne-Ossian Henry, found in the *U.S. Dispensatory*, a reference work Porter used when he worked in the prison pharmacy.

Stories he heard in prison were the germs of many of his narratives, among them the tale of Jimmy Connors, the thief-hero of "A Retrieved Reformation." But his work is most identified with New York City, which he liked to call "Bagdad-on-the-Subway." Among the collections of O. Henry stories are THE FOUR MILLION, *The Voice of the City* (1908), and *Options* (1909). *Works of O. Henry* (2 vols, 1953) includes all his stories and some of his poems. In 1918 the O. Henry Memorial Awards were established to be given annually to the best magazine stories, the winners and leading contenders to be published in an annual volume. See GIFT OF THE MAGI, THE; LAST LEAF, THE.

Henry, Patrick (1736–1799) American statesman and orator. As a member of the Virginia House of Burgesses, Henry offered a series of resolutions against the Stamp Act (1765). He later served in the Continental Congress and as governor of Virginia. Famous passages from his speeches include:

Caesar had his Brutus; Charles the First, his Cromwell; and George the Third—*may profit by their example.* If *this* be treason, make the most of it. (Virginia House of Burgesses, 1765)

Is life so dear, or peace so sweet, as to be purchased at the price of chains and slavery? Forbid it, Almighty God! I know not what course others may take; but as for me, give me liberty, or give me death! (Virginia Convention, 1775)

Henry Esmond, Esquire, The History of (1852) A historical novel by William Makepeace THACKERAY. It is narrated in the first person by Henry Esmond. He is brought up by Francis Esmond, heir to the Castlewood estate, with Francis's own children, Beatrix and Frank, and grows up in the belief that he is the illegitimate son of Thomas Esmond, the deceased viscount of Castlewood. On his deathbed, Francis confesses to Henry that he is the lawful heir, but Henry keeps the information secret. He and Frank Esmond are ardent supporters of James Edward, the (Old) PRETENDER, who falls in love with Beatrix and ruins his chances for the throne. When Beatrix joins the prince abroad, Henry, who has been in love with her, renounces the Pretender; he marries her mother, Rachel, Lady Castlewood, instead and takes her to America. The story of their descendants is related in Thackeray's THE VIRGINIANS.

Henry the Navigator (1394–1460)   Portuguese prince. The younger son of John I, Henry planned and directed a campaign of exploration and discovery that subsequently led to Portugal's extensive conquests in the Orient and the New World. From his residence at Sagres, which became the foremost center of navigation in Europe, he dispatched several vessels each year into the uncharted seas to the south and west, meeting only failure until 1434, when Cape Bojador was rounded. On later voyages Madeira and the Azores were discovered.

Hephaestus   In Greek mythology, the god of fire and metal-working. Later Hephaestus was identified with the Roman VULCAN. Hephaestus was either the son of ZEUS and HERA, or produced by Hera alone. HOMER related that Hera threw her lame son out of heaven, ashamed of his deformity. In revenge, Hephaestus wrought a golden throne from which Hera could not arise. In another story, Hephaestus took the part of Hera against Zeus, who then hurled him from heaven. He fell for nine days and was finally picked up, lamed for life, on the island of Lemnos.

Married to the unfaithful APHRODITE, he became known as the special patron of cuckolds. Hephaestus (or PROMETHEUS) delivered ATHENE from the head of Zeus with the stroke of an axe. Homer also depicts him as the maker of the AEGIS.

Heptaméron (1559)   An unfinished collection of seventy-two tales by MARGARET OF NAVARRE. Modeled on the *Decameron* (1353) of Boccaccio, the work is otherwise original. All but one of the tales were probably based on her own experiences. Though weak in literary style, the work is distinguished for its psychological perception and its didactic quality.

heptameter   In prosody, a line of verse containing seven metrical feet in any METER. It is usually identified together with the name of the meter: for example, iambic heptameter.

Hepworth, Dame Barbara (1903–1975)   British sculptor. Although Hepworth was a working sculptor as early as 1920, it was not until 1935 that she began the abstract stone and wood carvings for which she is known. She was influenced by Henry MOORE, Jean ARP, and Constantin BRANCUSI, and at times her sculptures have borne structural similarities to the works of each of these artists. Her best-known works are smooth, open forms, gracefully penetrated and folded, but her later works, cast in bronze, have a rougher, more monolithic character. *Biotite* (1949) is a typical work in the earlier style.

Hera   A Greek goddess, daughter of CRONOS and RHEA, and both sister and wife of ZEUS. Hera appears most often in myth as a jealous wife who persecutes her husband's many mistresses (SEMELE, IO, LETO, and others) or their children (DIONYSUS, HERACLES). Her worship, however, antedated that of Zeus in Greece, where she had important shrines at Argos and elsewhere. The Heraean Games for women were celebrated at Olympia long before the famous Olympic Games for men. She was the patroness of the ARGONAUTS.

Heracles (Latin name Hercules)   A mythical Greek hero of fabulous strength. Heracles was the son of ZEUS and ALCMENA, who caught Zeus' notice when her husband, AMPHITRYON, was away from Thebes. Amphitryon, however, returned the same night that Zeus had visited her, and in good time she gave birth to twins, Heracles and Iphicles, who was merely the son of Amphitryon. HERA, who had done everything possible to prevent the birth, did not give up. She sent two snakes to attack the twins, but Heracles strangled them in his crib. Heracles married the Theban king's daughter Megara, but, driven mad by Hera, he killed Megara and all their children. When he returned to his senses, he went into exile and bound himself to serve his cousin Eurystheus, the king of Mycenae, for twelve years. At the end of this time he would become immortal. Although he traveled far and wide for many of the famous Labors, Heracles' own home seems to have been at Tiryns. His Labors were as follows:

1. Killing the Nemean lion. This frightful beast, sent by Hera to ravage the Nemean plain and to annoy Heracles, he killed by clubbing and strangling it, although it was supposedly invulnerable. Henceforward he wore its skin.

2. Killing the HYDRA. This tremendous snake, one of the many delightful monsters spawned by Echidna, inhabited the Lernaean swamps. As soon as one of its numerous heads was lopped off, others grew in its place. Heracles persuaded his friend Iolaus to burn the stumps before the heads could grow and thus they disposed of the beast, as well as a crab sent by Hera to help it out. This crab became the constellation of Cancer.

3. Capturing the ERYMANTHIAN BOAR. Heracles brought this redoubtable beast back to Eurystheus and nearly scared him out of his wits.

4. Capturing the Hind of ARTEMIS. Heracles succeeded in capturing this sacred animal after a year's search, and Artemis permitted him to carry it off to Argos if he promised to let it go, which he did.

5. Killing the man-eating Stymphalian birds. Heracles chased them from their hiding in the woods by banging a bronze rattle, then shot them down one by one.

6. Cleansing the AUGEAN STABLES. These stables, belonging to King Augeas of Elis, had never been cleaned. Heracles accomplished the task in a day by redirecting a river through them.

7. Capturing the Cretan Bull. This bull, which may have been the father of the Minotaur, was taken alive and shown to Eurystheus, like the Hind, then released.

8. Capturing the horses of DIOMEDES, son of Cyrene and ARES. These horses were fed on human flesh by their owner, the king of the Bistonians. They suddenly became

tame when Heracles fed their master to them. He then took them back to Eurystheus and dedicated them to Hera.

9. Capturing the girdle of HIPPOLYTA. Either alone or with an army, Heracles defeated the AMAZONS and either killed Hippolyta or secured the girdle by holding one of her generals, Melanippe, for ransom.

10. Killing the monster GERYON. Heracles threatened Helios with his bow until the god gave him his golden cup, in which Heracles sailed the river Oceanus to the far west. There, after disposing of the herdsman Eurytion and the ferocious dog Orthrus, he killed Geryon himself, stole his cattle, and returned with them, either in the cup or by a long and arduous route through Spain, France, and Italy.

11. Capturing Cerberus. Heracles made his way down to HADES, dragged up Cerberus, the three-headed dog that watches the gates, showed him to Eurystheus, and duly returned him to his proper place. According to one story, Heracles actually fought with and wounded Hades himself.

12. Stealing the apples of the HESPERIDES. These apples grew on a tree guarded by a terrible dragon and belonged to the Hesperides, daughters of Night, who lived near the Atlas Mountains. There are various tales as to how Heracles plucked the apples: He either killed the snake or put it to sleep and took the apples himself, or he sent Atlas for them, holding the sky on his shoulders meanwhile.

Heracles had innumerable other adventures, either separately or incidentally to his main labors. He eventually died after donning the poisoned shirt dipped in the blood of the centaur NESSUS, which his wife Deianira had given him. He built himself a funeral pyre on Mount Oeta and persuaded Poeas with the gift of his bow and arrows to set it afire. After this he ascended to Olympus and married HEBE.

The last three labors of Heracles seem to indicate that he achieved immortality by his feats. A very considerable number of his adventures were added to his saga to explain the many places in which his cult flourished. Some authorities believe that the root of the Heracles saga is the adventures of an actual Mycenaean king of Tiryns who performed mighty feats at the bidding of his overlord, the high king of Mycenae. His feats were a favorite subject of art among the Greeks and in the Renaissance.

Heracles appears in two tragedies by SOPHOCLES, *Trachiniai* (*The Trachinian Women*) and *Philoctetes*; in two by EURIPIDES, *Alcestis* and *Heracles mainomenos* (*The Madness of Heracles*); and in SENECA's *Hercules furens*. Euripides' *Herakleidai* (*The Children of Heracles*) tells of the final defeat of Eurystheus, who had continued to persecute Heracles' family after his death.

Heraclitus (fl 500 BC) A pre-Socratic natural philosopher belonging to one of the ruling families of Ephesus. Heraclitus' single main work, *On Nature*, from which a good many fragments have survived, was one of the first pieces of Greek prose. It is written in an oracular style, striving to indicate rather than explicate truths. Heraclitus

saw that everything in the world is balanced by its opposite. Justice controls the conflicting opposites, hence nature is a unity. Accordingly, "Men do not understand how what is at conflict is at harmony with itself; it is an attunement of opposites like that of bow and lyre." His most famous fragment, "It is not possible to step twice into the same river," expresses his central belief that the only reality is that all things are in constant transition. His views on the mutability and fleeting character of all things led also to his partly humorous epithet, the "weeping philosopher," or the dark philosopher.

Herbert, Edward (first Baron Herbert of Cherbury, 1583–1648) English soldier, diplomat, and philosopher, brother of George HERBERT. His attempts, in such works as *De Veritate* (1624) and *De Religione Gentilium* (1663), to discover a rational and universally self-evident basis for religion make him the first of the English deists. Herbert also wrote an interesting *Autobiography*, which was discovered and published by Horace WALPOLE in 1764, and poetry in the metaphysical vein. See DEISM.

Herbert, Frank (1920–1986) American SCIENCE FICTION writer. Herbert was a newspaperman turned writer. His first novel was *The Dragon in the Sea* (1956), a psychologically intricate story of a search for a saboteur in an undersea war. *The Santaroga Barrier* (1968), about a utopian community, reveals Herbert's continued interest in the evolution of intelligence. He is best known for an ecology-minded series of heroic adventures that includes *Dune* (1965), the name of the desert planet that provides its setting, *Dune Messiah* (1970), *The Children of Dune* (1976), *The God Emperor of Dune* (1981), and *The Heretics of Dune* (1985). His other works include *Lazarus Effect* (1983) and, with his son Brian, *Man of Two Worlds* (1986).

Herbert, George (1593–1633) English poet of the metaphysical school (see METAPHYSICAL POETS). Herbert, who was a brother of Lord Herbert of Cherbury, came from a Welsh family famous for its soldiers and statesmen. For a long time he aspired to a government career, but a growing sense of religious vocation and the death of James I and other patrons led him to become an Anglican priest. In 1630 he was given the rural living of Bemerton, where he died a few years later, esteemed almost as a saint.

All of Herbert's poetry is religious, even that written during his period of secular ambition. In fact, a major theme of his work, revealed in poems like THE COLLAR and "Affliction (I)," is the conflict between his calling and his ambition, his pride in his descent and his attainments. Other poems, such as THE SACRIFICE, deal with every facet of religious life: the vicissitudes of a believer's hopes and fears; the nature of God, with emphasis on His love and suffering for man; the festivals, institutions, and doctrines of the Church. Herbert often expresses deep religious anxiety, but his characteristic mood is one of sweetness and equilibrium, a trusting, intimate friendliness with God. Technically, his work is marked by simple diction, striking colloquial rhythms, and the use of symbols and images from ecclesiastical ritual, farming, the trades, science, and everyday household pursuits. He is also known for his extraordinary metrical inventiveness and his occasional "pattern poems": poems whose lines are arranged to form a given shape like an altar or wings or a cross, such as the well-known "Easter Wings" (1633).

Herbert wrote one volume of poems, THE TEMPLE; a treatise on the life and duties of a country parson, A *Priest to the Temple* (1652); and several collections of proverbs. His work was highly popular in its day, but attacked in the later 17th century as over-elaborate in conceit and perversely ingenious. He had some admirers in the 19th century, but it was not until the 20th century, with the general revival of interest in metaphysical poetry, that his work was once more appreciated.

Herbert, [Albert Francis] Xavier (1901–1984) Australian novelist. Born in the rugged country of northwestern Australia, Herbert knew aborigines and their language from childhood. During his energetic and varied career as a cowboy, prospector, and railway roustabout, he produced four novels, a collection of stories, and his autobiography, *Disturbing Element* (1963). Herbert's novels, the best known of which is *Capricornia* (1939), are sprawling, vivid works with a powerful sympathy for the underdog.

Herbert, Zbigniew (1924–   ) Polish poet. Herbert, who fought in the Polish Resistance against the Nazis in World War II, rose to literary prominence in Poland toward the end of the 1950s and in the early 1960s, when the relaxation of the Soviet THAW was also felt in its satellite countries. On the surface, his poems appear restrained, balanced, and ironic, and deeply influenced by the Greek and Roman classics; on another level, they reveal the poet's indictment of totalitarian oppression. His works have appeared in two translations entitled *Selected Poems* (1968, 1977). Volumes in Polish include *Sturna światla* (*A String of Light*, 1956), *Hermes, pies i gwiazda* (*Hermes, Dog and Star*, 1957), and *Pan Cogito* (*Mr. Cogito*, 1974). Herbert's published works also include short plays and essays.

Herder, Johann Gottfried (1744–1803) German philosopher, historian, and critic. Herder is known as the most prominent representative of 18th-century irrationalism. His interest in the folk spirit (see VOLKSGEIST) was not confined to Germany, and his collection of *Volkslieder* (*Folk Songs*, 1778–79), which was prompted by Thomas Percy's *Reliques of Ancient English Poetry* (1765), included Nordic, English, and Romance songs, as well as German. His ideas about the value of intuition in both creation and criticism were taken up and developed by Goethe, with whom he was closely associated, and by German romanticism. His other works include *Von deutscher Art und Kunst* (*On German Character and Art*, 1773), *Auch eine Philosophie der Geschichte zur Bildung der Menschheit*

(*Another Philosophy of History for the Education of Mankind*, 1774), and *Briefe zur Beförderung der Humanität* (*Letters for the Furtherance of Humanity*, 1793–97). See STURM UND DRANG.

Heredia, José María de (1803–1839) Cuban poet. Exiled at twenty for revolutionary activity against the Spanish regime in Cuba, Heredia imbued his poetry with the disillusion and frustration that was the lot of many Cuban intellectuals of his generation. After spending two unhappy years in the U.S., he settled in Mexico, where, except for a brief trip to Cuba in 1836, he remained for the rest of his life. Although Heredia's poetry is classical in form, he has been called the first romantic poet of Hispanic America because of the subjectivity and intensity that characterize his verse. The two poems generally considered his best are "En el teocalli de Cholula" (1820), in which Heredia reflects on the impermanence of all earthly endeavor, and "Niagara" (1824), in which the poet describes the scene in a style as torrential as the falls itself, and then laments his solitude, so far from home.

Heredia, José Maria de (1842–1905) Cuban-born French poet. A pupil of Leconte de Lisle, Heredia was one of the first PARNASSIANS. His finest poetry is contained in the 118 sonnets of *Les Trophées* (1893), which are remarkable for the richness of their imagery, the sonorousness and cadence of their language, and the evocative character of their historical impressions.

Hergesheimer, Joseph (1880–1954) American novelist and short-story writer. A skillful popular writer, Hergesheimer won considerable acclaim with his novels *The Three Black Pennys* (1917), *Balisand* (1924), and *Java Head* (1919), which deals with the tragic marriage of a Yankee shipowner and a Chinese aristocrat.

Hermann und Dorothea (1797) An idyllic epic in hexameters by GOETHE, set during the French invasions of Germany that followed the French Revolution. Goethe explicitly avoids the heroic and concentrates on the bourgeois honesty and simplicity of the love between his two main characters, which he sees as a balance to the unrest of the times.

hermaphrodite A plant or animal containing both male and female organs of reproduction. The word is derived from the Greek myth of Hermaphroditus, son of HERMES and APHRODITE, as told in Ovid's METAMORPHOSES. The nymph Salmacis became enamored of him, and prayed that she might be so closely united that "the twain might become one flesh." Her prayer was answered, and the nymph and boy became one body.

Hermes Divine herald of Greek mythology. This ancient Arcadian deity was also a god of flocks, of roads, of trading, and of thieves, the inventor of the lyre, and the guide of souls on the way to HADES. The son of ZEUS and Maia, Hermes grew miraculously in both size and cunning, on the first day inventing the lyre and stealing APOLLO's flocks. He was widely worshiped in the form of the herm, a phallic pillar. The amusing story of his exploits on the day of his birth was told in the fourth Homeric hymn and in SOPHOCLES' satyr play, *Ichneutai*. The Romans identified him with MERCURY (Mercurius), their god of tradesmen.

Hermes Trismegistus (Gr, "the thrice-great Hermes")   A name applied by the Neoplatonists to the Egyptian god THOTH. Hermes Trismegistus was almost identical to the Greek god HERMES.

The name was also applied, from about the third century, to the supposed author of a body of alchemic, occult, and mystical writings. Until the 17th century he was thought to have been a contemporary of Moses, and his writings were considered Christian and almost as sacred as the Bible. Actually the Hermetic books were composed by a group of teachers who lived in Alexandria in the first two centuries BC or AD; they were a composite of Egyptian magical writings, Jewish mysticism, and Platonism. The 20th century saw a revival of interest in the Hermetic writings, notably in the work of the French SYMBOLISTS and the occult system of William Butler YEATS.

hermeticism   A name applied to a 20th-century school of Italian poets. It was first used by the noted Italian critic Francesco Flora to characterize the difficult, "occult-meaning" verse of a group of Italian poets headed by Salvatore QUASIMODO, Giuseppe UNGARETTI, and Eugenio MONTALE.

The verse of these poets originated in the French symbolist school of "pure poetry" as practiced by MALLARMÉ and VALÉRY. Decadent poetry entered Italy through the CREPUSCOLARI poets, and it is from them that "the hermetics" have evolved.

Typical of hermetic poetry is a deliberate rarefaction of poetic language; this is the result of the poet's attempt to verbalize a personal impression that seems to transcend common experience, in a language that conveys it with the maximum fidelity and immediacy. The hermetics reject rhetoric and the stylistic mechanics of formal traditional poetry. They adopt instead occult symbolism and a vocabulary that is extremely personal, idiosyncratic, and, to the uninitiated, abstruse and often meaningless.

Hermetic writings   See HERMES TRISMEGISTUS.

Hermione   (1) In Greek legend, the only daughter of MENELAUS and HELEN. Hermione became the wife of NEOPTOLEMUS, son of ACHILLES, but ORESTES assassinated him and married Hermione, who had already been betrothed to him. She appears in Euripides' ANDROMACHE as the cruel persecutor of the heroine. See Euripides' ORESTES.

(2) The virtuous and uncomplaining wife of Leontes, king of Sicilia, in Shakespeare's WINTER'S TALE.

Hernández, José (1834–1886)   Argentine poet. Born on a farm outside Buenos Aires, Hernández grew up as a genuine *gaucho* on the pampas. He worked as a secretary and civil servant and then founded a newspaper, *Río de*

la Plata (1869), which he used to lobby on behalf of the *gauchos*. Three years later he published the narrative poem on which his fame rests, MARTÍN FIERRO. The realism and accessibility of the poem made it as popular among the rural people of Argentina as Robert SERVICE's Yukon ballads were among the pioneers of the Pacific northwest. For years, Hernández suffered from a comparable disdain on the part of the more educated reader, but this changed greatly after the turn of the century.

Hernández, Miguel de (1910–1942)   Spanish poet and dramatist. Born in Orihuela, whose rural atmosphere influenced all his poetry, Hernández was a largely self-taught literary descendant of GÓNGORA and GARCILASO DE LA VEGA. With his first book of baroque and gongoristic verse, *Perito en lunas* (1933), his talent was recognized and encouraged by members of the GENERACIÓN DEL 27. In *El rayo que no cesa* (1936), a collection of sonnets of formal perfection, he sings of tormented love and sex, solitude, and death. He became an ardent Communist and fought for the Republicans in the Spanish Civil War, for which he later received a death sentence, commuted to life in prison. Patriotism, pain, poverty, and hope for the future are all elements of the stirring war poetry in *Viento del pueblo* (1937). *El hombre acecha* (1939) contains powerful poems about a bloody Spain and her sacrificial victims. Finally, in *Cancionero y romancero de ausencias* (1958; tr *Songbook of Absences*, 1972), poems written in the years of his imprisonment (1938–41), the despairing voice of a prisoner, near death and longing for his wife and son, is transmuted into an expression of love and mystical faith. He also wrote poetic dramas. Themes of melancholy, sensuality, violence, and despair alternate in this idealistic poet of the earth who fused traditional forms with a thoroughly modern consciousness, creating a poetry of extraordinary force and originality. Many critics equate his talent and subsequent influence with that of GARCÍA LORCA; like the great Andalusian poet, his life was snuffed out in its prime. Hernández died of tuberculosis in the prison hospital at Alicante at the age of thirty-two.

Herne, James A. (original name James Aherne, 1839–1901)   American dramatist. Herne was a pioneering realist. His best-known works include *Hearts of Oak* (1879), written with David BELASCO; *Margaret Fleming* (1890), a frank treatment of adultery that shocked contemporary audiences; *Shore Acres* (1893), a realistic study of Maine life; and *The Reverend Griffith Davenport* (1899), about a Methodist circuit rider in the South during the American Civil War.

Herne's Egg, The (1938)   A poetic drama by William Butler YEATS. Full of the symbolism and philosophy of Yeats's own occult system, it is the story of two warring Irish kings, their theft of the eggs of the sacred Great Herne, the raping of its priestess, and their death under a curse.

Herne the Hunter   See WILD HUNTSMAN.

Hero and Leander   The hero and heroine of a romantic Greek legend. Leander, who lived in Abydos, swam across the HELLESPONT every night to court Hero in Sestos. When he was drowned in a storm, she flung herself into the sea. A well-known treatment of the story is MARLOWE's *Hero and Leander* (1598).

Herod Antipas (d after AD 40)   Son of HEROD THE GREAT, tetrarch of Galilee and Peraea (4 BC–AD 39). Herod Antipas married his niece Herodias, who had been the wife of his half brother Herod Philip. This incestuous marriage was loudly denounced by JOHN THE BAPTIST and brought about John's beheading at the request of Herodias's daughter SALOME. It was before this Herod that Pontius PILATE sent Jesus; Herod "set him at nought, and mocked him, and arrayed him in a gorgeous robe, and sent him again to Pilate" (Luke 23:7–15). Herod was ultimately banished to Gaul in AD 39; Herodias voluntarily accompanied him.

Herodotus (c480–c425 BC)   A Greek historian, often called the Father of History. Herodotus was born at Halicarnassus, in Asia Minor, and traveled widely, living first at Samos and later at Athens. Herodotus was the first to carry on research into the events of the past and to treat them in a rational rather than a mythical manner. Although he lacked the political sense of Thucydides, his relation of incidents and anecdotes is extremely readable. His history of the Persian invasion of Greece until 479 BC is divided into nine books, named after the nine Muses. He is criticized for credulity, but admired for the charm of his narrative. The relation of the battles of Thermopylae, Salamis, and Plataea in Books VII, VIII, and IX is vivid, and his object, to perpetuate the memory of "great and wonderful deeds," is fully realized.

Herod the Great (73?–4 BC)   King of Judea under the Roman regime (37–4 BC). The birth of JESUS took place in the last year of his reign (an error in chronology first assigned it to AD 1), and it was he who ordered the Massacre of the INNOCENTS.

Herod had his wife Mariamne (and later their two sons) put to death because he suspected her of adultery, a suspicion which was without foundation. The story of Herod and Mariamne has been the subject of several tragedies, including VOLTAIRE's *Mariamne* (1724) and Friedrich HEBBEL's *Herodes und Mariamne* (1850). The expression "to out-herod Herod" means to surpass the worst of tyrants in violence and wickedness and refers to Herod the Great's tyrannical nature. He was the father of HEROD ANTIPAS.

heroic couplet   In English prosody, a rhymed couplet written in iambic pentameters, the English heroic (or epic) line. The neoclassical rules of the 17th and 18th centuries in England required that the heroic couplet express a complete thought and allowed no enjambment between the lines; it was a "closed" couplet. These requirements, however, were a phenomenon of that period, and both before it, as in CHAUCER's and SHAKESPEARE's work, and after, from the romantics on, the construction of sentences has been allowed to carry over from line to line and couplet to couplet; such couplets are called "open" or "run-on" couplets. The following is an example of POPE's use of the heroic couplet:

> But WHEN / to MIS/chief MOR/tals BEND / their WILL
> How SOON / they FIND / fit IN/struMENTS / of ILL.

Hero of Our Time, A (Geroy nashego vremeni, 1840)   A novel by Mikhail LERMONTOV. It portrays a young aristocrat during the reign of Tsar Nicholas I in the 1830s. The hero, Grigory Aleksandrovich Pechorin, faces the dilemma of all young men of his time: to serve the state or remain inactive. All other outlets for the talents and energies of the Russian aristocracy were closed. The willful and morbid Pechorin reacts to this situation by assuming the pose of a world-weary Byronic wanderer. His sinister air, however, is no pose. His aimless willfulness is a real threat to all who come near him. Serving as an army officer in the Caucasus, he has a love affair with a native woman, which indirectly leads to her death; briefly becomes involved with a band of smugglers, which almost leads to his death; and kills another young officer in a duel. Exciting as the adventures are, the most notable thing about the novel is the revelation and analysis of Pechorin's personality as rendered by his old army companion Maksim Maksimych, by a fictional narrator who meets Pechorin, and by the hero himself in his journal, which makes up the last three sections of the book. The portrayal is one of the best studies of the character of the superfluous man in 19th-century Russian literature. Lermontov's novel is ranked beside the works of the later great Russian novelists, whose narrative techniques and acute psychological analysis he anticipated.

Herrera, Fernando de (1534?–1597)   Spanish poet. Herrera spent his uneventful life in his native Seville, disturbed only by his platonic passion for Doña Leonor, countess of Gelves, to whom he addressed elegant Petrarchan sonnets. Known to his admiring contemporaries as *el Divino*, he sought to enrich and elevate Spanish lyric verse by the use of loftier themes and by verbal innovations. He unfolded his esthetic doctrines in his controversial *Anotaciones a las obras de Garcilaso de la Vega* (1580). His finest poems were inspired by patriotic sentiment. Among these are the song celebrating the Christian victory over the Turks at Lepanto; the ode to Don Juan of Austria, on the occasion of a Moorish revolt in the Alpujarras (1571); and the elegy on the death of King Sebastian of Portugal, killed at Alcázar Kebir in 1578. His other extant works include an account of the Cyprus war and the victory at Lepanto (1572) and a eulogy on the life and death of Thomas More (1592).

Herrera y Reissig, Julio (1875–1910)   Uruguayan poet. A representative of the "baroque" or extravagant wing of MODERNISMO, Herrera y Reissig was the leader of a Bohemian literary group that met in the attic of his father's home in Montevideo. His poetry, designed to appeal to the few, is characterized by experimentation in vocabulary and by unusual imagery, though his themes were often drawn from everyday life. A posthumous edition of his *Poesías completas* was published in 1945. All his poems are SON-NETS.

Herrick, Robert (1591–1674)   English poet, known for his pastoral and love lyrics. Herrick, though a clergyman, was a lover of London's society of poets and wits and, at first, regarded his appointment to a rural Devonshire living as bitter exile. However, his interest in country life produced contentment and much of his best poetry. A Royalist, Herrick lost his parish during the English Civil War. He lived happily in London until the Restoration, when he regained his old living and there spent the rest of his days.

Herrick was a CAVALIER POET, one of the sons of Ben, or poets who followed the tradition of Ben JONSON. Like his master, he was strongly influenced by the Latin poets, but his classicism is devoid of pedantry, rooted in a natural spiritual affinity to the Latin lyricists. At its best, Herrick's poetry has an unaffected simplicity, a gracefulness compatible with robustness and humor, vivid pictorial fancy, and unfailing command of form and feeling. Many of his short poems make ideal song lyrics: his famous TO THE VIRGINS, TO MAKE MUCH OF TIME became one of the most popular songs of the 17th century. Herrick writes of rustic rites and superstitions, flowers, fairies, country content, wine, the making of verse, and a number of imaginary mistresses and their clothing, as in DELIGHT IN DISORDER. He also wrote some excellent religious verse in the *Noble Numbers* section of his collection HESPERIDES.

Herrick is essentially a happy poet. While such poems as "To the Virgins," CORINNA'S GOING A-MAYING, and "To Daffodils" deal with the inevitability of age and death, the theme is treated with a gentle Epicurean melancholy which invites one to enjoy life's fleeting beauty. His love poems do not suggest passion's tragic possibilities, and his religious verse does not repudiate his secular poems in any absolute way. Poems dealing with aspects of religious anxiety, such as "To His Angry God," are honest and touching, but not cries from the depths. More characteristically, he expresses gratitude or simple piety.

Herrick published only one volume of verse, *Hesperides*, which—in spite of the popularity of some of his songs—was quickly forgotten. Only near the end of the 18th century was his work rediscovered and appreciated.

Herrick, Robert (1868–1938)   American novelist. A professor of English at the University of Chicago for thirty years, Herrick is known for his realistic novels describing the corruption of the middle-class soul by the commercialism of modern industrial society. His most widely read book was *The Master of the Inn* (1908), the story of a physician who cures mental illness. *The Common Lot* (1904) depicts the ways in which a young Chicago

architect succumbs to commercialism. Others of his novels include *One Woman's Life* (1913), about a selfish socialite; and *Chimes* (1926), which gives an unflattering picture of a large American university, presumably the University of Chicago.

Herries Chronicle, The   A series of novels by Hugh WALPOLE. Set chiefly in the English Lake District, the series comprises *Rogue Herries* (1930), *Judith Paris* (1931), *The Fortress* (1932), and *Vanessa* (1933). They form a romantic family saga, from the 18th to the first third of the 20th century.

Herriot, James (pseudonym of James Alfred Wight, 1916–   )   English veterinarian and author. Herriot's experiences as a Yorkshire country vet are the subjects of his engaging and immensely popular books, the titles of which are taken from an Anglican hymn: *All Creatures Great and Small* (1972), *All Things Bright and Beautiful* (1974), *All Things Wise and Wonderful* (1977), and *The Lord God Made Them All* (1981). *The Best of James Herriot*, a collection of his writings on four decades as a country animal doctor, appeared in 1982. In 1986 Herriot published *Dog Stories*, a charming collection of fifty tales about dogs.

Hersey, John [Richard] (1914–   )   American novelist and journalist. Hersey's early books of nonfiction, *Men on Bataan* (1942) and *Into the Valley* (1943), are direct reflections of his experiences as a war correspondent. Both his nonfiction and fiction usually deal with the effects of some major, often cataclysmic, event on people as individuals. His novel *A Bell for Adano* (1944, PULITZER PRIZE) was based on his careful observations of the American occupation of Italy. In 1946 Hersey visited Hiroshima and wrote an objective and horrifying account of the impact of the atomic bomb blast on six survivors. It was published in the same year in THE NEW YORKER and in book form as *Hiroshima*. Man's inhumanity and his courage are also themes of Hersey's most ambitious novel, THE WALL, the story of the extinction of the Warsaw ghetto. In 1985 he published *The Call*.

Hervey, John (Baron Hervey of Ickworth, 1696–1743)   English politician and lord privy seal (1740–42). He is the author of *Memoirs of the Court of George II* (3 vols, 1931; ed R. Sedgwick; repr 1970). Hervey was attacked by Alexander Pope, because of his well-known effeminacy, as "Sporus" in the EPISTLE TO DR. ARBUTHNOT: "that thing of silk, Sporus, that mere white curd of ass's milk."

Herzen, Aleksandr Ivanovich (1812–1870) Russian journalist and political thinker. The illegitimate son of a nobleman, Herzen very early interested himself in social and political problems. At Moscow University he became the leader of a group of students interested in politics. Such activity led in 1834 to his arrest and exile to the provinces. He was allowed to return to the capital in 1836 but was again exiled in 1840. Finally, in 1847, he obtained permission to emigrate from Russia and never returned. He witnessed the 1848 revolutions in western Europe with some disappointment and finally settled in London in 1852.

In 1857 Herzen began to publish his famous revolutionary periodical, *Kolokol* (*The Bell*), which had a large readership in Russia, even though it had to be smuggled into the country. Tsar Alexander II himself was reputed to be a regular reader of the publication. In the journal, Herzen carried on a spirited criticism of the social order in Russia and a constant advocacy of the need for Russia to adopt Western socialism.

Hesiod (8th century BC) A Greek poet known as the father of Greek didactic poetry. The most important works ascribed to him are *Works and Days* and *Theogony*. The first consists of moral maxims and precepts on farming as well as giving us what little is known of Hesiod's life. It is a rich source of information on primitive beliefs concerned with everyday life. The *Theogony* is an account of the origin of the world and of the gods.

If the statements made in *Works and Days* are authentic, Hesiod lived most of his life as a farmer in Boeotia. His father was an impoverished farmer who had taken to the sea to make ends meet. *Works and Days* was addressed to Hesiod's brother, supposedly a wastrel who had cheated Hesiod of much of his share of the family property.

Hesione In Greek legend, a daughter of LAOMEDON, king of Troy, and sister to PRIAM. Her father exposed Hesione to a sea-monster in order to appease the wrath of APOLLO and POSEIDON, but she was rescued by HERACLES, who made the stipulation that he should receive a certain reward. Laomedon did not keep his promise, so Heracles slew him, took Troy, and gave Hesione to TELAMON, by whom she became the mother of TEUCER. The refusal of the Greeks to give her up to Priam is given as one of the causes of the TROJAN WAR.

Hesperides Three sisters who guarded the golden apples that HERA received as a marriage gift. They were assisted by the dragon Ladon. HERACLES, as the last of his twelve labors, slew the dragon and carried some of the apples to Eurystheus. Many poets call the place where these golden apples grew the garden of the Hesperides. The apples are thought to have been a symbol of immortality.

Hesperides is the title of Robert HERRICK's collected poetry (1648), in allusion to the idyllic, pastoral character of most of his poems.

Hesse, Hermann (1877–1962) German novelist and poet. Hesse is known as a writer of engaging prose, rich in human sympathy, imagination, and ironic humor. As the title of his early verse collection, *Romantische Lieder* (1899), suggests, he was strongly influenced by GERMAN ROMANTICISM as a young man, particularly by the writings of NOVALIS. Romantic traits remained with him throughout his life: his intense interest in music, for example, and his tendency to combine the ideas of widely varying times

and cultures into a single whole. But the mature Hesse was by no means reliant on any school of writing; his later works are characterized by an individualized style and a strikingly original view of man and culture that combines, among other things, ideas from psychoanalysis and Eastern religion.

Two themes common to almost all of his work are the isolation of the artist and the fundamental duality of existence. His characters either represent opposite forces or struggle to find a point at which opposites can be reconciled. This is evident in his first major novel, DEMIAN, a book rich with symbolic paradoxes and heavily influenced by psychoanalytic thought. Here his protagonist, in an arduous process of self-discovery, discovers that the antithetical forces of light and darkness, good and evil, death and regeneration are all derived from the same force, personified by the demon-god Abraxas. In SIDDHARTHA, written, like *Demian*, in the form of a BILDUNGSROMAN, the way to self-fulfillment is unraveled through the teachings of Buddha. STEPPENWOLF is a more turbulent and perplexing novel, which treats the theme of artist as outsider and confronts the bestial aspects of human nature. The opposition of a contemplative, spiritual life to one that is active and sensual is the subject of *Narziß und Goldmund* (1930; tr 1959). The same theme is explored in MAGISTER LUDI, another *Bildungsroman*, considered by many to be Hesse's finest achievement.

Hesse's other writings in English translation include the essays *In Sight of Chaos* (tr 1923) and *My Belief: Essays on Art and Life* (tr 1974). Poems selected from his *Gesammelte Dichtungen* (1952) have been translated in *Poems* (1970) and *Crisis* (1975). *Stories of Five Decades* appeared in 1972, as did his *Autobiographical Writings*. Hesse's correspondence with Thomas MANN was published in 1975; his correspondence with Romain ROLLAND appeared in 1978. He was a Swiss citizen from 1921 until his death. He received the NOBEL PRIZE in 1946.

Hestia A Greek goddess, later identified with VESTA, the Roman goddess of the hearth. Originally one of the twelve Olympians, Hestia resigned her place to DIONYSUS.

hetaera Literally, a female companion or comrade. In ancient Greece, a courtesan of the better class. Some hetaeras were freed women or even women of free birth. LAIS and PHRYNE are the most famous ones.

He Who Gets Slapped (Tot kto poluchayet poshchochiny, 1914) A drama by Leonid ANDREYEV. The central character of the play is a disenchanted intellectual who seeks refuge as a clown in a circus. The clown, famous for the number of slaps he can endure, apparently symbolizes intellect being buffeted for the amusement of the coarse, uncomprehending mob.

hexameter In prosody, a six-foot line. The word usually refers to the dactylic hexameter line which was the epic verse of classical poetry, whereas the French epic line of iambic hexameter is usually called the ALEXANDRINE.

The hexameters of the ancients were imitated in English by Longfellow in EVANGELINE. The Authorized Version of the BIBLE furnishes a number of examples of "accidental" hexameters; the following are well known:

How art thou fallen from Heaven, O Lucifer son of the Morning.
Why do the heathen rage and the people imagine a vain thing?
God is gone up with a shout, the Lord with the sound of the trumpet.

Heyer, Georgette (1902–1974)   English novelist. Heyer wrote more than fifty immensely popular novels in three different genres: romantic, swashbuckling historical novels; detective stories; and "Regency" romances. Noted for her deft humor and encyclopedic knowledge of her chosen period, she had an enthusiastic following on both sides of the Atlantic and was translated into many languages. Among her many books are *The Grand Sophy* (1950), *The Reluctant Widow* (1946), *Friday's Child* (1944), and *Simon the Coldheart* (1925).

Heym, Georg (1887–1912)   German poet. With Ernst Stadler (1883–1914) and TRAKL, Heym is one of the great early poets of EXPRESSIONISM. He drowned in a skating accident at twenty-five, but already he had produced a body of work notable for its dynamism and sense of despair. In *Der ewige Tag* (*The Eternal Day*, 1911), he introduced a central metaphor: the big city (Berlin) as a demon which tortures and devours humanity. The other collection, *Umbra vitae* (1912), contains posthumous poems, which are modern "night thoughts." One of them, "The War," is an apocalyptic fantasy that became a reality in World War I. In his collection of prose pieces, *Der Dieb* (*The Thief*, 1913), he was one of the first to develop an expressionistic prose style.

Heyse, Paul (1830–1914)   German novelist, immensely popular in his time but not highly regarded today. Heyse's technical mastery of the novella form, however, is undisputed; the most effective among his numerous novellas is *L'Arrabbiata* (1855; tr *The Fury*, 1857), a love story set in Italy. He also outlined a theory of the novella in the preface to the collection *Deutscher Novellenschatz* (*Treasury of German Novellas*, 1871 et seq), which he edited. Among his novels, *Kinder der Welt* (1873; tr *Children of the World*, 1882) is respected; but his plays and lyric poetry are of little value. He received the NOBEL PRIZE in Literature in 1910, the first German to be so honored.

Heyward, DuBose (1885–1940)   American novelist, poet, and dramatist. Heyward is best known for PORGY, his first novel, which became a successful play and served as the basis for George GERSHWIN's opera *Porgy and Bess*. *Mamba's Daughter* (1929) was another novel of Charleston black life, and it was also successfully dramatized (1939). Heyward's other novels include *Peter Ashley* (1932), a story set in the Civil War, and *Star-Spangled Virgin* (1939), about the Virgin Islands and the New Deal. Heyward

began his career as a poet, publishing *Carolina Chansons* (1922) with Hervey ALLEN. He later published two more volumes of verse.

Heywood, John (1497?–?1580)   English poet, a friend of Sir Thomas MORE, and a court musician and entertainer under Henry VIII, Edward VI, and Queen Mary. Heywood made popular the court INTERLUDES that later became an important part of entertainment for royalty and the nobility in Elizabethan and Jacobean times. THE FOUR P'S is his most famous work of this type. He also wrote epigrams and proverbs, included in his *Works* (1562), and a satirical allegory on religion, *The Spider and the Fly* (1556).

Heywood, Thomas (c1570–1641)   English dramatist. One of the Henslowe group, Heywood wrote plays remarkable for their pictures of English domestic life. Among the best are A WOMAN KILLED WITH KINDNESS, THE FAIR MAID OF THE WEST: PARTS I AND II, *The Wise Woman of Hogsden* (c1604), *The Captives* (1624), and the masque *Love's Mistress* (1634). His other plays include *A Maidenhead Well Lost* (c1633), *A Challenge for Beauty* (c1635), *King Edward IV* (c1599), *The Royal King and the Loyal Subject* (c1602), *The English Traveller* (c1624), and a series of dramatizations of classical myths: *The Golden Age* (c1610), *The Silver Age* (c1610), *The Brazen Age* (c1610), and *The Iron Age: Parts I and II* (c1610).

Hezekiah   In the OLD TESTAMENT, a king of Judah for twenty-nine years. Hezekiah was noted for his efforts to abolish idolatry, which had flourished under his father Ahaz, and to restore the worship of JEHOVAH. The famous destruction of the Assyrian army (701 BC) under SENNACHERIB occurred during his reign (2 Kings 19).

Hiawatha (1855)   A long narrative poem by Henry Wadsworth LONGFELLOW. Hiawatha, an Ojibway Indian, is reared by his grandmother, Nokomis, daughter of the Moon. After detailing the hero's accumulation of wisdom, the poet recounts the deeds of Hiawatha in revenging his mother, Wenonah, against his father, the West Wind. Hiawatha eventually becomes the leader of his people, teaching peace with the white man. When his wife, Minnehaha, becomes ill, he goes with her to the land of the Northwest Wind. The poem has been endlessly parodied. See SCHOOLCRAFT, HENRY ROWE.

Hibbert, Eleanor [Burford] (1906–   )   English novelist. It was not until the late 1970s that readers discovered that Jean Plaidy, who wrote widely read romanticized biographies of England's royalty, Philippa Carr, the romance writer, Eleanor Burford, chronicler of domestic love stories, and Victoria Holt, the successful author of romantic gothic suspense novels, were, in fact, Eleanor Hibbert. Hibbert had used as many as seventeen pseudonyms in writing over one hundred novels, almost all of them set in England's past. Nearly all of the "Holt" novels, from *Mistress of Mellyn* (1960) to *The Devil on Horseback* (1977) and *The Spring of the Tiger* (1979), were best-sellers, featuring beautiful, resourceful young heroines who battle against all odds to find happiness. Hibbert's thorough research and her deft handling of character and plot offset the predictability of the gothic mode she so frequently employs.

Hickok, Wild Bill [James Butler] (1837–1876) American soldier, scout, and U.S. marshal. Hickok fought in many Civil War, frontier, and Indian battles. As marshal at Hays City and later in Abilene, Kansas, he faced some of the toughest men on the frontier, killing only in self-defense or in the line of duty. In 1872 he toured the East with Buffalo Bill (William Cody). Four years later, he was murdered by the notorious Jack McCall, and was buried in Deadwood, South Dakota. He became a legend during his lifetime, and after his death, a folk hero. Hickok's friend the poet scout Captain Jack Crawford dedicated a ballad to him, called "The Burial of Wild Bill."

Hicks, Granville (1901–1982) American author and literary critic. Hicks was known in the 1930s for his Marxist interpretation of literature. *Granville Hicks in the "New Masses"* (1974; ed J. A. Robbins) is a collection of his essays from 1933 to 1939, when he was literary editor of *New Masses*. His major works from this period are *The Great Tradition* (1933), *John Reed: The Making of a Revolutionary* (1936), *I Like America* (1938), and *Figures in Transition* (1939), a study of late-Victorian English literature. After the nonaggression pact between the U.S.S.R. and Nazi Germany, Hicks resigned from the Communist Party. In addition to several novels, he wrote an autobiography, *Part of the Truth* (1965), and *Literary Horizons: A Quarter of a Century of American Fiction* (1970).

Hidalgo y Costilla, Miguel (1753–1811) Mexican priest and revolutionary leader. Banished to the village of Dolores for his unorthodox views and irregular personal life, Hidalgo became the representative of the lower classes in Mexico's struggle for independence from Spain. On September 16, 1810, in the parish church, he uttered the *grito de Dolores*—"Long live Our Lady of Guadalupe, death to bad government, death to the Spaniards!"—which became the battle cry of the insurgents. At the head of an ill-kempt army of Indians and mestizos, Hidalgo won victories at Guanajuato and Guadalajara but, perhaps because of a lack of ammunition, failed to attack Mexico City. In March 1811, he was captured by the Spaniards and shot. Mexicans now celebrate September 16 as their Independence Day.

hieratic (fr Gr, *hieros*, "holy") Consecrated to sacred uses. The Greeks applied the term to an Egyptian cursive form of hieroglyphic writing which, though originally used for all literature, came to be reserved for religious texts when DEMOTIC writing was adopted for secular use.

High Church An unofficial division of the Church of England and the Episcopal Church in America. It is distinguished by the importance it places upon the priesthood, the sacraments, and, in general, the outward forms and ceremonies of liturgical ritual.

higher criticism The name applied to modern textual criticism of the Bible, treating such problems as authorship, authenticity, dates of composition. By those who accept the doctrine of the literal inspiration of the Bible, the term is used in a pejorative sense. The phrase was first used in 1787 in Eichhorn's *Einleitung in das Alte Testament*.

Highland Mary The most shadowy of Robert BURNS's sweethearts, but the one to whom he addressed some of his finest poetry, including "My Highland Lassie," "O, Highland Mary," "Thou Ling'ring Star" and—perhaps — "Will ye go to the Indies, my Mary?" She is believed to have been Mary Campbell, who died in 1788. The poem "To Mary in Heaven" was written on the first anniversary of her death.

High Wind in Jamaica, A (1929) A novel by Richard HUGHES, first published in the U.S. as *The Innocent Voyage*. A family of children living in Jamaica in the 19th century are sent to England after a hurricane has partly destroyed their home. Amiable pirates capture them by mistake, and the children bring about the pirates' ruin; one girl becomes a murderess. The irrationality and impenetrability of a child's amoral world and the horror of the whole situation are brilliantly conveyed.

Higuchi Ichiyō (1872–1896) Japanese novelist and poet, the first major woman writer of modern Japan. Higuchi's stories are marked by traditional Japanese lyricism on the one hand and by European-type realism on the other. The finest example is *Takekurabe* (1896; tr *Growing Up*, 1956), which describes a group of preadolescent children growing up near Tokyo's licensed quarter in the late 19th century.

Hildebrand (1) Hero of German legend, a follower of Theodoric the Great. In the *Hildebrandslied* (c800), a short poetic fragment, he is challenged to single combat by a young warrior. He discovers that the young man is his son Hadubrand, whom he has not seen for thirty years, and tries to stop the fight. Hadubrand, unbelieving, accuses him of a coward's evasive lie and insists on the battle, only to be slain by the older and better warrior. See the NIBELUNGENLIED for Hildebrand's role there.

(2) The original name of Pope GREGORY VII.

Hilton, James (1900–1954) English novelist. Hilton was a journalist and book reviewer before he published his two best-selling novels, *Lost Horizon* (1933), about the mythical land of SHANGRI-LA, and GOODBYE, MR. CHIPS. Thereafter he produced a steady stream of popular fiction, including *Random Harvest* (1941), about a man suffering from amnesia. In 1935 he moved to Hollywood, where he wrote a number of screenplays.

Himes, Chester [Bomar] (1909–1984) American novelist. Himes began writing while serving in Ohio State Penitentiary for armed robbery (1929–36). His account of the terrible 1930 Penitentiary fire that killed over three hundred men appeared in *Esquire* in 1932. From his first novel, *If He Hollers Let Him Go* (1945), Himes dealt consistently with the social and psychological burdens of being black in a white society. *The Third Generation* (1954) is an ambitious fictionalized history of oppression from the time of slavery to the mid-20th century. Beginning in 1953, Himes lived as an expatriate in Spain and France, where he met and was strongly influenced by Richard WRIGHT. It was in France that he began his best-known series of novels—including *Cotton Comes to Harlem* (1965) and *Run Man Run* (1966)—featuring the two Harlem policemen Grave Digger Jones and Coffin Ed Johnson. As with Himes's earlier work, the series is characterized by violence and grisly, sardonic humor. *A Quality of Hurt* (1972) and *My Life of Absurdity* (1976) are autobiographies.

Hind and the Panther, The (1687)   A poem by John DRYDEN in defense of the Catholic religion. The hind is the Church of Rome, and the panther is the Church of England. James II is the lion which protects the hind from the bear (Independents), the wolf (Presbyterians), the hare (Quakers), the ape (Freethinkers), the boar (Anabaptists), and the fox (Arians). One of Dryden's most celebrated works, the poem is notable for its wit, the brilliance of its argument, and its passages of rare eloquence and power.

Hindemith, Paul (1895–1963)   German-born composer and violist. One of the most prolific and versatile composers of his day, Hindemith had a style that was neo-classical in flavor, harmonically advanced, but decidedly tonal (he was the most articulate opponent of SCHOENBERG's atonal techniques). *Mathis der Maler* (*Matthias the Painter*, 1938; text by Hindemith) is probably his best-known opera. Other works include *Das Marienleben* (*The Life of Mary*, 1923; song cycle to poems by RILKE), *Ludus Tonalis* (1943; piano pieces), and diverse chamber music. He also wrote several theory texts. From 1940 until his death he taught at Yale University.

Hinduism   The predominant religion of India, claiming about eighty percent of the total population as at least nominal adherents. Hinduism evolved over thousands of years through the complex interaction of the religion brought by invading Aryan tribes (from 1500 BC), and a multiplicity of indigenous cults, many of whose deities, rituals, etc., were integrated into a broad and, to many, bewildering framework. With later accretions from BUDDHISM and JAINISM, particularly the emphasis on nonviolence (ÁHIMSA), Hinduism recognizes no single founder or group of founders, and there is little emphasis on credal purity.

There are innumerable Hindu sects, which differ from each other in some aspect of ritual practice or belief. There are, however, several distinguishing features that can be said to be common to all Hindus:

(1) Central to the entire Hindu socioreligious structure is the CASTE system.

(2) The essential truths of Hinduism are embodied in the sacred literature comprising the four VEDAS, to which are attached ritual texts, the *Brahmanas*; a variety of commentaries and interpretations of these; the philosophical treatises known as the UPANISHADS; a diverse collection of expositions and legends, the PURANAS; and the two great epics, the MAHĀBHĀRATA (with its crucial interpretation, the BHAGAVADGĪTĀ) and the RĀMĀYANA.

(3) Man is bound to an eternal cycle of birth, death, and rebirth through a process of reincarnation, or transmigration of souls (SAMSĀRA).

(4) The sacred scriptures recognize four legitimate ENDS OF MAN.

A central concept in Hindu religion and philosophy, as well as in the social system of caste stratification, is KARMA, the cosmic law of causality, according to which one's destiny in successive existences is determined by one's actions vis-à-vis *dharma*.

The vast Hindu pantheon is dominated by the TRIMURTI (trinity), composed of BRAHMĀ, the creator; VISHNU, the preserver; and SHIVA, the destroyer. The latter two, sometimes through their AVATARS and consorts, serve as the foci for the two major sects of Hinduism, Vaishnavism and Shaivism. A variety of animals, reptiles, and other objects are also worshiped in conjunction with the deities of "high" Hinduism. Often termed polytheistic, Hinduism can be considered monotheistic to the extent that most sects accept minor divinities as aspects of one great god, or essence.

For the six orthodox schools of Hindu philosophy, see DARSHANA.

Hippocrates (460?–?377 BC)   A Greek physician born on the island of Cos; known as Father of Medicine. According to tradition, he devised a code of medical ethics that imposed on his disciples the oath still administered to those about to enter medical practice and known as the Hippocratic Oath. Eighty-seven treatises are attributed to him.

Hippocrene (fr Gr, *hippos*, "horse," *krene*, "fountain")   The fountain of the MUSES on Mount HELICON, produced by a stroke of the hoof of Pegasus; hence, poetic inspiration.

hippogriff (fr Gr, *hippos*, "horse," *gryphos*, "griffin"; thus, a winged horse)   The flying steed whose father was a griffin and mother a filly. In ARIOSTO's ORLANDO FURIOSO, it carries RUGGIERO away from his beloved BRADAMANTE to the island of the enchantress ALCINA. It also takes ASTOLFO to Ethiopia, from whence he ascends to the moon to retrieve ORLANDO's lost wits. Further mention is made of the hippogriff in MILTON's *Paradise Regained*.

Hippolyta   An Amazon queen. When Eurystheus demanded Hippolyta's girdle, HERACLES went to fetch it. He succeeded either by killing her, or by holding her general Melanippe for ransom. This queen, or another of the same name, attacked Attica and was defeated with her Amazons by THESEUS. He married her and she bore him Hippolytus. Some, however, call her Antiope.

In Shakespeare's MIDSUMMER NIGHT'S DREAM, she is the proud and sophisticated woman who is betrothed to Theseus, duke of Athens. The play of the artisans is presented as a part of the celebration of the wedding.

Hippolyte   In Jean Racine's tragedy PHÈDRE, the stepson of Phèdre and the object of her guilty passion. Hippolyte rebuffs her advances, but his father, King Theseus, is convinced of his guilt and brings about his death by invoking Neptune against him.

Hippolytus (428 BC)   A tragedy by EURIPIDES. Hippolytus, the son of Theseus by the Amazon HIPPOLYTA, enrages Aphrodite by scorning the love of women. She avenges herself by causing THESEUS' wife PHAEDRA to fall in love with him. Though wasting away Phaedra will not tell Hippolytus of her passion, but, during Theseus' absence, her nurse gives the story away. Hippolytus is horrified, but will say nothing to Theseus. Humiliated, Phaedra hangs herself, leaving a message for Theseus claiming that Hippolytus has tried to violate her. Theseus returns and, refusing to listen to Hippolytus' denials, lays on him one of three unfailing curses given him by his father, POSEIDON. Hippolytus is soon killed when a bull rising from the sea frightens his horses. ARTEMIS, whose faithful servant Hippolytus has been, now reveals the truth to Theseus, who is grief-stricken over Hippolytus' death and his own guilt, although Hippolytus frees him of this guilt with his dying words.

This story was also told in Racine's masterpiece PHÈDRE, and in such lesser works as Seneca's *Phaedra*, Robinson Jeffers's dramatic poem "The Cretan Woman" (1954), and Mary Renault's novel *The Bull from the Sea* (1962).

Hiraoka Kimitake   See MISHIMA YUKIO.

Hiroshige   See ANDŌ HIROSHIGE.

Hiroshima   The Japanese city which was the target of the first atomic bomb used in warfare (August 1945). The bomb was dropped by the U.S. at the close of World War II. Hiroshima was largely destroyed by that attack, and afterward rebuilt. *Hiroshima* (1946), by John HERSEY, gave a factual and devastating account of the event. Since then, Hiroshima has become a symbol of the horror and devastation of nuclear war.

Hirschfeld, Georg (1873–1935)   German playwright. As a writer, Hirschfeld is identified with the movement of NATURALISM. His two best-known plays, both of which deal with women under extraordinary conditions of social pressure, are *Die Mütter* (*The Mothers*, 1896) and *Agnes Jordan* (1898).

Hishikawa Moronobu   See UKIYOE.

History   For many titles beginning with the words *History of . . .*, see the following proper names. For exam-

ple, *The History of Tom Jones, a Foundling* will be found under *Tom Jones, a Foundling, The History of.*

History of New York from the Beginning of the World to the End of the Dutch Dynasty, A (1809)   A satire by Washington IRVING. The book is presented as the work of a fictional character called Diedrich Knickerbocker. Beginning with a chapter on the creation of the world, the format of the volume mocks the pretensions of early historians. The burlesque became more pointed as Irving included many facts about the colony. The book contains lively descriptions of Dutch manners and morals. It was frequently reprinted after Irving expurgated racier passages, which offended descendants of the Dutch. The name Knickerbocker became a catchword to describe anyone of Dutch descent. See KNICKERBOCKER GROUP.

History of the Kings of Britain, The (Historia regum Britanniae, 1137)   A Latin prose chronicle in twelve books by GEOFFREY OF MONMOUTH. The work is of special importance in relation to the development of ARTHURIAN LEGEND, and also as a source book (partly by way of Holinshed's *Chronicles*) for Elizabethan dramatists. It purports to be a true account of events involved in the founding of the English nation, but is a mixture of fact and fantasy. It begins with the arrival in England of the mythical BRUTE, or Brutus, great-grandson of the Trojan Aeneas. In subsequent pages, there are accounts of such ancients as HENGIST AND HORSA, VORTIGERN, KING LEAR, Ferrex and Porrex, CYMBELINE, Gorboduc, many of whom turn up again in later literature, notably in the plays of Shakespeare.

The strongest influence of Geoffrey's work on other writers has been in the area of Arthurian legend. With the introduction of Merlin the magician, Uther Pendragon, and the building of Arthur into a towering national figure who conquers large chunks of Europe, the legends of Arthur achieved new impetus. Translations and adaptations of *The History of the Kings of Britain* soon appeared in other countries, the most notable of these being the French *Roman de Brut* (1155) of Wace.

Though Wace cautiously expressed doubts about the truth of Geoffrey's "history," the work was not seriously questioned by Englishmen for several centuries. Indeed, in the 16th century one claim to the throne was considerably strengthened by the popular belief that the claimant was directly descended from King Arthur.

Hitchcock, Sir Alfred (1899–1980)   British-born film director, often celebrated as the "master of suspense," though in fact his mastery extended to almost every technical aspect of cinema. During the 1920s and 1930s Hitchcock worked in England, establishing his reputation as a creator of stylish thrillers with *The Lodger* (1926). He directed Britain's first sound feature, *Blackmail* (1929), and between 1934 and 1938 he turned out half a dozen taut and witty melodramas, including *The 39 Steps* (1934) and *The Lady Vanishes* (1938), which rank among his finest work. In 1939 he moved to Hollywood, where most of his subsequent films were made. These were generally psychological hair-raisers laced with black humor, focusing on the adventures of a persecuted (or paranoid) hero. The best films of this period include: *Spellbound* (1945), *Rope* (1948), *Strangers on a Train* (1951), *Vertigo* (1958), *North by Northwest* (1959), and *Psycho* (1960). François TRUFFAUT's *Hitchcock* (1967), an extended interview with the director, is a classic source for information on the man and his films.

Hitler, Adolf (1889–1945)   Austrian Nazi Führer (leader). At the age of eighteen, Hitler tried twice to enter a Viennese school of art, but was rejected. He stayed in Vienna as a part-time construction worker and draftsman. At the outbreak of World War I, he joined a Bavarian regiment and fought at the Western front, receiving two medals for bravery. He was deeply embittered by Germany's defeat, blaming it on the treachery of Jews and Communists. Eager for political action, he remained in Munich after the war and built a tiny nationalist party, which was to become the Nationalsozialistische Deutsche Arbeiterpartei (National Socialist German Workers' Party, known as the Nazi Party).

Hitler's steady rise to power was interrupted only by the Beer Hall Putsch (1923), an unsuccessful attempt to overthrow the WEIMAR REPUBLIC. For his part in the abortive coup he was sentenced to jail, but also became widely known in an economically depressed and demoralized Germany. During the nine months of imprisonment that followed he wrote *Mein Kampf* (1924; tr *My Struggle*, 1940). This book contained autobiographical and reflective passages, rife with hysterical anti-Semitism and paranoia, as well as the program he intended to implement; for the West it was a warning that went unheeded.

Hitler was a master of demagogy and Machiavellian politics. He promised to avenge the shame suffered by Germany after World War I and to establish the dominion of the "master race" over the entire world. With an unshakable belief in his historic mission, a talent for organization, and tremendous energy, he pushed his party to prominence. In 1930 his election victories began; in 1933 he became chancellor; in 1934, president and supreme commander of the armed forces. He reintroduced compulsory military service, remilitarized the Rhineland, and in 1938 succeeded with the *Anschluss* (the joining of Austria to Germany). He also returned the Sudetenland, the border region of Czechoslovakia, to the Reich. When Hitler invaded Poland in 1939, Great Britain and France declared war on Germany.

Hitler welcomed the war, the ultimate goal of which was to defeat Russia and establish the inviolable supremacy of the master race. Initially his confidence seemed well-founded; he had defeated Poland and France in a surprisingly short time. In June 1941 he attacked Russia, advancing quickly on a front of two thousand miles to Leningrad

and Stalingrad. In November 1941 the great Russian offensives began, marking the turning point that led to his eventual defeat. Just after the Japanese attacked Pearl Harbor, Hitler and MUSSOLINI declared war on the U.S.

From that point on, Hitler's war was a war of protraction, demanding from all belligerents tremendous human sacrifices. As his plans for Germany's grandiose future faded, he stepped up a systematic program of extermination, murdering millions of people, most of them Jews. By the summer of 1944 it was clear that war would end in defeat for Germany. In April 1945 Germany finally collapsed and on April 29 Hitler committed suicide with his mistress, Eva Braun, whom he had married the day before. His name has become a byword for tyranny, cruelty, and insane anti-Semitism.

Hoagland, Edward (1932–   )   American novelist, journalist, and travel writer. Hoagland's fiction mainly deals with the struggles of lower-class characters, about whom he writes in a direct, colloquial prose. His novels *Cat Man* (1956), about circus life, and *The Circle Home* (1960), about boxing, are compassionate stories with vivid dialogue. His reputation rests mainly, however, on his essays and travel books. *Notes from the Century Before* (1969) is his journal of a trip through British Columbia. *African Calliope* (1979) describes a winter in the Sudan. Hoagland's interest is in the natural world and the people who interact with it, not with political matters. A collection of his essays appeared as *The Edward Hoagland Reader* (1979). *The Tugman's Passage* was published in 1982.

Hobbema, Meindert (1638–1709)   Dutch painter. After RUISDAEL, with whom he probably studied, Hobbema is considered the finest landscapist of the Dutch school. Although he was little known or appreciated during his lifetime, his work exerted a strong influence on English landscape painters. Like his masterpiece, *The Avenue at Middelharnis* (1689), his other paintings are inviting landscapes painted with subdued colors and engaging detail. A great many of his paintings are marked by the presence of a water mill.

Hobbes, Thomas (1588–1679)   English philosopher. Hobbes spent most of his long life as tutor and companion to the Cavendish family (the earls of Devonshire), though he once tutored Charles II in mathematics. He also spent a number of years in Europe, where he became acquainted with such thinkers as Galileo and Descartes. In England, his friends included Harvey, Ben Jonson, Cowley, and John Selden. An ardent Royalist, Hobbes defended secular monarchy in his best-known work, LEVIATHAN, OR THE MATTER, FORM, AND POWER OF A COMMONWEALTH, but its anticlericalism made his position difficult in Restoration England.

Hobbes has been called the father of materialism: his system reduces all events, even those of thought and memory, to some species of physical motion. He was a pioneer of modern political science, a forerunner of associational psychology, and a leader of modern rationalism, insisting on the complete separation of philosophy and theology. He was, in addition, the master of an unusually forceful and lucid prose style. His other works include *Elements of Law* (1651, 1655) and *Philosophical Rudiments* (1651), treatises on human nature and government.

Hobbit   A hairy-footed creature, ranging in height from two to four feet, an amiable inhabitant of "Middle Earth," created by J.R.R. TOLKIEN in *The Hobbit* (1937). The hero of *The Hobbit* is named Bilbo Baggins. Hobbits are, by nature, peace-loving and gentle, preferring well-farmed fields and bucolic pleasures to the complicated creations of "the Big Folk," as they call men. The Hobbits figure strongly in THE LORD OF THE RINGS.

hobgoblin   An impish, ugly, and mischievous sprite, particularly Puck or Robin Goodfellow. The word is a variant of *Rob-Goblin*, i.e., the goblin Robin, just as Hodge is the nickname of Roger.

Hochhuth, Rolf (1931–   )   German dramatist. Hochhuth was catapulted to international notoriety with his five-act play in FREE VERSE, *Der Stellvertreter* (1963; tr *The Deputy*, 1964), which contained a scathing indictment of Pope Pius XII for his failure to denounce the slaughter of the Jews in World War II. His next work of documentary theatre, *Die Soldaten* (1967; tr *Soldiers*, 1968), dealt with the ethics of saturation bombing, based on the Allied air attack on Dresden in 1945. In this play, Hochhuth lays the responsibility for atrocity directly at the feet of Winston Churchill, whom he depicts as a tragic figure, a leader of his times who lost touch with his own humanity. Hochhuth's conviction that history can be and is influenced by assertive individual action is echoed in his subsequent plays: *Guerrillas* (1970), about crime and corruption in American politics; *Die Hebamme* (*The Midwife*, 1972), his first piece of overt political satire; and *Lysistrate und die NATO* (*Lysistrata and NATO*, 1974), a modern adaptation of Aristophanes' antiwar comedy.

Hochwälder, Fritz (1911–   )   Austrian dramatist living in Switzerland. Born in Vienna, Hochwälder immigrated to Switzerland in 1938, a fugitive from HITLER. His classically constructed plays, written from a Christian socialist viewpoint, deal with fascism and the real sources of freedom in men. Frequently, he examines the social and political situation of the present through the perspective of history, as in his best-known play, *Das helige Experiment* (*The Holy Experiment*, 1943; staged on Broadway as *The Strong Are Lonely*, 1953), about a Jesuit community's armed resistance to the King of Spain's attempts to confiscate its rich Paraguayan territory in the 18th century, as well as with *Der öffentliche Anklager* (1947; tr *The Public Prosecutor*, 1958), set during the REIGN OF TERROR, and *Der Befehl* (*The Order*, 1967), set during World War II. Among his other plays are *Der Flüchtling* (*The Refugee*, 1945), *Die Herberge* (*The Inn*, 1957), *Donnerstag* (*Thursday*, 1959), and *Schicksalskomödie* (*Comedy of Fate*, 1960).

Hockney, David (1937–   )   British painter. Hockney inaugurated POP ART in England in the early 1960s, but thereafter he aspired to a more timeless appeal. His art is marked by a cool detachment and precise draftsmanship. His etchings illustrating *Grimm's Fairy Tales* (1969), *The Blue Guitar* (1977), and *Paper Pools* (1980) are witty and inventive, and are thought by some to be among his finest work. *Camera Works* was published in 1984.

Hoder   The Scandinavian god of darkness, called the blind old god, as opposed to his brother BALDER, the god of light. According to fable, LOKI urged Hoder to kill Balder with an arrow made of mistletoe. Hoder was in turn slain by Vali, the guardian of justice.

Hodgson, Ralph (1871–1962)   English GEORGIAN poet. His best-known poems, such as "The Bells of Heaven" and "The Bull," are passionate protests against cruelty to animals. His *Collected Poems* was published in 1961.

Hoffer, Eric (1902–1983)   American social philosopher. Hoffer, a longshoreman who wrote articles, books, and aphorisms in his spare time, was a self-taught philosopher whose style was strongly influenced by MONTAIGNE. He began reading voraciously at the age of fifteen when he regained his eyesight after seven years of blindness. During the 1920s and 1930s he worked as a migrant laborer in California, keeping a card at the public library of each town he passed through. Hoffer's writing is lucid and quotable, setting forth his belief in the potential for social change without revolution. His highly praised first book, *The True Believer* (1951), is an original study of the fanaticism of mass movements. *The Passionate State of Mind* (1955) and *Reflections on the Human Condition* (1973) are collections of aphorisms. Among later volumes is *Before the Sabbath* (1979), a collection of thoughts in journal form.

Hoffmann, E[rnst] T[heodor] A[madeus] (1776–1822)   German author, known especially for his fantastic and often humorous tales, two collections of which are the *Fantasiestücke* (*Fantasy-pieces*, 1814–15) and the *Nachtstücke* (*Night-pieces*, 1817). His MÄRCHEN style represents a new departure in romantic writing, for he weaves the fantastic closely into the real world—as opposed, for example, to Novalis, whose idealistic *Märchen* have nothing of the real world in them. Thus, Hoffmann may be said to stand between romanticism and the realism of the later 19th century. The same mixture of fantasy and realism characterizes his two novels, *Die Elixiere des Teufels* (*The Devil's Elixirs*, 1816) and the unfinished *Kater Murr* (*Tom-Cat Murr*, 1820). The latter, which is the fictional autobiography of a cat, also includes the story of Hoffmann's most famous character, a composer named Johannes Kreisler who is a typical example of ZERRISSENHEIT. Hoffmann himself was a composer as well as an author, and wrote the music for the opera UNDINE, based on a story by his friend Fouqué. See TALES OF HOFFMANN.

Hofmannsthal, Hugo von (1874–1929) Austrian playwright, poet, and essayist. Hofmannsthal's early writings (pre-1901) are typical of the movement of IMPRESSIONISM. Most of his lyric poetry, for example, was written during this period, and, like that of his friend Stefan GEORGE, it combines mysticism and exoticism in content with delicate balance in form. His language is characterized by the multivalence of key words and symbolism. Among his most famous poems are "Manche freilich . . ." ("Many, it is true . . ."), about the mystical unity of all human destinies, and "Vorfrühling" ("Early Spring"). The short plays that he wrote during this period, including *Der Tod des Tizian* (1892; tr *The Death of Titian*, 1973), *Das kleine Welttheater* (1897; tr *The Small World-Theater*, 1952), and DER TOR UND DER TOD, resemble his lyrics. They offer neither conflict nor action; their dialogues are the poetic expressions of a mood.

The essay *Brief des Lord Chandos* (1901; tr *Letter of Lord Chandos*, 1952), however, marks a clear turning point in Hofmannsthal's career. The fictitious lord explains that he no longer finds language adequate as a means of expression; even a common word like "apple" has so many different connotations for different people that one can never be certain that it will communicate the right one. Hofmannsthal had become discouraged with the lyrical poem as an expressive medium; and in many of his post-1901 dramas, he tried to compensate for the inadequacies of language by turning to traditional and mythical subject matter—that is, he attempted to communicate more directly with his audience by choosing themes that were part of the educated European's cultural heritage. Examples of this tendency are: *Elektra* (1903; tr 1908), adapted from Sophocles' tragedy; *Ödipus und die Sphinx* (1906); *Jedermann* (1911; tr *Everyman*, 1917), a revised medieval MORALITY PLAY; *Das Salzburger grosse Welttheater* (1923; tr *The Great World-Theater of Salzburg*, 1963), based on Calderón's EL GRAN TEATRO DEL MUNDO; and THE TOWER, a free adaptation of Calderón's LA VIDA ES SUEÑO. In these later plays, he makes extensive use of dramatic action and stage arrangements for expressive purposes, rather than relying on language alone. Finally, his search for better means of communication led him to combine his art with music in the opera librettos he wrote for Richard STRAUSS, including DER ROSENKAVALIER.

Hofmann von Hormannswaldau, Christian (1617–1679) German poet. Hofmann's style is characterized as "late baroque" or "manneristic," because of the self-conscious richness, sometimes highly overloaded, of his imagery and language. His writing does not have the stoic, ascetic quality that is found in Gryphius's works, but he was nonetheless a religious man, and the influence of German mysticism is felt in his verse. A characteristic poem is his sonnet "Auf den Einfall der Kirchen zu St. Elisabeth" ("On the Collapse of the Church in St. Elizabeth"), in which a rich, detailed picture of the ruined building is given, followed by a moral comparing it to the religion of the time.

Hofstadter, Richard (1916–1970) American historian. A professor at Columbia University for many years, Hofstadter made important contributions to the study of American social, political, and cultural history. *The Age of Reform* (1955), an unsentimental analysis of populism and progressivism, won a PULITZER PRIZE. He received the award again for *Anti-Intellectualism in American Life* (1963). Among his other major works are *Social Darwinism in American Thought* (1944; rev 1955); *The American Political Tradition* (1948); *The Paranoid Style in American Politics* (1965); *The Progressive Historians* (1968); and *America at 1750: A Social Portrait* (1971).

Hogarth, William (1697–1764) English painter and engraver. Hogarth is generally regarded as the greatest pictorial satirist of England. His reputation was established through the plates for Samuel Butler's *Hudibras* (1726). He then did a series of satirical paintings, *The Harlot's Progress* (1731), engravings of which he distributed the following year by subscription. They achieved a tremendous success, and Hogarth went on to do other series of narrative paintings, which he afterwards engraved. *The Rake's Progress* was distributed in 1735, *Marriage à la Mode* in 1745. Hogarth's fame rests on these satirical series, in which he expressed the hard morality of his age with sharpness and humor; however, his admirable portraits, with their strong sense of color and direct, free handling of paint, also make a claim to artistic greatness. His engravings are said to have furnished Henry Fielding with prototypes for his characters, and they inspired the libretto of W. H. Auden and Chester Kallman for Stravinsky's opera *The Rake's Progress* (1951).

Hogarth Press See WOOLF, VIRGINIA.

Hogg, James (known as the Ettrick Shepherd, 1770–1835) Scottish poet. Hogg was so called because he was born in Ettrick and inherited the occupation of shepherd from his family. Largely self-educated, he is known for his verse celebrating Scottish rural scenes and pursuits and for his treatments of the Celtic folklore tradition. He was encouraged by Sir Walter Scott and in his later life was associated with *Blackwood's Magazine*.

Hōjō ki See ACCOUNT OF MY HUT, AN.

hokku See HAIKU.

Holbein, Hans, the younger (1497–1543) German painter. His father (c1460–1524), after whom the son was named, was also a distinguished painter, noted for his altarpieces. The younger Holbein studied and worked in Basel and was led by the artistic depression ensuing from the Reformation to undertake a trip to England (1526–28), and finally to settle there in 1530. He executed smoothly finished, carefully detailed, precisely drawn, and richly colored portraits and religious paintings. His formal portraits preserve the features of Erasmus, Sir Thomas More and his family, Thomas Cromwell, and Henry VIII, in whose services he spent his last years.

Holbrook, David (1923–   )   English poet, novelist, and educator. Holbrook's literary and social criticism tends toward scathing attacks on individuals and social trends. *Llareggub Revisited* (1962) pillories Dylan THOMAS for infantile and fustian emotionalism. *Human Hope and the Death Instinct* (1971) takes FREUD, SARTRE, and R. D. LAING to task for promoting nihilism. His moral indignation at sexual explicitness is voiced in *The Case Against Pornography, The Pseudo-Revolution,* and *The Masks of Hate* (all 1972). Later criticism includes *Sylvia Plath* (1976) and *Lost Bearings in English Poetry* (1977). He has also written a novel, short stories, and several praised collections of poems, including the highly praised *Old World, New World* (1969).

Hölderlin, Friedrich (1770–1843)   German poet. In his predominant use of classical verse forms and syntax Hölderlin was a follower of KLOPSTOCK, but his language is more compressed and powerful than the older poet's. He was not directly affiliated with either of the two major literary movements of his time, Weimar classicism or romanticism, but his thought has elements in common with both. He shares the classicists' love of balance and repose, but couples it with a romantic yearning for complete oneness with nature and for a religion that could combine pantheism, Greek religion, and Christianity. SCHELLING and HEGEL, friends of his since their school days, expressed similar ideas at times.

Hölderlin's life was never settled or happy. He lacked both money and recognition, and these strains, combined with that of his entirely platonic but socially suspect love affair with a married woman (Susette Gontard, whom he calls "Diotima" in his poems), drove him insane in 1803, so that his actual career lasted only about a decade. Neither SCHILLER nor GOETHE recognized Hölderlin's greatness, but his lyric poetry and his novel HYPERION ODER DER EREMIT IN GRIECHENLAND are now counted among the greatest literary achievements in the language. Some of his finest lyrics (written 1800–1803) are "Brod und Wein" ("Bread and Wine"), an elegy celebrating both Jesus and Dionysus; "Der Archipelagus," an ode in which it is hoped that modern Germany will tend toward the character of ancient Greece; "Heidelberg" and "Der Rhein," odes on the city and the river, respectively; and the patriotic ode "Germanien."

Holinshed, Raphael (or Raphael Hollingshead, d c1580)   English historian. Holinshed is famous as the author of the CHRONICLES OF ENGLAND, SCOTLAND, AND IRELAND. A massive history of the world had been begun by Reginald Wolfe; when Wolfe died in 1573 Holinshed took over the project and, with the assistance of Richard Stanihurst and William Harrison, completed it on a somewhat smaller scale as a history of England. The work is memorable primarily as a source of plots for Elizabethan dramatists, particularly Shakespeare.

Hollow Men, The (1925)   A poem by T. S. ELIOT. Mixing nursery rhyme and liturgy, it presents Eliot's view of the spiritual emptiness and doom of the 20th century.

Holmes, Oliver Wendell, Sr. (1809–1894) American physician, professor, man of letters. By his own definition, Holmes was a New England Brahmin, a man of cultivated family and sufficient fortune. Holmes earned local recognition as a youth with the poem OLD IRONSIDES.

A man of immense energy, Holmes combined the practice of medicine and a Harvard professorship with the writing of verse. When *The Atlantic Monthly* began publishing under James Russell Lowell, Holmes gave it its name, and contributed THE AUTOCRAT OF THE BREAKFAST-TABLE, a series that combined fiction, essay, conversation, drama, and verse. The *Autocrat*, modeled on the work of Addison and Steele, made Holmes famous for wit and originality. THE CHAMBERED NAUTILUS, his most frequently anthologized poem, appeared there. He continued the essays in two further series: *The Professor at . . .* (1859), and *The Poet at . . .* (1872).

A conversationalist in the tradition of Dr. Johnson, Holmes was in great demand as a guest and speaker. He was a familiar figure at the dinners of the Saturday Club, of which Emerson, Longfellow, Whittier, Lowell, Agassiz, and Motley were members.

Holmes always rebelled against his Calvinist upbringing. As an enlightened scientist, he urged that criminals be educated rather than punished. His poem THE DEACON'S MASTERPIECE is a satire on tightly constructed dogmas. Holmes's "medicated" novels, such as ELSIE VENNER, continue his attack on Calvinist theology.

Holmes was not only ahead of his time in social thought, but his essay *The Contagiousness of Puerperal Fever* (1843) anticipated Semmelweis. He was the father of the great jurist Oliver Wendell Holmes, Jr.

Holmes, Oliver Wendell, Jr. (1841–1935) American jurist, son of the celebrated physician and author of the same name. Holmes was appointed to the U.S. Supreme Court in 1902 after teaching at Harvard Law School and serving on the Massachusetts Supreme Court; he is regarded as the leading exponent of law in Anglo-Saxon countries. Many of Holmes's pronouncements on such subjects as "judicial restraint" and free speech are regarded as legal landmarks. His vigorous and eloquent dissents on the First and Fourteenth Amendment cases earned him a reputation as "The Great Dissenter."

Holmes's publications include *The Common Law* (1881), a series of lectures which became a legal classic; *Speeches* (1891; rev 1913); and *Collected Legal Papers* (1920).

Holmes, Sherlock   One of the most famous of all fictional characters, this brilliant but eccentric detective was created by Sir Arthur Conan DOYLE, who introduced him in his *Study in Scarlet* (1887). His adventures are continued in *The Sign of the Four* (1889); *The Adventures of Sherlock Holmes* (1891); *The Memoirs of Sherlock Holmes* (1894); *The Hound of the Baskervilles* (1902); *The Return of Sherlock Holmes* (1904); *The Valley of Fear* (1915); *His Last Bow* (1917); and *The Case Book of Sherlock Holmes* (1927). Holmes has such brilliant analytical faculties and indefatigable interest in any detective problem that he regularly puts Scotland Yard to shame. He is abrupt in manner, master of the violin and a dozen obscure sciences, and a victim of the cocaine habit. His admiring friend, Dr. Watson, usually records his triumphs. Holmes's inveterate enemy is the malevolent Moriarty.

Holofernes   A tedious, pedantic schoolmaster in Shakespeare's LOVE'S LABOUR'S LOST. Holofernes and Sir Nathaniel are described as "arts-men" who "have been at a great feast of languages and stolen the scraps."

Holt, Victoria   A pseudonym of Eleanor HIBBERT.

Holtby, Winifred (1898–1935)   English novelist. Holtby's best novel was her last, *South Riding* (1936), a novel about Yorkshire life. She also wrote a study of Virginia Woolf (1932). She was memorialized in *Testament of Friendship* (1940), by Vera BRITTAIN.

Holy Fair, The (1786)   A poem by Robert BURNS ridiculing the Holy Fair at Mauchline. Three "sisters" —Fun, Superstition, and Hypocrisy—visit the Fair and view scenes of immorality.

Holy League   (1) Designation for an agreement arranged by Pope Julius II among the Italian and European powers. It was directed against France. The War of the Holy League (1511–13) put an end to French plans for the domination of Italy. Another league, called the Second Holy League, was an agreement among the Papacy, France, and the Italian powers directed against Spain. The War of the Second Holy League (1526–29), won by Spain, insured her control of Italy and the Papacy thereafter.

(2) An association formed in 1576 under the auspices of Henry, duke of GUISE, to defend the Roman Catholics against French Protestants and to win the French throne for the Guises. The league, which was subsidized by Philip II of Spain, was defeated by Henry IV of France at Arques and Ivry and lost its influence after his conversion to Catholicism.

Holy Living and Dying   A religious work by Jeremy TAYLOR. It was originally published in two parts: *The Rule and Exercise of Holy Living* (1650) and *The Rule and Exercise of Holy Dying* (1651).

Holy of Holies   The innermost quarter of the Jewish temple. In it the Ark of the Covenant was kept. Into this place only the high priest was allowed to enter, and that but once a year, on the Day of Atonement. The term, or its Latin equivalent, *sanctum sanctorum*, has been applied to any haven kept sacred from the world in general.

Holy Roman Empire   A loose confederation of German states ruled by various royal German houses who claimed the imperial authority of ancient Rome. The butt of generations of joking students ("it was neither Holy, Roman, nor an Empire"), the Holy Roman Empire lasted in name for over one thousand years (800–1806). It began when Charlemagne was crowned emperor by Pope Leo III and ended when Francis II (Francis I of Austria) abdicated. While the power of the emperor and the cohesion of the empire always existed more in theory than in practice, the Holy Roman Empire did give a certain unity to the many German states.

The first German emperor was Henry the Fowler, who was crowned in 919. Since the title was not hereditary, the emperor being elected by seven electors, the crown was held at various times by nearly all the royal German houses. The uninterrupted line of Hapsburg emperors began in 1438. The power and prestige of the Austrian Hapsburgs reflected on the empire as well. Under Maximilian I and Charles V the empire had its greatest strength. After Charles relinquished the crown in 1556, there began the steady decline that ended in 1806 with the empire's extinction.

Holy Sepulcher   The rock-hewn tomb in a garden outside the walls of Jerusalem, traditionally the burial place of the body of Jesus after the Crucifixion. Although the site of the tomb has never been precisely identified, rumor has fixed it in a cave under the edifice known as the Church of the Holy Sepulcher in Jerusalem, which was begun by Constantine the Great in the 4th century, destroyed and rebuilt—once during the Crusades—and reconsecrated in 1810 after extensive repairs.

Holy Trinity   See TRINITY, THE.

Holy Week   See EASTER.

Holz, Arno (1863–1929)   German poet, dramatist, and critic. In his early poems Holz showed himself an exponent of the early, idealistic phase of German NATURALISM. But during 1888–90, when he became a friend of Johannes Schlaf, he turned strongly toward what he called consistent realism, and attempted to reproduce everyday reality in his writing. At the same time, he turned away from lyric poetry to narrative and drama, and with Schlaf, coauthored the two starkly realistic works *Papa Hamlet* (1889), a collection of prose sketches which appeared under the pseudonym Bjarne P. Holmsen, advertised as a translation from the Danish, and the play *Die Familie Selicke* (*The Selicke Family*, 1890), about the troubles of a poor Berlin family. Shortly afterward, he wrote a theoretical work, *Die Kunst, ihr Wesen und ihre Gesetze* (*Art, Its Essence and Its Laws*, 1891), in which he strongly disputed the claim that art is a metaphysical absolute. Holz himself, however, turned away from naturalism and back to lyric poetry in his *Phantasus* (1898 et seq), and in a theoretical work, *Revolution der Lyrik* (*Revolution of Lyric Poetry*, 1899), he defended the use of completely free verse.

Homage to Mistress Bradstreet (1956)   A long poem by John BERRYMAN. This FREE VERSE, fifty-seven stanza composition is a tribute to Anne BRADSTREET, Puritan poet and wife of Massachusetts Bay Colony Governor Simon Bradstreet. Berryman created a moving portrait of this talented woman, whose life and verse exemplified a candor and explicit passion which were rare in her stern milieu. In the poem Anne Bradstreet speaks in first person; her rambling ideas are presented in a form resembling interior monologue. The imagery and syntax are discrete and random, simulating processes of human thought. The core of the poem dramatizes Bradstreet's conflict: her absolute devotion to God and family as opposed to her love of writing, which she fears is too "worldly" and self-indulgent.

Homer   Ionian poet. To him the ILIAD and the ODYSSEY are traditionally attributed. As early as the Hellenistic period, a few scholars insisted that the epics were the work of different authors. Orthodox opinion, however, claimed that Homer had composed both works, and numerous biographies were written of him. Eight of these are extant, but their dates and authors are unknown and they are regarded as largely invention. There was a further firm tradition that Homer was blind. A measure of the reliable information about Homer known to the ancients is the fact that seven cities claimed to have been his birthplace: Chios, Colophon, Smyrna, Rhodes, Argos, Athens, and Salamis. The fact is that nothing whatever is known about Homer the man, including the crucial point of whether he existed.

Nevertheless, modern scholars have learned a great deal about the works that the Greeks attributed to Homer. These were not only the *Iliad* and the *Odyssey*, but also the BATTLE OF THE FROGS AND MICE and the HOMERIC HYMNS, and certain epics from the EPIC CYCLE, known today only in brief fragments. It has long been accepted as certain that of these only the first two can be considered as genuinely "Homeric," although the Homeric hymns were clearly written in imitation of Homer's style. Today even most "unitarians," who believe the *Iliad* and the *Odyssey* each to be the work of a single author, do not consider them the work of the same author. The diction and language of the *Odyssey* show it to be a somewhat later work.

All scholars are aware that GREEK EPIC POETRY of the Homeric age was the end product of a long period of gradual accretion during which historical events, legends, and folk tales were stitched together by many generations of rhapsodes or bards. In the case of the *Iliad* and the *Odyssey*, this process probably covered four centuries, from shortly after the series of events known as the TROJAN WAR in the early 13th century BC to the mid-9th century BC, which seems the most likely date for Homer. The "analytic school" of Homeric scholars believe that this process continued up to the 6th century BC, when PISISTRATUS had the epics arranged for regular recitation at the Panathenaic festivals. This would mean that the epics were compiled and edited from bits and pieces rather than composed to a significant extent by a single individual.

Although analytic theories tended to dominate Homeric studies after the pioneer work of F. A. Wolf in 1795, there has been in recent years a strong resurgence of the unitarians. The most widely held position today is that, although both the *Iliad* and the *Odyssey* are made up of traditional materials, each bears the unmistakable imprint of a single artistic intelligence. This belief is supported by the remarkable structural, dramatic, and stylistic unity achieved in both epics, in spite of numerous and obvious anachronisms and other discrepancies. The *Odyssey*, in spite of—or perhaps in part because of—its broader scope and greater variety, evidences more clearly than the *Iliad* the work of a single poet. It is remarkable for its extraordinarily modern structure, which employs the techniques of the "flashback" and parallel lines of action common in the novel.

The *Iliad* and the *Odyssey* as they are known today are based on the texts edited in the 6th century BC for use in Athens. A considerable amount of tampering with the *Iliad* was done by the Athenians in order to increase their role in its events, and the texts were further edited in the 2nd century BC by two distinguished scholars in Alexandria: ARISTARCHUS of Samothrace and ARISTOPHANES OF BYZANTIUM. The extant texts are substantially those of Aristarchus.

Homer, Winslow (1836–1910)   American painter. Beginning as an illustrator, Homer was a Civil War correspondent for *Harper's Weekly*. About 1880 he gave up illustration for painting and settled on the Maine coast in 1884, often visiting Florida and the West Indies. His themes became the everyday lives of fishermen and the power of sea and wind. His paintings are remarkable for their realism and for their powerful yet subtle light effects. He is best known for his ocean paintings, such as *The Lookout—All's Well* (1896).

Homeric epithet   See EPITHET.

Homeric hymns   Poems in the epic style composed by poets known as Homeridae or sons of HOMER. Modeled after the works of Homer, these hymns, or Preludes, were presented by the Homeridae before their recitation of Homer at public festivals. Thirty-three poems are extant, among them hymns to DEMETER, PAN, APOLLO, and others.

Homme révolté, L'   See REBEL, THE.

Homunculus (Lat, "little man")   In Part II of Goethe's FAUST, a miniature man in a vial who is artificially created by WAGNER in an attempt to raise man above his dependency on sex for reproduction. Homunculus leads Faust and Mephistopheles to the classical WALPURGIS NIGHT.

Honegger, Arthur [Oscar] (1892–1955)   French composer, member of LES SIX. His best-known works include *Pacific 231* (1924; an orchestral imitation of a steam locomotive) and two cantatas: *Le Roi David* (*King David*, 1921; text by René Morax) and *Jeanne d'Arc au*

Bûcher (*Joan of Arc at the Stake*, 1938; text by Paul CLAUDEL). He also wrote chamber music and symphonies.

Honest Whore, The: Parts I and II (1604, 1605) A comedy by Thomas DEKKER. Hippolito, in love with Infelice, the daughter of the duke, believes that she is dead, and is inconsolable. Actually, she has been sent to a convent to separate her from Hippolito. Meanwhile, the constant Hippolito has been taken to the home of the courtesan Bellafont, whose advances he resists. She, however, falls madly in love with him and embarks on a life of chastity. Soon, Hippolito discovers that Infelice is alive and rushes to the convent to marry her. The duke arrives too late to prevent the match and becomes reconciled to the union. Bellafont, by order of the duke, is married to her first lover, Matheo. The subplot revolves around Candido, a linen draper, whom nothing perturbs. He is so mild and serene that his wife, in desperation, has him committed to an asylum. At the end, he is released, his brow gently furrowed with concern for his wife's sanity.

In Part II, the honest Bellafont's worthless husband Matheo is in prison, and she seeks help from Hippolito, who is struck by her beauty. When Matheo is released from prison, her sorrows only increase. Her husband stops at nothing, even suggesting that she return to her old profession to provide money; Hippolito presses her with his unwanted attentions. Meanwhile, Orlando Friscobaldo, Bellafont's father, has disguised himself and become Matheo's servant, in order to watch over his daughter. Soon, Bellafont is falsely arrested for prostitution, and Matheo accuses her of infidelity with Hippolito. However, her father, revealing himself, establishes her innocence, and Matheo is sternly warned to repent. Again the patient Candido appears, this time in the process of taming his second shrewish wife.

Hood, Thomas (1799–1845)   English poet and humorist. Hood suggested as his epitaph "Here lies one who spat more blood and made more puns than any man living." His actual epitaph reads "He sang the Song of the Shirt." Together they suggest something of the contradictory nature of his life and art: the long struggle with illness and poverty maintained with courage and gaiety, his unique standing as a poet both humorous and serious. He earned a livelihood through his light verse, which ranges from the penetrating but good-natured satire of "Miss Kilmansegg" (1841–43) to such pun-filled buffoonery as "Faithless Nelly Grey" (1834):

> O Nelly Grey! O Nelly Grey!
> Is this your love so warm?
> The love that loves a scarlet coat,
> Should be more uniform.

Among his serious works, his poems of social protest, such as "The Song of the Shirt" (1843), are most famous, but he wrote a wide variety of lyrics and ballads. Some of his collections are *Odes and Addresses to Great People* (1825), *The*

Midsummer Fairies (1827), and *Whims and Oddities* (1826, 1827).

Hooker, Richard (1554?–1600)   English theologian. Hooker took holy orders in 1581. As a result of a controversy with a strict Calvinist, he attempted to clarify the position of the Church of England and wrote his great work, *The Laws of Ecclesiastical Polity* (1593–97). The treatise treats church government from a philosophical and logical point of view, and anticipates the "common consent" grounds for government of Locke and Rousseau.

Hoover, Herbert [Clark] (1874–1964)   Thirty-first president of the U.S. (1929–33). After a successful career as a mining engineer and businessman, Hoover won an international reputation during World War I when he served successively as chairman of the American Relief Committee, chairman of the Commission for Relief in Belgium, and U.S. Food Administrator. As secretary of commerce (1921–28), he organized his department in order to make it serve business interests more efficiently. Elected president in 1928, he was faced by the Great Depression of 1929 soon after he entered the White House. Hoover, an advocate of self-help, was reluctant to use the power of the federal government to revive the economy, though he supported the Reconstruction Finance Corporation (1932) to extend loans to banks and other business enterprises. In 1932 he sought reelection but was defeated by Franklin D. ROOSEVELT. From 1947 to 1949 he headed a bipartisan commission to study ways of simplifying and improving the structure of the executive branch of the federal government. Hoover's books include *American Individualism* (1922), *The Challenge to Liberty* (1934), *Memoirs* (3 vols, 1951–52), *The Ordeal of Woodrow Wilson* (1958), and *An American Epic* (3 vols, 1959–61).

Hope, A[lec] D[erwent] (1907–   )   Australian poet. Hope has been called one of the two or three best poets writing in English. He is considered a controversial figure in Australian literature for his polemics against modernist movements in poetry. His own verse, though rooted in 17th- and 18th-century poetry and in traditional meter, expresses nonetheless a modern sensibility. *Collected Poems, 1930–1970* (1972) demonstrates the range of his work, from satires railing at modern angst, to lyrics seeking happiness in love and art, to mythic poems suggesting that the defense against chaos and loneliness lies in immemorial human rhythms and inner powers.

Hopkins, Gerard Manley (1844–1889)   English poet and Jesuit priest. Hopkins is known for his small number of brilliant poems on religion and nature, and for his revolutionary innovations in poetic technique. His poetry is distinguished by an intricate type of rhythm, which he called SPRUNG RHYTHM; by puns, internal rhymes, and intricate patterns of wordplay; and by an extremely individual technique of elliptical phrasing and compound metaphor capable of great concentration of meaning. His work is thought to be indebted to Old English ALLITERATIVE

VERSE, to the METAPHYSICAL POETS, especially George Herbert, and to traditional Welsh poetry.

Hopkins was a member of a large, artistically gifted family, and was himself talented in drawing and music as well as in poetry. He loved sensuous beauty; his earliest poems are lush and Keatsian, and for many years he kept diaries describing the beauties of nature. At Oxford University he was a student of Walter PATER and wrote a platonic dialogue, *On the Origin of Beauty*. He also came under the influence of Benjamin Jowett and Cardinal NEWMAN. Converted to Roman Catholicism in 1866, he was inducted into the Jesuit order in 1868. He received his theological training in North Wales. Hopkins tried to compensate for his sensuous nature by entering on an extremely ascetic course of life. It was not until 1875 that, at the wish of his rector, he broke a seven years' poetic silence and wrote THE WRECK OF THE DEUTSCHLAND, his first great poem. Subsequent poems celebrated the beauty and INSCAPE of God-made nature, and reflected his personal experience as a priest and his concern about social conditions and industrial materialism. He became a professor of Greek at Dublin University in 1884. His last poems include his "terrible" sonnets, which express his sense of alienation from God—a state commonly experienced by mystics.

Hopkins's poems were very much in advance of his time and none were published during his lifetime. He sent them, with long letters, to the poet Robert BRIDGES, his friend from Oxford days; Bridges published them in 1918. Because of the originality of his poetry and the date of its publication Hopkins tends to be regarded as a leading modern poet rather than as a Victorian. His techniques influenced a number of 20th-century British and American poets, notably W. H. AUDEN and Dylan THOMAS. Hopkins's letters, notebooks, and papers were published in four volumes from 1935 to 1938. These contain details of his metrical and aesthetic theories, accounts of his spiritual progress, and many descriptions of nature. Among Hopkins's best-known individual poems are "The Windhover," "Pied Beauty," "The Caged Skylark," "Felix Randall," "Spring and Fall," and "The Leaden Echo and the Golden Echo."

Hopper, Edward (1882–1967)   American painter. Hopper's paintings are precise representations, not only of scene, but also of mood, usually solitary detachment suggested by sharp, sometimes harsh light. Although he himself shunned avant-garde movements, his work, particularly the urban scenes, such as *Nighthawks* (1942), foreshadowed the POP ART and new realism movements of the 1960s.

Hopscotch   See RAYUELA.

Horace (full Latin name Quintus Horatius Flaccus, 65–8 BC)   Roman lyric poet and satirist. The son of a freed slave, Horace was born at Venusia in southern Italy. His father, a tax collector, spared no effort or expense to provide his son with the best possible education; he took

Horace to Rome to study under the best Roman grammarian. To complete his education, Horace, then a young man of twenty, enrolled at the University of Athens (45 BC). While he was there, word came that Caesar had been assassinated. Like many Roman intellectuals, Horace rallied to the cause of revolution and liberty, and, when Brutus appeared at Athens, he followed him, entering the senatorial army as a military tribune. After the defeat of Brutus at Philippi (42), Horace returned penniless to Rome and managed to get a job with the Roman civil service as a clerk.

Here he began writing his first successful poetry: a group of clever satires and a mélange of iambic poems after the manner of Greek lyrics. These poems won him the admiration of Vergil who, in 38 BC, introduced Horace to the influential patron MAECENAS. Thus began a lifelong friendship between the patron and the young poet, and, in 33 BC, Maecenas gave Horace a small estate in the Sabine hills. There he polished his satires (*The Sermones*) and his iambic poems (*The Epodes*); he published them in 30 BC.

His great poetic work was his four-book collection of odes (*The Carmina*), the first three books of which appeared in 23 BC. In them he displayed what Petronius termed a "painstaking felicity" of expression. Horace was the finished master of stanzaic meters, just as Vergil was the incomparable master of the larger and more sonorous dactylic hexameter. Horace's hexameters, as he used them in his satires and in his epistles (*The Epistulae*, composed 22–8 BC), were deliberately unmajestic; they employed everyday diction, interspersed with occasional slang, and were written in a conversational tone in which whole passages, nevertheless, have the feeling of elegant, musical prose. Throughout his poetry, his personality, though seldom obtrusive, is always evident. His poetry is, indeed, his own most vivid biography. Here we sense the presence of a sly but never ungenerous man, a sometimes aloof lover of independence who was also the devoted friend of the emperor Augustus, of Maecenas, and of Vergil; an epicurean in good times and a stoic in adversity; an artist and a country gentleman who had learned the advantages of cultivating his own garden in poetry as well as in politics.

Among Horace's other works are the *Carmen saeculare*, a liturgical hymn composed for the secular games held at Rome in 17 BC, and the ARS POETICA, which was adapted as a handbook on style by the neoclassicists of the 16th and 17th centuries. Horace died in 8 BC, only a few months after the death of his friend and supporter Maecenas, beside whose grave he was buried.

Horace (1640)   A tragedy by Pierre CORNEILLE. The material of the play is derived from Livy. Horace and his two brothers are chosen to represent Rome, Curiace and his two brothers to represent Alba, in a combat that will decide the war between the two cities. When his brothers are killed, Horace pretends to flee and thus contrives to kill each adversary separately. His sister Camille, the betrothed of Curiace, curses Rome. Infuriated, Horace kills her and is summoned before the king. Curiace's sister Sabine begs to be executed in Horace's place. His father pleads for him, and in view of his brave deed the king pardons Horace. See HORATII, THE THREE.

Horatian Ode upon Cromwell's Return from Ireland, An (1650)   A poem by Andrew MARVELL. It celebrates Cromwell as a kind of fated and elemental force, but with elements of pity for Charles I and strong suggestions of uneasiness about a future with Cromwell in supreme power.

Horatii, the three   In Roman legend, three brothers of the Horatia gens, or clan. They are celebrated for their combat with the three Curiatii, brothers from Alba Longa, to determine whether Rome or Alba was supreme. Two of the Horatii fell, while the Curiatii, though each was severely wounded, stood their ground. The surviving Horatius, unhurt, feigned flight. The Curiatii pursued him at unequal distances because of their wounds, and Horatius turned and killed them severally. He returned home in triumph bearing the bodies of the three Curiatii. His sister Horatia, recognizing one of the bodies as her betrothed, began to weep. Angered by her tears in his moment of triumph, Horatius plunged his sword into her breast, exclaiming: "So perish every Roman woman who bewails a foe." Horatius was condemned to death for this murder but was acquitted with a token punishment: a beam symbolizing a yoke was erected across the street, and Horatius passed under it with covered head, thus showing submission to Roman law. The beam came to be known as "sister's gibbet."

Horatio   In Shakespeare's HAMLET, the loyal friend and confidant whom the dying Hamlet adjures:

If thou didst ever hold me in thy heart,
Absent thee from felicity awhile,
And in this harsh world draw thy breath in pain,
To tell my story.

Horatius Cocles   Legendary hero of ancient Rome. When Lars PORSENA attacked Rome in the 6th century BC, Horatius and two companions defended a bridge across the Tiber against the entire Etruscan army, while the bridge behind them was destroyed by the Romans. Horatius then swam the river safely. In his honor a statue was erected, and he was given as much land as he could plow in a day. Another version has Horatius fighting alone and drowning in the Tiber.

Horatius's exploits are the subject of the poem "Horatius" in Macaulay's book of poems, *The Lays of Ancient Rome* (1842).

Horgan, Paul (1903–   )   American novelist, historian, and biographer. Horgan is a versatile and prolific writer of fiction, biography, children's books, plays, essays, and poetry. Much of his work is set in the southwest, particularly New Mexico. *Great River* (1954) is a PULITZER

PRIZE-winning history of the cultures that grew up along the Río Grande. Horgan's strong Roman Catholic beliefs are reflected in such novels as *The Saintmaker's Christmas Eve* (1955) and *Give Me Possession* (1957), the nonfiction *Rome Eternal* (1959), and *Lamy of Santa Fe* (1975), a biography of Father Jean Baptiste Lamy. The "Richard" novels—including *Things As They Are* (1964), *Everything to Live For* (1968), and *The Thin Mountain Air* (1977) —follow a boy's life from childhood to manhood.

Horn, King   Hero of a 12th-century French metrical romance and a 13th-century English one. Son of the king of Sudenne, Horn is set adrift by the Saracen pirates, who kill his parents. He comes to Westernesse, where he is brought up by the king and becomes the lover of the princess Rymenhild (or Rimel). A companion betrays the affair, and Horn is banished. As a disguised adventurer, he defeats a Saracen invasion in Ireland but declines the reward of marriage to the princess and returns to Westernesse to free Rymenhild from the threat of an unwelcome marriage, proving his identity by a magic ring she had given him. He leaves to recapture Sudenne from the Saracens, returns to release Rymenhild from a second unwelcome marriage, and finally takes her home to rule happily as king and queen of Sudenne. *Horn Childe* is a 14th-century English imitation with some variations. "Hind Horn" is a ballad describing Horn's return to Rymenhild disguised as a palmer.

Hornblower, Horatio   The courageous but sensitive hero of a series of popular novels by C. S. FORESTER. The novels, notable for their authentic historical background, follow Hornblower's naval career from midshipman to admiral in the wars against Napoleon.

Horovitz, Israel (1939–   )   American playwright. Horovitz earned early critical acclaim when four of his plays were produced off-Broadway during the 1967–68 season: *Line; It's Called the Sugar Plum; Rats;* and *The Indian Wants the Bronx.* The last of these, along with the farcical *The Primary English Class* (1976), depicts the comic and melancholy results of people's failure to communicate. *Alfred the Great* (1972), *Our Father's Failing* (1973), and *Alfred Dies* (1976), collectively known as *The Wakefield Plays,* are set in Horovitz's hometown in Massachusetts. They are mordant comedies with psychoanalytic overtones that unravel the mysteries and conflicts of a tormented family. *Mackerel* was published in 1979 and in that same year Horovitz successfully adapted DICKENS's "A Christmas Carol" for the stage.

Horse's Mouth, The (1944)   A novel by Joyce CARY, the third in his first trilogy. It is the story of Gulley Jimson, passionate artist and exuberant, rascally, comic old man, whose hero is William Blake.

Herself Surprised (1941) is about one of Gulley's mistresses, the fascinating, down-to-earth Sara Monday. She is successively cook, fine lady, housekeeper, thief, and respectable middle-class wife. *To Be a Pilgrim* (1942) is the story of Sara's other lover, the religious, near senile lawyer Mr. Wilcher. The central character of each book tells his own story in his own distinctive idiom.

Horus A major god of the ancient Egyptians, the son of OSIRIS and Isis, sometimes referred to as the god of silence. The Greeks called him Harpocrates and portrayed "Horus the Child" as a boy with a finger in his mouth. As one of the solar deities, Horus was represented by a hawk, or as a hawk-headed man; his emblem was the winged sun disk.

Hosea A prophet of the 8th century BC, and the OLD TESTAMENT book bearing his name. The book begins with an account of the unhappy life of Hosea with his unfaithful wife, which can be read as an allegory of God's trials with a sinful Israel. A catalogue of Israel's idolatrous impieties follows, ending with a call to repentance and the promise of God's blessing.

Hostage, The (L'Otage, 1909; tr 1917) A poetic drama by Paul CLAUDEL. It is the first of the plays which, with *Crusts* and *The Humiliation of the Father*, form a trilogy about the aristocratic Coufontaine family during the 19th century. Sygne de Coufontaine saves the pope by marrying her former servant Toussaint Turelure, an opportunist now become the most powerful man in France. However, she cannot complete her sacrifice by ceasing to hate her husband and their newborn son; consequently, when the cousin she loves tries to shoot Turelure, she intercepts the bullet and dies. In *Le Pain dur* (*Crusts*, 1914), the son Louis causes his father's death and marries a Jewish woman, Sichel. *Le Père humilié* (*The Humiliation of the Father*, 1916) describes the love between their blind daughter, Pensée, and the brothers Orian and Orso de Homodarmes.

Hostos, Eugenio María de (1839–1903) Puerto Rican educator and man of letters. Hostos was educated in Spain, where he wrote *La peregrinación de Bayoán* (1863), a political novel, and fought for the short-lived republic of 1868. His hopes that Puerto Rico might be granted autonomy with Santo Domingo and Cuba in a confederation of the Antilles were dashed by the imperialist attitude of the Spanish republicans. Hostos continued, however, to work for this goal in Santo Domingo, where he lived until 1889, establishing its first normal school. After a ten-year stay in Chile, he returned to Santo Domingo in 1900, bitterly disappointed at the results of the Spanish-American War, which finally doomed his dream of Antillean federation.

Hostos is remembered not only as a patriot, but also as an enlightened teacher, dedicated to progress and truth. His best-known work, *Moral social* (1888), is a guide to ethical social conduct, which was designed as a school text. He also wrote a famous essay (1872) on *Hamlet*.

Hotspur See PERCY, SIR HENRY.

Houdini, Harry (real name Erich Weiss, 1874–1926) American magician and writer. The most famous escape artist of all time, Houdini was celebrated for freeing himself from every kind of restraint: ropes, chains, handcuffs, sealed containers. An ardent debunker of spiritualistic "mediums," he exposed their methods in *Miracle Mongers and Their Methods* (1920) and *A Magician Among the Spirits* (1924).

Houdon, Jean Antoine (1741–1828) French sculptor. With an international reputation for his portrait busts, Houdon was the best-known sculptor in 19th-century France. His busts, which reveal his study of both anatomy and antique art, are animated, vigorously conceived, yet delicately executed. Among the many sculpted portraits he did were busts of Mirabeau (1791) and Rousseau (1779), and a full statue of Voltaire (1781). He also produced a bust of Benjamin Franklin (1779), through whose influence he visited the U.S. and executed a statue of George Washington (1705).

Hound of Heaven, The (1893) The best-known poem of Francis THOMPSON. In startling cosmic imagery and arresting cadences, it presents the "autobiography" of a fugitive from God's redemptive love.

houris Black-eyed damsels said to be the reward of the faithful in the Muslim Paradise. Possessed of perpetual youth and beauty, they can renew their virginity at pleasure and are always equal in age with their husbands. According to the KORAN, every believer will have seventy-two of these *houris* in Paradise and, depending on his wish, his intercourse may be fruitful or otherwise; if an offspring is desired, it will grow to full estate in an hour.

Hours, The (Gr, Horai) Greek goddesses of the seasons. In Greek, the word implies seasons, rather than hours, and these goddesses varied in number according to various concepts of the number of seasons in the year. HESIOD named them Eunomia, Dike, and Irene (Eirene).

House in Paris, The (1935) A novel by Elizabeth BOWEN. A story of complex love affairs, infidelities, and tragedy is revealed largely through two children who meet by chance at a house in Paris for a day. The boy, Leopold, the illegitimate issue of his mother's early love affair, is finally taken home to his mother and her new husband.

House of Fame, The (probably 1379 or 1380) An unfinished poem by Geoffrey CHAUCER, of 2,158 lines in octosyllabic couplets. It begins as a love-vision of the French type, but draws more on the works of OVID, VERGIL, and DANTE. In the first "book" the poet introduces his dream and describes finding himself in the Temple of VENUS. Here he finds engraved Vergil's story of DIDO and AENEAS. In the second book he conducts a lively conversation with a great shining eagle who carries him to the House of Fame, presumably to learn more about love. But the third section shows lady Fame in her house distributing fame and slander among some of her applicants and denying any renown to others, all with arbitrary capriciousness. Then the poet is taken to the House of Rumor, inhabited by shipmen, pilgrims, couriers, and other gossips, who increase the falsity of their tidings with each retelling.

House of Life, The   A sonnet sequence by Dante Gabriel ROSSETTI, written during the period between 1848 and 1881. Chiefly autobiographical, it was inspired by Elizabeth SIDDAL, the author's wife. The title refers to the house of human life in astrology.

House of Mirth, The (1905)   A novel by Edith WHARTON. Lily Bart, an orphan, tries to secure a wealthy husband, rejecting Lawrence Seldon, whom she loves but who lacks a fortune. Lily becomes involved with another man, who tries to blackmail her, and is falsely accused of an intrigue with another woman's husband. Her fortunes become progressively worse until she becomes a milliner and eventually takes an overdose of sleeping pills. The intention of the novel was to satirize and reveal the weaknesses of New York society.

House of the Dead, The (Zapiski iz myortvogo doma, 1861–1862)   An account of life in a Siberian prison by DOSTOYEVSKY. The work is based on Dostoyevsky's own experiences in the Omsk prison (1850–54), to which he was sentenced for having belonged to the Petrashevsky circle, a study group interested in French Utopian socialism.

House of the Seven Gables, The (1851)   A novel by Nathaniel HAWTHORNE. Iron-willed, grasping Colonel Pyncheon obtained the desirable land on which he built the pretentious House of the Seven Gables by accusing its humble owner, one Matthew Maule, of witchcraft. Old Maule, hanged for his crime, cursed the Colonel, saying, "God will give him blood to drink." That curse, reverberating down the generations, affects the whole family.

At the time of the story, the withered old spinster Hepzibah Pyncheon and her brother Clifford live in the house. Desperately poor, Hepzibah must open a cent-shop in order to refuse aid from Judge Jaffrey Pyncheon, the intellectual and moral heir of the old colonel. Clifford has just returned from an extended imprisonment for the murder of an uncle. The murder, in reality committed by Jaffrey, enabled the latter to gain control of the Pyncheon fortune. Clifford, a weak-willed aesthete, has been destroyed by the thirty-year sentence.

Phoebe, a visiting Pyncheon country cousin, and Holgrave, the young daguerreotypist boarding in the house, fall in love. Holgrave, a descendant of Matthew Maule, breaks the family curse, refusing to betray Phoebe by exercising his mesmeric powers. Hawthorne, in treating the weight of past guilt, once again reveals an unpardonable sin: the violation of another's soul.

Housman, A[lfred] E[dward] (1859–1936)   English poet and classical scholar. Housman's reputation as a poet grew from a single volume, A *Shropshire Lad* (1896). These lyrics, set against a background of the English countryside and showing the influence of both English ballads and classical verse, are marked by irony and a melancholy sense of the transitoriness of youth and love. Their tone has been ascribed to the poet's disappointment at his mediocre performance in his final examinations at Oxford and to his passionate love for a college friend, Moses Jackson, referred to in the poems as Terence. Housman became a professor of classics at Cambridge, edited Manilius's *Astronomica*, and refused even to talk about his verse. He published *Last Poems* in 1922; but these and others collected posthumously by his brother, Laurence HOUSMAN, in *More Poems* (1936), had been written during the same period as A *Shropshire Lad*. Two of the best-known poems are "Loveliest of trees, the cherry now . . ." and "Terence, this is stupid stuff . . ." In 1933 Housman emerged from silence to deliver a lecture, *The Name and Nature of Poetry*, at the Senate House in Cambridge. This, his first public utterance on the subject, was attended by many literary luminaries of the day and remains a unique exercise in criticism. His *Complete Poems* was issued in 1956.

Housman, Laurence (1865–1959)   English novelist, dramatist, and illustrator. He was the brother of A. E. HOUSMAN. Brilliantly versatile, Housman was a beautiful draftsman, a fine poet, and a delightful writer of fantastic stories. He was a prolific playwright; his greatest success was *Victoria Regina* (1934).

Houyhnhnmland (pronounced "whinnimland")   The country of Gulliver's fourth voyage in Jonathan Swift's GULLIVER'S TRAVELS, inhabited by Houyhnhnms, a race of horses. The Houyhnhnms, an embodiment of all that is good in mankind, are endowed with virtue and reason and live an idyllic existence. They hold in subjection the YAHOO, an inferior race whom Gulliver closely resembles. The Houyhnhnms consider Gulliver inferior, but he learns from them—so much so that, when he returns finally to his own country, he finds his fellow man so repellent that he becomes a confirmed misanthrope.

Howard, Sidney [Coe] (1891–1939)   American dramatist. Howard's first original play to attract attention was the PULITZER PRIZE-winning THEY KNEW WHAT THEY WANTED. The best known of his many later successes is *The Silver Cord* (1926), one of the earliest psychological studies of a dominant mother to be presented on stage.

Howards End (1910)   A novel by E. M. FORSTER. It deals with an English country house called Howards End and its influence on the lives of the materialistic Wilcoxes, the cultural and idealistic Schlegel sisters, and the poor bank clerk Leonard Bast. The Schlegels try to befriend Bast. Mr. Wilcox, whom Margaret Schlegel later marries, gives him financial advice which ruins him. Helen Schlegel becomes his mistress for a short time and bears his son; thereupon Charles Wilcox thrashes and accidentally kills him. The house passes from intuitive, half-mystical Mrs. Wilcox to her husband's second wife, Margaret Schlegel, to Margaret's nephew, Leonard Bast's son. Illustrating Forster's motto "Only connect," the house brings together three important elements in English society: money and successful business in the Wilcoxes, culture in the Schlegels, and the lower classes in Leonard Bast.

Howe, E[dgar] W[atson] (1853–1937) American editor and novelist. Primarily a newspaperman and small-town editor, he was called the "Sage of Potato Hill" for his cogent editorials. He is known for his first novel, *The Story of a Country Town* (1883), one of the early examples of REALISM in American fiction.

Howe, Irving (1920–   ) American literary critic and historian. Howe grew up speaking Yiddish; he learned English as a second language in New York City schools. His best-selling *World of Our Fathers* (1976), a comprehensive social and cultural history of eastern European Jews in America, includes a survey of the subculture of Jewish-American writers. Howe was one of the founders of the political magazine *Dissent* in 1954; he edited a selection of articles from that magazine in *Twenty-Five Years of Dissent* (1980). His literary criticism, which includes *Politics and the Novel* (1957) and *The Decline of the New* (1970), is concerned with how society influences the literary imagination. He has written a book-length essay, *Leon Trotsky* (1978), and edited numerous anthologies, among them several volumes of Yiddish literature. *A Margin of Hope: An Intellectual Autobiography* was published in 1982; it is a trenchant perspective on the New York intelligentsia in the 1945–60 period.

Howe, Julia Ward (1819–1910) American poet and reformer. In 1843 she married Samuel Gridley HOWE, the noted humanitarian and teacher of the blind, and helped him with such work as editing the Boston abolitionist paper *Commonwealth*. After her husband's death she continued his work, lecturing on prison reform and international peace, and becoming a force in the feminist movement. She was president of the American Woman's Suffrage Association, the New England's Woman's Club, and the Association for the Advancement of Women, and was an associate editor of the *Woman's Journal*. Although she is remembered chiefly for THE BATTLE HYMN OF THE REPUBLIC, she wrote several collections of verse, and is also the author of *Sex and Education* (1874), *Modern Society* (1881), and *Reminiscences* (1899). She was the first woman to be elected to the American Academy of Arts and Letters.

Howe, Samuel Gridley (1801–1876) American physician, teacher, and humanitarian. After receiving a medical degree from Harvard in 1824, Howe sailed to Greece, where he spent six years aiding the Greeks in their struggle for independence from Turkey. In 1831 he was named director of the school for the blind in Boston that later became the Perkins Institute; his best-known patient was the blind and deaf Laura Bridgman (1829–89), whom he trained by means of a raised type that he had devised and by other methods that later proved successful with Helen Keller. He was also interested in helping other handicapped persons. Active in the antislavery cause, he

founded, with his wife, Julia Ward HOWE, an abolitionist newspaper, *Commonwealth*.

Howells, William Dean (1837–1920) American novelist, editor, critic, and poet. Born and raised in Ohio, he had little schooling, but regularly contributed poems and tales to newspapers. Howells wrote of his boyhood and youth in the autobiographical *A Boy's Town* (1890) and *Years of My Youth* (1916). By the time he was twenty-three, he had published a book of poems, *Poems of Two Friends* (1860), and a campaign life of Abraham Lincoln. In 1860 he made a literary pilgrimage to Boston, where he was received by James Russell LOWELL and Oliver Wendell HOLMES.

The reward for his campaign biography was the consulship in Venice, where Howells spent the years of the Civil War. On his return, he published *Venetian Life* (1866), a series of travel letters and impressions. He worked for several magazines, finally becoming the editor of the *Atlantic Monthly* in 1871. A firm friend of Mark TWAIN, he also encouraged another admirer, the young Henry JAMES.

Howells's most important contribution to literary criticism is his theory of realistic fiction. He shared with George ELIOT a literary interest in the commonplace, and defined REALISM as "nothing more or less than the truthful treatment of material." Howells's bias is revealed, however, when he chooses Jane AUSTEN as the most truthful of writers. Among his own books, A MODERN INSTANCE and THE RISE OF SILAS LAPHAM illustrate his theory best.

Leaving the *Atlantic*, Howells wrote the "Easy Chair" column for HARPER'S. Influenced by TOLSTOY and the American socialist Laurence Gronlund, he supplemented his realism with liberal views. A HAZARD OF NEW FORTUNES and A TRAVELER FROM ALTRURIA are studies of American social institutions. Later in life, his militant liberalism subsiding, Howells continued to write realistic novels. From this period, *The Landlord at Lion's Head* (1897) and *The Kentons* (1902) approach his best earlier work in quality. He issued a number of collections of reviews and articles from magazines, the most important of which is *My Mark Twain* (1910).

Howells's reputation continued to grow; known as the dean of American letters, he was president of the AMERICAN ACADEMY OF ARTS AND LETTERS. Although he praised the posthumously published poems of Emily DICKINSON, and encouraged Stephen CRANE and Frank NORRIS, he was regarded as a genteel sentimentalist by Sinclair LEWIS, H. L. MENCKEN, and Theodore DREISER. Modern evaluation, restoring his reputation, grants him unquestioned historical importance in the history of American literature.

How Green Was My Valley (1939) A popular novel by Richard Llewellyn. Written in a lyrical style, it tells the story of a Welsh mining family.

Howl and Other Poems (1956) A collection of poems by Allen GINSBERG. The publication of *Howl* was surrounded by sensationalism. Obscenity charges were brought against it, but they were dismissed in court and the book became a *cause célèbre*. It was widely regarded as the "poetic manifesto" of the BEAT MOVEMENT.

The title poem consists of three sections and a footnote. The first section is a catalogue of nightmarish images which are meant to reflect brutalized contemporary America. The second section is Ginsberg's diatribe against the forces and institutions which abet such dehumanization. The third section, addressed to a mental hospital inmate, is an ironic commentary on society's diagnosis of "madness."

In technique, language, and tone *Howl* draws eclectically from scripture, Walt WHITMAN, and the visionary poetry of BLAKE and Christopher SMART. The biblical influence imbues the poem with a prophetic and admonitory mood. Ginsberg's debt to Whitman is evidenced in his use of the long line and the stylistic use of cataloguing and parallelism. The mystical aspects of the poem pertain to differentiated planes of reality in a context of timelessness and spacelessness. Ginsberg's approximation of meter is derived from what he refers to as "neural impulses."

How They Brought the Good News from Ghent to Aix (1845) A ballad by Robert BROWNING. Noted for its onomatopoeic effects, it describes a purely imaginary incident.

How to Win Friends and Influence People (1937) A practical guide to personality improvement by Dale Carnegie (1880–1958). This book was one of the most widely circulated in the history of American writing. Carnegie, a teacher of public speaking, was persuaded to convert his lectures into a book. "Six Ways to Make People Like You," "Twelve Ways to Win People to Your Way of Thinking," and "Seven Rules to Make Your Home Life Happier" are chapter titles representative of its style and content. The title itself has become a catch phrase for the success-oriented, self-improvement type of book and for a shallow approach to life's problems.

How to Write Short Stories (With Samples) (1924) A collection of stories by Ring LARDNER. The sardonic preface discloses that the purpose of this volume is to discuss the art of short-story writing. The "samples" included—among them such classic Lardner tales as "Alibi Ike" and "Champion"—were lampoons of current short-story conventions.

Hoyle, Sir Fred (1915–   ) English astronomer and SCIENCE FICTION writer. Hoyle, formerly professor of theoretical astronomy and experimental philosophy at Cambridge University, is the only scientist of real distinction to have produced a substantial body of work in science fiction. Beginning with *The Black Cloud* (1957), Hoyle's novels and stories are concerned with contemporary scientists and how they might respond to catastrophic events or new scientific developments. A scientific and a science-fictional treatment of Hoyle's views on the nature of time may be compared in two 1966 works, *Man in the Universe*, a

collection of lectures, and *October the First Is Too Late*, a novel. Some of Hoyle's novels have been written in collaboration with his son Geoffrey, and two, *A for Andromeda* (1962) and *Andromeda Breakthrough* (1964), originated as television scripts written with John Elliott.

Hsi Yü Chi See JOURNEY TO THE WEST.

Hsün Tzu Chinese Confucian work attributed to Hsün Ch'ing (c300 BC). It exerted considerable influence during the HAN period (202 BC–AD 220). The first Confucian text in expository form, it contradicts the MENCIUS by saying that man is by nature evil, and attacks superstition, extolling rationalism in its stead. It places great emphasis on the need for education.

Huang Ti (known as the Yellow Emperor, 2698–2598 BC) A legendary emperor of China. Worshiped as the god of agriculture, Huang Ti was a culture hero who is credited with many inventions and innovations.

hubris (fr Gr, *hybris*, "pride; insolence") A tragic flaw of pride, ambition, or overconfidence that leads a hero to ignore warnings of the gods or to disregard established moral codes, resulting in the hero's downfall, or NEMESIS. In general use, the term has come to mean wanton arrogance.

Huch, Ricarda (1864–1947) German novelist, poet, and essayist. In her time, Huch was considered the foremost woman of German literature. She was noted for an understanding of history, particularly evident in her novels about Garibaldi, *Die Geschichten von Garibaldi* (1906–7; tr *Defeat and Victory*, 1928, 1929), and the Thirty Years War, *Der große Krieg in Deutschland* (3 vols, 1912–14). Her work also includes passionate romantic verse in *Gesammelte Gedichte* (1929), and scholarly works on the Holy Roman Empire. Her studies of GERMAN ROMANTICISM are considered among the finest written in German.

Huckleberry Finn, The Adventures of (1884) A novel by Mark TWAIN. The sequel to *The Adventures of* TOM SAWYER, *Huckleberry Finn* is a PICARESQUE tale, told in Huck's own voice, of his adventures on a raft on the Mississippi River. It begins with Huck's escape from his drunken, brutal father to the river, where he meets up with Jim, a runaway slave. The story of their journey downstream, with occasional forays into the society along the banks, is an American classic that captures the smells, rhythms, and sounds, the variety of dialects and the human activity of life on the great river. It is also a penetrating social commentary that reveals corruption, moral decay, and intellectual impoverishment through Huck and Jim's encounters with traveling actors and con men, lynch mobs, thieves, and southern gentility. Through Jim, and through his own observations and experiences, Huck learns about the dignity and worth of human life. By the end, when Jim is recaptured, Huck is able to help Jim escape. Thus Mark Twain repudiates the moral blindness of the respectable slave-holding society whose decaying social order is portrayed so vividly throughout the novel. Huck Finn remains one of the greatest creations in American fiction.

Hudibras (1663, 1664, 1678)   A long satirical poem in three parts by Samuel BUTLER, directed against the hypocrisy and intolerance of the Puritans. Its hero, Hudibras, modeled after various Presbyterian worthies of the Commonwealth, is a country justice who sets out with his squire Ralpho, an Independent, to reform abuses and enforce the laws for the suppression of popular amusements. Like Don Quixote, Hudibras is of comical appearance, humpbacked and potbellied, with an untidy yellowred beard. He, too, rides a broken-down nag and receives much punishment in the performance of his exploits. The poem, written in jingling, doggerel couplets, gave rise to the adjective *hudibrastic*, meaning mock-heroic or in the style of *Hudibras*.

Hudson, Henry (d after 1611)   English navigator and explorer. Engaged by the Dutch East India Company to find a northern passage to the Orient, he sailed to America on the *Half Moon* and explored the river that now bears his name, reaching as far as Albany (1609). On a later voyage he was set adrift by his own men.

Hudson, Sir Jeffrey (1619–1682)   English dwarf, at one time page to Queen Henrietta Maria. When he was thirty years old, he was under two feet high, but later reached a height of about three feet nine inches. He was a cavalry captain in the Royalist army during the Civil War. Afterwards he was captured by pirates and sold as a slave in Barbary, but managed to escape. He is a character in Scott's PEVERIL OF THE PEAK.

Hudson, William Henry (1841–1922)   English naturalist and novelist, born in Argentina of American parentage. He became a naturalized British subject in 1900. He is best known for his writings on nature subjects, especially those with an Argentine background. His books include *The Purple Land* (1885), *Argentine Ornithology* (1888–89), *Nature in Downland* (1900), *El Ombú* (1902), *Little Boy Lost* (1905), and *A Shepherd's Life* (1910). He is best remembered for GREEN MANSIONS and his autobiographical *Far Away and Long Ago* (1918).

Hudson River School   The name given to a group of 19th-century U.S. artists who painted rural scenes, especially in New York's Catskill Mountains, after 1830. Romantic, poetic, or fantastic interpretations were given to these landscapes, which were popularized by Thomas COLE. Other painters of this school were Asher Durand (1796–1886), Frederic CHURCH, and Sandford Gifford (1823–80).

Hudson's Bay Company   A joint stock company chartered in 1670 by Charles II for the purpose of purchasing furs from the Indians. Its territory, the Hudson's Bay Territory or Rupert's Land, included all the streams flowing into Hudson's Bay. It was sold to the British government (1869) and incorporated with the Dominion of Canada (1870).

Hueffer, Ford Madox   See FORD, FORD MADOX.

Huerta, Vicente García de la   See GARCÍA DE LA HUERTA, VICENTE.

Hughes, [James] Langston (1902–1967)   American poet. Hughes, whose poetry was "discovered" by Vachel LINDSAY, was an important figure in the HARLEM RENAISSANCE. Marked by the rhythms of the blues and jazz, often documentary in tone, his poems deal with the tribulations and joys of the American black. His collections of verse range from *The Weary Blues* (1926), *The Dream Keeper* (1932), *Shakespeare in Harlem* (1942), and *One-Way Ticket* (1949) to *Ask Your Mama* (1961) and *The Panther and the Lash* (1967). From his own poem, "Cross," he made the play *Mulatto* (1935); this in turn was produced in a musical version called *The Barrier* (1950). He is also known for his humorous sketches, originally written for a black newspaper, which are collected in *Simple Speaks His Mind* (1950), *The Best of Simple* (1961), and *Simple's Uncle Sam* (1965). Hughes's other fiction includes the novels *Not Without Laughter* (1930) and *Tambourines to Glory* (1958), as well as *The Ways of White Folks* (1934) and *Something in Common* (1963), two collections of stories. He also wrote two volumes of autobiography: *The Big Sea* (1940) and *I Wonder As I Wander* (1956). *Good Morning Revolution* (1973) is a posthumous edition of his previously uncollected social protest writings. Hughes's importance in the development of black literature in America can hardly be exaggerated. His simplicity, directness, musicality, and willingness to employ black idiom, dialect, and speech patterns led both to his early vilification by contemporary black critics, who saw him as exemplifying all the aspects of black life they despised and feared, and later, to his recognition as an original voice true to himself and his race.

Hughes, Richard [Arthur Warren] (1900–1976)   English novelist, poet, and dramatist. The novel A HIGH WIND IN JAMAICA is generally considered his greatest achievement.

Hughes, Ted (full name Edward James Hughes, 1930–   )   English poet. One of the most individual poetic voices in England since Dylan THOMAS, Hughes owes much to his childhood in a Yorkshire milltown and his early introduction to the poetry of D. H. LAWRENCE. His reading in anthropology, mythology, and folklore has further enriched his work. Often set in Yorkshire or by the sea, his verse is noted for violence of feeling, for powerful nature and animal imagery, primitivism, and metrical virtuosity. His first volume, *The Hawk in the Rain* (1957), won immediate critical acclaim. Subsequent volumes include *Lupercal* (1960); *Wodwo* (1967), a collection of stories, verse, and prose poems; *Crow* (1970; rev 1972); *Selected Poems: 1957–1967* (1972); *Season Songs* (1975); *Cave Birds* (1977); and *Moortown* (1979). Hughes was married to the American poet Sylvia PLATH from 1956 until her suicide in 1963. In 1981 Hughes edited her *Collected*

Poems, and a further collection of his own verse, *Selected Poems, 1957–1981*, appeared in 1982. He has written poems for children, notably the award-winning *Under the North Star* (1981) and *What Is the Truth?* (1984). In 1984 Hughes succeeded Sir John Betjeman as POET LAUREATE.

Hugh of Lincoln, St. (c1246–1255)   English boy said to have been tortured and murdered by the Jews of Lincoln, a number of whom were hanged in consequence. Legends of miracles gathered around his name, such as the story that he spoke to his mother, though dead, and identified his murderer. His tragedy appears in Chaucer's THE PRIORESS'S TALE, *Alphonsus of Lincoln* (1459), Marlowe's *The Jew of Malta* (1589), and a number of ballads, such as "Sir Hugh," "Hugh of Lincoln," and "The Jew's Daughter."

Hugh Selwyn Mauberley (1920)   A poem in several sections by Ezra POUND. Although there has been much discussion on the exact relationship between Pound and his persona Mauberley, the poem represents Pound's farewell to London and is a vehement denunciation of a civilization marked by war, the commercialization of the arts, and a general and sexual sterility. The artist either prostitutes his art, as did Arnold Bennett ("Mr. Nixon"), or he barely manages to exist in a solitary and destitute state, as did Ford Madox Ford (the "stylist"). Mauberley himself is finally capable of only a refined and delicate art in such a corrupt civilization. It has been suggested that Mauberley represents the poet Pound would have become had he remained the simple imagist, unconcerned by the cultural and economic problems that from this point on were to occupy him.

Hugo, Victor [Marie] (1802–1885)   French poet, novelist, dramatist, and leader of the romantic movement in France. Like Chateaubriand, the literary figure he so admired, Hugo played an active part in political life. Serving first as a peer under the monarchy of Louis Philippe, he transferred his loyalties to the republicans in 1848 and was elected to the popular assembly. Deeply disturbed by the restoration of the Second Empire, in 1851 Hugo fled France, living in exile for eighteen years in the Channel Islands. His last public office was held under the Third Republic, in which he served as a senator. His love of liberty and his hopes for mankind were regarded, however, as a poet's dream, and Hugo had little real political influence during this period. If he lacked political influence, Hugo's influence upon French literature of the 19th century was unrivaled. In each genre he revealed himself as a romantic par excellence (see ROMANTICISM). The voice of his poetry is always musical, often highly personal, reflective, and sometimes characterized by gentle melancholy. Often considered France's greatest lyric poet, Hugo experimented with language and with rhythm, displaying a fine sensitivity to the sound and color of words. *Les Feuilles d'automne* (1831) and *Contemplations* (1856) both describe the moods and emotions of the poet in richly sonorous verse. In other volumes, however, such as *Les Châtiments* (1853), which attacked Napoleon III, or *Les Chants du crépuscule* (1835), Hugo conceived of the poet's role as public and prophetic. The poet should lead and guide the people, rather than express his own responses to nature's beauty or personal sorrow. This same strain appears again in Hugo's long novels, which reveal a humanitarian interest in the problems and suffering of the common man. Stylistically the novels are marked by violent melodrama, panoramic sweep, and the colorful use of language. These novels, best known of Hugo's work to the English audience, include *Han d'Islande* (*Hans of Iceland*, 1823), THE HUNCHBACK OF NOTRE DAME, LES MISÉRABLES, *Les Travailleurs de la mer* (*Toilers of the Sea*, 1866), *L'Homme qui rit* (*The Man Who Laughs*, 1869), and *Quatre-ving-treize* (*Ninety-Three*, 1879). His preface to his drama *Cromwell* (1827) became a manifesto adopted by the romantic dramatists. Hugo asserted the playwright's independence from the rigid rules of classicism. He suggested such innovations as a mixture of the comic and the tragic, colloquial dialogue, new freedom in meter and from the traditional unities of time and place. His own plays, historical melodramas filled with rather wooden, typically romantic personages, include *Hernani* (1830), *Ruy Blas* (1838), and *Les Burgraves* (1843). Some of these are better known today as sources for operatic librettos, notably *Hernani* and *Le Roi s'amuse* (1832), both set to music by Verdi in *Ernani* and *Rigoletto*, respectively, and *Angelo* (1835), which became Ponchielli's *La Gioconda*.

Huguenots   A term applied to French Protestants during the religious wars of the 16th and 17th centuries. The name was first applied to citizens of medieval Geneva who resisted the claims of the dukes of Savoy over the city; it is probably an adaptation of *Eidgenossen* (Ger, "confederates"). See NANTES, EDICT OF.

Hui-neng   See CH'AN BUDDHISM.

Huis clos   See NO EXIT.

Hulda   Old German goddess of marriage and fecundity who sent bridegrooms to maidens and children to the married. The name means "the Benignant," and is a euphemistic appellation.

Hull, Hell, and Halifax   An old beggars' and vagabonds' "prayer." As quoted by Taylor, the Water Poet (early 17th century), it was:

> From Hull, Hell, and Halifax,
> Good Lord, deliver us.

Hell was probably the least feared as being farthest from them; Hull was to be avoided because it was so well governed that beggars had little chance of getting anything without doing hard labor for it; and Halifax, because anyone caught stealing in that town was beheaded without intermediate proceedings.

Hull House   See ADDAMS, JANE.

Hulme, Thomas Ernest (1883–1917)   English critic and philosopher. Hulme is noted for *Speculations* (1924) and *Notes on Language and Style* (1929). He was killed in World War I, but his ideas were later widely popularized by T. S. ELIOT and Ezra POUND. Hulme distinguished classicism, which he considered true and "realistic," from humanism and romanticism, both of which he judged false and "unrealistic." Humanism, he claimed, erroneously described man as "naturally" good and capable of perfection; classicism, on the contrary, truthfully depicted man as "intrinsically bad or limited, but disciplined by order and tradition to *something fairly decent.*" Humanistic (and romantic) art, further, was undisciplined and imprecise, he concluded, while classic art was "clean, clearcut, and mechanical." See IMAGISM.

Human Age, The   A satirical prose epic by Wyndham LEWIS. It consists of *The Childermass* (1928), *Monstre Gai* (1955), and *Malign Fiesta* (1955). The subject is a surrealistic journey to a nightmare heaven. The description is macabre and imaginative; the language is obscure—full of allusion, wordplay, and parody.

humanism   An attitude of the mind that accompanied the flowering of the RENAISSANCE. The term refers to several varied literary and scholarly activities inspired by the study of antiquity but differing in aim and scope. Humanism in the Renaissance took its name from the *studia humanitatis*, those studies (grammar, rhetoric, poetry, history, and moral philosophy) that were thought to possess human value: the ability to make man a fully realized human creature, elevated and distinct from the lower animals. The ancient writers of Greece and Rome were particularly revered, as it was felt that they had excelled in such studies and would thus be of value in teaching the modern Christian how to attain the perfections of life. This aspect of humanism, sometimes called the REVIVAL OF ANTIQUITY, includes the study of the classics; editorial and philological work on ancient texts; the search of enthusiasts for unknown but extant manuscripts, statues, medals, and coins; the writing of modern works in classical Latin; and the teaching of the classics in universities and to the children of the nobility.

Our English term *humanists*, used to designate the participants in the above-mentioned activities, is derived from the Italian word *umanista*, which was first used in the late 16th century to describe a university teacher of the humanities. Renaissance humanists include scholars and poets such as PETRARCH, often called the first humanist; instigators of "the revival" such as the Greek scholar CHRYSOLORAS; the philologists VALLA and ERASMUS; archaeologists and antiquarians such as Poggio and CIRIACO; the educators VITTORINO of Feltre and GUARINO of Verona; philosophers, historians, and men of letters such as PIUS II and Leonardo BRUNI; and a host of secretaries, chancellors, legates, and other royal advisors who, having imbibed the spirit of the period, used their mastery of eloquence in

practical labors. Outstanding English humanists during the Renaissance were MORE, ELYOT, and ASCHAM.

The origins of humanism have been found to lie in the introduction of Greek studies into Italy by refugee and other visiting scholars from the Byzantine world and in the economic flowering of the Italian city-states, which provided the necessary wealth and leisure for cultural activities. From Italy, humanism spread north to France, England, the Netherlands, and Germany as well as Spain. By the time of its arrival in the northern countries, however, the purely cultural aims gave way to the needs of the Reformation; theological disputation and educational theory assumed greater importance than the study and imitation of pagan authors and text. In succeeding centuries, the influence of humanism persisted mainly in the school curricula.

Modern humanism (see NEW HUMANISM) only vaguely resembles the Renaissance brand, and is primarily a secular philosophy devoted to the propagation of a self-sufficient system of human values.

Humboldt, Baron Alexander von (1769–1859)   German naturalist. With Aimé Bonpland, a French botanist, he traveled throughout Latin America (1799–1804), studying physical geography and meteorology; in the Andes, he determined the relationship between altitude and temperature, and he also discovered the cool Peruvian current that now bears his name. The volumes in his *Voyage aux régions équinoxiales du Nouveau Continent* (1807 et seq) greatly influenced later explorers and give an excellent picture of political and economic conditions in Latin America on the eve of independence. His main work is *Kosmos* (1845–62), a description of the physical universe. He was the brother of Wilhelm von Humboldt, the philologist, educator, and statesman.

Humboldt's Gift (1975)   A novel by Saul BELLOW. Charles Citrine, an educated, mildly successful writer sapped of his energy by an endlessly proliferating world, falls under the spell of the wasted genius Von Humboldt Fleisher, a "poet, thinker, problem drinker" (partly modeled on Bellow's friend Delmore SCHWARTZ), and a sleazy operator named Rinaldo Cantabile. Citrine repeatedly attempts to resolve his conflicted feelings about art/poetry vs. power/success and the isolated life of artistic pursuits vs. rubbing shoulders with the "real world." Even though the character Humboldt dies part way through the book, his presence and influence are felt throughout. The book won a PULITZER PRIZE.

Hume, David (1711–1776)   Scottish philosopher and historian. Hume carried BERKELEY's "immaterialist hypotheses" to their logical extreme. He restricted all knowledge to the experience of ideas or impressions, maintaining that the mind consists only of accumulated perceptions (see EMPIRICISM). His philosophical skepticism, and his insistence that there is no knowledge other than what is directly observable, have been of extraordinary importance in the history of modern metaphysical thinking. His empirical outlook is clearly seen in his *Natural History of Religion* (1757) and *Dialogues Concerning Natural Religion* (1779), in which he assails anthropomorphism, denies the existence of miracles, and asserts that because God is only an idea in the mind of man, God cannot exist. His best-known philosophical works are *A Treatise of Human Nature* (1737–40) and *An Enquiry Concerning Human Understanding* (1748). He refuted the tenets of RATIONALISM and insisted that neither substance nor causal activity could be verified; they can only be inferred on the basis of perceived probability. Hume was the author of many essays and treatises, including a monumental *History of England* (1754–62) that for many years was the definitive text on the subject.

Humiliation of the Father, The   See HOSTAGE, THE.

humour   An obsolete medical term for the supposed four principal liquids of the body. In medieval times, these were supposed to be blood, phlegm, yellow bile, and black bile. They were thought to correspond to the four principal temperaments: the sanguine, the phlegmatic, the choleric, the melancholic. This idea was still popular in Elizabethan days. Ben Jonson's comedy EVERY MAN IN HIS HUMOUR has each character stereotyped with one ruling temperament. Albrecht DÜRER is said to have thought of the four temperaments and humours in connection with his paintings of the four evangelists. See COMEDY OF HUMOURS.

Humphrey Clinker, The Expedition of (1771) An epistolary novel by Tobias SMOLLETT. The letters are written by Matthew BRAMBLE, his sister Tabitha, their niece, their nephew, and their maid, Winifred Jenkins. Each correspondent has a highly individual style and caricatures himself unwittingly. The titular hero of this comic masterpiece, who plays a lesser role than the Brambles, is a workhouse lad who enters into their service by chance and who later becomes a Methodist preacher. He falls in love with Winifred, and is eventually found to be the natural son of Mr. Bramble. The "expedition" of the title is a family tour through England and Scotland, during which the correspondents express surprisingly varied reactions to the same events. Of particular note is the picture of Hot Wells (a sobriquet for the city of Bath), a fashionable watering place.

Hunchback of Notre Dame, The (Nôtre Dame de Paris, 1831)   A romance of medieval times by Victor HUGO centered on the life of the great Parisian cathedral. The principal characters are Esmeralda, a gypsy dancer in love with Captain Phoebus; Claude Frollo, the hypocritical archdeacon, whose evil passion for Esmeralda causes him to denounce her as a witch; and Quasimodo, the "Hunchback of Notre Dame," a deformed bellringer, whose devotion saves Esmeralda for a time when she seeks protection from the mob in the belfry of the cathedral. Esmeralda is finally executed, and Quasimodo throws Frollo from the heights of Notre Dame.

Hund des Generals, Der   See KIPPHARDT, HEINAR.

Hundred Days   The days between March 20 and June 28, 1815. On March 20 Napoleon reached the Tuileries after his escape from Elba; June 28 was the date of the second restoration of Louis XVIII. Napoleon left Elba February 26; landed near Cannes, March 1; entered Paris, March 20; and signed his abdication June 22, four days after the fateful battle at WATERLOO.

Hundred Years' War   The long series of wars (1337–1453) between France and England, beginning in the reign of Edward III and ending in that of Henry VI. The first battle was a naval action off Sluys, and the last the fight at Castillon. The war originated in English claims to the French crown, and resulted in the English being expelled from the whole of France, except Calais.

Huneker, James Gibbons (1860–1921)   American critic and man of letters. Huneker was preeminent as an in-depth music critic. His impressionistic but incisive criticism in all fields of art made him one of the most influential critics of his day.

Hung lou meng   See DREAM OF THE RED CHAMBER, THE.

Hunt, [William] Holman (1827–1910)   English painter. With John Everett MILLAIS and Dante Gabriel ROSSETTI, Hunt was a founding member of the PRE-RAPHAELITE BROTHERHOOD, and the one who adhered most faithfully to its principles. Among his best-known works are the richly detailed, symbolic religious paintings *Scapegoat* (1854) and *Light of the World* (1854). In 1905 he published his two-volume *Pre-Raphaelitism and the Pre-Raphaelite Brotherhood*.

Hunt, [James Henry] Leigh (1784–1859)   English journalist, essayist, poet, and political radical. For years, in the face of poverty, vilification, and official persecution, Hunt edited a series of one-man journals. From 1813 to 1815 he was imprisoned for attacking the future George IV in his *Examiner*, becoming a hero of the radicals. He is most important as an essayist and critic, an early champion of Shelley and Keats. Byron was briefly Hunt's patron, but the two were unable to get along; Hunt's *Lord Byron and Some of His Contemporaries* (1828) reflects some bitterness. Though much of his prose is perspicacious and graceful, his poetry tends to be slight and sentimental. A few shorter poems, such as "Abou Ben Adhem" (1834) and "Jenny Kissed Me" (1844), and parts of *The Story of Rimini* (1816), are still of interest. Among his other works are: *Critical Essays* (1807); *The Round Table* (1817, with William HAZLITT); *The Months* (1821); *Men, Women and Books* (1847); and *Autobiography* (1850).

Hunt, Violet (1866–1942)   English biographer and novelist. Hunt was the daughter of the Pre-Raphaelite painter Alfred William Hunt (1830–96) and, for some years, the companion of Ford Madox FORD. Her autobiography, *I Have This to Say* (1926), and her biography *The Wife of Rossetti* (1932) are valuable as firsthand accounts of the literary people of her day. She wrote novels, such as *White Rose of Weary Leaf* (1908), and macabre stories collected in two editions of *Tales of the Uneasy* (1910, 1925).

Hunter, Evan (1926–   )   American novelist. Hunter's first adult novel, *Cut Me In* (1954), written under the pseudonym Hunt Collins, was followed by his successful *The Blackboard Jungle* (1954), a sensational exposé of the brutal underworld of a big-city high school. A master of narrative, Hunter went on to write more than sixty novels. As "Ed McBain" he produced nearly thirty thrillers dealing with the 87th Precinct of an unnamed city, beginning with *Cop Hater* (1956).

Hurston, Zora Neale (1901–1960)   American folklorist, novelist, and short-story writer. As a student at Barnard College, Hurston studied anthropology under Columbia's Franz BOAS. She went on to write both novels and nonfiction books on folklore that illuminated aspects of black culture. *Mules and Men* (1935) is a study of black folkways in Florida. *Tell My Horse* (1938) records myth, magic, and music in Jamaica and Haiti. Novels like *Jonah's Gourd Vine* (1934), about a black preacher, and *Their Eyes Were Watching God* (1937), about the three marriages of a beautiful quadroon, were original and earthy stories of the black South. After a long eclipse of her literary reputation, a collection of Hurston's stories, essays, folklore, and novel selections was published in 1979 as *I Love Myself When I Am Laughing.*

Hurtado de Mendoza, Diego (1503–1575) Spanish historian and poet. A member of one of Spain's noblest families, Hurtado was a humanist who read Greek, Hebrew, and Arabic, as well as a distinguished diplomat who represented the king in Venice, Rome, and at the Council of Trent. A quarrel with another noble in 1568 led to his exile from Madrid. He retired to Granada, where he wrote his masterpiece, the *Guerra de Granada* (1627), a vivid history of the Morisco uprising of 1568–71, which was modeled on the works of Tacitus and Sallust. His poetry is of two types: his sonnets and the *Fábula de Adonis, Hipómenes y Atalanta* reveal the influence of classical and Italian verse, but he was more successful with Spanish forms, as is shown by his witty, sometimes cynical *redondillas.* The authorship of LAZARILLO DE TORMES has also been attributed to him. At his death he left all his books and manuscripts to the library of the Escorial.

Hu Shih (1891–1962)   One of modern China's greatest scholars. Hu Shih studied under John DEWEY (PhD, Columbia, 1917), returned to China, and was one of the most forceful advocates of the literary revolution which replaced the classical Chinese written language with everyday vernacular. He wrote widely on many subjects. He was ambassador to the U.S. (1938–42), and wrote *Collected*

Essays (1921–30) and *China's Place in the Present World Struggle* (1942).

Huss, John (or Jan Hus, c1371–1415)   Czech religious reformer. As a preacher and university professor, Huss launched an attack against the vices of the Catholic hierarchy; inspired by the teachings of John WYCLIF, he called for radical reform of the church. He was condemned as a heretic by the Council of Constance and burned at the stake.

Huss's followers in Bohemia, the Hussites, organized a successful military struggle against the papal armies and their domestic allies. In the end, the movement suffered defeat as a result of internal conflict between the radical Taborites and the more moderate Prague wing. However, the exclusive authority of the Catholic church could not be restored in Bohemia and the Czech Reformation continued throughout the 15th and 16th centuries.

Huss's life and death, as well as the victories and the final defeat of the Hussite armies, have been favorite topics of Czech historical fiction, drama, and poetry.

Husserl, Edmund (1859–1938)   German philosopher. He was a leader in the development of PHENOMENOLOGY as the basis for a new philosophical method. His work has had much influence on the existentialists, especially Jean-Paul Sartre, who studied under him from 1933 to 1934. His works include *Logische Untersuchungen* (*Logical Inquiries*, 1900–1901) and *Ideen zu einer reinen Phänomenologie und phänomenologischen Philosophie* (*Thoughts Toward a Pure Phenomenology and Phenomenological Philosophy*, 1922).

Hussonet   A character in Gustave FLAUBERT's novel L'EDUCATION SENTIMENTALE. A friend of the hero, Frédéric Moreau, Hussonet is an opportunistic journalist and editor. He voices firm support of the principles of 1848, but after Louis Napoleon's successful coup d'état, he rapidly becomes an ardent supporter of the empire.

Huston, John (1906–   )   American film director, actor, screenwriter, and son of the actor Walter Huston (1884–1950). A recurring theme in Huston's films is that man struggles to survive against all the odds, with little likelihood of success. Huston deals ironically with the flaws inherent in a male-dominated society; even the best-laid plans of his protagonists are undone by human weakness. Among his many successful films are *The Maltese Falcon* (1941), *The Treasure of the Sierra Madre* (1949), *The Asphalt Jungle* (1950), *The African Queen* (1951), *The Night of the Iguana* (1964), *The Man Who Would Be King* (1975), and *Wise Blood* (1979). In 1983 Huston successfully produced a film adaptation of Malcolm LOWRY's *Under the Volcano.* His autobiography, *An Open Book*, appeared in 1981.

Huxley, Aldous [Leonard] (1894–1963)   English novelist, essayist, and satirist. He is the grandson of Thomas HUXLEY, great-nephew of Matthew ARNOLD, brother of Julian HUXLEY, and half-brother of Andrew

Huxley (1917–   ), who won the 1963 Nobel Prize in Physiology. Huxley's early work differs sharply from that of his later years, the break reflecting his conversion to mysticism. His early novels are witty, despairing evocations of society in the 1920s, satirizing the intellectual pretensions and poses of the era. To this period belong CROME YELLOW, ANTIC HAY, *Those Barren Leaves* (1925), and POINT COUNTER POINT. Huxley's early short stories were collected in *Mortal Coils* (1922). In the 1930s he became increasingly interested in political and philosophical issues and wrote novels of ideas, including *Eyeless in Gaza* (1936), AFTER MANY A SUMMER DIES THE SWAN, and *Time Must Have a Stop* (1944). Preoccupation with mysticism dominates such later works as the novel *Island* (1962) and the essays HEAVEN AND HELL and *The Doors of Perception* (1954).

Huxley is noted for his interest in science; his last book was *Literature and Science* (1963). BRAVE NEW WORLD, perhaps his best-known novel, expresses his concern over the dangers of scientific progress; *Ape and Essence* (1948) is a satire about the world after an atomic war. His most important essays are *Music at Night* (1931), *Beyond the Mexique Bay* (1934), *The Perennial Philosophy* (1946), and *Brave New World Revisited* (1958).

Huxley studied medicine but was prevented from practicing by a disease of the eyes that temporarily blinded him. He was associated with J. Middleton MURRY and Katherine MANSFIELD in editing the *Athenaeum*. A friend and admirer of D. H. LAWRENCE, Huxley edited his letters in 1932; it was Lawrence who encouraged him to search for spiritual values when he was in despair. In 1947 he settled in southern California, his base for most of the rest of his life. He was associated for some time with the Ramakrishna Mission in Hollywood and pursued various occult studies.

Huxley, Julian Sorell (1887–1975)   English biologist and writer, brother of Aldous HUXLEY. A humanist, atheist, and scientific popularizer, Huxley was the author of, among many other books, *Essays of a Biologist* (1923), *The Science of Life* (with H. G. and G. P. Wells, 1929), *What Dare I Think?* (1931), *A Captive Shrew and Other Poems of a Biologist* (1932), *Evolution: The Modern Synthesis* (1942), *New Bottles for New Wine* (1957), *The Humanist Frame* (1961), and two autobiographical volumes: *Memories* (1970, 1972).

Huxley, Thomas Henry (1825–1895)   English biologist and teacher. Huxley is known for his defense of the theory of evolution held by Darwin, and for his lectures and writings popularizing science. His books include *Man's Place in Nature* (1863), *The Physical Basis of Life* (1868), *Lay Sermons, Addresses, and Reviews* (1870), *Science and Morals* (1886), *Essays upon Some Controverted Questions* (1892), and *Ethics and Evolution* (1893). Huxley was called "Darwin's Bulldog" and engaged in a controversy with the English statesman Gladstone on the question

of scientific evolutionary theories as opposed to biblical lore. He was the grandfather of Aldous and Julian HUXLEY.

Huysmans, Joris Karl (1848–1907)   French novelist. Of Dutch ancestry, Huysmans was born, lived, and died in Paris, where after a prolonged spiritual struggle, he became a convert to Roman Catholicism. His neurasthenia and perverse tastes mark Huysmans as a typical DÉCADENT. Stylistically, his work is characterized by vivid and concrete figures, fantastic description, and a gift for portraying the grotesque. Among his novels are *Marthe, histoire d'une fille* (1876), a naturalistic account of a young prostitute's life; AGAINST THE GRAIN; *Là-Bas* (1891), part of a spiritual autobiography; and *La Cathédrale* (1898).

Hyacinth (Greek name Hyakinthos)   In Greek mythology, a beautiful youth loved by APOLLO. ZEPHYR, the jealous west wind, spoiled Apollo's aim when he was throwing the discus; it struck Hyacinth and he died. From his blood sprang the hyacinth (not the modern flower), bearing on its petals the cry of grief, AI. Hyakinthos was, in fact, a pre-Hellenic local deity in Amyclae, antedating Apollo's appearance in Greece.

Hyde, Douglas (Gaelic name Dubhglas deh-Ide, 1860–1949)   Irish poet, scholar, and statesman. The first president of Eire (1938–45), he wrote much of his work in Gaelic and devoted himself to the restoration of Irish culture. He was one of the founders of the ABBEY THEATRE and wrote many books on Irish history, literature, and folklore. His *Love Songs of Connaught* (1894) is a classic compilation.

Hydra   A monstrous serpent of Greek mythology. It was born of TYPHON and Echidna. Living in the swamps of the river Lerna, it had many heads; when one was cut off, another grew in its place. HERACLES finally killed it by having his friend Iolaus burn the stumps with torches as soon as the heads were removed. Heracles poisoned his arrows with its blood.

Hydriotaphia, or Urn Burial (1658)   An essay by Sir Thomas BROWNE. In part a scientific report on some Roman burial urns that had recently been unearthed in Norfolk, the essay becomes a moving meditation on mortality and oblivion. The famous last chapter on death is considered an example of nearly flawless English prose.

Hyksos (fr Egyptian, *hikan Khasut*, "rulers of foreign lands"; erroneously, "shepherd kings")   An ancient, semi-nomadic Semitic race whose dominion, centered in Palestine, extended from the Euphrates to the Nile. Between 1720 and 1710 BC they defeated the Pharaohs of the Middle Kingdom and ruled Egypt until about 1570 BC (XV–XVIII dynasties). The Hyksos introduced the horse-drawn chariot and the composite bow into Egypt, as well as the Canaanite deities. In Egyptian art they are depicted as barbarians who misruled the country and debased its culture.

H*y*m*a*n K*a*p*l*a*n, The Education of   See ROSTEN, LEO.

Hymir   In Scandinavian mythology, a giant with a frosty beard who personified the inhospitable sea. He owned the kettle in which the gods brewed their ale, and it was he who took THOR in his boat and robbed him of his prey when the latter god sought to kill the MIDGARD serpent.

Hypatia (c370–415)   Member of the Neoplatonic School of philosophy at Alexandria, in the 5th century AD. A daughter of Theon, the mathematician, Hypatia was murdered by the Alexandrine mob. Her story is told in the historical novel *Hypatia* (1853), by Charles Kingsley. She is also known as the *Divine Pagan*.

hyperbole   In rhetoric, a figure of speech consisting of exaggeration or extravagance of statement. It is used deliberately for effect and not meant to be taken literally, as in "the waves were mountains high," or "I was fainting from hunger."

Hyperboreans   A happy people of early Greek legend. They were supposed to dwell on the other side of the spot where the North Wind had its birth, and therefore to enjoy perpetual warmth and sunshine. They were said to be the oldest of the human race, the most virtuous, and the most happy, dwelling for some thousand years under a cloudless sky, in fields yielding double harvests, and in the enjoyment of perpetual spring.

Later fable held that they had not an atmosphere like our own, but one consisting wholly of feathers. Both HERODOTUS and PLINY mention this fiction, which they say was suggested by the quantity of snow observed to fall in those regions.

Hyperion oder Der Eremit in Griechenland (Hyperion or The Hermit in Greece, 1797–1799)   An epistolary novel by Friedrich HÖLDERLIN. It is set in modern Greece but expresses an elegiac longing for the human and artistic perfection of ancient Greece.

Hypnos   In Greek mythology, the god of sleep.

I

Iachimo In Shakespeare's CYMBELINE, a Roman courtier who wagers with Posthumus Leonatus that he can seduce the latter's wife, IMOGEN. A worldly and affected libertine, he has no redeeming qualities.

Iago In Shakespeare's OTHELLO, the "ancient," or ensign, who is driven by bitterness against his master for having chosen CASSIO as his lieutenant. Though outwardly the epitome of "honesty and trust," he causes the downfall and near-death of Cassio and weaves the Machiavellian plot that plants in Othello's mind the false suspicion of his wife's infidelity with Cassio.

Ironically, one of Shakespeare's most famous speeches on honor is delivered by Iago:

> Good name in man and woman, dear my lord,
> Is the immediate jewel of their souls:
> Who steals my purse steals trash; 'tis something, nothing;
> 'Twas mine, 'tis his, and has been slave to thousands;
> But he that filches from me my good name
> Robs me of that which not enriches him
> And makes me poor indeed.

His also is the famous phrase:

> O, beware, my lord, of jealousy;
> It is the green-eyed monster, which doth mock
> The meat it feeds on.

iamb (or iambus) In English prosody, a metrical foot consisting of two syllables, the first unaccented, the second accented. The word *be*-TRAY is an iamb. The METER made up of such units is called iambic meter, and the following lines are a good example:

> As NIGHT / drew ON, / and, FROM / the CREST
> Of WOOD/ed KNOLLS / that RIDGED / the WEST,
> The SUN, / a SNOW/-blown TRAV/eller, SANK
> From SIGHT / beNEATH / the SMOTH/ering BANK.
> Whittier, *Snow-Bound*

Iambic meter is the most common English measure; insofar as one can generalize, it is the prevailing meter of natural English speech.

Ianthe A poetic name much in use in the 19th century. The Ianthe to whom Byron dedicated his *Childe Harold* was Lady Charlotte Harley, only eleven years old at the time. He borrowed it from Walter Savage Landor, who had thus etherealized the middle name of his early sweetheart, Sophia Jane Swift. Landor wrote many poems in her praise. Shelley gave the name to the maiden to whom the fairy queen appears in *Queen Mab*.

Iapetus In classical mythology, a TITAN son of URANUS and GE, father of ATLAS, PROMETHEUS, Epimetheus, and Menoetius, and ancestor of the human race.

Iberia Spain; the country of the Iberus, the ancient name of the river Ebro.

Iberville, Sieur d' (Pierre le Moyne, 1661–1706) French-Canadian commander and explorer. Born in Montreal, Iberville served in the French navy and took part in successful engagements with the English in the Hudson Bay area. In 1699 he organized and led an expedition which located the mouth of the Mississippi. In 1702 he established colonies at Biloxi and Mobile.

ibis A sacred bird of the ancient Egyptians. It was especially associated with the god THOTH, who, in the guise of an ibis, escaped the pursuit of TYPHON. Its white plumage symbolized the light of the sun, its black neck the shadow of the moon, its body a heart, and its legs a triangle. It was said to drink only the purest of water and to be so fond of Egypt that it would pine to death if transported elsewhere. The ibis was encouraged to make its nest in temples and was often mummified.

Ibsen, Henrik Johan (1828–1906) Norwegian poet and playwright. The son of a middle-class family that suffered severe financial reverses when he was a boy, Ibsen was apprenticed to a druggist in his teens, began to study medicine, but soon found his way into the theatre. In 1851 he was appointed manager and official playwright of the new National Theatre at Bergen, for which he wrote four plays based on Norwegian folklore and history, notably *Lady Inger of Östrat* (1855), dealing with the liberation of medieval Norway. He left the Bergen theatre for the post of

473

manager of the Norwegian Theatre at Christiania (now Oslo), remaining there until the theatre failed in 1864. To this period belong *The Vikings of Helgoland* (1858) and *The Pretenders* (1864), historical dramas, and *Love's Comedy* (1862), a satire. With the aid of a traveling scholarship, Ibsen began a period of self-imposed exile from his homeland, living until 1891 in various cities of the Continent, primarily Rome, Munich, and Dresden. In 1891 he returned to Christiania, where he lived until his death in 1906.

Ibsen's first two major plays, both in verse, were the symbolic tragedy *Brand* (1866) and the mock-heroic fantasy Peer Gynt. *The League of Youth* (1869), a political satire, was his first modern prose drama. It was followed by *Emperor and Galilean* (1873), a historical play in two parts on Julian the Apostate. *Pillars of Society* (1877) deals with the shady acts of a wealthy and hypocritical businessman. A Doll's House, a social drama on marriage, was alternately vilified and praised for its sympathy with women's rights shown when Nora Helmer slammed the door on her doll's house and her "duties" and went out in the world to learn how to be a human being. Ghosts touched on the forbidden subject of venereal disease and attacked social conventions and duty as destroyers of life and happiness. In *An Enemy of the People* (1882) Ibsen contrasted the enlightened and persecuted minority with the ignorant, powerful majority; Dr. Stockman is voted an "enemy of the people" because he insists that the town's famous and prosperous Baths are dangerously polluted and must be shut down for expensive repairs. The play was followed by the poetic and symbolic drama The Wild Duck; Rosmersholm, another play on the problems of idealism; and *The Lady from the Sea* (1888), a play with supernatural overtones and a happy ending. Hedda Gabler, one of Ibsen's greatest plays, is a striking study of a modern woman. The Master Builder deals symbolically with the plight of the artist. *Little Eyolf* (1894) concerns parental responsibility. Ibsen's last two works, the realistic John Gabriel Borkman and the highly symbolic When We Dead Awaken, both deal with men who are dead spiritually because they have sacrificed love.

Called the father of modern drama, Ibsen discarded the Scribean formula for the "well-made play" that had ruled the 19th-century theatre. He brought the problems and ideas of the day onto his stage, emphasized character rather than ingenious plots, and created realistic plays of psychological conflict. Throughout all his works, the social dramas as well as the symbolic plays, run the twin themes that the individual, not the group, is of paramount importance, and that the denial of love is the one unforgivable sin, tantamount to a denial of life.

Ibuse Masuji (1898–   )   Japanese novelist. Many of his works are marked by bittersweet humor as they depict human frailties emerging in small incidents of daily life. *Honjitsu Kyūshin* (1949; tr *No Consultations Today*, 1961) and *Yōhai Taichō* (1950; tr *Lieutenant Lookeast*, 1971) are stories representative of this category. *Jon Manjirō Hyōryūki* (1938; tr *John Manjiro*, 1940) and *Kuroit Ame* (1966; *Black Rain*, 1968) are both based on actual events, the former tracing the checkered life of a castaway and the latter drawing its material from the atomic bombing of Hiroshima.

Ibycus (6th century BC)   A Greek lyric poet. According to legend, Ibycus was murdered with only a passing flock of cranes as witnesses. In the presence of a large crowd one of the murderers betrayed himself, when he saw a flock of cranes pass overhead, by exclaiming: "The cranes of Ibycus!" This phrase signifies hence "unsuspected witnesses to a crime."

Icarius   In Greek legend an Athenian who was taught the cultivation of the vine by Dionysus. Icarius was slain by some peasants who had become intoxicated with wine he had given them and who thought they had been poisoned. They buried the body under a tree; his daughter Erigone, searching for her father, was directed to the spot by the howling of his dog Maera, and when she discovered the body she hanged herself for grief. Icarius became the constellation *Boötes*, Erigone the constellation *Virgo*, and Maera the star *Procyon*, which rises in July, a little before the dog star.

Icarus   In Greek mythology, son of Daedalus. Icarus flew with his father from Crete; but the sun melted the wax with which his wings were fastened on, and he fell into the sea, hence called the Icarian.

Icaza Coronel, Jorge (1906–1979)   Ecuadorian novelist, short-story writer, and playwright. Icaza began by writing plays when he was an actor with the National Theatre in the late 1920s. His literary reputation, however, is based on his story collections and novels. His novels belong to the *Indigenista* movement, which protested the abject conditions to which the Indian population of the Andes had been reduced by colonial and neocolonial rule. By far his best-known work is *Huasipungo* (1934; tr 1962, also tr as *The Villagers*, 1973), his first novel, which depicts with horrifying realism the appropriation of Indian lands, a brutal massacre to abort their protest, and the squalid conditions in which they are forced to exist.

Iceman Cometh, The (1939)   A play by Eugene O'Neill. Through the conversations of a group of derelicts in the backroom at the End of the Line Café, O'Neill pursues a recurring theme in his work: existence derives its meaning from the fantasies and pipe dreams we use to conceal the grimmer realities. Among the last and most important of O'Neill's plays, *Iceman* is autobiographical to the extent that the characters were modeled on people he knew in his youth. As in many of his other plays, O'Neill seems to conclude that, for those who face up to reality, all hope is lost; for those who keep their cherished illusions of themselves alive, there is at least the illusion of hope.

I ching   See Book of Changes.

ichthys (Gr, "fish")   An early symbol of Jesus. The word is an anagram of the phrase *Iesous CHristos, THeou Yios, Soter,* "Jesus Christ, Son of God, Saviour." This word, and the ichthys symbol, two facing curved lines which overlap at one end, are found on many early Christian seals, rings, urns, and tombs.

icon   In the Eastern Church, an image or representation of Jesus, a saint, or an angel. Icons are sacred and honored with relative worship (kissing, incense, light) but not with supreme worship, which is due to God alone. They range from elaborate works of art in the church buildings to humble enamel and niello objects venerated by the peasantry.

iconoclasts (Gr, "image breakers")   Reformers who rose in the Eastern Church in the 7th and 8th centuries, beginning under Emperor Leo III, the Isaurian. They destroyed sacred images, or icons, in the churches because they feared such visual representation would lead to pagan idol worship. The iconoclasts' crusade continued for 120 years under Constantine Copronymus, Leo the Armenian, Theophilus, and other Byzantine emperors, known as the *Iconoclast emperors.* Eventually, images were used in the Western Church, but in the Eastern Church sculptures are still excluded, though pictures are allowed.

A person who criticizes or seriously questions ideas and attitudes previously accepted as correct, just, and valuable by convention and tradition, rather than by independent examination and judgments, is also called an *iconoclast.*

Milton attacked the royal image of Charles II in his prose pamphlet *Eikonoclastes* (1649).

Ida, Mount   The highest mountain on Crete and, according to some legends, the birthplace of ZEUS. It is also the Trojan hill on which PARIS pastured his flocks and where he was forced to judge the relative beauty of ATHENE, APHRODITE and HERA.

Idaean Mother   CYBELE, who had a temple on Mount Ida, in Asia Minor.

Idalian   Pertaining to Idalium, an ancient town in Cyprus, or to APHRODITE, to whom the place was consecrated.

id, ego, and superego   See FREUD, SIGMUND.

ideologues   A group of materialistic and pragmatic philosophers and psychologists of the late 18th century. They believed that ideas originate in physical sensation and that morality is therefore physical in origin; they proclaimed the self-sufficiency of man. Their literary influence is found in the works of Benjamin CONSTANT and STENDHAL.

ides   In the Roman calendar, the 15th of March, May, July, and October, and the 13th of all the other months. The ides always fell eight days after the NONES.

According to Plutarch, Julius Caesar ignored a soothsayer's warning to beware the ides of March, the day on which he was slain.

Idiot, The (1868)   A novel by DOSTOYEVSKY. It is concerned with the effect of the saintly Prince Myshkin on worldly society in St. Petersburg. Myshkin's gentle, childlike nature and his refusal to take offense at anything have earned him the nickname of "the idiot." He himself admits to having been virtually an idiot for several years while under medical care in Switzerland. On the death of his benefactor, he returns to Russia to find himself heir to a large fortune. Almost immediately the trustful Myshkin is entangled in the affairs of the corrupt world of society. On the trip back to Russia he has already met the violently passionate ROGOZHIN, who is obsessed by the beautiful Natasha FILIPPOVNA, the victim in her youth of an older man who brought her up as his mistress. The shame Natasha feels has driven the proud girl to degrade herself even more. Only when she meets Myshkin does she feel she has encountered a sympathetic being. This feeling eventually drives her to greater self-torment, when she realizes that Myshkin's love is, in fact, pity.

Myshkin becomes involved with another woman, young Aglaya Epanchin, to whom he also cannot give the normal passionate love she wants, although he does ask her to marry him. His pity for Natasha, however, overcomes whatever love it is he feels for Aglaya, and he goes off to try again to redeem her. His vacillations manage only to hurt both women and, eventually, to enrage the jealous Rogozhin to the point of murder. The latter tries unsuccessfully to kill Myshkin and, at the end of the novel, he murders Natasha. Confronted by the scene, Myshkin relapses into idiocy.

Dostoyevsky's announced intention with the character of Myshkin was to portray a truly good man. The attempt has been viewed by critics as only partially successful, not only because Myshkin wreaks havoc with most of the characters he influences, but also because of the bloodless, abstract quality of the characterization itself. A more successful effort of this type is Aleksey Karamazov, in whose portrayal Dostoyevsky managed to blend harmoniously both human and Christlike attributes.

Dostoyevsky acknowledged that *The Idiot* was not completely successful but insisted that the book was, nevertheless, his personal favorite among his works. Besides the figure of Myshkin, the author included in the novel many of his ideas on the superiority of Orthodoxy to Western religion and on the connections between Roman Catholicism and socialism.

idyll   (1) A pastoral poem, usually brief, describing the picturesque in country life and conveying a mood of peace and contentment. The most celebrated idylls of antiquity are those of THEOCRITUS and VERGIL. Idylls may also be narrative poems, sometimes of epic stature, as in Tennyson's IDYLLS OF THE KING.

(2) Any bucolic, peaceful, romantic episode or period in life or literature which might be a suitable subject for an idyll.

(3) In music, a romantic pastoral composition.

Idylls of the King (1859–1885) A series of poems in ten books by Alfred Tennyson. Based on Arthurian legend, they comprise "The Coming of Arthur," "Gareth and Lynette," "Geraint and Enid," "Merlin and Vivien," "Lancelot and Elaine," "The Holy Grail," "Pelleas and Etarre," "The Last Tournament," "Guinevere," and "The Passing of Arthur." In interpreting the Arthurian legend, Tennyson focuses on the introduction of evil into the hitherto unblemished Camelot through Lancelot's sin of adulterous love for Guinevere. Because of this approach, some commentators have found Tennyson's conception of Arthur lacking in substance.

If It Die . . . (Si le grain ne meurt, 1926; tr 1950) An autobiographical work by André Gide. Written in 1920, it records Gide's experiences during his trips to North Africa in 1893 and 1894–95. In part a confession of homosexuality, the book was intended to force public discussion of an issue then normally avoided.

Ignatow, David (1914–) American poet and editor. Ignatow was among the poets who frequented Greenwich Village in the late 1930s and early 1940s and, under the tutelage of William Carlos Williams, espoused the tenets of Imagism. Daring in its use of meter and fantastic imagery, Ignatow's work is also marked by a keenly individual expression of humanism. His poems are primarily short, perceptive portraits or parables, centering on urban man's anxious existence, often doleful in tone. In 1967 he became the coeditor of the distinguished literary journal *Chelsea*. Three years later he published a collected edition of his work, *Poems: 1934–1969* (1970). He was awarded the Bollingen Prize for Poetry in 1977. *Tread the Dark* (1978), his seventh book of poems, contains some of his most purely expressed meditations on the human condition. *Open Between Us* was published in 1979; it was followed by *Whisper to the Earth* in 1982 and *Leaving the Door Open* in 1984.

Igraine, Queen In Arthurian literature the mother of King Arthur. In many versions, Igraine is the virtuous wife of Gorlois, duke of Tintagel, and she is innocently seduced by King Uther Pendragon when the magic of Merlin gives him the appearance of her husband. In other versions, Uther and Gorlois fight, and the latter is slain. Uther then besieges Tintagel Castle, takes it, and compels Igraine to become his wife. Nine months afterwards, Uther dies, and on the same day Arthur is born.

Ihara Saikaku (born Hirayama Tōgo, 1642–1693) Japanese novelist and story writer. After a period of work as a poet, he wrote many popular tales of merchant-class life that focus on two great human passions, sensual love and pecuniary avarice. His writings reflected the new bourgeois culture centering in Osaka. Among his noted works are *Kōshoku ichidai otoko* (1682; tr *The Life of an Amorous Man*, 1963), *Kōshoku gonin onna* (1686; tr *Five Women*

Who Loved Love, 1956), and *Seken munezan'yō* (1692; tr *Worldly Mental Calculations*, 1976).

Ihimaera, Witi (1944–) New Zealand novelist and short-story writer. As the first Maori novelist, Ihimaera's chief concern is to present Maori people and customs in as authentic a manner as possible. His novels *Tangi* (1973) and *Whanau* (1975), as well as his stories in *Pounamu, Pounamu* (1972) and *The New Net Goes Fishing* (1977), portray the traditions and familial bonds that hold the Maori people together and the European influences that tear them apart. He has also edited *Into the World of Light* (1980), a collection of contemporary Maori writing.

I.H.S. The first three letters of the Greek form of Jesus, and a widely used Christian symbol. In time, the long "e" (H) was mistaken by people of Latin culture for a capital H, and various phrases arose that used these letters as initials, such as *Jesus Hominum Salvator* ("Jesus, Savior of men") and *In hac salus* ("safety in this," i.e., the Cross).

Iliad Greek epic poem (9th century BC?) attributed to Homer. In twenty-four books of dactylic hexameter verse, it details the events of the few days near the end of the Trojan War, focusing on the withdrawal of Achilles from the contest and the disastrous effects of this act on the Greek campaign. The plot is as follows:

Book I. Agamemnon, commander-in-chief of the Greek forces, refuses to return his captive Chryseis to her father, Chryses, a priest of Apollo. An ensuing pestilence is divined to be the result of this unseemly act, and the Greeks insist that Agamemnon relinquish Chryseis. He grudgingly does so, but takes Achilles' captive Briseis in her place. Furious, Achilles refuses to fight with the Greeks. His mother, Thetis, persuades Zeus to turn the tide of battle so that the Greeks will see how much they need Achilles.

Book II. A false dream sent by Zeus leads Agamemnon to plan a battle. He tests his men by suggesting that they return home. To his dismay, they start to rush for the ships, and are only restrained when Odysseus beats their leader Thersites. The "Catalogue of Ships" lists the combatants and their forces.

Book III. Paris, whose abduction of Helen from Sparta was the cause of the war, now engages in single combat with her husband, Menelaus. About to be killed, Paris is spirited away by Aphrodite.

Book IV. Athene, who favors the Greeks, causes the Trojan Pandarus to break the truce by treacherously shooting Menelaus, and the battle is joined.

Book V. Diomedes is the hero of the day, killing Pandarus and many others and even wounding Aphrodite and (with Athene's help) Ares, who are helping the Trojans.

Book VI. Hector, the Trojan leader, returns to Troy, bids the women pray to Athene, and bids farewell to Andromache, his wife, and his infant son, in a touching scene. On the battlefield, Diomedes and Glaucus, finding that their godfathers were friends, refrain from fighting and exchange armor, Glaucus accepting bronze for gold.

Book VII. After an indecisive battle between the Trojan leader Hector and Great AJAX, there is a pause. Under pressure from the Trojans, Paris, though refusing to give up Helen, promises to make handsome restitution. The Greeks refuse his offer and build a wall to protect their ships.

Book VIII. Zeus orders the other gods not to interfere in the war. HERA and Athene at first defy him, but are chastened. The war turns in the Trojans' favor.

Book IX. Desperate, Agamemnon offers to return Briseis to Achilles and make further restitution. Odysseus, Ajax, and Phoenix, Achilles' old tutor, bear the offer to Achilles, but he indignantly refuses it and vows to start for home the next day.

Book X. Odysseus and Diomedes spy on the Trojans, and kill Dolon and the Thracian king, Rhesus.

Book XI. Agamemnon harries the Trojans, but he, Odysseus, Diomedes, and others are wounded. Achilles sends PATROCLUS to inquire about the course of the fighting. NESTOR urges him to beg Achilles to fight or to send Patroclus with Achilles' MYRMIDONS.

Book XII. The Trojans under Hector break through a gate in the Greek walls.

Book XIII. In spite of Zeus' commands POSEIDON rallies the Greeks under Idomeneus and the Ajaxes.

Book XIV. Hera amorously deceives Zeus and puts him to sleep, while Poseidon helps the Greeks. The Trojans are driven back and Hector is wounded.

Book XV. When Zeus awakes, Poseidon is forced to cease aiding the Greeks and APOLLO rouses Hector to lead the Trojans as far as the Greek ships, where he tries to burn them. Patroclus meanwhile begs Achilles to fight.

Book XVI. Achilles gives Patroclus his armor and tells him to repel the Trojan advance, but no more. Patroclus drives the Trojans to the walls of Troy, killing SARPEDON and Hector's charioteer; but there Hector kills him, with the aid of Apollo.

Book XVII. Hector takes Achilles' armor, but, in a violent fight, Menelaus and the Greeks recover Patroclus' body.

Book XVIII. In spite of Thetis' warnings that he is fated to die, Achilles determines to avenge Patroclus in battle. HEPHAESTUS makes him a new shield, richly engraved with many scenes.

Book XIX. Achilles announces that he will fight. Agamemnon makes amends. Achilles' immortal horses, Xanthus and Balius, warn him that this is the last time they will bear him safely from the field. Knowing that he is soon to die, Achilles goes into battle.

Book XX. Since Zeus' promise to Thetis now is fulfilled, the other gods are free to join in the war. Aligned with the Greeks are Athene, Hera, Poseidon, Hephaestus, and Hermes; with the Trojans, Apollo, Ares, Artemis, Aphrodite, and LETO. AENEAS fights with Achilles, but is rescued by Poseidon; similarly Hector is saved by Apollo.

Book XXI. Achilles routs the Trojans, killing many in the river Xanthus, which fights against him. Only Apollo saves the Trojans from destruction.

Book XXII. Hector waits alone outside the walls of Troy to meet Achilles. At first he flees from him three times about the city but then turns to fight. Abandoned by Apollo he is tricked by Athene and killed by Achilles, who drags his body behind his chariot to the ships, while his family and all Troy lament on the city walls.

Book XXIII. Achilles holds a great funeral for Patroclus, burning twelve Trojan youths with his body. Games are held in his honor.

Book XXIV. For days Achilles continues to heap indignities on the corpse of Hector, until Zeus warns him through Thetis that the gods will be angered. The Trojan king, PRIAM, begs the body from Achilles, who recognizes in him a fellow-sufferer, and consents. A funeral is held for Hector.

The Trojan war is now known, thanks to the discoveries of SCHLIEMANN and his successors, to have been a historical event of the 13th century BC, though hardly the glorious contest described in the *Iliad*. About that event there grew up a vast number of legends, which, during the succeeding centuries, were told and retold by the bards in accordance with the traditions of GREEK EPIC POETRY until a certain amount of order was imposed on the many variant strands. It was probably about four centuries after the war that a particular group of these myths were modeled into the dramatic and stylistic unit that became known as the *Iliad*. This work was attributed to an Ionian poet called Homer.

Controversy still rages on whether Homer was a single poet or many, but there is little question of the essential unity of concept that makes the *Iliad* a great poem. In spite of the monotonous similarity between one hand-to-hand combat and the next and in spite of the epithets and other bardic formulas that can apply as well to one hero as to another, the *Iliad* is far more than a vast, highly formalized panorama of battle. Many of the principal figures are considerably individualized: Achilles, Agamemnon, Nestor, Paris, Hector, Thersites, Dolon. There are amusing touches: the ignominious flight of the Greeks when Agamemnon tests their loyalty, Glaucus giving his gold armor in an access of hospitality; there are moving scenes: Hector's infant son frightened by the plume on his father's helmet, Achilles going into battle in spite of his horses' warning, Priam and Achilles weeping together over their mutual loss. All these scenes give the story a human significance that deeply involves the reader in its events. One of the most impressive qualities of the poem is the dramatic impact that the poet achieved by concentrating his attention not on the siege of Troy, but on the tragic results of one man's anger. In spite of Achilles' implacable and (to modern readers) childish resentment of a slight on his honor, he is a genuinely noble figure who knowingly embraces certain death rather than live a long life without glory.

The *Iliad* is written in the poetic line regularly associated with Greek epic, the dactylic hexameter. The dialect of the poem is primarily Ionic, with a strong subsoil of Aeolic, which had been the language of the earlier inhabitants of the part of Ionia from which Homer traditionally came. However, the language of the *Iliad*, or of epic in general, was more a traditional poetic diction than an actual speech.

The world of the Trojan War was very imperfectly remembered in the Homeric poem, written centuries later. Some of the traditional material, inherited and faithfully passed on by Homer, must have been incomprehensible to him: for example, the use of the Mycenaean full-length rectangular shield, which had long been obsolete. As a result, the soldiers in the *Iliad* are sometimes described as bearing the round bronze shield of the poet's day, whereas elsewhere they carry the ancient long shield. Such discrepancies as these have aided scholars in sorting out old and new material in the work. Other anachronisms are the result of deliberate tampering, in order to increase the role of Athens in the war and to diminish that of her enemies. This process may well have taken place in the days of PISISTRATUS, when the recitation of Homer became a regular part of the Panathenaic festival. The fact that certain barbarous customs, such as human sacrifice, torture, and mutilation, scarcely appear in the *Iliad* is probably also due to later expurgation.

I'll Take My Stand: The South and the Agrarian Tradition by Twelve Southerners   See FUGITIVES, THE.

illuminism   A pseudoscientific movement of mystics and visionaries in the 18th century which influenced literature in the 19th century. At first inspired by Christian doctrines, illuminists sought to live according to the Gospel and to regenerate their souls by direct contact with the divine. They also, however, believed in spiritism, magnetism, alchemy, and magic and professed to invoke the invisible and the arcane. Among the more famous illuminists were Swedenborg, who conversed with the dead; Lavater, a believer in black magic, who thought to contact God by magnetism; Claude de Saint-Martin ("the unknown philosopher"), who sought to hasten the coming of Christ by meditation and prayer; Mesmer; the Comte de Saint-Germain, who pretended to be several hundred years old and to possess the elixir of eternal life; Gall; and the famous Cagliostro, who evoked spirits. An almost instinctive reaction against 18th-century rational philosophies, illuminism under many names (e.g., millenarianism, syncretism, neopaganism, pythagorism, theosophy, etc.) influenced some writers of the romantic period. It revived a sense of religious exaltation and mystery and created, or re-

created, a need for the infinite, a belief in man's inner nature and a feeling for the mysteries of nature and of love.

Imaginary Invalid, The   See MALADE IMAGINAIRE, LE.

imagination   See FANCY AND IMAGINATION.

imagism   A theory of poetry adopted about 1910 by a number of English and American poets who followed the leadership of T. E. HULME and Ezra POUND. The movement admitted to several influences—including medieval philosophy, the aesthetics of Henri BERGSON, and Japanese poetry—but it was primarily a reaction against the stultified forms and bucolic sentimentality of the GEORGIANS. It demanded absolute precision in the presentation of the individual image, not mere description. In metrics it proposed the cadence of "the musical phrase," by which was meant a controlled FREE VERSE. Generally, imagist poems were short, pointed observations, often no more than four or five lines in length, and usually balanced on a single, radically original METAPHOR.

Pound and Hulme were joined by a number of other poets, notably Hilda DOOLITTLE, Richard ALDINGTON, William Carlos WILLIAMS, and, later, by Amy LOWELL. They called themselves *Imagistes*. In 1914 Pound edited the first of several imagist anthologies, *Des Imagistes*. While all those writers associated with imagism propagandized vigorously for their beliefs, Pound, who had become editor of Harriet Monroe's POETRY magazine, published therein a number of manifestoes as well as his own and his friends' poems. Pound later abandoned the movement and, with Wyndham LEWIS among others, began writing about VORTICISM. Although Amy Lowell carried on as leader for a few years, the movement, as an institutional force, expired by 1917 or 1918. It had, however, an enormous influence on the development of modern poetry, particularly in light of its encouragement of formal experimentation and its emphasis on concrete poetic image or metaphor. Apart from its direct influence on the work of such poets as T. S. ELIOT, Wallace STEVENS, and Hart CRANE, imagism provided the break with the immediate past that was necessary before new trends in poetry could develop.

Imbolc   February 1, one of the four great feast days of the ancient Celtic year. See BELTINE; LUGNASAD; SAMAIN.

Imhotep   In the mythology of ancient Egypt, the god of learning in general, and a physician later deified as god of medicine. He corresponds to the Greek ASCLEPIUS.

Imitation of Christ (De imitatione Christi, 1426) A religious treatise commonly ascribed to THOMAS À KEMPIS. It has been said that this book has had more influence on Christianity than any other book except the Bible. It is mystical in tone as it explores the inner life and the value of contemplation, yet remarkably clear in its simplicity. Other candidates for the authorship of this work are the brilliant chancellor of the University of Paris, Jean Gerson, and a Jean Gersen, who is identified only as the abbot of Vercelli.

Immermann, Karl Lebrecht (1796–1840)   German novelist and playwright. Immermann's *Die Epigonen* (*The Late-Comers*, 1836) is one of the earliest German social novels. It is set in the Germany of the 1830s, when, partly because of the stultifying political conservatism of Austria and Prussia, there was a widespread feeling of having been born too late for the great and exciting ages of humanity. His later novel *Münchhausen* (1838–39) consists of two main stories developed in alternating episodes; though connected, they are independent enough to be separated, and one, entitled *Der Oberhof* (*The Upper Manor*), is often printed alone. Immermann's best-known drama, *Merlin* (1832), is more romantic than either of the novels.

Immoralist, The (L'Immoraliste, 1902; tr 1930)   A tale by André GIDE. Michel takes his bride, Marceline, to North Africa, where he develops tuberculosis and becomes hyperconscious of physical sensations, particularly of his attraction to young Arab boys. Back on his French estate after being cured, he is encouraged by his friend Ménalque to rise above conventional good and evil and give free rein to all his passions. When Marceline falls ill with the tuberculosis she caught while nursing him, he takes her south. He neglects her demands on him more and more, however, in order to keep himself free, since his new doctrine demands that the weak be suppressed if necessary for the preservation of the strong. She dies, and he, guilt-ridden and debilitated by his excesses, tries to justify his conduct to a group of friends.

Imogen   In Shakespeare's CYMBELINE, the daughter of Cymbeline and the tender, faithful wife of Posthumus Leonatus. Attempting to find her husband, who erroneously believes that she has betrayed him, she disguises herself as a page and assumes the name of Fidele.

Importance of Being Earnest, The (1895)   A comedy by Oscar WILDE. It is noted for its witty lines, its clever situations, and its satire on the British nobility and clergy. It deals with the aspirations of Jack Worthing to the hand of Gwendolen Fairfax, daughter of Lady Bracknell. Lady Bracknell objects to the marriage because of the obscurity of Worthing's background; he was found in a handbag in Victoria Station and has no information as to who his parents were. Eventually matters are straightened out by the revelation that Worthing is actually the son of Lady Bracknell's sister and was left in the handbag as an infant through the absentmindedness of a governess. His name is actually Ernest John Moncrieff, and he is the brother of his friend Algernon Moncrieff. Worthing is particularly happy that his name turns out to be Ernest since he has created an imaginary younger brother of that name for the benefit of his ward Cecily Cardew (who eventually marries Algernon); this "Ernest," a purportedly rakish fellow whom Worthing had constantly to get out of scrapes, was Worthing's excuse for absenting himself from his country estate, where Cecily lived under the tutelage of Miss Prism, to go to London to see Gwendolen.

impressionism   A term applied originally to the work of a group of 19th-century French painters in Paris. Associated with NATURALISM, rebelling equally against the academic and romantic schools, the impressionists attempted to convey in painting the impression gained from direct observation of nature. They broke away from the traditional technique of continuous brush strokes. They sought instead to break up light into its component parts and to render its ephemeral play on various surfaces by a succession of discontinuous dabs of color. Paint colors were to be combined by the eye as colors are in nature. Much of the impressionists' work was done out-of-doors, thus continuing the tradition of their forerunners, the BARBIZON SCHOOL.

Claude MONET, RENOIR, and Alfred SISLEY are the most typical representatives of impressionism in its purest form, other important members of the group being MANET, DEGAS, PISSARRO, and CÉZANNE. When the work of several of these artists had been rejected by the Salon, they organized their own exhibition in 1874, calling themselves the *Société anonyme des artistes, peintres, sculpteurs, etc.* This first exhibition, as well as subsequent ones, was greeted with almost universal disapproval. Singling out Monet's *Impression: Sunrise* (1872) as particularly offensive, the critic Louis Leroy disdainfully labeled the group "*les impressionistes.*" The name was adopted by the artists for two of their eight exhibitions between 1874 and 1886. As each artist developed his own style, the association among them was marked by frequent altercations. The group had altogether disintegrated by their last show in 1886, although a spiritual unity continued to mark their highly individualized work.

Impressionism had an enormous effect on the subsequent history and development of painting both in and outside of France. Among American painters its influence can be seen in the works of James McNeill WHISTLER, John Singer SARGENT, Mary CASSATT, and Maurice PRENDERGAST.

In German literature in the late 19th and early 20th centuries, impressionism denotes a style of writing characterized by extreme precision of language and emphasis on accurately rendering, in all their complexity, subjective, individual experiences. Impressionism is therefore most commonly found in lyric poetry, particularly that of LILIENCRON, DEHMEL, and in the early works of HOFMANNSTHAL and RILKE; but it is also clearly an element in Thomas Mann's early prose style, especially in BUDDENBROOKS, and in the early dramatic writing of Arthur SCHNITZLER. The subjectivity of impressionistic writing constituted a reaction against both the materialism of mid-19th-century philosophy and the programmatic objectivity of naturalism. However, naturalism and impressionism had enough in common, particularly the wish to make words more precise and the tendency to concentrate on specific human situations, that several major writers, including HAUPTMANN, HOLZ, and Johannes Schlaf (1862–1941), were active in both movements. See EXPRESSIONISM.

In music, impressionism stresses sonorous effects for their own sake, i.e., the use of harmonies and instrumental timbres as musical "colors" that blend together to create a general mood. Most impressionistic pieces have literary or pictorial titles. Claude DEBUSSY, Maurice RAVEL, and Ottorino Respighi (1879–1936) are among those composers associated with impressionism.

Inadmissable Evidence (1964)   A play by John OSBORNE. Through a series of sardonic monologues this play unravels the nightmarish descent to a mental breakdown of Bill Maitland, an East London solicitor whose uneasy identity is further, and ultimately disastrously, eroded by the gradual desertion of all the people in his professional and private life. It is a stirring and painful character study in which even the egocentric and unpleasant protagonist succeeds in winning sympathy, if only for his inner struggle to live.

Inanna   A Sumerian goddess of erotic love and of war. She was a prototype of the goddess ISHTAR, who, under various names but with remarkably consistent nature, was the chief female goddess of the Near East for three thousand years. Many of her attributes caused her to be later identified with ARTEMIS, APHRODITE, and other Greek goddesses. The most important of the many myths in which she figures is that of her descent into the underworld.

Incas   A Quechua-speaking people who dominated pre-Columbian Peru. The name *Inca* was also given to their kings, absolute monarchs who were worshiped as descendants of the sun. See ATAHUALPA; GARCILASO DE LA VEGA; PIZARRO, FRANCISCO.

incunabula (Lat, "a cradle")   Works of art or industry of the infant stages in the development of a given field. In the history of bookmaking, books printed before 1500. They are sometimes called cradle books or fifteeners. In this sense the singular "incunabulum" can be used.

Indiana (1832)   A novel by George SAND. In this violently romantic work, which served as a springboard to establish George Sand's literary reputation, the events bear a provocative resemblance to those in the author's own life. Its heroine, a Creole named Indiana, abandons her old husband for a fascinating young lover.

Indra (also called Mahendra; fr Sans, *maha*, "great") In HINDUISM, the chief god in the pantheon of lesser deities. He is the god of battle and ruler over thunder, lightning, and storm. Several legends represent him as the destroyer of AHI, or Vrita (the drought demon). He is often depicted riding on his elephant, AIRĀVATA.

In Dubious Battle (1936)   A novel by John STEINBECK. It deals with the problem of labor organization among the migrant fruit-pickers in California. Mac, the leading character, is a veteran organizer for the Communist Party who allows nothing to interfere with his service to the cause, not even the murder of his friend Jim Nolan. Another important character is Doc Burton, an uncommitted sympathizer who helps the striking workers.

Inez, Donna   In BYRON's poem DON JUAN, the mother of Juan. After worrying her husband, Don José, to death by her prudery and want of sympathy, Donna Inez endeavors to raise Juan by the strictest rules of propriety and make him a model of all the virtues. Unfortunately, he is seduced by her best friend, the equally proper and intellectual Donna Julia.

Infant Phenomenon, The   The stage name of the allegedly ten-year-old Ninetta Crummles in Charles Dickens's NICHOLAS NICKLEBY. Actually, she is at least fifteen and her short stature results from being kept up late every night and "an unlimited allowance of gin and water."

Infernal Machine, The (La Machine infernale, 1934; tr 1962)   A tragedy by Jean COCTEAU. It uses the story of OEDIPUS as an example of a cosmic joke, "one of the most perfect machines constructed by the infernal gods for the mathematical annihilation of a mortal." Oedipus, who possesses the intuitive, imaginative qualities of Cocteau's ideal poet figure, is brutally crushed by a hostile external world.

Inferno (Hell)   Part I of the DIVINE COMEDY by DANTE. Vergil conducts Dante through the region of damnation, where the souls suffer eternal punishments appropriate to their sins. In the anteroom are those who did nothing in life, neither good nor evil. Then follow nine levels of Hell, descending conically into the earth. The first is Limbo, where are the blameless but unbaptized spirits, including the great men of pagan antiquity. The circles of the sins of incontinence, least terribly punished, include the carnal sinners (see PAOLO AND FRANCESCA), the gluttons, the misers and the spendthrifts, the wrathful and the sullen. With the sixth circle, that of the heretics, begin the horrible torments of the City of Dis, generally fiery. The seventh circle contains the violent against others (murderers), against self (suicides), and against God and Nature (blasphemers, perverts, and the like). The eighth level includes ten categories of the fraudulent (seducers, sorcerers, thieves, hypocrites, and various kinds of liars and evil counselors). The most odious of the fraudulent, the traitors, are frozen in the ice of the ninth circle: the betrayers of their own relatives or country (see UGOLINO) and, at the very center of the earth, Lucifer with three heads gnawing on Brutus and Cassius, the betrayers of Julius Caesar, and Judas Iscariot, the betrayer of Jesus Christ. Turning around at Lucifer's waist, Dante and Vergil emerge through a tunnel into the opposite hemisphere, which is covered with water, to approach the island of the mountain of Purgatory.

In Flanders Fields   See McCRAE, JOHN.

Informer, The (1925)   A novel by Liam O'FLAHERTY. It is a psychological melodrama describing the last day of Gypo Nolan, a destitute Irish revolutionary who turned a comrade in to the police for twenty pounds.

Ingalls, Rachel   See MRS. CALIBAN.

Ingamells, Rex [Reginald Charles] (1913–1955) Australian poet. Ingamells was founder of JINDYWOROBAK MOVEMENT with his pamphlet *Conditional Culture* (1938). His most ambitious work was an eight-thousand-line narrative poem, *The Great South Land* (1951), chronicling Australian history. He was killed in an automobile accident.

Inge, William (1913–1973)   American playwright. Often called the playwright of the Midwest, Inge worked as a teacher and a newspaper critic until 1945 when he met Tennessee WILLIAMS, who encouraged him to write plays. The result, *Farther Off from Heaven* (1947), was produced by Williams's friend Margo Jones in her Dallas theatre. The great success of his second play, *Come Back, Little Sheba* (1949), was matched by *Picnic* (1953; reworked by Inge as *Summer Brave*, 1962), which won a PULITZER PRIZE, *Bus Stop* (1955), and *The Dark at the Top of the Stairs* (1957), an expansion of *Farther Off from Heaven*. Then followed a series of critical failures—*A Loss of Roses* (1959); *Natural Affection* (1963); and *Where's Daddy* (1966)—eased only by the success of his screenplay, *Splendor in the Grass* (1961). Inge then wrote two novels, *Good Luck, Miss Wyckoff* (1970) and *My Son Is a Splendid Driver* (1971). His death in 1973 was apparently suicide.

Ingemann, Bernard Severin (1789–1862)   Danish poet and novelist. Ingemann was the author of a series of popular historical novels set in the Danish middle ages. A schoolteacher in the old town of Sorø, he acquired a lively sense of the past and a love for the ancient chivalric values. Among his novels are *Valdemar Seier* (*Waldemar, Surnamed Seir, or the Victorious*, 1826), *Erik Menveds Barndom* (*The Childhood of King Eric Menved*, 1828) and *Kong Erik og de Fredløse* (*King Eric and the Outlaws*, 1833). *Morgensange for Børn* (1837) and *Morgen og Aften sange* (1839) are collections of simple, delicate lyrics that express a naïve vision of the world.

Ingersoll, Robert G[reen] (1833–1899)   American lawyer, public official, and orator. Ingersoll was known as "the Great Agnostic" for his defense of free-thinking in religious matters. An active Republican, he became a sought-after orator when he eloquently nominated James G. Blaine for the presidency (1876). Influenced by Voltaire and Paine, Ingersoll is known for such aphorisms as these: "Many people think they have religion when they are merely troubled with dyspepsia"; "With soap, baptism is a good thing"; and "An honest God is the noblest work of man." Among Ingersoll's books are *The Gods* (1872), *Some Mistakes of Moses* (1879), and *Why I Am an Agnostic* (1869). After his death appeared *The Works of Robert G. Ingersoll* (12 vols, 1900). See BEN-HUR.

Ingres, Jean Auguste Dominique (1780–1867) French painter. Ingres painted religious, historical, and mythological subjects and was, for a time, the acknowl-

edged leader of the classical school. There was, however, a degree of sensuality present in many of his works, like the *Bather of Valpinçon* (1808), that set him apart from strict classicism. Of all his work, his portraits are most highly prized; many of them were painted during Ingres's long sojourn in Italy. The strong, refined purity of his drawing and the abstract grace of his form and line were deeply influential on such later painters as DEGAS, RENOIR, and PICASSO.

In Memoriam (Lat, "in memory of")   A long poem written between the years 1833 and 1850 by Alfred TENNYSON, in memory of his friend Arthur HALLAM, who died in 1833. It is considered one of the great English elegies and, on the whole, the poet's most impressive longer work. The poem not only deals with Hallam's death and Tennyson's enduring sense of loss, but also attempts to grapple with many of the intellectual and religious problems of the mid-19th century: the decline of faith, the rise of skepticism, and scientific materialism.

Innes, Michael   The pen name under which J. I. M. STEWART writes his detective stories.

Innocents, Massacre of the   The slaughter of the male children of Bethlehem "from two years old and under," when JESUS was born (Matt. 2:16). This was done at the command of HEROD THE GREAT in order to cut off "the babe" who was destined to become "King of the Jews." The Feast of the Holy Innocents commemorating this event is December 28.

Innocents Abroad, The, or, The New Pilgrim's Progress (1869)   A travel book by Mark TWAIN. It is based on a series of letters he wrote from Europe to San Francisco and New York newspapers as a roving correspondent. The book, which burlesques the sentimental travel books popular in the mid-19th century, was well received in Europe and the U.S., and made Twain famous. Twain looked at hallowed European landmarks from a fresh and humorous point of view without reverence for the past, and poked fun at both American and European prejudices and manners.

Innocent Voyage, The   See HIGH WIND IN JAMAICA, A.

Innommable, L'   See UNNAMABLE, THE.

Inns of Court   The four legal societies that have the exclusive right of calling candidates to the English bar. Dating from the late 13th century, the Inns are all in London, each consisting of a legal faculty governed by a board of "benchers," and each providing instruction and examination for candidates. They are: Lincoln's Inn, Gray's Inn, The Inner Temple, and The Middle Temple.

In Our Time (1924)   A collection of short stories by Ernest HEMINGWAY. First published in France and the following year in the U.S., many of the stories deal with the development of young Nick ADAMS, who bears some resemblance to the author himself. In "Indian Camp," Nick is introduced to the violence of life when he accompanies his doctor father; "Big Two-Hearted River" shows his mental state after he has been wounded in World War I. The stories alternate with imagistic "chapters" that give glimpses of the war and of bullfighting. See KILLERS, THE.

Inquisition   A court of the Roman Catholic Church devoted to the suppression of heresy, established in 1233 by Pope Gregory IX for the suppression of the Albigensians in southern France. Torture, first authorized in 1252, became common and those found guilty were handed over to the secular arm. Contrary to popular impression, the burning of heretics was not common in the Middle Ages: fines, imprisonment, and penance were the usual penalties. The suppression of heresy was used as a political weapon by secular rulers, as in the case of the TEMPLARS. The Inquisition was most active in southern France, Italy, and Germany. It was transformed into the Congregation of the Inquisition, also known as the Holy Office, in 1542 and thereafter is best known for its prosecution of GALILEO.

Inquisition, Spanish   A tribunal for suppressing heresy in Spain, established by Ferdinand and Isabella in 1478, with the reluctant consent of Pope Sixtus IV. The first Inquisitor-General was Tomás de Torquemada (c1420–98), a Dominican monk whose name has become a byword for cruelty and severity.

Though nominally under papal control, the Inquisition was actually an agency of the crown, which often used it for political purposes. The principal victims of the Inquisition in Spain were the converted Muslims and Jews, known respectively as *Moriscos* and *Marranos*. It also investigated crimes against morality, such as polygamy and rape. Its procedures were secret, and suspects were not told the identity of their accusers; torture was sometimes used. Penalties, which were announced at solemn public gatherings called *autos da fé*, ranged from reprimand and warning to "relaxation," i.e., being delivered to the secular authorities to be burned at the stake. The Inquisition was suppressed in 1808 and its successor, the Tribunal of the Faith, was abolished in 1834.

Insarov   The hero of Ivan TURGENEV's novel ON THE EVE. A Bulgarian revolutionary who lives only to free his country from Turkish oppression, the dedicated Insarov inspires love in the young Russian Elena Stakhova.

inscape and instress   Terms coined by the poet Gerard Manley HOPKINS. *Inscape* refers to the distinctive individual essence of a natural object or a scene in nature. When the quality of inscape is perceived clearly as, for example, in an EPIPHANY, the beholder becomes aware of an essential unity in all nature. *Instress* is the force which sustains the inscape and which makes the quality of inscape manifest in the mind of the beholder.

Inscription for the Entrance to a Wood (1817) A poem by William Cullen BRYANT. The poet finds solace in the woods for the guilt and misery of the world.

Inspector General, The (Revizor, 1836)   A comic drama by Nikolay GOGOL. It is regarded as one of the best plays in Russian literature. The action revolves around a case of mistaken identity. The central character, Khlestakov, a run-of-the-mill civil servant from St. Petersburg, is stranded in a small provincial town. The corrupt officials of the town, hearing that a government inspector is on the way there, convince themselves that Khlestakov is the man. Khlestakov quickly catches on and goes along with the error, bragging of his high connections in the capital, taking bribes, and wooing the mayor's daughter and wife. He is unmasked when a gloating letter he has written to a friend in St. Petersburg is read by the inquisitive postmaster, but before he is found out, Khlestakov has prudently left town. While the town officials are fuming about the ruse, the real inspector general arrives.

The play was taken as a social satire at the time of its production, and that view has remained the standard one in Russian criticism. There are, however, many fantastic aspects to the comedy, particularly in Khlestakov's inane chattering.

Instauratio Magna (Lat, "great renewal")   A projected work by Francis BACON designed to be a comprehensive survey of the principles, methods, and accomplishments of his "new philosophy" of experimental science. Bacon hoped to develop a theory of knowledge, based on inductive scientific methods, that would assure man's mastery over the natural world. Of the six projected parts, Bacon completed only two: THE ADVANCEMENT OF LEARNING and NOVUM ORGANUM.

Institutes of the Christian Religion (1536) The principal work of John CALVIN. It first appeared in Latin in 1536, and a French translation, made by Calvin himself, was published in 1541. Designed as a reply to attacks on Protestantism and as a guide to Scripture, the work states, with passionate conviction, the essential doctrines of the new religion.

instress   See INSCAPE AND INSTRESS.

Insulted and Injured, The (Unizhennye i oskorblyonnye, 1861)   A novel by DOSTOYEVSKY. The first of his full-length novels, it is also the first of his works clearly to express Dostoyevsky's characteristic ideas about the purifying function of suffering. The book has a conventional, melodramatic plot, with Ivan Petrovich (Vanya), who is in love with Natasha Ikhmeneva, trying to aid her in her wooing of Alyosha Valkovsky. Ivan, a young writer who bears some resemblance to the young Dostoyevsky, engages in philosophical duels with the cynical Prince Valkovsky, Alyosha's father, an early sketch of the "predatory type" more fully developed in SVIDRIGAILOV in CRIME AND PUNISHMENT and STAVROGIN in THE POSSESSED.

The sentimental atmosphere of the novel is heightened by the presence of a young girl, Nelly. Taken obviously from DICKENS, she undergoes harrowing experiences at the hands of the prince before she is rescued.

interior monologue   See MONOLOGUE; STREAM OF CONSCIOUSNESS.

interlude   A form of dramatic entertainment, originating during the reign of Henry VIII of England and popular at the Tudor court. The exact nature of the interlude is not known, but it is believed to have originated as a brief skit between the courses of a banquet. Court interludes, of which John HEYWOOD was the outstanding author, were usually lively and realistic and devoted chiefly to entertainment. Heywood's THE FOUR P'S is a typical example. There were also educational interludes, didactically teaching an edifying moral; these were usually written in Latin, using type characters and situations, and were performed at public schools, such as Eton. The interlude is considered a transitional form between the miracle plays and MORALITY PLAYS of the Middle Ages and fully developed ELIZABETHAN drama.

In the American Grain (1925)   A collection of essays by William Carlos WILLIAMS. This is a study of various figures out of the American past: COLUMBUS, CORTEZ, DE SOTO, Sir Walter RALEIGH, Benjamin FRANKLIN, and others. Focusing on a particular individual for each essay, Williams adopted a different style for each, creating the impression that the subject was speaking for himself. In some instances the heroes' own journals are in fact the text. For Williams, American history was not a matter of external conflicts or developments, but rather the outcome of individual confrontations within the continent.

In the Matter of J. Robert Oppenheimer   See KIPPHARDT, HEINAR.

In the Midst of Life (1892, rev 1898)   A collection of twenty-six stories by Ambrose BIERCE, published originally as *Tales of Soldiers and Civilians* (1891). In these tales of horror, Bierce implies that life is subject to accident and coincidence. The stories have twist endings rarely surpassed in literature. Ten of the tales deal with soldiers, and in every case, the young men die. Among the most famous are "An Occurrence at Owl Creek Bridge," "A Horseman in the Sky," and "The Eyes of the Panther."

In the Ravine (V ovrage, 1900)   A long story by CHEKHOV. A study of the brutal lives of the peasantry in a small provincial town, this work has long been considered one of Chekhov's best prose pieces. On its publication, it was unanimously acclaimed one of the outstanding works of Russian literature. The central characters of the story are the shopkeeper Tsybukin, his two sons, and their wives, Aksinya and Lipa. Aksinya is a rapacious creature who eventually takes over the household and shop, drives out the old man, and causes the death of Lipa's small son.

Intruder in the Dust (1948)   A novel by William FAULKNER. Lucas Beauchamp, an aging black who has long nettled the townsfolk of Jefferson by his refusal to adopt the black's traditionally servile attitude, is wrongfully accused of murdering a white man and is threatened with violent death at the hands of a mob. Through the efforts of sixteen-year-old Chick MALLISON, Aleck Sander, Chick's black friend, and seventy-year-old Miss Eunice Habersham, Lucas's innocence is proved and the real murderer captured. Because of his relationship with Lucas, Chick comes into manhood able to recognize other human beings as individuals, regardless of their color.

Invictus (Lat, "unconquered")   The title of a well-known poem (usually deplored by critics), written in a tuberculosis hospital, by William Ernest HENLEY. Its last lines read:

> It matters not how strait the gate
>   How charged with punishment the scroll,
> I am the master of my fate,
>   I am the captain of my soul.

Invisible Man (1952)   A novel by Ralph ELLISON. Although he wrote only two novels, *Invisible Man* firmly established Ellison's reputation. This powerful story is about a nameless black man's search for his own identity in a world that is essentially inimical to him. Through the narrator's transition from an initial acceptance of the guise invented for him by the whites in a Southern town, to his identification and eventual rejection of his role in a Black Nationalist Group in Harlem, where he becomes no more than a puppet and a pawn, Ellison portrays the irony of the black man's search for himself, a portrayal that avoids excessive emotionalism through the use of irony and wit. The narrator's struggle for identity, though perceived through the black/white racial dichotomy, becomes everyman's struggle to find himself, to give himself a name and a form that are uniquely his. In its perception of the absurdity of human existence, and its handling of this central existentialist theme, it has been ranked with the works of CAMUS and SARTRE. Ellison's other major novel was *Shadow and Act* (1964); in 1986 he published a collection of autobiographical writings, *Going to the Territory*, that shed further light on the particular era in the 1930s that is the backdrop for *Invisible Man*.

Io   In Greek mythology, a priestess of HERA. ZEUS seduced Io, then transformed her into a cow to save her from Hera's wrath. Hera, however, sent a gadfly which drove Io over Greece and much of Asia. In Egypt she finally regained human form and gave birth to twins, Belus and Agenor, who fathered many dynasties of Greece, Crete, and Asia Minor. She appears in Aeschylus' PROMETHEUS BOUND.

Ion (418 BC)   A drama by EURIPIDES. It treats the legend of Ion, son of Creusa and APOLLO. He ultimately became king of Athens and ancestor of the Ionian race. It is one of Euripides' most dramatic plays. It has been interpreted by some as a skeptical drama that questioned the sanctity of Apollo and the honesty of his Delphic oracle.

Ionesco, Eugène (1912–   )   Rumanian-French dramatist of the THEATRE OF THE ABSURD. Ionesco's earlier works are characterized by deliberate *non sequiturs*, the logic of nightmares, and strange metamorphoses. These grimly grotesque farces remain essentially comic because Ionesco is sympathetic to any human attempt, however inadequate, at communication and love.

Ionesco wrote his first play, THE BALD SOPRANO, in the same year (1950) that he wrote *La Leçon* (prod 1951; tr *The Lesson*, 1958) and *Jacques, ou la soumission* (prod 1955; tr *Jacques or Obedience*, 1958). In *La Leçon*, the caricatures of a professor and his student attempt to communicate through a very arbitrary yet absurdly logical language, which the professor wields as an instrument of power with which to dominate and finally to rape and kill the student. *Jacques, ou la soumission* depicts the humiliation and final submission of a young rebel to the conformism of orthodox thinking, especially to the bourgeois sense of embarrassment about sexuality. Its sequel was *L'Avenir est dans les oeufs* (1951; tr *The Future Is in Eggs*, 1960), which issues an insane exhortation to prolific reproduction. *Victimes du devoir* (1953; tr *Victims of Duty*, 1958) is an exploration into the subconscious mind and the meaning of existence in the form of a detective-story parody. Ionesco's first three-act play, *Amédée* (1954; tr 1958), portrays the lonely, bitter life of a couple who share their apartment with a corpse, symbol of their dead love, which grows to gigantic proportions as the play progresses.

Although the compassionate satire and the fantastic atmosphere remain, with *Tueur sans gages* (1957; tr *The Killer*, 1960)—the first of four long plays to feature Bérenger, a little Everyman who is also partly a projection of the author himself—Ionesco's plays begin to employ a more explicit symbolic technique and a more straightforward plot line. RHINOCEROS is an almost conventional allegory of the Nazi phenomenon, while *Le Roi se meurt* (1962; tr *Exit the King*, 1963) touches on metaphysical questions associated with the approach of death. Subsequent works include *Ce Formidable Bordel!* (1973), *Antidotes* (1977), *Un Homme en question* (1979), and *Thèmes et variations, ou Voyage chez les morts* (1980).

Ionesco's writings about the theatre have been collected in *Notes et contre-notes* (1962; tr *Notes and Counter Notes*, 1964). His *Journal en miettes* (1967–68) was partially translated in *Fragments of a Journal* (1968); *Présent passé passé présent*, a memoir that also appeared in 1968, was translated in 1971 as *Present Past, Past Present*. In 1970 Ionesco became a Chevalier of the LEGION OF HONOR; in 1971 he was elected to the venerable ACADÉMIE FRANÇAISE, and in 1985 he was awarded the T. S. Eliot Prize by the Ingersoll Foundation.

Iphicles   See HERACLES.

Iphigenia   In Greek mythology, the eldest child of AGAMEMNON and CLYTEMNESTRA. Iphigenia was sacrificed by her father in order to gain favorable winds for the Greek fleet on its way to Troy (see IPHIGENIA IN AULIS). Her mother used this act as an excuse for murdering Agamemnon on his return. Their son, ORESTES, driven mad after killing Clytemnestra, went to the savage land of Tauris and there found his sister, whom ARTEMIS had spirited away from her funeral pyre. Iphigenia saved Orestes and his friend PYLADES, and sailed away with them (see IPHIGENIA IN TAURIS).

Iphigenia in Aulis (c405 BC)   A tragedy by EURIPIDES. The seer Calchas has predicted that only the sacrifice of IPHIGENIA will save the Greeks from remaining trapped in the harbor at Aulis by unfavorable winds. AGAMEMNON has already sent for his daughter, pretending that she is to marry ACHILLES. He regrets his decision, but is dissuaded from altering it by the scorn of MENELAUS. When Iphigenia arrives, with her mother, CLYTEMNESTRA, and her brother, ORESTES, even Menelaus relents, but Agamemnon orders the sacrifice, sure that ODYSSEUS will force his hand in any case. Clytemnestra begs her husband to free his daughter, and Achilles, who has known nothing of the plot, offers to save her, but Iphigenia agrees to sacrifice herself for the Greeks.

The play was finished by Euripides' son after the playwright's death. An ending in which Iphigenia is saved when ARTEMIS carries her off and substitutes a deer on the altar is thought to be a later interpolation. An altered version of this story was made into an opera by Gluck, *Iphigénie en Aulide* (1772).

Iphigenia in Tauris (c414–412 BC)   A tragedy by EURIPIDES. After murdering his mother, CLYTEMNESTRA (see ORESTEIA), ORESTES has been pursued by the Furies (see ERINYES), and APOLLO has said he will be cured of madness only if he rescues the statue of ARTEMIS from the savage inhabitants of Tauris (the Crimea), who kill all Greeks they find in their country. With his faithful friend Pylades, Orestes arrives in Tauris. The two are promptly captured and are brought to the high priestess to be ritually prepared for their sacrifice. The priestess is Iphigenia, who had been transported to Tauris by Artemis (see IPHIGENIA IN AULIS). In a moving scene, she and Orestes recognize each other. After each of the friends has offered to die for the other, she manages by a ruse to save both and escape with them in a boat. They are driven back by the wind but saved when ATHENE appears and orders Thoas, the Taurian king, to let them leave. A version of this story was made into an opera by Gluck, *Iphigénie en Tauride* (1779).

Iphigenia in Tauris (prose version, 1779; final version in verse, 1787)   A play by GOETHE after EURIPIDES' play of the same title. Iphigenia, whom her father, AGAMEMNON, had wished to sacrifice in order to get good weather for the Greeks' voyage to Troy, has been snatched away by ARTEMIS and left in Tauris as a priestess. Her brother, ORESTES, tormented by the Furies, then comes unwittingly to Tauris, is joyfully reunited with his sister, and both sail home. Goethe, however, does away with Euripides' *deus ex machina* and makes the play's resolution arise from what he later called pure humanity, the inner core of emotional sympathy that unites men, transcends all boundaries of nationality or religion, and ultimately assuages all guilt. See STEIN, CHARLOTTE VON; WEIMAR CLASSICISM.

Iphigénie en Aulide (1679)   A tragedy by Jean RACINE. Its material is freely drawn from the play by EURIPI- DES. An oracle declares that only the sacrifice of Iphigénie can release the Greek fleet from Aulis, where unfavorable winds have stranded it. Priests force AGAMEMNON to send his daughter word that ACHILLES, her betrothed, desires her at Aulis for an immediate marriage. Achilles is incensed to learn of the ruse, but Iphigénie obediently awaits her fate. Remorseful, Agamemnon arranges for his daughter to escape, but the slave-girl Eriphile (a character invented by Racine), who loves Achilles, reveals the plan. The priest Calchas declares Eriphile the victim the gods require, for her name at birth was Iphigénie. Eriphile kills herself on the altar, and Iphigénie is spared.

Iqbāl, Sir Muhammad (1873–1938)   Indian poet and philosopher writing in Persian and Urdu. Iqbāl was considered the foremost Muslim thinker of his day and he was an early advocate of a separate Muslim state. His poetry was the vehicle for his religious, social, and political ideas. In *Asār-e khūdī* (1915; tr *The Secrets of the Self*, 1920), he urges the revitalization of Islam and the need for man to develop his potentialities, themes he developed in subsequent works. Although the long Persian poems were best suited to the development of his philosophical ideas, Iqbāl reached a wider audience in his own country and wrote his best poetry in Urdu. He is claimed by many Pakistanis as their national poet.

Ireland, David (1927–   )   Australian novelist and playwright. Ireland is essentially a political writer whose attacks on the materialism and apathy of Australian society reflect concern with the human condition rather than any specific ideology. His blackly humorous, surreal- istic works amass minutely described details to reveal an absurdist vision of an impersonal, dehumanized society. His novels include *The Chantic Bird* (1968), *The Unknown Industrial Prisoner* (1971), *The Flesheaters* (1972), *Burn* (1975), and *A Woman of the Future* (1979).

I Remember Mama (1944)   A play by John Van Druten (1901–57). A dramatization of Kathryn Forbes's *Mamma's Bank Account* (1943), it is the amusing and ten- der story of a Norwegian mother and father raising their children in America in the early days of the 20th century.

Iriarte, Tomás de (1750–1791)   Spanish fabulist and poet. Iriarte's best-known work is the collection of fables, seventy-six in all, entitled *Fábulas literarias* (1782), which satirizes contemporary literature in a series of apo- logues, including *El burro flautista* and *El oso y el mono*. Iriarte also completed a verse translation of Horace.

Iris   The Greek goddess of the rainbow, or the rain- bow itself. In classic mythology, she is called the messenger of the gods when they intended discord, and the rainbow is

the bridge or road let down from heaven for her accommo- dation. When the gods meant peace they sent HERMES.

Irish Renaissance   A term used to describe the outburst of creative activity at the turn of the last century, which grew out of the attempt to awaken the Irish people to the wealth and value of their native culture. The move- ment, which had been developing very slowly in the latter half of the 19th century, achieved its major impetus from the political martyrdom of the Irish leader Charles Stewart Parnell, an event which caused many thoughtful Irishmen to abandon the attempt to achieve a national identity within an English framework. The Gaelic culture with which the movement identified itself had been, prior to the English invasion in the 12th century, among the richest and most advanced in Europe, particularly distinguished by the enormous prestige with which it invested the tribal bard or storyteller.

The movement itself had two major developments: the activities of the GAELIC LEAGUE, an organization founded in 1893 by Douglas Hyde to restore Gaelic as the official language of Ireland; and the formation of the Irish National Theatre Society in 1901, out of which grew the famous ABBEY THEATRE Company. The leading figures of this latter movement were William Butler YEATS, Edward Martyn (1859–1927), George MOORE, Lady GREGORY, and the actors William (1872–1947) and Frank (1870–1931) Fay. The Abbey Theatre soon became (and remained for the next thirty years) a storm center, the result of the brilliant but, at the time, controversial plays of Yeats, John M. SYNGE, and Sean O'CASEY. Riots and vigorous protesta- tions greeted the productions of Synge's PLAYBOY OF THE WESTERN WORLD, Yeats's *Countess Cathleen* (1892) and O'Casey's *The Plough and the Stars* (1926) and JUNO AND THE PAYCOCK. Despite the protests at home, the Abbey soon developed an international reputation, and the play- ers, featuring such performers as Sara Allgood (1883–1950) and Barry Fitzgerald (1888–1961), enjoyed their greatest success, ironically enough, on tour in England. Other sig- nificant Abbey dramatists were Padraic Colum, Lennox Robinson, and Paul Vincent Carroll. Although the Abbey's greatest days are now past, its impact on the mod- ern theatre is still felt and its legacy may be seen in the work of two recent Irish dramatists of note, Brendan BEHAN and Samuel BECKETT.

In nondramatic literature, the revival was sparked by the poetry of Yeats and A.E. (q.v.), the fanciful and charming re-creations of Irish legends in the novels and poems of James STEPHENS, the more realistic treatment of contempo- rary life in the novels and short stories of Liam O'FLAHERTY, Sean O'FAOLAIN, and Frank O'CONNOR. The irony that marks so much of the Irish Renaissance—its great achievement lies, not in the restoration of Irish cul- ture, but in the immeasurable enrichment of English liter- ature—is nowhere so pronounced as in one of its greatest products: James JOYCE, who so steadfastly refused to be associated with the revival and yet whose work is saturated with Irish life.

Iron in the Soul   See ROADS TO FREEDOM, THE.

irony   In rhetoric, a deliberate dissembling for effect or to intensify meaning. In the most general sense, two categories of irony can be identified: verbal irony, in which it is plain that the speaker means the opposite of what he says; and circumstantial, or situational, irony, in which there is a discrepancy between what might reasonably be expected and what actually occurs—between the appearance of a situation and its reality. One of the most common forms of verbal irony is the use of praise when a slur is intended, as in JULIUS CAESAR when ANTONY insists in his funeral oration for Caesar that BRUTUS is "an honorable man." Ironic devices are favorite tools of satirists and dramatists and have been used by writers since before the time of PLATO. What is known as Socratic irony takes the form of pretended ignorance as a means of leading on and eventually confounding an opponent. Tragic irony results from a perception of the intensity of human striving and the indifference of the universe. In this sense, irony is related to the concept of the ABSURD. In DRAMATIC IRONY, a speaker may utter words that have a hidden meaning intelligible to the audience but of which he himself is unaware, as in SOPHOCLES' drama *Oedipus Rex* when OEDIPUS calls down curses on the slayer of Laius, not knowing that he is the guilty party. See ROMANTIC IRONY.

Irving, John [Winslow] (1942–   )   American novelist, short-story writer, and essayist. Irving concentrates on human relationships, particularly familial relationships, in his works. His early novels—*Setting Free the Bears* (1969), noted for its European voice, *The Water-Method Man* (1972), and *The 158-Pound Marriage* (1974)—were well received by critics but attracted little commercial attention. His fortunes changed with the publication of *The World According to Garp* (1978), the wild and humorous though violent and tragic story of T. S. Garp, a novelist. Filled with bizarre, sometimes absurd characters in an exaggerated world, *Garp* became an immediate best-seller. Neither of his subsequent novels, *The Hotel New Hampshire* (1981) and *The Cider House Rules* (1985), received the same critical acclaim as *Garp*. Critics argue over Irving's excessive use of violence and tragedy, but most agree that his mad preoccupation with language and unusual interpretation of everyday experience have made him a distinctive voice in American writing.

Irving, Washington (1783–1859)   American essayist, biographer, and historian. Although he prepared to be a lawyer, Irving was physically delicate, and his indulgent family allowed him to lead the life of a man of letters. His first published writing was a series of newspaper sketches appearing under the pseudonym of Jonathan Oldstyle, Gent. In 1807 in collaboration with his brother, William, and James Kirk Paulding, Irving wrote the SALMAGUNDI papers. These humorous and satirical pieces modeled on Addison brought him local renown in New York. His first book, A HISTORY OF NEW YORK FROM THE BEGINNING OF THE WORLD TO THE END OF THE DUTCH DYNASTY, supposedly by Diedrich Knickerbocker, created the character of the phlegmatic Dutchman. A quaint and humorous figure, Knickerbocker is a familiar byword, particularly in New York.

After the death of his fiancée, Irving sailed for Europe, where he remained for seventeen years. His best-known book, THE SKETCH BOOK OF GEOFFREY CRAYON, GENT., was published there in 1820, followed by BRACEBRIDGE HALL and *Tales of a Traveller* (1824), a collection of thirty-two tales and sketches. For financial reasons, Irving accepted a position in the U.S. embassy in Madrid. Fascinated by Spain, he enthusiastically wrote four works: HISTORY OF THE LIFE AND VOYAGES OF COLUMBUS, *The Conquest of Granada* (1829), *Companions of Columbus* (1831), and THE LEGENDS OF THE ALHAMBRA. He returned home, and journeyed across the prairies, recording his trip three years later in *A Tour on the Prairies* (1835). He contracted with John Jacob Astor to write the history of Astoria and produced a sequel, *The Adventures of Captain Bonneville* (1837). From 1842 to 1846 Irving served as U.S. minister to Spain. He then retired to Sunnyside, his home in Tarrytown, New York, where he wrote the collection of pieces entitled *Wolfert's Roost* (1855). As an old man, he wrote biographies of Goldsmith and Mahomet, and completed a five-volume biography (1855–59) of George Washington shortly before his death.

Irving took as his models Scott, Addison, and Goldsmith, never attempting to develop an original idiom. Though he rarely manifests moral or intellectual awareness, the charm, delicacy, and pictorial quality of his writing give it lasting value. Irving proved to skeptics at home and abroad that the world would read an American book. Further, among the delightful tales and sketches are a few that have become part of American folklore.

Irwin, Wallace [Admah] (1875–1959)   American newspaperman and writer of humorous verse and fiction. Irwin won national fame with *The Love Sonnets of a Hoodlum* (1902), a remarkable collection of Petrarchan verses in the American vernacular. He is also known for creating the character of Hashimura Togo, a Japanese schoolboy, under whose name he wrote epistolary stories for at least twenty years.

Isaac   In the OLD TESTAMENT, the only son of ABRAHAM and SARAH, the husband of REBEKAH, and the father of JACOB and ESAU. Isaac was nearly offered as a sacrifice to prove his father's faith, but at the last moment God intervened and told Abraham to slay a ram instead (Gen. 24–28).

Isabella   The beautiful and intensely virtuous religious novice who is the heroine of Shakespeare's MEASURE FOR MEASURE. Isabella is finally united with the introverted, philosophical Vincentio, duke of Vienna.

Isabella I (known as *la Católica*, "the Catholic," 1451–1504)   Queen of Castile. The daughter of John II of Castile, Isabella married FERDINAND II of Aragon in 1469. Her accession to the throne of Castile upon the death of her brother Henry IV in 1474 led to the permanent union of the two great kingdoms of Spain.

Isabella, or The Pot of Basil (1820)   A poem by John KEATS, adapted from a tale by Boccaccio. Set in Florence, it tells of Isabella's love for Lorenzo. Her brothers, discovering this love, revenge themselves by murdering Lorenzo in a forest. The ghost of Lorenzo appears to Isabella and tells her of the crime; she goes to the forest, digs up his head, and plants it in a pot of basil, keeping it by her and watering it with her tears. Her brothers discover her grotesque secret and steal the pot, leaving Isabella to die of grief.

Isaiah   A prophetical book of the OLD TESTAMENT. In its present form it is the work of at least three distinct authors in three successive stages of Jewish history from c750 to c450 BC. The first part is strongly political, the author having been a counselor of the Judaean kings. Urging peace with Israel's enemies, he can still foresee the coming tragedy of the Babylonian Exile. The middle chapters of Isaiah (40–55) were written after 586, when Jerusalem fell. They call on Israel not to lose faith in its god and prophesy the return of his loving care. The last part reflects the period of NEHEMIAH's return to Jerusalem and the rebuilding of the city and temple (c450). It is nationalistic and stresses the ritualistic side of Judaism.

All three parts of Isaiah are filled with Messianic hope. The life of the Messiah is told in Isaiah.

Isenbras, Sir (14th century)   Hero of a Middle English verse romance. Strong and prosperous but arrogant, Isenbras is offered the choice of suffering either in youth or in old age. Choosing the former, he is beset by great misfortunes, which humble him. After performing many deeds of generosity and bravery for twenty-one years, he is restored in happiness to all he had lost.

Iseult   The name of the heroine in the medieval cycle TRISTAN AND ISEULT. There are many other versions and parallels of this cycle, beginning with early Irish tales (see THE PURSUIT OF DIARMUID AND GRAINNE) and appearing in the modern world in such forms as the music drama of Richard Wagner. Iseult's name appears in various forms: Isolde, Isolt, Ysolt, etc. In general, Iseult the Fair is an Irish princess, wooed and won by TRISTAN for his uncle, King MARK of Cornwall. But in the process of journeying to the court of King Mark, both Iseult and Tristan drink a magic potion that causes them to fall in love with one another, a love which is completely binding, even in the face of death. The major part of this cycle is concerned with the adventures of the pair, after the marriage of Iseult to King Mark, in the name of their great love. Ultimately Tristan is banished and goes to Brittany, where he marries another, Iseult of the White Hands. When he is about to die, he sends for his love, Iseult the Fair, but she arrives too late. Lying beside the body of Tristan, she too dies. When the two lovers are buried next to one another, a briar grows up from the grave of Tristan and curves over to take root on the grave of Iseult. Three times it is cut down and three times it grows again, until King Mark commands that it be left alone. Iseult is depicted as very beautiful, gifted (among other things, she has great skill in healing wounds), shrewd, and something of a sorceress. In James Joyce's *Finnegans Wake* (1939), the wife and daughter of Earwicker represent the two Iseults of Tristan.

Isherwood, Christopher [William Bradshaw] (1904–1986)   English novelist, short-story writer, playwright, and memoirist. He was a member of the talented group of young left-wing writers of the 1930s that included W. H. AUDEN, C. DAY LEWIS, and Stephen SPENDER. Living in Germany during HITLER's rise to power, Isherwood brilliantly described the social corruption and disintegration in MR. NORRIS CHANGES TRAINS, *Sally Bowles* (1937), and *Goodbye to Berlin* (1939), published together as *Berlin Stories* (1946). *Goodbye to Berlin* was dramatized by John Van Druten (1901–57) as *I Am a Camera* (1952) and later formed the basis for the Broadway musical *Cabaret*. Isherwood and Auden collaborated on the verse plays *The Dog Beneath the Skin* (1935), *The Ascent of F6* (1937), *On the Frontier* (1938), and on *Journey to a War* (1939), about their journey to China and the Sino-Japanese war. At the outbreak of the European war, Isherwood, like Auden, immigrated to the U.S. Auden abandoned Marxism for Christianity; Isherwood, greatly influenced by Aldous HUXLEY, turned to Eastern religions. Much of his subsequent writing was devoted to popularizing aspects of HINDUISM; he translated the BHAGAVADGĪTĀ and other Hindu scriptures and wrote *Essentials of Vedanta* (1969) and *My Guru and His Disciple* (1979). He also translated Baudelaire's *Intimate Journals* (1930; repr 1978) and wrote several novels, including *Prater Violet* (1945). Isherwood's reminiscences of his friends in the 1930s are contained in *Christopher and His Kind* (1976).

Ishikawa Takuboku (1886–1912)   Japanese TANKA and free-style poet. A Buddhist priest's son, Ishikawa began writing poetry early, but had to struggle hard to earn a living after his father was excommunicated in 1904. Plagued by poverty, ill health, and his own temper, he became increasingly critical of the norms of both society and poetry. The *tanka* of his mature years, collected in *Ickiaku no suna* (1910; tr *A Handful of Sand*, 1934) and *Kanashiki gangu* (1912; tr *Sad Toys*, 1977), movingly express his frustrations through the unique three-line forms he invented.

Ishmael   (1) In the OLD TESTAMENT, the son of ABRAHAM and HAGAR, the half-brother of ISAAC. Because SARAH, Abraham's wife, was unable to conceive a child, she offered her servant, Hagar, as Abraham's concubine, which resulted in the birth of Ishmael. After Sarah bore Isaac, Hagar and Ishmael were sent off to the desert, where they were saved from starvation and thirst by the appearance of an angel of the Lord. Ishmael became a famous archer in Paran, married, and had twelve sons, from whom the Arab people are said to be descended. The name Ishmael, which means "may God hear," came to refer to any outcast from society because of the prophecy "And he will be a wild man; his hand will be against every man, and every man's hand against him" (Gen. 16:12).

(2) The narrator of Melville's MOBY-DICK.

Ishtar   The Babylonian goddess of love and war. Known to the Canaanites as Astarte, to the Israelites as Ashtoreth, to the Arabs as the god Athtar, Ishtar developed from the Sumerian goddess INANNA, and was the most widely worshiped of all the deities of the Near and Middle East. Though the goddess of erotic love, she was often warlike and, at best, had a remarkably irritable disposition. Her worship involved ritual prostitution, which was severely condemned by the Hebrew prophets. She may have been "the queen of heaven" mentioned by JEREMIAH; SOLOMON built a temple to her.

Of the many myths in which she figured, the most famous tells of her love for TAMMUZ, a young fertility god. In some unexplained way, her love caused his death. She mourned him extravagantly—her lamentations were ritually commemorated yearly when the summer sun dried up the vegetation—and finally descended into the underworld to bring back her lover. At each of the seven gates through which she passed, she was divested of one of her ornaments or pieces of clothing, until she stood naked before her terrible sister Ereshkigal, goddess of the underworld. She was imprisoned there, and the gods were powerless to help her, until EA fashioned a hermaphroditic creature called Asushu-Namir and sent it armed with magic spells against Ereshkigal. These were successful, and, after Asushu-Namir had poured over her "the water of life," Ishtar returned to earth, taking Tammuz with her. Ishtar's love for Tammuz and her struggle for him with the goddess of the underworld obviously influenced the myth of APHRODITE's rivalry with PERSEPHONE over ADONIS.

As Tammuz discovered, the love of Ishtar was a mixed blessing. In the *Epic of* GILGAMESH, the hero resists her advances and, employing many unflattering epithets, reminds her that her other lovers have regretted their good fortune, many being turned (literally or figuratively) into beasts. In her fury at this rude treatment, Ishtar induces her father, Anu, lord of heaven, to send the bull of heaven against Gilgamesh, but he and ENKIDU kill it. It is for this crime that Enkidu dies.

Isis   The principal goddess of ancient Egypt, forming with her husband-brother OSIRIS and son HORUS the major triad of deities. As the patron saint of mariners in Alexandria, she was often identified with the moon; the cow was sacred to her, its horns representing the crescent moon, which, in Egypt, appears lying on its back. Her chief temples were at Amydos, Busiris, and Philae. She is represented as a queen, her head being surmounted by horns and the solar disk or by the double crown.

The later Greeks and Romans also identified her with the goddess of nature, and Apuleius, in THE GOLDEN ASS, describes her as "the universal mother nature." Representations of Isis suckling Horus were possible prototypes of the Madonna and Child.

Milton, in PARADISE LOST, places Isis among the fallen angels. In THE FAERIE QUEENE, Spenser used the legend of Isis and Osiris to symbolize English equity and justice.

The expression *to lift the veil of Isis* means to pierce to the heart of a great mystery. PROCLUS mentions a statue of Isis, which bore the inscription "I am that which is, has been, and shall be. My veil no one has lifted. The fruit I bore was the Sun."

Iskander, Fazil Abdulovich (1929–   )   Soviet novelist, poet, and short-story writer. Born in Soviet Abkhazia, on the Black Sea, Iskander speaks Abkhazian and Russian and writes in Russian. Like Mikhail ZOSHCHENKO, Iskander satirizes bureaucracy and officialdom, using phrases and terms plucked from government; this has made him unpopular with the censors. Twice his novel *Sovezdiye kozlotura* (1966; tr *The Goatibex Constellation*, 1975) was nominated for a Lenin Prize, only to be rejected, presumably for its overt parody of Soviet interference in science. His second novel, *Sandro iz Chegema* (1979; tr *Sandro of Chegem*, 1984), has appeared unaltered only abroad. Iskander's whimsical and conversational prose style, as well as his focus on local themes of Abkhazia, has given a unique and exotic freshness to Soviet literature.

Islam   The religion of MUHAMMED, whose adherents are called Muslims, Moslems, Musulmans, Mohammedans. The word means "resignation" or "submission to the will of God." MUSLIMS believe every child is born in Islam and would continue in the true faith if not led astray.

Islam emphasizes five duties: (1) bearing witness that there is but one God and one prophet, Muhammed; (2) reciting daily prayers; (3) giving appointed and legal alms; (4) observing the Ramadan, a month's fast; and (5) making a pilgrimage to MECCA at least once in a lifetime. See HADJI; KORAN.

Islands of the Blessed   A mythical abode of dead heroes, called by the Greeks Happy Islands, and by the Romans Fortunate Islands. They are imaginary islands somewhere in the West, where the favorites of the gods are conveyed at death and dwell in everlasting joy.

Isla y Rojo, José Francisco de (1703–1781) Spanish Jesuit and satirist. Isla's best-known work is the *Historia del famoso predicador fray Gerundio de Campazas, alias Zotes* (1758), a satire aimed at bombastic and pedantic religious oratory. It was banned in Spain by the Inquisition, and the second part did not appear until after the expulsion of the Jesuits from Spain in 1767. Isla also wrote *Triunfo del amor y de la lealtad, o Día grande de*

Navarra (1746), a satirical treatment of a celebration in Pamplona upon the accession of Ferdinand VI.

Isle sonante, L' (The Ringing Island, 1562)   The title of the first edition of sixteen chapters of what is now known as Book V of Rabelais's GARGANTUA AND PANTAGRUEL. Ringing Island, which is the first of several islands visited by Pantagruel and his friends, is inhabited by variously colored birds named cardinjays, priestjays, etc., and one popejay, "unique in his species." Birds of passage who had migrated to the island from Nobreadland and Alltoomany, they pass their time in sumptuous living, warbling to the ringing of bells. The episode of these lucky folk who enjoy paradise "both in this world and the next" is a transparent satire on the luxurious living of the Roman Catholic clergy, who thus lured into their ranks many social outcasts and poverty-stricken people.

Ismene   In Greek legend, daughter of OEDIPUS and Jocasta. ANTIGONE was buried alive by the order of King CREON, for burying her brother POLYNICES, slain in combat by his brother Eteocles. Although she had actually been too timid to do so, Ismene declared that she had aided her sister and requested to be allowed to share the same punishment. The episode occurs in Sophocles' ANTIGONE.

Israel (Heb, "contender with God")   In the OLD TESTAMENT, it is the name given to JACOB after he wrestled with the angel of the Lord (Gen. 32:28). Thus, it is also the name given to the Jewish nation descended from him, frequently referred to as the *Children of Israel*.

Israel Potter: or, Fifty Years of Exile (1855)   A novel by Herman MELVILLE. The book is based on Henry Trumbull's biography *Life and Remarkable Adventures of Israel Potter* (1824). In search of freedom and adventure, Israel becomes involved in the battle of Bunker Hill. He meets three Americans: Benjamin Franklin, who robs him while masquerading as a friend; John Paul Jones, who genuinely befriends him; and Ethan Allen, who possesses America's most admirable characteristics. Israel's personality is a mixture of the virtues and faults of all three men. An archetypal American, he is taken prisoner by the English, exiled for fifty years, and returns home to die. Melville suggests, at the end of this satirical novel, that the best hope for America is in her pioneering West.

Issa   See KOBAYASHI ISSA.

italic   A style of type. *Italic type* or *italics* (the type in which the letters, instead of being erect, as in roman, slope upward from left to right, *thus*) was first used by Aldo Manuzio in printing the Aldine classics. It was called by him cursive, a running hand (from Lat, *curro*, "I run"). Vergil was the first author printed in this type (1501).

It Can't Happen Here (1935)   A novel by Sinclair LEWIS. It presents a fancied fascist dictatorship in the U.S., set up by Berzelius Windrip, a New England demagogue who is elected to the presidency. Doremus Jessup, a Vermont editor, fights Windrip, is arrested, escapes, and joins an underground movement in Canada headed by Walt Trowbridge, Windrip's opponent in the election.

Ithuriel   In Milton's PARADISE LOST, an angel who, with Zephon, is commissioned by Gabriel to search for Satan after the latter has effected his entrance into Paradise. Ithuriel is armed with a spear, the slightest touch of which exposes deceit.

Ivan IV (or Ivan the Terrible, 1530–1584)   Tsar of Russia (1533–84). Ivan engaged in a power struggle with the nobility (the boyars) throughout his reign. During this time, he consolidated the Muscovite state, the core of the future Russian empire, and gained an undying reputation for ferocious cruelty toward his enemies—a predilection which alternated with bouts of sensuality and piety. His squabbles with the boyars induced him to set up his own private state within the Muscovite state. Ivan's realm, called the Oprichnina, had its own courts, administration, and army. The rest of the country, called the Zemshchina, was ostensibly ruled by a prince appointed by Ivan, although the puppet ruler's power was slight.

Ivan's stormy career has provided the basis for many literary and dramatic works by Russian authors, as well as a two-part film by Sergey EISENSTEIN. Ivan's own literary legacy consists of several letters in an acrimonious correspondence with Prince Andrey Mikhailovich Kurbsky, who fled to Lithuania when the Tsar began his reign of terror in Russia.

Ivanhoe (1819)   A novel by Sir Walter SCOTT. The action occurs in the period following the Norman Conquest. The titular hero is Wilfred, knight of Ivanhoe, the son of Cedric the Saxon, in love with his father's ward Rowena. Cedric, however, wishes her to marry Athelstane, who is descended from the Saxon royal line and may restore the Saxon supremacy. The real heroine is REBECCA the Jewess, daughter of the wealthy Isaac of York, and a person of much more character and charm than the mild Rowena. Yet Ivanhoe finally rejects her in favor of Rowena. RICHARD the Lion-heart in the guise of the Black Knight and ROBIN HOOD as LOCKSLEY play prominent roles, and the novel is further emblazoned with a colorful entourage of chivalric knights and fair ladies. The frenzied variety of the action, with the pageantry of a tournament and a great flame-engulfed castle, makes this the most enthralling of Scott's works.

Ivanov, Vsevolod Vyacheslavovich (1895–1963)   Russian novelist and short-story writer. Ivanov ran away from home while in his teens and worked at a variety of jobs, including that of a circus clown and as a fakir and dervish. His first story was printed in a Siberian newspaper and attracted the attention of Maksim GORKY, who helped and encouraged the young writer. After the civil war, in which he fought first for the Whites and then for the Reds, Ivanov went to Petersburg and joined the SERAPION BROTHERS. His novels *Tsvetnye vetra* (*Particolored Winds*, 1922) and *Golubye peski* (*Azure Sands* 1922) and his stories, such as "Partizany" ("The Guerillas," 1921) and "Brone-poezd 14-69" (1922; tr "Armored Train 14-69," 1933), are exotic in both theme and treatment, written in the ornate prose style popular in the 1920s. Ivanov's depiction of primitivism as a constant factor in human behavior eventually displeased the Soviet critics, who felt he should concentrate on the social aspects of life. Ivanov then toned down the highly colored prose of his earlier work and made his stories more conventional, with some loss of vigor and excitement. His later works include an autobiographical novel, *Pokhozhdeniya fakira* (1934–35; tr *The Adventures of a Fakir*, 1935), and a war novel, *Vzyatiye Berlina* (*The Taking of Berlin*, 1945).

Ivanov, Vyacheslav Ivanovich (1866–1949) Russian poet. A classical scholar, Ivanov was the leader of the St. Petersburg branch of the SYMBOLISTS from 1905 to 1911, when he moved to Moscow. His earlier poetry is a compound of classical references and archaic Slavic diction, with an admixture of Nietzschean philosophy. His later *Rimskiye sonety* (*Roman Sonnets*), written just before World War II, dispense with ornateness and archaism, achieving powerful effects in simple, direct lines. Ivanov's study of DOSTOYEVSKY (1932) examines the novelist's work as creations of myth. Ivanov emigrated in 1924 and settled in Italy. He died in Rome, after becoming a Roman Catholic.

Ivanovna, Katerina In DOSTOYEVSKY's novel THE BROTHERS KARAMAZOV, the former fiancée of Dmitry KARAMAZOV. One of Dostoyevsky's "infernal woman" characters, Katerina refuses to abandon Dmitry because of her gratitude to him for helping save her father from disgrace. So tenacious is she that she is described as being in love with her own virtue. Ivan, the second brother, is in love with her, but their relationship is mainly a harrowing series of sadistic and masochistic scenes. Finally incensed at Dmitry's rejection of her, Katerina is instrumental in bringing about his conviction for his father's murder.

Ives, Charles [Edward] (1874–1954) American composer. Ives supported himself with a prosperous insurance firm as he composed some of the most original and inventive of all American music. His music was highly experimental but firmly rooted in traditional folk tunes, hymns, and Americana. Because of poor health, he stopped composing in the 1920s. He received little public attention until 1947, when he was awarded the PULITZER PRIZE for music. He has since been hailed as the archetypal American composer. In a style that is uniquely underivative, he wrote four symphonies, many songs, and choral and chamber music. Among his best-known pieces are the *Piano Sonata No. 2* (*Concord Sonata*, 1920) and the orchestral suite *Three Places in New England* (pub 1935).

Ixion In Greek mythology, a Lapith king. Ixion tried to seduce HERA, but ZEUS shaped a cloud in her likeness and Ixion lay with it. Zeus bound him to a fiery wheel that perpetually rolls through the sky. The phantom, later called Nephele, bore Centaurus, ancestor of the CENTAURS.

J

Jabberwocky   A well-known mock-heroic ballad by Lewis CARROLL, found in THROUGH THE LOOKING-GLASS. It contains a number of words coined by the author, including PORTMANTEAU WORDS such as *slithy*, a compound of *lithe* and *slimy*, *mimsy*, a compound of *flimsy* and *miserable*, etc. The Jabberwock is a species of dragon.

J'accuse (I Accuse, 1898)   The title of Emile ZOLA's famous open letter addressed to President Faure of France (first appearing in the newspaper *Aurore*, January 13, 1898), in denunciation of the Dreyfus affair. Zola used the phrase *"J'accuse"* several times in the letter, addressing himself to the injustices perpetrated by the war department. After a year of exile in England, Zola returned to France, a hero for the part he had played in this national crisis. See DREYFUS, ALFRED.

Jack and Jill   A well-known nursery rhyme. It is said to be a relic of a Norse myth, accounting for the dark patches in the moon. The two children are supposed to have been kidnaped by the moon while drawing water, and they are still to be seen with the bucket hanging from a pole resting on their shoulders.

Jack and the Beanstalk   A nursery tale. It is found among a wide variety of peoples from Icelanders to Zulus. Jack is a very poor lad, sent by his mother to sell a cow, which he parts with to a butcher for a few beans. His mother, in her rage, throws the beans away, but one of them grows during the night as high as the heavens. Jack climbs the stalk, and, by the direction of a fairy, comes to a giant's castle, where he begs food and rest. This he does thrice, and in his three visits steals the giant's red hen, which lays golden eggs, his money bags, and his harp. As he runs off with the last treasure, the harp cries out, "Master! master!" which wakes the giant, who runs after Jack. But the nimble lad cuts the beanstalk with an axe, and the giant is killed in his fall. As we know it, this story is of Teutonic origin. According to a frequently advanced theory, the "beanstalk" is the ash, Yggdrasil, of the *Eddas*, the giant is All-Father, whose three treasures are the wind,

the rain, and the red hen which lays golden eggs (the sun). Jack typifies Man, who avails himself of these treasures and becomes rich.

Jackson, Andrew (1767–1845)   Seventh president of the U.S. (1829–37), sometimes known as "Old Hickory." Jackson fought in the AMERICAN REVOLUTION at the age of thirteen, was imprisoned by the British, and later became a backwoods lawyer in what is now Tennessee. In 1791 he married Mrs. Rachel Robards in the erroneous belief that she had obtained a divorce from her husband. Although they were remarried immediately after the divorce was granted in 1793, Jackson's enemies used the scandal as a political weapon until Mrs. Jackson's death in 1828. From 1798 to 1804 he was a judge of the Tennessee supreme court. Commissioned a major general in the U.S. army during the WAR OF 1812, Jackson defeated the British at New Orleans (1815), an exploit that won him a national reputation. In 1818, as leader of an expedition to quell Indian depredations near the Georgia border, he entered Spanish-held East Florida and executed two British subjects. Although there were diplomatic repercussions, Jackson was not punished.

He was narrowly defeated for the presidency by John Quincy ADAMS in 1824 but was elected in 1828, after a campaign that portrayed Jackson as a symbol of the common man. During his first term, he introduced the "spoils system" on a large scale and relied heavily on a "kitchen cabinet" of unofficial advisers. At a Jefferson's Day dinner in 1830, he chagrined supporters of states' rights by proposing a toast to "Our Union: It must be preserved," to which Vice President John Calhoun replied, "The Union, next to our liberty, most dear." Jackson broke definitively with Calhoun the following year, partly as a result of a quarrel over the social status of Margaret Eaton, wife of the secretary of war. Jackson's opposition to the 2d Bank of the U.S., which he attacked as an organ of monopoly and privilege, was the main issue of the 1832 campaign. After his reelection, Jackson had federal funds withdrawn from the bank and deposited in state institutions that were known as pet banks. This policy contributed to the growing financial disorder which culminated in the Panic of 1837. By that time Jackson's successor, Martin VAN BUREN, had been inaugurated, and the ex-president had retired to The Hermitage, his estate near Nashville. Perhaps the most significant aspect of Jackson's administration was his expansion of presidential power.

Jackson, Helen [Maria Fiske] Hunt (1830–1885) American poet, novelist, and essayist. She is best known for her novel RAMONA. Her sympathetic attitude toward the Indians in the novel had earlier manifested itself in the tract *A Century of Dishonor* (1881). *Mercy Philbrick's Choice* (1876) is a novel supposedly dealing with the life of Emily Dickinson, who was a friend of the author.

Jackson, Laura (Riding)   See (RIDING) JACKSON, LAURA.

Jackson, Shirley (1919–1965)   American novelist and short-story writer. Jackson's most famous tale, THE LOTTERY, deals with ritualized murder in a small American town. Many of her stories and all her novels also deal with the fantastic and the terrifying. They include *Hangasman* (1951), *The Sundial* (1958), and *We Have Always Lived in the Castle* (1962). By way of contrast, *Life among the Savages* (1953) and *Raising Demons* (1957) are autobiographical, humorous descriptions of her life with her husband, Stanley Edgar Hyman, in a small Vermont town.

The Magic of Shirley Jackson (1966) and *Come Along with Me* (1968) are volumes of selected writings edited posthumously by her husband.

Jackson, Thomas Jonathan (known as "Stonewall" Jackson, 1824–1863)   American general. Considered one of the ablest Confederate generals in the Civil War, Jackson played an important role in both of the battles at BULL RUN and conducted a brilliant campaign in the Shenandoah Valley (1862), defeating the Union forces at Front Royal and Winchester. He died a few days after being accidentally wounded by his own men at CHANCELLORSVILLE. The words he supposedly said as he lay dying, "Let us cross the river and rest in the shade of trees," have inspired several poems and suggested the title of Ernest Hemingway's *Across the River and into the Trees* (1950). John Greenleaf Whittier paid tribute to Jackson after his death in BARBARA FRIETCHIE, based on an apocryphal incident.

Jacob   A biblical patriarch of the book of GENESIS, whose twelve sons were the founders of the twelve tribes of ISRAEL. As a young man, Jacob purchased the birthright of his brother ESAU for a mess of pottage and, by impersonating him, secured from his blind father, ISAAC, the blessing intended for Esau (see REBEKAH). To win RACHEL's hand, he served her father, LABAN, for seven years, but was then given her less attractive sister LEAH instead; whereupon he served another seven years, which "seemed to him but a short while so great was the love he bore her." Jacob is

famed for the shrewdness with which he accumulated wealth while in Laban's service (Gen. 24:34). For his later life, see BENJAMIN; JOSEPH.

Jacob's ladder refers to the ladder seen by Jacob in a vision (Gen. 28:12). *Jacob* is a slang name for a ladder; and steep and high flights of steps going up cliffs are often so called.

Jacob, [Cyprien-]Max (1876–1944)   French poet, prose writer, and painter. A friend of APOLLINAIRE, PICASSO, and the *avant-garde* Rue de Ravignon group, Jacob worked at a variety of odd jobs as he developed first as a painter, and later as a writer. He worked with futuristic literary and visual experiments well before SURREALISM became established as a movement, as in his prose poems *Le Cornet à dés* (1906). In 1915, following two visions of Jesus, he converted from Judaism to Catholicism, a process that had a profound effect on his life and work. *La Défense de Tartufe* (1919), the novel *Saint Matorel* (1909), *Les Oeuvres mystiques et burlesques de Frère Matorel* (1911), and *Le Siège de Jérusalem* (1912–14) all reflect the experience of his conversion. A strong element of Christian confession then found its way into his literary "nightmares and hallucinations." *Art poetique* (1922) contains his poetic aims and aesthetics. In 1944 he was taken by the Nazis to a concentration camp, where he died. The following year his *Derniers Poèmes en vers et en prose* (1945) were published.

Jacobean   Pertaining to the reign of James I of England (James VI of Scotland), 1603–25. With the accession of James I, a national spirit that had begun to make itself felt as early as 1600 (see ELIZABETHAN) became more pronounced. The dour and pedantic Scot who acceded to the throne had none of the symbolic value of his predecessor, "Good Queen Bess." The nation grew increasingly factious, particularly on the religious question. In 1605 the GUNPOWDER PLOT, an attempt by a group of Roman Catholics to blow up Parliament, increased the animosity. On the intellectual plane, the new discoveries in science and astronomy made it increasingly clear that the beautifully ordered universe of PTOLEMY, the large world of which man was the microcosm, was a pleasant fiction that would have to be traded in for the more realistic but less comforting world of COPERNICUS. Skepticism and doubt, together with an acute self-consciousness, became the dominant note, which SHAKESPEARE—who strode both Elizabethan and Jacobean ages like a Colossus—sounded in HAMLET and in MEASURE FOR MEASURE.

In prose the new mood was reflected in the reaction against the rhetorical, elaborate Ciceronianism of the Elizabethans. The new prose style, modeled after SENECA and TACITUS, was a more concise and flexible instrument, better suited to the new prose form, the essay. The essay, which had been developed by MONTAIGNE, was imported and perfected by Francis BACON, whose aphoristic style established the dominant tone of that form. But the prevailing mood was better represented by Robert Burton's massive THE ANATOMY OF MELANCHOLY, a detailed treatment of the affliction that characterized the age. Independently of these currents, the Jacobean age also witnessed one of the greatest achievements of English prose: the King James or Authorized Version of the BIBLE.

The poetry of the Jacobean age can be characterized in terms of the two poets who dominated it, Ben JONSON and John DONNE. The poetry of Jonson and his followers was generally derived from classical models and attempted to bring to English poetry the classical virtues of restraint, form, lucidity, and decorum. The CAVALIER POETS later in the century looked to Jonson's poetry as their chief English model. With John Donne, however, originates the more important direction pursued by the METAPHYSICAL POETS. In metaphysical poetry, the Jacobean reaction against the Elizabethan qualities of generous, rich profusion and abounding optimism is most clearly focused. In drama, "Jacobean melancholy" invaded both comedy and tragedy. In the comic area, it produced vivid, scathing satire of human rapacity in such plays as Ben Jonson's VOLPONE, OR THE FOX and THE ALCHEMIST and in John MARSTON's *The Malcontent* (1604). In tragedy, it resulted in some of the most memorable studies of evil in the history of drama. Webster's THE WHITE DEVIL and THE DUCHESS OF MALFI, Tourneur's THE REVENGER'S TRAGEDY, Ford's 'TIS PITY SHE'S A WHORE, and Middleton and Rowley's THE CHANGELING focus with an almost savage intensity on human, specifically sexual, corruption. Jacobean dramatists, heavily patronized by the pleasure-loving court, were called upon to create elaborate masques in the splendid settings of Inigo JONES as well as the courtly pastoral drama associated with BEAUMONT AND FLETCHER. Finally, it was in the Jacobean age that Shakespeare's greatest work was produced. The Jacobean element in Shakespeare is reflected in his refusal after 1600 to return to the charming simplicity of the early comedies or to the patriotic fervor of the histories. His mature work, whether the tragedies or the later "romances," never loses sight of the existence of evil as an operative force in life.

Jacobi, Friedrich Heinrich (1743–1819) German novelist and popular philosopher, who stressed feeling and the Christian faith against the rationalism of the age. Jacobi introduced the term and the concept of nihilism, which he considered a dangerous future possibility. His best-known work is the epistolary novel *Aus Edward Allwills Papieren* (*From the Papers of Edward Allwill*, 1776).

Jacobins (1) Name given the Dominican friars in France, because in Paris they first established themselves (1219) in the Rue St. Jacques.

(2) A political club, originally called the *Club Breton*, formed by liberal members of the National ASSEMBLY at Versailles (1789). On their removal to Paris, they met in the hall of an ex-convent of the Jacobins (hence their name). Although only moderately democratic in the beginning, they became increasingly radical and were a prime force in the Revolution. Many of their more moderate members broke off and formed their own clubs, notably the Feuillants. Among the best-known Jacobins are MIRABEAU, ROBESPIERRE, DANTON, and MARAT. The term *Jacobin* has come to denote a violent radical.

Jacobites The partisans of JAMES II and, after William III superseded him, the partisans of James's heirs. They maintained the indefeasible right of the house of Stuart to the throne and engaged in two fruitless rebellions: first to enthrone James's son ("the Old PRETENDER") and, later, his grandson (Bonnie Prince Charlie, or "the Young Pretender"). The Jacobites remained a powerful and disturbing political influence for generations. See FIFTEEN, THE; FORTY-FIVE, THE.

Jacobs, William Wymark (1863–1943) English short-story writer. His comic tales about sailors and rustics are collected in more than twenty volumes, including *Many Cargoes* (1896) and *Night Watches* (1914). He is best known for "The Monkey's Paw," a powerful horror story.

Jacobsen, Jens Peter (1847–1885) Danish poet and novelist. Jacobsen began his career as a student of botany and zoology; he introduced the scientific theories of DARWIN to Denmark. His body of creative work is small and was all produced after he retired to his native Thisted as a tubercular patient in 1873. Naturalistic in his subject matter, Jacobsen wrote in a careful, precise style. The novel *Fru Marie Grubbe* (1876) is a psychological study; *Niels Lynne* (1880) portrays an atheist in the modern world. His stories, noted for their skillful use of language, were published as *Mogens og andre Noveller* (*Mogens and Other Stories*, 1882).

Jacob's Ladder, The (1961) A collection of poems by Denise LEVERTOV. The imperative need for poetry to deal with human issues is the underlying motif of these lyrical poems. They are written in FREE VERSE, demonstrating Levertov's exceptional craftsmanship in this style. In a sequence entitled "During the Eichmann Trial," the poet ironically explores the banality of evil through the use of sensual nature imagery. In a sequence of travel pieces, "Five Poems from Mexico," the essence of place is realized through sparse, linear compositions that reveal the influence of IMAGISM on the poet's work.

Jacobson, Dan (1929–   ) South African novelist and short-story writer. Although Jacobson settled in England in 1954, most of his novels and stories are set in South Africa. His range as a writer is wide. His first novel, *The Trap* (1955), is a highly symbolic study of racial conflict. *The Price of Diamonds* (1957) is a light comedy employing the detective-thriller motif. *Evidence of Love* (1960) is a soberingly ironic investigation of the social and psychological pressures in an interracial love affair. Among

Jacobson's other novels are *A Dance in the Sun* (1956), *The Beginners* (1966), *The Wonder-Worker* (1973), and *The Confessions of Joseph Baisz* (1977). His highly regarded short stories are collected in such volumes as *The Zulu and the Zeide* (1959) and *Inklings* (1973).

Jacob's Room (1922)   A novel by Virginia WOOLF, her first original and distinguished work. The life story, character, and friends of Jacob Flanders are presented in a series of separate scenes and moments. The story of this sensitive, promising young man carries him from his childhood, through college at Cambridge, love affairs in London, and travels in Greece, to his death in the war. At the end, instead of describing his death, Virginia Woolf describes his empty room.

Jacopone da Todi (c1230–1306)   Italian poet. After ten years of penance following his wife's death in 1268, Jacopone became a Franciscan monk. His hymns reveal a fervent mysticism, and he is possibly the author of the *Stabat Mater Dolorosa*.

Jacquerie, La (1358)   An unsuccessful insurrection of the French peasants of Ile-de-France, provoked by their oppression under the noble class while King Jean II was in captivity in England. Acts of great violence and cruelty were committed first by the peasantry, who had sworn to kill every nobleman in France, and then by Charles the Bad of Navarre and his nobles in their suppression of the revolt and their reprisals. The name *Jacquerie* came from the 14th-century use of *Jacques* as a generic name for the peasant, connoting the humiliation of serfdom.

Jacques le fataliste (1796)   A novel by Denis DIDEROT. It was possibly Laurence STERNE's remark "Digressions, incontestably, are the sunshine; they are the life, the soul of reading" that inspired Diderot to write this, his last important work and longest novel. The story, intentionally disorderly in structure, is a burlesque recitation of Jacques's love affairs, as told to his master, but this framework in itself is of practically no importance, since it is interrupted constantly by digressions and stories within stories, in which the characters comment on their own tales, and even the reader is constantly brought into the narrative. Some of the interpolated stories are well known, for example, the tale of Mme de la Pommeraye who exacts vengeance from her faithless lover, or the tale of the immoral Father Judson, in which evil triumphs. In this complex work, Diderot is concerned with the problems of the novel as a literary medium to depict reality, with the philosophic problem of determinism versus fatalism, and with defining a mature attitude toward life.

Jade Emperor (Yü Huang)   The supreme deity of the Chinese Taoist pantheon, a popular, personal god who reigned in heaven as the emperor did on earth, with palaces, a court, and ministers.

Jahangir   See MOGUL EMPIRE.

Jainism   A religious system in India. Like BUDDHISM, Jainism is rooted in a 6th-century BC religious movement in opposition to the sacrifice-oriented, BRAHMIN-dominated, CASTE-segmented culture of early HINDUISM. Associated mainly with the sage Mahāvīra, Jainism stresses extreme asceticism and a most strict nonviolence (ÁHIMSA). Orthodox Jains eschew agriculture, lest animal life be inadvertently destroyed in the process of cultivation; for the same reason they filter water, wear surgeon-like masks across their faces, and lightly sweep their paths before them. Mahāvīra also insisted upon strict nudity, a practice observed by some of his followers but abandoned by others who wear simple white clothing. The former are known as *Digambaras* ("sky-clad"), the latter as *Svetāmbaras* ("white-clad").

James I (1566–1625)   Stuart king of England (1603–25). The son of Mary Queen of Scots and Lord Darnley, James ruled effectively in Scotland as James VI for twenty years before the death of Elizabeth, when he succeeded to the throne of England. There his awkwardness, pedantry, and Scottish accent were against him; his insistence on divine right and attempts to keep peace with Spain created a popular resentment which helped bring on the English Civil War. James was called "the English Solomon" and "the Wisest Fool in Christendom" on account of his impractical learning and literary ambitions. His most famous work was *Daemonologie* (1599), a treatise denouncing witches, but it was his *Essays of a Prentice in the Divine Art of Poesy* (1584), a critical treatise, and *Poetical Exercises at Vacant Hours* (1591) which led English poets to hope that he might become their patron; however, he is known to have assisted only Ben Jonson. He also wrote a well-known *Counterblaste to Tobacco* (1604), refuting the alleged virtues of the plant.

James II (1633–1701)   Stuart king of England (1685–88). The son of Charles I, he became a Roman Catholic and succeeded to the throne after the death of his brother, Charles II. Convinced that James planned to rule as absolute monarch and to restore Catholicism to England, seven representatives of the property-owning classes offered the throne to William of Orange, the king's Protestant son-in-law. After William had landed at Torbay in Devon (1688), James, finding himself without military and popular support, fled to France, where he was cordially received by Louis XIV. In an attempt to recover his throne, he landed in Ireland (1689), but was decisively defeated at the battle of the Boyne (1690). See GLORIOUS REVOLUTION.

James, Henry, [Jr.] (1843–1916)   American novelist, short-story writer, and critic. A major figure in the history of the novel, James is celebrated as a master craftsman who brought great art and fine perception to bear in the development of his abiding themes: the relationship between innocence and experience, especially as exemplified by the differences between the exuberant but uncultured Americans and the highly cultivated Europeans whose civilization was on the decline; the dilemma of the artist in an alien society; and the achievement of self-knowledge. With an approach to the art of fiction that resembled the research of a careful historian, James admitted into his stories and novels only that which could be represented as the experience or perception of his characters. With this approach to the problem of "point of view" in the novel, using what his brother William was the first to call "STREAM OF CONSCIOUSNESS" technique, James achieved reality and unity, and it is perhaps in this respect that he had the strongest effect on subsequent writers.

James came from a distinguished family: his grandfather was one of the first millionaires in America; his father, Henry James, Sr., a noted philosopher and theologian who became a Swedenborgian (see Emmanuel SWEDENBORG); his brother, the eminent and original psychologist William JAMES. Thus, the novelist grew up in an atmosphere that encouraged his becoming what he thought all novelists should be: "one on whom nothing is lost."

James entered Harvard Law School in 1862 but withdrew at the end of a year, determined instead to write. In 1864 his first story, "A Tragedy of Error," appeared in the *North American Review*. He soon caught the attention of William Dean HOWELLS who, as editor of the *Atlantic Monthly*, helped and encouraged him; in 1871 his first novel, *Watch and Ward*, was published serially in the *Atlantic*. Between 1864 and 1871 he wrote stories and reviews for both the *Atlantic* and the *Nation*. In 1869 he made his first independent trip to Europe as an adult (the James children had attended several European schools). This trip marked the beginning of Henry James's fascination with the theme of the American in Europe. During his second trip (1872–74), he wrote his best story to date: "A Madonna of the Future," the story of an artist who never manages to paint the perfect madonna. In 1875, after much thought, he decided to make his home abroad. He went first to Paris—where he knew MAUPASSANT, FLAUBERT, and TURGENEV—and in 1876 he settled in England. The 1870s saw the first real blossoming of James's talent. THE PASSIONATE PILGRIM AND OTHER STORIES appeared in 1875, followed in rapid succession by RODERICK HUDSON, THE AMERICAN, THE EUROPEANS, DAISY MILLER, and *Confidence* (1879). The major theme throughout this work—the confrontation of European and American civilizations—is posed unambiguously at this stage: Christopher Newman in *The American* is a naive innocent as he comes into contact with the sophisticated and evil DeBellegardes. In his later work, James was to see his theme in a more complex light: the innocently unaware may themselves be the cause of evil in others.

In 1879 James published *Hawthorne*, in which he pays tribute to Nathaniel HAWTHORNE as a writer who accomplished much despite the cultural aridity of his surroundings. WASHINGTON SQUARE, set in the New York of James's childhood, was published a year later. The climax of this period is THE PORTRAIT OF A LADY, considered by many to be not only James's finest but also one of the finest novels in English. The 1880s also saw the publication of THE BOSTONIANS, THE PRINCESS CASAMASSIMA, and THE ASPERN PAPERS.

In *The Tragic Muse* (1890), the intricate prose subsequently associated with James made its first impact. An interesting study of an actress, it preludes James's excursion into playwriting in the 1890s. The plays were all more or less unsuccessful, but the effect of them on his fiction was marked and decisive. His stories and novels of the late 1890s show a radical concern with experiment, maturing his characteristic late style of involved sentences in which every thought and image is qualified, each sentence in itself presented as a work of art. WHAT MAISIE KNEW, THE SPOILS OF POYNTON, THE TURN OF THE SCREW, THE AWKWARD AGE, and THE SACRED FOUNT are all products of these experiments.

Soon after the turn of the century, James entered into his last and most fruitful period, publishing in rapid succession three long and complex novels, THE WINGS OF THE DOVE, THE AMBASSADORS, and THE GOLDEN BOWL. Difficult as many have found them, they mark the pinnacle of James's art. This period also saw the publication of such famous short stories as "The Beast in the Jungle" (1903), a story of a man who waits for a special fate, only to find that his fate was to be the man "to whom nothing was to have happened"; "The Birthplace" (1903), the story of a couple who become caretakers of a Shakespeare-like birthplace; and "The Jolly Corner" (1908), a complicated tale of a man who meets his alter-ego as a ghost.

In 1904 James visited the U.S. and toured the country, producing on his return to England a travel book, *The American Scene* (1907). The major effort of these years, however, went into the task of writing the critical prefaces and, where needed, the revisions for the reissue of his works in the New York edition (1907–9), a venture that ultimately ran to twenty-six volumes. The prefaces, important comments on his work and craft, were later republished as *The Art of the Novel* (1934; ed R. P. BLACKMUR). After his brother William's death in 1910, James turned to another major undertaking—the writing of three autobiographical volumes, *A Small Boy and Others* (1913), *Notes of a Son and Brother* (1914), and the unfinished *The Middle Years* (1917). Two novels were left incomplete at his death, in 1916, *The Sense of the Past* and *The Ivory Tower*, both published in 1917. James became a British subject in 1915, as a measure of support for the British cause in World War I. More than a half century later, in 1976, he was one of a handful of Americans to be immortalized in the POET'S CORNER of Westminster Abbey. James's letters were edited and published (3 vols, 1974–80) by his biographer, Leon EDEL.

James, Jesse [Woodson] (1847–1882)   American bandit. After riding with Quantrill's guerrillas during the Civil War, Jesse and his brother Frank committed daring railroad and bank robberies in the Middle West during the 1870s, becoming popular heroes. When a large reward was offered for their capture, Robert Ford, a member of the James gang, earned it by shooting Jesse in the back. His death was narrated in an anonymous ballad, "Jesse James."

James, P. D. (pen name of Phyllis Dorothy James White, 1920–   )   English novelist. White was nearly forty when she began writing in her spare time. By day she was an administrator in the National Health Service; later she worked for the police as a specialist in juvenile delinquency. Her husband, a doctor, was largely confined in mental hospitals from his return from war service to his death in 1964. These circumstances are reflected in James's books, which reveal empathy with the sufferings of chronic illness and slow death as well as clear handling of medical detail. In *Cover Her Face* (1962; U.S. 1966) she introduced Detective Inspector Adam Dalgliesh, whose developing personality became a feature of her subsequent novels *A Mind to Murder* (1963; U.S. 1967), *Unnatural Causes* (1967), *Shroud for a Nightingale* (1971), *The Black Tower* (1975), and *Death of an Expert Witness* (1977). In *An Unsuitable Job for a Woman* (1972), Dalgliesh remains largely out of the picture, although his techniques are successfully employed by a young woman detective, Cordelia Gray. *Innocent Blood* (1980) clearly established James as a novelist not limited to the detective genre. *The Skull beneath the Skin* (1982) reintroduces Cordelia Gray in a house party murder marked, like all James's work, by first-rate characterization. *A Taste for Death* was published in 1986.

James, The General Epistle of   A NEW TESTAMENT book. It is a letter to the entire Christian Church. The date and authorship of this letter are not known. Traditionally it has been ascribed to James, the first bishop of Jerusalem and the brother of JESUS; this would date the work before AD 62, when James was martyred. Others feel that the epistle was written about the year 90 by an unknown church father. The writer reminds his readers of their moral obligations as Christians and calls not only for faith in Jesus but for Christian action in life.

James, William (1842–1910)   American philosopher, physiologist, psychologist, and teacher. The brother of Henry JAMES, he began to teach at Harvard in 1872. A gifted writer, he produced works on theology, psychology, ethics, and metaphysics, coining such phrases as "the bitch goddess success." He was distinctly American in the concepts he advanced, and his approach to metaphysics was frankly commonsensical. He objected to the pure and highly "logical" but unreal systems of Idealist metaphysi-

cians. Emphasizing the role of the nature of the knower in the character and validity of knowledge, he insisted that any view of the world is a compromise between the objectively given and the personally desired. He gave a series of lectures on PRAGMATISM at the Lowell Institute and later at Columbia University that was published as *Pragmatism* (1907) and *The Meaning of Truth* (1909). Turning away from abstractions, verbal solutions, fixed principles, and pretended absolutes, he looked for concreteness and facts, action and power. He argued that "the ultimate test for us of what a truth means is the conduct it dictates or inspires." The same attitude characterizes *The Varieties of Religious Experience* (1902), which contends that any article of religious faith is "true" when it provides emotional satisfaction. *The Principles of Psychology* (1890, 1892) shows James as a keen observer of sense data; one chapter, "The Stream of Thought," advances the concept of the STREAM OF CONSCIOUSNESS, later an important and revolutionary fictional technique. James's other books include *The Will to Believe* (1897), *Human Immortality* (1898), *The Sentiment of Rationality* (1905), and *A Pluralistic Universe* (1919). See PEIRCE, CHARLES SANDERS.

Jameson Raid   A raid on Johannesburg, South Africa, in 1895–96. Led by an Englishman, Leander Starr Jameson (1853–1917), it was an attempt to overthrow the Boer government during the troubles between the Boers and English in the gold mines. Jameson was captured and handed over to the British for trial, but was released shortly and later became prime minister of Cape Colony (1904–8). See BOER WAR.

James the Greater, St.   One of the twelve apostles of JESUS and the patron saint of Spain. James was the brother of JOHN and a son of Zebedee. Legend states that, after his missionary journey to Spain and his subsequent death in Palestine, his body was placed in a boat with sails set, and that next day it reached the Spanish coast; at Padron, near Compostela, they used to show a huge stone as the veritable boat. According to another legend, it was the relics of St. James that were miraculously conveyed to Spain in a ship of marble from JERUSALEM. A knight saw the ship sailing into port, his horse took fright, and plunged with its rider into the sea. The knight saved himself by "boarding the marble vessel," but his clothes were found to be entirely covered with scallop shells. The saint's body was discovered in 840 by divine revelation to Bishop Theodomirus, and a church was built at Compostela as a shrine for the relics. St. James is commemorated on July 25, and is represented in art sometimes with the sword by which he was beheaded and sometimes attired as a pilgrim, with his cloak covered with shells. He is also known as Santiago, a variation of St. James (Sp, *San Diego*).

James the Less, St.   One of the twelve APOSTLES of JESUS. His attribute as a saint is a fuller's club, in allusion to the instrument by which he was put to death after having been thrown from the summit of the temple at Jerusalem in AD 62.

Jamestown   The first permanent English settlement in the New World, founded (1607) on the site of the abandoned Spanish settlement of San Miguel, and named for King James I. It was the capital of Virginia until 1698. The first settlers suffered great hardships, especially during the starving years of 1609–10. John SMITH was an original settler, but left in 1609. Jamestown was burned down during Bacon's Rebellion (1676). Before its restoration in modern times, the only surviving relics were the tower of the church and a number of tombs. See POCAHONTAS.

Jammes, Francis (1868–1938)   French poet and novelist. Jammes's pastoral elegies describe his native region of the Pyrénées with sensuous and sentimental simplicity. The poems of *De l'angélus de l'aube à l'angélus du soir* (1897) were written during the time of his friendship with André GIDE. Then he drew closer to Paul CLAUDEL and was converted to Catholicism in 1905, after which his poems were more religiously inspired, such as *Clairières dans le ciel* (1906) and *Les Géorgiques chrétiennes* (3 vols, 1911–12).

Janaka   See SĪTĀ.

Jane Eyre (1847)   A novel by Charlotte BRONTË. In both heroine and hero the author introduced types new to English fiction. Jane Eyre is a shy, intense little orphan, never for a moment, neither in her unhappy school days nor her subsequent career as a governess, displaying those qualities of superficial beauty and charm that had marked the conventional heroine. Jane's lover, Edward Rochester, to whose ward she is governess, is a strange, violent man, bereft of conventional courtesy, a law unto himself. Rochester's moodiness derives from the fact that he is married to an insane wife, whose existence, long kept secret, is revealed on the very day of his projected marriage to Jane. Years afterward the lovers are reunited.

Janissaries (fr Turk, *yenitscheri*, "new corps") A celebrated militia of the Ottoman empire, raised by Orchan in 1326, originally, and for some centuries compulsorily recruited from the Christian subjects of the Sultan. In 1826, having become too formidable a threat to the state, they were abolished after a massacre in which many thousands of the Janissaries perished.

Jansenism   The doctrines of the sect of Roman Catholics known as Jansenists, derived from the teachings of Cornelius Jansen (1585–1638), professor of exegesis at Louvain and later the bishop of Ypres. An opponent of the Jesuits, Jansen advocated reforms based, he claimed, upon the teachings of St. AUGUSTINE. Posthumously published in *Augustin* (1640), his tenets included irresistible grace, original sin, and "the utter helplessness of natural man to turn to God." The Jansenists' declaration of man's personal relationship with God resembled Calvinist doctrine and influenced the thinking of both RACINE and PASCAL. LOUIS

XIV opposed the movement, whose influence was felt at court, in society, and in French letters (see PORT-ROYAL), and the Jansenists were finally put down by Pope Clement XI in his bull *Unigenitus* (1713).

Janus   One of the most ancient of Roman deities. Originally the god of light who opened the sky at daybreak and closed it at sunset, in time he came to preside over all beginnings and endings, all entrances and exits. He is often represented as having two faces, one in front and one behind, one to see into the future and one to see into the past. Doors (*ianuae*) were under his protection. The first month after the winter solstice, January, was sacred to him, and since 153 BC the first day of Janus's month has marked the beginning of the year. His principal temple was near the Roman forum. The doors of this temple were kept open in time of war and locked in time of peace. From the time of the earliest kings to the time of Augustus, these doors were closed only four times, twice during the latter's reign.

Japanese literature   The first literary works of Japan date from the NARA period (710–794). At that time poetry which had been preserved in an oral tradition was first recorded. This native poetry is represented by the MAN'YŌSHŪ, a collection of pre-Nara and Nara poems, many of which reflect indigenous Japanese moods and sentiments. In this period some of the first histories, based on Chinese models, were composed and much emphasis was laid on the study of Buddhist scriptures. The HEIAN period (794–1185) saw a great literary flowering, marked by the novels and diaries of women writers. Although Chinese literature, particularly poetry, continued to exert considerable influence, purely Japanese tendencies came to the fore. THE TALE OF GENJI by the celebrated court lady Murasaki Shikibu is regarded as the single greatest piece of Japanese literature; it has continued to influence the writers of Japan, even to the present time. Also popular were numerous diaries, some of them amusingly irreverent (see THE PILLOW-BOOK OF SEI SHŌNAGON or THE TOSA DIARY), which described the comings and goings and love affairs of the court. The succeeding KAMAKURA period (1185–1333) was a time of warfare and natural disaster. A military hegemony with its capital in Kamakura was established in 1185 by Minamoto no Yoritomo. The precedent of maintaining the imperial house in Kyoto, with government issuing from the military center in another city, was set by him. The literature of this period is colored by a pessimistic resignation, partly Buddhist inspired, to the uncertainty and transitory nature of life, as evidenced by AN ACCOUNT OF MY HUT. Tales of military valor, originally the transmitted stories of ballad singers, were written down in such works as THE TALES OF THE HEIKE and became a permanent part of the literature. Military unrest and natural calamities continued into the MUROMACHI period (1333–1600), although the country was more strongly unified under the Ashikaga shogunate. It was in this age that the

Nō drama evolved, under the sponsorship of the great *daimyo* (feudal lord). The Sengoku period, or Period of Warring States (1482–1588), saw the successive rise of three great military leaders: Oda Nobunaga (1534–82), ToYoTOMI Hideyoshi, and Tokugawa Ieyasu (1542–1616). These leaders established a feudal structure which unified and pacified the country.

The TOKUGAWA period (1616–1868), which saw Japan at peace after centuries of almost constant warfare, was an age of many new literary departures. The Tokugawa family, imposing a rigid feudal hierarchy based on neo-Confucian thought and ethics, set a firm and inflexible code of behavior. Studies of the Chinese FIVE CLASSICS were encouraged, and BUDDHISM, although still the official religion, was severely regulated. Meanwhile, the merchant class, which was formerly placed at the lowest of the four social strata, was responsible for a great new literary flowering. The merchants gained considerable wealth and with it the leisure and inclination to enjoy art and literature. A new culture developed, known as the "floating world" (*ukiyoe*), which was centered in the entertainment and theatre quarter. With it came new literature: the stories of IHARA Saikaku, detailing the lives of shopkeepers, courtesans, and humble people, and the BUNRAKU (puppet plays) and KABUKI theatre of CHIKAMATSU Monzaemon, which attained great popularity and continues to be performed. In art, the UKIYOE (wood-block prints) portrayed the "floating world" while poetry saw the rise of HAIKU under the direction of MATSUO Bashō, reflecting a sensitive approach to life and nature.

With the arrival of the Americans and Europeans in the mid-19th century, the Tokugawa regime declined and in 1868 the Imperial Court was returned to prominence with the Meiji Restoration. A great wave of Western influence swept Japan. All phases of life, including the literary scene, were influenced by the West. Vast numbers of European works were translated into Japanese, stimulating new approaches to writing and new literary forms. Nevertheless, works springing from the Japanese tradition continued to appear, especially in the period before World War II, when it was official government policy to encourage such trends and discourage, restrict, or prohibit things Western. In the period after World War II, the American influence on all aspects of life was strong. The latest Western materials, and thinking in all fields from archaeology to physics, appeared in Japanese. Throughout the 20th century Japan produced many novelists of exceptional talent and originality. Japan is a country of great literary productivity, and its people are voracious readers, which accounts for its being the second largest (after Russia) publisher of books in the world.

Japheth (1) In the OLD TESTAMENT, one of the sons of NOAH, brother of SHEM and HAM. He had seven sons whose descendants were said to occupy the "isles of the Gentiles" (Gen. 10:5), commonly thought to be the Mediterranean lands of Europe and Asia Minor.

(2) Milton's name for IAPETUS in PARADISE LOST.

Jaques In Shakespeare's AS YOU LIKE IT, a lord, attendant on the banished duke in the forest of Arden. A philosophical idler, cynical, melancholy, and contemplative, he has little to do with the plot, but his musings furnish some of Shakespeare's most frequently quoted lines, notably from the speech on "the Seven Ages of Man":

> All the world's a stage,
> And all the men and women merely players:
> They have their exits and their entrances;
> And one man in his time plays many parts,
> His acts being seven ages.

Jardiel Poncela, Enrique (1901–1952) Spanish playwright, novelist, and short-story writer. The author of over a hundred works, including seven volumes of plays and four novels, this tormented, bohemian, sensual descendant of QUEVEDO may well be the greatest Spanish humorist of the 20th century. An expert in the use of deformation, he foreshadows the THEATRE OF THE ABSURD.

Jarrell, Randall (1914–1965) American poet, novelist, and critic. A graduate of Vanderbilt University, Jarrell served in the Air Force in World War II, then became a professor of English. He emerged as a major poet after World War II with the dramatic and bitter war poems in *Little Friend, Little Friend* (1945). His poetry, whether dealing with war, art, or the loneliness of everyday living, is skillfully wrought and imaginative, often painfully sensitive. Other volumes of verse include *Losses* (1948), *The Seven-League Crutches* (1951), *Selected Poems* (1955), *The Woman at the Washington Zoo* (1960), and *Complete Poems* (1968). *Pictures from an Institution* (1954) is a novel satirizing life at a women's college. Jarrell's critical essays —hailed by some as a greater achievement than his poetry —have been collected in *Poetry and the Age* (1953), *A Sad Heart at the Supermarket* (1962), *The Third Book of Criticism* (1969), and *Kipling, Auden & Co.* (1980). During the last years of his life he concentrated on children's books.

Jarry, Alfred [-Henry] (1873–1907) French dramatist and novelist. Jarry is most famous for his epic burlesques UBU ROI and its sequels, and for the novel *Le Surmale* (1902; tr *The Supermale*, 1977). Both works are considered important precursors to SURREALISM and the THEATRE OF THE ABSURD.

Jason In Greek mythology, the son (christened Diomedes) of Aeson. Jason led the ARGONAUTS to recover the GOLDEN FLEECE. Saved by his mother from Aeson's brother PELIAS, who had seized the throne of Iolcus, he was reared by CHIRON. When he returned to claim the throne, he was sent to capture the Fleece. Thanks to the aid of MEDEA, he succeeded, killed Pelias, and became king of Ephyre (Corinth). Later, when he divorced Medea to marry Glauce, Medea killed her two children by Jason and escaped to Athens. Jason lost favor with the gods and wandered as an outcast until his old age, when the prow of his old vessel, the *Argo*, fell on him and killed him.

Jaspers, Karl (1883–1969)   German philosopher, one of the founders of modern EXISTENTIALISM. While a lecturer on psychology at Heidelberg, Jaspers published his first book, *Allgemeine Psychopathologie* (1913; tr *General Psychopathology*, 1962). Primarily a medical text, it also addressed itself to an existential theme: Man in *Grenzsituationen* ("extreme situations"). Shortly after World War I he published *Psychologie der Weltanschauungen* (1919; tr *Psychology of World Views*, 1919), which marked his transition from psychology to philosophy. Jaspers's interest in psychiatry provided the particulars for his search for a "perennial philosophy." His system is rigorously logical but acknowledges a transcendental power with which man seeks to communicate. Jaspers described his philosophy as a third way between religion and nihilism, but it has also been called the third way between theology and positivism (faith in the sciences as a sufficient and final account of all that man perceives). He combined his philosophy with profound political insight. *Die geistige Situation der Zeit* (1931; tr *Man and the Modern World*, 1933) is a politico-philosophical analysis of a national crisis so severe that the climate supporting a diabolical despotism would result. After publishing his three-volume *Philosophie* (1932) and several other works, he was stripped of his teaching post at Heidelberg by the Nazis in 1937. He was reinstated in 1945 and in 1946 published *Die Schuldfrage, ein Beitrag zur deutschen Frage* (tr *The Question of German Guilt*, 1947), which reflected his emphasis on man's involvement in his own times. In 1949 he took the chair of philosophy at the University of Basel in Switzerland, where he wrote *Die Atombombe und die Zukunft des Menschen* (1957; tr *The Future of Mankind*, 1961) and *Die großen Philosophen* (1957; tr *The Great Philosophers*, 1962), his best-known book in the U.S. Throughout his long life he remained a wise and passionate defender of democracy.

Jaurès, Jean Léon (1859–1914)   French socialist leader. Jaurès defended Captain DREYFUS in his newspaper *La Petite République*. With Briand, he founded (1904) and edited the daily *L'Humanité*. Jaurès was elected several times to membership in the Chamber of Deputies; in that capacity he expounded his socialist convictions eloquently. *Histoire socialiste* (1901–7), a history of France from the Socialist perspective, was written under his direction. In 1914, at the outbreak of World War I, Jaurès was assassinated by a French chauvinist.

Java Head (1919)   A novel by Joseph HERGESHEIMER. In his examination of the American past, Hergesheimer turned to the China trade that helped make New England rich. Gerrit Ammidon, the son of a famous Salem shipowner and retired captain, whose home is called Java Head, brings back from the Orient a Chinese wife, Taou

Yuen, of aristocratic family. But she is received with kindness only by the wife of her husband's brother and in addition arouses passion in a dissolute neighbor. Lured into a room, she commits suicide by taking opium in order to escape him. In the end, the bereaved husband marries a woman he had once been fond of and sails back to the Orient.

Jay, John (1745–1829)   American diplomat, jurist, and public official. After serving in the Continental Congress and as joint commissioner in making peace with Great Britain, Jay was secretary of foreign affairs under the Confederation. Upon the adoption of the Constitution, which he defended as one of the authors of THE FEDERALIST papers, he became chief justice (1789–95) of the Supreme Court. In 1794 he was made special envoy to Great Britain to settle differences that had arisen over British failure to comply with the Treaty of 1783. The resulting treaty, known in the U.S. as Jay's Treaty, provided for British evacuation of the Northwest Territory and set up machinery for settling other grievances, though it was silent about British violations of American neutral rights during the Anglo-French war. As Jay had foreseen, the treaty was extremely unpopular; he was denounced in the press and burned in effigy.

Jazz Age   A term used to designate the period of the 1920s in the U.S. At that time the apparent emotional abandon of jazz seemed best to express the spirit of determined unconventionality, gaiety, and dissipation of the American boom era that followed World War I. F. Scott FITZGERALD was one of the first to use this term by titling one of his works *Tales from the Jazz Age* (1922). Other writers of this period include John DOS PASSOS and James T. FARRELL.

Jean Christophe (10 vols, 1904–1912; tr 1913)   A novel series by Romain ROLLAND. The hero, Jean Christophe Kraft, is a German-born musician who travels through France and Germany, observing and criticizing contemporary civilization. A satire on modern society, the massive work is also a sensitive analysis of the artist's isolated position in his world. Rolland, speaking through his musician hero, proposes that the purpose of art is to express moral truth and thus to combat the disintegration of values.

Jean de Meun[g] (pen name of Jean Clopinel, c1250–c1305)   French poet and scholar. Jean de Meun's continuation of the ROMANCE OF THE ROSE satirizes most existing institutions of his day and makes Nature the standard for all moral and social judgments in a series of lucidly reasoned arguments.

Jean Santeuil (1952; tr 1955)   An unfinished novel, written 1895–99, by Marcel PROUST. It is largely an adapted version of his own life until 1895. Many of the characters and incidents are prototypes of those in his major work, REMEMBRANCE OF THINGS PAST, though none of the names are the same.

Jeeves   The perfect English valet. A man of infinite resource, Jeeves appears in many stories by P. G. WODE-HOUSE, usually engaged in extricating his master, Bertie Wooster, from some farcical predicament.

Jeffers, Robinson (1887–1962)   American poet. The son of a Presbyterian minister and educated in the classics from an early age, Jeffers drew extensively from biblical and classical sources. The Carmel/Big Sur region of California is the setting for many of his poems and the basis of much of his imagery: the intense and rugged beauty of the landscape is cast in opposition to the degraded and introverted condition of modern man. Jeffers was strongly influenced by NIETZSCHE's concepts of individualism and was therefore somewhat erroneously regarded as a nihilist. His poetry affirms the existence of God, but a God who has rejected humanity. Relying on the Greek idea of *moira* ("fate"), Jeffers's pessimistic verse suggests that man must endure a tortured and alienated existence.

After two romantic volumes, *Flagons and Apples* (1912) and *Californians* (1916), most of Jeffers's poems were strong, elemental narratives evoking rape, incest, or adultery to express moral despair. TAMAR, AND OTHER POEMS, which brought recognition of his unusual dramatic power, contains the verse play THE TOWER BEYOND TRAGEDY, based on AESCHYLUS. In "Roan Stallion," included in ROAN STALLION, TAMAR, AND OTHER POEMS, Jeffers uses an incident of a horse trampling his owner to contrast the primitive sexuality of the stallion with the degenerative lusts of man.

The Women at Point Sur (1927) deals with a minister driven mad by his conflicting desires. The title poem of *Cawdor and Other Poems* (1928) is based on the myth of PHAEDRA; *Dear Judas and Other Poems* (1929) is biblical. *Descent to the Dead* (1931) contains "At the Fall of an Age," a dramatic poem dealing with the execution of Helen by Polyxo twenty years after the fall of Troy. In the title poem of THURSO'S LANDING, Jeffers reveals, perhaps more than in any of his poems, his abhorrence of modern civilization. His many other volumes include *Solstice and Other Poems* (1935), containing an early use of the MEDEA story, to which he returned in his dramatized adaptation of Euripides' *Medea* (1946). His *Selected Poems* were published in 1965, and *The Selected Letters of Robinson Jeffers 1897–1962* (ed A. Ridgeway) appeared in 1968.

Jefferson, Thomas (1743–1826)   Third president of the U.S. (1801–9). A graduate of the College of William and Mary, Jefferson was admitted to the bar in 1767 and sat in the Virginia House of Burgesses from 1769 to 1775. As a delegate to the Continental Congress (1775–76), he drafted the DECLARATION OF INDEPENDENCE. While he was a member of the Virginia House of Delegates (1776–79), he supported the abolition of primogeniture and entail, the estab-

lishment of religious freedom, and the separation of church and state. After serving as wartime governor of Virginia and as a member of Congress, he succeeded Franklin as minister to France, where he published his *Notes on Virginia* (1784–85), still considered a valuable source of information about the natural history of Virginia as well as about 18th-century political and social life. He was named secretary of state under Washington, but resigned in 1793 as a result of long-standing political and personal differences with Alexander Hamilton and his supporters. Jefferson's championship of states' rights and agrarian interests distinguished him and his followers from the Hamiltonians and resulted in the emergence of the Democratic-Republican Party, of which Jefferson was the leader. He was the presidential candidate of the new party in 1796, but ran second to John ADAMS, the Federalist nominee, and, in accordance with the practice then followed, became vice-president. In 1798, Jefferson and James Madison prepared the Virginia and Kentucky Resolutions in reply to the Federalists' Alien and Sedition Acts, which were directed against propagandists for the French Revolution and the Democratic-Republican Party.

In the election of 1800, Jefferson tied with Aaron Burr in electoral votes and was chosen president by the House of Representatives with the support of Hamilton, who considered Jefferson the lesser of two evils. Important events of his administration were the Tripolitan War, the LOUISIANA PURCHASE, and the short-lived Embargo Act, designed to preserve American neutrality rights.

After forty years of public service, Jefferson retired permanently to his home at MONTICELLO in 1809, devoting much of his time to the creation of a university for Virginia. He was reconciled with his old political opponent, John Adams, and the two men, from 1811 to their deaths, carried on a voluminous correspondence, which is one of the most interesting in American letters. Perhaps the most versatile of the founding fathers, he is remembered for his faith in the capacity of the people to govern themselves through representative institutions. On his tombstone at Monticello is the inscription he ordered: "Author of the Declaration of American Independence, of the Statute of Virginia for religious freedom, and Father of the University of Virginia." His other writings include *A Summary View of the Rights of British America* (1774), *A Manual of Parliamentary Practice* (1801), and *Life of Captain [Meriwether] Lewis* (1817).

Jehovah   In the BIBLE, the Christian version of the word used for the name of God, the Almighty, the Supreme Being in the Hebrew Scriptures. It is a transliteration of the four Hebrew letters *Y, H, W, H,* which form the incommunicable name of God. These four letters are called the tetragram. Since the Jews consider the name of God too sacred to be pronounced, the tetragram is read aloud as Adonai or Elohim, when encountered in the

Scripture. The original form and pronunciation of the tetragram has been lost over the centuries; there is evidence that it may have been Yahweh or Yave, but certainly not Jehovah.

Jehu   In the OLD TESTAMENT, the tenth king of Israel, who overthrew the AHAB dynasty. Jehu slew King Jehoram, son of Ahab and king of Israel, and had the evil queen mother, JEZEBEL, put to death, along with all the prophets of BAAL. He also had Ahaziah, king of Judah, who was allied with Jehoram, killed. A *jehu* is a humorous appellation for a coachman, in reference to the swiftness with which Jehu drove his chariot (2 Kings 9:20).

Jellicoe, Ann (1927–   )   English dramatist and director. *The Sport of My Mad Mother* (1957), Jellicoe's first play, portrayed a society of bully-boys who express themselves in violence rather than words. In this experimental play, Jellicoe aimed at total engagement of the audience through visual action and through assault on the ear with noises and rhythms. *The Knack* (1961) combined her original techniques with more conventional comedy for a sensitive play about three men and a young woman. Several later plays were less well received.

Jellyby, Mrs.   In Charles Dickens's BLEAK HOUSE, an enthusiastic, unthinking philanthropist who forgets that charity should begin at home. Mrs. Jellyby would do anything for the poor fan-makers and flower girls of distant Borrioboola-Gha, but shamefully neglects her own children and would send away a poor beggar dying of starvation on her doorstep.

Jena romanticism   See GERMAN ROMANTICISM.

Jennie Gerhardt (1911)   A novel by Theodore DREISER. Jennie's harsh German father forces her to leave home when he discovers that she is pregnant; an Ohio senator had promised to marry her but died before he could carry out his intention. She becomes the mistress of the scion of a wealthy family, Lester Kane, who is finally forced by his family to give her up. He marries in his own class, becomes ill, and is nursed by Jennie. When he dies she steals in to his funeral, afraid to speak to his family. Jennie's daughter dies, and she is left to face life alone, but with the characteristic acceptance she has shown all along.

Jensen, Johannes Vilhelm (1873–1950)   Danish novelist, poet, and essayist. One of Denmark's first modernists, Jensen attained literary prominence with the publication of *Himmerlands historier* (*Himmerland Tales*, 1898–1910), stories of his native Jutland. *Kongens fald* (3 vols, 1900–1901; tr *The Fall of the King*, 1933), his first successful novel, paints a vivid and appreciative, although sometimes critical, portrait of Denmark and her people. Jensen was philosophically committed to Darwinism, which he wove into his novels and even into his lyric verse, and his epic fantasy, *Den lange rejse* (6 vols, 1908–22; tr *The Long Journey*, 1922), traces the evolution of man from the preglacial age to the time of Christopher Columbus. He is

famous for his "myths," subtle, poetic combinations of stories and essays. He was awarded the NOBEL PRIZE in Literature in 1944. He was the brother of the well-known feminist novelist Thit Marie Kirsten Jensen.

Jephthah   Known as "the Gileadite," a judge of Israel. Jephthah's story is told in JUDGES 11. His father was Gilead, his mother a harlot. When the sons and daughters of Gilead grew up, they cast Jephthah out of their father's household for his illegitimacy. Later, when Israel was threatened by the Ammonites, the elders of Gilead sought out Jephthah and beseeched him to be their captain. He accepted and made the rash promise that if he was successful he would sacrifice the first member of his household to greet him on his return. He was victorious in battle, and when he returned to his house his daughter and only child "came out to meet him with timbrels and with dances" (Judg. 11:34). To his dismay, Jephthah could not renege on his vow to the Lord and, after the two months requested by his daughter, she was sacrificed.

Jeremiah   A biblical prophet and the OLD TESTAMENT book that bears his name. Jeremiah was called to prophecy at an early age, and the book provides a moving record of his struggle with the burden of responsibility that God placed on him. The book contains many autobiographical sections, as well as descriptions of Jerusalem during the time of the fall of that city to the Babylonians (586 BC). In the midst of destruction and turmoil, Jeremiah discovers that the true root of religion is in the heart rather than in the temple. It is in the Book of Jeremiah that God promises the restoration of Israel and a "new covenant" with its people (Jer. 31:31–34). Because of his remarkable virtue and gentleness, it was thought by some that JESUS was the returned Jeremiah.

Jeroboam I   In the OLD TESTAMENT, the first king of the northern tribes after the division of Israel. Jeroboam plotted the overthrow of SOLOMON, but when his plans were discovered, he fled to Egypt. After Solomon's death, he led ten tribes in a revolt against Solomon's son and successor, REHOBOAM, and was made king of the new northern state. Because of his warlike ways and the idol worship he initiated, his name became a byword for wickedness. A very large wine bottle or flagon is called a *jeroboam*, in allusion to his power and strength.

Jerome, St. (full Latin name Sophronius Eusebius Hieronymus, c340–420)   One of the fathers of the Western Church and translator of the Latin version of the Bible known as the VULGATE. St. Jerome is generally represented as an aged man in a cardinal's dress, writing or studying, with a lion seated beside him. Legend has it that while St. Jerome was lecturing one day, a lion entered the schoolroom and lifted up one of its paws. All the disciples fled, but Jerome, seeing that the paw was injured, drew a thorn from it and dressed the wound. The lion, out of gratitude, showed a wish to stay with its benefactor.

Jerome, Jerome K[lapka] (1859–1927)   English novelist and playwright, best known as a humorist. Jerome's works include *Three Men in a Boat* (1889), a novel, and *The Passing of the Third Floor Back* (1908), a modern MORALITY PLAY set in a boarding house.

Jerusalem   A city in Israel. It is a holy city for Christians, Jews, and Muslims. A Canaanite city long before the arrival of the Israelites, Jerusalem was captured by DAVID (c1000 BC), who made it his capital city. David's son SOLOMON built his famous temple in Jerusalem, but after his death the city began to decline in importance. Under Solomon's son, REHOBOAM, the city was sacked by the Egyptians (920 BC). A weak city, it remained fairly secure for two centuries until the Assyrians began to invade Judah in the middle of the 8th century. Most of the kingdom was lost in ransom, but the city itself was spared until 586 BC, when it fell to the Babylonians, who destroyed it almost completely.

More than a century later (c420), Jerusalem was rebuilt under NEHEMIAH. The city was captured again by ALEXANDER THE GREAT in 332 BC. After a period of domination by the Seleucid kings of Antioch, the revolt of the MACCABEES restored rule of the city to the Jews.

Jerusalem became a Roman city in 46 BC under HEROD THE GREAT, who rebuilt it on a grand scale. Revolts in AD 66–70 and 132–135 saw the city leveled again. Under Byzantine control for five centuries, it fell to the Muslims in 638.

When the state of Israel was created in 1948, Jerusalem was divided between the Jews and Arabs. After the Arab-Israeli War of 1967, the Israeli government formally annexed Jerusalem and placed the city under a unified administration.

Jerusalem (1804)   A long, mystical poem by William BLAKE, in which he presents his theory that the world of imagination is a world of eternity after death.

Jerusalem (1901–1902)   A collection of stories by Selma LAGERLÖF, dealing with an old peasant family, the Ingmars of Ingmarson, and their devotion to the family farm in Sweden. The title refers to a pilgrimage to Jerusalem, for which the land is finally sold at auction by one member of the family. Another Ingmar, however, renounces his fiancée and marries a rich woman in order to save the farm.

Jesse   In the OLD TESTAMENT, the father of DAVID. A *Jesse tree* is a genealogical tree, usually represented as a vine or as a large brass candlestick with many branches, tracing the lineage of the house of David from Jesse to JESUS, it having been prophesied that the Messiah would be a "rod out of the stem of Jesse" (Isa. 11:1). Jesse is himself sometimes represented in a recumbent position with the vine rising out of his loins. A stained-glass window showing Jesse and the tree tracing the ancestry from him to Jesus is called a *Jesse window*.

Jessel, Miss   See TURN OF THE SCREW, THE.

Jesuits   A name applied to members of the Society, or Company, of Jesus, founded in 1534 by St. Ignatius of LOYOLA. From the first six disciples made by Ignatius, four of whom were Spaniards, the order had grown to over one thousand at the time of his death in 1556. Jesuits were particularly active in three fields: education, missionary endeavor in non-Catholic lands, and the development of deeper spiritual life.

The order was founded to combat the Reformation and to propagate the Roman Catholic faith among the heathen, but through its discipline, organization, and methods of secrecy it soon acquired such political power that it came into conflict with both the civil and religious authorities. It was driven from England in 1579, from France in 1594, from Venice in 1607, from Spain in 1767, from Naples in 1768; in 1773 it was suppressed by Pope Clement XIV, but was revived in 1814.

Owing to the casuistical principles maintained by many of the leaders of the older organization and attributed to the order as a whole, the name *Jesuit* acquired a very opprobrious signification both in Protestant and Roman Catholic countries. A *Jesuit* or *Jesuitical person* came to connote a deceiver or prevaricator.

Jesus (or Jesus Christ [Heb, "the Messiah"] or Christ Jesus)   Known also as Jesus of Nazareth. Born between 4 and 6 BC and crucified about AD 28. One of the world's major religious figures, Jesus is regarded by his followers as the Messiah predicted by the OLD TESTAMENT prophets (Isa. 9:2–6). The events of his life are recorded in the four Gospels of the NEW TESTAMENT. His genealogy is traced through DAVID to ABRAHAM.

Miraculous events occurred at his birth, but little is known of his youth and young manhood. He was born and lived in a time of distress and oppression. After his baptism by JOHN THE BAPTIST, he gathered twelve disciples (see APOSTLES) and began to teach his message of God's redeeming love for all mankind, the necessity of repentance, and the duty of the individual to God and to other men. Through his doctrine of salvation for mankind and his extraordinary healing powers, he had a large following among the common people. He became suspect with the authorities, both Roman and Jewish, because of his popularity and his attacks on the hypocrisy of the privileged. He foretold the advent of a new Kingdom of God, which the priests regarded as blasphemy and the Romans as sedition.

After his ministry in Galilee, Jesus went to Jerusalem for the observation of PASSOVER. There, after the LAST SUPPER, JUDAS ISCARIOT, one of the disciples, betrayed him to the authorities. He was arrested by the Roman soldiery, tried, and crucified. His followers believe that after three days he rose from the dead and later ascended to heaven to assume his rightful place with God.

The Christian Church was founded by the followers of Jesus, after his death. He is viewed as the word of God made flesh (John 1:14), the divine Incarnation that became fully human to redeem mankind. Through a series of Church councils, the nature of Jesus' exact relation to the Godhead was defined in the concept of the TRINITY, the three-person union of Father, Son, and Holy Spirit.

Jeune Fille Violaine, La   See TIDINGS BROUGHT TO MARY, THE.

Jeune Parque, La (1917)   A long poem by Paul VALÉRY. Written in a free-flowing version of classical rhymed Alexandrine couplets, it takes the form of a dramatic monologue. The young speaker is a maiden; she is simultaneously fearful of and fascinated by the desire awakening within her, for the violation of her self that will mark the beginning of her participation in the life process and her responsibility for new life.

Jewett, Sarah Orne (1849–1909)   American novelist and short-story writer. Jewett's familiarity with her native Maine countryside enabled her to become one of the most successful of the local-color writers. Her masterpiece, THE COUNTRY OF THE POINTED FIRS, a series of episodes taking place in a Maine seaport town, is considered a minor classic.

Jew of Malta, The (probably performed in 1589; quarto of 1633, first extant edition)   A romantic tragedy by Christopher MARLOWE. The Jew of Malta is essentially a dramatic portrait of one man, Barabas. At first the Jewish merchant, counting his "infinite riches in a little room," shares the longing for some extraordinary power and the ability to express his desire in stirring poetry that characterize other Marlovian heroes. He is a man of some dignity, unjustly persecuted by hypocritical Christians. But during the course of the play he degenerates from a human being who commands sympathy into a caricature of the grasping, greedy Jew dominated by his desire for gold. Barabas murders his daughter and an entire nunnery with poisoned porridge, performs other atrocities, and dies in an absurdly grotesque manner by falling into a bubbling caldron.

Jezebel   In the OLD TESTAMENT, the wife of AHAB. Jezebel is depicted as a pernicious, power-hungry schemer who worked tirelessly to establish the worship of BAAL during the reign of her husband and her sons, Ahaziah and Jehoram. She was finally put to death by JEHU.

Painted Jezebel refers to a flaunting woman of bold spirit and loose morals (see 2 Kings 9:30).

Jhabvala, Ruth Prawer (1927–   )   British novelist and short-story writer. Born in Germany of Polish- and German-Jewish parents, Jhabvala lived in England for twelve years before marrying an Indian architect and moving to New Delhi, where she remained until she moved to New York in 1976. Her subject is India, which she views as both an insider and an outsider, and with increasing distress at the poverty and misery surrounding her own com-

fortable life. She is concerned with social mores and psychological power struggles, and employs wit, nuance, and evocative descriptive detail. Her first novels, *To Whom She Will* (1955; U.S. *Amrita*, 1956), *The Nature of Passion* (1956), and *Esmond in India* (1957), deal with Indian arranged marriages and an East-West alliance. She has written a number of screenplays. Her later novels, such as *Heat and Dust* (1975), later made into a successful movie, show the influence of cinematic techniques. She has also published several volumes of short stories. *In Search of Love and Beauty* (1983) is a novel about German emigrés in 1930s New York.

Jibanananda Das (1899–1954)   Bengali poet. Jibanananda was born in East Pakistan. Considered to be the finest exponent of "pure poetry" in India, he taught English literature in a college in Calcutta. Of his published volumes, the finest is *Banalata Sen*, translated into English in 1962.

Jiménez, Juan Ramón (1881–1958)   Spanish poet. His work, which to a great extent introduced modernism to Spanish poetry, brought Jiménez the NOBEL PRIZE in Literature in 1956. Educated at Seville, the poet resided in Madrid for some years, where in 1892 he met Rubén DARÍO. His earlier volumes are lyrical, full of delicate metaphors, and stress folk motifs, but Jiménez later repudiated all his work written before 1917. That year marked the turning point in his career with the publication of *Diario de un poeta recién casado* (*Diary of a Recently Married Poet*), the poet's first venture into the field of "pure poetry." It is characterized, as is his later work, by a striving for simplicity, FREE VERSE, and intense concentration and condensation of form. Perhaps his best-known work is *Platero y yo* (1914; tr *Platero and I*, 1922, 1956), a series of autobiographical prose poems relating the wanderings of the poet and his donkey through Andalusia. Jiménez's numerous books of poetry appear in selected English translations, including *Three Hundred Poems: 1903–1953* (tr 1962), *Forty Poems* (tr 1967), and *Lorca and Jiménez: Selected Poems* (1973).

Jimson, Gulley   The passionate, comic artist hero of Joyce CARY's novel THE HORSE'S MOUTH.

Jindyworobak Movement   A school of Australian poets demanding fidelity to Australian environment and the employment of aboriginal themes. The name, meaning "to annex" or "to join" in aboriginal language, was applied by the founder, Rex INGAMELLS, in 1937.

Jingle, Alfred   In Charles Dickens's PICKWICK PAPERS, a strolling actor who imposes for a time on the members of the Pickwick Club. He is discovered to be a scoundrel and an imposter.

jinn (singular form *jinnee*)   Demons of Muslim legend thought to have been created from fire two thousand years before Adam was made of clay. Fable holds that they were governed by a race of kings named Suleyman, one of whom built the pyramids. Living chiefly in Mount Kaf, they assume the forms of serpents, dogs, cats, monsters, or even human beings and become invisible at will. Evil jinn are hideously ugly, while the good are exquisitely beautiful. See AFREET; EBLIS.

Jirásek, Alois (1851–1930)   Czech historical novelist and playwright. A professor of history, Jirásek departed from the traditional model of romantic historical fiction and created the realistic historical novel in Czech literature.

Joad, C[yril] E[dwin] M[itchison] (1891–1953) English philosopher. Joad was a distinguished rationalist philosopher at the University of London who became a religious convert. He was a popular lecturer and wrote many of his books for laymen. Among them are *Common Sense Ethics* (1920), *Matter, Life, and Value* (1929), and *Guide to Modern Thought* (1933). He wrote *Good and Evil* (1943) and *The Recovery of Belief* (1953) after his conversion.

Joad family   The central characters in John Steinbeck's novel THE GRAPES OF WRATH. Escaping from the dust bowl of Oklahoma during the depths of the Depression, they migrate to California as fruit pickers.

Joan, Pope   See POPE JOAN.

Joanna the Mad (or Joan the Mad; Spanish name Juana la Loca; 1497–1555)   Spanish queen. The daughter of Ferdinand and Isabella, Joanna married (1496) Philip the Fair of Flanders, whose infidelities probably aggravated her mental disorder. By him she bore the future Charles V. Although she inherited the crown of Castile upon the death of Isabella in 1504, the death of Philip (1506) increased her derangement, and Ferdinand sent her to live in seclusion in Tordesillas, while he became regent of Castile. At the time it was widely rumored that she was sane and was merely the victim of her family's machinations.

Joan of Arc (French name Jeanne d'Arc or Jeanne Darc; later known as the Maid of Orleans [Fr, La Pucelle]; 1412–1431)   French heroine. A deeply religious peasant girl of the village of Domrémy, Joan began at thirteen to have visions in which she identified the voices of St. Michael, St. Catherine, and St. Margaret. Henry VI of England had been crowned king of France in 1422, and when the English began their siege of Orleans in 1428, Joan became convinced that the saints had chosen her to repulse the English and conduct the French Dauphin to be crowned at the Reims cathedral. She finally convinced the Dauphin of her mission and, in male attire, led the French troops to victory at Orleans and elsewhere (May and June 1429) and stood beside Charles VII at his coronation in July. But then she was not given sufficient troops, and her military campaign began to fail; she was taken prisoner in May 1430 by the Burgundians, who sold her to their English allies six months later.

They did not want the English to execute her, however, until they could defame her in the eyes of the French peasants and troops, who regarded her as a saint. So she was turned over to the French ecclesiastical courts, the weak Charles not daring to interfere, and was tried on twelve charges of sorcery, wantonness in cutting her hair and wearing men's clothes, and blasphemous pride in regarding herself as responsible directly to God rather than to the Church. Worn out by the examination and condemned to the stake, she finally signed a recantation of her alleged sins; her sentence was commuted to life imprisonment. But in the next few days she resumed male attire and repudiated her recantation, so she was handed over to a secular English court and burned at the stake (May 30, 1431). After confused legal proceedings to shift the blame for her death, Joan was officially declared innocent in 1456; she was canonized as a saint in 1920.

The official records of her trial give the best account of the historical Joan. In literature she is treated variously as a witch, as in Shakespeare's *Henry VI*, reflecting contemporary English sentiment; with skepticism toward the mystic aura surrounding her belief in her voices, as in Voltaire's *La Pucelle* (1738, pub 1755); or with complete acceptance of the supernatural element, making her a romantic heroine, as in Schiller's tragedy *Die Jungfrau von Orleans* (1801). Famous accounts of her life include the one in Michelet's *History of France* (1833–67), Mark Twain's *Personal Recollections of Joan of Arc* (1896), and Anatole France's *Life of Joan of Arc* (1908). More recent plays about her include G. B. Shaw's *Saint Joan* (1923) and Jean Anouilh's *L'Alouette* (1953; tr by Christopher Fry as *The Lark*, 1955).

Job   An OLD TESTAMENT book. The greatest poetic drama in the Old Testament, it is one of the most philosophically involved books in the Bible. The unknown, undated author deals with the problem of undeserved suffering and God's justice in the framework of an antique folk legend. Job and his friends discuss the question of whether suffering is always the punishment for sin and conversely whether sin is always punished.

The Lord, confident of Job's faith, permitted SATAN to test him; thereupon, his wealth vanished, his children died, and he was smitten with boils. Yet, despite his wife's advice to "curse God and die," he remained steadfast, and his faith was rewarded. (See ELIHU.)

The expression *Job's comforter* refers to one who intends to sympathize with you in your grief but says that you brought it on yourself, thus in reality adding weight to your sorrow. *Job's post* means a bringer of bad news.

Jochumsson, Matthías (1835–1920)   Icelandic poet and playwright. Although he founded modern drama in Iceland, he is most famous as a fine lyric poet. Elegiac, religious, and nature poems appear in the collections *Ljóomoeli* (1884) and *Grettisljóo* (1897).

Joel   An OLD TESTAMENT book named for its author. A very approximate date of 350 BC has been assigned to its writing. The book describes a plague of locusts and a terrible drought that left the land barren. Repentance and fasting is urged, and a return of God's love is foretold and with it, the restored wealth of the land.

John (1167–1216)   King of England (1199–1216). The youngest son of Henry II and ELEANOR OF AQUITAINE, he was nicknamed "Lackland," because he had not shared in the division of Henry's territory; he was probably Henry's favorite son, however, and his subsequent rebellion against his father broke the old king's heart. John succeeded to the throne upon the death of his childless brother Richard I, successfully thwarting the claim of his nephew Arthur of Brittany. As a result of John's famous quarrel with Pope Innocent III over the selection of Stephen LANGTON as archbishop of Canterbury, England was laid under an interdict and the king was declared deposed; in 1213, however, John submitted to the pope, going so far as to make England a fief of the papacy. The following year John invaded France in an attempt to regain the provinces of Normandy, Anjou, and Touraine, which he had previously lost, but he was decisively defeated by Philip II of France at the battle of Bouvines. Meanwhile, John's arbitrary practices had aroused the ire of the English nobles, who compelled him to sign the MAGNA CARTA in 1215. He is the subject of KING JOHN, a play by Shakespeare, and is a character in Scott's *Ivanhoe* (1819).

John, St. (also St. John the Evangelist or St. John the Divine)   One of the twelve APOSTLES, frequently called "the beloved disciple," because he is referred to as "that disciple whom Jesus loved" in The Gospel According to St. JOHN. He was a son of Zebedee and brother of St. JAMES THE GREATER. Together with PETER, John and James witnessed the transfiguration of Christ (Matt. 17:1–13) and accompanied JESUS to GETHSEMANE (Matt. 26:36–46). John is usually represented as bearing a chalice from which a serpent issues, in allusion to his driving the poison from a cup presented to him to drink. Tradition says that he took the Virgin MARY to Ephesus after the Crucifixion, but there is no evidence to support this. Most scholars now agree that while John was an influential leader of the early Church, he was not actually the author of the fourth Gospel, The Epistles of John or THE REVELATION OF SAINT JOHN THE DIVINE. All of these works date after AD 80; Papias, a 2nd-century Christian writer, reports that John was killed in Palestine before AD 70.

John, The Epistles of   Three short books of the NEW TESTAMENT. As letters addressed to all Christians, the first two warn against false teachings, with a special condemnation of GNOSTIC ideas, and urge a strengthening of Christian faith, an adherence to the TEN COMMANDMENTS, and brotherly love. The third epistle praises an elder for his piety and shows concern for an arrogant, ambitious young church official, named Diotrephes. All three are held to be the work of one man, an elder of the church at Ephesus, named John (not to be confused with the APOSTLE). Stylistic similarities and a common outlook indicate that this man was also the author of The Gospel According to St. JOHN.

John, The Gospel According to St.   The fourth book of the NEW TESTAMENT. The most spiritual of the accounts of JESUS' life, its emphasis is more on interpreting the meaning of his life and death than on recording events. Of major importance to Christian theology is the book's emphasis on the incarnation: that Jesus was born truly man and truly God. The book recounts some of Jesus' teachings and miracles and then describes the betrayal of JUDAS, the Crucifixion, and the Resurrection. The book was traditionally ascribed to St. JOHN, although modern scholars tend to agree that it was probably written by the author of The Epistles of JOHN.

John Barleycorn   See SIR JOHN BARLEYCORN.

John Brown's Body (1928)   An epic poem by Stephen Vincent BENÉT. A narrative of the Civil War, it opens with a prelude on the introduction of slavery, which is followed by a description of John BROWN and his raid on Harpers Ferry. The poem, which considers both sides of the conflict with sympathy, includes sketches of famous participants, battles, the hardships of those on the home front, etc.

John Bull   The English nation personified, or the typical Englishman. Represented as a bluff, kind-hearted, bull-headed farmer, the character originated in John ARBUTHNOT's political satire *The History of John Bull*, which was first published in 1712 as *Law Is a Bottomless Pit*. In the early years of the 19th century, there was a scurrilous journal of this name, and in 1906 the name was adopted for a British weekly.

John Bull's Other Island (1904)   A play by George Bernard SHAW. It was written at the request of William Butler Yeats for the Irish Literary Theatre, the group that later became the Abbey Theatre, Dublin. As might be expected, the play deals with the conflict between the Irish and the English over home rule. The preface, written after the play, is strictly political, but the drama is subtle, having neither hero nor villain. The Irishman, Larry Doyle, is sensitive, imaginative, and more mature than his English friend Tom Broadbent. Broadbent's life is more straightforward, simpler than Doyle's; he is practical, adaptable, less bothered by thinking or feeling.

The conflict between the two men is in their characteristics, not their personalities. By the end of the play, Tom has assumed all of Larry's ties with his birthplace in Ireland: his girlfriend, his Parliamentary candidacy, even control of his property. This happens, not through conniving —Tom is too honest—but through Larry's reticence and Tom's blunt ambition.

John Gabriel Borkman (1896)   A play by Henrik
IBSEN. The story of a man who sacrificed love for ambition,
John Gabriel Borkman expresses Ibsen's belief that the only
unforgivable sin is "to murder the love-life in a human
soul." As a young man, Borkman dreamed of power and
broke his engagement to Ella Rentheim because Hinkel,
the man whose help he needed to succeed, wanted to
marry her. Borkman then married Ella's sister, but Ella
persistently refused Hinkel's proposals. Finally Hinkel
exposed Borkman's misappropriation of the bank's money,
and Borkman was sent to jail. The action of the play concerns the meeting, after many years, of Ella and Borkman,
and the attempts of Ella, Borkman, and Mrs. Borkman to
influence young Erhart Borkman to choose his duty to his
relatives, rather than his right to live for his own happiness.

John Gilpin (1782)   A humorous ballad by William
COWPER; its full title is "The Diverting History of John
Gilpin, Showing How He Went Further Than He
Intended and Came Safe Home Again." Gilpin, a successful London linen draper, goes on an excursion to
Edmonton with his wife and family. Unfortunately, he
elects to ride instead of joining them in the chaise, and the
horse bolts with him all the way to Ware, in Hertfordshire,
and then back to its stable in London. The ballad was
immensely popular, and there are many illustrated editions.

John Halifax, Gentleman (1856)   The only noteworthy novel of the prolific and popular Dinah Maria
Mulock Craik (1826–87). It is a moralistic tale concerning
an orphan who by perseverance and fortitude establishes
himself in life and marries the heroine. The book delivers a
mixed message in that the hero succeeds in spite of his
humble origin and proves himself the equal of any "gentleman born," but at the end of the book it is disclosed that
his parents were, in fact, gentry.

Johnny Got His Gun (1939)   An antiwar novel by
Dalton TRUMBO. The book is a first-person narrative by an
armless, legless, faceless, deaf war veteran, Joe Bonham.
Partly because of the shocking details of the hero's mutilation and its appearance just before World War II, the book
did not remain in print for long. However, it won the
National Book Award in 1939. It was reissued in 1970, and
a motion picture, directed by Trumbo, was made in 1971.

John of Gaunt, Duke of Lancaster (1340–1399)
English noble. The fourth son of Edward III and the father
of Henry Bolingbroke (later Henry IV), he was the founder
of the house of Lancaster and, during his lifetime, one of
the most powerful figures in England. In Shakespeare's
RICHARD II, he is an English nationalist who, upon his
deathbed, utters one of literature's most moving expressions
of patriotism:

> This royal throne of kings, this scepter'd isle,
> This earth of majesty, this seat of Mars,
> This other Eden, demi-paradise,

> This fortress built by Nature for herself
> Against infection and the hand of war,
> This happy breed of men, this little world,
> This precious stone set in the silver sea,
> Which serves it in the office of a wall,
> Or as a moat defensive to a house,
> Against the envy of less happier lands;
> This blessed plot, this earth, this realm, this England . . .

John of the Cross, St. (also known as San Juan de
la Cruz; religious name of Juan de Yepes y Alvarez; 1542–
1591)   Spanish mystic and poet. Known as the "ecstatic
Doctor," John became a Carmelite in 1563 and took an
active part in St. Teresa's efforts to reform the order. He
was canonized in 1726.

In his verse, he blended his religious ardor and his gift
for rich poetic imagery to produce what has been called
"the supreme expression of Spanish mysticism." His best-
known poems include *Noche oscura del alma*, *Llama de
amor viva*, and the *canciones* of *La subida al Monte
Carmelo*.

John o'Groat's House   Popularly considered the
most northerly point in Great Britain. It was on the coast of
Caithness, in Northern Scotland, near Duncansby Head; it
had an eight-sided room with a door in each side and an
octagonal table within. Supposedly it was built by John
o'Groat in the early 16th century to settle a quarrel over
precedence in his eight-household family.

Johns, Jasper (1930–   )   American painter,
sculptor, and printmaker. Johns was in large part responsible for shifting the emphasis of American art away from
ABSTRACT EXPRESSIONISM to a form of representational realism. Along with Robert RAUSCHENBERG, he is considered
the pioneer of POP ART. Most of his work involves his
attempts at viewing familiar objects (such as flags, targets,
numbers, beer cans, etc.) with a fresh vision.

Johnson, Andrew (1808–1875)   Seventeenth president of the U.S. (1865–69). A self-educated ex-tailor,
Johnson served as governor of Tennessee and as a member
of the House of Representatives. Elected to the U.S. Senate in 1856, he was the only senator from any of the eleven
seceded states who remained loyal to the Union when the
Civil War broke out. He was Abraham Lincoln's running
mate in 1864 and succeeded to the presidency after Lincoln's assassination. When Johnson attempted to carry out
Lincoln's conciliatory policies toward the defeated South,
he clashed with radical Republicans who demanded a harsher Reconstruction program under Congressional supervision. In 1868 he dismissed Secretary of War Edwin Stanton in defiance of the Tenure of Office Act (1867), which
forbade the removal, without Senate approval, of officials
whose appointments had been confirmed by the Senate. As
a result, Johnson was impeached by the House of Representatives, but in the Senate trial was acquitted by a single
vote, a two-thirds majority being needed for conviction.

Johnson, Esther (1681–1728)   Lifelong friend of Jonathan SWIFT, immortalized by him as "Stella" in JOURNAL TO STELLA. Their friendship began in 1689 when she was nine, in the home of Swift's patron, Sir William Temple (she may have been Temple's natural daughter), when Swift became her tutor, and they remained close friends until her death. There is unconvincing evidence that they were secretly married in 1716.

Johnson, Eyvind (1900–1976)   Swedish novelist. Largely self-educated—most of his twenties were spent wandering in Europe, particularly Paris—Johnson produced strikingly original fiction dealing with his impoverished upbringing and social or political problems. Among his most important works are the four semiautobiographical novels known collectively as *Romanen om Olof* (*Novels of Olof*, 1934–37), whose first volume has been translated as *1914* (1970). The allegorical trilogy *Krilon* (1941–43) voices his opposition to Nazism, and *Hans naades tid* (1960; tr *The Days of His Grace*, 1968) is an attack on totalitarianism set in the time of Charlemagne. In many of his novels, including *Strändernas svall* (1946; tr *Return to Ithaca*, 1952), a modern version of the ODYSSEY, and *Livsdagen lång* (1964), his experiments with time result in the same story taking place in several centuries simultaneously. An important influence on younger writers, Johnson shared the NOBEL PRIZE in Literature with Harry MARTINSON in 1974.

Johnson, James Weldon (1871–1938)   American poet and lawyer. The first black admitted to the Florida bar, Johnson was a vigorous and effective spokesman for his race. From 1906 to 1912 he served as American consul in Nicaragua and Venezuela. He helped found the National Association for the Advancement of Colored People and served as its secretary (1916–30). He compiled and edited *The Book of Negro Poetry* (1922), along with several collections of spirituals. He is also known for *God's Trombones* (1927), seven sermons in FREE VERSE, and for his novel, *The Autobiography of an Ex-Colored Man* (1912; 1927), first published anonymously. Among his other books are *Fifty Years and Other Poems* (1917); *Black Manhattan* (1930); *Along This Way* (1933), his autobiography; and *Selected Poems* (1936).

Johnson, Lionel [Pigot] (1867–1902)   English poet and critic. Johnson was a brilliant classical scholar, a disciple of Walter PATER, and a member, with his close friend W. B. YEATS, of the Rhymers' Club, an organization designed to promote pure poetry and the aesthetic cult of Pater. Among his books of verse are *Poems* (1895) and *Ireland and Other Poems* (1897). His critical works include *Postliminium* (pub 1911), essays on Pater, Charlotte Brontë, Blake, and others, and *The Art of Thomas Hardy* (1894).

Johnson, Lyndon B[aines] (1908–1973)   Thirty-sixth president of the U.S. (1963–69). A graduate of Southwest State Teachers College in San Marcos, Texas, in 1930, Johnson taught in the Houston public schools before going to Washington as secretary to a member of Congress. There he attracted the attention of President ROOSEVELT, who named him Texas state director of the National Youth Administration in 1935. He ran for Congress in 1937 and served in the House of Representatives until 1948, when he won a seat in the Senate. After an unsuccessful bid for the presidential nomination in 1960, Johnson accepted the vice-presidential spot on the ticket headed by John F. KENNEDY and succeeded to the presidency after Kennedy's assassination in 1963. He was elected to a full term in 1964. Johnson's vigorous domestic programs in the areas of civil rights and social welfare legislation were overshadowed by America's growing involvement in the Vietnam War. Massive riots in black ghettos across the United States also eroded the force of his presidency. In the spring of 1968, Johnson ordered a partial halt to the bombing of North Vietnam and announced that he would not seek reelection. He retired to Texas and wrote his memoirs: *The Vantage Point: Perspectives of the Presidency, 1963–1969* (1971).

Johnson, Pamela Hansford (1912–1981)   English novelist and literary critic, wife of C. P. SNOW. A prolific writer, Johnson produced many comic novels, including *This Bed Thy Centre* (1935), *An Error of Judgement* (1962), and *The Survival of the Fittest* (1968). *Six Proust Reconstructions* (1958) consists of sketches of some of PROUST's characters recast for radio; she also wrote studies of Thomas WOLFE and Ivy COMPTON-BURNETT. *Important to Me* (1974) is her autobiography.

Johnson, Philip [Cortelyou] (1906–   )   American architect. Johnson began his career as a critic and historian of architecture, serving from 1930 to 1936 as the first director of the architecture department at New York's Museum of Modern Art.

One of his best-known works is his own house in New Canaan, Connecticut (1949). The so-called "glass box house" was erected on a platform of glass and was thus isolated from nature, a characteristic that was repeated in other Johnson designs. With his mentor, Ludwig MIES VAN DER ROHE, he designed New York City's archetypal post–World War II skyscraper, the Seagram Building; his most controversial work is the AT&T Building with its parodistic "Chippendale" pediment. He is the author of *Machine Art* (1934) and *Mies Van Der Rohe* (1947).

Johnson, Samuel (1696–1772)   American philosopher, theologian, and teacher. The first native disciple of the 18th-century movement of rationalism, he is considered one of the most important thinkers of early America.

Johnson, Samuel (known as Dr. Johnson, 1709–1784)   English lexicographer, essayist, poet, and moralist, the major literary figure in the second half of the 18th century. Johnson was referred to as the GREAT CHAM OF

LITERATURE. After being a schoolmaster and a bookseller for six years in Lichfield, the town of his birth, he left for London in 1737, with his tragedy *Irene* under his arm, and remained there permanently. He was employed by Edward Cave, the founder of *The Gentleman's Magazine*, and regularly contributed essays, poems, Latin verses, and reports on Parliamentary debates to that publication. In 1738 he published his poem *London*, which was compared favorably with the maturer works of Pope; in 1749 *Irene* was produced and indifferently received, and in the same year appeared *The Vanity of Human Wishes*, a poem marked with the pessimism that pervaded his life.

Meanwhile, he was earning renown as a prose moralist, notably with his periodical essays THE RAMBLER and *The Idler*, and later with his philosophical romance RASSELAS, which, though not distinguished for its action, is a cogent presentation of Johnson's moral views and his abiding theme: the vanity of human wishes and the impossibility of human happiness in an imperfect world. His literary style, often referred to as "Johnsonese," is severely balanced, Latinate, and pithy.

The monumental DICTIONARY OF THE ENGLISH LANGUAGE (1755) secured his reputation as a scholar and, though faulty, it was highly useful. His edition of Shakespeare (1765), historical and interpretative in approach, greatly stimulated Shakespearean scholarship. His *Preface to Shakespeare* is sometimes considered one of his finest pieces of prose. In defending Shakespeare for not following the "rules," he makes a good case for imaginative truth while attacking the classical unities: "The objection arising from the impossibility of passing the first hour at Alexandria, and the next at Rome, supposes, that when the play opens, the spectator really imagines himself at Alexandria, and believes that his walk to the theatre has been a voyage to Egypt, and that he lives in the days of Anthony and Cleopatra. Surely he that imagines this may imagine more."

His last years were spent in the society of other great men. Of this facet of Johnson's career—that of conversationalist—we have BOSWELL's LIFE OF SAMUEL JOHNSON, LL.D., to inform us. In person slovenly, in manner abrupt and even rude, driven by fears of insanity and damnation, suffering from hypochondria, he yet emerges from Boswell's *Life* as a man of essential kindness, generosity, and sociability. He had married (1735) a woman twenty years his senior to whom he was devoted; her death (1752) may have caused him to seek more and more the society of men with whom he could indulge his fondness for conversation. In 1764 the Literary Club was founded, and here Johnson found an outlet for conversation; he cultivated the art consciously and even admitted that he sometimes talked for the sake of victory.

In 1773, at the age of sixty-four, he was prodded into taking a walking tour of the Hebrides with Boswell. His account of it, *A Journey to the Western Isles of Scotland* (1775), is overshadowed by Boswell's *The Journal of a Tour of the Hebrides with Samuel Johnson, LL.D.*(1785), which is the more lively for having Johnson as its subject. His last published work, in ten volumes, is the biographical and critical LIVES OF THE POETS. See THRALE, HESTER LYNCH.

Johnson, Uwe (1934–1984)　German novelist. Born in Pomerania, a descendant of Swedish immigrants, Johnson grew up in East Germany. When officials refused to allow publication of his first novel unless it was changed to conform more closely to the tenets of SOCIALIST REALISM, he moved to West Germany, where his modernist tendencies were admired. The division of Germany and his position as a "citizen of two worlds" are themes that pervade most of his fiction. Life between two imperfect modes of existence is directly treated in his best-known novel, SPECULATIONS ABOUT JAKOB, and again in TWO VIEWS. A two-year stay in New York (1966–68) provided the background for *Jahrestage I–III* (3 vols, 1970–73; Vol I tr as *Anniversaries I*, 1975), which continues the story of characters introduced in *Speculations about Jakob. Karsch und andere Prosa* (1964) is a collection of shorter fiction, the title story of which (tr as *An Absence*, 1969) provides the basis for the idea Johnson developed more fully in his novel *Das dritte Buch über Achim* (1961; tr *The Third Book about Achim*, 1966). In this novel, the West German journalist Karsch attempts to write an honest biography of a famous East German cyclist, Achim, but is frustrated by the cyclist's desire to be portrayed as a model Party member.

Johnston, George Henry (1912–1970)　Australian journalist and novelist. During World War II Johnston was a correspondent for *Time* and later for the *Saturday Evening Post*. His fictional "David Meredith" trilogy portrays a search for national identity in *My Brother Jack* (1967), for personal happiness in *Clean Straw for Nothing* (1971), and for ultimate patterns of life in *A Cartload of Clay* (1971).

John the Baptist, St. (d AD 29?)　The prophet who prepared the way for JESUS; much of his story is told in the SYNOPTIC GOSPELS. The priest Zacharias and his wife, Elizabeth, a cousin of MARY, the Virgin, were for many years unable to conceive a child. In their old age, the angel GABRIEL appeared to them and foretold the birth of their son, who would be called John and who would "give knowledge of salvation unto his people by remission of their sins" (Luke 1:77). John lived for a time as a NAZARITE in the desert, then brought his ministry to the Jordan valley, where he baptized repentant sinners and told of the coming Messiah. He baptized Jesus in the waters of the Jordan. John was an outspoken and fearless denouncer of the sins of his contemporaries. He was imprisoned by HEROD ANTIPAS because he opposed Herod's marriage to his brother's wife, Herodias, and was later beheaded at the request of SALOME, Herodias's daughter (Mark 6:17–28),

who had secured a promise from Herod to give her whatever she wished.

Joinville, Jean de (1224–1317)   French chronicler. As royal seneschal Joinville accompanied Louis XI on
his first crusade (1248–52). His *Histoire de saint Louis*
(1305–9) is a colorful first-person narrative of the events of
the crusade and of his friendship with the king.

Jolyon   A character in John Galsworthy's THE FOR-
SYTE SAGA. Young Jolyon is the most sensitive member of
the Forsyte family. He marries Soames Forsyte's former
wife, Irene.

Jonah   A biblical prophet and the OLD TESTAMENT
book that bears his name. Instructed by Jehovah to preach
in the great but wicked city of Nineveh, Jonah willfully
took ship in another direction. But the Lord sent a "mighty
tempest" that imperiled all aboard the ship. When Jonah
confessed that he was the cause of Jehovah's anger, the
sailors reluctantly cast him into the sea, whereupon he was
swallowed up by a "great fish." He lived in the belly of the
fish for three days and repented, after which he was "vomited out" onto dry land. Jehovah again commanded him to
go to Nineveh, which he did, preaching doom unless the
people fasted and repented their sins. Because of the storm
that Jonah caused, his name came to mean one who brings
bad luck.

Jonathan Wild the Great, The Life of (1743)
A novel by Henry FIELDING. Jonathan WILD was a famous
highwayman and receiver of stolen goods (1682–1725), but
his life has little relation to this satire on tyranny and political innocence. Wild is intended as an ironic representation
of Sir Robert WALPOLE.

Jones, David (1895–1974)   Anglo-Welsh artist and
writer. An accomplished painter and engraver, Jones produced many distinguished book illustrations. He is probably best known for his remarkable long poem on World
War I, *In Parenthesis* (1937), and *The Anathemata* (1952),
a long fusion of prose and poetry about the history of Britain.

Jones, D[ouglas] G[ordon] (1929–   )   Canadian poet and literary critic. Jones's poems express a passionate response to the enduring and life-giving aspects of
the natural world, in a style at once lyrical and spare.
Major volumes are *Frost on the Sun* (1957), *The Sun Is
Axeman* (1961), *Phrases from Orpheus* (1967), and *Under
the Thunder the Flowers Light Up the Earth* (1977). His
critical study *Butterfly on Rock* (1970) traces dominant
myths and symbols in modern Canadian writing. A *Throw
of Particles* was published in 1983.

Jones, Sir Henry Arthur (1851–1929)   English
playwright. Influenced by IBSEN, his plays deal with social
relationships and social problems.

Jones, Inigo (1573–1652)   English architect. Jones
is also well known for his designs of sets, costumes, and
stage machinery for court MASQUES written by Ben JONSON,
Thomas HEYWOOD, and Sir William DAVENANT. These
designs were of unprecedented elaborateness and ingenuity
and had considerable influence upon later theatre design.
The elegance and grace of his architectural work, which
was based on classical Renaissance elements, earned him
the title of "the English Palladio." Among the buildings
still in existence are the Banqueting Hall at Whitehall and
the Queen's House at Greenwich.

Jones, James (1921–1977)   American novelist.
Born in Robinson, Illinois, Jones enlisted in the peacetime
U.S. Army, which provided the material for his massive
and forceful first novel, FROM HERE TO ETERNITY. The
book, about four infantrymen in Honolulu just prior to the
attack on Pearl Harbor, won a National Book Award and
aroused a critical storm, many deploring the lurid language
and shocking incidents, others admiring its powerful vitality. Jones's second novel, *Some Came Running* (1957), is
concerned with the vagaries, mostly sexual, of small-town
life. *The Thin Red Line* (1962), a full-length sequel to
From Here to Eternity, is again concerned with the military, following three of the original four infantrymen
(under different names) through the Pacific war. *Whistle*
(1978), the final volume of Jones's trilogy, takes the same
three characters (renamed again) out of the Pacific to a
Tennessee Army hospital, crippled more in mind and emotions than in body. Jones died before the final chapters
were completed, but his friend Willie MORRIS pieced
together the end for posthumous publication. Jones also
wrote *Viet Journal* (1974), a nonfiction piece on combat
after a visit to Vietnam in 1963.

Jones, John Paul (1747–1792)   Scottish-born
American naval officer, famed for his exploits in the Revolution. In a naval engagement off the coast of England
(1779), Jones captured the British warship *Serapis*,
although his own vessel, the BONHOMME RICHARD, was
sunk. In response to a British demand for surrender during
the battle, Jones is said to have replied: "I have not yet
begun to fight!"

Jones, LeRoi   See BARAKA, IMAMU AMIRI.

Jones, Lady Roderick   See BAGNOLD, ENID.

Jong, Erica [Mann] (1942–   )   American poet
and novelist. Jong published two volumes of poetry before
her novel *Fear of Flying* (1973) created a sensation. The
novel, a picaresque romp through the sexual misadventures
of Isadora Wing, became a controversial best-seller largely
because Jong, as a woman writer, treated sex with such
explicit bravura. Somewhat less successful were the subsequent novels *How to Save Your Own Life* (1977) and
Parachutes and Kisses (1984). In 1987 she published *Ser-
enissima*. *Ordinary Miracles*, a collection of poems,
appeared in 1983.

jongleurs   Medieval entertainers, including acrobats, jugglers, and exhibitors of animals, as well as musicians and reciters of poetry. They entertained at the courts

of the nobility and also in public places, especially near the shrines and churches along the routes of pilgrimages. It was the jongleurs who sang the CHANSONS DE GESTE, FABLIAUX, and other romances and lyrics written by the TROUVÈRES, although sometimes a jongleur was also a trouvère: that is, he would be both poet and singer-musician. Jongleurs permanently employed by a court were called *ménestrels*, or minstrels, and the security they enjoyed allowed them to devote more time to literary composition, so that by the 14th century there was considerably more specialization of function between composers and performers.

Jonson, Ben (1573–1637)   English dramatist and poet. His father having died a month before his birth, Jonson was raised as the stepson of a bricklayer and briefly entered this trade after leaving school. Though considered the most learned of the Elizabethan dramatists, his formal education seems to have been limited to his years at the Westminster School, where he was sent at the expense of its master, William Camden. He spent a short time as a soldier in the Netherlands, returned to England, and, some time not later than 1592, married. During the next six years he probably existed as an actor and dramatic hack writer, reworking old plays. His first original play, EVERY MAN IN HIS HUMOUR, was performed in 1598, with Shakespeare as a member of the cast. A comedy that already gives evidence of Jonson's brilliant gift for caricature and comic realism, it presents a group of assorted characters, each dominated—almost possessed—by one overriding characteristic, or humour. Later in 1598, Jonson killed a man in a duel and was imprisoned and charged with manslaughter. While in prison he was converted to Catholicism, to which he adhered for twelve years. He narrowly escaped execution but was released by benefit of clergy, forfeiting his property and receiving a brand on his left thumb. This incident, however, seemed to have few untoward effects on him, and the following year a sequel to his first play, called *Every Man out of His Humour*, was produced at the Globe Theatre. Less coherent in plot, and containing more blatant caricatures, it assailed the morals and foibles of the age, and contained (in response to John MARSTON's satiric portrait of him in *Histriomastix*) veiled attacks on some of his fellow playwrights. *Cynthia's Revels*, which followed in 1600, was a flinging down of the gauntlet in the now-raging WAR OF THE THEATRES between Jonson, Marston, and Thomas DEKKER. Marston and Dekker retaliated with plays satirizing Jonson, and Jonson came back into the fray with *The Poetaster* (1601). Dekker answered with *Satiromastix, or The Untrussing of the Humorous Poet* in 1602, but Jonson did not take up the stage aspects of the war again. He turned to tragedy, writing the plays *Richard Crookbacke* and *Sejanus His Fall*, the latter performed at the Globe in 1603. A classical tragedy dealing with the attempt of the upstart Sejanus to overthrow the Emperor Tiberius, it lacks the verve and color of his comedies and the depth of char-

acterization and psychological insight requisite for tragedy. Jonson essayed only one more tragedy, *Catiline* (1611), also based on classical models.

After the accession of James I in 1603, Jonson turned most of his energies to writing MASQUES for the new court, working for a time with the architect Inigo JONES on sets and stage effects. He developed the antimasque, a satiric or grotesque interlude juxtaposed against the imaginative and usually lighthearted content of the rest of the work. His quarrel with his fellow playwrights was evidently patched up, for in 1604 he collaborated with Dekker on *The King's Entertainment* and with Marston and George Chapman on *Eastward Ho* in 1605. When Marston and Chapman were imprisoned because James I found some parts of the play unflattering to the Scots, Jonson voluntarily joined them.

Though his masques far outnumber his plays during the Jacobean period, the five comedies he then wrote are the crowning pieces of his dramatic career: VOLPONE, OR THE FOX; EPICENE, OR THE SILENT WOMAN; THE ALCHEMIST; *Bartholomew Fair* (1614); and *The Devil Is an Ass* (1616). Colorful, crowded canvases filled with all manner of contemporary English types, these comedies satirize hypocrisy and greed, exploiters and gulls, rogues and fools; as Jonson points out in the title of the last piece, the devil himself is a mere piker compared to humankind and its capacity for mischief.

In 1616 Jonson published the first folio edition of his collected works. Two years later he went on an extended holiday to Scotland, where he visited with the Scotch poet William Drummond. From this visit came Drummond's recollections of their *Conversations at Hawthornden*, a source of many of Jonson's opinions and an implicit portrait of the man as seen through the eyes of his friend.

The plays of Jonson's last period never reached the heights he had achieved before, though he remained until the end of his life the greatest figure of the English stage, the acknowledged leader of the gatherings of men of letters at the MERMAID TAVERN. His last plays include *The Staple of News* (1625); *The Magnetic Lady* (1632); and *Tale of a Tub* (1633). The lovely pastoral drama *The Sad Shepherd* (printed 1641) was left uncompleted at the time of his death.

A classicist who took the Roman writers for his models, a humanist who would engraft classical control and purity on English forms, and a moralist to whom the drama was a means of instruction and of criticism, Jonson both reflects the temper of his age and anticipates the more rock-ribbed classicism of the Augustan period. His poetry, notable for its balance, its control, its unadorned simplicity that is not without lyricism, prefigured the later lyrics of the 17th-century Cavalier poets, the "sons of Ben." Among his *Epigrams*, published in the first folio of 1616, are the two well-known poems mourning the deaths of his first daughter and his seven-year-old son; *The Forrest*, also in the first folio, contains the famous "To Celia," beginning "Drink to me, only, with thine eyes." The second folio, published in 1640, contains *Underwoods*, a collection of miscellaneous poems.

Jorrocks   A famous humorous character, a Cockney grocer passionately interested in foxhunting, created by Robert Smith SURTEES.

jōruri   Originally a genre of popular song in Japan, accompanied first by the *biwa* (Japanese lute) and later by the *samisen* (Japanese banjo), it was adapted as the musical narrative for the Japanese puppet theatre (BUNRAKU). The person who chants the *jōruri* is known as the *gidayu*. *Jōruri* is not a dramatic form, but rather is the chanted narration of tales often dramatic in nature.

Joseph   An OLD TESTAMENT hero of the book of GENESIS (Gen. 37–50). He was the eleventh of JACOB's twelve sons, and inspired the jealous hatred of his ten older brothers because he was his father's favorite. His brothers conspired against him and sold him as a slave to a caravan going to Egypt. There, he was sold to Potiphar, in whose service he rose to a position of responsibility because "his master saw that the Lord was with him, and that the Lord made all he did prosper in his hand" (Gen. 39:3). When he refused the advances of POTIPHAR'S WIFE, however, he was falsely accused and imprisoned (Gen. 39:7–20). After some years he was set free by order of the Pharaoh, who had heard of Joseph's ability to interpret dreams. He interpreted Pharaoh's dreams of seven lean cattle swallowing up seven fat cattle, and seven lean ears of corn devouring seven full ears, to mean that seven years of terrible famine would follow seven years of bounty. Joseph was then made governor of all the lands of Egypt that he might stockpile corn from the bountiful years to survive the coming famine. The famine struck in all lands and Jacob dispatched his ten oldest sons from CANAAN to purchase corn from Egypt. Joseph knew his brothers, who did not recognize him, and after a dramatic series of events (see BENJAMIN) Joseph revealed his identity, forgave his brothers, and brought about the migration of Jacob and all his family to Egypt. He was the father of Manasseh and Ephraim, founders of the two northern tribes of Israel. See JOSEPH AND HIS BROTHERS.

Joseph, St.   A descendant of DAVID and husband of MARY, the mother of JESUS. Joseph was a carpenter and is the patron saint of that trade. When he learned to his dismay that Mary was carrying a child before their marriage, an angel appeared to him in a dream saying, "fear not to take unto thee Mary, thy wife: for that which is conceived in her is the Holy Ghost. And she shall bring forth a son, and thou shalt call his name Jesus: for he shall save his people from their sins" (Matt. 1:20–21). After Jesus was born, the angel again appeared to Joseph in a dream telling him that HEROD THE GREAT would "seek the young child to destroy him" (Matt. 2:13). Joseph, Mary, and Jesus then fled to Egypt and did not return to Nazareth until Herod's death. Joseph's last recorded appearance in the NEW TESTAMENT is when Jesus was twelve (Luke 2:41–51). Because Jesus commended Mary to JOHN at the Crucifixion (John 19:26–27), it is thought that Joseph had already died by that time.

Joseph and His Brothers (Joseph und seine Brüder, 1933–1943)   A tetralogy of novels by Thomas MANN, on which he worked intermittently for sixteen years. Based on the biblical story of JOSEPH, the four novels are: *Die Geschichten Jaakobs* (1933; tr *The Tales of Jacob*, 1934), *Der junge Joseph* (1934; tr *Young Joseph*, 1935), *Joseph in Ägypten* (1936; tr *Joseph in Egypt*, 1938), and *Joseph der Ernährer* (1943; tr *Joseph the Provider*, 1945). In this massive BILDUNGSROMAN, Mann charts the development of Joseph from a young artistic character, aware of his isolation from the world, to the enlightened and judicious savior of his people. Mann expanded the original story tremendously, but most of the added episodes contribute not so much to the tale itself as to the characters' depth and symbolic significance. In its overall attitude, the Joseph tetralogy is neither ambiguous, like THE MAGIC MOUNTAIN, nor tragic, like DOKTOR FAUSTUS, but unqualifiedly redemptive. Joseph's return from the pit into which he is cast by his brothers is symbolically connected with Jesus' Resurrection, among other things, and indicates the redemption of man from death, whose realm is dominant in most of Mann's earlier writing.

Joseph Andrews (1742)   Hero and shortened title of *The History of the Adventures of Joseph Andrews and of his friend, Mr. Abraham Adams, written in Imitation of the Manner of Cervantes*, a novel by Henry FIELDING. Joseph Andrews, a prudent, brawny, pleasant young man, is intended to be the brother of Samuel Richardson's heroine PAMELA. His widowed employer, Lady Booby, dismisses him from his position as footman for refusing her advances, and he flees London to rejoin his own true love, Fanny Goodwill. On hearing the news of his disgrace, Fanny rushes to meet him. Both are set upon by thieves but are providentially rescued by Parson ADAMS, and the three return to their parish, where Joseph and Fanny, after comic-opera reversals and discoveries, are married in triumph. The time of the novel is coincident with *Pamela*, which it parodies and transcends.

Joseph of Arimathea   The rich Jew, probably a member of the Sanhedrin, who believed in JESUS but was afraid to confess it, and after the Crucifixion begged the body of Jesus and deposited it in his own tomb (Matt. 27:57–60). Legend relates that he was imprisoned for years, during which time he was kept alive miraculously by the Holy GRAIL, and that on his release by the emperor Vespasian (AD 9–79), about AD 63, he brought to Britain the Grail and the spear with which Longinus wounded Jesus, and there founded the abbey of GLASTONBURY, beginning the conversion of Britain.

The origin of these legends is to be found in a group of apocryphal writings of which the *Evangelium Nicodemi* is the chief one. These were worked upon at Glastonbury between the 8th and 11th centuries, and were further embellished by Robert de Boron in the 13th century; the latter version was used by Malory in his MORTE D'ARTHUR.

Josephus, Flavius (original name Joseph ben Matthias, AD 37–?95)   Jewish historian and general. Imbued with deep admiration for Rome and its institutions, he managed in his later years to live in the sunshine of the favor of the emperors Vespasian (AD 9–79) and TITUS. This was after the defeat of his people in their revolt (AD 66) against the Romans in Jerusalem, in which he had taken an active part. Among his writings are *History of the Jewish War* (seven books in Aramaic and Greek) and *Antiquities of the Jews* (in twenty books).

Joshua   In the OLD TESTAMENT, the successor of MOSES and the name given to the sixth book of the Old Testament. When the Israelites arrived at the border of Canaan in their flight from Egypt, Joshua was one of the twelve sent in to spy out the land. They came back reporting it was fruitful but inhabited by "giants, the sons of Anak," which so terrified the Israelites that they decided to return to Egypt, despite the plea of Joshua and Caleb, one of his fellow spies. In punishment for their lack of faith, the Lord decreed that the Israelites should wander forty years in the wildnerness and that of the adults only Joshua and Caleb should enter the PROMISED LAND. Joshua led the people in its conquest, in the course of which the walls of Jericho fell flat at the sound of his trumpets in one battle and the sun stood still in another.

Jotun[n]heim (or Utgard; ON, "outer ward")   In Norse mythology, one of the Nine Worlds, the home of the giants, situated at the northernmost edge of the universe. One of the roots of the ash tree Yggdrasill extends into it.

Jourdain, Monsieur   The title character of Molière's LE BOURGEOIS GENTILHOMME. Jourdain is the prototype of the bourgeois who, elevated by sudden wealth to the upper ranks, makes himself ridiculous by his attempts to imitate a gentleman's manners and accomplishments. Much of the fun of the play derives from the awkward figure M. Jourdain cuts as the pupil of dancing and fencing masters and professors of philosophy. One of his remarks is especially noted: he expresses his astonishment that he has been talking prose all his life and that he never knew it till his professor told him.

Journal of the Plague Year, A (1722)   A famous account by Daniel DEFOE of the epidemic of bubonic plague in England during the summer and fall of 1665. It purports to be an eyewitness report by a resident of London named "H. F.," and is remarkable in its convincingness as such, considering that Defoe was only five years old when the plague ravaged London. Some of the details, such as

the bell-man ringing his bell and calling, "Bring out your dead," seem more authentic than the original accounts reported in such works as the *Diary of Samuel Pepys*.

Journal to Stella   A private diary kept by Jonathan SWIFT from 1710 to 1713 in the form of letters addressed to "Stella," Swift's name for his friend Esther JOHNSON. The journal reveals the author's hopes, anxieties, social life, and political intrigues. Baby talk sprinkles the correspondence. See PPT; PRESTO.

Journey's End (1928)   A play by the English writer R. C. Sherriff (1896–1975). It is set in the British trenches of World War I. The three main characters are Stanhope, the once idealistic school-hero of eighteen-year-old Raleigh, who has just joined Stanhope on the front, and Osborne, a former teacher. Both Osborne and Raleigh are killed. Stanhope is still alive but drinks constantly to calm his shattered nerves and to hide his interminable fear. This realistic treatment of the debilitating effects of trench life was widely regarded as the most important drama about the war. It had long and successful runs in New York and London and was performed in every European language.

Journey to the End of the Night (Voyage au bout de la nuit, 1932; tr 1934)   A novel by Louis-Ferdinand CÉLINE. Ferdinand Bardamu, the cynical, disillusioned hero, wanders aimlessly through war-torn Europe, surrounded by destruction and putrefaction. Man, as Céline portrays him, attempts to flee from the solitude of his existence and the impossibility of helping his fellow humans but succeeds only in embracing evil and death. The novel caused a scandal when it was published because of the coarseness of its language and the unrelieved blackness of its pessimism. Yet the language is a highly original attempt to reproduce the proletarian *argot* that reflects the horror and intimacy of war, and the pessimism shows Céline's desire to arouse the reader and make him aware of his condition.

Journey to the West (Hsi yü chi)   A Chinese novel of the MING dynasty by Wu Ch'eng-en (c1500–1582). It describes the fictionalized adventures of a historical Buddhist priest, Hsüan-tsang (also known as Tripitika), on his quest to India in search of holy scriptures. He is accompanied on his pilgrimage by three magical helpers, one of whom, a monkey, is the most famous comic creation in Chinese fiction. The book is humorous and fantastic, but at the same time allegorical and deeply religious. It was partially translated by Arthur WALEY as *Monkey* (1943). See CHINESE LITERATURE.

Jouve, Pierre Jean (1887–1976)   French poet, novelist, and critic. At first closely associated with the ABBAYE GROUP, in 1924 Jouve renounced the influences of his past and turned to Catholicism and Freudian psychoanalysis. The resultant energetic mingling of religious and sexual imagery produced his best work: the poems of *Les Noces* (1928), *Le Paradis perdu* (1929), *Sueur de sang*

(1933), and *Kyrié* (1938) and the novels *Paulina 1880* (1925; tr 1973), *Le Monde désert* (1926), *Histoires sanglantes* (1931), and *La Scène capitale* (1935).

Jove   Another name for JUPITER.

Jovellanos, Gaspar Melchor de (1744–1811) Spanish statesman, economist, and man of letters. Appointed a magistrate in Seville (1767) and in Madrid (1778), he was banished to his native Asturias in 1790 because of his progressive views. He returned from exile to serve briefly as minister of justice, only to fall from favor again. From 1801 to 1808 he was a prisoner in Majorca.

His finest work is the well-known *Informe sobre la ley agraria* (1794), ostensibly a report on a projected code of agrarian law, but in reality an enlightened program for extensive economic reform. In *Defensa de la Junta Central* (1810), he outlined his moderate political ideas. Jovellanos also wrote verse in the classical tradition.

Joyce, James (1882–1941)   Irish novelist, short-story writer, and poet. Joyce is regarded as one of the greatest literary talents of the 20th century and is known for his revolutionary innovations in the art of the novel. Joyce's technical innovations include an extensive use of the interior monologue (see STREAM OF CONSCIOUSNESS) and other experimental narrative techniques; the use, in FINNEGANS WAKE, of a unique language of invented words, puns, and complex allusions; and the use of a complex network of symbolic parallels drawn from mythology, history, and literature. Joyce is also famous for his detailed rendering of Dublin life, his objective presentation of organic functions, his extraordinary psychological penetration, his robust humor, and his sensitivity to auditory impressions (he had a lifelong passion for vocal music). Before other writers had imitated his techniques and critics had explained his methods, his books were denounced as obscure, unintelligible, nonsensical, and obscene.

Joyce was raised in the kind of environment that might be least expected to produce a revolutionary genius. Son of an ordinary, chronically insolvent civil servant and a conventionally pious mother, and eldest of a family of ten children, Joyce's youth was marked by poverty and the struggle to maintain solid middle-class respectability. He was educated at a succession of excellent Jesuit schools, where he received a thorough training in Catholic and scholastic doctrines and in several languages. Joyce's rebellion against his family background, against Catholicism, and against Irish nationalism are described in his largely autobiographical novel A PORTRAIT OF THE ARTIST AS A YOUNG MAN. "I will not serve that in which I no longer believe," says the hero, Stephen Dedalus, "whether it call itself my home, my fatherland, or my church: and I will try to express myself in some mode of life or art as freely as I can, using for my defence the only arms I allow myself to use —silence, exile, and cunning." In 1902 the twenty-year-old Joyce left Dublin to spend the rest of his life in exile in

Paris, Trieste, Rome, and Zurich, with only an occasional brief visit to Ireland. But the world he had rejected remained basic to all his writing. From the short stories in DUBLINERS to *Finnegans Wake*, his subject matter is the city of Dublin, its streets, topography, history, and residents, and, to a somewhat lesser extent, biographical details of his own childhood and youth. The Catholicism he had rebelled against remained so ingrained in him that its doctrines and methods of thought, its symbolism and scholasticism, strongly color all his writings.

Joyce was always an admirer of Ibsen; his earliest publication was an essay, "Ibsen's New Drama," in the *Fortnightly Review* of 1900. He also wrote two collections of poems, *Chamber Music* (1907) and *Pomes Penyeach* (1927), and a play, EXILES.

Joyce had a difficult life. In 1904 he ran away to Trieste with Nora Barnacle, an almost entirely uneducated Dublin chambermaid, whom he met on June 16 of that year (the same day on which the action of ULYSSES takes place). On account of his antireligious principles they were not married until many years later. With their two children they wandered about Europe, while Joyce earned an inadequate living teaching languages and doing clerical work; he earned almost nothing from his writings until his last years. His poor eyesight deteriorated until he was almost blind; like Milton, he had to depend in his work on memory and the secretarial help of friends. His books were banned by censors, pirated by publishers, and misunderstood by the public. His much-loved daughter became insane and had to be confined in an institution.

A perfectionist who sought to fill his mature work with a network of complex internal echoes and allusions, Joyce toiled long hours at his writing and repeatedly revised and polished his work. *Ulysses* required seven years to complete (1914–21), and *Finnegans Wake*, which was known until its publication as *Work in Progress*, took seventeen years (1922–39).

Joyeuse   The name given to CHARLEMAGNE's sword in medieval romances.

Joyous Gard (Fr, La Joyeuse Garde)   In Malory's MORTE D'ARTHUR, the castle of Sir LAUNCELOT. It was given to him by King ARTHUR for defending Queen GUINEVERE's honor against Sir Mador. It is supposed to have been at or near Berwick-on-Tweed, but the Arthurian topography is very indefinite.

József, Attila (1905–1937)   Hungarian poet. Profoundly moved by the squalor of the proletarian milieu into which he was born, József was passionately hostile toward the established classes and authorities. Employing concrete imagery and intricate verse forms with energetic virtuosity, he voices an alienation and loneliness intensified by his own persecuted existence and bouts with schizophrenia. Despite the evidence of his early death by casting himself under a freight train, he believed in the beauty and inner harmony of life. József's poetry, considered blasphemous and subversive during his lifetime, had a profound effect on modern Hungarian poetry. *Selected Poems and Texts* (tr by J. Bátki) appeared in English in 1973.

J.R. See GADDIS, WILLIAM.

Juana Inés de la Cruz See CRUZ, SOR JUANA INÉS DE LA.

Juan Manuel, Infante Don (1282–?1349) Spanish statesman and writer. A nephew of Alfonso X, Juan Manuel was an important political figure as well as an outstanding prose writer. His masterpiece is *El Conde Lucanor* or *Libro de Patronio*; completed about 1335, it is a collection of fifty "exemplary tales," some of Oriental origin, which illustrate the counsels of Patronio to his pupil, Count Lucanor.

Juárez, Benito (1806–1872) Mexican statesman. A full-blooded Zapotec Indian, Juárez became the leader of *La Reforma*, a liberal, anticlerical movement for political, economic, and social reform. Named president in 1857, he fought the French-supported regime of MAXIMILIAN, whom he defeated in 1867, and ruled Mexico until his death. Though *La Reforma* was at best a qualified success, Juárez occupies a place in Mexican hagiography similar to that held by Lincoln in the U.S.

Jubal In the OLD TESTAMENT, the son of Lamech and Adah. As "father of all such as handle the harp and organ" (Gen. 4:21), he is said to have invented wind and stringed instruments. George ELIOT has a narrative poem of this title (1874).

Judah In the OLD TESTAMENT, the fourth son of JACOB; also, the name of the most powerful of the twelve tribes of Israel. After the death of SOLOMON, king of Israel, ten tribes seceded under JEROBOAM I, and the remaining kingdom, with its capital at JERUSALEM, was known thereafter as Judah.

Judas Iscariot The disciple who betrayed JESUS. Judas's specific act of betrayal was to cause the arrest of Jesus by the Roman soldiery by identifying him with a kiss in the Garden of GETHSEMANE. He was paid for this act thirty pieces of silver. MATTHEW (27:3–10) records that Judas returned the money to the Jewish priests and then hanged himself. The version in ACTS OF THE APOSTLES (1:16–20) has Judas dying by "falling headlong" after which "he burst asunder . . . and all his bowels gushed out."

Judas is known as one of the blackest villains in history. Dante in the INFERNO places Judas in the mouth of SATAN. There are numerous allusions to his crime in figures of speech: *a Judas kiss, thirty pieces of silver*, and the name itself all signify treachery and deception.

There have also been many attempts to explain the motives of Judas. Early Christians felt that Judas acted as he did for the silver; however, the amount he was paid was not any great fortune, thirty pieces being about the price of one slave. Modern theorists feel that Judas was dissatisfied

with Jesus' actions and wanted to force him into a situation where he would have to assert his divine powers and establish a glorious new order on earth.

Judas Maccabaeus The Hebrew patriot who gained decisive victories against the Syrians. In 165 BC, Judas Maccabaeus entered Jerusalem and reconsecrated the Temple; HANUKKAH, the Jewish feast of dedication, commemorates this event. See MACCABEES.

Jude, St. One of the twelve disciples of JESUS, also called Judas, or Thaddeus, brother of JAMES THE LESS. He is represented in art with a club or a staff, and a carpenter's square, in allusion to his trade. There is some dispute over whether or not he was the author of the last epistle in the NEW TESTAMENT, *The Epistle of Jude*, which is a general letter denouncing heretical teaching and immorality. Jude is invoked in prayer for cases which seem hopeless.

Jude the Obscure (1895) Thomas HARDY's tragic last novel. This story dramatizes the conflict between carnal and spiritual life, tracing Jude Fawley's life from his boyhood aspirations of intellectual achievement to his miserable, early death. His passions entangle him in marriage with Arabella, an insensitive, animalistic woman who gives birth to a son, but deserts them both. Jude then falls in love with his cousin, Sue Bridehead, an intelligent, sensitive, high-strung girl. She marries the decaying schoolteacher, Phillotson, but, finding him physically repellent, she flees to Jude. They both obtain divorces, but Sue, guilt-ridden over her desertion of her husband, cannot bring herself to take the step of marrying Jude, so they live together and have children, scorned by society. "Because there were too many," the children are killed by Arabella's son, a grotesque boy nicknamed Father Time, who subsequently hangs himself. Broken by this tragedy, Sue goes back to Phillotson and Jude returns to Arabella. Soon thereafter Jude dies.

Judges A book of the OLD TESTAMENT, a historical account of the tribes of Israel between the times of Joshua and SAMUEL (c1225–1020 BC). The Israelites had just invaded Canaan; the book tells of their attempts to subdue the former inhabitants and settle the land. Parts of the book are contemporaneous with the events; the rest are later additions. Judges had its present form by 500 BC.

Judgment Day See STUDS LONIGAN.

Judgment of Paris A mythological beauty contest of goddesses. It led to the TROJAN WAR. Angry at not having been invited to the famous wedding of THETIS, ERIS, the goddess of discord, threw into the gathering a golden apple bearing the inscription "For the fairest." It was claimed by HERA, ATHENE, and APHRODITE. They took it to PARIS, a son of PRIAM, who was then a shepherd on the slopes of Mount Ida. As the handsomest man in the world, he was regarded as an authority. Hera promised him greatness, Athene warlike prowess, and Aphrodite the love of the world's most beautiful woman in return for his vote. He awarded the apple to Aphrodite, and won for his pains the disastrous love of HELEN. This famous subject was a favorite with artists in both classical times and the Renaissance.

Judith   A legendary Jewish heroine of Bethulia whose story is told in the Apocryphal book bearing her name. To deliver her native city from the onslaught of Holofernes, general of the Assyrian king NEBUCHADNEZZAR, she entered his camp and slew him in his drunken sleep. When she showed the head of Holofernes to her countrymen, they rushed on the invading army and put it to complete rout.

In his tragedy *Judith* (1841), Friedrich HEBBEL deepens the story's psychological complexity by having Judith become intimate with Holofernes before murdering him. Jean GIRAUDOUX adapted the story for his play *Judith* (1931).

Judson, E[dward] Z[ane] C[arroll] (pen name Ned Buntline, 1823–1886)   American adventurer and dime novelist. Judson's career was more incredible than any of the four hundred dime novels he is said to have written. He was an inveterate duelist, led the Astor Place riots against the English actor MACREADY, was an organizer of the nativistic KNOW-NOTHING PARTY, and during the CIVIL WAR was dismissed from the Union army for drunkenness.

In the meantime, he was a prolific writer of dime novels, a genre that he is credited with originating. Some he published in a magazine he founded, *Ned Buntline's Own*; later he worked for the publishing firm of Beadle & Adams. On a trip to the West he met William F. CODY and wrote a play, *The Scouts of the Plains* (1872), for him; it was Judson who named the famous scout Buffalo Bill. Judson also wrote hymns and lectured on temperance.

He undoubtedly had an astonishing knack with words and once wrote a novel of more than six hundred pages in sixty-two hours. His dime novels have become collector's items. A few characteristic titles are *Magdalena, the Beautiful Mexican Maid* (1847), *The Black Avenger* (1847), and *Stella Delorme, or, The Comanche's Dream* (1860).

Juhász, Ferenc (1928–   )   Hungarian poet. The most prolific poet of his generation, Juhász is known for his demanding style. Based loosely on the forms of the BALLAD and folk song, his verse employs a torrent of images—personal, literary, and scientific—in an effort to give substance to his search for the elusive connection between microcosm and macrocosm which can give wholeness to the life of contemporary man in a divided society. Much of his most compelling work has been translated in *The Boy Changed Into a Stag: Selected Poems 1949–1967* (1970).

Julian, the Apostate (full Latin name Flavius Claudius Julianus, AD 331–363)   Roman emperor, nephew of Constantine the Great. Although educated in monastic schools, Julian renounced Christianity when he became emperor (361). He attempted to drive out Christi-

anity and to reinstate a polytheism based on Neoplatonic philosophy. He was, however, killed fighting in Persia before he could carry through his plans.

Juliet   (1) The passionate young heroine of Shakespeare's ROMEO AND JULIET. The love of this wildly romantic girl for Romeo, the son of her father's bitterest enemy, brings about her own death and that of her lover. Strong in spirit, she refuses to marry the husband that her family chooses and secretly weds Romeo. Her speeches contain some of Shakespeare's most beautiful and famous poetry:

> O Romeo, Romeo! wherefore art thou Romeo?
> Deny thy father, and refuse thy name;
> Or, if thou wilt not, be but sworn my love,
> And I'll no longer be a Capulet. . . .
>   O! be some other name:
> What's in a name? that which we call a rose
> By any other name would smell as sweet.

(2) In Shakespeare's MEASURE FOR MEASURE, the gentle, loyal betrothed of Claudio. Her pregnancy is the cause of Claudio's imprisonment for immorality.

Julius Caesar (c1599)   A tragedy by SHAKESPEARE. It deals with the conspiracy against Julius CAESAR, his assassination, and the defeat of the conspirators by Marc ANTONY and Octavius CAESAR.

The crafty and ambitious CASSIUS, envious of Caesar's political and military triumphs, forms a conspiracy against him. Although BRUTUS, a man of great integrity, loves Caesar, he is persuaded to join the conspiracy by Cassius, who argues that Caesar's power is a threat to Rome's freedom. Ignoring the entreaties of his wife, CALPURNIA, who has dreamed of his death, Caesar goes to the Senate on the IDES of March and is assassinated by the conspirators. When Antony discovers Caesar's body, he feigns friendliness toward the conspirators and asks only that he be allowed to speak at Caesar's funeral. His oration so inflames the people that the assassins are driven out of Rome. Antony, joined by LEPIDUS and Octavius, engages the conspirators in battle at Philippi. Cassius's rash suicide weakens the army and turns the tide of battle. Brutus is routed and falls on his own sword rather than be taken captive.

Shakespeare's source for the play was Sir Thomas North's translation (1579) of PLUTARCH's *Lives*.

Jung, Carl Gustav (1875–1961)   Swiss analytical psychologist. Jung studied at Basel (1895–1900) and received his M.D. degree from the university at Zürich in 1902. He then attended lectures by the pioneer French psychologist Pierre Janet in Paris and became an assistant at the Burgholzli Clinic under Eugen Bleuler, head of the Zürich school of depth psychology. Impressed by the work of his Viennese colleague Sigmund FREUD in the analysis of dream content and the treatment of neurosis, Jung met Freud in 1907. The association between the two men was of critical importance to each, but relatively short-lived. In

1909 they traveled together to Clark University in Massachusetts to lecture and receive honorary degrees. Jung broke from Freud four years later, not because they disagreed on fundamentals but because Freud could not agree with the broader applications which Jung was beginning to see for psychology.

With the publication in 1912 of *Wandlungen und Symbole der Libido* (tr 1916 as *Psychology of the Unconscious*; rev 1952 as *Symbols of Transformation* in *Collected Works*, Vol 5, 1956), Jung presented several important concepts that were divergent from Freudian theory. He advanced his definition of *libido* as embracing the totality of life's processes, not merely its sexual elements, as Freud had postulated. For Jung, Freud's emphasis on repressed sexuality did nothing to explain the relationship between an individual and the whole human culture of which he was a part. Jung enlarged Freud's notion of "personal" unconscious—of repression, sublimation, projection—to include what he called the *collective unconscious*, which was made up of universal, cross-cultural, and timeless elements of human experience. According to this theory, mankind shares a common and inborn unconscious life —not limited to the experience of any one individual —which is expressed in dreams, fantasies, and myths in the form of archetypal images and symbols. Jung conceived of an *archetype* as a conceptual equivalent of instinct; a way of organizing and symbolizing elements of the collective unconscious.

Jung's formal break with Freud thrust him into a long period of self-analysis, much of which is described in his autobiographical *Memories, Dreams, and Reflections* (1963; ed A. Jaffe). He developed the concepts of *shadow* (the repressed and guilt-laden part of personality) and *animus/anima* (the masculine and feminine components of the unconscious). Among other of Jung's many contributions to psychology are his formulation of *introvert* and *extrovert* types, found in *Psychological Types* (1923), and his development of analytical psychology. He developed a form of psychoanalysis that addressed itself as much to the creative potential as to the analysis of neurotic symptoms. He saw therapy as a process of the integration of the conscious and unconscious forces at work in an individual, resulting in a meaningful wholeness of life.

Jung's letters have been compiled in two volumes (1973 and 1976; ed G. Adler and A. Jaffe). *The Freud/Jung Letters* (ed W. McGuire) appeared in 1974. A twenty-volume edition, *The Collected Works of C. G. Jung*, was prepared by the Bollingen Foundation from 1953 to 1979.

Jung Deutschland (Ger, "Young Germany") A German literary movement of about 1830–48. Its name was coined by Ludolf Wienbarg (1802–72), who outlined its principles in his *Ästhetische Feldzüge* (*Aesthetic Campaigns*, 1834). He and the other important authors in the movement, Heinrich Laube (1806–84), GUTZKOW, and Theodor Mundt (1808–61), did not actually constitute a group until their names were linked in a Prussian edict (1835) prohibiting their writings. Their principal desire was to break away from the idealism that had characterized most previous German literature in the 19th century, for they felt that every literary work should take a stand on the real political and social problems of the day. Specifically, they advocated freedom of thought—which was by no means a fact under the oppressive Prussian and Austrian regimes of the time—emancipation of women, and, frequently, free love. See BIEDERMEIER; HEINE, HEINRICH.

Jünger, Ernst (1895–   ) German novelist, philosophical essayist, and diarist. Jünger was a highly decorated commander in World War I. Like other authors of war novels—REMARQUE, Ludwig Renn (1889–1979)—he described the horrors he experienced, but in contrast to them, he used his brilliant stylistic talents not in condemnation of war, but in praise of it. War was to him a cleansing of the soul, a metaphysical experience, as the titles of his early work suggest: *In Stahlgewittern* (1922; tr *Storm of Steel*, 1929) and *Der Kampf als inneres Erlebnis* (*The Struggle as Inner Experience*, 1920). Although his books were used by Nazi propagandists, Jünger opposed HITLER and wrote his best-known novel, *Auf den Marmorklippen* (1942; tr *On the Marble Cliffs*, 1947), as an attack on totalitarian power. His collected writings, *Sämtliche Werke*, appeared in eighteen volumes in 1978.

Jungle, The (1906) A novel by Upton SINCLAIR. Seldom has a book been the subject of more widespread discussion than this appallingly grim account of life in the Chicago stockyards. It depicts with vivid and brutal realism the experiences of a Slavic immigrant, Jurgis Rudkus, and his wife, Ona. Jurgis becomes debased and then, in accordance with Sinclair's own creed, turns to socialism.

Jungle Book, The (1894) A collection of animal stories for children, set in India and written by Rudyard KIPLING. The central figure of many of them is the human Mowgli, brought up as a wolf cub and instructed in the lore of the jungle. A sequel, *The Second Jungle Book*, was published in 1895.

Junker A member of the landed aristocracy of Germany, particularly east of the Elbe. The Junkers gained ascendency in Prussia during the early 18th century, when they represented a political philosophy of competent, military oligarchy, but with the development of the German national state in the 19th century, the Junkers became political and social reactionaries. It was not until after World War II that their large estates were redistributed.

Juno In Roman mythology, the wife of JUPITER and queen of the gods. Like her Greek counterpart, HERA, she was the special protectress of marriage and of women. In Vergil's AENEID, she is represented as the bitter foe of the exiled Trojans.

The Junonian bird was the peacock, dedicated to the goddess-queen.

Juno and the Paycock (1924)   A comitragedy by Sean O'CASEY. Against the background of the Irish Civil War of 1922, the action concerns the attempt of Juno Boyle to overcome the triple menace of war, poverty, and drunkenness which results in the destruction of her family. Juno's heroic posture, which is defined in terms of her unillusioned, long-suffering grasp of reality, is contrasted to that of her husband, the "Paycock," a vain, posturing—but extremely funny—weakling who hides from reality behind a bottle and a flow of fine language. The initial production, which starred Sara Allgood as Juno and Barry Fitzgerald as the husband, represented one of the finest triumphs of the ABBEY THEATRE.

Jupiter (fr early Lat, *Diespiter*, "Father of the sky") The ancient Italian sky god and the supreme deity of Roman mythology, also known as Jove and corresponding roughly to the Greek ZEUS. He was the special protector of Rome and, as Jupiter Capitolinus—his temple being on the Capitoline hill—presided over the Roman games. He knew and could influence the course of history and made known the future to man by means of signs in the heavens, by the flight of birds, and, most awesomely, by the stroke of his lightning bolt.

Justine   See ALEXANDRIA QUARTET, THE.

Justine (1791)   A novel by the Marquis de SADE, celebrating a sexually persecuted heroine.

Justinian I (called Justinian the Great, full Latin name Flavius Anicius Justinianus; 483–565)   Emperor of the BYZANTINE EMPIRE (527–565) during its most brilliant period. He married THEODORA (525). In 531 he bought a peace treaty with the Persians. In the West his generals Belisarius and Narses destroyed the Vandal kingdom in Africa and defeated the Ostrogoths in Italy, retaking Rome in 536.

Justinian's reign is highlighted by the amount of building that took place in the Empire (Sant' Apollinare in Classe and San Vitale, both in Ravenna, and Santa Sophia in Constantinople) and the code of laws he had published, the *Corpus juris civilis*, now called the Justinian Code. This codification is the foundation of the Roman law still used in many European countries.

Just So Stories (1902)   Animal stories for young children by Rudyard KIPLING, giving amusing and fanciful answers to such questions as why the leopard has spots or the elephant a trunk.

Jutland, Battle of   One of the greatest naval battles in history. It was fought in 1916 off Jutland peninsula between the German and British fleets. It won for England the undisputed control of the North Sea. Curiously, it was the British fleet that sustained the heavier casualties.

Juvenal (full Latin name Decimus Junius Juvenalis, AD 60?–?140)   Satirist of Roman vices under the empire. Of his life little is known, although most early accounts agree that he spent some time in military service and ended his life in exile for having criticized a popular stage performer who was a special favorite of the emperor Domitian. He is the author of sixteen satires, divided traditionally into five books. In these biting attacks on public manners and morals, Juvenal shows himself to have been a sharp observer of his fellow men. "Whatever men do," he announces in his first satire, "their devotion, their fear, their rage, their pleasure, their joys, their conversations —all these will make up the potpourri of my little work"; and he fulfills his pledge with the bitter gusto of an inspired cynic. Unlike Horace, the other great satirist of Roman letters, Juvenal seldom places himself among the foolish, the corrupt, and the frustrated; and while Horace's satires are conversational in tone and meter, Juvenal's are tight, rhetorical, and finely polished. He excels in sketching memorable vignettes and small portraits etched in vitriol. His satires abound in witty observations and terse proverbs, among which is the motto *mens sana in corpore sano*, "a sound mind in a sound body."

K

K., Joseph The hero of Kafka's THE TRIAL. As with K. in THE CASTLE, the initial is Kafka's own. This is an example of Kafka's method of introducing parts of his "inner biography" into his works. See SAMSA, GREGOR.

ka In Egyptian mythology, a double that survived after a man's death if a statue of him was made into which it might enter and certain other rites were performed. Such a statue, placed usually near the mummy in the tomb, came to be called a *ka*.

Kaaba (fr Arab, *kabah*, "a square house") The holiest shrine of the Muslims. Located at Mecca, in the center of the Great Mosque, it is said to have been built first by Adam, who received pardon there two hundred years after his expulsion from Paradise, and rebuilt by ISHMAEL and ABRAHAM after the Flood. In the northeast corner is the famous black stone. See HAJAR-AL-ASWAD.

Kabale und Liebe (Love and Intrigue, 1784) A bourgeois tragedy by Friedrich SCHILLER. The theme is the love across social barriers of Luise Miller, a musician's daughter, and Ferdinand von Walther, an aristocrat. Ferdinand's father opposes their love and, following the advice of a jealous schemer at court, unwittingly causes the lovers' death.

kabbalah See CABALA.

Kabīr (1440–1518) Indian religious reformer and poet. Opposed to all forms of religious sectarianism, ritual, and CASTE distinctions, Kabīr, a Muslim by birth, was banished from his native BENARES, and spent the rest of his life traveling in northern India. His poems, many of them translated by R. Tagore in *Poems of Kabīr* (1972), drew on both HINDUISM and ISLAM in their devotional and mystical aspects.

kabuki A form of Japanese drama. Developed out of BUNRAKU (puppet theatre) during the TOKUGAWA period, it catered to the tastes of the newly arisen merchant class. The plays are usually either historical dramas or domestic situations, performed by male actors only. The greatest kabuki playwright was CHIKAMATSU Monzaemon, who originally composed JŌRURI and whose plays were later rewrit-

ten for kabuki presentation. Kabuki is still performed extensively today. The lines are not spoken by the actors, who are mimes, but rather by narrators who sit to the side of the stage in full view of the audience and chant the lines. Kabuki is faster moving, somewhat more realistic, and much more colorful than Nō drama. See JAPANESE LITERATURE.

Kaddish (Aram, "holy") In Judaism, the prayer recited to hallow the name of God. Since medieval times, it has been repeated by mourners as a declaration of their faith. It is used in the synagogue to close a section of the service.

Kaddish and Other Poems: 1958–1960 (1961) A collection of poems by Allen GINSBERG. "Kaddish," the title piece, is a five-part prose poem. It is an elegy for the poet's mother, Naomi Ginsberg, who died in a mental institution in 1956. The poem draws upon two sources for its structure: the classical elegy, with its emotional transition from grief to reconciliation, and the Hebrew prayers chanted for the dead. Parts I and II are narrative in content. They enumerate in catalogue form the major events in Naomi's life, her various internments for delusional paranoia, and the devastating as well as mystical effect of her illness on the poet. Interspersed with graphic and sordid descriptions of Naomi are hymnal ejaculations of praise to her. Parts III, IV, and V are dramatically repetitive chants, intense in imagery and elliptical in syntax. The remaining poems in the volume celebrate the "Beat" themes found in all Ginsberg's writing: mystical hallucination through drugs, the homosexual experience, and criticism of contemporary American politics.

Kafka, Franz (1883–1924) Austrian novelist. Kafka is known for the visionary character of his novels, stories, parables, and sketches, all of which center on the problematic existence of modern man. He was born and raised in the German-Jewish enclave of Prague, the city where he spent most of his unhappy life. As a Jew, he encountered anti-Semitism; as a German-Austrian, the political resentment of the Czech population; and as the son of a well-to-do businessman, the class hatred of the poor. While he earned a law degree and then for fourteen years as he worked as a bureaucrat in a position he detested, Kafka lived in the house of his father, a robust, domineering man who misunderstood his son. In an undelivered letter, Kafka blamed his father for stripping him of all self-confidence and for developing in him "a boundless feeling of guilt." His strained family life, as well as his intense personal concern with religious questions, undoubtedly explains his repeated exploration of the utter incomprehensibility of God and the psychological ambivalence of family relationships, particularly between father and son. In his stories "Das Urteil" (1913; tr "The Judgement," 1945) and THE METAMORPHOSIS and in the novels AMERIKA, THE TRIAL, and THE CASTLE, fathers, father-figures, or authorities misunderstand, judge, misjudge, abuse, and even kill the young heroes.

Kafka scratched the surface of everyday existence to reveal a world of absurdity and paradox, of aimlessness and futility, in which man is tormented by an unrelieved and unexplained anxiety. His style is remarkably precise and lucid, despite the grotesque unreality of the occurrences that it is used to describe. His stories, in their combination of clarity and unreality, are masterpieces of dream-fiction.

When he died of tuberculosis, all his unfinished writings, including the three novels mentioned, were left to his friend Max Brod with instructions that they be burned. Instead, Brod edited and published the works, along with Kafka's diaries (tr 1948–49). With Brod's help, Kafka's work has been subjected to endless interpretation, which has created considerable critical disagreement as to his place in German or world literature. Central to the disagreement is the question whether Kafka's obscure, symbolic works were in fact profound existential or religious allegories or, as he expressed it, only about his "own dreamlike inner life."

Kahn, Louis I[sadore] (1901–1974)   Russian-born American architect. Educated in the Beaux-Arts tradition at the University of Pennsylvania, Kahn attempted vigorous three-dimensional facades, employing columns, arches, and unconventional solid forms. As an educator at Yale, Kahn gained a wide following with his fusion of idealism and practicality, urging students to "find out what the building wants to be." His best-known buildings include the Alfred Richards Medical Research Building at the University of Pennsylvania and the Yale University Art Gallery. Kahn's most significant contribution was the freeing of architecture from the restraints of post-BAUHAUS industrialism, inspiring an entire generation of architects.

Kaiser, Georg (1878–1945)   German playwright. Belonging to the movement of EXPRESSIONISM, Kaiser's plays turn, not on personal interaction among individualized characters, but rather on conflicts of ideas as exemplified in contrasting human types; often, in fact, his dramatis personae are nameless. His early writing (pre-1914), is of no significance, but, with the coming of World War I, he

was finally able to give effective expression to a deep longing for human redemption. In FROM MORN TILL MIDNIGHT, he depicts the complete emptiness of modern life, but in *Der Brand im Opernhaus* (*The Fire in the Opera-House*, 1918) he sees a possible solution for the individual in love. He preaches the salvation of peaceful society through individual sacrifice in *Die Bürger von Calais* (*The Burghers of Calais*, 1914), but he also envisions the possibility of an increasingly deindividualized society leading to ultimate cataclysm in his GAS trilogy. His later works follow the same general thematic lines.

Kalevala   Finnish national epic. It was compiled from popular songs and oral tradition by the Finnish philologist Elias Lonnrott (1802–84), who published his first edition of twelve thousand verses in 1835 and a second edition, nearly twice as long, in 1849. There is an account of the origin of the world, followed by the adventures of the three sons of Kaleva: the hero WAINAMÖINEN, Ilmarinen, and the gallant Lemminkainen. The plot takes them to Pohjola, a dismally cold land to the north, both to fight for the return of the lost SAMPO and to find a bride for Wainamöinen. It was written in unrhymed, alliterative, trochaic verse; and a German translation in the same meter suggested to Longfellow both the form and the epic style for his *Hiawatha* (1855).

Kali   Hindu goddess. The wife of SHIVA, Kali symbolizes the essence of destruction and bloodthirstiness, and the THUGS sacrificed their victims to her. Her naked idol is black and besmeared with blood; she has red eyes, four arms with blood-stained hands, matted hair, huge fanglike teeth, and a protruding tongue that drips with blood. She wears a necklace of skulls, earrings of corpses, and is girdled with serpents. She plays a major role in Thomas MANN's "legend of India," *The Transposed Heads* (1940), where she is also DURGA and Parvati, her two benign aspects. See SHAKTI.

Kālidāsa (fl c AD 400)   Indian dramatist and poet. Considered the greatest of all Sanskrit writers, Kālidāsa is renowned for his exquisite descriptions of nature and his facility for conveying the emotions felt by lovers. His greatest work, indeed the single most famous Sanskrit play, is SHĀKUNTALĀ, which elaborates on a story told in the MAHĀBHĀRATA. His surviving and authenticated work includes two other plays: *Vikramorvashīya*, about the love of the goddess Urvasī for the mortal king PURŪVARAS; and *Mālavikāgnimitra*, about a king who falls in love with his queen's maidservant. His verse includes the narrative epics RAGHUVAMSA and *Kumāra-sambhaua* (tr *The Birth of the War God*, 1887), and the lyrics *Meghadūta* (tr *The Cloud Messenger*, 1930) and *Ritusamhāra* (tr *The Cycle of the Seasons*, 1929).

Kama (also known as Kamadeva or Kandarpa)   In Hindu mythology, the god of love. He was shriveled into cinders by the eye of SHIVA, because Kama stirred passion in Shiva, who was practicing penance. Kama, or love, is also one of HINDUISM's four legitimate ENDS OF MAN, generally taken broadly to include physical pleasure in the broadest sense, not only sexual gratification. See KAMA-SUTRA.

Kamakura   Japanese historical period (1185–1333), following the HEIAN period and preceding the MUROMACHI. The military clans in eastern Japan gained ascendency, taking over rule that had been exercised in part by the emperor in Kyoto, in part by the Fujiwara family and its branches in Kyoto and to the north, and in part by the great estates with which the head temples of Buddhist sects had been endowed. New forms of BUDDHISM, notably AMIDISM and ZEN, arose during this era; new literary forms developed, centering on military chronicles that reflected the uncertainties of a period of incessant warfare and natural disasters. See JAPANESE LITERATURE.

Kama-sutra (fr Sans, *kama*, "love," *sutra*, "science") A detailed account of the art and technique of Indian erotics by the sage Vātsyāyana (1st century?).

Kamenev, Lev Borisovich (1883–1936)   Soviet Communist leader. With STALIN and ZINOVYEV, he formed the triumvirate ruling the Soviet Union after LENIN's death. By 1929, Stalin had taken the upper hand, and in 1936 he purged both his former colleagues.

Kandinsky, Vasily (1866–1944)   Russian painter. Kandinsky was a cofounder, with Franz Marc, of the BLAUE REITER and a pioneer in ABSTRACT EXPRESSIONIST painting. In 1910 he rejected representational art and evolved a style of turbulent, vividly colored abstractions. After 1920 his style gradually became orderly and strict. The works of this later period are limited to brightly colored dots, bundles of straight or broken lines, rectangles, and circular forms, but these shapes are handled with great freedom and inventiveness. From 1922 to 1933, Kandinsky taught at the BAUHAUS, where he did important work in his basic course on the theory of form and published *Punkt und Linie zu Fläche* (*Point and Line to Plane*, 1926).

Kangaroo (1923)   A novel by D. H. LAWRENCE. Set in Australia, it is notable for its vivid account of that country, largely drawn from Lawrence's own experience. The central characters of Richard Lovat Somers and Harriet Somers are closely based on Lawrence and his wife, Frieda LAWRENCE. The novel is largely concerned with their difficult marriage relationship, in which the husband keeps trying unsuccessfully to assert his will over his wife. Kangaroo is the nickname of an invented character, Benjamin Cooley, the leader of a political party whose platform is a combination of fascism and Lawrence's own doctrine of "blood-consciousness."

K'ang-hsi   Name of a Chinese emperor and of his reign period (1661–1722). It was a period of consolidation of CH'ING dynasty (1644–1911) rule, of great intellectual activity, and of extensive contact with Europeans.

Kannon   See KUAN-YIN.

Kant, Immanuel (1724–1804)   German philosopher. Kant's attempt to define precisely the domain of rational understanding is a landmark in Western thought. On the one hand, he opposed HUME's skepticism, the idea that pure reason is of no real use in understanding the world, and on the other, he challenged Enlightenment faith in the unlimited scope of reason. The basic formulation of what is called his critical philosophy is contained in the CRITIQUE OF PURE REASON, the CRITIQUE OF PRACTICAL REASON, and the CRITIQUE OF JUDGMENT. His ideas were used by SCHILLER as the basis for aesthetic theories and marked the beginning of German idealistic philosophy, which was developed by FICHTE, SCHELLING, and HEGEL. The quiet regularity of Kant's everyday life in Königsberg, where he was a university professor (1770–1804), became proverbial. According to an anecdote of Heinrich HEINE, the residents of the town set their watches by Kant's daily walks.

Kantemir, Antiokh Dmitryevich (1709–1744) Russian poet. Kantemir helped to form the classic tradition in Russian literature. He is known chiefly for his satires, written in imitation of those of HORACE and Boileau. Although he made Russians aware of European classical culture, Kantemir's own work had little direct influence. His prosody, based on the number of syllables in each line of verse, was supplanted by the accentual verse introduced by Mikhail LOMONOSOV.

Kantor, MacKinlay (1904–1977)   American novelist. Author of over twenty-five books, Kantor had his greatest success with novels dealing with the American past. *Andersonville* (1955), which won a PULITZER PRIZE, is a long and grimly realistic story of the infamous Confederate prison. Among his many other books are *Spirit Lake* (1961), an account of the massacre of thirty settlers in Iowa in 1857, and *Valley Forge* (1975), a striking tale of the Revolutionary War. Kantor also wrote many screenplays, including *The Best Years of Our Lives* (1947), which was an adaptation of his own novel *Glory for Me* (1945).

Kapital, Das (1867–1894)   A systematic critical study of capitalist economy by Karl MARX based on the ideas that he formulated, with Friedrich ENGELS, in THE COMMUNIST MANIFESTO. The first volume appeared in 1867; the second and third volumes were completed by Engels from Marx's notes (1885–94).

Karamazinov   In THE POSSESSED by DOSTOYEVSKY, a satirical portrait of Ivan TURGENEV, whose aesthetic posing and love of Western culture Dostoyevsky detested.

Karamazov, Fyodor Pavlovich   In THE BROTHERS KARAMAZOV by DOSTOYEVSKY, the father of the Karamazovs. He is a lustful, buffoonish character who thoroughly enjoys his sensual life and the sense of his degradation and only occasionally reveals contempt for himself. The shock and disapproval of others only inspire him to further antics. His sensual zest is contained in each of his sons in varying degrees, but none can match him for sheer animalism. He is a model of rampant irrationalism whose favorite mode of expression is the non sequitur.

Dmitry Fyodorovich Karamazov Dmitry, also known as Mitya, is the eldest of the Karamazov brothers. He has inherited more of his father's lustiness than his brothers, but is saved from the old man's depravity by his own innately noble nature. Accused of his father's murder, he refuses to defend himself adequately, because by so doing he would injure the reputation of his ex-fiancee, Katerina Ivanovna. The most full-blooded of the characters in the novel, Dmitry is also one of Dostoyevsky's most successful character creations.

Ivan Fyodorovich Karamazov The intellectual member of the Karamazov family, Ivan, also known as Vanya, is used by Dostoyevsky to represent the dead end to which he believed rationalism led. Tortured by the injustice and suffering in the world, Ivan "returns the ticket" to God, rejecting salvation from a Being who has allowed such a world to exist. Ivan both pities and despises man for his weakness. Both attitudes are revealed in his "Legend of the GRAND INQUISITOR," a parable he recites to Alyosha during their most prolonged discussion. Ivan's guilt at having wished for his father's death rends him, culminating in his hallucinatory conversations with a shabby devil who espouses Ivan's own ideas in a debased form, much as the bastard Smerdyakov does.

Aleksey Fyodorovich Karamazov The youngest son of Fyodor Pavlovich, Alyosha, as he is called, is a novice at a monastery but his mentor, the elder ZOSIMA, orders him to go into the world and serve God there. Although he is a mystic, Alyosha is much less removed from normal human concerns than Dostoyevsky's other famous mystic, Prince Myshkin of THE IDIOT. Despite his evident purity of heart, Alyosha admits to having a streak of the Karamazov sensuality in him. In the novel, he acts as the constant, sorrowful, and patient observer of his tormented father and brothers.

Smerdyakov The illegitimate son of Fyodor Pavlovich, who raped the boy's half-witted mother and later took the bastard into his house as a servant, Smerdyakov is a composite of cheap foppishness and second-rate intellect. He adopts Ivan's nihilistic ideas wholesale, perverts them in his own less fertile brain, and under their influence eventually commits the murder for which Dmitry is blamed.

Karamzin, Nikolay Mikhailovich (1766–1826) Russian writer and historian. Karamzin introduced the romanticism of both Jean Jacques ROUSSEAU and the early 19th-century English writers into Russian literature. His best-known works are *Pisma russkogo puteshestvennika* (*Letters of a Russian Traveler*, 1790–91), based on his journey through Europe; *Bednaya Liza* (*Poor Liza*, 1792), a sentimental love story; and the multivolume *Istoriya gosudarstva Rossiskogo* (*History of the Russian State*, 1818–24). Besides his introduction of new sensibilities and themes into Russian literature, Karamzin is important for his linguistic reforms. He attempted to make literary Russian less heavy in style by introducing French syntax and terms into the language.

Karatayev, Platon The wise peasant in Count Leo TOLSTOY's novel WAR AND PEACE. His message of the goodness of the natural, simple life affects the spiritual development of Pierre BEZUKHOV, one of the main characters of the book.

Karenina, Anna See ANNA KARENINA.

Karlfeldt, Erik Axel (1864–1931) Swedish poet. Karlfeldt's work is characterized by its purposely archaic style and its basis in folklore and custom, in such collections as *Fridolins visor* (1898), *Fridolins lustgård* (1901), and *Hösthorn* (1927). In 1918 he refused the NOBEL PRIZE in Literature, arguing that his work was unknown outside of Sweden. The prize was awarded to him posthumously in 1931.

karma (fr Sans, *karman*, "deed") The principle of causality, based on ethical merit, in the Hindu doctrine of reincarnation. Karma is regarded as binding man to the cosmos and to the cycle of birth and death, because whatever is done in one lifetime has its consequences in another. Freedom or release from this iron law, *moksha*, is the object sought in nearly all Indian philosophy and in the Buddhist faith.

Kārttikeya (also Skanda or Kumāra, "the youthful") In Hindu mythology the god of war. Kārttikeya is said to have been born without a mother and to have been adopted by Krittikas; hence he is sometimes called "the son of Krittikas." He rides on a peacock, with a bow in one hand and an arrow in the other. In south India, he is a special protector of BRAHMINS and is known as Subramanya or, in Dravidian, as Murugan.

Katayev, Valentin Petrovich (1897–   ) Russian novelist, playwright, and short-story writer. Born in Odessa, Katayev first wrote poetry and in 1912 published his first short stories. He was wounded in World War I, and later served in the Red Army. His tetralogy entitled *Volny chernogo morya* (*Black Sea Waves*) includes the novels *Beleyet parus odinoky* (1936; tr *Lonely White Sail*, 1937; U.S. *Peace Is Where the Tempests Blow*); *Khutorok v stepi* (1956; tr *Small Farm in the Steppe*, 1958); *Zimny veter* (*Winter Wind*, 1960), and *Za vlast Sovetov* (*For the Power of the Soviets*, 1947–61). A politically provocative work in the Soviet Union, this tetralogy has appeared in a number of revised editions. His later novels, such as *Svyatoy kolodets* (1966; tr *The Holy Well*, 1967) and *Trava zabyvaniya* (1967; tr *The Grass of Oblivion*, 1969), use methods of narration wholly at odds with the dictates of SOCIALIST REALISM: in *The Holy Well*, for example, the narrator roams freely through his memory, his mind altered by drugs. Katayev's works generally approach and sometimes transgress the literary bounds deemed acceptable by the Soviet authorities.

Katharina The fiery and ungovernable daughter of the bewildered Baptista in Shakespeare's TAMING OF THE SHREW. "Renowned in Padua for her scolding tongue," Katharina is wooed and won in wild and highhanded fashion by the equally high-spirited Petruchio.

Kathāsaritsāgara (11th century) A collection of poetic tales in Sanskrit written by SOMADEVA. It consists of twenty-two thousand verses in 124 chapters and constitutes a series of romantic adventure-tales, featuring the King Udayana. Somadeva's version is thought to be a recasting of the *Brihat-katha* ("great story") composed by Gunādhya several centuries earlier. The *Kathāsaritsāgara* has been translated as *Ocean of the Streams of Story* (10 vols, 1924–28).

Käthchen von Heilbronn, Das (pub 1810) A play by Heinrich von KLEIST. It is Kleist's most romantic work, a kind of dramatized fairy tale. Käthchen, apparently a young commoner, is drawn to the count von Strahl by a mysterious, irresistible love and refuses to leave his side. Her perfect devotion survives through a number of knightly and supernatural adventures, and it is finally discovered that she is the emperor's daughter. She and the count marry in the end.

Kaufman, George S[imon] (1889–1961) American playwright. Initially a theatre critic of considerable stature, Kaufman collaborated on over forty plays which ranged from rambunctious farce to serious theatrical satire. Between 1921 and 1944 he had an almost unbroken string of Broadway hits. His long series of collaborations include *Dulcy* (1921) and *Beggar on Horseback* (1924), with Marc CONNELLY; *The Royal Family* (1927), *Dinner at Eight* (1932), and *Stage Door* (1936) with Edna FERBER; with Morrie Ryskind he wrote the book for *Of Thee I Sing* (1931); and with Ring LARDNER he wrote *June Moon* (1929). Perhaps his most successful collaboration was with Moss HART. Together they wrote *Once in a Lifetime* (1930), a satire on Hollywood; YOU CAN'T TAKE IT WITH YOU; *I'd Rather Be Right* (1937); and THE MAN WHO CAME TO DINNER, among others. He also wrote the stage and screen adaptations of *The Late George Apley* (1944; with J. P. MARQUAND), *The Solid Gold Cadillac* (1954; with Howard Teichman), and the scripts for such Marx Brothers films as *The Coconuts* (1929) and *Animal Crackers* (1930).

Kaverin, Venyamin (pen name of Venyamin Aleksandrovich Zilberg, 1902–   ) Russian novelist and short-story writer. Kaverin was a member of the SERAPION BROTHERS, in which he joined Lev Lunts in advocating more attention to Western literary methods. His special favorite was Edgar Allan POE. His early stories, published in the collection *Mastera i podmasterya* (*Craftsmen and Apprentices*, 1923), show an attention to plot that sets them apart from the typical works of the time with their diffuse construction and ornate prose. Kaverin's best early novel is *Khudozhnik neizvesten* (1931; tr *The Unknown Artist*, 1947), the story of a young artist's problems in finding a place for himself in the new society after the revolution. Another novel with a similar theme, although less complex in its structure, is his *Ispolneniye zhelaniy* (1934–36; tr *The Larger View*, 1938). Kaverin's next novel, *Dva kapitana* (1938–44; tr *Two Captains*, 1942), is an adventure story of Arctic exploration with some detective elements thrown in.

In 1949 Kaverin published the first part of a novel entitled *Otkrytaya kniga* (1949–56; tr *An Open Book*, 1955), the story of a young girl who becomes a prominent bacteriologist. This fragment was not well received. In 1956, during the relaxed period following Stalin's death, Kaverin issued another part of the novel, a section entitled *Poiski i nadezhdy* (*Searches and Hopes*), which proved to be an outspoken criticism of Soviet scientific bureaucracy and the chauvinistic concern for Russian primacy in all fields, in this case, penicillin research. In 1976 he published *Osveshchennye okna*, an autobiographical novel about his youth. *Dvukhchasovaya progulka* (*The Two-Hour Walk*), a novel, appeared in 1979.

Kawabata Yasunari (1899–1972) Japanese novelist and literary critic, winner of the NOBEL PRIZE in Literature in 1968. Kawabata's typical works are pervaded by a sense of alienation and loss, and by a longing for pure, unearthly beauty often found in a maiden or a maidenly person. *Izu no odoriko* (1925; tr *The Izu Dancer*, 1964), *Yukiguni* (1948; tr *Snow Country*, 1957), *Sembazuru* (1952; tr *Thousand Cranes*, 1959), *Yama no oto* (1952; tr *The Sound of the Mountain*, 1970), *Nemureru Bijo* (1961; tr *The House of the Sleeping Beauties*, 1969), and *Utsukushisa to kanashimi to* (1965; tr *Beauty and Sadness*, 1975), all present a lonely man trying to find solace in the innate beauty and goodness of a young woman, though each story shows different thematic variations. Influenced by both Japanese and Western varieties of symbolist poetry, Kawabata's novels make their statement through symbolism as much as through plot and characterization. He committed suicide in 1972.

Kay, Sir In Arthurian legend, King ARTHUR's seneschal (steward). In the Welsh tale *Kulhwch and Olwen* (c1100), Sir Kay is a great hero—a wound from his sword, no physician might heal. In later tales, such as *Lancelot* (c1180) by Chrétien de Troyes and *Le Morte d'Arthur* (c1469) of Malory, he becomes the rude and boastful knight whose sharp tongue is always stirring up trouble and who is inept in combat; yet Arthur always defers to him. In *Le Morte d'Arthur*, he is the son of Sir Ector, King Arthur's foster father.

Kazakevich, Emmanuil Genrikhovich (1913–1962) Russian novelist and short-story writer. Born in the Ukraine, Kazakevich lived during the 1930s in the Jewish autonymous province of Birobidzhan and wrote his early works in Yiddish. After serving in the war, he drew from his experience behind the lines on reconnaissance missions in *Zvezda* (1947; tr *Star*, 1950) and *Dvoe v stepi* (*Two Men in the Steppe*, 1948), two stories which explore the dilemma peculiar among the allies to Soviet soldiers: the enemy lies ahead, while any show of cowardice will result in court-martial and subsequent execution at home. Laconic and dry yet highly psychological, they are fine representatives of early war literature. Kazakevich's later novels *Vesna na Odere* (tr *Spring on the Oder*, 1953) and *Dom na ploshchadi* (1956; tr *The House on the Square*, 1957) are rather unsophisticated works, portraying the Germans simplistically and the allied British and Americans with a distinct cold-war bias. With THE THAW, however, Kazakevich instilled his characters with greater complexity and assumed a more skeptical, ironic tone, as in the novellas *Pri svete dni* (*In the Light of Day*, 1961) and *Priezd ottsa v gosti k synu* (*The Father Visits His Son*, 1962).

Kazakov, Yury Pavlovich (1927–   )   Russian short-story writer. In the tradition of Turgenev's lyrical descriptions of nature and evocation of mood through natural imagery, Kazakov's stories deal with hunting, country life, and humble provincial people, avoiding any overt political content. For this lack of social implication, as well as for his focus on melancholy moods and alienated characters, Kazakov has been criticized, yet his poetic prose and subtle depiction of emotional life align him with Chekhov and distinguish him as a major writer of his generation. First recognized for his story *Arktur* (1958; tr *Arktur —Hunting Dog*, 1965), in which a blind dog, apparently fated to be an outcast, is adopted out of pity by a local doctor and becomes a famous hunter, Kazakov is known in Russia and abroad for his stories *Zapakh khleba* (1958; tr *The Smell of Bread*, 1964), *Adam i Eva* (1958; tr *Adam and Eve*, 1964), and *Trali-Vali* (1959; tr *Silly-Billy*, 1964).

Kazan, Elia (real name Elia Kazanjoglou, 1909–   ) American stage and film director and novelist. Kazan began as an actor and was for a time associated with the GROUP THEATRE and the development of naturalistic "method acting." Both these influences had a significant effect on his work as a filmmaker, particularly in his direction of *On the Waterfront* (1954). Most of his early films, including *Boomerang* (1947) and *Pinky* (1949), were indictments of social injustice. But Kazan, a former member of the Communist Party, appeared before the House Un-American Activities Committee in 1952 and "named names" of former Party associates. Thereafter, he made *Man on a Tightrope* (1952), denouncing communism, and *A Face in the Crowd* (1957), exposing the dangerous gullibility of the masses in the presence of a demagogue. During the same period he also adapted for the screen two plays by Tennessee WILLIAMS: *A Streetcar Named Desire* (1951) and *Baby Doll* (1956). Among his other films are *A Tree Grows in Brooklyn* (1945), *Gentlemen's Agreement* (1947), *East of Eden* (1955), *Wild River* (1960), and *Splendor in the Grass* (1961). His later films, many of them based on his own best-selling novels, tend to focus on autobiographical concerns, as with *America, America* (1964) and *The Arrangement* (1969). *The Anatolian* (1982), a novel, develops the theme of a young Greek immigrant growing up in America. He also directed a screen adaptation of F. Scott FITZGERALD's *The Last Tycoon* (1976).

Kazantzakis, Nikos (1883–1957)   Greek novelist, poet, dramatist, and thinker. Born in Crete, Kazantzakis took a law degree at Athens, then traveled widely for several years. From 1919 to 1947 he held a variety of governmental posts. In his novel *Toda Raba* (1929; tr 1964), he declared, "I am a mariner of Odysseus with heart of fire but with mind ruthless and clear." This essential ambivalence, the conflict between flesh and spirit, between DIONYSUS and APOLLO, was the fundamental subject of his art. This conflict is at the heart of ZORBA THE GREEK, the novel that established his reputation in America (later turned into a motion picture and a Broadway musical), and is also central to his next great novels, THE GREEK PASSION and *The Last Temptation of Christ* (1951; tr 1960). Kazantzakis' preoccupation with the dual nature of man and the meaning of existence found its ultimate expression in his monumental epic THE ODYSSEY: A MODERN SEQUEL.

Kazantzakis was influenced by philosophies as remote from one another as those of DANTE, LENIN, and BUDDHA. His principal mentors, however, were NIETZSCHE, whose works he read avidly, and BERGSON, under whom he studied in his youth. Like his hero, Odysseus, Kazantzakis valued freedom above all other blessings. Yet, he believed that the ultimate good is not freedom itself, which can never be achieved, but the passionate, often tragic *search* for freedom. Greatly admired during his lifetime, Kazantzakis was never awarded the NOBEL PRIZE, although he was nominated for that honor repeatedly. His autobiographical novel, *Anofora ston Greco* (1961; tr *Report to Greco*, 1965) was published posthumously.

Kazin, Alfred (1915–   )   American literary critic. Kazin's first book of criticism, *On Native Grounds* (1942), traced the development of American prose from the time of W. D. HOWELLS. Its sequel, *Bright Book of Life* (1973), continues his history and criticism from HEMINGWAY to Norman MAILER. Aside from such other books of criticism as *The Inmost Leaf* (1955) and *Contemporaries* (1962), Kazin has written three autobiographical works: *A Walker in the City* (1951), an appealing memoir of his boyhood in Brooklyn; *Starting Out in the Thirties* (1965), about his young manhood; and *New York Jew* (1978), a personalized literary and political history from the Hitler-Stalin pact (1939) to the 1970s. *An American Procession* (1984) is a critical appraisal of all the literary greats in American literature from THOREAU through POUND, FAULKNER, and HEMINGWAY.

Keaton, [Joseph Francis] Buster (1895–1966) American filmmaker and Charlie CHAPLIN's only significant rival in the art of silent film comedy. Keaton, whose hallmarks as a comedian were a deadpan face and an astonishing acrobatic skill, scripted and directed most of his own films. Typically, he plays the role of a "schlemiehl" character who, in spite of himself, survives or triumphs over the most unfavorable circumstances. His best pictures are distinguished by visual richness, fluent camerawork and editing, and a painstaking attention to detail. The short films *Cops* (1922) and *The Balloonatic* (1922) and the longer films *Sherlock Junior* (1924), *The Navigator* (1924), *The General* (1926), and *Steamboat Bill, Jr.* (1928) endure as classics of the golden age of silent comedy.

Keats, John (1795–1821)   English poet. The oldest of four children, Keats was born in London. His father, a livery-stable keeper, died when Keats was eight and his mother died six years later. The following year, when he was fifteen, he was withdrawn from school by his guardian and apprenticed to an apothecary-surgeon. In 1815 he entered a London hospital as a medical student, and though he received his certificate to practice, he soon gave up medicine in order to devote himself entirely to poetry. In the autumn of 1816 he gained the acquaintance of the influential editor of the *Examiner*, Leigh HUNT, who published his sonnet "On First Looking into Chapman's Homer" (1816) and through whom he later met SHELLEY and WORDSWORTH. The following year saw the publication of his first collection, *The Poems of John Keats*. He then began work on *Endymion* (1818), a long allegory of imagination in search of ideal beauty; the story is based on the Greek myth of the shepherd ENDYMION on Mount Latmos who was loved by SELENE, the goddess of the moon. Though Keats may have attached enough hopes to the poem to be troubled by the attacks of unfriendly critics, he was maturing rapidly both as a poet and as a critic of his own work and soon spoke of *Endymion* as "mawkish" and "slipshod." There is little truth in the popular belief, stimulated by Shelley's preface to his elegy ADONAIS, that Keats wasted away and died as a result of the "savage criticism" of *Endymion*, which "produced the most violent effect on his susceptible mind . . . [ending] in the rupture of a blood-vessel in the lungs."

In 1818 Keats had to cut short a walking tour because of a severe sore throat, possibly the first sign of his illness. He then nursed his brother Tom, suffering from tuberculosis, until Tom's death in the beginning of December. He had met Fanny Brawne in September, and he became engaged to her at Christmastime. Between the autumn of 1818 and the summer of 1819, Keats composed his finest poetry. He worked on *Hyperion*, a Miltonic blank-verse epic of the Greek myth of Creation, but left it after a little more than two books had been completed. The story was to deal with the Titan Hyperion, god of the sun, and his overthrow by APOLLO, representative of the new generation of gods headed by ZEUS.

In January 1819, he began THE EVE OF ST. AGNES; the story, which he probably got from Boccaccio, is based on the medieval belief that on St. Agnes's Eve a girl who follows certain rituals will see her future husband in her dreams. He wrote "La Belle Dame Sans Merci," a haunting and mysterious ballad, and began to compose his great odes—"Ode on Melancholy," ODE ON A GRECIAN URN, "Ode to Psyche," ODE TO A NIGHTINGALE—adapting elements of the rhyme-scheme of both Petrarchan and Shakespearean SONNETS. Notable for their sensuous imagery and sustained feeling, these odes are among the finest in English.

By summer he was at work on "Lamia," an allegorical poem based on a story, found in Burton's ANATOMY OF MELANCHOLY, of a youth who met a phantasm in the shape of a lovely woman and went to live with her. At their wedding, the woman was revealed to be a serpent (a LAMIA), and all her possessions mere illusions which, with her, vanished "in an instant." He began a revision of *Hyperion*, called *The Fall of Hyperion*, and "The Eve of St. Mark," both of which were left incomplete. By the fall of 1819 his tuberculosis had progressed until he could do little but revise and prepare his poems for publication. This third and final collection, *Lamia, Isabella, The Eve of St. Agnes and Other Poems*, appeared in July of 1820. In February of that year he had suffered his first hemorrhage. Bothered by financial problems, frustrated and unhappy in his unconsummated relationship with Fanny Brawne, he became progressively worse until a doctor warned that another English winter would kill him. In August he refused an invitation from Shelley, whom he knew slightly, to spend the winter at the Shelleys' villa in Italy. He borrowed money and sailed for Italy in September, accompanied by the young painter Joseph Severn, and died in Rome the following February.

Probably the most talented of the English romantic poets, Keats wrote a surprisingly large body of poetry before his early death. Practically all the finished poems of the 1818–19 group are the work of a mature poet, and a few of them, such as the magnificent "To Autumn," are among the finest examples of English lyric poetry. His letters are of particular interest not only for their biographical value but also for their poetic and philosophic insights. See ISABELLA, OR THE POT OF BASIL.

Keble, John (1792–1866)   Anglican clergyman and poet. Keble's Oxford sermon *National Apostasy* was considered by Cardinal NEWMAN to be the start of the OXFORD MOVEMENT. He was professor of poetry at Oxford (1831–41) and author of a popular collection of religious verse, *The Christian Year* (1827), as well as several volumes of sermons and essays.

Keller, Gottfried (1819–1890)   Swiss novelist and poet, writing in German. Keller is known especially for his ability to combine bourgeois good sense and humor with powerful symbolism and subtle psychological perception. After failing to realize his youthful ambition of becoming a painter, he turned to poetry in 1842. He was involved in the Swiss civil disputes of the time, and a number of his early poems are in the manner of such liberal political poets as Herwegh and Freiligrath. During 1848–55, he traveled and studied in Germany, completing his first major narrative work, the novel GREEN HENRY (*Der grüne Heinrich*; first version, 1854; second, 1879–80), which was shortly followed by a collection of stories, DIE LEUTE VON SELDWYLA. Most of his later years were spent comfortably in Zürich where, during 1861–76, he was a government official. Outstanding among his later works are the *Sieben Legenden* (*Seven Legends*, 1872), treating the early period of the Christian era. In them, he weaves a delicately ironic web of both Christian and pagan elements, by which he implies his own preference for a secularized view of religion, an idea that reflects the strong influence of FEUERBACH.

Keller, Helen [Adams] (1880–1968)   American memoirist, essayist, and counselor on international relations for the American Foundation for the Blind. Disease deprived Keller of sight and hearing at the age of nineteen months. Completely cut off from all communication, she was put in the care of Anne Sullivan Macy (1866–1936), who taught her the relationship between words and things and who remained her companion until her death. By the age of ten, she had learned to speak. She was graduated from Radcliffe College *cum laude* in 1904 and received numerous honorary degrees from universities all over the world. Among Helen Keller's books about her ordeals and triumphs are *The Story of My Life* (1903), *The World I Live In* (1908), *Out of the Dark* (1913), *My Religion* (1927), *Midstream* (1929), and *Teacher, Anne Sullivan Macy* (1955), which she subtitled "A Tribute from the Foster Child of Her Mind." A number of books have been written about her; in 1954 a movie called *The Unconquered* was based on her life story. *The Miracle Worker* (1959), a Broadway play, and later a movie, dramatized Anne Sullivan's first success in communicating with Helen as a child.

Kelly, Ellsworth (1923–   )   American painter and sculptor. Kelly is known as one of the purest representatives of "hard edge" painting. He developed a style using a literal abstraction of natural forms, eventually using color itself as his subject matter, as with his well-known "color panels" of the 1950s.

Kelly, George [Edward] (1887–1974)   American playwright. Originally a vaudeville actor and skit writer, Kelly became known on Broadway for his pungent satires of middle-class life. His fame rests principally on *The Show-Off* (1924), a parody of American success stories, and CRAIG'S WIFE, which won a PULITZER PRIZE. His plays were so popular in his day that "Aubrey Piper" (the main character in *Show-Off*) became a synonym for an insufferable braggart; and Harriet Craig (of *Craig's Wife*) for all ambitious women who sacrifice their families for material possessions.

Kelly, Robert (1935–   )   American poet and editor. Kelly founded and edited the literary journal *Chelsea* and, with George Economou, founded *Trobar*. A remarka-

bly prolific poet, he has published as many as six volumes of verse in a single year (1964). His poetry is emotional, esoteric, and sensual; in theme, he frequently returns to an awareness of the writer in the act of writing, and to the human voice in search of communication. His language is lively and dense and he moves easily between formal and free verse. His early works were primarily shorter lyrics: *Armed Descent* (1961) and *Her Body against Time* (1963). His later poetry is often composed in series, as in *Songs I–XXX* (1968), or in long narratives, as in *The Loom* (1975). In 1985 he published *A Transparent Tree*, a collection of short stories, and *Not This Island Music*, a volume of poetry.

Kelmscott Press   A cooperative publishing and printing enterprise established by William MORRIS on his English country estate in 1891. It was noted for the beauty of paper, binding, and typography in the books it published. The *Kelmscott Chaucer* is considered the masterpiece among these. See CHAUCER.

kelpie   In Scottish folklore, a spirit of the waters in the form of a horse. The kelpie was supposed to take delight in the drowning of travelers, but also occasionally to help millers by keeping the mill wheel going at night.

Kemp, William (fl c1600)   English comedian and dancer. Kemp acted in the plays of Shakespeare and Ben Jonson. He was an important member of Shakespeare's company until 1600, and later traveled widely on the Continent. Kemp's *Nine Daies Wonder* is an autobiographical account of his famous morris-dance from London to Norwich.

Keneally, Thomas [Michael] (1935–   )   Australian novelist. Although the forms and styles of Keneally's novels differ, each reveals his vivid historical imagination and his interest in characters at the point of emotional or psychological crisis. *Bring Larks and Heroes* (1967), the tragic story of an English intellectual and poet in a penal colony, and *The Chant of Jimmie Blacksmith* (1972), about a young aborigine driven mad by racial discrimination, are both set in Australia's past. *Blood Red, Sister Rose* (1974) is based on the story of Joan of Arc, and *Gossip from the Forest* (1975) treats the armistice of World War I in France. *Passenger* (1979) explores the origins of consciousness from the vantage point of a "supremely conscious fetus." *Confederates* (1979) is a moving historical novel about the American Civil War. It was followed by *Schindler's Ark* (1982; U.S. *Schindler's List*), a brilliant fictionalization of one man's extraordinary feat in saving lives during the Holocaust, which won Britain's Booker Prize in 1983, and *The Cut-Rate Kingdom* (1984); both novels are set against a backdrop of war, the perfect background for Keneally's revelations of character and the human spirit. In 1985 Keneally wrote another novel on the Holocaust, *A Family Madness*, which, like the earlier *Schindler's Ark*, takes place in Australia and examines the presence and power of the past in the present.

In late 1983, Keneally received the Order of Australia for his "service to literature."

Kenilworth (1821)   A novel by Sir Walter Scott, famous for its portrayal of Queen Elizabeth and her court. The other principal characters are Robert Dudley, the earl of Leicester, who entertains ambitions of becoming king-consort, and his beautiful, unhappy wife, Amy Robsart. She suffers neglect, insult, and finally death at his hands. Kenilworth is a magnificent castle near Stratford, now ruined.

Kennedy, John Fitzgerald (1917–1963)   Thirty-fifth president of the U.S. (1961–63). The son of Joseph P. Kennedy, Boston financier and former ambassador to England, and the grandson of a popular mayor of Boston, Kennedy was born into an atmosphere of wealth and prominence. After attending the London School of Economics (1935–36), he entered Harvard University, from which he graduated with honors in 1940. During World War II, Kennedy served as the commander of a PT boat in the South Pacific and was decorated by the navy for courage and leadership.

Kennedy's political career began in 1946 when he was elected to Congress as a representative from Massachusetts. He was reelected in 1948 and 1950, and in 1952 defeated Henry Cabot Lodge for a seat in the Senate. As a senator, Kennedy quickly became a leader of the moderate liberal wing of the Democratic Party. In 1956 he was a leading contender for the Democratic vice-presidential nomination, and in 1960, after impressive victories in a number of state presidential primaries, he became the Democratic nominee for president, winning the election by a narrow margin over Vice President Richard Nixon. He was the first Roman Catholic and the youngest man to be elected to the presidency.

During his brief administration, Kennedy launched the Peace Corps to aid underdeveloped areas, demanded the withdrawal of Soviet weapons from Cuba, and encouraged the black drive for full civil rights. On November 22, 1963, Kennedy was shot to death as he rode in a motorcade in Dallas, Texas. His accused assassin, Lee Harvey Oswald, was himself killed on November 24 by Jack Ruby, a Dallas nightclub operator, in full view of the nation's television audience.

Kennedy was the author of *Why England Slept* (1940), an analysis of the causes of England's failure to rearm before World War II; *Profiles in Courage* (1956), a Pulitzer Prize-winning collection of essays dealing with congressional leaders who, in historically critical moments, placed conscience over political expediency; and *The Strategy of Peace* (1960), which presented a statement of Kennedy's aims in international affairs.

Kennedy, Margaret (1896–1967)   English novelist, author of many popular novels including the best-selling The Constant Nymph.

Kennedy, William (1928–   )   American novelist. Born in Albany, New York, the son of working-class Irish Catholic parents, Kennedy has made the city the star of his best-known works, the "Albany cycle," a series of three novels. His Albany of the 1920s and 1930s has attained something of the mythic status of Joyce's Dublin or Farrell's Chicago. The first and second books of the cycle—*Legs* (1975), a fictional version of the life and times of Jack "Legs" Diamond, and *Billy Phelan's Latest Game* (1978), which centers around the kidnapping of the heir to the family that runs the city's Democratic machine—won critical but not popular acclaim. *Ironweed* (1983), the third novel in the series, is a haunting odyssey through the weekend of All Hallows Eve and All Saints Day in 1938 as seen through the eyes of Francis Phelan, a former baseball player now on skid row. It was awarded a Pulitzer Prize in 1984 and became a best-seller. Kennedy has also written the novel *The Ink Truck* (1969; repr 1984) and a collection of essays, *O Albany!* (1983), as well as the screenplay for Francis Ford Coppola's film *The Cotton Club* (1984).

Kenner, [William] Hugh (1923–   )   Canadian literary critic. Educated at Toronto and Yale, Kenner pursued an academic career that kept him in the U.S., where he became one of the most widely read, influential, and controversial critics of his generation. An early encounter with Ezra Pound profoundly influenced his approach to literature: typically he would concentrate on the words and sentences a writer put on the page rather than generalizing on a poet's "philosophy" or "spirit." Kenner's work is therefore distinguished for the clarity of his exegesis of what his subjects are saying. His subjects are the great figures of the literary revolution which took place during and after World War I, notably Joyce (*Dublin's Joyce*, 1955; *Joyce's Voices*, 1978), Lewis (*Wyndham Lewis*, 1954), T. S. Eliot (*The Invisible Poet*, 1959), Beckett (*A Reader's Guide*, 1973), and Pound (*The Poetry of Ezra Pound*, 1951; *The Pound Era*, 1971). In 1983 he published *A Colder Eye*, an account of the major figures of the Irish literary revival.

Kennicott, Carol   See Main Street.

kenning   In Anglo-Saxon and Norse poetry, a figure of speech using a descriptive figurative circumlocution in place of a common noun. Beowulf contains a number of excellent examples of kennings, as with "whale road" or "gannet's bath" for "sea"; "ash-wood" for "spear"; and "storm of swords" for "battle."

Kent, earl of   In Shakespeare's King Lear, the honest courtier banished by Lear for interceding on behalf of Cordelia. Under the assumed name of Caius, Kent continues to serve Lear.

Kenton, Simon (1755–1836)   American soldier and Indian fighter, famous in frontier legends. At one time a scout for Daniel Boone, he fought in the American Revolution and in the War of 1812. See Girty, Simon.

Kentucky Tragedy   A murder and suicide which took place in 1825. Anna Cook, a Kentucky woman who had been seduced by Col. Solomon P. Sharp, married an attorney, Jeroboam O. Beauchamp, in 1825. She made her husband take an oath to kill her seducer. Beauchamp stabbed Sharp to death the same year in Frankfort, Kentucky. He was tried, denied his guilt, but was convicted. The evening before his execution, Anna joined him, and both took laudanum. His wife died, but Beauchamp lived to be hanged the next day.

The dramatic possibilities of the crime inspired many works. Beauchamp wrote his own *Confession* (1826). Thomas Holley Chivers treated the theme in his verse drama *Conrad and Eudora* (1834); POE used it in *Politian* (1835–36); Charlotte Mary Barnes wrote a tragedy called *Octavia Bragaldi* (1837); Mary E. MacMichael wrote *The Kentucky Tragedy* (1838); and Charles Fenno Hoffman treated the same story in his romance *Greyslaer* (1849). The popular Southern novelist William Gilmore Simms wrote *Beauchampe* in 1842. More recently, two well-known works have been based on the story: Robert Penn WARREN's *World Enough and Time* (1950) and Joseph Shearing's *To Bed at Noon* (1951).

Kenyon Review, The   A distinguished quarterly founded by members of the Kenyon College (Ohio) faculty in 1939. John Crowe RANSOM was the first editor. The magazine stressed close structural criticism in keeping with the tenets of NEW CRITICISM and reviewed important new trends in the arts. The original advisory board included Allen TATE, Mark VAN DOREN, Robert Penn WARREN, and other writers of stature. In 1951 Ransom edited the anthology *The Kenyon Critics: Studies in Modern Literature from the "Kenyon Review."* The magazine suspended publication from 1970 to 1978 and began a new series in 1979, edited by Ronald Sharp and Frederick Turner. The expressed aim of the new series was to broaden the concept of literature to include many types of writing not ordinarily thought of as literary: writing from the fields of science, anthropology, philosophy, history, and politics, as well as fiction and poetry.

Kepler, Johannes (1571–1630)   German astronomer. Kepler helped to establish the validity of the Copernican system by his empirical formulation of the laws of planetary motion. Using the precise data of Tycho Brahe, he discovered that all planets move in elliptical orbits with the center of the sun as one of the foci, that the speed of a planet is related to its orbital position, and that the speeds of the different planets have a mathematical relationship to one another.

Kerensky, Aleksandr Fyodorovich (1881–1970)   Russian revolutionary leader. Kerensky became the head of the provincial government in 1917 after Tsar NICHOLAS II abdicated. He was overthrown by the BOLSHEVIKS in October 1917 because of his moderate policies, and he fled to Paris.

Kermode, [John] Frank (1919–   )   English critic and cultural historian. An English Renaissance scholar, Kermode combines his criticism of that period with his better-known work on modern literature. *Romantic Image* (1957) is a study of the use of image in literature by both SYMBOLISTS and romantics. In 1962 he published *Puzzles and Epiphanies*, a study of symbolism. *The Sense of an Ending* (1967) has as its underlying theme the idea that a sense of an ending gives form and order to both life and fiction. In later studies, such as *Continuities* (1968), *Renaissance Essays: Shakespeare, Spenser, Donne* (1971), and *Modern Essays* (1971), he has continued his study of the relationship between art and order. *The Genesis of Secrecy* (1979) is an inquiry into the nature of interpretation of narrative. *The Art of Telling* (1983) is a collection of writings on the novel.

Kern, Jerome [David] (1885–1945)   American composer of musical comedies. *Show Boat* (1927), with book and lyrics by Oscar HAMMERSTEIN 2nd, is regarded as an epochal work of American musical theatre. Some of his songs, such as "Ol' Man River" and "Smoke Gets in Your Eyes," have become standard favorites. Along with Irving BERLIN, Kern was in the top ranks of theatrical composers.

Kerouac, Jack (1922–1969)   American novelist and poet. Raised in Lowell, Massachusetts, Kerouac went to Columbia University on a football scholarship (1941). When a leg injury forced him off the team, his scholarship was dropped, and he withdrew from college. After a short stint in the merchant marine he was discharged as a "schizoid personality" and returned to live in New York City. There he renewed his seminal friendships with Allen GINSBERG and William S. BURROUGHS, whom he had met at Columbia, and began to write. His first novel, *The Town and the City* (1950), an account of his boyhood in Lowell, was well received, but it was not until the publication of ON THE ROAD seven years later that he became the rebel/cult hero who epitomized the style of living and writing associated with the BEAT MOVEMENT. Kerouac's books, written in loosely structured, spontaneous prose, are a blend of fiction and nonfiction. His fictional alter ego, Jack Duluoz, reflects his restless alienation and a pursuit of Zen *dharma* ("truth") through new experiences and drug, alcoholic, or sexual excesses. Kerouac recorded the real and fancied exploits of his generation of friends in such novels as *The Subterraneans* (1958), *The Dharma Bums* (1958), *Big Sur* (1962), *Desolation Angels* (1965), and *Satori in Paris* (1966). *Visions of Cody* (1972), published three years after his death, is an assortment of mood pieces, reminiscences, and conversations with his friend Neal Cassady and is held by many to be his best and most difficult work. *Mexico City Blues* (1959) is a volume of poetry. Kerouac was adversely affected by his own literary and personal notoriety. In the last years of his life, he drank heavily and, as he had at intervals throughout, lived alone with his mother and cut himself off from virtually all his friends.

Kesey, Ken [Elton] (1935–   )   American novelist. Kesey's literary reputation rests on two novels, *One*

Flew Over the Cuckoo's Nest (1962) and *Sometimes a Great Notion* (1964). *Cuckoo's Nest* employs STREAM OF CONSCIOUSNESS technique in a grim satire set in a mental institution. Distinctions between sanity and insanity and questions of freedom and responsibility are central issues in this highly acclaimed novel. *Sometimes a Great Notion* is a complex narrative saga of conflicts and loyalties in an Oregon logging family. On the heels of his literary success, Kesey became the leader of an itinerant band of hippies known as the "Merry Pranksters," whose exploits are described in Tom WOLFE's *The Electric Kool-Aid Acid Test* (1968). Kesey published *Demon Box* in 1986.

Ketch, John (known as Jack Ketch, d 1686)   English hangman and executioner, notorious for his barbarity. Ketch's name appeared in a ballad as early as 1678, and by 1702 it was associated with the executioner in Punch and Judy puppet-plays, which had recently been introduced from Italy.

Kevin, St.   An Irish saint of the 6th century. Legend relates that, like St. Senanus, he retired to an island where he vowed no woman should ever land. Kathleen tracked him to his retirement, but the saint hurled her from a rock, and her ghost never left the place while he lived. A rock at Glendalough (Wicklow) is shown as the bed of St. Kevin. Thomas Moore (1779–1852) has a poem on this tradition (*Irish Melodies*, iv).

Key, Ellen (1849–1926)   Swedish feminist and author. While Key was a prominent figure in Sweden, her works, proposing radical social views, gained her fame outside her own country. Her pacifist and feminist sympathies, as well as her broad humanitarian concerns, find expression in *Barnets århundrade* (1900; tr *The Century of the Child*, 1909), *Kvinnorörelsen* (1909; tr *The Woman Movement*, 1912), and *Kriget, freden och framtiden* (1914; tr *War, Peace, and the Future*, 1916).

Key, Francis Scott (1779–1843)   American lawyer and author of THE STAR-SPANGLED BANNER.

Keyes, Frances Parkinson (1885–1970)   American novelist. Keyes wrote dozens of successful novels in a long career that began with *The Old Gray Homestead* (1919). Her best-known work, *Dinner at Antoine's* (1948), is a murder mystery set in New Orleans a few weeks before Mardi Gras.

Keyne, St.   A Celtic saint, daughter of Brychan, king of Brecknock in the 5th century. Concerning her well, near Liskeard, Cornwall, it is said that if a bridegroom drinks therefrom before his bride, he will be master of his house, but if the bride gets the first draft, she will rule. Robert Southey (1774–1843) has a ballad, "The Well of St. Keyne" (1798), on this tradition. The man leaves his wife at the porch and runs to the well to get the first draft, but when he returns, his wife tells him his labor has been in vain, for she has "taken a bottle to church."

Keynes, John Maynard (first baron of Tilton, 1883–1946)   English economist. Originator of the so-called New Economics, Keynes lectured in economics at Cambridge from 1908 until his death, became an editor of the *Economic Journal* in 1912, and wrote such works as *The Economic Consequences of Peace* (1919), denouncing as unrealistic the reparations of the treaty of Versailles; *A Tract on Monetary Reform* (1923); *The End of Laissez-Faire* (1926); *A Treatise on Money* (1930); *The General Theory of Employment, Interest, and Money* (1936), his most influential and best-known work; and *How to Pay for the War* (1940).

Keynes served on the staff of the Treasury from 1915 to 1919 and was its principal representative at the Paris Peace Conference of 1919. During the 1930s, he advised wide government expenditure as a counter measure to deflation and depression. Though his suggestions were less followed in Great Britain, they became the foundation of President Roosevelt's recovery program in the U.S. At the close of World War II, Keynes was influential in planning for the World Bank and for the stabilization of international currency. Though his doctrine of deficit spending has been widely opposed, he was undoubtedly the most brilliant British economist of his time. Keynes was a member of the BLOOMSBURY GROUP.

Keyserling, Count Hermann Alexander (1880–1946)   Estonian social philosopher and mystic of German stock. Deprived of his estates by the Russian Revolution, he founded at Darmstadt the *Schule der Weisheit* ("School of Wisdom"). His thought was conditioned by contact with many cultures, the direct result of his far-flung travels, which earned him the well-deserved epithet "the wandering philosopher." His final ideal was a synthesis of the Western notion of "doing" with the Oriental concept of "being." His books include *Reisetagebuch eines Philosophen* (1919; tr *The Travel Diary of a Philosopher*, 1925) and *Schöpferische Erkenntnis* (1922; tr *Creative Understanding*, 1929).

Kezia   A little girl, the heroine of Katherine MANSFIELD's stories about her childhood in New Zealand.

Kgositsile, Keorapetse [William] (1938–   )   South African poet. Kgositsile went into voluntary exile in his early twenties and worked as a journalist in Dar Es Salaam before continuing his education in the U.S. The poems in *Spirits Unchained: Paeans* (1969), *For Melba* (1970), and *My Name Is Afrika* (1971) are personal and anguished; his verse revolves around the central paradox of seeking connection with others while recognizing the ultimate isolation of the individual.

Khadijah   MUHAMMED's first wife and, according to the KORAN, one of the four perfect women. The other three are FATIMA, the prophet's daughter, Mary, daughter of Imran, and ASIA, wife of the Pharaoh drowned in the Red Sea.

khedive   The title, from 1867 to 1914, of the ruler of Egypt, as viceroy of the sultan of Turkey. The word is

Turkish, derived from Persian, and means "prince" or "viceroy."

Khepera   An Egyptian solar deity represented by the beetle.

Khlebnikov, Velemir Vladimirovich (1885–1922)   Russian poet. One of the originators of FUTURISM in Russia, Khlebnikov was an inventive poet whose searchings for new poetic techniques helped revivify Russian poetry. His fellow futurist Vladimir MAYAKOVSKY described him as "the Columbus of new poetic continents now settled and cultivated by us." Khlebnikov, who loved old Slavic culture, replaced his original first name, Viktor, with the more archaic Velemir.

Khnemu   An Egyptian ram-headed deity, worshipped especially in the region of the five cataracts of the Nile.

Khrushchev, Nikita Sergeyevich (1894–1971)   Soviet government leader (1953–64). A factory worker, Khrushchev joined the Communist Party in 1918 and began a rapid rise through the ranks. In 1939 he was elected to the ruling body of the Soviet Union, the Politburo (renamed the Presidium in 1952). He was named, in 1949, as a secretary of the Communist Party Central Committee. After Stalin's death, he became the first secretary of the Party, sharing power with Georgy Malenkov, who was chairman of the Council of Ministers (the head of government). Malenkov resigned in 1955, and Nikolay Bulganin became head of state, to be ousted by Khrushchev in 1958. Khrushchev was deposed and disgraced in 1964. Two volumes of his memoirs, *Khrushchev Remembers* and *Khrushchev Remembers: The Last Testament*, were published in English in 1970 and 1974.

Khrushchev's speech at the twentieth Congress of the Communist Party in 1956 created a sensation by its violent attack on the memory of STALIN. The de-Stalinization campaign, thus instituted, created a freer atmosphere that was quickly reflected in Soviet literature and became known as THE THAW after the title of a novel by Ilya EHRENBURG. Khrushchev, however, kept a watchful eye on the work of Soviet writers and several times personally admonished them to maintain the correct spirit of loyalty to the Party and state.

Ki   In Sumerian mythology, the primeval earth goddess. Born of Nammu, the sea, she bore the air god ENLIL by her brother-consort AN, with whom she was originally joined as one. Enlil separated them, An becoming the upper sky. In religion she was supplanted by such younger counterparts as NINTU.

Kiblah   The point of adoration toward which Muslims turn when they worship; i.e., the direction of the KAABA at Mecca. In mosques, the direction is shown by the *mihrab*, a niche in the interior wall.

Kidd, William (known as Captain Kidd, 1645?–1701)   Scottish-born English pirate. Kidd was originally an affluent ship owner and sea captain who saw service against French privateers during King William's War and was later engaged by the British government to suppress piracy in the Indian Ocean. By 1699 a combination of circumstances, including a mutinous crew, had induced Kidd to turn to piracy; he captured several vessels and was declared a pirate by British authorities. Informed that he would be pardoned, he landed at Boston and was promptly arrested. He was sent to England, tried, and hanged at Execution Dock in London.

After his death, Kidd became a legendary figure in both England and the U.S. He became the hero of many ballads, his ghost was seen on several occasions, and numerous attempts were made to unearth a fabulous treasure which he supposedly buried in various points ranging from Oak Island, Nova Scotia, to Gardiner's Island, New York. James Fenimore COOPER referred to Kidd in several works, notably *The Water Witch* (1830), a novel. The influence of the Kidd legend is also evident in POE's short story "The Gold Bug" (1843) and STEVENSON's novel *Treasure Island* (1883).

Kidnapped (1886)   A historical novel by Robert Louis STEVENSON. It deals with the adventures of David Balfour, the young hero, and Alan Breck, a Jacobite who is considered one of Stevenson's most interesting and best-drawn characters. A sequel, *Catriona*, was published in 1893.

Kielland, Alexander Lange (1849–1907)   Norwegian novelist, short-story writer, and playwright. Although Kielland came from a wealthy merchant background, his writing was spurred by a strong sense of social protest. In *Arbeidsfolk* (1881) he attacked the bureaucracy; in *Sankt Hans Fest* (1887) he denounced the clergy. His best-known work, *Garman og worse* (1880; tr *Garman and Worse*, 1885), contains scathing attacks on hypocrisy and injustice but is tempered by lyrical nature descriptions and childhood memories.

Kiely, Benedict (1919–   )   Irish novelist, short-story writer, historian, and critic. Kiely's first book, *Counties of Contention* (1945), deals, as does much of his later work, with the spiritual and political consequences of the partition of Ireland. Two literary studies followed, and he also wrote novels, among them *In a Harbour Green* (1949) and *Honey Seems Bitter* (1952), both set in a small northern port; *There Was an Ancient House* (1955), based on his own religious novitiate; and *The Captain with the Whiskers* (1960), about the domestic tyranny of an Ulster patriot. Kiely then turned to the short-story form, of which he is an acknowledged master, writing for THE NEW YORKER for many years. His collections include *A Journey to the Seven Streams* (1963), *A Ball of Malt and Madame Butterfly* (1973), and *The State of Ireland* (1980). He published *Nothing Happens in Carmincross* in 1985.

Kierkegaard, Søren Aabye (1813–1855)   Danish philosopher. The early years of Kierkegaard's life were dark and cheerless, his home a lonely, gloomy place. Kierkegaard published his first philosophical works under pseud-onyms. In contrast to HEGEL's objective philosophy, he proposed, in such works as *Stadier paa Livets Vej* (*Stages on Life's Way*, 1845) and *Gjentagelsen* (*Repetition*, 1843), a system based on faith, knowledge, thought, and reality. In *Enten Eller* (*Either-Or*, 1843), he discusses the razor-edge decision made by man's free will, which determines his personal relation to God. In 1846 events in his private life led him to experience a deeper commitment to Christianity and to attack with new vigor orthodox, organized religion. For Kierkegaard the relation with God must be a lonely, agonizing experience of a man's inner solitude. During his lifetime he was not recognized in Denmark as a genius; a rebel against secure bourgeois morality, he was mocked and reviled for his unorthodox views and for the strange, ungainly figure he cut on the cheerful streets of Copenhagen. The 20th-century revival of Kierkegaard was initiated by the German philosophers HEIDEGGER and JASPERS, and furthered by members of the French existentialist movement, notably SARTRE and CAMUS.

Killers, The (1927)   A story by Ernest HEMINGWAY. One of Hemingway's most famous works, this story has as its protagonist Nick ADAMS. Two hired gunmen from the city enter a small-town lunchroom in search of Ole Andreson, an ex-prizefighter, whom they announce they are going to kill in revenge for a double-cross. Nick, a customer in the lunchroom, goes to warn Andreson in his boarding house. Andreson knows there is no final escape for him and refuses to help himself; his only remaining decision is when to go out and meet his death. The focus of the story is not so much city gangsters ("the killers") as it is Nick and the effect on him of Andreson's acceptance of violence. The story appeared in the collection MEN WITHOUT WOMEN.

Kilmer, [Alfred] Joyce (1886–1918)   American poet. Kilmer is remembered chiefly for his poem "Trees," which was published first in POETRY in August 1913, won its author national fame, and became the title poem of *Trees and Other Poems* (1914). He was killed in France during World War I.

Kim (1901)   A novel of Indian life by Rudyard KIPLING. The hero, Kimball O'Hara, is an Irish orphan raised as an Indian in Lahore. He attaches himself to a holy man, an old lama from Tibet who is on a quest for the mystic River of the Arrows, and together the pair roam about India. By accident Kim is recognized by his father's Irish regiment and, much against his wishes, is sent to school. During the long vacations he still tramps with his beloved lama. His intimate knowledge of India makes him a valuable asset to the English Secret Service, in which he wins renown while still a boy. The book abounds in brilliant descriptions of Indian scenes and deeply sympathetic portraits of her people.

King, Henry (1592–1669)   English poet and churchman, bishop of Chichester. An intimate friend of Donne and possibly his first editor, he was also close to Ben Jonson and Izaak Walton. King wrote two volumes of verse: *Psalmes of David Turned into Meter* (1651) and *Poems, Elegies, Paradoxes and Sonnets* (1657).

King, Martin Luther, Jr. (1929–1968)   American minister, civil rights activist, and writer. Born in Atlanta, Georgia, the son and grandson of middle-class Baptist ministers, King graduated from Morehouse College in 1951 and earned a Ph.D. from Boston University in 1955. King was influenced by the life and teachings of GANDHI, whose doctrines of nonviolence and passive resistance were to become his own guiding principles. King led a boycott by blacks of Montgomery's bus system in 1955, which culminated in a U.S. Supreme Court ruling that the Alabama laws on bus segregation were unconstitutional. King's account of the boycott was published as *Stride Toward Freedom* (1958). In 1957 King organized the Southern Christian Leadership Conference (SCLC) as the basis for a new civil rights movement based on nonviolence. Over the next thirteen years he helped lead numerous protests throughout the South; frequently arrested and jailed, he was stabbed once and had his house bombed three times. In 1963 he wrote the famous *Letter from Birmingham Jail*, replying to eight clergymen who had criticized his work. It was partly due to this that the great March on Washington in support of civil rights legislation took place on August 28, 1963, when King gave his memorable "I have a dream" speech. The following year King was awarded the Nobel Peace Prize, at thirty-five the youngest person to receive it.

As the 1960s wore on, King became the first to align the civil rights struggle with that against the rapidly escalating war in Vietnam, expressing his views on both subjects in *Where Do We Go from Here: Chaos or Community?* The civil rights movement itself became increasingly divided as many of the more militant black leaders felt that a creed of nonviolence was an insufficient response to white oppression. King continued to lead protests, however, such as the 1965 voter registration drive in Selma, Alabama. In 1968, in Memphis for a demonstration for striking sanitation workers, King was assassinated by a white man, James Earl Ray, who was subsequently sentenced to ninety-nine years in prison.

King, Stephen [Edwin] (1947–   )   American novelist and short-story writer. King is a phenomenally popular horror-fiction writer. His books have sold millions of copies and several have been made into successful films. Some consider his best novel to be his first, *Carrie* (1974), the story of an outcast schoolgirl, tormented by her classmates, who discovers she has amazing telekinetic powers with which she eventually exacts horrible revenge on her persecutors. King's other books include the novels *Salem's Lot* (1974), *The Shining* (1977), *Firestarter* (1980), *Cujo* (1981), *Christine* (1983), and the story collection *Night Shift* (1978).

Kingis Quair (1424; pub 1783)   A long poem written by James I of Scotland, while he was a prisoner in England. It laments his fortune and celebrates the beautiful woman, Lady Jane Beaufort, whom he married. *Quair* is an older form of *quire*, "booklet."

King John, The Life and Death of (c1595)   A historical play by SHAKESPEARE. The action concerns the efforts of the weak and despicable King JOHN to fend off the royal claims of Arthur, duke of Brittany, who is supported by the king of France. In spite of the able support of Philip FAULCONBRIDGE, John alienates the English nobility and runs disastrously afoul of the pope. In the end he is poisoned, and his son, Henry III, becomes king. An earlier play, *The Troublesome Reign of King John* (pub 1591), was once attributed to Shakespeare.

King Lear (c1605)   A tragedy by SHAKESPEARE. Seeking peace in his old age, the weary Lear, king of Britain, resolves to divide his kingdom among his three daughters, GONERIL, REGAN, and CORDELIA, but first he requires that they make declarations of their love for him. The first two, crafty and insincere, profess their love in the most grandiloquent terms and are each rewarded, in turn, by the bestowal of a third of the kingdom. Cordelia, the youngest and favorite, then disappoints Lear by stating that she loves him according to her bond, "nor more, nor less." Rage blinds him to the deeper, truer love of Cordelia, and he divides the portion designed for her between her sisters. Thus undowered, she is taken by the king of France for his wife. Lear now begins to suffer for his foolish vanity. It quickly becomes clear, as he spends a month first with one and then the other, that Goneril and Regan are grasping hypocrites and that they are bent on humiliating Lear. Goneril refuses to put up his entire retinue and demands that he reduce it to twenty-five; Regan puts Lear's servant, the faithful earl of KENT, in the stocks. In a famous scene, Lear goes out upon the heath in a raging storm and raves in an agony of madness. Cordelia, learning from Kent of her father's condition, brings an army from France to Britain's shores. Goneril and Regan unite against this threat. Cordelia sends attendants out after her father, and they are happily reunited in a tent in the French camp. In the battle that follows, Cordelia's army is defeated and they are taken prisoner. Goneril poisons Regan for love of EDMUND, the evil bastard son of GLOUCESTER, then stabs herself. By an order countermanded too late, Cordelia is hanged in prison and Lear, broken-hearted, dies soon after. A subplot, paralleling the main plot, involves Gloucester, who allows the jealous Edmund to turn him against his real son, EDGAR, who loves him. See FOOL; LEIR, KING.

King of the Wood (Lat, *Rex Nemorensis*)   The priest of Diana, who must pluck the golden bough (as Aeneas did before his descent into the underworld) and then slay his predecessor in a duel before entering on his office at Aricia on the shores of a lake (now Lago di Nemi) in the Alban Mountains, where the goddess had a sacred grove. A discussion of this myth is the opening passage in, and explains the title of, Sir James G. Frazer's THE GOLDEN BOUGH.

King Philip (d 1676)   Name given by English settlers to Metacomet, the son of Massasoit and chief of the Wampanoag tribe. During King Philip's War (1675–76), the most important Indian uprising in New England, Wampanoag, Narragansett, and Nipmuck warriors made sudden raids on frontier settlements; many towns were destroyed and captives taken, including the famous Mrs. Mary ROWLANDSON. Although the Indians were initially successful, the movement collapsed after Philip's death. See TOMPSON, BENJAMIN.

Kings, The First Book of and **The Second Book of**   Two books of the OLD TESTAMENT. Together these books—originally one—relate the history of Israel from the last years of DAVID to the Babylonian Exile. They record the glories of SOLOMON's reign (c960 BC) and the decline of the Southern Kingdom, which followed, ending with the destruction of the temple in Jerusalem in 586 BC.

king's evil   Scrofula. It was so called from a notion that prevailed from the reign of Edward the Confessor to that of Queen Anne that it could be cured by the royal touch. The Jacobites considered that the power did not descend to William III and Anne because the divine hereditary right was not fully possessed by them, but an office for such healing remained in the Prayer Book till 1719. The last person touched in England was Dr. Johnson, in 1712, when only thirty months old, by Queen Anne.

The French kings laid claim to the same divine power from the time of Clovis (AD 481). On Easter Sunday, 1686, Louis XIV touched sixteen hundred persons, using these words: *le Roi te touche, Dieu te guérisse.*

Kingsley, Rev. Charles (1819–1875)   English clergyman, novelist, and poet. Kingsley was much involved in the social reform movements of his time, having been strongly influenced by Carlyle. His earliest novels, *Alton Locke* (1850) and *Yeast* (1851), deal with Christian Socialism, a movement with which he was associated. His best-known books are the historical romances *Westward Ho!* (1855) and *Hereward the Wake* (1865) and his fairy tale THE WATER-BABIES. A review of his in *Macmillan's Magazine* led to the famous controversy with Cardinal Newman, which moved the latter to publish his *Apologia pro vita sua* (1864). Kingsley's brother, Henry, was also a novelist. See MUSCULAR CHRISTIANITY.

Kingu   A Babylonian demigod. Kingu was a general and consort of Tiamat, in the WAR OF THE GODS. After her defeat, Marduk killed him and fashioned man out of his blood and bones.

Kinnell, Galway (1927–   )   American poet, translator, and novelist. Kinnell is a poet of dark, tragic intensity. He acknowledges Walt WHITMAN and W. B. YEATS as his inspirations: Whitman for his ability to find the sacred in the ordinary and Yeats for his imagery and symbolism. Kinnell's own work eschews abstraction in favor of a fiercely personal expressiveness. In *Body Rags* (1968) and *The Book of Nightmares* (1971) he explores the primitive states of human consciousness, the mysterious struggle of the birth process, and man's dreadful journeys into nightmare. *The Avenue Bearing the Initial of Christ into the New World* (1974) is a collection of poems written between 1946 and 1964. The title is taken from a highly acclaimed poem that appeared in Kinnell's first collection, *What a Kingdom It Was* (1960). Kinnell's views on poetry, presented in a series of interviews, are contained in *Walking Down the Stairs* (1978). *Mortal Acts, Mortal Words* (1980) is a volume of poetry.

Kinsella, Thomas (1928–   )   Irish poet. Kinsella's earliest lyric poems and ballads deal with the pursuit of love. *Poems* (1956) and *Another September* (1958) combine charm and earthy wit with an elegiac tone that runs through his mature work, all against the dark backdrop of a divided Ireland. *Downstream* (1962) is concerned directly with the public brutality and moral complexities individuals face in daily life. *Wormwood* (1966) is a powerfully personal sequence about a marriage in crisis. *Nightwalker and Other Poems* (1968), his first volume after moving to the U.S., and *New Poems* (1973) combine the nostalgia of childhood memories with a deep foreboding of the erosion of public and private values. In the visionary *Butcher's Dozen* (1972), about "Bloody Sunday" in Londonderry, his troubled sense of a moral vacuum in Ireland complements his anger at England's destructive role there. In 1979 Kinsella published *Poems 1956–1973* and *Peppercanister Poems: 1972–1978*, which make available all of his work in its rich variety, including his brilliant translation of the saga of the legendary Irish hero Cú Chulainn in *The Tain* (1969). In 1985 he published *Her Vertical Smile*.

Kinsey, Alfred Charles (1894–1956)   American biologist and sex researcher known for his pioneering statistical studies of human sexual behavior, published in two volumes and known popularly as the Kinsey Report: *Sexual Behavior of the Human Male* (1948) and *Sexual Behavior of the Human Female* (1953). Both works attracted considerable attention and his work effectively opened up an entirely new field.

Kipling, Rudyard (1865–1936)   English short-story writer, poet, and novelist. Born in India of English parents, Kipling was brought up speaking both Hindustani and English; the impressions of his early years in India remained indelible. He was taken to England at the age of six and left to board with paid foster parents, a miserable experience later described in the story "Baa, Baa, Black Sheep," alleviated by his association with his uncle, Sir Edward Burne-Jones. In 1878 he entered an inferior boarding school for the sons of fathers in the Indian Services. His schoolboy experiences served as the basis for Stalky and Co. Four years later, at the age of seventeen, he returned to India, where his father had secured for him a position at the *Civil*

and Military Gazette of Lahore. Here he began his first stories about life in British-ruled India. The verses in *Departmental Ditties* (1886) and many of the stories collected in Plain Tales from the Hills and Soldiers Three were originally written for the *Gazette*. The stories he produced as editor, during his last two years in India, of the Allahabad *Pioneer* were collected in *The Phantom Rickshaw* (1889), which included the famous story The Man Who Would Be King.

In 1889 Kipling returned to England via Japan and America, writing letters during the trip that were to form *From Sea to Sea* (1899). Once in London he enjoyed spectacular success: all his Indian volumes were republished, and he followed up quickly with *Life's Handicap* (1891), a collection of Indian stories which included The Man Who Was; *The Light That Failed* (1891), a novel which demonstrated that Kipling's gift was for the short story; and Barrack-Room Ballads, a collection of poems that included Gunga Din, Fuzzy Wuzzy, Tommy, and "Mandalay." He also wrote a less successful romance, *The Naulakha* (1892), in collaboration with Woolcott Balestier, an American whose sister Caroline he married in the same year. They settled on her family's estate in Brattleboro, Vermont, and during the next five years Kipling published *Many Inventions* (1893), The Jungle Book, *The Second Jungle Book* (1895), *The Seven Seas* (1896), and *Captains Courageous* (1897). Dissatisfied with his life in America, Kipling moved back to England and settled in Sussex. Except for a brief visit to New York in 1899, when his daughter died of pneumonia and he almost died of the same disease, Kipling never returned to the U.S., and spoke of it with bitterness, despite his enormous popularity there. In the ensuing years he published a patriotic poem, Recessional, for Queen Victoria's Diamond Jubilee, *The Day's Work* (1898), *Stalky and Co.* (1899), Kim, Just So Stories, the only book he illustrated, *The Five Nations* (1903), *Traffics and Discoveries* (1904), *Puck of Pook's Hill* (1906), *Actions and Reactions* (1909), *Rewards and Fairies* (1909), *A Diversity of Creatures* (1917), *The Irish Guards in the Great War* (1923), a memorial to his only son, John, fallen in battle, *Debits and Credits* (1926), *Limits and Renewals* (1932), and *Something of Myself* (1937), an autobiography left unfinished at his death.

In 1907 Kipling became the first English writer to be awarded the Nobel Prize. Although his glorification of empire and his conviction that it was both the right and responsibility of the English to civilize the heathen of the world, memorably stated in his poem "The White Man's Burden" (1899; see white man's burden) antagonized some readers and many critics, particularly after his death, his worldwide popularity was phenomenal. Apart from the issue of imperialism, sophisticated readers recognize in Kipling an extraordinary ear for language, literary and vernacular, and a precise use of spare, vivid imagery.

Kipphardt, Heinar (1922–1982)   German dramatist. A practicing physician who was also chief dramaturg
(1950–59) at the Deutsches Theater in East Berlin,
Kipphardt moved to West Germany (1959), where his
independent Marxist views would not be imperiled. His
early plays were satires on political hypocrisy, but he
achieved distinction for his documentary dramas employing EPIC THEATRE techniques that reexamined the evidence
of disputed political-judicial cases. The first of these was
Der Hund des Generals (*The General's Dog*, 1962), in
which he indicts a German officer who sent a whole regiment into deadly fire because one of the men had accidentally killed his dog. Kipphardt believed that guilt is felt only
by those who will look at the truth; his concern in the play
was that the general in question, and others like him, were
living comfortably in a respected retirement. *Joel Brand*
(1963) focuses on Adolf Eichmann's dealings with the British and Americans over the deportation of Hungarian Jews.
In *In der Sache J. Robert Oppenheimer* (1964; tr *In the
Matter of J. Robert Oppenheimer*, 1967), an examination
of the testimony in the case of that eminent scientist shifts
from German guilt to universal responsibility for human
survival. In *Die Nacht, in der der Chef geschlachtet wurde*
(*The Night the Boss Was Slaughtered*, 1965) he returned to
satire, parodying the crass ideals of a German bourgeois
couple.

Kipps (1905)   A novel by H. G. WELLS. Arthur
Kipps, a wretched little draper's apprentice, suddenly
comes into a fortune. He marries an ambitious, upper-class
woman and is driven nearly mad by his (and her) efforts to
fit him into his new social world. He flees and finally marries a housemaid, the girl of his boyhood dreams. He finds
happiness only when he is eventually deprived of his
wealth by an embezzling solicitor and settles back down to
the simple life of a shopkeeper.

Kirby, William   See GOLDEN DOG, THE.

Kirilov, Aleksey Nilich   In DOSTOYEVSKY's novel
THE POSSESSED, a fanatically rebellious atheist who resolves
to commit suicide, asserting man's freedom from his terrible fate—death. The idea has been implanted in the half-
mad KIRILOV by STAVROGIN. The revolutionary Pyotr
VERKHOVENSKY tries to persuade Kirilov to leave a suicide
note confessing to the murder of SHATOV, who had been
killed by Verkhovensky's group.

Kirkup, James (1927–   )   English novelist, poet,
translator, and playwright. Among Kirkup's many collections of poetry are *The Drowned Sailor* (1947), *A Spring
Journey* (1954), *The Prodigal Son* (1959), and *The Body
Servant* (1971). They reflect his facility in different verse
forms and his keen eye for detail, turning commonplace
scenes into vividly evocative poetry. *The Love of Others*
(1962), his autobiographical first novel, is distinctive as a
happy record of his working-class childhood. *These Horned
Islands* (1962) and *Japan Behind the Fan* (1970) are about
Japan, where Kirkup lived and taught for many years.

Kirov, Sergey Mironovich (1886–1934)   Russian
revolutionary leader. One of STALIN's chief aides and a
member of the Presidium (1930–34), Kirov was the secretary of the Communist Party for the Leningrad area. His
assassination in 1934 set off the purges of 1936–37.

kismet (fr Turk, *qismat*, "portion; lot")   Fate; the fulfillment of destiny.

Kit-cat Club   A club formed in the beginning of the
18th century by the leading Whigs of the day, whose meetings were held in the house of Christopher Catt, a pastry
cook. Catt's mutton pies, which were eaten at the club,
were also called *kit-cats*, and probably gave the club its
name. The publisher Jacob Tonson was secretary, and the
members included Richard STEELE, Joseph ADDISON, William CONGREVE, Samuel Garth, John VANBRUGH, Robert
WALPOLE, and William Pulteney. Their portraits by Sir
Godfrey Kneller were reduced to three-quarter length in
order to accommodate them to the size of the clubroom
wainscot. Hence, a three-quarter portrait is still called a
kit-cat.

Kittredge, George Lyman (1860–1941)   American teacher and scholar. Kittredge, who taught at Harvard
University from 1888 to 1936, was an authority on Chaucer and Shakespeare. Among his important works were *The
Language of Chaucer's "Troilus"* (1894); *English and Scottish Popular Ballads* (1904), with H. C. Sargent; *Chaucer
and His Poetry* (1915); *Sir Thomas Malory* (1925); *Witchcraft in Old and New England* (1929); and an edition of
The Complete Works of Shakespeare (1936).

Kivi, Aleksis (pen name of A. Stenvall, 1834–1872)
Finnish novelist, playwright, and poet. Regarded as his
country's greatest 19th-century writer, Kivi found inspiration for his best work in the country life of Finland. In
Kullervo (1864) he dramatized an episode from the KALE-
VALA, while in the comedy *Nummisuutarit* (*Shoemakers of
the Heath*, 1864) and in the novel *Seitsemän veljestä*
(*Seven Brothers*, 1870), he depicted Finnish peasant life
with a realism and humor that have never been matched by
any other writer. He is also noted for his numerous collections of lyric verse.

Kjartan   See LAXDALE SAGA.

Klabund (pen name of Alfred Henschke, 1890–1928)
German novelist, playwright, and poet. Klabund was a versatile writer with expressionistic leanings and wide cultural
interests which are expressed in his historical novels,
Mohammed (1917), *Borgia* (1928), and *Rasputin* (1929).
Under the shock of World War I he wrote his best-known
novel, *Bracke* (1918), about a wise fool, similar to EULEN-
SPIEGEL, who fought for truth and justice at the time of the
REFORMATION. He is also known for his sensitive transla-
tions and adaptations of Chinese literature, particularly for
his play *Der Kreidekreis* (1924), an adaptation of the THE
CIRCLE OF CHALK that provided the basis for Brecht's CAU-
CASIAN CHALK CIRCLE.

Klaus, Peter   German legendary hero, the proto-type of RIP VAN WINKLE. Klaus is a goatherd of Sittendorf who is led into a deep dell, where he finds twelve knights silently playing skittles. He drinks of their wine and is over-powered with sleep. When he awakens, he is amazed at the height of the grass; and upon discovering how strange his village seems, he realizes he has been asleep for twenty years.

Klee, Paul (1879–1940)   Swiss painter. Generally considered one of the great masters of modern painting, Klee spent much of his life in Germany; he joined the BLAUE REITER group in 1912 and taught at the BAUHAUS from 1920 to 1929. Interested in the abstract meaning of pictorial representation, he was a highly original metaphys-ical painter who, by his playful line and subtle use of color, created an art of great whimsy and spontaneity.

Klein, A[braham] M[oses] (1909–1972)   Cana-dian poet. Klein was born in Montreal and educated at McGill University. A lawyer by profession and a student of Hebrew and rabbinical learning, he edited a Jewish period-ical and participated in Zionist and socialist politics. His love of Jewish folk culture and his strong concern with anti-Semitism are evident in three volumes of his poetry: *Hath Not a Jew* (1940), *Poems* (1944), and *Hitleriad* (1944). *The Rocking Chair* (1948) gives voice to Klein's sympathy for other persecuted minorities, including French Canadians, Indians, and poets. *The Second Scroll* (1951) is a religious parable in novel form.

Kleist, Heinrich von (1777–1811)   German dram-atist and novella writer, considered by many the greatest of all German authors in both genres. As a young man, Kleist was induced by his family to undertake a career in the Prussian army, but in 1799 he resigned his commission and began an intensive study of mathematics and philos-ophy in hopes of perfecting his mind and gaining intellec-tual control over his destiny. In 1801, however, after read-ing Kant, his faith in the perfectability of knowledge was shattered, and for the first time he turned decisively to a career in writing. During 1801–2 he worked on two plays, *Robert Guiskard* and *Die Familie Schroffenstein* (*The Schroffenstein Family*, pub 1803), a tragedy of errors influ-enced by Shakespeare's ROMEO AND JULIET. Though he never carried the latter beyond a fragmentary stage, he felt that it would be his *magnum opus*, and parts of it were highly praised by WIELAND; but in 1803, in a fit of despair, he destroyed the manuscript, and the fragment of it that he published in 1808 consisted only of some five hundred lines restored from memory. The year 1803, however, also saw the completion of his great comedy *Der zerbrochene Krug* (*The Broken Jug*, 1811). He then spent three years as a government official in Königsberg. But in 1807 he went to Dresden where, with his friend Adam Müller (1779–1829), he founded the periodical *Phöbus* (1808) in which his greatest novella, MICHAEL KOHLHAAS, appeared. By

1809 he had also completed several more plays: an adapta-tion of MOLIÈRE's *Amphitryon*, DAS KÄTHCHEN VON HEIL-BRONN, and PENTHESILEA.

Around 1808, along with the growing anti-Napoleonic movement in Germany, Kleist's interests became more patriotic. In 1810, again with Müller, he began editing the *Berliner Abendblätter* (*Berlin Evening News*), in which he took a firm stand against NAPOLEON; and in the same year he completed his last play, the strongly patriotic PRINZ FRIEDRICH VON HOMBURG. But in 1811, after his newspaper had been closed by the government, after all hope had faded of a successful German uprising against Napoleon in the near future, and in despair about his lack of literary recognition, he took his own life.

In form, Kleist's dramas show the clear influence of SCHILLER's classicism; but Kleist's characters, unlike Schil-ler's, have no clearly defined structure of moral principles and personal standards upon which to base their actions. They tend to vacillate unpredictably among various atti-tudes, to show some of the nervousness and insecurity of the modern individual. Some theoretical background to Kleist's dramatic style may be found in his essay *Über das Marionettentheater* (*On the Puppet-Theatre*, 1810), in which he suggested that man's self-consciousness hinders his freedom of action, that man cannot act purely and sim-ply in accordance with conscious ideas or standards.

Klimt, Gustave (1862–1918)   Austrian painter. Klimt was a painter primarily of decorative murals and pos-ters in Vienna and, in 1898, was a founder of the Vienna Secession, a group of painters working in the ART NOUVEAU style. His large paintings are characterized by richly orna-mented abstract backgrounds from which naturalistically rendered figures and details emerge. *The Kiss*, painted in 1908, exemplifies this style.

Kline, Franz (1910–1962)   American painter. Kline's early works were generally figurative portraits or urban scenes. By 1950 he had developed a completely abstract style using large white canvases covered with broad, forceful black strokes. His spontaneous, energetic approach to painting set him in the vanguard of ABSTRACT EXPRESSIONISM, along with his friend DE KOONING. By the end of his career, he reintroduced color into his work, as in *Dahlia* (1959), but he retained the tension and power of his black-white abstractions.

Klinger, Friedrich Maximilian (1752–1831)   German dramatist of the STURM UND DRANG, which took its name from the title of his play of 1776. His works are noted for boldness of expression and freedom of form. Goethe helped him through Giessen university.

Klingsor   An evil magician in medieval German legend. His small role in Wolfram von Eschenbach's *Par-zival* (13th century) is greatly expanded in Wagner's opera *Parsifal* (see PARZIVAL). He also appears in the stories of the WARTBURG singing contest.

Klondike   A region in the Yukon territory of Canada, famous for its gold mines. See SERVICE, ROBERT WILLIAM.

Klopstock, Friedrich Gottlieb (1724–1803) German poet in the movement of irrationalism. In Klopstock's preference for classical forms, especially the elegy and ode, and his virtually total rejection of rhyme, he was consciously attempting to develop for the German language a classical perfection of its own that would place it on a par with Greek and Latin. His major work is a religious epic in hexameters, *Der Messias* (*The Messiah*, 1773; final version, 1800), which shows the influence of Milton and pietism. He was deeply patriotic and hoped to be remembered as a prophet of his country's future greatness. This side of him appears in many of his lyrics and in his dramatic trilogy (1769–87) celebrating Hermann, the Germanic hero who defeated the Romans in the 1st century. His most famous prose work, *Die deutsche Gelehrtenrepublik* (*The German Republic of Letters*, 1774), proposes the outlines of a utopian state in Germany, and parallels the poet's more practical efforts toward the founding of a German Academy. See ARMINIUS; BODMER.

Knaben Wunderhorn, Des (The Boy's Wonderhorn; vol 1, 1805; vol 2, 1808; vol 3, 1818)   A collection of folk songs edited by Clemens BRENTANO and Achim von ARNIM, named for the first song in it. As opposed to Herder's earlier cosmopolitan collection of *Volkslieder* (*Folk Songs*, 1778–79), the *Wunderhorn* contains only German songs and was intended to draw attention specifically to the German folk spirit. It is not, however, a scholarly work, for Brentano and Arnim frequently made their own changes in the material they collected.

Knecht, Josef   The hero of HESSE's novel MAGISTER LUDI. Though Knecht rises to the position of master in the hierarchy of the glass-bead game, the fact that his name in German means servant is a central indication of the book's pervasive irony. Even as he dominates the game, he is dominated by it.

Kneller, Sir Godfrey (1646–1723)   German-born English portrait painter. Kneller was an exceedingly popular portraitist whose work won such favor with British aristocrats that he served as court painter to English kings from Charles II to George I.

Knickerbocker Group   A group of writers in and around New York during the first half of the 19th century. The name came from Diedrich Knickerbocker, the fictional character created by Washington IRVING as the "author" of A HISTORY OF NEW YORK FROM THE BEGINNING OF THE WORLD TO THE END OF THE DUTCH DYNASTY. The group's association was determined more by geographical proximity and friendships than by any commonly held literary principles. It was significant primarily because it marked the emergence of New York over Boston as a literary and cultural center. Among those associated with the group, besides Irving, were James Fenimore COOPER and William Cullen BRYANT.

Knight, G[eorge] Wilson (1897–1985)   English literary critic. His studies of Shakespeare's plays were original, controversial, and influential; in them he treats the plays as poems expressing cosmic ideas through patterns of imagery. Among his books are *The Wheel of Fire* (1930), *The Shakespearean Tempest* (1932), *The Golden Labyrinth* (1962), *Neglected Powers* (1971), *Shakespeare's Dramatic Challenge* (1977), and *Symbol of Man* (1979).

Knight of the Burning Pestle, The (c1607)   A comedy by Francis Beaumont. (See BEAUMONT AND FLETCHER.) A performance of a play called *The London Merchant* is interrupted by a grocer, who insists upon interspersing it with scenes from his own concoction, *The Knight of the Burning Pestle*, with his apprentice Ralph in the leading role. In the hilarious potpourri that follows, hackneyed sentimental scenes from bourgeois romance are laced with scenes from the grocer's effort, a parody of chivalric romance with Ralph cast as a kind of Don Quixote. The whole thing is continually interrupted with comments by the grocer and his wife.

Knights, The (Hippeis)   A comedy by ARISTOPHANES. Because of its political topicality, this play is less interesting to modern audiences than some others by Aristophanes. It is remarkable, however, for the freedom with which the playwright is able to attack the powerful Athenian demagogue Cleon and for the fact that it was awarded a first prize.

Knight's Gambit (1939)   A book of interrelated stories by William FAULKNER. Dealing with the various inhabitants of YOKNAPATAWPHA COUNTY, *Knight's Gambit* is a collection of detective stories in which Gavin STEVENS, the county attorney, ferrets out the real culprits and saves the innocent. The book is ingenious and skillfully narrated; perhaps the best story is "Monk," which deals with an idiot who is imprisoned for a murder he did not commit and who finally is incited to kill the warden who has befriended him.

Knight's Tale, The   One of THE CANTERBURY TALES of Geoffrey CHAUCER, a chivalric romance adapted from Boccaccio's TESEIDA. Theseus of Athens defeats Creon at Thebes, and the royal Theban cousins Palamon and Arcite are imprisoned in a tower. They see Emily, sister of Theseus' wife Hippolyta, walking in a garden; both fall in love with her. Arcite is released and banished from the territory, but he returns and works disguised as a court servant. Palamon escapes from prison, also determined to win Emily; the cousins meet by accident and determine to fight the next day in knightly regalia for the right to love her. Theseus interrupts the battle and orders that in a year the combatants will each bring one hundred knights to a tourney. Emily prays to Diana that both warriors will forget their quarrel and desert her, but her prayer is rejected. Palamon prays to Venus that he may win his beloved, while Arcite prays to Mars that he may triumph in the battle. Accordingly, Saturn arranges that Arcite be victorious in the joust but be thrown by his horse as he rides toward Emily. Dying, he yields Emily to Palamon, and after a suitable time the two are happily married.

Knights Templars See TEMPLARS.

Knowles, John (1926–   ) American novelist. Knowles was born in West Virginia and educated at Phillips Exeter Academy and at Yale. His early novels, reflecting his experiences at these schools, deal with the trials and confusions of adolescent rites of passage. His best-known novel is A *Separate Peace* (1960), about the friendship and treachery of two boys at an elite boarding school during World War II. This moving and accurate study of adolescence has enjoyed a continuing success that has overshadowed his subsequent books; in 1981 Knowles published *Peace Breaks Out*, a sequel to A *Separate Peace* that was unenthusiastically received.

Know-Nothing party In U.S. history, a popular name for the American party, which reached its greatest influence in 1854–55. Its program called for the exclusion of Catholics and foreigners from public office and for other nativist measures. It was originally a secret society whose members answered questions with "I don't know." The party split over the slavery issue and faded after the election of 1856.

Knox, John (1505–1572) Scottish reformer and founder of Presbyterianism. Knox was twice at Geneva in personal contact with Calvin (1554, 1556–58). He published six tracts dealing with religion in Scotland; the best known are his *Blasts of the Trumpet against the Monstrous Regiment of Women* (1st and 2nd, 1558). They were not meant for Queen Elizabeth but offended her deeply. Knox preached throughout Scotland against Mary Queen of Scots, whom he simply called "Jezebel," and against Catholicism in general.

kōan (Chin, *Kung-an*) In ZEN Buddhism, the problem or case to be meditated upon. Frequently paradoxical, and usually concerned with the sayings and actions of Chinese CH'AN (Zen) masters, it is one of the methods used for training in Japanese Rinzai Zen. The meditation on a seemingly nonsensical paradox such as "What is the sound of one hand clapping?" aims to disengage the mind from its traditional moorings in logical or consecutive thought and throw it back on the undifferentiated continuum of existence. A *kōan* is always studied under the guidance of a Zen master. There are some seventeen hundred *kōans*.

Kobayashi Issa (1763–1827) Japanese *haiku* poet. Kobayashi is noted for the humorous and simple treatment of his subjects. He was a prolific writer of both poetry and prose.

Kobayashi Takiji (1903–1933) Japanese novelist. Kobayashi was active as a member of the Communist Party and leader of the proletarian literary movement, but eventually he was arrested by the police and tortured to death.

His novel *Kanikōsen* (1929; tr *The Cannery Boat*, 1933) is generally considered the finest example of early Japanese left-wing literature.

Kober, Arthur (1900–1975) American writer. Kober is noted for his dialect-stories set in the Bronx or Hollywood. His famous "Bella stories" and others appeared regularly in THE NEW YORKER between 1926 and 1958 and were reissued in several books, including *My Dear Bella* (1941) and *Bella, Bella Kissed a Fella* (1951). His best-known book, *Having a Wonderful Time* (1937), the story of a group of vacationers in the Berkshires trying to improve themselves culturally, was made into a play (1937) and, later, a successful musical called *Wish You Were Here* (1952). His other contribution to the stage was the comedy A *Mighty Man Is He* (1959). Kober was married for a time to the playwright Lillian HELLMAN.

Kōbō Daishi See KŪKAI.

kobold In German folklore, a mischievous house spirit, similar to Robin Goodfellow or the Scottish Brownie. The kobold is also a gnome who works in the mines and forests.

Koch, Kenneth (1925–   ) American poet, playwright, and essayist. In the 1950s Koch was associated with the NEW YORK SCHOOL of poets. As is evident in *Poems* (1953) and the epic *Ko, or A Season on Earth* (1959), his work of this period was obscure and marked with preciosity. As he developed, his writing took on greater clarity, lyricism, social consciousness, and humor. *The Art of Love* (1975) was praised as a gracefully humorous book written in plain but beautiful language. *The Duplications* (1977) is an epic poem in the tradition of the Byronic OTTAVA RIMA. *The Burning Mystery of Anna in 1951* (1979) is a poetic reminiscence of Koch's life in New York in the early 1950s. As a teacher, Koch has communicated his delight in poetry to both the young and the very old. His teaching methods and samples of his students' work appear in *Wishes, Lies and Dreams: Teaching Children to Write Poetry* (1970), *Rose, Where Did You Get That Red?* (1973), and *I Never Told Anybody: Teaching Poetry Writing in a Nursing Home* (1977). In 1981, he edited (with Kate Farrell) *Sleeping on the Wing: An Anthology of Modern Poetry*.

Kochanowski, Jan (1530–1584) Polish poet. As one of the masters of Renaissance poetry, Kochanowski perfected Polish literary language and became the most prominent poet in Slavic literature of the 16th century. Traveling in Italy, he mastered Latin poetry, but upon his return to Poland, he wrote almost exclusively in Polish. Among his masterpieces were religious psalms, political poems, lyrical poetry, songs, and a series of nineteen *Laments* (*Treny*) commemorating the death of his daughter. He also wrote a poetic tragedy *Odprawa posłów Greckich* (1578; tr *The Dismissal of Grecian Envoys*, 1928). An English selection of his poetry, *Poems* (1928), is representative of his work.

Koestler, Arthur (1905–1983)   Hungarian-born English novelist and essayist. Koestler was raised in Vienna and began his career as a journalist and science writer. He went to Palestine as a reporter in 1926, where he became an ardent Zionist. His life in the Near East is described in his first volume of autobiography, *Arrow in the Blue* (1952). He joined the Communist Party in 1931 and withdrew at the beginning of the Stalinist purges in the late 1930s. In 1936 Koestler went to Spain to cover the Spanish Civil War for an English newspaper; he was arrested as a spy by the Fascists and sentenced to death. An account of his insights and reflections, until his release by British intervention, is stirringly recorded in *Spanish Testament* (1937). At the beginning of World War II he was arrested in France as a refugee and sent to the detention camp at Le Vernet, about which he wrote in *Scum of the Earth* (1941).

Koestler's second autobiographical volume, *The Invisible Writing* (1954), deals with his loss of faith in communism and describes the development of his profound concern with ethical problems. The conflict between true morality and social or political expediency became the focus of a sequence of novels that includes his chief work, DARKNESS AT NOON. *The Yogi and the Commissar* (1945), closed the cycle.

Thereafter, Koestler, the idealist who had been disillusioned by numerous ideologies, wrote from the vantage point of the "nonaligned left," covering an enormous range of topics, from a skeptical examination of Yoga and ZEN in *The Lotus and the Robot* (1961) to a new theory about the ethnic history of Eastern Europe, *The Thirteenth Tribe* (1975).

Koestler's works on science cover a vast range of subjects, from neurophysiology and molecular biology to behavioral psychology. He grew increasingly critical of scientific disciplines, however, as in *The Ghost in the Machine* (1967) and *The Case of the Midwife Toad* (1971), in which he reacted against a monolithic scientific view of man. In *Janus: A Summing Up* (1978), Koestler urged a transcendence beyond the need for clear answers and a receptivity to the "unknowable" around us. A man of penetrating and independent intelligence, Koestler earned a position as one of the important thinkers of his time. In 1983 Koestler, who had been ill for some time, and his wife took their own lives in a double suicide.

Kokoschka, Oskar (1886–1980)   Austrian painter and playwright. Known as an exponent of EXPRESSIONISM, Kokoschka is primarily significant as a painter. His plays, however, with their tendency to depict extreme human agony in almost abstract terms and with their use of an ecstatic and compressed diction, contributed considerably to the development of expressionist dramatic style. The best known are *Mörder, Hoffnung der Frauen* (*Murderer, Hope of Women*, 1907), *Hiob* (*Job*, 1917), and *Orpheus und Eurydike* (1910). In 1974 *My Life*, the translation of his autobiography (*Mein Leben*, 1972), appeared.

Kollwitz, Käthe [Schmidt] (1867–1945)   German graphic artist and sculptor. Kollwitz was deeply involved with and sympathetic to the struggles of the oppressed poor. In engravings, lithographs, and woodcuts she poignantly expressed her abhorrence of war, poverty, and exploitation. Death, as horror or as reprieve, was a recurring theme in her work and was the subject of an extensive series of prints executed in 1934 and 1935. Her best-known sculpture is a pair of mourning figures (actually herself and her husband) entitled *Memorial to the Fallen*, inspired by the death of her son Peter in World War I.

Konwicki, Tadeusz (1926–   )   Polish novelist and film director. A combatant in World War II, Konwicki often based his novels and films on the contrast between his war memories and postwar frustrations in a socialist country. *Sennik wspolczesny* (1963; tr *A Dreambook for Our Time*, 1969) was followed by a number of novels, among which *Kompleks Polski* (1977; tr *The Polish Complex*, 1982), describing "the Polish complex" in political terms, was banned and published illegally. The same fate met his next novel, *Mala apokalipsa* (1979; tr *A Minor Apocalypse*, 1983).

Kopit, Arthur L[ee] (1937–   )   American playwright. Kopit's plays are often characterized by dark humor, the juxtaposition of realistic and antirealistic elements, and some of the longest titles in theatrical history. His relationship to the THEATRE OF THE ABSURD is based more on these stylistic similarities than on a shared vision. While still an undergraduate at Harvard, he wrote nine plays, including *On the Runway of Your Life You Never Know What's Coming Off Next* (1957). He created a minor sensation with the production of *Oh Dad, Poor Dad, Mamma's Hung You in the Closet and I'm Feelin' So Sad* (1960), about an overprotective mother, Madame Rosepettle, who travels with her henpecked, retarded son, a pet piranha, man-eating Venus's-flytraps, and her dead husband in a coffin. After several unsuccessful plays and a time of relative obscurity, Kopit wrote *Indians* (1968), which established his reputation as a serious and inventive playwright. In *Wings* (1978) he suspended traditional narrative dramatic techniques to depict the fragmented perceptions of a stroke victim.

Koran   The sacred book of ISLAM. In Arabic, the word means "reading," from *quran*; the variant form, *Alcoran*, has a prefixed article. Written in the purest Arabic, it is considered the Word of God, the uncreated and eternal truth revealed to MUHAMMED by the angel GABRIEL. The tradition that the text should be transmitted orally had to be broken under the third Caliph, Othman, when the best Koran reciters had fallen in battle. There are 114 *Suras* or chapters in the Koran, unnumbered but individually named. Historically, the subject matter is of Jewish and, to a lesser extent, of Christian origin.

Korean War   The war between North and South Korea over the post-World War II balance of power in the peninsula. On June 25, 1950, North Korean troops, with Soviet military equipment and training, crossed the 38th parallel in a full-scale invasion of South Korea. In September the U.S., led by General Douglas MacArthur, entered the war to support the South and in October China entered the war for the North. After almost a year of advancing and retreating across the 38th parallel, MacArthur, who was defying presidential authority on foreign policy by advocating extending the war to China, was dismissed by Truman. On July 27, 1953, the armistice was signed during the EISENHOWER administration.

Perhaps the best-known novel to result from the Korean War is Richard Condon's *The Manchurian Candidate* (1959). Other works inspired by the war include James MICHENER's *The Bridges at Toko-Ri* (1953), S. L. A. Marshall's *Pork Chop Hill* (1956), and Richard Hooker's *M*A*S*H* (1968), which became a successful movie and even more successful TV series. See MAO TSE-TUNG; STALIN, JOSEPH; TRUMAN, HARRY S.

Kornbluth, Cyril M. (1923–1958)   American science fiction and fantasy writer. Kornbluth's early stories (1940–42) appeared under many pseudonyms. He is best known for his collaborations with Frederik POHL, *Wolfbane* (1959) and especially *The Space Merchants* (1952), a sharp satire of the future dystopian world of advertising. *Syndic* (1953) is his best solo novel.

Korniychuk, Oleksandr Yevdokimovich (1905–1972)   Soviet playwright. Noted for their use of Ukrainian themes and their strong nationalistic and militaristic devotion to the Soviet regime, Korniychuk's plays include *In the Ukrainian Steppes* (1941) and *Mr. Perkins's Mission to the Land of the Bolsheviks* (1944). He has won three Stalin Prizes.

Korobochka   A dull-witted woman landowner in Nikolay GOGOL's novel DEAD SOULS. Korobochka's fear that CHICHIKOV, the swindler-protagonist of the novel, may be cheating her (in their strange business deal) is instrumental in exposing him.

Korolenko, Vladimir Galaktionovich (1853–1921)   Russian writer and political radical. He was instrumental in helping the young Maksim GORKY get his start in literature. Korolenko, who was exiled to Siberia for six years by the Tsarist government, was also opposed to the Bolshevik regime. Korolenko's best works are "Son Makara" (1885; tr "Makar's Dream," 1892), a short story depicting the death of a Siberian native; "Bez yazyka" (1895; tr "In a Strange Land," 1925), a humorous story of three non-English-speaking peasants in America; and *Istoriya moyego sovremennika* (1922; tr *The History of My Contemporary*, 1972), an autobiographical work.

Korzybski, Alfred [Habdank] (1879–1950)   Polish-born American semanticist. Korzybski came to the U.S. about 1915. He propounded what he called "General Semantics," an approach to semantics that rejects the Aristotelian language structure, with its *is* of identity, as tending to confuse words with the things for which they stand, to see propositions as either "right" or "wrong," and to severely limit the levels of abstraction. Among his writings is *Science and Sanity: An Introduction to Non-Aristotelian Systems and General Semantics* (1933).

Kosinski, Jerzy [Nikodem] (1933–   )   Polish-born American novelist. Following his immigration to the U.S. in 1957, Kosinski taught himself English and wrote all his books in his adopted tongue. His first novel, THE PAINTED BIRD, won him international success. It was followed by *Steps* (1968), for which he received a National Book Award, and *Being There* (1971). His subsequent novels, including *The Devil Tree* (1973), *Cockpit* (1975), *Blind Date* (1977), *Passion Play* (1979), and *Pinball* (1982) continue to explore themes of sex, violence, power, and destruction as means to symbolic insights into a modern society in which conventional values and morality no longer apply. He has also written two works of a sociological nature about the Soviet mind—*The Future Is Ours, Comrade* (1960) and *No Third Path* (1962)—under the name "Joseph Novak."

Krafft-Ebing, Baron Richard von (1840–1902)   German neurologist and professor of psychiatry. Krafft-Ebing is widely known for his studies of sexual deviation and particularly for his collection of case histories, *Psychopathia Sexualis* (1886; tr 1892).

Krapp's Last Tape (1958; tr *La Dernière Bande*, 1960)   A one-act play by Samuel BECKETT. Its one character, Krapp, an old man, plays back tapes of monologues he recorded when young and ridicules the passions and ambitions of his youth and middle years, which have come to nothing. In the light of his broken-down old age, hope and optimism seem absurd, and we are made aware of the futility and meaninglessness of life.

Kraus, Karl (1874–1936)   Austrian satirist, essayist, poet, dramatist, journalist, and semanticist. Kraus is considered the greatest and most original satirist in German literature. At the age of twenty-four, Kraus started his own journal, *Die Fackel* (The Torch). Until 1911 he accepted contributions from like-minded writers, but from then on, to the year of his death, he was the sole contributor. In the 922 issues Kraus published, he attacked, with mordant wit and polemical skill, everything he considered corrupt in Austrian culture. A sensitive semanticist, he also attacked the misuse of language, particularly by the press, which, like ORWELL, he saw as both a symptom and a cause of a sick society. He is the author of a mammoth antiwar play, *Die letzten Tage der Menschheit* (1922; tr *The Last Days of Mankind*, 1974), and his entire oeuvre was published in *Werke* (14 vols, 1952–67). Several collections of his writing have appeared in English, including *In These Great Times* (1976, newly translated in 1984), and *No Compromise: Selected Writings* (1977).

Kremlin   A walled section of Moscow, containing cathedrals and palaces dating back to the 15th century.

There are twenty towers of various sizes and architectural styles. The largest building, the Great Kremlin Palace, is now used for sessions of the Supreme Soviet, the Soviet Union's governing body. Until Peter the Great moved the capital to St. Petersburg in 1712, the Kremlin was the residence of the Tzars. After the revolution, it became the seat of government and a symbol of Soviet power.

Kriemhild   Heroine of the NIBELUNGENLIED, known as Gudrun in the VÖLSUNGA SAGA and Gutrune in Wagner's *Ring des Nibelungen* (1876).

Krishna (Sans, "black")   One of the central deities in HINDUISM, often depicted as black or dark blue, the eighth AVATAR of VISHNU. According to one legend, when Kamsa, the demon-king of Mathura, committed great ravages, BRAHMĀ prayed to Vishnu to relieve the world of this distress. At this point, Vishnu plucked off one white and one black hair, the latter becoming Krishna. Another legend has Krishna born as a nephew of King Kamsa. Warned by a prophecy that the baby would slay him, the king sought to kill Krishna. The latter, smuggled away, was brought up by shepherds and later killed his uncle and became King of the Yadavas. He is often represented as playing on his divine flute and attracting the *gopis*, or milkmaids, to dance around him in the moonlight. In the BHAGAVAD-GĪTĀ, he appears as a charioteer to provide divine guidance to the troubled warrior Arjuna.

Kriss Kringle   The Pennsylvania Dutch Santa Claus. On Christmas Eve, arrayed in a fur cap and strange apparel, he goes to the bedroom of each good child, where he leaves a present in the stocking that is hung up in expectation of his visit. The word is a dialectal variant of High German *Christkindle*, "little Christ child," and has undergone such radical changes because it is no longer associated with either of its component parts.

Kristin Lavransdatter (1920–1922)   A trilogy of historical novels by Sigrid UNDSET. Recreating a woman's life in the devout Catholic Norway of the 13th and 14th centuries, this great romance appeared in successive volumes: *Kransen* (*The Bridal Wreath*, 1920), *Husfrue* (*The Mistress of Husaby*, 1921), and *Korset* (*The Cross*, 1922).

Kroetsch, Robert (1927–   )   Canadian novelist and poet. Kroetsch wrote a travel book (1968) about Alberta, the place of his birth. He created a series of PICA-RESQUE novels which, fusing unconventional literary techniques with a mood of comic playfulness, project a sardonic vision of Canadian prairie life. His major works are *But We Are Exiles* (1966), *The Words of My Roaring* (1966), *The Studhorse Man* (1969), *Gone Indian* (1973), and *Badlands* (1975). Kroetsch has published several volumes of poetry, including *Field Notes* (1981) and *Advice to My Friends* (1985).

Kropotkin, Prince Pyotr Alekseyevich (1842–1921)   Russian social philosopher and geographer. A leading theorist of anarchism, Kropotkin took part during the 1870s in the revolutionary movement against the tsarist government. To escape arrest, he immigrated to Europe and settled in England (1876). He returned to Russia in 1917 but was no friendlier to the Bolsheviks than he had been to the Tsars. His most famous book, *Zapiski revolyutsionera* (*Memoirs of a Revolutionist*, 1899), describes the social foment during the reign of Alexander II.

Krutch, Joseph Wood (1893–1970)   American critic, essayist, and teacher. Krutch was a drama critic for the *Nation* for many years, as well as an English professor at Columbia University and elsewhere. His critical works include *Edgar Allan Poe: A Study of Genius* (1926), one of the first psychoanalytical interpretations of literature; *Five Masters: A Study in the Mutations of the Novel* (1929); and *The American Drama since 1918* (1939; rev 1957). His essays are collected in *The Modern Temper* (1929), *The Measure of Man* (1954), and *Human Nature and the Human Condition* (1959), in which he discussed the need for humanistic values in a mechanized society. He was also an avid naturalist. *The Best Nature Writing of Joseph Wood Krutch* was published in 1970. *More Lives Than One* (1962) is his autobiography.

Krylov, Ivan Andreyevich (1769–1844)   Russian fabulist. In his early career both a dramatist and a journalist, Krylov published his collections of fables from 1809 on. They have become classics in Russian literature and were translated into English by the British historian Sir Bernard Pares in 1927.

kshatriya   A member of the warrior stratum (*varna*) in the four-fold division of the Hindu social hierarchy, below the BRAHMIN and above the VAISHYA and SUDRA. See CASTE.

Kuan-yin (Jap, *Kannon*)   The Chinese goddess of mercy, identified by the Buddhists with the masculine *Bodhisattva Avalokitesvara* in India. The object of much popular worship in China, Kuan-yin is often depicted in religious art.

Kubera   In Hindu mythology, the god of wealth. Kubera was the half brother of RAVANA, the demon-king of Ceylon.

Kublai Khan (1216–1294)   Mongol emperor of China after 1259 and grandson of Genghis Khan. Kublai Khan established his court at what is now Peking (1264) and founded the Yuan dynasty, which ended in 1368. His kingdom, finally extending as far as Russia, flourished under his patronage of commerce and culture. His reign was vividly described by Marco POLO, and the splendor of his court inspired S. T. Coleridge's poem KUBLA KHAN.

Kubla Khan (1797)   An unfinished poem by Samuel Taylor COLERIDGE. According to Coleridge, the poem was composed in an opium-induced sleep; when he awoke he immediately began to set it down, but was interrupted by a visitor, and when he returned to his task, he found that the rest of the poem had vanished from his memory. A precursor, to some extent, of both symbolism and surrealism, the poem is considered one of his best. See XANADU.

Kubrick, Stanley (1928–) American film director, resident in England after 1962. Kubrick's first important film, *The Killing* (1956), is an electrifying thriller comparable to the works of Alfred HITCHCOCK at his best. *Paths of Glory* (1957) is a powerful antiwar statement with a World War I setting. *Lolita* (1962), his first British-made film, captures the ironic tone of NABOKOV's novel and ranks among the most intelligent film adaptations of any work of modern fiction. *Dr. Strangelove* (1964) is an effectively hair-raising political satire about a diabolically power-mad scientist. This was followed by the provocative and innovative science fiction epic *2001: A Space Odyssey* (1968). Kubrick continued to explore an exceptionally broad range of genres in his subsequent four films, all of which are adapted from novels: the futuristic black comedy *A Clockwork Orange* (1971), from Anthony BURGESS's novel; the visually entrancing but static *Barry Lyndon* (1975), from a minor novel by THACKERAY; *The Shining* (1980), based on Stephen KING's horror novel; and *Full Metal Jacket* (1987), a nihilistic view of the experiences of young American Marines in the Vietnam War, based on *The Short-Timers* (1979) by Gustav Hasford.

Kuhn, Walt (real name William Kuhn, 1880–1949) American painter, illustrator, and cartoonist. Kuhn was a member of the ASHCAN SCHOOL, and an organizer-exhibitor of the ARMORY SHOW. His frontal portraits of circus figures (done in the 1920s) are the best examples of his attempts at portraying universal emotions by concentrating on the human figure against a neutral background.

Kūkai (774–835) Japanese priest, founder of Shingon Buddhism. The most literate scholar of his time, he was influential in the introduction of Chinese learning to Japan. His command of the Chinese language and the diversity of his writings mark him as one of the major literary figures of the early HEIAN period (794–1185). He is known posthumously as Kōbō Daishi.

Ku Klux Klan A name given to two white-supremacist American secret societies. The original Ku Klux Klan was an organization for ex-Confederates, formed about 1866, in Pulaski, Tennessee, to intimidate newly enfranchised blacks and prevent them from voting. At an 1867 convention in Nashville, the Klan declared its principles, which ostensibly were to protect the weak and aid the enforcement of the CONSTITUTION OF THE U.S. The Klan was formally disbanded in 1871, when it proved to be an instrument of violence and Congress passed acts to suppress it.

In 1915 the Klan was revived in Georgia with the avowed aims to maintain "pure Americanism" and white supremacy. It attacked blacks, Catholics, and Jews, as well as such ideas as birth control, Darwinism, PACIFISM, and the repeal of prohibition. By the early 1920s, the Klan was reputed to have a membership of twenty million through-

out the U.S. Membership declined after 1923, when its terroristic activities were exposed in newspapers. There was a revival in the South after World War II, and again in the 1960s in response to the civil rights movement; there were again sporadic revivals in the 1970s.

Many novelists have written about the Klan, both favorably and unfavorably. In Thomas Nelson PAGE's *Red Rock* (1898), the hero is a Klan leader. The sensational novel *The Clansman* (1905) by Thomas Dixon, Jr., was the basis of the motion picture *The Birth of a Nation* (1915) and is credited with reviving interest in the society. Two anti-Klan novels are Howard FAST's *Freedom Road* (1944) and Ward Greene's *King Cobra* (1940).

The name of the society is taken from the Greek word *kuklos*, "band; circle"; it is often referred to by the abbreviation KKK.

kulak A wealthy Russian peasant. The name, derived from the Russian word for "fist," was used derogatorily by the Soviet authorities who exterminated this class in the 1920s to make way for the collectivization of agriculture.

Kulhwch and Olwen (c1100) One of the tales in the Welsh MABINOGION. This prose narrative is especially important, being perhaps the earliest full-fledged Arthurian romance. Kulhwch, the hero, gains the help of Arthur and his followers in accomplishing the hard tasks set by the giant Ysbaddaden, whose beautiful daughter Olwen he seeks to win.

Kumarbi In Hurrian mythology, the supreme god. Kumarbi is probably best known for his role in the Hittite myth of the Stone Monster. After nine years as vizier of the sky god Anu, Kumarbi revolted. He won the ensuing battle by emasculating Anu with his teeth, but was soon alarmed to discover that Anu's two children were growing inside him. After a good deal of trial and error, Kumarbi managed to give birth to them. The second of these children promptly overthrew Kumarbi and replaced his true father, Anu, on the throne. On the advice of the lord of the sea, Kumarbi now impregnated a mountain, which, in due course, labored mightily and brought forth a baby made of stone. The delighted Kumarbi named the infant Ullikummi and arranged to have it placed on the right shoulder of UPELLURI, the giant who held up earth and heaven, standing in the midst of the ocean. The stone child grew most remarkably, and soon his immense size threatened to topple heaven itself. Neither the might of the gods nor the wiles of ISHTAR could prevail against it. Finally, EA, the god of wisdom, severed his legs at the ankles with a magic knife, and the stone monster fell into the sea. Thus ended Kumarbi's revolt.

Kundera, Milan (1929–) Czech novelist and short-story writer. Although he was a prominent figure in the liberalization that led to the Prague Spring and the Soviet invasion of Czechoslovakia (1968), Kundera writes fiction that on first reading appears to emphasize the personal and philosophical over the political. Comic irony and the erotic are also important in his work, beginning with the stories in *Smesné lásky* (1963, 1965, 1968; tr *Laughable Loves*, 1974) and in his first novel, *Žert* (1967; tr *The Joke*, 1969, new tr 1982). After 1969 Kundera was prevented from publishing in his homeland and his works appeared first in translation: *Život je jinde* (tr *Life Is Elsewhere*, 1974), *Valčík na rozloučenou* (tr *The Farewell Party*, 1976), *Kniha smíchu a zapomnění* (tr *The Book of Laughter and Forgetting*, 1980), and THE UNBEARABLE LIGHTNESS OF BEING, which was a major international success. Kundera has lived in France since 1975.

Kunitz, Stanley J[asspon] (1905–   )   American poet, editor, and translator. Dubbed a "poet's poet," Kunitz was regarded early in his career as one of America's best metaphysical poets. *Selected Poems 1928–1958* (1958) was awarded the PULITZER PRIZE. Thirteen years later, his new poems and some translations of Russian poets appeared in *The Testing-Tree* (1971). Kunitz here replaced his earlier third-person mode with a more directly personal style. A notable piece in this volume is "Journal for My Daughter," a conversation poem depicting the generation gap with passionate stoicism. *The Poems of Stanley Kunitz: 1928–1978* appeared in 1979. In 1985 he published a new volume of poems and essays, *Next-to-Last Things*.

Künstlerroman (Ger, "artist novel")   A type of novel popular in GERMAN ROMANTICISM. It is basically a BILDUNGSROMAN ("novel of education") in which the hero finally becomes an artist or poet, and thus the form reflects a characteristic romantic interest in the growth of the artist as a person. The most important examples are Tieck's *Franz Sternbalds Wanderungen* (*Franz Sternbald's Wanderings*, 1798) and Novalis's *Heinrich von Ofterdingen* (1802). In later literature, Joyce's *A Portrait of the Artist as a Young Man* (1916) is such an artist novel.

Kuprin, Aleksandr Ivanovich (1870–1938)   Russian novelist and short-story writer. Kuprin left Russia during the civil war but returned two years before his death. His work covers a wide range of subjects. Best known are the short novel *Poyedinok* (1905; tr *The Duel*, 1916), a story of army life in a provincial garrison; *Yama* (1909–15; tr *The Pit*, 1929), an account of a Russian brothel; *Shtabs-kapitan Rybnikov* (1906; tr *Captain Ribnikov*, 1916), a spy story; and *Granatovy braslet* (1911; tr *The Garnet Bracelet*, 1917), a sentimental love story.

Kurosawa, Akira (1910–   )   Japanese film director. Kurosawa gained international recognition with *Rashōmon* (1950), which won first prize at the Venice Film Festival the following year. His films are characterized by a bold handling of samurai epics in a style accessible to Western audiences. Other well-received films include *Ikiru* (1952), *Throne of Blood* (1957; an adaptation of *Macbeth*), *Seven Samurai* (1954; remade by Hollywood as *The Magnificent Seven*, 1960), *Yojimbo* (1961), and *Dersu Uzala* (1975). *Rān* (1985) received the National Film Critics Award for best picture of 1985.

Kurtz   See HEART OF DARKNESS.

Kuznetsov, Anatoly Vasilyevich (pen name since 1969 A. Anatoli; 1929–1979)   Soviet novelist and short-story writer. In 1969 Kuznetsov traveled to London in order to research a work on Lenin, bringing with him an uncensored copy of his most notable work, the documentary novel *Babiy Yar*. Depicting his childhood experience of the German occupation of Kiev and the Nazis' massacre of Jews there, *Babiy Yar* denigrates the stereotypical hero of SOCIALIST REALISM and was, therefore, censored in its Soviet edition. Kuznetsov requested and was granted asylum in Britain. The existence in the West of two versions of this work thus allowed a unique glimpse of Soviet censorship policy. Kuznetsov's first widely recognized notable work is *Prodolzheniye legendy: Zapiski molodogo cheloveka* (tr *Sequel to a Legend: Notes of a Young Man*, 1957), an account of his experiences as a construction worker in Siberia and a realistic portrayal of the problems facing Soviet youth.

Kvasir   See ODROVIR.

Kyd, Thomas (1557?–1594)   English dramatist. A scrivener by profession, Kyd became the author of the most popular drama of his day with his Senecan revenge-play THE SPANISH TRAGEDY (produced between 1584 and 1589). He may have written a lost play on the Hamlet theme and is thought to have worked on parts of SHAKESPEARE's plays TITUS ANDRONICUS and HENRY VI. *Arden of Feversham* is sometimes attributed to him, as is the anonymously published *Soliman and Perseda* (written c1588). In 1593 he was sharing a room with Christopher MARLOWE and was arrested with him for atheism and heresy. Possibly suffering from his imprisonment and disgrace, he died the following year.

Kyrie eleison (Gr, "Lord have mercy")   Originally an invocation to the Greek sungod. This petition is the first fixed chant in most Western Eucharistic liturgies and is also used in the liturgies of the Eastern churches.

L

Laban In the OLD TESTAMENT, the brother of ISAAC's wife, REBEKAH, and father of RACHEL and LEAH. When JACOB was sent by Isaac to seek out a wife from the family of Laban (Gen. 28:2), he fell in love with Rachel. Her father promised her to Jacob provided he worked for him for seven years. After that time, Laban substituted his older daughter, Leah, as Jacob's wife (Gen. 29:23). He then promised Rachel to Jacob if Jacob agreed to work for another seven years, which he did. When Jacob wished to return to the land of his father, Laban again urged him to stay in exchange for some livestock. Finally, after twenty years in Laban's service, Jacob stole away with his wives and children to return to Canaan. Laban, incensed, overtook them along the way, but the two men agreed to lay a boundary over which neither would cross again, and Laban returned to his own land (Gen. 31).

Labé, Louise (1524–?1566) French poet. Labé was celebrated for her talent and beauty. She was one of the best known of the school of French poets centered at Lyons. In the elegies and sonnets included in her *Oeuvres* (1555), she expressed in a direct, intense style the torments of a passionate nature which had been profoundly marked by an unhappy love. The wife of a wealthy rope-maker, she was sometimes called *la belle cordière*.

laberinto de la soledad, El See LABYRINTH OF SOLITUDE, THE.

Labiche, Eugène [Marin] (1815–1888) French playwright. Responding to the Second Empire's demand for farcical comedy, Labiche wrote a long series of popular plays including *Un Chapeau de paille d'Italie* (1851) and *La Poudre aux yeux* (1862). The delightful *Le Voyage de M. Perrichon* (1860)—perhaps his best-known comedy —was written in collaboration with Edouard Martin.

La Bruyère, Jean de (1645–1696) French writer and moralist of the neoclassical period. La Bruyère's sympathies lay with the ancients in their literary battle with the moderns, and, in addition to being conservative, his outlook was deeply misanthropic. His most famous work, *Caractères de Théophraste traduits du grec, avec les caractères ou les moeurs de ce siècle* (*Characters of Theophrastus Translated from the Greek, with Characters or the Manners of This Century*, 1688), is a piece of social satire in the manner of Theophrastus, combining maxims with character portraits of French social types and individuals of the day.

Labyrinth The palace of MINOS in Knossos, the Minoan capital of Crete, said to have been devised by DAEDALUS. According to the legend, it was a mazelike building in the center of which the MINOTAUR was imprisoned. The word has come to be applied to any structure with many confusing passages. The origin of the word is not known, but it may be connected with *labrys*, the double ax constantly used in the religious symbolism of ancient Crete.

Labyrinthine Ways, The See POWER AND THE GLORY, THE.

Labyrinth of Solitude, The (El laberinto de la soledad, 1950; tr 1961) A book by Octavio PAZ. This penetrating essay on Mexican history has probably been more widely read and is thus more influential than any of Paz's other essays or poetry. In search of the meaning of the Mexican and, by extension, the Latin American experience, Paz singles out the conquest of the Indians by Spanish invaders as the moment the true Mexico became isolated and obscured by masks. Silence, dissimulation, *machismo*, hermeticism, violence, and the cult of death are the masks adopted by the Mexican to disguise his fundamental historical solitude. Paz argues, however, that solitude has become a universal part of the human condition and that all men, like the poet himself, must become conscious of this condition in order to find, in the plentitude of love and creative work, a glimpse of the way out of the labyrinth of solitude.

Lacedaemon An ancient name of Laconia, and of SPARTA, its chief city.

La Chaise, Père François d'Aix de (1624–1709) French Jesuit confessor to Louis XIV. La Chaise's favorite retreat near Paris later became the site of the cemetery popularly known as the *cimetière du Père-Lachaise*.

Laclos, Pierre [Ambroise François] Choderlos de (1741–1803)   French artillery officer and author of the epistolary novel LES LIAISONS DANGEREUSES. The novel depicts the immorality of the times, particularly the corrupt and cynical seducers of innocence. Laclos was a member of the JACOBIN club, became a general, and played an important military role in the French Revolution.

Lady Chatterley's Lover (1928)   A novel by D. H. LAWRENCE, presenting the author's mystical theories of sex in the story of Constance, or Connie, the wife of an English aristocrat, who runs away with her gamekeeper. Her husband, Sir Clifford, has been rendered impotent by a war wound and is also an emotional cripple. The gamekeeper, MELLORS, is a forthright, individualistic man, uncontaminated by industrial society. Because of the frank language and detailed descriptions of love-making, the book was banned in England and the U.S. as obscene. After historic court cases the ban was lifted in the U.S. in 1959 and in England in 1960.

Lady Geraldine's Courtship (1844)   A poem by Elizabeth Barrett BROWNING. The lady falls in love with a peasant-poet, whom she marries. The poem contained a tribute to the poetry of Robert Browning, which prompted a warm letter from him and their subsequent meeting, romance, and marriage.

Lady into Fox (1922)   A novel by David GARNETT. It is a delicate, solemn fantasy about a man whose wife suddenly turns into a fox—and their consequent marital problems.

Lady of Pleasure, The (1635)   A comedy by James SHIRLEY. The good Sir Thomas Bornwell becomes increasingly alarmed at the growing extravagances of his wife, Aretina. Pretending to become converted to her spendthrift ways, he turns to gambling and begins paying attention to the beautiful widow Celestina, Lady Bellamour. Eventually, as he had hoped, Aretina becomes alarmed and returns to modesty and thrift.

Lady of the Fountain, The   A medieval Welsh tale from the MABINOGION in which are found King ARTHUR and his court. This tale has a remarkable parallel in the story *Yvain* by CHRÉTIEN DE TROYES.

Lady of the Lake   In ARTHURIAN LEGEND, an obscure, supernatural figure endowed with magical powers. In Malory's MORTE D'ARTHUR, the Lady of the Lake lives in a castle in the midst of a magical lake, which prevents access to her. She steals LAUNCELOT in his infancy and plunges with him into her home in the lake; hence, Launcelot comes to be called *Lancelot du Lac* (Launcelot of the Lake). When he has grown to manhood, she presents him to King ARTHUR. It is from the Lady of the Lake that Arthur receives the magical sword EXCALIBUR; he takes it from the mysterious arm extending above the surface of the lake.

She is also known as Nimuë or Vivien, the mistress of MERLIN, whom she ultimately imprisons forever in a tower. The Lady of the Lake appears in later works, notably in Tennyson's IDYLLS OF THE KING.

Lady of the Lake, The (1810)   A long narrative poem by Sir Walter SCOTT. It tells of Ellen DOUGLAS, who lives with her father near Loch Katrine, and of the varied fortunes of her suitors in troubled times of border warfare. One of her suitors is the king of Scotland, but she finally chooses the bold Malcolm Graeme.

Lady or the Tiger?, The (1882)   A short story by Frank R. Stockton (1834–1902). Stockton originally called the story "The King's Arena" and read it at a party given by a friend. Its reception there was so good that he elaborated it and sent it to the *Century Magazine*. It was the most famous story the magazine ever published; its plot is simple but unique. In a barbaric land a handsome youth is audacious enough to fall in love with the king's daughter and she with him. His offense is discovered, and he is condemned. In a great arena he must walk up to two doors and open one of them; behind one door is a beautiful maiden who would be given to him in marriage; behind the other is a ravenous tiger. The princess learns the secret of the doors and signals the young man to open the door on the right. Who comes out, asked Stockton, the lady or the tiger? Stockton wrote another story supposed to solve the puzzle, "The Discourager of Hesitancy" (1887), but it also cleverly left the query unanswered.

Lady's Not for Burning, The (1949)   A play in verse by Christopher FRY.

Lady Windermere's Fan (1892)   A comedy of manners by Oscar WILDE. Annoyed at her husband's persistent interest in Mrs. Erlynne, a woman of little reputation, Lady Windermere decides to leave him and run away with Lord Darlington. Mrs. Erlynne, actually Lady Windermere's mother, who deserted her husband and daughter years ago for a lover who then left her, finds the note and rushes to Lord Darlington's apartments. Here, without revealing her identity, she persuades Lady Windermere not to take this rash step and succeeds in rushing her off in a carriage just as Lord Darlington appears with Lord Windermere. Lord Windermere immediately notices his wife's fan; Mrs. Erlynne comes forth and generously assumes guilt, saying that she mistook it for her own, thus saving her daughter's reputation at the expense of her own. She succeeds, however, in convincing Lord Augustus Lawton that it was in his interests that she came to Lord Darlington's rooms, and the two marry.

Laertes   In Shakespeare's HAMLET, the son of Polonius and brother of Ophelia. A well-meaning but impetuous young man, he contrasts with the introspective and indecisive Hamlet, whose death he causes.

Laestrygonians   A fabulous race of cannibal giants who lived in Sicily. ODYSSEUS sent two of his men to request that he might land, but the king of the place ate one for dinner and the other fled. The Laestrygonians assembled on the coast and threw stones at Odysseus and his crew; they fled with all speed, but many men were lost.

LaFarge, John (1880–1963)   American Jesuit priest and writer. Son of the painter John LaFarge (1835–1910), he became known for his dedication to work in rural American missions and for his deep concern with racial problems. LaFarge served for many years as editor of the Jesuit weekly *America* and wrote several books on the Jesuits and on race issues. His highly praised autobiography, *The Manner Is Ordinary*, appeared in 1953. He was an uncle of poet and novelist Christopher LaFarge (1897–1953) and Oliver LaFarge.

LaFarge, Oliver [Hazzard Perry] (1901–1963) American anthropologist and writer. LaFarge was a leading authority on American Indians, particularly the Navajo. His well-known novels *Laughing Boy* (1929; Pulitzer Prize) and *The Enemy Gods* (1939) are both concerned with life among the Navajo. Many of his other novels and stories are also concerned with Indians. LaFarge's nonfiction includes a history of the American Indian, *As Long as the Grass Shall Grow* (1940), and his autobiography, *Raw Material* (1945). See also LaFarge, John.

La Fayette, Comtesse de (born Marie Madeleine Pioche de La Vergne, 1634–1693) French novelist. Although Comtesse de La Fayette borrowed the format of her early work *Zayde* from de Scudéry, her novels *La Princesse de Montpensier* (1662) and La Princesse de Clèves are unmarred by the sentimentality and extravagance that characterize the works of her predecessor. With these simply and soberly written romances, melancholy in mood, Comtesse de La Fayette originated the French novel of character.

Lafayette, Marquis de (Marie Joseph Paul Yves Roch Gilbert du Motier, 1757–1834)   French statesman and general, known as "the Hero of the Worlds." Lafayette served (1777–81) the American cause during the Revolutionary War as a major general in Washington's army. On furlough in France from 1778 to 1780, he did much to cement Franco-American relations. Active in French politics, he advocated moderation during the French Revolution. He was forced to flee to Austrian lines in 1792 after failing in his attempted coup d'état against the revolutionary government in Paris, and returned to Paris in 1799. He did not engage in politics during the Napoleonic era, but after the Bourbon Restoration (1815–30) he was one of the leaders of the liberal opposition. He persuaded the leaders of the 1830 revolution to accept Louis Philippe as their monarch, saying the famous words: "Take him, he will make the best of republics." At Lafayette's suggestion, Louis Philippe appeared on the balcony of the Hôtel de Ville, wrapped in the Tricolor, the national flag of France. Lafayette lived to regret his decision, becoming quite disappointed in the July Monarchy.

Lafcadio's Adventures (Les Caves du Vatican, 1914; tr 1927)   A satirical farce by André Gide. Also known in translation as *The Vatican Cellars* (1952), the book caricatures various types in society by means of three brothers-in-law and their many relations who comprise its major characters. The plot concerns the confusion resulting from a swindler's scheme to extort money by falsely reporting that the pope has been kidnapped and organizing a conspiracy to liberate him. The interest of the book, however, focuses on an *acte gratuit*—the apparently unmotivated murder of one of the brothers by Lafcadio, a bastard relative.

Lafitte, Jean (1780?–?1826)   French pirate and smuggler. Lafitte seems to have reached the neighborhood of New Orleans around 1809 as the head of a band of smugglers and privateers. During the War of 1812 he offered his services to Andrew Jackson and took part in the battle of New Orleans. Later he returned to his freebooting in Texas.

The subject of many legends, he was the hero of *Lafitte, The Pirate of the Gulf* (1836), a best-selling romance by Joseph Holt Ingraham. He also appears in Hervey Allen's novel *Anthony Adverse* (1933). Lord Byron, in a note to The Corsair, suggested some likeness between his hero and Lafitte.

La Follette, Robert M[arion] (1855–1925) American statesman. An opponent of Republican Party regulars in his native Wisconsin, La Follette was elected district attorney of Dane County in 1880 and served in Congress from 1885 to 1891. In 1900 he won the GOP gubernatorial nomination by acclamation and after his election instituted an extensive reform program that included opposition to political bosses, establishment of the direct primary, and regulation of the railroads. In the U.S. Senate (1906–25), he continued his battle against the "interests." As leader of the newly formed Progressive Party, he sought the 1912 presidential nomination but lost it to Theodore Roosevelt. He opposed President Wilson's foreign policy and argued against U.S. entry into the League of Nations. In 1924 he won nearly five million votes as the presidential candidate of the Progressives.

His son, Robert M. La Follette, Jr. (1895–1953), was appointed to the elder La Follette's Senate seat in 1925 and served until 1946 when he was defeated by Joseph R. McCarthy.

La Fontaine, Jean de (1621–1695)   French author. A prolific writer of comedies, lyrics, elegies, ballads, and licentious tales, La Fontaine is remembered primarily for his Fables choisies, mises en vers. Despite disputes with the French Academy, police condemnation of his ribald *Contes et nouvelles en vers*, and royal disfavor, La Fontaine was little distracted from his work and remained in the eyes of the world a vagabond, dreamer, and lover of pleasure, drifting happily from one patron to another throughout his highly productive literary career.

Laforgue, Jules (1860–1887)   French poet. Associated with the SYMBOLISTS, Laforgue, with Gustave Kahn, is considered to have invented *vers libre*, as free verse is known in the 20th century. His volumes of poetry include *Les Complaintes* (1885), *L'Imitation de Notre-Dame la lune* (1886), and *Le Concile féerique* (1886). *Moralités légendaires* (1887; tr *Moral Tales*, 1985) is a collection, published posthumously, of satires upon old tales. Taken more seriously by his British and American admirers than by his fellow countrymen, Laforgue exerted considerable influence upon ELIOT, POUND, JOYCE, CRANE, and STEVENS.

Lagado   In Jonathan SWIFT's satire GULLIVER'S TRAVELS, the capital of Balnibarbi, the continent neighboring LAPUTA. Lagado is celebrated for its Academy of Projectors, where scholars spend their time in such useless projects as extracting sunbeams from cucumbers and converting ice into gunpowder.

Lagerkvist, Pär (1891–1974)   Swedish novelist, playwright, and poet. Influenced in his formative years by the German expressionists and by his compatriot STRINDBERG, Lagerkvist was a moralist without a system of belief. Profoundly humanistic, his works probe the human heart and mind with an agonized honesty. Much of his philosophical orientation is revealed in the autobiographical *Gäst hos verkligheten* (1925; tr *Guest of Reality*, 1936). In such novels as *Bödeln* (*The Hangman*, 1933) and *Dvärgen* (1944; tr *The Dwarf*, 1945) he speaks out passionately against tyranny, violence, and totalitarianism. Later novels, including BARABBAS, *Sibyllan* (1956; tr *The Sibyl*, 1958), and *Pilgrim på havet* (1962; tr *Pilgrim at Sea*, 1964), deal symbolically with loneliness and man's search for belief.

Lagerkvist's style has a directness and spare beauty uniquely suited to his probings of the soul. He was awarded the NOBEL PRIZE in Literature in 1951.

Lagerlöf, Selma [Ottiliana Lovisa] (1858–1940)   Swedish novelist and short-story writer. Lagerlöf was uncomfortable with the literary realism in vogue in her day. She returned to the past for her stories and wrote in a romantic and imaginative manner, vividly evoking the peasant life and landscape of northern Sweden. With the publication of her novel GÖSTA BERLINGS SAGA, she became one of the most popular writers in Sweden. Her other major work is JERUSALEM, a collection of stories. *Nils Holgerssons underbara resa genom Sverige* (1906–7), the two volumes of which were translated as *The Wonderful Adventures of Nils* (tr 1907) and *The Further Adventures of Nils* (tr 1911), is a fanciful account, written for children, of a young boy's adventures as he travels across Sweden on the back of a goose. Lagerlöf was a committed pacifist and feminist but her social concerns rarely found their way into her novels. She was awarded the NOBEL PRIZE in Literature in 1909, the first woman to be so honored.

La Guma, Alex (1925–1985)   South African novelist and short-story writer. La Guma was born in Capetown, the son of the president of the South African Colored Peoples' Congress. He was a columnist for a Capetown newspaper and was among those accused in the South African "Treason Trials." His novels and short stories depict the atmosphere of racial tension and violence that characterizes the politics of apartheid, and reveal repeated indignities suffered by blacks and other nonwhites. His published works include *A Walk in the Night* (1962), *And a Threefold Cord* (1964), *The Stone Country* (1967; repr 1978), *In the Fog of the Season's End* (1972), and *Time of the Butcherbird* (1979).

Lahar   The Sumerian god of cattle.

La Hogue, Battle of   The successful naval operations of the English and Dutch fleets against the French off the coast of Normandy (May 19–23, 1692). La Hogue itself is a harbor which served as the base of Louis XIV's attempted invasion of England.

The escape of the French fleet after their defeat is recounted in BROWNING's poem "Hervé Riel."

lai (or lay)   A song or short lyric or narrative verse that originated in Europe during the Middle Ages. The term has been used to designate various verse forms in both French and English but probably originally referred to musical compositions sung by Breton minstrels. In medieval France, the *lai* took the form of a narrative, usually written in octosyllabic verse, recounting tales of COURTLY LOVE and the supernatural world of fairy kingdoms and enchanted islands. Many, such as those composed by MARIE DE FRANCE in the 12th century, dealt with subjects of Celtic origin, often drawing on ARTHURIAN LEGEND. The so-called BRETON LAIS that became popular in England in the 14th century were based on the earlier French models. The term should not be confused with the *Lais* (or *legs*, meaning "legacies") written by François VILLON.

Laing, R[onald] D[avid] (1927–   )   Scottish psychiatrist and writer. Laing's ability to see psychosis in positive and constructive terms became the foundation for several lucid and controversial studies that found a wide audience outside medical circles. In such books as *The Politics of Experience* (1967) and *The Facts of Life* (1976) he asserts that insanity can be seen as a sane response to an insane society. *The Politics of the Family* (1969; rev 1971) relates the psycho-social workings of the family to society as a whole. *Wisdom, Madness and Folly: The Making of a Psychiatrist* (1985) is an autobiographical account of the first fifty years of Laing's life.

Laïs   Name of two celebrated Greek HETAERAE or courtesans. The earlier was the most beautiful woman of Corinth, who lived at the time of the Peloponnesian War. The beauty of Laïs the Second so excited the jealousy of the Thessalonian women that they pricked her to death with their bodkins. She was the contemporary and rival of PHRYNE and sat for Apelles as a model. DEMOSTHENES claims that she sold her favors for ten thousand Attic drachmae.

laissez-faire (Fr, "let do," that is, "let people and things alone") The principal tenet of laissez-faire is that problems should be allowed to work themselves out without planning or regulation. It is, specifically, the principle of noninterference by government in commercial affairs. The phrase comes from the motto of the PHYSIOCRATS, a school of French economists of the mid-18th century: *Laissez faire, laissez passer* ("let do; let pass"). The physiocrats wished to have all customs duties abolished and demanded free circulation for their goods, thus anticipating the later free traders. Jean Claude Marie Vincent de Gournay (1712–59) is generally credited with being the author of the motto. Adam SMITH was the principal exponent of laissez-faire theories in England, from where they later spread to the United States.

Lajpat Rai, Lala (1865–1928) Militant Hindu nationalist leader, and one of the guiding spirits of the "Extremist" faction in the Indian National Congress. Lajpat Rai was a leader of the revivalistic Arya Samaj. He devoted himself to social and educational reform, reconversion of Muslims and others to HINDUISM, and the propagation of Hindi as the national language of India. He wrote extensively in English, mostly on Indian topics.

Lake poets (also called Lake School) A name applied to a group of poets in the 19th century, including WORDSWORTH, COLERIDGE, and SOUTHEY, making reference to their residences in the Lake District of England (Westmoreland, Cumberland, Lancashire). The name was first used as an epithet of derision by the *Edinburgh Review*, but has long since lost its disparaging connotations.

Lakshmi In Hindu mythology, the wife of the god VISHNU and mother of KAMA, the god of young love. Lakshmi is the goddess of beauty, pleasure, and especially wealth. The RĀMĀYANA describes her as springing, like APHRODITE, from the foam of the sea. She is extensively treated in Vishnu PURANAS.

Lallans A Scottish dialect used by some modern Scottish poets. It is a synthetic language, made up of the dialects of the Scottish lowlands and elements from the Scottish literary language of the past. See SCOTTISH RENAISSANCE.

Lalla Rookh (1817) A series of four Oriental tales in verse held together by a story in prose, by Thomas MOORE. The narrative tells of Lalla Rookh, daughter of the emperor of Delhi, who, on a journey to meet her betrothed, is entertained by the young Persian poet Feramorz; he relates four tales of romance and she falls in love with him. Ultimately she discovers that he is her betrothed.

The four tales he entertained her with are:

(1) *The Veiled Prophet of Khorassan* in which the chief figure is the prophet Hakem ben Haschem, who wears a silver gauze veil "to dim the luster of his face" or rather to hide its extreme ugliness.

(2) *Paradise and the Peri*, about a Peri who is told she will be readmitted to heaven if she brings the gift most dear to the Almighty. After a number of unavailing offerings she brings a guilty old man, who weeps repentantly. The Peri offers the Repentant Tear and the gates of Heaven fly open.

(3) *The Fire Worshippers*, about Hafed, the fire worshiper, who, when betrayed to the Muslims, throws himself in the sacred fire and is burned to death.

(4) *The Light of the Harem*, about Nourmahal, who regains the love of her husband, the Mogul Emperor Jehangir, by means of a magic spell.

lama A Buddhist monk or priest in Tibet. Prior to 1959, when he was forced to flee from the Chinese, the Dalai Lama ("superior priest") had been both the temporal and spiritual leader of the Tibetans. Ruling from the Potala, a huge palace-lamasery in Lhasa, the Dalai Lama is considered a reincarnation of Avalokitesvara, the ancestor of the Tibetan race. Great care is taken in the selection of successive Dalai Lamas. A baby is sought who will recognize the personal possessions of its predecessor in the office and take them as his own. When it is considered proven that the child is a reincarnation of the spiritual principle he rules under a regent and council.

Lamarck, Chevalier de (Jean Baptiste Pierre Antoine de Monet, 1744–1829) French naturalist. Lamarck advocated views on organic evolution which are sometimes mistakenly interpreted as representing Darwinism in a preparatory stage. In his *Philosophie zoologique* (1809), he held that an organism reacts to a new or changing environment by fitting developments; he did not hold, as did Darwin, that a new or changing environment permits the survival of the accidentally fittest. Lamarck also introduced new principles in the classification of animals and originated the terms *vertebrate* and *invertebrate*. See DARWIN, CHARLES ROBERT.

Lamartine, Alphonse Marie Louis de (1790–1869) French poet, writer, and statesman. Lamartine's work is marked by a preoccupation with nature, religion, and love, all subjectively presented (see ROMANTICISM). He is regarded as the first truly romantic poet in French literature. Among his published volumes are *Les Premières Méditations* (1820), *Les Nouvelles Méditations* (1823), and *Les Harmonies poétiques et religieuses* (1830). His narrative poems include *Jocelyn* (1836), dealing with a priest's love, and *La Chute d'un ange* (1838). A liberal in his beliefs, Lamartine tended toward radical republicanism in politics. Serving as a deputy for several years, he distinguished himself as an orator. A leader in the Revolution of 1848, he became the virtual chief of the provisional government, but fell from power upon the coup d'état of Napoleon III (1852).

Lamb, Lady Caroline (1785–1828) English novelist, the wife of William Lamb (later 2d Viscount Melbourne, prime minister to Queen Victoria). Lamb is better known for her nine-months' intrigue with Lord Byron than for any of her novels. She was neurotic and demanding, and Byron soon tired of her. She took revenge in an anonymous novel, *Glenarvon* (1816), which contains a caricature of the poet. After Byron's death she gave way to conduct of such impropriety that Melbourne was forced to separate from her.

Lamb, Charles (pen name Elia, 1775–1834) English essayist of the romantic period, a schoolmate of COLERIDGE, and friend of other figures of English romanticism. Lamb attempted work in the fields of drama and poetry, but was most successful in the personal essay. His writings in this form are known for their humor, whimsy, and faint overtones of pathos. He was also a perceptive critic with a special sympathy for the work of Elizabethan and early 17th-century writers: a sympathy that is reflected in his own vivacious, idiosyncratic style.

His essays are contained in the two series entitled *Essays of Elia*, which appeared in the *London Magazine* from 1820 to 1823 and from 1824 to 1825, being collected and published in 1823 and 1833, respectively. Outstanding single essays are: A DISSERTATION ON ROAST PIG; "A Chapter on Ears"; "Mrs. Battle's Opinions on Whist"; DREAM CHILDREN; and "The Supernatural Man." His most famous other works are *Tales from Shakespeare* (1807), adaptations for children written in collaboration with his sister, Mary Lamb, and *Specimens of English Dramatic Poets Contemporary with Shakespeare* (1808), his best-known critical work. Because he was most comfortable with short forms and took great pleasure in communicating with his friends, some of his best writing is in his letters, particularly those to Coleridge, which contain sharp, discriminating criticism of the work the poet had sent to him. An 1848 collection of letters was re-edited by E. V. LUCAS (3 vols) in 1905. *The Letters of Charles and Mary Lamb* (2 vols, ed E. W. Marrs) appeared in 1975–76.

Though he was much loved for his sweetness and humor, Lamb's life was marked by frustration and tragedy. A stammer kept him from qualifying for a university position, so he went to work as a clerk for the East India Company, where he remained until 1825. There was a strain of insanity in the family, and Mary Lamb, in a fit of madness, killed their mother. Lamb, who had himself spent time in a madhouse and who suffered from alcoholism, took lifelong care of his sister.

lamb In Christian art and imagery, JESUS is often symbolically represented as a lamb, in allusion to John 1:29, "Behold the Lamb of God, which taketh away the sins of the world." The reference is to his sacrificial act for the redemption of the sins of all men.

Lamech See JUBAL.

Lamentations of Jeremiah, The An OLD TESTAMENT book, traditionally ascribed to the prophet JEREMIAH, but probably the work of various authors. The book consists of five poems, the first four of which are alphabetical ACROSTICS. It laments the misery and suffering that attended the destruction of Jerusalem and offers a poignant repentance for the sins of the people in hopes that they will be restored to God's mercy.

Lament for the Death of a Bullfighter See GARCÍA LORCA, FEDERICO.

La Mettrie, Julien Offroy de (1709–1751) French physician and philosopher, the most notorious materialist of his day. La Mettrie's most famous work, *L'Homme machine* (1747), shows how thought depends on matter, not on God or the soul, and that though man is a machine, he is too complicated ever to be completely understood.

lamia A female phantom. Her name was used by the Greeks and Romans as a bugbear to children. She was a Libyan queen beloved by ZEUS, but robbed of her offspring by the jealous HERA. In consequence she vowed vengeance against all children, whom she delighted to entice and devour.

Witches in the Middle Ages were called lamioe, and KEATS's poem "Lamia" (1820), which relates how a bride when recognized returns to her original serpent form, represents one of the many superstitions connected with the race. Keats's story came (through Burton) from Philostratus's *De vita Apollonii*, Bk. iv. In Burton's rendering, the sage Apollonius, on the wedding night

found her out to be a serpent, a lamia. . . . When she saw herself descried, she wept, and desired Apollonius to be silent, but he would not be moved, and thereupon she, plate, house, and all that was in it, vanished in an instant; many thousands took notice of this fact, for it was done in the midst of Greece.—*Anatomy of Melancholy*, Pt. iii, sect. ii, memb. i, subsect. i.

Lammermoor See BRIDE OF LAMMERMOOR, THE.

Lamming, George (1927–   ) Barbadian novelist. Taken together, Lamming's early novels—*In the Castle of My Skin* (1953), *The Emigrants* (1954), *Of Age and Innocence* (1958), and *Season of Adventure* (1960)—form a continuum which moves from childhood to adulthood and from the island home (the imaginary San Cristobal) overseas. While these are political novels about Caribbean society, they also become a chronicle of emotional dislocation and personal development. His books deal with the responsibility of the artist to himself, his society, and the community of man, "his third world." Among Lamming's other works are *Water with Berries* (1971), *Natives of My Person* (1972), and a long essay, *The Pleasures of Exile* (1960), about the problems of the emigrant West Indian writer. Lamming has lived in England for many years.

Lampedusa, Giuseppe Tomasi, Prince of (1896–1957) Sicilian aristocrat, author of THE LEOPARD. Lampedusa was a member of an old, noble Sicilian family. He wrote his only novel late in life, within a few months in 1956 and 1957. Parts of the novel were submitted to at least two of Italy's major publishing houses, but were rejected largely on ideological grounds. Ultimately, the novel was brought to the attention of Giorgio BASSANI, then a consultant to Feltrinelli publishers, who finally issued it in book form several months after the author's death from cancer. The only other book of Lampedusa's writing, *Racconti* (1961; tr *Two Stories and a Memory*, 1962), contains short works of fiction and autobiographical fragments.

lampoon (fr Fr, *lampon*, fr the refrain *lampons*, "let's drink," in 17th-century French satirical drinking songs) A malicious, often scurrilous satirical piece, in prose or poetry, attacking an individual's character or appearance. The lampoon flourished in 17th- and 18th-century England. It fell into disuse as a result of a revulsion of public feeling, as well as of modern libel laws. The term is still in use, however, both as noun and verb, for any piece of pointed mockery of an individual or institution. A generalized use is seen in the name of the Harvard University humor magazine, *The Harvard Lampoon*.

Lancastrian A member or supporter of the English royal house of Lancaster during the Wars of the Roses.

Landor, Walter Savage (1775–1864) English poet, literary critic, and prose writer. Landor is best remembered for his interest in the classics and for the severity and intellectual coldness of his lyrics, many of which were written in direct imitation of Greek and Latin models. Among his works are *Gebir* (1797), an Oriental tale in blank verse; *Imaginary Conversations* (1824–53), a series of discussions between historical figures on a variety of subjects; and "Rose Aylmer," his best-known lyric.

In his youth, Landor was influenced by the revolutionary atmosphere of the time and was forced to leave Oxford because of his opinions. In 1808 he went off with a regiment he had raised to fight Napoleon in Spain. He tried to institute humanitarian reform on his estate in Wales but failed, and for a number of years lived in Italy. His poetry was never popular in his own time.

Landseer, Sir Edwin Henry (1802–1873) English painter. Landseer was a prodigy whose works were exhibited in London when he was thirteen. He became the most famous and popular of all VICTORIAN painters of animals. He painted highly detailed, humorous scenes of dogs and cats with anthropomorphic qualities as in *Dignity and Impudence* (1857) and sentimental works like *The Old Shepherd's Chief Mourner* (1837). He was a favorite of Queen VICTORIA, whose portrait he painted, and he also fashioned the four lions at the base of NELSON's Column in Trafalgar Square, London.

Lang, Andrew (1844–1912) Scottish scholar and man of letters. Lang wrote several books of graceful verse and collaborated with Samuel Henry Butcher on a well-known prose translation of the *Odyssey* (1879). He is now probably best remembered for the numerous volumes of fairy stories he edited. These volumes were named after colors, e.g., *The Red Fairy Book*.

Lang, Fritz (1890–1976) Austrian-born American filmmaker. In over fifty years of film work, Lang survived the two world wars (in the first, fighting in the Austrian army; before the second, escaping from the Nazis in 1933 and settling in the U.S. in 1934), bridged the change from silent movies to sound, and successfully adapted to the Hollywood studio system. His German expressionist films, more than his American productions, are acute in emotional content, cinematically innovative, and remarkably consistent in theme, dealing with the psychology of crime and death. Among his best-known German works are *Metropolis* (1927), now recognized as a cinematic milestone, *The Last Will of Dr. Mabuse* (1932), and *M* (1933). In Hollywood he made an anti-Nazi collaboration with Bertolt BRECHT, *Hangmen Also Die* (1943). His other well-known American films are *Ministry of Fear* (1944), *Scarlet Street* (1945), and *The Big Heat* (1953). See EXPRESSIONIST CINEMA.

Langer, Susanne K[nauth] (1895–1985) American philosopher. Langer was influenced by Alfred North WHITEHEAD's analysis of symbolic modes and by the work of the German philosopher Ernst Cassirer; her own concern, however, was primarily with aesthetics. In her major work, *Philosophy in a New Key: A Study of the Symbolism of Reason, Rite, and Art* (1942), she developed the distinction between discursive (scientific) and nondiscursive (artistic) symbols. Her other works include *Feeling and Form: A Theory of Art* (1953), *Problems of Art* (1957), *Philosophical Sketches* (1962), and *Mind: An Essay on Human Feeling* (2 vols, 1967, 1972).

Langland, William See PIERS PLOWMAN.

Langton, Stephen (c1150–1228) English prelate, statesman, and scholar, Archbishop of Canterbury (after 1207). King John refused to recognize his appointment until 1213, and Langton became the leader of the barons in their struggle against John, representing them with his signature on the MAGNA CARTA.

langue d'oc and langue d'oïl The two groups of medieval Romance dialects that emerged from Vulgar Latin in Gaul, named after the word for "yes" in each group. The *langue d'oc* was spoken in the region of southern France and northern Italy known as Provence. The *langue d'oïl* was spoken in France north of a line running approximately from the mouth of the Gironde River east to the Alps; it was the ancestor of standard modern French (in which *oïl* became *oui*).

Lanier, Sidney (1842–1881) American poet. After graduating from Oglethorpe University in his native Georgia in 1860, Lanier enlisted in the Confederate army and, in 1864, was captured and imprisoned for four months at Point Lookout, Maryland. He emerged from the war afflicted with the tuberculosis that remained with him for the rest of his short life. Prevented by economic necessity from devoting himself to literature, Lanier worked at odd jobs after the war. In 1873 he settled in Baltimore, becoming first flutist with the Peabody Symphony Orchestra.

Considered one of the most accomplished poets of the American South in the latter half of the 19th century, he tried to achieve in his work the auditory effect of music and experimented with varying metrical patterns and unusual imagery. Much of his poetry shows an affinity with that of the Pre-Raphaelites and Swinburne. His best-known poems include *The Symphony* (1875), a denunciation of industrialism designed to illustrate the close relationship between poetry and music; THE MARSHES OF GLYNN; and *The Song of the Chattahoochee* (1883), notable for its successful combination of alliteration, onomatopoeia, and melody. Lanier also wrote *Tiger Lilies* (1867), a novel based on his Civil War experiences, and three works of criticism, *The Science of English Verse* (1880), *The English Novel* (1883), and *Shakespeare and His Forerunners* (1902).

Laocoön   In Greek mythology, a Trojan priest who, having offended the gods, was strangled by sea serpents. In VERGIL's AENEID, he draws down the anger of ATHENE by warning the Trojans not to accept the TROJAN HORSE and by hurling his javelin into the hollow flank of the wooden statue dedicated to her. She sends two huge sea snakes to the shore where Laocoön, assisted by his two sons, is sacrificing to POSEIDON. The monsters choke the three to death.

The famous group of sculpture representing these three in their death agony, now in the Vatican, was discovered in 1506, on the Esquiline Hill in Rome. It is a single block of marble, and is attributed to Agesandrus, Athenodorus, and Polydorus of the school of Rhodes in the 2nd century BC. The discovery lent tremendous impetus to the renascence of interest in the classical period and had great impact on the art world.

In a famous treatise on the limits of poetry and the plastic arts (1766), LESSING uses this group as the peg on which to hang his dissertation, called LAOCOÖN.

Laocoön, or On the Limits of Painting and Poetry (Laokoon, oder Über die Grenzen der Malerei und Poesie, 1766)   An essay by Gotthold Ephraim LESSING. It seeks to dispute the idea that art criticism and literary criticism may be based on the same principles. The fundamental point is that a painting exists in space and all its parts are perceived simultaneously, whereas a work of literature exists in time and its parts are perceived one after another. On this basis, Lessing develops an extensive theory of the respective domains of painting and poetry, in which he challenges some of Winckelmann's ideas. Lessing uses the statue *Laocoön* as one of his central examples.

Laodicean   One indifferent to religion, caring little or nothing about the matter. The reference is to Rev. 3:14–18, where the Christians of the city of Laodicea are "lukewarm."

Laomedon   In classic myth, a king of Troy, the father of PRIAM. Laomedon is remembered chiefly for his ingratitude in refusing to give the rewards he had promised to APOLLO for pasturing his flocks on Mount Ida, to POSEIDON for building the walls of Troy, and to HERACLES for rescuing his daughter Hesione from the sea-monster sent by Poseidon. Heracles slew him and all his sons but Priam in revenge.

Lao She (pen name of Shu Ch'ing-ch'un, 1899–1966) Chinese writer. Born in Peking of Manchu parents, he began to write during a stay in England. On his return to China he occupied various educational posts and headed the Chinese Writers' Anti-aggression Association during the war years (1938–45). He was active in literature in the People's Republic of China but was denounced during the Cultural Revolution and was reportedly killed. His writing is known for its humorous and satirical approach and for its elegant use of the Peking dialect. His best-known work was translated into English as *Rickshaw Boy* (1945), a best-seller in America. Its original intent was distorted, however, by an unauthorized happy ending added by the translator.

Lao Tzu (6th century BC)   Legendary Chinese philosopher, supposedly an elder contemporary of CONFUCIUS. Lao Tzu is sometimes identified with a certain Lao Tan, an archivist of the state of CHOU, but this is uncertain, as are many other stories about him. He is revered as one of the founders of philosophical TAOISM. Lao Tzu is also the name of one of the basic Taoist texts, a book more commonly known in the West as the TAO TE CHING.

Lapiths   A Thessalian tribe. They were neighbors of the CENTAURS, with whom they had a famous battle. The Lapiths invited the Centaurs to the wedding of their king, Pirithous, to Hippodamia. Under the influence of wine, the Centaurs tried to carry off the Lapith women, including even the bride, but were roundly defeated. During the battle, an invulnerable Lapith leader named Caeneus was driven into the ground by the Centaurs, since he could not be killed. This Caeneus had been a girl until, upon being violated by Poseidon and granted a boon, she chose to become a man and invulnerable. The battle of Centaurs and Lapiths was a favorite subject for Greek artists. It appeared on the PARTHENON, the Theseum at Athens, and the temple of Apollo at Basso, as well as on numberless vases.

Lapointe, Paul-Marie (1929–   )   Quebec poet. Lapointe is at once one of the most broadly North American of Quebec poets and one of the most hermetic. His poems range from the surrealistic explosion of *La Vierge incendié* (1948) to the more public poems in *Pour les âmes* (1964) and *Tableaux de l'amoureuse* (1974). In Lapointe's vision, mechanism continually threatens spontaneous vitality and joyful sensuality. His is a poetry of revolt, spontaneity, and articulate improvisation, as in the exuberant *Choix de poèmes—arbres* (1960) and in the more tense and concise *Courtes pailles* (1965). His collected poems were published in *Le Réel absolu* (1971).

Laputa   The flying island which Gulliver visits in Jonathan SWIFT's GULLIVER'S TRAVELS. It is largely inhabited by abstract philosophers. In this third voyage, technical knowledge is extensively satirized. Laputans, in their preoccupation with the theoretical and with innovation in technical methods, are ill equipped for living in society. Swift regarded Laputan ingenuity as misplaced. See LAGADO.

Lardner, Ring[gold Wilmer] (1885–1933) American humorist and short-story writer. Lardner is known for his mordant wit, exemplified in satirical stories and sketches of American life in the early 20th century, told in the language of baseball players, boxers, songwriters, stockbrokers, stenographers, chorus girls, etc. A man who preferred listening to talking, he had an infallible ear for vernacular and an exceptional gift for parody. His first important work, YOU KNOW ME, AL, was followed by a series of books including *Gullible's Travels* (1917); HOW TO WRITE SHORT STORIES (WITH SAMPLES); *The Love Nest and Other Stories* (1926), a collection that included the famous story "Haircut"; and *The Story of a Wonder Man* (1927), a satirical autobiography; and *June Moon* (1929; with George S. KAUFMAN), a play satirizing the songwriters of Tin Pan Alley.

Lardner's four sons inherited his gift for writing. James died in the Spanish Civil War, but his letters revealed an unusual talent with words. David wrote for THE NEW YORKER before he, too, was killed in World War II. Before his death, the oldest son, John, applied the Lardner style to distinguished sportswriting. Ring, Jr. (1915–   ), whose term in jail for defying the House Committee on Un-American Activities inspired his novel *The Ecstasy of Owen Muir* (1955), collaborated on the screenplay for *Woman of the Year* (1942), for which he won an Academy Award, provided the script for *M*A*S*H* (1970), and wrote a thoughtful biography of his family, *The Lardners* (1976).

lares Household gods of the ancient Romans, usually referred to in the singular (*lar*), there being one lar to a household. The lares were protective, and were usually deified ancestors or heroes. The *lar familiaris* was the spirit of the founder of the house who, never leaving, accompanied his descendants in all their changes. See PENATES.

Lark, The (L'Alouette, 1953) A play by Jean ANOUILH about JOAN OF ARC. It was translated into English by Christopher Fry in 1955.

Larkin, Philip [Arthur] (1922–1985) English poet and novelist. Larkin came from a working-class background in the industrial north of England as a scholarship student to Oxford. The physical and human landscape of his past is reflected with lyrical grace in his first, Yeatsian volume of poems, *The North Ship* (1946), and in his two novels, *Jill* (1946) and *A Girl in Winter* (1947), both sensitive and accomplished works. After this Larkin returned permanently to verse and, with *The Less Deceived* (1955), established himself as the leader of the English anti-romantic movement, handling the old themes of childhood, love, and death with a searing wit and a sophisticated roughness

of style and feeling. He confirmed his hold on the English poetry-reading public with *The Whitsun Weddings* (1964) and *High Windows* (1974). He also published *All What Jazz* (1970), a collection of record reviews, and succeeded YEATS as editor of the *Oxford Book of Twentieth Century English Verse* (1973). *Required Writing: Miscellaneous Pieces, 1955–1982* (1984) won the 1984 W. H. Smith Literary Award.

La Rochefoucauld, Duc François de (1613–1680) French writer. In his *Mémoires* (1662), La Rochefoucauld records his political activities, describing his efforts to destroy the power of Cardinal RICHELIEU over the royal family and his participation in the battle of the FRONDE. After 1652 he abandoned politics for a sheltered intellectual life. The *Maximes* (*Maxims*, 1665) are concise and biting observations upon society and human nature, illustrating his conviction that self-interest is the spring of human conduct and that men delude themselves in pretending to virtue or disinterested behavior.

Larra [y Sánchez de Castro], Mariano José de (known as Fígaro, 1809–1837) Spanish journalist, literary critic, and author. Larra was famous for his satirical articles on Spanish regional life which appeared in the magazine *El pobrecito hablador* (1832–33), which Larra edited and wrote himself. His novel *El doncel de don Enrique el Doliente* (1834) and the drama *Macías* (1834) deal with the tragic loves of an actual medieval minstrel.

Larreta, Enrique Rodriguez (1875–1961) Argentine novelist. Larreta was a romantic who wrote with great technical precision. He recreated the Spain of Philip II in *La gloria de don Ramiro* (1908; tr *The Glory of Don Ramiro*, 1924). His dark and lyrical stories are remarkable for images which assault the reader's senses with colors, sounds, and smells. Other well-known works are two *gaucho* novels, *Zogoibi* (1926) and *En la pampas* (1955), and *El Gerardo* (1956), a two-part novel set in the Alhambra and Argentina, respectively, shortly after the Spanish Civil War.

Larsen, Wolf See SEA WOLF, THE.

Lars Porsena See PORSENA.

La Salle, Sieur de (Robert Cavelier, 1643–1687) French explorer in North America. La Salle descended the Mississippi River to the Gulf of Mexico (1682), claiming the entire valley for France. He named the region Louisiana after the French king Louis XIV.

Las Casas, Bartolomé de (1474–1566) Spanish-born Dominican missionary and historian. Las Casas came to Santo Domingo in 1502 and was the first priest ordained in the New World (1510). In 1514, Las Casas suddenly became aware of the injustice with which the Indians were being treated in America, and subsequently devoted himself entirely to promoting their welfare, usually with the support of the crown, but against the bitter opposition of the Spanish settlers. *Brevísima relación de la destrucción de las Indias* (1522), his vivid, but probably exaggerated, account of Indian sufferings, was instrumental in fostering the long-lived "black legend," which denigrated the colonial policies of Spain in America. His major work, *Historia general de las Indias* (1875), is an important source for the early period of colonization in Latin America.

Lasch, Christopher (1932–) American social critic and cultural historian. Lasch, a professor of history, is known for his penetrating analyses of contemporary American cultural and political phenomena. *The New Radicalism in America 1889–1963: The Intellectual as a Social Type* (1965) is a collection of critical and biographical essays detailing the psychological motivations of 20th-century social activism. In *The Culture of Narcissism* (1979), which became an unlikely best-seller, Lasch examined the effects of an increasingly self-centered worldview on the family and the community. He has consistently challenged contemporary Americans' reliance on experts to determine standards of behavior and thought. *The Minimal Self* (1984) examines individual freedom and privacy in the light of the agencies for social control in our lives. It is a study of the self through politics, culture, and psychoanalysis.

Laski, Harold J[oseph] (1893–1950) English political scientist. A Marxist, but not a Communist, Laski considered his political philosophy to be a logical outgrowth of Jeffersonian democracy. He believed that the state should be responsible for social reform and served as chairman of the Labour Party (1945–46). He was an authority on American politics, history, and law. Among his books are *The American Presidency* (1940), *The American Democracy* (1948), and *Liberty in the Modern State* (1948). His long and fruitful friendship with Justice Oliver Wendell HOLMES, Jr., is recorded in *The Holmes-Laski Letters* (2 vols, 1953).

Last Days of Pompeii, The (1834) A historical novel by Edward BULWER-LYTTON. The young Greek lovers, Glaucus and Ione, are thwarted in their intentions by Ione's rancorous guardian. The eruption of Vesuvius fortuitously allows them to escape to happiness.

Last Exit to Brooklyn See SELBY, HUBERT, JR.

Last Leaf, The (1907) A short story by O. HENRY. None of O. Henry's tales is more characteristic of his technique and sentiment than this account of a girl who lies, desperately ill of pneumonia, in a Greenwich Village apartment and makes up her mind to die as soon as the last leaf of five drops off the vine outside her window. One leaf hangs on, and she recovers—but there is a typical O. Henry twist to the ending.

Last of the Just, The See SCHWARTZ-BART, ANDRÉ.

Last of the Mohicans, The (1826) A novel by James Fenimore COOPER, the second of THE LEATHERSTOCKING TALES. The plot revolves around the efforts of Alice and Cora Munro to join their father, the British commander at Fort William Henry, near Lake Champlain.

Their course is blocked by Magua, the leader of a group of Hurons, who are leagued with the French against the British in the war. The schemes of Magua, an evil Indian, are frustrated by Uncas, the last of the Mohicans; his father, Chingachgook; and their friend Hawkeye (see Natty BUMPPO). The rhythm of the book is set by a series of thrilling attacks, captures, flights, and rescues. At the climax, Cora is killed by Magua and Uncas dies trying to save her.

Last Puritan, The (1936) A novel by George SANTAYANA. Subtitled *A Memoir in the Form of a Novel*, the book is a study of Oliver Alden, descendant of an old and wealthy New England family, who comprises in himself the Puritan characteristics of austerity, single-mindedness, gravity, and conscientious, scrupulous devotion to purpose. He is out of place in the civilization of the 20th century. In style, subject matter, and approach, *The Last Puritan* recalls the novels of Henry JAMES.

Last Rose of Summer, 'Tis the The title and first line of a song, used notably in the second act of the opera *Martha* (1847) by Friedrich von Flotow. It was written (1813) by Thomas Moore to the tune of an old air.

Last Supper The last meal shared by JESUS and his twelve APOSTLES. They celebrated the PASSOVER, then Jesus gave his followers bread and wine, thus instituting the sacrament of the EUCHARIST, also known as the Lord's Supper and Holy Communion. The original occasion has been the subject of many works of art, the most famous of which is a fresco by LEONARDO DA VINCI in the refectory of Santa Maria delle Grazie, Milan. It shows the consternation of the disciples when Jesus told them that he would be betrayed that night.

Late George Apley, The (1937) A novel by John P. MARQUAND. Subtitled *A Novel in the Form of a Memoir*, the story is told by Horatio Willing, a staid and polished annotator, who manages to satirize himself as he recounts the life of the recently deceased George Apley, a conventional, tradition-bound, but somewhat pathetic Bostonian. A highly successful book, it was awarded the PULITZER PRIZE and later dramatized (1946) by its author and George S. KAUFMAN.

Latimer, Hugh (1485?–1555) English bishop and Protestant martyr. Latimer was made bishop of Worcester in 1535, but resigned because he felt unable to accept the Act of the Six Articles of 1539. On the accession of MARY I he was committed to the Tower, and was burned at the stake for heresy in 1555.

Latinus The legendary king of the Latini, the ancient inhabitants of Latium. According to Vergil's AENEID, Latinus had been advised by an oracle to give his daughter, LAVINIA, in marriage to a stranger. Accordingly, he offers her to AENEAS, but Turnus, king of Rutuli, declares that she is betrothed to him. The contest between Aeneas and Turnus is settled by single combat, in which Aeneas is victorious.

Latitudinarians   Members of the liberal faction of the Church of England in the time of Charles II. They opposed the doctrinal rigidity of both the High Church and the Puritans. The term came to be applied to those persons who attach little importance to dogma and what are called orthodox doctrines.

Latmos, Mount   The mountain where ENDYMION pastured his flocks when SELENE, goddess of the moon, fell in love with him.

La Tour du Pin, Patrice de (1911–1975)   French poet. After the youthful and mainly religious lyrics of *La Quête de joie* (1933), he collected all his succeeding volumes into *Une Somme de poésie* (1946; tr *The Dedicated Life in Poetry*, 1947), a long and allusive work interspersed with prose speculations which give it a mythological and philosophical unity. The development of the adolescent concerned only with himself into an adult involved with the fraternity of men provides subject and pattern for the work. *Le Second Jeu* (1959) stresses again that the man is born only through the death of the child, and leads La Tour du Pin to the third stage, the Christian confrontation with the mystery of God.

Laud, William (1573–1645)   English prelate. The son of a clothier, he rose to the rank of Archbishop of Canterbury (1633) and became one of the foremost supporters of Charles I, representing absolutism in both Church and State. His attempts to impose High Church conformity in Scotland and England aroused the bitter opposition of the Puritans. Impeached for treason by the Long Parliament (1640), he was condemned and beheaded.

lauda   Religious songs popular in Italy during the medieval and early Renaissance periods. These used the *ballata* form, in which a stanza of varying length is followed by a two-line refrain, and were composed for lay confraternities. The outstanding early master of *lauda* was Jacopone da Todi (1230–1306). As the form developed in his hands and in those of his successors, it became increasingly dramatic, with dialogue, action, and setting assuming dominance. As such, it became the Italian equivalent of the mystery play, called SACRA RAPPRESENTAZIONE ("sacred representation"). Though plays of this type dwindled in popularity in the later Renaissance, they left their influence on the secular and neoclassical drama, which replaced them in popularity. During the Renaissance, some *lauda* were still written, but not for religious organizations; usually they were conceived as texts for musical setting, to be performed by individual artists or as part of religious services.

Launcelot, Sir   In ARTHURIAN LEGEND, the most famous of the knights of the Round Table. In the early Welsh legends of King Arthur, he does not appear, but almost seems a French innovation since we first find him figuring importantly in the 12th-century *Lancelot, or the Knight of the Cart* by Chrétien de Troyes. He comes to full growth, however, in Malory's *Morte d'Arthur* (c1469), as do so many of the other Arthurian characters.

In most versions he is the son of King Ban of Benwick, and his full title is Sir Launcelot du Lac (see LADY OF THE LAKE). In almost all versions in which he appears, he is the champion and lover of Queen GUINEVERE and the favorite of King Arthur. In Malory's version, he begets Sir GALAHAD by ELAINE, when he is deceived into believing that she is Guinevere, and he is then driven to madness for a long period by the jealousy of Guinevere. Most of his exploits are in the name of the queen, one way or another, and sometimes they take the form of rescuing her, as, for example, from being burnt at the stake. He is finally exiled by King Arthur, who afterwards comes to war with him at Benwick. In a combat with Sir GAWAIN, Launcelot mortally wounds that knight; then, going back to England, he finds King Arthur dead, the Round Table dissolved, and Queen Guinevere become a nun. He himself becomes a monk and dies not long after Guinevere. Launcelot is a major figure in Tennyson's *Idylls of the King* (1859–85). See JOYOUS GARD.

Laura   The beloved of PETRARCH and the subject of his collection of lyrics called *Rime* (*Verses*) or *Canzoniere* (*Song Book*). The poet says he first saw her in the church of St. Claire at Avignon on April 6, 1327, fell in love, and was inspired to write poetry. Her death, on the same date twenty-one years later, resulted in a profound spiritual crisis with which the poet struggled for the remainder of his life. Who Laura actually was is still a controversial matter. It was formerly thought that she was a certain Laure de Noves of Avignon, born in 1308, wedded to Hugues de Sede and the mother of eleven children, who died in the great plague of 1348. Modern scholars reject this identification in favor of the idea that Laura is a poetic fiction, a symbol of the poet's aspirations as well as a focal point of his psychological conflicts. In the poems, Petrarch frequently puns on the name because of its resemblance to the Italian words for *air* and *laurel* (hence, inspiration and fame). The name has been used by poets ever since, in love poems addressed to a similar idealized lady. Robert Tofte entitled his 1597 collection of love lyrics *Laura*; Lord Byron used the name for the Venetian lady who marries Beppo in the poem of the same name; and Schiller wrote a series of poems to Laura.

laureate   See POET LAUREATE.

Laurence, Friar   The wise and kindly Franciscan friar in Shakespeare's ROMEO AND JULIET who marries the young lovers. He hopes that the alliance will end the feud between the Montagues and Capulets.

Laurence, [Jean] Margaret [Wemyss] (1926–)   Canadian novelist. Born of Scots-Irish descent in Manitoba, Laurence married in 1947 and spent eight years in Africa, the setting of her early books: a novel, *This Side Jordan* (1960); a volume of short stories, *The Tomorrow-Tamer* (1963); and a travel book, *The Prophet's Camel Bell*

(1963; U.S. *New Wave in a Dry Land*, 1964). Settling in England in 1962, she began her series of "Manawaka" novels, set in her birthplace, which dramatize the lives of prairie women: *The Stone Angel* (1964), *A Jest of God* (1966), *The Fire Dwellers* (1969), and *A Bird in the House* (1970). *The Diviners* (1974) is a complex novel about a writer striving to understand herself as she faces middle age. Other books include a juvenile story, *Jason's Quest* (1970), and a collection of essays, *Heart of a Stranger* (1976).

Lauriers sont coupés, Les (1888; tr We'll to the Woods No More, 1938)   A novel by Edouard Dujardin. It is considered the first example in fiction of an intended interior monologue (see STREAM OF CONSCIOUSNESS). The story is told through the thoughts and impressions of the young protagonist, Daniel Prince, as he walks the streets and meets friends, sits in a restaurant, rides in a carriage, or visits Léah d'Arsay, an actress whom he courts but never wins. James Joyce is said to have read this book about 1901 and to have been partly influenced by it while writing ULYSSES. Dujardin himself claimed to have been influenced in his technique by Richard WAGNER's device of the musical LEITMOTIF, by the dramatic monologues of Robert BROWNING, and by the psychological monologues of DOSTOYEVSKY.

Lavengro: The Scholar, Gypsy, Priest (1851) A novel by George Borrow (1803–81). Mingling autobiography with fiction, the author relates the wanderings of a young man who is interested in philology and becomes intimate with a family of gypsies. His adventures are resumed in the sequel, *The Romany Rye* (1857). The name *Lavengro*, which means "philologist" in the language of the gypsies, was applied to Borrow in his youth.

Lavinia   (1) In Vergil's AENEID, the daughter of LATINUS. Lavinia is betrothed to Turnus, king of the Rutuli. When AENEAS lands in Italy, Latinus makes an alliance with the Trojan hero and promises to give him Lavinia as his wife. After Aeneas defeats the angry Turnus, he marries Lavinia and becomes by her the ancestor of ROMULUS, the mythical founder of Rome. The ancient city of Lavinium near Rome was said to have been built by Aeneas and named after her.

(2) See TITUS ANDRONICUS.

Lavransdatter, Kristin   See KRISTIN LAVRANSDATTER.

Lawler, Ray[mond Evenor] (1922–   )   Australian playwright. Lawler's most outstanding achievement is his quintessentially Australian play SUMMER OF THE SEVENTEENTH DOLL, for which he gained global recognition. Although many of his plays are set in England, the most successful are rooted in the Australian experience, as with *The Man Who Shot the Albatross* (1971), based on Captain Bligh of H.M.S. *Bounty*.

Law of Moses   See PENTATEUCH.

Lawrence, D[avid] H[erbert] (1885–1930) English novelist, short-story writer, poet, and essayist. Lawrence is known for his frequently misunderstood but basically idealistic theories about sexual relations and for his interest in primitive religions and nature mysticism. Lawrence regarded sex, the primitive subconscious, and nature as cures for what he considered modern man's maladjustment to industrial society. His philosophy, life history, and prejudices are inextricably involved in his writings; many of his views are expressed in WOMEN IN LOVE and LADY CHATTERLEY'S LOVER. SONS AND LOVERS is a partly autobiographical novel which deals with the author's boyhood and adolescence as the son of a coal miner. Lawrence struggled to become a teacher, then an established member of London's literary society, but he never ceased to rebel against Anglo-Saxon puritanism, social conventions, and mediocrity, a rebellion which led to his involvement in some of the most famous censorship cases of the 20th century. He was attracted to the Nietzschean idea of the superman and expressed his idea of the hero in his novels KANGAROO and THE PLUMED SERPENT.

Lawrence's work, of great volume and variety, is uneven in literary value. At its best it is marked by intensity of feeling, psychological insight, vivid evocation of events, places, and particularly nature. A controversial figure, he is regarded by some critics as the greatest of modern English novelists; most concede that he is a major writer in spite of his overfondness for preaching, his obscurantism, and his ranting attacks on the people and institutions he regarded as his enemies. Lawrence's other novels are *The White Peacock* (1911), *The Trespasser* (1912), THE RAINBOW, *The Lost Girl* (1920), *Aaron's Rod* (1922), and *The Boy in the Bush* (1924), in collaboration with M. L. Skinner. Among his short novels are *The Captain's Doll* (1923), *St. Mawr* (1925), THE MAN WHO DIED, and *The Virgin and the Gipsy* (1930). Lawrence's short stories, which do not have the faults of his novels, are widely admired. Among them are THE PRUSSIAN OFFICER, "Sun," "The Fox," THE WOMAN WHO RODE AWAY, "The Man Who Loved Islands," THE ROCKING-HORSE WINNER, and THINGS. His early fiction tends to be fairly conventional and realistic, while his later work is more immersed in the subconscious and rich in symbolism. Some of his later short stories, however, are taut and naturalistic.

Lawrence's first published works were poems (see MIRIAM). He began by writing in the school of imagism. His best-known poems are in free verse, about the individual, inner nature of animals and plants: "Fish," "Snake," "Mountain Lion," and "Bavarian Gentians" are among them. *Birds, Beasts and Flowers* (1923) is a well-known collection. *Look! We Have Come Through* (1917) is a collection of poems about his relationship with his wife, Frieda von Richthofen LAWRENCE. *Pansies* (1929) is a collection of didactic, satiric, and iconoclastic poems, which was seized as immoral by the English authorities on its first publication.

Lawrence's fine, vivid collections of travel sketches are *Twilight in Italy* (1916), *Sea and Sardinia* (1921), *Mornings in Mexico* (1927), and *Etruscan Places* (1927). His most influential book of criticism is *Studies in Classical American Literature* (1923), which contains brilliant, eccentric insights into American writers from Benjamin Franklin to Walt Whitman. *Psychoanalysis and the Unconscious* (1921) and *Fantasia of the Unconscious* (1922) are statements of his philosophy. He wrote a great many colloquial, iconoclastic essays, including *Pornography and Obscenity* (1930), *Reflections on the Death of a Porcupine* (1934), and *Democracy* (1936). He also wrote *Movements in European History* (1921), under the pen name of Lawrence H. Davidson, and a few unsuccessful plays. His outstandingly interesting *Letters* were edited by Aldous HUXLEY (1932), while an eight-volume series of his *Letters* began publication in 1979.

Even after Lawrence established himself in London literary circles—he was a close friend of Aldous Huxley (see POINT COUNTER POINT) and of Katherine MANSFIELD and J. Middleton MURRY—he still had many troubles. He suffered from tuberculosis, saw his books banned as obscene, and was persecuted during World War I for his supposed pro-German sympathies. Disgusted by England, he left it to travel with his wife, but he was continually disappointed in his quest for a homeland and congenial associates. At one time or another, Lawrence lived in Italy, Germany, Ceylon, Australia, New Zealand, Tahiti, the French Riviera, Mexico, and the southwestern part of the United States. In Taos, New Mexico, an artists' colony, he once dreamed of setting up an ideal social community. (See Mabel Dodge LUHAN.) At the end of his life, he was extravagantly admired by several women who called him Lorenzo, regarded themselves as his disciples, and engaged in jealous quarrels over his attentions. After Lawrence's death, a number of people who had known him published books and memoirs about him, both unfriendly and adulatory, often attacking each other. Among these remembrances were those of J. Middleton Murry, Mabel Dodge Luhan, Richard ALDINGTON, E. T. (see MIRIAM), and his wife. The perennial wrangling among critics about Lawrence's literary influence testifies to the complexity of his acknowledged genius.

Lawrence, Frieda von Richthofen (1879–1956) Aristocratic German wife of D. H. LAWRENCE. She was married to Professor Ernest Weekley, an English philologist, and had three children when she met Lawrence and eloped with him in 1912. Lawrence described their stormy, happy marriage in his writings, especially in the collection of poems *Look! We Have Come Through* (1917) and in the novels WOMEN IN LOVE and KANGAROO. She wrote *Not I, But the Wind . . .* (1934), a memoir of her husband. Her brother, Manfred von Richthofen, was a celebrated German aviator during World War I, still popularly known in the U.S. as The Red Baron.

Lawrence, T[homas] E[dward] (known as Lawrence of Arabia, 1888–1935) English soldier, archaeologist, and author. Lawrence is famous for his activities in arousing and directing a successful rebellion of the Arabs against the Turks during World War I, for his account of his exploits in *Seven Pillars of Wisdom* (1926), and for his enigmatic personality. During the war, he became an almost legendary figure in the Middle East; after the war, he received a number of honors and was offered but refused the Victoria Cross and a knighthood. He retired from public life to write the *Seven Pillars of Wisdom*, an abridgment of it called *The Revolt in the Desert* (1927), and a prose translation of Homer's *Odyssey* (1932). Meanwhile he sought still more obscurity by joining the Air Force as a private under the name of Shaw. His journal from this period was published as *The Mint* (1955). There has been much interest in and controversy about Lawrence's psychological motivations. B. H. Liddell-Hart, Robert GRAVES, and Richard ALDINGTON are among those who have written about him.

Lawrence, Sir Thomas (1769–1830) English portrait painter. A child prodigy, Lawrence succeeded Sir Joshua REYNOLDS as principal painter to the king in 1792. He was the graceful and romantic portraitist of the most brilliant society of England, and, after his reputation spread to the Continent, he painted the European princes and the heroes of the Napoleonic wars.

Lawrence of Arabia See LAWRENCE, T. E.

Lawson, Henry [Archibald Hertzberg] (1867–1922) Australian BUSH BALLADEER and short-story writer. Lawson was the son of a Norwegian seaman; he grew up with a troubled home life and deafness. His knockabout career was punctuated with periods of poverty, drunkenness, hospitalization, and imprisonment. *Poetical Works* (1925) contains Lawson's robust ballads, but his greatest contribution was his stories, collected in *Prose Works* (1935). These, with their advocacy of the underdog, their protests against privilege, and their focus on "mateship," create a classic picture of rural Australia in the 1890s.

Laxdale Saga An Icelandic saga of the early Middle Ages, dealing chiefly with the wilful, selfish Gudrun, who falls in love with Kjartan. While Kjartan is at the court of King Olaf, his cousin Bolli tells Gudrun that Kjartan has become friendly with Olaf's sister Ingebjorg. Vindictively, Gudrun marries Bolli; when Kjartan returns to Iceland and hears of the marriage, he marries Hrefna, also vindictively. He gives to Hrefna an ornate coif, which Ingebjorg had originally sent with him as a gift for Gudrun, and this causes Gudrun to precipitate a feud between the two families by having the coif stolen. There follows a series of raids and battles in which Kjartan is eventually killed through the machinations of the woman who really loved him and whom he loved.

Laxness, Halldór Kiljan (pen name of Halldór Gudjonsson, 1902–   ) Icelandic poet, novelist, and playwright. One of the great figures in modern Icelandic literature, Laxness passed through several spiritual stages during the course of his literary career. As a world traveler, he discovered EXPRESSIONISM in Germany and SURREALISM in France, both of which influenced his work, and he was converted to Catholicism in Luxembourg. The novels *Undir Helgahnúk* (*Under the Holy Mountain*, 1924) and *Vefarinn mikli frá Kasmir* (*The Great Weaver from Kashmir*, 1927) reflect his spiritual turmoil and the discontent that led him to the Church. A meeting with Upton SIN-CLAIR during a visit to the U.S. caused another conversion, this time to communism; when he returned to Iceland in 1930, he published *Alþýðubókin* (*The Book of the People*), a collection of essays expressing his new communist views. Laxness's finest work, however, appears in the three novels set in an Icelandic fishing village—*Þú vínvíður hreini* (1931) and *Fuglinn í fjörunni* (1932; both tr *Salka Valka*, 1936); *Sjálfstoett fólk* (2 vols, 1934–35; tr *Independent People*, 1945–46); and *Ljós heimsins* (4 vols, 1937–40; tr *World Light*, 1969). These novels are a rich blend of social criticism, vivid lyricism, and a turbulent, exciting prose style. The simple village girl, the sturdy farmer, and the victimized poet, who contains an inextinguishable spark of life, emerge as powerful symbols. Among his other highly intelligent, often irreverent works are *Paradísarheimt* (1960; tr *Paradise Reclaimed*, 1962) and *Kristnihald undir Jökli* (1968; tr *Christianity at the Glacier*, 1972). Laxness was awarded the NOBEL PRIZE in Literature in 1955.

lay See LAI.

Laye, Camara (1928–1980) Guinean novelist. Laye's father was a goldsmith, his mother the daughter of a goldsmith. A Muslim, Laye attended Koranic school and a French primary school in his native village, Kouroussa. He then studied mechanical engineering and automotive mechanics in France. His first book, *L'Enfant noir* (1953; tr *The Dark Child*, 1954), is a nostalgic autobiography written in Paris. It records with deep insight and affection his recollections of his childhood at the forge and on the farm in Kouroussa. This was followed by *Le Regard du roi* (1954; tr *The Radiance of the King*, 1956), an allegorical novel about man's search for God. A second (and autobiographical) novel, *Dramouss* (1966; tr *A Dream of Africa*, 1968), reintroduces characters from *L'Enfant noir*; it is a grim and horrifying picture of Guinean life from an adult perspective. Its unconcealed criticism of the regime of President Sekou Touré led to Laye's forced exile from his country.

Lay of the Last Minstrel, The (1805) A narrative poem by Sir Walter SCOTT. Lady Margaret of Branksome Hall, "the flower of Teviot," is beloved by Baron Henry of Cranstown, but a deadly feud exists between the two families. The poem celebrates the martial prowess and amorous success of the baron.

Lays of Ancient Rome (1842) A series of ballads by Thomas Babington MACAULAY. The chief ballads are "Horatius" (see HORATIUS COCLES), "The Battle of Lake Regillus," and "Virginia."

Layton, Irving (1912–   ) Rumanian-born Canadian poet. Layton's family settled in Montreal in 1913. He is known for his poems of protest against the social inequities he saw both in the countryside and in the city; often he shocked readers with harsh, "unpoetic" images. Among his works are *Here and Now* (1945); *In the Midst of My Fever* (1954); *The Bull Calf and Other Poems* (1956); *The Swinging Flesh* (1961), which includes short stories; *The Collected Poems of Irving Layton* (1977); and *Droppings from Heaven* (1979).

Lazarillo de Tormes, La vida de (1554) A PICA-RESQUE novel by an anonymous author, sometimes identified with Diego HURTADO DE MENDOZA. Divided into seven chapters, or *tratados*, it is the autobiography of the wily Lázaro, who describes his experiences with the various masters whom he served: the blind man, the miserly priest, the proud but hungry squire, the mendicant friar, the seller of indulgences. He ends his career as town crier of Toledo. Written with vigorous realism and irony, *Lazarillo* was enormously popular and inspired several sequels. It is considered the greatest Spanish work in this genre.

Lazarus (1) In the NEW TESTAMENT, the brother of MARTHA and Mary of Bethany, whom Jesus raised from the dead after four days (John 11–12).

(2) In one of Jesus' parables, the sick and starving man who begged daily at the gate of the rich man, DIVES (Luke 16:19). When he died, he was received into ABRAHAM'S BOSOM.

Lazarus, Emma (1849–1887) American poet and translator. Lazarus translated Heine's poems and published a novel, *Alide: An Episode in Goethe's Life* (1874). This early work, flowery and romantic, would not have won her a reputation. In 1882, however, her indignation was kindled by the Russian pogroms; she set out to defend and glorify the Jewish people. *Songs of a Semite* (1882) includes her best poem, "Dance to Death." Her sonnet "The New Colossus" (1883) is inscribed on the pedestal of the Statue of Liberty. *By the Waters of Babylon* (1887) showed the influence of Whitman.

Lazarus Laughed (1927) A drama by Eugene O'NEILL. It deals with LAZARUS after his resurrection by Jesus. The man to whom new life has been given goes about preaching a new religion of love and eternal life, symbolized by laughter. He eventually goes to Rome and causes a sensation there, finally being stabbed by CALIGULA in the great amphitheatre of the city but affirming until the last his belief in the triumph of life. Seven masked choruses, symbolizing varying periods of life, are used in this play.

Leacock, Stephen [Butler] (1869–1944) Canadian economist and humorist. As chairman of the Department of Economics and Political Science (1908–36) at McGill University, Leacock published numerous serious works in his field, as well as in history and biography. He is best known, however, for his collections of satirically humorous short stories and essays, including *Literary Lapses* (1910), *Nonsense Novels* (1911), *Moonbeams from the Larger Lunacy* (1915), *Frenzied Fiction* (1917), and *Winnowed Wisdom* (1926). His autobiography, *The Boy I Left behind Me* (1946), and a collection of essays, *Last Leaves* (1945), were published posthumously.

League of Nations   A league to promote international cooperation and peace, formed after World War I. Its headquarters were at Geneva, Switzerland. Its members were the signatories of the treaty of VERSAILLES on behalf of the Allies, with certain other states, including Germany and the U.S.S.R. Although it was created largely through the exertions of President Woodrow WILSON, the U.S. Senate refused to ratify the treaty of Versailles, and thus the U.S. was never a member of the league.

During the 1920s, the league was able to settle a few minor disputes between nations, and its contributions in the fields of refugee rehabilitation, public health, and international labor problems were considerable, but it had no power to enforce its policies in cases of war waged by important nations. It failed conspicuously to halt the invasion of Ethiopia by Italy (1935), of China by Japan (1937), and the Civil War in Spain (1936–39). Several members, including Italy, Japan, and Germany, resigned from the league in the late 1930s. It was formally dissolved on April 18, 1946, its material and moral heritage being taken over by the UNITED NATIONS.

Leah   In the OLD TESTAMENT, the daughter of LABAN and sister of RACHEL. She became one of the wives of JACOB.

Leander   See HERO AND LEANDER.

Lear, King   See KING LEAR.

Lear, Edward (1812–1888)   English painter and writer. He is known for his LIMERICKS and nonsense verse, marked by absurd humor, whimsy, and fantasy. These are inimitable of their kind and perennial classics of English humorous verse. "The Owl and the Pussycat" (1871) is his best-known set of verses. His books include *A Book of Nonsense* (1846), *Nonsense Songs, Stories, Botany, and Alphabets* (1871), *More Nonsense Songs* (1872), and *Laughable Lyrics* (1877). Lear was also the author of interesting illustrated travel books, such as a *Journal of a Landscape Painter in Greece and Albania* (1852), and so prominent a painter of landscape and animals that he once gave drawing lessons to Queen Victoria.

Leatherstocking Tales, The   A series of five novels by James Fenimore COOPER. The novels appeared in the following sequence: THE PIONEERS, THE LAST OF THE MOHICANS, THE PRAIRIE, THE PATHFINDER, and THE DEERSLAYER. The series follows the career of Natty BUMPPO from his youth (*Deerslayer*) to his death (*The Prairie*). An abridg-

ment of the five novels was made by Allan Nevins in a single volume called *The Leatherstocking Saga* (1954).

Leaves of Grass   A collection of poems by Walt WHITMAN. First published in 1855, it was revised and augmented every few years until the poet's death in 1892. The first edition, unsigned, contained only twelve untitled poems. The first and longest was later called SONG OF MYSELF. In 1855 the poems were preceded by a preface declaring Whitman's poetic credo. "The United States themselves," he said, "are essentially the greatest poem." The country's genius is the common people; the poet must be "commensurate" with the people and "incarnate" the spirit and geography of the States. Echoing *Walden* (1854), Whitman praises simplicity. A great poem, he says, is for "all degrees and complexions and all departments and sects." The poem's form was to be organic; it must grow out of the demands of its subject.

The book, radical in form and content, takes its title from the themes of fertility, universality, and cyclical life. Critics have noted the influence of Shakespeare and the Hebraic poetry of the Bible.

As he revised and added to the original edition, Whitman arranged the poems in a significant autobiographical order. In the final poems, the poet, though dead, survives in his work. In 1881, the permanent order of the volume was established; all later work was assigned to two annexes. The final or "death-bed" edition was issued in 1892.

Leavis, F[rank] R[aymond] (1895–1978) English literary critic, one of the CAMBRIDGE CRITICS, and editor of the influential quarterly SCRUTINY. An outspoken and confident man, Leavis made it his business to establish and maintain standards in English literature and criticism. He wrote controversial essays attacking what he considered mediocre and dilettantish work. Above all, he required literature to have moral value and to be centrally concerned with the health of society. He admired George ELIOT and D. H. LAWRENCE and praised them extravagantly. His chief works are *New Bearings in English Poetry* (1932), *Revaluation: Tradition and Development in English Poetry* (1936), *The Great Tradition: George Eliot, Henry James, and Joseph Conrad* (1948), *The Common Pursuit* (1952), *D. H. Lawrence, Novelist* (1955), and *The Living Principle* (1975).

Lebyadkin, Captain   In DOSTOYEVSKY's novel THE POSSESSED, the comical and unscrupulous brother of Marya Timofeyevna. He calls himself a retired army captain, although doubt is cast on the truth of this by the narrator. Lebyadkin, who callously mistreats his sister, continually tries to extort money from STAVROGIN for her support. He is murdered along with Marya at the end of the novel.

Lebyadkin, Marya Timofeyevna   In DOSTOYEVSKY's novel THE POSSESSED, the crippled half-wit whom STAVROGIN has married for obscure and perverse reasons. She is portrayed in the tradition of the Russian "holy fool" and, along with SHATOV, is the vehicle for the expression of many of Dostoyevsky's own religious ideas.

le Carré, John (pen name of David John Moore Cornwell, 1931–   ) English novelist. Widely known as the creator of George Smiley, the aging, diffident, indomitable secret service agent, le Carré draws on his background in the Army Intelligence Corps and Foreign Service to explore the moral problems of patriotism, espionage, and ends and means. Like Graham GREENE, he writes probing moral tales which are at the same time exciting stories. *The Spy Who Came in from the Cold* (1963), the story of a stale, worn-out agent who, in his last assignment, is brutally used and destroyed by his superiors, became an international best-seller. Others of his novels are *The Looking-Glass War* (1965), *Tinker, Tailor, Soldier, Spy* (1974), *The Honourable Schoolboy* (1977), *Smiley's People* (1980), *The Little Drummer Girl* (1983), and *A Perfect Spy* (1986). His style is precise and elegant and his novels are noted for subtle characterization, authenticity, and brilliant plotting. He vividly, often bitterly, describes the seedy aspects of espionage and examines the problems of men who are both the creators and victims of institutions which devour them. Many of his novels have been made into films.

Leçon, Le See IONESCO, EUGÈNE.

Leconte de Lisle, Charles Marie René (1818–1894) French poet, leader of the PARNASSIANS. A dislike for the excessive subjectivity and exaggerated emotionalism of the romantic writers caused him to write poetry that was objective in content and austere in style. Leconte de Lisle gave voice to dark pessimism, and his hatred for the ugly industrial civilization in which he lived led him to seek his subjects in the past or in strange, distant places. His works include *Poèmes antiques* (1852), *Poèmes barbares* (1862), *Histoire populaire du Christianisme* (1871), *Poèmes tragiques* (1884), and *Derniers Poèmes* (1895). His drama *L'Apollonide* (1888) and the verse tragedy *Les Erinnyes* (1889) are also well known.

Lecoq, Monsieur A brilliant detective created by Emile Gaboriau (1835–73), who pioneered the detective story in France. Lecoq, whose character was based on François VIDOCQ, a real-life Parisian chief of detectives, appears in several novels: *Monsieur Lecoq* (1869), *L'Affaire Lerouge* (1866), and *Le Dossier no. 113* (1867). He is one of the first of the famous detectives of literature and a precursor of Sherlock HOLMES.

Le Corbusier (real name Charles Édouard Jeanneret, 1887–1965) Swiss-born French architect and painter. Le Corbusier is known largely for his contributions to functionalism, a concept advocating the unity of aesthetics, form, and function. He believed that a new social and human order could be created by shaping an environment that would satisfy man's needs for light, order, and even joy. His ideas had a profound influence on the developing field of city planning. He accepted the machine as an object of absolute perfection and attempted to expand and humanize industrial concepts to construct "machines for living."

Among his best-known creations are the "Radiant City" in Marseilles, the students' pavilion at the Cité Universitaire in Paris, the main buildings of the new capital of Chandigarh in Punjab, India, and the graceful chapel of Nôtre-Dame-du-Haut in Ronchamp. Many of Le Corbusier's articles were published in *Vers un architecture nouveau* (1923; tr *Toward a New Architecture*, 1927), which along with his other writings had a considerable effect on the development of modern architecture.

Leda In Greek mythology, the wife of TYNDAREUS. She was the mother by ZEUS (who is fabled to have come to her in the shape of a swan) of two eggs, from one of which came CASTOR and CLYTEMNESTRA, and from the other Polydeuces and HELEN. There are, however, many versions of their birth. The subject of Leda and the Swan has been a favorite with artists; Paul VERONESE, CORREGGIO, and MICHELANGELO have all left paintings of it.

Leduc, Violette (1907–1972) French novelist. Of illegitimate birth, rejected by her mother, she had several lesbian affairs before her unrequited passion for the homosexual writer Maurice Sachs led her to write *L'Asphyxie* (1946; tr *In the Prison of Her Skin*, 1970). Her other novels are thinly veiled autobiographical confessions of ugly but sincere and lucidly poetic women who long for consolation and understanding: *Ma mère ne m'a jamais donné la main* (1945), *L'Affamée* (1949), *La Bâtarde* (1964; tr 1965), her first book to gain public attention, *La Femme au petit renard* (1965; tr *The Woman with the Little Fox*, 1966), *La Folie en tête* (1970; tr *Mad in Pursuit*, 1971), and *Le Taxi* (1971; tr *The Taxi*, 1972).

Lee, Ann (1736–1784) English mystic and founder of the American Shaker society in Watervliet, New York (1776). Lee claimed the power of discerning spirits and working miracles. She was known to her followers as "Ann the Word" or "Mother Ann" since they were convinced that she was the manifestation of the female counterpart of Christ.

Lee, Dennis (1939–   ) Canadian poet, editor, and literary critic. Lee's serious poetry, in *Kingdom of Absence* (1967) and *Civil Elegies* (1968; expanded 1972), contains anguished laments for the lost values and broken spirits he sees in modern Canada. In a different vein are his volumes of nonsense verse for children, *Nicholas Knock* and *Alligator Pie* (both 1974). *Savage Fields* (1977) is a work of literary criticism.

Lee, [Nelle] Harper (1926–   ) American novelist. Lee's first and only novel, *To Kill a Mockingbird* (1960), was published to almost unanimous critical acclaim. The story is narrated by Scout, a six-year-old Southern girl whose father, a lawyer, defends a black man accused of the rape of a white woman. The novel, which paints a vivid picture of life in a small southern town, won a PULITZER PRIZE in 1961.

Lee, Robert E[dward] (1807–1870) American soldier. The son of Henry Lee, a brilliant cavalry commander in the Revolutionary War, he was graduated from West Point in 1829, fought in the Mexican War, and commanded the marine detachment that quelled John Brown's abortive insurrection in 1859. Although Lee favored preservation of the Union, loyalty to his native Virginia, where his family had long been prominent, led him to refuse field command of the U.S. army in 1861 and to accept command of the state's forces. Named commander of the Army of Northern Virginia in 1862, he thwarted McClellan's Peninsula Campaign against Richmond in the Seven Days' Battles (1862), suffered a technical defeat at Antietam, and won engagements at Fredericksburg and CHANCELLORSVILLE. His defeat at GETTYSBURG began the attrition of Confederate strength that compelled him to surrender to Grant at Appomattox Courthouse on April 9, 1865. After the war, Lee became president of Washington College in Virginia, which was later renamed Washington and Lee University in his honor. An excellent strategist and leader of men, Lee is admired in both the North and the South for his courage and chivalry.

Le Fanu, J[oseph] S[heridan] (1814–1873) Irish novelist and short-story writer. Best known for his mystery novel *Uncle Silas* (1864), Le Fanu had begun writing ghost stories anonymously in 1839 with "Schalken the Painter," a story of the seduction of a young woman by a living corpse, a subtle and chilling precursor of modern occult tales. A contemporary of POE, with whom he is often compared, his treatment of the supernatural was distinguished by a black humor more characteristic of writers a century later than of his own time.

LeGallienne, Eva (1899–   ) English-born American actress, director, and producer. LeGallienne is known for her contributions to repertory theatre in the U.S. In 1926 she founded and directed the Civic Repertory Theatre in New York; twenty years later she co-founded the American Repertory Theatre. She translated many of Ibsen's plays, and in 1968 she directed her translation of THE CHERRY ORCHARD on Broadway. Her autobiographies, *At 33* (1934) and *With a Quiet Heart* (1953), were reprinted in 1974.

legend A narrative such as a story, song, verse, or BALLAD handed down from the past and often conveying the lore of a culture. It is distinguished from MYTH by its closer relation to historical fact than to the supernatural. The earliest legends recounted the lives of saints. The term also applies to the brief explanations of symbols used in pictures, maps, and charts.

Legend of Good Women, The (c1386) Unfinished poem by Geoffrey CHAUCER, of over twenty-seven hundred lines in decasyllabic couplets. In the prologue, which contains the best poetry, the poet describes his delight at wandering through the meadows on a May morning, especially celebrating the daisy. He falls asleep and dreams that the god of Love, attended by Queen ALCESTE, appears and berates him for having translated the *Romance of the Rose* and written *Troilus and Criseyde*, thereby discouraging men from the service of COURTLY LOVE. Alceste intercedes, pointing out Chaucer's exaltation of love in other works, and suggests that he be allowed to redeem himself by writing a collection of twenty lives of women who have served Love truly and well. There follow nine short narratives, modeled on stories by VERGIL and OVID, about women who suffered or died because they were faithful in love and (except for the first two stories) because men were treacherous: CLEOPATRA; Thisbe (see PYRAMUS); DIDO; Hypsipyle and MEDEA, both betrayed by JASON; Lucrece; ARIADNE; PHILOMELA; Phyllis, betrayed by Demophon; and Hypermnestra.

Legend of Sleepy Hollow, The (1819) A tale by Washington IRVING, collected in his SKETCH BOOK OF GEOFFREY CRAYON, GENT. The story takes place at Sleepy Hollow, now Tarrytown, New York. Ichabod CRANE, the local schoolmaster, courts Katrina Van Tassel. The affair is interrupted when Crane's rival, Brom Bones, masquerades as a headless horseman, and scares the schoolmaster out of town.

Legends of the Alhambra, The (1832; enlarged 1852) A group of tales and sketches on Spanish subjects by Washington IRVING. The book grew out of Irving's sojourn in Spain as a member of the U.S. Embassy, in 1826. The legends deal with the clashes between Spaniard and Moor. Irving, an admirer of Moorish civilization, invests the tales with glamor and mystery.

Léger, Aléxis St.-Leger See PERSE, ST.-JOHN.

Léger, Fernand (1881–1955) French artist whose paintings, murals, tapestries, mosaics, and stained glass windows exercised a profound influence upon his time. In 1917 Léger began to construct his compositions from mechanical elements such as radiators, railway wheels, or cogs; human figures were themselves treated as machines. Léger's art gradually became more human, achieving a liveliness and gaiety while retaining its monumental quality. His construction workers, mechanics, divers, or picnickers were constructed in bright flat colors increasingly dissociated from his strong and direct drawing but full of movement and power.

Legion of Honor (Légion d'honneur) A French order of distinction and reward instituted by Napoleon Bonaparte in 1802 for either military or civil merit. The order has continued to exist in France during the 19th and 20th centuries.

Legree, Simon The cruel plantation owner in Harriet Beecher STOWE's UNCLE TOM'S CABIN. He flogs Uncle Tom, causing his death, when the latter refuses to reveal the hiding places of two runaway women slaves. His name has become a synonym for a brutal taskmaster.

Le Guin, Ursula K[roeber] (1929–   ) American writer of SCIENCE FICTION and fantasy. Le Guin's early novels and stories fit into her "Hainish series," unified by her concept that an ancient civilization "seeded" the universe which then became inhabited by remotely related, vastly different forms of humanoids. Two particularly outstanding novels in the series are *The Left Hand of Darkness* (1969), which uses ambisexual aliens to comment on humans' sexual mores, and *The Dispossessed* (1974), in which the values of an anarchist world are contrasted with those of a world divided between capitalist and communist systems. Informed by a Taoist vision of wholeness and balance, Le Guin's stylistically precise and imagistically rich fiction transcends mere genre-writing and has gained serious critical attention. Her intricate allegorical trilogy intended for children, collected as *Earthsea* (1977), has also won a wide adult audience. *Always Coming Home* (1985) is a rich blend of magic realism, myth, technology, poetry, drama, and music.

Lehár, Franz (1870–1948) Hungarian composer of operettas. Lehár composed over thirty-five operettas, but none came close to the stupendous success of *Die lustige Witwe* (*The Merry Widow*, 1905). Also well known, however, are *The Count of Luxembourg* (1909) and *Das Land des Lächelns* (*The Land of Smiles*, 1929).

Lehmann, John [Frederick] (1907–   ) English editor and poet, brother of Rosamond LEHMANN. Lehmann was associated with Leonard and Virginia WOOLF's Hogarth Press. He also edited the influential left-wing magazine *New Writing* (1936–50) and *The London Magazine*, from its founding in 1954 to 1961. He published the work of his friends W. H. AUDEN, Stephen SPENDER, and Christopher ISHERWOOD, among others, and provided a forum for many younger writers. His autobiography, *In My Own Time* (1969), condensed from three earlier volumes, amounts to a literary history of his day. Lehmann's own poetry was published in such volumes as *Collected Poems 1930–1960* (1965) and *The Reader at Night* (1974). Among his other works are *Virginia Woolf and Her World* (1975) and *Thrown to the Woolfs* (1978).

Lehmann, Rosamond [Nina] (1901–   ) English novelist, sister of John LEHMANN. Lehmann's *Dusty Answer* (1927), a delicate treatment of the lesbian relationship of two young women in their college years, is the best known of a series of successful novels. *Invitation to the Waltz* (1932) describes the experiences and feelings of a girl at her first elegant party. *The Ballad and the Source* (1945) is an experimental novel in which the most violent events that afflict three generations of a tragically doomed family are narrated by a fourteen-year-old girl. Among her many other books are *The Gypsy's Baby* (1946; repr 1972), a collection of short stories; *The Echoing Grove* (1953); *The Swan in the Evening* (1967), a work of autobiography; and *A Sea-Grape Tree* (1976). A writer of grace and sensibility,

she has been compared with Virginia WOOLF and Elizabeth BOWEN.

Leibnitz, Baron Gottfried Wilhelm von (1646–1716) German philosopher, trained in mathematics and law. Leibnitz developed a philosophy of RATIONALISM by which he attempted to reconcile the existence of matter with the existence of God. He believed in a pre-established harmony between matter and spirit. Because there is only one world, a world created by God, he argued that it must be "the best of all possible worlds." Leibnitz was ridiculed by Voltaire in CANDIDE for the apparently irresponsible optimism of this view; however, Leibnitz intended a metaphysical concept that applied to a world of absolutely fixed, predetermined order. In his *Monadologie* (1714), Leibnitz maintained that the divine order of the universe is reflected in each of its parts, each part being called a *monad*. Monads are infinite in number and are arranged in an absolute hierarchical order. Rational monads are capable of self-consciousness, but because their position in the universe is fixed (i.e., there is no choice of action), there is no such thing as free will. Evil exists, but only to accentuate goodness; one cannot be without the other.

Most of Leibnitz's philosophical writings were not published until after his death. His contributions to mathematics, however, were also significant. Independently of NEWTON, he developed and published (1684) the system of differential and integral calculus which became the basis for modern mathematics.

Leipzig, battle of (also called the Battle of the Nations) A famous battle on October 16–18, 1813, where the French under Napoleon Bonaparte were badly defeated by the allied forces of Prussia, Austria, Sweden, and Russia.

Leir, King A central figure in a tale in the HISTORY OF THE KINGS OF BRITAIN by Geoffrey of Monmouth. His story is much the same as that found in Shakespeare's great tragedy KING LEAR. For his tragedy, Shakespeare seems to have made use of the version of Leir's story found in Holinshed's *Chronicles*.

leitmotif (Ger, "leading motif") In musical drama, a recurrent musical theme that coincides with each appearance of a given character, problem, emotion, or thought. It was used most notably by WAGNER and in Berg's Wozzeck (1925). The term has also been applied to a corresponding device in literature. In conscious emulation of Wagner, Thomas MANN employed the leitmotif technique in THE MAGIC MOUNTAIN. For example, each appearance of SETTEMBRINI in the novel is accompanied by the same brief description of his clothes. It is also a prominent feature of both ULYSSES and FINNEGANS WAKE.

Lely, Sir Peter (originally Pieter van der Faes, 1618–1680) Dutch-born English portrait painter. Lely immigrated to England c1642. In 1661 he became court painter to Charles II and produced a number of handsome portraits of Restoration figures. His studio became a school that introduced Dutch techniques of color and finish to the artistically isolated British, which were later adapted by Sir Joshua REYNOLDS.

Lem, Stanislaw (1921–   )   Polish writer of SCI-ENCE FICTION and theoretical criticism. Trained as a doctor, Lem is Poland's best-selling and most widely translated author. His books cover a broad stylistic and thematic range and employ science fiction as a narrative vehicle for the exploration of serious philosophical questions. *Solaris* (1961; tr 1970), his first novel to be translated into English, makes use of an alien sentient ocean to explore one of Lem's fundamental concerns, the anthropomorphic limitations of man. Though much of his work is in a lighter, satirical vein, like *Dzienniki gwiazdowe* (1957; tr *The Star Diaries*, 1976), nearly all of it is touched by a black humorist's sense of the grotesque along with a profound humanism and, always, paradox. Apart from his monumental nonfiction volume on futurology and socio-cybernetics, *Summa technologiae* (1964), his many novels include *Sledztwo* (1959; tr *The Investigation*, 1974), *Niezwyciezony i inne opowiadania* (1963; tr *The Invincible*, 1973), *Cyberiada* (1965; tr *The Cyberiad*, 1974), and *Doskonala próznia* (1971; tr *A Perfect Vacuum*, 1979), which contains parodic reviews of nonexistent books, spoofing purely rational and pedantic approaches to science and literature. *Fiasco*, a novel about cosmic travel, was published in 1987.

Lemnos   The island where HEPHAESTUS fell when ZEUS flung him out of heaven. One myth connected with Lemnos tells how the women of the island, in revenge for their ill-treatment, murdered all the men. The ARGONAUTS found the place an "Adamless Eden." They were received with great favor by the women; as a result of their few months' stay the island was repopulated, and the queen, Hypsipyle, became the mother of twins by JASON.

Lemonnier, Camille (1844–1913)   Belgian novelist, art critic, and playwright. The most influential of those writers associated with La Jeune Belgique, Lemonnier wrote many volumes of art criticism, over twenty collections of short stories, and thirty novels.

lemures   The name given by the Romans to the spirits of the dead, especially specters which wandered about at nighttime to terrify men.

Lemuria   The name given to a lost land that supposedly connected Madagascar with India and Sumatra in prehistoric times.

Lenau, Nikolaus (pen name of Nicolaus Franz Niembsch, Edler von Strehlenau, 1802–1850)   Hungarian-born Austrian poet, considered Austria's most important lyric poet. His lyrics are marked by a striking precision of imagery and morbid personal intensity that reflects his depressed, unstable temperament. His major works are two religious epics, *Savonarola* (1837) and *Die Albigenser* (1842), and the three-thousand-line verse-drama, *Faust* (1836), strongly derivative of GOETHE's work. In 1832 he immigrated to the U.S. hoping to begin a new,

idyllic existence, but returned, disillusioned, to Germany in 1833. In 1844 he suffered a complete mental breakdown from which he never recovered.

Lenclos, Anne (known as Ninon de Lenclos, 1620–1705)   French lady of fashion. Famous for her wit and beauty, she conducted a dazzling salon and numbered among her lovers the most distinguished men of the day. In the novel *Clélie*, her friend Madeleine de Scudéry drew a portrait of her under the name Clarisse.

Lenin, Nikolay (pseudonym of Vladimir Ilyich Ulyanov, 1870–1924)   Russian Communist leader. Lenin, who led the BOLSHEVIKS to power in 1917, was born in Simbirsk (now Ulyanovsk), the son of a provincial schoolmaster. His elder brother Alexander was executed in 1887 for an attempt on the life of Tsar Alexander III. Lenin attended the universities of Kazan and St. Petersburg where he became a profound student of Marxism and entered revolutionary activity in the 1890s. Much of his time was spent in Siberian exile or abroad. In 1903 he became a leader of the Bolshevik faction of the Social Democratic Party, having been largely responsible for the schism that split the party, the other faction being known as the Mensheviks. Lenin's drive and astuteness as a practical revolutionary led the Bolsheviks to power in the coup d'état of October (November by the Western calendar) of 1917. He became the head of the Soviet state and retained the post until his death. Like his colleague TROTSKY, Lenin had a background of bourgeois culture and apparently was little interested in the sort of manipulation of cultural life that took place under STALIN. His giant mausoleum in Red Square, Moscow, is a national shrine.

Lenormand, Henri René (1882–1951)   French dramatist. His plays, influenced by Freudian theory, show the psychological conflicts of men at the mercy of the forces of nature. *Le Temps est un songe* (1919), *Les Ratés* (1920), *Le Mangeur des rêves* (1922; tr *The Dream Doctor*, 1928), and *L'Homme et ses fantômes* (1924; tr *Man and His Phantoms*, 1928) are among his better-known works. His complete works for theatre appeared in ten volumes between 1921 and 1949.

Lent   The Christian period of fasting, penitence, and spiritual renewal preparatory to EASTER. Lent begins with ASH WEDNESDAY, the seventh Wednesday before Easter, and ends at midnight of Holy Saturday on the eve of Easter. The last two weeks of Lent are called Passiontide, commemorating Christ's redemptive suffering during his last days of human life and his crucifixion.

Lenz, Jakob Michael Reinhold (1751–1792)   German poet and dramatist of the STURM UND DRANG, admirer of Goethe. His plays, which are distinguished by a revolutionary realism and looseness of form, include *Der neue Menoza* (*The New Menoza*, 1774) and the comedies *Der Hofmeister* (1774) and *Die Soldaten* (*The Soldiers*, 1776). He also wrote lyric poetry and criticism, including

Anmerkungen über Theater (*Remarks on the Theatre*, 1774).

Lenz, Siegfried (1926–   )   German novelist, short-story writer, dramatist, and essayist. Lenz was born and raised in a small town in East Prussia. After naval duty in World War II (which he fled as a "conscientious defector"), unfinished university studies, and a brief stint as a journalist, he wrote his first novel, *Es waren Habichte in der Luft* (*There Were Hawks in the Air*, 1951), which introduced elements that were to figure prominently in his later works: considerations of conscience and heroism in a time of moral crisis, and the nature of oppression in its tyrannical interference with individual freedom and inner independence. The woodcutters, peasants, fishermen, and small craftsmen of his idyllic childhood memories (people Lenz calls "the simple gold of human society") are portrayed in his first volume of stories, *So zärtlich war Suleyken* (*That's How Tender Suleyken Was*, 1955). His best-known novel, *Deutschstunde* (1968; tr *The German Lesson*, 1971), is a forceful reexamination of the Nazi past which exposes the eternal barbarian in man. Other works of fiction include *Stadtgespräch* (1963; tr *The Survivor*, 1965), *Das Vorbild* (1973; tr *An Exemplary Life*, 1976), and *Heimatmuseum* (1978; tr *The Heritage*, 1981). *Einstein überquert die Elbe bei Hamburg* (1975) is a collection of stories written between 1966 and 1975.

Leonard, William Ellery (1876–1944)   American poet. Leonard is best known for his sonnet sequence *Two Lives* (1925), an autobiographical account of his tragic first marriage that ended in his wife's suicide. His other volumes of verse include *The Vaunt of Man and Other Poems* (1912), *The Lynching Bee* (1920), and *A Man against Time* (1945). *The Locomotive God* (1927) is his autobiography. His special interest in classical literature led to his translations of the poetry of Lucretius (1916) and a study of that poet's life (1942).

Leonardo da Vinci (1452–1519)   Italian painter, sculptor, architect, engineer, scientist, poet, and musician. A universal genius and one of the greatest intellects in the history of mankind, Leonardo was born at Vinci, near Florence, and became in 1468 an apprentice to Verrocchio. The latter's *Baptism of Christ* contains the head of an angel now universally acknowledged to be by his pupil, Leonardo, who was already his superior. In 1482 he went to Milan, where he worked for Lodovico Sforza as an engineer as well as a designer of costumes and scenery for court entertainments. He also made sketches for churches, painted the murals and ceiling pictures of the Sforza castle, and worked on problems of irrigation and central heating. In 1502 he served for a time as military engineer to Caesar Borgia. An offer from the French king, Francis I, took him to France in 1516, where he stayed until his death. Misfortune and Leonardo's own habit of endlessly experimenting with pigments have left few of his paintings to posterity. The best known are *The Adoration of the Magi*

(1481) in the Uffizi; *The Virgin of the Rocks* (1493) and *Mona Lisa* (also called La Gioconda, c1503–6), both in the Louvre; and the Last Supper (1495–?1498) in the Milan church of S. Maria delle Grazie. *The Battle of Anghiari*, done in 1505 at Florence in competition with Michelangelo, survives only in drafts. His style in painting is characterized by the use of *sfumato*, or blurring of outlines, the mysterious effects of chiaroscuro, the clarity of composition, and the overall tone of serenity. In sculpture, only sketches remain of the destroyed equestrian statue of Francesco Sforza and of the unfinished one of the *condottiere* Trivulzio. He left no architectural works, but his sketches for buildings and even whole cities were influential for his contemporaries. As engineer and scientist, Leonardo was led by his avid curiosity to speculate about and experiment with various mechanical devices, including guns and cannon, flying machines, parachutes, hydraulic works, submarines, and spiral staircases. In his notebooks there are some five thousand pages of sketches and comments that reveal his concern with anatomy, botany, and mathematics, including mechanical perspective drawings, studies of people and animals, caricatures, plant studies, and landscapes. He also left a treatise on painting, *Trattato della pittura* (1489–1518), which has been extracted from notebooks. Here he espoused again his favorite motif: fidelity to nature, which must be observed directly, not through abstractions or Aristotle or Galen. It was this attention to things themselves which produced the paradox of Leonardo's life, for he accomplished hardly a fraction of his schemes, so overwhelmed was he by the need to investigate and know everything. But even his most tentative ideas and experiments were years ahead of his time and simply beyond the capacities of his contemporaries.

Leonidas   A Spartan king and hero (fl early 5th century BC). Leonidas resisted the Persians at Thermopylae with only three hundred Spartans and was slain with all his forces at the pass. See Persian Wars; Simonides.

Leonov, Leonid Maksimovich (1899–   )   Russian novelist, playwright, and short-story writer. Leonov fought with the Red Army during the civil war. He published some short stories during the early 1920s, but first attracted attention in 1924 with a long story, *Konets melkogo cheloveka* (*The End of a Petty Man*). The story dealt with the acceptance of the revolution by a member of the older generation and foreshadowed a theme Leonov and others were to take up often in later works. Leonov's first novel, *Barsuki* (1924; tr *The Badgers*, 1947), deals with the conflict between the city and countryside during the civil war. The conflict is personified in two brothers, one of whom leaves the village for the city and eventually comes back at the head of an armed force sent to quell a revolt led by his brother. Leonov's second novel, considered by some critics his best work, is The Thief, which is set in the period of the New Economic Policy in Russia.

Leonov's other novels are *Sot* (1930; tr *Soviet River*, 1931), *Skutarevsky* (1932), *Doroga na okean* (1935; tr *Road to the Ocean*, 1944), and *Russkiy les* (1953; tr *The Russian Forest*, 1966). His best-known plays include *Polovchanskiye sady* (1938; tr *The Orchards of Polovchansk*, 1946), *Nashestviye* (1942; tr *Invasion*, 1944), and *Lyonushka* (1943). One of his best wartime works is the short novel *Vzyatiye velikoshumska* (1944; tr *Chariot of Wrath*, 1946), describing a Red Army offensive in the Ukraine.

Leonov is noted as one of the foremost stylists of Soviet prose. His rich and exuberant language and his predilection for complex plots have caused critics to cite him as a follower of Dostoyevsky, although this influence is plainly evident only in *The Thief*.

Leontes   In Shakespeare's WINTER'S TALE, the king of Sicilia, husband of Hermione and father of Perdita. Consumed with blind, unreasoning jealousy, he accuses his wife of adultery and tries to poison his friend Polixenes. When he finally realizes his folly, he is stricken with remorse.

Leopard, The (Il gattopardo, 1958; tr 1960)   A historical novel by Giuseppe Tomasi, Prince of LAMPEDUSA. It describes the impact of Garibaldi's invasion of Sicily and the subsequent unification of Italy on an aristocratic Sicilian family who had flourished under the Bourbon kings. The novel's depiction of the failure of the RISORGIMENTO created heated political debates when it was first published. However, the controversy subsided and the book was widely recognized as a penetrating psychological study of an age, written in a highly symbolic and richly poetic style.

Leopardi, Count Giacomo (1798–1837)   Italian poet. A self-taught prodigy, afflicted by physical deformity and spinal disease, he distinguished himself at an early age with the lyrical beauty and intense melancholy of his poetry. All his writings express belief in a cosmic nature that is unalterably hostile to man and the chief obstacle to human happiness. This pessimism provides the connective motif in the various collections of his verse: *Canzoni* (1824), *Versi* (1826), and *Canti* (1836). It is treated philosophically in the brief dialogue-essays *Le operette morali* (1824) and the miscellany of aphorisms *Pensieri* (1834–37).

Leopardi described himself as an ardent patriot and a confirmed classicist, but he revealed romantic tendencies in asserting that imagination rather than reason is the true source of poetic inspiration.

Lepanto, battle of   A naval engagement in the gulf of Corinth on October 7, 1571, fought between the forces of the Ottoman Empire and those of a Holy League comprising Spain, Venice, and the papacy. Under the leadership of Don John of Austria, the Christians overwhelmingly defeated the Turks, ending their naval domination of the Mediterranean. CERVANTES took part in the battle and was wounded in the left hand.

It is the subject of a stirring poem by G. K. CHESTERTON.

Lepidus, Marcus Aemilius (d 13 BC)   A member, with Octavius and Mark Antony, of the Second TRIUMVIRATE (43–33 BC). Lepidus was forced by Octavius into retirement.

leprechaun   An elflike creature in Irish folklore, often associated with shoemaking and the guarding of hidden treasure. He is usually characterized by small stature, supernatural qualities, and a puckish sense of humor.

Lermontov, Mikhail Yuryevich (1814–1841)   Russian poet and novelist. In his work and life he was the outstanding example of the influence of Byronic romanticism on Russian literature. His reputation as a poet in the 19th century was exceeded only by PUSHKIN's. Many of Lermontov's works are set in the Caucasus, where he was exiled for a poem denouncing court circles after Pushkin's death. He returned to St. Petersburg later, was exiled again for dueling, and was killed in a duel in the Caucasus. A few months before, he had described a death similar to his own in a short poem, "Son" ("A Dream"). His most famous poems are "Angel," "Demon," "The Novice," and "The Testament." Lermontov's only completed novel, A HERO OF OUR TIME, was important in the development of the Russian novel, marking a transition from the earlier form of a cycle of stories to the traditional novel form of the later 19th century. It consists of five stories, centering on the romantic hero Pechorin, which are presented out of their chronological sequence for purposes of suspense and retardation of the narrative, just as later novelists were to do. Lermontov's psychological analysis of the hero and realistic treatment of secondary characters also anticipate the work of the great 19th-century Russian realists.

Lesage, Alain René (1668–1747)   French novelist and dramatist. His early works are translations of Spanish authors, such as Rojas, Lope de Vega, Calderón, and others; these works caused no comment. His first original work, *Crispin, rival de son maître* (1707), a comedy, made him a reputation. It was soon followed by the novel *Le diable boiteux* (1707), an imitation and enlargement of Luis Vélez de Guevara's *El diablo cojuelo* (1641). ASMODEUS, as this novel is sometimes called in English translation, is an unrelated series of satirical tableaux, more descriptive than moralistic, of life in 18th-century France. His next play, *Turcaret, ou le Financier* (1708), is a bitter satire on money and financiers and caused a great scandal. After this comedy Lesage wrote some one hundred farces or comedies of manners, often interspersed with popular airs, for the Théâtre de la Foire. His masterpiece, *Histoire de* GIL BLAS DE SANTILLANE (definitive ed 1747), is considered by some critics to be the first novel of manners. Lesage wrote three other picaresque novels, *Don Guzman d'Alfarache* (1732), *Estevanille Gonzalès* (1734), and *Le Bachelier de Salamanque* (1736), and some inferior minor works of fiction. Celebrated for his animated style, and for his vivid and dramatic presentation of human foibles and absurdities, he had a marked influence on Fielding, Smollett, and Sterne, the English novelists.

lesbian   Pertaining to Lesbos, one of the islands of the Greek Archipelago. It pertains also to SAPPHO, the famous poet of Lesbos, and to the practices of female homosexuality (lesbianism) attributed to her.

Leskov, Nikolay Semyonovich (1831–1895) Russian novelist and short-story writer. Leskov, whose parents died when he was seventeen, supported himself as a civil servant, estate manager, and journalist in various provincial towns until, at the age of thirty, he became a journalist in St. Petersburg. His first large literary work, the novel *Nekuda* (*No Way Out*, 1864), won little critical acclaim. The radical critics held sway over literature at the time and Leskov had displeased them with some of his articles. His next novel, *Na nozhakh* (*At Daggers Drawn*, 1870–71), depicts young radicals in a manner that enraged them still more. Leskov was disinclined to placate the critics, even though their influence was able to delay his recognition as a major writer. He eventually attained this recognition with the general reading public for the humor and raciness of his stories and for his remarkable prose, which is full of puns, colloquial expressions, folk etymologies, and neologisms. Many of his most popular stories are set in the milieu of the clergy and OLD BELIEVERS, which Leskov had had ample time to observe during his early years in the provinces. Leskov was one of the early masters of SKAZ. He often placed the *skaz* narration in the framework of the story by having the recorder of the story meet a character who relates the tale in his own words.

Leskov's most popular works include the novel *Soboryane* (*Cathedral Folk*, 1872) and the tales "Zapechatlyonny angel" ("The Sealed Angel," 1873), "Ocharovanny strannik" ("The Enchanted Wanderer," 1874), "Melochi arkhiyereiskoi zhizni" ("Details of Episcopal Life," 1880), and "Skaz o tulskom kosom levshe i o stalnoi blokhe" ("The Left-Handed Smith of Tulsa and the Steel Flea," 1882).

Lespinasse, Julie Jeanne Eléonore de (1732–1776)   French letter-writer. She was the companion and protégée, from 1754 to 1763, of the blind Mme de DEFFAND. For a time, they conducted a sparkling literary salon together; later her own salon became a center for the *Encyclopédistes* (see ENCYCLOPÉDIE). She was a friend of d'Alembert, the marquis de Mora, and the comte de Guibert. To this latter are addressed her passionate love letters, *Lettres de Mlle de Lespinasse*, with their constant theme, *Je ne fais qu'aimer, je ne sais qu'aimer* (Fr, "I do nothing but love, I know nothing but love"). The letters were published by Guibert's widow in 1809.

Lessing, Doris [May] (1919–   )   English novelist and short-story writer, born in Persia and for many years a resident of southern Rhodesia. Lessing's first two published works, *The Grass Is Singing* (1950) and the stories in *This Was the Old Chief's Country* (1951), are set in Africa. She then began work on a series called "The Children of Violence"—including *Martha Quest* (1952), *A Proper Marriage* (1954), *A Ripple from the Storm* (1958), *Landlocked* (1965), and *The Four-Gated City* (1969)—that established her as a vividly realistic novelist, with an intense commitment to socialism and a particular capacity for identifying the social and emotional forces that shape women's lives. *The Golden Notebook* (1962), an ambitious experimental novel about a woman writer's struggle to discover the meaning of "self," has become a classic of feminist literature. While the primary interest in all her work has remained the delicate, often destructive interplay between men and women, Lessing has continually expanded both her field of focus and her stylistic experiments. *Briefing for a Descent into Hell* (1971) and *The Summer before the Dark* (1973) delve into aspects of neurotic disorders and madness. In the "Canopus in Argus: Archives" series, including *Shikasta* (1979), *The Marriages between Zones Three, Four, and Five* (1980), and *The Sirian Experiments* (1981), Lessing began a series of visionary, allegorical novels of the future in which archetypal images of men and women interact in a cosmos consisting of six zones, or "levels of being." *The Good Terrorist*, a novel, appeared in 1986. Lessing has also gained high praise as a writer of short stories. Among the most noteworthy of her collections are *African Stories* (1965), *The Habit of Loving* (1958), and *The Stories of Doris Lessing* (1978).

Lessing, Gotthold Ephraim (1729–1781)   German dramatist, aesthetician, and critic, a strong advocate of religious tolerance. Lessing's thought has roots in the enlightenment but is not cramped by a too strict rationalism. Perhaps more than any other, he was responsible for the emergence of German drama as a significant contribution to world theatre; in his critical work *Hamburgische Dramaturgie* (*Hamburg Dramaturgy*, 1767–69), he attacked the formalism of neoclassicism and called for a drama in which the form springs from the dramatist's vision of life. Among his more general works on aesthetics are the *Briefe, die neueste Literatur betreffend* (*Letters, Concerning the Most Recent Literature*, 1759–65), a periodical with Christoph Nicolai, which includes a Faust fragment; LAOCOÖN, OR ON THE LIMITS OF PAINTING AND POETRY; and *Wie die Alten den Tod gebildet* (*How the Ancients Represented Death*, 1769). Late in his life, he wrote a number of tracts on theological subjects, the best known of which is *Erziehung des Menschengeschlechts* (*Education of the Human Race*, 1780). His most famous dramas are *Miss Sara Sampson* (1755), MINNA VON BARNHELM, and NATHAN THE WISE.

Les Six   See SIX, LES.

Lesson, The   See IONESCO, EUGÈNE.

Lethe (fr Gr, *letho, latheo, lanthano,* "to cause persons not to know")   In Greek mythology, one of the rivers of HADES. The souls of all the dead are obliged to taste its water, that they may forget everything said and done when alive. See STYX.

Leto   In Greek mythology, a daughter of the TITANS Coeus and Phoebe and mother by ZEUS of APOLLO and ARTEMIS.

Letters from an American Farmer (1782)   A group of essays by CRÈVECŒUR, under the pseudonym of J. Hector St. John. They deal with farm life on the American frontier in the 18th century, sometimes idealizing it in the tradition of Jean Jacques Rousseau, yet depicting realistically the hard, unpleasant facts of the social life and customs in the American colonies. Crèvecœur sees America as a refuge for the persecuted and oppressed peoples of the world.

Let them eat cake   See MARIE ANTOINETTE.

Lettres de mon moulin (Letters from My Windmill, 1866)   A collection of short stories by Alphonse DAUDET depicting country life in Provence with skill and sympathy.

Leucadia's Rock   A promontory, the south extremity of the island Leucas or Leucadia in the Ionian Sea. According to legend, SAPPHO leapt from this rock when she found her love for Phaon unrequited. At the annual festival of APOLLO, a criminal was hurled from Leucadia's Rock into the sea; but birds of various sorts were attached to him in order to break his fall, and if he was not killed, he was set free.

Leucippus (fl 450 BC)   A Greek philosopher. His atomist theory held that all matter is composed of an irreducible and unchanging set of atoms. Always in motion, the atoms circulate in a void, and link to form an unlimited number of worlds. See DEMOCRITUS.

Leute von Seldwyla, Die (The People of Seldwyla; vol 1, 1856; vol 2, 1874)   A collection of humorous novellas by Gottfried KELLER, all set in the fictional Swiss town of Seldwyla. The two best-known ones are *Kleider machen Leute* (*Clothes Make the Man*), about a man who is taken for a Polish nobleman and, with an eye to his personal advantage, continues the pose, and *Spiegel, das Kätzchen* (lit, *Spiegel, the Little Cat*, tr as *The Fat of the Cat*), about a down-and-out cat who sells his cat-fat to a magician without fully realizing that in order to relinquish his fat, he must be killed.

Leutnant Gustl (1900)   A short narrative by Arthur SCHNITZLER. An early experiment in STREAM OF CONSCIOUSNESS technique, the story probes the mind of a conceited young officer who must decide between suicide or resignation from the army as restitution for his lost honor. This satire on the military honor code created such a controversy when published that Schnitzler was forced to resign his medical commission in the military reserves.

Levelers   In English history, a group of ultrarepublicans during the Civil War, who wanted to give all men the right to vote and to end class distinctions. John Lilburne (1614?–57) was one of the leaders of the sect, which was active from 1647 to 1649, when it was suppressed by Cromwell's troops.

In Irish history, an illegal association of 18th-century agrarian agitators, also called Whiteboys.

Leverkühn, Adrian   The hero of Thomas Mann's novel DOKTOR FAUSTUS. He is a contemporary composer, and in several places Mann has used actual music of Arnold Schoenberg to describe the fictional works of his protagonist. In order to achieve a breakthrough into the most sublime realms of art, Leverkühn, like the legendary FAUST, makes a pact with the powers of evil. Like Faust, he himself is utterly destroyed by the forces he has set in motion, but the magnificence of his music remains as a monument. The name *Leverkühn* suggests "one who lives boldly."

Levertov, Denise (1923–   )   American poet and essayist. Of Welsh and Jewish parentage, Levertov was born in England and worked there as a nurse in World War II. After the war she married the American writer Mitchell Goodman (1923–   ) and moved to the U.S. Her first book, *The Double Image* (1946), pervaded by the war experience, is couched in the traditional accentual-syllabic metrics of English poetry. In America, she abandoned these forms and her style became more lyrical and conversational in rhythm and vocabulary, owing in part to the influence of William Carlos WILLIAMS and the BLACK MOUNTAIN POETS. The volumes *With Eyes at the Back of Our Heads* (1959), *The Jacob's Ladder* (1961), and *O Taste and See* (1964) established her as a major poet of precise observation and realism. During the late 1960s and early 1970s, Levertov was preoccupied with political and social motifs. *Relearning the Alphabet* (1970) contains poems about Vietnam, starvation in Biafra, and riots in U.S. cities. *To Stay Alive* (1971) and *Footprints* (1972) are in a similar vein. Her political concerns are muted again in *Life in the Forest* (1978), poems about her own life. Selections from her first four volumes appear in *Collected Earlier Poems: 1940–1960* (1979). *Candles in Babylon*, a volume of verse, appeared in 1982; it was followed by a further collection, *Collected Poems 1960–1970* (1983). *Light Up the Cave*, prose writings, was published in 1982.

Levi   (1) In the OLD TESTAMENT, the third son of JACOB and LEAH (Gen. 29:34). His descendants are known as Levites, the priestly tribe of the Israelites (Deut. 21:15).

(2) Another name for MATTHEW (Luke 5:27; Mark 2:14) in the NEW TESTAMENT.

Levi, Carlo   See CHRIST STOPPED AT EBOLI.

Levi, Primo (1919–1987)   Jewish-Italian memoirist, novelist, short-story writer, and poet. His best-known works are *Se questo è un uomo* (1947; tr *If This Is a Man*, 1959; U.S. *Survival in Auschwitz*, 1961) and *La tregua* (1958; tr *The Truce*; U.S. *The Reawakening*, 1963), the first and second volumes of his autobiographical trilogy. Both are Holocaust memoirs distinguished by a combination of compassion and detachment and an extraordinary absence of personal bitterness. A chemist by profession, Levi gained international attention with his final volume of autobiography, *Il sistema periodico* (1975; tr *The Periodic Table*, 1984), a brilliant tour de force consisting of twenty-one imaginative pieces, each named after a chemical element, probing personal, social, and political experiences. After the appearance of *The Periodic Table* Levi attracted much more attention among English-language readers; several translations of his books have appeared, including *Se non ora, quando?* (1982; tr *If Not Now, When?*, 1985), a novel, and *The Monkey's Wrench* (1986).

leviathan   A word from the Hebrew, meaning literally "that which gathers itself together in folds," and given in the BIBLE to a mythical sea serpent (Job 41:1; Isa. 27:1; Ps. 104:26). The name is also applied to the whale and the crocodile, and by extension it has come to mean something vast and formidable of its kind.

Leviathan, or the Matter, Form, and Power of a Commonwealth, Ecclesiastical and Civil (1651)   A treatise on the origin and ends of government by Thomas HOBBES. This work, a defense of secular monarchy, written while the Puritan Commonwealth ruled England, contains Hobbes's famous theory of the sovereign state.

Hobbes, following the trend of his time, tended to regard politics as a branch of physical science, a kind of social physics. Comparing the motion of physical bodies to human behavior, he argued that just as physical things, when left to themselves, pursued their own direction, so individuals, when uncontrolled, naturally followed their own direction, their private self-interest. Thus, in his view, the first principle of human behavior was egoism, or self-interest, and it was this egoism that was the root of all social conflict. He believed that social peace could be achieved only within a stable government which had an absolute authority over its subjects and its institutions. Since the attainment of all desirable social ends was hindered by the "war of all against all," it was necessary that men agree among themselves, upon the basis of a social contract, to accept a common and absolute power that would protect them from themselves and from each other, keep the peace, and allow thereby a moderate satisfaction of human desires.

Levin, Ira (1929–   )   American novelist and dramatist. The best known of Levin's expertly crafted tales of horror and suspense is *Rosemary's Baby* (1967), in which the heroine bears the child of Satan. The book, along with the movie which was made from it, was credited with stimulating a revival of the occult in American fiction and films. Other novels include *A Kiss before Dying* (1953), a brilliant suspense novel, *This Perfect Day* (1970), *The Stepford Wives* (1972), and *The Boys from Brazil* (1976), which deals with Nazis in South America. His best play is probably *Deathtrap* (1978).

Levin, Konstantin   See ANNA KARENINA.

Levin, Meyer (1905–1981)   American novelist and newspaperman. Levin is known for his novels and nonfiction writings about American Jewish life. His novels—of which the best known is *Compulsion* (1956), his retelling of the 1924 Leopold-Loeb murder case—include *My Father's House* (1947), *Eva* (1959), *The Stronghold* (1965), and *The Settlers* (1972) and its sequel, *The Harvest* (1978). *The Obsession* (1973) is an account of Levin's twenty-year battle to get his dramatization of *The Diary of Anne Frank* published and produced.

Lévi-Strauss, Claude (1908–   )   French anthropologist. His major works include *Les Structures élémentaires de la parenté* (1949; tr *The Elementary Structures of Kinship*, 1969), *Tristes Tropiques* (1955; tr 1961, 1974), *Anthropologie structurale* (2 vols, 1958, 1973; tr *Structural Anthropology*, 1963, 1976), *La Pensée sauvage* (1962; tr *The Savage Mind*, 1966), *Mythologiques* (4 vols, 1964–71; tr *Introduction to a Science of Mythology*, 1969–81), and *L'Identité* (1977). His structuralist theories have been applied to a wide range of subjects from art to advertising to table manners and food. *Le Regard éloigné* (1983), *Paroles données* (1984), and *La Potière jalouse* (1985) are all developments of earlier themes. Lévi-Strauss is primarily concerned with such fundamental social and mental structures as kinship, myths, language, religion, and art. His basic premise is that the relationships among these phenomena, rather than the nature of the phenomena themselves, are of prime importance and can be shown through the structuralist methodology to be analogous (see STRUCTURALISM). The intellectual development of myth, for example, is similar in its patterns to the development of scientific thinking. He has had enormous influence on the structuralist school of literary criticism, particularly on such writers as Roland BARTHES and Jacques Derrida. He was elected to the ACADÉMIE FRANÇAISE in 1973.

Leviticus   A book of the OLD TESTAMENT traditionally ascribed to MOSES; the basic compendium of Jewish law. It was probably written about 475 BC and records the religious and ceremonial law of the Jews in the period after the rebuilding of the temple in 516 BC. Although it contains a few short narrative passages it is primarily a set of instructions to priests on procedures for sacrifices, the observance of certain ritual practices, rules of ethics, and penalties for transgressors.

Lewis, C[live] S[taples] (1898–1963)   English novelist, literary scholar, and essayist on Christian theological and moral problems. Lewis's critical studies include *The Allegory of Love* (1936), an examination of the relationships between literary language and medieval courtly love; *English Literature in the 16th Century* (1954); and *An Experiment in Criticism* (1961). He also wrote science fiction in the form of interplanetary fantasies which are really Christian allegories of good and evil: *Out of the Silent Planet* (1938), *Perelandra* (1943), and *That Hideous Strength* (1945). Also highly allegorical is his extremely popular series of books for children, "The Narnia Chronicle," beginning with *The Lion, the Witch, and the Wardrobe* (1950). *The Problem of Pain* (1940) and THE SCREWTAPE LETTERS are widely read works of Christian apologetics.

Lewis, Cecil Day   See DAY LEWIS, CECIL.

Lewis, D[ominic] B[evan] Wyndham (1894–1969)   Welsh-born English humorist, essayist, and biographer. Lewis is perhaps best known for an anthology of bad verse, *The Stuffed Owl* (1930), which he edited with Charles Lee. In addition, he wrote several scholarly yet colorful biographies, including *François Villon* (1928), *Doctor Rabelais* (1957), and *Molière: The Comic Mask* (1959). Despite the similarity in names, he is not related to the novelist and painter Wyndham LEWIS.

Lewis, Matthew Gregory (1775–1818)   English novelist and dramatist, author of the famous GOTHIC NOVEL *Ambrosio, or* THE MONK, for which he was known as "Monk Lewis." A lover of poetry, Lewis collaborated with Sir Walter Scott and Robert Southey in a collection of verse, *Tales of Wonder* (1801). Lewis's contributions included some of the earliest translations of the German romantics Goethe and Herder. He was a successful dramatist and a liberal who did his best to alleviate the condition of the slaves on his Jamaica plantation, where he died.

Lewis, Oscar (1914–1970)   American anthropologist. Lewis studied impoverished people in rural societies, earning particular recognition for his work with Mexicans and Mexican-Americans in *Five Families* (1959) and *Children of Sanchez* (1961) and with Puerto Ricans in *La Vida* (1966), which won a National Book Award in 1967. His books, distilled from hundreds of hours of tape-recorded conversations, attained a beauty and power that elevated them above mere documentary. In studying poverty as a culture unto itself, transcending national distinctions, Lewis created what has been called "the anthropology of poverty," which has had a major impact on subsequent social analysis. His final work was a massive oral history of the Cuban revolution, *Living the Revolution* (3 vols, 1977–78), based on interviews taken in 1969–70.

Lewis, [Harry] Sinclair (1885–1951)   American novelist. Born in Sauk Centre, Minnesota, Lewis was an awkward, lonely boy. After his graduation from Yale in 1908, he spent several years in newspaper and editorial work. His first novel, *Hike and the Aeroplane* (1912; written under the pseudonym Tom Graham), was a story for boys. He achieved moderate success with his early novels, and two of them—*Our Mr. Wrenn: The Romantic Adventures of a Gentle Man* (1914) and *The Job: An American Novel* (1917)—contain hints of the satire and realism that were to be characteristic of his best work.

The appearance of MAIN STREET in 1920 created a sensation. Although there were some howls of outrage, in general both the critics and the public were delighted with Lewis's devastating portrayal of the smugness and provin-

cialism of the American small town, as typified by Gopher Prairie, the novel's mythical locale. Lewis next directed his barbs at the American businessman in BABBITT, in many ways an extension of *Main Street*. In ARROWSMITH, often considered his best work, he attacked the venality and pettiness that impede the search for scientific truth. Although Lewis was awarded a PULITZER PRIZE for *Arrowsmith*, he promptly refused to accept it because the terms of the award state that it is to be given, not for literary merit, but for the best presentation of "the wholesome atmosphere of American life." Other successes of this period were ELMER GANTRY and *Dodsworth* (1929).

Lewis was awarded the NOBEL PRIZE in 1930, the first American writer to win such an honor. But his work declined in the 1930s, and his attitude to the former objects of his satire softened. *Ann Vickers* (1933) traces the career of a neurotic woman who starts as a social worker and ends as the mistress of a politician. *The Prodigal Parents* (1938) presents rebellious children in an unsympathetic light. Perhaps the most vigorous of Lewis's works in the 1930s was IT CAN'T HAPPEN HERE, a warning about the possibility of Fascism in the U.S. Among his later novels are *Cass Timberlane* (1945), the story of an older man's love for his unsuitable young wife; *Kingsblood Royal* (1947), about racial prejudice; and *The God-Seeker* (1949), about a missionary in Minnesota in the 1840s.

There is much disguised biography in Lewis's work, and many suggestions of Lewis himself in his characters. A romancer as well as a realist and satirist, he loved the Babbitts and Main Streets of America even as he deplored them.

Lewis, [Percy] Wyndham (1882–1957)   English novelist, essayist, and painter. A vitriolic satirist, Lewis wrote such notable satiric novels as TARR. He also wrote many essays in which he expressed his vehement political and literary opinions. Trained as an artist, he first attracted attention before World War I as the leading proponent of a cubist-related school of painting called VORTICISM, although he was also recognized as an accomplished painter in more traditional modes. With Ezra POUND, he edited the two issues of BLAST (1914–15), which published Pound's "vorticist manifesto" and promoted a return to classicism in the arts, blasting the current trends toward romanticism. Joined in this movement by T. S. ELIOT and James JOYCE, the four of them, with Ford Madox FORD, were known as "the men of 1914." Lewis later published his account of his experiences in World War I in *Blasting and Bombardiering* (1937). It was between the wars that Lewis's literary brilliance and satirical force was at its peak, producing *The Childermass* (1928), the first volume of the trilogy THE HUMAN AGE, and THE APES OF GOD. In the same period he was propounding neo-Fascist views, both political and literary, in such major essays as *The Art of Being Ruled* (1926), TIME AND WESTERN MAN, and *Hitler* (1931). *The Revenge for Love* (1937), a novel exploring the effects of extremism on character, signaled the beginning of a change in view which was more explicit in the critical essay *The Hitler Cult and How It Will End* (1939). At the outbreak of war Lewis and his wife moved to Canada for five unhappy years. There he wrote the self-critical novel *The Vulgar Streak* (1941; repr 1971). He would later describe the whole experience in *Self-Condemned* (1954). In 1949 Lewis began to go blind and in 1953 he lost his sight altogether. However, his productivity was unremitting, with *Rude Assignment* (1950), a second autobiography, *The Demon of Progress in the Arts* (1954), and the two final volumes of *The Human Age*, among other works. He also published *Poems* (1933) and several collections of short stories.

Lewis and Clark Expedition   An expedition across the U.S to the Pacific Ocean in 1804–6 led by Meriwether Lewis (1774–1809) and William Clark (1770–1838). Starting out from St. Louis in the spring of 1804, the party of twenty-three soldiers, three interpreters, and one slave ascended the Missouri River, spent the winter among the Mandan Indians of North Dakota, and descended the Columbia River to the Pacific late in 1805. The expedition showed that an overland route to the Pacific was feasible and provided scientific data about the previously unexplored region. *The Original Journals of the Lewis and Clark Expedition* were edited by R. G. Thwaites in 1904–5. See SACAJAWEA.

Lezama Lima, José (1912–1976)   Cuban poet, novelist, and essayist, a moving force behind a resurgence of Cuban poetry, which he fostered by publishing several literary reviews, notably *Orígenes* (1944–57). His own books of verse—including *Muerte de Narciso* (1937), *Enemigo rumor* (1941), *La fijeza* (1949), *Dador* (1960), and *Las eras imaginarias* (1971)—reveal his surrealist tendencies, making use of evocative metaphors, abrupt syntax, and literary allusions. His masterwork is his only novel, PARADISO, a complex exposition of a view of man fallen from grace and forever cut off from his full creative potential.

L'Hermite, François (known as Tristan l'Hermite, 1602–1655)   French author and playwright. The popularity of his tragedy *La Mariane* (1636) rivaled that of *Le Cid*, and *La Mort de Sénèque* (*The Death of Seneca*, 1644) is the finest French tragedy on a classical theme outside of Corneille's and Racine's.

Liaisons dangereuses, Les (1782)   An epistolary novel by Pierre Choderlos de LACLOS. The novel deals with the corruption of innocence and virtue by Valmont, a libertine, and his equally vicious and immoral mistress, Mme de Merteuil, for their own amusement. It is essentially a study of the fascination and power of evil, and one is struck by the absence of frivolity and sentimentality in this work; the battle of the sexes is depicted with utter seriousness and humorlessness. The style is Racinian in its brilliance, lucidity, and precision, diabolical in its impassivity.

Libedinsky, Yury Nikolayevich (1898–1959)   Russian prose writer and playwright. Born in Odessa, Libedinsky became an eminent proletarian writer for his first novel, *Nedelya* (1922; tr *A Week*, 1923), which depicts the imposition of Bolshevik authority in a small provincial town and largely set the standard for the depiction of Bolsheviks in later proletarian literature. His best-known play, *Vysoty* (*Heights*, 1929), warns against depending on ideologically suspect workers no matter how competent they may be.

liberal arts   In the Middle Ages, the seven branches of learning: grammar, logic, rhetoric, arithmetic, geometry, music, and astronomy. Biblical authority for fixing the number at seven comes from PROVERBS 9:1: "Wisdom hath builded her house, she hath hewn out her seven pillars." Such applied subjects as law and medicine were excluded from the liberal arts on the grounds that they were concerned with purely practical matters. In modern times, the liberal arts include languages, sciences, philosophy, history, and related subjects. The term is a translation of the Latin *artes liberales*, so called because their pursuit was the privilege of freemen who were called *liberi*.

Libertins   A sect of French freethinkers and skeptics of the 17th and 18th centuries, precursors of VOLTAIRE and the encyclopedists. Advocates of total freedom of thought and conscience, the *Libertins* questioned the doctrines and morality of all received religion and were continually accused of atheism and immorality. The greatest religious thinkers of the day, including Bossuet and PASCAL, denounced their views, and ultimately the *Libertins*' own poor conduct discredited their name.

liberty cap   A symbol of freedom. When a slave was manumitted by the Romans, a small Phrygian cap, usually of red felt, called *pileus*, was placed on his head; he was termed *libertinus* ("freedman"), and his name was registered in the city tribes. When Saturninus, in 100 BC, possessed himself of the Roman Capitol, he hoisted a similar cap on the top of his spear, to indicate that all slaves who joined his standard should be free; Marius employed the same symbol against Sulla; and, when Caesar was murdered, the conspirators marched forth in a body with a cap elevated on a spear, in token of liberty. In the French Revolution, the red cap of liberty was adopted by the revolutionists as an emblem of their freedom from royal authority.

licenciado vidriera, El   One of the tales in Cervantes's NOVELAS EJEMPLARES. It is really a collection of aphorisms, uttered by a demented law student who believes that he is made of glass but who, like Don Quixote, displays amazing insight and perspicacity.

Lichas   In Greek mythology, the friend of HERACLES who brought him Deianira's fatal tunic. He was thrown into the sea by Heracles.

Li-chi   See BOOK OF RITES.

Lichtenstein, Roy (1923–   ) American painter. Lichtenstein was an abstract expressionist in the 1950s, having studied with Reginald MARSH at the Art Students' League in New York. In the 1960s he became one of the innovators of the POP ART movement. He painted large-scale reproductions of comic book panels, stencilling on the dots that are used in printing and including typically vapid captions, parodying both the cartoons and life itself. In this same style, he imitated works of famous painters like MONDRIAN and MONET, and painted such commonplace objects as a light switch, a razor blade, and a ball of string. Lichtenstein's paintings are ambiguous comments on banality, simultaneously enshrining and disparaging objects and art.

lictor   In ancient Rome, an officer attending a magistrate. A dictator, for example, had twenty lictors, a consul twelve, a praetor six, and so on. The lictor bore the FASCES as the insignia of his office. He cleared the way, enforced respect for his superior, arrested offenders, and executed condemned criminals.

Lie, Jonas Lauritz Idemil (1833–1908)   Norwegian novelist, playwright, and poet. In 1870 Lie published *Den Fremsynte* (tr *The Visionary*, 1894); both this first novel and later volumes of stories, *Trold* (1891–92), mingle realistic with fantastic elements. His studies of family life in the middle classes—among them *Lodsen og hans hustru* (1874; tr *The Pilot and His Wife*, 1877), *Familjen paa Gilje* (1883; tr *The Family at Gilje*, 1920), and *Kommandørens døtre* (1886; tr *The Commodore's Daughters*, 1892)—represent his finest work.

Liebelei   See LIGHT O' LOVE.

Lied von Bernadette, Das   See SONG OF BERNADETTE, THE.

Li Fei-kan   See PA CHIN.

Life of Galileo, The (Leben des Galilei; written 1938–39, perf 1943, tr 1947)   A play in fifteen episodes by Bertolt BRECHT. The play concerns Galileo GALILEI's conflict with the church over the application of the Copernican system, which the church viewed as anathema. Brecht deliberately portrays Galileo as a self-serving and decidedly un-heroic character, willing to compromise his principles in the face of pressure. The play is not so obviously tendentious as most of Brecht's later works, but there are several episodes in which Marxist doctrine is propounded. The central question of the play revolves around Galileo's recantation of his theories before the Inquisition and his complex motivation for doing so.

Life of Samuel Johnson, LL.D., The (1791)   A biography by James BOSWELL, generally considered the greatest in the English language. Boswell met Dr. Samuel JOHNSON in 1763 in London and visited him periodically from that time, spending a great deal of time with him in the three years before Johnson's death. Boswell's method is of particular note: occasionally he made notes on the spot during Johnson's conversation; more often, however, from the habit of a lifetime, he made notes in his copious journals nightly on the events and conversation of the day, and for this, he had a prodigious memory to serve him. He questioned Johnson himself, prodding him into talk, and questioned Johnson's friends; after Johnson died, he was in constant quest of letters and anecdotes. He was greatly aided in his task by Edmund MALONE, who went over the last draft of the manuscript. Boswell's aim and achievement was completeness; no detail was too small for him, and on this very point Dr. Johnson remarked to him: "There is nothing, Sir, too little for so little a creature as man." Boswell's achievement is twofold: first, he was able, from his scrupulously accurate memory, to record faithfully the brilliance and wit of Dr. Johnson's conversation; second, he had the artistry to transform a painstaking, almost scholarly profusion of detail into a perceptive, lifelike portrait. The result is a study in depth of a complex and fascinating man who was the prime moving force in the literary world of his time. Although Boswell's *Life* is indisputably the finest of the many contemporary biographies of Johnson, Sir John Hawkins's *Life* (1787) is a better source for young Johnson, and Hester Lynch THRALE saw more of Johnson's intimate, domestic side.

Life on the Mississippi (1883)   An autobiographical account by Mark TWAIN. The first part of the book describes his apprenticeship as a river pilot, and the excitement of antebellum life on the Mississippi. The second half of the book, added seven years after the first half was published, records his return to the river in 1882. Conditions had greatly changed and the river was stripped of its romance while, with the growing competition from the railroads, the status of the riverboat pilot no longer was what it had been. Despite these elegiac, final impressions, the book is a graphic account of the heroic steamboat era.

Life Studies (1959)   A collection of poetry and prose by Robert LOWELL. This volume heralded a new poetic mode termed "confessional" by critics. In form and content *Life Studies* established standards for such CONFESSIONAL POETS as Snodgrass, Plath, Sexton, and Berryman. Drawing on autobiographical material, Lowell uses slanglike speech, personal anecdotes, place names, and actual events to evoke a dramatic sense of immediacy. The book is divided into four parts. Part One, the least subjective section, includes travel poems and occasional poems, such as "Inauguration Day: January 1953." Part Two, a prose fragment entitled "91 Revere Street," describes with moving candor Lowell's childhood in a family oppressed by Puritan ancestry. Part Three, a tribute to writers whose artistic commitment inspired Lowell, consists of poems dedicated to Hart CRANE, Delmore SCHWARTZ, SANTAYANA, and Ford Madox FORD. Part Four, itself subtitled "Life Studies," consists of family portraits. In this, the most technically innovative section, the poet attempts to reconcile his burdens and tensions with a bittersweet heritage. He also transforms his predicament as an individual into the social predicament of a decade which he labels the "tranquilized fifties." The prosodic features which distinguish *Life Studies* are open form, internal rather than conventional end-line rhymes, and colloquial or speech rhythm patterning as meter.

Life with Father (1935) A collection of sketches by Clarence DAY. In them the author recalls with delightful humor the not-always-easy life with his eccentric and domineering father. In spite of the elder Day's tyrannizing, however, his soft-spoken wife nearly always managed to get her way. Selections from this book and Day's companion volumes, *God and My Father* (1932) and *Life with Mother* (1937), formed the basis for Russel Crouse and Howard Lindsay's dramatization, *Life with Father* (1939), which enjoyed one of the longest runs in Broadway history.

Ligeia (1838) A tale by Edgar Allan POE. Ligeia, the narrator's mysterious dark-haired wife, dies after a lingering illness. He later remarries, though he does not love his fair Rowena. In the lavishly furnished English abbey to which they move, Rowena dies. The narrator, affected by opium, sees signs of life return to the corpse. Finally she rises; the Lady Rowena has been transformed into Ligeia.

Light in August (1932) A novel by William FAULKNER. The book reiterates the author's concern with a society that classifies men according to race, creed, and origin. Joe CHRISTMAS, the central character and victim, appears to be white but is really part black; he has an affair with Joanna Burden, a spinster whom the townsfolk of Jefferson regard with suspicion because of her New England background. Joe eventually kills her and sets fire to her house; he is captured, castrated, and killed by the outraged townspeople, to whom his victim has become a symbol of the innocent white woman attacked and killed by a black. Other important characters are Lena GROVE, who comes to Jefferson far advanced in pregnancy, expecting to find the lover who has deserted her, and Gail Hightower, the minister who ignores his wife and loses his church because of his fanatic devotion to the past.

Light o' Love (Liebelei, 1895; tr 1932) A play by Arthur SCHNITZLER, originally translated as *The Reckoning* (1907). The erotic theme of a man torn between two women, which had been treated lightly in *Anatol* (1891), appears here as a tragedy. A Viennese student, Fritz, engages in a *liebelei* ("lightly taken liaison") with Christine, the daughter of a simple musician, at the same time he is carrying on an affair with a married woman of high social standing. The naïve, sensitive Christine loves Fritz deeply. When she discovers that he has been killed in a duel over the other woman, she takes her own life.

light verse A loose term for poetry written with gaiety, elegance, wit, and technical virtuosity about trivial matters. The following forms can be placed in this category: PARODY, LIMERICKS, OCCASIONAL VERSE, EPIGRAMS, NONSENSE VERSE, CLERIHEWS, punning verses, and riddles. Among the many writers who have composed light verse are LOVELACE, HERRICK, Edward LEAR, and Lewis CARROLL.

Lihn, Enrique (1929–   ) Chilean poet and short-story writer. Lihn writes with a sense of irony that keeps even his most political work from becoming heavy-handed, and makes the author part of that world whose folly he describes. His images—in his stories as well as in his full-fleshed, richly lyrical poems—are among the most striking in the language. His books of poems include *La pieza oscura* (1963), *Poesía de paso* (1966), *Escrito en Cuba* (1969), *La musiquilla de las pobres esferas* (1969), and *Algunos poemas* (1972). A highly praised volume of short stories, *Aqua de arroz*, appeared in 1969. A selection of his poems in English translation, *The Dark Room and Other Poems* (1978), reveals his range of styles, from neorealist to antipoetry.

Li Ho (791–817) Chinese poet known in China as a poet of "devilish genius." Li Ho's work is unusually violent and morbid in its imagery. He has been relatively ignored in the more moderately inclined Chinese poetic tradition, but has attracted some notice in the West because of his peculiarities.

Liliencron, Detlev von (1844–1909) German lyric poet. Liliencron served as an officer in the Prussian army during three wars, and these experiences inspired his first and most popular volume of poems, *Adjutantenritte* (*An Adjutant's Rides*, 1883). In this book he emphasizes a subjective but realistic treatment of individual experience, as opposed to the formal polish and generalization typical of authors such as HEYSE. These characteristics made his writing important in the budding movements of NATURALISM and IMPRESSIONISM.

Lilith In Talmudic tradition, a demon, probably of Babylonian origin, said to haunt wildernesses in stormy weather and be especially dangerous to children and pregnant women. She is referred to as "the screech owl" in the King James Version and as "the night hag" in the Revised Standard Version (Isa. 34:14). Hebrew legend holds that she was created simultaneously with Adam and was his first wife, but, refusing to be considered his inferior, she left him and was expelled from Eden to a region of the air. In Arabic mythology, she married the Devil and became the mother of evil spirits. Superstitious Jews put in the chambers occupied by their wives four coins inscribed with the names of Adam and Eve and the words, "Avaunt thee, Lilith!" Goethe introduced her in his FAUST, and Dante Gabriel ROSSETTI in his "Eden Bower" (1870) made the serpent the instrument of Lilith's vengeance against Adam.

Lillibulero A political song, popular during the English revolution of 1688 and still the most savagely thunderous of British marching songs. The music is by Henry Purcell. The text by Thomas Wharton (c1686) satirizes James II and the Catholics, using the refrain "Lillibulero bullen a la" which is said to have been used as a watchword by the Irish Catholics in their massacre of the

Protestants (1641). The song was included by Bishop Percy in his *Reliques*.

Lilliput   The country of Gulliver's first voyage in GULLIVER'S TRAVELS by Jonathan Swift. The Lilliputians are about one-twelfth human size, and Gulliver is a giant among them. At first he falls in with their views, takes an interest in their disputes, helps them, and accepts their honors to him as real praise; he is soon disillusioned when the little creatures grudge him food and propose binding him lest he fend for himself. Their smallness is not merely a matter of stature; the pettiness of their lives is used by Swift to mirror the pettiness of human beings.

lily   A flower of innumerable varieties. There is a tradition that the lily sprang from the repentant tears of EVE as she went forth from Paradise. In Christian art, the lily is an emblem of chastity, innocence, and purity. In pictures of the Annunciation, GABRIEL is sometimes represented as carrying a lily branch, while a vase containing a lily stands before the Virgin, who is kneeling in prayer. St. JOSEPH holds a lily branch in his hand, indicating that his wife MARY was a virgin.

lily of France   The *fleur-de-lis* (Fr, "flower of the lily"; the iris). It is an emblem of France. The device of Clovis, Frankish king from 481 to 511, was three black toads, but the story goes that an aged hermit of Joye-en-valle saw a miraculous light stream one night into his cell, and an angel appeared to him holding an azure shield of wonderful beauty, emblazoned with three gold lilies that shone like stars, which the hermit was commanded to give to Clovis's queen, Clotilde. She gave it to her royal husband, whose arms were everywhere victorious, and the device was thereupon adopted as the emblem of France.

limbo (fr Lat, *limbus*, "border; edge")   The abode of souls that through no fault of their own are debarred from heaven. It is particularly identified with the souls of righteous men that lived before the coming of Christ and with the souls of unbaptized infants. Believed to be located near the region of hell, it is the setting for the first stage of the journey in Dante's DIVINE COMEDY. The word has come to refer more generally to the condition of being lost or confined to a state of neglect or oblivion.

limerick   A humorous, usually epigrammatic piece of verse in five lines of mixed iambic and anapestic meter, lines 1, 2, and 5 in trimeter and 3 and 4 in dimeter, rhyming a-a-b-b-a. The form, the origins of which are uncertain, was popularized by Edward LEAR in his *Book of Nonsense* (1846). Following Lear's practice, the first line of most limericks ends in a place name, usually the place of origin or residence of the protagonist of the verse. The last line, in most of Lear's limericks, repeated the place name instead of furnishing another rhyme upon it, but most modern limericks end with a rhyme word instead of a repetition. The subject of the typical limerick is likely to be somewhat ribald and puns and plays on words are often included. The limerick has a wide oral circulation and,

being a truly popular form of verse, is often of anonymous authorship. The following is an example:

> There once was a man from Nantucket
> Who kept all his cash in a bucket;
>   But his daughter named Nan
>   Ran away with a man,
> And as for the bucket, Nantucket.

Lin-chi   See CH'AN BUDDHISM.

Lincoln, Abraham (1809–1865)   Sixteenth president of the U.S. (1861–65). Born in a log cabin in Hardin (now Larue) County, Kentucky, Lincoln lost his mother, Nancy Hanks Lincoln, in 1818, while the family was living in Indiana. In 1831 he settled in New Salem, Illinois, where he studied law and worked as a storekeeper, postmaster, and surveyor; in 1836 he was admitted to the bar. From 1834 to 1841 he served in the state legislature as a Whig and supporter of Henry Clay. While Lincoln was living in New Salem, he met Ann Rutledge (1816–35), to whom he became engaged and who died in 1835; their romance has inspired many legends for which there is little concrete evidence. The truth about Lincoln's relationship to Mary Todd, whom he married in 1842, has also been distorted, largely as a result of the writings of William Herndon, Lincoln's law partner, who disliked Mrs. Lincoln intensely.

After serving one term (1847–49) in Congress, where he voiced his opposition to the Mexican War, Lincoln returned to his flourishing law practice in Illinois. Stirred to renewed political activity by the sectional agitation of 1854, Lincoln soon aligned himself with the newly formed Republican Party and ran for the U.S. Senate against Stephen A. DOUGLAS in 1858; although Lincoln lost the election, his famous debates with Douglas won him national prominence. In 1860 he won the Republican presidential nomination over such rivals as William Seward (1801–72) largely because of his conservative record on the slavery question, but the Southern states seceded from the Union soon after his election. His first Inaugural Address was conciliatory: he emphasized the indissolubility of the Union, but promised not to interfere with slavery where it already existed. During the Civil War, which began with the Confederate attack on Fort SUMTER, Lincoln did not hesitate to use his extensive powers as commander-in-chief, and although Northern Democrats and members of his own party often assailed his war policies, he handled his opponents with aplomb. In the election of 1864 he easily defeated George B. McCLELLAN, who had often tried his patience in the early days of the war. In his second Inaugural Address, he asked the nation "to finish the work we are in . . . with malice toward none, with charity toward all." Just after Lee's surrender, Lincoln was shot by John Wilkes BOOTH and died the following day.

Now transformed into a major American folk hero, Lincoln has been the subject of numerous literary works.

Among the best-known poems about him are Walt Whitman's O CAPTAIN! MY CAPTAIN! and WHEN LILACS LAST IN THE DOORYARD BLOOM'D. He is a character in many novels and stories, and his early life is the subject of Robert E. Sherwood's play ABE LINCOLN IN ILLINOIS. Edgar Lee MASTERS wrote a hostile biography, *Lincoln the Man* (1931), while another poet, Carl SANDBURG, offered a vivid portrayal in the six volumes of ABRAHAM LINCOLN. See EMANCIPATION PROCLAMATION; GETTYSBURG ADDRESS; LINCOLN, MARY TODD.

Lincoln, Mary Todd (1818–1882)   Wife of Abraham LINCOLN. Descended from a distinguished Kentucky family, Mary Todd was courted by Lincoln when she moved to Springfield, Illinois, in 1839 to live with her sister, Mrs. Ninian W. Edwards, who was the daughter-in-law of the state governor. There is no contemporary evidence for the story that the wedding was scheduled for January 1, 1841, and that the groom failed to appear; some emotional crisis in Lincoln's life, however, probably did lead him to delay the marriage, which took place in 1842. Despite the testimony of William Herndon, Lincoln's law partner, the Lincolns' married life was probably happy, though some difficulties arose after his election to the presidency, when Mrs. Lincoln was accused of extravagance and disloyalty to the Union cause. Her mind weakened by her husband's assassination and by the loss of three of her four sons, she was adjudged insane in 1875 but declared competent the following year.

Lincoln's Inn   See INNS OF COURT.

Lindbergh, Anne [Spenser] Morrow (1906–)   American writer and poet. Her books *North to the Orient* (1935) and *Listen! the Wind* (1938) are both accounts of flights taken with her husband, Charles LINDBERGH. *The Wave of the Future* (1940) is a tract influenced by her husband's isolationism, and *Gift from the Sea* (1955) is a highly personal series of essays addressed especially to married women. Of particular interest in "getting the record right and fair" about the tragedies and the controversies that swirled around the Lindberghs' lives are her diaries and letters compiled in five volumes: *Bring Me a Unicorn* (1972), *Hour of Gold, Hour of Lead* (1973), *Locked Rooms and Open Doors* (1974), *The Flower and the Nettle* (1976), and *War Within and Without* (1980).

Lindbergh, Charles A[ugustus, Jr.] (1902–1974)   American aviator. On March 21, 1927, Lindbergh became the first man to cross the Atlantic in a solo flight. *We* (1927) is an account of that flight in his plane, *The Spirit of St. Louis*. Following the kidnapping and death of their infant son, Lindbergh and his wife, Anne Morrow LINDBERGH, moved to Europe, where Lindbergh collaborated with Alexis Carrel on the development of an artificial heart. Convinced of the Germans' air superiority, Lindbergh returned to the U.S. in 1939 and became a vigorous opponent of America's entry into World War II. His views suggested a pro-Nazi bias to some and he resigned his commission in the Air Force Reserves. When the U.S. did enter the war, Lindbergh volunteered his services and flew combat missions in the Pacific. His writings include *Of Flight and Life* (1948), a PULITZER PRIZE-winning autobiography called *The Spirit of St. Louis* (1953), his *Wartime Journals* (1970), and *Autobiography of Values* (1978), a posthumous collection of notes and sketches.

Lindsay, Sir David (c1490–c1555)   Scottish poet. A courtier and diplomat, Lindsay was also a stern satirist whose principal target was the Catholic Church. In *Testament and Complaynt of Our Soverane Lordis Papyngo* (1538) the birds of prey who symbolize the clergy are criticized by the king's parrot. His most famous work, *Ane Pleasant Satyre of the Thrie Estatis* (1540), exposes the abuses of the political life of the time.

Lindsay, Jack (1900–   )   Australian poet, novelist, and classical scholar. Lindsay's strong socialist beliefs are reflected in most of his poetry and fiction. His work includes historical novels, polemical writings on Russia and Marxism, literary criticism, and biographies. His father was Norman LINDSAY.

Lindsay, Norman [Alfred William] (1879–1969)   Australian artist and writer. Lindsay spent many years as the chief cartoonist for the Sydney *Bulletin*. His pen-and-ink drawings, as well as paintings in oil and watercolor, won him an international reputation. His writings, caustic and high-spirited, include the novels *A Curate in Bohemia* (1913), *The Cautious Amorist* (1932), and *Age of Consent* (1938). He also wrote a classic book for children, *The Magic Pudding* (1918).

Lindsay, [Nicholas] Vachel (1879–1931)   American poet. Born in Springfield, Illinois, to a family of evangelical "Disciples of Christ," Lindsay had a crusading spirit that led him from temperance lectures to a troubadorian attempt at converting Americans to a love of poetry. Known for his dramatically effective readings, in 1912 he walked from Illinois to New Mexico preaching his "Gospel of Beauty" and exchanging his poems collected in *Rhymes to Be Traded for Bread* (1912) for meals and shelter. In the following year he published one of his best-known poems, GENERAL WILLIAM BOOTH ENTERS INTO HEAVEN, which was followed by THE CONGO and THE SANTA FE TRAIL. His work dealt mostly with American subjects and heroes, with patriotism and a mystic faith in the earth and in nature. Such other well-known poems as "The Eagle That Is Forgotten" (1913), "The Chinese Nightingale" (1917), "The Ghost of the Buffaloes" (1917), and "In Praise of Johnny Appleseed" (1923) contain Lindsay's unique synthesis of the folkways and lore of his time. Plagued by poverty, disillusionment, and depression, his poetic powers declined until, in 1931, he committed suicide by drinking poison.

Lingard, Captain   As a young man, the hero of Joseph Conrad's *The Rescue* (1920); in later life, in AN OUTCAST OF THE ISLANDS and *Almayer's Folly* (1895), a powerful white trader who takes Almayer and Willems for protégés.

linguistic philosophy   See LOGICAL POSITIVISM.

Linklater, Eric [Robert Russell] (1899–1974) Scottish novelist. The best known of his witty novels is *Juan in America* (1931), an amusing picaresque about a foreigner's adventures in the U.S.

Linnaeus, Carolus (Latinized name of Carl von Linné, 1707–1778)   Swedish botanist. In his *Systema naturae* (1735), Linnaeus outlined what was largely adopted as the *Linnaean classification* or *system* of plants. It is also known as the *sexual system*. It differs from Jussieu's system (1789), by which it was superseded, in that it makes no attempt to show the relationship of species and genera. Hence the name *artificial system* as opposed to Jussieu's *natural system*. Linnaeus's *Species plantarum* (1753) is considered the foundation of modern botanical nomenclature.

Lins do Rêgo, José (1901–1957)   Brazilian novelist. Reacting against the MODERNISMO tendency to disregard the past, Lins do Rêgo argued that there were in Brazil a land, a people, and a tradition worth knowing and preserving. His cycle of six novels that chronicle life in the great sugar plantations of northeastern Brazil stimulated a major revival of literary regionalism that began in the late 1920s. The first novels of the cycle—*Menino de Engenho* (1932), *Doidinho* (1933), and *Bagué* (1934)—were all three translated as *Plantation Boy* (1966). The series culminates in the author's masterpiece, FOGO MORTO.

Lin Yu-t'ang (usually Yutang in English, 1895–1976) Chinese writer. Following graduate work at Harvard and after receiving a Ph.D. from the University of Leipzig (1923), Lin returned to China to teach in Peking. He spent much of his time in the U.S. and wrote most of his books in English. Although he returned to China several times, he was at odds with the official view of literature as a means of political propaganda. Lin was distinguished as an editor of Chinese and American periodicals and textbooks, as the translator of such books as *Famous Chinese Stories* (1952), and as compiler and editor of such volumes as *The Wisdom of China and India* (1942) and *The Chinese Theory of Art* (1968). Among the best known of his many books interpreting China and her people are: *My Country and My People* (1935), *The Wisdom of Confucius* (1938), *A Leaf in the Storm* (1941), and *The Chinese Way of Life* (1959). His novels include *Chinatown Family* (1948), *Red Peony* (1962), and *The Flight of the Innocents* (1965).

lion   The "king of beasts." This animal figures perhaps more than any other in legend, symbolism, and heraldry. In religious art, the lion is an emblem of the Resurrection. According to tradition, the lion's whelp is born dead, and remains so for three days, when the father breathes on it and it receives life. Another tradition is that the lion is the only animal of the cat tribe born with its eyes open, and it is said that it sleeps with its eyes open.

St. MARK the Evangelist is symbolized by a lion because he begins his gospel with the scenes of St. JOHN THE BAPTIST and Christ in the wilderness. The device of Venice is the winged Lion of St. Mark. St. JEROME befriended lions. (See ANDROCLES, HERACLES, and UNA for legends of lions.)

Ever since 1164, when it was adopted as a device by Philip I, duke of Flanders, the lion has figured largely, and in an amazing variety of positions, as a heraldic emblem.

Li Po (or Li T'ai-po, 701–762)   Chinese poet of the T'ANG dynasty. Contemporary rumors make him of partly Turkic origin, perhaps a way of explaining his unconventional and unrestrained behavior. He never stood for the civil service exams required of most educated Chinese, and was exiled for a supposed role in the AN LU-SHAN REBELLION. His poetry shows his admiration for the folk songs of earlier periods. He wrote of wine, fabulous journeys, and palace ladies, but relatively little of himself. His great facility and the colorfulness of his verse bely its careful composition and high quality. He is one of China's greatest poets and one of the most frequently translated into English. A legend that is almost certainly false but often repeated says he died while drunkenly trying to embrace the moon's reflection in the water. Arthur WALEY translated some of his work in *The Poetry and Career of Li Po* (1950).

Lippi, Fra Lippo (or Fra Filippo Lippi, 1406–1469) Italian painter. A Florentine monk of the Carmelite order, he painted religious easel paintings and frescoes in a style stressing charm, imaginative detail, and sinuous outline. He was influenced primarily by MASACCIO, Fra ANGELICO, and DONATELLO, and in turn was the teacher of BOTTICELLI. Among his best-known works are *The Madonna with Saints* and the *Virgin and Child with Saints and Angels*. His restlessness as a monk, which caused him to leave his monastery, inspired Browning's famous poem FRA LIPPO LIPPI.

His son Filippino (1457–1504), who studied with his father's pupil Botticelli, also became famous as a painter of religious scenes. His masterpieces include the *Madonna Appearing to Saint Bernard*, the *Madonna and Child with Angels*, the *Allegory of Music*, and the frescoes of the Strozzi Chapel in the Florentine church of S. Maria Novella. He also finished the frescoes left incomplete by Masaccio in the Brancacci Chapel of the Carmine.

Lippmann, Walter (1889–1974)   American editor and essayist. One of the most influential and statesmanlike of American journalists, Lippmann was editor of the New York *World* from 1929 to 1931, after which he began writing his famous, widely syndicated column in the New York *Herald Tribune* (which moved to the Washington *Post* in 1962). He became a shaping influence on public opinion, particularly on matters of foreign policy. His position on domestic politics ultimately shifted from left-liberal to conservative, but his incisive articles remained throughout his life reasoned and free from polemics. Among Lippmann's many books are *A Preface to Politics* (1913), *Public Opin-*

ion (1922), *An Inquiry into the Principles of the Good Society* (1937), *The Cold War* (1947), *The Communist World and Ours* (1959), and *Western Unity and the Common Market* (1962). *The Essential Lippmann* (1963) was followed by a collection of *Early Writings* (ed Arthur SCHLESINGER, Jr.) in 1971.

Li Shang-yin (813–858)   Chinese poet. His poetry is extremely allusive, sometimes to the point of obscurity, but he is the acknowledged master of the difficult T'ANG dynasty style. His main theme seems to be of illicit and unhappy love.

Lisle Letters, The (1981)   Selections from the correspondence of Viscount Lisle, illegitimate son of Edward IV and courtier of HENRY VIII. Edited by Muriel St. Clare Byrne, the letters give an incomparably vivid and comprehensive picture of the political and domestic concerns of a high-ranking English family in the first half of the 16th century.

Lispector, Clarice (1925–1977)   Ukrainian-born Brazilian novelist. Lispector was trained as a lawyer, married to a diplomat, and usually lived abroad. Her novels and short stories—*Perto do Coração Salvagem* (1944), *Laços de familia* (1960; tr *Family Ties*, 1972), *Paixão segundo G.H.* (1964)—revolve around the existential anguish of women trapped in ancient female roles that are critically challenged by the rapid change of city life.

Liszt, Franz (1811–1883)   Hungarian composer and virtuoso pianist. A child prodigy, he first performed in public at the age of nine. He studied in Vienna under Czerny and Salieri, in Paris under Reicha. He lived in Geneva (1835–39) with the Comtesse d'Agoult, by whom he had three children, one of whom was Cosima, who later married Richard WAGNER. Liszt was court *kapellmeister* at Weimar from 1848 to 1859. In 1865 he entered the Franciscan order at Rome and was thenceforth known as Abbé Liszt. He died at Bayreuth in the midst of a Wagner festival. He was outstanding as a piano teacher, as well as being hailed as one of the greatest performing pianists of all time.

Much of his music, especially from the last twenty years of his life, is marked by daring innovations in form and harmonic relations, which have fascinated and influenced composers ever since. His works include the *Faust Symphony* (1853–61), the *Dante Symphony* (1856); twelve symphonic poems, including *Les Préludes* (after LAMARTINE); two piano concertos; much piano music, notably the *Anneés de Pèlerinage* (1855–83) and *20 Hungarian Rhapsodies* (1851–86); two oratorios, several masses, and other church music; songs and organ pieces. As a teacher and supporter of young composers, Liszt was extraordinarily open-hearted and generous. He never accepted payment from his students, and he was constantly conducting and performing the work of new composers, including BERLIOZ and Wagner.

Little Bear   See GREAT BEAR AND LITTLE BEAR.

Little Clay Cart, The (Mrichchhakatika)   A Sanskrit play ascribed to King Shudraka and variously assigned to the 3rd to 10th centuries. The hero is Charudatta, an impoverished Brahmin merchant, the heroine the lovely courtesan Vasantasena. The villain of the play, Sansthanaka, the king's brother-in-law, smothers Vasantasena in a remote garden and accuses Charudatta of the crime, but Vasantasena recovers and appears just in time to save her lover from execution. An important subplot is concerned with a successful conspiracy to overthrow the reigning monarch. GOETHE paraphrased the drama in his poem *Der Gott und die Bayadere*, and it was made the basis of a popular ballet, *Le Dieu et la bayadère*, which was staged throughout Europe about the year 1830.

Little Corporal   An epithet applied to Napoleon Bonaparte after the battle of Lodi in 1796. Bonaparte stood barely five feet two inches in height.

Little Dorrit (1855–1857)   A novel by Charles DICKENS. William Dorrit, with his three children, Edward, Fanny, and Amy (who is Little Dorrit), lives in prison where he is confined for debt. Little Dorrit was born in the prison, spends most of her life there, and ultimately chooses to be married there. The three children try to make a living outside the prison and bring back their earnings each night. Little Dorrit does her part by sewing for Mrs. Clennam. Suddenly, her father comes into a fortune and the whole family becomes as pretentious and despicable as they were formerly objects of compassion. Only Little Dorrit remains unchanged with her father's changing fortune, retaining her sweet and generous disposition. She grows to love Arthur Clennam, middle-aged son of Mrs. Clennam, who has recently returned from China. In Arthur's struggle with the civil service's CIRCUMLOCUTION OFFICE, Dickens levels an attack on bureaucracy. Arthur is sent to prison for debt and Little Dorrit labors to help him. Their love ends happily, and they are married in Marshalsea prison. This novel is one of Dickens's strongest attacks on bureaucratic inefficiency and the practice of imprisonment for debt. See BARNACLE.

Little Eva   A character in Harriet Beecher Stowe's UNCLE TOM'S CABIN.

Little Foxes, The (1939)   A play by Lillian HELLMAN. In telling the story of the Hubbard family, it depicts unfavorably the rise of industrialism in the South and condemns the new breed of Southerners as rapacious and ruthless—like "the little foxes who spoil the vines" of the biblical verse. *Another Part of the Forest* (1946) deals with an earlier stage in the Hubbards' career.

Little Gidding   The home of an Anglican lay religious community in England in the 17th century. It was composed of the family and friends of Nicholas Ferrar (1592–1637), who was intimate with the poets George HERBERT and Richard CRASHAW. It is the setting for the novel *John Inglesant*, by J. H. Shorthouse, and for T. S. ELIOT's poem "Little Gidding" (see FOUR QUARTETS). The community was dispersed by the Parliamentarians in 1647, during the Civil War.

Little John A chief follower of ROBIN HOOD in the English Robin Hood ballad cycle. He was a big stalwart fellow, first named John Little (or John Nailor), who encountered Robin Hood and gave him a sound thrashing, after which he was rechristened, Robin standing as godfather. He appears in Scott's novel *The Talisman* (1825).

Little Lord Fauntleroy (1886) A story for children by Frances Hodgson BURNETT, illustrated by Reginald Birch. The seven-year-old hero, Cedric Errol, is the son of a disinherited English father and an American mother. His title of Lord Fauntleroy he would normally inherit from his grandfather, an English earl, who has, however, never forgiven the boy's father for marrying an American. On the death of the father the boy is summoned to England, leaving his mother, whom he calls "Dearest," in the poverty-stricken quarters where they have been living in New York. He so completely wins the hearts of his English relatives that they are soon persuaded to extend to "Dearest" a cordial welcome. Little Lord Fauntleroy is a striking figure, dressed in black velvet with lace collar and yellow curls, and his name passed into common usage as referring either to a certain type of children's clothes or to a beautiful but pampered and effeminate small boy.

little magazines A name applied to small, noncommercial magazines of limited circulation whose original aim was to promote avant-garde writing. Such magazines have frequently been the only means of expression available to young, unknown writers, providing a forum for new ideas, experimental material, and for artistic, social, or political theories not in the mainstream of popular tastes. Little magazines, and the writers associated with them, have been at the center of numerous new literary movements; they were a major factor in the important literary developments in the first decades of the 20th century, both in England and America.

In America, the direct precursors to little magazines were published in the 19th century, notably the Transcendentalists' journal, THE DIAL (1840–44); *The Chapbook* (1894–98), which published work by Thomas Bailey ALDRICH, George Washington CABLE, Stephen CRANE, and others; *The Mirror* (1893–1920); and *The Philistine* (1895–1915). In England, comparable publications included *The Germ* (1850), published by the pre-Raphaelites, and Aubrey Beardsley's THE YELLOW BOOK (1894–97).

Beginning in 1912, with the founding of POETRY in America, little magazines began to appear in abundance; they proliferated further during World War I. Among the many published during this period were Alfred Kreymborg's *Others* (1915–19), which introduced IMAGISM to America, as did THE EGOIST (1911–19) in England. BLAST (1914), the vorticist journal, also appeared in England at this time. Notable among other American little magazines were THE LITTLE REVIEW (1914–29), which first published Joyce's ULYSSES in serial form, and THE SEVEN ARTS (1916–17), a monthly edited by James OPPENHEIM, Waldo Frank, and Van Wyck BROOKS.

During the 1920s a number of magazines were published abroad by American expatriates. Among the best known of these are: *Broom* (1921–24), edited by Kreymborg and Harold Loeb; THE CRITERION (1922–39), edited by T. S. ELIOT; *Exile* (1927), edited by Ezra POUND; and TRANSITION (1927–38), edited by Elliott PAUL and Eugene Jolas. Important American magazines started during this period were *The Dial* (1920–29; named for its forebear), which first published Eliot's THE WASTE LAND; William Carlos WILLIAMS's *Contact* (1920–32); *The Double Dealer* (1921–26), which published the early work of HEMINGWAY and FAULKNER; and *The Fugitive* (1922–25; see FUGITIVES).

Developing simultaneously were numerous little magazines with a left-wing political, rather than literary, orientation, as with THE MASSES (1911–17), *The Liberator* (1918–26), and *The New Masses* (1926–48). The late 1920s and 1930s also saw increasing numbers of quarterly reviews that combined critical essays, prose, poetry, and reports on new developments in the arts, such as *The Prairie Schooner* (begun 1927), THE PARTISAN REVIEW (begun 1934), THE SOUTHERN REVIEW (1935–42), THE KENYON REVIEW (1939–70), *Accent* (1940–60), *The Quarterly Review of Literature* (begun 1943), and *The Hudson Review* (begun 1948).

In reaction against the quarterlies, which were no longer avant-garde and were more critical than creative, a new group of little magazines appeared during the 1950s and 1960s in such ventures as *The Black Mountain Review* (1954–57), which published THE BLACK MOUNTAIN POETS, among others; *The Evergreen Review* (1957–73); Imanu Amiri BARAKA's *Yugen* (1958–62), closely associated with the BEAT MOVEMENT; and *Kulchur* (1960–65). Some, which combined new writing and criticism, like the *Paris Review* (begun 1953) and *Tri Quarterly* (begun 1958), prospered and became widely influential, particularly in academic quarters.

Antiestablishment feeling in the late 1960s stimulated another spate of independent publications. Throughout the decade of the 1970s little magazines continued to flourish as a medium for minority expression and literary experimentation. Although some failed as others began, by 1980 the number of little magazines in America alone was estimated at more than twelve hundred.

Little Orphant Annie (1885) A poem in Hoosier dialect by James Whitcomb RILEY. Orphant Annie works hard for her keep and tells hair-raising tales about the goblins. A comic strip by Harold Gray, based on the character, is called "Little Orphan Annie" and in 1977 the character was featured in a Broadway musical, *Annie*.

Littlepage Manuscripts, The (1845–1846) A series of three novels by James Fenimore COOPER: *Satanstoe*, *The Chainbearer*, and *The Redskins*. Presumably related by several generations of Littlepage men, the novels deal with the antirent controversy and its historical background. In this now forgotten issue, the tenants of the New York patroons, suffering hardships, refused to pay rent. Cooper defended the landlords' rights, insisting that the tenants had enjoyed years of advantages in the bargain. Cooper saw, in this controversy, a crisis in American democracy; if contracts could be broken by mob rule, democracy would turn to anarchy.

The three novels become progressively weaker, as Cooper's political principles outweigh those of his art. The trilogy marks the end of his most creative period.

Little Red Riding-Hood   A nursery tale. It comes to us from *Le Petit Chaperon rouge* (1697) of Charles PERRAULT (in his CONTES DE MA MÈRE L'OYE), though with slight alterations the story is common to France, Germany, and Sweden and probably originated in Italy. A little girl bringing a present to her grandmother is devoured by a wolf who has disguised himself in the old lady's ruffled nightcap. The brothers GRIMM added a happy ending to the tale: a huntsman slits open the wolf and restores the child and her grandmother to life.

Little Review, The (1914–1929)   An American literary periodical, considered one of the outstanding LITTLE MAGAZINES. It was published first in Chicago, later in New York and Paris, under the editorship of Margaret Anderson. It championed all the experimental movements that cropped up during its years of publication and published the work of such outstanding writers as T. S. ELIOT, Ezra POUND, Sherwood ANDERSON, and Ernest HEMINGWAY. It offered the first American publication of James Joyce's ULYSSES, in installments (1918–21); four issues containing that serialization were confiscated and burned by the U.S. Post Office.

Little Tragedies (Malenkiye tragedi, 1830)   Four short dramatic works in blank verse by Aleksandr PUSHKIN. The short dramas, which Pushkin referred to as "essays of dramatic investigation," are studies of character in four varied situations. *Kamyenny gost* (*The Stone Guest*) is a retelling of the DON JUAN legend. *Motsart i Salyeri* (*Mozart and Salieri*) depicts Salieri's jealousy of Mozart's artistic genius and his legendary poisoning of MOZART. *Skupoi rytsar* (*The Covetous Knight*) is a study of the effects of avarice. *Pir vo vremya chumy* (*The Feast during the Plague Year*), translated from the English drama *City of the Plague* by John Wilson, shows the evil effects on human behavior of imminent death. All four of the small dramas are regarded as being among Pushkin's most powerful poetic work.

Little Women, or Meg, Jo, Beth, and Amy (1868, 1869)   A widely read story for young people by Louisa May ALCOTT. The heroine is Jo March, the tomboyish and literary member of the family, who retires to the attic when "genius burns." Meg, her older, pretty sister, marries a young tutor, John Brooke, and reappears in the sequel, *Little Men* (1871), with her twins, Daisy and Demi. Gentle, music-loving Beth dies young. The fashionable and artistic Amy finally marries Laurie, a high-spirited boy who had long been Jo's boon companion, but who failed to persuade her to marry him. Jo herself becomes the wife of a kindly old German professor, Mr. Bhaer; in *Little Men*, she and the professor turn their home into a school for boys. *Jo's Boys* (1886) is a second sequel.

Litvinov   See SMOKE.

Lives of the Poets, The (1779–1781)   A collection of biographical and critical essays on fifty-two English poets from COWLEY to Johnson's contemporaries by Samuel JOHNSON. It is noted for its approach; Johnson was interested in establishing a causal relationship between the artist's life and his art:

To judge rightly of an author we must transport ourselves to his time, and examine what were the wants of his contemporaries, and what were his means of supplying them.—*Life of Dryden*

His criticism was vigorous and articulate. He considered DRYDEN, POPE, SWIFT, and ADDISON the most important authors of the RESTORATION and Queen Anne periods. Some of his critical opinion has been discredited with the perspective of time; the romantics deplored his failure to appreciate the odes of Thomas GRAY and MILTON's work, and his attack on METAPHYSICAL POETS, in the *Life of Cowley*, is not compatible with the modern view. However, Johnson's *Lives* remains an achievement beyond the "correctness" of its critical evaluations.

Livingstone, David (1813–1873)   Scottish-born English missionary and explorer in Africa. After working in a cotton mill from the age of ten, he went to college in 1837, received a medical degree in 1840, and left England for South Africa as a medical missionary. He discovered Lake Ngami (1849), the Zambesi River (1851), the Victoria Falls of the Zambesi (1855), and Lake Nyasa (1859). On his return to England (1864) he published *Narrative of an Expedition to the Zanzibar and Its Tributaries* (1865). Appointed British consul in central Africa, he went back with the express purpose of wiping out slave trade and determining the watershed of the Nyasa-Tanganyika region. Exhausted and near death, he spent some months in Ujiji; in 1871 an expedition was sent out under Sir Henry M. Stanley (1841–1904) to find Livingstone and their famous encounter began with Stanley's anticlimactic "Dr. Livingstone, I presume?" Livingstone died in an African village. His body was taken to England and buried in Westminster Abbey. His journals for the years 1866 to 1873 were published as *Last Journals of David Livingstone in Central Africa* (1873). Livingstone's example was followed by many missionaries and his influence was considerable in reducing slave trade.

Livy (full name Titus Livius, 59 BC–AD 17)   Roman historian. His *Ab urbe condita libri*, the history of Rome from the founding of the city, was written in 142 books of which only about thirty-six have been preserved. We have, however, summaries of all but two of the missing books; these outlines, written by an unknown scholar of the 4th century, give an indication of the vast scope of the work, which extended from the mythological beginnings of Rome down to AD 9. Though Livy's research must have been voluminous, it was unscholarly; his information is often inaccurate, and his facts are sometimes self-contradictory. But scientific history was not his primary objective. He wished to hold up to his countrymen the great panorama of their past, to recall to them the glories of their ancestors, and to urge them to abandon decadent ways. In this sense his aim was similar to that of Vergil in his *Aeneid*. Livy's style is one of polished rhetorical brilliance; the speeches which he puts in the mouths of historical personages are masterful, both as oratory and as character analysis.

A native of Patavium (Padua), Livy began his great work about 26 BC, but did not publish his first twenty-one books until AD 14. Excerpts were, however, in circulation much earlier, for Asinius Pollio, who died in AD 4, had occasion to criticize Livy's "patavinitas." This was apparently a reference to his provincial, Paduan manner of expression, evidence of which scholars have not been able to detect in Livy's prose.

Liyong, Taban lo (1938–) Ugandan poet, fiction writer, and critic. Liyong attended schools in Uganda and the U.S. and then took a graduate degree at the Writers' Workshop at the University of Iowa, the first African to do so. His volumes of poetry include *Eating Chiefs* (1970), *Frantz Fanon's Uneven Ribs* (1971), *Another Nigger Dead* (1972), and *Ballads of Underdevelopment* (1974). A novel, *In Limbo* (1970), was republished in a revised edition in 1977 as *Meditations. Fixions* (1968; repr 1978) is a collection of short stories. In his book of literary criticism, *The Last Word* (1969), he expounds his philosophy of "cultural synthesism," which maintains that the attainments of human intellectual endeavor—in philosophy and the arts —are accessible to any who choose to contemplate them. As opposed to the tenets of NÉGRITUDE, Liyong suggests that African culture and literature can be embraced by non-Africans just as other cultures can be embraced by Africans.

Llanto por Ignacio Sánchez Mejías   See GARCÍA LORCA, FEDERICO.

Llareggub   See UNDER MILK WOOD.

Lloyd George, David (1863–1945)   British statesman of Welsh descent. Lloyd George succeeded Asquith as prime minister (1916–22) and directed British policies during World War I and in the negotiation of peace terms. He instituted negotiations resulting in the establishment of the Irish Free State.

Lochinvar   A young Highlander, hero of a ballad in Scott's MARMION. Being in love with a lady already committed to an unenviable marriage, Lochinvar persuades her to dance one last dance, during which he swings her into his saddle and makes off with her before the bridegroom and his servants can recover from their astonishment.

Locke, John (1632–1704)   English philosopher. Educated at Christ Church, Oxford, Locke was a lecturer in Greek, rhetoric, and philosophy at that university and apparently practiced medicine, though he never received a medical degree. He became confidential secretary to the earl of SHAFTESBURY, who, as one of the proprietors of Carolina, induced Locke to write a well-known constitution for the colony in 1669. Suspected of complicity in Shaftesbury's plots against the government, Locke was forced to leave England, and he lived in the Netherlands from 1684 to 1689. He returned to England at the accession of William and Mary and was appointed commissioner of appeals.

Locke's most famous philosophical treatise is AN ESSAY CONCERNING HUMAN UNDERSTANDING, an inquiry into the nature of knowledge. In this work, he established the principles of modern EMPIRICISM and attacked the rationalist doctrine of "innate ideas." The human mind, Locke maintained, begins as a *tabula rasa* (Lat, "blank slate") and acquires knowledge through the use of the five senses and a process of reflection.

Locke's influence on political theory was enormous. His *Two Treatises on Government* (1690), written in defense of the GLORIOUS REVOLUTION, revealed his belief in the natural goodness and cooperative spirit of man and his theory that the state should operate according to natural laws of reason and tolerance. He advocated religious tolerance and rights to personal property. The American DECLARATION OF INDEPENDENCE, in particular, echoes his contention that government rests on popular consent and that rebellion is permissible when government subverts the ends—the protection of life, liberty, and property—for which it is established. Locke also wrote *Some Thoughts Concerning Education* (1693), *The Reasonableness of Christianity* (1695), and four *Letters on Toleration* (1689–92).

Lockhart, John Gibson (1794–1854)   Scottish editor and writer. At the age of twenty-three, Lockhart wrote for *Blackwood's Magazine* a series of four articles, signed "Z," dealing with the supposed COCKNEY SCHOOL of poetry and excoriating Leigh Hunt and John Keats. Though the tone of these articles is abusive and though to later generations many of Lockhart's adverse judgments seem as vicious as they are obtuse, especially in their confusion of enmity with criticism, Lockhart enjoys a high reputation in English letters, his life of his father-in-law Sir Walter Scott (7 vols, 1837–38) ranking second only to Boswell's *Johnson* among the great biographies in the language.

Locksley   In Scott's IVANHOE, a name assumed by Robin Hood, who appears as an archer at the tournament. It is said to have been the name of the village where the outlaw was born.

Locksley Hall (1842)   A poem by Alfred TENNYSON. The hero takes a last look at Locksley Hall, the remote seaside mansion where he spent his youth. Here he fell in love with his cousin Amy, who, yielding to social and parental pressure, married a rich "clown." Though disgusted by the weakness of women and the mercenary corruption of the age—he even considers exiling himself to some tropic island—his youthful belief in progress and in the high destiny of Europe reasserts itself. In 1886 Tennyson published "Locksley Hall Sixty Years After," a sequel.

Lodge, Thomas (1558?–1625)   English poet, playwright, and prose writer. The son of the Lord Mayor of London, Lodge was educated at Oxford and became one of the group in London known as the UNIVERSITY WITS. Considered by some to be the best of the imitators of LYLY and the Euphuistic style (see EUPHUISM), Lodge wrote several prose romances, including *Rosalynde, Euphues' Golden Legacie* (printed 1590), his most famous work, which provided SHAKESPEARE with the plot for AS YOU LIKE IT. Lodge's poetry includes *Scillaes Metamorphosis, Enterlaced with the Unfortunate Love of Glaucus* (1589; reissued as *Glaucus and Scilla*). As the first example of a classical story given romantic treatment in verse, it may have influenced Shakespeare's VENUS AND ADONIS. A *Fig for Momus* (1595), based on the satires of HORACE, is one of the earliest English verse satires.

Logan, John [Burton] (1923–   )   American poet, editor, and critic. Logan's work in poetry and prose manifests the dilemma of a religious sensibility in an anti-religious society. His poetry has the metaphysical quality of a mind steeped in the scholastic tradition. As such, it has been considered remote by many readers. He was poetry editor of *Choice, Critic,* and *The Nation,* and it was with this last-mentioned, politically oriented journal that he brought his moral, though acutely contemporary, sensibility most forcefully to bear on literary commentary. His best-known volume, *The Zigzag Walk: Poems 1963–1968* (1969), deals with that turbulent time in U.S. history. The volume *Only the Dreamer Can Change the Dream* (1981) and the selected poems in *The Bridge of Change* (1981) represent intensely personal probings of his own consciousness and unconsciousness.

logical positivism   A school of 20th-century philosophic thought, which maintained that philosophy is a logical and analytical discipline rather than a speculative or metaphysical one. It began with a group of Viennese philosophers in the 1920s, known as the Vienna Circle, who were very much influenced by the works of Ludwig WITTGENSTEIN. Their concern was with a logical analysis of thought and meaning; they maintained that nothing could be considered meaningful unless it could be empirically verified. The influence of the early logical positivists extended to England, where the study of meaning became inextricably linked with linguistic philosophy. A. J. AYER and the group known as the Oxford philosophers believed that human thoughts, ideas, and concepts are dependent on a command of language; hence philosophy must offer a logical analysis of language. Ayer's linguistic philosophy had a considerable influence on much English literary criticism, particularly that of the CAMBRIDGE CRITICS.

Lohengrin   A son of PERCIVAL or Parsifal in German legend, the Knight of the Swan. Lohengrin appears at the close of Wolfram von Eschenbach's PARZIVAL (c1210) and in other German romances, where he is the deliverer of Elsa, a princess of Brabant, who has been dispossessed by Telramund and Ortrud. He arrives at Antwerp in a skiff drawn by a swan, champions Elsa, and becomes her husband on the sole condition that she shall not ask his name or lineage. She is prevailed upon to do so on the marriage night, and he, by his vows to the Grail, is obliged to disclose his identity but at the same time to disappear. The swan returns for him, and he goes, but not before retransforming the swan into Elsa's brother Gottfried, who, by the wiles of the sorceress Ortrud, had been obliged to assume that form. Richard WAGNER has an opera based on the subject (1847).

Lohenstein, Daniel Caspar von (1635–1683)   German dramatist, poet, and novelist of the late baroque period. Like the poems of HOFMANN VON HOFMANNSWALDAU, Lohenstein's plays are rich and sensual in language and imagery. Unlike GRYPHIUS, who often gives his heroes a martyr's death, Lohenstein frequently ends his tragedies in suicide—showing less of an attempt to remain within Christian teachings. His most famous tragedies are *Cleopatra* (1661), *Ibrahim Sultan* (1673), and *Sophonisbe* (1680). His historical novel *Arminius* (1689) reveals many parallels with the actual political situation of the time and embodies the author's own views.

Loki   In Scandinavian mythology, the Satanic Aesir god of strife and evil who fathered the three monsters with the giantess Angerboda: the MIDGARD SERPENT, FENRISWOLF, and HEL. As enemy of the good gods, Loki artfully contrived the death of BALDER. He was finally bound to a rock by ten chains and tortured by drops of venom from a serpent overhead. One legend holds that he will remain captive until the Twilight of the Gods, when he will break his bonds. Another story says that he was freed at RAGNAROK when he and HEIMDALL slew each other.

Lo Kuan-chung   See ROMANCE OF THE THREE KINGDOMS.

Lolita (pub France 1955; U.S. 1958)   A novel by Vladimir NABOKOV. Humbert Humbert is a middle-aged intellectual who has a passion for girls between the ages of nine and fourteen. He falls in love with the twelve-year-old Dolores Haze, whom he calls Lolita. In his plot to seduce her, he marries Dolores's mother, whose accidental death then allows Lolita and Humbert to take off on an odyssey across the U.S. Humbert is surprised when, contrary to his schemes, Lolita seduces him and again when she leaves him and marries Clare Quilty, whom Humbert is forced to murder. The book presents a quest for eternal innocence, albeit in satirical terms. Its popular appeal as an erotic story thrust Nabokov into notoriety. It was banned in France and parts of the U.S., and its merits were debated in the British Parliament. Nabokov defended it as a moral rather than an obscene book. It combines parody, fanciful imaginative flights, literary puzzles, and a brilliant satirical overview of American culture. The book was made into a film and has been the subject of numerous critical studies, many of which, in reaction to its public reputation, try to minimize the novel's erotic aspects. A stage adaptation by Edward ALBEE was produced in 1981.

lo Liyong, Taban See LIYONG, TABAN LO.

Lollards A name given, sometimes disparagingly, to members of the 14th-century movement in England associated with John Wyclif and his demands for ecclesiastical reform. The Lollards held that the church in England had become so encrusted with false doctrine as to be virtually useless and that the only true way of life was one based on the Bible. They particularly objected to the wealth and power of the clergy and advocated that the church practice the poverty exemplified by Christ in the Gospels. The Lollards' rise into prominence during the latter half of the 14th century can best be understood in the historical context of the times: while the great mass of the people were plagued by warfare, pestilence, and poverty, the English clergy, by skillful abuse of ecclesiastical prerogatives, had amassed enormous power, wealth, and property. The Lollards reached the height of their strength in the decade following Wyclif's death: in 1395 it was said that one out of every two Englishmen was a Lollard. Under the house of Lancaster in the 15th century, they were more and more sternly repressed and, waning in numbers, responded to their loss of strength by ever-increasing fanaticism. Their decline was due in part to a loss of leadership. In the 16th century, to all intents and purposes, the Lollards had ceased to exist. Though it cannot be claimed that the Lollards sparked the English Reformation, the movement bore important fruit: the placing of the clergy under lay jurisdiction, the curbing of clerical abuses (especially in the form of the reduction in ecclesiastic holdings and possessions), and the insistence that the Bible through translation into the vernacular be made available to the reason of common men and women are all due, directly or indirectly, to the legacy left by the Lollards.

Lomax, John Avery (1872–1948) American folklorist and collector of folksongs, which he published in numerous books. His work was continued by his son Alan Lomax (1915–   ), who collected thousands of American and European folksongs by means of phonograph recordings, many of which are in the Library of Congress; some are also available on commercial recordings.

Lombard A banker or money-lender. They are so called because the first English bankers were from Lombardy and set up their businesses in Lombard Street (London), in the Middle Ages. The name *Lombard* is a contraction of *Longobard*. Among the richest of these Longobard merchants was the celebrated Medici family, from whose armorial bearings the pawnbrokers' insignia of three golden balls may have been derived (see St. NICHOLAS). The Lombard bankers exercised a monopoly in pawnbroking until the reign of Elizabeth I.

Lombard, Peter (c1100–c1164) Italian scholastic theologian. Lombard studied Aristotelian philosophy under Pierre ABÉLARD, then he himself became a teacher at Paris. He is often called Master of the Sentences (Lat, *Magister Sententiarum*) because of his compilation of the *Sententiarum libri quatuor* (*Four Books of Sentences*). These volumes contain quotations from the authorities on doctrinal questions, with objections and replies also from "the sayings of the fathers." The fourth volume, concerning the nature of the sacraments, was especially important at the time; the whole work became a theological textbook and inspired innumerable commentaries.

Lomonosov, Mikhail Vasilyevich (1711–1765) Russian scholar and poet. Lomonosov is considered the founder of modern literary Russian and the first to introduce what has become standard Russian prosody. The son of a fisherman, Lomonosov became one of the most versatile and brilliant Russians of his time. He made valuable contributions in chemistry, mathematics, grammar, and rhetoric. He formed modern literary Russian by establishing a working relationship between Old Church Slavonic and the Russian vernacular, producing a literary language that equals any other in richness and flexibility. Realizing that the old-style syllabic versification, based on the number of syllables in a line, was not fitted for Russian, Lomonosov introduced a system based on accents—alternating stressed and unstressed syllables. This system became the standard one used by the great classic Russian poets. Not until the early 20th century were new methods of versification introduced into Russian by Aleksandr BLOK.

London, Jack (real name John Griffith London, 1876–1916) American writer. An illegitimate child, London was raised in poverty in San Francisco by his mother, Flora Wellman, a self-styled spiritualist, and her husband, John London, a farmer. He began selling newspapers at ten and at fourteen worked in a cannery. By the age of sixteen, he had been both an oyster pirate and a member of the fish patrol in San Francisco Bay. At seventeen, he set off for a year at sea on a sealing schooner, and at eighteen he traveled the U.S. as a hobo. It is said that a particularly back-breaking job in a steam laundry hardened his resolve to become a writer and live by his wits. In a vigorous program of self-education, he read and wrote for up to twenty hours a day, voraciously ingesting the works of DARWIN, MARX, and NIETZSCHE, all of whom had a profound influence on the work he was later to produce. At twenty-one, he followed the gold rush north to the Klondike. Two years later, he sold his first story, "To the Man on the Trail," to THE OVERLAND MONTHLY for five dollars. In a year's time, he had sold enough to publish a collection, *The Son of the Wolf* (1900). His first novel, *A Daughter of the Snows* (1902), was a romance infused with his conviction of Anglo-Saxon superiority. Next he published THE CALL OF THE WILD, the classic story of the sled-dog Buck, which brought him instant celebrity and established his readership for generations through innumerable printings in sixty-eight languages. Then came THE SEA WOLF and, a year later, WHITE FANG. By the age of twenty-nine, London was the highest-paid and most widely read writer in America. The preoccupations evident in these early books pervade the rest of his work: an aggressive will to survive by being able to adapt and prevail; a compassion for the wounded, the mistreated, and the poor; visions of social justice through world revolution; and a predilection for raw, primitive power.

Among London's later novels are *The Iron Heel* (1907), a futuristic tale of fascist tyranny overthrown by socialist revolution, *Martin Eden* (1909), a partly autobiographical inversion of the American Dream, and *John Barleycorn* (1913), a tract against drinking, which also has autobiographical elements. *The Valley of the Moon* (1913), focusing on the advantages of agrarian life, was among the first novels to dwell on the dehumanizing effects of urbanization. London, unable to match the success of his earlier novels and plagued by bouts with alcoholism, uremia, and rheumatism, died of an overdose of drugs at the age of forty.

Best Short Stories of Jack London (1945) and *Tales of Adventure* (1956) are selections of his stories. *Essays of Revolt* (1926; ed L. D. Abbott) and *Jack London: American Rebel* (1947; ed P. S. Foner) are collections of his socialist writings.

Loneliness of the Long Distance Runner, The (1959)   A long short story by Alan SILLITOE. A boy who is sent to reform school for robbing a bakery narrates his own story. The corrupt society that has made him a delinquent is incidentally analyzed. The boy scores a triumph over the warden of the reformatory and the Establishment in general by deliberately losing in a long-distance race against another school.

Long, Huey [Pierce] (1893–1935)   American politician. Perhaps the most notorious as well as the most successful of American demagogues, Long began his career as a traveling salesman and later studied at Tulane University, completing the three-year law course in seven months. Having served as railroad commissioner of Louisiana, he was elected governor in 1928 and consolidated his power by placing his followers in strategic positions. After the failure of an attempt to remove him from office (1929), he was elected to the U.S. Senate in 1930 and, retaining the governorship until 1932, made himself master of the state; he provided Louisiana with good schools and highways during his term as governor, built a new state capitol at Baton

Rouge, and helped the state university. In 1934 he announced a Share-Our-Wealth program, intended to provide financial security for every American. After declaring himself a candidate for the presidency, he was assassinated on the steps of the state capitol by Dr. Carl A. Weiss, who was killed by Long's bodyguards.

Long's career inspired several novels, including Hamilton Basso's *Sun in Capricorn* (1942) and John DOS PASSOS's *Number One* (1943). Although Robert Penn WARREN has denied that the character of Willie Stark in his ALL THE KING'S MEN should be identified with Long, the similarity is striking.

Long Day's Journey into Night (1956)   A play by Eugene O'NEILL. An autobiographical drama, written before July 22, 1941, when O'Neill presented the manuscript to Carlotta, his third wife, it deals with the Tyrone family: the father, mother, and two sons. The only other character is Cathleen, a servant girl. The father is a celebrated actor; the older son is a drunkard and ne'er-do-well. A harrowing domestic tragedy, the play offers a clear insight into the character of O'Neill himself.

Longest Journey, The (1907)   A novel by E. M. FORSTER. Its main character is Rickie Elliot, a student at Cambridge University. Lame, an orphan, and weak-willed, he neglects his good friend, Stewart Ansell, to marry Agnes Pembroke. Agnes, a shallow girl, with her brother influences Rickie to cheat his half brother, Stephen Wonham. Rickie finally redeems himself when he loses his life in saving Stephen's. The novel is notable for its picture of the intellectual and social life of Cambridge students.

Longfellow, Henry Wadsworth (1807–1882) American poet, translator, romancer, and college professor. Longfellow is two poets: one, the popular schoolroom image of the wise but harmless old man who wrote "A Psalm of Life" (1839), THE CHILDREN'S HOUR, and THE VILLAGE BLACKSMITH; and the other, the serious but limited poet who wrote the sonnet "Mezzo Cammin" (1842) and was the subject of a study by the critic Newton Arvin.

Descended from old New England families, Longfellow went to Bowdoin College in Maine and then to Europe to study languages. On his return, he became professor of languages at Bowdoin and married Mary Potter. Dissatisfied with life in Maine, he turned to reminiscences. The result was his first book, the Irvingesque series of travel sketches *Outre-Mer: A Pilgrimage beyond the Sea* (1835). After another trip to Europe, he accepted the chair of modern languages at Harvard, succeeding George Ticknor. His wife had died in Rotterdam on the European trip.

At home, Longfellow wrote *Hyperion* (1839), a romance in which he modeled his heroine on Frances Appleton, whom he had met in Europe. In the same year, he published his first volume of poems, *Voices of the Night*, and, three years later, his second, *Ballads and Other Poems* (1842). In 1843, after another trip to Europe, he married Frances Appleton. Her father gave the pair the beautiful

Cambridge mansion Craigie House as a wedding present. Longfellow lived in the house for the rest of his life, and it is now dedicated to his memory.

Increasingly interested in narrative forms, he produced a series that helped to establish a native mythology: EVANGELINE, THE GOLDEN LEGEND, HIAWATHA, THE COURTSHIP OF MILES STANDISH, and TALES OF A WAYSIDE INN. To these he added a long prose romance of curious charm, *Kavanagh* (1849), an amusing and romantic vision of life in a small New England town.

In 1861, at the height of his fame, Mrs. Longfellow died. The poet's shock and sorrow prevented his working for several years. He finally finished his translation (1865–67) of *The Divine Comedy* and his religious poem, *Christus* (1872). In his last years, he added to his volumes, expanding earlier editions and writing a number of sonnets.

His poetry and values have been subject to great reversals in critical opinion. Never profound or powerfully original, he did have a sound lyric sense and an effective understanding of European culture. His work, however, is rooted in literature rather than life; there is always a feeling of aloofness in his lines. Longfellow's immense popularity did a great deal to develop audiences for poetry in America. See BUILDING OF THE SHIP, THE; WRECK OF THE HESPERUS, THE.

Longinus   The traditional name of the Roman soldier who stabbed JESUS with a spear at the Crucifixion.

Longinus, Cassius (c220–273)   Greek rhetorician and philosopher. A Neoplatonist and the teacher of PORPHYRY, Longinus is not to be confused with the unknown author of the treatise ON THE SUBLIME. Longinus taught at Athens and counseled Queen ZENOBIA at Palmyra. He was executed by Aurelian for his loyalty to the queen.

Long Parliament   In English history, the Parliament that assembled in November 1640, after the dissolution of the Short Parliament. The Long Parliament impeached the earl of STRAFFORD, passed the Grand Remonstrance (November 22, 1641), which listed the unconstitutional acts of Charles I and demanded reform, and, after the final rupture with CHARLES I in 1642, conducted the CIVIL WAR against the king's forces. In 1648 the members who were willing to come to terms with Charles were ousted during Pride's Purge. The remaining members constituted the RUMP PARLIAMENT, which was forcibly dissolved by Oliver CROMWELL in 1653 but was twice recalled in 1659. Early in 1660, after the Rump assembled and was joined by the members expelled in 1648, the Long Parliament declared itself dissolved.

Longus   See DAPHNIS AND CHLOË.

Lonigan, Studs   See STUDS LONIGAN.

Lonsdale, Frederick (1881–1954)   British playwright. Lonsdale is best known for his sophisticated comedies, such as *The Last of Mrs. Cheyney* (1925).

Look Back in Anger (1957)   A play in three acts by John OSBORNE. Jimmy Porter, a working-class man with a university education, finds that he has no place in the Establishment world his education had supposedly qualified him to enter. Bitterly resentful and at the same time contemptuous of that world, Jimmy takes a job in a street market and turns his frustrated fury at the English class structure against his middle-class wife, Alison. Learning that Alison is pregnant, Helena, a childhood friend, persuades her to leave Jimmy. Helena in turn becomes Jimmy's mistress and scapegoat, but, because she is incapable of real suffering, she proves an unworthy antagonist. When Alison returns in complete despair over the loss of her baby, she and Jimmy go back to their early childish make-believe and eventually achieve a real tenderness. See ANGRY YOUNG MEN.

Look Homeward, Angel: A Story of the Buried Life (1929)   A novel by Thomas WOLFE. It describes the childhood and youth of Eugene GANT in the town of Altamont, state of Catawba (said to be Asheville, North Carolina). As Gant grows up, he becomes aware of the relations among his family, meets the eccentric people of the town, goes to college, discovers literature and ideas, has his first love affairs, and at last sets out alone on a mystic and romantic pilgrimage. OF TIME AND THE RIVER is a sequel.

Loos, Anita (1893–1981)   American novelist and scriptwriter. Loos began writing film scripts for D. W. GRIFFITH at the age of fifteen and continued through a long career that included two successful plays, *Happy Birthday* (1946) and *Gigi* (1951; fr the novel by COLETTE). Her most famous work is the satirical novel GENTLEMEN PREFER BLONDES, which inspired a play (1926), two film versions (1928, 1953), and a musical comedy (1949). The sequel was a collection of stories, *But Gentlemen Marry Brunettes* (1928). Her autobiographical works, rich in the lore of Hollywood, include *This Brunette Prefers Work* (1956), *A Girl Like I* (1966), and *Kiss Hollywood Goodby* (1974). *The Talmadge Girls* (1978) is an amused and affectionate memoir of two stars of silent movies, Constance and Norma Talmadge.

López de Ayala [y Herrera], Adelardo (1828–1879)   Spanish statesman and dramatist. López de Ayala is best known abroad as an exponent of the moral tendency that infused 19th-century Spanish drama, in spite of the fact that he attained the rank of prime minister of the Spanish government. His plays include *El tanto por ciento* (1861), dealing with wealth and honor in love, and *Consuelo* (1870). His delicate and lyrical sonnets have also added to his reputation.

López de Ayala, Pero (or Pedro López de Ayala, also known as the Chancellor or el Canciller Ayala; 1332–1407)   Spanish statesman, poet, and historian. His chronicles of the reigns of Peter the Cruel, Henry II, John I, and Henry III are distinguished by their dramatic style and psychological penetration. As a poet, he is best known for *Rimado del Palacio*, a miscellaneous compilation containing religious verse as well as realistic satire on contemporary society. He also wrote a treatise on falconry and translated the works of Boethius, St. Isidore, and Boccaccio.

López Velarde, Ramón (1888–1921)   Mexican poet. A disciple of Leopoldo LUGONES, López Velarde wrote about love, religion, and his homeland in a style characterized by the use of eccentric, unexpected words and images. The poems in *La sangre devota* (1916) and *Zozobra* (1919) deal with the spiritual and carnal aspects of love, showing the poet's final disenchantment and dismay at his failure to satisfy either his physical appetites or the demands of his soul. *La suave patria*, his best-known poem, which appears in *El son del corazón* (1932), is an ironic but tender tribute to his native province.

López y Fuentes, Gregorio (1895–1966)   Mexican novelist. López y Fuentes's best-known novel is *El indio* (1935; tr 1937; repr 1961), in which he reveals the injustices inflicted upon Mexico's Indians in the early decades of the 20th century and realistically describes tribal customs and institutions.

Lorca, Federico García   See GARCÍA LORCA, FEDERICO.

Lord Jim (1900)   A novel by Joseph CONRAD. It is about a man's lifelong efforts to atone for an act of instinctive cowardice. The young Jim is one of the officers of the *Patna*, who frantically take to the boats when their ship appears to be sinking—leaving their passengers, eight hundred Muslim pilgrims, to apparently certain death. The ship, however, survives and is towed to port, and Jim becomes a wandering outcast. Eventually he wins a measure of self-respect in a busy, useful life among the natives of Patusan, who call him *Tuan Jim* ("Lord Jim"). His life comes to a second crisis when a group of white men whom he has befriended betray his trust and murder his best friend, Dain Waris, the son of the old chief Doramin. In spite of the pleas of the young native woman he loves, Jim immediately gives himself up to tribal justice and is killed by Doramin. Thus, he is able to win back his lost honor and triumph in death. The story is told obliquely through Conrad's familiar narrator, MARLOW.

Lord of the Flies (1955)   An allegorical novel by William GOLDING, about a group of boys stranded on an island after a plane crash. In spite of the efforts of a few leaders to form an organized society, the boys revert to savagery, complete with primitive rites and ritual murder. The book is a powerful combination of child's adventure story, anthropological insights, and the Christian concepts of Eden and ORIGINAL SIN.

Lord of the Rings, The   A trilogy of novels by J.R.R. TOLKIEN, consisting of *The Fellowship of the Ring* (1954), *The Two Towers* (1955), and *The Return of the King* (1956). The trilogy forms a sequel to Tolkien's *The Hobbit* (1937). Set in the remote, imaginary past, the story chronicles a magnificent battle between the forces of good and evil in the Third Age of Middle Earth, which has its own history, languages, geography, mythology, and population of men, elves, trolls, orcs, wizards, dwarfs, and HOBBITS. In Volume I, Frodo, one of the meek and comfort-loving hobbits, becomes the unwilling heir to the magical ring that was forged by Sauron, the Lord of Darkness. Sauron lost the ring, and it was recovered by Frodo's uncle, Bilbo Baggins. Although the ring gives long life and absolute power, it corrupts its users. At a great council, the hobbits decide to destroy it in the fires of Mount Doom, in which the ring was originally forged. A Fellowship formed for this mission sets out but is relentlessly pursued by Sauron's dark riders, who want to reclaim the ring and rule the world. The Fellowship is beset by calamities and is finally broken.

Volume II recounts the adventures of Frodo and his servant Sam Gamgee, who venture into the land of the enemy to complete their mission, while their companions in the Fellowship are betrayed and brought into battle in the terrible War of the Rings. The war is detailed in Volume III. The ring is eventually destroyed; good triumphs over evil, but only indefinitely. The Third Age of Middle Earth gives way to the Dominion of Man, which will either destroy or be destroyed by its own ring of power. This epic had a tremendous revival in the 1960s and has since become a well-loved contemporary classic.

Lord's Prayer   See PATERNOSTER.

Lord's Supper   See EUCHARIST.

Lord Ullin's Daughter (1809)   A ballad by Thomas CAMPBELL. Lord Ullin's daughter elopes with the Chief of Ulva's Isle and is pursued by her father with a party of retainers. The lovers reach a ferry and promise to give the boatman a silver pound to row them across the Lochgyle. The waters are very rough, and the father reaches the shore just in time to see the boat capsize and his daughter drowned.

Lorelei   The name of a rock cliff that juts into the Rhine near Bingen and whose reefs are known as a danger to shipping. Clemens BRENTANO, in his ballad "Lore Lay" (included in the novel *Godwi*, 1800–1801), was the first to associate the rock with a woman of the same name. The poem is so convincingly folklike in style that Brentano's invention came to be regarded as a genuine folk legend. But Brentano's Lore Lay is only a woman, and it was not until Heinrich HEINE's famous poem "Die Lorelei" (1827) that the now-popular idea of a siren sitting atop the rock and luring ships to their destruction by her singing was actually created.

Lorenz, Konrad (1903–   )   Austrian ethologist and author. A proponent of DARWIN's theories, Lorenz was the first to attribute to processes of natural selection the genetic evolution of behavior patterns. His theories, often criticized as unscientific, won popular acclaim through best-selling books, most notably *King Solomon's Ring* (1952), which was originally conceived as a children's book and was illustrated with the author's own humorous drawings. His *On Aggression* (1966) aroused considerable controversy by virtue of his contention that aggressive behavior is innate and for his comparisons of human and animal behavior. His pioneering work in ethology (the study of animal behavior) led to his being awarded the NOBEL PRIZE in Physiology or Medicine in 1973, with Nikolaas Tinbergen and the zoologist Karl von Frisch.

Lorenzini, Carlo   See PINOCCHIO, THE ADVENTURES OF.

Loretto, the house of   Santa Casa, the reputed house of the Virgin Mary at Nazareth. Supposedly it was miraculously translated to Fiume in Dalmatia in 1291, thence to Recanati in 1294, and finally to a plot of land belonging to a certain Lady Lauretta, near Ancona, Italy, around which the town of Loretto sprang up. The chapel contains bas-reliefs showing incidents in the life of the Virgin and a rough image traditionally held to have been carved by St. Luke. See CRASHAW, RICHARD.

Lorna Doone, a Romance of Exmoor (1869) A historical novel by R. D. Blackmore (1825–1900) set in 17th-century Devonshire at the time of the rebellion of the duke of MONMOUTH. The young hero, John Ridd, falls into the hands of the Doones, an outlaw clan. He is saved by Lorna Doone, a mere child, and, when he comes of age, he sets out to find her again. Because the Doones killed his father, he hates them, but he protects Lorna against them and finally, learning that she is the kidnapped daughter of a Scottish nobleman, marries her.

Lorrain, Claude (originally Claude Gellée, 1600–1682)   French landscape painter. At the age of twenty-seven, Lorrain established himself permanently in Rome, where he studied the surrounding countryside and the varying aspects it assumed with the passage of the day. Acknowledged a master during his lifetime, he permanently influenced the art of landscape painting. His serene and idyllic landscapes and seascapes are noted for his extraordinarily vibrant handling of light.

Los de abajo (1916; tr The Underdogs, 1929)   A novel by Mariano AZUELA. Ignored for years after its first appearance in a Spanish-language El Paso newspaper, *Los de abajo* is now generally regarded as the best of the many novels inspired by the Mexican Revolution. Written in a spare, colloquial style, the novel consists of a series of sharply etched vignettes that recount the career of Demetrio Macías, the leader of a band of ignorant, often bestial, peasants. Through Macías, Azuela brilliantly recreates the blind, apparently futile struggle of the nameless masses who took up arms for a cause they did not understand and, swept along by the turbulence of the revolution, continued fighting because they did not know how to stop.

lost generation   A term used to describe the generation of men and women who came to maturity between World War I and the Depression of the 1930s. Gertrude STEIN first heard the phrase from the proprietor of the Hotel Pernollet in Belley. Referring to a young mechanic repairing Stein's car, M. Pernollet used the expression *une génération perdue* to describe the dislocation, rootlessness, and disillusionment experienced in the wake of the war. Stein later expanded the meaning of the phrase in conversation with Ernest HEMINGWAY, saying that his was a decadent generation that was drinking itself to death. Hemingway, whose early books were prototypes for the lost generation of writers, recounts this conversation in a preface to THE SUN ALSO RISES and again in *A Moveable Feast* (1964). F. Scott FITZGERALD's TENDER IS THE NIGHT is a striking account of the spiritual climate of the time. Much of Malcolm COWLEY's work, notably *The Lost Generation* (1931), deals with the writers of that generation.

Lost Lady, A (1923)   A novel by Willa CATHER. The "lost lady" of the title is Marian Forrester, the charming young wife of a rugged pioneer and railroad-builder. She is seen, with a naïveté that becomes the most delicate irony and revelation, through the eyes of Niel Herbert, an adoring young boy. Her husband's death leaves Marian in financial difficulties, and she becomes the mistress of Ivy Peters, an aggressive businessman of the new generation. After Peters marries and moves into the Forrester mansion with his wife, Marian disappears and is heard of again only by rumor as the wife of a wealthy Englishman in South America.

Lost Weekend, The (1944)   A novel by the American novelist and short-story writer Charles Jackson (1903–68). It is a realistic study of an alcoholic who first resists then succumbs to his passion for liquor. On a five-day "lost weekend," much of his life flashes before him. The title has become a catch-word for a drunken fling of major proportions.

Lot   In the OLD TESTAMENT, the son of Haran and nephew of ABRAHAM, who accompanied his uncle to Canaan and divided the land with him. Lot, one of the inhabitants of the wicked city of SODOM, escaped by the intervention of an angel, just before the city was destroyed by fire and brimstone, but Lot's wife was turned into a pillar of salt for ignoring the warning not to look back at the city (Gen. 19:26).

Lot, King   In Arthurian romance, king of Orkney and one of the kings subdued by Arthur. In Malory's *Morte d'Arthur* (c1469), King Lot is the husband of MARGAWSE and father of the knights Gawain, Aggravaine, Gaheris, and Gareth.

Loti, Pierre (pen name of Louis Marie Julien Viaud, 1850–1923)   French novelist. Loti's career as a naval officer sent him to distant places, providing him with the exotic backgrounds for many of his novels, which were sentimental in theme and luxurious in setting. *Aziyadé* (1879) is set in Constantinople, *Le Mariage de Loti* (1880) in Tahiti, and *Madame Chrysanthème* (1888) in Japan. In his sensuous and impressionistic style, Loti gave voice to a persistent melancholy. Although his travel romances first brought him fame, it was the publication of his three novels of Breton life—*Mon Frère Yves* (1883), PÊCHEUR D'ISLANDE, and *Matelot* (1893)—that won him enduring acclaim.

Lottery, The (1949)   A short story by Shirley JACKSON. This quietly told tale describes an annual lottery held since time immemorial in a small American town. Only in the final lines of the story does it become apparent that the "winner" is to be stoned to death by the other townspeople.

lotus   A name of many plants. To the Egyptians, it was various species of water-lily; to the Hindus and Chinese, the Nelumbo (a water-bean, *Nymphaeaceae speciosum*), their sacred lotus; and to the Greeks, *Zizyphus Lotus*, a North African shrub of the natural order *Rhamneae*, the fruit of which was used for food.

According to MUHAMMED, a lotus tree stands in the seventh heaven, on the right hand of the throne of God. The Egyptians pictured God sitting on a lotus above the watery mud.

The lotus is a symbolic flower in Indian religion and literature. BRAHMĀ sits on a lotus and is himself born out of the lotus in VISHNU's navel. The BUDDHA is always depicted seated on a lotus; the Tibetan prayer chant is OM MANI PADME HUM ("I salute the jewel in the lotus"). Growing in stagnant village ponds, the flower stands for the emergence into light from the darkness and sensuality of the phenomenal world; the leaves, unaffected by water, symbolize the ATMAN ("self"), unpolluted by the attractions of the *gunas* ("senses"); and the daytime opening and nighttime closing of the flower suggest the timeless day and night of Brahmā in the context of Hindu metaphysical belief.

The Greek myth is that Lotis, a daughter of POSEIDON, fleeing from PRIAPUS, was changed into a tree, which was called Lotus after her. Another story has it that Dryope of Oechalia was one day carrying her infant son, when she plucked a lotus flower for his amusement and was instantaneously transformed into a lotus.

Lotus-eaters (or Lotophagi)   In Homeric legend, a people who ate the lotus-tree. The effect of this was to make them forget their friends and homes and lose all desire of returning to their native country, their only wish being to live in idleness in Lotus-land (ODYSSEY, ix).

Hence, a lotus-eater is one living in ease and luxury. TENNYSON wrote one of his best-known poems on this subject.

Lotus Sūtra (Sans, *Saddharma-pundarīka*; Chin, *Fahua ching*; Jap, *Hokke kyō*)   Buddhist scripture of great popularity in China and Japan. The T'ient'ai (Jap, TENDAI) and NICHIREN sects base their teachings on this work.

Louis XIV (called Louis the Great; *le Roi Soleil*, "the Sun King"; and *le Grand Monarque*; 1638–1715)   King of France (1643–1715). The greatest autocratic monarch that France has ever known, Louis XIV left his country bankrupt through his wars, conquests, and extravagances. His reign was marked by his lavish patronage of art, literature, and women, and it coincided with the greatest flowering of French civilization to date. Louis married Mme de MAINTENON, the last of his many mistresses, morganatically after the death of his first wife, Marie Thérèse of Spain.

Louis XVI (1754–1793)   King of France. Louis XVI married MARIE ANTOINETTE in 1770, and in 1774, on the death of his grandfather Louis XV, he began his reign; he was deprived of his powers by the Legislative ASSEMBLY in 1792 and was beheaded in 1793.

Louisiana Purchase   The acquisition of Louisiana from France in 1803 during the consulship of Napoleon by the U.S. for approximately $15 million. Alarmed by the threat implicit in Spain's retrocession of Louisiana to France in 1800, President Jefferson appointed James Monroe to purchase New Orleans and West Florida from the French. Napoleon, however, had abandoned his projects for a French empire in the New World and offered to sell the whole of Louisiana instead. The purchase of Louisiana, a vaguely defined tract of some 828,000 square miles lying between the Mississippi River and the Rocky Mountains, more than doubled the area of the U.S.

Louis Philippe (1773–1850)   King of France (1830–48). A son of Philippe Egalité, he was the first elected king of France. At the insistence of THIERS and LAFAYETTE, Louis Philippe was elected constitutional monarch after the deposition of Charles X. A partisan of the Revolution in his youth and democratic in the first years of his reign, he became more and more a typical Bourbon and absolutist. He himself abdicated the throne after the revolution of February 1848, and he died in exile at Claremont, England.

Louÿs, Pierre (pen name of Pierre Louis, 1870–1925)   French poet and novelist. A close friend of André GIDE and Paul VALÉRY, Louÿs still remained primarily a disciple of the Parnassian school of José-Maria de HEREDIA, whose daughter he married in 1899. *Astarte* (1891) is a collection of Hellenistic poetry; *Aphrodite* (1896) is a novel of Alexandrian manners. Although much of his fiction was intended to shock conventional morality, Louÿs was essentially a worshiper of form and beauty and was a moralist.

Love and Death in the American Novel (1960; rev 1966)   A critical study by Leslie A. FIEDLER, in which Fiedler attempts to identify a central tradition of innocence and new beginnings in American fiction. What makes Fiedler's analysis unique is his focus on the sexual dimension of American innocence. He argues, for example, that America's classic novels are written primarily for males and that fully developed female characters are virtually nonexistent, the woman being typically either goddess or whore. As a result, he suggests, American literature has tended to depict a kind of prepubescent male camaraderie instead of mature heterosexual relationships. Fiedler discusses American fiction in a broad cultural context, with frequent reference to the European novel. Essentially, Fiedler sees the American novel as a triumph of the romantic over the classical and of the Gothic over the sentimental.

Lovecraft, H[oward] P[hillips] (1890–1937)
American writer of horror tales in the POE tradition.
Lovecraft spent most of his life as a recluse in Providence,
Rhode Island. His work was first published (1919) in LITTLE
MAGAZINES, but, from 1923 to his death, it appeared most
frequently in *Weird Tales*. Only one book, *The Shadow
over Innsmouth* (1936), was published in his lifetime.
Notable are "The Colour Out of Space" (1927), "The
Dream Quest of Unknown Kadath" (1943), and "The Case
of Charles Dexter Ward" (1941).

Loved One, The (1948)   A novel by Evelyn
WAUGH. It is a very funny, biting satire on American life,
especially Hollywood mortuary practices, and on the more
universal themes of love and death. The hero finally cre-
mates the heroine in a dogs' cemetery.

Love for Love (1695)   A comedy by William CON-
GREVE. The extravagant Valentine agrees to relinquish his
inheritance to his sea-faring brother Ben if his father, Sir
Sampson Legend, will pay his debts. Valentine's attempts
to regain his inheritance are unsuccessful until the
resourcefulness of his devoted Angelica extricates him from
his predicament. Among the well-known lesser characters
are Prue, Angelica's rustic cousin, and Jeremy, Valentine's
enterprising servant.

Lovelace, Richard (1618–1658)   English poet.
One of the CAVALIER POETS, Lovelace was known for his
grace, his handsome appearance, and his aristocratic gallantry. A passionate Royalist, he was imprisoned twice by
Parliament during the Civil War and ruined himself supporting Charles I. He died in a London slum in great poverty.

Lovelace's poetry is very uneven: a large proportion of it
is lifeless, extravagant, and labored, but he wrote a few
lyrics whose nobility and grace equal anything of the
period. Such are TO ALTHEA FROM PRISON, "To Lucasta,
Going beyond the Seas" (1649), and TO LUCASTA, GOING
TO THE WARS.

Lover's Complaint, A   An anonymous poem. It
was attributed to Shakespeare on the basis of its inclusion
in the first edition of the *Sonnets of Shakespeare* in 1609.
The poem, which is somewhat wooden and stilted in its
manner, is not generally regarded as a legitimate item in
the Shakespearean canon.

Love's Labour's Lost (c1594)   A comedy by
Shakespeare. FERDINAND, king of Navarre, and his friends,
Berowne or Biron, Longaville, and Dumain, take an oath
to eschew the company of women and devote themselves to
study for three years. The charming princess of France
arrives with her three vivacious ladies, Rosaline, Maria,
and Katherine, on a diplomatic mission and, because of
Ferdinand's vow, is housed in a pavilion outside the city
gates. Despite their oath, the four gentlemen fall in love
with the four ladies: Ferdinand with the princess, Biron
with Rosaline, Longaville with Maria, and Dumain with
Katherine. Discovering each other's perfidy, the gentlemen

acknowledge love's power and decide to pursue the ladies,
who gently mock them for their conceit. Learning that the
king of France has died, the ladies are obliged to leave, but
they assign various penances to the four suitors and promise to return to them in a year.

The plot, which is based on current court life, cannot be
attributed to any early source and is presumed to be of
Shakespeare's invention. See HOLOFERNES.

Love Song of J. Alfred Prufrock, The (1915)
A poem by T. S. ELIOT. Said to have been written when
Eliot was still an undergraduate at Harvard, it was first published in *Poetry* magazine, after he had settled in England.
Through the person of the poem's narrator, J. Alfred
Prufrock, Eliot explores a kind of death in life and suggests
the spiritual decay of his society. Prufrock, a middle-aged
man of anonymous respectability, differs from those
around him only in his greater degree of self-awareness and
suffering. Conscious of the sterility of his world, he longs to
make some significant gesture but, lacking the necessary
will and passion, puts the matter off in introspection. The
poem ends on a note of hopelessness. Completely paralyzed by social habit and a sense of his own futility,
Prufrock will never escape and is finally identified with his
surroundings.

Loving (1945)   A novel by Henry GREEN. Set in an
Irish castle during World War II, it is a picture of the lives
of the owners and their many servants. On this level, the
book is a light, witty social comedy. Each of the characters
loves some person or idea, and the different kinds of love
are revealed by an ironical juxtaposition of scenes. The
central characters are Raunce, the butler, and Edith, a
maid, both of whom grow mature as their love develops.
This love is emphasized by various recurrent symbols, like
an imaginary cave of fairy gold. The gold is later replaced
by a valuable ring whose loss and recovery are a focal point
of the plot and a touchstone for the attitudes of the various
characters.

Lowell, Amy [Lawrence] (1874–1925)   American
poet, critic, and biographer. A member of an old and distinguished New England family, Lowell became a serious
student of poetic forms. She is known for her association
with and leadership in the imagist movement, in accordance with which she wrote numerous poems in free verse
and "polyphonic prose." Her first book was *A Dome of
Many-Coloured Glass* (1912). A year after its publication,
she met Ezra POUND and others in the imagist movement
in England and subsequently became the leader of the
movement in the U.S. Although Pound complained that
she converted IMAGISM into "Amygism," she did much to
sponsor imagist poets, and she edited a number of imagist
anthologies. Celebrated as a personality as well as an artist,
she was eccentric in behavior, keeping a troupe of dogs,
smoking large black cigars, and using language of extreme
frankness. One of her best single poems is "Lilacs" (1925);
several others, notably "Patterns" (1916), are familiar.

Among her books of poetry are SWORD BLADES AND POPPY SEED, *Men, Women, and Ghosts* (1916), *Can Grande's Castle* (1918), and *What's O'Clock* (1925). Among her critical works are *Six French Poets* (1915), *A Critical Fable* (1922), and a two-volume biography of Keats (1925). Her *Complete Poetical Works* (1955) were edited by Louis UNTERMEYER.

Lowell, James Russell (1819–1891) American poet, editor, critic, and diplomat. Although he was born into a distinguished Brahmin New England family, Lowell favored democratic ideas, attacked slavery, and was an early admirer of Lincoln. Trained for the law, he turned instead to journalism; he contributed to *The Dial* and founded a short-lived magazine, *The Pioneer*.

In 1844 Lowell married Maria White, poet and firm abolitionist. Four years later, he published THE BIGLOW PAPERS, First Series, which brought him to the notice of the literary world. The dialogue between the Yankee farmer Hosea Biglow and his friends was especially important for its use of authentic New England dialect. The interest in language was to remain with Lowell throughout his career. In the same year, his long poem, *The Vision of Sir Launfal* (1848), was published; long a favorite among schoolchildren, it is far from his most significant work. Lowell's satirical, often accurate, always amusing A FABLE FOR CRITICS was also published during this important literary year.

His reputation established, Lowell became a leader of what is now called the popular, conservative school of American letters. After travel abroad, he succeeded Longfellow to the chair of modern languages at Harvard and in 1857 was appointed as the first editor of *The Atlantic Monthly*. In 1861 he became coeditor with Charles Eliot Norton of the *North American Review*.

Lowell's active public life included the positions of minister to Spain and to England; in both countries, he was an able spokesman for democracy. See COMMEMORATION ODE.

Lowell, Robert [Traill Spense, Jr.] (1917–1977) American poet. A member of the prominent Lowell family of Boston and grand-nephew of James Russell LOWELL, Robert Lowell attended Harvard and transferred to Kenyon College, where he studied with Randall JARRELL and John Crowe RANSOM. Often associated with John BERRYMAN, Lowell has been regarded as one of the most important poets of his generation. His poetry is technically skillful, richly textured, and heavily symbolic. Lowell's intense concern with his ancestry, the minutiae of his family life, and personal struggles has led many critics to label him —along with Berryman—a CONFESSIONAL POET. *Land of Unlikeness* (1944) and *Lord Weary's Castle* (1946; PULITZER PRIZE) both contain a number of poems dealing with his conversion to Catholicism in 1940; so does *The Mills of the Kavanaughs* (1951). Lowell's earlier works are notably concerned with form and metrical exactness, but on the whole lack the explicit structural cohesiveness of his later

volumes. Lowell's autobiographical volume in prose and verse, LIFE STUDIES, marks an important development in his work. Similarly, his experiments with other poets' work, culminating in his translations of various European writers in *Imitations* (1961), did much to loosen his style and bring him closer to his own voice. During the same period, he wrote a trilogy of plays, *The Old Glory* (1964), based on two stories by HAWTHORNE and one by MELVILLE. Lowell reworked the loosely structured *Notebook of a Year* (1969) and produced *History* (1973) and *For Lizzie and Harriet* (1973). His next volume, *The Dolphin* (1973), won the Pulitzer Prize. Lowell's own edition of his *Selected Poems* (1976) represents a careful paring down of much of his previous work, revealing a poet of great stature and sensibility. *Day by Day* (1977), published just a month before his death, is considered by many critics to be the best of his work in verse autobiography. He was married for a time to Jean STAFFORD.

Lower Depths, The (Na dne, 1902) A drama by Maksim GORKY. The best known of Gorky's works, it is set among the derelicts of a sleazy flophouse. The theme of the play is the problem of whether to live without illusions and on one's own strength or to shield oneself from the pain of life by accepting a romanticized view of the world. These choices are supported by the thief Satin and the wandering pilgrim Luka. A strikingly similar theme was used by Eugene O'NEILL in his drama THE ICEMAN COMETH.

Lowry, [Clarence] Malcolm [Boden] (1909–1957) English novelist, whose literary quality became recognized only after his death. Lowry wrote several novels: *Ultramarine* (1933), an impressionistic, experimental sea story; UNDER THE VOLCANO, a subtle, semiautobiographical study of the last day in the life of an alcoholic living in Mexico, considered a modern masterpiece; and *October Ferry to Gabriola* (1970), an unfinished novel, published posthumously by his widow. *Lunar Caustic* (1958), a novella, describes Lowry's experiences in Bellevue Hospital, where he was treated for alcoholism, after being picked up drunk off the streets of New York City. *Hear Us O Lord from Heaven Thy Dwelling Place* (1961) and *Dark as the Grave Wherein My Friend Is Laid* (1968) are collections of short fiction. His *Selected Poems* appeared in 1962. Lowry died a suicide in Sussex, England.

Loyola, St. Ignatius of (1491–1556) The founder of the Society of Jesus (the order of JESUITS). Loyola is depicted in art with the sacred monogram I.H.S. on his breast, or as contemplating it, surrounded by glory in the skies, in allusion to his claim that he had a miraculous knowledge of the mystery of the Trinity vouchsafed to him. He was a son of the Spanish ducal house of Loyola, and, after being severely wounded at the siege of Pampeluna (Pamplona) in 1521, he left the army and dedicated himself to the service of the Virgin. His Order of the Society of Jesus, which he projected in 1534, was confirmed by Paul

III in 1540. His *Exercitia* (*Spiritual Exercises*, 1548), a manual of devotions and prayer, is considered a remarkable treatise on applied psychology as an inducement to mystic vision.

Lubitsch, Ernst (1892–1947)   German-born film director, who worked in Hollywood from 1922 until his death. Lubitsch was a master of the sophisticated comedy of manners, characterized by wit, frivolity, piquancy, and subtle innuendo, a European form that he transplanted to the American screen with brilliant success, beginning with *The Marriage Circle* (1924). At the start of the sound period, he made a series of charming musical comedies starring Maurice Chevalier, such as *The Love Parade* (1929). During the same period, he directed several other films, most notably *Trouble in Paradise* (1932) and *Design for Living* (1933), which established the vogue for Hollywood "screwball comedy." Among his most memorable later comedies were *Ninotchka* (1939), in which Greta Garbo, playing a straight-laced Russian commissar, falls in love with a "decadent bourgeois" playboy in Paris, and *To Be or Not to Be* (1942), in which a Polish company of Shakespearean actors outwit the Nazis in occupied Warsaw. Outstanding among Lubitsch's few serious films was *The Man I Killed* (1932), a poignant antiwar drama that demonstrates the true versatility of his directorial powers.

Lucan (full name Marcus Annaeus Lucanus, AD 39– 65)   Roman poet and prose writer. Lucan wrote the *Pharsalia*, an epic in ten books on the civil war between CAESAR and POMPEY. No other work of his is extant. He was, like BRUTUS and CASSIUS before him, an aristocrat and a rebel; like them, he regretted the lost republic and hated the regime of the Caesars. He joined PISO'S CONSPIRACY against NERO, was denounced, and, like SENECA, was ordered to commit suicide. He was only twenty-five when he took his own life.

Lucan enjoyed a great vogue during the Middle Ages but of late has been more criticized than praised for his exaggerated treatment of the war between Caesar and Pompey.

Lucas, E[dward] V[errall] (1868–1938)   English man of letters. Lucas wrote numerous charming essays in the manner of Charles LAMB, on whose work he was an authority. He published a biography of Lamb (1905) and an early edition of Lamb's correspondence with his sister Mary (1903–5). He was a prolific writer of novels, travel books, reminiscences, and essays, such as those collected in *Adventures and Misgivings* (1938).

Luce, Clare Boothe (1903–   )   American playwright and diplomat. Following her divorce from George T. Brokaw in 1929, Luce worked as an editor at *Vogue* and *Vanity Fair*. She published a novel, *Stuffed Shirts* (1933), under the name Clare Boothe Brokaw. In 1935 she married the publisher Henry LUCE. She is best known for a series of theatrical successes, including *The Women* (1936), *Kiss the Boys Goodbye* (1938), *Margin for Error* (1939), *Child of the Morning* (1951), and *Slam the Door Softly*

(1970). Luce's active political interests led her to public service. She served two terms (1943–47) in the House of Representatives from Connecticut and was ambassador to Italy from 1953 to 1956. She was confirmed as ambassador to Brazil in 1959 but resigned without serving because of controversy surrounding her confirmation.

Luce, Henry R[obinson] (1898–1967)   American editor and publisher. With Briton Hadden, Luce founded *Time*, the weekly newsmagazine, in 1923. *Fortune*, a monthly for businessmen, followed in 1930, and *Life*, the weekly picture magazine, appeared in 1936. Luce, whose second wife was author and diplomat Clare Boothe LUCE, also published *Sports Illustrated*, *Architectural Forum*, and *House and Home*. As one of the most powerful men in publishing history, Luce took the controversial position that "objective" reporting could not exist. He was often accused of imposing his own conservative political views on his publications.

Lucian (Loukianos, c120–200)   A Greek satirist. Lucian was the most brilliant wit of Greek letters under the Roman empire. A free-thinker, he was often referred to in his own time as the blasphemer and was later compared with Swift and Voltaire. He wrote rhetorical, critical, and biographical works, romances, dialogues, poems, and other works. His *Voracious History*, a mock narrative of travel, is the archetype of such books as Swift's *Gulliver's Travels*. His *Dialogues of the Dead* have been called brilliant satires of the living. He is regarded as the inventor of the satirical dialogue. His novel, *Lucius, or The Ass*, may have been based on a work by Lucius of Patrae that also served as a model for Apuleius's *The Golden Ass*.

Lucifer   The morning star. The Hebrew name for it was figuratively applied by ISAIAH to NEBUCHADNEZZAR, the proud but ruined king of Babylon: "Take up this proverb against the King of Babylon, and say . . . How art thou fallen, from heaven, O Lucifer, son of the morning!" (Isa. 14:4,12). It was later claimed that SATAN, before he was driven from heaven for his pride, was called Lucifer. In Marlowe's DR. FAUSTUS and Dante's INFERNO, Lucifer is the ruler of hell. In Milton's PARADISE LOST, Lucifer is called Satan after his fall.

Lucina   In Roman mythology, a goddess of childbirth. Lucina was sometimes identified with JUNO.

Lucinde   (1) The heroine of Molière's comedy *L'Amour médecin* (1665). Lucinde is the daughter of Sganarelle. As she has lost her spirit and appetite, her father sends for four physicians, who all differ as to the nature of the malady and the remedy to be applied. Lisette, her waiting woman, sends in the meantime for Clitandre, the lover of Lucinde, who comes disguised as a doctor. He tells Sganarelle that the disease of the young lady must be reached through the imagination and prescribes a mock marriage. As his assistant is in reality a notary, the marriage turns out to be a real one, and Lucinde, who has been pining because her father disapproved of her beloved, is cured.

(2) The heroine of Molière's LE MÉDECIN MALGRÉ LUI. Géronte, Lucinde's father, wants her to marry Horace, but, as she is in love with Léandre, she pretends to have lost the power of articulate speech, to avoid a marriage which she abhors. Sganarelle, the woodcutter, is introduced as a doctor specializing in dumb cases, and soon he sees the state of affairs. He takes with him Léandre as an apothecary; the young lady receives a perfect cure, an elopement.

Luck of Roaring Camp, The (1868)   A short story by Bret HARTE. This is a sentimental tale of gold-rush miners and their false toughness. Dying, Cherokee Sal, a prostitute who frequents the mining camps, gives birth to a child the miners adopt and name Thomas Luck. The following year, the camp is destroyed in a flood, and one of the miners, Kentuck, dies holding the infant in his arms. The story established Harte's fame after its first printing in his magazine, THE OVERLAND MONTHLY.

Lucky Jim (1954)   A best-selling novel by Kingsley AMIS. The title is ironic, since the story is about the comic misfortunes of Jim Dixon, a young lower-middle-class instructor at an English university. The book satirizes the academic "racket" and cultural pretensions. See ANGRY YOUNG MEN.

Lucretia   In Roman legend, the daughter of Spurius Lucretius, prefect of Rome, and wife of Tarquinius Collatinus. Lucretia was raped by Sextus, the son of the king, Tarquinius Superbus. Having avowed her dishonor in the presence of her father, her husband, and their friends Junius BRUTUS and Valerius, she stabbed herself. The outcome was an insurrection that changed the magistracy of kings to that of CONSULS. The story of Lucretia has been dramatized in French by Antoine Vincent Arnault in his tragedy *Lucrèce* (1792) and by François Ponsard in 1843; in Italian by Alfieri in *Brutus*; in English by Thomas Heywood in *The Rape of Lucrece* (1630), by Nathaniel Lee in *Lucius Junius Brutus* (17th century), and by John H. Payne in *Brutus or The Fall of Tarquin* (1820). Shakespeare selected the same subject for his poem *The Rape of Lucrece* (1594). See TARQUIN.

Lucretius (full name Titus Lucretius Carus, 98?–55 BC)   Roman poet. Lucretius was the author of the unfinished *De rerum natura* (*On the Nature of Things*), a didactic poem in six books, setting forth in outline a complete science of the universe, based on the philosophies of DEMOCRITUS and EPICURUS. The purpose of the work was to prove, by investigating the nature of the world in which man lives, that all things—including man—operate according to their own laws and are not in any way influenced by supernatural powers. Lucretius hoped thereby to free himself and all men from the yoke of religious superstition and the fear of death. The poem is arranged as follows:

Book I: All things are made up of eternal atoms that move through infinite space.

Book II: The entire world of material substances is produced through the joining together of these atoms.

Book III: The mind and the spirit are also an arrangement of atoms, in this case exceedingly more subtle. At death, the individual soul is dispersed as its imperishable atoms fly apart.

Book IV: Sensation, perception, and thought are all produced by the images emitted by external surfaces.

Book V: The world, as we know it, was created by a fortuitous concourse of atoms.

Book VI: All natural phenomena can be explained according to this atomic theory.

De rerum natura is the only large-scale poem written in dactylic hexameter that has come down to us from the period of the Roman republic and is, with the possible exception of VERGIL's epic AENEID, the most ambitious poem written in Latin. Its scientific and philosophical argumentation often rises to magnificent heights of emotional power, intensified by an eloquent simplicity of diction and by the great passion of the poet's conviction. Lucretius committed suicide before completing the final draft of the poem; CICERO was said to have prepared the manuscript for publication. TENNYSON's dramatic monologue "Lucretius" (1869) repeats the legend that the poet committed suicide in a fit of insanity induced by a love potion given him by his wife.

Lucullus (110–57 BC)   A wealthy Roman noted for his banquets and self-indulgence. On one occasion, when a superb supper had been prepared, being asked who were to be his guests, he replied, "Lucullus will sup tonight with Lucullus."

Ludwig, Otto (1813–1865)   German novelist and playwright, who popularized the term *poetic realism* as a description of the realistic trend in German literature of his time. Ludwig's own works, realistic in style, include the novel *Zwischen Himmel und Erde* (*Between Heaven and Earth*, 1856), about the tragic conflict of two brothers both in love with the same woman; *Der Erbförster* (*The Forester*, 1850), a domestic tragedy; and *Die Makkabäer* (1854), a play in verse about the revolt of the Maccabees.

Lug   In the Gaelic mythological cycle, a hero of the people called the TUATHA DÉ DANANN. Later, Lug becomes an important god for the Sons of Mil, who are said to be the first Celts in Ireland.

Lugnasad   August 1, one of the four great feast days of the ancient Celtic year. See BELTINE; IMBOLC; SAMAIN.

Lugones, Leopoldo (1874–1938)   Argentine poet. The outstanding exponent of MODERNISMO in Argentina, Lugones was a close friend of Rubén DARÍO, whom he resembled in verbal virtuosity and ingenuity. In his first books of poetry—*Las montañas de oro* (1897), *Los crepúsculos del jardín* (1905), and *Lunario sentimental* (1909) —he revealed a penchant for startling but beautiful imagery and rhythmical experimentation. His return to poetic orthodoxy was signaled by his *Odas seculares* (1910), written to commemorate the centenary of Argentine independence. In this and later works, including *Romancero* (1924) and *Poemas solariegos* (1928), he expressed his ardent love of country in a style that became progressively less personal and more realistic. His prose writings include *La guerra gaucha* (1905), poetic accounts of episodes in Argentina's war for independence, and *Las fuerzas extrañas* (1906), fantastic short stories.

Luhan, Mabel Dodge (1879–1962) American patroness of the arts and memoirist. Famous for her salons in Italy and New York in the early 20th century, Luhan cultivated close associations with D. H. LAWRENCE, John REED, Gertrude STEIN, and Carl VAN VECHTEN. She told of their lives and hers in a four-volume autobiography, *Intimate Memories* (1933–37). She had three husbands before she married a Pueblo Indian and settled in Taos, New Mexico, where she was a vital force behind the art colony there. She also wrote *Lorenzo in Taos* (1932), about her relationship with Lawrence.

Lu Hsun (also spelled Lu Xun; pseudonym of Chou Shu-jen, 1881–1936) Chinese short-story writer, essayist, and scholar. Educated in Japan as a medical doctor, Lu returned to China to use his writing to expose the superstitions and injustices of the early Republican period. He is China's greatest writer of the 20th century. Among his many works available in English are *Selected Stories of Lu Hsun* (1960) and a seminal scholarly work, *A Brief History of Chinese Fiction* (1959).

Lukács, György (1885–1971) Hungarian philosopher, aesthetician, and literary historian. Interpretations departing from Soviet orthodoxy contained in his voluminous writings extensively influenced Marxists in Western Europe long after he repudiated many of them. Some of his many works in English translation are *Soul and Form* (1911; tr 1974), *The Theory of the Novel* (1920; tr 1971), *History and Class Consciousness* (1923; tr 1971), *Essays on Thomas Mann* (1949; tr 1964), *Writer and Critic and Other Essays* (1970), and *Political Writings 1919–1929* (1972).

Luke, St. Author of The Gospel According to St. LUKE and the ACTS OF THE APOSTLES. Little is known of Luke's life other than what he reports of himself in these two books of the NEW TESTAMENT. He was a traveling companion to PAUL, who referred to him as "the beloved physician" (Col. 4:14). He was also said to be a painter; tradition holds that he painted a portrait of MARY, the Virgin. He is patron saint of painters and physicians; his feast day is October 18.

Luke, The Gospel According to St. The third book of the NEW TESTAMENT, almost certainly written by the Greek physician and painter St. LUKE, who was also the author of the ACTS OF THE APOSTLES. One of the SYNOPTIC GOSPELS, it was the third account of Jesus' life to be written, based, according to its author, on eyewitness accounts (Luke 1:2). Beginning with the conception of JOHN THE BAPTIST, the book recounts the birth of JESUS, his ministry in Galilee, his journey to Jerusalem, the Crucifixion, the Resurrection, and Jesus' ascension to heaven. The book has high literary merit and a strong humanitarian appeal.

Lully, Jean-Baptiste (1632–1687) Italian-born French composer. Known as the originator of French opera, Lully was appointed court superintendent of music by Louis XIV in 1653 and received his French naturalization in 1661. Out of the music that he composed for court entertainments, notably the ballets of Benserade and the *comédie-ballets* of MOLIÈRE, he developed French opera, with its characteristic accompanied recitatives, dramatic scoring, and balletic interludes. In 1672 Lully founded the Académie Royale de Musique, which later became the Paris Opéra and for which he composed twenty or more operas and ballets to libretti by QUINAULT. Reflecting the fashion of the day in their choice of classical subjects (*Alceste*, 1674; *Proserpine*, 1680), these works held the stage for almost a century.

Lunch Poems (1964) A collection of poems by Frank O'HARA, in which he details his random excursions through New York City during lunch hour. What seem to be inconsequential details and unrelated events, conversations, and memories actually constitute a cityscape in which the poet is a vital participant. O'Hara's technique is strongly influenced by the action paintings of Jackson POLLOCK and Larry RIVERS in its syntactic dislocation, abrupt time shifts, and synthesis of surrealistic imagery with realistic place names. The style achieves an effect of dizzying but vibrant actuality.

Lun-yü See ANALECTS.

Lupercalia In ancient Rome, an annual festival held on February 15, probably in honor of FAUNUS, worshiped under the name of Lupercal. The worshipers gathered at a grotto on the Palatine, where ROMULUS and his twin Remus were supposed to have been suckled by the wolf (Lat, *lupus*). It was a festival of expiation and purification, and goats and a dog were sacrificed. Youths smeared with sacrificial blood ran round the Palatine, carrying thongs of goat's hide (*februa*); women struck by them were supposedly made fertile. The ceremony survived into Christian times; it was suppressed in AD 494.

Lurie, Alison (1926–   ) American novelist. Lurie's experience in tthe academic world is reflected in her novels, most of which are witty, intelligent depictions of crises in the lives of well-educated upper-middle-class people who are often academics or connected to academia in some way. The best known of these is *The War Between the Tates* (1974), a brilliant dissection of the collapse of the apparently perfect marriage of a political-science professor and his wife, played out in an elaborate parallel with the concurrent progress of the VIETNAM WAR. Lurie's best-received book apart from *The Tates* was the novel *Foreign Affairs* (1984), a sharp comedy of manners concerning the relative fortunes of two English teachers on sabbatical in

London, which won a PULITZER PRIZE in 1985. Lurie's other novels include *Love and Friendship* (1962), *Imaginary Friends* (1967), and *Only Children* (1979); she has also written a work of nonfiction, *The Language of Clothes* (1981), and several books for children.

Lusíadas, Os (The Lusiads, 1572)   An epic poem by Luis de CAMÕES. It relates the historically illustrious actions of the Lusians, or Portuguese, but deals principally with the exploits of Vasco da GAMA and his comrades in their "discovery of India." Da Gama sailed three times to India. It is the first of these voyages (1497) that is the theme of the epic, but its wealth of episode, the constant introduction of mythological "machinery," and the intervention of Bacchus, Venus, and other deities make it far more than the mere chronicle of a voyage. Bacchus is the guardian power of the Muslims, and Venus, or Divine Love, of the Lusians. The fleet first sails to Mozambique, then to Quiloa, then to Melinda in Africa, where the adventurers are hospitably received and provided with a pilot to conduct them to India. In the Indian Ocean, Bacchus tries to destroy the fleet, but the "silver star of Divine Love" calms the sea, and da Gama arrives in India safely.

Interwoven in the poem are episodes based on notable events in Portuguese history, such as the death of Inés de CASTRO and the victory of Aljubarrota.

Lusitania   (1) The ancient name for Portugal.

(2) A British transatlantic liner torpedoed without warning by a German submarine off the coast of Ireland, on May 7, 1915. She sank in eighteen minutes with the loss of 1,198 lives, including those of 128 Americans. The *Lusitania* was unarmed but was carrying armaments to England. Germany, at first refusing responsibility, eventually paid reparations and agreed to discontinue sneak attacks on passenger ships, but the sinking aroused violent public indignation, which contributed to America's entry into World War I.

Lustra (1916)   A collection of poems by Ezra POUND. The title, from the Latin, refers to the offerings made by Roman censors "for the sins of the whole people." Pound also issued a collection called *Lustra of Ezra Pound* (1917), an extension of the earlier volume, containing *Near Perigord*.

Lutetia (fr Lat, *lutum*, "mud")   The ancient name of Paris, which, in Roman times, was merely a collection of mud hovels. Caesar called it *Lutetia Parisiorum* ("the mud town of the Parisii"), from which comes the present name.

Luther, Martin (1483–1546)   German religious reformer. Luther was an Augustinian monk and the professor of biblical exegesis at Wittenberg, where in 1517 he posted his critique of the Roman Catholic Church's practices, the NINETY-FIVE THESES, which are usually regarded as the original document of the REFORMATION. From then on, he was the center of a violent religious upheaval in Germany, where—among the humanists, for example —there had already been a great deal of feeling against

Rome. The most important of Luther's later contributions to the controversy were his pamphlets *An den Christlichen Adel deutscher Nation* (*Address to the Christian Nobility of the German Nation*, 1520) and *Von der Freiheit eines Christenmenschen* (*On Christian Liberty*, 1520). His principal contention was that man is justified by faith alone, and not by works. On the basis of this idea of a personal faith, he favored the abolition of many church rituals and challenged the supreme authority of the pope. He was excommunicated in 1521 and then appeared before the Diet of Worms, where he took a firm stand upon his views and was put under the ban of the Holy Roman Empire. The elector of Saxony, however, undertook to protect him; in a safe retreat, Luther began his translation of the Bible into German (New Testament, 1522; Old Testament, 1534). His other works include the *Sendbrief von Dolmetschen* (*Letter on Translation*, 1530), defending his rendering of the Bible, and forty *Kirchenlieder* (*Church-Songs*, 1524), among which is the famous hymn *Ein feste Burg ist unser Gott* (*A Mighty Fortress Is Our God*). His *Tischreden* (*Table-Talk*) is a valuable source of detail about his personality and beliefs. See MELANCHTHON, PHILIPP.

Lutrin, Le (The Lectern; cantos 1–4, 1674; cantos 5–6, 1683)   A mock-heroic poem by Nicolas Boileau (1636–1711). It satirizes a dispute between the treasurer and the choirmaster of the Sainte-Chapelle over the positioning of a choir lectern. The treasurer triumphs, but the poem ends with a reconciliation. Boileau not only lampoons clerical pomposity and pettiness with merciless irony but manages, by contriving a battle in a bookshop, to comment satirically upon the literary feud between the ancients and the moderns. See QUERELLE DES ANCIENS ET DES MODERNES.

Luzán Claramunt de Suelves y Gurrea, Ignacio de (1702–1754)   Spanish scholar and critic. A bilingual academician, Luzán is known for his championship of the neoclassic cause in Spanish literature. His ideas are contained in the treatise *Poética, o reglas de la poesía en general y de sus principales especies* (1737), which advocated a didactic poetry and adherence to the three unities in the drama. He also gained fame as a result of his Latin compendium of Descartes's ideas.

Lycaon   In classical mythology, a king of Arcadia. Desirous of testing the divine knowledge of Zeus, Lycaon served human flesh on his table, for which the god changed him into a wolf. His daughter, Callisto, was changed into the constellation Bear, whence this is sometimes called *Lycaonis Arctos*.

Lyceum   A grove and gymnasium on the banks of the Ilissus, in Attica. ARISTOTLE taught philosophy there as he paced the walks. The name is sometimes used to stand for Aristotle's philosophic school.

Lycidas (1637)   An elegiac poem by John MILTON, commemorating the death of Edward King (1612–37), a Cambridge schoolmate who was drowned in the Irish Sea.

The title is taken from the name of a shepherd in Vergil's third *Bucolic*. One of the most famous English elegies, *Lycidas* is not only concerned with King's untimely death but also attempts to deal with a world in which the good die young and false priests and poets prevail. Milton's solution is partly that of the Christian—ultimately God's justice will win out on earth; meanwhile virtue is rewarded in heaven —and partly that of the dedicated humanist poet—true genius is interconnected and immortal and enjoys a special relationship to and survival in the powers and beauties of the natural world. *Lycidas* has the strength and majesty of Milton's mature poetry and is consciously a poem of self-renewal and dedication to great work ahead.

Lydgate, John (c1360–c1451)   English poet and priest. Lydgate studied in both English and European universities and was ordained as a priest in 1397. He was a close friend of the son of CHAUCER and knew the elder poet, whose influence is obvious in much of Lydgate's work. An amazingly versatile and prolific writer, he is one of the few poets of merit in the 150 years between the death of Chaucer and the beginnings of the Elizabethan period. However, though his work was esteemed less than that of only Chaucer during the 16th century, his prolixity and medieval attitudes make him little read today. Among his numerous works are two allegorical poems, the *Complaint of the Black Knight* and the *Temple of Glass*; the *Troy Book* (1412–20), based on the *Historia Troiana* of Guido delle Colonne; *The Story of Thebes* (1420–22); *The Pilgrimage of Man* (c1424), a translation of a work by Guillaume de Deguileville; and the *Falls of Princes* (1430–38), based on a French prose version of Boccaccio's *De casibus virorum illustrum*.

Lyly, John (1554?–1606)   English prose writer, poet, and dramatist. Lyly gained a reputation as a wit at Oxford and took M.A. degrees both at Oxford and Cambridge. He went to London, where he became one of the UNIVERSITY WITS and tried to gain a place at court. Though associated with the court for a number of years, he never gained the position of Master of Revels, for which he had hoped. He came under the patronage of Edward Vere, earl of Oxford, and wrote the first part of his most famous work, *Euphues, the Anatomy of Wit* (1579), for which he was immediately acclaimed. The following year, he published the second part of this work, called *Euphues and His England*. The balanced, elegant, and highly artificial style of these pieces was very possibly Lyly's own invention. It was widely imi-tated for many years, notably by Robert GREENE and Thomas LODGE, and has come to be known as euphuistic (see EUPHUES; EUPHUISM).

Lyly succeeded in becoming the vice-master of the acting company of the Children of St. Paul's, for whom he wrote plays to be presented at court. Of the eight plays he wrote for the Children, the best known are *Alexander and Campaspe* (1584; reissued as *Campaspe*, 1591), *Endimion* (1591), and *Midas* (1592). He took his plots from Greek and Roman classic literature and transformed them into charming, ornate allegories of court flirtations and intrigues and the political affairs of the time, and he refined and intellectualized comedy from its former and cruder state. All but one of his plays (*The Woman of the Moon*, 1597) were written in euphuistic prose.

Lynd, Robert S. and **Helen M.**   See MID-DLETOWN.

Lyonnesse   A legendary land in medieval romance. It was located near Land's End, off the coast of England; at present, it is submerged "full forty fathoms under water." King Arthur came from this mythical country, and the battle of Lyonnesse was the final conflict between Arthur and Sir Mordred.

Lyrical Ballads (1798; 2nd ed 1800; 3rd ed 1802)   A volume of poems by Samuel Taylor COLERIDGE and William WORDSWORTH. It was the first important publication of the poetry of the romantic period in English literature and is considered one of the landmarks of literature. Wordsworth's contributions were his poems of country scenes and people, written in plain language and style, and his "Tintern Abbey." Coleridge's principal contribution was "The Rime of the Ancient Mariner." The second edition of *Lyrical Ballads* contains a preface by Wordsworth, explaining his theory that poetry should be drawn from the everyday life and speech of men; this preface came to be considered the manifesto of English ROMANTICISM.

Lysander (d 395 BC)   Spartan naval and military commander. Lysander defeated the Athenians at Aegospotami in 405 BC, thus ending the PELOPONNESIAN WAR.

Lysistrata (c415 BC)   The title and heroine of a comedy by ARISTOPHANES. It deals with an effective women's peace organization. In the twenty-first year of the Peloponnesian War, Lysistrata persuades the wives of Athens and Sparta to shut themselves up away from their husbands until peace shall be concluded. She has the satisfaction of dictating the terms.

M

Mab (or Queen Mab; perhaps fr Welsh, *mab*, "a baby") In 15th-century English and Welsh legend, the queen of the fairies, an honor later given to Titania. Mab is described in Shakespeare's *Romeo and Juliet* as the "fairies' midwife"—i.e., she is employed by the fairies as midwife to deliver man's brain of dreams. Excellent descriptions of Mab are given by Shakespeare (*Romeo and Juliet*, I:4), by Ben Jonson, by Herrick, and by Drayton in *Nymphidia* (1627).

Mabinogion, The A collection of medieval Welsh tales, first translated into English (1838–49) by Lady Charlotte Guest (1812–95). The tales, eleven in all, were preserved in two Welsh sources: *The White Book of Rhydderch* (1300–1325), and *The Red Book of Hergest* (1375–1425). Though the tales were, for the most part, not committed to writing until the 14th century, internal evidence indicates that they originated far earlier. KULHWCH AND OLWEN, for example, is at least early 11th century and reflects in language and custom an even more ancient time.

These eleven prose tales fall into three divisions. The first, called *The Four Branches of The Mabinogi*, includes "Pwyll," "Branwen," "Manawydan," and "Math." The second, called *Independent Native Tales*, includes "The Dream of Macsen Wledig," "Lludd and Llefelys," "The Dream of Rhonabwy," and "Kulhwch and Olwen," the last being the earliest Arthurian tale in Welsh. The third grouping consists of three comparatively late Arthurian romances: THE LADY OF THE FOUNTAIN; "Peredur, Son of Efrawg," an early PERCIVAL story; and "Geraint Son of Erbin."

Most of the stories are concerned with Celtic mythological subjects and filled with folk themes. Archaisms in custom and language reflect an ancient time when such tales were not written down but were memorized and transmitted orally from generation to generation.

The title word *Mabinogion* is a modern term appended to the collection by Lady Charlotte Guest. See ARTHURIAN LEGEND.

macaroni (fr Ital, *maccheróne*) A coxcomb. The word is derived from the Macaroni Club, instituted in London about 1760 by a set of flashy men who had traveled in Italy and introduced at Almack's subscription table the new-fashioned Italian food *macaroni*. By all reports, the macaronis were the most exquisite fops that ever disgraced the name of man; vicious, insolent, fond of gambling, drinking, and dueling, they were (c1773) the curse of Vauxhall Gardens.

There is a tradition that an American regiment raised in Maryland during the War of Independence was called The Macaronis, from its showy uniform. This may explain the allusion in the American song "Yankee Doodle."

macaronic verse Verses having words from various languages, often ludicrously distorted and jumbled. It seems to have been originated by Tisi degli Odassi (b 1450?) but was popularized by his pupil Teofilo Folengo, a Mantuan monk of noble family, who published a book entitled *Liber macaronicorum*, a poetical rhapsody made up of words of different languages and treating of "pleasant matters" (1520).

Macaronic Latin is a name for dog Latin, modern words with Latin endings, or a mixture of Latin and some modern language. Presumably the word *macaronic* comes from the Italian food, which was originally a mixture of coarse meal, eggs, and cheese.

MacArthur, Charles (1895–1956) American newspaperman and playwright. MacArthur's experiences as a newspaperman in Chicago and New York are reflected in *The Front Page* (1928), one of a number of plays on which he collaborated with Ben HECHT. His other collaborators included Edward SHELDON and Sidney HOWARD.

Macaulay, Dame Rose (1889–1958) English novelist. Macaulay's early novels were notable for their wit, urbanity, and mild satire. Among these are *Potterism*, (1920), *Told by an Idiot* (1923), *Crewe Train* (1926), and *Staying with Relations* (1930). *They Were Defeated* (1932; U.S. *The Shadow Flies*) is an excellent historical romance about Robert HERRICK and 17th-century intellectual life.

Her post-World War II novels are marked by irony and tenderness: *The World My Wilderness* (1950) is about a wild young girl in conflict with civilization, and her last novel, *The Towers of Trebizond* (1956), is a tragicomic story about a young man's personal and religious odyssey through Turkey. She also published two books of verse and critical studies of Milton (1934) and E. M. Forster (1938).

Macaulay, Thomas Babington (1800–1859) English statesman, poet, historian, essayist, and biographer. Macaulay is best known for his *History of England from the Accession of James the Second* (1848, 1855, 1861), a work extremely popular in his day, marked by a colorful style and vivid presentation. His LAYS OF ANCIENT ROME, narrative poems dealing with Roman heroes, were also popular. In addition, he wrote a number of well-known historical and biographical essays under the guise of book reviews for the *Edinburgh Review*, and a series of biographies of literary figures for the *Encyclopædia Britannica*. Macaulay was a staunch Whig and an advocate of moderate reforms. He served in the House of Commons, was a member of the Supreme Council of India, and was Secretary of War. In 1857 he was made Baron Macaulay of Rothley. Macaulay's prose style, much admired in its day, is somewhat pontifical and monotonous; similar qualities vitiate his poems. Much of his prose writing, however, in spite of stylistic faults, instances of insensitivity, prejudice, and exaggeration, remains interesting in itself and as an expression of Victorian tastes and standards. His essays are collected in *Critical and Historical Essays* (1843).

McAuley, James Phillip (1917–1976) Australian poet and critic. Impatient with the modern reliance on self, McAuley advocated Christian humanism to give order to individuals and society. *Collected Poems, 1936–70* (1971) generally employs traditional metrics and classically simple diction. McAuley was the author of a notorious literary hoax of the 1940s. To show up modernism as the fraud he believed it to be, he and a friend wrote sixteen poems —supposedly by a poet named Ern Malley who had died young—containing every fault of modernist writing as McAuley saw it. The magazine editor to whom the poems were submitted was completely taken in, and when the hoax was revealed modernist poetry became a laughingstock for many.

McBain, Ed Pseudonym of HUNTER, EVAN.

Macbeth (c1606) A tragedy by SHAKESPEARE. His shortest play, *Macbeth* has been described as a study in fear. It is thought that the play may have been written as a tribute to James I because of its emphasis on the supernatural, a subject in which the king was interested, and its flattering portrayal of the origins of the Stuart line, to which he belonged.

Two victorious generals, Macbeth and BANQUO, are accosted on a deserted heath by three mysterious witches, who prophetically hail Macbeth as thane of Glamis, thane of Cawdor, and future king of Scotland and then tell Ban-

quo that his sons will sit upon the throne. Macbeth is already thane of Glamis, and, when he learns that the title of the traitorous thane of Cawdor is to be bestowed upon him, his ambition to be king is kindled. When his wife, Lady Macbeth, hears of the prophecy, she urges Macbeth to kill King DUNCAN, caustically reproaching her husband for his scruples. Macbeth reluctantly acquiesces, murders Duncan, and is proclaimed king. Fearing the second part of the witches' prophecy, Macbeth engages two assassins to murder Banquo and his son FLEANCE, but Fleance escapes them. When Macbeth learns that the Scottish thane MACDUFF has joined Duncan's son Malcolm, who is raising an army in England to proceed against him, he orders the death of Lady Macduff and her children. Lady Macbeth, driven mad by her conscience, finally commits suicide, and Macbeth is slain by Macduff, who has returned to Scotland with the English forces. Malcolm is then proclaimed king.

The direct source of the play is Holinshed's *Chronicles* (1577). It records the career of a real Macbeth (d c1058), who killed Duncan of Scotland in 1040, seized the throne, and was overthrown by Malcolm, Duncan's son, seventeen years later.

The sleep-walking scene in Act V, in which Lady Macbeth, tormented by the memory of her victims, tries to wash imaginary bloodstains from her hands, is one of the most famous in Shakespeare.

MacBeth, George [Mann] (1932–   ) Scottish poet and novelist. MacBeth is best known for ingenious, explosive, witty, and often savage verse. Much affected by the early loss of his parents and by his Scottish background, he combines the macabre and the serious in his treatments of love, war, and death. His poetry has a strong aural quality (colloquial language, vivid imagery, and strong, regular rhythm), which is effectively utilized in his experiments with dramatic monologue in *A Doomsday Book* (1965). His first book, *A Form of Words* (1954), is typical of his precise and detached poetry. Other volumes include *The Broken Places* (1963), *A Poet's Year* (1973), *Buying a Heart* (1979), and *Poems of Love and Death* (1980). *The Survivor* (1977) recasts the major themes of MacBeth's poetry in a novel about a Japanese pilot in World War II who crashes on an island to live a nightmare of guilt and madness, tossed between illusion and reality. In the 1980s MacBeth has tended to focus more on prose than poetry, producing six novels and a book for children.

Maccabees The family of Jewish heroes descended from Mattathias the Hasmonaean and his five sons: John, Simon, Judas, Eleazar, and Jonathan. The Maccabees delivered the race from the persecutions of the Syrian king Antiochus Epiphanes (175–164 BC) and established a line of priest-kings, which lasted until HEROD THE GREAT's reign. Their exploits are told in 1 and 2 Maccabees, the last two books of the APOCRYPHA. See JUDAS MACCABAEUS.

MacCarthy, Sir Desmond (1878–1952) English critic and literary journalist. A member of the circle of Cambridge intellectuals surrounding G. E. MOORE and Bertrand RUSSELL and a friend of many members of the BLOOMSBURY GROUP, MacCarthy was influential as the literary editor of the newly founded *New Statesman*. Among his books are *Portraits* (1931), *Drama* (1940), *Shaw* (1951), and *Humanities* (1953).

McCarthy, Joseph R[aymond] (1908–1957) American politician. Elected to the U.S. Senate in 1946 from Wisconsin, McCarthy first drew national attention in 1950, when he charged that the State Department was infiltrated by Communist spies. He made further accusations but failed to produce evidence to validate his claims. As chairman of the Senate Permanent Investigations Subcommittee, he brought the public's fear of Communists and subversives to a peak and conducted an investigation of Communism in government that aroused great controversy because of his sensational methods and irresponsible charges. After a series of hearings (1953–54) on alleged subversion of the U.S. Army, McCarthy was formally condemned by the Senate. The term *McCarthyism* became synonymous with "witch hunts," blacklists, and the use of rumor, innuendo, and unsubstantiated charges to destroy reputations.

McCarthy, Mary [Therese] (1912–   ) American writer. Orphaned at the age of six, McCarthy was raised by relatives of various backgrounds, an experience chillingly recounted in *Memories of a Catholic Girlhood* (1957). Following her graduation from Vassar in 1933, she worked as a book reviewer for *The Nation* and *The New Republic*, which provided the basis for the short stories in *The Company She Keeps* (1942). As a drama reviewer for *Partisan Review*, she became known as a severe but extremely witty critic. Her theatre pieces are collected in *Sights and Spectacles, 1937–1956* (1956). After her divorce from Edmund WILSON, McCarthy taught for several years at colleges and produced the satirical novel *The Groves of Academe* (1952). Her scathing satires of American intellectual life acquire a particular effectiveness from being thinly disguised ROMANS À CLEF—*The Oasis* (1949) and *A Charmed Life* (1955), for instance—and from her fluid but precise prose style. She reached her widest audience with *The Group* (1963), a devastating account of the lives of eight Vassar graduates. McCarthy has also written many nonfiction books, including *Venice Observed* (1956), *The Stones of Florence* (1959), *Vietnam* (1967), *The Writing on the Wall* (1970), and *The Mask of State: Watergate Portraits* (1974). *Cannibals and Missionaries* (1979) is a novel about the hijacking of a plane carrying an ill-assorted group to the Shah's Iran. She was awarded the National Medal for Literature in 1984.

McCaslin A family in GO DOWN, MOSES and other works by William Faulkner. Among the first families to settle in YOKNAPATAWPHA COUNTY, the McCaslins evidence —more directly than any other Faulkner characters—the guilt of slaveholding, which continues to influence their lives after the Civil War. The founder of the family is [Lucius Quintus] Carothers McCaslin, father of Uncle Buck and Uncle Buddy (both white) and of Tomasina ("Tomey"), who is born a black slave. Incest is added to miscegenation when Carothers seduces Tomasina. Isaac ("Ike") McCaslin is the son of Uncle Buck and the last male McCaslin to bear the name. He is the principal character in the short story "The Bear." Unable to accept the family guilt, he refuses to inherit the family property, which then passes to Carothers McCaslin ("Cass") Edmonds, the great-grandson of the first McCaslin. Uncle Buck, who also appears in THE UNVANQUISHED, and Uncle Buddy do not believe in slavery and invent a system whereby their slaves can earn their freedom. Lucas Beauchamp, who also appears in INTRUDER IN THE DUST, is a part-black grandson of the first McCaslin; his friend and rival is his part-black cousin Isaac ("Zack") Edmonds, who temporarily steals Lucas's wife.

McClellan, George B[rinton] (1826–1885) American general. A West Point graduate who had become a railroad executive, McClellan was named commander of the Union forces in 1861. Although he had great organizing ability, his reluctance to take offensive action against the enemy exasperated President Lincoln, and he was relieved of one command after another until his retirement in 1863. In 1864 he was the unsuccessful Democratic candidate for president against Lincoln. There is still considerable controversy about McClellan; many historians have charged him with ineptitude and even with disloyalty, while others, notably J. G. Randall, have contended that he was the great Union general of the war.

McClure, James [Howe] (1939–   ) British novelist. Beginning with *The Steam Pig* (1971), McClure, who was born and brought up in South Africa before moving to England in the mid-1960s, wrote a series of police stories set in South Africa featuring Inspector Trompie Kramer, who is Cape Dutch, and Sergeant Mickey Zondi, who is a Bantu. Although the novels deal with a variety of themes, the background of ethnic tension is always present. In 1980 McClure published *Spike Island*, an important nonfiction work scrutinizing the daily work of a police division in Liverpool's besieged inner city.

McClure, Michael [Thomas] (1932–   ) American poet and playwright. McClure was associated with the BEAT MOVEMENT of writers based in San Francisco in the late 1950s and 1960s. His poetry embraces political radicalism, eastern mysticism, ecology, and sexual freedom. His work, which is frequently obscure, even incoherent, and hallucinatory, as well as highly visual, contains screeching utterances and uses language as an end in itself rather than as a means of expression. His plays, some of which incorporate obscenity and nudity, are technically reminiscent of the THEATRE OF THE ABSURD. His books of poetry include *Star* (1970) and *Jaguar Skies* (1975). Several of his most typical short plays are collected in *Gargoyle Cartoons* (1971).

McClure, S[amuel] S[idney] (1857–1949) Irish-born American editor. Having arrived in the U.S. in 1866, McClure studied at Knox College and later worked for the *Century Magazine*. In 1884 he created a revolution in publishing by starting the first newspaper syndicate, the purpose of which was to reprint in serial form material that had already been published.

In 1893 McClure founded *McClure's Magazine*, which became the most influential periodical in the country, particularly because of its muckraking articles. (See MUCKRAKERS.) In 1906, at its peak, McClure's partner, John S. Phillips, along with Ida M. TARBELL, Ray Stannard Baker, and Lincoln STEFFENS, resigned because of differences with McClure. They founded the *American Magazine*, which continued the policies of *McClure's* and became equally influential. In 1914 McClure suspended his own magazine, later reviving it briefly. It became part of the *New Smart Set* in 1929 and expired in 1933. McClure spent his last years in retirement. *My Autobiography* (1914) was ghost-written by Willa Cather.

McClure appears twice in fiction. R. L. STEVENSON, whom he helped to win an audience, presented him as Jim Pinkerton in *The Wrecker* (1892). Less friendly is the characterization of him as Fulkerson, an aggressive Westerner, in W. D. Howells's A HAZARD OF NEW FORTUNES.

McCrae, John (1872–1918) Canadian physician and poet. McCrae served as an army medical officer from 1914 until his death in France. His most famous poem was the inspirational "In Flanders Fields," published first in *Punch* (1915) and later as the title poem of a collection of McCrae's verse (1919).

McCullers, Carson [Smith] (1917–1967) American novelist and short-story writer. Recognized as one of the most talented literary artists of her generation, McCullers was born in Georgia and studied music in New York. Her first novel, *The Heart Is a Lonely Hunter* (1940), a parable on Fascism, was told as the story of a deaf-mute in a small Southern town. *Reflections in a Golden Eye* (1941) deals with violence at a peacetime army post in the South. With THE MEMBER OF THE WEDDING, her reputation, already established in literary circles, became widespread. *The Ballad of the Sad Café* (1951) contains the title novella, dramatized by Edward ALBEE in 1963, and a selection of short stories. It was followed by *The Square Root of Wonderful*, a play (1958); and *Clock without Hands*, a novel (1961). McCullers's work centers on the spiritual isolation of her characters. Her books are peopled with misfits and outcasts, whose terrible need for love is invested in the people least likely or able to fulfill it. She treats themes of longing and tormented loneliness with a delicate sensitivity that avoids sentimentality. *The Mortgaged Heart* (1971) is a

posthumous collection of her writings, from her first published story to her final autobiographical notes.

McCullough, Colleen (1937–) Australian novelist. McCullough is known for her novel *The Thorn Birds* (1977), a multigenerational saga of life, love, and death on an Australian sheep ranch. This fantastically successful book has sold over ten million copies in the U.S. alone and made publishing history when paperback rights were sold for a then record $1.9 million. McCullough has written three other novels: *Tim* (1974), *An Indecent Obsession* (1981), and A *Creed for the Third Millennium* (1985), and a novella, *The Ladies of Missalonghi* (1987).

MacDiarmid, Hugh (pen name of Christopher Murray Grieve, 1892–1978) Scottish poet and critic, a leading figure in the SCOTTISH RENAISSANCE. In the 1920s, he found his true lyrical voice in the Scots language, adopted the name MacDiarmid, and set about attempting a revival of Scots writing. Such early volumes as *Sangshaw* (1925) and *Pennywheep* (1926) are written in LALLANS, a language reconstructed from ancient Scots dialects. He was an ardent Marxist and cofounded the Scottish Nationalist Party in 1928. Much of his poetry is concerned with social and political themes, rich in images of the past, descriptions of the common people, and the hopes for a future under socialism. He turned again to English for the poetry in *Scots Unbound* (1932), *Stony Limits* (1934), and the *First* and *Second Hymn to Lenin* (1931; 1932). His *Collected Poems* appeared in 1962 (rev 1967). *Lucky Poet* (1943; rev 1972) and *The Company I've Kept* (1966) are autobiographical works. *Aesthetics in Scotland* (1984) is a study of poetry as bound up with Scottish nationalism. *The Letters of Hugh MacDiarmid* (1986) exhibits his polemical style.

Macdonald, Dwight (1906–1982) American essayist and critic. Macdonald's focus of interest moved gradually from Yale and his first job on *Fortune* magazine, to radical politics and a job on *Partisan Review*, to the founding of a journal of his own, *Politics* (1944–49), devoted at first to anarchist and pacifist views, with TROTSKY as a major influence, and finally to disillusioned criticism of any doctrinaire political stance. In 1952 he became a staff writer for THE NEW YORKER. *Memoirs of a Revolutionist* (1957; reissued as *Politics Past*, 1970) documents this progression. Macdonald's other works include *Henry Wallace: The Man and the Myth* (1948) and *Against the American Grain* (1962), a collection of essays that includes "Masscult and Midcult," Macdonald's controversial analysis of popular culture.

Macdonald, Flora (1722–1790) Scottish Jacobite heroine who aided Prince Charles Edward Stuart in his escape after the battle of CULLODEN. Macdonald resided in the United States (1774–79), where her husband, Allan Macdonald, was a brigadier general in the British Army during the American Revolution. See PRETENDER.

MacDonald, George (1824–1905)   Scottish novelist and poet. MacDonald's enduring reputation rests not on his serious work but on the juvenile fantasies *At the Back of the North Wind* (1871), *The Princess and the Goblin* (1872), and *The Princess and Curdie* (1882).

MacDonald, John D[ann] (1916–1986)   American mystery writer. MacDonald is best known as the creator of Travis McGee, a Florida-based private investigator. McGee is a mixture of the rough detective of HARD-BOILED FICTION and the compassionate investigator, like Ross MACDONALD's Lew Archer. MacDonald's plots are typically complex, the backgrounds investigated in depth. Among his many Travis McGee mysteries, all of which include a color in the title, are *The Deep Blue Good-By* (1964), *Nightmare in Pink* (1964), *The Dreadful Lemon Sky* (1975), *The Green Ripper* (1979), *Free Fall in Crimson* (1981), and *The Lonely Silver Rain* (1985). He has also written numerous other works of suspense and a novel of ecological concern, *Condominium* (1977).

Macdonald, [John] Ross (pen name of Kenneth Millar, 1915–1983)   American novelist. Macdonald was one of the few mystery writers whose books were consistently taken seriously by literary critics. His series of detective stories featuring private investigator Lew Archer began with *The Moving Target* (1949). Archer has a deep compassion for people in trouble and a reluctance to employ violent methods. Macdonald evidences deep psychological insight, frequently involving the pathological and the morbid, as in *The Underground Man* (1971), *Sleeping Beauty* (1973), and *The Blue Hammer* (1976), and a penchant for vivid metaphors and similes. His approach to the mystery novel was influenced by Raymond CHANDLER, with whom Macdonald shared the conviction that a well-written mystery is as artistically sound as any other type of fiction.

MacDowell, Edward Alexander (1861–1908)   American composer of symphonic poems, piano sonatas, and orchestral suites. Regarded in his day as the greatest of all American composers, MacDowell gradually fell from favor owing to the Germanic qualities of his music and its lack of a native "American" sound. In his memory, his widow founded the MacDowell colony for musicians, artists, and writers in Peterborough, New Hampshire, affording them the opportunity to work undisturbed the year round in picturesque surroundings. MacDowell's most popular work is *Woodland Sketches* (1896).

Macduff   In Shakespeare's MACBETH, the thane of Fife and a former friend of Macbeth. Horrified at the crimes Macbeth has committed and deeply loyal to his country, Macduff joins Malcolm in England and returns with him to Scotland to unseat Macbeth. Macduff, who was "from his mother's womb untimely ripp'd," slays Macbeth, thus fulfilling the witches' prophecy that no man born of woman could harm him.

Lady Macduff   The wife of Macduff. She and her children are murdered at Macbeth's order when it is discovered that her husband has joined Malcolm's forces.

MacEwen, Gwendolyn (1941–   )   Canadian poet and novelist. MacEwen emerged as an important Canadian poet with the publication of her mystical volumes of verse, *The Rising Sun* (1963), *A Breakfast for Barbarians* (1966), and *The Shadow-Maker* (1969). Her poetry employs striking manipulations of word and image and, like her fantasy novels, *Julian the Magician* (1964) and *King of Egypt, King of Dreams* (1971), reveals her fascination with the recurrent myths and archetypes in human experience. Other collections of her poetry include *Magic Animals* (1974) and *The Fire-Eaters* (1976).

M'Fingal   A verse satire by John TRUMBULL. The first canto was published shortly after Lexington and Concord in 1775; in 1782 Trumbull lengthened and reissued the poem, which was immensely popular. Modeled on Samuel Butler's *Hudibras* (1663–78), it ridicules extremism on both sides of the Revolution, especially the bombastic oratory of the Scotch-American Tory M'Fingal, who is tarred and feathered, repents, and prophesies final victory for the colonists.

MacFlecknoe (1682)   A satirical poem by John DRYDEN. It is directed against Thomas SHADWELL, who was to succeed Dryden as poet laureate in 1689. The title of the poem comes from the name of Richard Flecknoe (c1600–c1678), an Irish priest noted for his bad verse. Dryden depicts Shadwell as Flecknoe's successor in the monarchy of nonsense. Pope used the poem as a model for his *Dunciad* (1728–43).

McGee, Travis   See MACDONALD, JOHN D.

McGinley, Phyllis (1905–1978)   American writer of light verse. A frequent contributor to THE NEW YORKER and other magazines, McGinley was known for her clever and humorous poems about various aspects of modern life. Among her best-known collections of verse are *A Pocketful of Wry* (1940), *Love Letters* (1954), *Times Three: Selected Verse from Three Decades* (1960; PULITZER PRIZE), and *Christmas Con and Pro* (1971). She also wrote essays and numerous books for children.

McGuane, Thomas [Francis, III] (1939–   )   American novelist. McGuane's black humor, sometimes violent and alarming, is aimed at the pomposity and excesses of what he calls American "snivelization." His novels, *The Sporting Club* (1968), *The Bushwacked Piano* (1971), *Ninety-Two in the Shade* (1973), *Panama* (1978), *Nobody's Angel* (1981), and *Something to Be Desired* (1983), frequently feature crazy or crazed antiheroes in absurdly destructive situations. *An Outside Chance* (1980) is a collection of McGuane's writing on sports.

McGuffey, William Holmes (1800–1873)   American educator and textbook compiler. College teacher and president, McGuffey was known to thousands of Americans as the author of their first schoolbook. The series began in 1836, with the *First* and *Second Readers*. The *Primer, Third,* and *Fourth Readers* appeared in 1837, the *Speller* in 1838, the *Rhetorical Guide* in 1841, the *Fifth* and *Sixth Readers* in 1844 and 1857. He collaborated with his younger brother, Alexander Hamilton McGuffey, on the "Eclectic Series." The books have sold 122 million copies, with new editions issued as recently as 1920. McGuffey was a political conservative who supported the Hamiltonians rather than the Jeffersonians; his Readers reflect his point of view.

Mácha, Karel Hynek (1810–1836)   Czech poet and prose writer. The work of this greatest poet of Czech romanticism has never ceased to attract the attention of readers, critics, and poets. In contrast to the patriotic literature of his time, Mácha, influenced by the German, Polish, and English romantics, created a poetry dealing with fundamental existential and metaphysical themes. His major work, the lyrico-epic poem *Máj* (1836; tr *May*, 1932) was published shortly before his premature death. Its plot centers on the execution of a typically romantic hero, an outlaw and parricide, a victim of passions and alienation from society. The contrasting themes of blooming nature and violent death dominate the poem. The hero's fate is explicitly linked to that of his creator, the romantic poet.

Most of Mácha's work was published posthumously. His short novel *Cikáni* (*The Gypsies,* 1867) is the prose counterpart of *Maj,* while the short story "Marinka" (1862) develops a more realistic theme with a strong autobiographical element. Mácha's diary, published in 1929, is a record of his most intimate experiences; the romantic intertwining of life and literature makes it a most important document. See NERUDA, JAN.

Machado [y Ruiz], Antonio (1875–1939)   Spanish poet. Machado was one of the leading poets of the GENERACIÓN DEL 98. A trip to Paris in 1899 exposed him to the French SYMBOLISTS and to the MODERNISMO of Rubén DARÍO. The influence of both movements is evident in his first collection, *Soledades* (1903), which contains intimate, introspective reflections set against the somber background of Seville. His greatest and most characteristic verse is in the volume CAMPOS DE CASTILLA. This work contains such poems as "El dios iberico" and "Las encinas." His serious poetry is steeped in the landscape and history of Spain, with an accent on spiritual meditation. His final poetry became increasingly aphoristic, particularly in *Juan de Mairena* (1936; tr 1963), a philosophical miscellany of poetry and prose. Before they were estranged by taking opposing sides in the Spanish Civil War, he collaborated with his brother Manuel Machado, also a poet, on a number of plays. Antonio Machado contributed greatly to the Republican side of Spain's conflict. Forced to escape on foot to France in 1939, he died a month afterward. Among the translations of his work into English are *Eight Poems* (tr 1959) and *Sunlight and Scarlet* (tr 1973).

Machado de Assis, Joachim María (1839–1908) Brazilian novelist and poet. Widely regarded as Brazil's greatest novelist, Machado de Assis was the son of a black house painter and a Portuguese woman. He first earned his livelihood as a typesetter and as a journalist, but in his mid-twenties he began to be recognized for his poetry. In 1869 he married a Portuguese woman of distinguished family and, although afflicted by epilepsy, led a conventional private life until his death. In 1897 he founded and became first president of the Brazilian Academy of Letters.

In its musicality and detachment, his verse reflects the influence of the French PARNASSIANS. Two of his best-known poems are the ironical sonnet "Círculo Vicioso" and the perceptive "Mosca Azul," which appear in *Occidentaes* (1900). Other collections include *Chrysalidas* (1864) and *Phalenas* (1870).

The serenity that characterizes the poetry of Machado de Assis is also present in his novels; they have been compared to those of Henry JAMES in their psychological probing and to those of Laurence STERNE in their philosophical humor and whimsical digressions. In such works as *Memórias posthumas de braz cubas* (1891; tr *Epitaph for a Small Winner,* 1952), *Quincas borba* (1891; tr *Philosopher or Dog?,* 1954), and DOM CASMURRO, his masterpiece, Machado de Assis emerges as a skeptic who observes humanity with few illusions but great understanding.

Machau[l]t, Guillaume de (1300?–1377) French poet and composer. Machaut was in the service of the king of Bohemia until 1346, of the royal house of France thereafter, and was simultaneously holder of several ecclesiastical positions. Machaut was the chief of a school of lyric poets, including Eustache Deschamps and Jean FROISSART, establishing rigid forms for the BALLADE, CHANT ROYAL, RONDEL, and LAI. By introducing material from his personal life into his lyrics, he marked the transition from the impersonal conventions of troubadour poetry to the introspection of François VILLON.

His long narrative poems include *Jugement du roy de Navarre* (c1349); *Le Livre du voir-dit,* supposedly the true story of the love he inspired in a young girl because of his poetry; and *La Prise d'Alexandrie* (c1370). Chaucer borrowed from Machaut's *Livre de la fontaine amoureuse* for his BOOK OF THE DUCHESS and was probably significantly influenced by Machaut's work in general.

Machaut composed a great deal of secular and religious music, including the *Mass for Four Voices,* which is the earliest known polyphonic setting of the Mass Ordinary by one composer. But his principal contribution as a composer was to establish a tradition for the arrangement of vocal and instrumental parts in secular songs; it became the standard manner of setting rondeaux, virelais, and ballades for a century after his death.

Machen, Arthur [Llewellyn] (1863–1947) Welsh novelist and essayist. *The Great God Pan* (1894) was Machen's first novel and the first of many books about black magic and the horrors of the supernatural. He then began work on *The Hill of Dreams* (1907), with a semiautobiographical hero who sees visions of a terrifying Celtic and Roman past in an old fort. In the meantime, he also wrote other tales of the supernatural, such as *The Inmost Light* (1894) and *The White Powder* (1896), as well as a book of essays, *Hieroglyphics* (1902). In the 1920s, he was "discovered" by enthusiasts of the occult and remained a cult figure among them for several decades after his death.

Machiavelli, Niccolò (1469–1527)   Florentine statesman and political philosopher. Machiavelli is famous for his *Il principe* (THE PRINCE) and other political, historical, and literary writings. His early experience as an envoy for the Florentine republic filled him with firsthand knowledge of Italian political squabbles and intrigues and of powerful figures like Caesar BORGIA, all of which shaped his thought; the need to report these affairs precisely and economically shaped his style. At the same time, he read widely and deeply in ancient historical writers. In 1512 the return of the MEDICI to Florence left him without position, but the enforced exile gave him the time to compose *The Prince* and his other masterpiece, the *Discorsi* (*Discourses*, 1513–17). Other writings that followed include a book on the art of war, a discourse on the government of Florence, a life of the condottiero Castruccio Castracani, and a history of Florence. His literary efforts include *La mandragola* (*The Mandrake*, written c1518), one of the best comedies produced during the Italian Renaissance; the play *Clizia* (written 1525); a novella entitled *Belfagor*, in which an exiled devil investigates human matrimony; and a dialogue on the Italian tongue. *The Prince*, dedicated to a younger member of the Medici clan and in part motivated by a desire to show how useful its author could be as a political advisor, ranges from philosophical discussion of the nature and origins of principalities to realistic and practical comments on the relations between a prince and his subjects. The ruthlessness of Borgia toward his enemies is praised, but senseless cruelty is condemned; Italian politics are viewed with cynicism, but there is also an idealistic and stirring call to unity. Much emphasis is placed upon the military, especially the need for citizens rather than mercenaries to do the fighting necessary to protect any state.

In the more leisurely *Discorsi* on Livy, where the method is to compare ancient and modern events and draw from the comparison aphorisms of universal validity, Machiavelli makes clear his true republican sentiments. The ideal government is a republic in which the various social and political groups are given a say. *La mandragola*, his most famous literary work, tells a typical novella story in the dramatic manner of Roman comedy. Its young lovers triumph over an old fool through the assistance of a fiendish parasite and a nodding confessor. The cynicism of the play reinforced the reputation Machiavelli soon gained for being a teacher of treachery, intrigue, and immorality.

His criticism of contemporary Christianity earned him the censure of the Church and spurred the popular portrait of him as a diabolical anti-Christ. In Elizabethan England, where his influence reached Spenser, Raleigh, and Bacon, his name became a popular synonym, especially in the drama, for diabolical cunning. In later years, the term *Machiavellian* came to connote cynical politics; *The Prince* became a handbook for tyrants and dictators. Modern opinion has reversed this trend, so that he is now regarded as a pioneer of political science; his republicanism and patriotism are stressed; and, though the originality and value of his thought are now questioned, there is unanimous praise for his style and his literary genius.

Machine infernale, La   See INFERNAL MACHINE, THE.

MacInnes, Colin (1914–1976)   English novelist and essayist. The son of Angela Thirkell, MacInnes grew up in Australia, worked in British Intelligence during World War II, and in 1945 began writing for the BBC and London magazines. He is best known for the novels of his "London trilogy," the first of which, *City of Spades* (1957), is a vigorous and poignant picture of London's black community, as seen through the eyes of a young Nigerian. The next, *Absolute Beginners* (1959), examines the city's teenage culture in the person of an eighteen-year-old jazz lover who follows music from chic parties to the 1958 Notting Hill race riots. *Mr. Love and Justice* (1960), the subtlest of the three, focuses on the interplay between London police and street people.

MacInnes, Helen [Clark] (1907–1985)   Scottishborn American novelist. MacInnes is the prolific author of over twenty books, most of them suspense-thrillers with European settings. Beginning with *Above Suspicion* (1941), she wrote a best-selling series of adventure stories drawn from events in World War II, including *Assignment in Brittany* (1942), *Decision at Delphi* (1960), and *The Salzburg Connection* (1968). She is noted for the authentic depiction of her settings. Among her other works are *Message from Málaga* (1971), *Prelude to Terror* (1978), *The Hidden Target* (1980), and *Cloak of Darkness* (1982).

McKay, Claude (1890–1948)   Jamaican-born American poet and novelist. McKay, a major figure in the HARLEM RENAISSANCE of the 1920s, became the first black best-selling author with his *Home to Harlem* (1928), the story of a black soldier returning home after World War I. Among his other novels is *Banjo* (1929), a story of Marseilles. His verse was published in the collections *Songs of Jamaica* (1911), *Constab Ballads* (1912), *Spring in New Hampshire and Other Poems* (1920), and *Harlem Shadows* (1922).

MacKaye, Percy [Wallace] (1875–1956)   American poet and dramatist. MacKaye is known for his interest in the community theatre and his use of older literature as the point of departure for his plays. These include *The Scarecrow* (1908), a drama of a scarecrow brought to life, based on HAWTHORNE's "Feathertop," and *Caliban by the Yellow Sands* (1916).

McKenney, Ruth (1911–1972)   American journalist and humorist. McKenney is best known for her amusing novel *My Sister Eileen* (1938), whose characters are based on her sister and her brother-in-law Nathanael WEST. She also wrote a serious account of economic and social conditions in Akron, Ohio, from 1932 to 1936 in *Industrial Valley* (1939). Among her other humorous books is *The Loud Red Patrick* (1947), sketches about her grandfather.

Mackenzie, Sir [Edward Montague] Compton (1883–1972)   English novelist and nonfiction writer. Mackenzie was a convert to Catholicism and to the cause of Scottish nationalism and lived for many years on islands (Capri, two Channel islands, and Barra in the Outer Hebrides). He was knighted in 1952. His many and varied works include novels, essays, criticism, and autobiography. He is best known for his early serious fiction, especially *Carnival* (1912), SINISTER STREET, and *Guy and Pauline* (1915), and for the Scottish comedy *Whiskey Galore* (1947).

Mackenzie, Kenneth (pseudonym Seaforth Mackenzie, 1903–1954)   Australian novelist and poet. *The Young Desire It* (1937) is a classic study of passage from childhood to adolescence. His *Selected Poems* appeared in 1961. *Poems* (1972) is notable for a rich sensuality in fluent blank verse.

McKinley, William (1843–1901)   Twenty-fifth president of the U.S. (1897–1901). A veteran of the CIVIL WAR, McKinley was elected to Congress in 1876 and became known as a champion of high tariffs. After two terms as governor of Ohio, he was the Republican presidential nominee in 1896, defeating William Jennings BRYAN. The SPANISH-AMERICAN WAR occurred during his first term. Running on a platform that promised voters a "full dinner pail," he again defeated Bryan in 1900 but was assassinated by an anarchist, Leon Czolgosz, in Buffalo, New York. He was succeeded by Theodore ROOSEVELT.

Mackintosh, Elizabeth   See TEY, JOSEPHINE.

Macklin, Charles (c1700–1797)   English dramatist and actor. Macklin is remembered for his two fine comedies *Love à la Mode* (1759) and *The Man of the World* (1781). He was also one of the best actors of his time. See SHYLOCK.

MacLeish, Archibald (1892–1982)   American poet. After two early volumes of poetry, *Songs for a Summer Day* (1915) and *Tower of Ivory* (1917), MacLeish became an expatriate in Paris and remained there until 1928. During this period, he was greatly influenced by Ezra POUND, T. S. ELIOT, and the French SYMBOLISTS. He published two volumes of short lyrics, *The Happy Marriage* (1924) and *Streets in the Moon* (1926), both of which show his experiments in form and metrics. In *Nobodaddy* (1926), a verse play based on the story of Adam, Eve, Cain, and Abel, MacLeish turned to "the dramatic situation which

the condition of self-consciousness in an indifferent universe" presents.

In 1932 MacLeish published the narrative poem CONQUISTADOR, which was awarded a PULITZER PRIZE. Though he continued to publish verse, he became increasingly involved with world problems, writing verse plays with a political message: *Panic* (1935), about the Depression, and *The Fall of the City* (1937), written during HITLER's rise to power, showing the people of an unnamed city accepting through blind fear a conqueror whose power is only imagined; the latter, like *Air Raid* (1938), was written for radio.

MacLeish was appointed Librarian of Congress in 1939; during World War II he held several government posts, culminating in assistant secretary of state (1944–45), and wrote numerous essays dealing with social and political questions.

MacLeish won two more Pulitzer Prizes with *Collected Poems 1917–1952* (1952) and the verse drama *J. B.* (1958). *New and Collected Poems 1917–1976* (1976) spans MacLeish's remarkably varied career. Despite all his political involvements, MacLeish is best remembered as a serious lyric poet. *Reflections*, a series of interviews made during his final years, was published in 1986.

MacLennan, Hugh (1907–   )   Canadian novelist. MacLennan was among the first of his generation to write novels that attempted to define a uniquely Canadian national character. Beginning with *Barometer Rising* (1941), such novels as *Two Solitudes* (1945), *Each Man's Son* (1951), *The Watch That Ends the Night* (1959), and *Return of the Sphinx* (1967) treat Canadian themes and contemporary problems, such as Quebec separatism, with insight and conviction. His nonfiction includes *The Colour of Canada* (1967) and *On Being a Maritime Writer* (1984).

McLuhan, [Herbert] Marshall (1911–1980)   Canadian cultural critic and communications theorist. McLuhan established the Center for Culture and Technology at the University of Toronto to investigate the cultural and psychological consequences of mass media and technology. His first book, *The Mechanical Bride* (1951), probed, in a witty and epigrammatic style, the purposes and effects of modern culture, particularly advertising. Its successor, *The Gutenberg Galaxy* (1962), offered a theory of historical change based on major shifts in communications; the book compares "scribal man" (pre-1500) and "print man" (post-1500). *Understanding Media* (1964) considered the information explosion of the modern era and prophesied the liberation of "print man" into the boundless possibilities of "electronic man." If *Understanding Media* shook his readers with the assertion that electronic media were becoming an extension of the human nervous system, *The Medium Is the Massage* (1967), so called because "all media work us over completely," mystified them. Many, however, found in the mixture of wisecrack aphorisms and sharp insight a serious and stimulating argument about the effects of media on our age.

McMaster, John Bach (1852–1932)   American historian. Bach is best known for his eight-volume *History of the People of the United States* (1883–1913), in which he stressed the social and economic rather than the military aspects of the country's past, using newspapers and other contemporary materials as his sources.

McMurtry, Larry [Jeff] (1936–   )   American novelist. McMurtry's early novels present realistically detailed pictures of a vanishing way of life on the Texas plains. *Horseman, Pass By* (1961) and *Leaving Cheyenne* (1963) deal with the effects of government intervention and big business on ranchers and cowboys. The sense of a vanishing time and regional culture is also central to *The Last Picture Show* (1966), set in a small Texas town, which, like the later novel *Terms of Endearment* (1975), was made into a highly successful film. McMurtry's more recent novels include *Somebody's Darling* (1978), *Cadillac Jack* (1982), and *Lonesome Dove* (1985), an epic novel of the old West that won a PULITZER PRIZE in 1986.

MacNeice, Louis (1907–1963)   Irish-born English poet. MacNeice was associated with W. H. AUDEN and other left-wing poets during the 1930s but was not as closely committed to Marxist doctrines as they were. His poetry is characterized by its colloquial, sometimes humorous tone and its use of contemporary ideas and images. His volumes of poems include *Blind Fireworks* (1929), *Collected Poems* (1949), *Autumn Sequel* (1954), *Eighty-Five Poems* (1961), and *Solstices* (1961). MacNeice was a classical scholar and a lecturer in Greek and Latin; he wrote the verse translation *The Agamemnon of Aeschylus* (1936) and also translated (1951) Goethe's *Faust*. *Out of the Picture* (1937) is a verse drama in the Auden manner. He collaborated with Auden on *Letters from Iceland* (1937). From 1941 he wrote a number of works for the British Broadcasting Corporation; *The Dark Tower and Other Radio Scripts* appeared in 1947.

Macondo   See ONE HUNDRED YEARS OF SOLITUDE.

McPhee, John A[ngus] (1931–   )   American writer. McPhee worked as an editor for *Time* magazine, then became a staff writer for THE NEW YORKER, where all his books originally appeared. McPhee's precise and fascinated observation of detail brings alive the most diverse phenomena to an uninformed reader. His titles suggest the range of his interests: *Oranges* (1967); *The Pine Barrens* (1968); *The Deltoid Pumpkin Seed* (1973), about experimental aircraft; and *The Curve of Binding Energy* (1974), about the atomic bomb. He is most at home writing about his own experiences in the wilderness, as in *Encounters with the Archdruid* (1972); *The Survival of the Bark Canoe* (1975); and his long study of Alaska, *Coming into the Country* (1977). McPhee's other books include *A Roomful of Hovings* (1979), *Giving Good Weight* (1980), *Basin and Range* (1981), *In Suspect Terrain* (1983), and *La Place de la Concorde Suisse* (1984).

Macpherson, James (1736–1796)   Scottish poet, writer, and literary forger. In 1760 Macpherson published *Fragments of Ancient Poetry Collected in the Highlands of Scotland, and Translated from the Gallic or Erse Language*. Shortly thereafter, he published first *Fingal, An Ancient Epic* (1761) and then *Temora, An Epic Poem* (1763), purportedly translations from the Gaelic of the 3rd-century bardic hero OSSIAN. The Ossianic poems—in actuality, a literary hoax—aroused a great deal of interest, the author collecting funds from a number of well-known literary figures, such as John Home and Hugh Blair, to make a tour through the Highlands in search of epic material. The London critics, especially Samuel JOHNSON, soon became suspicious, however, and Macpherson failed to make further Ossianic "discoveries." After his death, investigation revealed that Macpherson had liberally edited traditional Gaelic poems and added passages of his own. These pseudo-Gaelic poems are written in poetic prose marked by rhapsodic descriptions of nature and an atmosphere of vague mystery and melancholy. Although critics do not now consider them to be of much literary value, they had an important influence on the development of romanticism in France and Germany.

MacPherson, [Jean] Jay (1931–   )   English-born Canadian poet. In relatively few volumes—*Nineteen Poems* (1951), *O Earth Return* (1954), *The Fisherman: A Book of Riddles* (1957), *The Boatman* (1957; repr and expanded 1968)—MacPherson developed a reputation as a master of poetic form. Like most of her work, *The Boatman* draws on symbols from the Bible and myth and employs a variety of poetic styles. Noah, as the boatman, represents the artist, whose function it is to rescue mankind from spiritual drowning. *The Four Ages of Man* (1962) is a prose collection of classical myths. *Welcoming Disaster*, a sometimes disturbing collection of poems, finally appeared in 1974; another long silence was eventually broken by *Poems Twice Told* (1981).

Macready, William Charles (1793–1873)   English tragedian, noted for his portrayals of MACBETH, CASSIUS, KING LEAR, HENRY IV, and IAGO, among others. By 1837 Macready was in the first rank of his profession. He made several trips to the U.S.; during the last of these the Astor Place Riot occurred (May 10, 1849), taking the lives of twenty-two persons and injuring thirty-six others outside the Astor Place Opera House in New York City. The riot involved partisans of Macready and Edwin Forrest, an American actor, and was occasioned by a resurgence of anti-British feeling.

McTeague (1899)   A novel by Frank NORRIS. Forbidden to practice dentistry when Marcus Schouler informs the authorities that he lacks both license and diploma, McTeague grows brutish and surly, while his wife, Trina, who had won $5,000 in a lottery, becomes a miser. He eventually murders Trina, steals her money, and is pursued into Death Valley by Schouler. McTeague kills Schouler, but not before the latter manages to handcuff their wrists. Tied to the corpse, McTeague is doomed to die of thirst in the desert.

Madame Bovary (1856)   A novel by Gustave FLAUBERT. With flawless style, Flaubert creates the life and fate of the Norman bourgeoise Emma Bovary. Unhappy in her marriage to a good-hearted but stupid village doctor, Emma finds her pathetic dreams of romantic love unfulfilled. A sentimental, discontented, and hopelessly limited person, she commits adultery, piles up enormous debts, and finally takes her own life in desperation. The novel's subject, the life of a very ordinary woman, and its technique, the amassing of precise detail, make *Madame Bovary* one of the crowning works in the development of the novel.

Madariaga [y Rojo], Salvador de (1886–1978) Spanish author, statesman, and academician. In the 1920s and 1930s, Madariaga held several diplomatic posts in the U.S. and Europe, finally settling in England, where he taught Spanish literature at Oxford and served as an articulate spokesman against the Franco regime in Spain. Writing in Spanish, English, and French, he was bent on opening up Spanish culture to foreign audiences. His wide range of interests is attested to by the variety of subjects he covered and genres he employed. He wrote novels and poetry but is better known for his literary criticism, including *Guía del lector del Quijote* (1926; tr *Don Quixote; A Psychological Study*, 1934) and especially his numerous historical works. These include *Hernán Cortés* (1941), *Bolívar* (1951), and his best-known book, *España* (1930; tr *Spain*, 1931). *Englishmen, Frenchmen, Spaniards* (1928) is a study in social psychology. His autobiographical *Memorias 1921–1936* was abridged and translated as *Morning without Noon* (1974).

mad as a hatter   A popular simile. The probable origin of this phrase is an occupational nervous disease that afflicted hatters, caused by prolonged exposure to the mercury used in the manufacture of felt. It was popularized by Lewis Carroll (*Alice's Adventures in Wonderland*, 1865), but it was well known earlier and was used by Thackeray in *Pendennis* (1849).

Madison, Dolley [Payne Todd] (1768–1849) Wife of James Madison, whom she married in 1794. Dolley Madison was unofficial first lady during the administration of Jefferson, a widower, and her fame as a charming, tactful hostess grew after her husband assumed the presidency. When the British burned Washington in 1814, she rescued many official papers and a portrait of George Washington from the White House. After Madison's death, she again became a social leader in Washington, though her last years were marred by financial difficulties.

Madison, James (1751–1836)   Fourth president of the U.S. (1809–17). After serving in the Continental Con-gress during the American Revolution, Madison was elected to the Virginia House of Delegates, where he helped secure passage of Thomas JEFFERSON's bill for religious freedom. As a member of the Constitutional Convention (1787), he played a dominant role in the framing of the Constitution, which he later defended in the FEDERALIST papers. He continued his close association with Jefferson, with whom he prepared the Virginia and Kentucky Resolutions, condemning the Alien and Sedition Acts, and under whom he served as secretary of state. After Madison's election to the presidency, continued friction with Great Britain over U.S. neutral rights led to the War of 1812, which found the U.S. unprepared and disunited. The war's opponents, especially in New England and New York, dubbed it "Mr. Madison's war." In the last years of his administration, Madison advocated tariff protection and a strong army.

Madonna, The   See MARY, THE VIRGIN.

madrigal   Italian literary and musical genre. In the 14th century, the poetic form of the madrigal consisted normally of two STROPHES of three lines each, followed by a strophe of two lines, called the *ritornello*. They were generally set to music in two or three vocal parts with the pattern a-a-b, reflecting the structure of the poem.

There is no connection between the madrigal of the 14th century and the much more widespread 16th-century type. Madrigalesque poetry in the 16th century consisted of a single stanza of seven or eleven syllable lines arranged in a free order, with no set rhyme scheme. The subject matter was usually amatory or pastoral, the style inspired by PETRARCH. The musical genre called madrigal in the 16th century consisted of settings for vocal ensemble, from three to eight voices, sometimes with instruments, of almost any lyric poetry, whether or not of the madrigal type; it might include sonnets, sestinas, canzoni, and so on. The 16th-century madrigal tradition developed a new expressive relationship between words and music. Rather than setting the poetry to music according to its poetic structure, as had been the case with earlier secular compositions, madrigal composers increasingly attempted to translate each word or phrase into an appropriately expressive musical setting. The competition between madrigal composers to outdo one another in text expression, often in multiple settings of the same poem, resulted in a rapid stylistic change that caused the genre to burn itself out very quickly. The entire rise, flowering, and decline of the madrigal may be placed between 1520 and 1620.

Late in the 16th century, the Italian madrigal became a vogue throughout Europe; this was especially the case in England, where composers adapted the ideas of such Italians as Luca Marenzio to their own madrigalesque compositions. Part of the musical significance of the madrigal comes from the fact that the modes of "word painting" in music invented by the madrigal composers were retained, with appropriate transformations, in much later music. Most vocal music of the Baroque era, from operas to the cantatas of J. S. BACH, would be inconceivable without the tradition of the madrigal.

Madwoman of Chaillot, The (La Folle de Chaillot, 1945; tr 1947)   A play by Jean GIRAUDOUX. A delightfully eccentric old woman manages to exploit and defeat the exploiters and financiers of Paris.

Maecenas, Gaius Cilnius (d 8 BC)   Roman statesman and patron of letters. As a friend and adviser of the young Octavius Caesar (later AUGUSTUS), Maecenas was instrumental in arranging the Peace of Brundisium (41 BC), which temporarily reconciled Octavius with Mark ANTONY. He was not a fawning creature of the emperor, for on one occasion he publicly reproved Octavius by warning him against becoming a common butcher (*carnifex*) of his own people. It was Maecenas who organized the cultural resources of the principate by subsidizing the work of young artists, among whom were VERGIL and HORACE. His munificence as a patron has made his name proverbial.

maenads   In Greek mythology, the female attendants of DIONYSUS. The word means mad or frenzied women, also called Bacchae. See BACCHANTS.

Maerlant, Jacob van (c1235–c1300)   Flemish poet who stimulated the cultivation of a Flemish literature distinct from the French. About 1264 Maerlant adapted a number of romances from the French; then he began metrical translations and adaptations of didactic works. His most important work, although he died before completing it, is the *Mirror of History* (begun 1284), a history of the world based on the *Speculum majus* of Vincent of Beauvais (d 1264).

Maeterlinck, Maurice (1862–1949)   Belgian poet, dramatist, and essayist. Maeterlinck's literary career began with the publication of two volumes of poetry: *Douze chansons* (1896) and *Serres chaudes* (1889), both mysterious and dreamy in subject matter and mood. His fame, however, rests on his symbolic dramas. *La Princesse Maleine* (1889), his first success, was followed by *L'Intruse* and *Les Aveugles* (1890), PELLÉAS ET MÉLISANDE, and *L'Intérieur* (1894). Antinaturalistic in its subject, Maeterlinck's drama portrayed the inner conflict of the individual, not the external struggle between man and his world. Antinaturalistic in method as well, it abandoned a realistic portrait of life as seen, for a symbolic expression of the inner life. The romantic melancholy of his early plays was succeeded by a faith in the spiritual life of all living things. The later plays, especially *L'Oiseau bleu* (1909), were more hopeful in mood, founded on that belief in the spirit expressed in the essays of *La Sagesse et la destinée* (1898) and *Le Temple enseveli* (1902). The mystery of human life and death that preoccupied Maeterlinck led him to write studies of flowers and animals who share in this mysterious existence: *La Vie des abeilles* (1901), *L'Intelligence des fleurs* (1907), and *La Vie des termites* (1927). In 1911 Maeterlinck was awarded the NOBEL PRIZE in Literature.

Maeztu y Whitney, Ramiro de (1875–1936)   Spanish man of letters. Originally a member of the GENERACIÓN DEL 98, Maeztu later abandoned their social program, turning to ardent support of traditional Roman Catholicism in Spain. This is best expressed in his most famous work, the essay *Defensa de la hispanidad* (1934).

Magda (Die Heimat, 1893; tr 1896)   A melodramatic play by Hermann SUDERMANN. When the prima donna Magda performs a concert in a small provincial town, she attempts a reconciliation with her estranged family, who live there. The drama emphasizes the conflicts between the mores of the provincial bourgeoisie and the bohemian life of urban artists.

Magdalene   See MARY MAGDALENE.

Magellan, Ferdinand (Portuguese name Fernando de Magalhães, 1480?–1521)   Portuguese navigator. After serving the king of Portugal in India and the Moluccas, or Spice Islands, Magellan fell into royal disfavor and offered his services to Charles V of Spain, from whom he won permission to sail to the Orient by a westward route. Leaving Spain in September 1519, with five ships, he sailed down the eastern coast of South America, exploring the estuary of the La Plata river. After wintering at Port St. Julian, where Magellan quelled a mutiny among his men, the expedition entered what is now known as the Strait of Magellan and sailed northwestward, reaching the Ladrones (now Mariana) Islands on March 6, 1521. A month later, Magellan discovered the Philippines. He made an alliance with a native chief and was killed on the island of Mactan while fighting on his behalf. His ships continued the voyage, but only one managed to return to Europe (1522), completing the first circumnavigation of the globe.

Maggie: A Girl of the Streets (privately printed, 1893; pub 1896)   A novel by Stephen CRANE. The first realistic American novel, *Maggie* is the story of a girl of the New York slums, doomed by family and environmental forces to a life that she is unable to escape. The tone of the novel is set in its opening scene of boys fighting in the streets. In this Darwinian jungle, even the toughest have difficulty in surviving. Maggie Johnson is the daughter of a brutal father and a drunken mother. She goes to work in a collar factory, falls in love with Pete, a bartender who is a friend of her brother Jimmie, and is seduced by him. Her mother disowns her; she becomes a prostitute; and in despair she finally kills herself. Her final degeneration becomes almost an allegory.

The novel, like THE RED BADGE OF COURAGE, is episodic in structure, relying on irony for its dramatic effect. Crane revised the original edition before the book was published in 1896, eliminating some of the more melodramatic sections.

Magi (Lat, plural of *magus*, "wise man")   The Three Wise Men of the East who brought gifts to the infant Jesus. Tradition calls them Melchior, GASPAR, and Balthazar, three kings of the East. The first offered gold, the emblem of royalty; the second, frankincense, in token of divinity; and the third, myrrh, a symbol of death.

Medieval legend calls them the Three Kings of Cologne, and the cathedral there claims their relics. They are commemorated on January 2, 3, and 4, and particularly at the Feast of the Epiphany.

Among the ancient Medes and Persians, the Magi were members of a priestly caste credited with great occult powers. After ZOROASTER's death, they adopted the Zoroastrian religion and spread its influence to Egypt and Asia Minor. In Camões's OS LUSÍADAS, the term denotes the Indian Brahmins.

Magic Mountain, The (Der Zauberberg, 1924; tr 1927)   A novel by Thomas MANN. Written in the tradition of the BILDUNGSROMAN, it is concerned with young Hans CASTORP and his personal development at Haus Berghof, a tuberculosis sanatorium in the Swiss Alps. In the book's symbolism, the sanatorium, with its international clientele, is a scale model of Europe on the eve of World War I; the pervasive atmosphere of sickness and death symbolizes a general European decadence, and the sanatorium's isolation indicates an unhealthy separation between artistic or intellectual life (the mountain) and the vital and active life below. Hans first comes there to visit his cousin Joachim Ziemssen, intending to stay only three weeks, but the place mysteriously attracts him, the discovery of a minute pulmonary defect induces him to remain, and he stays there for seven years. During this period, the other characters act upon him essentially as two forces; on the one hand, there are those like SETTEMBRINI, PEEPERKORN, and Dr. Behrens, the vigorous, outgoing head physician, who attract him to the side of reason and vital, nondecadent activity; on the other, such figures as Clavdia Chauchat, Leo NAPHTA, and Dr. Krokowski, the assistant physician interested in psychoanalysis, hypnotism, and spiritism, draw him toward the mysterious and decadent, occult and aesthetic aspects of life. Hans's development reaches a climax when he gets lost in the snow and has an internal vision in which he first sees a classical temple surrounded by a society of beautiful and enlightened men, but then finds that inside the temple two old hags are tearing apart and devouring a child. The import is that even the highest attainments of reason (the temple) must contain an element of deadly pagan decadence and that the two contradictory human tendencies toward enlightened, constructive activity and toward superstitious, destructive decadence are inseparable. Much later, Castorp leaves the sanatorium, healthy in body and mind. But it is 1914, the war has begun, and Castorp is last glimpsed with hundreds of young comrades in a barrage of shrapnel, exploding grenades, and gun-fire.

mágico prodigioso, El (The Wonder-Working Magician, 1637)   A drama by Pedro CALDERÓN DE LA BARCA, considered the best of his religious plays. It is the story, reminiscent of the FAUST legend, of the pagan philosopher Cipriano, who makes a pact with the devil to gain the love of Justina, a Christian who has previously rejected him. The devil tempts her in vain, and Cipriano, admiring her virtue, also becomes a Christian. The two then suffer martyrdom at the hands of the Roman governor of Antioch.

magic realism (Sp, lo real maravilloso)   A term introduced by Alejo CARPENTIER, in his prologue to El reino de este mundo (1949; tr The Kingdom of This World, 1957). The Cuban novelist was searching for a concept broad enough to accommodate both the events of everyday life and the fabulous nature of Latin American geography and history. Carpentier, who was greatly influenced by French SURREALISM, saw in magic realism the capacity to enrich our idea of what is "real" by incorporating all dimensions of the imagination, particularly as expressed in magic, myth, and religion.

Magister Ludi: The Glass-Bead Game (Das Glasperlenspiel, 1943; tr 1949, 1969)   A novel by Hermann HESSE. Written in the form of a BILDUNGSROMAN, the novel follows the intellectual and spiritual odyssey of Josef KNECHT, who lives in a utopian society in the 23rd century. The culture is dominated by a glass-bead game, practiced in its highest form (in which beads are not even used) by an intellectual elite. The game represents a balanced fusion of the active and contemplative disciplines; it is a combination of music and mathematics (art and science) but includes elements from virtually every cultural endeavor. Knecht becomes master of the game (Lat, Magister Ludi) but has doubts about the virtues of pure intellect. He renounces his order and departs to the outer world, where he eventually dies, the tragic result of a life dedicated entirely to the world of the spirit.

Magna Carta (or Magna Charta, 1215)   The "Great Charter" of England. It permanently guaranteed the principle that the king's power must be limited by law. The barons had long been embittered by King JOHN's misgovernment, his levying of heavy taxes to support his foreign wars, and his personal injustice and cruelty toward potential rivals among the nobility. Advised by Stephen LANGTON, the barons compelled John at Runnymede to sign a document clarifying their feudal relationship. Most of the provisions sought redress for grievances; the two later glorified as the basis of modern government and bills of personal rights were the clauses establishing the principle that the king could not levy taxes without the consent of a "counsel of the realm" and that he could not imprison a free man or deprive him of his property except by the judgment of his peers or the law of the land. Pope Innocent III suspended Langton for siding against the king and annulled the Charter, which incited a civil war; but, when John and the Pope died in 1216, Langton compelled a reissue of the Charter in Henry III's name and a confirmation of it when the young king came of age.

Magnificat The song of praise of the Virgin MARY, her response when she was greeted by her cousin Elizabeth in the house of Zacharias (Luke 1:46–55). It begins, "My soul doth magnify the Lord" (Lat, *Magnificat anima mea Dominum*). As a part of the vesper service of the Roman Catholic Church, it has been in use since the beginning of the 6th century, and, in the Anglican service, for over three hundred years.

It has been set to music numerous times, a famous version being Johann Sebastian BACH's *Magnificat in D* (1723), a superb cantatalike work for orchestra, chorus, and soloists.

Magritte, René (1881–1967) Belgian painter. Magritte was the first Belgian surrealist, having been attracted to the works of de CHIRICO around 1925. His work is characterized by bizarre juxtapositions of objects, painted in a restrained, realistic style. The contrast of his style with his fantastic subjects contributes to the unsettling quality of his paintings.

Magwitch, Abel In Charles Dickens's GREAT EXPECTATIONS, Pip's convict benefactor and father of Estella. Magwitch is a terrifying, simple man with a long memory for good and ill turns. When he returns illegally to England to see what kind of a gentleman his "dear boy" Pip has become, old enemies inform on him, and, after an abortive flight, he dies.

Mahābhārata One of the two great epic poems of ancient India (the other being the RĀMĀYANA), about eight times as long as the ILIAD and ODYSSEY together. It is a great compendium, added to as late as AD 600, although it had very nearly acquired its present form by the 4th century. Covering an enormous range of topics, the *Mahābhārata*, with its famous interpolation, the BHAGAVADGĪTĀ, has as its central theme the great war between the sons of two royal brothers, in a struggle for succession. The brothers are Dhritarāshtra and Pandū, their families being referred to respectively as the Kauravas and the Pandavas. The Pandavas ultimately prevail, the eldest of them, Yudhishtira, gains the throne, and Arjuna, one of his younger brothers and in many ways the hero of the entire epic (especially through the *Bhagavadgītā*), gains the hand of the lovely DRAUPADI and brings her home as the wife of all five brothers. The epic also contains the *Shantiparvan*, an important discourse on statecraft, and the famous *Savitri* episode, the tale of NALA and DAMAYANTĪ. In its totality, it is an encyclopedia of Hindu life, legend, and thought: "What is not in the *Mahābhārata*," says the *Mahābhārata*, "is not to be found anywhere else in the world."

Mahagonny See RISE AND FALL OF THE TOWN MAHAGONNY, THE.

Mahayana See BUDDHISM.

Mahdi (Arab, "the divinely directed one") The expected Messiah of the Muslims who is to lead the hosts of Islam to victory. A title often assumed by leaders of insurrection, it is applied especially to Muhammed Ahmed

(1843–85), who led the Sudanese uprising of 1883 and who is said to be sleeping in a cavern until the time he will return to life to overthrow Dejal ("Antichrist"). The Shiahs, or SHIITES, believe that the Mahdi has lived and that the twelfth Imam, who disappeared about 873, will someday come out of hiding to rule the Muslim world.

Mahendra See INDRA.

Mahler, Gustav (1860–1911) Austrian (i.e., Bohemian) conductor and composer. Mahler's compositions are classical-romantic in style, influenced strongly by BEETHOVEN, by way of BRUCKNER and WAGNER. He held Wagner in highest esteem and hoped for a career as a dramatic composer. Following the dismal failure of his early operatic endeavors, however, Mahler was forced, somewhat bitterly, to earn his living as a conductor. He wrote ten symphonies, the last unfinished, and a series of orchestral song cycles. As a reflection of his own musical credo that "the content must shape the form," Mahler's symphonies are generally not confined to the conventional four-movement scheme, and they make use of unorthodox instrumentation.

The second or *Resurrection Symphony* (1894) has a choral finale, using as its text an ode by KLOPSTOCK. The eighth or *Symphony of a Thousand* (1907) is entirely choral, in two vast movements, the second of which is a complete musical setting of the closing scene of Goethe's FAUST, Part Two. It is often said that Mahler's position as a significant composer rests principally on the last two works he completed: *Symphony No. 9* (1909) and *Das Lied von der Erde* (*The Song of the Earth*, 1908), a setting for solo voices and orchestra of a cycle of poems by the Chinese LI PO.

Maid Marian In the English ROBIN HOOD ballad cycle, the sweetheart of Robin Hood. In one version, Marian loved Robin Hood when he was the earl of Huntington. When he was outlawed for debt, she followed him into the forest, dressed as a page, and lived among his men as a virgin huntress until the marriage rites could be performed. This is a late version, arising in Tudor times. Originally she was the May queen in the early English May Day dances.

Maid of Orleans, The (Die Jungfrau von Orleans, 1801) A romantic tragedy by Friedrich SCHILLER, based on the life of Joan of Arc. Schiller emphasizes Joan's determined idealism and her refusal to be diverted from her transcendent goal by earthly temptations. He varies the usual story in that Joan dies in battle and not at the stake.

Maids, The (Les Bonnes, 1948; tr 1954) A play by Jean GENET. Two sisters, Claire and Solange, have betrayed their mistress's lover to the police, and, to complete their treachery, they poison her tea while she prepares to follow him to the penal colony. But Madame, learning that her lover has been freed, departs and leaves her tea undrunk. In order that her sister may join the elite of the criminal and the saint, Claire takes Madame's place as victim and forces Solange to poison her. The play illustrates two preoccupations central to Genet's work: human identity is seen exclusively as a shifting succession of masks, roles, and states, and moral values are systematically inverted, evil being assigned the hierarchical place more traditionally reserved for good.

Maid's Tragedy, The (c1611)   A tragedy by BEAUMONT AND FLETCHER. By order of the king, Amintor is forced to renounce his beloved Aspatia and marry Evadne, sister of his closest friend, Melantius, who has just returned a hero from the wars. But, on her wedding night, Evadne reveals that she is the king's mistress, a fact that Amintor later confides to Melantius. Enraged, Melantius plots against the king. He makes his sister repent and promise to kill the king, while he foments a successful revolution. Meanwhile, Aspatia, disguised as her brother, has been fatally wounded in a duel with Amintor. Evadne, after killing the king, kills herself when Amintor refuses to forgive her. Then Amintor discovers that the "man" he has slain is Aspatia and takes his own life. Melantius tries to follow his example but is restrained by the new king, who promises to abide by the lessons of these bloody events.

Mailer, Norman (1923–   )   American writer. Born in Brooklyn, New York, educated at Harvard, Mailer spent two years in the Pacific Theatre during World War II. While still at Harvard he wrote A Transit to Narcissus, a melodramatic novel set in a mental institution, not published until 1978. His army experiences provided the material for his first published novel, THE NAKED AND THE DEAD, generally considered one of the most important novels to come out of World War II, and one that catapulted its author into public and critical celebrity at the age of twenty-five. His next novel, Barbary Shore (1951), dealing with radical political ideologies, was less well received; but The Deer Park (1955), a sensational novel about Hollywood, reinforced Mailer's reputation as a powerful writer with a disturbing capacity to cut through to the bare bones of human nature. Advertisements for Myself (1959) is a collection of stories, essays, parts of novels, and articles held together by a "confessional" commentary. Mailer's persistent and outraged interest in sex, greed, and violence in America was given a strong voice by the semiautobiographical hero of his fourth novel, An American Dream (1965). As a social critic, Mailer has been actively engaged in the political turmoils of his time. Politics and financial need led him increasingly to journalism; his essays on social and political events were collected in such volumes as The Presidential Papers (1963), Cannibals and Christians (1966), and The Idol and the Octopus (1968). With his first-person account of the 1967 peace march on the Pentagon, Mailer created a landmark in American political journalism in a style that was soon dubbed "new journalism" (also practiced by Tom WOLFE and Truman CAPOTE). The Armies of the Night (1968; PULITZER PRIZE) combined acute factual reportage with the

novelist's wit, insight, and narrative sense. Subsequent efforts with the same techniques were less successful, until the publication of The Executioner's Song (1979), which won a Pulitzer Prize. In this study of a condemned murderer Mailer not only vividly portrays the character in a real-life drama but also invokes the whole history of westward migration of the Mormons of Utah. Ancient Evenings (1983), a novel about power, politics, and everyday life in ancient Egypt, and Tough Guys Don't Dance (1984), a murder mystery that also examines the essence of male/femaleness in the 20th century, are other works. As well as publishing over thirty works, the flamboyant and frankly egocentric Mailer also edited Dissent (1953–69), cofounded the Village Voice, experimented in filmmaking, and made an unsuccessful bid for Mayor of New York (1969).

Maillol, Aristide (1861–1947)   French sculptor. At first a painter and part of the symbolist Nabi group, Maillol later turned to sculpture and became famous for his massive nude figures of women.

Mains sales, Les   See DIRTY HANDS.

Main Street (1920)   A novel by Sinclair LEWIS. The book that first established Lewis's reputation as an important writer is both a satire and an affectionate portrait of Gopher Prairie, a typical American town, which was undoubtedly suggested by Sauk Centre, Minnesota, where Lewis was born. The heroine, Carol Kennicott, chafes at the dullness and sterility of her existence as the wife of the local doctor, and she tries unsuccessfully to make the townspeople conscious of culture and refinement. For a time, she leaves to lead her own life but eventually returns to make a kind of peace with "Main Street." The book aroused considerable controversy; Meredith Nicholson attacked it in Let Main Street Alone! (1921), and Carolyn Wells burlesqued it in Ptomaine Street, The Tale of Warble Petticoat (1921).

Maintenon, Marquise de (Françoise d'Aubigné, 1635–1719)   Mistress and second wife of Louis XIV. After the death of her husband, the crippled poet SCARRON, Mme de Maintenon became governess to the children of Louis XIV and Mme de Montespan. In 1674 she became the royal mistress and in 1684 the morganatic wife of the king. A Protestant by birth, she is thought to have exercised some religious influence over Louis.

Main-Travelled Roads (1891)   A collection of short stories and sketches by Hamlin GARLAND. These tales, set in the Dakotas and Iowa, are local-color stories realistically told in a manner that owes much to William Dean HOWELLS. Most of the stories depict the grim lives of farmers who are at the mercy not only of the elements but of rapacious landlords as well. "Under the Lion's Paw," a much-anthologized piece, is one of the most characteristic.

Major Barbara (1905)   A play by George Bernard SHAW. Barbara Undershaft is a major in the Salvation Army; her father is the millionaire owner of an armament company. When Undershaft and a whisky distiller donate money to the Army, Barbara cannot stand the hypocrisy of accepting this "tainted money," and she resigns. While never fully agreeing with her father, Barbara comes to accept his theory that poverty, not sin, breeds crime. The poor are not blessed, says Undershaft, they are cursed. This was advanced social theory in 1905, when complacent Edwardian England accepted the poor as a necessary evil.

All money is tainted, says Shaw; the problem then is to remove the taint and have a fairer distribution. Even with its moral and economic message, *Major Barbara* has a wealth of comic and arresting characters.

Making of Americans, The (1925)
A novel by Gertrude STEIN. Written between 1906 and 1911, it presents the history of three generations of the author's own family and, by extension, a history of America. Composed in a more readable style than much of Stein's work, it nonetheless ignores such conventional fictional devices as dialogue, plot, and action. It is marked by frequent verbal repetition to suggest what Stein called a "continual present." Her own prototype in the book is the character Martha Hersland. The book has been presented numerous times in fifty-hour uninterrupted readings in both Canada and the U.S.

Maksimov, Vladimir Yemelyanovich (1930–   )
Soviet novelist. Born in Leningrad, Maksimov published his first poetry in 1956. His focus in prose on the lower segments of Soviet society, juvenile homes and the criminal underworld, has made him a provocative writer for the censor. His short story best known in the Soviet Union, "Zhiv chelovek" (1962; tr "A Man Survives," 1963), depicts the fugitive life of criminals, and although this work was published in Russia, Maksimov's later works found a readership only in SAMIZDAT. His novel *Sem dnei tvoreniya* (1971; tr *Seven Days of Creation*, 1974), which portrays not criminal but everyday life, first appeared in print in West Germany. In 1973 Maksimov was ousted from the Union of Soviet Writers and then forced to immigrate in 1974 to Paris, where he became editor of the Russian emigré literary magazine *Kontinent*. During the same year his novel *Proshchanie iz neotkuda* (tr *Farewell from Nowhere*, 1978) appeared in an emigré publication, followed in 1979 by *Kovcheg dlya nezvannykh* (tr *Ark for the Uncalled*, 1985), which deals with the disastrous artificial settlement of the Kurile Islands after their seizure from Japan.

Malachi
The last book of the OLD TESTAMENT; and the name of the prophet who composed it. Written after the period of rededication of the temple in Jerusalem (516 BC), the book connects the economic hardships of the times with the moral laxness of the people. The priesthood is specifically criticized for its failure to abide by the Holy Covenant. All people are reproved for general indifference and apathy and for adultery and marriage to heathens. The book ends with a promise of blessing to those who fear the Lord and foretells the coming of the prophet Elijah before the "great and dreadful day of the Lord" (Mal. 4:5).

Malade imaginaire, Le (The Imaginary Invalid, 1673)
A COMÉDIE-BALLET by MOLIÈRE, his last play. The hypochondriac Argan allows himself to be victimized by the doctors Purgon and Diafoirus and, in order to have a doctor in the family, tries to force his daughter to marry Diafoirus's son. His second wife, however, who in reality does not love him but his wealth, schemes to send the daughter off to a convent. To test his wife's love, Argan pretends death and thus discovers his wife's greed and his daughter's loyalty. A final ballet with interpolated Latin doggerel parodies the admission of a doctor to the Paris faculty.

Malamud, Bernard (1914–1986)
American novelist and short-story writer. Malamud was born and raised in Brooklyn, New York, the setting for much of his work. Along with Saul BELLOW, he is one of the great masters of the Jewish-American idiom, treating the foibles of the "little man" with humor and compassion, often with the recurring theme of the possibility of human change and renewal and with an awareness of Jewish solidarity on one hand and of universal human loneliness on the other. His first novel, *The Natural* (1952), about the rise and fall of a baseball player, draws an allegorical parallel between baseball and the quest for the Holy Grail. *The Assistant* (1957) deals with a poor New York Jewish shopkeeper and a gentile hold-up man whom he takes on as his assistant. *A New Life* (1961), set in a college community in the Pacific Northwest, deals with a New York professor in search of himself. *The Fixer* (1966; PULITZER PRIZE) is a poignant novel about a Russian Jew falsely accused by the Tsarist government of murder. *The Tenants* (1971) deals with the tempestuous relationship of two writers, one a Jew, the other a black. In perhaps his most personal novel, *Dubin's Lives* (1979), Malamud portrays the private torments of a biographer in his late fifties. It was followed by another novel, *God's Grace*, in 1981. Malamud's collections of stories include *The Magic Barrel* (1958), *Idiots First* (1963), *Pictures of Fidelman* (1969), and *Rembrandt's Hat* (1973). He was awarded the American Academy and Institute of Arts and Sciences Gold Medal for fiction in 1984.

Malaprop, Mrs. (fr Fr, mal à propos, "out of place")
A character in Sheridan's comedy THE RIVALS, noted for her blunders in the use of words. "As headstrong as an *allegory* on the banks of the Nile" is one of Mrs. Malaprop's gross misapplications. She has given us the word *malapropism* to denote such mistakes.

Malatesta (Ital, "evil head")
The name of an Italian family that dominated the city and environs of Rimini during the Renaissance. The Malatesta symbol was an elephant. Of the several CONDOTTIERI it produced, the most infamous was Sigismondo Pandolfo Malatesta (1417–68), who combined a love of learning and patronage of the arts with a taste for cruelty and tyranny that earned him univer-

sal hatred. It was an earlier Malatesta, Giovanni, who murdered the lovers Paolo and Francesca, an event recalled by Dante in the famous episode of the *Inferno*.

Malavoglia, I (The Malavoglias, 1881)   A novel by Giovanni VERGA, also known in translation as *The House by the Medlar Tree*. It is celebrated for its sympathetic and perceptive portrayal of a Sicilian fisherfolk family (the Malavoglias) and its vivid depiction of the provincial town (Aci-Trezza) where they live. The Malavoglias are a family seemingly doomed by an ineluctable fate. When their vessel sinks, drowning Padron 'Ntoni's son, his grandson 'Ntoni joins the navy to support the family. The upshot of his first acquaintance with the world outside Trezza is his rebellion against family traditions. He refuses to continue the fishing trade, eventually refusing to work altogether. As a result, the family's meager fortune rapidly declines. 'Ntoni's mother and younger brother die, his proud grandfather Padron 'Ntoni dies in a pauper hospital, and 'Ntoni is forced by circumstances to leave Trezza without hope or destination.

Malcolm   See MACBETH.

Maldon, Battle of (late 10th century)   Old English poem, a fragment of 325 lines in ALLITERATIVE VERSE. In the heroic style, it describes the unsuccessful stand (991) of the English under Byrhtnoth against a Viking invasion.

Malebranche, Nicolas (1638–1715)   French philosopher, scientist, and theologian. Malebranche is known as one of the best prose writers of his century. In his principal work, *La Recherche de la vérité* (*The Search for Truth*, 1674–75), Malebranche took issue with the metaphysics of DESCARTES, though admiring his physics and method. Denying the interaction of spirit and matter, Malebranche declared that God arranges an exact correspondence between our notions of material objects and the motions of the objects themselves, for He is the sole source and cause of both. This ingenious solution to the Cartesian dualism antagonized the JANSENISTS and Bossuet, among others, because of its pantheistic overtones, and embroiled Malebranche in endless controversy; the doctrine also won him many disciples, including LEIBNITZ.

Malentendu, Le (1944; tr Cross Purpose, 1948)   A play by Albert CAMUS. It exposes the different ways in which men and women fail to face themselves and communicate with each other in their common plight before the unresponsiveness of the universe.

Malevich, Kazimir Severinovich (1879–1935) Russian painter. In 1913 Malevich derived from cubism the rigid geometrical abstractions called suprematism, in which all painting is reduced to the use of the square, the triangle, the circle, and the cross. *White Square on White Background* (1919) illustrates the subtlety that this simplification can attain in its extreme manifestation.

Malherbe, François de (1555–1628)   French writer. Malherbe, the official court poet, became the virtual literary dictator of France during the early 17th century. Of neoclassic tendencies, he advocated a poetry of order, rationality, and simplicity; opposing all colorful eccentricity in verse, he condemned the affectation, emotionalism, and decorative qualities of the late-baroque poets. Better known for his influence than for his own writings, Malherbe wrote the poem *Consolation de Monsieur du Périer sur la mort de sa fille* (*Consolation of Monsieur de Périer upon the Death of His Daughter*, 1598) and a sycophantic *Ode* (1600) to Marie de Médicis.

Malign Fiesta   See HUMAN AGE, THE.

Mallarmé, Stéphane (1842–1898)   French poet. Mallarmé is known as one of the leaders of the SYMBOLISTS and the formulator of their aesthetic theories. His own work shows the influence of BAUDELAIRE, POE, VERLAINE, and the PRE-RAPHAELITE BROTHERHOOD. Marked by elliptical phrases, Mallarmé's poetry employs condensed figures and unorthodox syntax. Each poem is built about a central symbol, idea, or metaphor and consists of subordinate images that illustrate and help to develop the idea. Often obscure, his work never fails to be evocative and exciting. *L'Après-midi d'un faune* (*The Afternoon of a Faun*, 1876), which inspired Debussy to write his well-known *Prélude*; LE CYGNE; *Hérodiade*; and "Le Tombeau d'Edgar Poe" are outstanding examples of Mallarmé's method.

Malle, Louis (1932–   )   French film director and scenarist of the NEW WAVE. Malle got an early start in film as an assistant to Robert BRESSON. He then codirected with Jacques Cousteau *The Silent World* (1956). In his subsequent films as an independent director, *Les Amants* (1958), *Zazie dans le métro* (1960), *Le Feu follet* (1963), *Le Souffle au coeur* (1971), and *Lacombe, Lucien* (1974), Malle produced a series of penetrating portraits, in which he frequently upset notions of conventional morality to expose often surprising new perspectives. His first American production was *Pretty Baby* (1978), set in a New Orleans brothel; it was followed by the critically successful *Atlantic City* (1980). In 1981 he directed *My Dinner with André*.

Mallea, Eduardo (1903–c1982)   Argentinian novelist, essayist, and short-story writer. Throughout his work, Mallea's theme is the spiritual apathy that he believes to be smothering modern life. He and his characters are involved in an existential pursuit of meaning and authenticity in life. Among his most important works of fiction are *Fiesta en noviembre* (1938), *Todo verdor perecerá* (1941), *Los enemigos del alma* (1950), and *Chaves* (1953), all of which are translated, along with other stories, in *All Green Shall Perish* (1966). His most completely developed character —perhaps one of the most finely drawn characters in modern literature—is Agata Cruz, the desolate, hopelessly lonely protagonist of *Todo verdor perecerá*. *Historia de una pasión Argentina* (1937; tr *History of an Argentine Passion*, 1983) and *La vida blanca* (1960) are studies of the Argentine mind. His *Obras completas* appeared in two volumes in 1965.

Mallet-Joris, Françoise (formerly Françoise Mallet, 1930–) Belgian-born French novelist. While still in her teens, Mallet-Joris wrote *Le Rempart des Beguines* (1950; tr *The Illusionist*, 1952), the story of a girl of fifteen who becomes the lesbian lover of her father's mistress. Like its sequel, *La Chambre rouge* (1955; tr *The Red Room*, 1956), it shows the defensive cruelty and cynicism that can overtake a love relationship. *Les Mensonges* (1956; tr *House of Lies*, 1957) and *L'Empire Céleste* (1958; tr *Café Céleste*, 1959) use a Flemish realism of detail and color to expose tragedies of self-delusion. Her other works include the elaborately structured *Les Personnages* (1961; tr *The Favorite*, 1962), set in the time of Louis XIII; *Cordélia* (1956; tr 1965), a collection of short novels; *Les Signes et les prodiges* (1960; tr *Signs and Wonders*, 1967), about the war with Algeria; *Le Jeu du souterrain* (1973; tr *The Underground Game*, 1974); *J'Aurais voulu jouer de l'accordéon* (1975); and *Allégra* (1976).

Malleus Maleficarum (Hammer of Witches, 1484) One of the most famous books of witchcraft and black magic, published in Cologne, by Henry Kramer and James Sprenger.

Mallison, Charles (or Chick Mallison) A character in several works by William FAULKNER. The nephew of Gavin STEVENS, Chick grows from childhood to young manhood in four of Faulkner's novels. As a child, he narrates part of *The Town*; as a sixteen-year-old boy he is instrumental in proving Lucas Beauchamp innocent of murder in *Intruder in the Dust*; and as a young man, he narrates part of *The Mansion* and is an interested observer in KNIGHT'S GAMBIT.

Malone, Edmund (1741–1812) Irish literary critic and Shakespearean scholar. Malone left Ireland for London to devote himself to literature and became a part of the literary and political scene, counting among his friends Dr. JOHNSON, Sir Joshua REYNOLDS, Bishop Percy, Edmund BURKE, and Horace WALPOLE. He was the first literary critic to establish a chronology of Shakespeare's plays in his *Attempt to ascertain the order in which the plays of Shakespeare were written* (1778), this work supplementing Johnson's edition of Shakespeare (1765). His own edition of Shakespeare was published in 1790. He also published an edition of Reynolds's works (1797) and an edition of DRYDEN (1800). A shrewd literary detective, he was one of the first to doubt the authenticity of Thomas CHATTERTON's Rowley poems and the purported Shakespearean works of William Ireland. He was probably the ablest research scholar of his day and provided invaluable aid to BOSWELL in his final draft of Johnson's biography.

Malone Dies (Malone meurt, 1951; tr 1956) A novel by Samuel BECKETT. As Malone, a bum, lies dying, alone in bed in a strange room, he remembers his past. By the end we realize that Malone was actually a murderer and that in his pathetic, senile, lonely state, he is an image for the condition of all men. Beckett uses the STREAM OF CONSCIOUSNESS technique throughout. The novel is part of the trilogy that also includes MOLLOY and THE UNNAMABLE. The three were published together as *Three Novels* (1959).

Malory, Sir Thomas (c1408–1471) English writer. Malory is the author of LE MORTE D'ARTHUR, the finest medieval prose collection of Arthurian romance. It was completed (c1469) while he was in prison; it was printed in 1485. Very little is known about Malory's life except for his rendering of the Arthurian romances. He was a member of Parliament (1445) and in 1451 was imprisoned for various offenses and remained in jail until his death.

Malraux, [Georges] André (1901–1976) French novelist and critic. In 1923 Malraux went to Indochina as an archaeologist but soon became active in the revolutionary upheavals in China. Returning to Europe on the eve of World War II, he sided with the Communists and other left-wing groups involved in anti-Fascist movements, an affinity that carried him into the Spanish Civil War as an aviator commanding a squadron in the Republican air force. He fought the Nazis in 1940 in the tank corps, was captured, escaped to join the Resistance, was recaptured, and escaped again. After the war, he allied himself with Charles DE GAULLE and, under the Fifth Republic, held the position of minister of culture.

Malraux's novels, like his life, are filled with adventures and political involvement, combined with a brooding pessimism about the destiny of Western man. The theme of social revolution dominates *Les Conquérants* (1928; tr *The Conquerors*, 1929), set in Canton, China, during the 1925 insurrection; MAN'S FATE; and *L'Espoir* (1937; tr *Man's Hope*, 1938), which takes place during the Spanish Civil War. Such revolutions are used as a symbol of oppressed man's struggle for dignity through revolt against his fate. By braving death for the life of their revolutionary doctrines, the leading characters transcend the individual self and accept a fate that binds them to all men. *La Voie royale* (1930; tr *The Royal Way*, 1935) is an intellectual thriller about two adventurers who flee a stagnant Europe and court death in the Indochinese jungle while trying to remove ancient religious sculptures. In *Le Temps du mépris* (1935; tr *Days of Wrath*, 1936), Malraux describes an underground Communist leader in Hitler's Germany, while *Les Noyers de l'Altenburg* (1943; tr *The Walnut Trees of Altenburg*, 1952) is a novel of ideas about human potential in the two world wars. Malraux departed from the fictional, storytelling aspect of his art in *La Tentation de l'Occident* (1926; tr *The Temptation of the West*, 1961), which is in the form of an ideological exchange between a Frenchman living in China and a Chinese in France who gives a lucid indictment of European sensibility.

After 1941 Malraux's career involved him more in political action and art criticism than in purely literary activity. As well as several volumes of autobiography, he wrote *The*

Psychology of Art (3 vols, 1947–50; adapted as *The Voices of Silence*, 1951), in which he argues that art—and not any social or moral system—is humanity's only permanent expression of the will to triumph over fate.

Maltese Falcon, The (1930)   A detective novel by Dashiell HAMMETT. It was one of the first examples of HARD-BOILED FICTION, and it marked the first appearance of Hammett's famous private eye, Sam SPADE. Dealing with the theft of a jewel-encrusted falcon, which originally belonged to the Knights TEMPLARS, the story was as romantic in content as it was realistic and tough in manner.

Malthus, Thomas Robert (1766–1834)   English political economist. In 1798, the year that he became a curate of the Church of England, Malthus published *An Essay on the Principle of Population as it affects the Future Improvement of Society, with Remarks on the Speculation of Mr. Godwin, M. Condorcet, and other Writers*, in which he set forth the Malthusian doctrine that population increases in a geometric ratio, while the means of subsistence increases in an arithmetic ratio, and that crime, disease, war, and vice are necessary checks on population. In the 1803 revision of his work, Malthus suggested moral restraint as a fifth check. Malthus's works also include *An Inquiry into the Nature and Progress of Rent* (1815) and *Principles of Political Economy* (1820).

Malvolio   In Shakespeare's TWELFTH NIGHT, the steward of Olivia. Malvolio is a smug, pompous fool who secretly aspires to his mistress's love. Annoyed by his conceit and priggishness, Sir Toby Belch, Sir Andrew Aguecheek, and Maria concoct a scheme to turn Olivia against him. Maria forges a letter in the handwriting of Olivia, leading Malvolio to believe that his mistress returns his love. He falls into the trap, and, when Olivia shows astonishment at his absurd conduct, he keeps quoting parts of the letter until he is shut up in a dark room as a lunatic.

Mamelukes (fr Arab, *mamluc*, "slave")   The slaves from the Caucasus in Egypt. Formed into a standing army, in 1254 they raised one of their body to the supreme power. They reigned over Egypt until 1517, when they were overthrown by the Turkish sultan Selim I. The country, though nominally under a Turkish viceroy, was subsequently governed by twenty-four Mameluke beys. In 1811 the Pasha of Egypt, Muhammed Ali, by a wholesale massacre, annihilated the Mamelukes.

Mamet, David (1947–   )   American playwright. Mamet made his Broadway debut in 1977 with *American Buffalo* (1975), a play about three small-time bungling crooks who plot the theft of a coin collection. In this and in *Sexual Perversity in Chicago* (1974), which features the various seductions of two couples, Mamet concentrates less on plot and action than on developing a vivid sense of character and atmosphere through the use of naturalistic, often profane language. His ear for the sounds and rhythms of street talk gives his plotters in *American Buffalo* a kind of pathetic eloquence. In *A Life in the Theater* (1977), two actors, one old and one young, reveal themselves to each other and the audience only in snippets as they try on and discard a variety of dramatic parts. Two other plays, *The Woods* (1977) and *Lone Canoe* (1979), were followed by *Glengarry Glen Ross* (1984), a PULITZER Prize winner, an embittered yet compassionate look at the savagely competitive world of a Chicago real-estate office.

mammon   An Aramaic word used in the NEW TESTAMENT to personify riches and worldliness; also, the god of avarice or cupidity. The word occurs in Matt. 6:24 and Luke 16:13 to represent the opposite of a God-fearing life: "No man can serve two masters: for either he will hate one and love the other; or else he will hold to one and despise the other. Ye cannot serve God and mammon." Both Spenser, with his cave of Mammon in the THE FAERIE QUEENE, and Milton, by identifying him with Vulcan in PARADISE LOST, make Mammon the epitome of the evils of wealth.

Mammon, Sir Epicure   A wealthy lecher in Jonson's comedy THE ALCHEMIST.

Man against the Sea   See MUTINY ON THE BOUNTY.

Man against the Sky, The (1916)   The title poem of a book of verse by Edwin Arlington ROBINSON. In this long elegiac work, man is symbolized as a lonely figure seen against the sky at sunset, the sunset itself representing death, World War I, and the universe described by modern science. Robinson examines five creeds that explain life and death, rejects them, and finally asserts a simple stoicism as a way of life.

Man and Superman (1905)   A play by George Bernard SHAW, subtitled *A Comedy and a Philosophy*. The comedy is the eternal pursuit of the male by the female; the philosophy is Shaw's brand of religion, creative evolution. These two elements are coordinated in the brilliant, discursive *Don Juan in Hell* scene in Act III.

John Tanner, rational, morally passionate, and defiant of tradition, is plotted for, chased after, and caught by Ann Whitefield, who, like most Shavian women, is instinctive, hypocritical, charming, and triumphant.

While in flight from Ann, Tanner dreams the scene of Don Juan in Hell. In a long, witty dialogue, Don Juan (Tanner), Doña Ana (Ann), the Statue from Mozart's opera *Don Giovanni*, and the Devil discuss the questions so far evoked by the action of the play. Don Juan describes the moral passion or "Life Force" that drives the universe forward. He explains to the sneering Devil that it is the idea of God's depending on man to get his will done that gives human life meaning. The superman of the title is the person who is able to detect and follow the will of the universe while suppressing his own. Don Juan is a superman; Tanner is not.

Man and Superman is usually performed without the Don Juan scene; however, the work has its essential unity in this episode. *Don Juan in Hell* has been acted separately and also has been given many dramatic readings.

Manchu   See CH'ING DYNASTY.

Manciple's Tale, The   One of THE CANTERBURY TALES of Geoffrey CHAUCER. In the *Prologue*, the Host and the Manciple tease the Cook for being drunk. Finally the Manciple shares his own wine with the Cook and begins his story, based on Ovid's version of a popular folk tale. The archer Phebus has a white crow that can sing as sweetly as a nightingale and can speak human language. One day the crow reports to Phebus that his beloved wife has entertained a lover in his absence. Phebus kills her with an arrow but afterward breaks his bow in remorse and grief. Then he turns bitterly on the crow for having disturbed, unasked, his unsuspicious bliss; he plucks the bird's feathers, turns him black, takes away his power of speech, changes his sweet song to a raucous croak, and flings him to the Devil, thus accounting for the present appearance of all crows and serving as a warning to all tattle-tales.

mandala   (Sans, "circle; round")   In BUDDHISM and HINDUISM, a mystical symbol in the form of a circle, a square, or some combination of a circle and other geometrical figures, used in meditation. It is generally associated with the representation of a deity or deities in a symmetrical design. The mandala symbol and its recurrence in many different cultures was studied extensively by the psychologist C. G. JUNG, who believed its appearance in dreams signified a stage of unity and balance in the process of individuation. It is also the name for each of the ten books of the RIG VEDA.

Mandarins, Les   (1954; tr 1957)   A novel by Simone de BEAUVOIR, which was awarded the PRIX GONCOURT. The novel, a ROMAN À CLEF, portrays leading existentialists during and after World War II. It includes a fictionalized version of the argument between Jean-Paul SARTRE and Albert CAMUS over the subjugation of philosophical ideals to the need to act.

Mandel, Eli[as] [Wolf]   (1922–   )   Canadian poet, editor, and literary critic. In *Fuseli Poems* (1960) and *An Idiot Joy* (1967), Mandel reveals a metaphysical cast of mind, much preoccupied with guilt and fear. His later works, especially *Out of Place* (1977), evoke his Jewish boyhood in an isolated Saskatchewan community. He has edited contemporary Canadian verse and a collection of writings about Canada, *Contexts of Canadian Criticism* (1971). His personal stance as a critic is the subject of the essays in *Another Time* (1977).

Mandelshtam, Osip Emilyevich   (1891–1938) Russian poet. Belonging to the early Soviet period, Mandelshtam's poetry is a model of the classically concise and finished work striven for in ACMEISM. His output was small, mostly contained in the collections *Kamyen* (*Stone*, 1913) and *Tristia* (1922). His obvious lack of enthusiasm for the Soviet regime ended in his arrest during the purges of the 1930s. He is believed to have died in a concentration camp.

Mander, Jane   (1877–1949)   New Zealand novelist. Mander's novels present vivid documents of rural and small-town New Zealand life. They reveal a concern for social and intellectual issues, which, at the time of their publication, made Mander a target for hostile criticism. Her best-known and most highly praised novel, *The Story of a New Zealand River* (1920), deals with the adjustment of an Englishwoman in a remote timber-mill settlement. *Allen Adair* (1925), a more skillfully constructed, less melodramatic novel, presents her hero's struggle against the middle-class aspirations of his family.

Mandeville, The Travels of Sir John   (c1371) A famous book of travels. It purports to be a guidebook for pilgrims to Palestine, but it goes on to describe the marvels that the author claims to have seen in Africa and the Orient: some real, such as the Pyramids; some highly fictitious, such as the people with no heads but eyes in their shoulders. According to the work itself, Sir John Mandeville (or Maundeville) was born at St. Albans, left England in 1322, roamed widely, and finally came under a new name to live at Liège in 1343, writing his *Travels* about 1357. He has been variously identified with French writers of Liège, such as Jean de Bourgoigne à la Barbe (d 1372) and Jean d'Outremeuse. Actually, the work was probably originally compiled (1366–71) in French, from early 14th-century travel books, and soon translated into Latin and English.

mandrake   An herb found in southern Europe and northern Africa. Its globose yellow berries were once believed to have aphrodisiac powers. The root of the mandrake often divides in two and presents a rude appearance of a man. In ancient times, human figures were cut out of the root and wonderful virtues ascribed to them, such as the production of fecundity in women (Gen. 30:14–16). It was said that mandrakes could not be uprooted without producing fatal effects upon the uprooter; and so a cord would be fixed to the root and tied around a dog's neck, and the dog, being chased, would draw out the mandrake and, theoretically, die. Moreover, it was believed that a small dose of mandrake made a person vain of his beauty, while a large one made him an idiot, and also that, when the mandrake was uprooted, it uttered a scream, in explanation of which Thomas Newton, in his *Herball to the Bible*, wrote, "It is supposed to be a creature having life, engendered under the earth of the seed of some dead person put to death for murder." Mandrakes were sometimes called love apples, from the old notion that they excited amorous inclinations; hence, Venus is called Mandragoritis, and the Emperor Julian, in his epistles, tells Calixenes that he drank mandrake juice nightly as a love potion. The narcotic and stupefying properties of the herb were well known to the ancients, and it was commonly said of a very indolent and sleepy man that he had eaten mandrake.

Manet, Edouard (1832–1883)   French painter. Manet is generally regarded as the originator of IMPRESSIONISM, although he never participated in the eight impressionist exhibitions between 1874 and 1886. He was, however, closely aligned with the impressionist painters, particularly MONET, and was one of the first French painters to abandon traditional three-dimensional uses of light and shadow in favor of subtle patches of color against a flat background. As early as 1863, he had executed two of his greatest and most controversial works: *Déjeuner sur l'herbe* and *Olympia*. Manet's painting was regarded as shocking and heretical, so much so that his friend Émile ZOLA was dismissed from his job as an art critic (1866) for praising Manet's honesty and originality. Despite nearly constant attacks on his work, he did manage to show his paintings in the annual Salons. The informal still lifes, landscapes, and scenes from contemporary life, for example *The Père Lathuile Restaurant* (1879), that he painted near the end of his career are among the finest examples of impressionist painting.

Man for All Seasons, A (1961)   A play by Robert Bolt (1924–   ). It is based on the life of Sir Thomas MORE and his controversy with Henry VIII.

Manfred (1817)   A dramatic poem by Lord BYRON. The hero, Count Manfred, sells himself to the Prince of Darkness and lives wholly without human sympathies in splendid solitude among the Alps.

Man Friday   A faithful, versatile, and willing attendant, from the young savage in DEFOE's novel ROBINSON CRUSOE. Found by Crusoe on a Friday, he was kept as his servant and companion on the desert island.

Manhattan Transfer (1925)   A novel by John DOS PASSOS. The book presents a picture of life in New York City during the 1920s through passages of impressionistic description and the simultaneous stories of several people from varying levels of society. The title, taken from the railroad station where people changed trains to get to and from the metropolis, is in itself suggestive of the shifting, variegated life of the city. Although the novel has no central hero, Jimmy Herf, a journalist divorced by his actress wife, is perhaps the character of greatest interest. Only slightly less important are Bud Korpenning, a young man who fails in the city and commits suicide; Joe Harland, a Wall Street gambler, who loses his fortune and becomes a beggar; and Ellen Thatcher Ogelthorpe, Herf's former wife, who is a successful actress but loses the man she loves and is unable to find happiness. The final effect of this panoramic impression of a swarming metropolis is one of frustration and defeat.

Mani (also Manes or Manichaeus, c216–c277)   The founder of Manichaeism, born in Persia. After repeated visions of an angel that was his double, Mani declared himself the prophet of a new religion. Although he drew heavily from aspects of Zoroastrianism, he was regarded as a heretic until Sapor I took the Persian throne in 240. Under Sapor's reign (240–72), Mani enjoyed considerable prestige and gained a substantial following. After 272 he was persecuted, and he died a martyr. He regarded himself as the last and greatest prophet of God, in a succession that included ZOROASTER, BUDDHA, and JESUS. See MANICHAEANS.

Manichaeans   Followers of the Oriental dualistic religion of Manichaeism, founded by MANI. Their principal doctrine concerns the conflict between Light, or goodness, and Darkness, identified with chaos or evil: the spirit of man was the creation of God, hence good, whereas the body was the creation of SATAN, hence evil. During the life of man, good and evil are merged, but ultimately, with the aid of a redeemer, man can achieve the subjugation of the body by the soul. Extreme asceticism and sexual abstinence were a means to this end. The system drew on diverse elements of ancient Babylonian and Persian nature worship, as well as aspects of Zoroastrianism and Christianity.

manifest destiny   A 19th-century slogan that expressed the conviction of many Americans that the U.S. was destined to rule the entire North American continent. The earliest known appearance of the phrase was in an editorial (1845) in *The United States Magazine and Democratic Review* by John L. O'Sullivan, who wrote that foreign powers opposed the annexation of Texas in order to hinder "the fulfilment of our manifest destiny to overspread the continent allotted by Providence for the free development of our yearly multiplying millions."

Manifold, John [Streeter] (1915–   )   Australian poet, folklorist, and musicologist. The influence of such different figures as "Banjo" PATERSON and Bertolt BRECHT is evident in the variety of Manifold's verse. *Collected Verse* (1978) demonstrates his range, from bush ballads to intricate sonnet sequences.

Manilov   In Nikolay GOGOL's novel DEAD SOULS, a character wholly given over to idle dreaming. The term *Manilovism* has since been used to describe indulgence in such vague reverie.

man in the iron mask   A mysterious French prisoner. He was held for over forty years by Louis XIV at Pignerol and other prisons, ultimately dying in the Bastille (November 19, 1703), with his identity still undisclosed. His name was given as "Marchiali" when he was buried. Subsequently, many conjectures as to his real identity were advanced. One possibility was General du Bulonde, who in 1691 raised the siege of Cuneo against the order of Catinat. In 1891 Captain Bazeriès published in *Le Temps* translations of some cipher dispatches, apparently showing that this was the solution, but Bulonde would have had to have taken the place of some earlier masked prisoner, for *l'homme au masque de fer* was at Pignerol in 1666 and was transferred to the island of St. Marguerite twenty years later, well before the siege of Cuneo.

Other persons who have been suggested are a twin brother of Louis XIV—or, perhaps, an illegitimate elder half brother, whose father is given as either Cardinal Mazarin or the duke of Buckingham—and Louis, duc de Vermandois, the natural son of Louis XIV by De la Vallière, who was imprisoned for life because he gave the dauphin a box on the ears.

Among the less likely possibilities that have been put forward are the duke of Monmouth; Avedick, an Armenian Patriarch; Fouquet, the disgraced French minister of finance; the duc de Beaufort, who disappeared at the siege of Candia in 1669; and Mattioli's secretary, Jean de Gonzague.

Since the private papers of Louis XIV and the correspondence of his minister Louvois and Barbezieux were made available to Franz Funck-Brentano, it has become apparent that the man in the iron mask was Count Girolamo Mattioli, minister to the duke of Mantua, a theory now widely accepted. In 1678 he acted treacherously toward Louis in refusing to give up the fortress of Casale—the key to Italy—after signing a treaty promising to do so, and in consequence was lured onto French soil, captured, and imprisoned at Pignerol.

It was in 1790 that the Abbé Soulavie put forth the theory that the mysterious personage was a twin brother of Louis XIV. This supposition was accepted in tragedies on the subject by Zschokke in German and Fournier in French. In Dumas's romance *The Iron Mask*—sometimes published separately but originally a part of his *Vicomte de Bragelonne*—a conspiracy to substitute the Man in the Iron Mask for his royal brother is all but successful.

manitou   A great spirit of the American Indians. The word is Algonquin and is used of both the great good spirit (Gitche-Manito) and the great evil spirit (Matche-Manito). The good spirit is symbolized by an egg, and the evil one by a serpent. (See Longfellow, *Hiawatha*, xiv.)

Manley, Mary de la Rivière (1672–1724)   English playwright and political pamphleteer. Manley is chiefly remembered as the author of *Secret Memoirs and Manners of Several Persons of Quality of Both Sexes from the New Atalantis* (1709, usually known as *The New Atalantis*) and its continuation, *Memoirs of Europe* (1710), both scandalous, licentious chronicles of contemporary politics and society; for these two works, she was arrested but subsequently released. She was active as a political writer during the Tory regime of 1710–14 and was well known to Jonathan Swift, whom she succeeded as editor of the periodical *Examiner* (1711). She was also the author of many plays and a romanticized autobiography, *Rivella* (1714).

Mann, Heinrich (1871–1950)   German novelist, elder brother of Thomas MANN. At the time of World War I, Mann's political and social attitudes were militantly liberal. This led to a serious rift with his still-conservative brother. Many of Heinrich Mann's novels satirize Germany's declining bourgeoisie and its unfounded nationalistic fervor; his trilogy *Das Kaiserreich* (*The Empire*, 1918–25) depicts the weaknesses of German society under Wilhelm II. Stripped of his German citizenship in 1933, he lived for a time in France and later in the U.S., near his brother. After World War II, Heinrich Mann hoped to return to Germany and in 1949 received an academic appointment in East Germany, but he died in Los Angeles before he was able to assume his post. His caricature of a corrupt and tyrannical schoolmaster, *Professor Unrat oder das Ende eines Tyrannen* (1905; tr *Small Town Tyrant*, 1944), was the basis for Josef Von Sternberg's famous film *The Blue Angel* (1930).

Mann, Horace (1796–1859)   American lawyer, educator, and legislator. After a childhood of hardship, Mann became a lawyer and practiced in Massachusetts, where he served as state representative (1827–33) and state senator (1833–37). In 1837 he turned from politics to education. As secretary of the state board of education, he labored successfully to improve the public schools, increase teacher salaries, and set up teacher-training schools.

After a spell in the House of Representatives, where he held firm antislavery views, he was appointed president of Antioch College. Although he struggled for four years to maintain the ideal of a liberal education for all, the college was sold for debt in 1859. In addition to twelve *Annual Reports*, Mann published *Lectures on Education* (1845).

Mann, Thomas (1875–1955)   German novelist and essayist. Awarded the NOBEL PRIZE in Literature in 1929, Mann is known for his many narrative psychological studies of the artistic temperament, for his extensive and penetrating explorations into Greek, Hebrew, Germanic, and Eastern mythology, and for the enlightened literary and social criticism found in both his imaginative and his discussive works. As a boy, Mann early became aware of the existence of two worlds between which his own life was divided: the solid, bourgeois, commercial world of his family and the more mysterious, spiritual world of his own artistic inclinations. This awareness in turn developed into a dualistic pattern of thought, which, in many variations and refinements, followed him throughout his career. The terms *Geist* ("spirit") and *Leben* ("life") are used to define this dualism: the realm of art, of imagination and the mind, of the decadent artistic personality, on the one hand, and that of everyday reality, of the relatively wholesome bourgeois temperament, on the other. The early influence of SCHOPENHAUER, WAGNER, NIETZSCHE, and the German romantic poets strengthened the belief that ordinary life and activity were not adequate for the artist's inner needs. In his first novel, BUDDENBROOKS, Mann treats this problem on a large scale, but his personal feelings are seen more clearly in the story TONIO KRÖGER, which, though it affirms art, is filled with a nostalgic longing for the solidity of bourgeois life. Mann wanted very much to affirm both spirit and life, and he achieved at least a fictional synthesis between them in his next novel, *Königliche Hoheit* (1909; tr *Royal Highness*, 1916), the story of a decadent young prince who eventually comes to grips with reality in his marriage to a rich but untitled American girl. Soon afterwards, however, Mann again began treating the tragic potentialities of artistic decadence, especially in the great novella DEATH IN VENICE; it was in this work also that his explorations of the vague borderline area between the psychological and the occult and of the continuing relevance to modern reality of ancient, mythical forces and configurations began to assume the form that became definitive for his later writing.

Concerned as he was with problems of a primarily spiritual nature, Mann remained aloof from the political controversies centering about World War I, though urged by his brother Heinrich MANN to make a liberal commitment. The essays in his *Betrachtungen eines Unpolitischen* (*Reflections of an Unpolitical Man*, 1918) reflect his attitude at this time, as does his novel THE MAGIC MOUNTAIN, in which political themes are treated as little more than a symbol for Europe's spiritual and intellectual condition. But the rise of Fascism and Nazism soon obliged him to take a more interested and liberal stand politically, which may be seen both in essays, such as the anti-Nazi *Appel an die Vernunft* (1930; tr *Appeal to Reason*, 1942), and in stories, such as MARIO AND THE MAGICIAN. In 1933 HITLER's government forced Mann into exile; in 1939 he came to the U.S. and in 1944 became an American citizen. During these years, he was active in many liberal pursuits, of which wartime broadcasts to the German people were only one. His post-World War II novel DOKTOR FAUSTUS reflects a deep and intense concern for the political fate of his native Germany. After the war, he made frequent trips to Europe; he died in Switzerland.

Mann's other important works include *Leiden und Größe der Meister* (1933; tr *The Sufferings and Greatness of the Masters*, 1947), literary essays; THE BELOVED RETURNS, a novel; *Die vertauschten Köpfe* (1940; tr *The Transposed Heads*, 1941), a short novel based on an Indian legend; JOSEPH AND HIS BROTHERS, a tetralogy of novels; and CONFESSIONS OF FELIX KRULL: CONFIDENCE MAN, a novel.

manna   The food miraculously supplied to the Children of Israel during their forty years of wandering in the Sinai Peninsula. What they took for God's gift is now believed to have been the sweet secretions of various insects that feed on desert trees.

mannerism   In general, an exaggerated adherence to a particular manner or style. More particularly, the term refers to a style originating in Italy and current in 16th-century European art and architecture. In mannerism, which was a reaction to the canons of the High Renaissance, imbalance and conflict became central; exaggeration and effects of illusion were important as methods of expression; and, in painting, spatial distortion and elongation of the human figure were used to emphasize the effect of

struggle. Elements of mannerism are evident in the work of CARAVAGGIO and El GRECO, among others. By the end of the century, mannerism had been superseded by the BAROQUE, a style that it directly foreshadowed.

Manning, Frederic (1882–1935)   Australian novelist. Manning's realistic *Her Privates We* (1930) is among the best novels in English on World War I. Private Bourne tries to understand himself and the chaotic war, but, like countless others, he is killed in action.

Manningoe, Nancy   A character in William Faulkner's short story "That Evening Sun Go Down" and in his REQUIEM FOR A NUN. Although it is mentioned in THE SOUND AND THE FURY that Nancy is murdered by her husband after the end of "That Evening Sun," she is resurrected by Faulkner to play an important part in *Requiem for a Nun*, in which she is Temple DRAKE's confidante and nursemaid to the latter's children. Because Nancy's past is as sordid as Temple's, Nancy is the one person whom Temple can trust. Unlike Temple, however, Nancy is able to face the question of guilt and responsibility honestly.

Mannyng, Robert (or Robert of Brunne, c1264–c1340)   English poet and chronicler, member of a Gilbertine monastery after 1288. Mannyng's works popularize religious and historical material in an early Middle English dialect of great importance in linguistic history. His best-known work is *Handlying Synne* (c1303), an adaptation in verse of William of Wadington's *Manuel des Pechiez* in which the homilies are illustrated with legends and anecdotes that give a vivid picture of his times. He also wrote a chronicle, *The Story of England* (c1338), based on WACE and Peter of Longtoft (d 1307?), continuing English history through the death of Edward I.

Man of Feeling, The (1771)   A novel by Henry Mackenzie (1745–1831), also used as an epithet for the author. The "man of feeling" is Harley, a sensitive, bashful, kind-hearted, and sentimental hero. The novel follows the style of Laurence Sterne in its structure of episodic adventures, keyed to moods and sentiments, and in its imitation of the dreamlike fantasy of *Tristram Shandy*. A companion piece, *The Man of the World* (1773), is the portrait of a villain.

Man of Law's Tale, The   One of THE CANTERBURY TALES of Geoffrey CHAUCER, based on an episode in Nicholas Trivet's *Anglo-Norman Chronicle* (c1335) and on John GOWER's version of it in his *Confessio Amantis* (1390). It is written in RHYME ROYAL and told in the manner of a medieval legend, Constance (or Custance) representing an extreme degree of resignation or uncomplaining fortitude. The Sultan of Syria becomes a Christian in order to wed Constance, daughter of the Emperor of Rome. His mother, however, successfully schemes to set Constance adrift in a rudderless boat. She is washed ashore in Northumberland, where a rejected suitor frames a murder charge against her. A miracle proves her innocence to King Alla (or Ella), who then makes her his queen. In his absence, she bears his son, Maurice, but the king's mother, anxious to rid the land of Christianity, has Constance set adrift once more with the child. They are rescued by a Roman senator and live with his family, until Alla, who had killed his mother as soon as he learned what had happened, discovers them by chance. The reunited family then return to live happily in Northumberland.

Man of Mode, The, or, Sir Fopling Flutter (1676) A comedy by Sir George Etherege (1634–91). It deals with the attempt of Dorimant to shed one mistress for another and his final match with yet another lady, the wealthy Harriet Woodvil, his equal in intellect and sophistication. Meanwhile Dorimant's friend Bellair wins the hand of his beloved Emilia, despite the rivalry of his own father. The most remarkable character in the play is Sir Fopling Flutter, the personification of dandyism. Part of the play's success was due to the fact that the characters were based on real people: Beau Hewitt, a notorious fop, was the model for Sir Fopling Flutter; Dorimant and Bellair are thought to be patterned on Lord ROCHESTER and Etherege, respectively.

Man of Property, The   See FORSYTE SAGA, THE.

man of sin   A phrase occurring in 2 Thess. 2:3, describing the ANTICHRIST, or one "Who opposeth and exalteth himself above all that is called God" (2 Thess. 2:4); his presence is said to antecede the second coming of Christ. The PURITANS used the phrase to apply to the pope; the Fifth Monarchy Men used it as a term of derision describing CROMWELL.

Manon Lescaut (1731) A novel by Abbé PRÉVOST, the full title of which is *L'Histoire du Chevalier des Grieux et de Manon Lescaut*. It is the story of a brilliant and talented young man who, as a student of philosophy with the brightest of futures, meets Manon Lescaut, a fascinating lower-class woman. She inspires in him a love for which he almost ruins his life in his efforts to satisfy her whims and expensive tastes; for her sake and in spite of the fact that she is rarely faithful to him, he steals, lies, borrows money, is imprisoned, exiles himself with her, and gravely wounds the son of the governor of Louisiana in a duel. She dies of exhaustion in his arms in the desert, where they have fled to escape the consequences of the duel. The novel inspired numerous other works, notably two operas: *Manon* (1884) by Massenet and *Manon Lescaut* (1893) by Puccini.

Manrique, Jorge (1440?–?1479)   Spanish poet and soldier. Manrique's fame rests on a single poem, *Coplas por la muerte de su padre*, an elegy written shortly after the death of his father, grand master of the military order of Santiago, in 1476. In simple, almost colloquial language, the grieving son describes his father's virtues, then submerges his personal sorrow to reflect on the impermanence of all earthly endeavor. Longfellow's translation of the poem (1833) is well known.

Man's Fate (La Condition humaine, 1933; tr 1934) A novel by André MALRAUX, also translated (1948) as *Storm over Shanghai*. It is very freely based on the Shanghai insurrection of 1927. The Communist Reds take over the city, in a shaky alliance with Chiang Kai-shek's Blues, who then turn against them and retake the city. Although the work moves swiftly, it is a probing psychological study of the men involved in the uprising.

Mansfield, Katherine (real name Kathleen Mansfield Murry, born Kathleen Beauchamp; 1888–1923) New Zealand-born short-story writer. Mansfield was one of the very few writers of the 20th century to devote her efforts in fiction exclusively to the short story. She had a passionate admiration for the work of Anton CHEKHOV; her own stories are notable for their poetic delicacy, psychological penetration, and her ability to provide sensitive renderings of very different kinds of characters, particularly children and women. Her stories usually follow the SLICE OF LIFE technique, describing a few typical hours in her characters' lives and focusing on some small but significant event that both captures the meaning of the whole story and clarifies the character of her protagonist. Among her best-known stories are BLISS, A DILL PICKLE, THE GARDEN PARTY, and "The Dove's Nest" (1923). A number of stories, beginning with "Prelude" (1918), evoke her New Zealand childhood.

Her first collection, *In a German Pension* (1911), was written when she was sent to Germany by her mother to bear an illegitimate child, who was stillborn. Much of her short life was clouded by unfortunate relationships. She had at least two unhappy lesbian affairs, and she became pregnant by the twin brother of a man she loved, at which point she impulsively married a musician, whom she abandoned on their wedding night. In 1915 she was shattered by the death of her brother in World War I. She married John Middleton MURRY in 1918; by this time, she was already so ill with tuberculosis that she was forced to make frequent trips to sanatoriums in France and Germany.

She collaborated with Murry on editing and writing criticism for a number of LITTLE MAGAZINES and for the *Athenaeum*. After her death, at thirty-five, Murry edited and published some additional stories, her poetry, a collection of her criticism, and her journals and letters. She was a friend of D. H. LAWRENCE, Aldous HUXLEY, and Virginia WOOLF, among other intellectuals of the day, and is said to be represented by the characters of Gudrun in Lawrence's WOMEN IN LOVE and Beatrice Gilray in Huxley's POINT COUNTER POINT.

Mansfield Park (1814) A novel by Jane AUSTEN. Fanny Price is adopted into the family of her rich uncle, Sir Thomas Bertram. Brought up with the four Bertram children, she is condescendingly treated as a poor relation by "Aunt Norris," a satirical portrait of a busybody. Of her cousins, only Edmund, a young clergyman, appreciates her fine qualities, and she falls in love with him. He unfortunately is irresistibly drawn to the shallow, worldly Mary

Crawford. In the meantime, Mary's attractive, unscrupulous brother Henry flirts violently with Maria Bertram, Edmund's sister, who is already engaged. Realizing his intentions are not serious, the disappointed Maria goes through with her marriage as planned. Henry turns his attentions to Fanny, falls in love with her, and proposes marriage. She refuses him. Henry then induces Maria to leave her husband and elopes with her. Mary Crawford takes this scandal very lightly, opening Edmund's eyes to her true nature. He turns to Fanny for comfort, falls in love with her, and marries her.

Mansion, The   See HAMLET, THE.

Mantegna, Andrea (1431–1506)   Italian painter and engraver. The great master of the early Renaissance, Mantegna worked principally in Padua and in Mantua. His study of classical sculpture and architecture, which he illustrated with archaeological accuracy, led to the evolution of a style that is austerely controlled and of a metallic intensity. Despite their ascetic flavor and sculptural quality, his works have brilliance of color and a feeling of movement and space. Their hitherto unknown realism and dramatic power, reinforced by the assimilation of Florentine discoveries of perspective and foreshortening, made Mantegna's works a magnet for other artists. His unusual line engravings influenced RAPHAEL, HOLBEIN, and DÜRER. His frescoes of the Gonzaga family in the Sala degli Sposi at Mantua, the earliest example of illusionist decoration of walls and ceilings, anticipated CORREGGIO, TIEPOLO, and the baroque penchant for trompe l'œil. The Venetian school founded by the BELLINI family owed its early inspiration to his work, for he was the brother-in-law of Giovanni and Gentile Bellini. Among the many artistic tragedies of World War II was the partial destruction of Mantegna's series of paintings *The Martyrdom of St. James* in the Eremitani Chapel at Padua.

Man That Corrupted Hadleyburg, The (1900)   A story by Mark TWAIN. A comic narrative with an unexpectedly grim ending, the story is an example of Twain's darker satire. A stranger leaves a sack of money in a bank in Hadleyburg, with a note instructing the cashier to give the sack to the person who makes a certain remark; secret letters then come to nineteen prominent townsmen, telling them the supposed remark. All prepare to claim the treasure, which turns out to be a sack of lead. They are all exposed, and the hypocrisy of the American small town is laid bare.

mantra (Sans, "formula")   In HINDUISM and BUDDHISM, a mystical syllable, word, phrase, verse, or short hymn believed to possess some religious or magical power, repeated during meditation. See OM; OM MANI PADME HUM.

Mantuan, The   Medieval epithet for VERGIL.

Mantuanus, Battista Spagnoli (1448–1516)   Mantuan humanist and Carmelite monk, widely known in Renaissance Europe for his Latin works. Of great importance are Mantuanus's ten *Eclogues*, derived from Vergil and Petrarch, which were used as texts in the classrooms of Europe. His style and treatment of the eclogue genre influenced such writers as Erasmus and Spenser, especially the latter's *Shepheardes Calender* (1579). Shakespeare probably studied the *Eclogues* in grammar school; in *Love's Labour's Lost*, Holofernes quotes a few words from the first eclogue and exclaims, "Old Mantuan, . . . who understandeth thee not, loves thee not."

Man Who Came to Dinner, The (1939)   A play by Moss HART and George S. KAUFMAN. A friendly burlesque on Alexander WOOLLCOTT, it deals with Sheridan Whiteside, a guest in the home of a Midwestern family. He is immobilized as the result of an accident, meddles in family affairs, and insults virtually everyone in town. His health regained, he prepares to leave—only to break his leg again.

Man Who Died, The (1929)   A short novel by D. H. LAWRENCE, first published under the title *The Escaped Cock*. It is a retelling of the story of Christ's resurrection. Rather than have Christ go to heaven, Lawrence has him mate with the priestess of Isis and declare that spiritual love and emphasis on death and heaven are a denial of life. The story is an ecstatic, symbolic presentation of Lawrence's personal religion.

Man Who Loved Children, The (1940)   English novel by Christina STEAD, about an American family. Samuel Clemens Pollit is "soft-soap Sam" to his coworkers in a Washington government office, "Sam the Bold" to his half dozen children, and "the great I-AM" to his bitter wife, Henrietta. Sam is the archetype of those good-natured, eternally kidding, naïvely optimistic, blandly egotistical American males who infuriate their wives and alienate their maturing children.

Man Who Was, The (1891)   One of Rudyard KIPLING's best-known short stories, published in *Life's Handicap* and later dramatized. The man, a mere "limp heap of rags," is living testimony to the cruelty of the Russians, who have kept him prisoner long after the Crimean War. Though amnesiac after his release, he recognizes his name in the regimental records, but he lives only a few days.

Man Who Was Thursday, The (1908)   A novel by G. K. CHESTERTON. It is a fantastic, witty allegory concerning anarchists, spies, and detectives. The theme, expressive of Chesterton's Catholicism, is the primacy and sanctity of order.

Man Who Would Be King, The (1889)   A short story by Rudyard KIPLING, originally published in his volume *The Phantom Rickshaw*. By dint of his natural shrewdness, the white trader Daniel Dravot sets himself up as god and king in Kafristan, dividing the kingdom with his companion, Peachey Carnehan. A woman discovers that he is human and betrays him. After suffering terrible torture, Peachey escapes to tell the tale, but Dravot is killed.

Man with the Golden Arm, The (1949)   A novel by Nelson ALGREN. Set in the slums of Chicago, the novel, which won a National Book Award in 1950, tells the story of Frankie Machine (Francis Majcinek), who is said to have a "golden arm" because of his sure touch with pool cues, dice, his drumsticks, and his heroin needle. Unable to free himself from his slum environment, Frankie is finally driven to suicide.

Man'yōshū (Collection of Myriad Leaves, c750) The first Japanese poetry anthology, containing some forty-five hundred poems written mostly during the 7th and 8th centuries. The poems reflect largely indigenous thought and beliefs and are one of the few literary sources for knowledge of Japan prior to the importation of the Chinese thought and culture of the T'ANG dynasty. See JAPANESE LITERATURE.

Manzoni, Alessandro (1785–1873)   Italian novelist, poet, and dramatist. The leader of the Italian romantic school, Manzoni is especially known for his great historical novel I PROMESSI SPOSI. Manzoni was a patriot, a liberal, and a Catholic whose poetic and religious sensibility found expression in his fiction; in his *Osservazioni sulla morale Cattolica* (1819), an essay on the power of Christian ethics to transmute human life; and in his five hymn-poems entitled *Inni sacri* (*Sacred Hymns*, 1822). His two tragedies, *Il Conte di Carmagnola* (1820) and *Adelchi* (1821), are noteworthy for their moral, religious, and patriotic themes and for the author's intentional disregard of the traditionally accepted Aristotelian unities.

In his historical fiction, Manzoni strove to synthesize historical fact and poetic imagination. His ultimate aim was to show the operation of divine providence in the everyday, seemingly insignificant actions of men. *I promessi sposi* became a model for subsequent Italian novels, for example, the work of D'Azeglio, Grossi, and Niccolini, and the refined modern Florentine that Manzoni used as a literary language established a precedent for modern Italian prose. Verdi honored his memory in his *Manzoni Requiem* (1874).

Mao Tse-tung (1893–1976)   Chinese revolutionary and statesman. Born in a peasant family in south-central China (Hunan), Mao was one of the founders of the Chinese Communist Party (1921) and a central figure in the period of struggle under Chiang Kai-shek. He participated in the Long March (1934–35) and the establishment of a secure base at Yenan, in north China. From here he directed the guerrilla war, first against Chiang, and then against the Japanese during the Sino–Japanese War (1937–45).

Chairman of the People's Republic of China (1949–59), he retained his post as party chairman, as well as his great influence and prestige, until his death. His contributions to Communist successes in China were immense. Against the early opposition of party colleagues, he stressed the role of peasants, of self-sufficiency, and of guerrilla warfare in the revolution. During the Yenan period, he made the People's Liberation Army into an effective educational and political tool. Since his death, there has been a reevaluation of his policies of the post-World War II period and of the "Cultural Revolution," which began in 1966 and resulted in the exile of most intellectuals and many now prominent political figures to menial jobs in the countryside.

The author of many books, his *Selected Works* appeared in four volumes (1954–56). Others of his works in English translation include *On Guerrilla Warfare* (1961), considered a definitive work on the subject; *Quotations from Chairman Mao Tse-Tung* (1966; ed S. R. Schram); *The Thoughts of Chairman Mao* (1967); and *Poems* (1972).

Map, Walter (c1140–c1209)   Welsh-born English courtier and satirist. Later archdeacon of Oxford (1197–1209), Map was a favorite at the court of Henry II. He was long considered the author of a lost prose version of the Launcelot story, on which later accounts of the Arthurian legends were partly based. But the only work he is definitely known to have written is *De nugis curialium* (*Courtiers' Trifles*, 1180–93), a collection of witty anecdotes, court gossip, and satirical denunciations. He was also reputed to be the author of large quantities of GOLIARDIC VERSE.

Maramzin, Vladimir Rafailovich (1934–   )   Soviet short-story writer. Born in Leningrad, Maramzin emigrated in 1935. Renowned for his masterful use of SKAZ, he is best known for *Istoriya zhenitby Ivana Petrovicha* (1975; tr *The Story of the Marriage of Ivan Petrovich*, 1976), in which the worker Dusya, in desperate need of money, sells herself to Ivan, who then falls in love with her. Another notable work by Maramzin is *Ya, s poshchochinoy v ruke* (1965; tr *A Slap in the Face*, 1975), a treatment of Soviet bureaucracy.

Marat, Jean Paul (1743–1793)   Swiss-born French politician and physician. At the beginning of the FRENCH REVOLUTION Marat published the paper *L'Ami du peuple* (1789), in which he advocated a republican form of government. With DANTON and ROBESPIERRE, he overthrew the GIRONDISTS. He was assassinated in his bath by Charlotte CORDAY on July 13, 1793.

Marathon   A plain in Attica, northeast of Athens. Here the Greeks won a victory over the Persians (490 BC) that ended Darius's Greek ambitions. According to tradition, the news of the victory was brought back to Athens by a runner, Pheidippides, whose feat is commemorated in the modern marathon races, usually fixed at 26 miles, 385 yards.

Marat/Sade   See WEISS, PETER.

Marble Faun, The (1860)   A novel by Nathaniel HAWTHORNE. Donatello, an Italian count, resembles the Faun of Praxiteles in appearance, as well as in his natural spirits. An innocent admirer of Miriam, the darkly beautiful, mysterious art student, he is driven to kill her strange pursuer, Antonio. The act catapults him into reality; sinning, he moves from innocence to experience. The murder scene is witnessed by Hilda, a pure, pale artist. Guilty through her inadvertent participation in the crime, Hilda must confess the secret to a Catholic priest; later she and the sculptor Kenyon reveal their love. Donatello, matured by his crime, becomes a moral being and turns himself over to the authorities. In telling his story, Hawthorne treats the theme of the fortunate fall. Setting the novel in Rome, the author employs the landscape of that center of art and faith to add to the richness of the work.

Marc, Franz   See BLAUE REITER, DER.

Marcel, Gabriel (1889–1973)   French philosopher, dramatist, and critic. Marcel introduced the writings of Søren KIERKEGAARD, by whom he was profoundly influenced, to France about 1925. A convert to Catholicism, he became the leading French exponent of "Christian existentialism," as presented in *Journal métaphysique* (1927; tr *Metaphysical Journal*, 1952), *Être et avoir* (1935; tr *Being and Having*, 1949), *Homo Viator* (1945; tr *Introduction to a Metaphysic of Hope*, 1951), *Le Mystère de l'être* (1951; tr *The Mystery of Being*, 1960), and *Du refus à l'invocation* (1940; tr *Creative Fidelity*, 1964). *The Existential Background of Human Dignity* (1963) is a collection of lectures delivered at Harvard in 1962. Among his many other works is a study of Martin Buber (1968). The importance of intuition and faith is also a recurrent theme in his plays, such as *La Grâce* (1914), *Un Homme de Dieu* (1925; tr *A Man of God*, 1958), and *Le Fanal* (1936). *L'Heure théâtrale* (1959) is a collection of his critical essays.

Märchen (Ger, "little tale")   A favorite narrative form in GERMAN ROMANTICISM. The term includes but has a wider range than the English fairy tale. It can refer to the *Volksmärchen* ("folk tale"), such as those collected by the brothers GRIMM, or to tales written in the folk style. The action is generally intense, the atmosphere is abstract, and the setting is removed from time and space. The key figure is frequently a hero who must go on a journey, during which he is put through tests and encounters various forms of evil. Generally, his tasks are three in number; symbolic numbers, superstition, supernatural creatures, and forms of magic are all important devices. In the end, the hero succeeds at his given tasks and is well rewarded, while his evil opponents are severely or fatally punished. The term *Märchen* can also refer to the deeply philosophical, allegorical form of the *Kunstmärchen* ("art tale"), the definitive example of which is GOETHE's *Das Märchen*. NOVALIS, BRENTANO, and E.T.A. HOFFMANN also employed this form for different effects. See FOLKLORE.

March Hare   A character in Lewis Carroll's ALICE'S ADVENTURES IN WONDERLAND. At a mad tea party, the March Hare offers Alice wine when there is none, and, when reprimanded for putting butter in the Hatter's watch, he replies, "It was the *best* butter." The fact that hares are unusually shy and wild during March, their rutting season,

gave rise to the popular expression "mad as a March hare." Carroll's March Hare is a burlesque of the expression.

Marco Millions (1928)   A play by Eugene O'NEILL. The Marco of O'Neill's play is Marco Polo, who is used as a whipping boy to express the dramatist's scorn for mercenary souls. His Marco is interested only in making his million; he does not see that Kublai Khan's daughter is in love with him. He serves her only for the bonus he hopes to receive. At last, he marries a fat, commonplace Venetian.

Marcus Aurelius (full name Marcus Aurelius Antoninus, 121–180)   Roman emperor (161–80) and Stoic philosopher. As emperor, Marcus Aurelius was beset by internal disturbances—famines and plagues—and by the external threat posed by the Germans in the north and the Parthians in the east. As, year after year, he witnessed the gradual crumbling of the Roman frontiers, he turned more and more to the study of Stoic philosophy. Between battles he wrote down the philosophical reflections that were later collected and published as *The Meditations of Marcus Aurelius*. This collection of precepts (written in Greek) is perhaps the most readable exposition of Stoic philosophizing that we possess.

Marcuse, Herbert (1898–1979)   German-born American political philosopher and sociologist. Already a noted sociologist, Marcuse fled Hitler's Germany in 1933 and immigrated to the U.S. in 1934. He taught at Columbia, Harvard, Brandeis, and the University of California at San Diego. Marcuse's dense and complex work attempted to apply the theories of MARX, FREUD, and HEGEL to modern technological society. In *Eros and Civilization* (1955), he relates sexual repression to political and social repression. In *One-Dimensional Man* (1964) he argues that the mass materialism of American culture stifles all diversity. Marcuse believed that revolutionary ideals of freedom can exist in a nonrevolutionary, industrial society. He saw American society as one that systematically impeded freedom, and believed that students and minority groups were the most effective agents of social change. Many of his radical libertarian ideals, sometimes imperfectly understood, were espoused by student radicals in the 1960s. Among Marcuse's other books are *Soviet Marxism* (1958), *Counterrevolution and Revolt* (1972), and *The Aesthetic Dimension* (1978).

Mardi and a Voyage Thither (1849)   A novel by Herman MELVILLE. His first literary treatment of metaphysical, ethical, and political problems, the book is overwhelmed by complexity. Begun as a narrative of adventure, it concludes as an allegory of mind.

A symbolic quest for Absolute Truth is undertaken by five men: Taji, the young monomaniacal hero; Babbalanja, a philosopher; Yoomy, a poet; Mohi, a historian; and King Media, a man of common sense. On King Media's boat, they sail through the island archipelagoes of Mardi (the world), stopping at various countries, including Vivenza, which represents the United States. Taji, who most resembles Melville, kills an island priest, Aleema, in order to rescue Yillah, a beautiful white woman of seeming prelapsarian innocence. Yillah disappears, and Taji's search for her becomes a search for truth and lost innocence. He in turn is sought by Hautia, the incarnation of sophisticated sexuality, who haunts him for the murder of Aleema. She becomes a symbol for guilt and the need for repentance. Taji, pursued and pursuing, is last seen alone, sailing on desperate seas. This is the first time Melville presents a questing hero involved in events that are more important on a symbolic than realistic level. The book anticipates problems explored in MOBY-DICK and PIERRE, OR THE AMBIGUITIES.

Mardi Gras (Fr, "fat Tuesday")   Last day of the pre-Lenten carnival in France, Shrove Tuesday. It is celebrated with all sorts of festivities. In Paris, a fat ox used to be paraded through the principal streets, crowned with a fillet and accompanied by mock priests and a band of tin instruments in imitation of a Roman sacrificial procession. In the U.S., New Orleans is famed for its Mardi Gras celebration. See SHROVETIDE.

Marduk   A Babylonian warrior god. Marduk was the son of EA, the god of water and wisdom. When the other gods are all terrified by the invasion of TIAMAT, the dragon of the sea, Marduk slays her. He makes heaven and earth of the two halves of her body and creates man of the bones and blood of Kingu, one of Tiamat's henchmen. Part of Marduk's supremacy in the pantheon of Assyria and Babylonia was due to the fact that he was the local BAAL of Babylon. See WAR OF THE GODS.

Margaret of Anjou (1430–1482)   French-born queen of England. The daughter of René I of Anjou, Margaret married Henry VI in 1445 and gave birth to her only son, Edward, in 1453, the same year in which Henry suffered a temporary fit of insanity. The rivalry between her and Richard, duke of York, who had been heir presumptive until the birth of Edward, brought on the Wars of the Roses between the houses of Lancaster and York. In 1471 she was captured, and Edward was killed at Tewkesbury, Henry dying in the Tower of London soon afterwards. She was freed in 1475.

In HENRY VI: Parts I, II, and III, Shakespeare chronicles her development into a savage and imperious woman, whom Richard Plantagenet calls:

> She-wolf of France, but worse than wolves of France,
> Whose tongue more poisons than the adder's tooth!

She also appears in RICHARD III.

Margaret of Navarre (also known as Marguerite de Navarre, Marguerite de Valois, and Marguerite d'Angoulême; 1492–1549)   French queen and author. The sister of Francis I of France, Margaret married Henri d'Albret, king of Navarre, after the death of her first husband and transformed her court into a refuge for humanists, among them Marot, Calvin, and Lefèvre d'Etaples.

Instilled with Platonic and Petrarchan mysticism, she devoted her life to culture and sacrifice for those she loved. She expressed her religious fervor and intimate joys and sorrows in such works of poetry as *Miroir de l'âme pécheresse* (1531) and *Les Marguerites de la Marguerite des princesses* (1547). In the HEPTAMÉRON she produced the first collection of French tales. Rabelais dedicated the third book of *Gargantua and Pantagruel* (1532–64) to her soul. She is sometimes referred to as *marguerite des marguerites* (Fr, "pearl of pearls"), the name by which Francis called her.

Margaret of Valois (known as Queen Margot or Reine Margot, 1553–1615)   French queen. The daughter of Henry II of France and Catherine de Médicis, Margaret married Henry of Navarre (later Henry IV of France) in 1572. The childless marriage was dissolved in 1599. Known for her learning and loose living, she was the author of interesting letters and *Mémoires* (1628).

Margawse, Queen   In ARTHURIAN LEGEND, the wife of King Lot and mother of the knights Gawain, GARETH, Gaheris, and Aggravaine. In Malory's *Morte d'Arthur* (c1469), Margawse is also the mother, by King Arthur, of Sir MORDRED. Margawse's son, Sir Gaheris, beheads her when he finds her with her lover, Sir Lamerok; Sir Gawain kills Lamerok. Margawse is Bellicent in Tennyson's *Idylls of the King* (1859–72).

Maria   Olivia's maid in Shakespeare's TWELFTH NIGHT. A lively, quick-witted shrew, Maria instigates the intrigues against Malvolio and eventually marries Sir Toby Belch, Olivia's uncle.

María (1867)   A novel by Jorge Isaacs (1837–95), Colombian poet and novelist. Perhaps the most widely read South American novel, *María* is a romantic idyll that describes the ill-starred love affair between the title character and her cousin Efraín. Although the plot is cloyingly sentimental by contemporary standards, the author's picture of life in Colombia's Cauca Valley, where the action takes place, retains its freshness and charm.

Maria Chapdelaine   See HÉMON, LOUIS.

Maria Magdalena (1844)   A play by Friedrich HEBBEL in the tradition of the bourgeois tragedy, which goes back ultimately to Diderot. It is the tragedy of a girl named Klara, who is pregnant by her worthless fiancé and becomes involved in a web of conflicting motives and obligations, including love for another man and fear of social reproach, that leads to her suicide.

In the preface to this play, Hebbel outlines his theory, largely influenced by Hegel, that great drama is produced only at moments in world history when an old order and a new order are in conflict. He believed that, in his own day, the world spirit was undergoing a crisis of self-consciousness that would eventually lead to a firmer, less superstitious basis for human institutions, and *Maria Magdalena* is intended to depict this crisis. The last words of the play, spoken by Klara's father, who is a representative of unbending tradition, are: "I don't understand the world anymore." The play's title refers to the fact that, in her tragedy, Klara is symbolically purged of evil as St. Mary Magdalene was.

Marías [Augilera], Julián (1914–   ) Spanish philosopher and essayist. An ardent defender of the philosophy of his teacher ORTEGA Y GASSET, Marías believes in the temporal aspects of philosophy and in the duty of man to create a personal metaphysics in order to determine the reality of individual life. In his major work, *Introducción a la filosofía* (1947; tr *Reason and Life*, 1956), he attempts to escape the tyranny of ideas, suggesting that the primary task of the 20th century involves the absorption of the philosophical past in order to obtain perspectives on the present. His other works include *Miguel de Unamuno* (1943; tr 1966), *El método histórico de las generaciones* (1949; tr *Generations: An Historical Method*, 1970), *El existencialismo en Epaña* (*Existentialism in Spain*, 1953), and *Los españoles* (*The Spaniards*, 1962). *Ortega y la idea de la razón vital* (1948) contains his endorsement of his mentor's theory of "vital reason."

Mariátegui, José Carlos (1895–1930) Peruvian essayist, one of the major thinkers of the Latin American left. Mariátegui's *Siete ensayos de interpretación de la realidad peruana* (*Seven Essays Interpreting Peruvian Reality*, 1928) constitutes an original and probing Marxist analysis of Peruvian life and literature and of the neocolonial social and economic factors that shaped both. He founded the literary journal *Amauta* (1926–30), where many of his own impeccably written essays were first published and which served as the intellectual nerve center of an entire generation. *Amauta* provided a forum for all manner of revolutionary aesthetic, religious, and political thought.

Maria Theresa (1717–1780) Archduchess of Austria and queen of Hungary and Bohemia (1740–80). The War of the Austrian Succession (1740–48) and the Seven Years' War (1756–63) were fought during Maria Theresa's reign, to defend the Hapsburg dominions, which she inherited. Among her many children were Marie Antoinette and Joseph II.

Marie Antoinette (1755–1793) Queen of France, wife of LOUIS XVI, whom she married when she was fifteen. As daughter of Maria Theresa of Austria, Marie Antoinette sought Austria's aid against French Revolutionaries. In 1791 she counseled Louis XVI to attempt flight from France, an attempt which ended in their imprisonment. They were regarded as traitors, and Marie Antoinette was guillotined on October 16, 1793. Her personal charm, her naïve ignorance of practical life, her extravagance, and her frank and courageous honesty contributed to her unpopularity both at court and with the French masses, who contemptuously called her *l'Autrichienne* ("the Austrian woman"). When she was told that a revolution was threatening because the people had no bread, she is said to have replied, "Let them eat cake." See BAKER, THE; DIAMOND NECKLACE AFFAIR.

Marie de France (c1200) French medieval poet, thought to have been the half sister of Henry II of England. Most of Marie's life seems to have been spent at the English court, and her writings had a considerable influence on English writers. She is famous for her Breton lais, verse-narrative romances full of Celtic atmosphere and often making use of Arthurian materials. Some fifteen of these lais are known, among them that of SIR LAUNFAL. She also wrote a collection of beast fables, based on Aesop, called *Ysopet* or *Isopet* (*Little Aesop*). See BRETON LAI.

Marie de Médicis (1573–1642) Italian-born queen of France. The second wife of Henry IV, whom she married in 1600, Marie was regent for her son Louis XIII from 1610 to 1617. She was forced to leave France in 1630 by her archrival RICHELIEU.

Marignano, battle of The meeting in 1515 at which the French king Francis I defeated Massimiliano Sforza, heir of the deposed Lodovico, duke of Milan, thus consolidating French control over Lombardy.

Marinism See MARINO, GIAMBATTISTA.

Marino, Giambattista (1569–1625) Italian poet. During a colorful lifetime spent mainly at Italian and French courts, Marino produced a collection of lyrics, *La Lira*; a group of iconographic poems, *La Galeria*; pastoral idylls, such as *La Sampogna*; and a sacred epic (1632) on the Massacre of the Innocents. His masterpiece is the *Adone* (1623), a long mythological poem centered around the love of Venus and Adonis. Its style, like that of his own earlier poems and that of the Marinists, his followers, features elaborate conceits, frequent plays on words, rhetorical devices, and a floridly sensuous tone. His extension of Petrarchan love motifs and his preference for themes from classical Roman mythology are also characteristic of Marinism. In the following centuries, a reaction against Marinism, seen as part of a larger decadence (*secentismo*, "17th-centuryism"), lowered his reputation to near oblivion. He has returned to literary discussion as a major example of the baroque style in poetry.

Mario and the Magician (Mario und der Zauberer, 1930; tr 1930) A story by Thomas MANN. The German narrator and his family have been asked to leave an Italian resort for allowing a small child to run naked on the beach. During their last night at the hotel, they watch the performance of a magician named Cippola, who brutally humiliates several members of the audience by hypnotic means. Mario, a young waiter who has been mocked in an especially cruel way, shoots and kills the magician when he awakens from his trance. The story is an allegorical condemnation of Fascism, which Mann saw as a violation of human dignity.

Marion, Francis (1732?–1795) American Revolutionary soldier. Marion was known as "the Swamp Fox" because of his skill in retreating, Indian-fashion, to swamps and forests after quick and effective raids on British forces. He participated in the battle of Eutaw Springs, South Carolina (September 8, 1781). William Cullen Bryant wrote "The Song of Marion's Men" (1831).

Maritain, Jacques (1882–1973)   French Catholic philosopher and man of letters. Reared as a Protestant, Maritain was converted to Roman Catholicism in 1906; Charles PÉGUY and Léon Bloy were influential figures in his spiritual development. Henri BERGSON, his teacher, was severely criticized by Maritain in *La Philosophie bergsonienne* (1914; tr *Bergsonian Philosophy and Thomism*, 1955); only the philosophy of St. Thomas AQUINAS, an ordered system that could reconcile faith and reason and acknowledge the coexistence of freedom and the divine in man, satisfied his needs. Systematically and energetically, he published critical studies of those philosophers whom he considered intellectually faulty or inadequate. *Antimoderne* (1922) and *Trois réformateurs* (1925; tr *Three Reformers*, 1928) were sharp attacks on LUTHER, DESCARTES, ROUSSEAU, and PASCAL for distorting modern thought. His own philosophy, neo-Thomism, is expounded in *Eléments de philosophie* (1923–30), *Distinguer pour unir, ou les Dégres du savoir* (1932; tr *The Degrees of Knowledge*, 1959), *Humanisme intégral* (1936; tr *True Humanism*, 1938), and *Confession de foi* (1941), first published in English as *I Believe* (1939). Maritain came to America after the fall of France in 1940 and taught at Columbia, Princeton, and the Institute of Medieval Studies in Toronto. Maritain also made significant contributions to the fields of aesthetics, ethics, and politics. *Art et scolastique* (1920) is a lucid attempt to use scholastic philosophy as the basis of an aesthetic.

Marius, [Caius] (157–86 BC)   Roman general, consul, and leader of republican Rome's popular party. Born of plebeian stock, Marius was a lifelong, fanatical foe of the privileged aristocracy. After a brilliant career as soldier and strategist, he won, in 107 BC, the Roman consulate. Soon after, he led a successful campaign against the African prince Jugurtha (107–105). It was here that his career first intercepted that of the aristocrat Lucius Cornelius SULLA, the man who was to become his mortal enemy. Through fifteen years (105–90), Marius and Sulla vied for popular acclaim. In 90, after the Social War had been successfully concluded, Roman civil war broke out. For four bloody years thereafter, Rome was the pawn of these two ruthless generals. As one rival recovered, the other's supporters were purged. The reprisals did not end with the death of Marius (86) but continued until Sulla was absolute master of Rome (82).

Marius the Epicurean (1885)   A philosophic romance by Walter PATER. The hero is a Roman noble of the time of MARCUS AURELIUS, and the book records his sensations and ideas rather than outward events. Though he makes no formal profession of Christianity, Marius is greatly drawn to it through his friend Cornelius and his own high principles and deeply religious nature. His death

is of such a nature that the Christian Church looks upon him as a martyr.

Marivaux, Pierre Carlet de Chamblain de (1688–1763)   French dramatist and novelist. Marivaux is most famous for those of his comedies that analyze the vicissitudes of the heart during courtship: timidity, jealousy, misunderstandings—in brief, the subtle psychological aspects of the game of love. Among this type of play are *Le Jeu de l'amour et du hasard* (1730), *Les Fausses Confidences* (1737), and *L'Epreuve* (1740). Other plays by Marivaux are mythological, social, philosophical, or romanesque in theme, and his treatment of them is strikingly fanciful. His subtly nuanced, precious language is so peculiar to him that the term *marivaudage* has been coined to describe it. Marivaux's two unfinished novels, *La Vie de Marianne* (1731–41), completed by Marie Jeanne Riccoboni (1713–92), and *Le Paysan parvenu* (1735), combine penetrating analyses of characters' states of mind and a vivacious, often realistic picture of all classes of Parisian society.

Mark, King   In the medieval legend of TRISTAN AND ISEULT, king of Cornwall, husband of Iseult, and uncle of Tristan. King Mark has the misfortune to be in the generally unsympathetic position of cuckold, but, in most versions, the drama of the tale in which his wife and favorite nephew are lovers is intensified by his nobility and sensitivity. In the version of Gottfried von Strassburg (c1210) particularly, the psychological conflict becomes more acute through the character of the king, whose understanding of the situation makes of him a tragic figure almost surpassing in importance the lovers themselves. In Malory's *Morte d'Arthur* (c1469), on the contrary, he is a base figure intent only on the death of Sir Tristram (Tristan). See TRISTRAM OF LYONESS, SIR.

Mark, St.   The author of The Gospel According to St. MARK. St. Mark is referred to as John, his Jewish name, or as Mark (or Marcus), his Roman name, or as "John, whose surname is Mark" (Acts 12:12). He accompanied BARNABAS and SAUL on their first missionary journey. He was at first distrusted by PAUL, who refused to have Mark with him on the second missionary journey (Acts 15:36-39), but was apparently later restored to favor, because he served as a missionary companion to both Paul (2 Tim. 4:11) and PETER (1 Pet. 5:13). He is the patron saint of Venice; his symbol is a winged lion. His feast day is April 25.

Mark, The Gospel According to St.   The second book of the NEW TESTAMENT. One of the SYNOPTIC GOSPELS, it is generally held to be the earliest account of JESUS' life. Tradition ascribes it to John Mark (Marcus), or St. MARK, the missionary companion first of BARNABAS and later of PETER and PAUL. The narrative is simple and, after a brief account of the ministry of JOHN THE BAPTIST and the baptism of Jesus, it recounts the teachings and miracles of Jesus. It describes the denial of Peter, the mocking of Jesus, and the Crucifixion, the Resurrection, and the Ascension. Biblical scholars generally agree that Mark was a source for the gospels of LUKE and MATTHEW.

Markandaya, Kamala (pseudonym of Kamala Purnaiya Taylor, 1924–   )   Indian novelist, writing in English. A journalist in Britain for many years, Markandaya is probably best known for her first novel, *Nectar in a Sieve* (1954), a poignant story of the hardships of Indian peasant life. Her insights into character are effectively put to use in such other novels as *Some Inner Fury* (1955), *A Silence of Desire* (1960), *The Coffer Dams* (1969), *Two Virgins* (1973), *The Golden Honeycombs* (1977), and *Shalimar* (1984). Among the most important modern Indian writers, Markandaya deals perceptively with the differences between Western and Oriental cultures.

Markham, Edwin (1852–1940)   American poet. Markham is best known for his spirited protest against exploitation of poor laborers in "The Man with a Hoe" (1899), a poem inspired by MILLET's painting of the same title. Another widely read poem was "Lincoln, the Man of the People," published in *Lincoln and Other Poems* (1901). Markham produced several other volumes of verse, including *The Ballad of the Gallows Bird* (1896), *Gates of Paradise* (1920), and *Collected Poems* (1940).

Marlborough, John Churchill, 1st duke of (1650–1722)   English military leader. The son of the impoverished Sir Winston Churchill, he was assisted in advancing his fortunes by his sister Arabella, who was the mistress of the duke of York, later James II. At the outbreak of the War of the Spanish Succession (1702–12), he was named commander of the English forces and defeated the French at the battles of Blenheim, Ramillies, Oudenarde, and Malplaquet. His wife, Sarah, the famous duchess of Marlborough, was Queen Anne's closest friend for many years.

Marlow   The narrator of a number of tales and novels by Joseph CONRAD. Marlow is a kind of detective of the conscience, who studies the moral dilemmas of other men in order to understand himself better. By using this character to narrate the stories (usually to his friends, at night, to the accompaniment of drinks and cigars), Conrad is able to develop the impersonal, oblique method of storytelling employed by Henry JAMES. Marlow describes and analyzes the various sources from which he has collected his information and comments on the significance of the events he narrates. Among the tales he tells are LORD JIM, YOUTH, HEART OF DARKNESS, and *Chance* (1913).

Marlowe, Christopher (1564–1593)   English dramatist and poet. Born at Canterbury, the son of a shoemaker, Marlowe attended Benet College (now Corpus Christi), where he took his B.A. in 1584, his M.A. in 1587. His life has become a legend, with its gay disdain for all convention, its irreverence, its reckless vitality. He was killed in a quarrel with a man named Ingram Frizer over the settlement of a tavern bill for supper and ale.

Considered the greatest figure in Elizabethan drama before Shakespeare, Marlowe raised the conventional, academic tragedy of his time, rigidly held within the limitations of the Senecan form, to a level of serious and emotionally gripping art. TAMBURLAINE THE GREAT, his first play, appeared in 1587. Blank verse, formerly stiff and wooden, sprang to life in his hands; the splendid utterances of the Scythian conqueror earned Marlowe's verse the praise of "mighty line." *The Tragical History of* DR. FAUSTUS, not entered on the *Stationer's Register* until 1601, was probably performed in 1588; THE JEW OF MALTA was probably produced in 1589. Each of these dramas is dominated by a single character whose force of personality alone gives unity to the play. Tamburlaine, Faustus, and Barabas are all gripped by a master passion, a Renaissance longing for infinite beauty or riches or power. In *Edward II*, entered on the *Stationer's Register* in 1593, Marlowe revealed a ripening and maturing of his dramatic and lyrical gifts. The play has less surface glitter and a graver, wiser understanding of human weakness and limitation. Not dependent on the superhuman power of one main figure for its coherence, *Edward II* contains several finely drawn characters and is skillfully plotted. Its poetry, too, is less startling but far more subtle in its varied use of the blank verse line. Marlowe may also have written *Dido, Queen of Carthage* (c1593, with Thomas NASHE), though the authorship of this play is disputed, and *The Massacre at Paris* (1593). Some scholars believe he may have had a hand in the writing of some of Shakespeare's plays, among them *Titus Andronicus*, *Henry IV*, and *Richard III*.

Marlowe's lyric poetry is graceful, musical, and warmly sensuous. It includes a translation (c1597) of OVID's *Amores*; *Hero and Leander* (1598), based on the poem by Musaeus, left unfinished at Marlowe's death, and completed by George CHAPMAN; a translation of the first book of LUCAN's *Pharsalia*, published in 1600; and the famous lyric beginning "Come live with me and be my love," published in *England's Helicon* (1600).

Marlowe, Philip   See CHANDLER, RAYMOND.

Marmeladov   A drunken, MICAWBER-like character in DOSTOYEVSKY's novel CRIME AND PUNISHMENT. His comicality is compounded with tragedy when he reveals to Raskolnikov that his daughter SONYA has been forced into prostitution to support the family. Marmeladov dies after being struck by a coach in the street.

Marmion, A Tale of Flodden Field (1808)   A romantic narrative poem by Sir Walter SCOTT, set in the time of HENRY VIII. Lord Marmion rejects his betrothed, Constance, and attempts unsuccessfully to secure the wealthy Lady Clare in marriage. Ultimately he is slain at the battle of FLODDEN FIELD (1513). See LOCHINVAR.

Marot, Clément (1496–1544)   French poet, known for his light and graceful lyrics. Marot's work marks the transition between medieval poetry, whose elaborate techniques were perpetuated by the RHÉTORIQUEURS, and the poetry of the Renaissance, which modeled itself after classical and Italian forms. He brought to the tortured poetic techniques of the Rhétoriqueurs a natural facility for playing with words and the sparkle of an engaging personality. He treated the modern forms, such as the Italian sonnet, which he introduced into French literature, with the same freshness and vivacity. A critical spirit led him to question traditional Catholic doctrines and to undertake his famous translation from Latin of the Psalms (1541–43). This religious independence caused him to be suspected of sympathizing with the Protestant reform movement and cost him imprisonment and periodic flights into exile in Navarre and Ferrara and in Calvin's Geneva (1542–43). His buoyant verve, satirical wit, and elegant, tactful gaiety endeared him, alone of all the 16th-century poets, to the classic poets of the 17th century.

Marple, Miss Jane   Creation of Agatha CHRISTIE. Miss Marple is an old lady, prone to knitting, who has lived all her life in the cozy English village of St. Mary Mead. A natural detective and amateur crime solver, she operates on the theory that human nature is universal and thus she finds the criminal through his resemblance to someone she has known in the village. She appears in over fifteen books, including *The Murder at the Vicarage* (1930), *A Pocket Full of Rye* (1953), and *The Mirror Crack'd* (1962), and has also been memorably portrayed on film and television by (among others) Margaret Rutherford.

Marprelate controversy   The name given to the vituperative pamphlet war (1588–90) between the Puritans and the Church of England. In 1588 appeared a number of pamphlets, printed by a secret press and purportedly written by one Martin Marprelate, attacking the Established Church and particularly the Episcopacy. Thinking that the best way to answer "Martin" would be in his own trenchant, witty style, the church authorities secretly hired writers, notably Robert GREENE and Thomas NASHE, to publish replies. In 1590 the Marprelate press was discovered and the printer, one Penry, executed. The real author may have been Job Throckmorton, who escaped execution. Seven of the Marprelate pamphlets, containing some of the best satirical writing of the time, are extant.

Marquand, J[ohn] P[hillips] (1893–1960) American novelist. Born in Delaware, Marquand was raised in Newburyport, Massachusetts, and attended Harvard College. He wrote a popular series of stories about the keen-witted Japanese detective Mr. MOTO, but he is best remembered for his amusing, lightly satirical novels about well-to-do New Englanders struggling to maintain their aristocratic, Puritan standards in the 20th century: THE LATE GEORGE APLEY; WICKFORD POINT; and *H. M. Pullman, Esq.* (1941).

Marquette, Jacques (known as Père Marquette, 1637–1675)   French Jesuit missionary in North America. Marquette accompanied Jolliet down the Wisconsin and Mississippi rivers and across Lake Michigan. He described the journey in *Voyage et découverte de quelques pays et nations de l'Amérique Septentrionale* (*Journey and Discovery of Several Countries and Nations of Northern America*, 1681).

Marquina, Eduardo (1879–1946)   Spanish poet and dramatist. Marquina was a leading exponent of modernism in Spanish poetry. His early works, *Odas* (1900) and *Vendimión* (1909), are somewhat romantic in tone and infused with a pantheistic flavor. Later the poet turned to social problems, as in *Canciones del momento* (1920) and *Tierras de España* (1914). As a playwright, he achieved success with his historical dramas, particularly with *Las hijas del Cid* (1908), *Doña María la Brava* (1909), and his masterpiece, *En Flandes se ha puesto el sol* (1910), which deals with the campaigns in the Low Countries during the reign of Philip II.

Marquis, Don[ald Robert Perry] (1878–1937) American newspaperman and humorist. In his early career an assistant editor to Joel Chandler HARRIS, who encouraged his tendency toward fantasy, Marquis was known for his columns "The Sun Dial" in the New York *Sun* and "The Lantern" in the New York *Tribune*. His most memorable writings are his stories and verses about ARCHY AND MEHITABEL. Among other characters Marquis created were Clem Hawley, the Old Soak, an uninhibited enemy of prohibition; Hermione and her Little Group of Serious Thinkers, all apostles of the platitudinous; and the Cave Man and his battered lady love.

Marriage of Figaro   See FIGARO.

Marriage of Heaven and Hell, The (1790) The chief prose work of William BLAKE, setting forth his doctrine of Contraries and emphasizing the negative side of his dualistic thinking. He writes: "Without Contraries is no progression. Attraction and repulsion, reason and energy, love and hate, are necessary to human existence." Blake denies matter as reality, eternal damnation, and the right of authority; specifically, he attacks the rationalism of 18th-century Protestantism for reducing moral complexities to oversimplified formulas.

Marryat, Captain Frederick (1792–1848)   English novelist. Marryat wrote his first novel, *Frank Mildmay, or the Naval Officer* (1829), in his late thirties, after a distinguished career in the British Navy. With his expert knowledge of nautical life and his vigor and humor, he produced some outstanding early specimens of the novel of the sea. Such books as *Peter Simple* (1834), *Mr. Midshipman Easy* (1836), and *Masterman Ready* (1841; first in a series of books for children) excel in the depiction of character and incident and still possess a considerable degree of vitality.

For many years, Marryat's books were favorites of boys all over the English-speaking world. He is also well known for his *Diary in America* (1839), a generally negative view of the United States, written during travels there.

Mars An Italian god of fertility whose month, March, began the spring season of growth and fruitfulness and who later took on the aspects of the Greek god of war, ARES. The great park and parade ground in Rome, the Campus Martius, was dedicated to him; when war was declared, the general would come before his legions and, striking a shield against the ground, would intone the words *Mars vigila!* ("Mars, awake!"). In Roman poetry, the word *Mars* is often used, through personification, as a synonym for war.

CAMÕES introduces him in the Portuguese epic OS LUSÍADAS as typifying divine fortitude; as BACCHUS, the evil demon, is the guardian of the power of Islam, so Mars is the guardian of Christianity.

Marseillaise, La The hymn of the FRENCH REVO-LUTION. Claude Joseph Rouget de Lisle (1760–1836), an artillery officer in the garrison at Strasbourg, composed both the words and music (April 24, 1792), with the title "Chant de guerre pour l'armée du Rhin." On July 30, 1792, volunteers from Marseilles entered Paris singing the song, and the Parisians, enchanted with it, called it the "Chant des Marseillais" and later "La Marseillaise." It has often been made use of by later composers, as for instance by SCHUMANN, in his music for Heine's poem "The Two Grenadiers" (1840), and by TCHAIKOVSKY, in his *Festival Overture, "1812"* (1880).

Marsh, Edward See GEORGIANS.

Marsh, Dame [Edith] Ngaio (1899–1982) New Zealand detective story writer. For her deftly written mysteries, generally set in England, Marsh often drew on her own experiences as an artist and theatrical producer. After her first book, *A Man Lay Dead* (1934), she published a series of successful crime novels, many of them featuring Detective Inspector Roderick Alleyn, including *Artists in Crime* (1938), *Night at the Vulcan* (1951), *Hand in Glove* (1962), *Black as He's Painted* (1975), and *Photo Finish* (1980). *Ngaio* (pronounced Nye-o) is Maori for "light on the water" or "flowering tree."

Marshall, George C[atlett] (1880–1959) American general and statesman. A graduate of Virginia Military Institute (1901), Marshall served in the Philippines and with the American Expeditionary Forces during World War I. From 1919 to 1924, he was an aide to General PERSHING. Named army chief of staff in 1939, he became the second non-West Pointer to hold this post and played a leading role in formulating Allied strategy during World War II. After going to China in 1945 as special ambassador in an unsuccessful attempt to mediate between Chiang Kai-shek and the Chinese Communists, Marshall was appointed secretary of state by President TRUMAN. On June 5, 1947, in a commencement speech at Harvard, he outlined the principles of the European Recovery Program, known as the Marshall Plan, by which the U.S. contributed to the postwar rehabilitation of Europe. Marshall also

served as secretary of defense from 1950 to 1951. In 1953 he was awarded the Nobel Peace Prize.

Marshall, John (1755–1835) American jurist. After serving as one of the commissioners in the X.Y.Z. Affair, Marshall was secretary of state for a short time. He was named chief justice of the Supreme Court in 1801. During his thirty-four years on the bench, he greatly increased the influence of the Supreme Court and interpreted the Constitution so as to strengthen the federal government at the expense of the states.

Marshes of Glynn, The (1878) A poem by Sidney LANIER, often considered his masterpiece. In this poem, notable for its skillful and varied use of anapestic measure, Lanier reached the height of his lifelong attempt to reconcile the techniques of music and poetry. Its lush imagery sensuously depicts the sea marshes of Glynn County, Georgia, visited by Lanier in 1875.

Marston, John (c1575–1634) English satirist and dramatist. Marston's plays are almost all concerned with depictions of unbalanced love and lust. In his best work, *The Malcontent* (1604) and THE DUTCH COURTEZAN, his satiric power is couched in a dramatic structure that, if not extraordinary, is at least adequate. In other works, such as *The Insatiate Countess* (pub 1613), dramatic structure all but disappears, and moral indignation degenerates to the level of hysteria. His other plays include *Antonio and Mellida* (1599), *Antonio's Revenge* (1600), and *Sophonisba* (c1605–1606), a tragedy.

Ben Jonson attacked Marston in *The Poetaster* (1601), but they were reconciled and collaborated with George Chapman on *Eastward Ho* (1605), a comedy. Because the play contained passages offensive to the Scottish followers of James I, the three playwrights were briefly imprisoned.

Marston also wrote *The Metamorphosis of Pigmalions Image* (1598) and *The Scourge of Villanie* (1598), coarsely satirical poems.

Marsyas A Phrygian flute-player. Marsyas challenged APOLLO to a contest of skill and, having been beaten by the god, was flayed alive for his presumption. From his blood arose the river Marsyas.

Martello tower A circular masonry fort. The word is a misinterpretation of the original *Mortella*, from *Cape Mortella* in Corsica, where a Martello tower repulsed an attack by the British fleet in 1794. In Joyce's ULYSSES, Stephen Dedalus and his friend Buck Mulligan live in a Martello tower in Dublin.

Martha The sister of LAZARUS and Mary of Bethany. When JESUS came to their house, Mary sat at his feet and listened, but Martha "was cumbered about much serving" and complained of her sister to Jesus. Jesus replied, "Martha, Martha, thou art careful and troubled about many things: But one thing is needful; and Mary hath chosen that good part, which shall not be taken away from her" (Luke 10:38–42). She is the patron saint of good housewives and is represented in art in homely costume, with a batch of keys at her waist and a ladle or pot in her hand. In later Christian literature, Martha was the symbol of activity, pragmatism, and self-reliance, as opposed to Mary, who was humble, contemplative, and dependent. Her feast day is July 29.

Martí, José [Julian] (1853–1895)   Cuban poet and essayist. Martí is famous not only as the "apostle" of Cuban independence but also as one of the most original and influential writers of Latin America. As a youth he was imprisoned and later deported from Cuba because of his opposition to Spanish rule; he remained an exile for most of his life. From 1881 to 1895, he resided in New York, earning a precarious livelihood as a newspaper correspondent, as Uruguayan consul, as a teacher and translator. At the same time, he tirelessly collected funds, made speech after speech, and founded the Cuban Revolutionary Party in order to prepare a military expedition that would drive the Spaniards from the island. In 1895 Martí decided to return to Cuba to take advantage of renewed revolutionary sentiment there. His journal, *Diario de Cabo Haitiano a Dos Ríos* (1941), and letters to family and friends record his emotions as he and General Máximo Gómez reached Cuba with four companions and joined other insurgents. During a skirmish at Dos Ríos, Martí disobeyed Gómez's order to retreat and was killed by Spanish soldiers.

Martí the poet is often regarded as a forerunner of MODERNISMO, though in reality his work belongs to no school. His verses, written in a fresh, uniquely personal style, deal ardently, sometimes mystically, with familial and romantic love, freedom, and death. His best-known poems are in three collections: *Ismaelillo* (1882), addressed to his young son; *Versos libres*, written mainly in 1882 but not published until the 20th century; and *Versos sencillos* (1891). Many of his prose works, such as the essays *Nuestra América* (1891) and *Simón Bolívar* (1893), express his faith in the future greatness of Hispanic America. A perceptive critic of the U.S., Martí also wrote articles such as "Coney Island" (1881), "Emerson" (1882), "Jesse James" (1882), and "Walt Whitman" (1887).

Martial (full name Marcus Valerius Martialis, AD 42?–?102)   Latin epigrammatist, born in Spain. Martial spent most of his life in Rome and, as a witty man of letters, was accepted in high imperial circles. His friends included the emperors TITUS, Domitian, and Trajan, as well as the litterateur PLINY the Younger. Martial's favorite form of writing was the epigram. His epigrams have come down to us in fifteen books and present a graphic picture of life and manners in 1st-century Rome. Unlike his satiric contemporary JUVENAL, Martial seems to have aimed more for elegant grotesquerie than for the exposure of moral evils.

Martin, St.   The patron saint of innkeepers and drunkards. Martin was born of heathen parents but was converted in Rome, and became bishop of Tours in 371, dying at Caudes forty years later. His day is November 11, the day of the Roman *Vinalia*, or Feast of BACCHUS, hence

his purely accidental patronage and hence also the phrase *Martin drunk*.

The usual illustration of St. Martin alludes to the legend that, when he was a military tribune stationed at Amiens, he once, in midwinter, divided his cloak with a naked beggar, who craved alms of him before the city gates. At night, the story says, Christ appeared to the soldier, arrayed in this very garment.

Martin Chuzzlewit, The Life and Adventures of (1844)   A novel by Charles DICKENS. Wealthy old Martin Chuzzlewit, Sr., is surrounded by a greedy, grasping, selfish family: Anthony Chuzzlewit, his brother; the villainous Jonas, Anthony's son; and Seth PECKSNIFF, a crafty hypocrite. Detecting incipient selfishness and greed in his grandson, young Martin, Chuzzlewit turns him from the house almost penniless; Martin is in love with Mary Graham, an orphan raised by the old Chuzzlewit. Thus turned away, Martin travels to the U.S. with his loyal friend and servant, Mark Tapley. Here he becomes an architect for the Eden Land Corporation, a fraudulent enterprise in which he loses everything. He contracts a fever and almost dies. He returns home to England, cured of his selfishness by his difficult experiences in America, his grandfather accepts him, and he and Mary Graham are married. A subplot deals with Jonas Chuzzlewit, who tries to poison his old father, murders Montague Tigg because Tigg knows his secret, and marries Mercy Pecksniff, making her utterly miserable. He commits suicide to save his neck from the gallows.

In *Martin Chuzzlewit*, Dickens slashes away at the ignorant provincialism of Americans (the section of the book which takes place in the U.S. was extremely offensive to the American public) and dissects the selfish, grasping nature of Englishmen of the Chuzzlewit variety. Sarah GAMP, one of Dickens's most memorable characters, appears in this novel.

Martin du Gard, Roger (1881–1958)   French novelist and dramatist. An objective narrative and rational analysis of the intellectual and moral problems of the pre–World War I generation characterize both *Jean Barois* (1913) and the eight-part series LES THIBAULTS. The novel *Vielle France* (1933; tr *The Postman*, 1954) is a satiric study of small-town life, as are the peasant farces for the stage *Le Testament du Père Luleu* (1914) and *La Gonfle* (1928). Martin du Gard's other works include the short novel *La Confidence africaine* (1931) and the drama *Un Taciturne* (1931). He received the NOBEL PRIZE in 1937.

Martineau, Harriet (1802–1876)   English author, a voluminous writer on religion, economics, and government. Deaf from early childhood, Martineau was raised in a stern, resolutely pious, and intellectual atmosphere. Her earliest works, such as *Devotional Exercises for the Use of Young Persons* (1823), were of a religious character, but she became famous for a series of stories illustrating the economic theories of such contemporary thinkers as Malthus,

Ricardo, and Mill. These tales, *Illustrations of Political Economy* (1832–34), *Poor Laws and Paupers Illustrated* (1833), and *Illustrations of Taxation* (1843), combine sentimental fiction with dreary paraphrases of fact and theory. Of continuing interest are her *Autobiography* (1877) and her unfavorable critiques of America, *Society in America* (1837) and *Retrospect of Western Travel* (1838).

Martínez de la Rosa, Francisco (1787–1862) Spanish statesman and dramatist. Although his political career carried him through the posts of emissary, ambassador, and prime minister, Martínez de la Rosa is better known as a dramatist, particularly as one representative of the drift from the classic to the romantic. He is credited with the first widely acclaimed romantic drama, *La conjuración de Venecia* (1834), which is set in 14th-century Venice. He is also the author of *Abén Huyeya* (1836), a historical drama containing romantic elements, which deals with the Christian campaign against the Moors in the Alpujarras.

Martínez Ruiz, José (known as Azorín, 1873–1967) Spanish essayist and novelist. Martínez Ruiz's sensitive use of the Castilian landscape links him to the GENERACIÓN DEL 98. In fact, he was the first to call the group by this name, in essays later collected in *Clásicos y modernos* (1913). Though he attempted nearly every literary genre, he excelled as an essayist. In *El alma castellano* (1900) and several later collections, including *Una hora de España* (1924; tr *An Hour of Spain 1560–1590*, 1930), he revealed the characteristics for which he is best known: an emphasis on the recurrence of time and a style employing short sentences and an accumulation of seemingly insignificant details.

He also wrote a trilogy of autobiographical novels consisting of *La voluntad* (1902), *Antonio Azorín* (1903), and *Las confesiones de un pequeño filósofo* (1904).

Martínez Sierra, Gregorio 1881–1947) Spanish dramatist. Although he was the author of novels and a volume of verse, Martínez Sierra's fame rests on his plays, especially the much-translated *Canción de cuna* (*Cradle Song*, 1911), written, as were most of his works, in collaboration with his wife, María. A skillful depiction of cloistered life, the play centers on an abandoned child discovered on the convent steps. In the second half, the child has come of age and prepares to leave the convent for the world.

Martín Fierro (1872) A narrative poem by José HERNÁNDEZ. What is now considered the Argentine national classic was not recognized as such until the subject of its tale, the gaucho, had historically disappeared. This masterpiece of GAUCHO LITERATURE follows the transformation of a brutally conscripted cowboy into an army deserter and outlaw. Martín Fierro, in the tradition of the minstrel, tells his own life story: his suffering injustice under the abusive power of law officers, his duels, and his final flight with his friend Cruz into the Indian-held terri-

tories. The second part, *La vuelta de Martín Fierro* (1879), portrays him ready to strike a pact with society. The political content of the poem was promptly acknowledged in Argentina. Its literary quality was first recognized by the Spanish poet Miguel de UNAMUNO, some twenty years after its publication. Drawing from the gaucho's oral tradition and expressing the gaucho's own sense of worth and rivalry with the educated folk from Buenos Aires, *Martín Fierro* became a favorite among the illiterate gauchos, who paid to hear it read in the camps and general stores of the *pampa*.

Martín-Santos, Luis (1924–1964) Spanish novelist. As director of a psychiatric institution, Martín-Santos published philosophical and psychoanalytic studies. His novel TIME OF SILENCE introduced the use of interior monologue and STREAM OF CONSCIOUSNESS techniques to the Spanish novel. His characters lead a tragic life in an absurd world, victimized by the Church, science, and sexuality. He also wrote *Apólogos* (1970), short stories and poematic sketches about life and death, and the unfinished novel *Tiempo de destrucción* (*Time of Destruction*, 1975), which also attacks institutions that curtail individual freedom. Both were published after he died in an automobile accident.

Martinson, Harry [Edmund] (1904–1978) Swedish novelist, poet, dramatist, and essayist. Martinson is one of the most important modern exponents of Swedish PROLETARIAN LITERATURE. Based largely on his own working-class background, his novels deal with indigent characters and their search, often futile, for freedom and personal integrity. Among the few works in translation are *Kap Farväl!* (1933; tr *Cape Farewell*, 1934) and *Vägen till Klockrike* (1948; tr *The Road*, 1955). His epic poem *Aniara* (1956; tr 1963) is about a spaceship's irreversible course into the void. A superb nature writer, Martinson has powerfully expressed his increasing unrest about the advancement of technology at the expense of humanity in *Gräsen i Thule* (1958) and *Vagnen* (1960). In 1974 Martinson shared the NOBEL PRIZE in Literature with Eyvind JOHNSON.

Marvell, Andrew (1621–1678) English poet. Balance and detachment, strong features of Marvell's poetry, characterize most of his life. During the English Civil War, he was a tutor in the household of Lord General Thomas Fairfax and later became assistant to John Milton, when the latter was Latin secretary of the Commonwealth, but he was also a good friend of Lovelace, who was a Royalist, and he never approved of the execution of Charles I. During the Commonwealth, he was elected to Parliament and served ably in public offices until his death. He was instrumental in saving Milton from punishment after the Restoration.

One of the METAPHYSICAL POETS, Marvell is best known for his early, largely lyric, poetry, including THE GARDEN, TO HIS COY MISTRESS, "Bermudas," THE DEFINITION OF

Love, An Horatian Ode upon Cromwell's Return from Ireland, and "A Dialogue between the Soul and Body." Typically, most of these poems represent a tacit, unresolved debate between two or more opposing values: contemplation versus activity, nature versus civilization, power versus justice. In his later days, he wrote satirical poetry directed against Stuart policies, such as "The Last Instructions to a Painter," a verse satire on the Dutch War. His work is distinguished by lyric grace, striking conceits and images, and a rare intellectual balance and subtlety. Most of his poems were not published until 1681 and the satires not until 1689, after the Glorious Revolution.

In the 18th century, Marvell was known as a satirist, Swift praising this aspect of his work. The romantics, Wordsworth and Lamb especially, appreciated his lyric poems, but it was the 20th century that saw a great revival of interest in him, in part through T. S. Eliot's influence as a critic.

Marx, Karl (1818–1883)   German socialist who, with Friedrich ENGELS, formulated the principles of DIALECTICAL MATERIALISM, or economic determinism. Marx used HEGEL's concept of the dialectic to explain history as a series of antitheses and syntheses, but, whereas the Hegelian dialectic describes the conflict of ideas leading to the development of reason and freedom, the Marxian dialectic operates in terms of economic forces. Marx maintained that economic structure is the basis of history and determines all the social, political, and intellectual aspects of life. The evils of capitalist society cannot be abolished by reform, therefore, but only by destruction of the whole capitalist economy and establishment of a new, classless society. (See THE COMMUNIST MANIFESTO.) Because of his revolutionary activities, Marx spent most of his life outside Germany, and his major work, DAS KAPITAL, was written in London, where he also organized the First International, an association of European socialists, in 1864. His ideas had great influence on Nikolay LENIN and the development of Russian communism.

Mary I (Mary Tudor, often called Bloody Mary; 1516–1558)   Queen of England (1553–58), daughter of HENRY VIII and Catherine of Aragon. Mary was declared illegitimate after her parents' marriage was dissolved but was nevertheless proclaimed queen after the death of her half brother, Edward VI, in 1553. She restored Catholicism in England, which had been Protestant for nearly twenty years. Despite strong popular opposition, she married Prince Philip of Spain, a Catholic and a foreigner. In 1555 the persecution and burning of Protestants began under the reinstated heresy laws; nearly three hundred persons went to the stake in the last years of her reign. She is the subject of Victor Hugo's tragedy *Mary Tudor* (1833) and Tennyson's play *Queen Mary* (1876).

Mary Barton (1848)   A novel by Elizabeth Cleghorn GASKELL. A work of great realism, it deals with the inhumanities suffered by the impoverished weavers of Manchester.

Maryland, My Maryland (1861)   A poem by James Ryder Randall (1839–1908). First printed in the New Orleans *Delta* (April 26, 1861), it was reprinted all over the South; sung to the tune of the German Christmas song "O Tannenbaum, O Tannenbaum," it was adopted as a favorite battle song by Confederate soldiers. The title of Edmund WILSON's study of the literature of the American CIVIL WAR, *Patriotic Gore* (1962), is taken from Randall's poem.

Mary Magdalene   In the NEW TESTAMENT one of the followers of JESUS. Mary Magdalene may have been the harlot whom Jesus rescued from her evil life (Mark 16:9). She is identified by the name of her home town, Magdala, which was famous for its immorality. Mary Magdalene was present at the Crucifixion and was one of the first to see the open tomb three days later.

Mary, Queen of Scots (Mary Stuart, 1542–1587)   Daughter of James V of Scotland, mother of JAMES I of England and VI of Scotland and titular queen of Scotland from six days after her birth until her abdication in favor of her son in 1567. Betrothed to the dauphin of France as a child and married to him in 1558, Mary did not actually reign in Scotland until after the death of her husband in 1560. In 1565 she married her cousin Henry, Lord Darnley, by whom she had a son, James. Darnley arranged the murder of David Rizzio, one of Mary's favorite councillors, and Darnley himself was murdered, possibly with Mary's complicity, shortly after (see CASKET LETTERS). The earl of Bothwell, who was probably responsible for Darnley's death, captured Mary, and after making a token resistance, she married him. The Scottish lords then rose up against Mary, and she was imprisoned and forced to abdicate. In 1568 she fled to England, where she was again put in prison. There were several Catholic plots to free Mary and put her on the English throne; from a Catholic point of view, Queen ELIZABETH was both illegitimate and a heretic, and Mary was the rightful claimant to the throne, both in terms of legitimate descent and faith. However, Mary was allowed to live in semiconfinement until the outbreak of BABINGTON'S CONSPIRACY, after which she was brought to trial for conspiring against the life of the queen. She was condemned and executed in 1587.

Mary is a prominent character in Sir Walter Scott's *Abbot* (1820), which deals with her flight to England. She is the subject of Schiller's tragedy *Maria Stuart* (1800); Björnstjerne Björnson's drama *Maria Stuart* (1864); Swinburne's trilogy of verse dramas *Chastelard* (1865), *Bothwell* (1874), and *Mary Stuart* (1881); and N. B. Morrison's biography *Mary, Queen of Scots* (1960).

Mary Stuart (Maria Stuart, 1800)   A tragedy by Friedrich SCHILLER. It treats the conflict between Elizabeth I and MARY, QUEEN OF SCOTS, while the latter is imprisoned in England. In Schiller's version, though Elizabeth wants Mary out of the way, she is unable to make a final decision about commanding her death, and, in the end, she contrives to make it seem as though a hasty official had been responsible for Mary's execution.

Mary, the Virgin The mother of JESUS, wife of JOSEPH. Jesus was Mary's first and possibly only child, although both MATTHEW (13:55) and MARK (6:3) mention other children as Jesus' siblings. The date of neither her birth nor her death is known. She was a cousin of Elizabeth, the mother of JOHN THE BAPTIST, and stayed with Elizabeth for three months during her pregnancy (Luke 1:39–56). She fled to Egypt with Joseph and Jesus and may have traveled with Jesus after their return to Nazareth; she was present at the Crucifixion, where Jesus entrusted her to the care of JOHN. Her last appearance in the NEW TESTAMENT is in ACTS OF THE APOSTLES (Acts 1:13), shortly after the Resurrection. She is the object of special veneration in the Roman Catholic Church, which adopted the doctrine of her Immaculate Conception (1854) and her bodily assumption into heaven (1950). She is an extremely important figure in religious painting and sculpture, in which she is usually called The Madonna.

Masaccio (real name Tommaso di Giovanni, 1401–1428) Florentine painter. Masaccio is often called "the true father of Renaissance painting," as his influence on his contemporaries was more immediate and fruitful than that of GIOTTO, of whom he was, however, the logical successor and modern embodiment. Masaccio stressed simplicity and evocative gesture rather than movement and brought about a revolution in painting through his ability, learned from BRUNELLESCHI, to construct convincing spatial relationships and through his mastery in creating the illusion of heaviness and weight by means of light and shade. His frescoes in the Brancacci Chapel of the Church of the Carmine in Florence, though unfinished, served as a training school for Florentine painters of succeeding generations, even to the time of MICHELANGELO.

Masaoka Shiki (1867–1902) Japanese poet and critic. Initially a prose writer, Masaoka Shiki devoted a major portion of his short life to the collection and composition of HAIKU. He advocated a naturalistic realism in the presentation of images, and, in such works as *Bashō zatsudan* (1894), he clarified the principles of the great haiku master, MATSUO BASHŌ. He restored the haiku to the prestige it had enjoyed during the TOKUGAWA period and became the greatest haiku poet of the 19th century. Using similar methods, he helped to modernize the TANKA.

Masefield, John (1878–1967) English poet, dramatist, and novelist. From 1930 to his death, Masefield was POET LAUREATE of England. He is best known for his sea poems, such as those collected in *Salt-Water Ballads* (1902); his poems "Sea Fever" and "Cargoes" appear in many anthologies. As a boy, he went to sea as a cadet officer. He then spent a number of years wandering around

the world, doing odd jobs, including working as a bartender's assistant in New York.

Masefield made his reputation with a long narrative poem, *The Everlasting Mercy* (1911). Like many of his other early poems, it is notable for its realistic, robust background of country life and its sometimes harsh, unpoetic language. Other narrative poems include *Reynard the Fox* (1919), *The Widow in the Bye Street* (1912), and *Dauber* (1913). He wrote a number of verse plays, including *The Tragedy of Nan* (1908). His novels are romantic adventure stories, packed with color and action. He also wrote journalism, literary criticism, and military and nautical history, as well as some classic children's books.

Masham, Lady Abigail (d 1734) Daughter of the London merchant Francis Hill, first cousin of the duchess of MARLBOROUGH, and a friend of Jonathan SWIFT. As a favorite of Queen Anne, superseding the duchess of Marlborough, Lady Abigail exercised much influence at court.

masochism A sexual abnormality in which one takes pleasure in being abused or tortured. See SACHER-MASOCH, LEOPOLD VON.

Mason, A[lfred] E[dward] W[oodley] (1865–1948) English novelist. Author of romantic tales of adventure and detection, often set in exotic countries, Mason wrote, among other works, *The Four Feathers* (1902), about the vindication of a man thought to be a coward.

Mason, Perry See GARDNER, ERLE STANLEY.

Mason, R[onald] A[lison] K[els] (1905–1971) New Zealand poet, editor, and dramatist. Most of Mason's poems were published before 1940. His tightly constructed, vigorous, but darkly pessimistic verse was hailed by Allen CURNOW as the first truly original New Zealand poetry. Among his best-known volumes are *No New Thing* (1934) and *This Dark Will Lighten* (1941). His *Collected Poems* appeared in 1962.

Mason and Dixon's line Originally the boundary line separating Maryland and Pennsylvania, laid (1763–67) by the English astronomers and surveyors Charles Mason and Jeremiah Dixon. It lies in 39° 43′ 26″ north latitude. At the time of the CIVIL WAR, the name was used to designate the line separating the free states from the slave states.

masque A form of dramatic entertainment. The masque, like drama itself, probably finds its origins in primitive fertility rites. It appears in a number of societies in a variety of forms, in almost all cases culminating in an impromptu dance, or *komos*, in which both spectators and performers engage. In the Middle Ages, the masque took the form of an unexpected visit to a friend's house by a group of masked players and musicians who would provide a spontaneous entertainment.

In England the masque had a dual development, on the one hand resulting in thinly disguised fertility rites, such as the St. George "Sword Dance" folk plays, and on the other in the elaborate court entertainments that make their first appearance in the early years of the 16th century, during the reign of Henry VIII.

These court festivities were continued (with considerably less profligacy) under the reign of Elizabeth, but it is not until the reign of James I (1603–25) and his pleasure-loving wife, Anne, that the masque in England develops the lavish, ornate, and elaborate spectacle for which it is known. The men who made the greatest contribution to the development of the masque were Inigo JONES and Ben JONSON. Jones, an architect trained in Italy and heavily influenced by Italian neoclassicism, was responsible for the magnificence of the spectacle. Jonson, who inherited a masque tradition that was essentially one of pantomime and in which there were no dramatic values, emphasized dialogue and song, giving the airy nothings of the Elizabethan masque a substantial literary framework. He also introduced the anti-masque, a comic interlude which parodied the major plot. The collaboration of Jonson and Jones ushered in the golden age of the masque. Together they achieved a balance of lyrical grace and sumptuous splendor that has never been equaled in stage entertainments. Inevitably, however, they quarreled over the relative importance of their contributions, and, with the dissolution of their partnership and, ultimately, the success of the Puritan Revolution, the masque disappeared from England.

Among Jonson's masques are *Hymenai* (1606), *The Masque of Beauty* (1608), *The Hue and Cry after Cupid* (1608), *The Masque of Queens* (1609), and *Oberon, the Faery Prince* (1611). Other writers of masques were George CHAPMAN, BEAUMONT AND FLETCHER, and Thomas MIDDLETON. John Milton's COMUS, though titled a masque, is often considered to be more of a pastoral drama.

Massacre of St. Bartholomew   The slaughter of French Protestants begun on the eve of St. Bartholomew's Day, August 24, 1572. Authorized by Charles IX at the instigation of his mother, Catherine de Médicis, the persecutions continued for several weeks and spread from Paris to the provinces. It has been estimated that some thirty thousand persons were killed, including Gaspard de Coligny and Pierre La Ramée.

Masses, The   A left-wing LITTLE MAGAZINE, founded in 1911. Max Eastman became editor in December 1912. Socialist and pacifist in viewpoint, it stressed literature, art, and the spoofing of the bourgeoisie. Eastman ran the magazine until its suppression by federal authorities in December 1917. Contributing editors included Floyd DELL, John REED, and Louis UNTERMEYER.

It was succeeded in March 1918 by the doctrinaire *The Liberator*, which Eastman edited for a while and which became associated with the Communist Party in 1922. The weekly *New Masses*, which appeared in 1926, was a successor to *The Liberator*; it became a monthly in 1948 under the name *Masses & Mainstream*. Samuel Sillen was editor, and Howard FAST, W.E.B. DU BOIS, and Paul ROBESON were among the contributing editors.

Massinger, Philip (1583–1640)   English dramatist. After attending Oxford, Massinger went to London, where he won the friendship of such men as Tourneur, Dekker, and Fletcher, with all of whom he later collaborated. His best-known play is the satiric comedy A NEW WAY TO PAY OLD DEBTS, whose principal character, the acquisitive Sir Giles Overreach, was long a favorite role among actors. Among the plays usually ascribed to Massinger alone are *The Duke of Milan* (1620), a tragedy; *The Maid of Honor* (c1621), a romantic drama based on a story told by Boccaccio; *The Great Duke of Comedy* (1627), a romantic comedy; and *The City Madam* (1632), a comedy. The religious emphasis of some of his works, notably *The Maid of Honor* and *The Virgin Martyr* (1622), on which he collaborated with Dekker, fostered the belief that he was converted to Roman Catholicism. With Nathan Field, he collaborated on the tragedy *The Fatal Dowry* (1619), and he may have shared in the writing of HENRY VIII and THE TWO NOBLE KINSMEN. The manuscripts of some of his lost plays were reputedly destroyed in the 18th century, when a cook in the household of Bishop John Warburton used them to line pie dishes.

Master Builder, The (1892)   A play by Henrik IBSEN. *The Master Builder* departs from the social subjects of the bulk of Ibsen's work and deals, both realistically and symbolically, with the spirit of the artist seeking to surpass its own limitations and the conflict between one's own needs and the needs of others. Master Builder Solness is afraid of being crushed by the younger generation of architects, as he himself has crushed the builders before him; yet he finds in the girl Hilda both the younger generation he fears and the strength of purpose he lacks. Through her urging, he attempts to do "the impossible": to climb, in spite of his vertigo, to the top of the high spire he has built on his new house, and then to build, with Hilda, "the loveliest thing in the world"—a castle in the air. He reaches the top of the spire but falls and is killed.

Masters, Edgar Lee (1868–1950)   American poet and novelist. Masters was a practicing lawyer in Chicago for nearly thirty years before he retired to New York in 1920. He published numerous collections of verse, beginning with *A Book of Verses* (1898), none of which attracted much attention. However, the publication in 1915 of SPOON RIVER ANTHOLOGY, a series of "auto-epitaphs" in FREE VERSE, giving a dramatic and realistic picture of village life in the Middle West, immediately gained Masters a large following and set him in the vanguard of the Chicago literary renaissance (see CHICAGO GROUP). His subsequent volumes of poetry include *Songs and Satires* (1916), *Starved Rock* (1919), *Domesday Book* (1920), *Poems of the People* (1936), and *Illinois Poems* (1941).

Masters wrote several novels, including the trilogy consisting of *Mitch Miller* (1920), *Skeeters Kirby* (1923), and

Mirage (1924). He also wrote biographies of Vachel Lindsay (1935), Walt Whitman (1937), and Mark Twain (1938). *Lincoln, the Man* (1931), the only one of his later books to attract wide attention, was sharply critical of the Civil War president. *Across Spoon River* (1936) was his autobiography. Masters was buried in the cemetery of Petersburg, Illinois, the village which, with Lewistown, Illinois, he had used as the scene of his most famous work.

Masters, John (1914–1983) India-born English novelist. A resident of the U.S., Masters is best known for his romantic novels on episodes in Indian history, such as *Bhowani Junction* (1954).

matadero, El (The Slaughterhouse, 1871) A story by Esteban ECHEVERRÍA. Written during the 1830s, "El matadero" is the unfinished draft of a novel denouncing the brutality of the dictatorship of Juan Manuel de Rosas. Its crude realism stands in sharp contrast to the romanticism that characterizes Echeverría's poetry; the story is set in a Buenos Aires slaughterhouse, where henchmen of Rosas murder a member of the opposition who passes by.

Matali In Hindu mythology, the charioteer of INDRA.

materialism In philosophy, the theory that matter is the basis of all reality, that all reality is capable of being perceived by the senses, and that all natural phenomena can be explained in terms of physical conditions alone. Strict materialists would maintain that nothing can exist independent of matter and that all things, including ideas and emotions, result from material activity. Classical materialism is usually identified with the atomistic theories of DEMOCRITUS and his teacher, LEUCIPPUS, who held that nothing exists but atoms and the void, that all is determined by the movements and collisions of atoms in space. EPICURUS applied Democritean principles to his theory that reality is determined by the senses, an idea that was not fully developed until the 17th century, by Pierre Gassendi (1596–1655) and Thomas HOBBES. Probably the greatest materialist theorizer of the 18th century was the German philosopher Paul Heinrich Dietrich d'Holbach (1723–89), whose major work, *Système de la nature* (1770), argued that all reality is nature and that nature is determined by matter—earth, fire, air, water—in motion. According to Holbach's constructs, even feelings are produced by certain arrangements and transformations of matter. In the 19th century, the idealist philosophy of Marx and Engels produced DIALECTICAL MATERIALISM, which marked a departure from classical theory, in that it allowed for the notion that, while mind is rooted in matter, it is also separate and distinct from matter. In a different vein, Darwin's theory of the order and organization of living creatures in ORIGIN OF SPECIES had a profound effect on the acceptance of a biological materialism. Materialist methodology has been applied not only to the sciences but also to fields as diverse as politics, parapsychology, and literary criticism.

Mather, Cotton (1663–1728) American clergyman, theologian, and writer. The grandson of Richard Mather and John Cotton, Mather was a child prodigy who entered Harvard at the age of twelve and became an erudite historian and folklorist, as well as a staunch Puritan and tireless writer on an encyclopedic range of subjects. Although he was inclined to believe in witchcraft and is often regarded as the epitome of Puritan fanaticism, he upheld the authority of reason and called Isaac Newton "our perpetual dictator." One of his many quarrels stemmed from his spirited defense of inoculation for smallpox, then a highly suspicious practice. Among his best-known works are *The Wonders of the Invisible World* (1693), a discussion of witches and the supernatural; *Magnalia Christi Americana* (1702); and *The Christian Philosopher* (1721), essays attempting to reconcile science with religion.

Mather, Increase (1639–1723) American clergyman and theologian. The son of Richard Mather, a leader in the establishment of the Congregational Church in America, and father of Cotton Mather, Increase Mather was a well-known preacher, served as president of Harvard College (1685–1701), and played an important part in the Salem witchcraft trials, though he criticized the extremism of the trials in *Cases of Conscience Concerning Evil Spirits* (1693). Among his better-known works are *Life and Death of Richard Mather* (1670), *A Brief History of the War with the Indians* (1676), and AN ESSAY FOR THE RECORDING OF ILLUSTRIOUS PROVIDENCES. Like his son, he was influenced by the growing scientific spirit of his time and upheld inoculation for smallpox.

Matisse, Henri [Émile] (1869–1954) French painter and sculptor. One of the greatest figures in modern painting, Matisse was the leader of LES FAUVES. Throughout his career, he sought to combine color and line so that each, while retaining its individual quality, would enhance the other. His style evolved from experiments with neoimpressionistic ideas (*Lux, calme, et volupté*, 1905), to the famous *Dance* and *Music* paintings (1909–10), to the sensuous *Odalisques* (1920–25), through to radically simplified color interiors with plants and women and the bold papercuts of his last years. Insisting that the painting itself must be considered apart from its subject, Matisse pursued the use of color as a sensual communication of the "feeling" of a subject rather than as a literal depiction. The line drawings and color cutouts from the end of his life stand with the finest graphic art produced in the 20th century. Similarly, his sculpture, in which the influences of both RODIN and black African art are clear, consists of bold, expressive abstract forms. As he used color in his paintings, Matisse used shape and structure in his sculptures to express enormous emotion.

Matsuo Bashō (1644–1694) Japanese HAIKU poet. Bashō is generally acknowledged as the developer and greatest master of this form. His *haiku* went through many phases, evolving from the pedantic verse of his early youth to the lighthearted poetry of his last years. The work of his peak period is characterized by evocations of man's ultimate harmony with nature. A wanderer for much of his life, Bashō also wrote travel sketches interspersed with *haiku*. *Oi no kobumi* (1688; tr *The Records of a Travel-Worn Satchel*, 1966) is famous for its opening passages, which reveal his basic beliefs, but the best work in this genre is *Oku no hosomichi* (1689; tr *The Narrow Road to the Deep North*, 1966), which, outwardly describing his journey to rural areas of northeastern Japan, inwardly traces his spiritual quest for simple primitive beauty all but lost in urban life.

Matsya   In Hindu mythology, an AVATAR (incarnation) of the god VISHNU, represented as a fish.

Matta Echaurren, Roberto [Sebastian Antonio] (1912–   )   Chilean painter. Originally a student of architecture, Matta worked in LE CORBUSIER's studio in the mid-1930s. Not long after his introduction to Salvador DALI, he began exhibiting paintings in the surrealist style. He developed the "accident" or spilled-paint technique and later carried SURREALISM to a level of abstraction unique in his time. His paintings portray his mystical belief in a cosmic unity, often depicting the interchangeability of man and machine. His abstract figures and iridescent colors create a vast sense of inner and outer space.

Matthew, St. (also called Levi)   One of the twelve APOSTLES of JESUS. St. Matthew was a publican (toll collector) at Capernaum by the Sea of Galilee when Jesus met him and called him to be one of his disciples (Matt. 9:9). The Gospel According to St. MATTHEW was originally attributed to him, but this has been seriously questioned by most modern biblical scholars. There is no information about his later life, but it is said that he was slain by the sword in Parthia. His feast day is September 21.

Matthew, The Gospel According to St.   The first book of the NEW TESTAMENT. It is unique among the SYNOPTIC GOSPELS in that it traces JESUS' ancestry back through DAVID to ABRAHAM and places strong emphasis on Jesus as the Messiah prophesied in the OLD TESTAMENT, referring to him in several instances as "King of the Jews." This internal evidence suggests that it was written for Jewish readers. This gospel also provides the most complete account of the sayings of Jesus, whereas The Gospel According to St. MARK, for example, is more a narrative of his actions. The date of its composition is usually placed after AD 75; its actual authorship is uncertain. Since it was written in Greek, it does not seem to be an eyewitness account, and there is some evidence to suggest that the author drew on the gospels of both Mark and LUKE. It is unlikely that, as traditionally ascribed, its author was actually Matthew, the APOSTLE.

Matthews, [James] Brander (1852–1929)   American teacher, critic, and author. Matthews's short but pioneering work *An Introduction to the Study of American Literature* (1896) stimulated the study of American literature as a legitimate field of interest. He taught English at Columbia University from 1891 to 1900, at which time he was appointed professor of drama, the first such post in America. Among his numerous influential works were *The Development of Drama* (1903), *Shakespeare as a Playwright* (1913), and *The Principles of Playmaking* (1919).

Matthiessen, F[rancis] O[tto] (1902–1950)   American teacher and critic. Matthiessen taught for several years at Yale and then at Harvard, from 1929 until his death. His significant contribution to literary criticism lay in his attempts at defining a unifying tradition of American literature. Always interested in the relationship of the social and political climate to the literature of a given era, he traced a line of American writing from HAWTHORNE to Henry JAMES to T. S. ELIOT and DREISER. His best-known works include *The Achievement of T. S. Eliot: An Essay on the Nature of Poetry* (1935), *American Renaissance: Art and Expression in the Age of Emerson and Whitman* (1941), and *Henry James: The Major Phase* (1944). In the year before his suicide, at the age of forty-eight, Matthiessen edited *The Oxford Book of American Verse* (1950) and began work on his posthumously published life of Theodore Dreiser (1951).

Matthiessen, Peter (1927–   )   American novelist, traveler, and nature writer. In 1951 Matthiessen cofounded and edited *The Paris Review*. As a writer, he is best known for perceptively drawn accounts of the people and wildlife he encountered on many expeditions: *The Cloud Forest* (1961), about the Amazon wilderness; *Under the Mountain Wall* (1962), observations of a New Guinea tribe; *Blue Meridian* (1971), an account of a search for the white shark off the coast of Australia; and *The Snow Leopard* (1978), which won a National Book Award, the chronicle of a trek through the mountains of Nepal, combining the delight of a naturalist with a meditation on man's fate, and the author's own, in relation to ZEN BUDDHISM. In all his travels, Matthiessen is acutely aware of the pernicious effects of civilization on primitive peoples and the natural wilderness. This theme runs through his impressions of Africa, *The Tree Where Man Was Born* (1972) and *Sand Rivers* (1981), and two of his novels, *At Play in the Fields of the Lord* (1965) and *Far Tortuga* (1975). *In the Spirit of Crazy Horse* (1983), a moral examination of racism as it relates to the American Indian, centers on a 1975 shootout between FBI agents and Native Americans in South Dakota. In 1986 he published *Men's Lives*, an account of life among the commercial fishermen of Long Island, New York.

Maturin, Charles Robert (1787–1824)   Irish novelist, one of the leading writers of the GOTHIC NOVEL. Maturin's most famous work is MELMOTH THE WANDERER, a story of the sale of a soul to the devil in exchange for prolonged life. In this book, Maturin achieves power and psychological validity, but generally his work is marred by excesses of horror and mystification. His other books include *The Fatal Revenge* (1807), *The Wild Irish Boy* (1808), *The Milesian Chief* (1811), *Women, or Pour et Contre* (1818), and *The Albigenses* (1824). He also wrote a successful play, *Bertram* (1816).

Matute, Ana María (1925–   ) Spanish novelist and short-story writer. One of Spain's foremost women writers, Matute also writes works for children. In her early writing, she treats the loss of innocence in a brutalized world. Her first major success, *Los hijos muertos* (1958; tr *The Lost Children*, 1965), describes the rebellious and frustrated young who suffer because of the war their elders created. "Historias de la Artámila" (1961), typical of her short stories, emphasizes existential themes of loneliness and isolation. Her major achievement, the trilogy of novels including *Primera memoria* (1960; tr *School of the Sun*, 1963), *Los soldados lloran de noche* (1964), and *La trampa* (1969) explores the psychological causes underlying the Spanish Civil War.

Maud Muller (1854) A narrative poem by John Greenleaf WHITTIER. It records a chance meeting between the wealthy judge and Maud, a rustic beauty. She laid aside her rake and gave him a drink from the spring. Each married someone of more suitable station in life but was tormented by regretful illusions:

> For of all sad words of tongue or pen,
> The saddest are these: "It might have been."

Maugham, W[illiam] Somerset (1874–1965) English novelist, short-story writer, and playwright. Although he used plots and material intended for popular appeal, Maugham's work is distinguished by his skillful craftsmanship, economy of expression, satire, and ironical detachment. His first novel, the naturalistic *Liza of Lambeth* (1897), was inspired by his experiences as a medical intern in a London slum. His other novels include *Mrs. Craddock* (1902); *The Magician* (1909), based on the character of Aleister CROWLEY; OF HUMAN BONDAGE, a partially autobiographical novel, generally considered his finest; THE MOON AND SIXPENCE; *Ashenden: or The British Agent* (1928), based on his experience as a secret agent in World War I; CAKES AND ALE; THE RAZOR'S EDGE; *Then and Now* (1946); and *Catalina* (1948).

Maugham's early reputation was based on his comedies of manners for the stage. Among the best remembered of his witty, cynical, and frankly commercial plays are *The Circle* (1921), *Our Betters* (1923), and *The Constant Wife* (1926). His economical technique and his ability to immerse a reader quickly in the action were ideally suited to the short-story form, with which his name was ultimately identified. Many of the stories, set in the tropics, were studies of mixed marriages, class differences, and the effects of the stress of climate on white people. His best-known stories include MISS THOMPSON, "Rain" (1921), and

"The Casuarina Tree" (1926). *The Art of Fiction* (1955) is a collection of introductions to ten great novels. Maugham was awarded the Order of Merit after his eightieth birthday.

Maundy Thursday The Thursday before EASTER. It commemorates the LAST SUPPER, at which Jesus instituted the EUCHARIST. After supper, Jesus washed his disciples' feet and gave them a new commandment (Lat, *mandatum*), that they love one another. For this reason, some churches still hold foot-washing ceremonies on this day.

Maupassant, Guy de (1850–1893) French short-story writer and novelist. A member of the naturalist school, Maupassant chose the subjects for his stories and novels chiefly from Norman peasant life, the Franco-Prussian War, the behavior of the bourgeoisie, and the fashionable life of Paris. A pupil of Gustave Flaubert, he brought the same careful attention to the writer's craft as did his master. Stories such as the famous "En famille," "Le Rendezvous," "The Necklace," and "The Umbrella" are built around simple episodes from the humble life of every day. In tone, the tales are marked by objectivity, detachment, and a fine use of irony. Maupassant's style is direct and simple, with attention to realistic detail. His vision of human existence is somber, for he sees clearly the toil, suffering, and the bitterly ironic happenings that twist human lives. Among his novels are *Une Vie* (1883), about the frustrating existence of a Norman wife; *Bel-Ami* (1885), which depicts an unscrupulous journalist; and *Pierre et Jean* (1888), a psychological study of two brothers.

Mauriac, Claude (1914–   ) French literary critic and novelist of the NEW WAVE; the son of François MAURIAC. He has written a number of critical studies of French writers but Mauriac's most significant contribution to literary ideas is *L'Alittérature contemporaine* (1958; tr *The New Literature*, 1959), in which he delineates the theories and techniques of the NOUVEAU ROMAN. He then began to write his own experimental novels, which record the simultaneous dialogue and thoughts of the characters but without building a plot or defining the time or setting in the traditional manner. His many novels include *Toutes les femmes sont fatales* (1957; tr *All Women Are Fatal*, 1964), *Le Dîner en ville* (1959; tr *The Dinner Party*, 1960), *La Marquise sortit à cinq heures* (1961; tr *The Marquise Went Out at Five*, 1962), and *Un Coeur tout neuf* (1980); the first three novels are part of a tetralogy entitled *Le Dialogue intérieur*. He has also written six volumes of memoirs, collectively titled *Le Temps immobile* (1970–78).

Mauriac, François (1885–1970) French novelist, essayist, and dramatist; father of Claude MAURIAC. His native Bordeaux is the setting for most of Mauriac's short novels, which present psychological analyses of middle-class characters tormented by lack of the grace of God. A Catholic, intensely concerned with the problem of sin and redemption, Mauriac presents the attempts and inevitable failures of those who seek satisfaction in money, property, and especially in human love. In his novels, sensual desire is always sinful and eventually destructive, and marriages are hateful duels between the partners.

Family relationships become enslaving bonds, and love breeds tragedy through its fiercely possessive jealousy and its attempt to manipulate another life. Yet those individuals whose passionate quests for self-fulfillment lead them deepest into sin are usually those whose capacity for self-knowledge eventually makes most capable of spiritual fulfillment. Those who pride themselves on their virtue remain most guilty of emotional coldness and spiritual sterility. Thus the women in *Génitrix* (1923; tr 1930) and *La Pharisienne* (1941; tr *A Woman of the Pharisees*, 1946) harm everyone around them with their "good" intentions. A father and son find that their romantic yearnings lead only to aridity in *Le Désert de l'amour* (1925; tr *The Desert of Love*, 1929); the family circle is further examined in *Le Noeud de vipères* (1932; tr *Vipers' Tangle*, 1933). Mauriac is best at describing the anguish of suffering, rather than suggesting possible solutions for man's quest. His most successfully drawn characters, as in *Le Baiser au lepreux* (1922; tr *The Kiss to the Leper*, 1930) and Thérèse Desqueyroux, cannot achieve either earthly happiness or the salvation of divine love.

His *La Vie de Jésus* (1936; tr *Life of Jesus*, 1937) and *Le Fils de l'homme* (1958; tr *The Son of Man*, 1960) present aspects of Jesus as human sufferer. The development of his own philosophy is revealed through his reactions to literature and life in *Dieu et Mammon* (1929; tr *God and Mammon*, 1936), his *Journal* (5 vols, 1934–53; partial tr *Second Thoughts*, 1961), and *La Pierre d'achoppement* (1948; tr *The Stumbling Block*, 1956).

Mauriac wrote many other novels; several plays, including *Asmodée* (1937); and collections of poetry, such as *Orages* (1925). He was awarded the Nobel Prize in 1952.

Maurois, André (pen name of Émile Herzog, 1885–1967)   French biographer, novelist, and essayist. The vastness of Maurois's fluent and intelligent output is remarkable in light of the fact that his first book was not published until he was thirty-three, and that he did not devote himself to writing until ten years later. In his first book, *Les Silences du Colonel Bramble* (1918; tr *The Silence of Colonel Bramble*, 1920), and in *Les Discours du Docteur O'Grady* (1922; tr *The Discourses of Doctor O'Grady*, 1965), Maurois presents humorous portraits of the British comrades with whom he served when a liaison officer in World War I. His many vivid biographies include *Ariel* (1923; tr 1930), about the poet Shelley; *Disraeli* (1927; tr 1928); *Proust* (1949; tr 1950); *Lélia* (1952; tr 1953), about George Sand; *Olympio* (1954; tr 1956), about Victor Hugo; *Les Trois Dumas* (1957; tr *The Titans*, 1957); and *Prométhée* (1965; tr *Prometheus*, 1965), about Balzac. *Histoire d'Angleterre* (1937; tr *The Miracle of England*, 1937) and *Histoire de la France* (1947; tr *The Miracle of France*, 1948) are popular historical works. His novels

include the autobiographical *Bernard Quesnay* (1926; tr 1927), *Climats* (1928; tr *Atmosphere of Love*, 1929), and *Le Cercle de famille* (1932; tr *The Family Circle*, 1932). His *Memoirs* appeared in 1970.

Maurras, Charles   See Action française, L'.

mausoleum   A tomb of great size. It is so called after Mausolus, king of Caria in the 4th century BC, whose wife Artemisia built for him a majestic sepulchral monument at Halicarnassus in Asia Minor. Parts of this sepulcher, which was one of the Seven Wonders of the Ancient World, are now in the British Museum.

Mauve Decade, The (1926)   A book by Thomas Beer (1889–1940), surveying the American literary and social scene of the 1890s. The color yellow had already been described as typical of the period in England, and Beer, trying similarly to capture the essence of the decade in America, chose mauve as the significant tone: "pink turning to purple."

Max   See Beerbohm, Sir Max.

maxim   A pithy statement, frequently drawn from experience, conveying some practical advice or general precept about human nature and conduct. An example, from La Rochefoucauld's *Maxims* (1665): "Old people are fond of giving good advice: it consoles them for no longer being capable of setting a bad example."

Maximilian (full name Ferdinand Maximilian Joseph, 1832–1867)   Archduke of Austria. The younger brother of Francis Joseph I, Maximilian was made emperor of Mexico (1864–67) by Napoleon III, who hoped to establish a French satellite in the Western Hemisphere. The opposition of Mexican liberals, U.S. protests, and political troubles in France led Napoleon to abandon Maximilian. After the withdrawal of the French forces, Maximilian was captured and shot by the Mexican leader Benito Juárez.

Maximus Poems, The   An epic-length poem by Charles Olson, published first as *The Maximus Poems* (1960), then as *The Maximus Poems IV, V, VI* (1970), and finally as the complete text, with manuscripts and fragments left behind at the poet's death (1975). This monumental composition, varying in form from free verse to pastoral ode to prose poem, is essentially a series of letters written by the persona Maximus to the coastal New England town of Gloucester. It is structurally similar to Pound's Cantos and Williams's Paterson and, like these works, came to conclusion only upon the death of the author. Maximus is not intended to be identified with the poet but is rather a ubiquitous and immortal voyager.

May, Phil (1864–1903)   English caricaturist. May is noted for his studies of London characters, such as the coster-girl, the street waif, etc. In 1896 he became a member of the staff of Punch.

maya (Sans, "cosmic illusion")   A central element in Hindu philosophy. *Maya* is the appearance that conceals the real, the many that conceal the one, the relative that conceals the absolute. Especially important in Vedantic philosophy, it refers to the ignorance that prevents man from realizing his identity with BRAHMAN, i.e., from comprehending that ATMAN is equivalent to brahman.

Maya A group of American Indians who inhabited parts of what are now Mexico, Guatemala, and Honduras. The "Old Empire" of the Mayas, which flourished between the 4th and 9th centuries, saw the rise of independent city states, such as Copán, Palenque, and Tikal, centered in southern Yucatán. For reasons that are still not clear, these were abandoned, and a "New Empire" later developed in northern Yucatán, which was dominated by the three cities of Chichén Itzá, Mayapán, and Uxmal. The greatest achievements of the Mayas were in the fields of astronomy, mathematics, and the calendar; their system of hieroglyphic writing was more advanced than that of any other American Indians. The Spaniards tried to subjugate the Mayas throughout the 15th century, but the conquest was not complete until the fall of Tayasal, the last Maya stronghold, in 1697. The investigations made by John Lloyd Stephens (1805–52), American diplomat and archaeologist, which he described in *Incidents of Travel in Central America, Chiapas, and Yucatán* (1841), did much to arouse interest in Maya civilization.

Mayakovsky, Vladimir Vladimirovich (1893–1930) Russian poet. Mayakovsky, the outstanding poetic talent of the early Soviet period, was born in Georgia, the son of a forester. The family moved to Moscow in 1906, after the death of his father. Mayakovsky joined the Social Democratic Party in 1908 and, for the next two years, spent much time in prison for his political activities. In 1910 he began to study painting but soon afterwards was convinced that his true talent was in poetry. In 1912 Mayakovsky signed the manifesto *A Slap in the Face of Public Taste*, issued by the futurists. The aims of FUTURISM that apparently most attracted him were its rejection of tradition in art and concern with formal experimentation in literature. He was not, however, so willing to neglect the content of his poetry as were some of the other futurist poets. Mayakovsky's first published work was a small book of four poems entitled *Ya* (*I*, 1913). This early work, with its startling imagery and powerful rhythms, created a stir, and Mayakovsky was marked as one of the more original young poets. He confirmed this estimate with his next work, *Oblako v shtanakh* (*A Cloud in Trousers*, 1914–15), a long poem that carried the depoetization of the language of poetry to an extreme limit. The characteristic features of Mayakovsky's work were all present: the declamatory nature of the verse, obviously fitted for being shouted from a platform, and its hyperbolic imagery, forceful rhythm, and often coarse language. Mayakovsky had virtually single-handedly overthrown the smooth, mellifluous poetry of the symbolists, going another step beyond the innovations of Aleksandr BLOK. While Blok had based his verse on a line that took into account the number of stresses, ignoring the number of unstressed syllables, Mayakovsky abandoned

metrical structure altogether, relying on rhythmic factors for the organizing principle of his poems. His chief means of poetic organization were the rhymes, often unusual and striking, that linked his irregular lines.

Mayakovsky triumphantly greeted the revolution with such works as *Oda revolyutsi* (*Ode to the Revolution*, 1918), *Levy marsh* (*Left March*, 1918), and the long poem *150,000,000* (1920). He also produced one of the first successful plays of the Soviet era, *Misteriya buff* (*Mystery-Bouffe*, 1918), a political satire in verse, predicting the downfall of capitalism.

Throwing himself into the work of establishing the revolution, Mayakovsky put his poetic talents at the service of the Russian telegraph agency and composed propaganda verses and read them before crowds of workers throughout the country. In 1923 he worked for LEF (Left Front), an organization of futurists who hoped to make their brand of art the standard one in the new Soviet society. Mayakovsky edited the journal of the organization, also called *LEF*, until 1925. The struggle between the radical approach of the LEF artists and the more conservative elements advocating realism in art finally ended in the closing of the journal. Mayakovsky went on an extended tour of Western Europe, Latin America, and the U.S. During his three-month stay in the U.S., he wrote an appreciative poem about the Brooklyn Bridge (1925). On his return to Russia in 1927, he attempted to revive the magazine under the title *The New LEF*. This venture lasted for just one year. A new conservative organization, RAPP (Association of Proletarian Writers), was gaining control of Soviet literature. Mayakovsky's awareness that the bureaucracy he had fought was triumphing is reflected in two satirical plays: *Klop* (*The Bedbug*, 1928) and *Banya* (*The Bathhouse*, 1929).

Mayakovsky continued his traveling and public readings. His troubles with literary opponents were compounded with unhappy romantic experiences, and in April 1930 Mayakovsky shot himself. Just five years earlier, he had harshly criticized the suicide of the poet Sergey YESENIN.

Among Mayakovsky's best-known longer poems are *Vladimir Ilyich Lenin* (1924), a eulogy to the Soviet leader; *Khorosho!* (*All Right!* 1927); and *Vo ves golos* (*With Full Voice*, 1929–30), an unfinished poem.

May Day The first day of May. VERGIL says that the Roman youths used to go into the fields and spend the *calends* (first) of May in dancing and singing in honor of Flora, goddess of fruits and flowers. The English consecrated May Day to Robin Hood and the Maid Marian, because the famous outlaw died on that day. Villagers used to set up and dance around a Maypole, crown a May queen, and spend the day in archery, morris dancing, and other amusements.

Mayerling A village in Austria, the site of the royal hunting lodge where the bodies of Archduke Rudolf, crown prince of Austria, and his mistress, Baroness Marie Vetsera, were found on January 30, 1889. Although the official report stated that they had committed suicide, it is generally believed that Rudolf, partly because of despair over his father's command to end the affair, shot the baroness and then killed himself.

Mayflower   The ship on which 102 Pilgrims sailed from Southampton, England, to Massachusetts in 1620. See MOURT'S RELATION.

Upon their arrival in America after the sixty-three-day voyage, the Pilgrims drew up the *Mayflower Compact*, an agreement binding them together in a "civil body politic" for the government of the colony. It remained the fundamental charter of the Plymouth Colony until its absorption by the Massachusetts Bay Colony in 1691.

Mayor of Casterbridge, The (1886)   A novel by Thomas HARDY. Michael Henchard, an unemployed farmhand, becomes very drunk at a fair and sells his wife and baby for five guineas to a sailor named Newson. The next day, remorse-stricken, he takes an oath not to drink for twenty years and begins a fruitless search for his family. Eighteen years later, when the reformed and prosperous Henchard has become mayor of Casterbridge, his wife, Susan, and Elizabeth-Jane, now eighteen, reappear. Newson had been reported dead at sea, and Susan has returned to be reunited with Henchard. After Susan dies, Henchard learns that his daughter died in infancy, and that Elizabeth-Jane is actually Newson's daughter, a fact which he conceals from her. A domineering, lonely man, he clings to her as his fortunes decline because of his differences with his astute Scottish assistant, Donald Farfrae. Then the memory of Henchard's sale of his wife is publicly revived, and he reverts to his drinking habits. Newson, not dead after all, returns to claim Elizabeth-Jane, who soon marries Farfrae, now the new mayor of Casterbridge. Henchard, deserted, wanders off and dies in dejection.

May school   See NERUDA, JAN.

Mazarin, Jules (1602–1661)   French cardinal and statesman of Italian birth. Succeeding RICHELIEU as prime minister in 1642, Mazarin was retained by the queen regent, Anne of Austria, after the death of Louis XIII. A wealthy collector of books, Mazarin bequeathed his library to France; his collection of theological and historical writings forms the core of the Bibliothèque Mazarine in Paris. See BIBLE, SPECIALLY NAMED EDITIONS.

Mazeppa, Ivan (1644–1709)   A famous Cossack hetman, hero of BYRON's poem *Mazeppa* (1819) and of PUSHKIN's drama *Pultowa*. Mazeppa was born of a noble Polish family in Podolia and became a page in the court of John Casimir, king of Poland. He intrigued with Theresia, the young wife of a Podolian count, who had the young page lashed naked to a wild horse, which was then turned loose. In the Ukraine, Mazeppa was released and cared for by Cossacks and in time became hetman and prince of the Ukraine under Peter the Great of Russia. Byron makes Mazeppa tell his tale to Charles XII of Sweden after the

battle of Pultowa, in which he had deserted to Charles and fought against Russia.

Mazzini, Giuseppe (1805–1872)   Italian patriot. An active member of the CARBONARI, Mazzini founded (c1831) the secret revolutionary society Young Italy, whose purpose was to liberate and unify Italy under a republican form of government. Later he fomented uprisings in Mantua, Milan, and Genoa. Although he gave every assistance to the expeditions of Garibaldi, he refused to support the monarchy established under Victor Emmanuel II of Sardinia, remaining a staunch republican to the end of his life.

Mead, Margaret (1901–1978)   American anthropologist. At the age of twenty-four Mead set off for Samoa to study adolescent girls in a noncompetitive, permissive culture. The results of her fieldwork were published in *Coming of Age in Samoa* (1928), which became a classic text in social anthropology. She made a number of later expeditions to study primitive peoples and their marriage rituals and sexual behavior, particularly in relation to rites of adolescence. Among her many books on these subjects are *Growing Up in New Guinea* (1930) and *Sex and Temperament in Three Primitive Societies* (1935). She applied her independent intelligence to a broad range of subjects, always examining the extent to which character is shaped by culture and vice versa. Her other important works include *Male and Female* (1949), *An Anthropologist at Work* (1959), and *Culture and Commitment* (1970). She lectured extensively, airing her progressive views on contemporary issues, and wrote frequently for both scholarly journals and popular magazines. *Aspects of the Present* (1980) is a selection from her articles that had appeared in *Redbook* magazine between 1969 and 1979. She also wrote a biography of her teacher and collaborator, *Ruth Benedict* (1974), and an autobiography, *Blackberry Winter* (1972). *Letters from the Field: 1925–1975* (1977) contains her own reflections on the methods of anthropological fieldwork that she developed.

Mean, The (Chung-yung)   One of the Chinese FOUR BOOKS. Originally one chapter from the BOOK OF RITES, it became important during the SUNG dynasty, when it became required reading for aspirants to Chinese officialdom. It discusses basic moral concepts.

Meander   The modern Menderes River in Asia Minor. It dried up when Phaëton drove the sun chariot. Its proverbial windings are comparable to those of the labyrinth of Minos.

Measure for Measure (c1604)   A comedy by SHAKESPEARE. After deputizing ANGELO to enforce Vienna's long-ignored laws, Duke Vincentio purports to leave the city but actually remains to observe the proceedings, disguised as Friar Lodowick. Angelo revives an old statute against fornication and sentences CLAUDIO to death for seducing JULIET, his betrothed. When Claudio's sister ISABELLA, a religious novice, pleads for his life, her beauty stirs

Angelo's repressed passions; he promises her Claudio's freedom if she will yield herself to him, a suggestion she angrily spurns. Claudio at first approves of her behavior but, overwhelmed by the thought of death, weakens and begs her compliance. Overhearing their conversation, Vincentio, still in monk's garb, proposes that Isabella pretend to accede to Angelo's request. In her place, however, he will send Mariana, who was formerly betrothed to Angelo but who has been spurned since the loss of her dowry. The plan is successful, and, although Angelo breaks his promise by demanding Claudio's life, Friar Lodowick manages to save him. Revealing his true identity, Vincentio castigates Angelo for his severity and orders him to marry Mariana, while he himself sues for the hand of Isabella.

The main source of the play is George Whetstone's *Promos and Cassandra* (before 1578), which is based upon a story in Giraldo Cinthio's *Hecatommithi* (1565).

Mecca   The birthplace of MUHAMMED and the holiest city of ISLAM. It is to Mecca that all pious Muslims are enjoined to make the *hadj*, or pilgrimage, at least once during their lifetime.

Meck, Nadezhda Filaretovna von   See TCHAIKOVSKY, PETER ILYICH.

Medal, The (1682)   A satirical poem by John DRYDEN. Like Dryden's ABSALOM AND ACHITOPHEL, it was aimed at the earl of Shaftesbury, who had recently been exonerated from a charge of high treason. His Whig followers had a medal cast to commemorate the event.

Medea   In Greek mythology, a sorceress and priestess of HECATE, daughter of the Colchian king Aeetes, and wife of JASON, later of AEGEUS. Falling in love with Jason, Medea helped him to steal the GOLDEN FLEECE and to murder her half brother Apsyrtus to delay their pursuers. (See ARGONAUTS.) Purified of murder by her aunt CIRCE and married to Jason among the Phaeacians, she returned with him to Iolcus. There she persuaded the three daughters of Jason's enemy PELIAS that she could rejuvenate him if they would cut him in pieces. ALCESTIS refused, but her sisters did so, and when Pelias was dead, Jason's Argonauts captured the city and placed Pelias' son ACASTUS on the throne.

Medea laid claim to the throne of Ephyre (Corinth), where Aeetes had once reigned, for Jason. Although he owed most of his successes to her, Jason later repudiated her in order to marry Glauce, daughter of CREON. Medea murdered her two children by Jason and escaped in a chariot drawn by winged serpents to Athens, where she married AEGEUS. After trying to poison his son THESEUS, she was banished and ultimately returned to Colchis.

Medea was sympathetically portrayed by Apollonius of Rhodes in his epic *Argonautica* and by EURIPIDES in his drama *Medea*, which told of her revenge on Jason, but neither forgot that she was both witch and barbarian. Robinson JEFFERS based his poetic drama *Medea* on the story of the Euripides play. The story has also been the subject of operas by M. A. Charpentier (1693) and Cherubini (1797), both entitled *Médée*.

Médecin malgré lui, Le (The Doctor in Spite of Himself, 1666)   A comedy by MOLIÈRE. Forbidden by her father, Géronte, to marry the penniless Léandre, Lucinde feigns dumbness. Géronte searches in vain for a skilled doctor to cure her. The woodcutter SGANARELLE, forced by his wife to masquerade as a specialist, earns an enormous fee from Géronte merely by reciting nonsensical medical jargon; he accepts a bribe from Léandre, takes the young man on as his ostensible apothecary, and restores Lucinde's speech so successfully that Géronte begs Sganarelle to make her dumb again. Sganarelle replies that he cannot do that, but he can make Géronte deaf. Lucinde elopes with Léandre, but Géronte is mollified upon learning that Léandre has inherited a fortune from his uncle. The character Sganarelle is one of Molière's supreme comic creations.

Médée (Medea, 1635)   The first tragedy of Pierre CORNEILLE. Modeled on those of Euripides and Seneca, it relates Medea's bloody vengeance upon the faithless Jason. While superior to earlier French tragedies, the play does not attain the simplicity and restraint of Corneille's later works.

Medici   A famous Florentine family that rose to prominence during the Italian Renaissance and remained powerful until the death of the last male member of the family, Gian Gastone de' Medici (1671–1737). Apart from the fact that members of the Medici family became prominent religious leaders (popes Leo X, Clement VII, and Leo XI) and queens of France (CATHERINE DE MÉDICIS and MARIE DE MÉDICIS), their greatest contribution was probably their generous patronage of the arts and their role in establishing Florence as a major cultural capital of the world.

Cosimo de' Medici (1389–1464)   After his death, Cosimo was given the official title *Pater Patriae*, "Father of the Country." Also called Cosimo the Elder, he was a vastly successful banker, who became the first Medici to actually rule Florence. A temperate leader, he endorsed a balance of power among the Italian states and dissolved old animosities between Florence and Milan by forging an alliance with the SFORZA family. With Cosimo began the long tradition of patronage of artists and encouragement of learning. He built the Medici Library, established a center for the study of Greek culture, headed by Marsilio FICINO, and supported such artists as BRUNELLESCHI, DONATELLO, and GHIBERTI.

Lorenzo de' Medici (1449–1492)   Called *Il Magnifico*, "the Magnificent," Lorenzo was the grandson of Cosimo and the most famous of all the Medici. He was patron to a host of Renaissance artists, including LEONARDO da Vinci and the young MICHELANGELO. Like his grandfather, he encouraged the study of Greek and Latin texts and supported such scholars and writers as FICINO and PICO DELLA MIRANDOLA. He himself wrote verse, sacred drama, and literary criticism, in which he encouraged the use of Italian in literature. An astute politician, he kept his city-state secure and Italy united through his expert use of diplomacy. He has been viewed by historians as the embodiment of much of the Renaissance spirit. At his death, he was succeeded for only two years by his son, Piero (1471–1503), whose weakness as a leader led to the temporary eclipse of Medici power under the rule of SAVONAROLA.

Giovanni de' Medici (1475–1521) A son of Lorenzo who, through his father's influence, was made a cardinal as a boy and later became Pope Leo X (1513–21). Although Giovanni was undistinguished as a church leader, he is remembered for his patronage of RAPHAEL and Bramante.

Giuliano de' Medici (1479–1516) The youngest son of Lorenzo, duke of Nemours. Giuliano was a minor poet, popular in the salons of his day, and was featured by Castiglione as an interlocutor in THE COURTIER. His statue was sculpted by Michelangelo.

Giulio de' Medici (1478–1534) Nephew of Lorenzo, who reigned as Pope Clement VII (1523–34). During his pontificate, Rome was sacked by the imperial forces of Charles V. After peace was secured, Clement crowned Charles emperor. He too was a patron of artists and writers, notably Michelangelo, Raphael, and CELLINI, whose autobiography includes a vivid account of Clement and the sack of Rome.

Giovanni de' Medici (1498–1526) Called Giovanni delle Bande Nere, he was the great-grandnephew of Cosimo and a famous military commander. Installed as commander of a troop by his relative Pope Leo X when he was only eighteen, Giovanni won a reputation as a charismatic leader with great tactical and strategic ability. He was also called the Invincible and won praise from Aretino, who was with him when he died of a wound received in battle. Though he was only twenty-eight at the time of his death, he has been called the greatest soldier of 16th-century Italy. It is not certain whether the epithet *Bande Nere* ("black bands") was derived from the black armor worn by his troops or from the black banners his troops carried into battle as a symbol of mourning at the death of Leo X.

médico de su honra, El (The Physician of His Own Honor, c1629) A drama by Pedro CALDERÓN DE LA BARCA, the most extreme of his honor tragedies. Doña Mencia, in love with Prince Enrique, is forced to marry Don Gutierre. However, the prince continues to pay her attention, although she tries to dissuade him. Don Gutierre, erroneously believing that his honor has been besmirched, has a surgeon bleed his wife to death. Since Don Gutierre has operated within the limits of the code of honor, the king condones his act.

Medina A city in Arabia, the second holy city of ISLAM. It was called Yathrib before MUHAMMED fled there from Mecca, but afterward Medinat-al-nabi, "the city of the prophet," from which its present name is derived. See FAERIE QUEENE, THE; HEGIRA.

Medium Is the Massage, The See MCLUHAN, MARSHALL.

Medmenham Abbey A ruined Cistercian abbey near Marlow on the Thames. It became the meeting place for the Hell-fire Club, founded by Sir Francis Dashwood in 1745, with John Wilkes and Bubb Dodington among its members. Its convivialities became orgies, and its ritual was a mockery of all religion.

Medusa The chief of the GORGONS of Greek myth. It is said Medusa dallied with POSEIDON in ATHENE's temple, and the goddess, outraged, changed Medusa's hair into serpents and made her face so terrible that it turned the beholder to stone. PERSEUS, with a sword given to him by the god HERMES, was able to cut off her head by looking only at her reflection in Athene's shield. From the dead Gorgon's blood sprang Pegasus, the winged horse, and Chrysaor, her children by Poseidon. Perseus used Medusa's head to rescue ANDROMEDA and later gave it to Athene in gratitude for her protection. Athene wears it on her shield or on her breastplate.

Mehta, Ved [Parkash] (1934–   ) Indian journalist, memoirist, and novelist, writing in English. Mehta was blinded at three, a result of meningitis. He was educated in India, America (where he lived from the age of fifteen), and England. He became a staff writer for THE NEW YORKER in 1961. His works of travel, fashion, autobiography, and contemporary journalism are distinguished by an elegant prose style and a precise apprehension of people, places, and moods. He wrote *Mahatma Gandhi and His Apostles* (1977), followed by *The New India* (1978), a collection of articles on Indira Gandhi's regime. *Face to Face* (1957), *Daddyji* (1972), *Mamaji* (1979), *A Family Affair* (1982), and *Vedi* (1982) are volumes of family biography.

Meiji The reign name of Japanese Emperor Mutsuhito (1852–1912). With the Meiji Restoration of 1868, the TOKUGAWA shōgunate collapsed and, with it, the entire feudal system of government. The Meiji period, which lasted from 1868 to 1912, marks the emergence of Japan as a modern state. Under the banner of the restoration of the imperial family, various leaders joined to bring an end to the Tokugawa shōgunate. This period saw an intense Westernization and modernization, with the introduction of Occidental scientific knowledge, culture, and literature. A constitution was established, parliamentary government was instituted, and Japan changed from an isolated feudal nation to a world power. Military victories were gained over China and Russia (1905), and Korea was annexed in 1910.

Mein Kampf See HITLER, ADOLF.

Meistersingers (Ger, "master singers") Members of German guilds of poets and singers who attempted to preserve the medieval art form of the MINNESINGERS during the 14th through 16th centuries. The Meistersingers, of whom the most famous were Hans SACHS and Hans Folz (c1450–c1510), usually formed organizations similar to the craft guilds of the day: the title of "master" was given only to those who had proven their creative and vocal talent, and singing contests were often held among the masters. In general, however, the *Meistergesang* ("master-singing") is regarded as a degeneration of the Minnesang, retaining the external form but relinquishing the immediacy and artistic power of the original.

mejor alcalde el rey, El (The King, the Greatest Alcalde, written 1620–1623) A historical drama by Lope de VEGA. It is based on an anecdote about King Alfonso VII (1126–57). In this work, Lope contrasts royal justice with feudal tyranny.

Sancho, a poor peasant, is in love with Nuño's daughter Elvira. Don Tello, a feudal lord of the region, consents to the marriage but, on seeing Elvira, determines to possess her himself and carries her off to his castle. When Don Tello ignores Sancho's protests, the injured youth goes to the king and begs him to send a strong *alcalde*, or judge, to see that justice is done. The king himself, disguised as an *alcalde*, orders Don Tello to release Elvira. When Don Tello refuses, the king, revealing his identity, orders the arrogant noble to be executed. First, however, he is forced to marry Elvira so that she may inherit his property as his widow and share it with Sancho.

Melampus In Greek mythology, a seer. Melampus understood the language of birds and beasts. This accomplishment saved his life when he overheard some woodboring worms remarking that the roof over his head was about to fall. He was the first mortal to practice the art of healing. He also appears to have been the first psychiatrist to recognize a castration complex. Phylacus, king of Phylace, had imprisoned Melampus for trying to steal Phylacus' famous cattle as a wedding gift for Melampus' brother Bias. Learning of Melampus' special gifts after the episode of the roof, he promised Melampus both freedom and the cattle if Melampus would cure Phylacus' son Iphiclus of impotence. Eavesdropping on a pair of vultures, Melampus learned that Iphiclus had been terribly frightened as a child on seeing his father approaching him with a gelding knife, bloodstained from some rams. Melampus fed Iphiclus a potion made of the rust of the knife, and he was cured.

Melanchthon, Philipp (Hellenized pseudonym of Philipp Schwarzerd [Ger, "black earth"], 1497–1560) German religious reformer, friend and follower of Luther, and nephew of Johann Reuchlin. A noted humanist scholar, Melanchthon began as a professor of Greek, and, because of his pedagogical endeavors, was known as *praeceptor Germaniae* ("the teacher of Germany"). His most important religious works are the *Loci communes rerum theologicarum* (*Common Topics in Theology*, 1524), the first extensive formulation of Protestant doctrine, and the *Augsburg Confession* (1531), which he helped to draft.

His desire to reconcile Roman Catholicism and Protestantism led to difficulties in his relationship with Luther.

Meleager A hero of Greek legend, son of Oeneus of Calydon and Althaea. Meleager was distinguished for throwing the javelin, for slaying the CALYDONIAN BOAR, and for being one of the ARGONAUTS. It was declared by the FATES that he would die as soon as a piece of wood then on the fire was burnt up, whereupon his mother snatched the log from the fire and extinguished it. After Meleager had slain his maternal uncles, who had tried to prevent him from giving the boar's head to ATALANTA for drawing first blood, his mother threw the brand on the fire again, and Meleager died.

Melibee One of THE CANTERBURY TALES of CHAUCER. It is told by Chaucer after the Host interrupts his narration of the rhyme of Sir THOPAS. It is a long prose didactic work, closely translated from a French adaptation of the Latin *Liber consolationis et consilii* by Albertanus of Brescia (c1193–c1270). Melibee (or Melibeus) returns from the fields to find that three of his enemies have beaten his wife Prudence and killed his daughter Sophie. Grieving, he rages about vengeance, but Prudence begins to reason with him, husband and wife both making extensive use of proverbs and quotations from scholastic authorities. Finally Prudence persuades him and his repentant enemies to come together in peace, and Melibee forgives them, hoping that God will likewise forgive human trespasses.

Mélisande See PELLÉAS ET MÉLISANDE.

Melissa A prophet in the ORLANDO FURIOSO of Ariosto, who lives in Merlin's cave. Bradamante, the warrior maiden, asks her to use an enchanted ring to rescue her beloved Ruggiero, who is in the power of the lovely witch Alcina. Assuming the form of Atlantes, Melissa rescues Ruggiero and Astolfo, then disenchants all the forms metamorphosed in the island. Later, posing as Rodomonte, she persuades Agramante to break the league that was to settle the contest by single combat, thus precipitating a general battle.

Mellors In D. H. Lawrence's novel LADY CHATTERLEY'S LOVER, the gamekeeper lover of the aristocratic heroine. Mellors is an ideal Lawrence hero, forthright, sexually potent, and close to nature. Lawrence himself was of working-class origin, and his wife, Frieda, of an aristocratic family.

Melmoth the Wanderer (1820) A horrific GOTHIC NOVEL by Charles MATURIN. The hero, Melmoth, sells his soul to the devil in exchange for prolonged life. The pact can be canceled if Melmoth finds anyone willing to accept the same terms, but no one, not even those in the worst of circumstances, is willing to make the bargain.

melodrama Literally, a play spoken with musical accompaniment. At one time the term was applied generally to opera. It has come to mean a play, with or without music, in which the emphasis is on spectacle and sensation, the plot is romantic, and the object is to stimulate the audience's emotions without regard to convincing character portrayal. The popular 19th-century English melodramas developed as a means of circumventing the Licensing Act of 1737, which restricted spoken dramas to a few theatres but did allow musical entertainments. Songs or instrumental music were then employed to disguise the dramatic nature of the productions.

Melpomene   One of the nine MUSES of classical mythology, the muse of tragedy and tragic poetry.

Melusina   A fairy in medieval French romance, who is turned into a water sprite, fish-shaped from the waist down. Melusina resumes human form when she marries Count Raymond of Poitiers, but he must promise never to see her on Saturdays, for then her mermaid appearance returns. He builds her the castle of Lusignan and others but one Saturday secretly observes her in her bath. Melusina is now forced to leave and wander as a spirit forever. Jean d'Arras wrote down the story in 1387.

Melville, Herman (1819–1891)   American novelist, short-story writer, and poet. A member of a once-prominent New York family, Melville was raised in an atmosphere of financial instability and genteel pretense. After the death of his father in 1832, he tried several jobs to help the family, among them clerking in a bank, teaching school, and going to sea.

His first voyage, to Liverpool, became the background for his fourth novel, *Redburn*. Next he sailed for the South Seas, where he deserted his ship, the *Acushnet*, and was a benignly treated captive among the cannibalistic Typees. After his rescue from this beguiling imprisonment, he became involved in a mutiny, worked on several Pacific islands, and finally sailed home with the navy in 1844. He had never considered writing as a career but, at the behest of friends, published his travel memoirs. TYPEE: A PEEP AT POLYNESIAN LIFE was a literary success, and the new author continued his adventures in a second book, OMOO.

Melville, who had been sporadically educated, now began reading widely to broaden his knowledge of the world's literature. Marrying Elizabeth Shaw in 1847, he moved to New York and then to a farm in the Berkshires, where his neighbor was Nathaniel HAWTHORNE. His next book, MARDI AND A VOYAGE THITHER, begins as an adventure story but ends in philosophical allegory. Melville, intoxicated by metaphysics, was no longer content with the comparatively simple aims of his earlier books. In MARDI AND A VOYAGE THITHER, Melville makes his first real use of a questing hero and a consciously symbolic level of meaning. Discouraged by the book's failure, the young author, now a father, dashed off *Redburn* (1849). Melville's only comic novel, the story of an adolescent's initiation into manhood, it drew on the experiences of the author's first voyage. Apparently a return to autobiographical adventure, *Redburn* was a financial success. The following year, Melville wrote WHITE-JACKET; OR, THE WORLD IN A MAN-OF-WAR, based on his life in the navy. Unable to wholly

ignore symbolic significance, he does introduce a deeper meaning in both books, especially in *White-Jacket*.

Melville traveled to England and arranged for the British publication of his books. In 1851 he completed his masterpiece, MOBY-DICK, OR THE WHALE. An epic of a literal and metaphysical quest, *Moby-Dick* belongs to no genre. Although characters appear and disappear without explanation and the point of view changes, the book succeeds. Melville's contemporaries did not appreciate it, however; mentally exhausted, he began PIERRE, OR THE AMBIGUITIES. A pessimistic, deeply personal book, *Pierre* mirrors its author's psychological state.

Melville supported his family during the 1850s by farming and by writing stories for magazines. Among these tales are BARTLEBY THE SCRIVENER and "Benito Cereno" (1856), both of which appeared in THE PIAZZA TALES. He also wrote a serialized novel, ISRAEL POTTER: OR, FIFTY YEARS OF EXILE, an ironic view of the state of American democracy. His last prose until his final years was the cynical and satirical novel *The Confidence-Man, His Masquerade* (1857).

Melville then traveled to England, where he saw his friend Hawthorne for the last time. Troubled and exhausted, he visited the Holy Land, returning to New York in 1857. After an unsuccessful attempt at lecturing, be became a customs inspector in New York, a job he held for twenty years.

Unnoticed by the literary public, Melville turned to writing poetry. Among his poetic works are BATTLE-PIECES AND ASPECTS OF THE WAR and CLAREL: A POEM AND PILGRIMAGE IN THE HOLY LAND. Two books were published posthumously: a volume of poetry called *Weeds and Wildings* (1924) and the novella BILLY BUDD, FORETOPMAN.

Like other American artists in the latter half of the 19th century, Melville was a member of the literary underground. He had a small coterie but was remembered, if at all, as the man who had lived with cannibals. It was not until the 1920s that he began to be recognized as one of the greatest of American writers.

Member of the Wedding, The (1946)   A novel by Carson McCULLERS. A perceptive study, it tells the story of a motherless girl, thirteen-year-old Frankie, who wants to accompany her brother and his wife on their honeymoon. The wedding is seen through her eyes; as a chorus to her remarks and thoughts, one hears her six-year-old cousin and the black cook. The author's highly successful dramatic version of the novel was produced in New York in 1950.

Memling, Hans (c1430–1494)   German-born Flemish painter. Memling is known for his altar pieces and sensitive madonnas, as well as his landscapes. His straightforward portraits tend to idealize the sitter and are noted for their meticulous attention to background detail.

Mémoires d'outre-tombe (Memories from beyond the Tomb, 1848–1850)   A volume of personal reminiscences by François René de CHATEAUBRIAND. Written during the period 1811–41, the work was first published in *La Presse*.

Memoirs of Barry Lyndon, Esq., Written by Himself, The (1844)   A novel by William Makepeace THACKERAY. The Irish narrator, Redmond Barry, an utter scoundrel, manages to involve himself in a steady succession of affairs, which he writes of as though he were invariably in the right, "the victim of many cruel persecutions, conspiracies and slanders." He courts and wins the widowed Countess Lyndon, spends her money, and keeps her in his power but finally goes from bad to worse and dies in the Fleet prison.

Mena, Juan de (1411–1456)   Spanish poet and scholar. Educated in Italy, Mena served as Latin secretary to King John II of Castile. His best-known work is *El laberinto de Fortuna* (or *Las trescientas*; 1444?), an allegory suggested by Dante's *Paradiso*, in which the poet is transported to the palace of Fortune, where he is offered a vision of the past, present, and future. Mena is also remembered for having introduced many neologisms of Latin origin into the Spanish language.

Men against the Sea   See MUTINY ON THE BOUNTY.

Menander (Menandros, 342–292 BC)   An Athenian comic playwright, perhaps the best-known writer of New Comedy. Menander's work was practically unknown until 1905, when considerable sections of three plays were discovered on a papyrus in Egypt. In 1957 the only extant complete play of Menander, *Dyskolos* (*The Bad-tempered Man*), was discovered in Egypt. Although he employed the type characters and standard plot devices of New Comedy, Menander was a sophisticated and witty playwright. Many of the better-known plays of Plautus and Terence were adapted from his works.

Mencius, The (Meng tzu)   One of the Chinese FOUR BOOKS, also known in translation as *The Book of Master Meng*. It contains the teachings of the Confucian philosopher Mencius (372–289 BC), second in importance after CONFUCIUS. Like other early philosophical texts, it is an unsystematic collection of sayings and dialogues, but its superb prose, the model of classical Chinese, and the profundity of its contents make it one of the most interesting of the early writings. After the SUNG dynasty, it became one of the basic texts of the Chinese educational system. Mencius lived in a time of great social change and constant warfare, and he advanced the doctrines of the goodness of man's nature and the necessity of a virtuous and benevolent king to bring order to the world.

Mencken, H[enry] L[ewis] (1880–1956)   American newspaperman, editor, and critic. Mencken began his career on the Baltimore *Herald*; he joined the Baltimore *Sun* papers in 1906 and remained with them for the rest of his life. In 1908 he became literary editor of the *Smart Set*; with George Jean NATHAN, he edited the magazine from 1914 to 1923. In 1924 he and Nathan founded the iconoclastic THE AMERICAN MERCURY, which became known for its "debunking" articles and its section entitled "Americana." Mencken excelled at framing insults, aimed at almost anyone. Since his chief target was complacent middle-class values, he elicited violent retorts from those he labeled the "booboisie." He flailed away tirelessly at Puritans, conservatives, communists, Christians, Jews, blacks, the Ku Klux Klan, and countless others, in a yeasty, exuberantly bad-tempered style. In 1918 he was diverted from his usual occupations by his developing interest in American English; in a detailed and well-organized volume called THE AMERICAN LANGUAGE, he opened up a new field of philological study. In 1933 Mencken withdrew from *The American Mercury* but continued his vitriolic attacks in his newspaper columns and numerous books of essays, including *A Book of Burlesques* (1916), *Damn: A Book of Calumny* (1917), and the aptly titled series *Prejudices* (6 vols, 1919–27; repr 1977). Critics credit Mencken with unusual satirical skill and admire the vigor and trenchancy of his attacks on the shams of his day, but they also call attention to his intolerance, frequent crudity, and misinformation.

He wrote many other books, among them poetry, plays, and such serious critical works as *George Bernard Shaw* (1905) and *The Philosophy of Friedrich Nietzsche* (1908), as well as *In Defense of Women* (1917) and *Treatise of the Gods* (1930). Mencken fell from favor after the Depression years. During that period, he wrote three lively autobiographies: *Happy Days* (1940), *Newspaper Days* (1941), and *Heathen Days* (1943; pub together, 1947).

A revival of interest in Mencken occurred two decades after his death. *The New Mencken Letters* (1975; ed Carl Bode) was followed in 1977 with the reissue of many of his books, including *Notes on Democracy* (1926), *Treatise on Right and Wrong* (1934), *The Bathtub Hoax and Other Blasts and Bravos* (1958), several biographies, and *A Choice of Days* (1980; ed E. L. Galligan), a selection of his writings.

Mencken appears as the character E. K. Hornbeck in the play *Inherit the Wind* (1955), by Jerome Lawrence and Robert E. Lee.

Mendel, Gregor [Johann] (1822–1884)   Austrian botanist and Augustinian monk. Through his breeding experiments with peas in the monastery garden, Mendel formulated the laws of heredity bearing his name and laid the foundation for modern genetics.

Mendelssohn[-Bartholdy], [Jacob Ludwig] Felix (1809–1847)   German composer, conductor, and pianist. Grandson of the philosopher Moses MENDELSSOHN, he pursued his musical career in a financially comfortable and sympathetic environment. As a conductor, Mendelssohn was largely responsible for the 19th-century revival of J. S. BACH, when in 1829 he performed the *Passion According to St. Matthew* for the first time since Bach's death.

A prolific composer, Mendelssohn wrote in all forms except opera. He was a champion of form and clarity; his works are generally unimpassioned and restrained in expression. *The Reformation* (1830), *Italian* (1833), and *Scotch* (1842) are the most enduring of his symphonies. He also wrote choral works, most notably, the oratorios *St. Paul* and *Elijah*; overtures, among them, *Midsummer Night's Dream* (1826) and the *Hebrides* (1830–32); chamber music; piano sonatas; and songs.

During his lifetime, Mendelssohn was one of the most popular composers in Europe, but succeeding generations dismissed his music as saccharine and lacking in strength. By the mid-20th century, his reputation had come almost full circle. Though he is not regarded as one of the great composers of all time, much of Mendelssohn's music is respected and frequently performed.

Mendelssohn, Moses (1729–1786)   German Jewish philosopher. With his friend Lessing, Mendelssohn was a staunch defender of religious tolerance. His major work is *Phädon* (1767), the title taken from Plato's *Phaedo*, which supports belief in the immortality of the soul. Felix Mendelssohn was his grandson.

Mendicant Orders   Orders of the Franciscans (Gray Friars), Augustines (Black Friars), Carmelites (White Friars), and Dominicans (Preaching Friars). So called from their begging, which was the only permitted means of support in the early years of the orders.

Mending Wall (1914)   A poem by Robert FROST. The dramatic situation of the poem is simple: once a year the poem's narrator and a neighbor mend the wall that separates their properties. The narrator contends that the wall is unneccessary, while the neighbor simply repeats the saying of his father, "Good fences make good neighbors."

Menelaus   In Greek mythology, a son of ATREUS, brother of AGAMEMNON, and husband of HELEN. Menelaus' wife's abduction by PARIS was the ostensible cause of the TROJAN WAR. Menelaus was king of Lacedaemon or Sparta. He appears prominently not only in the ILIAD but also in three plays by EURIPIDES: THE TROJAN WOMEN, *Helen*, and ANDROMACHE.

Menelek   See SHEBA, QUEEN OF.

Menen, Aubrey [Clarence] (1912–   )   English novelist and essayist, of Indian and Irish parentage, resident for many years in Italy. Much of Menen's work, such as the autobiographical essay *Dead Man in the Silver Market* (1953), is directed against nationalism and group prejudice. His novels are generally satirical in tone: *The Prevalence of Witches* (1947) is about the differences between tribal and British civil law in a remote Indian province; *The Abode of Love* (1956) is an ironic look at Victorian sexual mores. He has also written comedies of Italian life, including *The Duke of Gallodoro* (1952). His other works include *A Conspiracy of Women* (1965), *The Mystics* (1974), and *Four Days of Naples* (1979), about a street gang's resistance to German occupation of Naples during World War II. *Art*

and Money (1980) is a survey of art patronage from the 5th century BC to modern times.

Menéndez Pidal, Ramón (1869–1968)   Spanish literary historian. Menéndez Pidal was considered the chief Romance-language philologist and medieval authority of Spain; he was also a linguistics specialist of major repute. His works include *La leyenda de los infantes de Lara* (1896); his critical text in two volumes of the *Cantar de mio Cid* (1908–12), *La España del Cid* (*The Cid and His Spain*, 1930), and *Los orígenes del español* (1926). He founded the journal *Revista de filología española* (1914) and the Madrid Center of Historical Studies (1907).

Mennonite   A member of an evangelical Protestant sect. Originating in Switzerland during the 16th century, they took their name from Menno Simons (1492–1559), a Dutch religious reformer who belonged to the less fanatical wing of the ANABAPTISTS, from which they sprang. Personal regeneration by adult baptism, a refusal to bear arms and take oaths, and rejection of worldly concerns, as exemplified in a uniform plainness of dress, are among their characteristic tenets. The sect still exists in Holland and Germany, although most of its membership is now to be found in Canada and the U.S., the Amish Church being one of its major and strictest branches.

Men of Good Will   See ROMAINS, JULES.

Menotti, Gian Carlo (1911–   )   Italian-born American composer and librettist. Menotti's best-known operas are *The Medium* (1946), *The Telephone* (1947), *The Consul* (1950), *Amahl and the Night Visitors* (1951), and *The Saint of Bleecker Street* (1954). His conservative musical style hearkens back to PUCCINI and Italian *verismo*. Thoroughly grounded in theatrical technique, he stages his own works, which are replete with strong dramatic strokes.

Menshevik   See BOLSHEVIK.

Mentor   An old man, mentioned in the ODYSSEY. On embarking for the TROJAN WAR, ODYSSEUS left his son TELEMACHUS in Mentor's care. He appears prominently at the beginning of the *Odyssey*; his name has become synonymous with a wise and faithful counselor.

Men without Women (1927)   A collection of fourteen short stories by Ernest HEMINGWAY. The finest examples of Hemingway's mastery of description, dialogue, and atmosphere are to be found in this volume. The story most often anthologized is THE KILLERS, a narrative remarkable for its aura of impending doom and dramatic restraint. "The Undefeated" and "Fifty Grand" deal with one of Hemingway's favorite subjects—the courage of an aging man. "Hills Like White Elephants" and "A Simple Inquiry," both consisting of dialogue and a few vividly drawn descriptions, appear to be simple, almost trivial sketches, but they have a sinister and dramatic undertone.

Mephistopheles   Name of the demonic tempter in all the literary versions of the FAUST legend, although his characteristics vary among them. The derivation of the name is disputed, possibly Greek, "not loving the light" and thus the lord of the darkness, possibly Hebrew, "destroyer and liar." Mephistopheles inherits his varying form and personality both from the Christian system of demonology, in which he is one of the seven chief devils, and from the pagan Germanic tradition of the kobold, or mischievous familiar spirit. Thus he is never identified with the Devil, who is the fallen angel Lucifer, although he resembles him in part; he is more the pure fiend of pagan superstition in the earlier stories; and, by Goethe's time, the fiendish sneerer at all values has an air of urbane sophistication.

In Goethe's *Faust*, Mephistopheles is the tempting spirit of hell, who uses his supernatural powers in Faust's service after receiving a contract to the effect that Faust will sacrifice his soul to him at death. Mephistopheles characterizes himself as *"der Geist, der stets verneint"* ("the spirit who always negates"), that is, the spirit of absolute destruction, whose wish is that the entire world return to nothingness. Faust, on the other hand, never desires destruction for its own sake, but is always in some sense idealistic, despite the constant immorality of the means he employs for his ends. The pact between Faust and Mephistopheles, unlike that in other versions of the story, sets no time limit. Faust is to continue living with Mephisto as his servant until such time as he is so completely satisfied that he begs the present moment not to pass away.

He appears in Gounod's opera *Faust* and Boito's opera *Mefistofele*. He is mentioned by Shakespeare (*Merry Wives*, i.1) and Fletcher as *Mephostophilus* and appears prominently in Marlowe's *Dr. Faustus* as *Mephostopilis*.

Merchant of Venice, The (c1595)

A comedy by SHAKESPEARE. In order to finance BASSANIO's voyage from Venice to Belmont to win the hand of PORTIA, Antonio, a Venetian merchant, borrows money from the Jew SHYLOCK and signs a bond stipulating that, if the money is not repaid within three months, Shylock may cut a pound of flesh from Antonio's body. In Belmont, Bassanio is about to wed Portia when he learns that the ships from which Antonio would have obtained the money to pay Shylock have been lost and that Shylock is demanding his pound of flesh. After a hasty wedding, Bassanio returns to Venice to attend his friend's trial. Without telling her husband, Portia obtains legal advice and, accompanied by her maid, Nerissa, appears at the trial disguised as a lawyer. She wins the case by insisting that Shylock may take neither more nor less than the exact pound of flesh specified in the bond and that, if a single drop of blood is shed in the process, Shylock must pay for the infraction with his life. Because he had sought the life of a Venetian citizen, Shylock also loses half his property to Antonio, but the merchant returns it to him on the condition that it be bequeathed to Shylock's daughter Jessica, who has recently eloped with Lorenzo, a friend of Bassanio. The play ends happily as Portia reveals her identity to her astonished husband and Antonio's ships are recovered.

The sources of the plot are a play called *The Jew*, first mentioned in 1579, Fiorentino's *Il pecorone* (1558), and the *Gesta Romanorum* (c1472).

Merchant's Tale, The

One of THE CANTERBURY TALES of CHAUCER. The Merchant bewails his own unhappy marriage, then begins his tale with the arguments for wedded bliss that persuade the aged knight January to marry young May, despite anxious warnings from his friends. At the marriage feast, his squire Damyan falls sick of a passion for her, and she cures him by writing that she will respond. January becomes blind and possessively jealous, but May steals an impression of the key to January's private garden, and Damyan precedes the couple there one day and climbs into a pear tree. Meanwhile, in a marital argument between the rulers of Fairyland, Pluto says he will restore January's eyesight to let him see May betray him, and PROSERPINA vows to help her fool him anyway. May asks January to help her into the pear tree to taste the fruit. Soon January can see his wife happily sporting with Damyan, and he roars with rage. May replies that his new sight must be distorted as yet and complains that she had learned she might cure his sight by struggling with a man in a tree but now is getting no thanks for her successful undertaking. January is convinced, and in the *Epilogue* the Host exclaims bitterly over the slyness of women.

Mercury

The Roman equivalent of the Greek HERMES, son of Maia and JUPITER, to whom he acted as messenger. Mercury is probably of totally Greek origin, brought to Rome by Greek traders. He was the god of science and commerce, the patron of travelers and also of rogues, vagabonds, and thieves. Hence, the name of the god is used to denote both a messenger and a thief. Mercury is represented as a young man with winged hat and winged sandals (*talaria*), bearing the caduceus and sometimes a purse.

Mercury fig (Lat, *Ficus ad Mercurium*) The first fig gathered off a fig tree was devoted to Mercury by the Romans. The proverbial saying was applied generally to all first fruits or first works.

Mercutio

In Shakespeare's ROMEO AND JULIET, an elegant and high-spirited young nobleman, kinsman of Prince Escalus, and Romeo's friend. When Romeo refuses to quarrel with Tybalt, Mercutio, who does not know that Romeo's animosity toward the Capulets has diminished since his secret marriage to Juliet, draws his sword in exasperation and is slain by Tybalt.

Mercutio is one of the most highly coveted of Shakespearean roles, actors often preferring Mercutio's mocking wit to the blander and less biting lyricism of Romeo. His famous Queen Mab speech, in which he describes the nocturnal activities of the mischievous fairy queen, who delivers men of their dreams, is a masterpiece of spontaneous fancy:

O! then, I see, Queen Mab hath been with you.
She is the fairies' midwife, and she comes
In shape no bigger than an agate-stone
On the fore-finger of an alderman . . .

Meredith, George (1828–1909)   English novelist,
poet, and critic. Born into a family of naval outfitters, Meredith spent two years in a Moravian school in Germany
and there developed a cosmopolitan outlook and encountered the excesses of German romanticism. Twice married,
he supported himself until 1894 as a newspaper writer and
reader for a publisher. His poetry includes MODERN LOVE,
a marital tragedy based on his own unhappy first marriage;
Poems and Lyrics of the Joy of Earth (1883), a celebration
of evolutionary naturalism and his finest collection of verse;
and *Ballads and Poems of Tragic Life* (1887). His fiction
includes, among many others, *The Shaving of Shagpat*
(1855), an Oriental fantasy; THE ORDEAL OF RICHARD
FEVEREL, the partly autobiographical tragedy of an educational theory mistakenly applied; *Evan Harrington* (1860),
a romance of social climbing; *Rhoda Fleming* (1865), a
rural melodrama; THE EGOIST, a biting study of selfishness;
Diana of the Crossways (1885); *Lord Ormont and His
Aminta* (1894); *The Amazing Marriage* (1895); and an
unfinished novel, *Celt and Saxon* (1910). The influence of
Meredith's father-in-law, Thomas Love Peacock, is evident
in the writer's hatred of egotism and sentimentality, in his
affirmation of the intellectual equality of women with
men, and above all in his belief in the beneficial power of
laughter—a belief expounded in the critical work *The Idea
of Comedy and the Uses of the Comic Spirit* (1877), in
which he put forth the thesis that comedy corrected the
excesses of sentimentality, selfishness, and vanity. Though
Meredith's later novels are marred by an opacity of dialogue, narration, and style and though many of the ideas
that placed him politically and socially ahead of his time
now seem dated, the evolutionary philosophy of his poetry
and prose, the happy acceptance of life as a process of
becoming, has lost little of its power. In 1905 Meredith was
awarded the Order of Merit.

Merezhkovsky, Dmitry Sergeyevich (1865–
1941)   Russian historical novelist, poet, and critic. Merezhkovsky, who published his first collection of verse in
1888, was one of the Russian SYMBOLISTS. With his wife,
Zinaida Gippius, he opened a salon in St. Petersburg,
holding meetings of the Religious and Philosophical Society, which he founded. This group, whose purpose was to
spread mystical philosophical ideas, for a time attracted the
poets Aleksandr BLOK and Andrey BELY. Merezhkovsky's
own ideas of the dualism of flesh and spirit in human history were expressed in his trilogy of historical novels, entitled *Christ and Antichrist*. The separate volumes are *Smert
bogov: Yulian Otstupnik* (1896; tr *The Death of the Gods*,
1901); *Voskresshiye bogi: Leonardo da Vinci* (1901; tr *The
Forerunner*, 1902); and *Antikhrist: Pyotr i Aleksey* (1905; tr

Peter and Alexis, 1905). Merezhkovsky also used antithetic
contrast in his critical study *Tolstoy and Dostoyevsky*
(1901–2). He and his wife immigrated to France in 1919.

Mérimée, Prosper (1803–1870)   French novelist
and man of letters. Mérimée's fondness for literary hoaxes
showed itself at the outset of his literary career with the
publication of *Théâtre de Clara Gazul* (1825). These six
plays, presented to the public as translations from the work
of a Spanish actress, were actually Mérimée's own work.
He is known as a writer of vivid and skillful historical
novels. Although fiery passions are portrayed, in exotic settings, Mérimée uses irony to control his tone. His works
include *La Chronique du temps de Charles IX* (1829),
Colomba (1841), *Carmen* (1852), and *La Double Méprise*
(1833). A student of archaeology, Mérimée served as
Inspector General of historical monuments in France.
During the Second Empire, he held the position of senator. His novel *Carmen* was made by Georges Bizet into one
of the finest and most durable of all operas.

Merleau-Ponty, Maurice (1908–1961)   French
philosopher and essayist. First embracing, then renouncing
communism, Merleau-Ponty evolved from a politically
involved realist, with close ties to Jean-Paul SARTRE, to an
existential idealist who nonetheless never ceased defending
freedom and truth. His thought, often termed a philosophy
of ambiguity, is made up of hesitant enthusiasm and an
aesthetic fascination with visible, tangible reality. His
major works include *La Structure du comportement* (1941;
tr *The Structure of Behavior*, 1963), *Phénoménologie de la
perception* (1945; tr *Phenomenology of Perception*, 1962),
Humanisme et terreur (1947; tr *Humanism and Terror*,
1969), *Les Aventures de la dialectique* (1955; tr *Adventures
of the Dialectic*, 1973), and *Signes* (1960; tr *Signs*, 1964).

Merlin   The magician who plays an important role
in ARTHURIAN LEGEND. Merlin's origins seem distinctly
Celtic, and he figures prominently in early Welsh writings.
Perhaps the first known full-fledged treatment of him is to
be found in the *Libellus Merlini* (*Little Book of Merlin*;
c1135), a Latin tract written by Geoffrey of Monmouth,
which was later incorporated into his *History of the Kings of
Britain* (1137). In this work, Merlin has all the flavor of an
ancient Celtic druid, removing, for example, the great
stones of Stonehenge from Ireland to Amesbury by his
magic. Most important to the legends of Arthur, however,
it was Merlin in Geoffrey of Monmouth's work who
arranged for UTHER PENDRAGON to go to IGRAINE in the
likeness of her husband, for it was from that meeting that
Arthur was born. Merlin the magician was elaborated on
by Wace in *Roman de Brut* (1155) and achieved full
growth in Malory's *Morte d'Arthur* (c1469), where he is the
force behind Arthur's achievement of the throne and otherwise instructs Arthur, ensuring his continuing invincibility
and future greatness as king. Then the great seer and magician proceeds to fall in love with the LADY OF THE LAKE,

the sorceress who, soon tiring of him, imprisons him for eternity in an enchanted tower.

Merlin also appears in Spenser's *Faerie Queene* (1590–96), Tennyson's *Idylls of the King* (1859–85), T. H. White's *The Once and Future King* (1958), and C. S. Lewis's *That Hideous Strength* (1945). See ROUND TABLE.

Merlin (1874)   A poem by Ralph Waldo EMERSON. Analyzing the methods of the poet, Emerson advises waiting for inspiration rather than mechanically devising a form.

mermaid   A fabulous marine creature, half woman and half fish. The mermaid is allied to the SIREN of classical mythology. Popular stories of the mermaid probably arose from sailors' accounts of the manatee (dugong), a cetacean whose head has a rude approach to the human outline, and the female of which, while suckling her young, holds it to her breast with one flipper, as a woman holds her infant in her arm. If disturbed, she suddenly dives under water and tosses up her fishlike tail.

In Elizabethan plays, the term is often used for a courtesan. Cf. Massinger's *Old Law*, iv, 1, and Shakespeare's *Comedy of Errors*, iii, 2.

Mermaid Tavern   A famous English tavern of the early 17th century. In Bread Street, Cheapside, it was a meeting place for the wits, literary men, and men-about-town. Among those who met there were Ben JONSON, Sir Walter RALEIGH, Francis BEAUMONT, John FLETCHER, John SELDEN, and possibly SHAKESPEARE. In his "Lines to Ben Jonson" Beaumont wrote:

> What things have we seen
> Done at the Mermaid! Heard words that have been
> So nimble, and so full of subtile flame,
> As if that every one from whence they came
> Had meant to put his whole wit in a jest.

Merope   One of the PLEIADES. Merope is dimmer than the rest, because, according to Greek legend, she married SISYPHUS, a mortal. She was the mother of GLAUCUS.

Merovingians   The first dynasty of Frankish kings (r 428–751). Clovis I was the most important, establishing the capital at Paris; after 638 the nominal kings lost all real power to the officials called mayors of the palace, a position held by the CAROLINGIANS until they assumed the crown.

Merrilies, Meg   A brilliant and exotic character, the half-crazy queen of the gypsies, who appears in Scott's GUY MANNERING. Meg Merrilies is the nurse of the young heir before he is kidnaped, and she recognizes him when he returns as Brown. She is also the subject of a poem by Keats.

Merrill, James [Ingram] (1926–   )   American poet, novelist, and playwright. Merrill's early volumes, *The Country of a Thousand Years of Peace* (1959; rev 1970), *Water Street* (1962), and *Nights and Days* (1966), which won The National Book Award, established him as an art-

ful and urbane poet, noted for the formality, impersonality, and polish of his verse. With *Divine Comedies* (1976; PULITZER PRIZE), he began a series of Yeats-like communications with figures from the past. The hero of this epic poem is reincarnated and returns to earth in different places and eras, communicating with the poet through a Ouija board. This device of spectral communication is employed again in *Mirabell: Books of Number* (1978) and *Scripts for the Pageant* (1980), both of which were collected, together with a coda, *The Higher Key*, and republished under the title *The Changing Light at Sandover* (1982). This ambitious epic explores aspects of human evolution and man's place in the universe; it was awarded the National Book Critics Circle award in 1983. A selection, *From the First Nine: Poems 1946–1976* (1982), was followed by *Late Settings* (1985). Merrill received the Bollingen Prize for poetry in 1973.

Merry Wives of Windsor, The (c1598)   A comedy by SHAKESPEARE. Sir John FALSTAFF, knowing that Mrs. Ford and Mrs. Page control the purse strings in their respective households, decides to seduce them, but the two ladies learn of his scheme and resolve to make a fool of him. When he is informed of Falstaff's designs by the disgruntled NYM and PISTOL, Mr. Ford, who doubts his wife's fidelity, disguises himself as a Mr. Brook and, pretending to be another aspirant for Mrs. Ford's favors, engages Falstaff to intercede for him. After the unsuspecting Falstaff has undergone several misadventures—including a ducking in the Thames—in his pursuit of Mrs. Ford and Mrs. Page, the ladies and Mr. Ford, who by now knows of his wife's plan and is convinced of her virtue, reveal themselves to the old lecher and pardon him. A subplot deals with the romantic affairs of Mrs. Page's daughter Anne, who is courted by Slender, Dr. Caius, and Fenton, whom she loves and with whom she eventually elopes.

No single source for the play, which makes use of several comic devices, has been identified.

Merton, Thomas (1915–1968)   American poet, essayist, and religious writer. Ordained as a Catholic priest in 1949, Merton chose a solitary life as a Trappist monk, although he continued active involvement in the contemporary world through his writing, publishing nearly fifty books in his lifetime. His volumes of verse include *Thirty Poems* (1944), *Figures for an Apocalypse* (1948), *The Strange Islands* (1957), and the posthumous thousand-page *Collected Poems of Thomas Merton* (1977). He also published scores of essays. His religious writing shows the range of his interests, as in *Mystics and Zen Masters* (1967). Known for his critical and often satirical perspective on contemporary culture, Merton moves easily between the secular and the spiritual. His poems, though sometimes aphoristic, tend to be long, prosy, and autobiographical. His best-known prose is also autobiography, beginning with *The Seven Storey Mountain* (1948) and ending with an unfinished journal of a trip to the Far East in 1968, cut short in Thailand by his accidental death by electrocution.

Meru, Mount The OLYMPUS of Hinduism. It is a fabulous mountain in the center of the world, eighty thousand leagues high, the abode of VISHNU, and a perfect paradise. The name has been given to a real mountain in Tanzania.

Merwin, W[illiam] S[tanley] (1927–　　) American poet and translator. Merwin's poetry is remote, with stark metaphors and echoes of Eastern mysticism. In *The Moving Target* (1963), in an act of self-purification, both body and spirit are denied all defenses and possessions. Like William BLAKE, Merwin is acutely aware of man's inability to seize the present, and time and timelessness are major themes in *The Carrier of Ladders* (1970; PULITZER PRIZE) and *Writings to an Unfinished Accompaniment* (1973). In *The Compass Flower* (1977), surrealism is infused with a serenely meditative tone. *Houses and Travellers* (1977) is a collection of prose parables. *Unframed Originals: Recollections* (1982), a book of memoirs, recreates the author's life with other family members in rural Pennsylvania. Merwin's father, a prominent figure in these memoirs, appears again in *Opening the Hand; Poems* (1983). Merwin is also known for his translations, notably *The Poem of the Cid* (1959) and *The Song of Roland* (1963).

Méséglise Way See REMEMBRANCE OF THINGS PAST.

mesmerism A method of medical treatment by hypnosis developed by the Austrian physician Franz Anton Mesmer (1734–1815), who called it *animal magnetism*. He cured hysterical patients by what are now known to be hypnotic methods, but he attributed his success to a magnetic power, pervading the whole universe, which was concentrated in his own person.

Messalina, Valeria (d AD 48) Notorious Roman empress. The third wife of the emperor CLAUDIUS of Rome, Messalina was executed by order of her husband. Her name has become a byword for lasciviousness and incontinency. Catherine II of Russia (1729–96) has sometimes been called the modern Messalina.

Messer Gaster (Gr, "stomach") In Rabelais's GARGANTUA AND PANTAGRUEL, the prosperous master of arts who lives with Dame Pénie (Lat, "poverty"). Messer Gaster symbolizes Rabelais's view that progress and civilization are spearheaded by the energetic poor, who want more, not by the sluggish rich, whose wants are satisfied. Though Messer Gaster is monstrously greedy and his cult of gluttony is repulsive, it is precisely his vital need for bread that has led to the invention of all the arts.

Messiah (fr Heb, *māshīah*, "anointed one") In Judaism, a savior sent by God to the people of Israel as a redeemer, deliverer, and king. In the OLD TESTAMENT, the Messiah, or "the Lord's anointed," refers to a king descended from DAVID. In Christianity, Christ (fr Gr, *chris-*

tos, "anointed one," a direct translation from the Hebrew) is regarded as the redeemer prophesied in the Old Testament. A Messiah-like figure whose coming will rid the earth of evil and adversity appears in almost all religions, both ancient and modern, Eastern and Western.

Messiah (1742) The most popular oratorio in the English language, composed by George Frederick HANDEL, with libretto compiled from the Bible by the Rev. Charles Jennens. First performed in Dublin, it treats the life of Christ in a spiritual rather than a narrative manner.

Metamorphoses (c AD 8) A series of tales in Latin verse by OVID. Dealing with mythological, legendary, and historical figures, they are written in hexameters, in fifteen books, beginning with the creation of the world and ending with the deification of Caesar and the reign of Augustus. *Metamorphoses* is also the title of a satire by Apuleius, more commonly known as THE GOLDEN ASS.

Metamorphosis, The (Die Verwandlung, 1915; tr 1937) A story by Franz KAFKA. Often regarded as Kafka's most perfectly finished work, "The Metamorphosis" begins as its hero, Gregor SAMSA, awakens one morning to find himself changed into a huge insect; the story proceeds to develop the effects of this change upon Samsa's business and family life and ends with his death. It has been read as everything from a religious allegory to a psychoanalytic case history; it is notable for its clarity of depiction and attention to significant detail, which give its completely fantastic occurrences an aura of indisputable truth, so that no allegorical interpretation is necessary to demonstrate its greatness.

metaphor In figurative language, an implied comparison identifying the two things compared with each other. As distinguished from SIMILE, in which the comparison is stated, metaphor pretends that the two things compared are identical; the comparison is understood. Thus, in "the waves were soldiers moving," Wallace Stevens does not expect to be taken literally; he is comparing the waves, his first term, with moving soldiers, his second term.

metaphysical conceit See CONCEIT.

metaphysical poets A term generally applied to several English poets of the early 17th century. Their poetry is marked by highly complex and greatly compressed meanings, by complex and long-sustained CONCEITS, by a frequent avoidance of smooth and regular meter in order to achieve dramatic or conversational effects, and by unusual syntax and an unconventional type of imagery chosen from philosophy, religion, and theology, and the arts, crafts, sciences, and ordinary daily life of the period in which the poets lived.

The most famous of the metaphysical poets are John DONNE, George HERBERT, Richard CRASHAW, Francis QUARLES, Andrew MARVELL, Henry VAUGHAN, Thomas TRAHERNE, Abraham COWLEY, and John CLEVELAND. Donne is the founder of the school and is considered its greatest member; Herbert, Crashaw, and Marvell follow in importance; Cowley and Cleveland are regarded as the most culpable in the use of farfetched conceits.

These poets, among whom there is wide variation in individual style, represented a reaction against the tradition of the Elizabethan sonnet sequence of the late 16th century, the products of which had become feeble and over-conventionalized as the vogue died out, and a return in some ways to the cruder, more homely type of imagery in poetry of the middle of the 16th century, as well as to the scholasticism of the Middle Ages. The awakening interest in science in the early 17th century is also considered to have had an influence on metaphysical poetry. Its complex conceits, most popularly associated with the school, were paralleled and excelled in "fantastic" character in the baroque Spanish and Italian schools, and its use of imagery from the trades, professions, arts, and crafts was foreshadowed by practice in Italian and French poetry of the 16th century and by a critical recommendation in the DÉFENSE ET ILLUSTRATION DE LA LANGUE FRANÇAISE of Joachim du Bellay.

The term *metaphysical* was first derisively applied to this loosely associated group of poets by Samuel Johnson, in his study of Cowley in THE LIVES OF THE POETS, in which he condemned them for their excessive use of "learning" in their poetry.

Among the 19th-century poets whose work showed the metaphysical influence were Gerard Manley HOPKINS in England and Ralph Waldo EMERSON, Jones VERY, and Emily DICKINSON in America.

The 20th century saw a revival of interest in the metaphysical poets. Their work was highly praised by such English and American critics as T. S. ELIOT, I. A. RICHARDS, and Cleanth BROOKS, all of whom used metaphysical poetry, particularly that of Donne, as examples in their studies of poetic theory. Many 20th-century poets embraced different aspects of the metaphysical techniques and incorporated them in various ways in their own verse. Among those whose work has been described as metaphysical are T.S. Eliot, Elinor WYLIE, John Crowe RANSOM, Allen TATE, Wallace STEVENS, and Hart CRANE.

meter   In English verse, the measurement used in determining the rhythm of a line, insofar as it is established by the regular or almost regular recurrence of accented syllables. Meter is based on units called feet, each foot usually being a set relationship between one accented syllable and one or two unaccented syllables. The four most common feet in English verse are the IAMB, TROCHEE, ANAPEST, and DACTYL; occasional variations, such as the SPONDEE and PYRRHIC, occur. Verse lines are named according to the type of foot they contain and the number of feet in the line. A line made up of five iambs, for example, is called iambic PENTAMETER.

There are four types of metrical systems: *quantitative meter*, which depends on the length and number of syllables, used in classical and Sanskrit verse; *syllabic meter*, used in most Romance languages, in which there is a fixed number of syllables, with varying accents; *accentual meter*, the form of OLD ENGLISH and most Germanic versification, in which, regardless of the number of unstressed syllables, the number of accented syllables determines the basic metric unit; and *accentual-syllabic meter*, the form used in most English poetry, in which both the number of accents and the number of syllables are measured. See SCANSION.

Methodism   The doctrines of a Protestant denomination, originally of an evangelical nature, which grew from a loose religious association formed at Oxford University in 1729 by a group that included John and Charles WESLEY and George Whitefield. The name began as a term of derision applied by the Oxford students to the members of the association, because they displayed a methodical regularity in their meetings for Scriptural study and spiritual edification and in their fasts and prayers.

Methuselah   In the BIBLE, the son of Enoch. Methuselah is the oldest man mentioned in the Bible, where it states that he died at the age of 969 years (Gen. 5:27).

Metis   See ATHENE; ZEUS.

metonymy   A figure of speech in which the name of one thing is substituted for that of another with which it is commonly associated. Strictly speaking, the device of referring to a whole by one of its parts (*all hands* to mean *all sailors*) or to a whole for a part (*the nation* for *the people of the nation*) is called SYNECDOCHE. The term *metonymy* was originally reserved for less inseparable connections, such as the mention of a container for what it customarily contains ("He had one glass too many") or of a place for the person or persons who usually occupy it (*the throne* for *the reigning monarch*; *Capitol Hill* for *the U.S. Congress*). The distinctions between the two terms are, however, more subtle than they are significant, and *metonymy* is commonly used for both rhetorical devices.

Metternich, Prince Clemens von (1773–1859) Chancellor of Austria (1809–48). Metternich's reactionary policies dominated European diplomacy from the Congress of Vienna (1814–15) until the revolutions of 1848. He worked to maintain the security of Austrian power through a continental balance of power and suppression of nationalistic and liberal forces. During the insurrection of 1848 in Vienna, he fled to England.

Meursault   See STRANGER, THE.

Mexican War   A war between the U.S. and Mexico (1846–48), caused mainly by Mexican resentment against the annexation of Texas (1845) and by boundary disputes arising out of the annexation. During the war, California was conquered, and U.S. forces under General Winfield Scott captured Mexico City. By the terms of the treaty of Guadalupe-Hidalgo, Mexico gave up its claims to southern Texas and ceded to the U.S. all of Mexico north of the Rio Grande and the Gila River—about a million square miles of land. In return, the U.S. agreed to pay $15 million and to assume the claims of U.S. citizens against Mexico. Many Whigs opposed the war, claiming that it was motivated solely by the desire for territorial expansion. The war was an important training ground for many Civil War generals, including Grant, Sherman, and Lee.

Meyer, Conrad Ferdinand (1825–1898) Swiss poet and novella writer. Among German-language poets, Meyer was a pioneer in the use of symbolist techniques; that is, he often did not directly express his feelings and thoughts but tended to let them be tacitly implied in an objective description (see DINGGEDICHT). He is also famous for his historical ballads, and many of his novellas are based on historical material from the Italian Renaissance: for example, *Plautus im Nonnenkloster* (*Plautus in the Convent*, 1882) and *Die Hochzeit des Mönchs* (*The Monk's Wedding*, 1884). Like his poems, they are objective and realistic on the surface but deeply metaphysical in essence.

Meyerbeer, Giacomo (pen name of Jakob Liebmann Beer, 1791–1864) A composer of German birth, but of the French school. Immensely popular in their day, Meyerbeer's grand, somewhat grandiloquent operas have lost favor. Chief among them are *Robert le diable* (1831), *Les Huguenots* (1836), *Le Prophète* (1849), and *L'Africaine* (1865).

Meyerhold, Vsevolod Emilievich (1874–1940) Russian director and actor. Known for his stylized, highly theatrical productions, Meyerhold began his career as an actor with the Moscow Art Theatre. He later became manager of the Revolutionary Theatre in Moscow, where, in his staging of political propaganda plays, he introduced such innovations as dispensing with the theatrical curtain, the use of the bare stage, and purely symbolic scenery.

Meynell, Alice Thompson (1847–1922) English poet and essayist. Converted to Catholicism at twenty-five, Meynell began writing poetry that reflected her religious belief and sensibility, appearing first in *Preludes* (1875). Among her many subsequent volumes of verse is a complete collection published the year after her death. In 1877 she married Wilfrid Meynell, editor of a Catholic journal. She wrote articles for this and other periodicals, collected into numerous books of essays, including *The Rhythm of Life* (1893), *Ceres Runaway* (1910), and *Second Person Singular* (1921). The piety of her verse contrasts with the sometimes crusty liveliness of her often progressive essays. Among the Meynells' friends were Coventry PATMORE and Francis THOMPSON.

Meyrink, Gustav See GOLEM.

Micah The sixth Minor Prophet of the OLD TESTAMENT, whose prophecy is recorded in the book bearing his name. Micah predicted the fall of Israel and Judah but saw hope of redemption in the Messiah.

Micawber, Mr. Wilkins A well-known character in Charles Dickens's DAVID COPPERFIELD. Micawber is a great projector of bubble schemes sure to lead to fortune but always ending in grief. In spite of his indigence, he never despairs; he feels certain that something will "turn up." Having failed in every adventure in England, he immigrates to Australia, where he becomes a magistrate. Micawber is said to be drawn from Dickens's father.

Michael, St. The great prince of all the ANGELS and leader of the celestial armies.

And there was war in heaven: Michael and his angels fought against the dragon; and the dragon fought and his angels, and prevailed not.—Rev. 12:7–8

> Go, Michael, of celestial armies prince,
> And thou, in military prowess next,
> Gabriel; lead forth to battle these my sons
> Invincible; lead forth my armed Saints
> By thousands and by millions ranged for fight.
>   Milton, *Paradise Lost*

His day (St. Michael and All Angels) is September 29 (see MICHAELMAS DAY), and, in the Roman Catholic Church, he is also commemorated on May 8, in honor of his apparition in 492 to a herdsman of Monte Gargano. In the Middle Ages, he was regarded as the presiding spirit of the planet Mercury and bringer to man of the gift of prudence.

In art, St. Michael is depicted as a beautiful young man with severe countenance, winged, and clad in either white garments or armor, bearing a lance and shield, with which he combats a dragon. In the final judgment, he is represented with scales, in which he weighs the souls of the risen dead.

Michael Kohlhaas (1808) A novella by Heinrich von KLEIST. It is set in the 16th century, and Kleist calls its hero "one of the most upright and, at the same time, most terrifying men of his time." Kohlhaas, a common horse-trader, is tricked into leaving two of his best horses at the nearby castle of a dissolute young nobleman, and, when he returns, he finds that they have been ruined by being used in the fields. After failing to obtain restitution from the government, he takes the law into his own hands, gathers a band of men, razes the nobleman's castle, and burns several cities in his quest for justice. The book then develops into a constantly wider field, embracing the religious struggles and international politics of the time and the occult operations of fate. Finally Kohlhaas obtains twofold justice in that his horses are returned in perfect condition and he is executed for his crimes. The story is not based on historical fact.

Michaelmas Day September 29, the Festival of St. MICHAEL and All Angels. In England, it is one of the "quarter-days," when rents are due and when magistrates are elected. It also gives its name to the fall term of the English universities.

Michaux, Henri (1899–1984) French poet and painter born in Belgium. Although associated with the surrealists and the avant-garde in the early stages of his career, Michaux eventually came to be recognized as a unique and independent artist. One of the major themes in his writing is the conflict between inner feelings and the external world. Verbal humor and gusto, both playful and profoundly serious, characterize his stories and poems, as well as an extraordinary range of grotesqueness and fantasy. *Les Grandes Épreuves de l'esprit et les innombrables petites* (1966; tr *The Major Ordeals of the Mind and the Countless Minor Ones*, 1974), about the life of a manic-depressive, is considered by many to be his masterpiece. *Voyage en grande carbagne* (1941); *Ici, Poddema* (1946); and *Au pays de la magie* (1977) are also among his important works. *Une Certaine Plume* (1931), whose hero is a Chaplinesque figure embodying the weakness that exists in everyone, written in a much lighter vein, is often singled out by critics for special and affectionate mention. When Michaux's wife died in 1948, he created visionary drawings and watercolors, some reflecting psychic disturbances. He has produced numerous self-illustrated books of prose and poetry that explore the effects of hallucinogenic drugs; for instance, *L'Espace du dedans* (1944, rev 1966; tr *Selected Writings: The Space Within*, 1951) and *Connaissance par les gouffres* (1961; tr *Light through Darkness*, 1963).

Michelangelo [Buonarotti] (1475–1564)   Italian sculptor, architect, painter, and poet of the Renaissance. One of the greatest and most influential artists of all time, Michelangelo was born in Florentine territory and began his apprenticeship in the studio of the painter GHIRLANDAIO at Florence. Later, he studied antique sculpture under Bertoldo in the Medici academy, where he produced his first carving, the relief entitled *The Rape of Dejanira*. In the Florence of the time, he also absorbed the influence of GIOTTO, DANTE, SAVONAROLA, and the Neoplatonist circle of FICINO. His study of anatomy during this period was important for his later treatment of the human form. His first trip to Rome in 1496 produced the *Bacchus* statue and, in 1498, the famous *Pietà* of the Vatican. Having returned to Florence, he finished in 1504 the colossal statue *David* and the famous cartoon for the *Battle of Cascina*, in competition with LEONARDO DA VINCI. The painting was never finished, and only partial studies and copies remain, but CELLINI and VASARI assert that it was considered a marvel of the age. In 1504 Michelangelo also completed his *Holy Family*, one of his best-known paintings. Called to Rome again by Pope Julius II, for the purpose of executing the pope's tomb, he grew impatient with papal procrastination and left in a huff, refusing urgent pleas to remain. After a reconciliation with Pope Julius, he executed a huge bronze statue of him for the cathedral of Bologna (1507), but it was melted down shortly thereafter. In 1508 the pope diverted him from the tomb project to paint the ceiling of the Sistine Chapel, which was finally unveiled in 1512. This masterpiece consists of scenes from Genesis—the Creation to Noah—frescoed the length of the vault. Around these scenes, he painted architectural motifs (molding, ribs, pilasters), and where they intersected he inserted the Old Testament prophets, the sibyls, and, in the spandrels, the

Atlases—figures bursting with power and vitality. During the next three decades, the artist worked sporadically on the Julian tomb, which was finally abandoned. Its surviving elements include the colossal *Moses*, now in St. Pietro in Vincoli, and the unfinished figures of captives and slaves.

Back in Florence again, Michelangelo carved the Medici tombs for Lorenzo and Giuliano de' Medici in the new sacristy of St. Lorenzo, with the celebrated reclining figures of *Day, Night, Dawn,* and *Dusk* (1520–24). He also erected the Laurentian Library (1523–34) in this period. During the remaining decades of his life, spent mainly in Rome, he painted the celebrated *Last Judgment* on the end wall of the Sistine Chapel (1542), erected the Palazzo Farnese (1547), laid out the current plan of the Capitoline Hill, and erected the dome of St. Peter's, begun in 1547. Among his surviving literary works are letters and some two hundred poems, mainly sonnets, addressed to Vittoria COLONNA and the young boy Tommaso Cavalieri, to whom he was devoted. First published in bowdlerized form by his grandnephew in 1623, they were finally given to the world in their original state in 1863. They reveal Michelangelo's preoccupation with his art, his struggle to reconcile a Platonic sense of the beauty of the human form and of all material things, as a revelation of the soul within, and the Christian sense of sin. During the last week of his life, he worked on the so-called Rondanini *Pietà*, which, like several others done at this time, reveals the depth of his spiritual struggle. In addition to acknowledging with the past the greatness of individual works, modern opinion credits Michelangelo with having written the best lyrics of the Italian *cinquecento*, with being the inspiration of the stylistic movements known as MANNERISM and BAROQUE, and with being responsible for the direction taken by art for the two centuries after his death.

Michelet, Jules (1798–1874)   French historian. Michelet is noted for the vividness and penetration of his accounts of French history. He consistently expressed sympathy for the proletariat and the ideals of 1789 and consistently opposed the Church, the crown, and the bourgeoisie. His great work is *Histoire de France* (1833–67).

Michelet came from a background of poverty and secured his education through his own efforts. He lost his position as professor in the Collège de France because of his attacks on the Jesuits. Later, when Napoleon III assumed power and destroyed Michelet's hopes for liberty, he was dismissed from his employment in the national archives.

Michener, James A[lbert] (1907–   )   American novelist. Although he eventually became one of the most popular American writers of the post-World War II era, Michener was forty before he published his first novel. An immediate best-seller, *Tales of the South Pacific* (1947) won a PULITZER PRIZE and was made into the Broadway musical *South Pacific* (1949; Pulitzer Prize). Michener followed this success with a series of semidocumentary novels, each of which illuminates the history of a particular region: *Hawaii* (1959) celebrates America's fiftieth state; *The Source* (1965) is about Israel; *Centennial* (1974), about the state of Colorado; and *Chesapeake* (1978), about Maryland's Eastern Shore. *The Covenant* (1980) is an epic fictional journey through the history of South Africa. *Space* (1982), an adventure story about the American space program, celebrates man's exploratory instincts. *Poland* (1983), a novel, presents Polish history from the Middle Ages to the present, through life in a fictional Polish village. *Texas* (1985) is a blend of Texan history and fiction, written in the sweeping narrative saga style that made Michener's novels so popular with the general reading public, despite a generally cool reception by the critics of his more recent works.

Mickiewicz, Adam (1798–1855)   Polish poet. Mickiewicz studied at the Wilno University, where he was involved in a patriotic anti-Russian conspiracy. Exiled to Russia, he was released in 1829, and he settled in Western Europe. He lived mostly in Paris, where he became the spiritual leader of Polish emigrés, eventually exerting his influence on the whole nation enslaved by the foreign powers that occupied Poland in the 19th century. He died in Turkey; his body was eventually returned to Poland and buried with the Polish kings in Cracow. Mickiewicz was the first and a foremost Polish romantic poet. His collection of ballads and romances *Ballady i romanse* (1822) opened a new literary era. It was followed by a drama, *Dziady* (1823–32; tr *Forefathers*, 1968); together with a number of historical poems, a cycle of sonnets, and lyrical poetry, it represents the core of Polish romantic poetry at its very best. His best-known work is *Pan Tadeusz* (1834; tr *Pan Tadeusz or the Last Foray in Lithuania*, 1962), a long narrative poem regarded as a monument of Polish national literature.

Micromégas (1752)   A philosophic tale by VOLTAIRE that discusses the relativity of dimensions and the insignificance of mankind in the universe. Written in imitation of CYRANO DE BERGERAC's *Histoire comique* and of Jonathan SWIFT's GULLIVER'S TRAVELS, its protagonists are Micromégas, a 120,000-foot-tall inhabitant of the star Sirius, and his friend from Saturn, a "dwarf" 6,000 feet tall. They visit the earth and are impressed with the scientific knowledge of humans but are horrified by the stupidity of religious wars and dogmas. The work is a satire on the philosophic systems of DESCARTES, LEIBNITZ, and Nicolas de MALEBRANCHE.

Midas   A legendary king of Phrygia. Midas requested of the gods that everything he touched might be turned to gold. His request was granted, but, as his food became gold the moment he touched it, he prayed the gods to take this favor back. He was then ordered to bathe in the Pactolus, and the river ever after rolled over golden sands.

Another story about Midas tells that, when appointed to judge a musical contest between APOLLO and PAN, he gave judgment in favor of the satyr; whereupon Apollo, in contempt, gave the king a pair of ass's ears. Midas hid them under his Phrygian cap, but his barber discovered them, and, not daring to mention the matter, dug a hole and relieved his mind by whispering in it, "Midas has ass's ears," then covering it up again. The rushes forever after murmured the secret to the winds.

Middle Ages   The period of European history extending roughly from 476 (the fall of the Roman Empire) to 1453 (the capture of Constantinople by the Turks), although the dates vary with each nation. During this period, FEUDALISM was the characteristic form of social and economic organization. In the 8th century, the CAROLINGIANS established a connection between the Roman Catholic Church and the power of the kings and emperors as highest feudal lords. It was an uneasy alliance, however, resulting in a continuous struggle between the Church and the kings for supreme temporal authority.

The early part of the period (until about the 12th century) is occasionally referred to as the Dark Ages, because of the supposed extinction of culture and learning. Classical Greek and Roman manuscripts existed only in ecclesiastical libraries and were largely though certainly not totally ignored; the revival of general interest in classical learning and literature led to the RENAISSANCE. The Church dominated such education and scholarship as there was: compendiums of knowledge were written in the monasteries, and the great universities began as colleges of theology and divinity. By the 12th century, however, a fair amount of new literature was being written, largely under the patronage of the royal and ecclesiastical courts, based both upon the oral folklore traditions and upon scholastic learning.

Middle English   The English language as spoken and written roughly between the time of Norman conquest in England (1066) and the mid-15th century. There are two major linguistic distinctions between Middle English and OLD ENGLISH. First, the highly inflected character of Old English was replaced by a weaker, more regular inflectional system, in which many of the different case endings of Old English were reduced to a weakly accented and nondifferentiating -e. Second, Middle English incorporated many more words of Latin and French origin from the Norman French spoken by the ruling classes after 1066. Prior to the 14th century, little literature is known to have been written in Middle English, but, by the end of the century, when the use of French had effectively died out in England, such enduring works as PIERS PLOWMAN, SIR GAWAIN AND THE GREEN KNIGHT, and the works of CHAUCER and John GOWER had appeared.

Middlemarch: A Study of Provincial Life (1871–1872)   A novel by George ELIOT, with a double plot interest. The heroine, Dorothea Brooke, longs to devote herself to some great cause and, for a time, expects to find it in her marriage to Rev. Mr. Casaubon, an aging scholar. Mr. Casaubon lives only eighteen months after their marriage, a sufficient period to disillusion her completely. He leaves her his estate, with the ill-intentioned proviso that she will forfeit it if she marries his young cousin Will Ladislaw, whom he had seen frequently in Rome. Endeavoring to find happiness without Ladislaw, whom she has come to care for deeply, Dorothea throws herself into the struggle for medical reforms advocated by the young Dr. Lydgate. Finally, however, she decides to give up her property and marry Ladislaw. The second plot deals with the efforts and failure of Dr. Lydgate to live up to his early ideals. Handicapped by financial difficulties, brought about by his marriage to the selfish and ambitious Rosamond Vincy, and by the opposition of his medical associates, he drifts into cultivating a wealthy practice at the expense of his medical standards. There is a subplot dealing with the love affair of Rosamond's brother Fred Vincy and Mary Garth, the daughter of Caleb Garth, the builder.

Middle Temple   See INNS OF COURT.

Middleton, Thomas (1580–1627)   English dramatist. One of the most popular playwrights of his period, Middleton possessed considerable comic and satiric talents but seldom gave way to caricature. His observation was keen and balanced, so that his characterizations remain, on the whole, remarkably credible. His masterpieces are perhaps THE CHANGELING, written with William ROWLEY, one of the most powerful tragedies of the period, and A TRICK TO CATCH THE OLD ONE, one of the best comedies of manners. Among the finest of his other plays are THE ROARING GIRL, written with Thomas Dekker; *A Mad World, My Masters* (c1606); *Women, Beware Women* (c1623); *No Wit, No Help Like a Woman's* (1613?); *A Game at Chess* (1624); and a number of plays written in collaboration with William Rowley, in one of which, *The Spanish Gipsy* (1623), John FORD was also a collaborator.

Middletown (1929)   A classic sociological study of an American city, by Robert S. Lynd (1892–1970) and Helen M. Lynd (1897–1982). The community called Middletown was actually Muncie, Indiana. This study was among the first that demonstrated the discrepancy between American egalitarian beliefs and the class structure of an American community. It also focused on the conflict between the ideological emphasis on individualism and free enterprise and the demands created by the entry of this city into an industrialized and highly organized economy.

Midgard (fr ON, *mithgarthr*, "the yard in the middle")   In Scandinavian mythology, the region of earth. The abode of the first man and woman, ASK and Embla, Midgard was made from the body of YMIR and was joined to ASGARD by the rainbow bridge, BIFROST.

Midgard serpent (also known as *Jormungard*, "the earth's monster," and *Midgardsorm*, "the serpent of Midgard")   In Scandinavian mythology, the venomous serpent, fathered by LOKI, the spirit of evil, and the brother of HEL and the FENRIS-WOLF. The Midgard serpent lay at the root of the celestial ash until ODIN cast him into the ocean, where he grew so large that in time he encompassed the earth and was forever biting his own tail. THOR finally killed him with his hammer, but the serpent's flood of venom drowned the god.

Midrash   The rabbinical investigation into and interpretation of the OLD TESTAMENT writings. It began when the temple at Jerusalem was destroyed; it was committed to writing in a large number of commentaries between the 2nd and 11th centuries. Three ancient Midrashim contain both the HALACHAH, which deals with the legal sections of the BIBLE, and the HAGGADAH, treating the nonlegal.

midsummer day   June 24, the Feast of the Nativity of St. JOHN THE BAPTIST. Its eve (June 23) is called midsummer night. It occurs near the time of the summer solstice, which was associated with solar ceremonies long before the Christian era. The bonfires still lighted in parts of Europe on the eve are relics of these customs.

Midsummer Night's Dream, A (c1594)   A comedy by SHAKESPEARE. Plans are afoot for the wedding of THESEUS, duke of Athens, and the Amazon queen HIPPOLYTA, whom he has defeated in battle. Egeus, an Athenian, has promised his daughter Hermia to Demetrius, and, although she is in love with Lysander, the duke orders her to obey her father. The two lovers escape to the forest, followed by Demetrius and by Helena, who is in love with Demetrius. Here they are found by OBERON, king of the fairies, his queen, TITANIA, with whom he is extremely disgruntled, and the merry PUCK. Puck has a magic love-juice that will make the one whose eyelids are anointed fall in love with the first object he sees upon awaking. Since Puck uses the potion somewhat indiscriminately, a strange comedy ensues, but eventually Demetrius abandons Hermia to Lysander and devotes himself to Helena. At the duke's marriage feast, which celebrates three weddings in place of one, BOTTOM the weaver and his blundering group of players present as an interlude the play of PYRAMUS and Thisbe.

There is no single source for the play. The story of Theseus and Hippolyta is found in CHAUCER's KNIGHT'S TALE, as well as in PLUTARCH's *Lives*. The "tragical comedy" of Pyramus and Thisbe is a burlesque of the tale in OVID's METAMORPHOSES.

Mies van der Rohe, Ludwig (1886–1969)   German-American architect. Having established an international reputation with his design for the German pavilion at the Barcelona International Exposition (1929), Mies was appointed the last director of the BAUHAUS in 1930. After Nazi pressure forced the closing of the Bauhaus in 1933, he immigrated to the U.S. (1938), where, among other things, he designed a new campus for the Illinois Institute of Technology. Mies emphasized the credo "less is more" in design. His buildings, many of them with glass walls within a steel grid, became the standard for modern glass skyscrapers in the 1950s and 1960s. The Seagram Building in New York City, designed in collaboration with Philip JOHNSON, is an outstanding example of Mies's refinement of rectangular volume and surface proportion.

Mignon In GOETHE's novel *Wilhelm Meisters Lehrjahre*, a young girl whom Wilhelm finds in a troupe of side-show performers and buys from her brutal guardian. Mignon is Italian in origin and filled with a constant yearning to return to her sunny native land. Her complete devotion to her savior Wilhelm is too deep and mystical to be considered a simple manifestation of love between the sexes; in fact, everything about her is permeated with a sense of mystery. She wilts, finally, in her uncongenial northern surroundings, and dies. Her story, considerably altered, formed the basis for the once-popular opera *Mignon* (1866) by Ambroise Thomas. See WILHELM MEISTER.

Mihura [Santos], Miguel (1905–) Spanish playwright. Unlike his precursor JARDIEL PONCELA, Spain's other great comic genius, Mihura is more interested in human nature than in bizarre effects. Relying heavily on incongruous language and ridiculous situations, he criticizes the hypocrisy and false values of society. His first play, *Tres sombreros de copa* (tr *Three Top Hats*, 1968), though written in 1932, was not performed until 1952. Considered to be the best of his many plays, it satirizes bourgeois materialism while retaining compassion for human weakness and insisting that man must make his own individual choices.

Milbanke, Anne Isabella (called Annabella Milbanke, 1792–1860) English heiress and wife of Lord BYRON. A beautiful and rigorously moral woman, Milbanke was unsuited to a man of Byron's temperament. The two were married in 1815 and separated a year later, after the birth of their daughter, Augusta Ada. It was rumored at the time that the separation was caused by Lady Byron's discovery of an incestuous relationship between the poet and his half sister Augusta Leigh.

Miles, Josephine [Louise] (1911–1985) American poet and literary scholar. From her earliest volume, *Lines at Intersection* (1939), to her second collected edition, *To All Appearances* (1974), and the verse in *Coming to Terms* (1979), Miles's poetry is marked by freshness of vision, compassion, and wisdom, tempered with a gentle irony. Her contributions to serious literary study, particularly in *Continuity of Poetic Language, I–III* (1949–51) and *Eras and Modes in English Poetry* (1957; rev 1964), have been accepted as definitive studies of the history of English prosody.

Miles gloriosus (Boastful Soldier, c205 BC) A comedy by PLAUTUS. The hero is Captain Pyrgopolynices, a character who is the prototype of a long line of military braggarts in European and English drama.

Milesian School A school of Greek philosophers originating in Miletus, of the period preceding Plato. The Milesians tried to find a unifying principle for the universe in a basic "world-stuff" that maintained its integrity throughout all physical change. Water, air, and the infinite were suggested. The members of the school were THALES, Anaximander, and Anaximenes.

Milhaud, Darius (1892–1974) French composer, a member of LES SIX. Milhaud, a prolific composer of great versatility, explored the possibilities of jazz style and polytonality, as in the ballet *La Création du monde* (*The Creation of the World*, 1923), and Latin American music, as in *Saudades do Brazil* (*Souvenirs of Brazil*; piano suite, 1921). His operas include *La Brebis égarée* (*The Lost Sheep*, 1910; based on a novel by Francis JAMMES), *Cristophe Colomb* (1930, from a book by Paul CLAUDEL), and others based on Greek legends and plays, such as *Médée* (1939).

Mill, John Stuart (1806–1873) English philosopher and economist. A precocious child, Mill was put through a rigorous education by his grim and exacting father, James Mill (1773–1836), a utilitarian philosopher. In 1823 he entered India House as his father's assistant, became assistant examiner in 1828, was in charge of relations with native states (1836–56), and was made chief of office in 1856, retiring with a pension, when the East Indian Company dissolved in 1858.

Mill formed the Utilitarian Society (1823–26) for reading and discussing essays at the home of Jeremy BENTHAM. He was the chief contributor to the *Westminster Review* and was recognized as a leading proponent of UTILITARIANISM before the age of twenty. His first literary undertaking of note was the editing of Bentham's *Rationale of Judicial Evidence* (1825). After a severe mental crisis (1826–27), which was probably caused by the strict training by his father, he departed somewhat from the utilitarianism of Bentham and his father by humanizing it and adding a note of idealism.

James Mill died before his son's first major work, *System of Logic* (1843), appeared. Mill, in the meantime, had fallen in love with Harriet Taylor, who was already married. She remained so, technically, until her husband died in 1851. She and Mill married, but she was in poor health and died in 1859. Her daughter Helen took care of Mill for the rest of his life. It was largely through Harriet's influence that Mill wrote "The Enfranchisement of Women," an extraordinary article for that time. From this grew his radical and influential book, not yet finished when Harriet died, *The Subjection of Women* (1869). Mill also acknowledged Harriet's involvement in his famous essay *On Liberty* (1859). Others of his best-known works include *Thoughts on Parliamentary Reform* (1859), *Representative Government* (1861), *Utilitarianism* (1863), *Examination of Sir William Hamilton's Philosophy* (1865), *The Irish Land Question* (1870), and his *Autobiography* (1873). He was a member of Parliament (1865–68), voted with the Radical party, and became an outspoken advocate of women's suffrage. He lived the last years of his life at Avignon, in France. See EMPIRICISM.

Millais, John Everett (1829–1896) English painter. With Holman Hunt and Dante Gabriel Rossetti, Millais originated the PRE-RAPHAELITE BROTHERHOOD (1848). He illustrated the works of Trollope and of Tennyson and painted portraits of many of the distinguished men of his day. After 1870 his work deviated from Pre-Raphaelite style and subject matter.

Millay, Edna St. Vincent (1892–1950) American poet. After her graduation from Vassar and the appearance of her first book of poems, *Renascence and Other Poems* (1917), Millay went to live in Greenwich Village. For a time, she acted with the PROVINCETOWN PLAYERS, who produced some of the plays she had written in college, notably *Aria de Capo* (1920). During the 1920s, she also wrote satirical sketches, such as *Distressing Dialogues* (1924), under the pen name Nancy Boyd. It was also in this period that she wrote the poetry that made her one of the best-known poets of her time. Her second volume of poems, A FEW FIGS FROM THISTLES, celebrated Bohemian life, love, and moral freedom with lyrical gaiety and freshness. This was followed by such collections as the PULITZER PRIZE-winning THE HARP WEAVER AND OTHER POEMS and *The Buck in the Snow* (1928). Influenced by the ELIZABETHAN poets, by KEATS, and by Gerard Manley HOPKINS, she retained conventional forms in a brilliant and flexible style and was particularly noted for her sonnets, as in *Fatal Interview* (1931) and *Conversation at Midnight* (1937).

After her marriage in 1923 to Eugen Jan Boissevain, she lived mostly on their farm, Steepletop, in Austerlitz, New York, leaving only for occasional travel or public readings. Her later poetry, as with the war poem *The Murder of Lidice* (1942), became increasingly concerned with social and political themes. She wrote very little in the last decade of her life. Her *Collected Poems* was published in 1956. In 1975 her sister Norma Millay established the Millay Colony for the Arts at Steepletop.

Miller, Arthur (1915–) American playwright, short-story writer, and novelist. Miller began writing plays at the University of Michigan. Returning to New York, he published a novel, *Focus* (1945), an ironical study of race prejudice. *All My Sons* (1947), his first successful play, dealt with the emotional aftermath of World War II. The PULITZER PRIZE-winning DEATH OF A SALESMAN established Miller as one of the leading playwrights of his generation. The play exemplified Miller's contention that tragedy is possible in the modern theatre and that its proper hero is the common man. THE CRUCIBLE and A *View from the Bridge* (1955) confirmed his already secure reputation. His *Collected Plays* appeared in 1957. The screenplay for his film *The Misfits* (1961), which evolved from a short story published in *Esquire* (1957), was issued in book form in 1961. *After the Fall* (1964), an autobiographical drama that was the first production of the Lincoln Center Repertory

Theater in New York City, caused considerable controversy, partly because of the characterization of Maggie, supposedly modeled on Miller's second wife, the actress Marilyn Monroe.

Among his other plays are *Incident at Vichy* (1964), *The Price* (1968), *The Creation of the World and Other Business* (1972), and *The American Clock* (1980), a semiautobiographical reminiscence of a Jewish family during the Depression. *The Theater Essays of Arthur Miller* (1978) contains selected writings between 1949 and 1972. "*Salesman*" *in Beijing*, an account of Miller's experiences directing *Death of a Salesman* in China, was published in 1984. *Danger: Memory!*, two plays, followed in 1986.

Miller has collaborated with his wife, the photographer Inge Morath, on several books—including *In Russia* (1969) and *Chinese Encounters* (1979)—for which she took the pictures and he wrote the text.

Miller, Henry (1891–1980) American writer. Miller held a variety of jobs, including a position as employment manager for the Western Union Telegraph Company, before he settled for a nine-year period (1930–39) in France. During these years, he wrote and published the books usually considered his best: the controversial TROPIC OF CANCER; *Black Spring* (1936), stories and sketches, including the famous "The 14th Ward"; *Tropic of Capricorn* (1939), a counterpart to *Cancer*, beginning with his hilarious years at Western Union; and *Max and the White Phagocytes* (1938), a collection of stories, many of which were reprinted in *The Cosmological Eye* (1939). A garrulous and prolific writer, Miller combines elements of fictional narrative and autobiographical disclosure with bawdy humor, uninhibited fascination with sex, and rambling philosophical musings.

Miller traveled from Italy to Greece at the beginning of World War II. One product of that trip was *The Colossus of Maroussi* (1941), thought by many critics to be an example of his finest and most concentrated writing. In it, he proclaimed the genius of Greece to be not in its ruins but in the spirit of its people. He then returned to America, and, after a nationwide tour, published his critical reaction to the country in *The Air-Conditioned Nightmare* (1945) and its continuation, *Remember to Remember* (1947). Miller settled in the Big Sur region of California, where he wrote an autobiographical trilogy called *The Rosy Crucifixion*, which included *Sexus* (1949), *Plexus* (1949), and *Nexus* (1957).

Miller's anarchic dismissal of literary conventions and his revolutionary treatment of sex earned him the admiration of many writers, notably Lawrence DURRELL, who edited *The Henry Miller Reader* (1959), and Norman MAILER, who wrote about Miller in *Genius and Lust* (1976). Miller's correspondence with Durrell was published in 1963; his letters to Anaïs NIN appeared in 1965.

Miller, Joaquin (pen name of Cincinnatus Hiner Miller, 1837–1913) As a boy, Miller moved from Indiana to Oregon with his impoverished family. He led an adventurous life, teaching, editing, living with Indians, goldmining, practicing law, and establishing a Pony Express route between the Washington territory and Idaho. He wrote two volumes of poetry, *Specimens* (1868) and *Joaquin et al.* (1869), which received little attention. He then went to London (1870), where he cut a romantic and extravagant figure in cowboy boots and sombrero. It is said that he smoked three cigars at once and bit the ankles of debutantes, thus confirming the English image of American westerners. His *Songs of the Sierras* (1871), published in England, brought him wide renown. Miller wrote a prose autobiography, *Life among the Modocs* (1873), and published several other volumes of poetry. His most famous poems are "Columbus" and "Kit Carson's Ride," an extravagant celebration of the vigor of the West, learned by thousands of schoolchildren.

Miller, Perry [Gilbert Eddy] (1905–1963) American historian. A member of the faculty of Harvard University from 1931 until his death, Miller is best known for his two-volume analysis *The New England Mind* (1939–53), a work notable for its erudition, profundity, and wit, which examines the origins and implications of the religious, political, and social thought of the Puritans.

Miller, Walter M[ichael], Jr. (1923–   ) American science-fiction writer. Miller is the author of the highly respected novel *A Canticle for Leibowitz* (1959). In this, perhaps the best after-the-bomb novel ever written, a group of monks attempt to preserve the often indecipherable remnants of civilization. He has also published two collections of short stories, *Conditionally Human* (1962) and *The View from the Stars* (1964). *The Best of Walter M. Miller, Jr.*, appeared in 1980.

Miller's Tale, The One of THE CANTERBURY TALES of Geoffrey CHAUCER, based on a French *fabliau*. The Host asks the Monk to follow the Knight with a tale, but the drunken Miller insists on telling a ribald story. Alison, young wife of the old carpenter John, scorns the attentions paid her by Absolon, a foppish parish clerk, but would gladly return those of Nicholas, a young scholar boarding in their house. Nicholas convinces John that a second Flood is coming and persuades him to suspend three tubs in the attic so that they can float away in safety. John falls asleep in his tub, and Nicholas and Alison steal down from theirs to the bedroom. Absolon begs outside for a kiss, and Alison offers her rump at the dark window. Furiously insulted, Absolon borrows a hot brand from the smithy and returns, pretending to beg a second kiss in exchange for a gold ring. For a joke, Nicholas sticks his rump out this time and is thoroughly scorched. His cries for water awaken John, who thinks the Flood has come and cuts loose his tub; he crashes through to the ground and is thereafter considered a fool by the townsfolk.

Millet, Jean-François (1814–1875) French painter. Associated with the BARBIZON SCHOOL, Millet painted not only landscapes but also rural scenes celebrating the innocence and nobility of peasant life. Among his best-known works are the *Angelus* (1857–59) and *The Man with the Hoe* (1859–62), which, with his other peasant drawings, exerted a considerable influence on the works of VAN GOGH and SEURAT.

Millin, Sarah Gertrude (1889–1968) South African novelist and diarist. Millin's novels include *God's Step-Children* (1924), a tragic story of the Cape "colored" people; *The Dark Gods* (1941); and *The Wizard Bird* (1962). *The People of South Africa* (1951) is a history. Her diaries were published between 1945 and 1947; *The Measure of My Days* (1955) is her autobiography.

Mill on the Floss, The (1860) A novel by George ELIOT. The principal characters are Maggie Tulliver and her brother Tom, who grow up together at Dorlcote Mill, united by a strong bond in spite of their opposite temperaments. Maggie is loved by Philip Wakem, the deformed son of the lawyer responsible for the ruin of Maggie's father, but Tom's opposition makes the relationship impossible. Later she falls in love with Stephen Guest, the handsome and passionate fiancé of her cousin Lucy Deane. They go off together on impulse, and, although Maggie repents before it is too late, her return is misconstrued, and her life is made desperately unhappy. Only death reunites her with Tom; the two are drowned together in a great flood of the Floss.

Milne, A[lan] A[lexander] (1882–1956) English dramatist, novelist, and humorous journalist. Milne is best remembered for his children's books. First written for his son, CHRISTOPHER ROBIN, *Winnie-the-Pooh* (1926) and *The House at Pooh Corner* (1928) have a toy bear, POOH, as their hero. *When We Were Very Young* (1924) and *Now We Are Six* (1927) are collections of verse for children. Milne was also a successful dramatist of the 1920s.

Milosz, Czeslaw (1911–   ) Lithuanian-born Polish poet, essayist, and novelist. A member of the "catastrophist" school, Milosz established himself as Poland's leading avant-garde poet in the 1930s. He was active in the anti-Nazi underground in World War II and immediately after the war served his country as a diplomat. His disenchantment with communism led to his flight from Poland in 1951, first to Paris and then to the U.S., where he lived in voluntary exile for over thirty years. His exposure to totalitarianism led to a focus on ideology, consciousness, choice, and necessity in both his poetry and prose. He first received serious attention in the U.S. with *Zniewolony umysl* (1953; tr *The Captive Mind*, 1953), an examination of the power of communist ideology over Polish intellectuals. *Rodzinna Europa* (1959; tr *Native Realm*, 1981) is a moral and intellectual autobiography from childhood to the 1950s. In his poetry, which is classical, often almost biblical in style, Milosz created a mythic world, defined by memory and imagination, through which to view the realities and cruelties of man. *Selected*

Poems (1973; rev 1981) and *Bells in Winter* (1978) contain representative selections of his verse in translation. His fiction, also informed by acute moral awareness, includes *The Usurpers* (tr 1955) and *The Issa Valley* (1955; tr 1981), an autobiographical novel evoking the beauty of a Lithuanian countryside still insulated from the evils of the world. He also wrote *History of Polish Literature* (1969) and worked for years on a Polish translation of the Bible. Milosz was awarded the NOBEL PRIZE in Literature in 1980. *The Witness of Poetry*, a further volume of verse, was published in 1983. *The Land of Ulro* (1984) combines passages of intellectual autobiography with writings on literature and metaphysics.

Miltiades (540?–?489 BC)   A tyrant of the Thracian Chersonese. As a general of the Athenian forces, Miltiades defeated the Persians at MARATHON. He later died in prison, for having tricked the Athenians into giving him a large force of ships in order to settle a private grudge.

Milton (1804)   A symbolic poem by William BLAKE, in which the poet John Milton returns from heaven and corrects the misinterpretations given to his works on earth. Eventually he enters the spirit of Blake himself and preaches redemption and forgiveness.

Milton, John (1608–1674)   English poet and prose writer, one of the best-known and most respected figures in English literature.

Milton's father, a London notary who was raised a Catholic but became a convert to the Church of England, gave his talented son the best of educations. After private tutoring, the boy entered St. Paul's School and Cambridge, then was supported through five years of independent study, and finally was sent on a two-year tour of Europe to perfect his learning. During this period, Milton wrote some of his most brilliant poetry, including L'ALLEGRO and IL PENSEROSO, the masque COMUS, and the splendid elegy LYCIDAS, as well as other poems in English and Latin. He returned to England before the outbreak of the Civil War, for a while conducting a sort of private school and supporting the Puritan cause in various tracts and pamphlets. In 1649 his reputation as a learned controversialist won him the position of Latin secretary to Cromwell, in which office he handled correspondence with foreign nations and was apologist for the Commonwealth to the world at large. In 1657 Andrew MARVELL became his assistant, for by 1652 his grueling work had cost Milton his eyesight. After the Restoration, he was arrested and fined but escaped imprisonment or death, probably in part through Marvell's intervention. Aged, blind, his public career over, his hopes for a godly and republican England dashed, Milton turned to a cherished plan of composing a great national epic. In 1667 he published his masterpiece, PARADISE LOST, following it in 1671 with its sequel, *Paradise Regained*, and the fine dramatic poem SAMSON AGONISTES.

Milton was a noble and difficult man. Though he was a Puritan, morally austere and conscientious, some of his religious beliefs were unconventional to the point of heresy, and a number of his works, such as the AREOPAGITICA and the *Doctrine and Discipline of Divorce* (1644), came into conflict with the orthodox, or official, Puritan stand. He was also a humanist, convinced of the high possibilities of human nature, and he was a lover of music, literature, and the various amenities of civilized life. Milton's character was a paradoxical mixture that combined passion, sensuality, pride, and ambition with high idealism, self-discipline, self-sacrifice, and fortitude. He was least admirable in some of his personal relationships, specifically with Mary Powell, the first of his three wives, and with his three daughters, to whom he showed little understanding or consideration; in some of his controversial writings, he also revealed arrogance and coarseness.

Milton's writing reflects his rich and divided nature. Perhaps the most characteristic theme of his work is temptation—a theme running from "L'Allegro" and "Il Penseroso" down to *Samson Agonistes*, the temptations being sensual enjoyment, pride, and passivity, all of which must be met by the resolute, God-instructed and God-supported will. His style ranges from the fresh luxuriance of such works as *Comus* to the force and masculinity of his great sonnets to the sonority and lofty eloquence of *Paradise Lost*. His prose is complex and highly rhetorical, with passages of great power.

In addition to those mentioned above, the following works of Milton are of importance: "On the Morning of Christ's Nativity" (1629), such sonnets as "When I Consider How My Light Is Spent" ("On His Blindness"), "On the Late Massacre in Piedmont," "Methought I Saw My Late Espoused Saint" (all written between 1652 and 1658), and such prose writings as *Of Education* (1644), *Eikonoklastes* (1649), and *Defensio pro Publico Anglicano* (1651).

mime   An early form of comedy, probably originating in southern Italy, in which players combine dialogue with dancing and suggestive gestures. Sophron of Syracuse (fl 5th century BC) wrote ribald mime plays about daily life. Herodas (fl 3rd century BC) also wrote mime plays in verse that influenced THEOCRITUS, PLAUTUS, and TERENCE. Because of the frequently lewd nature of the presentations, the Church attempted to suppress the form. It was kept alive, however, by wandering players, and its influence spread through Europe and England. Traces of the form appear in medieval MYSTERY PLAYS, Renaissance DUMB SHOWS, and modern PANTOMIME.

Mimir   The Scandinavian god of wisdom, a water demon. Mimir was one of the most celebrated of the giants. The VANIR, with whom he was left as a hostage, cut off his head. ODIN embalmed it by his magic art, pronounced over it mystic runes, and ever after consulted it on critical occasions. Mimir dwelt under the roof of YGGDRASILL, where Mimir's Well (*Mimisbrunnr*) was located, in which all wisdom lay concealed, and from which Mimir drank with the horn Giallar. Odin gave one of his eyes to be permitted to drink of its waters and thereby became the wisest of the gods.

Mine Boy   See ABRAHAMS, PETER.

Minerva   The Roman goddess of wisdom and patroness of the arts and trades, fabled to have sprung, with a tremendous battle cry, fully armed from the head of JUPITER. Remarkably similar to the Greek ATHENE, Minerva became identified with her. She was one of the three chief deities, the others being Jupiter and JUNO. She is represented as grave and majestic, clad in a helmet, with drapery over a coat of mail, bearing the aegis on her breast.

Ming   Chinese dynasty (1368–1644). A native Chinese house that replaced the Mongols of the YÜAN dynasty. This era was famous for naval expeditions to Arabia and Africa and for the enormous number of printed works on all subjects. Blue and white Ming porcelain is highly valued. The Ming was followed by the CH'ING dynasty.

Minna von Barnhelm   (1767)   A comedy by Gotthold Ephraim LESSING. Major von Tellheim, because of a question of honor and military justice, refuses to marry Minna, whom he has long loved. To overcome his hesitation, Minna pretends to be poverty-stricken and in dire need, whereupon Tellheim rushes to her aid. In the end, Tellheim gets both Minna and satisfaction for his honor.

Minnehaha   (Sioux, "waterfall," lit "laughing water") In Longfellow's HIAWATHA, the Sioux maiden who becomes Hiawatha's bride.

Minnesingers   The lyric poets of the German courts in the 12th and 13th centuries. The *Minnesang* is by definition a song of love, although the Minnesingers also sang of religion and politics. Their poetry was greatly influenced by that of the Provençal TROUBADOURS and the tradition of COURTLY LOVE; they were succeeded by the MEISTERSINGERS. The most famous Minnesingers, usually men of the lower nobility, include Heinrich von Veldeke and Friedrich von Hausen (12th century), then Gottfried von Strassburg (early 13th century), WALTHER VON DER VOGELWEIDE, and WOLFRAM VON ESCHENBACH. See also WARTBURG.

Minos   In Greek mythology, the king and lawgiver of Crete. At his death, Minos became a judge in the underworld. The beginning of his reign was somewhat disturbed by the episode of the MINOTAUR, the end by the treachery of his daughter ARIADNE in helping THESEUS to kill the beast and release the Greek captives. In spite of this, another daughter, PHAEDRA, married Theseus, who had abandoned Ariadne. Theseus lived to regret it.

Minos may well have been the name given to a dynasty of priest-kings of Crete, whose magnificent palace at Knossos has been extensively excavated and restored. He gave his name to the Minoan period, about 2500 to 1400 BC, during which Crete was a predominant power in the Eastern Mediterranean area.

Minotaur   In Greek mythology, a monster with a bull's head on a human body. POSEIDON sent a bull from the sea as a sign to prove MINOS' right to become king of Crete, but Minos failed to sacrifice it to him. In revenge, the god caused Minos' wife PASIPHAË to conceive a passion for the bull. Aided in satisfying it by DAEDALUS, she bore the Minotaur, whose name was Asterius. It was shut up by Minos in the LABYRINTH. Every ninth year, it was fed with fourteen youths and maidens, a tribute exacted from Athens, until THESEUS killed it with ARIADNE's aid.

In Minoan Crete, a sacred bull was regarded as the animal form of the priest-king Minos, consort of the high priestess of the Mother-goddess, Pasiphaë. A version of the Minotaur story, based on the discoveries of modern archaeology and anthropology, is told in *The King Must Die* (1958), a popular novel by Mary RENAULT.

Mirabeau, Comte de   (Honoré Gabriel Victor Riqueti, 1749–1791)   French orator and revolutionary leader. In spite of his early notoriety as a pleasure-seeker, Mirabeau's unusual gift for oratory won him a firm and respected place in public life. One of the most important figures in the first two years of the Revolution, he advocated a limited, or constitutional, monarchy after the English model.

miracle plays   (or miracles, 13th–16th centuries) Medieval dramas presenting miracles of the Virgin Mary or the saints. There are about forty extant French miracle plays from the 14th century, all in octosyllabic couplets with a short prose sermon. Many of the English miracle plays were adapted from the French; there is more variation of metrical form, however. In English drama, the miracle plays also include what are now usually called the MYSTERY PLAYS, and the terms are generally interchangeable. See INTERLUDE; MORALITY PLAYS; PASSION PLAY.

Miranda   The innocent daughter of Prospero in Shakespeare's THE TEMPEST. Raised without human companions, Miranda is overcome with awe at the first men she sees:

> O, wonder!
> How many goodly creatures are there here!
> How beauteous mankind is! Oh, brave new world,
> That has such people in't!

She marries Ferdinand, son of Alonso, who is her counterpart in innocence and purity.

Miriam   (1) A Hebrew prophet of the OLD TESTAMENT, the elder sister of MOSES and AARON, who led the celebrative music and dances of the Hebrew women after Moses brought the Israelites across the Red Sea (Exod. 15:20).

(2) A mysterious, beautiful, and passionate art student in Rome in HAWTHORNE's "Marble Faun" (1860).

(3) In D. H. Lawrence's novel SONS AND LOVERS, the shy, intense farm girl who is the first love of Paul Morel. Miriam also occurs in Lawrence's early poems. The character is based on the young woman in Lawrence's own life who first encouraged his writing and submitted some of his

early poems to Ford Madox FORD, then editor of *The English Review*. She wrote *D. H. Lawrence, a Personal Record* (1936) under the initials E. T.

Miriam (1870)   A poem by John Greenleaf WHITTIER about a Christian maiden and her Muslim lord.

Miró, Joan (1893–1983)   Spanish painter, graphic artist, and ceramist. Although Miró remained closely tied to his homeland throughout his life, he spent enough time in Paris to feel the direct effects of the important artistic movements of his youth: LES FAUVES, CUBISM, DADA, and SURREALISM. Generally classified as an abstract surrealist, Miró created distinctive paintings containing a paradoxical mix of frivolous good humor and nightmarish vision.

Mirror for Magistrates, The   A work in verse on the fall of great men in English history, modeled after Boccaccio's *De casibus virorum illustrium* and Lydgate's *Falls of Princes*. The first edition (1559) contained nineteen tragedies written by various authors; each tragedy is purportedly narrated in the first person by the ghost of its subject. The second edition added eight more tragic histories, including Thomas Churchyard's *Shore's Wife* (see Jane SHORE) and Thomas Sackville's *Induction* and *Complaint* of the duke of Buckingham. The best piece in the collection, the *Induction* is one of the most important examples of early Elizabethan verse and is considered to be inaugural of a new age.

The Mirror for Magistrates was avowedly of moral rather than purely literary purpose, intended to warn contemporary rulers to study tragic stories and thereby learn to avoid tragedy. It is interesting primarily as a reflection of the new Renaissance conception of man, in which not only fickle Fortune but also moral flaws in a great man's character are responsible for his tragic end. The *Mirror* was very popular and appeared in numerous editions and expansions from 1559 to 1610.

Misanthrope, Le (The Misanthrope, 1666)   A comedy by MOLIÈRE. The play centers on ALCESTE, who has vowed to speak and act with complete honesty and no longer to adhere to the conventions of a hypocritical society. Pursued by the pretended prude Arsinoé, unable to accept the affection of the gentle and sincere Eliante, Alceste is in love with the sharp-tongued, vain coquette Célimène, epitome of all that he despises. After losing a lawsuit in which justice was on his side, Alceste resolves to abandon society and asks Célimène to accompany him. She refuses to give up her frivolous life, and he departs alone, gloomy and disillusioned.

Misérables, Les (The Miserable Ones, 1862)   A novel by Victor Hugo. The central figure of the tale is the convict Jean Valjean. One of society's victims, Valjean, originally an honest peasant, stole a single loaf of bread to feed his sister's starving family and was sentenced to five years in prison at hard labor. He was caught trying to escape and was given a nineteen-year term in the galleys. On his release, he has become a hardened criminal until he is befriended by a bishop and enabled to begin life anew. He becomes M. Madeleine, a successful industrialist and mayor of a northern French town, but, because of an impulsive, bitterly regretted former crime, he is discovered and compelled to return to prison by the implacable, ever-searching detective Javert. Escaping once again, Valjean befriends an unhappy woman of the streets, Fantine, and rescues her daughter, Cosette, from the abusive family with whom she has been living. The canvas of *Les Misérables* is an enormous representation of innumerable episodes and characters. Among the most famous chapters are the account of the battle of Waterloo and Valjean's flight through the Paris sewers.

Mishima, Yukio (pen name of Kimitake Hiraoka, 1925–1970)   Japanese novelist, playwright, and essayist. According to his autobiographical essay *Taiyō to tetsu* (1968; tr *Sun and Steel*, 1970), his lifelong concern was with the dichotomy between mind and body that he thought plagued modern civilization. His attempt to resolve the dichotomy is chronicled in his novels, beginning with *Kamen no kokuhaku* (1949; tr *Confessions of a Mask*, 1958) and ending with a tetralogy, *Hōjō no umi* (1965–71; tr *The Sea of Fertility*, 1971–74). Anti-intellectuals who succeed in overcoming the dichotomy are featured in *Shiosai* (1954; tr *The Sound of Waves*, 1956) and *Kinkakuji* (1956; tr *The Temple of the Golden Pavilion*, 1959). *Gogo no eiko* (1963; tr *The Sailor Who Fell from Grace with the Sea*, 1965) was filmed in 1974. Mishima himself chose to die as an anti-intellectual, committing ritual suicide in the traditional SAMURAI manner.

Mishnah (Heb, "repetition")   The collection of moral precepts, traditions, and law forming the basis of the TALMUD. Compiled by Rabbi Judah I (c135–220), the Mishnah is divided into six parts: (1) agriculture; (2) Sabbaths, fasts, and festivals; (3) marriage and divorce; (4) civil and penal laws; (5) sacrifices; (6) holy persons and things.

Miss Julie (1888)   A long one-act play by August STRINDBERG. Described by the author as a naturalistic tragedy, the play has twin centers of conflict in the love-hate relationship of men and women and in the social relationship of the upper and lower classes. Miss Julie is the daughter of a count. She has been brought up by her mother to hate men; when, to express her contempt for them, she forced her fiancé to jump over a horsewhip at her command, the man broke the engagement. As the play opens, Miss Julie joins in a servants' party and flirts with Jean, a footman. She seduces him and, unable to live with the conflicts this act creates in her, commits suicide.

Miss Lonelyhearts (1933)   A novel by Nathanael WEST. The story of a man who writes an "advice to the lovelorn" column, the theme of the book is the loneliness of the individual in modern society. The hero tries to live the role of omniscient counselor he has assumed for the paper, but his attempts to reach out to suffering humanity are twisted by circumstances, and he is finally murdered by a man he has tried to help.

Missouri Compromise   In U.S. history, an 1820 act of Congress by which Maine was admitted into the Union as a free state, Missouri as a slave state, and slavery was barred from the territory acquired in the Louisiana Purchase north of the line 36° 30′. This act, which kept the number of free and slave states equal, was the first of numerous attempts to settle differences between the North and South. It was repealed in 1854 with the passage of the Kansas-Nebraska Act.

Miss Thompson (1921)   A short story by W. Somerset MAUGHAM. The Reverend Alfred Davidson, a repressed missionary on a South Sea island during the rainy season, attempts to convert Sadie Thompson, a carefree young tart, to religion. His efforts are successful, but, when he seduces her, she reverts to her former ways. Guilty and despairing, he commits suicide.

The story was dramatized as *Rain* in 1922 by John B. Colton and Clemence Randolph.

Mistral, Frédéric (1830–1914)   French poet. Mistral was a leading figure in Le Félibrige, an association of Provençal poets. He gave new life to the language and literature of Provence through his own work and through his Provençal dictionary, *Trésor du Félibrige* (1879–86). In the tongue of his native region, he wrote the pastoral *Mireio*, the narrative poem *Lou Pouème deu rose* (1897), and the lyrics of *Lis Isclo d'or* (1875). He shared the NOBEL PRIZE in Literature in 1904 with the Spanish playwright José ECHEGARAY.

Mistral, Gabriela (pen name of Lucila Godoy Alcayaga, 1889–1957)   Chilean poet. The daughter of a rural schoolmaster who often composed songs and poems for village fiestas, Mistral also became a teacher. Her first verses were inspired by an unhappy romance, with a man who committed suicide; in 1914 she won a poetry contest in Santiago with her *Sonetos de la muerte*, which were later included in her first collection, *Desolacíon* (1922). All her work is a variation on the single theme of love. Initially she expressed her own tragic and frustrated passion, but, as she grew older, her vision became more universal. She was concerned especially with children and with the humble and persecuted everywhere. *Ternura* (1924) is a collection of children's songs and rounds. She donated the proceeds of *Tala* (1938) to the relief of Basque children orphaned in the Spanish Civil War. Acclaimed as an educator as well as a poet, she received the NOBEL PRIZE in Literature in 1945, the first woman poet and the first Latin American so honored. Her works for children are translated in English in *Crickets and Frogs: A Fable* (1972). Translations into English of her selected poems have been published by Langston Hughes (1957) and by Doris Dana (1972).

Mitchell, James Leslie (pen name Lewis Grassic Gibbon, 1901–1935)   Scottish novelist, archaeologist, and historian. Under his pen name, Mitchell wrote the

trilogy of novels *A Scots Quair* (1932–34), which is regarded as a major work of Scottish literature. (*Quair* is an older form of *quire*, "booklet.") See SCOTTISH RENAISSANCE.

Mitchell, Margaret (1900–1949)   American novelist. Mitchell's only book, the Civil War novel GONE WITH THE WIND, was written during a long period of hospitalization. Her correspondence about the extraordinary popular success of the book and its film version (1939) appears in *Margaret Mitchell's "Gone with the Wind" Letters, 1936–1939* (1976; ed Richard Harwell).

Mitchison, Lady Naomi [Margaret Haldane] (1897–   )   English writer of novels, short stories, plays, and poetry. A classical scholar as well as a political and educational reformer, Mitchison wrote a number of distinguished historical novels set mostly in ancient Greece or Rome. Among her many books, several of which portray aspects of Africa, a place that has absorbed her for years, are *The Conquered* (1923), *The Corn King and the Spring Queen* (1931), *Cleopatra's People* (1972), and *Solitary Three* (1975). *Small Talk* (1973), *All Change Here* (1976), and *You May Well Ask* (1980) are works of autobiography.

Mitford, Jessica [Lucy] (1917–   )   English-born American writer, sister of Nancy MITFORD. A lifelong commitment to civil rights, an unusual talent for investigative reporting, and a trenchant wit combine to make Mitford an effective assailant of fraud and corruption. In her best-known book, *The American Way of Death* (1963), she exposed the numerous ways in which the commercial funeral business bilks the bereaved. Mitford's volumes of autobiography, *Daughters and Rebels* (1960) and *A Fine Old Conflict* (1977), are spirited accounts of her wildly eccentric family, her flight from home, and her life as a left-wing political activist.

Mitford, Mary Russell (1787–1855)   English novelist and dramatist. Mitford's magazine sketches of country life, collected as *Our Village* (5 vols, 1824–32), are notable for their continuing freshness, sympathetic humor, and naturalism.

Mitford, Nancy (1904–1973)   English author. Mitford's witty, gaily satirical novels about her own eccentric upper-class family and contemporary English society include *The Pursuit of Love* (1945), *Love in a Cold Climate* (1949), and *The Blessing* (1951). She edited *Noblesse Oblige: An Enquiry into the Identifiable Characteristics of the English Aristocracy* (1956) and helped popularize the terms U ("upper class") and NON-U. She also wrote the biographies *Madame de Pompadour* (1954); *The Sun King* (1966), about Louis XIV; and *Frederick the Great* (1970). She was the sister of Jessica MITFORD.

Mithras   An ancient Persian sun god. In the 5th century BC, Mithras achieved a singular prominence in the Zoroastrian pantheon (see ZOROASTER), and his cult rapidly came to constitute a distinct and popular religion. By the 1st century BC, Mithraism had spread as far as Rome; in the

2nd century AD the emperor Commodus accepted Mithraism as an imperial cult.

Mithras is represented as wisdom, goodness, and light, engaged in a cosmic struggle against the powers of evil and darkness. He was also the agent of the creation of life, for, according to legend, all the goodness of the world and all living things sprang from the body of a sacred bull, captured and sacrificed by Mithras. The secret rituals of Mithras included baptism (honey, rather than water, being the medium of purification) and a sacred meal, in which the main elements were consecrated bread, wine, and water. The Mithraic priests were called Fathers and advocated a strict moral code emphasizing fasting and sexual restraint.

Mithraism was a source of extreme worry to the early Christians, as it was both similar to and more popular than Christianity. The Roman theologian Tertullian (c160–230) even speculated that it had been invented by the Devil to mock Christian rites. The Devil, however, had less than his usual success in this undertaking, for, by the 4th century, Mithraism had nearly died out and Christianity was flourishing.

Mithridate (Mithridates, 1673)   A tragedy by Jean RACINE. Drawn loosely from Roman history, it centers around Mithridate, the aged enemy of Rome, who is betrothed to the young Greek girl Monime. When he is reported dead in battle, his son Pharnaces attempts to force Monime into marriage. Monime begs Xiphares, Mithridate's second son, to protect her. When Mithridate returns and learns of Pharnaces's act, he orders his son to marry the princess of Parthia. Pharnaces refuses, is arrested, and reveals that Xiphares also loves Monime. Mithridate discovers that Monime returns Xiphares's love, and when Pharnaces leads a Roman attack against him, he orders Monime to poison herself and, believing defeat imminent, stabs himself. Xiphares routs his treacherous half brother and the Romans, and before dying, Mithridate bestows his blessing and his betrothed on his loyal son.

Mithridates   King of Pontus (120–63 BC). To guard against being poisoned by his enemies, he so accustomed his system to poisons of various sorts that when, on being conquered by the Romans, he wished to end his life by this means, it was impossible for him to do so. A. E. HOUSMAN uses his story in a poem.

Mittelholzer, Edgar Austin (1909–1965) Guyanan novelist. Of mixed Swiss and Creole heritage, Mittelholzer in his many novels treats themes of racial tension, psychological alienation, miscegenation, and violence. Determined from an early age to become a writer, Mittelholzer settled in London and eventually won critical attention with *Morning in Trinidad* (1950), a subtle exploration of the divisions created by race, color, and class, and with *Shadows Move among Them* (1951), an interesting satire and probably his best book. His greatest popular success was the Kaywana trilogy—*Children of Kaywana* (1952), *Hubertus* (1955), and *The Old Blood* (1958)—a fictionalized history of the Caribbean from 1612 to 1953. Near the end of his life, his books were increasingly concerned with isolation, disintegration, and suicide. Shortly before his final novel was published, he burned himself to death in a Surrey field.

Mnemosyne   Goddess of memory and mother by ZEUS of the nine MUSES of Greek mythology. Mnemosyne was the daughter of Heaven and Earth (URANUS and GE). A mere personification of memory, she was not worshiped.

Moberg, [Carl Arthur] Vilhelm (1898–1973) Swedish novelist. A major figure in Swedish PROLETARIAN LITERATURE, Moberg drew extensively on his own peasant background for the subject and the setting of many of his books. He viewed literature as a means for protesting social injustice. Outstanding among his works are the autobiographical novels included in the Knut Toring trilogy, translated together as *The Earth Is Ours* (1940), and *Soldat med brutet gevär* (1944; tr *When I Was a Child*, 1956). He is best known for his epic cycle dealing with the 19th-century Swedish immigration to America: *Utvandrarna* (1949; tr *The Emigrants*, 1951), *Invandrarna* (1952; tr *Unto a Good Land*, 1954), *Nybyggarna* (1956), and *Sista brevet till Sverige* (1959), the last two of which were abridged and translated together as *The Last Letter Home* (1961). A more ambiguous novel concerning the differences between the Old and New worlds is *Din stund på jorden* (1963; tr *A Time on Earth*, 1965), which is far more ruminative than his earlier work. Two volumes of Moberg's unfinished *History of the Swedish People* were translated in 1972.

Moby-Dick, or The Whale (1851)   A novel by Herman MELVILLE. The book begins as a straightforward narrative in realistic prose. After the first fifteen chapters, it becomes a complex combination of cetology, philosophy, and adventure narrative, written in rhapsodic metaphorical prose. A profound symbolic study of good and evil, and eventually regarded as the preeminent American novel, *Moby-Dick* was almost forgotten at the time of its author's death.

Moby-Dick, the great white whale, is pursued by the monomaniacal Captain Ahab, whose ivory leg is testimony to their previous encounter. The crew of Ahab's ship, the *Pequod*, is composed of a mixture of races and religions, including the God-fearing mate Starbuck; three primitive harpooners, Queequeg, Daggoo, and Tashtego; the black cabin boy Pip; and the fire-worshiping Parsee.

The whale, a symbol too complex for any one definition, but perhaps representing knowledge of reality, is hunted by Ahab at the cost of his own dehumanization and the sacrifice of his crew. It seems to be a sacrilegious quest, and only Ishmael, the narrator, who does not share the greed and pride of most of the others, is saved. Ishmael is borne up out of the vortex of the sinking ship on the coffin prepared by his friend Queequeg. Sustained by a belief in love and human solidarity, he alone remains to tell the tale. Ahab, determined to pierce the "pasteboard masks" of this world, to glimpse reality, is tied to the whale by his harpoon line, continuing his pursuit even in death.

mock epic (or mock heroic)   A literary form that combines a grand or elevated style with a trivial subject, so that both style and subject matter are burlesqued. The mock-Homeric BATTLE OF THE FROGS AND MICE was a model for the 18th-century mock epic. Classic examples in English literature are Dryden's MACFLECKNOE and Pope's THE RAPE OF THE LOCK and THE DUNCIAD.

Mock Turtle   A character in Lewis Carroll's ALICE'S ADVENTURES IN WONDERLAND. The Mock Turtle, who is always weeping, shows Alice how to dance the Lobster Quadrille. His conversation consists largely of puns and ingenious plays on words, and he himself is "the thing mock turtle soup is made from." The original illustrator of the book, John TENNIEL, accordingly gave the Mock Turtle the head, tail, and hooves of a calf.

Modern Chivalry   A once widely popular satirical novel by Hugh Henry BRACKENRIDGE, published in parts between 1792 and 1805 and reissued with final additions in 1815. It is a sort of American *Don Quixote*, in which the hero, Captain Farrago, and his man Teague O'Regan leave Pennsylvania to travel about and "observe human nature," meanwhile drawing an unflattering picture of manners in the early republic. The novel satirizes primarily the rule of political upstarts, of whom the scalawag Teague is chief. In Part II, when Farrago becomes governor of a backwoods community, the settlers are persuaded to give the vote to beasts as well as men and to make use of a monkey clerk and a hound lawyer. "The great moral of this book," Brackenridge concludes, "is the evil of men seeking office for which they are not qualified."

Modern Instance, A (1881)   A novel by William Dean HOWELLS. One of the first novels of social realism in America, it deals with problems of ethics and character in the context of marriage. It is the story of the fiercely possessive Marcia Gaylord and her self-indulgent writer-husband Bartley Hubbard. Bartley goes through a progressive moral decline, deserts his wife and child, and is not heard from for two years. When he tries to procure a divorce in Indiana, his attempt is frustrated by Marcia's enraged father. Squire Gaylord, after gaining a decree in his daughter's favor, dies in the law court. Bartley later dies in a brawl in a western town. Marcia and her child return to the East, where Ben Halleck, who has always loved her, debates the morality of marrying a divorced woman. On its publication, the book was considered daring for its open handling of the question of divorce.

modernismo   A literary movement that arose in Spanish America in the late 19th century and was subsequently transmitted to Spain. In their quest for pure poetry, the modernists displayed a dazzling verbal virtuosity and technical perfection that revolutionized Spanish literature.

According to some critics, the publication of José MARTÍ's *Ismaelillo* (1882) marks the beginning of the movement. Others assert that, while Martí exerted enormous influence on Spanish-American writing and thought, his poetry is so individual that he cannot be considered even a precursor of modernismo. There is no disagreement, however, as to the dominant role of Rubén DARÍO, whose work defined and stimulated modernism in America and in Spain. The publication of his *Azul* (1888) is sometimes said to signify the birth of modernismo, and *Prosas profanas* (1896) is held to show modernismo at its zenith. Other early modernist poets (often considered precursors of the movement) were Manuel GUTIÉRREZ NÁJERA, José Asunción SILVA, and Julián del Casal, the Cuban. Modernists of the later, post-1896 phase include Leopoldo LUGONES, José Enrique RODÓ, Julio HERRERA Y REISSIG, José Santos Chocano, Amado NERVO, and Rufino BLANCO FOMBONA.

In rebellion against romanticism, from which, however, they were not always able to free themselves, the modernists drew their initial inspiration and technique from European, particularly French, sources. From French PARNASSIANS and SYMBOLISTS, such as GAUTIER, Coppée, and VERLAINE, came their pessimism and melancholy, their belief in art for art's sake, their zeal for technical excellence and musicality, their love of exotic imagery and a vocabulary in which swans (one of Darío's favorite symbols), peacocks, gems, and palaces abound. Another distinctive characteristic of the modernists was their unceasing experimentation with old and new verse forms. In their desire to escape from the sordidness of reality, the early modernists usually shunned political and native themes. Their successors, however, inspired no doubt by the impassioned verses that Darío hurled at Theodore ROOSEVELT and by his ode to Argentina, turned increasingly to American subjects, as exemplified by Chocano's *Alma América* (1906). In prose writing, particularly the essay, modernismo fostered a new simplicity and elegance, the finest examples of which are to be found in the works of RODÓ.

Modern Love (1862)   A sequence of fifty poems by George MEREDITH. Containing sixteen lines each, they present the various thoughts and emotions of a married couple who perceive that their love for each other is dying, the husband occasionally speaking in the first person. The sequence is considered to have been based on Meredith's own difficulties in his unfortunate first marriage with Mary Ellen Nicolls.

Modern Painters (5 vols, 1843–1860)   A critical treatise on painting by John RUSKIN. The purpose of the first volume, which concentrated almost exclusively on landscape painting, was to prove the superiority of contemporary artists, especially Turner, over the old masters. Its brilliant style and original ideas established his reputation as an art critic. The four succeeding volumes cover a far wider area and expound Ruskin's views on the principles of true art in general.

Modest Proposal, A (1729)   The shortened title of *A Modest Proposal for Preventing the Children of the Poor People in Ireland from being a Burden to their Parents or Country; and for making them beneficial to their Publick*, a pamphlet by Jonathan SWIFT. The pamphlet, which is a masterpiece of bitterness and irony, turns the tables on a favorite theory of contemporary Whig economists: that people are the real wealth of a nation. The terrible suffering in Ireland is revealed in the mocking suggestion that the poor should devote themselves to rearing children to be killed and sold for eating. Swift gives recipes and six advantages of his proposal.

Modigliani, Amadeo (1884–1920)   Italian painter and sculptor. Modigliani became an artist because tuberculosis made it impossible for him to continue academic study. Influenced by African tribal sculpture and by the sculpture of BRANCUSI, he painted the female nude in an elongated, mannerist style. His usual subjects were Montmartre's poor, whose sadness he captured in delicate nuances of facial expression; a well-known example is *Gypsy Woman with Baby* (1918). His sculptures are rare, but he carved heads in limestone, elongated like his paintings and very obviously reminiscent of the African sculpture he admired. The decline in Modigliani's health was accelerated by alcohol and drug dependence; he died at what appeared to be the peak of his creativity.

Moe, Jørgen Engebretsen   See ASBJØRNSEN, PETER CHRISTIAN.

Mogul Empire   The Muslim-Tartar Empire in India. The Mogul Empire began in 1526 with Baber (1483–1530), a descendant of TAMERLANE, and broke up after the death of Aurangzeb (1618–1707), whose Islamic fanaticism and persecution of Hindus and SIKHS caused rebellions that weakened and ultimately collapsed the empire. The power passed to the Mahrattas and finally to the British. The emperor was known as the Great or Grand Mogul. Apart from those mentioned, the most noteworthy were AKBAR, his son Jahangir (1569–1627), and grandson Shah Jahan (1592–1666), who had the Taj Mahal built in Agra for his favorite wife.

Mohism   See MO TZU.

Molière (pen name of Jean Baptiste Poquelin, 1622–1673)   French comic dramatist. Born in Paris, son of an upholsterer who served the royal household of Louis XIV, Molière received his education under the Jesuits at the Collège de Clermont. In 1643 he became an actor and cofounder of the *Illustre Théâtre*, for which he wrote his first plays, notable among them *L'Étourdi* (*The Scatterbrain*, 1665) and *Le Dépit amoureux* (*The Amorous Vexation*, 1659). Initially unsuccessful in Paris, the company toured the provinces from 1645 to 1658, returning to the capital when the king granted it a theatre in the Louvre, the Théâtre du Petit-Bourbon.

The playwright's first success in Paris was also his first comedy of manners, LES PRÉCIEUSES RIDICULES, a one-act prose satire on the absurd affectations and pretensions displayed by members of such refined salons as the Hôtel de Rambouillet. Enormously popular, the play was followed by SGANARELLE, a one-act comedy in verse. The company moved to the Palais Royal the following year. *Dom Garcie de Navarre* (1661), its first production in its new home, was a failure. In the same year, Molière completed *L'École des maris* (*The School for Husbands*; see SGANARELLE) and the first of his many COMÉDIE-BALLETS, *Les Fâcheux* (*The Bores*, 1661); presented to the king during a sumptuous entertainment at his country mansion, the latter met with a delighted reception, won Molière a pension, and marked the beginning of the playwright's years as a royal favorite. A marriage to Armande Béjart, in 1662, proved unhappy and probably provided the embittering experience that led to the writing of one of Molière's masterpieces, LE MISANTHROPE. L'ÉCOLE DES FEMMES revealed a psychological penetration unprecedented in the comic theatre of the period, but the author's unsparing power of ridicule attracted the attention of disgruntled clergymen, courtiers, physicians, and rival dramatists—all victims of Molière's merciless wit—and Boileau and the king himself were forced to defend Molière against attacks. The *Critique de l'École des femmes* (*Criticism of the School for Wives*) and the *Impromptu de Versailles* (both 1663) constituted Molière's own reply to his critics and enemies, followed in 1664 by *Le Mariage forcé* (*The Forced Marriage*; see SGANARELLE) and *La Princesse d'Élide*. A three-act version of LE TARTUFFE produced the same year aroused clerical opposition and the play was forbidden until 1667, when, presented as *L'Imposteur* (*The Impostor*), it received a second interdiction. The ban was finally lifted in 1669, and *Le Tartuffe* enjoyed its deserved popularity and established itself as one of Molière's greatest comic achievements. Because of continuing attacks, DOM JUAN OU LE FESTIN DE PIERRE had to be taken out of the repertory, and, with *L'Amour médecin* (1665), LE MÉDECIN MALGRÉ LUI, and *Mélicerte, Pastorale comique*, and *Le Sicilien* (all written in the winter of 1666–67), the company passed through a period of financial hardship. *Amphitryon* (1668) was a success, and the company enjoyed a degree of good fortune for five years with L'AVARE, *Georges Dandin* (1668), *Monsieur de Pourceaugnac* (1669), LE BOURGEOIS GENTILHOMME, *Les Amants magnifiques* (*The Magnificent Lovers*, 1670), *Psyché* (1671), on which Molière collaborated, *Les Fourberies de* SCAPIN (*The Rogueries of Scapin*, 1671), *La Comtesse d'Escarbagnas* (1671), and LES FEMMES SAVANTES. After taking the part of Argan in the fourth performance of his last comedy, LE MALADE IMAGINAIRE, Molière collapsed from a sudden and severe hemorrhage and died the same day. At the insistence of the clergy, he was denied holy burial.

Sometimes called the father of modern French comedy, Molière rejected the Italianate farces and comedies of intrigue dear to his predecessors, for his was a theatre relying on sound observation of the foibles and complexities of human nature and on an incomparable skill in humorous presentation. Actor and director, as well as author, Molière could boast a total command of his art; few playwrights can equal his understanding of dramatic construction and effect, his sparkling verse or comic strength. His virtuosity ranged from the most buffoonish farce, full of gaiety and absurdity, to the highest comedy, where the subtlety of his observation rivals that of many tragedians. Molière's masterpieces are those plays in which, attacking hypocrisy and vice, he created characters that have become immortal types. His gallery of peasants, noblemen, servants, and bourgeois offers not only an astonishingly wide view of 17th-century French society but also a telling moral: the wise man observes moderation and remains within the bounds that good sense imposes on nature. Though many of the episodes and plots of his plays are borrowed, though —unlike Shakespeare—he dealt mainly in types rather than in individuals, and despite his occasionally arbitrary denouements and the faults of style inevitable in hasty writing, Molière's work triumphs over its weaknesses; a laughing yet compelling advocate of all that is natural and reasonable in man and an enemy of all that is false and pretentious, Molière remains to this day without rival in the comic exposition of human character.

Moll Flanders (1722)   The heroine and shortened title of *The Fortunes and Misfortunes of the Famous Moll Flanders, &c who was Born at Newgate, and during a Life of continued Variety for Threescore Years, besides her Childhood, was Twelve Year a Whore, five time a Wife (whereof once to her own Brother), Twelve Year a Thief, Eight Year a Transported Felon in Virginia, at last grew rich, liv'd honest, and died a Penitent. Written from her own Memorandums*, a PICARESQUE novel by Daniel DEFOE, written in the form of an autobiographical memoir. The extraordinary title-page gives one aspect of the novel—the providential escape of Moll from a continued course of wickedness —but it gives little idea of Defoe's sympathetic realism; it is one of the earliest social novels in English.

Molloy (1951; tr 1955)   A novel by Samuel BECKETT. The first part is the story of a disintegrating old cripple's odyssey to find his mother before he dies. The second part is an account of a search for him by the bullying petty official Moran and his young son, acting on the instructions of a Kafkaesque higher authority. None of them reaches his goal. The novel is a bitter, comic rendering of man's despairing condition and his quest for better things. It is part of the trilogy that also includes MALONE DIES and THE UNNAMABLE. The three were published together as *Three Novels* (1959).

Molnár, Ferenc (1878–1952)   Hungarian playwright, novelist, and short-story writer. Molnár's fiction effectively described life in Budapest, but his comedies, many of them translated into English, truly established his reputation in Hungary and abroad. *Az ördög (The*

*Devil,*1907) and *Liliom* (1909) are widely regarded as the most successful of his nearly thirty plays. Urbane and sophisticated, he invented suspenseful, often absurd situations involving violations of social conventions, and he wrote witty, epigrammatic dialogue. Not concerned with cosmic questions, he was content mainly with psychological probings of the moral ills of the upper-middle class. More often than not, his cunning characters triumph over decent ones. He made New York his permanent home in 1940.

Moloch (or Molech, fr Heb, *Mōlekh*, "the king")   A title for a Canaanite BAAL. Moloch was propitiated with the sacrifice of first-born children, who were killed or burned in the "high places." The great center of Moloch-worship was TOPHET. The Hebrew prophets of the OLD TESTAMENT inveighed against his widespread worship among the Israelites; 2 Kings 23:10 gives an account of the destruction of Tophet by Josiah.

Mommsen, Theodor (1817–1903)   German ancient historian. Mommsen's best-known work is his unfinished monumental history of Rome, *Römische Geschichte* (1854–56; tr 1870, 1900), based on extensive research of ancient writings and artifacts and notable for the aura of contemporaneity with which it recreates Roman life. A liberal thinker himself, Mommsen believed that history should both serve scholarly interests and promote political awareness. He was the first German to be awarded the NOBEL PRIZE in Literature (1902).

Momus   The sleepy god of the Greeks, son of NYX (Night). Momus was always railing and carping. Being asked to pass judgment on the relative merits of POSEIDON, HEPHAESTUS, and ATHENE, Momus rebuked them all. He said the horns of a bull ought to have been placed in the shoulders, where they would have been of much greater force; as for man, he said ZEUS ought to have made him with a window in his breast, whereby his real thoughts might be revealed.

Monday, Sara   The heroine of Joyce CARY's *Herself Surprised* (1941). See HORSE'S MOUTH, THE.

Mondrian, Piet[er Cornelius] (1872–1944)   Dutch painter. Influenced at first by CUBISM, Mondrian developed a progressively linear, nonobjective style, known as neoplasticism. He founded the STIJL school and formulated his ideas in the book *Le Neo-Plasticisme* (1920), which had an influence on the BAUHAUS group. Essentially, Mondrian believed that if cubist principles were followed to their logical extreme, painting would be reduced to the symbols of the square, the cube, and the right angle. His distinctive works consist mainly of horizontal and vertical lines forming various ninety-degree grids on a light background colored only with solid primary colors, as in his famous *Composition* series.

Monet, Claude [Oscar] (1840–1926)   French painter. Monet was one of the founders of IMPRESSIONISM; his view of Le Havre, entitled *Impression, Sunrise* (1872), gave its name to the movement. Developing techniques that became the hallmark of impressionist painters, Monet painted almost exclusively out-of-doors, catching spontaneous visual experiences with individual brushstrokes, emphasizing the play of light on subjects viewed from a distance. Although his work was viewed as offensively radical in his day, Monet came to be regarded as one of the greatest of all landscape painters.

Monk, The (1795)   The shortened title of *Ambrosio, or the Monk*, a GOTHIC NOVEL by Matthew Gregory LEWIS. Ambrosio, abbot of the Capuchins at Madrid, is renowned for his holy life. Matilda, a young noblewoman, is so smitten by his eloquence that she enters the abbey, disguised as a monk. Her passion, however, soon discloses itself; Ambrosio succumbs and goes from crime to crime, until he is discovered and condemned to death by the Inquisition. Supposedly following the example of Matilda (who is actually a demon in disguise), he now bargains with Lucifer for release. The Devil, as usual, barely performs his part by "releasing" Ambrosio in a desert waste. Ambrosio enrages him by a gesture of repentance, and the Devil dashes him to pieces against the rocks.

Monkey   See JOURNEY TO THE WEST.

Monkey Trial   See SCOPES TRIAL.

Monk's Tale, The   One of THE CANTERBURY TALES of Geoffrey CHAUCER. In the *Prologue*, the Host complains that his wife is not more like Prudence in the tale of *Melibee*; then he asks a merry tale of the Monk, jokingly lamenting that such a virile-looking man is forbidden procreation. The Monk says he can tell a hundred tragedies "of the falls of illustrious men." He tells seventeen tragedies in eight-line stanzas. These were written about 1374 (before *The Canterbury Tales* were begun), except for the account of Bernabo of Milan, murdered by his nephew in 1385, and possibly the accounts of Ugolino, Pedro of Spain, and Pedro of Cyprus. Besides these "modern instances" of the reverses of Fortune, there are examples taken from the Bible, mythology, and history: Lucifer, Adam, Samson, Heracles, Nebuchadnezzar, Belshazzar, Zenobia of Palmyra, Nero, Holofernes, Antiochus of Syria, Alexander the Great, Julius Caesar, Croesus of Lydia. In the *Prologue* to THE NUN'S PRIEST'S TALE the Knight interrupts the Monk, complaining of the "heaviness" of so much woe and wishing to hear about a rise to prosperity for a change.

Monmouth, James Scott, duke of (known also as James Fitzroy, James Crofts, and the Protestant Duke; 1649–1685)   Claimant to the throne of England. James was the son of Charles II, who named him duke of Monmouth in 1663. His religion, his clemency to the Scottish COVENANTERS, whom he defeated at Bothwell Bridge, as well as a persistent rumor that his mother had been secretly married to Charles led some Protestants to urge that he be named heir to the throne in place of James II, the king's brother, whose Roman Catholic sympathies were well

known. After the death of Charles, Monmouth led the unsuccessful uprising against James that is known as Monmouth's Rebellion, but he was defeated at Sedgemoor in Somerset and beheaded. He is the Absalom of Dryden's ABSALOM AND ACHITOPHEL. See BLOODY ASSIZES.

Monocle de Mon Oncle, Le (1923)   A poem in twelve sections by Wallace STEVENS. A dramatic monologue, the poem has been interpreted both as a commentary on the inspiration of youth and the sadness of age and as a celebration of "the faith of forty," an affirmation of the imagination of middle age as opposed to the invalid fancy of youth.

monologue   A speech or narrative presented entirely by a single person; also known as a soliloquy.

monometer   In prosody, a line of verse containing one metrical foot, in any METER; the line is usually identified together with the name of the meter, as iambic monometer, trochaic monometer, etc.

monosyllabic foot   In English prosody, a foot in accent meter composed of a pause and an accented syllable, or an accented syllable followed by a pause. An example is

O LONG / [*pause*] LONG / will the LA/dies STAND

from the ancient Scottish ballad "Sir Patrick Spens."

Monro, Harold [Edward] (1879–1932)   English poet and editor. Monro was a minor poet associated with the GEORGIANS. His entire poetic output was published together in *Collected Poems* (1933), with an introduction by T. S. ELIOT. He is best remembered for his three influential journals, *Poetry Review* (1911), *Poetry and Drama* (1913), and *Chapbook* (1919–25), and for his Poetry Bookshop, a haven for intellectuals, through which he provided generous encouragement to younger poets.

Monroe, Harriet (1860–1936)   American editor and poet. Monroe is known chiefly as the editor of POETRY, which she founded in Chicago in 1912. The magazine became immensely influential, publishing and often introducing the work of leading American and English poets. Monroe's own poetry, generally considered undistinguished, appeared in such volumes as *Valeria and Other Poems* (1892), *You and I* (1914), and *Chosen Poems* (1935). *The Passing Show* (1903) consists of five verse plays. She also edited, with Alice Corbin Henderson, an anthology entitled *The New Poetry* (1917). *A Poet's Life* (1938) is her autobiography.

Monroe Doctrine   A statement of U.S. foreign policy first presented to Congress by President James Monroe (1758–1831) in 1823. The presidential message resulted from a suggestion by George Canning, foreign secretary of Great Britain, that his country and the U.S. issue a joint declaration warning the quadruple Alliance not to attempt the restoration of Spanish rule in the newly independent republics of South America. At the urging of Secretary of State John Quincy ADAMS, who did not want the

U.S. "to come in as a cockboat in the wake of the British man-of-war," Monroe and the Cabinet decided on a unilateral statement. Scholars still disagree as to Adams's precise role in the wording of the doctrine, though he is often regarded as its chief architect. Monroe's statement declared in part that the U.S. would not permit Europe to extend its political system to the Western Hemisphere and that it would not interfere with existing European colonies in America or in the internal affairs of Europe.

Monsieur Ouine (1943; tr The Open Mind, 1945) A novel by Georges BERNANOS. Written as a series of fragmented episodes, this bitter and unhappy study of the depravity and anguish of modern man is widely regarded as Bernanos's masterpiece. Its hero is a man who comes to loathe his own flesh and to feel a tormented scorn for all mankind.

Monstre Gai   See HUMAN AGE, THE.

Montagu, Lady Mary Wortley (1689–1762) English BLUESTOCKING, best known for her lively and amusing correspondence, published in *Turkish Letters* (1763) and *Letters and Works* (1837). Montagu's other works include *Town Eclogues* (1716) and *Court Poems by a Lady of Quality* (1716). She introduced smallpox inoculation into England on her return from Constantinople, where her husband had been ambassador. She was the cousin and early patroness of Henry Fielding and was a close friend of Alexander Pope until their bitter quarrel of 1727–28. Pope, in his *Moral Essays* (1731–35), satirized her notorious slovenliness in the character of "Sappho."

Montaigne, Michel [Eyquem] de (1533–1592) French moralist and creator of the personal essay. His father, kindled by the enthusiasms of the Renaissance, hired a tutor who spoke only Latin to Montaigne until he was six and had him awakened every morning by music. He became a counselor in the Bordeaux *Parlement*, where he met Étienne de la Boétie, a young judge who encouraged his interest in philosophy and whose death affected him deeply. In 1571 he retired to his château in Dordogne and devoted himself to reading and writing until 1580, when he published the first two books of his ESSAYS. After a trip through Switzerland, Germany, and Italy, partly in search of treatment for gallstones, he served two terms as mayor of Bordeaux. As a result of an outbreak of the plague, he and his family spent six months wandering through the countryside, an experience he described in the third book of *Essays*.

Montale, Eugenio (1896–1981)   Italian poet, critic, and translator. With his first collection of poems, *Ossi di seppia* (1916; tr *Cuttlefish Bones*, 1970), Montale established himself, along with the older Giuseppe UNGARETTI, as one of the chief architects of modern Italian poetry. A style that effectively mixes archaic words with scientific terms and idioms from the vernacular is used to create new myths and move poetry into new directions. His poetry is concerned not with large events but with a whole "world" of objects, through which Montale defines philosophically the moral dilemmas of our tormented age. The best practitioner in Italy of what T. S. ELIOT was to call the "objective correlative," Montale focuses on the "pain of living" and on the unanswerable riddles of human existence, rejecting the consoling or diverting uses of poetry, so as to make literature an effective commentary on life.

With each new work, Montale gained wider recognition as one of the most perceptive and illuminating poetic voices of the 20th century, a recognition formally acknowledged in 1975, when he was awarded the NOBEL PRIZE in Literature.

Other writings include *Le occasioni* (1939; tr *Occasions*, 1970), *La bufera e altro* (1956; tr *The Storm and Other Things*, 1970), *Satura* (1963; tr 1969), *La farfalla di Dinard* (1956; tr *The Butterfly of Dinard*, 1970), *Auto-da-fé* (1966), a collection of critical essays, and *Diario del '71 e del '72* (1973). Selections in English translation include *Provincial Conclusions* (1970) and *New Poems* (1976). See HERMETICISM.

Montalvo, Garci Rodriguez de   See AMADÍS DE GAULA.

Montalvo, Juan (1832–1889)   Ecuadorian essayist. A bitter foe of tyranny, Montalvo attacked Ecuadorian dictator Gabriel García Moreno in the pages of his journal *El cosmopolita*. When he heard of García Moreno's assassination, Montalvo declared, "My pen has killed him!" His savage polemical essays, the *Catilinarias* (1880), were directed against a new dictatorship and contributed to his being banished from Ecuador. His best-known work, *Siete tratados* (1882), consists of seven treatises on moral and literary subjects, including a famous comparison between Washington and Bolívar. He also wrote *Capítulos que se le olvidaron a Cervantes* (1895), a successful imitation of Cervantes. Not considered a profound or original thinker, Montalvo is esteemed today largely because of the fecundity and vigor of his style.

Montargis, dog of   A dog named Dragon, in French legend. The dog belonged to Aubrey de Mondidier, who was murdered by the villain Richard de Macaire in 1371 near the castle of Montargis. Dragon's behavior drew suspicion on Macaire, and the king ordered a trial by combat between man and dog. Dragon defeated Macaire, who confessed. Guilbert de Pixerécourt (1773–1844) dramatized the tale as *Le Chien de Montargis* (1814).

Montefeltro, Guidobaldo da (1472–1508)   Italian nobleman. Duke of Urbino, Montefeltro married Elisabetta Gonzaga, who maintained his splendid court while he was ill. He is affectionately recalled by Castiglione in THE COURTIER, which is set in 1507 at the ducal court.

Montespan, Marquise de (born Françoise Athénaïs de Rochechouart, 1641–1707)   Mistress of Louis XIV of France and mother of eight of his children. Montespan performed notable service to French letters as a patroness of RACINE and Boileau.

Montesquieu, Charles Louis de Secondat, Baron de La Brède et de (1689–1755) French lawyer, philosopher, and man of letters. Montesquieu is noted for his *Lettres persanes* (1721), a series of 160 fictional letters exchanged, for the most part, between two Persians, satirizing Parisian institutions, individuals, gambling, religious intolerance, and royal power. Montesquieu's *Considérations sur la grandeur et la décadance des Romains* (1734) demonstrates how a democracy, once having lost those public virtues that constitute the very essence of its existence, perishes through tyranny. His most famous work, *De l'esprit des lois* (1748), analyzes the relation between human and natural law. See SPIRIT OF LAWS, THE.

Monteverdi, Claudio (1567–1643) Italian composer, the dominant figure in early Baroque music. Monteverdi began as a MADRIGAL composer in the Renaissance style; the technique and expressive gestures of the madrigal played an important part in all his works. His dramatic expressivity made his first opera, *Orfeo* (*Mantua*, 1607), the first great opera. He continued to write for the stage, but most of his work is lost, except for *Il ritorno d'Ulisse in patria* (*Ulysses's Return Home*; Venice, 1641) and *L'incoronazione di Poppea* (*The Coronation of Poppea*; Venice, 1642). He wrote eight books of madrigals, and his church music was also voluminous, including the *Vespers* of 1610 and a large number of works composed for St. Mark's in Venice, of which he was the musical director after 1613. Monteverdi's music is noted for its dramatic expression, rhythmic control, and adventurous harmonies.

Montezuma II (or Moctezuma II, 1480?–1520) Aztec emperor (1503–20). Having tried unsuccessfully to dissuade Cortés and the Spaniards from proceeding to the Aztec capital at Tenochtitlán, Montezuma was kidnapped and held as a hostage soon after their arrival. He continued to rule as chieftain and apparently won the affection of his captors. During an Indian uprising, he was struck on the forehead by a shower of stones as he was addressing his subjects, and he died a few days later.

Montgomery, L[ucy] M[aud] (1874–1942) A schoolteacher and minister's wife, Montgomery became a writer of popular juveniles almost by accident. Asked to prepare a short serial for a Sunday School paper, she drew on her girlhood memories of Prince Edward Island to produce the enormously successful *Anne of Green Gables* (1908), to which she wrote six sequels. Though her ventures into adult fiction were not a success, her books for girls have perennial appeal.

Montherlant, Henry de (1896–1972) French dramatist, novelist, and essayist. Montherlant's major theme, the haughtily superior male who both asserts and scorns his power, appears in his early novels, *Le Songe* (1922; tr *The Dream*, 1962), set in World War I, and *Les Bestiaires* (1926; tr *The Matador*, 1957), based on his own experience as a bullfighter. *Les Célibataires* (1934; tr *The Bachelors*, 1960) describes a decadent aristocracy in the ironic, elegant, and trenchant style for which Montherlant is noted. In later works, he goes on to portray the true aristocrat, the capable, courageous, virile man of rigorous integrity, doomed to intellectual and spiritual isolation if he would avoid the modern sin of mediocrity. Montherlant usually portrays women as selfish and inadequate creatures, who use love as a tool to destroy men and to undermine their sense of moral absolutes. The quartet of novels *Les Jeunes Filles* (1936–39; tr together in *The Girls*, 1968), which includes *Les Jeunes Filles* (1936), *Pitié pour les femmes* (1936), *Le Démon du bien* (1937), and *Les Lépreuses* (1939), develops this attitude by examining the relationship of four women to a writer whose work is his only imperative.

Montherlant's plays, set amid the wars, famines, and domestic turmoil of Renaissance Italy and Spain, seek a universality applicable to contemporary Europe. They include *La Reine morte* (1942), *Port-Royal* (1954), and *La Guerre civile* (1965; tr *Theatre of War*, 1967). Other works include *L'Histoire de l'amour de la rose de sable* (1954; tr *Desert Love*, 1957), selected writings based on his stay in Africa.

Month in the Country, A (Mesiats v derevne, 1850) A play by Ivan TURGENEV. Natalia, the bored wife of a provincial landowner, falls in love with her son's tutor, as does her ward, Vera. The rivalry remains unresolved, the tutor being sent away while Natalia lapses once again into ennui. In style and content, the play anticipates the dramas of Chekhov.

Monticello The home of Thomas JEFFERSON, situated on his estate three miles east of Charlottesville, Virginia. Jefferson himself designed the house and supervised its construction, which was begun in 1770.

Montolive See ALEXANDRIA QUARTET, THE.

Montpensier, Anne Marie Louise d'Orléans, duchesse de (1627–1693) French princess, known in her life and remembered as *La Grande Demoiselle*. Daughter of Gaston d'Orléans, the brother of Louis XIII, the duchesse de Montpensier was frustrated in her hope of marrying Louis XIV, when she sided against the royalists during the second FRONDE; she then spent a period in disgrace before returning to the court and asking permission to marry the French courtier and soldier, the future duc de Lauzun. The king objected to the match; Lauzun was imprisoned; and she was not able to obtain his release for ten years, and then only by ceding a huge portion of her estates to the king's bastards. She finally married Lauzun, was unhappy, and devoted herself to religious affairs and to the writing of her lively *Mémoires*, which were published in 1729, after her death. Her romance *La Relation de l'ile imaginaire* (*Account of the Imaginary Isle*) and *La Princesse de Paphlagonie* were published under the name of her secretary, Jean Segrais.

Mont-Saint-Michel and Chartres (privately printed, 1904; pub 1913) A historical and philosophical study by Henry ADAMS. The volume is subtitled *A Study in 13th Century Unity* and serves as a companion piece to his autobiographical THE EDUCATION OF HENRY ADAMS, which carries the subtitle *A Study in 20th Century Multiplicity.* Adams sees the century 1150–1250 as "the point in history when man held the highest idea of himself as a unit in a unified universe." At that point, according to Adams, philosophy, theology, and the arts were all informed by faith. The book begins with a discussion of the Norman style and spirit that went into the construction of the cathedral at Mont-Saint-Michel in the 12th century. From this, Adams moves to the culminating moment in the 13th century, when the statue of the Virgin of Chartres was a viable symbolic link between reason and intuition, science and religion. By 1250, in Adams's view, the scholasticism of St. Thomas AQUINAS, with its emphasis on reason, had begun to destroy this coherent world view.

Moodie, Susanna [Strickland] (1803–1885) English-born Canadian novelist. After her marriage to an English army officer, Moodie sailed with him and her sister, Catherine Parr TRAILL, to Canada in 1832. She described the hardships experienced by pioneers like herself in the Canadian wilderness in *Roughing It in the Bush* (1852). Moodie also wrote several poems and novels, including *Mark Hurdlestone* (1853) and *Geoffrey Moncton* (1856).

Moon and Sixpence, The (1919)   A novel by W. Somerset MAUGHAM. Based closely on the life of Paul GAUGUIN, it tells of Charles Strickland, a conventional London stockbroker, who in middle life suddenly decides to desert his wife, family, and business in order to become a painter. He goes to paint in Tahiti, where he takes a native mistress. Eventually Strickland dies of leprosy.

Moon for the Misbegotten, A (1943; pub 1952) A play by Eugene O'NEILL. A tragic story of the unfulfilled love between an alcoholic and a farm woman, the play continues the story of O'Neill's family begun in LONG DAY'S JOURNEY INTO NIGHT. In a highly fictionalized framework, O'Neill deals in this case with his alcoholic older brother. Although it was not well received when first produced, it had an enormously successful revival in 1973 and has come to be considered among the most important of O'Neill's mature works.

Moonstone, The (1868)   A novel by Wilkie COLLINS. It concerns the disappearance of the Moonstone, an enormous diamond that once adorned a Hindu idol and came into the possession of an English officer. The heroine, Miss Verinder, believes her lover, Franklin Blake, to be the thief; other suspects are Blake's rival and three mysterious Brahmins. The mystery is solved by Sergeant Cuff, possibly the first detective in English fiction.

Moore, Brian (1921–   )   Irish-born Canadian novelist. Moore was educated in Belfast in Northern Ireland and later immigrated to Canada and the U.S. A realistic observer, he treats failures, misfits, and outsiders with

wry humor and compassion. His prize-winning first novel, *The Lonely Passion of Judith Hearne* (1955), deals with a middle-aged spinster in a Belfast boarding house. Later works include *The Luck of Ginger Coffey* (1960), *Catholics* (1972), and *The Doctor's Wife* (1976). His more recent novels, such as *The Mangan Inheritance* (1979) and *Cold Heaven* (1983), are imbued with a darker and more gothic sensibility.

Moore, Douglas [Stuart] (1893–1969)   American composer. Moore preferred American themes, and the lyric stage inspired his best works. Among his operas are *The Devil and Daniel Webster* (1939), based on the story by Stephen Vincent BENÉT; *Giants in the Earth* (1951); *The Ballad of Baby Doe* (1955); and *The Wings of the Dove* (1961), based on the novel by Henry JAMES.

Moore, G[eorge] E[dward] (1873–1958) English philosopher. Moore was a professor of philosophy at Cambridge; his first major work was *Principia Ethica* (1903), which had a marked influence on contemporary intellectuals and writers (see BLOOMSBURY GROUP), as well as on his fellow philosophers. With his colleagues A. N. WHITEHEAD, Bertrand RUSSELL, and the younger Ludwig WITTGENSTEIN, he wrestled with problems of linguistic analysis and epistemology. Less exclusively focused on LOGICAL POSITIVISM than Wittgenstein, Moore came to be known as the father of analytic philosophy. His books include *Ethics* (1912), *Philosophical Studies* (1922), and *Some Main Problems of Philosophy* (1953). He edited the periodical *Mind* from 1921 to 1947.

Moore, George (1852–1933)   Irish novelist, playwright, poet, and critic. Moore was a cofounder of the Literary Theatre at Dublin, from which the Abbey Theatre developed, and author of the plays *The Strike at Arlington* (1893) and *The Bending of the Bough* (1900). His fiction, revealing traces of the influence of Balzac, Flaubert, and Zola, includes *Confessions of a Young Man* (1888) and *Esther Waters* (1894). *Memories of My Dead Life* (1906) and the trilogy *Hail and Farewell* (1911–14) are autobiographic in content, while *Héloïse and Abélard* (1921) and *Aphrodite in Aulis* (1931) are beautifully styled romances, the first historical, the second legendary. In his criticism, Moore was an influential defender of the impressionist school of painting and of the naturalist school of literature. His books of poetry include *Flowers of Passion* (1878) and *Pagan Poems* (1881). See BROOK KERITH, THE; IRISH RENAISSANCE.

Moore, Henry [Spencer] (1898–1986)   English sculptor. Moore's interest in ancient Egyptian and pre-Columbian sculptures is reflected in much of his work. Although he experimented with surrealist (*Composition,* 1931) and nonobjective (*Rectangular Form,* 1936) concepts, he developed his own style of bold, smooth, usually human forms relatively early in his career. Always respecting the inherent qualities of his sculpted materials (bronze, stone, concrete, and wood), Moore worked extensively on archetypal mother and child compositions, as well as reclining figures. The hollowing out of solid material to make space as much a part of sculpture as mass and the grouping together of two or more forms to create one sculptural entity are two techniques developed by Moore that characterize nearly all of his later works.

Moore, Marianne [Craig] (1887–1972) American poet. Born in St. Louis, Missouri, Moore was educated at Bryn Mawr College and was the acting editor of THE DIAL from 1925 to 1929. Her poetry is of the type called objectivist, presenting in each poem an object, scene, person, or bit of information precisely expressed and meticulously delineated (see OBJECTIVISM). Her work is distinguished by wit, irony, intellectual appeal, and compact, individual metrical patterns in syllabic verse. She was particularly fond of animals, and much of her imagery springs from the animal world.

Moore's first book, *Poems* (1921), was published without her knowledge by two friends, Hilda DOOLITTLE (H.D.) and Robert McAlmon. Her later works include *Observations* (1924), *Selected Poems* (1935), *Pangolin, and Other Verse* (1936), *What Are Years?* (1941), *Nevertheless* (1944), and *Collected Poems* (1951), awarded the Bollingen and PULITZER prizes. The definitive edition of her work, *The Complete Poems of Marianne Moore*, appeared in 1967.

Moore, Mrs. In E. M. Forster's novel A PASSAGE TO INDIA, an intuitive, half-mystical elderly woman with a sympathetic understanding of Indian people and religions.

Moore, Thomas (1779–1852) Irish poet of the romantic period. Moore is known for his graceful lyrics and Irish folk songs, set to traditional tunes, which he published in *Irish Melodies* (1807–35). Some of the famous songs of this collection are "The Harp That Once through Tara's Halls," "The Minstrel Boy," and "Believe Me, If All Those Endearing Young Charms." LALLA ROOKH, a narrative poem with an Oriental setting, was also very popular. Moore also wrote satires, a novel, a *History of Ireland* (1846), and several biographies, including one of Byron (1830), a close friend of Moore. Moore came to be regarded as the national poet of Ireland, and he was, next to Byron, the most popular writer of verse in the English romantic period. Subsequently, however, his work has been deprecated for its shallowness and sentimentality.

Moore, Thomas Sturge (1870–1944) English poet and art historian, brother of the philosopher G. E. MOORE. A friend of YEATS, Moore was associated with the GEORGIANS but was more strictly classical in his imagery and more experimental in technique than they were. His complete poetical works were published in four volumes between 1931 and 1933. He also translated the poetry of the French SYMBOLISTS and wrote *Dürer* (1905) and *Art and Life* (1910). His correspondence with Yeats was published in 1953.

Moorehead, Alan [McCrae] (1910–1983) Australian journalist and historical writer. Moorehead is well known for such books as *Gallipoli* (1956), about the ill-fated Gallipoli campaign of World War I; *No Room in the Ark* (1959), a report on animal life in Africa; and *The White Nile* (1960) and *The Blue Nile* (1962), both accounts of 19th-century exploration.

Mopsus A seer of Greek mythology and one of the ARGONAUTS. Mopsus interpreted many omens and the words of the Argo's talking prow. On the homeward journey, he was killed by a snake in Libya.

Moraes, Dom[inic Frank] (1938–) Indian poet and journalist, writing in English. Educated at Oxford, Moraes was awarded the Hawthornden Prize for his first volume of poems, *A Beginning* (1957). Subsequently he became established as one of India's leading poetic stylists. His selected poems from 1955 to 1965 appeared in *Poems* (1966). Other works include a book of travel writing, *Gone Away* (1960); an autobiography, *My Son's Father* (1968); *The People Time Forgot* (1972); *Mrs. Gandhi* (1980); and *Bombay* (1980). A volume of verse, *Absences*, appeared in 1983.

morality plays (or moralities or *moralités*; 15th–16th centuries) Allegorical dramas of the late Middle Ages. Although presented as popular pageants in the same way as MYSTERY PLAYS, they are different in that the characters are always abstract personifications (Mercy, Truth, Everyman, King, Church) rather than figures of Biblical history or individually characterized personalities. The mystery vividly portrays an event in religious history, whereas the morality is the dramatic presentation of a sermon. Most famous of the English morality plays is EVERYMAN; others include *The Pride of Life* (c1400), *The Castle of Perseverance* (c1405?), and *Wisdom* (c1460). The French *moralités* were often indistinguishable from FARCES, and, by the end of the 15th century, the English morality plays also included many scenes of broad comedy burlesquing the everyday life of the time or turning to political satire. Thus, in the 16th century, the morality play developed into the INTERLUDE.

Morante, Elsa (1916–1985) Italian novelist and poet. Morante's fascinating and unusual novels include *Menzogna e sortilegio* (1948; tr *House of Liars*, 1951), a tale of intrigue and deceit in the tradition of the 18th-century French novel; *L'isola di Arturo* (1957; tr *Arturo's Island*, 1959), which narrates the initiation of its protagonist into the adult mysteries of good and evil, and love and death; *La storia* (1974; tr *History: A Novel*, 1977), a long, ambitious novel that seeks to give an understanding of the human condition through the dramatization of various events between 1941 and 1947; and *Aracoeli* (1986), a novel that strongly displays the influence of Freud's theories on her work. She also published several volumes of poetry, fables, and short stories.

Moratín, Leandro Fernández de (1760–1828) Spanish dramatist. Moratín's early diplomatic career was ruined as a result of his collaboration with the Napoleonic invaders of Spain. After the fall of Joseph Bonaparte, he fled to France, where he remained in permanent exile.

Moratín's literary reputation rests on his five plays, which are notable for their successful blending of French classicism and the traditional drama of Spain. His masterpiece, *El sí de las niñas* (1806), is a charming comedy directed against parental tyranny. He also wrote *La comedia nueva* or *El café* (1792), a satire on contemporary dramatists; *La mojigata* (1804), an acute analysis of hypocrisy; and *La derrota de los pedantes* (1789), a prose satire on bad writers; and he translated Shakespeare's *Hamlet* and several works by Molière.

Moravia, Alberto (pen name of Alberto Pincherle, 1907–) Italian novelist, short-story writer, essayist, and playwright. Moravia was married to the Italian novelist Elsa MORANTE. The author of over thirty books, Moravia presents, from his early *Gli indifferenti* (1929; tr *The Time of Indifference*, 1953), through *La noia* (1960; tr *The Empty Canvas*, 1961), *L'attenzione* (1965; tr *The Lie*, 1966), and *La vita interiore* (1978; tr *Time of Desecration*, 1980), a compelling, thoroughly persuasive tableau of the decadence of the middle class and its shabby values. Through the ways his characters respond to the compelling drives for sex and money, there emerges an incisive dramatization of modern man's incapacity to understand and connect with reality. As is clear from the words in the Italian titles of his books (*indifference, mistaken ambitions, conformity, contempt, boredom*, and so on), Moravia is, in the last analysis, a moralist. He is an acknowledged leader of the neorealist school of novelists that emerged in Italy after World War II. Among his significant works are *La mascherata* (1941; tr *The Fancy Dress Party*, 1947), *L'amore coniugale* (1949; tr *Conjugal Love*, 1951), *Racconti romani* (1954; tr *Roman Tales*, 1956), and *La Ciociara* (1957; tr *Two Women*, 1958). He has also published collections of short stories, among them, *The Voice of the Sea* (1978) and *Erotic Tales* (1985).

Mordecai In the OLD TESTAMENT, the uncle of ESTHER. Through Mordecai's wise counsel to his niece when she became queen, he helped save the Jewish people from the plots of Haman.

Mordred, Sir In ARTHURIAN LEGEND, one of the knights of the ROUND TABLE, traditionally the treacherous one. In Malory's MORTE D'ARTHUR, he is the bastard son of King ARTHUR and Queen MARGAWSE and half brother of her other sons. When King Arthur goes to France on a military expedition, Sir Mordred usurps the throne and attempts to marry GUINEVERE, his stepmother. Upon receiving the news, Arthur hastens back to England to fight Mordred, and, in the ensuing battle, each gives to the other his death blow.

The name is spelled *Modred* in Tennyson's IDYLLS OF THE KING, where a much-altered version of the story is given. Here, Modred does not try to seduce Guinevere but rather to expose her liaison with Launcelot. With twelve other knights, he forces his way into the queen's chamber when Launcelot is there.

In the Welsh MABINOGION, Mordred appears as Medrawd. Like Arthur, Mordred may have originated in an actual historical figure. See ANNALES CAMBRIAE.

More, Hannah (1745–1833) English writer, reformer, and philanthropist. More's writings include *Percy* (1777) and *The Fatal Falsehood* (1779), tragedies; *Village Politics* and *Repository Tracts* (1792), religious tracts on reforming the poor; and *Coelebs in Search of a Wife* (1809), a novel.

More, Sir Thomas (1478–1535) English statesman, lawyer, humanist, poet, author, saint, and a friend of Erasmus, Colet, and other leading scholars of the time. A leading figure of English humanism, More was one of the most versatile and talented men of his age. His writings include a biography of Pico della Mirandola (1510) and *The History of Richard III* (c1513, posthumously pub 1543), which was based on an earlier account by Cardinal MORTON. UTOPIA (1516), his most famous literary work, was written in Latin. A loyal defender of Roman Catholicism, he engaged in vigorous controversies with the Protestant heretics of the time, especially with William TYNDALE, against whom he wrote *A Dialogue Concerning Heresies* (1528).

More held important positions in the government of his time, being a Member of Parliament, an envoy on several missions abroad, a court official, and ultimately Lord Chancellor, succeeding Cardinal Wolsey in 1529. Though he had been a long-time friend and favorite of HENRY VIII, More was a staunch Catholic and could not accept Henry's position, announced in 1531, that the king and not the Pope was the head of the Church in England. More resigned from the Chancellorship in 1532. He wrote a justification of his position in *An Apology of Sir Thomas More* (1533). Two years later, Parliament passed a bill requiring that all subjects take an oath acknowledging the supremacy of Henry over all other foreign kings, including the Pope. More refused, was imprisoned, and was finally executed a year later. He was beatified in 1886 and was canonized by Pope Pius XI in 1935.

He is the subject of a memorable biography, *The Life of Sir Thomas More* (1557?; repr 1935), by his son-in-law William Roper, and of a modern play, *A Man for All Seasons* (1961), by Robert Bolt.

Moreau, Frédéric The central character in Flaubert's novel L'EDUCATION SENTIMENTALE.

Morel, Charles A violinist in Proust's REMEMBRANCE OF THINGS PAST. The son of the servant of the narrator's great-uncle Adolphe, Morel becomes the homosexual lover of the Baron de CHARLUS and then of Robert de SAINT-LOUP, as well as a procurer of women for ALBERTINE.

Morel, Paul See SONS AND LOVERS.

Morgan, Charles (1894–1958) English novelist and playwright. Morgan wrote sensitive, difficult novels that drew a relatively small but enthusiastic audience. He won his first literary prize in France, where he was highly regarded, for *Portrait in a Mirror* (1929). Each of his novels deals with a specific moral problem, in a reflective, philosophical manner. *The Fountain* (1932) established his reputation in England and was followed by *Sparkenbroke* (1936), *The Voyage* (1940), *The Empty Room* (1941), *The Judge's Story* (1947), and *The River Line* (1949). He also wrote several plays, notably *The Burning Glass* (1954) and for many years was dramatic critic for the London *Times*.

Morgan, Sir Henry (1635?–1688)   Welsh buccaneer. During hostilities between England and Spain, Morgan captured Portobelo, Panama, and ravaged the coasts of Cuba and Maracaibo. Named commander-in-chief of the entire naval force of Jamaica, he captured Panama City after a bitterly fought battle (1671). He was later appointed lieutenant-general of Jamaica.

Morgan, J[ohn] Pierpont (1837–1913)   American financier and philanthropist. After inheriting the family fortune, Morgan turned it into a gigantic banking and industrial empire. He also helped to support many public institutions, particularly the Metropolitan Museum of Art. Morgan became a notable art and book collector, and his great library in New York City, separately housed in a beautiful building, contains valuable manuscripts and rare books. His son, J. Pierpont Morgan, Jr. (1867–1943), gave the library over to public use in 1924 as a memorial to his father.

Morgana   An enchantress, identified with the Lady of the Lake in ORLANDO FURIOSO and also with MORGAN LE FAY, the fairy sister of King Arthur. In the Orlando poem of Ariosto, she dwells at the bottom of a lake, where she keeps her treasure. In Boiardo's version of the Orlando story, she is simply Lady-Fortune but then takes on the attributes of a witch.

Morgan le Fay   One of the most mysterious figures in ARTHURIAN LEGEND and one who appears in most versions but in different guises. She is almost always a sorceress or in other ways has supernatural powers. Sometimes she is the sister of ARTHUR, sometimes his half sister, and almost always she is his enemy or the enemy of Guinevere. In Malory's MORTE D'ARTHUR, she is forever plotting against Arthur, and once she succeeds in stealing from him the sword EXCALIBUR, giving it to her lover in order that he might kill Arthur. In SIR GAWAIN AND THE GREEN KNIGHT, she is an unobtrusive old woman who remains in the background, for the most part, and is only revealed in the end to be "Morgan the goddess," who plotted the action of the tale. Oddly, however, with all her animosity toward Arthur, it is she, in some versions, who takes him to Avalon to be healed of his wounds after the great final battle. It is also to be noted that, in Malory's *Morte d'Arthur*, she is the only one of Arthur's enemies who is not ultimately vanquished by him. She also appears in ORLANDO FURIOSO, ORLANDO INNAMORATO, and OGIER THE DANE.

Morgante maggiore, Il (It, "The Great Morgante")   The comic masterpiece of the Florentine Renaissance poet Luigi Pulci (1432–84), it is a burlesque version of the Carolingian material, inspired by the style and technique of the Cantastorie. Completed in twenty-three cantos and published in 1470, it appeared in an edition of 1483 with five added cantos, hence the title. *Morgante* is the name of the giant who figures prominently in the plot. In 1822 Lord Byron's translation of the first canto of the poem appeared in his *The Liberal*, edited jointly with Leigh Hunt. The tale relates the adventures of Orlando, who leaves the Paris court of Charlemagne in anger at the instigation of Gano of Maganza (Ganelon). At the monastery of Chiaramonte, he defeats two giants but spares the third, Morgante, who becomes his shield-bearer and companion. The giant aids Orlando and the other paladins in their various adventures in pagan lands. They are also assisted by the magician Malagigi and the fiend Astarotte, who is a theologian and philosopher. When temporarily separated from Orlando, Morgante meets the demigiant Margutte, a charming fellow but an immense glutton who is proud of his ability as a thief and liar; he joins Morgante in several feats of appetite, treachery, and thievery until he dies in a fit of laughter at the sight of a monkey wearing Margutte's boots. Soon after, his loyal friend Morgante also dies, of a crab bite, and is buried by the grief-stricken Orlando. The final cantos of the poem retell the famous battle of Roncisvalle (Roncesvalles), the death of Orlando, the punishment of Gano, and the further adventures of Rinaldo. The final octaves praise the inspirer of the poem, Lucrezia Tornabuoni, mother of Lorenzo de' Medici, and ask God's mercy for its author.

Morier, James [Justinian]   See HAJJI BABA OF ISPAHAN, THE ADVENTURES OF.

Mörike, Eduard (1804–1875)   German poet, generally considered the greatest in the 19th century after Goethe. Gottfried Keller later characterized him as "this son of Horace and a fine Swabian lady," by which he meant that Mörike's poetry combines classical balance and monumentality (Horatian qualities), sophisticated charm and wit (the lady), and deep feeling for his Swabian homeland. Like the poets of Swabian romanticism, Mörike sometimes wrote folk-type lyrics, but he was also capable of a powerful classical style not unlike that of Klopstock and Hölderlin. His thought is generally close to that of the conservative BIEDERMEIER movement, with an affirmation of most bourgeois values. On the surface, his life was quiet and modest. He was educated in theology and served, at various times, as a Protestant pastor and a girls' school literature teacher. He was, however, never free of internal torment, the result of unhappy youthful loves, an unhappy marriage in 1851, religious doubts, and dissatisfaction with the clergy as a profession. This double character of his life is reflected in his verse, which, beneath the surface, beneath its careful consciousness of form and economy, often expresses an abysmal melancholy. He especially favors the theme of transience: the transience of love, as in "An eine Aols-harfe" ("To an Aeolean Harp," 1837) and "Ein Stündlein wohl vor Tag" ("A Little before Dawn," 1857); or of life in general, as in "Denk' es, o Seele" ("Remember, O My Soul," 1852). He was also highly skilled in description, and his "Auf eine Lampe" ("On a Lamp," 1846) is considered an early example of the DINGGEDICHT. His prose works include a highly sentimental novel, *Maler Nolten* (*Painter Nolten*, 1832), which in form is quite daring, embodying voluminous lyric and even dramatic insertions, and the masterful novella MOZART AUF DER REISE NACH PRAG.

Mori Ōgai (1862–1922)   Japanese physician and literateur. After studying medicine for years in Germany, Mori became a surgeon in the Imperial Army, eventually rising to the rank of surgeon-general. An indefatigable translator and writer of original works, he was one of the major contributors to the introduction of Western literature and ideas to Japan during the MEIJI period. Some of his stories, such as *Fushinchū* (1910; tr *Under Reconstruction*, 1961) and *Gan* (1922; tr *The Wild Geese*, 1959), treat problems related to Japan's westernization. Others are either autobiographical pieces like *Vita Sexualis* (1909; tr 1972) or historical tales like *Takese-bune* (1916; tr 1918). Works of his later years, including *Abe Ichizoku* (1913; tr *The Abe Family*, 1977) and *Sakai Jiken* (1914; tr *The Incident at Sakai*, 1977), are marked by their strict adherence to facts and by their unadorned prose style.

Morison, Samuel Eliot (1887–1976)   American historian. A prolific writer whose work is outstanding both for its scholarship and its felicity of style, Morison taught at Harvard from 1915 to 1955. As official historian of the university, he produced a three-volume history under the general title *Tercentennial History of Harvard College and University* (1936). Among his many works on early New England are *Harrison Gray Otis: Urbane Federalist* (1969; first pub 1913), *Builders of the Bay Colony* (1930; rev 1958), and *The Intellectual Life of Colonial New England* (1956; first pub *The Puritan Pronaos*, 1936). Morison did considerable work as a maritime historian, and, as official Navy historian during World War II, he wrote his fifteen-volume *History of the United States Naval Operations in World War II* (1947–62). He won Pulitzer Prizes for his masterly biography *Christopher Columbus, Admiral of the Ocean Sea* (2 vols, 1942) and for *John Paul Jones: A Sailor's Biography* (1959). His many other works include *The Oxford History of the American People* (1965) and a two-volume study, *The European Discovery of America* (1971; 1974).

Morituri te salutamus (Lat, "We [who are] about to die salute you")   A phrase with which, according to tradition, Roman gladiators greeted the emperor before they began their contests.

Morley, Christopher [Darlington] (1890–1957)   American writer and editor. After returning from England,

where he was a Rhodes Scholar, Morley worked on several magazines. He was one of the founders of the SATURDAY REVIEW, which he edited from 1924 to 1941. Morley was a prolific writer in many genres; in the 1930s, at the height of his literary celebrity, 175 pages were required to list his printed essays, articles, plays, novels, and poetry. He is best remembered for his novels *Parnassus on Wheels* (1917) and *Thunder on the Left* (1925) and for his enormously popular pot-boiler *Kitty Foyle* (1939), about a spirited, independent woman in the business world. *John Mistletoe* (1931) is his autobiography. Always fond of imbibing with his friends, Morley spontaneously founded dozens of "clubs," including the Three Hours for Lunch Club and the Baker Street Irregulars. At his death, he had published over fifty books, including two revised editions of *Bartlett's Familiar Quotations* (1937; 1948).

Morlocks   In H. G. Wells's THE TIME MACHINE, a future race of evil, underground monster-men.

Moro, César (pen name of Alfredo Quispez Asín, 1903–1956)   Peruvian poet. During his early years as a writer, Moro lived in Paris (1925–33) and became thoroughly immersed in SURREALISM; he wrote in French some of the most daring and fiery surrealist poetry of his time. He returned to Peru in 1934, then moved in 1938 to Mexico City, where he remained for ten years and where he published *Le Château de Grisou* (1943) and *Lettre d'amour* (1944). *Trafalgar Square* (1954) was the last book of verse published during his lifetime; his Spanish poems, *La tortuga ecuestre*, appeared posthumously in 1957. The despairing and hallucinatory eroticism of Moro's poetry introduced into an otherwise dry Spanish tradition a new vocabulary of desire and forbidden love. After his death, his bilingual poetry consistently gained the plaudits he failed to earn in his lifetime.

Morpheus   OVID's name for the son of sleep and the god of dreams; so called from the Greek word *morphe* ("form"), because he gives these airy nothings their form and fashion. Hence the name of the narcotics *morphine* and *morphia*.

Morris, Jan (before 1972, James Humphrey Morris; 1926–   )   British journalist and travel writer. After Oxford, Morris spent ten years as a foreign correspondent for the London *Times* and the Manchester *Guardian*, winning international acclaim for his coverage of Sir Edmund Hilary's ascent of Mount Everest. In newspaper pieces and travel books, Morris was highly regarded as one of the few authentic stylists in journalism. Morris again won high praise for a trilogy on the British empire, consisting of *Pax Britannica* (1968), *Heaven's Command* (1973), and *Farewell the Trumpets* (1978). Having long felt the "victim of a genetic mix-up," Morris underwent a sex-change operation in 1972, an experience that, as Jan Morris, she described in *Conundrum* (1974). Her subsequent works include *Travels* (1976); the *Oxford Book of Oxford* (1978); *Destinations* (1980), a collection of journalistic pieces; *Wales: The First*

Place (1982); and a collection of writings on fascinating cities of the world, *Among the Cities* (1985).

Morris, William (1834–1896) English artist, architect, designer, printer, poet, novelist, and social reformer. Endowed with protean talent and seemingly boundless energy and deeply troubled by the vulgarity and misery of the industrial age, Morris was one of the most productive and perennially influential of the eminent Victorians. He shared with Edward BURNE-JONES, his friend from their Oxford days, a passion for medieval art and architecture. Morris apprenticed himself to an architect, then, through Burne-Jones, studied painting with Dante Gabriel ROSSETTI. In 1858 he published his first book of verse, *The Defense of Guenevere and Other Poems*. That same year, he married the pre-Raphaelite painters' beautiful model, Jane Burden. Unable to find suitable furniture or fabrics for his house, he set up his own manufacturing and decorating firm (1861), which, as Morris & Co., revived the English tradition of hand-crafted, expertly designed furniture, wallpaper, textiles, ceramics, and stained glass. In 1890 he did the same thing for book design and typography, when he founded the Kelmscott Press.

Throughout, Morris continued to write poetry. *The Life and Death of Jason* (1867) was followed by *The Earthly Paradise* (1868–71), which ingeniously combines classical and medieval techniques. As a result of two trips to Iceland, he translated the great Norse sagas and wrote his masterpiece, the narrative poem *Sigurd the Volsung* (1876). Translations of *The Odyssey* (1875) and *The Aeneid* (1887), a morality play, *Love Is Enough* (1873), *The Water of the Wondrous Isles* (1897), and *The Story of the Sundering Flood* (1898) added to his formidable literary output.

Meanwhile his concern for social evils remained acute. He joined the Socialist Democratic Federation in 1883 but broke with it, two years later, for its preoccupation with parliamentary politics. In 1885 he helped found the Socialist League. When that organization was taken over by anarchists, he withdrew to the local Hammersmith Socialist Society, which had its meetings in his own house. The literary by-products of Morris's passionate socialist idealism include *The Dream of John Ball* (1888); *News from Nowhere* (1891), a classic in utopian fiction; and *Socialism, Its Growth and Outcome* (1893).

Morris, Wright (1910–   ) American novelist. Drawing effectively on his Midwestern background, Morris reveals through his fiction his fascination with the history and evolution of the American character. He is an accomplished photographer and his photographs complement the text in *The Inhabitants* (1946), *The Home Place* (1948), and *God's Country and My People* (1968). His best novels, including *The Works of Love* (1952), *Love among the Cannibals* (1957), *Ceremony in Lone Tree* (1960), *A Life* (1973), and *Plains Song* (1980), winner of the American Book Award, strike a delicate balance between tragedy and humor, pessimism and hope. *Will's Boy* (1981) is an autobiographical account of his early years in the Midwest; it was followed by *A Cloak of Light* (1985), the concluding volume of his memoirs.

Morrison, Toni (born Chloe Anthony Wofford, 1931–   ) American novelist and editor. Morrison's novels expose the formerly disregarded experience of the black American woman. Her language is musical and precise, creating evocative dialogue and merging mythical, supernatural elements with reality to paint a bleak and painful portrait of American life. Her first two novels, *The Bluest Eye* (1969) and *Sula* (1973), drawn from her own youth in the poor black sections of Midwestern steel towns, focus on the tragedy of black people raised with a divided (white and black) sense of themselves. In *Song of Solomon* (1977), a young black man leaves the North in search of hidden gold in the South, only to discover the richness of his own family's past. *Tar Baby* (1981) takes UNCLE REMUS's tale of the fox who fashions a tar baby to trap a rabbit, and puts it in modern terms, as a beautiful, educated black woman is hopelessly drawn to, but irretrievably cut off from, her own culture. In *Beloved* (1987), Morrison explores the tragedy of black American slavery and its aftereffects on the life of a woman who is a former slave living in Ohio in the years following the Civil War.

Mort dans l'âme, La See ROADS TO FREEDOM, THE.

Morte d'Arthur, Le (c1469) An English prose rendition of the legends of King ARTHUR, by Sir Thomas MALORY. It was first printed in 1485 by William CAXTON, who assembled the whole and presented it as one continuous narrative, entitling it *Le Morte d'Arthur*. The evidence of the Winchester Manuscript indicates, however, that Malory really wrote this famous work as eight separate romances, and a modern edition presents the material in that manner, under the title *The Works of Sir Thomas Malory*.

In these eight romances, ARTHURIAN LEGEND assumed ultimate and splendid shape. Malory's primary purpose in writing this material seems to have been simply the telling of a good story, and few will argue that he did not succeed. Even in his own era, the *Morte d'Arthur* enjoyed great popularity in many countries, and the influence it has had on subsequent generations cannot be overemphasized.

Written while Malory was in jail, the eight tales seem to have been taken from many English and French sources. One of them, called *The Tale of King Arthur*, retells the traditional story of Arthur's conception, birth, and coronation; in this tale are to be found Queen IGRAINE, UTHER PENDRAGON, Sir ECTOR, Sir KAY, and MERLIN, the great magician. The other seven tales are *King Arthur and the Emperor Lucius*, *Sir Launcelot du Lake*, *Sir Gareth*, *The Book of Sir TRISTRAM OF LYONESS*, *The Tale of the Sangreal*, *The Book of Sir Launcelot and Queen Guinevere*, and *Le Morte d'Arthur*. Malory used, as some titles suggest, materials not originally part of the Arthurian tradition;

however, the Tristan and Iseult legend and the quest for the Holy Grail are admirably intermingled with Arthurian materials.

Malory's tone in the *Morte d'Arthur* is primarily nostalgic: he is looking back to the days when knighthood was in flower and chivalry was the great social convention. Times past are brought to life again in his pages, full of the color of curious quests and the excitement of tournaments in which the knight rode to combat wearing a token of his chosen lady.

Malory's influence on later writers was very important: *Le Morte d'Arthur* was a source book for Spenser's *The Faerie Queene*, for example, and also for Tennyson's *Idylls of the King*, as well as for many other writers less well recognized.

Mortimer, Penelope [Ruth] (1918–　　) English novelist. Under the name Penelope Dimont (Charles Dimont was her first husband), Mortimer published her first novel, *Johanna* (1947), an account of adolescence. During her marriage to the playwright John Mortimer, she began to focus on the inner world of an individual's sexual and family relationships, writing of a couple's gradual disillusionment with each other in *A Villa in Summer* (1954), of the ups and downs of a woman trying to find her own identity through marriage in *The Pumpkin Eater* (1962), and of the despair of a woman awaiting divorce in *The Home* (1971). *About Time* (1979) is an autobiographical account of her youth. *The Handyman*, a novel, was published in 1983; it was followed by a biography, *The Queen Mother* (1986).

Morton, Thomas (1590?–1647) English-born American adventurer. Settling in Mount Wollaston (now Quincy), Massachusetts, Morton established a colony, which he named Ma-re Mount. The maypole revels of the colony's Anglican settlers, and their trade with the Indians, to whom they sold weapons, aroused the ire of the Puritans, and a force under Miles Standish was dispatched to oust Morton. He was arrested and shipped to England but later returned. Abroad, he published *New English Canaan* (1637), a caustic description of New England, dubbing Miles Standish "Captain Shrimp." His escapades are the subject of Hawthorne's allegorical short story "The Maypole of Merry Mount" (1836).

Mosby, John Singleton (1833–1916) American scout and ranger in the Confederate Army during the Civil War. After serving in the cavalry under General J.E.B. Stuart, Mosby left the regular forces early in 1863 and commanded an unofficial group of bold partisan adventurers, whose efficient operations foiled the Federal Army on numerous occasions. He is the author of *Mosby's War Reminiscences, and Stuart's Cavalry Campaigns* (1887) and *Stuart's Cavalry in the Gettysburg Campaign* (1908).

Mosca (Lat, "fly") In Ben Jonson's VOLPONE, OR THE FOX, the shrewd and rascally servant of Volpone. Mosca

believes that "almost all the wise world is little else, in nature, but parasites and sub-parasites."

Moscow Art Theatre A Russian theatrical organization, founded by Konstantin STANISLAVSKY and Vladimir Nemirovich-Danchenko in 1898. A repertory group, it became world-famous for its naturalistic, highly artistic productions. Closely identified with Anton CHEKHOV, whose major plays it first staged, and later with Maksim GORKY, the Moscow Art Theatre exercised an enormous influence on the course of 20th-century theatre.

Moses In the OLD TESTAMENT (Exod. 1; Deut. 34), the Hebrew lawgiver who led the Israelites out of Egypt through the wilderness and to the PROMISED LAND. Because Pharaoh had decreed that all Hebrew boy babies should be killed, Moses' mother put him in a basket and left him in the bulrushes, where he was found and adopted by Pharaoh's daughter. Later, he identified himself with his own people and, because he killed an abusive Egyptian taskmaster, was forced to flee the country. He returned, called down on Pharaoh's recalcitrant head the TEN PLAGUES, and led the Children of Israel out of Egypt, passing through the Red Sea on dry land. For forty years, he led his discontented, rebellious followers through the wilderness and was mediator for them with JEHOVAH, with whom he spoke on Mount Sinai when receiving the TEN COMMANDMENTS. Moses is spoken of in the BIBLE as the meekest of all men (Num. 12:3), but on one occasion he impulsively and vaingloriously struck a rock to bring water out of it, and he was punished for this sin by being forbidden to enter the Promised Land.

Moses, Grandma (sobriquet of Anna Mary Robertson Moses, 1860–1961) American primitive painter. Having lived and worked her whole life on farms in New York State, Grandma Moses began painting at the age of seventy-six. When her naïve renderings of rural community scenes were discovered by the art dealer Luís Caldor, she was catapulted into international recognition and became one of America's best-known folk artists.

Mosses from an Old Manse (1846) A collection of twenty-five tales and sketches by Nathaniel HAWTHORNE. One of the finest collections of stories in American literature, the book contains YOUNG GOODMAN BROWN, THE BIRTHMARK, RAPPACCINI'S DAUGHTER, and "The Celestial Railroad." The opening sketch describes the Concord parsonage in which Hawthorne wrote the tales.

Mother (Mat, 1907) A novel by Maksim GORKY. It depicts the regeneration of a frightened old woman when she throws herself into the revolutionary movement in Russia. Pelageya Nilovna gradually realizes that the cause that her son Pavel Vlasov serves is important and necessary. As she becomes more involved in the movement herself, her timidity disappears, and she emerges a live, fearless human being. The novel, which is less an artistic work than a Marxist propaganda tract, is cited by Soviet critics as a model of SOCIALIST REALISM.

Mother Courage and Her Children (Mutter Courage und ihre Kinder, 1939; perf 1941; tr 1941)   A play by Bertolt BRECHT, one of the first examples of his full employment of EPIC THEATRE techniques. The play covers twelve years of the THIRTY YEARS' WAR, in twelve episodes that reveal the utter horror and loss experienced by the people who survived. It describes the wanderings of Mother Courage, a woman who makes her living by following the armies and selling trifles to the soldiers. Despite her many admirable qualities, Mother Courage pays dearly for her economic dependence on war. One by one, each of her three children is caught up in the perversity of the war, and each eventually dies a violent death, leaving Mother Courage alone.

Mother Goose Tales   See CONTES DE MA MÈRE L'OYE.

Motherwell, Robert (1915–   )   American painter and printmaker. Motherwell was among the first American abstract expressionists to experiment extensively with collage. His idea that the creation of a picture is entrusted to the spontaneous, irrational movement of the unconscious had a profound effect on the ABSTRACT EXPRESSIONISM of the 1960s. He coined the term "automatic abstract art" and has been almost unique among painters, in that his style has remained consistently abstract throughout his career. *The Prints of Robert Motherwell*, cataloging all his prints to date, was published in 1984.

Motley, John Lothrop (1814–1877)   American historian and diplomat. After graduating from Harvard at eighteen and studying at Göttingen, Motley wrote *Morton's Hope: or, The Memoirs of a Young Provincial* (1839), a semiautobiographical novel. His best-known historical work is the three-volume *Rise of the Dutch Republic* (1856), in which he emphasized the conflict between William of Orange, who represented Protestantism and freedom, and Philip II of Spain, symbol of Catholicism and absolutism. Motley was minister to Austria (1861–67) and to Great Britain (1869–70).

Motley, Willard (1912–1965)   American novelist. Motley's first book, *Knock on Any Door* (1947), the story of the progressive criminal hardening of a boy in the Chicago slums, was a remarkably powerful and challenging novel. *We Fished All Night* (1951) and *Let No Man Write My Epitaph* (1958) also deal with poverty and crime. *Let Noon Be Fair* (1966) is about the experience of a black American living in Mexico, as Motley did for twelve years before his death.

Moto, Mr.   A clever Japanese sleuth, created by J. P. MARQUAND. Mr. Moto first appeared in stories published in the *Saturday Evening Post* and later in such collections as *Thank You, Mr. Moto* (1936) and *Stopover Tokyo* (1957).

Mo Tzu (470?–?391 BC)   Chinese philosopher. Mo Tzu advocated free will, universal love, and nonaggression and opposed the elaborate rituals of CONFUCIANISM on utili-tarian grounds. His doctrines, sometimes called *Mohism*, seriously challenge those of the Confucians, and he apparently had a large following in late CHOU times. His disciples were experts in siege and defensive warfare, and the writings of his school, although badly preserved, show an unusual interest in physics and the natural sciences. By HAN times, his school was extinct.

Mouches, Les   See FLIES, THE.

Mountain, the (Fr, *la Montagne*)   The extreme democratic party in the FRENCH REVOLUTION. The members, many of whom were Jacobins, were known as *les Montagnards* because they seated themselves on the highest benches of the hall in which the National Convention met. Their leaders were DANTON, ROBESPIERRE, MARAT, St. André, Legendre, Camille Desmoulins, Carnot, St. Just, and Collot d'Herbois. Extreme radicals in France in later times were often called *Montagnards*.

Mount Vernon   The home and burial place of George WASHINGTON, situated on the Potomac River near Alexandria, Virginia. Originally known as the Hunting Creek plantation, the estate was renamed by Lawrence Washington, George's half brother, in honor of Admiral Vernon of the British navy, under whom Lawrence served in an unsuccessful attack on Cartagena in 1740. The main part of the house was built by Lawrence, who died in 1752, and additions were made by George, who rented the estate until he inherited it upon the death of Lawrence's widow in 1761. The estate became a public monument in 1860.

Mourning Becomes Electra (1931)   A trilogy of plays by Eugene O'NEILL. Based on the ORESTEIA of AESCHYLUS, they are set in a stark New England, in which the Puritan conscience functions as the American equivalent of the Furies. AGAMEMNON is represented by Ezra Mannon, a general returning from the Civil War. His wife Christine corresponds to CLYTEMNESTRA; his daughter Lavinia is ELECTRA; his son Orin, ORESTES. Christine, assisted by her lover, Adam Brant, poisons her husband. Lavinia, also in love with Brant, persuades Orin to avenge their father's death. Brant is murdered, Christine commits suicide, and Orin and Lavinia travel to the South Seas in an unsuccessful attempt to forget. On their return, Orin too kills himself, and Lavinia retires to the Mannon house. The play's central theme is the conflict between Puritanism and romantic passion.

Mourt's Relation (1622)   The earliest narrative of the Plymouth Pilgrims. Known as *Mourt's Relation* from the name of the author of its preface, it consists mainly of letters from various colonists to their friends and families in England. Also included is a journal kept by William BRADFORD during the voyage of the *Mayflower* and the early days of settlement of Plymouth.

Mowat, Farley (1921–   )   Canadian writer. Born in Ontario, Mowat was first taken to the Arctic at the age of fourteen. After service in World War II, he spent two years there and became Canada's best-known popular authority on Arctic ecology, people, and seas. Two of his early books, *People of the Deer* (1952) and *The Desperate People* (1959), are passionate discourses on the destruction of the values and way of life of the Eskimo people, brought on by ignorant government bureaucrats and missionaries. Another of Mowat's passions, ocean sailing, led to *The Grey Seas Under* (1958), *The Serpent's Coil* (1961), and *The Boat Who Wouldn't Float* (1969). Among his many other works are *Sibir* (1970; U.S. *The Siberians*), *A Whale for the Killing* (1972), *The Snow Walker* (1975), a collection of short stories, and *And No Birds Sang* (1979), personal reminiscences of the war years.

Mowgli   An Indian baby brought up by Mother Wolf with her cubs in Kipling's JUNGLE BOOK. After a boyhood spent with the animals of the jungle, Mowgli finally becomes a man among men.

Mozart, Wolfgang Amadeus (1756–1791)   Austrian composer. Mozart's father, Leopold (1719–87), a gifted violinist and composer, began successful tours of Europe with Wolfgang and his sister Nannerl when Wolfgang was only seven years old. The boy was displayed like a trained pet, playing piano and violin and composing on demand, sometimes locked in a room alone to assure the genuineness of the composition, to the astonishment of spectators. In 1781 Wolfgang left the employ of the unmusical Archbishop of Salzburg, in an attempt to make his own way in Vienna. There he was plagued by constant financial hardship and ill health. He died, aged thirty-five, at work on his *Requiem Mass* and was buried in a pauper's plot in an unmarked grave. Although he never renounced Catholicism, he became an ardent FREEMASON.

Mozart composed over six hundred works, including forty-nine symphonies, nearly twenty operas, twenty-five piano concertos, twenty-three string quartets, forty-two violin sonatas, and many other chamber compositions. From his first years in Vienna, Mozart shared a close artistic relationship with HAYDN.

Mozart's fundamentally dramatic conception of musical structure explains in part why his piano concertos are among the supreme examples of the genre; he was able to treat the soloist like a character in a dramatic action confronting the orchestra. The last three symphonies (in E flat; G minor; and C, or "Jupiter"), all composed within the space of six weeks in the summer of 1788, and several of his string quartets and string quintets represent the zenith of classical form.

Mozart's operas reveal him to be among the supreme musical dramatists. Seldom has any composer had so acute an understanding of the psychology of his characters and at the same time possessed so rich a technique to project that psychology in music. Mozart penetrated deeply into the meaning of the libretto and enriched it with music that built a firm architectural structure, rich in details that support the ebb and flow of the drama. His best-known operas are *Le Nozze di Figaro* (*The Marriage of Figaro*, 1786),

Don Giovanni (1787), *Cosi fan tutte* (1790), and *Die Zauberflöte* (*The Magic Flute*, 1791).

Mozart auf der Reise nach Prag (Mozart on His Trip to Prague, 1856)   A novella by Eduard MÖRIKE. It is set in 1787 as MOZART and his wife are on their way from Vienna to Prague for the premiere of *Don Giovanni*. There is little plot, and the author concentrates primarily on depiction of mood, combining a feeling of essential joy in Mozart's creative energy with a sense of melancholy premonition about Mozart's impending death.

Mphahlele, Ezekiel (1919–   )   South African novelist and critic. Prevented from teaching because of his resistance to government policies on African education, Mphahlele left South Africa in 1957 and worked in Nigeria, Kenya, and the U.S. His imaginative prose includes the story collections *Man Must Live* (1947), *The Living and the Dead* (1961), and *In Corner B* (1967), and the novel *The Wanderers* (1971). Perhaps his most compelling work is his autobiography, *Down Second Avenue* (1959); written with the narrative structure of a novel, it is a dramatic chronicle of Mphahlele's personal struggle as a black from the Pretoria slums. *The African Image* (1962; rev 1972) is a mixture of autobiography, travel writing, and literary criticism; *Voices in the Whirlwind* (1972) is a volume of essays. *Chirundu*, a novel, was published in 1979. Mphahlele aslo published *The Unbroken Song* (1981) and *Bury Me at the Marketplace* (1984).

Mr. Bennett and Mrs. Brown (1924)   An essay by Virginia WOOLF. She attacks the naturalistic novelists Arnold BENNETT, John GALSWORTHY, and H. G. WELLS, asserting that their books are not truly realistic, because they disregard the moment-by-moment workings of the human mind.

Mr. Norris Changes Trains (1935; U.S., The Last of Mr. Norris)   A novel by Christopher ISHERWOOD. Set in Berlin during HITLER's rise to power, it is the story of the narrator's innocent friendship with odd, corrupt Mr. Norris. While pretending to be a sincere Communist, Mr. Norris is actually selling information to Fascists and foreigners. Mr. Norris's masochistic sexual aberrations add to the impression that he is a symbol of the whole corrupt, disintegrating society.

Mrozek, Slawomir (1930–   )   Polish dramatist and short-story writer. One of the most original and prolific of Polish writers for the stage, Mrozek uses biting satire in the absurdist tradition to present his mordant vision of the human drama. His plots tend to be built on paradoxes. In *The Police* (1958), his first play, a police force that has suppressed all crime is forced to break the law to avoid becoming obsolete. His major work, *Tango* (1964), is a grotesque family saga, in which the parents are the revolutionaries and the son, Arthur, is the reactionary, rejecting his parents as amoral. Arthur's attempt to create a structured world through power fails, and he is eventually killed by his mother's lover. Conspicuous in all Mrozek's plays is his ironic view of everyday life: he logically pursues realistic detail to a bizarre conclusion, demonstrating how tenuous is the division between the normal and the absurd.

Mr. Perrin and Mr. Traill (1911)   A novel by Hugh WALPOLE. Set in an English boys' boarding school, it is an account of the inbred, tense lives of the teachers, especially of the elderly Mr. Perrin. When young Mr. Traill arrives, is successful and popular with the boys, and becomes engaged to the young woman with whom Mr. Perrin is in love, the older man develops an obsession and tries to murder his young rival.

Mr. Polly, The History of (1910)   A novel by H. G. WELLS. Mr. Polly is a timid, middle-aged tradesman who escapes from his domineering wife and dreary small-town existence by setting his house on fire—intending, but comically failing, to commit suicide. Supposed dead, he wanders around the countryside, living a life of freedom and whimsical adventure. Eventually he serves the fat landlady of the Potwell Inn with comic chivalry and establishes a new life with her.

Mrs. Caliban (1982)   A novel by the American writer Rachel Ingalls. Originally published with little critical attention, *Mrs. Caliban* became a literary sensation when in 1986 it was chosen by the British Book Marketing Council as one of the top twenty American novels since World War II. This book's main character is Dorothy, a woman who has suffered the death of a young son and a miscarriage. She is married to an uncommunicative, morose, and unfaithful husband, and her best friend is neurotic and alcoholic. As if to compensate for these sorrows, Dorothy hears encouraging messages on the radio and is in love with an enormous humanlike amphibian named Larry. A novel of real human grief and fantastic consolations, *Mrs. Caliban* concludes in surrealistic action in which fact and fantasy mingle and unravel.

Mrs. Dalloway (1925)   A novel by Virginia WOOLF. It describes the events of one day in the life of Clarissa Dalloway, a middle-aged English society woman. As she busies herself with preparations for a party to be held that evening, she reflects on her life, her family, and her friends. Her sense that her life and love have been somehow misspent or her values misplaced is precipitated by the arrival from India of Peter Walsh, a man she had once passionately loved but whom she rejected in favor of security and stability. A complementary character is Septimus Warren Smith, who has retreated to a private world of madness and commits suicide the night of Mrs. Dalloway's party. The two never meet, but their lives are connected by external events, such as an airplane overhead and a bus passing both, and by the fact that they are both sensitive individuals who feel emotionally bankrupt.

Mrs. Warren's Profession (1893)   A play by George Bernard SHAW. Mrs. Warren's profession is prostitution, a secret she has kept from her twenty-two-year-old daughter Vivie. When Mrs. Warren does explain to Vivie

how she has been able to raise her in comfort and refinement, the daughter is, at first, sympathetic to her mother's candor and liberality. However, when Vivie learns that her mother not only was a madam but still is, she icily rejects her. Disillusioned but unsentimental, Vivie is ready to start her own life.

Because of its subject matter, *Mrs. Warren's Profession* caused a storm of protest from the public and was closed when it was first produced in New York (1905). It was not produced in England until 1925.

Much Ado about Nothing (c1598)   A comedy by SHAKESPEARE. There are two main plots. One concerns the love affair of BEATRICE and BENEDICK, who become betrothed as a result of the schemes of their friends, each one being told that the other is pining away in unrequited passion. The other plot deals with a conspiracy against CLAUDIO, who is engaged to Beatrice's gentle cousin Hero. Don John, who hates Claudio, stages a pretended assignation between Borachio, one of his followers, and Margaret, Hero's maid, who is garbed as her mistress. Claudio, who witnesses the scene and suspects Hero's virtue, rejects his bride at the altar, but, through the good offices of kindly Friar Francis, the matter is finally cleared up. Many sources have been suggested for the plot, since similar tales have been told by Bandello, Ariosto, and Spenser. See DOGBERRY.

muckrakers   In U.S. history, a group of reformers whose writings drew public attention to corruption in politics and business and to other social ills. The term was first used, in a deprecatory sense, by Theodore ROOSEVELT, who likened them to the character in PILGRIM'S PROGRESS who is so busy raking mud that he cannot perceive the celestial crown held above him.

Muckraking reached its height in the first decade of the 20th century. The spearhead of the movement was *McClure's Magazine*, with other mass-circulation periodicals, such as *Collier's* and *Cosmopolitan*, following its lead. Among the outstanding examples of muckraking literature are books based on articles that first appeared in these magazines: Ida M. TARBELL's *History of the Standard Oil Company* (1904), Lincoln STEFFENS's *Shame of the Cities* (1904), and Samuel Hopkins Adams's *The Great American Fraud* (1906). Other famous exposures include David Graham PHILLIPS's *The Treason of the Senate* (1906) and Ray Stannard Baker's *The Railroads on Trial* (*McClure's*, 1906). Many novelists also turned to muckraking, notably Upton Sinclair, who assailed the meat-packing industry in THE JUNGLE.

Mudrārākṣasa (Sans, "the minister's signet ring")   An ancient Sanskrit play by Viśākhadatta (fl 5th century AD?). It is a historical play dealing with political intrigue during the rise to power of Chandragupta Maurya, emperor of India in the 3rd century BC. The action takes place primarily between Chandragupta's wily minister Cānakya and Rākṣasa, the loyal minister of the Nandas, dynastic rulers of a neighboring kingdom. It is unusual in classical Indian drama for the absence of any central female characters.

muerte de Artemio Cruz, La   See DEATH OF ARTEMIO CRUZ, THE.

Muggeridge, Malcolm [Thomas] (1903–   ) English writer. As his two volumes of autobiography, collectively titled *Chronicles of Wasted Time* (*The Green Stick*, 1972; *The Infernal Grove*, 1973), document, Muggeridge had a varied career as a teacher, gossip columnist, novelist, editor of *Punch*, filmmaker, and social commentator. He embraced and rejected utopian socialism and Soviet communism and, by the mid-1960s, had become an apostle of nondenominational Christianity. Both his social and his spiritual concerns are evident in *Christ and the Media* (1977). Throughout his varied career, Muggeridge was known as a consistently polished and prolific writer and as a relentless iconoclast. *Things Past* (1978) is an anthology, arranged chronologically, of short stories and political and social commentary. Among his other notable works are *A Twentieth-Century Testimony* (1979) and *Like It Was* (1981), an edition of his diaries.

Muhammed (fr Arab, "the praised one"; also Mahomet or Mohammed, 570–632)   The founder of ISLAM, the Muslim religion. Muhammed was born in MECCA and was raised by his uncle. When he was twenty-four he married KHADIJAH, the first of his many wives, who bore him FATIMA. He lived as a wealthy man until, at the age of forty, he felt the calling to be the true prophet of God among the Arab people. This and many of his other revelations are contained in the KORAN. His preachings were unpopular in Mecca to the point that, under threat of murder, he fled to Yathrib (MEDINA). At this time of the HEGIRA, he adopted the name Muhammed. His original name is given as both Kotham and Halabi.

He lived the rest of his life in Medina, gaining converts from all over the Arab world. Because he claimed to be the last of the prophets and successor to JESUS, he was received with hostility by both Christians and Jews. His influence spread, however, and in 630 Mecca surrendered to him without resistance.

When Muhammed introduced his system to the Arabs, they asked for miraculous proofs. He then ordered Mount Safa to come to him but thanked God when it did not move, for "it would have fallen on us to our destruction," and he then went to the mountain to pray. This is the origin of the saying: "if the mountain will not come to Muhammed, Muhammed must go to the mountain," often used of one who bows before the inevitable.

Muir, Edwin (1887–1959)   Scottish poet, critic, and translator. Muir published *First Poems* in 1925 and his allegorical long poem *The Labyrinth* in 1949, but he was not recognized as an important 20th-century poet until his *Collected Poems* appeared in 1952. His work is characterized by a simple, direct style and by its use of dream imagery and archetypal myth and fable. Like many other

modern poets, Muir is indebted to the 17th-century META-PHYSICAL POETS and to the psychology of FREUD and JUNG. His autobiography, *The Story and the Fable* (1940; rev and expanded as *Autobiography*, 1954), provides a useful background to his poems. He was brought up on a poor Scottish farm until, when Muir was fourteen, his family was evicted, and they were forced to take up residence in a Glasgow slum. From that time, Muir earned his living as a clerk and later as a freelance writer. Besides several novels, he wrote nonfiction on travel, politics, and literature.

Muir, John (1838–1914)   Scottish-born American naturalist and writer. Muir, who migrated with his father to a Wisconsin farm, described his early experiences in *The Story of My Boyhood and Youth* (1913). Between 1863, when he left the University of Wisconsin, and 1868, when he settled for six years in Yosemite Valley, Muir traveled thousands of miles afoot through Wisconsin, Illinois, Indiana, and Canada; he also made a trip from Indiana to Mexico, the journal of which he published as *A Thousand Mile Walk to the Gulf* (1916).

Muir had the naturalist's keen eye, a poetic appreciation of nature, and a gift for style. A lover of animals, he repeatedly expressed his wonder and admiration for the intelligence of beasts. *Stickeen* (1909) is a loving tribute to the loyalty and resourcefulness of his little half-wild dog.

Much of Muir's life was devoted to saving the natural beauties of the West from destruction by commercial exploitation, and his letters report his constant, heartbreaking struggle to prevent man from ruining the beauties of nature. His other works include *The Mountains of California* (1894), *Our National Parks* (1901), and *The Yosemite* (1912).

Müller, Wilhelm (1794–1827)   German romantic poet. Müller's best-known work is the lyric cycle *Die schöne Müllerin* (*The Lovely Miller-Girl*, 1821), which was made famous by Franz SCHUBERT's musical settings. See GERMAN ROMANTICISM.

Mumford, Lewis (1895–   )   American social philosopher, writer, and teacher. Mumford's diverse books explore the relation of modern man to both the natural and the self-created environment. In *The Culture of Cities* (1938), *City Development* (1945), *The City in History* (1961), and *The Urban Prospect* (1968), Mumford demonstrates that the city is simultaneously an expression of civilization and a force shaping civilization's development. In *Technics and Civilization* (1934), *The Condition of Man* (1944), and *The Conduct of Life* (1951) and in the two volumes of *Myth and Machine* (1967, 1970), as in many other works, Mumford tackles the dehumanizing effects of modern technology, urging a return to humanitarian values and moral regeneration. He has also written on architecture and American literature. *My Works and Days: A Personal Chronicle* (1979) contains selected writings from 1914 to 1977 with autobiographical notes. It was followed by *Sketches from Life: The Early Years* (1982).

Munch, Edvard (1863–1944)   Norwegian painter and printmaker. A precursor of German EXPRESSIONISM, Munch was influenced by the postimpressionist painters, particularly VAN GOGH and GAUGUIN. His landscapes and portraits were more an expression of a tormented inner state than a representation of external reality. Recurring themes of his work before 1900 are awakening woman-hood, fear, desire, isolation, and death. His later works, following a nervous collapse (1908–9), are lighter and somewhat more optimistic in tone. Among his well-known paintings are *Summer Night*, *The Cry*, *The Sick Child*, and *Portrait of A. Strindberg*.

Munich Crisis   A European diplomatic crisis of September 1938. War was threatened by the demand of Adolf Hitler for the incorporation into Germany of a group of German-speakers living in the Sudetenland, a region that had been given to Czechoslovakia as part of its national territory by the Treaty of Versailles at the close of World War I. In an effort to prevent war, Neville Cham-berlain, prime minister of Great Britain, conferred with Hitler at Berchtesgaden and later made a peace treaty at Munich, Germany, permitting the annexation of the Sudeten region to Germany in return for a pledge by Hitler that the independence of the remainder of Czechoslovakia would be respected. Chamberlain believed that "peace in our time" had been achieved, but Hitler's pledge was not kept. The Munich agreement indirectly strengthened Hitler for his later aggression against Poland (September 1939), which brought about World War II.

Munonye, John (1929–   )   Nigerian novelist. Munonye's novels, all written in the realistic tradition, are about ordinary people beset by the difficulties of earning a living and realizing their modest dreams. *The Only Son* (1966) describes the opposing pull of Western religion and traditional ways; *Obi* (1969) is about village life; and *Oil Man of Obange* (1971) examines the tragic life of a palm oil trader. *A Wreath for the Maidens* (1973) deals with some of the consequences of the Nigerian civil war, and *A Dancer of Fortune* (1974) tells the story of a villainous seller of patent medicines.

Munro, Alice (1931–   )   Canadian novelist and short-story writer. Munro's stories in *Dance of the Happy Shades* (1968) and *Something I've Been Meaning to Tell You* (1974) sketch life in Jubilee, a fictional small town in southern Ontario. The typical semiautobiographical narra-tor of a Munro story is a girl of sensitive, precocious dispo-sition who observes the values, snobberies, and complex social relationships of her community. *Who Do You Think You Are?* (1979; U.S. *The Beggar Maid*) is a collection of ten interweaving stories, told from the point of view of a poor but gifted girl whose sharp eye for the illusions to which she and others cling leaves her finally with the feel-ing that real substance and honesty can never be fully grasped. *The Moons of Jupiter* was published in 1982.

Munro, Hector Hugh   See SAKI.

Mur, Le   See WALL, THE.

Murasaki Shikibu (978?–?1015)   Japanese court lady. Murasaki is the author of THE TALE OF GENJI, widely considered the world's oldest novel. This seminal work in Japanese literature established or refined many of the motifs, images, and sentiments that were later to become central to the literary tradition. She also wrote an impor-tant diary, *Murasaki Shikibu nikki* (1008–?1010; tr 1920), and a collection of TANKA. Little is known of her life except that she was a courtier-scholar's daughter and that she was married and had one child. After her husband's death, she served as a lady-in-waiting at the court, during which time she wrote her famous novel.

Murder in the Cathedral (1935)   A drama in verse by T. S. ELIOT. It deals with the assassination of St. THOMAS À BECKET, the archbishop of Canterbury who opposed King Henry II's attempt to limit the privileges of the clergy. In the play, Thomas is tempted by offers of worldly happiness, power, and influence, but he rejects them in order to obey what he regards as the laws of God, for which he is martyred. The language of the play is mostly ritualistic and liturgical, spoken in a chorus by the women of Canterbury and in monologues and formal exchanges by the other characters. The interlude is a ser-mon by Becket to his invisible congregation. The villains, four tempters in Part One and four knights and murderers in Part Two, are comic figures, expressing modern attitudes in colloquial language. The first work Eliot completed in his attempt to revive poetic drama on the English stage, *Murder in the Cathedral* is generally regarded as his best play.

Murders in the Rue Morgue, The (1841)   A story by Edgar Allan POE. A mother and daughter are bru-tally murdered in a crime that baffles the police. Poe's amateur detective, C. Auguste DUPIN, solves the mystery.

Murdoch, Iris (1919–   )   Irish-born novelist and philosopher. Murdoch's novels are noted for intricacy of plot and character, psychological penetration, and subtlety of style, with a wit that ranges from recondite irony to the crazily comic. Their structure is elaborate and unrealistic, often concerning a group of characters who become involved with each other through a complex network of love affairs. People's need for love and for freedom are explored as part of their greater need to affirm their own reality. In UNDER THE NET, THE BELL, and AN UNOFFICIAL ROSE, as in other Murdoch novels, the twin philosophical questions are posed: how free can man be and how much can he know himself? Among her many works are the novels *The Flight from the Enchanter* (1956), *The Sand-castle* (1957), *A Severed Head* (1961), *The Unicorn* (1963), *An Accidental Man* (1972), *Henry and Cato* (1977), *The Sea, the Sea* (1978; Booker Prize for literature), and *Nuns and Soldiers* (1980), as well as a study of SARTRE, *Romantic Rationalist* (1953), and *The Fire and the Sun* (1977), a dis-cussion of Plato's aesthetic theory. Her later novels are *The*

Philosopher's Pupil (1982) and *The Good Apprentice* (1985). In 1987 Murdoch was made a Dame of the British Empire.

Murfree, Mary Noailles (pen name Charles Egbert Craddock, 1850–1922)   American author of local-color stories and novels set in the Tennessee mountains. Murfree was one of the first to present the Southern mountaineer realistically, in her collection of dialect stories *In the Tennessee Mountains* (1884). *The Prophet of the Great Smokey Mountains* (1885) and *In the Clouds* (1887) also deal with the Great Smokies. In addition to her local-color books, Murfree wrote a series of Southern historical novels.

Murger, Henri (1822–1861)   French writer. Murger is best known for *Scènes de la vie de bohème* (pub 1848 serially; 1851 in book form), which formed the basis for Puccini's opera *La Bohème*. In it, Murger paints a picture of the world he knew well, that of the colorful but uncertain existence of the artist in Paris.

Murillo, Bartolomé Esteban (1617–1682) Spanish painter. After he completed eleven paintings of the Franciscan monastery in Seville (1645–46), Murillo was established as the most popular and respected painter of his day. He is best known for his slightly sentimental yet naturalistic religious paintings, particularly the *Inmaculadas* (*Immaculate Conceptions*).

Murnau, Friedrich Wilhelm (real name Friedrich Wilhelm Plumpe, 1888–1931)   German film director who worked in Berlin 1919–26 and in Hollywood 1927–31. As an innovator, an influence on and a creator of major films, Murnau surpasses even Fritz LANG, his only considerable rival in German silent cinema. The most famous films of his Berlin period are *Nosferatu* (1922) and *The Last Laugh* (1924). The former film, a version of the Dracula story, endures as one of the great atmospheric horror movies; the latter, the story of a humiliated petty bourgeois told with the barest minimum of insert titles, has frequently been singled out by critics as a masterpiece of purely visual narration.

Sunrise (1927), Murnau's first American film, arguably his greatest picture, used brilliant montage and a marvelously mobile camera to explore the psychic conflicts of the characters, in an adaptation of Hermann SUDERMANN's *Trip to Tilsit*. In 1931, shortly after completing the shooting of *Tabu* (codirected with Robert FLAHERTY), Murnau was killed in an automobile accident. See EXPRESSIONIST CINEMA.

Muromachi   Japanese historical period (1333–1616) that followed the KAMAKURA. Centralized rule declined, and there was widespread warfare throughout the country toward the end of the period. The era saw the development of ornate visual and dramatic art; the Nō drama developed during this period. During the unrest of the later years, there arose several able leaders whose efforts resulted in unification of the country and in transition to the TOKUGAWA period.

Murray, [George] Gilbert [Aimé] (1866–1957) Australian-born English classical scholar and writer. Murray is best known for his poetic translations of the great Greek dramas, in which he used heroic rhymes to preserve the original rhythms. Among his books, in which he attempted to set classical works within their historical social and political contexts, are *The Rise of the Greek Epic* (1907), *Euripides and His Age* (1918), *The Classical Tradition of Poetry* (1927), and *Hellenism and the Modern World* (1953). A deeply committed pacifist, he was a prominent promoter of the League of Nations and later of the United Nations. He wrote a number of books on international politics, such as *Liberality and Civilization* (1938).

Murray, Lindley (1745–1826)   Scottish-American grammarian, called the Father of English Grammar. Murray is best known for his *Grammar of the English Language* (1795).

Murry, John Middleton (1889–1957)   English critic and editor. As a young journalist recently down from Oxford, Murry met Katherine MANSFIELD in 1913; they married five years later. In 1919 he became editor of the *Athenaeum* and in 1923 founded his own literary journal, *Adelphi*. Many of the leading artists and writers of the day, who wrote for or were written about in his magazines, were close personal friends of the Murrys (see Huxley's POINT COUNTER POINT and Lawrence's WOMEN IN LOVE). After Mansfield's death in 1923, Murry brought out his edition of her *Letters* and *Journal* (2 vols, 1928; rev 1954) and *The Life of Katherine Mansfield* (1933). Notable among Murry's enthusiastic but somewhat ponderous literary studies are *The Problem of Style* (1922), *Keats and Shakespeare* (1925), *Son of Woman, The Story of D. H. Lawrence* (1931), *William Blake* (1933), and *Jonathan Swift* (1954). A pacifist (*The Necessity of Pacifism*, 1937) and a radical Christian with a mystic bent (*Life of Jesus*, 1926; *Christocracy*, 1942), he wrote the story of his own life in *Between Two Worlds* (1935).

muscular Christianity   Healthy or strong-minded Christianity, which braces a man to fight the battle of life bravely and manfully. The term was applied to the teaching of Charles KINGSLEY—somewhat to his annoyance, for he was less concerned with personal fortitude than with a program of vigorous social action by the church at large.

Muses   In Greek mythology, the nine daughters of ZEUS and MNEMOSYNE. There were originally only three, held to be goddesses of memory; nine were later identified with individual arts. The Muses were not worshiped as deities but were frequently invoked, particularly by poets who called on them for inspiration. The paintings of Herculaneum depict all nine with their respective attributes:

(1) CALLIOPE, Muse of epic poetry. Her symbols are a tablet and stylus, sometimes a scroll.

(2) CLIO, Muse of heroic poetry or history. Her symbol is a scroll or an open chest of books.

(3) ERATO, Muse of love poetry. Her symbol is a lyre.

(4) EUTERPE, Muse of music, particularly wind instruments. Her symbol is a flute.

(5) MELPOMENE, Muse of tragedy. Her symbols are a tragic mask, the club of HERACLES, and a sword. She wears the cothurnus, a boot worn by tragic actors, and her head is wreathed with vine leaves.

(6) POLYHYMNIA, Muse of sacred poetry and hymns. She has no single attribute but sits in a pensive posture.

(7) TERPSICHORE, Muse of choral song and dance. She is usually represented by a lyre.

(8) THALIA, Muse of comedy. Her symbols are a comic mask, a shepherd's crook, and a wreath of ivy.

(9) URANIA, Muse of astronomy. Her symbol is a staff pointing to a globe.

music of the spheres   A theory of PYTHAGORAS. Having ascertained that the pitch of notes depends on the rapidity of vibrations and also that the planets move at different rates of motion, Pythagoras concluded that the planets must make sounds in their motion according to their different rates and that, as all things in nature are harmoniously made, the different sounds must harmonize. In this originated the old theory of the harmony of the spheres. Kepler has a treatise on the subject. See SPHERES.

Music of Time, The   See DANCE TO THE MUSIC OF TIME, A.

Musil, Robert (1880–1940)   Austrian novelist. Musil's first novel, *Die Verwirrungen des Zöglings Törleß* (1906; tr *Young Törless*, 1955), was hailed as an early example of expressionistic writing. It is a grim depiction of adolescent psychosexual brutality, set in a Bohemian military academy. He is best known, however, for the extraordinary depth of psychological and cultural analysis built into his enormous, unfinished novel *Der Mann ohne Eigenshaften* (tr *The Man without Qualities*, 1953–60). The first two volumes of this monumental work were published in 1930 and 1932; a fragmentary third was published posthumously in 1942, and in 1952 the novel appeared, with additional chapters, in one volume. Apart from providing a brilliant, existential portrait of Ulrich, the scholarly, purposeless "man without qualities," the book is a vivid depiction of Austrian decadence before the outbreak of World War I. This single remarkable work established Musil as one of the most influential German-language novelists in the first half of the 20th century. Collections of his shorter fiction published posthumously in translation include *Tonka and Other Stories* (1965) and *Three Stories* (1970).

Muslim (or Moslem)   A follower of MUHAMMED. The word comes from the present participle of the Arabic *aslama*, "to be submissive to God; to be at rest," from which ISLAM is also derived.

Musset, Alfred de (1810–1857)   French poet, novelist, and dramatist. Musset's early poetry partakes of both Byronic wit and Byronic passion (see ROMANTICISM); it probes introspectively into the ecstasies and despairs of love. His celebrated love affair with George Sand ended disastrously in 1835, and this brought a darker coloring to his subsequent life and work. His poetic works include *Contes d'Espagne et d'Italie* (1830), *Premières poésies* (1829–35), and *Poésies nouvelles* (1836–52), which includes the series of lyrics for which he is best known, *Les Nuits*.

Musset's plays—comedies of manners called *comédies-proverbes*, as many of the titles were taken from proverbs popular at the time—also include fanciful comedies in the style of Shakespeare. Among his plays are *On ne badine pas avec l'amour* (1834), *Barberine* (1835), *Un Caprice* (1837), and *Il faut qu'une porte soit ouverte ou fermée* (1845). *La Confession d'un enfant du siècle* (1836) is an autobiographical novel.

Mussolini, Benito (1883–1945)   Italian dictator. Originally a socialist agitator, Mussolini later advanced a program of economic controls and national expansion that appealed to many Italians in the troubled years after World War I. In 1922 he led his followers in the famous march on Rome that resulted in his appointment as prime minister; he then proceeded to mold the Italian government to the ideals of FASCISM, stifling all opposition. Embarking on an aggressive foreign policy, he conquered Ethiopia (1935–36), withdrew from the League of Nations, and entered World War II on the side of Germany. After the Allied invasion of Italy, he was deposed and imprisoned but was rescued by the Germans, who installed him as head of a puppet state in northern Italy. Forced to flee, he was recognized by partisans and was shot, together with his mistress Clara Petacci.

Mussorgsky, Modest Petrovich (1837–1881) Russian composer. Mussorgsky is best remembered for his opera BORIS GODUNOV, based on the play by Aleksandr PUSHKIN. The work is famous for its choral passages, and it is sometimes said that the chorus rather than Boris is the protagonist. His other works include *Night on Bald Mountain* (1860–66) and *Pictures at an Exhibition* (1874), orchestrated by Maurice RAVEL, originally for piano. Mussorgsky was a close friend of Nikolay RIMSKY-KORSAKOV, who revised much of Mussorgsky's music after his death.

Mutiny on the Bounty (1932)   A historical novel by Charles NORDHOFF and James Norman HALL. This vivid narrative is based on the famous mutiny that members of the crew of the *Bounty*, a British war vessel, carried out in 1789 against their cruel commander, Captain William BLIGH. The authors kept the actual historical characters and background, using as narrator an elderly man, Captain Roger Byam, who had been a midshipman on the *Bounty*. The story tells how the mate of the ship, Fletcher Christian, and a number of the crew rebel and set Captain Bligh adrift in an open boat with the loyal members of the crew. The book was followed by two others: *Men against the Sea* (1934), which tells of Bligh and his men in the open boat, and *Pitcairn's Island* (1934), which describes the mutineers' life on a tiny Pacific island for twenty years.

My Ántonia (1918)   A novel by Willa CATHER. It deals with the life of Bohemian immigrant and native American settlers in the frontier farmlands of Nebraska. The heroine, Ántonia Shimerda, must work as a servant on the farms of her neighbors after her father kills himself. She elopes with a railway conductor but returns home and eventually becomes the patient and strong wife of a Bohemian farmer, Anton Cuzak, the mother of a large family, and a typical woman of the pioneer West. *My Ántonia* is notable particularly for its lucid and moving depiction of the prairie and the lives of those who live close to it.

My Last Duchess (1842)   A poem in the form of a dramatic monologue by Robert BROWNING. The speaker is the Renaissance duke of Ferrara, who, while negotiating a marriage with the daughter of a count, points out to the count's agent a portrait of his former wife, his "last Duchess." As he speaks of her, there is the intimation that, because she did not properly appreciate the honor bestowed upon her by his marrying her, he arranged for her murder.

My Life (Moya zhizn, 1896)   A long story by Anton CHEKHOV, subtitled *The Story of a Provincial*. The hero of the tale, Poleznev, rejects his position as a member of the intelligentsia and follows Tolstoyan teachings by supporting himself as a laborer. The story has been cited as Chekhov's criticism of TOLSTOY's preachings, but the tale at most seems to be an examination of their doctrinal effects.

My Lost Youth (1855)   A poem by Henry Wadsworth LONGFELLOW. Based on the author's boyhood in Portland, Maine, its continual refrain is:

A boy's will is the wind's will,
And the thoughts of youth are long, long, thoughts.

Robert Frost's "A Boy's Will" derives its title from this poem.

Myrdal, [Karl] Gunnar (1898–1987)   Swedish economist. Myrdal is known for his comprehensive economic and sociological analyses of a variety of issues, including population control (*Nation and Family*, 1934; tr 1941), developing nations (*Rich Lands and Poor: The Road to World Prosperity*, 1958), and political and economic problems in southern Asia (*Asian Drama*, 3 vols, 1968). An astute and objective observer of the United States, Myrdal conducted a monumental study of America's racial problems and wrote about his findings in his best-known work, *An American Dilemma* (2 vols, 1944), later condensed by his associate Arnold Rose as *The Negro in America* (1948). The book asserted that America's dilemma lay in the disparity between its high democratic ideals and its abusive, discriminatory treatment of blacks. Myrdal shared the NOBEL PRIZE in Economics in 1974 and received the Nehru Award in 1982. He has also published several other influential works, among them *The Challenge of World Poverty: A World Anti-Poverty Program in Out-* line (1970) and *Against the Stream: Critical Essays on Economics* (1972). In 1977 he published *Increasing Interdependence between States but Failure of International Cooperation*.

Myrmidons   In classic mythology, a people of Thessaly. The Myrmidons followed ACHILLES to the siege of Troy and were distinguished for their savage brutality, rude behavior, and thirst for rapine. They were originally ants, turned into human beings by ZEUS to populate the island of Oenone.

Myshkin, Prince   See IDIOT, THE.

Mysteries of Paris, The (Les Mystères de Paris, 1842–1843)   A romance by Eugène SUE. The kaleidoscopic life of Paris, painted in a lively and dramatic manner, serves as the subject of this novel.

Mysteries of Udolpho, The (1794)   A GOTHIC NOVEL by Mrs. Ann Radcliffe (1764–1823). The heroine, Emily de St. Aubert, has been brought up by a loving father in sunny Provence. On her father's death, she is left in the hands of her foolish aunt, Madame Cheron, who imprudently marries Montoni, an adventurer. The scene moves to Montoni's melancholy Gothic castle in the Apennines, from which he pillages the countryside. Emily's existence is enlivened by her aunt's death from Montoni's persecutions, by the attentions of Montoni himself, and by the discovery that there is a mystery surrounding her birth. Eventually, she escapes and returns to Provence, where she solves the mystery and marries her lover, the chevalier de Valencourt, from whom she had been estranged by her aunt's folly.

Mysterious Stranger, The (1898; pub 1916)   A story by Mark TWAIN. A boy in Eseldorf ("jackass village"), Austria, in the year 1590, is sitting with his two friends, when Satan makes their acquaintance. Disguised as a well-dressed and pleasing stranger named Philip Traum ("dream"), Satan convinces the boy of the falseness of morals, the kindness in killing a cripple, and the nonexistence of heaven. Destroying the boy's ideals, he vanishes. The book expresses Clemens's most pessimistic view of "the damned human race."

mystery plays (or mysteries; Fr, *mystères*, fr Lat, *mysterium*, fr Gr, *mustes*, fr *muein*, "to close the eyes or lips"; 13th–16th centuries)   Medieval dramas based on the Old and New Testaments and the Apocrypha. In English, the term is usually used interchangeably with MIRACLE PLAYS and thus can also include plays based on the lives of the saints. The mystery plays grew out of dramatically expanded presentations of the events of Christ's life in church liturgy. As these liturgical dramas were lengthened and enlivened with touches of realism and popular humor besides, they were moved to the porch or courtyard of the church; as the players were drawn more and more from the laity, the presentations moved to the public square or market place, although still given on the occasion of some religious holiday.

Most towns in England had at least a few presentations by their own craft guilds or parish clerks or by visiting players; about a dozen of the large towns developed large cycles of mystery plays after 1311, when the Corpus Christi day festival was confirmed, and the plays were given annually as commercial pageants under civic control. Each cycle presented a series of episodes beginning with the fall of Satan and continuing through biblical history, with particular development of the details of Christ's life and resurrection. Each play was performed by the members of an appropriate craft or trade guild: for instance, the story of Noah by the shipwrights, the Last Supper by the bakers. They used stage sets on wheels, so that the performance could be easily repeated in as many as a dozen different sections of a town during the day.

The plays are generally metrical, although of various verse forms. Their interpolation of wholly secular comic by-play into the religious material was the beginning of modern drama. There is the characterization of individuals, earthy and realistic humor, and a great deal of fairly coarse buffoonery. Aside from the individual plays unconnected with the cycles, there are four major collections: the forty-eight *York Plays* (early 14th century); the thirty-two TOWNELEY MYSTERIES (middle 14th–early 15th century, also called *Wakefield Mysteries*); the twenty-five *Chester Plays* (14th century), which are less dramatic and humorous and resemble more closely the serious French *mystères*; and the forty-two so-called *Coventry Plays* (15th century), which were probably actually performed by a traveling company. The plays by the unknown WAKEFIELD MASTER are considered the best.

The French *mystères*, usually Christmas or Easter pageants, were presented after 1371 by *confréries*, or fraternities of players. In 1402 the *Confrérie de la Passion* was given the royal commission for the presentation of the Easter Passion play, and it soon monopolized religious drama. However, it often joined forces with other groups who presented popular farces; comic scenes were thus introduced into the *mystères*, which continued to be given into the 16th century. Compare MORALITY PLAYS.

It is from the sense of closing the eyes or lips that the plays were called *mysteries*, though, as they were frequently presented by members of some single guild, or *mystery* in the sense (fr *ministerium*) of a trade, handicraft, or guild, even here the words were confused, and an opening was made for many puns.

myth Traditionally, a story belonging to any culture that is derived from primitive beliefs, presenting supernatural episodes to explain cosmic forces and the natural order. Regardless of the culture in which they originate, myths are generally concerned with the same themes and motifs: creation, divinity, the significance of life and death, natural phenomena, and the adventures of mythical heroes. See GODS OF CLASSICAL MYTHOLOGY.

Myth of Sisyphus, The (Le Mythe de Sisyphe, 1942; tr 1955)   An essay by Albert CAMUS. It is the first outline of his theory of the ABSURD: conscious man confronting an unintelligible universe. Man yearns to know, and absolute knowledge is impossible; thus the lucid man must live in the absence of hope. Yet, rejecting both despair and suicide, Camus urges that life and creation are possible within the narrow limits of what man does know. He makes the mythical SISYPHUS his hero of the absurd: to him, at least, belong his rock, his awareness of his fate, and his futile struggle toward the heights, which is enough to fill a man's heart and thus make him happy.

mythological cycle In GAELIC LITERATURE, a series of Old Irish sagas that survive in medieval manuscripts but date from much earlier. Here the exploits of the heroes of the TUATHA DÉ DANANN, the later gods of the Celts, are related. Among the major tales in the mythological cycle are *The Wooing of Etain*, *The Battle of Moytura*, and *The Nurture of the Houses of the Two Milk-Vessels*.

N

Naaman In the OLD TESTAMENT (2 Kings 5:1–27), a commander of the Syrian army, in service to the king in Damascus. He was stricken with leprosy and went to Samaria in Israel in search of a cure from the prophet ELISHA, of whose power he had heard from a captive Israelite servant. When he was cured, after dipping himself seven times in the Jordan river, he abandoned his worship of RIMMON and declared his conversion: "Behold, now I know there is no God in all the earth, but in Israel."

Nabi Painters, The (fr Heb, *nabis*, "prophets") A group of French symbolist painters working together in the last decade of the 19th century. They were united in their reverence for the philosophy of GAUGUIN and in their belief in a universal symbol-language of art. The group was founded by Paul Sérusier (1865–1927), the original disciple of Gauguin, and he and Maurice Denis (1870–1943) were its chief spokesmen. Their works appeared in the symbolist journal *La Revue blanche* and at several Nabi exhibitions, the last in 1899, after the group had disbanded. The Nabis included, besides Sérusier and Denis, K. X. Roussel (1867–1944), Edouard Vuillard (1868–1940), Pierre Bonnard (1867–1947), Félix Vallotton (1865–1925), and the sculptor Aristide MAILLOL. All except Bonnard and Vuillard took other vocations after the dissolution of the group.

Nabokov, Vladimir [Vladimirovich] (1899–1977) Russian-born American novelist and poet. Born of a noble Russian family, Nabokov was educated in England after 1917, lived in Europe, and immigrated to the U.S. in 1940, becoming an American citizen in 1945. From 1948 to 1959, he taught Russian literature at Cornell University. In 1959 he moved to Switzerland, where he remained for the rest of his life. Until 1938 Nabokov wrote his books in Russian, under the name Vladimir Sirin. Among the books from this period are *Mary* (1926; tr 1970), *King, Queen, Knave* (1928; tr 1968), *The Eye* (1930; tr 1965), and *Invitation to a Beheading* (1938; tr 1959). *The Real Life of Sebastian Knight* (1941), his first book in English, was followed by *Bend Sinister* (1947) and *Pnin* (1957), a comic account of a Russian teaching at an American college. Nabokov's greatest public success, and the work for which he is most widely known, is LOLITA, a brilliant satirical novel about an aging professor's obsession with a twelve-year-old nymphet. The theme of sexual preoccupation also appears in *Laughter in the Dark* (1932; tr 1938) and in ADA, OR ARDOR: A FAMILY CHRONICLE. Much of Nabokov's fiction represents variations on the form of the novel. As with the fantastic PALE FIRE and *The Gift* (1937; tr 1963), his last novel in Russian, Nabokov manipulates his readers as well as his characters, establishing one layer of reality and then interjecting another. For Nabokov, the creative act is a delicate interplay between the real world and the world the writer creates. Nabokov is known for his brilliant poetic imagination, pervasive sense of paradox, vivid wit, obscure literary allusions, and erudite word games. His skill at chess and his knowledge of lepidopterology also figure in much of his work. The novel *Look at the Harlequins!* (1974) is an "oblique biography" of himself; *Speak, Memory* (1951; rev 1966) is a remarkable and moving evocation of his childhood and youth. His spirited correspondence with Edmund WILSON was published in *The Nabokov-Wilson Letters* (1979). *Lectures on Literature* (1980), on six 19th-century English and American writers, is one of a series of lectures given at Cornell University.

Nabuco, Joaquim (1849–1910) Brazilian statesman and writer. The son of a wealthy landowner, Nabuco was a leader in the struggle against slavery, which he combated by political activity and in writings such as *O abolicionismo* (1883; tr *Abolitionism: The Brazilian Anti-slavery Struggle*, 1977). After the overthrow of the Brazilian monarchy, Nabuco retired from public life temporarily but later served as ambassador to the U.S. (1905–10). Cosmopolitan in outlook, he spent many years in France and England and was an enthusiastic supporter of the Pan-American movement. His finest literary work is probably his autobiography, *Minha formação* (1900), in which he gives a vivid portrait of slaveholding society in 19th-century Brazil.

Nadja (1928; tr 1960) A poetic novel by André BRETON. Breton's best-known novel, it is based on his love affair with a woman of psychic tendencies. The novel is a captivating mélange of bizarre and extraordinary events, woven into the fabric of mundane daily matters.

Nagai Kafū (1879–1959)   Japanese novelist. An admirer of ZOLA in his youth, Nagai Kafū helped to introduce French NATURALISM to Japan. However, after a visit to the U.S. and France, he became increasingly attracted to premodern Japanese culture, which, in his view, still survived in the lives of lower-class Tokyo women. His best works, such as *Ude kurabe* (1916; tr *Geisha in Rivalry*, 1965) and *Bokutō kidan* (1937; tr *A Strange Tale from East of the River*, 1965), vividly portray geisha, prostitutes, and other women against the background of a rapidly changing society.

Nahum   An OLD TESTAMENT prophet, and the book bearing his name. This short but poetic book begins by praising the majesty of the Lord and tells of His wrath against His enemies. It then prophesies the bloody destruction of Nineveh in graphic and ghastly detail. The book was probably written between 663 BC and the actual fall of Nineveh, in 612 BC. See JONAH.

naiads   In Greek mythology, water nymphs.

Naidu, Sarojini (1879–1949)   Indian poet writing in English. Naidu organized flood relief work in India (1908), was the first Indian woman president of the Indian National Congress (1925), and lectured in India and the U.S. (1928–29). Sometimes called "the nightingale of India," she exemplifies, in her light, delicate, sentimental verse, the romantic phase of Indian poetry in English. She is the author of *The Golden Threshold* (1905), *The Bird of Time* (1912), and *The Broken Wing* (1915–16).

Naipaul, V[idiadhar] S[urajprasad] (1932–   )   West Indian novelist and essayist. Naipaul was born in Trinidad of Hindu parents. He was educated in Trinidad and at Oxford and settled in London. With an exile's ambivalent sensibility, he is concerned in his writing with both the West Indies of his boyhood and his strong, if conflicted, identification with India. His first three novels, *The Mystic Masseur* (1957), *The Suffrage of Elvira* (1958), and *Miguel Street* (1959), are sharp, comic satires of the economic and intellectual poverty of the Caribbean. *A House for Mr. Biswas* (1961) and *The Mimic Men* (1967), also set in the Caribbean, offer a more compassionate picture and reveal that Naipaul's ironic perceptions grew out of an intense need for cultural and personal identity. His painful explorations of his Indian heritage are contained in the nonfiction accounts *The Middle Passage* (1962), *An Area of Darkness* (1964), and *India: A Wounded Civilization* (1977). These were followed by *Among the Believers: An Islamic Journey* (1981) and *Finding the Center: Two Narratives* (1985), which consists of two sections, one entirely autobiographical, the other a travel essay on the Ivory Coast. In 1983 Naipaul was awarded the Jerusalem Prize. Other novels include *Guerrillas* (1975), an ominous story of a senseless police murder in an unnamed republic,

clearly suggesting Naipaul's affinity with Joseph CONRAD; and *A Bend in the River* (1979), a dark political satire of the chaos of revolutionary politics, set in Africa. Also set in Africa is his collection of short fiction, *In a Free State* (1971), which won the Booker Prize. Naipaul is a superb stylist who writes with a studied detachment, yet whose satire is based on a moralist's outrage. His essays, many of which contain the seeds of his fiction, are collected in *The Overcrowded Barracoon* (1972) and *The Return of Eva Peron* (1980).

Naïve and Sentimental Poetry, On (Über naive und sentimentalische Dichtung, 1795–1796)   An essay by Friedrich SCHILLER. In it, he develops at length the distinction between the "naïve" poet, who seeks to depict objectively the balanced whole of life, and the "sentimental" poet, who is concerned more with depicting the ideals for which men should strive. Clearly enough, Schiller was thinking of GOETHE as the naïve poet and of himself as the sentimental poet. Parallel to this distinction, he describes two types of character: the realist, who acts in accordance with an objective view of reality, and the idealist, who bases his actions upon a subjective ideal. The importance of this essay in Schiller's dramatic development can be seen in the fact that, whereas all of his earlier heroes had been idealists, the heroes of his next two plays, WALLENSTEIN and *Mary Stuart* (1800), were realists.

Naked and the Dead, The (1948)   A novel by Norman MAILER. Based on Mailer's own experiences in World War II, it tells the stories of the members of an infantry platoon invading a Japanese-held island in the Pacific. It is widely regarded as the finest American novel to be written about the war. The book won such extensive popular and critical praise that Mailer became an instant literary celebrity at the age of twenty-five.

Naked Lunch   See BURROUGHS, WILLIAM S.

Nala   In Hindu legend, a king of Nishadha and husband of Damayantī, whose story is one of the best-known in the MAHĀBHĀRATA. Damayantī, through enchantment, falls in love with Nala without ever having seen him. The gods, however, want her for themselves and employ the unsuspecting Nala as their emissary and advocate; she declares that none but Nala shall possess her, whereupon the gods appear in Nala's shape, and Damayantī is obliged to make her choice, which she does, correctly. Nala is showered with magic gifts by the gods, and the wedding is celebrated. Nala later loses everything by gambling and becomes a wanderer, while Damayantī returns to her father's court. The lovers are reunited after many trials and adventures, in which magic plays a large part.

Nammu   See CREATION MYTHS.

Nana (1880)   A novel in the ROUGON-MACQUART series by Émile ZOLA. Nana, the heroine of this novel, is the daughter of Gervaise, central character in L'ASSOMMOIR. A product of the squalid atmosphere depicted in that novel, she becomes a prostitute and leads a similarly dissipated existence. One of Zola's themes in this series of novels is the transmission of traits through heredity; another is the significant influence of the environment in shaping human beings.

Nānak, Guru (1469–1538) Founder of the SIKH religion in India.

Nantes, Edict of A decree (1598) issued by Henry IV of France, establishing qualified religious toleration for French Protestants. They were granted liberty of conscience and the right to worship publicly in certain localities, as well as some political and juridical rights. The edict marked the end of France's religious wars. Louis XIV's revocation of the Edict of Nantes in 1685 ended toleration and was followed by a mass migration of Protestants to the Netherlands, England, and America.

Naphta, Leo In Thomas Mann's novel THE MAGIC MOUNTAIN, a tubercular Latin teacher in the Davos school near Haus Berghof. Naphta is an Austrian Jew who has been converted and become a Jesuit, and his attitudes, like his background, are a welter of violent contradictions. At various times, he seems to represent both spiritualism and materialism, both socialism and reaction. In his long debates with SETTEMBRINI, he upholds mysticism and faith against reason and empiricism, absolutism and authority against enlightenment and liberalism. His self-contradictory nature is epitomized when he meets Settembrini for a duel, and, rather than firing at the latter, kills himself.

Napoleon Bonaparte (Napoleon I, original name Napoleone Buonaparte; 1769–1821) Emperor of France (1804–15). Napoleon, born in Corsica and educated at French military schools, began his astoundingly successful military career as a very young man. Involved in the Revolution, he was imprisoned but managed to avoid the bloodletting of ROBESPIERRE's Reign of Terror. While serving the DIRECTORY, his victory in northern Italy during the campaign against Austria raised him to the position of national hero. His following campaign, in Egypt, was thwarted by the English victory of NELSON and the loss of the French fleet in the battle of the NILE. Returning to Paris at the time of a collapse in the government, Napoleon launched the coup d'état of 18 Brumaire (November 9, 1799) that set him firmly upon the path of destiny.

Now first consul, he was elected consul for life in 1802. Napoleon's coronation as emperor of France took place on December 2, 1804. The empire had been carved out of a series of military and political victories, but the Napoleonic dreams of glory and grandeur included the founding of a dynasty. In 1796 the Little Corporal had married Joséphine BEAUHARNAIS, but Napoleon divorced his wife, the first empress, when it became clear that she could not provide him with an heir, and he married Marie Louise, archduchess of Austria (1810). As emperor, Napoleon enacted various important internal reforms in the economy and the legal system, but it was the victories of the empire under the Old Guard, consisting of Marshal NEY, Davout,

Murat, and others, that made Napoleon a living legend and maintained his reign. The history of Europe during these years is the history of Napoleon's conquests, a chronicle of the gradual spread of his power throughout continental Europe.

Napoleon had captured the age, both in fact and in spirit, but there remained limits to even his sovereignty. After Nelson's second crushing defeat of the French fleet at Trafalgar, Napoleon was obliged to abandon any plans for the invasion of England. Furthermore, the English under WELLINGTON had landed an army on the Iberian peninsula, aiding the Spanish and the Portuguese, who were seeking to restore the Bourbon line and remove the economic weight of Napoleon's continental system, the blockade of England. Napoleon thus turned eastward, beginning the disastrous campaign on the Russian front that was to prove his undoing. At Borodino, he defeated the Russians under Kutuzov but paid a high price for his victory. Reaching Moscow, he found the city abandoned and in flames; the long retreat westward from Russia cost the Napoleonic Corps more than two-thirds of its men. Napoleon himself had returned to France to organize a new army. This force was defeated at the battle of Leipzig, which resulted in the fall of Paris to the coalition allies led by Wellington (1814). Forced to abdicate, Napoleon was banished to the island of Elba; ten months later, he escaped and returned to France in a final effort to regain power. But history's tide was no longer his to command; after the brief triumphant glory of the Hundred Days, he was crushed at the Battle of WATERLOO (June 18, 1815). His last years were spent in exile on the island of St. Helena.

A figure of great interest, not only to historians but to other writers as well, Napoleon has been the subject of an enormous amount of literature, including such works as SARDOU's *Madame Sans Gêne* and George Bernard SHAW's *Man of Destiny*.

Napoleon II (Napoleon François Charles Joseph Bonaparte, Duke of Reichstadt; 1811–1832) Son of NAPOLEON I and Marie Louise. At his birth, he was given the title of the king of Rome. Also known as *l'Aiglon* (Fr, "the Eaglet"), Napoleon was named by his father as his successor upon his abdication (1814), but he never ruled. From 1814 until his death, he lived at the court of Vienna, under the control of METTERNICH. Edmond ROSTAND made Napoleon II the hero of his drama *L'Aiglon* (1900).

Napoleon III ([Charles] Louis Napoleon [Bonaparte], 1808–1873) Emperor of France (1852–71). The third son of Louis Bonaparte, king of Holland, and Hortense Beauharnais, thus nephew of Napoleon I, Louis Napoleon was born in Paris but spent the early years of his career in exile (1815–30). Returning to France, he favored the Revolution of 1848. Elected to the National Assembly, he became president of the Republic in 1848. Louis Napoleon soon began to pursue his absolutist policies; suppressing the Republicans, he became dictator by coup d'état (1851). In

1852 he proclaimed himself Napoleon III. This period in French history is known as the Second Empire. EUGÉNIE Marie de Montijo de Guzmán became the bride of the emperor on January 29, 1853. Napoleon's plans for a Roman Catholic French empire in Mexico resulted in the disastrous MAXIMILIAN Affair (1863–67). This was followed by the FRANCO-PRUSSIAN WAR (1870–71). During the war, Napoleon III was captured at Sedan and held prisoner for the duration. In 1871 he was deposed by the National Assembly. Retiring to England with his wife and family, he spent the remainder of his life there.

Nara The first Japanese historical period (710–794) and the city that was its capital at that time. It is notable for the flowering of Buddhist art and learning and for the introduction of Chinese culture to Japan. Japan's earliest recorded histories, *Kojiki* (712) and *Nihongi* (720) are products of this age, as is the first anthology of ancient poetry, the MAN' YŌSHŪ.

Naraka The hell of Hindu mythology. By different accounts, it has various numbers of divisions, usually twenty-eight, each with its own name and with a punishment appropriate to the offense committed by those consigned to it. In Hindu conception, this is not an eternal hell, only a temporary one, where one pays for misdeeds before being reincarnated on a higher or lower level, according to one's KARMA.

Narasimha In Hindu mythology, an AVATAR of VISHNU, depicted as half man, half lion.

Narayan, R[asipuram] K[rishnaswami] (1906–) Indian novelist, writing in English. Through a succession of novels, Narayan has created an imaginary community, Malgudi, peopled by perceptively drawn characters whose very ordinariness provides fertile ground for Narayan's gentle humor. His early works, including *Swami and Friends* (1935), *The Bachelor of Arts* (1937), and *Mr. Sampath* (1949), were highly praised by Graham GREENE, who helped to establish Narayan's reputation in the West. *The Financial Expert* (1952) was his first novel to be published in the U.S. Subsequent novels include *The Man-Eater of Malgudi* (1961), *The Painter of Signs* (1976), and *A Tiger for Malgudi* (1983), a deceptively simple tale about the capture of a free-roaming tiger; the novel is ultimately an allegory of life, encompassing the complexities of Hinduism. *My Days* (1974) is a volume of memoirs. In 1978 he published a shortened modern prose version of the MAHĀBHĀRATA. *Under the Banyan Tree and Other Stories* appeared in 1985.

Narayana See VISHNU.

Narcisse parle (Narcissus Speaks) The title of two poems by Paul VALÉRY. First a sonnet (1890), then a longer monologue (1891), the idea was entirely rewritten to become *Fragments du Narcisse* (1922) and finally appeared as the libretto *Cantate du Narcisse* (1938). Narcissus, in love with his own reflection in the water, symbolizes the self seeking its own perfect image. The image, however, is shattered into fleeing ripples when Narcissus tries to kiss it.

Narcissus In Greek mythology, a beautiful youth. Narcissus was beloved by the nymph ECHO. When he repulsed her, caring for no woman's love, she caused him to fall in love with his own reflection in a pool. He pined away, longing for this image, and was changed into the flower that bears his name. The psychological term *narcissism*, describing a neurotic obsession with one's own person, is derived from this story.

Narrative of A. Gordon Pym, The (1838) A novella by Edgar Allan POE. A New England boy stows away on a whaler, surviving mutiny, savagery, cannibalism, and wild pursuit. At the end of the story, the hero drifts toward the South Pole in a canoe; before him, out of the mist, rises a great white figure. There is some confusion in detail, because Poe, serializing the story, often did not pick up the loose ends. Based on the factual travels of J. N. Reynolds, whose book Poe had reviewed, the tale deals with situations later to intrigue Melville.

Nash, Ogden [Frederick] (1902–1971) American writer of light verse. Nash is known for sophisticated whimsy and satire, marked by his adept use of the pun and distorted rhyme, and the inimitable cleverness of his FREE VERSE style. The foibles and pretensions of East Coast intellectuals and aristocrats were a favorite target. Most of his verse was first published in THE NEW YORKER, where he held an editorial post; Nash did much to establish that magazine's characteristic tone. His many collections of verse include *Free Wheeling* (1931), *Everyone but Thee and Me* (1962), *An Ogden Nash Bonanza* (5 vols, 1964), and *Bed Riddance* (1970).

Nashe, Thomas (1567–1601) English satirist and dramatist. A graduate of Cambridge and one of the UNIVERSITY WITS, Nashe was a brilliant and original writer and an outstanding personality of his time. His first published piece was the preface to the *Menaphon* of Robert GREENE (1589), in which he attacked pompous contemporary writers; he continued his assessment of contemporary literature in *An Anatomie of Absurdities* (1589). The Martin MARPRELATE CONTROVERSY gave him a further opportunity to exercise his lively wit under the pseudonym of "Pasquil"; later he entered a bitter controversy with Richard and Gabriel Harvey. This feud was brought to an end by ecclesiastical order in 1599.

Also among Nashe's writings is *The Unfortunate Traveller, or the Life of Jack Wilton* (1594). A prose romance of adventure, it is a precursor of the English novel and is notable for its detailed, journalistic style. Some critics consider it to be one of the finest examples of prose fiction of the period.

Only one of Nashe's plays has survived, a satirical masque called *Summer's Last Will and Testament* (1593). He may have collaborated with Christopher Marlowe on *Dido, Queen of Carthage* (c1593) and prepared the unfinished play for the stage after Marlowe's death, though the authorship of this play is now in doubt. He worked with Ben Jonson on *The Isle of Dogs* (1597, not extant), a comedy that resulted in Jonson's imprisonment for a time for having attacked the state.

Nast, Thomas (1840–1902)   German-born American cartoonist and illustrator. Nast's first political cartoon appeared soon after he joined the staff of *Harper's Weekly* in 1862. With his gift for devastating caricature, he chastized Andrew Johnson and supported Grant in two presidential campaigns. The greatest battle of his career, however, was his attack against Boss TWEED.

Always conservative and usually Republican, he came out strongly against race prejudice, while he attacked the income tax, inflation, and the reduction of the armed forces. He is credited with having been the first to use the donkey as a symbol for the Democratic Party and the elephant for the Republicans.

Nathan, George Jean (1882–1958)   American drama critic and editor. Nathan devoted most of his energies to the interpretation of the theatre; he was noted for his wit, cynicism, sophistication, and erudition. Nathan and H. L. MENCKEN, two scornful commentators, worked together on the *Smart Set* and later on THE AMERICAN MERCURY.

Nathan the Wise (Nathan der Weise, 1779)   A drama by Gotthold Ephraim LESSING. It is set in Jerusalem during the Crusades. The title character is a Jewish trader who has come to look upon all religions as forms of one great truth. A Christian knight falls in love with Nathan's adopted daughter Recha, and the development of this situation involves the Sultan Saladin, a Muslim, so that all three faiths are brought into close contact. In the end, it is discovered that the knight and Recha are actually brother and sister and that both are the children of Saladin's brother. The blood relationship among these three characters symbolizes the essential unity of the three religions.

National Institute of Arts and Letters   See AMERICAN ACADEMY OF ARTS AND LETTERS.

National Velvet (1935)   A novel by Enid BAGNOLD. The heroine of the book, a young girl called Velvet, is jockey of the winning horse in the Grand National, the famous English steeplechase. It was made into a successful movie in 1944.

Native Son (1940)   A novel by Richard WRIGHT. It is the story of a black youth, Bigger Thomas, the product of a Chicago slum, whom society victimizes because of his race. He commits two murders, is defended in court by a Communist lawyer, and is condemned to death. Wright's first novel, it stresses the sensational, but it is also highly forceful, moving, and skillful. It is based partly on Wright's own experiences and partly on the case of Robert Nixon, a Chicago black, who was electrocuted in 1938 for murder.

Natsume Sōseki (1867–1916)   Japanese novelist. A scholar in English literature, Natsume Sōseki was deeply concerned with moral problems resulting from Japan's Westernization, which he presented in his novels from a modern intellectual's viewpoint. The Westernization theme is most obvious in *Kusa makura* (1906; tr *The Three-Cornered World*, 1965). *Wagahai wa neko de aru* (1905; tr *I Am a Cat*, 1961) and *Botchan* (1906; tr 1972) treat the theme in a satirical vein, while later novels like *Kokoro* (1914; tr 1941) and *Michikusa* (1915; tr *Grass on the Wayside*, 1969) are more somber in tone, as they focus on the problem of egoism in modern individualistic society.

Natural, The   See MALAMUD, BERNARD.

naturalism   A movement in fiction begun in France in the latter half of the 19th century. Revolting against the subjectivism and imaginative escapism that seemed to characterize the romantic school, the naturalist writers were influenced by the biological theories of DARWIN and the social and economic determinism of TAINE and MARX. The new movement sought to depict human society and the lives of the men and women who compose it as objectively and truthfully as the subject matter of science is handled. STENDHAL, BALZAC, and FLAUBERT were forerunners of the movement; the GONCOURT brothers, MAUPASSANT, DAUDET, and, above all, ZOLA formulated the principles and engaged in the practices of naturalism. In technique, their work was marked by an objective, detached method of narration, meticulous accuracy of detail, and scholarly care in the documentation of historical background. Its subjects were drawn from the lower strata of society, and no detail of their sordid, unhappy lives was spared. Emphasis was placed on the social environment of the characters and on the totally subordinate relation of the individual human being to it. In the naturalistic novel, there is a pervading sense of the control exerted over the actions and destinies of the characters by impersonal social, economic, and biological forces. Human free will is shown as weak and almost completely ineffectual. Despite similarity of method, however, there was a difference in the aims of the naturalist writers. The Goncourt brothers engaged in a cold analysis of social misery, while Flaubert justified his minutely descriptive method on aesthetic grounds. Zola employed both his technique and his subject matter in the service of his passionate zeal for social reform.

In England, the novels of George GISSING, Thomas HARDY, and Samuel BUTLER show affinities with naturalist writings; Somerset Maugham's LIZA OF LAMBETH is in the tradition of Zola.

Naturalism in America, which appeared just before the turn of the 20th century, was to some extent an outgrowth of REALISM and was largely influenced by the spread of the theories of evolution, historical determinism, and mechanistic philosophy. The earliest naturalistic novel was Stephen Crane's MAGGIE: A GIRL OF THE STREETS, but Crane did not continue to work in this vein. Frank NORRIS and Jack LONDON, whose early naturalistic novels were the first to follow Crane's, became perhaps more famous as exponents of naturalism than as artists in their own right. Theodore DREISER is also considered a naturalist, as is James T. FARRELL in a later generation. The PROLETARIAN LITERATURE of the 1930s was in some ways an outgrowth of naturalism, though the similarities between the two are largely due to their common emphasis on the lower class.

Naturalism in German literature was a short-lived but important movement of about 1882–91. The most important documents from its early phase are the *Kritische Waffengänge* (*Critical Passages-at-Arms*, 1882–84) by the brothers Hart, a critical periodical; *Moderne Dichtercharaktere* (*Modern Figures in Poetry*, 1884), an anthology of verse edited by Hermann Conradi; and *Revolution der Literatur* (*Revolution of Literature*, 1886), a collection of essays by Karl Bleibtreu. In all these works, however, what the authors wanted was not *realism* and *objectivity* in style so much as simple *naturalness*, in opposition to what they saw as the classicistic posturing of such authors as HEYSE and Emanuel Geibel. They wanted genuine, heartfelt sentiment and expression in literature—which they found in LILIENCRON's poetry, for example—and they preferred genuine romantics to affected realists. In addition, they felt that German authors should concentrate on timely German subject matter; it was for this reason that they liked such writers as Anzengruber and Wildenbruch, while entirely rejecting the exotic "professorial novels" of DAHN and Ebers.

It was not until the later phase of the movement, with the early plays of Gerhart HAUPTMANN and the works on which HOLZ and Schlaf collaborated, that German naturalism tended toward an emphasis on exact and detailed realism. The basic elements of the dramatic technique of late naturalism may be summarized as follows: (1) emphasis on simple family situations rather than on heroism or historic events; (2) the complete avoidance of didacticism or artificiality in dialogue, and the use of dialect where appropriate; (3) the avoidance of monologues and asides; and (4) the avoidance, as much as possible, of obvious plot contrivance. Holz, in his *Die Kunst, ihr Wesen und ihre Gesetze* (*Art, Its Essence and Its Laws*, 1891), gives a theoretical justification for such realistic techniques.

Naturalism in Germany was quickly superseded, and, even in the works of such men as SUDERMANN, HALBE, and Max Kretzer, there are strong nonnaturalistic tendencies. But the naturalistic emphasis on genuineness of expression and respect for the unique individual experience as such strongly influenced IMPRESSIONISM and EXPRESSIONISM.

natural school   A Russian literary movement, particularly strong in the 1840s, which originated with the critic Vissarion BELINSKY. The school held that the task of literature was to give a truthful representation of reality, with the aim of criticizing society by depicting its true nature.

Nature (1836)   An essay by Ralph Waldo EMERSON. It is the best expression of the Transcendentalist philosophy. Emerson sees Nature as Commodity in its practical functions, as Beauty in the delight it arouses, and as Discipline in the education it gives the Reason and Understanding. The essay treats man's relationship with nature and its values. Behind every natural fact, the Transcendentalist finds a spiritual truth.

Nausea (La Nausée, 1938; tr 1965)   A novel by Jean-Paul SARTRE, also translated (1948) as *The Diary of Antoine Roquentin*. The historian Roquentin records the process of his "nausea," a violent feeling of disgust inspired by the overwhelming fact that things and people cannot help existing, and yet there is "absolutely no reason for existing." Rejecting concepts of a cosmic purpose or of human progress as illusions, he is horrified by the absurdity of human life and the ugliness of its pretenses. Anny, his former mistress, who returns to him, confesses similarly that she no longer experiences "perfect moments," which she used to feel when the opportunity offered by a "privileged situation" had been harmoniously completed. When she leaves him again, Roquentin discovers that, because there is no more reason to live, he is free—despite the deathlike loneliness of this freedom. He concludes that the only possible escape from the oppressiveness of the accident of existence is through the act of creation, and he contemplates writing a book so beautiful that he can accept himself.

Nausicaa   In Homer's ODYSSEY, the daughter of Alcinous, king of the Phaeacians. Nausicaa conducts ODYSSEUS to the court of her father when he is shipwrecked on the coast. Homer's portrait of this young lady is refreshingly human and believable.

Nazareth   The village in lower Galilee, Palestine (now north Israel), where JESUS lived as a boy and young man.

Nazarite (fr Heb, *nazar*, "to separate")   One who has made a vow to the Lord of separation and abstinence. Nazarites in the OLD TESTAMENT refrained from intoxicating liquor, from the use of a razor, and from contact with dead bodies. JOHN THE BAPTIST was a Nazarite, as were SAMSON and SAMUEL.

Nebuchadnezzar   The greatest king of Assyria. Nebuchadnezzar's reign lasted forty-three years (604–561 BC). He restored his country to its former prosperity and importance, practically rebuilt Babylon, restored the temple of BEL (Baal), erected a new palace, embanked the Euphrates, and was probably the ruler who built the celebrated Hanging Gardens. In the OLD TESTAMENT narrative, he besieges Jerusalem, is victorious, and carries the Jews away captive into Babylon. His name became the center of many legends. The story related in DANIEL (4:29–33), that he was one day walking in the palace of the kingdom of Babylon and said, "Is not this great Babylon that I have built . . . by the might of my power, and for the honor of my majesty?" and "the same hour . . . he was driven from men, and did eat grass as oxen, and his body was wet with the dew of heaven, till his hairs were grown like eagles' feathers, and his nails like birds' claws," is probably an allusion to the suspension of his interest in public affairs, which lasted, as his inscription records, for four years. Nebuchadnezzar was the king who, according to the account in Daniel, put the three Hebrews SHADRACH, Meshach, and Abednego into the fiery furnace.

Necessary Angel, The (1951)   A collection of essays on poetry by Wallace STEVENS. The major theme of the essays is the relation of the imagination—"the necessary angel"—to reality, and the way it invests reality with meaning.

Nechayev, Sergey Genadyevich (1847–1882) Russian revolutionary. Noted for his unscrupulous and audacious escapades, Nechayev provided the basis for the characterization of Pyotr VERKHOVENSKY in DOSTOYEVSKY's novel THE POSSESSED. It was Nechayev's manner of operation, however, rather than his actual achievements, that made him a legend in Russian revolutionary history. He allowed nothing to stand in the way of his revolutionary schemes. Friend and enemy alike were used as instruments to further his plans. The organizations and large numbers of followers that Nechayev claimed to lead were largely products of his imagination. For a short time, he managed to win the favor of the eminent revolutionary Mikhail BAKUNIN, but his unprincipled behavior eventually alienated the anarchist leader.

Necker, Jacques (1732–1804)   Swiss-born French banker and statesman. Necker succeeded Turgot (1727–81) as minister of finance in 1776. His *Account Rendered*, which dispelled any illusions about the economic equilibrium of the monarchy, brought about his dismissal in 1781. He resumed office in 1788–89 and again in 1789–90. He was the husband of Suzanne Necker, the famous literary hostess, and father of Mme de STAËL.

nectar   The drink of the gods of classical mythology. Like their food, AMBROSIA, it conferred immortality.

négritude   An attitude and aesthetic maintained by certain 20th-century French-speaking African authors, which upholds traditional African culture and values. The concept originated in reaction to the stereotyping of black Africans by European colonials, and it implies a total acceptance of pride in black heritage. The term was coined by Aimé CÉSAIRE and popularized by C. S. SENGHOR and Léon DAMAS.

Nehemiah   A Jewish patriot who, under the Persian king Artaxerxes, was appointed governor of Judea and was sent to help rebuild Jerusalem (c444 BC); also the OLD TESTAMENT book that bears his name. Usually considered in conjunction with the book of EZRA, Nehemiah contains an account of the rebuilding of the walls of Jerusalem after the Babylonian captivity, the reading of the law of MOSES by Ezra, the public confession of sin, the dedication of the walls, and the reforms instituted by Nehemiah and Ezra.

Nehru, Jawaharlal (1889–1964)   English-educated Indian political leader. Nehru joined GANDHI's movement and later became second only to Gandhi as a nationalist leader. He served as prime minister in the interim government and continued as prime minister from independence (1947) until his death. His best-known writings are his autobiographical books, *Toward Freedom* (1941) and *The Discovery of India* (1945), both written in prison.

Nekhlyudov, Prince   See RESURRECTION.

Nekrasov, Nikolay Alekseyevich (1821–1878) Russian poet and editor. Nekrasov was a prominent figure in the radical wing of literature during the middle of the 19th century. His first collection of poems appeared in 1840, but they received no special attention. His first literary success was as an editor. In 1846 he edited and published the popular *Peterburgsky sbornik* (*Petersburg Anthology*), which contained DOSTOYEVSKY's first novel, POOR FOLK. From 1847 to 1866, Nekrasov edited *Sovremennik* (*The Contemporary*), in which appeared the early works of TOLSTOY, GONCHAROV, and TURGENEV. *The Contemporary* was suppressed for political reasons, and in 1868 Nekrasov became editor of *Otechestvennye zapiski* (*Fatherland Notes*), which he made as popular and influential as *The Contemporary* had been.

Nekrasov's poetry typically shows concern with social rather than literary values, a concern that was characteristic of the literature of the period, especially among liberal writers. His verse tends to popular more than to literary usages of language and often contains elements based on or taken from folklore. His best-known poems are *Korobeiniki* (*The Pedlars*, 1861), *Moroz-Krasny Nos* (*Frost the Red-nosed*, 1863), and *Komu na Rusi zhit khorosho* (*Who Lives Well in Russia*, 1863–77).

Nekrasov, Viktor Platonovich (1911–   ) Soviet novelist and short-story writer. Nekrasov fought at Stalingrad during World War II; in 1946 he published *V okopakh Stalingrada* (1946; tr *Front-Line Stalingrad*, 1962), a novel based on his experiences there. His later work includes the novel *V rodnom gorode* (*In My Home Town*, 1954), set in Kiev after World War II. He has also written a series of travel sketches, *Po obe storony okeana* (1962; tr *Both Sides of the Ocean*, 1964), whose favorable comments on life in the U.S. drew Khrushchev's personal condemnation, and *Po obe storony steny* (1985).

Nelson, Horatio (Viscount Nelson, 1758–1805) English naval hero who, although he was victorious at the battle of Trafalgar (1805), was fatally wounded. Nelson's liaison with Emma, Lady HAMILTON was the subject of numerous books and plays. See NILE, BATTLE OF THE.

Nemerov, Howard (1920–   )   American poet, novelist, and short-story writer. Nemerov's poetry, which has a considerable range of style, has been collected in *The Image and the Law* (1947), *Mirrors and Windows* (1958),

The Winter Lightning (1968), *The Western Approaches: Poems 1973–1975* (1975), and *Inside the Onion* (1985). His *Collected Poems* (1977) won the PULITZER PRIZE and the National Book Award. The directness, wittiness, and apparent simplicity of much of his work conceals the complexity and power of his attempts to see into "the terror of each man's thought." His novels—including *The Melodramatists* (1949), *Federigo* (1954), and *The Homecoming Game* (1957)—treat moral dilemmas in an ironic and sometimes satirical way. Nemerov produced serious criticism in the highly respected *Poetry and Fiction* (1963), *Reflections on Poetry and Poetics* (1972), *Figures of Thought* (1978), and *New & Selected Essays* (1985).

Nemesis   The classical Greek personification of righteous anger. Nemesis exacts retribution from all who violate the natural order of things, whether by breaking a moral law, through an excess of riches or happiness, or through mortal arrogance (see HUBRIS). HESIOD calls her the daughter of Night. Other legends say she is the daughter of OCEANUS or of Dike (Justice). Her principal sanctuary was at Rhamnus in Attica, where there was a statue of her, said to have been carved by PHIDIAS from marble the Persians had brought to Marathon as the material for their trophy, presumptuously counting on victory in advance.

Nemo, Captain   The hero of TWENTY THOUSAND LEAGUES UNDER THE SEA by Jules Verne.

Nennius (c800)   An early medieval Welsh historian. Nennius is important in connection with the origins of Arthurian literature. He specifically mentions an Arthur, crediting him with a part in twelve victories over invading Anglo-Saxons and with killing 960 by himself. See ARTHURIAN LEGEND.

neoclassical period   See AGE OF REASON, THE.

neoclassicism   The revival or adaptation of classical taste and style. In English and French literature, the term is especially used to describe the spirit underlying much of the work of the 17th and early 18th centuries. RACINE, VOLTAIRE, ADDISON, SWIFT, and POPE are typically neoclassical in their approach to art. Their connection with the classical past is exemplified by their emphasis on traditionally classic values, such as sense of form, balance, discipline, dominance of reason, restraint, unity of design and aim, clarity, proportion, and a view that art should be focused on man.

neoimpressionism   A French artistic movement. Founded, about 1886, upon the recently formulated optical and color theories of such scientists as Edouard Root and Michel Eugène Chevreul, neoimpressionism sought to create a scientific method for the empirical division of tone used by the impressionists (see IMPRESSIONISM). The neoimpressionists carried the technique of division to its inherent extreme in their use of pointillism, which consisted of juxtaposing tiny dots of pure color upon a white canvas, thus allowing the eye alone to unite the strokes and create the impression of tone. Pointillism is best embodied in the work of Georges SEURAT. Paul Signac (1863–1935) was the leading spokesman of neoimpressionism.

neoplasticism   See STIJL, DE.

Neoplatonism   A 19th-century term to describe the philosophy of PLOTINUS, developed during the 3rd century. The last great Greek philosophic synthesis, it was influenced by PLATO in its division between sensible and intelligible and by ARISTOTLE in its equation of Being with intelligence. The basic impulse of Neoplatonism is man's return to God through reason. It asserts three levels of reality: that of non-Being, Nature, vegetative existence, sensible things; that of Being, Intellect (*Nous*), Plato's Ideas; and, finally, the level of Beyond Being, the One, the Good. It is with this last and, for Neoplatonists, most real level that union is to be achieved. The fundamental concept is unity. The philosophy is based on the assumption that there is Truth. One must awake from the sleep of this world into superconsciousness. This highest level of awareness is incommunicable by the intellect; it is an upward journey of the soul. These ideas were found highly congenial by the developing Christian philosophy. The relationship to St. AUGUSTINE has been indicated. There is evidence of the influence of Neoplatonism in the early German Idealism of HEGEL and BERGSON.

Neoptolemus (or Pyrrhus)   A son of ACHILLES. He was called Pyrrhus from his yellow hair and Neoptolemus because he was a new soldier, i.e., one who came late to the siege of Troy. According to VERGIL, it was this youth who slew the aged PRIAM. He married HERMIONE, daughter of HELEN and MENELAUS. On his return home, he was murdered by ORESTES at Delphi. He is an important and sympathetic figure in Sophocles' PHILOCTETES. See ANDROMACHE.

Neorealism   See NEW WAVE.

neorealist cinema   An Italian film movement that was in vogue from the early 1940s to the early 1950s. Neorealism was a reaction on the part of some film directors, scriptwriters, and cameramen against the artificiality of pre-World War II and Fascist cinema. The term was first used in a critical appraisal of Luchino VISCONTI's film *Obsession* (1942). Along with Visconti, such other directors as Roberto ROSSELLINI and Vittorio DE SICA strove to create a film art of authenticity that dealt with the physical, psychological, and social reality of humanity. Feeling that reality could better be conveyed through created situations than through the direct recording of actual events, they employed a synthesis of documentary and studio techniques, merging actual situations with a scripted story line. The essentials of neorealist films were the use of nonprofessional actors, authentic settings, naturalistic lighting, simple direction, and natural dialogue.

NEP   See NEW ECONOMIC POLICY.

Nepenthe (fr Gr, *ne*, "not," *penthos*, "grief")   An Egyptian drug mentioned in the ODYSSEY (iv. 228). Nepenthe was fabled to drive away care and make persons forget their woes. Polydamna, wife of Thonis, king of Egypt, gave it to HELEN, daughter of ZEUS and LEDA. Poe mentions it in THE RAVEN: "Quaff, oh quaff this kind Nepenthe and forget the lost Lenore."

Nephthys   An Egyptian goddess, sister and wife of SET. Both Nephthys and Set are associated with the ritual of the dead.

Neptune   The Roman god of the sea. Originally a water god of little importance, Neptune became an important deity through identification with the Greek POSEIDON, especially after Rome became a significant maritime power. The god was represented as an elderly man of stately bearing, bearded, carrying a trident, and sometimes riding a dolphin or a horse.

Nereids   The sea nymphs of Greek mythology. The Nereids were the fifty daughters of Nereus and gray-eyed Doris. The best known are Amphitrite, THETIS, and GALATEA.

Nero   (original name Lucius Domitius Ahenobarbus, AD 37–68)   Emperor of Rome (54–68). When he was adopted by CLAUDIUS, he took the name Caius Claudius Nero. At first acclaimed by all as a liberal and sober leader, the young emperor lost little time in correcting this impression. To please his mistress POPPAEA, he had his wife, Octavia, murdered, and, when Poppaea was pregnant, he killed mother and child by kicking her to death. He amused himself with playing the harp and taking part in athletics in the Circus, and he was always able to coerce a large attendance at both performances. In the summer of AD 64, a great fire destroyed a sizable portion of the city. The story that the mad emperor lit the fire "to see how Troy looked when it was in flames" and that he occupied himself musically "while Rome burned" is now generally held to be a legend. He did, however, blame the Christians for the fire and persecuted them cruelly for several years.

After the fire, Nero rebuilt Rome and erected for himself the Domus Aurea palace. In the meantime, conspiracies had been forming. One of them, PISO'S CONSPIRACY, involved the poet LUCAN and the philosopher SENECA, and both men were ordered to commit suicide. This they did, and their stoic deaths further incensed the populace against the emperor. In 68, after Nero returned from a concert tour of Greece, the armies installed Galba as emperor, declared Nero an enemy of the state, and would have executed him had he not first taken his own life. He is a prominent character in SIENKIEWICZ's novel QUO VADIS? See AGRIPPINA; BRITANNICUS.

Neruda, Jan   (1834–1891)   Czech poet, prose writer, journalist, and critic. Neruda was the most important representative of "the May school," which dominated Czech literature in the 1860s and 1870s. The group took its name from the title of MÁCHA's poem, thereby expressing its desire to break away from the narrow provincialism and nationalism of the preceding period; it emphasized general

human themes and sought connections with the contemporary developments in the European literatures.

Neruda grew up in a colorful part of old Prague called Malá Strana ("Little Quarter"); he lived as a bachelor and traveled widely in Europe and the Near East, recording his acute observations of foreign cultures in numerous *feuilletons*. He participated in all the cultural and political struggles of his generation and, as a sensitive critic, followed the rapid rise of contemporary Czech literature, theatre, and fine arts.

The atmosphere of Neruda's childhood and youth is captured in his most popular prose work, a collection of short stories, *Povídky malostranské* (1878; tr *Tales of the Little Quarter*, 1957), a major work of Czech realism. His six collections of poems, beginning with the early *Hřbitovní kvítí* (Cemetery Flowers, 1858) and *Knihy veršů* (Books of Verses, 1867), represent the highest achievement of premodernist Czech poetry; *Písně kosmické* (Cosmic Songs, 1878) contains reflexive poetry inspired by modern science; in *Prosté motivy* (Simple Motifs, 1883), Neruda created an intimate poetic diary; *Balady a romance* (Ballads and Romances, 1883) is a collection of epic poems with political and social themes; the posthumous *Zpěvy páteční* (Friday Songs, 1896) transposes patriotic themes into universal humanistic visions. With Neruda, Czech poetry acquired a truly modern poetic language, based on contemporary spoken Czech.

Neruda, Pablo   (pen name of Ricardo Neftalí Reyes, 1904–1973)   Chilean poet. After the appearance of *Veinte poemas de amor y una canción desesperada* (1924; tr *Twenty Love Poems and a Song of Despair*, 1969) had established Neruda as one of Chile's most promising poets, the Chilean government appointed him to various consular posts in Europe and Asia. In 1934 he was assigned to Madrid, where he mingled with Spanish writers, such as Manuel Altolaguirre, with whom he founded (1935) a literary review called *Caballo verde para la poesía*. In the same year, Neruda published a translation of William BLAKE's "The Visions of the Daughters of Albion" and "The Mental Traveller." His outspoken sympathy for the Loyalist cause during the Spanish Civil War led to his recall in 1937, but he soon returned to Europe to help settle republican refugees in America. From 1939 to 1943, he was Chilean consul in Mexico. Upon returning to Chile, Neruda became active in politics, was elected to the senate, and joined the Communist party. When the party was declared illegal in Chile, Neruda was expelled from the senate. After spending several years in exile, he returned to Chile in 1953.

Neruda's earliest poetry—*La canción de la fiesta* (1921), *Crepusculario* (1923), and *Veinte poemas* (1924)—is reminiscent of MODERNISMO in form and tone. In the poems of his next period, particularly in *Residencia en la tierra* (tr *Residence on Earth*, 1973), which appeared in two parts in 1932 and 1935, he gives full play to his intuition and experience. Written in an often surrealistic style, these poems depict an anguish-ridden world of chaos, desolation, and decay. The poet's experience in the Spanish Civil War and the impact of World War II turned him in new directions. In *Tercera residencia* (1947) and in such works as *Canto general de Chile* (1943), *Odas elementales* (1954), and *Estravagario* (1959; tr *Extravagaria*, 1972), Neruda—now a militant communist—became the people's poet and a polemicist. Though there is considerable debate over the merits of Neruda's later work, he is widely regarded as the greatest Spanish-American poet since DARÍO. Much of his poetry appears in translation in *The Selected Poems of Pablo Neruda* (1970).

He was awarded the NOBEL PRIZE in Literature in 1971. Stricken with cancer, which forced him to withdraw from the diplomatic position he had received under President Allende, he was living in Chile and suffered a fatal heart attack just twelve days after the successful right-wing coup in 1973. In his last days, between Allende's death and his own, Neruda completed his *Confieso que he vivido* (*Memoirs*, 1974), which appeared in translation in 1977.

Nervo, Amado Ruiz de (1870–1919)   Mexican poet. As a young man, Nervo studied for the priesthood, an experience reflected in the mysticism that characterizes much of his work. When he was forced to leave the seminary for financial reasons, he turned to journalism and became cofounder of the *Revista moderna*, an influential modernist review. From 1905 to 1918, he held a diplomatic post in Madrid and, at his death, was Mexican minister to Argentina and Uruguay.

Nervo's early works, such as *Perlas negras* (1898), *Poemas* (1901), and *Jardines interiores* (1905), place him in the mainstream of MODERNISMO. Subsequently, however, his poetry became more subjective and revealing, and such works as *Serenidad* (1914) and *Elevación* (1917) express the asceticism and tranquillity of his later years.

Nessus   In Greek mythology, the centaur responsible for the death of HERACLES. Heracles had ordered Nessus to carry his wife Deianira across a river; when the centaur attempted to carry her off, Heracles shot him. In revenge, Nessus gave Deianira his bloody tunic, telling her that it would preserve her husband's life. Later, when Heracles was unfaithful to her, she gave it to him as a present. The centaur's blood, together with the HYDRA's poison with which Heracles' arrow had been smeared, clung to his body, setting his flesh afire. The pain was so great that he immolated himself. Deianira hanged herself from remorse.

Nest of the Gentlefolk, A (Dvoryanskoye gnezdo, 1859)   A novel by Ivan TURGENEV. It tells the story of the tragic love affair between the hero, Fyodor Ivanovich Lavretsky, and Liza Kalitina. Lavretsky is about to marry Liza, when his first wife, whom he has believed dead, returns to him. Liza goes into a convent, and Lavretsky is left to his bleak duty. The novel, which poetically evokes the peaceful atmosphere of the provincial Russian feudal estate, had a great success on its publication.

Nestor   The oldest and wisest of the Greek generals who fought at Troy. The son of Neleus and king of Pylos, in the western Peloponnesus, Nestor was accustomed to offering sage advice at considerable length on every occasion. Robert GRAVES has ironically pointed out that Nestor's counsel, though highly respected, generally turned out to have disastrous consequences. Heinrich SCHLIEMANN, the famous amateur archeologist, thought that he had discovered Nestor's cup, described in detail in the ILIAD. Recent excavations on the site of Pylos prove that it was indeed a highly important center in Mycenaean times. Nestor appears in Shakespeare's TROILUS AND CRESSIDA.

Nestorians   Followers of Nestorius (d c AD 451), patriarch of Constantinople. Nestorius held the heretical view that Christ had two distinct natures and that MARY was the mother of His human nature, which was the mere shell or husk of the divine.

Nestroy, Johann (1801–1862)   Austrian playwright and actor. Nestroy is best known for his humorous satires, such as *Der böse Geist des Lumpacivagabundus oder Das liederliche Kleeblatt* (*The Evil Spirit of Lumpacivagabundus or The Dissolute Cloverleaf*, 1835). He also wrote parodies of such authors as Hebbel and Richard Wagner.

Nets to Catch the Wind (1921)   A book of poems by Elinor WYLIE. The first collection of her poetry to bear her name, it contained some of her most characteristic verse. Many of the poems are in the metaphysical vein, the title being taken from the 17th-century drama *The Devil's Law Case*, by John WEBSTER. "Velvet Shoes" and "The Eagle and the Mole," two of the author's best-known poems, were first printed in this volume.

Nevelson, Louise (1900–   )   Russian-born American painter. Nevelson's first works were terra-cotta portraits, but in the 1950s she began making the assemblages of found objects for which she is best known. These were contained in shallow boxes, spray-painted in black, white, or gold, and were ultimately stacked to form walls and even whole rooms, resulting in what were probably the first "environmental sculptures." In the late 1960s, she began using Plexiglas and sheet metal instead of found materials, adding the new dimension of light reflection and refraction to her work.

Never-Never-Land   See PETER PAN.

Neveu de Rameau, Le (Rameau's Nephew, 1891)   A satirical character sketch by Denis DIDEROT, written (1762) in the form of a dialogue between Diderot and Rameau, the nephew of the French composer Jean Philippe Rameau. In the most vivacious style, Diderot gives a character sketch of the nephew of the celebrated musician; Rameau is a lazy, original, hare-brained, sensual, utterly frank social parasite, whose gifts for pantomime, conversation, monologue, and music serve Diderot well in his biting satire on contemporary society and the artists who either pleased or displeased him.

Nevins, Allan (1890–1971)   American historian. A prolific writer and careful researcher, Nevins covered a wide range of historical topics but is best known for his PULITZER PRIZE-winning political biographies: *Grover Cleveland* (1932) and *Hamilton Fish: The Inner History of the Grant Administration* (2 vols, 1936), and his exhaustive study of the Civil War, published in the four volumes of *The War for the Union* (1959–73).

New Apocalypse   A short-lived romantic, surrealist movement in English poetry. It was formed by J. F. Hendry (1912–   ), G. S. FRASER, and Henry TREECE in 1939, in reaction to the socially committed poetry of W. H. AUDEN and others, which dominated the 1930s. The movement advocated a return to myth, eschewing all social, political, or literary doctrines, and published three anthologies: *The New Apocalypse* (1939), *The White Horseman* (1941), and *The Crown and the Sickle* (1944). George BARKER and Dylan THOMAS were among the few who wrote the kind of poetry the movement envisioned.

New Atlantis, The (1627)   A Utopian fable by Francis BACON, published in an unfinished state after his death. It is an account of a voyage to the island of "Bensalem" and of the government and manners of its people. Of particular interest is the Bensalem institution for scientific study, "Solomon's House," which provided inspiration for the founding of the Royal Society.

Newbery, John (1713–1767)   English publisher of newspapers and one of the first publishers of children's books. The Newbery Medal, established by Frederic Melcher, has been awarded annually since 1921 for the best children's book written by an American.

Newbolt, Sir Henry [John] (1862–1938) English poet. Newbolt wrote hearty, patriotic poems, such as "Drake's Drum" and "The Fighting Téméraire." He also wrote on naval history and was appointed official Naval Historian in 1923.

Newby, P[ercy] H[oward] (1918–   )   English novelist and short-story writer. Newby's novels tend to be farces, dealing with the meeting of two cultures. Among them are *The Picnic at Sakkara* (1955), *The Barbary Light* (1962), and *A Lot to Ask* (1973). *Saladin in His Time*, a biography of the sultan of Egypt and Syria in the 12th century, appeared in 1983.

New Comedy   See COMEDY.

Newcomes, The (1855)   A novel by William Makepeace THACKERAY. The plot is loose and complex, dealing with three generations of Newcomes. The lovable Colonel Thomas Newcome is a man of simple, unworldly tastes and the utmost honor. The colonel's son, Clive, an artist, is in love with his cousin Ethel Newcome, who, however, is urged by her brother to consider a more ambitious marriage. Clive, despairing of winning Ethel, marries Rosey Mackenzie, with whom he finds he is mismated. In

the course of time, however, Rosey dies, and Clive finally marries Ethel.

New Criticism   A movement in 20th-century American literary criticism. Although the term was first used by Joel SPINGARN in an address at Columbia University in 1910, it did not receive wide currency until John Crowe RANSOM used it as the title of a book on critical methods in 1941. The New Critics were united in their emphasis on dealing with the text directly; they insisted that a work of art be considered as an autonomous whole, without regard to biographical, cultural, or social speculations. Beyond this point, the New Critics differed widely: Kenneth BURKE emphasized literature as symbolic action; Yvor WINTERS was concerned with the moral aspects of form and style; R. P. BLACKMUR investigated the larger meanings of language; Cleanth BROOKS dealt with the ambiguity of poetic statement.

The New Criticism was derived in part from the critical writings of T. S. ELIOT and Ezra POUND and was closely related to a comparable movement in English literary analysis spearheaded by the CAMBRIDGE CRITICS. It tended to accept Eliot's definition of the English tradition in poetry, with its emphasis on the 17th century. With John Crowe Ransom at its center, the movement was also closely associated with THE FUGITIVES at Vanderbilt and was given further impetus in such periodicals as THE SOUTHERN REVIEW, THE SEWANEE REVIEW, and THE KENYON REVIEW.

Later, Yale University attracted several of the New Critics to its faculty. Although the movement was rejected in many quarters as being too limited, it left its mark on contemporary criticism: careful scrutiny of the text became an accepted approach, even by those embracing other critical methods.

New Deal   A name applied to the program of recovery and reform initiated by President Franklin D. ROOSEVELT in 1933, who first used the phrase in a speech to the Democratic convention on July 2, 1932, when he said, "I pledge you, I pledge myself, to a new deal for the American people."

The New Deal is generally divided into two phases. The first, lasting from 1933 to 1935, aimed at alleviating the economic hardships caused by the Depression following the stock-market crash of 1929. During the Congressional session known as the Hundred Days (March 9 to June 16, 1933), legislation was enacted to regulate banks and currency (Emergency Banking Relief Act), to curtail unemployment (Civil Conservation Corps Reforestation Relief Act), and to raise farm prices (Agricultural Adjustment Act); the Tennessee Valley Authority was created, to improve social and economic conditions in a seven-state area; and the National Industrial Recovery Act, which was declared unconstitutional in 1935, was passed to stimulate industry and lessen unemployment.

Roosevelt's message to Congress on January 4, 1935, in which he asked for social reform legislation, is regarded as the opening of the second phase of the New Deal (1935–39). This period saw the creation of the Works Progress Administration (1935), to relieve unemployment, and the enactment of the National Labor Relations Act (1935), which guaranteed unions the right to bargain collectively. Other legislation included a Social Security Act (1935), to provide unemployment compensation and old-age and survivors insurance, and the Fair Labor Standards Act (1938), establishing a minimum wage and a maximum work week.

Newdigate, Sir Roger (1719–1806)　English antiquarian and founder of the Newdigate Prize at Oxford for English poetry.

New Economic Policy (NEP)　A period of temporary return to capitalist trade and activity in the Soviet Union during the early 1920s. The policy was designed to help restore the war-damaged economy of the country. The period was one of disillusionment on the part of many Communists and of rife opportunism and chicanery in economic life. The atmosphere of the time is well rendered in Leonid Leonov's novel THE THIEF.

new economics　See KEYNES, JOHN MAYNARD.

New England Primer, The　A textbook used in early New England to teach children the alphabet and the rudiments of reading. The earliest extant edition is dated 1727, and millions of copies were sold as late as the 19th century. The author of the primer is unknown, but the pocket-sized book was similar to contemporary English volumes. Included in the 1749 edition were an alphabet with verses and illustrations, rules for behavior, several hymns, the prayer "Now I Lay Me Down to Sleep," and pious stories of several martyrs.

New Grub Street (1891)　A novel by George GISSING. It deals in grimly realistic fashion with the struggles and compromises of the modern literary world. The hero is Edwin Reardon, a novelist whose valiant attempts to maintain the standards of his art in the face of financial pressure are opposed by an unsympathetic wife. In sharp contrast to Reardon is his friend Jasper Milvain, a critic, whose cleverness and lack of moral or artistic integrity ultimately bring him great success.

new humanism　A movement in early 20th-century American literature and philosophy that upheld classical restraint and conservative values in an attempt to create new moral standards for judging art and literature. It was a reaction against what was regarded as the too narrowly scientific approaches of contemporary philosophy and psychology and especially against the excesses of NATURALISM, which, it was felt, overemphasized the animalistic qualities in man. The new humanism was at the height of its influence between 1920 and 1930.

new journalism　See MAILER, NORMAN; WOLFE, TOM.

Newlove, John (1938–　)　Canadian poet. The poetry in Newlove's earlier volumes—*Grave Sirs* (1962), *Moving in Alone* (1965; repr 1977), *Notebook Pages* (1965),

What They Say (1967)—depicts an alienated sensibility traumatized by a predatory environment. In *Lies* (1972) and *The Fat Man* (1977), the poet's focus shifts from intense self-scrutiny to a search for the truth about Canada's history and present dilemmas. Convinced that traditional poetic devices hinder authentic expression, Newlove uses direct statement, visual precision, and irony. Other works include *Dreams Surround Us* (1977) and *The Green Plain* (1981).

New Machiavelli, The (1911)　A novel by H. G. WELLS. Full of the author's ideas on politics and citizenship, it is almost a handbook of English political life on the eve of World War I.

Newman, Christopher　See AMERICAN, THE.

Newman, John Henry Cardinal (1801–1890) English churchman and author, famous as the leader of the OXFORD MOVEMENT. Newman took an outstanding part in the theological controversies involved in the movement and in 1845, after resigning the position that he held as Protestant vicar of St. Mary's, was converted to the Roman Catholic Church. In 1846 he was ordained a priest and in 1879 was made a cardinal. Throughout his career, he continued to engage in bitter controversies, especially with the Protestant clergyman and novelist Charles KINGSLEY and with the Catholic Cardinal Manning. His most famous work, *Apologia pro vita sua* (1864), a history of his intellectual development and conversion to Catholicism, was written to refute charges made against him by Kingsley. See DREAM OF GERONTIUS, A; TRACTS FOR THE TIMES.

New Masses　See MASSES, THE.

new novel　See NOUVEAU ROMAN.

Newsome, Chad　See AMBASSADORS, THE.

New Testament　The second part of the Christian BIBLE. It tells of the embodiment of God's covenant with man in the coming of JESUS Christ. The twenty-seven short books contain the four Gospels narrating the life of Jesus, the early history of the Church, letters by Church fathers to various congregations that have become cornerstones of Christian ethics, and the apocalyptic REVELATION OF SAINT JOHN THE DIVINE.

Newton, Sir Isaac (1642–1727)　English mathematician and natural philosopher. One of the greatest geniuses the world has known, Newton made three scientific discoveries of fundamental importance: first, the method of fluxions, which forms the basis of modern calculus; second, the law of the composition of light; and third, the law of universal gravitation, which he presented to the world in his major work, PRINCIPIA. Among his other works are *Method of Fluxions* (1693), *Optics* (1704), and *Chronology of Ancient Kingdoms Amended* (1728). The story that Newton's hypothesis on gravity was inspired by the fall of an apple was first told by Voltaire, who claimed to have heard it from the scientist's niece.

New Wave (Nouvelle Vague)　A literary and cinematic movement, originating in a cross-influence of the novel and film in France, beginning in the late 1950s. See NEW WAVE CINEMA; NOUVEAU ROMAN.

New Wave cinema   A loosely constituted group of French filmmakers who, after writing film criticism and devising the AUTEUR THEORY, began to produce their first feature films in the years 1958–60. Many of the New Wave directors had been associated with the prestigious film journal *Cahiers du cinéma*. Claude Chabrol's *Le Beau Serge* (1959) was followed in quick succession by Jean-Luc GODARD's *Breathless* (1959), François TRUFFAUT's *400 Blows* (1959), Eric ROHMER's *The Sign of Leo* (1959), Alain RESNAIS's *Hiroshima, mon amour* (1960), and Louis MALLE's *Zazie dans le métro* (1960). Each of these films marked a highly personal, spontaneous departure from the carefully scripted studio films that had preceded them. Holding to their own critical principles, these directors produced lively, partly improvised films, and each maintained complete command over the entire creative process, functioning as *auteurs*. Their effect was widespread, but, by the 1960s, their individual talents had developed in such different directions that they had only their origins in common.

New Way to Pay Old Debts, A (c1625)   A comedy by Philip MASSINGER. The avaricious Sir Giles Overreach, in order to obtain more money, has confiscated the property of his nephew Frank Wellborn and is planning to have his daughter Margaret marry the wealthy Lord Lovell against her wishes. Margaret, however, loves Tom, the stepson of Lady Allworth, who offers to aid the lovers. Lady Allworth pretends to be in love with Frank, who, on the basis of this splendid match, obtains money from his uncle. Margaret elopes with Tom, Lord Lovell marries Lady Allworth, and Sir Giles, from rage and despair, loses his mind.

New Yorker, The   An American weekly magazine, founded in 1925 by Harold ROSS. It specializes in short fiction, cartoons, verse, reviews, and sophisticated and literate commentary. Although avowedly "not for the old lady in Dubuque," it is widely read throughout the U.S. Leading contributors in the Ross days included James THURBER, E. B. WHITE, Robert BENCHLEY, Ogden NASH, John O'HARA, Dorothy PARKER, S. J. PERELMAN, J. D. SALINGER, Rebecca WEST, and Edmund WILSON. In 1951, after the death of Ross, William Shawn became the magazine's editor. Its tone and format remained the same, but its editorial involvement in public affairs increased, and it began to carry complete books of exceptional literary, artistic, or topical interest, usually in several installments. In 1987 Robert Gottlieb succeeded Shawn as editor.

New York Realists   See ASHCAN SCHOOL.

New York School   A group of poets living and writing in New York City during the late 1950s and early 1960s. Although their works are dissimilar in style, they share specific affinities: geographical setting, cosmopolitanism of spirit, and the influence of action painting, French SURREALISM, and European avant-gardism in general. In

1970 Ron Padgett (1942–   ) and David Shapiro (1947–   ) edited and published *An Anthology of New York Poets*. Its contributors included John ASHBERY, Frank O'HARA, Kenneth KOCH, James SCHUYLER, and Ted Berrigan.

The New York School originated at Harvard University, where Koch, O'Hara, and Ashbery met as students. Upon settling in New York, they became affiliated with painters, some of whom were engaged in action painting. Indeed, the free shapes of their poems partly derive from their familiarity with the techniques of Jackson POLLOCK, Willem DE KOONING, and Larry RIVERS. O'Hara, Ashbery, and Schuyler were on the staff of *Art News*, to which they contributed pieces on aesthetic relatedness between poetry and the pictorial arts. What all these poets shared was an absurdist or hallucinatory view of reality expressed in a style marked by disquieting, cryptic statements. Probably the most original and technically daring practitioners were O'Hara and Ashbery. O'Hara's poems of city life present a landscape of modernity that is brittle, dazzling, and mordantly witty. Ashbery's poems convert the ordinary into a self-conscious dream discourse that assembles images from contexts ranging from comics to Transcendentalism. The New York poets represented a shift away from the then popular CONFESSIONAL POETS, whose soul-baring they found distasteful.

For the group of painters also called the New York School, see ABSTRACT EXPRESSIONISM.

Nexö, Martin Andersen (1869–1954)   Danish proletarian novelist and short-story writer. Born in the slums of Copenhagen, Nexö worked as a herd boy and a shoemaker's apprentice. He developed a warm sympathy for the poor and a faith in the innate goodness of man. His convictions led him to practical action, first as a Social Democrat and later as a member of the Communist Party. *Pelle Erobreren* (1906–10; tr *Pelle the Conqueror: 1913–1916*, 1930) was the first of his novel series dealing with the struggles of the working classes. Its subject is the Danish labor movement and its hero, Pelle, is a trade union leader. In English, the work was divided into four parts: *Boyhood, Apprenticeship, The Great Struggle*, and *Daybreak*. *Ditte Menneskebarn* (5 vols, 1917–21; tr *Ditte: Girl Alive!*, 1920; *Ditte, Daughter of Man*, 1922; *Ditte: Towards the Stars*, 1923), his other great novel cycle, related the story of a poor servant girl.

Ney, Michel, Duc d'Elchingen, Prince de la Moskova (1769–1815)   French marshal and Napoleonic military commander. Although made a peer by Louis XVIII, Ney supported Napoleon after his return from Elba and commanded the Old Guard at WATERLOO. After the HUNDRED DAYS, he was condemned and shot for treason (December 7, 1815).

Nezhdanov   See VIRGIN SOIL.

Nezval, Vítězslav (1900–1958)   Czech poet, novelist, playwright, essayist, and translator. Nezval was the central figure of the interwar Czech avant-garde, promoting its aesthetic ideals in his literary work and in numerous theoretical essays and manifestos. His best-known work is the surrealist cycle *Básně noci* (*Poems of the Night*, 1930).

Ngugi wa Thiong'o (also called James Ngugi, 1938–   )   Kenyan novelist, dramatist, and essayist. Ngugi's first published novel, WEEP NOT, CHILD, introduced a tone of bitter disillusionment and fear that was to dominate his subsequent work. *The River Between* (1965) is a tragic story of young lovers separated and eventually destroyed by the fierce religious antagonism between their families. His third novel, A GRAIN OF WHEAT, dramatizes Kenya's struggle for independence during the Mau-Mau uprising. It was followed by *Petals of Blood* (1977) and *Devil on the Cross* (1982), both satirical and bitter indictments of the betrayal of Kenya by her postindependence leaders. Ngugi's stinging attacks on the government resulted in his imprisonment for nearly a year in 1978–79. He was the first of Kenya's intellectuals to be detained by the postindependence government.

Nibelungenlied, The   A Middle High German epic poem in four-line stanzas. It was probably written about 1190 or 1200, but the author and the exact original version are unknown. Although based on Scandinavian legends as told in the poetic EDDA and the VÖLSUNGA SAGA, it draws further on German legend and omits much of the supernatural material; Siegfried, for instance, is no longer a descendant of the Scandinavian god ODIN but rather the son of the king of the Netherlands and a typical hero of medieval romance.

Siegfried sets out for Worms to woo the famous beauty Kriemhild. Her three brothers, Burgundian kings, learn from their retainer Hagen that Siegfried is the hero who killed the Nibelung kings and took their name, their treasure of gold, and their cape of darkness, which makes the wearer invisible. Hagen also explains that Siegfried's skin is almost entirely invulnerable, for, except for a spot covered by a fallen leaf, it became horny when he bathed in the blood of a dragon he had slain.

Siegfried helps the three brothers fight the Saxons, then agrees to help one of them, Gunther, in courting Queen Brunhild of Iceland, on the condition of his own marriage to Kriemhild. Brunhild has vowed that she will marry the man who can best her at hurling a spear, throwing a stone, and jumping. Siegfried in his magic cape stands beside Gunther and invisibly accomplishes the difficult feats for him, so the double marriage is celebrated. But Brunhild is still suspicious about Gunther's strength, and, on their wedding night, she ties him in a knot and hangs him on the wall. He appeals to Siegfried, who, again invisible, wrestles her into pleased submissiveness and takes her girdle and ring, which he gives to Kriemhild. Then one day the two queens argue fiercely before the cathedral, and Kriemhild proves with the girdle and ring that Brunhild had been duped in accepting Gunther.

At this point, Brunhild's role, so important in the *Völsunga Saga*, becomes vague, and that of the retainer Hagen becomes dominant. Presumably jealous for Gunther's sake of Siegfried's glory, Hagen tricks Kriemhild into revealing Siegfried's one vulnerable spot. Hagen arranges a great hunt, during which he murders Siegfried. He seizes the treasure hoard, which had been Kriemhild's wedding gift from Siegfried, and sinks it in the Rhine, in collaboration with her brothers. The grieving widow broods on her wrongs, and when Etzel (Attila, king of the Huns) proposes marriage, she accepts, on condition that he aid her plans for vengeance. After the wedding, they invite her brothers for a visit, then attack them with the help of the heroes Hildebrand and Dietrich of Bern. When Hagen, the last living Burgundian, refuses to tell where the treasure is, Kriemhild kills him. At this point, horrified at the carnage caused by one woman, Hildebrand turns against her and kills her, leaving Etzel and Dietrich to lament the dead.

Wagner drew partly on this material for his opera DER RING DES NIBELUNGEN.

Nicene Creed   The creed formulated by the COUNCIL OF NICAEA (AD 325), on the basis of older wordings, which asserts the divinity of JESUS and contains a pronouncement of faith in the TRINITY. The Creed was specially designed to combat the heresy of ARIUS. The addition of the *Filioque* clause, which asserts that the Holy Ghost proceeds from the Son as well as the Father and which was recognized by the Council of Toledo in 589, touched off the Filioque controversy, the chief doctrinal cause of the schism between the Eastern Orthodox and Roman Catholic churches.

Nichiren   A Japanese Buddhist sect founded by the priest Nichiren (1222–82). It bases its teachings on the LOTUS SUTRA and claims that Japan is the true center of Buddhism and that the Lotus Sutra is the ultimate teaching of the historical BUDDHA. Noted for the fanaticism of its priests and adherents, it gained great strength during the KAMAKURA period. After World War II, a splinter group called Sōka Gakkai, reviving Nichiren's teachings, claimed over a million members. The Sōka Gakkai founded a political party, the Komeito ("Clean Government Party"), which has been largely concerned with domestic issues, particularly efforts to eradicate corruption from the political process.

Nicholas, St.   One of the most popular saints in Christendom, especially in the East. Nicholas was the patron saint of Russia, of Aberdeen, of parish clerks, of scholars (who used to be called clerks), of pawnbrokers (because of the three gold balls that he gave to the daughters of a poor man to save them from earning their dowers in a disreputable way), and of little boys (because he once restored to life three little boys who had been cut up and pickled in a salting tub to serve for bacon). He is invoked by sailors (because he allayed a storm during a voyage to the

Holy Land) and against fire. Finally, he is the original of SANTA CLAUS.

Little is known of the historical St. Nicholas, but he is said to have been bishop of Myra (Lycia) in the early 4th century. One story relates that he was present at the Council of Nicaea (325) and there buffeted Arius on the jaw. His day is December 6, and he is represented in episcopal robes with three purses of gold balls, or three small boys, in allusion to one of the above legends.

Nicholas I (Nikolay Pavlovich, 1796–1855) Tsar of Russia (1825–55). Nicholas's reign is noted for its extremely conservative, reactionary character, which was perhaps in part a direct result of the DECEMBRIST REVOLT, which occurred upon his accession to the throne. Two events that made Nicholas tighten his grip on the country even more were the Polish uprising of 1830–31 and the 1848 revolutions in Europe. The Tsar's determination to keep insurrection out of his country extended even to his personal censorship of the work of Aleksandr PUSHKIN. The closing years of Nicholas's reign were darkened by the debacle of the CRIMEAN WAR (1854–56), which clearly showed the corruption and inefficiency of the Tsarist government.

Nicholas II (Nikolay Aleksandrovich, 1868–1918) Tsar of Russia (1894–1917). Nicholas II's reign, filled with misfortunes and blunders, ended in the abolition of the monarchy and the revolution of 1917. The Tsar was not strong enough to deal with the social and political upheaval in his country, even if anything could have been done about it at such a late stage.

Even before World War I, the influence at court of such sinister characters as the monk Rasputin had made the supporters of the monarchy uneasy. The "Bloody Sunday" massacre in January 1905 also contributed to the revolutionary mood of the people. On this occasion, a large procession of workers, on their way to the Winter Palace to place their petitions before the Tsar, were fired upon by troops, and hundreds were killed and wounded. A general strike was called throughout the country, and the government all but toppled. Only the granting of the Constitution of 1905 and the promise of liberal reforms stopped the 1905 revolutionary movement from succeeding. During this period, the government also had the problem of the Russo-Japanese War (1904–5), with the destruction of the Russian fleet at Tsushima in May 1905 stirring general discontent.

The next and final test of the regime started in 1914, with Russia's entry into World War I. Defeats on the battlefield, combined with confusion and mismanagement at home, finally brought about Nicholas's abdication in March 1917. This was the first step in the Russian revolution, which culminated in October 1917, with the seizure of power by the Bolsheviks, who killed the Tsar and his family in July 1918.

Nicholas Nickleby (1838–1839) A novel by Charles DICKENS. When Nicholas's father dies, leaving

him penniless, his uncle Ralph Nickleby refuses to help him. Having his mother and his sister Kate to support, Nicholas sets about to make a living. He first serves as usher to Mr. Wackford SQUEERS, schoolmaster at Dotheboys Hall; the brutality of Squeers and his wife, especially toward a poor, half-witted boy named Smike, causes Nicholas to leave in disgust. Smike runs away from school to follow Nicholas, remaining his follower until he dies. Next Nicholas joins the theatrical company of Mr. Crummles, and finally he secures a good post in a counting house owned by the benevolent CHEERYBLE BROTHERS. In the meantime, Kate Nickleby has been working for Madame Mantalini, a milliner. Ralph Nickleby tries to lure her from her innocence by encouraging his friend Sir Mulberry Hawk to make unseemly advances toward her. He is foiled in this, and also in his plan to force Madeline Bray to marry his friend Gride, by Nicholas, who saves his sister from Mulberry Hawk and himself falls in love with Madeline Bray. Ralph tries to retaliate by injuring Nicholas through Smike, who finally dies. Ralph's final blow, the discovery that Smike was his son, causes him to commit suicide. Nicholas marries Madeline, and Kate marries the Cheerybles' nephew Frank.

This novel attacks schools and schoolmasters in much the same way that OLIVER TWIST attacks the workhouses. Dickens's ruthless exposure, through Dotheboys Hall, of actual conditions in many schools in England, where the pupils were half starved and taught nothing, led to the closing or reformation of many such institutions. See INFANT PHENOMENON, THE; NOGGS, NEWMAN.

Nichols, Anne See ABIE'S IRISH ROSE.

Nichols, Peter (1927–) English dramatist. Nichols deals, by way of black comedy, with the painful situations that boil up under the surface of family life. A Day in the Death of Joe Egg (1967) confronts on the stage the hitherto-taboo subject of what raising a severely spastic child can do to a marriage. Nichols next turned to The National Health (1969), a sweet-sour view of hospital life. In Forget-Me-Not Lane (1971), a middle-aged man looks back at his childhood, to see why his marriages have gone bad, and finds himself becoming his parents. Among Nichols's other works are The Freeway (1974), Born in the Garden (1979), Passion Play (1981), and Poppy (1982). Feeling You're Behind: An Autobiography appeared in 1984.

Nicodemus In the NEW TESTAMENT, a Pharisee and member of the Sanhedrin, the chief judicial council of the Jews from the 3rd century BC to AD 70, who came to visit JESUS by night (John 3:1–14). Jesus told Nicodemus that he must be "born again" to "see the kingdom of God." He was later rebuked by the Pharisees for suggesting that they should hear Jesus before judging Him (John 7:50–53). After the Crucifixion, he brought myrrh and aloes and helped JOSEPH OF ARIMATHEA with the burial of Jesus.

Nicol, Abioseh (pen name of Dr. Davidson Nicol, 1924–) Sierra Leonean poet, short-story writer, and essayist. Nicol had a distinguished career in medicine and as a university administrator before he was appointed his country's ambassador to the United Nations. His poems and short stories are published in such volumes as *The Truly Married Woman* (1965), *Two African Tales* (1965), and *West African Verse* (1967). Much of his writing reveals an interest in religious matters and in magic; his poems are lyrical celebrations of the African landscape.

Nicole, Pierre (1625–1695)   French theologian. An ardent Jansenist and a solitary resident at Port-Royal, Nicole defended JANSENISM against its enemies in a series of letters much in the manner of the *Lettres provinciales* of Pascal.

Nicolson, Sir Harold (1886–1968)   English critic, historian, diplomat, and journalist. Nicolson held diplomatic posts for the British Foreign Service from 1909 to 1929. He then retired and took up work as a journalist, later serving in the House of Commons (1935–45). He made his reputation as a critic and a biographer with the sympathetic studies *Paul Verlaine* (1921), *Tennyson* (1923), *Byron: The Last Journey* (1924), and *Swinburne* (1926). His books on diplomacy and public policy include *Curzon: The Last Phase* (1934), *Diplomacy* (1939), *The Evolution of Diplomatic Method* (1954), *The Age of Reason* (1960), and *Kings, Courts, and Monarchy* (1962). His son Nigel Nicolson edited his *Diaries and Letters* (1966–68) and wrote a memoir about Nicolson's marriage to Vita SACKVILLE-WEST in *Portrait of a Marriage* (1973).

Niebuhr, Reinhold (1892–1971)   American theologian. After thirteen years as pastor of the Bethel Evangelical Church in Detroit, during which he took an active interest in labor problems, Niebuhr joined the faculty at the Union Theological Seminary in New York, where he taught from 1928 to 1960. Allied with the socialist movement in the 1930s, Niebuhr dealt with questions of political morality and with the failure of Christianity to confront social problems in *Moral Man and Immoral Society* (1932). *The Children of Light and the Children of Darkness* (1944) contains his attack on the moral irresponsibility of those who fail to come to grips with the problem of power. Following World War II, Niebuhr's earlier radicalism was replaced by what he called "conservative realism"; but, in *Christian Realism and Political Problems* (1953), he maintained that the church was actively sanctioning social ills by refusing to confront them. He persistently emphasized the reality of sin and its bearing on the tragedy of man and saw the modern world as one to which power and technocracy have brought confusion and meaninglessness. Among his many books are *Beyond Tragedy: Essays on the Christian Interpretation of History* (1937), *Essays in Applied Christianity* (1959), and *A Nation So Conceived* (1963), an analysis of the American character. *Justice and Mercy* (1974; ed Ursula Niebuhr) is a posthumous collection of his sermons and addresses. Always invigorating, usually

controversial, Niebuhr was one of the most influential thinkers of his day.

Nietzsche, Friedrich (1844–1900)   German philosopher, classical scholar, and poet. Nietzsche is most famous for the theory of the ÜBERMENSCH ("superman"), which he developed in THUS SPAKE ZARATHUSTRA. As early as his *Unzeitgemäße Betrachtungen* (*Untimely Observations*, 1873–76), he had sharply criticized the systematic philosophy of the earlier 19th century, especially that of HEGEL; throughout his career, he continually sought to penetrate beyond all rational, systematic schemes to the irrational, human level beneath, as in his well-known BEYOND GOOD AND EVIL. His complete rejection of Christianity was based on the belief that Christianity leads man's thoughts away from this world and into the next, thus making him less capable of coping with earthly life; he said that Christianity teaches men how to die but not how to live. In his early career, especially in THE BIRTH OF TRAGEDY, his views were influenced by SCHOPENHAUER. His own lyrics strongly influenced the poetry of expressionism. Other well-known works are *Menschliches, Allzumenschliches* (*Human, All Too Human*, 1878), *Der Antichrist* (1888), and *Ecce Homo* (1888). In 1889 he went insane and remained so until he died.

Niflheim   In Norse mythology, the land of endless cold, darkness, and mists, the lowest region of the underworld. In contrast to VALHALLA, the abode of fallen warriors, Niflheim received all those who died of disease or old age. It was ruled by HEL. One of the roots of the sacred ash tree, YGGDRASILL, reached down from the world of men into Niflheim. In its center was the spring Hvergelmir, from which flowed ten rivers.

Nigger Heaven (1926)   A novel by Carl VAN VECHTEN. One of the first novels about black life in Harlem, the book takes its title from a slang term for the topmost gallery where blacks were required to sit in theatres. Set in the jazz era, the novel is filled with melodramatic episodes and ends with a murder, of which the hero is falsely accused. It is noteworthy as a true and understanding exploration of the black's suffering and aspirations, the more remarkable in that it was written by a white.

Nigger of the Narcissus, The (1897)   A novel by Joseph CONRAD. Less a narrative than a study of men's characters under stress, the story is centered on a black sailor, James Wait, who is dying of tuberculosis. The brooding presence of death brings out the best and the worst in the crew of the *Narcissus*. In this tense atmosphere, Donkin, a mean-spirited agitator, almost manages to stir the crew to mutiny.

Night before Christmas, The   See VISIT FROM ST. NICHOLAS, A.

Night Flight (Vol de nuit, 1931; tr 1932)   A novel by Antoine de SAINT-EXUPÉRY, reflecting the author's ideals of individual moral strength and devotion to duty. The hero, Rivière, director of an airline in South America, must impose harsh discipline on his pilots to raise them above self-centered concerns and to instill in them a will to challenge and overcome the dangers of their profession.

Nightingale, Florence (1820–1910) English nurse and hospital reformer, known as the Lady with the Lamp. Early interested in nursing, Nightingale inspected schools and hospitals throughout England and in Europe, and spent several months (1849–50) at a Roman Catholic hospital at Alexandria, Egypt. She trained (1850–51) as a nurse at the Institute of Protestant Deaconesses at Kaiserwerth, studied further in Paris, and in 1853 returned to London to take charge of a woman's hospital. At the news of the suffering of the wounded in the Crimean War, she volunteered her services and, at the head of a group of thirty-eight nurses, set up a hospital at Scutari in November 1854, soon after the battle of Balaklava. Here she set up stringent observance of sanitation, and by 1855 the death rate from cholera, typhus, and dysentery had fallen from about 50 percent to about 2 percent. She worked tirelessly and ceaselessly, making her nightly rounds with lamp in hand and performing administrative duties as well as nursing. After the war, with funds donated as a testimonial to her services, she founded (1860) the Nightingale home at St. Thomas's Hospital for the training of nurses, and thereafter, for thirty years, she worked to establish nursing schools in England. She was no longer able to participate actively in nursing, since her own health had been ruined during her war service. In 1907 she became the first woman to receive the Order of Merit.

nightingale For the classical legend, see PHILOMELA. There is a passage in T. S. Eliot's *The Waste Land* that confounds the nightingale with the nightjar:

> . . . yet there the nightingale
> Filled all the desert with inviolable voice
> And still she cried, and still the world pursues,
> "Jug Jug" to dirty ears.

This is unfair. No nightingale ever cried "Jug Jug." The goatsucker does; *nightjar*, not *nightingale*, is another name for the goatsucker.

Nightmare Abbey (1818) A novel by Thomas Love PEACOCK. In this book, Peacock satirizes the leading figures and concepts of romanticism in England in his day. Among the characters, Mr. Flosky is considered to represent Coleridge, Scythrop Glowry is understood to be Shelley, and the extravagant Mr. Cypress is a caricature of Lord Byron.

Night of the Iguana, The See WILLIAMS, TENNESSEE.

Night over Taos (1932) A regional drama by Maxwell ANDERSON. It deals with a clash between American frontiersmen and the Mexican patriarchate of Taos in 1847.

Night Thoughts on Life, Death and Immortality (1742–1746) A poem by Edward YOUNG, written in nine books in blank verse. Although its full title reads *The Complaint; or, Night-Thoughts on Life, Death and Immortality*, the poem is commonly referred to simply as *Night Thoughts*. It is the most specifically theological of the major works of the age. It contains the reflections of the poet late at night on "life, death and immortality," a long soliloquy urging an erring youth, Lorenzo, to turn to virtue, and a vision of the Judgment Day and eternity thereafter, with a description of the magnificence of the starry heavens. The poem contains many autobiographical allusions: Young refers to the successive deaths of his wife, his stepdaughter, and her husband. The characteristic theme in the poem, aside from its sentimental and orthodox elements, is upward progress through endless gradations of being:

> Nature revolves, but man advances; both
> Eternal; that a circle, this a line.

It is one of the outstanding examples of the melancholy "graveyard school" in 18th-century English literature.

Nihilism (fr Lat, *nihil*, "nothing") An extreme form of 19th-century revolutionism, indignantly disclaimed by Karl MARX, which took form in Russia in the 1850s and was particularly active in the 1870s and later, under BAKUNIN. It aimed at anarchy and the complete overthrow of the state, law, order, and all institutions, with the idea of reforming the world *de novo*. The code of the Nihilists was (1) annihilate the idea of God, or there can be no freedom; (2) annihilate the idea of right, which is only might; (3) annihilate civilization, property, marriage, morality, and justice; (4) let your own happiness be your only law. The name was given to them by TURGENEV, in his novel FATHERS AND SONS. Dostoyevsky portrays Nihilism in THE POSSESSED and THE BROTHERS KARAMAZOV.

Nile, battle of the A naval engagement fought in Abukir Bay, near Alexandria, Egypt (August 1, 1798). The British fleet under Horatio NELSON defeated the French fleet under Brueys. As a result of the victory, NAPOLEON's expedition to Egypt ended in failure, and Nelson earned for himself the epithet the Hero of the Nile.

Nimrod In the OLD TESTAMENT, the son of Cush, famous for his exploits as "mighty hunter before the Lord" (Gen. 10:9). Thus the name refers generally to any daring or outstanding hunter. Alexander POPE says of Nimrod that he was "a mighty hunter, and his prey was man" (*Windsor Forest*, 1713); so also does Milton interpret the phrase in PARADISE LOST.

Nims, John Frederick (1913–   ) American poet. Essentially a modernist poet, Nims makes use of elaborate wordplay and striking figures of speech. His verse deals primarily with aspects of modern, particularly urban, life. Among his volumes of poetry are *The Iron Pastoral* (1947), *Knowledge of the Evening: Poems 1950–1960* (1960), and *Of Flesh and Bone* (1967). He wrote *Western Wind* (1974), a book about poetry, and edited *The Poems of*

St. John of the Cross (1959; rev 1979) and the *Harper Anthology of Poetry* (1981). Among his other works are *The Kiss: A Jambalaya* (1982), *Selected Poems* (1982), and *A Local Habitation: Essays on Poetry* (1985).

Nin, Anaïs (1903–1977)   French-born American novelist and diarist. Although she had written over a dozen books, Nin was not widely known until the publication of *The Diary of Anaïs Nin 1931–1966* (7 vols, 1966–80). A record of avant-garde life in Paris and New York, with portraits of friends like Henry MILLER and Lawrence DURRELL, the diaries essentially chronicle a woman's coming to terms with her feminine identity. They served as the source of much of Nin's fiction, which shows the influences of SUR-REALISM and psychoanalysis. Her first novel, *House of Incest* (1936), is a prose poem dealing with psychological torments. The second, *Winter of Artifice* (1939), examines a daughter's relationship to her father. The series *Cities of the Interior* includes *Ladders to Fire* (1946), *Children of the Albatross* (1947), *The Four-Chambered Heart* (1950), *A Spy in the House of Love* (1954), and *Solar Barque* (1958). Both in her fiction and in her diaries, a dreamlike, sensuous prose expands personal concerns to a universal level. Nin's essays on literary theory include *Realism and Reality* (1946) and *The Novel of the Future* (1968). *The Delta of Venus* (1977) and *Little Birds* (1979) are books of erotica she wrote in the 1940s.

nine   A number regarded from the earliest times and by many peoples as having a peculiar mystical significance. Deucalion's ark, made on the advice of PROMETHEUS, was tossed about for nine days before it stranded on the top of Mount PARNASSUS. There were nine MUSES, frequently referred to merely as the Nine. There were nine Gallicenae or virgin priestesses of the ancient Gallic oracle; and Lars PORSENA swore by the nine gods.

There were nine rivers of hell; or, according to some accounts, the STYX encompassed the infernal regions in nine circles. MILTON makes the gates of hell "thrice three-fold; three folds are brass, three iron, three of adamantine rock." They have nine folds, nine plates, and nine linings.

In the early Ptolemaic system of astronomy (see PTOL-EMY), there were nine spheres; hence Milton, in his *Arcades*, speaks of the "celestial syrens' harmony that sit upon the nine enfolded spheres." In Scandinavian mythology, there were nine earths, HEL being the goddess of the ninth; there were nine worlds in NIFLHEIM, and ODIN's ring dropped eight other rings (nine rings of mystical import) every ninth night.

Nine appears many times in folklore. The ABRACADABRA was worn nine days and then flung into a river; in order to see the fairies, one is directed to put nine grains of wheat on a four-leaved clover; nine knots are made in black wool as a charm for a sprained ankle; if a servant finds nine green peas in a peasecod, she lays it on the lintel of the kitchen door, and the first man that enters in is to be her cavalier; to see nine magpies is most unlucky; a cat has nine lives;

and the nine of diamonds is known as the Curse of Scotland.

1984 (1949)   A satirical novel by George ORWELL. Set in the society of the future, toward which Orwell believed both extreme right- and left-wing totalitarianism were heading, it is the story of a middle-aged man and a young woman who rebel. In this terrifying society, there is no place for truth, for historical records are destroyed and propaganda replaces information. Thought and love are punished, while privacy is impossible. Placards everywhere say: "Big Brother is watching you." Big Brother represents Stalin, and the satire is chiefly directed against Russia.

1919 (1932)   A novel by John DOS PASSOS, the second of his trilogy *U.S.A.* (q.v.). It takes the characters introduced in THE 42ND PARALLEL, with a few additions, through World War I and presents a kaleidoscopic picture of the war years.

Like the other novels of the trilogy, *1919* uses the "newsreel" and "camera eye" techniques; it also contains brief biographical sketches of such public figures as Theodore ROOSEVELT, J. P. MORGAN, Woodrow WILSON, and the Unknown Soldier.

Ninety-five Theses   The original document of the Reformation, nailed on the door of the castle church at Wittenberg by Martin LUTHER on October 31, 1517. Essentially, it was an indictment of the venality of the Roman Catholic Church and, especially, of the common practice of selling indulgences in connection with the sacrament of penance. Luther contended that, after confession, absolution was dependent only upon the sinner's faith and divine grace, not upon the priest. At this point, Luther was not an advocate of actual separation from the church of Rome.

Nineveh   See JONAH.

Ningirsu   See NINURTA.

Ninlil   A Sumerian goddess of air, the wife of ENLIL. Following the sage advice of her old mother Nundarshegunu, Ninlil so delighted Enlil, the storm god, that he came to her in three different forms. The resulting offspring were Nergal, the king of the underworld, Ninazu, another underworld deity, and a third deity, who remains unknown.

Nintu (also called Ninhursag and Ninmah)   A Sumerian mother goddess. Possibly a later form of the ancient earth goddess KI, Nintu created human beings, molding six varieties of them from clay. To the water god ENKI, she bore Ninsar, who in turn bore him Ninkur, upon whom Enki fathered Uttu, the goddess of plants. When Enki ate the plants, he was cursed by Nintu, but he eventually persuaded her to remove the curse, in return for various gifts. See CREATION MYTHS.

Ninurta   Sumerian and Babylonian god of war, the south wind, and artificial irrigation. Ninurta is the hero of a fragmentary epic poem that tells of his successful war on the dragon Kur. Following the advice of his talking weapon

Sharur, Ninurta, a son of ENLIL, moves against Kur, a monster often associated with the underworld. At first defeated, Ninurta returns to the battle and destroys Kur completely. Kur's death, however, adversely affects the normal behavior of the waters, upon which the land depends for irrigation. Ninurta therefore guides the flood waters into the Tigris, and the fertility of the fields returns. Of the stones that were flung in his battle with Kur, Ninurta blesses those that had been on his side and curses the others. In many respects, this myth is the forerunner of innumerable others in which a hero slays a dragon. See POEM OF BAAL, THE; WAR OF THE GODS.

Ninus   Son of Belus, husband of the legendary SEMIRAMIS, and the reputed builder of Nineveh. In the Pyramus and Thisbe travesty in Shakespeare's MIDSUMMER NIGHT'S DREAM, the lovers meet at Ninus's tomb.

Niobe   In Greek mythology, the wife of AMPHION, king of Thebes. Niobe insulted the goddess LETO by boasting that she herself had produced more children. Leto's two offspring, APOLLO and ARTEMIS, avenged the affront to their mother by killing all or nearly all of Niobe's many sons and daughters. Inconsolable, Niobe went home to her native Lydia. There, at her own request, ZEUS turned her to stone on Mount Sipylus. A river of her tears forever flowed from the rock. Women who weep are occasionally likened to "Niobe, all tears."

Niord   The Scandinavian god of the sea, the protector of seafaring men. Niord ruled the winds, calmed the seas, and warded off fire. He was one of the AESIR and father, by his wife Skadhi, of FREY and FREYA. His home was Noatun, the place of ships. The name means "benefactor." See VANIR.

nirvana (Sans, "going out," as a light)   The Buddhist doctrine of release, analogous to the Hindu concept of moksha, or deliverance; meaning a positive state of bliss or a negation of existence. Among the early Buddhists, it was thought of as the extinction of all the fires of craving. As this was not only a snuffing out of all sensation but also a consummation devoutly to be wished, the later Mahāyāna Buddhists interpreted nirvana as a union with the Buddha nature following the destruction of one's KARMA.

Nixon, Richard M[ilhous] (1913–   )   American politician, lawyer, and 37th president of the United States (1969–74). Nixon graduated from law school in 1937, entered law practice in his home state of California, served in the navy during World War II, and after the war was elected to the U.S. House of Representatives and then the Senate. His reputation as an anti-Communist made him a desirable running mate for EISENHOWER in the 1952 presidential campaign, at the height of the cold war. Defeated by John F. KENNEDY in the 1960 presidential election and by Pat Brown in the California gubernatorial race, Nixon announced his retirement from politics and went to practice law in New York. During this hiatus, he published *Six Crises* (1962), an account of pivotal experiences during his political career. In 1968 he ran for president again, defeating Hubert Humphrey, and announced what came to be be known as the Nixon Doctrine, which reduced U.S. military forces abroad and used the funds to help smaller countries defend themselves; he also began withdrawing U.S. troops from Vietnam (see VIETNAM WAR). In 1972 relations with China were reopened and "détente" with the Soviet Union encouraged. The same year, Nixon defeated the Democratic challenger, George McGovern, in a landslide reelection victory and effectively ended U.S. participation in the war in Vietnam. The remainder of Nixon's second term was dominated by the WATERGATE scandal; when his own participation in the efforts to cover up the scandal became public, Nixon lost political support in his own party and in August 1974 became the first president to resign from office. He was later granted a pardon by President Gerald FORD, and he published his memoirs, *R.N.*, in 1978.

Nixon has been an object of fascination for many writers. Apart from Woodward and Bernstein's books on Watergate, *All the President's Men* (1974) and *The Final Days* (1976), views of Nixon have been expressed by very disparate writers in such works as Garry Wills's *Nixon Agonistes* (1970), Philip ROTH's *Our Gang* (1971), Theodore H. White's *The Making of the President* (1960, 1968, 1972), Robert Coover's *The Public Burning* (1977), and J. Anthony Lukas's *Nightmare* (1977).

NKVD   See CHEKA.

Nō   A form of Japanese drama. The plays deal largely with well-known historical themes and often have Buddhist overtones. The acting is highly stylized; masks, elaborate costumes, music, and a chorus are integral parts of the performance. Developed by the aristocratic and military societies of the MUROMACHI period, its greatest exponent was ZEAMI MOTOKIYO, who also formalized its aesthetic. It has long had great visual appeal to Western audiences, while YEATS and POUND acknowledged the influence of Nō in translation and in performance on their work.

Noah   A righteous man in the OLD TESTAMENT whom God chose to spare from the flood that covered the face of the earth. During the forty days and nights of the deluge, Noah lived in the ark, which he had built and where, with his own family, he had taken the animals, mostly two by two, following God's command. The ark finally came to rest on the mountains of Ararat, and Noah, with his three sons, SHEM, HAM, and JAPHETH, their families, and the various birds and animals, came out safely to repopulate the world. According to the biblical narrative, the first rainbow then appeared as God's promise to Noah that never again the world should be so destroyed (Gen. 6–9). See FLOOD MYTHS.

According to legend, Noah's wife was unwilling to go into the ark; the quarrel between the patriarch and his wife forms a prominent feature of *Noah's Flood*, in the Chester and Towneley MYSTERY PLAYS. In the KORAN, Noah's wife, known as Waila, tries to persuade the people that her husband is mad.

Noailles, Comtesse Anna de (born Princesse de Brincovan, 1876–1933)   French poet and novelist. Noailles published nine volumes of lyric and romantic poetry (1901–34), two novels, and an autobiography, *Le Livre de ma vie* (1932).

Nobel, Alfred Bernhard (1833–1896)   Swedish engineer and industrialist. Nobel amassed a great fortune from his discoveries of synthetics and explosives (especially dynamite) and their manufacture and from his interests in Baku oil fields. He was also an unsuccessful writer of novels and plays. When a newspaper accidentally printed his obituary, referring to him as a "merchant of death," Nobel realized that this was how he would be remembered. To avert this, in his will he set aside over $9 million for the establishment of the NOBEL PRIZES.

Nobel Prizes   Annual monetary awards of variable amounts (the average about $100,000) made to persons who have benefited mankind through their contributions in the fields of physics, chemistry, medicine, literature, and work for peace. They are paid out of a fund established for that purpose by the will of Alfred Bernhard NOBEL. The awards are presented in Stockholm each year, on December 10, the anniversary of Nobel's death, but they are occasionally reserved in one or more categories, especially the peace prize.

The literary awards are selected by the Swedish Academy of Literature. The recipients have been: 1901, René François Armand Sully Prudhomme (Fr); 1902, Theodor Mommsen (Ger); 1903, Björnstjerne Björnson (Norw); 1904, Frédéric Mistral (Fr) and José Echegaray (Sp); 1905, Henryk Sienkiewicz (Pol); 1906, Giosuè Carducci (Ital); 1907, Rudyard Kipling (Eng); 1908, Rudolf Eucken (Ger); 1909, Selma Lagerlöf (Sw); 1910, Paul von Heyse (Ger); 1911, Maurice Maeterlinck (Belg); 1912, Gerhart Hauptmann (Ger); 1913, Rabindranath Tagore (India); 1914, none; 1915, Romain Rolland (Fr); 1916, Verner von Heidenstam (Sw); 1917, Karl A. Gjellerup (Den) and Hendrik Pontoppidan (Den); 1918, none; 1919, Carl Spitteler (Switz); 1920, Knut Hamsun (Norw); 1921, Anatole France (Fr); 1922, Jacinto Benavente y Martínez (Sp); 1923, William Butler Yeats (Ir); 1924, Wladislaw S. Reymont (Pol); 1925, George Bernard Shaw (Eng); 1926, Grazia Deledda (Ital); 1927, Henri Bergson (Fr); 1928, Sigrid Undset (Norw); 1929, Thomas Mann (Ger); 1930, Sinclair Lewis (U.S.); 1931, Erik Axel Karlfeldt (Sw); 1932, John Galsworthy (Eng); 1933, Ivan Gasse Bunin (Russ); 1934, Luigi Pirandello (Ital); 1935, none; 1936, Eugene O'Neill (U.S.); 1937, Roger Martin du Gard (Fr); 1938, Pearl S. Buck (U.S.); 1939, Frans Eemil Sillanpää (Fin); 1940 to 1943, none; 1944, Johannes V. Jensen (Den); 1945, Gabriela Mistral (Chile); 1946, Hermann Hesse (Ger); 1947, André Gide (Fr); 1948, T. S. Eliot (Eng); 1949, William Faulkner (U.S.); 1950, Bertrand Russell

(Eng); 1951, Pär Lagerkvist (Sw); 1952, François Mauriac (Fr); 1953, Sir Winston Churchill (Eng); 1954, Ernest Hemingway (U.S.); 1955, Halldór Laxness (Icel); 1956, Juan Ramón Jiménez (P.R.); 1957, Albert Camus (Fr); 1958, Boris Pasternak (Russ, declined); 1959, Salvatore Quasimodo (Ital); 1960, Alexis Léger (Fr); 1961, Ivo Andric (Yugo); 1962, John Steinbeck (U.S.); 1963, Giorgos Seferis (Gr); 1964, Jean-Paul Sartre (Fr, declined); 1965, Mikhail Sholokhov (Russ); 1966, S. Y. Agnon (Pol-Isr) and Nelly Sachs (Ger-Sw); 1967, Miguel Angel Asturias (Guat); 1968, Yasunari Kawabata (Jap); 1969, Samuel Beckett (Ir-Fr); 1970, Aleksandr I. Solzhenitsyn (Russ); 1971, Pablo Neruda (Chile); 1972, Heinrich Böll (Ger); 1973, Patrick White (Austral); 1974, Harry Martinson (Sw) and Eyvind Johnson (Sw); 1975, Eugenio Montale (Ital); 1976, Saul Bellow (U.S.); 1977, Vicente Aleixandre (Sp); 1978, Isaac Bashevis Singer (U.S.); 1979, Odysseus Elytis (Gr); 1980, Czeslaw Milosz (Pol); 1981, Elias Canetti (Bulg); 1982, Gabriel García Márquez (Colom); 1983, William Golding (Eng); 1984, Jaroslav Seifert (Czech); 1985, Claude Simon (Fr); 1986, Wole Soyinka (Nigeria).

For author entries, see individual listings.

noble savage   The concept of a superior primitive man, uncorrupted by civilization. The first known use of the phrase occurs in DRYDEN's *Conquest of Granada* (1672), although idealized accounts of untainted savages have appeared as literary ARCHETYPES since the time of the ancient Greeks. The noble savage's supposedly simpler, purer, less inhibited emotional responses and religious life, uncomplicated by numerous conflicting dogmas or by persecution, served as subject matter for invidious comparisons between Occidental civilization and the more perfect savage cultures. Frequently the noble savage also supposedly lived under just and reasonable laws, which, when compared to European authoritarian governments, were made to seem infinitely more desirable. Literally hundreds of travel books describing such utopias were extremely popular from the 16th to 19th centuries and gave impetus to emigration from Europe to the New World. ROUSSEAU, though aware that a return to the primitive state was impractical, nevertheless used the myth of the noble savage to give substance to the anathemas he hurled against civilization. VOLTAIRE's *Ingénu* (1767) serves as an example of the convention of the noble savage. CHATEAUBRIAND's novels dealing with the American Indian, RENÉ, ATALA, and *Les Natchez*, portray the romantic, sentimentalized aspects of this myth; its influence is also to be found in the Indian novels of James Fenimore COOPER. See PRIMITIVISM.

Nod, Land of   A land referred to in the Bible. It is said that "Cain went . . . and dwelt in the Land of Nod" (Gen. 4:16). It was there that he found a wife. The phrase may mean merely "the land of wandering" rather than a definite locality.

No Exit (Huis clos, 1944; tr 1946)   A play by Jean-Paul SARTRE. The scene of the play is a drawing room into which a man and two women who have died are escorted. Unable to leave, they discover that "hell is other people." At the end, when the door is finally opened, they find they are inseparable and cannot leave.

Noggs, Newman   In Charles Dickens's NICHOLAS NICKLEBY, Ralph Nickleby's clerk. Noggs is a tall man of middle age with goggle eyes, set in a cadaverous face, and one miserable suit of clothes. This kind-hearted, dilapidated fellow "kept his hunter and hounds once" but ran through his fortune. He discovers a plot of Ralph, which he confides to the Cheeryble brothers; they frustrate it and then provide for Newman.

Nolde, Emil   (real name Emil Hansen, 1867–1956) German painter and, after 1910, a leader in the development of German EXPRESSIONISM. Nolde's expressionist paintings, with their harsh colors and masklike faces, recall the work of James Ensor. Like Ensor, he used African and Oceanic art as sources for his images. He was briefly affiliated with DIE BRÜCKE but finally opted for independence and solitude. He painted religious themes, such as his triptych *The Life of Christ* (1912), still lifes, and human subjects, such as *Teacher and Girl* (1916).

nom de plume   (Fr, "pen name")   A pseudonym, or fictitious name, used by an author.

nominalism   One of two rival doctrines in the disputes of the medieval schoolmen (see SCHOLASTICISM). It held that all abstractions, or universals, such as the general concept of a circle, of truth, of beauty, and the like, are mere names, rather than realities in themselves, and that only a particular and individual object or event has reality. Nominalism logically resulted in what was considered a heretical attitude toward the concept of the Trinity. See ABÉLARD, PIERRE; REALISM.

nones   (fr Lat, *nonus*, "ninth")   In the ancient Roman calendar, the ninth day before the IDES. In the Roman Catholic Church, Nones is the office for the ninth hour after sunrise, or 3:00 P.M.

nonsense verse   A form of LIGHT VERSE that does not make sense. It is often an entertaining poem with a strong rhythmic quality, lack of logical and consecutive development, and sometimes nonsensical neologisms. Limericks and tongue-twisters are frequently nonsense verses. The following lines from Lewis Carroll's JABBERWOCKY are an example of the form:

'Twas brillig and the slithy toves
Did gyre and gimble in the wabe;
All mimsy were the borogoves
And the mome raths outgrabe.

non-U   A term meaning "not upper-class," humorously popularized by Nancy MITFORD in *Noblesse Oblige: An Enquiry into the Identifiable Characteristics of the English Aristocracy* (1956). The term was first invented quite seriously by Professor Alan Ross in 1954 in a philosophical study that provides a set of rules for assessing an Englishman's class status by his speech habits.

Noon Wine   (1937)   A short novel by Katherine Anne PORTER. It was reprinted in the collection of three novels entitled PALE HORSE, PALE RIDER. In Porter's deceptively simple style, it tells the story of Mr. Thompson, an ineffectual farmer who kills a disagreeable stranger he imagines is attacking his eccentric but valuable hired man. Though acquitted of murder, Thompson commits suicide.

Nordhoff, Charles Bernard   (1887–1947) American writer. Nordhoff is best known for the trilogy narrating the story of the ship *Bounty*, on which he collaborated with James Norman HALL. Nordhoff drove an ambulance in France in 1916 and later joined the Lafayette Escadrille. In 1920 he went with Hall to Tahiti, where they remained for many years. See MUTINY ON THE BOUNTY.

Norns   In Scandinavian mythology, the three demigoddesses who presided over the fates of both men and gods. The three were known as Urdur, Verthandi, and Skuld, or Past, Present, and Future. Originally there was only one Norn, Urdur, but later the two others were added. They appeared at the cradle upon the birth of a child and dwelt at the root of the sacred ash, YGGDRASILL, sprinkling it from the fountain Norna to preserve it from decay. See FATES.

Norris, Aunt   A character in Jane Austen's novel MANSFIELD PARK. Aunt Norris is a satirical portrait of the typical busybody.

Norris, [Benjamin] Frank[lin]   (1870–1902) American novelist. Known for his naturalistic depictions of life in the U.S., Norris was born in Chicago. In his youth, he studied art in Paris and wrote medieval romances; at the University of California, he read Zola and began work on McTEAGUE. He later reported the Boer War, joined the staff of the San Francisco *Wave*, and went to Cuba to cover the Spanish-American War.

His first published novel was *Moran of the Lady Letty* (1898), a tale of adventure. *McTeague*, one of the first naturalistic novels in America, appeared the following year. After two more romances, Norris began a trilogy on the growth, sale, and consumption of wheat. Of the three volumes planned, only THE OCTOPUS, Norris's most ambitious work, and *The Pit* (1903) were written.

Norris explained his literary credo in his essay *The Responsibilities of a Novelist* (1903), in which he declared that the novelist must always be able to say, "I never truckled; I never took off the hat to Fashion and held it out for pennies. By God, I told them the truth." See NATURALISM.

Northanger Abbey   (1818)   A novel by Jane AUSTEN. Visiting Bath with her friend Mrs. Allen, an older but flighty, irresponsible woman, Catherine Morland falls in love with Henry Tilney, a young clergyman. Believing her to be wealthy, Henry's father invites Catherine to

Northanger Abbey, the Tilney home. Greatly influenced by her reading of Mrs. RADCLIFFE's novel *Mysteries of Udolpho*, Catherine sees Northanger Abbey as a house of nightmarish mysteries and is terrified by her own imagination. Her visions of medieval horror prove groundless, of course. However, she is soon ordered out of the house by Henry's dictatorial father when he discovers that she is not wealthy. Henry follows her and persuades her to marry him. The novel gives Austen an opportunity to satirize the Radcliffe school of romantic mystery and to treat a favorite theme of feminine self-delusion.

Northern and Southern Dynasties (AD 317–589)

Chinese historical period following the break-up of the HAN dynasty. During this time, north China was lost to a series of non-Chinese states, and the center of ethnic Chinese culture moved south. This period saw the entrenchment of BUDDHISM and innovations in the fields of poetry and literary criticism. After this period, China was reunited under the SUI dynasty. See SIX DYNASTIES.

Northwest Territory

An American territory northwest of the Ohio River, comprising practically all the land owned as unsettled territory by the thirteen colonies at the time of the Declaration of Independence. It was ceded to the federal government by the various states laying claim to it, and from it were formed the states of Ohio, Indiana, Illinois, Michigan, and Wisconsin.

Norton, Caroline Elizabeth Sarah (born Sheridan, 1808–1877)

English writer, granddaughter of Richard Brinsley SHERIDAN. Norton was famous for her wit, beauty, and marital troubles, the last of which occasioned her letter, addressed to the queen, in criticism of the divorce laws; she was influential in bringing about a change in attitude toward married women of the time. A strong vein of social protest and autobiography runs through her verse, such as *A Voice from the Factories* (1836), and her prose, such as *The Wife and Woman's Reward* (1835). She is said to be the original of George Meredith's heroine in *Diana of the Crossways* (1885).

Norton, Charles Eliot (1827–1908)

American teacher and man of letters. Professor of the history of fine art at Harvard, Norton was a frequent contributor to periodicals. In 1865 he helped to found and edit *The Nation*, and, with James Russell LOWELL, he edited the *North American Review*. Norton was active as translator, editor, biographer, and bibliographer. He edited the correspondence and reminiscences of Thomas CARLYLE and the poetry of John DONNE and Anne BRADSTREET. His friendships with famous men and women of his time make his *Letters* (1913) valuable documents.

Nostradamus (real name Michel de Nostre-Dame, 1503–1566)

French astrologer and physician. Nostradamus's famous *Centuries* (1555), a book of prophecies, caused much controversy and was condemned by the papacy in 1781.

Nostromo (1904)

A novel by Joseph CONRAD. Set in the South American republic of "Costaguana," it is an exciting, complicated story about capitalist exploitation and revolution on the national scene and about personal morality and corruption in individuals. Charles Gould's silver mine helps to maintain the country's stability and its reactionary government. Gould's idealistic preoccupation with the mine warps his character and makes him neglect his gentle wife, Dona Emilia. When the revolution comes, Gould puts a consignment of silver in the charge of Nostromo, the magnificent, "incorruptible" *capataz de cargadores* ("foreman of the dock workers"). A chance happening makes Nostromo decide to bury the silver and pretend that it was lost at sea. He is eventually killed on the island where his riches are buried, when he is mistaken by his fiancée's father for a prowler. Silver is the pivotal element of the story. It is the cause of the foreign capitalist intervention and exploitation, which in turn causes the revolution. It corrupts and destroys some men and reveals the strengths, weaknesses, and ruling passions of others. Conrad's characterization is strong; his narration is complex and oblique. The story starts halfway through the events of the revolution and proceeds by way of flashbacks and glimpses into the future.

Not by Bread Alone (Ne khlebom yedinym, 1956)

A novel by Vladimir DUDINTSEV. Noted for its criticism of the Soviet bureaucratic establishment, the story concerns the efforts of a young Soviet inventor, Lopatkin, to get his invention accepted by the authorities. He is blocked by an unscrupulous factory director, Drozdov, a careerist who has no interest in anything but his own cozy spot in the hierarchy. Through intrigue, Lopatkin is arrested and sent to a labor camp. When he is released, he finds Drozdov still in power. The authorities are at last ready to accept his invention, but Lopatkin is no longer interested in personally participating in a system that allows Drozdovs to go on prospering. He is left facing a continual struggle against such a system.

Notebooks of Malte Laurids Brigge, The (Die Aufzeichnungen des Malte Laurids Brigge, 1910; tr 1930)

A novel by Rainer Maria RILKE. The hero is a young Danish poet of noble birth who comes to Paris, where he lives in poverty. The novel is written as if it were a collection of diary entries, in which observations on the suffering and squalor of his immediate experience, reminiscences of his youth, and speculations on life and art are seemingly indiscriminately mixed. The book's overall structure, which emerges only gradually, is a symbolic repetition of the story of the PRODIGAL SON.

Notes from Underground (Zapiski iz podpolya, 1864)

A long story by DOSTOYEVSKY. Touching on many of the philosophical problems dealt with in his novels, the story is divided into two parts. The first part is a monologue in which the narrator philosophizes, poses, and then laughs at his posing, and defends himself in advance against criticism of his ideas; the second part is a recounting of adventures from the narrator's life, which illustrate some of the ideas propounded in the first part of the story. On one level, the work is a complex psychological portrait of the narrator, the underground man. On another level, it is a polemic against the positivist philosophy of the radical thinkers in Russia, who believed in the rationality of man and the possibility of social betterment through material progress. The narrator not only disagrees intellectually with the radicals; he himself embodies the irrationality that he insists is the essence of man. The story, one of Dostoyevsky's most powerful and original works, is usually considered the starting point of Dostoyevsky's literary maturity.

Notes toward a Supreme Fiction (1942)   A long poem by Wallace STEVENS. It marked his tendency to shift away from the rich metaphor and imagery of his earlier poetry toward a more abstract poetic statement about the nature of poetry. It is divided into three sections, labeled "It Must Be Abstract," "It Must Change," and "It Must Give Pleasure."

No Time for Comedy (1939)   A play by S. N. BEHRMAN. It is concerned with a playwright who has the urge to deal with the serious problems and tragedies of his time but has the talent only for light comedy.

Nourritures terrestres, Les   See FRUITS OF THE EARTH, THE.

nouveau roman (Fr, "new novel"; also called antinovel)   A French literary movement that started in the early 1950s and experimented with various forms of novelistic techniques. Although not considered a tightly knit "school," with their own aesthetic principles and doctrines, the new novelists—Alain ROBBE-GRILLET, Michel BUTOR, Nathalie SARRAUTE, Claude SIMON, Marguerite DURAS, and Claude MAURIAC—share common views and preoccupations. All are obsessed with the portrayal of time: how it passes, how it changes us, how our perception of it changes according to our moods and desires. They are also concerned with such specifically modern phenomena as the effects of technology and standardization and the mushrooming materialism of the 20th century.

Their novels, however, use a wide variety of narrative techniques. Both Sarraute and Simon scrutinize the consciousness of their characters, but, while the former depicts an elaborately lucid state of mind, the latter creates a deliberately distorted, depersonalized point of view. Robbe-Grillet excels at descriptions of objects seen through the sometimes disordered impressions of an anonymous narrator; Butor animates identifiable characters with dense ambiguities of thought set in constant counterpoint between past and present. Mauriac's telescoping and overlapping sequences and Duras's neutral, impressionistic style offer further contrasts in techniques.

Nouvelle Héloïse, Julie ou la (1791)   An immensely successful epistolary novel, by Jean Jacques ROUSSEAU. It is the moralistic story of a wife, Julie d'Etanges, beset by her former lover, SAINT-PREUX. Her husband, M. de Wolmar, invites him to live with them; Saint-Preux leaves because of the impossible situation but is recalled by the dying Julie. He promises to remain after her death to educate her children. It is a philosophic novel exalting virtue and the natural man, as opposed to hypocritical social morality.

Nouvelle Revue française, La   A review of literature and the arts, founded in 1909 by André GIDE, Jacques Copeau, and Jacques Rivière. Reflecting the independent spirit of its founders, the magazine sought to discover and to encourage new authors. Its interest in the new, however, was combined with a belief in permanent aesthetic values, transcending any contemporary trend. During the years before and after World War I, the *Nouvelle Revue française* exercised considerable influence in the French literary world. Its members began a publishing house, the *maison d'éditions de la nrf*, which has since been taken over by Gallimard.

Nouvelle Vague   See NEW WAVE.

Novalis (pen name of Friedrich Leopold, Freiherr von Hardenberg, 1772–1801)   German poet and novelist, the leading poet of early GERMAN ROMANTICISM. From the pietism of his parents, the mysticism of Jakob Böhme, and the ideals of his fellow romantics, Novalis developed a unique personal faith in the mystical unity of all things. He believed that man had once lived in complete union with nature and had been able to communicate directly with the world of animals, plants, and objects. This union, however, had been lost, and man's goal must be to regain it. His ideas about history were similar. In his essay *Die Christenheit oder Europa* (*Christianity, or Europe*, 1799), he urges that Europe strive toward the establishment of a new universal church and thus regain the spiritual unity of the Catholic Middle Ages, which had been lost in the Reformation. His young fiancée, whom he adored, died in 1797, and many of his subsequent works, including the prose-poems *Hymnen an die Nacht* (*Hymns to the Night*, 1800), express a mystical yearning for death. His unfinished novel HEINRICH VON OFTERDINGEN, a highly allegorical BILDUNGSROMAN, some sections of which are in the form of MÄRCHEN, treats the growth of a young poet in an idealized medieval Europe. It was also in this novel that the symbol of the Blue Flower, which was later taken to represent all romanticism, first appeared. Some of Novalis's religious poems have been included in Protestant hymnbooks. His friends F. Schlegel and Tieck edited his works after he died.

Novelas ejemplares (Exemplary Novels, 1613)   A collection of twelve tales by CERVANTES. To Cervantes and his contemporaries, the word *novela* meant a short story in the Italian manner, rather than a novel. He added the word *ejemplares*, however, to indicate that he had avoided the licentiousness of his Italian models. Although the stories vary in style and content, the best are those that give free rein to the author's personal experience and practical philosophy, such as RINCONETE Y CORTADILLO and "El coloquio de los perros." The other stories are "La gitanilla," "El amante liberal," "La española inglesa," "El licenciado vidriera," "La fuerza de sangre," "El celoso extremeño," "La ilustre fregona," "Las dos doncellas," "La señora Cornelia," and "El casamiento engañoso." Sometimes included in the collection is the ribald "Tía fingida," first published in 1814; its authenticity, however, is doubtful.

novella The Italian word for a short prose narrative, popular during the medieval and Renaissance periods. As the etymology suggests, the tales were originally news and concerned mainly the events of town and city life that were worth repeating—from a clever remark made by a local wit to a joke played on the town idiot by clever ruffians, from stories of clever seductions to tales of grim revenge taken by a husband on his betrayers. As these tales were gathered into collections, they were joined by other tales of a more literary type: legends and anecdotes from ancient and modern history, oriental folk tales, courtly and romantic episodes. The earliest known collection, *Le cento novelle antiche* (*The Hundred Ancient Tales*), also known as the *Novellino*, was of anonymous authorship; its tales are short and simple. But, as the form developed in the hands of artists such as Franco SACCHETTI, BOCCACCIO, Matteo Bandello, and Basile, the style, structure, length, and psychological subtlety of the stories made them popular with learned audiences throughout Europe. Their chief literary influence was on playwrights such as SHAKESPEARE, who used them for his plots. His ROMEO AND JULIET, for example, began as a *novella* by Da Porto.

In the modern period, the term is used in English to designate a serious fictional form that is somewhere between the novel and the short story in length. Also sometimes called the nouvelle, the novella probably contains from thirty to forty thousand words, as compared to a full novel of a minimum of sixty thousand words, and often of twice that and more.

Novikov, Nikolay Ivanovich (1744–1818) Russian satirical journalist. During the reign of CATHERINE THE GREAT, Novikov published *Truten* (*The Drone*, 1769–70), *Zhivopisets* (*The Painter*, 1772–73), and *Koshelyok* (*The Purse*, 1774), all of which were leading periodicals of the day, as well as a number of books. His jibes at Russian society and, what was worse, at the government displeased the empress, and in 1791 he was imprisoned. After his release in 1796 by order of Tsar Paul, he lived on his estate for the rest of his life.

Novum Organum (1620) A philosophical treatise written in Latin by Francis BACON. Its title means "new instrument." The second part of his projected INSTAURATIO MAGNA, it presents Bacon's statement of his inductive method of interpreting nature and organizing knowledge, by which the results of experience are studied and a general conclusion regarding them is reached. This method was the opposite of the procedure of reasoning deductively from a given postulate by means of the syllogism, which was the universal practice among the Scholastic philosophers of his day.

Nowlan, Alden (1933–) Canadian poet and fiction writer. Typically brief, lyrical, and colloquial, Nowlan's poems deal with incidents and characters drawn from his own experience of the harsh realities of life in Canada's Atlantic provinces, where the soil is barren, the economy chronically depressed, and escapism a way of life. Nowlan's chief collections include *The Rose and the Puritan* (1958), *A Darkness in the Earth* (1959), *Wind in a Rocky Country* (1961), *Bread, Wine, and Salt* (1967), *The Mysterious Naked Man* (1969), *Between Tears and Laughter* (1971), and *I'm a Stranger Here Myself* (1974). The short stories in *Miracle at Indian River* (1968) blame the hardships of life in the rural Maritimes for the eccentric, even pathological behavior of the characters. *Various Persons Named Kevin O'Brien* (1973) is an autobiographical novel based on Nowlan's upbringing in the poverty and isolation of Nova Scotia. *Campobello: The Outer Island* (1975) is a work of history.

Nox See NYX.

Noyes, Alfred (1880–1958) English poet, critic, and essayist. Decidedly antimodernist in viewpoint and style, Noyes is chiefly known for his narrative verse and ballads dealing with English history. His epic poem *Drake* (1906–8) appeared in BLACKWOOD'S MAGAZINE in serial form, each installment as eagerly awaited as a serial novel. His *Collected Poems* appeared in 1947; the best-known single poem is probably "The Highwayman." Noyes was a passionate convert to Catholicism, an experience he discussed in *The Unknown God* (1934).

Noyes, John Humphrey (1811–1886) American religious leader. A believer in perfectionism and the second coming of Christ, Noyes declared himself sinless in 1834 and was thereupon requested to withdraw from Yale; his license to preach was revoked, and Noyes wandered among groups of perfectionists in the country. He returned to his home in Putney, Vermont, and formed a community known as the Bible Communists (1836). This group adopted communism and published its religious views. Noyes soon asserted a belief in polygamy; complex marriage was practiced in Putney, Vermont, in 1846. Noyes was forced to flee to New York, where he and his followers established the prosperous ONEIDA COMMUNITY. During the following years, Noyes published several volumes, including *Bible Communism* (1848), *Male Continence* (1848), and *Scientific Propagation* (1873), as well as a *History of American Socialisms* (1870). His organizational skill made the Oneida Community the longest lasting and most successful of American utopian experiments. In 1879 Noyes was forced by public disapproval to flee to Canada.

Nozdryov A hard-drinking loudmouth bully in GOGOL's story DEAD SOULS. Nozdryov cheats at cards with

CHICHIKOV, the hero, then threatens to have the latter beaten for pointing out that fact. Nozdryov's coarseness makes him the only character who is totally immune to Chichikov's subtle wiles.

Numa Pompilius   See EGERIA.

Numbers   In the OLD TESTAMENT, the fourth book of the PENTATEUCH. It records the Israelites' trip through the wilderness from Mt. Sinai to Moab, on the border of the PROMISED LAND. The book contains much Mosaic law; MOSES is portrayed as a prophet to whom God speaks directly. The date of its composition is not known; it was once thought to be contemporaneous with the events it describes, but it is now dated from four hundred to eight hundred years later.

Nuns Fret Not at Their Convent's Narrow Room (1807)   A sonnet by William WORDSWORTH. It celebrates the pleasure of the poet in maintaining the discipline of the sonnet form.

Nun's Priest's Tale, The   One of THE CANTERBURY TALES of Geoffrey CHAUCER. The Host agrees with the Knight that THE MONK'S TALE is gloomy, and he turns to one of the priests accompanying the Prioress, to demand something merry. The Priest makes a mock-heroic epic of one of the episodes in the fables of REYNARD THE FOX. The cock Chauntecleer is described as belonging to a widow and ruling seven hens, his favorite being Pertelote. One dawn he wakes in fright, having dreamed a fox was after him. Pertelote calls him a coward and cynically suggests indigestion as the cause. He lectures her severely on the importance of dreams, citing numerous examples from scholarly authorities of people who dreamed accurately of coming disasters.

Nevertheless, he lets Pertelote distract him, but the fox Don Russell indeed awaits him. The fox flatters him that he only wants to hear if the cock has as fine a voice as his father. Chauntecleer closes his eyes to crow and is seized. Hearing the shrieks of Pertelote and the other wives, the widow sets many men and animals to chase the raider. Chauntecleer tricks Don Russell into opening his mouth to taunt his pursuers, and he flies into a tree, resisting all the fox's further enticements.

nurse, Juliet's   The garrulous old confidante of Juliet in Shakespeare's ROMEO AND JULIET. The nurse aids Juliet in her love affair with Romeo, badgering her all the while with good-natured raillery.

nursery rhymes   Brief verses, usually preserved orally or collected in anthologies for young children. The origins of the nursery rhyme are obscure, although most known to English-speaking children are well over two hundred years old. They include songs, NONSENSE VERSE, "counting-out" rhymes, riddles, proverbs, and rhymes accompanying games. The earliest collection of nursery rhymes, *Tom Thumb's Pretty Song Book*, appeared in England in 1744.

Nut-Brown Maid, The   An English BALLAD, given in Percy's RELIQUES OF ANCIENT ENGLISH POETRY, probably dating from the late 15th century. It tells how the "not-browne mayd" is wooed and won by a knight who pretends to be a banished man. After describing the hardships she would have to undergo if she married him, finding her love true to the test, he reveals himself to be a rich earl's son.

Nwapa, Flora (1931–   )   Nigerian novelist. Nwapa's novels, *Efuru* (1966), *Idu* (1970), *Never Again* (1974), and *One Is Enough* (1982), offer realistic treatments of the circumstances of women in modern Nigeria. Her women characters are highly individualized, yet also typical; their thoughts and experiences are conveyed with intelligence and sympathy. The most accomplished of the very few women writers in Africa, she has also written *This Is Lagos* (1971) and has published many short stories, some of which are collected in *Wives at War* (1980). She has also written fiction for children: *Mammywater* (1979), *Journey to Space* (1980), and *The Miracle Kittens* (1980) are some of her works.

Nyāya   See DARSHANA.

Nym   In Shakespeare's HENRY V, a rascally camp follower with the English forces. In THE MERRY WIVES OF WINDSOR, Nym appears as a crony of Sir John Falstaff.

Nyx   In Greek mythology, the goddess of night, daughter of CHAOS. Nyx was the mother of many mythological creatures, including the FATES, the HESPERIDES, THANATOS, HYPNOS, and NEMESIS. Her powers were revered even by ZEUS. For mankind she could be both blessing and curse, as she could bring darkness, sleep, or death at will. A very ancient personification, she was probably never worshiped as an anthropomorphic deity. She was called Nox by the Romans.

O

Oates, Joyce Carol (1938–   ) American novelist, short-story writer, poet, and critic. Beginning with her first collection of stories, *By the North Gate* (1963), Oates has produced a steady stream of novels, stories, poems, and critical essays. Her fiction runs from naturalistic stories of urban life to Gothic nightmares; her characters' search for love and identity is frustrated by unexpected violence and destructive forces. Typical of her work is the trilogy *A Garden of Earthly Delights* (1967), *Expensive People* (1968), and *them* (1969). This chronicle of three families from different economic strata paints a frightening picture of American life, from the Depression to the race riots of the 1960s. Among her many other novels are *Son of the Morning* (1978), which portrays the fanaticism of an evangelical preacher; *Bellefleur* (1980), a saga of several generations of a very wealthy family; *Angel of Light* (1981); *Mysteries of Winterthurn* (1984), a detective mystery novel; *Solstice* (1985); and *Marya: A Life* (1986). Collections of stories include *The Wheel of Love* (1970), *Crossing the Border* (1976), *A Sentimental Education* (1981), and *Last Days* (1984). Among her critical works are *The Edge of Impossibility* (1972), *New Heaven, New Earth* (1974), *Contraries* (1981), and *The Profane Art* (1983). In 1982 Oates published *Invisible Woman: New and Selected Poems, 1970–1982*, and in 1987 *On Boxing* appeared.

Oates, Titus (1649–1705) English perjurer and fabricator of the Popish Plot. An ordained Anglican minister, Oates was expelled from his living, became a Roman Catholic, and was later expelled from two Jesuit colleges. In 1678 Oates and Israel Tonge, a London clergyman, concocted what became known as the Popish Plot, charging that the Roman Catholics planned to assassinate Charles II, place the duke of York (later James II) on the throne, and turn the country over to the Jesuits. The story was widely believed; Oates was granted a large pension by the government, and, as a result of the public uproar, some thirty-five innocent persons were executed. After the accession of James II, Oates was convicted of perjury, flogged, and imprisoned, but he was pardoned by William III in 1689, and his pension was restored. In 1698 he became a Baptist but was soon expelled from the congregation for hypocrisy.

Oath of the Tennis Court The oath taken by the French National ASSEMBLY in 1789. After it had been prevented by Louis XVI from using its normal meeting place, the Assembly convened at the tennis-court building on June 20, 1789, where it took the oath never to disband until France had been given a constitution. As this negated the power of the king, the event is often considered the beginning of the FRENCH REVOLUTION.

Obadiah (1) A Minor Prophet of the OLD TESTAMENT; the name of the book that records his prophecy. Obadiah foretells the destruction of Edom, a traditional enemy of Israel, and prophesies the deliverance of Israel as a kingdom of the Lord.

(2) A slang term for a QUAKER.

Oberman (1804) A novel by Etienne Pivert de Sénancour (1770–1846). Written in the form of letters, it greatly influenced the romantic movement of the 19th century. The novel in part describes the author's wanderings in the forest of Fontainebleau and in Switzerland. Sénancour's restlessness, his disillusionment, and his torment of body and soul are, however, the real subject of his work. In its analytical, introspective concerns, *Oberman* foreshadows the development of modern fiction.

Oberon In medieval legend, the king of the fairies. Probably an outgrowth of Alberich, the king of the elves, Oberon appears in the medieval French romance *Huon de Bordeaux* (early 13th century), as the son of Julius Caesar and Morgan Le Fay.

In Shakespeare's MIDSUMMER NIGHT'S DREAM, Oberon is a strong-willed figure who resorts to a trick to obtain from Titania, his wife, the services of her changeling page. He dispatches Puck to anoint the sleeping queen with a love potion. In her drugged state, she makes love to Bottom and is so ashamed when she awakes that she agrees to Oberon's demand.

Obiter Dicta   Title of three books of essays by Augustine BIRRELL (1884; second series, 1887; *More Obiter Dicta*, 1924). An *obiter dictum* is an incidental and unbinding opinion given by a judge; hence, any incidental comment.

objectivism   (1) In literary usage, particularly in poetry, a term used to describe a theory of composition, in which a material object—or even a poem itself—is presented for its own sake rather than for its symbolic or emotional value. The term was first used by William Carlos WILLIAMS, whose poetry provides a good example of objectivism. In the 1930s, a group of poets including Charles REZNIKOFF, George Oppen (1908–84), and Louis ZUKOFSKY published, along with Williams, An *"Objectivist" Anthology* (1932). Essentially an outgrowth of IMAGISM, objectivism held that attention should be given to the poem as a unique and distinct structural entity, not to the symbolic intent of the poet. See SYMBOLISTS.

(2) In philosophy, a theory emphasizing external reality or the objective truth of human knowledge; in ethics, emphasis on the objectivity of moral good.

Oblomov (1859)   A novel by Ivan GONCHAROV. The work is one of the outstanding classics of Russian realistic fiction of the 19th century. The hero, Ilya Ilyich Oblomov, a Russian landowner living in St. Petersburg, is the embodiment of physical and mental laziness. His chief activities are indulging in reveries, while lying on his couch, and occasionally quarreling with his gloomy, coarse servant Zakhar. In the course of the book, Oblomov's robe and slippers, his almost constant apparel, become part of his character. Oblomov ignores his business affairs, although the estate on which he depends for his income and comfortable existence is being mismanaged and is rapidly going to ruin. Contrasted to Oblomov is his friend Andrey Shtolts, the model of the efficient man of business. All his efforts to rouse Oblomov to some kind of action end in failure. Not even the love offered by the young Olga Ilinskaya can move Oblomov to give up his way of life. Although he loves Olga, Oblomov chooses the peaceful, effortless existence he can have by marrying Agafya Pshenitsyna, his landlady. Olga marries Shtolts, and Oblomov, coddled by Agafya, sinks deeper into reverie and financial ruin until he dies.

Goncharov's novel occupies a secure place in classic Russian literature on the basis of the characterization of its protagonist. Oblomov has come to symbolize all that is slothful in human nature. The reasons cited by critics for his inactivity range from the social situation in Russia under serfdom, at one extreme, to Oblomov's superior sensibility, at the other. Since the well-known essay by the critic Nikolay DOBROLYUBOV "Chto takoye oblomovshchina?" ("What Is Oblomovshchina?," 1959) the main emphasis in Russian criticism has been on the social aspect of Oblomov's malady. The novel has also been regarded as a forerunner of later psychological discoveries, because of the hero's anxieties, his self-questioning, his reliving childhood in a dream, and the part these things are shown to play in his adult life.

O'Brien, Conor Cruise (1917–   )   Irish historian, critic, and diplomat. Ireland's ambassador to the United Nations (1956–60), O'Brien ended his diplomatic career after his controversial handling of the U.N. operations in Katanga Province in the Congo (Zaïre) in 1961, described in *To Katanga and Back* (1962). Thereafter he served as vice-chancellor of the University of Ghana (1962–65) and as a Labour member of the Irish parliament. His literary and political studies include *Writers and Politics* (1965), *Camus* (1969), *The Suspecting Glance* (1972), and *Across Three Oceans* (1985). He is also known for his books on the historical and contemporary struggles of a divided Ireland: *Parnell and His Party* (1957), *States of Ireland* (1972), *The Story of Ireland* (1972), and *Herod: Reflections on Political Violence* (1978). In 1985 O'Brien published *The Siege: The Saga of Israel & Zionism*, a survey of Israel in the context of Zionism and of the Arab-Israeli conflict that was provoked by the founding of Israel.

O'Brien, Edna (1932–   )   Irish novelist and short-story writer. From comic and charming beginnings in *The Country Girls* (1960), O'Brien moved in her mature work to more somber themes and more sophisticated settings. She is most concerned with women—alone, seeking communication and a sense of belonging, and finding neither response nor understanding in men. She portrays the Irish as violent, puritanical, and hypocritical; her books were banned in Ireland, partly because of her explicit treatment of sex. Among her novels are *The Lonely Girl* (1962), *Casualties of Peace* (1966), *Night* (1972), *Johnny I Hardly Knew You* (1977), *Returning* (1982), and *A Fanatic Heart* (1985). Characterized by stylistic elegance and humor, her writing is particularly suited to the short-story form. Her story collections include *The Love Object* (1968) and *Mrs. Reinhardt and Other Stories* (1978; U.S. *A Rose in the Heart*, 1979). She has also written plays, among them *A Pagan Place* (1970), *Virginia* (1980), and *Flesh and Blood* (1985).

O'Brien, Flann (pen name of Brian O'Nolan, 1911–1966)   Irish essayist, novelist, and playwright. O'Brien, who worked for the Irish Civil Service, was known during his lifetime as a brilliant columnist (under the pen name Myles na Gopaleen) for thirty years on the *Irish Times*. A selection of the columns appears in *The Best of Myles* (ed Kevin O'Nolan, 1968). His fame as a writer of novels, stories, and plays came posthumously. His highly original short novels include *At-Swim-Two-Birds* (1939), *The Third Policeman* (1967; written in 1940), *The Hard Life* (1961), and *The Dalkey Archive* (1964). Collections of his work are *Stories and Plays* (1973) and *A Flann O'Brien Reader* (1978).

O Captain! My Captain! (1865)   A poem by Walt WHITMAN. Commemorating the death of Abraham

Lincoln, it is written in conventional rhyme and meter. The Captain, who has brought the ship of state to a safe port, has "fallen cold and dead."

O'Casey, Sean (1884–1964)   Irish dramatist. Born and reared in a Dublin slum, O'Casey very early in life developed the two abiding concerns that were to characterize his life and work: a fierce, uncontrolled vitality of language and a rigid, uncompromising social conscience. The artistic fusion of these elements has resulted in two of the most powerful plays written in the 20th century, JUNO AND THE PAYCOCK and *The Plough and the Stars* (1926).

Hindered by bad eyesight, so that he was unable to read until the age of twelve, O'Casey compensated for his late start by developing a voracious appetite for books. At the same time, he became active in the revolutionary movement as an organizer of the transport strike of 1913 and a member of the Irish Citizens Army. He also joined the Gaelic League, learned the Irish language, and gained an entrée into the literary world.

The first of his plays to be produced was *The Shadow of a Gunman* (1923), presented by the ABBEY THEATRE, with which O'Casey was to be associated for the next six years. In 1924 the Abbey presented *Juno and the Paycock*. Regarded by many as O'Casey's masterpiece, it is a masterly blend of comedy and tragedy, set against the background of the Irish civil war. The production of *The Plough and the Stars* was greeted with rioting on the Dublin streets, as a result of the alleged anti-Irish sentiment of the play. In 1928 the Abbey Theatre rejected O'Casey's next play, *The Silver Tassie*, resulting in O'Casey's breaking his connection with the Abbey. The play, an expressionist drama dealing with World War I, was produced in London in 1929. *Within the Gates*, another play in the expressionist mode, appeared in 1933, revealing once again his strong sympathy with the lower classes. O'Casey's subsequent plays have been less successful, frequently hampered by the somewhat doctrinaire socialist message imposed upon them. Among these are *Purple Dust* (1940), *The Star Turns Red* (1940), and *Red Roses for Me* (1947).

In 1939 O'Casey published *I Knock at the Door*, the first book of his six-volume autobiography. It was followed by *Pictures in the Hallway* (1942), *Drums under the Window* (1945), *Inishfallen Fare Thee Well* (1949), *Rose and Crown* (1952), and *Sunset and Evening Star* (1954), highly lyrical, occasionally florid, always vivid accounts of his struggle to wrest some order and significance from the anarchic events of the first half of the 20th century. See IRISH RENAISSANCE.

Occam, William of (or William of Ockham, c1285–1349)   English scholastic philosopher and theologian, known as Doctor Invincibilis and Venerabilis Inceptor. Occam joined the Franciscans, was a partisan of strict observance in their controversy over evangelical poverty, and became general of the order in 1342. In his *Dialogus* (c1343) he summarizes many of his previous writings, con-

testing the temporal power of the Pope and asserting that a king has independent authority in civil affairs.

Occam's philosophy was greatly influenced by his teacher Duns Scotus, although later they were rivals in scholastic disputes. He revived a modified Nominalism, maintaining the distinction between concrete realities and the abstraction of universals. Thus he claimed that purely intellectual abstractions are not valid knowledge and that reasoning must be based on experimental proof. In this view, the basis of the later position known as theological scepticism, the existence and attributes of God are not susceptible of proof by human reason but can be approached only through intuition.

Occam's razor refers to his famous principle of economy in logic, expressed as "Entities [that is, assumptions used to explain phenomena] should not be multiplied beyond what is needed."

occasional verse   Poems written for a special purpose, to commemorate or celebrate a specific social, historical, or personal event. Funeral elegies, epithalamia, and birthday odes are all forms of occasional verse. Famous examples include Milton's LYCIDAS and Tennyson's THE CHARGE OF THE LIGHT BRIGADE.

Oceanus   In Greek myth, a river. Oceanus was believed to flow in a boundless circle around the earth. HOMER names Oceanus as the origin of all things, including the gods. In HESIOD's *Theogony*, he is a TITAN, son of URANUS and GE (Heaven and Earth). Oceanus and his wife TETHYS bore three thousand sons, the Rivers, and three thousand daughters, the Water Nymphs (Oceanides). He appears in Aeschylus' PROMETHEUS BOUND.

Ochs, Adolph Simon (1858–1935)   American publisher and editor. As a young man, Ochs worked as a newsboy and a printer's apprentice. By 1878 he had become publisher of the Chattanooga *Times*. In 1896 Ochs came to New York, having lost most of his money in the panic of 1893. He bought the *New York Times*, which had been nearly destroyed by the battles between the papers owned by William Randolph HEARST and Joseph PULITZER. To take his papers out of competition with the sensational dailies, Ochs instituted the slogan "All the news that's fit to print" and offered dignified, nonpartisan news stories. He added such features as book reviews and financial reporting and expanded the foreign news coverage. The paper rapidly increased its circulation and became one of the most influential and responsible newspapers in the country. Ochs also published the Philadelphia *Times* and the Philadelphia *Public Ledger* from 1902 to 1912. At Ochs's death, he was succeeded as publisher of the *New York Times* by his son-in-law, Arthur Hays Sulzberger.

Ocnus, rope of   Profitless labor. Ocnus, in Roman fable, was always twisting a rope of straw, but an ass ate it as fast as it was twisted.

O'Connell, Daniel (1775–1847)   Irish nationalist, statesman, and orator. O'Connell was a prominent lawyer who became known as an opponent of the Act of Union (1801), the Church of Ireland, and the civil disabilities placed on Catholics because of their religion. He founded the Catholic Association, which, gaining quietly and impressively in strength and numbers, was suppressed in 1825. O'Connell was elected to Parliament (1828) but refused to take his seat until Wellington's hard-won Catholic Emancipation Act (1829) went through Parliament. He was elected (1841) lord mayor of Dublin. When the Tory Sir Robert Peel became prime minister, O'Connell resumed his agitations for an independent Ireland. He reestablished the Catholic Association; Peel declared it illegal; O'Connell was tried and convicted for conspiracy; and the decision was reversed by the House of Lords. O'Connell's stay in prison, however, weakened his health, and he died on his way to Italy to convalesce. A radical group within the Catholic Association, YOUNG IRELAND, steadily gained adherents to the violent policy that O'Connell had consistently opposed.

O'Connor, [Mary] Flannery (1925–1964) American short-story writer and novelist. A native of Georgia, O'Connor used the South as the setting for most of her fiction. Her vivid descriptions, keen ear for dialect, and irreverent humor, combined with her intense Catholicism, produced a uniquely powerful body of work in a lifetime cut short by a degenerative disease. The characters in her novels *Wise Blood* (1952) and *The Violent Bear It Away* (1960) are bizarre religious fanatics driven to proving God's existence by acts of violence. This strange blend of strong religious faith and the grotesque characterizes as well the stories contained in *A Good Man Is Hard to Find* (1955) and *Everything That Rises Must Converge* (1965). Described as both a Southern Gothic and a "religious" novelist, O'Connor had a startling capacity to raise profound questions of belief against a backdrop of the Georgia backwoods. *The Complete Stories* appeared in 1971. *The Habit of Being* (1978) is a collection of her letters, edited and introduced by her close friend Sally Fitzgerald.

O'Connor, Frank (pen name of Michael O'Donovan, 1903–1966) Irish short-story writer and author of poetic translations from Gaelic. He was encouraged by A.E. (q.v.) and was for a time one of the directors of the ABBEY THEATRE. O'Connor's work is noted for its humor, its realism, and its poetic sensitivity. *Guests of the Nation* (1931) contains stories about the Irish-English troubles. *Dutch Interior* (1940) is a collection of separate stories that together paint a discouraging picture of Irish life. Later stories, such as "The Holy Door" and "Uprooted," are fine comedies. *An Only Child* (1960) and *My Father's Son* (1968) are autobiographical works. See IRISH RENAISSANCE.

octameter In prosody, a line of verse containing eight metrical feet, which may be in any METER, usually identified together with the name of the meter, as iambic

octameter, trochaic octameter, etc. Octameter is the longest line designated by a special term; beyond octameter, it would be necessary to speak of the nine-foot line, ten-foot line, and so on. Such lengthy lines, however, are rare.

octave See SONNET.

Octavia (1) Roman matron (d 11 BC). The sister of Octavius Caesar (later AUGUSTUS), Octavia married Mark ANTONY in 41 BC after the death of her first husband and Antony's first wife. Antony returned to CLEOPATRA in 36 BC and divorced Octavia in 32. One of her daughters by Antony became the mother of CALIGULA, and the other the grandmother of NERO. She appears as a character in Shakespeare's ANTONY AND CLEOPATRA, in which she is described as being "of a holy, cold, and still conversation," and in Dryden's ALL FOR LOVE.

(2) Wife of NERO, whom he had murdered to please his mistress.

October Revolution See BOLSHEVIK.

Octopus, The (1901) A novel by Frank NORRIS. The first of a projected trilogy on American wheat, the novel depicts the struggle for power between California wheat farmers and the railroad, "the octopus" that encircles and strangles them. With its epic sweep, the novel includes two love affairs, one involving the mystical Vanamee, and comes to a climax with a pitched battle between farmers and railroad men. *The Pit* (1903), its sequel, concerns an attempt to corner the Chicago wheat market in "the pit" of the stock exchange.

ode In prosody, a lyric poem of exalted emotion, devoted to the praise or celebration of its subject.

(1) The Pindaric ode was first composed in ancient Greece by PINDAR and other poets for choral recitation, written in units of three stanzas each, called respectively the STROPHE, antistrophe, and epode. The chorus moved up one side of the orchestra, chanting the strophe, down the other, chanting the antistrophe, and came to a stop before the audience to chant the epode. The ode continued in this way to its end. Modern poets using this form do not, of course, write for such performance, but they still use its basic construction. Their first three stanzas usually have rhyme and are constructed with great freedom and variety; the pattern then repeats these three stanza forms as a unit throughout the poem.

(2) The Horatian, or stanzaic, ode is written in a succession of stanzas that follow the pattern of the first stanza, which may be in any form. HORACE used this form, as did Keats in his ODE TO A NIGHTINGALE.

(3) The irregular ode is a modern invention and has no regular pattern at all; it came about through misunderstanding (by the English poet William Collins) of the Pindaric form. William Wordsworth's ODE: INTIMATIONS OF IMMORTALITY is perhaps the best-known example.

Ode: Intimations of Immortality from Recollections of Early Childhood (1807) A famous poem by William WORDSWORTH. It is based on the Platonic doctrine of "recollection," which asserts that the process of learning is actually only a recollection to the adult mind of knowledge gained in a preexistent spiritual realm and lost to the individual at birth. Wordsworth's poem celebrates the child, who, "trailing clouds of glory," still retains in infancy memories of his celestial abode. Although the mature man has forgotten this knowledge, we are told, he can regain it by heeding his intuition and remembering his own childhood.

Ode on a Grecian Urn (1819)   A famous ode by John KEATS. It describes the perfection and timelessness of art, as contrasted to the living world of change, suggested by the eternally still figures on a Greek urn, one of whom is a youth who, although he cannot possess his beloved, can never lose her:

> Bold lover, never, never canst thou kiss,
> Though winning near the goal, yet do not grieve:
> She cannot fade; though thou hast not thy bliss,
> Forever wilt thou love, and she be fair!

Odessa Tales (Odesskie rasskazy, 1927)   A collection of short stories by Isaak BABEL. Set in the Soviet writer's birthplace, the Black Sea city of Odessa, the stories are also known as *Jewish Tales* (*Yevreiskiye rasskazy*).

Ode to a Nightingale (1819)   A poem by John KEATS. It expresses the emotions of the poet as he listens to the song of the nightingale: his visions of sensuous beauty and his melancholy as he feels his own mortality in contrast to the immortality of the bird's song:

> Thou wast not born for death, immortal Bird!
> No hungry generations tread thee down;
> The voice I hear this passing night was heard
> In ancient days by emperor and clown:
> Perhaps the self-same song that found a path
> Through the sad heart of Ruth, when, sick for home,
> She stood in tears amid the alien corn;
> The same that oft-times hath
> Charm'd magic casements, opening on the foam
> Of perilous seas, in faery lands forlorn.

Ode to the West Wind (1820)   One of the best-known poems by Percy Bysshe SHELLEY. In it the poet addresses the wild, strong wind of autumn—as he was once, "tameless, and swift, and proud"—and implores that it may now inspire him with its force:

> Scatter, as from an unextinguished hearth
> Ashes and sparks, my words among mankind!
> Be through my lips to unawakened earth
> The trumpet of a prophecy! O, Wind,
> If Winter comes, can Spring be far behind?

Odets, Clifford (1906–1963)   American playwright. Odets was acclaimed in the 1930s as an outstanding proletarian dramatist. His first two plays, which are often considered his best, are concerned with the class struggle: WAITING FOR LEFTY and *Awake and Sing* (1935), which deals with the Bergers, a lower-class Jewish family in the

Bronx, most of whose disasters stem from the manipulations of a dominating mother. He continued to use socialist themes in his succeeding plays. *Till the Day I Die* (1935) deals with the Communist underground movement in Nazi Germany. *Paradise Lost* (1935) depicts the decline of a middle-class family. *Golden Boy* (1937) portrays a young Italian-American who should have been a violinist but who chooses the easier way to fame, through boxing. *Night Music* (1940) and *Clash by Night* (1941) are two later plays written before Odets turned to Hollywood. With *The Country Girl* (1950), he managed to repeat his early success. The play marks the end of his preoccupation with political themes; it centers on the struggle of a young woman to remain faithful to her dissolute husband. *The Flowering Peach* (1954) was less successful.

Odets was at first an actor with the Theatre Guild; in 1931 he became one of the founders of the GROUP THEATRE, which later produced his best-known plays.

Odette de Crécy   A cocotte in Marcel Proust's REMEMBRANCE OF THINGS PAST. At first "the lady in pink" introduced to the narrator by his great-uncle Adolphe, Odette becomes the mistress and then the wife of Charles SWANN, and by him the mother of Gilberte. After Swann's death, she marries his rival, de Forcheville; then, a widow again, she becomes the mistress of the duc de Guermantes.

Odin   The Scandinavian name of the Anglo-Saxon god Woden. Odin was the supreme god of the later Scandinavian pantheon, having supplanted THOR.

Odin was god of wisdom, poetry, war, and agriculture; on this latter account, Wednesday (*Woden's day*) was considered to be especially favorable for sowing. He was also god of the dead and presided over the banquets of those slain in battle. See VALHALLA. He became the *All-wise* by drinking from MIMIR's fountain but purchased the distinction at the cost of one eye, and he is usually represented as a one-eyed man wearing a hat and carrying a staff. His remaining eye is the sun.

The father of Odin was Bor. His brothers are VILI and VE. His wife is FRIGGA. His sons are THOR and BALDER. His mansion is Gladsheim. His court as war god is Valhalla. His two black ravens are Hugin (Thought) and Munin (Memory). His steed is Sleipnir. His ships are Skidbladnir and Naglfar. His spear is Gungnir, which never fails to hit the mark aimed at. His ring is called Draupnir, which every ninth night drops eight other rings of equal value. His throne is Hlidskjalf. His wolves are Geri and Freki. He will ultimately be swallowed up by the FENRIS-WOLF at Ragnarok.

Odin, Promise of   The most binding of all oaths to a Norseman. In making it, the hand was passed through a massive silver ring, kept for the purpose, or through a sacrificial stone, like that called the Circle of Stennis.

O'Donnell, Lillian [Uduardy] (1926–   )   American mystery writer. O'Donnell is the author of a series of police-procedural stories featuring Detective

Norah Mulcahaney Capretto of the New York Police Department. The stories are notable especially for their insight into the problems of a woman in a large city police force. The best-known books in the series are *The Phone Calls* (1972), *The Baby Merchants* (1975), *Aftershock* (1977), and *Wicked Designs* (1980). Among her other works are two nonmystery novels, *Tachi Tree* (1968) and *Dive into Darkness* (1971), and the novels *The Children's Zoo* (1981), *Cop Without a Shield* (1983), and *Casual Affairs* (1985).

Odrovir   The "poet's mead" of the Norse gods. Odrovir was made of Kvasir's blood mixed with honey, and all who partook of it became poets. Kvasir was the wisest of all men, and could answer any question put to him. He was fashioned out of the saliva spat into a jar by the AESIR and VANIR on their conclusion of peace, and he was slain by the dwarfs Fjalar and Galar.

Odysseus (called Ulysses by the Romans)   In Greek mythology, the king of Ithaca and hero of Homer's ODYSSEY. In both the ILIAD and the *Odyssey*, Odysseus is portrayed as shrewd and wily and also as a man of noble qualities. After Homer's day, Odysseus' reputation unaccountably declined, and he was generally presented (except in SOPHOCLES' *Ajax*) as a diabolically clever but unscrupulous man, who would stop at nothing to gain his ends. He appears in this light in Sophocles' *Philoctetes* and in many other works of the classical era. He was rehabilitated by Shakespeare in TROILUS AND CRESSIDA, in which Ulysses is almost the only noble character. Odysseus' complex character has never lost its fascination. He reappears as an old man in TENNYSON's poem "Ulysses"; in modern Dublin as Leopold Bloom, the unheroic hero of James Joyce's novel ULYSSES; and in fantastic surroundings in Nikos Kazantzakis' long poem THE ODYSSEY: A MODERN SEQUEL.

Odyssey (9th century BC)   An epic poem by HOMER. It recounts the adventures of ODYSSEUS on his way home to Ithaca after the TROJAN WAR. Though written in heroic verse, it has been called the first novel, because of its exciting narrative and the effective use of flashbacks to heighten the dramatic action. The poem opens on Ogygia, the far western island of the sea nymph CALYPSO, who has kept Odysseus imprisoned on her island for seven years, offering him immortality as an inducement to stay with her, but Odysseus insists on returning to his wife, PENELOPE. The story now turns to Odysseus' son TELEMACHUS, back home in Ithaca. Penelope's suitors have been eating them out of house and home. Resolving, under the influence of ATHENE, to act the man, Telemachus sets out to find his father. He consults first NESTOR in Pylos, then MENELAUS in Sparta; Menelaus tells Telemachus that he has learned of Odysseus' captivity in Ogygia.

Meanwhile, on ZEUS' orders, Calypso has released Odysseus. Shipwrecked on the Phaeacian island of Scherie, he is befriended first by the young Nausicaa, then by her parents, King Alcinous and Queen Arete. At a banquet, he reveals his identity and tells the story of his wanderings. After leaving Troy and making a raid on the Ciconians, he landed in the country of the LOTUS-EATERS. There some of his men ate the lotus, which made them forget their homes, and they had to be carried away by force. Next they landed on the island where the CYCLOPS lived; they were trapped by POLYPHEMUS in his cave, and those not eaten escaped by a trick after blinding the Cyclops. It is this deed that won the enmity of POSEIDON, the father of Polyphemus. Reaching the island of AEOLUS, Odysseus was given the unfavorable winds in a leather bag, so that his ships were blown straight toward home. But Odysseus' men, thinking that the bag held treasure, opened it, and they were blown back to Aeolus' island, where the god refused to help them again. The cannibal LAESTRYGONIANS destroyed all but one of Odysseus' ships. Odysseus and his crew reached Aeaea, where the enchantress CIRCE turned most of the men into swine. However, HERMES gave Odysseus a herb, called moly, which saved him, and he frightened Circe into changing his men back to their normal shapes. Next Odysseus descended into HADES to learn from the ghost of TIRESIAS how he would reach home. Following Circe's advice, he was able to avoid SCYLLA AND CHARYBDIS, with a loss of only six men, and sailed past the SIRENS without danger by putting wax in his men's ears. Odysseus, however, had himself tied to the mast so that he could enjoy their song. The crew would probably have reached Ithaca in safety, had not the men stolen the cattle of HELIOS on the island of Thrinacia, for which crime the ship was destroyed by a thunderbolt, and only Odysseus was saved, by being cast ashore on Ogygia.

When they hear this harrowing tale, the Phaeacians send Odysseus home to Ithaca on one of their ships, laden with rich presents. After he has landed, Poseidon avenges himself on the Phaeacians by turning the ship into stone. Disguised by Athene as a beggar, Odysseus stays in the hut of the faithful swineherd Eumaeus while he determines how to rid his house of suitors. He is recognized first by his old dog Argus, a bit later by his old nurse Eurycleia. He is ridiculed by the suitors and by the beggar Irus, whose jaw Odysseus breaks. With Telemachus' help, Odysseus hides the suitors' weapons, locks them in the great hall of the palace, and shoots them down with his bow. His wife and aged father are finally reunited to him, and he reestablishes himself as king of Ithaca, when Athene calms the resentment of the suitors' families.

The *Odyssey*, like the ILIAD, was attributed by the ancient Greeks to the poet Homer. Many modern scholars feel that this masterful dramatic structure and fairly consistent style are his work, for the most part at least. However, it is thought to be a somewhat later composition than the *Iliad*, although belonging to the same general period. Also, while the *Iliad* is a collection of mythical material that grew up about an event that seems actually to have occurred toward the end of the Mycenaean era, the *Odyssey* is largely a collection of folk tales, many of which are easily recognizable in the legends of other lands. These tales have been given continuity and coherence by attributing the adventures to a single hero and moreover by reworking each incident so that it contributes to a consistent picture of that hero. The consistency of the author's concept of Odysseus as a fictional character can be appreciated by comparing him with HERACLES, whose saga is also the result of a gradual accretion of unrelated tales but whose adventures were never told in a unified work of literature.

The monumental and complex figure of Odysseus and the chief work in which his adventures were told have had a perennial fascination for later writers. The most remarkable work that has been inspired by the *Odyssey* is James Joyce's novel ULYSSES, in which a single day's events in the life of Leopold Bloom, a notably unheroic Jewish citizen of Dublin, are made to conform to the pattern of the *Odyssey*. More recently, the Greek poet Nikos KAZANTZAKIS undertook to relate the further adventures of Odysseus in *The Odyssey: A Modern Sequel*.

Odyssey, The: A Modern Sequel (I Odysseia, 1938; tr 1958) An epic poem by Nikos KAZANTZAKIS. It was translated into English verse by Kimon Friar in 1958. The poem was begun in 1925 and reworked through seven versions and was intended as the summation of the author's philosophical attitudes. It contains twenty-four books, richly flavored with the idioms and rhythms of Greek folk songs and legends and with the earthy language of shepherds and fishermen. The poem's prologue and epilogue are invocations to the sun; fire and light supply the poem's dominant imagery. The journeys of Odysseus are presented as an agonized but ecstatic struggle toward freedom and purity of spirit.

The modern sequel is grafted to the Homeric epic at Book XXII, just after Odysseus has slain the suitors of Penelope. Although the mythological setting is retained for its hero's further adventures in Ithaca, Sparta, Crete, and down the length of Africa to his death at the South Pole, Kazantzakis has said that his *Odyssey* is "a new epical-dramatic attempt of the modern man to find deliverance by passing through all the stages of contemporary anxieties and by pursuing the most daring hopes."

Oe, Kenzaburō (1935–) Japanese novelist. Oe is widely read in his own country and considered by many to be Japan's finest writer of his generation. His first work, a novella called *Shiiku* (1958; tr *The Catch in the Shadow of the Sunrise*, 1966), describes the friendship between a Japanese boy and a black American prisoner of war. Published while Oe was still a student, it received the prestigious Akutagawa award. In Oe's early works, madness, abuse, perverse sex, and violence are commonplace. His fiction explores Japanese feelings of betrayal, dislocation, and alienation following Japan's surrender in World

War II, and his political writings focus on Japan's search for cultural and ideological roots. Oe's later works reflect his intense and painful experience as a father of a brain-damaged child: *Kojinteki na taiken* (1964; tr *A Personal Matter*, 1968); *Man'en gannen no futtobōru* (1967; tr *The Silent Cry*, 1974); and *Warera no kyōki o ikinobiru michi o oshieyo* (1969; tr *Teach Us to Outgrow Our Madness: Four Short Novels*, 1977). Oe's style has been described as innovative, wild, and vital and has angered certain critics by flouting prevailing Japanese literary conventions of delicacy and simplicity.

Oedipus In Greek mythology, the son of Laius, of the Theban dynasty founded by CADMUS, and of Jocasta (or Epicasta). Oedipus is the tragic hero of many dramas, most notably of SOPHOCLES' *Oidipous Tyrannos* (*Oedipus Rex*) and *Oidipous epi Kolonoi* (*Oedipus at Colonus*). His story is told also in the ILIAD and in the many works dealing with his sons (see SEVEN AGAINST THEBES).

In the most familiar version of the myth, Laius, having learned from an oracle that he would be killed by his own son, thrust a spike through the infant's feet and had him exposed on Mt. Cithaeron. Rescued by a shepherd, the boy was raised by the childless king Polybus of Corinth and his wife, Periboea (or Merope), as their own son. When he grew to manhood, Oedipus was warned by the Delphic oracle that he would kill his father and marry his mother. Avoiding Corinth in horror, he met Laius on the road, and, not knowing him, killed him in an argument. He proceeded to Thebes, which was then being ravaged by the SPHINX. When Oedipus answered her riddle, the Sphinx killed herself, and the regent CREON offered him the throne of Thebes and the hand of Laius' widow, Jocasta, who was Creon's sister. Later, famine struck Thebes, and the Delphic oracle advised Creon to cast from the city the slayer of Laius. The seer TIRESIAS and an old shepherd revealed Oedipus' identity, Jocasta committed suicide, and Oedipus blinded himself with her brooch.

Banished from the city and shunned by his sons, Eteocles and Polynices, he cursed them and wandered, an outcast, for many years. At last, his faithful daughter ANTIGONE led him to a grove at Colonus sacred to the Eumenides (see ERINYES). Creon tried to force his return to Thebes so that his body, buried outside the gates, would magically protect the city in war. But THESEUS, the king of nearby Athens, defended him. Dying, Oedipus promised that his tomb would guard Athens from harm.

The story of Oedipus was told also by SENECA in his tragedy *Oedipus* and by Jean Cocteau in his play THE INFERNAL MACHINE and in his libretto for Stravinsky's opera *Oedipus Rex*. In the 13th-century *Golden Legend* of Jacobus de Voragine and in other medieval works, the Laius-Jocasta-Oedipus myth was attached to the legend of JUDAS ISCARIOT. It is a theme common in folklore.

Oehlenschlaeger, Adam Gottlob (1779–1850) Danish poet and playwright. The leader of the romantic movement in Denmark, Oehlenschlaeger enjoyed a period of intense creativity during his early years. *Guldhorne (The Gold Horns*, 1802) is a romantic poem that exalted the glory of his country's past. His poetic dramas, based on Scandinavian myth and legend, include *Sanct-Hansaften-Spil (The Play of St. John's Eve*, 1803) and *Aladdin* (1805). Among his northern tragedies are *Hakon Jarl (Earl Hakon*, 1848) and *Baldur hin Gode (Baldur the Good*, 1808). In 1829 Oehlenschlaeger was crowned poet laureate of the Scandinavian countries.

Oenone   (1) In classical mythology, a nymph of Mount Ida. Oenone had the gift of prophecy and told her husband PARIS that his voyage to Greece would involve him and his country (Troy) in ruin. According to the legend, Paris came back to her beseeching her to heal his severe wounds, but she refused, changing her mind too late. When the dead body of old PRIAM's son was laid at her feet, she stabbed herself. This story forms the subject of TENNYSON's "Oenone" and "The Death of Oenone."

(2) In Jean Racine's tragedy PHÈDRE, the nurse of Phèdre. Oenone persuades her mistress to declare her passion to Hippolyte, and she later convinces King Theseus that Hippolyte made advances to Phèdre. Thus it is Oenone who brings about the ruin of Hippolyte and Phèdre. Realizing this, she kills herself.

O'Faolain, Sean (1900–   )   Irish novelist, short-story writer, and biographer. *Midsummer Night Madness* (1932) was his first volume of short stories. He followed it with the successful novel *A Nest of Simple Folk* (1933), a quietly compelling book about the movement of some ordinary Irish people to join the rebellion. In his next two novels, *Bird Alone* (1936) and *Come Back to Erin* (1940), and in such story collections as *The Man Who Invented Sin* (1947), *The Heat of the Sun* (1966), and *The Talking Trees* (1979), O'Faolain's gift for story telling and careful etching of character are brought to bear on his running theme, his painful sense that Irish religious inflexibility and unwillingness to face modern realities prolong the national agony. Among his other works are *Foreign Affairs, and Other Stories* (1976), *Selected Stories* (1978), a novel, *And Again?* (1979), and *The Collected Stories of Sean O'Faolain*, which appeared in three volumes in 1980–82. He wrote biographies of the Irish politician Eamon de Valera (1933) and the Irish patriot Daniel O'Connell (1938), and an autobiography, *Vive Moi* (1964). See IRISH RENAISSANCE.

Offenbach, Jacques (1819–1880)   German-born French composer of some ninety operettas. Offenbach virtually created the 19th-century operetta, and his influence, directly or indirectly, was responsible for its spread to Vienna (Johann STRAUSS the younger) and England (Arthur SULLIVAN). Many of his operettas parody classical subject matter, with reference to life under Napoleon III, among them *Orphée aux Enfers (Orpheus in the Underworld*, 1858) and *La Belle Hélène (Fair Helen*, 1864). The social criticism implicit in these and other works lends his

operas historical as well as musical interest. His fondest dream was to write a serious opera; the one work in which he departed substantially from the frivolous character of his operettas was the OPÉRA COMIQUE *Les Contes d'Hoffmann (The Tales of Hoffmann*), which was left partly unfinished at his death. It was completed by Ernest Guiraud and performed successfully in 1881; the work is based on three stories by E.T.A. HOFFMANN.

Of Human Bondage (1915)   A novel by W. Somerset MAUGHAM. Its hero is Philip Carey, a sensitive, talented, club-footed orphan who is brought up by an unsympathetic aunt and uncle. It is a study of his struggle for independence, his intellectual development, and his attempt to become an artist. Philip gets entangled and obsessed by his love affair with Mildred, a waitress. After years of struggle as a medical student, he marries a nice woman, gives up his aspirations, and becomes a country doctor. The first part of the novel is partly autobiographical, and the book is regarded as Maugham's best work.

O'Flaherty, Liam (1896–1984)   Irish novelist and short-story writer. Although he spent much time in adventurous, worldwide wanderings, O'Flaherty's fiction almost always deals with life among the poor in Ireland and in his native Aran Islands. THE INFORMER, his best-known book, is a psychologically acute study of an Irish revolutionary. Much of his finest work appears in his short stories, many of them masterpieces of bare, lyrical realism. Among his collections are *Two Lovely Beasts* (1948), *The Stories of Liam O'Flaherty* (1956), *The Wounded Cormorant* (1973), and *The Pedlar's Revenge* (1976). *Famine* (1937) is a historical novel. He wrote several "melodramas of the soul," novels compounded, like Graham GREENE's, of the thriller and the psychological case history: *The Black Soul* (1924), *Mr. Gilhooley* (1926), and *The Assassin* (1928).

Of Mice and Men (1937)   A novella by John STEINBECK, dramatized for the theatre in 1937. It deals with the friendship between two migrant workers in California: Lennie Small, a giant half-wit of tremendous strength, and George Milton, who acts as Lennie's protector. The two dream of owning a farm of their own one day, but Lennie accidentally kills a woman who tries to seduce him, and George is forced to shoot him to keep him from an angry lynch mob.

Of Thee I Sing (1931)   A musical comedy with book by George S. KAUFMAN and Morrie Ryskind, lyrics by Ira Gershwin, and music by George GERSHWIN. It satirizes American party politics, showing a presidential campaign conducted on a platform of love. John P. Wintergreen, the party candidate, is to marry the winner of an Atlantic City beauty contest. It was the first musical to win a PULITZER PRIZE.

Of Time and the River: A Legend of Man's Hunger in His Youth (1935)   A novel by Thomas WOLFE. It is a sequel to LOOK HOMEWARD, ANGEL, in which Eugene GANT, the hero, spends two years as a graduate student at Harvard, returns home for the dramatic death of his father, and teaches literature in New York City at the "School for Utility Cultures" (New York University). Eventually he tours France, returning home financially and emotionally exhausted. When the manuscript of the novel was submitted to Maxwell PERKINS of Scribner's, it was several thousand pages long. Perkins helped Wolfe to edit and divide the material into two sections, some of which was included in THE WEB AND THE ROCK.

Ogden, C[harles] K[ay] (1889–1957)   English scholar, inventor of BASIC ENGLISH. Ogden wrote, with I. A. Richards, *The Meaning of Meaning* (1923) and *The System of Basic English* (1934).

Ogham   The traditional alphabet of the ancient British and Irish people. It was used in writing on wood or stone and was supposedly invented by one Ogma. Ogham, and the language associated with it, were employed by the druids; it died out in the 5th century, with the coming of Christianity.

Ogier the Dane   A hero of medieval French romances, one of Charlemagne's paladins. Ogier is probably based on the Frankish warrior Autgarius, who first opposed Charlemagne, then joined him. According to tradition, however, he is held as hostage for his father, Geoffrey of Dannemarch (probably a region in the Ardennes, but later understood as Denmark). He gains Charlemagne's favor for his deeds in Italy, but he kills the queen's nephew to retaliate for the death of his own son in a quarrel and is pursued and imprisoned. Released to fight against the Saracens in Spain, he again wins favor and is eventually given the fiefs of Hainaut and Brabant.

According to another legend, MORGAN LE FAY has him brought to AVALON when he is a hundred years old. She introduces him to King Arthur, rejuvenates him, and sends him out to fight for France, but snatches him back before he can marry, to wait until he is next needed.

OGPU   See CHEKA.

O'Grady, Desmond [James Bernard] (1935–   )   Irish poet. Although O'Grady has lived abroad most of his life, he remains very much an Irish poet who has questioned but never shed his strict Catholic upbringing. He grew up in Limerick, as reflected in *Chords and Orchestrations* (1956), and went as a young man to Dublin; *Reilley* (1961) touches that event. His travels in Europe and the U.S. provided the material for much of the poetry in *Professor Kelleher and the Charles River* (1964), *The Dark Edge of Europe* (1967), *The Dying Gaul* (1968), and *Sing Me Creation* (1977). His poetry represents a need to connect previous with present lives and to connect the journey with the separation it creates. O'Grady also has done extensive translations of poetry, both classical and modern. *Off Licence: Translations from Irish, Italian and Armenian Poetry* (1968) is a well-known work. Other collections of verse include *Headgear of the Tribe* (1979), *His Skald-*

crane's Nest (1979), *These Fields in Springtime* (1984), and *The Wandering Celt* (1984).

ogres   In nursery and fairy tales, giants of very malignant disposition. Ogres live on human flesh. The word was first used (and probably invented) by Charles Perrault in his CONTES DE MA MÈRE L'OYE; it is thought to be made up from *Orcus*, a name of Pluto, the god of Hades.

O'Hara, Frank (1926–1966)   American poet, art critic, and playwright. O'Hara's first interest was in music, but he gave this up and began to write seriously after taking a job at the Museum of Modern Art in New York City. His first volume of poetry, *A City in Winter* (1952), attracted favorable attention, and his essays on painting and sculpture and his reviews for *Art News* were considered brilliant. O'Hara's association with the painters Larry RIVERS, Jackson POLLOCK, and Jasper JOHNS, among others, became a source of inspiration for his highly original poetry. He attempted to produce with words the effects these artists had created on canvas. In certain instances, he collaborated with the painters to make "poem-paintings," paintings with word texts, which are noted for their acid wit. O'Hara's most original volumes of verse, *Meditations in an Emergency* (1956) and *Lunch Poems* (1964), are impromptu lyrics, a jumble of witty talk, journalistic parodies, and surrealist imagery. Their disjunctive syntax simulates the chaotic and urgent quality of the modern cityscape. O'Hara was one of the most distinguished members of the NEW YORK SCHOOL of poets, which also included James SCHUYLER, Kenneth KOCH, and John ASHBERY. *Collected Poems* was published in 1971; *Collected Plays* appeared in 1978.

O'Hara, John [Henry] (1905–1970)   American short-story writer and novelist. Noted for his uncanny ear and skillful rendering of dialogue, O'Hara, who was born in Pottsville, Pennsylvania, began his career as a newspaperman. His short stories, many of which first appeared in THE NEW YORKER, tended, like most of his novels, to be set in the fictitious town of Gibbsville, Pennsylvania. Together they form an acute commentary on contemporary American morals and manners, written by a meticulous literary craftsman. Among his best-known story collections are *The Doctor's Son and Other Stories* (1935) and *Hellbox* (1947); his novel *Pal Joey* (1940) was made into a successful musical by RODGERS and HART. As a novelist, O'Hara established his reputation with *Appointment in Samarra* (1934), his famous first novel, and with *Butterfield 8* (1935), about the promiscuous Gloria Wandrous. His later books include *A Rage to Live* (1949), *Ten North Frederick* (1955), *From the Terrace* (1958), *Elizabeth Appleton* (1963), *Lovey Childs* (1969), and *The Ewings* (1972). *The Good Samaritan and Other Stories* (1974) contains many stories not previously published, written during the last ten years of his life. *Selected Letters of John O'Hara* (1978; ed M. J. Bruccoli) sheds light on a contradictory personality, devoted to the truth as he saw it and the unremitting work of maturing as a literary artist.

O'Hara [Alsop], Mary (1885–1980)   American writer. After writing screenplays in California, O'Hara moved to a ranch in Wyoming and wrote three novels about horses: *My Friend Flicka* (1941), a small classic; *Thunderhead* (1943); and *The Green Grass of Wyoming* (1946).

O'Hara, Scarlett   The willful and colorful heroine of Margaret Mitchell's historical novel, GONE WITH THE WIND.

Okara, Gabriel [Imomotimi Gbaingbain] (1921–   )   Nigerian poet and novelist. Okara studied journalism in the U.S. and served as chief information officer for the Biafran cause in the Nigerian civil war (1967–69). His poetry, which integrates Western forms with a distinctly Nigerian sensibility, is highly regarded for its precision and compression. Without sentimentality, he evokes the rich qualities of African life before it was diluted by Western colonizers. His published works include the novel *The Voice* (1964), a morality tale of Nigerian life, which recreates in the English language many of the verbal patterns and rhythms of his native Ijaw, and *The Fisherman's Invocation* (1978), a volume of verse. His *Poems 1957–1972* was published in 1973.

O'Keeffe, Georgia (1887–1986)   American painter. O'Keeffe was greatly encouraged in her work by Alfred STIEGLITZ, whom she met in 1916 and married in 1924; Stieglitz was the first to show her paintings. She became known for her huge close-up enlargements of flowers, which were gradually transmuted into abstract organic forms, the most famous of which is perhaps *Black Iris* (1926). After 1929 she lived in New Mexico, where she painted the landscapes and architecture of the Southwest, with desert-bleached skulls and bones and Mexican religious symbols. Her later works, many of which are aerial landscapes, became increasingly abstract. She wrote about the nature and process of her work in a spirited autobiography, *Georgia O'Keeffe* (1976).

Okigbo, Christopher (1932–1967)   Nigerian poet. Okigbo published two volumes of poetry in his lifetime: *Heavensgate* (1962) and *Limits* (1964). A posthumous volume, *Labyrinths* (1971), contains his complete poetic works. He acknowledged wide-ranging influences on his work—from his study of the classics to the work of T. S. Eliot, Ezra Pound, and the impressionist painters. To these he added his reflections on his own culture, producing a meditative and ritualistic poetry. A major in the Biafran army during the Nigerian civil war, he was killed in action.

Okudzhava, Bulat Shalovich (1924–   )   Soviet poet and prose writer. Widely popular in the Soviet Union for his ballads on war and life in Russia after the death of Stalin, Okudzhava is also known for his poetry, which first appeared in a collection entitled *Lirika* (1956), for his short story "Good Luck, Schoolboy," which was published in Konstantin Paustovsky's anthology *Tarusskiye stranitsy* (1961; tr *Pages from Tarusa*, 1964), and for his novels *The Extraordinary Adventures of Secret Agent Shipov in Pursuit of Count Leo Tolstoy in the Year 1862* (1973) and *Nocturne: From the Notes of Lt. Amiran Amilakhvan* (1978). Okudzhava's sharp commentary on Soviet society and his trenchant avoidance of convention perhaps spring from his personal encounter with Stalin's terror—his father died in the purges of 1937, and his mother was exiled at that time. Although born in Moscow, Okudzhava is of Georgian and Armenian parentage.

Old Believers   In Russian history, dissenters opposed to the 17th-century liturgical reforms of Patriarch Nikon. The disagreement resulted in a split in the Russian Church during the 17th century. One of the leaders of the dissidents was the priest Avvakum, who described in his autobiography the sufferings he endured for his cause. In 1667 a church council excommunicated Avvakum and his followers, branding them with the name *Raskolniki* ("schismatics"), by which the sect continued to be known.

Old Comedy   A style of Greek COMEDY, of which plays of ARISTOPHANES are the only surviving examples. Like TRAGEDY, Old Comedy evolved from the rituals in honor of DIONYSUS, and the two have in common the use of the CHORUS in PARODOS, EXODOS, and lyric interludes between episodes of dialogue. Comedy, however, apparently developed out of the parts of the Dionysiac festivals most directly concerned with fertility: ritual marriage and feast, bawdy jokes and songs. This ancient religious sanction accounts for both the obscenity and the freedom of political commentary in the plays. Other characteristics of Old Comedy are the *pnigos*, a kind of patter song sung by the chorus in one breath; the *agon* ("contest"), in which the two halves of the chorus argue violently over some contemporary question; and the *parabasis*, in which the chorus addresses directly to the audience an elaborate plea to reward the author with their approval. Old Comedy reached its end with the defeat of Athens in the Peloponnesian War, after which freedom of speech was greatly curtailed.

Old Curiosity Shop, The (1840)   A novel by Charles DICKENS. The heroine, Nell Trent, better known as Little Nell, lives with her grandfather, an old man who keeps a curiosity shop. In order to make some money for Little Nell, the grandfather borrows from the hunchback Daniel Quilp. An obsessive gambler, the grandfather loses all that he has, and Quilp takes over the Old Curiosity Shop. Little Nell and her grandfather leave and roam about the countryside as beggars. They meet Thomas Codlin and his traveling puppet show and work for Mrs. Jarley's Wax Works. Mr. Marton, a kindly schoolmaster, gives them a house near an old church, and Little Nell tends the graves. When Kit Nubbles, their only friend, and the grandfather's brother finally locate them after a long search, Little Nell is dead; her grandfather dies shortly thereafter. Kit marries Barbara and tells the story of Little Nell to his children. The Old Curiosity Shop is torn down to make way for a new building. Many modern readers have found Dickens overly sentimental about Little Nell. Some well-known characters from the book include Sampson and Sarah Brass, Dick SWIVELLER, and the Marchioness.

Oldenbourg, Zoé (1916–) Russian-born French historical novelist. Oldenbourg's novels are distinguished by her careful historical research and rich detail, through which she conveys a vivid picture of the era she describes. A specialist in the Middle Ages, she has written *Argile et cendres* (1946; tr *The World Is Not Enough*, 1948) and its sequel, *La Pierre angulaire* (1953; tr *The Cornerstone*, 1954), as well as *Les Brûlés* (1960; tr *Destiny of Fire*, 1961), about the Crusades. *Les Croisades* (1965; tr *The Crusades*, 1966) is a nonfiction documentation of the same period. *Réveillés de la vie* (1956; tr *The Awakened*, 1957) and its sequel, *Les Irréductibles* (1958; tr *The Chains of Love*, 1959), concern émigrés in pre- and post-World War II Paris. Among her other works to appear in English translation are *Catherine the Great* (1965) and *The Heirs of the Kingdom* (1971). Her memoirs appeared in two volumes: *Visages d'un auto-portrait* and *Le Procès du rêve* (1982). *Que nous est Hécube? ou un plaidoyer pour l'humain* (1986) won the Fémina Prize in 1985.

Old English The language of the Anglo-Saxon peoples in England, spoken from about the mid-5th century AD, when the Angles, Saxons, and Jutes first invaded the British Isles, until the early 12th century, after the Norman invasion of 1066. Part of the Germanic group of Indo-European languages, Old English was a highly inflected language with four major dialect divisions: Kentish, Mercian, Northumbrian, and West Saxon. There is a large body of writings in West Saxon, most of it dating from the 10th and 11th centuries. Well-known examples of Old English ALLITERATIVE VERSE survive in such volumes as BEOWULF and THE DREAM OF THE ROOD. See MIDDLE ENGLISH.

Old Fortunatus (1599) An allegorical comedy by Thomas DEKKER. An old beggar, offered wisdom, strength, health, beauty, long life, or riches by the goddess Fortune, chooses the latter. She gives him an inexhaustible purse, which brings little but trouble to the foolish old man and his equally silly sons; they wander through the world, buffeted by Vice and Virtue, until they perish miserably, and Fortune reclaims the purse.

Old Hickory See JACKSON, ANDREW.

Old Ironsides (1) Popular name for the U.S.S. CONSTITUTION.

(2) A poem (1830) by Oliver Wendell HOLMES. Written when Holmes read of the navy's plan to scrap the old frigate, the poem roused popular opinion, and the *Constitution* was saved.

Old Maid, The (1924) A novella by Edith WHARTON. One of the four books included in the volume OLD NEW YORK, it tells the story of Tina, Charlotte Lovell's illegitimate daughter, who is brought up by Charlotte's cousin in ignorance of her true origin. The dramatization by Zoë Akins in 1935 won a PULITZER PRIZE.

Old Man and the Sea, The (1952) A short novel by Ernest HEMINGWAY. It movingly depicts an old Cuban fisherman who has been eighty-four days without a catch. Far from port on the eighty-fifth day, he hooks a gigantic marlin, and, against great odds, in a battle lasting two days, brings the fish alongside and harpoons it. Soon sharks appear, and the old man breaks his knife after he has killed only a few; during the last night of the voyage home, the sharks devour all but the head of the great fish. The story has been interpreted as an allegory of man's inevitable defeat in the struggle with existence; in spite of defeat, however, man can fight with dignity, courage, and stoicism.

Old Man of the Sea A strange and alarming character in the story of SINBAD THE SAILOR in the *Arabian Nights*. A seemingly harmless if down-at-the-heels old man, he climbs onto the shoulders of the obliging Sinbad, then refuses to get off. He clings there for many days and nights, much to the discomfort of Sinbad, but the sailor finally escapes by making the old man drunk.

Old Masters An epithet for any of the great artists of the 13th to 16th centuries, usually those from Italy, Holland, or Belgium. The term is also applied to their works.

Old Mortality (1939) A short novel by Katherine Anne PORTER. It appeared in the collection PALE HORSE, PALE RIDER, which also included NOON WINE, as well as the title story. For many years, the child Miranda has heard her family speaking with a nostalgia that approaches reverence of her now-dead aunt, who had been known for her grace and beauty. In adolescence, however, Miranda comes to realize that her aunt was actually a totally self-centered woman to whose whims several other people had been sacrificed. Miranda, grown to young womanhood, is also the heroine of "Pale Horse, Pale Rider."

Old New York (4 vols, 1924) A series of four novellas by Edith WHARTON, each dealing with a decade in the years 1840 to 1880. *False Dawn* is about Lewis Raycie, who buys pictures so far in advance of his time that his father disinherits him. THE OLD MAID is considered the best of the group. The third volume, *The Spark*, deals with an elderly man who comes under the influence of Walt Whitman. In *New Year's Day*, a wife sacrifices herself to obtain money for a sick husband, only to be scorned by society.

Old Possum A name assumed by T. S. Eliot. It is used in his collection of comic and whimsical verse, *Old Possum's Book of Practical Cats* (1939).

Old Testament The first part of the Christian BIBLE, identical in content with the Hebrew scriptures. In the Hebrew canon, the Old Testament consists of twenty-four books in three divisions: the Law, or TORAH, comprising the first five books, known as the PENTATEUCH; the eight books of the PROPHETS, with the twelve Minor Prophets as one book; and the Writings, or Hagiographa, which includes the PSALMS, PROVERBS, JOB, SONG OF SOLOMON, RUTH, LAMENTATIONS, ECCLESIASTES, ESTHER, DANIEL, EZRA, and CHRONICLES. The English version of the Christian Bible divides the Old Testament into thirty-nine books, as follows: seventeen historical books (from GENESIS to Esther); five poetical books (from Job to Song of Solomon); and seventeen prophetic books (from ISAIAH to MALACHI).

The entire Old Testament was originally written in Hebrew, except for sections of Ezra, Jeremiah, and Daniel, which were in Aramaic. Its theme is God's covenant with Israel. It contains a history of Israel, its laws as given by God, its triumphs and failures as a nation, its return to God's love, and its eternal hope through righteousness.

Old Wives' Tale, The (1908) A novel by Arnold BENNETT. It is a naturalistic study of the environment and character development of two sisters, Constance and Sophia Baines, who are brought up together in their parents' store in Bursley, one of the Five Towns. Constance stays in Bursley, marries the good apprentice Samuel Povey, and inherits the business. The more adventurous Sophia elopes to Paris with a young ne'er-do-well who deserts her. She finally establishes herself as the successful keeper of a *pension*, and lives peacefully through the siege of Paris and other contemporary events. In her old age, she returns to Bursley to live—and die—with her widowed sister. The novel is remarkable for its sense of passing time and its detailed, sympathetic picture of ordinary women's lives.

Olesha, Yury Karlovich (1899–1960) Russian novelist and short-story writer. Olesha is best known for his short novel *Zavist* (1927; tr *Envy*, 1936), an outstanding work of Soviet prose fiction, which was initially well received but later condemned by Soviet critics for its preoccupation with personal emotions and its implied satire on Soviet methods. Undaunted by criticism, Olesha defended his right to choose his own subjects, but, after speaking at the first meeting of the Union of Soviet Writers, in 1934, he was rarely heard from again until 1957, when his reputation was rehabilitated, with the publication of a selection of his works. The collected stories of Olesha originally appeared in *Vishnovaya kostochka* (*The Cherry Stone*, 1930). He also wrote an adventure novel, *Tri tolstyaka* (*Three Fat Men*, 1928), and a play, *Spisok blagodeyeny* (*A List of Blessings*, 1931).

Olindo The lover of Sofronia in a famous episode of Tasso's GERUSALEMME LIBERATA. Olindo offers to substitute for her at the stake but is condemned to die with her instead. Finally they are both rescued by the warrior maiden Clorinda, and they marry.

olive In ancient Greece, a tree sacred to Pallas ATHENE, who was said to have made it her gift to the Athenians, thereby gaining their loyalty in preference to their previous patron, POSEIDON. It was a symbol of peace and also an emblem of fecundity: Athenian brides wore or carried olive garlands as ours do a wreath of orange blossom. A crown of olive was the highest distinction of a citizen who deserved well of his country and was the highest prize in the Olympic games.

The phrase "to hold out the olive branch," meaning to make overtures to peace, alludes, of course, to its ancient identification with peace. On some ancient Roman medals, the legendary King Numa is shown holding an olive twig, indicative of his peaceful reign.

Oliver Twist (1837–1839) A novel by Charles DICKENS, depicting the world of poverty, crime, and the workhouse of 19th-century London. The novel was written against the background of the new Poor Law of 1834, which ended the supplemental dole to the poor and forced husbands, wives, and children into separate workhouses, in the name of utilitarian efficiency.

Oliver, a foundling, is born in the workhouse, where he commits the unspeakable crime of asking for more gruel. He is apprenticed by Mr. BUMBLE to the undertaker Mr. Sowerberry, but he soon runs away, only to fall into the hands of a gang of thieves headed by FAGIN. With the aid of Jack Dawkins (the ARTFUL DODGER), Nancy, Bill SIKES, and Charley Bates, Fagin tries to make Oliver into a thief. The wealthy Mr. Brownlow tries to rescue Oliver, but, through the machinations of the evil Monks, who has a special interest in corrupting him, Oliver is kidnapped by Fagin's gang; he is forced to take part in a burglary, during the course of which he is wounded. He is nursed by Mrs. Maylie and her foster child Rose (later revealed to be Oliver's aunt). Eventually the secret of Oliver's parentage is disclosed; Monks is his half-brother and has tried to ruin Oliver in order to retain all their father's property. In the end, Monks, Fagin, and the gang are brought to justice. Mr. Brownlow adopts Oliver and educates him. In *Oliver Twist*, one of his most popular novels, Dickens illustrates that poverty breeds crime and that the road from the workhouse to Fagin's gang is a short and straight one.

Olives, Mount of A ridge east of Jerusalem. JESUS went to the Mount of Olives to pray and meditate in the evening. It was perhaps here that he taught his disciples the Lord's prayer (Matt. 6:9–13; Luke 11:2–4). At the foot of its western slope is the garden of GETHSEMANE.

Olivia The rich young countess wooed by Orsino in Shakespeare's TWELFTH NIGHT. Although she is in mourning for her dead brother and "hath abjured the company and sight of men," Olivia falls in love with Orsino's page, who is Viola in boy's disguise. She finally weds Viola's twin brother, Sebastian.

Olivier The close friend of ROLAND among the paladins of CHARLEMAGNE, gifted with the moderation and common sense that Roland lacks. His family is at war with Charlemagne, so that Roland and Olivier meet as dueling opponents. When their long and chivalrous battle is stopped by divine intervention, they become sworn friends, and Roland is engaged to Olivier's sister. The *Chanson de* ROLAND describes the death of all three.

As Oliviero, he appears prominently in Pulci's *Morgante Maggiore* and Boiardo's *Orlando Innamorato*. In Ariosto's *Orlando Furioso*, he joins Orlando (Roland) and Brandimarte in a great duel with the pagan leaders Agramante and Gradasso at Lipadusa; he is seriously wounded but survives.

Olney A country parish in England where William COWPER boarded with Mrs. Mary Unwin and received the religious ministrations of the Rev. John Newton, whom he assisted for a time in charitable activities in the parish. Newton, by forcing Cowper to incessant religious exercises, subjected the poet to a nervous strain, which brought on an attack of insanity in 1773. During this period, the *Olney Hymns* (1779) were written. The hymn "Light Shining out of Darkness" contains the famous stanza:

God moves in a mysterious way,
His wonders to perform;
He plants his footsteps in the sea,
And rides upon the storm.

Olson, Charles [John] (1910–1970) American poet, literary theorist, and scholar. Having taught at Clark University and Harvard, Olson went to Black Mountain College in North Carolina as instructor and rector (1951–56). It was there that he became the leader and theorist of the BLACK MOUNTAIN POETS. His seminal publication *Projective Verse* (1950) included a defense of new verse forms, initiated primarily by William Carlos WILLIAMS and, to a lesser degree, by the objectivist poets (see OBJECTIVISM). The book became the manifesto of practitioners of PROJECTIVE VERSE in Olson's time and afterwards. Olson based his theory on Williams's statement that a poem is a "field of energy." He amplified this concept in his theory of "composition by field," in which "form is never more than an extension of content." He contended that, in order to maintain the force and dynamism of speech, a poem should shy away from description and place emphasis on the syllable rather than on rhyme or meter. Olson himself wrote over twenty volumes of verse. The most significant of these is THE MAXIMUS POEMS, an epic-length collection that appeared in sequences from 1953 to 1976. His collected short poems are contained in *Archaeologist of Morning* (1970).

Olympic games The greatest of the four sacred festivals of the ancient Greeks. It was held at Olympia every fourth year, in the month of July. The festival commenced with sacrifices and included all kinds of contests of sport, ending on the fifth day with processions, sacrifices, and banquets to the victors, who were garlanded with olive leaves. In 1895 an international committee met in Paris in the interests of establishing the modern Olympic games, to which various countries should send contestants. The first games of the new series were held at Athens in 1896, and, after that date, they occurred every four years, with the exception of the duration of World Wars I and II.

Olympus The home of the gods of ancient Greece. There ZEUS held his court; the mountain is about ninety-eight hundred feet high, on the confines of Macedonia and Thessaly.

om A mystical syllable, or MANTRA, common to both HINDUISM and BUDDHISM. It is said to embody the essence of sacred teachings; the reiteration of the syllable is to produce powerful effects. Broken down into its three component sounds (A, U, M), it is also a representation of the Hindu TRIMURTI. See OM MANI PADME HUM.

O'Malley, Grace (Gaelic name Graine Ni Maille, fl 1550–1600) Irish princess. A member of a famous family of seafarers, Grace O'Malley commanded a large fleet of war galleys that preyed on English ships and coastal villages. There are numerous legends about her career, and she may have inspired one of the episodes in James Joyce's *Finnegans Wake* (1939).

Omar Khayyám (d 1123) Persian astronomer and poet. Born at Naishápúr, in Khorastan, Iran, as Abu-'l-fat'h 'Omar, son of Ibrahim the Tentmaker, Omar adopted as his poetic name the designation of his father's trade, Khayyám. He spent his whole life in his native town, where he studied under the celebrated teacher the Imam Mowaffak and was later granted a pension by the Vizier Nizam ul Mulk, a former schoolfellow, becoming known far and wide as a scholar and astronomer. He was one of a commission of eight appointed by Malik Shah to revise the calendar, and he was the author of astronomical tables and a book on algebra, as well as the celebrated collection of quatrains, the RUBÁIYÁT OF OMAR KHAYYÁM.

Never popular in his own country, Omar's poetry had been preserved only in mutilated manuscripts, among which the one in the library of the Asiatic Society, Calcutta, is perhaps the most nearly complete: it contains 516 *rubáiyát* (or *rubáis*). Edward FITZGERALD translated 101 of them from the original Persian into English. The *Rubáiyát* is a series of quatrains rhymed a-a-b-a (or sometimes a-a-a-a in the original), each one expressing a complete thought. Of Omar's thought, FitzGerald wrote: "Omar . . . pretending sensual pleasure as the serious purpose of Life, only diverted himself with speculative problems of Deity, Destiny, Matter and Spirit, Good and Evil, and other such questions."

omega See ALPHA.

omega point See TEILHARD DE CHARDIN, PIERRE.

om mani padme hum ("I salute the jewel in the lotus") A mystic formula, or MANTRA, of Tibetan and other northern Buddhists, the lotus symbolizing the universal being, and the jewel, the individuality of the speaker. These are supposed to be the first words taught to a child and the last uttered on the deathbed.

Omoo: A Narrative of Adventures in the South Seas (1847)   A novel by Herman MELVILLE. The book begins by recapitulating the end of TYPEE, in which the hero escapes on the whaler *Julia*. The crew of the *Julia* mutinies and is imprisoned on the island of Tahiti. The hero and his friend, Doctor Long Ghost, are released, and they explore the island together. *Omoo* is superior in style to *Typee*, with vivid characters and comic scenes. *Omoo* is a Polynesian word for a rover, one who wanders from island to island.

O'More, Rory   The name of three famous Irish rebel chiefs of the 16th and 17th centuries. The name appears frequently in Irish poetry.

Omphale   In Greek mythology, a queen of Lydia. HERACLES was sold to Omphale as a slave. For her, he rid Lydia of robbers and other pests, and they had several children. The idea that they changed clothes, Omphale wearing the lion's skin and Heracles woman's dress, was spread only by later writers, such as OVID.

On American Taxation   A famous speech by Edmund BURKE, delivered in the English Parliament on April 19, 1774, urging that the duty on tea imported into the American colonies be repealed. It was not successful.

On Conciliation with the American Colonies A speech by Edmund BURKE, delivered in the English Parliament in March 1775, in an effort to prevent disaffection between Great Britain and the colonies in America by granting them autonomy. Burke hoped for a system that might preserve both English superiority and colonial liberty. For his resolution in favor of conciliation, his speech won only fifty-eight votes.

One Day in the Life of Ivan Denisovich (Odin den Ivana Denisovicha, 1962; tr 1963)   A short novel by Aleksandr SOLZHENITSYN, describing in excruciating detail the struggle of one prisoner to survive a typical day in a Stalinist labor camp. Khrushchev personally sanctioned its publication in the Soviet magazine *Novy mir*, apparently finding its impassive depiction of degradation and suffering useful in his de-Stalinization campaign. Its appearance then opened a floodgate of prison memoirs by those who, like Solzhenitsyn, had once been incarcerated under Stalin; within a short time, writing on prison and forced labor once again became unpublishable in the Soviet Union.

One Day of the Year, The (1961)   A play by Alan SEYMOUR. For Alf Cook, a working-class ex-soldier, Anzac Day (a day honoring Australia's war veterans) renews his beleaguered sense of identity and "mateship." For his son Hugh, an idealistic university student, it is a day of disgrace, used by the "old diggers" as an excuse for drunken revelry. The play is a careful examination of both sides of the generation gap and the basic human need for illusions.

One Flew over the Cuckoo's Nest   See KESEY, KEN.

One Hundred Years of Solitude (Cien años de soledad, 1967; tr 1970)   A novel by Gabriel GARCÍA MÁR-QUEZ. In this masterpiece of MAGIC REALISM, García Márquez recounts the strange and lustful saga of seven generations of the Buendías, the founding family of the isolated, mythical town of Macondo. A Rabelaisian humor based on exaggeration and extravagance saturates the tragedy of a family irremediably inclined to the pleasures of incest and solitude.

Oneida Community   A perfectionist religious society established in New York state in 1847 by John Humphrey NOYES. An experiment in practical communism, the community developed an excellent school system, ran a nine-hundred-acre farm, and governed itself democratically. The original forty settlers grew to some three hundred; they manufactured steel traps and silver-plated ware. Their system of polygamy and polyandry, developed for the purpose of scientific propagation, aroused public disapproval. The community was abandoned in 1879 but reorganized as a business corporation two years later.

O'Neill, Danny   The hero of a series of novels by James T. FARRELL: *A World I Never Made* (1936), *No Star Is Lost* (1938), *Father and Son* (1940), *My Days of Anger* (1943), and *The Face of Time* (1953). Danny comes from a lower-middle-class Chicago Irish-Catholic background, similar to that of the hero of STUDS LONIGAN. Later he goes to live with more-well-to-do relatives and grows up to be a sensitive young man, becoming a student at the University of Chicago and rebelling against the life accepted by Studs. Danny, who is thought to be based on the author himself, also appears briefly in the Lonigan series.

O'Neill, Eugene [Gladstone] (1888–1953)   American playwright. O'Neill is, by common consent, one of the most significant forces in the history of American theatre. With no uniquely American tradition to guide him, O'Neill introduced various dramatic techniques, which subsequently became staples of the U.S. theatre. Among his notable innovations were the use of symbolic masks and costumes, the repetition of phrases or actions to underscore the thematic intent, and the use of archetypal themes drawn from classical mythology or religion. He also revived the Elizabethan devices of soliloquy and aside to reveal the inner state of his characters. Profoundly influenced by German EXPRESSIONISM, the works of STRINDBERG, and the ideas of NIETZSCHE and FREUD, O'Neill, in his grim and moving psychological dramas, marked a radical departure from the romantic conventions of theatre as entertainment.

The son of James O'Neill and Ella Quinlan, both actors, O'Neill was educated at parochial and private schools and, for a year, at Princeton. He then worked at odd jobs around the country and took several voyages as a merchant seaman, experiences which provided him with much material for his plays. In 1912 he contracted tuberculosis and entered a sanitarium, where he began reading and, eventually, writing plays. By 1914 he had written twelve one-act and two long plays. Of this early work, only *Thirst and Other One-Act Plays* (1914) was originally published. From this point on, O'Neill's work falls roughly into three phases: the early sea plays, written from 1914 to 1921; the experimental one-act plays, written in the fourteen years after 1921; and the last, great plays, written between 1934 and his death.

Crucial to his development were the year he spent as apprentice to George Pierce Baker in his Harvard Workshop (1914) and the association, beginning in 1916, with George Cram Cook, Susan Glaspell, and the PROVINCETOWN PLAYERS, who produced in that year *Bound East for Cardiff*, his one-act play about a dying seaman. The sailor's wistful dreams of leaving the sea to become a farmer marked the beginning of a theme—the life-sustaining pipe dream—that was to become central to O'Neill's later work. Other plays of the sea followed, including *The Long Voyage Home* (1917), concerning sailors in a London bar after a voyage; *Ile* (1917), the story of a captain who persists in his hunt for whale oil at the expense of his wife's sanity; *The Moon of the Caribbees* (1918), depicting the crisis on the steamer *Glencairn*, when women came aboard; and *Where the Cross Is Made* (1918), the tale of another obsessed captain. The plays of this era were collected in *Bound East for Cardiff and Other Plays* (1916) and *The Moon of the Caribbees and Other Plays* (1919). The critical interest they generated paved the way for the production of his first full-length drama, BEYOND THE HORIZON, which won a PULITZER PRIZE. In this early period, culminating in ANNA CHRISTIE, another play of the sea and also a Pulitzer Prize winner, O'Neill was greatly influenced by the naturalism of ZOLA. Also evident is an increasing interest in the characters' search for their own identity.

O'Neill's subsequent experiments with technique and thematic material show clearly the influences he was feeling. In THE EMPEROR JONES, sometimes called the first expressionist play in America, it was Strindberg. THE HAIRY APE, which continued the theme of a search for identity, combined the expressionistic with the naturalistic mode. DESIRE UNDER THE ELMS, a family tragedy set in New England, drew on Freudian psychology and the theories of Nietzsche. ALL GOD'S CHILLUN GOT WINGS, dealing with miscegenation, pointedly flouted the convention of caricaturing blacks in literature and helped destroy it. In these years, O'Neill also wrote THE GREAT GOD BROWN, MARCO MILLIONS, and LAZARUS LAUGHED, all of which make use of masks and deal with another recurring theme: the clash between spiritual and material values. The most important play to come out of this period was STRANGE INTERLUDE, winner of his third Pulitzer Prize. Notable for its innovative use of asides and soliloquy, it is an intricate psychological study of an emotionally barren woman. Following the great

trilogy MOURNING BECOMES ELECTRA, in which he attempted to translate the Greek concept of fate into psychological and environmental determinism, he produced the uncharacteristically light-hearted AH, WILDERNESS! After *Days Without End* (1934), in which two actors play the conflicting sides of the protagonist, no O'Neill play was seen until 1946.

In the interim, O'Neill had planned a nine-play series documenting the history of an American family over two hundred years. He saw America as "the greatest failure in the world," with materialistic obsessions and saccharine optimism covering up the ugly underbelly of a nation of lost souls. However, plagued by Parkinson's disease and consumed by a preoccupation with his own past, O'Neill abandoned his saga of America's failure and turned instead to an analysis of the failure of his own family. *A Touch of the Poet* (written 1943; pub 1957) and *More Stately Mansions* (unfinished; pub 1964), both posthumously produced, are all that survive of the "America" series. THE ICEMAN COMETH restored O'Neill to Broadway; this play and LONG DAY'S JOURNEY INTO NIGHT and A MOON FOR THE MISBEGOTTEN are all autobiographical. These last plays contain some of O'Neill's best writing, with the clear emergence of his authentic voice. He shed the earlier self-conscious symbolism and heavy use of myth and focused directly and realistically on penetrating close-ups of his characters. The themes developed throughout his career —of illusion and pipe dreams; of a tortured quest for some meaning or affirmation of life; of the struggle between materialistic and idealistic ends—were crystallized now with coherence and precision. However uneven the quality of O'Neill's work may seem to be, his extraordinary insight into character, his masterly use of language and bold technical innovations, combined with his brooding sense of tragedy, make him America's first truly great dramatist. O'Neill was awarded the NOBEL PRIZE in Literature in 1936. In 1976 the United States Government declared his California home, Tao House, a National Historic site, under the National Park Service. Only one other house, Carl SANDBURG's, has been similarly preserved solely because of its place in literary history.

One of Ours (1922)   A novel by Willa CATHER. It tells the story of Claude Wheeler, a boy who grows up on a Western farm, goes to a Western university, enters the army, and is killed in France. The book, which is based in part on the letters of a relative of Cather's who died in World War I, was awarded a PULITZER PRIZE.

Onetti, Juan Carlos (1909–   )   Uruguayan novelist and short-story writer. Onetti never completed his secondary education, but he is one of the most erudite and profound of contemporary novelists. He writes with a haunting mixture of sharply honed comedy and deep sadness about the loneliness of life, the futility of religions, and the crumbling of civilization. His books include a three-volume cycle of novels and stories often called the

"Santa Maria Sagas": *La vida breve* (1950; tr *A Brief Life*, 1976), *Los adioses* (1954), and *Una tumba sin nombre* (1959). *El astillero* (1961; tr *The Shipyard*, 1968), his most widely known book abroad, is also set in Santa Maria and draws on some of the same characters. *Juntacádaveres* (1965) takes the central character of *El astillero* back to a time before the beginning of the latter novel. Onetti's *Cuentos completos* was published in 1968 (rev 1974).

onomatopoeia   The formation of words imitating the sound of the object or action expressed, as in *buzz*, *hiss*, *clack*, *bang*, and *twitter*. In rhetoric, the figure of speech in which the writer deliberately reproduces in the sound of the words he selects the actual sound that he is describing or that is connected with his subject. The hissing passage in Milton's PARADISE LOST, where Satan's minions turn into snakes, and the famous frog's chorus in Aristophanes' satirical play THE FROGS are good examples of onomatopoeia.

On the Eve (Nakanunye, 1860)   A novel by Ivan TURGENEV. The heroine, Elena Stakhova, is wooed by three men: the scholar Bersenev, the sculptor Shubin, and the civil servant Kurnatovsky. Unmoved by all of them, she falls in love at first sight with the Bulgarian revolutionary Insarov. Elena feels that she has at last found her goal in life, to fight for social justice by Insarov's side. She leaves with him to continue the struggle for freedom in Bulgaria. Insarov dies on the way, but the inspired Elena goes on to carry on his work. Although he was attempting to show a young revolutionary acting in a positive manner, Turgenev was criticized by the radicals for portraying him as Bulgarian instead of Russian.

On the Road (1957)   A novel by Jack KEROUAC. Told by the autobiographical narrator Sal Paradise, it is a spontaneous chronicle of a hitch-hiking trip crisscrossing the U.S. Kerouac recreates the conversations and licit and illicit adventures of Sal Paradise and his cronies, Carlo Marx (based on the poet Allen GINSBERG) and Dean Moriarity (Neal Cassady), along with other assorted drifters, all of whom are alienated from "square" middle-class society. Ginsberg described its style as "bop prosody"; it was originally written as one paragraph, without punctuation, on a 250-foot roll of paper. Although violently attacked by some critics (Truman CAPOTE said: "This isn't writing; this is typing."), *On the Road* was highly acclaimed by the young and, with Ginsberg's HOWL, it was considered one of the classics of the beat movement.

On the Sublime (Peri hypsous)   A Greek treatise of unknown author and date. Attributed to Dionysius or Dionysius Longinus, it was probably written in the first half of the 1st century AD. The treatise finds five sources of the sublime in literature: significant thoughts, intense emotion, powerful figures of speech, excellence in choice of language, and effective organization. The author states that a passion for novelty often converts the sublime into the ridiculous. The sublime has universal appeal. The author

discusses the possibility of "noble error," saying that sublimity, not correctness, enables man to approach the gods. He cites HOMER, PLATO, and DEMOSTHENES as examples. The treatise was first published by Robortello in 1554 and was translated by Boileau in 1674. It was widely admired, particularly by DRYDEN, ADDISON, POPE, GOLDSMITH, REYNOLDS, FIELDING, and GIBBON.

Open Boat, The (1898)   A short story by Stephen CRANE. Often considered the greatest of his works in this form, it is based on a personal experience of the author. It deals with four men who have escaped in a small open boat from their sinking ship: the captain, the cook, an oiler, and a newspaper correspondent. They discuss the possibilities of being saved, sight land, and await help that does not come. After a whole night of drifting just off shore, they attempt to land the boat. In the process, three of the men come ashore successfully, but the oiler dies, just as he is about to reach safety. Told in a style of great understatement and economy, the story carries far more significance, weight, and drama than the slight plot would seem to indicate.

Open Mind, The   See MONSIEUR OUINE.

opera buffa   See OPÉRA COMIQUE.

opéra comique   A genre of opera in France, in which the dialogue between musical numbers is spoken rather than sung. It should be noted that the term does not designate "comic opera," since many works in the genre (e.g., Bizet's *Carmen*, Offenbach's *Les Contes d'Hoffmann*) are totally or predominantly serious in character. The correct term for a French opera that is primarily comic is *opéra bouffe*, the equivalent of the Italian *opera buffa*.

Ophelia   In Shakespeare's HAMLET, the young and innocent daughter of POLONIUS and sister of LAERTES. Dutifully, Ophelia obeys Polonius's request that she spurn Hamlet's advances and later permits her father to spy on her and Hamlet. After the death of Polonius, she loses her mind. The scene in which her madness is poignantly revealed is one of the most famous in literature.

Ophüls, Max (real name Max Oppenheimer, 1902–1957)   German-born film director. A great stylist, Ophüls made films in several European countries and in the U.S. His films are characterized by opulent decor, sweeping camera movements, and nostalgic, bitter-sweet recreations of life, love, and frivolity in old Vienna or the Paris of *La Belle Epoque*. Among his best films are *Liebelei* (1932), *Letter from an Unknown Woman* (1948), *La Ronde* (1950), *Le Plaisir* (1951), *Madame de . . .* (1953), and *Lola Montès* (1955). Ophüls's son Marcel (1927–   ) also became well known, as the director of *The Sorrow and the Pity* (1969) and *A Memory of Justice* (1976).

O Pioneers! (1913)   A novel by Willa CATHER. Her second novel and the first to be set in Nebraska, it tells of how Alexandra Bergson, on the death of her father, takes over the care of her family and the management of the farm. The other Bergsons are weak or dull, but Alexandra, energetic and courageous, succeeds in building up a prosperous farm. Her hopes for the future of her young brother Emil are blasted when he is killed by a jealous husband, but eventually her loneliness comes to an end, with her marriage to Carl Linstrum. Alexandra's deep devotion to the land dominates the novel.

Opitz, Martin (1597–1639)   Early German critic and baroque poet. Opitz is especially famous for his *Buch von der deutschen Poeterey* (*Book on German Poetry*, 1624), in which he set forth the poetic principles that were to be quite closely followed by subsequent baroque poets writing in German. Opitz, who was strongly influenced by RONSARD and the PLÉIADE, believed that poetry must be based on the models of classical antiquity, and he endeavored to show how the German language could be suited to these models. His own work includes many translations from Greek and Latin and many poems in classical forms, such as the elegy and ode.

Oppenheim, E[dward] Phillips (1866–1946) English novelist, popular and prolific writer of thrillers, many of which dealt with international diplomacy and espionage.

Optic, Oliver (pen name of William Taylor Adams, 1822–1897)   Adams edited the immensely popular children's periodical *Oliver Optic's Magazine* (1867–75). Volumes 1–14 were subtitled *Our Boys and Girls*, the title by which the magazine was frequently known; volumes 15–17 carried the subtitle *For Young and Old.*

oracle (Lat, *oraculum*, fr *orare*, "to speak; to pray") The answer of a god or an inspired priest to an inquiry respecting the future; the deity giving the response; or the place where the deity could be consulted. In ancient Greece, there were many oracles, some of which were consulted by men of other nations. Perhaps the best known was the DELPHIC ORACLE, but the oracle of ZEUS at DODONA, one of the most ancient, was also very highly respected. The oracle of TROPHONIUS, in Boeotia, was perhaps the most awesome. Other famous oracles were as widely separated as that of HERACLES at Gades, in Spain, that of Zeus (or Amen), in Libya, and that of ARES, in Thrace.

One reason for the reputation for infallibility enjoyed by many oracles was that their answers were given in such ambiguous terms that they were sure to be right, no matter what happened. A famous example of this, told by HERODOTUS, was the sad experience of CROESUS, who, on consulting the oracle about whether he should make war on Persia, was told that if he did, he would overthrow a great empire. He optimistically assumed that the empire was Persia—but it was his own empire of Lydia. Greek drama and myth is full of stories of oracles that turn out to be right, often after many years, and usually to the great sorrow of the recipient who has failed to accept the admonition.

Oracle of the Holy Bottle (Fr, *L'Oracle de la dive bouteille*)   In Rabelais's GARGANTUA AND PANTAGRUEL,

the oracle "near Cathay in Upper India" to which PANTAGRUEL, PANURGE, and Friar John journey in an effort to learn whether Panurge should marry. They approach the temple through vineyards, descend through subterranean passages, and eventually pass through the gates of the temple itself, over which is the inscription "In wine, truth." There the Pontiff Bacbuc (Heb, "bottle") leads Panurge unto a side chapel, where the Holy Bottle is sitting in the middle of a fountain. Bacbuc casts something into the fountain, whereupon the water begins to bubble, and the Bottle makes a cracking sound like "Trinch!" (Ger, *Trink!*, "Drink!"). Bacbuc declares this to be a perfect answer and gives Panurge what appears to be a book but is in fact a flask full of wine, so that he may interpret the oracle. The potion inspires Friar John and Panurge to recite doggerel. Bacbuc then sends the joyful party home, reminding the travelers that many secrets of nature are yet to be revealed by time and study.

orchestra   In ancient Greek theatres, the large, circular dancing floor occupied by the chorus. Surrounded on three sides by tiers of seats and on the fourth by a raised platform for the principal actors, it had an altar of DIONYSUS at its center. It was used by the chorus in their dances and songs and also for processions and pageantry.

Orczy, Baroness [Emmuska]   See SCARLET PIMPERNEL, THE.

ordeal (fr OE, *ordel*, related to *adoelan*, "to deal, allot, judge")   An ancient Anglo-Saxon and Teutonic practice of rendering justice in disputed questions of criminality by subjecting the accused person to a physical test, such as by battle, fire, water, or the like. This method of trial was based on the belief that God would defend the right, even by miracle if needful. All ordeals, except the ordeal by battle, were abolished in England by law in the early 13th century.

In *ordeal by battle*, the accused person was obliged to fight anyone who charged him with guilt. This ordeal was allowed only to persons of rank.

Ordeal by fire was also for persons of rank only. The accused had to hold in his hand a piece of red-hot iron or to walk blindfolded and barefoot among nine red-hot ploughshares laid at unequal distances. If he escaped uninjured, he was accounted innocent, *aliter non*. This might be performed by a deputy.

Ordeal by hot water was for the common people. The accused was required to plunge his arm up to the elbow in boiling water and was pronounced guilty if the skin was injured in the experiment.

Ordeal by cold water was also for the common people. The accused, being bound, was tossed into a river; if he sank he was acquitted, but if he floated he was accounted guilty. This ordeal remained in use for the trial of witches to comparatively recent times.

In the *ordeal by the bier*, a person suspected of murder was required to touch the corpse; if he was guilty, the "blood of the dead body would start forth afresh."

In *ordeal by the cross*, plaintiff and defendant had to stand with their arms crossed over their breasts, and he who could endure the longest won the suit.

The *ordeal by the Eucharist* was for priests. It was supposed that the elements would choke a guilty man.

Ordeal of Richard Feverel, The (1859)   A novel by George MEREDITH, with the subtitle *A History of Father and Son*. The plot concerns the tragic working out of Sir Austin Feverel's self-evolved system of education; in applying the precepts of this system to the upbringing and education of his son Richard, Sir Austin expects to create a perfect specimen of manhood. Richard is tutored at home by an uncle, Adrian Feverel, and is carefully protected from any untoward contact with the opposite sex. In spite of the system, however, Richard falls in love with Lucy Desborough, a girl beneath his station, and is forced to marry her. Sir Austin refuses to see Lucy and attempts to punish Richard by maneuvering to keep them apart, with the result that Richard succumbs to the attractions of a clever woman of low repute, while Lucy, in his absence, is approached by an aristocratic libertine. Bessie Berry, Richard's old nurse, a person much loved for her good judgment and large heart, finally succeeds in extricating Lucy from her difficulties. In the meantime, the repentant Richard lingers abroad, until his uncle Austin Wentworth, a man of tolerance and understanding, effects a reconciliation between Lucy and Sir Austin. Richard then returns, but, when he hears of the libertine's insult to Lucy's honor, he challenges him to a duel, is badly wounded, and on recovery learns that Lucy has died of brain fever. Richard is mentally broken, and the failure of his father's system is complete.

O'Reilly, Persse   In James Joyce's FINNEGANS WAKE, the author, hero, or singer of "The Ballad of Persse O'Reilly." Delivered in H. C. Earwicker's tavern, it is a merry, complex song having to do with Earwicker's misdeed in the park. The name is derived from the French *perce-oreille* ("earwig"); O'Reilly is therefore another incarnation of Earwicker himself. The ballad has often been anthologized.

Oresteia (458 BC)   A trilogy of plays by AESCHYLUS, the only extant trilogy of Greek dramas. It includes *Agamemnon*, *The Libation-Bearers*, and the *Eumenides*. See ATREUS, THE HOUSE OF.

Orestes   In Greek mythology, the son of AGAMEMNON and CLYTEMNESTRA. Aided or abetted by his sister ELECTRA, Orestes killed his mother and her lover Aegisthus to avenge his father, whom they had murdered. He appears in more Greek dramas than any other personage, notably in Aeschylus' ORESTEIA, Sophocles' ELECTRA, and Euripides' ELECTRA, IPHIGENIA IN TAURIS, ORESTES, and *Andromache*. See ATREUS, THE HOUSE OF.

Orestes (408 BC)   A drama by EURIPIDES. The main theme is the revelation of the character of ORESTES and his friends, who are shown to be bungling criminals. The play opens on Orestes asleep, tormented by the ERINYES for the murder of his mother. He and ELECTRA beseech MENELAUS to help them escape their city's death penalty, but he refuses on the urging of TYNDAREUS, the father of CLYTEMNESTRA and HELEN. Orestes and PYLADES set out for the Argive Assembly, where Orestes makes a fool of himself and ensures his condemnation. Electra, Orestes, and Pylades decide to kill Helen and hold HERMIONE, the daughter of Menelaus and Helen, as hostage against Menelaus. The most unusual messenger scene in Greek tragedy follows, in which a Phrygian slave from Helen's retinue jumps onto the stage and blurts out in jumbled language what has happened within. At the conclusion, Orestes and Pylades have set the palace afire and are preparing to murder Hermione; Electra is about to set fire to the whole city; Menelaus is shouting helplessly from below, calling the townspeople to his aid. Then, APOLLO appears from above and dictates the solution: Orestes is to marry Hermione; Electra and Pylades will be married; Menelaus must find himself a new wife, since Helen has been taken up into the sky as a beacon for sailors. The artificial DEUS EX MACHINA is convincing by its very absurdity; it is a fitting conclusion to a bitter play.

Orgon   See TARTUFFE, LE.

Oriane   See GUERMANTES, DE.

Oriani, Alfredo (1852–1909)   Italian poet, novelist, dramatist, and writer on history, politics, and social problems. Oriani's fiction is noted for its highly ornate and ponderous style, suggestive of that of Victor HUGO, Eugène SUE, and other French serial novelists in vogue during the second half of the 19th century.

Oriani had a taste for unusual plot situations that act as catalysts for the pathological states of mind common to his characters. Among his better-known novels are *Gelosia* (1894), which describes an unsuccessful *ménage à trois*; *La Disfatta* (1896), in which a child's death destroys all vestiges of love and hope in his parents; *Vortice* (1899), which describes in detail a planned suicide; and *Olocausto* (1902), whose protagonist is forced into prostitution at the age of sixteen and dies as a result of the loss of her childhood innocence.

A Hegelian idealist who subscribed to the mystique of national mission, Oriani often enunciated extremist views on nationalism and imperialism, which made him a precursor of fascism.

Among his political writings are *Fino a Dogali* (1889), inspired by the Italian campaign in Africa; *Il nemico* (1892); *La rivolta ideale* (1908); and *La lotta politica in Italia* (1892), a three-volume study of Italian political institutions from the Middle Ages to the 19th century.

Oriflamme (Fr, "flame of gold")   The ancient banner of the kings of France. First used as a national banner in 1119, it was a crimson flag cut into three triangular pennants to represent tongues of fire. It was carried on a gilt staff and a silken tassle hung between the flames. Originally the banner of St. Denis, the sacred Oriflamme became royal property in 1082. It was carried at Agincourt in 1415. It was said that the sight of it blinded any infidel. In the 15th century, the Oriflamme was succeeded by the blue standard powdered with fleur-de-lis, and the last mention of the original Oriflamme is in the inventory of the Abbey of St. Denis dated 1534.

Origen (c185–c253)   One of the Greek Fathers of the Church. The head of the catechetical school in Alexandria, in Caesarea, Origen wrote prolifically and collated the *Hexapla*, a collection of Old Testament texts.

Original Sin   The sin of all at birth. In orthodox Christian theology, the belief that all men are born with the taint of sin, resulting from the primal disobedience of ADAM AND EVE in eating the fruit of the forbidden tree. This sin is held to be removed by the Sacrament of BAPTISM.

Origin of Species (1859)   A work by Charles DARWIN, the full title of which is *On the Origin of Species by Means of Natural Selection, or the Preservation of Favoured Races in the Struggle for Life.* In it he develops his theory of evolution by natural selection. Darwin argues that every species develops or evolves from a previous one and that all life is a continuing pattern. His objects of study were the variations from generation to generation in domestic plants and animals. In the "struggle for existence," common to all life, an animal or plant that inherits an unfavorable variation is not likely to survive and produce offspring. The severe conditions in the environment tend to kill off individuals with unfavorable variations in favor of "the SURVIVAL OF THE FITTEST," that is, individuals with favorable variations. Darwin concludes that there exists a "natural selection" of favorable variations, which produces new varieties. While subsequent investigation has superseded some of Darwin's arguments, *Origin of Species* remains one of the most influential books ever published.

Orillo   A monstrous magician in Lodovico Ariosto's ORLANDO FURIOSO. Orillo is capable of reintegrating his body when it is cut to pieces. Astolfo, learning from a book given him by the enchantress Logistilla that Orillo's life depends on literally one hair of his head, decapitates him and, with the headless body in pursuit, plucks out each hair until he finds it; the head then dies and the body falls lifeless from its horse.

Orion   In Greek mythology, a famous hunter. In the many unreconciled variants of his story, Orion appears as an amiable if rather lustful giant. In one tale, he is blinded by Oenopion, king of Chios, to prevent his marriage to Oenopion's daughter, travels eastward toward the home of the sun, with a boy on his shoulders to guide him, and finally has his sight restored by the sun's rays. Two other legends, his pursuit of the PLEIADES and his death from a scorpion's sting as a result of trying to ravage ARTEMIS, are

astronomical myths that try to explain the relative positions of the constellations Orion, the Pleiades, and the Scorpion.

Orlando   (1) The courageous hero of Shakespeare's AS YOU LIKE IT, who challenges Duke Frederick's wrestler to prove his mettle. In love with Rosalind, who leads him a merry chase through the Forest of Arden, Orlando typifies the fashionable Elizabethan "lovesick swain," penning verses to Rosalind and hanging them on trees.

(2) The Italian name of Charlemagne's paladin ROLAND.

Orlando (1928)   A fantastic novel by Virginia WOOLF. Orlando begins as a young Elizabethan nobleman and ends, three hundred years later, as a contemporary young woman, based on the author's friend Victoria SACKVILLE-WEST. The novel contains a great deal of literary history and brilliant, ironic insights into the social history of the ages through which Orlando lives. Orlando starts life as a male poet and ends as an equally intense and able woman poet, in order to emphasize the author's belief that women are intellectually men's equals. The novel is thus a companion piece to the feminist essay *A Room of One's Own* (1929).

Orlando Furioso (Roland Mad)   A romantic epic by Lodovico ARIOSTO. It was published in 1516 with forty cantos and in a longer version of forty-six cantos in 1532. Its plot continues where BOIARDO broke off his ORLANDO INNAMORATO; like the earlier poem, the subplots involving CHARLEMAGNE's PALADINS and various pagan knights are interwoven (*intrecciatura*). The magic and enchantments of the earlier poem are continued and expanded, but with an ironic tone that contrasts strongly with the seriousness of Boiardo yet avoids the burlesque of Pulci and other popular treatments of the material.

The poem begins with the escape of ANGELICA from the custody of Duke Namo of Baviera, to whom Charlemagne had entrusted her in hopes of avoiding conflict between Orlando (see ROLAND) and his cousin RINALDO, both desperately enamored of her. She flees to the island of Ebuda, where she is captured and exposed to a sea monster, from which she is rescued by RUGGIERO. Orlando, who has dreamt of her plight, arrives at Ebuda to save Olimpia instead. Continuing his search for Angelica, he is detained in the enchanted castle of Atlante until his beloved rescues him. Angelica then disappears again and arrives at Paris, where a great battle has taken place; she meets the wounded Moorish youth Medoro, cares for him, and elopes with him to Cathay. Orlando goes mad with grief at this betrayal. ASTOLFO takes his winged horse to Ethiopia, then mounts the chariot of Elijah and, with Saint John as his guide, travels to the moon. There he recovers the lost wits of Orlando, who recovers upon sniffing the urn in which they lie. As the poem nears its end, the siege of Paris is broken, and Agramante killed. Ruggiero, converted to Christianity, wins his BRADAMANTE after defeating the last pagan warrior, RODOMONTE, in a furious battle.

Thus, despite its title, the poem is really centered on Ruggiero, with Bradamante the progenitor of the ESTE family. Like Boiardo, the poet flatters his patrons of the Ferrara court in this imaginary genealogy. Similar emphasis is given to descriptions of such delightful creatures as Astolfo's hippogriff and such memorable places as the grotto of the witch Melissa and the island of oblivion, ruled by the enchantress Alcina. Unlike his predecessors, Ariosto makes use of the opening octaves of each canto to set forth his personal views and critical comments.

The *Furioso* was the most influential of the early Orlando poems. In England, its popularity during the Renaissance is attested by Robert GREENE's play *The History of Orlando Furioso* (1594), Spenser's THE FAERIE QUEENE, and the translation done by Sir John Harington in 1591, presumably as a penance imposed by his godmother, Queen Elizabeth. Numerous artists have used the characters and incidents of Ariosto's poem for paintings and musical works, witness the *Alcina* (1735) of HANDEL.

Orlando Innamorato (Roland in Love)   A romantic epic of Matteo Maria BOIARDO, who first blended the chivalric material of the CAROLINGIAN stories with the amorous motifs of the ARTHURIAN cycle. Written in octaves, its first two books (of twenty-nine and thirty-one cantos, respectively) appeared in 1487; the third book was unfinished, breaking off at the ninth canto. The entire poem was rewritten by Berni in pure Tuscan, and ARIOSTO continued its plot in his ORLANDO FURIOSO.

At Paris, where thousands of knights have gathered for a tournament, the pagan princess ANGELICA suddenly appears. She has come from Cathay to sow discord in the ranks of the PALADINS and thus render them helpless before the Saracens, led by Agramante, emperor of Africa, and Gradasso, king of Sericana. One by one, CHARLEMAGNE's knights desert the court in pursuit of Angelica or each other. In the many subplots that follow, all interwoven (*intrecciatura*), the paladins Orlando (see ROLAND), his cousin RINALDO, ASTOLFO, and Brandimarte undergo various enchantments, combats with giants and pagan warriors, and timely rescues. The pagan warrior RUGGIERO, descended from the Trojans, is introduced as the forerunner of the ESTE family, who were Boiardo's patrons. When the poem breaks off, Ruggiero has not been reunited as yet with the warrior maiden BRADAMANTE, sister of Rinaldo and the object of his love. The pagan forces still threaten Charlemagne at Paris.

Ormuzd   The principal deity of the ancient Zoroastrians and modern Parsees. Ormuzd is the angel of light and good, the creator of all things, according to the Magian system. He is called *Ahura Mazda*, the good god, and is said to be in perpetual conflict with Ahriman, over whom he will ultimately triumph. The Latin form is *Oromasdes*. See ZOROASTER.

Orozco, José Clemente (1883–1949)   Mexican painter. Orozco was perhaps Mexico's greatest painter, known mainly for his frescos in Mexico and the United States and for his propagandist caricatures during the Mexican Revolution. His murals often depict the grim futility of war; thus he is sometimes called the Mexican Goya.

Orpheus   In Greek mythology, a fabulous musician. A son of the muse CALLIOPE and APOLLO or King Oeagrus, Orpheus was born in Thrace and was a devotee of DIONYSUS. He married Eurydice, a dryad, but she was killed by a snake while fleeing the advances of Aristaeus. Orpheus descended into HADES to find her. His playing of the lyre so delighted even Hades himself that Orpheus was permitted to take Eurydice back with him, provided that he did not look at her until they arrived in the upper world. When they were nearly there, however, he no longer heard her behind him, and he looked back. Eurydice returned to Hades.

Inconsolable, Orpheus would have nothing to do with other women. The Thracian women, outraged by this behavior, tore him to pieces in a bacchanalian revel—and Orpheus thus suffered the same fate as his god Dionysus. The fragments of his body were collected by the MUSES and buried at the feet of Mt. Olympus, but his head, which had been thrown into the river Hebrus, was carried into the sea and came ashore on the island of Lesbos. There it became a famous ORACLE.

The story of Orpheus and Eurydice has been a favorite subject for dramatists and composers. The first extant opera, by Jacopo Peri, was based on it, as were many others, including those by MONTEVERDI and HAYDN; the most famous is GLUCK's *Orpheus and Eurydice* (1762). Of the many dramatic versions of the story, one of the most unusual is *Orfée*, a motion picture (1950) by Jean COCTEAU.

orphism   A Greek mystic cult popular in the 6th century BC. Its mysteries were supposedly taught to men by ORPHEUS. They centered on the myth of Zagreus, son of ZEUS and PERSEPHONE, who was torn to pieces by the TITANS at HERA's orders. For this crime, Zeus destroyed the Titans and swallowed the heart of Zagreus, who was reborn of SEMELE in the person of DIONYSUS. The orphic rites apparently included the tearing and eating of animals representing Zagreus, whose myth was probably Thracian or Phrygian in origin. The notion, peculiar to the orphics, that human beings contained elements of both divinity and evil was explained by the fact that men were created from the ashes of the Titans, who, evil themselves, had nevertheless swallowed the divine Zagreus. Although orphism differed from both orthodox myth and popular cult, it influenced PLATO, PINDAR, and the PYTHAGOREANS.

Orsino   The sentimental duke of Illyria in Shakespeare's TWELFTH NIGHT. Orsino is in love with Olivia but finally marries Viola. His famous words open the play:

If music be the food of love, play on . . .

Ortega y Gasset, José (1883–1955) Spanish philosopher, essayist, and critic. One of the 20th century's leading thinkers, Ortega y Gasset received his early education with the Jesuits and took his doctorate at the University of Madrid. He then continued his studies in Germany, where he was strongly influenced by the philosophy of KANT. On his return to Spain, he was appointed to the chair in metaphysics at the University of Madrid, from which position he exerted an enormous influence on Spanish thinkers for half a century. His first book, *Meditaciones del Quijote* (1914; tr *Meditations on Quixote*, 1964) contained the seeds of much of the material he was to develop in later works. Here, in a metaphysical examination of the DON QUIXOTE figure, Ortega y Gasset contends that man, although powerless to affect his past, can affect his future by transcending his immediate circumstances and redefining the nature of individuality. His essays from 1916 to 1934 were published in eight volumes, collectively titled *El espectador*. Ortega y Gasset's conviction that historical patterns could explain and expose the ills of the present is manifest in *España invertebrada* (1921; tr *Invertebrate Spain*, 1937), in which he attempts to locate the roots of Spain's decadence. Another important work is *El tema de nuestro tiempo* (1923; tr *The Modern Theme*, 1931), in which he develops the concept of *razón vital*. The "vital reason" (embracing both thought and feeling) becomes the means by which life can transcend the restrictive elements of pure or mathematical reason. Ortega y Gasset's aesthetic theories are the subject of *La deshumanización del arte e ideas sobre la novela* (1925; tr *The Dehumanization of Art*, 1948). Perhaps his most popular and controversial work is *La rebelión de las masas* (1930; tr *The Revolt of the Masses*, 1932), in which he develops ideas from *España invertebrada* and suggests that Spain should be ruled by a benevolent intellectual elite, to avoid the decaying effects of mob control upon government and the arts.

Orton, Joe [John Kingsley] (1933–1967) English playwright. Perhaps closer in spirit to classic Greek comedy than any other modern playwright, Orton turned the outrageous and horrifying into farce. *Entertaining Mr. Sloane* (1964) is the story of a young murderer who manipulates both his landlady's and her brother's lust for him and who is in turn blackmailed by them. In *Loot* (1966), a bank robber uses his mother's corpse to conceal stolen goods. Set in a clinic, *What the Butler Saw* (1969) not only makes savage and bawdy fun of psychiatric practices, but also ingeniously parodies the farce form itself. In Orton's plays, nightmares come true; his characters are wounded psychologically and physically and sometimes killed. Orton's own life ended at thirty-four, when he was beaten to death by his lover, apparently in a fit of jealousy over Orton's success.

Orwell, George (pen name of Eric Arthur Blair, 1903–1950) English novelist, essayist, and critic. An independent socialist in adult life, Orwell was born in India, where his father was in the civil service. He won a scholarship to Eton but was financially unable to go on to Oxford or Cambridge. Instead he spent five years with the Imperial Police in Burma (1922–27). Much of his early work was at least partly autobiographical. His experiences in Burma provided the material for the novel *Burmese Days* (1934), an attack on British imperialism, and for the title essay in his collection *Shooting an Elephant* (1950). His years of impecunious vagabonding are described in *Down and Out in Paris and London* (1933). *The Road to Wigan Pier* (1937), an account of coal miners' lives in northern England, contains a clear statement of Orwell's liberal, socialist views. *Keep the Aspidistra Flying* (1936) and *Coming Up for Air* (1939) are comic novels with working-class characters.

Homage to Catalonia (1938) expresses Orwell's disillusionment during the Spanish Civil War, in which he fought on the Republican side. The book describes the internal dissension between the Republicans and their Communist allies, and it sharply criticizes Communist deceit and intellectual dishonesty. After that point, Orwell said that all his writings, both fiction and essays, were directed against totalitarianism in all forms. This commitment is manifest in his two best-known novels, ANIMAL FARM and 1984 (q.v.).

Orwell was known as a superb prose stylist who took a lucid, documentary approach to fiction. His *Collected Essays, Journalism and Letters* (4 vols) appeared in 1968.

Osborne, John [James] (1929–) English playwright. Osborne's first successful play, LOOK BACK IN ANGER, introduced a new strain of realism to British theatre and set the tone for the generation of anti-Establishment writers who became known as the ANGRY YOUNG MEN. Osborne described his own parents as "impoverished middle class," but his play deals with the frustrations, crude language, and squalid conditions of working-class life. His subsequent work made it clear, however, that it was human character rather than social action that intrigued him. In Archie Rice, the failed music-hall comic in *The Entertainer* (1957), Osborne draws a penetrating portrait of a man's brave but pathetic attempts to conceal his failure. *Luther* (1961) presents the great reformer as an intense, volatile, earthy man impelled by his own personality to upset the church establishment. The influence of BRECHT on Osborne's technique is apparent in those two plays and again in INADMISSABLE EVIDENCE, perhaps the most powerful of Osborne's character studies. Later plays include *West of Suez* (1971), *A Sense of Detachment* (1972), *Watch It Come Down* (1975), *You're Not Watching Me, Mummy*, and *Try a Little Tenderness* (both 1978), and *Too Young to Fight, Too Old to Forget* (1985). His autobiography, *A Better Kind of Person*, appeared in 1981. Osborne is also known for his screen adaptations, among them *Tom Jones* (1964), *Hedda Gabler* (1972), and *The Picture of Dorian Gray* (1973).

Osiris   The supreme god and king of eternity of ancient Egypt, whose name means "many-eyed." Osiris was thought to be judge of the dead, ruler of the kingdom of the Other World, creator, god of the Nile, and constant foe of his twin brother and son SET, the principle of evil. He was slain by Set, who cut his body into pieces, but Osiris was buried by his wife ISIS and revenged by HORUS and THOTH. Because he was resurrected to an eternal reign in heaven, he symbolized hope for life beyond the grave and fostered the process of mummification. He was usually depicted as a mummy wearing the crown of upper Egypt but was sometimes also shown as an ox.

Os Lusíadas   See LUSÍADAS, OS.

Osmond, Gilbert   See PORTRAIT OF A LADY, THE.

Osric   In Shakespeare's HAMLET, a court fop, contemptible for his affectations and sycophancy. Osric serves as umpire in the duel between Hamlet and LAERTES.

Ossian   The legendary Gaelic warrior, son of FIONN MAC CUMHAIL, who became a bard in his old age and is supposed to have lived about the end of the third century. It is to Ossian that James MACPHERSON ascribed the authorship of a group of poems published from 1760 to 1763; Macpherson claimed that he had translated them from manuscripts collected in the Scottish Highlands, and a great controversy as to their authenticity was aroused. The Ossianic poems, compared at the time to the works of Homer, could move the poet Thomas Gray to write, "Imagination dwelt many hundred years ago in all her pomp on the cold and barren mountains of Scotland." It was soon generally agreed, however, that Macpherson, although compiling from ancient sources, was the principal author of the poems as published.

Ostrovsky, Aleksandr Nikolayevich (1823–1886)   Russian playwright. Ostrovsky's plays laid the foundation for realistic Russian drama. He produced almost fifty in all, both tragedies and comedies, many of them set among the merchant class of Moscow. His first published play was *Bankrot* (*The Bankrupt*, 1847; prod 1850 as *Svoi lyudi—sochtiomsya*). His best-known works include: *Bednost ne porok* (*Poverty Is No Crime*, 1854), *Na vsyakogo mudretsa dovol'no prostoty* (*The Diary of a Scoundrel*, 1868), *Beshenie dengi* (*Easy Money*, 1870), *Les* (*The Forest*, 1871), and his masterpiece, *Groza* (*The Storm*, 1859). He also wrote a fairy tale in verse, *Snegurochka* (*The Snow Maiden*, 1873), which formed the basis for the opera by RIMSKY-KORSAKOV (1880).

Ostrovsky, Nikolay Nikolayevich (1904–1936)   Russian novelist. Ostrovsky wrote the popular *Kak zakayalas stal* (1932–34; tr *The Making of a Hero*, 1937), a largely autobiographical account of a disabled young man, Pavel Korchagin, who overcomes his handicaps to become a writer and teacher. Marxist moralizing in the novel has made it one of the most highly praised works of early Soviet literature.

O'Sullivan, Maurice (1904–1950)   Irish author. O'Sullivan's one book, *Twenty Years A-growing* (1933), is an autobiography in Gaelic of an Irish peasant from the Blasket Islands. It is a unique, authentic account of Irish culture, written with all the native vitality of the Irish oral tradition.

Otage, L'   See HOSTAGE, THE.

Othello, The Moor of Venice (c1604)   A tragedy by William SHAKESPEARE. Othello, a Moorish general in the service of Venice, appoints CASSIO as his chief lieutenant, unwittingly arousing the enmity of IAGO, his ensign, who thinks that he has a better claim to the post. Partly to avenge himself for the slight and partly out of sheer malice, Iago devises a scheme to undo both Cassio and the unsuspecting Othello, who regards Iago as a loyal, trustworthy friend. After causing the dismissal of Cassio by a trick, Iago hints to Othello that his bride, DESDEMONA, the daughter of BRABANTIO, has had illicit relations with Cassio. Although Othello is reluctant to believe Iago's accusations, his worst fears are confirmed when, as a result of Iago's machinations, a handkerchief that he had given to Desdemona is found in Cassio's possession. Enraged, Othello strangles Desdemona. EMILIA, Iago's wife and Desdemona's faithful servant, discovers her husband's plot and denounces him. Othello now realizes his horrible mistake and, after asking that he be remembered as one who "lov'd not wisely but too well," commits suicide. Iago is condemned to torture for his crimes.

The source of the play is Cinthio's *Hecatommithi* (1565). Two operas called *Otello*, one by ROSSINI (1816) and another by VERDI (1887), have been based on Shakespeare's play.

Other Voices, Other Rooms (1948)   A novel by Truman CAPOTE. The hero, thirteen-year-old Joel Knox, comes to his father's dilapidated mansion at Skully's Landing. There he comes in contact with the effeminate Randolph, with Jesus Fever and his daughter, and with his own invalid father. Beyond is the mysterious Cloud Hotel, where Joel achieves self-awareness and a sense of the emptiness of Skully's Landing. Sometimes described as a story of initiation, the book has also been interpreted as symbolizing a search for the Holy Grail and as a search for the father.

Otherwise Engaged   See GRAY, SIMON.

ottava rima   In prosody, a stanza of eight lines rhyming a-b-a-b-a-b-c-c. The form, which arose in Italy in the 14th century, was used by BOCCACCIO, TASSO, ARIOSTO, and many other Italian poets. In English it is usually written in iambic pentameters. It was used, for example, by Keats in ISABELLA; in DON JUAN, Byron strikes the mockheroic, almost burlesque note that has come to be associated with the form.

Ottone (Otho)   In Tasso's GERUSALEMME LIBERATA, a brave knight among the crusaders. When the infidel warrior Argante challenges the Christians to single combat,

Ottone is the first to accept; he is killed ruthlessly, in utter disregard of the laws of chivalry, by the ferocious Argante.

Otus and Ephialtes   In Greek mythology, giant twin sons of Aloeus (or POSEIDON) and Iphimedia. Enormous at nine years old, Otus and Ephialtes tried to pile Mount PELION on top of Mount Ossa in order to war with the gods on OLYMPUS, but ZEUS killed them. Before their death, they had managed to imprison ARES in a bronze bowl, where he stayed for more than a year.

Otway, Thomas (1652–1685)   English dramatist. Otway is best known for his heroic tragedy VENICE PRESERVED, one of the finest tragedies of the Restoration. With the exception of *The Orphan, or The Unhappy Marriage* (1680), a domestic tragedy, about twin brothers in love with the same woman, the rest of his plays are of little merit. See SCAPIN.

Our American Cousin (1858)   A comedy by Tom TAYLOR. A work of no particular merit, this play is remembered as the one Abraham Lincoln was watching when he was assassinated by John Wilkes Booth (April 14, 1865).

Our Mutual Friend (1864)   A novel by Charles DICKENS. The "mutual friend" is John Harmon, friend of Mr. Boffin and the Wilfers, who has been left a fortune on condition that he marry Bella Wilfer. Since he has never met Bella, has not been home for fourteen years, and is reported to have been murdered, he returns under the assumed name of John Rokesmith and acts as secretary to Mr. Boffin, who is to have the Harmon money if the will's conditions are not fulfilled. John and Bella fall in love, marry, and live for a time on John's earnings. Finally, Boffin turns over the fortune and Rokesmith again becomes John Harmon.

Some recent critics consider this novel as one of Dickens's finest from the point of view of conscious artistry, although it lacks the spontaneity of his earlier works. Dust as a symbol of money saturates the atmosphere of the book. Dust, deceit, and death fill the novel, reflecting Dickens's increasing pessimism about the responsibility of upper-middle-class society and life in general.

Our Town (1938)   A play by Thornton WILDER. The action takes place in a typical New England town, Grover's Corners, New Hampshire. The Stage Manager, a garrulous Yankee, sits at the side of the bare stage, talking intimately to the audience as the play unfolds. He describes the characters and the setting. Act I is entitled "Daily Life"; the citizens engage in their customary pursuits, while Professor Willard and Editor Webb comment on them objectively. In Act II, "Love and Marriage," Emily, daughter of Editor Webb, and George, son of Dr. Gibbs, fall in love and marry. In Act III, "Death," Emily dies in childbirth and is buried in the town cemetery. The ancient dead in the cemetery speak of their peace and their perception of eternal harmony in the universe. The play was awarded a PULITZER PRIZE.

Outcast of the Islands, An (1896)   A novel by Joseph CONRAD. It concerns the earlier lives of some of the characters in *Almayer's Folly* (1895). The "outcast" is Willems, who falls in love with the native girl Aissa; she is given him in return for his help in throttling Almayer's trade. Finally Aissa shoots Willems. See LINGARD, CAPTAIN.

Outcasts of Poker Flat, The (1869)   A short story by Bret HARTE. An eloping young couple fall in with a group of ne'er-do-wells—the gambler John Oakhurst, two prostitutes, and a drunkard—who have been expelled from a mining camp. A blizzard traps them all. The outcasts sacrifice themselves, one after another, so that the young people may live. This sentimental tale helped popularize local-color stories.

Out of Africa   See DINESEN, ISAK.

Out of the Cradle Endlessly Rocking (1859)   A poem by Walt WHITMAN. The poet, a child, walks on the beach at moonlight and hears the mourning song of a bird; no longer an innocent, he asks the sea for the secret, and the waves whisper the "low and delicious word death,/ And again death, death, death, death."

Overbury, Sir Thomas (1581–1613)   English poet and prose writer, one of the early 17th-century CHARACTER WRITERS. When Overbury's clever series of prose sketches, *Characters*, was published in 1614, his didactic poem "A Wife" was included in the same volume. Overbury was imprisoned in the Tower of London and killed by slow poison at the instigation of Lady Essex, whose marriage to his patron Robert Carr (later the earl of Somerset) he had opposed.

Overcoat, The (Shinel, 1842)   A short story by Nikolay GOGOL. Regarded as one of the major influences toward the development of realism in Russian literature, the story concerns a poor clerk in the St. Petersburg civil service, Akaky Akakyevich Bashmachkin. He is a miserable old man who is tormented by his callous fellow workers and who has only one thing to console him: his love of copying documents in his hovel at night. Copying is all he feels capable of doing, and when other, slightly more demanding work is offered him in the office, he refuses it. Akaky's life begins to change a little when he goes to the tailor to have his threadbare coat repaired for the coming winter. The coat is too ragged to be patched any more, and Akaky is persuaded to let the tailor make him a new coat. He saves his money carefully, buys the material and the imitation fur for the collar, and has the coat made. The new garment draws attention at the office, and Akaky is even invited to a party. On the way home from the party, delirious with wine and the happiness of his new status, he is robbed of his precious coat. His frantic appeals to the authorities are futile, and the heartbroken Akaky dies. Following his death, mysterious thefts of coats, right off the backs of honest citizens, begin in St. Petersburg. Even the official who had irascibly refused Akaky his aid is robbed of his coat. The story ends with a hesitant policeman approaching a man he believes to be the thief and being threateningly turned on by the man. The policeman timidly retreats, and the mysterious figure disappears in the night.

Gogol's story was hailed as one of the first pieces of literature to deal in a sympathetic way with the poor and downtrodden ordinary people of 19th-century Russia. DOSTOYEVSKY was quoted as saying about himself and his fellow writers: "We all came from beneath Gogol's 'Overcoat.'"

Overdone, Mistress A bawd in Shakespeare's MEASURE FOR MEASURE. Like the foolish Master Froth and the lusty tapster Pompey, Mistress Overdone embodies the rampant licentiousness that Angelo attempts to suppress in Vienna.

Overland Monthly, The An American magazine, published in California from 1868 to 1875 and from 1883 to 1933. It was edited, during its first two and a half years, by Bret HARTE, and it pictured a huge California grizzly bear on its cover. Harte printed THE LUCK OF ROARING CAMP, PLAIN LANGUAGE FROM TRUTHFUL JAMES, and other stories and verse in the magazine. The *Overland* also published other early California writers, among them Ambrose BIERCE, Edwin MARKHAM, and Jack LONDON. The magazine is portrayed as the *Transcontinental Monthly* in London's autobiographical novel *Martin Eden* (1909).

Over-Soul, The (1841) An essay by Ralph Waldo EMERSON. The writer expresses his concept of a primal Mind, a cosmic unity. This "soul of the whole," of which all men partake, is the keystone of Emerson's philosophic thought. The essay is included in his *First Series*.

Ovid (full Latin name Publius Ovidius Naso, 43 BC–AD 17) Roman poet, the first major writer to grow up under the empire. Although his parents had destined him for a career in law and had sent him to Athens to complete his studies, Ovid decided to become a poet. He returned to Rome and, in a short while, gained the reputation of being the most brilliant poet of his generation. His first series of poems were light, sophisticated love elegies, *Amores*. He followed this success with the *Heroides*, where he first displayed his unique gift for psychological insight by composing dramatic monologues in the form of love letters written between mythological lovers, such as Paris and Helen, Hero and Leander. His *Ars amatoria* (*The Art of Love*) was an instant success and established him, at the age of forty, as the undisputed arbiter of elegance for an upper-class Roman society that could no longer take itself seriously and that was generally disillusioned by the failure of the old Roman ideals to maintain the republic.

Ovid's greatest work, the METAMORPHOSES, reflects in its very theme the disillusionment of his generation. In fifteen books of legends, he wrote the history of the world from chaos to the apotheosis of Julius Caesar. This great historical epic is written neither in terms of the destiny of Rome, which was Vergil's concern, nor in terms of the gradual decline of Roman virtue, which Livy described in his history, but in terms of the instability of the forms of nature. A woman is transformed into a bird, stones become people, a girl becomes a laurel tree. The poems of metamorphosis are linked with transitions that are so smooth that the reader comes to accept each tale of sudden change, not as bizarre and fanciful, but as a comment on the unpredictable nature of things.

Ovid was himself doomed to suffer a severe "metamorphosis"—from the witty cosmopolitan, whom Rome had hailed as the fit successor to Vergil, to a tired, lonely old man living out the last ten years of his life among fur-clad barbarians. For some unknown indiscretion he was, in AD 8, exiled by Augustus to Tomi, a bleak fishing village on the northwest coast of the Black Sea. From there he sent poetic supplications to the Emperor and to his own influential friends that this sentence of banishment might be rescinded. These poems, sometimes sublime, often merely pathetic, were published as two collections of poetry, the *Tristia* (*Songs of Sadness*) and the *Epistulae ex Ponto* (*Letters from the Black Sea*). Despite his petitions, Ovid never returned to the city he loved. The greatest Roman poet of his age, he died in AD 17 on the bleak rim of the empire.

In the Middle Ages, the poetry of Ovid was one of the major sources of Western man's knowledge of his own antiquity. Again, Ovid became an arbiter of elegance—this time for the medieval courts of love. He was revered as the great preceptor of courtly love. Through the Renaissance up to modern times, his poetry has been respected as a treasury of mythic themes, the suggestiveness and psychological content of which have inspired the imagination of writers from Dante to Ezra Pound.

Owen, Robert (1771–1858) Welsh-born English manufacturer, pioneer in British socialism. A self-made businessman, Owen became manager and part owner of cotton mills in New Lanark, Scotland, in 1800. Here, for twenty-five years, he engaged not only in his business, but in educational, philanthropic, and propagandistic activities as well; he improved social conditions in the little mill town, laid particular stress on education, was the first to establish an infant school, inaugurated programs of adult education, and founded his Institution for the Formation of Character. His aim was to reorganize society on the basis of small, cooperative communities of from eight hundred to twenty-five hundred members, combining agriculture and industry and organizing production and consumption. In 1824 he went to the U.S. and founded (1825) the New Harmony Community in southern Indiana, which lasted only until 1827. Although his ideas were received enthusiastically in the U.S., the failure of his project cost him nearly all his fortune, and interest in his theories waned. Back in England, several other projects failed, but, undaunted, he continued the propagation of his ideas until his death at the age of eighty-seven.

Owen, Wilfred (1893–1918)   English poet. Owen is considered the best of the poets who wrote in and about World War I. Influenced by Siegfried SASSOON, whom he met in an army hospital, Owen wrote technically experimental poems expressing his hatred of war and savagely and ironically describing the cruelty and horror he saw about him at the battlefront. Among his best-known poems are DULCE ET DECORUM EST, "Anthem for Doomed Youth," and "Strange Meeting." His use of alliterative assonance instead of regular rhyme influenced younger poets, especially W. H. AUDEN. Owen, who was killed a week before the Armistice, published only four poems during his lifetime and was unknown as a poet until Siegfried Sassoon published his *Poems* in 1920. Owen's well-known poetic manifesto includes the statement "My subject is War, and the pity of War. The Poetry is in the pity."

Oxford, Edward de Vere, earl of (1550–1604) English courtier and poet, a favorite of Queen Elizabeth. Oxford was regarded as typical of the group of courtly lyric poets, which included Sir Philip SIDNEY and Sir Walter RALEIGH. Oxford was a patron of writers and actors; John LYLY served as his secretary and dedicated *Euphues and His England* (1580) to him. His verse is found in a number of poetic miscellanies, especially *A Hundred Sundry Flowers* (1573), which he may have edited. He has been one of the candidates for the "real" authorship of Shakespeare's plays.

Oxford Group Movement   An American evangelist, Frank Nathan Buchman (1878–1961), organized the Oxford Group Movement at Oxford, England (1921), sometimes called, in brief, the Oxford Movement or Buchmanism. It has no connection with the original Oxford Movement but emphasizes moral awakening through fellowship, public confession, and purity. Since 1939 the movement has been known as Moral Rearmament.

Oxford Movement   A movement in the Church of England, originating at Oxford around 1833 under the leadership of E. B. PUSEY, John Henry NEWMAN, and John KEBLE, which sought to bring back into the service of the Church much of the ritual and ornaments that had been dispensed with at the time of the Reformation, to emphasize neglected sacraments, practices, and doctrines, such as Confession, monastic or conventual life, and Apostolic Succession. A number of its followers ultimately became Roman Catholics, as did Newman. See TRACTS FOR THE TIMES.

oxymoron   In rhetoric, an apparent contradiction in terms deliberately employed for effect. An example is the use of a qualifying adjective whose meaning is contrary to that of the noun it modifies, such as strenuous idleness, wise folly, etc.

Oz, Amos (born Amos Klausner, 1939–   ) Israeli novelist and short-story writer, writing in Hebrew. Oz's highly acclaimed and successful books have caused controversy, challenging simplistic views of Zionism and the evolution of Israeli society and culture. His best-known book is probably *Mikhael sheli* (1968; tr *My Michael*, 1972), a painful examination of the gap between a comfortable husband and his despairing wife that is also a personification of the schizophrenic city of Jerusalem itself. Other works that have appeared in translation are the novels *Makon aher* (1966; tr *Elsewhere, Perhaps*, 1973), *La-ga'ath ba-mayim, la-ga'ath ba'ruah* (1973; tr *Touch the Water, Touch the Wind*, 1975), *Menuah nekhonah* (1982; tr *A Perfect Peace*, 1985), and a collection of stories, *Artzot ha'tan* (1965; tr *Where the Jackals Howl*, 1981).

Oz, The Land of   The setting for *The Wonderful Wizard of Oz* (1900) and other fantastic stories by Lyman Frank BAUM. The mythical kingdom was made extremely popular with American children both in the books and in the screen version of *The Wizard of Oz* (1939).

Ozick, Cynthia (1928–   )   American novelist and short-story writer. The determining influence on Ozick's moral and aesthetic vision is her identity as a Jew. She refers frequently to the sense of covenant among the Jewish people and to the effect of the diaspora on the Jewish experience. Her most ambitious work is her long first novel, *Trust* (1966), an experimental work written in richly allusive language. Her shorter fiction includes *The Pagan Rabbi and Other Stories* (1971), *Bloodshed and Three Novellas* (1976), and *Levitation: Five Fictions* (1981), tales of people who seek to transcend the limits of their own intelligence, but fail even at finding self-awareness.

In 1983 Ozick published *The Cannibal Galaxy*, a novel about an educator, Joseph Brill, who sets up a primary school with such an advanced curriculum that few students can be found for it. Through Brill, Ozick examines the theme of European intellectualism within a Jewish middle-American milieu. Ozick's *Art and Ardor*, an acclaimed collection of essays on everything from art to life to reminiscence, was also published that year.

Ozymandias (1818)   A famous sonnet by Percy Bysshe SHELLEY, first published by Leigh Hunt in his *Examiner*. It is an ironic commentary on the vanity and futility of a tyrant's power.

P

Pa Chin (pen name of Li Fei-kan, 1904–   ) Chinese writer. Born to a well-to-do family in southwest China, Pa Chin studied in Shanghai and France (1927–29), where he was influenced by anarchist ideas. His pen name is taken from parts of the names of two anarchist figures, *Ba*kunin and Kropot*kin*. He was active in cultural circles in the People's Republic of China but was forced to stop writing during the Cultural Revolution. In 1977 he was rehabilitated and allowed to publish again. His novels depict the struggles of young people with the traditional Chinese family and social system and had a large readership during the 1930s and 1940s. They are often naively romantic and heavy-handed in their ideological approach, but they are convincing in their sincerity and passionate commitment to change China. His best-known work, *The Family* (1931; tr 1958), was reprinted in a new English edition in 1972.

pacifism   Moral or religious opposition to warfare, militarism, and violence in general as a means of resolving political or social conflicts; refusal to participate in activities of organized violence. Modern formal pacifism took shape in the 19th century when the New York and Massachusetts Peace Societies were formed. The first international peace congress was held in 1843 in London.

In the twenty years following World War I pacifism grew to be a comparatively influential international movement, especially among the youth, and was supported by numerous religious and political organizations. The movement came to a head in the mid-1930s with the annual antiwar "strikes" held at a number of American universities. At Oxford University students initiated the Oxford oath, vowing not to fight in any war waged by their national governments. At the same time, the U.S. Congress enacted legislation to ensure American neutrality in time of war.

By the beginning of World War II, the influence of the pacifist movement had diminished, although legislation was secured in England and the U.S. permitting pacifists to become "conscientious objectors" (as defined by their religious beliefs), exempt from active military service. The Quakers have been outstanding among traditional pacifists.

Subsequent court interpretations of the law expanded the definition of "religious belief" to encompass a strong private moral or ethical conviction against all war.

Ironically, the two most outstanding pacifists of the 20th century died violent deaths. The Indian leader Mohandas K. GANDHI was shot by an assassin as was the American black leader Martin Luther KING, Jr., who had adopted Gandhi's technique of nonviolent resistance as a means of achieving racial equality.

During the Vietnam war, pacifists joined with other antiwar groups in massive protests and acts of civil disobedience in efforts to end the war.

Paderewski, Ignace [Jan] (1860–1941)   Polish pianist, composer, and statesman. Paderewski was one of the greatest and most popular pianists of his time. He donated a large part of the proceeds from his concerts to the cause of Polish nationalism. In 1919 he was chosen premier of the new Polish Republic, returned to the concert stage in 1920, but rejoined the Polish government as president of parliament after it was exiled by the invasion of 1939. Although his best-known composition is the *Minuet in G* for piano, he made his reputation as a composer with the opera *Manru* (1901). He is the subject of many biographies and panegyrics.

paean   From Paian, in Greek mythology the "healer of the gods"; the name was later applied specifically to the god APOLLO. In time it acquired the meaning of a song, hymn, or chant to Apollo, of a triumphant nature; hence, a triumphal song in general.

paeon   In classical prosody, a metrical foot which included three short syllables and one long syllable. They are distinguished as (1) the first paeon, with the first syllable long and the succeeding three short, (2) the second paeon, with the second syllable long and the first, third, and fourth short, and so on. In English prosody, the first paeon occasionally appears singly in accent meter in such words as "SHAdowiness" and "LINGeringly," in which an extra unaccented syllable seems crowded into the normal English limit of nonaccents.

Paganini, Nicolo (1782–1840)   Italian violinist and composer. A supreme virtuoso in technical accomplishment, Paganini was a performer and personality of extraordinary fascination. He wrote concertos and many other pieces for violin, notably the twenty-four *Caprices, Op. 1*, for solo violin. These works were translated for the piano in studies by LISZT and SCHUMANN and were the source of themes for piano variations by BRAHMS and RACHMANINOFF. *Harold in Italy* by BERLIOZ was commissioned by Paganini.

Page, P[atricia] K[athleen] (1916–   )   English-born Canadian poet. Page immigrated to Alberta with her parents in 1919. She began to write poetry in earnest in the 1940s in Montreal, where she was closely associated with A.J.M. SMITH and Ralph GUSTAFSON. Her first books, *As Ten As Twenty* (1946) and *The Metal and the Flower* (1954), reflect her protests against social injustice. In 1967, after a decade abroad, she published *Cry Ararat!*, a selection of poems concerned with human isolation and the alienated self, themes she treats both sympathetically and satirically. Subsequent works include *Poems Selected and New* (1974), *Evening Dance of the Grey Flies* (1981), and *The Glass Air* (1985). She has also edited an anthology of poetry, *To Say the Least: Canadian Poets from A to Z* (1979).

Page, Thomas Nelson (1853–1922)   American lawyer, novelist, essayist, historian, and diplomat. Page was deeply affected by the "Old Dominion" Virginia ideals of chivalry and family. His sentimental, nostalgic view of the antebellum South led to popular success in, among many other works, the story "Marse Chan" (1884), later included in a volume called *In Ole Virginia* (1887), and in his best-selling novel *Red Rock* (1898), which treats Southern resistance to the policies of Reconstruction.

pageant   Originally a scaffold or stage on wheels on which medieval MYSTERY PLAYS were presented. It later meant any play performed on this structure. By the 20th century, the term came to mean either a procession, including floats and tableaux celebrating specific events, or an outdoor exhibition consisting of several scenes, dialogue or recitation, music, and appropriate costumes to commemorate an event of local history.

Paghat   Sister of the hero in the Canaanite THE POEM OF AQHAT. She tracks down his killer and avenges her brother.

Pagnol, Marcel (1895–1974)   French playwright, screenwriter, and film director. Pagnol is widely known for his witty, sentimental trilogy of plays about life in Marseilles—*Marius* (1928), *Fanny* (1931), and *César* (1936) —in which he demonstrated a compassionate insight into the lives of ordinary people and captured the local scene by use of slang and dialect. Pagnol wrote the screenplays for all three when they were adapted for film (1931, 1932,

1934, respectively) and also was director of *César*. He wrote of his Provençal childhood in three volumes of memoirs, *La Gloire de mon père, Le Château de ma mère* (both 1957; tr together as *The Days Were Too Short*, 1960) and *Le Temps des secrets* (1960; tr *The Time of Secrets*, 1982). In an honor never before accorded a filmmaker, Pagnol was elected to the ACADÉMIE FRANÇAISE in 1946.

Pain dur, Le   See HOSTAGE, THE.

Paine, Thomas (1737–1809)   English pamphleteer and political radical. The son of a Quaker corsetmaker, Paine came to America in 1774. Famous for his activities in behalf of the colonies during the American Revolution, as well as in France during the French Revolution, he consistently urged revolt and independence instead of reform and tried to promote world revolution. Among his works are *The Case of the Officers of Excise* (1772), a plea for higher wages to excisemen, of whom he had been one; COMMON SENSE; THE AMERICAN CRISIS, a series of pamphlets supporting the American Revolution; *Public Good* (1780), in which he urged that western lands become the property not of one colony but of the nation; *Dissertations on First-Principles of Government* (1795), an attack on monetary inflation in the American colonies; THE RIGHTS OF MAN; and THE AGE OF REASON, for which he was denounced as an atheist.

Paine lived a turbulent career, beginning in a variety of humble occupations. He held several official positions in the colonies during the Revolution but made enemies and subsequently lost favor. In England he was tried for treason *in absentia* and outlawed because of some seditious passages in *The Rights of Man*. In France he was made an honorary citizen by the republican government (1792) and was a delegate to the Convention, until the more radical government of the Reign of Terror came into power and imprisoned him as an enemy Englishman. He died in the U.S. amid poverty and calumny, denounced as a radical, a drunkard, and an atheist, and was denied burial in consecrated ground. His remains were lost after being taken to England for reburial. In later years he came to be regarded as an American patriot and an important crusader for democratic rights.

Painted Bird, The (1965)   A symbolic novel by Jerzy KOSINSKI. The novel follows a small boy's odyssey through Eastern Europe during World War II. The ignorant and small-minded peasants whom the boy encounters believe him to be a gypsy or a Jew and subject him to horrible cruelty. Kosinski's command of realistic and imaginative effects makes *The Painted Bird*, with its total absence of dialogue, a haunting exploration of the primitive, elemental forces in man.

Painted Veil, The   See MAUGHAM, W. SOMERSET.

Painter, William (1540?–1594)   English prose writer. A clerk at the Tower of London and at one time a schoolmaster, Painter is best known for *The Palace of Pleasure* (1566–67), a collection of 101 tales translated from classic and contemporary sources, especially Boccaccio's *Decameron* and Bandello's *Novelle*. Widely read, the book supplied plots to the leading Elizabethan poets and playwrights. Shakespeare's *All's Well That Ends Well, Timon of Athens, Coriolanus, Romeo and Juliet*, and *Lucrece* may all derive from Painter's collection.

Pair of Blue Eyes, A (1873) A novel by Thomas HARDY. Elfride Swancourt, the daughter of a rector, is loved by Stephen Smith; she starts to elope with him, but changes her mind and returns home. Later she loves and is loved by Henry Knight, but Mrs. Jethway, a spying neighbor, writes Knight of Elfride's former experience, and the lovers quarrel. Sometime later the two men, each intending to be reconciled with Elfride, meet on a train, but they arrive only in time for her funeral. She has married, but, loving Knight, has pined away and died.

paladins Knights-errant, usually referring to the companions of Charlemagne in medieval romances. The twelve most illustrious were known as *The Twelve Peers* (Fr *Les Douze Pairs*), but the lists of their names vary widely. The *Chanson de* ROLAND lists Roland (Orlando), OLIVIER, Ivon, Ivory, Otton, Berengier, Samson, Anseis, Gerin, Gerier, Engelier, and Gerard. However, there are other important knights referred to as paladins in the *Chanson*, in Pulci's MORGANTE MAGGIORE, in Boiardo's ORLANDO INNAMORATO, and in Ariosto's ORLANDO FURIOSO: ASTOLFO, Florismart, FIERABRAS (Ferumbras), GANELON (Gan), Malagigi (Maugis), Namo (Nami), OGIER THE DANE, RINALDO (Renault), and Archbishop TURPIN. These and other knights are also the protagonists of lesser known CHANSONS DE GESTE.

Palamas, Koster (1859–1943) Major Greek poet of Missolonghiot origin, born in Patras. An erudite, profound, and prolific writer, Palamas had a great impact on Greek cultural life for decades. His complete works consist of eighteen volumes of poetry, fiction, drama, translation, criticism, and articles. He was honored as Greece's national poet and successor to Dionysios Solomos (1798–1857), whose practice of writing poetry in the vernacular he defended and expanded. Primarily inspired by the cultural and historical legacy of Hellas, Byzantium, and the heroic era of 1821, Palamas was influenced by both ancient and contemporary thinkers. Of the latter, NIETZSCHE and the French PARNASSIANS and SYMBOLISTS were the most influential. He wrote verse in most known forms in a highly rhetorical poetic language. His style and themes evolved from the folkloric and romantic, as in *Tragoudia tes patridos mou* (*The Songs of My Country*, 1886) and *O tafos* (1898; tr *The Grave*, 1930), a lyrical lament for his dead son, to the mystical, in *I asalefti zoi* (1904; tr *Life Immovable*, 1919). With *Ho Askraios* (*The Ascraean*, 1904) he entered the period of his great visionary epics: *O dodecalogos tou gyftou* (1907; tr *The Twelve Words of the Gypsy*, 1969, 1975) and *I floghera tou vasilia* (1910; tr *The King's Flute*, 1966). Often nominated for the NOBEL PRIZE,

Palamas failed to gain during his life the international reputation he deserved. His funeral in German-occupied Athens turned into a spontaneous and defiant demonstration against tyranny and the enemies of Hellenism.

Palamedes (1) One of the heroes against Troy. In Greek legend, Palamedes was the reputed inventor of lighthouses, scales and measures, the discus, dice, etc., and was said to have added four letters to the original alphabet of CADMUS. It was he who detected the madness assumed by ODYSSEUS to avoid entering the TROJAN WAR by putting his infant son TELEMACHUS in the way of the plow the supposed madman was driving. In revenge Odysseus achieved Palamedes' death.

(2) In Arthurian romance, a Saracen knight. Palamedes is overcome in single combat by TRISTAN. Both love Iseult, the wife of King Mark, and after the lady has been given up by the Saracen, Tristan converts him to the Christian faith, and stands as his godfather at the font.

Palazzo Vecchio The town hall of Florence, Italy. The austere, castlelike structure was built in the 13th and 14th centuries.

Pale Fire (1962) A novel by Vladimir NABOKOV. A satire on the pedantry and sterility of academic scholarship, the book consists of a 999-line poem and editorial commentary on the poem by a demented literary scholar who imagines himself to be the king of the mythical country Zembla. Charles Kinbote, the Zemblan scholar, is editing "Pale Fire," the last poem of the murdered American poet John Shade. The poem is Shade's autobiographical narrative in couplets and in itself has considerable literary merit. The humor of the novel comes from Kinbote's lunatic editing, in which he reads the poem as a chronicle of Zembla, and in each line sees a reference to his own life.

Pale Horse, Pale Rider (1939) A collection of three short novels by Katherine Anne PORTER. One of the stories, also titled "Pale Horse, Pale Rider," concerns a short-lived love affair during the influenza epidemic of the First World War between a young Southern newspaperwoman and a soldier. Like most of Porter's work, it is written in a limpid, somewhat spare style that suggests far more than it says. The two other works in the collection are NOON WINE and OLD MORTALITY.

Palestrina, [Giovanni Pierluigi da] (c1525–1594) Italian composer. His name comes from Palestrina, the city of his birth. Palestrina is best known for his more than one hundred masses and numerous motets, which have long been considered a yardstick of judgment for polyphonic music used in the Roman Catholic Church. His refined style, and especially his careful control of dissonance, have become a standard pedagogical model for student composers.

Paley, Grace [Goodside] (1922–   ) American short-story writer. Shortly after her first book, *The Little Disturbances of Man* (1959), was published, Paley began to have an enthusiastic underground following. Her reputation was enhanced by her second book, *Enormous Changes at the Last Minute* (1974), a collection of interrelated stories which can be read as an episodic novel, and by *Later the Same Day* (1985). Clearly, her identity as a woman, a Jew, and a political radical influences Paley's literary sensibility; however, she commands critical attention not for her thematic concerns, but for her commitment to exploring the enigmatic relationship between language and reality.

Paley, William (1743–1805)   English theologian and philosopher. Paley's theory of UTILITARIANISM differs from that of Jeremy Bentham in that it sanctions the supernatural. His most important treatises include *Principles of Morals and Political Philosophy* (1785), a Cambridge textbook; *Horae Paulinae* (1790); and *View of the Evidences of Christianity* (1794).

palindrome (fr Gr, *palin dromo*, "to run back again") A word or line the same backward and forward. Examples are *Madam, I'm Adam*, also *Roma tibi subito motibus ibit amor*. They have also been called Sotadics, from their reputed inventor, Sotades, a scurrilous Greek poet of the 3rd century BC.

Probably the longest palindrome in English is

Dog as a devil deified
Deified lived as a god;

and others well known are

Lewd did I live, evil I did dwel

and Napoleon's famous reputed saying,

Able was I ere I saw Elba.

A celebrated Greek palindrome is NIΨONANOMH-MATAMHMONANOΨIN. It means "wash my transgressions, not only my face."

palinode   A recantation or retraction. It is named for the poem by STESICHORUS in which he recanted his earlier harsh words about HELEN of Troy. Chaucer employs the palinode as a device in THE LEGEND OF GOOD WOMEN, written as an apology for his TROILUS AND CRISEYDE.

Palinurus   In Vergil's AENEID, the steersman of Aeneas' boat and the first Trojan to be killed in Italy. Overcome with sleep, he tumbles from the helm into the sea off the coast of Lucania and, after swimming to shore, is murdered by the natives. The persona was adopted by Cyril CONNOLLY for the narrator of *The Unquiet Grave* (1945). Connolly felt that Palinurus' fall from the ship represented a typically modern will to failure.

Palladio, Andrea (1508–1580)   Italian architect. Palladio's study of Roman architecture led him to develop an original style of design incorporating classical elements. Among his famous buildings are the churches of San Giorgio Maggiore and Il Redentore at Venice; the Villa Capra, or Rotonda, at Vicenza (c1567), which was the first modern example of integrated landscape and building; and

Palazzo Chiericati, also at Vicenza (1550). He also wrote a treatise, *Quattro libri dell'architettura* (*Four Books of Architecture*, 1570), that raised great interest throughout Europe and was translated into English by Inigo JONES; its drawings served to disseminate his ideas and to make the Palladian style the basis of English Georgian architecture in the 18th century.

Palladium   Wooden statue of Pallas ATHENE in the city of Troy. It was said to have fallen from heaven. It was believed that so long as this statue remained within the city, Troy would be safe, but if ever it were removed, the city would fall into the hands of the enemy. The statue was carried away by the Greeks, and the city burnt by them to the ground. Later, Argos, Sparta, and Athens all claimed to possess this statue.

Pallas   (1) An epithet of the Greek goddess ATHENE, and sometimes also of the Roman MINERVA. There are two main explanations of its origins. Apollodorus relates that Athene accidentally killed her playmate Pallas, daughter of the river god Triton, and that, in token of her grief, she placed her friend's name before her own. In another tale, Pallas was a giant and the father of Athene. When he attempted to violate his daughter, she flayed him and took his skin for her AEGIS, his wings for her shoulders, and his name to add to her own.

(2) In the THESEUS legend, the son of Pandion and the father of fifty sons, the Pallantids. He plotted to steal the throne of Athens from his brother Aegeus, Theseus' father, but he and all his sons were killed by Theseus.

Palma, Ricardo (1833–1919)   Peruvian writer. As a young man, Palma was a romantic poet and dramatist and deeply involved in politics. Disillusioned by the turbulence of Peruvian politics, Palma decided to devote himself exclusively to literature and history. In 1872 he published the first collection of his delightfully ironic TRADICIONES PERUANAS, the work upon which his reputation as a writer is based. From 1883 to 1912 he was director of Peru's national library, acquiring thousands of volumes to replace those that had been destroyed during the War of the Pacific (1879–83). At his death, he was generally regarded as Peru's foremost man of letters.

palmer   A pilgrim to the Holy Land who carried a palm staff and spent his life visiting holy shrines and living on charity. At the dedication of palmers, prayers and psalms were said over them as they lay prostrate before the altar; they were sprinkled with holy water and then they received the consecrated palm branch as a sign of their office.

Palmer, Vance [Edward] (1885–1959)   Australian novelist, short-story writer, poet, and dramatist. Seen during his lifetime as Australia's premier man of letters, Palmer sought to establish a specifically Australian body of literature. His stories appeared in such volumes as *Separate Lives* (1931) and *Let the Birds Fly* (1955). *Golconda* (1948), *Seedtime* (1957), and *The Big Fellow* (1960) comprise a trilogy chronicling the career of politician Macy Donovan. Palmer's best-known work is *The Passage* (1930), a novel of man's attunement to nature in a Queensland fishing village.

Palmerston, Henry John Temple, 3d Viscount (1784–1865) English statesman. Palmerston was prime minister from 1855 to 1858 and from 1859 to 1865. He opposed construction of the Suez Canal. He supported a policy of neutrality in the U.S. Civil War, but intervened successfully in a number of threatened and actual international conflicts in favor of the *status quo* or the restitution of liberal order.

Palm-Wine Drinkard, The See TUTUOLA, AMOS.

Palmyra The biblical Tadmor, a city east of Syria. After the revolt of its queen ZENOBIA, it was destroyed by the Emperor Aurelian (AD 273).

Pamela, or Virtue Rewarded (1740–1742) An epistolary novel in two parts by Samuel RICHARDSON, generally considered to be the first modern English novel. In the first part Pamela is *Aggressive Chastity*, in the second, *Provocative Prudence*. A simple, unsophisticated fifteen-year-old country girl, Pamela Andrews has a surprising tendency for self-analysis. She is the maidservant of a wealthy woman who dies and whose son, Mr. B., pursues her with base intentions. He kidnaps her and tries to seduce her but is deterred by the tenacity of her resistance. She then convinces him to marry her and sets about to reform him. The story is told in a series of letters from Pamela to her parents and reads like a private journal.

Pan (Gr, "all; everything") In Greek mythology, an Arcadian god of pastures, forests, flocks, and herds; also, the personification of the deity displayed in creation and pervading all things. Pan is represented with the lower part of a goat and the upper part of a man. He invented the musical pipe of seven reeds, which he named SYRINX.

Legend has it that at the time of the Crucifixion, just when the veil of the Temple was rent in twain, a cry swept across the ocean in the hearing of many, "Great Pan is dead," and that at the same time the responses of the oracles ceased forever. "The Dead Pan" (1844), a poem by Elizabeth Barrett BROWNING, is founded on this legend.

Panacea (Gr, "all-healing") In Greek mythology, the daughter of ASCLEPIUS, god of medicine. Panacea was merely a personification of the idea of a cure-all.

In the Middle Ages, the search for the panacea was one of the alchemists' self-imposed tasks. Fable tells of many panaceas, such as the Promethean unguent, which rendered the body invulnerable; ALADDIN's ring; the balsam of FIERABRAS; and Prince AHMED's apple.

Panchatantra (Sans, "book of five chapters") A collection of fables in Sanskrit. The compilation is supposed to have been ordered in the 5th century by a South Indian king for the edification of his sons. Attributed to Bidpai ("the favorite"), the fables were translated into Persian and

thereafter into European languages, where they served as the inspiration for LA FONTAINE, among others. An English translation by Arthur Ryder (1955) is available.

Pandarus In Greek legend, a Lycian leader, one of the allies of PRIAM in the TROJAN WAR. In the classic story, Pandarus is depicted as an admirable archer, slain by Diomedes and honored as a hero-god in his own country. In medieval romance, he is represented as such a despicable fellow that the word *pander* is derived from his name. In Boccaccio's FILOSTRATO, he is Criseida's young cousin. Chaucer, in his *Troilus and Criseyde* (see TROILUS), makes him Criseyde's uncle, a worldly wise, but sympathetic character. Shakespeare, in his drama TROILUS AND CRESSIDA, represents him as procuring for Troilus the good graces of Cressida, and in MUCH ADO ABOUT NOTHING, it is said that Troilus "was the first employer of panders."

pandemonium (Gr, "all the demons") A wild, unrestrained uproar; a lawless, infernal tumult. The word was first used by Milton, in PARADISE LOST, as the name of the principal city in Hell, "the high capital of Satan and his peers."

Pandora In Greek mythology, the first woman. PROMETHEUS had made an image and stolen fire from heaven to endow it with life. In revenge, ZEUS commanded HEPHAESTUS to make a woman, who was named Pandora (i.e., the All-gifted), because each of the gods gave her some power that was to bring about the ruin of man. Zeus gave her a vessel which she was to present to him who married her. Prometheus distrusted Zeus and his gifts, but Epimetheus, his brother, married the beautiful Pandora, and, against advice, accepted the gift of the god. As soon as he opened the jar, all the evils that flesh is heir to flew forth and have ever since continued to afflict the world. According to some accounts, the last thing that flew out was Hope, but others say that Hope alone remained. Some versions blame Pandora's curiosity for the disaster.

Pandora's box came to mean a present that seems valuable but is in reality a curse.

panegyric A speech or poem of praise. Originally it was a rhetorical form with specific rules laid down by MENANDER and Hermogenes. Panegyrics for living emperors were a popular form of oratory. A famous example is PLINY THE YOUNGER's speech in praise of the emperor Trajan.

Pangloss, Dr. (Gr, "all tongue") The pedantic old tutor to the hero in Voltaire's CANDIDE, OU L'OPTIMISME. Pangloss's distinguishing feature is his incurable and misleading optimism; he sees and endures all sorts of misfortune, but to the end he reiterates "All is for the best in this best of all possible worlds." He is said to have been based on the philosopher LEIBNITZ, but it is more likely that Voltaire had in mind the German philosopher Christian von Wolff (or Wolf, 1679–1754), who popularized Leibnitz's works, and whom Voltaire must have read.

Panini (c400 BC)   Indian grammarian. Panini is the author of the *Astadhyayi* (*Eight Chapters*), the oldest and most detailed systematization of Sanskrit. Panini's grammar established the rules by which Sanskrit was used thereafter. In eight chapters and thirty-two sections, he constructed nearly four thousand concise aphorisms that formulated the entire system of word formation in Sanskrit. As a work of structural linguistics it had no parallel until the 19th century.

Pan Michael   The third of a Polish historic trilogy by SIENKIEWICZ. See WITH FIRE AND SWORD.

Panova, Vera Fyodorovna (1905–1973)   Russian novelist and short-story writer. Panova's first successful work was *Sputniki* (1946; tr *The Train*, 1948), describing the lives of a group of people working on a hospital train during World War II. Its focus on the human elements of the situation and its high quality of craftsmanship, in characterization and language, are also to be found in some of Panova's later books, such as *Kruzhilikha* (1947; tr *The Factory*, 1949), which is set in a factory whose name gives the novel its title, and *Vremena goda* (1953; tr *Span of the Year*, 1957), about life in an industrial town. Panova is also well known for *Seryozha* (1956; tr *On Faraway Street*, 1968), a charming collection of stories of a little boy.

Pantagruel   The principal character of Rabelais's great satire GARGANTUA AND PANTAGRUEL. The name, meaning "all-thirsty," had originally been given to a little sea devil, in 15th-century MYSTERY PLAYS, who threw salt into the mouths of drunks to stimulate their thirst.

Capitalizing on the popularity of a contemporary CHAP-BOOK about a marvelous giant called Gargantua, Rabelais introduced Pantagruel, the son of GARGANTUA and Badebec, in *Les Horribles et Espovantables Faictz et prouesses du très renommé Pantagruel, Roy des Dipsodes, fils du grand géant Gargantua* (1532), which later came to be known as Book II of Rabelais's five-part satire. Born during a terrible drought, Pantagruel is covered with hair at birth, like a young bear, and is so strong that, though he is chained to his cradle, he breaks his bonds into five hundred pieces with a single blow of his infant fist. The tale goes on to recount his fabulous childhood feats, his tour of the universities and his life with PANURGE in the Latin Quarter of Paris, and his conduct of the war against the Dipsodes in Utopia. Aside from the realistic description of student life and the famous letter in which Gargantua, extolling the recent revolution in learning, instructs his son to immerse himself in all the new studies, the book remains on the whole faithful to medieval tradition.

In Books III–V Pantagruel continues as the hero, but he becomes less and less the fabulous giant and more a personification of the Renaissance man in search of knowledge and the good life.

Pantaloon   A COMMEDIA DELL'ARTE stock character. Always an emaciated old man in slippers, he is the father of COLUMBINE. He could give sound advice to the young and at the same time fall in love like an adolescent. His unconscious contradictions and childish behavior provoked great hilarity among audiences. He later became a figure in English PANTOMIME.

pantheism (fr Gr, *pan*, "all," *theos*, "god")   The doctrine that God is everything and everything is God. This monistic theory was elaborated by SPINOZA, who, by his doctrine of the Infinite Substance, sought to overcome the opposition between mind and matter, body and soul. During the romantic period and later, WORDSWORTH, SHELLEY, EMERSON, TENNYSON, and others expressed various doctrines of pantheism in their writings.

Pantheon (fr Gr, *pan*, "all," *theos*, "god")   A temple dedicated to all the gods; specifically, that erected at Rome by Agrippa, son-in-law to AUGUSTUS. It is circular, nearly 150 feet in diameter, and of the same total height; since the early 7th century, as Santa Maria Rotunda, it has been used as a Christian church.

The Panthéon at Paris was originally the church of St. Geneviève, built by Louis XV and finished in 1790. The following year the Convention gave it its present name and set it apart as the shrine of those Frenchmen whom their country wished to honor.

pantomime   Generally, a form of silent acting in which gesture, facial expression, and body movement are relied on to tell a story or express emotion. It is known to have existed in ancient cultures and was certainly a part of the Roman MIME plays. It is most familiar as the dramatic form that became popular in 18th-century England. The English pantomimes also featured singing and dancing and included COMMEDIA DELL'ARTE characters against elaborate backdrops. Children's stories, such as that of Dick WHITTINGTON and his cat and CINDERELLA, are favorite subjects for pantomime. See DUMB SHOW.

Panurge (Gr, "all-doer")   In Rabelais's GARGANTUA AND PANTAGRUEL, the high-spirited rogue who becomes Pantagruel's companion. In Book II, when Pantagruel first meets him in Paris, he is suffering from a chronic malady called "impecunitis," which he has sixty-three methods of curing, "the most honorable and ordinary of which was filching." He proves to be "a quarrelsome fellow, a sharper, a toper, a roisterer, and a profligate, if there ever was one in the city of Paris. In every other respect, he was the best fellow in the world." Later, in the war against the Dipsodes, he displays a remarkable talent for ruse and cunning.

It is his inability to decide whether or not to marry that forms the basis of the plot in Books III to V. Although he still displays dialectical genius in his defense of borrowers and debtors in Book III and cunning in dispatching the dishonest DINGDONG in Book IV, he is characterized chiefly by cowardice in these latter books. During the tempest in Book IV, for example, he is reduced to hysterical blubbering, which he later dismisses with the statement "I fear nothing but danger."

Panza, Sancho The squire of DON QUIXOTE in Cervantes's novel. Panza is a short pot-bellied rustic, full of common sense, but without a grain of "spirituality." He is famous for his proverbs. Panza, in Spanish, means *paunch*.

Paolo and Francesca Guilty lovers whose history is one of the most famous episodes in Dante's INFERNO. They are in the second circle, that of the carnal sinners, blown lightly about by stormy winds, as they had been by their passions when alive. Married to an unattractive man for political reasons, Francesca da Rimini had fallen in love with Paolo Malatesta, her husband's handsome brother, while they were innocently reading together the story of Launcelot. (See GALEOTO.) Her husband discovered their guilt and put them both to death (c1289). Another version, as in Stephen Phillips's poetic drama *Paolo and Francesca* (c1900), is that Paolo was sent by his brother to escort the bride from her home in Ravenna, with the same results. The story of the unhappy pair is also the subject of *Francesca da Rimini* (1901), a verse tragedy by Gabriele D'ANNUNZIO, which has passages of great lyric beauty. D'Annunzio dedicated this work to Eleonora Duse, who played the title role in its first production. There have been numerous other works on this theme.

Paphian Relating to VENUS, or rather to Paphos, a city of Cyprus, where Venus was worshiped; a Cyprian; a prostitute.

parabasis See OLD COMEDY.

parable A simple story that teaches a lesson or illustrates a moral principle. Like an ALLEGORY, details of a parable parallel the details of the situation calling for illustration. Jesus' parables are contained in the SYNOPTIC GOSPELS.

Paraclete (fr Gr, *parakletos*, "helper; advocate") The Holy Spirit as Comforter or Advocate. ABÉLARD gave this name to the oratory of his hermitage at Nogent-sur-Seine.

Parade's End A series of novels by Ford Madox FORD, consisting of *Some Do Not* (1924), *No More Parades* (1925), *A Man Could Stand Up* (1926), and *The Last Post* (1928), all published together as *Parade's End* in 1950. The series describes the adventures in love and war of Christopher Tietjens, an old-fashioned gentleman of the English governing class. Ford draws a brilliant picture of the social changes brought about by the First World War. Before the war, Tietjens is nobly faithful to his impossible wife. But trench warfare seems to him a symbol of the disintegration of his whole society. He has a mental breakdown, goes to live with a woman he loves, and gives up his position, wealth, and historic family ties.

Paradise Lost (1667) An epic poem in twelve books by John MILTON. Often considered the greatest epic in any modern language, it tells the story

Of Man's first disobedience and the fruit
Of that forbidden tree whose mortal taste

Brought death into the World, and all our woe,
With loss of Eden.

SATAN rouses the panic-stricken host of fallen angels with tidings of a rumor current in Heaven of a new world about to be created. He calls a council to deliberate what should be done, and they agree to send him in search of this new world. Passing the gulf between Heaven and Hell, Satan disguised as an angel enters the orb of the Sun, and, having obtained the information he seeks, goes to Paradise in the form of a cormorant. Seating himself on the Tree of Life, he overhears Adam and Eve talking about the prohibition made by God, and at once resolves upon the nature of his attack. GABRIEL sends two angels to watch over Paradise, and Satan flees. Sent to warn Adam of his danger, RAPHAEL tells him the story of Satan's revolt and expulsion from Heaven, and why and how this world was made. After a time, Satan returns to Paradise in the form of a mist, and, entering the serpent, induces Eve to eat of the forbidden fruit. Adam eats "that he may perish with the woman he loved." Satan returns to Hell to tell his triumph, and Sin and Death come into the world. As Michael leads the guilty pair out of the garden, he shows them a vision of humanity's misery—but, as he explains, the Son of God has already offered himself as ransom for man, and, in Him, man shall ultimately be victorious over Satan.

In 1671 *Paradise Regained* (in four books), written by Milton on suggestion of his Quaker friend Thomas Ellwood, was published. The subject is Jesus' triumphant resistance to Satan's temptation, regaining the Paradise lost by Adam and Eve. The New Testament narrative is followed and enlarged upon; Satan, for instance, appeals not only to hunger, ambition, and pride, but also to the love of humanistic learning and art. *Paradise Regained* has never been as popular as its predecessor. The earlier poem is distinguished by richness and sonority of style, heroic characterization, and action on a grand, cosmic scale, whereas the verse of the sequel is generally far more austere and simple, and its action is much more restricted. See BEELZEBUB; ITHURIEL; JAPHET; LUCIFER; PANDEMONIUM; URIEL.

Paradiso (Paradise) Part III of the DIVINE COMEDY by DANTE. BEATRICE and Dante are transported to the sphere of fire, where Dante first hears the musical harmony of the heavenly spheres. They move through the eight concentric heavens of the Moon, Mercury, Venus, Sun, Mars, Jupiter, Saturn, and the Fixed Stars, meeting in each heaven those of the blessed spirits notable for its appropriate virtue. Dante asks and Beatrice answers many specific questions about the nature of good and evil, original sin, transubstantiation, and the like. The ninth heaven is the Primum Mobile, divided into the nine orders of the angels. And beyond it is the Empyrean, a river of radiant light in the center of which is God's court, pictured as a white rose whose tiers of petals hold angels and beatified souls, united in the glorification of God. Here, as throughout the nine heavens, every participant is equally content with his position in the regions of bliss, but the closer a spirit is to God, the greater the intensity both of his joy and of the celestial light he reflects. Beatrice, who had originally been the one to petition that Dante be granted this extraordinary tour, now resumes her place in the rose, and is replaced by St. Bernard, who bids Dante to contemplate the Virgin Mary and himself prays her to allow the visitor a glimpse of the Godhead. Dante has been so thoroughly purified that, although still a mortal, his own will is totally merged in the Love and Will of the Creator, and he is thus capable of gazing for a moment on the supremely radiant light of the Trinity in Unity.

Paradiso (1966; tr 1977) A novel by José LEZAMA LIMA. Widely regarded as Lezama Lima's masterpiece, this richly poetic novel explores the development of the poet's artistic vision and his sensations, and chronicles his experiences in Havana in the first two decades of the 20th century.

paradox A statement or proposition seemingly contrary to common sense, yet possibly true in fact and full of significance, at least in part because of its contradictory qualities. "Waging the peace" is a concept that is paradoxical in this sense. Sometimes a paradox is implied, sometimes explicit. The paradox as a rhetorical device is full of surprises and often produces a memorable passage. Oscar WILDE and G. K. CHESTERTON were masters of the literary use of paradox. See IRONY.

Parashurama In Hindu mythology, an avatar of VISHNU, represented as a human with an axe.

Parcae The Latin name for the FATES. The three were Nona, Decuma, and Morta. Parcae is from the Latin *pars*, a "lot" in the sense of destiny; the corresponding Moirai of the Greeks is from the Gr *meros*, "a lot."

Pardo Bazán [de Quiroga], Emilia (1852–1921) Spanish novelist. The only child of the count of Pardo Bazán, she wrote numerous critical and scholarly works and was professor of modern romance literatures at the University of Madrid. Pardo's finest novels are *Los Pazos de Ulloa* (1886) and its sequel, *La madre naturaleza* (1887); these works, which describe the gradual degeneration of an aristocratic family, are notable for their evocation of the Galician countryside. Some of her best short stories of Galicia are collected in *Cuentos de Marineda* (1892).

Pardoner's Tale, The One of THE CANTERBURY TALES of Geoffrey CHAUCER. In the *Prologue* the Pardoner boastfully reveals both the fraudulent tricks he uses in selling supposedly holy relics and his own vices, particularly his hypocrisy in preaching primarily against cupidity when his own motives are purely avaricious. Then he gives a sample sermon, railing against gluttonous excess, drunkenness, gambling, and swearing. He uses as an *exemplum* the story, of Oriental origin, about three young revelers who determine to slay Death because he has just killed one of their comrades with the plague. Asked where they can find

Death, an old man directs them to a tree, where they find a great pile of gold. They draw lots and send the youngest back to town for food and wine. The remaining two plot to kill him, so as to split the gold only two ways, while he puts poison in the wine, so as to keep all the treasure himself. When he returns, they stab him, then drink the wine; thus all three indeed find Death. The Pardoner boldly follows his sermon with an attempt to sell his relics; he turns first to the Host, who repulses him rudely, so that the Knight has to intervene to prevent a quarrel.

Parini, Giuseppe (1729–1799) Italian poet. Highly didactic in tone and intention, Parini's poems are critical of the corruption and injustices of the 18th-century society, the moral being shown through subtly humorous satire. *Il giorno* (*The Day*, 1763–65, 1801) is a long poem in blank verse which ostensibly gives instruction in fashionable ways of spending time, but in reality pokes fun at the sterile life of the aristocracy.

Paris (1) In Greek legend, the son of PRIAM, king of Troy, and HECUBA; and through his abduction of HELEN, the cause of the siege of Troy. Before his birth Hecuba dreamed that she was to bring forth a firebrand, and, as this was interpreted to mean that the unborn child would bring destruction to his house, the infant Paris was exposed on Mount Ida. He was, however, brought up by a shepherd under the name of Alexander, and grew to perfection of beautiful manhood. When the golden APPLE OF DISCORD was thrown on the table of the gods, it was Paris who had to judge between the rival claims of HERA, APHRODITE, and ATHENE. (See JUDGMENT OF PARIS.) He awarded the apple and the title of "Fairest" to Aphrodite, who in return assisted him to carry off Helen, for whom he deserted his wife, OENONE. At Troy, Paris earned the contempt of all by his cowardice; he was fatally wounded with a poisoned arrow by PHILOCTETES at the taking of the city.

(2) In Shakespeare's ROMEO AND JULIET, a young nobleman to whom Juliet is betrothed against her will.

Paris, Matthew (c1200–1259) English historian, most famous of the chroniclers at the Benedictine monastery of St. Albans. Paris revised the chronicles of England kept by his predecessors, John of Cella (covering the period through 1188) and Roger of Wendover (through 1235), and continued a lively record of events in England and Europe until 1259, the whole work being called the *Chronica majora*. He abridged it (c1253) as the *Historia minor*, also called *Historia Anglorum*, covering the period 1067–1253. He also compiled and probably contributed to a series of lives of the abbots of St. Albans and lives of the saints.

Parker, Dorothy [Rothschild] (1893–1967) American writer of short stories, verse, and criticism. Parker was noted for her caustic wit, as drama critic of *Vanity Fair* and later book reviewer for THE NEW YORKER, and she became one of the luminaries of the ALGONQUIN ROUND TABLE. Her works in verse are equally sardonic, usually dry, elegant commentaries on departing or departed love. The collection *Enough Rope* (1926) contains the often-quoted "Resumé," on suicide, and "News Item," about girls who wear glasses. Her short stories, which were collected in *After Such Pleasures* (1932) and *Here Lies* (1939), are as imbued with a knowledge of human nature as they are deep in disenchantment; among the best known are "Big Blonde" and "A Telephone Call."

Parker, Sir Gilbert (1862–1932)   Canadian novelist. Parker settled in England in 1889, but most of his many novels are set in Canada, notably the best-selling *The Seats of the Mighty* (1896), about the fall of Québec in 1759, and *The Power and the Glory* (1925), about LaSalle and Frontenac.

Parker, Theodore (1810–1860)   American clergyman, writer, and abolitionist. A pastor of the Unitarian congregation of West Roxbury, Massachusetts, Parker was an active member of the Transcendentalist Club and wrote often on its doctrines. He rejected the church and scripture, relying on a personal intuition of God. An ardent abolitionist, he was constantly in trouble with the orthodox members of the church for his religious and later his social sentiments. See BROOK FARM.

Parkman, Francis (1823–1893)   American historian. Having contracted a severe case of what he called "Injuns on the brain" as a boy, Parkman made a trip to Wyoming in 1846, during which he lived with and studied the Sioux Indians, an experience he described in *The Oregon Trail* (1847). Upon his return to the East, Parkman suffered a physical and nervous breakdown and remained a semi-invalid for the rest of his life; afflicted with extremely weak eyesight, he constructed a wire frame that enabled him to write with his eyes closed. In 1851 he published *History of the Conspiracy of Pontiac*, the first volume of his series on the struggle between Great Britain and France for control of North America. To Parkman, the eventual success of the British represented the victory of progress over reaction. The other volumes of the series, which is distinguished by its documentation from original sources and by Parkman's virile style and narrative skill, are *Pioneers of France in the New World* (1865), *The Jesuits in North America* (1867), *LaSalle and the Discovery of the Great West* (1869), *The Old Regime in Canada* (1874), *Count Frontenac and New France under Louis XIV* (1877), *Montcalm and Wolfe* (1884), and *A Half-Century of Conflict* (1892). Parkman also wrote *Vassall Morton* (1856), a semiautobiographical novel.

Parliamentary novels   A series of novels about political life by Anthony TROLLOPE, including *Phineas Finn* (1869), *Phineas Redux* (1874), *The Prime Minister* (1876), and *The Duke's Children* (1880). The hero is Phineas Finn, a young Irishman, but Plantagenet Palliser, duke of Omnium, plays a prominent role.

Parliament of Fowls, The (c1382)   A poem by CHAUCER, almost seven hundred lines in RHYME ROYAL. After reading Cicero's account of Scipio Africanus's appearance to the younger Scipio in a dream, the poet himself dreams that Scipio Africanus conducts him to a garden where he sees the Temple of Venus. Then he comes to a hillside where all the fowls have gathered at the bidding of Nature to choose their mates, for it is Saint Valentine's Day. Nature declares that the royal tercel eagle has first choice, and he chooses the lovely formel eagle. Two tercels of lower rank contest the claim, one declaring he has loved her longer, the other that he loves her more truly. The other fowls begin a lively dispute over the three claims, each bird according to its character, until Nature finally refers the choice to the formel eagle, who asks for a year to make up her mind. The other birds quickly choose their mates, sing a rondel, and fly away.

Parmenides of Elea (fl 485 BC)   A Greek philosopher, founder of the Eleatic School. Parmenides maintained that the world is an unchanging whole, that motion and change are only illusion, and that unity is truth. In these beliefs, the Eleatic School opposed the MILESIAN SCHOOL.

Parnassians   A French school of poetry (active from about 1860 to 1880). Influenced by Théophile GAUTIER's theory of ART FOR ART'S SAKE, they reacted against the excessive emotion and subjectivity of ROMANTICISM. Instead, they advocated that poetry be calm, detached, and meticulously precise in technique. Their emphasis on precision and objectivity closely paralleled the growth of REALISM and NATURALISM in drama and fiction. The school's leader was Charles LECONTE DE LISLE, whose poetry appeared in the Parnassians' journal, *Parnasse contemporain* (1866–76), along with the work of others associated with the school: Théodore de Banville, François Coppée, SULLY PRUDHOMME, and Paul VERLAINE.

Parnassus   A mountain in Phocis, Greece. It has two summits, one of which was consecrated to APOLLO and the MUSES, the other to DIONYSUS. Owing to its connection with the Muses (though they were more often associated with Mt. HELICON), Parnassus came to be regarded as the seat of poetry and music. Delphi is located on the southern slope of Parnassus.

Parnell, Charles Stewart (1846–1891)   Irish nationalist leader, a Member of Parliament. Parnell ceaselessly agitated for Home Rule in Ireland, winning William Gladstone and the Liberal party over to his side and uniting a number of dissident elements in his own country, until his career was brought to an end by accusations, concerning his private life, made by his enemies. He was named corespondent in a divorce suit (1890) initiated by one Captain O'Shea against his wife, Kitty. Parnell is known for the devoted partisans and violent enemies that his policies and his personality created among the Irish people. He is referred to frequently throughout the works of James Joyce, to whom he was a political hero. See PHOENIX PARK.

Parnell, Thomas (1679–1718)   Irish poet and clergyman, a member of the SCRIBLERUS CLUB and a friend of

Steele and Addison. Parnell provided the preface, *Essay on the Life, Writings, and Learning of Homer,* to Pope's translation of the *Iliad* (1715–20). His major works include the meditative poems "A Hymn to Contentment" and "A Night Piece on Death," and the famous moral apologue "The Hermit." After Parnell's death, his poems were edited and published by Pope in 1721 with a dedicatory tribute to his poetic style.

parodos   In classical Greek drama, the first choral passage in a tragedy or comedy, recited or sung as the chorus enters the orchestra. It was named for the passageways between the sides of the raised stage and the ends of the tiers of the seats; through these two passageways the chorus entered, and later left in the EXODOS.

parody   In literature, a comic or satirical imitation of a piece of writing, exaggerating its style and content, and playing especially on any weakness in structure or meaning of the original. Familiar examples include Bret Harte's parody of other writers in *Condensed Novels* (1867) and FATHER WILLIAM by Lewis Carroll. The latter became so famous in its own right that it is scarcely remembered that it was written as a parody of Robert Southey's poem "The Old Man's Comforts" (1799).

Parolles   In Shakespeare's ALL'S WELL THAT ENDS WELL, a cowardly braggart and wastrel whose influence on Bertram is partially responsible for the latter's rejection of Helena. At one point in the play, Parolles is led blindfolded among his friends and, in the belief that he has been captured by the enemy, vilifies them to their faces.

Parr, Catherine (1512–1548)   The sixth and last wife of Henry VIII of England. Catherine took Henry as her third husband in 1543. An accomplished scholar and a woman characterized by piety and kindness, she was undoubtedly a wholesome influence on the king. She brought Mary and Elizabeth, who had been regarded as illegitimate for many years, back to court and treated them as princesses. She also tried to lessen the religious persecutions of the time. Shortly after Henry's death, she married Sir Thomas Seymour, a former suitor and the uncle of the new king, Edward VI. She died after the birth of her first child.

Parra, Nicanor (1914–   )   Chilean poet. Educated as a physicist at Brown University and Oxford, Parra has spent most of his adult life as a professor of theoretical mechanics at the University of Chile. His first book, *Cancionero sin nombre* (1937), is relatively traditional. *Poemas y antipoemas* (1954; tr *Poems and Antipoems*, 1967) signaled a sharp turn in the direction of his work, deliberately away from what he called the "formalism and rhetoric, grandiloquence, posturing, preciosity, limpness of character, softness" of much Spanish poetry. His antipoetry is carefully flat, nonsyllabic, antiromantic, and nonlogical, with the leap of association and surreal images as important elements.

Versos de salón (1962) is similar in tone and style to *Poemas y antipoemas.* In *Obra gruesa* (1969; tr in part as *Emergency Poems,* 1972), Parra cut back further the use of metaphor and the diction was even more matter of fact. Small, fragmentary poems, published intermittently as *Artefactos,* are distillations of the antipoetry principle so spare that the original antipoems seem almost lyrical in comparison.

Parra, Teresa de la (1895–1936)   Venezuelan novelist. De la Parra was born into a wealthy family and educated in Paris. Her partly autobiographical novels —*Ifigenia: diario de una señorita que escribió porque se fastidiaba* (1924) and *Memorias de Mamá Blanca* (1929; tr *Mama Blanca's Souvenirs,* 1959)—are evocative memoirs of the declining plantation aristocracy and the mysterious qualities of time and time passing. In a subtle and intimate way, de la Parra also comments on the second-class status of women of her position.

Parrington, Vernon L[ouis] (1871–1929) American teacher, historian, biographer, and critic. In 1927 Parrington published the PULITZER PRIZE-winning volume *The Colonial Mind.* This work became the opening section of his *Main Currents in American Thought* (1927–30), left unfinished at his death. His history has been attacked for its emphasis on social or economic themes, but despite these criticisms, *Main Currents* has been highly regarded by students of American literature.

Parsees (or Parsis)   The modern Zoroastrians who reside mainly in the Bombay section of India. They are descendants of a group of Zoroastrians who fled to India from Persia during the Muslim persecutions of the 7th and 8th centuries. Their name means people of Persia and is derived from the old Persian province of Parsa. Although influenced by the HINDUISM of India, they still maintain the main tenets of the Zoroastrian religion. A sacred fire is kept burning in their churches as a symbol of the Divine light that burns in man's soul. See ZOROASTER.

Parson's Tale, The   Last of THE CANTERBURY TALES of CHAUCER. It is a long prose sermon, replete with pious quotations, on the way of Penitence by which the soul may progress toward God. Contrition is followed by Confession, which involves awareness of the difference between venial and deadly sins. An exposition of the seven deadly sins is interpolated, with the various branches of each, and the virtues which serve as remedies against them. The discussion of the manner of Confession is then resumed, followed by an explanation of Satisfaction, or the undertaking of penances, which is the last stage of Penitence.

A short paragraph, known as Chaucer's *Retractions,* is attached to the end of this tale. Chaucer prays God's forgiveness for those of his works that are frivolous or sinful, including most of the *Canterbury Tales,* and hopes that his moral works—the translation of BOETHIUS, the homilies, and the lives of saints—will serve as penance.

Parthenon   The great temple on the Athenian Acropolis to Athene *Parthenos* (i.e., the Virgin). Many of its sculptured friezes and fragments of pediments are now in the British Museum among the Elgin Marbles. The Temple was begun by the architect Ictinus about 450 BC, and the embellishment of it was mainly the work of PHID-IAS, whose colossal statue of Athene, overlaid in gold and ivory, was its chief treasure.

Partisan Review   An American literary magazine founded in 1934. At first wholly identified with the radical left wing in politics, it diverged after 1937 from orthodox Marxism (see MARX) and became increasingly politically independent and concerned with intellectual, literary, and artistic questions. Edited by Philip Rahv, one of its founders, its staff at one time or another included Dwight MAC-DONALD, Mary MCCARTHY, and John ASHBERY. Always concerned with avant-garde writing, the magazine printed works by Samuel BECKETT, Gore VIDAL, and Norman MAILER and parts of James T. Farrell's STUDS LONIGAN before it appeared in book form. Other contributors have included Lionel TRILLING, Saul BELLOW, T. S. ELIOT, Wallace STEVENS, and Edmund WILSON. Its symposia on contemporary questions affecting writers and intellectuals became a notable part of the review. Several collections of material from the magazine have been published: *The Partisan Reader—1934–1944* (1946), *The New Partisan Reader* (1953), *Stories in the Modern Manner* (1953), and *More Stories in the Modern Manner* (1954).

Partridge, Eric [Honeywood] (1894–1979) New Zealand-born English lexicographer. Partridge approached the study of philology with enthusiasm and solid scholarship. His highly readable and comprehensive dictionaries and linguistic studies provided interesting insights into social trends as reflected by changes in the language. Particularly fond of the oddments of language, he produced such well-known works as *A Dictionary of Slang and Unconventional English* (1937; rev 1970), the first scholarly treatment of slang, and *A Dictionary of Catch Phrases* (1977).

Parzival (early 13th century)   A verse epic by WOLF-RAM VON ESCHENBACH, adapted from the *Perceval* of Chrétien de Troyes. Parzival is the guileless fool, totally innocent of sin and guilt. Leaving his wife, Kondwiramur, to visit his mother, he chances upon the castle of the Holy GRAIL, where its guardian Amfortas has been told that only a guileless fool's sympathy can heal his wound. But Parzival obeys the laws of courtly etiquette, rather than those of religion and humanity, and fails to ask the cause of his host's suffering. He thus must leave the castle and later that of King ARTHUR. He is determined now to win the Grail despite his disgrace but cannot until a hermit helps him renew his humility and his pure faith in God. Then his achievements allow him to be received at the Round Table, and he asks the questions which will cure Amfortas, becomes king of the Grail, and is reunited with his wife.

WAGNER's *Parsifal* is largely based on this material. For the Arthurian version see PERCIVAL.

Pascal, Blaise (1623–1662)   French philosopher, scientist, mathematician, and writer. At twelve years of age Pascal discovered Euclid's axioms unaided; at sixteen he wrote a treatise on conic sections, and at eighteen he invented a calculating machine. He formulated the first laws of atmospheric pressure, equilibrium of liquids, and probability, and invented the hydraulic press. In 1654 a mystical experience caused his conversion to JANSENISM, and a year later he retired to Port-Royal to end his days writing philosophical treatises. In the eighteen *Lettres provinciales* (1656–57), he sided with the Jansenists in a dispute over grace, and his argument in these eighteen letters, graceful and ironic in style, routed the Jesuit opposition, quoting them verbatim to their own disadvantage and greatly damaging the Jesuit cause. The PENSÉES, fragments of a projected apology for the Christian religion, appeared in their entirety (1844) only after Pascal's death.

Pascoli, Giovanni (1855–1912)   Italian poet and teacher, born into a family of farmers. Life in the fields coupled with the tragic murder of his father, and the early deaths of his mother, sister, and two brothers had a marked influence on Pascoli's poetry, as did his radical socialism. His teacher and mentor at the University of Bologna was Giosuè CARDUCCI, to whose chair he was appointed when Carducci retired. His first collection of poems, *Myracae* (*Tamarisks*, 1891), with its simplicity and naturalness, was greeted as a welcome change from the nationalistic rhetoric of Carducci and the baroque style of D'ANNUNZIO. Pascoli's early poetry excels in descriptions of nature and domestic life. His later work, while treating similar themes, is more experimental, enriched by considerations of broader significance. His reverence for the work of VERGIL, classical mythology, and rural life pervades all he wrote and exerted a lasting influence on the sensibility of younger poets, from the CREPUSCOLARI to MONTALE.

Other works include: *Canti di Castelvecchio* (1903), *Primi poemetti* (1904), *Odi e inni* (1906), and *Poemi del Risorgimento* (1913).

Pasiphaë   In Greek legend, a daughter of the Sun and wife of MINOS, king of Crete. Pasiphaë was the mother of ARIADNE, and also (through intercourse with a white bull given by POSEIDON to Minos) of the MINOTAUR.

Pasolini, Pier Paolo (1922–1975)   Italian poet, novelist, film director, and critic. Pasolini's poetry and his novels—*Ragazzi di vita* (1955; tr *The Ragazzi*, 1968) and *Una vita violenta* (1959; tr *A Violent Life*, 1968)—are significant for the ways in which the author makes use of dialects as a literary medium and for their focus on the unheroic qualities of the working classes. Pasolini addressed himself in all his work to ideological problems and the need for social reforms. His films often focus on the realities of a preindustrial age, using shocking juxtapositions of imagery to expose the vapidity of modern values. He received high praise for his direction of such films as *Accattone* (1961), adapted from *Una vita violenta*, *The Gospel According to St. Matthew* (1964), *Oedipus Rex* (1967), and *The Decameron* (1971).

Pasquier Chronicles See DUHAMEL, GEORGES.

Passage to India, A (1924) An ironic, compassionate novel by E. M. FORSTER about the difficulties of friendship between the races in British-ruled India. Adela Quested's hallucination that the friendly young Indian, Dr. Aziz, has assaulted her in the Marabar Caves gives rise to hysterical racial feeling in the community. In this atmosphere even Mr. Fielding, the liberal English principal of a local college, finds his friendship with Dr. Aziz shattered by a misunderstanding. Adela, who has come to India to visit her fiancé, the City Magistrate Ronny Heaslop, is traveling with his mother, Mrs. Moore, an intuitive, half-mystical woman, who has an instinctive understanding of Indians and India. Like Adela, she has an unpleasant experience in the ancient Marabar Caves; the echo in the cave seems to tell her of the worthlessness of life, and she has a nervous breakdown. However, she remains an influence for good, persuading Adela to take back her accusation against Dr. Aziz. Ronny breaks off his engagement with Adela, who he feels has betrayed the English by putting the truth above racial prejudice.

The novel is notable for its strong mystical flavor and its treatment of Indian religions. Mrs. Moore passes from sympathy with poetic Islam, Dr. Aziz's religion, to Hinduism, the religion of destruction and creation which is practiced by the odd Professor Godbole.

Passionate Pilgrim and Other Stories, The (1875) A collection of stories by Henry JAMES, about American adventures in Europe. The title story was one of a number of pieces stimulated by James's trip abroad in 1869–70. It tells of Clement Searle, who goes to England, long the object of his dreams, to claim a rich estate. He is penniless, ill, and morbid; his misadventures lead to his death just at the moment when his desire was on the point of being gratified. The tale is ironic and tragic, but full of James's own passionate love of England.

passion play (Ger, *Passionspiel*) A dramatic presentation of the suffering, crucifixion, and resurrection of Jesus, usually performed during Holy Week. Similar to the MIRACLE PLAY, such representations developed during the 13th to 16th centuries and are still common. The most famous is that given every ten years (with a few omissions) by the village of Oberammergau in Bavaria. It was first performed there in 1633, when the villagers vowed to repeat it regularly, in gratitude for escape from a plague epidemic.

Passover (Heb, *Pesach*) The most important Jewish feast. It commemorates the events recorded in the OLD TESTAMENT (Exod. 12) when JEHOVAH killed the Egyptian first-born while sparing the Israelites. This was the last of the TEN PLAGUES and the one that forced Pharaoh to release the Jews from their bondage.

On the first evening of the Passover the family celebration of SEDER takes place; symbolic foods are served, and the story of the EXODUS is read by the head of the household.

Pasternak, Boris Leonidovich (1890–1960) Russian lyric poet and novelist. Pasternak, the son of a well-known portrait painter, was educated at the universities of Moscow and Marburg, majoring in philosophy. He published his first poetry in 1912. Two collections of his lyrics, in 1922 and 1923, *Sestra moya zhizn* (*My Sister, Life*) and *Temy i variyatsi* (*Themes and Variations*) brought him recognition as one of the most important young poets of the early Soviet period. He was connected, for a while, with the literary group of futurists led by Vladimir MAYAKOVSKY but soon went his own way. For Pasternak, this involved writing a difficult, personal poetry that displeased the Soviet censors, who were gaining more and more control of literature during the 1930s. After publishing two long poems, *1905* (1926) and *Leitenant Schmidt* (*Lt. Schmidt*, 1927), Pasternak turned to translations for almost a decade, rendering some excellent Russian versions of Shakespeare's tragedies, as well as works from the German, French, and Georgian. During these years Pasternak was also at work on a novel. The work was rejected for publication in Russia but appeared in 1957 in an Italian translation and in English in 1958. This novel, DOCTOR ZHIVAGO, created a sensation in the West, principally because of its obvious rejection of Marxism and its general disaffection from the Russian revolution. In 1958 Pasternak was awarded the NOBEL PRIZE in Literature, but the furor stirred up in the Soviet Union forced him to reject the award. After living for years in peaceful and productive obscurity, he became the object of everyone's attention, hounded by newsmen from the West in search of sensational copy and by literary watchdogs in his own country who demanded his exile from Russia. His example of courage and fortitude in the face of both onslaughts and the deep humanism so forcefully expressed in his work made him the idol of the younger generation of Russian poets and writers. He died after a brief illness in 1960, and his funeral assumed the character of a protest demonstration against the regime that had sought to silence him.

Besides his novel, Pasternak's prose work includes an autobiographical sketch, *Okhrannaya gramota* (1930; tr *Safe Conduct*, 1945), and several short stories, including the memorable *Vozdushnye puti* (1924; tr *Aerial Ways*, 1945).

Pasteur, Louis (1822–1895) French chemist. Pasteur is famous for his discoveries in applied bacteriology. His most sensational work concerned the development of a curative treatment for hydrophobia. Popularly, his name is associated with the process called *pasteurization*, which he developed, which causes the destruction of pathogenic organisms in milk and other liquids.

Paston Letters (1422–1509)   A series of letters and legal documents written by and to three generations of the Paston family in Norfolk, England. They are a valuable source of information about English history, as well as the business and social customs of the upper-middle class of the time.

pastoral   A term now applied to almost any kind of work depicting a more or less idealized rural life. In a stricter sense, it is a kind of poetry dealing with shepherds and country folk, first written by the Greek poet THEOCRITUS.

As part of the general revival of classical literature, Italian poets of the Renaissance period cultivated the ancient pastoral types and stirred a renewed interest and activity in them throughout Europe. Latin ECLOGUES were written by DANTE, PETRARCH, and BOCCACCIO, mostly in imitation of VERGIL; PONTANO and other humanists later continued to write in Latin, but the Italian eclogues of Rota (1509–75), BOIARDO, and CASTIGLIONE paved the way for a vernacular treatment of the form. The pastoral romance, pioneered by Boccaccio's *Ameto* (1341), was later revived with great influence by Sannazzaro (1456–1530) in his *Arcadia* (1501). There was no classical precedent except the primarily mythological SATYR PLAY for a pastoral drama. But the interest in pastoral generally, and in the drama, led to the advent of the pastoral play. The first wholly pastoral play was Beccari's *Sacrificio* (1554). Tasso's AMINTA and Guarini's IL PASTOR FIDO were the climax of the trend.

Of less importance but equally in the tradition were the many pastoral lyrics (short poems, especially sonnets, with pastoral settings, characters, or brief incidents) written by such poets as Bernardo Tasso, Luigi Tansillo (1510–68), and MARINO. The so-called pastoral IDYLL, a short narrative poem dealing with an erotic episode from mythology, always included pastoral elements, but these are more correctly called mythological poems or Ovidian narratives.

Although pastoral poetry, almost by definition, always represents country life in a good light, it may be fairly true to the facts of rural existence. However, according to the conventions of the genre, which were largely established by sophisticated urban poets, the country is the abode of innocence and health, eloquent and musical shepherds, proud and beautiful maidens. Such a vision has provided a convenient setting for motifs of romantic love, either because the innocence of the shepherd's world lent itself to a special kind of erotic titillation—as in Longus's DAPHNIS AND CHLOE, where the lovers, after embracing, are too naive to know what to do next—or because Arcadia could be so much kinder to ideals of romantic love than the real world —as in most pastoral poetry of the Elizabethan and Spenserian schools, where the lady is perfectly beautiful, the lover infinitely devoted, the world always at spring.

Another use to which the pastoral has been put stemmed from the early identification of the piping shepherd with the poet. A pastoral poem, such as "October" from Spenser's THE SHEPHEARDES CALENDAR, could serve as a vehicle for discussion of the poet's craft and place in society. This identification also gave rise to the pastoral elegy, in which the poet, in the role of a shepherd, mourns the death of a gifted colleague. Milton's LYCIDAS, Shelley's ADONAIS, and Matthew Arnold's THYRSIS are notable examples of this form, reserved exclusively for dead poets.

A final, major function of pastoral has been the implicit or explicit criticism of the corruption, sterility, and falseness of life in city or court. This aspect is significant in the work of many classical authors, including Vergil in his BUCOLICS and GEORGICS, and is recurrent throughout English literature, gaining a new emphasis with the romantic movement.

Pastoral Symphony, The (La Symphonie pastorale, 1919; tr 1931)   A tale by André GIDE. A Swiss pastor adopts and educates the blind orphan Gertrude but tries to keep her from falling in love with his son Jacques, ostensibly from Christian scruples. On the eve of an operation which may restore the girl's sight, frightened that she may love him less than Jacques when she can see, the pastor yields to the desire which he has suppressed under self-deceptive hypocrisy and seduces the girl. Her sight restored, Gertrude understands for the first time the truth about the people around her and the suffering which she has indirectly caused the pastor's wife and children. She commits suicide. Written in the form of the pastor's diary, the tale is remarkable for its restrained and oblique irony and for the sharpness of the author's observations on the hypocrisy which masquerades as Christian pity and duty.

pastor fido, Il (The Faithful Shepherd, 1590)   A Renaissance pastoral play by Giambattista GUARINI, begun in 1580. Its author called it a tragi-comedy, a new genre that combined a tragic plot with a happy ending, thus precipitating a major literary debate at the time. The plot stems from the lingering anger of Diana with the people of Arcadia. To placate the goddess, the oracle says, two people of divine descent must wed and a faithful shepherd must be found. The two Arcadians of divine descent are Silvio and Amarilli, but the former prefers hunting to women, and the latter is loved by and loves the shepherd Mirtillo. Amarilli's rival, Corisca, arranges to have her condemned for breaking her vows to Silvio. Finally, the revelation of Mirtillo's divine descent enables him to marry Amarilli; and his willingness to die for her, also, satisfies the goddess's other demand. At the same time, Silvio consents to marry Dolinda, who has made him fall in love at last, and Corisca is pardoned.

Patanjali (c2nd century BC)   Indian philosopher, author of the *Yogasūtra*, the basic text of yoga, one of the six DARSHANAS in Hindu philosophy. He is probably also the author of the *Mahabhasha*, a commentary on the renowned Sanskrit grammar by PANINI.

Patchen, Kenneth (1911–1972)   American poet and novelist. Patchen is known primarily as a poet. His work ranges from humor, fantasy, and love lyrics to poems of social protest. His style is distinguished by striking imagery, original language, and free forms. Often described as a surrealist, Patchen illustrated his verse with his own abstract paintings and, in the early 1950s, began reading his poems to a jazz accompaniment. Among his over thirty volumes are *Before the Brave* (1936), *Panels for the Walls of Heaven* (1947), *Red Wine and Yellow Hair* (1949), *Because It Is* (1960), *Hallelujah Anyway* (1966), *Love and War Poems* (1968), and *In Quest of Candlelighters* (1972). His *Collected Poems* appeared in 1969.

Pater, Walter [Horatio] (1839–1894)   English essayist and critic. A leader in the 19th-century revival of interest in Renaissance art and humanism, Pater was a formulator of the doctrine that art and aesthetics are in themselves one of the ends of life. His works, noted for their stylistic purity and precision, include *Studies in the History of the Renaissance* (1873); the philosophic novel MARIUS THE EPICUREAN, generally considered his masterpiece; *Plato and Platonism* (1893); the partly autobiographical *The Child in the House* (1894); *Greek Studies* (1895); and the five posthumously published chapters of *Gaston de Latour* (1896), a novel left unfinished at his death. See ART FOR ART'S SAKE.

paternoster (Lat, "our father")   The Lord's Prayer; from the first two words in the Latin version.

Paterson (Books I–V; 1946, 1948, 1950, 1951, 1958) A philosophical epic in verse by William Carlos WILLIAMS. The complete edition of Books I–V appeared in 1963. Notes for a projected Book VI were found among the poet's papers after his death in 1963. *Paterson* stands with Ezra Pound's CANTOS and T. S. Eliot's THE WASTE LAND as one of the major achievements of 20th-century American poetry.

Paterson, the protagonist of the poem, is a mythic being, a projection of the poet himself, and also a metaphor for the city of Paterson (New Jersey). In this compound role, Paterson wanders about his environs and reflects on the past history of the "locale" as well as on its contemporary scene. Book I introduces the theme of language, from which contemporary man is said to be "divorced." The poem's incorporation of newspaper fragments, snatches of living dialogue, letters, etc., is intended to restore a sense of continuum or belonging to contemporary man. Book II is a commentary on Paterson as brutalized by industrial chaos and social inequity. Book III is an indictment of the American literary tradition, which the poet feels is grounded in European conventions. Book IV is a version of the Theocritan pastoral idyll, warped in modern life by such phenomena as usury, divorce, and sterile sophistication. Book V is a coda which reviews earlier motifs and resolves them into a new affirmation. The "New World" becomes a place of promise through the transcendence of artistic imagination and the human spirit. The work sums up the writer's sense of the poet's essential ordering function in the chaos of modern life.

Paterson, Andrew Barton "Banjo" (1864–1941) Australian BUSH BALLADEER. Australia's most popular poet at the turn of the century, Paterson was a superb storyteller whose vigorous verse celebrated the heroes and idealists of the Australian outback. His WALTZING MATILDA, along with other high-spirited ballads, appears in *Collected Verse* (1921).

Pathelin, La Farce de maistre Pierre (c1470) An anonymous medieval French FARCE famous for the artfully cheating lawyer Pathelin (or Patelin). Having cheated the woolen-draper Joceaume, he comes to court to defend the shepherd Aignelet, charged with stealing Joceaume's sheep. Joceaume gets so confused in making his complaints that the judge keeps demanding, *"revenons à ces moutons"* ("let us get back to these sheep"), a line later quoted by Rabelais that since has become a proverbial plea to get back to the subject.

Pather Panchali   See BANERJI, BIBHUTI BHUSAN.

pathetic fallacy   A phrase invented by John RUSKIN to designate the illusion that external objects seem actuated by human feelings, particularly when one is under great emotional strain. Thus when a poet is tormented by grief, he is apt to ascribe to inanimate nature either sympathy or heartless cruelty. Tennyson's IN MEMORIAM, Shelley's ADONAIS, and other elegies are especially noteworthy for eloquent effects gained by the use of the pathetic fallacy.

Pathfinder, The, or The Inland Sea (1840)   A novel by James Fenimore COOPER, in THE LEATHERSTOCKING tales. The story takes place in the Lake Ontario region in 1760, during the French and Indian Wars. Pathfinder, or Natty BUMPPO, relinquishes his claim to Mabel Dunham's hand, when he discovers that she loves Jasper Western. Jasper, suspected of being a traitor, is finally vindicated. The best episode in the book involves Dew-of-June, Cooper's most successful Indian heroine, and the siege of the blockhouse.

pathos   The quality in art or literature that evokes sympathy, tenderness, or sorrow in the viewer or reader. Desdemona's death in OTHELLO is an example.

Patmore, Coventry [Kersey Dighton] (1823–1896)   English poet. As a young man, Patmore was an associate of the Pre-Raphaelites and contributed to *The Germ*. His best-known works are *Angel in the House* (1854–63), a long poetic celebration of married love; *The Unknown Eros* (1877); and several fine sonnets. After the death of his first wife in 1864, he was converted to Roman Catholicism.

Patmos   The Greek island of the Sporades in the Aegean Sea (now called Patmo or Patino). On this island an unknown exile, a prisoner of Rome, wrote THE REVELATION OF SAINT JOHN THE DIVINE.

Paton, Alan [Stewart] (1903–   )   South African novelist and humanitarian. One of the founders of the

Liberal Association of South Africa, Paton wrote *Cry, the Beloved Country* (1948), *Too Late the Phalarope* (1953), and *Ah But Your Land Is Beautiful* (1981), novels about the tragedy of South African racism, as well as several nonfiction treatments of the same theme. He has also published a volume of short stories, *Tales from a Troubled Land* (1961), and a collection of occasional writings, *Knocking on the Door* (1975). *Towards the Mountain* (1980) is a memoir of his life up to the time he published *Cry, the Beloved Country*.

patrician   Properly speaking, one of the *patres* (fathers) or senators of Rome, and their descendants. As they held for many years all the honors of the state, the word came to signify the magnates or nobility of a nation, the aristocrats.

Patrick, St. (c373–464)   The apostle and patron saint of Ireland. St. Patrick was born at what is now Dumbarton in Scotland; his father was Calpurnius, a deacon and Roman official. As a boy he was captured in a Pictish raid and sold as a slave in Ireland. He escaped to Gaul about 395, where he studied under St. MARTIN at Tours before returning to Britain. There he had a supernatural call to preach to the heathen of Ireland, so he was consecrated and in 432 landed at Wicklow. He at first met with strong opposition, but, going north, he converted first the chiefs and people of Ulster, and later those of the rest of Ireland. He founded many churches, including the cathedral and monastery of Armagh, where he held two synods. He is said to have died at Armagh and to have been buried either at Down or Saul. One tradition gives Glastonbury as the place of his death and burial; Downpatrick Cathedral claims his grave.

Many legends exist of St. Patrick's miraculous powers: perhaps the best-known tradition is that he cleared Ireland of its vermin. In commemoration of this, St. Patrick is usually represented banishing the serpents. He is shown with a shamrock leaf, in allusion to the tradition that when explaining the TRINITY to the heathen priests on the hill of Tara, he used this as a symbol.

Patriot for Me, A   See OSBORNE, JOHN.

Patroclus   In Homer's ILIAD, a loyal friend of ACHILLES. Achilles, angry at AGAMEMNON, refused to fight with the Greeks, but, seeing them hard pressed, Patroclus begged to be allowed to join them, and Achilles finally gave him his own armor. Leading the MYRMIDONS into the battle, Patroclus was slain by HECTOR. Grief and fury over Patroclus' death caused Achilles to reenter the fighting.

patroons   The name given to a class of large landholders in New Netherland, those who within a four-year period had established a settlement of fifty persons. The patroons held their feudal privileges until the Anti-Rent War of the 1840s.

Patterson, [Horace] Orlando (1940–   )   Jamaican novelist and sociologist. Patterson, who teaches at Harvard University, has written on the history and psychology of Jamaican slavery in *The Sociology of Slavery* (1967) and on the impulse to conformity in *Ethnic Chauvinism* (1977) and *Slavery and Social Death: A Comparative Study* (1982). His novels include *The Children of Sisyphus* (1964), about a West Indian back-to-Africa movement, and *An Absence of Ruins* (1967) and *Die the Long Day* (1972), both dealing with an existential battle between survival, identity, and futility.

Paul, St. (d AD 64?)   The great APOSTLE and missionary of Christianity, author of the principal Epistles of the NEW TESTAMENT. As Saul of Tarsus, he was a devoted Jew and a bitter persecutor of the early Christians. On his way to Damascus to subdue Christians there, he was stopped by a vision of JESUS; he was temporarily blinded and his conversion was immediate. On his three missionary journeys, which are described in ACTS OF THE APOSTLES, he encountered much hardship, pain, and persecution. He was imprisoned in Rome (AD 60), and tradition has it that he was beheaded five or six years later, after having converted one of NERO's favorite concubines, although some scholars set his death at AD 62.

He was accompanied on his first missionary journey by BARNABAS and, for a time, by John MARK. It is said that he changed his name to Paul on that journey after his conversion of the Roman proconsul Sergius Paulus, in Cyprus (Acts 13:6–12).

The PAULINE EPISTLES are among the most important documents of early Christian theology. His symbols are a sword and an open book, the former the instrument of his martyrdom, and the latter to represent the new law propagated by him as the apostle of the Gentiles. He is commemorated, along with St. Peter, on June 30.

Paulding, James Kirke (1778–1860)   American novelist, dramatist, and historian. Early in his life, Paulding became friendly with Washington Irving and his brother William; they formed the nucleus of a literary group whose most important production was SALMAGUNDI. Paulding's early writings were satirical and violently anti-British. They include *The Diverting History of John Bull and Brother Jonathan* (1812). He also wrote a number of long poems and serious histories. Among his novels are *Königsmarke, the Long Finne* (1823) and *The Dutchman's Fireside* (1831).

Paulding served as naval commissioner and secretary of the navy (1838–41).

Paul et Virginie (1787)   An idyllic, highly successful romance by BERNARDIN DE SAINT-PIERRE. Paul and Virginia, two fatherless children, are brought up on the Isle of France (now Mauritius) by their mothers in virtuous poverty and ignorance, far from corrupt civilization. They fall in love during their adolescence. When a long-forgotten aunt summons Virginia by letter to Paris, she is loath to leave Paul. She does go, however, remaining away from the island two years. Unable to adjust either to her aunt or to civilization, Virginia returns, but a storm sinks her ship, and she dies within sight of Paul, who dies of grief later. The nostalgic evocation of a lost paradise and the sumptuous descriptions of nature and landscapes have assured this work enduring success.

Pauline Epistles Epistles in the NEW TESTAMENT written by or attributed to St. PAUL. Probably the earliest was Paul's Epistles to the THESSALONIANS, dating from Corinth in AD 52 or 53. Most scholars agree that these were almost certainly the work of the apostle, as were 1 and 2 CORINTHIANS, GALATIANS, ROMANS, EPHESIANS, PHILIPPIANS, COLOSSIANS, and PHILEMON. The so-called Pastoral Epistles, directed primarily at the Christian clergy, are 1 and 2 TIMOTHY and Titus; it is generally agreed that they are the work of one writer, but most modern scholars doubt that it was Paul. Attribution to Paul of the Epistle to the HEBREWS has been almost unanimously refuted.

Paul's teachings established clear theological doctrines about God as father, both to Jesus and to all creation, about ORIGINAL SIN, and the existence of the Holy Spirit. The Epistles also formed the basis for later Christian interpretations of forgiveness and grace, justification by faith, and the use of the SACRAMENTS.

Paul Revere's Ride (1861) A narrative poem by Henry Wadsworth LONGFELLOW telling of the midnight ride of the Revolutionary patriot Paul REVERE, to spread the news of an expected British raid.

Paul's Case See YOUTH AND THE BRIGHT MEDUSA.

Paustovsky, Konstantin Georgiyevich (1892–1968) Soviet short-story writer and journalist. After his war service, Paustovsky worked in Odessa, where he became a friend of Isaak BABEL. Paustovsky was encouraged in his literary career by Maksim GORKY, for whom he worked on a journal from 1929 to 1937. He is the author of many romantic pieces, nature stories, tales for children, and a six-volume autobiography, *Povest o zhizni* (1946–64; tr *Story of a Life*, 1964–69). He was consistently outspoken in his defense of liberalism in Soviet literary policy, and was one of the chief defenders in 1956 of Vladimir DUDINTSEV, who was under attack for his novel NOT BY BREAD ALONE. For years Paustovsky ran a seminar for young writers; his anthology of their and others' work, *Tarusskie stranitsy* (*Pages from Tarusa*, 1961), was one of the literary highlights of Khrushchev's THAW.

Pavese, Cesare (1908–1950) Italian poet, novelist, editor, and translator. Along with Elio VITTORINI, Pavese was responsible for translating and commenting on the works of major American writers. The dominant themes of his own work are the contrast between city and country life, man's solitude and his need to establish a rapport with other human beings, and the necessity to rediscover one's roots. In his novels, he strove to give life to human suffering, alienation, and violence while at the same time fashioning a style that could yield poetic effects without being academic or too literary. He wrote of his own experience as a political exile in *Il carcere* (1949; tr *The*

Political Prisoner, 1950); of love, lust, and violence in *Paesi tuoi* (1941; tr *The Harvesters*, 1961); about World War II in *La casa in collina* (1948; tr *The House on the Hill*, 1961); and about the meaning of returning home in *La luna e i falò* (1950; tr *The Moon and the Bonfires*, 1953). His poems were published in a single omnibus volume, *Poesie edite e inedite* (1962). His tormented diary, which tells much about his long-contemplated suicide, is entitled *Il mestiere di vivere* (1952; tr *The Burning Brand: Diaries 1935–1950*, 1961).

Pavlova, Anna (1885–1931) A Russian ballerina of immense popularity. She was particularly famous for her performance of *The Dying Swan*, choreographed by Michel Fokine.

Payne, John Howard (1791–1852) American actor, playwright, and poet. Perpetually impoverished, Payne created a sensation as an actor both in New York and London and wrote several plays, his triumph being *Clari, The Maid of Milan* (1823). This play included the song "Home, Sweet Home," with music by Sir Henry Bishop. It became highly popular, but Payne, having sold the play outright, was not able to collect royalties.

Paz, Octavio (1914–   ) Mexican poet, essayist, social philosopher, and critic. Paz published his first book of poems, *Luna silvestre* (1933), when he was only nineteen. Along with his lifelong absorption in literature, Paz had a profound interest in the Mexican past, a keen social and political consciousness, and a somewhat mystical philosophical bent. After twenty-five years in the diplomatic service Paz resigned his post as ambassador to India in 1968 to protest his government's suppression of a student-worker demonstration.

His poetry is lyrical and erotic and expresses his sense of the deep loneliness of man, which can be transcended only through attempts at communion, through sexual love, compassion, and faith. It is rich with images of Mexico's landscape and allusions to his Indian past. His books of poems include *Aguila o sol?* (1951; tr *Eagle or Sun?*, 1970); *Piedra de sol* (1957; tr *Sun Stone*, 1963), perhaps his most important long poem, addressed to the planet Venus; *Salamandra* (1962); *Ladera este* (1969); and *Poemas 1935–75* (1979). Among the English translations selected from various books are *Selected Poetry* (1963) and *Early Poems 1935–1955* (1973; both translated by Muriel RUKEYSER) and *A Drift of Shadows* (1979). A further collection of poems, *Selected Poems* (ed Eliot Weinberger), was published in 1984. His outstanding prose work is THE LABYRINTH OF SOLITUDE, a compelling, highly original, and influential study of the Mexican national character. Along with studies of Claude LÉVI-STRAUSS (1967; tr 1970) and Marcel DUCHAMP (1968; tr 1970), he has also written the critical essays on poetry *El arco y la lira* (1956; tr *The Bow and the Lyre*, 1973); *Conjunciones y disjunciones* (1969; tr *Conjunctions and Disjunctions*, 1974), essays on sex and religion; *Posdata* (1970; tr *The Other Mexico*, 1972), written after his resignation from the diplomatic corps; and *El orgo filantrópico* (1979), essays on modern history.

p'Bitek, Okot (1931–1982) Ugandan poet. P'Bitek's literary reputation was established with the publication of *Song of Lawino* (1966), his own English rendering of a tale he had written in his native Lwo vernacular. The "song," a poignant and dispassionate metaphor for the African situation in general, treats the domestic upheaval experienced by Lawino, an African woman, and her husband, Ocol, who turns away from his cultural roots and tries to assimilate Western styles and values. It was followed by *Song of Ocol* (1970). Other prose-poems are *Song of a Prisoner* (1971), *Two Songs* (1971), and *Horn of My Love* (1974). *Hare and Hornbill* (1978) is a collection of animal tales and legends. In 1973, responding to what he saw as negative outside influences on African artistic traditions, he wrote *Africa's Cultural Revolution*.

Peace, The (Eirene, 421 BC) A comedy by ARISTOPHANES. Trygaeus, a farmer, flies up to heaven on a huge dung beetle to find out from Zeus what has happened to the goddess Peace, who has been so long away from Greece. He finds that War has hidden her in a pit under a heap of stones. Farmers and workingmen from every part of Greece help Trygaeus to rescue the goddess. The play ends with a great feast, demonstrating the joys of peace. It was written when Athens and Sparta had been long at war.

Peacock, Thomas Love (1785–1866) English novelist and poet. Satirical and critical in subject and often extravagant in style, Peacock's novels include HEADLONG HALL, *Melincourt* (1817), NIGHTMARE ABBEY, CROTCHET CASTLE, and *Gryll Grange* (1860–1). Peacock caricatured contemporary figures by the device of bringing a group of thinly disguised eccentrics together and letting their conversation, often ridiculous, fill the book. Peacock's satirical essay "The Four Ages of Poetry" (1820) provoked Shelley to write a serious rebuttal in his *Defense of Poetry* (1821).

Peacock Throne A throne built (1628 to 1635) at Delhi, India, for the Indian ruler Shah Jehan. He also built the Taj Mahal. Each of its twelve pillars was decorated with two peacocks glittering with gems. A century later (1739), Nadir Shah took it to Persia.

Peale, Charles Willson (1741–1827) American painter. Peale was the leading colonial painter of portraits and genre scenes (most notably, *The Staircase Group*, 1795) and was instrumental in founding the Pennsylvania Academy of Fine Arts. He was the father of seventeen children, five of them artists. Raphaelle Peale (1774–1825) was a still-life and trompe-l'oeil painter whose most famous work was *After the Bath* (1823); Rembrandt Peale (1778–1860) was a painter of portraits and historical tableaux. Charles Peale's brother James (1749–1831) was also a noted portrait painter, whose daughter Sarah (1800–1885) was a leading portrait painter in Baltimore, Washington, D.C., and St. Louis.

Pearl The illegitimate child of Arthur Dimmesdale and Hester Prynne in Hawthorne's THE SCARLET LETTER.

Pearl, The (1947) A novelette by John STEINBECK. Kino, an Indian pearl-fisher in the Gulf of California, and his wife, Juana, have a baby who is bitten by a scorpion. Kino finds a large pearl to pay the doctor, but it brings only tragedy.

Pearl Poet (late 14th century) Supposed author of a manuscript containing four alliterative poems in a West Midland dialect of Middle English: *The Pearl*, *Purity* (or *Cleanness*), *Patience*, and SIR GAWAIN AND THE GREEN KNIGHT, although it is not certain that *Sir Gawain* was actually composed by the same author as the first three. *Purity* and *Patience* are didactic poems drawing heavily on biblical stories; *The Pearl* is an allegorical tale capped with a description of the New Jerusalem. There are indications that the Pearl Poet was also familiar with the French and Italian literature of the time.

Pearse, Patrick H[enry] (1879–1916) Irish writer and patriot. Pearse's stories, poems, and plays (collected and published in 1917) were all dedicated to the cause of Irish nationalism, as were his numerous political writings (collected and published in 1922). Most of his writings were in Gaelic. He was commander-in-chief of the Irish republican forces during the EASTER REBELLION of 1916, for which he was executed by a British firing squad.

Peasant Bard An epithet applied to Robert BURNS.

Peasants (Muzhiki, 1897) A long story by Anton CHEKHOV. Its somber picture of peasant life in Russia stirred up a heated debate, generally divided according to political convictions, about the accuracy of Chekhov's portrayal.

Pease-Blossom In Shakespeare's MIDSUMMER NIGHT'S DREAM, one of four fairies of Titania who serve as personal attendants to Bottom. The others are Cobweb, Moth, and Mustardseed.

Peau de chagrin, La (The Wild Ass's Skin, 1830) A novel, part of LA COMÉDIE HUMAINE, by Honoré de BALZAC. The hero, Raphael, receives a piece of magic skin that will ensure the gratification of his every desire. The skin, however, and the life of its owner, grow smaller with each wish. After a brief hedonistic fling, Raphael seeks frantically for some way to stretch the skin. His attempts fail, and while yet a young man he dies.

Pêcheur d'Islande (An Iceland Fisherman, 1866) A novel by Pierre LOTI. Each year the fishermen who live on the coast of Brittany make a voyage to the waters off the shores of Iceland for the long fishing season. Loti describes the loneliness of this existence and the bitter struggle between the men and the sea from which they draw their livelihood. The element of romantic adventure which characterizes Loti's popular, earlier work is not absent, however, for the hero becomes involved in the war between France and China and dies in Singapore before reaching home.

Pechorin   See HERO OF OUR TIME, A.

Pecksniff   In Charles Dickens's MARTIN CHUZ-ZLEWIT, a canting hypocrite who is eventually exposed and denounced by Chuzzlewit, Sr., for trying to force Mary Graham to marry him. His two daughters are Charity and Mercy. The first is a thin shrew eventually jilted by a young man who really loves her sister. Mercy is pretty and true-hearted and is made miserable in her marriage to Jonas Chuzzlewit.

Pecos Bill   See TALL TALE.

Peder Victorious   See GIANTS IN THE EARTH.

Peele, George (1558?–?1597)   English playwright and poet. The holder of an M.A. degree from Oxford, a UNIVERSITY WIT notorious for his dissipated life, Peele wrote numerous works, including plays, pageants, lyrics for use in his plays, and verse celebrating various occasions of honor in the lives of noble patrons. The influence of John LYLY can be seen in his plays, notably *The Arraignment of Paris* (perf c1581, printed anonymously 1584), *The Old Wives' Tale* (1595), and *The Love of King David and Fair Bethsabe* (written c1588, perf 1599).

Peeperkorn, Pieter   In Thomas Mann's novel THE MAGIC MOUNTAIN, a rich Dutch coffee planter who comes to Haus Berghof with Clavdia Chauchat. Peeperkorn is the novel's single representative of a robust and active, rather than lax and decadent, life of the senses. He has a huge appetite and speaks in broken, incoherent sentences, which suggest that his basic energy defies all discipline. Under his influence, Hans CASTORP begins to think of leaving the sanatorium and leading a normal life. But Peeperkorn does not last long; deeply aware that he is past his physical prime, he soon commits suicide by poison.

Peeping Tom of Coventry   See GODIVA, LADY.

Peer Gynt (1867)   A verse drama by Henrik IBSEN. A satiric fantasy, the play takes as its hero the legendary Peer Gynt of Norse folklore. The boastful, capricious, irresponsible Peer goes through life thinking quite well of himself, though there is no more reality to his personality than there is to an onion when one has peeled all the layers away. Peer has many amazing adventures in many lands, alternately ships missionaries and idols to China, makes and loses money, saves his own life in a shipwreck by letting another drown, and finally comes up before the Button Molder, who tries to melt him in his ladle. Peer is horrified at the idea of losing his precious identity, though he has no true self. However, he is saved by Solveig, who has always loved him and in whose mind he has existed as a real personality. Incidental music to accompany the play was composed by Edward GRIEG.

Pegasus   In classical mythology, the winged horse of the MUSES. Pegasus was born of the sea foam and the blood of the slaughtered MEDUSA. He was caught by BELLEROPHON, who mounted him and destroyed the CHIMAERA. But when Bellerophon attempted to ascend to heaven, he was thrown from the horse, and Pegasus mounted alone to the skies to become the constellation of the same name.

Peggotty, Clara   In Dickens's DAVID COPPERFIELD, the faithful nurse of David, who, with the other members of her family, is a great aid and comfort to him in his early childhood.

Dan'el Peggotty   Clara's brother. Dan'el is a Yarmouth fisherman, living with his nephew Ham Peggotty and his brother-in-law's child Little Em'ly, in an odd, ship-like house where David loves to visit as a child. He is a bachelor, and Mrs. Gummidge keeps house for him.

Em'ly Peggotty   Daughter of Dan'el's brother-in-law, better known as Little Em'ly. She is engaged to Ham, but, being fascinated by David's old schoolmate STEERFORTH, is seduced by him and runs off with him. She is later reclaimed and immigrates to Australia with Dan'el and Mrs. Gummidge.

Ham Peggotty   Dan'el's nephew. Ham loves Little Em'ly, but loses her to Steerforth. A simple, honest, warmhearted fisherman, he is drowned attempting to rescue Steerforth from the sea.

Péguy, Charles (1873–1914)   French poet and essayist. Of peasant stock, Péguy became an ardent polemicist for the causes of Catholicism, nationalism, and socialism. In *Marcel* (1898) he projected the idea of the perfect socialist state based on the harmonious union of Christianity and France. He founded the bimonthly review *Cahiers de la quinzaine* (1900–1914), which introduced a number of important new authors in addition to publishing Péguy's polemics on contemporary affairs, notably his defense of Charles DREYFUS. He absorbed in his native Orleans the story of JOAN OF ARC, who became for him the symbol of the unity of Catholicism and France, which he exalted in his poems *Jeanne d'Arc* (1897) and *Le Mystère de la charité de Jeanne d'Arc* (1909; tr *The Mystery of the Charity of Joan of Arc*, 1950). Other poems include *Le Porche du mystère de la deuxième vertu* (1911), *Le Mystère des saints innocents* (1912; tr *Mystery of the Holy Innocents*, 1956), and *Eve* (1913). Collections of his work in English translation are *Basic Verities: Prose and Poetry* (1943), *Men and Saints* (1944), and *God Speaks: Religious Poetry* (1945). Péguy's principal English translator was Julien GREEN.

Peg Woffington (1853)   A novel by Charles READE, first brought out as a drama entitled *Masks and Faces* (1852). Its heroine is the famous Irish actress Margaret Woffington (1714?–60). In both play and novel, proof of her art is given in two extraordinary impersonations: she first imitates a famous tragic actress of the day so skillfully that she deceives an entire dramatic company, and she later substitutes her own face for the face of her portrait, which has been painted by James Triplet and is being inspected by a group of critics. The plot centers on the relations of Peg and Ernest Vane, a married man who falls in love with her during a sojourn in town. When she learns that he is already married and has no serious intentions, she determines on revenge but, won over by the naiveté and charm of Mrs. Vane, renounces her purpose.

Peirce, Charles [Santiago] Sanders (1839–1914)   American philosopher and scientist. Son of the great American mathematician and astronomer Benjamin Peirce (1809–80), he was brought up from earliest childhood tackling logical and mathematical problems designed by his father. At Harvard, he studied under J.L.R. AGASSIZ and took Harvard's first advanced degree in chemistry. Uncomfortable with the restrictions of the academic establishment, Peirce spent much of his working life at the U.S. Coast and Geodetic Survey, becoming a world figure in astronomy and geodesy. From time to time he taught, lecturing on the philosophy of science at Harvard and on logic at Johns Hopkins. It was Peirce who made the first full statement of PRAGMATISM, a term he coined in an article entitled "How to Make Our Ideas Clear" (1878), appearing in *Popular Science Monthly*. William JAMES, to whom pragmatism owes its fame as a philosophical movement, first used the term in 1898 and credited Peirce as its originator. Peirce also wrote on religion and history, and translated philosophic and scientific works from four languages, but the only book published in his lifetime was *Photometric Researches* (1878). After his death, Harvard's philosophy department housed his papers, a mass of disorganized material. With the publication of *The Collected Papers of Charles Sanders Peirce* (8 vols, 1931–57; ed C. Hawthorne and P. Weiss), the full significance of his work began to be widely recognized. Four volumes of his mathematical papers, *The New Elements of Mathematics* (ed Carolyn Eisele), appeared in 1976.

Pekkanen, Toivo (1902–1957)   Finnish novelist. Pekkanen was a major figure in Finnish PROLETARIAN LITERATURE. His work evolved from the naturalistic *Isänmaan ranta* (*On the Shores of Finland*, 1937) to the realistic, autobiographical tale of a poor family in *Lapsuuteni* (1953; tr *My Childhood*, 1966), his masterwork. He also wrote four plays and a volume of verse, *Lähtö matkalle* (1955).

Peleus   In Greek mythology, a son of AEACUS, king of Aegina. With his brother TELAMON, Peleus killed their half brother Phocus to prevent his inheriting the kingdom. Banished, he became ruler of a part of Phthia, but accidentally killed his co-ruler Eurytion as they hunted the CALYDONIAN BOAR. Fleeing to Iolcus, he rejected the advances of ACASTUS' wife, Cretheis, and she accused him of trying to violate her, but CHIRON helped him escape Acastus' treacherous revenge. HERA arranged for him to marry THETIS, and she bore him ACHILLES. As she was placing the child in the fire to immortalize him, Peleus cried out in horror, and she deserted both in anger. Later Peleus sailed with the ARGONAUTS. He outlived his son and his grandson NEOPTOLEMUS. As an old man he appears in Euripides' tragedy ANDROMACHE, defending the heroine from persecution.

Pelias   In Greek mythology, a son of POSEIDON. Pelias seized the throne of Iolcus from his half brother Aeson. When Aeson's son JASON claimed the throne, Pelias sent him with the ARGONAUTS to recover the GOLDEN FLEECE. Jason returned with MEDEA, who tricked Pelias' daughters into killing Pelias.

pelican   In Christian art, a symbol of charity. It is also an emblem of JESUS, "by whose blood we are healed." St. JEROME gives the story of the pelican restoring its young ones destroyed by serpents, and his salvation by the blood of Jesus. The old popular fallacy that pelicans fed their young with their blood arose from the fact that when the parent bird is about to feed its brood, it macerates small fish in the large bag against its breast and transfers the macerated food to the mouths of the young.

Pelion and Ossa   Mountains in Thessaly. In Greek mythology, the giant sons of Aloeus or POSEIDON, OTUS and EPHIALTES, planned to pile Ossa on Mount OLYMPUS and Pelion on Ossa, in order to carry on their somewhat obscure quarrel with the gods. ZEUS, however, struck them down while they were still in their downy-cheeked youth. This story is told by HOMER; later writers often confused them with the GIANTS and the TITANS, who also warred on heaven. "Heaping Pelion upon Ossa" has come to mean adding difficulty to difficulty.

Pelléas et Mélisande (1892)   A drama by Maurice MAETERLINCK. Mélisande is found wandering wretchedly about in the forest by Golaud, a grandson of King Arkel who, although she will disclose nothing about herself, marries her and takes her to court. Her sadness and charm win her first the sympathy and then the love of Pelléas, Golaud's brother. While talking with Pelléas, she loses her wedding ring, and at the same moment, Golaud meets with an accident. Mélisande nurses him back to health. Golaud's son by a former marriage, Yniold, unwittingly confirms his father's growing suspicions. Finally, Pelléas and Mélisande decide to part and meet for the last time, but the jealous Golaud kills Pelléas. After the birth of her child, Mélisande also dies. Claude DEBUSSY made this play into an opera in 1902.

Pelles, King   In Malory's MORTE D'ARTHUR, the father of ELAINE, grandfather of Sir GALAHAD and related to JOSEPH OF ARIMATHEA.

Pellico, Silvio (1789–1854)   Italian writer and patriot. The editor of the liberal periodical *Il conciliatore*, Pellico was arrested as a suspected member of the CARBONARI in 1820 and was shuttled between prisons in Milan and Venice and the notorious Spielberg dungeon (Moravia), until his release in 1830. He narrated his prison experiences in *Le mie prigioni* (1832), wherein he tells how adversity confirmed his previously wavering Christian faith. A spirit of Christian forgiveness pervades the book, so that Cesare Balbo observed that it was more damaging to Austria than the loss of a battle. He also wrote poetry, several verse tragedies, and made a translation of Byron's *Manfred*.

Pellinore, King   In Malory's MORTE D'ARTHUR, the hunter of the Questing Beast. Pellinore is the father of Lamerok, Percival, Agglovale, Dornar, and Torre, all knights of the ROUND TABLE. Sir GAWAIN kills him in revenge for the death of his own father, King LOT.

Peloponnesian Wars   A struggle (431–404 BC) between Athens, a democratic sea power, and Sparta, an oligarchical, conservative state. THUCYDIDES, who fought in the war, considered the cause to be Athens's rise to greatness; later historians have thought that the conflict arose out of commercial rivalries involving Corinth. The Spartans won an important victory at the battle of Mantinea (418 BC). The defection of ALCIBIADES during the ill-omened expedition to Sicily (415 BC) gave Sparta increased strength. When the Athenian fleet was destroyed at Aegospotami (405 BC), Sparta succeeded in reducing Athens to a second-rate power. Most of our information about the war comes from Thucydides' history; the later years are related in XENOPHON's *Hellenica*. ARISTOPHANES lampooned warmongers and demagogues repeatedly in his comedies. EURIPIDES' THE TROJAN WOMEN was in part a protest against atrocities committed in the war.

Pelops   In Greek mythology, a son of TANTALUS. The Peloponnese was named after him. As an infant, Pelops was served at a banquet given by his father for the gods. Failing to notice, DEMETER ate a part of his shoulder, but the other gods were horrified. They condemned Tantalus to torture in HADES and revived Pelops by boiling him; Demeter gave him a new shoulder of ivory. Making the beautiful child his favorite, POSEIDON took him to OLYMPUS.

As a young man, Pelops sued for the hand of Hippodamia, the daughter of Oenomaus, king of Pisa. Her suitors were required to flee with her in their chariots while Oenomaus pursued them, armed. Many had been killed thus, but Pelops persuaded Oenomaus' charioteer Myrtilus to place linchpins of wax in the chariot. Oenomaus was killed, but, when Myrtilus demanded the payment agreed on, a night with Hippodamia, Pelops killed him also, and was cursed by him.

Pelops subjugated much of the northern Peloponnese. Unable to subdue Stymphalus, king of Arcadia, he invited him to a banquet, where he treacherously killed him. The crime caused a famine throughout Greece, which was ended only by the prayers of AEACUS. Hippodamia bore many children by Pelops, including Atreus and Thyestes (see the House of ATREUS) and Pittheus. Through jealousy she caused the death of his son by the nymph Astyoche, Chrysippus, whom Laius carried off to Thebes. The sanctuary of Pelops at Olympia was one of its most sacred spots.

penates   In ancient Rome, guardian deities of the household and of the state, usually referred to in the plural. They were personifications of the natural powers, and whereas the LARES protected and warded off danger, it was the duty of the penates to bring wealth and plenty.

Pendennis, The History of (1848–1850)   A novel by William Makepeace THACKERAY. The hero, Arthur Pendennis, known as Pen for short, is spoiled by his mother and by Laura Bell, a distant relative of his own age with whom he grows up. He goes through the university, enters London society, writes a successful novel, becomes editor of the *Pall Mall Gazette*, and is involved in love affairs of varying character. He finally marries Laura, who has always loved him, and whom he has grown to love.

Pendragon   An ancient British title, denoting chief leader or king. It was conferred on a chief when he was invested with the supreme power in times of danger and is particularly identified with Uther Pendragon, father of King Arthur. The word is derived from the Welsh *pen*, "head," and *dragon* (the reference being to the war chief's dragon standard). It corresponds to the Roman *dux bellorum*.

Penelope   The wife of ODYSSEUS and mother of TELEMACHUS in the ODYSSEY. While Odysseus was away from Ithaca during the TROJAN WAR and on his subsequent wanderings, Penelope was besieged by suitors. She put them off by various devices, the cleverest being to say that she would decide on which she would marry when she had finished weaving a shroud for her father-in-law. At night she raveled out what she had woven by day. The suitors eventually discovered the ruse, but Odysseus fortunately returned to slay them all and rescue Penelope from her dilemma.

Penguin Island (L'Ile des pingouins, 1908)   A novel by Anatole FRANCE. It deals with French history in a satiric manner. The old Breton monk Saint Maël lands on an island and in his semiblindness fails to perceive that the inhabitants whom he baptizes are penguins and not men. They are, however, changed to men by God, and the island is carefully towed back to shore by the monk. A highly ironic and imaginative account of the development of civilization comprises the remainder of the novel.

Penitentes   A religious order in New Mexico. It puts on an annual passion play, in the course of which the practice of self-flagellation is indulged in. The Penitentes are Roman Catholics, though the practice is condemned by the Church. See FLAGELLANTS.

Penitential Psalms   Seven psalms expressive of contrition. In the Christian tradition they have been recited together as a devotion. They are PSALMS 7, 32, 38, 51, 102, 130, and 143. All except the first are one number lower in the Latin numbering.

Penn, Arthur (1922–   )   American film and stage director. Penn moved to films from the theatre, where he had a long list of distinguished Broadway productions to his credit. In many of his films, Penn examines violence as a reaction to a rigid society. *Bonnie and Clyde* (1967), *Alice's Restaurant* (1969), and *Little Big Man* (1970) detail the conflict between varying degrees of lawlessness in America and portray a series of charismatic antiheroes at odds with a hostile society. Penn did not direct another feature film until *Night Moves* (1975), a detective thriller. *The Missouri Breaks* (1976) is set in the American West of the past.

Penn, William (1644–1718)   English Quaker, founder of Pennsylvania. In 1681 Penn obtained a grant of land from James II, where Quakers might live without fear of religious persecution. In the new colony, which was named Pennsylvania in honor of Penn's father, he established a liberal government, permitted religious freedom, and maintained friendly relations with the Indians. A prolific writer, Penn is best known for *Some Fruits of Solitude* (1693), a collection of religious and moral maxims.

penny dreadful   Any cheaply printed paperbound book of adventure or mystery popular in England and America, particularly in the 19th century. As with the DIME NOVEL, penny dreadfuls were inexpensive and known more for the sensationalism of their stories than for any literary merit.

Penrod (1914)   A novel by Booth TARKINGTON. This account of the humorous adventures and escapades of Penrod Schofield, a typical twelve-year-old boy in a Midwestern community, has been widely read and highly popular; it was followed by *Penrod and Sam* (1916) and *Penrod Jashber* (1931). All three were collected in the omnibus volume *Penrod: His Complete Story* (1931).

pensée   The French word for thought, it originated as a literary form with Pascal's posthumously published PENSÉES. Generally, it is an idea set in the form of an APHORISM, MAXIM, or short sentence, although *pensées* can run to several pages. DIDEROT used the form in his *Pensées philosophiques* (1746) and his *Pensées sur l'interpretation de la nature* (1753).

Pensées (Thoughts, 1844)   A collection of reflections on religion by Blaise PASCAL, found in fragmentary form after his death. The first edition (1670) abridged the *Pensées* in order to soften their strongly Jansenist tone, but the edition of 1844 is faithful to the original manuscript. It is Pascal's view that man—less than God yet more than the animals—is a helpless creature suspended between the great unknown of past and future, birth and death. A frail reed in a vast universe, he is yet a thinking reed: *"L'homme n'est qu'un roseau, le plus faible de la nature, mais c'est un roseau pensant."* The Christian telling of man's fall from grace and the possibility of redemption must be true, because only thus can the contradictions in man's nature be explained. Faith cannot be gained by reason alone, for logic must be aided by God's grace, which speaks to the heart: *"Le coeur a ses raisons que la raison ne connaît pas."* ("The heart has its reasons, which reason does not know.") A testament of religious faith, the fragmentary *Pensées* offer perceptive insights into the human condition, revealing Pascal's power of lucid reasoning and the depth of his Christian belief.

Penseroso, Il (1632)   A poem by John MILTON. It celebrates the "pleasures" of melancholy, contemplation, solitude, and study. The thematic opposite of its companion piece L'ALLEGRO, it shares the latter's qualities of style: rich verbal music and an extraordinary range and opulence of fancy.

pentameter   In prosody, a line of verse containing five metrical feet in any METER, usually identified together with the name of the meter, such as iambic pentameter, trochaic pentameter, etc. The iambic pentameter is the English heroic line; it is also the standard line in English BLANK VERSE, the HEROIC COUPLET, the SONNET, and other forms.

Pentateuch (fr Gr, *penta*, "five," *teuchos*, "tool; book")   The first five books of the OLD TESTAMENT, traditionally ascribed to MOSES, and often called the Law of Moses. Consisting of GENESIS, EXODUS, LEVITICUS, NUMBERS, and DEUTERONOMY, the Pentateuch relates the history of the Jews from the Creation to the death of Moses. Beginning with Exodus, the prevailing theme is the migration of the Jews, their deliverance from Egypt, and their entry into the PROMISED LAND.

The Samaritan Pentateuch   The Hebrew text as preserved by the Samaritans; it is said to date from 400 BC. See ELOHISTIC AND JEHOVISTIC SCRIPTURES.

Pentecost (fr Gr, *pentekostos*, "fiftieth")   Originally, in the OLD TESTAMENT, a feast celebrating the harvest of wheat and barley, held in the late spring. It later came to commemorate the giving of the Tablets of Law to MOSES. It was adopted as a Christian festival, also called WHITSUNDAY, to commemorate the appearance of the Holy Ghost to the APOSTLES, causing them to "speak with other tongues, as the Spirit gave them utterance" (Acts 2:4).

Penthesilea   In classical mythology, a queen of the AMAZONS. Penthesilea was slain by ACHILLES when she came to the aid of the Trojans after the death of HECTOR. Her beauty and courage won for her a sincere lament from her slayer.

Penthesilea (pub 1808)   A tragedy by Heinrich von KLEIST, in which both PENTHESILEA and ACHILLES die. It was on the basis of this play that GOETHE made his notoriously unfair judgment of Kleist as a "hypochondriac northerner," by which he meant that, in his opinion, Kleist concentrated too strongly on the violently passionate, tragic potentiality of human nature and overlooked possibilities for wholesome balance.

Pentheus   A king of Thebes and grandson of CADMUS. Pentheus' tragic fate at the hands of his mother, AGAVE, is recounted in Euripides' drama THE BACCHANTS.

People of the City (1954)   By Cyprian Ekwensi, a popular Nigerian writer, the first West African novel to be published overseas and therefore widely considered the first modern African novel. It tells the story of the experiences of Amusa Sango, by day a crime reporter, by night a highlife band leader, in Lagos. Sango's experiences with bribery and corruption, murder and the occult, love and death, are recorded in a series of episodes that reflect the variety of the lives of the people of Lagos.

Pepin the Short   See FRANCE, RULERS OF.

Pepys, Samuel (1633–1703)   English politician, best known for his *Diary*. The son of a tailor, Pepys had as a patron Sir Edward Montagu, the earl of Sandwich, and was in a position to meet the outstanding personalities of his day. He was secretary of the admiralty from 1673 to 1688 and also served in Parliament and as president of the Royal Society. After the accession of William III, he lost all his offices and was briefly imprisoned for his Stuart sympathies.

Written in shorthand between 1660 and 1669 and not deciphered until 1825, when it was published in part, the *Diary* was never intended for the public eye. It not only presents a vivid picture of an age, but is also a uniquely uninhibited and spontaneous revelation of its author's life and character.

Percival   (1) In ARTHURIAN LEGEND, one of the most famous knights of the ROUND TABLE, figuring especially in the quest for the GRAIL. Percival's first appearance in literature is in the French poem *Perceval, ou le conte du Graal*, written c1175, by CHRÉTIEN DE TROYES. *Peredur, Son of Efrawg*, a medieval Welsh tale of Arthurian romance included in THE MABINOGION, is parallel to Chrétien's *Perceval*. From the time of Chrétien on, he appears in almost all the Arthurian romances; he is Sir Percival in Malory's MORTE D'ARTHUR and the PARZIFAL of the German versions.

In general, his story begins with his boyhood in the forest and his complete ignorance of the ways of knights and warriors and of courtly manners. He then goes to King Arthur's court, where he commits one gaucherie after another; he is trained as a knight, however, and goes on to become one of the best knights of the Round Table. His quest for the Grail is the main incident of the story and ends with his being awarded a sight of it. Late versions of his story usually present him as a virgin knight. Malory's *Morte d'Arthur* was Tennyson's source for his version in IDYLLS OF THE KING.

(2) In Virginia Woolf's novel THE WAVES, the childhood friend of the six leading characters. Percival does not appear in the novel but acts as a unifying force, since he is admired deeply by all the others. He is a symbol of balance and pleasantness and all that the other characters aspire to be. He is killed in a fall from a horse in India, and his death serves as a symbol for the death which all the characters approach.

Percy, Sir Henry (known as Hotspur, 1364–1403) English soldier, eldest son of Henry Percy, first earl of Northumberland. Percy joined Owen Glendower's rebellion against Henry IV and was killed at the battle of Shrewsbury. Called Hotspur because of his fiery and uncontrollable temper, he contrasts with the cool-headed Prince Hal in Shakespeare's HENRY IV: PART I.

Percy, Bishop Thomas   See RELIQUES OF ANCIENT ENGLISH POETRY.

Percy, Walker (1916–   )   American novelist. Percy was born, and spent most of his life, in the moneyed, leisured, upper-class South. He studied medicine but stopped practice during his internship after he contracted tuberculosis. He used his convalescence to study the philosophers of EXISTENTIALISM, whose ideas were to have conspicuous effects on his future works. He converted to Catholicism and for many years wrote articles on psychiatry, philosophy, and language theory, many of which are collected in *The Message in the Bottle* (1975). It was not until his mid-forties that he published his first novel, *The Moviegoer* (1961), which won the National Book Award. This novel and those that followed—*The Last Gentleman* (1966), *Love in the Ruins* (1971), *Lancelot* (1977), and *The Second Coming* (1980)—share a primary concern: the struggle of an alienated individual to find faith and human connection in a world without apparent meaning. Percy's vivid characterizations, written with a mixture of humor and compassion, serve as the vehicle for his serious philosophical preoccupations. With its thrillerlike plot, *The Thanatos Syndrome* (1987), which continues the adventures of the hero of *Love in the Ruins*, is considered more accessible than much of his earlier work.

Perdita   The virtuous and beautiful daughter of Hermione and Leontes, king of Sicilia, in Shakespeare's WINTER'S TALE. As an infant Perdita is abandoned by her father's orders and is raised by a shepherd as his daughter. Despite her supposedly humble birth, the nobility of her nature is apparent, and Polixenes says of her:

> This is the prettiest low-born lass that ever
> Ran on the green-sord: nothing she does or seems
> But smacks of something greater than herself,
> Too noble for this place.

Mary Robinson, who played the role of Perdita at Drury Lane in 1779 and became the mistress of the prince of Wales, later George IV, adopted the name as a pseudonym.

Pereda, José María de (1833–1906)   Spanish novelist. A conservative defender of tradition, Pereda wrote primarily of his native province, Santander, and is at his best as a landscapist. *Sotileza* (1885) has been called the finest Spanish novel of the sea; it contains vivid description, as does *Peñas arriba* (1895), dealing with paternalistic rural squires and peasants. Vignettes of local customs are found in *El sabor de la tierruca* (1882), *Escenas montañesas* (1864), and *Tipos y paisajes* (1871).

Père Goriot, Le (1834)   A novel, part of LA COMÉDIE HUMAINE, by Honoré de BALZAC. Père Goriot's consuming passion is his devotion to his two ungrateful daughters, Mme de Nucigen and Mme de Restaud. He deprives himself of everything for them, including his self-respect. Married to wealthy men, the two sisters are ashamed of their father's bourgeois manners, but they expect him to extricate them from financial difficulties. After sacrificing his last silver plate, Goriot dies of apoplexy. In a characteristic gesture, the daughters send empty carriages to the funeral. See RASTIGNAC, EUGÈNE DE.

Peregrine Pickle, The Adventures of (1751) A PICARESQUE novel by Tobias SMOLLETT. The hero, an imaginative young man with a flair for practical jokes whose rascality often shades into villainy, grows up under the tutelage of his aunt, Grizzle Pickle, and her madcap husband, a one-eyed veteran, Commodore Hawser Trunnion. After an ignoble attempt to seduce his friend's sister, Amanda, he dissipates the fortune inherited from Trunnion on false friends and extravagances and is reduced to poverty, jail, and misanthropy. Upon his father's death, however, he is left a second fortune, and he marries Amanda.

Père humilié, Le　See HOSTAGE, THE.

Perelman, S[idney] J[oseph] (1904–1979) American humorist. Perelman published his first and highly successful book, *Dawn Ginsbergh's Revenge*, in 1929, then moved to Hollywood to do gag writing and scriptwriting. There he wrote extensively for the Marx Brothers and eventually won an Oscar for the script of *Around the World in Eighty Days* (1956). Most of Perelman's work was published in magazines, most frequently THE NEW YORKER, before it appeared in book form. In it he satirized, by way of outrageous puns and uproarious *non sequiturs*, almost every aspect of contemporary society. Among his more than twenty books are *Strictly from Hunger* (1937), *Westward Ha! or, Around the World in 80 Clichés* (1947), *The Swiss Family Perelman* (1950), *The Road to Miltown; or, Under the Spreading Atrophy* (1957), *The Rising Gorge* (1961), and *Vinegar Puss* (1975). Beneath Perelman's high-spirited assaults on language and conventions was a sense of both anger and sadness. His ebullient humor was all the more affecting because of the underlying seriousness.

Perez de Ayala, Ramón (1881–1962)　Spanish novelist, critic, essayist, poet, and journalist. Perez de Ayala is known for his skillful use of language and his intellectual liberalism. His poetry includes *El sendero innumerable* (1916) and *El sendero andante* (1924); his best-known criticism is found in the two-volume work *Las máscaras* (1917–19), which includes portraits of many of those involved in the contemporary Spanish theatre. The real basis of Perez de Ayala's fame, however, is his novels, which developed from a form of autobiographical realism to a symbolic philosophical depiction of the human condition. Early works in the realistic vein include *A.M.D.G.* (1910), a satirical picture of a Jesuit boarding school. He then wrote a series of "poematic novels" which identified him most closely with the GENERACIÓN DEL 98: *Prometeo, Luz de domingo,* and *La caída de los Limones* (all 1916). His major work is *Belarmino y Apolonio* (1921), in which

he experiments with multiple perspectives, particularly the opposing philosophies of the two title characters, both cobblers.

Pérez Galdós, Benito (1843–1920)　Spanish novelist and dramatist. A native of the Canary Islands, Pérez Galdós devoted himself to writing after the publication of his first novel, *La fontana de oro*, in 1870. Often compared to BALZAC, he was an enlightened progressive who sought to reproduce in his work every facet of human existence.

In the forty-six novels of his *Episodios nacionales* (1873–1912), he traced Spanish history from the battle of Trafalgar to the restoration of the monarchy in 1875; thoroughly documented, they reveal the author's ability to evoke the spirit of a bygone age. Simultaneously, Pérez Galdós was writing several thesis novels which reflect his liberal, mildly anticlerical views. Among these are *Doña Perfecta* (1876), showing the tragic effects of religious bigotry; *Gloria* (1877), about a young Roman Catholic woman who is unable to marry the Jew she loves; and *La familia de Léon Roch* (1879), which describes a marriage ruined because of the religious differences between husband and wife. Some of Pérez Galdós's finest works are in the series called *Novelas españolas contemporáneas*, which includes *Fortunata y Jacinta* (4 vols, 1886–87), a masterly study of the bourgeoisie of Madrid; the trilogy *Nazarín, Holma,* and *Angel Guerra* (1891), an analysis of modern mysticism; and *Misericordia* (1897), about the "underworld" of Madrid's paupers and beggars.

With *Realidad* (1892), *El abuelo* (1897), and *Casandra* (1905), Pérez Galdós created a new genre, the dialogue novel, in which the author's intrusions are totally suppressed, and the characters portray themselves only by their words and deeds. Later he adapted these works for the stage. His approximately twenty dramas include *La loca de la casa* (1893) and *Electra* (1901).

Peribáñez y el comendador de Ocaña (c1614) A drama by Lope de VEGA. It takes place during the reign of Enrique III (1309–1406). The *comendador*, or governor, of Ocaña is attracted to Casilda, bride of the peasant Peribáñez, but she spurns his advances. After making Peribáñez captain of a peasant company and sending him away, the *comendador* tries to take Casilda by force but is surprised in the act by Peribáñez, who has returned unexpectedly. Peribáñez kills the *comendador*, then recounts the whole affair to the king, who pardons him.

Pericles (c500–429 BC)　An Athenian statesman. Pericles dominated Athens from about 460 BC to his death. Influenced by the philosopher Anaxagoras, he lost the superstitious beliefs held by many of his countrymen. His political ideal was a democratic Athens, leader of the Greek world. To this end he attempted to bring about a Greek union, but, when resisted by Sparta, he converted the Delian Confederacy into an Athenian empire. He pursued an imperialistic policy, while instituting democratic reform in Athens. A striking innovation was the payment of salaries to the *archons* and members of the Assembly. As a result of this reform, the qualification of wealth for the holding of public office could be dropped. Further, the *Areopagus*, or council of former *archons*, which had had the power of supervising the administration and judging crime, was relieved of these powers. Its censorial powers over the private lives of citizens were also abolished, and the wealthy and conservative institution was limited to duties without political significance.

In 430 BC Pericles was charged with misuse of public funds; it was thought that he used the treasury of the Delian League for the beautification of Athens. However, he was reelected general the following year and died in 429 BC, a victim of the plague.

Athens owes the Parthenon, Propylaea, the long wall of Piraeus, and many temples to Pericles' program of civic embellishment. He was also widely known for his eloquence, which is reported by Thucydides. The historian records Pericles' *Funeral Oration*, supposedly delivered by the general in honor of the Athenians who died in the Battle of Samos (440 BC). Pericles also led the Athenians in battle at the opening of the Peloponnesian War.

He took as mistress the *hetaera*, or courtesan, ASPASIA (fl 440 BC), who was famous for her beauty and intelligence. Her home became the center of the literary and philosophical life of Athens. It is said that she aided Pericles in matters of public policy, and helped to compose his speeches. She was condemned to death for impiety, but the eloquence of Pericles saved her life. Their son was later legitimatized and made a citizen by the Athenians.

The period 460–429 BC is often referred to as the Periclean Age or the Golden Age of Athens.

Pericles, Prince of Tyre (c1608)   A drama by SHAKESPEARE and another author, presumably George Wilkins. The plot is believed to be derived from Lawrence Twine's *Pattern of Painful Adventures* (1576) and John GOWER's *Confessio Amantis* (1390). Gower himself is a character in the play, appearing as the Chorus.

At Antioch, Pericles arouses the enmity of King Antiochus by guessing that the king has an incestuous love for his daughter. Pursued by the wrath of Antiochus, he is forced to leave his own kingdom of Tyre and go on a journey. At Pentapolis, where he has been shipwrecked, he wins a tournament for the hand of King Simonides' daughter Thaisa, whom he marries. Hearing of Antiochus' death, Pericles sets sail for Tyre with his wife, who gives birth to a daughter during a storm at sea but falls into such a deep state of unconsciousness that she is presumed dead. Her body is placed in a chest, which is thrown overboard and is later washed ashore at Ephesus. Thaisa is revived by Cerimon, an Ephesian lord, and, believing her husband to be dead, becomes a votaress in the temple of Diana. Meanwhile, Pericles leaves his infant daughter, Marina, in Tarsus to be reared by Cleon and his wife, Dionyza. Sixteen years later, the jealous Dionyza tries to kill Marina, but the

girl is saved by pirates, who place her in a brothel in Mytilene. Lysimachus, governor of the city, is so struck by her beauty and virtue that he purchases her freedom. Pericles, who has been told that Marina is dead, finds her in Mytilene and blesses her union with Lysimachus. Guided by the goddess Diana, who has appeared to him in a vision, Pericles then goes to Ephesus, where he is finally reunited with Thaisa.

Peripatetic School   The school of philosophy founded by ARISTOTLE. It was so named because Aristotle used to walk about as he taught his disciples. The covered walk of the LYCEUM was called the *Peripatos*. THEOPHRASTUS and Strato led the school after Aristotle's death, and gradually turned it wholly to scientific research. After 1 BC, the Peripatetics produced expositions of Aristotle's work. Finally the school turned to Neoplatonism.

periphrasis   Circumlocution, or an indirect and unnecessarily roundabout way of expressing a thought that could be more simply stated. "It would appear that there is an atmospheric perversion in the form of precipitation" is a periphrastic way of saying "It's raining."

periquillo sarniento, El (1816; tr The Itching Parrot, 1942)   A PICARESQUE novel by José Joaquín FERNÁNDEZ DE LIZARDI. Modeled on ALEMÁN's GUZMÁN DE ALFARACHE and Lesage's GIL BLAS, the book relates the adventures of Periquillo, an engaging rogue, in a pungent, colloquial style; the result is a realistic picture of Mexican society on the eve of independence. Interspersed throughout the narrative are didactic essays in which Fernández denounced the sloth of the middle class, the abuses of the clergy, the defects of the educational system, and other evils.

Perkins, [William] Maxwell [Evarts] (1884–1947)   Editor. The best known of 20th-century American editors, Perkins, in the course of a long career at Charles Scribner & Sons, was the discoverer and mentor of many of the finest writers of his day, including F. Scott FITZGERALD, Ernest HEMINGWAY, Marjorie Kinnan RAWLINGS, and James JONES. Especially notable was his association with Thomas WOLFE, whose enormous, sprawling manuscripts were shaped into books with considerable editorial help and advice from Perkins. A fine biography, *Max Perkins, Editor of Genius*, by A. Scott Berg was published in 1978.

Perrault, Charles (1628–1703)   French writer and critic. In his day Perrault took a leading role in the controversy between the ancients and the moderns. His *Parallèles des Anciens et des Modernes* (*Parallels between the Ancients and the Moderns*, 1688–97) is a series of dialogues pointing out the superiority of the writers of Perrault's own day over those of the past. He is now remembered chiefly as the collector and publisher of a book of fairy tales, LES CONTES DE MA MÈRE L'OYE.

Perry, Matthew Calbraith (1794–1858)   American naval officer. Chosen by President Fillmore to negotiate a treaty with Japan, which at that time refused to have contact with the West, Perry arrived in Yedo Bay with his naval squadron in 1853 and succeeded in delivering a letter from Fillmore to the emperor. The following year he returned and concluded a treaty of peace, amity, and commerce, bringing about the entrance of Japan into world affairs.

Perry, Oliver Hazard (1758–1819)   American naval officer. After serving in the Tripolitan War, Perry was given command of the U.S. naval forces on Lake Erie during the War of 1812. On September 10, 1813, he decisively defeated the British fleet on Lake Erie and announced the victory to Gen. W. H. Harrison in a famous message, "We have met the enemy and they are ours." Perry, who was the older brother of Matthew Calbraith Perry, died of yellow fever after concluding a diplomatic mission to Venezuela.

Perse, St.-John (pen name of [Marie-René] Alexis Saint-Léger Léger, 1887–1975)   French poet and diplomat. Perse's childhood on a family-owned island near Guadalupe is reflected by the recurrence of sea imagery in his poems. His travels as ambassador to the Far East (1916–21) and his studies of geology and early pagan mythology perhaps account somewhat for his work's exotic flavor and colorful settings, such as the Asiatic lands in *Anabase* (1924; tr 1930) and the imaginary Oriental kingdom by the sea in *Amers* (1957; tr *Seamarks*, 1958). The poems are written in lines of irregular length, ranging from a single word to a short paragraph, with a fluid, resonant rhythm like that of an incantation.

Indeed, Perse's work as a whole has a hymnlike tone of mystery and passion, devoted not to God, but to the vast scope of human experience and the triumphal joy of man's exploration and conquest of the universe and of himself. The poet as creator is a dominant theme, as in *Exil* (1942; tr *Exile*, 1949), in which he is prince of lands which are void until he gives them existence in a poem. Panoramas of mankind's history and natural landscapes blend through a rich vocabulary and occasionally unusual syntax in a symphonic progression of images. The thematic unity of each piece is symbolized by one dominant image, as in *Pluies* (1943; tr *Rains*, 1945), *Vents* (1946; tr *Winds*, 1953), *Chronique* (1960; tr 1961), and *Chant pour un equinoxe* (1971; tr *Song for an Equinox*, 1977). Early poems include *Éloges* (1911; rev 1925, 1948; tr 1944) and *Amitié du Prince* (1924). His *Collected Poems* appeared in English translation in 1971; his *Oeuvres complètes* in French in 1972. He was awarded the NOBEL PRIZE in Literature in 1960. Among others, T. S. ELIOT and Archibald MacLEISH translated his poems into English, Rainer Maria RILKE into German.

The other half of Perse's "double life" was as Alexis Léger, who entered the French foreign service in 1914, specialized in Far Eastern affairs, and became one of France's most widely known and respected diplomats. In 1940 when the Nazis occupied Paris, he fled to London, where he met and declined to join up with De Gaulle. Instead, he lived in exile in the U.S., stripped of his citizenship by the Vichy government, and did not return to France until 1959. Throughout his life he labored to keep his two identities—the poet and the diplomat—separate. He was circumspect about his work and remained steadfastly apart from literary associations, although his friendships included Paul CLAUDEL and Francis JAMMES. As revealed in the selected translations of his *Letters* (1979), while he allowed bilingual editions of his work to be published abroad, he curtailed such publication in France from 1925 to 1947. In spite of this, his reputation increased steadily with age until, at his death, he was among the most highly regarded poets of his era.

Persephone (also known as Kore)   In Greek mythology, both queen of the underworld and goddess of the reviving crops. In the latter capacity, Persephone is identified as the daughter of DEMETER, abducted by HADES. With her mother, she plays an important role in the ELEUSINIAN MYSTERIES. Her Roman counterpart was called Proserpina.

Perseus   A hero of ancient Greece. He was worshiped as divine at Athens. Epics relate that he was the son of ZEUS by DANAË, daughter of King ACRISIUS of Argos. The Delphic oracle had predicted that Danaë would bear a son who would kill his grandfather, so Acrisius cast Danaë and Perseus adrift in a chest. Zeus caused the waves to carry them to the isle of Seriphus, where Dictys, a fisherman and the brother of King Polydectes, rescued them. When Perseus was a young man, Polydectes desired Danaë and, wanting to get rid of her son, tricked him into promising the head of the Gorgon MEDUSA as a gift, a hopeless task. But Perseus, aided by the gods, killed Medusa and secured the head, which turned all who looked on it to stone. He rescued ANDROMEDA with its help and, returning with her to Seriphus, turned Polydectes and his friends to stone. Later, while taking part in the games at Larissa, he accidentally killed his grandfather Acrisius with a discus, thus bringing the early prophecy to pass. Perseus and Andromeda founded the family of the Perseids, from whom HERACLES descended.

Pershing, John J[oseph] (1860–1948)   American general. A graduate of West Point, Pershing served in Cuba during the Spanish-American War. In 1913 he suppressed an insurrection in the Philippines and in 1916 commanded the border campaign against the Mexican bandit and revolutionary Francisco Villa. That year he became a major general. In 1917 he was placed in command of the American Expeditionary Forces in France. When the great offensive of July 1918 began, the American army under Pershing opened the way for the collapse of the German forces. He served as army chief of staff from 1921 until his retirement in 1924. In 1931 he published *My Experiences in the World War* (2 vols), a work for which he received a PULITZER PRIZE in history.

Persians, The (Persai, 472 BC)   A tragedy by AES-
CHYLUS. In this play, Aeschylus relates the humiliating
return of XERXES to his capital, Susa, after his defeat in the
Persian wars. A principal figure in the play is Xerxes'
mother, Atossa. It is remarkable for the compassion that
Aeschylus, who himself had fought the Persians, shows for
his former enemies in their defeat, which he attributes to
the pride and arrogance of Xerxes. *The Persians* is the only
extant Greek tragedy that dealt with figures of recent history, instead of ancient myth.

Persian Wars   Wars between Persia and Greece
(500–c449 BC). The Persian king Darius, enraged at the
defiance of Athens and Eretria, which had delayed his conquest of the Ionian cities of Asia Minor, moved against the
two cities in revenge. Hippias, the exiled son of Pisistratus,
traitorously led thirty thousand Persians to the plain of
Marathon, terrain supposedly favorable to the Persian cavalry. There eleven thousand Greeks under Miltiades, fighting in close array, won a glorious victory (490 BC). This
battle ended the first Persian War, and Darius, busy putting down revolt in Egypt, did not live to return to Greece.
After his death in 485 BC, his successor, Xerxes, spent three
years preparing for the second Persian War. Athens was
then under the leadership of Themistocles, and the Greek
states had joined in a defensive confederation. At the invasion of Xerxes, the Spartan Leonidas and an army of six
thousand Greeks defended the narrow pass of Thermopylae
(480 BC). Betrayed by the traitor Ephialtes, Leonidas
detached most of his army and, with three hundred
Spartans and seven hundred Thespians, held back the Persians until all were slain. Simonides wrote a famous epitaph for the valorous Greeks. Upon hearing the news of the
defeat at Thermopylae, the Greek fleet retired to Salamis.
There they encountered the Persians and routed them. See
THEMISTOCLES. After the defeat at Salamis, Xerxes left his
army under the leadership of Mardonius. In 479 BC the
Greeks won a complete victory in the battle of Plataea.
Further battles were fought during the next thirty years, but
the Greeks had assumed the aggressive position. Some
mark the end of the Persian Wars at 479 BC; others consider
the final date to be 449 BC, when the Peace of Callias was
established. Our knowledge of the Persian Wars comes
from the history of HERODOTUS, which covers the course of
the wars to 479 BC.

Persius (full name Aulus Persius Flaccus, AD 34–62)
Roman satiric poet. Persius was a friend of Lucan and
greatly influenced by Horace. He is the author of six satires
which expound the tenets of Stoicism.

persona (Lat, "mask")   In ancient times, the *persona*
was a mask worn by actors. In literary usage, the *persona* is
the "I" created by an author and through whom the author
unravels his perceptions of characters and events. Thus,
the narrator, Marlowe, is Conrad's *persona* in HEART OF
DARKNESS, as is the "I" in Keats's ODE TO A NIGHTINGALE.

Personae (1909)   A volume of poems by Ezra
POUND. The title, literally translated from the Latin, means
"masks of the actor," recalling YEATS's demand that the
poet objectify his experience through an imagined personality, a mask. The second book of his poems published, it
also reveals Pound's indebtedness to the monologues of
BROWNING's *Men and Women*. Pound also used *Personae* as
the title for later collections of verse.

personification   A figure of speech attributing
human characteristics or feelings to nonhuman organisms,
inanimate objects, or abstract ideas. ALLEGORY frequently
employs personifications; the Giant Despair in John
Bunyan's PILGRIM's PROGRESS, for example, is a personification, in which the abstract concept of despair is represented as a person. But the use of personification is by no
means confined to allegory. Keats, for example, personifies
the Grecian urn in his ODE ON A GRECIAN URN as a "Syl-
van historian," an "unravished bride of quietness," and a
"foster-child of silence and slow time."

Persuasion (1818)   A novel by Jane AUSTEN. The
heroine, Anne Elliott, and her lover, Captain Wentworth,
were engaged for eight years before the story begins, but
Anne broke the engagement in deference to family and
friends. Upon being thrown into her company again,
Wentworth realizes that he is still drawn to Anne. When
he is certain that she, too, still loves him, he renews his
offer of marriage and the two lovers are united. Anne is
gentle, sensitive, and charming; the author wrote of her,
"She is almost too good for me."

Peshkov, Aleksey Maksimovich   See GORKY,
MAKSIM.

Peste, La   See PLAGUE, THE.

Peter, St.   One of the twelve disciples of JESUS,
noted for his impulsive nature. More incidents are related
to Peter in the Gospels than to any other disciple. He was
first called Simon but, when introduced to Jesus by his
brother ANDREW, Jesus called him Cephas (Aram, "stone"),
which was translated into the Greek Petros (Gr *petra*,
"rock"). His position as first bishop of Rome led to the
Roman Catholic belief that all popes are his successors.
Jesus addressed to him the words on which papal authority
is based: "Thou art Peter, and upon this rock I will build
my church; and the gates of Hades shall not prevail against
it; I will give unto thee the keys of the kingdom of heaven;
and whatsoever thou shalt bind on earth shall be bound in
heaven; and whatsoever thou shalt loose on earth shall be
loosed in heaven" (Matt. 16:18–19). From the passage also
derived the popular conception of St. Peter as keeper of the
gates of heaven, to whom saints and sinners present themselves for admittance.

Peter was one of the leading disciples and often served as
their spokesman. With James and John he witnessed the
Transfiguration (Matt. 17:1–13) and Jesus' despair in GETH-
SEMANE (Matt. 26:36–45). After the LAST SUPPER, Jesus predicted that Peter would deny him three times before the

cock crowed. When Jesus was arrested, Peter denied his association with him three times and "he went out and wept bitterly" (Matt. 26:69–75).

After the Crucifixion, Peter became widely known for his miracles and his missionary activities, in ACTS OF THE APOSTLES. He is the patron saint of fishermen, having been a fisherman himself, and is usually represented as a bald old man with a flowing beard, dressed in a white mantle and blue tunic and holding a book or scroll. His symbols are the keys and a sword. Tradition tells that he confuted Simon Magus, a magician at NERO's court, and that he was crucified (c AD 67) with his head downward at his own request, as he said he was not worthy to suffer the same death as Jesus.

Peter, The General Epistles of   Two books of the NEW TESTAMENT traditionally ascribed to St. PETER although most modern scholars dispute the ascription. The first epistle offers encouragement to Christians who suffered persecution. It outlines moral and ethical responsibilities as a means to holiness and teaches that suffering will be rewarded with salvation. The second epistle denounces moral laxity in the Church and warns of false teachers. It stresses that only through knowledge of Jesus can one grow in grace and hope for salvation.

Peter Pan, or The Boy Who Wouldn't Grow Up (1902)   A dramatic fantasy by J. M. BARRIE. The boy-hero, Peter Pan, has run away to Never-Never-Land to escape growing up; here he lives as the leader of a group of lost children. While in search of his lost shadow, he encounters the Darling children—Wendy, Michael, and John—whom he instantly befriends, teaches to fly, and takes back with him to Never-Never-Land. They have many adventures, particularly at the hands of Peter's enemy, Captain Hook, leader of a band of pirates. The Indian princess Tiger Lily and the invisible fairy Tinker Bell protect the children. After Peter rescues the Darlings from the clutches of Captain Hook, all the children realize that they must go home. Although Peter is very attached to the children, he decides he cannot accept their invitation to stay with them in the world where children grow up; Wendy, however, promises to return to Never-Never-Land each year to look in on the lost children and Peter.

Peter Quince at the Clavier (1923)   A poem by Wallace STEVENS. It is built on a musical analogy; the poet, seated at the clavier, retells part of the biblical story of Susanna and the Elders in the Apocrypha. He draws the conclusion that "beauty is momentary in the mind . . . / But in the flesh it is immortal."

Peter Schlemihl's wundersame Geschichte (Peter Schlemihl's Remarkable Story, 1814)   A story by Adalbert von CHAMISSO. It tells, with both sympathy and humor, the adventures of a young man who gives up his shadow to a gray stranger in return for Fortunatus's purse. The careful balance between the fantastic subject and the

matter-of-fact style in which it is treated is the story's chief merit.

Peter the Great (or Peter I; born Pyotr Alekseyevich; 1672–1725)   Tsar of Russia (1689–1725). More than any previous ruler, Peter Europeanized Russia, when necessary forcibly imposing Western ideas and customs on his subjects. He visited Western Europe in 1697–98, gathering information and hiring teachers and technicians to take back to Russia. Peter's energy was unlimited, and his interests covered a wide range. He founded the Russian navy, reorganized the army on Western lines, instituted obligatory service to the state by gentry class, bound administration of the church to that of the state, reformed the Russian alphabet, and gained Russian outlets on the Baltic Sea by driving out the Swedes. On the marshes at the mouth of the Neva River on the Baltic, he built Russia's "window on the West," St. Petersburg, making it the capital instead of Moscow. In 1721 the title of emperor was taken by Peter. The designation was also used by succeeding rulers.

Peter's reforms created Russian civilization and set its direction for the next two hundred years. His introduction of Western ways to the gentry classes laid the basis for the split between the upper classes and the peasantry that was to plague Russian society until the 1917 revolution. Besides the far-reaching effects of his action on Russian society, Peter's personality also had a strong impact. The chief response in literature to this impact is PUSHKIN's poem THE BRONZE HORSEMAN. Another of Pushkin's poems, *Poltava*, deals with Peter's victory in 1709 over Charles XII of Sweden. The Tsar is the subject of Aleksey TOLSTOY's historical novel *Pyotr Pervyi* (*Peter the First*, 1929–45).

Peter the Hermit (known as Peter of Amiens and Pietro l'Eremita, 1050?–1115)   French monk. Peter was one of the instigators of the First Crusade (1096–99), which he preached widely and enthusiastically. He actually led one segment of the crusade to Asia Minor in 1096. He is introduced by Tasso in the epic GERUSALEMME LIBERATA, where he advises and exhorts the Christian forces against the infidel armies.

Petrarch (Italian name Francesco Petrarca, 1304–1374)   Italian poet and scholar. A major force in the development of the Renaissance and European culture generally, Petrarch was born at Arezzo and spent much of his early life at Avignon and Carpentras, the former city being the seat of the papacy during the so-called Babylonian captivity. Although he studied law at Bologna, his primary interests were in Latin and Greek literature and in writing. As scholar and poet, he soon grew famous enough to be crowned at Rome on April 8, 1341, with the coveted laurel, in a ceremony that had not been seen since ancient times. The latter part of his life was spent in wandering restlessly from city to city in northern Italy, despite the welcome he received everywhere as an international celebrity. Like his friend Boccaccio, he was avidly interested in classical antiquity and fostered its revival. His learning, sound scholarship, and critical spirit made him a founder of Renaissance HUMANISM. Several factors set him apart from his medieval contemporaries and later earned him the designation of the first modern man: his love of nature, evidenced by the descriptions of Vaucluse in his writings and the then unusual feat of mountain climbing; his frank confession of and meditation on psychological conflicts; his preference for Plato over Aristotle; and most of all, his human treatment of his love for LAURA, which transcended the conventions of courtly love. A prolific correspondent, he wrote many important letters. Among his Latin works are *De viris illustribus* (*On Illustrious Men*); the epic poem *Africa*, which has Scipio Africanus as its hero and the love of Masinissa and Sophonisba as its key romantic episode; the dialogue *Secretum*, which reveals in a debate with St. Augustine Petrarch's "secret" conflict—his love of Laura and the laurel (fame) opposed to his spiritual yearnings; an incomplete treatise on the cardinal virtues, *Rerum memorandarum libri*; *De vita solitaria* (*On the Solitary Life*); *De otio religioso* (*On the Virtue of the Religious Life*); *Bucolicum carmen*, twelve eclogues; *Invecta contra medicum* (*Invective Against Doctors*); *De remediis utriusque fortunae* (*Remedies Against One and the Other Fortune*), his most popular Latin prose work, translated into English in 1579 by Thomas Twyne; an *Itinerarium*, or guide book, to the Holy Land; and *De sui ipsius et multorum ignorantia* (*On His Own Ignorance and That of Others*), against the Aristotelians.

Equally influential, especially during the Renaissance, were his Italian poems, collected in a *canzoniere*, or songbook. Usually called *Rime* or *Rime sparse* (*Scattered Lyrics*), they include sonnets, canzoni, sestine, ballate, and madrigals, divided by later editors into two parts: *In vita* and *In morte di Madonna Laura* (*During the Life* and *After the Death of My Lady Laura*). Modern scholars do not believe that Laura was a real woman, but it is admitted that she is more realistically presented than the conventional lady of the Provençal troubadours and the literature of courtly love, that she is less ethereal than the *donna angelicata* ("angelic lady") of his immediate Italian predecessors, the *stil-novisti* (followers of Dante's "sweet new style"), and especially Beatrice. Some of the poems are addressed to friends; others deal with contemporary personages and affairs; still others are religious; but the dominant theme is Laura, whose beauty and actions enamor the poet and cause him both joy and despair, for she is unattainable, and the poet would be a lesser man and a lesser poet were his desire to be fulfilled. This conflict is recorded in detailed psychological terms, albeit formalized by figurative language and the other devices of literary style. Upon her death, the poet finds that his grief is as difficult to live with as was his former despair, but the mood and the tone become more spiritual and a consolatory note appears. These poems were the source of European Petrarchism, which everywhere dominated lyric poetry for centuries

after. Petrarch's other vernacular work, the *Trionfi*, is in terza rima and partly inspired by Dante. It describes allegorical processions, or "triumphs," of Love, Chastity, Death, Fame, Time, and Eternity, including historical and literary persons, among whom Laura appears again. The poet was still revising the work when he died in 1374.

His immense influence in England began with Chaucer, who used for his *Clerk's Tale* Petrarch's translation into Latin of the *Griselda* story in the *Decameron*, as well as a poem from the *Rime* for the *cantus Troili* in *Troilus and Criseyde*. Later, English Petrarchism started its long journey in the poems of Wyatt and Surrey, and from there continued to exert its power through the 19th century. During the English Renaissance, when every lyricist was touched by the *Rime*, there was also great interest in the *Trionfi*, as the translation of Henry Parker, Lord Morley, in 1550 reveals. Shelley's poem *The Triumph of Life* indicates its later impact. Among the Latin works, the *De remediis* proved especially popular with English readers and authors.

Petrarchan sonnet   See SONNET.

Petrie, Sir [William Matthew] Flinders (1853–1942)   English archaeologist, and renowned Egyptologist. His excavations in Egypt and Palestine, the most important of which were at Memphis at the apex of the Nile, led to many discoveries in archaeology and anthropology. He was the author of numerous books on ancient civilizations and archaeology, among them *A History of Egypt* (6 vols, rev 1923–27) and *Methods and Aims in Archaeology* (1904).

Petrified Forest, The (1935)   A play by Robert E. SHERWOOD. Set in the Arizona desert, the drama deals with Alan Squier, an unsuccessful New England author who is hitchhiking to California. Arriving at a gasoline station and cheap lunchroom, he persuades a gangster to kill him, first revising his insurance policy. He makes the daughter of the lunchroom proprietor his beneficiary, so that she can escape from her sordid environment.

Petronius, Gaius (d AD 66)   *Arbiter Elegantiae* ("judge of elegance"), as Tacitus calls him, at the court of Nero. Petronius is probably the author of the *Satyricon*, a fragmentary manuscript in prose and verse which is considered one of the first examples of the novel form and gives a vivid, sardonic, and extremely realistic picture of the luxuries, vices, and social manners of the imperial age of ancient Rome. Almost the only historical evidence of Petronius's existence is to be found in the sixteenth book of the *Annals* of Tacitus, where it is reported that he committed suicide to escape being put to death by Nero. He figures importantly in *Quo Vadis?* (1896) by Sienkiewicz. See TRIMALCHIO.

Petruchio   In Shakespeare's TAMING OF THE SHREW, a highhanded gentleman of Verona who undertakes to tame the haughty Katharina, the title character. Petruchio marries her and reduces her to lamblike submission with his wit, spirit, and vigor.

Peveril of the Peak (1822)   The longest of Sir Walter SCOTT's novels. Julian Peveril, a Cavalier, is in love with Alice Bridgenorth, a Roundhead's daughter, and the action is interwoven with the "Popish Plot" of 1678. The 108 characters include a gallery of memorable historical figures.

Pevsner, Antoine   See CONSTRUCTIVISM.

Peyrefitte, Roger (1907–   )   French novelist. After almost fifteen years (1931–45) in the French diplomatic corps, Peyrefitte gained wide acclaim with his first novel, *Les Amitiés particulières* (1945; tr *Special Friendships*, 1950), which treated the secret and tragic friendship of two boys in a Jesuit boarding school. He went on to write many witty, satirical novels, often set in diplomatic or clerical milieux.

Phaedo   A dialogue by PLATO. In it, Phaedo, a disciple of SOCRATES, describes the last hour of his teacher's life. Socrates and his friends discuss the possibility of the immortality of the soul. The doctrine of ideas and the theory of reminiscence are the most important arguments.

Phaedra   In Greek mythology, a daughter of MINOS and PASIPHAË and wife of THESEUS. Theseus had previously abandoned her sister ARIADNE. She fell in love with her stepson Hippolytus. When he scorned her, she committed suicide but left a message for Theseus claiming that Hippolytus had tried to violate her. This story is the subject of Euripides' tragedy HIPPOLYTUS, Racine's masterpiece PHÈDRE, and many other works, including Mary RENAULT's historical novel *The Bull from the Sea* (1963).

Phaedrus   A dialogue by PLATO. In it Socrates and his friend Phaedrus discuss the difference between conventional rhetoric, which attempts to persuade regardless of truth, and true rhetoric, based on dialectic. As illustration, the subject of love is discussed in both styles. The dialogue includes the famous simile in which the soul is compared to a charioteer (the rational element) driving a black steed (the irrational appetites) and a white steed (the spiritual element).

Phaëthon (Gr, "the shining one")   In classical myth, the son of HELIOS or Phoebus, the Sun. He undertook to drive his father's chariot, but was upset and thereby caused Libya to be parched into barren sands, and all Africa to be injured, the inhabitants blackened, and vegetation nearly destroyed. He would have set the world on fire had not ZEUS transfixed him with a thunderbolt.

Pharisees (Heb, *perushim*, fr *perash*, "to separate")   An ascetic, separatist Jewish sect that arose after the revolt of the MACCABEES. The Pharisees attempted to regulate their lives according to the strict orthodoxy of the TORAH and the OLD TESTAMENT ideal of the oral law given by God to MOSES. Because the Pharisees were highly self-righteous and refused contact with all who were not their kind, the term "Pharisee" developed a negative connotation. They refused to accept JESUS as the Messiah and were cuttingly described by the NEW TESTAMENT writers. In The Gospel According to St. MATTHEW, Jesus condemns them as hypocrites who "bind heavy burdens and grievous to be borne, and lay them on men's shoulders; but they themselves will not move them with one of their fingers" (Matt. 23:4).

Phèdre (1677)   A tragedy by Jean RACINE. It is based upon Euripides' *Hippolytus*, but with the emphasis shifted from Hippolytus to PHAEDRA. During the absence of her husband, King THESEUS, Phèdre conceals her passion for her stepson HIPPOLYTE, but receiving false word of Theseus' death, she is urged by her nurse OENONE to declare her love. Horrified, Hippolyte repulses her and upon Theseus' return asks permission to leave the court. Oenone convinces the king that Hippolyte made advances to her mistress, and Theseus calls upon NEPTUNE, his protector, to destroy his son. Hippolyte refuses to accuse the queen directly, but inflames her jealousy by declaring his love for Aricie, a captive princess (the character is Racine's invention). In despair, Phèdre commits suicide, but the disclosure of her guilt comes too late, for Neptune has already destroyed Hippolyte.

Pheidippides   See MARATHON.

phenomenology   In philosophy and metaphysics, the description and classification of *phenomena*, or acts of perception, as the only objects of knowledge possessing ultimate reality. In the 20th century the phrase is particularly identified with the work of Edmund HUSSERL, who sought to establish a foundation for all the sciences by describing the formal structure of phenomena.

Phidias   Greek sculptor of the 5th century BC. Phidias is known for his colossal statues, notably the *Zeus of Olympia* and the gold and ivory *Athena Parthenos*. He was supervisor of PERICLES' program for rebuilding the ACROPOLIS. Although little of his work survives, contemporary descriptions indicate the magnitude of his accomplishment. Phidias died in prison under a charge of sacrilege, brought by the enemies of Pericles, for having represented Pericles and himself on the shield of Athena.

Philadelphia Story, The (1939)   A comedy by Philip BARRY. Tracy Lord, a young heiress, finds her old Philadelphia family traditions too restrictive, especially after an escapade with a reporter on the eve of her second marriage. When everything becomes mixed up on the morning of the wedding, C. K. Dexter Haven, Tracy's first husband, takes the place of the pompous bridegroom and remarries Tracy.

Philaster, or Love Lies A-Bleeding (1609)   A tragi-comedy by BEAUMONT AND FLETCHER. Philaster, heir to the throne of Sicily, is forced to live at the court of the usurping king of Calabria and Sicily. Arethusa, the king's daughter, who loves Philaster, is about to be married to the lecherous Pharamond, prince of Spain. However, Pharamond's lecheries become known, and the engagement is broken off. Pharamond avenges himself by accusing Arethusa of having an affair with Bellario, Philaster's page now in her service. The distracted Philaster first offers his life to Arethusa and Bellario and then tries to kill them. He is arrested and entrusted to the custody of Arethusa, who saves his life by marrying him. Arethusa's honor is finally cleared when it is revealed that Bellario is really a young girl who entered Philaster's service because of her infatuation for him. Meanwhile, an uprising forces the king to restore Philaster's titles and lands.

Philemon, The Epistle of Paul to   A NEW TESTAMENT book. A short personal letter from PAUL to the master of a runaway slave who carried the letter on his return trip. Paul asks Philemon to forgive Onesimus, the slave. It is the only personal letter to an individual in the New Testament; it shows the new Christian social order, which harmoniously included reformed slaves, rabbis, and pagans.

Philemon and Baucis   In Greek and Roman mythology, poor cottagers of Phrygia, husband and wife. In Ovid's account in METAMORPHOSES, they entertained JUPITER so hospitably that he promised to grant them whatever request they made. They asked that both might die together, and it was so. Philemon became an oak, Baucis a linden tree, and their branches intertwined at the top.

In the second part of Goethe's FAUST, Philemon and Baucis are an old couple who refuse to sell their home at any price. Because theirs is a part of the land that he is redeeming from the sea, Faust, with the aid of MEPHISTOPHELES, dispossesses them, and they die of the shock.

Philip II (382–336 BC)   King of Macedon (359–336 BC). Philip assumed charge of the Macedonian government as regent for his nephew Amyntas, whom he later set aside. The first few years of his reign were marked by his successful dispersal of rivals for the throne. Philip reorganized the Macedonian army on the basis of the phalanx. He extended Macedonian territory to include the gold mines of Mt. Pangaeus. Attempting to push into Greece, he eased Athens out of her possessions on the Thermaic Gulf. He married Olympias, who gave birth to Alexander in 356 BC.

On the capture of Olynthus, Athens sent envoys to Philip to negotiate the peace of Philocrates, which was disapproved by DEMOSTHENES. Philip soon broke the treaty and overran Thrace. The combined forces of Thebes and Athens were defeated, but Philip, who admired the Athenians, was lenient in his treatment of prisoners. About to move against Persia, he was assassinated by an agent of Olympias, who was jealous of his new consort. It is said that Alexander knew of the plot. Philip's reign marked the end of the city-state in Greece, paving the way for a Greek nation. Philip's aim, frustrated by his death, was to bring Greek culture to Macedon.

Philip II (1527–1598)   King of Spain. The son of Charles V and Isabella of Portugal, Philip succeeded to the throne in 1556 upon his father's abdication. His first wife was Mary of Portugal, who died giving birth to the ill-starred DON CARLOS; in 1554 he married MARY I of England and upon her death (1558) was an unsuccessful suitor for the hand of ELIZABETH I. He arrived in Spain in 1559, never again to leave the Iberian Peninsula.

The most powerful monarch in Christendom, Philip ruled not only Spain, but also the Netherlands, Franche Comté, Sicily, Sardinia, Naples, and Milan, as well as the Spanish possessions in America. In 1580, upon the extinction of the Aviz dynasty, he also acquired the crown of Portugal. This vast empire he ruled virtually alone, making all decisions, whether trivial or important, himself.

Often pictured, especially by northern European writers, as a tyrannical religious bigot, Philip was determined to strengthen royal power in Spain and to unify the peninsula, a policy which led him to suppress religious heterodoxy there and to curtail the traditional "liberties" of Aragon. The outbreak of a serious Protestant revolt in the Netherlands in the 1560s led him to aim at the subjugation of England, a design that was thwarted by the astute diplomacy of Elizabeth and the defeat of the Spanish ARMADA in 1588. He also intervened actively in the religious and dynastic struggles of France, but his efforts to control that country were checked by the accession of HENRY IV, though the latter's conversion to Catholicism represented a partial victory for Philip. He also warred with the powerful Ottoman Empire, winning a signal victory at LEPANTO in 1571. The burden of paying for this ambitious foreign policy rested almost entirely on Spain, especially Castile, which continually skirted financial disaster despite the influx of American treasure and suffered a serious economic decline.

A bibliophile and a patron of art, Philip amassed a fine collection of rare books and paintings at the ESCORIAL, where he died and lies buried.

Philippi   A town in Macedonia, the scene of the defeat of the forces of BRUTUS and CASSIUS by those of Octavius (later AUGUSTUS) and Mark ANTONY in 42 BC.

Philippians, The Epistle of Paul the Apostle to the   A NEW TESTAMENT book. It is a letter of thanks and encouragement written by PAUL to the church at Philippi. Paul was in prison and had received presents from the Philippians; he writes to thank them and to encourage them in the face of persecution. The letter is filled with joy and a sense of triumph, and it indicates the strength of Paul's faith.

Philip Sparrow (c1500)   A long, quick-running, rambling, tenderly humorous elegy for a pet bird by John Skelton, employing fragments from the office for the dead. The poem was probably suggested by Catullus's dirge for a dead sparrow. Philip is the traditional name for sparrows, derived from the sound of the bird's chirp.

Philip the Apostle   One of the original twelve disciples of JESUS. Although he was active during the ministry of Jesus, Philip is not mentioned after the Resurrection. He is traditionally supposed to have preached in Hierapolis. During the Middle Ages, Philip the Apostle was confused with Philip the Evangelist. The latter was one of the seven deacons ordained by the apostles as recorded in ACTS OF THE APOSTLES.

Philistines In the OLD TESTAMENT, the inveterate enemies of the Israelites, fought against by SAMSON, DAVID, and other Jewish heroes. In modern usage, the term refers to ignorant, ill-behaved persons lacking in culture or artistic appreciation and only concerned with materialistic values. Matthew ARNOLD first used the word in this sense by adapting it from the German *Philister*, the term applied by the university students to the townspeople, or "outsiders." This usage is said to have arisen at Jena, because after a "town and gown" row in 1689, which resulted in a number of deaths, the university preacher took for his text "The Philistines be upon thee" (Judg. 16).

Phillips, David Graham (pen name John Graham, 1867–1911) American journalist and novelist. Phillips is known for his muckraking articles, especially the series entitled *The Treason of the Senate*, which appeared in *Cosmopolitan* in 1906 (see MUCKRAKERS). Phillips wrote numerous novels exposing political corruption and social problems. Several of the novels, as well as his only play, *The Worth of a Woman* (1908), deal with his era's changing attitudes toward women. His most important novel was *Susan Lenox: Her Fall and Rise* (1917), a realistic, well-documented account of a country girl who becomes a prostitute and later a successful actress. Phillips was murdered by a madman who thought that he had been maligned and slandered by the author's *The Fashionable Adventures of Joshua Craig* (1909).

Phillips, Wendell (1811–1884) American abolitionist and reformer. Phillips dismayed the exalted Boston circles in which he moved by becoming an ardent antislavery agitator in the mid-1830s. A long-time ally of William Lloyd Garrison, Phillips was particularly noted as a superb speaker whose informal, direct delivery contrasted with the bombast then in vogue. After the Civil War, he devoted himself to economic reform, denouncing "the present system of finance which robs labor and gorges capital. . . ."

Philoctetes Greek hero in the TROJAN WAR. On the way to Troy Philoctetes was bitten by a serpent. The stench from the wound proved so noxious and his pain so great that his companions abandoned him on the island of Lemnos. He remained there for ten years, nursing his wound and his hatred of the Greeks. Ultimately, however, his former companions learned from the captured Trojan seer Helenus that Troy could fall only before the arrows of HERACLES. These had descended to Philoctetes from his father, Poeas, who had received them for the service of lighting Heracles' funeral pyre. ODYSSEUS and NEOPTOLEMUS (or Diomedes) sailed to Lemnos. According to SOPHOCLES' tragedy *Philoctetes*, they would have tricked him into going with them or taken him by force except for the compassion of Neoptolemus. In the end, Heracles appeared and commanded Philoctetes to go. He was cured by Machaon, the son of ASCLEPIUS. Philoctetes then killed PARIS with one of the arrows and Troy soon fell.

Philomela In Greek legend, daughter of Pandion, king of Attica. According to one version of the story, Tereus, king of Thrace, brought Philomela to visit his wife, Procne, who was her sister. He dishonored her, and cut out her tongue that she might not reveal his conduct. Tereus told his wife that Philomela was dead, but Philomela made her story known by weaving it into a peplus, which she sent to Procne. In another version Tereus married Philomela, telling her that Procne was dead, and it was Procne whose tongue was cut out and who wove the telltale story. In each case the end is the same. Procne, in revenge, cut up her own son Itys, or Itylus, and served the flesh to Tereus. The gods changed all three into birds. In the Greek legend Tereus became the hoopoe, Philomela the swallow, and Procne the nightingale. In the Latin versions, followed by most succeeding English poets, it is Philomela who becomes the nightingale, which is still called Philomel (lover of song) by the poets. Matthew ARNOLD's "Philomela," COLERIDGE's "Nightingale," and SWINBURNE's "Itylus" are among the best-known poems based on the tale, while Tereus appears in his form as a hoopoe in Aristophanes' THE BIRDS.

philosophers' stone The hypothetical substance which, according to the medieval alchemists, would convert all baser metals into gold. Its discovery was the prime object of all the alchemists, and to the wide and unremitting search that went on for it we are indebted for the birth of the science of chemistry, as well as for many inventions.

philosophes A group of 18th-century French thinkers, scientists, and men of letters. They held that human reason ought to be the supreme guide in human affairs and therefore opposed those institutions and creeds which they found irrational, constraining, or superstitious. Though the *philosophes* differed widely in their separate views, they were united in their skeptical attitude toward religious and political authority and helped induce a climate of popular disrespect for government and church which contributed directly to the FRENCH REVOLUTION. Despite censorship difficulties, the *philosophes* were able to publish their great work, the ENCYCLOPÉDIE, a systematic classification of all human knowledge marked by its rigorous rationality, its utter contempt for superstition, and its blunt skepticism toward religion. In addition to DIDEROT, who was chief director of the *Encyclopédie*, the most important *philosophes* were d'Alembert, BUFFON, Condillac, Condorcet, HELVÉTIUS, Marmontel, ROUSSEAU, Turgot, and VOLTAIRE, many of whom were at one time or another imprisoned or otherwise persecuted for expressing their views too freely.

Philostratus (fl c210) Greek author, also known as the Athenian. To Philostratus, the third of his family to bear the name, are attributed two important works: *Lives of the Sophists* and a fictional biography of a philosopher, *Apollonius of Tyana*. The latter work was the subject of religious controversy between Christians and pagans.

Phineus In classical mythology, a blind soothsayer. Phineus was tormented by the HARPIES. Whenever a meal was set before him, the harpies came and carried it off. The ARGONAUTS delivered him from these pests in return for his information respecting the route they were to take in order to obtain the GOLDEN FLEECE. He also appears in the *Argonautica* of Apollonius of Rhodes.

Phiz (pen name of Hablot Knight Browne, 1815–1882) English illustrator and caricaturist. Famous for his illustrations of the works of Charles DICKENS, Phiz first made his reputation when, in 1836, Robert Seymour died and he succeeded him as illustrator of *Pickwick Papers*. He was also noted for his contributions to *Punch*.

Phobos Literally, "panic fear." It is personified by the ancient Greeks as one of the sons of ARES, god of war, the other being Deimos (terror). The twin satellites of the planet Mars, Phobos and Deimos, were discovered in 1877.

Phoebus (fr Gr, *phoibos*, "bright") An epithet of APOLLO, particularly in his quality as the god of light. The name often stands for the sun personified.

Phoenician Women, The (Phoinissai, 410 BC) A drama by EURIPIDES. In this, the longest extant Greek play, Euripides treated the events of the war of THE SEVEN AGAINST THEBES, and more. Oedipus lives imprisoned in the palace; Creon's son Menoceus kills himself when Tiresias predicts that his death will save the city; Jocasta kills herself on failing to separate the brothers; Creon declares that Antigone shall marry his son Haemon, but she defies him and goes into exile with Oedipus. Parts of this story also were told in Aeschylus' SEVEN AGAINST THEBES, SENECA's *Phoenissae*, and STATIUS' epic *Thebais*. Parts of it are found in Sophocles' ANTIGONE and Euripides' THE SUPPLIANT WOMEN.

phoenix A mythical Arabian bird, the only one of its kind. At the end of a certain number of years, it was said to make a nest of spices, sing a melodious dirge, flap its wings to set fire to the pile, consume itself in the ashes, but come forth with new life to repeat the former one.

It is to this bird that Shakespeare refers in CYMBELINE and in his poem THE PHOENIX AND THE TURTLE.

The phoenix was adopted as a sign over chemists' shops because of its association with alchemists. It was also regarded as a symbol of immortality.

The *phoenix period*, or *cycle*, is the period between the transformations of the phoenix, generally supposed to be five hundred years but sometimes estimated as high as fifteen hundred years.

Phoenix and the Turtle, The (1601) A poem by SHAKESPEARE. It was published with a group of poems in a volume called *Loves Martyr: Or Rosalin's Complaint* by Robert Chester. An obscure, enigmatic, but strikingly effective work, it has provoked a great deal of critical speculation as to its merit and its meaning.

Phoenix Nest, The (1593) A poetic miscellany edited by "R. S. of the Inner Temple, gentleman." One of the finest of Elizabethan collections, it contains poems by LODGE, Breton, RALEIGH, and others.

Phoenix Park An amusement area in Dublin, where on May 6, 1882, the then newly appointed lord secretary of Ireland, Lord Frederick Cavendish, and his under-secretary, Thomas H. Burke, were murdered by members of the FENIAN movement. In retaliation the English government instituted severe repressions and attempted to implicate the Irish parliamentary leader Charles Stewart PARNELL. In James Joyce's ULYSSES, the Phoenix Park murders are discussed in the scene in the newspaper office. In FINNEGANS WAKE, Phoenix Park is the site of Earwicker's sexual transgression.

phooka (also pooka or púca) A many-shaped hobgoblin of Irish folklore, whom some see as akin to Shakespeare's Puck. Samain (the first of November) is of special importance to him, and it was said that he used to appear on this day out of a certain hill as a great and terrible horse, able to speak in a human voice and answer the questions of passersby. A pooka plays a prominent part in Flann O'BRIEN's comic masterpiece *At-Swim-Two-Birds*.

Phoreys See GORGONS.

Phrixus See GOLDEN FLEECE.

Phryne (4th century BC) A famous Athenian courtesan. Phryne acquired so much wealth by her beauty that she offered to rebuild the walls of Thebes if she might put on them this inscription: "Alexander destroyed them, but Phryne the hetaera rebuilt them." She is said to have been the model for PRAXITELES' Cnidian Venus, and also for Apelles' picture of Venus rising from the sea.

Phrynicus (6th century BC) An Athenian playwright. Only fragments of Phrynicus' many plays remain, but he was highly regarded by his contemporaries and for generations thereafter. It is said that one of his plays proved so distressingly moving to the Athenians that he was fined. According to tradition, he was the first playwright to introduce female characters in his plays, though the parts were played by men.

Physician's Tale, The One of THE CANTERBURY TALES of CHAUCER. After a digression on the raising of young girls, the Physician tells the story of the judge Apius and VIRGINIA, purportedly from Livy, but resembling more the version in the 13th-century *Romance of the Rose*. According to the Physician, Virginia's father tells her at home that she must die by his hand or else be shamed by the lecherous Apius. She weeps but voluntarily accepts her death. Apius condemns her father to be hanged, but the people revolt, and the judge commits suicide in prison.

physiocrats Name given to a French school of economic theorists of the latter part of the 18th century.

François Quesnay (1694–1774) is considered to be the founder and leader of physiocracy, though many of his ideas are to be found in the writings of earlier French economists, such as Jean Claude Vincent, sieur de Gournay; Sébastien Vauban; and Pierre de Boisguilbert. Among other economists who subsequently elaborated on Quesnay's thought are the marquis de Mirabeau, Mercier de la Rivière, Anne Turgot, and Pierre Samuel Du Pont de Nemours.

The term *physiocrat* combines two Greek words meaning "nature" and "rule," and implies the economic view that only natural resources constitute national wealth, that only agriculture and mining are really productive, and that industry and commerce, though not to be neglected, add nothing to national wealth. Agricultural methods, according to this doctrine, should be scientifically improved, since only abundant production coupled with fair prices can create prosperity. Absolute freedom of trade, and an economic policy of *laissez faire* (free competition) will establish a natural economy, from which all other benefits will flow. A single tax is to be levied at the very source of wealth, i.e., on the land, and any tax on manufacturers and traders would be futile, since they would pass their tax burden on to the farmer. Though physiocracy died partly because of its failures, and possibly because of ridicule on the part of contemporaries, it did influence the classical school of economists, notably Adam Smith. The founder of the single-tax movement in America, Henry George, was directly influenced by the physiocrats.

Piaget, Jean (1896–1980)   Swiss psychologist and educator. Piaget's study of the psychology of learning has been compared in scope and impact with FREUD's development of psychoanalysis. He was the author of over a hundred books, most of them based on his analyses of children and their emergent reasoning processes. The most significant and widely read of these are *Le Langage et la pensée chez l'enfant* (1923; tr *The Language and Thought of the Child*, 1926), *La Psychologie de l'intelligence* (1947; tr *The Psychology of Intelligence*, 1950), and *De la logique de l'enfant à la logique de l'adolescent* (1955; tr *The Growth of Logical Thinking from Childhood to Adolescence*, 1958). His theories have been summarized for the lay reader in many books, the best known being *The Essential Piaget* (1977), a collection of excerpts and essays by Piaget himself.

Piaget's theories center on his discovery that children perceive the world differently from adults and that their development proceeds in genetically determined stages which always follow the same sequence.

Piazza Tales, The (1856)   A collection of six long stories by Herman MELVILLE. All of the tales, with the exception of the introductory piece, "The Piazza," were published individually in magazines and are among his finest stories. In "The Bell Tower," the artist Bannadonna attempts to rival the power of God, but is destroyed by his own creation. In "The Lightning-Rod Man," a lightning-rod salesman is refused a sale by an unwilling customer who believes that man, who cannot control God, should not fear Him. "The Encantadas, or The Enchanted Isles" is a collection of ten descriptive sketches based on Melville's 1841 voyage to the Galápagos Islands. *The Piazza Tales* concludes with the two excellent stories "Benito Cereno" and BARTLEBY THE SCRIVENER.

picaresque   An adjective from the Spanish *pícaro* ("rogue") used to describe a genre of literature in which the life and adventures of a rogue are chronicled. Although the picaresque takes many forms—for example, memoirs, plays, ballads—its best expression is found in the novel.

The picaresque novel is typically a realistic depiction of the criminal element in society; it is usually an autobiographical account of a peripatetic rogue of "loose" morals. The retelling of his adventures in the service of a series of masters, and of his various ways of outwitting them, affords the author an opportunity to make humorous, satiric sketches of types in various levels of society. Moralizing, in greater and lesser degrees of serious intent, is also characteristic. Stylistically, the picaresque novel usually displays plainness of language and faithfulness to petty detail; the tone is often cynical. The structure is that of a series of loosely connected episodes; there being no plot, these could end at any time or go on endlessly, since neither character nor incident is treated developmentally. The hero, or picaroon, who may be thought of as an ANTI-HERO, need not be a man; it may be a woman or an animal.

Picaresque elements are found in the *Satyricon* of PETRONIUS, in THE GOLDEN ASS of Apuleius, in the medieval FABLIAUX and animal epics, and in the work of François VILLON. It was not established as a genre, however, until the publication of the anonymous *La vida de* LAZARILLO DE TORMES, which was one of the most widely read books of the 16th century. The next picaresque novel was GUZMÁN DE ALFARACHE by Mateo ALEMÁN. CERVANTES took up the manner with the stories "El coloquio de los perros" and "Rinconete y Cortadillo" in his NOVELAS EJEMPLARES, and elements of the picaresque are to be found in DON QUIXOTE. *Historia de la vida del Buscón* (1626) by Francisco de QUEVEDO is a further example of the genre.

The picaresque novel in Spain declined after the mid-17th century; the last of the Spanish series is usually given as *Periquillo el de las gallineras* (1668). Early in the 18th century the picaroon appeared in France, notably in Lesage's GIL BLAS, which was highly popular. Initially the genre was so firmly established as Spanish that the French writers gave their novels Spanish settings and their characters Spanish names, but inevitably the form underwent many modifications. By the time the English picked it up, in the 18th century, the picaroon's criminality was often mere prankishness; he was crafty and lived by his wits; and although hard-hearted, he was often lovable and essentially good. Outstanding examples are Defoe's MOLL FLANDERS and the novels of Smollett, notably *The Adventures of* RODERICK RANDOM and *The Adventures of* PEREGRINE PICKLE; the middle section of Fielding's TOM JONES may also be considered picaresque. Some latter-day novels—for example, Mark Twain's HUCKLEBERRY FINN and Saul Bellow's THE ADVENTURES OF AUGIE MARCH—are sometimes loosely described as picaresque.

Picasso, Pablo [Ruiz y] (1881–1973)   Spanish artist. Picasso was the most influential painter of the 20th century, hailed as having instigated the greatest revolution in aesthetics since the Renaissance. A figure of protean diversity, he contributed to virtually every mode of visual expression—painting, drawing, graphics, sculpture, ceramics, and theatrical design.

Born in Málaga, the son of a Basque art teacher, he studied in Barcelona and Madrid, and traveled in 1900 to Paris, where he was influenced by TOULOUSE-LAUTREC. Shortly thereafter, he began his famous "blue period" (1901–4), painting the indigent and sick in cool, sorrowful blue tones. *The Old Guitarist* (1903), with its gaunt subject bent in fatigue and despair, epitomizes this period. This was followed by the "rose period" (1904–6), when he favored acrobats, harlequins, and children as subjects, painting them in pinks and grays.

In 1907, influenced by his study of CÉZANNE and of African sculpture, he painted the pivotal *Demoiselles d'Avignon*, which anticipated the advent of CUBISM in 1908. Picasso and his cubist colleagues advanced the notion that the artist's conception of a subject, not its external appearance, is its reality. His *Seated Nude* (1909) is a classic cubist interpretation.

In the period following the cubist revolution, from 1914 to the early 1920s, he developed paper cutouts, called *papiers collés*, collages, and various techniques of applying bits of reality to his otherwise highly abstract canvases. He was expanding and departing from cubist thought in such works as *Three Musicians* (1921), various paintings of massively modeled men and women in classical dress, and a series of eminent still-lifes, including *Mandolin and Guitar* (1924).

The bombing of the Basque capital in the Spanish Civil War inspired the monumental painting *Guernica* (1937), which depicted not the actual bombing but rather the agony of war and the imminence of doom. It also marked the beginning of a series of expressionist paintings he executed in the 1940s.

He subsequently became less influential but continued to work prodigiously. Inspired by the birth of a son, Claude, and a daughter, Paloma, he produced his series of sentimental *maternités*. He also worked extensively in ceramics at this time and, in the 1950s, painted a series of variations on famous works by DELACROIX, VELÁZQUEZ, and MANET. In the last twenty years of his life, he continued to produce an extraordinary variety of works, including innumerable sketches, linocuts, painted landscapes and still-lifes, and whimsical sculptures. No artist in the 20th century rivaled his creative versatility and influence.

Pickwick, Samuel   In Charles Dickens's PICKWICK PAPERS, the founder of the Pickwick Club. An unsophisticated, innocent man, he is caught up in a breach of promise suit against him by Mrs. BARDELL. When he refuses to pay damages, he is put into Fleet Prison, accompanied by Samuel WELLER. When released, he dissolves the club and retires to a house outside London with Sam Weller and Weller's bride, who acts as housekeeper.

Pickwick Papers (1836–1837)   A humorous novel by Charles DICKENS, first published serially under the pseudonym BOZ. Originally intended as mere prose sketches to accompany the illustrations of the popular caricaturist Seymour, *The Posthumous Papers of the Pickwick Club* (the series's formal title) was an almost immediate success, and made Dickens famous. The book is made up of letters and manuscripts about the club's activities. The chief character is Samuel PICKWICK, founder of the club, a most naïve and benevolent elderly gentleman. As chairman of the Pickwick Club, he travels about with his fellow club members and acts as their guardian and advisor. The book is one of Dickens's most quoted and it contains many of his well-known characters, or caricatures, including Mrs. BARDELL, Serjeant BUZFUZ, Alfred JINGLE, and Samuel WELLER.

The expression *in a Pickwickian sense* refers to words or epithets usually of a derogatory or insulting kind, which, in the circumstances in which they are employed, are not to be taken as having quite the same force or implication as they normally would have. The allusion is to the scene in chapter I where Mr. Pickwick accuses Mr. Blotton of acting in a "vile and calumnious manner," whereupon Mr. Blotton retorts by calling Mr. Pickwick a humbug. It finally is made to appear that both use the offensive words only in a Pickwickian sense and that each has, in fact, the highest regard and esteem for the other.

Pico della Mirandola, Count Giovanni (1463–1494)   Italian humanist, philosopher, and author. In 1484 Pico came to Florence and joined the so-called Florentine Academy, actually a literary gathering sponsored by the MEDICI family. Pico knew Latin, Greek, Hebrew, and Arabic, and was one of the first Christian scholars of the CABALA. Unlike his friend FICINO, he was interested in the more esoteric writing of the philosophical tradition. It was his idea that all knowledge could be reconciled and systematized. In 1486, at the age of twenty-three, he published a series of nine hundred conclusions, or theses, ranging from logic to the Cabala, and offered to take on all challengers of his ideas. After the church found thirteen of them heretical, he fled to France for a time but returned to continue his studies. His best-known work in modern times is the Latin oration *De dignitate hominis* (*On the Dignity of Man*), which was prefaced to his nine hundred theses as the opening salvo in the expected debate. It has been regarded as a typical RENAISSANCE expression of the renewed faith in the power and stature of the human creature. In England, he was especially influential on John Colet (1466–1519) and Sir Thomas MORE, the latter having translated some of his work and written his biography.

Picrochole (Gr, "who has a bitter bile")   In Rabelais's GARGANTUA AND PANTAGRUEL, the despot of Lerne, who declares war on the kingdom of Grandgousier, Gargantua's father. When the power-mad tyrant, using a quarrel between his bakers and Grandgousier's shepherds as a pretext for attack, begins ravaging the countryside, Grandgousier is obliged to send for Gargantua, who leaves his studies in Paris to defend his homeland. Gargantua and Friar John win the war, Picrochole and his counselors flee, and peace is restored. The war is waged in the vicinity of Chinon, where Rabelais was born, and the narrative faithfully portrays its people and their customs. In describing the war, Rabelais expressed his own humanist ideal of reasoned and benevolent government as opposed to unbridled tyranny.

Picture of Dorian Gray, The (1891)   A fantastic, moral novel by Oscar WILDE. The plot concerns a beautiful youth, Dorian Gray, who has his portrait painted by Basil Hallward. Hallward introduces Dorian to Lord Henry Wotton, who initiates the youth in a life of vice. The painting, it turns out, has supernatural powers, and while Dorian remains young and beautiful throughout his deterioration, the portrait changes, reflecting his real state of degeneracy. Finally Dorian kills Hallward and then stabs the painting; he is then found dead with a knife through his heart, his face the very picture of corruption while the portrait, restored to what it was, hangs over him portraying a young, innocent, handsome man.

Pied Piper of Hamelin   A magician in German folklore. According to legend, the town of Hamelin was plagued with rats in 1284. A mysterious stranger in particolored clothes appeared and offered to rid the town of the destructive vermin for a specified sum of money. The leaders of the town agreed to the contract, and the stranger began to play his pipe. The rats came swarming from the buildings and followed him to the river Weser, where they drowned. But then the town leaders refused to make the agreed payment, so the Pied Piper returned, once more playing his pipe. Only this time it was all the children of the town whom he enchanted and lured away, to vanish behind a door in the Koppenberg hill.

Robert Browning told the story in his poem "The Pied Piper of Hamelin" (1842).

Piercy, Marge (1936–   )   American poet and novelist. Piercy's poetry and fiction treat political and personal themes with equal intensity. The poems in *Breaking Camp* (1968) combine to form an angry indictment of American poverty; *To Be of Use* (1973) addresses issues of feminism; *The Twelve-Spoked Wheel Flashing* (1978), less polemical, includes poems on nature and domesticity. Among her other verse collections are *Circles on the Water*

(1982), *Stone, Paper, Knife* (1983), and *My Mother's Body* (1985). Piercy's novels tend to be realistic narratives about people who are either on the fringes of American society or active in the movement for social change. Among them are *Going Down Fast* (1969), *Dance the Eagle to Sleep* (1971), *Small Changes* (1973), *Woman on the Edge of Time* (1976), *The High Cost of Living* (1978), *Vida* (1980), *Braided Lives* (1982), and *Fly Away Home* (1984).

Pierian spring   Inspiration, from Pieria, where the MUSES were born.

Piero della Francesca   See FRANCESCA, PIERO DELLA.

Pierre, or The Ambiguities (1852)   A novel by Herman MELVILLE. *Pierre* is a deeply personal and pessimistic book in which Melville projects his own psychological conflicts. Pierre Glendinning, a young writer, leaves his ancestral home and rejects his mother and his fiancée, Lucy Tartan, in an effort to protect the interests of Isabel, a beautiful woman who has convinced him that she is his illegitimate sister. They move to New York, where Pierre's recognition of incestuous desires transforms him from an innocent to a stormy cynic. Disowned, forced to live in poverty, and struggling to write, he eventually commits suicide in prison. In pursuit of truth, he has caused the deaths of his mother, Isabel, and Lucy.

Pierrot (Fr, "Little Peter")   A favorite character of the old Italian drama and of PANTOMIME, a sort of clown lover. Pierrot is traditionally played by a tall, thin young man with his face and hair covered with white powder or flour. He wears a white gown with very long sleeves and a row of big buttons down the front. Pierrot is the lover of Pierrette, or sometimes of COLUMBINE. From the simple figure of the early pantomime, poets and artists have gradually evolved another, more romantic Pierrot, an artist-lover of soaring imagination, who grimly hides his real passions behind a comic mask.

Piers Plowman (c1362–c1387)   Middle English poem, the full title of which is *The Vision of William Concerning Piers Plowman*, usually attributed in whole or in part to a hypothetical William Langland or Langley (c1332–c1400). Actually, there are three different versions of the poem (c1362, 2,579 lines; c1377, 7,241 lines; c1387 or 1393?, 7,353 lines), by at least two and perhaps even five different writers. Although contemporary with Chaucer's work, it is written in ALLITERATIVE VERSE like Old English poetry and uses a deliberately rustic and archaic dialect.

It is an allegorical moral and social satire, written as a "vision" of the common medieval type. The poet falls asleep in the Malvern Hills and dreams that in a wilderness he comes upon the tower of Truth (God) set on a hill, with the dungeon of Wrong (the Devil) in the deep valley below, and a "fair field full of folk" (the world of living men) between them. He describes satirically all the different classes of people he sees there; then a lady named Holy Church rebukes him for sleeping and explains the meaning of all he sees. Further characters representing abstract personification (Conscience, Liar, Reason, etc.) enter the action; Conscience finally persuades many of the people to turn away from the Seven Deadly Sins and go in search of St. Truth, but they need a guide. Piers (Peter), a simple Plowman, appears and says that because of his common sense and clean conscience he knows the way and will show them if they help him plow his half acre. Some of the company help, but some shirk; and Piers becomes identified with Jesus, trying to get men to work toward their own spiritual salvation, as well as toward their own material relief from the current abuses of worldly power. In the last section of the poem, much less coherent, the dreamer goes on a rambling but unsuccessful summer-long quest, aided by Thought, Wit, and Study, in search of men who are Do-Well, Do-Bet, and Do-Best.

pietism   The name given to a vague and widespread Protestant movement in 18th-century Germany, which stressed emotional piety and the pure Christian life, as opposed to rationalism and outward formalization in religion. The principal pietistic sect was the Moravian Brethren.

pig in a poke   A blind bargain. The French phrase is *acheter chat en poche* ("to buy a cat in a pocket"). The reference is to a common trick in days gone by of trying to palm off on a greenhorn a cat for a suckling pig. If he opened the sack he "let the cat out of the bag," and the trick was disclosed.

Pilate, Pontius   A roman procurator (governor) of Judaea in the first half of the 1st century, before whom JESUS was tried. Failing to persuade the mob of Jesus' innocence, he yielded, washing his hands before them and condemning Jesus with the words, "Take ye him, and crucify him: for I find no fault in him" (John 19:6). Tradition has it that Pontius Pilate's later life was so full of misfortune that, during CALIGULA's time, he committed suicide in Rome. Another legend has it that both he and his wife became penitent, embraced Christianity, and died peaceably in the faith.

Pontius Pilate is a term used for one who disavows his personal moral convictions and submits to the pressure of the mob or to his superiors: one who "washes his hands of the matter."

Pilgrims   The name given to the English Puritans who sailed to America on the MAYFLOWER and, by extension, to any early Puritan settlers of New England. The *Mayflower* Pilgrims, unlike the other Puritans of Massachusetts, were Separatists, in that they sought complete independence from the Established Church of England. Originally from Scrooby, England, they first immigrated to the Netherlands (c1606), where they could worship freely. More than half of this group sailed to America on the *Mayflower*.

Pilgrim's Progress from This World to That Which Is to Come, The (Part I, 1678; Part II, 1684)

A prose ALLEGORY by John BUNYAN. The author purports to have a dream in which he sees Christian, who is weeping and wondering what to do to avoid the destruction of himself, his family, and his town that is prophesied in the Bible. Evangelist comes, warns Christian to flee, and tells him to journey to the Wicket-gate beneath the shining light in the distance. Closing his ears to the entreaties of his family and neighbors to remain, Christian flees the City of Destruction and sets out for the Celestial City beyond the Wicket-gate. He wanders into the Slough of Despond, from which he cannot get out because of the weight of the burden of sin on his back, until at last he is rescued by Help. He meets Mr. Worldly-Wiseman, who urges him to give up his dangerous journey, have his weighty burden removed by Mr. Legality, and settle down in the comfortable village of Morality nearby; Christian is ready to follow Mr. Worldly-Wiseman's counsel, but is rescued by Evangelist, who warns him against being led astray again. At the Wicket-gate, Christian is let in by Mr. Good-will and shown the straight and narrow way that leads to the Celestial City. He comes to the Cross, and his burden of sin falls from his back and rolls into the Holy Sepulchre nearby. Soon he comes upon three men, fettered and asleep, called Simple, Sloth, and Presumption; they give no heed to his warnings to wake and seek the Celestial City. Then he comes upon Hypocrisy and Formalist, climbing over the Wall to get on the narrow way; Christian warns them that they may be counted as thieves and trespassers because they have not come through the Wicket-gate. They go on together until they come to the Hill Difficulty; Christian takes the narrow road over the steep hill, while his two companions take the easier paths, called Danger and Destruction, around it. At the top of the Hill he meets Timorous and Mistrust, who turn back because they fear greater difficulties ahead. He rests at the House Beautiful, where he talks with the damsels Discretion, Prudence, Piety, and Charity. They show him the Delectable Mountains ahead, and send him on his way armed against attackers. He goes down into the Valley of Humiliation, where he meets the fiend Apollyon; they fight for more than half a day before Christian, himself wounded, vanquishes the enemy. He then must pass through the Valley of the Shadow of Death, which is full of Hobgoblins, Satyrs, and Dragons of the Pit. He meets a pilgrim named Faithful, and they describe their journeys to one another. Evangelist appears and predicts the troubles they will encounter in the town of Vanity, where a year-round fair sells all the empty things of the world. At Vanity Fair the two pilgrims cause a great hubbub by their refusal to buy anything and are arrested. Faithful is tried and sentenced to be burned at the stake, after which a heavenly Chariot carries him off into the clouds. Christian escapes and is joined by Hopeful, who had been converted by the example of Faithful. They come to the plain of Ease and beyond it the Hill of Lucre, where they are tempted to dally with a free silver mine.

Soon they come to a pleasant river, which runs alongside the narrow way for a while, but before long the path goes away from the River and becomes rough, and Christian leads Hopeful into a more pleasant path nearby. Night falls and they become lost, and in the morning they are near the Doubting Castle, where they are caught by the Giant Despair. He locks them in a dungeon and beats them, until finally Christian remembers that he has a key called Promise, which will unlock the door. They go back to the narrow way, which soon leads them to the Delectable Mountains, where they talk with the shepherds called Knowledge, Experience, Watchful, and Sincere. Going on, they enter the Enchanted Ground, on which they have been warned not to sleep, and they converse to stay off drowsiness. At length, they come to the country of Beulah, which is within sight of the Celestial City. Two angels tell them that to get to the City they must cross the River of Death; in the water Christian is afraid, but he is encouraged by Hopeful. On the other side they are met by angels who lead them to the gate of heaven.

Pilgrim's Progress, with its vivid characterization, direct and colorful style, and beauty of language, has been one of the most widely read books in the English language. Because of its immense popularity, Bunyan was encouraged to write a second part, which, unfortunately, has not the power of the original book. Part II deals with the pilgrimage to the Celestial City of Christian's wife, Christiana; accompanying her are their children; Mercy, a neighbor; and Mr. Great-heart, who is given them for a guide.

pillars of Hercules   The opposite promontories at the entrance of the Mediterranean, one in Spain and the other in Africa. The tale is that they were bound together till Hercules (see HERACLES) tore them asunder in order to get to Gades (Cadiz). The ancients called them Calpe and Abyla; we call them Gibraltar and Mount Hacho.

The ancients supposed that these rocks marked the utmost limits of the habitable globe, hence the expression *I will follow you even to the pillars of Hercules*.

Pillow-Book of Sei Shōnagon, The (Makura no Sōshi)   A Japanese miscellany of the HEIAN period. Its author, known as Sei Shōnagon, was a lady-in-waiting at the empress's court during the last decade of the 10th century. Witty and brilliantly written, the work occupies a unique position in Japanese literature. An abridged translation by Arthur Waley (1928) and a complete one by Ivan Morris (1967) have been published. See JAPANESE LITERATURE.

Pilnyak, Boris (pen name of Boris Andreyevich Vogau, 1894–1941)   Russian novelist. One of the outstanding practitioners of the rich, ornamental prose style popular with Soviet writers in the 1920s, Pilnyak was a victim of the purges in the 1930s. His first novel, *Goly god* (1921; tr *The Naked Year*, 1928), is an account of the revolution. *Krasnoye derevo* (1929; tr *Mahogany*, 1965) depicts

the period of the New Economic Policy (NEP) in 1921–28, when a return to a limited form of capitalism was allowed in the Soviet Union. Pilnyak was reprimanded when *Mahogany* was published abroad before being approved by the Soviet authorities. He revised the work and included part of it in a longer novel, *Volga vpadaet v Kaspiyskoye more* (1930; tr *The Volga Falls to the Caspian Sea*, 1931), which deals with the first Five-Year Plan. Pilnyak was arrested in 1937 and sent to a labor camp. He died four years later.

Pincher Martin (1956)   A novel by William GOLDING, published in the U.S. as *The Two Deaths of Christopher Martin*, about a shipwrecked man and his struggle to keep alive on a bare rock. He remembers his selfish past life with the "eat or be eaten" principles, and in his dying delirium imagines he is eaten himself (perhaps, ironically, by God). In a surprise ending Golding shows that his hero actually died in the wreck, so that the rock has been either a dream or a kind of purgatory. The name Pincher is from the slang "pinch," to steal.

Pindar (522 or 518–432 or 438 BC)   Greek poet also known as the Dircaean Swan. Pindar was born near Thebes, and his works, about one fourth of which survive, are mainly EPINICIA composed on commission to celebrate famous victors at the Olympian, Pythian, Nemean, or Isthmian games. They were mainly intended to be sung by a chorus at some later celebration in honor of the victor, rather than immediately. Pindar was immensely admired both in his own day and in centuries to come.

His works combine gravity of manner with strikingly bold images. The onrushing beat of his verse has been compared to that of Kipling. Pindar was aristocratic in his sympathies and conservative in both politics and religion. He refused, for example, to credit the famous story of TANTALUS feeding his son PELOPS to the gods, for he could not believe that the gods would be cannibals. Since Pindar's Epinicia are generally concerned with mythical subjects, reserving praise of the mortal victor for the end of the ode, his works are a fine source of legend. According to tradition, he was criticized by Corinna, a popular poet, for having failed to use myth in his first poem. In his next he used it so extravagantly that she warned him to "sow with the hand, not with the sack."

Pinero, Sir Arthur Wing (1855–1934)   English dramatist, actor, and essayist. Pinero worked as an actor (1874–81, 1885) in both modern and Shakespearean roles, but then began writing wildly successful farces. With THE SECOND MRS. TANQUERAY his plays became more seriously concerned with social issues in a modest but, at the time, daring way. Among his other plays *The Notorious Mrs. Ebbsmith* (1896), *Trelawney of the Wells* (1898), *The Gay Lord Quex* (1899), *Iris* (1901), and *Mid-Channel* (1909) are the best known.

pin money   A lady's allowance of money for her own personal expenditure. At one time pins were a great expense to a woman, and in 14th- and 15th-century wills there are often special bequests for the express purpose of buying pins.

Pinocchio, The Adventures of (Le avventure di Pinocchio, 1883)   A children's story by Collodi, the pen name of Carlo Lorenzini (1826–90), a native of Florence, Italy. The hero of the tale is Pinocchio, a puppet come-to-life, whose many escapades serve to teach him (and his young readers) to distinguish right from wrong. The puppet's nose grows larger when he tells a lie and returns to normal size when he tells the truth. Walt DISNEY produced a full-length animated cartoon of the story (1943).

Pinter, Harold (1930–   )   English dramatist. Beginning his career as an actor and later as a writer for television, Pinter went on to establish himself as one of the most original voices in the English-speaking theatre, though his debt to Kafka and, above all, Beckett is clear. His plays are characterized by unexplained circumstances and an ever-present aura of menace; he steadfastly refuses to provide rational justifications for action or clear-cut conclusions. Instead, he offers existential glimpses of bizarre or terrible moments in people's lives. His characters, typically, are engaged in a struggle for survival or identity. In such plays as *The Room* (1957), THE BIRTHDAY PARTY, THE DUMB WAITER, and *A Slight Ache* (1961), which was originally written for radio, the action takes place among a few people in one room. In each case, the sanctuary of apparent order of familiar surroundings is shattered by the random intrusion of an outsider or an outside presence. In THE CARETAKER, Pinter's first popular success, themes of domination, isolation, and role changing are explored in the uneasy relations of two brothers and a tramp. Dominance, again, and the impossibility of verifying the truth are treated in THE COLLECTION and *The Lover* (1963). In *The Homecoming* (1965), the battle for dominance in a sexual context is played out as a professor is talked into leaving his new wife with his father, brother, and nephews for their own use. Similar motifs recur in *Landscape* and *Silence* (both 1969) and in *Old Times* (1971). In *Monologue* (1973) and *No Man's Land* (1975), the characters use words as their weapons in their struggles, not only for survival but also for sanity. Pinter's ear for the rhythms of speech—broken sentences, repetitions, non sequiturs, silences—not only suffuses his plays with a mordant humor but also gives them the subtlety and force of poetry. One of Pinter's least enigmatic plays, *Betrayal* (1980), works backwards in time through the complicated affair of a wife with her husband's best friend. In *Family Voices* (1981) a mother and son, through simultaneous monologues, reveal their terrible sense of entrapment in family relationships. *One for the Road* appeared in 1985.

Pinter's screenplays include *The Servant* (1963), *The Quiller Memorandum* (1966), *Accident* (1967), *The Go-Between* (1971), and *The French Lieutenant's Woman* (1981). He also wrote and published a screen treatment of REMEMBRANCE OF THINGS PAST, *The Proust Screenplay* (1977).

Pioneers, The, or the Source of the Susquehanna (1823)   A novel by James Fenimore COOPER. The character of Natty BUMPPO here makes his first appearance in print as an older man, who has witnessed the coming of civilization to the wilderness. The story takes place in upper New York State, in the village of Templeton, founded by Judge Temple. The central conflict in the book concerns the opposition between the laws of nature, upheld by Natty, and the laws of civilization. Symbolic of this opposition are two incidents; in the first, Natty kills a deer for food, in Indian fashion. The white settlement seeks to punish him for failing to respect the seasonal hunting laws it has established. On the other hand, there is the wholesale slaughter of pigeons by the civilized inhabitants of Templeton, with no purpose but sport. A second moral question involves the true ownership of Judge Temple's lands. The marriage of Elizabeth Temple and Edward Effingham, heir of the true owner, resolves the difficulty. Natty, like Huck Finn, heads for the far West to escape confining civilization. See LEATHERSTOCKING TALES, THE.

Pipes, Tom   In Tobias Smollett's novel PEREGRINE PICKLE, a taciturn, battered, retired boatswain's mate, who speaks chiefly in whistles.

Pippa Passes (1841)   A poetic drama by Robert BROWNING. Pippa is a poor child who works all year, except for one holiday on New Year's Day, in the silk mills at Asolo in Italy. The drama hinges on her chance appearance "at critical moments in the spiritual life-history of the leading characters in the play." Pippa passes, singing some song, and her voice and words alter the destinies of the men and women who overhear her. Her own life is altered by her final song. Her famous first song, which ends,

God's in His heaven—
All's right with the world!

while often quoted as revealing naïve optimism on Browning's part, is actually mainly an expression of Pippa's innocent and trusting character.

Pirandello, Luigi (1867–1936)   Italian dramatist and novelist. Pirandello is one of the major figures of modern theatre, celebrated for his symbolical dramas and satires, which aroused much controversy because of their alleged obscurity in the 1920s.

He also introduced some radical changes in the structure of his plays by making them open-ended and curtailing the fiction of the sets. In some cases the action takes place on a bare stage, as in SIX CHARACTERS IN SEARCH OF AN AUTHOR, or among the spectators (as in *Tonight We Improvise!*, 1932).

In both his dramas and his fiction, Pirandello explored the many faces of reality. His characters are invariably confronted with the "problems" of several "truths" or "realities," depending upon the individual point of view. The relentless pessimism that pervades his work is aptly articulated by a character in the stort story "La veglia" ("The Wake"): "I'm not suffering on my account, or on your account. I'm suffering because life is what it is."

Pirandello's oeuvre includes some memorable novels, chiefly *Il fu Mattia Pascal* (1904; tr *The Late Mattia Pascal*, 1964) and *Uno, nessuno, e centomila* (1926; tr *One, None, and a Hundred Thousand*, 1933). He wrote over two hundred short stories (*Novelle per un anno*, 1922–36) and several essays, of which "L'umorismo" ("On Humor") is fundamental to an understanding of his art.

During much of his early career, Pirandello was professor of literature at a women's teachers college. After his success, he founded his own theatre in Rome, with the financial backing of Mussolini's government, and took his own acting company on tours throughout Europe. He was awarded the Nobel Prize in Literature in 1934.

Other plays include: *Così è se vi pare* (1918; tr *Right You Are! If You Think So*, 1923); *Enrico IV* (1923); *Come tu mi vuoi* (1930; tr *As You Desire Me*, 1931); *La nuova colonia* (1928; tr *The New Colony*, 1958); *I giganti della montagna* (1937; tr *The Mountain Giants*, 1958).

Piranesi, Giovanni Battista (1720–1778)   Italian architect and engraver. Piranesi is best known for his engravings. His *Views of Rome*, executed from 1745 to 1756, are prominent among over two thousand known works by him in this medium. His most inventive works, however, are the *Imaginary Prisons* (1745), fantastic variations of Roman architecture, crowded with stairways, ladders, and implements of torture. He is also noted for his writings on aesthetics, wherein he stated, in opposition to the prevailing view of Joachim Winckelmann, that Roman and Etruscan art and architecture were superior to their Greek counterparts. He founded his own publishing house, where he produced *Concerning the Magnificence of Roman Architecture* (1761) and subsequent written and engraved works.

Pirithous   King of the Lapiths in Thessaly, and friend of Theseus. He was the husband of Hippodamia, at whose wedding feast the Centaurs offered violence to the bride, thus causing a great battle.

Pisan Cantos, The (1948)   Ten sections of the Cantos of Ezra Pound, thought by many to be the most brilliantly executed section of his epic work. This section was written during Pound's imprisonment in an American stockade in Pisa, following his arrest on charges of treason for his radio broadcasts on behalf of the Italian Fascists. Pound turns back to essential things, to nature, to regain his lost emotional and spiritual balance, frequently referring to his fellow prisoners, guards, and the physical surroundings at Pisa. The awarding of the Bollingen Prize to Pound for the *Pisan Cantos* created an intense literary controversy.

Pisarev, Dmitry Ivanovich (1840–1868)   Russian radical journalist. Although born a member of the gentry

class, Pisarev became a leading spokesman for the young nihilists of the 1860s. Most of the articles that established Pisarev's reputation were written while he was in prison, from 1862 to 1866, for publishing illegal pamphlets. Pisarev's ideas on literature and art were even more extreme than those of the radical critics Chernyshevsky and Dobrolyubov. While these two men saw art as a worthy pursuit when it served a social purpose, Pisarev tended to deny any value at all to art. He attacked Pushkin's work as a waste of time and once claimed that a pair of boots was more important than a play by Shakespeare. Elements of the nihilist ideology remained in radical thinking, but the force of the movement began to wane after Pisarev's accidental death by drowning.

Piscator, Erwin   See Epic Theatre.

Pisemsky, Aleksey Feofilaktovich (1820–1881) Russian novelist, dramatist, and short-story writer. The son of an impoverished nobleman, Pisemsky spent his early life in the provinces. There he acquired the intimate knowledge of provincial life and of peasant character that became a prominent feature of his literary works. His interest in literature began early, and he was already writing stories before he finished secondary school. After graduation from Moscow University, he entered government service and remained a civil servant for most of his life. Pisemsky's first published work was the short novel *Tyufyak* (*The Muff*, 1850), a somberly realistic study of a family tragedy. The combination of an objective narrative manner and a pessimistic attitude toward his subjects and toward life marked most of Pisemsky's writings. His best-known works are *Ocherki iz krestyanskogo byta* (*Sketches from Peasant Life*, 1856), a collection of short stories; the novel A Thousand Souls; and the drama A Hard Lot.

Pisgah   In the Bible, the mountain in Moab, northeast of the Dead Sea, from which Moses, unable to enter Canaan, was allowed to view the Promised Land (Deut. 34:1). Mount Nebo was one of its summits.

Pisistratus (612?–527 BC)   The greatest of the tyrants of Athens. Although Pisistratus respected and, for the most part, retained the constitution of his predecessor Solon, he made himself tyrant in 560 BC and, except for brief periods of exile, held that position for the rest of his life. His reign was characterized by stability, prosperity, and cultural advancement. He either instituted or significantly altered the festival called the Greater Panathenaea, at which he introduced contests of bards. Tradition says that he arranged for the editing of the works of Homer, which had many variant forms. Dramatic contests were added to the festival of Dionysia, and it may have been at this time that Thespis' plays were performed.

Piso's conspiracy   A plot in AD 65 against the life of the tyrannical emperor Nero instigated by Caius Calpurnius Piso. When the plot was discovered, Piso committed suicide. Many distinguished persons involved in the conspiracy, including LUCAN and SENECA, were ordered to commit suicide and took their own lives.

Pissarro, Camille (1830–1903) French painter. Born in the Virgin Islands, and intended by his family for a career in business, Pissarro finally convinced his father of his absorbing interest in painting and went to Paris at the age of twenty-five. There, he was a student of COROT, whose influence is reflected in many of his early works. He then became associated with IMPRESSIONISM and remained loyal to that movement despite great personal hardship; he was, in fact, the only painter to exhibit in all eight impressionist shows. Recognition did not come to Pissarro until he was nearly sixty years old, although he was a much-admired teacher of GAUGUIN, CASSATT, and CÉZANNE, among others. He was never extreme or daring in technique; fine, small strokes and subtle tonal shading characterize his delicate, dappled landscapes.

Pistol A cowardly braggart, in the tradition of the *capitano* of the COMMEDIA DELL'ARTE, whose bombastic speech is filled with quotations from old plays. He appears in Shakespeare's HENRY IV: PART II and THE MERRY WIVES OF WINDSOR as Sir John Falstaff's ensign. He is promoted to lieutenant in HENRY V. His wife is Mistress Nell QUICKLY.

Pit, The See OCTOPUS, THE.

Pit and the Pendulum, The (1842) A story by Edgar Allan POE. The narrator, a victim of the Spanish Inquisition, is condemned to death by torture. He narrowly escapes death by falling into the pit, as he moves around his dark cell. Bound to a board, a pendulum swings a knife across his body. He escapes by enticing the prison rats to gnaw through his ropes. Then the walls of his cell become molten; as they close in around him, he is forced to the edge of the pit. Fainting, about to fall, he is rescued by the successful opposing army.

Pitcairn Island A Polynesian island. It was colonized by refugee mutineers from the H.M.S. *Bounty* (see MUTINY ON THE BOUNTY), who were the ancestors of its present natives. It was named after the British midshipman Robert Pitcairn (1747?–?70), who first sighted the island (July 2, 1767) from the H.M.S. *Swallow*.

Pitkin, Lemuel See WEST, NATHANAEL.

Pitt, William, 1st earl of Chatham (called the Elder Pitt, 1708–1778) English statesman and orator; "the Great Commoner." Pitt entered Parliament in 1735 as a Whig and was made paymaster-general under the duke of Newcastle. When Newcastle resigned (1756), George II asked Pitt to form a new government, but Pitt was unsuccessful. When Newcastle returned (1757) and Pitt was made secretary of state, success was achieved; Newcastle kept Parliament in line, and Pitt vigorously pursued the Seven Years' War. Pitt resigned in 1761, returned as head of government in 1766, but resigned (1768) because of ill health. Pitt recognized the foolishness of George III's policies toward the American colonies, and although he did

not wish to grant them their independence, he tried to use his influence on their behalf.

Pitt, William (called the Younger Pitt, 1759–1806) English statesman, second son of William PITT, 1st earl of Chatham, and considered by many to have been the greatest of England's prime ministers. He entered Parliament in 1780; by 1782 he was chancellor of the exchequer and leader of the House of Commons. In 1783 he became prime minister and remained in office until 1801, one of the longest ministries in English history. During this period he effected major reforms in financing the public debt, in customs duties, and in the administration of India, which he took out of the hands of the East India Company. He resigned in 1801, resumed office in 1804, and retired in 1806, just two weeks before his death.

Pitti Palace A palace in Florence, Italy, completed in the 16th century by Cosimo de' MEDICI. It is now one of the world's outstanding art galleries.

Pizarro, Francisco (1470?–1541) Spanish conqueror of Peru. The illegitimate son of a Spanish army officer, Pizarro was a swineherd before he left for America, where he settled in Panama. In 1522 he formed a pact for the conquest of Peru with Diego de Almagro and Fernando de Luque, a priest. After two unsuccessful expeditions, Pizarro won the support of Charles V, who named him governor and captain-general of Peru while Almagro was relegated to a secondary position. In 1531 Pizarro left for Peru, leaving Almagro in Panama to recruit additional men. Reaching the city of Cajamarca, Pizarro and his men seized ATAHUALPA, the Inca emperor, and slew a large number of Indians. Although Atahualpa complied with Pizarro's demand that he produce a huge ransom, he was later executed. By 1535, when Pizarro founded Lima, the Inca empire had been vanquished; however, he now had to contend with Almagro, who claimed the city of El Cuzco for himself. Almagro was defeated and killed at the battle of Las Salinas (1538), but his partisans assassinated Pizarro in Lima three years later.

Plague, The (La Peste, 1947; tr 1948) A novel by Albert CAMUS. The Algerian port of Oran is overwhelmed by an epidemic of bubonic plague, although modern medicine does its best to quarantine the city and isolate the stricken and the dead within. The emergency forces many to make character-revealing decisions; yet death plays no favorites, and life continues much the same after the calamity. The doctor Bernard Rieux represents those who, despite everything, simply do what they can for the cause of human life and hope for the possibility of occasional human joy.

plagues of Egypt See TEN PLAGUES.

Plaideurs, Les (The Litigants, 1668) A comedy by Jean RACINE. The magistrate Dandin, driven mad by his mania for judging, is kept locked up by his son and hears cases from the attic and cellar windows, among them those arising from neighborhood and household quarrels. The farcical highlight of the play is the trial of Dandin's own dog for eating a chicken. After an elaborate prosecution and defense, Dandin condemns the dog to death, but he commutes the sentence out of compassion for the pups. The play abounds in burlesques of the legal corruption and pomposity of Racine's day.

Plaidy, Eleanor   A pseudonym of Eleanor HIB-BERT.

Plain Language from Truthful James (1870) A humorous narrative poem by Bret HARTE. Bill Nye and "Truthful" James attempt to get the better of a Chinese named Ah Sin in a card game. Ah Sin is too good for them until they discover he has twenty-four jacks up his sleeve. The poem parodies SWINBURNE and shows influences of KIPLING. It has often been reprinted under the title *The Heathen Chinee*, and was unsuccessfully dramatized as *Ah Sin* by Harte and Mark TWAIN in 1887.

Plain Tales from the Hills (1888)   A volume of stories of life in India by Rudyard KIPLING, first published in the Lahore (India) *Civil and Military Gazette* on which Kipling worked. It contains the first story about the famous trio of Otheris, Learoyd, and Mulvaney, whose exploits were continued in SOLDIERS THREE.

planets   The heavenly bodies that revolve around the sun in approximately circular orbits. They are so called because, to the ancients, they appeared to wander (Gr, *planasthai*, through Lat and OF, "to wander") among the stars, instead of having fixed places.

Only five of the planets were known to the ancients (the earth, of course, not being reckoned): Mercury, Venus, Mars, Jupiter, and Saturn; to these were added the sun and the moon, making seven in all. Among the astrologers and alchemists, the Sun (Apollo) represented gold, the Moon (Diana) represented silver, Mercury represented quicksilver, Venus represented copper, Mars represented iron, Jupiter represented tin, and Saturn represented lead. According to astrology, some planet, at the birth of every individual, presides over his destiny. Some of the planets, such as Jupiter, are lucky; others, such as Saturn, are unlucky.

Plantagenet (fr OF, *planta genista*, "sprig of broom") The surname, originally a nickname, of the Angevin line of English kings (1154–1399). As a family cognizance, it was first assumed by Geoffrey, count of Anjou (d 1151), during a pilgrimage to the Holy Land, as a symbol of humility. By his wife Matilda, daughter of Henry I of England, he was father of Henry II, the first of the house of Plantagenet to occupy the throne. See ENGLAND, RULERS OF.

Platen, August, Graf von (1796–1835)   German poet. Platen's verse, though classicistic and highly form-conscious, often expresses a deep pessimism. His collected *Gedichte* (*Poems*, 1828, expanded 1834) include many sonnets and poems in Oriental forms. Heinrich Heine, in his *Die Bäder von Lucca* (*The Baths of Lucca*, 1830), uses Platen's homosexuality as the basis for a witty but vicious attack on him.

Plath, Sylvia (1932–1963)   American poet and novelist. Plath's brief and tragic life was marked by prolific creativity. Her influence was widespread, especially on the work of women writers of the 1960s. Plath studied with Robert LOWELL in 1959 and assimilated the doctrines of the CONFESSIONAL POETS, but she went on to mark confessionalism with her own decidedly feminist imprint.

Plath won prizes for her writing while she attended Smith College, and scholarly excellence earned her a Fulbright fellowship to England in 1955. There she met and married the poet Ted HUGHES and spent the rest of her life in England. Her first book of poetry, *The Colossus* (1960), showed remarkable talent, but was somewhat timid and self-consciously aware of craftsmanship. Nevertheless, the themes that were to darken the pages of ARIEL, *Crossing the Water* (1971), and *Winter Trees* (1972), all posthumous works, were already discernible. After *The Colossus*, Plath became less inhibited by poetic models and plunged headlong into the visionary terrain of her encroaching schizophrenia. The poems written between 1960 and 1963, when she took her life, are terrifying. Although the imagery in these late poems is graphically macabre, they are rescued from sensationalism by their honesty, ironic wit, and technical control. They are also objectified as correlatives to contemporary civilization; thus one woman's nightmare becomes the collective experience of the Nazi holocaust. Plath wrote one novel, *The Bell Jar*, which was published under the pseudonym Victoria Lucas in 1963, and with proper attribution in 1971. The novel is largely autobiographical and deals with the efforts of its young heroine to avert compulsive suicidal tendencies.

Selected Poems, edited by Ted Hughes, was published in 1985.

Plato (c427–c348 BC)   A Greek philosopher and prose writer. Born at Athens of a noble family, Plato aspired to political activity. Dismayed at the inequities of the Athenian tyranny, and later at the execution of his teacher Socrates under the democracy, he turned toward philosophy in search of an alternative to the unstable and unjust public life of the time. He also sought unity behind the changing impressions of the visible universe.

After Socrates' death, Plato went to Megara and possibly visited Egypt and Cyrene. During this decade the dialogues that emphasize the personality of Socrates are supposed to have been written. At the age of forty, Plato visited Sicily and Italy, and twice returned there later in life, hoping vainly to influence Dionysius II, tyrant of Syracuse, to establish a Platonic government. On his return to Athens, Plato founded the Academy, at which discussion and research were stimulated in mathematical and astronomical fields, in practical legislation, in the art of definition, and in natural history.

All Plato's writing, except for the *Apology* and the *Letters*, is in the dialogue form. Of the thirty-five dialogues, twenty-nine are considered genuine. In the earliest dialogues, Socrates is the principal figure. This group includes the *Charmides, Crito, Euthyphro, Hippias Minor, Ion, Laches,* and *Lysis.* The *Apology* records Socrates' defense at his trial. These dialogues are philosophically inconclusive, but are considered best to represent the historical Socrates. In a second group, Socrates is the spokesman for Plato's views or Plato's interpretation of Socrates. These include *Alcibiades, Cratylus, Ethydemus, Gorgias, Menexenus, Meno, Parmenides, Phaedo, Phaedrus, Protagoras, Republic, Symposium,* and *Theaetetus.* A third group of dialogues, written in Plato's later years, includes *Critias, Philebus, Politicus, Sophist, Timaeus,* and *Laws.* The last was unpublished at Plato's death.

The dialogue, as Plato used it, is a literary form, not merely a vehicle for the expression of a philosophical system. Plato's philosophy emerges not in a systematic or didactic way, but through the use of dramatic setting and myth. Therefore, summary or paraphrase easily distorts Plato's thinking.

The core of his philosophy is the doctrine of ideas. Form and idea are used interchangeably to designate that which remains the same through all the manifestations of a material thing or a virtue. An idea for Plato, contrary to its common English usage, is something outside the mind. He posited a realm of truth or being in which the ideas reside, as distinct from the world of opinion, or *Doxa.* Through the soul, the mediator between the ideas and appearances, we may obtain knowledge.

Tradition has it that Plato was originally named Aristocles, and only later called Plato ("broad") because of his wide forehead, his robust physique, the quality of his writing, or a variety of other explanations.

Platonov, Andrey Platonovich (1889–1951)
Russian prose writer, poet, and critic. Although Platonov fought for the BOLSHEVIKS in the Civil War, his satirization of bureaucracy and somewhat anarchistic bent have elicited critical attacks and periodically caused his works to be banned. He left the Communist Party in 1921, but his early work, which mostly focuses on the role of machinery in the transformation of nature, aligns him best with the proletarian movement. His satire *Gorod Gradov* (1927; tr *The City of Gradov,* 1973) probes the emerging dominance of bureaucracy and technology; in *Kotlovan* (1968; tr *The Foundation Pit,* 1973) Platonov investigates the ramifications of complete centralization. Among Platonov's other notable works are *Chevengur* (1972; tr 1978), *Fro* (1936; tr 1970), *Tretiy syn* (1936; tr *The Third Son,* 1970), *Dzhan* (1964; tr 1970), and *Semya Ivanova* (1946; tr *Homecoming,* 1970). His portrayal of social readjustment after the war was officially denounced as slanderous to Soviet society. Platonov's reputation has been only partially rehabilitated,

for several of his early works remain absent from Soviet editions of his writing.

Plautus, Titus Maccius (254?–184 BC)
The greatest comic playwright of Rome. Son of a peasant family, Plautus worked as a stagehand in a traveling theatrical troupe. This job afforded him nothing but experience, and when the group disbanded, he was left penniless. He was obliged to return to Rome and work in a flour mill; here he found the time to compose his first verse comedies. He subsequently wrote and produced about 130 plays, of which 21 are still extant in more or less complete form. In them he Romanized many of the plots and characters of New Greek Comedy (see MENANDER). Through his plays, he introduced to the non-Greek world characters which have since become part of traditional Western European comedy, among them the braggard soldier (in his MILES GLORIOSUS) and the sly servant (in his *Pseudolus*). In his treatment of stock comic plots, he displayed a mastery of language and meter, and a seemingly inexhaustible supply of wit—sometimes subtle, often humorously coarse.

Plautus's play the *Menaechmi* was the source for Shakespeare's THE COMEDY OF ERRORS; and his comedy about the old miser and his pot of gold, the *Aulularia,* supplied the model for Molière's L'AVARE.

Playboy of the Western World, The (1907)
A play by John Millington SYNGE. Christy Mahon, a timid, pleasant boy, flees home, convinced that he has killed his cruel, bullying father with a blow to the head. His presumed act is treated by the people to whom he flees as a piece of heroic audacity, and his lionization results in the transformation of his personality. When his father appears with bandaged head and they have another scuffle, the opinion of the townspeople is reversed. The plot, however, is a mere backdrop for the most fertile and vigorous poetic dialogue written for the stage since Shakespeare. The play's fierce humor offended Irish patriots, culminating in the "Playboy riots" that took place in Dublin after its production at the ABBEY THEATRE.

Pléiade
A group, first known as the Brigade, of young 16th-century French poets. Led by Pierre de RONSARD, they boldly asserted themselves with the publication of Joachim DU BELLAY's DÉFENSE ET ILLUSTRATION DE LANGUE FRANÇAISE. Condemning the poetry of the RHÉTORIQUEURS and of Clément MAROT, they sought to revitalize French literature through study and imitation of Greek and Roman writers. Later on they modified some of their principles, avoiding too servile an imitation of classical models, and by 1555 they were truly representative of French Renaissance poetry. The members of the Pléiade were Ronsard, Du Bellay, Jean Antoine de Baïf, Etienne Jodelle, Pontus de Tyard, Rémy Belleau, and Jean Dorat, their former teacher who had first revealed to the poets the treasures of classical literature. With the success of the group's efforts, and because their number was seven, Ronsard

changed the name of the Brigade to *La Pléiade* after the PLEIADES.

Pleiades   The most prominent cluster of stars in the constellation Taurus. Especially, it includes the seven larger ones out of the great number that compose the cluster; so called by the Greeks, possibly from Gr *plein*, "to sail," because they considered navigation safe at the return of the Pleiades, and never attempted it after those stars disappeared.

In Greek mythology, the *Pleiades* were the seven daughters of ATLAS and Pleione. They were transformed into stars, one of which is invisible and known as the lost Pleiad. Some say this star is ELECTRA, mourning over the destruction of the city and royal race of Troy. Others say it is Merope, ashamed to show herself because she married a mortal, SISYPHUS.

Plekhanov, Georgy Valentinovich (1857–1918) Russian philosopher and critic. Plekhanov helped to found the Emancipation of Labor Party and participated in the struggles between the Mensheviks and BOLSHEVIKS but eventually came to shun both parties and even denounced the October Revolution itself. He is best known for his early systematization of Marxist artistic theory, which, although largely conventional in ideology, was forgotten under Stalin because of its emphasis on the disinterested enjoyment of art and on certain anthropological elements of Darwinism unusual in Marxist theories. His most notable works include *Pisma bez adresa* (1899–1900; tr *Letters without Addresses*, 1953), *Frantsuzskaya dramaticheskaya literatura i frantsuzskaya zhivopis XVIII veka s tochki zreniya sotsiologii* (1905; tr *French Drama and Painting of the Eighteenth Century*, 1936), and *Iskusstvo i obshchestvennaya zhizn* (1912–13; tr *Art and Social Life*, 1936). In the 1970s Plekhanov came to be recognized once more as a major Soviet Marxist theoretician.

Pliny the Elder (full Latin name Caius Plinius Secundus, AD 23–79)   Latin author. Pliny is known for his *Historia naturalis* (*Natural History*), which was regarded as a scientific source book during the Middle Ages. His zeal for scientific research led him to Pompeii, in AD 79, where he studied the eruptions of Mt. Vesuvius; here he died when the city was destroyed.

Pliny the Younger (full Latin name Caius Plinius Caecilius Secundus, AD 62–113)   The nephew and adopted son of PLINY THE ELDER, he rose to a high and respected rank in imperial society. His friends included QUINTILIAN, MARTIAL, SUETONIUS, TACITUS, and the emperor Trajan (AD 52?–117). His collected letters give a vivid account of the social, literary, and political life of his times.

Plomer, William [Charles Franklin] (1903–1973)   South African novelist, short-story writer, and poet. Plomer traveled and lived in many parts of the world, spending most of his adult life in England. While still a young man in South Africa, he worked with Roy CAMPBELL on the outspoken review *Voorslag*, and wrote his first novel, *Turbott Wolfe* (1925), an angry denunciation of South Africa's racist policies, a theme that was echoed in his stories *I Speak of Africa* (1927). He then lived in Japan, where his objective insight into national character was revealed in *Paper Houses* (1932), stories, and in the novel *Sado* (1931). Plomer's English novels, *The Case Is Altered* (1932), *The Invaders* (1934), and *Museum Pieces* (1952), are ironic glimpses of the tragic and funny effects of British class distinctions. It was Plomer's poetry, however, that best expressed his concomitant sense of horror and absurdity of life. The poems in *Taste and Remember* (1966), *Celebrations* (1972), and *Collected Poems* (1973), many of them ballads, are gentle, satirical expressions of a man of great sensibility. *Electric Delights* (1978) is a posthumous collection of poetry and short fiction. *Double Lives*, an autobiography, appeared in 1943, and *At Home*, another memoir, appeared in 1958; they were republished together as *The Autobiography of William Plomer* in 1976.

Plotinus (c204–c270)   A Greek philosopher of Neoplatonism. After studying in Alexandria with Ammonius Saccas, Plotinus settled in Rome. He persuaded his friend the Emperor Gallienus to build a city for philosophers, to be governed according to the laws of PLATO. Plotinus' own philosophy had no political significance; he lived in a time of political chaos and mystery religions. Porphyry, his biographer and student, relates that he refused to eat meat, and that he attained the state of mystical union with God four times while Porphyry knew him. The treatises, arranged into Enneads, or groups of nine, were written during the last seventeen years of Plotinus' life. He broke his vow of silence with regard to Ammonius' doctrines only because other students were reporting them mistakenly. Plotinus is reported by Porphyry as ashamed of his bodily existence and reticent about revealing biographical information.

Plough and the Stars, The   See O'CASEY, SEAN.

Plumb, J[ohn] H[arold] (1911–   )   English historian. Plumb is a specialist in 18th-century English history. His political biographies are distinguished by his enthusiastic approach to his subjects and by his meticulous research of original materials. His two-volume biography of Sir Robert Walpole—*The Making of a Statesman* (1956) and *The King's Minister* (1961)—is a compassionate yet objective study of that controversial figure. *The Origins of Political Stability, 1675–1725* (1967) is a landmark study of political history. His lectures and essays have also been collected in *The Death of the Past* (1969) and in *The Light of History* (1972). *Georgian Delights* (1980) documents the pursuits of pleasure in 18th-century England. *Royal Heritage* (1980) studies the reign of Queen Elizabeth II. In 1982, Plumb published (with Neil McKendrick and John Brewer) *The Birth of a Consumer Society*.

Plumed Serpent, The (1926)   A novel by D. H. LAWRENCE. It is a powerful, vivid evocation of Mexico and its ancient Aztec religion. Kate Leslie, an Irish visitor to

Mexico, goes to a bullfight and is horrified by the vulgar cruelty of modern Mexico. But then she meets Don Ramón, a scholar and political leader, and General Cipriano, a military leader, and becomes involved in their resurrection of the ancient Mexican religion. For Lawrence, this religion is characterized by "blood consciousness," emotional and symbolic depth, and sex awareness. It is marked by dominance of the male over the female and the political leader over the masses, a Nietzschean type of superman. Don Ramón, the sexual, political, and religious hero of the book, is regarded as the reincarnated Quetzalcoatl, the Plumed Serpent that the Aztecs used to worship. He rises to lead the people, drawing them away from "outworn" Christianity toward the Aztec religion. Eventually the cult spreads over the whole of Mexico and Kate, too, comes under its spell. She marries General Cipriano, who is regarded as Huitzilopochtli, god of war, and in spite of the rebelliousness of her European character, she passively submits to his male domination. The views Lawrence expresses in it are typical of his later period.

Plurabelle, Anna Livia   See ANNA LIVIA PLURABELLE.

Plutarch (AD c46–c120)   A Greek biographer. Except for some meager details—that he was born at Chaeronea, that he visited Rome and Athens, and possibly Alexandria, but spent most of his life in Chaeronea as a priest of the Delphic Apollo—nothing is known of Plutarch's life. His biographical and philosophical writings show that he was one of the most erudite men of his age. His surviving works are confined to the *Moralia*, a book of essays on many subjects, and the famous *Parallel Lives*, arranged mainly in pairs in which a Greek and a Roman are contrasted. His subjects, who include Demosthenes and Cicero, were statesmen or generals. In the process of writing about them, he invents dialogue and describes the emotions of the personages involved. Shakespeare's *Julius Caesar, Coriolanus*, and *Antony and Cleopatra* are based on Plutarch in the famous translation made by Thomas North in 1579. The *Moralia* is concerned with an amazing range of subjects, including the education of children, advice on marriage, the oracles, the face in the moon, and the reasoning of animals.

Pluto   See HADES.

Plutus   In Greek mythology, the god of riches—originally the fertility of the earth. Hence the phrase *rich as Plutus*, and the term *plutocrat*, meaning one who exercises influence or possesses power through his wealth. The legend is that he was blinded by ZEUS so that his gifts should be equally distributed and go only to those who merited them. *Plutus* is the name of ARISTOPHANES' last extant play.

Plymouth Rock   The ledge in the harbor of Plymouth, Massachusetts, where the *Mayflower* Pilgrims landed (December 21, 1620). They had previously landed at Provincetown, Massachusetts, on Cape Cod.

Plyushkin   An incredibly miserly landowner in Nikolay Gogol's DEAD SOULS. After completing his business transactions with him, the hero CHICHIKOV is almost subjected to the hospitality of the house: a year-old Easter cake that Plyushkin has been saving for a special occasion.

pnigos   See OLD COMEDY.

Pocahontas (c1595–1617)   Daughter of Powhatan, an Indian chief of Virginia. Her real name was Matoaka, Pocahontas being a pet name meaning "playful." She is said to have rescued Captain John SMITH, a member of the governing board of the English settlement in Jamestown, who was to be put to death in January 1608, by order of her father. She later (1614) married the tobacco planter John Rolfe (1585–1622), an alliance that brought the colonists peace with the Indians for eight years. She converted to Christianity, was baptized under the name Rebecca, and went with Rolfe to England in 1616. She was presented at court as a princess and became an object of curiosity, admiration, and of frequent allusion in contemporary literature.

Pocahontas appears in numerous literary works, notably J. N. Barker's drama *The Indian Princess* (1808) and John Davis's *The First Settlers of Virginia* (1805) and J. E. Cooke's *My Lady Pokahontas* (1885), both novels.

Po Chü-i (or Po Lo-t'ien, 772–846)   Chinese poet of the T'ANG dynasty. Po is most famous for his long narrative poems *The Lute Song* and *The Song of Everlasting Regret*, as well as for his poems critical of corrupt officials and the hard lives of the common people. He is also a poet of everyday life and a chronicler of his own old age. He was Arthur WALEY's favorite Chinese poet and the one most translated by that great Orientalist.

Podhoretz, Norman (1930–   )   American editor, critic, and essayist. Podhoretz began his career as a literary critic—he wrote *Doings and Undoings: the 50's and After in American Writing* (1964) and edited *The Commentary Reader* (1966)—but became known as a political spokesman for the left. As editor in chief of *Commentary*, Podhoretz initially led the journal's political orientation to the left; as he moved to the right, however, *Commentary* followed his lead and has become, under his guidance, a neoconservative vehicle designed to battle the New Left. In 1968 he published *Making It*, an autobiography and a confessional on literary success. It was poorly received. His second volume of autobiography, *Breaking Ranks* (1979), which examines his growing disaffection with the left, met with even greater disapproval and accusations of betrayal of his former political and literary allies. His books continue to reflect his drift to the right: In *The Present Danger* (1980), Podhoretz argues that the United States faces the danger of political and economic subordination to the Soviet Union, and *Why We Were in Vietnam* (1982) sanctions American participation in the VIETNAM WAR on a moral basis. In 1986 he fused his earlier interest in literary criticism with politics in *The Bloody Crossroads: Where Literature and Politics Meet.*

Poe, Edgar Allan (1809–1849)   American poet, critic, and short-story writer. Poe's stormy personal life, further confused by an unscrupulous literary executor, postponed honest evaluation of his place in American literature.

The child of theatrical parents, Poe was orphaned early in life. He was taken into the home of John Allan, who did not adopt him, but became his godfather. From 1815 to 1820 the Allans lived in England, where Poe studied at a classical academy. During the next decade Poe and John Allan quarreled more and more frequently. When Mrs. Allan died, and her widower remarried, the two severed relations. Up to 1831, when he went to New York for a brief period, Poe had entered and left several schools, including West Point, and had enlisted in the Army. He had already published *Tamerlane and Other Poems* (1827) and *Al Aaraaf* (1829).

In 1831 he published his *Poems*; content and preface show the influence of the English romantic poets. He won a story contest with "MS. Found in a Bottle," and began to write the poetic drama *Politian* (1835–36). His newly established reputation gained him the position of editor of the *Southern Literary Messenger* in Richmond. He contributed such stories as BERENICE and "Hans Pfaal," raising the circulation of the magazine from five hundred to thirty-five hundred, and began the serialization of THE NARRATIVE OF A. GORDON PYM in 1837. Leaving the *Messenger*, he went to Philadelphia to work on *Burton's Gentleman's Magazine.*

In 1836 Poe married his thirteen-year-old cousin, Virginia Clemm. She died eleven years later, and he addressed the famous ANNABEL LEE to her. Issuing TALES OF THE GROTESQUE AND ARABESQUE, he then began writing his tales of ratiocination.

Poe went again to New York in 1845 and worked on the *Evening Mirror*, in which his poem THE RAVEN was published. The poem established Poe's national reputation. He became coeditor, and then proprietor, of his own paper, *The Broadway Journal*, which collapsed in 1846.

Virginia Clemm died of tuberculosis in 1847. Poe, cared for by Mrs. Clemm and his female admirers, continued to write several important pieces, among them "The Philosophy of Composition" (1846), "Ulalume" (1847), and EUREKA. A series of drinking bouts left him exhausted. In October of 1849 he was found seriously ill by a friend, and he died several days later, at the age of forty.

Although Poe felt that he was primarily a poet, his tales of horror and ratiocination have become increasingly popular. He is respected for his books of criticism, as well as for the day-to-day newspaper reviews he turned out.

Poe exercised the greatest influence on the French poet Charles BAUDELAIRE, who wrote several articles about him, and translated his work. Through Baudelaire, his influence extended to MALLARMÉ, VALÉRY, RIMBAUD, and others of the symbolist school. See CITY IN THE SEA, THE; GOLD BUG, THE; MURDERS IN THE RUE MORGUE, THE; PIT AND THE PENDULUM, THE; PURLOINED LETTER, THE; TELL-TALE HEART, THE.

Poem of Aqhat, The   A Canaanite epic poem. It was discovered during the excavation of the ancient city of Ugarit (now Ras Shamra) in Syria in the early 1930s. It was written in an early Semitic script in cuneiform characters on clay tablets dating from about the 14th century BC. Though less clearly associated with religious ritual than THE POEM OF BAAL, found in Ugarit at the same time, it nevertheless contains many of the basic elements commonly found in seasonal rites. It is also an astronomical myth similar to that of ORION, in which the physical juxtaposition of certain constellations apparently resulted in their association in legend.

At the beginning of the poem, an old chieftain named Danel (or Daniel) observes an elaborate rite beseeching Baal to grant him a son. Baal intercedes with the chief deity EL on his behalf, and El consents. Danel celebrates his good fortune, and in due time Aqhat is born to his wife Danatiya. Sometime thereafter, the divine artisan Koshar-wa-Khasis is entertained by Danel as the god is returning from his Egyptian forge with a load of new bows for the gods. In return, Koshar presents his host with one of the bows as a present for Aqhat.

Unfortunately, this bow had (as well as can be judged from the fragmentary remains of the poem) been intended for the goddess Anat, a warlike Canaanite counterpart of the Greek Artemis. She offers Aqhat (now a youth) wealth and immortality in return for the bow, but he spurns them. With threats she wins El's permission to take vengeance on Aqhat. Seductively, she lures the youth to the city of the moon god, and there her henchman Yatpan kills him. She then weeps for Aqhat and promises to revive him. The clumsy Yatpan drops and breaks the divine bow, so Anat's efforts have been in vain. Moreover, the murder has brought famine on the land, which lasts for seven years.

Danel learns of Aqhat's death. Shooting down the eagles that hover about, he finds his son's remains and buries them with proper ceremony, at the same time cursing the unknown murderer. After seven years of mourning, Aqhat's sister Paghat sets out to avenge him. Hiding clothes and weapons of a soldier under her dress, she seeks out the professional assassin Yatpan, who, under the influence of drink, reveals himself as the murderer of Aqhat.

Although the rest of the poem is lost, it is generally agreed, on the basis of numerous parallel myths of the death and resurrection of a young god, that Aqhat too was eventually revived.

Poem of Baal, The   A Canaanite epic poem of undetermined antiquity. Lengthy fragments of this poem were discovered at the site of ancient Ugarit (now Ras Shamra) in Syria in the early 1930s. The clay tablets on which it appears date from about the 14th century BC, but the poem itself was probably several centuries older. It was written in cuneiform characters in Semitic dialect that was deciphered within a few years after its discovery. The poem relates the myth that grew out of certain important Canaanite religious rituals. These myths include a combat between fertile and infertile seasons of the year, and the death and revival of a young god: elements common to most parts of the eastern Mediterranean area.

The epic begins with a fragmentary section that apparently describes rivalry for dominion over the earth between Yam, the dragon god of the sea and all inland waters, and Ashtar, the young god of artificial irrigation. Ignoring the warning of the sun goddess Shapash, Ashtar demands of the Bull God El (the supreme deity) that Yam be deposed in Ashtar's favor, but El confirms Yam's supremacy, on the grounds that Ashtar is inadequate to this exalted position. Soon, however, El's son Baal, the rain god and spirit of fertility, challenges the power of Yam. Emissaries from Yam to the divine assembly frighten the other gods, but Baal boasts that he will destroy Yam. Although El has to pacify Yam's messengers, Baal causes the divine smith Koshar-wa-Khasis to make him two thunderbolts for weapons. In a protracted battle, Baal subdues Yam.

Baal now complains that, although he rules the earth, he has no palace there. After driving Yam back into the sea, the war goddess Anat, Baal's ally, accompanies him to the abode of the mother of the gods, Asherat, El's consort, in order to present his plea. On their approach, Asherat is at first alarmed, but becomes friendly when she sees the rich gifts that they have brought, and promises Baal that his dominion will continue. After feasting her guests, Asherat presents Baal's case to El, who agrees that he may have his palace. Koshar-wa-Khasis plans the palace, but cannot persuade Baal to allow him to put windows in it, for Baal feels that Yam will steal away his young brides. When he has finally disposed of Yam, however, Baal consents to the windows. When he opens them, the windows of heaven will open likewise and rain will fall on the earth, fertilizing it. Baal feasts the gods and makes a royal progress about his kingdom, the earth.

In his pride, Baal now challenges a more formidable enemy than Yam: Mot, the god of death and the underworld, and of aridity, which means death to vegetation. He sends his messengers Gupan and Ugar (Vine and Field) to Mot's abode beyond the northern mountains, to demand that he confine himself henceforward to the underworld and the deserts of the earth. Mot, however, invites Baal to banquet with him in the underworld. Though terrified at the prospect, Baal feels that he cannot refuse. By way of precaution, he smears himself with red ochre to warn off demons and gains strength (and a son) by copulating eighty-eight times with a heifer. He then descends into the underworld and is reported dead.

El mourns for Baal in sackcloth and ashes, and even with self-mutilation. Anat does likewise, but afterwards she determines to seek him in the underworld. With the aid of Shapash (who, as the sun, visits there every night), she recovers Baal's body. His burial is accompanied with numerous animal sacrifices. Ashtar now sits on Baal's throne, but his feet do not reach the footstool and he realizes that he is not adequate to take Baal's place. Anat roams through the earth in search of Baal, and demands that Mot release him, but he repeatedly refuses. After some months she slays Mot in a fury.

El dreams that Baal is alive and rejoices in his imminent return. On his orders, Anat sends Shapash to find Baal. Resurrected, Baal subdues his enemies, including the revived Mot, who at last surrenders. Anat takes savage vengeance on Mot's allies but is finally persuaded by Baal, who again reigns supreme, that peace must be restored to earth and heaven.

Apart from its intrinsic interest, *The Poem of Baal* is of great importance for the light it sheds on primitive myth and ritual, and on certain hitherto obscure passages in the Old Testament. Considerable parts of the books of Joel and Zephaniah seem to have been deliberate satires on Canaanite myth and ritual, which the Hebrews regarded as heathen. In other cases, they ascribed to Yahweh feats that are here attributed to Baal, such as the conquering of the dragon of the sea by the storm god: "Awake, awake, put on strength, O arm of the Lord; awake, as in the ancient days, in the generations of old. Art thou not it that hath cut Rahab, and wounded the dragon? Art thou not it which hath dried the sea, the waters of the great deep?" (Isaiah 51:9–10). There are shades of Greek myth too: the dominion over earth, sea, and underworld among Baal, Yam, and Mot, is identical with the division among Zeus, Poseidon, and Hades; Anat's mourning for the dead fertility god Baal is similar even in phraseology to the accounts of the mourning of Aphrodite for Adonis, or Demeter for Persephone. The unexplained hostility of El, Asherat, and many other gods toward Baal in the poem recalls the relegation of the older gods to positions of lesser importance when Cronos was conquered by Zeus, and the resulting wars with Giants and Titans, offspring of Ge, who, like Asherat, was the mother of the gods.

Poeta en Nueva York   See García Lorca, Federico.

poetaster   A derogatory term describing an incompetent and inferior poet.

Poetaster, The (1601)   A satirical comedy by Ben Jonson. In it he attacked Thomas Dekker and John Marston during the War of the Theatres.

poète maudit (Fr, "accursed poet")   In a collection of essays entitled *Les Poètes maudits* (1884), Verlaine called attention to such poets as Corbière, Rimbaud, and Mallarmé, all of whom were little known at the time. From this, the phrase came to be used to describe gifted poets who are either maligned, ignored, or misunderstood by society.

Poetics (Peri poietikes, 335–322 BC)   A treatise by ARISTOTLE. It was composed over a period of time. All the arts, says the philosopher, have their origin in imitation, or *mimesis*. Poetry springs from this instinct for imitation and from the instinct for harmony and rhythm. Aristotle makes the famous observation that poetry is more philosophical than history, since it expresses the universals rather than particulars.

The objects of imitation in poetry are men in action. If they are presented as better than they are in actual life, the genre is TRAGEDY; if worse, it is COMEDY. Epic poetry and tragedy have the same characteristics, except that epic admits only the narrative meter. Further, epic has no limits of time, whereas tragedy confines itself to a single revolution of the sun. Tragedy excites the emotions of pity and fear, effecting a release, or *catharsis*. Elements of the tragic plot are reversal of situation and recognition. The hero's fortunes fall from good to bad as a result of his tragic flaw, or *hamartia*. Aristotle disapproves of the use of the DEUS EX MACHINA, saying that the unraveling of the plot must arise out of the action of the plot itself.

This exhaustive treatise, the first devoted wholly to literary criticism, has influenced all Western literatures, most notably the 17th-century French classical drama. Aristotle's definitions have become a part of our critical language.

poet laureate   In England, an official court poet, appointed by the sovereign. Originally, his duty was to compose odes in honor of the sovereign's birthday and in celebration of state occasions, in return for £200 a year and a butt of sack.

The first poet officially recognized as such was Ben JONSON, for he was the first to carry out the duties of the office; but the first to bear the actual title was Sir William DAVENANT. In earlier times there had been an occasional *Versificator Regis*; CHAUCER, SKELTON, SPENSER, and Samuel DANIEL were each called poet laureate, though not appointed to that office.

The term arose from the ancient custom in the universities of presenting a laurel wreath to graduates in rhetoric and poetry. In France, authors of distinction continue to be crowned with a wreath when elected to the ACADÉMIE FRANÇAISE. The following is a list of the English poets laureate:

Ben Jonson	1619–1637
Sir William Davenant	1638–1668
John Dryden	1668–1688
Thomas Shadwell	1688–1692
Nahum Tate	1692–1715
Nicholas Rowe	1715–1718
Laurence Eusden	1718–1730
Colley Cibber	1730–1757
William Whitehead	1757–1785
Thomas Warton	1785–1790
Henry James Pye	1790–1813
Robert Southey	1813–1843
William Wordsworth	1843–1850
Alfred Tennyson	1850–1892
Alfred Austin	1896–1913
Robert Bridges	1913–1930
John Masefield	1930–1967
Cecil Day Lewis	1968–1972
Sir John Betjeman	1972–1984
Ted Hughes	1984–

Poetry: A Magazine of Verse   An American magazine founded in Chicago in 1912 by Harriet MONROE and edited by her until her death. It was one of the first and most enduring LITTLE MAGAZINES to appear in America in the 20th century. Devoted to the publication of poetry, it introduced the work of numerous poets, including members of the CHICAGO GROUP, the imagist poets (see IMAGISM), Marianne MOORE, Wallace STEVENS, William Carlos WILLIAMS, and many others. Ezra POUND, as foreign editor, had an inestimable effect on shaping the magazine's destiny. Many important spokesmen for new movements in American literature served as associate, foreign, or contributing editors, among them Yvor WINTERS, Peter DeVRIES, Hayden Carruth, and Karl SHAPIRO.

Poet's Corner   The southern end of the south transept of Westminster Abbey. It is said to have been first so called by Oliver Goldsmith because it contained the tomb of Chaucer. Addison had previously (*Spectator*, No. 26, 1711) alluded to it as "the poetical Quarter." Besides Chaucer's tomb, it contains that of Spenser, and either the tombs of or monuments to Drayton, Ben Jonson, Shakespeare (a statue), Milton (a bust), Samuel Butler, Davenant, Cowley, Prior, Gay, Addison, Thomson, Goldsmith, Dryden, Dr. Johnson, Sheridan, Burns, Southey, Coleridge, Campbell, Macaulay, Longfellow, Dickens, Thackeray, Tennyson, and Browning.

Pogodin, Nikolay (pen name of Nikolay Fyodorovich Stukalov, 1900–1962)   Russian playwright. Pogodin's early plays, such as *Temp* (1930; tr *Tempo*, 1934) and *Poema o topore* (*Poem about an Axe*, 1930), deal with the problems encountered during the first Five-Year Plan. One of his most successful plays was *Aristokraty* (1934; tr *Aristocrats*, 1937), about the rehabilitation of a band of outcasts and undesirables at a labor camp in northern Russia. Two plays portraying Lenin are *Chelovek s ruzhiom* (*Man with a Gun*, 1937) and *Kremlyovskiye kuranty* (1941; tr *The Chimes of the Kremlin*, 1946). A later interesting play by Pogodin is *Sonet Petrarki* (1957; tr *Petrarchian Sonnet*, 1968), published during the period of the thaw after Stalin's death. The play treats the question of love in Soviet society and broadly hints that there are areas, such as those of the emotional life of a person, that the Party would do well to avoid.

Pohl, Frederik (1919–   ) American SCIENCE FICTION writer, anthologist, and editor. Pohl has served various magazines and book publishers as an editor and compiled numerous anthologies. The dystopian, satiric nature of his own writing is suggested by the title of one of his best story collections, *The Case Against Tomorrow* (1957). He collaborated on stories and novels with a number of writers, including five books with C. M. KORNBLUTH, notably *The Space Merchants* (1953), which depicts a future world dominated by advertising agencies. In nearly all of his works Pohl uses science fiction scenarios to point up the foibles of the present. His solo productions include *Man Plus* (1976), about a man turned into a cyborg to survive on Mars; *Gateway* (1977); *JEM* (1979); *Beyond the Blue Event Horizon* (1980); *Midas World* (1983); *Heechee Rendezvous* (1984); and *Black Star Rising* (1985). He has written a memoir, *The Way the Future Was* (1979).

Point Counter Point (1928)   A novel by Aldous HUXLEY. It presents a satiric picture of London intellectuals and members of English upper-class society during the 1920s. Frequent allusions to literature, painting, music, and contemporary British politics occur throughout the book, and much scientific information is embodied in its background. The story is long and involved, with many characters; it concerns a series of broken marriages and love affairs, and a political assassination. The construction is elaborate, supposedly based on Bach's *Suite No. 2 in B Minor*. It is also a novel within a novel. Philip Quarles, a leading character in the novel, is himself planning a novel, which echoes or "counterpoints" the events going on around him. Quarles is a critical portrait of Huxley himself. The only sympathetic characters in the novel are Mark Rampion and his wife, Mary, idealized portraits of D. H. LAWRENCE and his wife, Frieda. The diabolical, sexually depraved Spandrell is said to be based on BAUDELAIRE, and Everard Webley, whom he assassinates, on Sir Oswald Mosley, leader of the British Fascist movement. Denis Burlap and Beatrice Gilray are said to represent J. Middleton MURRY and Katherine MANSFIELD.

pointillism   See NEOIMPRESSIONISM.

Poirot, Hercule   The internationally famous Belgian detective created by Agatha CHRISTIE. Poirot, small in stature, was known for his oversized ego, his charm, his broken English, and his vanity. He retired from the Belgian police force in 1904 and began an illustrious career as an exceptionally acute amateur sleuth. He finally died in *Curtain* (written 1930s, pub 1975), a victim of severe arthritis and a weak heart.

Politick Would-Be, Lord   An English nobleman residing in Venice in Jonson's comedy VOLPONE, OR THE FOX. The principal figure in a subplot that is often omitted from modern performances of the play, he is a caricature of a pompous Englishman living abroad.

Pollock, Jackson (1912–1956)   American painter. Pollock painted murals for the W.P.A. in the 1930s, but he is most famous for his revolutionary "action paintings." His emotion-charged technique involved standing over his canvases and dripping industrial paint, covering them with an overall rhythmic design and sometimes adding cigarette butts, tacks, and other such objects for textural enhancement. Always iconoclastic, his methods and his paintings were objects of unprecedented public ridicule, but he came to be highly respected as a pioneer of ABSTRACT EXPRESSIONISM.

Pollux   See CASTOR AND POLYDEUCES.

Pollyanna (1913)   A novel by Eleanor H[odgman] Porter (1868–1920), an American. The child heroine of the story is an expert at her favorite "Glad Game" of always looking at the bright side in her numerous trials. The word *Pollyanna* has become a synonym for the fatuous, irrepressible optimist who always makes the best of things for himself and other people. Porter herself wrote *Pollyanna Grows Up* (1915), but several other sequels by other writers followed.

Polo, Marco (c1254–1324)   Venetian traveler and adventurer. About 1263, Nicolo and Maffeo Polo (the father and uncle of Marco) visited the court of Kublai Khan, the first Europeans to do so. They returned to Venice in 1269 and, with Marco, left for the East again in 1271. After arriving at the mouth of the Persian Gulf, they abandoned their plan of traveling by sea and turned north, traversing Persia and Turkmen until they reached the Oxus River. They crossed the plain of Pamir and traveled on through the Gobi Desert until they reached Tangut, in the extreme northwest of China. Early in 1275 the three Polos were cordially received at Shangtu by the great Khan, who became especially fond of Marco. The young Polo studied the various native languages, and in 1277 he became a second-class commissioner in the Mongol bureaucracy. Traveling throughout the empire on missions for the Khan, he journeyed from Tibet to Burma and as far as the southern states of India.

So popular at court were the Polos that Kublai Khan would not tolerate their leaving. However, in 1292 they escorted a Mongol princess to Persia. The journey by sea took two years. The Polos went on through Constantinople to Venice, arriving unrecognized late in 1295.

While engaged in a sea battle with the city of Genoa in 1298, Marco Polo was captured and spent nearly a year in prison, during which time he dictated his *Book of Marco Polo* to Rustichello of Pisa.

Polonius   In Shakespeare's HAMLET, a garrulous courtier, typical of the pompous, sententious old man. He is the father of Ophelia and Laertes and lord chamberlain to the king of Denmark. His advice to his son, however, is justly famous. The speech contains this admonition:

> This above all: to thine own self be true,
> And it must follow, as the night the day,
> Thou canst not then be false to any man.

Polybius (202?–120 BC)   A Greek historian of the Roman world. Taken as a hostage by the Romans in the Third Macedonian War, Polybius, a Greek statesman of prominence, became a tutor to the young Publius Scipio Aemilianus and his brothers. Though later free to return home, he accompanied Scipio to Carthage in the Third Punic War and was present when the city fell. He later saw the fall of Corinth. He wrote a reliable history of Rome from 262 BC to 120 BC in forty books, of which only five are extant. Undistinguished as literature, this work is a sound book for Roman history of this period.

Polycleitus   The name of two Greek sculptors, often confused, both of whom worked in Argos. The elder, who flourished in the 5th century BC, was a contemporary of PHIDIAS and was held in the same high esteem. His most famous statue, *Doryphorus* (*Spear-bearer*), was the embodiment of his ideas on the sculptural perfection of the human form, which became the standard for many generations of Greek artists. The younger, who probably lived into the 4th century BC, was known both as a sculptor and as the architect of the theatre at Epidaurus.

Polycrates (6th century BC)   A tyrant of Samos. Polycrates was known and feared for his unfailing success in all his ventures. He won a number of wars with other Greek islands and even withstood an attack from the combined forces of Sparta and Corinth. For a time he was allied with Amasis, the king of Egypt, but Amasis grew so uneasy at his success that (according to the legend) he superstitiously demanded that Polycrates deliberately throw away one of his most valued possessions. Polycrates obligingly threw his favorite ring into the sea and in a few days received it back again in the belly of a fish. Amasis broke off their alliance. A patron of the arts, Polycrates is particularly known for his friendship with the lyric poet Anacreon. His luck finally broke when, lured to the mainland by the envious Oroetes, satrap of Sardis, he was ignominiously crucified.

Polydorus   In classical mythology, the youngest son of PRIAM and HECUBA. According to Homer (ILIAD, xx. 470), he was killed by ACHILLES, but other legends state that he was committed to the care of Polymestor, king of Thrace, who treacherously slew him. His ghost appears in Euripides' tragedy HECUBA, which tells of her revenge on Polymestor.

Polyeucte (1641)   A tragedy by Pierre CORNEILLE. Derived from the *Vitae sanctorum* of the 16th-century monk Surius, the play is set in Armenia in the early Christian era. Polyeucte, a newly baptized Christian, reviles the pagans and is imprisoned. Desiring martyrdom, he surrenders his wife, Pauline, to her first lover, Severus, but she refuses to comply if her husband dies. Severus bravely attempts to save Polyeucte, but Pauline's father, Felix, the Roman governor of the province, orders the execution of his son-in-law. Polyeucte's martyrdom subsequently provokes the conversions to Christianity of both Pauline and the repentant Felix.

Polyhymnia   In classical mythology, the MUSE of sacred poetry and hymns. Polyhymnia is most frequently pictured seated, in a thoughtful mood.

Polymestor   See HECUBA.

Polynices   In Greek legend, a son of Oedipus and Jocasta. See SEVEN AGAINST THEBES, THE.

Polyphemus   The best known of the CYCLOPS of Greek mythology. A cyclops had a single eye in the middle of his forehead. ODYSSEUS, landing in Sicily with his crew during their wanderings described in Homer's ODYSSEY, comes to Polyphemus' cave. The monster imprisons them by pushing a stone against the entrance and dines on six of them. They manage to blind him and escape holding onto the undersides of Polyphemus' sheep. However, Polyphemus prays to his father, POSEIDON, and the god's enmity is the main cause of Odysseus' long wanderings. This story is humorously told in EURIPIDES' satyr play *Cyclops*.

According to OVID, this same Polyphemus was in love with the nymph Galatea, who, however, preferred the handsome ACIS. Polyphemus crushed him under a rock, from which thereafter flowed the river Acis, near Mount Aetna.

polyphonic prose   A type of FREE VERSE resembling prose in its thought sequence and published as a prose passage. Its use is outstanding in the poetry of Amy LOWELL.

Pomona   In Roman mythology, the goddess of fruit trees. Pomona was wooed and won by Vertumnus, god of the seasons.

Pompadour, Jeanne Antoinette Poisson, Marquise de (1721–1764)   Mistress of Louis XV. She was established at Versailles (1745) and given the estate of Pompadour. She had great influence over the king, especially in internal affairs. Opposed to RICHELIEU's foreign policy, she was instrumental in bringing on the Seven Years' War, which ended in disaster for France. She protected writers on the ENCYCLOPÉDIE and spent enormous sums to pay artists to decorate her residences.

Pompey the Great (full Latin name Gnaeus Pompeius Magnus, 106–48 BC)   Roman general and statesman. Pompey organized the First TRIUMVIRATE with Julius Caesar and Crassus in 60 BC. He became a champion of the Senatorial Party. When Caesar crossed the RUBICON, Pompey and his followers fled to northern Greece; Caesar pressed them, and they were decisively defeated at Pharsalus (48). Pompey then fled to Egypt, where Ptolemy had him murdered. The earliest English tragedy based on the story of Pompey is *Pompey the Great, his faire Cornelia's Tragedy* (1595), a translation into blank verse by Thomas Kyd from the French of Garnier.

Ponce de León, Juan (c1460–1521)   Spanish explorer. Ponce de León may have sailed to America on the second voyage of Christopher Columbus. In 1508 he conquered the island of Puerto Rico and subsequently became its governor. Seeking a legendary fountain of youth, supposedly located in a land called Bimini, he sighted the North American mainland on Easter Sunday, 1513, and upon landing called the region Florida, probably for *Pascua florida* ("flowery Easter"). After exploring much of the Florida coast, he returned to Puerto Rico. During a second expedition to Florida, he was wounded in a skirmish with the Indians and was taken to Cuba, where he died.

Pons Asinorum (Lat, "the asses' bridge")   The fifth proposition, Bk. I, of EUCLID. The first difficult theorem, which dunces rarely get over without stumbling.

Pontano, Giovanni (also known as Jovianus Pontanus, 1426?–1503)   Italian humanist and poet. Born in Umbria, Pontano moved to Naples in 1447 to begin his career as author and public figure. He was a founder and leading light of the Neapolitan academy, and many of its members appear as interlocutors in his dialogues. Of his Latin prose and verse, the group of poems entitled *De amore coniugali* (*On Married Life*) is outstanding. His eclogues, sensual lyrics, and didactic poems were widely admired and imitated, notably in England by George Chapman. He is considered an outstanding humanist and the author of some of the most natural Latin writing of the Renaissance.

Pontoppidan, Henrik (1857–1943)   Danish novelist. Pontoppidan is most famous for three novel series, *Det forjœttede Land* (3 vols, 1891–95; tr *Emanuel, or Children of the Soil*, 1892, and *The Promised Land*, 1896); *Lykke-Per* (8 vols, 1898–1904); and *Dœes Rige* (5 vols, 1912–16). In his books he paints a somber, pessimistic portrait of Denmark and the Danish people. With Karl GJELLERUP he received the NOBEL PRIZE in Literature in 1917.

Pooh   The toy bear of A. A. MILNE's classic children's stories *Winnie-the-Pooh* (1926) and *The House at Pooh Corner* (1928). The kindly, lovable Pooh is one of an imaginative cast of animal characters which includes Eeyore, the wistfully gloomy donkey, Tigger, Piglet, Kanga, and Roo, all living in a fantasy world presided over by Milne's young son, CHRISTOPHER ROBIN. Many of the animals are drawn from figures in Milne's life, though each emerges as a universally recognizable type. The *Pooh* books have sold millions of copies in over eighteen languages.

Poor Clares   Nuns of the order founded by St. Clare of Assisi (1194–1253). It is the equivalent for women of the Friars Minor (Franciscans).

Poor Folk (Bednye lyudi, 1846)   A short novel by DOSTOYEVSKY. The author's first published fictional work, written in the form of an epistolary novel, it tells of the hopeless love of Makar Alekseyevich Devushkin, a poor, timid clerk, for Varvara Alekseyevna Dobroselova, a poor young woman who lives in the building across the way

from him. Despite Devushkin's frantic efforts to save Varvara, interspersed with the clerk's despairing bouts of drunkenness, Varvara is married to a wealthy landowner who carries her away. The work is remarkable for the vivid characterization, especially of Devushkin, solely by means of his letters to Varvara and her answers to him.

Poor Richard's Almanack   Composite name given to the ALMANACS issued from 1732 to 1757 by Benjamin FRANKLIN under the pen name of Richard Saunders. From 1732 to 1747 their title was *Poor Richard*; the later numbers were called *Poor Richard Improved*. To *Poor Richard* are attributed most of Franklin's famous adages:

Make haste slowly.

God helps them that help themselves.

Early to bed and early to rise,
Makes a man healthy, wealthy, and wise.

Poor Robin   A series of almanacs published in England from 1662 to 1828. The poet Robert HERRICK is said to have assisted with the first numbers.

pop art   An international movement in art, beginning in America in the late 1950s. In an attempt to minimize the distance between everyday life and art, and in reaction to the nonrepresentational forces of ABSTRACT EXPRESSIONISM, such artists as Jasper JOHNS and Robert RAUSCHENBERG began by attaching real objects to their paintings or by painting the objects themselves. Based in commercial art, the pop artists dealt with the banal, often vulgar, products of mass production. Such artists as Andy WARHOL created visual clichés by repeated use of ordinary objects such as soup cans; Roy LICHTENSTEIN represented his views of American popular culture in giant, simulated comic strips; Claes Oldenburg (1929–   ) produced "soft" versions of mechanical devices, like typewriters and toilets, in plaster, paint, and plastics. Although styles and techniques vary, the personal stamp of the artist is almost always either consciously eliminated or secondary to the object portrayed, in an attempt to force the spectator to explore other levels of reality beyond the familiar facade of commercial products.

pope   The title of the spiritual ruler of the world's Roman Catholics. His other titles include bishop of Rome, Vicar of Christ, Supreme Pontiff of the Universal Church, Patriarch of the West, primate of Italy, archbishop and metropolitan of the Roman Province, and sovereign of the State of Vatican City.

The title "pope" came into use in the 4th century; until that time the usual title was bishop of Rome. According to tradition, St. PETER went from Antioch to Rome c AD 41 and was martyred there c67. The papal see has since remained at Rome, except that in 1309 King Philip of France persuaded Clement V (who had been elected by a college of cardinals dominated by the French) to move to

Avignon; the "Babylonian captivity" of the popes, as the era is called, lasted until 1377. For centuries, the popes were powerful temporal rulers. The Papal States, which grew out of a nucleus of land grants in the 4th century and eventually spread over vast areas of Italy, were finally absorbed in 1870 by Victor Emmanuel II. The Lateran Treaty of 1929, however, granted the popes full sovereignty over Vatican City, an enclave in the heart of Rome.

According to the theory of Petrine succession, the popes are the rulers of all Christendom, by virtue of their succession to the see of St. Peter, the vicar (vicegerent) of Jesus. This claim has always been rejected by the Protestant churches, and was the principal reason for the disunion (schism) of the Church of Rome and the churches of the Eastern (Orthodox) rite, which became definite in 1054, when Pope Leo IX condemned the patriarch of Constantinople.

Popes are elected at an assembly of the college of cardinals known as the conclave. Balloting ends when one name has received two thirds plus one of the votes cast. In theory any Catholic, even a layman, is eligible for election; in practice the cardinals have always selected one of their own number, and he has most often been an Italian, though John Paul II, elected 1978, being Polish, is a notable exception. The last previous non-Italian pope was Adrian VI of Utrecht, elected in 1522; the sole English pope was Adrian IV (Nicholas Breakspear), elected in 1154.

Pope, Alexander (1688–1744)   English poet and satirist, literary dictator of his age and regarded as the epitome of English neoclassicism. Pope was born a Roman Catholic at a time when England was violently anti-Catholic and was educated largely at home; a severe illness in boyhood caused permanent damage to his health and disfigurement of his body. Pope's metrical skill was apparent very early in his *Pastorals* (1709), which he said he wrote when he was sixteen. Known for its skillful use of the heroic, or closed, couplet, his poetry is characterized by technical finish, invective, and wit; it is satiric, epigrammatic, and didactic. Pope's best-known works include AN ESSAY ON CRITICISM, which made him famous at the age of twenty-three; THE RAPE OF THE LOCK; "Messiah," a Vergilian paraphrase of the Book of Isaiah, first published in *The Spectator* in 1712; *Windsor Forest* (1713), in praise of the Tory peace of Utrecht; "An Elegy to the Memory of an Unfortunate Lady" and "Epistle from Eloisa to Abelard" (1717), two passionate though rhetorical poems; translations of the *Iliad* (1715–20) and the *Odyssey* (1725–26); an edition of Shakespeare (1725); THE DUNCIAD; *Moral Essays* (1731–35); AN ESSAY ON MAN; and EPISTLE TO DR. ARBUTHNOT. The first complete edition of Pope's works was that published by William Warburton, his literary executor, in 1751. In his *Essay on the Writings and Genius of Pope* (1756), Joseph Warton argued that Pope's claim to poetic greatness was limited by his cultivation of didacticism and

wit, rather than sublimity and pathos, but that "in the species of Poetry wherein Pope excelled, he is superior to all mankind." Pope was wont to attack his contemporaries, often spitefully, as, for example, his attack on Joseph ADDISON in *Epistle to Dr. Arbuthnot*; because of this he was called the Wicked Wasp of Twickenham, from the name of the villa in which he lived. He was a Tory in politics, a friend of John GAY and Jonathan SWIFT, and a member of the SCRIBLERUS CLUB.

Pope Joan   A mythical female pope, fabled in the Middle Ages to have succeeded Leo IV in 855. The legend first appeared in *The Seven Gifts of the Holy Spirit* by a French Dominican, Stephen de Bourbon (fl mid-13th century), at a time when there was much opposition to the extravagance of the papacy. The legend tells of a girl of English or German origin, named Joan, who went to Rome disguised as a man to be with her lover, the monk Folda. Her extraordinary learning led to her ordination as a priest. In rapid succession, she was raised to the College of Cardinals and then elected pope under the name of John. She was exposed when, during a ceremonial procession, she went into labor and delivered a child before the astonished eyes of the people.

Popeye   A character in William Faulkner's SANCTUARY. An embodiment of pure evil, Popeye is a reptilian and perverted gangster and murderer who rapes Temple DRAKE and kills the half-wit Tommy. Popeye is finally hanged in Alabama for a murder he did not commit, having been busy, at the time of the supposed crime, murdering a man in Memphis. As repulsive as this degenerate representative of urban culture is, he, too, is in part the victim of his environment.

Poppaea   The mistress and later the wife of the Roman emperor NERO. Poppaea is a character in SENECA's Latin tragedy *Octavia*, appears in SIENKIEWICZ's historical novel *Quo Vadis?* (1896), and is the heroine of MONTEVERDI's opera *L'incoronazione di Poppea* (1642).

Popper, Karl R[aimund] (1902–   )   Austrian-born British philosopher. Born in Vienna, Popper spent the years between 1937 and 1945 in New Zealand and in 1945 immigrated to England, where he became professor of logic and scientific method at the London School of Economics. At the age of seventeen, he formulated (and eventually answered) a major question in the philosophy of science: how do we distinguish between science (such as astronomy) and pseudoscience (such as astrology)? Although he was influenced by the logical positivists of the Vienna School (see LOGICAL POSITIVISM), Popper's philosophical positions differ from theirs. For Popper, truth can be uncovered and established as truth only after it has been subjected to logical refutation. Among his best-known works are *Logik der Forschung* (1935; tr *The Logic of Scientific Discovery*, 1959), *The Open Society and Its Enemies* (1945), *The Poverty of Historicism* (1957), *Conjectures and Refutations: The Growth of Scientific Knowledge* (1962),

Objective Knowledge: An Evolutionary Approach (1972), and *The Self and Its Brain* (1977; with J. C. Eccles). His autobiography, *Unended Quest*, appeared in 1976. He was knighted in 1965.

Poppins, Mary   See Travers, P. L.

Popular Front   A term of the later years of the 1930s, during the Spanish Civil War (1936–39) and again after the beginning of World War II (1939–45). It signified an alliance between the capitalist democracies (especially the U.S. and Great Britain) and the U.S.S.R. against Nazi Germany, Fascist Italy, and, later, Japan. The Popular Front became a reality only after the German invasion of the U.S.S.R. in June 1941. The term is also applied to coalitions of certain progressive parties in Spain and France during the late 1930s.

Populisme   A French literary movement. It advocated a literature written for and about the common working man. Essentially a revolt against mannered, aristocratic literature, *Populisme* defined its aims in two manifestos, of August 1929 and January 1930. Naturalistic in their minutely descriptive method and in their humble subject matter, the chief writers of the school were Eugène Dabit (1898–1936), Léon Lemonnier (1892–1953), André Thérive (1891–1967), and Louis Guilloux (1899–1980). The novels that best embodied the goals of *Populisme* were Dabit's *Hôtel du Nord* (1929), *Femme sans péché* (1931) by Lemonnier, *Sans âme* (1928) and *Le Charbon ardent* (1929) by Thérive, and Guilloux's *Le Pain des rêves*. An annual *Prix populiste* is still awarded.

Populist Party (or People's Party)   In U.S. history, a political party established in 1892 in Omaha, Nebraska, by farmers and laborers, primarily from the West, who were dissatisfied with Eastern financial and commercial policies. The Populists nominated James B. Weaver of Iowa as their presidential candidate and adopted a platform calling for the free and unlimited coinage of silver and gold at the ratio of sixteen to one; government ownership of transportation and communications facilities; direct election of U.S. senators; and a graduated income tax. Their aim was "to restore the government of the Republic to the hands of the 'plain people,' with which class it originated." Weaver received over one million votes in the election of 1892. In 1896 the Populists endorsed the candidacy of William Jennings Bryan, the Democratic nominee, and subsequently disappeared as a national political party.

Porch, The   Another name for the Stoic school of Greek philosophy. See Stoicism.

Porgy (1925)   A novel by DuBose Heyward. Set in Charleston, South Carolina, it deals with blacks along Catfish Row. Central to the story is Porgy, a crippled beggar who becomes involved in a murder. Other characters include Bess, Sportin' Life, Crown, and Serena. With his wife, Dorothy, Heyward adapted the novel as a play (1927). The play in turn became the basis of George Gershwin's *Porgy and Bess* (1935), a folk opera which has become an American classic.

Porgy, Captain   A comic character created by William Gilmore Simms. He appears in Simms's trilogy about the American Revolution—*The Partisan* (1835), *Mellichampe* (1836), and *Katharine Walton* (1851)—and in *The Forayers* (1855) and Woodcraft. Porgy combines a Falstaffian paunch and love for food and drink with the more typical Southern virtues of bravery, gallantry, and generosity. He is bawdy, humorous, inventive, and a tireless practical joker. Many critics felt Simms was at his best when describing the exploits of Porgy, although others, notably Poe, found Porgy "an unsufferable bore."

Porphyry (233–c301)   Greek Neoplatonist, the student and biographer of Plotinus. Porphyry is the source for all our information about his teacher. He arranged Plotinus' treatises into six groups of nine treatises (*Enneads*), and seems to have faithfully respected the text. He also wrote a life of Pythagoras and an introduction to Aristotle's *Organon*.

Porsena, Lars   In the 6th century BC, king of Clusium in Etruria. Porsena led an expedition against Rome, but was stopped from entering the city by the bravery of Horatius Cocles. After laying siege to Rome, he finally made peace on condition that the Romans give up some captured land and supply hostages.

This is the Roman legend. Scholars feel that it is an attempt to cover up a greater tragedy inflicted on Rome by the Etruscans as they, the Etruscans, moved southward before the invading Celts, passing through Rome as they fled.

Porte étroite, La   See Strait Is the Gate.

Porter, Cole (1893–1964)   American composer and lyricist. One of the most sophisticated of popular composers, Porter wrote bewitching melodies and intricately crafted, witty lyrics which combined to make most of his musicals box office and critical successes. The long list of these includes *Anything Goes* (1934), *Born to Dance* (1936), *Kiss Me Kate* (1948), and *High Society* (1956). Unlike other great American composer-lyricists, Porter did not get his start in Tin Pan Alley. He was a wealthy midwesterner, with degrees from Yale and Harvard Law School, who circulated with the artists and intellectuals living in the U.S. and Europe after World War I.

Porter, Edwin Stratton (1870–1941)   American film pioneer; inventor of the art of motion picture editing. Porter was probably the first filmmaker to shoot a movie at night (*Panorama of Esplanade by Night*, 1901), but his lasting contributions to film are more evident in *The Life of an American Fireman* (1902) and *The Great Train Robbery* (1903). In making the former picture, he discovered that, through editing, authentic stock footage could be combined with synthetic, or staged-action, footage to create a continuous and seemingly homogeneous narrative. *The Great Train Robbery*, sometimes acclaimed as the first

Western, demonstrated for the first time the dramatic effectiveness of a moving camera and of various angle shots; it also established the shot as the basic unit of film editing. This film and *The Kleptomaniac* (1905), in which Porter experimented with parallel action editing, exerted immense influence on the development of D. W. GRIFFITH.

Porter, Eleanor H.   See POLLYANNA.

Porter, Gene[va] Stratton (1863–1924)   American novelist. Porter is noted for the enormous popularity of her sentimental romances, set in the great Limberlost Swamp of Indiana, notably *Freckles* (1904) and *A Girl of the Limberlost* (1909).

Porter, Hal [Harold] (1911–1984)   Australian short-story writer, novelist, dramatist, and poet. Porter was among Australia's most outstanding and versatile writers. A skillful stylist, fascinated with the eccentricities of everyday life, Porter wrote an enormous number of stories, the best of which are collected in *A Bachelor's Children* (1962), *The Cats of Venice* (1965), and *Selected Stories* (1971). His autobiographical works—*The Watcher on the Cast-Iron Balcony* (1963), *The Paper Chase* (1966), *Criss-Cross* (1973), and *The Extra* (1975)—offer lively, detailed insights into Australian life.

Porter, Jimmy   See LOOK BACK IN ANGER.

Porter, Katherine Anne (1890–1980)   American short-story writer and novelist. Although she published relatively little, Porter firmly established herself among the top ranks of American short-story writers. Her work is noted for its stylistic elegance and technical accomplishment; it is rich in psychological insight and heavily weighted with symbolic elements. Two of her best-known collections of stories are *Flowering Judas* (1930), which established her reputation, and *The Leaning Tower* (1944). PALE HORSE, PALE RIDER contains three short novels: the title story, NOON WINE, and OLD MORTALITY. Porter's one long novel, SHIP OF FOOLS, the product of twenty years' work, was hailed as a major achievement of allegorical writing. Her *Collected Stories* (1965) received both a PULITZER PRIZE and a National Book Award. An augmented version of her *Collected Essays and Occasional Writings* (1970) offers an interesting self-portrait and explains her concept of the function of a writer.

Porter, William Sydney   See HENRY, O.

Porthos   One of the famous trio of Dumas's THE THREE MUSKETEERS, and a prominent character in its sequels *Twenty Years After* (1845) and *The Viscount of Bragelonne* (1848–50). In physical stature the good-hearted Porthos is a giant; intellectually he is somewhat less impressive.

Portia   The clever and wise young heroine of Shakespeare's MERCHANT OF VENICE. Disguised as Balthazar, a young lawyer, Portia defends Antonio against SHYLOCK's demand for a pound of his flesh. At first she tries to soften Shylock by pleading for mercy:

> The quality of mercy is not strain'd,
> It droppeth as the gentle rain from heaven
> Upon the place beneath: it is twice bless'd;
> It blesseth him that gives and him that takes.

Although this appeal fails to move Shylock, she manages to outwit him and win the case for Antonio. See BASSANIO.

portmanteau word   A completely new word combining parts of two or more words. The word thus created expresses a combination of the meanings of its parts, as in the now common word *brunch*, created by combining the "br" of *breakfast* with the "unch" of *lunch*. Lewis Carroll introduced portmanteau words in THROUGH THE LOOKING GLASS; he says *slithy* means *lithe* and *slimy*, *mimsy* is *flimsy* and *miserable*, etc. Carroll called these portmanteau words because in them two meanings were "packed up" in one bag, as it were. Modern writers have made liberal use of such words, notably James Joyce in his FINNEGANS WAKE.

Portrait of a Lady (1917)   A poem by T. S. ELIOT. It is about the lack of communication between a woman and a man who are trapped by the conventions of a dying social order. Both are conscious of their isolation, yet are equally unable to escape it. The lady of the poem is driven by her loneliness to reach out to the man but realizes that she has nothing left to give. Her life, she knows, is an empty shell determined by empty forms and devitalized by social rituals. He, evading her demands, seeks solace in humdrum habits and conventions.

Portrait of a Lady, The (1881)   A novel by Henry JAMES. The motives that lead Isabel ARCHER, a romantic and independent American woman who inherits an English fortune, to refuse other suitors and marry Gilbert Osmond are skillfully analyzed, and her subsequent disillusionment is traced in devastating detail. Osmond is an impoverished dilettante of exquisite tastes, living in retirement in Italy with his daughter, Pansy. After Isabel's marriage she discovers that she has only served the purposes of her quasi-friend, Madame Merle, who, as Osmond's mistress and the mother of Pansy, brought the two together for the sake of Isabel's fortune. Osmond's fine sensibilities are likewise seen to be but the expression of an intensely egocentric nature. The novel has been considered one of James's finest works.

Portrait of the Artist as a Young Man, A (1916)   A largely autobiographical novel by James JOYCE. It portrays the childhood, school days, adolescence, and early manhood of Stephen Dedalus, later one of the leading characters in ULYSSES. Stephen's growing self-awareness as an artist forces him to reject the whole narrow world in which he has been brought up, including family ties, nationalism, and the Catholic religion. The novel ends when, having decided to become a writer, he is about to leave Dublin for Paris. Rather than following a clear narrative progression, the book revolves around experiences that are crucial to Stephen's development as an artist; at the end of each chapter Stephen makes some assertion of identity. Through his use of the STREAM OF CONSCIOUSNESS technique, Joyce reveals the actual materials of his hero's world, the components of his thought processes. *Stephen Hero*, the first version of the book, was written about 1904 and published in 1944. It is longer and more conventional in form.

Port-Royal   A French Cistercian convent near Versailles, which in the 17th century became the center of JANSENISM. Its teachings greatly influenced both religion and literature, and Jesuit rivals induced Pope Innocent X to condemn certain Jansenist doctrines. In 1660 Louis XIV suppressed the community. Springing again into prominence, Port-Royal was razed in 1710 and permanently condemned three years later in the papal bull *Unigenitus* of Clement XI.

Poseidon   The chief sea god of the ancient Greeks. According to the usual story, he was the son of CRONOS and brother of ZEUS, HADES, and other gods. When dominion over the universe was divided among these three gods, Poseidon was given the sea. He was also a god of horses, and may even have had a horse shape originally, and of earthquakes. He was married to Amphitrite. Inclined to be ill-tempered, it was Poseidon whose anger at ODYSSEUS for blinding his son POLYPHEMUS so long prevented that hero's return to Ithaca, in the ODYSSEY. It was enmity against PRIAM's father, LAOMEDON, who had refused to pay Poseidon and APOLLO for building the walls of Troy, that made the god side with the Greeks in the TROJAN WAR. In a contest with ATHENE for the patronship of Athens, Poseidon lost when the goddess's gift of the olive tree was judged a more valuable boon than Poseidon's horse.

positive hero (Russ, *polozhitel'nii geroi*)   A type of protagonist designed by Soviet literary critics in accordance with the tenets of SOCIALIST REALISM. As opposed to the 19th-century SUPERFLUOUS MAN, who was alienated from society, the positive hero was to be an active participant in the advancement of Communist ideals: a healthy and productive individual who welcomed personal sacrifice as a means of building a truly socialist society. The creation of such heroes stemmed from the Soviet perception that it is the writer's duty to put his art at the service of the movement toward communism.

Positivism   A philosophical movement of the 19th century. It was developed under the influence of the new discoveries in the science of the period, particularly outstanding in the thought of Auguste COMTE, regarded as its founder. Its chief principles call for: a study of the various sciences and an arrangement of them in a "scale of subordination," with those of greater complexity placed near the top of an ascending series; the assignment of sociology, with its study of past history and contemporary society and its attempts to solve persistent social problems, to a position at the summit of hierarchy; and a belief in the progress of mankind toward a superior state of civilization by means of

the science of sociology itself. In the later years of his career, Comte, turning toward mysticism, attempted to convert sociology into a literal Religion of Humanity, with a set creed, rituals, and ceremonies for private and public use, the worship of great men and women of the past, saints' days, etc. As a church, Positivism lasted in France into the 20th century, although this development of his philosophy alienated a number of early admirers from the side of Comte. J. S. MILL and George Henry Lewes (1817–78) were among the leading disciples of early Positivism in England. George ELIOT's poem "The Choir Invisible" (1867) expresses its aspiration. Herbert Croly, first editor of the *New Republic*, was the first American child to be christened in the faith.

Possessed, The (Besy, 1871–1872)   A novel by DOSTOYEVSKY, also known in translation as *The Devils* and *The Demons*. It has two plot lines, one depicting the revolutionary movement in Russia and the other tracing the strange career of Nikolay STAVROGIN, the enigmatic central character of the novel. Stavrogin is a brilliant, attractive, but emotionally sterile young nobleman, afflicted with a genuine spiritual nihilism as contrasted to the affected nihilism of the revolutionaries portrayed in the book. Stavrogin indulges in crime and debauchery, infects SHATOV and KIRILOV with ideas in which he himself does not believe, and accepts the love of Lizaveta Nikolayevna Tushina without being able to return it. On a whim he marries the cripple Marya Timofeyevna LEBYADKIN. The leader of the small revolutionary group, Pyotr VERKHOVENSKY, whose character was modeled on that of Sergey NECHAYEV, tries to persuade Stavrogin to join the conspiracy, knowing what an attraction Stavrogin would be as a figurehead. Verkhovensky manages to have Shatov, who has belonged to the revolutionary group and is attempting to break with it, murdered. This incident was based on one of Nechayev's notorious exploits. See SHIGALYOV.

The ending of the novel is bloody, with Marya Timofeyevna and her brother being murdered and their home burned, ostensibly by the terrorists. Lizaveta is the victim of mob vengeance, and both Kirilov and Stavrogin commit suicide.

Dostoyevsky intended the novel to show how a lack of organic ties with the Russian people and adherence to Western political ideas wreak havoc with the Russian upper classes, represented by Stavrogin and the hapless revolutionaries. This aim was in part realized—that is, with Stavrogin but not with the revolutionary group, which is a caricature, not a portrayal, of the reality in Russia at the time. Dostoyevsky's own hope for the salvation of his country is expressed by Shatov. The aristocracy must return to the Orthodox faith, which the people have never abandoned, and must lead the people in attaining the high destiny assigned to Russia: saving the world by revealing to it the "new world" of universal love and brotherhood contained in Orthodoxy.

Although he satirized the nihilists, Dostoyevsky also feared their effect and took them seriously. The epigraph to the novel, from which the title comes, refers to the demons cast out by Jesus into the Gadarene swine. The nihilists in this case are regarded as the swine into which the demons haunting Russian society are cast.

postimpressionism   A term coined by Roger FRY to denote the work of a number of artists who sought independent self-expression and a pictorial reality distinct from the concentration on light effects that characterized IMPRESSIONISM. These artists, including CÉZANNE, VAN GOGH, and GAUGUIN, did not subscribe to any one theory but, as a group, are considered the forerunners of LES FAUVES and CUBISM. The term has a different application than that of Seurat's NEOIMPRESSIONISM.

Postman Always Rings Twice, The   See CAIN, JAMES M.

Potemkin, Grigory Aleksandrovich (1739–1791)   A Russian field marshal and favorite of Empress Catherine of Russia, influential in her councils.

Potiphar's wife   In the OLD TESTAMENT and the KORAN, the wife of Joseph's master in Egypt. JOSEPH fled from her advances, leaving his robe behind him, whereupon she accused him of evil and had him cast into prison (Gen. 34). Some Arabian commentators have called her Rahil, others Zuleika. The theme of this story is familiar in the myth and folklore of many lands, notably in the myth of PHAEDRA.

Pot of Earth, The (1925)   A long poem by Archibald MACLEISH. It is based on the description of an ancient fertility rite in Sir James Frazer's THE GOLDEN BOUGH. Several themes are woven into the story, including that of the sexual maturation, marriage, and death in childbirth of a 20th-century woman.

Potok, Chaim (1929–   )   American novelist. Potok is an ordained rabbi whose popular novels deal with the incompatibility of religious and artistic life, particularly in the American-Jewish context. His books include *The Chosen* (1967), *The Promise* (1969), *My Name Is Asher Lev* (1972), *In the Beginning* (1975), *The Book of Lights* (1981), and the nonfiction *Wanderings* (1978), a highly personal history of the Jews.

Potter, Beatrix (1866–1943)   English writer and illustrator of stories for children. As a young woman she was kept a virtual recluse by her father. She eventually bought a farm in Sawrey, in the Lake District, where she lived with her husband, William Heelis. Her subjects were the rabbits, ducks, squirrels, hedgehogs, and cats that she observed in and around her home. The stories were enhanced by her own drawings and watercolors, which were said to have the emotional feeling of CONSTABLE's landscapes. Among her many books, twenty-three in all, are *The Tale of Peter Rabbit* (printed privately 1900; pub 1902), *The Tale of Benjamin Bunny* (1904), *The Tale of Tom Kitten* (1907), *The Roly-Poly Pudding* (1908), and

Jemima Puddleduck (1910). Her *Journals 1881–1897* were published in 1966.

Poulenc, Francis [Jean Marcel] (1899–1963) French composer. The youngest member of LES SIX, Poulenc is known mainly for his songs, choral works, and operas. The songs include settings of texts by APOLLINAIRE and ÉLUARD; the operas are based on plays by COCTEAU (*Le Voix humaine*, 1959), BERNANOS (*Les Dialogues des Carmélites*, 1957) and Apollinaire (*Les Mamelles de Tirésias*, 1947); and the choral works include a *Mass in G* (1937), *Stabat Mater* (1951), and *Gloria* (1959). Poulenc's music is personal and basically melodic. His first major success was *Les Biches* (1924), written for DIAGHILEV's Russian ballet company.

Pound, Ezra [Loomis] (1885–1972)   American poet, editor, and critic. One of the most influential and controversial figures in modern literature, Pound was born in Hailey, Idaho, of New England stock. After graduate work at the University of Pennsylvania, where he met William Carlos WILLIAMS and Hilda DOOLITTLE, Pound went to live in Europe: first in England (via Italy), then in France, and finally in Italy again. His first book, a small collection of poems entitled *A Lume Spento* (1908), was published in Venice. In England he was the guiding spirit and chief promoter of IMAGISM, a poetic movement that stressed the direct treatment of the object without unnecessary rhetoric, the free phrase rather than the forced metric, and utter clarity of image and metaphor. During his years in England (1908–20), Pound edited the first anthology of imagist poetry, *Des Imagistes* (1914), founded and edited the vorticist magazine BLAST, served as foreign editor of POETRY, and as London editor (1917–19) of THE LITTLE REVIEW. His importance in the development of modern poetry can scarcely be overstated. Through his extensive involvement with LITTLE MAGAZINES, he found publishers for the early works of T. S. ELIOT, Wyndham LEWIS, James JOYCE, William Carlos Williams, Ernest HEMINGWAY, Marianne Moore, and many other distinguished, but then unknown, writers.

His own poetry during this period was published in *Exultations* (1909), PERSONAE, *Provença* (1910), *Canzoni* (1911), *Ripostes* (1912), and LUSTRA. While in England he became deeply interested in Oriental literature, publishing in *Cathay* (1915) his adaptations of the translations by Ernest Fenollosa (1853–1908) of the great Chinese poet LI PO. He also published a work on Japanese classical drama, *Noh; or, Accomplishment* (1916). In 1917 "Homage to Sextus Propertius" appeared. This was his first major poetic work, a broad adaptation of the Latin poet, in which he specifically disparaged the trend toward politically conscious poetry that began to appear as Europe entered World War I. Pound was, however, increasingly distressed by the inherent failures of Western democracies. In 1920 he decided to move to France. HUGH SELWYN MAUBERLEY marked Pound's farewell to England and to a period in his own life. Thereafter his poetry became progressively "engaged." In *Mauberley*, he expressed his hatred of war, his dissatisfaction with the commercialism he felt was smothering the arts, and his growing concern with economic questions. These themes pervade the CANTOS, Pound's unfinished epic work, which he began as early as 1913—publishing the first sections in 1925—and continued to write throughout his life.

While in Paris, Pound remained an influential associate of many important writers, particularly of Gertrude STEIN and Ernest Hemingway. In 1924 he moved to Italy, intent on devoting himself to his *Cantos*. As his concern with economic problems increased throughout the 1920s and 1930s, he developed views, stemming in part from social credit theories, which eventually propelled him into an obsessive anti-Semitism, and an unquestioning acceptance of HITLER, MUSSOLINI, and Fascism. During World War II he made over three hundred broadcasts of Fascist propaganda to the U.S. from Rome, an act that led to his arrest in May 1945 by American forces and his temporary confinement at Pisa (see THE PISAN CANTOS). At his treason trial in the U.S. he was judged insane and was committed to St. Elizabeths Hospital in Washington, D.C. He remained there from 1946 to 1958, when his release was secured (thanks largely to the persistent intercession of major literary figures), and he was allowed to return to Italy.

Pound's essays and works of criticism are almost as important as his poetic output. He was a voluminous contributor to magazines and published numerous works of prose, often intensely polemical, including *The Spirit of Romance* (1910; rev 1952); *Pavannes and Divisions* (1918); *Instigations* (1920); *Indiscretions* (1923); *Antheil and the Treatise on Harmony* (1924); *How to Read* (1931); *ABC of Reading* (1934); *Polite Essays* (1937); *Guide to Kulchur* (1938; rev 1952); *Literary Essays of Ezra Pound* (1954; with an introduction by T. S. Eliot); and *Selected Prose 1909–1965* (1973). His letters to James Joyce were published in 1967.

Although Pound's erudition was often attacked—as needlessly obscure from the layman's point of view, as seriously flawed from the scholar's—there is no question that he was instrumental in promoting a renewed general interest in the poetry of the places and periods with which he was concerned. His translations from the Greek, Chinese, Egyptian, Provençal, Anglo-Saxon, and other languages appeared in *The Translations* (1954; rev 1963). Pound was also instrumental in helping to create a poetic revolution in the first decades of the 20th century. His importance was in his total effect as a literary critic, essayist, promoter, editor, and adviser, as well as creator, practicing craftsman, and articulate innovator.

Poussin, Nicolas (1594–1665)   French painter. The great master of the classical school, Poussin worked chiefly at the studio he established in Rome. In his rational, clearly composed paintings of mythological, historical, and religious scenes, he imitated the measured gestures of antique sculpture and the clean draftsmanship and effortless order of RAPHAEL. His work, which exerted an enormous influence on the course of art, embodies the ideal of the classical school, but his principles were later turned into sterile academism by his imitators.

Powell, Anthony [Dymoke] (1905–   )   English novelist. Beginning with *Afternoon Men* (1931), *Venusberg* (1932), *Agents and Patients* (1936), and *What's Become of Waring?* (1939), Powell wrote comedies of manners and mild social satires directed against the worlds of fashion, the arts, and the upper classes. Powell's masterwork is a series of twelve novels written over a period of more than twenty-five years, collectively titled A DANCE TO THE MUSIC OF TIME, a massive, detailed chronicle beginning at the end of World War I and proceeding to the late 1960s. Powell's four volumes of memoirs, *Infants of the Spring* (1977), *Messengers of the Day* (1978), *Faces in My Time* (1980), and *The Strangers All Are Gone* (1982), were published under the collective title *To Keep the Ball Rolling*. In 1983 O, *How the Wheel Becomes It!* was published.

Power and the Glory, The (1940)   A novel by Graham GREENE, first published in the U.S. as *The Labyrinthine Ways*. Its hero, a drunken, lecherous priest in Mexico, withstands political persecution and dies a Christ-like death.

Power of Darkness, The (Vlast tmy, 1886)   A tragedy by Count Leo TOLSTOY. The epigraph of the play, "when one claw is caught, the whole bird is doomed," refers to Nikita, a young peasant, who perpetrates a series of crimes. He seduces a young girl, Marina; poisons Peter, a wealthy peasant; and marries Peter's wife, Anisya. He then seduces Anisya's stepdaughter, and, when Akulina gives birth to his child, he kills the baby and buries it in the cellar. His conscience finally impels him to make a public confession of his crimes.

One of the outstanding peasant dramas in Russian literature, the play demonstrates that, despite Tolstoy's love for the peasants, he was not blind to their faults. The only character free from the crime and vice so vividly presented is Akim, Nikita's father; he is described as "God-fearing."

Power of Sympathy, The (1789)   A novel generally regarded as the first to be written in the U.S. Long attributed to Sarah Wentworth MORTON because a subplot resembles an incident in her sister's life, it was probably written by William Hill BROWN. In a series of letters, it tells how Harrington, the hero, is prevented from marrying the charming but socially inferior Harriot Fawcett by the discovery that she is his half sister. The shock of the discovery kills Harriot, and Harrington commits suicide. Brown's purpose was to illustrate "the dangerous Consequences of Seduction" and "the Advantages of Female Education."

Powys, J[ohn] C[owper] (1872–1963)   English novelist, essayist, and poet. He was the elder brother of

Theodore Francis POWYS and Llewelyn Powys, both writers; all three brothers had a mystical love for nature. In John Cowper's best-known novel, *Wolf Solent* (1929), the romantic hero retreats from the city to find happiness in the Dorset countryside. Powys was the author of more than forty volumes, including *A Glastonbury Romance* (1932).

Powys, T[heodore] F[rancis] (1875–1953) English novelist and short-story writer, the most original and best remembered of the three Powys brothers (see John Cowper POWYS). Powys, who spent his whole life in the same Dorset village, wrote of village life with realism, grim humor, and a sense of life's tragedy, oddness, and mystery. Among his novels are *The Left Leg* (1923), *Mr. Tasker's Gods* (1925), *Mr. Weston's Good Wine* (1927), *Unclay* (1931), and *The Two Thieves* (1932). *God's Eyes A-Twinkle* (1947) is a collection of short stories.

Ppt In Jonathan Swift's JOURNAL TO STELLA, a cryptic abbreviation and pet name for Stella. It recurs throughout James Joyce's *Finnegans Wake*, where H. C. Earwicker uses it as a pet name for his daughter Isobel. See PRESTO.

Prado The national museum of painting and sculpture in Madrid, Spain. It is next to the famous fashionable promenade of the same name. The word means "meadow."

praetor In ancient Rome, one of eight magistrates whose duty was to administer justice. They correspond roughly to U.S. Supreme Court justices. After his year in office, the praetor often went as propraetor to govern a province. See CURSUS HONORUM.

Praetorian Guard In Roman history, the imperial bodyguard. It was organized by AUGUSTUS on the basis of the older praetorian cohorts, the bodyguards of the praetors. The Praetorian Guard grew more and more powerful, and many emperors were hardly more than its puppets. It survived to the time of Constantine the Great.

pragmatism (fr Gr, *pragma*, "deed") The philosophical doctrine that the only test of the truth of human cognitions or philosophical principles is their practical results. It does not admit "absolute" truth, as all truths change their trueness as their practical utility increases or decreases. The word was introduced in this connection about 1875 by the American logician C. S. PEIRCE and was popularized by William JAMES, whose *Pragmatism: A New Name for Some Old Ways of Thinking* lectures delivered at the Lowell Institute and Columbia University (1906–7) were published in 1907. Aspects of Jamesian pragmatism were also taken up by John DEWEY.

Prairie, The (1827) A novel by James Fenimore COOPER, in THE LEATHERSTOCKING TALES series. The story centers on the death of the aged Natty BUMPPO. Cooper contrasts the noble, disinterested Natty with the squatter Ishmael Bush and his family. Lawless and self-seeking, the squatters portend ill for the future of democracy. Cooper's prairie descriptions, which include an effective buffalo stampede and prairie fire, are derived from the *Journals* of Lewis and Clark.

Pratt, E[dwin] J[ohn] (1883–1964) Canadian poet. A native of coastal Newfoundland, Pratt set much of his poetry on or near the sea. He was highly regarded as one of Canada's foremost writers of narrative verse. Among his best-known epics are *The Roosevelt and the Antinoe* (1930), a dramatic poem about a rescue at sea; *Brébeuf and His Brethren* (1940), about the Jesuit martyrs of North America; and *Towards the Last Spike* (1952), about the building of Canada's first transcontinental railway. Pratt's poetry, written in a lucid, lively style, reflects his belief in the heroic qualities of man. Two volumes of his *Collected Poems* appeared in 1944 and 1958. *Selected Poems* (1968) was published posthumously.

Praxiteles (4th century BC) Athenian sculptor. One of the greatest Greek sculptors, Praxiteles worked in marble and is noted for a relaxed, sensuous style, distinct from the idealized forms of PHIDIAS or the mathematically symmetrical proportions devised by POLYCLEITUS. The hallmark of his statues is the so-called Praxitelian curve, seen in his *Hermes and Dionysus* and often admired and imitated in later sculpture.

Preacher The author of the Old Testament book ECCLESIASTES, once reputed to be Solomon.

Précieuses Ridicules, Les (The Ridiculous Snobs, 1659) A one-act prose comedy by MOLIÈRE. The first of Molière's satires on a foible of contemporary society, it narrates how Madelon and Cathos, daughters of a provincial bourgeois and ardent admirers of the affectations of Parisian society, reject their suitors as insufficiently ornate in speech and dress; they will have no proposals without the garnish and flamboyance described in the novels of Madeleine de SCUDÉRY. The suitors avenge themselves by sending their valets to call on the ladies disguised as a marquis and viscomte. The ladies are ravished by the extravagant behavior of their visitors, whom they take for men of the highest fashion, but when the trickery is revealed they are suitably mortified.

Precious Bane (1925) A novel by Mary Webb (1881–1927). Set in the English county of Shropshire, it is a story of harsh farming life, and fierce, morose country people. Prudence Sarn, the narrator, finds a husband who appreciates her in spite of her harelip. The novel became extremely popular when Stanley Baldwin, then prime minister, wrote an introduction to it in 1928. See also COLD COMFORT FARM. The title is from Milton's PARADISE LOST:

> Let none admire
> That riches grow in Hell; that soil may best
> Deserve the precious bane.

Prelude, The (1850) A long autobiographical poem by William WORDSWORTH. It shows the growth of a poet's mind by tracing his own life from childhood. Completed in 1805, it underwent many revisions before it was published. Wordsworth originally dedicated the poem to his friend Samuel Taylor COLERIDGE.

Premchand (pen name of Dhanpat Rai Srivastav, 1880–1936) Indian short-story writer and novelist in Urdu and Hindi. Premchand originally wrote in Urdu, but in order to reach a wider audience he changed to Hindi, to become the greatest fiction writer of that language. He was an ardent social critic, and his novels sometimes betray a dogmatic idealism. His best writing is in his short stories, over 250 collected in eight volumes. Together they provide a vivid record of life in north India. His last and best novel, *Godān* (1936; tr *The Gift of a Cow*, 1968), is a harrowing tale of the vicissitudes of the Indian peasant.

Prendergast, Maurice [Brazil] (1859–1924) Canadian-born American painter. An original member of the ASHCAN SCHOOL, and exhibitor in the ARMORY SHOW, Prendergast was a pioneer postimpressionist.

Pre-Raphaelite Brotherhood A group of artists and poets formed in London in 1848, originally consisting of Holman HUNT, John Everett MILLAIS, and Dante Gabriel ROSSETTI. Their endorsement of the detailed and idealized depiction of nature in early Italian painting led them to adopt the title of Pre-Raphaelites, and to stress their rejection of academicism, which they traced to RAPHAEL and the High Renaissance. The Brotherhood's publication, *The Germ*, was started in 1850 under the editorship of Rossetti's brother, William Michael, but only four numbers were issued. Its aim was "to enforce and encourage an entire adherence to the simplicity of nature," a principle they applied to the writing of poetry as well as painting.

The artists in the Brotherhood painted scenes of the childhood of Jesus and the Virgin and represented contemporary scenes with a moral message; as a whole, the group had a strongly religious and moralizing cast. The poetry of the Brotherhood—most notably that of Christina ROSSETTI —tended to treat medieval or mystical themes in a sensuous, symbolic narrative verse, rich in pictorial detail. The group broke up in 1854 but enjoyed a brief revival through the support of William MORRIS and Edward BURNE-JONES in 1856 at Oxford.

Presbyterian Pertaining to one of the Churches of Calvinistic origin. In it, as in the early Christian Church, the presbyters, or elders, are the medium through which the members govern the church.

Prescott, William Hickling (1796–1859) American historian. Prescott lost the use of his left eye in his junior year at Harvard, when it was struck with a hard crust of bread thrown by a playful classmate. Shortly after his graduation, his right eye was seriously impaired. Wealthy enough to pay assistants and aided by a device called a noctograph, he was able to devote his life to historical research and composition. Prescott's high standards of scholarship and his ability to write dramatic, exciting narrative are most evident in the *History of the Conquest of Mex-*

ico (1843) and *History of the Conquest of Peru* (1847), the works for which he is best known. He also wrote *History of the Reign of Ferdinand and Isabella* (1838) and *History of the Reign of Philip the Second* (1855–58).

President of the U.S. The chief executive of the U.S. According to the Constitution, he must be a native-born American and must be at least thirty-five years of age. The original document did not impose restrictions on the number of four-year terms a president might serve, but no president had served more than two until Franklin Delano Roosevelt violated the tradition in 1940 by running for and winning a third term; as a result of the ratification (1947) of the 22nd amendment, the president is now limited to two terms. A list of the presidents follows:

George Washington	1789–1797
John Adams	1797–1801
Thomas Jefferson	1801–1809
James Madison	1809–1817
James Monroe	1817–1825
John Quincy Adams	1825–1829
Andrew Jackson	1829–1837
Martin Van Buren	1837–1841
William Henry Harrison	1841
John Tyler	1841–1845
James K. Polk	1845–1849
Zachary Taylor	1849–1850
Millard Fillmore	1850–1853
Franklin Pierce	1853–1857
James Buchanan	1857–1861
Abraham Lincoln	1861–1865
Andrew Johnson	1865–1869
Ulysses S. Grant	1869–1877
Rutherford B. Hayes	1877–1881
James A. Garfield	1881
Chester A. Arthur	1881–1885
Grover Cleveland	1885–1889
Benjamin Harrison	1889–1893
Grover Cleveland	1893–1897
William McKinley	1897–1901
Theodore Roosevelt	1901–1909
William Howard Taft	1909–1913
Woodrow Wilson	1913–1921
Warren G. Harding	1921–1923
Calvin Coolidge	1923–1929
Herbert C. Hoover	1929–1933
Franklin D. Roosevelt	1933–1945
Harry S. Truman	1945–1953
Dwight D. Eisenhower	1953–1961
John F. Kennedy	1961–1963
Lyndon B. Johnson	1963–1969
Richard M. Nixon	1969–1974
Gerald R. Ford	1974–1977
James E. Carter	1977–1981
Ronald Reagan	1981–

Prester John (or John the Presbyter) A legendary Christian king and priest, supposed in medieval times to have reigned in the 12th century over a wonderful country somewhere in the heart of Asia. He appears in Ariosto's

ORLANDO FURIOSO, having furnished materials for a host of medieval legends, including that of the Holy GRAIL.

Presto   The name frequently applied by Jonathan Swift to himself in his JOURNAL TO STELLA.

Pretender   Called the Old Pretender, James Francis Edward Stuart (1688–1766), only son of JAMES II. He played one of the principal roles in the JACOBITE cause. He appears as a character in Thackeray's HENRY ESMOND. See FIFTEEN, THE.

The Young Pretender   Charles Edward Louis Philip Casimir Stuart (1720–88), son of "the Old Pretender" and grandson of James II, sometimes called "the Chevalier" or "Bonnie Prince Charlie." As a result of his unsuccessful attempt to seize the Hanoverian throne (see THE FORTY-FIVE), the hereditary jurisdiction of the Highland chiefs was taken away. He appears as a character in Scott's WAVERLEY and *Redgauntlet* (1824).

Prévert, Jacques (1900–1977)   French poet and screenwriter. Prévert wrote lyrical and accessible poetry that earned him enormous popularity. Many of his verses were written as songs for cabarets such as "Barbara" and "Les Feuilles mortes." At times his lyricism is turned to a mockingly satirical purpose; at others it is tender, wistful, evocative of gentle melancholy. In the poems of *Paroles* (1945) and *Spectacle* (1951), he ridicules the conformity and conventions of his world, while he praises the simple joys of love, of color, and of smell and sound. Prévert wrote screenplays for several of the films of Marcel Carné, among them *Les Enfants du paradis* (1945) and *Les Portes de la nuit* (1946). His poems have been translated in several volumes: *Selections from Paroles* (1958), *To Paint the Portrait of a Bird* (1971), and his collected poems, *Words for All Seasons* (1979).

Prévost d'Exiles, Antoine François (known as Abbé Prévost, 1697–1763)   French novelist and journalist. Prévost vacillated in his youth between a career in the army and one in the church, but, after entering the Benedictine order, his taste for a worldly life won. He feared ecclesiastical reprisals and fled to Holland (1729) and to England (1733) but returned to France in 1734. In order to earn money, he wrote the seven-volume work *Mémoires et aventures d'un homme de qualité* (1728), the last volume of which contains his most famous story, *L'Histoire du Chevalier des Grieux et de* MANON LESCAUT (1731).

Priam   In Greek legend, king of Troy when that city was sacked by the Greeks, husband of HECUBA, and father of fifty children. Among the children were HECTOR, Helenus, PARIS, Deiphobus, Polyxena, TROILUS, CASSANDRA, and POLYDORUS. When Hector was slain, the old king went to the tent of ACHILLES and made a successful plea for the body of his dead son. After the gates of Troy were thrown open by the Greeks concealed in the wooden horse, NEOPTOLEMUS, the son of ACHILLES, slew the aged Priam. See TROJAN WAR.

Priapus   In Greek mythology, the ithyphallic god of reproductive power and fertility (hence of gardens) and protector of shepherds, fishermen, and farmers. In later times he was regarded as the chief deity of lasciviousness and obscenity.

Price, [Edward] Reynolds (1933–)   American novelist and short-story writer. Price's characters are firmly rooted in the landscape and traditions of the North Carolina cotton country where Price has spent most of his life. He employs complex narrative forms to unravel the symbolic and mythical elements of his characters' efforts to reconcile their hopes and ideals with reality. In the novels *A Long and Happy Life* (1962) and *A Generous Man* (1966) and in the lead story in *The Names and Faces of Heroes* (1963), Price applied his talent for clean characterization to several members of the Mustian family. In *Love and Work* (1968), a novelist and teacher uses his compulsiveness about work to attain what he hopes is a freedom from pain, only to discover that true freedom derives from one's capacity to share oneself with others. Price reset his focus on the family in *The Surface of Earth* (1975) and *The Source of Light* (1981), in which he applied the biblical theme of the sins of the fathers being visited on the sons. In 1986 he published *Kate Vaiden* to critical acclaim.

Prichard, Katharine Susannah (1883–1969)   Australian novelist. Born in Fiji, Prichard was brought to Tasmania at the age of three, and in time became the most distinctively Australian of writers. She taught in outback schools in Victoria and New South Wales and spent six years in London, where the condition of the working class deeply stirred her sympathies. These experiences led to her becoming an apostle of what one critic called "extreme democracy"; in addition, she was a founding member of the Australian Communist Party. During a literary period of thirty-six years, she published nine novels, two volumes of short stories, and several plays. Her books include *The Pioneers* (1915); *The Black Opal* (1921), a study of social relationships in the opal-mining community; *Working Bullocks* (1926), often considered her best novel; *Coonardoo, the Well in the Shadow* (1929), a story of the relations between whites and aborigines at an isolated northwest cattle station; *Haxby's Circus* (1930; U.S. *Fay's Circus*, 1931); and *Intimate Strangers* (1937). *The Wild Oats of Han* (1928), written for children, is largely autobiographical and has been called an Australian *Huckleberry Finn*.

Pride and Prejudice (1813)   A novel by Jane AUSTEN. The story concerns the middle-class household of the Bennets. The empty-headed and garrulous Mrs. Bennet has but one aim in life: to find a good match for each of her five daughters. Mr. Bennet, a mild and indolent man given to witty cynicisms, refuses to take this vulgar project seriously; he ridicules his wife instead of giving her support in her schemes. One of the daughters, Elizabeth, becomes prejudiced against her future suitor, Darcy, because of his arrogance and his uncalled-for interference with his friend

Bingley's courtship of her sister Jane. In interfering with Jane and Bingley, Darcy is influenced by Mrs. Bennet's undisguised husband-hunt and her impropriety in general; he mistakenly believes that Jane is only seeking an advantageous match and that her feelings are not sincere. In spite of his disapproval of the Bennet family, Darcy cannot keep himself from falling in love with Elizabeth, and he proposes to her. The tone of the proposal (it is evident that his love for Elizabeth is a blow to his pride) and her own prejudice cause Elizabeth coldly to reject him. His subsequent support of a renewal of Bingley's suit with Jane and his sensitive assistance throughout the foolish elopement of young Lydia Bennet with an officer, Wickham, show Darcy's ability to recognize and correct his own false pride, and Elizabeth's prejudice dissolves. The two are reconciled, and the book ends with their marriage and the marriage of Bingley and Jane. The novel contains two of Jane Austen's best-known minor characters, Mr. COLLINS and Lady Catherine de BOURGH.

Priest, Judge   A well-known character appearing in a number of stories by Irvin S. COBB. A wise Kentucky judge, Priest acts as a local Solomon in getting people out of trouble and solving their problems with deep insight into human nature. *Old Judge Priest* (1915), the first of these books, was followed by *Down Yonder with Judge Priest and Irvin S. Cobb* (1932). *J. Poindexter, Colored* (1922) is a novel about the judge's servant Jeff. *Judge Priest Turns Detective* was published in 1937.

Priestley, J[ohn] B[oynton] (1894–1984)   English novelist, playwright, and essayist. Priestley, who wrote over one hundred novels, plays, and essays, is best known as the author of the novel THE GOOD COMPANIONS. He is also known for *Angel Pavement* (1930) and some of his later works, including *Festival at Farbridge* (1951), *Lost Empires* (1965), and *The Image Men* (1968), which look satirically at his country and countrymen. He was nevertheless a fervent believer in the goodness of life, people, England, and humor, and many of his most successful works are happy comedies, full of Dickensian characters.

Priestley's plays fall in two groups. Some are middle-class domestic comedies with some mild social commentary, such as *Dangerous Corner* (1932) and *An Inspector Calls* (1946). Others, influenced by the time theories of John William DUNNE, are experimental dramas concerned with problems of time: *I Have Been Here Before* (1937), *Time and the Conways* (1937), and *Johnson over Jordan* (1939). In 1963 he collaborated with Iris MURDOCH on a stage version of her novel *A Severed Head*.

Priestley also wrote voluminously on literature, politics, and social issues, and published autobiographical works, including *Midnight on the Desert* (1937), *Rain upon Godshill* (1939), and *Instead of Trees* (1977). In 1977 he was awarded the Order of Merit, an honor limited to twenty-four "living greats," one of the highest honors in England.

primitivism   The persistent tendency in European literature, art, and thought since the 18th century to attribute superior virtue to primitive peoples. J. J. ROUSSEAU was the first notable primitivist, with his doctrine of the "natural man" and the widespread 18th-century veneration of the NOBLE SAVAGE, of which the American Indian was a favorite example. This doctrine had an important influence on romanticism. Later, primitivism expanded to include among the objects of its enthusiasm the violent, crude, undeveloped, ignorant, naive nonintellectual or subintelligent of any kind.

Primrose, Dr. Charles   The hero of Oliver Goldsmith's novel THE VICAR OF WAKEFIELD. He is a guileless, charitable, and unworldly clergyman.

primum mobile (Lat, "prime mover")   In the classical concept of the order of the heavens, the ninth heaven. In the Middle Ages it was generally held that the earth was the center of the universe enclosed by invisible SPHERES around which the heavens continuously revolved. ARISTOTLE postulated eight revolving heavens: the moon, Mercury, Venus, the sun, Mars, Jupiter, Saturn, and the heaven of stars. Ptolemy postulated a ninth heaven, the *primum mobile*, or "prime mover," of all the other heavens. The *primum mobile* was conceived as ordaining by its motion the daily revolution of the other heavens.

When the Fathers of the Church came to Christianize the Ptolemaic system, they naturally postulated the existence of the *primum mobile* in the mind of God, and this concept of the *primum mobile* was of extreme importance to medieval theology. DANTE, in the *Convivio* and the DIVINE COMEDY, offers the most lucid account of it to be found in nontechnical literature.

Prince, The (Il Principe)   A controversial political treatise by Niccolò MACHIAVELLI. Written during an enforced exile and dedicated to the MEDICI, it was completed in 1517 in twenty-six chapters. The opening chapters discuss the various types of principalities and in particular the difficulties of maintaining power in a newly acquired state. Examples of how rulers of the past and present handled new conquests suggest that one must often be ruthlessly despotic as well as cunningly magnanimous to keep corrupt human nature in obedience. Cesare BORGIA is offered as a model prince; through the exercise of *virtù* (personal dynamism) and the adoption of force and fraud, he was able to maintain territories originally obtained through the influence of his father, Pope Alexander VI. His eventual failure is attributed to malign fortune, which influences the affairs of men, even though it would be better to act on the assumption that it does not.

The importance of the soldiery and the use of citizen soldiers instead of militia and auxiliaries are defended in the middle chapters. Then the author takes up the character of the ruler, asserting that, although it is desirable to have a reputation for virtue, it is foolish to act in such a way that public applause comes before retention of power.

Cruelty is sometimes mercy in disguise; it is much safer to be feared than loved. It is laudable to keep faith, but if necessary one must combine the cunning of the fox and the violence of the lion. A prudent prince avoids flatterers and sycophants.

In his final chapter, Machiavelli exhorts the princes of Italy to unite and expel the barbarians who are occupying its land.

Prince and the Pauper, The (1881) A novel by Mark TWAIN. Edward VI of England and a little pauper change places a few days before Henry VIII's death. The prince wanders in rags, while Tom Canty suffers the horrors of princedom. At the last moment, the mistake is rectified. The book, dedicated to Twain's two daughters, is a favorite among children.

Prince of Parthia, The (pub 1765) A tragedy in blank verse by Thomas GODFREY. The first play written by an American, it was produced at the Southwark Theatre in Philadelphia on April 24, 1767. The plot deals with a villainous Parthian prince who murders his father and deprives his elder brother of the throne.

Princess Casamassima, The (1886) A novel by Henry JAMES. The Princess Casamassima is the former Christina Light, who appeared in RODERICK HUDSON; now separated from her husband, she decides to make a first-hand study of poverty and radicalism in London. The hero of the book is Hyacinth Robinson, the illegitimate son of an English nobleman and a Frenchwoman; though brought up in the London slums and a member of a radical underground movement, he makes his way into upper-class society, and meets the Princess. He is selected by the revolutionaries to commit an assassination, but having understood the values of civilization, he is torn between the opposing interests of socialism and society and ends his life in suicide.

Princesse de Clèves, La (1678) A novel by the comtesse de LA FAYETTE. It deals with the struggle of the princess of Clèves to remain loyal to her husband though drawn to the duc de Nemours. She eventually confesses her feelings to the prince, who dies in bitterness and despair. Focusing upon the characters' states of mind, the book is a precursor of the psychological novel and, as such, is of considerable importance in French literary history.

Principia (1687) A work by Sir Isaac NEWTON. Its full title is *Philosophiae naturalis principia mathematica* (*The Mathematical Principles of Natural Philosophy*). The book is divided into three parts: "The Motion of Bodies," "The Motion of Bodies in Resisting Media," and "The System of the World." Because of its presentation of the law of gravitation and of Newton's rules for reasoning from physical events, its appearance signified the beginning of a new era in scientific investigation.

Prinz Friedrich von Homburg (1821) A play by Heinrich von KLEIST. Prince Friedrich, cavalry general under the elector of Brandenburg in a war against the Swedes, dreams on the night before a crucial battle that he will be crowned with glory and will win the hand of the elector's niece Natalie. In the battle itself, however, he is confused and excited by the apparent nearness of his greatest desires; he attacks before the order is given, and though his charge carries the day, he is condemned to death for insubordination. He breaks down and begs for pardon, but when the decision about his fate is put in his own hands, he realizes the justice of the sentence and resigns himself to death. It is then that he is pardoned and, in a nearly exact repetition of the first dream scene, his dreams come true.

Prior, Matthew (1664–1721) English poet and diplomat, known chiefly for his epigrams, satires, and "society" verse. Prior took part in several important European treaty negotiations of his time, including the Treaty of Ryswick (1697) and the Peace of Utrecht (1713), known as "Matt's peace."

Prioress's Tale, The One of THE CANTERBURY TALES of Chaucer, a legendary miracle of the virgin told in RHYME ROYAL. After an invocation to the Virgin Mary, the Prioress piously tells the story of a seven-year-old schoolboy who learns a hymn in honor of Mary and sings it on his way through the Jewish ghetto to school. Satan inspires the Jews to cut his throat and cast him in a pit; but Christ and Mary take pity on his anxious mother, and the child miraculously begins to sing again, so that his body is found and the murderers are hanged. The boy explains that Mary has laid a grain upon his tongue and commanded him to sing until it is removed, when she will take him to her. The abbot removes the grain, and the martyr gives up the ghost and is buried. The Prioress concludes with an allusion to the slaying of St. HUGH OF LINCOLN.

Prisoner of Chillon, The (1816) A poem by Lord BYRON. It is freely based on the imprisonment of François de Bonnivard, a 16th-century Genevan prelate and politician, in the dungeon of Chillon on the edge of Lake Leman. In the poem, he and his two brothers, victims of religious persecution, are chained in a lightless cell. The brothers die and are buried in the floor of the cell; years later the survivor is released—it hardly matters to him:

> My very chains and I grew friends
> So much a long communion tends
> To make up what we are—even I
> Regain'd my freedom with a sigh.

Prisoner of Grace, A (1952) The first novel in a trilogy by Joyce CARY. The story of Chester Nimmo, dynamic liberal politician, is told by his wife, Nina, who is completely under his spell. *Except the Lord* (1953) is Nimmo's own story of his early struggles and ideals. *Not Honour More* (1955) is an account of Nimmo by Nina's second husband, Jim Latter, who views his predecessor as a ruthless, time-serving hypocrite.

Prisoner of Zenda, The (1894)   A popular English romance by Anthony Hope Hawkins (1863–1933). For three months the English hero, Rudolf Rassendyl, impersonates the king of RURITANIA, who is being held captive in the castle of Zenda. Rudolf finally secures the king's release, surrendering the crown and the hand of his beloved Princess Flavia to the rightful ruler. Though not the first novel of its kind, *The Prisoner of Zenda* began a trend of best-seller romances of high political adventure, a trend that lasted for ten years.

Prisonnière, La   See REMEMBRANCE OF THINGS PAST.

Pritchett, Sir V[ictor] S[awdon] (1900–   ) English novelist, short-story writer, biographer, and critic, one of 20th-century England's most urbane men of letters. Pritchett's early short stories, such as those in *Marching Spain* (1928), were set in the Spain he knew well in his younger days and wrote about later in *The Spanish Temper* (1954). He is a master of the short story, able to distill the essence of character; his other collections include *When My Girl Comes Home* (1961), *Blind Love* (1969), *The Camberwell Beauty* (1974), *Selected Stories* (1978), and *On the Edge of the Cliff* (1979). Many of these have been assembled in *Collected Stories* (1982) and *More Collected Stories* (1983). Of his novels, *Mr. Beluncle* (1951), a compassionate study of a Puritan eccentric, is considered his masterpiece. A *Cab at the Door* (1968) and *Midnight Oil* (1971) are memoirs. His biographies *Balzac* (1973) and, of TURGENEV, *The Gentle Barbarian* (1977), are also works of characteristically discerning literary criticism, more of which is evident in *The Myth Makers* (1979). *The Tale Bearers* (1980) consists of twenty-three sketches of writers from Samuel PEPYS to Saul BELLOW. He has edited a highly acclaimed anthology, *The Oxford Book of Short Stories* (1981).

Private Life of the Master Race, The (Furcht und Elend des Dritten Reiches, 1938; tr 1944)   A loose collection of twenty-four dramatic scenes by Bertolt BRECHT. As a literal translation of the title ("Fear and Misery of the Third Reich") indicates, it is an open attack on the terror and suffering inflicted by HITLER's regime between 1933 and 1938. Each scene begins with a rhymed introduction and then opens into dialogue in which actual atrocities are reported.

Private Papers of Henry Ryecroft, The (1903) A novel by George GISSING. The first part of the book is a brief biography of Ryecroft, whose diary Gissing is ostensibly publishing. The diary itself is divided into four sections: Spring, Summer, Autumn, and Winter, which contain reflections, or *pensées*, on the human condition.

Prix Goncourt   The most sought after and highly respected French literary prize. Established in 1903 under the terms of the will of Edmond GONCOURT, it is given annually to the best volume of imaginative work in prose published during the year. In the case of a tie, novels are to be given preference over collections of short stories or sketches. The awarding of the prize is decided by the Académie Goncourt, an institution founded in 1896 in compliance with Goncourt's specifications. Consisting of ten members, whose annual salary of sixty new francs has never varied, the academy seeks to recognize and reward new original efforts in thought or form, as opposed to the more conservative awards by the ACADÉMIE FRANÇAISE.

The recipients of the Goncourt prize since its inception are: 1903, John Antoine Nau, *La Force ennemie*; 1904, Léon Frapié, *La Maternelle*; 1905, Claude Farrère, *Les Civilisés*; 1906, Jérôme and Jean Tharaud, *Dingley l'illustre écrivain*; 1907, Emile Moselly, *Terres Lorraines*; 1908, Francis de Miomandre, *Écrit sur de l'eau*; 1909, Marius-Ary Leblond, *En France*; 1910, Louis Pergaud, *De Goupil à Margot*; 1911, Alphonse de Chateaubriant, *Monsieur des Lourdines*; 1912, André Savignon, *Filles de la pluie*; 1913, Marc Elder, *Le Peuple de la mer*; 1914, Adrien Bertrand, *L'Appel du sol*; 1915, René Benjamin, *Gaspard*; 1916, Henri Barbusse, *Le Feu*; 1917, Henri Malherbe, *La Flamme au poing*; 1918, Georges Duhamel, *Civilisation*; 1919, Marcel Proust, *À l'ombre des jeunes filles en fleurs*; 1920, Ernest Pérochon, *Nène*; 1921, René Maran, *Batouala*; 1922, Henri Béraud, *Le Vitriol de lune*; *Le Martyre de l'obese*; 1923, Lucien Fabre, *Rabevel*; 1924, Thierry Sandre, *Le Chèvrefeuille*; 1925, Maurice Genevoix, *Raboliot*; 1926, Henri Deberly, *Le Supplice de Phèdre*; 1927, Maurice Bedel, *Jérôme, 60° latitude nord*; 1928, Maurice Constantin-Weyer, *Un Homme se penche sur son passé*; 1929, Marcel Arland, *L'Ordre*; 1930, Henri Fauconnier, *Malaisie*; 1931, Jean Fayard, *Mal d'amour*; 1932, Guy Mazeline, *Les Loups*; 1933, André Malraux, *La Condition humaine*; 1934, Roger Vercel, *Capitaine Conan*; 1935, Joseph Peyré, *Sang et lumières*; 1936, Maxence Van der Meersch, *L'Empreinte du Dieu*; 1937, Charles Plisnier, *Faux Passeports*; 1938, Henri Troyat, *L'Aroigne*; 1939, Philippe Hériat, *Les Enfants gâtés*; 1940, Francis Ambrière, *Les Grandes Vacances* (awarded 1946); 1941, Henri Pourrat, *Vent de Mars*; 1942, Marc Bernard, *Pareils à des enfants*; 1943, Marius Grout, *Passage de l'homme*; 1944, Elsa Triolet, *Le Premier Accroc coûte deux cents francs*; 1945, Jean-Louis Bory, *Mon village à l'heure allemande*; 1946, Jean-Jacques Gautier, *Histoire d'un fait divers*; 1947, Jean-Louis Curtis, *Les Forêts de la nuit*; 1948, Maurice Druon, *Les Grandes Familles*; 1949, Robert Merle, *Week-end à Zuydcoote*; 1950, Paul Colin, *Les Jeux sauvages*; 1951, Julien Gracq, *Le Rivage des Syrtes*; 1952, Béatrice Beck, *Léon Morin, prêtre*; 1953, Pierre Gascar, *Le Temps des morts*; 1954, Simone de Beauvoir, *Les Mandarins*; 1955, Roger Ikor, *Les Eaux mêlées*; 1956, Romain Gary, *Les Racines du ciel*; 1957, Roger Vailland, *La Loi*; 1958, Francis Walder, *Saint-Germain ou la négociation*; 1959, André Schwarz-Bart, *Le Dernier des justes*; 1960, award rescinded; 1961, Jean Cau, *La Pitié de Dieu*; 1962, Anna Langfus, *Les Bagages de sable*; 1963, Armand Lanoux, *Quand la mer se retire*; 1964, Georges Conchon, *L'État sauvage*; 1965, Jacques Borel, *L'Adoration*; 1966, Edmonde Charles-Roux, *Oublier Palerme*; 1967, André Pieyre de Mandiargues, *La Marge*; 1968, Bernard Clavel, *Les Fruits de l'hiver*; 1969, Félicien Marceau, *Creezy*; 1970, Michel Tournier, *Le Roi des aulnes*; 1971, Jacques Laurent, *Les Bêtises*; 1972, Jean Carrière, *L'Epervier de Maheux*; 1973, Jacques Chessex, *L'Ogre*; 1974, Pascal Lainé, *La Dentellière*; 1975, Emile Ajar, *La Vie devant soi*; 1976, Patrick Grainville, *Les Flamboyants*; 1977, Didier Decoin, *John l'enfer*; 1978, Patrick Modiano, *Rue des boutiques obscures*; 1979, Antoinette Maillet, *Pelagie-La-Charette*; 1980, Yves Navarre, *Le Jardin d'acclimatation*; 1981, Lucien Bodard, *Anne-Marie*; 1982, Dominique Fernandez, *Dans la main de l'ange*; 1983, Frederick Tristan, *Les Egarés*; 1984, Marguerite Duras, *L'Amant*; 1985, Yann Queffelec, *Les Noces barbares*; 1986, Michel Host, *Valet de nuit*.

Proclus (c410–485)   A Greek Neoplatonic philosopher. Also known as the Successor because of his position as head of the Platonic Academy, Proclus presented the fullest systematization and extension of the Neoplatonic position. He was the last important pagan Greek philosopher; Proclus' life was related by his student Marinus. Forty-four years after Proclus died, the Emperor Justinian closed the schools of philosophy.

Procrustes   In Greek legend, a robber of Attica. He placed all who fell into his hands upon an iron bed. If they were longer than the bed he cut off the redundant part; if shorter, he stretched them till they fitted it. He was slain by THESEUS. He is also called Damastes.

prodigal son   A repentant sinner from the parable of the prodigal son who "wasted his substance with riotous living" in a far country, but returned to his father's house and was forgiven (Luke 15:11–32). It has become a familiar motif in literature, as evidenced, for example, in Prince Hal's repentant behavior in Shakespeare's HENRY IV, PART II.

Professor Bernhardi (1912; tr 1927)   A satirical comedy by Arthur SCHNITZLER. In order to prevent a young girl from learning of her impending death, a Jewish medical professor prevents a priest from administering Extreme Unction. The play is concerned with the religious and political consequences of this action, and develops into a critique of many trends in the society of the time, particularly of anti-Semitism.

Professorenroman (Ger, "professor's novel")   In German literary history a very convenient term applied to novels that are crammed full of reliably correct historical detail but which remain absolutely devoid of literary inspiration.

Projective Verse (1950)   An essay on prosody by Charles OLSON, first published in the journal *Poetry New York*. One of the most influential contemporary writings on poetry, it rejected the constraint of closed, traditional forms

and offered instead what Olson termed "composition by field," where the poet puts himself into the open in the act of writing, not knowing ahead of time what form the poem will take.

The essay is in two parts: the first concerning principles of writing, the second, the philosophy that must guide the poet's awareness. Both were an articulation of the basic principles of the BLACK MOUNTAIN POETS as well as Olson's own poetics. The term "projective" is derived from a combination of projectile, percussive, and prospective.

Prokofiev, Sergey Sergeyevich (1891–1953)   Russian composer and pianist. Prokofiev's best-known works include *Classical Symphony* (1917), the opera *Love for Three Oranges* (1921; based on a comedy by Carlo Gozzi), and a fairy tale for narrator and orchestra, *Peter and the Wolf* (1936). His later works are mostly unsuccessful attempts to comply with the Soviet ideal of SOCIALIST REALISM.

proletarian literature   A type of literature, at the height of its influence in the 1930s, particularly in the U.S., that had as its aim a sympathetic portrayal of the lives and sufferings of the working class. Many, but not all, of the leading writers of the genre were either sympathetically or actively involved with the Communist Party, and their work represented a sincere response to an era of economic depression and to obvious social injustices.

In its subject matter and sympathetic approach to characters, proletarian literature had its forerunners among such humanitarian novelists of the 19th century as Charles DICKENS, George ELIOT, and Victor HUGO. Its social perspective was preceded by the French naturalists FLAUBERT and ZOLA, and by their American disciples Stephen CRANE and Frank NORRIS. Norris's THE OCTOPUS and Upton Sinclair's THE JUNGLE were landmarks in establishing a tradition of novels that advocated social reform. The bitter or idealistic rebellion that animates its most characteristic examples had a precedent among the English and American romantics—Robert BURNS, the early WORDSWORTH, SHELLEY, EMERSON, THOREAU, and WHITMAN. Walt Whitman's exaltation of the "common man" was continued particularly by such American poets as Carl SANDBURG and Muriel RUKEYSER.

With the growth of the international ambitions of Nazi Germany and Fascist Italy, anti-Nazi and anti-Fascist works by such writers as Ralph Bates and Ignazio SILONE came to be included under the umbrella of proletarian literature. Leading outlets for the work and views of proletarian writers were the magazines *New Masses*, *The Anvil*, and PARTISAN REVIEW (in its early period of publication only). A school of proletarian criticism also developed, which advocated that literature should concern itself with social and economic injustice and participate actively in the "class struggle," impelling its readers to action rather than giving them pleasure or turning them to escapist contemplation. It vigorously condemned theories of ART FOR ART'S SAKE.

Of the many writers and works that fall under the category of proletarian literature, the following are considered outstanding examples: Steinbeck's IN DUBIOUS BATTLE and THE GRAPES OF WRATH, Dos Passos's U.S.A. (q.v.), Farrell's STUDS LONIGAN, and Wright's NATIVE SON. Odets's WAITING FOR LEFTY is probably the best-known example of proletarian drama.

promessi sposi, I (The Betrothed, 1827) A romantic historical novel by Alessandro MANZONI, often considered the greatest Italian novel of modern times. The story tells of the attempts of Renzo and Lucia, two peasants in 17th-century Lombardy, to marry despite the bullying threats of a local grandee, Don Rodrigo. The lovers are assisted in their plight by their saintly confessor, Fra Cristoforo, and by Cardinal Borromeo, who personifies Manzoni's ideal of the moral perfection of Catholic doctrine and practice. Their situation is worsened by the cowardice of their parish priest, Don Abbondio, who typifies what the author considers a common type of human failing. The Nun of Monza figures as the willful sinner whose maliciousness harms the lovers and confirms her own moral turpitude. The "Unnamed" Signore (L'Innominato) represents the repentant sinner whose conversion protects Renzo and Lucia from Don Rodrigo and facilitates their marriage and the book's happy outcome.

The author's stated purpose in the novel is to show the workings of divine providence in history, specifically, in the day-to-day events in the life of a common man; hence the obvious moralizing of the text and the moral lessons implicit in the personalities of the characters. Among the many remarkable scenes in the book is that describing the plague in Milan.

Prometheus (Gr, "forethought") In Greek mythology, a Titan, the son of Iapetus and THEMIS. Prometheus stole fire from heaven. A champion of men against the gods, he tricked ZEUS into choosing fat and bone as the god's portion of sacrifices, leaving the flesh for men. Angrily Zeus withheld fire from men, but Prometheus stole it in a fennel stalk. As a punishment, Prometheus was nailed to a mountain, where an eagle tore out his liver by day and it grew again by night. Eventually HERACLES rescued him, or he was saved by ZEUS himself. Man, meanwhile, had been afflicted by Zeus with innumerable ills through PANDORA. According to some stories, Prometheus was the creator of man, molding him of mud. It is likely that he was a pre-Hellenic fire god who was replaced by HEPHAESTUS. In Aeschylus' PROMETHEUS BOUND, he is a heroic figure, as he was in Shelley's narrative poem PROMETHEUS UNBOUND.

Prometheus Bound (Prometheus desmotes) A tragedy of unknown date by AESCHYLUS. Prometheus, who has stolen fire from heaven for man, is punished by ZEUS by being fastened to a Scythian mountain by HEPHAESTUS. He tells a chorus of sympathetic ocean nymphs how he had once helped Zeus in his war with the TITANS. The old god OCEANUS enters, riding a strange, winged animal, and advises Prometheus to defy Zeus no longer. IO, now a heifer, enters and tells of her sorrow. Prometheus foretells a happy outcome after her further wanderings. He then says that Zeus himself will be destroyed by a son yet to be born to him, but only Prometheus knows who will be its mother. When Io is gone, HERMES tries to force Prometheus to reveal his secret, but he refuses unless he is released. With lightning and an earthquake, Zeus plunges Prometheus into TARTARUS.

In this monumental play, Aeschylus deals with the theme of men's relation to the gods. *Prometheus Bound* was the first play of a trilogy. The other two, *Prometheus Unbound* (*P. lyomenos*) and *Prometheus, the Fire-Bearer* (*P. pyrphoros*), are lost, but a fragment of the second shows that Prometheus remained in Tartarus for thirty thousand years.

Prometheus Unbound (1820) A lyrical drama by Percy Bysshe SHELLEY, inspired by the Greek myth of PROMETHEUS. In Shelley's work, the chained and tormented Prometheus is a symbol of humanity; JUPITER, the usurper, represents the tyranny of kings and civil institutions; Demogorgon, the son of Jupiter and THETIS, is the Primal Power of the world and the spirit of Necessity or Destiny; Asia, Prometheus' wife, is ideal Love or Nature. Demogorgon drives Jupiter from his throne, Prometheus is released by Hercules (HERACLES) and reunited with Asia, and a golden age, where love and beauty reign, begins.

Promised Land CANAAN or Palestine, so called because God promised ABRAHAM, ISAAC, and JACOB that their offspring should possess it (Gen. 12:7, 26:3, 28:13).

Propertius, Sextus (49–15 BC) Roman poet and master of elegiac verse. Propertius's three books of poetry deal with his experiences in love as well as etiological myths and Roman history. The 20th-century American poet Ezra POUND made several modern imitations of him in "Homage to Sextus Propertius."

Prophet (1) In the KORAN, the special title of MUHAMMED. According to the Muslims there have been 200,000 prophets, or interpreters, of God's will, but only six of them—ADAM, NOAH, ABRAHAM, MOSES, JESUS, and MUHAMMED—brought new laws.

(2) In the OLD TESTAMENT, men called on by God to speak God's will, particularly during the periods of the Northern and Southern Kingdoms and the Babylonian captivity. Because their writings were more extensive, ISAIAH, JEREMIAH, EZEKIEL, and DANIEL are known as the Major Prophets. The Minor Prophets were HOSEA, JOEL, AMOS, OBADIAH, JONAH, MICAH, NAHUM, HABAKKUK, ZEPHANIAH, HAGGAI, ZECHARIAH, and the author of MALACHI.

Prophet, The (1923)   A prose poem in sections by Kahlil GIBRAN which presents the elements of his mystical faith.

propos   See ALAIN.

Proserpina   The Roman counterpart of the Greek goddess PERSEPHONE.

prosody   The broad study or science of how language is handled in the composition of poetry. The term encompasses VERSIFICATION (meter, rhyme, traditional forms); Anglo-Saxon poetics; syllable-count methods and forms; FREE VERSE; distortion and dissonance applied to traditional methods; SPRUNG RHYTHM; and any specific stylistic rules or requirements of special poetic movements.

Prospero   The rightful duke of Milan, who reigns over an enchanted island in Shakespeare's THE TEMPEST. Almost superhuman in his attributes, he is wise, firm, and philosophical, meting out justice to friend and enemy. His magical skills symbolize the power that man may attain by the use of his mind, though he is often impeded by the baser aspects of his nature. His is one of the most famous of Shakespeare's speeches:

> Our revels now are ended. These our actors,
> As I foretold you, were all spirits and
> Are melted into air, into thin air:
> And, like the baseless fabric of this vision,
> The cloud-capp'd towers, the gorgeous palaces,
> The solemn temples, the great globe itself,
> Yea, all which it inherit, shall dissolve,
> And like this insubstantial pageant faded,
> Leave not a rack behind. We are such stuff
> As dreams are made on; and our little life
> Is rounded with a sleep.

Prospero is often said to embody the philosophy at which the dramatist arrived toward the end of his life.

Prospice (1864)   A poem by Robert BROWNING. Written soon after his wife's death, it expresses an optimistic and courageous attitude toward death. The title, taken from Latin, states the theme: "Look forward!"

protagonist   Originating in early Greek drama, the term was applied to the first actor and leader of the CHORUS. The antagonist was the second most important character and the other contender in the *agon*, the dispute or debate that formed part of a Greek tragedy. Protagonist is now used generally to denote the main character of a play or story and is sometimes used interchangeably with *hero*.

protasis (Gr, "stretching forward")   A term used by grammarians of late antiquity for the introductory act or exposition of classical Greek drama. See CATASTASIS; CATASTROPHE; EPITASIS.

Protesilaus   The first Greek to die in the TROJAN WAR. At the siege of Troy an oracle prophesied that the first Greek to step on land would be killed. Protesilaus took the honor upon himself and was promptly slain. His faithful wife, Laodameia, who had kept a wax statue of him always beside her, now prayed that he should return for a brief while. His ghost appeared to animate the statue for three hours, but she willingly returned with him to HADES at the end of that time. According to another story, she killed herself when her father took away the statue.

Protestant ethic   The moral code associated with Protestantism, and especially Calvinism (see John CALVIN), which stresses hard work, asceticism, and the rational organization of one's life in the service of God. The term was made famous by Max WEBER in the *Protestant Ethic and the Spirit of Capitalism* (1904–5). Weber concluded that the motivating force for the rise of capitalism was provided by the development of the Protestant ethic.

Calvinism, in particular, provided the complex of psychological sanctions that drove men to hard work even in the absence of need. Hard work was an outward sign of one's inner faith. The material success produced by work came to be taken as a sign of faith and probable salvation.

Proteus   In Greek legend, Poseidon's herdsman, an old man and a prophet. Proteus was famous for his power of assuming different shapes at will. When caught, however, he was helpful to many Greek heroes by his foreknowledge. Proteus lived in a vast cave, and his custom was to count over his herds of sea-calves at noon, and then go to sleep. There was no way of catching him but by stealing upon him at this time and binding him; otherwise he would elude anyone by a rapid change in shape. In Euripides' HELEN, he is referred to as a former king of Egypt.

prothalamion   A song or poem in celebration of a marriage.

Prothalamion (1596)   Lyric poem by Edmund SPENSER. It was written to celebrate the double wedding of Lady Elizabeth and Lady Katherine Somerset, daughters of the earl of Worcester.

Proudhon, Pierre Joseph (1809–1865)   French socialist and anarchist. Proudhon's most famous work, *Qu'est-ce que la propriété?* (*What Is Property*, 1840), denounces private property as an institution which perpetrates inequality and injustice. A fiery reformer, Proudhon fled France in 1858 when his *La Justice dans la Révolution et dans l'Eglise* (1858), a work violently critical of church and state, was angrily received.

Proudie, Bishop and **Mrs.**   Two of the best-known characters in Anthony TROLLOPE's Chronicles of BARSETSHIRE. Mrs. Proudie is a formidable woman who propels her husband through life with unrelenting vigor. See BARCHESTER TOWERS.

Proust, Marcel (1871–1922)   French novelist. Son of an eminent Catholic doctor and his Jewish wife, Proust grew up in their permanent home in Paris near the Champs-Elysées. His memories of visits to relatives in Auteuil and in Illiers were the material for the imaginary village of COMBRAY, the setting for the early part of his long and most important novel, REMEMBRANCE OF THINGS PAST. He suffered his first attack of asthma when he was nine; thereafter, his summer visits were to shore resorts on the

English Channel, which he combined into the BALBEC of the novel.

In 1889 he joined the army for a year as a subofficer. The following year, to satisfy his father's insistence that he should have a regular career, he entered the Sorbonne as a student of both law and political science. His real interest was philosophy, however; he was much influenced by the lectures of Paul Desjardins and of Henri BERGSON, whose theories about time as subjectively lived contributed to Proust's.

At the Lycée Condorcet, his schoolfellows and he had produced in 1887–88 a number of ephemeral handwritten little magazines. In 1892 the same group founded the printed review *Le Banquet*, which lasted for eight issues. Proust was one of the most prolific contributors of sketches and short stories, but his artificial although graceful style did not impress even his colleagues, except as revealing his apparently snobbish fascination with titled society. And indeed, the young Proust was steadily and deliberately making his way, despite his bourgeois origins, into higher and higher circles of the Faubourg St. Germain, the social elite of Paris. Similarly, although Anatole FRANCE wrote an introduction for *Les Plaisirs et les jours* (1896; tr *Pleasures and Regrets*, 1948), a collection of sketches, stories, and poems in a variety of imitative styles, the book was received as the elegant but slight work of a literary dilettante.

In 1895 Proust began working on a long novel, which was published posthumously as JEAN SANTEUIL, finally abandoning it about 1899. These were also the years of the Dreyfus Case, during which Proust with Anatole France and other intellectuals actively protested the miscarriage of justice and demanded a retrial.

The aesthetic theories of John RUSKIN attracted Proust, who, in 1899, began a serious study of his works, translating *La Bible d'Amiens* (1904) and *Sésame et les lys* (1906), with notes and prefaces. Ruskin's descriptions of architecture inspired Proust to make a number of trips to see the important buildings of France, Holland, and Venice.

After his father died in 1903 and his mother in 1905, Proust began to relinquish almost all his social ties, although he continued to travel a bit and to write for newspapers and reviews. In 1907 he moved to the apartment on Boulevard Haussmann, famous for the cork-lined bedroom from which, in later years, he almost never stirred, partly to prevent serious asthmatic or nervous attacks, partly to avoid being distracted from his writing. By 1908 he had conceived and begun writing his life work, *Remembrance of Things Past*. The narrator of the novel is very like Proust in character and background. A neurotic, hypersensitive, asthmatic young man, who is even called in one place "Marcel," he courts fashionable society and romantic experiences, records his observations in great detail, introspectively analyzes his responses to them, and finally discovers his vocation in the writing of this novel. In shaping the narrator's personality, Proust omitted his own Jewish back-

ground, homosexuality, and hypochondria. All these attributes, transposed to other characters, are extensively analyzed, however, and the narrator's generalized conclusions about love, snobbery, art, literature, etc., are assumed to be Proust's own.

The only significant interruption to direct work on his masterpiece was the writing (1908–10) of *Contre Sainte-Beuve* (1954; tr *By Way of Saint-Beuve*, 1958). Proust began this as a critical study, but it soon digressed into an analysis of his own processes of memory, thought, and emotion, and thus like *Jean Santeuil* was an exploratory preparation for his masterpiece. The first draft of *Remembrance of Things Past* was completed by 1912, and the first volume in print by 1913, but World War I delayed further publication, giving Proust time for "revisions" that expanded the work to nearly twice its original length. Proust died before the last three books were published.

proverb   A pithy saying expressing a general truth or practical observation about life or human behavior. Proverbs are frequently preserved by oral tradition, and consequently may employ archaisms or unfamiliar idioms. The following are examples: "time and tide wait for no man"; "forewarned is forearmed"; "a stitch in time saves nine." The best-known collection is the book of PROVERBS in the OLD TESTAMENT.

Proverbs   A book of the OLD TESTAMENT, appearing directly after PSALMS. As the title suggests, it contains a collection of MAXIMS and pithy statements about sin and righteousness and universal aspects of the human condition, based on common sense and practical observation rather than on revelation. Many sections of the book were traditionally ascribed to SOLOMON; it is more likely a compilation of many people's writing.

Provincetown Players   A group of actors, producers, and playwrights, known for its encouragement of native writers and its part in promoting a resurgence in the American theatre after World War I. The group started as an acting company in Provincetown, Massachusetts, under the direction of George Cram Cook. It produced plays by Cook and by his wife, Susan GLASPELL, and also by other dramatists, notably Eugene O'NEILL. The Players was organized in 1915; after moving to New York, the group continued to work until 1929. O'Neill was its most important discovery, but it eventually produced almost one hundred plays by some of the most famous playwrights of the period.

Prufrock, J. Alfred   See LOVE SONG OF J. ALFRED PRUFROCK, THE.

Prussian Officer, The (1914)   A short story by D. H. LAWRENCE. It is about a sadistic Prussian army officer and his victim, a young orderly, who is finally driven to kill his tormentor.

Prynne, Hester   The heroine of Hawthorne's THE SCARLET LETTER.

Psalms   The nineteenth book of the OLD TESTA-
MENT, containing 150 hymns, or songs, to God. Many of
them are ascribed to DAVID, who was called "the sweet
psalmist of Israel" (2 Sam. 23:1).

Psyche (Gr, "breath"; hence, life or soul)   The heroine of the myth of CUPID (Eros) and Psyche, an episode in
THE GOLDEN ASS of Apuleius, 2nd century AD. Psyche was
a beautiful maiden beloved by Cupid, who visited her
every night, but left her at sunrise. Cupid bade her never to
seek to know who he was, but one night curiosity overcame
her prudence; she lit the lamp to look at him, a drop of hot
oil fell on his shoulder, and he awoke and fled. The abandoned Psyche wandered far and wide in search of her lover.
She became the slave of VENUS, who imposed on her
heartless tasks and treated her most cruelly. But ultimately
she was united to Cupid and became immortal. The kernel
of the story, the lover who must not be named, is a common theme in folklore.

psychoanalysis   See FREUD, SIGMUND.

Ptolemy (full Latin name Claudius Ptolemaeus, 2nd
century)   Alexandrian astronomer and geographer. In his
Almagest, he described a new system of astronomy that was
accepted until the 16th century. The Ptolemaic system, as
it is called, stipulates that the sun, the planets, and the stars
revolve around the earth. The movements of the heavenly
bodies were plotted by a complicated arrangement of epicycles (small circles with their centers on the circumference
of a larger one). Whenever a planet or star was observed
moving out of its prescribed path, it was assumed that it
had entered a new series of epicycles. By continually adding epicycles, the Ptolemaic system was made to work;
however, it had become insanely complex with dozens of
epicycles for a single planet when COPERNICUS advanced
his uncomplicated theory of heliocentricity in 1530.

Puccini, Giacomo (1858–1924)   Italian composer
of opera. VERDI regarded Puccini as the most talented Italian dramatic composer of his time and by the end of his
life, Puccini's popularity rivaled that of Verdi. Among Puccini's operas are *Manon Lescaut* (1893); *La Bohème* (1896);
and *Tosca* (1900), which brought him recognition as
Verdi's successor. *Madama Butterfly* (1904), at its premiere, was Puccini's worst failure, only to become, within
the year, one of his best-loved works. Others included *The
Girl of the Golden West* (1907) and *Turandot*, first performed in 1926.

Puck   A mischievous sprite of popular folklore, also
called Robin Goodfellow. Originally an evil demon, he
was transformed and popularized in his present form by
Shakespeare, who depicts him in A MIDSUMMER NIGHT'S
DREAM as a merry wanderer of the night, "rough, knurly-
limbed, faun-faced, and shock-pated, a very Shetlander
among the gossamer-winged" fairies around him.

Pudd'nhead Wilson, The Tragedy of (1894)
A novel by Mark TWAIN. David Wilson is called
"Pudd'nhead" by the townspeople, who fail to understand

his combination of wisdom and eccentricity. He redeems
himself by simultaneously solving a murder mystery and a
case of transposed identities.

The mystery revolves around two children, a white boy
and a mulatto, who are born on the same day. Roxy, the
mother of the mulatto, is given charge of the children; in
fear that her son will be sold, she exchanges babies.

The mulatto turns out to be a scoundrel. He sells his
mother, and murders and robs his uncle. He accuses
Luigi, one of a pair of twins, of the murder; Pudd'nhead, a
lawyer, undertakes Luigi's defense. On the basis of finger-
print evidence, he exposes the real murderer, and the white
boy takes his rightful place.

The book is an implicit condemnation of a society that
allows slavery. It also includes a series of brilliant epigrams,
each the headpiece of a chapter, which are distillations of
Twain's wit and wisdom.

Pugin, Augustus Welby Northmore (1812–
1852)   English architect and designer. Pugin, whose
father, Augustus Charles Pugin (1762–1832), was also an
architectural draftsman and writer on Gothic architecture,
was the most prominent theorist of the great Gothic Revival in England in the first half of the 19th century. In *Contrasts* (1836) he called for a return to the morally superior
social order of the Middle Ages, as embodied in the architecture of that period. He argued for authenticity of Gothic
reproductions in *The True Principles of Pointed or Christian Architecture* (1841) and worked with Charles Barry
(1795–1860) on the design, furnishing, and decoration of
England's Houses of Parliament.

puja (Sans, "adoration")   The main external form of
Hindu worship, *puja* involves the recitation of prayers,
chanting of hymns, the burning of incense, and a token
offering to the gods, either in one's home or in a temple or
sacred place. It replaced *yajna*, or sacrifice, which was the
central element of religious ritual in the VEDAS.

Pulci, Luigi   See MORGANTE MAGGIORE, IL.

Pulitzer, Joseph (1847–1911)   Hungarian-born
American journalist. Pulitzer began his career in 1868 as a
reporter for the German daily *Westliche Post* in St. Louis
and soon became its part-owner. He was also a lawyer
active in politics, first as a liberal Republican and later as a
Democrat. In 1878 he bought the St. Louis *Dispatch*,
which was soon merged with the *Evening Post* to become
the *Post-Dispatch*. He bought the New York *World* in
1883, founded the *Evening World* in 1887, and made both
of them prosperous enterprises by adding cartoons, crusades, news stunts, and illustrations. Their prestige and circulation declined after a sordid war of yellow journalism
with the dailies of William Randolph HEARST in the late
1890s. Pulitzer had retired from active control in 1890
because of ill health, but his directives eventually restored
the papers to respectability. See PULITZER PRIZES.

Pulitzer Prizes   Annual awards in journalism and
letters made by the trustees of Columbia University. They

were endowed by the will of Joseph PULITZER, who also left money to found the University's School of Journalism. The nominees are screened by juries appointed in each category and recommended to the trustees by the Advisory Board on the Pulitzer Prizes.

There are eight journalism awards: to a newspaper, for public service, and for "distinguished examples" of editorial writing, cartooning, news photography, and national, international, local spot news, and local investigative reporting. In letters, the awards are for distinguished works by American authors in the fields of fiction, U.S. history and biography, drama, poetry, and (since 1962) for a work not eligible in any other existing category. There are also a prize for a larger musical work, and four fellowships.

Literary works awarded the Pulitzer Prize are:

Fiction 1918, Ernest Poole, *His Family*; 1919, Booth Tarkington, *The Magnificent Ambersons*; 1920, none; 1921, Edith Wharton, *The Age of Innocence*; 1922, Booth Tarkington, *Alice Adams*; 1923, Willa Cather, *One of Ours*; 1924, Margaret Wilson, *The Able McLaughlins*; 1925, Edna Ferber, *So Big*; 1926, Sinclair Lewis (author declined), *Arrowsmith*; 1927, Louis Bromfield, *Early Autumn*; 1928, Thornton Wilder, *Bridge of San Luis Rey*; 1929, Julia M. Peterkin, *Scarlet Sister Mary*; 1930, Oliver La Farge, *Laughing Boy*; 1931, Margaret Ayer Barnes, *Years of Grace*; 1932, Pearl S. Buck, *The Good Earth*; 1933, T. S. Stribling, *The Store*; 1934, Caroline Miller, *Lamb in His Bosom*; 1935, Josephine W. Johnson, *Now in November*; 1936, Harold L. Davis, *Honey in the Horn*; 1937, Margaret Mitchell, *Gone With the Wind*; 1938, John P. Marquand, *The Late George Apley*; 1939, Marjorie Kinnan Rawlings, *The Yearling*; 1940, John Steinbeck, *The Grapes of Wrath*; 1941, none; 1942, Ellen Glasgow, *In This Our Life*; 1943, Upton Sinclair, *Dragon's Teeth*; 1944, Martin Flavin, *Journey in the Dark*; 1945, John Hersey, *A Bell for Adano*; 1946, none; 1947, Robert Penn Warren, *All the King's Men*; 1948, James A. Michener, *Tales of the South Pacific*; 1949, James Gould Cozzens, *Guard of Honor*; 1950, A. B. Guthrie, Jr., *The Way West*; 1951, Conrad Richter, *The Town*; 1952, Herman Wouk, *The Caine Mutiny*; 1953, Ernest Hemingway, *The Old Man and the Sea*; 1954, none; 1955, William Faulkner, *A Fable*; 1956, MacKinlay Kantor, *Andersonville*; 1957, none; 1958, James Agee, *A Death in the Family*; 1959, Robert Lewis Taylor, *The Travels of Jaimie McPheeters*; 1960, Allen Drury, *Advise and Consent*; 1961, Harper Lee, *To Kill a Mockingbird*; 1962, Edwin O'Connor, *The Edge of Sadness*; 1963, William Faulkner (posthumous), *The Reivers*; 1964, none; 1965, Shirley Ann Grau, *The Keepers of the House*; 1966, Katherine Anne Porter, *Collected Stories of Katherine Anne Porter*; 1967, Bernard Malamud, *The Fixer*; 1968, William Styron, *The Confessions of Nat Turner*; 1969, N. Scott Momaday, *House Made of Dawn*; 1970, Jean Stafford, *Collected Stories*; 1971, none; 1972, Wallace Stegner, *Angle of Repose*; 1973,

Eudora Welty, *The Optimist's Daughter*; 1974, none; 1975, Michael Shaara, *The Killer Angels*; 1976, Saul Bellow, *Humboldt's Gift*; 1977, none; 1978, James Alan McPherson, *Elbow Room*; 1979, John Cheever, *The Stories of John Cheever*; 1980, Norman Mailer, *The Executioner's Song*; 1981, John Kennedy Toole, *A Confederacy of Dunces*; 1982, John Updike, *Rabbit Is Rich*; 1983, Alice Walker, *The Color Purple*; 1984, William Kennedy, *Ironweed*; 1985, Alison Lurie, *Foreign Affairs*; 1986, Larry McMurtry, *Lonesome Dove*; 1987, Peter Taylor, *A Summons to Memphis*.

Drama 1918, Jesse Lynch Williams, *Why Marry?*; 1919, none; 1920, Eugene O'Neill, *Beyond the Horizon*; 1921, Zona Gale, *Miss Lulu Bett*; 1922, Eugene O'Neill, *Anna Christie*; 1923, Owen Davis, *Icebound*; 1924, Hatcher Hughes, *Hell-Bent for Heaven*; 1925, Sidney Howard, *They Knew What They Wanted*; 1926, George Kelly, *Craig's Wife*; 1927, Paul Green, *In Abraham's Bosom*; 1928, Eugene O'Neill, *Strange Interlude*; 1929, Elmer Rice, *Street Scene*; 1930, Marc Connelly, *The Green Pastures*; 1931, Susan Glaspell, *Alison's House*; 1932, George S. Kaufman, Morrie Ryskind, and Ira Gershwin, *Of Thee I Sing*; 1933, Maxwell Anderson, *Both Your Houses*; 1934, Sidney Kingsley, *Men in White*; 1935, Zoë Akins, *The Old Maid*; 1936, Robert E. Sherwood, *Idiot's Delight*; 1937, George S. Kaufman and Moss Hart, *You Can't Take It With You*; 1938, Thornton Wilder, *Our Town*; 1939, Robert E. Sherwood, *Abe Lincoln in Illinois*; 1940, William Saroyan, *The Time of Your Life*; 1941, Robert E. Sherwood, *There Shall Be No Night*; 1942, none; 1943, Thornton Wilder, *The Skin of Our Teeth*; 1944, none; 1945, Mary Chase, *Harvey*; 1946, Russel Crouse and Howard Lindsay, *State of the Union*; 1947, none; 1948, Tennessee Williams, *A Streetcar Named Desire*; 1949, Arthur Miller, *Death of a Salesman*; 1950, Richard Rodgers, Oscar Hammerstein II, and Joshua Logan, *South Pacific*; 1951, none; 1952, Joseph Kramm, *The Shrike*; 1953, William Inge, *Picnic*; 1954, John Patrick, *Teahouse of the August Moon*; 1955, Tennessee Williams, *Cat on a Hot Tin Roof*; 1956, Frances Goodrich and Albert Hackett, *The Diary of Anne Frank*; 1957, Eugene O'Neill, *Long Day's Journey Into Night*; 1958, Ketti Frings, *Look Homeward, Angel*; 1959, Archibald MacLeish, *J. B.*; 1960, George Abbott, Jerome Weidman, Sheldon Harnick, and Jerry Bock, *Fiorello!*; 1961, Tad Mosel, *All the Way Home*; 1962, Frank Loesser and Abe Burrows, *How to Succeed in Business Without Really Trying*; 1963, none; 1964, none; 1965, Frank Gilroy, *The Subject Was Roses*; 1966, none; 1967, Edward Albee, *A Delicate Balance*; 1968, none; 1969, Howard Sackler, *The Great White Hope*; 1970, Charles Gordone, *No Place to Be Somebody*; 1971, Paul Zindel, *The Effect of Gamma Rays on Man-in-the-Moon Marigolds*; 1972, none; 1973, Jason Miller, *That Championship Season*; 1974, none; 1975, Edward Albee, *Seascape*; 1976, conceived by Michael Bennett, *A Chorus Line*;

1977, Michael Cristofer, *The Shadow Box*; 1978, Donald L. Coburn, *The Gin Game*; 1979, Sam Shepard, *Buried Child*; 1980, Lanford Wilson, *Talley's Folly*; 1981, Beth Henley, *Crimes of the Heart*; 1982, Charles Fuller, *A Soldier's Play*; 1983, Marsha Norman, *'Night Mother*; 1984, David Mamet, *Glengarry Glen Ross*; 1985, Stephen Sondheim and James Lapine, *Sunday in the Park with George*; 1986, none; 1987, August Wilson, *Fences*.

Poetry 1922, Edwin Arlington Robinson, *Collected Poems*; 1923, Edna St. Vincent Millay, *The Ballad of the Harp-Weaver, A Few Figs from Thistles*, and other poems; 1924, Robert Frost, *New Hampshire: A Poem with Notes and Grace Notes*; 1925, Edwin Arlington Robinson, *The Man Who Died Twice*; 1926, Amy Lowell, *What's O'Clock*; 1927, Leonora Speyer, *Fiddler's Farewell*; 1928, Edwin Arlington Robinson, *Tristram*; 1929, Stephen Vincent Benét, *John Brown's Body*; 1930, Conrad Aiken, *Selected Poems*; 1931, Robert Frost, *Collected Poems*; 1932, George Dillon, *The Flowering Stone*; 1933, Archibald MacLeish, *Conquistador*; 1934, Robert Hillyer, *Collected Verse*; 1935, Audrey Wurdemann, *Bright Ambush*; 1936, Robert P. Tristram Coffin, *Strange Holiness*; 1937, Robert Frost, *A Further Range*; 1938, Marya Zaturenska, *Cold Morning Sky*; 1939, John Gould Fletcher, *Selected Poems*; 1940, Mark Van Doren, *Collected Poems*; 1941, Leonard Bacon, *Sunderland Capture*; 1942, William Rose Benét, *The Dust Which Is God*; 1943, Robert Frost, *A Witness Tree*; 1944, Stephen Vincent Benét, *Western Star*; 1945, Karl Shapiro, *V-Letter and Other Poems*; 1946, none; 1947, Robert Lowell, *Lord Weary's Castle*; 1948, W. H. Auden, *The Age of Anxiety*; 1949, Peter Viereck, *Terror and Decorum*; 1950, Gwendolyn Brooks, *Annie Allen*; 1951, Carl Sandburg, *Complete Poems*; 1952, Marianne Moore, *Collected Poems*; 1953, Archibald MacLeish, *Collected Poems 1917–1952*; 1954, Theodore Roethke, *The Waking*; 1955, Wallace Stevens, *Collected Poems*; 1956, Elizabeth Bishop, *Poems, North and South*; 1957, Richard Wilbur, *Things of This World*; 1958, Robert Penn Warren, *Promises; Poems 1954–1956*; 1959, Stanley Kunitz, *Selected Poems, 1928–1958*; 1960, W. D. Snodgrass, *Heart's Needle*; 1961, Phyllis McGinley, *Times Three: Selected Verse from Three Decades*; 1962, Alan Dugan, *Poems*; 1963, William Carlos Williams (posthumous), *Pictures from Brueghel*; 1964, Louis Simpson, *At the End of the Open Road*; 1965, John Berryman, *77 Dream Songs*; 1966, Richard Eberhart, *Selected Poems*; 1967, Anne Sexton, *Live or Die*; 1968, Anthony Hecht, *The Hard Hours*; 1969, George Oppen, *Of Being Numerous*; 1970, Richard Howard, *Untitled Subjects*; 1971, William S. Merwin, *The Carrier of Ladders*; 1972, James Wright, *Collected Poems*; 1973, Maxine Winokur Kumin, *Up Country*; 1974, Robert Lowell, *The Dolphin*; 1975, Gary Snyder, *Turtle Island*; 1976, John Ashbery, *Self-Portrait in a Convex Mirror*; 1977, James Merrill, *Divine Comedies*; 1978, Howard Nemerov, *Collected Poems*; 1979, Robert Penn Warren,

Now and Then; 1980, Donald Rodney Justice, *Selected Poems*; 1981, James Schuyler, *The Morning of the Poem*; 1982, Sylvia Plath (posthumous), *The Collected Poems*; 1983, Galway Kinnell, *Selected Poems*; 1984, Mary Oliver, *American Primitive*; 1985, Carolyn Kizer, *Yin*; 1986, Henry Taylor, *The Flying Change*; 1987, Rita Dove, *Thomas and Beulah*.

History 1917, J. J. Jusserand, *With Americans of Past and Present Days*; 1918, James Ford Rhodes, *History of the Civil War*; 1919, none; 1920, Justin H. Smith, *The War with Mexico*; 1921, William Sowden Sims, with Burton J. Hendrick, *The Victory at Sea*; 1922, James Truslow Adams, *The Founding of New England*; 1923, Charles Warren, *The Supreme Court in United States History*; 1924, Charles Howard McIlwain, *The American Revolution: A Constitutional Interpretation*; 1925, Frederick L. Paxton, *A History of the American Frontier*; 1926, Edward Channing, *History of the U.S.*; 1927, Samuel Flagg Bemis, *Pinckney's Treaty*; 1928, Vernon Louis Parrington, *Main Currents in American Thought*; 1929, Fred A. Shannon, *The Organization and Administration of the Union Army, 1861–65*; 1930, Claude H. Van Tyne, *The War of Independence*; 1931, Bernadotte E. Schmitt, *The Coming of the War: 1914*; 1932, Gen. John J. Pershing, *My Experiences in the World War*; 1933, Frederick J. Turner, *The Significance of Sections in American History*; 1934, Herbert Agar, *The People's Choice*; 1935, Charles McLean Andrews, *The Colonial Period of American History*; 1936, Andrew C. McLaughlin, *A Constitutional History of the United States*; 1937, Van Wyck Brooks, *The Flowering of New England*; 1938, Paul Herman Buck, *The Road to Reunion 1865–1900*; 1939, Frank Luther Mott, *A History of American Magazines*; 1940, Carl Sandburg, *Abraham Lincoln: The War Years*; 1941, Marcus Lee Hansen, *The Atlantic Migration 1607–1860*; 1942, Margaret Leech, *Reveille in Washington*; 1943, Esther Forbes, *Paul Revere and the World He Lived In*; 1944, Merle Curti, *The Growth of American Thought*; 1945, Stephen Bonsal, *Unfinished Business*; 1946, Arthur M. Schlesinger, Jr., *The Age of Jackson*; 1947, Dr. James Phinney Baxter 3d, *Scientists Against Time*; 1948, Bernard De Voto, *Across the Wide Missouri*; 1949, Roy F. Nichols, *The Disruption of American Democracy*; 1950, O. W. Larkin, *Art and Life in America*; 1951, R. Carlyle Buley, *The Old Northwest, Pioneer Period 1815–1840*; 1952, Oscar Handlin, *The Uprooted*; 1953, George Dangerfield, *The Era of Good Feelings*; 1954, Bruce Catton, *A Stillness at Appomattox*; 1955, Paul Horgan, *Great River: The Rio Grande in North American History*; 1956, Richard Hofstadter, *The Age of Reform*; 1957, George F. Kennan, *Russia Leaves the War*; 1958, Bray Hammond, *Banks and Politics in America —From the Revolution to the Civil War*; 1959, Leonard D. White and Jean Schneider, *The Republican Era: 1869–1901*; 1960, Margaret Leech, *In the Days of McKinley*; 1961, Herbert Feis, *Between War and Peace: The Potsdam*

Conference; 1962, Lawrence H. Gipson, *The Triumphant Empire, Thunder-Clouds Gather in the West*; 1963, Constance Green, *Washington, Village and Capital*; 1964, Sumner Chilton Powell, *Puritan Village: The Formation of a New England Town*; 1965, Irwin Unger, *The Greenback Era*; 1966, Perry Miller, *Life of the Mind in America*; 1967, William H. Goetzmann, *Exploration and Empire: The Explorer and Scientist in the Winning of the American West*; 1968, Bernard Bailyn, *The Ideological Origins of the American Revolution*; 1969, Leonard W. Levy, *Origins of the Fifth Amendment*; 1970, Dean Acheson, *Present at the Creation: My Years in the State Department*; 1971, James McGregor Burns, *Roosevelt: The Soldier of Freedom*; 1972, Carl N. Degler, *Neither Black nor White. Slavery and Race Relations in Brazil and the United States*; 1973, Michael Kammen, *People of Paradox: An Inquiry Concerning the Origin of American Civilization*; 1974, Daniel J. Boorstin, *The Americans: The Democratic Experience, Vol. 3*; 1975, Dumas Malone, *Jefferson and His Time*; 1976, Paul Horgan, *Lamy of Santa Fe*; 1977, David M. Potter (posthumous), *The Impending Crisis: 1841–1861*; 1978, Alfred D. Chandler, Jr., *The Invisible Hand: The Managerial Revolution in American Business*; 1979, Don E. Fehrenbacher, *The Dred Scott Case: Its Significance in Law and Politics*; 1980, Leon F. Litwack, *Been in the Storm So Long*; 1981, Lawrence A. Cremin, *American Education: The National Experience, 1783–1876*; 1982, C. Vann Woodward, editor, *Mary Chestnut's Civil War*; 1983, Rhys L. Isaac, *The Transformation of Virginia, 1740–1790*; 1984, none; 1985, Thomas K. McCraw, *The Prophets of Regulation*; 1986, Walter A. McDougall, *The Heavens and the Earth*; 1987, Bernard Bailyn, *Voyagers to the West: A Passage in the Peopling of America on the Eve of the Revolution*.

Biography   1917, Laura E. Richards and Maude Howe Elliott, assisted by Florence Howe Hall, *Julia Ward Howe*; 1918, William Cabell Bruce, *Benjamin Franklin, Self-Revealed*; 1919, Henry Adams, *The Education of Henry Adams*; 1920, Albert J. Beveridge, *The Life of John Marshall*; 1921, Edward Bok, *The Americanization of Edward Bok*; 1922, Hamlin Garland, *A Daughter of the Middle Border*; 1923, Burton J. Hendrick, *The Life and Letters of Walter H. Page*; 1924, Michael Pupin, *From Immigrant to Inventor*; 1925, M. A. DeWolfe Howe, *Barrett Wendell and His Letters*; 1926, Harvey Cushing, *Life of Sir William Osler*; 1927, Emory Holloway, *Whitman, An Interpretation in Narrative*; 1928, Charles Edward Russell, *The American Orchestra and Theodore Thomas*; 1929, Burton J. Hendrick, *The Training of an American: The Earlier Life and Letters of Walter H. Page*; 1930, Marquis James, *The Raven* (Sam Houston); 1931, Henry James, *Charles W. Eliot*; 1932, Henry F. Pringle, *Theodore Roosevelt*; 1933, Allan Nevins, *Grover Cleveland*; 1934, Tyler Dennett, *John Hay*; 1935, Douglas Southall Freeman, *R. E. Lee*; 1936, Ralph Barton Perry, *The Thought and Character of William James*; 1937, Allan Nevins, *Hamilton Fish: The*

Inner History of the Grant Administration; 1938, divided between Odell Shepard, *Pedlar's Progress*, and Marquis James, *Andrew Jackson*; 1939, Carl Van Doren, *Benjamin Franklin*; 1940, Ray Stannard Baker, *Woodrow Wilson, Life and Letters*; 1941, Ola Elizabeth Winslow, *Jonathan Edwards*; 1942, Forrest Wilson, *Crusader in Crinoline*; 1943, Samuel Eliot Morison, *Admiral of the Ocean Sea*; 1944, Carleton Mabee, *The American Leonardo: The Life of Samuel F. B. Morse*; 1945, Russel Blaine Nye, *George Bancroft: Brahmin Rebel*; 1946, Linnie Marsh Wolfe, *Son of the Wilderness*; 1947, William Allen White, *The Autobiography of William Allen White*; 1948, Margaret Clapp, *Forgotten First Citizen: John Bigelow*; 1949, Robert E. Sherwood, *Roosevelt and Hopkins*; 1950, Samuel Flagg Bemis, *John Quincy Adams and the Foundations of American Foreign Policy*; 1951, Margaret Louise Coit, *John C. Calhoun: American Portrait*; 1952, Merlo J. Pusey, *Charles Evans Hughes*; 1953, David J. Mays, *Edmund Pendleton 1721–1803*; 1954, Charles A. Lindbergh, *The Spirit of St. Louis*; 1955, William S. White, *The Taft Story*; 1956, Talbot F. Hamlin, *Benjamin Henry Latrobe*; 1957, John F. Kennedy, *Profiles in Courage*; 1958, Douglas Southall Freeman (posthumous), *George Washington*, vols I–VI, John Alexander Carroll and Mary Wells Ashworth, vol VII; 1959, Arthur Walworth, *Woodrow Wilson, American Prophet*; 1960, Samuel Eliot Morison, *John Paul Jones*; 1961, David Donald, *Charles Sumner and the Coming of the Civil War*; 1962, none; 1963, Leon Edel, *Henry James: The Conquest of London and the Middle Years*; 1964, Walter Jackson Bate, *John Keats*; 1965, Ernest Samuels, *Henry Adams*; 1966, Arthur M. Schlesinger, Jr., *A Thousand Days*; 1967, Justin Kaplan, *Mr. Clemens and Mark Twain*; 1968, George F. Kennan, *Memoirs, 1925–1950*; 1969, B. L. Reid, *The Man from New York*; 1970, T. Harry Williams, *Huey Long*; 1971, Lawrance Thompson, *Robert Frost: The Years of Triumph, 1915–1938*; 1972, Joseph P. Lash, *Eleanor and Franklin; The Story of Their Relationship Based on Eleanor Roosevelt's Private Papers*; 1973, W. A. Swanbert, *Luce and His Empire*; 1974, Louis Sheaffer, *O'Neill, Son and Artist*; 1975, Robert A. Caro, *The Power Broker: Robert Moses and the Fall of New York*; 1976, Richard W. B. Lewis, *Edith Wharton: A Biography*; 1977, John E. Mack, *A Prince of Our Disorder*; 1978, Walter Jackson Bate, *Samuel Johnson*; 1979, Leonard Baker, *Days of Sorrow and Pain: Leo Baeck and the Berlin Jews*; 1980, Edmund Morris, *The Rise of Theodore Roosevelt*; 1981, Robert K. Massie, *Peter the Great*; 1982, William S. McFeely, *Grant: A Biography*; 1983, Russell Baker, *Growing Up*; 1984, Louis R. Harlan, *Booker T. Washington*; 1985, Kenneth Silverman, *The Life and Times of Cotton Mather*; 1986, Elizabeth Frank, *Louise Bogan: A Portrait*; 1987, David J. Garrow, *Bearing the Cross: Martin Luther King, Jr., and the Southern Christian Leadership Conference*.

General Nonfiction 1962, Theodore H. White, *The Making of the President, 1960;* 1963, Barbara W. Tuchman, *The Guns of August;* 1964, Richard Hofstadter, *Anti-Intellectualism in American Life;* 1965, Howard Mumford Jones, *O Strange New World;* 1966, Edwin Way Teale, *Wandering Through Winter;* 1967, David Brion Davis, *The Problem of Slavery in Western Culture;* 1968, Will and Ariel Durant, *Rousseau and Revolution;* 1969, Rene Jules Dubos, *So Human an Animal,* and Norman Mailer, *The Armies of the Night;* 1970, Erik H. Erikson, *Gandhi's Truth;* 1971, John Toland, *The Rising Sun;* 1972, Barbara W. Tuchman, *Stilwell and the American Experience in China, 1911–1945;* 1973, Frances FitzGerald, *Fire in the Lake: The Vietnamese and the Americans in Vietnam,* and Robert M. Coles, *Children of Crisis,* vols 1 and 2; 1974, Ernest Becker, *The Denial of Death;* 1975, Annie Dillard, *Pilgrim at Tinker Creek;* 1976, Robert N. Butler, *Why Survive? Being Old in America;* 1977, William W. Warner, *Beautiful Swimmers: Watermen, Crabs and the Chesapeake Bay;* 1978, Carl Sagan, *The Dragons of Eden;* 1979, Edward O. Wilson, *On Human Nature;* 1980, Douglas R. Hofstadter, *Gödel, Escher, Bach: An Eternal Golden Braid;* 1981, Carl E. Schorske, *Fin-de-Siècle Vienna: Politics and Culture;* 1982, Tracy Kidder, *The Soul of a New Machine;* 1983, Susan Sheehan, *Is There No Place on Earth for Me?;* 1984, Paul Starr, *Social Transformation of American Medicine;* 1985, Studs Terkel, *The Good War: An Oral History of World War II;* 1986, Joseph Lelyveld, *Move Your Shadow,* and J. Anthony Lukas, *Common Ground;* 1987, David K. Shipler, *Arab and Jew: Wounded Spirits in a Promised Land.*

pun   A wordplay in which two meanings appear in one word or in two words of identical sound. Used as a rather low form of wit, often in playful humor, a pun sometimes has deeply serious implications.

> Ask for me tomorrow and you shall find me a grave man.
> Shakespeare, *Romeo and Juliet*

Punch   An English comic weekly magazine, founded in 1841. The title came from the clever and irascible figure of the PUNCH AND JUDY puppet show. In the magazine Punch was transformed into "the laughing philosopher and man of letters; the essence of all wit, the concentration of all wisdom," and the titular "editor" of the magazine. *Punch* soon became an English institution to which eminent artists, humorists, and writers contributed. The format is a blend of humor, serious comment, and views on topical and controversial subjects presented in text and illustration. In its long career, *Punch* has done much to expose various shams, fads, affectations, and forms of ostentation. The present use of the word "cartoon" originated with *Punch,* which is known especially for its bitingly satirical illustrations.

Punch and Judy   The hero and heroine—and the title—of countless English puppet shows. In the traditional story, Punch, in a fit of rage, kills his infant child and bludgeons Judy, his wife, to death; although he is imprisoned, he manages to escape. Later he encounters and outwits several other characters, including the Devil. The irascible, hump-backed, hook-nosed Punch is thought to be derived from Pulcinella, the Neapolitan servant of the COMMEDIA DELL'ARTE, who was also a great favorite in Italian puppet shows. By about 1650 this character was appearing in puppet shows in France; transformed into the witty Polichinelle reaching England at the time of the RESTORATION, he became known as Punchinello or Punch. In their present form, Punch and his wife, Judy, who was originally called Joan, date from about 1800.

Punic Wars   The three wars fought between Rome and Carthage in the 3rd and 2nd centuries BC. The First Punic War (264–241 BC) was waged by Rome to prevent Carthaginian supremacy in Sicily. The second (218–202 BC) was fought over the Carthaginian advances in Spain, and it was during this war that HANNIBAL crossed the Alps with his army and ravaged Italy for nearly fifteen years. At its conclusion, Carthage was stripped of all its territories except its own city, and Rome was left mistress of the Mediterranean. The Third Punic War (149–146 BC) ended in the complete destruction of Carthage. See CATO THE ELDER.

puppet plays, Japanese   See BUNRAKU.

Puranas (Sans, "ancient stories")   A class of Sanskrit works written at various times between 500 BC and AD 1000, serving as secondary scriptures of HINDUISM. The *Puranas* deal with a wide range of topics, including religious customs and mythology. The eighteen so-called *Great Puranas* focus mainly on the gods BRAHMĀ, VISHNU, and SHIVA, and their incarnations. Especially important are the *Bhagavata* and *Vishnu Puranas.*

Purcell, Henry (c1659–1695)   Outstanding English Baroque composer. Purcell's early work consisted largely of sacred music, hymns, and anthems. After 1689, when he wrote his exquisite opera *Dido and Aeneas,* he concentrated almost exclusively on music for the stage. *King Arthur* (1691; libretto by DRYDEN), *The Fairy Queen* (1692; based on A MIDSUMMER NIGHT'S DREAM), and *The Indian Queen* (1695; libretto by Dryden and Sir Thomas Howard) are among his best-known MASQUES. He also composed chamber music, such as *Fantasias for Strings* (1680) and many songs and odes, notably *Hail, Bright Cecelia* (1692) and *Come Ye Sons of Art* (1694; written on the occasion of Queen Mary's birthday). The prodigious output of his short life was extremely well received by his contemporaries.

Purdy, Al[fred Wellington] (1918–   )   Canadian poet. Born near Belleville, Ontario, Purdy spent his early adult years traveling and working in factories. In the 1950s he began writing poems which powerfully evoke the landscapes and peoples of Canada, both past and present. Major volumes are *Poems for All the Annettes* (1962; rev 1968), *The Cariboo Horses* (1965), *North of Summer*

(1967), and *Wild Grape Wine* (1968). His *Selected Poems* appeared in 1972. *No Other Country* (1977) is a collection of prose pieces. *Moths in the Iron Curtain* (1978), *The Stone Bird* (1981), and *Piling Blood* (1984) are other volumes of verse.

Purdy, James (1923–   ) American novelist and short-story writer. Purdy's work was first recognized in England by Dame Edith SITWELL, who called his novella *63: Dream Palace* "a masterpiece," and who saw to its publication, along with short stories, in *Color of Darkness* (1957). A controversial figure, Purdy writes black allegorical parodies depicting a world of twisted or negated morals in which people are incapable of communication. Beginning with his first stories, and again in such novels as *Malcolm* (1959), *The Nephew* (1961), and *Cabot Wright Begins* (1964), he treats young men, either orphaned or fatherless, who are led through terror and perversion by predatory and exploitative adults. In *Jeremy's Version* (1970), *The House of the Solitary Maggot* (1974), *Narrow Rooms* (1978), *Mourners Below* (1981), and *On Glory's Course* (1984), he continued with grim glimpses of ruined communities, failed relationships, and unbearable loneliness. A book of plays, *The Berry Picker/Scrap of Paper* (1981), and several story and play collections, including *Children Is All* (1962) and *A Day After the Fair* (1977), are among his other works.

Pure Land Buddhism   See AMIDISM.

Purgatorio (Purgatory)   Part II of the DIVINE COMEDY by DANTE. Vergil conducts Dante up the mountain of Purgatory, or purification. At the foot in Ante-Purgatory are the negligent who for some reason delayed repentance for their sins and must wait as long as they delayed before beginning their ascent. A terrace makes an ascending spiral up the mountain, and repentant spirits toil forward on it bowed beneath burdens appropriate to the sins of which they must be purged, and learning the corresponding virtues. The higher on the mountain the spirit is climbing, the less grievous the sin of which he is being cleansed, and the easier his progress, until at last he will be ready to join the blessed in Paradise. Dante must join in the labors of this ascent—although his progress is much more rapid than others—and he meets successively those doing penance for pride, envy, wrath, sloth, avarice, gluttony, and lust. Vergil explains that an instinct to love and desire is natural in man, and properly leads the soul to God. The first three sins are perversions of that instinct; sloth is the failure to pursue it; and the last three sins, although exercising the instinct, deflect it toward worldly objects and thus, at least temporarily, away from God.

Having guided Dante as far as human intellect can go, Vergil leaves him at the entrance to the Earthly Paradise. Here Matilda, representing the perfect active life, conducts him through an Edenlike garden to BEATRICE, who represents the perfect contemplative life, or divine grace and revelation. After a series of allegorical appearances and adventures, representing the crises of the Roman Catholic Church, Beatrice prepares Dante for the ascent to Paradise.

Purgatory (1939)   A short verse play by William Butler YEATS. For Yeats, purgatory is the condition of a spirit so obsessed by remorse or some other emotion that it constantly relives the crisis of its life in its old home. An old man and his son watch the ghost of the old man's mother in such a purgatory. The conversation between father and son reveals the family history and melodrama; at the end, the father kills his son in order to give his mother peace and put an end to the family's polluted blood.

Purim   See ESTHER.

Puritans   Originally, seceders from the Church of England in the time of Queen Elizabeth I. They were so called because as radical, or Calvinistic, Protestants, who acknowledged only the authority of the "pure Word of God" as expressed in the BIBLE, they wished to "purify" the church of its Catholic heritage of doctrines, rites, and organization. Early persecution drove them to immigrate in large numbers to Europe and New England; later they played a major role in the social and religious conflicts of the 17th century. In both England and America, the rigid morals of the Puritans and their stern suppression of various forms of recreation and art have made the word *puritanical* synonymous with narrow-mindedness. See CALVIN, JOHN.

Purloined Letter, The (1845)   A story by Edgar Allan POE. A woman of royal rank is blackmailed by a cabinet minister on the basis of a compromising letter. The police, failing in the search, turn to the amateur C. Auguste DUPIN, who is able to locate the purloined letter.

purple patches   Highly colored or ornate passages in a literary work that is, generally speaking, otherwise undistinguished. The allusion is to Horace's *De arte poetica*:

Inceptis gravibus plerumque et magna professis,
Purpureus, late qui splendeat, unus et alter
Adsuitur pannus.

(Often to weighty enterprises and such as profess great objects, one or two purple patches are sewed on to make a fine display in the distance.)

Pursuit of Diarmuid and Gráinne, The   An early Irish tale from the FENIAN CYCLE. It is a variant of the Deirdre story and an early parallel to the Tristan and Iseult legend. Diarmuid, nephew of FIONN MAC CUMHAIL, runs off with Fionn's second wife, Gráinne. The major part of the story concerns the life of the lovers in the wilderness, fleeing from Fionn and his forces, and finally being caught by Fionn.

Pururavas and Urvasi   A Hindu myth similar to the classical myths of CUPID and PSYCHE or APOLLO and DAPHNE. The heavenly nymph Urvasi decided to live on earth as a mortal. On first sight, the King Pururavas fell hopelessly in love with her and begged her to marry him. She consented, imposing certain conditions to which he agreed. When, because of mischief on the part of Urvasi's celestial colleagues, Pururavas was forced to violate the conditions, Urvasi disappeared. Pururavas, inconsolable, wandered everywhere to find her. Ultimately he succeeded, and they were indissolubly united. The best-known version of the story is found in KĀLIDĀSA's Sanskrit drama *Vikramorvashiyā*.

Purusha (Sans, "man; male")   In HINDUISM, the primeval man, who was sacrificed, the universe issuing from various parts of his body. The basic fourfold division of Hindu society (see CASTE) is expressed in this myth of creation.

Pusey, E[dward] B[ouverie] (1800–1882) Anglican theologian, associated with John KEBLE and John Henry NEWMAN in the OXFORD MOVEMENT. Perhaps the staunchest controversialist and most learned theologian in the movement, Pusey became its virtual leader after Newman's conversion to Roman Catholicism, effecting many changes in the churches of England, such as the establishment of Anglican nunneries and the revival of private confession. His works consist mainly of controversies or doctrinal writings. See TRACTS FOR THE TIMES.

Pushkin, Aleksandr Sergeyevich (1799–1837) Russian poet, playwright, novelist, and short-story writer. Russia's greatest poet, whose standing in his own country is equivalent to SHAKESPEARE's in England or GOETHE's in Germany, Pushkin almost single-handedly created a classical literary heritage for Russian writers, producing outstanding work in almost every major genre.

Pushkin was the descendant on his father's side of an ancient noble family. On his mother's side he was a great-great-grandson of an Abyssinian black, Gannibal, who served under Peter the Great. Pushkin's poetry attracted attention even before he graduated from the Lyceum in 1817. He obtained a sinecure in the foreign ministry in St. Petersburg, led a fast-paced social life, and wrote *Ruslan i Lyudmila* (*Ruslan and Ludmilla*, 1820), a long poem based on folklore motifs, which established him as one of the distinguished young poets. Because of some politically indiscreet verses, Pushkin was transferred in 1820 to southern Russia. He traveled in the Caucasus, served in Bessarabia and Odessa, and continued his poetic work, which at this point shows the influence of BYRON in theme and treatment: *Kavkazsky plennik* (*The Captive of the Caucasus*, 1822), *Bakhchisaraisky fontan* (*The Fountain of Bakhchisaray*, 1824), and *Tsygany* (*The Gypsies*, 1827). He also began his greatest work, EUGENE ONEGIN, a novel in verse.

Pushkin's trouble with the authorities continued. In 1824 he was expelled from the government and banished to his family estate. While there he wrote his famous historical tragedy BORIS GODUNOV. Pushkin was on the family estate when the DECEMBRIST REVOLT of 1825 took place.

Several of his friends were involved in the affair, but he apparently had no connection with it. In 1826 Pushkin was given permission by Tsar NICHOLAS I to return to St. Petersburg, where he resumed the active social life interrupted six years before. In 1829 he met sixteen-year-old Natalya Goncharova, whom he married two years later. In the autumn of 1830, while stranded by a plague quarantine on his country estate at Boldino, Pushkin wrote *Tales by Belkin*, began LITTLE TRAGEDIES, and completed *Eugene Onegin*. After his marriage, he had little peace for such intense creative activity. His wife's frivolous social life was a constant source of irritation, and a growing family necessitated added income. In 1836 he founded the literary journal *Sovremennik* (*The Contemporary*). Jealousy over his wife's attachment to a guards officer, Baron George D'Anthes, led to a duel, in January 1837, in which Pushkin was fatally wounded.

Besides the poems mentioned, Pushkin produced a large body of lyric verse, as well as numerous long poems, including *Graf Nulin* (*Count Nulin*, 1825), *Domik v Kolomne* (*The Little House in Kolomna*, 1830), and THE BRONZE HORSEMAN. His prose work includes, besides the *Belkin* tales, *Dubrovsky* (1832–33), THE QUEEN OF SPADES, and *Kapitanskaya dochka* (*The Captain's Daughter*, 1836), an account of the Pugachev rebellion of the 1770s.

Much of Pushkin's work had an immense influence on later Russian literature. He was the master for all the poets after him in both lyric and narrative poetry. His character of Ivan Belkin, the narrator of the *Belkin* tales and of the prose fragment *Istoriya sela Goryukhina* (*History of the Village of Goryukhino*, 1830), is one of the initial models of realistic depiction of character in Russian literature. Eugene Onegin is one of the original SUPERFLUOUS MEN of Russian literature, the ancestor of LERMONTOV's Pechorin and of many of TURGENEV's heroes. Tatyana, the heroine of *Onegin*, has been regarded as the ideal of Russian womanhood, and many later writers, notably Turgenev, have modeled their heroines after her.

Pushkin's early poetic style was influenced by the classical styles of such 18th-century French writers as VOLTAIRE, Evariste Perny, and André CHÉNIER. The smoothness and balance of Pushkin's diction in his early works partly derives from these authors and from his own compatriots who imitated them: ZHUKOVSKY and Konstantin Nikolayevich Batyushkov (1787–1855). *The Captive of the Caucasus* and *The Fountain of Bakhchisaray* are perhaps the best examples of Pushkin's early manner. In a letter of 1823, Pushkin wrote: "I don't like grafting European graces and French subtleties onto our language. Roughness and simplicity suit it better." Pushkin's poetic style from this time on reflects these thoughts. His language becomes more concise than before, and it loses its mellifluent qualities, reaching the limits of simplicity in such late works as *Poltava* (1828–29) and *The Bronze Horseman*. The shift in poetic style was accompanied by a change in Pushkin's relationship to his work: from that of a narrator who is sometimes subjectively involved in the work to that of an objective creator who is always outside the work. This objectivity is particularly evident in Pushkin's prose works. In these works, the language is extremely simple and straightforward, and instances can be found in the prose where Pushkin changed the ordinary Russian syntax to make the language simpler. Although many of his prose pieces—such as the *Belkin* tales, *The Queen of Spades*, and *The Captain's Daughter*—have been quite influential in Russian literature because of their themes and characterizations, Pushkin's prose language was too experimental a medium to be more than a starting point for later writers.

Puss in Boots   A famous tale with many sources, it is best known from Charles PERRAULT's tale "Le Maître-chat ou le chat botté" (1697), and also STRAPAROLA's *Le piacevoli notti* (1550–53). The cat is marvelously accomplished and by ready wit or ingenious tricks secures a fortune and royal wife for his master, a penniless young miller who passes under the name of the Marquis de Carabas. In the Italian tale, Puss is called "Constantine's cat." Ludwig TIECK's play *Der gestiefelte Kater* (1797) also treats this theme.

Putain respectueuse, La   See RESPECTFUL PROSTITUTE, THE.

Puzo, Mario (1920–   )   American novelist. Puzo's first novel, *The Dark Arena* (1955), set in Germany, was followed by a semiautobiographical novel about an Italian immigrant family, *The Fortunate Pilgrim* (1964). He did not become widely known, however, until the publication of *The Godfather* (1969), which became a bestseller and was made into a successful motion picture. It is the story of Don Vito Corleone, the head of a New York crime syndicate, and of the desperate struggles among the underworld bosses for power. *Fools Die* (1978) describes the life of a street-wise boy turned successful novelist in Las Vegas and Hollywood. *The Sicilian* (1984), set in Sicily after World War II, again takes up the themes of crime and power as personified by the Mafia.

Pygmalion   A sculptor and king of Cyprus in Greek legend, who, though he hated women, fell in love with his own ivory statue of APHRODITE. At his earnest prayer, the goddess gave life to the statue, and he married his own creation.

The story is told in Ovid's METAMORPHOSES, and appeared in English in John MARSTON's *Metamorphosis of Pygmalion's Image* (1598). William Morris retold it in *The Earthly Paradise* (1868–70). In W. S. GILBERT's comedy *Pygmalion and Galatea* (1871), the sculptor is a married man and his wife, Cynisca, is jealous of the animated statue Galatea, which, after considerable trouble, returns to its original state. George Bernard Shaw's play PYGMALION takes its name from this legendary figure.

Pygmalion (1913)   A play by George Bernard SHAW. Based on the classical legend, Shaw's work is about human relations and the delicate modern social order. The Pygmalion of the play is Professor Henry Higgins, a teacher of phonetics. He takes on Eliza Doolittle, a Cockney flower girl, as his student. She is transformed from a guttersnipe into an elegant woman, but then, like the statue of the legend, having come to life, she falls in love with Higgins. His is the responsibility for having made her a lady; she cannot return to her former life, but Shaw makes it clear that she does not marry the professor. *Pygmalion* was made into a successful musical comedy, *My Fair Lady* (1956).

pygmies (fr Gr, *pygme*, the length of the arm from elbow to knuckles)   The name used by HOMER and other classical writers for a supposed race of dwarfs. They were said to dwell somewhere in Ethiopia. Fable has it that every spring the cranes made war on these creatures and devoured them. The pygmies required axes to cut down cornstalks. When HERACLES went to the country, they climbed up his goblet by ladders to drink from it, and while he was asleep two whole armies of them fell upon his right hand, and two upon his left. They were rolled up by Heracles in his lion's skin. Jonathan Swift used this legend in his GULLIVER'S TRAVELS.

The term is now applied to certain dwarfish races of Central Africa, unknown until late in the 19th century, and of Malaysia.

Pylades   The son of Strophius and loyal friend of ORESTES. Pylades appears in several Greek dramas about Orestes, often as a mute character, but plays a noble role in Euripides' *Iphigenia in Tauris*. He married ELECTRA. His friendship for Orestes, like that of DAMON AND PYTHIAS, is proverbial. See ATREUS, HOUSE OF; IPHIGENIA.

Pym, Barbara (pen name of Barbara Mary Pym Crampton, 1913–1980)   English novelist. An editor of *Africa*, an anthropological review, for many years, Pym published her first novel, *Some Tame Gazelle*, in 1950. Subsequent novels, including *Excellent Women* (1952), *A Glass of Blessings* (1958), and *No Fond Return of Love* (1961), were widely praised for their elegant high comedy and their portraits of genteel and solitary women, kindly serving tea while taking a cool look at the world which has ignored them. In the 1960s, however, changing tastes pushed Pym out of literary circles; no one would publish her. In 1977 the *Times Literary Supplement* celebrated its 75th anniversary by asking well-known writers to name the writers they considered most over- and underrated. Barbara Pym was the only one mentioned twice as underrated, and from then on her fortunes changed and she was able to be published again. In 1978 *Quartet in Autumn* appeared, a gentle and ironic treatment of four unmarried people on the verge of retirement. *Excellent Women* was reissued in the same year. This was followed by *The Sweet Dove Died*, written in 1968 but not published until ten years later, dealing with loneliness and the inability to love. Her last novel was *A Few Green Leaves* (1980). Another earlier novel, *Less Than Angels* (1955), was reissued in 1981. Two novels, *An Unsuitable Attachment* (1982), an elegant novel about a young vicar and his wife's efforts at matchmaking, and *Crampton Hodnet* (1985), were published posthumously; an autobiographical work, *A Very Private Eye*, appeared in 1984.

Pym, John (1584–1643)   English Parliamentary statesman and orator. As leader of the anti-Royalist extremists in the Long Parliament, Pym prosecuted the case against the earl of STRAFFORD and sponsored the Grand Remonstrance, the protest passed by the House of Commons on Nov. 22, 1641, that listed the unconstitutional acts of Charles I and demanded reform. His intransigence contributed to the outbreak of the Civil War.

Pynchon, Thomas (1937–   )   American novelist. Pynchon's complex, pessimistic novels depict a world in which humanity is locked in a losing battle with the inanimate powers of technology, a world of human isolation that is both unbearable and impossible to understand. The novels are virtual floods of factual detail—physics and electronics, history, cybernetics, information theory, etc. —the very density of which renders irrelevant any distinctions between what is true or false. Pynchon's first novel, *V.* (1963), is a parody of the BLACK HUMOR techniques it employs. The multiple plots involve the *schlemiel* Benny Profane, a hunter of alligators in New York's sewers, and Herbert Stencil, who becomes obsessed by his pursuit of V., an initial he found in his dead father's notebooks. V.'s various manifestations include a femme fatale, a spy, and a hag who happened to be present at every significant event in Europe from 1890 to World War II. *The Crying of Lot 49* (1966), an equally complicated but more compact novel, follows Oedipa Maas in her efforts to untangle the mystery of a sinister communications system called "Tristero." Pynchon's best-known work, GRAVITY'S RAINBOW, is an immense, dark novel involving a Faustian quest for a secret missile. In *Gravity's Rainbow*, Pynchon develops the full force of the apocalyptic paranoia and theory of entropy that were treated in his earlier novels. It was followed by *Low-Lands* (1978), *The Secret Integration* (1980), and *The Small Rain* (1980). *Slow Learner*, a collection of stories, appeared in 1984.

Pyramus   A Babylonian youth in classical legend (Ovid's METAMORPHOSES), the lover of Thisbe. Thisbe was to meet Pyramus at the white mulberry tree near the tomb of Ninus, but she was scared by a lion and fled, leaving her veil, which the lion smeared with blood. Pyramus, thinking she had been killed, committed suicide. When Thisbe returned she found her lover dead and stabbed herself. The legend says that their blood stained the white fruit of the mulberry tree to its present color.

The "tedious brief scene" and "very tragical mirth" presented by the rustic tradesmen in Shakespeare's MIDSUMMER NIGHT'S DREAM is a travesty of this legend.

Pyrrha   See DEUCALION'S FLOOD.

pyrrhic   The shortest metrical foot in classical verse. It is a foot of two unstressed syllables. It is also known as a *dibrach* and is the opposite of a SPONDEE. It is uncommon in English versification and is represented mainly by a double ANACRUSIS, as in "O my / MARi/ON'S a / BONNY / LASS."

Pyrrhonism   A school of Greek philosophy named after Pyrrho (c365–275 BC). Pyrrho believed that virtue is the only good, and all other things are indifferent. Realizing the eternal nature of good helped him to achieve a tranquil state called *ataraxy*. In the field of action, Pyrrho relied upon convention and custom; only in the sphere of truth did he refuse to rely on human cognition. The attitude of Pyrrho was later refined and referred to as SKEPTICISM.

Pyrrhus   See NEOPTOLEMUS.

Pythagoras   (6th century BC)   A Greek philosopher and mathematician. Almost nothing is known of Pythagoras' life, except that he was born on the island of Samos; it is probable that he studied with Pherecydes, and he may have visited Egypt. Reliable information even on his teachings is scant, but he is known to have been interested in mathematics, especially in relation to weights and measures, and musical theory. He is best known for his doctrine of the transmigration of souls and the harmony of the spheres, although the proof of the so-called Pythagorean theorem (the 47th proposition of Euclid, Book I) is also attributed to him. He founded a semimonastic school of philosophy in Crotona, Italy, where he apparently practiced divination, among other arts. He was regarded by his contemporaries with mingled awe and suspicion, and many wild tales grew up of his supernatural powers. The meeting place of Pythagoras' secret society was set afire and the sect suppressed almost everywhere. Whether Pythagoras himself died at this time or later is uncertain. Among the tales told of him are that he had a golden thigh, that he recalled previous existences, including one as Euphorbus, who fought at Troy, and that he was an incarnation of the Hyperborean Apollo.

Pythia   The title of the priestess of the famous DELPHIC ORACLE.

Python   The monster serpent hatched from the mud of DEUCALION'S FLOOD. It was slain near Delphi by APOLLO. It was the ancient guardian of the shrine of the DELPHIC ORACLE and probably an oracular serpent.

Q

Q   See QUILLER-COUCH, SIR ARTHUR THOMAS.

quaestor   In ancient Rome, one of twenty treasury officials. See CURSUS HONORUM.

quair   See KINGIS QUAIR.

Quakers   A familiar name for members of the Society of Friends, a Christian religious sect founded by George FOX. They have no definite creed and no regular ministry but are guided by their doctrine of inner light. Their tenets include PACIFISM, a refusal to take oaths, and originally a characteristic simplicity in dress and speech (e.g., use of the archaic "Thee" and "Thou"). "Justice Bennett, of Derby," says Fox, "was the first to call us Quakers because I bade him quake and tremble at the word of the Lord."

Quare Fellow, The   See BEHAN, BRENDAN.

Quarles, Francis (1592–1644)   English poet of the metaphysical school (see METAPHYSICAL POETS). Quarles's religious poetry, similar to that of George Herbert, is marked by an elliptical, colloquial, or hortatory style and by striking imagery chosen from the everyday pursuits and interests of his time. He is best known for *Emblems* (1635), a book of poems accompanied by appropriate pictures, which won enormous popularity in its day. His other works include A *Feast for Worms* (1620), *Argalus and Parthenia* (1629), *History of Samson* (1631), *Divine Fancies* (1632), and *Hieroglyphics* (1638). See EMBLEM BOOKS.

Quasimodo   See HUNCHBACK OF NOTRE DAME, THE.

Quasimodo, Salvatore (1901–1968)   Italian poet, critic, and translator. Quasimodo's work falls roughly into two periods, divided by World War II. Beginning with the nostalgic poems about Sicily in *Acque e terre* (1930), the first, or "hermetic," period is characterized by a recondite style and metaphysical content (see HERMETICISM), as exemplified by the verse in *Oboe sommerso* (1932), *Erato e Apollion* (1936), and *Poesie* (1938). The poems in *Poesie nuove* (1942) contained hints of what he was to produce in the "engagé" period after World War II, in which his poetry was more concerned with the interpretation of contemporary history, social conditions, and the frustrations

and aspirations of the common man, as in such works as *Giorno dopo giorno* (1947), *La vita non è sogno* (1949), *La falso e vere verde* (1956), and *La terra impareggiabile* (1958). He was awarded the NOBEL PRIZE in Literature in 1959. His last book of verse was *Dare e avere* (1966; tr *To Give and to Have*, 1969; also tr *Debit and Credit*, 1972). He also translated Greek and Roman lyric and epic poems, as well as works of MOLIÈRE, SHAKESPEARE, and E. E. CUMMINGS, among many others, into Italian.

quatrain   In prosody, a stanza containing four lines in any meter or rhyme scheme, the most frequently used stanzaic form in European verse.

quattrocento (Ital, "four hundred")   The Italian way of designating the 15th century. The term thus refers to the early RENAISSANCE, the age of HUMANISM, and the period of the REVIVAL OF ANTIQUITY, and, in art history, to the century and the style of such artists as MASACCIO, BOTTICELLI, Fra ANGELICO, GHIBERTI, BRUNELLESCHI, and DONATELLO.

Queen, Ellery (pen name of Frederic Dannay, 1905–1982, and Manfred B. Lee, 1905–1971)   American detective-story writers and editors. The two were cousins, whose fictional sleuth Ellery Queen exercised his ratiocinative powers in numerous successful novels and stories from his first appearance in *The Roman Hat Mystery* (1929) to his last in A *Fine and Private Place* (1971). Under the pseudonym Barnaby Ross, they also occasionally wrote about detective Drury Lane. In 1941 the cousins began to edit *Ellery Queen's Mystery Magazine*, making it the finest and best-known periodical in the field.

Queen of Hearts   A character in Lewis Carroll's ALICE'S ADVENTURES IN WONDERLAND. Every time she is crossed or defeated during her mad croquet match, the queen shouts "Off with his head!" at the offender. When Alice points out that the trial of the Knave of Hearts, alleged to have stolen some tarts, is being absurdly conducted, the queen replies irrefutably, "Off with her head!"

Queen of Spades, The (Pikovaya dama, 1833)   A short story by Aleksandr PUSHKIN. Although it belongs to the Gothic tradition of horror, the tale is unusual for the calm, matter-of-fact manner in which the breakdown of the gambler Germann is related. Pushkin's prose style in this story is at its barest and most simple. TCHAIKOVSKY based an opera on the story.

Queirós, Rachel de (1910–   ) Brazilian novelist and journalist. Queirós's starkly realistic novels deal not only with the socioeconomic problems of the Brazilian northeast, but, most centrally, with the position of women in a class- and race-conscious society. The most socially oriented of her novels, *O quinze* (1930), chronicles the struggle for survival in the terrible drought of 1915. Her other novels, including *João Miguel* (1932), *Caminho de pedras* (1937), and *As três Marias* (1939; tr *The Three Marias*, 1963), deal with different manifestations of feminine love and the sacrifices often necessitated by rigid social convention. Her association with the other great novelists of the region is evident in *Brandão entre o mar e o amor* (1942), a collaborative novel with chapters by de Queirós, Jorge AMADO, José LINS DO RÊGO, and Graciliano RAMOS. Following a period in which her published work was written primarily for newspapers and the stage, she returned to the novel with *Dôra Doralina* (1975).

Quem quaeritis trope A text in the medieval Easter liturgy, named for the Latin question "Whom seek ye?" It was in the form of a dialogue between the women and the angel at the empty tomb of the risen Jesus. At about the beginning of the 11th century it began to be acted out during the service of Matins. The brief scene was gradually expanded, with priests, nuns, and choirboys taking the parts. From this simple beginning grew the medieval drama. SEE MYSTERY PLAYS.

Queneau, Raymond (1903–1976) French novelist, poet, and critic. Queneau is a difficult author to classify. He straddles the line between serious humor and simple entertainment. He retained from the surrealist movement, of which he was briefly a member, a dislike for established grammatical rules and a fondness for puns, parody, and orthographic fantasy. *Exercices de style* (1947; tr *Exercises in Style*, 1958, 1981) was a spoof on various literary conventions in which he rewrote the same story in ninety-nine different ways. Among his many novels, the best known are *Le Chiendent* (1933; tr *The Bark Tree*, 1968) and *Zazie dans le métro* (1959; tr *Zazie*, 1960).

Quennell, Peter [Courtney] (1905–   ) English biographer, poet, and literary critic. Quennell is an authority on BYRON and RUSKIN; he wrote highly readable personal histories of these men in *Byron: The Years of Fame* (1935), *Byron in Italy* (1941), and *John Ruskin* (1949). He also wrote studies of Baudelaire (1929) and Alexander Pope (1968). His poetry, written mostly when he was a young man, includes *Masques and Poems* (1922) and *Poems* (1926). His autobiographies, *The Marble Foot* (1977) and *The Wanton Chase* (1980), were praised for their grace and elegance of style. *Customs and Characters*

(1982) is a portrayal of contemporary men and women Quennell has admired and/or known, among them T. S. ELIOT, Cecil Beaton, Greta Garbo, Elizabeth BOWEN, and Virginia WOOLF.

Quental, Antero Tarquínio de (1842–1891) Portuguese poet. Born in the Azores, Quental studied at the university of Coimbra, where he became a leader of the "Coimbra generation" of students, who sought to revivify Portuguese literature. His famous pamphlet *Do bom senso e bom gosto* (1866) sparked the *questão Coimbra*, a bitter literary dispute in which the younger generation rebelled against the sterile romanticism, divorced from contemporary reality, that was exemplified by the works of the blind poet António Castilho. Influenced by HEGEL and PROUDHON, Quental was a socialist for a time but failed to find a creed that would satisfy his spiritual and moral aspirations. Having retired from public life in 1874, he returned in 1891 to his native island, where he took his own life in a public park.

As a poet Quental is best known for his sonnets, which constitute a spiritual autobiography of his tortured existence. About 150 of these are collected in *Sonetos completos* (1886). He also wrote *Raios de Extinta Luz* (1859–63) and *Primaveras românticas* (1871), poems representative of his early romantic phase, and *Odas modernas* (1865), in which he gave expression to his revolutionary views.

Quentin Durward (1823) A romantic novel by Sir Walter SCOTT, set in 15th-century France. Durward, a gallant young member of Louis XI's Scottish Guards, seeks the hand of Isabella, countess of Croye. His suit prospers when he saves the king's life in a boar hunt.

Querelle des anciens et des modernes (Quarrel of the Ancients and the Moderns) A French literary battle of the late 17th century between the ancients (classicists), who believed that literature should adhere to models and even to themes of antiquity, and the moderns, who did not wish literature to be thus restricted. The first leading spokesman for the moderns, Desmarets, was promptly condemned by Boileau. The ensuing dispute engaged the entire world of French letters and ended at the turn of the century with Boileau's partial capitulation. See BATTLE OF THE BOOKS, THE.

Quetzalcoatl The nature god of various Indian tribes in Mexico prior to the Spanish conquest. His symbol was the feathered serpent.

Quevedo [y Villegas], Francisco Gómez de (1580–1645) Spanish satirist, moralist, and poet. Born in Madrid of a good family, Quevedo studied at Alcalá. After a hasty flight from Spain to escape the consequences of a duel in which he had slain a noble (1611), Quevedo entered the service of the duke of Osuna in Italy. When Osuna fell from favor, Quevedo was exiled to his estate in La Mancha. In 1639 he was accused of having slipped into the king's napkin a satiric poem against the royal favorite, the count-duke of Olivares, and was imprisoned in the monastery of San Marcos in Leon. He was released in 1643, his health shattered.

A prolific writer who essayed nearly every genre, Quevedo is remembered mainly for his vitriolic satires, in which he mercilessly exposed the follies and vices of mankind. The best known are the picaresque novel El BUSCÓN and the SUEÑOS, a series of burlesque descriptions of Hell. His other prose works include *Política de Dios* (1626), a treatise on Christian rule; *Marco Bruto* (1644), a commentary on Plutarch's life of Brutus; a life of St. Paul (1644); and translations from Seneca, Epictetus, and St. François de Sales.

In poetry as in prose Quevedo excelled as a satirist. Over eight hundred of his poems have been preserved, but the best of these are the picaresque ballads and light verses that enable him to display his wit and familiarity with low life. An excellent stylist, he used CONCEPTISM to good effect, though it sometimes marred his most ambitious works.

Quickly, Mistress Nell In Shakespeare's HENRY IV: PART I and PART II and HENRY V, the excitable and stupid hostess of the Boar's Head Tavern in Eastcheap, frequented by Prince Hal, Sir John Falstaff, and their disreputable crew. In THE MERRY WIVES OF WINDSOR, she becomes servant of all work to Doctor Caius and devotes her boundless energy to securing a husband for Anne Page. Her husband is PISTOL.

Quiet Don, The (Tikhiy Don; 4 vols, 1928–1940) A novel by Mikhail SHOLOKHOV. Regarded as the outstanding work of early Soviet literature, this four-volume work is an epic of the intrusion of the revolution into the Don Cossack region of Russia and of the struggle between the old and new ways of life, both on the battlefields and in men's hearts. The hero of the work, a young Cossack named Gregor Melekhov, unlike the positive hero demanded by the Soviet literary doctrine of SOCIALIST REALISM, vacillates between two choices. He is at first convinced that the BOLSHEVIKS are right, then he gives up this view and fights with the Whites in the civil war, intending to help the Cossacks maintain their independence after the fighting is over. At the end of the novel, Melekhov is tending to favor the Bolsheviks again, but he is still not firmly convinced which side is best. His hesitation is set against the fanatical conviction of such Communists as Ivan Bunchuk, who is killed by Cossacks siding with the Whites. Even such characters as Bunchuk, however, are treated by Sholokhov as multidimensional human beings, rather than as the undeviating automatons that Soviet literary theorists would have preferred. There is reason to believe that Soviet authorities expected Sholokhov to convert Melekhov into a believing Communist by the end of the novel. By the time the fourth volume was finished, they realized that the work was too popular to condemn severely and that they had to accept the novel as a literary classic, as it deserved to be for its artistic merits.

The first half of *The Quiet Don* was published as *And Quiet Flows the Don* (1934) and the second half as *The Don Flows Home to the Sea* (1941).

Quietism A form of religious mysticism based on the doctrine that the essence of religion consists in the withdrawal of the soul from external objects and in fixing it upon the contemplation of God. Specifically, the term is applied to the creed professed by the Spanish mystic Miguel Molinos (1640–96), who taught the direct relationship between the soul and God. His followers were called Molinists or Quietists.

Quiller-Couch, Sir Arthur [Thomas] (pen name Q., 1863–1944) English man of letters. Especially known as editor of the *Oxford Book of English Verse* (first pub in 1900) and several other anthologies in that series, Quiller-Couch was, from 1912 until his death, professor of English literature at Cambridge.

Quinault, Philippe (1635–1688) French playwright. Ill-starred love provides the subject for Quinault's tragedies: *La Mort de Cyrus* (The Death of Cyrus, 1656), *Amalasonte* (1657), and *Astrate, Roi de Tyr* (1664). Quinault supplied librettos for many of the ballets and operas of LULLY, and it is for his contributions to the French lyric theatre that he is best remembered. His operas include *Alceste* (1674) and *Armide* (1686).

Quint, Peter See TURN OF THE SCREW, THE.

Quintana, Manuel José (1772–1857) Spanish poet and statesman. Two ideals—patriotism and liberalism—guided Quintana's public life and literary work. He denounced the Napoleonic invaders of Spain and took an active part in the Central Junta, only to be imprisoned by the reactionary Ferdinand VII. During the liberal period of 1820–23 he served as director of public instruction.

His best-known poems are his patriotic odes, notably *A España, después de la revolución de marzo* and *Al armamento de las provincias españolas contra los franceses* (both 1808), in which nationalist fervor is wedded to classical form.

Quintilian (full Latin name Marcus Fabius Quintilianus, c AD 35–c99) Spanish-born rhetorician and teacher of oratory in Rome (from AD 68). Quintilian's most important work is his *De institutione oratoria* (On the Training of an Orator), which he published in 96 after a long and successful career of oratory and teaching. Like Cicero in his *De oratore*, Quintilian proposes to give an educational schedule for the training of the ideal orator. Throughout, he emphasizes the importance of personal integrity and honest conviction in the art of public persuasion. The book is a valuable source for us today, for it describes, in minute detail, the educational advantages available to the well-to-do Roman youth of the 1st century, and includes, as good and bad examples, selections from the works of Latin authors whose writings would otherwise have been entirely lost.

Quiroga, Horacio (1878–1937)   Uruguayan short-story writer. Although Quiroga wrote poetry and novels, he found his greatest success in the short story. He never lost his initial tendencies toward MODERNISMO, but his prose became clearer and his narrative technique more realistic. His best-known stories are set in the jungles of Misiones territory in Argentina, where he spent many years. In some, such as those collected in *Cuentos de la selva* (1918; tr *South American Jungle Tales*, 1922; repr 1950) and *Anaconda* (1921), the protagonists are animals. The stories are characterized by haunting, imaginative depictions of the forces of nature, which seem to dwarf the fears and passions of his characters. Other collections include *Cuentos de amor, de locura y de muerte* (1917) and *La gallina degollada y otros cuentos* (1925; tr *The Decapitated Chicken and Other Stories*, 1976).

Quo Vadis? (1896; tr 1960)   A historical novel by H. SIENKIEWICZ. It deals with the Rome of Nero and the early Christian martyrs. The Roman noble PETRONIUS, a worthy representative of the dying paganism, is perhaps the most interesting figure, and the struggle between Christianity and paganism supplies the central plot, but the canvas is large. A succession of characters and episodes and, above all, the richly colorful, decadent life of ancient Rome give the novel its chief interest. The beautiful Christian Lygia is the object of unwelcome attentions from Vinicius, one of the Emperor's guards, and when she refuses to yield to his importunities, she is denounced and thrown to the wild beasts of the arena. She escapes and eventually marries Vinicius, whom Peter and Paul have converted to Christianity. *Quo Vadis?* has been translated into nearly every language.

R

Ra   In ancient Egyptian religion, one of the most frequent names given to the sun god, the supposed ancestor of all the Pharaohs. He was worshiped as the creator and protector of men and the vanquisher of evil; it was said that men and women were made from his tears. He is usually represented with the head of a falcon and crowned with the solar disk and uraeus, the symbol of power over life and death.

Raabe, Wilhelm (1831–1910)   German realistic novelist. Raabe is known for the pessimistic irony and cultural criticism found in the three novels that established his fame: *Der Hungerpastor* (1864; tr *The Hunger-Pastor*, 1885), *Abu Telfan* (1868; tr *Abu Telfan's Return from the Mountains of the Moon*, 1881), and *Der Schüdderump* (1870). His style, however, often shows a benign, forgiving humor about his characters. In his later works, for example, *Stopfkuchen* (1891), he began to experiment more with the form of the novel, and often created complicated time-structures.

Rabbi Ben Ezra (1855)   A famous poem on old age by Robert BROWNING. First published in the collection *Dramatis Personae* (1864), it opens with the well-known lines:

Grow old along with me!
The best is yet to be,
The last of life, for which the first was made.

The supposed speaker, Rabbi Ben Ezra, or, properly, Abraham ben Meïr ibn Ezra (c1092–1168), was one of the most distinguished Jewish literati of the Middle Ages.

Rabbit, Run (1960)   A novel by John UPDIKE. Contemporary in setting and tone, and brilliant in its evocation of everyday life in America, the novel is about Harry ANGSTROM ("Rabbit"), a salesman who, on an impulse, leaves home, his alcoholic wife, Janice, and his child, Nelson, to find freedom. After several escapades and a liaison with an ex-prostitute, he returns to his wife and child and attempts to settle down again. In this novel, Updike conveys the longings and frustrations of family life. Rabbit's malaise is not so much a yearning for freedom as, perhaps, a yearning

for guiding spiritual values and meaning. At the end, still dissatisfied and guilt-ridden because of the responsibility he feels for the death of his second child, he begins running again.

Rabe, David [William] (1940–   )   American playwright. Rabe established his reputation with two plays (both produced in 1971) deriving from his experience in the Vietnam War: *Sticks and Bones* (written 1968) and *The Basic Training of Pavlo Hummel* (written 1967). Both plays depict not only the horrors and absurdities of the military ethos but also the tragic results of unquestioning acceptance of dubious values. *The Orphan* (1973) is a modern musical interpretation of the Oresteia story. *In the Boom Boom Room* (1973; rev 1974) is a woeful saga of a go-go dancer. *Streamers* (1976), again war-related, deals with a senseless tragedy in an army barracks. Rabe wrote the screenplay for *I'm Dancing as Fast as I Can* (1982); this was followed by another play, *Hurlyburly*, in 1984.

Rabelais, François (1494?–1553)   French scholar, humanist, physician, and author of the robust and outspoken GARGANTUA AND PANTAGRUEL. Having first entered the Franciscan and then the Benedictine order, Rabelais left the confining environment of the monastery to study, practice, and teach medicine in Montpellier and Lyons. Twice he accompanied Jean du Bellay, bishop of Paris and later cardinal, to Rome, where he made archeological and botanical studies. From 1550 to 1553, Rabelais, who is sometimes known as "the curate of Meudon," held the parishes of Saint-Martin-de-Meudon and of Saint-Christophe-du-Jambet in the diocese of Mans, though he probably did not reside there. Throughout his life he published various works on medicine and translations in addition to his literary masterpiece. *Gargantua and Pantagruel* is filled with allusions to Rabelais's personal life, as well as to the contemporary French scene, humanistic studies which interested him, and observations he had made on his visits to Italy. *Rabelaisian* has come to mean coarsely and boisterously satirical in the Gallic comic tradition; grotesque, extravagant, and licentious in language; reminiscent of the literary style of Rabelais.

Rachel (1) In the OLD TESTAMENT, the daughter of LABAN and wife of JACOB. Jacob had been promised Rachel's hand in marriage if he worked seven years for her father. At the end of that time, he was tricked into marrying her sister LEAH and was forced to serve another seven years for Rachel (Gen. 29–33). She was childless for a long time but finally bore JOSEPH. She later died in childbirth bearing BENJAMIN. The phrase "Rachel weeping for her children refused to be comforted for her children, because they were not," which appears in Jeremiah 31:15, was later taken by MATTHEW to be a prophecy of HEROD's massacre of the INNOCENTS after the birth of Jesus (Matt. 2:18).

(2) An actress in Proust's REMEMBRANCE OF THINGS PAST. At first offered to the narrator as a prostitute, Rachel becomes the demanding mistress of Robert de SAINT-LOUP. At that time she is scorned by society, but later she is launched as a great actress by the duchess de GUERMANTES.

Rachmaninoff, Sergey Vasilyevich (1873–1943) Russian-born composer and pianist. Rachmaninoff's music, often rhapsodic and impassioned, is quite popular on the concert stage, especially his *Prelude in C-sharp minor* (1892) and the piano concertos. Although an expatriate after 1917, he was greatly admired in the Soviet Union.

Racine, Jean (1639–1699) French playwright. Born at La Ferté-Milon, near Soissons, the son of a petty official, Racine was orphaned at an early age and left in the care of a Jansenist grandmother who sent him in 1655 to the schools of Port-Royal. There he acquired a thorough education in doctrine, as well as in classical literature, and the combination of the Jansenist concept of original sin with the Greek concept of Fate was to exert considerable influence upon his later work. In 1658 Racine went to the Collège d'Hancourt, part of the university of Paris, where he discovered and delighted in the profane world of actors and the theatre. He became a protégé of Chapelain and, after writing an ode on the marriage of Louis XIV—*La Nymphe de la Seine* (*The Nymph of the Seine*, 1660)—he managed to obtain a small pension. Fearful for the state of his soul and hoping to persuade him to enter the church, his family sent him to Uzès to live with a clergyman uncle, but Racine returned to Paris in 1662 to publish further odes and to cultivate the friendship of such men as Boileau, MOLIÈRE, and LA FONTAINE. Molière produced Racine's first two tragedies: *La Thébaïde* (*The Thebaid*, performed 1664) and *Alexandre le Grand* (1665). Though not his finest work, these plays established Racine's reputation. ANDROMAQUE achieved as great a success as Corneille's LE CID, and after the comedy LES PLAIDEURS, a satire on the judiciary and one of his few treatments of a contemporary subject, Racine challenged Corneille with BRITANNICUS, a historico-political tragedy very much in the older playwright's genre, and BÉRÉNICE, based on the same subject as

Corneille's *Tite et Bérénice* and appearing at virtually the same time. The public held Racine the victor in the contest, and the young playwright, now at the height of his powers and of his career, went on to produce his greatest plays: BAJAZET, MITHRIDATE, IPHIGÉNIE EN AULIDE, and PHÈDRE. Racine was elected to the French Academy in 1673. In 1677, the year of his marriage, he retired from the theatre, discouraged by the elaborate intrigue conducted by his enemies against *Phèdre*, tempted by an appointment to the post of historiographer to Louis XIV, and reconciled with the Jansenists of Port-Royal. Racine devoted himself fully to his new duties, and aside from two biblical plays, ESTHER (1689) and ATHALIE (1691), commissioned by Madame de Maintenon for the schoolgirls of St. Cyr, he never again wrote for the theatre. The works of his last years include four *Cantiques spirituels* (*Spiritual Hymns*) and the *Abrégé de l'histoire de Port-Royal*, published after his death.

Racine's tragedies resemble those of Corneille in their rigid adherence to a single theme shorn of all irrelevancies, in their loyalty to the classical unities, and in their careful exposition of character and depiction of powerful spiritual conflicts. He was no mere imitator, however, but rather the inheritor and modifier of a tradition. Though Racine's Hellenism is apparent in his frequent culling of themes from Greek originals, his main thematic preoccupations are passion and women. His depiction of the emotions and especially of the subverting, destructive power of love was severely criticized during his lifetime as being unnecessarily realistic. Compared to Corneille's, Racine's characters are ordinary beings, subject to superhuman passions but also to human doubts and fears; far from possessing the extraordinary determination of, for example, Corneille's Cid, they are subject to the fluctuations of feeble and uncertain wills, and in this respect reveal the influence of Racine's Jansenist upbringing. His most memorable characters are the fierce and tender women of his great tragedies; in these creatures, Racine accomplished the humanization of classical French drama. Many might agree with La Bruyère, but few would regard his remark as condemnation, when he said that Corneille showed men "as they ought to be" and Racine "as they are." More would perhaps echo Brunetière, who praised Racine as the first to write "the literature of the passions of the heart."

Radcliffe, Ann (born Ann Ward, 1764–1823) English novelist, known for her tales of terror in the convention of the GOTHIC NOVEL. Besides THE MYSTERIES OF UDOLPHO, her most popular novel, Radcliffe's books include *The Italian, or the Confessional of the Black Penitents* (1797), whose best-drawn character, the implacable, villainous monk Schedoni, is one of the prototypes of the Byronic hero.

Radiguet, Raymond (1903–1923) French novelist and poet. At once lyrical and cynical in his accounts of the adolescent's emotional initiation, Radiguet showed a precocious talent in his two novels, *Le Diable au corps* (1923; tr *The Devil in the Flesh*, 1932), about a young man's attraction to an older woman, and *Le Bal du Comte d'Orgel* (1924; tr *Count's Ball*, 1929; *Count d'Orgel*, 1952). He also wrote a volume of poetry, *Les Joues en feu* (1920). Although Radiguet's style was undeveloped (he died of typhus at age twenty), his writing conveyed a clear sense of the prevailing disillusionment in the wake of World War I.

Radishchev, Aleksandr Nikolayevich (1749–1802)   Russian writer. Radishchev's politically liberal book, *Puteshestviye iz Peterburga v Moskvu* (*A Journey from Petersburg to Moscow*, 1790), created a sensation during the reign of CATHERINE THE GREAT. Radishchev was educated at the University of Leipzig, where he picked up the liberal ideas prevalent in Europe at the time. He returned to Russia and became a customs official. His book, describing an imaginary trip between the two Russian cities, was an outspoken indictment of serfdom and the government. The Empress, already upset by the French Revolution, was enraged at the exposures and ordered Radishchev sentenced to death, but this punishment was commuted to exile in Siberia. He was released on the accession of Paul I in 1801. Broken in physical and mental health, he committed suicide the following year. Radishchev was also the author of some technically fine poetry, including "Ode to Liberty" (1781–83), which forcefully expressed the liberal sentiments of his book.

Raeburn, Sir Henry (1756–1823)   Scottish portrait painter. Largely self-taught, Raeburn established himself in Edinburgh, where he became known as "the Scottish REYNOLDS." He painted directly on the canvas with no preliminary sketches, thus achieving a strong, spontaneous style. He was knighted in 1822; in 1823 King George IV appointed him King's Limner for Scotland.

Raffles   The hero of a series of novels by E. W. Hornung. He is a debonair, witty, and cricket-loving gentleman thief.

raga   In Indian music, a basic melodic scale, each raga being associated with a particular time of day and/or mood, upon which the singer or instrumentalist elaborates extensively.

Raggedy Man, The (1890)   A poem by James Whitcomb RILEY. Written in the Hoosier dialect of a little boy, it tells of his admiration for the farm's hired man. The Raggedy Man is also the beau of Lizabuth Ann, in Riley's *Our Hired Girl*.

Raghuvamsa (Sans, "the race of Raghu"; c 3rd century)   A narrative poem in nineteen cantos by KĀLIDĀSA. It tells of the life and history of Rāma, the hero of the Hindu epic, RĀMĀYANA, tracing his lineage back to the legendary king of the solar dynasty, Raghu.

Ragnarok   In Scandinavian mythology, the Twilight of the Gods, or day of doom. Ragnarok will result in the destruction of the universe: the heavens will disappear, the earth will be swallowed up by the sea, and fire will

consume the elements. There will be a final battle between the gods of evil, LOKI, HEL, FENRIS-WOLF, and the MID-GARD SERPENT, and the good gods, ODIN and his companions, during which all will be slaughtered. After Ragnarok there will be a regeneration of all things; a new world will arise repopulated by Lif and Lifthrasir. Ragnarok is translated into German as *Götterdämmerung*, which is the title of the fourth work in Wagner's RING DES NIBELUNGEN. See BIFROST; VALI.

Ragtime (1975)   A novel by E. L. DOCTOROW. Set in New York between the turn of the century and the beginning of World War II, the novel revolves around three interlocking groups of characters: a family of Jewish immigrants from the Lower East Side, their upper-class WASP counterparts from New Rochelle, and a black piano player, Coalhouse Walker, and his wife. Walker is probably based on the character of rag composer Scott Joplin. The evocation of America before World War II is enriched by the interaction of Doctorow's fictional characters with such real-life figures as Harry Houdini, J. P. Morgan, Booker T. Washington, and C. G. Jung. Doctorow's prose conveys a sense of his story by maintaining a contrapuntal, ragtime cadence.

Rahab   In the OLD TESTAMENT, the woman of Jericho who protected the two Israelite spies sent by Joshua and managed their escape (Josh. 2). When the city was later to be destroyed, Joshua commanded that "only Rahab the harlot shall live, she and all that are with her in the house" (Josh. 6:18). She lived among the Israelites for a long time afterward.

Rahu   The demon who, according to Hindu legend, causes eclipses. Rahu drank some of the nectar of immortality one day, but was discovered by the Sun and Moon, who informed against him, and VISHNU cut off his head. But he had already taken some of the nectar into his mouth, as a result of which the head was immortal; ever afterward he hunted the Sun and Moon, causing eclipses when he occasionally caught them.

Rai, Lala Lajpat   See LAJPAT RAI, LALA.

Raimund, Ferdinand (1790–1836)   Austrian playwright, associated with the highly successful People's Theatre of Vienna. Many of Raimund's plays, such as *Der Alpenkönig und der Menschenfeind* (*The Alp-King and the Misanthrope*, 1828), were popular primarily because of their light-hearted humor and songs; but some, such as *Der Verschwender* (*The Squanderer*, 1834), laid more stress on serious moral teachings.

Rain   See MISS THOMPSON.

Rainbow, The (1915)   A novel by D. H. LAWRENCE. It is about the emotional life and loves of three generations of the Brangwen family, farmers and craftsmen of Nottinghamshire, Lawrence's childhood home. Tom Brangwen, a farm youth, marries Lydia Lensky, a Polish widow of a political exile. Anna, Lydia's daughter by her first marriage, grows up as Tom's own child and marries her cousin, Will Brangwen, a strong-willed, morose man with a passion for wood carving. Most of the novel is about Ursula, daughter of Anna and Will. A sensitive, high-spirited rebel, she escapes from her confining environment, as Lawrence himself did, by going to college and becoming a teacher. Her emotional life consists of a love affair with Anton Skrebensky, a Polish exile and officer in the British army, and an intense attraction to Winifred Inger, an older teacher. Winifred, an athletic, intellectual woman and a feminist, marries Ursula's uncle; Ursula rejects Skrebensky. Ursula's story is continued in WOMEN IN LOVE, a sequel. When *The Rainbow* was published it was denounced as obscene, and a whole edition was destroyed by court order.

Raine, Kathleen [Jessie] (1908–   )   English poet and scholar. A romantic, mystical poet who combines Platonic idealism with exact natural description, Raine produced her first book of verse, *Stone and Flower*, in 1943. *Collected Poems* (1956) preceded ten years of scholarly research on William BLAKE which resulted in several books on the visionary poet-artist, in particular *Blake and Tradition* (2 vols, 1968), as well as *From Blake to "A Vision"* (1978) and other works. She has also written books on the work of the Welsh poet David Jones. Other books of poetry include *The Lost Country* (1971), *The Oval Portrait* (1977), and *Collected Poems* (1981). In 1985, she published *Yeats to Initiate: Essays on Certain Themes in the Writings of W. B. Yeats*. She has also written three volumes of autobiography: *Farewell Happy Fields* (1973), *The Land Unknown* (1975), and *The Lion's Mouth* (1977).

Rake's Progress, The   A series of engravings by William HOGARTH. Depicting the career of a wealthy, foolish young gentleman that carries him through the pleasure houses of London to the madhouse of Bedlam, the engravings served as the basis of the libretto that W. H. AUDEN and Chester Kallman wrote for Igor Stravinsky's opera *The Rake's Progress* (1951).

Rakosi, Carl (1903–   )   American poet. Rakosi worked for many years as a social worker and psychotherapist. During the 1930s, when he was still unpublished, he was loosely connected with the objectivists (see OBJECTIVISM). In practice, however, Rakosi's own work was more reminiscent of IMAGISM, with short epigrammatic verse forms similar to the Japanese HAIKU. His first book, *Selected Poems* (1941), as well as his better-known volumes, *Amulet* (1967) and *Ere-VOICE* (1971), contains bitter commentary on the corruption that so frequently accompanies the pursuit of the American dream. Many of the poems evolve into thoughtful maxims for coping with success-oriented modern life. *Ex Cranium, Night* (1975), a kind of poet's diary, is a collection of poems, aphorisms, and sketches that demonstrate Rakosi's broad-ranging concerns and gentle humor. His other works include *My Experiences in Parnassus* (1977), *History* (1981), *Spiritus I* (1983), and *Collected Prose* (1984).

Raleigh, Sir Walter (1552?–1618)   English explorer, courtier, poet, and prose writer. One of the favorites of Queen Elizabeth between 1581 and 1592, Raleigh helped his friend Edmund SPENSER arrange for the publication of the first three books of *The Faerie Queene*; also during this period he sent several expeditions to North America, though the Queen would not allow him to make the voyages himself. He fell from Elizabeth's favor in 1592, according to legend, because of his seduction of one of her maids of honor. He took advantage of being in the Queen's bad graces by making in 1595 an expeditionary voyage to South America, which he described in the colorful (and fanciful) *Discovery of Guiana*. He was reinstated at court during the last years of Elizabeth's reign, but at the accession of James I he was imprisoned on a flimsy charge of treason. He narrowly escaped execution, and was detained in the Tower (though in reasonable comfort) for the next thirteen years. In 1616 he was released on the promise to James I to discover gold in South America, providing that he neither intruded on Spanish possessions nor pirated Spanish ships. Unfortunately, Raleigh attacked a Spanish settlement, and on his return to England was condemned and executed.

A true courtier poet, Raleigh did not publish his poetry but had it circulated in manuscript. As a result, only a few of his poems have come down to the present day. "Cynthia," a long poem in honor of the Queen, was highly praised by Spenser, but only a fragment has survived. Among his best-known poems are "The Nymph's Reply to the Shepherd," an answer to Christopher Marlowe's "Passionate Shepherd"; "The Lie"; "The Passionate Man's Pilgrimage"; and the sonnet beginning "Methought I saw the grave where Laura lay," prefixed to Spenser's *Faerie Queene*. In addition to a prose *History of the World* (of which only one volume was completed), Raleigh wrote a narrative of the sea battle between the *Revenge* and a Spanish warship in which his cousin, Sir Richard Grenville, was killed; Tennyson's ballad "The Revenge" is largely based on Raleigh's account. The legend of the courteous Sir Walter spreading his cloak over a puddle that the Queen might cross dry-shod is mentioned by Sir Walter Scott in *Kenilworth*.

Ralph Roister Doister (perf c1553; pub 1566) The earliest English comedy, written by Nicholas Udall (or Nicholas Uvedale; 1504?–56). Based on Latin models, it has five acts and is written in rhymed doggerel. The titular hero is a swaggering, blustering fellow who, urged on by Mathew Merygreeke, tries unsuccessfully to win Dame Christian Custance, a rich widow.

Rāmāyana (Sans, "relating to Rama") The history of Rama, the great epic poem of ancient India, ranking with the MAHĀBHĀRATA. It is ascribed to the poet VALMIKI, and, as now known, consists of twenty-four thousand stanzas in seven books. Parts of the *Rāmāyana* date from 500 BC. The young hero, Rama, according to the PURANAS the seventh incarnation (*avatar*) of the deity VISHNU, wins his bride, SĪTA, by bending the great bow that had belonged to the god RUDRA. When about to be named heir-apparent of Ayodhya, Rama is exiled for fourteen years through the jealousy of Kaikeyi, one of his father's wives, who desires the throne for her son, Bharata. Sita is carried off by RAVANA, the demon-king of Ceylon. A great part of the narrative is concerned with Rama's efforts to win her back. He secures the assistance of Vibhishana, Ravana's own brother, and of HANUMAN, the great monkey-god, whose monkeys construct a bridge to Ceylon. After this alliance rescues Sita, Rama is welcomed back as the monarch of Ayodhya. But both Rama and the people fear that Sita has been defiled by her sojourn with the demon-king, and although she successfully undergoes an ordeal by fire, Rama sends her away. She wanders into the forest, finds shelter in the hut of Valmiki, and there gives birth to Rama's two sons, whom she brings up to be brave and noble youths. Eventually she is found by Rama and received back as his wife.

Rambler, The (1750–1752)   A series of semi-weekly essays written by Samuel JOHNSON, dealing with mores and literature. They were thought, at first, too difficult for a public trained on Addison's SPECTATOR. Some even found them dull, as did Lady Mary Wortley Montagu, who remarked that the *Rambler* "follows the *Spectator* with the same pace that a pack horse would a hunter."

Ramona (1884)   A historical romance by Helen Hunt JACKSON. The heroine, Ramona, of mixed Scottish and Indian blood, elopes with the noble Indian, Alessandro. The proud young man comes to a tragic end as a result of harassment by whites. The book helped to create a marked change in the attitude of whites toward the Indian.

Ramos, Graciliano (1892–1953)   Brazilian novelist. Sometimes considered the finest Brazilian novelist since MACHADO DE ASSIS, Ramos wrote about the northeastern state of Alagoas, where he was a merchant and public official. His first novel, *Caetés* (1933), was written in the mid-1920s and was published after the vivid style and sardonic tone of one of his official reports had won him national attention. Later, his radical political views brought him persecution and imprisonment. He spent his last years as a proofreader for a newspaper in Rio de Janeiro.

Ramos's novels are characterized by acute, though dispassionate, insight into the human mind and awareness of the inequities of social and economic conditions in northeast Brazil. *São Bernardo* (1934) is a first-person account of an unfeeling parvenu in the cane-growing littoral of Alagoas. In *Angústia* (1936; tr *Anguish*, 1946; repr 1972), he utilized a STREAM OF CONSCIOUSNESS technique to weave the story of a man who is led to destruction through thwarted sexual desire. Set on the arid *sertão*, or backcountry, of Alagoas, *Vidas Sêcas* (1938; tr *Barren Lives*, 1965) is an episodic work about a cowherd whose lot is difficult but who is uncontaminated by the corruption of the littoral.

Ramsay, Mr. and **Mrs.**   The central characters in Virginia Woolf's novel TO THE LIGHTHOUSE. Mrs. Ramsay is a personification of creative womanhood; Mr. Ramsay is a typical intellectual male.

Ramuz, Charles-Ferdinand (1878–1947)   Swiss novelist. Ramuz produced over twenty novels, most of which dealt with peasant life in his native canton of Vaud. His works include *Le Règne de l'esprit malin* (1917; tr *The Reign of the Evil One*, 1922), *Présence de la mort* (1922; tr *The End of All Men*, 1944; *The Triumph of Death*, 1946), and what is widely held to be the pinnacle of his achievement, *Derborence* (1936; tr *When the Mountain Fell*, 1947), about a young man who survives an avalanche.

Ran   In Norse mythology, goddess of the sea, wife of Aegir, and mother of nine daughters of the waves. Her name signifies robbery, and it was Ran who caught seafarers in her net and drew them down to her dwelling beneath the water.

Rand, Ayn (1905–1982)   Russian-born American novelist. Ayn Rand's novels, which include *We the Living* (1936), THE FOUNTAINHEAD, and *Atlas Shrugged* (1957), are polemical and melodramatic vehicles for her ideas. In her objectivist philosophy, she defends capitalism and attacks government and other controls for inhibiting the self-interested individuals whom she has pictured in her novels and expatiated on further in *For the New Intellectual: The Philosophy of Ayn Rand* (1961) and other works of nonfiction.

Ranke, Leopold von (1795–1886)   German historian. Outstanding for his scientific approach to history, Ranke relied entirely on contemporary, firsthand sources, which he subjected to the most rigorous analysis. His best-known work is his *Die römischen Päpste* (*History of the Popes*, 1834–39).

Ransom, John Crowe (1888–1974)   American poet and critic. Ransom attended and, after two years as a Rhodes scholar, taught at Vanderbilt University (1914–37), where he was a leading member of THE FUGITIVES. With Allen TATE, Robert Penn WARREN, and others, he founded and edited the influential LITTLE MAGAZINE *The Fugitive* (1922–25). A staunch believer in southern agrarianism, he also contributed to *I'll Take My Stand* (1930), a symposium of essays defending the South against the encroachment of industrialism. Though he later reversed his position, the dream of the agrarians left its imprint on Ransom's later work; in one way or another, its aim was to prove that only in a traditional, rural society such as the antebellum South can human beings achieve mental and physical completeness. From 1937 to 1958 he taught at Kenyon College and founded THE KENYON REVIEW, which he edited for twenty years.

The bulk of Ransom's poetry can be found in *Chills and Fever* (1924), *Two Gentlemen in Bonds* (1927), and *Selected Poems* (1945; rev 1963, 1969). Central to his poetry, which shows the broad influence of the METAPHYSI-

CAL POETS, is the theme of decay, be it decay of society, values, or the individual. His verse is marked by irony, realism, and a spare, classic style. As a critic, Ransom gave currency to the term and the ideas of NEW CRITICISM in *The New Criticism* (1941). His literary essays, discussing the nature and function of poetry, appear in *God Without Thunder* (1930), *The World's Body* (1938), and *Beating the Bushes: Selected Essays 1914–1970* (1972).

Ransome, Arthur (1884–1967)   English writer. Ransome, who began his career as a war correspondent in Russia for English newspapers during the First World War and the Russian Revolution, is best known for his realistic books written for and about children. *Swallows and Amazons* (1931) was the first of a series of twelve children's novels about vacations spent sailing boats or exploring. Ransome's perennially enthusiastic readers are treated to innocent adventures and detailed practical descriptions of sailing, knot-tying, camp-cooking, and bird watching.

Rao, Raja (1909–   )   Indian novelist, writing in English. Rao's involvement in the nationalist movement is reflected in his first two books, the novel *Kanthapura* (1938) and the story collection *The Cow of the Barricades* (1947), both of which deal with the effect of GANDHI's movement on south Indian villagers. His semiautobiographical novel, *The Serpent and the Rope* (1960), dealing with a young Indian's growing self-awareness in France, established Rao as one of the finest Indian stylists writing in English. His third novel, *The Cat and Shakespeare: A Tale of India* (1965), is a "metaphysical comedy" that reveals Rao's profound religious concerns. *Comrade Kirillov* (1976) and *The Policeman and the Rose* (1977) are among his other works.

Rape of Lucrece, The (1594)   A long poem by SHAKESPEARE, dealing with LUCRETIA.

Rape of the Lock, The (1714)   A mock-heroic poem, often considered the best in the English language, by Alexander POPE. The first sketch of two cantos was published in 1712; the final version was in five cantos. The poem was based on a real incident: Lord Petre, in a thoughtless moment of frolic gallantry, cut off a lock of Arabella Fermor's hair, and this liberty gave rise to a feud between the two families. In his treatment of the incident, Pope employed an elaborate and elevated style from the classical epic: the description of a card game as a battle, the final combat between beaux and belles, and the journey to the Cave of Spleen. The heroine, called BELINDA, indignantly demands back the ringlet, but after a fruitless charge it is affirmed that it has been transported to heaven, and henceforth shall "midst the stars inscribe Belinda's name."

Raphael   One of the principal ANGELS of Jewish angelology. According to the apocryphal book of TOBIT, Raphael traveled with TOBIAS, instructing him how to marry Sara and drive away the wicked spirit, ASMODEUS. In his PARADISE LOST, Milton calls him "the sociable spirit" and "affable archangel," and it is he who is sent by God to advise ADAM of his danger. Raphael is usually distinguished in art by a pilgrim's staff, or is shown carrying a fish; this alludes to the fish he helped Tobias catch which miraculously cured Tobit's blindness.

Raphael (real name Raffaelo Sanzio or Raffaelo Santi, 1483–1520)   Italian painter. The son of a painter, Raphael was born in Urbino and studied under Perugino (1445–1523), although he quickly surpassed his master. In about 1504 he traveled to Florence, where he encountered the works of LEONARDO DA VINCI and MICHELANGELO, under whose influence he solidified his own style. During his stay in Florence (1504–8), he made many paintings of the Holy Family, notable for their subjects' outward humanity and the serene holiness they radiated. From 1509 to 1517, he was commissioned to decorate three Vatican apartments, the first of these being the famous Stanza della Signatura, whose frescoes epitomize High Renaissance ideals of human nobility. Many of his paintings were copied and published by the engraver Marcantonio Raimondi (c1480–c1534), thus accounting for Raphael's immediate, immense popularity. In the period from 1514 until his death in 1520, he made cartoons for tapestries to be hung in the Sistine Chapel, many half-figure portraits, such as that of Baldessare Castiglione (c1515), and executed the design for St. Peter's Cathedral, in addition to his work on the Vatican stanzas.

RAPP   The initials of the Russian Association of Proletarian Writers, an organization that virtually controlled Soviet literature from 1929 to 1932. The group was first formed in 1925 as VAPP (All-Russian Association of Proletarian Writers) and then was changed in 1928 to RAPP. The organization hounded writers with orders to heed and fulfill the "social command" with their work, that is, to produce works that reflected the times. After the first Five-Year Plan was over, RAPP had its power taken away by the newly formed Union of Soviet Writers.

Rappaccini's Daughter (1844)   A story by Nathaniel HAWTHORNE. Rappaccini, a doctor and devoted man of science, nourishes his beautiful daughter, Beatrice, on poisons, so that she, invulnerable, may aid him in his experiments with dangerous plants. Physically deadly, but pure in spirit, Beatrice drinks the antidote given her by a faithless suitor, knowing it will kill her. She reproaches her father for subordinating heart to head, depriving her of human existence. This theme is frequent in Hawthorne's work.

Raskolnikov   See CRIME AND PUNISHMENT.

Rasputin, Grigory Yefimovich (1871–1916)   Russian monk in the household of Tsar NICHOLAS II. Despite his notoriously bad reputation, Rasputin wielded power at the court through his influence over the Tsarina. He was assassinated by a group of Russian nobles on December 30, 1916.

Rasselas, Prince of Abyssinia, History of (1759)   A philosophical romance by Samuel JOHNSON, hastily written within a month of his mother's death to meet her funeral expenses. Rasselas is the youngest son of an Oriental despot who confines his children in the Happy Valley, a paradise. Rasselas, longing for the novelty of the world outside, escapes with his sister, Nekayah, and his mentor, Imlac. They go to Cairo where Rasselas is warned by one example after another that romantic reverie, romantic love, the flights of the imagination, the daring speculations of philosophy, the great discoveries of science, all harm man by giving him an unrealistic estimate of what life has to offer and by encouraging false hopes. Ranging through all that nature and society have to offer, they find nothing that promises the happiness they expected, and they return to the Happy Valley.

The attack in *Rasselas* is directed against the optimism of the 18th century or, more generally, against all simple formulas that profess to lead man to happiness, against all glib generalizations about the goodness of nature and the satisfactions of solitude, learning, or social life. *Rasselas* has often been compared with Voltaire's *Candide*; the two works were published only a few weeks apart.

Rastignac, Eugène de   One of Balzac's best-known characters, appearing in several of the novels of *La Comédie humaine*, notably LE PÈRE GORIOT and LA COUSINE BETTE. Introduced as a struggling young law student who has come to Paris to make his fortune, Rastignac quickly acquires practicality. He determines to conquer society by giving up his ideals and taking advantage of circumstances. By installing himself as the lover of Mme de Nucingen, the daughter of his fellow-boarder Père Goriot, he manages to better his fortunes. Later, he marries Augusta de Nucingen, the daughter of his former mistress, and becomes a prominent statesman, peer, and millionaire. Rastignac finally epitomizes ruthless, cynical ambition.

rationalism   A term applied to a trend in philosophic thinking toward emphasis on reason and intellect over emotion or imagination. ARISTOTLE and St. Thomas AQUINAS are considered rationalists, although the term is most frequently used to apply to the philosophic school of the 17th and early 18th centuries, the most ardent proponents of which were DESCARTES, SPINOZA, and LEIBNITZ. Rationalism, in this sense, is contrasted with EMPIRICISM, the view that the chief, or only, source of substantial knowledge is experience.

Rattigan, Sir Terence [Mervyn] (1911–1977) English playwright. A meticulous craftsman, Rattigan enjoyed enormous popular success as a master of the WELL-MADE PLAY. Audiences, both in England and America, flocked to his early comedies and period pieces, such as *French without Tears* (1936) and *While the Sun Shines* (1943). *The Winslow Boy* (1946), about a father's struggle to clear his son of an accusation of petty theft, and *The Browning Version* (1948), set in a boys' school and showing considerable psychological penetration, established his rep-

utation as a serious playwright; SEPARATE TABLES, a study of loneliness set in a seaside resort, confirmed it. Outstanding among his later plays is *Ross* (1960), based on the life of T. E. LAWRENCE.

Rauschenberg, Robert (1925–)   American artist, among the most important in POP ART. Rauschenberg uses sophisticated techniques of photomontage and silk-screening. He championed the theory that the essential nature of creativity is not in the object produced but in the concept and the process of creation.

Ravana   In HINDUISM, a ten-faced demon-king of Lanka (Ceylon). Ravana was fastened between heaven and earth for ten thousand years by SHIVA's leg, because he audaciously attempted to move the hill of heaven to Lanka. He is best known from the Hindu epic, the RĀMĀYANA, where he is the abductor of Rama's wife SĪTĀ.

Ravel, Maurice Joseph (1875–1937)   French composer. Some of Ravel's best-known works are the song cycle *Shéhérazade* (1903; text by Tristan Klingsor), the operas *L'Heure espagnole* (*The Spanish Hour*, 1910; libretto by Franc-Nohain) and *L'Enfant et les sortilèges* (*The Child and the Enchantments*, 1925; libretto by Colette), and the ballets *Daphnis et Chloe* (1912) and *Boléro* (1928). Accused of imitating DEBUSSY throughout his career, Ravel has since been recognized as one of France's most distinguished modern composers.

raven   A bird of ill omen. It is fabled to forebode death and bring infection and bad luck generally. The former notion arises from ravens' following an army under the expectation of finding dead bodies; the latter notion is a mere offshoot of the former, since it was noted that pestilence kills as fast as the sword. In Christian art, the raven is an emblem of God's Providence, in allusion to the ravens that fed ELIJAH.

The fatal raven, consecrated to ODIN, the Danish war god, was the emblem on the Danish standard, *Landeyda* ("desolation of the country"), and was said to have been woven and embroidered in one noontide by the daughters of Regner Lodbrok, son of Sigurd, that dauntless warrior who chanted his death song (the *Krakamal*) while being stung to death in a horrible pit filled with deadly serpents. If the Danish arms were destined to defeat, the raven hung his wings; if victory was to attend them, he stood erect and soaring as if inviting the warriors to follow.

Raven, The (1845)   A famous poem by Edgar Allan POE. Lost in melancholy memories of his dead love, the poet is startled by a tapping at his chamber door. A raven enters and, perching on the bust of Pallas Athene, answers the tormented questions of the bereaved lover with the mysterious, unchanging "Nevermore."

Rawlings, Marjorie Kinnan (1896–1953)   American novelist. Originally a syndicated journalist, Rawlings moved to Cross Creek, Florida, in 1928, which became the setting for most of her work. She is best known for her novel THE YEARLING. Her other fiction includes her first novel, *South Moon Under* (1933), *Golden Apples* (1935), and *The Sojourner* (1953). *Cross Creek* (1942) is a humorous account of her life in the backwoods of Florida.

Raw Youth, The (Podrostok, 1875)   A novel by DOSTOYEVSKY. In this book the author examines directly the reasons for what he sees as the "chemical decomposition" of Russian society in the late 19th century. The central character is Arkady Makarovich Dolgoruky, a young man in his early twenties, who tries to find something solid to cling to in the disorder and chaos of the times. He settles on the idea of becoming a Rothschild, as he terms it: he wants to amass vast wealth, not for the sake of the monetary value of the money, but for the sense of power it will give him.

Arkady is the illegitimate son of the nobleman VERSILOV, who has been living with Arkady's mother for some years. His nominal father, Makar DOLGORUKY, has become a religious pilgrim. The youthful Arkady goes to St. Petersburg to see Versilov, full of mixed love and hate for his father. The nobleman—a brilliant, twisted product of the acceptance of Western ideas—charms the boy. Their closeness is short-lived, however, for Arkady learns that his father is his rival for Katerina Nikolayevna Akhmatovo. After a siege of brain fever, the anguished Arkady begins to find peace, when the pilgrim Makar Dolgoruky arrives for a visit. The old man preaches love for all of God's creation and the need for all men to strive for seemliness in their relations with themselves and one another. Arkady abandons the idea of becoming a Rothschild for the goal of attaining seemliness.

Ray, Man (1890–1976)   American artist. Ray's friendship with Marcel DUCHAMP, begun in New York in 1915, was of critical importance to his work as an artist. He was the only American to participate fully in the DADA movement and SURREALISM from their earliest beginnings. He moved to Paris in 1921 and became immediately involved with the writers and artists of the so-called LOST GENERATION. He made various mixed-media objects and surrealist paintings and created the "Rayogram," or photogram, an image made by placing objects directly onto light-sensitive photographic paper. His characteristic wit is evident in his *New York 1920* (1920), a jar filled with ball bearings in oil. Of his several surrealist films, the most successful was *L'Étoile de mer* (1928).

Ray, Satyajit (1921–   )   Indian filmmaker. Born to a wealthy Bengali family, Ray became India's most internationally lauded director. His masterpiece is the so-called Apu Trilogy—*Pather Panchali* (1955), *Aparajito* (*The Unvanquished*, 1956), and *Apu Sansar* (*The World of Apu*, 1959)—based on B. B. BANERJEE's novels about a group of impoverished Bengali characters. These films are characterized by a slow, contemplative pace, by human compassion, and by a sensitive depiction of the total Bengali environment.

Raymond IV (called Raymond de Saint-Giles, d 1105)   Count of Toulouse (1088–1105). As a historical personage, Raymond led a major force in the First CRUSADE (1096). In Torquato Tasso's GERUSALEMME LIBERATA he appears as Raimondo di Tolosa, one of the leading veterans among the Crusaders, especially noted for his Nestor-like wisdom.

Rayuela (1963)   A novel by Julio CORTÁZAR. Oliveira, an Argentine intellectual, leads a bohemian existence in the boulevards and attics of Paris. Two accidents change his life: falling in love with la Maga, a childlike woman, and finding the manuscripts of the revered Morelli. Tired of Oliveira's pretended irresponsibility, la Maga leaves him. He returns to Buenos Aires, where eventually his games of alienation lead to madness, although we could choose to believe that, in his room in the insane asylum, he alone has found the window that opens onto the beyond. The story is narrated in jarring segments interspersed, in a sort of hopscotch, with Morelli's ironic reflections on the death of the contemporary novel. One of the most influential novels of the 1960s, *Rayuela* was translated by Gregory Rabassa as *Hopscotch* (1966).

Razor's Edge, The (1944)   A novel by W. Somerset MAUGHAM. The hero is a worldly young man who is converted to Hinduism and leaves his inheritance for the holy life.

Razumov   The central character in Joseph Conrad's novel UNDER WESTERN EYES. Razumov is a Russian, a student, and an unsuccessful spy.

Read, Sir Herbert [Edward] (1893–1968)   English poet, art critic, and literary critic. Read wrote a distinctively modern verse, often associated with IMAGISM, and his development as a poet and thinker owed much to the romanticism of WORDSWORTH and, among his contemporaries, to T. E. HULME, Ezra POUND, William Carlos WILLIAMS, and his lifelong friend T. S. ELIOT. Several versions of his *Collected Poems* have been published (1926, 1946, 1966). His criticism, reflecting a more classical and intellectual vision, was highly tolerant and welcomed new ideas, and is well represented in *Collected Essays in Literary Criticism* (1938). He was a constant champion of art and its role in education and industry, and his most influential book, *Education Through Art* (1943), had an incalculable effect on secondary educators and education following World War II.

Read, Miss (pen name of Dora Jessie Saint, 1913–   )   English novelist. As a schoolteacher Saint began by writing journalism, including articles about schools, under her own name. When a publisher suggested she turn her graceful and unsentimental accounts into fiction, the persona "Miss Read," headmistress, was conceived. She began with a trilogy about a school in the fictional village of Fairacre: *Village School* (1955), *Village Diary* (1957), and *Storm in the Village* (1958). *The Market Square* (1966), *The Christmas Mouse* (1973), and *Return to Thrush*

Green (1978), among others, chronicle the lives of the townspeople of Thrush Green, another imagined town in southern England.

Reade, Charles (1814–1884)   English novelist. Reade is best known for his medieval romance THE CLOISTER AND THE HEARTH. In his other novels, he often deals with social problems and exposes social abuses.

Reagan, Ronald W[ilson] (1911–   )   American actor, politician, and fortieth president of the United States. Born in Illinois, Reagan had a short career as a radio sports announcer before he went to Hollywood in 1937, where he appeared in fifty productions—many of them "B" movies—over the next twenty-five years. Twice president of the Screen Actors Guild and an active liberal in the years immediately after World War II, by the early 1950s he had moved well to the right and was investigating possible Communist influence in the film industry. He joined the Republican Party in 1962 and in 1966 was elected governor of California. In 1965 he published a memoir, *Where's the Rest of Me?*, with Richard G. Hubler.

In 1980 Reagan ran for president and defeated the incumbent, Jimmy CARTER, and in 1984 was reelected in a landslide victory. He became the first president to appoint an official resident biographer, Pulitzer Prize winner Edmund Morris.

realism   In philosophy, one of two rival doctrines in the disputes of the medieval Schoolmen (see SCHOLASTICISM). Derived from the theories of PLATO, it held that only universal concepts, such as roundness, beauty, and the like, have reality, since they exist before any particular circle or beautiful object. See ABÉLARD, PIERRE; NOMINALISM.

The term *realism* is also used to describe literature that attempts to depict life in an entirely objective manner, without idealization or glamor, and without didactic or moral ends. Realism may be said to have begun with such early English novelists as DEFOE, FIELDING, and SMOLLETT, and to have become a definite literary trend in the 19th century. In America, realism became an important movement in the 1880s with William Dean HOWELLS as its leading theorizer and Henry JAMES as one of its main practitioners. It contributed to the growth of NATURALISM, with which it is sometimes identified, at the turn of the century. At present it is such a pervasive element in literature that it scarcely retains any distinct import.

Rebecca   In Scott's IVANHOE, the real heroine, daughter of Isaac the Jew. Rebecca loves Ivanhoe, who has shown great kindness to her and her father. When Ivanhoe marries Rowena, both Rebecca and her father leave England for the Continent.

Rebecca of Sunnybrook Farm (1903)   A children's story by Kate Douglas Wiggin (1856–1923). The ten-year-old heroine, Rebecca Randall, goes to live with her two maiden aunts, Miranda and Jane. Aunt Miranda, particularly, is a great trial, but Rebecca finds a friend in

Emma Jane Perkins and a hero and admirer in Adam Ladd. The book ends with her graduation from Wareham Academy, in Maine. There was a sequel, *New Chronicles of Rebecca*, in 1907. *Rebecca of Sunnybrook Farm* was successfully dramatized in 1910, and made into a movie with Shirley Temple in 1938.

Rebekah   In the OLD TESTAMENT, the wife of ISAAC and mother of JACOB and ESAU. The meeting at the well between Rebekah and ABRAHAM's servant, sent to seek a wife for Isaac, is one of the celebrated pastoral love stories (Gen. 24). It was Rebekah who helped her favorite son Jacob secure the birthright that should have been Esau's (Gen. 27:6).

Rebel, The (L'Homme révolté, 1951; tr 1953)   A long philosophical essay by Albert CAMUS. It expands the theory of the ABSURD first treated in THE MYTH OF SISYPHUS and explores the possible responses man can make in attitude and in action, rejecting equally suicidal despair and all promises of complete personal or social salvation. Camus distinguishes between philosophical rebellion, proper to the man of the absurd, and historical or political revolution, which promises salvation but consists merely of murder and a new tyranny.

Récamier, Jeanne Françoise Julie Adélaïde (born Bernard, 1777–1849)   French leader of society. The wife of a Paris banker and close friend of Mme de STAËL, Mme Récamier was known for her wit and beauty. Mme Récamier's salons were filled with the most important people of her time, both in the arts and in politics. In later years, CHATEAUBRIAND became the indisputed center of this group and the object of Mme Récamier's devotion.

Recessional (1897)   A famous poem by Rudyard KIPLING. It was written to celebrate the sixtieth anniversary of the accession of Queen Victoria. The title refers to the hymn that is sung at the close of a church service. The poem includes a warning to the British people not to become overconfident, but to remember their obligations during their hour of greatest glory.

recherche du temps perdu, À la   See REMEMBRANCE OF THINGS PAST.

Recognition, The   See GADDIS, WILLIAM.

Records of the Historian   See SSU-MA CH'IEN.

Red and the Black, The (Le Rouge et le noir, 1830)   A novel by STENDHAL. The author's most celebrated work, it is equally acclaimed for its psychological study of its protagonist—the provincial young romantic Julien SOREL—and as a satiric analysis of the French social order under the Bourbon restoration. Its intensely dramatic plot is purposively romantic in nature, while Stendhal's careful portraiture of Sorel's inner states is the work of a master realist, foreshadowing new developments in the form of the novel.

Red Badge of Courage, The: An Episode of the American Civil War (1895)   A novel by Stephen CRANE. More the story of the battle that rages inside the hero, Henry Fleming, than of that between Confederate and Union soldiers, the novel is, as its author said, a psychological study of fear. Young Fleming has romantic notions of the hero he will be when he enters his first battle, but his illusions are soon destroyed and he turns and runs. Ironically, he receives his "red badge" when a fellow soldier strikes his head with the butt of a gun. He sees a friend die and tries to find security in a secluded spot in the forest. After attempting to stop the advancing troops he thinks are doomed, Fleming returns to his comrades. During the battle on the next day, he gives up his illusions, merges with the great body of soldiers, and becomes, temporarily at least, a hero.

Crane's realism is remarkable, especially in view of the fact that he had not seen a battle at the time he wrote the book. His insight into the feelings and fears of soldiers provided a new experience to a public unaccustomed to reading about the seamier aspects of war. *The Red Badge of Courage* established Crane's reputation and remains his most popular work.

Red Cavalry (Konarmiya, 1926)   A collection of short stories by Isaak BABEL. It is based on the Soviet author's experiences with Budenny's cavalry regiment during the civil war in Russia.

Red Cross Knight, The   Central character of Book I of Spenser's THE FAERIE QUEENE. He is identified with St. George, the patron saint of England, and is a symbol of holiness.

Red Gloves   See DIRTY HANDS.

Redskins, The, or Indian and Injin   See LITTLEPAGE MANUSCRIPTS.

reductio ad absurdum   A proof of inference arising from the demonstration that every other hypothesis involves an absurdity. In common parlance, the phrase has come to signify the opposite: an argument that brings out the absurdity of a contention made.

Reed, Sir Carol (1906–1976)   British film director. Reed's best work belongs to the late 1930s and 1940s: *The Stars Look Down* (1939), a grimly realistic account of a mine disaster; *The Way Ahead* (1944), a seriocomic, but authentic, study of a group of conscripts adjusting to army life; *The Third Man* (1949), a taut Cold War melodrama; and *Outcast of the Islands* (1951), a vivid adaptation of Joseph CONRAD's novel. Reed's acknowledged masterpiece is *Odd Man Out* (1947), the poignant story of the last hours of a dying Irish revolutionary. Most of Reed's films of the 1950s and 1960s were not up to his earlier standards, although *The Agony and the Ecstasy* (1965) enjoyed a measure of popular success, and *Oliver!* (1968) was awarded an Academy Award.

Reed, Ishmael (1938–   )   American novelist and poet. Reed's writing reflects his belief that the black American writer should function as a kind of conjurer of what Reed calls "neo-Hoodoo," an attempt to pry the distinct qualities of Afro-American culture loose from Euro-

American culture. In a language composed of black dialects, standard English, and hip jargon, he writes angry satires on an American society corrupted by racism and runaway technology. Among his novels are *The Free-Lance Pallbearers* (1967), *Mumbo Jumbo* (1972), *Flight to Canada* (1976), and *The Terrible Twos* (1982). His verse collections include *Conjure* (1972) and *Secretary to the Spirits* (1975). *Shrovetide in Old New Orleans* (1978) is a collection of occasional writings. He has also written a play, *Hell Hath No Fury* (1980).

Reed, John (1887–1920)   American journalist, poet, and radical leader. Reed came from a wealthy Oregon family. After graduating from Harvard (1910), he worked as a journalist, became friendly with Lincoln STEFFENS, and in 1913 joined the staff of THE MASSES. He became profoundly interested in social problems and labor struggles and, through his journalistic assignments, became increasingly radicalized. His experiences as a correspondent during the Mexican Revolution provided the material for his first book, *Insurgent Mexico* (1914). He covered the Eastern Front in World War I, then went to Russia where he became an active supporter of the Bolsheviks. His eloquent eyewitness account of the Russian Revolution, *Ten Days That Shook the World* (1919), is considered his best work.

After helping to found the Communist Labor Party (a spin-off from the Socialist Party) in America, he returned to Russia, where he worked for the bureau of propaganda. He died in Russia and was buried in the Kremlin.

Reeve's Tale, The   One of THE CANTERBURY TALES of Geoffrey CHAUCER, based on a French *fabliau* (see FABLIAUX). Oswald the Reeve takes THE MILLER'S TALE as a personal insult, for he is also a carpenter, and retaliates in kind with his tale. The young scholars John and Alan resolve to watch carefully and stop the miller Simkin's gross cheating of their college. But Simkin lets loose their horse, so that they give chase, and proceeds to steal more grain than ever. When they return late, he scornfully offers them a bed for the night in the same room with his family. But in the dark Alan steals over to the lovely daughter's bed, and John, by moving the infant's cradle, tricks the wife into his own bed. The daughter tells Alan where the stolen grain is hidden, and he goes to wake John and boast of his exploits, but is also misled by the cradle and wakes Simkin instead. In the confused fight that follows, the wife knocks out Simkin by mistake, and the scholars escape with all their grain and a little more.

Reflections on the French Revolution (1790) A treatise by Edmund BURKE, written in the form of a letter to a Frenchman. It attacks the leaders and principles of the French Revolution for their violence and excesses, and urges reform, rather than rebellion, as a means of correcting social and political abuses. This work was, in turn, attacked by Thomas PAINE. Burke had interpreted the Glorious Revolution (1688) and the American Revolution as just assertions of rights guaranteed by the British Constitution; he opposed the French Revolution because, he thought, it broke the framework of tradition altogether.

Reformation   The great 16th-century movement against the authority of the Roman Catholic Church that brought about the establishment of Protestantism. The chief religious leaders of the Reformation were Martin LUTHER, John CALVIN, Ulrich ZWINGLI, and John KNOX. Although the movement originated as a protest against religious abuses, it had profound political implications as well. See COUNTER-REFORMATION; THIRTY YEARS' WAR.

Reform Bill   In English history, a bill that enlarges the number of voters in elections for the House of Commons, reducing inequalities in representation. The first of these, the Reform Bill of 1832, disfranchised boroughs of very few inhabitants (called rotten boroughs), giving increased representation to large towns and extending the number of holders of the county and borough franchise. The Reform Bill of 1867 went further in the same direction, and the Franchise Bill (1884) extended suffrage to nearly all men. In 1918 suffrage was given to all men over twenty-one and to women over thirty; in 1928, all persons over twenty-one were eligible to vote. The background of George Eliot's *Middlemarch* is the Reform Bill of 1832.

Regan   In Shakespeare's KING LEAR, the second daughter of Lear. Like her older sister, Goneril, Regan refuses to house her father's large entourage and later aids her husband, Cornwall, in plucking out Gloucester's eyes when he shelters Lear. After her husband's death, she plans to marry Edmund, but is poisoned by the jealous Goneril.

Regenta, La   See ALAS Y UREÑA, LEOPOLDO.

Régnard, Jean François (1655–1709)   French comic dramatist. Régnard was once captured by pirates and sold as a slave in Constantinople. He traveled extensively, settling finally in Paris, where he wrote his autobiographical *Voyages* (1731). Among his more celebrated comedies in verse are *Le Joueur* (*The Gambler*, 1696), *Les Folies amoureuses* (*Amorous Follies*, 1704), *Les Ménechmes* (1705), and his masterpiece, *Le Légataire universel* (1708). Régnard's plays are simply witty and sparkling, with no attempt at being profound; indeed, human sympathy is conspicuously absent.

Régnier, Henri de (1864–1936)   French poet and novelist. As a member of the SYMBOLISTS and a disciple of Mallarmé, Régnier wrote verse, such as that published in *Tel qu'en songe* (1892) and *Les Jeux rustiques et divins* (1897), which was musical and skillful in its use of vers libre. In his later work—such volumes as *Les Medailles d'argile* (1900) and *La Sandale ailée* (1906)—he returned to classical forms and sought themes for his poetry in antiquity. Régnier's best-known novel is *La Double Maitresse* (1900).

Rehoboam   A Hebrew king in the OLD TESTAMENT, the son and successor of SOLOMON. During Rehoboam's leadership, the northern tribes revolted and, retaining the name Israel, formed a new kingdom under JEROBOAM I. His remark, "My father . . . chastised you with whips, but I will chastise you with scorpions" (1 Kings 12:14), cost him the allegiance of the greater part of his kingdom; only the tribe of JUDAH and part of the tribe of BENJAMIN remained loyal.

Reign of Terror   A term applied to the period of anarchy, bloodshed, and confiscation in the FRENCH REVOLUTION. It may be considered to have begun on January 21, 1793, with the execution of Louis XVI, or after May 31, 1793, when the GIRONDISTS fell; it extended to the overthrow of ROBESPIERRE and his accomplices on July 27, 1794. During this period thousands of persons were put to death. The name is also applied to similar cataclysms in the histories of other nations, such as the Red Terror of the Russian Revolution (March–September 1917).

Reineke Fuchs (1794)   An epic poem in hexameters by GOETHE, which retells the story of REYNARD THE FOX. Goethe lays stress upon the fact that the amoral man, even though his crimes may be harmful to others, is still useful to society because of his superior resourcefulness, and necessary to society as a balance to the gradual stultification of unchallenged morality.

Reinhart, Carlo   See BERGER, THOMAS.

Religio Laici (1682)   A poem by John DRYDEN in defense of the Anglican religion. It preceded his famous defense of Catholicism, *The Hind and the Panther*, by only three years. The work is a witty and cogent argument for the middle way of Anglicanism.

Religio Medici (1643)   The best-known work of Sir Thomas BROWNE, who called it "a private Exercise directed to myself." Published only after a pirated edition had appeared, it represents Browne's attempt to arrive at a warm and vital faith, one without cant or a spirit of exclusiveness, acceptable to a scientist; its Latin title means "a doctor's religion." It is one of the great achievements in the ornate style of English prose.

Reliques of Ancient English Poetry (1765)   A collection of ballads, sonnets, historical songs, and romances published by Thomas Percy (1729–1811); more properly, it is one of the earliest histories of literature. It contains metrical romances and traditional ballads from the 15th through the 18th centuries, all arranged in chronological order. In it appeared, for the first time, such famous ballads as "Sir Patrick Spens" and "Edward, Edward."

Remarque, Erich Maria (1898–1970)   German journalist and novelist. Like most of his generation, Remarque was deeply affected by World War I, which is the subject of his most successful novel, ALL QUIET ON THE WESTERN FRONT. The best known of his other novels is *Zeit zu Leben, Zeit zu Sterben* (1954; tr *A Time to Love and a Time to Die*, 1954). Remarque left Nazi Germany in 1932 and settled in the U.S. in 1939.

Rembrandt [Harmenszoon van Rijn] (1606–1669)   Dutch painter and etcher. Born in Leyden, Rembrandt settled in Amsterdam in 1631 and quickly established himself as the finest portrait painter of the city. His wife died in 1642, leaving him a considerable fortune, but his popularity declined as his art became increasingly divergent from popular taste, and he sank into financial difficulties. A declaration of bankruptcy in 1656 was followed by the sale of his property, including his art collection.

The range of Rembrandt's art is unusually extensive. He painted numerous portraits, both of individuals and groups, and he is well known for his dramatic use of light and shadows in such paintings as *The Company of Captain Franz Banning Cock*, popularly known as the *Night Watch* (1642). His series of nearly one hundred known self-portraits beautifully chronicle the gradual alteration of his features, as well as the many facets of his character. In his paintings of sacred themes, he created a style of representation which was at once poignantly human and deeply religious, as, for example, the *Supper at Emmaus* (1648).

Mention must also be made of his extraordinary etchings. The grandeur of his conception of the Crucifixion and of other scenes from the life of Jesus is enhanced by the intense realism with which his subjects are represented. Also greatly prized are his pen-and-wash drawings, brief notations of great vigor and expressiveness, which further reveal this master as a great landscapist.

Remembrance of Things Past (À la recherche du temps perdu; 16 vols, 1913–1927)   A long novel in seven parts by Marcel PROUST. Except for *The Past Recaptured*, which is translated by Stephen Hudson, the English translation (1922–31) is the work of C. K. Scott-Moncrieff. Proust's own French title indicates this great work's subject and theme; the narrator is "in search of lost time," and he finds in involuntary memories stimulated by some object or circumstance the true meaning of past experience. He could not appreciate this meaning at the time of the experience itself; and conscious attempts at recollection only serve to change his view of the experience, according to the perspective of the new self he has meanwhile become. But certain "privileged moments" of memory, evoked by unconscious associations, mean simultaneous existence in the past and present; they thus permit a glimpse of the essence common to both, a transcendental reality independent of time.

Otherwise, time invariably produces a kaleidoscopically changing series of patterns in people and their emotions, as well as in society and its fashions. The novel exposes the illusory nature of the narrator's early ideals, especially those regarding the permanence of love and the absoluteness of any hierarchy of values. Love, at first inspired by unattainability, becomes boring after consummation, unless continually stimulated by jealousy. Even the inhabitants of the fashionable and exclusive Faubourg St. Germain greatly disappoint the bourgeois narrator, once he has climbed carefully from salon to salon to view their supposedly gallant splendor and cultivated wit. In structure, the novel first introduces as opposite paths the Méséglise Way, which leads past Swann's bourgeois estate, and the Guermantes Way, leading toward a royally titled estate —both at first impossible for the narrator to enter. But he gradually discovers the personal relationships that increasingly connect these families and the ways of life they represent. Eventually, even the superficial appearances of difference degenerate and take new shapes, until Swann's daughter—by a cocotte whom the Guermantes had formerly refused to meet—has married a Guermantes and offers her daughter by this marriage to the narrator as a mistress.

The analysis of love includes male and female homosexual relationships, showing their essential similarity to heterosexual ones. The analysis of snobbery exposes pathetic self-delusion as much as deliberate hypocrisy. In regard to artists and their work, as to everything else, anticipated pleasure always exceeds the actual pleasure at first meeting; but, after assimilation of the work of the actress BERMA, the writer BERGOTTE, the composer VINTEUIL, and the painter Elstir, the narrator does conclude that art can occasionally —as can dreams, but never life—express the associations that make perceptible the world of essential reality, which lies outside of lived Time.

Swann's Way (*Du côté de chez Swann*)   After the *Overture* introduces most of the themes of the entire novel, the narrator recalls his childhood at home in Paris and with his relatives at COMBRAY, including his idealized love for SWANN's daughter, Gilberte. He then recounts the story of Swann's love for ODETTE many years before, which is intertwined with the beginning of the rise of the VERDURINS.

Within a Budding Grove (*À l'ombre des jeunes filles en fleurs*)   In Paris the narrator's love for Gilberte slowly ends. Two years later, when he is at BALBEC, he falls in love with a little band of frolicsome girls and particularly with ALBERTINE.

The Guermantes Way (*Le Côté de Guermantes*)   The narrator, whose family have been tenants in the large GUERMANTES home in Paris, conducts his laborious ascent to the summit of high society, finally attending the duchesse de Guermantes's reception. He also describes SAINT-LOUP's passion for RACHEL, and the death of his own beloved grandmother.

Cities of the Plain (*Sodome et Gomorrhe*)   The narrator discovers Baron CHARLUS's homosexuality and the changing nature of socially fashionable opinions—regarding the DREYFUS Case, for instance. After a reception given by the princesse de Guermantes, he returns to Balbec, where Charlus is launching MOREL at the Verdurins' *soirées*. He is about to break with Albertine when suspicions of her lesbian tastes arouse his horror and jealousy, and revive his love.

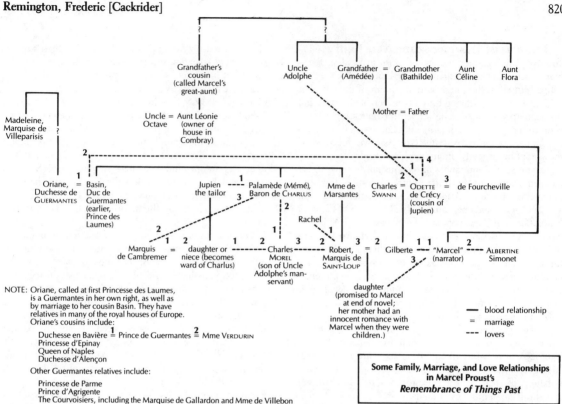

Some Family, Marriage, and Love Relationships
in Marcel Proust's
Remembrance of Things Past

NOTE: Oriane, called at first Princesse des Laumes,
is a Guermantes in her own right, as well as
by marriage to her cousin Basin. They have
relatives in many of the royal houses of Europe.
Oriane's cousins include:

Duchesse en Bavière [1] = Prince de Guermantes [2] = Mme VERDURIN
Princesse d'Epinay
Queen of Naples
Duchesse d'Alençon

Other Guermantes relatives include:

Princesse de Parme
Prince d'Agrigente
The Courvoisiers, including the Marquise de Gallardon and Mme de Villebon

— blood relationship
= marriage
--- lovers

The Captive (*La Prisonnière*)   Albertine is living in the narrator's Paris home, where he attempts to keep complete watch on her activities. The Verdurins provoke a scandalous rupture between Morel and Charlus. Albertine suddenly flees, just as the narrator is ready to dismiss her.

The Sweet Cheat Gone (*Albertine disparue*)   The narrator seeks the return of Albertine, but after her death he observes the gradual encroachment of oblivion on grief until, on a trip to Venice, he finds his pain completely cured. Gilberte has become the social-climbing Mlle de Forcheville; she marries Saint-Loup, who is now Morel's lover.

The Past Recaptured (*Le Temps retrouvé*)   World War I accelerates the kaleidoscopic changes in society. The narrator attends a reception of the new princesse de Guermantes, actually the former Mme Verdurin, and finds most of his acquaintances almost unrecognizable. He has enjoyed three "privileged moments" of memory, and in contemplating them discovers that his vocation is to be the shaping of his experiences into a literary work of art.

Remington, Frederic [Cackrider] (1861–1909) American artist. Remington popularized the American West in his dramatic, animated paintings and sculptures of life on the plains, such as the bronze *Bronco Buster* (1895).

Remizov, Aleksey Mikhailovich (1877–1957) Russian novelist. Remizov, whose ornate prose style influ-

enced such writers as Boris PILNYAK, Isaak BABEL, and Yevgeny ZAMYATIN, left Russia in 1921 and lived in Paris for the remainder of his life. His works include *Prud* (*The Pond*, 1907), *Pyataya yazva* (1912; tr *The Fifth Pestilence*, 1927), and *Plamennaya Rossiya* (*Flaming Russia*, 1921).

Renaissance   From the French word for *rebirth*. First used by 19th-century historians, it is a label for the period dating approximately from the mid-14th to the end of the 16th centuries. During the period itself, the idea of a revival or rebirth of culture after the barbarism of the Dark Ages and the medieval period was a favorite notion of the Humanists; but they did not use the word itself. It was used at the time by such art historians as VASARI, whose reference was exclusively to the fine arts. With MICHELET and BURCKHARDT, the term and the concept of the Renaissance came into general use. Since their day, controversy has centered on denigration of the Middle Ages, on the chronological limits of the period, on its applicability to science and philosophy of the time, on its causes, and even on its value as a term for widely differing phenomena in Europe, especially outside Italy. There is essential agreement, however, on the main ingredients of the era. These include the REVIVAL OF ANTIQUITY, the REVIVAL OF LEARNING, the activity of the Humanists, the increased secularization of social life, the burst of creativity in the fine arts, the cultivation of the arts, the growth of individualism in private as well as public life, the expansion of scientific and philo-sophical horizons, the creation of new social, political, and economic institutions, and the arrival of a new view of man and his world. In the literary sphere, the men of letters and the works of the period, from PETRARCH to SHAKESPEARE, represent an impressive roster unmatched before or since. There is a continuity of themes and forms as the wave of inspiration passed from Italy to France and Spain, then to England, where the novelle of BOCCACCIO and the sonnets of Petrarch were being read and imitated two centuries after their composition. See ELIZABETH I; FRENCH RENAISSANCE; HUMANISM; QUATTROCENTO.

Renan, Ernest (1823–1892)   French critic, writer, and scholar. Raised in poverty, Renan was a student pre-paring for the priesthood when he lost his faith in orthodox religion. Renan later became a relativist. From a tolerant, skeptical point of view, he realized that no one system of religious, scientific, or historical knowledge could claim absolute truth. A professor of Hebrew at the Collège de France, Renan's major influence was felt in the field of religion. In 1863 he published *La Vie de Jésus* (*The Life of Jesus*), the first work in a series called *Histoire des origines du Christianisme* (*History of the Origins of Christianity*, 1866–81). This study offered a new perspective on religious history, approaching the subject matter not merely in a fac-tual, historical manner but as biography and psychology. Renan also published *Histoire du peuple d'Israël* (*History of the People of Israel*, 1887–95), *Histoire générale des langues sémitiques* (*General History of the Semitic Languages*, 1855), and *Dialogues philosophiques* (1876). His work was widely influential.

Renault, Mary (pen name of Mary Challans, 1905–1983)   English novelist. Renault began a long string of successful books with novels on contemporary subjects, drawing largely on her experience as a hospital and war nurse. *Promise of Love* (1939), the first of these, treated the nurse-loves-doctor theme with a freshness and intensity that signaled Renault's promise as a writer. *The Charioteer* (1953) was a well-received and compassionate study of a homosexual soldier. *The Last of the Wine* (1956), set dur-ing the wars between Athens and Sparta, was greeted as a superb historical novel. The next, *The King Must Die* (1958), recreating the myth of THESEUS and the minotaur, is generally considered her greatest achievement. Her later vivid reconstructions of the ancient world include *Fire from Heaven* (1969), about ALEXANDER THE GREAT, its sequel, *The Persian Boy* (1972), and *The Praise Singer* (1978), the story of SIMONIDES, the Greek lyric poet.

René (1802)   A romance by François René de CHA-TEAUBRIAND, published first in *Le Génie du Christianisme*, and as a separate volume in 1805. Set in America, the story concerns a violently unhappy, morbidly introspective youth whose posture is typically romantic.

Renoir, [Pierre] Auguste (1841–1919)   French painter. In the early impressionist years, Renoir painted charming, ethereal scenes of women, children, and gar-dens, such as the popular *Girl with Watering Can* (1876). He was responsible for a number of innovations, among them the use of pure, unmixed colors, which became inte-gral elements of impressionist technique.

In his later years, Renoir retained his fondness for lovely scenes painted in luminous hues, but in pictures like his portrait of the collector Paul Durand-Ruel (1910), Renoir, now crippled by arthritis, revealed greater freedom, vigor, and originality than in his earlier works. See IMPRESSION-ISM.

Renoir, Jean (1894–1979)   French motion picture director. Widely acknowledged as one of the greatest of filmmakers, Renoir is noted for the rich humanity of his work and his portrayal of life's confusion, its muddle of farce and tragedy. Among the most famous of his films is *Grand Illusion* (1937), a perennially moving antiwar film, voted by an international jury in 1958 as one of the ten best films ever made. *The Rules of the Game* (1939), *The Diary of a Chambermaid* (1946), and *The River* (1950) represent the varieties of mood and feeling with which Renoir invests his basically simple plots. The son of Pierre Auguste RENOIR, he is also the author of *Renoir, My Father* (1962), a vivid and affectionate biographical reminiscence of the famous impressionist painter.

Representative Men (1850)   A series of biograph-ical sketches by Ralph Waldo EMERSON. The men dis-cussed are SHAKESPEARE, the Poet; PLATO, the Philosopher; GOETHE, the Writer; SWEDENBORG, the Mystic; NAPOLEON, the Man of the World; and MONTAIGNE, the Skeptic. The essays are preceded by an introduction dealing with the "uses of great men." The book is modeled on CARLYLE's *On Heroes, Hero Worship and the Heroic in History*. The two volumes reveal the difference in their authors' feelings about democracy. Unlike Carlyle, Emerson believed that great men are representative of their time, rather than apart from it.

Reprieve, The   See ROADS TO FREEDOM, THE.

Republic, The   A dialogue by PLATO. The dialogue begins with an attempt at the definition of justice. SOCRA-TES remarks that before justice can be found in the individ-ual, it must be sought in the state. Describing the ideal state, Plato's Socrates divides the citizens into three classes: the guardians, the soldiers, and the workers or producers. Democracy and tyranny are both rejected. Temperance and restraint must characterize all three classes. Political justice would confine each to his proper function.

Requiem for a Nun (1951)   A novel by William FAULKNER. Written in three prose sections, which provide the background, and three acts which present the drama in the courthouse and the jail, the novel centers on Temple DRAKE, one of the main characters of SANCTUARY. In the interval of the eight years separating the events of the two books, Temple has married Gowan Stevens and borne two children; she is being blackmailed by Pete, brother of her lover in *Sanctuary*, and is planning to run away with him when Nancy MANNINGOE, her black servant, kills Temple's youngest child. Her attempts to gain a pardon from the governor for Nancy finally bring out Temple's own involvement in and responsibility for the crime.

Resnais, Alain (1922–   )   French film director. Resnais began by making documentary films, two of which, *Nuit et brouillard* (1955), about the Nazi concentration camp Auschwitz, and *Toute le mémoire du monde* (1956), about the Bibliothèque Nationale, were particularly highly regarded. He then became known for several films made in close association with writers of the NEW WAVE: *Hiroshima, mon amour* (1960; written by Marguerite DURAS) and *L'Année dernière à Marienbad* (1962; written by Alain ROBBE-GRILLET). His other films, with the possible exception of the more romantic *La Guerre est finie* (1966), are characterized by an intellectual and objective approach to both characters and settings. Among them are *Je t'aime, je t'aime* (1968), *Stavisky* (1974), *Providence* (1977), and *Mon Oncle d'Amérique* (1980).

Respectful Prostitute, The (La Putain respectueuse, 1946; tr 1949)   A play by Jean-Paul SARTRE. It is set in the American South. Lizzie does not want to lie to help build a case against an innocent black. But the senator's son Fred needs a scapegoat for his cousin Thomas, who killed another black, and Lizzie is finally so thoroughly confused about relative rights and wrongs that she agrees.

Restif de la Bretonne, Nicolas Edmé (or Nicolas Edmé Rétif de la Bretonne, 1734–1806)   French novelist and dramatist, often labeled as the "Rousseau of the Gutter," or the "Voltaire of Chambermaids." Restif wrote some 250 volumes, many of which describe peasant life and lower-class women. To gather material for his works he was wont to prowl around Paris at night. In 1775 he published *Le Paysan perverti ou les dangers de la ville*, a four-volume novel about the corrupting influences of Paris on a young peasant. From 1780 to 1785 he published his forty-two-volume work on the lives of contemporary women, *Les Contemporaines ou Aventures des plus jolies femmes de l'âge présent*. His intimate knowledge of women is reflected in his self-appraisal: "Without women, I was a nonentity, without vigor, without energy, in a word, without a soul." *La Vie de mon père* (2 vols, 1779) is perhaps his masterpiece. He also wrote a series of works under the general title *Les Idées singulières* (1769–89), in which he advocated reforms in education, prostitution, the theatre, and spelling. In his novels Restif presents a faithful picture of the last thirty years of the French monarchy, but some readers find his style coarse and the subject matter melodramatic and occasionally obscene.

Restoration   In English history, the period after the fall of the Commonwealth, when the Stuart dynasty returned to England in the person of Charles II, who became king in 1660. In its reaction to Puritan austerity and its imitation of French manners, the period gained a reputation for licentiousness and frivolity. It is marked in the field of English letters by characteristic developments in the drama (DRYDEN, CONGREVE, WYCHERLEY, FARQUHAR), particularly in the prose COMEDY OF MANNERS; by the flourishing of song and verse satire (Dryden, ROCHESTER); and by the productions of numerous diarists (PEPYS, EVELYN). These forms, though they confirm the worldliness and dissoluteness of the Restoration, are only a partial expression of the age, which also saw remarkable accomplishments in prose composition, science, philosophy, and religion.

Resurrection (Voskreseniye, 1899)   A novel by TOLSTOY. The story deals with the spiritual regeneration of a young nobleman, Prince Nekhlyudov. In his earlier years, he seduced a young girl, Katyusha Maslova. She became a prostitute and later became involved with a man she is accused of poisoning. Nekhlyudov, serving on the jury, recognizes her and decides that he is morally guilty for her predicament. He decides to marry her, and when she is convicted he follows her to Siberia to accomplish his aim. Maslova is repelled by his reforming zeal. She marries another prisoner, but is finally convinced of Nekhlyudov's sincerity and accepts his friendship.

The novel, which is the weakest of Tolstoy's three large works, was very popular at the time of its publication. Tolstoy used the money received from it to help the Russian religious sect of Dukhobors to immigrate to Canada.

Retrieved Reformation, A (1909)   A short story by O. HENRY. It relates the ironic fate of Jimmy Valentine, a burglar who decides to reform but is foiled when he shows his skill in opening a safe during an emergency. Jimmy is said to have been modeled on Jimmy Connors, one of O. Henry's fellow prisoners in the Ohio state penitentiary.

Return of the Native, The (1878)   A novel by Thomas HARDY. Clym Yeobright, tired of city life, returns from Paris to open a school on Egdon Heath and, in spite of the opposition of his mother, marries Eustacia Vye, a passionate, pleasure-loving girl who hopes to persuade him to return to Paris. She has been in love with reckless Damon Wildeve, who, to spite her, married Clym's cousin, Thomasin. Clym's eyesight fails and he becomes, for the time being, a furze cutter. With the idea of becoming reconciled to her son, Mrs. Yeobright walks over the heath to his cottage, but Eustacia, entertaining Wildeve, does not answer the door until Clym's mother leaves in despair. Overcome with fatigue, she sinks down and is found by Clym, unconscious and dying of an adder bite. Clym learns enough to blame Eustacia, who subsequently drowns herself at a midnight rendezvous with Wildeve, who also drowns attempting to rescue her. Thomasin later marries Diggory Venn, the reddleman, and Clym becomes an itinerant preacher.

Retz, Gilles [de Laval] de (or Gilles [de Laval] de Rais, 1404?–1440)   A Marshal of France who fought with

JOAN OF ARC against the English. A generous patron of the arts, Retz turned to alchemy and sorcery to recoup his fortune, and, at his trial in an ecclesiastical court, confessed to the kidnapping, torture, and murder of more than one hundred children. He was tried and executed for heresy and murder. It used to be thought that his history was the origin of the story of BLUEBEARD.

Reuchlin, Johann (1455–1522)   German jurist and humanist, famous for his Greek and Hebrew studies. Reuchlin's *De verbo mirifico* (*The Miraculous Word*, 1494), a defense of Jewish literature and philosophy, brought him into conflict with the Dominicans and the apostate Jew Pfefferkorn, who advocated the destruction of Jewish books. Other humanists, in the EPISTOLAE OBSCURORUM VIRORUM, supported Reuchlin in the dispute.

Revelation of Saint John the Divine, The The only purely apocalyptic book in the NEW TESTAMENT. The unknown author, a prisoner of Rome on the island of PATMOS, saw a vision of the end of the world and the final triumph of JESUS. The book is highly symbolic and employs mystic numbers. See ANTICHRIST.

Revenger's Tragedy, The (1607)   A Senecan tragedy by Cyril TOURNEUR. It tells of the revenge taken by Vendice upon a duke who had poisoned Vendice's mistress when she refused his advances. The play describes in almost grotesque detail the incredible degeneracy of the duke and his court.

Revenons à nos moutons (Fr)   Literally, "Let us come back to our sheep," a phrase used to express, "Let us return to our subject." It is taken from the 14th-century French comedy *La Farce de Maître Pathelin*, or *L'Avocat Pathelin* (line 1282), in which a woolen-draper charges a shepherd with ill-treating his sheep. In telling his story he keeps running away from his subject, and to throw discredit on the defendant's attorney (Pathelin) accuses him of stealing a piece of cloth. The judge must pull him up every moment with, "*Mais mon ami, revenons à nos moutons.*" The phrase is frequently quoted by Rabelais.

Reverdy, Pierre (1889–1960)   French poet and essayist. A friend of APOLLINAIRE, PICASSO, BRAQUE, JACOB, and other artistic innovators at the beginning of the century, Reverdy founded the journal *Nord-Sud* in 1916 as a forum for experimental poetry. In his own contributions to poetic theory, collected in *Le Gant de crin* (1926), he formulated important ideas about the poetic image that had considerable influence on SURREALISM and subsequent poetic movements. His poetry is characterized by fantastic, illogical, and disturbing images. Reverdy's early work (1915–22) is collected in *Plupart du temps* (1945), his later work in *Main-d'oeuvre* (1949).

Revere, Paul (1735–1818)   American patriot and craftsman. A successful silversmith by trade, Revere is best remembered for his midnight ride from Boston to Lexington on April 18–19, 1775, to warn the colonists that British soldiers were on the march. Revere's exploit is described in Longfellow's popular, though inaccurate, ballad "The Midnight Ride of Paul Revere" (1863).

Revival of Antiquity   One of the key aspects of the RENAISSANCE and a leading activity of the advocates of HUMANISM in Italy during the 14th and 15th centuries. It refers specifically to the search for lost manuscripts, the recovery of statues, medallions, coins, and other artifacts of classical civilization, a renewed interest in the available remnants of Greek and Roman art, especially its sculpture and architecture, its philosophy, and its literature. Finally, the term refers to the putting into practice of classical precepts and ideals in education, in political and social life, and in the creation of works of art and literature.

Revival of Learning   Sometimes identified with the RENAISSANCE and HUMANISM. More accurately, the term refers to the quickening pace of activity in philology, scholarship, criticism, and education that occurred in Italy from the mid-14th through the 16th centuries, and in other European countries shortly thereafter. Modern theory attributes the revival to the economic and political conditions of the Italian city-states and petty kingdoms, where a craving for culture was a characteristic of the individual as well as the society.

revolutionary romanticism   See SOCIALIST REALISM.

Rexroth, Kenneth (1905–1982)   American poet, critic, and translator. Rexroth was at the center of numerous literary movements—particularly the BEAT MOVEMENT—in or near San Francisco, where he lived for many years. Central to both his prose and poetry is a denunciation of the dehumanizing forces in modern society and a call for visionary union with nature. His volumes of verse include *The Phoenix and the Tortoise* (1944), *The Signature of All Things* (1950), *The Heart's Garden, the Garden's Heart* (1968), and *The Morning Star* (1979). Much of his work has been consolidated in *Collected Shorter Poems* (1967) and *Collected Longer Poems* (1968). Largely self-educated, Rexroth was influenced by Chinese and Japanese BUDDHISM. He produced distinguished translations of Oriental poetry, such as in *One Hundred Poems from the Japanese* (1955) and *One Hundred Poems from the Chinese* (1956). In addition to a volume of verse plays and a ballet, he wrote such books of essays as *Bird in the Bush* (1959) and *The Alternative Society* (1970). His *An Autobiographical Novel* (1966), about his youth in Chicago, is an excellent introduction to Rexroth's intellectual and philosophical preoccupations.

Reyes, Alfonso (1889–1959)   Mexican essayist and poet. One of the young Mexican intellectuals who formed the circle known as the *Ateneo de la Juventud*, Reyes left his homeland soon after receiving his law degree in 1913. He lived in Spain until 1924 and subsequently served as a Mexican diplomat in France, Argentina, and Brazil. He returned permanently to Mexico in 1939.

Often considered the finest prose stylist of Spanish America since RODÓ, Reyes was also an authority on the literature of Spain's golden age. He eschewed pedantry, and his work is remarkable for its subtlety, grace, and insight. His best-known book is probably *Visión de Anahuac, 1519* (1917), a depiction of Aztec civilization just before the Spanish Conquest. His collections of essays include *Capítulos de literatura española* (1939; 1945), *Pasado immediato y otros ensayos* (1941), *Ultima Tule* (1942), and *Tentativas y orientaciones* (1944). He also wrote *El deslinde* (1944), an introduction to literary theory; *Letras de la Nueva España* (1948), on the culture of colonial Mexico; and *La X en la frente* (1952), an interpretation of Mexico. *Ifigenia cruel* (1924) is a dramatic poem based on the classical legend. Collections of his essays in English translation are *Mexico in a Nutshell* (1964; tr by C. Ramsdell) and *The Position of America* (1971; tr by H. de Onís).

Reyles, Carlos (1868–1938) Uruguayan novelist. Independently wealthy, Reyles was able to devote his life to writing and other intellectual pursuits. His early novels are naturalistic and emphasize psychological analysis. Among these works are *Beba* (1894), about the evil effects of consanguinity on both men and animals; *La raza de Caín* (1900), a study in abnormal psychology; and *El terruño* (1916), a story of ranch life. His best-known work is probably *El embrujo de Sevilla* (1922; tr *Castanets*, 1929), a sensuous, lyrical novel, in which the Andalusian city itself is the dominant figure. He also wrote *El gaucho florido* (1932), another realistic portrayal of rural life.

Reymont, Wladyslaw Stanislaw (1867–1925) Polish novelist. Before he became a writer, Reymont worked on many jobs, gaining the experience later to be explored in his fiction. His first novel, *Komediantka* (1896; tr *The Comedienne*, 1920), presented theatrical life at the turn of the century, while his *Ziemia obiecana* (1899; tr *The Promised Land*, 1920) is among the first European novels to deal with the problems created by rapid industrialization and its effects on society. Reymont's masterpiece, *Chlopi* (1904–9; tr *The Peasants*, 1924), presents a complex and colorful picture of the life of peasants in a remote Polish village. His historical trilogy, *Rok 1794* (1913–18), recreates the year 1794 when the partition of Poland led to an insurrection against the invading Russian armies. He received the NOBEL PRIZE in Literature in 1924.

Reynard the Fox A medieval beast fable in French, Flemish, and German literature. It satirizes contemporary life by endowing animals with human personality traits, the major plot concerning the struggle for power between the cunning fox Reynard and the physically powerful wolf Isengrim (or Ysengrin): sly wit usually wins. Other characters for Reynard to outwit include King Noble the lion, Sir Bruin the bear, Tibert the cat, and Chanticleer the cock.

The ever-changing cycles of episodes derived from the countless animal fables circulating in Europe, Aesop's and others, as in MARIE DE FRANCE's *Ysopet*. From the 12th to the 14th centuries the tales were circulated in numerous forms, with constant additions and changes. By the 15th century the folktale quality and often the humor were being subordinated to each author's specific didactic purpose; a gloss would accompany the text, explaining the political significance of the characters and events, interpreting the power struggle, for instance, as that between the Church, the Barons, and the King. Goethe published a modern German version, REINEKE FUCHS, as did Jacob GRIMM in 1834.

Before CAXTON's translation of 1481, portions of the tale had been known in England as *Vox and the Wolf* (13th century), and CHAUCER used part of the French material in his NUN'S PRIEST'S TALE.

Reynolds, Sir Joshua (1723–1792) English painter. Reynolds was a leading proponent of painting in the "Grand Manner" as exemplified by the Italian Renaissance works of MICHELANGELO, RAPHAEL, and TITIAN, which he studied extensively while in Rome from 1750 to 1752. In his fifteen *Discourses* as first president of the Royal Academy (1768–89), he set forth many of the ideals of 18th-century aesthetics, eschewing realistic detail in favor of what were considered eternal, noble qualities. He was the leading British portrait painter of his century and painted a number of his literary contemporaries, such as Samuel JOHNSON, Edmund BURKE, and Richard SHERIDAN.

Reznikoff, Charles (1894–1976) American poet and novelist. The imprint of Reznikoff's urban Jewish background is found in much of his work. The influence of both IMAGISM and OBJECTIVISM is also evident in all he wrote. His poems are generally short, with sharply etched images, in which the meaning is not spelled out but suggested by objective details and, as he put it, by "the music of the verse . . . without the artifice of regular meters." His major collections include *By the Waters of Manhattan* (1962; also the title of his first novel, 1930), *By the Well of Living and Seeing* (1974), selected poems from 1918 to 1973, and *Holocaust* (1975), which drew on the testimony given at the Nuremberg Trials. *The Complete Poems*, published in two volumes, appeared in 1976 and 1978.

Rhadamanthus In Greek mythology, son of ZEUS and EUROPA and brother of MINOS. Rhadamanthus reigned in the Cyclades with such impartiality that at death he was made one of the judges of the infernal regions, with Minos and AEACUS.

Rhea In Greek mythology, the wife and sister of CRONOS, and mother of ZEUS and other Olympians. One of the TITANS, born of GE (earth) and URANUS (sky), Rhea married her brother Titan Cronos and gave birth to HESTIA, DEMETER, HERA, and POSEIDON. Cronos, having learned from his mother that one of his sons would dethrone him, swallowed them as soon as they were born. In order to avoid this fate for Zeus, Rhea bore him secretly and gave him to Ge, who arranged for his upbringing in

Crete. Rhea, meanwhile, gave Cronos a stone wrapped in swaddling clothes, which he swallowed in place of Zeus.

Though a somewhat shadowy figure herself, Rhea was widely worshiped under other names, or identified with local earth-mother goddesses with similar functions. Her most famous counterpart is the Asian goddess CYBELE.

Rhétoriqueurs, Grands   A school of French poets which originated in the duchy of Burgundy toward the end of the 15th century and extended as a medieval anachronism well into the Renaissance of the 16th century. Its representatives were the last to compose on the medieval themes of courtly love and chivalry, but medieval poetic lyricism having died out with the passing of knighthood, the apparatus of allegory and mythology served now only to cloak banal moralizing by such poets as Olivier de la Marche (c1422–1502) or Georges Chastellain (c1405/15–1475). This degeneration in content was accompanied by increasing complexity of technique. The *Art de rhétorique vulgaire* (1493) by Jean Molinet (1435–1507) and the *Grand et vray art de pleine rhétorique* (1521) by Pierre Fabry (c1460–before 1520) described the infinite variations in rhythm and rhyme scheme then in fashion.

Rhinoceros (1959)   A play by Eugène IONESCO. The central character is a man caught by the fear of remaining a human being when his fellow citizens are achieving animalistic conformity by turning into rhinoceroses.

Rhoda Fleming (1865)   A novel by George MEREDITH. The plot concerns the tireless efforts of the titular heroine, aided by her lover Robert Armstrong, to set right the affairs of her sister, Dahlia, who has been seduced by Edward Blancove, an irresponsible young nobleman. Rhoda obstinately believes in her innocence through a long series of revealing episodes, and, when she learns the truth, as obstinately forces her sister to marry a worthless man under the conviction that her only hope lies in becoming a married woman.

Rhodes, Cecil John (1853–1902)   British financier. Rhodes amalgamated the diamond mines around Kimberley in South Africa under a corporation called the De Beers Consolidated Mines (1888). As prime minister of Cape Colony (1890–96), he sought to establish a federal South African dominion under Great Britain. He instigated the JAMESON RAID (1895) in pursuit of his imperialistic aims, and its failure compelled him to resign as premier. He is now best remembered for the Rhodes scholarships, which have enabled students from all over the British Empire, from the U.S., and from Germany to study at Oxford University.

rhyme   In English prosody, the repetition of identical or similar accented sound or sounds. Full or perfect rhyme occurs when differing consonant sounds are followed by identical, accented vowel sounds, and any sounds that may come after are also identical. Foe, toe; meet, fleet; buffer, rougher are perfect rhymes.

Rhyme is classified according to the number of syllables contained in the rhyme as follows: masculine rhyme, in which the final syllables are accented and after differing initial consonants the sounds are identical (lark, stark; support, resort); feminine rhyme, in which accented, rhyming syllables are followed by identical, unaccented syllables (revival, arrival; flutter, butter); and triple rhyme, a kind of feminine rhyme in which accented, rhyming syllables are followed by two identical syllables (machinery, scenery; tenderly, slenderly).

Rhyme is also distinguished according to its position in the poem as follows: end rhyme, in which the rhyme occurs at the ends of lines; internal rhyme, in which at least one rhyme occurs within the line (as in Wilde's "Each narrow *cell* in which we *dwell*"); initial rhyme, in which the rhyme occurs as the first word or syllable of the line; cross rhyme, in which the rhyme occurs at the end of one line and in the middle of the next; and random rhyme, in which the rhymes seem to occur accidentally in any combination of the foregoing, often mixed with unrhymed lines.

Near rhyme or slant rhyme is the repetition of similar sounds instead of identical sounds or the coupling of accented-unaccented sounds that would be perfect rhymes if they were both accented. Because they involve degrees of identity of sound combinations, ALLITERATION, ASSONANCE, and CONSONANCE are considered to be near rhymes.

Historically, rhyme is a latecomer to poetry, having first come into use in the Western world around AD 200 in the Church Latin of North Africa; rhyme was unknown in classical prosody. It first became popular in medieval Latin poetry. The word rhyme comes from Provençal *rim* and was originally spelled rime, and still often is. The usual English spelling, rhyme, comes from a false identification with the Greek *rhythmos*, rhythm.

rhyme royal   In prosody, a stanza form containing seven lines of heroic (i.e., iambic pentameter) verse rhymed a-b-a-b-b-c-c. It is also known as the Troilus stanza because Chaucer popularized it in his poem TROILUS AND CRISEYDE; Chaucer also used it in his *Ballad of Good Counsel* and part of THE CANTERBURY TALES. Written in later periods by SHAKESPEARE and others, it supposedly received its name after James I of Scotland, who was both king and poet.

Rhys, Jean (1894–1979)   English novelist and short-story writer. Born in the West Indies, Rhys was the daughter of a Welsh doctor and a Creole mother. She was sent to England to school when she was sixteen, but her father died shortly thereafter, leaving her penniless. After a variety of jobs she married a Dutch journalist who took her to Paris. There she met Ford Madox FORD, who encouraged her writing and wrote the introduction to her first book, *The Left Bank and Other Stories* (1927). Her lifelong theme was the victimized woman, lonely, seeking but never finding compassion in a world where men are masters. Her style is spare and direct, her tone detached and sardonic. Her novels *After Leaving Mr. Mackenzie* (1930), *Voyage in the Dark* (1934), and *Good Morning, Midnight* (1939), all tracing the dilemma of women forced by financial need to be dependent on men who use and discard them, brought great literary celebrity. With World War II and its aftermath she was lost to public view until 1958, when the BBC dramatized *Good Morning, Midnight*. Her next novel, *Wide Sargasso Sea* (1966), was an enormous success, winning three of the most coveted literary awards in Britain. In it she takes the character of the mad Creole heiress who was Rochester's hidden wife in JANE EYRE and imagines her childhood and calamitous marriage. Her books were reissued and new collections of stories were subsequently published: *Tigers Are Better-Looking* (1968; U.S. 1974) and *Sleep It Off, Lady* (1976). Her unfinished autobiography, *Smile Please* (1979), was published posthumously.

Ribbentrop, Joachim von (1893–1946)   Diplomat in Nazi Germany. Ambassador to Great Britain (1936–38) and foreign minister during World War II, von Ribbentrop was sentenced to death at the Nuremberg Trials.

Ricardo, David (1772–1823)   English economist. It was reading Adam Smith's WEALTH OF NATIONS that caused Ricardo to devote himself to the study of political economy. *Principles of Political Economy and Taxation* (1817) is the most systematic exposition of his theory of rent, property, and wages, as well as the quantity theory of money.

Rice, Elmer (1892–1967)   American playwright. Rice is known for his use of experimental technique, his realism, and his portrayal of the problems of his time, especially social injustice. Rice is best remembered for the expressionistic *The Adding Machine* (1923) and for the realistic STREET SCENE. *The Left Bank* (1931) deals with American expatriates. The Depression and the Nazi and Soviet menaces provided subjects for *We, the People* (1933), *Judgment Day* (1934), *Between Two Worlds* (1934), *Two on an Island* (1940), and *Flight to the West* (1940). *Dream Girl* (1945), a comedy, and the operatic version of *Street Scene*, for which Kurt WEILL supplied the music and Langston HUGHES the lyrics (1947), were notably successful with the public. Rice also wrote novels and an autobiography, *Minority Report* (1963).

Rich, Adrienne [Cecile] (1929–   )   American poet. Rich expresses in her poetry a concern with sexuality as determined by centuries of acculturation. The formal achievement of her early works, marked by conciseness of metrics and diction, shifted, with *Snapshots of a Daughter-in-Law: Poems 1954–1962* (1963), to a hard-hitting, explosive FREE VERSE. Her subsequent volumes, all dated to document her changing attitudes, chart her development as a radical feminist and as a major force in American poetry. Her insights into life, love, sexuality, and revolution are chronicled in *Necessities of Life: Poems 1962–1965* (1966),

Leaflets: Poems 1965–1968 (1969), *The Will to Change: Poems 1968–1970* (1971), and *Diving into the Wreck: Poems 1971–1972* (1973). *The Dream of a Common Language: Poems 1974–1977* (1978) is less turbulent in tone and focuses on an often joyful affirmation of woman's being. A *Wild Patience Has Taken Me This Far: Poems, 1978–1981* (1981) continues in a similar vein. Poems spanning her entire writing career have been collected in *The Fact of a Doorframe: Poems 1950–84* (1984). Further poems appeared in *Your Native Land, Your Life* (1986). Rich's most important work in prose is *Of Woman Born* (1976), which is at once a moving account of the experience of mothering and a feminist polemic against the "institution" of motherhood. Selected essays and speeches are collected in *On Lies, Secrets, and Silence* (1979).

Rich, Penelope (born Penelope Devereux, 1562?–1607)   Beloved of Sir Philip SIDNEY, the "Stella" of his sonnet sequence *Astrophel and Stella* (1591).

Richard I (called Coeur de Lion or the Lion-Hearted, also Richard Yea and Nay; 1157–1199)   King of England (after 1189), son of Henry II and ELEANOR OF AQUITAINE. Richard I spent only six months of his ten-year reign in England, but the troubadours and later writers glorified his courage, romanticizing his exploits as leader of the Third Crusade (1190–92), his captivity in Austria (1192–94) while his brother John was plotting to supplant him, and his wars against Philip II to protect his French possessions. He is the hero of the anonymous metrical romance *Richard Coeur de Lion* (c1300) and is prominent in Sir Walter Scott's historical novels *The Betrothed*, THE TALISMAN, and IVANHOE.

Richard II (1367–1400)   King of England (1377–99). The son of Edward the Black Prince, Richard II succeeded his grandfather Edward III while still a child. During his minority, the country was governed by his uncles, JOHN OF GAUNT, duke of Lancaster, and Thomas of Woodstock, duke of Gloucester. He is remembered for the bravery and presence of mind he displayed when he faced an angry mob during TYLER'S REBELLION of 1381. Overthrown by Henry Bolingbroke, John of Gaunt's son and later HENRY IV, Richard was probably murdered at Henry's castle of Pontefract. In Shakespeare's RICHARD II, he is depicted as an engaging man but an ineffective ruler.

Richard III (1452–1485)   King of England (1483–85). The third son of Richard, duke of York, and brother of Edward IV, Richard III took an active part in the Wars of the Roses. Upon Edward's death in 1483, he seized his nephews, the young Edward V and his brother Richard, and had himself declared protector. Later he assumed the crown, announcing that the two princes had died in the Tower of London. Richard was defeated and killed at the battle of Bosworth Field by Henry Tudor, earl of Richmond (later Henry VII).

One of the most controversial figures in English history, Richard was often denigrated, especially in works of the

Tudor era, such as Thomas More's *History of Richard III*, which was a source of Shakespeare's RICHARD III. Horace Walpole sought to vindicate him in *Historic Doubts on the Life and Death of Richard III* (1768) and Josephine TEY presented the case for the defense in the guise of a mystery novel, *The Daughter of Time* (1951). He now tends to be regarded not as a blood-thirsty monster but as a capable ruler who often behaved ruthlessly in a ruthless age.

Richard II, The Tragedy of (c1595)   A historical tragedy by SHAKESPEARE. The action begins with a conflict between Henry Bolingbroke and Thomas Mowbray, which King Richard resolves by banishing both. Upon the death of Bolingbroke's father, JOHN OF GAUNT, Richard confiscates Henry's inheritance to finance the Irish war. While Richard is in Ireland, Bolingbroke boldly invades England, and upon Richard's return, imprisons him. After Bolingbroke's coronation as HENRY IV, Richard is murdered by Sir Pierce of Exton, acting on a hint from the new king. Professing horror at the deed, Henry plans a pilgrimage to the Holy Land to do penance. The play is based upon the account in Holinshed's *Chronicles* (1577).

Richard III, The Tragedy of King (c1594)   A historical tragedy by SHAKESPEARE. A scheming Richard, duke of Gloucester and younger brother of Edward IV of the house of York, resolves to inherit the crown of the ailing king and systematically plans the extermination of all who hinder his succession. He causes the death of his brother George, duke of CLARENCE, and marries the Lady Anne, daughter-in-law of Henry VI. When Edward dies, Richard imprisons the two young sons of the late king in the Tower of London and, with the help of the duke of BUCKINGHAM, seizes power. In order to strengthen his position, he orders the murder of the princes and, after disposing of his wife, sues for the hand of Elizabeth, daughter of Edward IV. Meanwhile, the earl of Richmond, the representative of the rival house of Lancaster, has invaded England. At Bosworth Field, Richard's forces are defeated by Richmond; his horse having been killed, Richard fights desperately on foot, shouting "A horse! A horse! my kingdom for a horse." He is slain by Richmond, who is recognized as Henry VII and announces his intention of marrying Elizabeth, thus ending thirty years of conflict between the houses of York and Lancaster.

Shakespeare depicts Richard as a crafty villain whose soul is as deformed as his body, though the blackness of the portrait is relieved somewhat by Richard's courage, his wit, and his freedom from self-delusion. Written while Elizabeth, the granddaughter of Henry VII, ruled England, the play was enormously popular in its day and is largely responsible for the ill-repute in which Richard has long been held. It is Colley Cibber's alteration (1700) of the play that contains the line "Off with his head! so much for Buckingham!" which is often searched for in vain in the Shakespearean version.

Richard Carvel (1899)   A historical novel by Winston CHURCHILL. One of the most popular novels ever written about the American Revolution, *Richard Carvel* is an account, narrated by the hero, of his adventures aboard a slaver from which he is rescued by John Paul Jones. The book describes sea warfare, a London interlude, and a successful love affair.

Richards, I[vor] A[rmstrong] (1893–1979) English critic, linguistics scholar, educator, and poet. A pioneer in the analytic method of criticism later associated with the CAMBRIDGE CRITICS, Richards collaborated with C. K. OGDEN in developing "a science of meaning," later known as semantics, in their ground-breaking book *The Meaning of Meaning* (1923). The relevance of this study was demonstrated by Ogden with the almost simultaneous development of BASIC ENGLISH, and by Richards in *Principles of Literary Criticism* (1925), *Science and Poetry* (1926), and *Practical Criticism* (1929). These were the basic texts of the close textual analysis which became the "new wave" in the reading, teaching, and criticism of both prose and poetry. William EMPSON and F. R. LEAVIS were among his early pupils. Richards moved on to study the nature of imagination in *Mencius on the Mind* (1932) and *Coleridge on Imagination* (1934). He also wrote *Basic English and Its Uses* (1943), a Basic English translation of Plato's *Republic* (1942), and *So Much Nearer: Essays Toward a World English* (1968). In the meantime, this distinguished expositor of poetry had himself become a poet with such volumes as *Goodbye Earth* (1958) and *New and Selected Poems* (1979). *Beyond* (1974) is an examination of man's greatest poetic endeavors, focusing on the ILIAD, the Book of JOB, and THE DIVINE COMEDY.

Richardson, Dorothy (1873–1957)   English novelist. Richardson was a pioneer and outstanding exemplar of the STREAM OF CONSCIOUSNESS school. Her novels are grouped together under the general title *Pilgrimage* (12 vols, 1915–38). In describing the thoughts, sense impressions, memories, and feelings that pass through one woman's mind, Richardson is a forerunner of JOYCE and WOOLF.

Richardson, Henry Handel (pen name of Henrietta Richardson; original name Ethel Florence Lindesay Richardson; 1870–1946)   Anglo-Australian novelist. Born in Melbourne and trained as a pianist, Richardson frequently employed musical themes, notably in her first novel, *Maurice Guest* (1908), and in *The Young Cosima* (1934). Her early books were influenced by French and Russian models, but with her third novel, *Australia Felix* (1917), her style became more surely her own. This was the first of a trilogy of novels with the general title FORTUNES OF RICHARD MAHONY, finished in 1930, which was regarded by many critics as an outstanding realistic achievement.

Richardson, Samuel (1689–1761)   English novelist. Richardson is known for his expansion of the novel, for his interest in the psychological aspects of character, and for his highly emotional tone. He was one of the most successful printers of his day, having risen from an apprenticeship as a boy. In 1739, while working on a manual of letter-writing that two booksellers had asked him to prepare, Richardson took time off to write PAMELA, OR VIRTUE REWARDED. *Pamela* is generally considered to be the first modern English novel. CLARISSA HARLOWE and *Sir Charles Grandison* (1753), whose hero is an ideal 18th-century gentleman, the male counterpart of Clarissa, are his two other major novels; all three are epistolary in form.

Richelieu, Armand Jean du Plessis, duc de (known as Cardinal Richelieu, 1585–1642) French statesman and prelate. As chief minister under Louis XIII, Richelieu was largely responsible for the downfall of Protestantism and for the entrenchment of monarchic autocracy in France. An undistinguished writer himself (as is seen in *Testament Politique*), he was a patron of the literary arts, founding the ACADÉMIE FRANÇAISE (1635) and employing five authors, among them CORNEILLE, to write plays under his direction. Richelieu appears as a character in de VIGNY's *Cinq mars* (*The Fifth of March*, 1826), in BULWER-LYTTON's historical drama *Richelieu, or the Conspiracy* (1838), and in Dumas's *Les Trois Mousquetaires* (*The Three Musketeers*, 1844). See DUPES, DAY OF.

Richler, Mordecai (1931–   ) Canadian novelist. Richler's fiction reflects his early years in the poor Jewish section of Montreal. *Son of a Smaller Hero* (1955) and *The Apprenticeship of Duddy Kravitz* (1959) dramatize the tensions, both tragic and comic, of that background. *The Street* (1969) is a collection of semiautobiographical pieces about the same time and place. Life in Paris and London between 1951 and 1972 added an international perspective to *Cocksure* (1968) and *St. Urbain's Horseman* (1971). Characteristic of all Richler's writing is a strong sense of the ridiculous, a mordant mixture of humor and anger, and a keen eye for the hypocrisies and corruption of modern life, all of which are exuberantly combined in his novel *Joshua Then and Now* (1980). His other writings include *Images of Spain* (1977) and *Home Sweet Home: My Canadian Album* (1984). *The Street*, a volume of memoirs with the same title as the earlier story collection, appeared in 1975.

Richter, Conrad [Michael] (1890–1968) American novelist and short-story writer. Richter was primarily a historical novelist, dealing with the settlement and development of the American Southwest. His first novel, *The Sea of Grass* (1937), written after years as a journalist, is the story of a cattle baron of the old Southwest and his hopeless battle against progress. His most ambitious work was a trilogy entitled *The Awakening Land*, depicting a pioneer family and a settlement's slow evolution from virgin wilderness to an organized community: *The Trees* (1940), *The Fields* (1946), *The Town* (1950; PULITZER PRIZE winner). His other books include *The Light in the Forest* (1953), about a Pennsylvania boy brought up by Indians; *The*

Water of Kronos (1960), a symbolic fantasy; and *The Aristocrat* (1968).

Richter, Jean Paul Friedrich (pen name Jean Paul, 1763–1825) Popular German novelist and aesthetician. Both the ironic humor of Richter's style and the sometimes excessive sentimentality of his stories show the influence of Laurence Sterne. Also like Sterne, he often tinkered with the novel's structure, and with his *Vorschule der Ästhetik* (*Introduction to Aesthetics*, 1804) he became one of the first theorists of the novel. He rejected both Weimar classicism and romanticism; the former because he felt it to be too cold, the latter because of its one-sided emotional idealism. His best-known novels are *Leben des vergnügten Schulmeisterlein Maria Wuz* (*Life of the Complacent Little Schoolmaster Maria Wuz*, 1790), *Siebenkäs* (1796–97), *Titan* (1800–1803), and *Flegeljahre* (*Years of Indiscretion*, 1804–5).

Richthofen, Frieda von See LAWRENCE, FRIEDA VON RICHTHOFEN.

(Riding) Jackson, Laura (1901–   ) American poet, critic, and novelist. A native of New York City, Riding spent her post-college years abroad, moving in the literary circles of Paris and London during the 1920s and 1930s. Her early work showed the influence of Gertrude STEIN, not so much for technical innovations as for its tone of self-confidence and its interest in poetic diction. She greatly influenced Robert GRAVES, with whom she lived from 1927 to 1939. She co-wrote a study of poets of the 1920s, *A Survey of Modernist Poetry*, with Graves in 1927. Many of the poets championed in this text have been consigned to oblivion by time, whereas others deemed worthless—such as William Carlos WILLIAMS and the objectivists (see OBJECTIVISM)—were to gain growing recognition. Ironically, Riding's own poetry came to seem increasingly archaic. In 1938 she published *Collected Poems*. She was not to publish verse again for over thirty years, when she brought out *Selected Poems* (1970), all of which were taken from the 1938 volume. *A Trojan Ending*, a brilliant historical novel, was published in 1937. Among her other well-known works are *Lives of Wives* (1939; repr 1985), *The Telling* (1972) and *Communications of Broad Reference* (1983).

Riefenstahl, [Bertha Helene] Leni [Amalie] (1902–   ) German filmmaker; the most celebrated woman film director. Riefenstahl began as an actress, rising to stardom in the late silent-movie period in such mountaineering adventure films as *The White Hell of Pitz Palu* (1929). As a director, she glorified Hitler and the Nazis in an epic documentary, *Triumph des Willens* (*Triumph of the Will*, 1934) and the strength and beauty of the human body in *Olympia* (1936), perhaps the most magnificent sports film ever made. Her association with the Nazis blighted her career as a filmmaker after World War II. *Schwarze Fracht* (1956), a documentary on the East African slave trade, was left unfinished. Subsequently she turned to photography and in 1973 published a widely acclaimed and highly controversial volume of photographs, *The Last of the Nuba*, a pictorial study of a tribe of African "supermen."

Righetti, Carlo   See SCAPIGLIATURA, LA.

Right, Declaration of (1689)   An instrument submitted to William and Mary and accepted by them, setting forth the fundamental principles of the English constitution and limiting royal power. According to its provisions, the Crown cannot levy taxes without the consent of Parliament, nor keep a standing army in times of peace. In addition, Roman Catholics are barred from the throne. The document was confirmed by Parliament as the Bill of Rights.

Rights of Man, The (1791–1792)   A political work by Thomas PAINE, defending the FRENCH REVOLUTION against attacks made on it by Edmund BURKE. In it Paine argues that civil government exists only through a contract with a majority of the people for the safeguarding of the individual, and that if man's "natural rights" are interfered with by the government, revolution is permissible. As a result of this tract, Paine was forced to flee to France and was tried in England *in absentia* as a traitor.

Rig Veda (Sans, "the Veda of praise")   The oldest and most sacred of the VEDAS, consisting of 1,028 hymns in ten books, or mandalas. The hymns of the Rig Veda were composed and transmitted orally over a period of several hundred years beginning around 1500 BC, and are considered to be SHRUTI, that is, divinely revealed to ancient seers.

Riis, Jacob [Augustus] (1849–1914)   Danish-born American journalist and reformer. Arriving in America at the age of twenty-one, Riis worked at odd jobs and learned at first hand of the squalor of New York slums. Later he became a police reporter for the New York *Tribune*, and waged a single-handed battle against the terrible conditions in the New York City tenements. Finally his book *How the Other Half Lives* (1890) attracted the attention of Theodore ROOSEVELT; the result was an improved water supply, child labor laws, playgrounds, the closing of police lodging houses, and the elimination of the worst slum, the notorious Mulberry Bend. *The Making of an American* (1901) is Riis's own account of his life and crusades; it is his most famous book.

Riley, James Whitcomb (1849–1916)   American poet, lecturer, and newspaperman. Known as the Hoosier poet, Riley acquired his real education not in school, but as a journalist, traveling artist, actor, and musician, in his native Indiana. He had an ear for the local Hoosier speech and he published a series of poems in dialect for the Indianapolis *Journal*. The poems were collected as *The Old Swimmin' Hole and 'Leven More Poems* in 1883, and made him not only famous, but also the wealthiest American writer of his time. He increased his income by lecturing and writing humorous sketches. He is remembered for his dialect poems, among them LITTLE ORPHANT ANNIE, THE

RAGGEDY MAN, and "When the Frost Is on the Punkin" (1883), which have been called "comforting, familiar platitudes restated in verse."

Rilke, Rainer Maria (full name René Wilhelm Josef Maria Rilke, 1875–1926)   German poet, born in Prague. Rilke is considered the most significant figure in 20th-century German poetry. In his youth, he unhappily attended military school, a trade school, and eventually the University of Prague, which he left after a year. He traveled extensively and in 1901 married the German artist Clara Westhoff. Finding family responsibilities incompatible with his passion to write, he left his wife and infant daughter after eighteen months. His early works were effusively emotional and showed a strong tendency to seek escape from the real world in a subjective realm of half-religious, half-aesthetic anguish and ecstacy. His elevation of art to a personal religion, at this stage, reflects the strong influence of both French and GERMAN ROMANTICISM.

If particular experiences can be identified as the shaping forces of the creative process, two in Rilke's case would be his trips to Russia (1899, 1900) and his association with Auguste RODIN in Paris. He returned from Russia deeply affected by the brooding Slavic soul, the Russian landscape, and an almost mystical conception of the relationship between God, man, and nature. The result was *Das Stundenbuch* (1905; tr *Poems from the Book of Hours*, 1961), poems written as if they were the reflections of a Russian monk.

After the dissolution of his marriage, Rilke ended up in Paris, where, for a time, he was Rodin's secretary. Rodin taught him that art was not merely the outpouring of emotions but also a means by which an object, feeling, or experience is brought into focus and communicated with precision. In his two volumes of "new poems," *Neue Gedichte* (1907; tr in *Poems 1906–1926*, 1957) and *Der neuen Gedichte anderer Teil* (1908; dedicated to Rodin), Rilke broke away from his youthful subjectivity and created a body of visually brilliant, verbally precise DINGGEDICHTE ("thing-poems").

His last and most famous works, THE DUINO ELEGIES and THE SONNETS TO ORPHEUS, represented still another departure. In these intensely personal visions, he developed an individualized style in which the most minute shades of meaning, not only in every word but even in prefixes, suffixes, and individual sounds, are carefully considered and made to contribute to the structure of the poem. Rilke's extraordinary capacity to manipulate words to communicate images in both poetry and prose introduced a plasticity to the German language that had a profound impact on younger writers. His novel, THE NOTEBOOKS OF MALTE LAURIDS BRIGGE, abounds in the same kind of daring but meticulously chiseled imagery that characterizes his poetry.

Rimbaud, Arthur (1854–1891)   French poet. Rimbaud, a member of the SYMBOLISTS, became a forerunner of the surrealist school. His poetry is characterized by dramatic and imaginative vision, particularly in the realm of hallucination. Subtle and infinitely suggestive, his work uses words for tone-color, as in his famous "Sonnet des voyelles" and is partially written in free verse. Stylistically the poetry is marked by a distortion of common meaning and syntax and by the grouping of images about a single central metaphor. His best-known works are *Les Illuminations* (1886), *Le Bâteau ivre* (*The Drunken Boat*, 1871), and UNE SAISON EN ENFER. A striking and enigmatic personality, Rimbaud was raised in a poor and strictly religious home by his mother. He was an industrious, quiet, and irreproachably mannered student in a provincial school until the age of fifteen. Then suddenly, in savage rebellion, he ran away to Paris. He studied occult writings, Plato, the cabbala, and Buddhist scriptures in order to make himself a seer. Believing the role of poetry to be one of mystic revelation, he deliberately debauched himself in order to reach a transcendent world through sin and suffering. For two years, he was closely associated with Paul VERLAINE and had a powerful influence—morally corruptive but aesthetically fruitful—on the older poet. All of Rimbaud's known poetry was written prior to the age of twenty, and he apparently spent the remainder of his short life as a trader in Africa. A poetic prodigy, Rimbaud is of vital import to 20th-century poetry.

Rime of the Ancient Mariner, The (1798)   A poem by Samuel Taylor COLERIDGE. It deals with the supernatural punishment and penance of a seaman who heartlessly shot an albatross, a bird of good omen, in the Antarctic regions. The story is told by the Mariner himself —part of the penance is its periodic repetition—to the reluctant, fascinated listener, a man who was on his way to a wedding.

Rimmon   A Babylonian storm god. It was Rimmon who was worshiped by NAAMAN before his conversion to the worship of Yahweh. In PARADISE LOST, Milton identifies Rimmon as one of the fallen angels. See SATAN.

Rimsky-Korsakov, Nikolay Andreyevich (1844–1908)   Russian composer, a member of the nationalist "Five." Rimsky-Korsakov was a professor of composition (1871) at the St. Petersburg Conservatory, and in 1902 he met STRAVINSKY, who became his pupil. He is best known for his symphonic suites *Antar* and *Scheherazade*, and the *Russian Easter* overture. His operas based on Russian legends include *Le Coq d'Or*.

Rinaldo   One of the great heroes of medieval romance (also called Renault of Montauban, Regnault, Reynold, etc.), a paladin of Charlemagne and cousin of Orlando. One of the four sons of Aymon, Rinaldo rides the famous horse Baiardo, or Bayardo. Though brave and ingenious, he is often given to violent and unscrupulous behavior. His rapacious instincts often lead him to act like a common plunderer. He appears in Luigi Pulci's MORGANTE MAGGIORE, in Matteo Maria Boiardo's ORLANDO INNAMORATO, and in Lodovico Ariosto's ORLANDO FURIOSO.

Rinconete y Cortadillo   One of the tales in Cervantes's NOVELAS EJEMPLARES. Containing many elements of the PICARESQUE, it deals with two youths who travel to Seville, where they receive thorough training in crime and roguery at the thieves' school of Monipodio.

Rinehart, Mary Roberts (1876–1956)   American novelist. *The Circular Staircase* (1908; later dramatized as *The Bat*, 1920) and *The Man in Lower Ten* (1909) established Rinehart's reputation as a writer of mystery novels that combined humor and ingenuity. Others of her popular works of mystery fiction include *The Door* (1930), *The Yellow Room* (1945), and *The Swimming Pool* (1952). She also wrote numerous stories about a dauntless spinster called Tish and her middle-aged cronies, Aggie and Lizzie, collected in such volumes as *The Amazing Adventures of Letitia Carberry* (1911), *Tish* (1916), and *The Best of Tish* (1955). *My Story* (1931; rev 1948) is her autobiography.

Ring and the Book, The (1868–1869)   A long poem in twelve books by Robert BROWNING. Based on an Italian murder case of 1698, the story is presented in dramatic monologues spoken by twelve characters, each of whom approaches it from a different point of view. Guido Franceschini, a Florentine nobleman of shattered fortune, marries Pompilia Comparini, whom he believes to be an heiress. Pietro and Violante Comparini, learning that Guido is not wealthy as they believed, sue for the return of Pompilia's dowry, claiming that she is not really their daughter. Guido treats her so brutally that Pompilia, who is about to have a child, flees to Rome under the protection of Caponsacchi, a young priest. They are caught by her husband, and Caponsacchi, charged with adultery, is banished for three years; Pompilia is sent to a nunnery. Two weeks after her child is born, Pompilia and her supposed parents are murdered by Guido. He is arrested and admits his crime, and though he claims that Pompilia's alleged adultery justified him, he is condemned and executed.

The "Book" of the title is an ancient record of the case which Browning found in Florence. The "Ring" refers to an Etruscan ring that had belonged to Mrs. Browning. In order to shape it, an alloy had been added to the gold; when the ring was finished the alloy was burned off with an acid, and the pure gold remained. Thus, the facts of the case in the old manuscript were the gold that could be given form only when mixed with a "baser metal," the poet's imagination and interpretative fancy.

Ring des Nibelungen, Der   A prologue and three music-dramas, or operas, by Richard WAGNER. They are based on Scandinavian legends and were first performed together at Bayreuth in 1876. Although Wagner's principal source was not the NIBELUNGENLIED but the VÖLSUNGA SAGA, the *Nibelungenlied*, the *Elder* and *Younger Eddas*, and the *Eckelied* were also drawn upon for material. The interest centers about the magic ring made from the Rhine gold and the curse it brought to all who owned it.

The four operas may be briefly summarized as follows:

Das Rheingold (*The Rhinegold*, 1869) In the bottom of the Rhine is a hoard of gold guarded by the Rhine maidens. Alberich, the dwarf, forswears love to gain this hoard, which confers boundless power upon its possessor. From it he makes a magic ring. Meanwhile, Wotan, chief of the gods, has given Freya, the goddess of youth and love, to the giants Fasolt and Fafner as payment for their labor in building for him the castle Valhalla. Without Freya, everything grows old, even the gods. To get her back, Wotan and Loki steal the ring and the hoard from Alberich and trade them for the goddess. Alberich has put a curse on the ring; and accordingly, almost immediately the giant Fafner kills his brother Fasolt. As the opera ends, the gods go over the rainbow bridge to Valhalla.

Die Walküre (*The Valkyrie*, 1870) Wotan is the father of two children, Siegmund and Sieglinde, who grow up on earth in ignorance of each other but who, by the desire of Wotan, are to mate in the interest of the coveted ring. Sieglinde has married Hunding, but when Siegmund comes, she goes with him into the forest. Wotan's wife, the goddess of marriage, insists that Siegmund be punished, and Wotan finally yields and entrusts the Valkyrie Brunhilde with the task. In spite of her orders, Brunhilde tries to protect Siegmund, but Hunding, finally aided by the angry Wotan, kills him. She succeeds, however, in escaping with Sieglinde, who is about to give birth to the hero Siegfried. Wotan punishes Brunhilde by making her a mortal woman asleep on a mountain peak surrounded by magic fire through which only a hero may pass.

Siegfried (1876) Siegfried, since the death of his mother, Sieglinde, has been brought up to the trade of the smithy by Mime, the dwarf, whom he hates. He remakes his father's sword and slays a dragon who is really the giant Fafner. A drop of dragon's blood on his tongue makes him understand the language of the birds. Acting on the information they give him, he kills the treacherous Mime, secures the magic ring, and finds Brunhilde and marries her.

Götterdämmerung (*The Twilight of the Gods*, 1876) Siegfried leaves the magic ring with Brunhilde and goes to seek adventure. At the court of Gunther and his sister Gutrune, their half brother Hagen, son of the dwarf Alberich, gives Siegfried a magic potion that causes him to forget Brunhilde and become a suitor for the hand of Gutrune. He even agrees to secure Brunhilde for Gunther and does so. Unable to understand his fickleness, Brunhilde denounces him and enters into schemes for revenge with the wily Hagen. At a hunting feast, just as Siegfried is remembering his past and calling for Brunhilde, he is killed by a thrust in the back from Hagen. The hero's body is burned on a funeral pyre; Brunhilde sacrifices herself in the flames; the Rhine overflows its banks; Gunther and Hagen perish in the struggle for the ring, which now returns to the Rhine Maidens; and Valhalla, with all the gods, is destroyed by fire.

Rinzai See ZEN BUDDHISM.

rios profundos, Los See ARGUEDAS, JOSÉ MARÍA.

Ripley, George (1802–1880) American editor, reformer, and literary critic. A Unitarian minister in Boston, Ripley edited *Specimens of Foreign Standard Literature* (14 vols, 1838–52), translations of the philosophers whose work forms the basis of the American Transcendentalist movement. On April 1, 1841, Ripley and twenty other members of the Transcendental Club moved to West Roxbury, Massachusetts, where be became president of the community at BROOK FARM. After the disastrous fire of 1846, Ripley moved to Flatbush, Long Island, and as a literary critic for the New York *Tribune* was soon recognized as an important influence in American letters.

Rip Van Winkle (1819) A tale by Washington IRVING, collected in his SKETCH BOOK OF GEOFFREY CRAYON, GENT. Certainly the most popular piece Irving ever wrote, the story is based on a folk tale. Henpecked Rip and his dog Wolf wander into the Catskill mountains before the Revolutionary War. There they meet a dwarf, whom Rip helps to carry a keg. They join a group of dwarfs playing ninepins. When Rip drinks from the keg, he falls asleep and awakens twenty years later, an old man. Returning to his town, he discovers his termagant wife dead, his daughter married, and the portrait of King George replaced by one of George Washington. Irving uses the folk tale to present the contrast between the new and old societies.

The story was adapted many times for the stage and opera house. The most famous adaptation was done by Dion Boucicault for the actor Joseph Jefferson, who played Rip for almost forty years (1865–1904).

Rise and Fall of the City Mahagonny (Aufstieg und Fall der Stadt Mahagonny, 1929; tr 1956) A play by Bertolt BRECHT set to music by Kurt WEILL in a style similar to that of their best-known collaboration, THE THREEPENNY OPERA. Set in the U.S., it is strongly Marxist in thought, and is intended as an object lesson about bourgeois decadence. The city of Mahagonny, founded and populated entirely by pleasure-seekers, eventually collapses because of inherent economic and human contradictions. The play is an example of what Brecht called EPIC THEATRE.

Rise of Silas Lapham, The (1885) A novel by William Dean HOWELLS. Silas, a self-reliant businessman who has become wealthy, moves to Boston. Building a pretentious home on Beacon Hill, he disgraces himself by drinking too much at a dinner party given by the social elite. Originally careless of the morality of his money-getting methods, Silas begins to recognize ethical standards. Although he is financially ruined by the end of the book, his "rise" reflects this change in attitude. Persis, his helplessly provincial wife, has been unable to guide her daughters' social careers; Penelope Lapham finally marries Tom

Corey, member of a Brahmin family, and the two escape to Mexico. The novel is generally considered Howells's best.

Risorgimento (Ital, "revival; resurrection") The political movement, starting about 1831, whose objective was the liberation and unification of Italy. Its three great leaders were MAZZINI, GARIBALDI, and Camillo Benso di Cavour (1810–61). *Risorgimento* was the name of a newspaper founded (1847) by Count Cavour.

Ritsos, Yannis (1909–   ) Greek poet. Plagued by tuberculosis, family misfortunes, and repeated persecution for his Communist views, Ritsos spent many years in sanatoriums, prisons, or in political exile while producing dozens of volumes of lyrics, dramas, and translations.

Beginning as a follower of the updated demotic tradition, Ritsos went through a phase of militant, doctrinaire poetry, as in *Trakter* (1934) and *O Epitaphios* (1936). He eventually achieved a personal, humanitarian medium devoid of anger and recrimination. In long poems like his celebrated *Romiosyne* (1947; tr *Romiosini*, 1969) and most of his later volumes, Ritsos writes with compassion and hope, celebrating the life, toil, and dignity of peasants in an unadorned and direct language. Among Ritsos's books in English are *Selected Poems* (1974), *Gestures & Other Poems* (1971), *Eighteen Short Songs of the Bitter Motherland* (1974), *The Fourth Dimension* (1977), *Chronicle of Exile* (1977), *Ritsos in Parentheses* (1978), and *Scripture of the Blind* (1978).

Rivals, The (1775) A comedy by Richard Brinsley SHERIDAN. Though less well known in name, this play is considered by some to be better than THE SCHOOL FOR SCANDAL. The plot is complicated: Sir Anthony Absolute wishes his son Captain Absolute to marry Lydia Languish. He does not know that Captain Absolute is already wooing her in the guise of the impecunious Ensign Beverly, a guise taken on to please Lydia's romantic dream of an elopement rather than marriage with a well-to-do baronet's son. Lydia's aunt Mrs. MALAPROP, disapproving of the penniless Beverly, threatens to take away half of Lydia's fortune if she marries him. She wishes Lydia to marry Captain Absolute. The plot is further complicated by the fact that Captain Absolute's friend Bob Acres is also in love with Lydia and challenges Beverly to a duel (not knowing that Beverly is really Absolute). Things get straightened out in the end, however, and Lydia, after scolding Captain Absolute for ruining her hopes of a romantic elopement, happily agrees to marry him.

Rivas, Angel Saavedra y Ramírez de Baguedano, duque de (1791–1865) Spanish poet and dramatist. As a youth Rivas was seriously wounded while fighting against the French during the Napoleonic invasion of Spain. Exiled in 1823 by Ferdinand VII because of his liberal tendencies, he lived in London, Paris, and Malta and was introduced to English romanticism. After his return to Spain in 1834, he inherited the title and held a number of important positions.

A champion of Spanish romanticism, with his prose-and-verse drama, DON ALVARO O LA FUERZA DEL SINO, first presented in 1835, Rivas had an impact on the Spanish theatre comparable to that of Hugo's *Hernani* in France five years earlier. He also wrote, among other poems, *Romances históricos* (1841), a series of ballads on important events in Spanish history.

Rivera, Diego [Maria] (1886–1957) Mexican painter. Rivera's paintings were influenced by French POST-IMPRESSIONISM, but in the revolutionary murals for which he is most famous, he evolved a popular propagandist style derived from Mexican folk art. In bright, simplified images, his murals depict Mexican history from a controversial communist perspective.

Rivera, José Eustacio (1889–1928) Colombian novelist and poet. As a lawyer, Rivera's work took him to the largely ignored flatlands and jungles of Colombia, where he encountered the horrible exploitation of people in the cattle and rubber production businesses. His reactions to the barbarisms he witnessed constitute the core of his only novel and masterpiece, LA VORÁGINE. Rivera's terse, Parnassian verse, *Tierra de promisión* (1921), was all but forgotten in the shadow of his epoch-making novel.

Rivers, Larry (originally Larry Grossberg, 1923–   ) American painter and sculptor. Rivers was a poet and a jazz saxophonist before he became a painter. While he was drawn to the free and spontaneous brushwork of ABSTRACT EXPRESSIONISM, he also greatly admired the minute realism of the Old Masters and sought to combine those elements in his work. His close relationship with Frank O'HARA was of pivotal importance to both men; they collaborated on a number of works, notably a series of lithographs entitled *Stones* (1958). Rivers also made life-size sculptures and numerous portraits, both of his friends and of historical American figures.

Rizal, José (1861–1896) Philippine novelist and national hero. Rizal was sent into exile by the Spanish government because of his novel *Noli me tangere* (1886, tr *The Lost Eden*, 1961), in which he criticized both the Spanish regime and the clergy. In 1896, on his return to the Philippines, he was charged with fomenting revolution and executed. Before his death he wrote a remarkable poem, *Mi último adiós*.

Rizzio, David (1533?–1566) An Italian musician in the service of MARY, QUEEN OF SCOTS. Rizzio became her private foreign secretary, arranged her marriage with Darnley, and finally attained such influence that he was attacked and killed in Queen Mary's apartment at Holyrood Palace in Edinburgh by Darnley, Morton, and Lindsay. SWINBURNE treats this event in *Mary Stuart: A Tragedy* (1881).

Road Not Taken, The (1915) A poem by Robert FROST. One of Frost's best-known poems, it describes how the narrator coming to a fork in the road is undecided which way to go. Both roads seem very much alike. He takes the one less traveled—and "that has made all the difference."

Roads to Freedom, The (Les Chemins de la liberté)   A trilogy of novels by Jean-Paul SARTRE. *L'Age de raison* (1945; tr *The Age of Reason*, 1947), set in 1938, presents Mathieu, a professor of philosophy trying to maintain his ethical freedom. *Le Sursis* (1945; tr *The Reprieve*, 1947), is a panorama of the eight days preceding the Munich Pact in September 1938. *La Mort dans l'âme* (1949; tr *Troubled Sleep*, 1951; also tr as *Iron in the Soul*, 1950), shows varied reactions to the fall of France in 1940.

Roanoke Island   An island off the coast of North Carolina, site of an ill-fated English colony (1584–91), sponsored by Sir Walter Raleigh. Although previous attempts at settlement had failed, a group of new colonists arrived in 1587. The ships that sailed back to England for supplies did not return until 1591 and found no trace of the settlers, except for the word "Croatoan," the name of a friendly tribe of Indians, carved on the bark of a tree. The fate of the colony has never been discovered. Paul Green's historical pageant, *The Lost Colony* (1937), is presented annually on the island. See DARE, VIRGINIA.

Roan Stallion, Tamar, and Other Poems (1925)   A collection of poems by Robinson JEFFERS. The title poem deals with the almost religious love of a woman named California for a magnificent red stallion, in which she sees godlike power and beauty. She permits the horse to trample her brutal husband to death, but then shoots the beast "out of some obscure human fidelity."

Roaring Girl, The (c1610)   A comedy by Thomas MIDDLETON and Thomas DEKKER. The marriage of Mary Fitzallard and Sebastian Wengrave is opposed by the latter's arrogant and avaricious father, Sir Alexander. In order to force his father's compliance, Sebastian pretends to pay court to "the roaring girl," Moll Cutpurse. A woman who combines a knowledge of London's lowlife with a sort of manly virtue, Moll agrees to help Sebastian and act as go-between with Mary. Sir Alexander sends his spidery servant, Trapdoor, to gain Moll's confidence and bring about her downfall. However, Moll eludes the trap and succeeds, by pretending momentarily to be Sebastian's bride, in bringing about the wedding of the happy pair while gulling Sir Alexander into the bargain.

Robbe-Grillet, Alain (1922–   )   French novelist and critic. Robbe-Grillet first described the NOUVEAU ROMAN, or new novel, in 1956 (he later published *Pour un nouveau roman*, 1963; tr *Towards a New Novel*, 1965), and thus became the leading exponent of the NEW WAVE in literature. His own novels reflect a preoccupation with sexual aberrations and experiments with space and time. Plots are nonexistent or only remotely evident. The changing appearance of what the protagonist actually sees is the subject matter of his novels, conveying the sense of decomposition or destruction of reality that the author perceives as the state of man's consciousness. *Les Gommes* (1953; tr *The*

Erasers, 1964), the story of a detective who ends up killing the supposed victim of a murder he is assigned to investigate, is full of imagined events, repetition, and contradiction, intermingled with minute description of objects. In *Le Voyeur* (1955; tr *The Voyeur*, 1958), we watch a rape and murder by a traveling salesman, and in *La Jalousie* (1957; tr *Jealousy*, 1959), we observe the powerful obsession of a banana plantation owner with his wife and his neighbor. As well as many other works of fiction, Robbe-Grillet has also written several *ciné-romans* (movie-novels), beginning with *L'Immortelle* (1963; tr *The Immortal One*, 1971), and screenplays, the best known of which is *L'Année dernière à Marienbad* (1961; tr *Last Year at Marienbad*, 1962).

Robbers, The (Die Räuber, 1782)   A play by Friedrich SCHILLER. Karl Moor, the hero, is cheated out of his inheritance by his brother, and feeling himself cast out of human society, he forms a band of robbers. Some of the men who gather around him are mere opportunists, but others are genuine victims of social injustice. Thus, Schiller depicts the robber band in a morally ambiguous light, giving a possible justification for it as a protest against social evil. But in the end, Karl recognizes that antisocial action is not justifiable and gives himself up to the authorities.

Robbia, Luca della (1400–1482)   Italian sculptor. Working in Florence in the early RENAISSANCE, della Robbia was inspired by his contemporaries DONATELLO and GHIBERTI. He was an accomplished sculptor in marble but is more famous for his works in glazed terra-cotta, typically white figures modeled in relief on a blue background. This innovation was further utilized by his son Giovanni (1469–c1529) and his nephew Andrea (1435–1525) in the della Robbia workshop, which flourished into the 1700s.

Roberts, Sir Charles G[eorge] D[ouglas] (1860–1943)   Canadian poet and fiction writer. Roberts's early books of poetry, *Orion* (1880) and *Songs of the Common Day* (1893), began an important trend in their reliance on indigenous Canadian sources. Roberts became the first of his countrymen to be knighted for his contribution to Canadian letters. A representative sampling of his poetic works was published in *Selected Poems* (1936 and 1955).

Roberts, Elizabeth Madox (1886–1941)   American novelist. A regional writer, Roberts is noted for her treatment of the pioneers and "poor whites" of Kentucky and the Virginias. Although her talent and insight were highly poetic and she wrote several books of verse, including *Under the Tree* (1922) and *Song in the Meadow* (1940), she is known primarily for her distinguished works of prose. *My Heart and My Flesh* (1927) is the story of a Southern girl and her attempt to find happiness through three different love affairs. *The Great Meadow* (1930) is a novel dealing with the settlement of Kentucky.

Roberts, Kenneth [Lewis] (1885–1957)   American historical novelist. Roberts is best known for his excellent novels of the colonial and Revolutionary periods, especially *Arundel* (1930) and *Rabble in Arms* (1933), both dealing with the career of Benedict Arnold, and *Northwest Passage* (1937), which describes Major Robert Rogers's 1759 expedition in search of an overland route to the Northwest. Roberts based his novels on facts unearthed after careful research; the journals of men accompanying Benedict Arnold, which Roberts used for *Arundel*, were edited by him in *March to Quebec* (1939).

Robeson, Paul (1898–1976)   American actor and singer. Born in Princeton, New Jersey, the youngest son of an escaped slave, Robeson was a Phi Beta Kappa student and all-American football star at Rutgers University and a graduate of Columbia Law School. A man of imposing presence and magnificent bass-baritone voice, he appeared on Broadway in *Taboo* in 1922. In 1924 he joined the PROVINCETOWN PLAYERS, with whom he starred in Eugene O'Neill's ALL GOD'S CHILLUN GOT WINGS, and then in the title role of O'Neill's THE EMPEROR JONES. His dramatic successes in plays like DuBose Heyward's PORGY (1928) were matched by his appeal as a singer in Jerome Kern's SHOW BOAT (1927; film 1936), where he sang, most notably, "Ol' Man River," and put him much in demand as a concert performer. He played the title role in OTHELLO in London (1930) and again in New York (1943–45). Always politically conscious and outspoken on racial issues, during the Cold War years Robeson was branded a radical. Although he repeatedly disclaimed membership in the Communist Party, life in the U.S. became increasingly difficult for him after he was awarded the Stalin Peace Prize in 1952. In 1958 he moved to London, the same year in which he published his autobiography, *Here I Stand*. He continued to be enthusiastically received in performances abroad but was forced by illness to return to the U.S. in 1963, where he lived in seclusion until the end of his life.

Robespierre, Maximilien François Marie Isidore de (1758–1794)   French revolutionist. Undisputed master of the JACOBIN Club, Robespierre was called by the Parisians "the Incorruptible" for his uncompromising honesty and revolutionary fervor. In the year 1793–94, he dominated the COMMITTEE OF PUBLIC SAFETY which instituted the REIGN OF TERROR. While head of the committee, he and his two lieutenants, Louis de SAINT-JUST and Georges Couthon, gave every appearance of being masters of France. Robespierre was overthrown by the Convention of July 27, 1794. He and his fellow terrorists were sent to the guillotine without a trial, as they had sent so many others. During the 19th century the Robespierre legend enjoyed a revival among the working classes as a champion of social revolution; others consider him to have been an ambitious demagogue and dictator. See FRENCH REVOLUTION.

Robin Hood   A legendary English outlaw and popular hero, best known through a cycle of ballads. It is said that Robin Hood was born (c1160) at Locksley, Nottinghamshire; he is also said to have been the outlawed earl of Huntington, Robert Fitzooth, in disguise. He lived in the forest, either out of choice or because he was outlawed for debt. His chief haunt was Sherwood Forest in Nottinghamshire. Ancient ballads abound with anecdotes of his personal courage, his skill in archery, his generosity, and his great popularity. It is said that he robbed the rich to give to the poor, and that he protected women and children with chivalrous magnanimity. According to tradition, he was treacherously bled to death by the prioress of Kirkley; as an old man he had gone to her to be bled, and she let him die.

Robin Hood's companions in Sherwood Forest and Barnsdale, Yorkshire, were LITTLE JOHN, FRIAR TUCK, Will Scarlet, Allan-a-Dale, Will Stutly, and MAID MARIAN. According to one tradition, Robin Hood and Little John were two heroes defeated with Simon de Montfort at the battle of Evesham. Robin Hood became a stock figure in the MAY DAY plays and festivities.

Robin Hood has long figured in English literature. He is first mentioned in a 1377 edition of *Piers Plowman*. The most important ballad series of which he is the hero is A *Lytell Geste of Robyn Hode* (1510), a near epic of 456 four-line stanzas.

Robinson, Edwin Arlington (1869–1935) American poet. Robinson is known for his long narrative poems and objective psychological portraits of New England characters, usually written in blank verse, and for his creation of Tilbury Town, whose prototype was Gardiner, Maine, where he spent his boyhood. Robinson privately printed three hundred copies of *The Torrent and the River* (1896), his first book of poems, and, encouraged by the warmth of its critical reception, determined to make a career of writing. Published the following year with some changes, as *The Children of the Night*, the volume contained several of what were to become Robinson's best-known poems, among them "Luke Havergal," "Richard Corey," and "Two Men." The poet moved to New York, and worked at various uncongenial occupations, hounded by poverty and depression. After the publication of *Captain Craig* (1902), Theodore Roosevelt, impressed by his work, secured a position in the New York City custom house for him. In 1910 *The Town Down the River*, which included "Miniver Cheevy," appeared, and thereafter Robinson earned his living by writing, spending his summers at the MacDowell Colony in Peterboro, New Hampshire. With the publication of THE MAN AGAINST THE SKY his reputation was firmly established. Although there are long narratives and dramatic monologues among them, the majority of the poems in these collections are short lyrics and character sketches.

Robinson's *Collected Poems* (1921) won the first PULITZER PRIZE to be awarded for poetry. He won the Pulitzer Prize again in 1925 for *The Man Who Died Twice* (1924) and in 1928 for *Tristram* (1927). This long poem, which followed *Merlin* (1917) and *Lancelot* (1920), was the final volume of Robinson's Arthurian trilogy, and had a very considerable popular success.

Despite the irony and pessimism of his work, Robinson is usually considered 19th century in tone. His poetry forms an important bridge from Walt WHITMAN and Emily DICKINSON to the truly modern poets of the 20th century.

Robinson Crusoe (1719–1720)   The hero and shortened title of *The Life and Strange Surprising Adventures of Robinson Crusoe, of York, Mariner,* a novel by Daniel DEFOE. Robinson Crusoe runs away to sea, is wrecked, and leads a solitary existence on an uninhabited island near the Orinoco river for twenty-four years. He meets the difficulties of a primitive existence with wonderful ingenuity and finds consolation in reading the Bible. At length he meets a human being, a young native whom he saves from death at the hands of cannibals. He calls him "MAN FRIDAY," because he met him on a Friday, and makes him his companion and servant. Crusoe and Friday share in a variety of adventures which include a fierce battle with cannibals, culminating in their recapturing a mutinous ship and returning to England. *Robinson Crusoe* is a manual of the qualities that have won the world from barbarism—courage, patience, ingenuity, and industry. Defoe founded this story on the adventures of Alexander SELKIRK. In a commentary, *Serious Reflections of Robinson Crusoe* (1720), Defoe claims that the novel is an allegory of his own life.

Roblès Emmanuel (1914–   )   Algerian-born French novelist and dramatist. In the years before World War II, Roblès became a member of the "school of Algiers," led by Albert CAMUS. He is known for his proletarian novel, *Travail d'homme* (1943; tr *The Angry Mountain*, 1948), and particularly for a later novel, *Cela s'appelle l'aurore* (1952; tr *Dawn on Our Darkness*, 1954), a critical and popular success centering around the violent love affair of a doctor working among desperately poor Sardinian peasants. Roblès also wrote *Montserrat* (1948), a play set in Venezuela in 1812, which was translated and adapted by Lillian HELLMAN in 1950.

Rob Roy (nickname of Robert Macgregor, 1671–1734) Scottish outlaw, comparable to England's Robin Hood. He was given the name Roy because of his red hair. He is the title character of *Rob Roy* (1817), a novel by Sir Walter SCOTT.

roc   An enormous white bird in Arabian folklore. Said to be of such size and strength that it could carry elephants to its mountain nest where it devoured them, it appears in the *Arabian Nights,* most notably in the story of SINBAD THE SAILOR, where it transports Sinbad from the Valley of Diamonds.

Rochambeau, Jean Baptiste Donatien de Vimeur, comte de (1725–1807)   French soldier. Rochambeau joined, as commander of a French force, Washington's Continental Army in 1781; he helped besiege Cornwallis at Yorktown, and, with the French fleet, forced his capitulation in 1781. He was made marshal of France in 1791.

Rochester, John Wilmot, 2nd earl of (1647–1680)   English courtier and poet. A favorite of Charles II, Rochester was known in his day as "the Wicked Earl" for his profligate life, atheism, and obscene verse. Rochester, who died worn-out and repentant at the age of thirty-two, was nevertheless a man with some amiable characteristics and a highly talented poet, author of a number of graceful lyrics and a few biting satires. His best-known poem is *A Satire against Mankind* (1675), a brilliant attack on *homo sapiens* and his pretensions to rationality.

Rocinante   In Cervantes's DON QUIXOTE, the steed of Don Quixote, "lean, lank, meagre, drooping, sharp-backed, and raw-boned." The name implies "that the horse had risen from a mean condition to the highest honor a steed could achieve, for it was once a cart-horse, and rose to become the charger of a knight-errant."

Rockefeller, John D[avison], Sr. (1839–1937) American oil magnate and philanthropist, founder of the Rockefeller family fortune. He, his son, and his five grandsons have made their name famous not only for their wealth but also for the scope and scale of their philanthropy.

Rocking-Horse Winner, The (1933)   A short story by D. H. LAWRENCE. It is about a small boy, the son of greedy parents, who rides himself to death on a demonic toy rocking horse which prophesies the winners in the horse races.

Rockwell, Norman (1894–1978)   American illustrator. Rockwell's illustrations depicting idealized, nostalgic, everyday scenes of middle-class America were enormously popular. He is best known for his cover illustrations for the *Saturday Evening Post.*

rococo   A late style of BAROQUE art, architecture, and interior decorating originating in France in the first quarter of the 18th century. It was characterized by extreme freedom, playfulness, and grace, achieved by a liberal use of flowing curves, irregular or broken rhythms, and elaborate ornament. The painting and sculpture of the period was characterized by delicacy of form, a graceful, ornamental style and often a certain frivolity in subject matter. BOUCHER and FRAGONARD were among those who painted in the rococo style. The term is now applied to any flamboyant and excessively ornamental style.

Roderick (or Rodrigo)   A Spanish hero around whom many legends have collected. The thirty-fourth and last of the Visigothic kings, Roderick came to the throne in 710 and was routed and probably slain by the Moors under Tarik in 711.

One legend tells that he is befriended by a shepherd who is then rewarded with the royal chain and ring. Roderick passes the night in the cell of a hermit, who tells him that he must do penance by living for some days in a tomb full of snakes, toads, and lizards. After three days, the hermit goes to see him, and he is unhurt, "because the Lord kept his anger against him." The hermit goes home, spends the night praying, and goes again to the tomb. Roderick says, "They eat me now, they eat me now, I feel the adder's bite." His sins thus atoned for, he dies. According to other versions, he does not die but will come again in time of need. In one legend, he reappears at the Battle of Covadonga with the old rallying cry "Roderick the Goth! Roderick and victory!" and saves the day, but is seen no more. Another famous Spanish hero named Roderigo is the Cid.

Roderick Hudson (1876)   A novel by Henry JAMES. In this, the first of James's novels published in book form, the titular hero is a talented young American sculptor. Going to study in Rome under the aegis of a wealthy benefactor, he becomes gradually disillusioned about his art and utterly demoralized by his experience. Christina Light, with whom he falls disastrously in love, reappears as a character in THE PRINCESS CASAMASSIMA.

Roderick Random, The Adventures of (1748) A PICARESQUE novel by Tobias SMOLLETT modeled on Lesage's GIL BLAS. The titular hero, a young Scottish scapegrace in quest of fortune, narrates a succession of adventures. At one time he revels in prosperity, at another he is in utter destitution. Fleeing prosecution for having killed an officer in a duel, Roderick, accompanied by his comrade Hugh Strap, runs off to sea and becomes a surgeon's mate. He subsequently meets and falls in love with Narcissa; her suitors, Sir Timothy Thicket and Lord Quiverwit, impede the progress of the romance. Thwarted in his plans, he flees to France and, supported by Strap's money, plans to marry Miss Melinda Goosetrap. Failing in these plans, he goes to sea with his uncle Tom Bowling and lands in South America, where he meets the wealthy Don Rodrigo, who turns out to be his long-lost father. The triumphant exile returns, marries Narcissa, repurchases the family estate, and shows scorn for those relatives who had earlier scorned him.

Rodgers, Richard (1902–1979)   American composer of musical comedies. Rodgers enjoyed different careers with a series of lyricists. Working first with Lorenz Hart (1895–1943), he produced a string of memorable songs and shows culminating in *Pal Joey* (1940; based on stories by John O'HARA), considered the first significant American musical with fully integrated lyrics, score, and book. Rodgers continued in the direction of unified dramatic form in his musicals with Oscar HAMMERSTEIN II, especially *Oklahoma!* (1943), *Carousel* (1945; based on Molnar's *Liliom*), *South Pacific* (1949), and *The King and I* (1951). After Hammerstein's death in 1960, Rodgers continued writing shows with a variety of lyricists, but none of them achieved the success of his two earlier collaborations.

Rodin, [François] Auguste [René] (1840–1917) French sculptor. A prolific and innovative sculptor whose works ranged from the meticulous realism of his *Age of Bronze* (1877) to the controversial roughness of his monolithic tribute to BALZAC (1898). During the last twenty years of Rodin's life, he worked on *The Gates of Hell*, inspired variously by the DIVINE COMEDY of Dante, GHIBERTI's *Paradise Gate*, and the art of William BLAKE. Comprised of 186 figures and never completed, it provided the basis for many of Rodin's most famous individual sculptures, among them *The Kiss* (1886) and *The Thinker*. He bequeathed most of his works to the French government, forming the collection housed in the Rodin Museum in Paris. There is also a Rodin Museum in Philadelphia.

Rodó, José Enrique (1871–1917)   Uruguayan essayist. Rodó spent most of his uneventful life in Montevideo, where his home became a mecca for Latin-American intellectuals, especially after the publication of ARIEL, his most influential essay. *Los motivos de Proteo* (1909; tr *The Motives of Proteus*, 1928) is a series of related essays, undoubtedly influenced by Bergson, in which the dominant note is the unlimited possibility for the development of the human spirit. The essays on Montalvo and Bolívar in *El mirador de Próspero* (1913) are also well known. Regarded as the foremost prose writer of MODERNISMO, Rodó wrote in a style remarkable for its serenity and purity.

Rodomonte   A Saracen hero in Carolingian legends, who appears as king of Sarza or Algiers in Matteo Maria Boiardo's ORLANDO INNAMORATO and Lodovico Ariosto's ORLANDO FURIOSO. Called the "Mars of Africa," Rodomonte is the Saracen Achilles, commander of the armies sent against Charlemagne and the Christians by Agramante.

Roethke, Theodore (1908–1963)   American poet. The son of a florist, Roethke wrote verse which is essentially an interplay between a quest for the self and extensive horticultural imagery. Stylistically, his poetry ranges from witty, rational poems in strict forms to mystical verse in free form with almost surrealistic imagery. The latter are noted for their affecting evocations of childhood and old age. He received the PULITZER PRIZE for his *Collected Poems* (1954) and a Bollingen Prize for *Words for the Wind* (1958). His last book, *The Far Field* (1964), is an excellent example of Roethke's sensitive use of landscape to depict various states of mind. Other well-known volumes of verse are *Open House* (1941), *Praise to the End* (1951), and *The Waking* (1953). *On the Poet and His Craft* (1965) is a collection of his lectures and essays.

Rogers, Robert (1731–1795)   American frontier captain and dramatist. Rogers's company of rangers became famous in 1756. As a loyalist, he was imprisoned at the start of the Revolution, but escaped and organized the Queen's Rangers. He fled to England (1780), where he received a pension from the government. Rogers wrote a drama about Pontiac's Conspiracy, *Ponteach* (1766), the first tragedy written on a native American subject. He is the central figure of Kenneth ROBERTS's novel *Northwest Passage*.

Rogers, Samuel (1763–1855)   English poet and patron of men of letters. A friend of Wordsworth, Scott, and Byron, Rogers was noted for his biting, sarcastic wit in conversation. Much of Rogers's table talk is preserved in Alexander Dyce's *Recollections* (1856) and G. H. Powell's *Reminiscences* (1859). His carefully lifeless 18th-century-style poetry has not stood the test of time, though it was highly regarded in its day. His best-known poetic work is *The Pleasures of Memory* (1792).

Rogers, Will[iam Penn Adair] (1879–1935) American humorist. Rogers joined the Ziegfeld Follies in 1915. His widely popular act consisted of swinging a lasso while making seemingly naive, but actually shrewd, comments on society and politics. He wrote books with such titles as *The Cowboy Philosopher on Prohibition* (1919) and *The Illiterate Digest* (1924), and appeared in a number of motion pictures. From 1926 on, he wrote an extremely popular syndicated column, selections from which were published by Donald Day in *Sanity Is Where You Find It* (1955). Typical of his quips was "I don't make jokes, I just watch the government and report the facts." An early aviation enthusiast, he was killed while flying in Alaska with the noted flier Wiley Post.

Rogozhin   In Dostoyevsky's novel THE IDIOT, the sinister rich young man who has an insane passion for Natasha Filippovna. Violent as he is, Rogozhin is fascinated by the gentle Prince Myshkin. When he begins to see that Myshkin is a rival for Natasha's love, he attempts to kill the prince. His jealousy finally drives him to murder Natasha.

rogue literature   A type of prose literature, popular in Elizabethan England, and regarded as a forerunner of the English novel. It dealt realistically and exuberantly with the lives and adventures of thieves, vagabonds, and tricksters of the London underworld and rural highways, often expanding from fact to fiction. Robert GREENE and Thomas NASHE were outstanding authors of rogue literature.

Rohmer, Eric (real name Jean-Marie Maurice Scherer, 1920–   )   French filmmaker and writer. One of the best known of the NEW WAVE directors, Rohmer was an early editor of the highly influential film journal *Cahiers du cinéma*. The best known of his many films are his six *contes moraux* ("moral tales"), which explored variations on the theme of a man and a woman deciding if, when, and how to love each other, while creating a lively, often contradictory, interplay between thoughts, words, and actions. The last three films in the series—*My Night with Maud* (1968), *Claire's Knee* (1970), and *Chloe in the Afternoon* (1972)—have earned Rohmer an enthusiastic following in both Europe and America.

Roi Soleil, Le (The Sun King)   A title adopted by LOUIS XIV when he took the sun as his emblem.

Rojas [Sepúlveda], Manuel (1896–1973)   Chilean novelist. Rojas's realistic fiction chronicles the complexity of urban life in Chile and Argentina. In the short stories of *Hombres del sur* (1927) he sketches, from first-hand experience, his central concern, the lives of rugged working people. *Hijo de ladrón* (1951; tr *Born Guilty*, 1955), the first of an autobiographical trilogy of novels, tells the exploits of a young orphan whose faith in the solidarity of men is not deterred by hunger, pain, or violence. His unswerving will to taste the sweetness of life is finally rewarded in *Mejor que el vino* (1958). Rojas's *Obras completas* appeared in 1961.

Rojas Zorrilla, Francisco de (1607–1648)   Spanish dramatist. A native of Toledo and a member of the order of Santiago, Rojas was strongly influenced by Calderón. His finest play, *Del rey abajo ninguno* or *García del Castañar*, deals with a peasant who mistakenly believes that the king has violated his honor; despite some gongoristic traits, the drama is vigorous and direct. Rojas also wrote the amusing *Entre bobos anda el juego* and *Cada cual lo que le toca*, notable for its unconventional approach to feminine honor. His plots were borrowed by French dramatists such as CORNEILLE, LESAGE, and SCARRON.

Roland (or Orlando)   The most famous of Charlemagne's paladins in medieval romances. Roland's story grew up around the name of Hruotland of Brittany, historical leader of Charlemagne's rear guard in the defeat at RONCESVALLES. Tradition makes Roland the nephew of Charlemagne, his mother being the king's sister. He is the most perfect type of the devotedly loyal and courageous knight who sacrifices himself in service to his king. He is apt to be too trusting and unsuspicious in his dealings with others, too impetuous and determined in his decisions. These tendencies, however, are not treated as flaws, but as the necessary attributes of his pride and his admirably frank, straightforward nature. His close friend OLIVIER is thus his complement, being cooler and wiser in his advice.

Roland's story seems to have entered the tradition of French ballads by the 9th century and is said to have been sung by TAILLEFER in 1066. The *Chanson de Roland* (*Song of Roland*) is a French CHANSON DE GESTE, probably written in the middle of the 11th century in Brittany. It has 4002 decasyllabic lines using assonance rather than rhyme, divided into lays or stanzas of unequal length. As the *Chanson* tells the story, Charlemagne has, in seven years of fighting, conquered all of Spain except Saragossa. The Saracen leader Marsile asks for a meeting to discuss a settlement in exchange for Charlemagne's departure from Spain. Roland warns of a trap, but the king accepts GANELON's advice to send a messenger to Marsile at Saragossa. Roland then successfully urges that Ganelon be the messenger. The angry Ganelon goes, but decides to accept Marsile's bribes and betray Roland. He has Roland appointed commander of the rear guard and informs Marsile of the planned route through the pass of Roncesvalles. Accordingly, Roland's twenty thousand men are ambushed by four hundred thousand Saracens. Olivier begs Roland to sound his ivory horn and recall the main body of the army, but Roland refuses. The valorous deeds of the twelve PALADINS during this unequal contest occupy much of the poem. When only sixty men are still alive, Roland finally sounds his horn, at the third blast cracking it and bursting the veins of his own neck; but it is too late to save anyone. Roland and Olivier exchange farewells and are blessed by the Archbishop TURPIN; all are dead on the arrival of Charlemagne and his army, who then avenge the dead by defeating the Saracens. Aude, the sister of Olivier and the betrothed of Roland, dies upon learning of the disaster. Ganelon is found guilty and punished by quartering.

There are many episodes involving Roland that appear not in the *Chanson*, but in other *chansons de geste*: fights with giants, various accounts of how he acquired his sword DURENDAL and his horn Olivant, and the like. Two important 12th-century Latin versions of the Roland story are the *Chronicle of Charlemagne*, erroneously attributed to the Archbishop TURPIN, and the anonymous poem *De proditione Guenonis* (*Ganelon's Betrayal*).

Roland became known in Italian minstrelsy as Orlando, and by the 15th and 16th centuries his loves and his adventures against the Saracens, along with those of the other paladins, had been thoroughly reshaped in Pulci's MORGANTE MAGGIORE, Boiardo's ORLANDO INNAMORATO, and Ariosto's ORLANDO FURIOSO.

Rolfe, Frederick [William Serafino Austin Lewis Mary]

(1860–1913)   English novelist. Rolfe used the name Baron Corvo, which he said had been given him as a gift. A versatile, eccentric, learned, and bitterly witty man, he lived his entire life in penury. He was a convert to Catholicism and tried unsuccessfully on a number of occasions to become a priest. His novel, *Hadrian the Seventh* (1905), is a bizarre tale of a failed writer who is elected Pope, providing a compensation for Rolfe's rejections and a vehicle for savage revenge on his "enemies." In *The Desire and Pursuit of the Whole* (1934), his genius for invective is directed against his publisher. His other works include *Chronicles of the House of Borgia* (1901), a passionately written history, and *In His Own Image* (1901), a retelling of the legends of Catholic saints.

Rolfe, John   See POCAHONTAS.

Rolland, Romain

(1866–1944)   French novelist, dramatist, essayist, and musicologist. Disturbed by the materialism of contemporary civilization, Rolland began in 1889 to write his long novel series JEAN CHRISTOPHE, a satirical criticism of the world he saw about him. His intellectual and spiritual development was greatly influenced by TOLSTOY and by his friendship with Malwida von Meysenburg, who had known both WAGNER and NIETZSCHE. He evolved his own philosophy, a faith in humanity based on pantheistic religion. An active participant in the DREYFUS case, Rolland collaborated with another Dreyfus sympathizer, Charles PÉGUY, on the bimonthly review *Cahiers de la quinzaine*. He advocated a new form of

drama built on the traditions of French history and accessible to the masses and wrote twenty plays on the theme of revolutionary heroism, among them *Les Loups* (1898; tr *The Wolves*, 1937), *Danton* (1900), *Le Quatorze juillet* (1902; tr *The Fourteenth of July*, 1918), and *Robespierre* (1938). Outstanding among his writings about the theatre is *Le Théâtre du peuple* (1903; tr *The Peoples' Theatre*, 1918). Rolland was a professor of music at the Sorbonne (1900–1912) and published numerous works on music, along with biographies of musical figures, notably *Beethoven* (6 vols, 1928–45). Selections from five of his books on music were translated in *Essays on Music* (1948). During World War I he acted on his strongly held pacifist views and wrote *Au-dessus de la mêlée* (1915; tr *Above the Battle*, 1916), an influential essay of pacifist protest. Combined with his other literary accomplishments, this led to his being awarded the NOBEL PRIZE in Literature in 1915. *L'Âme enchantée* (7 vols, 1922–33; tr *The Soul Enchanted*, 1925–34) is a second major novel series, with a woman as its central character. *D'une rive à l'autre* (1972; tr *Hermann Hesse and Romain Rolland*, 1978) is a collection of his correspondence with the German novelist, which offers extensive insight into his philosophical and literary aims.

Rolle of Hampole, Richard

(c1290–1349)   English hermit and mystic. Rolle wrote about the soul's approach to the mystic state through Purgation of worldliness, Illumination through meditation and prayer, and finally joyful Contemplation of the presence of God in *Incendium amoris* (*The Fire of Love*) and *Emendatio vitae* (*The Mending of Life*) in Latin and paraphrases of the Psalms, with commentaries, and *The Form of Living* in English. His emphasis on individual spiritual experience rather than the forms of religion had great influence. However, he was best known for the *Prick of Conscience*, the most popular poem in 14th-century England, which he probably did not write.

Rölvaag, Ole Edvart

(1876–1931)   Norwegian-born American novelist. Rölvaag is known for his dramatic and realistic accounts of the life of Norwegian pioneers in the Dakotas, marked particularly by psychological studies of the characters. Rölvaag immigrated to the U.S. in 1896; all his work was written first in Norwegian, then translated into English. His best-known work is the trilogy that consists of GIANTS IN THE EARTH, *Peder Victorious* (1929), and *Their Father's God* (1931). *The Boat of Longing* (1933), inspired by the death of his youngest child, contrasts the scenery of Norway with the sordidness of the American city.

Romains, Jules

(pen name of Louis Farigoule, 1885–1972)   French novelist, dramatist, essayist, and poet. Romains was a leading exponent of UNANIMISM in such early poetry as *La Vie unanime* (1908) and in the novels *Mort de quelqu'un* (1911; tr *The Death of a Nobody*, 1914) and *Les Copains* (1913; tr *The Boys in the Back Room*, 1937). He defined his belief in the collective spirit of groups in *Manuel de déification* (1910) and celebrated the soul of the city (one such group) in the prose poems *Puissances de Paris* (1911) and in the verse plays *L'Armée dans la ville* (1911) and *Cromedeyre-le-Vieil* (1920). His greatest achievement, which led to his election to the ACADÉMIE FRANÇAISE in 1946, was the twenty-seven-novel cycle *Les Hommes de bonne volonté* (1932–46; tr *Men of Good Will*, 1933–48), chronicling aspects of French life between 1908 and 1933. Subsequent works included *Examen de conscience des français* (1954; tr *A Frenchman Examines His Conscience*, 1956) and *Situation de la terre* (1961; tr *As It Is on Earth*, 1962). *Ai-je fait ce que j'ai voulu?* (1964) and *Amitiés et rencontres* (1970) are autobiographical works. Collections of his correspondence with his literary colleagues Gide (1976) and Copeau (1978) appeared posthumously.

roman à clef   Literally, a novel with a key, or secret meaning. Such a work of fiction contains one or more characters and situations based upon actual persons and their lives. Often such novels skirt dangerously close to infringement of the libel laws. Contemporary novels that might be mentioned are POINT COUNTER POINT, by Aldous Huxley, and LES MANDARINS, by Simone de Beauvoir. See SCUDÉRY, MADELEINE DE.

romance   In medieval literature, a verse narrative (originally written in Old English or Provençal, which were "Romance" languages) recounting the marvelous adventures of a chivalric hero. Such medieval romances fall into three main cycles: the Arthurian, based upon the life of King ARTHUR and his Knights of the ROUND TABLE; those recounting the life and deeds of CHARLEMAGNE and his most celebrated paladin, ROLAND; and those devoted to the exploits of ALEXANDER THE GREAT. Romances were written in English and German as well as in French; the vast majority of them were connected with one of these cycles, but German romances in particular drew upon Scandinavian and other sources as well.

In modern literature, i.e., from the latter part of the 18th through the 19th centuries, a romance is a work of prose fiction in which the scenes and incidents are more or less removed from common life and are surrounded by a halo of mystery, an atmosphere of strangeness and adventure. The GOTHIC NOVELS, such as Horace Walpole's THE CASTLE OF OTRANTO, are typical English romances. The American romance is typified by the novels of Nathaniel Hawthorne, who presented a theory of romance in his preface to THE HOUSE OF THE SEVEN GABLES.

In linguistics, the term is applied to languages developed from Latin, including Spanish, Portuguese, French, Italian, Rumanian, and Provençal. English is made up of both Romance and Germanic elements, with a small Celtic element as well.

Romance of the Rose (Roman de la Rose, 13th century)   Medieval French poem in two parts. The first four thousand lines were written by Guillaume de Lorris

about 1230 and form an allegory of the Art of Love modeled on OVID's. The Lover is conducted by Idleness to a garden of roses where he meets such characters as Pleasure, Riches, and Sweet-Looks. He is attracted to one particular rosebud and tries to pluck it, but the god of love (Cupid) stops him with an arrow and explains to him the sufferings required by the code of COURTLY LOVE. Resolved to return to his Rose, the Lover is encouraged by Welcome but obstructed by Danger, Shame, and Slander. Reason urges him to abandon the attempt, but Pity and Venus finally help him attain a kiss. Thereupon Slander rouses Jealousy, who builds a wall around the Rose and imprisons Welcome, leaving the Lover to grieve.

The continuation of over eighteen thousand lines was written by JEAN DE MEUN about 1275. Hypocrisy overcomes Slander; Nature allows the fire of Venus to drive away Danger, Shame, and Fear; and the Lover wins his Rose. The events of the story, however, are subordinate in this section to the long digressions in which the author flaunts the extent of his learning with a number of quotations. Here the main point is a series of satires from the bourgeois point of view: against the holders of political and economic power, against the friars, against popular superstitions, against women, and particularly against the artificial glorification of women in the aristocratic tradition of courtly love that had originally inspired Guillaume de Lorris's poem. Instead, Jean de Meun glorifies Nature, asserting that only the natural is good, whether in matters of love or of social institutions.

The *Romaunt of the Rose* attributed to CHAUCER is a translation, with additions, of the Guillaume de Lorris section and about one sixth of the Jean de Meun section. However, this is probably a 15th-century version of which only the first seventeen hundred lines are actually Chaucer's.

Romance of the Three Kingdoms (San-kuo chih yen-i)   A Chinese novel by Lo Kuan-chung (c1330–1400). It is a vast historical novel depicting the struggles between the contending states of the THREE KINGDOM period. Its seemingly endless episodes and the stratagems and personalities of the generals and kings involved have entered into Chinese folklore. See CHINESE LITERATURE.

Romancero gitano (1928; tr Gypsy Ballads, 1953)   A collection of eighteen ballads by Federico GARCÍA LORCA. The collection, Lorca's second, brought him immediate fame, although he was unhappy with his popular designation as the "gypsy poet." In it he combines the traditional *romancero* or ballad form with brilliant, imaginative metaphor and sophisticated symbolism to express his tragic view of life. With the gypsies representing the free force of primitive sexual drives repressed by puritanical Spain, personified by the Civil Guard, he draws a sensuous, lyrical, and violent portrait of his native Andalusia. As with much of his work, suppressed erotic passion becomes aggressive, producing a close association of love and death.

Roman de Brut (1155)   A verse chronicle in French by the Norman poet WACE. It is an adaptation of the Latin Chronicle HISTORY OF THE KINGS OF BRITAIN by Geoffrey of Monmouth. In his interpretation of ARTHURIAN LEGEND, the ROUND TABLE motif is introduced for the first time. See BRUT, THE.

Roman Empire, rulers of   The Empire was inaugurated 27 BC, when Octavius received from the Senate the title "Augustus." He had been actual ruler since 31 BC, when the SECOND TRIUMVIRATE was dissolved after the battle of Actium. The Republican constitution remained in force, but only formally; Augustus gradually assumed the titles of all the major offices. His reign is sometimes called the principate, from *princeps* (first citizen), the title he favored.

The empire in the West ended 476, when Romulus Augustulus was banished by the barbarian Odoacer. Zeno continued to rule in the East until 491. The Byzantine empire lasted until 1453, when Constantinople fell to the Turks. Charlemagne was crowned Emperor of the West in 800, the date usually accepted as the founding of the HOLY ROMAN EMPIRE.

roman-fleuve (Fr, "river novel")   A novel or, more frequently, a series of novels dealing with a set of characters over a long period of time. It came to be characteristic of much French fiction during the first half of the 20th century. Outstanding examples include Romain Rolland's JEAN CHRISTOPHE; REMEMBRANCE OF THINGS PAST by Proust; and Roger Martin's LES THIBAULTS. C. P. Snow's STRANGERS AND BROTHERS is an example of the form in English.

Romanov   The last Russian royal house. The Romanovs descended from Andrey Romanov (14th century). The first Romanov tsar was Mikhail, who was elected by a conference of nobles (boyars) in 1613. The direct male line ended with Peter II in 1730 and the direct female line in 1762 with Elizabeth. Peter III, who succeeded Elizabeth, was her nephew; his wife, Catherine the Great, was a German princess. The dynasty ended in July 1918 when Nicholas II, his wife, and his children were killed by the revolutionaries.

Romans, The Epistle of Paul the Apostle to the   A book of the New Testament. It is a long letter written by Paul in AD 56 to the Christians in Rome. It is sometimes called the "Gospel of Saint Paul," being his most profound exposition of the nature of Christianity. In this letter is the core of Pauline thought: Christianity is a religion for the whole world, having its roots in the older prophetic religion of the Jews.

Romantic Comedians, The (1926)   A novel by Ellen Glasgow (1874–1945). Like Glasgow's *They Stooped to Folly* (1929), this novel is an ironical comedy of manners. The elderly Judge Honeywell, who belongs to the generation before World War I, marries eighteen-year-old Annabel Upchurch. The juxtaposition in age, manners, and values produces a rich comedy, told by Miss Glasgow

with wit and compassion. Eventually Annabel runs away with Dabney Birdsong, leaving the judge looking longingly at the young nurse sent to take care of him.

romantic irony   A literary technique first specifically defined by Friedrich SCHLEGEL. Romantic irony is basically the introduction of paradox into a literary work, as, for example, when the hero of a novel suddenly announces that the author of the novel has died and that he, the hero, will carry on the work, a situation that occurs in BRENTANO's *Godwi* (1800–1801). Another common ironic technique is for statements *about* a literary work to be included *within* the work. Examples of this are TIECK's play *Der gestiefelte Kater* (*Puss in Boots*, pub 1797), in which a fictitious audience is put on the stage to criticize the play, and Schlegel's own novel *Lucinde* (1799), which embodies a theory of the novel.

romanticism   A term applied to the movement in literature and the arts that began in Europe toward the end of the 18th century. In emphasizing the imagination and emotions over intellect and reason, the movement was a reaction against NEOCLASSICISM.

The rise of romanticism was so gradual, and exhibited so many phases, that a clear definition is nearly impossible. Generally speaking, romanticism might be said to involve the following characteristics: a belief in the innate goodness of man in his natural state; individualism; reverence for nature; PRIMITIVISM; philosophic idealism; a paradoxical tendency toward both free thought and religious mysticism; revolt against political authority and social convention; exaltation of physical passion; the cultivation of emotion and sensation for their own sakes; and a persistent attraction to the supernatural, the morbid, the melancholy, and the cruel.

Jean Jacques ROUSSEAU is considered the father of romanticism, although its first manifestation as an organized movement appeared in Germany in the work of SCHILLER, GOETHE, NOVALIS, KLEIST, and TIECK, and particularly in the idealist philosophies of KANT, FICHTE, SCHELLING, and HEGEL. In England early forerunners of romanticism were Thomas GRAY, William COLLINS, William COWPER, Robert BURNS, Thomas CHATTERTON, William BLAKE, and the emergence of the GOTHIC NOVEL. The movement was given impetus with the publication of Percy's RELIQUES OF ANCIENT ENGLISH POETRY and Mac-Pherson's OSSIAN, and was powerfully stimulated by the FRENCH REVOLUTION. English romanticism flowered (1789–1832) in the work of WORDSWORTH, COLERIDGE, SHELLEY, BYRON, KEATS, SOUTHEY, Sir Walter SCOTT, Charles LAMB, William HAZLITT, and Thomas DE QUINCEY.

In France, Mme de STAËL and CHATEAUBRIAND were forerunners of romanticism, but there was no definite movement there until the 1820s, lasting until about 1843. Led by Victor HUGO, the major French romantic poets included LAMARTINE, MUSSET, VIGNY, and GAUTIER, and the novelists, George SAND, DUMAS PÈRE, STENDHAL, and MERIMÉE.

In the U.S., romanticism developed later, and was less well defined, exhibiting modifications from the peculiar nature of American culture at the time with a strong emphasis on humanitarianism and reform. Among the American romantic writers were Charles Brockden BROWN, James Fenimore COOPER, Washington IRVING, William Gilmore SIMMS, William Cullen BRYANT, POE, EMERSON, THOREAU, HAWTHORNE, MELVILLE, LONGFELLOW, WHITTIER, and WHITMAN. TRANSCENDENTALISM is regarded as the clearest example of romanticism in the U.S.

Romanticism in music is exemplified by BEETHOVEN, BERLIOZ, SCHUBERT, MENDELSSOHN, and SCHUBERT, and by DELACROIX, INGRES, COROT, and MILLET in painting.

The romantic movement was arrested in its development in England after 1832, with only a brief revival under the PRE-RAPHAELITE BROTHERHOOD; in the U.S. it was rapidly absorbed by native tendencies and other influences. In France, dominant romantic characteristics were developed by BAUDELAIRE and, through him, passed on to the DÉCADENTS, the SYMBOLISTS, and, ultimately, the surrealists (see SURREALISM). In Germany, it persisted, continuing especially in the philosophies of SCHOPENHAUER and NIETZSCHE, in the fiction of Thomas MANN, and in the poetry of Stefan GEORGE and RILKE. See GERMAN ROMANTICISM.

Romany   A gypsy; or the gypsy language, the speech of the Roma or Zincali. The word is from Gypsy *rom*, "man" or "husband." A *Romany rye* is one who enters into the gypsy spirit, learns their language, and lives with them as one of themselves. *Rye* is gypsy for "gentleman."

romanzo (Ital, "romance")   Italian term for the genre of the romantic epic. In Italy this took the form of a long poem in OTTAVA RIMA, dealing with the chivalric adventures and romantic loves of the knights of Charlemagne and of King Arthur. Sung on the streets by minstrels as well as written in the study by learned poets, the *romanzi* reached their artistic peak in the work of BOIARDO and ARIOSTO, who wrote on the Orlando theme. TASSO's *Gerusalemme liberata* is an attempt at a stricter emulation of the classical epics of Homer and Vergil, but its variety of characters and incidents, its interweaving of plots, and its reliance on the marvelous and the magical make it the last of the Italian Renaissance *romanzi*. Mock *romanzi* that poked fun at the absurdities of the genre, especially IL MORGANTE MAGGIORE, also appeared during the period. In the same vein, the *Gargantua and Pantagruel* of Rabelais and the *Don Quixote* of Cervantes utilize the ingredients of the popular romantic epics in a satiric manner. In England, the chief influence of the *romanzo* can be seen in Spenser's *Faerie Queene*.

Rome (known as the Eternal City)   A city in central Italy, the capital of the Republic of Italy. In ancient times Rome was the capital and center of the Roman Empire. It then became, through Peter, the first bishop of Rome, the home of the pope and the capital of early Christendom. Today the pope lives in the VATICAN CITY, which is wholly within the city's precincts, and Rome remains the center of the Roman Catholic religion.

Traditionally the city was founded by ROMULUS in 753 BC. By 265 BC Rome controlled the entire Italian peninsula, having subjugated all the neighboring tribes. Victory in the three PUNIC WARS with Carthage (264–241, 218–202, 149–146 BC) gave Rome domination of the Mediterranean and made her the most powerful state in the ancient world.

As a republic (753–31 BC), Rome had flourished. Under the dictatorship of Julius CAESAR and later under the emperors AUGUSTUS, Trajan, and HADRIAN, Rome became the capital of an empire that included virtually all the known world.

From the early days of the empire, various emperors had contemplated moving the capital from republican-minded Rome to an eastern city. In AD 330, CONSTANTINE THE GREAT moved the seat of empire to Byzantium on the Bosphorus, renaming it Constantinople. The Visigoths sacked Rome in 410. The city was repeatedly pillaged by barbarian tribes until JUSTINIAN I restored imperial power (536).

During this period the popes (as bishops of Rome) began to assume temporal power over the city. In 756 the Frankish king Pepin donated Rome to Pope Adrian I.

Medieval Rome was a dingy, mud-filled city with animals grazing in the Imperial Forum. The population shrank as low as two thousand people. Even the papacy moved to France (1309–77).

A new period of splendor began in the 15th century under the Renaissance popes. New churches and public buildings were erected, often using material from the ruinous buildings of Imperial Rome that littered the city. In 1527 the imperial armies of Charles V, inspired by the zeal of Protestant mercenaries from the northern countries, destroyed and pillaged the city. Pope Clement VII took refuge in the Castel Sant' Angelo and later fled the city. However, this only temporarily halted the rebuilding. The modern city is still dominated by the lavish baroque and rococo churches and places built in the 16th, 17th, and 18th centuries.

The popes lost sovereignty of the city in 1870, when Rome became the capital of the united nation of Italy. A symbolic temporal power was restored to the popes in 1929, with the creation of the Vatican City as an independent state.

Rome's outstanding feature as a city is the fact that its history as a center of political and religious importance is unparalleled in duration. This is visually evident in its abundance of historic architecture. Roman buildings from the classical age can be seen standing between a Renaissance church and a modern apartment house.

The expression *When in Rome, do as Rome does* means to conform to the manners and customs of those among whom you live. St. Monica and her son St. Augustine said to St. Ambrose: "At Rome they fast on Saturday, but not so at Milan; which practice ought to be observed?" To which St. Ambrose replied, "When I am at Milan, I do as they do at Milan; but when I go to Rome, I do as Rome does!"

Romeo and Juliet (c1596)   A tragedy by SHAKE-SPEARE. Romeo, the young heir of the Montagues, attends the great ball of the Capulets in disguise and falls in love with JULIET, the daughter of the house. (See CAPULET AND MONTAGUE.) Because of the deadly feud between the Montagues and Capulets, the lovers are married secretly in the cell of Friar LAURENCE. During a street brawl, Romeo's friend MERCUTIO is killed by Juliet's cousin Tybalt. Enraged by his friend's death, Romeo kills Tybalt and is banished from Verona. In desperation Juliet, who is about to be married to Paris against her will, takes a sleeping potion given her by the friar to bring on a semblance of death. Romeo, hearing of her death before the friar's explanation reaches him, returns and drinks poison at Juliet's tomb. When she wakes up a few moments later to find him dead, she stabs herself. Realizing that their hatred has caused the tragedy, the two houses make a tardy, sorrowful peace.

Sentimental, romantic, and given to poetic expression of his love, Romeo is typical of the youthful Elizabethan swain. His best-known speech occurs in the famous balcony scene with Juliet:

> But, soft! what light through yonder window breaks?
> It is the east, and Juliet is the sun!
> Arise, fair sun, and kill the envious moon,
> Who is already sick and pale with grief,
> That thou her maid are far more fair than she.

The first written version of the story of the ill-fated lovers appears in the *Novellino* (1476) of Masuccio Salernitano. The story was retold in Arthur Brooke's poetic *Tragical History of Romeus and Juliet* (1562) and in William Paynter's *Palace of Pleasure* (1567). Shakespeare most closely follows Brooke's version.

GOUNOD wrote an opera, *Roméo et Juliette* (1867), based on the Shakespearean plot, and Jean ANOUILH has written a bitter and very realistic version of the story in his *Roméo and Jeanette*.

Romola (1863)   A historical novel by George ELIOT. After her marriage to the hedonistic Tito Melema, Romola, a young Florentine woman, comes under the influence of Savonarola; she finds peace through faith and dedication.

Romulus   Legendary and eponymous founder of Rome (753 BC) and its first king (753–716 BC). Descendants of AENEAS, Romulus and his twin, Remus, were sons of Mars and Rhea Silvia; Numitor, Rhea's father and king, was ousted by his brother Amulius, who made Rhea a vestal virgin. Accordingly, when she gave birth she was put to death and her two babies were thrown into the Tiber. They

were washed ashore, suckled by a she-wolf, and found by a herdsman and his wife who brought them up. They were eventually recognized and overthrew Amulius, restoring Numitor as king. They then set about to found a city; they quarreled over the site for the city, and Romulus killed his brother in anger. Romulus's settlement prospered, but there were no women, so he invited the SABINES for a festival. During the celebrations, the young Romans seized the Sabine women and drove off the men. The ensuing war was settled by making Sabines and Romans equal in the new settlement. Romulus ruled wisely for thirty-seven years. When he died, JUPITER permitted MARS to come down and take Romulus off to the heavens in his chariot. Romulus was thereafter worshiped as a god among the Romans under the name Quirinus.

Roncesvalles   A pass in the Pyrenees mountains. The rear guard of CHARLEMAGNE's army, returning from a campaign in Spain, was ambushed and badly defeated there in 778 by Basque mountaineers. In medieval romances such as the *Chanson de* ROLAND, however, the ambush is attributed to the treachery of one of Charlemagne's knights, the Basques become an army of 400,000 Muslims, and the defeat of the rear guard is followed by the return of Charlemagne's main army and the retaliatory defeat of the Muslim Saracens, to the glory of Christendom.

Ronde, La (Reigen; written 1896; pub 1903; first perf 1920)   A play by Arthur SCHNITZLER, consisting of ten scenes, each ending before ten different couples have sexual intercourse. The scenes are interlocking—thus, for example, after a scene between a young girl and a married man comes a scene between the man and his wife, followed by a scene with the wife and her lover—and the whole play forms a circle beginning and ending with a prostitute. This circular form symbolized both the unending frenetic quality and the sameness of human erotic behavior. The play contains touches of sophisticated comedy. It was translated into English as *Hands Around* (1920) and is well known from the French film version, *La Ronde* (1950).

rondeau   A lyric poem of fifteen lines, in three stanzas of uneven length. The rondeau is characterized by a refrain, at the end of the second and third stanzas, made up of a fragment taken from the first line of the first stanza; the fragment may consist of a phrase, a clause, or as little as a single word. The rondeau form arose in France and its rules were enunciated in the 16th century. The rhyme scheme is: a-a-b-b-a, a-a-b-R, a-a-b-b-a-R, the R being the refrain. The following is an example:

> In after days when grasses high
> O'ertop the stone where I shall lie,
>   Though ill or well the world adjust
>   My slender claim to honoured dust,
> I shall not question or reply.

I shall not see the morning sky;
I shall not hear the night wind sigh;
    I shall be mute, as all men must
        In after days!

But yet, now living, fain were I
That some one then should testify,
    Saying—*He held his pen in trust*
    To art, not serving shame or lust.
Will none?—Then let my memory die
        In after days!

                                    Austin Dobson, "In After Days"

See CHAUCERIAN ROUNDEL; RONDEL; ROUNDEL.

rondel   A verse form containing fourteen lines and two rhymes. The rondel arose in France in the 14th century, was written in English as early as the 15th century, and revived in the 19th century. A two-line refrain is repeated in the rondel three times in its entirety. The rhyme scheme is A-B-b-a-a-b-A-B-a-b-b-a-A-B, or sometimes A-B-a-b-b-a-A-B-a-b-a-b-A-B (A-B represents the refrain). There is also a rondel form of thirteen lines which omits either one of the last two refrain lines. The following example has thirteen lines:

Love comes back to his vacant dwelling,—
    The old, old love that we knew of yore!
    We see him stand by the open door,
With his great eyes sad and his bosom swelling.

He makes as though in our arms repelling,
    He fain would lie as he lay before;—
Love comes back to his vacant dwelling,
    The old, old love that we knew of yore!

Ah, who shall help us from over-spelling
    That sweet, forgotten, forbidden lore!
    E'en as we doubt in our heart once more,
With a rush of tears to our eyelids welling,
Love comes back to his vacant dwelling.

                                    Austin Dobson, "The Wanderer"

See CHAUCERIAN ROUNDEL; RONDEAU; ROUNDEL.

Ronsard, Pierre de (1524?–1585)   French poet and leader of the PLÉIADE. Ronsard was destined by his father for a diplomatic career, but after spending four years as a page in the service of Francis I, he was struck by deafness and turned to humanistic studies and poetry. Inspired by the teaching of Jean Dorat at the Collège de Coqueret in Paris, Ronsard and his fellow-students Joachim DU BELLAY and Jean Antoine de Baïf conceived a new program for French poetry, which Du Bellay elaborated in the DÉFENSE ET ILLUSTRATION DE LA LANGUE FRANÇAISE.

The succession of Ronsard's works testifies to his steady development and great versatility. Although his *Odes* (1550) were closely modeled after the work of HORACE and PINDAR, the *Amours de Cassandre* (1552), a collection of Petrarchan sonnets published with musical accompaniment, was characterized by the light, graceful style for

which he is best known. The *Folâtries* (1553), *Mélanges* (1555), *Odes* (1555), and *Amours de Marie* (1555) are simple, sensual love poems which celebrate rustic pleasures and evoke the gentle atmosphere of Ronsard's native countryside. In the *Hymnes* (1555) he expressed his awe before the mysteries of the universe. With the outbreak of the religious wars, Ronsard the patriot produced the *Discours des misères de ce temps* (1562) and other political works that at first were conciliatory but became increasingly hostile to the HUGUENOTS. He made an unsuccessful attempt at epic poetry with *La Franciade* (1572). His last and perhaps best collection of love poetry, *Sonnets pour Hélène* (1578), was written in the prevailing platonic style and betrayed the profound melancholy which dominated Ronsard as he saw death approaching.

Although widely acknowledged throughout Europe as the "Prince of poets," Ronsard, mindful of posterity's verdict, never ceased polishing and perfecting his work. After his death, his reputation suffered an eclipse until he was rediscovered by the 19th-century Romantics.

Room at the Top (1957)   A best-selling novel by John BRAINE. It is the story of a young man's hypocritical efforts to rise in his job and marry his boss's daughter—at the cost of his mistress's life.

Room of One's Own, A (1929)   A feminist essay by Virginia WOOLF on the status of women and the difficulties of a woman artist. See ORLANDO.

Room with a View, A (1908)   A novel by E. M. FORSTER. It is set mostly in Italy, a country which represents for the author the forces of true passion. The heroine, upper-class Lucy Honeychurch, is visiting Italy with a friend. When she regrets that her hotel room has no view, lower-class Mr. Emerson offers the friends his own room and that of his son. Lucy becomes caught between the world of the Emersons and that of Cecil Vyse, the shallow, conventional young man of her own class to whom she becomes engaged on her return to England. Finally, she overcomes her own prejudice and her family's opposition and marries George Emerson. The book was made into a highly successful film in 1986.

Roosevelt, [Anna] Eleanor (1884–1962)   American humanitarian and wife of President Franklin D. ROOSEVELT. A niece of Theodore ROOSEVELT, she married Franklin, who was a distant cousin, in 1905, and, after his election to the presidency, became the most active first lady in American history; she engaged in social welfare work, took part in Democratic politics, served as assistant director of the Office of Civilian Defense (1941–42), and conducted a newspaper column, *My Day*. After her husband's death, she was chairman of the Commission on Human Rights of the UN Economic and Social Council and represented the U.S. in the UN General Assembly from 1949 to 1952. In her last years, she was a leader in New York City reform politics. Her books include *This Is My Story* (1937), *My*

Days (1938), *This I Remember* (1948), *On My Own* (1958), and *The Autobiography of Eleanor Roosevelt* (1961).

Roosevelt, Franklin Delano (1882–1945) Thirty-second president of the U.S. (1933–45). Roosevelt was a fifth cousin of Theodore ROOSEVELT, who was also his wife's uncle. Educated at Groton and at Harvard University, he attended Columbia University Law School and married Eleanor ROOSEVELT in 1905. After his admission to the bar, he entered politics in 1910 as the leader of a group of insurgents against Tammany Hall in New York and won election to the state legislature. He supported Woodrow Wilson in 1912 and in 1913 was made an assistant secretary of the navy under Josephus Daniels. In 1920 he was nominated as the vice-presidential candidate on the Democratic ticket with James M. Cox and battled eloquently for the League of Nations. In August 1921, he was stricken with poliomyelitis; he went to Warm Springs, Georgia, to take the cure but, although his condition was somewhat improved, he remained disabled for the rest of his life. He later established a foundation at Warm Springs to aid other victims of the disease.

After serving two terms as governor of New York, he ran for the presidency in 1932, defeating Herbert HOOVER. Declaring in his first inaugural address that "the only thing we have to fear is fear itself," he dedicated his first term to a NEW DEAL that would alleviate the economic distress caused by the depression of 1929. In 1936 he defeated Alfred Landon of Kansas to win reelection by a landslide, losing the electoral votes of only Maine and Vermont. Domestic matters occupied much of Roosevelt's second term, during which he lost his fight to enlarge the Supreme Court, but the worsening situation in Europe brought a new concern with foreign affairs as the president sought to sway public opinion in favor of international cooperation against aggressor nations, a policy that was bitterly attacked by isolationists.

Roosevelt defied a long-standing tradition in 1940 when he decided to run for a third term, defeating Wendell Willkie. Soon after his inauguration, he secured enactment of the Lend-Lease Act to aid Great Britain and met with Winston CHURCHILL to frame the Atlantic Charter, a statement of Anglo-American aims for the future. When the U.S. entered World War II after the Japanese attack on Pearl Harbor on December 7, 1941, which Roosevelt described as "a day which will live in infamy," he directed American mobilization and acted to ensure hemispheric solidarity; in 1944 he won an unprecedented fourth term by defeating Thomas E. Dewey. At the Casablanca conference (1943), Roosevelt and Churchill announced that the war would continue until the enemy surrendered unconditionally; at the Yalta meeting (1945) with Premier STALIN, several concessions were made to the Soviet Union in exchange for her entry into the war against Japan. Two months later Roosevelt was dead of a cerebral hemorrhage.

One of the most colorful and controversial presidents in American history, Roosevelt greatly expanded the scope of the federal government, particularly in the field of social and economic legislation. His enemies, however, accused him of dictatorial tendencies and denounced his encroachments on private enterprise. His extraordinary gift for communication was best shown in his press conferences, of which transcripts were always made, and in his famous radio "Fireside Chats."

Roosevelt's writings include *Looking Forward* (1933) and *On Our Way* (1934). Samuel I. Rosenman edited his *Papers and Addresses* from 1928 to 1945. Playwright Robert E. SHERWOOD, who was one of Roosevelt's speech writers, wrote about the president in *Roosevelt and Hopkins* (1948). FDR's early struggles against polio are described in Dore Schary's drama *Sunrise at Campobello* (1959).

Roosevelt, Theodore (1858–1919) Twenty-sixth president of the U.S. (1901–9). After his graduation from Harvard, Roosevelt turned to writing history, in which he was intensely interested all his life. His first book was *The Naval War of 1812* (1882). Then he entered politics and served from 1882 to 1884 as a Republican member of the New York legislature. When his first wife, Alice Lee, and his mother died within a few hours of each other, the grief-stricken Roosevelt went to the Dakota Territory, where he ranched and won the approbation of the local residents. In 1886 he married Edith Carow.

Returning to politics, Roosevelt served as a member of the U.S. Civil Service Commission and as police commissioner of New York City, displaying in these posts the vigor and determination that were his hallmarks. At the same time he was writing his four-volume *Winning of the West* (1889–96), an account of U.S. expansion after the Revolution.

He was assistant secretary of the navy in 1898 when the Spanish-American War broke out, and he resigned to form the Rough Riders, a volunteer cavalry group that was to become famous for its charge up San Juan Hill in Cuba. After Roosevelt had been elected governor of New York in 1898, Republican Party bosses who feared his independence and liberal views secured his nomination as William McKinley's running mate in 1900, only to see him become president upon McKinley's death in 1901. As chief executive, Roosevelt gained a reputation as a "trust-buster," particularly for his dissolution of the Northern Securities Co. (1902); he encouraged conservation of national resources and secured the passage of the Pure Food and Drug Act (1906) and the Hepburn Act (1906) to ensure stricter regulation of the railroads.

An advocate of a venturesome foreign policy, he effected the construction of the Panama Canal, won the Nobel Peace Prize for his successful intervention in the Russo-Japanese War (1905), and dispatched the U.S. Fleet on a round-the-world tour (1907–9). His motto was "Speak softly and carry a big stick."

After the inauguration of his "lieutenant," William Howard TAFT, in 1909, Roosevelt traveled in Africa and Europe and returned to find a growing split between Republican conservatives and progressives. Breaking with Taft and unable to win the Republican nomination in 1912, he organized the "Bull Moose" Party, ran against Taft and Woodrow WILSON, and took enough votes away from Taft to ensure Wilson's election.

In 1914 he led an expedition to South America and explored Brazil's River of Doubt, which was renamed Rio Teodoro in his honor. Later, he favored U.S. entry into World War I on the side of the Allies and was deeply disappointed when President Wilson prevented him from raising a volunteer division. His son Quentin was killed in action; in World War II his sons Kermit and Theodore died in active service.

Roosevelt's other writings include *The Strenuous Life: Essays and Addresses* (1900), *The New Nationalism* (1910), and *Theodore Roosevelt, An Autobiography* (1913). See SINCLAIR, UPTON.

Rootabaga Stories (1922)   A book of children's stories by Carl SANDBURG. Written in a style nearer poetry than prose, it is rich in the language and cadence of folk song. It was followed by *Rootabaga Pigeons* (1923).

Roots of Heaven (Les Racines du ciel, 1956; tr 1958)   A novel by Romain GARY. A passionate plea on behalf of the protection of wildlife, it is about the idealist Morel's fight to save the elephants—symbol of liberty —from extinction.

Rosales [Comacho], Luis (1910–   )   Spanish poet and literary critic. Born in Granada, Rosales became one of the leading members of the GENERACIÓN DEL 36. His volume of poetry *Abril* (*April*, 1935) signals that group's return to Renaissance influences, particularly that of GARCILASO DE LA VEGA. A graceful, lyric outpouring of love for God and nature, *Abril* uses strange imagery, verging at times on the irrational. In 1940 Rosales published *Retablo sacro del nacimiento del Señor*, which expresses his pure religious sentiment. *La casa encendida* (1949; rev 1967) contains introspective FREE VERSE musings on time and approaching old age. *Rimas* (1951, 1971) continues his interior search and *Canciones* (1973) contains short verses about man, truth, knowledge, and death.

Rosalind   The courageous, witty, and charmingly sportive heroine of Shakespeare's AS YOU LIKE IT.

Rosas, Juan Manuel de (1793–1877)   Argentine dictator. Named governor of Buenos Aires province in 1829, Rosas controlled the entire country until 1852 when he was defeated at the battle of Caseros. This was a period of great intellectual ferment in Argentina, and many writers, usually from exile in Chile or Uruguay, produced literary works attacking the despotism and terror of the Rosas regime. Among these were Sarmiento's FACUNDO, Mármol's *Amalia* (1851–55), and Echevarría's EL MATADERO.

rose   A flower of many symbolic connotations. Medieval legend asserts that the first roses appeared miraculously at Bethlehem as the result of the prayers of a "fayre Mayden" who had been falsely accused and was sentenced to death by burning. The burning brands changed to roses and she was saved.

The rose has been an emblem of England since the time of the Wars of the Roses, a contest that lasted thirty years, in which eighty princes of the blood, a large portion of the English nobility, and some one hundred thousand common soldiers were slain. It was a struggle for the crown between the houses of York (the white rose) and Lancaster (the red). When the parties were united in the person of Henry VII, the united rose was taken as his device.

Rose and the Ring, The (1845)   A burlesque fairy tale by William Makepeace THACKERAY. The action revolves around a magic rose and ring, both of which make their possessors seem both lovely and lovable. After various trials and mishaps, a happy ending is brought about by the efforts of Fairy Blackstick.

Rose Bernd (1903; tr 1913)   A tragedy by Gerhart HAUPTMANN. Rose is engaged to August Keil but becomes pregnant by the town magistrate. After she postpones her marriage, she is seduced by a mechanic who then publicly maligns her. Rose's father initiates a lawsuit against the mechanic which will require Rose to offer testimony that can only bring more pain. She conceals her pregnancy from all but the wife of the magistrate who fathered the child. She gives birth to the child alone and outdoors, and smothers it. In the end, when all have turned away from her, she confesses to killing her child and is arrested. Only Keil understands that she has been condemned by a society that brutally misused her.

Rosenberg, Isaac (1890–1918)   English poet and painter. Rosenberg was killed in action in World War I, ending the career of what many critics thought to be one of the most promising poets of his generation. He wrote passionate, original, muscular verse, the best of which grew directly out of his wartime experiences. His *Collected Works* were published in 1937 and again in 1979, when there was a substantial revival of interest in his work.

Rosencrantz and Guildenstern   In Shakespeare's HAMLET, two time-serving courtiers. They are willing to undertake any commission, however iniquitous, to please the king.

Rosencrantz and Guildenstern Are Dead See STOPPARD, TOM.

Rose Tattoo, The (1951)   A play by Tennessee WILLIAMS. Set in a Sicilian community on the Gulf Coast, the play deals with Serafina Delle Rose, a passionate and warm-hearted dressmaker, whose truckdriver husband has just been killed. Serafina, unwilling to believe rumors of her husband's infidelity, keeps his ashes in a marble urn in the house and remains a frustrated widow, until three years later she meets a younger truckdriver who, like her dead husband, has a rose tattoo on his chest. The play has a clownish humor not generally found in Williams.

Rosetta stone   A stone found in 1799 by M. Boussard, a French officer of engineers, in an excavation made at Fort St. Julien, near Rosetta, in the Nile delta. It has an inscription in three different languages: the hieroglyphic, the demotic, and the Greek. It was erected in 195 BC, to honor Ptolemy Epiphanes, because he remitted the dues of the sacerdotal body. The great value of this stone is that it furnished the French Egyptologist Jean François Champollion the key whereby he deciphered the Egyptian hieroglyphics.

Rosh Hashanah (Heb, "head of the year")   The Jewish New Year, Rosh Hashanah is a solemn festival that is celebrated on the first day of the Hebrew month of Tishri, usually late in September or early October. The holiday begins the ten days of penitence that end on Yom Kippur, the DAY OF ATONEMENT; this period is called the Days of Awe. The three central sections of the Rosh Hashanah liturgy are concluded by cycles of blasts on the *shofar* (ram's horn). It is regarded as the Day of Judgment, when all mankind stands before the Lord, who determines each man's fate for the coming year, and as the Day of Remembrance, recalling God's goodness to the patriarchs during their time of need. In the TALMUD and MIDRASH, Rosh Hashanah celebrates the anniversary of creation and is called the Birthday of the World.

Rosicrucians   A mystical society of religious reformers, who first appeared in Germany in the early 17th century and who were said to have a knowledge of magical secrets. Their symbol was a red rose upon a cross.

Rosmersholm (1866)   A play by Henrik IBSEN. Johannes Rosmer has freed himself intellectually, but is unable to cut his emotional ties to the life-destroying conventions embodied in Rosmersholm, his ancestral home. His invalid wife, Beata, has committed suicide to leave him free to marry the vital and strong-willed Rebecca West, but when Rosmer learns that Rebecca has subtly led Beata to believe that she must sacrifice herself, his faith in himself and his idealism die. He refuses to believe that Rebecca truly loves him unless she agrees to go the way of Beata; she consents willingly, and together she and Rosmer end their lives by leaping into the millrace.

Ross, Harold [Wallace] (1892–1951)   American editor. A dynamic, contradictory personality, Ross edited THE NEW YORKER from its founding in 1925 until his death. James THURBER, long associated with the magazine, wrote of him in *The Years with Ross* (1959).

Ross, Martin   See SOMERVILLE, E. O.

Ross, [James] Sinclair (1908–   )   Canadian novelist and short-story writer. Born in rural Saskatchewan, Ross combined a career of banking with a life of writing. His early stories about prairie farm life during the 1930s are collected in *The Lamp at Noon* (1968). Two novels, *As for Me and My House* (1941) and *Sawbones Memorial* (1974),

dramatize the physical and spiritual trials of prairie town dwellers during the 1930s. Other novels are *The Well* (1958) and *Whir of Gold* (1970). In 1982 Ross published a collection of short stories, *The Race.*

Rossellini, Roberto (1906–1977)   Italian film director and producer. Rossellini began his film career by working on a number of documentaries for the Mussolini regime. In 1944, while the Germans were preparing to evacuate Rome, he began work on his famous film *Open City* (1945), in which he recreated, as closely as possible, the heroic action of the Roman peoples' resistance. His sensitive merging of fictional human stories and the reality of an actual historical event was a crucial step in the development of Italian NEOREALIST CINEMA. Rossellini's next film, *Paisan* (1948), dealt vividly with the Italian experience of World War II, and *Germany Year Zero* (1947) with the war's aftermath in ruined Berlin. *L'Amore* (1948), a pair of films, featured the great Italian actress Anna Magnani. In 1950 Rossellini married the Swedish actress Ingrid Bergman; together they made what were probably Rossellini's most personal films: *Stromboli* (1949), *Europa '51* (1952), and *Viaggio in Italia* (1953). After their divorce in 1958, he concentrated on documentaries, and at the end of his life he worked on films on Italian history.

Rossetti, Christina Georgina (1830–1894) English poet of Italian parentage, sister of Dante Gabriel and William Michael ROSSETTI. She is known for her ballads and her mystic religious lyrics, marked by symbolism, vividness of detail, and intensity of feeling. Among her works are *Goblin Market, and Other Poems* (1862); *The Prince's Progress* (1866); and *Sing-Song* (1872), a collection of verse for children. "A Birthday," "When I Am Dead," and "Up-Hill" are probably her best-known single works. Her first poems were published in *The Germ*, the Pre-Raphaelite publication, and she often modeled for painters in the PRE-RAPHAELITE BROTHERHOOD. After a serious illness in 1874, she was left an invalid and withdrew from the world, rarely receiving visitors or leaving her home. Her *Complete Poems* appeared in 1979.

Rossetti, Dante Gabriel (full name Gabriel Charles Dante Rossetti, 1828–1882)   English poet and painter of Italian parentage, brother of Christina and William Michael Rossetti. He was the driving force of the PRE-RAPHAELITE BROTHERHOOD. As a painter he had little formal training, revealed little technical ability, and is noted chiefly as a colorist. His best-known painting, *Ecce Ancilla Domini* (1850), is an emotive representation of the Annunciation.

His lyric poems are distinguished by richness and vividness of detail, mysticism and fantasy, and the frequent use of modified ballad form. His books of poetry include *The Early Italian Poets* (1861), translations of the lyrics of Dante, his contemporaries, and predecessors; *Poems* (1870), a collection that was at first buried in the coffin of Elizabeth SIDDAL, Rossetti's wife; and *Ballads and Sonnets*

(1881). His best-known single works are THE BLESSED DAM-
OZEL, "Sister Helen," "Troy Town," and THE HOUSE OF
LIFE. He also made a number of translations from the Italian, German, and French, the most outstanding of which
is THE BALLAD OF DEAD LADIES of François Villon.

Rossetti, William Michael (1829–1919)   Art
critic and author, brother of Dante Gabriel and Christina
Rossetti. He was one of the original members of the PRE-
RAPHAELITE BROTHERHOOD, serving as editor of *The Germ*.
He wrote a translation of Dante (1865) and a *Life of Keats*
(1887); he also wrote memoirs of both his brother (1895)
and his sister (1904).

Rossini, Giacchino Antonio (1792–1868)   The
dominant operatic composer of the early 19th century.
Rossini's more than forty serious and comic operas were all
written between 1810 and 1829, after which he wrote little
but the *Stabat Mater* (1842) and the *Petite Messe solenelle*
(1864). His most important operas are *The Barber of Seville*
(1816), *Otello* (1816), *La Cenerentola* (*Cinderella*, 1817),
Semiramide (1823), and *William Tell* (1829). Rossini established the standard musical forms for Italian romantic
opera which were followed by all Italian composers to midcentury and the works of the mature VERDI.

Rostand, Edmond (1868–1918)   French playwright. Rostand's plays provided absorbing light entertainment and were enthusiastically received by audiences less
inclined to the brooding thoughtfulness of naturalistic theatre. *Cyrano de Bergerac* (1897; tr 1937; filmed 1950) is the
most famous example of the poetic, romantic drama he
created. A colorful and exciting portrait of the reign of
Louis XIII, with an aspiring poet-lover for its hero, the play
enjoyed tremendous popularity. The actress Sarah Bernhardt made famous the title roles of *La Princesse lointaine*
(1895; tr *The Princess Faraway*, 1921), *La Samaritaine*
(1897; tr *The Woman of Samaria*, 1921), and *L'Aiglon*
(1900; tr 1927), the story of Napoleon's son.

Rosten, Leo [Calvin] (1908–   )   Polish-born
American humorist, political scientist, and teacher. The
author of scholarly works, film scripts, novels, stories,
essays, and assorted nonfiction, Rosten is best known for
The Education of H*y*m*a*n* K*a*p*l*a*n* (1937), a
series of amusing sketches of a night school for adult immigrants, which he wrote under the name Leonard Q. Ross.
The Joys of Yiddish (1968) and *Hooray for Yiddish: A Book
About English* (1982) are subsequent humorous writings.

Rostova, Natasha   The heroine of Tolstoy's novel
WAR AND PEACE. One of Tolstoy's greatest characterizations, Natasha matures in the course of the book from a
charming but ingenuous girl into a woman of poise and
devotion. Her tragic love affair with Prince Andrey
BOLKONSKY takes much of the joy out of her life, but her
eventual marriage to Pierre BEZUKHOV is a happy one.

Roswitha (c935–c1002)   German poet, dramatist,
and historian. A nun in a Benedictine convent in Saxony,
Roswitha was among the first to adapt classical drama to a
Christian purpose: she wrote six prose comedies revealing
an effective sense of theatre, modeled on the Latin comedies of Terence but devoted to the lives of saints, especially
virgins. She also wrote eight narrative poems on religious
subjects and a poetic chronicle in epic style celebrating the
career of Otto I.

Roth, Henry   See CALL IT SLEEP.

Roth, Philip [Milton] (1933–   )   American
novelist and short-story writer. After the critical and popular success of his novella *Goodbye, Columbus* (1959),
which won The National Book Award, and several short
stories, Roth became established as a leading writer of his
generation. He then followed with the novels *Letting Go*
(1962) and *When She Was Good* (1967). His fame was
secured with the publication of *Portnoy's Complaint*
(1969), an irreverently funny account of a modern man
torn between the repressive, traditional values embodied by
his Jewish mother, his passion for WASP women, and his
desperate desire to be released from the past to create himself as a human being out of his own nothingness. As in his
other novels—*The Breast* (1972), *The Great American
Novel* (1973), and *The Professor of Desire* (1977)—Roth
deals with aspects of contemporary Jewish identity with wit
and irony, pointing to both its grotesque and its poignant
features. His characters are nonheroes who deal, sometimes heroically, sometimes pathetically, with unreconciled feelings of self-love and self-hate; some critics have
accused him of "Jewish anti-Semitism." *My Life as a Man*
(1974), *The Ghost Writer* (1979), *Zuckerman Unbound*
(1981), *The Anatomy Lesson* (1983), *Zuckerman Bound*
(1985), and *The Counterlife* (1986) all deal with the adventures of the Jewish writer Nathan Zuckerman, a typical
Rothian hero. In 1976 Roth became general editor of a
Penguin series, "Writers from the Other Europe," which
publishes writers from behind the Iron Curtain, a project
stimulated by Roth's sense of debt to Franz KAFKA.

Rothko, Mark (1903–1970)   Russian-born American painter. Although he was originally a figurative painter
influenced by Max WEBER, Rothko's later, abstract works
are his most famous. In these, rectangles of subtly layered
colors appear to float in a space of infinite depth, evoking
intimacy and contemplation. He was an important shaping
force in ABSTRACT EXPRESSIONISM.

Rouault, Georges (1871–1958)   French painter
and printmaker. Rouault's paintings, primarily religious
scenes with black outlines and luminous color, recall his
early apprenticeship as a stained-glass maker. Although he
was involved with LES FAUVES, his work was more expressionist, and he rejected the bright, flat colors favored by
CÉZANNE and MATISSE. His chief prominence was as a
printmaker, particularly for his series of fifty-eight plates,
executed in various techniques, comprising his *Miserere et
guerre* (1916–27).

Rouget de Lisle, Claude Joseph   See
MARSEILLAISE, LA.

Rougon-Macquart, Les (1871–1893)   A series of twenty novels by Émile ZOLA. He characterized the work as the natural and social history of a family under the Second Empire. This enormous work, exhaustive in its treatment of events, describes the world of the Rougon-Macquart family in minute detail. The characters are depicted with brutal realism, sparing no detail of their sordid lives. The novels provided Zola with a laboratory in which he could experiment with his new naturalistic theories of fiction. A reformer at heart, Zola uses his naturalistic technique to dramatize the desperate need for social change. The thick volumes vary in their merit, but such works as L'ASSOMMOIR, NANA, LA TERRE, and GERMINAL are widely read. See NATURALISM.

roundel   An eleven-line poem of particular structure. It is a variation of the French RONDEAU attributed to SWINBURNE, who popularized it in his *A Century of Roundels*. The first part of line one is repeated as a refrain in lines four and eleven. The rhyme scheme goes a-b-a-R, b-a-b, a-b-a-R.

Roundheads   English Puritans of the reign of Charles I, and later, especially Cromwell's soldiers. They were so called because they wore their hair cut short, while that of the Royalists or Cavaliers was worn long, covering their shoulders.

Round Table   The table, in ARTHURIAN LEGEND, fabled to have been made by MERLIN at Carduel for Arthur's father, UTHER PENDRAGON. Uther gives it to King Leodegraunce of Camiliard, who in turn gives it to Arthur when Arthur marries his daughter, GUINEVERE. To prevent any jealousy on the score of precedency, it was circular and seated 150 knights, with a place left in it for the GRAIL. The first reference to it is found in Wace's ROMAN DE BRUT, but the fullest legendary details are from Malory's MORTE D'ARTHUR.

Knights of the Round Table   According to Malory, there were 150 knights who had sieges (chairs) at the table. (See SIEGE PERILOUS.) Among the best known of the knights of the Round Table are LAUNCELOT, TRISTRAM, Lamerok, the three bravest; Torre, the first made; GALAHAD, the chaste; GAWAIN, the courteous; GARETH, the big-handed; PALAMEDES, the Saracen or unbaptized; KAY, the rude and boastful; and MORDRED, the traitor.

Rourke, Constance M[ayfield] (1885–1941) American writer. A specialist in American folklore and humor, Rourke is best known for the highly original *American Humor: A Study of the National Character* (1931). Her central interest was to establish the relationship of all aspects of American art to American culture, which was considered in her posthumously published volume *The Roots of American Culture and Other Essays* (1942). Among her other books were *Trumpets of Jubilee* (1927), *Davy Crockett* (1934), *Audubon* (1936), and *Charles Sheeler: Artist in the American Tradition* (1938), all of which were characterized by originality of thought, sound historical research, and a lucid literary style.

Rousseau, Henri [Julien Felix] (also known as Le Douanier, 1844–1910)   French painter. Rousseau was a customs official (hence his nickname) until he retired in 1885 to devote himself fully to painting. Although his direct and intuitive approach (he was completely self-taught) led to his being called a "primitive" painter, his original vision, sophisticated use of color, and philosophical themes suggest a more complex artistic sensibility. He painted portraits, still lifes, and scenes of Paris life, but he is best known for such metaphorical, often surreal representations as *Sleeping Gypsy* (1897), *Snake Charmer* (1907), and *The Dream* (1910), set in exotic, junglelike or desert locations.

Rousseau, Jean Jacques (1712–1778)   Swiss-born French philosopher, author, political theorist, and composer. The son of a watchmaker, Rousseau set out on a life of wandering at the age of sixteen; he went to Turin, where he was converted to Catholicism and served as footman to a wealthy family. He left Turin in 1731 and spent most of the next ten years at Chambéry, Savoy, with Mme de Warens, his benefactress. In 1741 he set out for Paris, became a secretary in the French embassy in Venice, but resigned and returned to Paris, where he became acquainted with the writers of the ENCYCLOPÉDIE, for which he wrote the article on musical notation. During this period he began his liaison with the half-literate servant girl Thérèse Le Vasseur, by whom Rousseau said he had five children, all of whom he put in an orphan asylum. She later became his common-law wife, and accompanied him throughout his life. During his stay in Paris he wrote the ballet *Les Muses galantes* (*The Gallant Muses*) and light opera *Le Devin du village* (*The Village Soothsayer*, 1752). Rousseau became famous overnight after the publication of his first essay, *Discours sur les sciences et les arts* (*Discourses on the Sciences and Arts*, 1750), in which he reacts against the 18th-century view that progress in the sciences and arts increases man's happiness; he argued that, on the contrary, they corrupt mankind. His second philosophical essay, *Discours sur l'origine et les fondements de l'inégalité parmi les hommes* (*Discourse on the Origin and Bases of Inequality among Men*, 1754), celebrates the "natural man" and indicts private property and the political state as causes of inequality and oppression. Rousseau returned to Geneva (1754), became a Protestant again, and returned to Paris. He lived at the Hermitage, a cottage built for him at Montmorency by Mme d'Epinay. He fell in love with Comtesse d'Houdetot, Mme d'Epinay's sister-in-law, who was herself in love with another man. Rousseau's persecution complex began to show itself, for he quarreled with his friends and left the Hermitage to live nearby in the château of the duc de Luxembourg. Here he finished his immensely popular novel JULIE OU LA NOUVELLE HÉLOÏSE while still partially under the influence of his unrequited love affair. Here, too, Rousseau wrote his most famous and influential work, THE SOCIAL CONTRACT, and his ÉMILE. This latter, because of its religious view, incurred the censure of the Sorbonne and the *Parlement*, and Rousseau was banished from France. He escaped to Switzerland, settling finally, at the invitation of David HUME, in England, where he started his CONFESSIONS, written from 1766 to 1770. Suspecting Hume, as he had suspected most of his friends, of a conspiracy against him, Rousseau quarreled with him and left England in 1767. Until 1770 he wandered with Thérèse and her mother from province to province, prey to intermittent delirium, finally returning to Paris, where he lived in a state of poverty and near solitude. Here, protected from prying eyes by Thérèse, he wrote *Rêveries d'un promeneur solitaire* (*Daydreams of a Solitary Stroller*, 1776–78), published in 1782, and a draft for a constitution for Poland, at the request of a Polish count. His only friend and contemporary disciple was BERNARDIN DE SAINT-PIERRE. He died at Ermenonville, near Paris; in 1794 his remains were transferred to the Panthéon in Paris.

Rousseau's closeness to nature, his sensitivity, individualism, rebellion against the established social and political order, his imagination, and his glorification of the emotions make him the father of French ROMANTICISM. William Godwin and the leaders of the French Revolution of 1789 were among those influenced by his political ideas; LAMARTINE and de MUSSET were influenced by his style, as was CHATEAUBRIAND.

Rousseau, Théodore   See BARBIZON SCHOOL.

Roussin, André (1911–   )   French dramatist. Roussin's farcical comedies, such as *Les Oeufs de l'autruche* (1950), *Lorsque l'enfant paraît* (1952), and *La Petite Hutte* (1950; tr *The Little Hut*, 1951), generally revolve about the familiar romantic triangle. A skilled dramatic craftsman, Roussin enlivens his plays with light, witty dialogue.

Rovani, Giuseppe   See SCAPIGLIATURA, LA.

Rover Boys   The heroes of a popular series of books for boys about life in preparatory school and college. The series included more than thirty titles, the first of which appeared in 1899. The books were written by Edward STRATEMEYER under the pen name Arthur M. Winfield. Stratemeyer also created Tom SWIFT.

Rovetta, Gerolamo (1851–1910)   Italian novelist and dramatist. Rovetta is noted for his satirical treatment of the cultural and social values of the Italian bourgeoisie in the period following the RISORGIMENTO. An uncompromising and pessimistic social critic, he was inspired by BALZAC to write a "human comedy" pointing out the sordid economic and political interests that underlie the most praiseworthy ideals. His skill as a narrator is exceptional; his descriptions are precisely realistic; his language synthesizes dialect (usually Milanese) and colloquial modes of expression; his tone is at once satirical and cynical.

Rovetta's forte is his psychological analysis of character types. For example, Pompeo Barbarò, the protagonist of *Le lagrime del prossimo* (1887), is a pitiless moneylender and shrewd investor whose rapid rise to social and financial prominence is sparked by a remark he heard as a poor young man, that the real gentleman is one who knows how to steal. Among Rovetta's numerous plays might be cited *La trilogia di Dorina* (1889), *I disonesti* (1892), *La realtà* (1895), *Romanticismo* (1903), and *Re burlone* (1905).

Rowe, Nicholas (1674–1718)   English poet and dramatist. Rowe is best known for such tragedies as *Jane Shore* (1714), *The Fair Penitent* (1703), *Tamerlane* (1701), and *Lady Jane Grey* (1715). He also edited Shakespeare's plays and was POET LAUREATE (1715–18).

Rowlandson, Mary (1635?–1678)   American pioneer and author of the first Indian-captivity narrative. The wife of a minister, Rowlandson was taken captive with her six-year-old daughter in 1675 during King Philip's War, after an Indian attack on Lancaster, Massachusetts. Her account of the event is *The Sovereignty and Goodness of God . . . Being a Narrative of the Captivity and Restauration of Mrs. Mary Rowlandson* (1682). One of the most popular American prose works of the 17th century, reprinted many times since, it gives a hair-raising picture of frontier perils.

Rowlandson, Thomas (1756–1827)   English caricaturist. Rowlandson is especially well known for his series of plates entitled *Tours of Dr. Syntax* (1812, 1820, 1821). He also illustrated books by SMOLLETT, GOLDSMITH, STERNE, and others.

Rowley, William (c1585–c1637)   English dramatist, best known for his collaboration with Thomas MIDDLETON on THE CHANGELING. Rowley's own plays include *All's Lost by Lust* (1622) and *A Match at Midnight* (1633). He also collaborated with John FORD, Philip MASSINGER, John FLETCHER, John WEBSTER, and possibly, on a play now lost, with SHAKESPEARE.

Rowse, A[lfred] L[eslie] (1903–   )   English literary historian, critic, and poet. One of England's most prominent Elizabethan scholars, Rowse is noted for his careful research and a highly readable style that won broad popular success for such books as *The Use of History* (1946; rev 1963), *The Elizabethan Age* (3 vols, 1950–1972), and *William Shakespeare: A Biography* (1963). His more than fifty books include studies of Swift, Arnold, and Milton, numerous volumes of poetry, and a series of memoirs. It is for his studies of Shakespeare, however—*Shakespeare the Man* (1973), *Shakespeare the Elizabethan* (1977), *The Annotated Shakespeare* (3 vols, 1978)—that he is best known. It is this subject, however, that embroiled him in the thickest controversies of a controversial career—one in which he has been criticized for arrogance, for highly personal interpretations of history and literature, and occasionally for a somewhat cavalier attitude to the rules of traditional historical scholarship. In particular, argument has raged around the identity of the person to whom Shakespeare's sonnets are addressed. Among his other well-known works on Shakespeare are *Prefaces to Shakespeare's Plays* and *Shakespeare's Self-Portrait*, which were both published in 1984. *Glimpses of the Great*, a collection of essays, was published in 1985.

Roxane The wicked sultana in Jean Racine's tragedy BAJAZET. The heroine of Rostand's CYRANO DE BERGERAC is also named Roxane.

Roy, Gabrielle (1909–1983) Canadian novelist, writing in French. Roy's greatest success was her first novel, *Bonheur d'occasion* (1945; tr *The Tin Flute*, 1947), a compassionate story of a Montreal slum family at the outbreak of World War II. Her pioneer childhood in the Manitoba plains was the basis for many of her later stories and novels.

Royal Society of London for Improving Natural Knowledge, The An English scientific academy, founded in 1660 for the purpose of studying the whole field of knowledge and still in existence. Abraham COWLEY and the chemist Robert BOYLE had presented plans for such an organization, and among its members were included some of the leading literary, diplomatic, and scientific figures of the day. Samuel PEPYS, who was admitted to the society in 1665 and later became its president, has a number of references to its meetings and its experiments in his famous diary. Isaac NEWTON was president from 1703 to 1727, and John WINTHROP and Cotton and Increase MATHER were leaders of a group of New England correspondents of the Royal Society. Thomas Sprat, bishop of Rochester, was historian of the organization, which sought, among other aims, to improve the English prose style of the time, making it simpler, clearer, and more suited to the needs of scientific exposition than the usual literary style then current.

The Royal Society was satirized in numerous contemporary works, including Swift's GULLIVER'S TRAVELS.

Royce, Josiah (1855–1916) American philosopher, teacher, and essayist. *The Religious Aspect of Philosophy* (1885) established Royce's famous theory of the Absolute. He held that if one admits the presence of evil in the world, it then necessarily follows that there is also an absolute principle of Truth, an all-knowing Mind or Universal Thought. Royce, the leader of the post-Kantian idealistic school in the U.S., also wrote *The Spirit of Modern Philosophy* (1892), *The Concept of God* (1897), *The Problem of Christianity* (1913), *Lectures on Modern Idealism* (1919), and other volumes.

Rozanov, Vasily Vasilyevich (1856–1919) Russian writer, critic, and philosopher. Rozanov is best known for his views on the central place that sexuality holds in man's nature. His views were expressed in the collections of aphorisms entitled *Uyedinyonnoye* (1911; tr *Solitaria*, 1927) and *Opavshiye listya* (1913–15; tr *Fallen Leaves, Bundle One*, 1929). An avid admirer of DOSTOYEVSKY,

Rozanov published a penetrating study of the novelist, *Legenda o velikom inkvisitore F. M. Dostoyevskogo* (1894; tr *Dostoyevsky and the Legend of the Grand Inquisitor*, 1972), in which he was the first to note the importance of Dostoyevsky's short work, NOTES FROM UNDERGROUND. Rozanov married Polina Suslova, the former mistress of Dostoyevsky.

Różewicz, Tadeusz (1921–   ) Polish poet and playwright. A representative of the generation that came to maturity during and immediately after World War II, Różewicz expresses the anxieties created by the war and its aftermath in terse, simple, and almost prosaic poems built around the questions of survival and the loss of innocence (*The Survivor and Other Poems*, 1976). His dramas, often grotesque and seemingly absurd, render the moral problems of the postwar era with similar intensity and tension, as in the English-language collection *The Card Index and Other Plays* (1969).

Rubáiyát of Omar Khayyám (early 11th century) A collection of epigrammatic quatrains by OMAR KHAYYÁM, the title of which comes from Arabic *rubai*, "quatrain." Of the twelve hundred quatrains attributed to Omar, experts have authenticated fewer than five hundred. The poems are more widely known in English than in the original Persian, primarily through the brilliant translation by Edward FITZGERALD. FitzGerald selected 101 quatrains, arranged them with a thematic coherence, and published them in 1859. In FitzGerald's rendering, the *Rubáiyát* sings of the fact that because man has no understanding of an afterlife, he must allow his senses the fullest possible appreciation of life on earth. Although FitzGerald's translation remains true to the spirit of the original, it was regarded as a masterpiece of English poetry in its own right. The sensual grace of the FitzGerald *Rubáiyát* helped establish the mood of *fin de siècle* poetry in England.

Rubens, Peter Paul (1577–1640) Flemish painter. Born in Westphalia and educated in Antwerp, Rubens is considered the greatest of the northern BAROQUE painters. Revered as an unsurpassed draftsman, he was known in his day not only as a painter but also as a scholar, businessman, and diplomat. From 1600 to 1608, he worked in Italy and during this time studied and copied the works of MICHELANGELO, TITIAN, CARAVAGGIO, and other Renaissance painters. From this, and from his knowledge of Greek and Roman antiquity, came much of the inspiration for future paintings, such as *The Raising of the Cross* (1611). In Antwerp, he operated with a large studio of assistants, including Anthony VAN DYCK, thus accounting for his prodigious output. After the death of his first wife, when he was fifty-three years old, he married sixteen-year-old Helen Fourment, who subsequently became his best-known model. She appeared in many works depicting the artist's family, such as *Helen Fourment and Her Children* (1636), but also represented saints, goddesses, and angels in many of his other works. His second marriage marked also the development of a new serenity and lyricism in his style and a reintroduction of landscape painting into his repertoire, exemplified in *Landscape with the Castle of Steen* (1636).

Rubicon A small river separating ancient Italy from Cisalpine Gaul, the province allocated to Julius CAESAR in the First TRIUMVIRATE. Fearing Caesar's growing power in Gaul, POMPEY and the senate ordered Caesar to return to Rome without his army. When, in defiance of this order, Caesar crossed the Rubicon with his army (49 BC), he passed beyond the limits of his province, thereby becoming an invader of Italy and precipitating civil war. Hence, "to cross the Rubicon" is to take an irrevocable step.

Rückert, Friedrich (1788–1866) German poet, known especially for his pioneering efforts in popularizing Oriental poetic forms and philosophical ideas in Germany. Rückert's works include *Geharnischte Sonette* (*Harnessed Sonnets*, 1814), a collection treating political themes of the day; a collection of *Kindertotenlieder* (*Songs on Children's Deaths*, 1872), set to music by MAHLER; and *Die Weisheit des Brahmanen* (*The Wisdom of the Brahman*, 1836) and collected translations from Oriental literature.

Rudin (1856) A novel by Ivan TURGENEV. It traces the ineffectual career of the hero, Dmitry Nikolayevich Rudin. Typifying the philosophically inclined idealists whom Turgenev had encountered in his student days in Berlin, Rudin impresses almost everyone with his brilliant and high-minded talk. The hero does well when talking or dreaming, but decisive action is not in his line. The demands of a love offered him by Natalya Alekseyevna frighten him away. Rudin eventually does try to act and loses his life for it. During the 1848 revolt in Paris, he is shot while standing on top of a barricade, futilely waving a sword and trying to rally the retreating insurgents. Rudin has been characterized as one of the SUPERFLUOUS MEN in Russian literature, a man unable to find a suitable cause to serve or a proper outlet for his energies. Another view is that his nature would make him unable to act in any conditions.

Rudkin, David (1936–   ) English playwright. Rudkin weaves strands of his evangelical Christian upbringing, his classical education, and his mixed Anglo-Irish heritage throughout his work. His plays mix naturalistic speech with lush imagery and sardonic humor; his characterization often combines realistic portraiture with figures from religious mythology and science fiction. His first play, *Afore Night Come* (1962), about the gruesome ritual murder of an Irish vagrant by Midlands fruit pickers, established his reputation as a dramatist of power and subtlety. Subsequent plays include *The Sons of Light* (1966), *The Filth Hunt* (1972), and *Ashes* (1972), a painful study of a childless couple. He has also written numerous highly acclaimed plays for television.

Rudra (perhaps fr Sans, *rud-*, "to weep," *-dra*, "to run") In Hindu mythology, the father of tempest gods and an archer-god whose arrows brought disease. Rudra was also the protector of curative herbs, and thus could bestow favors upon those who pleased him.

Rugby A public school in England, founded in 1567. Its headmaster from 1828 to 1842 was Thomas Arnold, the father of Matthew ARNOLD. The book *Tom Brown's Schooldays* (1857) by Thomas HUGHES concerns the school in the 19th century. A poem by Matthew Arnold is called "Rugby Chapel." The game of Rugby football originated at this school.

Ruggiero A leading figure in Carolingian legends and in Matteo Maria Boiardo's ORLANDO INNAMORATO and Lodovico Ariosto's ORLANDO FURIOSO. Ruggiero is the brother of Marfisa (Marphisa) and the ward of the magician Atlante (Atlantes). After the slaying of his mother, he was nursed by a lioness. From Atlante he receives an enchanted sword of such dazzling splendor that it numbs all who look upon it, but he casts it into a well because he regards it as unchivalrous. At first he fights with the pagan forces of Agramante, the African king, against Charlemagne and the Christian knights. Later, having met and fallen in love with the warrior maiden Bradamante (Bradamant), he becomes converted to Christianity and marries her. Ariosto's poem ends with their marriage feast and his election to the crown of Bulgaria. From their union comes the house of Este, the princely patrons of both poets at the court of Ferrara.

In Torquato Tasso's GERUSALEMME LIBERATA, Ruggiero is a Norman, son of Roberto Guiscardo. A member of the crusading army led by Goffredo (Godfrey) against the Saracens, he is killed by Tisaphernes in the final canto.

Ruggles of Red Gap See WILSON, HARRY LEON.

Ruisdael, Jacob van (c1629–1682) Dutch painter. Born in Haarlem, the son of a painter and framemaker, Ruisdael soon established himself independently as one of the greatest Dutch landscapists. His paintings are characterized by swirling clouds and waterfalls, and even the more peaceful canvases, such as the famous *Windmill at Wijk Bij Duurstede* (c1670), are energized by dramatic lighting. His best-known work, *The Jewish Cemetery* (c1655), displays all these elements, as well as a sense of brooding that is common to much of his work.

Ruiz, Juan (also known as the archpriest or arcipreste of Hita, c1283–?1350) Spanish poet. Little is known about the life of the archpriest, considered the greatest poet of medieval Spain, except what Ruiz himself relates in his realistic and humorous autobiography in verse, *El libro de buen amor*, which may have been composed while he was in prison. His purpose, the poet wrote, undoubtedly with tongue in cheek, was to warn readers of the pitfalls of *loco amor*, or foolish love. The contents of the work are varied; included are hymns to the Virgin and animal apologues as well as picaresque accounts of the author's love affairs and a description of a battle between Lord Flesh and Lady

Lent, in which the latter is vanquished. Among the outstanding characters is the old hag Trotaconventos.

Rukeyser, Muriel (1913–1980) American poet, biographer, and fiction writer. Rukeyser's political activism in the 1930s led to her arrest during the Scottsboro trial in Alabama. In the title poem of her first volume of verse, *Theory of Flight* (1935), she used the airplane as a symbol of man's longing for freedom, a theme that runs throughout her work. In *U.S.1* (1938) the poet tested the influences of other poets, particularly Hart CRANE and W. H. AUDEN, in her search for a more personal statement. The poems in her mature works *Beast in View* (1944) and *The Green Wave* (1948) are marked by intense imagery and a fluid line. The two editions of her collected works, *Waterlily Fire: Poems 1932–1962* (1962) and *The Collected Poems* (1978), offer the full range of her social commitment and mystical faith. The title poem of *The Gates* (1976) concerns her efforts on behalf of an imprisoned Korean poet, revealing again that for Rukeyser the concerns of poetry are inseparable from the concerns of life.

Rulfo, Juan (1918–1986) Mexican novelist and short-story writer. In a quiet, unpretentious prose, rough with the common expressions of the people, Rulfo tells the stories of Mexico's downtrodden, landless, and forgotten. His stories are set in the poverty-scarred region of Jalisco, where he was born. His reputation rests primarily, and firmly, on his one novel, *Pedro Páramo* (1955; tr 1959). He is also known for *El llano en llamas* (1953; tr *The Burning Plain and Other Stories*, 1967). Both works present vivid pictures of the desolate life of the rural poor.

Rumpelstiltskin A deformed dwarf in German folktale. A king tells a miller's daughter he will marry her if she can really spin straw into gold. Helpless, she accepts the dwarf's offer to do it in exchange for her first child. Once queen, she grieves so bitterly when the child is born that the dwarf agrees to relent if in three days she can guess his name, which no one knows. On the third day he is so sure he will win the child that he is overheard muttering his name triumphantly to himself. When he hears his name from the queen, he destroys himself in his rage at losing.

Rump Parliament In English history, a derisive nickname given to the fragment of the LONG PARLIAMENT that remained after Pride's Purge (1648). The sixty to seventy members of the Rump voted for the execution of Charles I.

Runciman, Sir Steven [James Cochran Stevenson] (1903–   ) English historian. A scholar of Byzantine history, Runciman is known for his lucid prose style and for his ability to write clearly about even the most chaotic historical subjects. His *History of the Crusades* (3 vols, 1951–54) is widely accepted as the definitive work on the subject. Other important works are *The Fall of Constantinople* (1965), *The Great Church in Captivity* (1968), *The Last Byzantine Renaissance* (1970), *Byzantine Style*

and Civilization (1975), and *Mistra: Byzantine Capital of the Peloponnese* (1980).

Runeberg, Johan Ludvig (1804–1877) Finnish poet. Though he wrote in the Swedish language, Runeberg was a leader of the Finnish nationalist literary movement of the 19th century. In addition to lyric poems and philological works, he wrote *The Elk Hunters* (1832), an epic of Finnish rural life; *King Fjalar* (1844), a Norse epic; and *Tales of Ensign Stål* (1848, 1860), a collection of prose and verse glorifying the Finnish soldiers of the 1808–9 Russo-Finnish war. The *Tales* were instrumental in accelerating Finland's awareness of herself as a nation separate from Sweden and Russia, and they contain the poem "Vårt Land" ("Our Land"), which has become Finland's national anthem.

runes Letters in various alphabets used by Teutonic peoples, especially in Scandinavia and the British Isles from the 2nd century to the 12th. The runic alphabets were adaptations of a Greek alphabet, simplified for facility in carving inscriptions on wood, stone, and metal. Each rune is the initial letter of its name (as the *m* letter is called *man*), and the name is also a common word (*man, horse, thorn, sun*); thus the runes were used as characters in ordinary spelling, but also as idea-symbols in composing magical incantations or charms.

Runnymede An island (Charter Island) in the Thames in Surrey, where King JOHN, on June 19, 1215, was forced to sign the MAGNA CARTA. Cf. KIPLING's poem "The Reeds of Runnymede." Some say the document was signed in the meadow on the south side of the Thames.

Runyon, [Alfred] Damon (1884–1946) American journalist and short-story writer. Runyon is famous for stories about such colorful Broadway characters as the Lemon Drop Kid and Harry the Horse. His style, so individual that it is called Runyonese, relies on Broadway slang, outrageous metaphors, and constant use of the present tense. Among his books are *Guys and Dolls* (1932) and *Blue Plate Special* (1934). He wrote only one play, *A Slight Case of Murder* (1935), with Howard LINDSAY; but many of his stories were made into successful film and stage productions.

Ruritania An imaginary Central European kingdom. It is the locale of THE PRISONER OF ZENDA and *Rupert of Hentzau* (1898) by Anthony Hope Hawkins and has become a synonym for any extravagantly romantic, highly colored country.

Rushdie, [Ahmed] Salman (1947–   ) Indian novelist and critic who lives in England. Rushdie's second novel, *Midnight's Children* (1981), was a resounding success and won him much critical acclaim and the British Booker McConnell Prize for fiction. Critics hailed the novel as the voice of contemporary India, rid of the influences of British classicists such as Kipling. The novel is about Shiva and Saleem, two of the 1,001 babies born in the hour following independence at midnight on August

15, 1947. It is notable as much for its portrayal of contemporary politics in India as for the brilliance of its style and insights into human nature and mind. *Grimus* (1975), Rushdie's first novel, tells the story of an immortal American Indian who undertakes an odyssey to find life's meaning; a fantasy, hard to classify, it has been called an engrossing work of science fiction by a number of critics. *Shame* (1983), which examines the concepts of honor and shame in an unnamed country that strongly resembles Pakistan, and whose central characters reflect the careers and regimes of Bhutto and General Zia, was almost as well received as its predecessor and has been compared to *Candide, Gulliver's Travels,* and *Tristram Shandy. The Jaguar Smile* (1987) concerns the revolution in Nicaragua.

Ruskin, John (1819–1900) English writer and critic. The son of a wealthy merchant, Ruskin benefited from extensive travel and private drawing lessons during his youth. In the first volume of MODERN PAINTERS he included a spirited defense of the then much-misunderstood landscape painter John Turner, attracting attention with his clear style and his novel approach to art criticism. The four later volumes of this series, along with *The Seven Lamps of Architecture* (1849) and *The Stones of Venice* (3 vols, 1851–53), a study of the development of Byzantine and Gothic architecture in Venice and of the city's moral, vital, and artistic decline, established Ruskin as a leading critic and stylist. Several of his lectures on art were published in *Lectures on Art* (1870), *Aratra Pentelici* (1871), *The Eagle's Nest* (1871), *Ariadne Florentina* (1873–76), *Val d'Arno* (1874), and *Lectures on Landscape* (1898). He developed and expressed his philosophy of art in these and other works, including *St. Mark's Rest: The History of Venice* (1877–84), *Morning in Florence* (1875–77), and *The Bible of Amiens* (1880–85). Believing that the "greatest picture" was the one that conveyed "to the mind of the spectator the greatest number of the greatest ideas" and classifying the greatest ideas in the categories of Power, Imitation, Truth, Beauty, and Relation, Ruskin advocated a basically religious aesthetic, in which moral perception of beauty was superior to the merely sensuous and beauty itself revealed the attributes of God. His conviction that faith, morality, education, and good social conditions were prerequisites to the creation of good art led him to take up the cause of social and economic reform in such works as *The Political Economy of the Arts* (1857), *Unto This Last* (1862), *Essays on Political Economy* (1862–63), the widely read *Sesame and Lilies* (1865), and *Fors Clavigera: Letters to the Workmen and Laborers of Great Britain* (1885–89). Ruskin's views deeply influenced the British socialist movement, just as his art history and criticism brought about the revival of interest in Gothic architecture. A scholar of enormously varied interests, he wrote works on botany, *Proserpina* (1875–86); ornithology, *Love's Meinie* (1873–78); and geology, *Deucalion* (1875–83); and an unfinished autobiography, *Praeterita* (1885–89).

Ruskin's personal life was less successful. His boyhood had been mother-dominated, and when in 1848 he married the beautiful Euphemia Gray, he was unable to consummate the union. Annulment followed in 1854, and Effie married John Everett MILLAIS, the Pre-Raphaelite painter. Ruskin's emotional and mental instability increased with age and from 1878 on he suffered from episodes of insanity.

Russell, Bertrand [Arthur William] (3rd Earl Russell, 1872–1970) English philosopher, mathematician, and iconoclastic social reformer. Russell's books on mathematics, philosophy, and logic include *Principia Mathematica* (1910–13), with A. N. WHITEHEAD as coauthor, which became a classic; *Introduction to Mathematical Philosophy* (1919); *The Analysis of Mind* (1921); and *An Inquiry into Meaning and Truth* (1940). He wrote a number of essays on philosophic and scientific problems in a semipopularizing vein; among these are *The ABC of Relativity* (1925), *Religion and Science* (1935), and *A History of Western Philosophy* (1945). He also wrote numerous books expressing his unorthodox views on war, politics, sociology, and religion, and on such domestic matters as education, sexual relations, and marriage. Russell's writing is remarkable for its clarity and ease. In 1944 he was awarded the British Order of Merit, and in 1950 the NOBEL PRIZE in Literature. Such works as *Common Sense and Nuclear Warfare* (1959), *Has Man a Future?* (1962), and *Unarmed Victory* (1963) show the concern of a lifelong pacifist with the threat of a nuclear Armageddon.

Intent on putting his beliefs into practice, articulate, and supremely self-confident, Russell was a center of controversy for most of his ninety-eight years. Toward the end of his life, internationally acclaimed as an important 20th-century thinker, he had become more notorious than ever. During World War I, he was fined and imprisoned in England for his pacifist views. An experimental school, Beacon Hill, that he ran with his wife, Dora Russell, from 1927 to 1932 was severely criticized. An appointment to teach at the City College of New York was withdrawn because it was felt that his teachings were immoral. When over ninety years old, he founded the Committee of 100 in England, an influential militant group which campaigned, through civil disobedience, for nuclear disarmament and international morality. Russell was married four times; one of his books is entitled *Is Modern Marriage a Failure?* (1930). His *Autobiography* appeared in three volumes (1967–69).

Russell, George William See A. E.

Russell, Sir William Howard (1820–1907) English journalist, one of the first and best-known war correspondents, reporter for the London *Times* in the Crimean, American Civil, and Franco-German wars. In the Crimean War, Russell coined the phrase "the thin red line," applied to British Infantry at Balaclava. His *The War from the Landing at Gallipoli* (1855–56), about the Crimean

War, and *My Diary North and South* (1862), about the Civil War, are of particular interest.

Russian Primary Chronicle, The (Nachalnaya letopis)   Historical annals of medieval Russia, also known as *Povest vremennykh let* (*The Tale of Bygone Years*), covering events from 852 to the early 12th century. The chronicle contains descriptions of historical occurrences, legends, and tales from folk tradition. Kiev was the center of the Russian nation when these annals were compiled, and their authorship was for years attributed to Nestor, a monk in a Kiev monastery. Nestor's authorship is now doubted by most scholars. Chronicles also survive from other cities, such as Tver, Pskov, and Novgorod.

Russian Revolution   The events that began with the abdication of Tsar NICHOLAS II in the spring of 1917 and ended with the seizure of power by the BOLSHEVIKS in November 1917. An earlier, unsuccessful attempt at revolution had taken place in 1905, when a series of strikes had obliged the tsarist regime to promise full civil rights to the people and the establishment of Russia's first legislative body, the DUMA. After the storm had blown over, however, the government managed to avoid fulfilling most of its promises.

Early in 1917 military defeats by the Germans and internal chaos led to a series of strikes and mutinies among workers and soldiers, particularly in the capital of St. Petersburg. After the Tsar abdicated in March 1917, power was divided between a provisional government under Prince Lvov, set up by a committee of the Duma and the Soviet (council) of workers' deputies in St. Petersburg. Soviets also existed in Moscow and other cities. Lvov's government was replaced in July by a coalition government under Kerensky, which was repeatedly attacked by the Bolsheviks. LENIN had returned from exile to Russia in April and immediately began agitation for the overthrow of the provisional government and the seizure of power by the Bolsheviks. In September the Bolsheviks won majorities in both the St. Petersburg and Moscow Soviets. Some Bolshevik leaders wanted to content themselves with this electoral gain, but Lenin's urging for a coup d'état prevailed. Shortly before the convening of a constituent assembly in November, the Bolsheviks seized power. The new regime, under Lenin, signed a peace treaty with Germany in March 1918 and turned to defend itself against its enemies, known as the Whites, who had massed armed forces in the Volga region, the south, and in western Siberia. The ensuing civil war raged until late 1920, when the last remnants of the White army under General Wrangel were forced from the Crimea.

The outstanding literary work based directly on the revolution is Aleksandr Blok's long poem THE TWELVE. Many works have been devoted to the civil war, the most notable being those of Mikhail SHOLOKHOV, Isaak BABEL, Aleksandr FADAYEV, Boris PILNYAK, and Vsevolod IVANOV.

Ruth   The Moabite heroine of the OLD TESTAMENT book that bears her name. After the death of her husband, Ruth loyally refused to desert Naomi, his Hebrew mother: "Entreat me not to leave thee, or to return from following after thee; whither thou goest, I will go; and where thou lodgest, I will lodge; thy people shall be my people, and thy God my God" (Ruth 1:16). After accompanying Naomi to Bethlehem, Ruth became a gleaner in the fields of the wealthy Boaz, whom she married.

Ruysbroeck, Jan van (1293–1381)   A Flemish mystic, called the Ecstatic Doctor. Ruysbroeck wrote mystical works in Flemish and Latin.

Ryder, Albert Pinkham (1847–1917)   American painter. Ryder lived as a recluse in New York City, working for years on glowing compositions in which he developed unerring patterns and rhythms. His subjects were drawn from the depths of his imagination and from the works of SHAKESPEARE, CHAUCER, and the BIBLE. His moonlit seas and night scenes evoke mystery and power, and have the distinction of having been labored over more extensively than the works of almost any other American artist.

Ryle, Gilbert (1900–1976)   English philosopher. Ryle was Waynefleet Professor of Metaphysical Philosophy at Oxford (1945–68) and editor of the philosophical review *Mind* (1947–71). He was a leading figure in the British school of linguistic philosophy. In "Systematically Misleading Expressions" (1931), a highly influential article, and in other essays appearing in *Mind*, he laid the foundation for his system of philosophy, which saw parallels and distinctions between rules of grammar, word usage, and logic. *The Concept of Mind* (1949), which challenges the Cartesian distinction between mind and body, became a classic in modern philosophy. His *Collected Papers*, two volumes including *Critical Essays* and *Collected Essays, 1929–1968*, appeared in 1971.

S

Saarinen, Eero (1910–1961)   Finnish-born American architect. Spectacular shapes, such as the graceful winglike curves of the Trans World Airline terminal at New York's Kennedy Airport (1962), dominate the work of this architect and designer. With Charles Eames (1907–78) in 1940, Saarinen designed classic furniture, including the famous molded-plywood "Eames chair." His best-known other project was the parabolic Gateway, or Jefferson Memorial Arch, in St. Louis, Missouri (1967).

Sábato, Ernesto (1911–   )   Argentinian novelist and essayist. After his initial encounter with SURREALISM, in Paris in the 1930s, Sábato abandoned his career as a physics professor and turned to writing. His first book, *Uno y el universo* (1945)—along with subsequent essays and criticism like *Heterodoxia* (1953) and *El escritor y sus fantasmas* (1963)—addresses complex existential and metaphysical concerns which are echoed in his fiction. His novels *El túnel* (1948; tr *The Outsider*, 1950), the confession of a convicted murderer, *Sobre heroes y tumbas* (1961; tr *On Heroes and Tombs*, 1981), an existential tragedy of incest, fire, and death, and *Abaddón, el exterminador* (1974) portray man as an alienated creature, obsessed with and plagued by guilt. In 1984, Sábato was awarded the Spanish-speaking world's highest literary accolade, the Cervantes Prize in Literature.

Sabbatical year   Originally, one year in seven when the ancient Jews allowed all their land to lie fallow for twelve months. The practice was based on a law found in the books of EXODUS, LEVITICUS, and DEUTERONOMY. The phrase now applies to a year's furlough or vacation taken by a missionary or academician.

Sabines   An ancient Italian people, subjugated by the Romans about 290 BC. The rape of the Sabine women, an important incident in the legendary history of Rome, was instigated by ROMULUS who needed wives for his men and solved the problem by telling them to help themselves to Sabine virgins after he had lured the male population away.

Sabrina   Latin name of the river Severn, named from the daughter of Estrildis and Locrine in Geoffrey of Monmouth's HISTORY OF THE KINGS OF BRITAIN. Sabrina and her mother are drowned in the river Severn by Gwendolen. In John Milton's COMUS, Sabrina is a nymph of the Severn.

Sacajawea (1787?–1812)   American Indian woman, probably of the Snake or Shoshone tribe. She served as a guide and interpreter for the Lewis and Clark Expedition (1805), during which she bore a son to a Canadian trapper whom she had married by Indian rites.

Sacchetti, Franco (c1330–1400)   Italian poet and prose writer. Born in Dalmatia of Florentine parents, Sacchetti spent most of his life in Florence as a public official. His writings include sonnets, *canzoni*, *sestine*, and *ballate*, as well as the then less familiar madrigals, *cacce*, and *frottole*. Many of these varied lyrics were intended for musical setting, since he composed himself and was associated with musicians writing in the *ars nova* style. His most famous poem is the pastoral *ballata* beginning "O vaghe montanine pasturelle" ("O lovely mountain shepherdesses"). In prose, his masterpiece is the *Libro delle trecentonovelle* (*Book of Three Hundred Tales*), a collection of novelle, of which some two hundred pieces are extant. Unlike the *Decameron*, there is no structure or framing story to knit the tales together.

Sacco-Vanzetti case   A celebrated murder trial in May–July 1921 in which two Italian anarchists, Nicola Sacco and Bartolomeo Vanzetti, were convicted and condemned to death for the murder of a paymaster and a guard and the theft of over $15,000 at a shoe factory in South Braintree, Massachusetts, on April 15, 1920. Both men denied any knowledge of the crime, and it was widely believed that they had been convicted largely because of their radical political views. The case aroused intense public interest, both in the U.S. and abroad, and defense committees succeeded in obtaining many stays of execution. In July 1927, Governor Fuller of Massachusetts appointed a committee headed by President Lowell of Harvard to review the case; it upheld the original verdict, and Sacco and Vanzetti were executed the following month.

The case inspired numerous literary works, including Edna St. Vincent MILLAY's poem "Justice Denied in Massachusetts" (1927), Upton SINCLAIR's novel *Boston* (1928), and two plays by Maxwell ANDERSON, *Gods of the Lightning* (1928) and *Winterset* (1935). During their imprisonment, the two accused men wrote hundreds of letters which possess considerable literary power. Vanzetti's final appeal has become a classic. A collection of the *Letters of Sacco and Vanzetti* appeared in 1928.

On the fiftieth anniversary of their execution, the governor of Massachusetts issued a proclamation declaring that the Sacco-Vanzetti trial was unfair and that any stigma or disgrace should be removed from the names of their families and descendants. In the same year Katherine Anne PORTER published her recollections of the trial in *Never-Ending Wrong* (1977).

Sacher-Masoch, Leopold von (1836–1895)
Austrian novelist whose name is the source of the word MASOCHISM. This abnormality is portrayed in many of Sacher-Masoch's works, such as *Das Vermächtnis Kains* (*The Legacy of Cain*, 1870–77) and *Falscher Hemelion* (*False Ermine*, 1873).

Sachs, Hans (1494–1576)
German poet and dramatist, by trade a shoemaker, most skillful and famous of the MEISTERSINGERS. In addition to his more than four thousand mastersongs, Sachs wrote many poems on moral and religious subjects, the most famous being *Die Wittenbergisch Nachtigall* (*The Nightingale of Wittenberg*, 1523), an allegory in praise of Martin LUTHER, and an *Epitaphium* (1546) on Luther's death. His enormous dramatic production includes tragedies on classical, biblical, and medieval subjects, dialogues in defense of Protestantism, and many Shrovetide-plays, a genre which he carried to its highest perfection. He appears as a leading character in Richard WAGNER's opera *Die Meistersinger von Nürnberg* (1868).

Sachs, Nelly (1891–1970)
German-born poet and playwright. Born in Berlin as the only child of upper-middle-class Jewish parents, Sachs was well schooled in the arts from an early age. Her first book, *Legenden und Erzählungen* (*Legends and Stories*, 1921), went largely unnoticed. She lived under HITLER's reign of terror until 1940, when she fled with her mother to Sweden, aided by the intervention of Selma LAGERLÖF, with whom Sachs had corresponded for years. The rest of her family perished in Nazi concentration camps. From that time on, her poetry developed a depth of feeling and expression that established her as the leading poetic voice lamenting the fate of the Jewish people. The unrhymed poems in her first cycle after World War II, *In den Wohnungen des Todes* (*In the Dwellings of Death*, 1947), catalogued the horrors of the Holocaust. In subsequent volumes, her poems reflect a deepening religious sense and expanded concern with the mysteries of universal human suffering. These collections include *Und niemand weiß weiter* (*And No One Knows Where to Go*, 1957), *Flucht und Verwandlung* (*Flight and Metamorphosis*, 1959), and *Fahrt ins staublose* (*Journey into a Dustless Room*, 1961). She was awarded the NOBEL PRIZE in Literature with S. Y. AGNON in 1966. Works in English translation include *O the Chimneys* (1967) and *The Seeker and Other Poems* (1970).

Sackville, Thomas (1st earl of Dorset and Baron Buckhurst, 1536–1608)
English poet and statesman. Sackville is known for his authorship (with Thomas Norton) of *The Tragedy of* GORBODUC, an important work in the history of English drama; and especially for his *Induction* to the 1563 edition of THE MIRROR FOR MAGISTRATES. The latter piece is the most famous part of the *Mirror*, and one of the most outstanding poems written in England between the death of Chaucer and the publication of Spenser's *Shepheardes Calender* (1579). The *Induction* is patterned after the classical Descent into Hades; in it the poet meets the personification of Sorrow, who leads him to Hell and shows him the ghosts of men ruined by their ambition. The *Induction* then introduces Sackville's *Complaint* of Henry, duke of Buckingham.

In later life, Sackville devoted himself to a public career, serving variously as a Member of Parliament, ambassador, member of the Privy Council, Lord Treasurer, and Chancellor of Oxford University.

Sackville-West, Victoria [Mary] (1892–1962)
English novelist, poet, and critic. Sackville-West's best-remembered novels are *The Edwardians* (1930), a sensitive portrait of an era, and *All Passion Spent* (1931), an account of an unusual marriage and aging. She is particularly noted for her feeling for English history and the English countryside. This is notable in her long poem *The Land* (1926) and the verse in *The Garden* (1946). She was a member of an old aristocratic family whose ancestral home was Knole Castle, originally a gift from Queen Elizabeth I to her forebear, Thomas SACKVILLE. ORLANDO, by Virginia Woolf, a close friend, was said to be a portrait of Sackville-West and of Knole. She herself wrote *Knole and the Sackvilles* (1922), a family history. Her other books include *The Eagle and the Dove* (1943), a biographical study of St. Teresa of Avila and St. Thérèse of Lisieux, and *The Easter Party* (1953). She married Nigel NICOLSON. Their close but unconventional relationship is described in the memoir *Portrait of a Marriage* (1973), by their son, Nigel NICOLSON.

sacrament (fr Lat, *sacrare*, "to consecrate")
Originally, a military oath taken by Roman soldiers not to desert their standard, turn their back on the enemy, or abandon their general. The early Christians used the word to signify a "sacred mystery" and applied it to any number of ritual church practices. St. AUGUSTINE defined a sacrament as "the visible form of an invisible grace." The Roman Catholic Church set the number of sacraments at seven: BAP-

TISM, Penance (Confession), the EUCHARIST (Lord's Supper), Confirmation, Holy Orders, Matrimony, and Extreme Unction. Most Reformed and Protestant churches recognize only the two sacraments instituted by Jesus, namely baptism and the Lord's Supper.

sacra rappresentazione (Ital, "sacred representation") The Italian equivalent of the English and French MYSTERY PLAY, especially popular during the early RENAISSANCE. Developed from the dramatic religious song called the LAUDA, these sacred dramas were elaborately performed by the young men and boys of religious organizations, with appropriate scenery and props. The subject was exclusively biblical and the favorite from the OTTAVA RIMA. The strict classicism of the later Renaissance ended the influence and popularity of the sacred representation.

Sacred Fount, The (1901) A novella by Henry JAMES. The title refers to the theory of the narrator that in an unequal marriage, or liaison, the older or weaker partner is refreshed and invigorated at the "sacred fount" of the younger or stronger personality, which in turn becomes depleted. At an English house party, the narrator attempts, by the use of his theory, to discover the relationships among his fellow guests.

sacred thread In Hindu custom, a cotton thread of three strands (the *upavita*), given at a special initiation ceremony (the *upanayana*), to Hindu boys of the first three CASTES, usually between the ages of eight and twelve. It symbolizes their entry into the spiritual community, and this, coupled with the natural birth, is the reason for terming the top three castes "twice-born."

Sacrifice, The (1633) A long poem by George HERBERT. It is a dramatic first-person account of the Crucifixion in which Jesus repeatedly stresses the paradoxes of His situation: His goodness to man, man's ingratitude; His actual power, His seeming weakness, etc.

Sade, Donatien Alphonse François, comte de (known as marquis de Sade, 1740–1814) French author. Sade's works, because of their pornographic and blasphemous subject matter, have been denied official publication by the French courts as recently as 1957. After completing his Jesuit education, Sade acquired various military ranks and took part in the Seven Years' War. Soon after his marriage at twenty-three, much of the rest of his life was punctuated by violent scandals over his sexual conduct and by feuds with enemies, netting him several prison sentences totaling some thirty years. After seven years of liberty from 1794 to 1801, he was again arrested for writing licentious books; he remained in prison to the end of his life. His works, many of which were written in prison, include *Justine ou les Malheurs de la vertu* (1791), *La Philosophie dans le boudoir* (1795), *Aline et Valcour* (1795), *Juliette* (1797), and *Les 120 Journées de sodome* (1931–35) —in all, a dozen two- to ten-volume novels, about sixty short stories, twenty plays, and many smaller works. Approximately one fourth of his manuscripts were burned

by the police during the Consulate and the Empire. For years his works were considered to be the monstrous ravings of a delirious criminal mind, but recent criticism and psychiatric analysis have viewed him as a precursor of NIETZSCHE and FREUD and of such 20th-century movements as EXISTENTIALISM, and as a writer whose originality of thought and language warrants his being given a permanent high place in French literature. See SADISM; WEISS, PETER.

Sa'dī (pen name of Musharrif-uddīn, c1184–1291) Persian poet. As a young man Sa'dī studied in Baghdad, returning to Persia about the time the ruler, Sa'd, was deposed by the Mongol invaders. It was in his honor that the poet took his pen name, Sa'dī. Depressed by conditions in Persia, Sa'dī became a wanderer, traveling in other countries for thirty years. While in exile his life varied from that of a renowned sheikh to that of a prisoner condemned to forced labor. In 1256 he returned to his birthplace in Shiraz, Persia, where he lived, according to tradition, to the advanced age of 107.

Sa'dī is perhaps the most popular Persian poet of all time. His *Būstān* (*Fruit Garden*), GULISTAN (*Rose Garden*), and *Dīwān*, or collection of lyrics, are classics of Persian poetry. Sa'dī's polished style and the wit and poignancy of his sentiments have delighted readers everywhere.

sadism A type of sexual perversion in which gratification is found by torturing the object of love. It is so called from comte (known as marquis) de SADE, the French writer whose works first brought such practices to public attention. The term has come to be popularly applied to any delight in causing suffering to others, sex not necessarily being involved. Sadism is usually associated with MASOCHISM.

saga A long narrative EPIC, indigenous to Iceland and Ireland. The prose form of the saga differentiates it from the normally poetic epic.

The Old Norse sagas may be roughly divided into two groups. The less numerous of these, called the *fornaldarsögur* ("sagas of the olden times"), recount mythical or legendary events prior to the colonization of Iceland by Norse chieftains in AD 870. The other group, far more numerous and better known, are called *aettirsögur* ("family sagas"). These sagas depict the migration to Iceland, the occupation and settlement of the different regions of the new country, Viking expeditions to Europe and the New World, feuds among families and clans, and bitter disputes about personal property and prestige. Although the action of the stories takes place primarily between 930 and 1050, the sagas themselves were written down much later, during the 13th century.

The Irish saga, a much older genre than the Icelandic, concerns legendary heroes and kings of Ireland. See CATTLE-RAID OF COOLEY; ULSTER CYCLE.

Sagan, Françoise (pen name of Françoise Quoirez, 1935–   ) French novelist and playwright. Sagan was catapulted to fame at the age of nineteen with the publication of her first novel, BONJOUR TRISTESSE, an international best-seller. In such subsequent novels as *Un Certain Sourire* (1956; tr *A Certain Smile*, 1956), *Aimez-vous Brahms?* (1959; tr 1960), and *Des Bleus à l'âme* (1972; tr *Scars on the Soul*, 1974), she also presents, in a subdued, unemotional style, innocents in search of experience and their half-despairing, half-cynical disillusionment. The same theme is echoed in her plays.

Sahitya Darpana (The Mirror of Literature)   A Sanskrit treatise. Written by Visvanath Kaviraj, who lived in the court of King Narasingha, East India, in the 15th century, it explains the nature and forms of literary expression.

Saikaku   See IHARA SAIKAKU.

Saint, The   In novels by the English popular novelist Leslie Charteris (1907–   ), the nickname, taken from his initials, of the gentleman-burglar Simon Templar. He appears in *Enter the Saint* (1930), *The Saint Goes West* (1942), *The Saint to the Rescue* (1959), *The Saint Returns* (1968), *Send for the Saint* (1978), and many other works. The popular television series *The Saint* was based on these novels.

Saint-Amant, Marc Antoine de Gérard (1594–1661)   French poet. An original member of the ACADÉMIE FRANÇAISE but subsequently condemned by Boileau, Saint-Amant was an uninhibited freethinker and wrote verse that was by turns outlandish, fanciful, and realistic. In addition to sonnets and lyrics, he produced satires, burlesques, and tavern songs, as well as an epic, *Moïse* (*Moses*, 1653).

Saint-Denys-Garneau, Hector (1912–1943)   Quebec poet, the great-grandson of François-Xavier GARNEAU. Saint-Denys-Garneau's *Regards et jeux dans l'espace* (1937) marks the beginning of modern poetry in Quebec and is the most extreme exploration of a traditional Jansenist Christianity. Flexible and spare, his poems vary from the delicately impressionistic to symbolist and metaphysical; extended mathematical conceits dramatize the barrenness of a world emptied of spiritual presence. His works are contained in *Poésies complètes* (1949; tr *Complete Poems*, 1975) and *Journal* (1954; tr 1954).

Sainte-Beuve, Charles Augustin (1804–1869)   French literary critic and man of letters. Sainte-Beuve's career as a critic can be divided into three periods. When he first began to practice journalism, writing for the *Globe* in Paris, he spoke out warmly and enthusiastically in favor of the romantic school. His passionate love affair with the wife of Victor HUGO, celebrated in the love lyrics of *Le Livre d'amour* (1843), engendered a certain coldness between the poet and the young critic. His interest in ROMANTICISM considerably diminished, Sainte-Beuve was writing for the *Revue de Paris* and the *Revue des deux mondes* by 1831. During this second period, he developed his biographical and psychological approach, studying a literary work through the life and personality of its author.

The third period saw Sainte-Beuve writing for the *Constitutionnel* and using a naturalistic method of criticism, placing emphasis upon historical background and social environment. Among his published works are *Portraits contemporains* (1869–71), *Portraits littéraires* (1862–64), *Chateaubriand et son groupe littéraire* (1861), and his collected weekly critical articles, *Causeries du lundi* (1851–62) and *Nouveaux lundis* (1863–70). His criticism favors moderation, artistic unity, truth in the portrayal of life, and good taste. A strange individual, Sainte-Beuve was erratic in both his personal friendships and intellectual affiliations. He became caught up, at various times, in the swirling intellectual currents of his day: Saint-Simonism, liberal Roman Catholicism, Swiss Calvinism, scientific skepticism, and positivism.

Saint-Evremond, Charles de Marguetel de Saint-Denis, seigneur de (1613–1703)   French wit and man of letters. Saint-Evremond attacked Mazarin's treaty with Spain in his *Lettre sur le traité des pyrénées* (*Letter on the Pyrenees Treaty*, 1656) and was forced in 1661 to flee to England. Well received by Charles II, he became a permanent member of the English court. In his critical essays, his poems, and his play *Comédie des académistes* (*The Academists' Play*, 1643) Saint-Evremond displays a keen wit coupled with natural elegance.

Saint-Exupéry, Antoine de (1900–1944)   French novelist, essayist, and aviator. A commercial pilot in West Africa and South America, Saint-Exupéry was a pioneer in exploring flight over the desert, the Andes, and at night. His barely fictionalized experiences became the novels *Courrier-Sud* (1928; tr *Southern Mail*, 1933) and NIGHT FLIGHT. Regretfully the pilots abandon the terrestrial order of things, partially represented by women and their love, in order to discover the hidden treasures of experience represented by the stars, courageously accepting discipline and risk in a quest for the spiritual fraternity of mankind.

Already the prose poet of the new world of the skies, Saint-Exupéry then rediscovered men's earth in WIND, SAND, AND STARS. *Pilote de guerre* (1942; tr *Flight to Arras*, 1942) is an autobiographical account of a dangerous wartime mission, which becomes an introspective analysis of the pilot's mind and philosophy.

Lettre à un otage (1943; tr *Letter to a Hostage*, 1945) and the posthumous publication of his unfinished notebook of reflections, *Citadelle* (1948; tr *The Wisdom of the Sands*, 1954), give further exposition of his moral philosophy. *Le Petit prince* (1943; tr *The Little Prince*, 1944) is a fairy tale whose mode of whimsy and fantasy cloaks a wise understanding of the significant values in human life.

Saint-Exupéry disappeared while on a reconnaissance flight over occupied southern France in July 1944.

Saint-Gaudens, Augustus (1848–1907)   American sculptor. Saint-Gaudens is noted for his monuments, symbolic figures, and portrait plaques in low relief. His *Reminiscences* were published in 1913.

Saint Joan (1923)   A play by George Bernard SHAW. Produced three years after the canonization of St. JOAN OF ARC, Shaw's play shows her as an early nationalist and the prototype of the Protestant thinker who put her conscience before the judgment of the Church. She died because her new ideas were dangerous to both the Church and feudal society. In an epilogue Joan is surprised to learn of her sainthood; when she offers to return to earth she is again rejected, the usual fate of saints and geniuses according to Shaw.

St. John, Henry, Viscount Bolingbroke (1678–1751)   English statesman, orator, and man of letters, who, during the reign of Queen Anne, was the leader of the Tory party in association with Robert Harley. Bolingbroke later propagandized his opposition to the government of Sir Robert Walpole in *The Craftsman* (1726), a periodical. His major works include the DISSERTATION UPON PARTIES; the *Idea of a Patriot King* (1749), an essay; and the *Letters on the Study of History*, published posthumously in 1752. As a patron, Bolingbroke formed literary friendships with SWIFT, John GAY, John ARBUTHNOT, and POPE. An adherent of DEISM, he furnished Pope with many of the philosophical ideas used in the groundwork of AN ESSAY ON MAN.

Saint-Just, Louis Antoine Léon de (1767–1794)   French revolutionary leader and intimate of ROBESPIERRE. Saint-Just was known as "the archangel of the Revolution" because of his incorruptibility and good looks. He was active in overthrowing the GIRONDISTS and instrumental in bringing on the REIGN OF TERROR. He was arrested and guillotined with Robespierre in 1794.

Saint-Loup, Marquis Robert de   A close friend of the narrator in Marcel Proust's REMEMBRANCE OF THINGS PAST. Saint-Loup is one of the GUERMANTES, and his relatives deplore his passion for the prostitute RACHEL. Eventually he marries Gilberte, although he has become a homosexual, and is killed in World War I.

St. Nicholas   A monthly magazine for children published from 1873 to 1940. Mary Mapes Dodge edited the magazine from its beginning until 1905. Among its contributors were Louisa M. ALCOTT, Mark TWAIN, Rudyard KIPLING, Palmer Cox (the founder of the Brownies), Howard Pyle (1853–1911), and others. Anthologies of selections from the magazine were published in 1948 and 1950.

St. Patrick's Purgatory   A cave on Station Island in Lough Derg (a lake in Donegal). A penitential pilgrimage to this site has existed since the early Middle Ages, though its connection to St. Patrick is purely legendary.

St. Paul's Cathedral   An Anglican cathedral in London. The original Gothic building was destroyed in the Great Fire of 1666. Christopher WREN designed the present St. Paul's, completed 1701. Its huge dome is a London landmark. Inside are tombs of DONNE, WELLINGTON, NELSON, and other notables, including that of the architect.

St. Peter's Basilica   The largest church in Christendom. It can accommodate fifty thousand people, and in it most of the important papal functions are held. Donato BRAMANTE laid out the plan in the form of a Greek cross. This was modified, but MICHELANGELO used Bramante's ideas in bringing the plan to completion. The famous dome is Michelangelo's work. BERNINI designed the colonnades of the *piazza* and the ornate baldacchino over the high altar.

Saint-Preux   The hero of Rousseau's novel LA NOUVELLE HÉLOÏSE. Saint-Preux is Julie's tutor and lover, and is drawn chiefly from Rousseau himself, who bore the same relation to comtesse d'Houdetot, Julie's prototype.

Saint-Saëns, [Charles] Camille (1835–1921)   French composer of operas, symphonies, chamber music, and choral works. Saint-Saëns's works include the opera *Samson et Dalila* (1877), the humorous suite *Le Carnaval des animaux* (composed in 1886 as a musical joke; he did not permit its performance in public while he lived), and five well-known piano concertos.

Saint-Simon, Claude Henri de Rouvroy, comte de (1760–1825)   French philosopher and social reformer. Saint-Simon's social doctrines were developed by his disciples into a system called Saint-Simonianism. Within this system, all property is owned by the state, while the worker shares in it according to the amount and quality of his work. The basic principle of the state is that of association for the good of all. Surprisingly modern in their ideas, the Saint-Simonians not only advocated social equality, increased attention to education, and the abolition of hereditary rights, but also demanded disarmament.

Saint-Simon, Louis de Rouvroy, duc de (1675–1755)   French courtier and writer. An aristocrat embittered by the frustration of his own political ambitions, Saint-Simon was sharply critical of bourgeois royal officialdom. His *Mémoires*, which present a vivid and candid picture of the life and the personalities of the fashionable court of LOUIS XIV, are colored by the tart disposition of their author, who admits that he cannot be impartial. Claimed by his creditors at his death and sequestered by the state, the manuscript was not published until 1829, and an accurate edition did not appear until 1879.

Saison en enfer, Une (A Season in Hell, 1873)   A prose-poem by Arthur RIMBAUD. Called a psychological autobiography, the work, consisting of nine fragments, describes the poet's tortured spiritual experiences.

Saki (pen name of Hector Hugh Munro, 1870–1916)   Scottish-born writer. Known for his very witty and very short stories, Saki also wrote two novels, three plays, and one book of history. Two young men, Reginald and Clovis, are heroes of a series of short stories in which they gaily take revenge on the conventional adult world. Other stories are somber and macabre, such as "Sredni Vashtar," "The Muse on the Hill," and "Esme." *The Unbearable Bassington* (1912), a long-underrated novel, features an extraordinarily fresh characterization of Francesa Bassington, a woman ahead of her time. *Reginald* (1904), *The Chronicles of Clovis* (1912), *Beasts and Super Beasts* (1914), and *The Square Egg* (1924) are collections of stories. Saki was killed in action in World War I, having volunteered for service at the age of forty-four. His work, full of paradox, has extraordinarily durable appeal. *The Complete Works of Saki* (1976) contains all but his earliest book, *The Rise of the Russian Empire* (1899), and some of his war reporting.

sakti   See SHAKTI.

Sakūntala   See SHĀKUNTALĀ.

Salacrou, Armand (1899–   )   French dramatist. In an era of naturalistic theatre, many of Salacrou's early plays anticipated avant-garde techniques, using flashbacks, disjointed time sequences, and dream-fantasy. His best plays reveal a humanistic concern with man's sense of the chaos of life, and sympathy for his anguished need to believe in God in the face of death's inevitability. His best-known plays include *L'Inconnue d'Arras* (1935), an exploration of a suicide's life; *Les Nuits de la colère*, a moving work on the French Resistance; the antifascist *La Terre est ronde* (1938; tr *The World is Round*, 1967) and *Histoire de rire* (1939; tr *When the Music Stops*, 1967).

Salamis   An island off the coast of Greece, not far from Athens. It is famous for the naval victory won by the Greeks over the Persians (480 BC) in the bay between it and Attica. See PERSIAN WARS; THEMISTOCLES.

Salammbô (1862)   A historical novel by Gustave FLAUBERT. Set in ancient Carthage, the action of this book is colorfully romantic. Before writing it, Flaubert made a voyage to Tunisia, thus carrying out literally his artistic theories of precise and accurate documentation.

Salavin, Louis   See DUHAMEL, GEORGES.

Salem witch-hunt   A hysterical persecution of witches and wizards in Salem, Massachusetts, in 1692. It began when several young girls accused some old women of bewitching them. Hundreds of persons were accused; many were brought to trial at a special court; nineteen were hanged; and one, Giles Corey, was pressed to death. All the witches were exonerated by a decree of 1711. The episode has frequently been described in literature: e.g., John Neal's *Rachel Dyer* (1828), a novel; LONGFELLOW's "Giles Corey of the Salem Farms," a dramatic poem in *The New England Tragedies* (1868); and Arthur Miller's THE CRUCIBLE, a play. See also MATHER, COTTON; MATHER, INCREASE; SEWALL, SAMUEL.

Salinas [Serrano], Pedro (1891–1951)   Spanish poet, critic, and scholar. A well-known academician, Salinas taught both at home and in France and finally in the U.S., where he lived out his exile from the Franco regime. He was the oldest member of the GENERACIÓN DEL 27 and is best known as a poet. His finest writing can be found in *La voza a ti debida* (1933; tr *My Voice Because of You*,

1976) and *Razón de amor* (1936), investigations into the expression of love.

Salinger, J[erome] D[avid] (1919–   )   American novelist and short-story writer. Salinger won wide acclaim with his first novel, THE CATCHER IN THE RYE, which captivated a whole generation of young people. His collection of short fiction, *Nine Stories* (1953), a majority of which originally appeared in THE NEW YORKER, deals mainly with sensitive and troubled adolescents and children who are strongly contrasted with the empty world of their parents. In this collection, Salinger introduces the Glass family, notably in "A Perfect Day for Bananafish," in which Seymour Glass, the oldest son, commits suicide. Members of the Glass family are also the subject of *Franny and Zooey* (1961) and *Raise High the Roof-Beam, Carpenters; and Seymour: An Introduction* (1963), long stories also originally published in *The New Yorker*.

Salinger's style is clean and concise, and he is particularly noted for his faithful reproduction of colloquial speech. Perhaps no other writer of so few works has been the subject of so many scholarly analyses. He has lived as a recluse and published nothing since the mid-1960s.

Sallust (full Latin name Gaius Sallustius Crispus, 86–34 BC)   Roman historian. Sallust's *Bellum Catilinae*, on the conspiracy of Catiline, and his *Bellum Jugurthinum*, on the war with Jugurtha, are extant. Sallust was the first artistic writer of Roman history. Like his Greek model Thucydides, he strove to give a vivid dramatic structure to a historical situation, and included brilliant speeches which, though they are fictitious, reveal the character of his historic personages with amazing force and subtlety. His style differs sharply from the rhetorical orchestration of Cicero; it is more like the style of the elder Cato—straightforward, condensed, and paradoxical.

Salmagundi; or, The Whim-Whams and Opinions of Launcelot Langstaff, Esq. and Others (1807–1808)   A humorous periodical published by Washington IRVING, his brother William, and James Kirk PAULDING. It was collected in book form in 1808 and is an American link between *The Spectator* and *Pickwick Papers*. Under fantastic pseudonyms, the writers discussed politics, theatre, fashions, and manners in order to "instruct the young, reform the old, correct the town, and castigate the age." The papers were an immediate success; their bias was Federalist and conservative. Their wit makes them readable today. Paulding went on to do a second series, but it lacks the spontaneity and vitality of the first.

The word *salmagundi* first appeared in the 17th century; it refers to a spicy stewlike concoction, whose ingredients are as various as the contents of the book.

Salome   In the BIBLE, the daughter of Herodias and Herod Philip. When Salome's mother divorced her husband and married his brother HEROD ANTIPAS, governor of Judaea, the prophet JOHN THE BAPTIST was imprisoned for denouncing the marriage. According to the NEW TESTA-

MENT narrative, Salome so pleased Herod by her dancing at his birthday feast that he promised her "whatsoever she would ask." She followed her mother's advice and demanded the head of John the Baptist on a platter (Matt. 14:6–11).

According to medieval legend, Herodias had been in love with John. Modern treatments of the story, such as Hermann SUDERMANN's tragedy *The Fires of St. John* (1897) and Oscar WILDE's *Salomé* (1894), make Salome also infatuated with the prophet and Herod infatuated with Salome. The opera *Salome* (1905) by Richard STRAUSS is based on Wilde's play. FLAUBERT has a short narrative called *Herodias, the Story of Salomé* (1877).

Saltykov, Mikhail Yevgrafovich (pen name N. Shchedrin, 1826–1889)   Russian novelist and satirist. At eighteen Saltykov joined the Petrashevsky circle, a group of young intellectuals interested in the theories of the French utopian socialists of which the novelist DOSTOYEVSKY was also a member.

The radical tone of one of Saltykov's early short novels, *Zaputannoye delo* (*A Complicated Affair*, 1848), attracted the attention of the Tsarist censor, and Saltykov was exiled to Vyatka in eastern Russia. His exile saved him from the more severe treatment dealt to the Petrashevsky circle in 1849, when the members were imprisoned, subjected to a mock execution, and sent to Siberia. Saltykov languished in Vyatka until 1856, when amnesty following the death of Nicholas I released him. One result of his exile was *Gubernskiye ocherki* (*Provincial Sketches*, 1856), a collection of satirical pieces on provincial life, published under the pseudonym of N. Shchedrin.

From 1857 to 1862, Saltykov was again in the provinces, serving as vice-governor in Ryazan and Tver. Returning to St. Petersburg, he became the editor of the journal *Sovremennik* (*The Contemporary*) when its previous editor, Nikolay CHERNYSHEVSKY, was exiled. In 1868 Saltykov took over the journal *Otechestvennye zapiski* (*Fatherland Notes*) in collaboration with the poet Nikolay NEKRASOV. He continued to work on this journal until 1884. During this period he produced his best-known works. These include *Istoriya odnogo goroda* (*The History of a Town*, 1869–70), a satirical history of an imaginary town; the novel *Gospoda Golovlyovy* (*The Golovlyov Family*, 1872–76), considered Saltykov's masterpiece; and *Skazki* (*Fables*, 1880–85), in which Saltykov used the fable form for incisive comments on man and society.

Salvation Army   A religious and charitable organization that grew out of the Christian Mission in London, established by the Methodist evangelist William Booth in 1865. From the beginning it devoted itself largely to work among the urban poor, criminals, alcoholics, and other neglected classes. The name Salvation Army, together with its semimilitary organization, was adopted in 1878. George Bernard SHAW has depicted the group in his MAJOR BARBARA.

Samael   In rabbinical legend, the prince of demons who, in the guise of a serpent, was said to have tempted Eve. Samael was also known as the angel of death. See ADAM AND EVE.

Samain   November 1, the New Year's feast of the ancient Celtic year. Samain Eve, October 31, corresponds to the more modern HALLOWE'EN, and in early Irish tales this was the time that the fairy mounds of Ireland opened, allowing supernatural beings to come out into the world. By the same token, Samain Eve was the time when the mysterious mounds became accessible to Irish heroes in search of glory and hidden treasure. With the coming of Christianity, Samain became ALL SAINTS' DAY.

Samaritan, Good   In the NEW TESTAMENT, a compassionate character who aids a man robbed and injured by thieves (LUKE 10:30–34). The expression applies, in general, to any philanthropist who relieves the poor.

Sam Hill   A mythical individual of American origin, frequently referred to in such phrases as *fight like Sam Hill*, *swear like Sam Hill*. According to F. J. Wilstach, author of *A Dictionary of Similes*, the expression *what in Sam Hill* occurred at least as early as 1839 (in the Elmira, New York, *Republican*), and seems to have been well established in usage at that time. This date excludes a theory that Sam Hill was Sam Hall, the murderous chimney sweep of an English song popular in 1848–49. Mr. Wilstach is inclined to derive the fighting, swearing Sam Hill from the daemon Samael, and to see in references to him a satisfactory Puritan substitute for profanity. A simpler, not necessarily less probable, explanation treats the name as a playful euphemism for "hell."

Samhitas   See VEDAS.

samizdat   A Russian term designating manuscripts that are typed or photocopied and circulated from reader to reader without official approval of the Soviet authorities. The word derives from the Russian word *sam*, meaning "self," and the word *izdaniye*, meaning "edition."

Sampo   A precious object in the KALEVALA, usually described as a magic mill that grinds out meal, salt, and gold.

Sampson, Dominie   An extremely well-drawn character in Scott's GUY MANNERING. Tutor to the hero, Harry Bertram, Sampson is described as "a poor, modest, humble scholar, who had won his way through the classics, but fallen to the leeward in the voyage of life." He is overfond of the exclamation "Prodigious!"

Samsa, Gregor   The hero of Kafka's THE METAMORPHOSIS. A traveling salesman, Samsa awakens one morning to find himself changed into an insect. His name is a code form of the author's own, for by the substitution of *k* for *s* and *f* for *m*, Samsa becomes *Kafka*. See K., JOSEPH.

samsara (Sans, "general flow")   A word evidently first appearing in the UPANISHADS, *samsara* refers to the cycle of transmigration: birth, death, and rebirth. The law of KARMA determines the nature of the rebirths, and the samsaric cycle is broken up upon attainment of *moksha*. See HINDUISM.

Samson In the OLD TESTAMENT, a judge of Israel famous for his prodigious strength and the many remarkable feats by which he routed his enemies, the PHILISTINES. Samson's birth was foretold by an angel of God, who said that he would live as a NAZARITE. He became infatuated with a Philistine woman, DELILAH, who discovered that the secret of his strength lay in his uncut hair, a symbol of the Nazarite's covenant with God. She coaxed him to sleep on her lap and called for a Philistine to shave off his locks; Samson awoke to find that both God and his strength had left him. He was captured and blinded by the Philistines and was sent to grind meal in the prison-house at Gaza. When, at the feast of DAGON, he was brought to the temple to be mocked, he prayed to Jehovah for a return of his strength. This was granted and he pulled down the two supporting pillars of the edifice, killing himself and all present (Judg. 13–16).

He is the hero of Milton's tragic poem SAMSON AGONISTES.

Samson Agonistes (1671) A tragedy in blank verse by John MILTON. It deals with the captivity of the blinded Samson among the Philistines, his repudiation of the faithless Delilah, and his destruction of the Philistine temple. The agon, or struggle about which the play centers, is Samson's effort to renew his faith in God's support and his own mission. In structure the drama is closely modeled on Greek tragedy: there is a chorus; the action is confined to a single day; and the climactic event (the destruction of the temple) occurs offstage and is related by a witness.

Samuel A judge and prophet, the religious and political reformer of early Israel, after whom are named two books of the OLD TESTAMENT. At his birth, Samuel was consecrated to temple service by his mother, HANNAH, and, when still a child, heard JEHOVAH's voice in the night. He preserved the work of MOSES in reuniting the people and established schools devoted to the cultivation of sacred poetry and song. After a long life as NAZARITE priest and leader, Samuel was forced to yield to the people's demand for a king and established SAUL on the throne, though he prophesied loss of liberty. He also anointed DAVID as future king.

samurai A Japanese warrior, member of a military caste which arose in the wars of the KAMAKURA period (1185–1333) and was finally abolished only in the MEIJI period (1868–1912). A samurai was always a retainer of a higher-ranking member of the same class, the hierarchy extending from foot soldier up to the SHŌGUN, or military ruler. If the samurai's lord died with no successor or was divested of rank, the samurai was reduced to the status of *ronin*, or masterless, samurai; he would have to seek another master, or face the fate of becoming either an outlaw or member of the agricultural class.

Sánchez, Florencio (1875–1910) Uruguayan dramatist. Considered the outstanding dramatist of the Río de la Plata region, Sánchez turned to the theatre after working as a journalist and participating in anarchist agitation. He wrote his first play, *M'hijo el dotor* (1903), in less than three weeks in order to earn enough money to marry his sweetheart, whose parents viewed his bleak prospects with disfavor. Dealing with the conflict between an old gaucho and his urbane, self-centered son, the play met with notable success. The struggle between the old order and new is also the theme of other plays by Sánchez, notably *La Gringa* (1904), which is concerned with racial animosity between native Argentines and Italian immigrants, and *Barranca abajo* (1905), a poignant elegy on the gaucho threatened by "progress." Sánchez's work has been likened to IBSEN's because of its realism and emphasis on contemporary problems. His most important plays have been translated into English in *Representative Plays of Florencio Sánchez* (1961; tr by W. K. Jones). See GAUCHO LITERATURE.

Sanctuary (1931) A novel by William FAULKNER. Horace Benbow, an ineffectual intellectual, becomes involved in the violent events centering on Temple DRAKE, a young coed. Temple is raped by POPEYE, who murders a man trying to protect her. Carried off to a Memphis brothel by Popeye, Temple later protects him and testifies against Lee Goodwin, who is accused of the murder. Benbow defends Goodwin at the trial and unsuccessfully tries to give shelter to Goodwin's common-law wife. Temple's testimony ends all hope for Goodwin, who is lynched by the townspeople. Temple's story is continued in REQUIEM FOR A NUN.

Sand, George (pen name of Amandine Lucie Aurore Dupin, Baronne Dudevant, 1804–1876) French writer. George Sand is as famous for her "unfeminine" independence, her habit of wearing men's clothes, and her love affairs with such prominent artistic figures as Alfred de MUSSET and Frédéric CHOPIN, as she is for her writings. In 1831 she left her husband, Baron Dudevant, and established herself in Paris. Her work is usually divided into three distinct periods, the first of which, intensely romantic, corresponds to her affair with Musset (see ELLE ET LUI). The novels of this period plead the right of free love for both men and women, and include such works as INDIANA, *Lélia* (1833), and *Valentine* (1832). During the next decade George Sand became interested in various humanitarian reform movements and published such works as CONSUELO and *Le Meunier d'Angibault* (1845). Her last group of novels, sentimental studies of nature and of rustic manners, includes *La Mare au diable* (1846), *La Petite Fadette* (1848), and *François le Champi* (1850).

Sandburg, Carl (1878–1967) American poet. Sandburg is known for his FREE VERSE poems celebrating industrial and agricultural America, American geography and landscape, great figures in American history, and the American common people. Strongly influenced by Walt WHITMAN, he made use of contemporary slang and colloquialisms. He was born in Galesburg, Illinois, left school at thirteen and took odd jobs, traveled West as a hobo, served in the Spanish-American War, and then worked his way through Lombard (now Knox) College in his hometown. He was an advertising writer, a newspaper reporter, a correspondent in Sweden and Norway, and an editorial writer for the Chicago *Daily News*. Early in his career he evinced socialist sympathies; he worked for the Social-Democrat Party in Wisconsin and later was secretary to the first Socialist mayor of Milwaukee.

After an early pamphlet, *In Reckless Ecstasy* (1904), Sandburg began publishing his poems in Harriet Monroe's POETRY, becoming part of the Chicago literary renaissance (see CHICAGO GROUP). With *Chicago Poems* (1916) and CORNHUSKERS, his reputation was established. These volumes were followed in the 1920s by SMOKE AND STEEL, *Slabs of the Sunburnt West* (1922), *Selected Poems* (1926), and *Good Morning, America* (1928). During the same period, Sandburg's energies were directed into three other areas. The most important of these was the beginning of his monumental study ABRAHAM LINCOLN. The second was his collection of American folklore, the ballads in THE AMERICAN SONGBAG, and its successor, *The New American Songbag* (1950). The third area was writing books for children. ROOTABAGA STORIES, the best known of these, was followed by three others.

In the 1930s Sandburg continued his celebration of America with *Mary Lincoln, Wife and Widow* (1932), *The People, Yes* (1936), and the second part of his Lincoln biography, *Abraham Lincoln: The War Years* (1939). For this he was awarded a PULITZER PRIZE; later he received a second Pulitzer Prize for his *Complete Poems* (1950). His final volumes of verse were *Harvest Poems, 1910–1960* (1960) and *Honey and Salt* (1963).

Sandel, Cora (pen name of Sara Margarethe Fabricius, 1880–1974)   Norwegian novelist. Sandel's books all deal with women's struggles to lead independent and fulfilled lives. She is best known for her trilogy, *Alberte og Jacob* (1926; tr *Alberta and Jacob*, 1962), *Alberte og friheten* (1931; tr *Alberta and Freedom*, 1963), and *Bare Alberte* (1939; tr *Alberta Alone*, 1965). Her masterpiece, *Kranes konditori* (1945; tr *Krane's Café*, 1968), about the pressures on a woman in a small town, is a technical tour de force, compressed into a single place and a time frame of two days. *Kjøp ikke Dondi* (1958; tr *The Leech*, 1960) is more experimental and uses dialogue heavily to tell its story.

Sandoz, Mari[e Susette] (1896–1966)   American biographer and historical writer. A native of Nebraska, Sandoz is known especially for her biography of her pioneer father, *Old Jules* (1935), and for such nonfiction narratives as *Crazy Horse* (1942), *Cheyenne Autumn* (1953), and *The Battle of the Little Big Horn* (1966). She also wrote several novels.

Sangreal   See GRAIL.

Sangster, Charles (1822–1893)   Canadian poet. An outstanding pre-Confederation poet, Sangster is remembered as one of the first poets to make appreciative use of Canadian subjects. His works include *The St. Lawrence and the Saguenay and Other Poems* (1856), dealing with themes of love and nature; and *Hesperus and Other Poems* (1860), poems frankly patriotic in tone.

Sankhya   See DARSHANA.

San Martín, José de (1778–1850)   Argentine general and revolutionary leader. After taking part in Argentina's struggle for independence from Spain, San Martín became governor of Cuyo province (1814–17), where he organized an army to lead against Chile and Peru, the stronghold of Spanish power in South America. After an arduous trek across the Andes, San Martín and the Chilean patriot Bernardo O'Higgins defeated the Spaniards at Chacabuco and Maipu and declared the independence of Chile. Rejecting the political honors which the grateful Chileans offered him, San Martín turned to the liberation of Peru. Although he was able to declare Peru's independence in 1821, most of the territory included in the viceroyalty of Peru still remained in royalist hands, and San Martín, who was named dictator of Peru, resolved to seek the aid of Bolívar. After a famous meeting between the two liberators at Guayaquil (1822), San Martín, perhaps in the belief that his continued presence in Peru would delay the final victory, resigned his post and left the country, leaving a clear field for Bolívar. He spent his last years in Europe and died in France. His achievements were belatedly recognized by his countrymen, who had ignored or vilified him during his lifetime, and in 1880 his remains were brought to Argentina for final burial in Buenos Aires.

Sannazzaro, Jacopo (1456–1530)   Neapolitan poet. Known also by his academic name of Actius Syncerus, Sannazzaro devoted most of his life to the service of the house of Aragon. His writings include Latin elegies, epigrams, and piscatorial (or maritime) eclogues, the latter being the first attempts at the genre since Theocritus. His religious poem *De partu virginis* (*On the Virgin's Parturition*) was one of several Renaissance attempts at writing Vergilian epic on Christian subject matter and eventually influenced Milton. In Italian he wrote sonnets and *canzoni*, but his masterpiece is the *Arcadia* (1501–4), a pastoral romance immensely popular and influential throughout Europe. Written between 1480 and 1485, it is divided into twelve prose chapters, each accompanied by twelve poems, and tells of the adventures of Sincero, who visits Arcadia to observe the pastoral life of its inhabitants. He returns to Naples in search of his beloved Fillide, only to find her dead. The *Arcadia* was imitated by many European writers; in England, Spenser and Sidney are only two of his adapters, the latter using its title and some details for his own prose romance.

sannyāsin   In HINDUISM, one who has renounced all worldly concerns and devotes himself entirely to asceticism and meditation. For orthodox Hindus it is the fourth and final stage of life, or ASHRAMA. It is more generally applied to any religious mendicant.

Sanskara   The ten essential rites of Hindus of the first three castes. They take place at the conception of a child; at the quickening; at birth; at naming; when carrying the child out to see the moon; when giving him his first food to eat; at the ceremony of tonsure; during investiture with the sacred thread; at the close of his studies; at the ceremony of "marriage," when he is qualified to perform the sacrifices ordained.

Sansom, William (1912–1976)   English novelist and short-story writer. Sansom is the author of sinister, Kafkaesque works such as his first novel, *The Body* (1949), an account of a paranoid delusion narrated by its victim, and the short stories collected in *Fireman Flower* (1944) and *Something Terrible, Something Lovely* (1948). His other novels include *The Face of Innocence* (1951), *Goodbye* (1966), and *A Young Wife's Tale* (1974). *The Passionate North* (1950) and *The Ulcerated Milkman* (1966) are collections of stories.

Sanson, Charles Henri (1740–?1795)   Official executioner in Paris from 1788 to his death. Sanson executed Louis XVI. His son and colleague, Henri, executed Marie Antoinette.

Santa Anna, Antonio López de (1795?–1876)   Mexican general and political leader. Now generally regarded as a self-seeking opportunist who betrayed every cause he espoused, Santa Anna dominated Mexican politics for over twenty-five years. After serving as president (1834–35), he led the Mexican assault at the Alamo. Taken prisoner at the battle of San Jacinto shortly afterwards, he was released when he promised to recognize the independence of Texas. He was provisional president and commander of the Mexican forces during the Spanish-American War, but was deposed after the American victory. Again made president in 1853, he was exiled in 1855. In 1874 he was permitted to return to Mexico, where he died penniless and alone.

Santa Claus   The patron saint of children and bearer of gifts on CHRISTMAS Day. His name is a corruption of the Dutch form of St. NICHOLAS. His feast-day is December 6, and the vigil is still held in some places, but for the most part his name is now associated with Christmastide. The old custom used to be for someone, on December 5, to assume the costume of a bishop and distribute small gifts to good children.

Santa Fe Trail, The: A Humoresque (1914)   A poem by Vachel LINDSAY. It contrasts industrial civilization at the beginning of the 20th century with the Rachel-Jane bird, which sings of love and eternal youth. It is notable for its radical sound effects.

Santayana, George (1863–1952)   Spanish-born American philosopher, poet, novelist, and critic. Santayana was known for his cosmopolitan viewpoint, his philosophic skepticism and materialism, his interest in the systems of PLATO and ARISTOTLE, and his fondness for Greek and Roman classical ideals of beauty.

Santayana studied at Harvard University and later returned there to teach philosophy; among his students were Conrad AIKEN, Robert BENCHLEY, Felix FRANKFURTER, Walter LIPPMANN, and T. S. ELIOT. In 1912 Santayana resigned from the university and went to live and travel in Europe, spending winters in Rome and summers in Paris. At the outset of World War II, he moved to a Roman Catholic nursing home in Rome, where he spent the rest of his life.

Santayana himself divided his work into two groups: the poetic, or personal, and the academic. The first group includes such works as *Lucifer: A Theological Tragedy* (1899), *Dialogues in Limbo* (1925), and THE LAST PURITAN. Santayana's memoirs, *Persons and Places*, were published in three volumes: *The Background of My Life* (1944), *The Middle Span* (1945), and *My Host the World* (1953).

In the academic group are *The Sense of Beauty* (1896), an outline of an aesthetic theory; *The Life of Reason, or, The Phases of Human Progress*, a five-volume work including *Introduction and Reason in Common Sense* (1905), *Reason in Society* (1905), *Reason in Religion* (1905), *Reason in Art* (1905), and *Reason in Science* (1906), all based on a materialistic view of nature; *Skepticism and Animal Faith* (1923); and *Realms of Being*, including the four volumes *The Realm of Essence* (1927), *The Realm of Matter* (1930), *The Realm of Truth* (1937), and *The Realm of Spirit* (1940). In addition to many other works, Santayana dealt with the American scene in *Character and Opinion in the United States* (1921) and *The Genteel Tradition at Bay* (1931).

Santillana, Iñigo López de Mendoza, marqués de (1398–1456)   Spanish poet. The nephew of the chancellor Ayala, Santillana was a great feudal lord who fought against the Moors and conspired against Alvaro de Luna, the powerful favorite of John II. Italian influences are evident in his two allegorical poems, *La comedieta de Ponza* and *Infierno de los enamorados*, and in his forty-two sonnets, a form which he introduced to Spain. He is best known, however, for his charming *serranillas*, or mountain songs, such as the one about his encounter with the milkmaid of Finajosa. He also wrote *Proemio e carta*, a letter on the nature of poetry addressed to the constable of Portugal, which is regarded as the first example of literary criticism in Spain.

Sapphic   A four-lined verse-form of classical lyric poetry. It is named after the Greek poetess SAPPHO, who employed it, the fourth line being an Adonic. There must be a caesura at the fifth foot of each of the first three lines, which run thus:

$$-\smile|--|-||\smile\smile|-\smile|-\smile$$

The Adonic is

$$-\smile\smile|-\smile \; or \; --$$

All the night sleep came not upon my eyelids,
Shed not dew, nor shook nor unclose a feather,
Yet with lips shut close and with eyes of iron
  Stood and beheld me.

                        Algernon Charles Swinburne

Sapphira   A female liar.

Sappho (b 612 BC)   One of the most famous lyric poets of all time, a native of Lesbos. Except for a period of some years in Sicily, Sappho lived in Lesbos all her life. Married and with a daughter, she was the leader of some kind of group of young girls who were devotees of music and poetry, and perhaps of Aphrodite. To some of these girls are addressed many of Sappho's poems. Classical writers called Sappho the tenth Muse. Although her poems survive only in fragments, their lyrical intensity and economy prove that her reputation was not exaggerated. The legend that she flung herself into the sea on being rejected by the beautiful youth Phaon has been the subject of many works, from a section of Ovid's *Heroides* to plays by John Lyly (1584) and Percy MacKaye (1907), both of which are named *Sappho and Phaon*.

Sara   See ASMODEUS.

Sarah (originally Sarai)   In the OLD TESTAMENT (Gen. 12–23), the wife of ABRAHAM. Unable to bear children, she gave her handmaiden, HAGAR, to Abraham to produce a child. When a very old woman, she became pregnant through divine intervention and bore Abraham's son, ISAAC. At this point her name was changed to Sarah. Jealous of Hagar and her son ISHMAEL, Sarah convinced Abraham to send them off to the desert to die. This Abraham reluctantly did only after he was told by God that Ishmael would begin a great nation. Sarah died at the age of 127 and was buried in the cave of Machpelah in Hebron.

Sardanapalus   The mythical last king of Assyria. His legend, as it grew up among the Greeks, combined the name of one historical ruler, Assurdanin-pal, with some of the exploits of another, ASSUR-BANI-PAL. An effete ruler, he nevertheless was said to have fought bravely against the rebellious Medes. When faced with inevitable defeat, he burned himself, his wife, and his treasures in the year 880 BC.

Sardou, Victorien (1831–1908)   French dramatist. The author of comedies and historical dramas that won him enormous popularity during his lifetime, Sardou excelled at clever plot construction. His light, shallow comedies of manners include *Les Pattes de mouche* (A Scrap of Paper, 1860), *Nos Intimes* (Peril, 1861), and *La Famille Benoîton* (1865). Sarah Bernhardt played the lead-

ing role in several of his historical dramas, including *Fédora* (1882), in which she triumphantly returned to the stage of Paris, and *La Tosca* (1887), on which Puccini based his opera.

Sargent, John Singer (1856–1925)   American painter. Born in Italy, Sargent studied in Florence and Paris, and lived mostly in London. A painter of fashionable and elegant portraits, he recorded his subjects in natural settings with brilliant brushwork, if admittedly little insight. His *Portrait of Madam X* (1884), with its revealing dress and blatant sensuality, scandalized Paris society. He was a distinguished watercolorist and muralist, completing in 1916 the historical murals in Boston's public library, after twenty-six years of research, sketching, and painting.

Sargeson, Frank (1903–1982)   New Zealand novelist and dramatist. One of New Zealand's most respected writers, Sargeson did not complete his first short novel, *That Summer* (*That Summer and Other Stories*, 1946), until he was thirty-eight. His early work is characterized by the creation of a New Zealand idiom: a first-person monologue in an accurate vernacular, recounted by an outsider or social misfit. His ability to communicate the thoughts and feelings of the inarticulate and his flexible use of language increasingly accommodate a more complex vision, moving from the naturalistic short stories of *Conversation with My Uncle* (1936) and *A Man and His Wife* (1940) to richly textured longer fiction, often concerned with the search for identity, exemplified by *Joy of the Worm* (1969).

Sarmiento, Domingo Faustino (1811–1888)   Argentine statesman, educator, and writer. Completely self-educated, Sarmiento once wrote that he had tried to pattern himself on Benjamin Franklin. His political career began when he opposed the dictatorship of Juan Manuel de Rosas, whom he denounced in his greatest work, FACUNDO. He spent many years as an exile in Chile, where he became known as an innovative educator. He returned to Argentina after Rosas had been overthrown and held several important political posts, including minister to the U.S., a country he unabashedly admired. Elected president of the republic in 1868, he reformed the country's educational system, encouraged large-scale immigration, and furthered advances in transportation and communications. He was, however, unable to diminish the personalism in Argentine politics, and when his term ended the country was divided by civil war.

A prolific writer whose complete works fill fifty-two volumes, Sarmiento was a romantic in style and literary outlook. Other important works are *Viajes* (1849), an account of a trip to Europe, Africa, and the U.S., and *Recuerdos de provincia* (1850), an engaging memoir of his childhood.

Saroyan, William (1908–1981)   American short-story writer, novelist, and playwright. Born in California of Armenian parents, Saroyan found his strongest themes in the poignant spiritual rootlessness of the immigrant. He is known for his impressionistic stories and sketches, which exalt personal emotion and freedom and assert kindness and brotherly love as human ideals. His reputation was first established with the ebullient short story collection *The Daring Young Man on the Flying Trapeze* (1934). Thereafter he published in leading magazines a vast number of stories that were collected in book form almost annually for many years. One of the most notable collections is the autobiographical *My Name Is Aram* (1940). Saroyan also wrote numerous plays. *My Heart's in the Highlands* (1939) was a major success. It was followed quickly by THE TIME OF YOUR LIFE, unquestionably Saroyan's most popular play; it won a PULITZER PRIZE, which its author refused, believing that commerce should not patronize art.

The Human Comedy (1943) was his first novel. He wrote eight more, including *The Laughing Matter* (1953), his most sustained effort at a tragic theme, and *One Day in the Afternoon of the World* (1964). He also wrote many autobiographical works, memoirs, and sketches, including *The Bicycle Rider in Beverly Hills* (1952) and *Here Comes, There Goes, You Know Who* (1961).

Sarpedon (1) A brother of MINOS and RHADAMANTHUS and son of EUROPA. Sarpedon was driven from Crete when Minos claimed the throne for himself alone.

(2) In the ILIAD, king of Lydia, son of ZEUS and Laodameia. He fought with the Trojans in the TROJAN WAR. Learning that he was fated to die at the hands of PATROCLUS, Zeus wept for him.

Sarraute, Nathalie (1902–) Russian-born French novelist and playwright. With *Tropismes* (1939; tr *Tropisms*, 1964), Sarraute began to experiment with presenting the fluctuations of human feelings and motivations by concentrating on the minutiae of impulses that fill the subconscious and conscious mind. In his preface to her *Portrait d'un inconnu* (1948; tr *Portrait of a Man Unknown*, 1958), Jean-Paul SARTRE described the work as an "anti-novel." In the essays collected in *L'Ère du soupçon* (1956; tr *The Age of Suspicion*, 1963), first published between 1947 and 1955, Sarraute analyzed the techniques of what was to be called the NOUVEAU ROMAN. Her later novels include *Martereau* (1953; tr 1959), *Le Planetarium* (1959; tr 1960), and *Les Fruits d'or* (1963; tr *The Golden Fruits*, 1964). In 1984, Sarraute published her autobiography, *Childhood*.

Sarto, Andrea del (real name Andrea Vanucci, 1486–1531) Italian painter. Sarto was known as *Andrea senza errore* (Andrea the faultless) because of his technically flawless fresco paintings. Under the influence of RAPHAEL, he painted such notable works as *Madonna of the Harpies* (1517) and the fresco *Nativity of the Virgin* (1514). His paintings, though still classically balanced in High Renaissance style, contain the germ of MANNERISM to be seen in the later works of his pupils Jacopo Carucci da Pontormo (1494–1556) and Fiorentino Rosso (1494–1540). He is the

speaker in Robert Browning's famous dramatic monologue "Andrea del Sarto" (1855).

Sarton, May (1912–) Belgian-born American poet and novelist. Beginning with her first book of verse, *Encounter in April* (1937), Sarton wrote in traditional forms about intimate relationships, failures of communication, and loneliness. Her *Collected Poems, 1930–1973* (1974), *Selected Poems* (1978), and *Letters from Maine* (1984) are extensive volumes reflecting similar themes. Like her verse, her novels deal with the relationship between love and the creative process and between creativity and identity. Among her novels are *Shadow of a Man* (1950), *The Small Room* (1961), *Mrs. Stevens Hears the Mermaids Singing* (1965), *A Reckoning* (1978), and *The Magnificent Spinster* (1985). She also wrote the autobiographical works *I Knew a Phoenix* (1959) and *Plant Dreaming Deep* (1968) and a series of journals.

Sartoris (1929) A novel by William FAULKNER. The book tells the story of the descendants of Colonel John SARTORIS, especially that of young Bayard, who returns from World War I haunted by guilt feelings for the death of his brother, John. Driven by an urge for self-destruction, Bayard has a series of accidents. Because of his reckless driving, his grandfather, old Bayard Sartoris, rides with him in an attempt to force him to drive carefully, but young Bayard runs the car off the road and his grandfather dies of a heart attack. Young Bayard marries Narcissa Benbow, the sister of Horace Benbow who figures so prominently in SANCTUARY, but his suicidal drive leads him to become a test pilot in Ohio, and he is killed. This is the first of Faulkner's novels to deal with YOKNAPATAWPHA COUNTY. The early history of the Sartoris family is described in THE UNVANQUISHED.

Sartoris, Colonel John A leading character in William Faulkner's THE UNVANQUISHED and other novels and stories, and ancestor of the family treated in the novel SARTORIS. His many descendants and kinsfolk make up one of the important aristocratic families of Faulkner's imaginary world. He is believed to be reminiscent of Colonel William C. Falkner, the novelist's great-grandfather.

Sartor Resartus (1833–1834) A philosophical satire by Thomas CARLYLE, the Latin title of which means "tailor retailored." It purports to review a work on the philosophy of clothes by Diogenes Teufelsdröckh, an eccentric old professor of Things in General at Weissnichtwo (Ger, "know not where"). Passages supposedly translated from the German and the editor's running comments weave a narrative of Teufelsdröckh's life, often considered of autobiographical interest. A restless, impressionable youth, he passes through one disillusioning experience after another. He attends the university, studies law, and falls in love with the Rose Goddess, Blumine, who discards him for a more eligible suitor. After years of despair and wandering, he realizes that "here, in this poor, miserable, hampered, despicable Actual, wherein thou even now standest, here or nowhere is thy ideal. . . ."

Sartre, Jean-Paul (1905–1980)   French philosopher, dramatist, novelist, and critic. Born and educated in Paris, Sartre began his career by teaching. He also traveled widely, and while in Germany (1933–34) he studied under the philosophers Edmund HUSSERL and Martin HEIDEGGER. Before World War II he wrote several original psychological studies and a series of articles on contemporary literature which did much to popularize in France the works of American novelists such as FAULKNER, HEMINGWAY, DOS PASSOS, and STEINBECK. In 1938 Sartre published his first novel, the autobiographical NAUSEA, and the next year, the short stories in *Intimacy*, both books dramatizing the discovery of the meaninglessness of human life, the precondition for the philosophy of EXISTENTIALISM as Sartre later developed it.

He joined the French army in 1939 and was taken prisoner in 1940. After nine months he escaped to Paris and to an active part in the underground Resistance movement, writing for such clandestine publications as *Combat*. During the German occupation of France, he began writing plays. The production of THE FLIES in 1943, despite Nazi censorship, emphasized that the apparent pessimism of *Nausea* did not lead to nihilism for Sartre, but to the active assumption of moral responsibility—the position Sartre described as being *engagé*, or actively engaged in the business of shaping one's life. The same year, he published BEING AND NOTHINGNESS, the major exposition of his analysis of man's condition and potentialities.

The following year NO EXIT was produced and, after the liberation of France, Sartre organized (1945) the politico-literary review LES TEMPS MODERNES. He became internationally famous as the leader of a group of intellectuals described in many of the works of his intimate friend and associate of fifty years, Simone de BEAUVOIR. The Café Flore, where they gathered for conversation and argument, attracted tourists as well as disciples, and for the rest of the decade existentialism became a popular fashion as well as a serious and important influence on contemporary writers.

Albert CAMUS, whom Sartre had met along with de Beauvoir at the elite École Normale Superieure in the 1920s, was one of the friends in Sartre's circle. Although Camus's philosophical thinking started from similar assumptions, he was not an existentialist and disagreed publicly with Sartre on a number of issues, particularly that of ends and means. Sartre dramatized this issue in the controversial play DIRTY HANDS, which reflects his troubled sympathy with Communism. He defended this sympathy on occasion on the grounds that one must be *engagé*, supporting the least undesirable of the inevitably flawed contemporary political movements. After the Soviet intervention in Hungary in 1956, however, Sartre publicly announced his final disillusionment with Soviet communism.

Other important plays by Sartre include THE RESPECTFUL PROSTITUTE, an indictment of racism in the U.S.; *Le Diable et le bon Dieu* (1951; tr *The Devil and the Good Lord*, 1960), which deals with action versus complacency under tyranny; and *Les Séquestres d'Altona* (1959; tr *The Condemned of Altona*, 1961), about a former Nazi plagued by the view history will take of his acts. *Les Jeux sont faits* (1947; later revised as a novel; tr *The Chips Are Down*, 1948); and *L'Engrenage* (1948; tr *In the Mesh*, 1954) are film scenarios. Sartre's writings about the theatre were collected in *Un Théâtre de situation* (1973; tr *Sartre on Theatre*, 1976).

Sartre's other works include the novel trilogy THE ROADS TO FREEDOM and the essays *L'Existentialisme est un humanisme* (1946; tr *Existentialism and Humanism*, 1949); biographies, *Baudelaire* (1947) and *Saint Genet* (1952), exploring the life of Jean GENET, whom Sartre considered the prototypical ANTI-HERO; and the culmination of his political philosophy, *Critique de la dialectique* (1960). His essays were collected in the ten volumes of *Situations* (1947–72), which have been translated in such volumes as *Situations* (1965) and *Life/Situations* (1977).

Sartre remained until the end of his life a committed supporter of leftist causes. In 1964 he was awarded the NOBEL PRIZE in Literature, an honor he declined to accept on the grounds that commitment can be undermined by homage. His final major work was a three-volume biography of Gustave Flaubert, *L'Idiot de la famille* (1971–72).

Sassoon, Siegfried (1886–1967)   English poet and autobiographer, best known for his verse exposing the horrors of war. Sassoon's volume *Counter-Attack and Other Poems* (1918) contains angry, violent, and satirical poems about World War I, in which he fought as an officer, was wounded twice, and received two medals for bravery. He is also known for his three-volume fictional autobiography, at first published anonymously under the collective title *The Memoirs of George Sherston* (1928–36). The first volume, *Memoirs of a Fox-Hunting Man*, is a particularly vivid evocation of the life of the English country gentry before World War I. *The Old Century and Seven More Years* (1938), *The Weald of Youth* (1942), and *Siegfried's Journey* (1945) are explicit autobiography. His *Collected Poems* appeared in 1961.

Sastre, Alfonso (1926–   )   Spanish dramatist. The author of works of theatrical criticism, Sastre emphasizes the didactic function of drama. Most of his plays —which frequently went unproduced in his own country for many years under Franco—involve solitary protagonists, in conflict with an absurd world of false values, who end in failure. In such plays as *Escuadra hacia la muerte* (1953; tr *The Condemned Squad*, 1961), *La mordaza* (1954), and *Guillermo Tell tiene los ojos tristes* (1955; tr *Sad Are the Eyes of William Tell*, 1970), he pleads for justice and individual liberty while pondering the moral ambiguities involved in modern life. *Crónicas romanas* (*Roman*

Chronicles, 1968) represents a turn to the EPIC THEATRE in the Brechtian mold.

Satan (Heb, "adversary")   In Judeo-Christian belief, the chief spirit of evil in the universe. Satan entered into Jewish religious thought during the Exile under the influence of the dualistic Persian theology of Zoroastrianism, and continued in Christian doctrine. It was Satan who, in opposition to God, tested JOB and tempted JESUS in the wilderness. In early Christian writings, he appeared as Christ's chief adversary. Many strange doctrines concerning Satan's continuing war with God were later considered heretical, but belief in the DEVIL was an important factor in daily life throughout the Middle Ages and was common up until modern times, though it no longer plays a widespread role in Christian theology.

The gods of one religion have often become the devils of an opposing religion. Following this principle, the Christian Devil acquired many characteristics of various "heathen" deities. In the early days of the Church, popular superstition added a whole company of demons to Satan's entourage. Later, many traits of Norse and Germanic gods and spirits enhanced his powers, notably the capacity to assume many forms, human and animal. See DIVINE COMEDY; PARADISE LOST; SATANISM.

Satanism   The worship of SATAN. A survival of heathen fertility cults, Satanism gained impetus in about the 12th century from the secret rebellion against the Church. The central ritual of the cult was the Black Mass, an insulting and sometimes grisly parody of the Christian Mass. Traditionally it was performed by an unfrocked priest, with the nude body of a reclining woman as the altar. The Host was sometimes stolen from a church; at other times it was said to be made from the ashes and blood of murdered children. These practices, often connected with witchcraft, were supposed to have magical efficacy. They gave rise to the legend of the WITCHES' SABBATH, or WALPURGIS NIGHT.

Satanstoe   See LITTLEPAGE MANUSCRIPTS, THE.

sati (Sans, "devoted wife")   A woman who goes to her own death at the funeral of her deceased husband, most commonly by immolation on the funeral pyre. The practice was commended rather than commanded by sacred scripture and was observed only on a limited scale. Considered an intolerable barbarism by the British and many Indians, it was officially abolished in 1829 in those areas under direct British control.

Satie, Erik[-Alfred-Leslie] (1866–1925)   Unorthodox French composer whose early rebellion against the ideals of ROMANTICISM earned him the adulation of LES SIX and others. In addition to his piano works, Satie collaborated with COCTEAU and PICASSO on the ballet *Parade* (1917), which was described as a "cubist manifesto."

Satin Slipper, The (Le Soulier de satin, 4 vols, 1928–1929; tr 1931)   A poetic drama by Paul CLAUDEL, revised for the stage in 1943. The never-consummated passion of Don Rodrigue and Doña Prouheze blazes across a baroque pageant of 16th-century Spain. The love they cannot exchange is transmuted during their lives into the energy that explores a continent or holds an embattled fortress, and thus fulfills God's purpose. Because they accept the difficult challenge of bearing their separation loyally and nobly, their passion becomes the annealing flame that prepares them for spiritual joy; the symbol of this is the free-spirited Doña Sept-Epées, who is actually Prouheze's daughter by her second husband but spiritually the child of Rodrigue.

satire   A manner or spirit employing any number of literary and rhetorical devices that expose human or institutional vices and in which a corrective is either implied or directly proposed. In his DICTIONARY OF THE ENGLISH LANGUAGE, Dr. Johnson wrote that satire is a "poem in which wickedness or folly is censured." Satire, however, is not limited only to poetry, nor can it be labeled strictly as a literary form.

The protean forms and enormous range of satire recall that the word originally meant "a dish of mixed fruits." Some scholars connect its origins with the ritual exercises of primitive cultures to drive away evil spirits. Classical Greek and Roman literature offers a rich tradition of satiric writing in the work of ARISTOPHANES, JUVENAL, HORACE, MARTIAL, and PETRONIUS. In fact, from the classical examples, satire has been classified into two general types: Juvenalian satire, a biting, morally indignant exposé of evil and corruption; and Horatian, a gently humorous satire that aims to correct through laughter.

Although satiric writing has been prevalent in European literature since the Middle Ages, it found its greatest expression in the 17th and 18th centuries. Outstanding examples from the period include Molière's TARTUFFE and others of his plays, Voltaire's CANDIDE, Swift's GULLIVER'S TRAVELS, Dryden's ABSALOM AND ACHITOPHEL and MACFLECKNOE, and Pope's THE DUNCIAD and THE RAPE OF THE LOCK. In poetry, the HEROIC COUPLET was the favored satiric form of the age and, during the English RESTORATION, the COMEDY OF MANNERS was a popular form of satirical drama. Targets of satire are as various as the forms it takes. Hypocrisy, ambition, greed, piety, pride, materialism, and pretension are among the many weaknesses of the human character that have been pinpointed and ridiculed by the satirist's pen. Swift, whose grim depiction of human nature in *Gulliver's Travels* could be called Juvenalian satire, once wrote that "Satire is a sort of glass wherein beholders do generally discover everybody's face but their own, which is the chief reason for that kind of reception it meets with in the world, and that so very few are offended with it" (from the Preface to THE BATTLE OF THE BOOKS).

satori   Enlightenment in ZEN BUDDHISM. It is attained in Rinzai Zen through successful intensive meditation and KŌAN practice; in Sōtō Zen, through meditative sitting. An adept may experience *satori* many times in the course of his Zen training.

Saturday Night and Sunday Morning (1958)
A novel by Alan SILLITOE. Arthur Seton, the hero, is a
rebellious young loner whose weekdays are spent working
at a dull job in a foul-smelling factory. Although he doesn't
particularly mind his work, he treats it with an intentional
indifference, because if he were to work hard, his labors
would only reward the managerial class for whom he
harbors considerable contempt. His Saturday nights are
devoted to boozing, brawling, and promiscuity; on Sunday
mornings he nurses his hangover at a peaceful fishing spot
in the country. He eventually succumbs to the almost-
secure life of marriage with a nice, very ordinary woman.
Sillitoe's realistic, unsentimental characterization of working-class life in this novel led to his public identification
with the ANGRY YOUNG MEN.

Saturday Review   A weekly literary review
founded in 1924 by Henry Seidel Canby, Christopher
MORLEY, Amy Loveman, and William Rose BENÉT. Originally called *The Saturday Review of Literature*, it changed
its name in 1952 when it extended its coverage to other
arts, the mass media, and increased social commentary.
For many years it was identified with Norman COUSINS,
who guided the magazine as editor and then as editor-pub-
lisher from 1940 to 1978. As with other independent magazines, it was beset with financial difficulties in the 1960s
and 1970s and changed its format and editor several times
in the 70s and 80s.

Saturn   An Italian god of agriculture, later identified
with the Greek CRONOS. Saturn was the husband of Ops,
goddess of plenty identified with the Greek RHEA. As a legendary king of Rome, Saturn was remembered for introducing agriculture, and his reign, considered a golden age,
was commemorated by the SATURNALIA.

Saturnalia   A time of unrestrained disorder and mis-
rule. In ancient Rome, it was the festival of SATURN, and
was celebrated from the 17th to the 19th of December.
During its continuance no public business could be trans-
acted; the law courts and schools were closed; no war could
be started, and no malefactor punished. Presents were
exchanged and everyone, even slaves, was freed from customary restraints. Under the empire, the festival was
extended to seven days.

satyagraha (Sans, *satya*, "truth," *graha*, "firm grasping")   A term, sometimes rendered as "soul force,"
applied to the nonviolent civil disobedience campaigns
organized by Mahatma GANDHI in India.

satyr play   A semiserious form of classical Greek
drama. Presented at the end of a trilogy of tragedies by the
same author, a satyr play apparently brought comic relief to
the great festivals of drama. It treated serious mythological
events in a grotesquely comic manner, but had the form of
tragedy. The only surviving satyr plays are *Cyclops* by
EURIPIDES and a long fragment of SOPHOCLES' *Ichneutai*.
The first tells the famous story of POLYPHEMUS and ODYS-
SEUS, the second the miraculous growth of the infant HER-

MES. As in all satyr plays, the chorus is made up of SATYRS.
Because of its comic scenes with the drunken HERACLES,
Euripides' ALCESTIS resembles a satyr play.

satyrs   In Greek legend, a race of goat-men who
dwelt in the woodlands. The most famous satyr was SILE-
NUS. They were often shown as followers of DIONYSUS and
spent much of their time in amorous pursuit of the
nymphs.

Saul   (1) In the OLD TESTAMENT (1 Sam. 9–31), the
first king of Israel, anointed by SAMUEL when the people
demanded a king. Saul's reign was marked by repeated
conflicts with the PHILISTINES. In his moods of despair, he
was calmed by the harp playing of DAVID, whom he loved
and who became Saul's armor-bearer. Saul, however,
became increasingly jealous of David's friendship with
Saul's son, Jonathan, and of his growing popularity with
the people and sought to have David killed. In a battle with
the Philistines, after his sons were slain and after receiving
a prophecy of defeat from the WITCH of Endor, Saul killed
himself on Mt. Gilboa.

(2) PAUL, the apostle, who was known in Hebrew as Saul
of Tarsus.

Saul (1845)   A dramatic monologue by Robert
BROWNING.

Saunders, Richard   Benjamin FRANKLIN's pen
name, under which he wrote the maxims in POOR RICH-
ARD'S ALMANACK.

Savage, Richard (1697–1743)   English playwright
and poet, who claimed to be the illegitimate son of the
countess of Macclesfield and Richard Savage, fourth Earl
Rivers. Savage's friend Dr. Samuel Johnson wrote his biography in THE LIVES OF THE POETS, although the account
there of his birth and ill treatment is now generally disbe-
lieved. Some of his plays were acted in Drury Lane. In one
of them, *Sir Thomas Overbury* (1723), he himself played
the title role. Savage edited *Miscellaneous Poems and
Translations* (1726), a well-known collection, and wrote
The Wanderer (1729), a poem. He had an adventurous life,
and died in debtor's prison.

Savonarola, Fra Girolamo (1452–1498)   The
celebrated monk of Ferrara who came to Florence and
preached reform. From the Dominican monastery of San
Marco and the pulpit of the cathedral, Savonarola's sermons and exhortations engulfed the city in a tidal wave of
piety. After the ouster of the MEDICI family, he held political as well as spiritual power over the city; heeding his call
to reform and purify, the people burned vanities, eschewed
paganism, and practiced repentance. Finally, charges of
disobedience, then heresy, brought his excommunication
from the Church and his burning at the stake. His surviving sermons give some indication of why he was able to
win adherents among the people and among such artists as
BOTTICELLI, PICO DELLA MIRANDOLA, FICINO, and the
young MICHELANGELO. Savonarola is a leading character in

George Eliot's ROMOLA, and appears in Harriet Beecher Stowe's *Agnes of Sorrento* (1862).

Savoy Operas   See GILBERT AND SULLIVAN OPERAS.

Sayers, Dorothy L[eigh] (1893–1957)   English detective-story writer and essayist on medieval and Christian subjects. Sayers earned first-class honors in medieval studies, among the first women to be granted an Oxford degree. Her witty, sophisticated detective novels and stories, most of them featuring the urbane aristocrat-sleuth Lord Peter Wimsey, are perennially popular. Among her many carefully plotted thrillers are *Whose Body?* (1923), *Strong Poison* (1930), *The Nine Tailors* (1934), and *Busman's Honeymoon* (1937). She also wrote plays, mostly religious in nature, notably *The Man Born to Be King* (1942); essays on Christianity such as *Creed or Chaos* (1947); and translations of most of Dante's *Divine Comedy* (1949, 1955).

Sayre, Zelda   See FITZGERALD, F. SCOTT.

scalds   Court poets and chroniclers of the ancient Scandinavians.

Scaligero, Giulio Cesare (known as Julius Caesar Scaliger, 1484–1558)   Italian literary critic. Scaligero was born and spent his youth as soldier and student in northern Italy. In 1525 he moved to France as a physician and stayed there to become a leading advocate of the moralist approach to literature. His *Poetices* (1561), ostensibly a manual for writing Latin poetry, served to spread his critical ideas throughout Europe.

Scamander (or Xanthos)   A river near the ancient city of Troy. It figures largely in the accounts of the TROJAN WAR.

scansion   A system for determining the METER of a piece of poetry. Detailed scansion is accomplished by marking each syllable according to whether it is accented or not and analyzing the patterns. Any piece of writing or speech can be scanned.

scapegoat   A sacrificial animal symbolically bearing the sins of a group. Part of the ancient ritual among the Hebrews for the DAY OF ATONEMENT laid down by Mosaic law (Lev. 16) was as follows: Two goats were brought to the altar of the tabernacle and the high priests cast lots, one for the Lord, the other for AZAZEL. The Lord's goat was sacrificed; the other was the *scapegoat*. After the high priest, by confession, had transferred his sins and the sins of the people to it, it was taken into the desert and allowed to escape.

The word has come to mean anyone who bears the blame for a group or another person.

Scapigliatura, La (Ital, "the disheveled ones")   An avant-garde literary circle that flourished in Milan c1860–75. The name was coined by one of its founding members, Cletto Arrighi, pen name of Carlo Righetti (1830–1906).

The Scapigliatura counted among its adherents Arrigo BOÏTO; Giuseppe Rovani (1812–74), its chief exponent; Emilio Praga (1839–75); and Iginio Ugo Tarchetti (1841–69), "the Italian Edgar Allan Poe." These writers had a common objective in their declared war against the classical and Arcadian as well as against the moralistic traditions in Italian literature. They proposed BAUDELAIRE and the budding school of French SYMBOLISTS as models for Italian writers. POE (known through Baudelaire's translations) was another model, as were E.T.A. HOFFMANN and other German romantic writers of the bizarre and macabre.

The result of the Scapigliatura's antibourgeois, antitraditionalist stand was a fusion of interest in pathological characters and a preference for realistic descriptions expressed in a direct, unaffected, and nonclassical language. VERGA, Emilio De Marchi (1851–1901), and CAPUANA were influenced by the Scapigliatura during their literary apprenticeships in Milan. The circle disbanded, having realized its *raison d'être*, when Capuana published his novel of psychological realism, *Giacinta* (1879), and Verga published his exemplar of realistic narrative, I MALAVOGLIA.

Scapin   The central character in Molière's comedy *Les Fourberies de Scapin* (*The Rogueries of Scapin*, 1671). A clever and intrepid valet whose roguery provides the interest of the drama, Scapin is the direct literary descendant of Scapino, the lively rascal who had long been one of the stock characters of the Italian stage. In Molière's comedy, he is the valet of Léandre, the nominal hero of the play, whose complicated amorous difficulties he resolves in a masterful manner.

Scaramuccia (Fr, Scaramouche; Eng, Scaramouch)   A stock character of the Italian COMMEDIA DELL'ARTE. Scaramuccia is sometimes considered one of the *zanni*, or servants, though he may have more closely resembled the braggart soldier.

Scarlatti, Alessandro (1660–1725)   Italian composer, the outstanding figure of the Late Baroque period in Italy. Scarlatti's many operas are an important milestone on the way to modern opera, and he also wrote over six hundred cantatas for solo voices, as well as church music. His son Domenico Scarlatti (1685–1757), long resident in Spain, was a virtuoso harpsichordist and composer, famous for his sonatas for the harpsichord.

Scarlet, Will   See ROBIN HOOD.

Scarlet Letter, The (1850)   A novel by Nathaniel HAWTHORNE. Hester Prynne is condemned to wear the scarlet embroidered letter A on her breast, as punishment for her adultery. She resists all attempts of the 17th-century Boston clergy to make her reveal the name of her child's father. Her husband, an old physician who had remained in Europe, arrives in America to see her on the pillory. Assuming the name of Roger Chillingworth, he seeks revenge. Soon correctly suspecting the respected young minister, Arthur Dimmesdale, he constantly torments him without revealing the full extent of his knowledge. Pearl, the elfin child, is a constant trial to her mother; perverse, wild, an "outcast of the infantile world," she is the brilliant product of sin. Chillingworth succeeds in frustrating the escape of Hester, Arthur, and Pearl. In the final scene, the minister mounts the pillory with Hester and their child, revealing his guilt and the scarlet letter that remorse had etched on his breast. By this act, he finally escapes Chillingworth's Satanic power and dies in Hester's arms. The child, transfigured by the sorrowful scene, sheds tears for the first time. Kissing her father, she gives proof of her humanity.

The book treats Hawthorne's favorite themes. First, all men are guilty of secret sin. Second, greater than Dimmesdale's is Chillingworth's sin, for he has invaded the sanctity of another's soul.

Scarlet Pimpernel, The (1905)   A novel, the first in a series by the Hungarian-born English novelist Baroness ORCZY (1865–1947). It is an adventure story of the French Revolution. The apparently foppish young Englishman, Sir Percy Blakeney, is found to be the daring Scarlet Pimpernel, rescuer of distressed aristocrats.

Scarlet Woman (or Scarlet Whore)   The woman seen by the author of the book of Revelations in his vision "arrayed in purple and scarlet color," sitting "upon a scarlet colored beast, full of names of blasphemy, having seven heads and ten horns," "drunken with the blood of the saints, and with the blood of the martyrs," upon whose forehead was written, "Mystery, Babylon the Great, the Mother of Harlots and Abominations of the Earth" (Rev. 17:1–6). The author was probably referring to Rome, which, at the time he was writing, was "drunken with the blood of the saints." Some Protestants have applied the words to the Church of Rome; and some Roman Catholics, to the Protestant churches generally.

Scarron, Paul (1610–1660)   French novelist. Scarron's *Roman comique* (*Comic Novel*, 1651), an account of a troupe of wandering comedians, is believed by scholars to be based upon the troupe of Molière. Scarron's realism and satire constituted a revolt against the artificial and excessively mannered writing of his time. Crippled by rheumatism at the age of thirty, Scarron married François d'Aubigné, who later became Mme de MAINTENON.

Scève, Maurice (1510?–?1564)   French poet. The first of a group of French poets whose center was at Lyons, Scève wrote love poetry that reveals a profound spiritual uneasiness. His most famous collection of poems, the *Délie* (1544), betrays the Petrarchan influence—the conception of love progressing from the senses to pure idea. In fact, Scève was involved in the discovery of what was thought to be the tomb of PETRARCH's Laura in Avignon (1543). His verse is marked by a subtle musicality which 19th-century symbolism (see SYMBOLISTS) was quick to appreciate. The symbolist poets brought Scève back into literary prominence after two centuries of neglect.

Schahriah   In the ARABIAN NIGHTS, the Sultan for whom the tales are told. When both his own wife and that of his brother prove unfaithful, Schahriah, imagining that no woman is virtuous, resolves to marry a new wife every night and have her strangled at daybreak. But Scheher-

azade, the Vizier's daughter, marries him in spite of his vow and contrives, an hour before daybreak, to begin a story to her sister, Dinarzade, in the Sultan's hearing, always breaking off before the story is finished. The Sultan grows interested in these tales and, after 1001 nights, revokes his decree, bestows his affection on Scheherazade, and calls her the liberator of her sex.

Scheherazade   See SCHAHRIAH.

Schelling, Caroline (born Caroline Michaelis, 1763–1809)   Influential figure in German literary life during the period of romanticism. After the death of her first husband (1788), Schelling's erotic attachment to a French officer involved her in serious political trouble, from which she was rescued by August Wilhelm SCHLEGEL, whom she then married in 1796. It is thought that she helped him with some of his essays on Shakespeare, and perhaps with his translations. Friedrich Schlegel was also deeply attached to her, and though he yielded to his brother, she clearly inspired many of his ideas on feminine emancipation. In 1803 she divorced A. W. Schlegel and was married, for the last time, to the young philosopher SCHELLING. Her letters later appeared in a collection entitled *Briefe aus der Frühromantik* (*Letters of Early Romanticism*, 1871) and offer many personal and literary insights into the romantic movement.

Schelling, Friedrich Wilhelm Joseph von (1775–1854)   German philosopher and aesthetician of romanticism. Schelling's commitment to a pantheistic view of the universe is seen in his *Von der Weltseele* (*Of the World-Soul*, 1798) and *System des transcendentalen Idealismus* (*System of Transcendental Idealism*, 1800). He saw the universe as an organic, living whole pervaded by a single spirit, and contended that "nature is visible spirit and spirit is invisible nature." He believed that the creative act of the artist is analogous to the act of world creation, since it comprehends both the material and spiritual aspects of the world. Hegel and Hölderlin were both schoolmates and close friends of his, and all three shared the wish to see man and nature as parts of a single whole. See GERMAN ROMANTICISM; SCHELLING, CAROLINE.

Schiele, Egon (1890–1918)   Austrian painter. Schiele was an expressionist painter influenced by ART NOUVEAU, especially by his teacher, Gustave KLIMT. He painted landscapes, portraits, and nudes with an intensity evinced by their vibrant colors and angular black lines. His career was short, and he died impoverished in the 1918 influenza epidemic.

Schiller, [Johann Christoph] Friedrich von (1759–1805)   German dramatist, poet, and historian. From 1794 until his death, Schiller was closely associated with Goethe, and the two authors, almost alone, led the movement known as WEIMAR CLASSICISM. The two men's tendencies, however, were considerably different. Whereas Goethe's main strength was broad, epic development, always striving to comprehend the balanced wholeness of life, Schiller's talent lay in the treatment of fast-moving, dramatic action. He had more skill in creating and maintaining theatrical interest than Goethe did, and though his characters are often not as deep, they are usually more sharply defined than Goethe's.

Schiller's early prose plays are in the style of the STURM UND DRANG, but tend to deal with more specific social problems than Goethe's early plays. THE ROBBERS and KABALE UND LIEBE are examples. But after DON CARLOS, the play in which this period culminated, Schiller began to have serious misgivings about the value of his writing and felt the need for a reappraisal of his aesthetic and philosophical principles. For the next decade he wrote no plays at all, and his most important writings were several treatises on aesthetics, all influenced by Kant, including *Über Anmut und Würde* (*On Grace and Dignity*, 1793); *Briefe über die ästhetische Erziehung des Menschen* (*Letters on the Aesthetic Education of Man*, 1795), in which art is defined as the expression of a human play-drive, and its value seen in the cultivation of this drive; and *On Naïve and Sentimental Poetry* (1795–96). These aesthetic writings provided the theoretical groundwork for his later dramatic style, which first appeared in WALLENSTEIN. He had now given up much of his earlier unquestioning and tendentious idealism in favor of a more realistic, Goethean technique, which is also observable in MARY STUART. But Schiller never entirely forsook his basic tendency toward idealism, and in fact took a strong turn back in that direction in his last plays, including THE MAID OF ORLEANS and WILHELM TELL. These plays, however, are more polished and classical in form than his early *Sturm und Drang* works, and put more emphasis on general, moral ideas.

As a lyric poet, Schiller is more famous for his long didactic poems, including *Die Götter Griechenlands* (*The Gods of Greece*, 1788) and *Die Künstler* (*The Artists*, 1789). By profession Schiller was a historian and in 1791 was made a professor of history at the University of Jena. His most famous scholarly work is *Die Geschichte des Dreißigjährigen Krieges* (*History of the Thirty Years' War*, 1791).

Schism, Great   The period (1378–1417) when the Roman papacy was challenged by antipopes who reigned at Avignon.

Schlegel, August Wilhelm von (1767–1845) and his brother **Friedrich** (1772–1829)   German romantic poets and critics. August Wilhelm's poetry is of little significance, but he was an extremely able critic and scholar. His lectures at Berlin University, *Über schöne Literatur und Kunst* (*On Literature and Art*, delivered 1801–2), and those at Vienna, *Über dramatische Kunst und Literatur* (*On Dramatic Art and Literature*, delivered 1807–8), were instrumental in formulating and publicizing the ideas of his fellow romantics. He also accompanied Madame de STAËL on her travels in Germany, and many of her ideas are borrowed from him. Among his other works are translations of CALDERÓN under the title *Spanisches Theater* (1803), and translations of seventeen plays of SHAKESPEARE (1797). His German *Shakespeare* was later continued by TIECK (1825) and is still read today.

Friedrich Schlegel was a more original and creative spirit than his brother, but often lacked the latter's gift of stylistic clarity. He wrote hundreds of brilliant philosophical and critical aphorisms, which include many important statements about the romantic movement. It was he who defined romantic poetry as a "progressive universal poetry," and it was he who first clearly defined the concept of romantic IRONY. In his novel *Lucinde* (1799), he advocated free love, but not on a purely sexual basis; he believed in full equality of the sexes and felt that a man and a woman should not live together except on terms of complete spiritual and sexual union. He was a competent classical scholar and wrote a *Geschichte der alten und neuen Literatur* (*History of Ancient and Modern Literature*, 1815). Among his close friends were NOVALIS, Tieck, and SCHLEIERMACHER; like his brother, he was a lifelong admirer of GOETHE, but fell out with SCHILLER, whom he attacked critically on occasion.

The two brothers together edited the romantic periodical *Athenäum* (1798–1800). Central among the ideas they held in common was a distinction between classical (ancient) poetry as a "poetry of accomplishment," and romantic (modern) poetry as a "poetry of yearning." Goethe makes a similar distinction in *Faust* (see HELEN). The Schlegels are also credited with a large part in the establishment of modern literary critical techniques, in that they opposed the 18th-century ideal of the critic as a *judge* of art and insisted that the critic must first of all *understand* and *appreciate* the literary work on its own terms. Both brothers, finally, were pioneers in the fields of Romance philology and Sanskrit studies. See GERMAN ROMANTICISM; SCHELLING, CAROLINE; WEIMAR CLASSICISM.

Schlegel, Margaret   The cultured, idealistic heroine of E. M. Forster's novel HOWARDS END. Her sister Helen is also an important character.

Schleiermacher, Friedrich Ernst Daniel (1768–1834)   German philosopher and Protestant theologian, important in GERMAN ROMANTICISM. In his *Reden über die Religion* (1799; tr *Speeches on Religion*, 1892), he developed the idea that every individual must establish an entirely personal attitude to religion. With his friend Friedrich von SCHLEGEL, he was a staunch advocate of equality of the sexes. Of his *Idee zu einem Katechismus der Vernunft für edle Frauen* (*Ten Commandments for Noble-minded Women*, 1801), the ninth reads: "Thou shalt not give false testimony for men; thou shalt not defend their barbarities with words and deeds." The tenth reads: "Thou shalt covet men's education, art, wisdom, and honor."

Schlemmer, Oskar (1888–1943)   German painter and sculptor. Schlemmer is known for the rigid geometric structure of much of his work and for sculptures which are gleaming, meticulously symmetrical representations of the human body. From 1920 to 1929, Schlemmer taught at the BAUHAUS, where he influenced the course of theatre and stage design, as well as painting and sculpture.

Schlesinger, Arthur M[eier] (1888–1965) American historian. Schlesinger taught at Ohio State University and the University of Iowa before joining the faculty of Harvard University in 1924. His many important historical works include *The Colonial Merchants and the American Revolution* (1918), *New Viewpoints in American History* (1922), *The Rise of the City* (1933), *Paths to the Present* (1949), and *Prelude to Independence: The Newspaper War on Britain, 1764–1776* (1958). *In Retrospect: The History of a Historian* (1963) is autobiographical.

Schlesinger, Arthur [Meier], Jr. (1917–   ) American historian. The son of Arthur SCHLESINGER, he served on the faculty of Harvard from 1946 to 1962. His well-known book *The Age of Jackson* (1945) stimulated a reexamination of the Jacksonian era of American history and won a PULITZER PRIZE. Known as a political liberal, Schlesinger wrote a sympathetic and highly praised three-volume analytic history of the New Deal, *The Age of Roosevelt* (1957–60). In 1961 he was appointed special assistant to President John F. KENNEDY. His account of the Kennedy White House years, *A Thousand Days* (1965), also won a Pulitzer Prize. His other works include *The Politics of Hope* (1963); *The Bitter Heritage* (1967); and *The Imperial Presidency* (1973), about the Nixon administration. *Robert Kennedy and His Times* (1978) is at the same time a biography and a reexamination of the Kennedy era in light of evidence not available when A *Thousand Days* was written. *The Cycles of American Parties* (1986) is a further collection of writings on politics.

Schlesinger, John (1926–   )   English film director. Schlesinger's films tend to feature characters who don't fit comfortably in the mainstream, are aware of their loneliness, and hide their fears beneath a mask of worldliness or sophistication. His most important films are *Billy Liar* (1963), *Darling* (1965), *Far From the Madding Crowd* (1966), *Midnight Cowboy* (1969), and *Sunday, Bloody Sunday* (1971). *An Englishman Abroad* (1983) was awarded the British Academy Award for best picture.

Schliemann, Heinrich (1822–1890)   German amateur archaeologist, famous for having found ancient Troy. Near the Turkish village of Hissarlik Schliemann excavated the fabled city between layers of older and younger settlements. Even though he considered the wrong layer to be the Homeric Troy, his achievement remains one of the greatest in the history of archaeology. He also discovered the tombs of Mycenaean kings. His monumental discoveries are largely the result of his belief, then considered absurd, that the Homeric legends were to a considerable degree historical fact.

Schloß, Das   See CASTLE, THE.

Schnitzler, Arthur (1862–1931)   Austrian playwright and novelist. Schnitzler is known for his stylistic experiments in both prose and drama and for his brilliance of psychological observation and depiction. Both of these qualities are found in his two best-known works, LEUTNANT GUSTL, a short novel, and LA RONDE, a play. His early play *Anatol* (1891) is filled with characteristically Viennese wit and a vigorously amoral attitude toward erotic situations, which form the atmospheric background in many of his subsequent works. But though he continued to favor erotic themes, he became increasingly aware, in plays such as LIGHT O' LOVE and *Der grüne Kakadu* (*The Green Cockatoo*, 1899), of problems inherent in his early carefree attitude. Only once, in the play PROFESSOR BERNHARDI (1918), did he treat a completely nonsexual theme. Before turning to writing, Schnitzler had studied medicine and done research in psychiatry, which accounts in part for his ability to probe characters in depth.

Schoenberg, Arnold (1874–1951)   Austrian-born composer and teacher. Schoenberg is the inventor of the twelve-tone or serial method of composition to provide a basis for unity and coherence in atonal music (see ATONALITY). His method and his music, as well as his personal philosophy, which he expounded in many essays and several books such as *Style and Idea* (1950), have had a great impact on composers and musicians of many nations. Several of his students are major composers in their own right, among them Alban BERG and Anton von WEBERN. When Thomas MANN described the twelve-tone method in *Doktor Faustus*, Schoenberg demanded and received credit for his idea. The composer is also identified with the expressionism that affected various arts at the beginning of the 20th century. His works include *Verklärte Nacht* (*Transfigured Night*, 1899), *Pierrot lunaire* (*Moonstruck Pierrot*, 1912; for voice and instruments), *Suite for Piano* (1924, the first work based entirely on twelve-tone techniques), and *Ode to Napoleon* (1942, for speaker, strings, and piano; based on Lord BYRON's poem).

Scholar-Gipsy, The (1853)   A poem by Matthew ARNOLD. According to an old story current in Oxford, a student of that university, who years before wandered off to learn the gypsy traditions, still roams about. Arnold makes this lonely wanderer, whose life he regards as enviable in many ways, the hero of his poem.

Scholasticism (fr Lat, *schola*, "school")   The philosophical system of the Schoolmen of the Middle Ages. In schools first established under the Carolingians and usually attached to monasteries or cathedrals, the Schoolmen, as distinct from the practicing clergy, were involved in trying to synthesize a Christian system of logic and philosophy based on ARISTOTLE and other ancient scholars. Their work was made even more difficult by the fact that very often the classical texts they had at their disposal were poor Latin translations from Arabic sources, which were in turn dubious translations from the original Greek. Hampered by the

Church's insistence that their results be reconcilable with Christian doctrine, the Schoolmen were often reduced to hair-splitting quibbles over methodology and terminology. Their most significant contribution to modern philosophy was their argument over the priority of essence or existence, which was the problem behind the opposition of NOMINALISM and REALISM. The climax of the first period (9th to 12th century) was reached in the work of Peter LOMBARD and Pierre ABÉLARD; the best of the second period was summarized by St. Thomas AQUINAS and John DUNS SCOTUS.

Scholem, Gershom [Gerhard] (1897–1982) Jewish historian, philologist, and scholar. Born in Berlin, Scholem immigrated to Palestine in 1923 and became the pioneer and leading authority in the field of Jewish mysticism and the KABBALAH, which he established as a major discipline by placing its study on a solid philological basis. His textual analysis, philosophical insight, and historical understanding set new standards and added new perspectives to Jewish studies as a whole. His most important works include *Major Trends in Jewish Mysticism* (1941); *Jewish Gnosticism, Merkabah Mysticism and Talmudic Tradition* (Hebrew, 1960); *Sabbatai Sevi: The Mystical Messiah* (1973); and *Kabbalah* (1974). The selected essays in *On Jews and Judaism in Crisis* (1977) include autobiographical accounts as well as Scholem's reflections on Zionist thinking.

scholia (Lat plural, fr Gr, *scholion*, "leisure; ease; learned discussion; school") A body of marginal notes to a classical text. When Alexandrian scholars wrote commentaries on classical authors (particularly the poets), they compiled lists of explanations of specific wording. Material from these glossaries was eventually excerpted into the margins of the manuscripts. Successive owners of a manuscript often transcribed more *scholia* from other commentaries and added critical notes of their own. The result is that a late medieval manuscript of HOMER or SOPHOCLES, for example, is likely to contain largely anonymous *scholia* whose sources range all the way from the Alexandrian commentaries to interpretations by Byzantine scholars in the 12th century. *Scholia* frequently provide valuable information on matters relating to the text and are often used as guides in correcting "corrupt" texts.

Schongauer, Martin (c1430 or 1445–1491) German painter and engraver. Schongauer was the undisputed master of late German gothic art, evidently influenced by Rogier van der WEYDEN. The only painting unquestionably painted by him is *The Madonna of the Rose Bower* (1473); he is best known as an engraver. His engraved works, all signed M + S, were dispersed throughout Europe and used extensively by later artists. He executed religious themes, such as *The Temptation of St. Anthony*, with unsurpassed depth of interpretation. Schongauer's work was the model for DÜRER, who further elevated the status of engraving as an art form.

Schoolcraft, Henry Rowe (1793–1864) American ethnologist, explorer, geologist, and writer. After serving as geologist to the Lewis Cass expedition (1820) to Lake Superior, Schoolcraft was appointed Indian agent there. In 1832 he discovered the source of the Mississippi. Married to the daughter of a Chippewa chief, he gathered much of his Indian lore from his wife. As superintendent of Indian affairs for Michigan (1836–41), he wrote his explorations and researches in a number of highly influential books. The first white man to translate Indian poetry, he was among the first seriously to study Indian legend and religion. Among Schoolcraft's books are *Travels in the Central Portions of the Mississippi Valley* (1825), *Algic Researches, Comprising Inquiries Respecting the Mental Characteristics of the North American Indians* (2 vols, 1839), and *Personal Memoirs of a Residence of Thirty Years with the Indian Tribes* (1851). Schoolcraft's writings made a profound impression on LONGFELLOW; repeating Schoolcraft's error, the poet confused the Iroquois HIAWATHA with the Chippewa Manabozho, and set his famous verse narrative on the shores of Lake Superior, instead of in central New York.

School for Scandal, The (1777) A comedy, one of the most popular in the English language, by Richard Brinsley SHERIDAN. Lady Sneerwell and a group of friends meet often at her house for the purpose of creating and spreading malicious gossip. Lady Teazle, attractive young wife of the much older Sir Peter, is a member of the circle. By making overtures to Lady Teazle, Joseph Surface, a hypocritical young man, tries to gain access to Maria, Sir Peter's ward. Although Maria is in love with Joseph's brother, Charles, Sir Peter favors a match with Joseph. Joseph tells Lady Teazle that he is indifferent to Maria; after a quarrel with Sir Peter, Lady Teazle keeps an appointment at Joseph's rooms. Suddenly Sir Peter is announced, and Joseph hides Lady Teazle behind a screen. Sir Peter tells Joseph that he thinks his wife is in love with Charles and also speaks of the handsome settlement he intends to make on her. Overhearing this, Lady Teazle is full of remorse. Moments later Charles is shown in, and Sir Peter hides in a closet; he is thus able to hear Charles tell Joseph that his interest is entirely in Maria. Sir Peter comes out of hiding, and, while Joseph is called away, the screen topples, exposing a much chastened Lady Teazle. Meanwhile Sir Oliver Surface, wealthy uncle of Joseph and Charles, has returned from India with a plan to test the mettle of his nephews' characters. First, disguised as Mr. Premium, a usurer, he calls on Charles. Charles and his friends auction off the family portraits to Premium, but Charles refuses to sell the portrait of his Uncle Oliver. He sends some of the money to Stanley, an old relative who has asked him for assistance. Uncle Oliver, pretending to be Stanley, then calls on Joseph to ask for assistance and is refused; Joseph tells him that he can't help him because Uncle Oliver is so stingy. Joseph's duplicity is brought to light; Sir Peter and Lady Teazle are reconciled; and Maria and Charles are united.

School for Wives, The   See ÉCOLE DES FEMMES, L'.

Schoolmaster, The (1570)   A celebrated treatise by Roger ASCHAM, expressing the author's ideas on the education of the English youth of his time. It opposes foreign schooling, especially in Italy, favors the incorporation of athletics into the curriculum, and attacks English verse meter, while defending the use of English prose.

Schoolmen   See SCHOLASTICISM.

Schopenhauer, Arthur (1788–1860)   German philosopher whose extreme pessimism is expressed in *Die Welt als Wille und Vorstellung* (*The World as Will and Idea*, 1819). Schopenhauer maintained that the desires and drives of men, as well as the forces of nature, are manifestations of a single will, specifically the will to live, which is the essence of the world. Since operation of the will means constant striving without satisfaction, life consists of suffering. Only by controlling the will through the intellect, by suppressing the desire to reproduce, can suffering be diminished.

Schorer, Mark (1908–1977)   American novelist and critic. The best known of Schorer's fourteen books is his monumental biography *Sinclair Lewis: An American Life* (1961). Among his critical works are *William Blake: The Politics of Vision* (1946), *D. H. Lawrence* (1969), and *The World We Imagine: Selected Essays* (1968).

Schreiner, Olive [Emilie Albertina] (pen name Ralph Iron, 1855–1920)   South African novelist and essayist. Schreiner is best known for her semiautobiographical novel, THE STORY OF AN AFRICAN FARM. With very little formal education, she was a fervent rationalist, feminist, and extreme liberal. Most of her later books were concerned with social problems, as in *The South African Question* (1890) and *Women and Labor* (1911).

Schubert, Franz [Peter] (1797–1828)   Austrian composer. Schubert was perhaps the finest composer of art songs the world has known; his catalogued works number nearly a thousand, of which nearly six hundred are songs with piano. His favored poets were GOETHE and SCHILLER, but he also set SHAKESPEARE and Sir Walter SCOTT, among others. He wrote much piano music, six masses, other church music, operas, and nine symphonies, of which *No. 8*, the "Unfinished" in B minor, and *No. 9*, the "Great" in C major are the most remarkable. His *Quintet in C major* is generally regarded as his greatest piece of chamber music. Though twenty-seven years his junior, Schubert died the year after BEETHOVEN. They are buried next to each other in Vienna.

Schulberg, Budd (1914–   )   American novelist and short-story writer. The son of a film producer, Schulberg first attracted notice with his very successful satire of the rise of a Hollywood mogul, WHAT MAKES SAMMY RUN? Among his other well-known novels are *The Harder They Fall* (1947), the story of a prizefighter; and *The Disenchanted* (1950), whose alcoholic central character is based on F. Scott Fitzgerald. He wrote the screenplay for *On the Waterfront* (1954), and has written an autobiography, *Moving Pictures: Memories of a Hollywood Prince* (1981).

Schumann, Robert (1810–1856)   German composer, pianist, and music critic, a representative and leader of the romantic school. Among Schumann's works are highly imaginative song cycles based on poems by HEINE (*Dichterliebe*), CHAMISSO (*Frauenliebe und Leben*), and others, four symphonies, one piano concerto, and many sets of piano pieces with titles such as *Papillons* (*Butterflies*), *Carnaval*, *Kinderscenen* (*Scenes from Childhood*), and *Nachtstücke* (*Nightpieces*). He founded, in 1833, and edited the *Neue Zeitschrift für Musik* (*New Chronicle of Music*). His wife, Clara Schumann, born Clara Wieck (1819–96), was a fine pianist and a masterly interpreter of her husband's works. Schumann's last years were darkened by mental illness.

Schütz, Heinrich (1585–1672)   Outstanding German composer of the 17th century. A pupil in Italy of Giovanni Gabrieli (1555–1612), and later influenced by Claudio MONTEVERDI, Schütz introduced many of the new practices of Baroque music to Germany. He wrote the first German opera, *Dafne* (1627, music lost), but he is best known for his masterly setting of German Bible texts for use in services of the Lutheran Church.

Schuyler, James [Marcus] (1923–   )   American poet, novelist, and playwright. A member of the NEW YORK SCHOOL, Schuyler was closely involved with modern painting, both as a member of the staff of The Museum of Modern Art and as a writer for *Art News*. His verse is highly visual. The poems in *Salute* (1960), *Freely Espousing* (1969), and *The Crystal Lithium* (1972) are collages of overheard conversations, imaginary scenes, personal recognitions, and "hints that are revelations," assembled to create a lively and varied texture. *The Home Book* (1977), a collection of both prose and poetry, includes such traditional forms as the SONNET and VILLANELLE, which Schuyler handles in a relaxed, conversational manner. Together with John Ashbery, Schuyler has written the novel *A Nest of Ninnies* (1969), and in 1978 he published his own novel, *What's for Dinner?*, about mental illness and the sickness of "normal" life. In 1981 he was awarded the PULITZER PRIZE for *The Morning of the Poem* (1980).

Schwartz, Delmore (1913–1966)   American poet, short-story writer, and critic. Regarded by his peers as one of the most gifted writers of his generation, Schwartz wrote highly allusive and ironic poetry. It deals with themes of personal alienation, guilt, and an awed awareness of the weight of history and time. His first major book of verse and prose, *In Dreams Begin Responsibilities* (1938), was followed by the verse play *Shenandoah* (1941) and the autobiographical poem *Genesis* (1943). With the publication of *Summer Knowledge: New and Selected Poems 1938–1958* (1959), Schwartz became the youngest poet to be awarded the BOLLINGEN PRIZE in poetry.

His sensitive stories, many of them rooted in problems of Jewish life, are collected in such volumes as *The World Is a Wedding* (1948) and *Successful Love, and Other Stories* (1962). His criticism, on subjects ranging from T. S. ELIOT to Ring LARDNER, is collected in *Selected Essays* (1970). He also published an impressive translation of Rimbaud's *A Season in Hell* (1939) and served as an editor of *Partisan Review* from 1943 to 1955. Schwartz's life and work had an important impact on such other writers as Bernard MALAMUD, John BERRYMAN, and Saul BELLOW; Bellow depicted a Schwartz-like character in HUMBOLDT'S GIFT. In his last years he grew bitter, alcoholic, and withdrawn. Previously uncollected and unpublished poems written at the end of his life appeared in *The Last Poems of Delmore Schwartz* (1979). He was the subject of a highly praised biography, *Delmore Schwartz* (1977), by James Atlas.

Schwarz-Bart, André (1928–   ) French novelist. Schwarz-Bart's parents were Polish Jews who immigrated to France in 1924; in 1941 they were deported to an extermination camp by the Nazis. Soon after, Schwarz-Bart joined the French Resistance at the age of fifteen. His semihistorical novel *Le Dernier des justes* (1959, PRIX GONCOURT; tr *The Last of the Just*, 1960) traces the martyrdom of the Jews through thirty-six generations of the Levy family, culminating with the death of Ernie in the Auschwitz concentration camp. He also wrote *La Mulâtresse Solitude* (1972; tr *A Woman Named Solitude*, 1973), the title novel of a projected series of seven dealing with the racial issues associated with NÉGRITUDE and Judaism.

Schweik (or Švejk) The hero of Jaroslav HAŠEK's satirical novel *Osudy dobrého vojaka Švejka za světové války* (1921–23; tr *The Good Soldier Schweik*, 1930). Schweik was called an "ingenious idiot" for his skills at using absurd, idiotic methods to survive the most difficult situations. Schweik, with his pattern of behavior, was interpreted as a typical product of a historical and geopolitical situation in which a small nation has to face much stronger enemies. In Czechoslovakia Schweik's pronouncements became part of the folk wisdom, his favorite tavern a tourist attraction, and his figure, in the form of paintings (by the painter Lada) or puppets (by the filmmaker Trnka) a popular emblem.

Schweitzer, Albert (1875–1965) Alsatian philosopher, musician, theologian, and medical missionary. In 1913 Schweitzer, who held degrees in medicine and theology and was a noted expert on the music of BACH, founded a medical mission at Lambaréné, Gabon (then French Equatorial Africa). Except for a few lecture and concert trips, he devoted his life to the mission.

His philosophy expounds what he called "reverence for life," an ethical system based on the mutual respect of all living things that calls for the full development of human resources.

Among his works are *Philosophy of Civilization* (1923), *The Quest of the Historical Jesus* (1906), and *Out of My Life and Thoughts* (1932). He was awarded the 1952 Nobel Peace Prize.

science fiction A literary genre. Historically, science fiction began to split from the broader field of fantasy when writers combined the established narrative forms of utopia and the imaginary voyage with speculative accounts of future-science. Its first lasting myth grew out of the Faustian theme employed in Mary Shelley's FRANKENSTEIN, OR THE MODERN PROMETHEUS. As a genre, however, it did not gain a separate identity until it began to document future wars, beginning with the anonymous publication of *The Battle of Dorking* (1871) in BLACKWOOD'S magazine. Its development has taken two basic directions: Jules VERNE and such early enthusiasts as Hugo GERNSBACK emphasized infatuation with the machine, while such cautionary tales as H. G. Wells's THE TIME MACHINE explored man's precarious place in the universe. A growing disenchantment with technology led to a predominantly dystopian mood in the 1950s and 1960s. Writers became more concerned with the social, psychological, and ecological implications of science and technology. This in turn led to an increased emphasis on characterization rather than on plot. In all its diversity, the genre includes such writers as Ray BRADBURY and Brian ALDISS, who have criticized technology, Isaac ASIMOV, who continued to celebrate it, as well as writers of science fantasy like Edgar Rice Burroughs (see TARZAN), whose books often pitted man against the physical perils of an alternate world. Arthur C. CLARKE, H. P. LOVECRAFT, Frederik POHL, and Olaf STAPLEDON are among the many other well-known practitioners of the genre.

Scipio Africanus, Publius Cornelius (known as Scipio the Elder, 237–183 BC) Roman general and politician. Scipio's successful invasion of Carthage in the Second PUNIC WAR caused the Carthaginians to recall HANNIBAL from Italy. Scipio decisively defeated Hannibal at Zama (202 BC).

Sciron A robber of Greek legend. Sciron was slain by THESEUS. He infested the parts about Megara, and forced travelers over the rocks into the sea, where they were devoured by a giant turtle.

Scobie (1) In Graham Greene's novel THE HEART OF THE MATTER, the hero who is torn between love and religious duty.

(2) In Lawrence Durrell's novels THE ALEXANDRIA QUARTET, a comic old homosexual sailor.

Scopes trial A court trial in Dayton, Tennessee, in July 1925 in which John Scopes, a high school biology teacher, was found guilty of violating a state law that forbade teaching the theory of evolution. Clarence DARROW defended Scopes, and William Jennings BRYAN directed the prosecution. Although Scopes was convicted, Bryan's was a Pyrrhic victory; taking the stand as an expert on the Bible, he was subjected to relentless cross-examination by Darrow, who ridiculed his simple fundamentalist creed; Bryan died five days after the trial. H. L. MENCKEN reported on the "monkey" trial in some famous sardonic dispatches. The trial was the basis of the play *Inherit the Wind* (1955) by Jerome Lawrence and Robert E. Lee.

Scot, Michael (or Michael Scott, 1175?–1234) Scottish-born medieval scholar. After studying at the universities of Oxford, Paris, and Toledo, Scot became attached to the court of Frederick II of Sicily; there he served as physician and astrologer and, with others, translated the works of ARISTOTLE and Averroës into Latin. Famed for his occult learning, even in his own lifetime he was said to possess miraculous powers; after his death this reputation spread, and he became known as a wizard and magician. He is mentioned by DANTE in the *Inferno* and by Sir Walter SCOTT in *The Lay of the Last Minstrel* (1805).

Scotland Yard The headquarters of the London Metropolitan Police. From this office all public orders to the force proceed. The original Scotland Yard was a short street near Trafalgar Square, so called from a palace on the spot, given by King Edgar (about 970) to Kenneth II of Scotland when he came to London to pay homage and subsequently used by the Scottish kings when visiting England. New Scotland Yard was close by, on the Thames Embankment near Westminster Bridge. In 1967 Scotland Yard moved to new quarters in the same area.

Scots, Wha Hae (1794) A patriotic poem by Robert BURNS, celebrating the victory of Robert Bruce over the English King Edward II at the Battle of Bannockburn in 1314, and hailing liberty and independence for the Scottish nation. It is believed that Burns was strongly influenced in the writing of this poem by the French Revolution.

Scott, Duncan Campbell (1862–1947) Canadian poet and short-story writer. Scott worked for fifty-three years in the Department of Indian Affairs in Ottawa. His poetry, including *The Magic House* (1893), *New World Lyrics and Ballads* (1905), *Lundy's Lane* (1916), and *The Green Cloister* (1935), ranges from ballads and descriptive verse about Indian life to FREE VERSE. His *Selected Poems* (1951) reflect his recurrent concern with man's struggles with the forces of nature. He also wrote two volumes of stories.

Scott, F[rancis] R[eginald] (1899–1985) Canadian poet and lawyer. A member in the 1920s of the "Montreal School," a group of poets influenced by T. S. ELIOT, Scott contributed experimental poetry to *New Provinces: Poems of Several Authors* (1936), which helped to establish the modernist movement in Canadian poetry. His poems range from concise, often lyrical evocations of his native Quebec to high-spirited satires on Canadian society. He edited, with A.J.M. SMITH, *The Blasted Pine* (1957; rev

1967), a collection of satirical verse. His *Selected Poems* appeared in 1966, and in 1973 he published a collection of his own verse and translations, *The Dance Is One.*

Scott, Sir Walter (1771–1832) Scottish novelist and poet of the romantic period. Deriving most of his material from Scottish history and legend, and influenced by medieval French romance, popular ballads, and the Gothic novel, Scott wrote narrative poetry at first; but when overshadowed in this field by BYRON, he turned to the novel. His great achievement here lay in his exploitation of history as material for the novel, and with WAVERLEY he began the long series of works which proved him the master of the historical novel. In these romances he displays an arresting ability to recreate the atmosphere of an age in all its pageantry and detail. He was a skillful portrayer of character; his most brilliant figures are generally eccentric Scottish peasants; his romantic lovers, usually aristocratic, tend to be somewhat uninteresting. His novels are written with an immense vigor, and achieved for him a vast public in England and on the Continent, where he strongly influenced BALZAC and TOLSTOY. Although by far the most popular novelist of his day, he has lost favor, partly because of the improbability of his plots, which he admitted to turn on "marvellous and uncommon incidents," and partly because his romanticism now seems rather cloying.

His more notable poetic works include *Minstrelsy of the Scottish Border* (1802–3), a collection of ancient Scottish ballads; THE LAY OF THE LAST MINSTREL; MARMION; and THE LADY OF THE LAKE. The best known of his novels are *Waverley*, GUY MANNERING, THE ANTIQUARY, THE HEART OF MIDLOTHIAN, ROB ROY, THE BRIDE OF LAMMERMOOR, IVANHOE, KENILWORTH, PEVERIL OF THE PEAK, QUENTIN DURWARD, and THE TALISMAN.

Scott also wrote several dramatic works and a number of studies in biography and in the history, legends, and antiquities of Scotland. He contributed some articles to the *Encyclopaedia Britannica* and also had a part in the foundation of the *Quarterly Review.*

As his fortune increased, he built the baronial mansion of Abbotsford on the banks of the Tweed. In 1813 he refused the laureateship in favor of SOUTHEY. He was almost ruined when the publishing firm of Ballantyne, in which he was a partner, went into bankruptcy in 1826, and spent the rest of his life working to pay off the debts.

Scott was known to the readers of his day as The Wizard of the North. See WAVERLEY NOVELS.

Scottish Renaissance A 20th-century revival of Scottish literature, chiefly in poetry. It is characterized by its use of Scottish themes usually written in the Scottish poetic dialect of LALLANS. The movement originated in the *kailyard* group of Scottish writers, who, in the 1890s, wrote partly in dialect on humble, homespun topics. The leading figure of the Scottish Renaissance was the poet Hugh MACDIARMID; James Leslie MITCHELL was the most prominent novelist associated with the movement.

Scotus Erigena, Johannes (9th century) Christian theologian and philosopher, probably born in Ireland of Scottish parents. Scotus Erigena came to the court of the Carolingian emperor Charles II before 847, directed the palace school, and greatly influenced later scholasticism. He wrote a treatise on predestination (c851), asserting the fundamental identity of philosophy and religion, and freedom of the will in both God and man; he was soon under attack for lack of orthodoxy. His translation, with commentary (c858), of the neo-Platonic treatise *On the Heavenly Hierarchy*, by Dionysius the Areopagite, was similarly controversial, although important in the development of medieval mysticism. His major work, the *Divisions of Nature* (*De divisione naturae*, c865–870), is also neo-Platonic, establishing God as the supreme intellect through whose will archetypal ideas are made manifest as created things; but it was attacked for pantheism because it made Nature the totality of all things and forces, whether creating or created, or both or neither.

Scourge of God Epithet for Attila (406?–453), king of the Huns. He was so called by medieval writers because of the widespread havoc and destruction caused by his armies. The term was also applied to Genseric, king of the Vandals (d 477), and to Tamerlane.

Screwtape Letters, The (1942) A popular work on Christian moral and theological problems by C. S. LEWIS. It is in the form of a series of letters in which a devil, Screwtape, advises his nephew, Wormwood, on how to deal with his human "patients."

Scriabin[e], Aleksandr Nikolayevitch (1872–1915) Russian composer and pianist. Scriabin's mysticism led to experimentation with synesthesia and dissonance, reflecting his conviction that all forms of art should be synthesized in service of religion. *The Poem of Ecstasy* (1908) and *Prometheus—The Poem of Fire* (1911) are among his best-known works; the score of the latter work includes a special color keyboard intended to project changing colors during the performance of the piece. His music is a complex departure from traditional harmonic structures.

Scribe, Augustin Eugène (1791–1861) French dramatist. Scribe, a prolific and popular playwright, wrote nearly four hundred plays, many in collaboration with other writers. Bright, spirited comedies of manners, his dramas were constructed with skill but had little substance. Almost devoid of characterization, they depended on farcical plots. Among his most successful comic efforts were *Le Mariage de raison* (1826), *Le Mariage d'argent* (1828), *Le Camaraderie ou la courte échelle* (1837), and *Une Chaîne* (1841). He is known also for his many opera libretti.

Scriblerus Club An association formed in 1714 by John ARBUTHNOT, Alexander POPE, Jonathan SWIFT, John GAY, Thomas PARNELL, and Robert Harley, earl of Oxford. The group met in Arbuthnot's apartments in St. James's Palace. Arbuthnot and Pope were the principal instigators of the project to combat pedantry and the abuses of learning. Although meetings ceased within the year, the spirit of Scriblerus lived on, kept alive by Pope's correspondence. Pope's THE DUNCIAD and the third book of Swift's GULLIVER'S TRAVELS are the most important works which sprang from this association.

Scrooge, Ebenezer A character in Charles Dickens's A CHRISTMAS CAROL. Ebenezer Scrooge is a miserly old man who is converted to loving benevolence by a series of visions depicting Christmases past, present, and future. He is remembered, however, for his meanness rather than for his change of heart, and the name Scrooge has come to be applied to anyone tight-fisted and grasping.

Scrutiny An English literary review edited in Cambridge by F. R. LEAVIS, published from 1932 to 1953. It provided an influential forum for the outspoken critical views of Leavis and others of the CAMBRIDGE CRITICS. In 1963 it was republished in twenty volumes, with an introduction by Leavis.

Scudéry, Madeleine de (1607–1701) French novelist. Scudéry was also known as Sapho, the name she gave herself in *Artamène, ou le Grand Cyrus* (10 vols, 1649–53). This novel and CLÉLIE, HISTOIRE ROMAINE intermix adventurous historical narrative with portraits of contemporary society, friends, and even the author herself in Persian, Greek, and Roman disguise, abounding in conversations expressing the author's opinion on a variety of practical subjects (see Anne LENCLOS). Scudéry is considered to have brought the sentimental romance to the height of its popularity with her enormous novels, which include *Ibrahim, ou l'Illustre Bassa*, the first *roman à clef* (1641), and *Almahide, ou l'Esclave reine* (*Almahide, or the Slave as Queen*, 1660–63). She and her brother, the dramatist Georges de Scudéry, were associated with the Hôtel de Rambouillet, and her elaborate salons with their competitions in *précieux* gallantry were satirized in Molière's *Les Précieuses ridicules*.

Scylla In Greek legend, a daughter of King Nisus of Megara. The daughter of Nisus promised to deliver Megara into the hands of her lover MINOS and, to effect this, cut off a golden hair on her father's head while he was asleep. Minos despised her for this treachery and Scylla threw herself from a rock into the sea. At death she was changed into a lark and Nisus into a hawk.

Scylla and Charybdis In Greek mythology, two monsters. They endangered shipping through the narrow Straits of Messina between Italy and Sicily. Scylla, a female monster with twelve feet, six heads, each on a long neck and each armed with three rows of pointed teeth, barked like a dog as she sat on her rock on the Italian side of the straits. HOMER called her a daughter of Crataeis, but later accounts make her a nymph who, because she was beloved by GLAUCUS, was changed by the jealous CIRCE into a monster. Across the straits, Charybdis supposedly lived under an immense fig tree; thrice every day he swallowed the waters of the sea and thrice threw them up again. In post-Homeric legends he is said to have stolen the oxen of HERACLES, been killed by lightning, and changed into the whirlpool that bears his name.

The phrase *between Scylla and Charybdis* came to mean "between two equal difficulties, between the devil and the deep sea." HORACE says that an author trying to avoid Scylla drifts into Charybdis: i.e., in seeking to avoid one fault, he falls into another.

sea deities   In classical mythology, besides the fifty NEREIDS, the Oceanides (daughters of OCEANUS), the SIRENS, the Tritons, etc., a number of deities presiding over or connected with the sea. The chief of these are:

Amphitrite, wife of Poseidon, daughter of Nereus and Doris, queen goddess of the sea.

GLAUCUS, a fisherman of Boeotia, afterward a marine deity.

Ino, who threw herself from a rock into the sea, and was made a sea-goddess.

Nereus and his wife Doris. Their palace was at the bottom of the Mediterranean; his hair was seaweed.

OCEANUS and his wife Tethys (daughter of URANUS and GE). Oceanus was god of the ocean, which formed a boundary round the world.

Portuminus, the protector of harbors.

POSEIDON, the chief sea god.

PROTEUS, who assumed every variety of shape.

THETIS, a daughter of Nereus and mother of Achilles.

Seafarer, The (8th century)   Old English poem of about one hundred lines in ALLITERATIVE VERSE. It speaks alternately of the joys and the sorrows of life at sea, then compares the pleasures of earth to those of heaven.

Sea Gull, The (Chaika, 1896)   A play by Anton CHEKHOV. A four-act work, it established Chekhov as a major dramatist and was one of the first successful productions of the MOSCOW ART THEATRE. Two years earlier, the play had been presented in St. Petersburg with such poor results that Chekhov nearly abandoned writing for the stage. The plot deals with young Konstantin Gavrilovich Trepliov, his literary ambitions, and his love for Nina Mikhailovna Zarechnaya, a girl who aspires to become a great actress. Trepliov's hopes for literary greatness suffer a setback when a private performance of his play proves to be a failure, arousing mostly laughter from his audience. He fears that Nina has lost her love and respect for him, and is angered at her attentions to Trigorin, a well-known writer who has been a lover of Trepliov's mother, Irina Nikolayevna Arkadina. Trepliov, in his despair, kills a gull at the lake and places it at Nina's feet as a symbol of his ruined hopes. Nina leaves with Trigorin, after the stricken Trepliov has made an unsuccessful suicide attempt. Two years pass, during which Trepliov finally achieves his aim of becoming a capable writer. Nina returns, having been cast aside by Trigorin. In a semicoherent speech, she compares herself to the gull destroyed by a man's mere momen-

tary whim. Nina leaves, and Trepliov, with his old griefs stirred once more, succeeds in his second suicide attempt.

Seaman, Elizabeth Cochrane (pen name Nelly Bly, 1867–1922)   American journalist. As a MUCKRAKER for the New York *World*, Seaman had herself committed to the city's insane asylum on Blackwell's Island, and her account of the horrifying conditions there resulted in great improvements. Her most famous feat (1889) was her round-the-world trip in seventy-two days, six hours, eleven minutes, a record beating that of Jules VERNE's hero in *Around the World in Eighty Days* (1873).

Seami Motokiyo   See ZEAMI MOTOKIYO.

Seasons, The (1726–1730)   A descriptive poem in blank verse by James THOMSON, in four parts—*Winter* (1726), *Summer* (1727), *Spring* (1728), and *Autumn* (1730). The poem reflects the author's main convictions: his belief in progress, his fascination with the ideal of the Golden Age, his deistic views, and, above all, his sense of a universe ordered by divine harmony and reason.

Sea Wolf, The (1904)   A novel by Jack LONDON. Humphrey Van Weyden, a wealthy literary critic, is shipwrecked while crossing San Francisco Bay. He is rescued by the ruthless Wolf Larsen, captain of the *Ghost*, an outward-bound sealing schooner. "Hump" is forced to work with frequent abuses, as cabin boy. The beautiful poet Maude Brewster is also rescued and draws the attentions of both Humphrey and the dangerous "Sea Wolf." Later the *Ghost* itself is wrecked; Humphrey and Maude swim to a deserted island. When the hulk of the ship is washed ashore, its only occupant is the blinded Larsen, who thwarts Humphrey and Maude's efforts to repair the ship. He dies, blind and paralyzed, but as indomitable and angry as ever. Humphrey and Maude are rescued and return to civilization.

Sebastian   (1) The twin brother of VIOLA in Shakespeare's TWELFTH NIGHT. Sebastian is mistaken for Viola, who has assumed male disguise, and led off to the altar by the infatuated Olivia.

(2) The weak-willed but ambitious brother of Alonso, the king of Naples, in Shakespeare's THE TEMPEST. Prodded by the evil ANTONIO, Sebastian makes a feeble attempt to assassinate his brother, but is stopped in time by ARIEL.

Sebastian, St. (fl 3rd century?)   A Roman martyr. A centurion in DIOCLETIAN's army, Sebastian was bound to a tree and shot at with arrows when it was discovered that he was a Christian. He survived the first attack but was later beaten to death. He is the patron saint of archers and soldiers and, because the arrows were said to have stuck in his body as thickly as pins in a pin-cushion, he was also made patron saint of pin makers.

Second Mrs. Tanqueray, The (1893)   A play by Arthur Wing PINERO, one of his most successful works. Paula, the titular heroine, is a woman "with a past" and, in spite of Aubrey Tanqueray's hopes and efforts, is not very cordially accepted by his friends or by his nineteen-year-old daughter, Ellean. Ellean goes to Paris with a friend and there becomes engaged to Captain Ardale, a former lover of Paula. Paula tells Aubrey, who then forbids Ellean to see Ardale again. Ellean suspects Paula of ruining her love, and tells her that she always knew what kind of a woman she was. In the end Paula kills herself.

Second Nun's Tale, The   One of THE CANTER-BURY TALES of CHAUCER. Although written in 1373 before he thought of the plan for the *Tales*, it was included. It is an adaptation in RHYME ROYAL of the life of Saint CECILIA as told by medieval Latin sources. Cecilia, born of Roman nobility and raised a Christian, warns her bridegroom Valerian that an angel guards her at all times. Valerian goes to Saint Urban to be christened and finds on his return that he can see the angel, who gives Cecilia a crown of roses and him a crown of lilies, adjuring them to live a pure life. Cecilia also converts Valerian's brother Tiburtius, and they all perform many miracles. The pagan Almachius tries to make them sacrifice to Jupiter, but they refuse and are killed. Cecilia is the last; the executioner strikes her three times in the neck while she is in her bath, but she continues to preach and convert for three days. Saint Urban buries her body when she dies.

Second Sex, The   See BEAUVOIR, SIMONE DE.

Second Shepherd's Play, The (Secunda pagina pastorum)   A medieval English MYSTERY PLAY written in the late 14th or early 15th century, generally considered to be the creation of the WAKEFIELD MASTER. It is the second in the cycle of TOWNELEY MYSTERIES to present the adoration of the shepherds at Jesus' nativity, but its success is probably due to the long, lively prefatory episode about the exposure of a sheep thief, who pretends that a stolen sheep concealed in a cradle is his wife's newborn baby.

Secret Agent, The (1907)   A novel by Joseph CONRAD. Set in a London back street, amid a group of anarchists, it is the story of Verloc, an agent-provocateur. He persuades his stupid, trusting brother-in-law Stevie to blow up the Greenwich Observatory. When Stevie blows himself up in the attempt, Verloc's wife, Winnie, who was devoted to her brother, kills Verloc. After a revolutionary steals her money while helping her to escape, she commits suicide.

Secret Sharer, The (1912)   A short story by Joseph CONRAD. A young captain takes on board, hides, and saves a murderer who is physically and psychologically his "double."

Section: Rock-Drill 85–95 de los Cantares (1956)   A section following THE PISAN CANTOS in the longer CANTOS of Ezra POUND. After the purgatorial tone of the Pisan section, the *Cantos* move into a new phase, in which Pound begins to describe his paradise.

Sedaine, Michel Jean (1719–1797)   French dramatist and librettist. Sedaine was the first to recognize the possibilities of combining a comic play with music, and is considered the founder of comic opera. His most famous

play, *Le Philosophe sans le savoir* (1765), is the best example of the BOURGEOIS DRAMA.

Seder (fr Heb, *sedher*, "order; division")   Usually the ritual meal of the Jewish PASSOVER celebration, held in commemoration of the flight of the Jews from Egypt led by MOSES. Each portion of the Seder is fixed by law and custom. See HAGGADAH.

Sedgemoor   See MONMOUTH.

Seeger, Alan (1888–1916)   American poet. Seeger enlisted in the French Foreign Legion at the outbreak of World War I and was killed in action. A thoroughgoing romantic, Seeger is best known for his famous poem "I Have a Rendezvous with Death," which appeared in his *Collected Poems* (1916).

Seferis, George (pen name of Georgios Seferiadis, 1900–1971)   Greek poet and diplomat. Born in Smyrna, Seferis and his family settled in Athens in 1914 to escape the devastation of World War I. After law studies in Paris, he joined the Greek foreign service and eventually retired as ambassador to England. Influenced by the French SYMBOLISTS, and later by T. S. ELIOT and Ezra POUND, Seferis wrote most of his twelve books of poetry, essays, translations, diaries, and fiction while posted overseas. *Strophe* (*Turning Point*, 1931) marked the advent of modernism in Greece. His work was translated by Henry MILLER, Lawrence DURRELL, and Rex WARNER, among others. He was awarded the NOBEL PRIZE in Literature in 1963, the first Greek to be so honored. *Collected Poems, 1924–1955* (1967), *Three Secret Poems* (1969), *On the Greek Style* (1966), and *Days of 1945–1951* (1974) are among his English editions. His verse is spare, hermetic, and characterized by a profound knowledge of Greek history and classical mythology and a deep understanding of Greece's past and its relevance to her present and future. Several of his finest poems—"In the Manner of G.S.," "Helen," "Against Whitethorns"—are prophetic of momentous political events. In the words of the Swedish Academy, Seferis's verse symbolizes "all that is indestructible in the Hellenic acceptance of life."

Segal, George (1924–   )   American artist. Segal was originally a figurative painter. In the 1960s he began making plaster sculptures of people in environments that seem to be an outgrowth of his earlier work. His technique was to cast a living person, clothes and all, in plaster and then set this eerily realistic but lifeless figure in a natural and commonplace setting. The pieces are often ambiguous expressions of despair and sarcasm, a famous example being *Woman Shaving Her Leg* (1963).

Seghers, Anna (pen name of Netty Radványi, born Netty Reiling, 1900–1983)   German novelist with socialist convictions. Seghers left Germany during World War II and, afterwards, returned to East Berlin. Her most famous novel is *Das siebte Kreuz* (1942; tr *The Seventh Cross*, 1943), about the escape, recapture, and crucifixion of prisoners of war.

Seifert, Jaroslav (1901–1986)   Czech poet. Seifert, whose first book of poetry, *Město v slzach*, was published in 1921, became internationally known only when he was awarded the NOBEL PRIZE in Literature in 1984. Author of over thirty volumes of poetry, he has been revered in his own country for many years both as a poet and as a symbol of freedom of expression in the face of political oppression. His poetry is difficult to translate and very few of his books have appeared in English. Seifert's verse, which has spoken out against repression under several different regimes, has been praised for its conversational style, humor, and sensuality, and for its celebration of Prague and Czechoslovakia's cultural heritage. In 1977 he was one of the signatories of Charter 77, which protested the suppression of human rights in Czechoslovakia. Among his many volumes of verse are *Samá láska* (1923), which speaks of youth's longing for revolution; *Slavík zpívá spatne* (*The Nightingale Sings Badly*, 1926), strongly influenced by DADA and SURREALISM; and *Zhasněte světla* (*Put Out the Lights*, 1938), whose title poem, about the Nazi threat hanging over Prague, is one of Seifert's most famous. *Morový sloup* (1977; tr *The Plague Column*, 1982, also *The Plague Monument*, 1984), a single long poem divided into numbered lyrics, refers to a three-hundred-year-old Prague monument as a symbol for Czech fate and history: a small country that can never hope to escape invasion and occupation; *Odlévání zvonů* (1967; tr *The Casting of Bells*, 1983) and *Děstník z Piccadilly* (1979; tr *An Umbrella from Piccadilly*, 1985) are his most recently translated works.

Sei Shōnagon   See PILLOW-BOOK OF SEI SHŌNAGON, THE.

Selby, Hubert, Jr. (1928–   )   American novelist. Selby became widely known when his first novel, *Last Exit to Brooklyn* (1964), became the subject of an obscenity trial in England. It is a series of intricately linked sketches portraying thugs, homosexuals, and hookers in scenes of urban violence and degradation. The prose is energetic and relentlessly realistic; some critics saw the book as a vigorous moral exposé of urban decay. It was followed by *The Room* (1971), the monologue of an imprisoned psychopath and his fantasies of revenge; *The Demon* (1976), the story of a sexually obsessed executive; and *Requiem for a Dream* (1978), about the living hell of four drug addicts.

Selden, John (1584–1654)   English jurist, scholar, and Orientalist, known for his treatises, many of which were written in Latin and dealt with questions of law. Of humble birth, Selden was an outstanding lawyer and became especially known for his collection of Oriental manuscripts, which he willed to the Bodleian Library.

His scholarly publications include *De Diis Syriis* (1617), a study of Oriental religion, and *History of Tithes* (1618), which was suppressed because of the objections of the English clergy. Perhaps his best-known work is *Table Talk* (1689), a collection of his sayings compiled after his death by his secretary, Richard Milward.

Seldon, Lawrence   See HOUSE OF MIRTH, THE.

Selene   The moon goddess of Greek mythology, daughter of Hyperion and Thea, and sister of HELIOS (the sun), corresponding to the Roman Luna. Selene had fifty daughters by ENDYMION, and several by ZEUS, one of whom was called "The Dew." Selene is usually shown in a chariot drawn by two white horses. Late Greek mythographers identified her with ARTEMIS.

Self-Portrait in a Convex Mirror (1975)   A collection of poems by John ASHBERY. The title poem is the longest and most elaborately developed in this thirty-five-poem volume. It is a long meditative piece evolving from the experience of viewing the Renaissance painter Francesco Parmigianino's portrait of himself reflected in a barber's convex mirror. The portrait, which is distorted in perspective and depicts the painter's right hand as "bigger than the head," is a metaphor for man's ways of depicting reality. A "self-portrait" that considers a famous self-portrait, the poem ironically investigates the role of a self in the world: ". . . this / 'Not-being-us' is all there is to look at / In the mirror." This brilliantly imaginative, FREE VERSE composition is the description of a philosophical exploration. What Ashbery finds is at once both ephemeral and solid: "Affirmation that doesn't affirm anything." The volume was awarded the PULITZER PRIZE for poetry in 1976.

Self-Reliance (1841)   An essay by Ralph Waldo EMERSON. The writer, in some of his best-known epigrammatic sentences, instructs his listener to discover his relationship with Nature and God, and then to trust his own judgment above that of all others. The essay is collected in Emerson's *Essays, First Series*.

Seljuks   A Perso-Turkish dynasty of eleven emperors over a large part of Asia. It lasted 138 years (1056–1194).

Selkirk, Alexander (1676–1721)   A Scottish sailor whose narrative of his actual experience as a castaway suggested Daniel Defoe's ROBINSON CRUSOE. As the sailing-master of the privateer *Cinque Ports Galley*, Selkirk, at his own request, was left on the desolate island of Juan Fernández off the coast of Chile for four years and four months (1704–9). His rescue and return to England by Captain Woodes Rogers caused the publication of many narratives of his history.

Selvon, Samuel [Dickson] (1923–   )   Trinidadian novelist. Selvon moved to London in 1950 and soon thereafter began to write and to publish, while supporting himself by working as a clerk in the Indian embassy. Whether set in Trinidad—as in *A Brighter Sun* (1952), *An Island Is a World* (1955), *Turn Again Tiger* (1958), and *I Hear Thunder* (1963)—or in London—as in *Lonely Londoners* (1956) and *The Housing Lark* (1965) —Selvon explores the mistrust and prejudice between races with a compassionate humor and with a keen ear for dialect. Among his other works are the stories in *Ways of Sunlight* (1958; repr 1979) and the novels *Those Who Eat the Cascadura* (1972) and *Moses Ascending* (1975).

Semele In Greek mythology, the daughter of CADMUS and Harmonia and mother of DIONYSUS by ZEUS. Six months pregnant by her unknown lover, Semele was persuaded by the jealous HERA to insist that he reveal himself. Zeus appeared as a thunderbolt and she died, but the unborn Dionysus was saved by HERMES. Semele was later rescued from HADES by her son under the name of Thyone. The raising of Semele, symbolizing the return of vegetation in the Spring, was widely celebrated. Semele seems to have been a Greek adaptation of Zemelo, a Phrygian earthgoddess.

Semiramis (or Sammuramat) Assyrian queen. All that is known of the historical queen, Sammuramat, is that she was the mother of the Assyrian king Ninus and a woman of immense importance through more than one reign. Perhaps Babylonian herself, she introduced a Babylonian god, Nebo, into the Assyrian pantheon. She fought effectively against both Medes and Chaldeans.

The legendary queen, Semiramis, on the other hand, is a figure known to various Greek writers, who believed her to be the daughter of the Syrian goddess Atargatis. Various legends claimed that she was fed as a child by doves (which fact later identified her with ISHTAR), married King Ninus, and after his death built Babylon and other great cities and monuments. At her death she became a dove. It was this fabulous creature, rather than the human queen, who was the heroine of Voltaire's tragedy *Sémiramis*, a drama by Calderón, and Rossini's opera *Semiramide*.

Semites The descendants of SHEM (Gen. 10), who later came to include the Akkadians, Arameans, Canaanites, Arabs, and Ethiopians. They were identifiable chiefly because their languages—the so-called Semitic languages—were derived from a common base. Their lands extended from southern Babylonia to the Egyptian border, including portions of Mesopotamia, Syria, and Palestine. The term Semitic is commonly used as a synonym for Jewish.

Sender, Ramón José (1902–1982) Spanish novelist and essayist. A revolutionary activist who served in the Republican forces during the Spanish Civil War and escaped to France in 1938, Sender lived first in Mexico and then for some three decades in New Mexico and California. A prolific writer, he combines realism and fantasy, occasional propaganda, and existential concerns, often with considerable autobiographical content, as in *Imán* (1930; tr *Pro Patria*, 1935), dealing with his war experience in Morocco; *Siete domingos rojos* (1932; tr *Seven Red Sundays*, 1936); and *Contraataque* (1937; tr *Counter-attack in Spain*, 1937), picturing respectively the political and military struggle in Spain. *Epitalamio del prieto Trinidad* (1942; tr *Dark Wedding*, 1943) is the fruit of his sojourn in the Caribbean. *La esfera* (1939; tr *The Sphere*, 1949), his most ambitious work, failed with critics because of philosophical vagueness and didacticism. *Crónica del alba* (1942; tr *Chronicle of Dawn*, 1944), a personal memoir,

begins a long novelistic cycle wherein the protagonist is Sender's double. One of his most admired novels is *El rey y la reina* (1947; tr *The King and the Queen*, 1948).

Seneca (full name Lucius Annaeus Seneca, 4 BC–AD 65) Roman philosopher and playwright. In AD 49 Seneca, a Spanish-born scholar, was chosen to become the tutor of the future emperor NERO. Seneca spent the major portion of his life studying and writing and instructing his disciple Nero on the art of government and the virtues of a Stoic philosopher-king. When the young prince ascended the imperial throne in AD 54, Seneca remained his most trusted advisor and three years later, in 57, was honored by the conferral of a consulship. However, Seneca lost favor with the emperor and prudently withdrew from imperial politics and court society in 62. In 65 he was implicated in PISO's CONSPIRACY to assassinate Nero and was commanded by his one-time pupil to kill himself. With Stoic composure, the philosopher had his veins opened and bled to death.

As a Roman philosopher, Seneca is second only to CICERO; and like Cicero, he was an adherent of the philosophy of STOICISM. He wrote the first and only Roman textbook on physics, the *Quaestiones naturales* (*Investigations in Natural Science*), which was an important source of knowledge (and misinformation) in the Middle Ages. His influence on Renaissance drama was considerable. Eight tragedies are ascribed to him; they are *Hercules*, *Troacles*, *Phoenissae*, *Medea*, *Phaedra*, *Agamemnon*, *Oedipus*, and *Thyestes*. Marked by violence and bloodshed, and characters of little individuality or differentiation, they had an important influence on the tragic drama of Italy, France, and, especially, of Elizabethan England.

Senghor, Léopold Sédar (1906–) Senegalese poet and statesman. President of the Republic of Senegal (1960–80). Senghor writes in French of the rich African folklore and popular traditions of his country. Along with Aimé CÉSAIRE, Senghor was largely responsible for establishing the concept of NÉGRITUDE, a positive affirmation of black African culture, exemplified in his important and influential anthology *Anthologie de la nouvelle poésie nègre et malgache* (1948). His works of poetry include *Chants d'ombre* (1945), *Chants pour Naëtt* (1949), *Ethiopiques* (1956), and *Nocturnes* (1961). Volumes of his *Selected Poems* appeared in English in 1964 and 1977.

Sennacherib (d 681 BC) Assyrian king. Most of Sennacherib's reign was consumed by struggles to keep order in the embattled Assyrian empire. He revived the capital at Nineveh. He destroyed Babylon and, during the reign of HEZEKIAH, he captured many of the cities of Judah. Jerusalem, however, was spared when an angel of God descended in the night and destroyed Sennacherib's army. He was then forced to return to Nineveh, where he was murdered by two of his sons, who were angered by his choice for a successor (2 Kings 19).

Byron made the destruction of his army the subject of his famous lyric THE DESTRUCTION OF SENNACHERIB, based on the account in 2 Chron. 32.

Sennett, Mack (original name Michael Sinnott, 1884–1960) Canadian-born American motion picture producer and director. After acting for a time under the direction of D. W. GRIFFITH, Sennett started his own Keystone Company in 1912. Here he began to produce his famous slapstick movies, which delighted audiences with pie-in-the-face comedy and madcap chase scenes featuring the Keystone Kops. It was in Sennett's films that the young Charlie CHAPLIN first developed his Tramp character. His autobiography was aptly titled *King of Comedy* (1954).

senryū Japanese satiric verse. It follows the same syllabic system as HAIKU, but deals with subjects of a lighter vein.

Sense and Sensibility (1811) A novel by Jane AUSTEN in which two sisters, Elinor and Marianne Dashwood, represent sense and sensibility, respectively. Each is deserted by the young man from whom she has been led to expect an offer of matrimony. Elinor bears her deep disappointment with dignity and restraint, while Marianne violently expresses her grief. Elinor soon discovers why her suitor, Edward Ferrars, has left her: he has been secretly engaged to Lucy Steele for four years, and, while he regrets the connection now, he feels honor bound to marry her. When his mother discovers his engagement to Lucy, a girl of inferior social standing, she disinherits him, settling her property on his younger brother, Robert. The sly Lucy, at this turn of events, shifts her interest to Robert. Thus released, Edward proposes to Elinor and is accepted. On the other hand, Marianne, with characteristic impetuosity, follows her suitor John Willoughby to London, where she only becomes more disillusioned with him. As she gradually recovers from her foolish love, she is able to see, for the first time, the quieter attractions of her old admirer, Colonel Brandon, whom she finally marries.

Sensitive Plant, The (1820) A poem by Percy Bysshe SHELLEY. The sensitive plant is a variety of mimosa; its outer leaves curl up when touched. The poem relates the mystic love of the plant for the "lady of the garden" and its death in the general ruin of the garden following the lady's demise.

Sentimental Education See ÉDUCATION SENTIMENTALE, L'.

Sentimental Journey, A (1768) An unfinished narrative by Laurence STERNE. Attacking sentimentalism in the guise of a tour through France and Italy, it is itself didactic in its sentimental emphasis on natural benevolence and philanthropy. Here Sterne moralizes so playfully as to present an almost delicate caricature of moralizing. It was long read seriously, even in such famous episodes as YORICK weeping over an ass chewing a thistle. Its first illustrator was William HOGARTH.

Separate Peace, A See KNOWLES, JOHN.

Separate Tables (1954) A play by Terence RATTIGAN. The play is actually two one-acts, *Table by the Window* and *Table Number Seven*, both set in the same English resort hotel run by Miss Cooper. The minor characters remain the same in both acts; only the male and female leads change. The common theme is the frustration and misunderstanding caused by the artificial social barriers erected between individuals. The loneliness and isolation of the guests in the hotel is suggested by their separate tables in the dining room.

sepoy The Anglicized form of the Hindu and Persian *sipahi*, "soldier," denoting a native Indian soldier trained and disciplined in the British manner, especially one in the British Indian Army.

Sepoy Mutiny A revolt of the Sepoy troops in British India during the transference of the administration of India from the East India Company to the British crown.

seppuku See HARAKIRI.

September Massacres An indiscriminate slaughter, during the FRENCH REVOLUTION, of Loyalists confined in the Abbaye and other prisons, lasting from September 2 to 5, 1792. As many as eight thousand persons died.

Septuagint The oldest translation from Hebrew to Greek of the OLD TESTAMENT, originating in Alexandria c250 BC. Also called version of the seventy or simply LXX, its name comes from the story that it was translated by seventy-two men in seventy-two days. The first translation was of the PENTATEUCH, and this was the version used by early Christians; it is still used in the Greek Orthodox Church. Greek translations of the other books and the APOCRYPHA were added later.

seraglio In a general sense, a harem, or the part of a royal or noble Muhammedan household where the wives and concubines are confined. It also specifically refers to the former palace of the Sultan of Turkey at Constantinople. Situated on the Golden Horn, it is enclosed by walls seven and a half miles in circuit.

Serao, Matilde (1856–1927) Italian novelist and journalist. Serao was the most prolific and accomplished of Italy's women writers at the turn of the century. In her many journalistic pieces, some of which were collected in *Il ventre di Napoli* (1884), and in her novels, she described Neapolitan life in a vivid and sympathetic manner. Her best-known novel, *Il paeso di Cuccagna* (1891; tr *The Land of Cockayne*, 1902), is a humorous depiction of the Neapolitan passion for the national lottery.

seraphim ANGELS. Seraphim belong to the highest order of angels, according to medieval angelology, especially distinguished by the ardency of their zeal and love. In the BIBLE, each seraph had six wings: "with twain he covered his face, and with twain he covered his feet, and with twain he did fly" (Isa. 6:2). Elizabeth Barrett BROWNING wrote a poem entitled "The Seraphim" (1838).

Serapion Brothers   An organization of writers formed in Russia during the 1920s. The group, which had no definite program, came together chiefly to advocate the right to nonconformity and freedom in literature. It especially reacted against the growing demands for literature to concern itself with political themes. Included in the group were Yevgeny ZAMYATIN, the oldest member and leading spirit, and younger writers such as Venyamin KAVERIN, Konstantin FEDIN, Mikhail ZOSHCHENKO, and Vsevolod IVANOV. The name of the group was taken from a story called "The Serapion Brothers" by E. T. A. HOFFMANN, in which one of the characters advocates unlimited freedom in literary work.

Serapis   An Egyptian deity, combining the attributes of Apis and OSIRIS. The temples of Serapis were called Serapea. The most famous Serapeum, at Memphis, was the burial place of the sacred bull Apis.

sergas de Esplandián, Las   See AMADÍS DE GAULA.

Sergeyev-Tsensky, Sergey Nikolayevich (pen name of Sergey Nikolayevich Sergeyev, 1875–1958) Russian novelist. Sergeyev-Tsensky began publishing in 1898, producing poetry, short stories, and novellas until 1908, when his first novel, *Babayev*, appeared and established his predominant genre as the historical novel. He was widely recognized for *Preobrazhenniye* (1914; tr *The Transfiguration*, 1926), a novel depicting the intelligentsia of Russia in the early 20th century. This work lent its title to an enormous cycle of novels called *The Transfiguration of Russia*, consisting of twelve novels, three novellas, and two études, all written between 1914 and 1958. Sergeyev-Tsensky also wrote a formidable novel on the Crimean War called *Sevastopolskaya strada* (*The Ordeal of Sevastopol*, 1937–39).

Sermon on the Mount   In the NEW TESTAMENT, the sermon given by Jesus to the multitudes and his disciples (Matt. 5–7), where he explains the essence of the true disciple and enunciates his teachings of love and righteousness. See BEATITUDES.

Sertões, Os (Rebellion in the Backlands, 1902)   A book, considered the chief classic of Brazilian literature, by Euclides da Cunha (1866–1909). Sometimes called "the Bible of Brazilian nationality," the work defies classification. It is partly a geographical and sociological treatise that gives a brilliant description of the drought-ridden *sertão*, or hinterland, and its backward, poverty-stricken inhabitants. It is also a fast-paced, moving, and suspenseful narrative that can be read as a novel. The book recounts the heroic, though ill-fated, attempt of a religious zealot, "Antônio the Counsellor," and his followers to resist the authority of the central government in 1896–97. In their settlement at Canudos, three hundred miles northwest of Salvador, the rebels stubbornly held out against government troops until the last man was dead. Da Cunha was an engineer and journalist of Darwinian convictions who accompanied one of the military expeditions to Canudos as a newspaper correspondent. He turned the story of the rebels into a remarkable document, an indictment of Brazilian society for its neglect of the *sertão* as well as a stirring account of human misery and courage. The English translation by Samuel Putnam appeared in 1944 (repr 1970).

Sérusier, Paul   See NABI PAINTERS.

Service, Robert W[illiam] (1874–1958)   English-born Canadian poet. Intrigued by adventure and travel, Service wrote popular ballads about the rugged life of the frontier. He is best known for "The Shooting of Dan McGrew," contained in his most popular collection, *Song of a Sourdough* (1907; retitled *The Spell of the Yukon*, 1915). *Collected Verse* appeared in 1960. *Ploughman of the Moon* (1945) and *Harper of Heaven* (1948) are the two volumes of his autobiography.

Sesha   In Hindu mythology, the thousand-headed serpent who supports the world on his head. In some creation myths, it is Sesha who destroys the world with fiery breath at the end of each age for VISHNU who will then create the world anew. He is also called Ananta (Sans, "the endless").

Sesshū (1420–1506)   Japanese painter. A Zen priest, Sesshū specialized in black and white landscape painting. Noted for his originality, simplicity, and sensitivity, his work greatly influenced later artists.

Sessions, Roger [Huntington] (1896–1985) American composer. Early works by Sessions are in a STRAVINSKY-influenced, "neoclassical" style, but he adopted some elements of SCHOENBERG's twelve-tone system after its appearance early in the century. Nonetheless he has remained strongly independent of systems, both as composer and as teacher. His music is dense in texture, with emphasis on independent, long, contrapuntal lines. His major works include incidental music to *The Black Maskers* (1923), eight symphonies (between 1927 and 1968), a violin concerto (1935), three piano sonatas, two string quartets, two cantatas, and the operas *The Trial of Lucullus* (1942; libretto by Bertolt BRECHT) and *Montezuma* (1941–62; libretto by G. A. BORGESE). He has written on musical aesthetics.

sestet   See SONNET.

sestina   In prosody, a lyric poem of six stanzas of six lines each and an ENVOI, or *tornada*, of three lines. A specialized form of the Provençal *canso* and the Italian CANZONE, the sestina was developed sometime toward the end of the 13th century by the famed Provençal troubadour Arnaut Daniel. Admired and written by DANTE and PETRARCH in Italy, it was hardly used in France and England before the 19th century.

Instead of rhyme, the sestina uses a pattern of repetition of the six words which terminate the six lines of the first stanza. (Not content with this, SWINBURNE invented a rhymed form of the sestina.) Such modern poets as Ezra

seven

POUND and W. H. AUDEN wrote the sestina with notable success.

The arrangement of repetition is as follows:

Stanza I.	1–2–3–4–5–6
Stanza II.	6–1–5–2–4–3
Stanza III.	3–6–4–1–2–5
Stanza IV.	5–3–2–6–1–4
Stanza V.	4–5–1–3–6–2
Stanza VI.	2–4–6–5–3–1

The envoi contains inner repetition, as well as terminal repetition. Line one has word 2 in the middle and 5 at the end. Line two has word 4 in the middle and 3 at the end. Line three has word 6 in the middle and 1 at the end.

Set The Egyptian god of darkness, prototype of the Greek TYPHON, the god of evil. Set was the brother-son and deadly enemy of OSIRIS, whom he slaughtered and cut into pieces. Representations of Set portray him with a human body and the head of some unidentified mythological beast with pointed muzzle and high square ears.

Seton, Anya (1916–   ) American novelist. The daughter of Ernest Thompson SETON, Anya Seton is the author of many best-selling historical novels. Much of her best-known earlier work is drawn from the American past, including *My Theodosia* (1941), about Aaron Burr's daughter; *Dragonwyck* (1944); and *Foxfire* (1951). *Katherine* (1954) is a romance based on the 14th-century love affair of CHAUCER's sister-in-law and JOHN OF GAUNT. She has also written a number of best-selling gothic novels set in England. Most of her novels have been translated into many languages and enjoy worldwide popularity.

Seton, Ernest Thompson (real name Ernest Seton Thompson, 1860–1946) English-born American artist and naturalist. Seton's well-known book of stories and paintings, *Wild Animals I Have Known* (1898), was a staple of primary school nature study in the early 20th century. He also founded the Woodcraft League, a precursor of the Boy Scouts.

Seton-Watson, [George] Hugh [Nicholas] (1916–1984) English historian. An authority on Eastern European and Russian culture and political history, Seton-Watson is known for such works as *Eastern Europe between the Wars* (1945) and *The Decline of Imperial Russia* (1952). He later turned to an examination of trends in contemporary world history in *Neither War nor Peace* (1960), *Nations and States* (1977), and *The Imperialist Revolutionaries* (1978).

Settembrini, Ludovico In Thomas Mann's novel THE MAGIC MOUNTAIN, an Italian tubercular patient who befriends Hans CASTORP. Settembrini is concerned lest the young man succumb to the decadent atmosphere of Haus Berghof and frequently urges him to leave. He represents the classical European tradition of enlightened humanism and political liberalism.

Seurat, Georges (1859–1891) French painter. One of the founders of NEOIMPRESSIONISM, Seurat had a deep interest in the theoretical aspects of color and form in painting that led him to the development of *pointillism*, wherein color tones were represented by uniform dots of pure color on a white background; this method was subsequently adopted by PISSARRO and Paul Signac (1863–1935). His paintings often possessed scientifically derived geometric proportions. His most famous work is *Sunday Afternoon on the Island of La Grande Jatte* (1886), the product of over sixty preparatory drawings and paintings.

Seuss, Dr. (pen name of Theodor Seuss Geisel, 1904–   ) American writer and illustrator of scores of immensely popular, humorous children's books, such as *And to Think That I Saw It on Mulberry Street* (1937), *Horton Hears a Who* (1954), and *The Cat in the Hat* (1957), the first in a series of Beginner Books (a publishing company founded by Geisel) that uses a limited vocabulary for very young readers. Geisel's alternative to the Dick-and-Jane reading primers revolutionized early reading. *How the Grinch Stole Christmas* (1957), *Green Eggs and Ham* (1960), *Hunches in Bunches* (1982), *The Butter Battle Book* (1984), an undisguised polemic against the arms race, and *You're Only Old Once!* (1986) are some of his other well-known books.

Sevastopol Sketches (1855) Three stories by Count Leo TOLSTOY. They are based on his own experiences and observations at the siege of Sevastopol during the CRIMEAN WAR. Tolstoy, who was an army officer at the time, was in the thick of the fighting at the most exposed point in the town's fortifications. The stories were a departure from the usual war descriptions; Tolstoy stripped away the tinsel and showed war, not as a heroic and glorious pastime, but as a dangerous, tedious, and bloody succession of horrors. In these stories, Tolstoy first used the stream-of-consciousness technique that he developed in his later work. In an article about the sketches, the Russian critic Nikolay CHERNYSHEVSKY called the technique an internal monologue, the first time this term was used in relation to the literary device.

The three stories are separately entitled "Sevastopol v dekabre mesyatse" ("Sevastopol in the Month of December"), "Sevastopol v maye" ("Sevastopol in May"), and "Sevastopol v avguste 1855 goda" ("Sevastopol in August 1855"). At the end of the second story appear the famous lines: "The hero of my story, whom I love with all the strength of my soul, whom I have tried to reproduce in all his beauty and who always was, is, and will be beautiful, is truth."

seven A mystic or sacred number. It is composed of four and three, which, among the Pythagoreans, were, and from time immemorial have been, accounted lucky numbers. Among the Babylonians, Egyptians, and other ancient peoples, there were seven sacred planets. The Hebrew verb for "to swear" means literally to come under the influence of seven things; thus, seven ewe lambs figure in the oath between Abraham and Abimelech at Beersheba (Gen. 21:28); and Herodotus describes an Arabian oath in which seven stones are smeared with blood.

There are seven days in Creation, seven days in the week, seven graces, SEVEN DEADLY SINS, seven divisions in the Lord's Prayer, and seven ages in the life of man; climacteric years are seven and nine with their multiples by odd numbers; and the seventh son of a seventh son was held noble.

Among the Hebrews, every seventh year was sabbatical, and seven times seven years was the jubilee. The three great Jewish feasts lasted seven days; and between the first and second were seven weeks. Levitical purifications lasted seven days; BALAAM would have seven altars, and sacrificed on them seven bullocks and seven rams; NAAMAN was commanded to dip seven times in Jordan; ELIJAH sent his servant seven times to look out for rain; ten times seven Israelites went to Egypt, the exile lasted the same number of years, and there were ten times seven elders. Pharaoh in his dream saw seven kine and seven ears of corn; JACOB served seven years for each of his wives; seven priests with seven trumpets marched round Jericho once every day, but seven times on the seventh day. SAMSON's wedding feast lasted seven days; on the seventh he told his bride the riddle, he was bound with seven withes, and seven locks of his hair were cut off. NEBUCHADNEZZAR was a beast for seven years.

In the Apocalypse, there are seven churches of Asia, seven candlesticks, seven stars, seven trumpets, seven spirits before the throne of God, seven horns, seven vials, seven plagues, a seven-headed monster, and the Lamb with seven eyes.

The old astrologers and alchemists recognized seven so-called planets. According to the Muslims, there are seven heavens.

Seven Against Thebes (Hepta epi Thebas, 467 BC) A tragedy by AESCHYLUS. It deals with the war between the sons of OEDIPUS for the throne of Thebes. It is the last play of a trilogy that included *Laius* and *Oedipus*, both now lost. The ending was changed by an unknown poet to conform to Sophocles' popular tragedy *Antigone* and the original ending is lost. Static in action, the play is martial in spirit; it may have been in part a tract urging Athens to fortify its acropolis. For the story, see THE SEVEN AGAINST THEBES.

Seven against Thebes, The Seven mythical Argive champions. They waged war on Thebes. Cursed by OEDIPUS for consenting to his banishment, his sons, Eteocles and Polynices, agreed to occupy the Theban throne on alternate years. But Eteocles banished his brother; Polynices fled to Argos, where, with the help of ERIPHYLE, he won the support of King Adrastus, whose daughter he married. Their force was led by seven champions: Adrastus; his brother-in-law, the seer Amphiaraus, who foresaw that only Adrastus would survive the war; Adrastus' son-in-law

Tydeus, a hero from Calydon; Parthenopaeus; Hippomedon; Capaneus; and Polynices (though some accounts add the Argives Mecisteus and Eteoclus in place of the foreign leaders, Polynices and Tydeus).

Tydeus was sent ahead to demand Theban surrender; Eteocles refused and Tydeus was ambushed but killed his fifty attackers and escaped. On the way to Thebes, the seven were dismayed by the death of the infant Opheltes, which they regarded as an ill omen. Each of the champions stationed himself at one of the seven gates of Thebes; Eteocles assigned a general to defend each, reserving for himself the one menaced by Polynices. In the ensuing battle, the Argives were almost totally destroyed. ZEUS struck Capaneus from a scaling ladder for his impious boasting; Amphiaraus was swallowed by the earth; ATHENE would have saved the wounded Tydeus, but refused when she saw him eating the brains of an enemy; and the other Argive leaders died, except for Adrastus, who was saved by his horse Arion. Polynices and Eteocles met in single combat and killed each other.

The story of the war was told by Aeschylus in his SEVEN AGAINST THEBES, by Euripides in his PHOENICIAN WOMEN and THE SUPPLIANT WOMEN, by SENECA in his *Phoenissae*, and by STATIUS in his epic poem *Thebais*. See ANTIGONE; EPIGONI.

Seven Arts, The (1916–1917) An American monthly periodical of literature and opinion. Founded by James Oppenheim and edited in various issues by Van Wyck BROOKS and Waldo FRANK, it was one of the best known and shortest lived of the LITTLE MAGAZINES. Its aim was to provide a vehicle for the expression of ideas and literary experimentation to which the more conservative journals of the day were closed. It attracted many of the writers who were later to be celebrated as the vanguard of the new renaissance in American writing. Partly because of its strongly held pacifist views in the midst of the war years, it was unable to obtain adequate funding and ceased publication scarcely a year after it began. It published the first work of Eugene O'NEILL and the early stories about Winesburg, Ohio, by Sherwood ANDERSON, along with the works of many other important young writers.

Seven Champions of Christendom, The Famous History of the (1596) A romance by Richard Johnson (1573–?1659) about the national patron saints of England, Scotland, Wales, Ireland, France, Spain, and Italy.

seven deadly sins Seven sins, or vices, discussed authoritatively by St. Thomas AQUINAS. They are anger, covetousness, envy, gluttony, lust, pride, and sloth and are distinguished not by their inherent gravity but by their potential for causing other sins. Aquinas considered pride to be the chief of the deadly sins.

seven heavens (Arab, *sabā samawatin*) A concept of ultimate spiritual bliss based upon some verses in the KORAN and further elaborated by Muslim commentators.

Muslims believe that ALLAH created seven heavens, one above another, and that the Prophet Muhammed was carried there on his horse Borak.

seven last words of Christ   (1) "Father, forgive them; for they know not what they do." (2) "Today shalt thou be with Me in paradise." (3) "Woman, behold thy son!" etc. (4) "My God, My God, why hast Thou forsaken Me?" (5) "I thirst." (6) "It is finished." (7) "Father, into Thy hands I commend My spirit."

Seven Pillars of Wisdom   See LAWRENCE, T. E.

Seven Sleepers   According to early Christian legend, seven noble youths of Ephesus, who fled the city in the Decian persecution (AD 250) to a cave in Mount Celion. Their pursuers walled up the cave, but rather than starve to death, miraculously, the youths fell asleep. After 230 years or, according to some versions, 309 years, they awoke, but soon died, and their bodies were taken to Marseilles in a large stone coffin, still shown in St. Victor's church. The legend is said to be of Syrian origin and occurs in the KORAN. See TALISMAN.

Seventeen (1916)   A novel by Booth TARKINGTON. Its hero is William Sylvanus Baxter, Silly Billy, an adolescent in the throes of his first love affair. The object of his attention is Lola Pratt, whose chief occupation is lavishing baby talk on her pet dog Flopit and on her numerous admirers.

Seven Wonders of the Ancient World   A list of man-made wonders compiled by Hellenistic travelers. The first extant list was that made by Antipater of Sidon in the 2nd century BC; a better-known list by Philo of Byzantium was made somewhat later. The Seven Wonders included the pyramids of Egypt; the HANGING GARDENS OF BABYLON; the statue of ZEUS at Olympia, carved by PHIDIAS; the temple of ARTEMIS OF EPHESUS; the tomb of king Mausolus (hence the term MAUSOLEUM) at Halicarnassus; the COLOSSUS of RHODES; and any one of the following three: the Pharos, the walls of Babylon, or the palace of Cyrus.

Seven Years' War (1756–1763)   The war against Frederick the Great of Prussia waged by France, Austria, and Russia. England aided Frederick with subsidies and Hanoverian troops. The war ended with the treaty of Hubertusburg, by which Frederick retained all his dominions. The war carried with it the struggle between France and England overseas, which was settled in the Peace of Paris of 1763, leaving England predominant in India and America. See FRENCH AND INDIAN WAR.

Sévigné, marquise de (born Marie de Rabutin-Chantal, 1626–1696)   French letter writer and lady of fashion. In letters to her daughter, Mme de Grignan, and to a circle of intimate friends, Sévigné described the life of the court, city, and countryside, her domestic affairs, and her reading. These writings afford not only a picture of an age but also a portrait of the woman herself—wise and witty, imaginative and affectionate.

Sewall, Samuel (1652–1730)   English-born American statesman of early New England. Known for his liberal views and for his *Diary* (1878–82), written between 1674 and 1729, Sewall gives a vivid picture of life and personalities in the Boston of his day. Among his other writings are *The Revolution in New England Justified* (1691), which seeks to justify the deposition of the dictatorial English governor Andros; *The Selling of Joseph* (1700), one of the first antislavery tracts written in America; and *A Memorial Relating to the Kennebeck Indians* (1721), a brief appeal for charitable treatment of the Indians.

Sewall, who held a number of political offices in the Massachusetts colony, was one of the judges at the Salem witchcraft trials but later repented publicly in church while his confession was read to the congregation.

Sewanee Review, The   A quarterly magazine founded in 1892 at the University of the South at Sewanee, Tennessee. Though concerned with Southern affairs and Southern writers, under the editorship of Allen TATE (1944–46) it became known as an organ of the NEW CRITICISM and of avant-garde writing in general. See LITTLE MAGAZINES.

Sewell, Anna   See BLACK BEAUTY.

Sexton, Anne (1928–1974)   American poet. A native of New England, Sexton worked in the Boston literary milieu which included the confessional poets Robert LOWELL and Sylvia PLATH, and was greatly influenced by the poet W. O. Snodgrass. After her volume of verse *Live or Die* (1966) won the PULITZER PRIZE, she taught creative writing in several universities. Although Sexton enjoyed continued recognition from her first book, *To Bedlam and Part Way Back* (1960), to the last published in her lifetime, THE DEATH NOTEBOOKS, her years were clouded with mental illness, hospitalization, and suicide attempts. Her popularity with readers was attributable to the candor with which she documented her life, unabashedly dealing with taboo topics in startling terms. She used a simple metrical beat, often that of nursery rhymes. Interspersed with her poems on madness are others which openly yearn for religious faith. The theme so dominates Sexton's posthumous volume *The Awful Rowing Toward God* (1975) that the bawdy tone of her verse begins to seem merely a cover to conceal the painful intensity of this need. Sexton was never able to resolve her creative and personal conflicts and took her own life at the age of forty-six. Several other posthumous collections have been published, including *45 Mercy Street* (1976) and *Words for Dr. Y* (1978).

Seymour, Alan (1927–   )   Australian playwright, novelist, and scriptwriter. Seymour is best known for his neorealist drama THE ONE DAY OF THE YEAR. Although he experiments with dramatic forms, Seymour writes plays that are generally either realistic, quasi-comic scenes in the lives of ordinary people or bizarre, almost surrealistic happenings, as in *Swamp Creatures* (1957).

Seymour, Jane (1509?–1537)   Third wife of Henry VIII of England, mother of Edward VI. A lady in waiting to Catherine of Aragon and then to Anne BOLEYN, Jane caught the fancy of the king in 1535. The following year Anne Boleyn was executed, and less than two weeks after her death Henry and Jane were privately married. She gave birth to Henry's only son in 1537, an event that was met with great public rejoicing, but she died twelve days later.

Sforza   Italian family that ruled in the second half of the 15th century at Milan. From their obscure origins as soldiers of fortune, they established themselves as a princely house and one of the leading powers of Italy. Among those noted for their cultivation of the arts and their patronage of learning were Francesco Sforza (1401–66) and his son Lodovico Sforza (1451–1508), both dukes of Milan. Lodovico, surnamed *il Moro* (the Moor) because of his swarthy complexion, is especially known for his employment of LEONARDO DA VINCI.

Sganarelle   In the comedies of Molière, a favorite name for the cowardly, domineering, or unpleasant character:

(1) The titular character in *Sganarelle, ou Le Cocu imaginaire* (*The Imaginary Cuckold*, 1660). This farce hinges on the consequences of Sganarelle's finding and confiscating the miniature of a gentleman, which he thinks his wife has dropped. In reality, the miniature was dropped by Clélie, and the portrait is not that of Sganarelle's imaginary rival but that of Lélie, her sweetheart.

(2) In *L'École des maris* (*The School for Husbands*, 1661), Sganarelle and his brother Ariste are the guardians of the two young orphans, Isabelle and Léonore. The conceited and domineering Sganarelle expects to marry Isabelle but forces her to lead such a dull, strict life that she dupes him and marries Valère instead.

(3) In *Le Mariage forcé* (*The Forced Marriage*, 1664), Sganarelle is a rich man of sixty-four who promises marriage to Dorimène, a young girl in her teens. He decides at the last moment to withdraw from the alliance, but Dorimène's brother beats him ruthlessly until he consents to go to the altar.

(4) In *L'Amour médecin* (*Love, the Doctor*, 1665), Sganarelle is the selfish father of Lucinde.

(5) In DOM JUAN OU LE FESTIN DE PIERRE, Sganarelle is Don Juan's rather foolish, cowardly valet.

(6) In LE MÉDECIN MALGRÉ LUI, the last of the Sganarelle plays, of which *Le Cocu imaginaire* is logically the sequel, Sganarelle is a woodcutter. Martine, his wife, wanting to get even for the blows he has dealt her, tells some inquirers who are looking for a doctor that he is a noted specialist but so eccentric that he will deny it until they beat him well. Sganarelle, beaten, is taken to the house of the apparently dumb Lucinde. The shrewd Sganarelle sees through her ruse and brings her lover Léandre to her in the guise of an apothecary.

Shadow-Line, The (1917)   A short novel by Joseph CONRAD. Its hero is a young captain who grows mature in the experience of taking his sailing ship through a difficult calm.

Shadrach, Meshach, and Abednego   In the OLD TESTAMENT, three Hebrews who, because of their refusal to worship a golden image, were cast by the command of NEBUCHADNEZZAR into a fiery furnace. But although the furnace was made burning hot, the three men "came forth of the midst of the fire" unharmed, convincing Nebuchadnezzar of the power of their God (Dan. 3:12–30).

Shadwell, Thomas (c1642–1692)   English dramatist and poet. Shadwell is best known as Dryden's original for the titular hero of MACFLECKNOE and for Og in *Absalom and Achitophel* (1682). These satirical portraits were inspired by Shadwell's *The Medal of John Bayes* (1682), a savage attack on Dryden as a member of the court party. Shadwell later became poet laureate when Dryden was deprived of the position upon the accession of William III. His best plays, distinguished equally by their coarseness and acute observation of manners of the day, are *Epsom Wells* (1672) and *The Squire of Alsatia* (1688).

Shaffer, Peter [Levin] (1926–   )   British playwright. Shaffer's widely diverse plays show persistent concern with a theme that corresponds to his interest in the use of masks and ritual: deception of the self or others. In his first big success, *Five Finger Exercise* (1958), a young tutor is almost destroyed by evasions and lies in the family he serves. In Shaffer's most successful farce, *Black Comedy* (1965), an apartment blackout serves to blend deliberate deceptions with confusions of space and identity, while in *The Royal Hunt of the Sun* (1964), the false Christian promise of saving pagan civilizations and the deceit used by the Spanish conquistadors to pillage the Inca empire are central to the plot. *Equus* (1973) presents a disturbed boy who acts out his violent fantasies on the horses he worships and on his psychiatrist, whose professional competence masks an arid personal life. *Amadeus* (1980), adapted successfully as a film in 1984, deals with Antonio Salieri's struggle to reconcile his own aspirations to be great with Mozart's real greatness. *The Collected Plays of Peter Shaffer* appeared in 1982. Shaffer's other work includes plays for radio and television and several novels written in collaboration with his twin brother, Anthony Shaffer, under the pseudonym Peter Anthony.

Shaftesbury, Anthony Ashley Cooper, 1st earl of (1621–1683)   English statesman. A Royalist during the Civil War, Shaftesbury was a member of the CABAL after the Restoration and was named lord chancellor in 1672. A fomenter of the Popish Plot and a supporter of the duke of Monmouth, he was satirized by Dryden, who made him the Achitophel in his ABSALOM AND ACHITOPHEL. See MEDAL, THE.

Shah Jahan   See MOGUL EMPIRE.

Shahn, Ben (1898–1969)   Lithuanian-born American artist. Shahn's fame derives from his work as an artist of social protest, a champion of the politically oppressed. His most famous work was a series of *gouache* (watercolor) paintings, *The Passion of Sacco and Vanzetti* (1932). He was also a noted photographer, working for the Farm Security Administration during the Depression (1935–38).

Shah-nama (The Book of Kings)   Persian epic poem by FIRDOUSĪ. The poet labored for thirty-five years on this work, finishing it in 1010. It consisted of sixty thousand couplets, but not all have survived. A legendary treatment of Persian history, it immediately became the national epic. It chronicles the entire history of Persia from the creation of man to the Sasanian empire (AD 226–641). By writing this epic, Firdousī preserved material that was on the verge of oblivion; he used now lost written sources and the dying oral traditions for his material. While *Shah-nama* has many heroes, its main theme is an expression of Persian pride and glory.

Shakers   A celibate sect of Second Adventists, founded in the 18th century in England by a secession from the QUAKERS and transplanted to the U.S. by Ann LEE. Their official name is The United Society of Believers in Christ's Second Appearing, or The Millennial Church. Their popular name was originally derisive and refers to the contortions they made during the religious dances of which their public form of worship chiefly consisted. Theologically, they hold that God is dual, comprising the eternal father and eternal mother, the parents of angels and of men.

Shakespeare, William (1564–1616)   English poet and dramatist of the Elizabethan and early Jacobean period; the most widely known author in all English literature. Shakespeare was born at Stratford-on-Avon, the son of John Shakespeare, a man who attained some prominence in town affairs, and Mary Arden, a woman of good family. William was probably educated at the King Edward IV Grammar School in Stratford, where he learned Latin and a little Greek and read the Roman dramatists. At eighteen he married Anne Hathaway, some seven or eight years his senior, who bore him a daughter, Susanna, in 1583, and twins, Hamnet (who died in boyhood) and Judith, in 1585. There is no record of Shakespeare's activities between 1585 and 1592, when he is known to have been in London and is alluded to as an actor and playwright in a bitter passage in Robert Greene's A GROATSWORTH OF WIT. There is some speculation that Shakespeare may have taught school during this period, but it seems more probable that in 1585, or shortly after, he went to London and began his apprenticeship as an actor.

The London theatres were closed from June 1592 to April 1594, because of the plague. How Shakespeare earned his living during this period is not precisely known, though he probably had some income from his patron, Henry Wriothesley, earl of Southampton, to whom he dedicated his first two poems: VENUS AND ADONIS and THE RAPE OF LUCRECE. *Venus and Adonis* is a long narrative poem based on Ovid and dealing with Adonis' rejection of the goddess of love, his death, and the consequent disappearance of beauty from the world; it was immensely popular, and went through six editions in nine years. Contemporary sources, however, indicate that the more conservative elements objected to what they considered the poem's glorification of sensuality, and it may have been in response to this that Shakespeare wrote *Lucrece*, which praises chastity. The story of the rape of the Roman matron LUCRETIA by Tarquin, it is based on tales found in OVID, Livy, and Chaucer's LEGEND OF GOOD WOMEN, and written in rhyme royal. Though a more polished and in some senses a better poem than *Venus and Adonis*, it suffers from excessive length and never found the popularity of the earlier poem.

In 1594 Shakespeare appears in contemporary records as a member of the Lord Chamberlain's company of actors. The most popular of the companies acting at Court, it lasted through the reign of Elizabeth and became the company of the King's Men under the patronage of James I. In 1599 a group of the leading actors of Chamberlain's Men —Shakespeare among them—formed a syndicate to build and operate a new playhouse; it was named the GLOBE, and became one of the most famous theatres of its time. Largely from his share of the income of the Globe (and of BLACK-FRIARS, in which he also had an interest) Shakespeare became a moderately wealthy man. As early as 1597 he purchased New Place, a large house in Stratford.

By 1597 Shakespeare had written at least a dozen plays: comedies, patriotic histories, and one tragedy in the bloody-revenge style popular in the Elizabethan theatre. The dates of these plays, and their order of composition, cannot be definitely established. The earliest plays include, among the histories, HENRY VI (Parts I, II, and III, 1590–92), RICHARD III (1594), RICHARD II (1595), and KING JOHN (1596–97); among the comedies, THE COMEDY OF ERRORS (1590–92), TWO GENTLEMEN OF VERONA (c1592), THE TAMING OF THE SHREW (c1593), LOVE'S LABOUR'S LOST (1593–94), and A MIDSUMMER NIGHT'S DREAM (1595–96); and, among the tragedies, TITUS ANDRONICUS (1590–92). The earliest plays, as might be expected, show the greatest influence of contemporary and classical models; the early comedies are conventional, artificial, filled with ingenious conceits, puns, and other elaborate wordplay, but they foreshadow his later, great comedies in their careful structure. The *Henry VI* plays, though faulty in themselves, developed into an early triumph in *Richard II*. *Titus Andronicus*, Senecan in style and strongly influenced by Thomas Kyd's *The Spanish Tragedy*, is so unlike Shakespeare's mature tragedies that some critics dispute his authorship of it.

ROMEO AND JULIET (1596), Shakespeare's second tragedy, is a transitional work; like the early comedies, it tends to be artificial, but in its lyricism and its development of character it indicates the direction of Shakespeare's growth. His plays in the last years of the 16th century are primarily comedies and histories: the so-called joyous comedies, namely, THE MERCHANT OF VENICE (1596), THE MERRY WIVES OF WINDSOR (1597–1600), MUCH ADO ABOUT NOTHING (1598–99), AS YOU LIKE IT (1599–1600), and TWELFTH NIGHT (1599–1600); and the histories of HENRY IV (Parts I and II, 1597–98) and HENRY V (1598–99). It is in these plays that Shakespeare's great gift for character portrayal becomes evident as he brings to life SHYLOCK, FALSTAFF, JAQUES, and a host of memorable figures.

The great period of Shakespeare's tragedies is ushered in at the turn of the century with JULIUS CAESAR (1599–1600). In the intensely drawn character of Brutus from this play, there is a foreshadowing of the heroes of the first two of the great tragedies: HAMLET (1600–1601) and OTHELLO (1604). These profound explorations of the human spirit are developed with even larger range in KING LEAR (1605–6), generally regarded as his greatest work, and with a sharper focus in MACBETH (1606) and ANTONY AND CLEOPATRA (1607–8). TIMON OF ATHENS (1607–8) and CORIOLANUS (1608–9) are his final tragedies, and their enigmatic quality is shared by the other plays of this period: TROILUS AND CRESSIDA (1600–1602), a play variously described as a comedy or a tragedy and now generally regarded as a serious satire; and ALL'S WELL THAT ENDS WELL (1602) and MEASURE FOR MEASURE (1604–5), two of the "dark comedies."

The plays of Shakespeare's last period are sometimes described as comedies, but might be better termed romances or tragicomedies; clearly experimental, they are light-hearted and yet serious, romantically fanciful and yet symbolic. They include PERICLES (1608–9), CYMBELINE (1609–10), THE WINTER'S TALE (1610–11), and THE TEMPEST (1611–12).

HENRY VIII, a history play, is the final work attributed to Shakespeare; it is generally considered to be an inferior piece, and many scholars believe much of it to have been written by John FLETCHER. Eighteen of Shakespeare's plays were published separately in quarto editions during his lifetime; a complete collection of his works did not appear until the publication of the FIRST FOLIO in 1623.

Shakespeare's achievements did not go unnoticed among his contemporaries. In 1598 Francis Meres cited "honey-tongued" Shakespeare for his plays and poems. With Shakespeare as their leading dramatist, the Chamberlain's Men rose to become the leading dramatic company in London and in 1603 were installed as members of the royal household, bearing the title of the King's Men.

Sometime after 1612, Shakespeare apparently retired from the stage and returned to Stratford. In January 1616 he had his will drawn up; it included the famous bequest to his wife of his "second best bed." On April 25 of that year, he was buried at Stratford Church, and the monument over his tomb lists the day of his death as April 23, 1616.

Although Shakespeare was ranked among the foremost dramatists of his time by his contemporaries, evidence indicates that both he and his world looked to poetry, not playwriting, for enduring fame. In the years following the publication of *Venus and Adonis* and *Lucrece*, Shakespeare continued to write poems; his sonnets (see THE SONNETS OF SHAKESPEARE) were composed between 1593 and 1601, though not published until 1609. In 1599 there appeared a volume of twenty poems called THE PASSIONATE PILGRIM; Shakespeare's name was given on the title page, but only five of the poems (I, II, III, V, and XVII) are now believed to be his. A poem called THE PHOENIX AND THE TURTLE, attributed to Shakespeare, was published in Robert Chester's *Loves Martyr* (1601). A LOVER'S COMPLAINT, published at the end of the 1609 edition of the sonnets, is written in the same meter as *Lucrece* but seems to belong to a different period. Not all scholars agree that it is the work of Shakespeare.

During the 17th and early 18th centuries Shakespeare suffered at the hands of those—including Alexander POPE—who would "improve" him; his plays were frequently staged, but apparently he was not widely read. There was, however, a considerable upsurge of interest in his works, beginning in the middle of the 18th century and continuing with the enthusiastic criticism of Samuel Taylor COLERIDGE, Charles LAMB, and William HAZLITT. The 19th century also saw the growth of the theory that someone other than Shakespeare—usually Sir Francis BACON—wrote his plays (see BACONIAN CONTROVERSY).

Shakespearean sonnet   See SONNET.

shakti (Sans, "power; energy")   In HINDUISM, the dynamic, energizing aspect of a god, personified by his consort, particularly the consorts of SHIVA. By the 5th century, a distinct cult had evolved within Hinduism that based its worship on the fertile, productive energy of the feminine force, personified most often by KALI and DURGA. Some of the rituals of Shaktism include the communal breaking of Hindu taboos (see TANTRAS) to bring about complete bodily and spiritual communion with the particular deity being worshipped. This is carried to such extremes that the uninitiated consider the practices merely orgiastic.

Shākuntalā   In Hindu mythology, the daughter of Visvamitra and Menaka. She is the heroine of KĀLIDĀSA's Sanskrit drama *Shākuntalā*. She was abandoned on the banks of the river Malini and brought up by the hermit Kanva. While hunting one day King Dushyanta meets Shākuntalā, falls in love with her, and persuades her to marry him. He gives her a ring before returning to his throne. Shākuntalā gives birth to a son and sets out with him to find Dushyanta. She loses the ring while bathing and the king, enchanted by Durvasas's curse, does not recognize her. The ring is subsequently recovered by the king in the stomach of a fish he has caught. He then recognizes his wife and proclaims her his queen. Their son, Bharata, becomes the heir to the throne and later the founder of the race of the Bharatas.

The play, written in both poetry and prose, follows a highly traditionalized style. Like Attic Greek drama, the plot is taken from mythology, and there is no effort to use suspense or to introduce elements into the story that are not already known to the sophisticated audience. Through his poetry and music, the playwright seeks to evoke states of being and to elicit the emotions in his audience: love, mirth, energy (the heroic emotion), terror, disgust. Each scene is supposed to engender some emotional flavor, but not to run counter to the dominant emotion of the play, which in the case of *Shākuntalā* is erotic.

Shākyamuni   See BUDDHA.

Shallow, Justice Robert   A weak-minded country justice in Shakespeare's HENRY IV: PART II, HENRY V, and, more prominently, in THE MERRY WIVES OF WINDSOR. A braggart, he is fond of endlessly recounting his imaginary exploits.

shamanism   A primitive form of religion. Those who practice it believe that the world and all events are governed by good and evil spirits who can be propitiated or bought off only through the intervention of a witch doctor, or *Shaman*. The word is Slavonic; it comes from the Samoyeds and other Siberian peoples, but is now applied to American Indian and other primitive worship.

Shamash   The Babylonian sun god. The son of SIN, the moon god, and brother of ISHTAR, he was a divine dispenser of justice. In this role it was he from whom HAMMURABI claimed to have received sanction for his code of laws. His wife was Aya, the Dawn.

Shang (or Yin)   The first historical Chinese dynasty (c1523–1027 BC). Centering on the Yellow River with its capital at Anyang, it possessed a highly developed civilization. Exquisite Chinese bronzes and oracle bones, inscribed with an advanced form of writing, which date to this period were unearthed in excavations in the late 1920s. The Shang was followed by the CHOU dynasty.

Shangri-La   In James HILTON's popular novel *Lost Horizon* (1933), a mythical land of eternal youth and safety from war, supposedly situated somewhere in the interior of Tibet. Shangri-La has come to mean any ideal refuge.

Shantiparvan   See MAHĀBHĀRATA.

Shapiro, Karl [Jay] (1913–   )   American poet, critic, and editor. Shapiro's reputation as a poet was established with his early volumes, which stemmed from his experiences as a soldier and a Jew in World War II: *Person, Place, and Thing* (1942), *The Place of Love* (1942), *V-Letter and Other Poems* (1944; PULITZER PRIZE), and *Trial of a Poet* (1947). His subsequent poetry, in which he eventually broke with traditional forms in favor of the FREE VERSE of Walt WHITMAN and the BEAT MOVEMENT, is collected in *Poems: 1940–1953* (1953), *Selected Poems* (1968), and *Collected Poems: 1940–1977* (1978). *Love and War, Art and God* appeared in 1984. In addition to his philosophical discourse in verse, *Essay on Rime* (1945), Shapiro has written several books of criticism, including *Beyond Criticism* (1953), *In Defense of Ignorance* (1960), and *To Abolish Children and Other Essays* (1968). His essays, as well as his poetry, oppose academicism and stress the aesthetic and cultural values of verse. He was editor of POETRY magazine from 1950 to 1956 and later edited *Prairie Schooner*.

Sharp, Becky   The central character in the novel VANITY FAIR by William Makepeace Thackeray. She is a cool, unprincipled, selfish girl, whose only object is to rise in the world from her obscure and poverty-stricken origins. "She was small and slight in person, pale, sandy-haired, and with green eyes, habitually cast down, but very large, odd, and attractive when they looked up."

Shatov, Ivan Pavlovich   In Dostoyevsky's novel THE POSSESSED, an earnest, awkward former student and friend of STAVROGIN, whose father had been a servant in the household of Stavrogin's mother. He has become obsessed with the idea of the mission of Russia in saving the world with the unsullied Christianity preserved in Orthodoxy, a notion once casually dropped by Stavrogin. Shatov is a member of VERKHOVENSKY's revolutionary group. When he tries to quit, Verkhovensky has him murdered.

Darya Pavlovna Shatova   Ivan's sister, a ward in the household of Varvara Petrovna, Stavrogin's mother. The open-hearted Darya is in love with Stavrogin and immediately agrees to go away with him to begin a new life elsewhere. Before the plan is carried out, Stavrogin hangs himself.

Marya Ignatyevna Shatova   Ivan's wife, who returns to him on the evening of his murder and gives birth to a child, presumably fathered by Stavrogin.

Shaun the Postman   In James Joyce's novel FINNEGANS WAKE, the name by which Kevin, one of H. C. EARWICKER's twin sons, is generally known. He represents the man of action. SHEM THE PENMAN is his opposite.

Shaw, George Bernard (1856–1950)   Irish dramatist, critic, and social reformer. Idealistic, prudish, afraid of intimacy, often shy, Shaw's public image was his own created caricature: "G.B.S." The beard, the mysticism, the eccentricities all belonged to G.B.S., whom Shaw used as the spokesman for his social, moral, and literary theories. Political and economic socialism, a new religion of creative evolution, antivivisection, vegetarianism, and spelling reform were a few of his causes. His plays and essays, never written solely to entertain, were the vehicles for Shaw's theories; G.B.S. was his press agent.

Shaw had written five unsuccessful socialist novels by 1884 when he met William Archer, who urged him to write modern, purposeful dramas as IBSEN had done. Through Archer, Shaw became music critic for a London newspaper. He was well known for his music reviews long before he became famous as a dramatist. He began to write for the stage in 1885. With most of his early plays either banned by the censor or refused production, Shaw sought a reading audience with his first published collection, *Plays Pleasant and Unpleasant* (1898), the pleasant plays being ARMS AND THE MAN, *Candida*, *The Man of Destiny*, and *You Never Can Tell*; the unpleasant, *The Philanderer*, MRS. WARREN'S PROFESSION, and his first play, *Widowers' Houses*. It was for this volume that Shaw began the practice of writing the challenging, mocking, eloquent prefaces to his plays, the prefaces sometimes being longer than the plays themselves and covering a diversity of topics.

By 1900, some of Shaw's plays had been produced in the U.S. and in Germany, but not in England. His next collection of plays, *Three Plays for Puritans* (1900), contained THE DEVIL'S DISCIPLE, CAESAR AND CLEOPATRA, and *Captain Brassbound's Conversion*.

Before the outbreak of the World War I, and largely through the efforts of H. GRANVILLE-BARKER, Shaw had been accepted in England; his position as a playwright was secure, and his fame, worldwide.

Because of his attacks on British policy during the war and his continual irritation to reactionary elements in England, Shaw was widely unpopular for a time, but his international fame allowed him to speak his mind and write what he pleased.

Shaw wrote his best plays prior to, during, and shortly after World War I. They include MAN AND SUPERMAN, JOHN BULL'S OTHER ISLAND (written at the request of William Butler YEATS for the Irish Literary Theatre), MAJOR BARBARA, *Fanny's First Play* (1912), *Androcles and the Lion* (1912), PYGMALION, HEARTBREAK HOUSE, BACK TO METHUSELAH, and SAINT JOAN. He received the NOBEL PRIZE in Literature in 1925.

A member of the FABIAN SOCIETY from its founding (1883), Shaw wrote many essays on socialism, politics, and economics and one longer work, *The Intelligent Woman's Guide to Socialism and Capitalism* (1928).

He wrote less as he grew older, but never stopped completely; he was at work on a comedy when he died at the age of ninety-four. His last full-length play, *Buoyant Billions*, was produced in Zurich in 1948 "before a respectful if uncomprehending audience."

Always outspoken, with a barbed humor and wit, never satisfied with the conventional, Shaw conducted himself so that the adjective *Shavian* is descriptive of an iconoclastic way of life, rather than a literary form.

His fame and popularity rest on his plays, but John Mason Brown has observed, "This astonishing Mr. Shaw has been greater than anything even he has written."

Shaw, Irwin (1913–1984)   American novelist, short-story writer, and playwright. Shaw began writing serials for radio and, later, successful scenarios for Hollywood, but it was his antiwar play *Bury the Dead* (1936), that first attracted wide attention. He followed it with *The Gentle People: A Brooklyn Fable* (1939), another dramatic fantasy, this one dealing with the threat of fascism. Shaw wrote

other plays, but his narrative skill ensured the greatest success with the short story and novel forms. Among his distinguished volumes of stories, many of which first appeared in THE NEW YORKER, are *Sailor off the Bremen* (1939), *Mixed Company* (1950), *Love on a Dark Street* (1965), *God Was Here, But He Left Early* (1973), and *Short Stories: Five Decades* (1978). His first novel was THE YOUNG LIONS. Subsequent novels include *Two Weeks in Another Town* (1960); *Rich Man, Poor Man* (1969), which was made into a very successful series of movies for television; *The Top of the Hill* (1979); and *Bread Upon the Waters* (1981).

Shchedrin, N.   See SALTYKOV, MIKHAIL YEVGRAFOVICH.

Shchepkin, Mikhail Semenovich (1788–1863) Russian actor. Generally considered the finest of 19th-century Russian actors, Shchepkin with his realistic style paved the way for the drama of OSTROVSKY and CHEKHOV and the acting theories of STANISLAVSKY.

Sheba, queen of   The queen who visited King SOLOMON (1 Kings 10), known to the Arabs as Balkis, queen of Saba. According to the OLD TESTAMENT story, she came to Solomon "to prove him with hard questions," but on seeing him in all his glory and wisdom, had "no more spirit in her." One version of the story holds that she bore Solomon a son, Menelek, from whom the Abyssinians were descended.

Sheed, Wilfrid [John Joseph] (1930–   ) English-born American novelist and journalist. Sheed's parents were the founders of the Roman Catholic publishing house Sheed and Ward (London and New York). As a result, he received his schooling on both sides of the Atlantic, and attended Oxford University. He then settled in New York and worked as a book and theatre reviewer. Selected essays and reviews were collected in *The Morning After* (1971). His fiction, lightly satirical in tone, is drawn largely from his own experience. *Transatlantic Blues* (1978), perhaps the most directly autobiographical of his novels, is the satirical sketch of a man who can neither accept nor abandon his Catholicism and who lives in both Britain and the U.S. but feels rooted in neither. Among his other works are *Clare Boothe Luce* (1982) and a memoir of his publisher parents, *Frank and Maisie* (1985).

Sheeler, Charles (1883–1965)   American painter and photographer. His paintings, explorations of geometrical and architectural form, had a lasting effect on the development of ABSTRACT EXPRESSIONISM. His series of paintings and photographs of the Ford Motor Company River Rouge plant, more than any other single piece, opened the eyes of his generation to the severe beauty of functional engineering design.

Sheldon, Edward Brewster (1886–1946)   American playwright. His best-known plays were melodramas based on the social problems current in the early 20th century. *The Nigger* (1909) created a furor because its hero is a white man with African blood, whose fiancée does not reject him.

Shelley, Mary Wollstonecraft (born Mary Godwin, 1797–1851) English novelist, daughter of William GODWIN and Mary WOLLSTONECRAFT, and second wife of Percy Bysshe SHELLEY. Mary Shelley wrote in the convention of the GOTHIC NOVEL. FRANKENSTEIN, OR THE MODERN PROMETHEUS is her best-known work. Other romances are *Valperga* (1823), *The Last Man* (1826), and *Lodore* (1835).

Shelley, Percy Bysshe (1792–1822) English poet. Although he was the son of a conservative country squire, Shelley was influenced early in life by the doctrines of the Enlightenment, ardently championing liberty and rebelling against the strictures of English politics and religion. While at Oxford he wrote and circulated a pamphlet called *The Necessity of Atheism*, and was expelled for "contumacy in refusing to answer certain questions" about it. In 1811, when he was nineteen, he eloped with sixteen-year-old Harriet WESTBROOK, and the pair spent the following two years traveling in England and Ireland, distributing pamphlets and speaking against political injustice. By 1814, however, an estrangement was growing between them, and they were separated. At about the same time, he met William Godwin, whose *Political Justice* had strongly influenced the early direction of his thinking, and soon fell in love with Godwin's daughter Mary (see Mary SHELLEY). In the summer of 1814 he and Mary eloped to the Continent; though they did not believe in marriage because of its exclusiveness and limitations, they were married after Harriet committed suicide in 1816. Their household, however, was scarcely conventional, and after 1818 they lived exclusively in Italy, where Shelley did his best work.

Shelley's early poetry includes *Queen Mab*, written in 1812–13, a long work inveighing against orthodox Christianity and secular tyranny, and *Alastor, or the Spirit of Solitude* (1816), an allegory of a youth seeking in vain for a being equal to his most perfect imaginings. His "Hymn to Intellectual Beauty," conceived during a voyage to Lake Geneva with Byron in 1816, reflects Shelley's Platonism. He revised the early "Laon and Cythna," an allegorical poem on the French Revolution, and renamed it *The Rise of Islam*; somewhat similar in ideological content to *Queen Mab*, it was the last poem Shelley wrote before leaving for Italy in 1818. He was working on *The Cenci* (1819), a blank-verse drama on the unfortunate Beatrice CENCI, when news came of the Peterloo Massacre, which was the result of a government-ordered cavalry charge on a working-class rally at Manchester; inspired by outrage and pity, he wrote the *Mask of Anarchy* (pub 1832). He soon began working on PROMETHEUS UNBOUND, a lyric and symbolic drama for which he adapted elements from the Greek myth of Prometheus.

In 1819 the Shelleys moved to Pisa, where Shelley composed many of his shorter lyrics, among them THE CLOUD, "To a Skylark," ODE TO THE WEST WIND, and THE SENSI-

TIVE PLANT; with the earlier OZYMANDIAS, these poems have become the most famous among Shelley's works, though their popularity has obscured his general recognition as a philosophical poet.

Among Shelley's last works are EPIPSYCHIDION, a passionate love poem addressed to Emilia VIVIANI; and ADONAIS, an elegy on the death of KEATS, modeled after the elegies of Bion and Moschus and frequently considered to be, of elegies in English, second only to Milton's *Lycidas*. In 1821, in response to Thomas Love PEACOCK's disparaging comments on the value of poetry in *The Four Ages of Poetry*, Shelley wrote his famous *Defence of Poetry*. Based somewhat on Sir Philip SIDNEY's essay, and drawing on ideas contained in the *Symposium* and *Ion* of PLATO, the *Defence* is interesting primarily for the light it throws on Shelley's philosophical thought and his analysis of the value of the creative imagination.

In 1822 the Shelley household, which now included Jane and Edward Williams, moved to the Bay of Lerici, where Shelley wrote the poems addressed to Jane and sailed with Edward. He was at work on a long poem, *The Triumph of Life*, which was left incomplete when his boat was caught in a storm and he and Edward Williams were drowned. Their bodies were washed ashore at Viareggio, where, in the presence of Lord BYRON and Leigh HUNT, they were burned on the beach.

A thorough student of Greek, Shelley was a Platonist and a humanist, looking to the Athens of the time of PERICLES as the ideal toward which present-day civilization should be directed. Though his enthusiasms had the spontaneity and impulsiveness of an adolescent, there can be little question of the sincerity of his beliefs or his dedication to his liberal ideals. Never an atheist, he rejected orthodox Christianity but always held to the idea of some "pervading spirit co-eternal with the universe"; and he rejected all conventions that he believed stifled love and human freedom. His poetry, typically abstract and allegorical, reflects his concern with the nature of transcendent reality.

Shem In the book of GENESIS, the oldest of the three sons of NOAH, said to be the eponymous ancestor of the SEMITES. His brothers were JAPHETH and HAM.

Shem the Penman In James Joyce's novel FINNEGANS WAKE, the name by which Jerry, one of H. C. EARWICKER's twin sons, is known. He represents the artist. His brother, SHAUN THE POSTMAN, is his opposite.

Shenstone, William (1714–1763) English poet. Although he is known for his pastoral verse, including songs, odes, ballads, and elegies, Shenstone's major work is a poem, *The Schoolmistress* (1742), written in Spenserian stanzas.

Shepard, Sam (1943–   ) American playwright. Shepard had had over thirty plays produced in New York before he was thirty. Early plays like *Cowboys* (1964), *The Rock Garden* (1964), *Icarus's Mother* (1965), and *Red Cross* (1966) have in common with such subsequent plays as

Operation Sidewinder (1970), *The Tooth of Crime* (1972), and *The Curse of the Starving Class* (1976) a despairing preoccupation with the sinister forces that erode the strength and vitality of the American spirit. In his surrealistic and allegorical plays, Shepard repeatedly examines the moral anomie and spiritual starvation that characterize modern times. Among his many other plays are *Buried Child* (1978; PULITZER PRIZE), *True West* (1980), *Motel Chronicles* (1982), and *Fool for Love* (1984).

Shepheardes Calender, The (1579)   Twelve eclogues by Edmund SPENSER, one for each month of the year. The first and last eclogues are laments by the shepherd Colin Clout (a persona of Spenser), because the fair Rosalind does not return his love. The remaining ten are dialogues on love and other subjects among the shepherds.

Sheridan, Richard Brinsley (1751–1816)   Irishborn English dramatist, orator, and statesman. Sheridan wrote brilliantly polished, satirical comedies of manners that returned to the general vein of the Restoration period, although critics have pointed out that the moral tone of his works is not to be found in the drama of 17th-century England. He established himself as a versatile playwright within one year (1775) with the Covent Garden Theatre productions of THE RIVALS, *St. Patrick's Day*, and *The Duenna*, a light opera. In 1776 he succeeded David Garrick as manager of the Drury Lane Theatre. His other plays include THE SCHOOL FOR SCANDAL, *The Critic* (1779), and *Pizarro* (1799), a melodramatic tragedy.

Sherman, William Tecumseh (1820–1891)   American general. After succeeding Grant as commander of the Union forces in the West during the Civil War, Sherman captured Atlanta on September 1, 1864, and began his famous March to the Sea, which cut the Confederacy in half. His men lived off the country, destroying enemy supplies, buildings, and railroads, and so devastated the region that Sherman's name is still anathema in the South. After the war he performed important services in the West. When Republican leaders attempted to nominate him for the presidency in 1884, he replied, "I will not accept if nominated, and will not serve if elected." The remark that "war is hell," usually attributed to Sherman, probably stems from a speech (1880) in which he said, "There is many a boy here today who looks on war as all glory, but, boys, it is all hell."

Sherwood, Robert E[mmet] (1896–1955)   American playwright and editor. Wounded in World War I, Sherwood early resolved to do all he could to stop future wars. This attitude appears in his first Broadway play, *The Road to Rome* (1927), a comedy satirically attacking the concept of military glory, and *Idiot's Delight* (1936), a PULITZER PRIZE-winning drama. Among his many other plays are *Reunion in Vienna* (1931), a romantic comedy; *The Petrified Forest* (1935), an Arizona melodrama; ABE LINCOLN IN ILLINOIS; and *There Shall Be No Night* (1940),

another Pulitzer Prize winner, about the Russian invasion of Finland.

Sherwood was extremely vocal in warning of the dangers of European totalitarianism. During World War II, he was at various times special assistant to the secretaries of war and the navy and director of the overseas operation of the Office of War Information. He helped write some of Franklin D. ROOSEVELT's speeches and later won a Pulitzer Prize with *Roosevelt and Hopkins: An Intimate History* (1948).

She Stoops to Conquer, or, The Mistakes of a Night (1773)   A comedy by Oliver GOLDSMITH. The story concerns young Marlow, a bashful young man who feels easy only with barmaids and serving girls. It is with reluctance that he sets forth to win the hand of Miss Hardcastle. Tricked into believing that the home of Mr. Hardcastle is a village inn, he treats her enraged father as if he were an impudent landlord. Miss Hardcastle takes advantage of the situation, posing first as the barmaid, then as a poor relative and thus conquers Marlow. The mistakes of the evening unravel with the arrival of Marlow's father who had arranged the match. Mr. Hardcastle forgives young Marlow and all ends happily. This comedy is noted for its rich characterizations.

shibboleth   The password of a secret society; the secret by which those of a party know each other; also, a worn-out or discredited doctrine. The Ephraimites could not pronounce *sh*, so when they were fleeing from Jephthah and the Gileadites (Judges 12:1–16) they were caught at the ford on the Jordan because Jephthah caused all the fugitives to say the word shibboleth (which means "a stream in flood"), which the Ephraimites pronounced as sibboleth.

Shigalyov   In Dostoyevsky's THE POSSESSED, a member of VERKHOVENSKY's revolutionary group. He is a burlesque portrait of a political theorist. Reporting on his plan for the new order after the revolution, the bewildered Shigalyov admits that in working out his ideas he began with unlimited freedom in the system and ended with unlimited despotism.

Shih chi   See SSU-MA CH'IEN.
Shih-ching   See BOOK OF ODES.
Shih-t'ou chi   See DREAM OF THE RED CHAMBER.
Shiites (Arab, *shiah*, "sect")   Those Muslims who regard Ali as the first rightful Imam or Caliph (rejecting the three Sunni Caliphs), and do not consider the SUNNA, or oral law, of any authority, but look upon it as apocryphal. There are numerous Shiite sects, all of them regarded as heretical by the orthodox SUNNITES. Because of the Shiite doctrine of the MAHDI, a twelfth Imam who is supposedly living in concealment through the centuries but is expected to rule Islam, the Shiites have had a political as well as a religious influence on the development of ISLAM as evidenced in the overthrow of the Shah of Iran in 1979 and

the subsequent rise of Shiite fundamentalism in other countries of the Middle East.

Shimazaki Tōson (1872–1943)   Japanese poet and novelist. The poetry of Shimazaki's youth, inspired by English romanticists and written in a new, freer style, set off a movement that eventually liberated Japanese verse from the agelong dominance of TANKA and HAIKU. He later became a novelist, producing *Hakai* (1906; tr *The Broken Commandment*, 1974) and *Ie* (1911; tr *The Family*, 1976), among others. The former is a provocative story exposing social discrimination, while the latter, a novel tracing the disintegration of two old families, has been acclaimed as a masterpiece of naturalistic fiction.

Shinto   The native religion of the Japanese. Animistic, it has always emphasized the worship of natural objects, legendary deities, and national heroes. From the NARA period (710–794), it coexisted with BUDDHISM, and many of its gods were incorporated into the Buddhist pantheon. Although without a scripture or fixed tenets, it has always held a firm place in Japanese religious life. The MEIJI government accorded it state sponsorship (1868) and officially divorced it from Buddhism. The word *Shinto* means literally "the way of the gods."

Shipman's Tale, The   One of THE CANTERBURY TALES of CHAUCER, based on a popular *fabliau*. The monk John has claimed cousinship with a rich merchant in order to frequent his house and be near his wife. Just before the merchant departs on a business trip, the wife complains bitterly to John about her husband's miserliness and begs the loan of one hundred francs to pay a debt for fine clothes. John then asks the departing merchant for a loan, takes the money to the wife, and spends the night with her. When the merchant returns, John thanks him for the loan and says he has already returned it to his wife. She, when questioned, claims she understood the money was meant as a gift because of the two men's friendship. The merchant decides the case is hopeless and accepts her offer to pay him back in their marriage bed.

Ship of Fools   Title of a number of allegorical satires lashing the weakness and vices of their times. The first popular one was Sebastian BRANT's *Das Narrenschiff* (1494), a poem in rhymed couplets, assembling on a ship bound for Narragonia, the land of fools, representatives of every age, class, and quality among men. In exposing, among other things, abuses within the Church, it helped prepare the way for the Protestant Reformation. Written in an Alsatian dialect, it was almost immediately translated and adapted throughout Europe; in English the most famous versions were Alexander Barclay's *The Ship of Fools* (1509) and the anonymous *Cock Lovell's Bote* (c1510).

Ship of Fools (1962)   A novel by Katherine Anne PORTER. It is an allegorical account of a voyage of the German ship *Vera* from Veracruz, Mexico, to Bremerhaven in 1931. The title of the book, taken from Brant's *Das Nar-* *renschiff*, represents a "simple almost universal image of the ship of this world on its voyage to eternity."

Shirer, William L[awrence] (1904–   )   American journalist and historian. Shirer vividly depicted the rise of Nazism in his CBS radio reports from Germany and in his *Berlin Diary* (1941). His massive and controversial history, *The Rise and Fall of the Third Reich* (1960), was followed by two works for children on the subject, *The Rise and Fall of Adolf Hitler* (1961) and *The Sinking of the Bismarck* (1962), and by *The Collapse of the Third Republic* (1969). He has published two volumes of memoirs, *20th Century Journey: The Start* (1976) and *The Nightmare Years* (1984). He has also written a biography of GANDHI (1980), whom he knew as a young reporter.

Shirley (1849)   A novel by Charlotte BRONTË. The story is set in Yorkshire at the end of the Napoleonic Wars. The depressed wool industry of the time and the strife between workers and the hero, a mill owner named Robert Gerand Moore, figure in the plot. The heroine, Shirley Keeldar, was drawn from Charlotte's sister, Emily.

Shirley, James (1596–1666)   English dramatist. Shirley was often called "the last of the Elizabethans" because he was the last important dramatist writing when the theatres were closed by Parliament in 1642. He is best known for his comedies of manners, such as THE LADY OF PLEASURE, *The Witty Fair One* (1628), *Hyde Park* (1632), and *The Gamester* (1633), although he wrote at least two noteworthy tragedies: *The Cardinal* (1641) and *The Traitor* (1631). He wrote more than thirty plays and masques, including *The Triumph of Peace* (1634) and *Cupid and Death* (1653).

Shiva (or Siva)   In HINDUISM, the Supreme Spirit represented as the destroyer in the Hindu trinity, TRIMURTI. Since in Hindu philosophy restoration is involved in destruction, Shiva is also the reproductive or renovating power. Shiva is a worker of miracles through meditation and penance, and hence is a favorite deity with ascetics. He is a god of the fine arts and of dancing. The Siva Nataraja, the dancing Shiva, is probably the most famous single representation of this deity. Shiva is also known as *Hara* and as *Mahadeva* (the great god). His principal consort is KALI.

Shklovsky, Viktor Borisovich (1893–1984) Russian prose writer and critic. Shklovsky was a founder of the formalist school of literary criticism (see FORMALISM). In his essay *Iskusstvo kak priyom* (1917; tr *Art as Device*, 1965), Shklovsky promulgated his concept of *ostraneniye*, or defamiliarization, as the process by which literary art makes new and strange that which is familiar and therefore incompletely recognized. As the formalist movement came under increasingly sharp attack from the social critics of the 1920s, Shklovsky compromised and synthesized a new literary approach encompassing elements from both his earlier work and the rising social critics, producing studies such as *Material i stil v romane L. N. Tolstogo Voyna i mir* (*Material and Style in L. Tolstoy's War and Peace*, 1928).

In 1930, in his notorious article "A Monument to Scientific Error," he capitulated somewhat to the nascent doctrine of SOCIALIST REALISM, conceding that formalism could allow for social and economic factors, though he refused to declare himself a Marxist. Shklovsky then turned to film criticism, scriptwriting, and memoirs, the best known being *O Mayakovskom* (1940; tr *Mayakovsky and His Circle*, 1972). Some of his best books are his autobiographical fiction, such as *Sentimentalnoye puteshestviye* (1923; tr *A Sentimental Journey*, 1970) and *Zoo, ili pisma ne o lyubvi* (1923; tr *Zoo, or Letters Not about Love*, 1971), which recounts in epistolary form the author's own romantic experiences, presumably with the Russian-born French writer Elsa TRIOLET. Shklovsky's critical chef d'oeuvre, *Khudozhestvennaya proza: Razmyshleniya i razbory* (*Literary Prose: Reflections and Analyses*, 1959), added to his growing postwar reputation as one of the Soviet Union's great original critical thinkers.

Shogun   The title of the military rulers of Japan from the 12th century to the MEIJI Restoration in 1868. The Shogunate was a hereditary position at the apex of the military class. As commander in chief of the military and with the power to enforce a fairly centralized rule, the shogun governed the country for some six centuries. The successive shogunates always maintained the emperor and court in Kyoto; the emperor thus remained, in name at least, the source of spiritual legitimacy.

Sholokhov, Mikhail Aleksandrovich (1905–1984)   Russian novelist. Sholokhov's famous multivolume novel THE QUIET DON is considered one of the most important major literary works published since the revolution. Born in the Don Cossack region of southern Russia, Sholokhov published his first volume of stories, *Donskie rasskazy* (tr *Tales from the Don*, 1961) in 1925. The next year he began work on his major novel, *The Quiet Don*, a study of the conflicting loyalties among the Don Cossacks during the revolution. The four-volume work was immensely popular, selling millions of copies in Russia and abroad. In 1936 Sholokhov was elected to the Supreme Soviet, the legislative body of the nation, and in 1939 he was awarded the Order of Lenin. He was awarded the NOBEL PRIZE in Literature in 1965.

Between the publication of the third and fourth volumes of *The Quiet Don*, Sholokhov worked on a novel dealing with the collectivization of agriculture during the Five-Year Plan in Russia. This work, *Podnyataya tselina* (1932, rev 1953; vol 1 tr *Virgin Soil Upturned*, 1935; vol 2 tr *Harvest on the Don*, 1960), was less artistically successful than his masterpiece, but it gave a good picture of the misery caused by collectivization.

Toward the end of his life, Sholokhov published very little (possibly due to problems with censorship) and publicly vilified several writers not adhering to the principles of SOCIALIST REALISM or identified with the dissident movement such as Boris PASTERNAK, Andrey SINYAVSKY, Yuly

DANIEL, and Aleksandr SOLZHENITSYN; he was also charged (by Solzhenitsyn and others) with plagiarizing at least part of *The Quiet Don*.

Sholom Aleichem   See ALEICHEM, SHOLOM.

Shore, Jane (1445?–1527)   Mistress of Edward IV. Shore left her husband, a London goldsmith, in 1470 to become the mistress of the king, and through her wit and beauty exerted great influence. After the death of Edward, she continued to have political influence, thereby incurring the hatred of RICHARD III, who accused her of practicing witchcraft. She was put to public penance and became a prisoner in London, remaining in poverty and disgrace until her death.

Thomas Churchyard, in 1563, and Nicholas ROWE, in 1714, wrote tragedies based upon her life, both entitled *Jane Shore*. She is also the heroine of a ballad included in Percy's RELIQUES OF ANCIENT ENGLISH POETRY and appears in Shakespeare's RICHARD III, Thomas HEYWOOD's *Edward IV*, and many other works of literature.

Short Happy Life of Francis Macomber, The (1938)   A short story by Ernest HEMINGWAY. In this compact, taut, and dramatic story, the Macombers, an American couple, are on a safari in Africa with the Englishman, Wilson, as their guide. When confronted with a wounded lion, Macomber proves himself a coward, is saved by Wilson, and earns his wife's utter contempt. On the next hunting expedition the following day, Macomber feels a gathering strength, and his wife, who has always found gratification in his weakness, is suddenly frightened by this new Macomber. His second chance comes with a wild buffalo. Cowardice vanishes, and, as he heroically tries to fell the onrushing beast, a bullet fired by his wife kills Macomber. The tale infuses Hemingway's favorite theme, cowardice as opposed to courage, with tragic overtones.

Shostakovich, Dmitry Dmitryevich (1906–1975)   Russian composer. Shostakovich's *First Symphony* (1926) was very popular; later works were criticized in Russia for their Western decadence, especially the opera *Lady Macbeth of Mtsensk* (1934; based on a story by LESKOV). Official Soviet approval was restored with the performance of his famous *Symphony No. 5* (1937). His *Symphony No. 7* (1942), depicting the German siege of Leningrad, was frequently played by the Allies during World War II. His *Symphony No. 13* for orchestra, chorus, and solo bass (1962; text by YEVTUSHENKO) aroused considerable controversy because the text recalled the Nazi slaughter of Jews of Kiev at Babi Yar and warned against residual anti-Semitism in the Soviet Union.

Show Boat (1926)   A novel by Edna FERBER. In this popular book three theatrical generations appear: Captain Andy Hawks, who runs a showboat on the Mississippi and marries Parthy Ann, a prim New England schoolmarm; their daughter, Magnolia, who becomes an actress and runs off with the leading man Gaylord Ravenal; and their daughter Kim, who grows up to be a Broadway star. In

1927 the novel was made into one of the best known of all American musicals, with music by Jerome KERN and libretto by Oscar HAMMERSTEIN, 2nd.

Shropshire Lad   See HOUSMAN, A. E..

Shrovetide   A period of carnival and merrymaking ending with Shrove Tuesday, the last day before the beginning of the penitential season of LENT. The name of Shrove Tuesday derives from the fact that on this day the people are shriven, or absolved of their sins.

shruti (Sans, "that which is revealed")   In the literature of HINDUISM, this comprises the VEDAS, *Brahmanas*, *Aranyakas*, and UPANISHADS. It is considered to be of divine origin and to have been made known to man through revelation to ancient privileged seers (*rishis*). See SMRITI.

Shui hu chuan   Chinese novel. It developed out of 14th-century folk storytellers' accounts of the adventures of a band of 108 robber-heroes who prey on the wicked to help the poor and oppressed. The episodic story describes a large array of different social types and an endless number of battles and journeys. The novel exists in several versions, the most popular dating from 1641. Translated by Pearl BUCK as *All Men Are Brothers* (1937), it is also known as *The Water Margin*.

Shukshin, Vasily Makarovich (1929–1974) Russian short-story writer, novelist, and film scriptwriter. Born in Siberia, Shukshin retains themes of his birthplace in his works, portraying country life frankly and from an insider's view. He is best known for his novel *Kalina krasnaya* (1973; tr *Snowball Berry Red*, 1979), which depicts a repentant thief and was made into a successful film in which Shukshin himself played the leading role. Many of Shukshin's film scripts are collected in *Kinopovesti* (1975), and his other works may be found in *Izbrannye proizvedeniya* (1975). A collection of his short stories has been translated into English as *Roubles in Words, Kopeks in Figures* (1985).

Shute, Nevil (pen name of Nevil Shute Norway, 1899–1960)   English novelist. An aeronautical engineer and managing director of an airplane factory, Shute concocted his very popular novels out of technological detail and exciting plots. His early adventure stories include *Pied Piper* (1941) and *No Highway* (1948). Later novels were set in Australia: *A Town Like Alice* (1950; U.S. title *The Legacy*) and *On the Beach* (1957), which shows Australians awaiting inevitable death by radiation poisoning after an atomic war has depopulated the rest of the world.

Shylock   The avaricious Jewish moneylender in Shakespeare's MERCHANT OF VENICE. When his daughter Jessica elopes, taking some of his money with her, he is more concerned with the loss of his ducats than the loss of his daughter. His hatred for the merchant Antonio is so great that he persists in obtaining a pound of flesh as forfeit for his bond, until he is outwitted by PORTIA in the Venetian court.

One of the most controversial of Shakespearean roles, Shylock was played as a low-comedy character until Charles Macklin electrified London audiences in 1741 by making the despised usurer a tragic, dignified figure. His performance drew from Alexander POPE the comment, "This was the Jew that Shakespeare drew."

Although Shylock cannot be described as a likable or attractive character, he utters the moving speech:

Hath not a Jew eyes? hath not a Jew hands, organs, dimensions, senses, affections, passions? . . . If you prick us, do we not bleed? if you tickle us, do we not laugh? if you poison us, do we not die?

Sibelius, Jean (1865–1957)   Finnish composer. A fervent nationalist, Sibelius wrote music—symphonies, songs, and choral works—that captures the spirit of Finnish mythology: remote, melancholy, and grand. The tone poem *Finlandia* (1899) is the most popular of his works.

sibyl   A prophetess of classical legend, who was supposed to prophesy under the inspiration of a particular deity. The name is now applied to any prophetess or woman fortuneteller. There were a number of sibyls, and they had their seats in widely separate parts of the world: Greece, Italy, Babylonia, Egypt, etc.

PLATO mentions only one sibyl, the Erythraean, identified with Amalthaea, the Cumaean sibyl, who was consulted by AENEAS before his descent into HADES and who sold the SIBYLLINE BOOKS to TARQUIN. Martianus Capella speaks of two, the Erythraean and the Phrygian; Aelian of four, the Erythraean, Samian, Egyptian, and Sardian. Varro tells us there were ten, the Cumaean, the Delphic, Egyptian, Erythraean, Hellespontine, Libyan, Persian, Phrygian, Samian, and Tiburtine.

The medieval monks adopted the sibyls, as they did so much of pagan myth; they made them twelve in number and gave to each a separate prophecy and distinct emblem.

Sibylline Books   A collection of oracles of mysterious origin, preserved in ancient Rome and consulted by the Senate in times of emergency or disaster. According to LIVY, there were originally nine of these books; they were offered in sale by Amalthaea, the SIBYL of Cumae, to TARQUIN; the offer was rejected, and she burned three of them. After twelve months, she offered the remaining six at the same price. Again being refused, she burned three more, and after a similar interval asked the same price for the three left. The sum demanded was then given, and Amalthaea never appeared again.

The three books were preserved in a stone chest underground in the temple of JUPITER Capitolinus, and committed to the charge of custodians chosen in the same manner as the high priests. The number of custodians was at first two, then ten, and ultimately fifteen. AUGUSTUS had some two thousand of the verses destroyed as spurious and placed the rest in two gilt cases under the base of the statue of APOLLO, in the temple on the Palatine Hill, but the whole perished when the city was burnt in the reign of NERO.

A Greek collection in eight books of poetical utterances relating to JESUS, compiled in the 2nd century, is entitled *Oracula Sibylina* or the *Sibylline Books*.

sic (Lat, "thus") A word sometimes inserted [sic] to indicate that the preceding word or phrase is reproduced exactly as in the original text, calling attention to the fact that it is wrong in some way.

Sic et non (Yes and No, 12th century) A compilation of theological arguments by Pierre ABÉLARD. It is notable as being an unprejudiced listing of all the arguments, pro and con, on the doctrinal questions of the Middle Ages with no attempt to draw conclusions.

Siddal, Elizabeth [Eleanor] (d 1862) Wife of Dante Gabriel ROSSETTI who both before and after her marriage posed for his paintings and served as an inspiration for his poetry, notably *The Blessed Damozel* (1850). A frail, lilylike beauty, she died just two years after her marriage. Rossetti, beside himself with grief, buried with her in her coffin the sole copy of a manuscript of poems dealing with their love and marriage; in 1869 the manuscript was recovered and published. *The House of Life* was contained in the collection.

Siddhartha The given name of the BUDDHA, whose more common name, GAUTAMA (or Gotama), is that of his family. The occasionally used name Shākyamuni signifies that he was a sage of the Shakya tribe, to which his family belonged.

Siddhartha (1922; tr 1951) A novel by Hermann HESSE. Set in India, it is the story of a young Brahmin's search for ultimate reality, reflecting Hesse's interest in Oriental mysticism. Siddhartha's search, which takes him through both profligacy and asceticism, reinforces the idea that wisdom cannot be taught; it must come from one's own inner struggle. The story contains parallels to BUDDHA's life, but it is not a fictionalized life of Buddha; Hesse uses the Buddha parallels instead to give his work a legendary and symbolic quality.

Sidney, Sir Philip (1554–1586) English poet, scholar, soldier, and courtier. Regarded by many as the perfect example of the Renaissance gentleman, Sidney came from a noble family, traveled extensively on the Continent, and was one of the most admired of Elizabeth's courtiers. With his uncle, the earl of Leicester, Sidney took part in a military expedition to the Low Countries and was fatally wounded at Zutphen. According to the traditional story told by his friend and biographer Fulke Greville, the wounded Sidney gave his own water bottle to a dying foot soldier, saying, "Thy necessity is greater than mine." His death was greatly mourned and celebrated in a number of elegiac poems, the best of which is Edmund SPENSER's "Astrophel."

Only two of Sidney's poems were published during his lifetime, but his works were read and circulated among his friends. His essay entitled AN APOLOGIE FOR POETRIE (c1580; pub 1595) is perhaps the most eloquent and solid critical work of the Elizabethan period. *Arcadia* (c1580; pub 1590) is a pastoral romance in prose, interspersed with lyrics, which established that genre in England. ASTROPHEL AND STELLA (1580–84; pub 1591) created a vogue for the sonnet sequence in England. Sidney's poetry, though making much use of conventional Petrarchan elements, is distinguished by its metrical skill, its poignant, grave, and virile tone.

Siege Perilous (also called The Perilous Seat) In ARTHURIAN LEGEND, especially Malory's MORTE D'ARTHUR, a vacant chair at the ROUND TABLE of King Arthur, reserved for the one predestined to achieve the quest of the GRAIL. It was the death of any other who sat in the chair. At the appointed time, the name of GALAHAD is found on the Siege Perilous; he takes the chair and later goes on to win the Grail.

Siegfried Hero of the first half of THE NIBELUNGEN-LIED and the second half of Wagner's RING DES NIBE-LUNGEN. He is known as Sigurd in the VÖLSUNGA SAGA.

Sienkiewicz, Henryk (1846–1916) Polish novelist. After his travels in the U.S. in 1876–78, later depicted in his *Portrait of America* (tr 1959), Sienkiewicz emerged as Poland's foremost historical novelist with the publication of WITH FIRE AND SWORD, followed by two more novels on 17th-century Poland. Another major historical novel, *Krzyzacy* (1900; tr *The Teutonic Knights*, 1943), deals with a 15th-century war between Poland and the German invaders. The most popular among Sienkiewicz's works is QUO VADIS?, a historical novel about first Christians in ancient Rome. He also wrote a number of short stories and contemporary novels. He won the NOBEL PRIZE in Literature in 1905.

Signac, Paul See NEOIMPRESSIONISM.

Sigurd See GUDRUN; SIEGFRIED; SWANHILD.

Sikes, Bill In Charles Dickens's OLIVER TWIST, a brutal, violent housebreaker and thief. The only rudiment of a redeeming feature he possesses is a kind of affection for his dog. His murder of his mistress, Nancy, is a horrible but celebrated incident in the novel.

Sikh (Hindi, "one who is learning; disciple") A member of a religious community that broke away from HINDUISM in Punjab in the 16th century, under the leadership of Guru Nānak (1469–1538). In an effort to forge some reconciliation between Hindu and Islamic beliefs, the Sikhs believed in one supreme God, the essential commonness of all religions, and denied the divisions of the CASTE system. They were guided by a succession of gurus after Nānak and eventually developed as a military community, assuming formal independence in 1764. From 1849 to 1947 the Sikhs, as part of India, were ruled by the British. Reinforced by a code of the highest ascetic and moral ideals, the Sikh religion enjoins on all its truly faithful the strict observance of the five K's: *kesha* (long hair); *kanga* (the hair comb); *kaccha* (the undergarment); *kada* (the steel bangle); and *kirpan* (a short dagger). Their sacred scriptures, compiled by the fifth guru, Arjun, are known as the *Adi Granth.*

The orthodox Sikh neither smokes nor drinks. Sikhs are famous for their courage and fighting ability, and they have been a major component of the Indian army, both under the British and after independence. However, extremist agitation for a separate Sikh state led to much communal violence between Sikhs and Hindus in the mid-1980s and the assassination of Prime Minister Indira Gandhi.

Silas Marner, or the Weaver of Raveloe (1861)

A novel by George ELIOT. The author says that the book "is intended to set in a strong light the remedial influences of pure, natural, human relations." Silas is a lonely, embittered handloom weaver who long ago was accused of a theft of which his best friend was guilty and so was robbed of the girl he loved. He has no friends in Raveloe, the village to which he has come, and cares only to add a little more gold to the pile in his humble cottage. In close succession two strange events occur: he is robbed of his gold and finds by chance a little yellow-haired baby girl whom no one claims. Gradually he is brought back into a more wholesome, normal life through his love for little Eppie. In the meantime, much of the story is concerned with the affairs of the two sons of Squire Cass, Dunstan and Godfrey. Dunstan, who is a wild reckless fellow, always in debt, disappears. Godfrey marries the young woman of his choice, Nancy Lammeter. At last, after sixteen years Silas's lost gold is found, together with the skeleton of Dunstan Cass. Godfrey now confesses that Eppie is the offspring of his earlier, secret marriage to a common woman who died the night Eppie was found; he asks Eppie to come and live with him and Nancy, but Eppie chooses to stay with Silas and eventually marries a village boy whom she has always known.

Si le grain ne meurt   See IF IT DIE. . . .

Silence

A country justice in Shakespeare's HENRY IV: PART II. When sober, he is dull and asinine; drunk, he is outrageously funny.

Silenus

In Greek mythology, an elderly follower of DIONYSUS. Originally there were many *sileni*, male spirits of the woods who became associated with the worship of Dionysus. Later, Silenus was differentiated, and usually represented as a sly, cowardly, and often drunken old man. As such he appears in innumerable paintings of the Renaissance. He is a leading character in EURIPIDES' satyr play *Cyclops.*

Silhouette, Etienne de (1709–1767)

French controller general of finances (1759). Silhouette's rigid economies were ridiculed by certain members of the nobility who applied his name sarcastically to any mode or fashion that was plain or cheap; eventually it was used only in the restricted sense to apply to portraits in which the painter's expensive art is replaced by a profiled outline in plain black; hence, *silhouette.*

Sillanpää, Frans Eemil (1888–1964)

Finnish novelist and short-story writer. Sillanpää's novels, which are sensitively written and reveal keen psychological insight into characters and a profound reverence for nature, include *Hurskas kurjuus* (1919; tr *Meek Heritage,* 1938) and *Nuorena nukkunut* (1931; tr *Fallen Asleep While Young,* 1933). In 1939 Sillanpää received the NOBEL PRIZE in Literature.

Sillitoe, Alan (1928–   )

English novelist. A factory worker who left school at fourteen, Sillitoe is a critical realist who writes best about the lives of contemporary workers and their families in industrial towns. He first drew attention in the late 1950s with the publication of SATURDAY NIGHT AND SUNDAY MORNING and THE LONELINESS OF THE LONG DISTANCE RUNNER. In both books his working-class heroes live with a barely contained rage derived from constant struggles with class oppression, conventional morality, rotten jobs, and the Establishment, leading to Sillitoe's reputation as one of the most able and articulate of the so-called ANGRY YOUNG MEN.

Among several later novels are *The Widower's Son* (1976), in which Sillitoe chronicles the life and psychotic breakdown of Master Gunner William Scorton, whose disastrous flaw is that he has never learned to feel; *The Lost Flying Boat* (1983); and *Down from the Hill* (1984). He has also written short stories and several volumes of poetry, including *The Second Chance* (1981) and *Sun Before Departure: Poems 1974–1982* (1984).

Silone, Ignazio (original name Secondo Tranquilii, 1900–1978)

Silone lived in a small village in central Italy until it was destroyed by an earthquake that took the lives of his mother and all but one of his brothers. He became active in socialist causes during World War I and in 1921 joined the Communist Party. In 1922, while he was working as editor of the labor newspaper *Il lavoratore* in Trieste, the paper was raided by Fascists. His brother was seized and subsequently beaten to death in prison, but Silone escaped, finding shelter among the Italian peasantry, with whose life and cause his own work was so movingly and consistently identified. From 1930 until the fall of the Fascist regime, he lived in exile in Switzerland, during which time he wrote his first three, and probably greatest, novels: *Fontamara* (1930; tr 1934; rev 1958), BREAD AND WINE, and *Il seme sotto la neve* (1941; tr *The Seed Beneath the Snow,* 1942). Coincident with his exile, he went through a profound spiritual and ideological crisis and broke with the Communist Party in 1931. His essay "Emergency Exit" in Richard Crossman's *The God That Failed* (1950) describes his gradual disillusionment.

Although he remained committed to a kind of Christian-socialist ideal, he curtailed his political activities and devoted himself to writing. Among his many other works are *La scuola dei dittatori* (1938; tr *The School for Dictators,* 1938), a satirical treatise on the training of despots, and the novels *Una manciata di more* (1952; tr A *Handful of Blackberries*, 1953), *Il segreto di Luca* (1956; tr *The Secret of Luca*, 1958), and *La volpe e le camelie* (1960; tr *The Fox and the Camelias*, 1961). *Ed egli si nascose* (1944; tr *And He Hid Himself*, 1946) and *L'avventura di un povero cristiano* (1968; tr *The Story of a Humble Christian*, 1971) are plays.

Silva, José Asunción (1865–1896)   Colombian poet, considered a precursor of MODERNISMO. A tragic figure of acute sensibility, Silva felt oppressed by the smug provincialism of his native Bogotá, against which he rebelled in bitter, though highly lyrical, verse. The death of a beloved sister is said to have inspired his best-known poem, "Nocturno III," which displays the musicality and morbid melancholy, akin to POE's, that distinguish his poetry. Another characteristic note is the nostalgic yearning for the past that is evident in the short poem "Vejeces." He died by his own hand. An edition of his *Obra completa* appeared in two volumes in 1968.

Silver, Long John   The villainous, one-legged sea cook and pirate in Stevenson's TREASURE ISLAND. A man of considerable intelligence and force of character, Silver is sly enough to impress Squire Trelawney with his devotion to duty, while at the same time plotting mutiny. He is always accompanied by his parrot, Cap'n Flint.

Silver Cord, The (1926)   A play by Sidney HOW-ARD. It is one of the earliest psychological studies of a dominant mother to be presented on the stage. Mrs. Phelps has two sons, one of whom is unable to break away from her, while the other succeeds only through the help of his wife.

Simenon, Georges (1903–   )   Belgian-born French novelist. One of the most skillful and literate writers of detective fiction, Simenon is best known for his long series of novels featuring Inspector Maigret, begun in 1931. In the series, Simenon combines his moral objectivity, compassion, and psychological insight to create characters that are wholly credible. Later he also wrote more ambitious psychological analyses of modern man, among them *La Neige était sale* (1948; tr *The Stain on the Snow*, 1953), *La Mort de belle* (1952), *Lettre à mon juge* (1947), and *L'Ours en peluche* (1960; tr *Teddy Bear*, 1971). Simenon's prodigious output, over three hundred novels, also includes numerous autobiographical works and diaries.

Simeon Stylites   See STYLITES.

Simic, Charles (1938–   )   Yugoslavian-born American poet and translator. Simic's verse is a combination of influences sifted through an original sensibility: French SURREALISM and the pastoralism of Russian poets like Boris PASTERNAK are joined by a Jungian focus on the dream side of man's psyche. His early volumes, *What the Grass Says* (1967) and *Somewhere Among Us a Stone Is Taking Notes* (1969), are collections of poems in open form, and were followed by the highly acclaimed *Dismantling the Silence* (1971), incorporating many of the poems from these two earlier collections. *Return to a Place Lit by a Glass of Milk* (1974) uses macabre, erotic imagery, as in

"Pornographer's Psalm," to present reality in a wry, morbidly comic light. Simic has also written a number of surrealistic parables in verse, including *Charon's Cosmology* (1977) and *Classic Ballroom Dances* (1980). *Shaving at Night* (1982), *Austerities* (1982), and *Weather Forecast for Utopia and Vicinity: Poems 1967–1982* (1983) are among his other verse collections.

simile   In rhetoric, a figure of speech: a comparison between two things of a different kind or quality, usually introduced by "like" or "as." Simile is one of the two main figures of speech, the other being METAPHOR; in simile, the comparison made is explicit, whereas in metaphor it is implied. The object of both simile and metaphor is double: to achieve clarity and exactness of meaning and to achieve vividness of presentation and style. An example of simile is:

Now the chimney was all of the house that stood,
Like a pistil after the petals go.

Robert Frost

Simms, William Gilmore (1806–1870)   American novelist and poet. Born in Charleston, South Carolina, Simms had a varied career, marked by numerous misfortunes. Although he considered himself primarily a poet and published eighteen volumes of verse up to 1860, his reputation rests on his historical novels. The first of these, *Guy Rivers* (1834), which deals with a fiendish Georgia bandit, was an outstanding success. Also included in the series known as "the Border Romances" are THE YEMASSEE and *The Cassique of Kiawah* (1859), in which Indians figure prominently, and two novels based on the KENTUCKY TRAGEDY: *Beauchampe* (1842) and its sequel, *Charlemont* (1846). The series called "the Revolutionary Romances" includes *The Partisan* (1835) and its sequels, *Mellichampe* (1836) and *Katharine Walton* (1851); *The Kinsmen* (1841), later revised as *The Scout* (1854); *The Sword and the Distaff* (1853), later issued as WOODCRAFT; and *The Forayers* (1855) and its sequel, *Eutaw* (1856).

In his romances, Simms was a loyal follower of Sir Walter Scott and James Fenimore Cooper. His stories preserve a wealth of local tradition and vividly express many aspects of the American Revolution in South Carolina. An ardent defender of the Southern ideal of agrarian life, he was also steeped in Elizabethan literature, and one of his best characters, Captain PORGY, has been called "the American Falstaff."

A member of the Charleston School of Southern writers, Simms was surrounded by a coterie of young men in his later years, chief among them Paul Hamilton HAYNE.

Simon   In the NEW TESTAMENT: (1) One of the original disciples of JESUS, also called Simon the Canaanite or Simon Zelotes (the Zealot). Almost nothing is known of his life except that at one time he had been a member of the Zealots, an ultranationalistic Jewish group (Matt. 10:4).

(2) The original name of the apostle PETER.

(3) A PHARISEE who entertained Jesus and criticized him for forgiving the sins of a woman of the street who anointed his feet (Luke 7).

(4) A sorcerer of Samaria, called Simon Magus, rebuked by Peter for his attempt to buy the power of the Holy Spirit (Acts 8), which is the origin of the term *simony*, the buying of ecclesiastical power.

(5) A leper of Bethany in whose house Jesus was anointed (Matt. 26:6).

(6) A man of Cyrene who was compelled to carry Jesus' cross on the way to the Crucifixion (Matt. 27:32).

Simon, Claude (1913–   )   French novelist born in Madagascar. A major novelist in the genre of the NOUVEAU ROMAN, Simon writes in a fluid style, using long, convoluted sentences. His novels give extremely detailed and precise descriptions of sensual impressions, yet often leave their essence or significance obscure. His novels include *Le Vent* (1957; tr *The Wind*, 1959) and *L'Herbe* (1959; tr *The Grass*, 1960), both set in the rural south of France, and *La Route de Flandres* (1960; tr *The Flanders Road*, 1961), in which three soldiers remember the fall of France in 1940. *Le Palace* (1962; tr *The Palace*, 1963) relates the suicide of an anonymous Frenchman serving the Loyalists during the Spanish Civil War. These last three, along with *Histoire* (1967; tr 1968), form part of a single work connected by recurring characters and incidents. Simon's essay *Orion aveugle* (1970) deals with his theory and methods of writing. Simon was relatively unknown until he won the NOBEL PRIZE in Literature in 1985.

Simon, [Marvin] Neil (1927–   )   American playwright. Simon is without rival as the most commercially successful playwright in Broadway history. Beginning with *Come Blow Your Horn* (1960; written with his brother Danny), *Barefoot in the Park* (1963), and *The Odd Couple* (1965) he established himself as a master of superficial but tightly structured domestic comedies, featuring a clash of opposing temperaments. In a succession of hits from 1968 to 1976 Simon's characters use wisecracks and biting humor to avoid the pain of marital failure, impotence, nymphomania, adultery, alcoholism, or other byproducts of paralyzing middle-class values. An autobiographical element is evident in *Chapter Two* (1978), *I Ought to Be in Pictures* (1980), *Brighton Beach Memoirs* (1984), *Biloxi Blues* (1985), and *Broadway Bound* (1986), the last three concerned with the growing up of Eugene Morris Jerome, a stand-in for Neil Simon.

Simonides (c556–468 BC)   Greek poet. Born at Ceos, Simonides was the first Greek poet to make a living from his writing. He was highly admired by classical writers. He is said to have either invented or perfected the EPINICION, but is better known for his elegiac epigrams and GNOMIC POETRY. Particularly famous is his epitaph for those who died at Thermopylae:

> Go, tell the Spartans, thou who passest by
> That here obedient to their laws we lie.

See PERSIAN WARS.

Simon Lee (1798)   A poem by William WORDS-WORTH, subtitled *The Old Huntsman with an Incident in Which He Was Concerned*. The incident is that the poet helps Simon dig up the root of a tree, which causes him to relate the simple story of the old huntsman's life.

Simonov, Konstantin [Kirill] Mikhailovich (1915–1979)   Russian novelist, playwright, journalist, and editor. Simonov was born in Leningrad and studied at the Gorky Literary Institute in Moscow. He became well known during World War II as a war correspondent for the newspaper *Krasnaya zvezda* and is now remembered for his war poetry, some of which endorses a wholly merciless attitude toward the enemy and utilizes a highly emotional and lyrical tone. Simonov wrote the novel *Dni i nochi* (1943–44; tr *Days and Nights*, 1945), a patriotic depiction of the battle of Stalingrad, and served as editor in chief of both *Novy mir*—from which he was dismissed for publishing such liberal works as DUDINTSEV's NOT BY BREAD ALONE—and *Literaturnaya gazeta*. He was also secretary of the Union of Soviet Writers (1946–59, 1967).

Simple Cobler of Aggawam in America, The (1647)   A tract by Nathaniel WARD, published under the pseudonym Theodore de la Guard. The book is a satirical denunciation of England and New England for being tolerant of England for the quarrel between Parliament and the Crown and of the human race in general and women in particular for being silly. Ward's vitriolic, witty style has been compared to that of Elizabethan pamphlet writers such as GREENE and NASH. Aggawam was an early name for Ipswich, Massachusetts.

Simple Heart, A (Un Coeur simple, 1877)   A short story by Gustave FLAUBERT. Originally published in the volume *Trois Contes*, it portrays the life of Félicité, the servant of Mme Aubain—a smalltown, bourgeois widow and mother of two children. Flaubert reveals himself as a true master of the genre in the careful strokes that picture the endless self-denial of Félicité's existence; only faith remains upon the canvas at the completion of the work.

Simplicissimus (1668, continuations 1670, 1672)   The popular title of a novel by Hans GRIMMELSHAUSEN. Its full title is *Der abenteuerliche Simplicissimus* (*The Adventurous Simplicissimus*). A PICARESQUE story set during the THIRTY YEARS' WAR, which had ended twenty years earlier, it treats the development of its hero's originally simple soul toward resignation and wisdom. It is well known as a panorama of contemporary events, of the horrors and injustices of war, but its treatment of psychological development has also caused some critics to give it a place in the growth of the BILDUNGSROMAN.

Simplicissimus   A satirical weekly, founded (1896) by Thomas T. Heine in Munich. Many of the leading

German writers of the early 20th century contributed to its pages until it ceased publication in 1944. It was revived in 1954 but did not regain the stature it had enjoyed in the pre-Hitler era.

Simpson, Louis [Aston Marantz] (1923–   ) American poet. Born in Jamaica, Simpson came to the U.S. in 1940 and, after interrupting his studies in 1943 to serve in the army for three years, during which time he saw active service in Europe and subsequently had a nervous breakdown, eventually earned a degree at Columbia University. His inventive poems, which have gradually moved away from strict meter and rhyme, frequently deal with personal experience as well as interpretations, usually ironic, of mythic subjects. Among his volumes of verse are *The Arrivistes: Poems 1940–49* (1949), *A Dream of Governors* (1959), *At the End of the Open Road* (1963; PULITZER PRIZE), and *Adventures of the Letter I* (1972). His *Selected Poems* appeared in 1965. *Riverside Drive* (1962) is a novel; *North of Jamaica* (1972) is autobiographical. He has also written critical studies of James HOGG (1962) and of Ezra POUND, T. S. ELIOT, and William Carlos WILLIAMS in *Three on the Tower* (1975). *A Revolution in Taste* (1978) contains reflections on the work of Dylan THOMAS, Allen GINSBERG, Sylvia PLATH, and Robert LOWELL. Other verse collections include *Caviare at the Funeral: Poems* (1980), *A Company of Poets* (1981), *The Best Hour of the Night* (1983), and *People Live Here: Selected Poems 1949–1983* (1983).

sin Failure to attain to the standard of behavior attributed to God's moral requirements. In Roman Catholic theology sins are distinguished as *venial* (those that do not forfeit the state of grace) and *mortal* (those that forfeit the state of grace and can be removed only by confession and absolution). According to St. Thomas AQUINAS there are SEVEN DEADLY SINS.

In Milton's PARADISE LOST, Sin is the Keeper of the Gates of Hell, together with death. Described as half woman, half poisonous serpent, she sprang full grown from the head of SATAN.

The Man of Sin (referred to in 2 Thess. 2:3) is generally held to signify the ANTICHRIST. However, it was applied by the old Puritans to the Roman Pope, by the Fifth Monarchy men to CROMWELL, and by many 19th-century theologians to "that wicked one" (identical with the "last horn" of Dan. 7), who was immediately to precede the second advent of Christ.

Sin The Babylonian moon god. An old man, he was the first of the astral deities and father by Ningal of SHAMASH (the sun god), ISHTAR, and Nesku (the fire god). He rode in his moon boat through the sky at night. He is much like Nanna, the moon deity of Sumerian Ur.

Sinbad the Sailor A well-known story in the *Arabian Nights*. Sinbad is a Baghdad merchant who acquires great wealth by going on seven voyages. He describes these to a poor discontented porter, Hindbad, to show him that wealth can only be obtained by enterprise and personal exertion.

First Voyage Being becalmed in the Indian Ocean, he and some others of the crew visit what they suppose to be an island, but which is really a huge whale asleep. They light a fire on the whale and the heat wakes the creature, which instantly dives under water. Sinbad is picked up by some merchants and in due time returns home.

Second Voyage Sinbad is left on a desert island, where he discovers a ROC's egg fifty paces in circumference. He fastens himself to the claw of the bird and is deposited in the Valley of Diamonds. The next day, some merchants come to the top of the crags and throw into the valley huge joints of raw meat to which the diamonds stick; when the eagles pick up the meat, the merchants scare them from their nests and carry off the diamonds. Sinbad then fastens himself to a piece of meat, is carried by an eagle to its nest, and, rescued by the merchants, returns home laden with diamonds.

Third Voyage This is the encounter with the Cyclops. See POLYPHEMUS.

Fourth Voyage Sinbad marries a lady of rank in a strange island on which he is cast; when his wife dies, he is burned alive with the dead body according to the custom of the land. He makes his way out of the catacomb and returns to Baghdad, greatly enriched by valuables rifled from the dead bodies.

Fifth Voyage The ship in which he sails is dashed to pieces by huge stones let down from the talons of two angry rocs. Sinbad swims to a desert island, where he throws stones at the monkeys who throw back coconuts in return. On this island, Sinbad encounters and kills the OLD MAN OF THE SEA.

Sixth Voyage Sinbad visits the island of Serendip (Sri Lanka) and climbs to the top of the mountain where ADAM was placed on his expulsion from Paradise.

Seventh Voyage Sinbad is attacked by corsairs, sold into slavery, and employed in shooting at elephants from a tree. He discovers a tract of hill country completely covered with elephants' tusks, communicates his discovery to his master, obtains his liberty, and returns home.

Sinclair, Emil See DEMIAN.

Sinclair, May (1865–1946) English novelist. The best of Sinclair's popular books were experimental in technique and based on the new Freudian psychology. A feminist, she wrote her first novels about the lives of women. *The Divine Fire* (1904), a study of a temperamental Cockney genius supposedly drawn from the poet Ernest Dowson, made her famous.

Sinclair, Upton [Beall] (1878–1968) American writer of novels and nonfiction. Sinclair, a remarkably prolific author, with over eighty books to his credit, is known for his steady espousal of socialism and his concern with social and political problems. His best-known book, THE JUNGLE, created a sensation when published; it shocked

President Theodore ROOSEVELT, who invited Sinclair to the White House, and influenced the passing of the Pure Food and Drug Act (1906).

Sinclair used his earnings from *The Jungle* to found the cooperative Helicon Home Colony, near Englewood, New Jersey. The project, in which Sinclair LEWIS participated briefly, was abandoned after a mysterious fire in 1907. In 1915 Sinclair moved to California. In 1934 he was the Democratic candidate for governor of the state, running on the famous EPIC (End Poverty in California) platform; after an acrimonious campaign, he was narrowly defeated.

Meanwhile, Sinclair continued to write steadily. Among his later novels are *King Coal* (1917), *Oil!* (1927), and *Boston* (1928), the latter two based respectively on the TEAPOT DOME scandal and the SACCO-VANZETTI CASE. His nonfiction works include *The Brass Check* (1919), a highly critical treatise on journalism, based on his own experiences, and *American Outpost: A Book of Reminiscences* (1932). His *Autobiography* appeared in 1962.

With the rise of Fascism and Communism in Europe, Sinclair became more interested in foreign affairs. He wrote a long series of popular novels, beginning with *World's End* (1940), which deal with Lanny Budd, scion of a wealthy family, who takes it upon himself to right the world's wrongs and becomes a prominent figure in international politics and intrigue.

Singer, Isaac Bashevis (1904–   )   Yiddish novelist, short-story writer, critic, and journalist. Born in Poland, Singer received a traditional rabbinical education, concentrating on the study of Talmudic law and KABBALAH. Rather than becoming a rabbi, he opted for the life of a writer and immigrated in 1935 to the U.S., where he wrote for the New York paper *The Jewish Daily Forward*, using a variety of pseudonyms. Singer's stories are characterized by a magical, grotesque atmosphere, often dominated by demonic forces; yet his style is powerfully realistic and his characters are molded with a Balzac-like precision. His works combine elements of misanthropy and profound compassion, as well as a fusion of Jewish and universal world culture. Written in Yiddish, his stories are often set in the Poland of the past, as are the novellas *Satan in Goray* (1935; tr 1955), *The Magician of Lublin* (1960), and *The Slave* (1962). *The Family Moskat* (1950), one of his best-known works, is a realistic novel about the decline of traditional Jewish values in Warsaw before World War II. *Shosha* (1978) is also a novel set in Warsaw before the Holocaust, while *Enemies* (1966; tr 1972) marks something of a departure in its setting of America after World War II. His many collections of short stories include *Gimpel the Fool* (1957), *The Spinoza of Market Street* (1961), *Passions* (1975), *Old Love* (1979), and *The Image* (1985). Singer's belief in a world full of endless mysteries makes him an ideal writer for children. *Mazel and Schlimazel* (1966), *The Fools of Chelm and Their History* (1973), and *Stories for Children* (1984) are among his numerous books for young

readers. His memoirs, including *In My Father's Court* (1956; tr 1966), *A Little Boy in Search of God* (1976), *A Young Man in Search of Love* (1978), *Lost in America* (1981), *The Golem* (1982), *The Penitent* (1983), and *Love and Exile* (1984) offer further insights into the conflicting strains of cynicism and mysticism that mark Singer's works. He was awarded the NOBEL PRIZE in Literature in 1978.

Singer, Israel Joshua (1893–1944)   Yiddish novelist, playwright, and journalist. Born in Poland, the older brother of Isaac Bashevis SINGER, Israel Singer became a U.S. citizen in 1939. He is best known as a master of the family novel, portraying a whole society or epoch. Among his important works translated into English are: *Blood Harvest* (tr 1935), *Yoshe Kalb* (tr 1965), and *The Family Carnovsky* (tr 1969). His best-known novel is *The Brothers Ashkenazi* (tr 1936).

Singh, Khushwant (1915–   )   Indian historian and novelist, writing in English. Notable among his numerous studies of the Sikh religion is his two-volume *A History of the Sikhs* (1963, 1966). His fiction constitutes a vivid, sometimes sardonic chronicle of a world undergoing the upheavals of change, as in his best-known novel, *Train to Pakistan* (1956), an account of the horrors of partition. *The Mark of Vishnu* (1950) and *Black Jasmine* (1971) are collections of stories. *The Sikhs* and *Punjab Tragedy* appeared in 1984.

Singspiel   German term (literally, "sing play") for a kind of opera in which spoken dialogue occurs between musical numbers; it is similar to the French OPÉRA COMIQUE. A Singspiel could be either comic or serious; MOZART's *Die Zauberflöte* (*The Magic Flute*, 1791), BEETHOVEN's *Fidelio* (1805), and WEBER's *Der Freischütz* (*The Freeshooter*, 1821) are all examples of the genre. It was not until the time of WAGNER that German opera was usually composed with music throughout.

Sinis   In Greek mythology, a robber of the Isthmus of Corinth known as the Pine-Bender. Sinis used to fasten his victims to two pine trees bent toward each other so that they were rent asunder by the rebound. He was eventually captured by THESEUS and put to death in this same way.

Sinister Street (1913–1914)   The best-known title in a series of novels by Compton MACKENZIE. An early archetype of the novel of growing up, it describes the childhood and youth of Michael and Stella Fane, illegitimate children of wealthy parents. The book was published in two volumes in England, and appeared in the U.S. as *Youth's Encounter* (1913) and *Sinister Street* (1914). *Plashers Mead* (1917), *Sylvia Scarlett* (1918), and *Sylvia and Michael* (1919) continue the story up to Michael's marriage.

Sinyavsky, Andrey Donatovich (pen name Abram Tertz, 1925–   )   Russian novelist, short-story writer, and critic. Born in Moscow and educated in philology at Moscow University, Sinyavsky became a noted literary critic and scholar, producing with A. Menshutin a long essay, *The Poetry of the First Years of the Revolution; 1917–1920* (1964), and a book on Picasso (1960) written with I. Golomshtok. Sinyavsky's faith in Marxism began to falter as the enormity of Stalin's crimes became known, and he began to publish essays and Gogolesque fiction in the West; the manuscripts circulated in Russia in SAMIZDAT.

In his essay *Chto takoye sotsialistichesky realizm?* (1959; tr *On Socialist Realism*, 1960), he advocates a "phantasmagoric art, with hypotheses instead of a Purpose, an art in which the grotesque will replace realistic descriptions of ordinary life." This style of fantastic realism, in direct opposition to officially sanctioned SOCIALIST REALISM, is expressed in the short novel *Sud idyot* (1960; tr *The Trial Begins*, 1960), and in his other pseudonymous works, including *Mysli vrasplokh* (1966; tr *Unguarded Thoughts*, 1972), *Fantasticheskiye povesti* (1961; tr *Fantastic Stories*, 1963), and *Lyubimov* (1964; tr *The Makepeace Experiment*, 1965), about a bicycle mechanic who for a short time establishes a utopian state in the town of Lyubimov.

The Soviets eventually traced the authorship of these works to Sinyavsky and, after bringing him to trial with Yuly DANIEL in 1966, sentenced him to seven years at hard labor. During his time in prison Sinyavsky wrote a study of Pushkin as well as the material—consisting of notes and letters mailed to his wife—that he shaped into perhaps his best book, *Golos iz khora* (1973; tr *A Voice from the Chorus*, 1976), after he was released. Sinyavsky's own meditations are interrupted by comments from the other prisoners, the "chorus." He was released in 1973 and allowed to immigrate to France, where he accepted a teaching position at the Sorbonne.

Sion   Another name for Mount Hermon in the Anti-Lebanon. It is to be distinguished from ZION.

Sirat, Al (Arab, "the path")   In Muslim legend, a bridge said to span the distance between earth and paradise, yet be no wider than a spider's thread. Sinners fall into the abyss below.

Sir Charles Grandison   See RICHARDSON, SAMUEL.

siren (fr Gr, *seiren*, "entangler")   A mythical monster, half woman and half bird. Sirens were said by Greek poets (see ODYSSEY) to entice seamen by the sweetness of their song to such a degree that listeners forgot everything and died of hunger. Odysseus escaped their blandishments by filling his companions' ears with wax and lashing himself to the mast of his ship.

In Homeric mythology, there were but two sirens; later writers name three, Parthenope, Ligea, and Leucosia; and the number was still further augmented by later writers. According to one tale, the ARGONAUTS safely passed the sirens because ORPHEUS sang more ravishingly than they. Chagrined, they either flew away forever or committed suicide.

Sir Gawain and the Green Knight (c1370)   A Middle English poem in ALLITERATIVE VERSE written by an unknown called the PEARL POET. The poem is one of four (all by the same writer) which appear in a single manuscript of the Cotton Collection.

Perhaps the greatest single ARTHURIAN LEGEND in English, this masterpiece of Middle English writing concerns the ordeal of the ideal knight, Sir Gawain. Two major motifs are utilized in the unfolding action: the so-called Beheading Game and the Temptation to Adultery.

Into the midst of New Year festivities at King Arthur's court bursts a green giant on horseback. He dares any of Arthur's knights to chop off his head on condition that in one year he be allowed to return the blow. Sir Gawain accepts the challenge, wields the axe successfully (the Green Knight calmly scoops up his head and leaves), and twelve months later sets out in search for the Green Chapel, where he is to keep the bargain. After a long, bitter journey, he comes to a marvelous castle where he is entertained by Lord Bercilak, his beautiful wife, and an ugly old lady who quietly hovers in the background. Bercilak suggests to his guest an exchange-of-gifts game: every day he will bring to Sir Gawain what he gains hunting, and Sir Gawain will give him what he has won in the castle during the absence of the host. For two days, Sir Gawain is tempted to adultery by the beautiful wife of Bercilak; he resists, and each night, in accordance with their game, exchanges with Bercilak the kisses of the lady for animals from the hunt. On the third day, however, he accepts a supposedly magic sash of green silk from the lady, believing that it will save him from the Green Knight. That evening he fails to mention the sash during the exchange of gifts.

At the appointed time, he leaves the castle and goes for his tryst at the Green Chapel. Three times the Green Knight strikes at his neck. The first two strikes do not touch him because he twice resisted temptation, but the third blow nicks his neck slightly, marking his failure with regard to the green sash.

The Green Knight turns out to be Bercilak, in the service of the ugly old lady who is really MORGAN LE FAY and who planned the entire affair.

Returning to King Arthur's court at Camelot, Sir Gawain swears always to wear the green sash around his waist as a reminder of moral lapse. His fellow knights, in tribute to Sir Gawain's courage, also place green sashes around their waists, to wear thereafter.

Sirin, Vladimir   See NABOKOV, VLADIMIR.

Sir John Barleycorn   An old song. As it was written down by Robert Burns, his neighbors vowed that Sir John should die, so they hired ruffians to "plough him with ploughs and bury him"; this they did and afterward "combed him with harrows and thrust clods on his head," but they did not kill him by these or by numerous other means that they attempted. Sir John bore no malice for this ill usage but did his best to cheer the flagging spirits even of his worst persecutors. The song seems to recall fertility rites at corn-planting time.

Jack London wrote an autobiography called *John Barley-corn* (1913), which he described as his "alcoholic memories."

Sir Launfal   A 12th-century BRETON LAI by MARIE DE FRANCE. In this narrative verse romance, Sir Launfal is one of the knights of King Arthur's court. He falls in love with a beautiful fairy who brings him great wealth and happiness but pledges him to secrecy regarding the source. But the oath is violated when the envious Queen Guinevere goads him into admitting his love for someone else. Infuriated, Guinevere accuses him, as Potiphar's wife did Joseph, of having insulted her. Thereupon King Arthur swears that unless Sir Launfal can defend himself at trial, he will be either burned or hanged. Being told that he might save himself by producing his fairy mistress, Sir Launfal has to admit that by breaking his oath to her, he may never again expect her aid. Faced with a most miserable fate, he is, however, dramatically rescued by the beautiful fairy and carried off by her to Avalon.

There have been many adaptations of this romance, one of the best known being a 14th-century English version bearing the same title. The material was also used centuries later in *The Vision of Sir Launfal* (1848) by James Russell Lowell.

Sir Patrick Spens   The title of a medieval Scottish sea ballad. It is a tragic tale of shipwreck based on the voyage of the titular Scottish hero. Though warned of a terrible storm, Sir Patrick Spens puts out to sea with his companions, and then:

> . . . O lang, lang may the ladies stand,
>   Wi thair gold kems in their hair
> Waiting for thar ain deir lords,
>   For they'll se thame na mair. . . .

Sir Thomas More (1595)   A CHRONICLE PLAY. Probably it was written by Anthony Munday (c1553–1633). It deals with three significant episodes in the life of Thomas MORE. One of these, an account of More's role in pacifying a rioting mob, was apparently rewritten by another playwright whom many reputable scholars believe to be SHAKESPEARE. Since the play is extant in manuscript form, it is further argued that the relevant passages are in Shakespeare's handwriting.

Sisera   In the OLD TESTAMENT, the Canaanite captain defeated by Barak and DEBORAH. Taking refuge in the tent of Jael, Sisera was killed by her with a tent pin (Judg. 4–5).

Sisley, Alfred (1839–1899)   French impressionist painter. Sisley rejected a career in business, and, in 1862, went to study in the studio of Gleyre, where he met MONET and RENOIR. His landscapes are usually set in the countryside near Paris or near his birthplace of Moret, as in *Le Canal* and *La Barque pendant l'inondation*. The play of light over natural forms in his work is subtle and delicate. Muted blues, greens, and browns, his characteristic colors,

contribute to a quiet, sometimes gently wistful, mood. See IMPRESSIONISM.

Sister Carrie (1900)   A novel by Theodore DREISER. The author's first novel, it was officially published in 1900 but was not made publicly available until 1912 because of its outspoken frankness and supposed immorality. It is considered by many to be Dreiser's finest work. It tells the story of Carrie Meeber, an innocent country girl, who is exposed to the impersonal cruelty of Chicago in the 1890s. From this life of bleak poverty and loneliness, she is rescued by a traveling salesman, Charles Drouet. Later, a wealthy married man, George Hurstwood, virtually absconds with funds in order to take her to New York. There Carrie goes on the stage, but as her star rises, Hurstwood's sinks, until finally, unknown to Carrie, he commits suicide, a destitute Bowery bum, while Carrie herself fails to find happiness despite her success.

Sister Helen (1870)   A BALLAD by Dante Gabriel ROSSETTI about a young woman who destroys a false lover by melting a waxen image of him.

Sisters, The   The first story in James Joyce's DUBLINERS. It is about a boy confronted with death for the first time. Through the conversation between his aunt and the two sisters of the dead man (a paralyzed old priest, his former teacher), the boy learns of the priest's insanity and finds a new, dubious light shed on the Catholic religion.

Sisyphus   In Greek mythology, a son of AEOLUS and founder of the city of Ephyre, later Corinth. Sisyphus appears as a rogue and a trickster in numerous classical legends. When AUTOLYCUS stole his cattle, he avenged himself by stealing Autolycus' daughter and thus became, by some accounts, the true father of her son ODYSSEUS.

He is best known for the punishment he received for revealing ZEUS' rape of Aegina to her father, the river Asopus: in HADES he is condemned to roll a huge stone up a hill, only to have it roll down again each time. Albert Camus used this myth as a metaphor for man's fate in his essay THE MYTH OF SISYPHUS.

Sītā (Sans, "furrow")   In Hindu mythology, wife of RĀMA and heroine of the Hindu epic, the RĀMĀYANA, which is largely concerned with her faithfulness in the face of misfortune. She was not born, but arose from a furrow when her father, Janaka, king of Videha, was plowing. Because of her behavior in the *Rāmāyana*, Sītā is regarded as the ideal of Hindu womanhood. She is also regarded as an AVATAR of LAKSHMI.

Sitting Bull (1834?–1890)   American Sioux Indian chief. Sitting Bull was the leader of the Indian forces during the Sioux War of 1876–77 and was present at the battle of the Little Big Horn, during which a U.S. contingent under George A. CUSTER was wiped out. Forced to flee to Canada, he returned to the U.S. in 1881 and was settled on a reservation. He was killed by Indian police while trying to escape arrest.

Sitwell, Dame Edith (1887–1964)   English poet and prose writer. Sitwell is known for the brilliant, experimental patterns of sound and imagery in her poems. From 1916 she edited *Wheels*, an annual anthology that printed light-hearted, experimental, near-nonsense poems by herself, by her brothers, Osbert and Sacheverell (qq.v.), and by other writers. *Clowns' Houses* (1918) was her first successful volume of poetry. Her public reading of her long, difficult poem *Façade* in 1922 caused a sensation. *Gold Coast Customs* (1929) is a satirical poem. During World War II she began to write emotional, passionate, and religious poetry; "Still Falls the Rain," which combines thoughts of the crucifixion with impressions of a London air raid, is one of her best poems. Collections of poetry include *Gardeners and Astronomers* (1953) and *Music and Ceremonies* (1963). Her historical and critical works include *Alexander Pope* (1930), *Bath* (1932), *The English Eccentrics* (1933), and *A Poet's Notebook* (1943). *I Live under a Black Sun* (1937) is a novel about Jonathan SWIFT. Born into a noble and ancient family, Sitwell, who was converted to Roman Catholicism in 1954, maintained a reputation for aristocratic eccentricity, habitually dressing in medieval costume. She was made dame of the British Empire in 1954. Her autobiography, *Taken Care of*, was published in 1965.

Sitwell, Sir [Francis] Osbert [Sacheverell] (1892–1969)   English poet and writer. Brother of Edith and Sacheverell SITWELL. Osbert Sitwell's most remarkable achievement is his five-volume autobiography, which is an interesting account of the Sitwell family background and an evocation of the aristocratic England of his own childhood and youth. The volumes are *Left Hand! Right Hand!* (1944), *The Scarlet Tree* (1945), *Great Morning* (1947), *Laughter in the Next Room* (1948), and *Noble Essences* (1950). *Tales My Father Taught Me* (1962) consists mainly of autobiographical anecdotes about the author's eccentric father. Sir Osbert's poetry, collected in *Argonaut and Juggernaut* (1919) and other volumes, is largely satirical, concerned with war and types of English character. He also wrote fiction, plays, essays, and literary criticism.

Sitwell, Sacheverell (1897–   )   English poet and writer. Brother of Edith and Osbert SITWELL, Sacheverell has written on art and travel. Among his volumes of poetry are *The Hundred and One Harlequins* (1922), *Doctor Donne and Gargantua* (1926), *Selected Poems* (1948), *Agamemnon's Tomb* (1972), and *An Indian Summer: 100 Recent Poems* (1982). He has also written of the baroque period, music, and travel from the art-lover's point of view. *For Want of the Golden City* (1973) is an autobiography.

Siva   See SHIVA.

Six, Les   A group of French composers: Darius MILHAUD, Arthur HONEGGER, Francis POULENC, Georges Auric (1899–1983), Louis Durey (1888–1979), and Germaine Tailleferre (1892–1983). A music critic coined this soubriquet in comparing these composers with "The Five" Russians. Although they joined Erik SATIE, their mentor, and Jean COCTEAU, their spokesman, in decrying the pretentiousness of Romanticism and admiring the directness of popular music, they seldom met, and developed different musical styles.

Six Characters in Search of an Author (Sei personaggi in cerca d'autore, 1921; tr 1922)   A play by Luigi PIRANDELLO. The action takes place on an unprepared stage, where a company of actors is being assembled for a rehearsal. Six persons appear, announce that they are the incomplete, unused creations of the author's imagination, and demand that they be permitted to perform the drama that was never written for them but is implied in their lives. The life stories of all six characters are then presented.

Six Dynasties (AD 222–589)   Chinese historical period following the HAN dynasty. The succession of six short-lived dynasties with their capital at Chien-k'ang (present-day Nanking) gives this era its name. This was a period of interregnum and complex political and social change. It includes the shorter NORTHERN AND SOUTHERN DYNASTIES period. After this period China was reunited under the SUI dynasty.

1601 (1939)   A sketch written about 1876, by Mark TWAIN. The piece is subtitled "Conversation as It Was by the Social Fireside in the Time of the Tudors." An amusing essay on manners, it was printed only privately for many years because of its free use of Anglo-Saxon vocabulary.

Sixteen-string Jack   The almost affectionate nickname of a famous highwayman whose real name was John Rann and who is referred to in Boswell's LIFE OF SAMUEL JOHNSON. He was renowned for his affectation of fine clothes, and his nickname was an allusion to the many strings or ribbons he wore at his knees. He was hanged in 1774.

Sjöwall, Maj (1935–   )   Swedish mystery writer. In collaboration with her husband, Per Wahlöö (1926–75), she wrote the series about Chief Inspector Martin Beck of the Swedish National Police, beginning with *Roseanna* (1965) and concluding with *The Terrorists* (1975). The novels are characterized by clarity of insight into the police subculture and a disillusioned, somewhat bitter, picture of a socialist society.

skald   An Old Norse court poet. Unlike eddic poetry (see EDDA), which narrated heroic and mythological stories, skaldic verse was composed to glorify princes or commemorate events in the lives of great men. The most popular skalds were those who would devise new and intricate kennings, whose meanings were not intended to be understood immediately, but to provide the substance for an evening's discussion. See KENNING.

Skanda   See KARTTIKEYA.

Skanderbeg (c1404–1468)   Albanian national hero. The self-proclaimed prince of Albania, Skanderbeg led the resistance to the Turkish invasion of Albania with support from Pope Pius II. Although he forced a ten-year truce with the Turks, Albania fell when Skanderbeg died in 1468. Skanderbeg themes and biographies have recurred frequently throughout Albanian nationalist literature.

skaz A term in Russian prosody designating the recreation by a narrator of indigenous oral speech in cadence, rhythm, and diction. Masterful use of the technique appears in the works of Nikolay GOGOL, Aleksey REMIZOV, Mikhail ZOSHCHENKO, and Nikolay LESKOV.

skeleton at the feast An Egyptian custom. PLUTARCH says that toward the close of Egyptian banquets, a servant brought in a wooden skeleton, about eighteen inches long, and cried aloud to the guests, "Look on this! Eat, drink, and be merry; for tomorrow you die!"

Skelton, John (c1460–1529) English poet. Skelton is known for his satire, humorous and realistic verse, and short, "breathless" lines and irregular rhyme-scheme, called Skeltonic meter. His surviving works include *A Garland of Laurel* (c1520), an allegorical poem dealing with the crowning of Skelton himself as a great poet; PHILIP SPARROW (c1500), a lyric mourning the death of a sparrow, the pet of a young girl; *Colin Clout* (c1519), a satire on the abuses of the Church; *The Bowge of Court*, a satire in allegory on life at the English court; *Magnificence, a Morality Play*; *The Tunning of Elinour Rumming*, a coarse and humorous work, giving a realistic picture of contemporary low life; and *Why Come Ye Not to Court?* (c1523) and *Speak, Parrot*, satires on Cardinal Wolsey. Skelton received the title of Poet Laureate from both Oxford and Cambridge universities and held an unofficial position as Laureate under Henry VIII. He was ordained a priest, but spent most of his time at court, where he made many enemies by his outspokenness. As a result of the hostility between him and Cardinal Wolsey, he was forced to seek refuge with the abbot of Westminster, with whom he stayed virtually as a prisoner until his death.

Skelton is considered a poet of the transition between England of the Middle Ages and the Elizabethan period, writing in the tradition of CHAUCER, GOWER, and LYDGATE, and the medieval Latin poets. Interest in his work was revived in the 20th century by Robert GRAVES, and Skeltonic meter is parodied in the early verse of W. H. AUDEN.

Skepticism A movement in Greek philosophy. It was based on careful examination and deliberately suspended judgment. There were two main types of Skepticism, PYRRHONISM and Academic Skepticism. The last, beginning in the Platonic Academy c250 BC, was founded by Arcesilaus. He believed that philosophic assent should always be withheld, because reasons can be adduced for any side of every question. The Skeptics believed that it was impossible to attain certainty; all that one can do is assess probabilities. They continued to influence Greek philosophy until the 3rd century of the Christian era.

Sketch Book of Geoffrey Crayon, Gent., The (1819, 1820) A collection of tales and sketches by Washington IRVING. The book marked the beginning of the short story in America. At the time of publication, Irving's sketches of English landscape and customs were most popular; but the best loved and most permanently valuable tales in the collection are THE LEGEND OF SLEEPY HOLLOW and RIP VAN WINKLE.

Skinner, B[urrhus] F[rederic] (1904–   ) American psychologist. The leading proponent of behaviorism—the belief that man is controlled by external factors and that autonomy and free will do not exist—in such books as the novel *Walden Two* (1948) and *Beyond Freedom and Dignity* (1971), Skinner attempted to show how behaviorist principles could be applied to create an ideal society. Several of Skinner's mechanical inventions became famous. These included the "Skinner box" for observing animals' stimulus-response behavior, teaching machines, and, especially, the air crib or mechanical baby-tender. In spite of the controversy and largely negative popular response generated by Skinner's books and inventions, his ideas have had a profound impact on the fields of psychology and education. *Particulars of My Life* (1976), *The Shaping of a Behaviorist* (1979), and *A Matter of Consequences* (1983) are volumes of autobiography.

Skinner, Cornelia Otis (1901–1979) American author and actress. The daughter of actor Otis Skinner (1858–1942), Cornelia Otis Skinner won a reputation with her "monodramas," one-woman shows about famous figures, written and acted by herself. In 1937 she made a play of Margaret Ayer Barnes's novel *Edna His Wife* and acted all the parts. She wrote several other plays, including the highly successful *The Pleasure of His Company* (1958; with Samuel Taylor), and was the author of several collections of humorous essays, such as *The Ape in Me* (1959). With Emily Kimbrough she wrote the best-selling memoir *Our Hearts Were Young and Gay* (1942).

Skin of Our Teeth, The (1942) A play by Thornton WILDER. Unconventional in structure, it gives a panoramic picture of George Antrobus (man), his family, and their maid Sabina (the eternal temptress), who manage to survive world upheavals from prehistoric times until the 20th century. Wilder was awarded his third PULITZER PRIZE for this play.

Skuld See NORNS.

Škvorecký, Josef [Václav] (1924–   ) Czech novelist, essayist, scenarist, translator, and publisher. Škvorecký became extremely popular when his first novel, *Zbabělci* (written 1949; tr *The Cowards*, 1970), was published in Prague in 1958. Its young hero, a jazz enthusiast, bears many autobiographical traits and reappears in Škvorecký's later writings. The novel became the center of a *cause célèbre* when, because of its unorthodox description of the last days of World War II in a provincial Czech town, it was attacked and confiscated by Party officials. In the 1960s Škvorecký's short stories and film scenarios made him one of the most popular writers of his generation. His last novel published in Czechoslovakia, *Lvíče* (1969; tr *Miss Silver's Past*, 1973), depicted backroom intrigues in a Prague publishing house. In 1970 he moved to Canada, became a professor of English at the University of Toronto, and founded, with his wife, a successful publishing house of Czech literature. His subsequent works, including the biting antimilitary satire *Tankový prapar* (*The Tank Regiment*, 1971), *Mirákel* (*Miracle*, 1972), and the novel for which he is best known in the West, *The Bass Saxophone* (1977), show his undiminished gusto for a bizarre story with a sharp political edge. Another novel, *Pribeh inženyra lidskych duši* (1977), was published in 1984 as *The Engineer of Human Souls*.

Slap in the Face of Public Taste, A   See FUTURISM.

Slaughterhouse-Five or the Children's Crusade: A Duty-Dance with Death (1969)   A satirical novel by Kurt VONNEGUT, Jr. After surviving the firebombing of Dresden by British and American forces during World War II, the naive optometrist Billy Pilgrim returns from the war to Illium, New York. On the eve of his daughter's wedding, Billy is kidnapped by aliens from the planet Tralfamadore, who teach him that there is a fourth dimension where time is an eternal present. He is then allowed to return to Illium, to try to teach the earthlings his new knowledge. As Billy becomes "unstuck in time," he travels back and forth between past and future, reliving the horror of his wartime experiences.

Slavophilism   A 19th-century school of thought in Russia which stressed the uniqueness of Russian life and culture. The Slavophiles claimed that the Russian way of life, based on the faith of the Orthodox Church, was superior to that of the West, whose rationalism and weak religious faith doomed it to decay. The leading Slavophile thinkers included Aleksey Stepanovich Khomyakov (1804–60), Ivan Vasilyevich Kireyevsky (1806–59), Yury Fedorovich Samarin (1819–76), and Konstantin and Ivan Aksakov, sons of the author Sergey Timofeyevich AKSAKOV. Although he was not an adherent of the movement, DOSTOYEVSKY manifested some Slavophile tendencies in his work.

The Slavophiles were opposed to the so-called Westerners, who believed that Russia should adopt the social, political, and cultural ways of the West. Outstanding members of this group were Vissarion BELINSKY, Aleksandr HERZEN, and the novelist Ivan TURGENEV.

Slawkenbergius, Hafen   An imaginary author, distinguished for the great length of his nose, in Laurence Sterne's novel TRISTRAM SHANDY. Slawkenbergius is referred to as a great authority on all lore connected with noses, and a curious tale, filled with sexual symbolism, is introduced from his hypothetical works about a man with an enormously long nose. Gogol based a short story called "The Nose" on Slawkenbergius's tale.

Slessor, Kenneth (1901–1971)   Australian poet and journalist. A war correspondent during World War II, Slessor became the literary editor for the Sydney *Sun* in 1944. In the 1920s he had begun writing verse that was to put him among the foremost Australian poets. His work, highly individualistic, rich in imagery and unconventional rhythms, reveals a keen zest for life. His publications include *Thief of the Moon* (1924) and *Earth Visitors* (1926), collections of antimodern, anti-intellectual verse in Victorian and Edwardian forms. The later volumes, such as *Cuckooz Contrey* (1932) and *Five Bells* (1939), an elegy on the death of a dear friend, are influenced by such modernists as POUND and ELIOT; here Slessor applies technical innovation to distinctly Australian themes. His work is collected in *One Hundred Poems, 1919–1939* (1944) and *Poems* (1957; rev 1962).

slice of life   A phrase used to describe the work of naturalistic writers, such as ZOLA, who attempt to present a chunk of life complete, not modified by any selection or arrangement of material. The phrase is used for short stories that have no plot, climax, or structured form, but instead give an impression of the characters' daily life.

Sloan, John (1871–1951)   American painter. One of the ASHCAN SCHOOL, Sloan was a teacher and an organizer of the ARMORY SHOW and other independent shows. He was art editor of *The Masses* and contributed to *Harper's* and *Collier's*. His reminiscences and ideals are set forth in his book *The Gist of Art* (1938).

Sloper, Catherine   See WASHINGTON SQUARE.

Slough of Despond   See PILGRIM'S PROGRESS.

Sly, Christopher   The principal character in the Induction to Shakespeare's TAMING OF THE SHREW. He is a keeper of bears and a tinker, the son of a peddler, and a drunken sot; he may have been an actual person from the village of Wincot, near Stratford-on-Avon. Sly is found dead drunk by a lord, who commands his servants to put Sly to bed, and on his waking to attend him like a lord and deceive him into thinking himself a great man. The play is performed for his entertainment.

Small Souls, The Book of the (De boeken der kleine zielen, 4 vols, 1901–1904; tr 1914)   The first of a series of novels by the Dutch author Louis COUPERUS. They deal with the Van Lowe family, a large and diverse group, many of them united by little except the custom of pleasing old Granny Lowe by spending Sunday evenings together at her home. The other novels of the series are *The Later Life* (tr 1915), *The Twilight of the Souls* (tr 1917), and *Dr. Adrian* (tr 1918).

Smart, Christopher (1722–1771)   English poet and journalist. In 1756 a religious mania overtook him and Smart was confined to an asylum. During this period he wrote his best-known work, *Song to David* (1763), a rhapsodic poem in praise of God. His religious concepts are close to those of William BLAKE.

Smerdyakov See KARAMAZOV.

Smetana, Bedřich (1824–1884) Bohemian composer. Smetana's opera *The Bartered Bride* (1866) is considered the national opera of Czechoslovakia. His best orchestra music is *Má vlast* (*My Country*, 1879), a set of six musical landscapes, of which *Vltava* (*The Moldau*) is best known.

Smith, Adam (1723–1790) Scottish moral philosopher and political economist. Smith was educated at Glasgow and Oxford and gave a series of lectures on English literature at Glasgow that were so popular that they had to be repeated the two following years. He was elected to the chair of logic at Glasgow in 1751, which he exchanged for the chair of moral philosophy the following year. With the publication of *Theory of Moral Sentiments* (1759), in which he expressed his ethical views, he won recognition as a contemporary writer of the first rank. His major work, THE WEALTH OF NATIONS, was the first systematic formulation of classical English economics. Adam Smith's name is popularly associated with his belief that self-interest would operate to bring about the healthiest economic conditions for all citizens, hence a laissez-faire economy. His *Essays on Philosophic Subjects* (1795) was published posthumously.

Smith, A[rthur] J[ames] M[arshall] (1902–1980) Canadian poet, critic, and anthologist. Born in Montreal and educated at McGill University, Smith was one of the moving spirits, with F. R. SCOTT, of the modern poetry group there. Though he spent most of his working life at Michigan State University, his poetry, criticism, and anthologies exerted a profound influence on contemporary Canadian literature and helped establish it as a subject worthy of serious study. In his introduction to *The Book of Canadian Poetry* (1943; rev 1948, 1957) he called for an end to parochialism, insisting on judging Canadian poetry by the highest standards. His own poetry, intense in feeling, complex, and often cryptic, reflects the varying influences of the METAPHYSICAL POETS, the French SYMBOLISTS, and such 20th-century figures as T. S. ELIOT and Ezra POUND. His volumes of verse include *News of the Phoenix* (1943), *A Sort of Ecstasy* (1954), *Collected Poems* (1962), *Poems: New and Collected* (1967), and *The Classic Shade* (1978). A collection of his criticism is found in *Towards a View of Canadian Letters* (1973).

Smith, Betty [Wehner] See TREE GROWS IN BROOKLYN, A.

Smith, David (1906–1965) American sculptor. One of the most influential and innovative sculptors of the 20th century, in his work Smith mingled themes of social injustice with his fascination with mechanical devices. His many pieces in steel and other media combined aspects of European CONSTRUCTIVISM, SURREALISM, and CUBISM with his purely American freshness of vision.

Smith, E[dward] E[lmer] (1890–1965) American SCIENCE FICTION author. He was known as Doc Smith because the famous editor Hugo GERNSBACK attached the Ph.D. he had earned in food chemistry to his name on some early stories. He is the progenitor of space opera, stories of galactic, interstellar adventure, beginning with *The Skylark of Space* (1946), which was first serialized (1928) in *Amazing Stories* and had three "Skylark" successors. His other major cycle was the "Lensman" series, beginning with *Triplanetary* (1948), which was serialized in *Astounding* in 1934, and concluded six volumes later with *Masters of the Vortex* (1960); the series chronicled the conflicts between two diametrically opposed civilizations. A selection of his stories appeared in *The Best of E. E. "Doc" Smith* (1975).

Smith, Ernest Bramah (pen name Ernest Bramah, 1869–1942) English author. Smith wrote detective stories. He also wrote the suave, witty, and ironic Kai Lung books, about Chinese life and traditions: *The Wallet of Kai Lung* (1900) and *Kai Lung's Golden Hours* (1922).

Smith, H[arry] Allen (1907–1976) American humorist. Originally a newspaperman, Smith turned his irreverent view of the world into a career as one of America's most popular humorists. He followed his first big success, the enormously popular *Low Man on a Totem Pole* (1941), with more than thirty-five books of anecdotal humor that took potshots at all forms of pomposity and pretension. Among his many books are *Rhubarb* (1946), *The Compleat Practical Joker* (1953), *A Short History of Fingers, and Other State Papers* (1963), and *Low Man Rides Again* (1973). *The Best of H. Allen Smith* was published in 1972. *To Hell in a Handbasket* (1962) is his autobiography.

Smith, John (1580–1631) English explorer and soldier of fortune. Smith came to Jamestown, Virginia, in 1607 and became president of the governing council of the colony. The legend of his rescue from death by Pocahontas is based on his own story, told in *Generall Historie of Virginia, New-England, and the Summer Isles* (1624). He also made several expeditions to New England and helped to promote interest in the region. *A True Relation of . . . Virginia* (1608) is sometimes called the first American book.

Smith, Joseph (1805–1844) American religious leader and Mormon prophet. In 1820 Smith began to have supernatural visions, which appointed him prophet of a new religion; in 1827, according to his account, he got from the angel Moroni a book written in strange characters on golden plates. He translated the message as the *Book of Mormon* (1830), and on this book the Church of the Latter-Day Saints was founded the same year. Smith decided to move westward from Vermont with his followers; he went to Ohio (1831), Missouri (1838), and finally to Nauvoo, Illinois. There on July 12, 1843, he proclaimed the doctrine of polygamy. Much opposition was aroused, especially in the columns of the Nauvoo *Expositor*. When Smith's followers destroyed the press of this paper, a warrant for his arrest was issued. He resisted, but was placed in jail at Carthage. An angry mob invaded the jail and killed him. His son, Joseph Smith, Jr. (1832–1914), headed the Church of Jesus Christ of Latter Day Saints in Missouri, and his nephew, Joseph Fielding Smith (1838–1918), later became a leader of the Utah Mormon Church.

Smith, Lillian (1897–1966)   American writer. Born in the South, and for a time a music teacher in a mission school in China, Smith worked as a social worker in Georgia and published a quarterly, *South Today*. She is best known for her vividly written and perceptive books dealing with racial problems: *Strange Fruit* (1944; adapted for stage, 1945), a novel dealing with the hopeless love of a white boy and a black girl; and *Killers of the Dream* (1949; rev 1961), a penetrating nonfiction analysis of growing up with a double racial standard. Her other nonfiction includes *The Journey* (1954), *Now Is the Time* (1955), and *One Hour* (1959). *The Winner Names the Age* (1978) is a posthumous collection of essays on civil rights and the role of women in a male-dominated society.

Smith, Seba (1792–1868)   American humorist and poet. Born in Maine, where he attended school and contributed to various newspapers, Smith adopted the persona of Major Jack Downing, a semiliterate Yankee oracle, in contributing satirical letters to the Portland *Courier* (1830). Smith first attacked the local legislature and Maine customs, then went on to Washington and President Jackson.

Smith, Stevie (pen name of Florence Margaret Smith, 1902–1971)   English poet and novelist. Smith lived with her maiden aunt in an Edwardian house at the edge of London until the latter died, aged 96, in 1968. Always intent on writing poetry, Smith wrote her first novel at the suggestion of a publisher who rejected her verse. The result was *Novel on Yellow Paper* (1936), a spirited, amusing, and rather bizarre monologue in a style full of digressions and non sequiturs that many likened to Gertrude STEIN's. Later novels, such as *The Holiday* (1949), about a doomed love affair, preserved the style but followed a more coherent plot line. Her first published volume of poetry, *A Good Time Was Had by All* (1937), was accompanied by her "Thurber-ish" line drawings, which some dismissed as mere doodles; as she continued to write, her short, light poems focused on deeper and darker ideas, particularly on the language and bases of Christianity. By the time her *Selected Poems* appeared in 1962, however, she was highly regarded as a serious poet. Two years before her death, she was awarded the Queen's Gold Medal for Poetry (1969). Her *Collected Poems* was published in 1976.

Smith, Thorne (1892–1934)   American humorist. Smith is known for his ribald and impish books, especially *Topper* (1926), the story of a sober gentleman transformed into an adventurous romantic by two ghosts. *Topper Takes a Trip* (1932) is its sequel.

Smoke (Dym, 1867)   A novel by Ivan TURGENEV. It combines the story of a love triangle with strictures on Russia's need to turn to the West for her civilization. The hero Litvinov, in love with Tanya, is distracted by an old lover, Irina, who manages to break up the romance; the interjections of social comment are mostly made by Turgenev's mouthpiece in the book, Potugin.

Smoke and Steel (1920)   A collection of poems by Carl SANDBURG. The title poem is an attempt to find some kind of beauty in modern industrialism, with particular reference to the steel mills.

Smollett, Tobias [George] (1721–1771)   Scottish-born English novelist and surgeon. After a vain attempt to sell a tragedy in London, Smollett served as surgeon's mate on board the *Chichester*, took part in an ill-fated attack on the Spanish at Cartagena (1741), and lived for a few years on the island of Jamaica. On his return to England, he began writing his PICARESQUE novels, including *The Adventures of* RODERICK RANDOM and *The Adventures of* PEREGRINE PICKLE, both satiric works patterned on LESAGE; *The Adventures of Ferdinand Count Fathom* (1753), the memoirs of a Gothic villain; *The Expedition of* HUMPHREY CLINKER, an epistolary novel; and *The Adventures of Launcelot Greaves* (1760), an attempt to adapt DON QUIXOTE to 18th-century England. He was fined and imprisoned for a libel that appeared in the *Critical Review*, which he edited from 1756 to 1763. He also published a *History of England* (1757–58); *Travels through France and Italy* (1766), a sardonic account of his travels; and *The Adventures of an Atom* (1769), a somewhat gross and virulent political allegory. During his last illness, he returned to Italy, where he died.

Smollett is noted for his well-drawn eccentric characters, particularly those of a nautical type; these at times grotesque caricatures often draw interest away from the main plot to the incidental and to comic relief. Smollett expressed his conception of what a novel should be in his preface to *Ferdinand Count Fathom*:

A novel is a large diffused picture, comprehending the characters of life, disposed in different groups, and exhibited in various attitudes, for the purpose of an uniform plan, and general occurrence, to which every individual figure is subservient. But this plan cannot be executed with propriety, probability, or success, without a principal personage to attract the attention, unite the incidents, unwind the clue of the labyrinth, and at last close the scene, by virtue of his own importance.

smriti (Sans, "remembered")   In the literature of HINDUISM, the body of scriptures said to have been handed down by tradition. *Smriti*, as opposed to the divinely revealed SHRUTI, were written and passed on by real historical personages such as VYĀSA and VALMIKI. Consequently, the PURANAS, the RĀMĀYANA, and the MAHĀBHĀRATA are all included in *smriti* scriptures.

Smuts, Jan Christian (1870–1950)   A famous Boer leader in the Boer War. During World War I, Smuts organized the South African forces. Prime minister of the

Union of South Africa (1919–24; 1939–48), he was most influential in World War II.

Snopes   A family in several novels and stories by William Faulkner, notably THE HAMLET, *The Town* (1957), and *The Mansion* (1959). Residents of YOKNAPATAWPHA COUNTY, the Snopeses typify the vicious and inhuman aspects of modern commercial civilization. The first Snopes to be mentioned is Ab, who is involved with a gang of horse thieves and killers in THE UNVAN-QUISHED; he reappears in the story "Barn Burning" and in *The Hamlet*. Ab's son, Flem, is a central character in the trilogy of which *The Hamlet* is the first volume. Flem works his way up from clerkship in a store to the presidency of a bank, is largely responsible for his wife's suicide, and drives her lover from town. Mink Snopes, who spends forty years in prison for murdering Jack Houston, is a central character in *The Mansion* and is Flem's murderer. Eula VARNER Snopes, Flem's wife, carries on an eighteen-year-long love affair with Manfred De Spain and later kills herself to keep her daughter, Linda, from scandal. Linda is a Snopes in name only; she is the illegitimate child of Eula and Hoake McCarron. Byron Snopes, who appears in *The Town* and SARTORIS, writes anonymous letters to Narcissa Benbow and robs the Sartoris bank. Clarence, the son of I. O. Snopes, appears in SANCTUARY and *The Mansion* and is an unscrupulous state senator. Other members of the family are I. O., a schoolteacher noted for his lengthy use of proverbs; Ike, the idiot ward of Flem who has a pathetic and tender attachment to Jack Houston's cow; Eck, an honest man and not a true Snopes; Montgomery Ward, who runs a French postcard peep-show before being run out of town; and Wallstreet Panic, who, like his father, Eck, is honest and not truly a Snopes.

Snorri Sturluson (1178–1241)   Icelandic historian. Snorri's HEIMSKRINGLA is a record of the kings of Norway from earliest times to 1177, as well as a collection of the sagas and poems. He expanded one of its sections into a separate *Olaf's Saga*. He also wrote *Prose Edda* (see EDDA).

Snow, C[harles] P[ercy] (Baron Snow of Leicester, 1905–1980)   English novelist and scientist. Snow took his Ph.D. in physics at Cambridge; he taught at that university and served as a scientific advisor to the British government on several occasions. His chief work of fiction is the related series of partly autobiographical novels, collectively titled STRANGERS AND BROTHERS, dealing with the ethics of power and questions of morality in a modern, scientific society. Always interested in the relationship of science to society, he argues in his essay THE TWO CULTURES that scientists are too little appreciated and understood in Britain. In such novels as *The Search* (1934) and *The New Men* (1954), he gives a picture of scientists and the problems of their work. His years of research at Cambridge also gave him the opportunity to observe the workings of power in a small community, his reflections of which form the basis for *The Masters* (1951) and *The Affair* (1960). His best-known

novel is *Corridors of Power* (1964), an examination of parliamentary politics. Snow's numerous and varied writings include biographical studies, essays, lectures, and several plays on which he collaborated with his wife, the novelist Pamela Hansford JOHNSON.

Snow, Edgar [Parks] (1905–1972)   American journalist. Snow first won recognition for *Red Star over China* (1937), in which he reported the growing power of the Communists. During his career as a correspondent, he traveled widely and wrote numerous books, but his central interest was always China; he became friends with MAO TSE-TUNG and wrote about him extensively.

Snow-Bound, A Winter Idyll (1866)   A long poem by John Greenleaf WHITTIER. An excursion into Whittier's boyhood, *Snow-Bound* evokes the memory of being snowed in on his father's Massachusetts farm. Sharply depicted details bring out the wondrous metamorphosis of the barnyard as the snow falls, and the cozy, homely indoor scene around the fire. Whittier nostalgically pays tribute to his family and their guests and adds a prayer for peace and brotherhood.

Snows of Kilimanjaro, The (1938)   A short story by Ernest HEMINGWAY. With a wealthy woman who has been keeping him, Harry, a writer, goes on a safari in Africa. There he hopes to "work the fat off his mind," so that he can set to work on all the things he has dreamed of writing. This dream is shattered when he develops gangrene in his leg. In the knowledge of death he reviews his life, and in a dream just before he dies he sees a legendary, gigantic, frozen leopard on the summit of Mt. Kilimanjaro.

Snyder, Gary [Sherman] (1930–   )   American poet and essayist. Snyder's reverence for nature and for the simple life suggest a modern THOREAU with Buddhist overtones. Reared in the logging camps of the Pacific northwest, he studied Chinese philology and T'ang poetry at the University of California at Berkeley and became associated with the BEAT MOVEMENT in San Francisco. In 1959 he went to Japan as a novice in a Zen Buddhist monastery. The Eastern influence is evident in his verse, which in its sparse and clear imagery deals with common sensory experience and a reverent dedication to the land. He draws deeply also from American Indian culture. His most important volumes of verse are *The Back Country* (1967), *Regarding Wave* (1970), and *Turtle Island* (1974), which was awarded the PULITZER PRIZE. His other writings include a collection of essays, *The Old Ways* (1977), *The Real Work* (1980), and *Passage through India* (1984).

Sobakevich   A bearlike character in Nikolay Gogol's novel DEAD SOULS. Everything about Sobakevich is huge and solid: his person, his furniture, and especially his appetite. At a banquet for the artful schemer CHI-CHIKOV, Sobakevich creates a sensation by devouring a grandiose sturgeon that was to have served as the main course.

Sobre los ángeles (1929; tr Concerning the Angels, 1967) A volume of poems by Rafael ALBERTI, among the major titles of Spanish SURREALISM. Written in a period of personal crisis, it combines classical elements with FREE VERSE to express a sense of loss and danger, of conflict with unknown or mysterious adversaries, in an atmosphere of human and cosmic anguish. The perspective is at once that of the patient on the psychiatrist's couch and that of the psychiatrist who listens, observes, and interprets.

Social Contract, The (Le Contrat social, 1762) Chief work of Jean Jacques ROUSSEAU, a treatise on the origins and organization of government and the rights of citizens. Rousseau's thesis states that, since no man has any natural authority over another, the social contract, freely entered into, creates natural reciprocal obligations between citizens. The individual, as the basic political unit, surrenders his rights to the State, and is legally equal to all other members. The third book is a discussion of three forms of government: democratic, which Rousseau distrusts; aristocratic, which, if elective, is acceptable; and monarchic, which is preferable, if headed by an ideal ruler. Like MONTESQUIEU, Rousseau states that practical, moral, and theoretical considerations should determine the best form of government for any people. That all minorities must submit to the general will or be banished is the conclusion of the fourth book. Though an individualistic work, it reveals Rousseau as a firm collectivist. Some critics assert that the injustices of collectivism and "democratic despotism" during the French Revolution and later in the 19th and 20th centuries were, in part, derived from this work.

socialism A term used since the 1830s to describe any theory or social or political movement predicated upon communal or government ownership and control of production and distribution of goods. Socialism does not necessarily imply the abolition of private property, though it is characterized by public ownership of property directly affecting public interests. The societies advocated in Plato's REPUBLIC and Sir Thomas More's UTOPIA are socialist in nature, and the early Christian community has been held to have been socialist in that all property was communally owned. Socialist theories have been advanced by Robert OWEN in England and François Fourier (see FOURIERISM) in France, advocating the organization of society into cooperative communities. In 1847 Marx and Engels's THE COMMUNIST MANIFESTO laid down the principles of their own brand of scientific socialism. The FABIAN SOCIETY in England attempted to popularize the socialist cause. There have been many nominally socialist governments in various countries since World War II, particularly in northern Europe, but in virtually all of them the impact of reality has profoundly modified socialist theory.

socialist realism The officially supported artistic doctrine that has been more or less obligatory for Soviet writers and artists since 1932. The resolution of the Communist Party's Central Committee, which set up the Union

of Soviet Writers, declared that "Socialist realism is the basic method of Soviet literature and literary criticism. It demands of the artist a truthful, historically concrete depiction of reality in its revolutionary development. . . . [This] must be combined with the task of reforming the ideas of the toilers and of educating them in the spirit of socialism." The writer Maksim GORKY was one of the early theoreticians of the doctrine, but Gorky's ideas about the relationship of literature to life contained elements of romanticism that later critics have tended to label "revolutionary romanticism," rather than realism. As the grip of Soviet control tightened on literature, the freedom of the artist to depict reality as he or she saw it or wished it to be was—officially, at least—subordinated to the demand for an art that showed the steady progress of Soviet society toward its socialist goal. Concomitant with the general depiction of a progressive society, there was also a demand for the creation of the POSITIVE HERO in Soviet literature. This was a sharp break with the literature of the 19th century, in which the protagonists were most often SUPERFLUOUS MEN, alienated from society and unable to find a useful purpose for their lives. The Soviet hero, on the contrary, was to be an active, healthy man or woman, without hesitations and scruples about his role in society. This rigid formula resulted in the deadness of much of Soviet literature for three decades. Gorky's novel MOTHER, held up as an early example of socialist realism, fell more within the scope of Gorky's revolutionary romanticism. Another novel often cited as a model of socialist realism, Sholokhov's THE QUIET DON, also fails to meet the test. Its hero, Gregor Melekhov, resembles the 19th-century superfluous man more than he does a positive hero.

Obviously, Soviet writers have had trouble adhering to the prescribed formula while producing readable literature. Some openly question the possibility of writing within such a narrow framework or the validity of such a doctrine. Andrey SINYAVSKY, in a pseudonymous SAMIZDAT essay, *On Socialist Realism*, asks: "What is the meaning of this strange and jarring phrase? Can there be a socialist, capitalist, Christian, or Mohammedan realism? Does this irrational concept have a natural existence? Perhaps it does not exist at all, perhaps it is only the nightmare of a terrified intellectual during the dark and magical night of Stalin's dictatorship? Perhaps a crude propaganda trick of Zhdanov or a senile fancy of Gorky?" Despite the rebellion of large numbers of Russia's best writers, notably PASTERNAK and SOLZHENITSYN, the doctrine is still officially in force.

sock and buskin Forms of footwear used in classical drama. The sock and buskin have come to be used as terms to differentiate COMEDY and TRAGEDY, respectively. Tragic actors wore a high, thick-soled boot, or buskin, intended to add stature and heroic grandeur to the wearer. The actors of comedy wore a low slipper, or sock, for the opposite effect.

Socrates (c470–399 BC)   Greek teacher of wisdom. Socrates himself left no writings, and is known to us through the *Dialogues* of PLATO, ARISTOTLE's treatises, and XENOPHON's discourses. His interest was in ethics. He is represented as believing that virtue is knowledge; all wickedness, he said, is due to ignorance. In his teaching, Socrates sought the universal definition of virtue through particulars. Aristotle credits him with developing inductive method. With self-knowledge the foundation for inquiry, Socrates would save men from leading "unexamined" lives. The Socratic method of teaching consisted in asking questions, and drawing out the answers from the student. Socrates himself pretended to be ignorant of the subject. The purpose of the method, which Plato called midwifery, was to show the student that the answers are contained in his own mind. Socrates always understated the truth, giving rise to the expression "Socratic irony." In 399 BC the Athenians tried Socrates on a charge of impiety and corruption of youth. He was sentenced to death, and drank hemlock, as described by Plato in the PHAEDO.

The only unfavorable view of Socrates occurs in Aristophanes' comedy THE CLOUDS, where he is caricatured as a representative of the Sophistic profession. The play, however, is professedly fictional, and is not accepted as history. See also XANTIPPE.

Söderberg, Hjalmar (1869–1941)   Swedish novelist, short-story writer, and playwright. Söderberg was a frank, naturalistic writer who early understood the teachings of FREUD, a fact that is particularly evident in his novel *Doktor Glas* (1905; tr *Doctor Glas*, 1963). His other novels, including *Martin Bircks Ungdom* (1901; tr *Martin Birck's Youth*, 1930), are usually grimly pessimistic stories set in Stockholm. The stories in *Historietter* (1898) are regarded among the best in Swedish literature.

Sodom and Gomorrah   In the OLD TESTAMENT, the two principal of the five Cities of the Plain. They were destroyed by heaven with fire and brimstone because of their wickedness, which took the form of homosexual debauchery. ABRAHAM persuaded JEHOVAH to spare Sodom if ten righteous men could be found there, but this condition could not be fulfilled. LOT and his family were the only inhabitants who escaped the doomed city, but Lot's wife became a pillar of salt because she looked back.

Sodome et Gomorrhe   See REMEMBRANCE OF THINGS PAST.

Sohrab and Rustum (1853)   A narrative poem in blank verse by Matthew ARNOLD, dealing with the legendary Persian hero Rustum and his son Sohrab. The two meet in single combat, in ignorance of their relationship, and Sohrab is slain.

Sōka Gakki   See NICHIREN.

Soldiers, The   See HOCHHUTH, ROLF.

Soldiers Three (1888)   A volume of short stories of Anglo-Indian life by Rudyard KIPLING. The three soldiers of the title are Otheris, Learoyd, and Mulvaney, the famous trio who first appeared in PLAIN TALES FROM THE HILLS.

Solemn League and Covenant   A league of the General Assembly of the Church of Scotland, the Westminster Assembly of English Divines, and the English Parliament in 1643, for the establishment of Presbyterianism and suppression of Roman Catholicism in both countries. Charles II swore to the Scots that he would abide by it, and therefore they crowned him in 1651 at Dunbar; but at the Restoration, he not only rejected the Covenant but had it burnt by the common hangman.

soliloquy   See MONOLOGUE.

Sologub, Fyodor (pen name of Fyodor Kuzmich Teternikov, 1863–1927)   Russian novelist, poet, and short-story writer. Sologub was a schoolteacher until the success of his novel *Melkiy bes* (1907; tr *The Little Demon*, 1916) allowed him to devote himself entirely to writing. Its protagonist, the evil and vindictive school teacher Peredonov, is one of the most striking and grotesque characters in Russian fiction. The novel expresses Sologub's sense of the evil reality of the world, stifling an ideal of good which is only sporadically glimpsed. Similar ideas are found in his finely wrought poetry, in his stories, and in his other novels, *Tyazhiolye sny* (*Bad Dreams*, 1896) and *Tvorimaya legenda* (1907–13; tr *The Created Legend*, 1916). His poetry places him with the Russian SYMBOLISTS.

Solomon   In the OLD TESTAMENT, the wisest and most magnificent of the kings of Israel and the son of DAVID and BATHSHEBA. When asked by JEHOVAH to be granted any wish, Solomon wisely chose "an understanding heart" by which to judge the people (1 Kings 3:9). He is perhaps most celebrated for his building of the famous temple which bore his name and for his lavish entertainment of the queen of SHEBA. (See 1 Kings 2–11.) The glory of his reign gave rise to many legends in the TALMUD and the KORAN. See CARPET, MAGIC; SOLOMON'S TEMPLE, SONG OF SOLOMON, THE.

judgment of Solomon   A famous example of SOLOMON's wisdom. Two harlots came before the king bearing a live and a dead baby, and each claimed the live baby as her own. Solomon ordered that the live child be cut in half and shared between the two. One woman begged the king to give the living child to the other woman rather than kill it. Solomon at once knew that she was the true mother, and the people knew that "the wisdom of God was in him, to render justice." See CIRCLE OF CHALK, THE.

Solomon's Temple   The central place of Jewish worship. It was erected by SOLOMON and his Tyrian workmen (probably on Phoenician models) on Mount Moriah, Jerusalem, about 1006 BC. It was destroyed at the siege of Jerusalem by NEBUCHADNEZZAR (586 BC), and some seventy years later the Temple of Zerubbabel was completed on its site. In 20 BC HEROD THE GREAT began the building of the last Temple—that of the NEW TESTAMENT—which was utterly destroyed during the siege of Jerusalem by Vespasian and TITUS in AD 70. For many centuries the site has been covered by the splendid Muslim mosque, Haram esh Sherif.

Solon (c640–c558 BC)   A Greek statesman and poet. Solon was elected *archon* (594–593 or 592–591 BC) on order to mediate between the oppressed poor and the rich few. He carried out extensive reforms to this end, but his true title to fame rests on his constitutional reforms. Although he retained a class system, he added the lowest class, the Thetes, and gave them a part in the Assembly and in the choice of magistrate. His radical measure was establishing courts of justice, Heliaea, administered by all the citizens. Even the magistrates, after they resigned their office, could be accused before the people.

Solon's reforms won him the title of founder of Athenian democracy. A man of moderation, a poet, legislator, traveler, and merchant, he embodied the best characteristics of the Greeks. He survived to see his reforms partially thrust aside under the tyranny of PISISTRATUS.

Soloukhin, Vladimir Alekseyevich (1924–   ) Russian poet, journalist, short-story writer, and novelist. Better known for his prose than his poetry, Soloukhin is best characterized as a "village writer": he, like Vasily SHUKSHIN, concentrates on peasant traditions and a return to rural, natural values; his depiction of man's relationship with nature is strongly reminiscent of the work of Sergei AKSAKOV. His story *Vladimirskiye prosyolki* (1958; tr *A Walk in Rural Russia*, 1967) is both a travel sketch of and a search for roots in his native area, while *Chornye doski* (1969; tr *Searching for Icons in Russia*, 1971) depicts his growing concern for the preservation of old Russian art. The unspoken conclusion is that the new society has been unable to replace the culture it destroyed. Like the other "village writers," Soloukhin evinces certain Christian tendencies in his work provocative to Soviet authorities. Since 1967 he has been chief editor of the journal *Molodaya Gvardiya*.

Solovyov, Vladimir Sergeyevich (1853–1900) Russian religious philosopher and poet. His mystic doctrine of Sophia (the eternal feminine, the divine wisdom) had a large influence on the symbolist poets Aleksandr BLOK and Andrey BELY. Much of Solovyov's poetry reflects his mystical thought, although some of it is riotously witty nonsense verse. His major prose work is *Tri razgovory* (*Three Conversations*, 1899).

Solzhenitsyn, Aleksandr Isayevich (1918–   ) Russian novelist. Born in Kislovodsk in the Caucasus, Solzhenitsyn graduated from the Department of Physics and Mathematics of Rostov University in 1941. He promptly joined the army, serving as an officer until he was arrested in February 1945 for having referred to Stalin as "the boss" (*pakhan*) in criminals' slang. After eight years in prison camps, he was exiled to Kazakhstan, where he taught physics and mathematics in a rural school. He was allowed to return to European Russia in 1957, and in 1962

his first published work, ONE DAY IN THE LIFE OF IVAN DENISOVICH, appeared in the Soviet magazine *Novy mir*. Also published in *Novy mir* were the stories "Sluchay na stantsii Krechetovka" (1963; tr "Incident at Krechatovka Station," 1963), "Matryonin dvor" (1963; tr "Matryona's House," 1963), and "Zakhar Kalita" (1966; tr "Zakhar the Pouch," 1969).

The relatively liberal atmosphere of the early 1960s made such publication possible, yet by 1965 some of Solzhenitsyn's work began to appear only in the West. His novel THE FIRST CIRCLE was accepted by *Novy mir* but never appeared, while the novel CANCER WARD elicited heated controversy at a meeting of the Board of Soviet Writers but also never appeared in print in the Soviet Union. These works, and especially their appearance abroad, began to evoke charges that Solzhenitsyn was slandering the Soviet state. His open letter denouncing censorship, which he sent to the Fourth Congress of Soviet Writers, further enraged the authorities, and in 1969 Solzhenitsyn was expelled from the Writers' Union. In 1970, however, he was awarded the NOBEL PRIZE in Literature for the "ethical force" his works have imparted to contemporary Soviet literature.

Cancer Ward and *The First Circle* appeared in the West without Solzhenitsyn's permission, but his historical novel of the first eleven days of World War I, *Avgust Chetyrnadtsatogo* (1971; tr *August 1914*, 1972), appeared in Paris in 1971 with his consent. Then in 1973, the KGB confiscated a manuscript of THE GULAG ARCHIPELAGO and Solzhenitsyn, no longer able to protect those named in the book, allowed its publication in the West. He was arrested, and on February 13, 1974, he hastily departed for West Germany. Thus exiled, Solzhenitsyn published his *Pismo vozhdyam Sovetskogo Soyuza* (1974; tr *Letter to the Soviet Leaders*, 1974), in which he advocates the end of Communist rule in the Soviet Union and the right of non-Russian states within the Soviet Union to secede. Solzhenitsyn moved to the United States in 1976, settling into a secluded existence in Cavendish, Vermont, where he has continued to write, exploring his views of the evolution of the Soviet Union through history in such works as *Lenin in Zurich* (1976) and *The Oak and the Calf* (1980).

Solzhenitsyn is the latest in the long line of Russian writers from the Slavophiles (see SLAVOPHILISM) through DOSTOYEVSKY and TOLSTOY to PASTERNAK and MANDELSHTAM who have seen Russia as having a unique moral and religious destiny which is undermined by Western rationalism and secularism, of which Marxism is merely the latest and most effective manifestation.

In his works Solzhenitsyn has trenchantly sought to restore to Soviet society its memory. The unspeakable terror of Stalin's reign, long a forbidden topic, finds impassioned expression in much of Solzhenitsyn's work, particularly in *The Gulag Archipelago*, which in its relentless march of grisly detail leaves no reader unmoved nor fails to evoke in the reader its author's own moral indignation. Literary art, as Solzhenitsyn explains in his Nobel lecture, serves to battle lies, preserving the cultural and moral history of a society without the transitory and debasing rhetoric of bureaucrats and dictators.

Soma   An intoxicating drink. It was brewed by Hindu priests in ancient times, with accompanying mystic rites and incantations, from the juice of some Indian plant, and was drunk by the BRAHMINS, as well as offered as libations to their gods. It was fabled to have been brought from heaven by a falcon or by the daughters of the Sun, and it was itself personified as a god. Soma is one of the most important of the old Vedic deities, a sort of Hindu BACCHUS. All the 114 hymns in the ninth book of the RIG VEDA are invocations in his honor. In later mythology, Soma represented the moon, which was supposed to be gradually drunk up by the gods and then filled up again.

The expression *to drink the Soma* means to become immortal, or as a god.

Somadeva (11th century)   Indian writer in Sanskrit, famous for his poetic folk stories in KATHĀSARITSĀGARA. Somadeva's tales gave a vivid picture of the life and customs of India and served as the basis for much subsequent Sanskrit literature. The *Vētalapanchavimsati* is a particularly popular set of tales frequently excerpted from the body of the main work.

Somerville, E[dith Anna] O[eone] (1861–1949)   Irish novelist who collaborated with Martin Ross, the pen name of Somerville's cousin Violet Florence Martin (1865–1915), on a series of humorous novels about the rural Irish gentry. Among their collaborative efforts were *The Real Charlotte* (1894), *Some Experiences of an Irish R. M.* (1899), and *In Mr. Knox's Country* (1915).

Sometimes a Great Notion   See KESEY, KEN.

Somnus   In Roman mythology, the god of Sleep, the son of Night (Nox), and the brother of Death (Mors).

Sondheim, Stephen [Joshua] (1930–   )   American lyricist and composer of musical comedies. He first appeared on Broadway as a lyricist with *West Side Story* (1957; music by Leonard Bernstein) and *Gypsy* (1959; music by Jule Styne). After that he preferred to write his own music; he has contributed a series of innovative musicals to the Broadway theatre. His lyrics are intricately crafted with much use of internal rhyme; they project the ambiguities and uncertainties of human relationships. His songs have been among the most complex ever written for the commercial theatre. His principal musicals include *A Funny Thing Happened on the Way to the Forum* (1962), *Company* (1970), *Follies* (1971), *A Little Night Music* (1973), *Pacific Overtures* (1976), *Sweeney Todd, the Demon Barber of Fleet Street* (1979), and *Sunday in the Park with George* (1984; PULITZER PRIZE).

Sonette an Orpheus, Die   See SONNETS TO ORPHEUS, THE.

Song of Bernadette, The (Das Lied von Bernadette, 1941; tr 1942)   A novel by Franz WERFEL, concerning the life of Saint BERNADETTE OF LOURDES. Werfel, who was in France when the Germans invaded in 1940, is said to have taken refuge in the church of St. Bernadette and to have vowed to dedicate a book to the saint if he should escape. He did escape to the U.S. in 1940, and the novel appeared shortly afterward.

Song of Igor's Campaign, The (Slovo o polku Igorevye, late 12th century)   An anonymous Russian heroic poem, also known as *The Igor Tale*. Describing the ill-fated campaign of a Russian prince against the roaming Polovtsy tribes in 1185, it is regarded as one of the greatest literary masterpieces in Russian written before PUSHKIN's work. Rather than strictly an epic poem, the work is a mixture of epic, lyric, and sometimes oratorical styles. The only manuscript of the poem was discovered in the late 18th century. An edition of it was published in 1800, and the original manuscript was destroyed in the Moscow fire of 1812. Some scholars have expressed doubts about its genuineness, although a literary forger with such poetic talents could hardly have remained anonymous. The work is now generally accepted as authentic.

Song of Lawino   See P'BITEK, OKOT.

Song of Myself (1855)   A poem by Walt WHITMAN. Nearly two thousand lines long, it is probably Whitman's most important poem, containing his major themes. The poet celebrates himself; encompassing all, he gives everything significance. The poet-prophet sees the equality and the beauty of all things and all people; in his huge catalogues, he moves through space and time, the poet of wickedness as well as goodness. The grass, "a uniform hieroglyphic" transpiring from the graves of men and women, testifies to immortality and cyclical rebirth. Sounding his "barbaric yawp," Whitman departs, dissolving into the universe. If he is sought, he advises, "look for me under your bootsoles." His *Song*, containing the "origin of all poems," direct experience of life, is "good health" to its reader.

Song of Solomon, The   One of the books of the OLD TESTAMENT, "the song of songs." A love IDYLL, it was universally ascribed to SOLOMON until the 19th century; critics now consider it of later date. It is interpreted as an allegory of the union between Jesus and his Church more frequently than as a type of Oriental love poem.

Song of the Lark, The (1915)   A novel by Willa CATHER. The author said this was both her favorite novel and the one that satisfied her least. It tells the story of Thea Kronborg, a Colorado girl, the daughter of a Swedish clergyman, who has a talent for music. She goes to Chicago to study, has an unhappy love affair with Fred Ottenburg, a wealthy young man who cannot obtain a divorce to marry her, and eventually becomes a soprano at the Metropolitan Opera House in New York City, famous for her Wagnerian roles. Thea is to some extent drawn from the famous Wagnerian singer Olive Fremstad.

Song of the Open Road (1856)   A poem by Walt WHITMAN. The road on which the poet travels, and on which he encounters and accepts all things, becomes symbolic of life. The universe itself is a road "for traveling souls."

Songs of Innocence (1789) and **Songs of Experience** (1794)   Two series of poems, subtitled *Showing the Two Contrary States of the Human Soul*, by William BLAKE. The first group exults in the omnipresence of divine love and sympathy, even in face of sorrow; the second group, gloomy in tone, opposes the first and deals with the power of evil. Innocence and experience are two opposing states of the human soul; the poems of one group are set against the poems of the other. Thus we have "Infant Joy" against "Infant Sorrow," "The Blossom" against "The Sick Rose," "The Lamb" against THE TIGER, and "The Divine Image" against "The Human Abstract." Often the same subject is treated in each group, as in "The Chimney Sweeper" and "A Little Boy Lost." This dualistic thinking, so characteristic of Blake, is set forth in his most important prose work, THE MARRIAGE OF HEAVEN AND HELL.

sonnet   In prosody, a fourteen-line poem of a set rhyme scheme and movement. In English the sonnet is written in heroic verse, i.e., iambic pentameter. The earliest sonnet form was the Italian or Petrarchan sonnet, so called after PETRARCH, its earliest major practitioner. Apparently the form developed after long experimentation from a kind of "little song" (*sonetto* in Italian and *sonet* in Provençal, from Latin *sonus*, "sound"). The 13th-century Italian poet Guittone of Arezzo (1230–94) established its rules. In structure it falls into the octave, or first eight lines, which state the proposition, and the sestet, or last six, which contain the resolution. A break between the octave and the sestet, and a minor thought-division between lines four and five and eleven and twelve, are standard in the form. The rhyme scheme is a-b-b-a, a-b-b-a in the octave, and either c-d-e, c-d-e or c-d-c, d-c-d in the sestet. The Italian sonnet form was introduced in England early in the 16th century by Wyatt and Surrey, and sonnets and sonnet sequences, usually upon the subject of love, were soon a literary fashion.

However, English writers were not satisfied with the Italian form, and soon were experimenting with what became the English, or Shakespearean, sonnet, so called because SHAKESPEARE was the greatest writer to use the form. As in the Italian sonnet, the rhyme scheme largely determines its movement. Rhymed a-b-a-b, c-d-c-d, e-f-e-f, g-g, it usually retains the Italianate break in thought between octave and sestet, but the epigrammatic force of the final couplet is so strong that it changes the whole character of the form; a major break comes between the twelfth and thirteenth lines, and this sometimes becomes the main thought division of the poem.

Writers of sonnet sequences in the 16th century include Sir Philip SIDNEY, Michael DRAYTON, Edmund SPENSER,

and Shakespeare. MILTON, WORDSWORTH, KEATS, Elizabeth Barrett BROWNING, and Christina ROSSETTI have written notable sonnets and sonnet sequences, in both the Italian and the Shakespearean forms. In the 20th century the sonnet has lost none of its popularity, having been written by Edwin Arlington ROBINSON, Edna St. Vincent MILLAY, E. E. CUMMINGS, W. H. AUDEN, and many others.

The two kinds of sonnet, first the Italian and then the Shakespearean, are illustrated in the following examples:

> Much have I travell'd in the realms of gold,
> And many goodly states and kingdoms seen;
> Round many western islands have I been
> Which bards in fealty to Apollo hold.
> Oft of one wide expanse had I been told
> That deep-brow'd Homer ruled as his demesne:
> Yet did I never breathe its pure serene
> Till I heard Chapman speak out loud and bold:
> Then felt I like some watcher of the skies
> When a new planet swims into his ken;
> Or like stout Cortez, when with eagle eyes
> He stared at the Pacific—and all his men
> Look'd at each other with a wild surmise—
> Silent, upon a peak in Darien.
>   John Keats, "On First Looking into Chapman's Homer"

> Shall I compare thee to a summer's day?
> Thou art more lovely and more temperate:
> Rough winds do shake the darling buds of May,
> And summer's lease hath all too short a date:
>
> Sometime too hot the eye of heaven shines,
> And often is his gold complexion dimm'd:
> And every fair from fair sometime declines,
> By chance, or nature's changing course, untrimm'd.
>
> But thy eternal summer shall not fade
> Nor lose possession of that fair thou owest;
> Nor shall Death brag thou wanderest in his shade,
> When in eternal lines to time thou growest:
>
> So long as men can breathe, or eyes can see,
> So long lives this, and this gives life to thee.
>   Shakespeare, Sonnet XVIII

sonnet sequence   A collection of SONNETS in which there is a discernible, if only vague, narrative or psychological development. The effect is like STANZAS in a long poem, but each sonnet retains its own force and independence. In PETRARCH's *Rime* (*Verses*), the antecedent of most European and English sequences, the sonnets are mixed with MADRIGALS and *canzoni* (see CANZONE), but they are the chief vehicles of the story of the poet's love for Laura. Outstanding examples in English include Sidney's ASTROPHEL AND STELLA, Spenser's *Amoretti* (1595), and THE SONNETS OF SHAKESPEARE.

Sonnets from the Portuguese (1850)   A collection of sonnets by Elizabeth Barrett BROWNING, expressing the poet's love for her husband, Robert BROWNING, and presented to him as a gift. The basis for the title is probably the series of sonnets of the great 16th-century Portuguese poet Luiz de CAMÕES. The forty-third sonnet in Mrs. Browning's series begins with the well-known line, "How do I love thee? Let me count the ways."

Sonnets of Shakespeare, The (printed 1609)   A series of 154 sonnets by SHAKESPEARE. Probably composed between 1593 and 1601, they are written in the form of three quatrains and a couplet that has come to be known as Shakespearean (see SONNET). Influenced by, and often reacting against, the popular sonnet sequences of the time, notably Sir Philip Sidney's ASTROPHEL AND STELLA, Shakespeare's sonnets are among the finest examples of their kind. They fall into two groups, Sonnets 1–126 addressed to a beloved friend, a handsome and noble young man, and Sonnets 127–152 to a malign but fascinating "Dark Lady" whom the poet loves in spite of himself and in spite of her unworthiness. It is frequently suggested that the stolen mistress of Sonnets 40–42 is the Dark Lady; the poet's complaint in the second group indicates that she has been false to him with his friend. Several themes recur throughout the series, notably the inevitable decay brought by Time, and the immortalization of beauty and love in poetry. The final two poems (153–154), which do not seem to fit anywhere, are adaptations of a Greek epigram and were possibly early poetic exercises.

Critics disagree as to whether the *Sonnets* form a coherent and unified sequence, and whether they are simply fictional pieces written according to the Petrarchan conventions of the day or deep expressions of Shakespeare's intimate life. Perhaps the safest general conclusion is that the *Sonnets* fall into several related groups within the two main divisions, and that, because of their intensity of feeling, many if not most of them sprang out of the poet's personal experience. The dedication of the 1609 printing to a "Mr. W. H." has led many scholars to identify the beloved youth of the first group as Henry Wriothesley, earl of Southampton, to whom Shakespeare had dedicated *Venus and Adonis* (1593) and *The Rape of Lucrece* (1594). Another theory is that William Herbert, earl of Pembroke, is the object of the dedication (as he was of the First Folio edition of Shakespeare's plays in 1623), although he was only in his teens during the period in which the poems were probably written.

Sonnets to Orpheus, The (Die Sonette an Orpheus, 1923; tr 1936)   A cycle of sonnets by Rainer Maria RILKE. The sonnets are free and varied in form and center about the myth of ORPHEUS. One of the main ideas in the cycle is that in order to realize his true essence, man must make his nature fluid, must be capable of constant inner metamorphoses in order to exist on a par with the varied and changing world about him. Death is only one metamorphosis among many. Similar ideas may be found in the later poetry of Stefan GEORGE.

Son of the Middle Border, A (1917)   An autobiographical narrative by Hamlin GARLAND. Garland tells of the westward migration of the Garland and McClintock families and of his own boyhood in the Middle West. Although he writes feelingly of the grandeur of the prairie, he also describes the bleakness and hardship of farm life that forced men like his father into what was by then a fruitless quest from frontier to frontier. The book was the first of an eight-volume autobiography.

Sons and Lovers (1913)   A novel, autobiographical in character, by D. H. LAWRENCE. It deals with the family background, childhood, adolescence, and young manhood of Paul Morel, sensitive and talented son of an English coal miner in Nottinghamshire. His mother, Gertrude, the educated daughter of Puritanical middle-class parents, has married the miner in the heat of physical attraction. The marriage soon disintegrates; Walter Morel takes to drink and beats his wife and children, and Mrs. Morel pours all her possessive love upon her sons, especially Paul. The novel is concerned with Paul's painful introduction to the commercial world, his discovery of books and art, his growing discontent with his background of poverty and gloom, and his developing talent for painting. It records his love affairs with MIRIAM and with Clara Dawes. Because of the strong bond of love between him and his mother, he is never able to give his affection wholly to either of the women. After his mother dies, he sets out on an independent life and rejects both Miriam and Clara.

The novel, which was attacked on its publication because of its frankness in dealing with sexual matters, is more naturalistic than Lawrence's later work. It is remarkable for its portrayal of English mining life, its vivid characterizations, and its poetic descriptions of nature.

sons of Ben   English poets such as Thomas CAREW, Robert HERRICK, Richard LOVELACE, and John SUCKLING, who acknowledged Ben JONSON as their literary "father." Like him, they emulated the ease and polish of the Latin lyricists. The group is also called "the tribe of Ben" or (most commonly now) the CAVALIER POETS. It was their custom to meet with Jonson regularly at the Apollo Room of the Devil Tavern in London, membership in the "tribe" implying a certain convivial as well as poetic relationship.

Sons of Mil   See TUATHA DÉ DANANN.

Sontag, Susan (1933–   )   American essayist, philosopher, novelist, short-story writer, and filmmaker. Sontag is a leading observer of new trends in literature, art, film, photography, and culture. Her elucidation of the word "camp" in *Partisan Review* (1964) was widely quoted and later collected along with other essays in *Against Interpretation* (1966). The title essay is a plea for less analysis of works of art and more reliance on the sensory pleasures they afford. *On Photography* (1976) is an investigation of photography as a communicative medium, while *Illness as Metaphor* (1978) examines the ways in which sickness (specifically cancer) is viewed in literature and in modern society. Her novels *The Benefactor* (1963) and *Death Kit* (1967), short fiction collected in *I, Etcetera* (1978), and films *Duet for Cannibals* (1970) and *Brother Carl* (1974) can be seen as experimental applications of her theories of art. *A Susan Sontag Reader* appeared in 1982.

Sonya   The heroine of Dostoyevsky's CRIME AND PUNISHMENT, a saintly, gentle young woman who has been forced into prostitution to support her father, the drunken MARMELADOV, her stepmother, and their children.

Sophists   Greek philosophers of the 5th century BC, masters of the arts of rhetoric and persuasion. They are considered the first professional teachers of Greece and the first to give practical help in politics. Since rhetorical training was the key to political power, these teachers emphasized the arts of persuasion. Originally, *sophist* was the Greek term for any skilled craftsman or artist; however, it was later applied to anyone who devoted himself to wisdom. Early Sophists such as GORGIAS and Protagoras of Abdera were conservative: they affirmed things as they were and stood for the rule of law and order. The later Sophists, Hippias, Antiphon, Callicles, and Thrasymachus, were more radical; they opposed "nature" or man's individual instincts and desires to law or convention, and were the first to set forth the doctrine, later criticized by PLATO, THUCYDIDES, and ARISTOTLE, that might makes right. Because the Sophists were in the service of the rich, a class inimical to democracy and held in contempt by Plato and Aristotle, the word Sophist was given a pejorative sense by these two men: they thought the object of the teachers was not genuine knowledge, and sophist in the general sense has come to mean anyone who makes the worse reason appear the better. The Sophists and their methods were caricatured in THE CLOUDS by Aristophanes, who erroneously placed SOCRATES among them.

Sophocles (496–406 BC)   Greek tragic dramatist. He was born at Kolonos, near Athens, and in his own day was probably the most generally admired of the three great Athenian dramatists. He was known not only for his poetic and dramatic gifts, but also for his musical skill and his fine appearance; he was the CHORAGOS when the victory over Xerxes at SALAMIS was celebrated in Athens in 480 BC. In addition to his work as a playwright, he also held military and political positions, and was a priest of ASCLEPIUS. He was only twenty-seven when, with his first tragedy, he defeated AESCHYLUS in the playwrights' contest. Evidence of his special position in the public esteem is the fact that ARISTOPHANES, who ridiculed EURIPIDES and, to some extent, Aeschylus in THE FROGS, spoke only with the greatest respect of Sophocles.

Although Sophocles wrote well over one hundred plays, only seven tragedies and a part of a SATYR PLAY remain. Best known of the plays are the three about OEDIPUS and his children—*Oedipus Tyrannos, Oedipus at Colonus*, and ANTIGONE—and the ELECTRA. He also wrote plays on AJAX,

The Women of Trachis (see HERACLES), *Philoctetes*, and the *Ichneutai*, his fragmentary satyr play about the birth of HERMES. It was Sophocles who added a third speaking actor to the two used by Aeschylus, increased the size of the chorus, and abandoned the use of the trilogy in favor of single plays—his three plays on Oedipus were written over a period of forty years.

Whereas both Aeschylus and Euripides, in different ways, may be said to have had a progressive attitude toward religion and social custom, Sophocles was more conservative. His chief interest was in the search for truth and self-understanding on the part of the individual in relation to the existing moral order, as in the case of Oedipus' relentless seeking after the murderer of Laius, even though that knowledge brings with it his own destruction. His best dramas have never been excelled in their power and economy of expression.

A doubtful but highly popular tradition about Sophocles is that at the age of ninety he was hailed into court by his son Iophon as too senile to manage his own affairs. To prove the absurdity of this contention, Sophocles merely read a choral ode he had just written for the *Oedipus at Colonus*. As a matter of fact, Iophon himself became a tragic dramatist, as did Sophocles' grandson by his second son.

Sophonisba (d 204 BC)   Daughter of Hasdrubal of Carthage, sister of HANNIBAL. Like her brother, Sophonisba was reared to detest Rome. Originally affianced to Prince Masinissa of Numidia, she was married, for political reasons, to Syphax, Masinissa's rival. Masinissa defeated Syphax in battle and captured Sophonisba, but was compelled by Rome to give her up. Rather than fall into Roman hands, she willingly took the poison given to her by Masinissa. She is the subject of tragedies by CORNEILLE, VOLTAIRE, TRISSINO, ALFIERI, and John MARSTON, among others.

Sorbonne   The institution of theology, science, and literature in Paris founded by Robert de Sorbon, canon of Cambrai, in 1252. In 1808 the buildings, erected by RICHELIEU in the 17th century, were given to the University, and since 1821 it has been called the *Académie universitaire de Paris*.

Sordello (c1200–c1270)   Italian TROUBADOUR who wrote in Provençal. Sordello wrote a conventional didactic poem, *L'Ensenhamen d'onor*, and a bitter complaint against poor rulers, *Serventese* (1237), written on the death of his patron Blacatz. His fame, however, comes from his appearance in Dante's *Purgatorio* as a too zealous patriot and in Robert Browning's psychological poem SORDELLO.

Sordello (1840)   A poem by Robert BROWNING. Against the background of restless southern Europe of the 13th century, it projects the conflicting thoughts of a poet about the best way of making his influence felt, whether by personal action or the power of song. TENNYSON said that he had done his best with *Sordello*, but there were only two lines he understood—the first and the last—and they were both untrue:

Who will, may hear Sordello's story told.

Who would has heard Sordello's story told.

Sorel, Agnès (also called Mlle de Beauté, 1422–1450)   Politically influential mistress (1444–50) of the French king Charles VII.

Sorel, Georges (1847–1922)   French advocate of social progress. A proponent of revolutionary syndicalism, Sorel published his most famous work, *Réflexions sur la violence*, in 1908. A spiritual revitalization of all sectors of society would occur, he believed, through spontaneous outbreaks of violence which would engender widespread enthusiasm and release human energy. His revolutionary doctrine did not depend upon an ideology; he emphasized not the source of the violence, whether proletariat or bourgeois, but its effect. At the turn of the century, he looked to the labor unions for revolutionary action, and later published *Matériaux pour une théorie du prolétariat* (1919). In an abrupt shift of sympathies, he collaborated with royalists and nationalists and finally transferred his allegiance to LENIN and MUSSOLINI. Among Sorel's works are *Le Procès de Socrate* (1889), an anti-intellectualist tract; *Introduction à l'économie moderne* (1903), a hopeful view of technology controlled and used to good purpose by man; and *Les Illusions de progrès* (1908).

Sorel, Julien   The protagonist of Stendhal's novel THE RED AND THE BLACK. Julien Sorel is a young man motivated by boundless ambition. Calculating and egotistical, he uses his love affairs to serve his drive for power. *Le Rouge* represents the red of the military while *Le Noir* is the black of the clergy, which for Julien, living in the aftermath of the Napoleonic dreams of glory, represents the one channel then open for advancement.

Sorrows of Young Werther, The (Die Leiden des jungen Werthers, 1774; final version 1787)   A short novel by GOETHE, the first great popular success of his career. It is the story, in Goethe's words, of an artistically inclined young man "gifted with deep, pure sentiment and penetrating intelligence, who loses himself in fantastic dreams and undermines himself with speculative thought until finally, torn by hopeless passions, especially by infinite love, he shoots himself in the head." Werther's infinite love for an uncomplicated girl named Lotte who, however, marries a man with a much steadier, more bourgeois temperament than Werther's, at least partly reflects Goethe's own experiences. In its epistolary form, the book was influenced by Samuel RICHARDSON, and in its imagery and language by MACPHERSON's *Ossianic Poems*. The book caused a wave of suicides among young German romantics. See ZERRISSENHEIT.

Sōtō   See ZEN BUDDHISM.

Sot-weed Factor, The (1960; rev 1967)   A ribald pastiche of various 18th-century literary conventions by John BARTH. The novel centers on the PICARESQUE adventures of young Ebenezer Cooke, who, having devoted himself to poetry and chastity, journeys from England to the New World to take charge of "Malden," a tobacco plantation on Maryland's eastern shore. In a series of convoluted plots and counterplots filled with unbelievable coincidences, disguises, and reversals, the questing hero finds himself in the middle of political intrigue and a bawdy celebration of physical appetites.

Soulier de satin, Le   See SATIN SLIPPER, THE.

Sound and the Fury, The (1929)   A novel by William FAULKNER. Often considered Faulkner's best novel, the book is a radical experiment in form and technique. Three of the novel's four sections are the interior monologues of the three COMPSON brothers. With their hypochondriac mother and their vanished sister, Caddy, they are the last members of a decaying aristocratic family in Mississippi. The first section, seen through the eyes of the idiot Benjy, is literally "a tale told by an idiot, full of sound and fury." The second follows the thoughts of Quentin, a Harvard student whose world, built on a dying view of family honor and on his abnormally close ties to his sister, Caddy, has been shattered by her seduction and hasty, loveless marriage.

The third section is a first-person narrative by greedy, petty-minded Jason, who has kept for himself the money Caddy has been sending for the support of her illegitimate daughter, Quentin. The final section is a third-person narrative focused on Dilsey, the black cook, whose patience and compassion are implicitly contrasted with the self-absorption and self-destructiveness of the Compsons.

Soupault, Philippe (1897–   )   French poet, novelist, and critic. At first closely associated with DADA, Soupault and André BRETON founded SURREALISM with the publication of *Les Champs magnétiques* (1921). He later left the group, though he remained faithful to surrealist principles, and wrote novels describing the social and moral degeneration of the 1920s, such as *Les Dernières Nuits de Paris* (1928; tr *Last Nights of Paris*, 1929). *Le Temps des assassins* (1945; tr *Age of Assassins*, 1946) is the story of his imprisonment by the Nazis. His critical works include books on William Blake (1928), Charlie Chaplin (*Charlot*, 1931) James Joyce (1944), and Alfred de Musset (1956). Much of Soupault's verse is collected in *Poèmes et poésies* (1973).

Sousa, John Philip (1854–1932)   American bandmaster and composer of marches. Among the best known of these are "Stars and Stripes Forever" (1897) and "El Capitan," from Sousa's comic opera of that name (1896). He was known as the "March King."

Souster, Raymond (1921–   )   Canadian poet and editor. Souster helped to disseminate new Canadian poetry in the 1940s and 1950s, especially through the Contact Press of Toronto. He is himself the undisputed poet of that city, which he celebrates in short poems of strong rhythm and colloquial manner. His major collections are *The Color of the Times* (1964), *Ten Elephants on Yonge Street* (1965), *So Far So Good* (1969), and *Selected Poems* (1972). Later volumes include *Double-Header* (1975) and *Extra Innings* (1977). His entire oeuvre has been collected in five volumes (1980–84).

Southampton, Henry Wriothesley, 3rd earl of (1573–1624)   English politician and soldier, patron of SHAKESPEARE and other Elizabethan poets. Shakespeare's VENUS AND ADONIS and RAPE OF LUCRECE are dedicated to Southampton. He was imprisoned for his part in Essex's rebellion (1601), but was released by James I. In 1605 he helped to equip an expedition to Virginia.

Southern, Terry (1926–   )   American novelist, short-story writer, and screenwriter. Southern is a satirist who relies on shock tactics and outrageous humor. He is best known as the coauthor of *Candy* (1958; with Mason Hoffenberg), first published in Paris under the pseudonym Maxwell Kenton, and later (1964) a best-seller in the U.S. A parody of CANDIDE, it chronicles the bizarre sexual generosity of an innocent coed in search of her father. His other work includes *The Magic Christian* (1959), *Blue Movie* (1970), and short stories collected in *Red-Dirt Marijuana and Other Tastes* (1967). He has written, or helped write, several screenplays, including *Dr. Strangelove* (1963), *Barbarella* (1968), *Easy Rider* (1968), and *End of the Road* (1969).

Southern Review, The (1935–1942)   American literary quarterly founded at Louisiana State University, the third magazine in the South to bear such a title. Under the editorship of C. W. Pipkin, Cleanth BROOKS, and Robert Penn WARREN, it became one of the most distinguished of the LITTLE MAGAZINES of the 1930s, printing articles on literary criticism—particularly those on NEW CRITICISM—philosophy, and politics, as well as stories and poems by outstanding contemporary authors. Kenneth BURKE, Katherine Anne PORTER, John Crowe RANSOM, and Allen TATE were among its regular contributors. The magazine was revived in 1965 by Lewis P. Simpson and Donald C. Sanford. The new series continued to publish verse and short fiction but retained a primary interest in criticism.

Southey, Robert (1774–1843)   English romantic poet, one of the so-called LAKE POETS. Though a leader in his day, he is considered by 20th-century critics to have been of mediocre talent. He wrote a great deal of verse, including epic and didactic poems, but is now remembered chiefly for his place in literary history, as the author of the much-anthologized ballad "The Battle of Blenheim" (1798), and for his prose criticism and short biographies of NELSON (1813), WESLEY (1830), and COWPER (1833). In his youth, Southey joined with Coleridge in the utopian scheme of *pantisocracy* and married Edith Fricker, whose

sister married Coleridge. His early liberalism was superseded by a conservatism that was attacked in satire by BYRON. Southey was POET LAUREATE (1813–43). In the last years of his life his mind gave way.

South Sea Scheme (or South Sea Bubble)   A stock-jobbing scheme devised by Sir John Blunt, a lawyer, in 1710, and floated by the earl of Oxford in the following year. The object of the company was to buy up the national debt in return for the sole privilege of holding an extensive trade monopoly in the South Seas and in South America. Spain refused to give trading facilities, so the money was used in other speculative ventures and, by careful "rigging" of the market, £100 shares were run up to over ten times that sum. The company at times rivaled in influence even the Bank of England (incorporated in 1694); but the highly inflated value of its stock caused, in 1720, England's first great stock-market panic, in which thousands were ruined.

Southwell, Robert (c1561–1595)   English poet and author of religious writings. Southwell was ordained a Jesuit priest in Rome in 1584; two years later he was sent, at his own request, as a missionary to England, where his presence (after forty days) was legally treason. In 1592, after six years of secret service to English Catholics, he was arrested. He was imprisoned and repeatedly tortured for three years, and hanged in 1595. His religious tracts, such as *Mary Magdalen's Funeral Tears* (pub 1609), were written before his imprisonment and probably fairly widely circulated in manuscript. Most of his poetry, which is concerned with the spiritual life, was composed while he was in prison. *Saint Peter's Complaint* was published anonymously in 1595 and followed shortly by *Maeoniae*, a supplementary volume. A *Fourfold Meditation of the Four Last Things* was published in 1606. THE BURNING BABE, which was highly praised by Ben JONSON, is Southwell's best-known poem.

South Wind (1917)   A novel by Norman DOUGLAS. It is set on the Capri-like island of NEPENTHE, and is concerned with the group of exotic, odd, and learned characters who live there during a spring "season." The novel is less a story than a symposium—a series of long hedonistic and skeptical discussions of ethics, religion, art, food, and many other matters. These discussions are interspersed with Douglas's lightly satirical essays on the island's history and mythology.

Soyinka, Wole (pen name of Akinwande Oluwole Soyinka, 1934–   )   Nigerian poet, playwright, and essayist. Soyinka was educated at the universities of Ibadan and Leeds. While in England, he was associated with the English Stage Company and the Royal Court Theatre. He returned to Nigeria and became instrumental in developing an indigenous theatre. To that end, he founded two theatre companies (the 1960 Masks and the Orisun Repertory), directed the school of drama at Ibadan, and contributed numerous plays, many of which are preoccupied with the themes of sacrifice and martyrdom and draw heavily on Nigerian folk motifs, such as *A Dance of the Forests* (1960), *The Lion and the Jewel* (1962), *The Road* (1965), *Kongi's Harvest* (1966), *Madmen and Specialists* (1970), *Death and the King's Horseman* (1975), and *A Play of Giants* (1984). A man of prodigious literary talent, Soyinka is one of Africa's most productive writers. His works reflect his ardent concern with the health of the state and the freedom of individuals (he has been jailed on several occasions for his insistence on personal liberty). Among his volumes of sensitive, highly rhythmic poetry are *Idanre and Other Poems* (1967), *Poems from Prison* (1969; U.S. *A Shuttle in the Crypt*, 1972), and *Ogun Abibiman* (1976). *The Interpreters* (1965) and *The Season of Anomy* (1974) are novels. He has also edited various literary journals, most notably, *Transition*, and the volume *Poems of Black Africa* (1974). *Myth, Literature and the African World* (1976) is a collection of his essays. *Aké: The Years of Childhood*, an autobiography, appeared in 1981. In 1986 he was awarded the NOBEL PRIZE in Literature.

Spade, Sam   A private detective created by the novelist Dashiell HAMMETT. His first and most significant appearance was in THE MALTESE FALCON. Spade, a rough, tough, realistic man, was a far cry from the dilettantes who had been featured in most detective fiction up to his appearance.

Spanish-American War   A war in 1898 between the U.S. and Spain, stemming from a native revolt on the Spanish-held island of Cuba, in which Americans had long had a political and economic interest. The sensational reports of the "yellow press" about Spanish atrocities in Cuba aroused American resentment against Spain, as did the publication of a letter written by Dupuy de Lôme, Spanish minister to the U.S., in which he referred to President McKinley in derogatory terms. War hysteria reached its height when an explosion destroyed the U.S. battleship *Maine* in Havana harbor with the loss of two hundred sixty lives; although a naval court of inquiry could not discover who was to blame for the disaster, it was popularly attributed to Spanish agents. Although McKinley had previously followed a peaceful policy, he asked Congress to declare war on April 11, 1898. U.S. victories in the Philippines and Cuba led Spain to sue for peace in July. According to the terms of the treaty of Paris, Spain agreed to Cuban independence and ceded the Philippines to the U.S. for $20 million, as well as Puerto Rico and Guam. The conflict marked the emergence of the U.S. as a world power. See ROOSEVELT, THEODORE; WHITE MAN'S BURDEN.

Spanish Tragedy, The (prod between 1584 and 1589)   A drama by Thomas KYD. A bloody tragedy of revenge in the popular Senecan style, *The Spanish Tragedy* deals with political intrigue between the Spanish and the Portuguese that explodes in the murder of Horatio, the son of the marshal of Spain, Hieronimo. Horatio, in the arbor with his beloved Bel-Imperia, is slain by her brother and

the prince of Portugal, who wants to marry her. Horatio's body is left hanging in the arbor, where Hieronimo finds it and goes mad with grief. Finally Hieronimo conspires with Bel-Imperia to stage a play at a royal party at which the murderers are present. The villains are lured into taking parts in the play and are killed, and Hieronimo, to prevent himself from being tortured into naming his confederates, kills himself. In 1592 a prologue was added to the play, called *The First Part of Jeronimo* [sic], *or the Warres of Portugal*. This gives a somewhat different version of the story and is thought by some critics to be the work of someone other than Kyd.

Spark, Muriel (1918–   )   Scottish novelist, poet, and critic. Spark's early critical studies include *Child of Light* (1951), about Mary SHELLEY, *John Masefield* (1953), and *Emily Brontë* (1953). In 1954 she converted to Roman Catholicism, and later turned to the writing of witty, highly satirical novels, including *Robinson* (1958), *Memento Mori* (1958), *The Ballad of Peckham Rye* (1960), and *The Girls of Slender Means* (1963). Her books are carefully structured and, despite a sometimes glib surface, are concerned with serious moral issues. Her best-known novel is *The Prime of Miss Jean Brodie* (1961), about a schoolteacher and her girl students, which was successfully adapted for the stage and film. Her other novels include *The Mandelbaum Gate* (1965), an ambitious work set in divided Jerusalem; *The Abbess of Crewe* (1974), about a Watergate-like power struggle among nuns; *The Takeover* (1976), which shows the rich coping with shifts in global monetary power; *Territorial Rights* (1979), a gracefully plotted novel of Venetian intrigue; and *Loitering with Intent* (1981), which shares with her other works a fascination with the balance of good and evil, but deals, more than most of her other works, with the world of the writer's mind. *The Only Problem* (1984), a novel about the sufferings of a millionaire Canadian writer living in France whose estranged wife becomes involved with terrorists, conveys the subtle underpinnings of suspense, wit, and verbal skill that characterize Spark's novels.

Sparks, Jared (1789–1866)   American historian and editor. After his undergraduate years at Harvard, Sparks was ordained (1819) in a Unitarian church by William Ellery CHANNING. He served as pastor in Baltimore for four years, in two of which (1821–23) he was also chaplain of the U.S. House of Representatives. He returned to Boston as owner-editor (1824–30) of the *North American Review*, making it the most influential magazine in the U.S. Meanwhile, he had begun to compile his twelve-volume edition of *The Writings of George Washington* (1834–37). He also edited *The Works of Benjamin Franklin* (1836–40) and two series of *The Library of American Biography* (1834–38; 1844–47), to which he contributed several sketches. Although his editorial methods were often faulty, Sparks rescued many important documents from oblivion and stimulated interest in American history. In 1839 he joined the Harvard faculty as the first professor of American history in any American university. From 1849 to 1853 he served as president of Harvard.

Sparta (or Lacedaemon)   The ancient capital of Laconia, in the southeast corner of the Peloponnesus. The victorious opponent of Athens in the PELOPONNESIAN WAR, Sparta was also opposed to that city in spirit. Aristocratic, conservative, and militaristic, the Spartans took pride in their courage, endurance, frugality, and discipline. Boys were taken from their mothers at the age of seven and lived in barracks until they were thirty. No deformed Spartan children were allowed to live, and the newborn were washed in icy mountain streams. The Spartans were frugal even in speech, a fact that gave us the word laconic. Two famous figures of legend illustrate Spartan attitudes: the Spartan mother who, handing her son the shield he was to carry into battle, told him to come back either with it or on it; and the boy who, having hidden a stolen fox under his tunic, permitted it to gnaw his vitals rather than confess his theft. These characteristics were peculiar to the Dorian Sparta of Classical times. In the Mycenaean period, Sparta was known primarily as the capital of Menelaus' dominions, from which Helen was abducted by Paris.

Spartacus (d 71 BC)   Roman slave and gladiator. Spartacus led an insurrection of slaves (73–71 BC), during which he routed several armies; he was finally defeated and killed by the army of Crassus.

Sparti (Gr, "sown men")   Armed men. They grew from the dragon's teeth sown by CADMUS and by JASON (see ARGONAUTS). The dragon had guarded the sacred spring of ARES at Thebes. Both heroes defeated the Sparti by throwing a stone among them, which set them fighting each other to the death.

Specimen Days and Collect (1882)   A collection of notes and essays by Walt WHITMAN. The book begins with an account of the poet's youth, but concentrates on his Civil War experiences. Much of the material is adapted from notebooks Whitman kept during the period. Some reminiscences of his old age are included. The "Collect" is a group of literary essays.

Spectator, The (March 1711–December 1712)   A famous series of essays by Joseph ADDISON and Richard STEELE. In these essays, purportedly edited by the members of the fictional Spectator Club, Mr. Spectator, a shy, observant gentleman who has settled in London, provides a picture of the social life of the times, while the individual concerns of the club's other members, Sir Roger de COVERLEY, Will Honeycomb, Andrew Freeport, and Captain Sentry, add narrative depth and interest.

Speculations about Jakob (Mutmaßungen über Jakob, 1959; tr 1963)   A novel by Uwe JOHNSON consisting of pieced-together conversations, accounts, reflections, and speculations about Jakob Abs's life and his violent death. Jakob, a quiet, conscientious yard inspector for the East German railway, is committed to the socialist system,

although he has some reservations about the ways in which it is implemented by his government. He is in love with Gesine Cresspahl who has gone, however, to West Germany to work for NATO. Jakob is politely but persistently encouraged to persuade her to engage in espionage in the East. It is 1956, the Hungarian revolt is crushed, and Jakob joins Gesine in West Germany. Soon England and France drop bombs on Egypt in connection with the Suez crisis, and Jakob, again disillusioned, returns to East Germany. On the morning of his return he is crushed between two trains, one East-bound, one West-bound. Johnson leaves it to the reader to speculate on the reasons for Jakob's death and to consider the consequences of life in a divided world.

Speculum Meditantis (also known as Speculum Hominis or Mirour de l'omme, c1378?)   Norman-French poem by John GOWER, of thirty thousand lines in twelve-line stanzas. A didactic work, it describes the contest for men's souls between the seven vices, with all their offspring by the Devil, and the seven virtues, with their offspring by Reason. In doing so, it gives a detailed "mirror of men" of all classes in contemporary life. It concludes that all men are corrupt and must turn to the Virgin Mary for mercy and aid.

Spencer, Herbert (1820–1903)   English philosopher and social scientist. Spencer is known for his application of the scientific doctrines of evolution to philosophy and ethics, with a central principle, the "persistence of force," as the agent of all change, form, and organization in the knowable universe. In education, he scorned the study of the liberal arts and advocated that science be the chief subject of instruction.

Spencer's best-known works include *Principles of Psychology* (1855), and the ten-volume *System of Synthetic Philosophy*, the general title of the series that he announced in 1860 and to which he devoted the rest of his life. His *Autobiography* appeared in 1904.

Spender, Stephen [Harold] (1909–   )   English poet. Spender was a leading member of a group of English poets—including W. H. AUDEN, Christopher ISHERWOOD, Cecil DAY LEWIS, and Louis MACNEICE—who were Marxists in the 1930s. His poetry, especially in its later development, is more personal, lyrical, and romantic than that of his associates. Much of his work is characterized by imagery appropriate to an industrial and mechanical civilization, but it deals chiefly with his own emotional reactions as he contemplates poverty, suffering, and injustice or visualizes betterment of life in a socialist state. His *Selected Poems* appeared in 1964. His autobiography, *World within World* (1951), is particularly valuable for its portraits of his poet-friends and account of his own political beliefs and intellectual development. *The Thirties and After* (1978), a collection of criticism, essays, and journal entries, encapsulates fifty years of literary and political history.

Spender also wrote *Trial of a Judge* (1938), a poetic, political allegory. His works of fiction include two collections of short stories, *The Burning Cactus* (1936) and *Engaged in Writing and the Fool and the Princess* (1958), and a novel, *The Backward Son* (1940). He is also a prolific and sensitive author of criticism, such as the volumes *The Destructive Element* (1935), *The Creative Element* (1953), and *The Making of a Poem* (1962). He coedited (with Cyril CONNOLLY) the magazine *Horizon* during World War II, and coedited the Anglo-American magazine *Encounter* from 1953 to 1965. *Collected Poems: 1928–1985* appeared in 1986.

Spengler, Oswald (1880–1936)   German philosopher of history. Spengler's noted work *Der Untergang des Abendlandes* (*The Decline of the West*, 1918–22) reflects the pessimistic atmosphere in Germany after World War I. Spengler maintained that history has a natural development, in which every culture is a distinct organic form that grows, matures, and decays. He predicted a phase of "Caesarism" in the further development of Western culture, which, he believed, was in its last stage.

Spengler's attitude became very popular with the Nazi government, but he refused to enter into their persecution of the Jews. Being independently wealthy, he managed to exist in Germany, somewhat under a cloud, until the end of his life.

Spenser, Edmund (1552?–1599)   One of the greatest English poets, and the first major English writer to arise after CHAUCER. Born in London, Spenser was educated at the Merchant Taylors' School and Pembroke Hall, Cambridge. He was well acquainted with PLATO and ARISTOTLE, whose influences are clear in his works, with the Greek and Latin poets, and with the great Italian epics of TASSO and ARIOSTO. As early as 1569 he contributed some translations of PETRARCH and the French poet DU BELLAY to the *Theatre for Worldlings*, an edifying volume of anti-Catholic propaganda. Also in his youth he wrote the hymns "In Honor of Love" and "In Honor of Beauty" (not published until 1596), which show his debt to Platonism. While at Cambridge he met Gabriel Harvey, a scholar and something of a pedant, but nevertheless a faithful and helpful friend, and the model for Hobbinol in THE SHEPHEARDES CALENDER. Harvey may have introduced Spenser to Sir Philip SIDNEY, the nephew of the earl of Leicester; in any event, in 1578 Spenser became a member of Leicester's household, and during this time formed with Sidney, Dyer, and others a literary club known as the Areopagus. Probably from the discussions of this club came the theories expressed in Sidney's *Apologie for Poetrie* and Spenser's *The English Poete*, a critical work which is not extant. In 1579 Spenser published his first important work, *The Shepheardes Calender*. Dedicated to Sidney, it contained twelve eclogues in the style of VERGIL and MANTUANUS and is particularly notable for its use of various

meters and its vocabulary, enriched both by foreign borrowings and a reviving of older English words.

By this time Spenser had probably begun to work on his great epic, THE FAERIE QUEENE. Most of the following years were spent in Ireland, where he first went in 1580 as secretary to Lord Grey of Wilton, who had been appointed lord deputy of Ireland. In about 1587, Spenser was given possession of Castle Kilcolman in County Cork, and it was here that he wrote "Astrophel," an elegy on the death of Sidney. In 1589 he was visited by Sir Walter RALEIGH, who urged him to go to London to arrange for the publication of the first three books of *The Faerie Queene*, and promised to present him to Queen ELIZABETH. When Spenser returned to Ireland after an absence of nearly two years, he wrote his autobiographical pastoral COLIN CLOUTS COME HOME AGAINE (published, with "Astrophel," in 1595), in which he allegorically describes his voyage with Raleigh, his admiration for Elizabeth, and includes an attack on the intrigues at court. During his visit to London, meanwhile, Spenser had been received with favor by Elizabeth, had seen the publication (1590) of the first three books of *The Faerie Queene*, and had been granted a royal pension of fifty pounds a year. The year 1591 saw the publication of his *Complaints*, which included revised versions of some of the poems that had appeared in the *Theatre for Worldlings*; it also contained "The Teares of the Muses," a complaint on the current status of poetry, "The Ruines of Time," a lament on the deaths of Sidney and Leicester (see Robert DUDLEY), and "Mother Hubberds Tale," a satire in the form of an animal fable thought to be directed against Lord Burghley and the proposed marriage of Elizabeth to the French duc d'Alençon.

Spenser's courtship of Elizabeth Boyle probably occasioned most of the eighty-eight sonnets in the *Amoretti*, and his marriage to her in 1594 inspired his magnificent EPITHALAMION (pub with *Amoretti* in 1595). The PROTHALAMION, another marriage-poem, was written for the double wedding of the daughters of the earl of Worcester. In the same year appeared *Four Hymns to Love and Beauty*, the first two the early poems to earthly love and beauty, the latter two on their celestial counterparts. During the winter of 1595–96, he was again in London arranging for a reissuing of Books I–III of *The Faerie Queene* and the publication of the next three books. In 1598 he was recommended as sheriff of Cork; however, it was not long until the outbreak of Tyrone's rebellion, during which Castle Kilcolman was burned and Spenser forced to flee. He died shortly after in London, apparently in bad straits but probably not "for lack of bread," as Ben Jonson reported. He left two cantos and two stanzas on mutability (pub 1609), thought to have been intended for a future book of *The Faerie Queene*. A *View of the Present State of Ireland*, a prose defense of the repressive policy of Lord Grey of Wilton in Ireland, was not published until 1633.

A Protestant and a Platonist, Spenser was deeply concerned with the religio-historical problems of his age, and reflected in his work the Renaissance conception of poetry as the highest instrument of moral teaching. Deliberately archaic in style, he looked to Chaucer as the pure "well of English undefiled," but he was no mere imitator of his master, and gave to English poetry both an enriched, romantic language, lines marked by their running sweetness of diction, and stanzas—called Spenserian—adapted from ottava rima but made particularly his own. Both the SPENSERIAN STANZA and the archaic language contribute to the mythic romance of *The Faerie Queene*, enveloping the scenes of chivalry and adventure with a singularly appropriate mistiness of style. An epic to compare with the great epics of the classical world and of Renaissance Italy, *The Faerie Queene* is simultaneously a nationalistic paean to the greatness of Elizabeth and her England, an imaginative romance, and a moral allegory of the soul of man on his quest for salvation.

Spenserian school   A group of English poets, including William Basse, William Browne, Sir John DAVIES, and George Wither, who flourished in the first part of the 17th century. In opposition to a growing fashion for more self-conscious, intellectual, and ingenious verse, they preserved the simpler lyric and pastoral tradition of the early Elizabethans, their chief model being Edmund SPENSER. Their typical form was the PASTORAL or pastoral dialogue (ECLOGUE), and their verse was characteristically musical, pictorial, and allegorical.

Spenserian stanza   Stanza devised by Edmund Spenser for THE FAERIE QUEENE. Adapted from the Italian OTTAVA RIMA, it is a stanza of eight decasyllable lines concluded by a ninth, six-foot iambic line, or ALEXANDRINE, and rhymes a-b-a-b-b-c-b-c-c:

> A Gentle Knight was pricking on the plaine,
> Ycladd in mightie armes and silver shield,
> Wherein old dints of deepe woundes did remaine,
> The cruell markes of many a bloody fielde;
> Yet armes till that time did he never wield:
> His angry steede did chide his foming bitt,
> As much disdayning to the curbe to yield:
> Full jolly knight he seemed and faire did sitt,
> As one for knightly giusts and fierce encounters fitt.
>
> (*The Faerie Queene*, I, i)

It has the advantage of tending to be less rapid and more sonorous than the Italian form, while still retaining a sense of motion suitable for a long poem dealing with heroic exploits. It was later used by Byron in his CHILDE HAROLD'S PILGRIMAGE.

spheres   A particular concept in the Ptolemaic system of astronomy. The earth, as the center of the universe, was supposed to be surrounded by nine spheres of invisible space, the first seven carrying the "planets" as then known: (1) Diana or the Moon, (2) Mercury, (3) Venus, (4) Apollo or the Sun, (5) Mars, (6) Jupiter, and (7) Saturn. The

eighth, the Starry Sphere, carried the fixed stars, and the ninth, the Crystalline Sphere, was added by Hipparchus in the 2d century BC to account for the precession of the equinoxes. Finally, in the Middle Ages, was added a solid barrier that enclosed the universe and shut it off from Nothingness and the Empyrean. These last two spheres carried neither star nor planet. See MUSIC OF THE SPHERES.

Sphinx   (1) In Egypt, the Sphinx was usually represented as a wingless lion with the head and breast of a man, typifying the sun god, RA. Thousands of sphinxes were carved from stone in ancient Egypt. The most celebrated, the Great Sphinx (c2550 BC) probably erected by Khafre, is one of the earliest and measures two hundred feet in length.

(2) A monster of Greek mythology with the face of a woman, the body of a lion, and the wings of a bird. The offspring of Echidna and TYPHON or Orthus, she flew to Mount Phicium, near Thebes. There she propounded a riddle and devoured those young men who could not answer it. The most familiar version of this riddle, a common theme in folklore, is as follows: What walks on four legs in the morning, on two at midday, on three in the evening? When OEDIPUS gave the correct answer (man, who crawls as an infant, walks upright as an adult, and uses a staff in old age), the Sphinx killed herself in chagrin.

EMERSON has a poem entitled "The Sphinx" (1841), as does Oscar WILDE.

Spielhagen, Friedrich   (1829–1911)   German author of many realistic, politically liberal novels about the problems of his time, the most famous of which is the four-volume *Problematische Naturen* (1861; tr *Problematic Characters*, 1869), set during the revolution of 1848. As a literary theorist, Spielhagen advocated realism in his influential *Beiträge zur Theorie und Technik des Romans* (*Contributions to the Theory and Practice of the Novel*, 1883).

Spillane, Mickey   (full name Frank Morrison Spillane, 1918–   )   American detective story writer. Spillane developed a particularly violent form of HARD-BOILED FICTION known for its blend of sex and sadism and written in a blunt narrative prose. His chief character is the detective Mike Hammer. *I, the Jury* (1947) is one of his best-known works; others include *Kiss Me, Deadly* (1952), *The Girl Hunters* (1962), *The Twisted Thing* (1966), *The Delta Factor* (1967), *Survival: Zero* (1970), and *Tomorrow I Die* (1984).

Spingarn, Joel E[lias]   (1875–1939)   American critic. A student of Benedetto CROCE, and influenced by the work of SANTAYANA in America, Spingarn helped shift critical emphasis away from such external considerations as history and biography, and focus it solely on the work of art itself. He first outlined his views in an address called "The New Criticism," delivered at Columbia University in 1910, which anticipated the NEW CRITICISM of the 1930s and 1940s. In 1931 he compiled the most significant critical studies of three decades and published them as *Criti-*

cism in America: Its Function and Status. Among his other writings are *A History of Literary Criticism in the Renaissance* (1899), *Creative Criticism* (1917; rev 1931), and *Critical Essays of the 17th Century* (3 vols, 1908–9). In 1913 he established the Spingarn Medal, an annual award recognizing outstanding achievement by a black in service to his race.

Spinoza, Baruch (or Benedict Spinoza, 1632–1677) Dutch philosopher, born of Portuguese-Jewish parents. An insistently independent thinker, Spinoza declined offers of academic posts and pursued his individual philosophical inquiry, earning his living as a grinder of lenses. He was a major figure in 17th-century RATIONALISM and is regarded today as the most eminent expounder of the doctrine of PANTHEISM. He read the mathematical and philosophical works of DESCARTES; however, unlike Descartes, he saw no separation between God, mind, and matter. For Spinoza, God, the universe, and all of nature are one, and everything in the universe is part of God. Man can be conscious of his acts, but he cannot determine them—there is no free will. What man *can* do is to understand the processes at work in him and find joy in his union with God. By increasing his own sense of well-being, man can increase the well-being of others. *A Treatise on Religious and Political Philosophy* (1670) was the only one of Spinoza's works to be published during his lifetime, partly because his pantheistic views were held to be heretical. His major work, *Ethics,* was probably completed by 1665 but was not published until 1677, as was his *Opera Posthuma,* which contained letters as well as philosophical treatises.

Spirit of Laws, The (*De l'esprit des lois,* 1748) A treatise on the principles and historical origins of law by Charles de MONTESQUIEU. Its theme may be understood in part by the whole title: "Concerning the spirit of laws, or the relationship which laws must have to the constitution of each government, to mores, religion, commerce, etc." Underlying man-made laws are natural, or universal, laws which may be broadly described thus: universal peace in all nature; the need for food; the need to reproduce in kind; and gregariousness. Once society is formed, it is necessary for human beings to formulate positive laws to govern that society. These positive laws are not deduced a priori but must take into account natural law, and, as the subtitle suggests, such considerations as the mores, climate, religion, commerce, population, and customs of each different society to which the laws apply. In seeking to establish positive laws perfectly just to all peoples, Montesquieu reveals himself to be a universal humanist for whom justice is the supreme political virtue. In this connection, it is interesting to note that he speaks out against slavery, aggressive war, cruel punishments, and religious intolerance. Of the three types of government which he analyzes, monarchic, republican, and despotic, Montesquieu shows a preference for a constitutional monarchy for France. He also admires the English constitution for its separation of powers. The last five books are a technical treatise on the Roman and Germanic origins of French law.

The somewhat incoherent plan of the work does not lessen its value as the first authoritative example of a comparative study of social institutions; it also, by implication, exposed grave abuses in the French monarchy and defects in contemporary civilization. For example, Montesquieu advocated separation of Church and State in legal matters and believed that civil law should not be used to condemn men for heresy or witchcraft. It is generally considered one of the most important political treatises in existence; its influence on practically every constitution in the world (e.g., the U.S. Constitution and Catherine II's efforts to recodify Russian law) cannot be overestimated. Its literary style makes it eminently readable today.

spirituals The religious folksongs of the American black slaves. While some spirituals are exuberant, the most characteristic express the slaves' misery in bondage and their yearning for freedom, generally in Old Testament terms borrowed from the tales of the captivity of Israel, which the slaves saw as analogous to their own. Spiritual melodies are often built on the pentatonic or other scales, closer to Greek or Hungarian modes than to the standard major and minor scales of Western music, and their free treatment of the third and seventh degrees occasionally results in the so-called blue note. While they are eminently susceptible to the simple tonic-subdominant-dominant harmonizations typical of the hymnbook, their rhythms retain the freedom, subtlety, and complexity common in African music. Not surprisingly, these traits were carried over into black secular song and dance music and became basic components of early jazz.

Spitteler, Carl [Friedrich Georg] (pen name Carl Felix Tandem, 1845–1924) Swiss poet and novelist. Spitteler was insistently independent of the prevailing literary tendency of his day toward REALISM. His masterpiece, the epic *Olympischer Frühling* (*Olympian Spring*; 2 vols, final version 1910), is a vast and original work for which he even evolved his own metrical scheme. It is an allegory of the human condition based on the organization of the Greek gods on Olympus. As with his other works, particularly *Prometheus und Dulder* (1924), there is a strong emphasis on the importance of ethical values. He received the NOBEL PRIZE in 1919.

Spoils of Annwn, The A 10th-century Welsh poem that briefly mentions King ARTHUR.

Spoils of Poynton, The (1897) A novel by Henry JAMES. The "spoils" of the title refer to a great art and furniture collection in a house at Poynton. When Owen Gereth, owner of the house, is unwilling to marry Fleda Vetch, his mother's choice, Mrs. Gereth removes the art treasures. After Owen's marriage to Mona Brigstock, he offers Fleda any object in the collection. She arrives at Poynton to find that the house has been destroyed in an accidental fire.

spondee In English prosody, a foot of two accented syllables; in classical prosody, of two long syllables. The form in English is rare since most polysyllabic words contain a primary accent; when the spondee does occur, it is usually as two monosyllabic words, such as "ah, joy." In examining the subject, POE found only three or four instances where spondee occurs in a single word; "football," "bookcase," and "heartbreak" are examples. See METER.

Spooner, William Archibald (1844–1930) English dean and later warden of New College, Oxford. Spooner acquired a (probably exaggerated) reputation for his "spoonerisms," witty or unwitting transpositions of sounds, technically known as metathesis: for example, "There is a roaring pain" for "There is a pouring rain." Spoonerisms form part of Joyce's technique in *Finnegans Wake*.

Spoon River Anthology (1915) A volume of verse epitaphs by Edgar Lee MASTERS. The men and women of Spoon River narrate their own biographies from the cemetery where they lie buried. Realistic and sometimes cynical, these free-verse monologues often contradict the pious and optimistic epitaphs written on the gravestones. The poems made their first appearance in *Reedy's Mirror* in 1914 and 1915, and William Marion Reedy himself was partly responsible for their inception: he gave Masters a copy of J. W. Mackail's *Select Epigrams from the Greek Anthology*, and the style of the Greek poems impressed Masters deeply. *New Spoon River* (1924) was a less successful sequel.

Sportsman's Sketches, A (Zapiski okhotnika, 1852) A collection of short stories by Ivan TURGENEV. Portraying the life led on one of the typical great feudal estates in Russia, the *Sketches*, with its perceptive descriptions by a fictional narrator of what he encountered on his rambles through the countryside, brought Turgenev his first fame as an author. Because of the sympathetic attitude shown to the peasants and the often explicit condemnation of the landowners, the work has been interpreted as an attack on serfdom, which was abolished about ten years after the book's publication.

Sporus A favorite of the emperor Nero. The name was applied by Alexander Pope in his *Epistle to Dr. Arbuthnot* (1735) to Lord Hervey, and implied effeminacy.

Spring and Autumn Annals (Ch'un ch'iu) One of the Chinese FIVE CLASSICS. It is a CHOU dynasty chronicle of the feudal state of Lu for the years 722–481 BC. It is extremely terse and dry in its style and owes its high position in the Confucian canon to the fact that CONFUCIUS was said to have compiled it and read great moral significance into it. Its name, *Spring and Autumn*, is the Chinese term for historical annals.

sprung rhythm A combination of ACCENT METER with certain stylistic devices. It is the term by which Gerard Manley HOPKINS designated his approach to rhythm in

poetry. The word "sprung," he said, connoted for him something like "abrupt." Instead of the intense musicality of most poetry in accent meter, Hopkins sought the sense of halt, of impediments to smoothness. He used such stylistic devices as ALLITERATION, a preponderance of Anglo-Saxon vocabulary, the deliberate use of archaic and provincial words and turns of phrase, and inversion of natural order, in order to suggest the power of Anglo-Saxon poetry, which greatly influenced him.

Spurgeon, Caroline (1869–1942) English literary scholar. Spurgeon is known primarily for her influential study *Shakespeare's Imagery and What It Tells Us* (1935).

Spyri, Johanna See HEIDI.

Square, Mr. [Thomas] One of two tutors to Tom and Blifil in Henry Fielding's TOM JONES. Deistic in thought, Square spouts the "natural beauty of virtue." Actually, he is a great hypocrite. Both Square and Thwackum, the other tutor, satirize theological pedantry in education.

Squeers, Mr. Wackford In Charles Dickens's NICHOLAS NICKLEBY, the vulgar, conceited, ignorant schoolmaster of Dotheboys Hall. He steals the boys' money, clothes his son in their best suits, half starves them, and teaches them next to nothing. Ultimately, he is transported for purloining a deed.

Mrs. Squeers Squeers's wife, a raw-boned, harsh, heartless virago, without one spark of womanly feeling for the boys in her charge.

Squire, Sir J[ohn] C[ollings] (1884–1958) English poet and editor. Squire was literary and, later, general editor of the *New Statesman*, until he took on the editorship of the *London Mercury* (1919–34), in which he published a good deal of the work of the GEORGIAN poets. His own poetry was squarely in the Georgian tradition (*Collected Poems*, 1959). He also wrote fine parodies (*Collected Parodies*, 1921) and collaborated on writing a number of plays, including *Berkeley Square* (1928; with J. L. Balderston).

Squire's Tale, The One of THE CANTERBURY TALES of CHAUCER, an unfinished medieval romance. The first part tells of the birthday feast of the Tartar king Cambuscan, to whom a mysterious knight brings four magical gifts—a brass horse, a mirror, a ring, and a sword—and explains their workings. In the second part Cambuscan's daughter Canacee goes out next morning wearing the ring, which enables the bearer to understand and speak with birds. She takes pity on a bitterly distressed falcon, who tells her how her tercelet lover has deserted her for a kite. The section ends with a promise to describe the adventures of Cambuscan and his two sons, and the fights for Canacee's hand in marriage, but Chaucer never continued the tale. Spenser wrote a continuation in the fourth book of his *Faerie Queene*.

S.S. The abbreviated name of the Nazi *Schutzstaffel* (Elite Guard), organized in 1929 by Heinrich Himmler

(1900–1945). Members of the S.S., selected from the larger S.A., served as bodyguards for high officials and as supervisors of the concentration camps. They were also called Blackshirts.

Ssu-ma Ch'ien (145?–?90 BC)   Chinese historian, author of the *Shih chi*, or *Records of the Historian*, the first major Chinese historical work. Son of a scholar, Ssu-ma served in the Imperial Court. He organized and edited ancient source materials, writing a masterpiece that covers Chinese history from legendary times to the author's day and set the pattern for all later DYNASTIC HISTORIES. He was castrated for having incurred the emperor's displeasure but continued his work until its completion. See Burton Watson, *Ssu-ma Ch'ien: Grand Historian of China* (1958).

Stabat Mater (Lat, "The Mother was standing") Opening words of a medieval Latin hymn which describes the suffering of the Virgin Mary at the foot of the Cross of Jesus. It is ascribed to the 13th-century Franciscan JACOPONE DA TODI. It has been set to music by many major composers.

Staël, Mme de (born Anne Louise Germaine Necker, 1766–1817)   Swiss-French belle-lettrist. Staël's father, Jacques NECKER, was the French minister of finance; her husband, the Baron de Staël-Holstein, was Swedish ambassador to France. She is known for her celebrated salons, which were attended by leading literary and political figures, for her charm, talent for conversation, vigorous mind, and for her influence on ROMANTICISM in France. Among her works are *Lettres sur les écrits et caractère de Jean-Jacques Rousseau* (1788); *De l'influence des passions* (1796); *Essai sur les fictions* (1795); and *Considérations sur la Révolution française* (1818). DELPHINE and CORINNE are considered by some critics to be the first "modern" feminist, psychological, romantic novels; they anticipate the works of George SAND. In her *De la littérature considérée dans ses rapports avec les institutions sociales* (1800), Mme de Staël attempted, among other things, to establish that literature develops qualitatively as social and political freedom increase. It was unanimously criticized because of its superficiality and simplistic literary prophecies. In *De l'Allemagne*, suppressed by NAPOLEON in 1811, but later published in London in 1813, she makes invidious comparisons between German and French culture and politics; in it she introduced German romanticism into France, thereby influencing greatly European thought and letters.

Mme de Staël was an outspoken critic of Napoleon, and was exiled from Paris several times. She traveled in Germany, Russia, England, Switzerland, and Sweden—hence her cosmopolitan attitude toward literature and politics. Her marriage was disappointing, and she had several love affairs. She inspired, in part, her Don-Juan-like lover, the Swiss novelist Benjamin CONSTANT DE REBECQUE, to write his ADOLPHE. Her influence has been found in the works of LAMARTINE, Victor HUGO, and Charles Nodier.

Stafford, Jean (1915–1979)   American novelist and short-story writer. A serious writer and admirable stylist, Stafford is particularly noted for evocative presentations of childhood and adolescence. Her first novel, *Boston Adventure* (1944), depicts Boston as perceived by the young daughter of immigrants. It was followed by *The Mountain Lion* (1947), a study of a brother and sister in the years between childhood and adolescence; *The Catherine Wheel* (1952); and a novella, *A Winter's Tale* (1954). *Children Are Bored on Sunday* (1953) and *Bad Characters* (1966) are collections of short stories. Her *Collected Stories* (1969) was awarded a PULITZER PRIZE. She was married for a time to Robert LOWELL.

Stafford, William [Edgar] (1914–   )   American poet and editor. Stafford was born and educated in Kansas and subsequently taught on the West Coast. He first received widespread recognition with his third book of verse, *Traveling through the Dark* (1962; National Book Award). This collection, like his others, has a wry and balanced moral vision, often integrating the human and animal worlds. *The Rescued Year* (1966) is largely autobiographical. Stafford uses everyday language, stretched taut for poetic purposes, and writes in a formal meter. Later volumes, such as *Someday, Maybe* (1973), are concerned with such issues as ecology and the rediscovery of the American Indian. *Stories That Could Be True: New and Collected Poems* appeared in 1977.

Stakhova, Elena   The heroine of Ivan TURGENEV's novel *On the Eve* (1860). Falling in love with the Bulgarian revolutionary Insarov, Elena leaves the comfort and safety of her home to follow him into the dangers of the battle for freedom in Bulgaria.

Stalin, Joseph (real name Iosef Visarionovich Dzhugashvili, 1879–1953)   Russian political leader. Stalin, who succeeded LENIN as the ruler of the Soviet Union and thenceforth governed with an iron hand until his death, was born in Georgia. The son of a shoemaker, he attended a theological seminary in Tiflis for a short time. He joined the Social Democratic Party and actively entered the revolutionary movement in the late 1890s, often thereafter being imprisoned for his activities. In 1903 he sided with the BOLSHEVIK faction, and in 1912 he went to St. Petersburg as a member of the Central Committee. He was imprisoned (1913–17), but at the start of the revolution he was freed and became Lenin's lieutenant. After the revolution, he served as commissar of nationalities until 1922, when he was made general secretary of the Central Committee of the Communist Party. From this position he carefully built his power, and when Lenin died in 1924, he was able to eliminate the opposition of TROTSKY, KAMENEV, ZINOVYEV, and other rivals. By 1927 he was in uncontested command of the Party and the government. Instead of actively attempting to spread international revolution, Stalin concentrated on building Russia's strength, forming his national policy around the doctrine of "socialism in one country" as a base from which Communism could spread. He initiated the Five Year Plan for industrial construction and the collectivization of agriculture. In the cultural field, he exercised a paternal watchfulness over writers and artists, exhorting them with such platitudes as "writers are engineers of the human soul." One of his most direct acts in the literary sphere was his declaration that the greatest Soviet poet was Vladimir MAYAKOVSKY—a pronouncement that was quickly heeded by Soviet critics. Stalin himself was the object of countless eulogistic writings, which fail to earn any attention as literature.

Stalin purged the government and the army so thoroughly in the 1930s that he had complete control of Russia at the outbreak of World War II. In 1936 Russia had supported the Loyalists in the Spanish Civil War, in opposition to Italy and Germany, the two fascist nations that helped Franco establish his government. Nevertheless, in 1939, Russia and Germany signed a nonaggression pact. When Hitler violated that treaty and invaded Russia in 1941, Stalin assumed command of the Russian armed forces. Russia suffered tremendous losses in the war, but upon defeating Germany, Russia became one of the two great powers in the world, dominating the Eastern hemisphere as no modern nation had done before. In his last years, Stalin was loved, hated, and feared as no other living man.

Stalky and Co. (1899)   A collection of boys' stories by Rudyard KIPLING. Largely autobiographical, they narrate the pranks and adventures of three schoolboys: Arthur Corkran, otherwise known as "Your Uncle Stalky," the Irish McTurk, and Beetle. Beetle is usually taken to be Kipling himself. McTurk is George Charles Beresford (d 1938), and Stalky is Major General Lionel Charles Dunsterville (1866–1946).

Stallings, Laurence   See WHAT PRICE GLORY?

Stampa, Gaspara (c1523–1554)   Italian Renaissance poet. Stampa spent most of her brief life in Venice. Here she recorded the emotional experiences of that life in a series of sonnets, madrigals, and elegies published as her *Rime* (1554). This work entitles her to a high place among the poets of the Renaissance period.

Stamp Act   A revenue act, known as Grenville's Stamp Act, passed by the English Parliament in 1765. It required that all legal documents, newspapers, almanacs, and commercial papers in the American colonies carry stamps showing that a tax had been paid on them. Led by Samuel ADAMS and James Otis, the colonists protested against the measure, and the Stamp Act Congress, the first intercolonial congress, petitioned the king to repeal the act. The request was granted in 1766.

Standard, Battle of the   Battle fought near Northallerton in 1138. The English defeated the Scots under King David I, who was contesting King Stephen's right to the English throne on behalf of his niece Matilda.

Standish, Miles (1584?–1656)   Military leader of the Pilgrims. Standish was largely responsible for the colonists' friendly relations with the Indians and led the party which arrested Thomas MORTON of Merrymount. He is the title character of Longfellow's THE COURTSHIP OF MILES STANDISH, for which, however, there is no historical foundation.

Stanhope, Lady Hester [Lucy] (1776–1839)   English eccentric who established herself in the Levant and became legendary during her lifetime. From 1803 until his death in 1806, Stanhope was secretary and housekeeper for her uncle, William Pitt. Four years later, leaving England forever, she made a pilgrimage to Jerusalem, and thereafter traveled widely in the Levant, camping among the Bedouin tribes, until she finally settled among the Druses on Mt. Lebanon. Adopting Eastern dress and practicing her own peculiar brand of religion, based partly on astrology, she gained such influence over the half-civilized tribes by her prophecies and pronouncements that they believed her divinely inspired—a view that came to be shared by certain English mystics and, eventually, by Lady Hester herself. Her life on Mt. Lebanon is described in *Eöthen, or Traces of Travel Brought Home from the East* (1844) by Alexander Kinglake.

Stanislavsky, Konstantin (stage name of Konstantin Sergeyevich Alekseyev, 1865–1938)   Russian actor and director. Cofounder (with Vladimir Nemirovich-Danchenko) and director (1898–1938) of the famous Moscow Art Theatre, Stanislavsky is also known for his theories of acting, which he set forth in such works as *An Actor Prepares* (1926), *Building a Character* (1950), and the autobiographical *My Life in Art* (1924). He rejected purely external theatrics in favor of a realistic style in which the actor seeks to identify with, or "live," his role, using his own psychological reactions. Sometimes called the Stanislavsky system, his theories have been widely accepted by modern actors.

Stanley, Sir Henry Morton (1841–1904)   Famous explorer, chiefly remembered for his expedition into Central Africa to find David Livingstone. The expedition was commissioned by the New York *Herald*. Stanley reached Livingstone in November 1871, greeting him with the now famous words, "Dr. Livingstone, I presume?" He published a number of books, including *Through the Dark Continent* (2 vols, 1878); *The Congo and the Founding of Its Free State* (2 vols, 1885); *In Darkest Africa* (2 vols, 1890); etc.

Stanton, Elizabeth Cady (1815–1902)   American woman suffragist. The first woman's rights convention was held in Stanton's home in Seneca Falls, New York, in 1848. With Lucretia Mott, she was one of the first agitators for woman suffrage. She was the first president of the National Woman Suffrage Association (1869–90) and edited, with Susan B. ANTHONY, a militant magazine called *Revolution*. Also with Anthony and Matilda Gage, she wrote A *History of Woman Suffrage* (6 vols, 1881–1922). Elizabeth Cady Stanton's autobiography, *Eighty Years and More*, was published in 1898.

stanza In prosody, a division of a poem containing one or more lines, separated by spacing from other like units; a group of lines standing together, apart from other such groups. Stanzas are defined according to the number of lines they contain as in the terms couplet; triplet or tercet; quatrain; quintet or cinquain; sestet, sextet, or sextain; septet; octave or octet. There are also numerous traditional stanza forms of a set length and rhyme scheme that have names, as: the ballad stanza, RHYME ROYAL, OTTAVA RIMA, the SPENSERIAN STANZA, TERZA RIMA, etc.

Stanzas may be of arbitrary length and plan, as in regular stanza forms, or they may be free and irregular, as in the irregular ode or most FREE VERSE forms. The thought may be continued from one stanza to another, or the stanza may be a closed thought unit. One stanza may, and frequently does, constitute a complete poem. On the other hand, many longer poems written in BLANK VERSE or HEROIC COUPLETS are not divided into stanzas at all, but consist of an unbroken flow of lines divided, if at all, into larger parts such as numbered sections or cantos.

Stapledon, [William] Olaf (1886–1950) English philosopher, essayist, and novelist. Stapledon published a number of philosophical works, but he is best remembered for nine "novels" that have had great influence on the development of SCIENCE FICTION. They include *Odd John* (1935), widely regarded as the best of all novels on the superman theme; *Sirius: A Fantasy of Love and Discord* (1944), which tells of the trials and tribulations of a dog whose intelligence has been artificially raised to the human level; and two books best described as "future histories," *Last and First Men* (1930) and *Star Maker* (1937). His science fictional concepts had a direct influence on Arthur C. CLARKE and many other science fiction writers.

Stark, [Dame] Freya [Madeline] (1893–   ) English travel writer. Most of Stark's adventurous traveling was done in the Middle East. Her books include *The Valleys of the Assassins and Other Persian Travels* (1934), *A Winter in Arabia* (1940), *East Is West* (1945), *The Lycian Shore* (1956), *The Minaret of Djam* (1970), *A Peak in Darien* (1976), and *Rivers of Time* (1982). Her work is notable for its shrewd observation, original thought, and sympathetic receptivity to foreign cultures. Her collected *Letters* were published in five volumes (1974–78).

Stark, Willie See ALL THE KING'S MEN.

Star Spangled Banner The national anthem of the United States. The poem was written by Francis Scott KEY in 1814, during the WAR OF 1812. During the British bombardment of Fort McHenry, the gateway to the Baltimore defenses, Key was aboard a British man-of-war, detained on a mission to obtain the exchange of an American prisoner. The bombardment lasted throughout the night from September 13 to 14. A part of the poem was scribbled on the back of an envelope when, after a long night of anxious waiting, "by the dawn's early light," Key could see that the Stars and Stripes were still flying over the fort. It was sung to the tune of *To Anacreon in Heaven*, ascribed to the English composer John Stafford Smith (1750–1836). "The Star Spangled Banner" became the national anthem in 1931 by an act of Congress, although it had long held that position unofficially.

Stations of the Cross (Lat, *Via Crucis*, "the Way of the Cross") A medieval devotion based on the events of Jesus' Crucifixion. It originated in Jerusalem, where pilgrims followed the supposed path of JESUS, stopping at the places where specific events had taken place; prayers were said at each station, which number fourteen. Later, frescos, pictures, or sculptural representations were made of these events and placed in churches so that those who could not go to the Holy Land could make the devotion. The events:

1. Jesus is condemned to death.
2. He is made to bear His cross.
3. His first fall under the cross.
4. Jesus meets His sorrowing mother.
5. Simon of Cyrene helps to bear the cross.
6. Veronica wipes the face of Jesus.
7. Jesus falls the second time.
8. Jesus speaks to the daughters of Jerusalem.
9. Jesus falls the third time.
10. He is stripped of his garments.
11. He is nailed to the cross.
12. He gives up the Ghost.
13. He is taken down from the cross.
14. Jesus is laid in the sepulcher.

Statius, Publius Papinius (c45–96) Latin poet. Statius is the author of the *Thebais* (c91), an epic in twelve books dealing with the SEVEN AGAINST THEBES. He also wrote *Achilleis*, about the life of Achilles, and the five books of the *Silvae*, occasional poems. Statius appears as a character in Dante's *Purgatorio*.

Stavrogin, Nikolay Vsevolodovich The central character in DOSTOYEVSKY's novel THE POSSESSED. A young nobleman tormented by spiritual sterility, Stavrogin returns to his native provincial town after several years of listless debauchery and crime in Moscow and abroad. He has capriciously married a crippled half-wit, Marya Timofeyevna Lebyadkin, and has become associated with the revolutionary plotter Pyotr VERKHOVENSKY, who wants Stavrogin as a figurehead for his movement. Unable to lose himself in either crime or political activity, or to find any solace in religion, Stavrogin is also unable to respond to the love offered by Lizaveta Tushina. For a while he considers starting a new life with the adoring Darya Shatova, but he is unable to make the effort. He is haunted by the memory of a horrible crime which he finally confesses to the monk

Tikhon. Some years before, he had violated a young girl and then allowed the frightened, tormented girl to hang herself. (The chapter containing this confession was not allowed to be published when the novel first appeared.) Finally, unable to live with his guilt, Stavrogin hangs himself.

Stead, Christina [Ellen] (1902–1983)   Australian novelist. Apart from *Seven Poor Men of Sydney* (1934) and *For Love Alone* (1944), both of which have Australian settings, Stead is not an Australian writer in either setting or style. An immensely cosmopolitan writer, her works reflect her own varied experiences living in Europe, England, and the U.S. In all her novels, particularly THE MAN WHO LOVED CHILDREN, *Letty Fox* (1946), and *Dark Places of the Heart* (1966; U.K. as *Cotter's England*), she combines an acute awareness of social and political strains with a searing insight into individual characters. A common thread is her treatment of subtly destructive obsessions.

Stedman, Edmund Clarence (1833–1908) American poet, critic, anthologist, and businessman. Stedman was considered one of the leading poets of his time, but his sonorous verse has not worn well. His chief literary importance rests on his criticism and anthologies. His two large volumes of criticism, *Victorian Poets* (1875) and *Poets of America* (1885), were supplemented by two anthologies: *A Victorian Anthology* (1895) and *An American Anthology* (1900). The American volumes, significant for the estimation of POE and WHITMAN, were early studies in American literature, a field hitherto barely explored. Stedman's work became very popular, and he was often referred to as the literary dean of his day.

Steegmuller, Francis (1906–   )   American novelist, short-story writer, critic, biographer, and translator. Steegmuller has published many novels, including detective stories and light comedies, under a variety of pseudonyms. He is, however, best known for his meticulous translations of French literature and such distinguished biographies as *Flaubert and Madame Bovary* (1939), *Maupassant* (1949), and *Cocteau* (1970). He also selected, edited, and translated *The Letters of Gustave Flaubert 1830–1857* (1980) and *The Letters of Gustave Flaubert 1857–1880* (1983).

Steele, Richard (1672–1729)   Irish-born English playwright and essayist, known for his writing in the periodicals THE TATLER and THE SPECTATOR in association with Joseph ADDISON. Steele took the initiative in the founding of these two journalistic enterprises, serving as the first editor of *The Tatler* under the name of Isaac BICKERSTAFF, and contributing the majority of the essays published in *The Tatler*. Other works by Steele include *The Christian Hero* (1701), an attack on dueling published as a pamphlet, and several plays. Steele was more journalistic than Addison: his subjects are lighter and less varied.

Steele, Wilbur Daniel (1886–1970)   American short-story writer and novelist. Steele is best known for his short stories. Of his many collections, four won O. Henry Memorial Awards: *For They Know Not What They Do* (1919), *Bubbles* (1926), *The Man Who Saw Through Heaven* (1925), and *Can't Cross Jordan* (1931). Among his novels are *Storm* (1914), *Undertow* (1930), *That Girl from Memphis* (1945), and *Their Town* (1952). He also wrote several one-act plays and, with his second wife, Norma Mitchell, a full-length drama, *Post Road* (1934).

Steendam, Jacob (1616–1672)   Dutch merchant-poet, the first poet of colonial New York. After a trip to the Gold Coast for trade and adventure, he settled in New Amsterdam in 1649, buying property in Long Island and Manhattan. His chief works are the rhetorical *Klacht van Niew Nederlandt tot haar moeder* (*Complaint of New Netherlands to Her Mother*, 1659), a verse allegorical history of the colony; and *'T lof van Niew Nederlandt* (*The Praise of New Netherlands*, 1661), a three-hundred-line idealized picture of colonial New York, designed to encourage immigration.

Steerforth   In Charles Dickens's DAVID COPPERFIELD, David's hero at CREAKLE's school. Steerforth leads Em'ly PEGGOTTY astray; when he tires of her, he proposes that she marry his valet. Later he is shipwrecked off the coast of Yarmouth, and Ham Peggotty, who tries to rescue him, is drowned with him. Steerforth cuts a dazzling, attractive figure, but is arrogant, selfish, and heartless.

Steffens, [Joseph] Lincoln (1866–1936)   American journalist. Born in San Francisco, Steffens had a restless youth. After studying in Europe, he became a journalist in New York City in 1892. He was managing editor of *McClure's Magazine* (1902–6) and associate editor of the *American Magazine* and *Everybody's Magazine* (1906–11).

Best known as one of the first MUCKRAKERS, Steffens exposed business and government corruption in articles that were collected in such works as *The Shame of the Cities* (1904), *The Struggle for Self-Government* (1906), and *The Upbuilders* (1909). He also wrote a candid and entertaining *Autobiography* (1931).

Stegner, Wallace [Earle] (1909–   )   American writer. Stegner's distinguished novels of American rural life include *On a Darkling Plain* (1940), about the 1918 influenza epidemic in Saskatchewan; *The Big Rock Candy Mountain* (1943), a family's odyssey through the Western frontier; and *The Preacher and the Slave* (1950), about the labor leader Joe Hill. Stegner's novels and many of his stories are richly written, with a strong evocation of place and well-researched factual detail and a preoccupation with ethical behavior. *Angle of Repose* (1971), set in the American West, is about a young engineer and his strong but compassionate wife, whose marriage nevertheless is not a complete success. The book won a PULITZER PRIZE in 1972. *The Spectator Bird* (1976), about a seventy-year-old arthritic literary agent in California, won the National Book Award in 1977. Also known for his nonfiction,

Stegner has written *One Nation* (1945), about religious tensions in the U.S., *Mormon Country* (1941), and *The Gathering of Zion* (1964), a story of the Mormon trail, as well as numerous essays and biographies.

Steichen, Edward (1879–1973)   American photographer. He is most noted for his pioneering efforts toward the establishment of photography as a fine art. He was a founder of Photo-Secession (1902), a group of photographers sharing that objective and, in 1905, founded with his friend Alfred STIEGLITZ the Gallery "291." As director of The Museum of Modern Art's photography department (1947–62), he vastly enlarged that collection and organized many influential exhibitions, notably *The Family of Man*, which, along with the book in which the photographs were published (1955), brought artistic and documentary photography to the attention of millions.

Stein, Charlotte von (1742–1827)   The beloved of GOETHE, probably the most important woman in his life. Stein was married to an equerry who was much her intellectual inferior, and Goethe fulfilled her need for spiritual companionship. Goethe, in turn, when he came to Weimar in 1775, was in need of a sobering, stabilizing influence upon his character and it was this that she provided. Austere, highly intelligent, and older than the poet, she resisted his sensual tendencies and taught him the art of renunciation of personal desire. Though the intimate details of their love are not known, it is certain that even if she later did become his mistress, their relationship still remained primarily a spiritual one. Their love lasted unbroken from 1775 until Goethe's departure for Italy in 1786. In Italy, he experienced a sensual reawakening and when he returned, he and Charlotte had little left in common.

Her influence upon him, though, was lasting. The character of Iphigenia in his *Iphigenia in Tauris* (1787) is an adoring portrait of her, and the Princess in his *Torquato Tasso* (1790), though not a character as completely admirable, seems also to have been modeled after her. And finally, the theme of renunciation, which is extremely important in all Goethe's later works, is largely based on his experience with her.

Stein, Gertrude (1874–1946)   American poet, novelist, and critic. For many years a prominent expatriate in Paris, she was at the center of a celebrated literary and artistic circle and was herself the subject of wide literary controversy in the 1920s. Her unique style, which was influenced by the psychological theories of William JAMES and by modern French painting, was intended as a verbal counterpart to CUBISM. She used words for their associations and sounds rather than for their meaning, frequently employing an intricate system of repetition and variation on a single verbal theme. She avoided conventional punctuation and syntax, placing her emphasis on the presentation of impressions and a particular state of mind rather than the telling of a story. In an effort to liberate language

and thinking from the bonds of convention, she created improbable juxtapositions of common language and concentrated on concrete, spare diction in a basically monosyllabic vocabulary.

Stein was raised in a wealthy family in Pennsylvania. She studied psychology under William James at Radcliffe College and later began studies in medicine at Johns Hopkins University. In 1903 she settled in Paris with her brother and Alice B. Toklas (1877–1967), her secretary and companion for forty years. She returned to America only once, in 1934, for a brief and successful lecture tour. Her home in Paris became a center for such artists as PICASSO, MATISSE, BRAQUE, and Juan GRIS, whose work she collected, and for such writers as HEMINGWAY, FITZGERALD, and Sherwood ANDERSON, among many others.

THREE LIVES was her first book. In part an example of primitivistic writing, it is regarded by many critics as her best. *Tender Buttons* (1914) is a poetic series of paragraphs about objects, often witty, often close to automatic writing. In 1925 she finally published her longest and most complex work, THE MAKING OF AMERICANS, which she had written between 1906 and 1911. Among her many later works are *Matisse, Picasso and Gertrude Stein, with Two Shorter Stories* (1933); two operas with music by Virgil THOMSON, FOUR SAINTS IN THREE ACTS and *The Mother of Us All* (1947); *In Savoy, or "Yes" Is for a Very Young Man* (1946), which was produced on Broadway in 1949; and *Four in America* (1947), essays on George Washington, U. S. Grant, Wilbur Wright, and Henry James.

Stein's work has never been met with indifference: it is either celebrated as the work of a genius (an appraisal with which she heartily concurred) or dismissed as tedious and hopelessly obscure. By any measure, her influence on other writers was significant; she forged new pathways of experimental writing and helped bring wide attention to avant-garde movements in literature and art. Many of her lines became famous, most notably, "A rose is a rose is a rose." She also gave currency to the phrase "the LOST GENERATION," which described the expatriates after World War I. One of her least experimental and most widely read works is her autobiography, which she titled THE AUTOBIOGRAPHY OF ALICE B. TOKLAS.

Steinbeck, John [Ernst] (1902–1968)   American novelist and short-story writer. Born in Salinas, California, Steinbeck was awarded a PULITZER PRIZE in 1940 and the NOBEL PRIZE in Literature in 1962. A writer of proletarian sympathies, he is noted for his realistic studies of life among the depressed economic classes of the U.S., especially the itinerant farm laborers of California.

Steinbeck's first book, *Cup of Gold: A Life of Henry Morgan, Buccaneer, with Occasional References to History* (1929), reflected his long interest in the sea. He had specialized in marine biology at Stanford University, and he later published two other books about sea life: *Sea of Cortez*, with Edward F. Ricketts (1941), and *The Log of the*

Sea of Cortez (1951), a reissue of the narrative part of the earlier volume with a biographical sketch of Ricketts.

The Pastures of Heaven (1932), a collection of short stories about the inhabitants of the valley of that name, is the first example of Steinbeck's interest in simpleminded people, the "unfinished children of nature." *To a God Unknown* (1933) presents Steinbeck's strongest statement about man's relationship to the land. Tortilla Flat and In Dubious Battle established Steinbeck's reputation. Of Mice and Men, first conceived as a play, was dramatized the year of its publication. *The Long Valley* (1938) is a book of short stories set in the Salinas valley, which includes "The Red Pony" (published separately 1937).

The Grapes of Wrath, Steinbeck's major novel, is perhaps the best example of the proletarian literature of the 1930s. Realistic and naturalistic, it also expresses Steinbeck's mystical affirmation that all life is holy. A war correspondent during World War II, Steinbeck published three nonfiction works and a novel dealing with that conflict.

Cannery Row and its sequel, *Sweet Thursday* (1954), hark back to *Tortilla Flat* in their sentimental rendering of the lives of simple people, and *The Wayward Bus* (1947) reflects the same attitude. The Pearl is a parable of a Mexican pearl fisher. Steinbeck's most ambitious work after *The Grapes of Wrath* was East of Eden, a long family novel based partly on the story of Cain and Abel. Steinbeck's later works include a satirical novelette, *The Short Reign of Pippin IV* (1957); *The Winter of Our Discontent* (1961); *Travels with Charley* (1962), an account of his trip across the U.S. in the company of an elderly poodle; and *America and Americans* (1966). *Steinbeck* (1975) is a collection of letters and notes for the "big novel" that he never wrote. In the last few years of his life, Steinbeck was preoccupied with his free translation of Thomas Malory's *The Acts of King Arthur and His Noble Knights*. His unfinished manuscript and letters concerning the work were published in 1976.

Steinberg, Saul (1914–   )   Romanian-born American artist. His drawings for The New Yorker have been collected in several volumes. They are witty, technically innovative graphic creations, often employing rubber stamps, photographs, and popular symbols in fantastic and satirical images.

Steiner, [Francis] George (1929–   )   French-born American critic and fiction writer. Steiner ranges from political commentary to criticism in all areas of the humanities. His literary studies focus on the relationship between thought and feeling and between literature and society. *Tolstoy or Dostoevsky* (1958) examines those two writers in terms of their opposing views of life. *The Death of Tragedy* (1960) surveys the rise and fall of the Western tragic tradition. Other volumes of essays include *Language and Silence* (1967), *Extraterritorial* (1971), *In Bluebeard's Castle* (1971), *After Babel* (1975), and *On Difficulty*

(1978). Steiner published a volume of poetry in 1953 and a collection of stories, *Anno Domini*, in 1964; *The Portage to San Cristobal of A. H.* (1981) is a work of imagination about Adolf Hitler.

Stella   Lady Penelope Devereux, the object of Sir Philip Sidney's affection, celebrated in his sonnet series Astrophel and Stella. She married Lord Rich.

Stendhal (pen name of Marie Henri Beyle, 1783–1842)   French novelist and critic. Stendhal, one of France's greatest literary artists, played a major role in the development of the modern novel. His place lies somewhere between the romantic and realistic schools, for his plots and subjects are often violently melodramatic, yet his treatment of them is painstakingly realistic. Pointing the way toward the psychological novel, his probing, analytical studies of character deal with proud and egotistical natures involved in love and war. A great admirer of Napoleon Bonaparte and Lord Byron, Stendhal himself participated in several campaigns of the Napoleonic Wars, and his works are in part autobiographical. His most noted works are *Le Rouge et le noir* (The Red and the Black), *La Chartreuse de Parme* (The Charterhouse of Parma), *Armance* (1827), and the unfinished *Lucien Leuwen* (1894). *Racine et Shakespeare* (1823) is a critical discussion of classicism and romanticism, and *De l'amour* (1822) is a series of notes on the effects of love on a variety of temperaments.

stentor, the voice of a   A very loud voice. Stentor was a Greek herald in the Trojan War. According to Homer's Iliad, his voice was as loud as that of fifty men combined; hence, stentorian, loud voiced.

Stephansson, Stephan (1853–1927)   Icelandic-born Canadian poet and novelist. In 1873 he left Iceland and went to Alberta, Canada, with his family. Directly influenced by the realist movement, Stephansson produced a novel series, *Bréf og ritgeroir* (4 vols, 1938–48), which criticized existing social conditions. He also wrote many sensitive and beautiful nature poems. *Úti á vidavangi* (1894), *Andovökur* (6 vols, 1909–38), *Kolbeinslag* (1914), and *Vigslóöi* (1920) are among his collections of verse.

Stephen, Sir Leslie (1832–1904)   English man of letters. Although Stephen took orders as a young man, he later became an agnostic, explaining his views in his *Essays on Free Thinking and Plain Speaking* (1873) and his *Agnostic's Apology* (1876). After having edited the *Cornhill Magazine* from 1871 to 1882, he became the first editor of the *Dictionary of National Biography* in the latter year. His books include *The History of English Thought in the Eighteenth Century* (1876), *The English Utilitarians* (1900), and *English Literature and Society in the Eighteenth Century* (1904). Stephen's first wife was Harriet Marian, the younger daughter of Thackeray. He was the father of Virginia Woolf; another daughter, Vanessa, married the English art critic Clive Bell. The daughters were later the nucleus of the Bloomsbury Group, which met in Sir Leslie's house after his death. In 1977, an autobiographical account of his marriage and family life was published as *Sir Leslie Stephen's Mausoleum Book*. It provides much of the factual background for Virginia Woolf's To THE LIGHT-HOUSE.

Stephen Hero See EPIPHANY; PORTRAIT OF THE ARTIST AS A YOUNG MAN, A.

Stephens, James (1882–1950) Irish poet and fiction writer. He is best known for his whimsical tales and adaptations from Irish legend. *The Crock of Gold* (1912), a novel that combines humor, realism, and fantasy, is his best-known work. Stephens was associated with the IRISH RENAISSANCE.

Steppenwolf, Der (1927; tr Steppenwolf, 1929) A novel by Herman HESSE. It is a treatment of the artist as an outsider, a common theme in Hesse's fiction. The hero, Harry HALLER, exemplifies in modern terms the typical disintegration of German romantic characters (see ZERRIS-SENHEIT). He is torn between his own frustrated artistic idealism and the inhuman nature of modern reality, which, in his eyes, is characterized entirely by philistinism and technology. It is his inability to be a part of the world and the resulting loneliness and desolation of his existence that cause him to think of himself as a "Steppenwolf" (wolf of the Steppes). The novel, which is rich in surrealistic imagery throughout, ends in what is called the magic theatre, a kind of allegorical sideshow. Here, Haller learns that, in order to relate successfully to humanity and reality without sacrificing his ideals, he must overcome his own social and sexual inhibitions. He realizes, however, that unrestrained release leads to chaos.

Sterne, Laurence (1713–1768) English novelist and clergyman. When, in 1759 at the age of forty-seven, he published the first two volumes of TRISTRAM SHANDY, he emerged like a comet on the literary world from the complete obscurity of the small Yorkshire vicarship he had held since 1739. Though *Tristram* was denounced by Dr. JOHNSON, Samuel RICHARDSON, GOLDSMITH, and others on both literary and moral grounds, Sterne was well received in London. Successive volumes of *Tristram* appeared until 1767, accompanied by volumes of *Sermons of Mr. Yorick* (1760–69), as well as by A SENTIMENTAL JOURNEY. This tremendous output was accomplished in the face of the throes of consumption from which Sterne was to die—an autobiographical circumstance which he treats in volumes seven and eight of *Tristram*. Two views of his character have held sway: Sterne the accomplished scoundrel and Sterne the sentimental humorist. He was both by turns, although it is only fair to say that he did all in his power to propagandize the second. See ELIZA; YORICK.

Stesichorus (c640–555 BC) Greek lyric poet, born in Sicily. The fragments that remain of his works justify the high reputation he bore in classical times: LONGINUS called him "most like Homer." His unusual achievement was to write of heroic subjects with epic sweep but in lyric verse.

According to legend, he wrote unflatteringly about HELEN's role in causing the TROJAN WAR. Helen (who was also a goddess) punished him with blindness. He recovered his sight only when he composed a PALINODE retracting his claim and suggesting that it was a "phantom-Helen" who had caused the war.

Stevens, Gavin A character in several works by William FAULKNER. Educated at Harvard and Heidelberg, Stevens is a lawyer and later the county attorney in Jefferson, Mississippi; he comments philosophically on events in YOKNAPATAWPHA COUNTY, although he is rarely directly involved in them. He develops a hopeless love for Eula Varner SNOPES in *The Town* (1957) and later for her daughter, Linda, in *The Mansion* (1959) (see THE HAMLET). He solves murders in KNIGHT'S GAMBIT and is a somewhat ineffectual but philosophic presence in INTRUDER IN THE DUST. Finally, to cure himself of his unrewarded love for Linda Snopes, he marries Melisandre Backus Harriss, a wealthy widow who appears in the title story of *Knight's Gambit*.

Stevens, Wallace (1879–1955) American poet. Although critically regarded as one of the most significant American poets of the 20th century, Stevens did not receive widespread recognition until the publication of his *Collected Poems* (1954; PULITZER PRIZE). A lawyer by training, Stevens was associated for nearly forty years with the Hartford Accident and Indemnity Company, serving as its vice-president from 1934 until his death. The wholly individual poetry that he wrote in his spare time was notably influenced both by the French SYMBOLISTS and the English romantic poets, particularly WORDSWORTH and COLERIDGE.

Part of the poetic renaissance shortly before World War I, Stevens's first poems were published in POETRY in 1914, but it was not until he was nearly forty-four that his first book of poems, *Harmonium*, appeared. He wrote little during the 1920s, adding only a few poems to the reissue of *Harmonium* in 1931. The volumes that followed—*Ideas of Order* (1935), *Owl's Clover* (1936), *The Man with the Blue Guitar* (1937), *Parts of a World* (1942), NOTES TOWARD A SUPREME FICTION, *Esthétique du Mal* (1945), *Three Academic Pieces* (two poems and a prose address, 1947), *Transport to Summer* (1947), and *The Auroras of Autumn* (1950)—show the progressive development of his poetic style. Stevens gradually turned away from the intricate stylization, recondite vocabulary, and lavish, tropical imagery that characterized much of his early work to a more exacting, moderate, though abstract style and a profound concern with aesthetics. Central to all Stevens's work is the primacy of the creative imagination: in a universe devoid of clear spiritual definition, the imagination creates form, order, and understanding, hence, knowledge. Although his later work is often more carefully studied, such earlier poems as "The Emperor of Ice Cream," PETER QUINCE AT THE CLAVIER, SUNDAY MORNING, Le Monocle de Mon Oncle, and "Hibiscus on the Sleeping Shores" are among his best known.

The body of Stevens's work is contained in *The Necessary Angel* (1951), his essays on imagination, *Collected Poems* (1954), and *Opus Posthumous* (1957). The *Selected Letters of Wallace Stevens* (1966) and selections from his journals, *Souvenirs and Prophecies* (1977), are edited by his daughter, Holly Stevens. Because of his highly visual imagery, his metaphors of brilliant originality, and his inimitable style, Stevens's influence on younger poets has been almost more as a philosopher of aesthetics than as a poetic model.

Stevenson, Adlai E[wing] (1900–1965) American statesman. The grandson and namesake of a former vice-president of the U.S., the darling of the liberal wing of the Democratic Party, Stevenson had a long and distinguished career in various government capacities. During his unsuccessful bids for the presidency in 1952 and 1956, his campaign speeches—collected in *The Speeches of Adlai Stevenson* (1952), *Major Campaign Speeches* (1953), and *Call to Greatness* (1954)—earned him a reputation as one of the most brilliant political orators in U.S. history. Noted for their clear language, incisive humor, and fairness to opponents, Stevenson's books include *What I Think* (1956), *Friends and Enemies* (1959), *Putting First Things First* (1960), and *Looking Outward: Years of Crisis at the United Nations* (1963).

Stevenson, Robert Louis [Balfour] (1850–1894) Scottish novelist, poet, and essayist. A sickly child, Stevenson was tubercular all his life, in spite of which he lived adventurously, traveling widely. He studied civil engineering and prepared for the bar but never took up the practice of law. A trip to Europe supplied the materials for *An Inland Voyage* (1878) and *Travels with a Donkey in the Cévennes* (1879). In France he met Fanny Osbourne, followed her to the U.S., and married her, returning to Scotland in 1880. In rapid succession he published the collections of essays *Virginibus Puerisque* (1881) and *Familiar Studies of Men and Books* (1882); a collection of tales, *New Arabian Nights* (1882); *Silverado Squatters* (1883), his recollections of California; and the novel TREASURE ISLAND, one of his most popular books and the one which brought him fortune and renown. The following year, 1885, saw the publication of A CHILD'S GARDEN OF VERSES, *The Body Snatcher*, and *Prince Otto*, and in 1886 came THE STRANGE CASE OF DR. JEKYLL AND MR. HYDE and the historical romance KIDNAPPED, both of which have retained their popularity with readers. In 1887, after a series of disappointing visits to European health spas, the Stevensons went to America; while at Saranac Lake, Stevenson wrote *The Master of Ballantrae* (1888). He and his wife moved on to the West Coast and set out for the South Seas; except for one trip to Sydney, Stevenson spent the last five years of his life on Samoa, living as a planter and chief of the natives. It was there that he wrote *The Wrecker*, in collaboration with his stepson Lloyd Osbourne (1892), *Island Nights Entertainments* (1893), and *Catriona* (1893), a

sequel to *Kidnapped*. While dictating his WEIR OF HERMISTON, Stevenson died suddenly of apoplexy. He was buried on his beloved island.

During his life Stevenson wrote half a dozen plays with various collaborators, among them his wife and stepson, none of them successful; his *Letters* were published in 1895, after his death. Though his novels are perhaps less successfully accomplished than his briefer tales and stories, his work is marked by his power of invention, his command of horror and the supernatural, and the psychological depth which he was able to bring to romance.

Stewart, Douglas [Alexander] (1913–   ) New Zealand-born Australian poet, dramatist, and critic. As literary editor of the Sydney *Bulletin* (1940–60), extensive editor of Australian literature, influential critic, and prolific poet, Stewart became one of the most important modern literary figures in Australia. His *Collected Poems, 1936–1967* (1967) and *Selected Poems* (1973) show enormous range, most interestingly in his sharp, perceptive images of Australian landscapes. *The Fire on the Snow* (1941), about the tragic Scott expedition to Antarctica, has proved one of the most frequently broadcast of radio verse dramas. He has written several books of criticism, including *The Flesh and the Spirit* (1948) and *The Broad Stream* (1975). His autobiography, *Springtime in Taranaki*, appeared in 1984. He has also edited collections of Australian short stories, verse, bush songs, and ballads and written memoirs of such eminent Australians as Norman LINDSAY and Kenneth SLESSOR.

Stewart, J[ohn] I[nnes] M[ackintosh] (pen name Michael Innes, 1906–   ) English novelist, scholar, and literary critic. Under his own name Stewart is the author of a number of serious novels including a quintet of novels collectively titled *A Staircase in Surrey* (1974–78). In his capacity as scholar at Christ Church, Oxford, he wrote *Character and Motive in Shakespeare* (1949) and *Eight Modern Writers* (vol XII of the *Oxford History of English Literature*, 1963), as well as biographies of Rudyard KIPLING (1966), Joseph CONRAD (1968), and Thomas HARDY (1971). As Michael Innes he has written over thirty detective novels featuring the erudite Inspector Appleby. Among these books are *Hamlet, Revenge!* (1937), *The Man from the Sea* (1955), *Picture of Guilt* (1969), *The Gay Phoenix* (1976), *Going It Alone* (1979), *Sheiks and Adders* (1982), *Appleby and Honeybath* (1983), and *Carson's Conspiracy* (1984).

Stewart, [Lady] Mary [Florence Elinor] (1916–   ) English novelist. A storyteller of many dimensions, Stewart was a lecturer in English at Durham University, and writing poetry, when she met her geologist husband. He encouraged her to write her first novel, *Madam, Will You Talk?* (1955), and became an enthusiastic collaborator in her search for the authentic settings which are a distinctive feature of all her books. Time and place are unusually integrated with plot and character in Stewart's popular suspense stories. Among the best known of her long list of romances of the natural and supernatural are *The Ivy Tree* (1961), *Airs above the Ground* (1965), *The Gabriel Hounds* (1967), *Touch Not the Cat* (1976), and *The Wicked Day* (1983). Stewart's interest in myth led her to produce her own version of ARTHURIAN LEGEND in a trilogy about the magician Merlin and his life up to the crowning of King Arthur. Consisting of *The Crystal Cave* (1970), *The Hollow Hills* (1973), and *The Last Enchantment* (1979), this trilogy remains her major work. Among her books for children are *The Little Broomstick* (1971), *Ludo and the Star Horse* (1975), and *A Walk in Wolf Wood* (1980).

Stieglitz, Alfred (1864–1946)   American photographer. Stieglitz did a great deal to bring about the recognition of photography as an art form through his own work and through his landmark quarterly, *Camera Work* (1903–17), of which he was editor and publisher. At his Gallery "291," he and Edward STEICHEN exposed Americans to the new movement of modernism in painting and sculpture by supporting and exhibiting such American artists as John Marin and Arthur Dove and such French avant-gardists as RODIN, MATISSE, PICASSO, and TOULOUSE-LAUTREC. His wife, the painter Georgia O'KEEFFE, is depicted in more than four hundred of his photographs in *Portrait of O'Keeffe.*

Stifter, Adalbert (1805–1868)   Austrian novelist. Stifter's style reflects the tendency, found in much German literature of the time, away from romantic idealism and toward realism. His attachment to the common people and his sometimes excessive emphasis on the preservation of tradition align him, as well, with the conservative BIEDERMEIER movement. In the preface to his collection of narrative sketches, *Bunte Steine* (*Colored Stones*, 1853), he states that a boiling teakettle interests him as much as a volcano, that in even the most trivial phenomena, provided one knows how to look at them, the universal harmony of nature may be recognized. It is primarily this "gentle law," depicted in Stifter's writing, by which all things, small and great, are connected, that accounts for his extensive treatment of seemingly insignificant events and characters. His novel *Der Nachsommer* (*Indian Summer*, 1857) is one of the finest examples of the BILDUNGSROMAN.

Stijl, de (Du, "Style")   A movement in 20th-century Dutch art and architecture towards a distillation of pure form, also called *neoplasticism.* The principles of the movement were spelled out by its founders, Piet MONDRIAN and the versatile writer and artist Theo van Doesburg (1883–1931), in the avant-garde periodical, *De Stijl*, that was published from 1917 to 1931. In its final form, *de Stijl* reduced artistic elements to the basic forms of the cube and the rectangle and to unmixed primary colors (red, yellow, blue) and non-colors (black, white, gray). While the movement itself was relatively short-lived, it had a considerable

influence on the BAUHAUS, as well as on contemporary painting, typography, and commercial design.

Stilnovisti   A late 13th-century Tuscan school of Italian poets. They introduced what DANTE called a *dolce stil nuovo* ("sweet new style") in lyrical poetry. Reacting against the stylized conventions of the Provençal TROUBADOURS and the tradition of COURTLY LOVE, they achieved greater simplicity and sincerity in portraying the psychology of love and sorrow. Their poetry of love, however, is imbued with metaphysics and religion; the beloved lady becomes idealized as an "angelic woman," while love for her becomes an emotionally and spiritually ennobling experience that prepares a man for love of beauty and truth and God. This trend began with Guido Guinicelli; its leading exponents were Guido CAVALCANTI and Dante.

Stockton, Frank R.   See LADY OR THE TIGER?, THE

Stoic, The (1947)   The last novel in a trilogy by Theodore DREISER. See TITAN, THE.

Stoicism   A school of Greek philosophy. It was founded by Zeno of Citium (c362–c264 BC) around 308 BC. The Stoics were austere, advocating freedom from passions and desires. They equated the real with the material and defined the active principle in the universe as Force or God. They sought to be in harmony with nature and the divine will, and their philosophy is characterized by a detachment from the outside world. The Stoicism later taught by EPICTETUS had more of a religious emphasis. Zeno's school was continued by Cleanthes and Chrysippus and derived its name from the *Stoa Poikile*, a painted colonnade or porch at Athens in which Zeno and his successors lectured. Stoicism was highly congenial to the Roman temperament and influenced Roman Law. See MARCUS AURELIUS.

Stoker, [Abraham] Bram (1847–1912)   English writer. Stoker is best known for *Dracula* (1897), a wild tale of vampires and werewolves. It has been made into several motion pictures and sequels. Stoker was also, for several years, business manager of the famous actor Sir Henry IRVING.

Stoker, The   See AMERIKA.

Stone, Irving (1903–   )   American writer. A highly successful writer of popular fictionalized biography, Stone created a sensation with his second book, *Lust for Life* (1934), the life of Vincent VAN GOGH. He also edited some of Van Gogh's writings in *Dear Theo: The Autobiography of Vincent Van Gogh* (1937). He next wrote *Sailor on Horseback* (1938), about Jack LONDON, and *Clarence Darrow for the Defense* (1941). Among his many other best-selling books are *Adversary in the House* (1947), about Eugene V. DEBS, *Love Is Eternal* (1954), about Mary Todd LINCOLN, *The Agony and the Ecstasy* (1961), about MICHELANGELO, *The Origin* (1980), about Charles DARWIN, and *Depths of Glory* (1985).

Stone, Lucy (Mrs. Henry Brown Blackwell, 1818–1893) American woman suffragist. Stone insisted upon retaining her own name after marriage. Her first opponent in her battle for women's rights was her father, who refused her financial aid toward higher education. After several years of teaching, she was able to go to Oberlin College. After her graduation, she lectured against slavery and for woman suffrage. Although she had not intended to marry, she relented when Henry Blackwell promised to devote himself to her cause. With her husband, Lucy Stone edited the *Woman's Journal* (1872–93). She helped to form the American Woman Suffrage Association in 1869.

Stonehenge The great English prehistoric (Neolithic or early Bronze Age) monument on Salisbury Plain. The monument originally consisted of four concentric series of stones, circled by a ditch: an outer circle of thirteen-foot sandstones connected by lintels; next, a circle of single standing blue stones; then, a horseshoe-shaped ring; and, finally, an inner ovoid ring around a central block of blue marble, eighteen feet by four feet, known as the Altar Stone. It was originally believed to be a Druid construction, but it is now known that Druids arrived in Britain after its erection. It is generally agreed that the stones had a religious purpose, and in 1963 astronomer Gerald Hawkins claimed that the stones were astronomical instruments that measured solar and lunar movements.

Stoppard, Tom (original name Tom Straussler, 1937–   ) Czech-born English playwright. Stoppard moved to England with his family when he was nine and became a journalist at seventeen. His first staged play, *Rosencrantz and Guildenstern Are Dead* (1967), took the theatre world on both sides of the Atlantic by storm. The originality of the idea which put Hamlet's two insignificant friends centerstage was matched by the brilliance of the dialogue between these bewildered nonentities. Stoppard's mordant wit, experimental spirit, and instinct for stagecraft are evident in the subsequent products of his barbed and active pen. These products include *Jumpers* (1972) and *Travesties* (1974), a brilliant and hilarious concoction of pastiche, paradox, and political and intellectual history which combines Lenin, James Joyce, and the dadaist Tristan Tzara, all living in Zurich in 1917, with an amateur production of The Importance of Being Earnest. *Every Good Boy Deserves Favour* (1977), the story of a political dissident incarcerated in a mental hospital, and *The Real Thing* (1984), a less exuberant, though still witty, study of the problems and possibilities of love and commitment, have maintained Stoppard's reputation as a brilliant wit and parodist concerned with problems of alienation and free will.

Stopping by Woods on a Snowy Evening (1923) A lyric poem by Robert Frost. The poet stops his horse to contemplate the beauty of the scene and then continues his journey:

> The woods are lovely, dark and deep.
> But I have promises to keep,
> And miles to go before I sleep . . .

It is one of Frost's most famous and most frequently discussed poems; he himself once said that he would like to have it printed on one page, followed by "forty pages of footnotes."

Storey, David [Malcolm] (1933–   ) English novelist and playwright. The son of a Yorkshire miner, Storey earned his living as a professional rugby player and teacher before his first novel (the eighth he had written) was published. The novel, *This Sporting Life* (1960), is a compelling story about a rugby player's struggle not to be destroyed by the off-field aspects of professional sports. Subsequent novels include *Flight into Camden* (1961), *Radcliffe* (1963), *A Temporary Life* (1974), and *Saville* (1976). His fiction bears some relation to the early D. H. Lawrence in its North Country, working-class background and its concern with class, problems between generations in a changing society, and the complexity of love. Like Lawrence, he writes with power and brilliant imagery. His plays, beginning with *The Restoration of Arthur Middleton* (1966), are notable for their intensity and powerful use of dialogue. *In Celebration* (1969) takes three successful miner's sons home for a wedding anniversary, where they find themselves envying their father's sense of significance while they, each differently, feel injured and crippled. Among his other plays, all successes in Britain and the U.S., are *The Contractor* (1969), *Home* (1970), about the alienation and emptiness of life in a mental home, *The Changing Room* (1971), *Mother's Day* (1976), *Early Days* (1977; U.S. 1981), *A Prodigal Child* (1982), and *Present Times* (1984).

Storm, Theodor (1817–1888) German poet and novella writer. Storm is an unparalleled master of the so-called frame-technique of narrative writing: that is, he often has a character in a story tell another story, so that the second is framed by the first. His novellas, most of which are permeated by a strong feeling for his North German homeland, include *Immensee* (1850), in which the romantic melancholy of Storm's early period may be seen; *Aquis Submersus* (*Sunken in the Water*, 1876), which, like *Immensee*, is a story of lost love but is more realistic; and *Der Schimmelreiter* (*The White-Horse Rider*, 1888), a strongly realistic and deeply symbolic story about the man responsible for the dikes upon which his community's safety depends.

Storm, The (Groza, 1860) A drama by Aleksandr Ostrovsky. It depicts the tragedy of a young wife, Katerina, who tries unsuccessfully to break out of the stifling atmosphere of her life. No longer in love with her husband and weary of the dull merchant-class milieu in which they live, Katerina seeks a change by having a love affair with Boris, a young man who is unable to provide her with the escape she needs. Katerina confesses her infidelity, is hounded by her cruel mother-in-law, and, finally, commits suicide.

Storni, Alfonsina (1892–1938)   Argentine poet. Her poetry is guided by a thwarted eroticism and a deep resentment against a male world that left no role, other than submission, for women of talent. Although she desperately sought love, love became for her the simultaneous experience of hope, disillusion, and disgust. The tortured erotic poetry in *Dulce daño* (1918) and *Ocre* (1925) registered a uniquely feminine and feminist note. In a later volume, *El mundo de siete pozos* (1934), her erotic themes gave way to a more balanced, intellectual poetry. She drowned herself in 1938, the same year in which her final, haunting poems were published in *Mascarilla y trébol* (*Death-Mask and Clover*). Her *Obra poética completa* appeared in 1961.

Story of a Bad Boy, The (1870)   A semi-autobiographical novel by Thomas Bailey ALDRICH. The hero, Tom Bailey, is not really bad; he is, as the author explains, "a real human boy." The book tells of Tom's youth in New Hampshire and his early years in New Orleans with distant relatives. In Rivermouth, Tom gets into all kinds of mischief. This popular book was a forerunner of Mark Twain's *The Adventures of Tom Sawyer* (1876).

Story of an African Farm, The (1883)   A novel by Olive SCHREINER, published under the pseudonym Ralph Iron. Most of the action takes place on a Boer farm in South Africa in the late 19th century. The principal characters are three childhood playmates: Waldo, son of the kindly, pious German overseer; Em, the good-hearted stepdaughter of Tant' Sannie, owner of the farm; and Lyndall, Em's talented orphan cousin. Lyndall grows into a woman of great beauty and power, but her life is unhappy. She separates Em from her lover, has a child by a man whom she refuses to marry, and soon afterward dies. Waldo, who has always loved her, outlives her only a short while.

Story of the Stone, The   See DREAM OF THE RED CHAMBER.

Stout, Rex [Todhunter] (1886–1975)   American detective-story writer. Stout is famous as the creator of Nero Wolfe, the 286-pound sedentary sleuth and orchid-fancier who solves nearly all of his cases from his New York brownstone. Relying solely on logic and his keen wit, Wolfe employs the amiable and brash Archie Goodwin to do his legwork. Wolfe made his debut in *Fer-de-Lance* (1934) and continued his triumphs in forty-six novels, ending with *A Family Affair* (1975), written when Stout was eighty-eight. One of Stout's most controversial books —though, as detective fiction, not his best—was *The Doorbell Rang* (1965), in which he pitted Nero Wolfe against the F.B.I. and its then director, J. Edgar Hoover. *Justice Ends at Home* (1977) is a posthumous collection of previously unpublished stories written between 1913 and 1917.

Stow, [Julian] Randolph (1935–   )   Australian novelist and poet. Most of Stow's books are set around his birthplace in Western Australia. His reputation was established with his third novel, *To the Islands* (1958), the story of an old man's Lear-like journey to his death, accompanied by an old aborigine. *Tourmaline* (1963) depicts the eccentric citizens of an almost abandoned mining town as a microcosm of a world desperately seeking rebirth. *The Merry-Go-Round in the Sea* (1965), written in New Mexico, follows two cousins through World War II and the even more difficult years of readjustment in Australia after the war. Stow's novels, like the verse in *Act One* (1957) and *A Counterfeit Silence* (1969), contain lyrical evocations of the Australian landscape. *Visitants* (1979), *The Girl Green as Elderflower* (1980), and *The Suburbs of Hell* (1984) are among his other works.

Stowe, Harriet Beecher (1811–1896)   American novelist. Stowe had two major interests: writing and religion. The daughter of a prominent Congregationalist clergyman, Lyman BEECHER, and the wife of another, Calvin Stowe, she was both attracted and repelled by orthodox doctrine. Although she finally became an Episcopalian, at several periods during her difficult life she turned to different kinds of spiritualism.

She was born in Connecticut, but her father moved the family to Cincinnati, where Harriet was married in 1836. She and her husband returned to New England, where she was visited, in 1848, by the vision that inspired UNCLE TOM'S CABIN. The book brought her immediate fame and fortune; the following year, she and her husband traveled abroad and were well received. During Stowe's stay in England, she vigorously championed the cause of Lady BYRON in a series of articles and books.

After the publication of articles and a sequel to *Uncle Tom's Cabin*, she based a number of books on her husband's childhood reminiscences of rural New England. These books, including *The Pearl of Orr's Island* (1862), *Old-Town Folks* (1869), and *Poganuc People* (1878), are among the first examples of local color writing in New England. The other important book by Stowe is *The Minister's Wooing* (1859), in which local color is mixed with a religious theme.

Strabo (c 58 BC–c AD 24)   Greek geographer. Born in Pontus, Strabo traveled widely through the Roman world and wrote a description of it in seventeen books, *Geographia* (*The Geography*), nearly all of which are extant. His history of Rome in forty-seven books, beginning where Polybius's history ended, is lost.

Strachey, [Giles] Lytton (1880–1932)   English biographer and historian. A member of the BLOOMSBURY GROUP, Strachey revolutionized the art of biography by writing humanized criticism, not panegyric, especially about the Victorians. His urbanity, irony, and witty malice are seen best in his most famous work, *Eminent Victorians* (1918). He also wrote *Landmarks in French Literature*

(1912), *Queen Victoria* (1921), *Books and Characters* (1922), and *Elizabeth and Essex* (1928).

Strafford, 1st earl of (Sir Thomas Wentworth, 1593–1641) English statesman, favorite and chief adviser of Charles I. In 1640 Strafford was named commander of the royal forces against a Scottish army that had invaded northern England. His failure to repel the Scots gave his enemies in Parliament, led by John Pym, an opportunity to accuse him of treason. He was condemned by a bill of attainder, which the king reluctantly signed, and executed. He is the central figure of Robert Browning's drama *Strafford* (1837).

Strait Is the Gate (La Porte étroite, 1909; tr 1924) A novel by André GIDE. Jerome woos his cousin Alissa, but, although she accepts and returns his spiritual love, she will not marry him. Alissa says that she prefers to please God by sacrificing her own worldly happiness to that of her sister, but she is fearful, too, of passion. When the sister no longer needs her sacrifice, Alissa fears that God does not think her capable of such holy selflessness and says she must continue to renounce her own happiness—and Jerome's—in order to prove her sincerity. She dies without even coming close to the mystic joy she sought.

strambotto Italian folk lyric popular during the Middle Ages and the Renaissance with both rustic and aristocratic poets. Of uncertain etymology, the word may reflect an original link with folk dance. Its subject is love, treated either seriously or lightheartedly; its form consists of a stanza of eight eleven-syllable lines rhyming a-b-a-b-a-b-a-b or a-b-a-b-a-b-c-c (as in *ottava rima*). The former scheme was preferred among the Sicilian poets of the 13th century; the latter, by the Tuscan writers of the Renaissance, who also called the form a *rispetto*, perhaps because the poet pays his respects to the lady in these poems. In addition to single stanzas, there were also chains, or longer poems, made up of *strambotti* or *rispetti*. It differed from the *ottava rima* stanza mainly in content, the latter being regularly used for long narrative poems rather than single lyrics. But some *rispetti* also varied the rhyme scheme to a-b-a-b-c-c-d-d. Among the better-known writers who used the form were Angelo Poliziano (1454–94) and Lorenzo de' MEDICI.

Strand, Mark (1934–   ) Canadian-born American poet, editor, and translator. Strand turned to poetry after studying painting at Yale; the graphic quality of his poems attests to his training in the visual arts. He is a poet of restlessness and dark sensibility; the tone of his poetry is brooding and introspective, conveying at times a sense of terror reminiscent of ROETHKE. Strand's translation, *18 Poems from the Quechua* (1971), exposed him to the illusionist techniques of Latin American writers. His own verse in *The Story of Our Lives* (1973) reveals this influence, particularly in its shifting boundaries of reality. Among his other books of verse are *Sleeping with One Eye Open* (1964), *Darker* (1970), and *The Late Hour* (1978), poems

about the past, loss, and the power of love. *Selected Poems* appeared in 1980. He has edited a book of essays on art, *Art of the Real: Nine American Figurative Painters* (1983). His other publications include two books for children, *The Planet of Lost Things* (1982) and *The Night Book* (1985), and a collection of short stories, *Mr. and Mrs. Baby* (1985).

Strand, Paul (1890–1976) American photographer. Strand was a student of the documentary photographer Lewis W. Hine (1874–1940) and, through him, met Alfred STIEGLITZ. His photographs were subsequently exhibited at Stieglitz's "291" gallery and published in *Camera Work*. Strand's photographs of this period already displayed the penchant for geometric abstraction that was to pervade his later work. They immediately set him in the vanguard of artistic photography, while firmly aligning his own work with the cubist innovations of the European painters whom Stieglitz alone exhibited and promoted in the U.S. at that time. In the 1920s, Strand made many pictures of machine parts, like *Double Akely* (1922), that show the influence of the futurist styles of Picabia and DUCHAMP. His most famous later works were eloquent portraits of peasants and villagers he encountered while traveling in France, Italy, and the Outer Hebrides in the 1950s.

Strange Case of Dr. Jekyll and Mr. Hyde, The (1886) A novel by Robert L. STEVENSON, the disturbing tale of the dual personality of Dr. Jekyll, a physician. A generous and philanthropic man, he is preoccupied with the problems of good and evil and with the possibility of separating them into two distinct personalities. He develops a drug that transforms him into the demonic Mr. Hyde, in whose person he exhausts all the latent evil in his nature. He also creates an antidote that will restore him to his respectable existence as Dr. Jekyll. Gradually, however, the unmitigated evil of his darker self predominates, until finally he performs an atrocious murder. His saner self determines to curtail these alternations of personality, but he discovers that he is losing control over his transformations, that he slips with increasing frequency into the world of evil. Finally, unable to procure one of the ingredients for the mixture of redemption, and on the verge of being discovered, he commits suicide.

The novel is of great psychological perception and strongly concerned with ethical problems.

Strange Interlude (1928) A play in nine acts, by Eugene O'NEILL. The plot concerns the emotional and especially the sexual reactions of Nina Leeds, who subconsciously hates her father; she holds him responsible for preventing her from sleeping with her fiancé before he was killed in France in World War I. She becomes a nurse and marries good-natured Sam Evans, but when she learns she is about to have a child, she resorts to abortion, ostensibly because of a strain of insanity in his family. However, she has an affair with Dr. Darrell, becomes pregnant, and pretends their child is Evans's. When Evans dies, Nina marries a childhood admirer who reminds her of her father. The play caused a sensation by its use of a STREAM OF CONSCIOUSNESS technique. The characters speak in asides to reveal their true thoughts, in contrast to their conversation.

Stranger, The (L'Étranger, 1942; tr 1946)   A novel by Albert CAMUS. It reveals the ABSURD as the condition of man, who feels himself a stranger in his world. Meursault refuses to "play the game," by telling the conventional social white lies demanded of him or by believing in human love or religious faith. The unemotional style of his narrative lays naked his motives—or his absence of motive—for his lack of grief over his mother's death, his affair with Marie, his killing an Arab in the hot Algerian sun. Having rejected by honest self-analysis all interpretations which could explain or justify his existence, he nevertheless discovers, while in prison awaiting execution, a passion for the simple fact of life itself.

Strangers and Brothers (1940–1970)   A series of eleven novels written by C. P. SNOW over the course of more than thirty years. The hero and narrator of most of the series is Lewis Eliot, a lawyer and government administrator, whose development in many ways paralleled Snow's own. The novels are *Strangers and Brothers* (1940), *The Light and the Dark* (1947), *Time of Hope* (1949), *The Masters* (1951), *The New Men* (1954), *Homecoming* (1956), *The Conscience of the Rich* (1958), *The Affair* (1959), *Corridors of Power* (1964), *The Sleep of Reason* (1968), and *Last Things* (1970). Written in a direct prose, the novels all deal variously with power struggles and conflicts between private conscience and public life, in science and government.

Straparola, Giovan Francesco (c1480–1557) Italian writer. A native of Lombardy, Straparola is the author of two books of *novelle*, *Le piacevoli notti* (*The Pleasureful Nights*, 1550–53). Of the seventy-five *novelle*, some twenty are folk tales, marking the first appearance in European literature of a large group of such stories. Included among these folk tales are such favorites as BEAUTY AND THE BEAST, PUSS IN BOOTS, and "The Singing Apple."

Stratemeyer, Edward L. (1862–1930)   American writer of over four hundred books for young readers, under more than twenty pen names. Stratemeyer began writing magazine stories in 1884 and DIME NOVELS under the name Jim Bowie. He began his immensely popular series "The ROVER BOYS," with the pseudonym Arthur M. Winfield, and the adventure series about Tom SWIFT. He provided his public with a steady stream of books in series-form and started a syndicate with a stable of ghost writers for whom he provided outlines and ideas. Stratemeyer continued to write and personally edited all the work of the syndicate. Two other perennial favorites were his "Hardy Boys" series for boys and the "Nancy Drew" series for girls (Stratemeyer himself wrote nine of the former and three of the latter). At his death, over six million of his books had been sold. The

syndicate was then managed by his two daughters, primarily by Harriet S[tratemeyer] Adams, who took over the Nancy Drew series.

Strauss, David Friedrich (1808–1874)   German theologian. In *Leben Jesu* (*Life of Jesus*, 1835), which was translated into English by George ELIOT, he attributed a secular, mythical origin to the miraculous narrative of the gospels. See FEUERBACH, LUDWIG.

Strauss, Johann (1825–1899)   An Austrian composer and conductor, known as "The Waltz King." He succeeded to the conducting post of his father, Johann Strauss (1804–49), also a well-known composer. Many of the younger Strauss's waltzes are still famous—among them the *Blue Danube* and *Tales of the Vienna Woods*. His operetta *Die Fledermaus* (*The Bat*, 1874) remains a perennial favorite.

Strauss, Richard (1864–1949)   German composer and conductor. He extended the musical ideas of Richard WAGNER and Franz LISZT to their limits in tone poems such as *Don Juan* (1889), *Till Eulenspiegels lustige Streichen* (1895), and *Don Quixote* (1898); and in his greatest operas, *Salomé* (1905; based on Oscar WILDE's play), *Elektra* (1909), *Der Rosenkavalier* (1911), and *Ariadne auf Naxos* (1912). Strauss collaborated with Hugo von HOFMANNSTHAL on many of his operas.

Stravinsky, Igor [Fyodorovich] (1882–1971) Russian-born composer. Stravinsky's creative output spanned and deeply affected the entire development of modern music, from impressionism to neoclassicism and from tonality to polytonality and atonality. His first significant works, commissioned by Sergei DIAGHILEV's Russian Ballet, were *L'Oiseau de feu* (*The Firebird*, 1910), *Petrouchka* (1911), and *Le Sacre du printemps* (*Rite of Spring*, 1913). The latter so startled its first audience that it provoked a riot. Later works seem restrained by comparison: *Histoire du soldat* (1918; a pantomime, with narrator and instruments); *Oedipus Rex* (1927; an "opera-oratorio" using the Jean Cocteau version of Sophocles' play in a Latin translation in order to dissociate the text's sound from its meaning); *Symphony of Psalms* (1930); *Symphony in C* (1940); *The Rake's Progress* (1951), an opera to a libretto by W. H. AUDEN and Chester Kallman; *Agon* (1957; ballet). Stravinsky attempted to explain his musical aesthetic in his autobiography, *Chronicles of My Life* (1936), and in *Poetics of Music* (1948), a group of lectures.

Strawberry Hill   The estate of Horace WALPOLE at Twickenham, Surrey, England. It was here that he established his private printing press (1757–89) in the house he converted into "a little Gothic castle."

stream of consciousness   A narrative technique. This device was developed toward the end of the 19th century, often confused with interior monologue, and employed to evoke the psychic life of a character and depict subjective as well as objective reality. The term "stream of consciousness" was first used by William JAMES in his *Prin-*

ciples of Psychology (1890); the concept behind it—that ideas and consciousness in general are fluid and shifting, rather than fixed—contributed to a new approach to the novel. This approach was also given impetus by the new Freudian theories of the conscious and unconscious mind and the Bergsonian concept of time as duration and of consciousness as an indivisible flux. As a literary term, "stream of consciousness" generally refers to the presentation of a character's thoughts, feelings, reactions, etc., on an approximated preverbal level and with little or no direct comment or explanation by the author. It is frequently difficult to distinguish absolutely between stream of consciousness and interior monologue, and the terms are sometimes used as if they were interchangeable. In general, the term "stream of consciousness" is used as the description of mental life at the borderline of conscious thought and is characterized by the devices of association, reiteration of word- or symbol-motifs, apparent incoherence, and the reduction or elimination of normal syntax and punctuation to simulate the free flow of the character's mental processes. "Interior monologue" refers to a presentation of thoughts more consciously controlled and on a level closer to direct verbalization. The French writer Edouard Dujardin claims to have been the first to use the interior monologue in his LES LAURIERS SONT COUPÉS. Another innovator was Dorothy Richardson, who recorded the psychic experience of one character in her twelve-volume *Pilgrimage* (1915–38). James Joyce brought the stream-of-consciousness approach to its highest form in ULYSSES and FINNEGANS WAKE. In America, William Faulkner's THE SOUND AND THE FURY is often given as a leading example of stream-of-consciousness writing, though only the first two sections of the book can be described as such; the third section, however, provides a good example of an interior monologue according to the differentiation made above. In England, Virginia Woolf adapted the stream-of-consciousness technique to slightly different uses in TO THE LIGHTHOUSE, MRS. DALLOWAY, and THE WAVES. It is no longer the "experimental" form it was once considered, and aspects of stream-of-consciousness techniques are evident in the work of most of the important writers to appear since the 1930s.

Streetcar Named Desire, A (1947)

A play by Tennessee WILLIAMS. The winner of a PULITZER PRIZE, it is set in the French Quarter of New Orleans where two streetcars named Desire and Cemetery run on a single track. It is the story of Blanche DuBois, a faded Southern belle, who comes to live with her sister, Stella, and the sister's husband, Stanley. Annoyed at her pretensions to gentility and her flirtatious behavior, Stanley eventually warns a friend who had thought of marrying Blanche. With her hopes of marriage destroyed, Blanche confronts Stanley, who rapes her. Finally, with her illusions still strong, she is taken away to a mental institution.

Street Scene (1929)

A play by Elmer RICE. The play, using a naturalistic setting, presents life in a slum tenement and reaches its climax in a double murder. One of the first stage productions to include realistic sound effects throughout the performance, it was the winner of a PULITZER PRIZE. Later it was given a musical score by Kurt WEILL (1947).

Strephon

The shepherd in Sir Philip Sidney's *Arcadia* who makes love to the beautiful Urania. It is a stock name for a pastoral lover, while the name Chloe is frequently given to a Strephon's beloved.

Strindberg, [Johan] August (1849–1912)

Swedish playwright, novelist, and poet. The son of a serving woman and a bankrupted ex-gentleman, Strindberg knew poverty and misery from childhood. Later, he was variously employed as a journalist, a tutor, and an assistant at the Royal Library. His first significant play was *Master Olaf* (written in 1874 in prose, rewritten in verse in 1878, and first performed in the original version in 1881). It was followed by *Lucky Per's Travels* (1880), reminiscent of Ibsen's PEER GYNT, and *Sir Bengt's Wife* (1882), an answer to Ibsen's A DOLL'S HOUSE, which Strindberg hated. In 1879 Strindberg first became the subject of literary excitement with his satirical novel *The Red Room*, which many critics consider the first example of modern Swedish realism. With the publication of the stories in *Married* (1884–86), his fame became unpleasant notoriety, for these satirical, bitter narratives involved their author in a prosecution for blasphemy. He was acquitted, but the experience contributed to his feelings of persecution that culminated in his breakdown of 1896.

Strindberg embarked on the first of his unfortunate marriages in 1877. His relations with his wife, the former Siri Wrangel, probably formed the basis for the conflicts in the major plays of his realistic-naturalistic period: THE FATHER, *Comrades* (1888), and *The Creditors* (1890). These three works are centered on the duel between the sexes: the woman, ruthless and aggressive, asserts herself as the equal —if not the superior—of the man, usurps his masculine prerogatives of decision and leadership, and destroys him. Not until many years later, in the powerful THE DANCE OF DEATH, did Strindberg write of a husband who enslaves and torments his wife. In MISS JULIE, probably the best known of the plays of this period, Strindberg depicts both sexual antagonism and class conflict in the figure of the aristocratic young woman who seduces her father's footman.

In 1891 Strindberg's first marriage ended in a painful divorce. He married again in 1893, but this union lasted only a few years. He was beginning to show increased evidence of emotional disturbance, and his feelings of persecution were intensified by his difficulties in getting his plays produced; he had been forced to establish his own Experimental Theatre in Copenhagen to have *Miss Julie* and *The Creditors* performed. He became interested in the physical sciences, but his experiments in chemistry were soon transformed into delvings into alchemy, occultism, and mysticism. In July of 1896 he suffered a psychological crisis which brought him to the edge of madness, an experience which he recorded in the autobiographical *Inferno* (1897) and *Legends* (1898), and expressed dramatically in the mystical and symbolic plays *To Damascus* (Parts I and II, 1898; Part III, 1904), *Advent* (1899), and *There Are Crimes and Crimes* (1899). This period of crisis marks the beginning of what is perhaps the most interesting phase of his creative life; in order to give dramatic form to his new vision of life—a vision in which the inner world has as much, if not more, claim to reality than external experience—he wrote the haunting, surrealistic "dream-plays" that became the forerunners of modern expressionism. Gentler and less bitter than the plays of his realistic period, these dramas have a scope that ranges from the mystic surrealism of *A Dream Play* (1902) to the nearly naturalistic but tenderly mystical *Easter* (1901). As his emotional health improved, he turned again to Swedish history and wrote a series of dramas probably inspired by the historical plays of Shakespeare. Among them are *The Saga of the Volsungs*, *Gustavus Vasa* (a continuation of the story of the Vasa dynasty begun in *Master Olaf*), *Erik XIV*, and *Gustavus Adolphus*. In 1907 he and August Falck established the Intimate Theatre in Stockholm, for which Strindberg wrote a series of four "Chamber Plays"; of these, only *The Spook Sonata* (1907) achieved marked success.

Strindberg's collected writings—plays, fairy tales, poems, short stories, prose sketches, essays, autobiographical writings, novels—fill fifty-five volumes. Particularly interesting are his autobiographical works, including *The Son of a Servant* (1886), *A Fool's Defense* (1893), and *Alone* (1903).

Stroheim, Erich von (real name Erich Oswald Stroheim, 1885–1957) Austrian-born film director. Stroheim's motion pictures (all made in the U.S.) represent the pinnacle of realism in the American silent cinema. The "von" was an assumed title: he was the son of a Jewish hat merchant from Silesia, not of a Viennese aristocrat. An extra in D. W. GRIFFITH's *The Birth of a Nation* (1915), Stroheim first leapt to fame playing the dastardly Hun, in a series of movies made during World War I. His directorial career began with *Blind Husbands* (1918), which, together with his second film, *The Devil's Passkey* (1919), injected a new cynical-realistic strain into what has been called the cinema's "age of innocence." With his third film, *Foolish Wives* (1921), an incisive study of moral corruption in Monte Carlo after World War I, he established a reputation for reckless extravagance which would ultimately contribute to the termination of his career as film director. With the same film, he also ran afoul of the censors on the first of many occasions. But *Greed* (1923–24), his masterpiece and one of the summits of film art, was hacked from its original forty-two reels down to ten—not by the censors but at the behest of the studio executives. A close adaptation of Frank Norris's novel MCTEAGUE, *Greed*, even in

the drastically abridged form in which it survives, demonstrates Stroheim's unparalleled ability to create a rich visual and dramatic fabric out of the accumulation of carefully observed details. His later films, though similarly mutilated or left uncompleted, reveal the same unfaltering mastery of the medium. They include *The Wedding March* (1926–28) and *Queen Kelly* (1928). *Walking Down Broadway* (1932–33), his only talkie, brought his directorial career to a close. Thereafter, he established his reputation as an actor on both sides of the Atlantic, playing memorable roles in such films as *As You Desire Me* (1932), *La Grande Illusion* (1937), *Five Graves to Cairo* (1943), and *Sunset Boulevard* (1950).

strophe (Gr, "turn") Originally, that part of an ODE which was sung by the Greek dramatic CHORUS as it moved in one direction, followed by an antistrophe when the chorus reversed the direction of its movement. Hence, in prosody, a STANZA.

structuralism A method of intellectual inquiry. Broadly multi- and interdisciplinary, structuralism provides a framework for organizing and understanding any area of study concerned with the production and perception of "meaning": primarily philosophy, mathematics, linguistics, psychology, anthropology, and literary criticism, but several other fields as well. Its fundamental assumption is that all human behavior arises from an innate structuring capacity which gives rise to language, myths, and social patterns. "Structure," in the structuralist sense, denotes the mutual relation of constituent parts of a whole, governed by a system of transformations that is entirely self-regulating. Totalities take logical priority over individual elements, relationships over entities, the hidden or "deep" over the apparent. Claude LÉVI-STRAUSS is the most important structural anthropologist. Other notable structuralists and their major works include the psychoanalyst Jacques Lacan (*Écrits*, 1966), the linguists Ferdinand de Saussure (*Cours de linguistique générale*, 1916) and Noam Chomsky (*Language and Mind*, 1968), the philosophers Jacques Derrida (*L'Écriture et la différence*, 1967) and Michel FOUCAULT (*Les Mots et les choses*, 1966), and the group of mathematicians known as Nicholas Bourbaki.

Literary structuralism relies on the premise that literature is simply a language having a system of signs which must be exposed and analyzed so that the meaning of a work can be conveyed. Evaluation of the "truth" or "message" of a novel or play is not the goal of structuralist criticism so much as the enumeration of underlying patterns of discourse and the laws which control them. Thus both the comic-book character Superman and RACINE have been objects of ingenious and often rewarding structuralist scrutiny. Critics and their works who have influenced or been associated in one way or another with structuralism are Gaston BACHELARD (*La Poétique de l'espace*, 1958; *La Poétique de la rêverie*, 1960), Maurice BLANCHOT (*L'Espace littéraire*, 1955; *Le Livre à venir*, 1959), Lucien Goldmann

(*Le Dieu caché*, 1956), and Georges Poulet (*Études sur le temps humain*, 4 vols, 1950–68). Structuralists proper include Roland BARTHES (*Le Degré zéro de l'écriture*, 1953; *Sur Racine*, 1963), René Girard (*La Violence et le sacré*, 1972), Julia Kristeva (*Semeiotike*, 1970), Paul de Man (*Blindness and Insight*, 1971), Philippe Sollers (*Logiques*, 1968), and Tzvetan Todorov (*Littérature et signification*, 1967).

Strugatsky, Arkady Natanovich (1925–   ) and **Boris Natanovich** (1933–   )   Russian science-fiction writers. Widely popular in the Soviet Union, the Strugatskys often combine high adventure with social and political criticisms provocative to Soviet censors. Marxist theory is questioned in the story *Trudno byt bogom* (1966; tr *Hard to Be a God*, 1973), and the novel *Khishchnye veshchi* (1965; tr *The Final Circle of Paradise*, 1976) warns against the positivism of science and the ideal of complete material satisfaction. Other notable works of the Strugatskys include *Ponedelnik nachinaetsya v subbotu* (1966; tr *Monday Begins on Saturday*, 1977), *Skazka o troike* (1968; tr *Tale of the Troika*, 1977), and *Obitayemy ostrov* (1969; tr *Prisoners of Power*, 1977).

Stuart, Gilbert [Charles] (1755–1828)   American painter. After seventeen years in England and Ireland, where he studied with Benjamin WEST and began a successful career, he returned to America in 1792. He gained fame for his portraits, among which is the well-known, unfinished "Athenaeum" head of George WASHINGTON in the Boston Museum of Fine Arts.

Stuart, [Hilton] Jesse (1907–1984)   American poet, novelist, and short-story writer. Stuart is known for his many books dealing with the mountain region of Kentucky and its people. Besides verse and short stories, Stuart wrote over thirty novels, beginning with *Trees of Heaven* (1940).

Stubbs, George (1724–1806)   British painter. Self-taught as a painter of portraits and animals, Stubbs began as an anatomist. His drawings illustrated many medical texts, and he was at one time a hospital lecturer in anatomy. He gained lasting international fame for his monumental *Anatomy of a Horse* (1766), a book which he researched, wrote, illustrated, and engraved single-handedly over a period of twelve years. Although he was known for a century and a half primarily as a painter of horses, Stubbs's reputation has grown remarkably in the second half of the 20th century, and he is now valued as much for his sensitive depiction of grooms, menagerie keepers, and the gentry seated in their carriages as for his painting of the animals themselves. *Horse Frightened by a Lion* (1770) is one of his best-known paintings.

Stuckenberg, Viggo (1863–1905)   Danish poet. With his friends Sophus Claussen (1865–1931) and Jens Johannes Jørgensen (1866–1956), Stuckenberg initiated the neoromantic movement in Denmark. His poem "Den Vilde Joeger" ("The Wild Huntsman," 1894), mystical and medieval in its mood, marked a departure from the realistic school and its social concerns. Gentle melancholy, wistful tenderness, and a love for nature characterize his verse. Among Stuckenberg's collections of poetry are *Flyvende Sommer* (1898), *Aarsens Tid* (1905), and *Sidste Digte* (1906).

Studs Lonigan (1935)   A trilogy by James T. FARRELL, consisting of *Young Lonigan*, *The Young Manhood of Studs Lonigan*, and *Judgment Day*. In relentlessly naturalistic style it presents the boyhood, adolescence, early manhood, and, finally, the death of William (Studs) Lonigan, the son of lower-middle-class Irish Catholic parents in Chicago. Although Studs as a boy displays sparks of vigor and ambition, the combined influences of his social and economic environment, his swaggering and vicious associates, and his narrow family, educational, and religious background serve to aggravate his weaknesses and lead him into a life of futile dissipation, which he recognizes as unsatisfactory, but from which he is unable to escape. The language of the streets, the monotony and crudity of the thought processes of Studs and his associates, and their numerous sordid sexual adventures are all frankly and faithfully reproduced, and there is extensive documentation in the depiction of the social background in the U.S. during the period between 1912 and the early 1930s.

Young Lonigan (1932) introduces Studs as a boy of fifteen graduating from a Roman Catholic grammar school and starting out on the typical career of his class and time. He dreams of becoming a "great guy" and takes care to conform to the pattern of conduct set for him by his associates. Notable events are his initiation into the mysteries of sex (in which he is assisted by Iris, a promiscuous adolescent girl of the neighborhood) and his first sentimental attachment, of which Lucy Scanlan is the object.

In *The Young Manhood of Studs Lonigan* (1934), the career of Studs is carried through the period of the 1920s, during which he works as a house painter with his father and participates in the dissipations of the time. The culmination of the novel is a wild New Year's Eve party at which a girl named Irene is raped by Weary Reilley, one of Studs's companions.

Judgment Day (1935) records Studs's declining health, futile dissipation, love affair with Catherine Banahan, fruitless search for a job, and ultimate death from pneumonia. The climax of the novel is a dramatic death scene against the background of family lamentations and quarrels and of Roman Catholic prayers for the dead.

Sturm und Drang (Ger, "storm and stress")   A literary movement in late 18th-century Germany that led to GERMAN ROMANTICISM. The movement, which took its name from the title of a play by Maximillian KLINGER, was particularly rich in its drama and lyric poetry. Goethe's GÖTZ VON BERLICHINGEN was hailed as an outstanding example of *Sturm und Drang* drama. Other major figures were the young SCHILLER, Reinhold LENZ, Heinrich Wagner, and Gottfried Bürger. The drama of the *Sturm und Drang* emphasized social injustices and the need for reform. In lyric poetry, the writers celebrated natural feeling, reacting against the formalism of NEOCLASSICISM. They stressed the energetic Promethean quality of the individual in opposition to the rationalistic ideal of the ENLIGHTENMENT. The representatives of the *Sturm und Drang* greatly admired SHAKESPEARE, and the effect of HERDER's writing on them can be seen in their frequent interest in folk material and the German past.

stylites (or pillar saints; fr Gr, *stylos*, "pillar") A class of early and medieval ascetics. Chiefly of Syria, they lived on top of pillars from which they never descended. The most celebrated were Simeon Stylites of Syria and Daniel the Stylite of Constantinople. Simeon (d 596) spent sixty-eight years on different pillars, each loftier and narrower than the preceding, the last being sixty-six feet high. Daniel (d 494) lived for thirty-three years on a pillar and was not infrequently nearly blown from it by the storms from Thrace.

Tennyson wrote a poem, "St. Simeon Stylites" (1842). Paphnutius in Anatole France's *Thaïs* becomes a stylite for a time.

Stymphalian birds   See HERACLES.

Stymphalus   See PELOPS.

Styron, William [Clark, Jr.] (1925–) American novelist. Born and raised in Virginia, Styron first drew critical notice with *Lie Down in Darkness* (1951), his long novel about the disintegration of a Southern family. His use of the STREAM OF CONSCIOUSNESS technique in this novel reveals the influence of FAULKNER and Thomas WOLFE. His next book, *The Long March* (1957), is an economically written account of the clash between liberal ideals and military values. *Set This House on Fire* (1960), dealing with American expatriates in Italy, was less successful than his powerful and controversial next novel, *The Confessions of Nat Turner* (1967; PULITZER PRIZE), a fictionalized treatment of the 1831 slave rebellion in southern Virginia. In 1972 he wrote a play, *In the Clap Shack*, set in the VD ward of a World War II Navy hospital. Always preoccupied with the complex nature of evil, he spent his next five years working on *Sophie's Choice* (1979), an intricate, soul-searching novel about a love affair between a beautiful Polish woman who survived Auschwitz and a young American writer. *This Quiet Dust and Other Writings* (1982) is a collection of essays, reviews, and miscellaneous pieces.

Styx   A river of the underworld across which CHARON ferried the dead. According to classical mythology, it flowed seven times round the infernal regions. The five rivers of Hell are the Styx, ACHERON, Cocytus, Phlegethon, and LETHE. Styx is also the deity of the river, a daughter of OCEANUS and Tethys, and mother of Zelus (Zeal), Nike (Victory), Bia (Strength), and Kratos (Power).

Dante, in his DIVINE COMEDY, places the rivers in different circles of the Inferno. Thus, he makes the Acheron

divide the borderland from Limbo. The former realm is for the "praiseless and the blameless dead"; Limbo is for the unbaptized. He places the Stygian Lake of inky hue in the fifth circle, the realm of those who put no restraint on their anger. The fire-stream of Phlegethon he fixes to the eighth steep, the Hell of burning, where it snows flakes of fire and where blasphemers are confined. He places the frozen river of Cocytus in the tenth pit of Malebolge, a region of thick-ribbed ice, the lowest depth of Hell, where JUDAS and LUCIFER are imprisoned. Lethe, he says, is no river of Hell at all, but it is the one wish of all those in the infernal regions to get to it, that they may drink its water and forget their torments. It being, however, in Purgatory, they can never reach it.

sub rosa (Lat, "under the rose") In strict confidence. The origin of the phrase is wrapped in obscurity, but the story is that CUPID gave a rose to Harpocrates, the god of silence, to bribe him not to betray the amours of VENUS. Hence the flower became the emblem of silence. In 1526 it was placed over confessionals.

Subtle   A character in Ben Jonson's comedy THE ALCHEMIST. An artful quack, Subtle is an "alchemist" who pretends to be on the eve of discovering the Philosopher's stone. Sir Epicure Mammon, a rich knight, is his principal dupe but by no means his only one.

Such Is Life   See FURPHY, JOSEPH.

Suckling, Sir John (1609–1642) English poet, courtier, and soldier. Suckling was known in his day for his wit, gaiety, extravagance, and love of gaming. He was implicated in the plot to rescue the earl of Strafford from the Tower of London in 1641 and died a fugitive in France, possibly a suicide, possibly the victim of a vengeful servant.

One of the CAVALIER POETS, Suckling was, however, influenced in some superficial effects by Donne. His poetry has the kind of ease, knowledgeability, and unaffected simplicity of diction that has traditionally formed, in England, the ideal of gentlemanly speech. In his poems he could play both the ardent lover and skeptic—although the latter pose gave more scope for the wit which distinguishes lyrics like the song "Why so pale and wan, fond lover?" from his play *Aglaura* (1637). Other works by Suckling include "Session of the Poets" (1637), a poem containing descriptions of Ben JONSON, Thomas CAREW, and other contemporary writers, and *Brennoralt, or The Discontented Colonel* (1639), a play.

Sucre, Antonio José de (1795–1830) Venezuelan general and patriot. Considered one of the most high-minded of Hispanic America's revolutionary heroes, Sucre was the chief lieutenant and friend of Simón BOLÍVAR. In 1822 Sucre's victory at Pichincha drove the Spaniards from Ecuador. In Peru he commanded the revolutionary army that defeated the Spaniards at Ayacucho, virtually ending the wars for independence. He assisted in the creation of an independent Bolivia and reluctantly became its first president in 1826, only to resign in 1828. He was returning to his home in Quito after an unsuccessful attempt to keep Venezuela in Gran Colombia when he was mysteriously murdered near Pasto, Colombia.

Suddenly Last Summer   See WILLIAMS, TENNESSEE.

Sudermann, Hermann (1857–1928)   German playwright and novelist. With the exception of his stories in *Litauische Geschichten* (1917; tr *Excursion to Tilsit*, 1930), Sudermann is remembered primarily for his earlier works in both drama and fiction. In his plays, which include *Die Ehre* (1889; tr *Honor*, 1915), *Sodoms Ende* (1891; tr *The Man and His Picture*, 1903), and *Die Heimat* (tr MAGDA), he exercised a searching social criticism aimed particularly at the Prussian aristocracy; this led critics to associate him with NATURALISM. His dramatic technique, however, is far from naturalistic; his plots are contrived, and he makes frequent use of monologues and asides. His novels include *Frau Sorge Frau Sorge* (1887; tr *Dame Care*, 1891), *Der Katzensteg* (1889; tr *Regine*, 1894), and *Das hohe Lied* (1908; tr *Song of Songs*, 1909); all of them, like his plays, deal with social questions.

sudra   A member of the menial CASTE (*varna*). In the fourfold division of the Hindu social hierarchy, sudra is below the BRAHMIN, KSHATRIYA, and VAISHYA. Unlike the others, the sudra is not in principle supposed to have access to the sacred myths and rituals of HINDUISM and is not of *dvija* (twice-born) status.

Sue, Eugène (real name Marie Joseph Sue, 1804–1857)   French novelist. A ship's doctor, Sue found the material for such sea stories as *Plik et Plok* (1831) and *La Vigie de Koatven* (1833) among his own adventures. Best known for his popular and sensational romances in the manner of Dumas père, Sue had a prolific and highly successful career. Among his works are THE MYSTERIES OF PARIS and *Le Juif errant* (*The Wandering Jew*, 1844–45).

Sueños, Los (1627)   A series of prose satires by Francisco de QUEVEDO. Supposedly a description of the author's visits to Hell, they are notable for their incisive caricature of the men and institutions of contemporary society. Usually included in the series are *El sueño de las calaveras*, *El alguacil alguacilado*, *Las zahurdas de Plutón*, *El sueño del mundo por de dentro*, *La visita de los chistes*, *El discurso de todos los diablos*, and *La hora de todos*.

Suetonius (full name Gaius Suetonius Tranquillus, AD 75?–?150)   Roman biographer and historian. Suetonius was private secretary to the emperor HADRIAN from about AD 119 to 121. The work for which he is principally remembered is *De vita Caesarum* (*Lives of the Caesars*), a detailed account of the life and times of the first twelve emperors from CAESAR to Domitian. Suetonius is also the author of a work on literary history, *De viris illustribus* (*Famous Men*). Of this work we possess only the biographies of TERENCE and HORACE, and a fragment on the life of LUCAN.

Sufis   A Muslim sect of mystics, mentioned, for instance, by OMAR KHÁYYÁM. They are so named, from the Arabic word *suf* "wool," because they wore woolen garments to symbolize their renunciation of worldly comforts. Their ultimate goal is blissful union with the Supreme Being who may be reached by following the Law, the Way, and the Truth.

Suggs, Captain Simon   A rapscallion character created by the American humorist Johnson Jones Hooper (1815–62). Hooper's reputation as a humorist is founded chiefly on his account of *Some Adventures of Captain Simon Suggs, Late of the Tallapoosa Volunteers* (1846). It was Suggs's guiding principle "to be shifty in a new country." The rowdy tales ridiculed many folkways of the South. Hooper wrote several other books and became secretary of the Provisional Congress of the Southern States when the Civil War broke out. In his *Flush Times of Alabama and Mississippi* (1853), J. G. Baldwin, another Southern humorist, introduced a character named Simon Suggs, Jr., Esq., "a good trader and the mean boy of the school."

Sui   Chinese dynasty (590–618) founded by Yang Chien (541–605). A vast canal system was established during this dynasty and the country reunited after a period of disunity following the HAN dynasty. This set the stage for the T'ANG dynasty which followed.

Sukhovo-Kobylin, Aleksandr Vasilyevich (1817–1903)   Russian playwright. Sukhovo-Kobylin is known for his trilogy *Svadba Krechinskogo* (*Krechinsky's Wedding*, 1855), *Delo* (*The Affair*, written 1857, prod 1881), *Smert Tarelkina* (*The Death of Tarelkin*, written between 1857 and 1869, full version prod 1917).

Suleiman I (known as Suleiman the Magnificent, 1496?–1566)   A famous Turkish ruler. Suleiman encouraged the arts and sciences.

Sulla, Lucius Cornelius (surnamed Felix, 138–78 BC)   Roman general, dictator, and reformer. Sulla took part in various campaigns and was elected consul (88 BC). During the civil struggle between Sulla and MARIUS (88–82), Sulla led for the first time an army of Romans against Rome (88). In 81 he was appointed dictator. He reorganized the senate and the judiciary of Rome and was the first in Roman history to use the weapon of proscription.

Sullivan, Sir Arthur [Seymour] (1842–1900)   English composer. Sullivan is best known for his collaboration with W. S. Gilbert on the GILBERT AND SULLIVAN OPERAS. He was also an accomplished organist and composed sacred and orchestral music and one serious opera, *Ivanhoe* (1891). His songs "The Lost Chord" and "Onward Christian Soldiers" are widely known.

Sullivan, Frank [Francis John] (1892–1976)   American columnist and humorist. Long a columnist for the New York *World*, Sullivan contributed his pieces of gentle humor to many newspapers and magazines. His famous character, "Mr. Arbuthnot," and his annual

Christmas poem (1932–74) were regular features in THE NEW YORKER. Sullivan's writings have been collected in such volumes as *The Life and Times of Martha Hepplethwaite* (1926), *A Pearl in Every Oyster* (1938), *A Rock in Every Snowball* (1946), *The Night Old Nostalgia Burned Down* (1953), and *Moose in the Hoose* (1959).

Sullivan, Louis (1856–1924)   American architect. A pioneer in the use of steel frames for high buildings, Sullivan practiced principally in Chicago. Sullivan's famous dictum, "form follows function," influenced many architects, among them Frank Lloyd WRIGHT. His theories are contained in the books *Autobiography of an Idea* (1924) and *Kindergarten Chats*, which was serialized in 1901 and published in its entirety in 1934.

Sullivan, Mark (1874–1952)   American journalist and historian. First winning recognition as a MUCKRAKER, Sullivan is best known for his lively six-volume history, *Our Times: The United States, 1900–1925* (1926–36).

Sully, duc de (Maximilien de Béthune, 1560–1641) French statesman. As finance minister under Henry IV, Sully reformed France's fiscal system by curtailing expenditures and correcting abuses. His *Mémoires des sages et royales oeconomies d'estat, domestiques, politiques, et militaires de Henry le Grand*, often referred to as the *Economies royales* (*Royal Economies*, 1638) include a discussion of Henry's well-known though probably apocryphal plan to ensure permanent peace by means of a federation of European states. These writings are an invaluable historical source.

Sully, Thomas (1783–1872)   English-born American painter. Sully settled in Philadelphia in 1808, and, after a trip to England (1809–10), where he was profoundly influenced by Sir Thomas LAWRENCE, he returned to become one of the most popular and prolific portraitists in America. His portraits and lesser-known historical scenes are noted for their sensitive use of color and striking lighting effects. His canvases, over two thousand of them, include portraits of most of the notable Americans of his day, including five presidents, Benjamin Franklin, and Daniel Boone. One of his most famous paintings is *Washington at the Passage of the Delaware* (1819).

Sully Prudhomme (pen name of René François Armand Prudhomme, 1839–1907)   French poet. Sully Prudhomme's early work—*Stances et poèmes* (1865), *Les Solitudes* (1869), and *Les Vaines tendresses* (1875)—is lyrical and expresses a delicate melancholy. Later volumes, however, such as *La Justice* (1878) and *Le Bonheur* (1888), stress impersonality and objectivity—favored techniques of the PARNASSIANS. In 1901 Sully Prudhomme received the NOBEL PRIZE in Literature.

Sumarokov, Aleksandr Petrovich (1718–1777) Russian playwright and writer. The founder of classical drama in Russia and an important reformer of the poetic language, Sumarokov wrote in almost every classical genre. Among his ten tragedies is an adaptation of HAMLET. In reaction to the "high" style of solemn odes based on the theory and practice of Mikhail LOMONOSOV, Sumarokov insisted on greater naturalness in poetic language. He was instrumental in introducing what became the modern love lyric into Russian poetry. He is best known for two classical plays, *Khorev* (1747) and *Zemir* (1751).

Sumer   An ancient nation of Mesopotamia. It is the oldest civilization known in the Near East, but its origins are still a mystery. Its language is neither Semitic nor Indo-European. It dominated most of Mesopotamia during the fourth millennium before Jesus. Excavations at UR, Nippur, and other ancient cities have demonstrated that Sumer had a very rich culture. The Sumerian language continued as the hieratic language of Babylonia and Assyria for many centuries after the Sumerians themselves had disappeared and were forgotten. The very existence of Sumer was unknown until the relatively recent decipherment of ancient tablets bearing the cuneiform writing that was probably the invention of the Sumerians and the ancestor of Phoenician script. For much that has been learned of the Sumerian mythology, on which was based much of the mythology of Babylon and Assyria, see AN; ENKI; ENLIL; INANNA; NINTU; ZIUSUDRA.

Summa theologica (c1265–1274)   Major philosophical treatise by St. Thomas AQUINAS, the full title of which is *Summa totius theologiae*. A "summary of all theology," it is still recognized as the doctrinal basis for all such teachings in the Roman Catholic Church. It applies the methodology of Aristotelian logic to problems of Christian doctrine, systematizing and quoting from the works of both classical and early Christian thinkers. Aquinas emphasizes the importance of logical argument in matters of reason but the supremacy of revelation through scriptural and Church pronouncements in matters of faith. The work is in three sections: the first concerns the existence and nature of God and His universe; the second develops a moral philosophy, treating the virtues and vices from the practical viewpoint of society as well as from the theoretical aspect; the third discusses the role of Jesus and the sacraments in the salvation of the soul. Aquinas died before he could finish the third section, but his follower Reginald of Piperno completed it later according to Aquinas's design.

Summer and Smoke   See WILLIAMS, TENNESSEE.

Summer of the Seventeenth Doll (prod 1955, pub 1957)   Drama by Australian playwright Ray LAWLER. The title refers to an annual souvenir doll, marking seventeen years of holidaying for sugar-cane-cutters Barney and Roo. It explains the disillusionment of middle age as Barney's propositioning evokes only feminine derision, while Roo, broke, is bumped from the canefield gang by the younger Johnnie Dowd. The play satirizes the macho mystique of the swaggering outdoors workman and the mateship (brotherhood) theme. At the same time, it presents an authentic picture of the Australian working class.

Summoner's Tale, The   One of THE CANTER-BURY TALES of CHAUCER. The Summoner, very angry at THE FRIAR'S TALE, retorts that all friars are consigned to the most repulsive spot in Hell. He then tells a scatological tale of the comeuppance given a particularly greedy and hypocritical friar. Thomas, sick in bed, grows increasingly angry at the friar's use of pious argument to get gold from him, ostensibly for the convent where prayers are being said for the recovery of the invalid. The friar now exhorts him against his ire, telling numerous stories demonstrating how evil anger is. Thomas finally pretends to offer the friar a precious gift if he promises to divide it equally among his fellow friars, instructing him to reach under the covers behind his back because the gift is hidden with him in bed. The friar eagerly complies, and Thomas coarsely revenges himself. The friar rages to the lord of the village about the insult offered his order. The lord and his family, however, simply ridicule him by holding a mock-scholarly discussion as to how the roar and odor of the offering can be equally divided, as stipulated, among the friar's colleagues.

Sumner, Charles (1811–1874)   American statesman. After lecturing at Harvard Law School and spending several years in Europe, Sumner became active in Massachusetts politics and in various reform movements. In the U.S. Senate, where he served from 1851 until his death, he was an outspoken opponent of slavery. In 1856 he delivered a speech, later known as "The Crime against Kansas," in which he denounced several proslavery senators, including Andrew Butler of South Carolina. A few days later, Butler's nephew, Rep. Preston Brooks, attacked Sumner in the Senate chamber, raining blows on him with his cane. As a result of his injuries, Sumner was not able to return to the Senate until 1859. During the Civil War, he favored emancipation and later opposed the Reconstruction policy of President Johnson. In 1861 he was named chairman of the Senate Foreign Relations Committee, a post from which he was removed in 1872 after he made his "Naboth's Vineyard" speech against the proposed annexation of Santo Domingo.

Sumter, Fort   A fort in the harbor of Charleston, South Carolina, and the site of the first military engagement of the U.S. Civil War. After the secession of South Carolina in December 1860, Major Robert Anderson, U.S. commander in Charleston harbor, withdrew his men to Fort Sumter. The administration then had to decide whether to evacuate the fort or to send reinforcements. Delaying a final decision, President Lincoln dispatched provisions. When state authorities demanded that Anderson surrender, he offered to surrender when his supplies ran out. The South Carolinians, who knew that provisions would soon arrive, rejected Anderson's offer, and shore batteries under Pierre G. T. Beauregard opened fire on April 12, 1861. Historians still disagree as to Lincoln's role in the events preceding the attack, some arguing that he deliberately maneuvered South Carolina into firing the first shot of the Civil War.

sun   The source of light and heat and, consequently, of life to the whole world. Hence it is regarded as a deity and worshiped as such by all primitive peoples. It has a leading place in all mythologies. SHAMASH was the principal sun god of the Assyrians, *Merodach* of the Chaldees, ORMUZD of the Persians, RA of the Egyptians, *Tezcatlipoca* of the Mexicans, and HELIOS (known to the Romans as *Sol*) of the Greeks. Helios drove his chariot daily across the heavens, rising from the sea at dawn and sinking into it in the west at sunset. The Scandinavian sun god *Sunna*, who was in constant dread of being devoured by the FENRIS-WOLF (a symbol of eclipses), was similarly borne through the sky. In later times APOLLO was also a sun god of the Greeks, but he was the personification not of the sun itself but of its all-pervading light and life-giving qualities.

Sun Also Rises, The (1926)   A novel by Ernest HEMINGWAY. Considered by many critics to be his finest long work, it deals with the LOST GENERATION of Americans who had fought in France during World War I and then had expatriated themselves from the America of Calvin COOLIDGE. The story is told by Jake BARNES, rendered impotent by a war wound. Lady Brett ASHLEY, who is divorcing her husband, is possibly in love with him. These two go to Spain with a group that includes Michael Campbell, whom Brett plans to marry; Bill Gorton, a friend of Jake; a Greek nobleman; and Robert Cohn, an American-Jewish writer. Brett has an affair with Romero, a bullfighter whom the others respect for his grace and control in the face of danger; she eventually leaves him and returns to Michael. The fact that at the end nothing has really changed for any of the characters is the point of the novel: for these disillusioned people, life can have no direction, no point toward which to develop.

Sunday Morning (1923)   A poem by Wallace STEVENS. The narrator debates with a woman who feels "the need of some imperishable bliss." The lady must learn that "Death is the mother of beauty," that there is no transcendence, and that the earth is "all of paradise that we shall know."

Sung   Chinese dynasty (960–1279). Following the T'ANG dynasty, this era saw the gradual weakening of the empire and the loss of its northern territories to the Jürched Chin in 1126. This date is the dividing line between the Northern and Southern Sung dynasties. The Sung was a period of cultural ferment in which great urban centers developed for the first time and in which CH'AN BUDDHISM became dominant and CHU HSI established a revitalized Confucianism (Neo-Confucianism) as the principal political and moral force. It was conquered by the YÜAN dynasty.

Sunken Bell, The (Die versunkene Glocke, 1896; tr 1900)   A five-act fairy-drama in verse by Gerhart HAUPTMANN. Heinrich, the bell-maker/artist, is caught between the world of nature and the world of man and between paganism and Christianity. A malicious forest spirit caused the bell that he had forged for a church on the mountain to tumble into the lake below. Injured and in despair over his lost creation, Heinrich succumbs to the charms of the beautiful sprite, Rautendelein, who has nursed him back to health. He leaves his family and the gloomy village in the valley and lives in seraphic happiness with Rautendelein. He begins work on a wonderful chime that will celebrate the joys of nature rather than the sins of man. The village parson visits and pleads with him to return to his wife, saying, as Heinrich protests, that he will regret his choice and that the sunken bell will toll again. His grief-stricken wife throws herself into the lake and rings the bell to remind him of his guilt. Heinrich returns to the valley and finds that his wife is dead and that he cannot forget the freedom and creative joy of the mountain. When he returns to the mountain, he finds that Rautendelein has married a water sprite. After a tragic reconciliation in which Heinrich realizes he cannot exist in either world, he accepts a lethal potion and dies in Rautendelein's arms. Along with HANNELE, this play signals Hauptmann's departure from NATURALISM.

Sun King, The   See LOUIS XIV.

Sunna (Arab, "custom; divine law")   (1) The sayings and example of MUHAMMED and his immediate followers. Insofar as they conform to the KORAN, they are applied to the collections of legal and moral traditions attributed to the Prophet, supplementary to the Koran, as the Hebrew MISHNAH is to the PENTATEUCH.

(2) In Scandinavian mythology, a personification of the sun. See SUN.

Sunnites   The orthodox and conservative body of Muslims who consider the SUNNA as authentic as the KORAN itself and acknowledge the first four caliphs as the rightful successors of MUHAMMED. They form the largest section of Muslims and are divided into four sects: *Hanafites, Hanbalites, Malikites,* and *Shaflites.* See SHI-ITES.

Sun Yat-sen (1866–1925)   Chinese statesman. Sun Yat-sen is considered in China as the father of his country. He traveled abroad early, spending time in Hawaii, Hong Kong—where he studied medicine—and London. His contacts with overseas Chinese were helpful in gaining support for his anti-Manchu revolutionary activities in China. He founded the *Kuomintang* and assumed provisional presidency of the Chinese republic in 1912 but retired in favor of Yuan Shih-k'ai. He later headed a southern government at Canton. Under the influence of the Comintern agent Mikhail Borodin, he consolidated the organization of the *Kuomintang* along Leninist lines and elaborated his political philosophy of the *Three Principles of the People*: nationalism, democracy, and socialism. A large park and mausoleum were built in his honor in Nanking.

superego   See ID, EGO, AND SUPEREGO.

superfluous man   A term used to describe a specific type of protagonist in 19th-century Russian literature. Such a man is exemplified by Pushkin's EUGENE ONEGIN, Goncharov's OBLOMOV, Turgenev's RUDIN, and Lermontov's Pechorin in A HERO OF OUR TIME. Characteristics of the type are an inability to act decisively in personal or social matters and a lack of contact or involvement with the life of the society in which he lives. The condition is usually engendered by a combination of private inadequacies or maladjustments and the deadening effect of a restrictive political or social system. The radical critics of the 19th century proposed replacing the socially useless superfluous man with an exemplary POSITIVE HERO. This task was finally accomplished by decree after the Soviet regime exerted its power in literary affairs and proclaimed the doctrine of SOCIALIST REALISM.

Supervielle, Jules (1884–1960)   Uruguayan-born French poet, fiction writer, and dramatist. In both his prose and poetry, Supervielle treats questions of cosmic scope with disarming simplicity. Far more accessible than the surrealist poets, whose influence he denied, his works deal extensively with elements of myth, dream, and allegory. His best verse is included in *Gravitations* (1925), the moving *Les Poèmes de la France malheureuse* (1941), and *Oublieuse Mémoire* (1949). Among his prose fantasies are *Le Voleur d'enfants* (1944; tr *The Colonel's Children*, 1949) and *L'Enfant de la haute mer* (1931; tr *Along the Road to Bethlehem*, 1933). *La Belle au bois* (1932) and *Bolivar* (1936) are plays. An edition of his *Selected Writings* appeared in English in 1967.

Suppliant Women, The (Hiketides, 421 BC)   A drama by EURIPIDES recounting the successful plea of the mothers of the SEVEN AGAINST THEBES that THESEUS, king of Athens, bury the bodies of their sons.

Suppliant Women, The (Hiketides, c490 BC)   The earliest surviving play by AESCHYLUS and the first play of a trilogy. It concerns the flight of Danaus and his fifty daughters from Aegyptus, his brother, who has usurped the throne of Egypt. They plead for protection from the people of Argos, where their ancestress IO was born. King Pelasgus grants their request and defies the herald of Aegyptus, who arrives with his fifty sons to demand that the maidens marry them. The play is the first of a trilogy that told the myth of the murder on their wedding night of all but one of the young men by the Danaid brides. The other two plays are lost.

Suprematism   See MALEVICH, KAZIMIR SEVERI-NOVICH.

Sura   In Arabic, any one ethical revelation; thus each chapter of the KORAN is a Sura.

surrealism   A literary, artistic, and philosophical movement, founded in France in 1924. Surrealism sought a reality above or within the surface reality, usually through efforts to suspend the discipline of conscious or logical reason, aesthetics, or morality in order to allow for the expression of subconscious thought and feeling.

Since the rise of the SYMBOLISTS, there had been a growing interest in the irrational and in the technique of producing impressions through startling juxtapositions of images. RIMBAUD, MALLARMÉ, JARRY, and Lautréamont (1846–70) were considered the leading precursors of surrealism, and Guillaume APOLLINAIRE seems to have coined the name in describing his own poem "Oniro-critique." World War I heightened the sense of protest against a purely scientific and materialistic world view and strengthened the conviction that the intellect alone could not achieve a complete understanding of life. While the DADA movement was an artistic response to such disillusionment, André BRETON and Philippe SOUPAULT began to outline surrealist principles in *Les Champs magnétiques* (1921). The surrealist group then announced themselves with Breton's *Manifeste du surrealisme: Poison soluble* (1924). Based on FREUD's theory of the unconscious, it claimed that through "automatic" writing and painting, the subconscious would dictate images and symbols in combinations which, however unexpected and incongruous to the conscious mind, would actually reveal the true nature and content of the human soul. A second manifesto (1930) stressed the importance of investigation of dreams and psychic states.

Breton, with Louis ARAGON, René Crevel, Robert Desnos, Paul ÉLUARD, Soupault, and others, converted (1924) the dada review *Littérature* to *La Révolution surréaliste*. In 1930 the title was again changed, to *Surréalisme au service de la revolution* (until 1933), in an attempt to claim that the movement was the representative of Communism in the arts. Communist leaders, however, disavowed surrealism, which resulted in Aragon's defection from the Party in 1932 and Eluard's in 1938.

In England, Herbert READ tried to introduce "super-realism" as a manifestation of the principle of romanticism, but the original name survived, carried on most notably by the English surrealists David Gascoyne (1916–   ) and Hugh Sykes DAVIES. Giorgio di CHIRICO and Salvador DALI became the leading surrealist painters; others include Yves Tanguy (1900–1955) and Max ERNST.

Few other writers and artists produced primarily surrealistic works, but many either were actively associated with the movement for a time or were greatly influenced by it: to list a few, in painting Paul KLEE, Joan MIRÓ, PICASSO, and Pavel TCHELITCHEV; in literature, Jean COCTEAU, Saint-John PERSE, Jacques PRÉVERT, and Raymond QUENEAU (France); Dylan THOMAS (England); E. E. CUMMINGS, Henry MILLER, Anaïs NIN, and William Carlos WILLIAMS (U.S.); and GARCÍA LORCA (Spain).

Surrey, Henry Howard, earl of (1517?–1547) English poet and courtier attached to the court of Henry VIII. Surrey won various distinctions, particularly during the years (1540–42) that his cousin, Catherine Howard, was married to the king. After her execution, however, his enmity with the Seymours finally led to his arrest on a trumped-up charge of treason. He was executed early in 1547. With Sir Thomas WYATT, Surrey helped introduce new Italian and French verse forms into English. His blank verse translations of Books II and IV of Vergil's AENEID represent the first use of unrhymed iambic pentameter in English, and he is responsible for what is now known as the "Shakespearean" form of the SONNET. Forty of his poems were published in TOTTEL's MISCELLANY. His metrical smoothness and elegance led critics, until recent times, to regard him as superior to Wyatt, but many 20th-century critics favor Wyatt's poetry for its greater intensity of feeling.

Sursis, Le   See ROADS TO FREEDOM, THE.

Surtees, Robert Smith (1803–1864)   English novelist and sports writer. Surtees wrote the humorous fox-hunting sketches *Jorrocks' Jaunts and Jollities* (1838), which suggested the original plan of Dickens's *Pickwick Papers* and other works of light fiction dealing mainly with the hunt. These include *Handley Cross* (1843), *Hillingdon Hall* (1845), and *Mr. Sponge's Sporting Tour* (1853). Although of minor literary value, his books preserve the spirit of the old English sporting life. See JORROCKS.

survival of the fittest   A concept of the Darwinian theory of evolution (see ORIGIN OF SPECIES). This principle maintains that the biological species best adapted to its environment will be the one to survive and perpetuate in its offspring. A popular misconception of this idea was that the species surviving was the one able to overcome its rivals in a literal, tooth-and-nail struggle. The phrase itself is said to have been coined by Herbert SPENCER in a study on Darwinian natural selection.

Surya   In Hindu mythology, the god of the sun. In the older legends Surya presides over the gods of the sky, sharing the government of nature with AGNI, lord of the gods of the earth, and INDRA, lord of the gods of the air. The famous Sun Temple of Konarak, also known as the Black Pagoda, was constructed in the ninth century in eastern India to glorify Surya; its erotic friezes symbolize the multitudinous fertility of the sun, source of all energy.

Susanna and the Elders   A favorite subject among Renaissance and later artists. The *Story of Susanna*, one of the books of the Old Testament Apocrypha, tells how Susanna was accused of adultery by certain Jewish elders who had unsuccessfully attempted her chastity, how her innocence was proved by DANIEL, and the Elders put to death.

Sut   See EBLIS.

Sutpen   A family in William Faulkner's ABSALOM, ABSALOM! Thomas Sutpen is the head of the family. Descended from poor whites, Sutpen acquires land in Mississippi from the Indians in 1833 and later marries Ellen Coldfield, daughter of a Jefferson merchant, in order to establish his respectability. Two children, Henry and

Judith, are born of the marriage. Henry becomes a close friend of Charles Bon but kills him when he discovers that Bon, who wants to marry Judith, is their half brother and part black, the son of Thomas Sutpen and Eulalia Bon, who is part black. After Bon's death, Judith brings up his son, Charles Etienne St.-Valery Bon.

Other characters connected with the Sutpen story are Rosa Coldfield, Ellen's sister, who is at one point engaged to Thomas Sutpen; Clytie (Clytemnestra) Sutpen, the daughter of Thomas and a black slave; Jim Bond, the idiot son of Charles E. St.-Valery and the last descendant of Thomas; and Wash Jones, who murders Thomas after the latter rejects the illegitimate child borne to him by Jones's granddaughter.

sutras   Ancient Hindu aphoristic manuals probably developed from 500 to 200 BC. They give the rules of systems of philosophy, grammar, and other disciplines, and contain directions concerning religious ritual and ceremonial customs. They form a link between the Vedic and later Sanskrit literature and are so called from the Sanskrit *sutra* (thread), the aphorisms being, as it were, threaded together themselves and threading together other things.

In BUDDHISM *sutras* refer to the preachings of the historical Buddha. There are, however, hundreds of *sutras* composed after his death and many apocryphal ones composed in China. As the sayings of the Buddha they are venerated and are the most important sections of the TRIPITAKA.

suttee   See SATI.

Su Tung-p'o (or Su Shih, 1037–1101)   Chinese poet and painter of the SUNG dynasty. He is noted for his *tz'u*, or musical poetry, and for a happy combination of CONFUCIANISM and BUDDHISM in his philosophical outlook.

Suzuki, Daisetz T.   See ZEN BUDDHISM.

svayamvara   See DAMAYANTĪ.

Svengali   A Hungarian musician in George du Maurier's novel TRILBY. He controls Trilby's stage singing through his hypnotic power. Hence, a Svengali is one who can exercise a sinister, mesmeric influence over another.

Svevo, Italo (pen name of Ettore Schmitz, 1861–1928)   Italian novelist. Svevo's hopes to devote himself entirely to writing were dashed when his father's mental breakdown required him to support his family at nineteen. He eventually became a successful businessman, but his first love remained writing. His first two novels, published at his own expense, were virtually ignored by the literary establishment: *Una vita* (1893; tr *A Life*, 1963), which centers on the ineptness of a modest bank clerk who, unable to cope with life and his own shortcomings, commits suicide; and *Senilita* (1898; tr *As a Man Grows Older*, 1968), in which an insurance agent falls in love with, and idealizes, a prostitute. It was twenty-five years before his next and greatest novel, *La conscienza di Zeno* (1923; tr *The Confessions of Zeno*, 1958), was published. Clearly influenced by Freudian ideas, the novel is presented as a statement of self-analysis by the protagonist, Zeno, for his psychiatrist.

Due largely to the efforts of Svevo's friend James JOYCE, the book received considerable critical attention in Europe, and its author was compared with PROUST, MANN, and Joyce himself. Svevo was credited with introducing an entirely new, experimental strain into Italian fiction and was considered a master of psychological portrayal.

Svidrigailov   A sinister profligate in Dostoyevsky's CRIME AND PUNISHMENT. Svidrigailov admits to having violated young girls and to having caused the death of one of them. His final attempted seduction is of Raskolnikov's sister, Darya, whom he has followed to St. Petersburg after having tormented her when she was employed in his household. Svidrigailov shows no remorse for his acts until one night, after saying he is going off to America, he shoots himself.

Swabian school   See GERMAN ROMANTICISM.

Swanhild   An old Norse legendary heroine, the daughter of Sigurd and GUDRUN. She is falsely accused of adultery with the son of the king who is wooing her, and the king has his son hanged. She is sentenced to die by being trampled to death by wild horses but is so beautiful that she must be blanketed before the horses will perform their task.

Swann, Charles   A neighbor and friend of the narrator's family in Marcel Proust's REMEMBRANCE OF THINGS PAST. Swann, who is part Jewish, has an affair with ODETTE DE CRÉCY, whom he later marries, and is the father of Gilberte, the narrator's first love. Himself a member of high society, he grieves that Odette is not similarly accepted.

Swann's Way   See REMEMBRANCE OF THINGS PAST.

swan song   The song fabled to be sung by swans at the point of death. Figuratively, it means the last work of a poet, composer, or other creator. The superstition that the swan, known as the bird of APOLLO or ORPHEUS, sings beautifully just before death is very ancient, though baseless.

Swedenborg, Emanuel (1688–1772)   Swedish theologian, scientist, and philosopher. During the first half of his career, he devoted himself to scientific research and spent several years studying in Europe and in England. In 1716, Swedenborg published Sweden's first scientific journal, *Daedalus Hyperboreus*, and was appointed to the Royal Board of Mines. During his twenty-five years as an active member of this board, he published scientific books and articles in almost every field: mathematics, geology, anatomy, physiology, chemistry, and physics. The most important works of this period were *Opera Philosophica et Mineralia* (1734), *Oeconomia Regni Animalis* (1740), and *Regnum Animale* (1744–45). Between the years 1743 and 1745, Swedenborg experienced a spiritual crisis. Turning away from his former interests, he spent the last twenty-five years of his life in biblical study and the writing of religious philosophy. His most significant theological works are *Arcana Coelestia* (8 vols, 1749–56), *Doctrina Vitae pro*

Nova Hierosolyma (*Divine Love and Wisdom*, 1763), and *Vera Christiana Religio* (*The True Christian Religion*, 1771). After his death his followers formed the New Church or New Jerusalem Church. Swedenborg's accounts of his mystical visions have influenced a number of writers, among them the English poet William BLAKE.

Sweeney   A figure in several poems by T. S. ELIOT. Sweeney is symbolic of the sensual, brutal, and materialistic man of the 20th century. In "Sweeney Erect" and "Sweeney among the Nightingales," rhyming, semicomic poems, he is set against the dignity and beauty of the classical past. *Sweeney Agonistes, Fragments of an Aristophanic Melodrama* (1932) is part of a play, striking in its use of music-hall rhythms and slang speech.

Sweet Cheat Gone, The   See REMEMBRANCE OF THINGS PAST.

Swenson, May (1919–   )   American poet. Born in Utah of Swedish parents, Swenson moved to New York City after college. Editorial jobs, poetry awards, and teaching fellowships came her way in quick succession after *Another Animal: Poems* (appearing in *Poets of Today I*, 1954) attracted praise for its virtuosity of technique and vivid images. Her first book, *A Cage of Spines* (1958), confirmed an early reputation for ingenuity without self-consciousness. *Half Sun Half Sleep* (1967) is a mixture of witty descriptions of life in New York and in Europe and her own translation of six contemporary Swedish poets. *Iconographs* (1970) carries on an experiment she had tried briefly in her first book with "shaped poems," in which the typographical appearance on the page suggests the shape of the subject of the poem. *New and Selected Things Taking Place* (1978) is a sampling displaying Swenson's clever, sophisticated style and her precise, objective eye for detail.

Swift, Jonathan (1667–1745)   English satirist, poet, political writer, and clergyman. Born in Dublin of English parents, Swift received his education in Ireland. In 1689 he went to England and became secretary to Sir William Temple, retired at Moor Park from his distinguished political career. It was here that Swift met Esther JOHNSON; it was also here that he learned a great deal about politics and wrote his first important prose: THE TALE OF A TUB, a Rabelaisian and allegorical satire on the divisions in the Christian religion, and THE BATTLE OF THE BOOKS. Swift was the major political writer for the moderate Tories in their brief reign (1710–14) under Robert Harley, producing the *Examiner* (1710), a newspaper in the Tory interest, and *The Conduct of the Allies* (1711), a masterly pamphlet of his party's plan for peace in the war of the Spanish Succession. His life during these years is reflected in his JOURNAL TO STELLA, a series of letters written for Esther Johnson. He was appointed dean of St. Patrick's Cathedral in Dublin (1713) by Queen Anne and remained in Ireland, except for brief excursions, for the rest of his life. He returned to politics again in 1724, this time as an Irish patriot in the person of "M. B. Drapier"; *Drapier's Letters* (1724–25) were

designed to incite the Irish against a new coinage, and a reward of £300 was soon offered for discovering the author. It was well known that Swift was the author, but proof was needed and never obtained, for, by now, he was greatly loved in Dublin; his birthday thereafter was celebrated by Dubliners with the ringing of bells and bonfires. By this time, Swift had almost finished his masterpiece, GULLIVER'S TRAVELS, which contained his bitterest denunciation of mankind. Of his many minor satires, the most celebrated are *An Argument against Abolishing Christianity* (1708) and A MODEST PROPOSAL, both in prose; and *The Day of Judgment* (1731) and *Verses on the Death of Dr. Swift* (1739). The 19th-century notion of a demonic, cynical Swift, an exaggeration used to explain the savage indignation of his satire, ignores his playfulness and love of fun, qualities evident throughout his work. Though he called himself a misanthrope, he always wrote for the betterment of mankind. He valued reason as a human attribute and became bitter at its abuse. A master impersonator, Swift often became the person in which he wrote: now he is "Isaac BICKERSTAFF," a clairvoyant astrologer; now the urbane "CADENUS"; now the playful "PRESTO"; now "M. B. Drapier"; now "Lemuel Gulliver." The "true Swift" is still, and perhaps always will be, uncertain. See SCRIBLERUS CLUB.

Swift, Tom   A boy inventor, hero of a long series of novels for boys. Tom's hair-raising adventures with all kinds of contrivances, some of which anticipated actual inventions, became widely popular and brought considerable wealth to his creator, Edward L. STRATEMEYER, who also originated the ROVER BOYS series.

Swinburne, Algernon Charles (1837–1909) English poet and man of letters. Swinburne is known for his rebellion against Victorian social conventions and religion, his active sympathies with the movements and leaders of political revolution of his time, and the pagan spirit and musical effects of his poetry. He was an intense admirer of SHELLEY and Victor HUGO, and was influenced in his own work by Greek legend and Roman classic literature, medieval romance, and Elizabethan drama.

In his early career, Swinburne's behavior was eccentric, violent, and dissipated, calculated to shock the respectable people of his time. A masochist and epileptic as well as an alcoholic, Swinburne was on the point of collapse when he was taken into the home of Theodore Watts-Dunton (1832–1914), the critic and man of letters, in 1879. He stayed there for the rest of his life in what amounted to protective custody.

Swinburne's first published volume, *The Queen Mother. Rosamund. Two Plays* (1860), attracted no attention. With the publication of ATALANTA IN CALYDON, a drama in classical Greek form, he won fame. In the same year he published *Chastelard* (1865), the first of three dramas on Mary Queen of Scots. This was followed closely by *Poems and Ballads: First Series* (1866), lyrics dealing chiefly with sensual love, which caused a scandal and was severely censured by some. A *Song of Italy* (1867) and *Songs before Sunrise* (1871) deal with the cause of Italian union and independence. The second drama of the Mary Queen of Scots trilogy was *Bothwell: A Tragedy* (1874), and *Poems and Ballads: Second Series* was published in 1878. *Mary Stuart*, the last of the trilogy, appeared in 1881, and *Tristram of Lyonesse*, an Arthurian poem in rhymed couplets, considered by some his finest work, in 1882. In *Marino Faliero* (1885) Swinburne reworks a theme previously treated by Byron. His last volumes of poems are *Astrophel* (1894), *A Tale of Balen* (1896), and *A Channel Passage* (1904). *The Duke of Gandia* (1908), a tragedy, is his last work. His prose works include *Essays and Studies* (1875), *Miscellanies* (1886), and astute critical writings on many modern writers including BLAKE, the BRONTËS, and DICKENS. His later work is not considered to be as fine as the earlier. Among his best-known single poems are "Hymn to Artemis," "Hymn to Proserpine," "Hertha," "Laus Veneris" and "The Triumph of Time." He wrote two novels dealing with the complexities of love, *Love's Cross Currents* (1905) and *Lesbia Brandon*, posthumously published (1952).

Swiss Family Robinson, The (Der schweizerische Robinson, 1813; tr 1920)   A story for young people by J. R. Wyss, the Swiss writer and philosopher. It relates the adventures of a Swiss clergyman, his wife, and four sons, who are wrecked on a desert island.

Swiveller, Mr. Dick   In Charles Dickens's THE OLD CURIOSITY SHOP, a dirty, smart young man, living in apartments near Drury Lane. His language is extremely flowery and interlarded with quotations. He is forever humming some dismal air.

sword   A long-bladed weapon used for cutting or stabbing. The sword was the chief weapon of the romances. In the days of chivalry, a knight's horse and sword were his most treasured and carefully kept possessions, and his sword as well as his horse had its own name. The old romances, especially those of the CHARLEMAGNE and ARTHURIAN cycles, are full of these names, among the more noteworthy of which are:

Angurvadal (Stream of Anguish), Frithiof's sword.

Ar'ondight, the sword of LAUNCELOT of the Lake.

Balmung, one of the swords of SIEGFRIED, made by WIELAND.

Colada, the CID's sword.

Courtain (the Short Sword), one of the swords of OGIER the Dane; *Sauvagine* was the other, and each took Munifican three years to make.

DURANDAN, *Durandal*, or *Durandana* (the Inflexible), ORLANDO's sword.

EXCALIBUR, the sword of King ARTHUR (fr Lat, *ex cal[ce] liber[are]*, "to liberate from the stone").

Flamberge or *Floberge* (the Flame-Cutter), the name of one of Charlemagne's swords, and also that of RINALDO and Maugis or Malagigi.

Glorius, OLIVER's sword, which hacked to pieces the nine swords made by Ansias, Galas, and Munifican.

Gram (Grief), one of the swords of Siegfried.

Joyeuse (Joyous), one of Charlemagne's swords; it took Gallas three years to make.

Mimung, the sword that Wittich lent Siegfried.

Morglay (Big Glaive), Sir Bevis's sword.

Nagelring (Nail-Ring), Dietrich's sword.

Philippan, the sword of ANTONY, one of the triumvirs.

Sword Blades and Poppy Seed (1914)   A collection of poems by Amy LOWELL. The second book of poetry that she published, it was especially important in its use of free verse and in containing the first English examples of polyphonic prose—rhythmical prose characterized by all the devices of verse except strict meter.

Sybarite   An inhabitant of Sybaris, in South Italy, proverbial for its luxurious living and self-indulgence. The Sybarites piped their chief product, wine, down to the sea, so that they would not have to transport it. A tale is told by SENECA of a Sybarite who complained that he could not rest comfortably at night and, being asked why, replied that he found a rose leaf doubled under him, and it hurt him. Sybaris was destroyed as a significant power in a war with nearby Crotona. Fable has it that the Sybarites taught their horses to dance to a pipe. When the Crotonians marched against Sybaris, they played on their pipes, whereupon all the Sybarite horses began to dance; disorder soon prevailed in the ranks, and the victory was quick and easy.

Sybil, or The Two Nations (1845)   A novel by Benjamin DISRAELI. The two nations are the rich and the poor working class in England during the 1840s. The novel deals with the Chartist movement and the distressed condition of the laboring class during this period.

Sycorax   The evil witch who originally inhabited the island of PROSPERO in Shakespeare's THE TEMPEST. Sycorax imprisoned ARIEL in a pine rift and left to posterity her son, the subhuman CALIBAN. When Prospero reaches his island, she is already dead.

sylphs   Elemental spirits of air. They are so named in the Middle Ages by Paracelsus (1493–1541) and others, possibly from the Greek *silphe*, a kind of beetle, or a grub that turns into a butterfly. Any mortal who has preserved inviolate chastity may enjoy intimate familiarity with these gentle spirits. Deceased virgins were said to become sylphs, "and sport and flutter in the fields of air." Sylphs play an important part in Pope's RAPE OF THE LOCK.

symbolists (Fr, *symbolistes*)   A group of French poets who were active during the last thirty years of the 19th century. Although the work of each writer was unique, and neither the aims nor the techniques of the movement were at all rigid, the poets did share certain basic convictions and used similar poetic methods. Symbolism in France began as a revolt against the cold impersonality of the realistic novel and its minute descriptions of an objective, external reality. The rebel poets turned inward, in order to explore and express the shifting, subtle states of the human psyche. They believed that poetry should evoke and suggest, raising itself above the level of objective description only; hence, they sought poetic techniques that would make possible the recreation of human consciousness. The symbol and the METAPHOR enabled them to suggest mysterious and inexpressible subjective emotion. Often the symbols were highly personal, and their use resulted in obscure, esoteric verse. At its finest, however, symbolist poetry achieved a richness of meaning and created an awareness of the mystery at the heart of human existence.

As symbolism sought freedom from rigidity in the selection of subject matter, so it desired to free poetry from the restrictions of conventional versification. The art that seemed most to resemble poetry was not that of the sculptured precision of plastic forms but music; fluid melody and delicate lyricism characterized symbolist poetry. POE and BAUDELAIRE were admired by the symbolists; RIMBAUD, VERLAINE, and MALLARMÉ are generally considered the leaders of the school. Other members included Gustave Kahn, Henri de RÉGNIER, Jules LAFORGUE, E. J. CORBIÈRE, and Maurice MAETERLINCK. Among the numerous symbolist reviews were *Vogue* (1886–89), *Revue indépendante* (1886–95), *Ermitage* (1890–1906), and *Revue blanche* (1891–1903).

Symbolism, as a literary movement, was predominant in Russia from about 1896 to 1910. Its characteristics were an interest in mysticism and exotic lore, an intense concern with the aesthetic aspects of art, and an impressionistic poetic style. The main sources and influences on the group were the French symbolists, the Russian poets TYUTCHEV and FET, and the philosophical ideas of Vladimir SOLOVYOV. The earlier symbolists included Valery BRYUSOV, Konstantin Balmont, Dmitry MEREZHKOVSKY, and Fyodor SOLOGUB. Best known among the younger generation were Vyacheslav IVANOV, Andrey BELY, and Aleksandr BLOK, the greatest poet to emerge from the movement.

Symbolism did much to add new life to Russian poetry, which had fallen into decline during the last part of the 19th century because of the preponderance of great prose writers. The great amount of fine work produced by the symbolist poets earned the symbolist period—the most fruitful period since the time of PUSHKIN—the name of "the second golden age" (or "the silver age") of Russian poetry.

During the 20th century the use of symbolism became a major force in British literature. Symbolist poetry was introduced and popularized by Arthur SYMONS. George MOORE imitated it; W. B. YEATS was influenced by it in his early career and based his mature style on it; T. S. ELIOT adapted it in the development of his individual style and praised it in his criticism, influencing the critical tenets of the CAMBRIDGE CRITICS and the New Critics (see NEW CRITICISM). But the most outstanding development of symbolism was in the art of the novel. The great 20th-century British novelists, James JOYCE especially, but also Joseph CONRAD, D. H. LAWRENCE, E. M. FORSTER, and Virginia WOOLF, wrote novels in which much of the meaning is conveyed through patterns of images and ideas and central suggestive symbols rather than through the traditional method of narrative and overt discourse.

Symonds, John Addington (1840–1893) English historian, scholar, and translator. Symonds is best known for his *History of the Renaissance in Italy* (1875–86), a study, often consisting of a series of impressionistic essays on separate subjects under the main heading, of the politics, culture, art, and literature of Italy in the 15th and 16th centuries. He also translated the *Autobiography of Benvenuto Cellini* (1888) and did other translations, notably of the Greek poets and the Italian Renaissance poets. In addition, he wrote verse and literary criticism. *The Memoirs of John Addington Symonds* was published in 1984.

Symons, Arthur (1865–1945) English critic and poet. His most important critical work was *The Symbolist Movement in Literature* (1899), which, along with his translations, introduced English readers to the work of the French SYMBOLISTS. It particularly influenced Symons's friend W. B. YEATS.

Symons, Julian [Gustave] (1912–   ) English novelist, poet, and critic. Symons writes crime stories rather than detective fiction, emphasizing motivation more than mystery. His characters are often ironically portrayed as men conditioned by the pursuit of success and power to commit irrational acts of violence. Among his best-known books are *The 31st of February* (1950), *The End of Solomon Grundy* (1964), and *The Man Who Lost His Wife* (1970). His interest in the Victorian era provided the background for *The Blackheath Poisonings* (1978) and *Sweet Adelaide* (1980). Among his other works are *The Great Detectives* (1981), *Classic Crime Omnibus* (1984), and a biography, *Dashiell Hammett* (1985).

Symplegades The "clashing rocks." They guarded the entrance to the Black Sea and crushed ships between them by moving quickly together. When the ARGONAUTS passed through them safely, by the advice of PHINEUS and the help of HERA, the rocks became fixed to the sea bottom and were harmless thereafter.

Symposium A dialogue by PLATO. Each guest at the banquet speaks in honor of love, mainly between males. Phaedrus treats love mythically, Pausanias sophistically, Agathon poetically, and ARISTOPHANES comically. SOCRATES says that the priestess Diotima has taught him that love may take an intellectual form, creating the desire to produce things of beauty; poets and legislators experience this sort of love. The dialogue ends with the speech of ALCIBIADES, praising Socrates.

synecdoche A figure of speech, or METAPHOR, giving the part to represent the whole, as in "fifty head" for "fifty cattle," or "all hands" to signify "all working men."

synesthesia A medical (or psychological) term describing the occurrence when stimulating one sense organ causes another to respond. It is as though in eating one were to receive strong visual sensations of color rather than, or along with, sensations of taste. As a literary device, synesthesia has been used in certain types of poetry of the 19th and 20th centuries, especially that of the SYMBOLISTS. RIMBAUD's "Sonnet des voyelles," expressing the sounds of the common vowels in terms of colors, is an excellent example of the use of this device.

Synge, John Millington (1871–1909) Irish dramatist. Synge's tragically brief career established him as the foremost dramatist of the IRISH RENAISSANCE. He began his career by settling in France, where he spent his time translating the poetry of MALLARMÉ and other French SYMBOLISTS. Here he met William Butler YEATS, who persuaded him to return to the Irish countryside, where the peasants' speech still exhibited vigorous, exuberant, poetic qualities unmatched elsewhere in the world. Synge followed Yeats's advice with the result that he claimed his plays amounted to literal transcriptions of the language of western Ireland's peasants. His plays include *In the Shadow of the Glen* (1903); *Riders to the Sea* (1904), a one-act trag-

edy which achieves an almost Aeschylean starkness and grandeur; *The Well of the Saints* (1905); PLAYBOY OF THE WESTERN WORLD, generally regarded as his masterpiece; *The Tinker's Wedding* (1907); and the nearly completed *Deirdre of the Sorrows* (1910), one of the most distinguished recreations of Irish myth of the Celtic revival.

Synoptic Gospels The first three books of the NEW TESTAMENT: The Gospel According to St. MATTHEW, The Gospel According to St. MARK, and The Gospel According to St. LUKE. They are so called from the Greek word *synoptikos*, meaning "general view." These three accounts of JESUS' life are similar in substance, language, and order. Mark is thought to be the oldest; both Luke and Matthew use it as a source. A lost book containing the sayings of Jesus was also used by the authors of Matthew and Luke. This lost book, called *Q* (fr Ger, *Quelle*, "source") was one of the earliest Christian documents. Since it was probably only an anthology of Jesus' wisdom, Bible scholars have postulated that Mark was written to accompany *Q* and supply biographical material.

Syrinx An Arcadian nymph of Greek legend. On being pursued by PAN, Syrinx took refuge in the river Ladon and prayed to be changed into a reed. The prayer was granted, and of the reed Pan made his pipes. Hence, the name is given to the Pan pipe or reed mouth organ and also to the vocal organ of birds.

T

Tabernacles, Feast of   A Jewish festival. It lasts eight days, beginning on the 15th of Tishri (toward the end of September). It is kept in remembrance of the sojourn in the wilderness.

Tacitus, Cornelius (AD 55?–117)   Roman historian. Tacitus's most ambitious works were the *Historiae*, a history of his own times, from AD 69 to 96, and the *Annales*, a detailed account of events from the death of Augustus to the year 69. These two historical works were originally published in thirty books, only eleven of which have been preserved in complete form while four have survived in fragments. Tacitus is also famous for his *Germania*, a careful study of the manners and mores of the peoples of Germany. As a reporter and historian, he always sought to be scrupulously impartial, and, not content with a simple narration of events, he searched constantly for causes. His style, especially in his later work, is colored now and then with poetic diction, but is at the same time tightly organized, precise, and epigrammatic.

Taft, William Howard (1857–1930)   Twenty-seventh president of the U.S. (1909–13). After graduating from Yale University and Cincinnati Law College, Taft held several posts in the Ohio and federal judiciaries.

As the first civil governor of the Philippines (1901–4), he introduced various reforms and established limited self-rule. He served as secretary of war (1904–8) under Theodore ROOSEVELT and was the latter's choice to succeed him in the presidency. During his term in office, Taft continued his predecessor's policies and strongly enforced the antitrust laws, but he later broke with Republican progressives and with Roosevelt himself. In 1912 he ran unsuccessfully for a second term against Woodrow WILSON and Roosevelt, who had founded the Bull Moose Party after failing to receive the Republican nomination. In 1913 Taft became professor of constitutional law at Yale and served until 1921 when he was named chief justice of the Supreme Court.

Tagore, Rabindranath (also written Ravindranath Thakura, 1861–1941)   Indian poet, novelist, story writer, and essayist in Bengali, awarded the NOBEL PRIZE in Literature in 1913. Tagore is known in his country for his lyrics and songs on nature, love, and childhood, and for his *Ravindrasangeet*, or poems set to music. In the West he is generally considered a poet of mysticism and religious feeling, and for three decades after the Nobel Prize, Tagore coteries and cults tended to misinterpret much of the fine poetry as Oriental mysticism. His early work strongly impressed Ezra POUND, who found in it a "new Greece," and W. B. YEATS, who wrote the introduction to *Gitanjali* (1912). Since then Tagore's influence in the West has steadily declined, though in his homeland it is a massive literary phenomenon. He was also an educationist, founder of the "world university" Santiniketan, one hundred miles from Calcutta. In his "dance dramas" (such as *Valmiki Prativa*) he employed opera for the purposes of the Bengali stage; in his last years he emerged as a symbolist painter of startling vividness and richness. He was knighted in 1915, but in 1919 resigned the honor in protest against the British repressive measures in Jallianwala Bagh in the Punjab. English translations of his work include: *The Crescent Moon* (1913); *One Hundred Poems of Kabir* (1914); *Chitra* (1916), a play; *The Gardener* (1917); *Lectures on Personality* (1917); *Red Oleanders* (1925); *Fireflies* (1928); *The Religion of Man* (1931), on his ideas of God; *Broken Ties, and Other Stories* (1925); *The Child* (1931); *The Golden Boat* (1932); *Collected Poems and Plays* (1936, 1973); and *Farewell My Friend* (1940).

Ta-hsüeh   See GREAT LEARNING, THE.

Taillefer (d 1066)   Norman minstrel. According to WACE, Taillefer rode with WILLIAM THE CONQUEROR's invading army, singing the deeds of CHARLEMAGNE and ROLAND, and died at the battle of HASTINGS. It is uncertain whether he actually knew the *Chanson de Roland* or simply another version of the legend.

Taine, Hippolyte [Adolphe] (1828–1893)   French philosopher, literary critic, and historian. Taine was influenced by HEGEL, the positivism of COMTE, and the English Utilitarians (see UTILITARIANISM). He is known for his emphasis on the role of scientific determinism in literature and history, particularly as exemplified in hereditary and environmental influences. One of Taine's most famous doctrines is that of the *faculté maîtresse*, or dominant trait, from which the critic hoped to deduce an author's career geometrically. His other significant theory is that of *race, milieu, et moment*, which linked Taine with the naturalistic school. Essentially this is the proposition that a literary or historical figure might be fully understood by considering the three forces that composed his biological inheritance: environment, the configuration of tradition, and the dominant trends at the time of his appearance. Among Taine's works are *La Philosophie de l'art* (1865–69), *Histoire de la littérature anglaise* (1864), *Nouveaux essais* (1865), *Origines de la France contemporaine* (1875–94), and *De l'intelligence* (1870).

Taishō   Japanese period (1912–26). The name given to the reign of Emperor Yoshihito (1879–1926).

Tale of a Tub, The (1704)   An allegorical satire by Jonathan SWIFT, written in 1696–98. A ridicule of religious extremists, it is the tale of three brothers: Peter (the Roman Catholic Church), Jack (English dissenters or extreme Protestants), and Martin (the Lutheran or Anglican Church). The title comes from the nautical practice of throwing empty wooden tubs into the sea to divert whales who threaten a vessel. The tale is interspersed with ironic digressions, best known of which is the *Digression of Madness*, revealing that the author himself, who impersonates a Grub Street hack writer, is an inmate of Bedlam. Along with *The Tale of a Tub* were published two separate pieces, THE BATTLE OF THE BOOKS and *Discourse concerning the Mechanical Operation of the Spirit*. All three are thematically related. The book gave Thomas Carlyle, in the next century, the idea for SARTOR RESARTUS.

Tale of Genji, The (Genji monogatari)   A Japanese novel of the HEIAN (794–1185) period by MURASAKI SHIKIBU. This vast chronicle of court life centers on the career of Prince Genji and the women with whom he was associated. Its style is highly ornate and the work is rich in poetry and elaborate wordplay. Reflecting pure Japanese traditions, it has had a tremendous influence on subsequent literature and is regarded unreservedly as the greatest single work in Japanese fiction. It was translated first by Arthur WALEY (1925–33) and then by Edward Seidensticker (1976).

Tale of Two Cities, A (1859)   A novel by Charles DICKENS. The two cities are London and Paris; the background is the French Revolution, descriptions of which Dickens obtained from his friend Thomas Carlyle's FRENCH REVOLUTION.

Dr. Alexander Manette, unjustly imprisoned for eighteen years in the Bastille because of his knowledge of an attack on a peasant girl by the marquis de St. Evrémonde, is released from prison and waits in an attic above the wine shop of M. and Madame DEFARGE for his rescuers to take him back to England. Reunited with his daughter, Lucie, he safely returns to London. Years later they are called to the Old Bailey to testify that they saw a young man named Charles Darnay on the boat from France to England. A nephew of St. Evrémonde who has rebelled against his family and immigrated to England, Darnay is now falsely accused of treasonable activities. He is saved by the presence of Sydney CARTON, a dissolute young man, who bears a striking resemblance to Darnay; Stryver, the defense counsel, points out the resemblance, stating that legal identification is impossible. Darnay and Carton become friends; both are frequent callers on the Manettes and both love Lucie. Darnay marries Lucie, and they have a baby. Some time later, he hears from Paris that an old faithful servant has been unjustly imprisoned and hastens to his aid. In the revolution-torn city, Darnay, as a member of a hated aristocratic family, is imprisoned and sentenced to the guillotine. Sydney Carton now appears and intervenes; with bribery, and aided by his resemblance to Darnay, he drugs the latter, spirits him out of prison to safety, and takes his place on the guillotine. This he does out of his great love for Lucie and complete cynicism about himself. Darnay and Lucie are happily reunited in England.

Tales of a Traveller   See IRVING, WASHINGTON.

Tales of a Wayside Inn (1863)   A collection of narrative poems by Henry Wadsworth LONGFELLOW. The work's structure is modeled on Chaucer's *Canterbury Tales* and Boccaccio's *Decameron*. Each of the tales is narrated by one in a group seated around the fireside of a New England tavern. Many of the stories reflect Longfellow's interest in the Middle Ages. Even when the event related is not ancient, as in the popular "Paul Revere's Ride," it is presented as though it occurred long, long ago. Some of the more interesting tales include "Elizabeth," "The Battle of Carmilhan," "Emma and Eginhard," and "The Saga of King Olaf."

Tales of Hoffmann (1881)   A fantastic opera by Jacques OFFENBACH, based on three tales by the German author E.T.A. HOFFMANN. The successive acts deal with the love affairs and other adventures of the poet Hoffmann, which he recalls over wine in a Nuremberg tavern.

Tales of the Grotesque and Arabesque (1840)   A collection of short stories by Edgar Allan POE. His first book of tales, it includes THE FALL OF THE HOUSE OF USHER and BERENICE. In the preface, Poe explains that he based his tales not on German Gothicism, but on the terror of the soul.

Tales of the Heike, The (Heike monogatari)   Japanese epic detailing the dramatic rise of the Taira (Heike) family to a position of dominance in Japanese society during the late 12th century, their hubristic rule, and their crushing defeat at the hands of the Minamotos, a rival clan. Based on history, the work fills the place in Japanese literature occupied by the Homeric epics in the literature of the West. Stemming from oral tradition and incorporating

Buddhist themes of the transience of human endeavor, it achieved its present form in the mid-13th century during the Kamakura period. It was first translated into English in 1918 and 1921.

Taliesin (Welsh, "shining brow") A quasi-mythical figure traditionally said to be the greatest of the early Welsh bards (fl 550?). Taliesin is said to be the first bard to acquire the secret of prophetic poetry; according to legend he could divine the future and strike less gifted poets dumb. He is mentioned in Tennyson's IDYLLS OF THE KING and figures prominently in Thomas Love PEACOCK's *Misfortunes of Elphin* (1829). Frank Lloyd WRIGHT gave the name *Taliesin* to his residences in Wisconsin and Arizona.

talisman (Arab, *tilasman*, fr late Gr, *telesma*, "mystery") A charm, magical figure, or word, such as the ABRAXAS, which is cut on metal or stone under the influence of certain planets. It is supposed to be sympathetic to these influences, which it communicates to the wearer.

In Arabia, a talisman consisting of a piece of paper on which are written the names of the SEVEN SLEEPERS and their dog is used to protect a house from ghosts and demons. In order to free any place of vermin, a talisman consisting of the figure of the obnoxious animal is made in wax or consecrated metal, in a favorable planetary hour.

Talisman, The (1825) A historical novel by Sir Walter SCOTT, relating the adventures of Sir Kenneth, prince royal of Scotland, as a knight in disguise in the Holy Land under RICHARD I. Richard and his noble enemy Saladin are leading characters. The talisman is an amulet of singular healing powers with which Saladin effects the cure of Richard's sickness.

Talleyrand-Périgord, Charles Maurice de (1754–1838) French statesman, commonly known as Talleyrand. He was minister of foreign affairs from 1797 to 1807, and was made grand chamberlain (1804) by NAPOLEON. He opposed Napoleon's Russian and Spanish policies, and after Napoleon's fall he helped restore the BOURBONS. Louis XVIII made him minister of foreign affairs (1814) and grand chamberlain (1815). He represented France at the Congress of VIENNA (1815), where his diplomatic tact succeeded in maintaining his country's territorial integrity. He resigned after Napoleon's defeat at WATERLOO. In 1830 he became ambassador to Great Britain and helped form the Quadruple Alliance (1834). His *Mémoires* were published in 1891. See VERNON, MME DE.

tall tale A FOLKLORE genre, originating on the American frontier, in which the physical attributes, capabilities, and exploits of characters are wildly exaggerated for comic effect. Davy CROCKETT's *Narrative of the Life of David Crockett* (1834) is rich in tall tales, boasting not only of his own bold feats but also those of the "king of the flatboatmen," Mike Fink, and Daniel BOONE. Legendary folk heroes, like the phenomenally strong railroad man John HENRY or the gargantuan logger Paul BUNYAN, provided ample material for fertile imaginations. Washington

IRVING and Mark TWAIN are two of many American writers who incorporated tall tales in their fiction.

Talmud (Heb, "instruction") The body of Jewish civil and religious law, not contained in, but largely derived from, the PENTATEUCH. The Talmud is divided into the MISHNAH and the Gemara. The Mishnah gives a simple statement of a law or precept; the Gemara presents the discussion and debate on it.

When the Talmud is spoken of without any qualification, the reference is to the Babylonian Talmud, one of the two recensions of the Gemara. The other is the Palestinian Talmud, which is only one fourth the size of the Babylonian and is considered by Jews to have less authority.

Work on the Mishnah began in the time of the MACCABEES. The four thousand rules and postulations were codified and arranged by subject by Rabbi Judah I (c135–220). The schools in Palestine had codified their Gemara by the 4th century; the Babylonian scholars finished their Gemara in the 6th century.

Talus (1) In Greek myth, the guardian of Crete; a giant of brass fashioned by HEPHAESTUS for MINOS. Talus kept strangers off the island by throwing huge rocks at approaching ships, or he would make himself red-hot and burn trespassers to death in his embrace. A single vein of blood ran from his head to his foot, where it was closed with a nail. MEDEA, coming to Crete with the ARGONAUTS, charmed the nail out by her magic, and Talus bled to death. In Spenser's THE FAERIE QUEENE (Book V) he is the "yron man" attendant upon Sir Artegal and represents executive power—"Swift as a swallow, and as lion strong."

(2) An apprentice of DAEDALUS, also known as Perdix. Daedalus, according to a Greek myth, grew jealous of Talus' skill as an artisan and threw him into the sea, but he was saved by being turned into a partridge (*perdix*). The invention that incited Daedalus' enmity is said to have been the saw.

Tamar and Other Poems (1924) A collection of poems by Robinson JEFFERS. The title poem is loosely based on the biblical story of Tamar, the daughter of King David, who was seduced by her brother. It deals with a modern Tamar living on the Monterey coast, who seduces her brother, a neighbor, and her father, communicates with the dead, and finally brings destruction to her entire family.

Tamburlaine the Great (in two parts; probably acted first in 1587, pub in 1590) A romantic tragedy by Christopher MARLOWE, based on the history of TAMERLANE. A Scythian shepherd who becomes a fierce bandit and finally the victorious conqueror and king of Persia, the Tamburlaine of Part I is an embodiment of the Renaissance spirit: bold, defiant, eager to explore the possibilities of human life. Marlowe creates a hero who is free to act, unhampered by fate or external circumstance. At the end of Part I, he is at the height of his glory; in Part II, however, his lust for power and his cruelty finally end in ruin.

Tamerlane (or Tamburlaine, corruption of Timur i Leng [Timur the Lame]; 1336–1405) Mongol conqueror, great-great-grandson of Genghis Khan. After establishing his capital at Samarkand, Tamerlane conquered great parts of Russia, Persia, India, and central Asia, and died while preparing to invade China.

TAMBURLAINE THE GREAT, a blank verse tragedy, was Christopher Marlowe's first play. In it Tamburlaine becomes a bloodthirsty, inhuman villain, and the action consists of one atrocity after another.

In Nicholas Rowe's play *Tamerlane* (1702), the warrior appears as a calm, philosophic prince, out of compliment to William III. There is an early poem called "Tamerlane" by Edgar Allan POE.

Taming of the Shrew, The (c1593) A comedy by SHAKESPEARE. The "shrew" is KATHARINA, a maiden of such violent whims and tempers that it seems unlikely she will ever find a husband. Her father, Baptista, refuses to allow her lovable younger sister, Bianca, to marry any of her numerous suitors until Katharina is off his hands. Finally PETRUCHIO appears, marries Katharina in short order, and by his own abrupt highhandedness "tames" her to such good effect that he wins a bet with two other men on a test of their wives' obedience. Meanwhile, Lucentio, through the ruse of becoming Bianca's tutor while his servant Tranio assumes his name and clothing and presses his suit with her father, has succeeded in winning her hand. The entire play is enacted for the benefit of Christopher SLY, a drunken tinker who, in the opening "induction" scene, is taken to a nobleman's castle where he is fooled into thinking he is the nobleman himself.

The relationship of Shakespeare's play to an earlier, anonymous play, *The Taming of a Shrew*, is disputed by scholars, but the plot elements of the two plays are similar. The opening episode, concerning the induction of the drunken Sly, is a common one in folk tales, as old as the *Arabian Nights*. The subplot involving Bianca and Lucentio is based on ARIOSTO's *I suppositi*, translated by Gascoigne in 1566.

tamizdat A Russian term for literary works published abroad without permission of the Soviet authorities. The word derives from the Russian word *tam*, meaning "there," and the word *izdaniye*, meaning "edition."

Tammany Hall The headquarters (formerly on Union Square) of the controlling organization of the Democratic Party in New York City and State; hence, the party itself. As this has been the political target for so-called party abuses, the term "Tammany" is figuratively employed for municipal malpractice.

Tammany was the name of a 17th-century Delaware chief, and the patriotic, anti-British leagues of pre-Revolutionary days adopted the name "St. Tammany" to ridicule the titles of loyalist organizations—societies of St. George, St. Andrew, and so on. After the Revolution, these leagues became antiaristocratic clubs, but all soon died a natural

death except "Tammany Society, No. 1," which was that of New York. This flourished, and was converted into a political machine by Aaron Burr in his conflict with Alexander Hamilton (c1798), and in 1800 played a prominent part in the election of Jefferson to the presidency.

Tammuz A Near Eastern god of fertility. In some obscure manner, ISHTAR's love for him caused his death, and Tammuz descended into the underworld, leaving the earth barren. Ishtar mourned him, and eventually followed him into the underworld, from which, with the help of EA, she rescued him. With his father, Ningishzida, he became a gatekeeper at the palace of Anu, the god of heaven.

Tammuz was important, under one name or another, throughout the Near East. His earliest known form was the Sumerian shepherd-god DUMUZI. He was most widely known in later times in the modified form of ADONIS.

Tam o'Shanter (1791) A narrative poem by Robert BURNS, based on the legend that no manner of spirit or sprite could cross the middle of a running stream. On his way home one night, a little drunk, Tam sees witches and warlocks dancing in the Kirk of Alloway. Delighted, he calls out to one "winsome wench" among the beldams, "Weel done, CUTTY SARK!" Immediately the lights go out, and the witches come down on Tam, who rides for his life until he has reached the middle of the bridge over the DOON. Being past the middle of the stream, he is out of the witches' power, but his mare's tail is not, and Cutty Sark catches hold of this and pulls it off.

Tancred (known as Tancred of Altavilla or of Sicily, d 1112) Norman soldier and crusader. During the First Crusade (1096–99), Tancred took part in the siege of Jerusalem and the battle of Ascalon; he eventually became ruler of the principalities of Edessa and Antioch.

The character of Tancredi in Tasso's GERUSALEMME LIBERATA is based on him. He was the subject of an opera, *Tancredi* (1813), by ROSSINI and a musical drama, *Il combattimento di Tancredi e Clorinda* (1624), by MONTEVERDI.

Tancred, or the New Crusade (1847) A novel by Benjamin DISRAELI. Tancred is a young and highborn visionary who leaves the social circles of 19th-century London to travel in the East. In the Holy Land he experiences the great Asian mystery, which is to work regeneration for the West.

Tandem, Felix See SPITTELER, CARL.

T'ang Chinese dynasty (618–906), following the SUI dynasty. It was the golden age of Chinese civilization, which saw vast expansion of the empire, the origins of CH'AN BUDDHISM, and many new developments in literature, science, and the arts. There was much contact with the outside world, and there was a passion for foreign things and ideas. ISLAM, NESTORIAN Christianity, and Zoroastrianism (see ZOROASTER) entered China at this time. Poetry reached heights unequaled in later centuries. Among the most famous poets are WANG WEI, LI PO, TU FU, PO CHÜ-I, LI HO, and LI SHANG-YIN. Prose writing returned to the direct and powerful style of the ancient philosophers of the late CHOU, and turned away from the elaborate conceits of the SIX DYNASTIES style. The compilation of dictionaries and encyclopedias made great advances and the prototypes of later drama and fiction can be traced to this period. The AN LU-SHAN REBELLION drove the imperial court out of north China temporarily and marked the beginning of the great decline in the political fortunes of the empire. Li Po and Tu Fu were among the poets caught up in the disaster, which became a popular subject of poetry and drama. Japan was greatly influenced by all aspects of the culture of the T'ang dynasty. It was succeeded by the SUNG dynasty.

Tanglewood Tales (1853)   A book for children by Nathaniel HAWTHORNE. The author retells six Greek myths, dealing with the same themes—revenge, the effects of time, and strange transformations—that interest him in his major work. The book is a sequel to A *Wonder-Book for Boys and Girls* (1852).

Taniguchi Buson (1716–1783)   Japanese painter and HAIKU poet. Generally ranked next to MATSUO BASHŌ as the greatest haiku poet of the TOKUGAWA period, he created delicate, carefully wrought haiku that sought to elevate the form to the highest aesthetic standards. As a painter, he also idealized his subjects rather than portraying the commonness of everyday life. Some of his verse was published in *Buson Shichibushū* (1908).

Tanizaki Jun'ichirō (1886–1965)   Japanese novelist. Tanizaki's works are characterized by skillful storytelling and by a deep concern with the psychic forces rooted in human sexuality. This is especially evident in his last two novels, *Kagi* (1957; tr *The Key*, 1960) and *Fūten rōjin nikki* (1961; tr *Diary of a Mad Old Man*, 1965), but is also true of his earliest stories, such as *Shisei* (1910; tr *Tattoo*, 1961). The works of his middle period, notably *Tade kuu mushi* (1928; tr *Some Prefer Nettles*, 1955), *Shunkin shō* (1933; tr *A Portrait of Shunkin*, 1965), and *Sasame yuki* (1943–48; tr *The Makioka Sisters*, 1957), reveal Tanizaki's fascination with classical Japanese culture, which he thought had succeeded in taming these psychic forces and creating unique beauty. His admiration for traditional aesthetics is also expounded in his essay *In'ei raisan* (1933; tr *In Praise of Shadows*, 1977).

tanka   The classic form of Japanese poetry, fixed centuries ago as five lines with 5, 7, 5, 7, 7 syllables. It reduces, through the strict limits of its form, all poetic raw material to the concentrated essence of one static event, image, mood, etc. An example by Saigo Hoshi:

Now indeed I know
that when we said "remember,"
and we swore it so,
it was in "we will forget"
that our thoughts most truly met.

See HAIKU.

Tannhäuser (13th century)   A minor German MINNESINGER, or lyrical poet. Tannhäuser led a wandering life and went on a Crusade to the Holy Land. He was associated with the knight Tannhäuser of popular ballads, which relate how he discovers Venusberg (or Hörselberg), a magic land reached through a subterranean cave, and stays to enjoy its pleasures with the goddess Venus. At last he becomes conscious of having sinned, and journeys to the upper world to ask the Pope for absolution. The Pope replies that he should no more expect God's forgiveness than he could expect the papal scepter to bring forth green leaves. Tannhäuser departs in despair, but on the third day the papal staff bursts into blossom. Messengers are sent after him, but the knight has disappeared, having returned to Venusberg.

In WAGNER's adaptation for his opera *Tannhäuser* (1845), the hero returns from Venusberg to the court of the landgrave of Thuringia, where the landgrave's niece Elizabeth has been faithful to her love for him. His friend WOLFRAM VON ESCHENBACH persuades him to take part in the singing contest, for the winner is to marry Elizabeth. The last to sing, Tannhäuser bursts unwillingly into a song in praise of Venus, so wildly pagan that the other knights draw their swords to kill him. Elizabeth begs for his life, and he departs with a group of pilgrims to seek forgiveness at Rome. The Pope gives the legendary reply, and Tannhäuser returns weak and dejected. He is just in time to see the funeral of Elizabeth, who has died despairing that he would never return. He falls sorrowfully, dying, on the bier, just as more pilgrims arrive, carrying the Pope's leaf-bearing staff.

Tantalus   In Greek mythology, a son of ZEUS or Tmolus and progenitor of the house of ATREUS. Tantalus is best known for the punishment he suffers in HADES: suffering hunger and thirst, he stands in the midst of a lake, but when he bends to drink, it dries up; a fruit-laden bough flies up when he reaches for it; and an overhanging stone threatens to crush him. The word *tantalize* recalls his tortures.

The punishments were inflicted for various crimes. A favorite of Zeus, Tantalus betrayed his secrets and gave AMBROSIA to his friends. Offering a banquet to the gods on the Lydian Mount Sipylus, he served his dismembered son PELOPS. His theft of the golden dog that had watched over the infant Zeus caused Zeus to crush him under Sipylus. By Euryanassa, he was the father of Pelops, NIOBE, and BROTEAS.

Tantras   Sanskrit religious writings, forming the holy scriptures associated with the Hindu sect Shaktism (see SHAKTI). The adherents worship the divine power in its female aspect (*sakti*). The *Tantras* consist of magical formulas, for the most part in the form of dialogues between Shiva and his wife, Kali, and deal with the creation and ultimate destruction of the world, divine worship, the attainment of superhuman power, and final union with the

Supreme Spirit (*purusha*). They are of comparatively recent date (6th or 7th century). *Tantra* is Sanskrit for thread, or warp, and is used here as groundwork, order, or doctrine of religion.

T'ao Ch'ien (or T'ao Yuan-ming, 365–427)   Chinese poet of the Six Dynasties period. Unhappy with government service, he withdrew into country retirement, where he wrote poetry praising wine and the simple pleasures of his farm and garden. He was deeply influenced by Taoist ideas, although he was clearly still under the influence of Confucian concepts of history and fate. He has always had great popularity in Japan and has been much translated into English.

Taoism   A Chinese philosophical and religious system. Philosophical Taoism is based on the writings of Lao Tzu and Chuang Tzu and called for a return to primitive, preliterate social forms and abandonment of the conventional value system of their times. It opposed the ritualistic and moralistic social order of Confucianism. Its mystical and poetic ideas were a source for much of later imaginative literature, and its rejection of the conventional materialistic world provided a refuge for scholar-officials burdened with the orthodox Confucian view of life. Much of the vocabulary and conceptual imagery of Taoism was used to adapt early Buddhism to Chinese patterns of thought. Another strain, religious Taoism, grew out of cosmological speculation and alchemy, and involved the search for longevity drugs, yogic practices, Yin and Yang theory, and a vast pantheon of gods. Beginning in late Chou and early Han times, this school grew to be a syncretic and popular religion with admixtures of Buddhism and Confucianism.

Tao te ching   Chinese Taoist text attributed to Lao Tzu. A brief work in eighty-one paragraphs in both verse and prose, it probably dates from the 4th or 3rd century BC, although some believe it may be as early as the 6th century BC. The meaning is obscure and subject to many interpretations, the two principal ones being that it is a mystical book about union with the absolute, and that it is a political handbook on how to rule and survive in chaotic times. It advocates following the *Tao*, or Way, which precedes and underlies all things; adopting an attitude of humility, passivity, and inaction (*wu-wei*); and returning to a primitive preliterate form of society. Good translations are D. C. Lau, *Lao Tzu: Tao Te Ching* (1963) and Wing-tsit Chan, *The Way of Lao Tzu* (1963). See Taoism.

Tara   A site in Meath, Ireland. There the kings, the clergy, the princes, and the bards used to assemble in a large hall to consult on matters of public importance. The name Tara's Psaltery or Psalter of Tara was given to the great national register or chronicles of Ireland, read to the assembled princes when they met in Tara's Hall in public conference.

Taras Bulba (1835)   A short novel by Nikolay Gogol. It is set during the 17th-century wars between the Poles and the Cossacks in the Ukraine. The old Cossack Taras Bulba, and his two sons, Andri and Ostap, join the Cossacks in a campaign against the Poles. Andri falls in love with a Polish woman and deserts his comrades to be with her inside a besieged Polish fortress. Meeting Andri in a skirmish outside the fort, Taras kills his traitorous son. Meanwhile Ostap is captured and tortured to death by the Poles. Taras later suffers the same fate. The novel is rich not only in battle scenes but also in the language in which the Ukrainian countryside is described. The work ends with a famous description of the Dniester River, with a wild duck, called in Russian a *gogol*, included in the scene.

The story has a biographical connection with Gogol. One of his Cossack ancestors, named Ostap Gogol, sided with the Poles during the 17th-century wars and once surrendered a fortress to them.

Tarasov-Rodionov, Aleksandr Ignatiyevich (1885–1938)   Russian novelist. Born in Astrakhan, Tarasov-Rodionov studied law at Kazan University. He joined the Communist Party in 1905 and thereafter served both in the Red Army and in the Communist court system. He was also an early organizer of the Russian Association of Proletarian Writers (RAPP). His best-known work, the novel *Shokolad* (1922; tr *Chocolate*, 1932), appeared in the magazine *Young Guard* and became immediately popular, although its frank depiction of "revolutionary justice" elicited heated controversy. Through intrigue and pity for a "class enemy," the chief of the local Security Police (Cheka) comes to pardon a prostitute who, in gratitude, returns the favor by giving his wife some chocolate gotten from a suspected English spy. Later the chief of police is charged with bribe-taking and collaboration with a class enemy. In 1936 Tarasov-Rodionov was expelled from RAPP as a Trotskyite and executed in 1938, although his reputation was rehabilitated after the death of Stalin.

Tar Baby (1880)   One of the best-known stories of Joel Chandler Harris. It first appeared in book form in Uncle Remus, His Songs and His Sayings and later in *The Tar Baby Story and Other Rhymes by Uncle Remus* (1904). A tar doll set up by the roadside so irritates Brer Rabbit by its unresponsiveness that he strikes it until he is stuck tight.

Tarbell, Ida M[inerva] (1857–1944)   American journalist. Famous for her exposés in *McClure's Magazine* (1894–1906), Tarbell was one of the leading Muckrakers of her day. Aside from biographies of Napoleon (1895), Lincoln (1900), Judge Gary (1925), and Owen D. Young (1932), she is known for her two-volume *History of the Standard Oil Company* (1904), one of the best accounts of corporate monopoly of the day. *All in the Day's Work* (1939) is her autobiography.

Tarkington, [Newton] Booth (1869–1946)   American novelist and playwright. After studying at Princeton, where he founded the Triangle Club, Tarkington served in the Indiana House of Representatives in

1902–3; his concern for politics is reflected in *The Gentleman from Indiana* (1899), his first novel, and *In the Arena* (1905). He also is noted for his stories of childhood and adolescence, particularly PENROD and SEVENTEEN. The title *Growth* (1927) was later given to his trilogy about urban life in the Midwest, which appeared as *The Turmoil* (1915); *The Magnificent Ambersons* (1918), for which he was awarded a PULITZER PRIZE; and *The Midlander* (1923). He received another Pulitzer Prize for ALICE ADAMS. His other novels include *Monsieur Beaucaire* (1900) and *The Conquest of Canaan* (1905). He also wrote twenty-five plays, notably *The Man from Home* (1907), which contrasts American innocence with European sophistication. *The World Does Move* (1928) is his autobiography.

Tarpeian Rock   An ancient rock or peak (now no longer in existence) on the Capitoline Hill, Rome. The name comes from Tarpeia, a vestal virgin and daughter of Spurius Tareius, governor of the citadel. According to legend, he agreed to open the gates to the Sabines if they would give his daughter "what they wore on their arms" (meaning their gold bracelets). The Sabines, thereupon, crushed her to death with their shields, and her body was hurled from the Tarpeian Rock. Subsequently, traitors were cast down from this rock, and so killed.

Tarquin   The family name of a historical and legendary line of Etruscans who ruled early Rome. Ancient sources do not clearly differentiate among the exploits of the Tarquins. The legend of the SIBYLLINE BOOKS has been attributed to both Tarquinius Priscus, the fifth king of Rome (616–579 BC) and the builder of the Circus Maximus, and to Tarquinius Superbus, the seventh and last Roman king (534–510 BC), a tyrannical despot who was expelled from the city. Sextus, the son of Tarquinius Superbus, raped LUCRETIA, the wife of Tarquinius Collatinus, in revenge for which the Tarquins were expelled from Rome, and a republic established. Collatinus was one of the first consuls of the republic.

Tarr (1918)   A novel by Wyndham LEWIS. It is a psychological drama about a group of Paris art students of various nationalities. The hero is Frederick Tarr, an Englishman, but the center of interest is Otto Kreisler, a German student through whom Lewis attacks German romanticism, nihilism, and militarism.

Tartarin   A famous comic character created by Alphonse DAUDET. He is the hero of *Aventures prodigieuses de Tartarin de Tarascon* (1872) and *Tartarin sur les Alpes* (1885). Tartarin, a native of Provence, is an amusing braggart who bubbles over with good humor and with hilarious, fantastic tales of his own escapades.

Tartarus   The infernal regions in classical mythology. Used as equivalent to HADES by later writers, by HOMER it was placed as far beneath Hades as Hades is beneath the earth. It was here that ZEUS confined the TITANS.

Tartuffe, Le (1664)   A witty comedy by MOLIÈRE. The religious hypocrite Tartuffe worms his way into the household of Orgon, a credulous fool who deeds all his property to the imposter and intends to marry his daughter to him. Orgon's wife, Elmire, tricks Tartuffe, who is unaware that Orgon is watching, into trying to seduce her; Orgon, finally understanding Tartuffe's true nature, orders him from the house. But Tartuffe, owning the house, evicts the family instead and arranges Orgon's arrest. The king intervenes at the last moment and Tartuffe is hauled off to jail. The word *tartufe* has come to mean religious hypocrite in the French language. The play itself was twice suppressed before permission to perform it freely was finally given.

Tarzan   A fabulous character by Edgar Rice Burroughs (1875–1950). Although Burroughs wrote many other stories about the fantastic and unearthly, his main claim to fame is the Tarzan series. First appearing in *Tarzan of the Apes* (1914), this 20th-century folk hero is depicted as the son of an English nobleman, abandoned in Africa in his infancy. He is brought up by apes, learns to speak their language (and that of other animals as well), and goes through a long series of breathtaking adventures. Eventually Tarzan marries, has a son, and finally a grandson. Millions of copies of the Tarzan books have been sold, and they have been translated into fifty-six languages. Many films have been made of his adventures, and he has long been a comic-strip favorite.

Task, The (1785)   A long poem by William COWPER, its purpose being, according to a statement by the author, "to discountenance the modern enthusiasm after a London life, and to recommend rural ease and leisure as friendly to the cause of piety and virtue." In its six books ("The Sofa," "The Time-piece," "The Garden," "The Winter Evening," "The Winter Morning Walk," and "The Winter Walk at Noon"), it deals with a number of subjects in which the author was interested, such as nature, rural life, animals, simple hard-working people, and social reform. Cowper's Christian orthodoxy—his insistence on the fallen state of man and on a God found necessarily in revelation and not merely in nature—makes him bitterly hostile to Deism and limits his sympathy and scientific discovery to prove divine design. In its recollections of the inspiring and healing qualities of nature, and in its use of blank verse, it is considered a forerunner of some of the poetry of Wordsworth. The poem contains Cowper's perhaps most famous aphorism: "God made the country and man made the town."

Tasso, Torquato (1544–1595)   Italian poet. He was born at Sorrento and educated by the Jesuits at Naples and by his father, Bernardo Tasso, himself a distinguished man of letters. At Padua, he studied law, then philosophy and eloquence under the influence of Speroni. When eighteen, he wrote a romantic epic, *Rinaldo*, about the adventures of the hero, a cousin of Orlando (Roland) the paladin. In 1565, he went to Ferrara to serve the Este family and began work on his masterpiece, the GERUSALEMME LIBERATA. During the decade he composed several discourses on the art of poetry and wrote AMINTA, first performed at the Este court in 1573. A few years later, his physical and mental health began to disintegrate as his sensitive nature was racked by doubts about the critical and religious orthodoxy of his work and by suspicions of hostility toward him on the part of patrons and friends. In 1579 the duke of Ferrara placed him in an asylum, where he languished for seven years in misery, despite such visitors as MONTAIGNE and many expressions of sympathy from the literary world. The fact that his writings in the asylum reveal an anguished rather than a deranged mind prompted later writers like Goethe to picture him as the victim of a romantic but forbidden attachment to the duke's sister Leonora (see TORQUATO TASSO). In 1586, upon his release, he found himself honored for his *Jerusalem*, which had appeared during his imprisonment. Despite further wanderings and continuing poor health, he completed in 1586 a tragedy, *Torrismondo*, and a creation poem, *Mondo creato* (1607), as well as more critical treatises and many letters. In 1593, he completed a revised version of his masterpiece, called *Gerusalemme conquistata* (*Jerusalem Conquered*), to meet critical and ecclesiastical objections. But in Italy and elsewhere, the first version was and remains the celebrated work; the second version has lived only as a document of biographical value. In 1594 Pope Clement VIII planned to crown him with the laurel on the Capitol in Rome, but the poet died in April 1595, before the projected ceremony. From the time of Edward Fairfax's translation into English of *Jerusalem Delivered* (1594, 1600), Tasso strongly influenced English poets, from SPENSER to BYRON.

Tassoni, Alessandro (1565–1635)   Italian poet. Tassoni wrote a celebrated mock-heroic epic, *La secchia rapita* (*The Rape of the Bucket*, 1624). It is made up of twelve cantos of octaves that narrate in epic style a struggle between the cities of Bologna and Modena over possession of a bucket.

Taste of Honey, A   See DELANEY, SHELAGH.

Tate, [John Orley] Allen (1899–1979)   American poet and critic. In a career extending over half a century, Tate was early associated with the agrarian-oriented FUGITIVES (he was a student of John Crowe RANSOM at Vanderbilt University) and was one of the founders of their seminal literary magazine, *The Fugitive* (1922–25). He also edited *Hound and Horn* (1931–34) and THE SEWANEE REVIEW (1944–46). Like the other agrarians, Tate tended toward social and political conservatism and a serious devotion to a nonindustrial South. The lifeblood of Tate's work was always poetry, although he also wrote biography, letters, one novel (an acute psychological study, *The Fathers*, 1938), and important criticism. His verse, beginning with *Mr. Pope, and Other Poems* (1928), is marked by a classical

severity of form, by intellectual complexity, satire, and a tendency to use religious symbolism. A recurrent theme is the decline of values and manners in the new industrial South. His verse is collected in such volumes as *Poems: 1922–1947* (1948), *Poems* (1960), *The Swimmers and Other Selected Poems* (1971), and *Collected Poems: 1919–1976* (1977). Among his most widely anthologized poems are "Ode to the Confederate Dead," "The Mediterranean," and "The Oath."

Tate wrote two excellent biographies, *Stonewall Jackson* (1928) and *Jefferson Davis* (1929), but his most distinguished prose appears in his critical essays. An important exponent of NEW CRITICISM, he published *Reactionary Essays on Poetry and Ideas* (1936), *Essays of Four Decades* (1969), and *Memoirs and Opinions 1926–1974* (1975). His theories of poetry influenced many younger poets, notably John BERRYMAN and Robert LOWELL.

Tate, Nahum (1652–1715)   English playwright and poet. Tate is best known for his bowdlerized versions of works of more famous authors, particularly for his adaptation (1681) of Shakespeare's KING LEAR, which gave the play a happy ending and remained the standard acting version until 1840. He collaborated with Dryden on the second part of ABSALOM AND ACHITOPHEL and with Nicholas Brady on a *New Version of the Psalms* (1696), a widely used hymnal. His best independent work is *Panacea, a Poem on Tea* (1700). Tate was POET LAUREATE from 1692 to 1715.

Tatler, The   A series of periodical essays started by Richard STEELE under the pseudonym Isaac BICKERSTAFF (1709–11). Joseph ADDISON and Jonathan SWIFT were also contributors. The essays are predominantly light satires and allegorical criticisms of contemporary mores and fall into five categories: entertainment, poetry, domestic and foreign news, and miscellaneous subjects. *The Tatler* was succeeded by THE SPECTATOR.

Taunay, Viscount Alfredo d'Escragnolle (1843–1899)   Brazilian novelist and historian. Of French ancestry, Taunay fought in the Paraguayan war (1864–70); *A retirada da Laguna* (1871), which was originally written in French as *La Retraite de Laguna*, is an epic account of a famous retreat during the war. His fiction, which reflected the growing interest of Brazilian intellectuals in social problems, tends toward realism. *Inocência* (1872), his best-known novel, is a tragic love story, notable for its depiction of the Brazilian hinterland.

Tawney, R[ichard] H[enry] (1880–1962)   English economic historian. Tawney was one of the foremost students of the development of capitalism. His first important work was *The Agrarian Problem in the 16th Century* (1912), which shows early changes in systems of production and English class structure foreshadowing capitalist growth. *Religion and the Rise of Capitalism* (1926) is a classic study of the relationship between Protestantism and economic development in the 16th and 17th centuries. Other important works are *The Acquisitive Society* (1920) and *Land and Labour in China* (1932).

Taylor, A[lan] J[ohn] P[ercivale] (1906–   ) English historian. Taylor has written particularly about 19th- and 20th-century European history and the events leading up to the two world wars in such books as *The Course of German History* (1945), *Rumours of Wars* (1952), *The Struggle for Mastery in Europe, 1848–1918* (1954), and *Bismarck, the Man and Statesman* (1955). *The Origins of the Second World War* (1962) sparked a well-known historiographical controversy between Taylor and, among others, H. R. TREVOR-ROPER. In asserting the historical reasons for Germany's expansion in the 1930s, Taylor was accused of exonerating Hitler and "throwing the baby out with the bathwater"; some praised Taylor for his courage and clearsightedness, others abused him for "standing history on its head" and giving comfort to neo-Nazis. *The War Lords* (1977) is a collection of lectures on world leaders during World War II. *Revolutions and Revolutionaries* (1980) and *Politicians, Socialism, and Historians* (1980) are works aimed at a general rather than a scholarly audience. He is also a frequent contributor to public discussions of the background of post-war diplomatic crises. Taylor's autobiography, *A Personal History*, was published in 1983.

Taylor, Bayard (1825–1878)   American man of letters. The author of extremely popular travel books and several novels and a translator of Goethe, Taylor thought of himself primarily as a serious poet. Most of his verse is romantic; the best known is "Bedouin Song."

Taylor, Edward (1642–1729)   English-born American poet and clergyman. In 1668 Taylor sailed to Massachusetts, entered Harvard College, and in 1671 became a minister in the frontier town of Westfield, Massachusetts. An ultraconservative in theology, Taylor began to write pamphlets attacking the liberal ideas of Solomon Stoddard, the grandfather of Jonathan Edwards. In 1682, at the age of forty, he began to compose the *Preparatory Meditations*, 217 poems in six-line stanzas, written over a period of years. The poems, intended to "stir up" the affections before observing the Lord's Supper, celebrate in the metaphysical manner the glory, and also the difficulty, of man's relation to God. Around 1685, Taylor began his major long poem GOD'S DETERMINATIONS TOUCHING HIS ELECT.

Only two of Taylor's poems were published in his lifetime. A selection from his verse first appeared in 1939, but no complete edition of the *Meditations* was published until 1960. Still in manuscript are Taylor's sermons, and his *Metrical History of Christianity*. Most critics of American literature now consider Taylor the most important American poet before the 19th century.

Taylor, Elizabeth (1912–1975)   English novelist and short-story writer. Widely read on both sides of the Atlantic, Taylor wrote stories and novels distinguished by a singular moral delicacy. Loneliness and the ways in which

people cut themselves off from each other and deceive themselves and others are recurrent themes. Her writing is understated and controlled, containing little external action but a keen eye for detail and a flair for evocative description and imagery. Among her novels are *A Wreath of Roses* (1949), *A Game of Hide-and-Seek* (1951), *The Soul of Kindness* (1964), *The Wedding Group* (1968), *Mrs. Palfrey at the Claremont* (1971), and the highly acclaimed, post-humously published *Blaming* (1976). Collections of her stories, many of which first appeared in THE NEW YORKER, include *The Blush and Other Stories* (1958), *A Dedicated Man* (1965), and *The Devastating Boys* (1972).

Taylor, Jeremy (1613–1667)   English clergyman and writer. Taylor's best-known work is the devotional book HOLY LIVING AND DYING. His prose is noted for its warmth and eloquence, its splendor of cadence, and its vividness of metaphor.

Taylor, John (1580–1653)   English author, known as "the Water Poet" because he worked for a time as a waterman on the Thames River. Taylor wrote a vast number of pamphlets and poems on a variety of subjects, which were first collected in 1630. Among his best-known prose works is *The Penniless Pilgrimage* (1618), an amusing account of a journey from London to Edinburgh. Taylor was known for his eccentric exploits, one of which was sailing on the Thames in a boat made of brown paper.

Taylor, Tom (1817–1880)   English dramatist. Some of Taylor's better-known plays include the comedies *Masks and Faces* (1854, written with Charles Reade) and *Our American Cousin* (1858); the latter was a success in the U.S., and it was the play LINCOLN was watching when he was assassinated at Ford's Theater in Washington by John Wilkes BOOTH. Taylor's serious melodrama *Ticket of Leave Man* (1863) is notable for its celebrated character Detective Hawkshaw.

Tchaikovsky, Pyotr Ilyich (1840–1893)   Russian composer. Tchaikovsky's music, while having definite Russian characteristics, is not as fiercely nationalistic as that of his contemporaries "The Five" of St. Petersburg, consisting of Mily Balakirev (1837–1910), BORODIN, César Cui (1835–1918), MUSSORGSKY and RIMSKY-KORSAKOV. His music owes much to French and German models. The composer himself recognized his greatest weakness when he said, "I cannot complain of lack of inventive power, but I have always suffered from want of skill in the management of form." His strong points, warm and expansive melodies and moments of intense dramatic expression, have made many of his works popular with a wide audience.

Tchaikovsky was an intensely complicated man, and his life was a series of soaring successes and crashing failures. He embarked on a disastrous marriage, which lasted only weeks, and found his most stable and enriching relationship with a woman who insisted they never meet. She was Nadezhda Filarelovna von Meck (1831–94), a wealthy widow, who commissioned a number of pieces and provided the composer with a substantial annual allowance. Their correspondence was regular and intimate until three years before Tchaikovsky's death, when she wrote to say that she could no longer afford to support him.

Tchaikovsky's best-known works are his three last symphonies (*No. 4 in F minor*, 1877; *No. 5 in E minor*, 1888; No. 6 in B minor, the *Pathétique*, his last work, 1893); the first piano concerto, in B-flat minor (1875); the violin concerto (1878); symphonic poems, especially *Romeo and Juliet* (1869, 1880); and his three ballets: *Swan Lake* (1876), *Sleeping Beauty* (1889), and the *Nutcracker* (1891–92). The most popular of his eleven operas are *Eugene Onegin* (1879) and *The Queen of Spades* (1890), both based on works by PUSHKIN.

Tchelichev, Pavel (1898–1957)   Russian-born American painter. Forced to flee Russia during the revolution, Tchelichev worked first in Berlin (1921–23) and then in Paris, where he designed sets for DIAGHILEV. He eventually immigrated to the U.S. in the 1930s. Best known for his work in America, he experimented with simultaneous images, multiple perspectives, and radical foreshortening to explore perceptual ambiguities. He often created textural interest by embedding coarse material, such as sand or coffee grounds, in his canvases. In his most famous painting, *Hide and Seek* (1942), the space between images of infants and children forms a gnarled tree, which itself conceals images of old age and death. References to ancient mystical symbols appear frequently in his work.

Teapot Dome   A tract of oil-bearing government land in Wyoming which figured in a major scandal of the Harding administration. A Senate investigating committee revealed that the Teapot Dome reserve and one at Elk Hills, California, had been transferred from the navy to Secretary of the Interior Albert B. Fall, who in turn had secretly leased the fields to private oil operators in 1922. It was also disclosed that the oilmen had lent Fall substantial sums of money. The leases were later canceled by the government, and Fall was convicted of bribery. The scandal inspired Upton SINCLAIR's novel *Oil!* (1927).

Teasdale, Sara (1884–1933)   American poet. Known for the evocative intensity of her lyrics, Teasdale was, for a time, associated with the group that gathered around Harriet MONROE in Chicago. She received a special PULITZER PRIZE for her *Love Songs* (1917). Other collections of her poetry include *Sonnets to Duse and Other Poems* (1907), *Helen of Troy and Other Poems* (1911), *Rivers to the Sea* (1915), *Flame and Shadow* (1920), *Dark of the Moon* (1926), and *Strange Victory* (1933). More and more withdrawn as the years went by, she committed suicide.

Tecumseh (1768?–1813)   Shawnee chief, considered one of the greatest American Indian leaders. Determined to check the westward expansion of U.S. settlers, Tecumseh and his brother, the Prophet, formed a league of Northwest Indian tribes, which was supported by British officials in Canada. While Tecumseh was away, General William Henry Harrison defeated the Indians at the battle of Tippecanoe (1811) in what is now Indiana. During the War of 1812, Tecumseh, who had allied himself with the British, was killed at the battle of the Thames in Canada.

Tegnér, Esaias (1782–1846)   Swedish poet, scholar, and bishop. After a university education at Lund, Tegnér was appointed a lecturer in aesthetics in 1803. By 1812 he was a professor with a chair of Greek; the leader of an intellectual circle, he remained at the university until 1826. Tegnér had been ordained in 1812, and he left the academic life to devote himself to his duties as bishop of Växjö. His finest poetry appeared in the collections *Krigssång för skånska lantvärnet* (1808), *Sång till solen* (1813), *Hjälten* (1813), *Nattuardsbarnen* (1820; tr by Henry Wadsworth Longfellow, *The Children of the Lord's Supper*, 1842), and *Frithiofs Saga* (1825), based on the old Norse sagas and one of the masterpieces of Scandinavian romanticism. Although he is noted for the clarity of language and expression in his philosophical lyrics, Tegnér also wrote some fine love poetry.

Teilhard de Chardin, Pierre (1881–1955)   French theologian and paleontologist. Teilhard was ordained a Jesuit priest in 1911 and earned a doctorate in paleontology eleven years later. Throughout his life he endeavored to reconcile his Christian beliefs with his scientific knowledge. Because his order considered his philosophical and metaphysical writings (particularly with regard to evolutionary theory) improper, he was forbidden to publish anything other than purely scientific papers on mammalian paleontology during his lifetime. His best-known works, all published posthumously, are *Le Milieu divin* (1957; tr *The Divine Milieu*, 1960), *Le Phénomène de l'homme* (1955; tr *The Phenomenon of Man*, 1959), *L'Apparition de l'homme* (1956; tr *The Appearance of Man*, 1965), *La Vision du passé* (1957; tr *The Vision of the Past*, 1966), *Comment je crois* (1969; tr *How I Believe*, 1969), and *Le Coeur de la matière* (1976; tr *The Heart of the Matter*, 1979). In these and other works, he argues that evolution is a process of continual converging toward an ultimate unity or "omega point." He also argues that living things tend to produce increasingly complex descendants —biologically, socially, and spiritually—so that the final convergence will represent the fulfillment of creation: Parousia, or the Second Coming of Jesus.

Telamon   In Greek mythology, a son of AEACUS, king of Aegina. With his brother PELEUS, Telamon killed their half brother Phocus to prevent his inheriting the kingdom. Banished, Telamon became king of Salamis. He was one of the ARGONAUTS and hunted the CALYDONIAN BOAR. He became the father of Great AJAX and TEUCER.

Tel-el-Amarna   Ruins of an Egyptian city. It was built in the 14th century BC by the great Egyptian ruler Ikhnaton. About four hundred clay tablets, representing the diplomatic correspondence between Ikhnaton and Amenhotep III and the kings of Babylon and Assyria, inscribed in cuneiform, were discovered there in 1887. The tablets were translated into English and reveal much about ancient Egypt and the Middle East.

Telemachus In classical legend, the only son of ODYSSEUS and PENELOPE. As a babe Telemachus was thrown in front of his father's plow as a test of that hero's pretended madness. When Odysseus had been absent from home nearly twenty years, Telemachus went to Pylos and Sparta to gain information about him. NESTOR received him hospitably at Pylos, and sent him to Sparta, where MENELAUS told him the prophecy of PROTEUS concerning Odysseus. Telemachus then returned home, where he found his father and assisted him in slaying his mother's suitors. Telemachus was accompanied on his voyage by ATHENE, the goddess of wisdom, under the form of MENTOR, one of his father's friends. He is the hero of TÉLÉMAQUE, a French prose epic by Fénelon. This once widely read story is based on the old legends but adds many incidents, notably Telemachus' love affair with the nymph CALYPSO, who had been so violently enamored of his father.

Télémaque (1699) A didactic romance by François de Salignac de la Mothe FÉNELON, written for his pupil the duc de Bourgogne. Ostensibly relating the adventures of Telemachus, the son of Ulysses, the book bears no relation to the actual *Odyssey*: it is an imaginative narrative, a pretext for dissertations on politics, morals, education, and religion. Fénelon's proposals for fair economic and legal systems offended Louis XIV, and the book brought its author into disfavor. It proved, nevertheless, the prototype of the religious and political tract disguised as a novel later employed by the PHILOSOPHES.

Telesio, Bernardino (1500–1588) Italian philosopher. One of the key figures in the Renaissance trend toward the modern scientific approach to nature, Telesio was influenced by the naturalistic school of Padua, where he studied and taught. His major work, *De rerum natura iuxta propria principia* (*The Phenomena of Nature According to Its Own Principles*, 1565–86), outlined his approach.

Telipinu Hittite god of fertility. The harsh, infertile winter was ascribed to Telipinu's sleep, and seasonal rituals were performed to wake him and calm his anger at being awakened, thereby bringing fertility back to the earth. A myth explaining these rituals in terms of divine precedents was discovered on clay tablets in the ancient Hittite capital Hattusas, now Boghazköy, Turkey. The earliest of the tablets are from the 15th century BC, but the myth itself is far older.

Tell, Wilhelm (or William Tell) The legendary national hero of Switzerland. In the 14th-century Swiss uprising against Austrian rule, Tell was supposedly a popular leader. Because of his refusal to salute the cap of Gessler, the imperial governor, as a sign of allegiance to

Austria, he was forced to attempt to shoot an apple from the head of his own son with his crossbow. He succeeded in doing so, but afterward dropped an arrow from his jacket. When Gessler asked him what the second arrow was for, Tell replied, "To shoot you, if I had killed my son." Gessler then ordered his imprisonment, but he was rescued by the peasantry and led his country to freedom from Austrian domination.

This legend is the subject of plays by, among others, SCHILLER (1804) and of ROSSINI's opera *William Tell* (1829).

Saxo Grammaticus tells a similar story about the Danish Toki who killed Harald, and many other variations of the legend are found in Scandinavian and English folklore.

Telling the Bees (1858) A poem by John Greenleaf WHITTIER. The title is derived from the New England custom of telling the bees and draping their hives when a member of the family has died. A young man, coming to visit his beloved, sees that the hives are being covered. He assumes that her grandfather has died, but discovers that it is the young woman herself.

Tell-Tale Heart, The (1843) A story by Edgar Allan POE. The murderer of an old man buries the dismembered body beneath the floor in his room. While the police are investigating, he begins to hear the heartbeats of his victim. He confesses in a frenzy. When the body is recovered, the murdered man's watch is found to be ticking.

Tellus (Lat, "earth") An ancient goddess of Rome; the symbol of fertility.

Tel quel French literary review published by the Editions du Seuil. It is associated primarily with authors of the NEW WAVE and with structuralist and other avant-garde criticism. See STRUCTURALISM.

Temora, An Epic Poem See MACPHERSON, JAMES.

Tempest, The (c1611) The last play of SHAKESPEARE. PROSPERO, magician and philosopher, reigns over an enchanted island with his daughter, MIRANDA. By use of magic, Prospero raises a tempest, causing a boat and its occupants to be washed ashore on the island. The boat contains the enemies who usurped Prospero's dukedom of Milan twelve years previously and cast him adrift on a bark with Miranda. The plot, planned by his brother Antonio and Alonso, the king of Naples, miscarried through the kindliness of Gonzalo, an old counselor, who had fitted Prospero's bark with supplies, unbeknownst to his masters. FERDINAND, son of Alonso, is feared drowned by the others, but has landed alone on another part of the island, discovered Miranda, and fallen in love with her. Alonso, Antonio, and the others are led by the music of ARIEL, the invisible sprite who serves Prospero, as they search for Ferdinand. At last they meet Prospero, who chastises them and orders them to right their wrongs. Alonso, rejoicing at finding Ferdinand alive, blesses the union of the young lovers and restores Prospero to his dukedom, whereupon Prospero renounces his magic and frees Ariel from his spell.

The play contains some of Shakespeare's most famous lines and is among his most beautiful works. The existence of analogues to the play in Italian literature and elsewhere suggests the possibility of a source now lost. Prospero's speech renouncing magic was taken from a passage in Arthur Golding's translation (1565–67) of Ovid's *Metamorphoses*, well known to Elizabethans. See CALIBAN; SEBASTIAN.

Templars (or Knights Templars)   An order of knighthood founded about 1118 to guard the passage of pilgrims to Jerusalem. Begun in poverty—the seal shows two knights riding on one horse—it was joined by many noblemen who brought great wealth to the order. Their independent conduct on the battlefield eventually became an embarrassment rather than an aid to the king of Jerusalem, and their wealth and political power a threat to the kings in Europe. Thus the order was savagely crushed by many rulers, notably Philip IV of France, and officially suppressed by the Pope in 1312.

Temple, Sir William   See SWIFT, JONATHAN.

Temple, The (1633)   A collection of 160 religious poems by George HERBERT. Deeply influential in its day, it inspired such works as Richard Crashaw's *Steps to the Temple* (1646).

Temps modernes, Les   French literary and philosophical review. Founded by Jean-Paul SARTRE, Simone de BEAUVOIR, and other writers in 1945, it became the principal forum for the discussion of and dissemination of existentialist viewpoints and doctrines.

Temps retrouvé, Le   See REMEMBRANCE OF THINGS PAST.

Tenant of Wildfell Hall, The (1848)   A novel by Anne BRONTË. It concerns a marriage destroyed by a dissipated husband.

Ten Commandments   The Decalogue (Gr, "ten words"), or the laws revealed at Mount Sinai to MOSES on the third month after the Israelites' deliverance from Egypt. The Ten Commandments forbid polytheism, idolatry, murder, adultery, theft, false testimony, and covetousness, while commanding that God's name be revered, the Sabbath kept holy, and one's father and mother honored (Ex. 20:1–17). They were received by Moses on two tablets of stone.

Tendai   A Japanese Buddhist sect. It teaches an elaborate, comprehensive form of BUDDHISM. Introduced in Japan by Saichō (767–822), it is based on the Chinese sect T'IEN-T'AI and emphasizes the teachings of the LOTUS SUTRA. Its headquarters were at Enryakuji at Mt. Hiei, near Kyoto. The popularity of esoteric Shingon Buddhism obliged Tendai to incorporate Shingon's doctrines during the HEIAN period (794–1185). Mt. Hiei was long the center of Japanese learning and culture, and the leaders of almost all of the sects of Japanese Buddhism had their early training there.

Ten Days That Shook the World   See REED, JOHN.

Tender Is the Night (1934)   A novel by F. Scott FITZGERALD. In a hedonistic setting in Europe after World War I, a wealthy mental patient, Nicole, falls passionately in love with her young psychiatrist, Dick Diver. She finds her cure in marrying him, but as she achieves mental stability and emotional independence, he deteriorates. Finally Nicole leaves him for a man who will be her lover and not her caretaker, and Dick begins an irreversible decline into alcoholism and dissolution. Diver is perhaps a reflection of Fitzgerald himself, who had painful experiences with his mentally disturbed wife, Zelda. Despite the book's many terrifying scenes, the warm tenderness of its writing lifts it into the realm of genuine tragedy. Fitzgerald kept reworking the book after its publication and initial failure with the public. After Fitzgerald's death, Malcolm COWLEY made a new version (1951), in which the episodes were placed in chronological order, and the flashback technique of the original version was abandoned.

Tendryakov, Vladimir Fyodorovich (1923–1984)   Soviet short-story writer and novelist. In his handling of suspense and crisis, Tendryakov has distinguished himself as a masterful author in the genre of the short story and novella. In his story "Troyka, semyorka, tuz" (1960; tr "Three, Seven, Ace," 1967, 1973), the intrusion of an ex-criminal disrupts the peace of a logging camp and reveals Tendryakov's focus on questions of morality. Two other notable works by Tendryakov are *Chrezvychaynoye* (*An Extraordinary Affair*, 1962) and *Podyanka—vek korotkiy* (*Creature of the Day*, 1967), in which the quota system encourages a crime.

Tennant, Kylie (1912–   )   Australian novelist. Tennant is a lively and warmly humorous writer whose books have nearly all grown out of her personal experiences. Her first novel, *Tiburon* (1935), is a grimly realistic story of the Depression. *The Battlers* (1941), *Lost Haven* (1946), and *The Honey Flow* (1956) all contain vivid evocations of the Australian countryside, whereas *Foveaux* (1939), *Ride On, Stranger* (1943), and *Time Enough Later* (1943) deal with the struggles and corruptions of city life. Tennant has also written criticism, including *The Australian Essay* (1968), and a biography, *Evatt: Politics and Justice* (1970). Among her other writings are *The Man on the Headland* (1971) and *Tantavallon* (1983).

Tenniel, Sir John (1820–1914)   English illustrator and cartoonist on the staff of *Punch*. Tenniel is best known as the illustrator of *Alice's Adventures in Wonderland* and *Through the Looking Glass* by Lewis CARROLL. His illustrations have defined Carroll's characters in the public mind as sharply as the author's own descriptions. The cheery chubbiness of Tweedledum and Tweedledee, the outsized head of the Duchess, the calf's head and feet of the Mock

Turtle, and the Hatter's hat with its price tag, "In this style 10/6," are all the products of the illustrator's fancy. Tenniel's pictures so perfectly capture the illogic and whimsy of the text that few editions of the books have been printed without them.

Ten Nights in a Bar-Room and What I Saw There (1854)

A story by Timothy Shay Arthur (1809–85), American editor and reformer. A melodramatic temperance tale, it was a favorite among American readers for more than twenty years; in 1858, Arthur's book was dramatized by William W. Pratt. As a play, it was more in demand than any other, with the exception of *Uncle Tom's Cabin*. An important influence in the passage of many temperance laws, its climax was little Mary's song at the saloon door, "Father, dear Father, come home with me now."

Tennyson, Alfred (1st Baron Tennyson, commonly called Alfred, Lord Tennyson; 1809–1892)

English poet. Appointed POET LAUREATE in 1850, Tennyson is considered highly representative of the Victorian age in England. In his early career, Tennyson was influenced by the English romantic poets, particularly John KEATS. His poetry reflects the sensibility and the intellectual and moral values of his time and of the dominant Victorian social class, and is a characteristic response of his time and class to the encroachments of science in the domain of religious faith. He was the favorite target for the attacks of English and American poets of the late 19th and early 20th centuries who, rebelling against Victorian standards, denounced him for sentimentality, insipidity, intellectual shallowness, and narrow patriotism. Later critics have praised him for his metrical skill and the distinguished imagery of some of his brief lyrics; his longer poems, however, are still regarded as suffering the aforementioned weaknesses.

Tennyson's works include the following: *Poems by Two Brothers* (1827), early verse with his brother Charles Tennyson Turner; *Poems, Chiefly Lyrical* (1830); *Poems* (1832); *Poems* (1842); LOCKSLEY HALL; *The Princess* (1847), which is especially notable for its songs; IN MEMORIAM, often considered his greatest poem, though long; *Ode on the Death of the Duke of Wellington* (1852); *Maud, and Other Poems* (1855); IDYLLS OF THE KING; ENOCH ARDEN; *Queen Mary* (1875), *Harold* (1876), and *Becket* (1884), historical tragedies in verse; *Tiresias, and Other Poems* (1885); *Locksley Hall Sixty Years After* (1886); *Demeter, and Other Poems* (1889); and *The Death of Oenone* (1892).

Tennyson was immensely popular and successful throughout his later career; the one enduring shadow in his life, aside from those inspired by his sensitive and somewhat melancholy temperament, was caused by the death of his friend Arthur HALLAM. This early bereavement led not only to *In Memoriam*, but to a lifelong conflict between faith and doubt. See BREAK, BREAK, BREAK; CHARGE OF THE LIGHT BRIGADE, THE; CROSSING THE BAR.

Tenochtitlán

The capital of the Aztec empire and the site of modern Mexico City. Founded about 1325, the city was built on two marsh-bound islands in Lake Texcoco, which were connected to the mainland by a system of causeways; the islands were subsequently enlarged by means of floating gardens. It is said that CORTEZ wept when he saw the ruins of the city, completely destroyed in 1521 as a result of bitter fighting between Aztecs and Spaniards.

Ten Plagues

In the OLD TESTAMENT, plagues called down upon Egypt by Jehovah through MOSES to facilitate the escape of the Jews from bondage (Ex. 7–12). Although most of the plagues were natural phenomena, they occurred with such severity and in such rapid succession that the Pharaoh was convinced that they were miraculous works of God. They were: (1) the turning of water to blood (a flood of red silt from the Abyssinian headwaters of the Nile); (2) the plague of frogs; (3) the plague of lice; (4) the plague of flies; (5) the plague of murrain, in which all but the Israelites' cattle perished; (6) the plague of boils on man and beast; (7) the plague of hail; (8) the plague of locusts; (9) the plague of darkness; and (10) death to firstborn Egyptians. A recitation of the ten plagues is part of the PASSOVER ritual.

Tenth Muse Lately Sprung Up in America, The (1650)

The first volume of poems written in North America, by Anne BRADSTREET. Included in the collection are "A Dialogue between Old England and New" and the ambitious "Four Elements," "Four Constitutions," "Four Ages of Man," "Four Seasons," and "Four Monarchies," the last an incomplete attempt at writing universal history. "Contemplations," which appeared in 1678 in the second edition of *The Tenth Muse*, is generally considered her best work; it is a meditative and descriptive poem, probably influenced by Edmund SPENSER and Giles FLETCHER.

tercet

In prosody, a synonym for triplet or a STANZA of three lines. Specifically, a tercet is a three-line stanza used in the TERZA RIMA form and in the two three-line divisions of the sestet of the Italian SONNET.

Terence (full Latin name Publius Terentius Afer, 185?–159 BC)

Comic playwright of ancient Rome, second only to PLAUTUS. Born in Carthage within a year of the death of Plautus, Terence was taken as a young man of twenty-one to Rome as the slave of the senator Terentius Lucanus. Impressed by the wit and learning of the young Carthaginian, his master set him free and helped him to continue his studies. His first play, the *Andria* (*Maid of Andros*), won him entry into what was called "the Scipionic Circle," the group of artists which was subsidized and encouraged by Scipio Africanus the Younger and his friend Laelius. His better-known works include the *Eunuchus*, the *Phormio*, and the *Adelphi*. He died at the age of twenty-six.

Unlike his predecessor Plautus, Terence wrote thoughtful, psychologically refined comedies. He did not aim at strong wit or farcical effect but at sharp delineation of character and elegance of form. His faults stem, accordingly, from his virtues: he is sometimes dry and excessively refined, and often his plots display more skill than wit.

Teresa, St. (or St. Theresa; known as Santa Teresa de Jesús or St. Teresa of Avila; real name Teresa de Cepeda y Ahumada; 1515–1582) Spanish nun and mystic. Born near Avila, Teresa was devout even as a child and ran away from home at the age of seven to seek martyrdom among the Moors. In 1534 she became a Carmelite, later becoming mother superior of the order and the foundress of seventeen new convents. The story of her intense spiritual life, with its moments of ecstasy and depression, and of her struggles to reform the order is told in her letters, over four hundred of which have been preserved, and in the autobiographical *Libro de su vida* and *Libro de las fundaciones*. She was canonized in 1622.

Her finest mystical work is *El castillo interior* (*The Interior Castle*, 1583), in which she guides the reader through the "abodes" of the human soul until he reaches the innermost chamber, the dwelling place of God. She also wrote the *Camino de perfección* (*Way of Perfection*, 1583), which discusses ways of achieving perfection in the religious life.

Though her meaning is occasionally obscure, her style is artless and vivid, offering an excellent example of colloquial Castilian of the 16th century.

Tereus See PHILOMELA.

Termagant The name given by the Crusaders, and by the authors of medieval romances, to a Saracen idol or deity. The Saracens were popularly supposed to worship the Termagant. He was introduced into the Morality plays as a most violent and turbulent person in long, flowing Eastern robes, a dress that led to his acceptance as a woman, whence the name came to be applied to a shrewish, violently abusive virago.

Terminus The Roman god of bounds. A boundary stone with a bust of the god was called a *terminus*.

Terpander (c675 BC) A Greek musician who established the first Greek school of music at Sparta.

Terpsichore One of the nine MUSES of classical mythology, the Muse of dancing and the dramatic chorus; hence the adjective Terpsichorean, "pertaining to dancing." She is usually represented holding a lyre.

Terre, La (The Soil, 1888) A novel by Emile ZOLA. One of the ROUGON-MACQUART series, it deals with greed for land. The characters, French peasants, are portrayed with merciless realism.

Terre des hommes See WIND, SAND, AND STARS.

Tertullian See ABSURD.

Tertz, Abram See SINYAVSKY, ANDREY DONATOVICH.

terza rima An Italian verse form in chain-rhymed TERCETS, the second line of each STANZA rhyming with the first and third of the next. The poem or division of a poem in terza rima concludes either with an extra line added to the last stanza or with a separate couplet rhyming with the second line of the last stanza. The rhyme scheme is thus a-b-a, b-c-b, c-d-c, d-e-d-e, or a-b-a, b-c-b, c-d-c, d-e-d, e-e. Terza rima may be written in any meter, but iambic pentameter is preferred in English. Dante's DIVINE COMEDY was written in this form, which was introduced into England by Sir Thomas WYATT in the 16th century and has been used by SHELLEY, BYRON, and other English poets.

Teseida The first Tuscan epic, written in octaves by Giovanni BOCCACCIO. Two friends, Arcita and Palemone of Thebes, vie for the love of Emilia, sister to the queen of Athens, where they are prisoners. THESEUS, king of Athens, orders a tournament to settle the quarrel; the wounded Arcita wins, but dies soon after his betrothal to Emilia. As Arcita wished, Emilia then marries Palemone.

In addition to prefiguring the ORLANDO poems of BOIARDO and ARIOSTO, the *Teseida* was used by Chaucer for THE KNIGHT'S TALE, by Fletcher in THE TWO NOBLE KINSMEN, and by DRYDEN for his *Palamon and Arcite*.

Tess of the D'Urbervilles; A Pure Woman (1891) A novel by Thomas HARDY. Tess Durbeyfield, urged by her dissipated father and the necessities of a poverty-stricken household, takes service with the wealthy Mrs. D'Urberville. Here Alec, the son of the house, forces Tess into sexual relations with him, and she becomes pregnant. The child, however, dies in infancy, and Tess hires herself out as a dairymaid on a farm. She falls in love with Angel Clare, a rector's son, and they marry. On their wedding night they indulge in mutual confessions. Though he expects to be forgiven for his own sinful past, Angel cannot forgive Tess for her past, in which she was victimized rather than sinful, and he deserts her. Some time later, Alec, now a preaching fanatic, entreats Tess to return to him. She does so in the belief that Angel will never relent, and in the face of growing poverty. When the repentant Angel returns and, finding Tess with Alec, prepares to leave once again, Tess stabs and kills Alec in desperation. She and Angel hide out for a time, but finally Tess is arrested and hanged.

Teternikov, Fyodor Kuzmich See SOLOGUB, FYODOR.

Tethys In Greek mythology, a Titaness and a sea goddess, wife of OCEANUS; hence, the sea itself. Tethys was the daughter of URANUS and GE and mother of the river gods.

tetragrammaton (Gr, "four letters") The Hebrew letters *Y*, *H*, *W*, *H*, which spell the name of God. See JEHOVAH.

tetrameter In prosody, a line of verse containing four metrical feet in any METER. Usually it is identified together with the name of the meter, as iambic tetrameter, trochaic tetrameter, etc.

Teucer In the ILIAD, the son of TELAMON, and stepbrother of Telamonian Ajax. Teucer went with the allied Greeks to the siege of Troy, and on his return was banished by his father for not avenging on ODYSSEUS the death of his brother. He was the best archer among the Greeks.

Tey, Josephine (pen name of Elizabeth Mackintosh, who also wrote as Gordon Daviot; 1896–1952)   Scottish novelist and playwright. Under the pseudonym of Gordon Daviot, Mackintosh wrote several novels and the highly successful historical drama *Richard of Bordeaux* (1933). As Josephine Tey, she produced a series of perennially popular, carefully crafted mystery novels, notably *Miss Pym Disposes* (1946); *The Franchise Affair* (1948); and *The Daughter of Time* (1951), in which the detective-hero reinterprets the evidence against King RICHARD III in the case of the princes in the tower.

Thackeray, William Makepeace (1811–1863) English novelist and satirist, best known for his satirical and moralistic studies of upper- and middle-class English life. Born in India of a wealthy merchant family, Thackeray moved to England at the age of six upon the death of his father. Leaving Trinity College, Cambridge, without a degree, he read law but abandoned the idea of the bar in order to explore journalism and art. Losing his inheritance in 1833, he spent three years in Paris studying unsuccessfully to be a painter. In 1836 he married Isabella Shawe and returned to England, resolved to try his luck as a writer. Thackeray gained a degree of recognition as a contributor of sketches to the *Times* and to *Fraser's Magazine* and as the author of such works as *The Yellowplush Correspondence* (1838), *A Shabby Genteel Story* (1840), and *The Fitz Boodle Papers* (1842–43). His literary success, however, had been tragically offset in 1840, when his wife, having borne him three daughters, lost her sanity and never recovered it, though she survived Thackeray by thirty years.

From 1842 to 1851 Thackeray was on the staff of PUNCH, to which he contributed the satires later published as *The Book of Snobs* (1848). With the appearance of this work and of VANITY FAIR, he won a popular and critical reputation that he went on to consolidate with such novels as PENDENNIS; HENRY ESMOND and its sequel, THE VIRGINIANS; and THE NEWCOMES. His other works include THE MEMOIRS OF BARRY LYNDON; several Christmas books, among them *Rebecca and Rowena* (1850) and THE ROSE AND THE RING; *The English Humourists of the Eighteenth Century* (1851) and *The Four Georges* (1855), lectures delivered in Great Britain and the U.S.; *The Adventures of Philip* (1862); and *The Roundabout Papers* (1863), essays written for the *Cornhill Magazine*, of which Thackeray was editor from 1860 to 1862. A novel, *Denis Duval* (1864), was left unfinished at his death. Shortly before he died, Thackeray was reconciled with Charles DICKENS, with whom he had been feuding since 1858. His younger daughter, Harriet, married Sir Leslie STEPHEN and became the mother of Virginia WOOLF.

Thaïs (1890)   A novel by Anatole FRANCE. Inspired by one of the tales in THE GOLDEN LEGEND, it is an ironic story of Paphnutius, a young Alexandrian debauché turned monk. Leading an ascetic life in the desert, he interprets his voluptuous dreams of the famous courtesan Thaïs as a call to convert her to Christianity. He succeeds in this aim, and she lives a short but saintly life as a hermit. Paphnutius, however, still dreams of her. In his attempt to hide from himself his lust for her, he mortifies his flesh relentlessly, and even spends some time as a STYLITE atop a high pillar. Finally he realizes his true feelings and tries to persuade her to flee the convent with him. As she dies, the abbess sends him away, horrified at the savagery that is finally revealed on his face.

Thales (c624–c546 BC)   A Greek philosopher of the MILESIAN SCHOOL. Regarded by some as the founder of Greek philosophy, Thales was considered one of the seven wise men of ancient Greece. He made several discoveries in geometry and astronomy, on one occasion accurately predicting an eclipse. Not satisfied with the answers provided by mythology, he searched for the primary substance in the universe, so that he could explain change as well as stability. He believed that water was this substance.

According to tradition, Thales replied to the charge of being an impractical philosopher by going into the olive-oil business and becoming very wealthy.

Thalia   One of the MUSES, generally regarded as the patroness of comedy. Thalia was supposed by some, also, to preside over husbandry and planting, and is represented holding a comic mask and a shepherd's crook. She was also, by some accounts, one of the GRACES.

Thammuz (or Tammuz)   The Syrian and Phoenician name of ADONIS. Thammuz's death occurs on the banks of the river Adonis, and in summer the waters become reddened with the hunter's blood. In the BIBLE, reference is made to the heathen "women weeping for Tammuz" (Ezek. 8:14). See SATAN.

Thanatopsis (1817)   A poem by William Cullen BRYANT. Inspired by the English Graveyard School of poetry, Bryant's poem seeks comfort in Nature for death. The earth, tomb of mankind, will cover all who now laugh or chase their "favorite phantoms." The poet advises, then, that when our time comes to join the "innumerable caravan":

> . . . approach thy grave,
> Like one who wraps the drapery of his couch
> About him, and lies down to pleasant dreams.

Thanatos   In Greek mythology, Death represented as a person. Thanatos appears in Euripides' ALCESTIS. Sleep (Hypnos) was his twin brother.

Thatcher, Becky   A young girl in Mark Twain's ADVENTURES OF TOM SAWYER. She is lost in the cave with Tom.

thaw, the   The name applied to the period of relative relaxation in Soviet life and culture following the death of Stalin in 1953. The name was taken from the title of a novel by Ilya ERENBURG, which was one of the first of a growing stream of works criticizing aspects of Soviet life. The unaccustomed freedom of writers to comment openly, if carefully, on their society reached its peak in 1956 with the publication of such works as Dudintsev's NOT BY BREAD ALONE and Aleksandr YASHIN's story "Levers." Previously outlawed writers such as Yury Olesha, Isaak BABEL, and Anna AKHMATOVA were reprinted at this time. By 1966, however, with the trial and imprisonment of Yuly DANIEL and Andrey SINYAVSKY, the thaw had for the most part ended, and dissent became, once again, a dangerous affair.

Theaetetus   A dialogue by PLATO on the nature of knowledge. Theaetetus, an Athenian mathematician, has been mortally wounded in the Corinthian War, and the news recalls to a friend a conversation Theaetetus and SOCRATES had once had. Varying definitions of knowledge are considered, but all are rejected. The subject is resumed in the dialogue called the *Sophist*, which includes Socrates' comment that he is the midwife of men's thoughts.

Theale, Milly   See WINGS OF THE DOVE, THE.

theatre of cruelty   A form of ritualistic theatre designed to assault the senses and sensibilities of the audience. It takes its name from a theatrical manifesto written in 1932 by Antonin ARTAUD. Artaud attempted to provide a framework in which the theatrical experience would profoundly affect the audience through its senses rather than by words. He felt that the spectator should be "inundated" to the point of participating in the cruelty that underlies every dramatic action. Cruelty to Artaud was an awareness of the determinism of evil, the devouring forces of love, the eroticism of death, and of man's obsessions and criminal tendencies. The theatre would deal with man's instinctual preoccupations in order to liberate them, and it aimed to do this through gesture and scenery. Words were subordinated to action in an attempt to restore the ceremonial and purgative powers of drama.

theatre of the absurd   An avant-garde dramatic convention that emphasizes the illogical and purposeless nature of existence. Often violent, grotesque, and outrageously funny, it strips language of traditional poetic and utilitarian functions, and instead conveys its meaning through masks, ritual, sounds, gestures, costumes, or stylized actions. The DADA and surrealist movements, the experiments and theoretical writings of Antonin ARTAUD and Roger VITRAC, and such plays as Alfred Jarry's UBU ROI and Guillaume APOLLINAIRE's *Les Mamelles de Tirésias* (1917) are directly related to the theatre of the absurd.

The main concern of the major dramatists of the ABSURD —Samuel BECKETT, Jean GENET, and Eugène IONESCO—is to project onto the stage a personal, concrete image of a situation that epitomizes man's fundamental helplessness in a contradictory and alienating universe. Sometimes, social criticism is embedded in these authors' works, but this is less important than their portrayal of human reaction to the essential realities: death, self, time, loneliness, communication, and freedom. These ancient themes are presented in ways that are intended to shock the audience so that the viewer assumes a more detached and critical attitude than in conventional drama; it is a theatre of alienation rather than a theatre of identification. Other dramatists of the absurd include Fernando ARRABAL, Max FRISCH, Günter GRASS, Harold PINTER, and Edward ALBEE.

Thebes   (1) Called "The Hundred-Gated," the chief town of the Thebaid, on the Nile in Upper Egypt, said to have extended over twenty-three miles of land. HOMER says out of each gate the Thebans could send forth two hundred war chariots.

It is here that the vocal statue of Memnon stood, and here too are the tombs of the kings, the temple of Karnak, and large numbers of sculptures, sphinxes, etc. The village of Luxor now marks the spot.

(2) Called "The Seven-Gated," the chief city of Boeotia, according to legend named after the nymph Thebe (see AMPHION). Founded, according to legend, by CADMUS, it was the birthplace of DIONYSUS and the scene of the tragic events that began with the birth of OEDIPUS and continued through the wars of his sons (see SEVEN AGAINST THEBES) and grandsons, the EPIGONI. It was still an important city in classical times.

Their Father's God   See GIANTS IN THE EARTH.

Thélème, abbey of   (Gr, "will; pleasure")   In Rabelais's GARGANTUA AND PANTAGRUEL, the abbey given by Gargantua to FRIAR JOHN for the aid he rendered in the war against PICROCHOLE. Built like a magnificent castle, it was the very reverse of a convent or monastery. Thélèmites were free to leave when they chose; they could marry, own wealth, and lived in perfect freedom. The only rule was "Do as thou wilt."

Themis   In Greek mythology, one of the TITANS, and goddess of natural law and justice. Themis was regarded as an earth goddess, and was one of the earliest patronesses of the DELPHIC ORACLE.

Themistocles   (c528–c462 BC)   An Athenian statesman and general. THUCYDIDES spoke of him as a man of genius. Themistocles persuaded the Athenians to concentrate on the development of sea power, building up their fleet to two hundred triremes. When the Persians, led by XERXES I, invaded Greece, Themistocles tried vainly to persuade the united Greeks to engage them by sea in the Bay of SALAMIS, where their more maneuverable vessels would have a tactical advantage. He then sent a message to the Persians that the Greeks were about to flee in disunity. The message had the intended effect, and the Persians at once surrounded the deliberating allies at Salamis. The battle (480 BC) was a great victory for the Greeks.

It was on Themistocles' advice that the Athenians rebuilt the walls of Athens and erected a walled way to her port at Piraeus. After the war, Themistocles became unpopular; he was vain and reportedly accessible to bribes. Ostracized, he moved to Argos, but was accused of treason. In time, he fled to the Persian court of Artaxerxes, where he was awarded the Asian kingdom of Magnesia. At his death, the Magnesians erected a statue of the "savior of Greece" in their market place.

Theocritus (early 3d century BC)   Greek poet. Theocritus was probably born in Syracuse. He is regarded as the inventor of the PASTORAL. Only about thirty of his works are extant; they include mainly the *Idyls*.

Theodora (508?–548)   Empress of the Byzantine Empire, wife of JUSTINIAN I. Theodora was an actress and noted for her beauty. She had great influence over Justinian and on the political and religious thinking at court.

Theodoric the Great (c454–c526)   A king of the Ostrogoths who invaded Italy, then ruled it in peace after 493. Theodoric is the origin of the heroic Dietrich of Bern in Germanic legends such as the *Heldenbuch* and the *Nibelungenlied*, but there he is described as fleeing from Italy to the court of Etzel (Attila, king of the Huns).

Theognis (fl 6th century BC)   Greek poet. Known as a writer of GNOMIC POETRY Theognis composed elegiac verse expressing his distaste for the lower classes and his belief in loyalty, moderation, and honor. Some of the work originally ascribed to him is now known to have been written by other poets.

Theophrastus (c370–285 BC)   A Greek philosopher, successor to Aristotle. Originally named Tyrtamus, he was called Theophrastus, or divine speaker, by Aristotle, because of his eloquence. As the leader of the Peripatetic School, he continued the work of Aristotle in natural history and botany. The surviving fragments show little originality. His best-known work is *Characters*, thirty satiric depictions of typical work weaknesses. See CHARACTER WRITERS.

Theory of the Leisure Class, The (1899)   An economic treatise by Thorstein VEBLEN. Veblen held that the feudal division of classes continued into modern times, with the lords employing themselves uselessly while the lower classes labored at industrial pursuits to support the whole of society. The leisure class, Veblen said, justifies itself solely by practicing "conspicuous leisure and conspicuous consumption"; he defined waste as any activity not contributing to material productivity. Veblen antagonized many opponents, notably H. L. MENCKEN, who called the economist's theory of conspicuous waste "one per cent platitude and 99 per cent nonsense." Veblen's unorthodox views and his vigorous, pointed style made the book one of the most popular of American scholarly works. His analysis of business cycles and prices, and of the emerging technocracy, was to seem increasingly prophetic as 20th-century industrial society evolved.

theosophy (fr Gr, *theos*, "divine," *sophia*, "wisdom")   A philosophical system of mystical speculation that provides for a complete belief in the existence of God as all-knowing and all-good; evil exists only because of man's insistence on temporal rewards. Theosophists maintain that a deeper understanding of nature is derived from a direct knowledge of God and a sense of the complete spirituality of the universe. Elements of theosophical thought were embraced by the Cabalists (see CABALA) and the GNOSTICS, although modern theosophy is largely based on the writings of Jakob BÖHME. The term was later adopted by Mme BLAVATSKY and others, who founded the Theosophical Society (1875) in New York. Their aims included the study of Eastern religions and sciences, and a study of the occult and the latent faculties in man. Eastern religions offered particular appeal to theosophists for the belief in a single, unifying spiritual principle.

Thérèse Desqueyroux (1927)   A novel by François MAURIAC. The title character, feeling herself stifled by the bourgeois proprieties of her marriage, attempts to poison her husband. She is acquitted at her trial, however, through her family's efforts to avoid scandal.

There Shall Be No Night   See SHERWOOD, ROBERT E.

Thermidor (fr Gr, *thermē*, "heat," *doron*, "gift")   Eleventh month in the French Revolutionary calendar, containing thirty days beginning July 19. It was on Thermidor 9 (July 27, 1794) that ROBESPIERRE was overthrown and the REIGN OF TERROR ended.

Theroux, Paul [Edward] (1941–   )   American novelist and travel writer. As a teacher in Malawi, Uganda, and Singapore, Theroux experienced life in the postcolonial Third World firsthand. He has explored the social and personal effects of this life on Europeans or Americans in several novels, including *Saint Jack* (1973) and *The Consul's File* (1977). *The Family Arsenal* (1976) is a thriller that becomes much more, a brilliant if depressing portrait of urban life in Britain in the 1970s; *Picture Palace* (1978) is a novelistic reflection on the differences between life and art. *The Mosquito Coast* (1982) and *O-Zone* (1986) are deeply pessimistic and scathing accounts of, respectively, a man's attempt to colonize an exceedingly unhospitable corner of Central America, and a partly devastated United States a few years into the future. Theroux has also written two travel books based on train journeys, one through Europe and Asia in *The Great Railway Bazaar* (1975), the other through North and South America in *The Old Patagonian Express* (1979). *World's End* (1980) and *The London Embassy* (1982) are collections of stories. *Sunrise with Seamonsters* (1985) is a collection of autobiographical pieces.

Thersites   In Homer's ILIAD a deformed, scurrilous officer in the Greek army at the siege of Troy. Thersites was always railing at the chiefs; hence the name is applied to any dastardly, malevolent, impudent railer against the powers that be. ACHILLES felled him with his fist and killed him. In Shakespeare's TROILUS AND CRESSIDA he is "a slave whose gall coins slanders like a mint."

These Thirteen (1931)   A collection of short stories by William FAULKNER. This volume contains one of the best known of all of Faulkner's stories, "A Rose for Emily." It tells of an aristocratic, eccentric, and aging Southern spinster, Miss Emily Grierson, who has been courted by Homer Barron, a Yankee construction worker, who then disappears. When Miss Emily dies years later, having become a legend, the townspeople find the skeleton of Barron locked in an upstairs bedroom. The volume also contains two stories dealing with the Indians who inhabited the land before the white settlers arrived: "Red Leaves" and "A Justice."

Theseus   The chief hero of Attica in ancient Greek legend; son of AEGEUS and the performer of innumerable exploits. Theseus is sometimes also described as the son of POSEIDON. He was brought up by his mother, Aethra, but when he became strong enough to lift the stone under which his father's sword was hidden, he was sent to the court of Athens, where, in spite of the efforts of his father's wife, MEDEA, he was recognized as heir to the throne. Among his deeds were the slaying of PROCRUSTES, SCIRON, SINIS, and the Crommyonian sow; the capture of the Marathonian bull; the slaying of the MINOTAUR with the aid of ARIADNE, whom he subsequently deserted in Naxos; his war against the AMAZONS; and his part in the expedition of the ARGONAUTS and the hunt for the CALYDONIAN BOAR. He defends OEDIPUS in Sophocles' *Oedipus at Colonus*.

There are numerous versions of his war against the Amazons. He married the Amazonian queen who opposed him, known as either Antiope or HIPPOLYTA (according to some accounts there were two sisters of these names), and took her home with him. After the death of this queen, he married PHAEDRA, whose ill-fated infatuation with her stepson HIPPOLYTUS has formed the subject of many tragedies in which Theseus plays a part. In his old age, he became unpopular with his people and was so foully murdered by Lycomedes in Scyros, where he had taken refuge. He is the hero of two fine historical novels by Mary RENAULT, *The King Must Die* (1958) and *The Bull from the Sea* (1962).

According to medieval legend, Theseus' title was duke of Athens and his duchess was Hippolyta. Under this title he plays a part in Chaucer's KNIGHT'S TALE and in Shakespeare's MIDSUMMER NIGHT'S DREAM.

Thesmophoriazusai (The Women Who Celebrate the Thesmophoria, 411 BC)   A comedy by ARISTOPHANES. The play is based on the notion that the women of Athens plan to kill Euripides for presenting them in so harsh a light in his plays—a crime of which, in real life, Euripides was not guilty. He tries to persuade the effeminate tragic poet Agathon to attend in women's dress the annual festival of Athenian women, the Thesmophoria, in order to plead Euripides' case. Agathon refuses, but lends his women's clothes to Euripides' father-in-law, Mnesilochus. The women of Athens resent Mnesilochus' arguments and, on penetrating his disguise, threaten to burn him. Euripides comes to the rescue and both men play several roles from Euripides' plays in hilarious attempts to outwit the women

and a guard. Finally Euripides is reconciled with the women.

Thespis (6th century BC)   An Attic poet, regarded as the father of Greek tragedy. His chief contribution to drama, of which he may be considered the inventor, seems to have been that he gave to specific members of the chorus lines of dialogue in dramatic narratives, hitherto entirely performed by the whole chorus. Thus he would have performed a service similar to that of the unknown priests who first assigned the QUEM QUAERITIS? line from the Easter gospel to individual voices, thereby giving birth to medieval drama.

Thessalonians, The Epistles of Paul the Apostle to the   Two epistles of the NEW TESTAMENT believed to have been written by St. PAUL c AD 52. The first letter is possibly the oldest portion of the New Testament to be preserved in its original form. It reviews the founding of the church in Thessalonica, assures the people of Paul's love for them, and exhorts them to be strengthened by their faith. Both epistles take up the matter of Jesus' second coming; the second epistle contains a description of the ANTICHRIST and his destruction before the final judgment.

Thetis   Greek sea goddess, daughter of Nereus. Thetis was loved by ZEUS and POSEIDON, but, when THEMIS or PROMETHEUS disclosed that she was fated to bear a son greater than his father, Zeus quickly wedded her to the hero PELEUS. Their wedding was a brilliant celebration attended by the gods, but marred by the incident of the APPLE OF DISCORD. Thetis bore ACHILLES and proceeded to immortalize him by dipping him in the river Styx; only the heel by which she held him remained mortal. In another version, she held him in the fire, but when Peleus saw her and cried out, she dropped the child on the floor and left the house forever. When Achilles was grown to manhood, she warned him to return home from Troy in order to live a long life, but he preferred a short, glorious one. The tragic events recorded in the ILIAD resulted in part from her plea to Zeus to punish the Greeks for having offended her son. It was Thetis and Euronyme who caught HEPHAESTUS when he was thrown out of heaven. She aided the ARGONAUTS to pass through the Clashing Rocks.

Thévenin, Denis   See DUHAMEL, GEORGES.

They Knew What They Wanted (1924)   A play by Sidney HOWARD. Tony Patucci, a California winegrower, misleads his mail-order bride-to-be, Amy, by sending her a picture of his handsome young hired man Joe. On their wedding day Tony breaks both his legs, and Amy, humiliated and confused, allows Joe to seduce her and becomes pregnant. Tony nearly kills the younger man, but finally allows Amy to stay. The play was awarded a PULITZER PRIZE. It was later filmed, and still later became the basis of the musical *The Most Happy Fella* (1956) by Frank Loesser.

Thibaults, Les (1922–1940; tr The World of the Thibaults, 1939–1940)   Novel series by Roger MARTIN DU

GARD. In the tradition of the 19th-century naturalists, this work is marked by objectivity and by the amassing of precise detail. Two brothers, Jacques and Antoine Thibault, react as individuals to their bourgeois environment. Antoine leads a simple, dutiful existence while Jacques succumbs to his rebellious, adventurous temperament. The personal histories of the two main characters are set against a sweeping backdrop of world violence and chaos; both men die in World War I.

Thief, The (Vor, 1927; tr 1931)   A novel by Leonid LEONOV. The book is set during the time of the NEW ECONOMIC POLICY in Soviet Russia. The hero of the novel, Mitka Vekshin, has fought courageously during the civil war but emerges from the combat with inner conflicts about whether the killing was worthwhile. Disaffected with the humdrum life of building a society he is not sure he wants, he becomes a thief. The picture of the Moscow underworld, with its odd characters and the psychological probing of their personalities, reveals DOSTOYEVSKY's influence on Leonov in this work. A further similarity is to be found in the frenetically paced prose of the novel. The disillusionment with Soviet society implied in Leonov's description of life during the NEP period caused the novel to be severely criticized by Soviet reviewers. For years the work was not included in Leonov's collected works, and it was only after he revised it that it was printed at all.

Thiers, Louis Adolphe (1797–1877)   French statesman and historical writer. A leader of the liberals (1863–70) against Napoleon III, Thiers negotiated the peace treaty with Germany in 1871. He disposed of the Paris Commune, and was elected the first president (1871–73) of the Third Republic. His most famous works are *Histoire de la Révolution française* (1823–27) and *Histoire du consulat et de l'empire* (1845–62).

thing-poem   See DINGGEDICHT.

Things   A short story by D. H. LAWRENCE, originally published in *The Lovely Lady* (1933). It is the cynical account of two American "idealists" who try to devote their lives to art, beauty, Buddhism, and European culture. They only succeed, however, in collecting material "things."

Things Fall Apart (1958)   A novel by Chinua ACHEBE. Set in eastern Nigeria during the British expansion into Igboland, the novel recounts the tragedy of Okonkwo and his clansmen under British colonialism. When Okonkwo, a respected tribal leader, accidentally kills one of his clansmen, he is banished from his village for seven years. On his return, he finds his village subject to colonial laws and his tribal beliefs replaced by Christianity. Okonkwo opposes these new practices but finds the villagers divided. In a moment of rage, he kills a messenger from the British District Officer, only to find that his clansmen will not support him. He hangs himself in despair. The first novel by an African to attain the status of a con-temporary classic, *Things Fall Apart* has been translated into many languages.

Third Book About Achim, The   See JOHNSON, UWE.

third estate   The third of the social classes, or "estates," according to political theory of medieval and feudal times. It comprised peasants, serfs, yeomen, and the early bourgeoisie; the nobles and clergy constituted the first two estates. In France the third estate was known as *tiers état* and was without representation until the Revolution of 1789, at which time it declared itself to be the National ASSEMBLY. The three estates together formed the *états-généraux*, or States-General, which was something like the English Parliament.

Third Man, The (1950)   A thriller by Graham GREENE. Concerned with love and intrigue in cold war Vienna, it was originally written as the screenplay to a 1949 film by Carol REED.

Third Reich   The name given to Germany by HITLER during his dictatorship. In his terminology, the HOLY ROMAN EMPIRE was the First Reich and the German Empire of Bismarck the Second. The Third Reich, Hitler prophesied, would last a thousand years; it lasted just over twelve. It is possible that Hitler took the name from the nationalist German writer Müller van den Bruck, who published *Das dritte Reich* in 1924.

Thirteen Questions of Love   An episode in Giovanni Boccaccio's prose romance FILOCOLO. The hero, shipwrecked at Naples, is invited to join a party in a garden. One of the young ladies, FIAMMETTA, is chosen to preside over a discussion of love problems and to render a decision in each case. Since the statement of the problem involves the telling of stories, the whole scene is THE DECAMERON's frame story in embryo.

Thirty-Nine Articles, The   The articles of faith of the Church of England, the acceptance of which is obligatory on its clergy. They were originally issued in 1551 as forty-two, but in 1563 were modified and reduced to their present number. They received parliamentary authority in 1571.

Thirty-Nine Steps, The (1915)   An adventure romance by John BUCHAN. Its hero and narrator, Richard HANNAY, uncovers a spy ring and forestalls an invasion of Britain. It was filmed by Alfred HITCHCOCK.

Thirty Tyrants   (1) The thirty magistrates appointed by Sparta over Athens at the termination of the PELOPONNESIAN WAR. This reign of terror, after one year's continuance, was overthrown by Thrasybulus (403 BC).

(2) In the Roman empire, those military usurpers who endeavored, in the reigns of Valerian and Gallienus (253–268), to make themselves independent princes are also called the Thirty Tyrants. The number must be taken with great latitude, as only nineteen are given, and their resemblance to those of Athens is extremely fanciful.

Thirty Years' War (1618–1648)   A war that devastated central Europe, especially Germany, and eventually involved most of the nations of Europe. It was originally a religious conflict between Protestants and Roman Catholics; northern Germany supported the former, and southern Germany, led by Austria, supported the latter. Later, political issues overshadowed religion as Sweden and France entered the struggle in an effort to crush the power of the HAPSBURGS. The immediate cause of the war was a revolt (1618) of Bohemian Protestants whose religious rights had been violated by Austria. The Peace of Westphalia (1648) made territorial concessions to France and Sweden, recognized the independence of Switzerland and the Netherlands, and upheld the autonomy of the states of the German empire. It also confirmed the Peace of Augsburg (1555), which granted freedom of worship to the princes and free cities of Germany, and extended its provisions to include Calvinists.

Thisbe   See PYRAMUS.

This Side of Paradise (1920)   A novel by F. Scott FITZGERALD. Amory Blaine, a handsome, wealthy, spoiled and snobbish young man from the Middle West, attends Princeton University and acquires a refined sense of the proper "social" values. Lacking all sense of purpose, he interests himself primarily in literary cults, vaguely "liberal" student activities, and a series of flirtations with some rather predatory young ladies that culminate in a genuine but ill-fated love for Rosaline Commase, who rejects him to marry a wealthier young man. During the war Amory serves as an officer in France, and upon his return home he embarks upon a career in advertising, world-weary, cynical, regretful, and not yet thirty years old. Virtually a record of the "LOST GENERATION" in its college days, the novel treats Fitzgerald's characteristic theme of true love blighted by money lust and is remarkable for its honest and detailed descriptions of the early "Jazz Age." The book established Fitzgerald's reputation.

Thomas, St.   One of the twelve original disciples of JESUS, also called Didymus. When the other disciples warned Jesus that he might be in danger if he went to Bethany to heal LAZARUS, Thomas alone suggested "Let us also go, that we may die with him" (John 11:16). Because he did not believe in the Resurrection until Jesus appeared to him (John 20:24–29), he was called "doubting Thomas" in popular accounts.

He is traditionally credited as the author of the apocryphal Gospel According to St. Thomas. According to the apocryphal Acts of St. Thomas, he worked as a missionary in India and was finally martyred at Meliapore. His feast day is December 21.

One legend has it that Gondoforus, king of the Indies, gave him a large sum of money to build a palace. St. Thomas spent it on the poor, "thus erecting a superb palace in heaven." Hence he is the patron saint of masons and architects, and his symbol is a builder's square.

Thomas, Dylan [Marlais] (1914–1953)   Welsh poet and prose writer. Thomas's poetry is remarkable for its lyrical power, its surrealism, its compact, vivid metaphors, its use of Christian and Freudian imagery, and its puns and intricate patterns of sound and meaning, influenced by the work of Gerard Manley HOPKINS. It expresses Thomas's personal religion, celebrating the glory and wonder of procreation, growth, and death. He published his first volume of poetry, *Eighteen Poems*, in 1934; the leaders of the NEW APOCALYPSE movement in poetry imitated and advocated his visionary style. His *Collected Poems* appeared in 1952. Among Dylan Thomas's best-known individual poems are "And death shall have no dominion," "Altarwise by owllight" (a sonnet sequence), "A Refusal to Mourn the Death, by Fire, of a Child in London," "Do not go gentle into that good night," "In My Craft and Sullen Art," and "Fern Hill."

Thomas's earliest prose works were surrealistic short stories; they were not published until 1955, when they appeared as *Adventures in the Skin Trade*. In the 1940s he worked on film and radio scenarios; he began to write more popular and humorous but still poetic prose, expressing his exuberant love of life. *Portrait of the Artist as a Young Dog* (1940) is a collection of stories about his childhood and youth; the title reflects Thomas's admiration for James JOYCE. UNDER MILK WOOD is a radio play for voices. He also wrote *Quite Early One Morning* (1954) and *A Prospect of the Sea* (1955).

Through his radio work and his poetry readings in England and the U.S., Thomas achieved wide popular appeal. His reputation thrived on the storms of his private life, his tempestuous marriage with his wife, Caitlin, and his alcoholism. His death in New York in 1953 was regarded as an international event, symbolic of the plight of the artist in modern society.

Thomas, [Philip] Edward (1878–1917)   English poet and critic. Associated with the GEORGIANS, Thomas was for some years dismissed as just another old-fashioned nature poet, but he was subsequently rediscovered as an original writer about life and the human consciousness. He was a friend of Robert FROST, and the two poets' work is in many ways alike. He was killed in action during World War I. His *Collected Poems*, with a preface by Walter DE LA MARE, appeared in 1920; among his best-known single poems are "Old Man," "Adlestrop," and "The Glory."

Thomas, Hugh [Swynnerton] (1931–   )   English historian and novelist. After two novels, work in the Foreign Office, and a brief stint as a parliamentary Labour candidate, Thomas began work on his best-selling *The Spanish Civil War* (1961; rev 1977), a comprehensive political, diplomatic, and military history that traces the study from the early 1920s to the fall of Barcelona in 1939. Notable among his other works is his massive political and social history *Cuba, or, The Pursuit of Freedom* (1971) and

A History of the World (1979). *Havannah*, a novel, appeared in 1984.

Thomas, Norman [Mattoon] (1884–1968) American political leader and socialist. A graduate of Princeton University and an ordained Presbyterian minister, Thomas founded and edited *World Tomorrow* from 1918 to 1921. Eventually he resigned his ministerial duties to devote his entire time to writing and speaking for social reform and pacifism. As a Socialist Party candidate he ran unsuccessfully for many offices, including the presidency (1928–48). His books include *The Challenge of War* (1923), *Mankind at the Crossroads* (1936), *A Socialist's Faith* (1951), and *Great Dissenters* (1961).

Thomas, R[onald] S[tuart] (1913–) Welsh poet. An Anglican priest and a classics scholar, Thomas became rector (1942) of a church among the hill farms of central Wales. His poems reflect the rugged landscape, his parishioners' almost mystical attachment to it, and his own compassion for their hard and joyless lives. His collections of poems include *The Stones of the Field* (1946), *Poetry for Supper* (1958), *The Bread of Truth* (1963), *H'm: Poems* (1972), and *Selected Poems 1946–1968* (1973). Thomas is admired for the profundity of his vision, for the taut power of the verse which expresses it, and for the poetic discipline which gives his diction its apparent ease and naturalness.

Thomas à Becket (also known as St. Thomas Becket or Thomas of London, 1118?–1170) English prelate, archbishop of Canterbury (1162–70). Against the lay interference of Henry II, Becket defended the rights of the Church without compromise. In 1164 he was forced to flee to France. Papal pressure brought about the king's reconciliation with him, but, after his return to England in 1170, he was murdered on December 29 in Canterbury Cathedral by four overzealous knights of Henry's court. Two years later he was canonized. His shrine was plundered by Henry VIII, and his name erased from the English church calendar. The lively company in Chaucer's THE CANTERBURY TALES are making a pilgrimage to St. Thomas à Becket's shrine. His martyrdom is the subject of T. S. Eliot's play MURDER IN THE CATHEDRAL and of Jean ANOUILH's play *Becket* (1959).

Thomas à Kempis (more correctly Thomas Hammerken von Kempen, c1380–1471) German monk and writer. Kempis is generally regarded as the author of the IMITATION OF CHRIST. He entered the Augustinian monastery of Mt. St. Agnes in 1407, where he spent the rest of his life in meditation and writing.

Thomas Aquinas See AQUINAS, ST. THOMAS.

Thompson, Dorothy (1894–1961) American journalist. One of the most able newspaperwomen of her generation, Thompson established her reputation as a foreign correspondent in Germany and Vienna during the 1920s. Later she wrote the widely syndicated column *On the Record*, in which she discussed foreign and domestic affairs. From 1928 to 1942 she was married to Sinclair

LEWIS; their marriage is the subject of *Dorothy and Red* (1963), an account by Vincent Sheean (1899–1975).

Thompson, Francis (1859–1907) English poet. Thompson studied medicine in his early youth, but never received a degree. He was extremely unpractical and was unable to make a living for himself in London, failing at such diverse attempts as shoe-making, errand-running, and match-selling. He became addicted to opium, starved, and attempted suicide. During this period of misery, he wrote his earliest poems, some of which were accepted for publication by Wilfrid Meynell in his magazine *Merry England*. Thereafter, Thompson lived with Wilfrid and Alice MEYNELL, who nursed him and encouraged him in his writing.

His *Poems* (1893) contains his famous poem "The Hound of Heaven"; later publications include *Sister Songs* (1895), *New Poems* (1897), and the prose pieces *Life of St. Ignatius Loyola* (1909) and *Essays on Shelley* (1909). In color and imagery, Thompson's work shows the marked influence of KEATS and SHELLEY, and in spirit and tone it is often akin to that of the METAPHYSICAL POETS. A devout Roman Catholic, Thompson frequently presented ecstatic visions of heaven in his mystical poetry.

Thompson, Sadie See MISS THOMPSON.

Thomson, James (1700–1748) Scottish-born English poet, known as a forerunner of romanticism in a period when neoclassicism held sway in literature, and except for Alexander POPE, the most celebrated poet of the first half of the 18th century. Thomson's best-known works are THE SEASONS and THE CASTLE OF INDOLENCE. Both poems are marked by their love of nature, fantasy, and sensuous imagery, all romantic qualities unique at the time of composition. Thomson was one of the first to write nature poetry in the manner of the later romantics. He also wrote *A Poem Sacred to the Memory of Sir Isaac Newton* (1727); *Sophonisba* (1731), a tragedy; *Liberty* (1735–36), a long poem, which he considered his best work, setting forth the view that political liberty was attained in Greece, lost in the Middle Ages, and regained in Great Britain; and the masque *Alfred* (1740), in which he collaborated with David Mallet, and which contains the famous "Rule, Britannia."

Thomson, James (1834–1882) English poet. Known for his savage melancholy, atheism, and political radicalism, Thomson had an extremely unhappy life. His alcoholic father was paralyzed when the poet was six; two years later his mother, who had suffered from acute religious melancholy, died. The virtually orphaned child was sent to an institution. For a time he was an army instructor in Ireland, there meeting the love of his life, a beautiful sixteen-year-old girl, Matilda Weller, who died before they could be married. Later he became a radical journalist and held a number of miscellaneous, precarious jobs. His death came as the result of chronic alcoholism. The despair engendered by his experiences (and the philosophical pessimism of the late 19th century as well) is best expressed in his THE CITY OF DREADFUL NIGHT, in which the poet pursues the enigma of fate through a magnificently realized, terrifying city of nightmare. Much of Thomson's work is in this vein, but some poems, such as his accounts of Cockney life in "Sunday at Hampstead" (1863) and "Sunday up the River" (1865), reveal a humorous, realistic side of his talent. His volumes of poetry include *Vane's Story and Other Poems* (1881); *Insomnia* (1881); and the posthumous *A Voice from the Nile* (1884). Many of his poems were published under the pseudonym Bysshe Vanolis, or B.V., a compound of the names of Percy Bysshe SHELLEY and NOVALIS. He also wrote critical studies of WHITMAN, HEINE, and numerous English writers, as well as notable translations of LEOPARDI.

Thomson, Virgil [Garnett] (1896–   ) American composer and music critic. An intimate friend of Gertrude Stein, Thomson wrote two operas to her libretti: FOUR SAINTS IN THREE ACTS and *The Mother of Us All* (1947), the latter based on Susan B. ANTHONY's fight for women's rights. His witty and perceptive music criticism is the basis of several books.

Thopas, Sir   One of THE CANTERBURY TALES of Chaucer, a stanzaic parody of minstrel romances, begun by Chaucer when the Host asks him for a tale. In greatly exaggerated detail, Sir Thopas is described as an exemplary knight of Flanders who rides out, determined to love no one but an elf-queen. He meets the giant Olifaunt, escapes the stones thrown at him, and goes home to get his armor so he can give battle. At this point the Host interrupts, calling the rhyme "doggerel" and worse. Chaucer then offers to tell a "little thing in prose": see MELIBEE.

Thor   In Norse mythology, the AESIR god of thunder, second in importance to his father, ODIN. Perhaps the most widely worshiped of the gods, Thor was popular as the benevolent protector of man. His most precious possessions are his magic hammer, the thunderbolt Mjollnir, a belt of strength, and a pair of iron gloves. The giant who built the residence for the gods was paid by Thor with his hammer. When this had fallen into the possession of the giant Thrym, Thor recovered it by dressing himself in FREYA's clothes, pretending to be the fair goddess whom the giant wanted to be his bride in exchange for the hammer. Thor killed the MIDGARD SERPENT with his hammer but was drowned in his flood of venom. He was represented as a vigorous, red-haired youth, whose goat-drawn chariot created the thunder as it rolled by. From his name comes the word *Thursday*.

Thoreau, Henry David (1817–1862)   American essayist, naturalist, and poet. Born at Concord, Massachusetts, and educated at Harvard, Thoreau began his career as a teacher. Through his older friend and neighbor, Ralph Waldo EMERSON, he became a part of the Transcendentalist circle (see TRANSCENDENTALISM).

During Emerson's trip abroad in 1843, Thoreau took over the editorship of *The Dial*. Later that year he went to New York to tutor the children of Emerson's brother, Wil-

liam. He quickly returned to Concord, finding it a far more congenial place to live.

In 1845 Thoreau built a cabin at Walden Pond, on land owned by Emerson. He lived there for two years, two months, and two days; the experience was later described in his best-known work, WALDEN. During his stay at the pond, Thoreau was no hermit. He visited and entertained friends, worked his small plot of land, recorded observations of natural phenomena, and wrote an account of a trip with his brother, John. This first book, *A Week on the Concord and Merrimack Rivers*, was published in 1849.

During Thoreau's stay at Walden, he spent a night in jail, when he refused to pay his poll tax. He performed the gesture of civil disobedience to indicate his disapproval of the Mexican War. Later he explained his action in his essay CIVIL DISOBEDIENCE.

Since his first book had sold so poorly, Thoreau was unable for five years to find a publisher for *Walden*. During this period he worked as a laborer and a surveyor and served in the family pencil business. He traveled to Maine, Canada, Cape Cod, and New York; these excursions were the basis of a series of posthumously published books and essays, including *A Yankee in Canada*, *The Maine Woods*, and *Cape Cod*.

Speaking publicly against the Fugitive Slave Law, he eloquently defended John BROWN after Brown's capture in 1859. He died of tuberculosis in 1862, soon after his return from a trip to Minnesota. Politically the most conscious of the Transcendentalists, an acute observer of natural and social facts, Thoreau was an outstanding prose stylist. The *Journal* he kept from 1837 to the end of his life, the source of all his books, is an important literary document.

Thoth   In Egyptian religion, the god of wisdom, and inventor of arts, sciences, and the system of hieroglyphics. Thoth is represented with the head of an ibis on a human body. Sometimes he is shown holding in his hand the heart and tongue of RA, the sun god, to symbolize his control of the intelligence of that great deity. The Greeks and Romans identified him with HERMES or MERCURY. See IBIS.

Thousand and One Nights, A   See ARABIAN NIGHTS' ENTERTAINMENT, THE.

Thousand Souls, A (Tysyacha dush, 1858)   A novel by Aleksey PISEMSKY. It traces the career of Kalinovich, an ambitious young man determined to make his way however he can. The title of the novel refers to the one thousand serfs, or "souls," belonging to the woman Kalinovich marries to further his career.

Thrale, Hester Lynch (born Hester Salusbury, 1741–1821)   English BLUESTOCKING. Thrale met Samuel JOHNSON in 1764, and became perhaps his closest confidante until 1784, when, after the death of her first husband, he broke with her over her marriage to the Italian musician Gabriel Piozzi. After Johnson's death she published the *Anecdotes of Johnson* (1786) and *Letters to and* *from Johnson* (1788). Her diaries, published under the title *Thraliana* (1942), form a valuable source for Johnson's biography, as well as a delightful record of her volatile personality. Her letters to Queeny, her oldest daughter, are particularly notable.

three   The perfect number of the philosopher PYTHAGORAS. It is expressive of "beginning, middle, and end," wherefore he makes it a symbol of Deity. A Trinity is by no means confined to the Christian creed. The Hindu TRIMURTI consists of Brahma, the Creator; Vishnu, the Preserver; and Siva, the Destroyer. The world was supposed by the ancient Greeks to be under the rule of three gods: ZEUS (heaven), POSEIDON (sea), and HADES (underworld). The FATES are three, the Furies three, the GRACES three, the HARPIES three, the SIBYLLINE BOOKS three times three (of which only three survived); the fountain from which Hylas drew water was presided over by three nymphs; the MUSES were three times three; the PYTHIA sat on a three-legged stool, or tripod; and in Scandinavian mythology we hear of the Mysterious Three: Har the Mighty, the Like-Mighty, and the Third Person, who sat on three thrones above the rainbow.

Man is threefold (body, soul, and spirit); the world is threefold (earth, sea, and air); the enemies of man are threefold (the world, the flesh, and the devil); the Christian graces are threefold (Faith, Hope, and Charity); the kingdoms of nature are threefold (mineral, vegetable, and animal); the cardinal colors are three in number (red, yellow, and blue); and so on.

Threefold Refuge   See THREE TREASURES.

Three Kingdoms (AD 221–264)   Chinese historical period. After the fall of the HAN dynasty (206 BC–AD 220) China broke up into three mutually hostile kingdoms: Wei, Shu Han, and Wu. The period is the subject of many legends and literary works, most significant among them the vast adventure novel ROMANCE OF THE THREE KINGDOMS by Lo Kuan-chung (c1330–1400).

Three Lives (1909)   A book of three stories by Gertrude STEIN. Written in a clear and masterly style, free from any of its author's later stylistic mannerisms, it consists of three character studies of women. "The Good Anna" deals with a kindly but domineering German servingwoman; "Melanctha" is concerned with an uneducated but sensitive black girl; and "The Gentle Lena" is about a pathetically feebleminded young German maid.

Three Musketeers, The (Les Trois Mousquetaires, 1844)   A famous historical romance by Alexandre DUMAS. With its sequels *Twenty Years After* (1845) and *The Viscount of Bragelonne* (1848–50), the novel covers the period of French history from 1625 to 1665. The central figure, D'Artagnan, is a historical personage (Charles de Baatz d'Artagnan, 1623–73), and much of the story's material is drawn from his memoirs. His three friends also have counterparts in history, even to their names. D'Artagnan, a carefree young Gascon, arrives in Paris on a rawboned, yellow pony, with only three crowns in his pocket. Determined to become one of Louis XIII's guardsmen, he immediately involves himself in duels with Athos, Porthos, and Aramis, three of the most renowned fighters of the day. They welcome him into the fellowship of the Three Musketeers, and the narrow escapes and amazing exploits of these four friends form the subject matter of Dumas's exciting narrative.

Threepenny Opera, The (Die Dreigroschenoper, 1928; tr 1933)   An EPIC THEATRE ballad-opera by Bertolt BRECHT, with music by Kurt WEILL. It is an adaptation of John Gay's THE BEGGAR'S OPERA, the principal differences being Brecht's biting attack on the bourgeoisie and the fact that it is set in London almost two hundred years after the time depicted in Gay's opera. In Brecht's version, it is the decadent capitalist society of the day that is responsible for creating a criminal underworld.

Three Sisters, The (Tri sestry, 1901)   A play by Anton CHEKHOV. Written in four acts, it is regarded by some critics as the best drama of the 20th century. The Prozorov sisters, Olga, Masha, and Irina, along with their brother, Andrey, drag out a dull existence in a small provincial garrison town. Only the diversions afforded by the officers and the ever-present dream of someday moving to Moscow keep the sisters going from one drab day to the next. Andrey, who has had dreams of becoming a professor, makes a bad marriage that thwarts his ambition and adds to his sisters' troubles. His wife, Natalya Ivanovna, becomes a domestic despot. Masha, who is married to the pedantic schoolmaster Kulygin, tries to find happiness in a love affair with the officer Vershinin. The youngest sister, Irina, attempts to escape the drabness of her life by marrying Baron Tuzenbakh, another officer. The removal of the regiment from the town undoes Masha's plan, because Vershinin is married and cannot take her with him. Tuzenbakh is killed in a duel. The three sisters are left as they were at the beginning, deriving some faint pleasure from the cheerful sounds of the regimental band as it marches away, still clinging to their hopes for a better life.

Three Soldiers (1921)   A novel by John DOS PASSOS. The book deals with three representative soldiers in the American army during World War I: Dan Fuselli, an Italian-American; Chrisfield, a farm boy from Indiana; and John Andrews, a sensitive musician who longs to be a composer. Dos Passos was interested mainly in the story of Andrews, who joins the army hoping to find comfort by contributing to a righteous cause. Instead he encounters tyranny, aimlessness, red tape, and boredom. Eventually he deserts, and in the French countryside he begins to write music, only to be captured and taken away, leaving the sheets of his unfinished composition to be scattered and destroyed. The part of society represented by the military is the real villain of the book; it is possible to see in this early novel seeds of the later *U.S.A.* (q.v.).

Three Treasures (Sans, *tritatna*; or Threefold Refuge, *trisharana*)   In BUDDHISM, the three treasures or "jewels" consist of the Buddha himself; the law (DHARMA); and the order of monks (*sangha*). See TRIPITAKA.

three worlds   The concept of the universe in Hindu (Vedic) mythology. The *triloka* (Sans, *tri*, "three," and *loka*, "world"), or the universe, was visualized as consisting of the earth, the middle space or atmosphere, and the ether or sky. By another interpretation it may also signify the world of men, of semi-divine creatures, and of gods. It sometimes refers to heaven, earth, and the territory of the demons. The three-forked river mentioned in Kalidasa's play SHĀKUNTALĀ refers to the descent of the holy river Ganges from heaven into the matted hair of SHIVA, who, in the midst of his severe practice of penance, received it on the earth.

Through the Looking Glass (1872)   A children's tale by Lewis CARROLL. A sequel to *Alice's Adventures in Wonderland*, the book tells of Alice's experiences when, curious about the world behind the mirror, she climbs over the mantel through the glass. In looking-glass country, everything is reversed, just as reflections are reversed in a mirror. Brooks and hedges divide the land into a checkerboard, and Alice finds herself a white pawn in the whimsical and fantastic game of chess that constitutes the bulk of the story. On her trip to the eighth square, where she at last becomes a queen, Alice meets talking flowers, looking-glass insects, a man in a white paper suit, such nursery-rhyme characters as Humpty Dumpty and the Lion and the Unicorn, and many others, including Tweedledum and Tweedledee and the WHITE KNIGHT. When, after her coronation, Alice begins shaking the red queen, the red queen turns into Alice's cat, and Alice awakens from her dream. The ballad JABBERWOCKY is found in the tale.

Thrym   See FREYA; THOR.

Thucydides (c460–400 BC)   An Athenian historian. Thucydides became a general and was sent to defend the Greek city of Amphipolis in Thrace (424 BC). Failing in his mission, he was exiled from Athens for twenty years. He was recalled in 403 BC; he is supposed to have been assassinated soon after.

During Thucydides' exile he wrote a history of the PELOPONNESIAN WAR admirable for its objectivity in discussing contemporary events, its direct and descriptive style, and the author's grasp of cause and effect. It begins by tracing the history of the Hellenic race, and ends, unfinished, in 411 BC, seven years before the wars ended. The best-known passages are those relating PERICLES' *Funeral Oration*, the plague at Athens, and the Sicilian expedition. The painstaking reporting and acute political analysis vindicate Thucydides' claim that the work is a "possession for all time."

thug   Originally, a member of a religious body of northern India. KALI, the goddess of death in her aspect worshiped by this sect, could be propitiated only by human victims who had been strangled. Hence, the thugs became a professional fraternity of stranglers who supported themselves by the plunder obtained from those they strangled. Their native name is *p'hansigars* ("stranglers"); that of *thug* ("cheat") was given them in 1810. Their methods were rigorously suppressed under British rule, and they were practically extinct by 1840. The word is now used in English for any ruffian.

Thule   The ancient name of an island or point of land six days' sail north of Britain. It was considered to be the extreme northern limit of the world. The name is first found in the account by Polybius (c150 BC) of the voyage made by Pytheas in the late 4th century BC. PLINY says, "It is an island in the Northern Ocean discovered by Pytheas, after sailing six days from the Orcades." Others consider it to be Shetland, in which opinion they agree with the descriptions of PTOLEMY and TACITUS. Still others assert that it was some part of the coast of Norway. The etymology of the name is unknown. Ultima Thule means the end of the world, the last extremity.

thumbs down (Lat, *pollice verso*)   A sign ordering death for a fallen gladiator. At the gladiatorial contests in ancient Rome, the winning gladiator turned to the spectators to ask whether he should kill his fallen enemy. If the spectators held out their arms with thumbs down, the victim must die; thumbs up meant that he was to be spared.

Thurber, James [Grover] (1894–1961)   American essayist, short-story writer, humorist, and artist. Thurber began his career as a journalist; in 1927 he met E. B. WHITE, who introduced him to Harold ROSS, the editor of the newly founded magazine THE NEW YORKER. Thurber joined Ross's staff (1927–33) and was a prominent contributor for many years. During his years with *The New Yorker*, Thurber did much to establish the tone, style, and popularity of the magazine. Thurber applied his sardonic humor and psychological acuity to examining the follies of men and women, revealing these in a deadpan prose and inimitable line drawings. Missing no human frailty, he nonetheless managed to affirm the power of love in a fantastic, often nightmare world. His famous story "The Secret Life of Walter Mitty," later made into a movie, describes the fantasies of a mild and retiring man who imagines himself a hero. Among Thurber's books are *Is Sex Necessary?* (1929; with E. B. White), a spoof on pop psychology; *The Seal in the Bedroom and Other Predicaments* (1932); *The Middle-Aged Man on the Flying Trapeze* (1935); *Let Your Mind Alone* (1937); *The Male Animal* (1940), a play written with Eliott Nugent; *Fables for Our Time* (1940); *The Thurber Carnival* (1945); and *Alarms and Diversions* (1957). *The Thirteen Clocks* (1950), a story for children, is a triumphant blend of nonsense and morality tale. *The Years with Ross* (1959) is a memoir of the redoubtable editor at *The New Yorker. Lanterns and Lances* (1961) was his last book of essays, written after he had lost his long battle with blindness.

Thurso's Landing (1932)   A narrative poem by Robinson JEFFERS. The poem deals with Helen Thurso's ambivalent attitudes toward her husband, whom she alternately loves and hates; toward her crippled brother-in-law, who loves her; and toward death itself, which simultaneously fascinates and repels her.

Thus Spake Zarathustra (Also sprach Zarathustra, 1883–1892)   A philosophical narrative by Friedrich NIETZSCHE in which the ancient Persian philosopher Zarathustra (see ZOROASTER) is used as a mouthpiece for the author's views. In it, Nietzsche develops his doctrine of the ÜBERMENSCH, and the quasi-biblical style he uses underlines the prophetic character of his ideas.

Thyrsis   A herdsman introduced in the *Idyls* of THEOCRITUS, and in Vergil's seventh BUCOLIC. It has become a conventional name for any shepherd or rustic.

> Hard by, a cottage chimney smokes
> From betwixt two aged oaks,
> Where Corydon and Thyrsis, met,
> Are at their savoury dinner set.
>
> Milton, *L'Allegro* (1638)

thyrsus   A long pole with an ornamental head of a fir cone. It was carried by the votaries of DIONYSUS at the celebration of his rites. It has been suggested that the fir tree was an earlier source of intoxicating beverages than the vine.

Tiamat   In Babylonian mythology, the primeval sea seen as a dragon goddess. The wife of Apsu (see ABZU), the ancient god of the fresh waters, Tiamat was the mother of all the gods. In the famous creation myth of the WAR OF THE GODS, she fights against the younger gods, but is killed by MARDUK, who, splitting her body, makes heaven of the upper half and earth of the lower.

Tiber   The river that flows through Rome to the Tyrrhenian Sea.

Tiberinus   In Roman myth, the god of the River Tiber.

Tiberius (full name Tiberius Claudius Nero, 42 BC–AD 37)   Roman emperor (AD 14–37). The historians TACITUS and SUETONIUS labeled Tiberius a cruel tyrant, although modern scholars recognize his reign as one of sound administration and of benefit to the empire. He was emperor when JESUS was crucified.

Ticknor, George (1791–1871)   American historian and scholar. An innovative professor of languages at Harvard for more than twenty-five years, Ticknor resigned his post to write his great three-volume *History of Spanish Literature* (1849, 1872). On his death, Ticknor left his collection of rare books on Spanish literature to the Boston Public Library.

Tidings Brought to Mary, The (L'Annonce faite à Marie, 1912; tr 1916)   A poetic drama, revised 1948, by Paul CLAUDEL. An adaptation of Claudel's *La Jeune Fille Violaine* (1892; rev 1898), it symbolizes the struggle and the bond between spiritual devotion and the claims of human life and love. Pierre de Craon, architect of cathedrals, is set apart from life by his leprosy. Violaine Vercors kisses him in pity, and the affliction makes her a recluse, separated from earthly happiness and devoted to a religious vocation. Her fiancé, Jacques Hury, marries her sister Mara. But one Christmas Eve their infant dies, and Mara comes to Violaine, desperately demanding that Violaine hold the child and through her faith restore its life. Although Mara takes home a living baby, she notices that its eyes are now the color of Violaine's, and later murders her sister.

Tieck, Ludwig (1773–1853)   German author. In Tieck's early career, he was a leading representative and popularizer of GERMAN ROMANTICISM, but later turned to realism. He contributed some sections to the pace-setting romantic work of his friend WACKENRODER, *Herzensergießungen eines kunstliebenden Klosterbruders* (*Outpourings of the Heart of an Art-loving Lay Brother*, 1797); his play *Der gestiefelte Kater* (*Puss in Boots*, pub 1797) is a classic example of romantic IRONY; his novel *Franz Sternbalds Wanderungen* (*Franz Sternbald's Wanderings*, 1798) is the definitive German KÜNSTLERROMAN; and he also wrote a number of MÄRCHEN (tales). The most significant work from his realistic period is the novella *Des Lebens Überfluß* (*Life's Overflow*, 1837). Among his friends were NOVALIS and the brothers SCHLEGEL.

T'ien-t'ai   Chinese Buddhist sect. Founded by a Chinese monk, Chih-i (538–597), it developed the concept of relative levels of truth as a way of reconciling conflicting Buddhist doctrines. It popularized the LOTUS SŪTRA, the most widely read Buddhist scripture in East Asia. Most important in China from the 6th to 8th centuries, it was introduced to Japan in the HEIAN period (794–1185) as TENDAI.

Tiepolo, Giovanni Battista (1696–1770)   Italian painter. Tiepolo decorated churches and palaces in Venice, Milan, Würzburg, and Madrid with religious scenes in the ROCOCO style. His frescoes, such as those adorning the ceiling of the Kaisersaal of the Würzburg Episcopal Palace (1751), created the illusion of vast open space with their luminous colors and radically foreshortened figures. His works and those of his son Giovanni Domenico Tiepolo (1727–1804) influenced the painting of GOYA.

Tietjens, Christopher   The hero of PARADE'S END by Ford Madox Ford. This series of novels is sometimes known as the Tietjens tetralogy.

Tiffany, Louis Comfort (1848–1933)   American designer. He was the son of Charles Tiffany (1812–1902), proprietor of the famous New York silver and jewelry store. Tiffany was an accomplished painter of Middle Eastern scenes, but was attracted, in the 1870s, to the so-called arts and crafts revival in Europe. It was then that he formed the prestigious interior design firm which became, in 1885, the Tiffany Glass Company. He invented a process for making opalescent glass, called *favrile*, which he used extensively in the ART NOUVEAU vases and lamps for which he is best known.

Tiger, The (1794)   A poem by William Blake, included in his SONGS OF EXPERIENCE, celebrating the mystery and triumph of the creation of life. The well-known first stanza is as follows:

Tiger! Tiger! burning bright
In the forests of the night,
What immortal hand or eye
Could frame thy fearful symmetry?

Tiger at the Gates (La Guerre de Troie n'aura pas lieu, 1935)   A play by Jean GIRAUDOUX. It was translated into English by Christopher FRY in 1955. The setting of the play is Troy just before the outbreak of the TROJAN WAR. Peace-loving HECTOR keeps repeating that "the Trojan War will not take place," eventually persuading PARIS, HELEN, and even the willing but dubious ULYSSES to cooperate in avoiding battle. But the Trojan people have been inflamed for various reasons, and it is finally not the leaders' decision but a warmonger's lie that precipitates the war.

Tilbury Town   See ROBINSON, EDWIN ARLINGTON.

Tillich, Paul [Johannes] (1886–1965)   German-born American theologian and philosopher. Forced to leave Germany because of his opposition to Nazism, Tillich came at the invitation of Reinhold NIEBUHR to New York, where he taught at the Union Theological Seminary from 1933 to 1955. He then taught at Harvard until 1962, when he joined the faculty at the University of Chicago. A liberal theologian of marked originality and force, Tillich embraced aspects of depth psychology and EXISTENTIALISM in his interpretation of Christian doctrine. He based his theology on the estrangement of existence from its essence —of man from the divine—an estrangement he felt was symbolized by the story of the Fall. He felt that the ultimate concern of man is to be reunited with the divine through faith. Rather than conceptualizing Jesus as a historical personage or as a social or ethical reformer, he saw Jesus as the Christ, the bearer of the New Being, or creative power, capable of reconciling existence with essence. His major work is *Systematic Theology* (3 vols, 1951, 1959, 1963). Among his other influential books are *The Courage to Be* (1952), *Love, Power, and Justice* (1954), *The New Being* (1955), *Biblical Religion and the Search for Ultimate Reality* (1955), *Theology of Culture* (1959), and *My Search for Absolutes* (1967).

Time and Western Man (1927)   A political and artistic manifesto by Wyndham LEWIS. He attacks Henri BERGSON and the STREAM OF CONSCIOUSNESS technique in the novel. Lewis advocates fixity rather than flux, intelligence and the external rather than intuition and the internal, and classicism rather than romanticism.

Time Machine, The (1895)   A science-fiction story by H. G. WELLS. The inventor of the time machine travels into the future and visits stages in the evolutionary degeneration of life. He sees the stage when the evil, ape-like MORLOCKS (the descendants of our age's industrial workers) live underground and farm and eat the beautiful but frivolous aristocrats, the Eloi. He witnesses, too, the stage when giant crabs are the only surviving living things, and the sun and the earth are dying.

Time of Silence (Tiempo de silencio, 1962; tr 1964)   A novel by Luis MARTIN-SANTOS. An unsparing analysis of all levels of Spanish society after the Civil War, this nihilistic and furiously ironic novel, which burlesques the conventional mythology of Church and sex, changed the course of Spanish fiction with its introduction of Joycean narrative techniques (see James JOYCE). The protagonist, Pedro, a young research scientist, is falsely accused of the responsibility for the death of a young woman who has had an abortion after an incestuous relationship with her father and whose injuries he had tried to treat. He is cleared, but is dismissed from the cancer institute where he works, and his fiancée is murdered by the boyfriend of the dead woman. Alone and despairing, Pedro leaves for the provinces to practice medicine, condemned to silence by an ABSURD world in which there is no such thing as free choice.

Time of Your Life, The (1939)   A play by William SAROYAN. A blend of social consciousness and poetic symbolism, it is set in a waterfront saloon and takes as its themes the need to make the most of life, to be compassionate to the weak, and to oppose the enemies of life. A collection of lovable eccentrics represents the weak and Detective Blick of the Vice Squad personifies the forces of evil. The play was given the New York Drama Critics' Award and also the PULITZER PRIZE for 1940, which Saroyan refused.

Times, The   A London newspaper (so named since 1788) founded by John Walter (1739–1812) as *The Daily Universal Register* in 1785.

Timmermans, Felix (1886–1947)   Flemish novelist, poet, and playwright. Timmermans is best known for his romantic regional novels, *Pallieter* (1916; tr 1924) and *Boerenpsalm* (*Peasant Psalm*, 1935). With books written to entertain rather than instruct, he enjoyed great popularity during his lifetime and became one of the most widely read Flemish novelists outside Belgium.

Timon of Athens (c1607)   A tragedy by SHAKESPEARE, perhaps written only in part by him. Timon, a generous host and patron of the arts, finds himself in financial difficulties and discovers, as the cynical Apemantus had predicted, that the so-called friends who had previously fawned on him now refuse to help him. Cursing mankind, Timon leaves Athens and settles in a cave where he finds a buried treasure of gold. There he meets ALCIBIADES, a general who had been banished by the Athenian senate when he pleaded for the life of a condemned soldier. Timon finances an expedition that Alcibiades is preparing against

Athens and rewards his faithful servant Flavius, exhorting him to show charity to no one. When word reaches Athens of Timon's gold, the senate sends a delegation to ask his aid against Alcibiades, but Timon rejects the request. Alcibiades, however, negotiates with the Athenians and is allowed to enter the city when he agrees to seek vengeance only from his and Timon's enemies. Just as the peaceful compromise is reached, it is learned that Timon has died in his cave, still inveighing against the human race.

The principal source of the play is Plutarch's *Life of Marcus Antonius*, translated into English (1579) by Sir Thomas North and retold also in Paynter's *Palace of Pleasure* (1567), though the story of Timon the Misanthrope was well known to Elizabethans.

Timotheus (446–357 BC)   A renowned Greek musician and poet, referred to in *Alexander's Feast* by John DRYDEN.

Timothy   In the NEW TESTAMENT, an early Christian who became a trusted associate of St. PAUL. Along with his mother and grandmother, he was converted on the first missionary journey. He accompanied Paul on the second journey and was left for a time in Berea, where he and Silas bolstered the new church. He rejoined Paul and traveled with him until Paul established him at Ephesus, where he was eventually martyred. It is to Timothy that two of the pastoral epistles attributed to Paul are addressed.

Timothy, The Epistles of Paul the Apostle to   Two books of the NEW TESTAMENT. With the Epistle of Paul to Titus, they are called the Pastoral Epistles because of their theme of "care of the church." They are traditionally ascribed to PAUL, but scholars believe they were written by a disciple of Paul after his death. Together, they outline a course for church action, detail such administrative functions as the selection of bishops and ministers and the treatment of the unfaithful, and provide guidelines for the duties of Christians. See PAULINE EPISTLES.

Timrod, Henry (1828–1867)   American poet and journalist. A member of the Charleston School of Southern writers, Timrod is known for his intensely emotional poems written in classical forms. During the Civil War, Timrod earned the title Laureate of the Confederacy. His *Collected Verse* was published in 1873. Timrod's best-known poems are "The Cotton Boll" and "Ethnogenesis."

Timur   See TAMERLANE.

Tin Drum, The (Die Blechtrommel, 1959; tr 1962) A novel by Günter GRASS, generally acclaimed as the first major literary work to be published in Germany since the 1930s and the first German novel to attract an international audience since the works of Thomas MANN. Narrated in the first person by the grotesque hunchback Oskar Matzerath, it consists of his recollections of the bizarre events in his (and Grass's) hometown of Danzig, before, during, and after the HITLER era. Oskar, fearful and distrustful of the adult world, decides at the age of three that he will grow no more. He is very attached to a tin drum, on which he beats

masterfully, thus finding relief for his feelings of anger, anxiety, and contempt for the petty bourgeois adults who foster the rise of Nazism. From his unique perspective, he observes and comments on the freakishness and hypocrisy of his elders and contemporaries.

Tin Pan Alley   A popular and journalistic term applied to the section of New York City frequented by writers and publishers of popular songs. Later, this term was applied by extension to the industry as a whole. Tin Pan Alley was at first located in the district around 14th Street, but later moved uptown to the Times Square area.

Tintern Abbey   A medieval abbey dating from the 13th century, located in Monmouthshire, England, on the river Wye. An ivory-covered ruin, it is well preserved except for the vaulting. WORDSWORTH wrote a poem, "Lines Composed a Few Miles above Tintern Abbey, on Revisiting the Banks of the Wye," popularly though somewhat inappropriately known as "Tintern Abbey."

Tintoretto (real name Jacopo Robusti, 1518–1594) Venetian painter. Called *Il Furioso* because of the extreme rapidity with which he painted, Tintoretto executed fine portraits and large decorative canvases, mainly in the Scuola di San Rocco and in the doge's palace of his native city. His vast imagination often took a mystical turn as he experimented with the mysterious effects of barely lighted interior and exterior scenes. A master of movement, he used perspective and foreshortening to give drama and excitement to his scenes from the New Testament. His leading works include the San Rocco frescoes—the largest collection of works by one painter in a single building to be found anywhere. The best known of these are *The Annunciation* and *The Agony in the Garden*. In the ducal palace are *Four Allegories of Venice* and *Bacchus and Ariadne*. In the Venetian Accademia are the paintings *Legend of the Body of St. Mark*. Having painted a *Crucifixion* from a revolutionary side view, he turned to the theme of the Last Supper and avoided frontality by setting the table in diagonal perspective. The latter painting, perhaps his single best-known work, is in the Church of San Giorgio Maggiore in Venice. Tintoretto's influence was immediately felt by RUBENS and REMBRANDT.

Tiresias   In Greek mythology, a Theban seer. Tiresias' predictions played an important part in the lives of OEDIPUS and his descendants. Blinded in his youth at seeing ATHENE bathing, he received second sight as a consolation. He was transformed for a time into a woman as a result of seeing snakes coupling. As a result of this unusual experience, he was asked to settle an argument between ZEUS and HERA as to whether men or women more deeply enjoyed the pleasures of love. He voted nine to one in favor of women. His blinding was recounted in *The Baths of Pallas*, a poem by Callimachus; in Euripides' BACCHANTS, he is a convert to Dionysian rites. For his prophecies, see OEDIPUS, SEVEN AGAINST THEBES, and ANTIGONE. After prophesying the fall of Thebes before the EPIGONI, he died, his life having spanned seven generations. His bisexuality appears as a theme in T. S. Eliot's THE WASTE LAND and in APOLLINAIRE's play *Les Mamelles de Tirésias* (1903).

Tir et Sidon (Tyre and Sidon, 1608)   A tragedy in two parts by the French playwright Jean de Schelander (c1585–1635). Set in Phoenicia during the war between Tyre and Sidon, this long play centers on the ill-starred love of Belcar, prince of Sidon, and Méliane, princess of Tyre. Though originally culminating in four deaths, the play was rewritten twenty years later as a tragicomedy in the manner of Alexandre HARDY, a happy ending being substituted for the earlier catastrophe. The preface to the revised play, written by the cleric François Ogier, defends the mixing of comic and tragic elements on the stage as being closer to life than either the dramas of the ancients or those of their modern imitators.

Tirso de Molina (pen name of Fray Gabriel Téllez, c1583–1648)   Spanish dramatist. Born in Madrid, Tirso studied at Alcalá and became a Mercenarian friar in 1601. Thereafter he lived in Toledo, Santo Domingo, Salamanca, and Barcelona, rising to important positions in the order. In 1625 the Council of Castile recommended that he be enjoined from writing any more plays because of the scandal they were causing.

An avowed disciple of Lope de Vega, Tirso geared his plays to popular taste. He is said to have written more than three hundred dramas, of which about eighty are extant. The finest of these is EL BURLADOR DE SEVILLA, in which the now universally known character of Don Juan was definitively delineated. His other plays include *El condenado por desconfiado*, considered the best religious drama of Spain; *La prudencia en la mujer*, a historical work dealing with the dowager queen Doña Maria, whose wisdom saves the throne for her son, Ferdinand IV; *Don Gil de las calzas verdes*, a cloak-and-sword play; and *Marta la piadosa*, about a female hypocrite. He also wrote two collections of miscellaneous verse, drama, and stories: *Los cigarrales de Toledo* (1624) and *Deleitar aprovechando* (1635).

Tisiphone   One of the three ERINYES. Covered with a bloody robe, Tisiphone sits day and night at hell-gate, armed with a whip. Tibullus says her head is coifed with serpents in lieu of hair.

'Tis Pity She's a Whore (c1627)   A tragedy by John FORD about the fatal attraction of Giovanni for his beautiful sister, Annabella. Annabella returns his affection and hesitates to choose among her suitors: Soranzo, Grimaldi, and Bergetto. Soranzo has been having an affair with Hippolita, the wife of Richardetto, and has sworn to marry the lady, should she become a widow. When word comes that Richardetto has been lost at sea, Soranzo rejects his pledge and continues to press his suit with Annabella. Meanwhile, Richardetto, disguised as a physician, has returned to watch his wife with her lover. When Annabella chooses Soranzo for her husband, Richardetto and the jeal-

ous Grimaldi join forces to kill him but murder the innocent Bergetto by mistake. At the wedding feast, Hippolita, double-crossed by Soranzo's servant Vasques, drinks a cup of poisoned wine she had intended for her erstwhile lover. Soon the reason for Annabella's marriage becomes apparent—she is pregnant by Giovanni. Soranzo plans to avenge himself by revealing the facts at a splendid banquet. To save her honor, Giovanni kills Annabella, proclaims her death at the banquet, stabs Soranzo, and is himself killed by Soranzo's followers.

Titan, The (1914)   A novel by Theodore DREISER. *The Titan* is the succeeding volume to THE FINANCIER and the second in the trilogy dealing with Frank Cowperwood. Having married Aileen Butler, his former mistress, and moved to Chicago, Cowperwood almost succeeds in his dream of establishing a monopoly of all public utilities. Dissatisfaction with Aileen leads him, however, to a series of affairs with other women. When the Chicago citizenry frustrate his financial schemes, he departs for Europe with Berenice Fleming, the lovely daughter of the madam of a Louisville brothel. Cowperwood, a powerful, irresistibly compelling man driven by his own need for power, beautiful women, and social prestige, at last experiences "the pathos of the discovery that even giants are but pigmies, and that an ultimate balance must be struck." In the final volume, *The Stoic* (1947), which was published posthumously, Dreiser concludes "the trilogy of desire" with an account of Cowperwood's life in England and his death after his return to the U.S.

Titania   The queen of the fairies and wife of OBERON in Shakespeare's MIDSUMMER NIGHT'S DREAM. Her name is mentioned by OVID as an alternative for DIANA, the moon goddess.

Titanic   The White Star liner that struck an iceberg in the Atlantic on April 14, 1912, during her maiden voyage and sank with the loss of over fifteen hundred lives. A fabulous vessel whose fifteen watertight bulkheads supposedly made her "unsinkable," the *Titanic* carried only enough lifeboats for fifty-two percent of the 2,207 persons on board. Walter Lord's *A Night to Remember* (1955) is a minute-by-minute account of the disaster.

Titans   In Greek mythology, offspring of URANUS and GE. The Titans appear to have been pre-Hellenic nature deities, consigned to near oblivion by the new pantheon headed by ZEUS. Their names are CRONOS, OCEANUS, and IAPETUS, males, and RHEA, TETHYS, and THEMIS, females. Under the leadership of Cronos, they emasculated Uranus, who had hidden all but Cronos in the womb of earth. Rhea and Themis were both earth goddesses; Oceanus and his wife, Tethys, were the progenitors of the sea gods—according to some accounts, all the gods. Besides the six above-mentioned Titans named in HESIOD's *Theogony*, there were Hyperion, a sun god; Coeus, Crius, Theia, Phoebe, and MNEMOSYNE. In many sources, their descendants are also called Titans. It is generally believed that the protracted

war that the Titans fought with Zeus, after he had overcome his father, Cronos, with the aid of his mother, Rhea,
reflects the prolonged conflict between the ancient Pelas-
gian inhabitants of Greece and their Hellenic conquerors.

Tite et Bérénice (1670)   A tragedy by Pierre COR-
NEILLE. The emperor Titus is about to marry Domitia, who
is actually in love with his brother Domitian, when the
arrival of Bérénice, queen of Judea, reawakens his love for
her. Realizing that her presence places Titus in jeopardy,
Bérénice abandons hope of marrying him and departs.
Titus in his turn surrenders Domitia to Domitian, who
loves her. It is believed that the duchesse d'Orléans
encouraged RACINE and Corneille to write plays on this
subject, each in ignorance that the other was doing the
same. Corneille's intricacies of plot contrasted poorly with
the simplicity of Racine's treatment, and Corneille's play
was judged inferior. See BÉRÉNICE.

Tithonus   A beautiful Trojan of Greek legend, son
of LAOMEDON, and beloved by Eos, goddess of the dawn. At
his prayer, the goddess granted him immortality, but, as he
had forgotten to ask for youth and vigor, he grew old, and
life became insupportable. He now prayed to Eos to
remove him from the world. This, however, she could not
do, but she changed him into a grasshopper. TENNYSON has
a poem entitled "Tithonus."

Titian (real name Tiziano Vecelli, c1477–1576)   Italian painter. Titian was the greatest master of the Venetian
school and one of the most influential artists in history.
During a long and productive life, he gained a mastery of
color that enabled him to achieve increased movement by
disregarding symmetry of composition while restoring unity
through chromatic balance. He also relied on color, rather
than on the intensity of tone, to model forms and to
describe lavish textures. Among his celebrated religious
works are the Louvre *Entombment*, the Frari *Assumption*,
the Pesaro *Madonna*, and the moving *Pietà* of his final
phase. His mythological works include the *Rape of Europa*,
Bacchus and Ariadne, *Nymph and Shepherd*, and *Diana
and Acteon*. Of his allegories, the best known are *Sacred
and Profane Love* and *The Three Ages*. A superb portraitist,
Titian did many versions of his patron, the Emperor
CHARLES V, as well as the celebrated portrait of Pietro Aretino. He is regarded as an important link between Renaissance and baroque painting, through his influence on such
followers as RUBENS, and in his appeal to the impressionists.

Titus (full name Titus Flavius Sabinus Vespasianus, AD
39–81)   Roman emperor (79–81). Titus completed the
Colosseum and erected the triumphal arch known as the
Arch of Titus. On this arch (still standing in modern
Rome), the emperor had friezes carved to represent his
conquest of the Jews (70) and looting and destruction of
SOLOMON'S TEMPLE.

Titus and Gisippus   A tale from Boccaccio's
DECAMERON. Titus, a Roman youth studying philosophy at
Athens, falls in love with Sophronia, the betrothed of his
best friend, the Athenian Gisippus. The latter decides to
give her up to Titus, who replaces him in the darkened
nuptial chamber. Despite the clamor of outraged relatives,
Sophronia accepts Titus as her husband, and the two leave
for Rome. Gisippus is left to face the combined anger of
family and friends; this takes the form of rejection, which,
coupled with poor luck in his affairs, soon reduces him to
abject poverty. He then goes to Rome in a wretched state,
hoping to find Titus; but, when he meets his friend, the
latter fails to recognize him. Believing himself snubbed, he
decides to end his life by accepting the guilt for a murder
committed by another. As Gisippus is being tried by the
triumvir Octavianus Caesar, Titus wanders into the court
and soon realizes the identity of the defendant. Titus
promptly tells Octavianus that he, not Gisippus, is guilty.
This magnanimity stirs the true murderer to confess his
crime, whereupon all three are freed. Finally, Gisippus
marries Titus's sister, and the two couples live together in
perfect joy and harmony thereafter.

Titus Andronicus (c1590)   A tragedy by William
SHAKESPEARE, based on Senecan models (see SENECA). The
aging Titus Andronicus returns to Rome after a victorious
war against the Goths, bringing as captives their queen
Tamora and her three sons, one of whom is sacrificed by
Titus to appease the souls of the slain members of his fam-
ily. Declared emperor through Titus's intercession,
Saturninus claims Titus's daughter Lavinia as his wife.
When Saturninus's brother Bassanius abducts Lavinia,
Saturninus marries Tamora, who has sworn to avenge the
death of her son. Through the intrigues of Tamora and her
Moorish lover Aaron, Tamora's sons kill Bassanius, rape
Lavinia, and cut off her tongue and hands. Two of Titus's
sons are accused of murder and executed; another son,
Lucius, is banished and proceeds against Rome with a
Gothic army. Determined to exact vengeance for the
crimes against his family, Titus kills Tamora's sons and
serves their remains to her in a pie. After he has killed
Lavinia to end her shame and has stabbed Tamora, Titus is
slain by Saturninus, who is himself killed by Lucius.
Lucius then tells the tale of his family's wrongs and is proclaimed emperor.

Neither the direct source of the play nor the extent of
Shakespeare's share in the authorship has been clearly
determined.

To Althea from Prison (1649)   A poem by Richard LOVELACE. The poet maintains that true liberty, which
comes from freedom of soul, cannot be threatened by
chains or fetters. The last stanza contains the well-known
lines:

Stone walls do not a prison make,
   Nor iron bars a cage.

To a Waterfowl (1815)   A poem by William Cullen BRYANT. The poem describes the flight of a bird, which renewed Bryant's belief in divine guidance.

Tobacco Road (1932)   A novel by Erskine CALDWELL. Jeeter Lester is an impoverished Georgia sharecropper who lives on Tobacco Road with his starving old mother, his sickly wife, Ada, and his two children, sixteen-year-old Dude and Ellie May, who has a harelip. A third child, Pearl, has been married at the age of twelve to Lov Bensey, a railroad worker. When Jeeter's widowed preacher sister, Bessie Rice, induces Dude to marry her by buying him a new automobile, Dude accidentally wrecks the car and kills his grandmother. Pearl runs away from Lov Bensey; Ellie May happily goes to live with him; and Jeeter and Ada, left alone one night, perish when their shack burns down. The hapless Lesters, at once comical and shockingly degenerate, became widely familiar to the public through Jack Kirkland's dramatization (1933), which ran for 3,182 performances on Broadway, and the book's title has become a symbol of slovenly poverty and depravity.

Tobias   In the APOCRYPHA, the son of TOBIT. Tobias left Nineveh to collect a loan for his father. Guided by the archangel RAPHAEL, in disguise as Azarias, Tobias fell in love with and married his cousin Sara, seven of whose betrothed lovers had been carried off by the evil spirit ASMODEUS. With Raphael's aid, Tobias drove Asmodeus away.

Tobit   The principal character of the Book of Tobit, a romance included in the APOCRYPHA. As a Jew in captivity at Nineveh, Tobit buried the Hebrew dead, despite civil bans. Growing impoverished, miserable, and blind, he sent his son TOBIAS to collect a loan. When he returned, Tobias cured his father's blindness by applying to his eyes the gall of a fish, which had attacked him on the Tigris and which the archangel RAPHAEL had helped him catch.

Tocqueville, Count Alexis [Charles Henri Maurice Clérel] de (1805–1859)   French historian. De Tocqueville is known for his studies of the nature and operation of democracy. He sought to advance the rule of the people while simultaneously controlling undesirable tendencies. One of his best-known works, *Démocratie en Amérique* (*Democracy in America*, 1835–39), is considered the first impartial and systematic study of American institutions. *L'Ancien Régime et la Révolution* (*The Old Regime and the Revolution*, 1856), a history of the French Revolution, was left unfinished at the time of his death. De Tocqueville held a number of official positions in the French government, at one time serving on a special mission to the U.S. He was later a deputy and then a minister under Louis NAPOLEON, a position from which he retired after the *coup d'état* of December 2, 1851.

Tod in Venedig, Der   See DEATH IN VENICE.

toga   The outer garment worn by Roman citizens when appearing in public. Hence, the Romans were known as the *gens togata*, or togaed people. The toga con-

sisted of a single piece of undyed woolen cloth, cut almost in a semicircle and worn in a flowing fashion around the shoulders and body.

toga picta   The toga embroidered with golden stars that was worn by the emperor on special occasions and by a victorious general at his triumph.

toga praetexta   The toga with a purple border that was worn by children, by those engaged in sacred rites, by magistrates, and by others.

toga virilis   The plain white toga worn by men (Lat, *virilis*, "manly"); it was assumed by boys when they reached fifteen years of age.

To Have and Have Not (1937)   A novel by Ernest HEMINGWAY. It deals with the effort of Harry Morgan, a native of Key West, to earn a living for himself and his family. He has operated a boat for rental to fishing parties, but, during the Depression of the 1930s, he is forced to turn to the smuggling of Chinese immigrants and illegal liquor. While assisting a gang of bank robbers to escape, he is shot and mortally wounded. He dies gasping, "One man alone ain't got . . . no chance."

To His Coy Mistress (1650)   A poem by Andrew MARVELL; one of the great English love lyrics. The poet requests the lady's immediate favor; he would like to spend an aeon in compliment:

> But at my back I always hear
> Time's wingèd chariot hurrying near;
> And yonder all before us lie
> Deserts of vast eternity.

Toklas, Alice B.   See AUTOBIOGRAPHY OF ALICE B. TOKLAS, THE.

Tokugawa   Japanese period (1616–1868), succeeding the MUROMACHI period and ending with the MEIJI Restoration. Under the leadership of Tokugawa Ieyasu (1542–1616), the country was unified under a feudal government (the Shōgunate) located in Edo (Tokyo), and the perpetual warfare of the previous centuries was replaced by a peace that lasted over 250 years. The imperial court was without power, foreigners were excluded, and Christianity was banned. A rigid feudal system, based on Neo-Confucianism (see CONFUCIANISM), assured a strict control of the nation by the Tokugawa family. A new bourgeois, or merchant-oriented, literature arose in Osaka, the commercial capital. The KABUKI and BUNRAKU plays of CHIKAMATSU Monzaemon, the HAIKU of MATSUO Bashō, the stories of IHARA Saikaku, and the UKIYOE wood-block prints were all products of this time. Economic decline, the rise of the merchant class, and the arrival of Western nations (particularly the Americans, under Admiral Matthew PERRY) all contributed to the restoration of the imperial rule, with the establishment of the Meiji government in 1868.

Tolkien, J[ohn] R[onald] R[euel] (1892–1973) English philologist, writer of fantasies, and professor of medieval literature. Ironically, Tolkien's much-loved and widely read fantasies grew out of his philological studies at Oxford. While still a student, he began to create "Elvish," a language with its own laws, roots, and inflections. He then created a mythology around Elvish, which he developed fully in *The Hobbit* (1937) and the trilogy THE LORD OF THE RINGS. The first book introduced the gnomelike HOBBITS, their cosmology, and the beginnings of their struggles with good and evil. In the three books of the *Ring* trilogy, the world of Middle Earth comes to life in a vivid narrative depicting additional creatures, their habits, dispositions, and history; and the humble hobbits become involved in great deeds that determine the course of their society's fate. *The Simarillion*, described by the author as a "prequel" to the entire series, was published posthumously in 1977, edited by his son, Christopher Tolkien, also a medievalist.

Tolkien was also admired as a serious philologist. Among his scholarly works are *A Middle English Vocabulary* (1922), an edition of *Sir Gawain and the Green Knight* (1925), and *Beowulf: The Monster and the Critics* (1937).

Toller, Ernst (1893–1939)   German dramatist and poet, associated with EXPRESSIONISM. Toller advocated a social revolution to follow World War I. Fighting in that war, he entered the German army as a volunteer but soon underwent a change of heart and, after his discharge in 1916, was imprisoned for his part in pacifist movements. His own development is reflected in that of the hero in his first play, *Die Wandlung* (1919; tr *Transfiguration*, 1935), who is prompted by the horrors of war to renounce his patriotism and commit himself to the cause of peace and a people's revolution. Toller, a passionate believer in socialist ideology, was well aware that mass movements often injure the social and moral ideals that they seek to promote. This problem is the theme in both the highly abstract *Masse Mensch* (1920; tr *Man and the Masses*, 1924) and a historical drama about rioting weavers, *Die Maschinenstürmer* (1922; tr *The Machine-Wreckers*, 1923). Moving away from the simple ideal of revolution, in another play, *Hinkemann* (1924; tr *Brokenbow*, 1926), he all but left the realm of ideas to concentrate on the tragic human problems faced by a returning soldier. Finally, in *Hoppla, wir leben!* (1927; tr *Hoppla! Such Is Life*, 1935), a kind of political panorama, he expressed complete disillusionment with post-World War I Europe. Later, driven into exile by the Nazis, he committed suicide in New York.

Tolstoy, Aleksey Nikolayevich (1883–1945) Russian novelist, short-story writer, and playwright. Born a count, Tolstoy was distantly related to Count Leo TOLSTOY and, on his mother's side of the family, to Ivan TURGENEV. He fought with the Whites during the civil war, emigrated in 1919, and returned to the Soviet Union in 1923, where his writings became extremely popular. His best-known works of fiction are *Khozhdeniye po mukam* (1921–40; tr *Road to Calvary*, 1946), which is a trilogy describing the

years before, during, and just after the revolution, and *Pyotr pervy* (1929–43; tr *Peter the First*, 1959), a highly regarded historical novel. Tolstoy became one of the first Soviet science fiction writers with the publication of *Aelita* (1924), an account of a Russian landing on Mars.

Tolstoy, Count Leo (Lev Nikolayevich Tolstoy, 1828–1910)   Russian novelist and moral philosopher. Best known for his novels, Tolstoy also wrote short stories, plays, and essays. With DOSTOYEVSKY, Tolstoy made the realistic novel a literary genre that ranks in importance with classical Greek tragedy and Elizabethan drama. Aside from his literary prominence, Tolstoy holds an important place in his own country's cultural history as an ethical philosopher and religious reformer. He is especially known, both inside and outside Russia, as an early champion of nonviolent protest and the source of much of that doctrine's moral force. He was an influential factor in the social restlessness that swept Russia before the 1917 revolution.

Tolstoy was born, one of four brothers, on the family estate of Yasnaya Polyana, south of Moscow. His father, Count Nikolay Ilyich Tolstoy, was a veteran of the 1812 Russian campaign against NAPOLEON. His mother died when Tolstoy was not yet two years old. In 1837 the family moved to Moscow so that the boys could receive a formal education. That same year their father died, and the care of the children passed to their aunts. The story of his happy childhood and the later years were described by Tolstoy in his autobiographical trilogy, *Childhood* (1852), *Boyhood* (1854), and *Youth* (1857).

In 1844 Tolstoy enrolled in the University of Kazan, intending to study Oriental languages. His interest flagged, however, and he left the university in 1847 to settle on the Yasnaya Polyana estate. While at the university, he had acquired the habit of keeping a diary of his thoughts, plans, and accomplishments. This diary, maintained throughout his life, has been an invaluable source of information for his biographers. Entries for 1847 show that Tolstoy intended to follow a rigorous course of self-study while living on the estate. Instead he turned his attention to running the estate and improving the condition of the peasants. Encountering the serfs' mistrust, he soon gave up this idea also. The next few years were spent enjoying the pleasures of Moscow society. His diary shows that this enjoyment was often followed by periods of self-castigation and vows to improve himself. (The first full English version of his diaries was published in 1985.)

In 1851 Tolstoy went to the Caucasus, joined the army, and took part in the Russian efforts to suppress the rebellious Caucasian mountain tribes. During the next year, he completed and published *Childhood*, the first volume of his trilogy. This was published in the journal *Sovremennik* (*The Contemporary*). In 1854 he was transferred to Sevastopol, where he took part in the defense of the city against the British and French in the CRIMEAN WAR. During these years, he completed several short works, including *Nabeg*

(*The Raid*, 1853), *Boyhood*, and *Rubka lesa* (*The Woodfelling*, 1855). His greatest success, however, was his stories based on the defense of Sevastopol—"Sevastopol v dekabre mesyatse" ("Sevastopol in the Month of December," 1855), "Sevastopol v maye" ("Sevastopol in May," 1855), and "Sevastopol v avguste 1855 goda" ("Sevastopol in August 1855," 1855). These stories, generally known as the SEVASTOPOL SKETCHES, made their author famous and opened St. Petersburg's literary circles to him. Tolstoy's aristocratic aloofness and youthful bravado alienated many of the literati, including the novelist Ivan TURGENEV, with whom Tolstoy was to have intermittent quarrels for years.

In 1857 Tolstoy made his first European trip. Western life made a bad impression on him. He recorded his reactions in a short piece entitled *Lucerne* (1857). After his return to Yasnaya Polyana, Tolstoy became interested in education for the children of peasants. He opened a school for them on the estate in 1859 and took another trip abroad that year to study European educational methods.

In 1862 Tolstoy married Sofya Andreyevna Behrs. She was then eighteen years old and he was thirty-four. The following year, he published one of his best early works, THE COSSACKS, on which he had been working for several years. He also began writing his great novel WAR AND PEACE, with which he had been occasionally occupied since 1860. He had originally planned to set the book in the 1850s and to make the hero one of the Decembrist rebels who had been exiled to Siberia in 1825. This plan gradually changed. Tolstoy moved the time of the main action to 1825, the year of the Decembrist revolt, and finally to the period before the 1812 invasion by Napoleon.

Tolstoy's next major work was ANNA KARENINA, his second great novel. While at work on this book, he was beset with those metaphysical torments that he described in A CONFESSION. Following his rejection of orthodoxy and his conversion to a religion of love based on a literal interpretation of the SERMON ON THE MOUNT, Tolstoy concentrated more on philosophical and religious writings than on pure literature. Even the works of fiction he produced are weighted with didactic messages. One outstanding work that successfully carries such an extraliterary burden is the story THE DEATH OF IVAN ILYICH. Tolstoy's belief in the simple life of poverty and toil had its counterpart in his new attitude toward art, which he expressed in WHAT IS ART? The didactic moral element is also particularly noticeable in such works as *Kreitserova sonata* (*Kreutzer Sonata*, 1890), *Otets Sergey* (*Father Sergey*, 1898), the novel RESURRECTION, and *Falshivy kupon* (*The False Coupon*, 1904).

Tolstoy's main interest was in working out his religious and philosophical ideas. He wrote commentaries on the gospels and made translations of them and produced many tracts and pamphlets on religious subjects. His larger works on these subjects include *Kritika dogmaticheskogo bogosloviya* (*A Criticism of Dogmatic Theology*, 1885), *V chiom*

moya vera (*What I Believe*, 1883), and *Tak chto zhe nam delat?* (*What Then Must We Do?*, 1886).

Tolstoy stressed the moral and ethical side of Christianity; he believed in the mystical doctrine of the inner light. He rejected the divinity of JESUS, regarding him only as the greatest of ethical teachers. He also rejected the ideas of an afterlife or a personal God. The main principles on which he based his teachings were love for all of mankind and freedom from all forms of hatred and violence, including the hatred and violence generated by the appetites of greed, anger, and lust. From these principles sprang his doctrine of passive resistance to evil (with all its corollaries of war and of the demands of the state, both of which he regarded as forms of violence). Tolstoy condemned capitalism, private property, and the division of labor. Civilization in general he regarded as bad, emphasizing the need to make life as simple and primitive as possible. He extolled the virtues of physical labor, of earning one's livelihood by the sweat of one's brow. Tolstoy undertook to make his own shoes and wore simple peasant blouses. While some of his followers tried to build social utopias on the basis of his ideas, Tolstoy himself was generally content to criticize the existing society in their light. He was an effective and fearless critic and his strictures on the government and on the church were answered by these two closely connected powers in 1901, in the form of Tolstoy's excommunication from the Russian Church. Instead of harming his standing with the general public, this action seemed to make Tolstoy more popular. When the tsarist government executed numbers of people after the 1905 revolution, Tolstoy issued a scathing criticism of the policy in *Ya ne mogu molchat* (*I Cannot Be Silent*, 1908).

Besides his moral and religious writings, Tolstoy produced a number of moralizing tales for the people. Several of these are small masterpieces, despite their didacticism. They include "Bog pravdu vidit, da ne skoro skazhet" ("God Sees the Truth but Waits," 1872), "Chem lyudi zhivut?" ("What Men Live By," 1881), "Dva starika" ("Two Old Men," 1885), and "Alyosha Gorshok" (1905). These stories were written in the simple, plain narrative manner that Tolstoy conceived as the best style for all good literature. Despite his self-restrictions regarding style, Tolstoy managed to produce several fine works of art in his later years. These include *Khozyain i rabotnik* (*Master and Man*, 1895) and the short novel HADZHI MURAD. He also wrote three major plays: THE POWER OF DARKNESS, *Plody prosveshcheniya* (*Fruits of Enlightenment*, 1890), and *Zhivoy trup* (*The Living Corpse*, 1900).

Tolstoy's ideas and way of life after his conversion put a strain on his family life. His views on the evil of private property and his desire to put all his literary work in the public domain especially irritated his wife, who knew that only the royalties from Tolstoy's books supported the large family. After years of estrangement from his wife and all his children except for his youngest daughter, Alexandra, Tolstoy left Yasnaya Polyana in November 1910, accompanied by Alexandra and his doctor. He was on his way to a monastery, but he was taken ill during the train journey and died at the small railway junction of Astapovo.

To Lucasta, Going to the Wars (1649)   A poem by Richard LOVELACE. In it the poet asks his lady to forgive him for leaving her to go to war. The poem closes with the famous lines:

> I could not love thee, Dear, so much,
>   Lov'd I not Honour more.

The Lucasta to whom Lovelace addressed this and other poems is said to have been his fiancée, Lucy Sacheverell.

Tomasi di Lampedusa, Giuseppe   See LAMPE-DUSA, GIUSEPPE TOMASI, PRINCE OF.

Tom Brown's School Days (1857)   A famous book for boys by Thomas Hughes, an English reformer and jurist. It portrays life in an English public school. When Tom enters Rugby, he is a shy, homesick chap, but he is soon drawn into the life of the school and develops robust, manly qualities. A sequel, *Tom Brown at Oxford*, appeared in 1861.

Tom Jones, a Foundling, The History of (1749)   A novel by Henry FIELDING, generally considered one of the masterpieces of English literature. Squire Allworthy, who lives with his sister Bridget, returns home after a long absence to find an infant on his bed. Suspecting his servant Jenny Jones to be the mother, he names the baby Tom Jones, determines to rear him himself, and Jenny leaves town. Soon after, Bridget marries Captain Blifil, a fortune-hunter; they have a son, and Captain Blifil dies. Tom and young Blifil are raised together, taught by Square and Thwackum. Blifil, a malevolent boy, seizes every opportunity to misrepresent Tom and get him into trouble. Tom is a lusty, imprudent boy, but essentially benevolent. A rivalry over the attentions of Sophia Western, daughter of the neighboring Squire WESTERN, arises between them. Because of an affair with the gamekeeper's daughter and because of Blifil's treachery, Tom is sent packing by Squire Allworthy. In the PICARESQUE section that follows, Tom meets with many adventures, some of them of a dissipated nature, on the road to London. Sophia, in the meantime, flees to London to escape the marriage which her father is trying to force with Blifil, who is interested only in her fortune. Soon the whole cast of characters is on the scene; Jenny Jones turns up to reveal that Squire Allworthy's sister Bridget, not she, is the mother of Tom. Blifil's cruelties to Tom over the years are exposed. Tom, promising to mend his ways, marries Sophia, and becomes the heir of Squire Allworthy. As a hero, Tom Jones is not overly heroic; he is perhaps a model of generosity and manly spirit, but mixed with dissipation. Lord Byron called him "an accomplished blackguard."

Tomlinson, [Alfred] Charles (1927–   )   English poet, critic, and translator. To Tomlinson, a much traveled poet, four areas became almost equally important: the southwest and the Midlands in England, the Italian coast of Liguria, and the American Southwest. He is noted for his precise diction, natural rhythms, and emotionally powerful yet detached verse. Unlike many of his contemporaries, he sought a return to and continuation of the broad European perspective of YEATS, T. S. ELIOT, and Ezra POUND. He was also profoundly influenced by the American modernists Wallace STEVENS, Marianne MOORE, William Carlos WILLIAMS, and the BLACK MOUNTAIN POETS. His first published verse was *Relations and Contraries* (1951), which was followed by *The Necklace* (1955; rev 1966), written in Italy, and *Seeing Is Believing* (1958). *A Peopled Landscape* (1963) was written after his first visit to the U.S. Other major collections are *American Scenes* (1966), *The Way In* (1974), and *Notes from New York and Other Poems* (1984). *Some Americans* (1981) contains prose sketches and reminiscences of the American poets who so strongly influenced his work. *Poetry and Metamorphosis* (1983) is a series of lectures on the creative imagination's preoccupation with legends and myths of metamorphosis. He has also translated the work of the Russian poet Fyodor TYUTCHEV (1961) and of the great Castilian Antonio MACHADO (1963), and he has edited *The Oxford Book of Verse in English Translation* (1981).

Tommy (or Tommy Atkins)   A British private soldier, as a Jack Tar is a British sailor. At one time, all recruits were given manuals in which were to be entered the name, age, date of enlistment, length of service, wounds, medals, and so on of the holder. With each book was sent a specimen form showing how the one in the manual should be filled in, and the hypothetical name selected, instead of the lawyer's *John Doe* or *Richard Roe*, was *Thomas Atkins*. The nickname was popularized by Kipling:

> For it's Tommy this, and Tommy that, and "Tommy wait outside";
> But it's "Special train for Atkins" when the trooper's on the tide.
>
> "Tommy" (*Barrack-Room Ballads*)

Tom o' Bedlam   A mendicant who asks charity on the plea of insanity. In the 16th and 17th centuries, applications for admission to BEDLAM became so numerous that many inmates were dismissed half cured. These "ticket-of-leave" men wandered about chanting mad songs and dressed in fantastic costumes to elicit pity. Posing as these harmless innocents, a band of sturdy rogues appeared. Called Abram men, they committed great depredations.

Tompson, Benjamin (1642–1714)   Puritan poet and teacher, the first native-born American to publish a volume of poems in America. Born in Braintree (now Quincy), Massachusetts, and brought up by foster parents, Tompson graduated from Harvard in 1662 and five years later became master of the Boston Latin School. In 1676 he published *New England's Crisis*, modeled on Francis QUARLES's *History of Sampson* (1631). The title poem of the collection describes the towns of New England at the time of KING PHILIP's War. It is especially notable for its use of pidgin English and Indian dialect and for its concluding picture of a group of women building a fortress to protect Boston. Tompson was the first poet in colonial America to make extensive use of the contemporary scene.

Tom Sawyer, The Adventures of (1876)   A novel by Mark TWAIN. Tom, a shrewd and adventurous boy, is at home in the respectable world of his Aunt Polly, as well as in the self-reliant, parentless world of Huck Finn. The two friends, out in the cemetery under a full moon, attempt to cure warts with a dead cat. They accidentally witness a murder, of which Muff Potter is later wrongly accused. Knowing that the true murderer is Injun Joe, the boys are helpless with fear; they decide to run away to Jackson's Island. After a few pleasant days of smoking and swearing, they realize that the townspeople believe them dead. Returning in time to hear their funeral eulogies, they become town heroes. At the trial of Muff Potter, Tom, unable to let an innocent person be condemned, reveals his knowledge. Injun Joe flees. Later Tom and his sweetheart, Becky Thatcher, get lost in the cave in which the murderer is hiding. They escape, and Tom and Huck return to find the treasure Joe has buried.

Mark Twain wrote three sequels to this popular book: *The Adventures of* HUCKLEBERRY FINN, *Tom Sawyer Abroad* (1894), and *Tom Sawyer, Detective* (1896).

Tom Thumb   The pygmy hero of an old nursery tale, popular in the 16th century. "The History of Tom Thumb" was published by R. Johnson in 1621, and a similar tale by PERRAULT ("Le Petit Poucet") in 1697. The American midget Charles Sherwood Stratton (1838–83), exhibited at sideshows by P. T. Barnum, was popularly called "General Tom Thumb."

Tone, [Theobald] Wolfe (1763–1798)   Irish revolutionist, one of the founders of the UNITED IRISHMEN. Tone set forth his policy of unity for Ireland in *A Review of the Conduct of Administration* (1790), *Hibernicus* (1790), and *An Argument on Behalf of the Catholics of Ireland* (1791). Tone negotiated for a landing of the French in Ireland, but the fleet was scattered by a storm in 1796. The British captured him with a small French squadron off Lough Swilly in 1798 and were preparing to prosecute him for treason when Tone committed suicide.

Tonio Kröger (1903; tr 1913)   A story by Thomas MANN. When he is a boy, Tonio Kröger's mixed ancestry (a fiery southern mother, a staid Nordic father), his sensitivity, and his literary interests make him sharply aware of the gulf between himself and his "blond and blue-eyed" classmates, who ridicule his name and his tastes. He endures two unrequited loves—for Hans Hansen, whose eyes are bright and clear and never clouded by dreams, and later for the beautiful, blond Ingeborg Holm. He becomes

a famous writer and ultimately realizes that his unrequited love for the uncomplicated vitality of "normal" and "ordinary" people is the source of his own inner strength and the true value of his art.

Tono-Bungay (1909)   A novel by H. G. WELLS. The narrator is George Ponderevo, son of the housekeeper on a large estate, who is apprenticed to his uncle, Edward Ponderevo, a small-town druggist. His fantastic uncle soon moves to London and makes a fortune from his quack medicine Tono-Bungay. George helps his uncle, ironically observes his rise in the world, and uses some of his money to set himself up as an airplane designer. George resembles H. G. Wells himself—the son of a housekeeper, apprenticed to a druggist, a socialist, and a man with a vision of progress through properly used science.

Toomer, Jean   See HARLEM RENAISSANCE.

Tophet   A valley south of Jerusalem, at the extremity of GEHENNA or the Valley of Hinnom, where children were burnt alive in idolatrous rites as sacrifices to MOLOCH. There, the reformer-king Josiah threw dead bodies, ordure, and other unclean things, to prevent any further use of the place for religious purposes (2 Kings 23:10); it was also the site of the destruction of SENNACHERIB's army (Isa. 30:31–33). A perpetual fire was kept burning in Tophet to consume the bodies, filth, etc., deposited there; hence, it was taken as symbolical of Hell. The name is Hebrew and may mean "a place to be spat upon" or may be connected with *toph*, "a drum," in allusion to the drowning of the murdered children's cries by the beating of drums.

Torah   A Hebrew word, originally referring to oral teachings. In the OLD TESTAMENT, *torah* is used to mean "law," specifically the law handed down to MOSES by God; hence in Jewish scriptures, the Torah is the PENTATEUCH. In Jewish literature, it refers to God's total revelation. It is also used to designate the scroll, always present in a synagogue, on which the Pentateuch is handwritten.

Torquato Tasso (1790)   A play by Johann Wolfgang von GOETHE, based on the life of the 16th-century Italian poet. Though classical in form, like his earlier *Iphigenia in Tauris, Tasso* is not as optimistic about the ultimate solution of all human conflicts. Basically, it treats the incompatibility of the poet's inner nature with life in the external world: a theme not unlike that of THE SORROWS OF YOUNG WERTHER, except that there is no suicide. The play ends ambiguously, and it is not clear whether or how this disharmony is eventually resolved. See WEIMAR CLASSICISM: ZERRISSENHEIT.

Tortilla Flat (1935)   A novel by John STEINBECK. It deals with the poor but carefree Danny and his friends Pillón, Pablo, Big Joe Portagee, Jesús María Corcoran, and the old Pirate, all of whom gather in Danny's house. Steinbeck insists the meeting of these friends "was not unlike the Round Table." The novel contrasts the complexities of modern civilization with the simple life of these men.

Tor und der Tod, Der (1893; tr Death and the Fool, 1913)   A one-act lyric drama by Hugo von HOFMANNSTHAL, written when he was nineteen. Claudio, a young nobleman, feels death approaching and laments his overcultivated, empty life. Death appears to him as a "great god of the soul" and places before the young aesthete three accusers. First appears his mother, who gave her entire life to this son who failed to notice it. She is followed by a girl who loved him deeply and died when he cast her aside. Finally appears his friend, whose violent death was caused by Claudio's indifference. As he follows his visitors, Claudio finally glimpses life's meaning: "To be bound to others, yes, and to bind others firmly to oneself." The basic motif is the medieval DANCE OF DEATH, which here becomes an indirect praise of fulfilled life, or the "authentic existence," as Martin HEIDEGGER was later to call it.

Tory   A word of Irish origin meaning "pursuer." First applied to Irish outlaws, it later became a nickname for those who opposed the exclusion of the duke of York (later James II, a Roman Catholic) from succession to the Crown. After 1689, the English Tories continued to incline toward the Stuarts, but, after George III came to the throne, their policy became one of upholding the established church and state and of opposing liberalism. In this way, Tory became the name of one of the two great English Parties (see WHIG). Today the Tory Party has given place in English politics to the Conservative, to which the nickname Tory is still applied. In the American colonies and during the Revolution, British loyalists were called Tories. A U.S. source of 1777 defines a Tory as "a thing whose head is in England, whose body is in America, and whose neck ought to be stretched."

Tosa Diary, The (Tosa nikki)   One of several famous diaries written during the HEIAN period in Japan. It is attributed to Ki no Tsurajuki (d 946). Humorous and elegant in style, it describes a trip from the province of Tosa to Kyoto in 936. It was much imitated by later writers. See JAPANESE LITERATURE.

totemism   Belief in a sacred relationship between an object (especially some species of animal) and a human kinship group, or clan. The sacred object, called a totem (derived from the term used by the Ojibwa Indians), is representative of the kinship group. Although the members of the group may in fact be related by blood only distantly or not all, they regard themselves as members of the same family, united by their relationship to the totem. Often the totem is regarded as the ancestor of the clan or as having had a supernatural relationship to the putative human ancestor of the clan. Any object can be a totem, its sacred character being ascribed to it by kinship group rather than derived from any intrinsic qualities.

Totemism exists in a wide variety of forms and in all parts of the world. One of its most common characteristics is that the totem, by virtue of its sacred nature, is regarded as taboo. A totem animal must not be killed and eaten as food, except on special occasions when totemic rites are being performed. A man and woman bearing the same totem are forbidden to marry, this being a form of incest taboo.

To the Finland Station   See WILSON, EDMUND.

To the Lighthouse (1927)   A novel by Virginia WOOLF. With the techniques of STREAM OF CONSCIOUSNESS and symbolism (see SYMBOLISTS), this novel has little plot, but a great deal of atmosphere, emotion, and poetry. The characters' moment-by-moment actions, sense impressions, and thoughts are described. The first section, called "The Window," describes a day during Mr. and Mrs. Ramsay's house party at their country home by the sea. Mr. Ramsay is a distinguished scholar and, in the eyes of Woolf, a typical male, whose mind works rationally, heroically, and rather icily. He is drawn from her father, Sir Leslie STEPHEN. Mrs. Ramsay is a warm, creative, intuitive woman, the center of the household. Among the various guests is Lily Briscoe, an artist. The Ramsays have arranged to take a boat out to the lighthouse the next morning, and their little son James is bitterly disappointed when a change in the weather makes it impossible. The second section, called "Time Passes," describes the seasons and the house, unused and decaying, in the years after Mrs. Ramsay's death. In the third section, "The Lighthouse," Mr. Ramsay and his friends are back at the house. He takes the postponed trip to the lighthouse with his now sixteen-year-old son, who is at last able to communicate silently with him and forgive him for being different from his mother. Lily Briscoe puts the last touches to the painting Mrs. Ramsay once inspired. The lighthouse, everyone's goal, symbolizes many things to many people. More like a prose poem than a conventional novel, the whole book is a statement about time and death and the permanence of art.

To the Virgins, to Make Much of Time (1648)   A poem by Robert HERRICK, the theme of which is explicit in the title. It was set to a number of melodies, and the first lines gained proverbial familiarity:

> Gather ye rosebuds while ye may,
> Old time is still a-flying
> And this same flower that smiles to-day
> Tomorrow will be dying.

Tottel's Miscellany (1557)   Popular title for *Songs and Sonnets*, a "miscellany" or collection of poems by various authors, published by Richard Tottel in England. It contained 271 poems, chiefly lyrics, although EPIGRAMS, ELEGIES, SATIRES, PASTORALS, and narrative verse were included, as well as translations of Latin, Italian, and French poems. It introduced the use of TERZA RIMA, OTTAVA RIMA, RONDEAU, the first English SONNETS, and possibly the first original English BLANK VERSE. In the collection were ninety-seven poems attributed to Sir Thomas WYATT, forty to the earl of SURREY, forty to Nicholas Grimald, and ninety-four to "Uncertain Authors." The majority of these poems had never before appeared in print, for courtier-poets, such as Wyatt and Surrey, circulated their verse among the court in manuscript. It was not considered fashionable for them to publish their own work (this rule did not hold in the case of translations of poems from foreign languages) and as a result contemporary poetry reached the general public only rarely, if at all.

The first publication of its kind, *Tottel's Miscellany* was extremely popular. It went through eight editions in thirty years, and was followed by a host of imitators, which are known generally as the Elizabethan anthologies. They are of lesser importance than the original, which is considered to mark the beginning of modern English poetry.

Touchstone   In Shakespeare's As You Like It, a court jester who accompanies Rosalind to the Forest of Arden. Touchstone is a witty, cynical fellow who lists "the seven degrees of affront" in a famous speech: (1) the retort courteous, (2) the quip modest, (3) the reply churlish, (4) the reproof valiant, (5) the countercheck quarrelsome, (6) the lie circumstantial, and (7) the lie direct. His wit is realistic and biting, usually aimed at the foibles of mankind, and he openly insults his betrothed Audrey, who is too stupid to realize it.

Toulouse-Lautrec [Monfa], Henri [Marie Raymond] de (1864–1901)   French painter. Descended from an old French family and physically misshapen, Toulouse-Lautrec became the supreme portrayer of Montmartre night life, with its dancers, actresses, singers, and women of the demimonde. He probed the emotional significance of his subjects, picturing them with an elegant, nervous, expressively revealing line. At first influenced by Edgar DEGAS and Japanese prints, he soon developed his own original style. His decorative posters and lithographs are also highly distinguished.

Tourgée, Albion W[inegar] (1838–1905) American novelist. Born in Ohio, Tourgée served in the Federal army and in 1865 moved to North Carolina, where he played an active part in the work of the Reconstruction. Tourgée wrote several novels, among them *A Fool's Errand* (1879) and *Bricks without Straw* (1880), which describes the problems and inevitable failure of the Reconstruction.

Tourneur, Cyril (c1575–1626)   English dramatist. Tourneur is the probable author of the bloody Senecan tragedy THE REVENGER'S TRAGEDY and of the somewhat milder *Atheist's Tragedy* (1611).

Toussaint L'Ouverture, Pierre François Dominique (1743–1803)   Haitian black soldier and liberator, a self-educated slave. In 1791 he led a successful revolt against white rule in San Domingo (Hispaniola [Haiti and the Dominican Republic] of today) and, through his administration, brought law and order to the island by 1801. When he asked Napoleon for approval of a constitutional form of government, Napoleon sent a French expedition against him under General Leclerc. Captured and taken to France, he was imprisoned and died there ten

months later. He is the central figure of a historical novel, *The Hour and the Man* (1840), by Harriet MARTINEAU, and *Citizen Toussaint* (1944; reprinted 1965) by Ralph Korngold. He is also the subject of poems by WORDSWORTH, WHITTIER, and LAMARTINE.

Tower, The (Der Turm, 1925; tr 1963)   A verse play by Hugo von HOFMANNSTHAL. It is freely adapted from Calderón's LA VIDA ES SUEÑO. The most important of Hofmannsthal's additions to the original work is the character of Olivier, a demagogical dictator who assumes power after the old king's deposition and executes Prince Sigismund. Thus, Sigismund's final triumph, which is real in Calderón's work, becomes entirely symbolic in Hofmannsthal's.

Tower Beyond Tragedy, The (1924)   A play in verse by Robinson JEFFERS. This drama is based on *Agamemnon* and *The Libation Bearers*, the first two plays of the ORESTEIA trilogy of Aeschylus, but Jeffers gives an enlarged role to Cassandra, the prophetess, and emphasizes the contrast between the incestuous desires of Electra and the desire of Orestes to break away from her and from all ties with humanity.

Tower of London   A famous London prison for political prisoners. William the Conqueror and the monarchs who followed him built the various buildings included in the name *Tower of London*, which stand by the Thames. The Tower has been a prison for many distinguished persons, including kings and queens, and the site of many executions.

Town, The   See HAMLET, THE.

Towneley Mysteries (or Towneley Plays)   One of the important cycles of English medieval MYSTERY PLAYS. They are also known as the Wakefield Mysteries, because they were probably acted at the fairs of Widkirk, near Wakefield. They have a more popular, lively, and even jocular tone than the plays of the other cycles. See WAKEFIELD MASTER.

Toy Cart, The   See LITTLE CLAY CART, THE.

Toynbee, Arnold [Joseph] (1889–1975)   English historian and student of international affairs (he was a member of the British delegation to the Paris Peace Conference in 1919), and father of Philip Toynbee (1916–), a novelist and critic. From 1924 to 1938, Toynbee helped write and edit the yearly *Survey of International Affairs*. He wrote on many historical and international subjects, but his greatest work was his twelve-volume *A Study of History* (1934–61), a condensed version of which became a best-seller. Comparing the history of twenty-one different civilizations, he traced a cyclical pattern of growth, maturity, and decay in them all. He believed that societies thrive best in response to challenge and that society's most important task is to create a religion. Though he saw Western civilization as in its decay stage, he saw hope for the future formation of one spiritually oriented world community. Despite his encyclopedic knowledge, Toynbee was more a poet, mythologist, and metaphysician than an empirical historian.

Toyotomi Hideyoshi (1536–1598)   First unifier of Japan. Arising from peasant stock, Toyotomi Hideyoshi served the famous warrior Oda Nobunaga (1534–82), gaining and consolidating military control after the latter's death. He engaged in extensive campaigns against Korea, which proved inconclusive. A patron of the arts, he is revered in folklore and legend as one of Japan's greatest military geniuses. His successors lost control of the nation to Tokugawa Ieyasu (1542–1616), founder of the TOKU-GAWA shōgunate.

Tozzi, Federigo (1883–1920)   Italian novelist. Tozzi's works are characterized by their descriptions of the author's unhappy adolescence in his native Siena (Tuscany). His most outstanding novels are *Con gli occhi chiusi* (1919), an idyllic tale about the love of two sensitive adolescents; *Tre croci* (1920; tr *Three Crosses*, 1921), the title of which refers to the crosses that mark the graves of three brothers whose lack of moral fiber led them to three varieties of catastrophe; and *Il podere* and *Ricordi di un impiegato*, both published posthumously in 1921.

Tracts for the Times (1833–1841)   A series of ninety papers on theological and liturgical subjects, sometimes called the Oxford Tracts. They consist of extracts from 17th-century High Church divines and church fathers and of contributions from John Henry NEWMAN, Richard Hurrell Froude (1803–36), E. B. PUSEY, John KEBLE, and Isaac Williams (1802–65). The tracts were launched with the object of arresting "the advance of Liberalism in religious thought" and reviving "the true conception of the relation of the Church of England to the Catholic Church at large." The series came to an end (at the request of the bishop of Oxford) with Newman's Tract No. 90, in which he stated that it is possible to interpret some aspects of the Thirty-Nine Articles of the Church in a manner not inconsistent with the Council of TRENT. This tract was condemned by several bishops and heads of colleges, and a group of Tractarians, including Newman, entered the Roman Catholic Church. See OXFORD MOVEMENT.

Tracy, Honor [Lilbush Wingfield] (1913–   )   British novelist. Born and educated in England, of an old Anglo-Irish family, Tracy worked as a foreign correspondent before moving to Ireland to write her observant and satirical novels. *The Straight and Narrow Path* (1956) is a hilarious account of the eccentricities of an Irish village as seen by a visiting English anthropologist. Subsequent novels, including *A Number of Things* (1960), *Men at Work* (1966), *The Man from Next Door* (1977), *The Ballad of Castle Reef* (1979), and *The Heart of England* (1983), satirize the bizarre and pretentious in settings all over the world. Tracy's vigorous exposure of whatever she considers nonsense, combined with her acute powers of observation, have made her a first-rate travel writer. *Kakemono: A*

Sketchbook of Postwar Japan (1950), while attacking the American occupation, gives a vivid introduction to Japanese life and culture. *Mind You, I've Said Nothing* (1950) is about Ireland. She has also written three highly acclaimed books on Spain: *Silk Hats and No Breakfast* (1957), *Spanish Leaves* (1964), and *Winter in Castile* (1974).

Tradiciones peruanas (1827–1906)   The aggregate title of ten volumes by Ricardo PALMA, consisting of *tradiciones*, or traditions, a literary form that Palma himself originated. Virtually defying classification, Palma's traditions are short sketches combining history, anecdote, and satire. Using a formula that called for a *soupçon* of truth, a great deal of invention, and painstaking attention to style, Palma covered virtually every aspect of the Peruvian past, though he was most at home describing the intrigues and amorous escapades of 18th-century Lima. Written in a pungent, ironical style reminiscent of that of the 17th-century Spaniard Francisco QUEVEDO, Palma's traditions have often been imitated but never equaled.

Tradition and the Individual Talent (1919)   An essay by T. S. ELIOT. In this influential poetic manifesto, the author asserts that a poet cannot write significant poetry in the 20th century unless he is steeped in the tradition and poetry of the past. The past will teach him to avoid romantic, autobiographical writing and to concentrate on technique and impersonal, detached poetry.

tragedy (fr Gr, *tragoidia*, "goat song")   A Western literary form, chiefly dramatic, which evokes strong emotions in the audience by presenting an often superior and noble being who demonstrates great courage and perseverance while facing and struggling against certain defeat. Like COMEDY, dramatic tragedy grew out of the celebrations in honor of the Greek god DIONYSUS. These celebrations evolved from ritualistic presentations to the great tragic dramas of SOPHOCLES, EURIPIDES, and AESCHYLUS. In describing these classical plays, Aristotle, in the POETICS, arrived at what is considered the most generally acceptable definition for an almost undefinable form: a dramatic presentation that arouses pity and fear in the audience, thus stimulating a *catharsis* of these emotions.

The classical tragic hero was usually a person of stature or significance who is undone either by some personal flaw, such as HUBRIS, or by the will of the gods. In another period of great tragic writing—the late 16th and early 17th century in England (MARLOWE, SHAKESPEARE, WEBSTER), in Spain (CALDERÓN, Lope de VEGA), and in France (CORNEILLE, RACINE)—the heroes were often kings, princes, or noblemen. More contemporary tragedies include middle-class heroes and heroines, such as Ibsen's HEDDA GABLER and Arthur Miller's DEATH OF A SALESMAN. In modern tragedy, the emphasis is not so much on a struggle against fate or some tragic flaw but on a conflict with social, hereditary, psychological, or environmental forces.

The forms of tragedy have changed to reflect the beliefs, values, and conventions of the age in which they are produced. However, the fundamental tragic vision remains the same: the spectacle of a human being of nobility, idealism, and courage in conflict either with his or her own frailty or with a hostile or indifferent universe. See THEATRE OF THE ABSURD.

Tragical History of Dr. Faustus, The   See DR. FAUSTUS, THE TRAGICAL HISTORY OF.

tragic flaw   The defect or error of a tragic hero that leads to his or her downfall. The Greeks called it *hamartia*.

Traherne, Thomas (1636–1674)   English poet and clergyman. One of the later METAPHYSICAL POETS, Traherne is known for his emphasis on what he regarded as the direct and untutored apprehension of truth on the part of children. His work is marked by simple direction and a vivid presentation of the common things of everyday life as the vehicles of mystical revelation. Traherne was not discovered as a poet until early in the 20th century; his manuscripts, which were recovered in 1895 from a London bookbarrow, were at first ascribed to Henry Vaughan. His best-known verse is included in *Poetical Works* (1903) and *Poems of Felicity* (1910). *Centuries of Meditations* (1908) is a collection of his prose sketches.

Traill, Catherine Parr [Strickland] (1802–1899) English-born Canadian writer and naturalist. Traill came to Canada with her husband and her sister, Susanna MOODIE, in 1832 and settled near Rice Lake, Ontario. The two sisters wrote of the many trials and occasional rewards of frontier life with a frankness and dry humor, designed to disillusion the dupes of land agents.

Trakl, Georg (1887–1914)   Austrian poet. Trakl was influenced by the French SYMBOLISTS and, with HEYM, was one of the early and most influential poets associated with EXPRESSIONISM. *Gedichte* (*Poems*, 1913), the only volume of his poems published during his lifetime, revealed a poet of exceptional sensitivity and lyric power, overcome by an apocalyptic vision of the decay of civilization. In World War I, he worked as a pharmacist in the German army and died in a military hospital, probably by his own hand. Among the posthumous works published are *Der Herbst des Einsamen* (*The Autumn of the Lonely*, 1920) and *Gesang des Abgeschiedenen* (*Song of the Desperate*, 1933). His complete works were published in German in three volumes (1948–51).

Transcendentalism   An American philosophic and literary movement centered in New England during the 19th century. A reaction against scientific rationalism, it relied upon intuition as the only way to comprehend reality in a world where every natural fact embodies a spiritual truth. Its chief spokesman, Ralph Waldo EMERSON, expressed the Transcendentalist belief that everything in man's world is a microcosm of the universe when he stated that "the world globes itself in a drop of dew." Emerson thus stressed the essential unity of all things, which are ordered by a Supreme Mind or Over-Soul. Man's soul is identical with the Over-Soul; it is this belief in the divinity of man that allowed Transcendentalists to disregard external authority and tradition, and to rely on direct experience. "Trust thyself," Emerson's motto, became the code of Henry David THOREAU, Bronson ALCOTT, Margaret FULLER, and other members of the Transcendental Club, an informal group organized in 1836 by the Rev. George RIPLEY.

An idealistic philosophy, Transcendentalism was shaped by the ideas of PLATO and PLOTINUS. It took its name and many of its ideas from Kant's CRITIQUE OF PRACTICAL REASON. The American writers were influenced by Continental thinkers, including HEGEL, SCHELLING, FICHTE, and GOETHE. The doctrines of the German Transcendentalists were reflected in the works of CARLYLE, COLERIDGE, and WORDSWORTH, to whom the Americans owe a great debt. Emanuel SWEDENBORG's mystical doctrines of contact with the spiritual world also profoundly influenced the New England writers.

Basic statements of Transcendental belief may be found in Emerson's essay *Nature* (1836) and in his lecture "The Transcendentalist" (1842). See DIAL, THE.

transition (1927–1938)   A monthly literary magazine founded in Paris with Elliot Paul and Eugene Jolas as editors. As with other LITTLE MAGAZINES, its purpose was to encourage experimental writing, which it did by publishing works by such writers as Gertrude STEIN, E. E. CUMMINGS, Hart CRANE, and Archibald MACLEISH. From 1927 to 1930, it published sections of James Joyce's FINNEGANS WAKE, then known as *Work in Progress*.

Traveller from Altruria, A (1894)   A novel by William Dean HOWELLS. Aristides Homos has just returned from the utopian Altruria, where the socialistic regime is democratic and Christian. In a series of amusing conversations, Homos finds the American system inferior to the Altrurian.

Traven, B. (d 1969)   Novelist. The man who wrote under the name of B. Traven guarded the secret of his identity all his life. Although he is known to have lived his final years in Mexico, the details of his early life are shrouded in mystery. The two most common conjectures are that he was either born in Chicago in 1890 and named Berick Traven Torsvan or born in Germany in 1882 and named Ret Marut. More fanciful interpretations identify him as everyone from Jack LONDON to the illegitimate son of Kaiser Wilhelm. It is not even known in what language Traven's novels were originally written. Whatever his identity, he left a legacy of hard-boiled proletarian novels. The most famous, *The Treasure of the Sierra Madre* (1935), is a brilliant psychological study of human greed, which became an award-winning motion picture. His major work was the *Caoba Cycle*, a series of six novels about the gruesome conditions that led to the Revolution of 1910 in Mexico.

Travers, P[amela] L[yndon] (1906–   ) Australian writer. Travers's books, starting in 1934, about the adventures of the magic-working nanny Mary Poppins, are delightful and popular stories for children. Among her other works are *About Sleeping Beauty* (1975) and *Two Pairs of Shoes* (1980).

Treason of the Intellectuals, The (La Trahison des clercs, 1927; tr 1928) An essay by Julien Benda (1867–1956), the rationalist philosopher, that denounces the tendency of intellectuals to engage in politics as the defeatist surrender of intelligence to propagandistic ideology. Their engagement, Benda says, necessitates the abdication of their responsibility to consider abstract truth and justice. The essay has also been translated as *The Great Betrayal* (1934).

Treasure Island (1883) A romance by Robert Louis STEVENSON. The story is told by Jim Hawkins, a young boy who learns of the whereabouts of a buried treasure from the papers of an old sailor staying at his mother's inn. He shows the treasure map to Dr. Livesey and Squire Trelawney, and the three determine to find it. They fit out a ship, the schooner *Hispaniola*, hire hands, and set off for Treasure Island. Among the ship's crew are Long John Silver and some of his followers, who are after the treasure for themselves. Jim Hawkins overhears their plans to mutiny, and with the rest of the crew is able to thwart them in the bloody battle that ensues. Finally they reach the island and retrieve the treasure with the help of the marooned sailor Ben Gunn.

trecento (Ital, "three hundreds") The Italian way of designating the 14th century, the age of DANTE, PETRARCH, and BOCCACCIO.

Treece, Henry [William] (1912–1966) English poet and novelist. Treece was associated with the NEW APOCALYPSE movement of poetry. Among his collections of verse are *Invitation and Warning* (1942) and *Collected Poems* (1946). Treece wrote a critical study of Dylan Thomas (1949), whom he and his associates admired greatly. He is probably best known for his numerous historical novels, including *The Dark Island* (1952) and *Oedipus* (1964), and for the extremely high standard of his historical novels for children.

Tree Grows in Brooklyn, A (1943) A novel by Betty Smith (1904–72). This best-selling, warm-hearted book tells of the life of the sensitive child Francie Nolan, growing up in a city slum, and of Francie's parents, her lovable drunkard father and her tender, determined mother.

Treitschke, Heinrich von (1834–1896) German historian. A strong partisan of German unification under Prussia and an ardent nationalist and anti-Semite, Treitschke is best known for his *Deutsche Geschichte im XIX. Jahrhundert* (*German History in the Nineteenth Century*, 1879–94).

Trelawny, Edward John (1792–1881) English biographer and traveler. Trelawny's life included episodes of naval service, privateering in the Indian Ocean, and action in the Greek rebellion of 1823. He was a close friend of BYRON and SHELLEY, and it was he who recovered Shelley's and Edward Williams's bodies after they had drowned. He is best known for his autobiographical *Adventures of a Younger Son* (1831) and *Recollections of the Last Days of Shelley and Byron* (1858).

Trelawny of the Wells (1898) A comedy by Arthur Wing PINERO. The actress heroine, Rose Trelawny, becomes engaged to a young aristocrat, but breaks her engagement to return to the stage. Not daunted, her lover follows and becomes an actor.

tremendismo   See CELA, CAMILO JOSÉ.

Trench, Richard Chenevix (1807–1886) The Anglican archbishop of Dublin (1863–84) and a noted philologist and poet. Trench was active in the Philological Society, which supported his scheme for beginning the Oxford *New English Dictionary*. He was the author of *Poems from Eastern Sources* (1842), *The Study of Words* (1851), *English Past and Present* (1855), and *Alma and Other Poems* (1865).

Trent, Council of   A council of the Roman Catholic Church. It met intermittently from 1545 to 1563 in reaction to the Protestant Reformation (see COUNTER-REFORMATION). Its discussions and its conclusions influenced art, including literature, in the period immediately following.

Trent's Last Case (1912) A classic detective novel by E. C. BENTLEY. Philip Trent, an English painter, poetry lover, and amateur detective, successively uncovers three different plausible solutions to the murder of an American millionaire.

Trevelyan, G[eorge] M[acaulay] (1876–1962) English historian, son of the distinguished historian Sir George Otto Trevelyan (1838–1928), great-nephew of Thomas Babington MACAULAY. Professor of modern history at Cambridge from 1927 to 1951, Trevelyan believed that history should be written as literature, that is, to be read, and that historical evidence should be measured with a humanistic eye as well as with a scientist's calculation. His great scholarly works were a study of GARIBALDI (1907–11) and the three-volume *England under Queen Anne* (1930–34). He is better known for his one-volume *History of England* (1926); his numerous biographies, such as *Grey of Fallodon* (1937); and *English Social History* (1942), published in an illustrated four-volume edition (1949–52).

Trevor, William (pen name of William Trevor Cox, 1928–   ) Irish novelist, short-story writer, and dramatist. Trevor first achieved notice with his second novel, *The Old Boys* (1964), which was distinguished for its stylized comic dialogue among eight old men at a class reunion. His writing is distinguished by its spare, subtle humor and by a kind of unsentimental nostalgia. He has dealt with old people in several of his other novels, including *The Boarding-House* (1965) and *Miss Gomez and the Brethren* (1971). *Other People's Worlds* (1980) deals with a middle-aged wife who becomes involved in trying to salvage the lives of women ruined by her loutish younger husband. Among his other works are *Fools of Fortune* (1983) and *A Writer's Ireland* (1984). His short stories, many of which have been adapted for television, are collected in such volumes as *The Day We Got Drunk on Cake* (1968) and *Lovers of Their Time* (1979).

Trevor-Roper, H[ugh] R[edwald] (1914–   ) English historian. Regius Professor of Modern History at Oxford, Trevor-Roper has a range of interests that runs from a book on Archbishop Laud (1940), the most controversial of early-17th-century prelates, to *The Hermit of Peking* (1977), a detective biography of the fraudulent 20th-century sinologist Sir Edmund Backhouse. During World War II, Trevor-Roper was in British Intelligence. Out of this experience came the classic *The Last Days of Hitler* (1947) and, in 1978, his edition of the diaries of Joseph Goebbels, Hitler's minister of propaganda, *Final Entries: 1945*. Among his other works are *The Gentry, 1540–1640* (1953), *The Rise of Christian Europe* (1965), *The Crisis of the Seventeenth Century: Religion, the Reformation, and Social Change* (1967), *The Plunder of the Arts in the 17th Century* (1970), and *Princes and Artists: Patronage and Ideology at Four Hapsburg Courts, 1517–1633* (1976). His books combine impeccable research with a vivid and readable style. In 1962 he became embroiled in a controversy with A.J.P. TAYLOR over Taylor's book *The Origins of the Second World War* (1962), which Trevor-Roper and others felt exonerated Hitler of blame for starting the war.

Trial, The (Der Prozeß, pub posthumously, 1925; tr 1935)   An unfinished, fragmentary novel by Franz KAFKA. Insofar as it depicts the confrontation of an individual and a baffling bureaucracy, it is similar to Kafka's THE CASTLE. The hero, a bland bank assessor named Joseph K., lives without joy and without yearning for anything beyond professional advancement. He awakens one morning to find himself accused by a mysterious legal authority, headquartered in a rundown tenement, of an unnamed crime of which he knows nothing. The novel treats his many fruitless attempts to obtain justice from an authority with which he cannot effectively communicate, and it culminates in his utter frustration, his complete loss of human dignity, and his cruel death by stabbing. Like *The Castle*, this novel lends itself to innumerable allegorical interpretations. Whereas *The Castle* was seen as a struggle for divine grace, *The Trial* has been seen as a quest for divine justice. On another level, Joseph K.'s relationship to his judges has been seen as symbolic of psychological (and perhaps autobiographical) feelings of existential guilt. Other interpretations suggest that the novel is a modern version of the book of JOB, a treatment of the mystery of original sin, an attack on the bureaucracy of old Austria, a prophetic warning of

the coming Nazi terror, a clinical study of the psychological effect of tuberculosis on a dying man, etc. A short section of the book was completed and published separately in 1919 under the title V*or dem Gesetz* (*Before the Law*) in the collection *Ein Landarzt* (1919; tr *A Country Doctor*, 1962).

tribune   In ancient Rome, one of ten magistrates whose duty was to represent the will of the plebeian populace. A tribune had the right to veto any decree of the Senate, any law of the comitia, and any public action of a magistrate. Their persons were considered sacred, and no one was allowed to hinder them in the performance of their official duties. See CURSUS HONORUM.

Trick to Catch the Old One, A (c1606)   A comedy by Thomas MIDDLETON. A penniless rake, Theodorus Witgood, connives to get money from his avaricious uncle, Pecunius Lucre, by pretending to be engaged to the wealthy Widow Medler, who is really a courtesan in disguise. Immediately, Widow Medler is the focus of all attention. Old Walkadine Hoard, Lucre's equally avaricious enemy, is first among those who wish to cut out Witgood and win the wealthy widow for themselves. Meanwhile, Witgood's creditors, anticipating prompt payment, lend him additional sums to finance his suit with the widow. On Witgood's advice, the widow assures her future by marrying old Hoard. To protect himself from his creditors, Witgood counters with a breach-of-promise suit, which Hoard settles by paying Witgood's debts. At the wedding feast, the widow is unmasked but promises to make Hoard a good wife. At the same time, Witgood announces that he has married Mistress Joyce, Hoard's niece. All are reconciled in the joy of the celebration.

tricoteuses (Fr, "knitters")   Parisian women who, during the French Revolution, used to attend the meetings of the Convention and other popular assemblies. While they went on with their *tricotage* ("knitting"), they encouraged the leaders in their bloodthirsty excesses. The royalists called them the "furies of the guillotine." Madame DEFARGE in Dickens's A TALE OF TWO CITIES typifies such a woman.

Trifonov, Yury Valentinovich (1925–1981) Soviet writer. Born in Moscow, the son of a prominent Bolshevik and party member who died in one of Stalin's purges in 1937, Trifonov, ironically, won a Stalin Prize for his first novel, *Studenty* (1950; tr *Students*, 1953), which already demonstrated his enduring focus on morality and life in Soviet society. Unlike many Soviet writers in the period after World War II, Trifonov appears to have made a conscious decision to remain in his own country and to write in a way that would permit him to be published. In this he succeeded, and even works such as *Obmen* (1969), *Predvaritelnye itogi* (1970), *Dolgoe proshchanie* (1971; all tr in *The Long Goodbye*, 1978), and *Drugaya zhizn* (1975; tr *Another Life*, 1983), the "Moscow novellas," which seem obvious indictments of the alienation, loss of ideals, and plain amorality produced by life in contemporary Soviet society, were successfully published, though not without semiofficial criticism. Trifonov's most complex novel, *Dom na naberezhne* (1976; tr *The House on the Embankment*, 1983), the story of the life of a successful literary bureaucrat who has conformed and compromised all his life to save his skin, also met with a great deal of official criticism, but was a huge success with the public. *Starik* (1978; tr *The Old Man*, 1984) is also a fierce examination of moral corruption and shallow values.

Trilby (1894)   A novel by George DU MAURIER. Trilby O'Ferrall, a young artist's model in Paris, is beloved by three English art students. Her engagement to one of them, William Bagot, known as Little Billee, is broken off, and she falls into the hands of a sinister Hungarian musician, SVENGALI. She becomes a great singer under his mesmeric influence, but she loses her voice when he suddenly dies of heart failure. She sickens and dies soon after.

Trilling, Lionel (1905–1975)   American critic and scholar. Trilling graduated from Columbia University in 1925 and later became professor of literature there, an association with the university that lasted over forty-four years. As a critic, he employed a wide range of disciplines—literature, history, philosophy, psychology—to establish the essential interaction between culture and a work of art. His first published work was *Matthew Arnold* (1939), followed by *E. M. Forster* (1943). Trilling's critical essays, collected in, among others, *The Liberal Imagination* (1950), *The Opposing Self* (1955), *Beyond Culture* (1965), *Sincerity and Authenticity* (1972), and *Mind in the Modern World* (1973), established him as one of the dominant critical voices of his day. These works embody his theory that the function of criticism is to search for the ideas by which every age can be evaluated. Among his other works are short stories, a novel, and several studies of FREUD. His wife, Diana Trilling, has edited a twelve-volume posthumous edition of Trilling's complete works (1978–80).

triloka   See THREE WORLDS.

Trim, Corporal   In Laurence Sterne's novel TRISTRAM SHANDY, UNCLE TOBY's orderly. Trim is, like his master, a devotee of military ways, but, in sharp contrast to Uncle Toby, he is also extremely eloquent.

Trimalchio   The vulgar and ostentatious multi-millionaire of PETRONIUS' *Satyricon*. Trimalchio is the subject of allusion on account of the colossal and extravagant banquet that he gave. He was the literary prototype of Jay Gatsby in F. Scott Fitzgerald's novel *The Great Gatsby* (1925), which was originally to be entitled *Trimalchio's Banquet*.

trimeter   In prosody, a line of verse containing three metrical feet in any METER. It is usually identified together with the name of the meter, as iambic trimeter, trochaic trimeter, etc.

trimurti (Sans, "three forms")   In HINDUISM, the threefold aspect of the supreme spirit made up of BRAHMĀ,

the creator, VISHNU, the preserver, and SHIVA, the destroyer. Brahmā has been largely ignored as a focus of worship, the vast majority of Hindus being devotees of Vishnu, Shiva, or their AVATARS.

Trinity (also called the Holy Trinity)   In Christianity, the name of God as he exists in his three persons or hypostases: the Father, the Son, and the Holy Spirit. They are coequal, coeternal, and indivisible. The Father is thought of especially as the Creator, the Son as the Redeemer, and the Holy Spirit as the Enlightener. The Trinitarian doctrine was evolved and enunciated in early Church councils; its various definitions have caused great controversies and schisms. The question of whether the Holy Spirit proceeds from the Father alone or from the Father and the Son, known as the *Filioque* controversy, still divides the Eastern and Western churches, the Eastern Church holding the former position.

The Latin word *trinitas* was first used c180, when the doctrine began to take form. The three-person nature of God is nowhere expressly stated in the OLD TESTAMENT. In the NEW TESTAMENT, however, the doctrine of the Trinity is expressly and frequently taught, as, for example, in 1 John 5:7.

The essence of the Trinity is considered a mystery by the Church: a full understanding is not possible through human intelligence. The Trinity can be known only through divine revelation.

The concept of a three-person god is not unique to Christianity: such a relation exists in Hindu mythology (see THREE; TRIMURTI).

Triolet, Elsa (1896–1970)   Russian-born French novelist, wife of Louis ARAGON. Triolet's novels range widely, encompassing poetic tenderness, inventive humor, and exciting adventure, as well as Marxist ideological polemic. Among her many novels are *Le Cheval blanc* (1943; tr *The White Charger*, 1946), the novel cycle *L'Age de nylon* (1959–63), *Le Grand Jamais* (1968), and *Écoutez-voir* (1968). *Le Premier Accroc coûte 200 francs* (1945; tr *A Fine of 200 Francs*, 1947) is a well-known collection of stories.

tripitaka (Pali, "three baskets")   A three-part set of sacred Buddhist writings, including the *Vinayapitaka*, rules of discipline for Buddhist monks and nuns; the *Suttapitaka*, aphorisms and parables for laymen; and the *Abhidhammapitaka*, an analytic study of consciousness and metaphysics.

Triple Alliance   (1) A treaty among England, Sweden, and Holland against Louis XIV in 1688. It ended in the treaty of Aix-la-Chapelle.

(2) A treaty among England, France, and Holland against Spain in 1717. In the following year, when Austria joined, it became the Quadruple Alliance.

(3) A military alliance initiated between Germany and Austria-Hungary in 1879, which Italy joined in 1882. It lasted until the outbreak of World War I.

triplet   In prosody, a STANZA containing three lines; also called TERCET.

Trissino, Giangiorgio (1478–1550)   Italian poet and dramatist. Born in Vicenza, Trissino wrote the first modern tragedy on Greek rather than Roman models, the SOPHONISBA. In 1547 he published a "correct" Homeric epic, *L'Italia liberata dai Goti* (*Italy Liberated from the Goths*), which had taken him twenty years.

Tristan (or Tristram)   Hero of the great medieval cycle TRISTAN AND ISEULT, and sometimes a knight of the Round Table in the legends of King Arthur (see LE MORTE D'ARTHUR). Tristan is generally depicted as a great lover, great warrior, great musician, champion dragon killer, skillful hunter, excellent seaman, poet, and marvelous teller of tales (some insist that he was an expert liar). In addition, he is supremely handsome. Due to the accidental drinking of a magic potion, his life is governed by an undying love for ISEULT the Fair, even though she is married to his uncle, King MARK of Cornwall. See PALAMEDES; TRISTRAM OF LYONESS, SIR.

Tristan and Iseult   A great medieval cycle of tales revolving about the figures of TRISTAN and ISEULT. Evolving from Celtic sources, with a theme irresistible to writers up to the present day, this legend has been called one of the world's greatest love stories. The core motif is the Celtic tale of elopement of the king's nephew with the wife of the king (see DEIRDRE; THE PURSUIT OF DIARMUID AND GRÁINNE). Tristan goes to Ireland to bring the beautiful princess Iseult to Cornwall, where she is to become the bride of his uncle, King MARK. On the way, the pair drink a potion that causes them to become eternally in love with one another; this love gives rise to the drama of the cycle. The cycle incorporates many folk themes. No major, complete version of the cycle survives. Malory's MORTE D'ARTHUR incorporates the Tristan and Iseult legend into ARTHURIAN LEGEND.

The story of Tristan and Iseult has been used by Tennyson in his *Idylls of the King*, by WAGNER in the music drama *Tristan and Isolde*, and by Edwin Arlington Robinson in TRISTRAM, to name a few. See TRISTRAM OF LYONESS, SIR.

Tristes Tropiques   See LÉVI-STRAUSS, CLAUDE.

Tristram (1927)   A narrative poem in blank verse by Edwin Arlington ROBINSON. The third of Robinson's Arthurian trilogy, preceded by *Merlin* (1917) and *Lancelot* (1920), the poem emphasizes and contrasts Tristram's love for Isolt, the wife of his old uncle, and his neglect of his own wife, Isolt of Brittany. The longed-for is unattainable, and the attainable, neglected.

Tristram of Lyoness, Sir   In *The Book of Sir Tristram of Lyoness*, from Malory's MORTE D'ARTHUR, one of the most valiant knights of the Round Table. The story was drawn from the TRISTAN AND ISEULT tradition, a cycle originally separate from the legends of Arthur. Malory makes Tristram a knight of the Round Table, second only to Sir Launcelot. In this version, King MARK is a vengeful and ignoble enemy.

Tristram Shandy (1759–1767)   A novel by Laurence STERNE, the full title of which is *The Life and Opinions of Tristram Shandy, Gentleman*. Sterne declared that his one rule was to be spontaneous and untrammeled. The novel, ostensibly a chaotic account by Tristram of his life from the time of his conception to the present, shows how much Sterne was influenced by John LOCKE's theory of the irrational nature of the association of ideas. The historian, however (except for a few brief flashes), never gets beyond the second or third year of his life. In between are sandwiched his "opinions," long-winded and philosophical reflections on everything under the sun, including his novel, and accounts of the lives of YORICK; his father, Walter Shandy; his mother; and his UNCLE TOBY. The form of the book is in fact the character of Tristram himself, doomed by improbably fantastic fatalities to write a hodgepodge instead of a history, to spend two years describing one, to describe events whose chain of causation is cosmic but whose significance is comically petty for all but the exasperated historian.

For Sterne, the actual content of consciousness, what passes through the mind of the character at a given moment, "writing to the moment," and the accompanying reactions and gestures are of primary importance.

The novel is sprinkled with many typographical eccentricities, such as a profusion of dots, dashes, asterisks, one-sentence chapters, blank pages, and unfinished sentences. See SLAWKENBERGIUS, HAFEN; TRIM, CORPORAL.

Triton   In Greek mythology, a merman. Tritons are usually depicted as blowing on conch horns and appear as minor figures in Greek legends.

Triumph of the Egg, The (1921)   A collection of "impressions from American life" by Sherwood ANDERSON. Widely held to be among Anderson's best works, the stories depict the quiet desperation of people who are unable to find in others a release from and solace for their inner loneliness. Throughout the volume, the characters' search for innocence in a world already too complicated is rendered in a poignant manner, both comic and pathetic. The title story refers to a chicken farmer whose failure is symbolized by his inability to perform a simple trick with an egg.

Triumvirate, First   In Roman history, an alliance formed (60 BC) by CAESAR, POMPEY, and Crassus to divide the power among them. Caesar received the consulship for the year 59 and a command in Cisalpine GAUL (extended to Transalpine Gaul) and Illyricum. Pompey received assignment of lands for his veterans and administration of the grain supply for himself. By a renewal of the Triumvirate in 56, Pompey received the consulship and command in Spain; Crassus obtained the consulship and command in the East, where he was killed in 53. The alliance between Pompey and Caesar was formally broken with the outbreak of civil war in 49. See RUBICON.

Triumvirate, Second   In Roman history, an alliance formed (43 BC) by Octavius (later AUGUSTUS), Mark ANTONY, and LEPIDUS. The triumvirs were to have consular power for three years; they appointed magistrates, and their decrees were valid as laws. The empire was divided among them: Octavius obtained Africa and the islands; Antony, Gaul; Lepidus, Spain and Narbonensis. The alliance was followed by the overthrow of the republicans under CASSIUS and BRUTUS at Philippi (42). Eventually, Lepidus, whose position in the alliance was minor, was banished; by the Treaty at Brundisium, Octavian received the West and Antony the East. Their union was broken in 31, and Antony was defeated at Actium. This left Octavius sole ruler, and, in gradual steps, he completed the transformation of Rome from a republic to an empire, as Augustus, its first emperor.

trochee   In English prosody, a metrical foot consisting of two syllables, the first accented and the second unaccented. The word CARE-*ful* is a trochee. The METER made up of such units is called trochaic meter, of which the following lines are a good example:

TELL me / NOT in / MOURNful / NUMbers
LIFE is / BUT an / EMPty / DREAM
FOR the / SOUL is / DEAD that / SLUMbers . . .

Longfellow ("Psalm of Life")

troglodytes   The cave dwellers in Letters XI–XIV of MONTESQUIEU's *Lettres persanes*. Their behavior illustrates satirically Montesquieu's belief that man must have a sense of justice if he is to organize and maintain society.

Troilus   In classical mythology, one of the sons of Priam. Troilus was killed by Achilles in the TROJAN WAR. The loves of Troilus and Cressida, celebrated by SHAKESPEARE and CHAUCER, form no part of the old classical tale. Their story appeared for the first time in Dares Phrygius and Dictys Cretensis, then about the 12th century in Benoît de Sainte-Maure, and in the 13th century in Guido delle Colonne. Later it passed to Boccaccio, whose IL FILOSTRATO—where PANDARUS first appears in his role of pander—was the basis of Chaucer's TROILUS AND CRISEYDE. Shakespeare's drama by the same name, TROILUS AND CRESSIDA, follows the general outline of Chaucer's narrative. In the earliest versions, Cressida, or Cressid, daughter of Calchas, a Grecian priest, is beloved by Troilus. They vow eternal fidelity to each other, and, as pledges of their vow, Troilus gives the maiden a sleeve, and Cressid gives the Trojan prince a glove. Hardly has the vow been made when an exchange of prisoners is agreed to. Diomed gives up three Trojan princes and is to receive Cressid in lieu thereof. Cressid vows to remain constant, and Troilus swears to rescue her. She is led off to the Grecian's tent, and soon gives all her affections to Diomed, even bidding him wear the sleeve that Troilus gave her in token of his love. Hence Cressida has become a byword for infidelity.

Troilus and Cressida (c1601)   A tragedy by William SHAKESPEARE. During a truce between the Greeks and Trojans in the eighth year of the Trojan siege, Troilus, a Trojan prince, pursues his beloved Cressida (see CRISEYDE), though she pretends indifference. At last, through the offices of PANDARUS, an assignation is arranged, and the two consummate their love, vowing eternal fealty. Meanwhile, Calchas, Cressida's father, who has gone over to the Greeks, accomplishes her exchange for a Trojan prisoner. She is brought to the Greek camp by Diomedes, who is taken with her beauty. After the Greeks and Trojans join in a friendly feast in ACHILLES' tent, Troilus discovers that Cressida is being unfaithful to him with Diomedes.

The subplot concerns the efforts of the Greeks to end the war and the insubordination of Achilles, who has been sulking moodily in his tent. Achilles finally bestirs himself when PATROCLUS, his closest friend, is killed by the great HECTOR, Troilus' eldest brother. After Achilles has slain the unarmed Hector, the Trojans sadly return to their city, led by Troilus, who castigates Pandarus for his lecherous offices.

The play's sources are Chaucer's TROILUS AND CRISEYDE and John LYDGATE's *Siege of Troy* (c1420).

Troilus and Criseyde (c1385)   A poem by Geoffrey CHAUCER, of 8,239 lines in RHYME ROYAL. Although based on Boccaccio's IL FILOSTRATO, Chaucer's tale has considerably more individual characterization and humor. In the first book, the Trojan prince TROILUS falls hopelessly in love with CRISEYDE, daughter of the Trojan prophet Calchas, who has fled to the Greeks, and PANDARUS offers to help him. He convinces Criseyde (Book II) that Troilus is dying of his love for her, encourages the pair to exchange letters, then arranges a meeting at a dinner given by Troilus' brother Deiphobus. Criseyde gives Troilus permission (Book III) only to serve her in the COURTLY LOVE tradition, but Pandarus soon manages to have them spend the night together in his own house. Calchas persuades the Greeks (Book IV) to demand his daughter in exchange for the return of Antenor to Troy, and the lovers bewail their separation; Criseyde promises, however, that she will contrive to return in ten days. Troilus sees her off (Book V), then immediately begins to grieve and worry. Criseyde, on the contrary, is seduced on the tenth day by the Greek Diomedes; though sincerely grieved at her infidelity to Troilus, she remains. Troilus dreams of her betrayal, hears it described by his sister CASSANDRA, the prophetess, receives evasive answers from Criseyde when he writes, but is not convinced until he sees on a piece of Diomedes' armor the brooch he himself had given Criseyde. Then he rages into battle and fights frequently with Diomedes but is finally killed by ACHILLES.

Trojan Horse   A wooden horse in which, according to legend, the Greeks entered the city of Troy during the TROJAN WAR. Unable after ten years to take the strongwalled city by force, the Greeks resorted to strategy. Under the supervision of the artisan Epeios, they built a huge, hollow wooden horse, secreted some of their best soldiers inside it, and left it before the gates of Troy. They then sailed away, leaving behind one of their number named Sinon. Pretending to hate the Greeks, who had supposedly ill-treated him, he told the Trojans that the horse was an offering to ATHENE; if brought inside the city, it would make Troy invulnerable. LAOCOÖN, a priest of APOLLO, warned them of a trick but was immediately killed, with his sons, by a pair of sea serpents. CASSANDRA's warnings also were, as usual, unheeded. The Trojans dragged the horse inside, making a breach in the wall. At night the hidden Greeks left the horse and unlocked the city's gates, and, after the other Greeks returned, Troy was quickly captured. The story was told by Homer in the ODYSSEY and by Vergil in the AENEID.

Trojan War   A war fought between Greek invaders and the defenders of Troy, probably near the beginning of the 12th century BC. The archaeological discoveries of Heinrich SCHLIEMANN and others have shown that the classical tradition that began with HOMER was based on an actual struggle for control of the important trade routes through and across the Hellespont, which were dominated by the city of Troy. About the events of this war and the return to their homes of the Greek generals, there grew up a body of myth that was recounted in the ILIAD, the ODYSSEY, a number of lost epics, plays by the Athenian dramatists, and many other works down to the present day.

According to the more familiar versions of this complex myth, the cause of the war was the episode of the golden apple (see APPLE OF DISCORD), which resulted in the abduction of HELEN, the wife of MENELAUS, king of Sparta, by the Trojan prince PARIS. Earlier, most of the rulers of Greece had been suitors for Helen's hand, and her father, TYNDAREUS, had made them swear to support the one chosen. Accordingly, they joined Menelaus and prepared to move against Troy under the leadership of AGAMEMNON, king of Mycenae. (See ATREUS, THE HOUSE OF.)

After forcing Agamemnon to sacrifice his daughter IPHIGENIA to insure fair weather, they sailed from Aulis. In the tenth year of the siege of Troy, ACHILLES withdrew from the fight in an argument with Agamemnon over possession of a female captive, but, grieved by the death of his friend PATROCLUS, he rejoined the fray and killed the Trojan leader HECTOR, son of PRIAM. By the use of the TROJAN HORSE, Greek leaders gained entrance to the walled city, and Troy was overthrown and destroyed. Except for AENEAS and his clan, most of the Trojan men were killed and the women taken captive.

Among Greek dramas dealing with the war or its aftermath are Aeschylus' *Agamemnon*, Sophocles' PHILOCTETES, and four plays by Euripides, IPHIGENIA IN AULIS, THE TROJAN WOMEN, *Helen*, and ANDROMACHE. Homer and most later Greek authors wrote of the war in a heroic vein, but Euripides consistently, if mainly by implication, attacked it as the cause of senseless horror and suffering. The fall of Troy is also recounted at the beginning of Vergil's AENEID, which claimed AENEAS as the founder of Rome.

The custom of claiming noble Trojan ancestry was widespread among European nations for a thousand years. As late as Elizabethan times, Albion (England) was said to have been founded by Brutus, a descendant of Aeneas. In the Middle Ages, the legends of the Trojan War were best known through two Latin works attributed to Dictys Cretensis and Dares Phrygius, two supposed contemporaries of the war. On these two books Benoît de Sainte-Maure (12c) based a long romance called the *Roman de Troie*, which became immensely popular and was the source in turn for many other medieval romances. See TIGER AT THE GATES.

Trojan Women, The (Troades, 415 BC)   A tragedy by EURIPIDES. It relates the fate of the family of PRIAM at the fall of Troy. Priam and HECTOR are dead; their widows, HECUBA and ANDROMACHE, and the mad CASSANDRA are to be slaves. Troy is in flames; yet the Greek generals, fearful of the future, sacrifice Hector's sister Polyxena to the ghost of ACHILLES and fling his son Astyanax from the walls to end the royal line. In the midst of the horrors, HELEN appears and, through sheer sexual attraction, easily sways her husband, MENELAUS, from his intention to kill her. Her presence, vain and frivolous as ever, demonstrates the futility of the war that was fought for her sake.

In this play, which portrays the Greeks as cruel and cowardly, Euripides implicitly rebuked the Athenians for their recent brutal slaughter of the natives of Melos for remaining neutral in the war with Sparta. It is one of the most powerful indictments of war ever written.

Trollope, Anthony (1815–1882)   English novelist, son of Frances TROLLOPE and brother of Thomas TROLLOPE. Although a post office official for many years, Trollope was a prolific writer, producing a large number of novels dealing with Victorian life. He declared that "a novel should give a picture of common life enlivened by humor and sweetened by pathos," which is a fair estimation of his own work. His best-known novels are those included in two series, the so-called Chronicles of BARSETSHIRE and the PARLIAMENTARY NOVELS, which were overshadowed by DISRAELI's popular novels of the same type. Among his other novels are *The Claverings* (1867) and *The Eustace Diamonds* (1873). He also wrote a number of travel books, a study of W. M. THACKERAY, and an *Autobiography* (1883). See BARCHESTER TOWERS.

Trollope, Frances (born Frances Milton, 1780–1863)   English author of novels and travel books, mother of Anthony and Thomas Trollope. Her first book, the famous and derogatory *Domestic Manners of the Americans* (1832), was written after a three-year stay in the United States. Thereafter she wrote many travel books and novels.

Trollope, Thomas Adolphus (1810–1892) English novelist and essayist, son of Frances TROLLOPE and elder brother of Anthony TROLLOPE. His books, which deal mainly with Italian life and history, include A *Decade of Italian Women* (1859), *Marietta* (1862), and *Beppo the Conscript* (1864).

trolls In Teutonic mythology, the dwarfs who were said to live in underground caverns or beneath hills. Trolls were represented as stumpy, misshapen, humpbacked, inclined to thievery, and fond of carrying off children and substituting their own. Because THOR used continually to fling his hammer after them, these hill people were especially averse to noise. The Troll King is a character in Ibsen's PEER GYNT.

trope (1) In rhetoric, a figure of speech employing a word or phrase out of its ordinary usage in order to give life to an idea; the most important types are METAPHOR, METON-YMY, SYNECDOCHE, and IRONY.

(2) In music, (a) historically, in liturgical music, a final melodic or verse phrase added as decoration in Gregorian chant or the sung parts of the medieval Mass; and (b) a basic group of chords in the twelve-tone scale, used by Josef Hauer (1883–1959).

Trophonius Architect. Trophonius is celebrated in Greek legend as the builder of the temple of APOLLO at Delphi. With his brother Agamedes, he also built a treasury for King Hyrieus in Boeotia but so constructed it that they could easily steal from it. When Agamedes was trapped there, Trophonius cut off his head so that he might not be recognized. After his death, Trophonius was deified and had an oracle in a cave near Lebadeia, Boeotia, which was so awe-inspiring that those who entered and consulted the oracle never smiled again. Hence a melancholy or habitually terrified man was said to have visited the cave of Trophonius.

Tropic of Cancer (1934) An autobiographical book by Henry MILLER. Originally published in Paris, *Tropic of Cancer* was immediately banned by U.S. customs officials on the grounds of obscenity. When the first American edition (1961) appeared, it became a best-seller. The book is a history of Miller's life in Paris during the early 1930s. Penniless and starving, he underwent a complete physical and spiritual degradation. The numerous philosophical ruminations that intrude on his story explain the poet's "heroic descent to the very bowels of the earth, the dark and fearsome sojourn in the belly of the whale." The poet's ascent from this abyss and his final emergence as "a bright, gory sun god cast up on an alien shore" are intended to inspire the reader with the same joy of life that Miller found after his sufferings.

Trotsky, Leon (real name Lev Davidovich Bronstein, 1879–1940) Russian Communist leader. First arrested in 1898 for his revolutionary activities, he was sent to Siberia but escaped under the alias of Leon Trotsky, the name he used for the rest of his life. After his escape, he went to London, where he worked with the exiled LENIN. Trotsky returned to Russia in 1905 to take part in the revolutionary attempt of that year. Once more he was arrested and sent to Siberia; once more he escaped. He spent the next twelve years in exile in Europe and America.

When Tsar NICHOLAS II abdicated in 1917, Trotsky again made his way home to Russia. After the BOLSHEVIKS seized power, Lenin and Trotsky emerged as the two top men in the new government, the latter becoming the commissar for foreign affairs. Trotsky negotiated the treaty of Brest-Litovsk with Germany. In 1918 he was replaced as foreign minister. As commissar for war, a position he held until 1924, he organized and directed the armies that repelled invasion on four fronts. Lenin, supported by STA-LIN, and Trotsky began to differ on ideological points as early as 1919. When Lenin died, in 1924, Stalin openly attacked Trotsky and appointed him to increasingly less important positions. In 1927 Trotsky was exiled to Turkistan and in 1929 was banished from the U.S.S.R. In 1940 Ramón Mercader murdered Trotsky with an alpenstock in Mexico City; the possibility that Mercader acted on Stalin's behalf was not substantiated at the murder trial.

Trotsky viewed the Russian Communist Party as an instrument of international revolution. He differed from Lenin and Stalin in that he was not satisfied to concentrate on the consolidation of the Russian state and withdraw active support to the cause of immediately exporting the revolution beyond the borders of the Soviet Union.

Of brilliant intellect, Trotsky wrote many important books and pamphlets on the Communist revolution. His works include *The Defence of Terrorism* (1921), *Literature and Revolution* (1925), *My Life* (1930), and *The History of the Russian Revolution* (3 vols, 1932).

Trotwood, Miss Betsey In Charles Dickens's DAVID COPPERFIELD, great-aunt of David. Miss Betsey lives with the likable lunatic Mr. Dick. Her snappishness and briskness conceal great tenderness of heart. She takes in the runaway David, defends him against Mr. Murdstone, and becomes devoted to him.

troubadours Poet-musicians of Provence in the 11th, 12th, and 13th centuries. The troubadours wrote short poems in the LANGUE D'OC, following elaborate formal conventions, principally celebrating chivalry and the tradition of COURTLY LOVE. The leading troubadours, Bertran de Born and Bernard de Ventadour, were received at the court of ELEANOR OF AQUITAINE. Through her influence Provençal poetry was introduced at the courts of northern France, and its emphasis on romantic love began to enter the verse epics there (see TROUVÈRES). Other troubadour poets include Geoffrey Rudel, Peire Vidal, Guiraut de Bornelh, and Guilhem de Cabestan.

Troubled Sleep See ROADS TO FREEDOM, THE.

trouvères Medieval poets of northern France. The trouvères wrote in the LANGUE D'OÏL, principally narrative poems like the CHANSONS DE GESTE and shorter lyrics some-

what influenced by the Provençal poetry of the TROUBA-
DOURS.

Troyat, Henri (real name Lev Tarassov, 1911–   )
Russian-born French novelist and biographer. Troyat met
with considerable success early in his career: his first novel,
Faux Jour (1935), was awarded the Prix Populiste (see
POPULISME), and his third, *L'Araigne* (1938), won the PRIX
GONCOURT; in 1959 he was elected to the ACADÉMIE FRAN-
ÇAISE. An extremely prolific author, very popular in France
and the U.S., Troyat was influenced particularly by TOL-
STOY and the sweep of history in his novels. Troyat's own
novel cycles include *Tant que la terre durera* (1947–50; tr
While the Earth Endures, 1951–58), a trilogy of
semiautobiographical novels tracing the effect of the Russian Revolution on an upper-class Russian family, and
their immigration to Paris. He is also well known for his
richly detailed biographies of Russian literary and historical
figures, among them *Dostoïevski* (1940; tr *Firebrand*,
1946), *Pouchkine* (1946; tr *Pushkin*, 1970), *Tolstoï* (1965; tr
Tolstoy, 1967), and *Catherine la grande* (1977; tr *Catherine
the Great*, 1980).

Truce of God   A Church attempt in 1041 to limit
private war. The Church decreed that there should be no
hostilities between Lent and Advent or from the Thursday
to the next Monday at the time of great festivals. This
Truce of God was confirmed by the Lateran Council in
1179 and was agreed to by England, France, Italy, and
other countries; however, little attention was ever paid to it.

Truffaut, François (1932–1984)   French film
director, one of the leading directors of the NEW WAVE,
and the original exponent of the AUTEUR THEORY. Truffaut,
like several other noted French directors of his generation,
began as a critic writing for *Cahiers du cinéma*. He was
largely responsible for the close study of and revival of
interest in Hollywood directors of the 1940s and 1950s and
was himself particularly influenced by Alfred HITCHCOCK
and Jean RENOIR. More than any other New Wave director, Truffaut communicates through his films his love for
the cinema; in fact, *Day for Night* (1973) is a film about
filmmaking, in which he acts the part of a director. His
best films reveal, with deep sensitivity and visual lyricism,
the problems, pleasures, and ecstasies of children, adolescents, and misfits. A sequence of four features the autobiographical character Antoine Doinel: *The 400 Blows* (1959),
Stolen Kisses (1966), *Bed and Board* (1970), and *Love on
the Run* (1978). Other well-known Truffaut movies
include *Shoot the Piano Player* (1960), *Jules and Jim*
(1961), *The Wild Child* (1970), *The Man Who Loved
Women* (1977), and *The Last Metro* (1981). His classic
book *Hitchcock*, an account of Truffaut's dialogues with
Alfred Hitchcock, first published in 1966, was revised and
republished in 1984.

Truman, Harry S (1884–1972)   Thirty-third president of the U.S. (1945–53). Unable to obtain a college
education, Truman managed his father's farm and clerked
in a bank. He served in the armed forces during World
War I, then started an unsuccessful business venture as a
haberdasher. Through the influence of Thomas J. Pender-
gast, the political boss of Kansas City and the surrounding
region, he won a series of public offices: county judge, presiding judge of the court, U.S. Senator from Missouri. He
had attended the Kansas City Law School for two years.

Having been elected vice president as Franklin D.
ROOSEVELT's running mate in 1944, Truman succeeded to
the presidency when Roosevelt died on April 12, 1945. He
made many momentous decisions toward the end of World
War II, perhaps the most important of which was the use of
the atomic bomb to end the war against Japan. He gave
unwavering support to the UNITED NATIONS and formulated
the Truman Doctrine of aid to the free peoples of the world
"resisting attempted subjugation by armed minorities or
outside pressures." He generally followed his predecessor's
policies in domestic matters.

In the 1948 election, Truman surprised most experts by
defeating Thomas E. Dewey. In what he regarded as his
own presidency, he gave U.S. aid to the U.N. when North
Korea, assisted by Russia and China, invaded South Korea
in 1950. To him must be credited the Marshall Plan,
designed to aid European rehabilitation and check Communist expansion. Refusing to seek a third term, Truman
returned to his home in Independence, Missouri, where he
prepared his memoirs, published as *Year of Decisions*
(1955) and *Years of Trial and Hope* (1956). He also wrote
Mr. Citizen (1960; repr *Harry Truman Speaks His Mind*,
1975).

Trumbo, Dalton (1905–1976)   American screenwriter and novelist. One of Hollywood's highest paid writers in the 1930s and 1940s, Trumbo was blacklisted and
served a prison term for his refusal—as one of the "Hollywood Ten"—to answer questions about Communist affiliations posed by the House Committee on Un-American
Activities in 1947. Living in Mexico, he continued to write
popular movie scripts, such as *Exodus* (1960), *Spartacus*
(1960), *The Sandpiper* (1965), and *The Fixer* (1968),
although some of his work in the 1950s had to be credited
to pseudonyms. He published four novels, including
JOHNNY GOT HIS GUN, all of which expressed his populist
attitudes.

Trumbull, John (1750–1831)   American poet, a
member of the HARTFORD WITS, known as the author of
satires and bombastic patriotic poems in the neo-classic
style. Trumbull's works include *The Progress of Dulness*
(1772–73), a satire on contemporary methods of education;
An Elegy on the Times (1774), a patriotic piece; M'FINGAL,
an anti-British satire, issued in more than thirty editions in
its time; essays in the style of *The Spectator*; several anonymous revolutionary essays; and a number of incidental
poems. He also collaborated with Joel BARLOW and other
members of the Hartford Wits on THE ANARCHIAD.

Trumbull, in his time the most widely read poet of the Hartford school, came of an outstanding Connecticut family and was a child prodigy. He learned to read and write at the age of two, passed the Yale entrance examinations at seven, and entered the college at thirteen. During the period just before the Revolution, he studied law in the office of John ADAMS in Boston and took part in the political agitation of the times. Later he was a representative in the Connecticut legislature and a judge in the superior and supreme courts of that state.

Ts'ao Hsueh-ch'in   See DREAM OF THE RED CHAMBER, THE.

Ts'ao-tung   See CH'AN BUDDHISM.

Tsvetayevna, Marina Ivanovna (1892–1941) Russian poet. Much of Tsvetayevna's verse was published abroad, where she lived after 1922, having supported the Whites in the civil war. Some of her best poetry, which is typically written in powerful, staccato rhythms, is based on folk literature and legends. Tsvetayevna returned to the Soviet Union in 1939; she committed suicide two years later. Her poetry was admired by Boris PASTERNAK.

Tuatha Dé Danann (Gael, "the peoples of the goddess Dana" or "Danu")   In the Gaelic MYTHOLOGICAL CYCLE, one of the five original races to invade and inhabit prehistoric Ireland. They defeated the people before them, the Fir Bolg, and also were victorious on several occasions over the Fomorians, notably in the Battle of Moytura. Ultimately they themselves were conquered by the next invaders, the Sons of Mil, last of the five races. After defeating the Tuatha Dé Danann, the Sons of Mil came to worship them as gods. Traditionally, they were given the lower half (underground) of Ireland, and they are said to dwell there, in the mounds, to this day. Among the heroes of the Tuatha Dé Danann who later were worshiped as gods by Sons of Mil are Dadga, LUG, Mananaan Mac Lir, Morrigan, and Ogma. In modern folklore, the Tuatha Dé Danann are the Irish faeries and come out of the mounds on SAMAIN Eve.

Tubalcain   In the OLD TESTAMENT, the third son of Lamech and Zillah. Tubalcain was the first smith, "an instructor of every artificer in brass and iron" (Gen 4:22).

Tuchman, Barbara W[ertheim] (1912–   ) American historian. Tuchman's histories are noted for their narrative power and for their portrayal of the protagonists in world dramas as believable human beings. Meaning, in her view, emerges not from preconceived design but from the aggregation of details and events that fall into a pattern. Tuchman won her first PULITZER PRIZE for *The Guns of August* (1962), a detailed military and diplomatic history of World War I. Her second came with *Stilwell and the American Experience in China, 1911–1945* (1971), a careful review of the shaping of America's China policy. A *Distant Mirror* (1978), which began as a study of the bubonic plague in Europe, became an exhaustive account of France in the 14th century. Among her other works are

Practicing History (1981) and the best-selling *The March of Folly* (1984), a historical examination of four situations mismanaged by governments, from the Trojan Horse and Britain's loss of its colonies to the war in Vietnam.

Tudor period   The period in English history from 1485 to 1603, when the throne was occupied by the Tudor family. It includes the English RENAISSANCE. The monarchs were HENRY VII, HENRY VIII, EDWARD VI, MARY I, and ELIZABETH I. See ELIZABETHAN.

Tu Fu (712–770)   Chinese poet of the T'ANG dynasty. Tu Fu is considered by the Chinese to be their greatest poet and is almost always mentioned in the same breath with LI PO, whom he knew and greatly admired. His poetry exploits fully the difficult forms of verse popular during the T'ang dynasty and contains many poignant descriptions of his personal misfortunes during the AN LU-SHAN REBELLION. Tu Fu's CONFUCIANISM and sober dedication to government service contrast strongly with Li Po's Taoist exuberance (see TAOISM).

Tuileries   One of the oldest palaces in Paris. Its superb gardens were laid out by LOUIS XIV. The original palace, begun by CATHERINE DE MÉDICIS, is no longer in existence. The name means "tileyard," from the previous use of the site it occupies.

Turgenev, Ivan Sergeyevich (1818–1883)   Russian novelist. Turgenev was born in Orel, in south-central Russia, and raised on the family estate at Spasskoye. His childhood was troubled by continual ill will between his mother and father. His mother's feelings of resentment were often taken out on the children and servants.

In 1837 Turgenev graduated from the University of St. Petersburg, and the following year he went to Germany to continue his studies at the University of Berlin, concentrating on classical languages, literature, and especially philosophy. Among his fellow Russian students at the university was Nikolay Stakevich (1813–40), who had headed one of the famous philosophical circles of students at Moscow University in the early 1830s. Another fellow student was the future anarchist leader Mikhail BAKUNIN. The intense interest in philosophical questions, the incessant talk, and the personality of Bakunin were all used to some extent in Turgenev's first novel, *Rudin* (1855). In 1841 Turgenev returned to Russia, intending to have a career as a philosopher. The government abolished the teaching of philosophy, however, and the idle scholar spent his time going to the theatre, carrying on a romance with Tatyana Bakunin, Mikhail's sister, and meeting the leaders of the intelligentsia. In 1843 he met the renowned Vissarion BELINSKY, with whom he established a close friendship. Turgenev's mother objected to his idleness, and in June he obtained a minor appointment in the civil service, a job he held for almost two years.

During the winter of 1843, Turgenev had one of the most fateful meetings of his life, with Pauline Viardot-Garcia, a singer married to the French writer Louis Viardot.

Turgenev fell in love with her almost at once, and the unrequited relationship continued for the rest of Turgenev's life. Pauline continued to live with her husband and to pursue her singing career, returning to Russia for concerts in each of the winters between 1843 and 1846. She did not return in 1846, however, and Turgenev went to France to see her. He lived on the Viardot estate and in Paris from 1847 to 1850. During this period, he wrote the work that was to bring him his first literary success, A SPORTSMAN'S SKETCHES. He also wrote some of his best plays at this time, including A MONTH IN THE COUNTRY.

Turgenev's mother having died in 1850, he was financially independent and was freed from having to write all the time for a living. He became a member of the editorial board of *Sovremennik* (*The Contemporary*), which was headed at that time by the poet Nikolay Nekrasov. Turgenev left this literary milieu in 1856 to go abroad again; he returned to Russia in 1858, and during that summer he lived on his estate at Spasskoye, completing his second novel, A NEST OF GENTLEFOLK. In 1860 appeared his third novel, ON THE EVE, and the autobiographical story "Pervaya lyubov" ("First Love"). *On the Eve* did not appear in *The Contemporary*, as had most of Turgenev's previous work. The journal had virtually been taken over by the radical critics CHERNYSHEVSKY and DOBROLYUBOV. Turgenev disagreed with their utilitarian view of literature, and they thought him too much of an aesthete. Another literary quarrel beset Turgenev in 1860. The novelist Ivan GONCHAROV, whose mental health was in decline, accused Turgenev of having plagiarized his novel *Obryv* (*The Precipice*, 1859) for parts of *On the Eve* and of having intercepted his letters to steal his ideas. Turgenev demanded that a panel of three literary men judge the case. This was done, and Turgenev was cleared. The novelist had more trouble to face, however, when his major novel, FATHERS AND SONS, was published. The depiction of the central character, Bazarov, outraged both conservatives and radicals. The furor of criticism induced Turgenev to leave Russia, and thereafter he returned to his native land only for short visits. His next novel, SMOKE, was in part a retaliation against the radicals and the conservatives. Neither, Turgenev maintained, were on the right track. There was nothing in Russia or in the Russians worth working with. The salvation of the country would come, Turgenev claimed, by turning to the civilization of the West. *Smoke* was, naturally, not well received in Russia, a fact that further embittered Turgenev. The novel also was the central point of a famous argument in Baden-Baden between Turgenev and DOSTOYEVSKY. The two men had not been on good terms since the 1840s, when both had been in the circle of young writers gathered around the critic Belinsky. At that time, Turgenev had reputedly outraged the sensitive Dostoyevsky with his barbed wit, and now Dostoyevsky supposedly paid back Turgenev by needling him about the poor reception of *Smoke*.

Turgenev's best work of his late years is the short novel *Veshnye vody* (*Torrents of Spring*, 1872). His last attempt at a novel, VIRGIN SOIL, was another effort to deal with the revolutionaries in Russia, and again Turgenev met hostile criticism. Ill with cancer of the spine, he made a few visits to Russia in his last years. On one of these visits, he made peace with TOLSTOY after a rift of almost twenty years. In 1882 *Stikhotvoreniya v proze* (*Poems in Prose*), his last notable work, was published. Turgenev died in 1883 on the estate at Bougival, France, which he shared with the Viardots. Pauline Viardot was at his bedside.

Turgenev was the first major Russian novelist of the late 19th century to become well known outside his own country. His reputation in the West diminished somewhat when the more powerful talents of Tolstoy and Dostoyevsky were revealed, but the esteem accorded Turgenev's artistic ability remained high.

Turm, Der   See TOWER, THE.

Turner, Frederick Jackson (1861–1932)   American historian. Turner is best known for his "frontier hypothesis," which he first presented at a meeting of the American Historical Association in 1893, in a paper called *The Significance of the Frontier in American History* (1894). Rejecting the traditional emphasis on the influence of the East and of Anglo-Saxon political institutions, Turner claimed that the form and spirit of American democracy were the direct product of the frontier, with its free land, its stimulation of ingenuity and resourcefulness, and its dominant individualism. His thesis was immediately recognized as a historical idea of great importance, and it opened up a new area for historical investigation; later historians, however, have challenged many of his interpretations.

Turner, Joseph Mallord William (1775–1851)   English painter. His earliest successes were accurately represented landscapes, influenced by Claude LORRAIN and by 17th-century Dutch marine painting. In the early 1800s, however, inspired by a visit to Paris, where he saw the artworks plundered by Napoleon, he began to paint the romantic landscapes for which he became famous. *Crossing the Brook* (c1815) exemplifies this development. Subsequent visits to Italy resulted in his increased concern with the power of light and atmosphere and in his growing tendency toward abstraction. This later style, epitomized in his *Rain, Steam and Speed* (1844), though at the time generally rejected by critics and public alike, was extolled by John RUSKIN in his famous *Modern Painters* (1843) and was supported by a few loyal patrons. The true impact of these controversial works could be seen only in retrospect, as they had anticipated the impressionist movement by some forty years.

Turn of the Screw, The (1898)   A novella by Henry JAMES. It is told from the viewpoint of the leading character, a governess in love with her employer, who goes to an isolated English estate to take charge of Miles and

Flora, two attractive and precocious children. She gradually realizes that her young charges are under the evil influence of two ghosts, Peter Quint, the ex-steward, and Miss Jessel, their former governess. At the climax of the story, she enters into open conflict with the children, as a result of which Flora is alienated and Miles dies of fright. Some critics, notably Edmund Wilson, have interpreted the ghosts as products of the disordered mind of the governess, but most critics now agree that James intended them to have actual, objective existence, even though their exact nature remains ambiguous. The story was dramatized by William Archibald as *The Innocents* (1950) and was made into an opera by BENJAMIN BRITTEN (1954) and a movie in 1961.

Turpin, Archbishop (d 800?)   French churchman, elected archbishop of Reims about 753. According to some legends, such as the *Chanson de* ROLAND, Turpin was the religious leader among CHARLEMAGNE's paladins and died with Roland at Roncesvalles in 778. More frequently, he is erroneously considered the author of the *Historia de vita Caroli Magni et Rolandi* (usually called the *Chronicle of Charlemagne*), a Latin history of Charlemagne's exploits in Spain, actually written by monks in the 11th and 12th centuries.

Turpin, Richard (known as Dick Turpin, 1706–1739)   English highwayman. Turpin has been the subject of many ballads and legends. The incident of his famous ride from London to York in a single night on his steed, Black Bess, to establish an alibi first appeared in the novel *Rookwood* (1834), the fictionalized account of Turpin's life by Harrison Ainsworth. Turpin was finally hanged at York, having been convicted of horse stealing.

Tushina, Lizaveta Nikolayevna   In Dostoyevsky's THE POSSESSED, the young woman who gives herself to STAVROGIN, only to learn that he is incapable of returning love to anyone. She is murdered by a rampaging mob at the scene of the fire where the Labyadkins are killed.

Tutuola, Amos (1920–   )   Nigerian novelist. Tutuola, who received little formal education, was the first African writer to achieve international fame. This came with the publication of his first novel, *The Palm-Wine Drinkard and His Dead Palm-Wine Tapster in the Dead's Town* (1952), an immensely imaginative allegorical epic, mingling the mythical and the magical with the trappings of the real world to create a unique modern fantasy. Tutuola's ungrammatical English, initially an embarrassment to African critics, has come to be appreciated as an unusually expressive use of the language. His other novels include *My Life in the Bush of Ghosts* (1954), *Simbi and the Satyr of the Dark Jungle* (1958), *The Brave African Huntress* (1958), *Feather Woman of the Jungle* (1962), *Ajaiyi and His Inherited Poverty* (1967), *The Witch-Herbalist of the Remote Town* (1981), and *The Wild Hunter in the Bush of Ghosts* (1982).

Tuwhare, Hone (1922–   )   New Zealand poet. Tuwhare is the most prominent Maori poet writing in English. His immensely popular volume *No Ordinary Sun* (1964) successfully combined traditional Maori verse with English forms. The title refers to the atomic bomb. Among his other volumes of verse are *Making a Fist of It* (1978), *Selected Poems* (1980), and *Year of the Dog* (1982).

Tvardovsky, Aleksandr Trifonovich (1910–1971)   Russian poet and editor. Tvardovsky's first book of poems was *Put k sotsializmu* (*The Road to Socialism*, 1931). In 1936 he published *Strana Muraviya* (*The Land of Muravia*), a long narrative poem for which he received a Stalin Prize. His best-known work, *Vasily Tyorkin* (tr 1975), another narrative poem about a jovial, courageous soldier, was published between 1941 and 1945 in installments. At the height of the THAW, Tvardovsky published parts of a long poem, *Za dalyu dal'* (*Horizon beyond Horizon*, 1956), which advocates literary freedom. He was editor of *Novy mir*, the Soviet literary journal known for its often liberal tendencies during its greatest years, 1958–70, when it published such works as Solzhenitsyn's ONE DAY IN THE LIFE OF IVAN DENISOVICH.

Twain, Mark (pen name of Samuel Langhorne Clemens, 1835–1910)   American humorist, newspaperman, lecturer, and writer. Born in Florida, Missouri, Twain drew on his boyhood along the Mississippi River for many of the characters and incidents in his work. His formal schooling ended early, and he learned the printing trade. In 1853, after writing for newspapers in Hannibal, Missouri, he left for St. Louis, Philadelphia, and New York. He returned to the river in 1857 and became a Mississippi steamboat pilot until the Civil War put an end to river traffic. He wrote of this period in LIFE ON THE MISSISSIPPI. He took his pen name from river slang for "two fathoms deep."

In a Nevada mining camp, Twain met Artemis WARD and learned from him the technique of giving successful, humorous lectures. Next he went to California as a roving correspondent and worked for Bret HARTE. His fame as a humorist and storyteller was established with the publication of THE CELEBRATED JUMPING FROG OF CALAVERAS COUNTY. Lecturing increased his reputation, but it was THE INNOCENTS ABROAD, the product of a European trip, that gave him a firm place in the world of letters. The success of this book also gave him enough financial security to marry Olivia Langdon.

Twain also wrote the autobiographical *Roughing It* (1872), TOM SAWYER, *1601* (q.v.), *The Gilded Age* (1873), *A Tramp Abroad* (1880), THE PRINCE AND THE PAUPER, HUCKLEBERRY FINN, and A CONNECTICUT YANKEE IN KING ARTHUR'S COURT. After a protracted European lecture tour, during which one of his daughters died, he returned to write such books as *The Tragedy of* PUDD'NHEAD WILSON, THE MAN THAT CORRUPTED HADLEYBURG, and THE MYSTERIOUS STRANGER. These and his other writings of the time revealed a growing misanthropy. In his last years, Twain became a bitter satirist, famous for cynical epigrams. He had by this time lost his second daughter and his wife.

A careful and conscious artist, Twain as a humorist was a master of the techniques of exaggeration, irreverence, and deadpan solemnity. He was unsurpassed as a creator of character, preeminently in the immortal Huck Finn, and as a keen observer of the social scene. Sensitive to the sound of language, he introduced colloquial speech into American fiction.

'Twas the Night Before Christmas   The popular title of A VISIT FROM ST. NICHOLAS.

Tweed, William Marcy (1823–1878)   American politician, head of TAMMANY HALL. Known as "Boss" Tweed, he and the Tweed Ring of politicians swindled the treasury of New York City out of millions of dollars. Thomas NAST's remarkable cartoons in *Harper's Weekly* and the editorial views of the *New York Times* (1870) were significant influences in arousing public opinion against this corruption.

Tweedledum and Tweedledee   Names created by John Byrom (1692–1763), satirizing two quarreling but negligibly different schools of musicians; hence, names used to indicate people whose persons or opinions are "as like as two peas."

Lewis Carroll introduced Tweedledum and Tweedledee, in the persons of two quarrelsome but identical schoolboys, in THROUGH THE LOOKING GLASS, where they sing the famous ditty "The Walrus and the Carpenter."

Twelfth Night   January 5, the eve of Twelfth Day, the Feast of the EPIPHANY, twelve days after Christmas. It was formerly a time of great merry-making, as the end of the secular celebration of Christmas.

Twelfth Night; or What You Will (c1600)   A comedy by SHAKESPEARE. The main plot hinges on the physical likeness between Sebastian and his twin sister, Viola, who are separated after a shipwreck off the coast of Illyria, each believing the other to be dead. Disguising herself as a boy and taking the name of Cesario, Viola becomes the page of ORSINO, the duke of Illyria, and falls in love with him. The duke, however, cherishes a hopeless passion for Olivia, who is in mourning for her dead brother and, aided by her pompous steward MALVOLIO, has forced her entire household to share her grief. When Cesario is sent by the duke to further his suit, Olivia is instantly smitten with the disguised Viola. Arriving in Illyria, Sebastian is mistaken for the page by Olivia, who sends for a priest and marries the astonished young man. The ensuing confusion is cleared up when Viola and Sebastian meet and recognize each other. Yielding Olivia to Sebastian, the duke decides to marry Viola, who has confessed her love for him.

The subplot concerns the machinations of MARIA, Sir Toby BELCH, and Sir Andrew AGUECHEEK against the pretentious Malvolio. The efforts to remove him from Olivia's favor result in some of the finest low comedy in Shakespeare.

The play is based on an old Italian comedy, *Gl'ingannati* (1537), and later versions of it by Bandello, Belleforest, and Barnabe Riche.

Twelve, The (Dvenadtsat, 1918)   A long poem by Aleksandr BLOK, which is regarded as one of the best literary works produced by the RUSSIAN REVOLUTION. The scene is the chaotic streets of St. Petersburg in the early days of the revolution. The chaos is indicated by a striking mixture of poetry, bits of popular songs, and coarse colloquialisms. The twelve are a detachment of Red Guards patrolling the snowy streets. An ambiguous note was introduced when Blok inserted the figure of JESUS at the end of the poem. Blok's own explanation for this insertion did little to clarify its meaning.

Twenty-six Men and a Girl (Dvadtsat shest i odna, 1899)   A short story by Maksim GORKY. A group of wretched, slaving bakery workers have a glimpse of joy each day when a pretty young girl comes to buy their buns. Their adoration for her turns to bitter rage when a swaggering boor bets them he can seduce the girl and succeeds.

Twenty Thousand Leagues under the Sea (Vingt Mille Lieues sous les mers, 1870)   A romance by Jules VERNE, remarkable for its prognostication of the invention of deep-sea submarines. The central characters of the tale, in the process of exploring marine disturbances, are captured by the megalomaniacal Captain Nemo. An undersea tour in a strange craft and their ensuing escape conclude the work.

Twenty Years After   See THREE MUSKETEERS, THE.

Twice-Told Tales (1837, 1842)   A collection of tales and sketches by Nathaniel HAWTHORNE. The name of the volume is probably derived from the line in Shakespeare's *King John*: "Life is as tedious as a twice-told tale." Among the most interesting pieces are "Howe's Masquerade," "The Grey Champion," "The Great Carbuncle," and "The Minister's Black Veil."

Twicknam Garden (1633)   A poem by John DONNE. The poem concerns the grief caused the poet by the paradoxes of fidelity and falseness in love. It is notable for its intensity of feeling and brilliance of conceit.

Two Cultures, The (1959)   A controversial speech and pamphlet by C. P. SNOW. It claims that scientists are not sufficiently appreciated and that English society is divided into two cultures: the scientific on the one hand, and the literary and humanistic, on the other. The literary and humanistic culture is of upper-middle-class origin, part of the ESTABLISHMENT, and conservative. The scientific culture is of lower-middle-class origin but at the center of progress.

Two Deaths of Christopher Martin, The   See PINCHER MARTIN.

Two Gentlemen of Verona, The (c1592)   A comedy by SHAKESPEARE. The "two gentlemen" are Valentine and Proteus, close friends at first but later rivals for the hand of Silvia, daughter of the duke of Milan, who wants her to marry the foolish and cowardly Thurio. Proteus forgets his old love, Julia, plays his friend false, and brings about his banishment. Silvia escapes to the forest to join Valentine, who has become an outlaw, and is pursued by Proteus and his page, who is really the doting Julia in disguise. Proteus finds Silvia and is about to make her submit to him when she is rescued by Valentine, who generously forgives his wayward friend. The duke then arrives on the scene and, impressed by Valentine's manly conduct, freely bestows his daughter upon him, while the repentant Proteus contents himself with marrying Julia.

The play is one of Shakespeare's lesser comedies. Its principal source is Jorge de Montemayor's *Diana* (1559), and its form is based on the early Italian comedies.

Two Noble Kinsmen, The (pub 1634)   A romantic drama by John FLETCHER, which was probably written in collaboration with SHAKESPEARE. The play takes place in Athens after the defeat of Thebes by THESEUS. Two valiant Theban knights, Palamon and Arcite, spy Theseus' sister-in-law Emilia from their prison window. Each immediately falls in love with her. Later Arcite is released, and Palamon escapes with the help of the jailer's daughter. They meet and duel in a forest, where they are discovered by Theseus, who plans a great tournament. The winner will have the hand of Emilia; the loser will be executed. Palamon loses the tournament and is about to be beheaded when word comes that Arcite has been killed in a fall from his horse. With his last breath, Arcite relinquishes his right to Emilia's hand in Palamon's favor. The story of Palamon and Arcite was first told in Boccaccio's TESEIDA. See MASSINGER, PHILIP.

Two Serious Ladies (1943)   The only novel by Jane BOWLES. The two protagonists, Christina Goering and Frieda Copperfield, who meet each other only twice, pursue the parallel but opposite goals of sainthood (Goering) and self-fulfillment (Copperfield). In a series of surreal encounters with strange characters, the fates of the two women are ironically juxtaposed, as Miss Goering entertains a succession of men who are ineffectual failures, and Mrs. Copperfield discovers the world of sensuality through a Panamanian prostitute. The book enjoyed a considerable underground popularity and was reissued in Bowles's *Collected Works* (1966) and again in *My Sister's Hand in Mine* (1978).

Two Views (Zwei Ansichten, 1965; tr 1966)   A novel by Uwe JOHNSON. In chapters alternating the man's and the woman's point of view, the book describes the tenuous attachment, established by a casual night of love, between a West German photographer and an East German nurse. When she wishes to leave the East for personal reasons, he helps her to escape. Once in West Germany, however, she returns to her profession, refuses marriage, and leaves him to his vacuous life. The novel is a fairly direct statement of the impossibility of real communication and understanding between the two Germanys.

Two Years before the Mast (1840)   A narrative by Richard Henry DANA, Jr. It is based on his own journal, written while he was a sailor. The book dwells on the brutality of the ship's captain and the sailors' lack of redress. It did much to arouse public opinion and led to legal action. In 1859 Dana added a final chapter, describing a second trip to California. He continues the stories of several men he mentioned in the earlier part of the narrative. The book influenced both MELVILLE and CONRAD.

Tybalt   See ROMEO AND JULIET.

Tyche   Literally "Fortune." Originally the Greek goddess of chance. Later in antiquity, she was worshiped as the goddess of good fortune, who allots wealth and power to mortals. She is variously represented with a horn of plenty, a wheel, a rudder, or a ball.

Tydeus   In classical mythology, one of THE SEVEN AGAINST THEBES.

Tyler, Moses Coit (1835–1900)   American literary historian and reformer. Tyler was called to Cornell in 1881 to occupy the first chair of American history established in the U.S. One of the first scholars to examine American literature critically, he wrote *A History of American Literature 1607–1765* (1878), *Three Men of Letters* (1895), and *The Literary History of the American Revolution, 1763–1783* (1897).

Tyler, Royall (1757–1826)   American jurist, dramatist, and novelist. Tyler is remembered as the virtual founder of American drama. His play *The Contrast* (1787) was the first comedy to be written by a native-born American. Tyler also wrote *The Georgia Spec, or Land in the Moon* (1797), a comedy satirizing the *Yazoo* real estate fraud, and *The Algerine Captive* (1797), a novel noted chiefly for its preface, which contains the first significant plea for native American fiction.

Tyler's Rebellion (also called the Peasants' Revolt)   Insurrection in 1381 of the peasants of Kent and Essex. They demanded abolition of serfdom, the poll tax, and all restrictions on the freedom of labor and trade. Under the leadership of Wat Tyler, they sacked Canterbury and several official buildings in London. The young Richard II met with Tyler and was having charters drawn up acceding to his demands, but Tyler insolently presented fresh demands the next day, and in the fighting that ensued Tyler was killed by William Walworth, Lord Mayor of London. In 1382 Parliament revoked the concessions that Richard had made. John Gower described the revolt in his VOX CLAMANTIS; Robert SOUTHEY, in his dramatic poem *Wat Tyler* (1817).

Tynan, Kenneth Peacock (1927–1980)   English drama critic. Immensely influential during the 1950s and '60s, Tynan eloquently supported the raw new drama of the ANGRY YOUNG MEN and was a leading figure in the post-World War II renaissance of the British theatre. He was literary manager of the National Theatre for most of the 1960s and published several books, including *Tynan Right and Left* (1967). He devised and co-wrote the musical *Oh! Calcutta!* (1969), which ran for many years in London and New York.

Tyndale, William (d 1536)   English Protestant preacher, known for his translation of the Bible into English. It was first printed at Cologne in 1525. Tyndale sent copies of his translation into England for distribution, but they were condemned by the bishops and burned. Tyndale also wrote pamphlets supporting the authority of the Bible and the king over the power of the Church and the Pope, and for a while was favored by King HENRY VIII, although he soon lost this favor when he disapproved of the king's divorce. He carried on a vigorous controversy with Sir Thomas MORE. In 1536, Tyndale was strangled and burned at the stake in Antwerp as a heretic. See BIBLE, ENGLISH VERSIONS.

Tyndareus   Mythical king of Sparta, husband of LEDA. After years in exile, Tyndareus was restored to the Spartan throne by HERACLES. There is considerable debate as to whether Tyndareus or ZEUS was the father of Leda's children, HELEN, CLYTEMNESTRA, and CASTOR AND POLYDEUCES. APHRODITE is said to have turned his daughters into adulteresses to punish Tyndareus for forgetting her at a sacrifice. Helen left MENELAUS with PARIS; Clytemnestra, with her lover Aegisthus, murdered her husband, AGAMEMNON.

Tynyanov, Yury Nikolayevich (1894–1943) Russian literary critic and prose writer. After studying at the University of St. Petersburg, Tynyanov joined the Petrograd Society for the Study of Poetic Language, or OPOYAZ. He became a prominent supporter of the formalist movement in Russian literary criticism, while lecturing on poetry at the Petrograd State Institute of Art History. Of his works translated into English, *O literaturnoy evolyutsii* (1927; tr *On Literary Evolution*, 1971) best represents Tynyanov's critical focus on the dynamics of literary history. As the 1920s proved increasingly hostile to formalist methods, Tynyanov turned to historical fiction. He produced *Smert Vazir Mukhtara* (1929; tr *Death and Diplomacy in Persia*, 1938), a novel depicting the demise of GRIBOYEDOV, and *Podporuchik Kizhe* (1927; tr *Second Lieutenant Asfor*, 1965), a satire of tsarist bureaucracy.

Typee: A Peep at Polynesian Life (1846)   A novel by Herman MELVILLE. Based on Melville's own experiences, the story tells of the hero and his friend Toby, who jump ship in the Marquesas Islands and wander mistakenly into the valley of Typee, which is inhabited by cannibals. The Typees become their benevolent captors, refusing to allow them to leave. Toby escapes, while the hero, suffering from a leg wound, remains to be nursed by the lovely Fayaway. Tempted to enjoy a somnolent, vegetative

existence, the moral American chooses, with regret, to return to civilization. The novel is a disjointed romance, adventure story, and travelogue, Melville's apprentice work before writing the more successful OMOO.

Typhon   A fire-breathing monster, the father of the SPHINX, the CHIMAERA, and other monsters. Typhon is often identified with Typhoeus, a son of Tartarus and GE, who begot the unfavorable winds or, according to other stories, is himself one of them. As one of the Hundred-handed Giants (Hekatoncheires), he warred against the gods and was banished by ZEUS to TARTARUS, under Mount Aetna. Typhon is also the name used by the Greeks for the Egyptian SET, the god of evil, who killed his brother (or father) OSIRIS.

Typhoon (1903)   A short novel by Joseph CONRAD. The stolid, seamanly Captain MacWhirr rides out a tempest and brings his crew and his cargo of Chinese passengers to safety.

Tyr   The god of battle in Nordic legend, second in importance to his brother THOR. Tyr was one-handed since the day FENRIS-WOLF bit off the hand he had placed in its mouth as a pledge; thus, in battle, he could give victory only to one side. Also patron of athletic sports, he possessed a magic sword, which was said to insure victory.

tyrant   An absolute ruler. In ancient Greece, the tyrant was merely the absolute ruler, the despot of a state. At first the word had no implication of cruelty or what we call tyranny. Many of the Greek tyrants were excellent rulers, such as PISISTRATUS and PERICLES, of Athens; Periander, of Corinth; Dionysius the Younger, Gelon, and his brother Hiero, of Syracuse; Phidion, of Argos; POLYCRATES, of Samos. The word *tyrannos* soon, however, obtained much the same meaning that "tyrant" has today.

Tyrtaeus   A lame schoolmaster and elegiac poet of Athens. Tyrtaeus is said so to have inspired the Spartans by his songs that they defeated the Messenians (7th century BC).

Tyutchev, Fyodor Ivanovich (1803–1873)   Russian poet. After graduating from Moscow University in 1821, Tyutchev entered the diplomatic service and spent twenty years abroad, mostly in Germany. While there he became the friend of HEINE and SCHELLING. He was one of the first Russian translators of Heine. Tyutchev wrote and published in literary journals during his years in the diplomatic service. It was not until the mid-1850s that his work was issued in a separate volume. From that time on, he was held in high esteem as a poet. His renown faded somewhat toward the end of the 19th century. It was revived through the influence of the SYMBOLIST poets, who considered Tyutchev one of their precursors. A distinctive feature of his work is his nature poetry, which often deals with the duality caused by the apparent order of the universe and the chaos that lies just beneath this order. This idea is expressed clearly in one of his most famous lyrics, "Ne to chto mnite vy priroda" ("Nature Is Not What You Think,"

1836). A duality of feeling is also evident in Tyutchev's love poems, where love is sometimes called "the key of life" and sometimes an "unequal struggle of two hearts." Many of his finest love lyrics were occasioned by his affair with Elena Aleksandrovna Deniseva, his children's governess. Among the more famous of Tyutchev's poems are "Silentium" (1833) and "Son na more" ("Dream at Sea," 1836).

Tzara, Tristan (pen name of Samuel Rosenfeld, 1896–1963)   Romanian-born French poet, best known for having founded the DADA movement in 1916. The first dada text, Tzara's *La Premiere Aventure céleste de M. Antipyrine*, was published in 1916. Tzara went on to write a great many more dramatic or epic poems in a surrealistic style, among them *L'Homme approximatif* (1931; tr in *The Approximate Man and Other Writings*, 1973), *La Fuite* (1947), *La Face intérieure* (1953), and *Parler seul* (1956).

U

Übermensch (Ger, "superman") A term in Nietzsche's THUS SPAKE ZARATHUSTRA. The word, which had first occurred, only in passing, in Goethe's FAUST, was used by Nietzsche to designate the goal of human existence. Despite the Nazi interpretation of his works, Nietzsche did not believe that the Germans were a race of supermen, nor did he believe that self-discipline and training, or racial purity, would ever develop such a race. The substance of his belief was simply that whereas every distinct human culture has its own unique goals, there exists a single universal human goal, the sum of all particular cultural goals, and this is the "Übermensch." He believed that man should completely commit himself to his earthly goals, that he should sacrifice his life for them, and that out of the self-destruction resulting from such sacrifice, the "Übermensch" would arise. It is not clear whether Nietzsche conceived of the "Übermensch" as an actual being or as an idea.

Ubu roi (1896; tr Ubu Roi, 1951) A play by Alfred JARRY which grew out of a farce written with a classmate at fifteen to ridicule a pompous math teacher. A stylized burlesque, this play satirizes the tendency of the successful bourgeois to abuse his authority and to become irresponsibly complacent. The hero's scatological language and absurdly inappropriate posturings, along with his grotesque physical proportions, anticipated characteristics of the DADA movement and, later, of the THEATRE OF THE ABSURD. Jarry wrote other, less successful parodies in the Ubu cycle collected in *Tout Ubu* (1962; tr *Ubu Plays*, 1969).

Uccello, Paolo (real name Paolo di Dono, 1397–1475) Florentine painter. Uccello's works, such as *St. George and the Dragon*, have the charming simplicity of a toylike world because of their decorative use of simplified forms and sharply outlined patterns of color. His best-known works are the three battle scenes he painted to commemorate the defeat of the Sienese by the Florentines at San Romano in 1432.

Udall, Nicholas See RALPH ROISTER DOISTER.

Ugly Duckling, The A fairy tale by Hans Christian ANDERSEN about a cygnet hatched among ducklings and mocked as an ungainly member of the brood, until finally he grows into a swan.

Ugolino, Count of Pisa (c1220–1289) Guelph leader whose history is one of the most famous episodes in Dante's *Inferno*. He is found frozen in the ice of the ninth circle, that of the traitors, gnawing on the head of the Ghibelline Archbishop Ruggiero, who was Ugolino's ally in the betrayal of Pisa, then turned on him and imprisoned him with his four sons until they starved to death.

Uhland, Ludwig (1787–1862) German romantic poet. He is most famous for his ballads in folk style. He was a serious student of folklore, and his collection of *Alte hoch- und niederdeutsche Volkslieder* (*Old South and North German Folk-Songs*, 1844–45) is an important scholarly work. His dramas, *Herzog Ernst von Schwaben* (*Duke Ernst of Swabia*, 1818) and *Ludwig der Bayer* (*Ludwig the Bavarian*, 1819), seek to further both regional and national cultural awareness in Germany. Uhland himself was a politically active liberal. See GERMAN ROMANTICISM.

ukiyoe Japanese woodblock prints. The name means, literally, "pictures of the floating world," referring to the ephemeral nature of the pictures themselves and to the transience of the people and scenes they depicted. Originally anonymous genre paintings in the 16th century, the movement evolved over the next two centuries to encompass popular woodblock prints depicting, for instance, prostitutes, circuses, and the kabuki theatre.

Beginning with the black-and-white line illustrations of Hishikawa Moronobu (c1625–c1695), and later hand-tinted black-and-white prints, the art of *ukiyoe* culminated in the sophisticated and meticulously executed color prints called *benizuri-e*. These prints inspired Western painters of the 19th century, such as WHISTLER, CASSATT, and MONET, and the popular fashion and design trend of *japonisme*. The prints were designed to appeal to the masses; they were shunned by contemporary intellectuals and members of the upper classes. In spite of their beauty and the intricacy of their production, which represented a collaboration of skilled artists, engravers, and printers, their cost was minimal. After the art declined in the 19th century, they became attractive to Western connoisseurs and increased in value.

Ulalume (1847)   A poem by Edgar Allan POE. It was composed at the request of an elocutionist who wanted a poem for recitation. The narrator and his soul walk in a "ghoul-haunted woodland" on Halloween. They are stopped, as they follow the planet Venus, by the door of the forgotten tomb of the narrator's beloved, the lost Ulalume.

Ullikummi   See KUMARBI.

Ulster   The northernmost province of Ireland. It was forfeited to the Crown in James I's reign in consequence of the rebellions of Tyrconnel and Tyrone, and colonized (1609–12) by English and Scottish Protestant settlers, who were forbidden to sell land to any Irishman. Since then the Ulstermen have been intensely anti-Irish in sentiment and action and have refused on any terms to coalesce with the original Catholic inhabitants who have ever been anti-British. When Ireland gained its independence in 1920, six of the nine Ulster counties chose to remain united with England under the name of Northern Ireland. The Irish Republic never accepted this partition as permanent and in 1968 violence erupted in the north, leading to a prolonged period of terrorism and repression.

Ulster cycle   In GAELIC LITERATURE, a group of pagan sagas and romances that survive in medieval manuscripts but deal with much earlier periods. The sagas are peopled with the legendary heroes of Ulster, among whom are King Conchobar, Medb and Ailill, Fergus, Cu Roi, Finnabair, DEIRDRE, Noisi, Emer, Bricriu Poison-tongue, Cathbad the Druid, Etain, Da Derga, Mac Datho, Conaire, Conall Cernach, and CÚ CHULAINN, the greatest hero of all. The most important tale from this cycle is CATTLE-RAID OF COOLEY.

Ulyanov, Vladimir Ilyich   See LENIN, NIKOLAY.

Ulysses   The Roman name of the Greek ODYSSEUS, hero of Homer's ODYSSEY and a prominent character in the ILIAD. He is called Ulysses in most English poetry, including the earlier translations of Homer. TENNYSON wrote a poem, "Ulysses" (1842), in which the hero in his old age speaks of his still active longing for adventure. In a modern reincarnation as Leopold BLOOM, he is the hero of James Joyce's novel ULYSSES.

Ulysses (1922)   A novel by James JOYCE. First published in Paris, and banned in the U.S. until 1933, this novel is now generally recognized to be the greatest 20th-century novel written in English. Its obscurity has made it the subject of much controversy. Virginia WOOLF, William Butler YEATS, and Ezra POUND admitted to their confusion upon a first reading; T. S. ELIOT, immediately recognizing its greatness, said the book would be a landmark because it destroys our civilization.

In *Ulysses*, Joyce has shifted from the personal, lyrical style of A PORTRAIT OF THE ARTIST AS A YOUNG MAN to the detached and impersonal style of the epic. Whereas his earlier book is affirmative in tone, *Ulysses* is a disillusioned study of estrangement, paralysis, and the disintegration of society.

The novel records the events of one average day, June 16, 1904, in the lives of its three leading characters: Leopold BLOOM; his wife, Molly; and Stephen Dedalus. The chronological pattern of these events provides the only narrative sequence in the book. Journeys about the city of Dublin are matched by inward journeys into the consciousness (see STREAM OF CONSCIOUSNESS), which Joyce expresses through journeys into the nature of language itself. On one level Joyce's style is as unrelentingly naturalistic as a movie reel; every detail, from a newspaper ad to a bodily function, is recorded and dispassionately analyzed. But by means of these details, he captures the chain of stimulus and response—the material of experience—with a degree of accuracy and immediacy never before achieved in fiction. And by means of careful orchestration, these details become significant as symbols and raise the work above the level of simple naturalism.

It has been said that in order to fully understand *Ulysses* one must, at the very least, be familiar with the theology of the Roman Catholic Church, the history of heresy, Irish legend, European history, mythology, astronomy, Hebrew, Latin, Gaelic, and Gypsy slang. Joyce's method relates the time-world of Dublin to the timeless patterns of myth, history, and religion. The plan of the book parallels the ODYSSEY. Ulysses' nineteen years of wandering are paralleled by the one-day pilgrimage of Bloom, an advertisement canvasser. The commonplace occurrences of his day echo episodes in the *Odyssey*. Stephen is related to TELEMACHUS, and Molly BLOOM to PENELOPE, although through a complex network of literary and historical allusions, each character is associated with many other figures as well. The central theme, that of exile, is one that preoccupied Joyce. Both Stephen and Bloom are exiled from their home and family life, their country, and their religion. However, Stephen is rejected because of his rejection of his dying mother—in a larger sense his rejection of Ireland—while Bloom is rejected by Ireland as a Jew. Bloom—in a sense a symbol for humanity—searches for fulfillment in social, political, and ethical terms, while Stephen—the artistic and uncompromising mind—searches for spiritual and emotional values. Whereas Ulysses on his odyssey gradually discovers the truth about himself and his relation to the gods and finally returns to his homeland, Joyce's two exiles cannot find the key to their loneliness and frustration, and their potentialities for growth seem fated to be stunted by their environment. But the final section of the book belongs to Molly Bloom, an embodiment of the feminine, regenerative principle of the universe. Her famous soliloquy, in one uninterrupted long sentence, ends with the word "yes"—her affirmation of life and love.

Believing that man is rooted in matter, Joyce was the first novelist to give physical actualities the importance they have in life. In *Ulysses* he perfected the interior monologue. Throughout the book he parodies a variety of literary styles.

Una   The heroine of the first book of Spenser's THE FAERIE QUEENE. Una personifies Truth, her name being derived from the Latin *unus*, "one." She is believed to represent Protestantism and Queen Elizabeth, as well as abstract truth; in this connection she is strongly contrasted with DUESSA.

Unamuno [y Jugo], Miguel de (1864–1936) Spanish philosopher, poet, novelist, playwright, and essayist. The leading member of the GENERACIÓN DEL 98, Unamuno is a major figure in the history of modern thought. The conflict of reason and faith, religion and science, and the problem of life and death anguished him and led him to conclusions which anticipated EXISTENTIALISM. A vision of the tragic nature of life, its absurdity, and man's radical solitude is conveyed in his major philosophical works *Del sentimiento trágico de la vida en los hombres y en los pueblos* (1913; tr *The Tragic Sense of Life*, 1958) and *La agonía del cristianismo* (1924; tr *The Agony of Christianity*, 1960). He also explored the problem of 20th-century materialism.

After the failure of his first novel, *Paz en la guerra* (1897), Unamuno invented the "nivola," the best example of which is *Niebla* (1914; tr *Mist, A Tragicomic Novel*, 1928). *Tres novelas ejemplares* (1920; tr *Three Exemplary Novels*, 1930) and *San Manuel Bueno, mártir* (1931; tr *St. Manuel Bueno, Martyr*, 1954) are his most popular works of fiction. Unamuno experimented with the autonomous character. In *Mist* the protagonist proclaims his own reality to be equal to that of the author. His novels abound with philosophy, as do his other works.

One of Spain's major 20th-century poets, Unamuno's best-known works include *El Cristo de Velázquez* (1920; tr *The Christ of Velázquez*, 1951) and *Cancionero* (1953, a posthumous poetic diary).

unanimism   A French school of thought. In the early 20th century (c1907), this was a theory based on the idea that the group is of prime importance and that the individual, especially the poet, can attain power and significance only by merging himself with a social aggregation of one kind or another. He himself was considered far less important than the collective whole. Georges DUHAMEL and Jules ROMAINS were among the literary men associated with the school. Unanimism spread through the ABBAYE GROUP. In 1908 Romains published a volume of poetry entitled *La Vie unanime*. The unanimist influence is considered to be found in the collective emphasis of his *Men of Good Will* (1932–47).

Unbearable Lightness of Being, The (1984) A novel by Milan KUNDERA, written in Czech under the title *Nesnesitelná lehkost bytí* and originally published in French—as have been all of Kundera's novels since he became resident in France—as *L'Insoutenable Légèreté de l'être* (1984). Set in Czechoslovakia after the 1968 Soviet invasion, it follows two couples who are redefining their relationships. Tomas is a distinguished, well-respected surgeon in Prague and a lover of women. Although he tries to settle down with Tereza, a bartender, his philandering instincts draw him toward other women. Among them is a free-spirited artist, Sabina, who is having an affair with a married university professor, Franz. Among the novel's many themes are the desolate nature of life within a totalitarian state, the metaphysical conflict between body and soul, and the ultimate sense of weightlessness that afflicts us when we confront the meaninglessness of life. Divided into seven sections, the novel interweaves different motifs as in a musical composition.

Uncle Remus, His Songs and His Sayings (1880)   A famous book of folk tales by Joel Chandler HARRIS. They are told to a small white boy by whimsical, lovable Uncle Remus, an aging black servant, whose stories are based on traditional fables of his race. The tales, which include the story TAR BABY, are ones that Harris himself heard as a boy and are fine examples of dialect and regional writing. Many of the characters are animals endowed with human qualities.

Uncle Sam   A commonly accepted personification of the U.S. government. This name was originally a derogatory nickname for the federal government, used by New Englanders opposed to its policies during the WAR OF 1812. Uncle Sam may have been inspired by the nickname of a government inspector in Troy, N.Y., one Samuel Wilson (1766–1854), or it may represent an extension of the initials of the U.S. *The Adventures of Uncle Sam* (1816) by "Frederick Fidfaddy" seems to be the earliest use of the name in a book. The familiar tall, lean, bearded figure, dressed in a top hat and a suit made from the American flag, was introduced in the 1870s in cartoons by Thomas NAST.

Uncle Toby   The lovable but almost totally inarticulate military uncle of the hero in Laurence Sterne's TRISTRAM SHANDY. His principal activity (he is incapacitated by a wound in his thigh) is to reconstruct all the military campaigns of MARLBOROUGH in miniature on a small bowling green. His speech is largely the whistling of tunes and the vain attempt to communicate his ideas through military palaver. See TRIM, CORPORAL; WADMAN, WIDOW.

Uncle Tom's Cabin, or, Life Among the Lowly (1852)   A novel by Harriet Beecher STOWE. The book relates the trials, suffering, and human dignity of Uncle Tom, an old black slave. Cruelly treated by a Yankee plantation owner, Simon Legree, Tom dies as the result of a beating. Uncle Tom is devoted to Little Eva, the daughter of his white owner, Augustine St. Clare. Other important characters are the mulatto girl Eliza; the impish black child Topsy; Miss Ophelia St. Clare, a New England spinster; and Marks, the slave catcher. The setting is Kentucky and Louisiana. The two most famous scenes are the death of Little Eva and the pursuit of Eliza and her baby over the Ohio River's ice floes. Eliza's husband, George, later joins her by using the UNDERGROUND RAILROAD.

The book, which Mrs. Stowe said was written by God, was a contribution to the abolitionist movement, but treats the situation in a balanced manner. There is admiration for the best of Southern gentility; the villain is a Vermonter. The book, extraordinarily popular, was followed by sequels and answers and counteranswers before 1860.

Uncle Tom's devotion to his white master led to the use of the pejorative term "Uncle Tomism," meaning undue subservience to white people on the part of blacks.

Uncle Vanya (Dyadya Vanya, 1899)   A play by Anton CHEKHOV, subtitled *Scenes from Country Life in Four Acts*. Uncle Vanya, Ivan Petrovich Voinitsky, for years has managed the estate of his brother-in-law, Aleksandr Vladimirovich Serebryakov, a retired professor. Vanya has given up his own dreams and ambitions to provide support for Serebryakov, who he thinks is a great scholar. When he finally realizes that the old professor is something of a fraud, Vanya feels cheated. His rancor against Serebryakov is increased by his love for the professor's young second wife, Elena Andreyevna—a love that is not returned. He is thrown into fury and despair by Serebryakov's plan to sell the estate that Vanya has labored to make profitable. He unsuccessfully attempts to shoot the professor, then contemplates suicide. Serebryakov agrees not to sell the estate, and Vanya, reconciled to his lot, prepares to continue his drudgery.

underground railroad   The organized secret system for transporting slaves to freedom before the CIVIL WAR. Blacks were frequently hidden on vessels bound from the South to New England, where they were helped farther north, sometimes even to Canada. The program was supported by contributions from Northern abolitionists; many of its agents were Quakers.

Under Milk Wood (1954)   A radio play for voices by Dylan THOMAS. Written in poetic, inventive prose, this play is full of humor, a joyful sense of the goodness of life and love, and a strong Welsh flavor. It is an impression of a spring day in the lives of the people of Llareggub, a Welsh village situated under Milk Wood. It has no plot, but a wealth of characters who dream aloud, converse with one another, and speak in choruses of alternating voices.

Understanding Media   See McLUHAN, MARSHALL.

Under the Net (1954)   A novel by Iris MURDOCH. This novel recounts the adventures of Jake Donaghue, who gets himself involved in filmmaking, horse racing,

blackmailing, and dog-stealing. Finally he becomes a hospital orderly. Unable to build for himself the kind of structured, successful life all his friends lead, he remains free —the goal of the existentialist. The "net" of the title refers to both the cage in which society tries to trap him and the falsifications it constructs through illogical words and theories.

Under the Volcano (1947)   A novel by Malcolm LOWRY. Through the central character, Geoffrey Firmin, an ex-British consul and alcoholic living in Mexico, Lowry explores the gradual disintegration of a human being in despair. The book, which uses a variety of experimental techniques, is notable for its stylistic brilliance, as well as for the subtlety and depth of its characterizations. It was made into a film by John HUSTON in 1984.

Under Western Eyes (1911)   A novel by Joseph CONRAD. This novel depicts the 19th-century Russian police state and extremist revolutionaries. Razumov betrays to the authorities his fellow student Haldin, who has assassinated an official. Sent to Geneva as a government spy, Razumov falls in love with Haldin's sister Nathalie. He confesses the truth to the revolutionaries and is beaten, deafened, and run over by a tram car; finally he returns to Russia. The "Western eyes" are those of an Englishman who reads and comments on Razumov's journal.

Undine (1811)   A tale by the German romantic author Friedrich von Fouqué (1777–1843) about the tragic love between the water spirit Undine and a knight. Fouqué later made it into a libretto which was set to music by E. T. A. HOFFMANN. This musical work was first performed in 1816. Jean GIRAUDOUX adapted the story of Undine in his play *Ondine* (1939).

Undset, Sigrid (1882–1949)   Norwegian novelist. She is best known for her novels dealing with life in the Scandinavian countries during the Middle Ages. Undset presented a vividly realistic picture of the past, combining scholarly knowledge with a keen sense of psychological analysis and a powerful style. Among Undset's historical works are KRISTIN LAVRANSDATTER, *Olaf Audunsson* (4 vols, 1925–27; tr *The Master of Hestviken: The Axe*, 1928; *The Snake Pit*, 1929; *In the Wilderness*, 1929; and *The Son Avenger*, 1930), and *Den braendende busk* (1930; tr *The Burning Bush*, 1932). Undset's novels of the modern era concern themselves with social and psychological problems; her conversion to Roman Catholicism in 1924 is reflected in her fiction and in such studies as *Norske helgner* (*Saga of Saints*, 1934). Her personal life, too, was patterned on her medieval interests—she spent the later years of her life in a restored house dating from the year 1000, and she dressed in the gown of a Norse matron of the Middle Ages. In 1928 Sigrid Undset was awarded the NOBEL PRIZE in Literature.

Ungaretti, Giuseppe (1888–1970)   Italian writer, poet of the metaphysical "Hermetic" school (see HERMETICISM). Born and raised in Alexandria, Egypt, and educated partly in France, Ungaretti is one of the major figures of 20th-century Italian letters. In his verse, traditional rhyme schemes were at first abandoned (to reappear in his later work) and the perception of the music and rhythm of poetry visibly changed. His reduction of his work to its essentials produces an effect of innocence and purity, and it has great evocative power. Ungaretti sees man as a suffering pilgrim, vulnerable and defenseless, proud and yet humble. In 1970 his poetic work was published in a "definitive" edition, with the title *Vita d'un uomo: Tutte le poesie*. An excellent English rendition appears in *Selected Poems* (1975).

unicorn (fr Lat, *unum cornu*, "one horn") A fabulous animal. It is represented by medieval writers as having the legs of a buck, the tail of a lion, the head and body of a horse, and a single horn—white at the base, black in the middle, and red at the tip—jutting from the middle of its forehead; its body is white; head, red; and eyes, blue. The earliest author to describe it is Ctesias (400 BC). The medieval notions concerning it are summarized in the following extract:

The unicorn has but one horn in the middle of its forehead. It is the only animal that ventures to attack the elephant; and so sharp is the nail of its foot, that with one blow it can rip the belly of the beast. Hunters can catch the unicorn only by placing a young virgin in his haunts. No sooner does he see the damsel than he runs towards her, and lies down at her feet, and so suffers himself to be captured by the hunters. The unicorn represents Jesus Christ, who took on Him our nature in the virgin's womb, was betrayed to the Jews, and delivered into the hands of Pontius Pilate. Its one horn signifies the Gospel of Truth.—*Le Bestiaire Divin de Guillaume, Clerc de Normandie* (13th century)

The heraldic supporters in the old royal coat of arms of Scotland are two unicorns. When James VI of Scotland came to reign over England (1603), the unicorn supplanted the red dragon, representing Wales, as one of the supporters of the English shield, the other being the lion. The animosity that existed between the lion and the unicorn is allegorical for that which once existed between England and Scotland. A battle between the Lion and the Unicorn is an episode in THROUGH THE LOOKING GLASS by Lewis Carroll, and Spenser mentions it in THE FAERIE QUEENE.

Unitarianism A Christian denomination. Unitarianism states that God exists in one being. It rejects the doctrine of the TRINITY. The father of English Unitarianism was John Biddle (1615–62), whose anti-trinitarian views were written in *Twelve Arguments Drawn Out of Scripture* (1645). The principles of Unitarianism involve an affirmation of reason and conscience, of religious tolerance, of freedom of religious belief, and of a faith in the universal brotherhood of mankind.

United Irishmen An Irish revolutionary organization. Founded in 1791 by Theobald Wolfe TONE, this group was committed to the forcible overthrow of English rule in Ireland. In its formative years the organization was identified as an essentially middle-class, Protestant faction, but its consistent support of Catholic enfranchisement enlisted many Catholics to its ranks. In 1794 the organization was outlawed and began to function as an underground movement. Increasing suppression resulted in an attempt on the part of the United Irishmen to engage in an alliance with Napoleon and to attempt to stage a rebellion in 1798. The rebellion, however, had been anticipated by the English, and, by the time the French forces arrived to assist the rebels, the uprising had been put down. Wolfe Tone, who later committed suicide in prison, and the other Irish leaders were captured. The rebellion's chief effect lay in hastening the political union of England and Ireland. This union occurred in 1800.

United Nations An international organization set up after World War II succeeding, in principle, the LEAGUE OF NATIONS. The foundation for the U.N. was established during the war when the Allied Powers agreed upon the need for creating "a world family of democratic nations." At its initial meeting in San Francisco in 1945, with 51 nations in attendance, the U.N. Charter was drafted and adopted. Within five years the U.N. had permanent headquarters in New York City and, by 1963, it had more than doubled its original membership, largely as a result of the admission of many newly independent African and Asian countries. By 1987 membership had increased to 159 nations.

The general aims of the U.N. are to develop amicable relations between nations, to promote and preserve peace, to mediate in international disputes, and to ensure international cooperation in solving social, economic, cultural, and humanitarian problems.

unities, three dramatic The rules governing socalled classical drama. They are founded on RENAISSANCE interpretations of passages in Aristotle's POETICS, and are hence sometimes styled the Aristotelian unities. Their principles are that in drama there should be (1) unity of action, (2) unity of time, and (3) unity of place. Aristotle lays stress on unity of action, meaning that an organic unity, or a logical connection between the successive incidents, is necessary; but unity of time was deduced by Castelvetro, the 16th-century Italian scholar and critic, from the passage in the *Poetics* where Aristotle, in comparing epic poetry and tragedy, says that the former has no limits in time but the latter "endeavors, as far as possible, to confine itself to a single revolution of the sun, or but slightly to exceed this limit." The unity of time thus established, the unity of place followed almost perforce.

The theory of the three unities was formulated in Italy nearly a century before it was taken up in France, where it became, after much argument, the cornerstone of drama. Its first modern offspring was *La Sophonisbe* (1629) by Mairet, though it was not till Corneille's triumph with LE CID that the convention of the three unities can be said to have been finally adopted. The principle had little success in England, despite the later championship of Dryden (cf. his ESSAY ON DRAMATIC POESY), ADDISON (as exemplified in his *Cato*), and others. Ben Jonson's *The Alchemist* (1610) is perhaps the best example of the small class of English plays in which the unities of place and time have been purposely adhered to. In France, on the other hand, the three unities were much more strictly observed, and not until the momentous performance of Victor HUGO's *Hernani* (1830) did the old classical theories really give way to those of the modern romantic movement.

University Wits   A name for a group of young English writers of the later years of the 16th century. All had received their training at Oxford or Cambridge and came to London to embark on careers in literature. They were primarily pamphleteers and dramatists; many of them took part in the MARPRELATE CONTROVERSY and contributed to the growth of English satire. As dramatists they developed the Senecan revenge tragedy, the use of bigger-than-life characters, the CHRONICLE PLAY, and the romantic comedy. Chief among them was Christopher MARLOWE; others were Robert GREENE, John LYLY, Thomas NASHE, Thomas LODGE, and George PEELE.

Unnamable, The (L'Innommable, 1953; tr 1958) A novel by Samuel BECKETT. It is an account, through the technique of STREAM OF CONSCIOUSNESS, of the empty existence of the most immobilized of Beckett's characters: in one of his self-descriptions, he lives legless and armless in a large jar outside a restaurant. The novel is part of a trilogy, which also includes MOLLOY and MALONE DIES, all published together as *Three Novels* (1959).

Unofficial Rose, An (1962) A novel by Iris MURDOCH. When an elderly gentleman becomes a widower and tries to return to his former mistress, his action precipitates a general round of "change partners" among his family and friends. His son Randall decides to leave his dull wife, Ann, the unofficial or hedge rose of the title, for a more exotic woman. But the comedy and irony of the story are that no one decides anything through the exercise of free will, but is manipulated by circumstances and by other self-interested persons. Randall finds he has merely exchanged one servitude for another, and will probably return to Ann. This comic, philosophic novel qualifies the existentialist idea of freedom expressed in UNDER THE NET.

Unruh, Fritz von (1885–1970) German playwright and short-story writer, a major figure in EXPRESSIONISM. He was educated for military service and served as an officer in World War I but became known for his passionate denunciations of war in such plays as *Ein Geschlecht* (A Family, 1917) and its sequel, *Platz* (The Square, 1920). His best-known piece of narrative prose, *Opfergang* (1919; tr *The Way of Sacrifice*, 1928), written at Verdun in 1916, is a powerful description of the horrors of war. He attempted to further his democratic and humanistic ideals as a member of the Reichstag, but the rise of Nazism forced him to leave his homeland from 1932 to 1948. *Der*

nie verlor (1947; tr *The End Is Not Yet*, 1948) is a novel about HITLER.

Untermeyer, Louis (1885–1977) American poet and anthologist. Untermeyer is widely known for over fifty-six anthologies, which include *Modern American Poetry* (1919), *The Book of Living Verse* (1932), *A Treasury of Great Humor* (1972), and *Fifty Modern American and British Poets* (1973). He was the first to expose a wide readership to poets as various as Robert FROST and Erica JONG. His own poems appear in such volumes as *Burning Bush* (1928) and *Selected Poems and Parodies* (1935). He also wrote several volumes of criticism; short stories; a novel; a collection of compact biographies, *Makers of the Modern World* (1955); and two works of autobiography, *From Another World* (1939) and *Bygones* (1965). He wrote or edited numerous books for children, including several volumes of fairy tales.

untouchable In HINDUISM, a member of one of the many low CASTES. The touch of such persons is considered to be ritually defiling or polluting by those of a higher caste. They are also known as Pariahs, and Gandhi, who attempted to break down the discrimination against them, named them Harijans (children of God).

Unvanquished, The (1938) A collection of interlocking stories by William FAULKNER. Set during the Civil War, these stories deal with the Sartoris family, whose modern history Faulkner recounted in SARTORIS. Composed of seven stories, which first appeared separately in magazines, the book centers primarily on the adventures of Bayard Sartoris and his black companion, Ringo. Colonel John SARTORIS and Miss Rosa, Bayard's grandmother, also figure prominently.

upanayana See SACRED THREAD.

Upanishads The oldest speculative literature of the Hindus (composed from about 600 to 300 BC), a collection of treatises on the nature of man and the universe, forming a part of the Vedic writings. These writings reveal great subtlety and sophistication, and combine abstract discussion with dialogue and illuminating metaphor. The basic Upanishadic principles are (1) that the supreme Godhead, because it is completely attributeless, is uncommunicable, but "realizable"; (2) that the individual self, ATMAN, is also the universal self, BRAHMAN, but is unaware of this identity; (3) that the phenomenal world of appearance exists on the relative plane of the lower truth and appears to be real without being so; (4) that *yoga*, or physical and spiritual discipline, is necessary to effect the union of *atman* and *brahman*.

Updike, John [Hoyer] (1932–   ) American novelist, short-story writer, and poet. Following his graduation from Harvard, Updike worked for a time on the staff of THE NEW YORKER, to which he contributed reviews, poems, and stories. Although he has published several volumes of poetry—among them *The Carpentered Hen and Other Tame Creatures* (1958), *Midpoint* (1969), *Sev-*

enty Poems (1972), and Facing Nature (1985)—Updike is at his best in prose. His novels and stories, characterized by a precise, highly individual style and gentle realism, tend to deal with the tensions and frustrations of middle-class suburban life and their effect on love and the institution of marriage. After his first novel, The Poorhouse Fair (1959), he published the widely acclaimed RABBIT, RUN, a novel whose central character tries desperately to avoid the responsible choices that might give him some clear definition as a human being. In direct contrast to Rabbit, Run, The Centaur (1963) deals with a protagonist who is overburdened with a sense of responsibility and guilt. "Rabbit" reappears in Rabbit Redux (1971) to confront the volatile problems facing America in the 1960s and again in Rabbit Is Rich (1981; PULITZER PRIZE, 1982). Updike dealt again with various aspects of love and responsibility, mostly painful, in such novels as Of the Farm (1965), Couples (1968), and Marry Me (1976). In The Coup (1978), he departed from his familiar suburban milieu for the mythical African state of Kush. The strange cultural juxtapositions and his uncharacteristic choice of characters caused many to regard it as his funniest book. He returned to the suburban milieu in The Witches of Eastwick (1985), a novel about three Rhode Island women whose marriages have collapsed and who turn to devil worship and witchcraft. Roger's Version, a novel that revolves around a discussion of proving the existence of God through scientific means, was published in 1986.

Collections of Updike's short stories include Pigeon Feathers (1962), The Music School (1966), Bech: A Book (1970), Problems (1979), Too Far to Go (1979), a chronological arrangement of previously published stories about Joan and Richard Maple, the prototypical Updike couple, The Beloved (1982), Bech Is Back (1982), and Trust Me (1987). Updike is a first-rate literary journalist whose critical essays and miscellaneous prose pieces have been published in Assorted Prose (1965), Picked-Up Pieces (1975), and Hugging the Shore: Essays and Criticism (1983), a collection of literary evaluations of novelists, historians, scientists, theologians, and diarists from all over the world. He has also written a play, Buchanan Dying (1974), about President James Buchanan, and edited (with S. Ravenel) The Best American Short Stories 1984 (1984).

Upelluri   In Hittite mythology, a giant who holds earth and heaven on his shoulders. Like the Greek ATLAS described by HOMER, Upelluri carries earth as well as heaven, and stands in the middle of the ocean. Also like Atlas, he is not very intelligent and, consequently, is easily exploited. He is unaware that earth and sky are being piled on his shoulders and does not notice when the gods separate them with a magic knife. Later, he is equally ignorant of the fact that the stone monster Ullikummi has been placed by its father, KUMARBI, on his right shoulder and is growing to stupendous size.

Up from Slavery   See WASHINGTON, BOOKER T.

Ur   Sumerian city dating from 4000 BC. In Ur's long history it rose and fell, was destroyed and rebuilt many times. The changing course of the Euphrates River finally robbed it forever of its greatness, leaving Ur stranded in the desert.

Urania   The MUSE of astronomy in Greek mythology, usually represented pointing at a celestial globe with a staff. Milton (PARADISE LOST vii 1–20) makes her the spirit of the loftiest poetry and calls her heavenly born (the name means "the heavenly one") and sister of Wisdom.

Uranus   (or Ouranos)   The ancient Greek personification of Heaven; son and husband of GE and father of the TITANS, the CYCLOPES, and the "hundred-handed" giants Cottus, Briareus, and Gyes. Uranus hated his children and confined them in the depths of the earth, but his son CRONOS, with the help of Ge, castrated him with a sickle and took his place.

Urdur   See NORNS.

Urfé, Honoré d'   (1568–1625)   French writer. He is best known as the author of L'Astrée (1607–27), a vast pastoral romance in prose which enjoyed great popularity and influenced the development of the PASTORAL genre.

Uriel   One of the seven ARCHANGELS of rabbinical angelology, sent to God to answer the questions of Esdras (2 Esd. 4). In Milton's PARADISE LOST, he is "the Regent of the Sun," and "sharpest-sighted spirit of all in heaven." The name means "flame of God" or "angel of light."

Uris, Leon [Marcus]   (1924–   )   American novelist. Uris left school at seventeen to join the Marines, and his first novel, Battle Cry (1953), describes the training and combat of Marines during World War II. A storyteller rather than stylist, Uris's forte is the panoramic semihistorical novel. His three best-known books of this type are Exodus (1957), about the Jewish resettlement of Palestine and the creation of the state of Israel; Trinity (1976), a fictional version of the Protestant-Catholic battles in Northern Ireland; and The Haj (1984), a novel about a Muslim's pilgrimage to Mecca, set against a contemporary Palestinian background.

Urizen   In William BLAKE's personal mythology, appearing in his mystical poetry and particularly in THE BOOK OF THEL and THE MARRIAGE OF HEAVEN AND HELL, the figure of JEHOVAH but also a symbol of man in bondage. It represents the limiting mental power of reason, an analytical and destructive force which dominates man and against which man must struggle. Urizen is never destroyed, but is periodically regenerated by a union with Los (or the imagination) and Luvah (or passion).

Urn Burial   See HYDRIOTAPHIA.

Ursa Major and Ursa Minor   See GREAT BEAR AND LITTLE BEAR.

Urvasī   See PURŪRAVAS AND URVASĪ.

U.S.A.   (1938)   A trilogy of novels by John DOS PASSOS. These novels, THE 42ND PARALLEL, 1919 (q.v.), and THE BIG MONEY, give a panoramic picture of life in the

U.S. from just before World War I through the first years of the Great Depression. The tone is bitter; the only victors are unscrupulous opportunists; the only heroes, those few among the radicals who succeed in preserving some measure of personal integrity.

Ushant (1952; repr 1971) An autobiographical prose work, written in the third person by Conrad AIKEN. The title comes from the name of an island off the coast of Brittany. The book mingles personal references with mention of literary associates in a kind of waking dream suggestive of psychoanalytic free association.

Usigli, Rodolfo (1905–) Mexican playwright. Usigli writes historical drama and social and political satire. In his *Tres comedias impoliticas* (1933–35), he questions the pervading demagoguery of the Mexican political system. *El gesticulador* (1937), his best-known play, concerns the lack of authenticity of Mexican life. His antihero Cesar Rubio, a failed teacher, decides to impersonate General Cesar Rubio, a hero of the Mexican revolution of 1910. Ironically the impostor comes to believe in the general's ideals and is murdered by the same assassin. In *Corona de luz* (1956; tr *Two Plays: Crown of Light, One of These Days,* 1971), Usigli focuses on the birth of the cult of the Virgin of Guadalupe as a symbol of national consciousness in Mexico. Other plays include *Corona de sombras* (1942; tr *Crown of Shadows,* 1946), dealing with the empire of Carlotta and Maximilian; and *Buenos días, señor Presidente!* (1972). *Mexico in the Theatre* (tr 1976) is a collection of essays.

Uslar Pietri, Arturo (1906–) Venezuelan novelist and essayist. Influenced by MAGIC REALISM, his prose is rich in symbols and metaphors. His two most important historical novels are *El camino de El Dorado* (1948), a fictionalized biography of the conquistador Lope de Aguirre, and *Las lanzas coloradas* (1931; tr *The Red Lances,* 1963). In both books Uslar Pietri depicts people who, failing to find meaningful points of contact in their lives, move irreversibly toward a tragic end. The unwoven quality of the action in *Las lanzas coloradas,* a reconstruction of the wars of independence in Venezuela, can be taken as a metaphor for the chaos that enveloped the country after Bolivar's death.

Ussher, James (1581–1656) Irish prelate and scholar. Named archbishop of Armagh and primate of Ireland in 1625, he wrote *Annales Veteris et Novi Testamenti* (1650–54), a scheme of biblical chronology. He had a remarkable library and left his books and manuscripts, among them the famous Book of Kells, to Trinity College, Dublin.

Ustinov, Peter [Alexander] (1921–) British playwright, actor, novelist, short-story writer, director, and essayist. Ustinov was born in London of Russian, French, and German ancestry. His plays *The Love of Four Colonels* (1951), *Romanoff and Juliet* (1956), and *The Unknown Soldier and His Wife* (1967) are all set in imaginary Euro-

pean countries and have an internationalist viewpoint. His mordant wit takes aim at the social, political, and literary pretensions of people and nations. Among his other works are *The Frontiers of the Sea* (1966), a collection of short stories, *The Wit of Peter Ustinov* (1969), *Krumnagel* (1971), a novel, and *Dear Me* (1977), his autobiography. His writings also include *Overhead* (1981) and *My Russia* (1983), a further volume of memoirs and travel writings.

U Tam'si, Tchicaya (real name Gérald Felix Tchicaya, 1931–) Congolese poet. U Tam'si had most of his education in France. In poetry that draws on African themes and imagery, he points out the essential sadness and isolation of man, sometimes in a wryly humorous way. His collections include *Le Mauvais Sang* (1955), *Feu de brousse* (1957; tr *Brush Fire,* 1964), *À triche-coeur* (1958), and *Épitomé* (1962). His work has also appeared in English translation in *Selected Poems* (1970).

Utgard See JOTUNHEIM.

Utgard-Loki In Norse mythology, the chief of the giants living in the infernal regions. Disguised as Skyrmir, he conducted THOR, Thialfi, and LOKI to Jötunheim. There Fire, disguised as Logi, ate faster than Loki; Thought, disguised as Hugi, ran faster than Thialfi; Old Age, disguised as Elli, was stronger than Thor. When Utgard-Loki had told Thor about his tricks, he escaped the god's wrath by vanishing.

Uther Pendragon The father of King ARTHUR, in Geoffrey of Monmouth's HISTORY OF THE KINGS OF BRITAIN (c1137) and other versions of the story of Arthur's birth and conception. With the help of Merlin, the magician, Uther visits IGRAINE in the guise of her husband, and, from that union, Arthur is subsequently born.

utilitarianism An ethical doctrine. Actions are right or good in proportion to their usefulness or as they tend to promote happiness, the doctrine that the end and criterion of public action is "the greatest happiness of the greatest number." John Stuart MILL coined the word *utilitarianism,* but Jeremy BENTHAM, the official founder of the utilitarian school, employed the word utility to signify the doctrine that makes "the happiness of man" the one and only measure of right and wrong.

Utnapishtim The Babylonian NOAH. An ancient sage, living with his wife on an island at the end of the earth, beyond the ocean of death, he tells the hero GILGAMESH the story of a great flood in which he played a role almost identical to that of Noah. With his wife, he was made immortal by the gods. He tells Gilgamesh the secret of a plant that restores youth—a herb that he himself has apparently never tasted, since he is described as very old. He is probably a Babylonian development of the Sumerian ZIUSUDRA.

Utopia (fr Gr, *ou,* "not," *topos,* "a place") "Nowhere," the name given by Sir Thomas MORE to the imaginary island in his political romance of the same name, written in Latin (1516). Book I of *Utopia* is a dialogue, which presents a perceptive analysis of contemporary social, economic, penal, and moral ills in England; the second book is a narrative describing Utopia, a country run according to the ideals of the English humanists, where poverty, crime, injustice, and other ills do not exist. The classic English translation of *Utopia* is by Ralph Robinson (1551).

The name of this fictitious place, Utopia, has since been applied to all such ideal projections, including even those which antedated More's, such as Plato's REPUBLIC. Others are Francis Bacon's NEW ATLANTIS, Samuel Butler's EREWHON, and several conceived by H. G. WELLS, including his *A Modern Utopia* (1905). In Rabelais's GARGANTUA AND PANTAGRUEL, Pantagruel goes to the kingdom of Utopia.

Utrillo, Maurice (1883–1955) French painter. He was the illegitimate son of the painter Suzanne Valadon (1867–1938) and took his name from the Spanish journalist Miguel Utrillo, who adopted him. An alcoholic as early as 1900, he began painting as a form of therapy under his mother's instruction. In these early years his work reflects the influence of the impressionists, primarily PISSARRO. Between 1910 and 1920 he produced paintings of Paris and its suburbs at a frenzied rate. In this, his most successful period, the paintings are carefully controlled in technique, but the bleakness of the landscapes, the subdued, melancholic color tones, and the tiny human figures dwarfed by towering buildings reflect the artist's own unhappiness.

Uz In the OLD TESTAMENT, the home of Job, a land east of Palestine (JOB 1:1).

Uzziel One of the principal ANGELS of rabbinical angelology, the name meaning "strength of God." Uzziel was next in command to GABRIEL and appears in Milton's PARADISE LOST.

V

V. See PYNCHON, THOMAS.

Vaché, Jacques   See BRETON, ANDRÉ.

vade mecum   A portable manual or handbook. The phrase is Latin and means "go with me."

Vailland, Roger [François] (1907–1965)   French novelist, essayist, and dramatist. An ironic iconoclast, concerned with the rules according to which a "man of quality" must "play the game." The central tension in Vailland's life and work was between the acceptance of ideological commitment and the pursuit of individual pleasures. He joined the Communist Party after World War II, in which he had been a member of the French Resistance, but left it in 1956, after Khrushchev's denunciation of Stalin at the 20th Party Congress. His first important work, *Drôle de jeu* (1945; tr *Playing with Fire*, 1948), was set during the Resistance. He was awarded the PRIX GONCOURT for *La Loi* (1957; tr *The Law*, 1958), set in a southern Italian seaport. His other works include the antireligious play *Héloïse et Abélard* (1947) and the novels *Les Mauvais Coups* (1959; tr *Turn of the Wheel*, 1962), *La Fête* (1960; tr *Fête*, 1961), and *La Truite* (1964; tr *The Trout*, 1965).

vaishya   Hindu caste. A member of the producer-commercial CASTE (*varna*) in the four-fold division of the Hindu social hierarchy, it is below the BRAHMIN and KSHATRIYA and above the SUDRA.

Valente, José Angel (1929–   )   Spanish poet. Much of Valente's precise, almost austere poetry reveals his preoccupation with death, memory, faith, and the coming to terms with the mystery of creation. In his masterpiece, *La memoria y los signos* (*Memory and Marks*, 1966), the poet investigates metaphysical hope through love and faith in man, in the face of political, historical, and existential reality.

Valentine, Jimmy   The burglar hero of O. Henry's short story A RETRIEVED REFORMATION.

Valera y Alcalá Galiano, Juan (1824–1905)   Spanish novelist, critic, and diplomat. Valera's literary works reflect his urbanity and refinement, qualities that stemmed from his extensive reading and from his distinguished diplomatic career, during which he served as Spanish minister at Lisbon, Washington, and Brussels. His lucid and harmonious style is considered a model of 19th-century Castilian.

His first and best-known novel, *Pepita Jiménez* (1874), resulted from his mystical readings. Written partly in the form of letters, it is a psychological study of the inner struggles of a seminarist who falls in love with an attractive widow and eventually renounces the priesthood. He also wrote *El comendador Mendoza* (1877), *Doña Luz* (1879), and *Juanita la larga* (1895). Among his other works of fiction are the short stories "El pájaro verde" and "Parsondes" (both 1860) and the dialogue *Asclepigenia* (1878). Valera also exerted considerable influence as a critic, though his writings in this field are thought to be marred by excessive politeness.

Valéry, [Ambroise] Paul[-Toussaint-Jules] (1871–1945)   French poet and critic. While studying for a law degree, Valéry met Pierre LOUŸS and André GIDE and with them began (1891) attending MALLARMÉ's symbolist salons. The poem NARCISSE PARLE reflects the beginning of Valéry's concern with the interior drama of man's conflicting selves. He began an independent course of self-education in science, the arts, and history. *Introduction à la méthode de Leonard da Vinci* (1895; tr 1929) launched his theory that the processes of the creative mind are all analogous, whether the mind be turned toward science or toward any of the arts. In 1896 he wrote the first of the sketches collected as *Monsieur Teste* (1947), in which the central character represents the pure mind, or consciousness.

Valéry wrote very little more until 1912, when Gide, Louÿs, and the publisher Gaston Gallimard persuaded him to collect and revise the poetry he had written in the 1890s; in thus preparing his *Album de vers anciens* (1920), he again became interested in writing poetry. In 1913 he began his masterpiece, LA JEUNE PARQUE, and, after 1917, he wrote the poems in *Charmes* (1922), including LE CIMITIÈRE MARIN, "La Pythie," "Ébauche d'un serpent," and

"Fragments du Narcisse." All are dramatic monologues in fairly conventional poetic forms, worked and reworked by the poet in an attempt to reach his ideal "crystal systems" of "pure poetry"; all symbolize some aspect of the tension between rational intellectual control and irrational possession by inspiration or passion—that is, between the freedom of detached contemplation and the surrender to involvement in life. This theme also inspired two prose dialogues: *L'Âme à la danse* (1921; tr *Dance and the Soul*, 1951) and *Eupalinos, ou l'architecte* (1923).

Valéry wrote dramatic libretti and fragments of two theatrical variations on the FAUST legend, *Lust* and the ironical *Le Solitaire*, which were published posthumously in *Mon Faust* (1946).

After Valéry was elected to the ACADÉMIE FRANÇAISE in 1925, he became an internationally known public lecturer and administrator of artistic affairs. His numerous essays range from artistic and literary criticism to political comment. Particularly valuable for insights into his analysis of creative processes and his own methods of inquiry are the copious notebooks he kept throughout his life, published as *Cahiers* (29 vols, 1957–61).

Valhalla   The hall of slain warriors in Scandinavian mythology. The largest palace in ASGARD, Valhalla has 450 gates so wide that eight hundred men can enter abreast. Here ODIN feasts on mead and boar's meat with the heroes brought from mortal battles by the VALKYRIES. The heroes go out every morning to fight with each other for sport, but their wounds are healed by the time they return for their banquet. See RING DES NIBELUNGEN, DER.

Vali   (1) The guardian of justice in Scandinavian mythology, who was said to have grown to full stature in a day. The second son of Orin, Vali avenged the death of BALDER by using an arrow to kill his blind murderer, HODER. Typifying new light after darkness, he was one of the few expected to survive RAGNAROK, or the Twilight of the Gods, for justice was not to be banished from the earth.

(2) This was also an alternative name of the Scandinavian *Lifthrasir* (Desiring Life), who, with her mate, *Lif* (Life, also called *Vidar*), was to repeople the earth after Ragnarok. Lif slew the FENRIS-WOLF at Ragnarok to avenge ODIN's death.

Valkyries   The maidens of Old Norse mythology. The Valkyries chose those warriors who were to die heroically in battle. They are also the attendants of ODIN in VALHALLA. Usually nine to twelve in number, they are the sometimes divine, sometimes mortal princesses who have become immortal. Brilliantly adorned, they ride into battle and select those heroes who are worthy of dining with Odin. They conduct those selected to Valhalla and serve them as cupbearers.

In earlier mythology they are maidens who can take the shape of swans and are associated with white clouds. The most familiar image of the Valkyrie is the Brunhild of the VOLSUNGA SAGA and Wagner's RING DES NIBELUNGEN; they

no longer are the bloodthirsty creatures of Old Norse legend but rather lusty Amazonian virgins reputed to be the wisest of women.

Valle-Inclán, Ramón María del   (1869–1936) Spanish novelist, dramatist, poet. A colorful eccentric who was a legend in his own time, Valle-Inclán has emerged as one of the most innovative and significant Spanish writers of the 20th century. His early "modernistic" work, the four-volume *Sonatas* (1902–5), recounts the adventures of the fictitious Marqués de Bradomín. Each volume bears the name of a season of the year and symbolizes a "season" of love corresponding to that time of life. *Corte de amor* (1902), *Jardín umbrío* (1903), and *Flor de santidad* (1904) contain works of short fiction set in his native Galicia and reflect its atmosphere of mystery and superstition. *Aromas de leyenda* (1907) and *La pipa de Kif* (1919), poetry, recreate his changing aesthetics, from symbolism and emphasis on vague beauty to delight in the grotesque. *Aguila de blasón* (1907), *Romance de lobos* (1908), and *Cara de plata* (1922), a dramatic trilogy, together with his novelistic trilogy on the Carlist wars, *La guerra Carlista* (1909–10), constitute an intermediate stage.

Valle-Inclán's most original inventions are the short, expressionistic dramas called *esperpentos*, a mingling of horror and satire, caustic humor and grotesque deformation, of which excellent examples are *Divinas palabras* (1920), *Los cuernos de Don Friolera* (1921), *Luces de Bohemia* (1924), and *El retablo de la lujuria, la avaricia y la muerte* (1927). A novel produced with the same aesthetic principles is *Tirano Banderas* (1926), a satire of revolution in an imaginary Latin American dictatorship, one of the best works of Valle-Inclán's later period, which was followed by *La corte de los milagros* (1927) and *Viva mi dueño* (1927).

Vallejo, César   (1892–1938)   Peruvian poet. Vallejo lived most of his life in a close battle with hunger and illness, and his poems increasingly spell out the bitterness and anguish he felt as he approached his early death. Always intimately identified with the downtrodden and involved in efforts to end political oppression, his poetry managed to combine the force of his passionate personal voice with his intense social commitment. Shortly after the publication of his first book of poetry, *Los heraldos negros* (*The Dark Messengers*, 1918), he was imprisoned on trumped-up political charges. While in jail, he wrote many of the poems in the striking volume *Trilce* (1922; tr 1971), in which he broke through all convention and produced a broadside of poetic rebellion as free in syntax and logic as it is in rhyme and meter. He sailed to Paris in 1923, never to return to Peru, although his feeling for his homeland never disappeared from his writing. Two trips to Russia (1928 and 1929) strengthened his leftist convictions, and he was finally deported from France as a Communist. He went to Spain, where he soon found himself working with Pablo NERUDA to raise support for the Loyalists.

He wrote several novels, notably *Tungsteno* (1931), but a somewhat self-conscious socialist realism tended to weaken the impact of his fiction (collected in *Novelas y cuentes completas*, 1967). As a poet, however, he was remarkably inventive, constantly attempting to discover new possibilities of expression. He is widely considered to be one of the greatest poets of the 20th century. Most of his poetry was collected after his death, in such stirring volumes as *Poemas humanos* (1939; tr *Human Poems*, 1968) and *España, aparta de mi este cáliz* (*Spain, Take Thou This Cup from Me*, 1940). An English edition, *The Complete Posthumous Poetry*, appeared in 1978.

Vallon, Annette   A young Frenchwoman with whom WORDSWORTH had a brief affair while visiting France in 1792. A daughter, Caroline, was born, and Wordsworth corresponded with Annette for a while thereafter. It is believed that the poet returned to France to meet with the mother and child sometime in 1802, shortly before his marriage to Mary Hutchinson. The affair was kept secret by the Wordsworth family and became publicly known only in the 20th century.

Valmiki   The legendary author of the Hindu epic the RĀMAYĀNA. Valmiki was born a BRAHMIN, and is supposed to have lived by stealing until set right by Narada, the adviser of the gods. According to one story, he composed the *Rāmayāna* in a single inspired burst when he saw a hunter's arrow shoot down a mating bird; from *soka* ("sorrow") flowed *sloka* ("poetry").

Valmouth (1918)   A novel by Ronald FIRBANK. Valmouth is Firbank's fantastic English village, where Mrs. Yajñavalka provides Eastern massage and cultured conversation, where society ladies practice religion and pursue men, and where the homosexual hero comes home with a black bride. It was adapted into a successful musical comedy in 1958.

Valois   The name of the French royal house (1328–1589) that preceded the Bourbons.

Vamena   See VISHNU.

vampire   A fabulous being. Supposed to be the ghost of a heretic, excommunicated person, or criminal, the vampire returns to the world at night in the guise of a monstrous bat and sucks the blood of sleeping persons, who, usually, become vampires themselves. Probably the most famous of modern vampires is Count Dracula, the hero of the novel *Dracula* (1897) by Bram Stoker. First filmed as *Nosferatu* (1922), later as *Dracula* (1931), this story was the first of a seemingly unending series of movies about vampires. The word is applied to one who preys upon his fellows: a "blood sucker." In the early 20th century, *vampire*, or *vamp*, meant a *femme fatale*, a beautiful but heartless woman who lures men to moral destruction.

Vanbrugh, Sir John (1664–1726)   English dramatist. His plays of the early 18th century mark the end of the Restoration and the beginning of the change from satirical wit to respectability on the English stage. They include *The*

Relapse (1697), *The Provoked Wife* (1697), *The Confederacy* (1705), and *The Provoked Husband* (1728). Vanbrugh was also an architect and designed a number of buildings, including Blenheim Palace and the Clarendon Building, Oxford.

Van Buren, Martin (1782–1862)   Eighth president of the U.S. (1837–41). The leader of a New York political faction known as the Albany Regency, Van Buren served in the U.S. Senate (1821–28) and as secretary of state (1829–31) under Andrew Jackson. Elected to the vice presidency in 1832 as Jackson's running mate, Van Buren defeated William Henry Harrison in the presidential election of 1836, but his popularity declined as a result of the economic distress engendered by the Panic of 1837. In the famous campaign of 1840, the Whigs appealed to the common man by presenting Harrison as a homespun frontier hero content with his log cabin and jug of hard cider while Van Buren was depicted as an aristocrat who dined off gold plate; Harrison won 234 electoral votes to Van Buren's sixty. In 1844 the Democrats passed Van Buren over after he declared his opposition to the immediate annexation of Texas.

Vančura, Vladislav (1891–1942)   Czech novelist, short-story writer, playwright, and filmmaker. The most prominent prose writer of the Czech avant-garde between the world wars, he was executed by the Nazis.

In his novels and short stories, Vančura departed radically from the traditional realistic model, concentrating on the elaboration of new narrative devices and on a poetic language for fiction. Among his many novels and stories are *Konec starých časů* (1934; tr *The End of the Old Times*, 1965) and a monumental cycle of stories recreating, in modern narrative forms, the events of Czech history: two volumes (*Obrazy z dějin národa českeho*) appeared in 1939 and 1940; the third volume, never completed, was published posthumously in 1948.

Van der Post, Laurens [Jan] (1906–   )   South African novelist and travel writer, of Boer and Dutch-French ancestry. Having grown up on a ranch deep in the South African countryside, Van der Post felt a strong bond with the blacks who surrounded him. With Roy CAMPBELL and William PLOMER he founded the outspoken antiapartheid magazine *Voorslag* and was later forced out of the country for his progressive racial views. He went to Japan, where he became fluent in Japanese and wrote his first novel, *In a Province* (1934), about a black boy's ruinous encounter with the city. He joined the British Army when war was declared in 1939, and served with the commandos all over southeast Asia until he was captured by the Japanese in 1943. As a prisoner, he stored up material for the searing stories in *The Seed and the Sower* (1963) as well as *A Portrait of Japan* (1968) and *The Prisoner and the Bomb* (1971). From 1948 to 1965 he was concerned with promoting agriculture in South Africa, where he farmed his own land. It was during this period that he produced the major works *Venture to the Interior* (1951), *The Dark Eye in Africa* (1955), *The Lost World of the Kalahari* (1958), and *The Heart of the Hunter* (1961), the last two being the record of Van der Post's search for and discovery of a dying tribe of desert Bushmen. In all his books Van der Post combines evocative descriptions of the places and peoples he encounters with personal reflections on the spiritual and intellectual parallels that he perceives. His conviction that peoples of all colors have shared a common humanity through all stages of human history was amplified by his involvement with the work of C. G. JUNG, about whom he wrote in *Jung: The Story of Our Time* (1975). Among his many other works are *A Story Like the Wind* (1972), *A Far-Off Place* (1974), *First Catch Your Eland: A Taste of Africa* (1977), and *Yet Being Someone Other* (1982).

Van der Valk, Piet   See FREELING, NICHOLAS.

van de Velde, Henry   See ART NOUVEAU.

van de Wetering, Janwillem (1931–   ) Dutch novelist. Beginning with *Outsider in Amsterdam* (1975), van de Wetering has produced a series of police procedurals unique in their incorporation of elements of Eastern religions and surrealism into ostensibly "straight" detective fiction. Zen principles are applied in *Tumbleweed* (1976); the surrealistic element, in the form of recurrent dreams and bizarre imagery, predominates in *The Japanese Corpse* (1977), *The Blond Baboon* (1978), and *The Mind Murders* (1981).

Van Doren, Carl [Clinton] (1885–1950) American editor, critic, and biographer. The brother of Mark VAN DOREN, he served on the Columbia University faculty from 1911 to 1930. He acted as managing editor of the *Cambridge History of American Literature* (3 vols, 1917, 1918, 1921) and was a member of the committee on management of the *Dictionary of American Biography* (1926–36). Van Doren helped to give the study of American literature a systematic place in university curricula and wrote widely on literary and historical subjects. His biography *Benjamin Franklin* (1938) won a PULITZER PRIZE.

Van Doren, Mark (1894–1972) American poet, critic, and novelist. Van Doren taught at Columbia University (1920–59) and numbered among his students Lionel TRILLING, John BERRYMAN, and Allen GINSBERG. He served as an editor and critic for the *Nation* in the 1920s and 1930s. He was a prolific and versatile writer; his works include the critical biographies *Henry David Thoreau* (1916), *John Dryden* (1931; rev 1946), *Shakespeare* (1939), and *Nathaniel Hawthorne* (1949); numerous anthologies; *Collected Stories* (1962, 1965, and 1968); and several novels. His scholarly works include *American and British Literature Since 1890* (1939), written with his brother Carl VAN DOREN. He also wrote an autobiography (1958) and a play, *The Last Days of Lincoln* (1959). Van Doren's meditative verse is strongly influenced by the English romantic poets, particularly WORDSWORTH. Among the many collections of his poems are *Collected Poems 1922–1938* (1939;

PULITZER PRIZE), *Collected and New Poems 1924–1963* (1963), *That Shining Place* (1969), and his last poems, *Good Morning* (1973). *The Essays of Mark Van Doren* appeared in 1981.

Van Dyck, Sir Anthony (or Sir Anthony Vandyck; 1599–1641)   Flemish painter. Van Dyck studied briefly under Peter Paul RUBENS and was then influenced by TITIAN while in Italy (1621–26). He settled in England in 1632, becoming court painter to Charles I, whom he depicted in numerous portraits. He was knighted the same year, and his name was anglicized to Vandyke. Although he painted some biblical and historical scenes, he is best known as a portrait painter, particularly of full-length courtly figures, such as *Charles I Hunting* (c1635). The freedom of his drawing, the elegance and ease of his work, and his brilliant representation of rich fabrics exerted a tremendous influence on 18th-century English portraiture.

Van Gogh, Vincent (1853–1890)   Dutch painter. Before painting, he worked intermittently in various clerical jobs and in 1878 went to work as a Calvinist missionary among the coal miners of Borinage, Belgium. He was overzealous and unsuccessful as an evangelist, but the experience provided the inspiration for many of his paintings, including the famous *Potato Eaters* (1885). Largely self-taught as an artist, he began by imitating Jean François MILLET and later encountered the impressionists, whose influence is evident in his many Provençal paintings of the late 1880s, particularly *Souvenir de Mauve*, a memorial to his uncle and mentor Antoine Mauve (1838–88). Impressionist methods proved restrictive to his expression, however, and he evolved the vibrant, often violent, technique for which he is best known. Characterized by bold, slashing strokes in thick impasto, his later paintings relate his inner turmoil through their intensity. The technique can be seen in his most famous paintings, such as the still-life *Sunflowers* (1888) and *Starry Night* (1889), and in his many deeply introspective self-portraits.

In spite of a short artistic career variously interrupted and intensified by mental illness, Van Gogh left a vast and enormously varied oeuvre. His life and struggles were chronicled in a continual correspondence with his brother Theo, which was fortunately saved and published in three volumes in 1959 as *Complete Letters*. He took his own life at the age of thirty-seven.

Vanir   The Norse nature gods, once at war with the AESIR. After an exchange of hostages, the two races of gods made peace, and the Vanir were received in ASGARD. NIORD, the water god, was the chief. His son was FREY; his daughter, FREYA; and his wife, Skadi. Noatun was their home.

Vanity Fair   In Bunyan's PILGRIM'S PROGRESS, a fair established by BEELZEBUB, Apollyon, and Legion in the town of Vanity and lasting all year round. Here are sold houses, lands, honors, preferments, titles, countries, kingdoms, and all sorts of worldly pleasures.

Vanity Fair, a Novel without a Hero (1848)   A novel by William Makepeace THACKERAY. The author said of the novel while he was writing it: "*What I want to make is a set of people living without God in the world (only that is a cant phrase), greedy, pompous men, perfectly self-satisfied for the most part, and at ease about their superior virtue. Dobbin and poor Briggs are the only two people with real humility as yet. Amelia's is to come.*"

The two boarding-school friends Amelia Sedley and Becky SHARP are in marked contrast throughout the novel. Becky Sharp, clever, scheming, determined to get on in the world, first plays her cards to win Amelia's rich and stupid brother, Joseph Sedley. Failing that, she secretly marries Rawdon Crawley, a younger son of Sir Pitt Crawley, at whose house Becky is governess. Rawdon, however, is disinherited, but the undaunted Becky manages to live at the height of fashion on a small income with the help of Lord Steyne. Rawdon finally becomes suspicious of his wife's relations with Steyne, and, when at last he discovers the truth, he departs to become the governor of Coventry Island, leaving his son by Becky to the care of his brother Pitt. This causes Becky to be completely ostracized, and she is forced to live by her wits on the Continent.

In the meantime Amelia, loved by George Osborne and William Dobbin, has married the former, but he is killed in the battle of WATERLOO. Because of her poverty, Amelia is forced to give her son, Georgy, into the care of his grandfather, Mr. Osborne, who will, however, have nothing to do with her. On Mr. Osborne's death, Georgy is left a fortune. Amelia and her brother, traveling on the Continent, now meet Becky Sharp, and the latter gradually regains her old influence over Joseph Sedley. The faithful Dobbin, who has loved Amelia through thick and thin, is at last rewarded with her hand.

Van Loon, Hendrik Willem (1882–1944) Dutch-born American journalist and historian. Van Loon is best known for his many illustrated popularized histories, such as *Ancient Man* (1920), *The Story of Mankind* (1921), and *The Story of the Bible* (1923). He also taught history at several American colleges, worked as a correspondent for the Associated Press, served as an editor of the Baltimore *Sun*, and was a distinguished radio commentator.

Van Vechten, Carl (1880–1964)   American critic and novelist. A leading music critic and the author of five volumes of music criticism, Van Vechten is best known for his witty, satirical, and sophisticated novels of life among New Yorkers in the 1920s. Van Vechten's best novel is NIGGER HEAVEN, a book about Harlem.

Vanzetti, Bartolomeo   See SACCO-VANZETTI CASE.

Varāha   An avatar of VISHNU, represented as a boar.

Varchi, Benedetto (1503–1565)   Florentine historian. He wrote a history of his native city and a treatise on language, the *Ercolano*. Posterity is indebted to him primarily because of his good sense in refusing the request of

CELLINI that he revise the style of the celebrated autobiography.

Vargas Llosa, [Jorge] Mario [Pedro] (1936–)   Peruvian novelist. Officials at a school Vargas Llosa had attended in Lima ceremonially burned hundreds of copies of his first novel, *La ciudad y los perros* (1963; tr *The Time of the Hero*, 1966), when they recognized the setting for this blistering treatment of military academies. The novel was the first of several about political corruption, violence, and exploitation. In his public statements as well as in his books, Vargas Llosa speaks as a voice of society's conscience. He left his country for Europe in 1959, living in Paris, London, and Barcelona, but his writing is always, at heart, about Peru, its powerful and powerless, and its dramatic and tragic history. His next novel was *La casa verde* (1966; tr *The Green House*, 1968), a vast and complicated book in which his numerous characters struggle in vain to extract themselves from the degenerative mire of social and economic forces that have shaped their lives. This was followed by *Conversación en La Catedral* (1969; tr *Conversation in The Cathedral*, 1975), a densely written exploration of the hypocrisy and corruption of Peruvian business and politics; and *Pantaleón y las visitadoras* (1973; tr *Captain Pantoja and The Special Service*, 1978), a farcical novel about a military brothel in the Peruvian Amazon. After this Vargas Llosa turned to a novelistic examination of writing itself and the relationship between a creative work and its inspiration in *La tía Julia y el escribidor* (1977; tr *Aunt Julia and the Scriptwriter*, 1982). In stark contrast, *The War of the End of the World* (1984) is a historical novel about the popular rebellion in the impoverished northeast of Brazil against the military government and the eventual crushing of the rebels by the army. *Historia de Mayta* (1985) appeared in English as *The Real Life of Alejandro Mayta* in 1986. Vargas Llosa's novels are so vast in scope and so structurally complex that both plot and character often are secondary. He expands the conventional narrative form with such devices as shifting points of view, jumbled time sequences, and intricately layered, multiple plot lines. His short stories are carefully structured, well crafted, and filled with suspense. The first collection of his stories to appear in English translation was *Los cachorros* (1967; tr *The Cubs*, 1979). He has written numerous essays and a critical study of his friend Gabriel GARCÍA MÁRQUEZ in *García Márquez: Historia de un deicidio* (1971).

varna   See CASTE.

Varner, Eula   A rural Helen of Troy in William Faulkner's trilogy beginning with THE HAMLET. A mindlessly voluptuous woman married to the impotent Flem SNOPES, she is beloved of nearly every man in the town of Jefferson and is the mistress of Manfred De Spain. Ultimately, however, she has the courage to commit suicide in order to save her daughter Linda from the shame of scandal over her mother.

Varuna In the early Hindu mythology of the RIG VEDA, the lord of the universe; with INDRA the greatest of the gods of the Vedic times (4000 BC). Varuna is invoked as the night sky, and his double, Mitra, as the day sky. In the later Vedic period his power is more and more confined to this one aspect of nature. In the post-Vedic period, however, he becomes the Hindu NEPTUNE, represented as an old man riding a sea monster with a club in one hand and a rope in the other.

Vasari, Giorgio (1511–1574) Italian painter, architect, and art historian. He painted mannerist portraits and religious themes in the 1530s and 1540s and was the architect of the Uffizi in Florence (1560–80), but he is best known as the author of *Lives of the Most Eminent Painters and Sculptors* (1550, enlarged 1568). Although sometimes inaccurate and always subjective, the *Lives* are a valuable source of information on Italian artists and, more importantly, on RENAISSANCE thought and aesthetics. The concept of the Renaissance as a rebirth of fine art was first set forth in the *Lives*, and thus the work can be seen to have greatly influenced the course of the Renaissance itself.

Vasconcelos, José (1882–1959) Mexican educator, philosopher, and writer. Trained as a lawyer and being a leading member of the intellectual group known as the *Ateneo de la Juventud*, Vasconcelos took an active part in the revolutionary movements that swept Mexico after 1910. As minister of education under President Alvaro Obregón, he initiated an outstanding program of mass education, especially in rural areas, that reflected his own passion for enlightenment. In 1929 he ran for the presidency, denouncing the corruption and militarism that infected Mexican politics; after winning only a small number of votes, he charged fraud and was forced into exile. He was permitted to return in 1939.

During his years of exile, he wrote several works, notably *Etica* (1932) and *Estética* (1936), expounding his philosophical system, which was strongly influenced by SCHOPENHAUER. At the same time he produced what may be his most enduring work—an impassioned, often bitter, autobiography consisting of five volumes: *Ulises criollo* (1935; tr *Mexican Ulysses*, 1963, repr 1972), *La tormenta* (1936), *El desastre* (1938), *El proconsulado* (1939), and *La flama* (1959). In these books, which reflect his increasingly conservative views and his conversion to Catholicism, he extolled Mexico's Hispanic tradition and berated the U.S. Among his many other works are *Prometeo vencedor* (1920), a drama, and *La raza cósmica* (1925), in which he predicted the appearance of a new "cosmic race" of human beings in Latin America.

Vashti In the OLD TESTAMENT, the proud queen of King AHASUERUS before the days of ESTHER. Merry with wine, the king commanded his chamberlains to bring Vashti into the banquet hall to show the guests her beauty; when she refused to obey the insulting order, the angered king divorced her (Esther 1:10–19).

Vassilikos, Vassilis (1933–) Greek writer. A militant defender of political freedom and a sophisticated critic of the "age of affluence," Vassilikos has produced several dozen books of avant-garde fiction, poetry, essays, and translations, plus a new "cinematic" genre, in which he blends fiction and documentary. The best example of this genre is *Zeta* (1966; tr *Z*, 1968), a fictionalized account of a leftist deputy's murder by reactionaries in the 1960s which was made into a film by the Greek director Costa-Gavras. Vassilikos spent the years between 1967 and 1974 in self-imposed exile to protest the military's seizure of political power in Greece. His prose works include *To phyllo; to pegadi; t'angeliasma* (1961; tr *The Plant, the Well, the Angel*, 1964); *Hoi photographies* (1964; tr *The Photographs*, 1971); *Outside the Walls* (1973), a collection of newspaper articles; *O Monarchis* (*The Monarch*, 1976); and several short stories.

Vathek, an Arabian Tale (1786) A GOTHIC NOVEL by William Beckford (1759–1844). Vathek, the ninth caliph of the Abbasside dynasty, is a haughty, effeminate monarch, induced by his sorceress mother, the Greek Carathis, and by his own curiosity and egotism to offer allegiance to Eblis, the Devil, in the hope of obtaining the throne of the pre-Adamite sultans. This he gains, only to find that it is a place of torture and that he is doomed to remain in it forever. In the final scene the hearts of the newly damned are set aflame with infernal fire.

This story of how the sadistic young caliph sold his soul to the devil is a notable contribution to the literature of horror that also includes THE MONK by Matthew Lewis. Beckford's Orientalism is largely derived from the ARABIAN NIGHTS.

Vatican Cellars, The See LAFCADIO'S ADVENTURES.

Vatican City A city-state enclave in Rome, Italy, ruled by the pope. The Vatican City contains the basilica of St. Peter, the offices of the Papal See, and the Vatican Palace, the residence of the pope, which also houses the famous papal libraries and museums.

This tiny state (108.7 acres), which is fully independent, was established by the Lateran Treaty with Italy (1929).

Vatican Swindle, The See LAFCADIO'S ADVENTURES.

vaudeville A light entertainment, also called variety, consisting of a succession of unrelated acts such as songs, dances, comedy routines, acrobatics, etc. The name comes from Vau-de-Vire (in Normandy, France), where a kind of light, satirical song, designated as "vaudeville," originated.

In 1865, when theatre manager Tony Pastor (1837–1908) opened his Opera House in New York, he introduced this kind of entertainment to the United States. The Palace Theater in New York became the principal home of vaudeville until it closed in 1932.

Vaugelas, Claude Favre, sieur de (1585–1650) French grammarian. An original member of the ACADÉMIE FRANÇAISE, Vaugelas sought in *Remarques sur la langue française* (*Remarks on the French Language*, 1647) to formulate principles of correct French writing and speech based upon the example of the best writers and court speakers of his day. While he had no intention of fixing the French language in perpetuity, he had a lasting influence on the Académie's approach to linguistic reform.

Vaughan, Henry (1622–1695) Welsh-born English poet. Vaughan is often called "the Silurist" because he was born in South Wales, whose inhabitants were known as Silures in ancient times. One of the last of the METAPHYSICAL POETS, he wrote two volumes of secular verse, *Poems* (1646) and *Olor Iscanus* (1651), before turning to religious poetry. His best-known work is *Silex Scintillans* (1650–55), which includes "The Retreat," "The World," and "They Are All Gone into the World of Light." His poetry is characterized by a mystical view of nature and is believed to have exerted considerable influence on WORDSWORTH.

Vaughan Williams, Ralph (1872–1958) English composer, considered the most important of his generation. Vaughan Williams's music displays a distinctly English character consciously derived from the English folk and classical tradition. This quality is evident in the operas *Hugh the Drover* (1911) and *The Pilgrim's Progress* (1949), and in many other works, such as *A London Symphony* (1914; rev 1920), the second of his nine symphonies, and *Fantasia on a Theme from Thomas Tallis* (1909). His best-known composition is probably the Fantasia on "Greensleeves," an arrangement of an excerpt from his opera *Sir John in Love* (1924; after Shakespeare's MERRY WIVES OF WINDSOR).

Vazov, Ivan (1850–1921) Bulgarian writer. Following Bulgaria's liberation from Turkey in 1878, Vazov almost single-handedly filled the void of a national literature. Extraordinarily prolific, he wrote in every genre, virtually setting a standard for subsequent literary developments in his homeland. His writings are imbued with a strong sense of the strength and the suffering of his countrymen before independence. His many volumes of poetry include *Izbavlenie* (*Liberation*, 1878), *Pod nashete nebe* (*Under Our Heaven*, 1900), and *Ne shte zagine* (*It Will Not Perish*, 1920). His internationally famous novel, *Pod igoto* (1893; tr *Under the Yoke*, 1894), about the beginnings of the Turkish revolt, is a landmark in patriotic literature.

Ve The brother of ODIN and VILI in Scandinavian mythology. He was one of the three deities who took part in the creation of the world, his role being to give the senses to the first man and woman, ASK and Embla. He, Odin, and Vili slew Ymir and drowned the whole race of the frost giants in his blood.

Veblen, Thorstein B[unde] (1857–1929) American economist and social philosopher, known for his trenchant criticism of 19th-century capitalism. Born in Wisconsin of Norwegian immigrant parents, Veblen studied at Carleton College, Johns Hopkins, and Yale, and taught at several American universities. His first published book, THE THEORY OF THE LEISURE CLASS, became an American classic in economics and sociology. His ability to understand the psychological bases of social and economic institutions made him an innovative and influential social critic. He also wrote *The Theory of Business Enterprise* (1904), *The Instinct of Workmanship* (1914), and *The Vested Interests and the State of the Industrial Arts* (1919).

Vedānta See DARSHANA.

Vedas (Sans, "knowledge; lore") The four most sacred books of HINDUISM, recognized by most Hindus as the authoritative source of spiritual truths. They are the RIG VEDA, or Veda of the stanzas, the oldest and most important, consisting of prayers and hymns in verse; the *Yajur Veda*, or Veda of liturgical formulae, consisting of prayers in prose; the *Sama Veda*, or Veda of melodies, containing prayers (most of which come from the *Rig Veda*) for musical chanting; and the *Atharva Veda*, consisting largely of magical spells and incantations.

These four Vedas are collectively referred to as Samhitas. Also considered part of Vedic literature in general are the prose interpretations later appended to the *Vedas*, the *Brāhmanas*; the treatises on meditation, the *Aranyakas*; and the speculative treatises, the UPANISHADS.

Vega [Carpio], Lope [Félix] de (1562–1635) Spanish dramatist and poet. Lope's achievement is considered second among Spanish writers only to that of Cervantes. The world's most prolific playwright, he is also known as *El Fénix de los Ingenios* and *Monstruo de la Naturaleza* ("Prodigy of Nature"), the latter a name given to him by Cervantes. His reputation was such that the phrase "Es de Lope" became a synonym for perfection. According to his contemporary biographer, Montalbán, he wrote about 1800 *comedias*, or plays, 400 AUTOS SACRAMENTALES, and many short sketches, interludes, and simple compositions accompanied by songs, which were woven into many of his plays. Surviving works include 426 *comedias* and 42 *autos*.

Virtually alone, Lope created the Spanish national drama, blending the most effective elements of earlier times. He elaborated some of his essential ideas in *El arte nuevo de hacer comedias* (*The New Art of Writing Plays*, 1609), a poetical essay in which he gave the rules for a new kind of play (*comedia nueva*), whose principal characteristics were violation of the unities, division of the play into three acts, with the *dénouement* beginning about the middle of the last act, and the use of a variety of metrical forms in each play.

Lope's restless sensibility and ever-changing and contradictory personality made him understand the Spanish people, especially the masses, better than any other playwright. His works reflect his violent character and tumultuous existence, crowded with love affairs, elopements, abductions, and several marriages; his religious intolerance; and his profound love for his family. Even when he took holy orders (1614) after a religious crisis, he did not curtail his profane writing or his amorous proclivities.

Lope's plays, like those of Shakespeare, reveal him as a writer of artistic integrity as well as an ingenious craftsman who utilized dramatic themes and devices that would appeal to a mass audience. He knew that the people would applaud a play like *El niño inocente de la Guardia* because of its anti-Semitic theme, just as they would like *El remedio en la desdicha* and *Pedro Carbonero*, in which Moors are portrayed sympathetically, in accordance with popular sentiment.

Lope's characters are not given to reflection, unlike those of CALDERÓN's more intellectual dramas. Instead, his personages are spontaneous, paradoxical, and unreasonable; accordingly, they are more engaging than Calderón's. It is difficult, in many of Lope's plays, to find a single central character. Sometimes there are two or three, a nobleman and common people, as in *El caballero de Olmedo*; sometimes the people themselves constitute the protagonist, as in FUENTEOVEJUNA.

Lope's most important and representative works are his historical plays based on national events, such as *Fuenteovejuna*, PERIBÁÑEZ, and EL MEJOR ALCALDE, EL REY. In these three plays, the common people and the king are arrayed against a corrupt feudal nobility. Other well-known historical dramas are *El caballero de Olmedo*, *Porfía hasta morir*, *Las grandezas de Alejandro*, and *Roma abrasada*. He also wrote numerous heroic plays based on Spanish legends and chronicles, such as *El último godo*, dealing with Rodrigo, the last Visigothic king of Spain; *Las mocedades de Bernardo del Carpio*; *Las almenas de Toro*, about El Cid; and *El bastardo Mudarra*, about the legend of the seven *infantes* of Lara.

Among his COMEDIAS DE CAPA Y ESPADA are *El acero de Madrid*, *Los melindres de Belisa*, *El perro del hortelano*, and *La moza del cántaro*.

His religious plays include *El vaso de elección*, *Barlaam y Josafat*, *El divino africano*, and *El serafín humano*. Among his *autos* are *El auto de los cantares*, *La siega*, *La locura por la honra*, and *El hijo pródigo*.

Although Lope is remembered chiefly for his plays, he also essayed other types of literature. LA DOROTEA, a long prose romance, is his best nondramatic work. His other prose works include *La Arcadia* (1598), a pastoral romance in which Lope appears as Belardo and the duke of Alba as Anfriso, and *El peregrino en su patria* (1604). His finest lyrics are collected in *Rimas sacras* (1614) and *Rimas humanas y divinas* (1634). He also wrote narrative poetry: the historical epics *Jerusalén conquistada* (1609), based on the Third CRUSADE but containing much legendary material, *La Dragontea* (1598), which is directed against England and Sir Francis DRAKE, and *Corona trágica* (1627), about MARY STUART; the romantic epic *La hermosura de*

Angelica (1602), a sequel to Ariosto's ORLANDO FURIOSO; and the burlesque epic *Gatomaquia* (1634), a witty and ironic parody of the Italian epic, dealing with the romantic affairs of a trio of cats. *Los pastores de Belén* (1612) is a prose-and-verse improvisation about the Holy Family.

Velázquez, Diego Rodríguez de Silva y (1599–1660)   Spanish painter. His early pictures represent common people with a naturalism reminiscent of CARAVAGGIO. In 1623 he became court painter to Philip IV, whom he continued to serve all his life, doing portraits and paintings, among which *The Surrender of Breda* (1634) and *The Maids of Honor* (*Las Meninas*, 1656), both in the Prado, are among the most celebrated. Velázquez is renowned for his objectivity and for the dignity and reserve of his portraits. A sensitive observer of reality, he represented surface textures with a sketchy touch that is more suggestive than imitative, and revealed in his work a sure sense of color, creating both delicate and varied harmonies of tone.

Vélez de Guevara, Luis (1579–1644)   Spanish dramatist and novelist. Born in Ecija, Vélez de Guevara was a page in the household of the archbishop of Seville. He also served in the army in Italy and Africa. Although he later won the favor of Philip IV, who appointed him usher of the king's chamber in 1625, he teetered continually on the brink of penury. His reputation for wit and merriment was such that CERVANTES dubbed him *Quitapesares* ("Dispeller of cares").

He is said to have written some four hundred plays, only eighty of which have survived, most of them dealing with historical subjects. The best known of these is *Más pesa el rey que la sangre*, dealing with Guzmán el Bueno, who placed loyalty to his king above love for his son. In *Reinar después de morir* he retold the story of Inés de CASTRO.

The finest work by Vélez de Guevara is probably the satirical novel *El diablo cojuelo* (1641), which describes the adventures of Cleofás Leandro Pedro Zambullo, a student who releases a "limping devil" from a bottle in which he had been confined by a magician. To repay the kindness, the devil takes Cleofás on an aerial tour of Spain; he makes the roofs transparent, revealing the vices and follies of the citizens and offering a splendid framework for the author's witty commentary. The novel achieved great popularity in Europe as a result of LESAGE's French imitation, *Le Diable boiteux* (1707).

Venerable Bede   See BEDE.

Venice Preserved, or A Plot Discovered (1682)   A tragedy in blank verse by Thomas OTWAY. Jaffeir, a Venetian gentleman now in reduced circumstances, has married Belvidera, daughter of the senator Priuli, who retaliates by disowning her. Jaffeir's friend Pierre persuades him to join a conspiracy to overthrow the Venetian government. After Renault, another of the conspirators, makes advances to Belvidera, Jaffeir reveals the plot to her and, at her urging, warns the senate. Although the senators promise to pardon Jaffeir and his fellow conspirators, they are condemned to death. At the scaffold Jaffeir stabs Pierre to save him from an ignoble death and then kills himself. Belvidera, who has gone mad, also dies. Among the actresses well known for their interpretation of Belvidera were Elizabeth Barr, who created the role and with whom Otway was hopelessly in love, and Sarah Siddons.

It is believed that in the character of the foolish old senator Antonio, Otway was satirizing the earl of Shaftesbury.

Veni, Creator Spiritus (Lat, "Come, Creator Spirit") An 18th-century Latin hymn in honor of the Holy Ghost, author unknown. This hymn was set by MAHLER as the first movement of his *Symphony of a Thousand*, and was set several times by J. S. BACH.

veni, vidi, vici (Lat, "I came, I saw, I conquered") The words with which, according to PLUTARCH, Julius CAESAR announced to his friend Amintius his victory at Zela (47 BC), in Asia Minor, over Pharnaces, son of MITHRIDATES, who had rendered aid to POMPEY. SUETONIUS, however, says that the words were displayed before Caesar's title after his victories in Pontus and does not ascribe them to Caesar himself.

Venizelos, Eleutherios (1864–1936) A Greek statesman. Venizelos forced the abdication of King Constantine (1917) and brought Greece into World War I on the side of the Allies. He took part in the Peace Conference at Paris (1919), advocated a republic in Greece, was several times premier, and finally (1935), having opposed the government, was forced into exile. King George II, after his return to the throne (1935), granted him an amnesty.

Venus In Roman mythology, the goddess of beauty and love. Originally of minor importance, she became, through identification with the Greek APHRODITE, one of the major characters in classical myth.

Venus and Adonis (1593) A long poem by William SHAKESPEARE.

Venusberg In German legend, a magic land of pleasure where VENUS keeps her court. See TANNHÄUSER. William MORRIS modernizes the setting in his poem "The Hill of Venus," included in *The Earthly Paradise* (1868–70).

Vercors (pen name of Jean [Marcel] Bruller, 1902–   ) French novelist and essayist, founder of Les Editions de Minuit, a clandestine publishing house during the Resistance that became one of the most important French publishers of avant-garde writing after World War II. His short novels include the classic *Le Silence de la mer* (1942; tr *The Silence of the Sea*, 1944) and *La Marche à l'étoile* (1943; tr *The Journey to the Star*, 1946) dramatically implied the need for intellectual resistance during the Occupation. His later works include *La Bataille du silence: Souvenirs de minuit* (1967; tr *The Battle of Silence*, 1968), about the founding and operation of Les Editions de Minuit, and the novels *Sylva* (1961; tr 1962) and *Le Radeau de la Meduse* (1969; tr *The Raft of the Medusa*, 1971).

verdad sospechosa, La (The Truth Suspected, c1619) A comedy by Juan Ruiz de ALARCÓN. The hero is Don García, a handsome young aristocrat who is an inveterate liar. Because of this flaw, he ends by losing the woman he loves. This play was the model for CORNEILLE's *Menteur* (1643).

Verdi, Giuseppe (1813–1901) The most important Italian opera composer of the 19th century. All but a few of Verdi's works are operas. More a practical musician than a theorist, he at first completely accepted Italian operatic tradition, with its emphasis on vocal coloratura and beautiful melodies supported by conventional orchestral complements and its reliance on the set forms of recitative and aria. Only as he matured did he develop his unique form of *arioso* as the basis of his style. This form is evident in his last two operas, *Otello* (1887) and *Falstaff* (1893).

Verdi was an ardent nationalist and was associated with the struggle for Italian independence. The death of the poet and patriot MANZONI led him to write his famous *Requiem Mass* in 1874. Among his other operas are *Rigoletto* (1851), *Il trovatore* (1853), *La traviata* (1853), *Simon Boccanegra* (1857; rev 1881), *La forza del destino* (1862), *Don Carlo* (1867), and *Aida* (1871).

Verdurins The name of a *nouveau-riche* couple in Marcel Proust's REMEMBRANCE OF THINGS PAST. Insignificant themselves in the social hierarchy, the Verdurins affect scorn for the GUERMANTES and other aristocrats who ignore them. Fiercely possessive toward the little clan who attend their almost nightly *soirées*, they pride themselves on attracting and launching literary, artistic, and musical celebrities. Gradually there is a narrowing of the social gulf between them and the elite, and Mme Verdurin eventually marries the prince de Guermantes.

Vere, Edward de, earl of Oxford See OXFORD, EDWARD DE VERE, EARL OF.

Verga, Giovanni (1840–1922) Italian novelist and leader of the naturalistic school (called *verismo* in Italy). A regionalist writer, he is at his best when he describes the environment with which he was most familiar: the land and people of Sicily. As a young man, Verga left his native Catania and resided for a time in Florence and in Milan, where the action of his early novels takes place. His short story "Nedda" (1874) initiated his naturalistic depiction of Sicilian peasant life.

After Verga's return to Sicily (1879) appeared two collections of short stories: *Vita dei campi* (1880) and *Novelle rusticane* (1883), the former containing the novella *Cavalleria rusticana*, which Pietro Mascagni reworked as an opera (1890).

The great novels of this period are I MALAVOGLIA and *Maestro Don Gesualdo* (1889). They were to be the first two novels of a projected five-novel cycle that was intended to depict man's struggle for material existence from the lowest, most primitive level of impoverished fisherfolk (*I Malavoglia*) to the highest pinnacle of wealth and power, embodied in the "man of luxury" (the planned, but never realized, *L'uomo di lusso*). See DE ROBERTO, FEDERICO; SCAPIGLIATURA, LA.

Vergil (full Latin name Publius Vergilius Maro, 70–19 BC)   Roman poet. He was born in Andes, a small village near Mantua. After a preliminary education at Cremona, his father, a fairly prosperous farmer, sent him to Rome to study rhetoric and the physical sciences. The seventeen-year-old farm boy was, however, too shy and frail to stand up well in the competitive city. After several years, he gave up the ambition of becoming an advocate and, retiring to his father's farm, spent his time studying Greek philosophy and poetry.

Vergil was twenty-five in 44 BC when Julius Caesar was assassinated. All of the Roman world, even the small village of Andes in quiet, rustic Transpadane Gaul, was plunged into political chaos. Like all periods of political revolution in Roman Italy, the period from 44 to 40 BC was marked by large-scale confiscations and bloody reprisals —what the Romans termed proscriptions. In one of these mass confiscations (41 BC), all the land in the neighborhood of Mantua and Cremona was confiscated, the owners were given notice to vacate, and their farms were resettled by veterans of Antony's army. Fortunately, however, through the influence of the gifted administrator and man of letters Asinius Pollio, Vergil was not dispossessed. Instead, his poetry was taken by Pollio to MAECENAS, who was already what would be known today as the minister of culture. Maecenas was enthusiastic over these short pastoral compositions, then known generically as *eclogae* (see ECLOGUE), and urged the poet to organize them into publishable form. After several years of painstaking polishing, during which Vergil added two or three more poems and fitted them into the arrangement of ten idyls, he published the work under the title *Bucolica* (37). The BUCOLICS, apparently only artful variations on a theme by THEOCRITUS, are, however, imbued with the spirit of postrepublican Rome, a spirit which looked back longingly to simpler times and forward with desperate hope to a new era of peace.

His fame now well established by the *Bucolics*, Vergil accepted the invitation of Maecenas to come and live on his estate in Naples and there begin work on a much more ambitious project, which Vergil had already outlined. The poet worked for seven years (37–30) on what was to be the great didactic poem of Rome: the *Georgica*, or "poems of farm life," also known as the GEORGICS. While Octavius Caesar (see AUGUSTUS) was busy with the reconstruction of Rome's moral and political life, Vergil was occupied with the portrait of that archetypal builder and civilizer, the farmer. Like his *Bucolics*, Vergil's *Georgics* are superficially based on a Greek classic, HESIOD's *Works and Days*, but, again like his first work, they are filled with an intense historical sense of the past and present and with the hope that Rome, under Octavius, would enter an era of peace.

After finishing the *Georgics*, Vergil immediately began work in the most exalted genre of classical literature, the epic. He gave consideration to several possible legends before he finally decided on the story of AENEAS, the Trojan prince whose descendants were supposed to have founded Rome and whom the Julian family, of which Octavius was a member, claimed as their great ancestor. Again he made use of an ancient model, this time the ILIAD and the ODYSSEY of Homer, and again created a work that was, in every sense, Roman. In this great twelve-book myth, his countrymen were to see not only a symbolic summation of their history but a statement of their noblest aspirations for the future. The epic was never wholly completed. The poet died on September 21, 19 BC, after returning from a voyage to Athens. His unfinished AENEID was not destroyed, as he had wished, but was edited by his friends Varius and Tucca and, at last, published. Despite its minor imperfections—several obscure passages, a number of unfinished lines, and two or three inconsistencies in narrative—the *Aeneid* was at once accepted as the supreme epic of the Roman world.

Vergil was popular during the Middle Ages, partly because of his acceptance by the early Christians as an inspired poet and partly because of the medieval habit of making magicians out of the poets and sages of antiquity. Dante, in his DIVINE COMEDY, has Vergil lead him through the infernal and purgatorial regions, considering him the wisest and most closely Christian of the ancient pagan poets.

Verhaeren, Emile (1855–1916)   Belgian poet. At the opposite pole from MAETERLINCK's contemplative sensibility, Verhaeren's verse is characterized by energy and unflagging vitality. He was influenced by the French SYMBOLISTS and became one of the most important exponents of FREE VERSE associated with *La Jeune Belgique*. Beginning with *Les Flamandes* (1883), a robust celebration of peasant life, Verhaeren used his painter's eye for detail to produce over thirty volumes of varied and powerful verse. Before World War I he entertained a faith in the possibility of universal brotherhood and in human progress. *Les Visages de la vie* (1899), *Les Forces tumultueuses* (1902), and *Les Rhythmes souverains* (1910) all express this faith. Essentially socialist in outlook, he expressed his despair at the collapse of rural life and the encroachment of cities in *Les Villes tentaculaires* (1895), a grim picture of the destruction of nature and human quality by technology. His most refined and lyrical verse is contained in a trilogy of love poems to his wife: *Les Heures claires* (1896; tr *The Sunlit Hours*, 1916), *Les Heures d'après-midi* (1905; tr *Afternoon*, 1917), and *Les Heures du soir* (1911; tr *The Evening Hours*, 1918). *Les Ailes rouges de la guerre* (1916) is a bitter attack on the ravages of war, which brutally destroyed his hope in the future.

Veríssimo, Érico [Lopes] (1905–1975)   Brazilian novelist. Veríssimo's novels are set in his native state of Rio

Grande do Sul and in its capital city, Porto Alegre, and are rich in characterization and extensive in scope. His best-known works include *Caminhos cruzados* (1935; tr *Cross-roads*, 1943), which describes five days in the lives of the inhabitants of a suburban street in Porto Alegre; *Olhai os lírios do campo* (1938; tr *Consider the Lilies of the Field*, 1945), about a wealthy doctor who reviews his past at the deathbed of a former mistress; and *O resto é silêncio* (1942; tr *The Rest Is Silence*, 1946), which studies the effect of a girl's suicide on seven people who witness her act. *O tempo e o vento* (1949; tr *Time and the Wind*, 1951) is the title of a trilogy tracing the development of Rio Grande do Sul in the history of the Terra-Cambará family from the 18th through the 20th centuries.

Verkhovensky, Pyotr Stepanovich   In Fyodor Dostoyevsky's THE POSSESSED, the leader of the revolutionary terrorist group. Pyotr, whose portrayal was partially based on the character of the infamous Sergey NECHAYEV, is depicted as cold and ruthless in his methods and strictly self-seeking in his goals. His aim is destruction for the pleasure of destruction, with no real interest in improving the lot of the oppressed people he claims to be helping. Personally he is shown to be an obnoxious boor. He is fascinated by the sinister STAVROGIN and quickly realizes the magnetism the man would exert as a figurehead of the revolutionary movement. He is unable, however, to persuade Stavrogin to lend himself to such a purpose. Verkhovensky's most diabolic act in the novel is the murder of SHATOV, who had been trying to resign from the revolutionary group. The incident was based on a real event from Nechayev's career.

Stepan Trofimovich Verkhovensky, the father of Pyotr Stepanovich, lives in retirement on the estate of Varvara Petrovna, Stavrogin's mother. Stepan is a representative of the mildly radical generation of the 1840s, who read Fourier and SAINT-SIMON, talked incessantly, and took no real action against the government (see FOURIERISM). Stepan is, however, convinced that the authorities regard him as a dangerous radical and are constantly watching his every move. His harmlessness is contrasted to the menace represented by his nihilist son, Pyotr. The implication seems to be that such men as Stepan, who wholeheartedly accepted Western ideas, prepared the ground for the growth of nihilism.

Stepan's distance from the ways of the new generation is emphasized during a literary evening at which he passionately defends the value and autonomy of art against the ridicule of the young radicals, whose views on such matters are strictly utilitarian.

Verlaine, Paul (1844–1896)   French poet. Associated with the early SYMBOLISTS, Verlaine is noted for the grace, delicacy, and musical suggestiveness of his lyrics. Among his books are *Poèmes saturniens* (1866), a volume in the style of the Parnassians; *Fêtes galantes* (1869), written in a Watteau-like, 18th-century mood, and *Romances*

sans paroles (1874). *Sagesse* (1881) contains poems of religious sentiment that reflect the poet's conversion to Roman Catholicism. Verlaine's personal life was disordered and tragic. He abandoned his young wife and in 1872 began his unhappy liaison with the young poet RIMBAUD. This relationship, which ended in Brussels with a prison term for Verlaine and a bullet wound for Rimbaud, marked the beginning of a pitifully debauched existence that continued until the poet's death without, however, affecting his honesty and childlike simplicity of spirit.

Vermeer, Jan (or Jan Van der Meer, 1632–1675) Dutch painter. Vermeer, who was born in Delft and lived there all his life, was the creator of some thirty-five highly prized known paintings. The work of a master colorist, these quiet interior scenes are characterized by an absence of sentimentality, by outstanding color harmonies, and by an appreciation of light effects that led to the frequent inclusion of an open window as a source of light. Among his famous genre paintings are *The Lacemaker* (c1664) and *The Artist in His Studio* (c1665–70).

Vermeylen, Auguste (1872–1945)   Flemish essayist and critic. A guiding force in the influential literary journal *Van nu en straks*, Vermeylen's nationalist opinions had a remarkable influence on both the literary tastes and the religious, social, political, and moral attitudes of the Flemish. He wrote a number of essays on the Flemish movement and published an important critical history of Flemish literature, *De Vlaamse letteren van Gezelle tot heden* (4th ed, 1949). His novel *De wandelende Jood* (*The Wandering Jew*, 1906), a symbolic treatment of a man's search for truth, became the model on which novels of succeeding generations were based.

Verne, Jules (1828–1905)   French writer. Verne's startling imaginative powers produced a number of semi-scientific adventure stories that proved to be not only universally popular with young people but also almost unbelievably prophetic. He is best known for *Voyage au centre de la terre* (A *Voyage to the Center of the Earth*, 1864), *The Mysterious Island* (1870), TWENTY THOUSAND LEAGUES UNDER THE SEA, and AROUND THE WORLD IN EIGHTY DAYS.

Vernon, Mme de   The mother in Mme de Staël's DELPHINE. A cool-headed, intriguing egotist, she is considered to be a satirical, vengeful portrait of TALLEYRAND in feminine guise.

Veronese, Paolo (real name Paolo Cagliari, 1528–1588)   Italian painter. Born in Verona, he excelled in large, brilliantly colored, and detailed paintings; these adorn the palaces and churches of his adopted city, Venice. He favored the pageantry of a lively multitude of richly costumed figures in both his religious and allegorical works. His *Rape of Europa* (1576) and *Apotheosis of Venice* (c1585), the latter a spectacular essay in illusionist ceiling decoration, may be seen in the palace of the Doges. His *Feast at the House of Simon* (1573) caused him to be arraigned before the INQUISITION for iconographic violations. He avoided punishment by changing the title to its present one, *Christ in the House of Levi*, and making a historic plea for artistic freedom in the handling of religious themes.

Veronica, St. A late medieval legend says that a maiden handed her handkerchief to Jesus on his way to Calvary. He wiped the sweat from his brow, returned the handkerchief to the owner, and went on. The handkerchief was found to bear a perfect likeness of the Saviour, and was called *Vera-Icon* ("true likeness"); the maiden became *St. Veronica*, and is commemorated on February 4. Milan Cathedral, St. Sylvester's in Rome, and St. Bartholomew's in Genoa all lay claim to the handkerchief.

Verrazano, Giovanni da (c1485–c1528) Florentine navigator who located the mouth of the Hudson River (1524) while seeking a northwest passage to Asia.

Verrocchio, Andrea del (real name Andrea di Michele di Francesco de' Cione, 1436–1488) Florentine sculptor, painter, and goldsmith. Few of his works survive, but his *Baptism of Christ* (c1470), in which his young pupil LEONARDO DA VINCI participated, and other paintings reveal his innovation in the depiction of three-dimensional space. His greater fame as a sculptor rests mainly on the bronze *David* (1476) and the celebrated equestrian statue of the condottiere Colleoni in Venice (1479).

Versailles, treaty of The treaty formally ending World War I, signed on June 28, 1919, by the Allied powers and Germany in the Hall of Mirrors of the palace of Versailles. Similar treaties were accepted by Austria and Bulgaria on September 12, 1919.

versification The practice of verse composition using the traditional mechanical elements of poetry: METER, RHYME, rhythm, accent, STANZA form, etc. The narrower meaning of the term refers only to the structural form of a verse. See PROSODY.

Versilov In Fyodor Dostoyevsky's novel THE RAW YOUTH, the natural father of the central character, Arkady DOLGORUKY. Versilov is a representative of the "predatory type" of the Russian 19th-century man. Infected with Western ideas, without real religious faith, and cut off from a living contact with the Russian people, Versilov is shown as a weak and artificial man, as opposed to Makar Ivanovich DOLGORUKY, the religious pilgrim.

Very, Jones (1813–1880) American poet. Licensed as a Unitarian minister, Very lived a withdrawn life with his sisters in Salem, Massachusetts. At one time he was committed to the McLean Asylum but secured a release partly through the help of Ralph Waldo EMERSON, who declared him "profoundly sane." The only volume of his writings to appear during his lifetime, *Essays and Poems* (1839), was edited and published by Emerson and received high praise. His essays resembled the work of MONTAIGNE, and his fervently religious sonnets showed a clear relationship to the METAPHYSICAL POETS. Two posthumous collections appeared: *Poems* (1883) and *Poems and Essays* (1886).

Vespucci, Amerigo (1451–1512) Florentine navigator. He visited the mouth of the Amazon in 1499 and explored what is now the coast of Brazil in 1501. On the basis of these two voyages (and two others, probably fictional), described in his letters, and because of his assertion that the South American continent was not part of Asia but a new world, his name was given to the land. The designation "AMERICA" was first made by the German cartographer Martin Waldseemüller (1470–1518) in 1507, when he published two maps showing North and South America as distinct land masses separate from Asia; the maps were based on Vespucci's letters, which Waldseemüller also published.

Vesta The virgin goddess of the hearth of Roman mythology, corresponding to the Greek HESTIA, one of the twelve great Olympians (see GODS OF CLASSICAL MYTHOLOGY). She was custodian of the sacred fire brought by AENEAS from Troy, which was never permitted to go out lest a national calamity should follow. See VESTALS.

vestals The six spotless virgins consecrated to VESTA. They tended the sacred fire brought by AENEAS from Troy and preserved by the state in a sanctuary in the Forum in Rome. They were subjected to very severe discipline, and in the event of losing their virginity were buried alive. The vestal virgins also prepared from the first fruits of the May harvest the sacrificial meal for the LUPERCALIA, the Vestalia, and the Ides of September.

The word *vestal* has been figuratively applied to any woman of spotless chastity.

Via Dolorosa The way to the place of the Crucifixion. This was the way that Jesus followed from the Hall of Judgment to Golgotha, about a mile in length. See STATIONS OF THE CROSS.

Vian, Boris (1920–1959) French novelist and dramatist. A poet and existentialist playwright, Vian is best known for the tough and bloody thrillers in the American vein which he wrote under the name of Vernan Sullivan: *J'irai cracher sur vos tombes* (1946), *Les Morts ont tous la même peau* (1947), and *On tuera tous les affreux* (1947). He then turned to a coldly lyrical humor in *L'Écume des jours* (1947; tr *Moon Indigo*, 1973) and *L'Arrache-coeur* (1953; tr *Heartsnatchers*, 1968).

Vicar of Christ A title given to the pope, symbolizing his claim to be the representative of Christ on earth.

Vicar of Wakefield, The (1766) A pastoral novel by Oliver GOLDSMITH. The story is told by Dr. Charles Primrose, an unworldly, generous, and kindly vicar. With his wife, a woman with aspirations to gentility, his two daughters, Olivia and Sophia, and his sons, George, Moses, and two smaller boys, he lives in quiet contentment until he loses his independent income. They move to humbler dwellings near the estate of Squire Thornhill, and there begins a series of misfortunes: Olivia is abducted and seduced by Squire Thornhill after a mock marriage ceremony; the vicar's house burns down and he is imprisoned for debt; Sophia is abducted by an unknown villain; and George, in attempting to avenge Olivia, is imprisoned. The intervention of Sir William Thornhill, the squire's uncle, straightens out the vicar's tangled affairs, which he himself has borne with remarkable fortitude. Sir William not only rescues Sophia, but marries her.

The book early became and has remained a classic, perhaps most of all because it reflects so truly the mellow wisdom and gentle irony of its author.

Viceroys, The   See DE ROBERTO, FEDERICO.

Vice-Versa, or a Lesson to Fathers (1882)   A fantastic novel by F. Anstey (1856–1934). It tells of the transformation of a father into his son and of the schoolboy son into his father.

Vico, Giambattista (or Giovanni Battista Vico, 1668–1744)   Italian philosopher and historian. An opponent of Cartesian rationality, Vico anticipated HEGEL's philosophy. Studies in the comparative history of law led him to formulate a concept of the relativity and evolution of human achievements, which he applied to all the arts and sciences and to ideas in general. In *The New Science* (*La scienza nuova*, 1725–30) he propounds a natural law of growth, decay, and regrowth through which all nations and civilizations must pass.

Victoria (full name Alexandrina Victoria, 1819–1901) Queen of Great Britain and Ireland, empress of India. Victoria's long reign (1837–1901) began on the death of William IV. In 1840 she married ALBERT, prince of Saxe-Coburg-Gotha, who died in 1861. Her name is used to describe the literature, and the characteristics, qualities, and attitudes of the period of her reign. See VICTORIAN.

Victoria, Tomás Luis de (c1548–1611)   The most important Spanish Renaissance composer. Victoria was educated in Rome at the expense of King Philip II. He remained there nearly thirty years, then returned to Madrid in the service of the Empress Maria, Philip's sister. Victoria was a priest, and his work was totally directed to the church; his music is full of the ardor and exaltation of Spanish mysticism.

victoria de Junín, La: Canto a Bolívar (1825) An ode by José Joaquín Olmedo (1780–1847), Ecuadorian poet and statesman. Dedicated to Simón Bolívar, the poem was inspired by the patriots' victories at Junín and Ayacucho, which virtually terminated the South American struggle for independence. In form and structure, the work reveals Olmedo's familiarity with the classics, and the opening lines closely imitate one of the odes of HORACE. However, Olmedo's exuberance, imagination, and extravagant metaphors, which Bolívar himself satirized, make the poem one of the forerunners of the romantic movement in Latin America.

Victorian   Of or pertaining to the sixty-three-year reign (1837–1901) of Queen Victoria of England, to the English people of the period, to their sentiments, beliefs, tastes, and accomplishments. In both literary and social history, Victoria's reign may be divided into two phases, each roughly thirty years long: the first period characterized by moderate and gradual political reforms, by the rapid growth of industry, by an enormous increase in population, by the rise to power of the industrial middle class, whose struggles with the working class and with the old aristocracy were to form the dominant theme of Victorian literature; and the second period characterized by a declining birth rate, by an increasingly jingoistic nationalism, by the looming specter of mass unemployment and economic crisis, by the tendency of the new science to undermine deeply held religious convictions, by the reflection in literature of a growing disillusionment with traditional moral values.

In the first half of Victoria's reign, England enjoyed unparalleled material prosperity and political stability. Prince ALBERT was sufficiently impressed by the achievements of his new country to urge that they be publicly compared with those of the other nations of the world. He became an active promoter of the "Great Exhibition of the Works and Industries of All Nations," held in London in 1851 under the glass arch of the Crystal Palace. Six million persons came from all parts of the kingdom and from nearly every corner of the world to view this great monument to Progress.

Such was the complacent mood during the first half of Victoria's reign: a combination of pride in the stable constitutional government, of optimism generated by increasingly industrial prosperity, of an as yet unshaken confidence in the inherent rightness of the liberal and evangelical virtues of industriousness, self-reliance, temperance, piety, charity, and moral earnestness. William Makepeace THACKERAY, though a self-proclaimed republican, composed odes to the Crystal Palace. TENNYSON, after riding in the first train to travel from Liverpool to Manchester, wrote "Let the great world spin for ever down the ringing grooves of change." Lord MACAULAY began his *History of England* (1848, 1855, 1861) with the suggestion that "the general effect of this checkered narrative will be to excite thankfulness in all religious minds, and hope in the breasts of all patriots. For the history of our country during the last hundred and sixty years is eminently the history of physical, of moral, and of intellectual improvement." In the writings of lesser men, this characteristic pride, optimism, and confidence would often be transformed into a shoddy self-satisfaction, a naïve equating of success with right, and an arrogant belief in the inherent superiority of all things English—sentiments that later generations were to associate, rightly or wrongly, with the word *Victorian*.

The first half of Victoria's reign was a stable and prosperous period, but it was not stagnant. Well before Tennyson and Macaulay so eloquently celebrated the accomplishments of the age, others were diligently exposing its defects. In the 1830s KEBLE, NEWMAN, and PUSEY, as leaders of the OXFORD MOVEMENT, had sought to restore to the Anglican

Church its original spiritual power and ritualistic beauty, to rid it of a bleak and literal evangelical "enthusiasm," to make it once again "more than a merely human institution." Throughout the 30s, 40s, and 50s an increasing number of able writers turned their attention to current social evils that had been recently highlighted by Chartist (see CHARTISM) agitation. The plight of the poor, the trials of the workingman, the evils of child labor, and the incessant conflict of the middle and working classes were examined in books such as Dickens's OLIVER TWIST and HARD TIMES, Mrs. Gaskell's MARY BARTON, Charlotte Brontë's SHIRLEY, and Disraeli's SYBIL and CONINGSBY.

In 1859 Charles Darwin's ORIGIN OF SPECIES was published. Despite the caution with which he presented his conclusions, they were immediately construed by those of orthodox views to be not only a challenge to the prevailing literal biblical interpretation but also to be an affront to the best achievements of an age. Whether he had intended to do so or not, Darwin hastened the undermining of traditional Victorian values. Also published in 1859 was John Stuart MILL's brilliant essay On Liberty. Although he was once a Benthamite, Mill no longer believed that the good society could be based solely upon the crude doctrines of laissez-faire. He advocated a long series of reforms "to fit mankind by cultivation for a state of society combining the greatest personal freedom with that just distribution of the fruits of labour, which the present laws of property do not profess to aim at." And by questioning whether communal ownership or private property would best serve this end, he challenged no less effectively than Darwin the underlying Victorian assumptions.

Throughout the 60s, 70s, and 80s, the assaults upon mid-Victorian values increased in frequency and intensity. Matthew Arnold bitterly attacked the barbarians and Philistines in his Essays in Criticism (1865) and in CULTURE AND ANARCHY. John RUSKIN extolled the beauties of nature and art and decried the ugliness of the industrial age in Sesame and Lilies (1865). Thomas HUXLEY expounded, with somewhat less reticence than Darwin, the implications of evolution in Man's Place in Nature (1863) and in The Physical Basis of Life (1868). Eventually Herbert SPENCER became the only remaining political thinker to advocate the doctrine of laissez-faire, and in Man versus the State (1884) he justified his position by appealing not to the old creed of self-reliance and industry, but to Darwin's theories of evolution.

By the last decade of the 19th century there was no respectable philosophical refuge in which one disposed to cling to his mid-Victorian intellectual heritage could take shelter. The old verities were being assaulted skillfully and with devastating effect from every possible angle by English authors, such as BUTLER, CONRAD, WILDE, WELLS, and SHAW, and by a growing number of foreign writers as well, including ZOLA, MAUPASSANT, and DOSTOYEVSKY. The average reader could either follow them in new and often

disturbing directions or find relief from his humdrum existence by escaping to the South Seas with Robert Louis STEVENSON and to the far-flung outposts of the empire with Rudyard KIPLING.

Victory (1915)   A novel by Joseph CONRAD. Axel Heyst, a man who has deliberately avoided all ties and commitments, lives the life of a self-exiled wanderer in the South Seas. Although he distrusts the world, he is a man of integrity and generosity who can be moved by pity, not love, to help those in trouble. One such is the unhappy young woman Lena, whom he takes to his island retreat. Schomberg, the manager of a hotel where Lena had worked, desires her and tells the unscrupulous adventurer Jones and his followers that Heyst has treasure hidden on his island. The band of ruthless men invade Heyst's sanctuary and Lena is killed in an effort to save herself and Heyst. The only "victory" is Heyst's final recognition of love and his newfound purpose in life through Lena's death.

Vida, Girolamo (or Marco Girolamo Vida, c1485–1566)   Italian poet. Cremona was his birthplace, but he spent most of his life in Rome in the service of his church, which made him bishop of Alba in 1532. He was famous for his Latin poetry, especially De ludo sacchorum (The Game of Chess) and Christias, or Christiad, an epic poem in the Vergilian manner on the life of Christ and the foundation of the Church. In 1527 he wrote De arte poetica, the first of many Renaissance treatises on the art of poetry. In England, GOLDSMITH translated the Ludo, MILTON imitated the Christias, and POPE praised Vida in Essay on Criticism.

vida es sueño, La (Life Is a Dream, c1636)   A play by Pedro CALDERÓN DE LA BARCA, considered one of the outstanding Spanish dramas of all time. This allegorical and philosophical play, through the symbolical character of the hero, Segismundo, explores the mysteries of human destiny, the illusory nature of mundane existence, and the conflict between predestination and free will.

Segismundo, a Polish prince, has been confined in a tower under the care of Clotaldo because astrologers had predicted that he would harm his father, King Basilio. After some years, the king decides to test the character of his son. Segismundo is drugged and brought to the palace, where, since he is unaccustomed to human society, he behaves in a crude and violent fashion. Consequently, he is sent again to his confinement, convinced that the episode in the palace was a dream. Later the people revolt, liberate the prince, who is at first fearful that his new experience may not be real, and seize the kingdom. Segismundo is proclaimed king and, having learned that all life is a dream, decides that only virtue and nobility will give meaning to the dream.

Vidal, Gore (1925–   )   American novelist, playwright, and essayist. Vidal is known for his polished, sophisticated, and bitter satire of public and private corruption. It runs through all his work, from such plays as Visit to a Small Planet (1957) and An Evening with Richard Nixon (1972), to his many novels, which include Myra Breckinridge (1968) and Two Sisters (1970). Julian (1964), Burr (1973), 1876 (1976), Lincoln (1984), and Empire (1987) are novels which probe the personal lives of historical figures. Vidal is reliably outspoken and irreverent; some of his essays, political and otherwise, are collected in Rocking the Boat (1962), Reflections upon a Sinking Ship (1969), Collected Essays 1952–1972 (1972), and Matters of Fact and Fiction (1977). Views from a Window (1980) is a series of conversations (with Robert Stanton). Vidal has also written several entertaining mysteries under the pseudonym Edgar Box.

Vidocq, François Eugène (1775–1857)   French chief of detectives in Paris (1809–27; 1832). Himself a clever criminal, his force consisted of ex-criminals who knew the ways of the underworld. On one occasion Vidocq organized a robbery himself and then investigated it as a police officer. M. LECOQ, a character created by Emile Gaboriau, is based on his character.

Vieira, Antônio (1608–1697)   Portuguese-born Brazilian clergyman, orator, diplomat, and writer. Brought to Brazil at the age of six, Vieira soon identified himself with his new country, although he later spent many years in Europe and became an important adviser to King John IV of Portugal. As a Jesuit preacher and missionary, he dedicated himself to the education and defense of the Indians; he also aroused the suspicions of the Inquisition because of his efforts on behalf of Portuguese Jews. His literary reputation rests largely on his letters and on his fiery, sometimes bombastic, sermons.

Vienna, Congress of   The congress (1814–15) by the powers of Europe after Napoleon's first abdication. It was called to settle the question of new boundaries. France kept the frontiers she had had in 1792; Prussia's territory was much increased; Poland was made into a new kingdom under the tsars.

Vienna Secession   See KLIMT, GUSTAVE.

Vietnam War   The war, fought primarily in South Vietnam, between government forces aided by the United States and insurgents aided by North Vietnam. The conflict between the two Vietnams grew out of the political, religious, and ideological legacies of the defeat of the French colonial regime at Dienbienphu in 1954, when the country was divided along the 17th parallel into a north section, assisted by China, the Soviet Union, and other Communist states, and a south section, aided by the United States. In 1957 the Communist-led insurgents, known as the Vietcong, began a brilliant campaign of guerrilla warfare against South Vietnam; in the United States, the concerns of the Kennedy and Johnson administrations about the "domino theory"—that once a country fell to a Communist regime, its neighbors would also fall—led to increased direct American involvement. As the war continued, however, the conviction grew in Washington, D. C.,

that victory was impossible; at the same time opposition across the U.S. increased as many turned against the war because of its length, the high number of casualties, and revelations of American involvement in war crimes. In January 1973 the U.S. and all Vietnamese parties signed a cease-fire agreement, although fighting between Communist and South Vietnamese forces ended only in 1975 with the fall of Saigon (now Ho Chi Minh City).

A large number of factual and imaginative books have been written about the Vietnam War, including Graham GREENE's The Quiet American (1955); Norman MAILER's The Armies of the Night (1968); Frances FitzGerald's Fire in the Lake (1972); David Halberstam's The Best and the Brightest (1972); Philip Caputo's A Rumor of War (1977); James Jones's Viet Journal (1974); Larry Heinemann's Close Quarters (1977); Michael Herr's Dispatches (1977); and Tim O'Brien's Waiting for Cacciato, which won the National Book Award in 1978. Later books, including Jayne Anne Phillips's Machine Dreams (1984), Bobbie Ann Mason's In Country (1985), and Philip Caputo's Indian Country (1987), tended to concentrate on the effects of the war on families and communities back home rather than on the soldier's experiences in Vietnam.

Vigny, Comte Alfred Victor de (1797–1863) French poet, playwright, and novelist. One of the leaders of the romantic school, although not entirely typical of it in either his life or work, de Vigny wrote poetry marked by stoical despair and a bare, restrained classicism. Bleak and bitter, his work possesses a unique dignity. During the later years of his life, he retired almost entirely from public life, leading an isolated existence in what Sainte-Beuve called his tour d'ivoire ("ivory tower"). His volumes of poetry include Poèmes (1822), Poèmes antiques et modernes (1826), and Les Destinées (1864). Chatterton (1835) is highly esteemed by critics as an example of romantic drama, while Cinq Mars (1826) is an interesting pioneer attempt at a French historical novel. See ROMANTICISM.

Vikings   Danish and Norwegian sea pirates and adventurers of the 8th to 10th century (not to be confused with sea-kings, who were royal Norse chieftains). They were called Norsemen or Normans ("north-men") by the Europeans whose coasts they plundered. They made important permanent settlements in England, France, and Iceland. Henrik IBSEN wrote a drama called The Vikings (1858).

Vildrac, Charles   See ABBAYE GROUP.

Vili   In Norse mythology, a mighty archer who, with his brothers ODIN and VE, slew the giant YMIR and created the world out of his body. When the first man and woman, ASK and Embla, were made, Vili gave them reason and motion.

Villa, Francisco (or Pancho Villa; real name Doroteo Arango; 1877–1923)   Mexican revolutionary leader. Originally a peon in the northern state of Chihuahua, Villa turned to cattle-rustling and became a romantic hero to the local peasantry. With the outbreak of the Mexican Revolution, he joined in the struggle against Porfirio Díaz and Victoriano Huerta, and later vied with Venustiano Carranza for supreme power. He was defeated by Alvaro Obregon, Carranza's lieutenant, at the battle of Celaya in 1915. Hoping to embarrass the Carranza government, Villa led a raid on Columbus, New Mexico, in 1916, killing several Americans. President Wilson responded by dispatching a punitive force under John J. PERSHING into Mexico, and the two nations came close to war. Villa eluded capture and subsequently retired to a hacienda given to him after the successful revolt against Carranza in 1920. He was assassinated three years later. Martín Luis GUZMÁN draws an excellent portrait of him in *The Eagle and the Serpent* (1928).

Village, The (1783)   A long poem by George CRABBE. It was written partly as a realistic response to the artificialities of the pastoral convention, particularly as exemplified in Oliver Goldsmith's THE DESERTED VILLAGE, which Crabbe considered a sentimentalized picture of rural life. *The Village* describes, in realistic terms, the hardships, evils, sordidness, and misery of the lives of country-dwellers of the day.

Village Blacksmith, The (1839)   A poem by Henry Wadsworth LONGFELLOW. Melodic and very popular, it describes a New England smithy.

villanelle   A lyric poem written in TERCETS and a closing QUATRAIN, characterized by two refrain lines. These refrain lines are stated in the first STANZA as lines one and three and return alternately in the succeeding stanzas as line three until the last stanza, where they are repeated in order as lines three and four. The rhyme scheme is A^1-b-A^2, followed by a-b-A^1, a-b-A^2 as many times as desired, completed by a-b-A^1-A^2. The most frequent length is five tercets and a closing quatrain.

Originally a round-song of farm laborers, the name *villanelle* comes from Latin *villa*, "farm." Medieval French villanelles were irregular in form, but in the 16th century the form became fixed. Such famous modern lyrics as "Do not go gentle into that good night," by Dylan THOMAS, are villanelles. The following is an example by Oscar WILDE:

O Singer of Persephone!
  In the dim shadows desolate
Dost thou remember Sicily?

Still through the ivy flits the bee
  Where Amaryllis lies in state,
O Singer of Persephone!

Simaetha calls on Hecate
  And hears the wild dogs at the gate;
Dost thou remember Sicily?

Still by the light and laughing sea
  Poor Polypheme bemoans his fate,
O Singer of Persephone!

And still in boyish rivalry
  Young Daphnis challenges his note;

Dost thou remember Sicily?
Slim Lacon keeps a goat for thee;
  For thee the jocund shepherds wait;
O Singer of Persephone,
Dost thou remember Sicily?

Oscar Wilde, "Theocritus"

Villari, Pascuale (1827–1917)   Italian historian. His best-known works are *Storia di Girolamo Savonarola e de' suoi tempi* (1859–61) and *Niccolò Machiavelli e i suoi tempi* (1877–82).

Villehardouin, Geoffroy de (c1150–c1213) French court adviser and historian. He took part in the Fourth Crusade, and his *Conquête de Constantinople*, considered one of the earliest important works in French prose, recounts the events from 1202 to the capture of Constantinople in 1207.

Villette (1853)   A novel by Charlotte BRONTË. Based on the author's experiences at the Brussels school where she lived and studied in 1842–44 and her deep but frustrated attachment to Constantine Héger, the proprietor, Brontë's novel tells of Lucy Snowe, an English girl who teaches at a girls' boarding school in the city of Villette. After a series of ups and downs revolving around her secret love for a young doctor, Lucy comes to recognize her true destiny in the love of the embittered headmaster, to whom she becomes engaged.

Villiers de L'Isle-Adam, Comte Jean Marie Mathias Philippe Auguste de (1838–1889) French writer of fiction and drama. Born into an aristocratic family in Brittany, he went as a young man to Paris, where he led the life of a bohemian artist. In his dramas *Axël* (1890), *Elen* (1865), and *Morgane* (1866), Villiers de L'Isle-Adam displays flagrant romanticism. His tales, collected in *Contes cruels* (1883) and *Nouveaux Contes cruels* (1888), are written in a fantastic, macabre manner. His writing, often freighted with philosophical ideas, obscure and highly poetic, is generally considered as the immediate predecessor of the French SYMBOLIST movement.

Villon, François (originally called François de Montcorbier or François de Loges, 1431–?)   French poet, considered the finest poet of the late Middle Ages. Villon adopted the last name of his patron, the chaplain of a university church who adopted him about 1438. A brilliant student, he received a Master of Arts degree from the Sorbonne before he was twenty-one (hence the title "Master Villon" occasionally used). However, he also excelled in the rowdier side of the student life of the time, cultivated disreputable society, and was involved in a number of brawls, in one of which he killed a priest (1455). Thereafter he was repeatedly under arrest, sentenced to prison or to exile, or he was wandering to escape arrest for a series of brawls, robberies, and other illegal escapades. His *Petit Testament* (1456) is a series of *lais*, or "legacies," facetiously parodying the style of a legal testament; it explains that he is leaving Paris because of a broken heart (he was probably fleeing arrest) and bequeaths a number of worthless items to his friends and enemies.

But the *Grand Testament* (1461), the poem of two thousand lines that made him famous, is melancholy and pathetic in some of its bequests, bitterly humorous in others. It includes a self-castigating review of his life as a beggar and thief, but also derides the vanity of all human life, whether or not overtly dissipated like his own. It is interspersed with *ballades* and *rondeaux*, including the "Ballade des dames du temps jadis" (translated by Dante Gabriel ROSSETTI as "The Ballad of Dead Ladies") and the "Ballade pour prier Nostre Dame," addressed as a request to his mother to pray for him. In 1462 he was present at a street fight involving a death and was sentenced to be hanged. This inspired him to write his own epitaph, the "Ballade des pendus," or ballad of the hanged men, denouncing the justice of men and appealing for divine justice. His friends succeeded in having the sentence commuted in 1463 to ten years of banishment. Villon disappeared, and nothing further is known of him. His poems were first printed in 1489.

In the 19th century, Villon became popular as a romantic rogue-hero, a colorful and sympathetic outlaw; episodes from his life (mostly legendary) appear frequently in literature, as in R. L. STEVENSON's short story "Lodging for the Night." D. G. Rossetti and A. C. SWINBURNE translated many of his ballads, and Bertolt Brecht adapted some of them for the lyrics of his *Threepenny Opera* (1928). J. H. Huntley made a largely fictitious Villon the hero of *If I Were King* (1901). This was adapted by Rudolf Friml for his operetta *The Vagabond King* (1925), and D. B. Wyndham LEWIS wrote a popular biography, *François Villon* (1928).

Villon, Jacques   See DUCHAMP, MARCEL.

Vilmorin, Louise [Levecque] de (1902–1969) French novelist and poet. Vilmorin is known for her elegantly witty and perceptive fantasies and comedies of manners, such as the novels *Erica's Return* (1948), *Julietta* (1951), *Madame de . . .* (1951), *Les Belles Amours* (1954), and *La Lettre dans un taxi* (1958). Her verse was collected in *Poèmes* (1970).

Vinteuil   A great composer of music in Marcel Proust's REMEMBRANCE OF THINGS PAST. He is an idealized composite of a number of 19th-century French composers. The "little phrase" from one of his sonatas, a recurrent motif in the novel, closely resembles one by SAINT-SAËNS. Vinteuil's daughter is revealed to be a lesbian and a sadist.

Viola   The heroine of Shakespeare's TWELFTH NIGHT and the twin sister of Sebastian. Disguising herself as a boy and taking the name of Cesario, she becomes page to Duke Orsino, with whom she falls in love. When her identity is revealed, Orsino weds her.

Viollet-le-Duc, Eugène Emmanuel (1814–1879) French architect. A leader of the Gothic revival, he was responsible for the restoration of many of France's most

historic cathedrals and medieval buildings. He is most famous for his great standard works, *Dictionnaire raisonné de l'architecture française du XIe au XVIe siècle* (10 vols, 1854–69) and *Dictionnaire du mobilier français* (1855). His use of iron for structural reinforcement and design enhancement and his notion that beauty in architecture relies on its conformance to function anticipated 20th-century architectural thought and design.

Virginia   A young Roman plebeian of great beauty, decoyed by Appius Claudius Crassus, one of the decemvirs, and claimed as his slave. According to tradition, her father, L. Virginius, on hearing of it, hastened to the Forum just as Virginia was about to be delivered up to Appius. He seized a butcher's knife and stabbed his daughter to the heart, crying, "There is no way but this to keep thee free." He rushed from the Forum and raised a revolt in which the decemvirs were overthrown and the old order of government was restored (449 BC). The story is told by LIVY and has been retold by PETRARCH and by CHAUCER in the *Doctor's Tale*.

Virginia (1913)   A novel by Ellen GLASGOW. This story of a Southern woman is set in the years between 1884 and 1912. Virginia's marriage is unhappy; she is unable to adapt herself to a new environment, loses the respect of her husband and daughters, but manages to retain the love of her son. The book is, in essence, an analysis of social change and the new world facing women in the early 20th century.

Virginian, The (1902)   A novel by Owen Wister (1860–1938). Portraying cowboy life in Wyoming and in many ways the prototype of the modern Western, the story deals with the enmity between its unnamed hero and a local bad man called Trampas. When Trampas accuses the Virginian of cheating at poker and impugns his ancestry, the latter lays his pistol on the table and utters the immortal retort: "When you call me that, smile!" Trampas is eventually vanquished in a gun duel that constitutes the first "walkdown" in American literature, and the Virginian marries Molly Wood, a New England schoolteacher whom he has rescued from a marooned stagecoach.

Virginians, The (1857)   A novel by William Makepeace THACKERAY. A sequel to HENRY ESMOND, it relates the story of George and Harry Warrington, the twin grandsons of Colonel Henry Esmond. The novel takes the two brothers, of differing tastes and temperaments, through boyhood in America, through various experiences in England, where they are favorites of their wicked old aunt, Baroness Bernstein (the Beatrix of *Henry Esmond*), and through the American Revolution, in which George fights on the British side and Harry on the side of his friend George Washington.

Virgin Mary   See MARY, THE VIRGIN.

Virgin Queen   See ELIZABETH I of England.

Virgin Soil (Nov, 1877)   A novel by Ivan TURGENEV. This novel concerns the revolutionary movement in Russia. The student Nezhdanov, who believes himself committed to the people's cause, carries off Marianna, the daughter of a government official. She wants to "go to the people" with him and work for the freedom of the peasants. Nezhdanov discovers that he is not really fitted to be a revolutionary leader and in despair kills himself. The stronger Marianna marries again; she and her husband, Solomin, go off to work for a democratic Russia in a more gradual and realistic way.

Vischer, Friedrich Theodor (1807–1887)   German critic and aesthetician, known for his attempts to provide a theoretical basis for literary realism. Among his works are *Kritische Gänge* (*Critical Paths*, 1844), a collection of essays, and a more systematic work, *Ästhetik* (*Aesthetics*, 1846).

Visconti, Luchino (full name Luchino Visconti de Mondrone, 1906–1976)   Italian film director. Visconti's *Ossessione* (*Obsession*, 1942), based on James M. CAIN's novel *The Postman Always Rings Twice*, is regarded as a pioneer work of Italian NEOREALIST CINEMA, a movement that reached one of its peaks with the same director's *La terra trema* (1948). But Visconti's commitment to neorealism was transitory. A wide-ranging stylist, Visconti embraced lyricism and romanticism in *Senso* (*Sense*, 1954) and *Le notti bianche* (*White Nights*, 1957), "classical" realism in *Rocco e i suoi fratelli* (*Rocco and His Brothers*, 1960), and contrapuntal complexities in *Death in Venice* (1971), adapted from Thomas MANN's novella. His development can be seen as persistent movement away from neorealist concerns with the inexorable pressures of environment and society toward a profound interest in the problems and passions of individual and familial relationships—exemplified by such films as *Bellissima* (*The Most Beautiful*, 1951), *Il gattopardo* (*The Leopard*, 1962), adapted from the novel by LAMPEDUSA, and *La caduto degli dei* (*The Damned*, 1969).

Vishnu   In HINDUISM, the supreme spirit represented as the Preserver in the TRIMURTI. He has had nine incarnations, or AVATARS: Matsya, a fish; Kurma, a tortoise; Varāh, a boar; Narasimha, a half man, half lion; Vamena, a dwarf; Parashurama, a human with an axe; Rāma, a human, hero of the epic RĀMĀYANA; KRISHNA, a human; and the BUDDHA. There is one, Kalki, yet to come in the form of a white horse with wings, to destroy sin, the sinful, and all the enemies of the natural, stable, cosmic order. Vishnu, also known as Hari and Narayana, is usually depicted as four-armed, carrying a club, a shell, a discus, and a LOTUS, with a bow and sword slung at his side. Vishnu in his various forms and aspects is perhaps the most popular of the many Hindu deities. As the preserver of the *trimurti* he is at all times a kindly god, in contrast to an intellectualized BRAHMĀ and a destructive SHIVA. His devotees are known as Vaishnavas or Vaishnavites.

Vishnu Purana   See PURANAS.

Vision, A (1925)   A book by William Butler YEATS, important for understanding some of the ideas in his poetry. He claimed that the spirits dictated much of it in automatic writing to his wife, the medium Georgie Hyde Lees. It states that history is cyclical and recurrent, proceeding for the individual as well as for mankind in a gyre, or corkscrew pattern. At death, men's souls transmigrate into other bodies and continue the pattern. It also states that all human personality types have their opposite, antithetical selves, or masks, and that the complete man should learn to assimilate the characteristics of his mask.

Visit, The   See VISIT OF THE OLD LADY, THE.

Visit from St. Nicholas, A (1823)   A poem by Clement Clarke Moore (1779–1863), often referred to by its first line, "Twas the night before Christmas." First published anonymously in the Troy, New York, *Sentinel*, the poem was widely appreciated. Moore reprinted it in *Poems* (1844). His retelling of the visit of the jolly old man, with his descent through the chimneys, became the standard version of the legend for his many readers. Moore was a scholar who taught Oriental and Greek literature at the General Theological Seminary in New York from 1823 to 1850.

Visit of the Old Lady, The (Der Besuch der alten Dame, 1956; tr 1958)   Play by Friedrich DÜRRENMATT. An old billionairess returns to her destitute hometown and offers a huge sum of money for the life of the man who had been her lover but who cruelly betrayed her to "marry a shop" when they both were young and poor. The citizens at first indignantly refuse to commit the murder, but eventually the temptation becomes too great and at a full town meeting they ritualistically execute the man. The play was performed in New York as *The Visit*, with Lynn Fontanne and Alfred Lunt in the main roles.

vita nuova, La (The New Life, c1293)   A short work by DANTE, collecting his early sonnets and *canzoni* with prose commentaries. They are connected by an autobiographical prose narrative of the love for BEATRICE which inspired the poems. He meets her only twice, when he is nine and eighteen, but adores her from afar. He feigns love for another woman to protect his true love, observes Beatrice's grief at the death of her father, foresees her death, finds consolation after it happens with "a compassionate lady," but soon rededicates himself entirely to love of the memory of Beatrice. Finally a "new perception" of her in a vision makes clear the mystic significance of all these events, and he understands that he is not yet worthy to write about her ultimate meaning for him, but that he will —an intimation of her role to come in the DIVINE COMEDY. Both the poetry and the commentary, considering love for a woman as the first step in the soul's spiritual improvement toward a capacity for divine love, make the book a major work of the new poetic school of the STILNOVISTI. Dante Gabriel ROSSETTI wrote a popular English translation (1861).

Vitrac, Roger (1899–1952)   French dramatist. Vitrac continued in Alfred JARRY's style of bitterly satirical farce, combined it with a strong surrealist influence, and ended as a striking precursor of the THEATRE OF THE ABSURD. His best plays are *Les Mystères de l'amour* (1927), *Victor ou les enfants au pouvoir* (1928), and *Le Loup-garou* (1940).

Vittorini, Elio (1908–1966)   Italian novelist, critic, and translator, who, with Cesare PAVESE, pioneered the study of modern American writers through his translations and essays. A politically "engaged" writer, he worked in the anti-Fascist underground in World War II. His first full-length novel, *Il garofano rosso* (written 1934, pub 1948; tr *The Red Carnation*, 1952), attempts to suggest the link between fascism and violence. *Erica* (written 1936; pub 1956; tr 1960) treats the theme of poverty and hypocrisy. His major work is *Conversazione in Sicilia* (1941; tr *Conversation in Sicily*, 1961), a striking departure, in language, theme, and structure, from his earlier books. This allegorical tale revolves around the voyage of its hero, Silvestro, a young linotype operator, to his native Sicily in search of "truth" and of ideals that will sustain him in the days to come. Vittorini also wrote *Il sempione strizza l'occhio al Frejus* (1947; tr *The Twilight of the Elephant*, 1951), *La Garibaldina* (1950; tr 1960), and the "collective novel" *Le donne di Messin* (1949; rev 1964; tr *The Women of Messina*, 1973).

Vitus, St.   A Sicilian youth. He was martyred with Modestus, his tutor, and Crescentia, his nurse, during the Diocletian persecution (303). In Germany it was believed in the 16th century that good health for a year could be secured by anyone who danced before a statue of St. Vitus on his feast day. This dancing developed almost into a mania, and came to be confused with chorea, which was subsequently known as St. Vitus's dance, the saint being invoked against it.

Vivaldi, Antonio (c1675–1741)   Italian composer and violinist, known familiarly as *il prete rosso* (the red-haired priest). Vivaldi wrote more than four hundred concertos for various instruments and combinations of instruments, thirty-eight operas, nearly all of which are lost, and church music, of which the *Gloria* (c1726) is well known. The *Four Seasons* is one of his most popular secular pieces.

Viviani, Emilia   The daughter of an Italian nobleman. Emilia was placed against her will in the convent of St. Anna, near Pisa. Percy Bysshe SHELLEY met her in 1820, was attracted by her beauty and was sympathetic toward her plight, and took her as a flesh-and-blood symbol of Ideal Beauty. He addressed his EPIPSYCHIDION to her in 1821.

Vladimov, Georgy Nikolayevich (1931–   )   Soviet novelist. Born in Kharkov, Vladimov graduated from Leningrad University's law school but never practiced. He became an editor of the literary journal *Novy mir* (1956–59), which published his first novella, *Bolshaya ruda* (1961; tr "The Ore" in *Four Soviet Masterpieces*,

1965), whose truck-driver hero is killed by his own ambition, the quality of which goes unrecognized by the collective. *Novy mir* also published Vladimov's next novel, *Tri minuty molchaniya* (1969; tr *Three Minutes' Silence*, 1986), about the danger to a fishing trawler and its sailors when the negligent officers decide to ignore damage to its hull. Heavily cut by the censors, the book was still tremendously popular; Vladimov, however, publicly opposed the censorship and began to be persecuted and isolated by the authorities. He was unable to publish his next novel, *Verny Ruslan* (1975; tr *Faithful Ruslan*, 1979), in the U.S.S.R.; this, his artistically most brilliant book, the story of a labor-camp guard dog that is, ironically, helpless and confused when the camp is closed and he is set free, is plainly a portrait of Soviet man. After more years of suppression and resistance, Vladimov immigrated to West Germany in 1984.

Vlaminck, Maurice de (1876–1958)   French painter. Originally a violinist, he joined his friend André DERAIN in a painting studio and began painting in earnest at the turn of the 20th century. His early paintings, such as *The Seine River at Nanterre* (1902), reflect his infatuation with the art of VAN GOGH, and his work of this period united him with LES FAUVES. In 1908, however, he began to paint more in the style of CÉZANNE, using somber colors and solid forms, as in his *Still Life with Lemons* (1913–14). He was known as a radical in his time, and his thoughts are revealed in his writings, *Dangerous Turning* (1929), *Good Manners* (1931), and *Portraits Before the Decease* (1943).

Voinovich, Vladimir Nikolaevich (1932–   )   Soviet short-story writer and novelist. As a child Vladimir Voinovich had a frequently interrupted education and an even more interrupted relationship with his father, who was sentenced to a labor camp in the 1930s for criticizing Stalin's doctrine of "socialism in one country" and then had to leave to fight the Germans. Voinovich began to write while an army recruit; his first story, "My zdes' zhivem," was published in the journal *Novy mir* in 1961. In 1965 Voinovich and many other writers protested against the trial of SINYAVSKY and DANIEL and, as a result, was harassed by the authorities and compelled to circulate his works—in particular the hilarious and famous satirical novel about a Soviet SCHWEIK, *Zhizni neobychainye priklyucheniya soldata Ivana Chonkina* (1975; tr *The Extraordinary Adventures of Private Ivan Chonkin*, 1977)—in SAMIZDAT; in 1974 he was expelled from the Writers' Union and, unable to publish officially, condemned as a "parasite." The second volume about Chonkin, *Pretendent na prestol* (1979; tr *Pretender to the Throne*, 1981), was written to be published abroad; by this time Voinovich knew he had no hope of publication at home. In 1980 life in the Soviet Union had become intolerable and he was forced to emigrate. Voinovich's other translated works include *Ivankiada* (1976; tr *The Ivankiad*, 1977), a brilliant mock-epic satirizing Soviet bureaucracy in a battle to get control of a two-room apartment, and *Putem vzaimnoi perepiski* (tr *In Plain Russian*, 1979), a collection of various fiction and nonfiction pieces.

Vol de nuit   See NIGHT FLIGHT.

Volksbuch (Ger, "folk book")   A term popularized by the scholar and political writer Joseph von Görres (1776–1848), referring to the many cheap, easily understood books that were produced for the people in 15th- and 16th-century Germany, roughly equivalent to the English chapbook. The most important folk books are those containing prose narratives, some of which, like EULENSPIEGEL and the FAUSTBUCH, assumed great importance in subsequent literary history.

Volksgeist (Ger, "folk spirit")   The national character or genius of a people, as distinguished from the entirely rational sense of humanity accepted during the Enlightenment. This concept, which was formulated by HERDER, gained wide currency during the romantic era.

Volpone, or the Fox (1606)   A comedy by Ben JONSON. Aided by his servant Mosca (the Fly), the avaricious Volpone (the Fox), who is a childless Venetian nobleman, devises a new method of adding to his hoard of gold. He pretends a lengthy illness in order to pique the expectations of his rascally associates, all of whom aspire to inherit his fortune: Voltore (the Vulture), a lawyer; Corbaccio (the Carrion Crow), a miserly old man; and Corvino (the Raven), a knavish merchant. Mosca assures each, one by one, that he is in line for the fortune—thanks to Mosca's own efforts. Finally, Mosca whispers abroad that Volpone is near death. They rush to Volpone with rich gifts, in order to assure themselves of his favor. Corbaccio disinherits his own son in Volpone's favor; Corvino goes so far as to offer his wife to ensure his goodwill. After a series of complications, as logical as they are hilarious, Volpone, who is about to be outwitted by his own servant, reveals the whole plot in court, and all the participants are punished according to their crimes or their station in life. In 1928 Jules ROMAINS and Stefan ZWEIG made a new adaptation of the play, which ends with Mosca inheriting all Volpone's money from the false will. Volpone, who will be executed if he turns out not to be dead, slinks away penniless. This version was employed by George Antheil in his opera *Volpone* (1953). Jonson's play is generally recognized as one of the finest comedies of the Jacobean period.

Völsunga Saga   A Scandinavian prose cycle of legends, going back to the West Germanic, most likely Frankish, heroic LAIS, which were also the base of the German NIBELUNGENLIED. The Völsunga Saga is the main source of Wagner's opera cycle DER RING DES NIBELUNGEN, although names and plot details vary. The saga takes its name from Völsung, grandson of the god ODIN and father of Sigmund. The hero, Sigurd (Siegfried), is Sigmund's son. He kills the dragon Fafnir, present guardian of a gold treasure and a magic ring, which carry the curse of their original owner, from whom they were forcibly taken by the god LOKI.

Sigurd then begins his travels, taking the treasure and the magic horse Grani, given him by Odin.

He awakens the sleeping Valkyrie maiden Brunhild, and they become betrothed; but he leaves her in search of adventure and becomes the friend of the three sons of a Rhine king, and their sister Gudrun (Kriemhild, Gutrune). He is given a magic potion, which makes him forget Brunhild, and it is arranged that Sigurd will marry Gudrun if he helps her brother Gunnar (Gunther) win the hand of Brunhild, who has surrounded herself with a circle of fire that a prospective suitor must cross, since she assumes that none but Sigurd can do so. Sigurd rides through on his magic horse, but takes on Gunnar's appearance while winning Brunhild's promise of marriage. After he resumes his own shape, the double marriage is celebrated; but one day during a jealous argument Gudrun tells Brunhild about the deception. The enraged Brunhild has Sigurd killed, although still in love with him, then commits suicide. Gudrun eventually marries Atli (Attila, or Etzel, king of the Huns), who determines to get the treasure hoard, now in the hands of Gudrun's brothers. They sink the gold in the Rhine and die fighting in refusal to reveal where it is hidden. Gudrun avenges them by killing Atli and the sons she has borne him.

William MORRIS retold the saga in his *Sigurd the Völsung* (1876).

Voltaire (pen name of François Marie Arouet, 1694–1778)   French satirist, philosopher, historian, dramatist, and poet. He is known for his enmity to organized religion and to fanaticism, intolerance, and superstition (which he attacked under the slogan *Ecrasez l'infâme!* [Fr, "Crush the infamous thing!"]). Equally characteristic are his biting wit and his prejudices, his generosity in helping the poor and oppressed, his personal vigor in spite of chronic ill health, his clever and swiftly moving philosophic tales, and his contributions to the objective study of history. His merciless satire and unorthodox ideas were a constant source of irritation to the political and religious authorities of his time.

One of the most famous and influential men in the history of thought, Voltaire had an extremely turbulent life. His early reputation was made as a dramatist and wit, the latter gift earning him a beating at the hands of the lackeys of the chevalier de Rohan, a nobleman whom he insulted. He was subsequently imprisoned for a few days (1725), and thereafter immediately exiled to England, where he spent three years (1726–29). There Voltaire met, and came under the influence of, POPE and SWIFT; he was much drawn to English political thought, and, in particular, to NEWTON and LOCKE, whose ideas he propagated in France. On his return to his native land, he enthusiastically introduced English literature, and particularly SHAKESPEARE, to the French public. (In time, however, he was to regard Shakespeare's influence on drama as deplorable.) After the publication of his *Lettres philosophiques* (1734), Voltaire was again pursued by the government. He took refuge with Mme du CHÂTELET at Cirey, in Lorraine, where he remained, for the most part, from 1734 to 1749, writing historical works and dabbling in science. It was during this period, through the influence of Mme de POMPADOUR, that Voltaire was made royal historiographer (1743) of Louis XV and a member of the ACADÉMIE FRANÇAISE. After the death of Mme du Châtelet, Voltaire accepted FREDERICK II's invitation to visit him at his court in Berlin, where he stayed for three years until, in 1753, the two men became estranged. Their quarrels are celebrated: one of Voltaire's duties was to correct the monarch's attempts at French poetry. Angry at thus being treated as a subordinate, Voltaire on occasion referred to this chore as "washing the king's dirty linen." He fled from Prussia, not without first experiencing imprisonment: Frederick's revenge for the publication of Voltaire's *Diatribe du docteur Akakia*, a satire of Frederick's highly placed functionary Pierre Moreau de Maupertuis. Unwelcome elsewhere in Europe, Voltaire returned to Colmar, in eastern France; in 1775 he retired to a home in Geneva known as *Les Délices*. Here he continued publishing philosophic works and contributed articles to the ENCYCLOPÉDIE. Because of the violent religious controversies he stirred up with reference to the article "Geneva" in the *Encyclopédie*, he thought it better to purchase an estate called FERNEY in 1758. It was just across the French border, near Geneva, and there, safe from both the Swiss and the French governments, he could and did live comfortably for nearly all the rest of his life. Here he spent his time corresponding with the major figures of the time; receiving homage from innumerable visitors; managing his estate, where he instituted social reforms; writing and producing plays; and publishing treatises (many anonymously), which violently denounced the cases of intolerance and injustice that came to his attention. Specifically, he aided many persons who were victims of injustice, notably the family of Jean Calas. It was from Ferney that Voltaire quarreled with ROUSSEAU and inveighed against the Roman Catholic Church and Calvinism, winning fame all over Europe.

When he returned once more to Paris, just before his death, he was entertained sumptuously and honored as befitted a great man at the performance of his play *Irène* (1778). It proved too much for the eighty-four-year-old man, and he died shortly thereafter, on the thirtieth day of May. The Church denied him a Christian burial, but an abbot of his acquaintance brought his body to his own abbey in Champagne. In 1791, after the FRENCH REVOLUTION, on which Voltaire had had such an important influence, his remains were transferred to the Panthéon in Paris.

Voltaire's major dramatic works, chiefly neoclassical in form (see NEOCLASSICISM), include *Oedipe* (1718), his first tragedy; *Brutus* (1730); *Zaïre* (1732), an Oriental drama of love and jealousy, considered one of his best plays; *Alzire, ou les Américains* (1736); *Mahomet, ou le Fanatisme* (1742); *Mérope* (1743); *L'Orpheline de la Chine* (1755); and *Tancrède* (1760). Among his polemic and philosophic writings are the *Lettres philosophiques* (definitive edition 1737, known also as *Lettres sur les Anglais* and *Lettres anglaises*, in the 1734 edition), in which he praises the religious practices of the Quakers, English politics, philosophy, science, and literature, and, by implication, criticizes authoritarian France. The letters had been translated and published in England in 1733. In them Voltaire is impressed with England's progress in scientific thinking, and especially with the importance given to the experimental method in the works of BACON, Locke, and Newton. The French *parlement* was quick to sense the heresy in these letters and ordered them burned in 1734.

Other philosophic works are the *Traité de métaphysique* (1734), in which Voltaire insists that metaphysical matters are beyond human understanding; the *Discours en vers sur l'homme* (1738); the *Traité sur la tolérance* (1763), written as part of Voltaire's campaign to rehabilitate Jean Calas's memory; the *Dictionnaire philosophique portatif, ou la raison par alphabet* (1764); the *Sermon des cinquante* (before 1753), said to be one of the most violent pamphlets ever to have come from the pen of a major writer; *Le Philosophe ignorant* (1766); and *Les Questions de Zapata* (1767), which points out contradictions in Christian dogma. His philosophical poems include *Epître à Uranie* (known also as *Le Pour et le contre*, 1722?), in which Voltaire shows that he conceives of God more abstractly than do revealed religions; *Le Mondain* (1736), which is both an apology for the epicurean way of life and an economic theory proclaiming the usefulness of luxury; *Poème sur le désastre de Lisbonne* (1756), which treats the problem of evil in nature and the earthquake at Lisbon in 1755; and *Poème sur la loi naturelle* (1756), the aim of which is to establish the existence of a universal morality independent of any revealed religion.

It is in the *Epître CIV à l'auteur du livre des trois imposteurs* (1769) that Voltaire wrote his oft-quoted observation on religion: "If God did not exist, it would be necessary to invent him." Of his historical works, the greatest are considered to be the *Histoire de Charles XII* (of Sweden) (1731); *Le Siècle de Louis XIV* (1751), in which Voltaire celebrates the progress of the arts, sciences, and letters of that epoch, giving wars a subordinate place; *Essai sur les mœurs et l'esprit des nations* (1756/69), which is regarded as the first history of civilization; *La Philosophie de l'histoire* (1765); and *Le Pyrrhonisme de l'histoire* (1770). His best-known philosophical tales, which have become the most popular of his works, are ZADIG; *Bacbouc, ou le Monde comme il va* (1748); *Memnon, ou la Sagesse humaine* (1750); MICROMÉGAS; CANDIDE; *Jeannot et Colin* (1764); *L'Ingenu* (1767); *L'Homme aux 40 écus* (1767), a satire on

French economic legislation; and *Le Taureau blanc* (1774), a satire on the Old Testament. Outstanding among his poems are LA HENRIADE; *Le Temple du goût* (1733), a satiric allegorical voyage in the realm of taste; and *La Pucelle* (1755, definitive edition 1762), an irreverent burlesque of Joan of Arc.

Voltaire also wrote numerous light and witty verses on a variety of subjects. His more than twelve thousand letters are still being edited in over sixty volumes by Theodore Besterman at the present date.

The name Voltaire is simply an anagram of Arouet l.j. (*le jeune*—Fr, "the younger," his having an elder brother), which Voltaire adopted in 1718.

Volumnia   In Shakespeare's CORIOLANUS, the "Junolike" mother of Coriolanus. In contrast to the gentle Virgilia, Coriolanus's wife, she is proud and fearless and has exerted great influence on her son's development. In Roman accounts of the story, the name Volumnia is given to the wife of Coriolanus, and his mother is called Veturia.

Volund   See WAYLAND.

Vonnegut, Kurt, Jr. (1922–   )   Popular and prolific American novelist and essayist. Born in Indianapolis, Indiana, Vonnegut worked for the General Electric Company before becoming a free-lance writer in 1950. Although his early pieces appeared in various SCIENCE FICTION magazines, his work cannot be delimited by that generic label. Indeed, in a series of character- and scene-linked novels such as *The Sirens of Titan* (1959), in which Earth's history is discovered to have been manipulated by aliens, *Cat's Cradle* (1963)—the first book to bring Vonnegut to the attention of the general public—in which the world comes to a frozen end thanks to a product called Ice Nine, and *Slaughterhouse Five* (1969), which mixes a fictionalized account of the author's experience of the fire bombing of Dresden with a compensatory fantasy of the planet Tralfamadore, the science-fiction element is progressively dominated by the overall concerns of satire, black humor, and absurdism. Central to Vonnegut's method is his adoption of a childlike, paratactic style. *Slapstick* (1976), *Jailbird* (1979), and *Deadeye Dick* (1982) are among his other works.

von Stroheim, Erich   See STROHEIM, ERICH VON.

Vorágine, La (1924; tr The Vortex, 1935)   The only novel by José Eustacio RIVERA. Arturo Cova, a poet, flees his hometown with his lover, Alicia, and ventures into the cattle country of Colombia. For a variety of reasons he is drawn further and further into the jungle, only to discover how thin is the veneer of civilization in the face of the fierce and terrifying life of the Amazon basin. Ultimately, Cova and all his associates succumb to madness, leaving behind them a feverish documentary of blood and death. The delirious lyricism of the tale is made credible through Cova's despair at not having lived to become a poet.

Vortex, The   See VORÁGINE, LA.

vorticism   A movement in English painting. Led by the painter and novelist Wyndham LEWIS, vorticists used abstracted machine forms in their work. The movement, an offshoot of Italian FUTURISM, produced two issues of its journal *Blast* (1914), with contributions from the writers T. S. ELIOT, Ezra POUND, and Rebecca WEST, and the philosopher T. E. HULME. The movement died in 1915 in the unfavorable climate caused by the start of World War I; it resurfaced briefly in 1920 as Group X.

Vortigern   One of the kings cited by Geoffrey of Monmouth in the HISTORY OF THE KINGS OF BRITAIN. He was ultimately betrayed by HENGIST AND HORSA, a fate foretold him by the wizard MERLIN.

Vox Clamantis (c1382–1384)   Latin poem by John GOWER, of ten thousand lines. The first third gives a vivid description of TYLER'S REBELLION of 1381, which serves as the occasion for the allegorical denunciation of the corruptness of men of all classes, particularly with regard to their political responsibilities.

Voznesensky, Andrey (1933–   )   Soviet poet. One of the leaders of the poetic renaissance in Soviet literature in the early 1960s, Voznesensky studied architecture in Moscow, but gave up that career when his drawings were destroyed in a fire. His poetry, full of technical virtuosity even early on, attracted the attention of Boris PASTERNAK, and he became Pasternak's protégé. Voznesensky's collections of verse include *Parabola* (1960), *Mozaika* (*Mosaic*, 1960), and *Treugolnaya grusha* (*The Triangular Pear*, 1962). *Nostalgia for the Present*, a collection of English translations of his poetry, was published in 1978. After a period of poetic flamboyance and political reticence, Voznesensky's poetry has become more complex, thoughtful, and restrained as his willingness to stand up for literary freedom has increased; in 1979 he was one of the contributors to *Metropol*, the anthology that attempted to publish semiofficially while avoiding censorship. *An Arrow in the Wall*, a selection of Voznesensky's poetry and prose, appeared in a bilingual edition in 1987.

Vronsky, Count Aleksey   See ANNA KARENINA.

Vulcan   In Roman mythology, a son of JUPITER and JUNO. Originally a destructive god of fire, he became identified with the Greek artisan god HEPHAESTUS; thus he became the patron of smiths and other craftsmen. He was sometimes called *Mulciber*, "the softener."

Vulgar Errors (1646)   The popular title of a treatise by Sir Thomas BROWNE. With an impressive display of recondite learning, he confutes various errors and misconceptions in science, history, geography, etc. Its original title was *Pseudodoxia Epidemica, or Enquiries into Very Many Received Tenets and Commonly Presumed Truths.*

Vulgate   A Latin version of the BIBLE made by St. JEROME, under the commission of Pope Damasus (366–

384). Jerome began his work in 382, using Greek and Hebrew sources. It is a liberally free, highly literate translation and is still the authorized Latin text of the Roman Catholic Church. Jerome's text was used in the first printed Bible, the Mazarin Bible (see BIBLE, SPECIALLY NAMED EDITIONS).

Vyāsa   A Sanskrit word meaning "compiler," applied specifically to the legendary, semi-divine sage to whom authorship of the MAHĀBHĀRATA is attributed.

W

Wace (c1100–c1175)   Norman poet from Jersey. Wace is especially important in Arthurian literature for his ROMAN DE BRUT. This graceful verse chronicle is an adaptation into French of the Latin HISTORY OF THE KINGS OF BRITAIN, written by Geoffrey of Monmouth, which exalts the deeds of King ARTHUR.

Wacht am Rhein, Die (Ger, "the watch on the Rhine")   A German national song, written in 1841 by Max Schneckenburger and set to music by Karl Wilhelm (1854). It provided the name for WATCH ON THE RHINE, Lillian Hellman's distinguished play about Nazism.

Wackenroder, Wilhelm Heinrich (1773–1798)   German author. Wackenroder's most important work, some parts of which were written by his friend Ludwig TIECK, is *Herzensergießungen eines kunstliebenden Klosterbruders* (*Outpourings of the Heart of an Art-loving Lay Brother*, 1797). This revolutionary book deals for the most part with Renaissance painting, and, because of its elevation of art to a religion, in opposition to the rationalistic art criticism of the 18th century, it may be considered the original work of GERMAN ROMANTICISM. Toward the end of the book, Wackenroder also treats music and prepares the way for the later romantic appraisal of music as the queen of the arts.

Waddell, Helen [Jane] (1889–1965)   English scholar, best known as a student of medieval literature. Among her well-known books on that period are *The Wandering Scholars* (1927); *Mediaeval Latin Lyrics* (1929), translations; and *Peter Abelard* (1933), a novel.

Wadman, Widow   In Laurence Sterne's novel TRISTRAM SHANDY, a comely widow who wishes to secure UNCLE TOBY for her second husband. The Widow's wiles are disconcerted by Toby's total innocence, and her purpose is perplexed because she, like the reader, is uncertain of the severity of the wound in Toby's thigh. Sterne introduces the Widow by a blank page, on which the reader can write his own description.

Wägner, Elin (1882–1949)   Swedish novelist and journalist. An active feminist and pacifist, Wägner wrote a number of novels supporting feminist causes and her antiwar views. Her masterwork, the provincial novel *Åsa-Hanna* (1918), concerns basic moral and spiritual questions rather than specific contemporary problems.

Wagner, Richard (1813–1883)   German composer, conductor, and author. Wagner's operas (which he called music dramas) form the major part of his output. He always wrote his own librettos. These sometimes fail to reach poetic heights, but his music generally overcomes their deficiencies. He developed the concept of the LEITMOTIF. As a reformer, he did away with the excessive *coloratura* and artificiality of the prevailing operatic style, much as GLUCK had done before him. The subject matter of most of his works is drawn from Norse and Teutonic mythology and from history. In all cases, he adapted the source material with the utmost freedom to his own artistic purposes.

One of the major themes running through much of Wagner's work—beginning with *Der fliegende Holländer* (*The Flying Dutchman*, 1841) and continuing in TANNHÄUSER and LOHENGRIN—is the search for a woman who will give ideal, unquestioning devotion to the hero, a devotion perfect enough to encompass his salvation.

From *Lohengrin* on, Wagner's works are composed with continuous music, rather than the older alternation of aria and recitative. His most extensive work, the four-part cycle DER RING DES NIBELUNGEN, required more than a quarter century to finish. Its composition was interrupted by two other operas, one tragic, one comic. Intended to be small, practical potboilers that would provide an income for the completion of the *Ring*, both of these operas substantially outgrew their original conception, to become two of the most demanding operas ever written: *Tristan und Isolde* (1865; see TRISTAN AND ISEULT) and *Die Meistersinger von Nürnberg* (*The Mastersingers of Nuremberg*, 1868; see MEISTERSINGERS). During this time, Wagner thoroughly absorbed the philosophy of SCHOPENHAUER, which colored his mature operas. The complete *Ring* cycle was first performed in 1876 at the theatre that Wagner, in his massive egotism, had constructed in Bayreuth for the sole purpose of producing his works (a function that it has fulfilled ever since, with an annual summer Wagner festival run by his descendants). His final work, *Parsifal* (1882; see PARZIVAL), was also composed for Bayreuth.

In his lifetime, Wagner was not only famous for his music but notorious for his extreme egotism, nationalism, and financial and emotional irresponsibility. At the same time, he was extremely well read and was familiar with the literature and philosophy of many countries. He wrote voluminously on almost every conceivable question—artistic, social, or political; among his writings are notorious anti-Semitic tracts.

His second wife, Cosima (1837–1930), a daughter of Franz LISZT, was instrumental in securing funds for the Festspielhaus (Festival Playhouse) at Bayreuth and ran the festival until her death. Their son, Siegfried Wagner (1869–1930), conducted his father's works at Bayreuth. The composer's grandson, Wieland Wagner (1917–66), was the stage director at Bayreuth and proved a radical innovator in his simplified manner of staging Wagner's operas to emphasize their archetypal elements.

Wagner had a stronger influence on writers than perhaps any other 19th-century composer. NIETZSCHE fell totally under his spell for a time. There was an extraordinary Wagner vogue in French literary circles, which affected BAUDELAIRE and MALLARMÉ. D'ANNUNZIO's *Trionfo della morte* (*Triumph of Death*) reflects *Tristan*. Thomas MANN referred to Wagner and Wagnerian images in many of his works, notably DEATH IN VENICE. Joyce's ULYSSES and T. S. Eliot's THE WASTE LAND are also filled with Wagnerian allusions.

Wahabites   A Muslim sect, particularly strong in Saudi Arabia, whose object is to bring back the doctrines and observances of Islam to the literal precepts of the KORAN. Their name is derived from their founder, Ibn Abdul Wahab (d 1787).

Wahlöö, Per   See SJÖWALL, MAJ.

Wahlverwandtschaften, Die (The Elective Affinities, 1809)   A novel by GOETHE, originally planned as a novella and intended for insertion into *Wilhelm Meisters Wanderjahre* (see WILHELM MEISTER). The title is a term from chemistry referring to the fact that, when certain compounds are mixed, their component elements change partners, as it were. Likewise, in the novel, the marriage of two characters, Eduard and Charlotte, collapses when each of them finds a more suitable partner. Ottilie, Charlotte's young niece, arrives at their estate, and Eduard falls immediately and passionately in love with her, while Charlotte's practical, sober nature is attracted to a captain who is also their house guest. Ottilie is the book's central character, and, like MIGNON in *Wilhelm Meister*, she is felt to be somehow in tune with mysterious natural forces in a way that others cannot understand. She is magnetically drawn to Eduard, as he is to her, but his passionate impatience is

too much for her, and she finally rejects him. Ottilie and Eduard both die and are buried together.

Wain, John [Barrington] (1925–   )   English novelist, poet, and critic. Wain's best-known novel is his first, *Hurry on Down* (1953; U.S. *Born in Captivity*), a picaresque satire of the British class system that earned him a dubious critical identification with the so-called ANGRY YOUNG MEN. While Wain is committed to the rights of an individual in a mass society, he was not himself a member of any movement. Among his other novels are *Living in the Present* (1955), *The Young Visitors* (1965), *A Winter in the Hills* (1970), and *The Pardoner's Tale* (1978), based on CHAUCER's tale. He also writes dry, witty poetry, in such volumes as *Weep Before God* (1961) and *Feng* (1975). *Professing Poetry* (1977) is a collection of lectures on contemporary poetry. Wain has edited *Everyman's Book of English Verse* (1981) and *An Edmund Wilson Celebration* (1978), a collection of essays and studies; he has written biographies or critical studies of, among others, Gerard Manley HOPKINS (1959), Arnold Bennett (1967), and Samuel JOHNSON (1974).

Wainamöinen   Known as the wise enchanter or singing musician. Wainamöinen is the hero of Finland's epic KALEVALA, and plays the role of the Finnish ORPHEUS.

Waiting for Godot (En attendant Godot, 1952; tr 1954)   A play by Samuel BECKETT. It is a tragicomedy about two tramps, in which nothing happens except trivial events and conversations that suggest the meaninglessness of life. The two tramps Vladimir (Didi) and Estragon (Gogo) are continually aware of cold, hunger, and pain as they wait for Godot, who sends a boy to them each day to tell them he will come the next day. The tramps quarrel and contemplate suicide, separation, and departure, but they remain dependent on each other and never do anything. Their condition is reflected in the relationship between Pozzo and Lucky, the only passersby, whom they at first mistake for Godot. Pozzo is a rich man who cruelly mistreats his servant, Lucky, driving him as if he were an animal. One of the most brilliant passages in the play is Lucky's monologue when he is forced to "think" for his master: it is a satirical and pitiful mixture of Christian, would-be profound, and banal, mechanical thought. Ironically, the pair are as dependent on one another as the two tramps are; on their second appearance, Lucky, now dumb, is leading Pozzo, who has become blind. The play ends with the tramps still waiting for Godot to come. Though the play is bleak and despairing, it is also richly humorous, asserting the human will to live in spite of everything.

Waiting for Lefty (1935)   A play by Clifford ODETS. Its subject is a taxi drivers' strike. Using an impressionistic flashback technique, Odets presents the situations of six people involved in the strike. At the climax, the news that the popular committeeman Lefty has been murdered rouses the men to decisive action. *Waiting for Lefty* was one of the best known of the proletarian plays of the 1930s.

Wajda, Andrzej (1926–   )   Polish filmmaker. In films that are basically pessimistic, Wajda suggests that the heroic aspirations of humanity are doomed to failure in a monolithic society. He is best known for his trilogy about Poland in World War II, which includes *Generation* (1954), *Kanal* (1956), and *Ashes and Diamonds* (1958). Here, the theme is the psychological ordeal of young soldiers (and Poland) fighting to survive the war. Wajda is known for his depiction of violence and grotesque imagery, a visual style that gives such later films as *Lotna* (1960) and *Landscape after Battle* (1970) a harsh brilliance. His most introspective exercise was *Everything for Sale* (1968). Other films include *Man of Marble* (1976), in which a student discovers a bricklayer's sculptures and paintings and gradually uncovers his life; *Without Anesthesia* (1978), in which a successful journalist's life is smashed when his wife leaves him and he loses his job; and *Man of Iron* (1981), an explicitly political film about Poland's labor-leader hero Lech Walesa.

Wakefield Master (fl 15th century)   Conjectural author of leading works in the English medieval TOWNELEY MYSTERIES. He is thought to have been a man of humble birth, though well educated, and probably a secular priest. He is called the Wakefield Master because internal evidence in the plays suggests that these plays were performed by the local guilds of Wakefield, in southern Yorkshire. Thirteen plays are attributed to him, including *Noah*, *Herod*, *The Way of the Cross*, and the *First* and SECOND SHEPHERD'S PLAY; they are distinguished by a nine-line stanza and a rhyming verse scheme of QUATRAIN, COUPLET, TRIPLET. Because of their humor, the unknown author has been called the "first great comic dramatist in English literature."

Walcott, Derek [Anton] (1930–   )   West Indian poet and playwright from St. Lucia. One of the most distinguished poets of the West Indies, Walcott writes with a dramatic mixture of island rhythms and English verse forms. After his first major collection, *In a Green Night* (1962), he published *Selected Poems* (1964), *The Castaway* (1965), *The Gulf* (1969), and the long narrative poem *Another Life* (1973). *The Star Apple Kingdom* (1979) is a collection of narrative poems rich with the imagery and history of the Caribbean and *The Fortunate Traveller* (1982) is a collection of verses Walcott wrote while living in the U.S. and elsewhere. The fifty-four lyrics in *Midsummer* (1983) recount a year's passing in the poet's life, from summer to summer. Walcott has done a great deal to promote the development of an indigenous West Indian theatre, to which he has contributed his own plays, among them *Henri Christophe* (1950), *Drums and Colours* (1958), *Dream on Monkey Mountain* (1970), *Ti-Jean and His Brothers* (1971), *The Jokes of Seville* and *O Babylon!* (both 1978), and *Remembrance* and *Pantomime* (both 1980).

Walden, or, Life in the Woods (1854)   A book by Henry David THOREAU. Convinced that "the mass of men lead lives of quiet desperation," Thoreau lived alone in a cabin at Walden Pond, outside Concord, New Hampshire, from 1845 to 1847. His aim was to "front only the essential facts of life," to emancipate himself from slavery to material possessions. After giving these reasons for his experiment, Thoreau goes on to describe his observations and habits at Walden Pond, where he watched the seasons unfold. He does not encourage everyone to live in the woods but rather urges that life be simplified so that its meaning may become clear.

Waley, Arthur (1889–1966)   English scholar and translator of Oriental literature. Born Arthur David Schloss, Waley took his mother's maiden name in 1914. It is ironic that Waley, who did more to expose the Western world to the classical writings of the Orient than anyone before him, never set foot in Asia. His translations of Chinese and Japanese poetry, originally published in such volumes as *One Hundred and Seventy Chinese Poems* (1918) and *Japanese Poetry* (1919), possess an intrinsic excellence and influenced numerous British and American poets (notably William Butler YEATS and Ezra POUND). Equally distinguished are Waley's translations in prose. Among them are *The Nō Plays of Japan* (1921), Lady Murasaki's novel THE TALE OF GENJI (6 vols, 1925–33), THE PILLOW-BOOK OF SEI SHŌNAGON (1928), and the Chinese Buddhist tale *Monkey* (1942). He also wrote a number of books on Chinese painting and literature, a study of Taoism in *The Way and Its Power* (1934), and *The Secret History of the Mongols, and Other Pieces* (1964), his last book, a miscellany including some of his own poetry and short stories.

Walker, Alice (1944–   )   American novelist, short-story writer, and poet. Walker's work deals with personal and family relationships and, in particular, with the strengths and sensibilities of black women in a society pervaded by sexism and racial oppression. Her poetry, published in such volumes as *Once* (1968) and *Revolutionary Petunias* (1973), is pared down and unsentimental. Her first novel, *The Third Life of Grange Copeland* (1970), examines the strains of racism on three generations of a black share-cropping family. *Meridian* (1976), also a novel, depicts the courage and strength of a black woman in the civil rights movement. The subtle and often destructive interplay of racial, social, and political tensions is a recurrent theme in her collections of stories, *In Love and Trouble* (1973) and *You Can't Keep a Good Woman Down* (1981). These were followed by the highly acclaimed novel *The Color Purple* (1982), which won a PULITZER PRIZE in 1983 and was made into a successful film in 1985. Set in the American South, early in the 20th century, it tells the story of Celie, a fourteen-year-old who is repeatedly raped by a man she thinks is her father. The resulting offspring are adopted by a missionary family in Africa. Celie's sister,

Nettie, works for the missionary family, and the novel takes the form of a series of letters between Celie and Nettie. Celie eventually returns to her childhood home, which had always belonged to her real father and which she inherits after his death. There she is reunited with her children and her sister. Walker has also published a collection of feminist writings, *In Search of Our Mothers' Gardens* (1983).

Walker, Margaret [Abigail] (1915–   )   American poet and novelist. In her first book of poetry, *For My People* (1942), Walker was an early celebrant of black identity. She continued to publish precise, graphic poems in the volumes *Prophets for a New Day* (1970) and *October Journey* (1973). Her most celebrated book, however, is the monumental historical novel *Jubilee* (1965), a fictionalization of her great-grandmother's life during and after slavery. Subsequent works include *A Poetic Equation: Conversations Between Nikki Giovanni and Margaret Walker* (1974) and *The Daemonic Genius of Richard Wright* (1982).

Wall, The (Le Mur, 1939; tr 1948)   A collection of short stories by Jean-Paul SARTRE. In the title story, the central character awaits death in a Fascist prison during the Spanish Civil War. Offered a reprieve if he tells where his leader is hiding, he decides to lie, not out of loyalty, for he has decided that the sacrifice of one man for another is meaningless, but simply to defy his captors. Soon released, he is surprised to learn that his leader had changed his hideout and has been captured at the spot he had named.

Wallace, Edgar (1875–1932)   English writer of popular fiction. Apart from being a prolific journalist, Wallace wrote more than 170 books, most of which, after *The Four Just Men* (1905), were best-sellers. He wrote primarily thrillers dealing with crime and detection, notably *The Terror* (1930), as well as scenarios for films, such as *King Kong* (1933), and plays.

Wallace, Lew[is] (1827–1905)   American lawyer, novelist, and soldier. Wallace served in the Union army, in which he rose to the rank of major general. During his political career, he was governor of New Mexico and Indiana and minister to Turkey. Two of his many novels achieved great popularity: *The Fair God* (1873), based on Cortez's conquest of Mexico and the result of thirty years of research and writing, and BEN-HUR: A TALE OF THE CHRIST.

Wallace, Sir William (1272?–1305)   Scottish patriot, known as the Hammer and Scourge of England. Wallace was a hero in the struggle against England for Scottish independence and was associated with Robert BRUCE. He led Scottish insurgents in a series of engagements against the English, but was ultimately betrayed to them. He was tried at Westminster Hall in London, was found guilty, and was hanged, drawn, and quartered.

Wallenstein   A trilogy of dramas by Friedrich SCHILLER, including *Wallensteins Lager* (*Wallenstein's*

Camp, 1798), *Die Piccolomini* (*The Piccolominis*, 1799), and *Wallensteins Tod* (*Wallenstein's Death*, 1799), based on the fall of the German general Count Albrecht von Wallenstein (1583–1634). In Schiller's version, Wallenstein, as the principal general of Emperor Ferdinand II in the Thirty Years' War, is tempted by the enormous strength he has built up to entertain the idea of deserting the emperor and establishing his own political power. He never actually intends to commit treason, but the idea intrigues him, and he begins to correspond with the Swedish enemy. Jealous elements in the Viennese court discover this correspondence and use it to induce the emperor to outlaw Wallenstein. Wallenstein flees but is murdered by one of his generals.

Waller, Edmund (1606–1687)   English poet. Waller was known for the smoothness and harmony of his verse, which was highly praised by Dryden. Two of his best-known poems are "On a Girdle" and "Go, Lovely Rose," love lyrics from his *Poems* (1645). Although Waller was banished from England for participation in a Royalist plot during the Civil War, he later wrote a panegyric on Cromwell and a lament for his death. In the Restoration period, he wrote verse praising Charles II.

Walpole, Horace (fourth earl of Orford, 1717–1797) English author and historian. Walpole's *Memoirs*, covering the years 1746 to 1791, are among the most important and accurate sources of the period. Selections were published in 1822 and 1846. His *Anecdotes of Painting in England* (1762–71) is the earliest attempt at a history of art in English; his estate at STRAWBERRY HILL in Twickenham, Surrey, in the process of rebuilding and remodeling (1754–94) set a taste for refined Gothic architecture and gardening in England. He is best remembered for his encyclopedic *Correspondence*—noted not only for the superb style of the letters but also for the wide range of its matter—and for THE CASTLE OF OTRANTO, reputedly the earliest English GOTHIC NOVEL. His other major works include a *Catalogue of Engravers in England* (1763), *Historic Doubts on Richard III* (1768), and *A Letter from XoHo, a Chinese Philosopher at London to His Friend Lien Chi at Peking* (1757), an essay that influenced Oliver Goldsmith's THE CITIZEN OF THE WORLD. Although he was the son of Sir Robert WALPOLE and served as a member of Parliament (1741–67), Walpole took little interest in politics. His life was dedicated to literature and art, as a writer, as a collector, and as the founder of Strawberry Hill Press, which he opened in 1757. His great contribution was a minute history of himself, his friends, and his contemporaries. Leslie STEPHEN has said, "The history of England throughout a very large segment of the 18th century is simply a synonym for the works of Horace Walpole."

Walpole, Sir Hugh [Seymour] (1884–1941) New Zealand-born English novelist. Walpole wrote short stories, criticism, miscellaneous essays, travel books, and plays, but he is best known for his many popular novels.

They encompass a wide range of subjects and styles, from romances to bizarre fantasies; generally, however, he was a traditionalist in a time of modernist experimentation. His novels include MR. PERRIN AND MR. TRAILL, a remarkable study of morbid psychology; *Jeremy* (1919), a semiautobiographical novel about the daily life of a small boy; *Portrait of a Man with Red Hair* (1925), a horror story; and four novels of THE HERRIES CHRONICLE. The character of Kear in Somerset Maugham's CAKES AND ALE is said to be a satirical portrait of Walpole.

Walpole, Sir Robert (first earl of Orford, 1676–1745)   English statesman. A leader of the Whig party in England, secretary of war (1708–10), and treasurer of the navy (1710–11), Walpole was twice prime minister and chancellor of the exchequer. He restored credit after the SOUTH SEA BUBBLE and abolished tariff duties on many articles. He stood for peace among France, England, and Spain. An expert in finance and especially commerce, he laid the basis for free trade in England. His ministry fell in 1742 because of his mismanagement of the war with Spain and also because of generally corrupt methods, particularly in rigged elections. He was the father of Horace WALPOLE.

Walpurgis Night (Ger, *Walpurgisnacht*)   In German tradition, a WITCHES' SABBATH held on the Brocken, highest peak of the Harz Mountains, the night preceding May 1. The name comes from St. Walpurga (c710–c777), an English missionary nun who aided St. Boniface in Germany. Although she was actually believed to be a protectress against magic, her May 1 feast day became associated with the pagan traditions earlier assigned to that day. According to these, May 1 marked the official beginning of the agricultural season for men, so the witches held rendezvous with the devil the night before to celebrate the beginning of their own increase in activity.

In Part I of his FAUST, Goethe uses the witches' festival as the background for a scene that shows at length the chaotic, magical realm in which MEPHISTOPHELES is at home. In Part II, as a parallel to this scene, there is a classical Walpurgis Night set in Greece, where Faust searches for Helen of Troy. In Thomas Mann's THE MAGIC MOUNTAIN, the chapter dealing with the Shrovetide festival is also entitled "Walpurgis Night"; by using this title, Mann stresses the similarity of his chapter to both Goethe's scene and the popular legend.

Walser, Martin (1927–   )   German novelist and playwright. Walser is known as a sharp, often sarcastic critic of the greed and hypocrisy of modern Germany's consumer society. His two main goals as a writer are the critical representation of the German upper-middle class and formal perfection. In such novels as the trilogy comprising *Halbzeit* (*Half-Time*, 1960), *Das Einhorn* (1966; tr *The Unicorn*, 1971), and *Der Sturz* (*The Crash*, 1973), his heroes lose sight of their values and principles as they strive for social acceptability. His plays include *Eiche und Angora* (1962; tr *The Rabbit Race*, 1963), a sharply ironic satire of

Germany after World War II, and *Die Zimmerschlacht* (*The Homefront*, 1967), a dramatization of the battle between the sexes.

Walsh, Peter   See MRS. DALLOWAY.

Walsingham, Sir Francis (1530?–1590)   English statesman and spymaster. Walsingham was made secretary of state by Elizabeth in 1573 and, with Lord Burghley, he shared most of the administrative responsibilities of the government. Described as "exceeding wise and industrious," he persistently urged resistance to Spain in the Netherlands. He built up an effective network of spies, who unmasked BABINGTON'S CONSPIRACY and the evidence that led to the execution for treason of MARY, QUEEN OF SCOTS, as well as keeping the government posted as to the progress of the Spanish ARMADA.

Walther von der Vogelweide (c1170–c1230)   German MINNESINGER, the most famous of the medieval lyric poets. Walther was attached to the Viennese court but later became a wandering minstrel. He is noted for very often breaking with the conventions of traditional love poetry and for making his poems a vehicle for his strong religious and political opinions, even at the risk of his patrons' disfavor. The German national song "Deutschland, Deutschland über alles" is an adaptation of one of his lyrics of patriotism and friendship. He appears as a contestant in the singing tourney in Wagner's opera *Tannhäuser* (1845).

Walton, Izaak (1593–1683)   English writer, best known for THE COMPLEAT ANGLER, a discourse on the quiet pleasures of fishing. Walton followed the trade of ironmonger and in his youth became a close friend of John DONNE and Ben JONSON. In his later years, he spent much of his time at his beloved avocation, fishing, in the company of various eminent clergymen, to whom his sweet and pious nature endeared him. Besides *The Compleat Angler*, Walton wrote biographies, usually called *Walton's Lives*, of such literary figures of his day as Donne (1640), Sir Henry WOTTON (1651), Richard HOOKER (1665), George HERBERT (1670), and Bishop Robert Sanderson (1678). All his prose work is distinguished by great simplicity, grace of style, earnestness, and humor.

Walton, Sir William [Turner] (1902–1983)   English composer. Walton's standing as a composer was first established with *Façade* (1923; arr for orchestra 1926), which he wrote as music to accompany poems by Edith SITWELL. He wrote the opera *Troilus and Cressida* (1954), the oratorio *Belshazzar's Feast* (1931), and many other works.

Waltzing Matilda (1895)   A ballad by Andrew Barton ("Banjo") PATERSON. In the verse, a swagman (hobo) steals and butchers a jumbuck (sheep), then leaps to his death in a billabong (pond after heavy rains) when pursued by the squatter (landowner) and police. The hobo's pack, bouncing as he hikes, is nicknamed "waltzing Matilda." The ballad's rollicking verse epitomizes Australian gusto, and the theme is the outcry of the little man against the repressive Establishment. It has been adopted as Australia's unofficial national anthem.

Wanderer, The (8th century?)   Old English poem of over one hundred lines in ALLITERATIVE VERSE. It is the poignant dramatic monologue of a warrior, now homeless and kinless, who laments the passing of his former glories and companions, singing an elegy of the times gone by.

Wandering Jew, The   A legendary Jew condemned to wander the world until Jesus' second coming. Although there are numerous variants of the story, the Jew is always said to have urged Jesus to go faster in carrying the cross to Calvary, cruelly refusing him a moment's rest, and Jesus' reply is that he goes, "but thou shalt tarry till I come." The Jew thereafter is periodically rejuvenated to the age of thirty. His character changes, however; he is now extremely wise, and, in his repentance, he uses the time of his wandering to exhort other men to be mindful of their sins and avoid the wrath of God.

Wang Wei (699–759)   Chinese poet of the T'ANG dynasty. Wang's limpid and placid poetry expresses well the BUDDHISM of members of the scholar-official class to which he belonged. He is famous also as a writer of prose pieces and as a painter, although no paintings survive that can be positively attributed to him.

Wang Yang-ming (or Wang Shou-jen, 1472–1529) Chinese MING dynasty high official and philosopher. Wang's school of neo-Confucianism is known as the school of Idealism (*hsin-hsueh*, "learning of the mind"). It advocated intuitive knowledge to be gained by meditation and opposed the elaborate investigation of the philosophy of poet-sages and of external things advocated by CHU HSI's school of neo-Confucianism. Wang Yang-ming, although anti-Buddhist because of his CONFUCIANISM, was strongly influenced by CH'AN thought.

War and Peace (Voina i mir, 1864–1869)   A novel by Count Leo Tolstoy. Regarded as the author's masterwork, the story covers roughly the years between 1805 and 1820, centering on the invasion of Russia by NAPOLEON's army in 1812 and the Russian resistance to the invader. Over five hundred characters, all carefully rendered, populate the pages of the novel. Every social level, from Napoleon himself to the peasant Platon Karatayev, is represented. Interwoven with the story of the war are narrations of the lives of several main characters, especially those of Natasha ROSTOVA, Prince Andrey BOLKONSKY, and Pierre BEZUKHOV. These people are shown as they progress from youthful uncertainties and searchings toward a more mature understanding of life. Natasha exemplifies the instinctual approach to life that Tolstoy was later to preach as the way to true happiness. She is one of the most successfully drawn characters in the book and perhaps ranks as Tolstoy's greatest achievement in character. Everything from her girlish excitement at her first ball through her experiences of first love and her final role as wife and mother is depicted with consummate skill. The two main male characters, Prince Andrey Bolkonsky and Pierre Bezukhov, represent contrasting approaches to life. Prince Andrey's struggles to find the meaning of life through his intellect end in the belated triumph of his calm acceptance of death as a natural and necessary end to life. Pierre, on the other hand, manages to find a sort of peace in living, chiefly with the aid of the simple wisdom preached to him by the peasant Karatayev. This wisdom, which was a large part of Tolstoy's later philosophy, was that life should be experienced emotionally and accepted naturally rather than twisted into artificial forms by man's imperfect intellect. Prince Andrey and Pierre have one other thing in common, besides their searchings. Both are romantically connected with Natasha. Prince Andrey is engaged to her, then loses her to the rake Anatol Kuragin. He is reunited with her shortly before his death. After the war is over, Natasha becomes Pierre's wife.

While some writers have criticized the inclusion of the disparate themes of the historical, social, and personal in the novel, the book derives much of its strength from this mixture. The alternation of chapters describing the personal lives of the characters with those depicting battles and dealing with Tolstoy's philosophy of history is well handled and carefully planned. The monumental size of *War and Peace*, its hundreds of characters, the variety of its action and scenes, all combine to make it an accurate portrait of the entire Russian nation. Far from being a static tableau, it has a vibrant animation and conveys the movement of people and events in history.

Ward, Artemus (pen name of Charles Farrar Browne, 1834–1867)   American humorist, newspaperman, editor, and lecturer. After working for several New England newspapers, Browne moved to Ohio, where he contributed his first Artemus Ward letters to the Cleveland *Plain Dealer* in 1858. Ward, a shrewd and supposedly illiterate showman, wrote in Yankee dialect of adventures and misadventures with his traveling museum of wax figures (also a few "snaiks and other critturs"). The letters brought Browne a wide reputation, and he was made city editor of the *Plain Dealer*. After difficulties with the manager, he resigned in 1860; by that time, his character was so well known that he had become merged with his creator. From Cleveland, Ward (better known than Browne) went to New York, where he wrote for *Vanity Fair*. Among the sketches he contributed was a fictitious interview with Lincoln that delighted the President. At this time, Ward published his first collection, *Artemus Ward, His Book* (1862), which sold forty thousand copies in a short time.

Ward's first lecture, "Babes in the Woods," was a great success when it was delivered in 1861. A master of the dead-pan expression and the sudden pause, he amused his audience by the incongruity of his remarks. In the course of his travels, Ward met Mark TWAIN in Virginia City, Nevada. In 1866 he departed for England, where he was made an editor of PUNCH, and later died of tuberculosis. He had published only one more volume in his lifetime, *Artemus Ward, His Travels* (1865). Posthumously appeared *Artemus Ward in London* (1869), *Artemus Ward's Lectures* (1869), and *Artemus Ward: His Works Complete* (1875, 1890, 1910). Ward's most familiar techniques include cacography, or humorous misspellings, and what he himself called "ingrammaticisms." He loved puns and plays on words, burlesque and anticlimax, and pure absurdity. He exerted an important influence on Mark Twain and other American humorists.

Ward, Mrs. Humphry (born Mary Augustus Arnold, 1851–1920)   English novelist, granddaughter of Thomas Arnold. Ward wrote popular novels and was inclined toward philanthropy, social work, and religious polemics.

Ward, Nathaniel (1578?–1652)   New England Puritan clergyman, born in England but forced to leave during the period of Puritan persecution. Ward is known for two works: THE BODY OF LIBERTIES, a code of laws for Massachusetts, in the preparation of which Ward figured most prominently, and THE SIMPLE COBLER OF AGGAWAM IN AMERICA, written under the pseudonym Theodore de la Guard. Ward returned to England about 1647.

Ward No. 6 (Palata nomer shest, 1892)   A long story by Anton CHEKHOV. It depicts the gradual disintegration of Dr. Andrey Yefimovich Ragin, the head of a mental hospital. Neglecting the miserable condition of the patients, he withdraws more and more into private study, thought, and alcohol. He finally reaches the point where he is unable to communicate with anyone except one of the inmates, Ivan Dmitrich Gromov, with whom he holds long talks on philosophical subjects. Ragin's unscrupulous assistant uses the doctor's eccentric behavior as a pretext for committing him to the hospital, where Ragin experiences the maltreatment he has allowed the patients to undergo for so many years. The realization of his part in the horror in which the patients live comes to him just before his death.

Warens, Mme Louise Elénore de (1700–1762)   The first benefactress, mistress, and *chère maman* of Jean Jacques ROUSSEAU, whom she took under her protection and installed as her companion at her farm Les Charmettes near Chambéry in the early years of his career (1729–40).

Warhol, Andy [Andrew] (1928?–1987)   American painter, graphic artist, and filmmaker. Among the most prominent examples of POP ART, Warhol's work reproduced ordinary images (dollar bills, soup cans, celebrity photographs, etc.) in an objective fashion, intentionally avoiding a strong stamp of the artist's perceptions. A fundamental aspect of his silkscreens and paintings, as well as the films he began making in the 1960s, was repetition. His work was mass-produced in his New York studio (called, appropriately, The Factory), rendering the process as mechanized and impersonal as the result. His film *Chelsea*

Girls (1966) was the first so-called underground film to be shown in commercial theatres. He wrote autobiographical/photographic works, among them *The Philosophy of Andy Warhol: From A to B and Back Again* (1975), *Exposures* (1979), *POPism* (1980), and *America* (1985), a collection of 350 photos and essays. Warhol will undoubtedly also be remembered for his pronouncement that "everyone will be famous for fifteen minutes," a state that he himself managed greatly to exceed.

War Is Kind (1899)   A volume of poems by Stephen CRANE. His second volume of verse, it contains epigrammatic parables similar to those in the earlier THE BLACK RIDERS AND OTHER LINES but has a more pronounced vein of cynicism. The title poem, "Do Not Weep, Maiden, for War Is Kind," often considered one of Crane's best, is a good illustration of the dramatic irony that Crane used so successfully in both his poetry and prose.

Warner, Charles Dudley (1829–1900)   American essayist, editor, and novelist. Warner is remembered today chiefly for his collaboration with Mark Twain on the novel *The Gilded Age* (1873). He was editor of the American Men of Letters Series and, with others, a multivolume *Library of the World's Best Literature*. He also was the author of such charming essays as *My Summer in a Garden* (1871).

Warner, Rex (1905–   )   English novelist, poet, translator, and critic. *The Professor* (1938) and *The Aerodrome* (1941), Warner's two best-known novels, are fantastic social and political allegories in the style of Franz KAFKA. He has also translated and written extensively on the Greek classics, producing such works of historical imagination as *Imperial Caesar* (1960) and *Pericles the Athenian* (1963).

Warner, Sylvia Townsend (1893–1978)   English novelist, short-story writer, and poet. The distinctive mixture of fantasy and realism in Warner's writing came naturally to a woman who was an expert on Tudor music, an authority on the supernatural, and the possessor of a social conscience that led to her participation in the Spanish Civil War. Central to all her novels is a compassion for people who are forced to live constricted lives, and into her stories, no matter how earthy in substance, a strong streak of the fanciful is woven. Her first novel, *Lolly Willowes* (1926; repr 1979), the story of a woman who forsakes a stifling middle-class life in London to become a witch in a rural village, had the distinction of being the first selection of the then newly formed Book-of-the-Month Club. *The Corner That Held Them* (1948), considered by many her masterpiece, examines life in a medieval convent. *The Flint Anchor* (1954) tells of a man weighed down with possessions and family responsibilities. Warner wrote a great many short stories, 144 of which appeared in THE NEW YORKER. In one collection, *Kingdoms of Elfin* (1977), fairy tales are vehicles for subtle social criticism. Warner published five volumes of poetry and two volumes of nonfiction. Her works include a study of Jane Austen (1951), to whom she is often compared, and a biography of T. H. WHITE (1967).

War of 1812   A war between Great Britain and the U.S., sometimes called the second American war for independence. The conflict was caused mainly by British violations of American neutral rights during the Napoleonic wars, though the desire of some Americans for territorial expansion, especially in Canada, was also a factor. Although the U.S. won several naval engagements, attempts to take Canada failed, and the British burned Washington in 1814. The treaty of Ghent (December 24, 1814) restored peace but said nothing about the issues that had caused the war. Andrew Jackson's defeat of the British at New Orleans, the greatest U.S. land victory of the war, occurred two weeks after the signing of the peace treaty. See CONSTITUTION; LAWRENCE, JAMES; MADISON, JAMES; PERRY, OLIVER HAZARD; STAR SPANGLED BANNER, THE.

War of the Gods   A Babylonian epic poem. A myth of the creation of the world and the establishment of the divine hierarchy, it formed a part of the New Year festival, in which it may have been acted out. It is known as the *Enuma elish*, from its opening words. The first gods were Apsu (see ABZU) and his wife, TIAMAT, personifications respectively of the fresh and salt waters. From their union sprang two obscure gods of the deep, Lahmu and Lahamu, who in turn gave birth to Anshar and Kishar. These were the parents of Anu, the sky. Anu was the father of EA, the god of wisdom. After his birth, a multitude of other gods came into being, but they were such a rowdy lot that Apsu, against Tiamat's advice, determined to destroy them all. Ea, however, drugged Apsu and his dwarfish counselor Mummu, killed Apsu, and imprisoned the dwarf. Tiamat promptly took the god Kingu for her consort.

Ea now married Damkina, who bore him MARDUK, the storm god. A mighty prince, he was given to such pranks as putting the winds on a leash. Many of the gods grew resentful and asked the primal mother, Tiamat, to destroy him. She created a variety of hideous monsters and, placing Kingu at the head of her forces, prepared to make war on the principal gods, who supported Marduk. Ea and Anu were both quickly routed, but Anshar sent Marduk to fight Tiamat. Arming himself with bow and arrows, a bludgeon of thunder, and a flail of lightning, the young storm god marched against the ancient goddess. After a terrible battle, he destroyed her and imprisoned her monsters in the depths of the earth. Splitting Tiamat's body into two pieces, he formed the firmament from one half, the foundations of the earth from the other. He then determined the spheres of the chief gods: Anu was to rule the area above the firmament; Enlil, that between firmament and earth; and Ea, the waters below the earth. In order to find someone to serve the gods, he finally created a puppet, man, out of the blood and bones of Kingu, who was killed

for the purpose. In gratitude, the gods built the city of Babylon, which was crowned by a great shrine for Marduk.

This story, one of the oldest known creation myths, bears striking parallels to Greek myth, in which the primal father (URANUS) is destroyed by a descendant (CRONOS), and later the young storm god (ZEUS) defeats various monsters spawned by the primal mother (GE) and imprisons them in the earth. Marduk's killing of Tiamat has its counterpart in Baal's killing of Yam, the dragon of the sea, in the Canaanite POEM OF BAAL.

War of the Theatres   A feud involving several Elizabethan playwrights. A personal quarrel between Ben JONSON, on the one hand, and John MARSTON and Thomas DEKKER, on the other, was carried into the theatres when Jonson wrote *Cynthia's Revels* (1600) for the Children of the Revels at the Blackfriars Theatre. A little later, he attacked Marston (who had apparently answered him with a play of unknown name, produced by Paul's Boys) in the *Poetaster* (1600–1601). Thomas Dekker then attacked Jonson in *Satiromastix* (1601), played by the Chamberlain's Men. The war of satire was popular with the public for two or three years but quickly died out. It is referred to in *Hamlet* by the Player King.

War of the Worlds, The (1898)   A science-fiction story by H. G. WELLS. It describes an invasion of England by Martians. Orson Welles's radio dramatization of it in 1938 caused widespread panic in the U.S.

Warren, Mercy [Otis] (1728–1814)   American writer. A friend of the best-known public figures of her time, including John and Samuel ADAMS and Thomas JEFFERSON, Warren devoted her literary talents to the service of the American republic. Her works include *The Adulateur* (1773) and *The Group* (1775), two satirical dramas criticizing British rule in America, *Poems Dramatic and Miscellaneous* (1790), and a *History of the Rise, Progress, and Termination of the American Revolution* (1805).

Warren, Robert Penn (1905–   )   American poet and novelist. Born in Kentucky, Warren was identified with THE FUGITIVES as a young man. His sympathies with agrarian orthodoxy were confirmed by his contributions to *The Fugitive* (1922–25), his unsympathetic account of the abolitionist John Brown in *The Making of a Martyr* (1929), and by his essay in the agrarian anthology, *I'll Take My Stand* (1930). With Cleanth BROOKS, he helped found and edit THE SOUTHERN REVIEW; with Albert Erskine, he coedited two anthologies of Southern writing: *A Southern Harvest* (1937) and *A New Southern Harvest* (1957).

Also with Brooks, Warren wrote the perennially influential texts *Understanding Poetry* (1938), *Understanding Fiction* (1943), and *Modern Rhetoric* (1949), which, combined with his critical pieces in *Selected Essays* (1958), established him as a leading exponent of the NEW CRITICISM. Warren's initial conservatism—both literary and political—developed into a liberal voice in *Who Speaks for the Negro?* (1965) and *Homage to Theodore Dreiser* (1971).

Warren's reputation rests on his poetry, which is noted for its vivid metaphor and brilliant description. His verse is collected in such volumes as *Thirty-Six Poems* (1935), *Selected Poems: 1923–1943* (1944), *Promises* (1957; PULITZER PRIZE), *Now and Then: Poems 1976–1977* (1978; PULITZER PRIZE), *Being Here: Poetry 1977–1980* (1980), and *New and Selected Poems 1923–1985* (1985). Although Warren is ranked among the foremost American poets, his novels won him a far wider audience. Beginning with *Night Rider* (1939), a story of the Kentucky tobacco war, his novels tend to deal with the effects of corruption and violence on people's lives. After *At Heaven's Gate* (1943), he published his two best-known books, ALL THE KING'S MEN and *World Enough and Time* (1950), a historical novel based on the KENTUCKY TRAGEDY. Other novels include *Band of Angels* (1955), a story of miscegenation in the Civil War era; *The Cave* (1959); *Wilderness* (1961), about a Bavarian Jew in the Civil War; *Flood* (1964); *Meet Me in the Green Glen* (1971); and *A Place to Come To* (1977). The body of Warren's work, which also includes a volume of short fiction, *The Circus in the Attic* (1948), reveals an intense intelligence dealing with the profound moral dilemmas of modern life. In 1985 Warren was named the first Poet Laureate in America.

Wars of the Roses (1455–1485)

A series of encounters between members of the house of York and the house of Lancaster, contesting possession of the English throne. The wars take their name from the roses, white for York and red for Lancaster, that were the emblems of the opposing factions. The parties were united after the Lancastrian Henry Tudor, earl of Richmond, defeated the Yorkist Richard III at the Battle of Bosworth (1485). Henry was proclaimed king (HENRY VII) and married Elizabeth of York, the eldest daughter of Edward IV.

Wartburg

A castle near Eisenach in Germany. Landgrave Hermann of Thuringia (d 1217) welcomed wandering entertainers at his court there and, according to legend, sponsored a *Sängerkrieg*, or minstrels' contest, in 1207 among WALTHER VON DER VOGELWEIDE, WOLFRAM VON ESCHENBACH, HEINRICH VON OFTERDINGEN, and other illustrious MINNESINGERS. This merged with another legend, in which KLINGSOR, helped by the Devil, competes with Wolfram von Eschenbach, who victoriously represents Christendom. These traditions, popularized in the poem *Der Wartburgkrieg* (*The Battle of Wartburg*, 13th century), were used by WAGNER for the singing contest in his opera *Tannhäuser*.

Warton, Thomas (1728–1790)

English literary historian, critic, and POET LAUREATE (from 1785), son of Thomas Warton (c1688–1745), noted poet and teacher. Warton's *History of English Poetry* (1774–81) extends to the end of the Elizabethan age. It is the first history of English literature that still merits our attention. Like Richard Hurd, Warton regretted the loss of the medieval imaginative world:

> We have parted with extravagancies that are above propriety, with incredibilities that are more acceptable than truth, and with fictions that are more valuable than reality.

This sentiment is reflected in his poetry as early as the *Pleasures of Melancholy* (1747).

Washington, George (1732–1799)

First president of the U.S. (1789–97), known as the Father of His Country. Washington had little formal education but early showed an aptitude for mathematics and, by the time he was fifteen, was a skilled surveyor. From 1753 to 1759, he was a British officer in the French and Indian War. He was elected to the Virginia House of Burgesses in 1758 and was successively reelected until the house was dissolved by the colonial governor in 1774. During the decade before the American Revolution, Washington became progressively more dissatisfied with British rule, particularly with the commercial regulations that required him and other Virginia planters to trade exclusively with Britain, under conditions that he felt to be unfair to the colonists.

Washington was one of Virginia's delegates to the first and second Continental Congresses in 1774 and 1775, and was elected commander of the Continental Army in June 1775. He was faced with the problem of directing an untrained and inexperienced army, composed primarily of militiamen whose terms of enlistment were short; his task was further complicated by a lack of supplies and the hesitancy on the part of Congress to establish the long-term enlistments necessary for a permanent army. In spite of his handicaps, once the war had begun, his leadership and success in the field were remarkable, and he won brilliant victories at Trenton and Princeton, New Jersey (1776–77), and at Yorktown (1781).

Having retired to his estate at MOUNT VERNON after the war, Washington returned to public life to preside at the Constitutional Convention in 1787. In 1789 he was unanimously elected president. During his administration, he followed Hamilton's financial program, observed neutrality in the European wars, and crushed the WHISKY REBELLION, firmly establishing the authority of the new government. He declined a third term—setting a precedent that lasted until 1940—and prepared, with the help of several friends, his famous FAREWELL ADDRESS.

Numerous myths later grew up around the figure of Washington. The most famous of these was created by Mason Locke Weems, whose biography of Washington (1800) contained the story that the boy Washington admitted having cut down a cherry tree because he could not tell a lie and that he was immediately forgiven by his astonished father. Another widely repeated story had Washington throwing stones (some claimed silver dollars) across the Rappahannock River.

Washington Square (1881)   A novel by Henry JAMES. As a boy, James had lived on Washington Square in New York City, a fashionable residential district at that time. The novel concerns Catherine Sloper, the shy daughter of wealthy, urbane, sardonic Dr. Austin Sloper. When young Morris Townsend, who is courting Catherine for her money, learns that her father will disinherit her if she marries him, he leaves her. Townsend renews his courtship after the doctor's death but is rejected by Catherine, who lives on at Washington Square unmarried. She has achieved her own kind of self-realization, freeing herself from the two men who had victimized her. The theme of the young, defenseless person trying to escape from the tyranny of an older, often more knowledgeable adult became a favorite theme for James. The novel was dramatized as *The Heiress* (1947) and filmed in 1949.

Wasps, The (Sphekes, 422 BC)   A comedy by ARISTOPHANES. *The Wasps* is an attack on Aristophanes' favorite butt, the Athenian demagogue Cleon, who had recently initiated the practice of paying citizens for jury duty. Philocleon ("Cleon-lover"), a foolish old man, suffers from an inordinate passion for jury duty. He resorts to all manner of ruses to escape from his house, where his sensible son Bdelocleon ("Cleon-hater") is trying to keep him confined for his own good. Finally, the young man persuades his father to hold trials at home. In the first, a hilarious parody of legal proceedings, a dog is tried for stealing cheese. In spite of all his son's efforts, Philocleon remains unregenerate to the last.

Wassermann, Jakob (1873–1934)   German-born Austrian novelist. Wassermann was a prolific if uneven writer, whose novels achieved international popularity in the 1920s and 1930s. The intense psychological realism in such novels as *Christian Wahnschaffe* (2 vols, 1919; tr *The World's Illusion*, 1920) invited comparisons with DOSTOYEVSKY. Among his other novels are *Die Juden von Zirndorf* (1897; tr *The Dark Pilgrimage*, 1933), *Caspar Hauser* (1908; tr 1928), and *Der Fall Maurizius* (1928; tr *The Maurizius Case*, 1929). He also wrote essays, biographies, and an autobiography, *Mein Weg als Deutscher und Jude* (1921; tr *My Life as German and Jew*, 1933).

Waste Land, The (1922)   A long poem by T. S. ELIOT. Completely breaking from conventional modes of poetic expression in its condensed use of language, its wealth of literary and historical references, and its lack of narrative sequence, the poem occasioned a violent literary controversy on publication and has been the subject of an endless amount of critical explication ever since. In five sections, it explores the different psychic stages of a soul in despair, struggling for redemption. The waste land, throughout the poem a central image of spiritual drought, is contrasted with sources of regeneration relied upon in the past, such as fertility rituals and Christian and Eastern religious practices. The dominant imagery in the poem is drawn from Jessie L. Weston's *From Ritual to Romance* (1920), a study of some of the themes of medieval romances and legends, such as the GRAIL story, which probably originated in ancient fertility religions. In medieval legend, the waste land and its ruler, the FISHER KING, rendered sterile by a curse, were cured by a knight who underwent purifying ordeals. But doubt remains the burden of Eliot's poem, and there is no resolution at the end, when, in a decaying twilight world, the poet shores up his ruins with literary and religious fragments. Each one echoes a hope of rebirth, but they are in a medley of foreign languages, suggesting that they are nothing more than unassimilated memories.

The publication of *The Waste Land* was an important event in the development of modern English poetry. The technique of the poem was as radically new as and in some ways similar to that of Joyce's ULYSSES. Both contrast the spiritual stagnation of the present with the myths of the past; both use the city as a major symbol of paralysis; both are full of scenes, phrases, and references that have little meaning in themselves but that echo and explain one another; and both depend upon the reader's knowledge of many works of literature, of various religions, and of history.

Following Ezra POUND's suggestion, Eliot reduced *The Waste Land* to about half its original length. The first version, with Pound's revisions, was published in 1971.

Watch on the Rhine (1941)   A play by Lillian HELLMAN. A German refugee in the U.S., whom Nazi agents want to intercept, is recognized by a hanger-on at the German embassy. The refugee kills the informer and, in so doing, helps to awaken the American conscience to the danger of tyranny. It was one of the first successful anti-Nazi plays on the American stage.

Water-Babies, The, A Fairy Tale for a Land-Baby (1863)   A highly moralistic fantasy by Charles KINGSLEY. This tale concerns the adventures of little Tom, the chimney-sweep, who falls into a river and is transformed into a kind of miniature merman.

Watergate   Political scandal arising during the 1972 presidential election campaign. In June 1972 five men who broke into the Democratic Party national headquarters at the Watergate Hotel in Washington, D.C., were arrested and charged with burglary and wiretapping; they and the men who hired them were all employees of CREEP, the Committee to Re-elect the President (Richard M. NIXON). The burglars' connection to the White House was soon revealed, and the discovery of Nixon's secretly taped conversations regarding the break-in confirmed suspicions of the President's involvement in the cover-up. The House Judiciary Committee voted to impeach Nixon, and he resigned from office in August 1974. By 1975 more than sixty people had been convicted of criminal charges stemming from Watergate. Nixon was pardoned by his successor, Gerald R. FORD.

A number of books have been written about Watergate, including Carl Bernstein and Bob Woodward's *All the President's Men* (1974) and *The Final Days* (1976); John Dean's *Blind Ambition* (1976); Jimmy Breslin's *How the Good Guys Finally Won* (1975); Charles Colson's *Born Again* (1976); H. R. Haldeman's *The Ends of Power* (1978); John Ehrlichman's *The Company* (1976) and *Witness to Power* (1982); and G. Gordon Liddy's *Will* (1980).

Waterloo, battle of   A decisive victory gained near Waterloo, a village south of Brussels, by the Allies over NAPOLEON BONAPARTE on June 18, 1815. The French numbered about seventy-two thousand; the combined forces of the British, the Dutch, and the Germans, under Arthur Wellesley, duke of WELLINGTON, numbered about sixty-seven thousand; the Prussians, under Gebhard Leberecht von Blücher, made an additional fifty thousand. The Allies lost about twenty-two thousand and the French about thirty-seven thousand men. Waterloo is the climax of the HUNDRED DAYS, which commenced with Napoleon's escape from Elba; his seizure of power ended, however, with the restoration of Louis XVIII on June 28, 1815.

The triumph of the "Iron Duke" over the "Man of Destiny" made Waterloo one of the most famous names of the period—second only to that of Bonaparte. Today it has come to mean failure and tragic, hope-shattering defeat. More than a battle, Waterloo marks the end of almost twenty years of European war and of the Napoleonic dreams of glory.

Water Margin, The   See SHUI HU CHUAN.

Watkins, Vernon [Phillips] (1906–1967)   Welsh poet. Watkins, who spent most of his adult life working as a bank clerk, is known for his musical, visionary verse. Among his volumes of poetry are *The Ballad of the Mari Lwyd* (1941), *Cypress and Acacia* (1959), and *Affinities* (1962). His *Selected Poems* was published in 1967.

Watteau, Antoine (1684–1721)   French painter. Watteau was instrumental in developing a Parisian style of painting distinct from Italian influences. His own work derived much from the exuberance of RUBENS, whose works he had copied and whose *Garden of Love* (1634) is vividly recalled in Watteau's *Embarkation for Cythera* (1717). This and other charmingly informal and ethereal scenes, called *fêtes champêtres* or *fêtes gallantes*, as well as his genre paintings, such as *Italian Comedians* (c1705), were emulated by the ROCOCO painters of the 18th century.

Watts, Isaac (1674–1748)   English nonconformist theologian, hymn writer, author, and pastor. Watts is best known for his sacred poems, *Horae Lyricae* (1706), *Psalms of David* (1719), and *Divine and Moral Songs for Children* (1720). He also wrote theological and philosophical works. He revolutionized the Protestant hymn, and many of his hymns are still sung today. He is the author of the famous lines "How doth the little busy bee," from one of his instructive poems for children.

Watts-Dunton, [Walter] Theodore   See SWINBURNE, ALGERNON CHARLES.

Waugh, Auberon [Alexander] (1939–   )   English novelist and journalist. The son of Evelyn WAUGH, Auberon Waugh achieved prominence as a reporter, reviewer, and political and social columnist with his acerbic commentary on aspects of contemporary experience. His first novel, *The Foxglove Saga* (1960), is a satire on Catholic boarding schools and the British army. Other novels, often thought to straddle the line between satire and invective, are *Path of Dalliance* (1963), about life at Oxford; *Consider the Lilies* (1968), about Anglican clergymen; and *A Bed of Flowers* (1972), concerning those who reject the modern world. Among his mockingly autobiographical writings are *Auberon Waugh's Yearbook* (1981) and *The Diaries of Auberon Waugh: A Turbulent Decade, 1976–1985* (1985), collected from his columns in the satirical magazine *Private Eye*.

Waugh, Evelyn [Arthur St. John] (1903–1966)   English novelist. Waugh's earliest and most famous novels are witty, sophisticated satires of fashionable London society, the English upper classes, and the young intellectuals of the 1920s, with all of whom he consorted. DECLINE AND FALL, *Vile Bodies* (1930), BLACK MISCHIEF, A HANDFUL OF DUST, *Scoop* (1938), and THE LOVED ONE established his reputation as a master of mordant comedy—cruel, funny, and right on target. Waugh was converted to Catholicism in 1930, and BRIDESHEAD REVISITED, perhaps his most popular and least satirical novel, is also one of the most thoroughly Catholic in viewpoint. He served as an officer in the army through World War II, an experience that provided the material for the trilogy consisting of *Men at Arms* (1952), *Officers and Gentlemen* (1954), and *Unconditional Surrender* (1961; U.S. *The End of the Battle*), whose central character is Guy Crouchback. These books project a more sober view of life, which at times verges on misanthropy. The novel *The Ordeal of Gilbert Pinfold* (1957) is a complex, paranoid self-portrait, with an account of a hallucination actually experienced by Waugh as a result of too much alcohol and too many sleeping pills. Waugh also wrote travel books with an aristocratic, imperialistic flavor and a number of biographies, notably *Rossetti* (1928) and *Edmund Campion* (1935). *The Diaries of Evelyn Waugh* appeared in 1976; *The Letters* in 1980. *A Little Order* (1981) is a collection of his journalistic pieces.

Waugh, Hillary [Baldwin] (1920–   )   American novelist. One of the pioneers of the police procedural detective story, Waugh has created two series characters: Fred Fellows, police chief of a small Connecticut town, introduced in *Prisoner's Plea* (1963); and Detective Frank Sessions of Manhattan Homicide, introduced in "*30*" *Manhattan East* (1968). Before he began either series, Waugh wrote *Last Seen Wearing* (1952), considered a classic of realistic police fiction. Waugh's stories, including *Madman at My Door* (1978), *The Veronica Dean Case*

(1984), and *The Priscilla Copperwaite Case* (1985), are characterized by a clear knowledge of law enforcement procedures and by tightly woven, suspenseful plots.

Waverley (1814)   The first of Sir Walter SCOTT's historical novels, which established him as the foremost romantic novelist of the time and which gave a name to an entire series of his novels. The chief characters are Prince Charles Edward, the Young PRETENDER; the noble old baron of Bradwardine; and Captain Edward Waverley, the hero. The background is the JACOBITE rebellion of 1745.

Waverley Novels   A series of thirty-two novels and tales by Sir Walter SCOTT. The first of these, WAVERLEY, gave the series its name. The novels were published anonymously "by the author of Waverley," who became famous as the Great Unknown. Originally Scott published the books anonymously because he feared that novel writing was beneath his dignity as a clerk of court; he discovered that his anonymity increased sales and kept it up for eleven years, until 1825, when his identity, by then generally known, was disclosed.

Waves, The (1931)   A novel by Virginia WOOLF. Highly original, unconventional, and poetic, it describes the characters, lives, and relationships of six persons living in England. The book is composed of interior monologues (see STREAM OF CONSCIOUSNESS), spoken by the six characters in rotation, and of interludes describing the ascent and descent of the sun, the rise and fall of the waves, and the passing of the seasons. These natural cycles symbolize the progress of time, which carries the individual from birth to death.

As children, the six live in the same house by the seashore and take lessons from the same governess. Their early experiences influence their developing personalities and remain valuable memories for the rest of their lives. They have two reunions: one with PERCIVAL, their childhood friend, in a restaurant, and one, in middle age, at Hampton Court. The characters' life stories are revealed only incidentally, but their monologues throw brilliant, subtle light on their various personalities. The three men are various types of the artist: Bernard is a life-loving storyteller; Neville is a meticulous perfectionist; and Louis, an Australian with an inferiority complex, is vain, driving, and nourished by tradition. The women, too, differ widely in character: Susan is domestic and maternal—she loves Bernard but marries someone else; Jinnie is a flirtatious society beauty and, like Neville, who loves only Percival, does not marry; Rhoda, timid and mystical, becomes the mistress of the other outsider, Louis, and finally commits suicide. In a final monologue, Bernard, as an elderly man, reviews the lives of himself and his friends and feels himself flowing into their consciousnesses like a wave into other waves. He thinks that the six of them together make up one complete person.

Wayland   A wonderful and invisible smith of English legend. Wayland is the English form of the Scandina-

vian Volund or Volunder, a supernatural smith and king of the elves. In *Frithiof's Saga* (13th century), Volund forges the armor of Thorsten, Frithiof's father, particularly a golden arm-ring, which descends to Frithiof as one of his most precious possessions. According to the legend, King Nidud or Nidung of Sweden cut the sinews of Volund's feet and cast him into prison to avail himself of his workmanship, but the smith made his escape in a feather boat. Scott introduced Wayland or Wayland Smith into his novel *Kenilworth* (1821). He is said to have lived in a cromlech near Lambourn, Berkshire, since called Wayland Smith's Cave, and legend relates that, if a traveler tied up his horse there, left sixpence for a fee, and retired from sight, he would find the horse shod on his return. Kipling has the tale "Weland's Sword" in his *Puck of Pook's Hill* (1906).

Way of All Flesh, The (1903)   A novel by Samuel BUTLER, published posthumously. The hero, Ernest, is the son of an English clergyman, Theobald Pontifex. Few clergymen in fiction are as unsympathetic as this pious bully, nor is his docile, sanctimonious wife, Christina, any more lovable. The story deals with one of Butler's favorite themes, the relations between parents and children, and is autobiographical in many details. It is, moreover, a keenly satirical criticism of middle-class English family life. Ernest's school and university days are not happy. He struggles with the problem of orthodoxy, goes to live in the slums, is thrown into prison for impulsive advances to a respectable young woman, and marries the extremely vulgar Ellen, who had been his mother's maid. He is freed from this marriage by the fact that Ellen is already married. Receiving an inheritance from an aunt, he is able to devote his life to literature and finally wins some measure of self-respect and genuine success.

Way of the Cross   See STATIONS OF THE CROSS.

Way of the World, The (1700)   A comedy by William CONGREVE. The plot revolves around the efforts of the urbane and witty Mirabell to marry the equally quick-witted Millamant, despite the opposition of her aunt, Lady Wishfort, to whom he has feigned passion in order to disguise his suit for her niece. In the famous "bargaining" scene, Mirabell and Millamant decide to marry, after negotiating an intricate agreement on their various rights and responsibilities. The play is now considered Congreve's greatest work; however, the comparatively poor reception it received contributed to Congreve's decision to give up writing for the stage.

We (My, 1924)   A novel by Yevgeny ZAMYATIN. Describing a regimented totalitarian society in the 26th century, it is an ancestor of such novels as Aldous Huxley's BRAVE NEW WORLD and George Orwell's 1984 (q.v.). Written in 1920, it was first published abroad, in 1924. The publication of a Russian edition in Prague in 1929 led to Zamyatin's expulsion from the Federation of Writers and to his eventual departure from the Soviet Union.

Wealth of Nations, The (1776)   An influential work on economics by Adam SMITH, the full title of which is *Inquiry into the Nature and Causes of the Wealth of Nations*. It is in this work that Smith outlines a system of LAISSEZ-FAIRE economics, based on an absolutely free economy.

Weavers, The (Die Weber, 1892; tr 1899)   A play by Gerhart HAUPTMANN, considered among the finest works of German NATURALISM. Based on Hauptmann's grandfather's eyewitness account of the Silesian weavers' rebellion in 1844, the play offers a compassionate glimpse of the ghastly conditions and economic plight of the Silesian weavers. One version, *Die Waber*, was written entirely in dialect; the version most often performed is in High German, though it is heavily spiced with dialect. Rather than giving the play an individual protagonist, Hauptmann makes the weavers themselves the collective hero.

Web and the Rock, The (1939)   A novel by Thomas WOLFE. Wolfe follows his autobiographical hero, George Webber (called Eugene Gant in LOOK HOMEWARD, ANGEL and OF TIME AND THE RIVER), to the "Enfabled Rock" of New York, where, in the midst of his youthful literary struggles, he meets the gifted scenic designer Mrs. Esther Jack. During their love affair, George is at first entranced by and then disillusioned with the magic of the city that is so much a part of Esther's personality. At length George breaks from Esther's web of devotion and flees abroad to seek in an older culture the stability he could not find in the American city. YOU CAN'T GO HOME AGAIN is a sequel.

Webb, [Martha] Beatrice [Potter] (1858–1943) and **Sidney [James]** (1859–1947)   British historians, social and political activists, and Fabians—socialists dedicated to reforming society gradually without revolutionary upheaval. Beatrice Webb's *The Co-operative Movement in Great Britain* (1891) is a thorough account of the subject. Following their marriage in 1892, Beatrice and Sidney Webb collaborated on standard studies of the socialist movement and trade unionism in Britain. *The History of Trade Unionism* (1894), their first joint work, is a penetrating analysis of the growth and development of British trade unionism. Among their other works are *Industrial Democracy* (1897), *History of English Local Government* (9 vols, 1906–29), and *Soviet Communism: A New Civilization?* (2 vols, 1935). They founded the London School of Economics in 1895 and *New Statesman* magazine in 1913.

Webb, Mary   See PRECIOUS BANE.

Weber, Karl Maria von (1786–1826)   German composer, best known as the founder of German romantic operas. *Der Freischütz* (1821) is based on the old legend of the hunter whose bullets, charmed by the devil, cannot miss. *Oberon* (London, 1826; sung in English) is based on the poem of the same name by WIELAND. Weber employed the LEITMOTIF technique, which was later developed by Richard WAGNER. Weber also wrote much piano and chamber music, but his reputation rests chiefly on his operas.

Weber, Max (1864–1920)   German sociologist and historian. Weber's attempts at developing a systematic methodology for cross-cultural studies had a significant influence on the development of modern social science. In his best-known and most controversial work, *Die Protestantische Ethik und der Geist des Kapitalismus* (1905, 1922; tr *The Protestant Ethic and the Spirit of Capitalism*, 1930), he opposed the Marxist concept of DIALECTICAL MATERIALISM and related the rise of capitalist economy to the Calvinist belief in the moral value of hard work in the fulfillment of one's worldly duties.

Weber, Max (1881–1961)   Russian-born American artist. An avant-garde painter early in the 20th century, Weber reflects, in his paintings of this period, such as *Chinese Restaurant* (1915), his association with CÉZANNE and the cubist-futurists. As a sculptor, he created the first totally nonobjective works in America, among them *Spiral Rhythm* (1915). In the 1940s, he painted scenes, first realistic and later somewhat expressionistic, of the Hasidic Jews, whose mysticism and fervor had impressed him as a child in Russia. His writings include *Cubist Poems* (1914), *Essays on Art* (1916), and *Primitives* (1926).

Weber, Die   See WEAVERS, THE.

Webern, Anton von (1883–1945)   Austrian composer. Along with Alban BERG, Webern was the most famous pupil of Arnold SCHOENBERG. His studies in Renaissance music, as well as his penchant for abstract musical reasoning, led to a style of extraordinary conciseness and intricacy, employing Schoenberg's twelve-tone technique in a highly condensed manner. During his lifetime, he exerted little influence, but following his death (he was accidentally shot by an American military policeman shortly after the end of World War II), other composers seized upon his music as the basis for new developments.

Webster, Daniel (1782–1852)   American statesman and orator. A native of New Hampshire, Webster was admitted to the bar in 1805. As a member of the House of Representatives (1813–17), he attacked the War of 1812. He moved to Massachusetts in 1816 and, after two more terms in the House, was elected to the Senate in 1827. A champion of nationalism, as opposed to state sovereignty, he engaged in a famous debate (1830) with Senator Hayne of South Carolina, during which he extolled "Liberty *and* Union, now and forever, one and inseparable!" After two futile attempts to win the Whig presidential nomination, he served as secretary of state (1841–43), negotiating the Webster-Ashburton Treaty with Great Britain, which settled the dispute over the Maine boundary. In 1844 Webster was again elected to the Senate, where he favored the COMPROMISE OF 1850 in his Seventh of March speech, which began, "I wish to speak today, not as a Massachusetts man, nor as a Northerner, but as an American." His moderate stand cost him the support of abolitionists, and John

Greenleaf WHITTIER denounced him in his poem "Ichabod" (1850). Whittier later condoned Webster's action in "The Lost Occasion" (1880). Webster is also a prominent character in Stephen Vincent Benét's THE DEVIL AND DANIEL WEBSTER.

Webster, John (1580?–?1625)   English dramatist, noted for his passionate tragedies of revenge. Webster's most famous plays are THE WHITE DEVIL and THE DUCHESS OF MALFI, both of which deal with actual events that occurred in Italy. He made additions to MARSTON's *The Malcontent* and collaborated with Thomas DEKKER on *Westward Ho* and *Northward Ho*, both of which were published in 1607. He also wrote *The Devil's Lawcase* (pub 1623), a tragicomedy, and the tragedy *Appius and Virginia* (pub 1654), to which Thomas HEYWOOD probably contributed. He is perhaps the Elizabethan dramatist most frequently compared with SHAKESPEARE, because of the dynamism and poetic lyricism that characterize his best work.

Webster, Noah (1758–1843)   American lexicographer and author. A man of varied interests, Webster was a teacher, lecturer, journalist, lawyer, judge, scientist, gardener, and traveler. In politics, he was an ardent partisan of Federalism, advocating the adoption of the Constitution and a strong central government. While a resident in Amherst, Massachusetts, he was president of the Amherst Academy (1820–21) and helped to found Amherst College.

Webster believed that the American nation needed a language and literature of its own; he wrote a three-volume *Grammatical Institute of the English Language*. Parts II (1784) and III (1785) were a grammar and a reader, but Part I, commonly known as *Webster's Spelling Book* or the *Blue-Backed Speller* (1783), became a best-seller in its own right. Used in all schools, it sold some sixty million copies in the course of the century and helped to make American orthography uniform.

Webster's great work, *An American Dictionary of the English Language* (1828), was revised in 1841. Upon Webster's death, George and Charles Merriam acquired the unsold copies and publishing rights to the work, which has been revised many times and in many versions and is still popular.

Wedekind, Frank (1864–1918)   German playwright and actor. The scion of a wealthy family, destined for a career in law, Wedekind left school and took jobs advertising soup and later as secretary to a traveling circus. Having absorbed the divergent influences of HAUPTMANN's realism and STRINDBERG's symbolism, he caused a sensation with the production of *Frühlings Erwachen* (1891; tr *The Awakening of Spring*, 1909), which dealt with the problems created by adolescent ignorance of sex. The uproar aroused by that play was surpassed with the appearance of *Der Erdgeist* (1895; tr *Earth Spirit*, 1914) and its sequel, *Die Büchse der Pandora* (1903; tr *Pandora's Box*, 1918), both of which treated sexual themes with a revolutionary frankness. They were the basis for Alban BERG's libretto for his opera *Lulu*. Wedekind's plays were as important for their style as for their content; they are regarded as the forerunners of German EXPRESSIONISM in drama.

Wedgwood, Dame C[icely] V[eronica] (1910–   )   English historian. Wedgwood is known for her distinguished studies of English and European history in the 17th century. Her works include *The Thirty Years' War* (1938); *Oliver Cromwell* (1939; rev 1973); the two volumes of the *Great Rebellion, The King's Peace: 1637–1641* (1955) and *The King's War: 1641–1647* (1958); *A Coffin for King Charles* (1964); *Milton and His World* (1969); and *The Political Career of Peter Paul Rubens* (1975). She was created Dame of the British Empire in 1968. In 1984 she published the first volume of her History of the World series, *The Spoils of Time*.

Weems, Mason Locke (1759–1825)   American clergyman, biographer, and bookseller. Known as Parson Weems, he was an itinerant evangelist and book agent. In 1800 he wrote a *History of the Life, Death, Virtues and Exploits of George Washington*. Vastly popular in its own day, the book was accepted as semifiction and then took its place in American mythology. In its fifth edition (1806), the earliest known version of young Washington and the cherry tree is related. Aside from his other "biographies," of Franklin, Penn, and Marion, Weems wrote a number of moral tracts, among them *God's Revenge Against Murder* (1807) and *The Drunkard's Looking Glass* (1812).

Weep Not, Child (1964)   A novel by NGUGI WA THIONG'O. Set in the period immediately before and during the Mau-Mau uprising in Kenya, 1952–56, the novel tells the story of the family of Ngotho and how the emergency affects them. The story is told from the point of view of Njoroge, the youngest son, whose dream of a better life for himself and his country is shattered by the tragedies occasioned by the struggle for independence.

Wei   See THREE KINGDOMS.

Weidman, Jerome (1913–   )   American novelist, short-story writer, and playwright. Weidman's first novel, *I Can Get It for You Wholesale* (1937), was an enormously popular account of unscrupulous characters in New York's garment industry, which the author adapted into a successful musical in 1962. The novel was followed by a sequel, *What's in It for Me?* (1938). Most of Weidman's novels are witty and irreverent accounts of the urban Jewish scene. Among them are *Other People's Money* (1967); *The Temple* (1975); *A Family Fortune* (1978), which picks up the rags-to-riches theme of his first novel; and *Counselors-at-Law* (1980). He has also written several collections of stories; plays, including the musical *Fiorello!* (1959; PULITZER PRIZE), with George ABBOTT; and essays. *Praying for Rain*, a memoir, was published in 1986.

Weil, Simone (1909–1943)   French philosopher. A brilliant and precocious student, Weil studied philosophy with ALAIN in her teens and gained entrance to the École

Normale Supérieure. Though she was Jewish, she developed a strong interest in Hellenic traditions of mystic spirituality and in Catholicism. Her writings are passionate essays, reflecting her profound concerns with pacifism, social freedoms, and religion. Painfully aware of the oppression and suffering around her, she came to see suffering itself as a means to spiritual unity with God. Her early death, at the age of thirty-four, was recorded as suicide by starvation.

Apart from a few essays, all of her works were pieced together and published posthumously. Most notable among them are *La Pesanteur et la grâce* (1947; tr *Gravity and Grace*, 1952), *L'Enracinement* (1949; tr *The Need for Roots*, 1955), *L'Attente de Dieu* (1950; tr *Waiting for God*, 1959), *La Connaissance surnaturelle* (1950), and *Cahiers* (1951–55; tr *Notebooks*, 1956). Notes from her lecture course in philosophy appeared in *Légon de philosophie* (1959; tr *Lectures of Philosophy*, 1978).

Weill, Kurt (1900–1950)   German-born composer, known especially for his operas and musical comedies. Under the influence of Bertolt BRECHT, Weill adopted a superficially popular style, while retaining subtle techniques of modern music. With Brecht, he wrote his most famous work, THE THREEPENNY OPERA. In the United States, Weill worked with Maxwell ANDERSON on *Knickerbocker Holiday* (1938; based on Washington IRVING's *Father Knickerbocker*) and *Lost in the Stars* (1949; based on Alan PATON's *Cry, the Beloved Country*). He also composed *Lady in the Dark* (1941; libretto by Moss Hart, lyrics by Ira GERSHWIN) and the "folk opera" *Down in the Valley* (1948; libretto by Arnold Sundgaard).

Weimar classicism (Ger, *Weimarer Klassik*)   A literary movement in Germany, usually dated from GOETHE's return from Italy (1788) until SCHILLER's death (1805). During most of this period, Goethe was in Weimar itself, and Schiller was in Jena, a small university town only a few miles away. From 1794 on, the two poets worked together closely, and, in the main, it is their thinking and writing, their cooperative effort to establish and develop a new poetic humanism, that form the backbone of the movement. Wilhelm von HUMBOLDT, who was a friend of both poets, also contributed a good deal of critical thought to their endeavors, and, though the brothers SCHLEGEL are usually thought of in connection with romanticism, they both influenced and were themselves influenced by the classical strivings of Goethe and Schiller.

The ideal of the Weimar classicists was one of harmony and balance, for which they took the ancient Greeks as their models, following WINCKELMANN. But neither Goethe nor Schiller believed in the rationalistic harmony of the Enlightenment. Both sought instead an emotional and organic harmony based on the inward sympathy that unites all men and on an unstrained, optimistic view of the relationship between man and the world. They thought that the ordinary man in his actions, as well as the artist in his works, should exercise restraint but never at the expense of his essential humanity.

Goethe and Schiller cooperated on a collection of *Xenien* (1797; see XENION), in which, with a good deal of satire about other authors, they stated their own position within the literature of the time. Among Goethe's works, other central documents of Weimar classicism are IPHIGENIA IN TAURIS, TORQUATO TASSO, *Wilhelm Meisters Lehrjahre* (see WILHELM MEISTER), and HERMANN UND DOROTHEA. Among Schiller's works, the essays on aesthetics are important for the movement, as are a number of lyric poems, including "Der Spaziergang" ("The Walk," 1795), an imaginary excursion through the whole progress of human culture; "Würde der Frauen" ("Dignity of Women," 1795), which attempts to define the eternal and unchanging spiritual relationship between man and woman; and "Das Lied von der Glocke" ("The Song of the Bell," 1799), which takes the making of a town's church bell as the occasion for a eulogy on the communal spirit in human society.

Weimar Republic   The unofficial name for the first German state with a democratic parliamentary government. Formed in the wake of defeat in World War I, it began with the formulation of its constitution in the city of Weimar in 1919 and lasted until HITLER seized power in 1933. The republic was unpopular in Germany from the beginning, largely because it accepted what many felt were the unfair terms of the Treaty of VERSAILLES. The German middle class did not accept their country's defeat; many believed that Germany had been treacherously disarmed by socialist and Jewish agitators on the home front. The republic was also unable to control rampant inflation and massive unemployment, which produced a bitter and despondent population, susceptible to a broad spectrum of extremist rhetoric that promised bloody revenge and a utopian future. Shaky coalition governments were established, and the President was granted emergency powers that preempted legislative functions, bringing the republic within one step of dictatorship. Hitler took that step in 1933, when he became Chancellor and then secured dictatorial powers from a collapsing parliament, upon the death of President Hindenburg, combining the offices of President and Chancellor under the title of Führer.

Weir of Hermiston (1896)   An unfinished novel by Robert Louis STEVENSON. Left unfinished at his death, this work promised to be Stevenson's masterpiece and contains some of his best writing. It is the story of Archie Weir, banished by his severe father, a judge, to live in solitude in the village of Hermiston. Here he meets Christina, with whom he falls in love. The novel breaks off at this point; Stevenson intended to have Archie forced to commit a murder because of his love for Christina, tried and sentenced to death by his own father, and rescued by some relatives of Christina. Archie's father was to die of shock after his condemnation of his son.

Weiss, Peter [Ulrich] (1916–1982)   German-born Swedish dramatist, novelist, painter, and film director. In a number of autobiographical novels, most notably *Fluchtpunkt* (1962; tr *Vanishing Point*, 1966), Weiss chronicles the growing political awareness that informed his artistic and social attitudes. His early surrealist plays, *Der Turm* (*The Tower*, 1948) and *Die Versicherung* (*The Insurance*, 1952), foreshadowed his preoccupation with revolution and the necessity of violence. This theme dominated his most famous play, *Marat/Sade* (1964; full title *Die Verfolgung und Ermordung Jean Paul Marats dargestellt durch die Schauspielgruppe des Hospizes zu Charenton unter Anleitung des Herrn de Sade*; tr *The Persecution and Assassination of Jean-Paul Marat as Performed by the Inmates of the Asylum of Charenton under the Direction of the Marquis de Sade*, 1965). This play within a play, which contains elements associated with both the THEATRE OF THE ABSURD and the THEATRE OF CRUELTY, consists of a debate, set in a lunatic asylum, between the French revolutionary MARAT and the eccentric individualist the Marquis de SADE. Weiss's other work includes a long Marxist drama about Vietnam, *Diskurs über . . . Viet Nam* (1967; tr *Discourse on Vietnam*, 1970), beginning with the struggles of the Vietnamese in 500 BC. Most of Weiss's plays are written in verse; the prose play *Trotzki im Exil* (1970; tr *Trotsky in Exile*, 1972) most clearly spells out his revolutionary principles.

Weld, Theodore Dwight (1803–1895)   American abolitionist. Weld helped to found Lane Seminary in Cincinnati, an abolitionist school whose president was Lyman BEECHER. According to Harriet Beecher Stowe, Weld inspired her to write UNCLE TOM'S CABIN.

Weller, Samuel   The center of comic interest in Charles Dickens's PICKWICK PAPERS. Sam Weller is a bootblack at the White Hart and afterward servant to Mr. PICKWICK, to whom he becomes devotedly attached. When Pickwick is sent to the Fleet Prison, Sam Weller, rather than leave his master, gets his father to arrest him for debt. His colorful speech and his cunning on behalf of his master make him one of Dickens's most amusing characters. "Bless his old gaiters . . ." Sam Weller cries about Pickwick, "I never seen such a fine creetur in my days. Blessed if I don't think his heart must ha' been born twenty-five year arter his body, at least!"

Welles, [George] Orson (1915–1985)   American film director, actor, and producer. Welles's abundant energy, active intelligence and imagination, and forceful personality led to his early reputation as the precocious *Wunderkind* of stage and radio theatre. In 1937 he founded, with John Houseman, the Mercury Theatre. A year later, on the Mercury Theatre of the Air, Welles and his collaborators stunned radio listeners with their adaptation of H. G. Wells's WAR OF THE WORLDS, a realistic broadcast purporting to report the landing of aliens on earth. Taken seriously by many, the program created a

chaos of panic across the country the night it was aired. Welles is best known, however, for his monumental cinematic achievement *Citizen Kane* (1941), a profound and brilliant film written (with Herman Mankiewicz), directed, produced, and starred in by Welles. The innovative technical mastery of the film medium, as well as its highly complex treatment of characters and symbols, made *Citizen Kane* a landmark in cinema history that inspired countless subsequent directors in both the U.S. and Europe. Welles's work after *Citizen Kane* never again displayed the full deployment of his talent. Among his later films were *The Magnificent Ambersons* (1942), *The Lady from Shanghai* (1948), *Touch of Evil* (1958), and *Chimes at Midnight* (1966), as well as several that Welles abandoned and left to studios to complete. He appeared as an actor in numerous pictures, notably *The Third Man* (1949), *Compulsion* (1959), and *Crack in the Mirror* (1960).

Wellington, Arthur Wellesley, first duke of (known as the Iron Duke, 1769–1852)   English general and statesman. Wellington was chief in command, after the death of Sir John Moore (1761–1809), in the Peninsular War (1809), represented England at the Congress of Vienna (1814–15), and defeated Napoleon at WATERLOO. Thereafter he was a member of repressive TORY governments, was Prime Minister in 1828–30, and was so unpopular as to be the target of rioting mobs. He is buried in St. Paul's Cathedral.

well-made play   A term applied to any play that is neatly constructed out of the following components: a plot that revolves around some unknown but decisive factor; a framework of mounting suspense; a climax (or obligatory scene) in which the unknown factor is revealed, usually in such a way as to save the hero from a perilous situation; and a DÉNOUEMENT in which all actions and events are satisfactorily explained. The French dramatist Eugène SCRIBE is popularly credited with originating the form, which had a considerable influence on much 19th-century drama.

Wells, H[erbert] G[eorge] (1866–1946)   English novelist and journalist. Wells is known for his science fiction, his satirical novels, and his popular accounts of history and science. He was a vigorous advocate of socialism, feminism, evolutionism, nationalism, and the advancement of science. The first great writer of science fiction, Wells produced THE TIME MACHINE, *The Island of Dr. Moreau* (1896), *The Invisible Man* (1897), THE WAR OF THE WORLDS, and *The First Man in the Moon* (1901), among many others. Coming down to earth in his next period, he wrote such realistic novels as KIPPS, TONO-BUNGAY, *The History of Mr. Polly* (1910; see MR. POLLY), and THE NEW MACHIAVELLI. Most of these novels are concerned with improving people's living conditions and their attitudes toward life. Among his later works were such popular nonfiction as the *Outline of History* (1920) and its compressed version, *A Short History of the World* (1922). Throughout Wells's enormously productive life, he was deeply concerned with the survival of society. From *Mankind in the Making* (1903) and *A Modern Utopia* (1905) to *Men Like Gods* (1923), he tried to depict an ideal world. *The Open Conspiracy* (1928) proposed government by supermen and a new world religion based on physics; *The World of William Clissold* (1926) is a long didactic novel on the subject. However, just before his death, he reached a point of despair in *Mind at the End of Its Tether* (1946), suggesting that man's scientific advances were fatally outdistancing his intellectual and social development.

The son of a housekeeper on a large estate, Wells worked his own way through the University of London, where he studied under the great biologist Thomas HUXLEY. He then became a teacher and a FABIAN socialist. The works of his middle period contain many autobiographical elements, and in 1934 he wrote *Experiment in Autobiography*. He was married several times; by his own account, the alliance most important to his life and work was with Rebecca WEST.

We'll to the Woods No More   See LAURIERS SONT COUPÉS, LES.

Welsh, Jane Baillie (1801–1866)   Scottish-born wife of Thomas CARLYLE, whom she married in 1826. An exceptionally intelligent and charming woman, Welsh is said to have suffered much from her husband's irritability, neglect, and ambition. J. A. Froude edited a collection of her *Letters* in 1883, and additional volumes have since been published.

Welty, Eudora (1909–   )   American short-story writer and novelist. Born in Jackson, Mississippi, Welty is known for her compressed portraits of people and life in the deep South. Such books as *A Curtain of Green* (1941), *The Wide Net* (1943), *The Golden Apples* (1949), *The Bride of the Innisfallen* (1955), and *Thirteen Stories* (1965) make extensive use of myth, symbols, and literary references to explore the mysteries of individuals' "separateness." *The Collected Stories of Eudora Welty* was published in 1980. Although at her best in stories, Welty writes novels—*Delta Wedding* (1946), *The Ponder Heart* (1954), *Losing Battles* (1970), and *The Optimist's Daughter* (1972; PULITZER PRIZE)—that are also distinguished by her perception of the Southern character in the midst of change, her uncanny ear for colloquial speech, her eye, even her sense of smell, and her rich sense of humor, which give her pictures of small-town Delta life a universal reality. Like her literary mentors, Katherine Anne PORTER and Anton CHEKHOV, she sees in each life a piece of all life. In *The Eye of the Story: Selected Essays and Reviews* (1978), her first collection of nonfiction, she discusses her craft and some writers she admires. *One Writer's Beginnings* (1984), an autobiographical account of her childhood in Jackson, describes those elements that profoundly affected the direction of her writing and shows her vibrant literary style.

werewolf (or werwolf; fr OE, *wer*, "man," *wulf*, "wolf")   A legendary creature, a man who, according to

medieval superstition, was turned—or could at will turn himself—into a wolf (the *loup-garou* of France). This creature had the appetite of a wolf and roamed about at night devouring infants and sometimes exhuming corpses. Its skin was proof against shot or steel, unless the weapon had been blessed in a chapel dedicated to St. Hubert.

This superstition was once common to almost all Europe and still lingers in certain remote areas. In the 15th century, a council of theologians convoked by the Emperor Sigismund gravely decided that the werewolf was a reality.

OVID tells the story of Lycaon, king of Arcadia, turned into a wolf because he tested the divinity of JUPITER by serving up to him a "hash of human flesh." HERODOTUS describes the Neuri as having the power of assuming once a year the shape of wolves. PLINY relates that one of the family of Antaeus was chosen annually by lot to be transformed into a wolf, in which shape he continued for nine years; and St. Patrick, we are told, converted Vereticus, king of Wales, into a wolf.

Werfel, Franz (1890–1945)   Austrian novelist, poet, and playwright, born in Prague. Among the best-known expressions of his religiously based yearning for a brotherhood of man are his realistic novels *Barbara; oder Die Frömmigkeit* (1929; tr *The Pure in Heart*, 1931), *Die vierzig Tage des Musa Dagh* (1933; tr *The Forty Days of Musa Dagh*, 1934), and THE SONG OF BERNADETTE. The same message, in an earlier, more expressionistic stage, is found in his collections of verse: *Die Weltfreund* (*Friend to the World*, 1911), *Wir sind!* (*We Are!* 1913), and *Einander* (*Each Other*, 1915). His early plays, such as GOAT SONG and *Juarez und Maximillian* (1924), contain many expressionistic elements and tend toward a tragic view of human conflicts. Such subsequent dramas as *Der Weg der Verheißung* (1936; tr *The Eternal Road*, 1936), a triumphant dramatic unfolding of Jewish history, and *Jacobowsky und der Oberst* (1944; tr *Jacobowsky and the Colonel*, 1944), a comedy, are more optimistic. Werfel fled Germany and the Nazis in 1938; he immigrated to the U.S. in 1940 and died in California five years later.

Werner, Zacharias (1768–1823)   German dramatist. Werner's plays, the most famous of which are *Der 24. Februar* (*The 24th of February*, 1810) and *Martin Luther; oder, Die Weihe der Kraft* (*Martin Luther; or, The Consecration of Strength*, 1807), concentrated on the would-be tragic but actually contrived workings of fate, spawning imitators who made up the "fate-tragedy" school. After divorcing his third wife, he became a Catholic priest (1814).

Wertmuller, Lina (1928–   )   Italian filmmaker and screenwriter. One of the first major women film directors, Wertmuller began her career as an assistant to FELLINI on $8\frac{1}{2}$. She uses irony, satire, and farce to portray an oppressed class, particularly women, as imprisoned by poverty and marriage. Her most important films released in the U.S. are *Love and Anarchy* (1971), *The Seduction of Mimi*

(1972), *Swept Away* (1974), *Seven Beauties* (1976), and *Revenge* (1979).

Wescott, Glenway (1901–1987)   American novelist and poet. Wescott was born in Wisconsin and, though he was for many years an expatriate, his most esteemed work is concerned with the puritanism and pioneering spirit of his native region. He published two volumes of poetry, *The Bitterns* (1920) and *Natives of Rock* (1925), but he is better known for his fiction. His first novel, *The Apple of the Eye* (1924), was originally published serially in THE DIAL. *The Grandmothers* (1927), a portrait of a pioneering Wisconsin family, stands as a minor classic. Equally strong are some of the stories contained in *Good-bye, Wisconsin* (1928). His other novels include *The Babe's Bed* (1930), *The Pilgrim Hawk* (1940), and *Apartment in Athens* (1945). *Images of Truth: Remembrances and Criticism* (1962) contains personal reminiscences and portraits of various writers.

Wesker, Arnold (1932–   )   English playwright. The son of poor Jewish émigré parents, Wesker began writing at twelve. He left school at sixteen, working at odd jobs until his play *Chicken Soup with Barley* was produced in 1958. This play, *Roots* (1959), and *I'm Talking about Jerusalem* (1960) constitute a trilogy about a family of left-wing Jewish intellectuals. Wesker, who was identified with the group of playwrights that included John OSBORNE, Brendan BEHAN, and David STOREY, won a wide audience with such subsequent productions as *Chips with Everything* (1962), about an air force rebel who eventually yields to pressure and takes his place in the hierarchy, and *Their Very Own and Golden City* (1964). As a working-class playwright with strong socialist convictions, Wesker was something of a maverick in the West End theatre world of London. With trade union support, he founded and directed Centre 42, a theatre, gallery, and studio, through which he hoped to involve London's lower classes in the arts; it was open from 1962 to 1970. Wesker's other plays include *The Wedding Feast* (1974), *The Journalists* (1975), and *The Merchant* (1976), which is based on Shakespeare's *The Merchant of Venice*. In addition to his plays, Wesker has written short stories and essays; *Fears of Fragmentation* (1970), a collection, contains a discussion of the establishment and failure of Centre 42. Wesker's *Collected Plays and Stories* appeared in five volumes in 1980.

Wesley, Charles (1707–1788)   English Methodist clergyman and hymn writer, brother of John WESLEY. Charles Wesley composed some sixty-five hundred hymns and left a *Journal* (pub 1849); he also accompanied his brother John on his missionary trip to Georgia, U.S.

Wesley, John (1703–1791)   English evangelist and theologian, famous as the founder of METHODISM. In 1735, accompanied by his brother Charles WESLEY, he went to the U.S. as a missionary to the Indians and colonists in Georgia. Returning to England (1738), he established the Methodist Church. In 1763 he drew up a legal deed stating that Methodist preachers should preach no other doctrine than that contained in his *Notes on the New Testament* and the first four volumes of his sermons. John Wesley was a powerful preacher, traveling all over England on horseback. He published his prose *Works* in 1771–74. His *Journal* was published in 1909–11.

West, Anthony [Panther] (1914–   )   English novelist and critic, the son of Rebecca WEST and H. G. WELLS. West moved to the U.S., where he wrote the novels *Heritage* (1955), which explores the mind of a growing boy who, like West, is the son of two famous people who are not married to each other, and *The Trend Is Up* (1960), about how a nineteen-year-old man ruthlessly reaches his goal of becoming a millionaire before the age of thirty, and a collection of stories, *David Rees, Among Others* (1970). *Principles and Persuasions* (1957) is a collection of literary essays. His mother's treatment of him during his childhood, at a time when the existence of illegitimate offspring was usually concealed, led to lifelong bitterness and in 1984 to his writing *H. G. Wells: Aspects of a Life*, in which West attacks his mother and defends his father.

West, Benjamin (1738–1820)   American painter. West was noted for his portraits and historical scenes and for his drawings, such as *Head of an Apostle* (c1818). At the age of twenty-two, he left America to study painting in Europe, probably the first of the many American artists to do so. In Europe, he affected the popular neoclassical style, provoking considerable controversy with his *Death of General Wolfe* (1771), in which his subjects wore contemporary clothing. Toward 1800 he began painting in a romantic manner, achieving perhaps his greatest acclaim for the melodramatic *Death on a Pale Horse* (1802). The measure of his importance in his day is reflected by his being selected in 1763 as history painter to King George III and his election to the presidency of the Royal Academy in 1792, succeeding Joshua REYNOLDS. West's influence was considerable, particularly on the many Americans who traveled to England to study with him.

West, Morris L[anglo] (1916–   )   Australian novelist. Although primarily a novelist, West made his reputation with *Children of the Shadows* (1957), his nonfiction study of street urchins in Naples. All his books are infused with a devout sense of Catholic principle. Two of his best-selling novels, *The Devil's Advocate* (1959) and *The Shoes of the Fisherman* (1963), deal directly with religious issues. West has also written a number of political thrillers. Among his many works are *The Clowns of God* (1981) and *The World Is Made of Glass* (1983).

West, Nathanael (pen name of Nathanael Wallenstein Weinstein, 1904–1940)   American novelist. An unusual and highly original talent, West was one of the first and best American writers of black comedy. The four books that constitute the *Complete Works of Nathanael West* (1959) are a scathing indictment of the horror and emptiness of the American Dream. His first novel, *The Dream Life of Balso Snell* (1931), a bitter, surrealistic chronicle of personal despair, is important primarily as an indication of what was to follow. MISS LONELYHEARTS and THE DAY OF THE LOCUST are his most compelling and effective works. *A Cool Million* (1934) is an overt parody of the Horatio Alger myth, in the innocent character of Lemuel Pitkin. West and his wife, Eileen McKenney, the subject of Ruth MCKENNEY's *My Sister Eileen* (1938), were killed in an automobile accident in California. West was not generally acknowledged as a writer of distinction until the 1950s.

West, Dame Rebecca (real name Cicily Maxwell Andrews, born Fairfield, 1892–1983)   English novelist, critic, and political journalist. Her novels tend to be psychoanalytic studies, the best known being *The Judge* (1922), *The Thinking Reed* (1936), *The Fountain Overflows* (1956), and *The Birds Fall Down* (1966). Her substantial reputation, however, rests on her nonfiction. Her criticism includes *Henry James* (1916), *St. Augustine* (1933), and *The Court and the Castle* (1958). *Black Lamb and Grey Falcon* (2 vols, 1942), a study of Yugoslavia, is widely considered a masterpiece of sociopolitical journalism. Her later virtuoso pieces of reportage covered treason trials in the wake of World War II, *The Meaning of Treason* (1947; rev as *The New Meaning of Treason*, 1964), and *A Train of Powder* (1955). West was an ardent feminist and social reformer in her youth; her writing is notably without sexual prejudice. Anthony WEST is her son by H. G. WELLS.

Westbrook, Harriet (1795–1816)   English schoolgirl who became the first wife of Percy Bysshe SHELLEY. A friend of Shelley's sisters, Harriet was unhappy at school and at home, and Shelley, possibly in an attempt to "rescue" her, eloped with her to Edinburgh in 1811. When they separated in 1814, she had borne him one child and was expecting another. She drowned herself in the Serpentine, a lake in London's Hyde Park, in 1816.

Western, Squire   An irascible, hare-hunting Tory squire, father of the heroine of Henry Fielding's TOM JONES. Squire Western is singularly unlearned and very prejudiced and countrified, but he is fond of his daughter, Sophia.

western   A piece of fiction set in the frontier American West, dealing with the adventures of cowboys, scouts, Indians, lawmen, and the like. Westerns were popular fare for DIME NOVELS and pulps, which featured tales romanticizing the white man's conquest of the Indian territories. The western hero embodied rugged individualism and enforced his own kind of frontier justice. Because of the mass consumption of western stories and the generally facile plots, the genre has not been regarded as one of high literary distinction. Apart from the perennially popular novels of Zane GREY, notable examples of western fiction include Walter van Tilburg CLARK's *The Ox-bow Incident* (1940), Max Brand's *Destry Rides Again* (1930), and Owen

Wister's THE VIRGINIAN. Cooper's THE PRAIRIE, with its lone hero, prairie fires, and buffalo stampedes, is loosely considered to be one of the earliest westerns.

Weston, Edward (1886–1958)   American photographer. Weston started his career in Chicago as a portrait photographer, working in the painterly, soft-focused style that characterized much of early artistic photography. After traveling to the West Coast in 1915, however, he became interested in sharp focus and the natural subjects for which he became famous. Perhaps his greatest contribution to photography was his affirming its complete independence from painting, establishing it as a modern art in its own right. His most famous works are minutely detailed, richly toned close-ups of peppers, shells, and cypress trees. In 1931 he joined Ansel ADAMS in founding f/64, an influential group of photographers dedicated to the magnificently detailed prints resulting from the use of a large camera with a very small aperture. His philosophy, theories, and much autobiographical information are contained in his *Daybooks*, published in 1961.

Weston, Jessie L[aidley]   See WASTE LAND, THE.

Weyden, Rogier van der (c1400–1464)   Flemish painter. Van der Weyden's paintings, famous for their richness of emotional expression, influenced virtually every northern artist of the 15th century, most notably Hugo van der Goes (1440–82) and Martin Schongauer (1430–91). His best-known painting, *Descent from the Cross* (c1435), abundantly displays the pathos for which his works are known. His portraits were also influential. The most famous of these, the *Portrait of Francesco d'Este* (c1455), reveals, although more subtly than his highly emotional religious scenes, his concern with expressing the inner qualities of his subjects.

Wharton, Edith [Newbold Jones] (1862–1937)   American novelist and short-story writer. A follower of Henry JAMES, Wharton is known for her studies of the tragedies and ironies of life, especially among the members of middle-class and aristocratic New York society in the 19th and early 20th centuries. Her work is marked by an interest in psychological characterization, a preoccupation with manners and morals, and an adherence to aristocratic form.

Born into one of New York's most prominent families, she was at first criticized for her intellectual pursuits. Her first real success came with *The Valley of Decision* (1902), a novel of 18th-century Italy. In THE HOUSE OF MIRTH, she satirized the New York society that she knew so well. In 1907 she moved permanently to Europe, where she wrote *Madame de Treymes* and *The Fruit of the Tree* (both 1907), but she soon returned to American settings in her work, using the New England scene for what many consider her best and least typical work, ETHAN FROME.

After a minor novel, *The Reef* (1912), Wharton wrote THE CUSTOM OF THE COUNTRY, about the breakdown of traditional New York culture. During World War I, she received the Cross of the Legion of Honor for her relief work in Paris. *The Marne* (1918) and *A Son at the Front* (1923) show the influence of her wartime experiences. *Summer* (1917) is a novel about the summer romance of a New England girl. In 1920 appeared THE AGE OF INNO-CENCE, her highly successful novel of manners.

Of her later work, perhaps the best is OLD NEW YORK, a series of four novelettes that includes THE OLD MAID. *Hudson River Bracketed* (1929) and its sequel, *The Gods Arrive* (1932), deal with family problems. Of her several volumes of short stories, the best known is *Xingu and Other Stories* (1916). *A Backward Glance* (1934), her autobiography, is well known for its picture of Henry James, her close friend and literary mentor.

What Is Art? (Chto takoye iskusstvo?, 1897–1898) A treatise on aesthetics by TOLSTOY. Tolstoy considered art an extension of morality and felt that it should be suffused with a morally uplifting spirit. To be good, in Tolstoy's terms, a work of art must also be simple enough to be understood by everyone, not only by the well educated. The feelings of the artist should be obvious in his work. In the Christian era, these feelings should reflect a religious view of man's place in the world and his relation to God.

As examples of literature that transmit such feelings, Tolstoy lists Charles Dickens's A TALE OF TWO CITIES, A CHRISTMAS CAROL, and *The Chimes* (1845); Victor Hugo's LES MISÉRABLES; Harriet Beecher Stowe's UNCLE TOM'S CABIN; and works by DOSTOYEVSKY, SCHILLER, and George ELIOT.

As examples of "universal art" that convey "the simplest feelings of common life accessible to all men in the whole world," Tolstoy cites Cervantes's DON QUIXOTE; the comedies of MOLIÈRE; Dickens's DAVID COPPERFIELD and PICK-WICK PAPERS; and works by GOGOL, PUSHKIN, and MAUPAS-SANT.

Tolstoy's views on art and aesthetics became the framework for the doctrine of SOCIALIST REALISM in Soviet literature, which uses extraliterary standards to judge works of art.

What Maisie Knew (1897) A novel by Henry JAMES. Always interested in the "small expanding consciousness" of a child, James deals in this novel with twelve-year-old Maisie Farange, whose divorced parents have each subsequently remarried. Because custody of the child had been awarded to each of the parents for alternating periods of six months, Maisie presently learns that her stepfather and her stepmother are having adulterous affairs, just as earlier she had been aware of her own parents' infidelities. Instead of corrupting her, this knowledge endows her with a precious understanding of the adult world; ultimately she decides to live with her old governess, Mrs. Wix, instead of with either of her parents.

What Makes Sammy Run? (1941) A novel by Budd SCHULBERG. The hero, Sammy Glick, is a tough

New York youth who works his way into a position of power in the motion-picture industry, where his harshness and crude manners are not out of place. A fast-paced novel, it is filled with much realistic detail of life in the movie colony.

What Price Glory? (1924) A play by Maxwell ANDERSON and Laurence Stallings (1894–1948). This is one of the first realistic American treatments of World War I. Centered on the rivalry of Captain Flagg and Sergeant Quirt for the favors of a French girl, the play caused a sensation by its frank presentation of the profanity and brutality of the professional soldiers and the wearying ugliness of war.

Wheatley, Phillis (or Phyllis Wheatley, 1753?–1784) African-born American poet, the first black woman writer in the U.S. In 1761 she was brought to America from Africa and purchased as a slave by John Wheatley, a Boston merchant. As a child, she showed unusual intelligence and was given an education. Famous in her day, Wheatley was received in London aristocratic circles, and her poetry was praised by George WASHINGTON. Thomas JEFFERSON, however, stated that her *Poems on Various Subjects* (1773) "were below the dignity of criticism."

When Lilacs Last in the Dooryard Bloom'd (1867) A poem by Walt WHITMAN. With the return of lilacs in the spring, the poet mourns again the death of Abraham Lincoln. The thrush pours forth his carol of death, as the coffin slowly journeys through the land to its place of rest. A western star, sailing in the sky, "dropt in the night, and was gone." The song of death becomes victorious; the poet finally glorifies the "strong deliveress."

When We Dead Awaken (1900) A play by Henrik IBSEN. The play is a symbolic statement of a theme that can be found in almost all of Ibsen's dramas: that spiritual death is the price of denying love. The sculptor Rubek meets Irene, who had been the model for his masterpiece many years before but whom he had not dared to love for fear that love would interfere with his art. She tells him that they both have been dead for many years. In an attempt to regain a life of the spirit, they go up into the wild mountains; pressing on to the peak and the sunrise, they are swallowed up in a storm.

Where Angels Fear to Tread (1905) A novel by E. M. FORSTER. The first-published of Forster's novels, written when he was twenty-six, it is set principally in Italy. Its theme is the effect of that land's culture and atmosphere on insular British personalities. Lilia Herriton, a widow of thirty-three, has gone to Italy and married the irresponsible twenty-one-year-old Gino Carelli. She dies in childbirth, and her Herriton relatives decide that her infant son must be properly brought up in England. However, Gino refuses to relinquish his son; the Herritons' offer of a bribe is of no avail. Harriet, Lilia's grimly self-righteous sister-in-law, attempts to impose her will. She abducts the baby, and the child is accidentally killed. The title of the novel is taken from a line in Alexander Pope's ESSAY ON CRITICISM: "For fools rush in where angels fear to tread."

Whig (abbr of *whiggamore*, fr Scot, *whig*, "to drive," *mere*, "mare") (1) A name first derisively applied to raiding parties in western Scotland about 1648, then to Scottish Presbyterians. In 1679, Whig became the name for those who opposed the succession of the Catholic James II to the throne, and after that it was applied to one of the two chief political parties in England, the other being the TORY party. The Whigs were generally identified with industrial concerns, social reform, and their interest in curbing royal power in favor of increased Parliamentary power. In the latter part of the 19th century, the Whigs were replaced by the Liberal Party.

(2) A U.S. political party. For a short time in the mid-19th century, there was an American Whig Party; it was superseded by the Republican Party in 1854.

Whilomville Stories (1900) A collection of thirteen stories by Stephen CRANE. Set in a town usually thought to be Port Jervis, New York, these tales are realistic and unsentimental sketches of childhood. Several are partly based on incidents from Crane's own youth. The title might be translated as "once-upon-a-time town," but the stories are less nostalgic than most stories about childhood. "Lynx-Hunting," a comedy in which Jimmie Trescott, the principal character, shoots a cow, has as one of its characters Henry Fleming, the hero of THE RED BADGE OF COURAGE and of the story "The Veteran."

Whisky Rebellion (1794) An outbreak in western Pennsylvania, resulting from an attempt by the federal government to enforce an excise law passed in 1791, imposing duties on domestic distilled liquors. The rebellion was halted, proving the power of the new government to enforce its laws.

Whistler, James [Abbott] McNeill (1834–1903) American painter. Whistler spent most of his life abroad, especially in France, where he met Gustave COURBET, the dominant influence on his early work. A subsequent alliance with the Pre-Raphaelites (see PRE-RAPHAELITE BROTHERHOOD) influenced such works as his *Symphony in White: The White Girl* (1862). This and other musical titles reflect his preoccupation with aesthetic considerations over social or literary significance—ART FOR ART'S SAKE—as well as his comparison of color harmonies to those in music. His admiration for Japanese art, shared with such contemporaries as MONET and MANET, is evident in the restrained palette and geometric simplicity of the famous *Arrangement in Gray and Black No. 1*, popularly known as *Whistler's Mother* (1871).

In 1877 he became embroiled in a bitter and costly libel suit against the critic John RUSKIN, who had violently denounced his impressionistic *Nocturne in Black and Gold: The Falling Rocket* (1874). The case, which Whistler won, ironically left him nearly penniless but drew wide attention to his wit and character. His character is more

fully disclosed in the collection of his early writings, *The Gentle Art of Making Enemies* (1890).

white A color symbolically denoting purity, simplicity, and candor; innocence, truth, and hope. The ancient Druids and indeed the priests generally in antiquity used to wear white vestments, as does the clergy of the Church of England. The head of OSIRIS, in ancient Egypt, was adorned with a white tiara; all his ornaments were white, and his priests were clad in white.

The priests of JUPITER and the Flamen Dialis of Rome were clothed in white and wore white hats. The victims offered to Jupiter wore white. The Roman festivals were marked with white chalk, and, at the death of a Caesar, the national mourning was white; white horses were sacrificed to the sun; white oxen were selected for sacrifice by the Druids; and white elephants were held sacred in Siam. The Persians affirmed that the divinities are habited in white.

In MOBY-DICK, Melville, in discussing the significance of the whale's unusual color, includes a long essay on white.

White, Antonia (1899–1980) English novelist, translator, and journalist. White is the author of sensitive, partly autobiographical novels, usually dealing with Catholicism. Among them are her first novel, *Frost in May* (1933), a minor classic about a young girl in an Edwardian convent school, and the trilogy about Clara Batchelor: *The Lost Traveller* (1950), *The Sugar House* (1952), and *Beyond the Glass* (1954). She also translated more than thirty books from the French, including many of COLETTE's works, and published a collection of letters, *The Hound and the Falcon: The Story of a Reconversion to the Catholic Faith* (1965).

White, E[lwyn] B[rooks] (1899–1985) American humorist and essayist. White's association with The NEW YORKER, which began in the 1920s, was marked for the public by his regular contributions to the "Talk of the Town." His sharp satirical style and graceful prose gave a distinction to the editorial essay that has been much imitated but seldom equaled. White's influence was felt by a generation of writers, including his colleague on *The New Yorker*, James THURBER, with whom he collaborated on *Is Sex Necessary?* (1929). He also conducted the "One Man's Meat" department for HARPER's from 1938 to 1943. In addition to his essays collected in *The Wild Flag* (1946) and *The Points of My Compass* (1962), White wrote humorous commentary and stories in *Alice Through the Cellophane* (1933), *Quo Vadimus?* (1939), and *The Second Tree from the Corner* (1954). He also wrote poetry—*The Lady Is Cold* (1929) and *The Fox of Peapack* (1938)—and the classic children's books *Stuart Little* (1945), *Charlotte's Web* (1952), and *The Trumpet of the Swan* (1970). In 1959 he edited a revision of *The Elements of Style* by William Strunk, Jr. The *Letters of E. B. White* were published in 1976, and the *Essays of E. B. White* in 1977. *Poems and Sketches of E. B. White* appeared in 1981.

White, Gilbert (1720–1793)   English clergyman and naturalist, known for his *Natural History and Antiquities of Selborne* (1789), a classic scientific work in the field of ornithology.

White, Patrick [Victor Martindale] (1912–   ) Australian novelist. Although born in London, White came from four generations of Australians. He spent his childhood in Sydney and in the outback, where the eerie landscape haunted his imagination and later became the literary and spiritual inspiration for his work. After an unhappy stint in an English boarding school, he returned to Australia and worked for two years on a New South Wales sheep station. Then he returned to England, where he received his university education at Cambridge and lived for a time in London. He spent nearly a year in New York, where he negotiated the U.S. publication of his first novel, *Happy Valley* (1939), an ironically titled, scathing analysis of a small Australian community.

Both the cosmopolitan influences of his extensive travels and the fact that he was relatively affluent set White apart from other Australian writers, who were traditionally poor and who wrote realistic novels on Australian subjects. White's style, which reveals the influence of James JOYCE and Gertrude STEIN, exploits the STREAM OF CONSCIOUSNESS technique but is at the same time uniquely his own. Throughout his work there is a very serious effort, in his words, "to find reason in apparent unreason, and how to accept a supernatural force which on one hand blesses and on the other destroys."

Among his novels are *The Tree of Man* (1955), about the struggles of a dairy-farming family; *Voss* (1957), about a man who disappears into the wild Australian interior to test himself and to gain some sort of psychic regeneration; and *The Eye of the Storm* (1973), in which a woman's attempts to have a serene death are interfered with by the greed and egocentricity of her heirs. *The Cockatoos* (1974) is a collection of stories. A *Fringe of Leaves* (1976) explores the various forms of bondage to which people are subjected or to which they subject themselves. *The Twyborn Affair* (1979) involves the confusions of sexual and spiritual identity. White's autobiographical works are *Flaws in the Glass: A Self-Portrait* (1981) and *Memoirs of Many in One* (1986). He was awarded the NOBEL PRIZE in Literature in 1973.

White, T[erence] H[anbury] (1906–1964)   English writer, best known for *The Once and Future King* (1958), a tetralogy based on ARTHURIAN LEGEND. It began with *The Sword in the Stone* (1939), a witty and erudite fantasy of Arthur's boyhood, which combines affectionate satire on 20th-century English manners and mores with broad humor and a deep knowledge of both nature and the Middle Ages. The other novels in the series are less fanciful and high-spirited. They include *The Witch in the Wood* (1940; repub as *The Queen of Air and Darkness*), *The Ill-Made Knight* (1941), and *The Candle in the Wind* (1942). A fifth volume, published posthumously as *The Book of*

Merlyn (1977), was different in tone, not truly part of the series. White also wrote *The Age of Scandal* (1950) and *The Scandal-mongers* (1952), both 18th-century social history; *The Goshawk* (1951), on falconry; *A Book of Beasts* (1954), a translation of a medieval Latin bestiary; *Mistress Masham's Repose* (1947), a fantasy; and two works of autobiography, *England Have My Bones* (1936) and *The Godstone and the Blackymor* (1959).

White, Theodore H[arold] (1915–1986)   American writer and journalist. White was a student of Chinese history and language at Harvard, and his first journalistic assignment was to China before and during World War II. The result was *Thunder out of China* (1946; with Annalee Jacoby), which met with instant acclaim. *Fire in the Ashes* (1953), an analysis of post-World War II Europe, was also much respected. Subsequently White became known for his highly successful accounts of U.S. presidential campaign politics. Following the PULITZER PRIZE-winning *The Making of the President: 1960* (1961), he wrote similarly titled accounts of the presidential elections of 1964 (1965), 1968 (1969), and 1972 (1973), though these were received increasingly badly by the critics. He also wrote *Breach of Faith* (1975), his documentation of Richard Nixon's political demise. *The View from the Fortieth Floor* (1960), his only novel, is about the New York magazine world. *In Search of History* (1978) is a personal memoir of his years in journalism. In 1982 White published *America in Search of Itself: The Making of the President 1956–1980*.

White, Walter [Francis] (1893–1955)   American novelist and black leader. Executive secretary of the NAACP from 1931 to his death, White worked tirelessly against racial injustice and violence in America. An account of his efforts is contained in his autobiography, *A Man Called White* (1948). His novels and other books with racial themes include *Fire in the Flint* (1924), *Flight* (1926), *Rising Wind* (1945), and the posthumously published *How Far the Promised Land* (1955).

White Devil, The, or Victoria Corombona (pub 1612)   A tragedy by John WEBSTER. It is based on the story of Vittoria Accoramboni (c1557–85), whose husband was murdered so that she might marry the duke of Bracciano. In the play, Vittoria's affair with Brachiano, as the duke is called, is encouraged by her diabolical brother, Flamineo. He and Brachiano dispose of Vittoria's husband, Camillo, and the duke's wife, Isabella. After being tried for murder and adultery, Vittoria is confined in a house for fallen women but is rescued by Brachiano, with whom she elopes. To avenge Isabella's murder, her brother Francisco, duke of Florence, instigates a plot that results in the deaths of Brachiano, Vittoria, and Flamineo.

White Fang (1905)   A novel by Jack LONDON. Written as a complement to CALL OF THE WILD, which describes the reversion of a tame dog to the wild, *White Fang* features a wolf-dog that is gradually domesticated. After being brutally treated by his first owner, who wants a ferocious fighting dog, White Fang is rescued by Weedon Scott, a mining engineer, who tames the dog and takes him to his home in California. White Fang proves his worth when he is gravely wounded while defending his master's family against an escaped convict.

White Goddess, The (1948; rev 1952, 1961) An anthropological and mythological study by Robert GRAVES. Graves claims that the White Goddess, the ancient female, fertility, and mother goddess, and goddess of the moon, became the Muse of poetry and that poetry originated in the ritual worship of this goddess in primitive societies.

Whitehead, Alfred North (1861–1947) English philosopher and mathematician. Whitehead's idealistic and mystical philosophy, which is aimed at a knowledge of God the Absolute, is based on his mathematical ideas. His best-known book, *Science and the Modern World* (1925), is a clear layman's history of the development of science and an exposition of his own philosophy. Among Whitehead's other works are *Principia Mathematica* (1910–13), with Bertrand RUSSELL as coauthor, *The Aims of Education* (1929), and *Adventures of Ideas* (1933).

White Horse [of Uffington] A huge figure of a horse, incised on a hill in Berkshire, England, by cutting away the turf covering the white chalk downs. It is 374 feet long and was traditionally supposed to have been the emblem of the Saxons under ALFRED the Great, cut into the hill to commemorate their victory over the invading Danes at Ashdown (871). It may actually have been cut by Belgic Gauls in the days of the Roman occupation. Thomas Hughes, the author of TOM BROWN'S SCHOOL DAYS, describes the periodic festival of cleaning the turf away from the figure in *The Scouring of the White Horse* (1859). In his poem "The Ballad of the White Horse" (1911), G. K. CHESTERTON makes the horse symbolic of Christianity under Alfred, battling against Norse paganism.

White Jacket, or The World in a Man-of-War (1850) A novel by Herman MELVILLE. Melville reveals his distaste for the brutal and inhumane practices of the ship officers in a realistic account of life aboard a U.S. Navy man-of-war. Some of the flogging scenes later persuaded Congress to abolish that punishment. The white jacket, for which the narrator is named, symbolic of his isolation and innocence, threatens to drown the hero when he falls from the mast into the water. Regaining his buoyancy, White Jacket frees himself from the jacket and rises to the surface, while the hated garment sinks forever. A memorable character in the novel is Jack Chase, captain of the foretop; a natural leader and a sensitive and intelligent man, he reappears in many of Melville's works.

White Knight A well-known character in Lewis Carroll's THROUGH THE LOOKING GLASS. A participant in the chess game that gives the story its structure, the knight is a kindly and chivalrous but vague and incompetent old man. He rescues Alice from the Red Knight but is forever falling off his horse, and he wears spiked anklets "to guard against the bites of sharks."

White Ladies A species of *fée* in many countries. Their appearance generally forbodes death in the house. The belief is a relic of old Teutonic mythology, and the White Ladies represent Holda, or Berchta, the goddess who received the souls of maidens and young children.

white man's burden A euphemism for the type of imperialism predominant in continental Europe, America, and especially Great Britain at the end of the 19th and beginning of the 20th century. It was justified by many of its supporters as a moral duty devolving upon the "superior" white nations in their newly acquired colonies. The term is from the title of a poem by Rudyard KIPLING (1899). Addressed to the American people on the occasion of their assuming control of the Philippines at the end of the Spanish-American War, it exhorts them to "send forth the best ye breed" in paternalistic care of "your new-caught, sullen peoples." It gives an excellent impression of the British imperialism of that date, and of the author's own views at the time of its composition.

white rabbit A character in Lewis Carroll's ALICE'S ADVENTURES IN WONDERLAND. The white rabbit astonishes Alice when he rushes past her, worriedly consulting his watch. Curious to know why he has a watch and where he is hurrying, Alice chases him and falls down a rabbit hole into Wonderland, where her adventures begin.

Whiting, John [Robert] (1917–1963) English playwright. A writer of fierce individuality, Whiting blazed a trail for younger dramatists, such as John OSBORNE and Harold PINTER, with such plays as *A Penny for a Song* (1950) and *Saint's Day* (1951). Whiting's early plays failed to attract a wide following, perhaps because they seemed out of step with theatrical fashion. His aloof, uncompromising heroes, his strong sense of the past, and his angry pessimism made them difficult to embrace. Ironically, it was his last play that won him acclaim. Set in the 17th century, based on *The Devils of Loudon* by Aldous HUXLEY, *The Devils* (1961) concerns Grandier, a libertine priest, who is denounced by a sexually obsessed nun.

Whitman, Walt[er] (1819–1892) American poet, journalist, and essayist. Born near Huntington, Long Island, of mixed Dutch and English ancestry, Whitman early adopted the nickname Walt to distinguish himself from his father. After a few years of schooling, he learned the printing trade and worked in Brooklyn and Manhattan. For the next fifteen years, he alternated between printing and writing jobs, with an interval as a country schoolteacher. In 1842 he wrote his only novel, the temperance tract *Franklin Evans*. By 1846 he had become editor of the Brooklyn *Eagle*, a Democratic paper; in 1848 he lost his position because of his support of the Free Soil Party. After a trip to New Orleans on a short-lived journalistic venture, he founded his own paper, the *Freeman*; it folded in a year because of conservative Democratic pressure.

Whitman then held several odd jobs, working as a carpenter and contractor, and published a few poems. None of these hinted that in 1855 he would publish a striking original book of poetry, LEAVES OF GRASS. The volume, with its twelve untitled poems, was not well received; it offended most delicate sensibilities with its ostensible vulgarity, but EMERSON, a more perceptive critic, greeted Whitman "at the beginning of a great career." An expanded edition was published the following year.

In 1860, after a period of association with the bohemian group in New York, Whitman added two sections, CHILDREN OF ADAM and CALAMUS, to the third edition of his book. In 1862, when his brother George was wounded in the Civil War, Whitman went to Virginia to nurse him. He stayed on in Washington, volunteering to nurse in army hospitals. He published his war impressions in *Drum Taps* (1865), the sequel of which included the elegy for Lincoln, WHEN LILACS LAST IN THE DOORYARD BLOOM'D. Much of this wartime prose is included in SPECIMEN DAYS AND COLLECT.

When *Leaves of Grass* became more popular, its author was dismissed from his government clerkship for having written an immoral book. His supporters rallied, and William D. O'Connor wrote a defense called *The Good Gray Poet* (1866). From this title came Whitman's unfortunate nickname, implying that he was a benevolent but harmless old man. By 1868 his poems were becoming known in England through the appreciation of William ROSSETTI. In 1871 a new edition of *Leaves of Grass* was issued, containing the poem "Passage to India." Shortly after, Whitman wrote DEMOCRATIC VISTAS.

After a paralytic stroke, he moved to Camden, New Jersey. He lectured in the East, visited Colorado and Canada, and published new editions of *Leaves of Grass*. He purchased a house on Mickle Street in Camden and entertained writers and artists from all over the world. The house became the center of a band of disciples, who included Horace Traubel, Dr. R. M. Bucke, and Thomas Harned. At the time of Whitman's death, he had become a legend.

In Whitman's unorthodox form, the line is the rhythmical unit; meter is disregarded, but Whitman employs parallelism and tries to achieve a musical effect. His major themes include the sacredness of the self, the beauty of death, the equality of all people, the love of comrades, and the immortality of the soul. The popular poems that caused him to be admired as "the bard of democracy" have become secondary to CROSSING BROOKLYN FERRY, SONG OF MYSELF, OUT OF THE CRADLE ENDLESSLY ROCKING, and others that identify him as a major poet. Whitman's collected writings appeared in numerous editions. His correspondence (ed E. H. Miller) appeared in four volumes between 1961 and 1969; his prose works (ed F. Stovall) appeared in two volumes in 1963 and 1964; three volumes of *Daybooks and Notebooks* appeared in 1978. See BUR-

ROUGHS, JOHN; O CAPTAIN! MY CAPTAIN!; SONG OF THE OPEN ROAD.

Whitsunday   The Christian feast of PENTECOST. This old English name derives from the white garments traditionally worn by those who were baptized on this Sunday. It and the two days following are the chief early summer holiday in England.

Whittier, John Greenleaf (1807–1892)   American poet and editor. Whittier's formal education was slight, but he read assiduously; before he was twenty, he had published enough verse to bring him to the attention of editors and readers in the antislavery cause. A Quaker devoted to social causes and reform, Whittier worked zealously in behalf of a series of abolitionist newspapers and magazines. His first book, *Legends of New England in Prose and Verse*, was published in 1831; from then until the Civil War, he wrote essays and articles as well as poems, almost all of which are concerned with abolition. See WEBSTER, DANIEL.

The Civil War inspired the familiar poem BARBARA FRIETCHIE, but the important change in his work came after the war. From 1865 until his death, he wrote of religion, nature, and New England life; he became the most popular rural New England poet. He was the poet of the country folk, whose vigorous speech is mirrored in his SNOW-BOUND.

In old age, Whittier turned toward religious verse; many hymns still sung are excerpted from his long religious poems. His finest work was done in the rural poetic genre and includes *Snow-Bound*, TELLING THE BEES, THE BAREFOOT BOY, and MAUD MULLER.

Whittington, Dick (d 1423)   Familiar name of Richard Whittington, lord mayor of London (1397–98, 1406–8, 1419–20). According to popular legend, Dick Whittington was a poor orphan country lad who heard that London was "paved with gold" and went there to earn a living. When he was reduced to starvation, a kind merchant gave him employment in his family as the cook's helper, but the cook so ill-treated him that he ran away. While resting on the roadside, he heard the Bow bells, and they seemed to him to say "Turn again, Whittington, thrice lord mayor of London," so he returned to his master. His master permitted him, with the other servants, to contribute to a ship bound for Morocco. Richard had nothing but a cat; this, however, he sent. It happened that the king of Morocco was troubled by mice, which Whittington's cat destroyed, and this so pleased the king that he bought the mouser at a fabulous price. Dick commenced business with this money, soon rose to great wealth, married his master's daughter, was knighted, and was thrice elected lord mayor of London. Except for Whittington's three elections as mayor, the legend bears little relationship to the recorded facts of his life.

whore of Babylon   An epithet for the Roman Catholic Church, used by the early PURITANS and some of their descendants. In the NEW TESTAMENT (Rev. 17–19), Babylon is the city of the ANTICHRIST.

Who's Afraid of Virginia Woolf? (1962)   A play by Edward ALBEE. The play is a virulent unveiling of the relationship between George, a history professor, and his wife, Martha, the college president's daughter. Another couple, Nick and Honey, get caught in the crossfire of George and Martha's verbal and emotional lacerations, and it becomes clear that each character is engaged in an isolated struggle through a personal hell. Albee has stated that he took the title from a graffito scrawled on a men's room wall.

Wickford Point (1939)   A novel by John P. MARQUAND. It deals with a declining upper-class family that lives near Boston in tarnished splendor, supported by a trust fund and by obliging creditors. Arrogant and indolent, they rely completely on their vanished distinction.

Wiebe, Rudy [H.] (1934–   )   Canadian novelist, short-story writer, and essayist. Wiebe's fiction explores the implications of his Mennonite ancestry and his own active Christian faith against the background of his native Canadian west. His most ambitious work, *The Blue Mountains of China* (1970), is a large-scale parable of modern life based on the Mennonites' trek in search of paradise on earth. Among his other works are *The Temptations of Big Bear* (1973) and *The Scorched-Wood People* (1977), set in prairie Canada at the time of the Riel Rebellion. These vigorous characterizations of Canadian Indians are stories of man's inhumanity to man. *The Mad Trapper* (1980) is a novel about a legendary trapper hunt in 1931. In 1982 *The Angel of the Tar Sands*, a collection of short stories, was published.

Wied, Gustav Johannes (1858–1914)   Danish novelist, playwright, and short-story writer. One of Denmark's finest humorists, Wied produced work marked by sharp cynicism and bitter wit. His amused scorn for the absurdity of human existence is mingled with a tender compassion. Wied's novels include *Sloegten* (1898), *Livsens Ondskab* (1899), and *Knagsted* (1902). *Menneskenes Børn* (2 vols, 1894) and *Circus Mundi* (1909) are collections of stories; *Det svage køn* (1900), *Dansemus* (1905), *Første Violin* (1898), and *Ranke Viljer* (1906; tr 2 × 2 = 5, 1923) are among his plays.

Wieland, Christopher Martin (1733–1813) German poet and novelist. Wieland's work represents a blending of ENLIGHTENMENT and ROCOCO styles. His translations of twenty-two of Shakespeare's plays (1762–66) introduced the English bard to German readers and provided one of the most cherished models for the writers of the STURM UND DRANG. He also contributed to German classicism with translations of HORACE and, particularly, LUCIAN, who attacked religious superstition and bigotry, which were also targets of Wieland's satire. Many of his novels, including his psychological BILDUNGSROMAN, *Die Geschichte des Agathon* (1766–67; tr *The History of*

Agathon, 1773), used Greek settings. His most enduring novel is *Die Abderiten* (1774; tr *The Republic of Fools*, 1861), a political satire with modern applications, on the foolishness of the ancient Abderans. The famous episode of the trial of the donkey's shadow in this novel found a contemporary counterpart in Kafka's THE CASTLE. It first appeared in *Der deutsche Merkur* (*The German Mercury*), a periodical he edited (1773–89), which was a pioneering effort in German literary journals. Of his verse, his most outstanding effort was the fairy-epic *Oberon* (1780).

Wienbarg, Ludolf   See JUNG DEUTSCHLAND.

Wiesel, Elie (1928–   )   Rumanian-born Jewish American novelist and essayist. Winner of the Nobel Peace Prize in 1986, Wiesel has achieved prominence as an important writer on the Holocaust and a world-renowned spiritual leader. Wiesel is a survivor of the Nazi concentration camps at Auschwitz and Buchenwald, where he lost his parents and a sister. At the urging of François Mauriac, Wiesel wrote his first memoir-novel, *Un di velt hot geshvign* (1956), an account of his family's death-camp sufferings and of his own guilt about his survival, subsequently published in a shorter version in French (*La Nuit*, 1958) and English (*Night*, 1960). In his more than twenty-five books, Wiesel probes themes related to the Holocaust: survival, human cruelty, and lack of justice. His books have won many prestigious literary awards. Most were originally written in French and include many novels: the strongly autobiographical *Le Jour* (1961; tr *The Accident*, 1962), *La Ville de la chance* (1962; tr *The Town Beyond the Wall*, 1964), *Les Portes de la forêt* (1964; tr *The Gates of the Forest*, 1966), *Le Testament d'un poète juif assassiné* (1980; tr *The Testament*, 1981), and *Le Cinquième Fils* (1983; tr *The Fifth Son*, 1985). His nonfiction includes *The Jews of Silence* (1966), an eyewitness report of Jewish persecution in the Soviet Union originally published in Hebrew as a series of newspaper articles; *Le Chant des morts* (1966; tr *Legends of Our Time*, 1968); *Entre deux soleils* (1970; tr *One Generation After*, 1970), and *Un Juif aujourd'hui* (1977; tr *A Jew Today*, 1978). Wiesel also examines Jewish biblical figures and legends in several volumes, among them *Célébration hassidique* (1972; tr *Souls on Fire*, 1972).

Wife of Bath's Tale, The   One of THE CANTERBURY TALES of Chaucer. It is famous for its long *Prologue*, in which the Wife of Bath first argues against the virtues of virginity, and then uses an account of her life with five successive husbands to prove that the married state is happiest when the wife has the sovereignty. She boasts of all the tricks she used to keep her first four husbands in hand. The fifth, half her age, she married for love rather than money; when he made life difficult by reading antifeminist tales to put her in her place, she precipitated a fight and pretended he had nearly killed her, so that he repentantly offered to let her run everything—and thereafter they were tender to each other and never quarreled.

Her tale makes the same point. One of King ARTHUR's knights is condemned to death for ravishing a maid, but the ladies of the court intervene, and he is given a year to find out "what women most desire" and thus save his life. A foul witch offers to exchange the answer for his obedience to her next request. Accordingly, he pleases the court ladies with the answer that women most desire sovereignty over their husbands and their love, and the hag demands that he marry her. He takes her miserably to bed, and, after a long lecture, she offers him a choice: she can remain foul and guarantee loving fidelity, or she can become young and fair and probably make him a cuckold. He wisely says that she should make the choice, whereupon she is transformed into a beauty and promises fidelity as well.

Wigglesworth, Michael (1631–1705)   English-born American poet and clergyman. For most of his life, Wigglesworth served as Congregational minister and physician at Malden, Massachusetts. In 1662 he published his most popular poem, THE DAY OF DOOM, based on a dream he had had nine days earlier. He also wrote *Meat out of the Eater* (1669), a cycle of short theological poems almost as popular in its day as *The Day of Doom*, and lesser poems on religious subjects. Another long poem, *God's Controversy with New England*, left in manuscript at his death, was published in 1871. Considered by some critics Wigglesworth's best work, it is a bitter denunciation of backsliders in the Puritan colony.

Wilbur, Richard [Purdy] (1921–   )   American poet. Wilbur's carefully wrought poetry shows the influence of the METAPHYSICAL POETS, particularly Andrew MARVELL, and of Wallace STEVENS. Usually rhymed and metrically regular, Wilbur's verse is distinguished by its elegantly reasoned attempts at defining the essences of experience. Among the most important of the post-World War II "traditionalist" poets, his verse collections include *The Beautiful Changes* (1947), *Things of This World* (1956; PULITZER PRIZE), *The Poems of Richard Wilbur* (1963), *Walking to Sleep: New Poems and Translations* (1969), and *The Mind-Reader* (1976). Wilbur is also known for his translations of RACINE and MOLIÈRE.

Wild, Jonathan (1682–1725)   A famous criminal, hanged at Tyburn for housebreaking. Tales of Wild's six wives and of his gang of subordinates have become popular legend. Daniel DEFOE wrote a romance, *Jonathan Wild* (1725), and Henry Fielding a satire, *The Life of* JONATHAN WILD THE GREAT. In these works, he is a coward, traitor, hypocrite, and tyrant, unrelieved by human feeling and never betrayed into a kind or good action. The character is historic, but the adventures are in a measure fictitious.

Wild Duck, The (1884)   A play by Henrik IBSEN. A satire on meddling, half-baked idealists, a poetic fantasy of illusions, and a realistic tragedy of human weakness, all unified by the symbolism of the wild duck, the play is one of Ibsen's most complex and compelling dramas. Hjalmar Ekdal is a weak, kindly, self-deluding man who believes

himself to be on the verge of discovering a great invention; Gregers Werle, his old schoolfriend, is a crackpot idealist who is determined to free Hjalmar of his comforting—and necessary—illusions. Finally, through Werle's revelations, Hjalmar comes to believe that his beloved daughter, Hedvig, is not his own child. He rejects the girl, and Werle tries to persuade her that her adored father will come back to her if she sacrifices the thing she loves best—the wild duck. Hedvig, crushed by her father's rejection of her, kills herself.

Wilde, Oscar [Fingal O'Flahertie Wills] (1854–1900)   Irish-born poet, dramatist, and novelist. During his undergraduate years at Oxford and as a disciple of Walter PATER, Wilde became the leader of an aesthetic movement that advocated ART FOR ART'S SAKE. He attracted a great deal of attention with his aestheticism, and by wearing long hair, dressing eccentrically, and carrying flowers in his hands while lecturing—idiosyncrasies later satirized in Gilbert and Sullivan's *Patience* (1881). Wilde was accused of homosexual practices, was tried and found guilty, and was sentenced to imprisonment (1895–97) with hard labor. On his release, physically, spiritually, and financially ruined, he went to Paris, under the name of Sebastian Melmoth. There he lived in bitterness and despair until his death.

Wilde's works include *Poems* (1881); two collections of fairy stories, *The Happy Prince, and Other Tales* (1888) and *The House of Pomegranates* (1891); THE PICTURE OF DORIAN GRAY, a novel; and many brilliantly witty plays, including LADY WINDERMERE'S FAN; *A Woman of No Importance* (1893), *Salomé* (1893), written originally in French and used as the basis for Richard Strauss's opera of the same title; *An Ideal Husband* (1895); and THE IMPORTANCE OF BEING EARNEST, often considered his masterpiece. THE BALLAD OF READING GAOL and *De Profundis* (1905) are the fruits of his imprisonment. See DE PROFUNDIS; DOUGLAS, LORD ALFRED.

Wildenvey, Herman Theodore (1886–1959)   Norwegian poet. With the publication of his first collection, *Nyinger* (1907), Wildenvey began a long career as a popular lyric poet. Unlike most Norwegian poetry, his verse is light, graceful, and tinged with humor. Among his volumes of verse are *Prismer* (1911), *Kjoertegn* (1916), *Ildorke stret* (1923), and *Fiken av tistler* (1925).

Wilder, Thornton [Niven] (1897–1975)   American novelist and playwright. An enormously successful writer—all his novels, after the first, were best-sellers—Wilder was the subject of much critical controversy during his lifetime. He was applauded by such critics as Edmund WILSON for his treatment of universal themes and was attacked by others for his lack of social consciousness. Wilder's concern was with the quintessential elements of human nature, about which he wrote in an elegant but simple style.

In 1926 he published a mannered novel about decadent Italian nobility, *The Cabala*. In the same year, his first play, *The Trumpet Shall Sound*, was produced and well received. The appearance of his PULITZER PRIZE-winning novel THE BRIDGE OF SAN LUIS REY brought him instant international acclaim. This initial success was followed by two other novels and a collection of plays. Wilder's next novel, *The Ides of March* (1948), set in the time of Julius Caesar, was his last for nearly twenty years, until he published *The Eighth Day* (1967), a novel with biblical overtones, which won the National Book Award in 1968. *Theophilus North* (1973), his last piece of fiction, is a humorous account of a young man's summer in Newport, Rhode Island.

Unlike his novels, which followed conventional forms, Wilder's plays broke with traditional theatrical practices. His first major theatrical success came with the production of OUR TOWN, which won him a second Pulitzer Prize. Though the play uses no scenery, very few props, and follows no clear course of action, it has become a classic of American theatre. THE SKIN OF OUR TEETH, also a Pulitzer Prize winner, treated the story of EVERYMAN in a similarly unorthodox manner. Wilder's other works for the stage include *The Angel That Troubled the Waters* (1928); *The Merchant of Yonkers* (1938), which was revised as *The Matchmaker* (1954) and later adapted as the Broadway musical *Hello, Dolly!* (1963); and a cycle of one-act plays, *Plays for Bleecker Street* (1962). In the early 1950s, he also wrote a trilogy inspired by Euripides, *The Alcestiad*. Wilder's plays and fiction both contain his essentially optimistic view of mankind and his assertion that whatever "truth" there is will be discovered in the lives of ordinary people.

Wild Goose Chase, The (1621)   A comedy by John Fletcher. (See BEAUMONT AND FLETCHER.) It chronicles the attempts of the beautiful Oriana to win the love of the rakish Mirabel. She tries to provoke Mirabel's jealousy by having her disguised brother woo her, and she tries to awaken his pity by feigning madness. Finally, disguised as the daughter of a man whose life Mirabel once saved, she is able to trick him into a declaration of love. Meanwhile Mirabel's companions Pinac and Belleur have, after many false steps, fallen for the charms of Rosalura and Lillia Bianca.

Wild Huntsman   A spectral hunter of medieval legend who, according to some versions, is condemned to hunt forever for his violation of the Sabbath. Another account has it that the Huntsman was a Jew who would not suffer JESUS to drink out of a watering trough but pointed to some water in a hoofprint as good enough for "such an enemy of Moses." With a pack of spectral dogs, he frequents certain forests and occasionally appears to mortals.

The Germans place him in the Black Forest; the French in the Forest of Fontainebleau; in England, he became identified with Herne the Hunter, once a keeper in Wind-

sor Forest, who "walks" in wintertime at about midnight and blasts trees and cattle.

Wilhelm Meister   The central character of two novels by GOETHE, *Wilhelm Meisters Lehrjahre* (*Wilhelm Meister's Apprenticeship*, 1795–96) and *Wilhelm Meisters Wanderjahre, oder Die Entsagenden* (*Wilhelm Meister's Travels, or the Renunciants*, 1829). The first, which is the original and classic example of the BILDUNGSROMAN, relates Wilhelm's progress from a naïve, excitable youth to responsible manhood. He has dreams of becoming a great playwright and actor, but, under the unobtrusive guidance of a mysterious Tower Society, whose existence he does not even suspect, he gradually comes to adopt a more modest and objective view of himself, and in the end is accepted to membership in the society. The second novel is less of a connected narrative than the first and serves, like Part II of FAUST, to allow Goethe to develop his ideas on a wide variety of subjects. In its course, Wilhelm finally discovers his true calling as a surgeon. See MIGNON.

Wilhelm Tell (1804)   A play by Friedrich SCHILLER, based on the legend of the famous Swiss hero Wilhelm TELL. Schiller uses the play and the figure of Tell primarily as a vehicle for his own moral and political idealism.

Wilkes, John (1727–1797)   English political reformer. In writing for *The North Briton*, a newspaper that he founded in 1762, Wilkes savagely attacked George III and his government, and his paper was suppressed. Repeatedly elected a member of Parliament, he was prevented from taking his seat until 1774 by a charge of seditious libel. Notorious for his dissipation, a member of the Mad Monks of MEDMENHAM ABBEY, Wilkes is remembered for his support for the liberties of the American colonies, for freedom of the press, and for the electoral rights of the people, as opposed to royal privilege.

Willard, George   See WINESBURG, OHIO.

William of Malmesbury (c1090?–c1143)   English historian, librarian at the monastery of Malmesbury. William wrote a Latin history of England, the famous *Gesta regum Anglorum* (*Chronicle of the Kings of England*, c1120–28), and continued it to 1142 in the sequel *Historia novella* (*Modern History*): both books are important sources of information and lively anecdote, particularly on the period since the Norman conquest in 1066. He also wrote a *Gesta pontificum Anglorum* (c1125), a history of the bishops and leading monasteries of England, as well as other works of ecclesiastical history and lives of the saints.

Williams, Charles [Walter Stansby] (1886–1945)   English novelist, poet, playwright, and critic. Williams wrote romantic thrillers with Christian-mystical overtones, such as *Descent into Hell* (1937) and *All Hallows' Eve* (1945). They deal with the conflict between good and evil in terms of sensational adventure, psychology, black magic, and fantastic miracles. Peter Stanhope, the hero of *Descent into Hell*, is said to be based on T. S. ELIOT, whom Williams knew. His best poetry is his strange, original, symbolic treatment of ARTHURIAN LEGEND in *Taliessin through Logres* (1938) and *Arthurian Torso* (1948), coauthored by C. S. LEWIS. His *Collected Plays* appeared in 1963.

Williams, [George] Emlyn (1905–   ) Welsh stage and screen actor and playwright. Williams's plays include *A Murder Has Been Arranged* (1930), *Night Must Fall* (1935), and *The Corn Is Green* (1938). After World War II, he was more active as actor than as writer, touring England and America with dramatic readings of DICKENS and Dylan THOMAS. *George* (1961), a delightful autobiography of his childhood, was followed by *Emlyn: An Early Autobiography 1927–1935* (1973).

Williams, John A[lfred] (1925–   ) American novelist. Williams is best known for his fourth novel, *The Man Who Cried I Am* (1967). The book consists of the bitter recollections of a dying black American writer on a short trip to Amsterdam. To his horror, he discovers a U.S. government plan to annihilate American blacks in the event of a racial revolution. The novel, a chronicle of frustrated hopes and disillusionment, includes fictional portraits of such figures as James BALDWIN, Richard WRIGHT, Malcolm X, and Martin Luther KING, Jr. Williams's other novels—including *The Angry Ones* (1960; repr as *One for New York*, 1975), *Night Song* (1961), *Sons of Darkness, Sons of Light* (1969), and *Captain Blackman* (1972)—all deal to some extent with the effects of racism on black consciousness. His nonfiction includes *Africa: Her History, Lands, and People* (1962) and *Flashbacks* (1973), a collection of articles and essays. *The Junior Bachelor Society* (1976) and *!Click Song* (1982) are among his other works.

Williams, Ralph Vaughan   See VAUGHAN WILLIAMS, RALPH.

Williams, Raymond [Henry] (1921–   ) British novelist and critic. A professor at Cambridge, Williams is best known for his distinctive literary and social criticism. Such works as *Culture and Society* (1958), *The Country and the City* (1973), *Problems in Materialism and Culture* (1980), and *Culture* (1981) have strongly influenced those who see literature as the continual record of cultural attitudes. His other works include *Towards 2000* (1983), *Writing in Society* (1984), and *Loyalties* (1985).

Williams, Roger (1603–1683)   English-born religious leader, founder of the Rhode Island colony. Immigrating to America in 1631, Williams settled in Massachusetts, but his unorthodox religious views and his defense of the Indians resulted in his expulsion from the colony. With a few followers, he founded a settlement at Providence, Rhode Island (1636), where he befriended the Indians and instituted a democratic form of government. He was also the first advocate of complete religious toleration in America.

Williams's writings include *A Key into the Language of America* (1643), a study of Indian languages; *Queries of Highest Consideration* (1644), a plea addressed to the Eng-

lish Parliament, against the establishment of a national church; THE BLOUDY TENENT, his most famous work; and *George Fox Digged Out of His Burrowes* (1676), an attack on the Quakers, uncharacteristic of his tolerant views.

Williams, Tennessee (born Thomas Lanier Williams, 1911–1983)   American playwright. Williams was born in his grandfather's Episcopal rectory in Columbus, Mississippi, moving with his family to St. Louis, Missouri, when he was twelve. He left college for financial reasons, worked in a shoe factory, and then became ill. He returned to his grandparents, who had retired to Memphis, Tennessee. On the money he earned from his writing, mostly lyric pieces, he completed his college education and received a degree from the University of Iowa. He was twenty-six when he wrote his first play. Known for the primitive violence in his dramas, a quality he believed lurks beneath the surface of modern life, and for his realistic settings that, nevertheless, make use of symbolic and mythological allusions, Williams is often considered the foremost American dramatist of the post-World War II era. He is likely to be best remembered for the works of "poetic realism" he wrote between 1944 and 1961. His first important play, *Battle of Angels* (1940), was unsuccessful; he later rewrote it as *Orpheus Descending* (1957). With THE GLASS MENAGERIE, which won the New York Drama Critics' Circle Award, Williams established himself as an important playwright. The lonely woman inhabiting a world of dreams was to remain one of his most powerful themes, one to which he later gave a violent turn in the PULITZER PRIZE-winning A STREETCAR NAMED DESIRE. *Summer and Smoke* (1947) deals with a woman who, lost in dreams of her purity, is unable to respond to the man she loves and is driven into lonely spinsterhood. *The Rose Tattoo* (1951) is a humorous and sympathetic treatment of a Sicilian-American woman. More controversial was *Camino Real* (1953), an experimental play featuring such characters as Don Juan, Casanova, and Kilroy, the ubiquitous American G.I. CAT ON A HOT TIN ROOF, which also won a Pulitzer Prize, deals with the tensions and pretensions of a wealthy Southern family. *Suddenly Last Summer* (1958), produced in a double bill with *Something Unspoken* under the title *Garden District*, concerns a possessive mother and her homosexual son, who use others for their own selfish purposes; the son is killed and devoured by a mob of starving children. Other plays from this fertile period of Williams's career include *Sweet Bird of Youth* (1959); *Period of Adjustment* (1960), his first social comedy; and *The Night of the Iguana* (1961). Subsequent and progressively less successful works for the stage include *The Milk Train Doesn't Stop Here Anymore* (1963) and *The Eccentricities of a Nightingale* (1965), which Williams considered two of his best and most difficult plays. Later plays include *The Seven Descents of Myrtle* (1968); *In the Bar of a Tokyo Hotel* (1969); *Small Craft Warnings* (1972); *A Lovely Sunday for Creve Coeur* (1979), a comedy; and *Clothes for a Summer Hotel* (1980), about Zelda and F. Scott FITZGERALD.

Much of Williams's work is based on the stresses of his early family life and on those springing from his homosexuality. Williams's plays are not dramas of reconciliation, although he sometimes leaves a hint of hope. His characters are unhappy creatures, plagued by loneliness, by fear of death and God, and by profound sexual anxiety—all of which troubles generally remain unresolved. He wrote one novel, *The Roman Spring of Mrs. Stone* (1950), and collections of stories, such as *Hard Candy* (1954), *The Knightly Quest* (1967), and *Eight Mortal Ladies Possessed* (1974). *Memoirs* was published in 1975, and selected personal essays, *Where I Live*, in 1978.

Williams, William Carlos (1883–1963)   American poet. Williams's prolific and highly influential writing of poetry, plays, essays, and fiction is all the more remarkable for the fact that he sustained a lifelong medical practice in his birthplace, Rutherford, New Jersey, the "Paterson" of his poems. Although not altogether ignored during his lifetime, it was not until the 1950s that Williams began to be seen as a "patron saint" of American poets. An early friend of Ezra POUND, Williams was influenced by IMAGISM but scorned Pound both for his expatriatism and for his role as aesthete. An even more provocative, if negative, influence was T. S. ELIOT, whom Williams decried as "the man who gave poetry back to the academics." Williams's poetry is firmly rooted in the commonplace detail of everyday American life. He conceived of the poem as an object: a record of direct experience that deals with the local and the particular. He abandoned conventional rhyme and meter in an effort to reduce the barrier between the reader and his consciousness of his immediate surroundings. The first volumes of verse to show the seeds of Williams's poetic philosophy were *The Tempers* (1913), *Kora in Hell* (1920), and *Sour Grapes* (1921). The body of his subsequent verse is in *Collected Poems* (1934); *Collected Later Poems* (1950); *Collected Earlier Poems* (1951); *Pictures from Brueghel and Other Poems* (1963; PULITZER PRIZE); and a five-volume epic, PATERSON, an impressionistic exploration of the role of the poet in historical and contemporary contexts. His experiments in prosody led him to develop the "variable foot" to express the rhythms, cadences, and sounds of American speech, a technique he refined and used with great delicacy in the three-line units of such late poems as "Asphodel, That Greeny Flower." His theories about poetry and the creative life are set forth in *Selected Essays* (1954); *Selected Letters* (1951); and, more personally, in his *Autobiography* (1951).

All through his life, Williams also wrote novels and short stories and tried his hand at plays as well. His novels include *A Voyage to Pagany* (1928) and the "Steche" trilogy, about an immigrant family's struggle with the exploitative demands of American life: *The White Mule* (1937), *In the Money* (1949), and *The Build Up* (1952). His

stories have been collected in *The Farmer's Daughters* (1961), and his experimental plays in *Many Loves and Other Plays* (1961). Other prose works include *The Knife of the Times* (1932), *Life along the Passaic River* (1938), IN THE AMERICAN GRAIN, and *Embodiment of Knowledge* (1974).

Williams's original approach to poetry, his insistence on the importance of the ordinary, and his successful attempts at making his verse as "tactile" as the spoken word had a far-reaching effect on American poetry. Ironically, this rigorously independent poet, who spurned all "schools" of thought, whose central theory of poetry was "no ideas but in things," became the most widely imitated poet of the century.

Williamson, Henry (1897–1977)   English novelist and nature writer. Williamson's most popular works are the classic animal stories *Tarka the Otter* (1927) and *Salar the Salmon* (1935). He also wrote two series of novels: the tetralogy *The Flax of Dream* (1921–28); and the monumental fifteen-novel *Chronicle of Ancient Sunlight* (1951–69), the story of three generations of a contemporary English family. *The Children of Shallowford* (1939), *The Story of a Norfolk Farm* (1941), and *A Clear Water Stream* (1958) are autobiographical.

William the Conqueror (William I, known as William the Norman and the Bastard of Normandy; c1027–1087)   King of England (after 1066). The natural son of Robert the Devil, duke of Normandy, William was a relative of Edward the Confessor, the reigning king of England, and married a descendant of ALFRED the Great. Harold, earl of Wessex, had been forced by William (c1064) to swear to help him obtain the English succession. When Harold took the crown himself upon Edward's death, William invaded England and won the battle of HASTINGS (1066); as King William I, he completed the "Norman Conquest," replacing the English nobility with Norman-French, thus changing the social and eventually the cultural structure of England.

Willingham, Calder [Baynard, Jr.] (1922–   )   American novelist and screenwriter. Willingham's first novel, *End as a Man* (1947), is an angry and ironic picture of life in a Southern military academy. Subsequent works revealed Willingham as a writer of "mock novels" characterized by cruel humor, a strong sense of the absurd, and irreverent satire, which anticipated the black-comic fictions of such writers as John BARTH and Thomas PYNCHON. In *Reach to the Stars* (1951), the frailties and pretensions of Willingham's typically antiheroic characters are exposed in fragmented comic episodes interspersed with bizarre science-fiction stories. *Eternal Fire* (1963) is a fierce parody of the conventions of the Southern Gothic novel. Willingham's most autobiographical work is *Rambling Rose* (1972), a nostalgic account of a boyhood in the South. *The Big Nickel* (1975) and *The Building of Venus Four* (1977) are among his other works.

willing suspension of disbelief   A term coined by Samuel Taylor Coleridge in BIOGRAPHIA LITERARIA. It describes the receptivity, or "poetic faith," of a reader or member of an audience, the act of suspending reason and accepting either the fictive element in a literary work or the climate created in a theatrical production.

Will's Coffee-House   A famous coffeehouse of Queen Anne's time that stood at the corner of Bow Street and Russell Street, in Covent Garden, sometimes referred to as "Russell Street Coffee-House" and "The Wit's Coffee-House." It was the meeting place of the most prominent wits and literary men of the day. It was well known to ADDISON, who established his servant Button in another coffeehouse, which eventually, as Button's, became the headquarters of the WHIG *literati*, as Will's had been of the TORY.

Willy, Colette   See COLETTE.

Wilson, Sir Angus (born Frank Johnstone-Wilson, 1913–   )   English novelist, short-story writer, and biographer. Wilson's collections of stories, *The Wrong Set* (1949), *Such Darling Dodos* (1950), and *A Bit off the Map* (1957), introduced a writer with a satirical eye for the British middle-class social scene and an acute ear for the tensions that reverberate through dialogue. During the same period, he also wrote a successful play, *The Mulberry Bush* (1955). *Hemlock and After* (1952), his first novel; *Anglo-Saxon Attitudes* (1956), considered by many critics to be his finest; and *The Middle Age of Mrs. Eliot* (1958) all depict the complex social relationships of his protagonists —respectively, a masochistic novelist, a spiritually troubled historian, and an attractive, painfully uprooted widow. In all of them, Wilson combines ironic observations of his characters' moral self-deception with unexpected compassion. *The Old Men at the Zoo* (1961) is a political satire, a nightmare-fantasy about an imagined war and occupation. His later novels are increasingly experimental in form. They include *No Laughing Matter* (1967), a three-generation family saga, and *Setting the World on Fire* (1980), a subtle, many-layered story, told with the assured wit and elegance of Wilson's mature work. His distinguished nonfiction includes *Emile Zola* (1952; rev 1964); *The Wild Garden* (1963), in which he explores the sources of his own creativity; *The World of Charles Dickens* (1970); *The Strange Ride of Rudyard Kipling* (1977); and *Diversity and Depth in Fiction* (1984), a selection of his critical writings.

Wilson, Colin [Henry] (1931–   )   English critic, novelist, and writer on philosophy, psychology, and the occult. Wilson was the precocious author, at twenty-five, of a best-selling philosophical study of alienation, *The Outsider* (1956), the first of six volumes of his "new existentialism." Wilson rejects the despair of some existentialists and devotes his novels to his search for "values in a universe of chance." All his novels, beginning with *Ritual in the Dark* (1960), are about "outsiders" trying to find relief from boredom or meaninglessness in some sort of authentic inner experience. Among his many nonfiction works are a number of serious critical studies of literature, philosophy, and music, including *Anti-Sartre* (1981) and *Existential Essays* (1985); several systematic studies of murderers; *Voyage to a Beginning* (1969), an autobiography; companion volumes on parapsychology, *The Occult* (1971) and *Mysteries* (1978); and *A Criminal History of Mankind* (1984), a survey of human criminal behavior from about 2350 BC to the present.

Wilson, Edmund (1895–1972)   American literary and social critic, novelist, short-story writer, and poet. Following his graduation from Princeton, Wilson worked briefly as a reporter, served in World War I in France, and returned to New York to work as an editor and writer for *Vanity Fair* (1920–21), *The New Republic* (1926–31), and THE NEW YORKER (1944–48). Wilson was a man of immense intelligence, with an unappeasable curiosity; his catholic interests led him from studies of foreign languages and cultures to scholarly inquiries into the literary imagination. In 1917 he wrote in a letter, "My single aim has been literature."

Influenced by the ideas of MARX and FREUD, as well as the French thinkers TAINE and MICHELET, Wilson embraced in his approach to literature most of the social, political, and psychological conceptions that shaped contemporary literary thought. Among his most important works of literary analysis are *Axel's Castle* (1931), a seminal work on symbolism; *The Triple Thinkers* (1938); *The Wound and the Bow* (1941), concerned with the relationship of neurosis to the creative imagination, based on the myth of PHILOCTETES; *The Shores of Light* (1952), about the 1920s and 1930s; *Patriotic Gore* (1962), dealing with the literature of the Civil War era; and *The Bit between My Teeth* (1965), a literary chronicle of the years 1950–65. The last work he himself compiled was *The Devils and Canon Barham: Ten Essays on Poets, Novelists, and Monsters* (1973). Wilson also wrote two books on social history: his classic study of revolutionary ideology, *To the Finland Station* (1940); and *The American Earthquake* (1958), about the Great Depression. Wilson's imaginative work is not on the same plane as his criticism. It includes a novel, *I Thought of Daisy* (1929); short stories in *Memoirs of Hecate County* (1946); plays, collected in *Five Plays* (1954) and *The Duke of Palermo* (1969); and a volume of poetry, *Poets, Farewell* (1929). He also edited his friend F. Scott FITZGERALD's posthumous *The Crack-Up* (1956). Wilson's cultural studies and travel writings include *Travels in Two Democracies* (1936); *The Scrolls from the Dead Sea* (1955); *Red, Black, Blond, and Olive* (1956); and *O Canada* (1965). His somewhat circumspect autobiographical writings—*A Piece of My Mind* (1957), *A Prelude* (1967), and *Upstate* (1971) —have been supplemented by numerous posthumous publications. Among them are *Letters on Literature and Politics, 1912–1972* (1977); *The Nabokov-Wilson Letters* (1979); and sequential volumes of his notebooks and diaries edited by Leon EDEL, beginning with *The Twenties* (1975) and including up to *The Fifties* (1986).

Wilson, Ethel [Davis Bryant] (1888–1980) Canadian fiction writer. Wilson was born in South Africa but lived in England until orphaned at the age of eight, when she went to relatives in Vancouver. She received most of her education in England but returned to Vancouver and married in 1921. Though unknown in her adopted country before her first novel, *Hetty Dorval*, appeared in 1947, she had been publishing stories in English magazines for ten years. Many of these humorous stories were reprinted in *Mrs. Golightly, and Other Stories* (1961). Wilson's world is one of chaotic unpredictability and potential disaster, which she accepts whimsically and without question, the better to minimize its effects. Her novels, including *The Innocent Traveller* (1949), *The Equations of Love* (1952), *Swamp Angel* (1954), and *Love and Salt Water* (1957), are known for their narrative skill, ironic wit, perceptive analyses of character, and a wise yet unpretentious view of human behavior.

Wilson, Harry Leon (1867–1939) American novelist and playwright. Wilson is best known for *Ruggles of Red Gap* (1915), a humorous novel about an English butler in a Western town, and *Merton of the Movies* (1922), about a small-town clerk who finally reaches Hollywood. *Merton* was dramatized in 1922 by Marc Connelly and George S. Kaufman. Wilson collaborated with Booth TARKINGTON on *The Man from Home* (1907), a play.

Wilson, John Dover (1881–1969) English Shakespearean scholar. Wilson wrote a number of critical studies and was chief editor of the New Cambridge edition of Shakespeare's plays (from 1921). His works include *Life in Shakespeare's England* (1911), *What Happens in "Hamlet"* (1935), and *Shakespeare's Happy Comedies* (1962).

Wilson, Lanford (1937–   ) American playwright. Wilson's plays explore, often with quiet humor, the spiritual and physical decay of individuals, families, segments of society, and entire cultures. His plays tend to be highly verbal productions, blending conversations, direct audience address, and soliloquy. Family conflicts are probed in *The Gingham Dog* (1968), *Lemon Sky* (1970), and *Serenading Louie* (1970). In such one-act plays as *Home Free!* (1964), *Ludlow Fair* (1966), *The Great Nebula in Orion* (1970), and *Brontosaurus* (1977), he plays subtle variations on the theme of loneliness. *Balm in Gilead* (1965) depicts the bleak world of New York whores, junkies, and homosexuals; *The Rimers of Eldritch* (1965) presents deterioration within a small Midwestern town. In *The Hot l Baltimore* (1973), a group of transient social outcasts subsist in a condemned hotel. In a series of plays set in his Missouri hometown, Wilson returned to his fascination with the family, depicting, in a general sense, the effect of historical events on ordinary people. The first play, *The Fifth of July* (1978), set in the post-Vietnam era, deals with the lost ideals and passions of the Talley family,

one of whose members lost his legs in the war. The second, *Talley's Folly* (1979; PULITZER PRIZE), set in 1944, is a touching romantic comedy about a day in the courtship of a young Talley daughter and a middle-aged German-Jewish immigrant. *A Tale Told* (1981; rev as *Talley and Son*, 1985), which takes place on the same day as *Talley's Folly*, explores the slightly hackneyed conflicts and evasions of the other members of the family in a less interesting manner.

Wilson, Sloan (1920–   ) American novelist. The characters who populate Wilson's novels are, by and large, middle-aged, upper-middle-class New Englanders. His people live in the suburbs and hold responsible jobs. Not infrequently, they feel that the world is no longer theirs to shape and that life is passing them by. Like John CHEEVER, Wilson knows these people and writes with care about their triumphs and agonies. His second novel, *The Man in the Gray Flannel Suit* (1955), was by far his most successful and became a standard metaphor in the American cultural lexicon. Thirty years later, Wilson published its sequel, *The Man in the Gray Flannel Suit II*. Other novels include *A Summer Place* (1958), *All the Best People* (1970), *Small Town* (1978), and *Ice Brothers* (1979). His autobiography, *What Shall We Wear to This Party?*, was published in 1976.

Wilson, [Thomas] Woodrow (1856–1924) Twenty-eighth president of the U.S. (1913–21). Born in Staunton, Virginia, Wilson took his B.A. at Princeton University, studied law at the University of Virginia, and obtained a Ph.D. in history and political science at Johns Hopkins University; his doctoral dissertation was *Congressional Government* (1885). In 1890 he became professor of jurisprudence and political economics at Princeton and in 1902 was unanimously chosen president of the university. While there, he did much to improve its academic standards and to democratize its social system.

Always keenly interested in politics, Wilson resigned from Princeton in 1910 to become the Democratic candidate for governor of New Jersey. Though he was supported by the state's conservative machine, he won the election on a reform platform; during his brief term, he waged a successful fight against his former backers and enacted several liberal, social, and economic measures. At the Democratic national convention in 1912, Wilson was nominated after William Jennings BRYAN threw his support to him, and he won the election as a result of the feud between Theodore ROOSEVELT and William Howard TAFT, which split the opposition.

Wilson was a moderate on political and economic questions, but his banking and tariff reforms were regarded as radical. As president, he gave new meaning to the "general welfare" clause of the Constitution, supplied vigorous executive leadership to Congress and to his party, and fought privilege. He was unable to complete his projects for domestic reform because of the outbreak of the European war in 1914. Although Wilson tried to avoid U.S. participation in the conflict and won reelection in 1916 with the slogan "He kept us out of war," repeated German violations of American neutrality led him to ask Congress for a declaration of war in 1917, affirming that "the world must be made safe for democracy." (See LUSITANIA.) On January 8, 1918, he announced a program of Fourteen Points as the basis for world peace.

After the cessation of hostilities, Wilson attended the Paris Peace Conference at the head of an American delegation, which was conspicuous for the absence of senators and for the inclusion of only one Republican. Although he was the idol of the European masses, he was forced to make numerous concessions at the conference table in order to salvage his dream of a LEAGUE OF NATIONS that would ensure world peace. But the U.S. Senate refused to ratify the treaty of VERSAILLES, and Wilson, who refused to compromise with "the little group of wilful men" who were blocking the treaty, decided to take his case to the people. During a strenuous speaking tour, he suffered a stroke at Pueblo, Colorado, and never fully recovered.

Wilson's writings include *The State* (1889), *Division and Reunion* (1893), *George Washington* (1897), *A History of the American People* (1902), and *Constitutional Government* (1908). His early essays and lectures were collected in *An Old Master and Other Political Essays* (1893) and *Mere Literature and Other Essays* (1896).

Wimsey, Lord Peter   See SAYERS, DOROTHY L.

Winckelmann, Johann Joachim (1717–1768) German classical scholar, especially interested in painting and sculpture. Winckelmann originated the concept of classical Greece as the home of *"edle Einfalt und stille Größe"* ("noble simplicity and silent greatness"), an ideal that influenced WEIMAR CLASSICISM. The final step in the destruction of Winckelmann's conception of Greece was taken by Friedrich Nietzsche in THE BIRTH OF TRAGEDY.

Wind in the Willows, The (1908)   A classic fantasy for children by Kenneth GRAHAME. The characters are Mole, Water Rat, Mr. Toad, and other small animals, who live and talk like humans but have charming individual animal characters. The book is a tender portrait of the English countryside.

windmills, to fight with   To face imaginary adversaries, combat chimeras. The allusion is to the adventure of DON QUIXOTE, who, when riding through the plains of Montiel, approaches thirty or forty windmills, which he declares to Sancho Panza are "giants, two leagues in length or more." Striking his spurs into Rosinante, he drives at one of the "monsters dreadful as Typhoeus." His lance lodges in the sail, and the windmill lifts both man and beast into the air. When the valiant knight and his steed fall, they are both much injured, and Don Quixote declares that the enchanter Freston, "who carried off his library with all the books therein," changed the giants into windmills.

Wind, Sand, and Stars (Terre des hommes, 1939; tr 1939)   A series of tales and reflections by Antoine de SAINT-EXUPÉRY. With concise, elegant imagery, Saint-Exupéry expresses a faith in the potential courage, nobility, and love of men, including the tiller of the earth as well as the explorer of unknown skies.

Windsor, duke of (1894–1972)   Former king of Great Britain. The son of George V and Queen Mary, he ascended the throne as Edward VIII upon the death of his father in 1936. He abdicated before his actual coronation, in order to marry Wallis Warfield Simpson, a twice-divorced American woman. Thereafter he was known as the duke of Windsor. The duke recounted his life up to 1936 in *A King's Story* (1951).

Winesburg, Ohio (1919)   A novel by Sherwood ANDERSON, consisting of twenty-three thematically related sketches and stories. The narrative is united by the character of George Willard, a young reporter, who is still undergoing the shifts and uncertainties of adolescence, and who is in revolt against the narrowness of small-town life. Other inhabitants of Winesburg, whom Anderson dubs the "grotesques," offer their own tales, of sterility and thwarted creativity, but the book is essentially an episodic BILDUNGSROMAN about Willard's developing "wholeness." It is written in a simple, realistic language illuminated by a controlled lyric beauty.

Wings of the Dove, The (1902)   A novel by Henry JAMES. Kate Croy is in love with the English journalist Merton Densher but will not marry him until he is financially secure. When she discovers that her friend Milly Theale, an American heiress, has not long to live, she tells Densher to take an interest in Milly, who promptly falls in love with him. Before her death, Milly learns of Kate and Densher's true relationship, but she nevertheless leaves Densher her money. When the legacy, in the form of a check, arrives, Densher is anxious to refuse it. Kate, however, demands that he accept the money or promise that he is not in love with Milly's memory. When Densher can agree to neither of these, their romance is terminated.

Winnie-the-Pooh   See POOH.

Winters, [Arthur] Yvor (1900–1968)   American critic and poet. A member of the English department at Stanford for forty years, Winters was known first as a critic and teacher, secondarily as a poet. A man with controversial views, irascibly expressed, Winters was generally identified with the NEW CRITICISM in his close analysis of a literary work, but he differed from the other critics in his insistence on moral evaluation. Opposed to romanticism and symbolism, Winters maintained that a poem must contain a rational statement about human experience. His most important work of criticism is *In Defense of Reason* (1947), which contains three earlier studies: *Primitivism and Decadence* (1937), *Maule's Curse* (1938), and *The Anatomy of Nonsense* (1943). In addition to the studies *Edwin Arlington Robinson* (1946), *The Poetry of W. B.*

Yeats (1960), and *The Poetry of J. V. Cunningham* (1961), Winters's other major critical work is *The Function of Criticism* (1957). Winters's poetry, in *Collected Poems* (1960) and *The Early Poems of Yvor Winters: 1920–1928* (1966), represents his attempts to put his critical theories into practice. He was awarded the BOLLINGEN PRIZE in 1960.

Winterset (1935)   A verse drama by Maxwell ANDERSON. Based on the SACCO-VANZETTI case, it deals with the son of an Italian radical whose father was executed for a murder he did not commit. In seeking to avenge himself on the actual murderer, the son, Mio, falls in love with Miriamne, the sister of one of the criminals. Through her love, Mio is saved from the need for revenge, but both are killed by gangsters. Anderson had used the Sacco-Vanzetti theme unsuccessfully in an earlier play, *Gods of the Lightning* (1928; with Harold Hickerson).

Winter's Tale, The (c1611)   A comedy by SHAKESPEARE. Polixenes, king of Bohemia, is invited to Sicilia by King Leontes and unwittingly excites the jealousy of his friend because he prolongs his stay at the entreaty of Queen Hermione. Leontes orders Camillo to poison the royal guest, but, instead of doing so, Camillo flees with him to Bohemia. Leontes now casts Hermione into prison and orders that her infant daughter be abandoned on some deserted shore. Although the Delphic oracle asserts Hermione's innocence, Leontes remains unconvinced. After falling into a deep swoon, Hermione is reported dead. Leontes, now deeply repentant, goes into mourning. Sixteen years later, FLORIZEL, the son of Polixenes, falls in love with PERDITA, Leontes's lost daughter, who has been reared by a shepherd who found her near "the coast of Bohemia." When Polixenes forbids his son to marry a lowly shepherdess, the lovers, aided by Camillo, flee to Sicilia. There the identity of Perdita is revealed, and the lovers are married. Leontes and Polixenes, who has followed the fugitives, resume their friendship. Only the memory of the wronged Hermione mars the happiness of Leontes. He is then shown a perfect statue of Hermione, which turns out to be the queen herself, who has been living in seclusion.

The play is based on Robert Greene's romance *Pandosto: The Triumph of Time* (1588), and the character of the rogue AUTOLYCUS is derived from the second of Greene's "Cony-catching" pamphlets (1591–92).

Winthrop, John (1588–1649)   English-born leader of the Puritan exodus to America and governor of the Massachusetts Bay Colony twelve times. Using the Bible as proof, Winthrop combatted the idea of democratic government and argued that there was "no such government in Israel." More than any other man, he shaped the character of early New England. His *Journal*, partly published in 1790, appeared in full as *The History of New England from 1630 to 1649* (1825–26). He is portrayed in Hawthorne's THE SCARLET LETTER.

Wishes to His Supposed Mistress (1646)   A poem by Richard CRASHAW. Addressed to an ideal mistress, it presents a radiant though somewhat humorous picture of her physical beauty and gifts of spirit.

Wister, Owen   See VIRGINIAN, THE.

witch   A possessor of malevolent supernatural powers. In Anglo-Saxon culture, the typical witch is pictured as an old hag who uses black magic, rides on a broomstick, and is accompanied by a black cat. Witchcraft originated in Europe with pre-Christian cults.

There are many celebrated witches of history and legend, beginning perhaps with the *Witch of Endor*, who, according to the biblical narrative, called up the prophet SAMUEL from the dead to answer King SAUL's questions concerning the fateful battle in which he would meet his death. The most famous witches in English literature are the Three Weird Sisters, whose prophecies concerning MACBETH started him on his ambitious and tragic course.

Pope Innocent VIII issued the celebrated bull *Summis desiderantes* in 1484, directing inquisitors and others to put to death all practitioners of witchcraft and other diabolical arts, and it has been computed that as many as nine million persons have suffered death for witchcraft since that date. In the Massachusetts colony, most accused witches in Salem were hanged; Giles Corey was pressed to death. This communal hysteria was the subject of Arthur Miller's THE CRUCIBLE.

witches' Sabbath   The supposed night-time muster of witches and demons to concoct mischief. It was common belief that, alone in her house, the witch anointed her feet and shoulders with the fat of a murdered baby, then mounted a broomstick, distaff, or rake, and made her exit by the chimney, to ride through the air to meet the rest of the coven. The assembled witches feasted together and concluded with a dance, in which they all turned their backs to each other. James Joyce's ULYSSES and Thomas Mann's MAGIC MOUNTAIN contain scenes based on the tradition of the witches' Sabbath. Hawthorne's YOUNG GOODMAN BROWN is a famous short story about a New England witches' Sabbath. See WALPURGIS NIGHT.

With Fire and Sword (Ogniem i mieczem, 1884; tr 1958)   The first novel in a historical trilogy by Henryk SIENKIEWICZ, dealing with the history of Poland from 1648 to the time of King John III (John Sobieski) at the end of the 17th century. The novel describes a war between Poland and the Ukraine, while its sequel, *Potop* (*The Deluge*, 1886), deals with the Swedish invasion of Poland. *Pan Wolodyjowski* (*Pan Michael*, 1888) concludes the trilogy with the theme of a Polish-Turkish war. The trilogy has been on the best-seller list in Poland ever since its publication.

Within a Budding Grove   See REMEMBRANCE OF THINGS PAST.

Witkiewicz, S[tanislaw] I[gnacy] (pen name Witkacy, 1885–1939)   Polish dramatist. Born in Warsaw,

Witkiewicz wrote over forty plays before 1926 but was almost unknown in his lifetime. He was one of the innovators of the THEATRE OF THE ABSURD, writing grotesque comedies about societies that dehumanize people through enforced uniformity. Having experienced the Russian Revolution firsthand, he shot himself the day after the Russians marched into Poland in 1939. Until a collected edition was published in 1962, only a few of his plays were performed or appreciated. Most of them are antirealistic, using distortion in color and stage design to contrast with a dialogue abounding in philosophical discussion. His experiments in theatre emphasized the cruelty of man, in the kind of black comic terms that have come to be associated with such writers as BECKETT and GENET. Among his most influential plays are *Kurka wodna* (*The Water Hen*, 1921), *Szalona lokomotywa* (*The Crazy Locomotive*, 1923), *Wariat i zakonnica* (*The Madman and the Nun*, 1923), and *Szewcy* (*The Shoemakers*, 1931–34).

Witla, Eugene   See "GENIUS," THE.

Wittgenstein, Ludwig (1889–1951)   Austrian philosopher and professor at Cambridge University. In his seminal books *Tractatus Logico-Philosophicus* (1922) and *Philosophical Investigations* (1953), Wittgenstein proposed a critical method of linguistic analysis as the solution to most philosophic problems, which were the result, he argued, not of difficulty or inadequate knowledge but of the systematic misuse of language by philosophers. "Philosophy," he said, "is a battle against the bewitchment of our intelligence by means of language." His work was central to the development of LOGICAL POSITIVISM.

Wizard of Oz   See BAUM, L. FRANK; OZ.

Wodehouse, P[elham] G[renville] (1881–1975) English writer and humorist. Wodehouse's blithe popular stories and novels about whimsical upper-class characters feature the Honourable Bertie Wooster; Psmith; Mr. Mulliner; Jeeves, the valet; and assorted peers, notably the absent-minded Lord Emsworth of Blandings Castle. Much of Wodehouse's humor derives from the contrast between the efficient servant Jeeves and the idle, dimwitted, but charming gentleman Wooster. His books contain fantasy, affectionate satire, and absurd farce. The style is rich with mock-pomposity, verbal ingenuity, and unexpected slang. Among his best-loved books are *Leave It to Psmith* (1923), *Jeeves* (1925), *The Code of the Woosters* (1938), *French Leave* (1956), and *The Plot That Thickened* (1973). *Performing Flea* (1953) and *Over Seventy* (1957) are amusing autobiographical works. Wodehouse also wrote and collaborated on a number of successful plays and musical comedies. *Sunset at Blandings* (1977), his unfinished last novel, was published posthumously, as were collections of his early stories, *The Uncollected Wodehouse* (1976) and *The Scoop* (1979). Wodehouse's naïvely conciliatory broadcasts from his internment in Nazi Germany aroused sharp criticism during and after World War II, leading George Orwell to write his essay *In Defense of P. G. Wodehouse*.

Wodehouse eventually immigrated to the United States, where he became a U.S. citizen in 1955. He was knighted in 1975, shortly before his death.

Woden   The Anglo-Saxon form of ODIN, chief of the Scandinavian gods. From his name is derived the word *Wednesday* ("Woden's Day").

Woe from Wit (Gore ot uma, 1822–1824)   A comic drama in verse by Aleksandr GRIBOYEDOV. A young nobleman, Aleksandr Andreyevich Chatsky, returns homesick to his native land after a tour of Europe. The pettiness of Russian society is all the more apparent to his eager eyes, and he loudly complains of his disenchantment. His outspokenness causes him to be ostracized. In the end, he stands alone, rejected by his sweetheart and buffeted by malicious rumors that he is insane. One of the outstanding features of the play is its biting, pungent language in rhymed iambic verse. Many of the lines have become popular proverbial phrases.

Wolfe, James (1727–1759)   English general who defeated Montcalm in the battle of the Plains of Abraham at Quebec. Both Wolfe and Montcalm were fatally wounded. Wolfe is a prominent character in Thackeray's THE VIRGINIANS and in PARKMAN's *Montcalm and Wolfe*.

Wolfe, Nero   See STOUT, REX.

Wolfe, Thomas [Clayton] (1900–1938)   American novelist. Intense individualism, exuberance of spirit, frequently extravagant rhetoric, and the mystical celebration of youth, sex, and America characterize Wolfe's highly autobiographical writing. At fifteen, he entered the University of North Carolina, where he wrote two plays: *The Return of Buck Gavin* (1924) and *The Third Night* (1938). He then went to Harvard to study playwriting under George Pierce Baker. Before Baker succeeded in discouraging him from writing for the theatre, he had begun *Mannerhouse* (1938), a play about the disintegration of a Southern family, and produced, at Harvard, *Welcome to Our City* (1923). The city in the play was "Altamont," which was to reappear in Wolfe's mammoth first novel, LOOK HOMEWARD, ANGEL, representing his hometown, Asheville, North Carolina.

Look Homeward, Angel was the result of six years of work under the editorial guidance of Maxwell PERKINS at Charles Scribner's Sons. The book is a thinly veiled, often cruel portrait of town and family, in which Wolfe is the character he calls Eugene Gant. After writing a short novel, *A Portrait of Bascom Hawke* (1932), Wolfe presented Perkins with a massive sequel to Gant's story. This was pared down and published as OF TIME AND THE RIVER. Wolfe then severed connections with Perkins and Scribner's and began an editorial relationship with Edward C. Aswell at Harper & Brothers. In 1935 he published a collection of short stories, *From Death to Morning*, and a year later, *The Story of a Novel*, from a lecture he had given on his own writing. In 1938 he died after a brief illness, leaving his new editor with an eight-foot pile of manuscript. From this Aswell assembled two more novels—THE WEB AND THE ROCK and YOU CAN'T GO HOME AGAIN—and a collection of stories, *The Hills Beyond* (1941). Wolfe's last two novels, also autobiographical, depict himself as "George Webber"; George Pierce Baker as "Professor Hatcher"; Maxwell Perkins as "Foxhall Edwards"; and Aline Bernstein, the noted stage designer, with whom Wolfe lived, as "Esther Jack." The four novels, powerful, lyrical, shot through with a young man's longing for some kind of faith, add up to an American epic.

Wolfe, Tom (pen name of Thomas Kennerly, Jr., 1931–   ) American journalist. Wolfe is a major exponent of "new journalism," a form of nonfiction reportage that combines detailed description, analysis, dialogue, and a strong sense of the writer's presence to create the pace, tone, and mood of fiction. He has captured movements and eras in single phrases such as "radical chic" and "the me decade." His sketches and essays, collected in such volumes as *The Kandy-Kolored Tangerine-Flake Streamline Baby* (1965), *The Pump House Gang* (1968), and *Mauve Gloves & Madmen, Clutter & Vine* (1976), constitute a perceptive record of American popular culture, written in kinetic, highly descriptive prose. The *Electric Kool-Aid Acid Test* (1968) is an account of the psychedelic escapades of Ken KESEY and his Merry Pranksters. *The Right Stuff* (1979), which was made into a successful movie, focuses on the men involved in America's first manned space program. *In Our Time* (1980) is a collection of his drawings; *From Bauhaus to Our House* (1981), an entertaining, somewhat rhetorical, and highly opinionated discourse on modern architecture, argues that contemporary architects have failed to reflect the essence of contemporary America and raises the controversial issue of the relationship between architecture and society. *The Purple Decades* (1982) is a selection of Wolfe's writings from the 1960s and 1970s, compiled by the author.

Wolfram von Eschenbach (c1170–c1220) German MINNESINGER, or lyric poet. Wolfram is known for three verse epics, PARZIVAL, *Willehalm*, and *Titurel*, as well as a collection of love lyrics. His handling of chivalric themes often rebukes the usual traditions of knighthood and COURTLY LOVE, for, instead of making women necessarily either sinful temptations or the objects of a grand but adulterous passion, he glorifies married love and a calmer kind of real affection.

Wolfram becomes a major character in WAGNER's opera *Tannhäuser*; he is a close friend of Tannhäuser, although he is also secretly in love with Elizabeth. See WARTBURG.

Wollstonecraft, Mary (1759–1797) English author. Wollstonecraft is best known for *Vindication of the Rights of Woman* (1792), the first great feminist manifesto. In 1797 she married William GODWIN and died when their daughter, Mary, later Mary Wollstonecraft SHELLEY, was born.

Wolsey, Thomas (c1475–1530) English Cardinal and Lord Chancellor. Wolsey became Privy Councillor to HENRY VIII in 1511 and was appointed Cardinal in 1515, the same year that he became Lord Chancellor. He had ambitions to become Pope and cultivated a friendship with the Emperor CHARLES V to gain that end, but he failed to be elected. When Henry wished to divorce Catherine of Aragon, Wolsey attempted to secure a divorce from the Pope—a course doomed to slow failure because Charles V, Catherine's nephew, effectively controlled the Papacy. Henry, displeased with Wolsey's conduct of the affair, deprived him of his offices (1529). A moving account of Wolsey's dismissal is given in Shakespeare's HENRY VIII, in which Wolsey's famous farewell is, however, generally thought to be the work of John FLETCHER.

Woman in White, The (1860) A mystery novel by Wilkie COLLINS. The plot hinges on the resemblance of Laura Fairlie, an English heiress, to Anne Catherick, a mysterious woman in white, confined in a lunatic asylum. In order to secure Laura's money, the unscrupulous Sir Percival Glyde thrusts her into the asylum in place of the dying Anne, but this villainy is finally exposed by her faithful lover, Walter Hartright. A subsidiary villain is the subtle, sardonic Count Fosco.

Woman Killed with Kindness, A (1603) A tragedy by Thomas HEYWOOD. Mistress Anne, the sister of Sir Francis Acton, is married to John Frankford. Frankford unwittingly admits to his home the charming Master Wendoll, who succeeds in seducing Anne. Hearing rumors of this, Frankford surprises the two and banishes Anne forever from his sight, although he provides for her care and maintenance. Carrying the burden of her own guilt and her husband's "kindness," Anne pines and dies, having been reconciled with her husband on her deathbed.

Woman Who Rode Away, The (1928) A short story by D. H. LAWRENCE, about a lonely and bored American woman in Mexico. Riding off alone into the mountains, she comes to a strange Indian tribe, who imprison her and then sacrifice her to their god. The heroine is said to be based on his friend and patron Mabel Dodge LUHAN.

Women in Love (1920) A novel by D. H. LAWRENCE. Containing some of the clearest statements of Lawrence's own beliefs, it is a sequel to THE RAINBOW and describes the later life of Ursula BRANGWEN and her sister Gudrun, a sculptor. Gudrun falls in love with Gerald Crich, a mining industrialist, but their relationship is marred by their possessive, destructive approach to love. In contrast, Ursula marries Rupert Birkin, a school inspector and spokesman for Lawrence, with whom she achieves an ideal sensual union. Birkin says that modern man exists in a living death because he allows his passionate, unconscious, true self to be imprisoned by his intellect and by the pressures of industrial society. Man's salvation lies in his making a good, passionate marriage in which the lovers recognize each other's true separateness. He must complete his happiness by a different but similarly deep friendship with another man. Birkin offers this friendship to Gerald, who rejects it. When his affair with Gudrun ends, Gerald destroys himself in the mountains of the Tyrol, where they are all on vacation. The novel has a minimum of plot and action but a great deal of philosophical discussion and description of the characters' emotional states and unconscious drives. Many of the ideas are expressed through symbolism. The characters and relationships in the novel are probably partially based on those of Lawrence and his wife, Frieda Lawrence, and John Middleton MURRY and his wife Katherine MANSFIELD. The friends shared a house in England in 1914–15.

Wood, Clement (1888–1950)   American writer. Wood is the author of *Hunters of Heaven* (1929), a discourse on American poetry, and *The Complete Rhyming Dictionary and Poet's Craft Book* (1936). Deeply interested in social and racial injustice, Wood won considerable fame with his poem "De Glory Road," the title poem of his 1936 collection. *The Greenwich Village Blues* (1926) is an earlier poetry collection.

Wood, Grant (1892–1942)   American painter. Inspired by the meticulous detail of Flemish paintings and by the American midwestern landscape and people, Wood is noted for his stark, often ironic regionalist paintings, such as *American Gothic* (1930) and *Daughters of the American Revolution* (1932).

Wood, Mrs. Henry (born Ellen Price, 1814–1887) English novelist. Wood's enormously successful, frequently dramatized novel EAST LYNNE came to epitomize the ludicrous, tear-jerking melodrama of the later 19th century. No longer read now, she was a crude, sensational, prolific, and highly popular writer in her day.

Woodcock, George (1912–   )   Canadian man of letters. Woodcock was educated in England, where he came in contact with the anarchist movement of the 1930s and 1940s and began to publish first poetry, then biographical studies of libertarian thinkers in *William Godwin* (1946) and *The Anarchist Prince* (with I. Avakumovic, 1950), about Peter KROPOTKIN. He returned to Canada in 1949 and continued to write prolifically and on many topics. *Anarchism* (1962) is the standard work on the subject. He has also written critical studies of Canadian and English writers, historical studies, critical essays, and numerous travel books, including *Orwell's Message* (1984), *Strange Bedfellows* (1985), and *The Walls of India* (1985). A collection of his writings appeared in *A George Woodcock Reader* (1980). His poetry has been gathered in *Collected Poems* (1983). He also founded the influential journal *Canadian Literature*, which he edited from 1959 to 1977.

Woodcraft, or The Sword and the Distaff (1854)   A novel by William Gilmore SIMMS. The book is set in the Charleston, South Carolina, area during 1782. The withdrawal of the British troops in December of that year is the chief historical event. Captain PORGY and his demobilized but loyal fellow soldiers return to his plantation to repair wartime devastation. Porgy rescues his slaves and those of the charming widow, Mrs. Eveleigh, from the scheming British officers and their dishonest American coconspirators. He also pays the widow ardent but unsuccessful court. Because of Simms's favorable treatment of the lives of the slaves under their old masters, the book has been called his answer to UNCLE TOM'S CABIN.

wooden walls   Ships of wood. When XERXES I invaded Greece (480 BC), the Greeks sent to ask the DELPHIC ORACLE for advice and were cryptically told to seek safety in their wooden walls.

Woodham-Smith, Cecil (1896–1977)   English biographer and historian. Woodham-Smith's scholarly studies of figures in the Crimean War—*Florence Nightingale* (1950) and *The Reason Why* (1954)—were highly esteemed and very readable works. *The Great Hunger* (1962) is a vivid study of the Irish potato famine of the 1840s.

Woodhull, Victoria Claflin (1838–1927)   American reformer and lecturer. As a child, Victoria Woodhull gave spiritualistic performances, sold patent medicines, and told fortunes with her traveling family. Twice married, she moved to New York with her sister, Tennessee Celeste Claflin. The two sisters were befriended by Cornelius Vanderbilt, Sr., and founded *Woodhull and Claflin's Weekly* (1870–76), a periodical devoted to social and political reform; they defended women's rights and free love. The first English translation of the *Communist Manifesto* (1872) and the story of the notorious Beecher-Tilton affair appeared in the *Weekly*. The Equal Rights party nominated Victoria Woodhull for President in 1872, with Frederick DOUGLASS as her running mate. Moving to England, she married the scion of a wealthy banking family; her sister, Tennessee, married a baronet. With her daughter, Zulu Maud Woodhull, Victoria Woodhull published a periodical entitled *Humanitarian* (1892–1901). Among the articles and pamphlets Victoria Woodhull wrote are *Origins, Tendencies and Principles of Government* (1871), *Stirpiculture* (1888), and *The Alchemy of Maternity* (1889). She and her sister are regarded as the models for Audacia Dangereyes in Harriet Beecher STOWE's novel *My Wife and I* (1871).

Woolf, [Adeline] Virginia (1882–1941)   English novelist, critic, and essayist, the wife of Leonard Woolf. An exact contemporary of James JOYCE, Woolf too is known as an experimenter and innovator in novel writing, particularly in her use of the techniques of interior monologue and STREAM OF CONSCIOUSNESS. Her novels are noted for their poetic and symbolic quality; emphasis is not on plot or action but on the psychological realm occupied by her characters. The books are also known for their delicacy and sensitivity of style, their evocation of place and mood, and their background of historical and literary reference.

Many of her novels are concerned with time, its passage, and the difference between external and inner time.

Her first two novels, *The Voyage Out* (1915) and *Night and Day* (1919), are fairly conventional and realistic. These were followed by JACOB'S ROOM, MRS. DALLOWAY, TO THE LIGHTHOUSE, ORLANDO, THE WAVES, *The Years* (1937), and BETWEEN THE ACTS. Her short stories were published in *Monday or Tuesday* (1921) and *A Haunted House* (1944). Woolf also wrote a great deal of literary criticism and numerous essays, including *Mr. Bennett and Mrs. Brown* (1924); *The Common Reader* (1925, 1932); A ROOM OF ONE'S OWN; *Flush* (1933), on Elizabeth Barrett BROWNING's pet spaniel; *Three Guineas* (1938), which gave voice to her ardent feminism; *Roger Fry* (1940), a biography; *The Death of the Moth* (1942); and *A Writer's Diary* (1953; ed Leonard Woolf).

In the home of her father, Sir Leslie STEPHEN, Virginia Woolf was reared in an atmosphere of literature and learning, receiving her education in her father's own extensive library and meeting many of the outstanding literary and intellectual figures of the day. After Sir Leslie's death, Virginia and her sister, Vanessa, hosted gatherings of artists and writers who had been friends at Cambridge University. This began what came to be known as the BLOOMSBURY GROUP. Vanessa Stephen married one of these friends, Clive BELL. Virginia married another, Leonard Woolf, a writer on politics and economics, in 1912. Five years later, with a single hand-press, the Woolfs founded the Hogarth Press, which became a successful publishing house. It printed the early works of Katherine MANSFIELD, E. M. FORSTER, T. S. ELIOT, and Virginia Woolf's own first short stories. Among its other pioneering productions was the first English edition of FREUD.

Virginia Woolf's books draw largely on her own life experience. Her childhood provides the background for her novel *To the Lighthouse*; the sudden death of her favorite brother in 1906 is reflected in the deaths of PERCIVAL in *The Waves* and Jacob in *Jacob's Room*. Almost all of her characters are members of her own leisured, intellectual, upper-middle class. Many of the novels are set in London, where she lived most of her life. In 1941, profoundly depressed by the war and afraid of the recurrence of a nervous breakdown, she committed suicide by drowning.

The publication of her *Diaries* (5 vols, 1975–79; ed A. O. Bell) and her *Letters* (6 vols, 1977–80; ed Nigel Nicolson, J. Trautman) coincided with a proliferation of critical and biographical studies of Woolf and others of the Bloomsbury Group. A definitive biography of Virginia Woolf (1972) was written by her nephew, Quentin Bell (1910–).

Woollcott, Alexander [Humphreys] (1887–1943)   American journalist, drama critic, and writer. Born in a commune called the North American Phalanx in Red Bank, New Jersey, Woollcott became a drama critic for the *New York Times* (1914–22) and later for the New York *World* (1925–28). He also carried on a radio show, "The Town Crier" (1929–42), which, combined with his writings for THE NEW YORKER, established his reputation for wit, sentimentality, egotism, and insult. He was a leading member of the Algonquin Round Table, a group consisting of such writers, musicians, and artists as Harpo Marx, George S. KAUFMAN, Dorothy PARKER, and Robert BENCHLEY, who met regularly in the Algonquin Hotel. By the 1930s, Woollcott was one of the best-known people in America and an arbiter of popular literary tastes. He was the model for Sheridan Whiteside, the impossible and egotistical title character in *The Man Who Came to Dinner*, by George S. Kaufman and Moss HART. Far from taking offense, Woollcott played the role himself until he was stopped by the first of the series of heart attacks that eventually killed him.

Worde, Wynkyn de (real name Jan van Wynkyn, d 1534?)   English printer and stationer. Worde was born in Alsace and early in his career was an apprentice to William CAXTON. He published a number of well-known books of the time, including the fourth edition (1498) of Chaucer's THE CANTERBURY TALES.

Wordsworth, Dorothy (1771–1855)   English writer and younger sister of William WORDSWORTH. Her *Journals* (1798, 1874, 1889, 1897, 1904, 1924), *Recollections of a Tour Made in Scotland* (1803), *Journal of a Mountain Ramble* (1805), and other similar works are records of her impressions and travels, many undertaken in the company of her brother, and are not only notable for their excellent style but also useful to Wordsworth students and biographers for their wealth of information on the poet. Dorothy Wordsworth wrote several short poems herself, which were included in various editions of her brother's poetic works. She spent the last twenty-five years of her life struggling against physical and mental illness.

Wordsworth, William (1770–1850)   English poet. Wordsworth is known for his worship of nature, his humanitarianism, his early sympathy with democratic liberalism, and his interest in the lives, the daily pursuits, and the common speech of common people. With his friend Samuel Taylor COLERIDGE, he was one of the early leaders of English ROMANTICISM. Wordsworth was particularly interested in instituting reform in poetic diction, which would employ, as he proposes in his famous preface to LYRICAL BALLADS, "a selection of language really used by men." His most ambitious works are THE EXCURSION, actually the first part of the uncompleted poem "The Recluse," and THE PRELUDE, both long philosophical poems of autobiographical character. His earliest works, *An Evening Walk* and *Descriptive Sketches*, were published in 1793; the bulk of his best-known poetry is contained in *Lyrical Ballads* (1798), which he published jointly with Coleridge. Among his better-known shorter works are "Alice Fell," "Michael," SIMON LEE, the *Lucy* poems, "Resolution and Independence," "The Solitary Reaper," "Peter Bell," "The

Idiot Boy," "I Wandered Lonely as a Cloud," "Elegiac Stanzas," NUNS FRET NOT AT THEIR CONVENT'S NARROW ROOM, "The World Is Too Much with Us," "Lines Composed a Few Miles Above Tintern Abbey," and ODE: INTIMATIONS OF IMMORTALITY.

In his early youth, Wordsworth was deeply influenced by the ideas of Jean Jacques ROUSSEAU and William GODWIN, and he enthusiastically supported the FRENCH REVOLUTION. He visited France in 1792 and had a love affair with Annette VALLON, evidence of which was not uncovered until the 20th century. As he grew older, he lived peacefully in the Lake Country of northern England and became increasingly conservative in his political views and orthodox in his religion. In 1843 he was appointed poet laureate, succeeding Robert SOUTHEY. He is buried in the churchyard at Grasmere. See DAFFODILS, THE; DOVE COTTAGE.

Work in Progress   See FINNEGANS WAKE.

Works and Days   See HESIOD.

World Enough and Time   See WARREN, ROBERT PENN.

World I Never Made, A   See O'NEILL, DANNY.

World War I   The European war that began with Austria-Hungary's declaration of war on Serbia on July 28, 1914. The major belligerents were the Central Powers —Germany, Austria-Hungary, Turkey, and Bulgaria—and the Allies—Great Britain, France, Russia, Italy, and the U.S.

Although the spark that set off the conflict was the assassination of Archduke FRANCIS FERDINAND of Austria by a Serbian nationalist on June 28, Europe had been on the verge of war for years as a result of the political, economic, and military rivalries of the great powers. Complicating the situation were such factors as the disintegration of the Turkish empire, the turbulence of the Balkans, and France's desire to avenge its defeat in the Franco-Prussian War of 1870–71.

After Austria's declaration of war on Serbia, Russia ordered mobilization of her forces, and, on August 1, Germany declared war. Commencing hostilities against France, the Germans invaded Belgium in order to reach Paris from the northwest; the attack on Belgium, whose neutrality had been guaranteed by Germany, brought England into the war on August 4. In the east, the Germans smashed the Russian armies. Italy, an erstwhile ally of Germany and Austria, abandoned them and joined the Allies in 1915; Turkey came into the war on the German side, thus extending the area of conflict to the eastern Mediterranean.

In the U.S., President Woodrow WILSON sought to preserve American neutrality, but popular feeling gradually ran in favor of the Allies, particularly after the sinking of the LUSITANIA. When, after an interval of nonbelligerence toward America, Germany resumed unrestricted submarine warfare, after February 1917, the U.S. severed diplomatic relations with Berlin; in April war was declared. The

entrance of American troops on the western front ended the stalemate. After a series of reverses, the German armies retreated; the Berlin government fell; rebellion broke out in Germany; an armistice was negotiated and signed on November 11, 1918.

The war killed millions, civilians as well as soldiers; it impoverished most of the world; it created a number of new nations, when the German, Austrian, and Turkish empires were dismembered; and it hastened the RUSSIAN REVOLUTION of 1917. The treaty of VERSAILLES, moreover, carried within it the seeds of World War II.

The war inspired many literary works. Among the best novels dealing with the war are John Dos Passos's THREE SOLDIERS, Jaroslav Hašek's *The Good Soldier Schweik* (see SCHWEIK), E. E. Cummings's THE ENORMOUS ROOM, Erich Maria Remarque's ALL QUIET ON THE WESTERN FRONT, and Ernest Hemingway's A FAREWELL TO ARMS. Poets who wrote about the war include Alan SEEGER, Wilfred OWEN, Siegfried SASSOON, John MCCRAE, and Rupert BROOKE. Plays on this theme include WHAT PRICE GLORY? by Maxwell Anderson and Laurence Stallings and JOURNEY'S END by Robert Cedric Sherriff. The poet Robert GRAVES described his war experiences in *Goodbye to All That* (1929), and T. E. LAWRENCE wrote about the Arab campaign against the Turks in his *Seven Pillars of Wisdom* (1926). See CLEMENCEAU, GEORGES; LLOYD GEORGE, DAVID; ORLANDO, VITTORIO; PERSHING, JOHN J.

World War II   The global conflict that began officially with the German invasion of Poland on September 1, 1939. The major belligerents were the axis powers —Germany, Italy, and Japan—and the Allies—Great Britain, France, the U.S.S.R., China, and the U.S.

The causes of World War II were intimately connected with those of WORLD WAR I and with the unfavorable conditions that obtained after the treaty of VERSAILLES. Economic distress, together with the unpopularity and weakness of the WEIMAR REPUBLIC in Germany, led the way to the growth of FASCISM and the rise of Adolf HITLER. The LEAGUE OF NATIONS, the first world organization established to maintain peace and settle international disputes, was drastically weakened by the refusal of the U.S. to join. When the league did nothing but formally condemn Japan for its invasion of Manchuria in 1931–32, many countries felt the need to protect themselves by building up armaments. In 1935 the league failed to prevent Italy's invasion of Ethiopia. Under Hitler, Germany began to rearm and sent troops into the Rhineland (1936) in violation of the Versailles treaty; Germany seized Austria in 1938 and, in August 1939, entered into a nonaggression pact with Russia.

After defeating Poland in 1939, the Germans invaded Norway and Denmark; the British were driven from the Continent; and France fell. On June 22, 1941, Germany attacked Russia.

On December 7, 1941, the Japanese bombed Pearl Harbor in Hawaii and destroyed the greater part of the U.S. fleet there. The subsequent declarations of war by the U.S. included Germany and Italy, both of which had made prior declarations of war on the U.S., as well as Japan. The latter country followed up the Pearl Harbor attack with others in the Pacific region, and the war involved all the continents and all the oceans. The Japanese captured Wake, Guam, the Philippines, and other strategic islands before the Allied offensive, begun in the fall of 1942, began to dislodge them. However, it was not until President Harry S TRUMAN authorized the dropping of the first atomic bombs (on Hiroshima, August 6, 1945; on Nagasaki, August 9, 1945) that Japan was forced to surrender (September 2, 1945).

After an Allied invasion of southern Italy, the Italian army and navy surrendered (September 3, 1943), but German forces in Rome and to the north were not dislodged until the summer of 1944. On June 6, 1944, an immense invasion army of men and supplies, under the direct supervision of General Dwight D. EISENHOWER, landed in France and eventually forced the Germans to retreat across the Rhine. Germany surrendered unconditionally on May 7, 1945.

Among the best-known novels dealing with the war are Thomas Heggen's *Mister Roberts* (1946), Norman Mailer's THE NAKED AND THE DEAD, Irwin Shaw's THE YOUNG LIONS, James Jones's FROM HERE TO ETERNITY, and Herman WOUK's *The Caine Mutiny*. Other novelists who have written about the war include John HERSEY, André SCHWARZ-BART, Erich Maria REMARQUE, and Konstantin SIMONOV. *There Shall Be No Night* (1940) by Robert E. Sherwood and THE DEVIL'S GENERAL by Carl Zuckmayer are plays dealing with the war. *The Diary of Anne Frank* was written by a Jewish girl in Nazi-occupied Holland (see Anne FRANK). Winston CHURCHILL, prime minister of England from 1940 to 1945, wrote a six-volume history of the war called *The Second World War* (1948–54). See DE GAULLE, CHARLES; MACARTHUR, DOUGLAS; MARSHALL, GEORGE C.; MUSSOLINI, BENITO; ROOSEVELT, FRANKLIN D.; STALIN, JOSEPH.

Worthies, Nine   Nine heroes, three from the BIBLE, three from the classics, and three from romance. They were frequently bracketed together, as in the burlesque Pageant of the Nine Worthies in Shakespeare's *Love's Labour's Lost*. They are Joshua, DAVID, and JUDAS MACCABAEUS; HECTOR, ALEXANDER THE GREAT, and Julius CAESAR; ARTHUR, CHARLEMAGNE, and Godfrey de Bouillon (see GOFFREDO).

Wotan   The Old High German form of ODIN, chief of the Scandinavian gods. This is the form used in the operas of Wagner's RING DES NIBELUNGEN, in which Wotan the Mighty plays a leading role.

Wotton, Sir Henry (1568–1639)   English diplomat and poet. Wotton served as ambassador to Venice and later became provost of Eton College. He was an intimate friend of John DONNE and a fishing companion of Izaak WALTON, whose brief biography of Wotton was included in *Reliquiae Wottonianae* (1651), a posthumous edition of the latter's work. Wotton wrote poems of considerable charm, such as "On His Mistress, the Queen of Bohemia" (1624), and was the author of the statement "An Ambassador is an honest man sent to lie abroad for the good of his country."

Wouk, Herman (1915–   )   American novelist. Wouk's most famous work, *The Caine Mutiny* (1951), a PULITZER PRIZE-winning novel about World War II, was followed by another best-seller, *Marjorie Morningstar* (1955), the story of a middle-class Jewish girl who temporarily rejects her upbringing in her infatuation with the world of show business. Among Wouk's other novels are the ambitious and popular *The Winds of War* (1971), about the coming of World War II in Europe and the Pacific. In that book, Wouk created the fictional Henry family, which he continued to follow through the horrors of HITLER and MUSSOLINI in the sequel *War and Remembrance* (1978). *Inside, Outside* (1985) again looks at the importance of religious roots to American Jews in the story of a Jewish presidential advisor.

Would-be Gentleman, The   See BOURGEOIS GENTILHOMME, LE.

Woyzeck (1836?; pub 1879)   A fragmentary play by Georg BÜCHNER, about an imbecilic army private who murders his unfaithful common-law wife. It depicts, with powerful realism, the social and economic injustices that led to both the wife's faithlessness and Woyzeck's murder of her; as such, it is a socialistic document. In style, it is extremely compact, a quick succession of short, meaningful scenes. For this reason and because of its tendency to treat typical rather than individual phenomena, to depict human agony in the pure state, it has been regarded as a forerunner of expressionism. Alban Berg's twelve-tone opera *Wozzeck* (1925) is based on the play.

Wreck of the Deutschland, The (1875)   A poem by Gerard Manley HOPKINS. Its subject is the death of five nuns, drowned off the Welsh coast while seeking refuge in the U.S. from religious persecution in Germany. In intricate stanzas, full of complex metaphor and allusion, the poet deals with the problem of suffering, man's relationship with God, the decline of religion, and the nuns' happiness in dying in God's hands.

Wreck of the Hesperus, The (1841)   A ballad by Henry Wadsworth LONGFELLOW. It was inspired by a newspaper account of an actual wreck at sea.

Wren, Sir Christopher (1632–1723)   English architect. Following the Great FIRE OF LONDON in 1666, Wren was entrusted with the reconstruction of many churches and public buildings, notably St. Paul's Cathedral (1675–1710). His work is characterized by decorative interiors ornamented with designs and by graceful spires known for their inventive variety and for the technical resourcefulness of the construction. Wren is buried under the choir of St. Paul's; the tablet erected to mark the spot bears the Latin inscription *Si monumentum requiris, circumspice* ("If thou seekest a monument, gaze around").

Wright, Frank Lloyd (1869–1959) American architect, probably the most influential of the 20th century. A student and disciple of Louis SULLIVAN, Wright is known both for his industrial architecture and for his private dwellings. In his large-scale projects, he used poured reinforced concrete extensively as a decorative as well as structural device. Notable among these buildings, characterized by their organically curved surfaces, are the Johnson Wax Company in Racine, Wisconsin (1950), and the inverted-spiral Guggenheim Museum (1959). His many prestigious houses were revolutionary in their use of cantilevered horizontal masses, as in the famous Kaufmann house in Bear Run, Pennsylvania (1936), precariously perched over a rushing waterfall. Wright incorporated into these designs an admiration for the fluidity and geometric simplicity of Japanese architecture and a desire for total harmony—on the outside and with surrounding landscape, and on the inside with the furnishings, which he often designed himself. To this end, he used natural materials, like brick and unvarnished wood, and a low, gently spreading profile, known in the 1930s as the Prairie Style. The famous Robie House in Chicago (1909) embodies all these principles.

At Taliesin West, his home in Scottsdale, Arizona, he formed the Taliesin Fellowship, as a school where architects could come to work and learn. Wright's ideals are set forth in *An Autobiography* (1943; repr 1977), *A Testament* (1957), and his biography of Sullivan, *Genius and the Mobocracy* (1949).

Wright, James [Arlington] (1927–1980) American poet. Wright's poetry is often identified with the "deep image" school of writers, including Robert BLY and Jerome Rothenberg. During the late 1950s these poets advocated the use of subjective imagery deeply imbued with unconscious elements. In his first book, *The Green Wall* (1957), Wright employed a polished verse and skillfully drawn dramatic portraits. His second volume, *Saint Judas* (1959), had fewer personae and focused more on a central I. Increasingly his work dealt with a homeless, lonely self confronted by an overwhelming, godless universe. The plain-spoken poems in *The Branch Will Not Break* (1963) represented a change in tone and technique, although the thematic focus remained on the self. After the publication of his *Collected Poems* (1971) he was awarded the PULITZER PRIZE for poetry.

Wright, Judith [Arundell] (1915–   ) Australian poet and critic. One of Australia's best-known poets, Wright evokes both her country's past and its landscape through her verse. Beginning with *The Moving Image* (1946), her poetry is a progressive exploration of the mysterious dynamics of human and biological relationships. *Col-*lected Poems 1942–1970 appeared in 1971. Apart from her critical writings, children's books, and short stories, she has also written *The Generations of Men* (1959), about her pioneering grandparents' settlement of Australia. *The Double Tree* (1977) is an updated selection of her poetry.

Wright, Richard [Nathaniel] (1908–1960) American novelist. Born on a farm near Natchez, Mississippi, Wright, largely self-educated, began to write after he moved to Chicago in 1934. Often associated with Nelson ALGREN, James FARRELL, and the Chicago realists, he wrote powerfully dramatic books exploring the ways in which blacks have been shaped and misshaped by white society. His first published work, *Uncle Tom's Children* (1938), a collection of four novellas, was followed by NATIVE SON, which became a minor classic and was made into a film in 1951 and again in 1986. Wright was a member of the Communist Party from 1932 to 1944, lived in Mexico for much of the 1940s, and moved to Paris in 1946, where he remained until his death. In his autobiography *Black Boy* (1945) Wright comes to terms with the ways in which the black can act as his own enemy as well as with the predicament of the artist in society. The second part of Wright's autobiography, *American Hunger*, was not published until 1977. Other works include *The Outsider* (1953), a philosophical novel; *White Man, Listen!* (1957); *The Long Dream* (1958), a novel; and *Eight Men* (1961), a collection of stories published posthumously, which contains some of his finest writing.

Wu See THREE KINGDOMS.

Wuthering Heights (1847) A novel by Emily BRONTË, first published under the pen name Ellis Bell. Mr. Earnshaw, father of Catherine and Hindley, finds a waif on the streets of Liverpool and brings him home to raise with his own children. From the beginning, HEATHCLIFF, a strange, uncouth, passionate creature, is a disruptive influence in the Earnshaws' lonely moorland home, Wuthering Heights. Catherine forms a passionate attachment to him, while Hindley hates him, regarding him as a usurper and a rival for his father's affection. After Mr. Earnshaw's death, the household degenerates. In spite of her love for Heathcliff, Catherine lets fall a remark, which he overhears, that it would degrade her to marry him; the furious Heathcliff steals off, disappearing for three years, and Catherine marries the well-to-do Edgar Linton. Years later, Heathcliff, mysteriously transformed into a wealthy and polished man, returns and is invited by Hindley, who has money troubles, to make his home at Wuthering Heights. Heathcliff accepts but deceitfully elopes with Edgar's sister, obviously to avenge himself on Catherine and her husband. Barred from the house, Heathcliff still manages a final meeting with Catherine before she dies in premature childbirth. Seventeen years later, Heathcliff, now a widower, forces Catherine's daughter to marry his sickly son Linton, and, upon the deaths of Edgar and of Linton, he gains control of Wuthering Heights and of the young girl Cathy. When

Heathcliff dies, the girl is at last free: she devotes herself to her young cousin Hareton, the uncouth and ignorant son of her uncle Hindley. The story, told by characters within the narrative and, to an extent, chronologically reshuffled, attains an almost mystical intensity. The adjective *wuthering* is a Yorkshire word referring to turbulent weather.

Wyatt, Sir Thomas (1503?–1542)   English poet. Wyatt held a number of official positions under Henry VIII, including those of Member of the Privy Council, Ambassador to Spain, Member of Parliament, and Commander of the Fleet. During an official trip to Italy in 1527, he became acquainted with the work of the Italian love poets. Later, his translations of PETRARCH introduced the sonnet into England. He was a friend of the earl of SURREY and had a strong influence on the writing of the younger man; together Wyatt and Surrey are credited with being the founders of the school of English lyric poetry that flourished during the remainder of the 16th and continued into the 17th century.

Wyatt's poetry is often characterized by extreme irregularity of rhythm, which 19th-century scholars regarded as evidence of crude technique. In the 20th century, however, critics began to point out that this irregularity was often important in the total effect of the poems, comparing it with the dramatic rhythm in the work of John DONNE. Critics also have praised the vigor and authentic intensity of feeling in Wyatt's best poems, such as "They Flee from Me," "My Lute, Awake," and "In Eternum." His work appeared in several anthologies, among them *The Court of Venus* (1542), *Seven Penitential Psalms* (1549), and TOTTEL'S MISCELLANY.

Wycherley, William (1640–1716)   English comic dramatist of the Restoration, noted for the savagery of his satire, his cynical realism, and his coarse, mordant wit. Educated in France and at Oxford, Wycherley briefly contemplated a legal career. His first comedy, *Love in a Wood, or St. James' Park* (1671), won him the favor of the duchess of Cleveland, mistress of CHARLES II. This play was followed by *The Gentleman Dancing Master* (1672?) and his best works, THE COUNTRY WIFE and *The Plain Dealer* (1676). He incurred the king's displeasure by his secret marriage (c1680) to the widowed countess of Drogheda; after her death, he became involved in lengthy litigation over her estate and spent seven years in a debtor's prison. Charles refused to help Wycherley out of his financial difficulties, but JAMES II, who, it is said, had greatly admired *The Plain Dealer*, came to his rescue by paying his debts.

Wyclif, John (or John Wycliffe or Wiclif, d 1384) English theologian and reformer. Called The Morning Star of the Reformation, Wyclif was one of the earliest antagonists of papal encroachments on secular power. He felt that all Christians should have access to the Bible in the vernacular, and he instigated the first complete English translation, which was probably done by his followers. The translation was completed c1388 but was not published

until 1850. In addition to resisting the growth of the secular power of the papacy, Wyclif condemned monasticism and attacked the foundations of medieval orthodoxy in his denial of the dogma of transubstantiation, from which the priesthood derived the basis of its power. He taught that all ecclesiastical and secular authority is derived from God and is forfeited when one is in a state of mortal sin. The followers of Wyclif were known as Wyclifites; however, the LOLLARDS, with whom they are often grouped, were not, strictly speaking, followers of Wyclif.

Wyeth, Andrew [Newell] (1917–   )   American painter. Wyeth's photographic realism and advocacy of traditional values make him immensely popular, but his tempera paintings of Maine and Pennsylvania also possess considerable depth of emotion and elegance of composition. His best-known work is *Christina's World* (1948). In 1986 Wyeth revealed that he had secretly made over 240 drawings and paintings of Helga Testorf, his neighbor, between 1971 and 1985. Known as the "Helga Pictures," this series of drawings and watercolors is particularly valued because it dwells on a single subject over a long period of time.

Wylie, Elinor [Hoyt] (1885–1928)   American poet and novelist. Known for the precise and vivid imagery in her lyrics and the subtle analysis of emotion in her later love poems, Wylie established a considerable reputation in less than two decades of writing. She published *Incidental Numbers* (1912) anonymously but thereafter used her own name on such volumes of verse as NETS TO CATCH THE WIND, *Black Armour* (1923), *Trivial Breath* (1928) and *Angels and Earthly Creatures* (1929), all of which show the influence of the Elizabethan and METAPHYSICAL POETS. Her third husband, William Rose BENÉT, edited her *Collected Poems* (1932) and *Collected Prose* (1933). Her *Last Poems* appeared in 1943.

Her fanciful historical novels include *Jennifer Lorn* (1923), a satire of a pompous aristocrat, seen through the eyes of his wife, in 18th-century England and India; *The Venetian Glass Nephew* (1925); *The Orphan Angel* (1926), an imaginative story of what would have happened to Shelley had he been saved from drowning by an American ship; and *Mr. Hodge and Mr. Hazard* (1928).

Wyndham, John (pen name of John Wyndham Parkes Lucas Beynon Harris, 1903–1969)   English SCIENCE FICTION writer, who concocted a variety of pseudonyms from his wealth of given names. The English countryside provides a cozy backdrop for the catastrophic events of his fiction, and his best novels use the Wellsian technique of domesticating threats: perambulating plants in *The Day of the Triffids* (1951); ocean-occupying aliens in *The Kraken Wakes* (1953; U.S. *Out of the Deeps*); post-nuclear war mutants in *The Chrysalids* (1955; U.S. *Rebirth*); and alien inseminators in *The Midwich Cuckoos* (1957; U.S. *The Village of the Damned*). Several collections were published posthumously, including *The Best of John Wyndham* (1973) and *The Man from Beyond* (1975).

wyrd (OE, "fate") The Anglo-Saxon concept of fate that manifests itself chiefly in a hero's willingness to test fate by matching his courage against heavy odds. It was felt that sooner or later fate would decree a hero's death but that courage in the face of danger could defer that end. As BEOWULF said, "Fate often saves an undoomed man when his courage is good." Once a man's doom had been decreed by fate, however, courage could no longer save him.

X

Xanadu A province or region in China mentioned by Coleridge in his KUBLA KHAN as the site of the Khan's pleasure garden. *The Road to Xanadu* (1927) by the American John Livingston Lowes (1867–1945) is a study of the workings of the imagination, using Coleridge as an example.

Xantippe The wife of the Greek philosopher SOC-RATES. Xantippe's shrewish nature has made her name proverbial.

Xavier, St. Francis (1506–1552) Spanish Jesuit missionary, the "Apostle of the Indies." As a student in Paris Xavier became a friend of Ignatius of Loyola and helped him establish the Society of Jesus (1534). He worked in Japan for several years. He was canonized, together with his master and friend, in 1622.

Xenion (Gr, "stranger") A two-line, usually satirical poem in the form of the classical epigram. Goethe's and Schiller's *Xenien* (1797; see WEIMAR CLASSICISM) are examples. "Xenien" is the German plural of the word.

Xenophon (c430–c355 BC) Athenian writer. In 401 BC Xenophon joined the force of mercenary Greeks recruited by Cyrus the Younger for the purpose of dethroning his older brother Artaxerxes. Cyrus was killed, and Xenophon led the ten thousand Greeks through Persian territory to the Black Sea. His account of the expedition is known as the *Anabasis*, in which he portrays himself as the hero of the affair. Xenophon, who had a great love for Sparta, fought with the Spartans against Athenians and Thebans in 394 BC. The Athenians exiled him for this activity, and he subsequently lived in Sparta and Corinth. Among his other works, all of which seem to have survived in full, are the *Hellenica*, a continuation of Thucydides' history of Greece; the *Memorabilia of Socrates*, a popular philosophy; and the *Cyropedia*, a biography of Cyrus modified to suit Xenophon's didactic purpose. A famous part of the *Anabasis* is Xenophon's record of the Greeks crying "*Thalassa, thalassa,*" as they caught the first glimpse of their beloved sea.

Xerxes I (c519–465 BC) King of Persia, the son of Darius and Atossa. Concluding from a dream that the gods demanded war on the Greeks, Xerxes gathered a huge army and fleet. He constructed a bridge of boats over the Hellespont and reached Athens but had to retreat after the battle of Salamis. He is an important figure in Aeschylus' tragedy THE PERSIANS. See PERSIAN WARS.

Y

Yahoo In the fourth voyage of GULLIVER'S TRAVELS by Jonathan Swift, a race of filthy, loathsome brutes tamed by, and contrasted to, the virtuous and reasonable Houyhnhnms. Gulliver is discomfited by their resemblance to the human race. While the Houyhnhnms represent the highest attributes of mankind in their purest form, the beastly Yahoos represent Swift's conception of man living in a degenerate state of nature. See HOUYHNHNMLAND.

Yam The Canaanite god of the sea and inland waters. Yam is represented as a dragon. At the beginning of THE POEM OF BAAL, he has dominion over earth as well as sea, but after a protracted struggle, BAAL, with the aid of his sister Anat, supplants him as lord of the earth. There are numerous references to this legend in the OLD TESTAMENT, where Yam is referred to as Rahab or simply as the dragon, who was destroyed by Yahweh.

Yama The god of the dead in Hindu mythology. According to legend he was the first mortal to die, and was thereafter made into a god. In some versions, he is the judge of the dead, with the power to punish; in others he merely conducts the dead to their ancestors. He is depicted as green in color, with blood-red clothes, holding a club and a noose, astride a buffalo.

Yañez, Agustín (1904–   ) Mexican novelist. One of the earliest Mexican writers to employ NOUVEAU ROMAN techniques, Yañez writes a lyrical prose which is enriched by his personal memories of rural Mexico. The town in *Al filo del agua* (1947; tr *The Edge of the Storm*, 1963), his tenth and most important novel, lives under the weight of a morbid, narrow, and collapsing religious order. The spontaneity of the young is repressed by the fear of gossip, and his characters agonize in a seesaw of guilt and eroticism which eventually explodes, fanned by the fresh winds of the Mexican revolution of 1910. Yañez does not draw realistic characters. Like an impressionist painter, he creates a slow-moving, blurry atmosphere through which one discerns the feelings of a people on the verge of revolution. Among his other novels are *La creación* (1959), *La tierra pródiga* (1960), *Las tierras flacas* (1962; tr *The Lean Lands*, 1968), and *Ojerosa y pintada* (1967).

Yang Chien See SUI.

Yankee Properly, a New Englander or one of New England stock. The term was extended to mean, first, an inhabitant of the North as apart from the South and, later, to comprise all citizens of the U.S. In the South, Northerners were often referred to as "Damyankees."

The word is generally taken to be a North American Indian corruption of *English* or of the French *Anglais*. There is also the story that in 1713 one Jonathan Hastings, a farmer of Cambridge, Massachusetts, used the word as a puffing epithet, meaning "genuine," "what cannot be surpassed," as in Yankee horse, Yankee cider, and so on. The students at Harvard, catching up the term, called Hastings "Yankee Jonathan." It soon spread, and became the jocose pet name of the New Englander.

Yankee Doodle A quasi-national song of the U.S. Both the tune and several stanzas of "Yankee Doodle" were current early in the British colonies; the catchy tune seems to have inspired innumerable verses. The origin of the tune is disputed, and the words have traditionally been ascribed to Dr. Shuckburgh, a British army surgeon. The song seems to have been deliberately used by the British to provoke the American troops during the Revolution; the Americans, however, adopted the song as their own and created an image of the American in a rustic mold. The song was first printed in America in 1795.

Yarrow A river in Scotland. SCOTT and HOGG have celebrated its legends, and Wordsworth wrote a poem called "Yarrow Revisited" (1835). "The Braes of Yarrow" is the title of an old Scottish ballad.

Yashin, Aleksandr (pen name of Aleksandr Yakovlevich Popov, 1913–1968) Russian poet and short-story writer. For *Alyona Fomina* (1949), his long poem glorifying work of the collective farm, Yashin received a Stalin prize. Most of his early work deals with themes of peasant and village life. His short story "Rychagi" ("Levers," 1956) was one of the most discussed works of the THAW period in

Soviet literature. The story depicts the tyrannical behavior of Communist Party members toward subordinates on a collective farm.

Yatpan The killer of the young hero in the Canaanite THE POEM OF AQHAT. Yatpan is hired by the goddess Anat to dispose of Aqhat and recover the divine bow which the youth refuses to give her. Yatpan, a most inefficient assassin, kills Aqhat, but promptly drops and breaks the bow, and, moreover, reveals his guilt to Aqhat's sister Paghat after drinking too much wine.

Ydalir See ASGARD.

Yearling, The (1938) A novel by Marjorie Kinnan RAWLINGS. Set in the scrub country of northern Florida, it recounts one year in the lives of a backwoods farmer, his wife, and his young son, Jody, who adopts an orphaned fawn and finds in the animal the love and companionship he craves. When the fawn begins to eat the family corn, Jody is ordered by his father to shoot him. The tragedy lifts Jody out of his boyhood and into a more mature relationship with his parents. It was awarded a PULITZER PRIZE.

Yeats, William Butler (1865–1939) Irish poet and dramatist. Yeats is generally considered to be one of the greatest poets of the 20th century. The three major concerns of his life—art, Irish nationalism, and occult studies—are also central to his poetry and drama. His greatest work is in the poetry of his maturity and old age; it is characterized by its lyrical and dramatic qualities, its use of symbolism and the mythology of Irish folklore and the occult, its autobiographical and political themes, and its sensuous beauty, realism, precision, and economy.

He was the son of John Butler Yeats, a well-known Irish painter, and he himself studied painting for three years. Yeats's early poetry is characterized by a romantic affectation of melancholy and a preoccupation with "the Celtic twilight." "The Wanderings of Oisin" (1889), a long, mystical narrative poem based on Irish legend, and "The Lake Isle of Innisfree" (1893) date from this period.

In London, Yeats was a founding member of the Pre-Raphaelite Rhymer's Club, whose aims were to promote pure poetry and the aesthetic cult of Walter PATER. On his return to Ireland in 1896, he became a leader of the IRISH RENAISSANCE. Believing that the Irish poet's task was to communicate with the Irish people, he wrote simple, direct poetry; *The Wind Among the Reeds* (1899) and *In the Seven Woods* (1903) are collections written during this period. Yeats met Maud GONNE when he was twenty-three and became indirectly involved in her political activities. He was in love with her during much of his life and used her as a central symbol in his poetry.

With Lady GREGORY, George MOORE, and others, Yeats founded, in 1899, the theatre society that was later to become the celebrated ABBEY THEATRE. He encouraged Lady Gregory and SYNGE to write plays for it, and he himself wrote many works for it, including THE COUNTESS CATHLEEN, *The Land of Heart's Desire* (1894), *Cathleen ni*

Houlihan (1902), and *Deirdre* (1907). Under the influence of Ezra POUND, whom Yeats met in 1912, he began to write ritualistic, symbolic dramas, with dance and music, in imitation of the Japanese Nō plays. These plays, in prose and verse, often make symbolic use of Irish heroic legends, especially those about Cú CHULAINN. Usually, like most of Yeats's work, they are concerned with peasants, aristocrats, beggars, wandering minstrels, and kings and queens, and they are based on his mystical and occult ideas. THE HERNE'S EGG and PURGATORY are characteristic plays of this period.

Yeats had been interested in magic and occult philosophy since his Dublin days with A.E. (q.v.), and when he met Madame BLAVATSKY in London in 1887, he became a devoted disciple. He did not believe in any orthodox religion, but since he felt that he needed some system of supernatural belief to give depth to his life and poetry, he half-accepted the doctrines of THEOSOPHY, Hermetism (see HERMES TRISMEGISTUS), and spiritualism. In 1917 he married Georgie Hyde Lees, a spiritualist medium, and with the help of her trances and automatic writing composed A VISION, a prose work that combined a system of magic, philosophy of history, and a philosophy of personality. Yeats's esoteric ideas provided a mythical background and a system of symbols for all his poetry, but especially for his later work.

In technique, Yeats's mature poetry was influenced by the work of John DONNE, Walter Savage LANDOR, and Ezra Pound. It appeared in the volumes *The Green Helmet* (1910), *Responsibilities* (1914), *The Wild Swans at Coole* (1917), *Michael Robartes and the Dancer* (1921), *The Tower* (1928), and *The Winding Stair* (1929). Yeats prepared *The Collected Poems* (1933) himself, rewriting many of his early poems in accordance with his later stylistic ideas. Among the best-known individual poems are "Byzantium" and "Sailing to Byzantium"; "Easter 1916," a commemoration of an incident during the Irish rebellion (see Padraic PEARSE); "A Prayer for My Daughter"; "Leda and the Swan"; "Among School Children"; "Lapis Lazuli"; "Long-Legged Fly"; and CRAZY JANE, a series of poems.

Yeats's prose works include *Fairy and Folk Tales of the Irish Peasantry* (1888); occult works, such as *The Celtic Twilight* (1893) and *The Secret Rose* (1897); collections of essays such as *Ideas of Good and Evil* (1903), *The Cutting of an Agate* (1912), and *Essays* (1937); and *Autobiographies* (1926). He edited the works of William BLAKE (1893).

At the end of his life Yeats was widely honored as one of the most important poets of the century. He was elected a senator of the Irish Free State in 1922 and was awarded the NOBEL PRIZE in Literature in 1923.

yellow (fr OE, *geolu*, connected with Gr, *chloros*, "green") A color symbolically indicating jealousy, inconstancy, and treachery. In France the doors of traitors used to be daubed with yellow. In some countries the law ordained that Jews must be clothed in yellow, because they betrayed Jesus; hence Judas, in medieval pictures, is arrayed in yellow. In Spain the vestments of the executioner were either red or yellow: the former to denote bloodshedding; the latter, treason.

In heraldry and in ecclesiastical symbolism, yellow is frequently used in place of gold.

Yellow Book, The A quarterly consisting of short fiction, poetry, essays, and illustrations published in England between 1894 and 1897. Its literary editor was the American expatriate novelist Henry Harland (1861–1905); Aubrey BEARDSLEY served as art editor for the first two years and was primarily responsible for setting the exotic, sometimes bizarre tone of the publication. Among its many contributors were Oscar WILDE, William Butler YEATS, and Arnold BENNETT. In form and content, *The Yellow Book* anticipated the LITTLE MAGAZINES of the first decades of the 20th century.

Yemassee, The (1835) A historical novel by William Gilmore SIMMS. The book deals with the conflict between the South Carolina Yemassee Indians and the British in 1715. Occonestoga, the son of Sanutee, chief of the Yemassee, betrays his tribe, and is killed by his mother, Matiwan. Dying in the attack on Charleston, Sanutee is defeated by the novel's hero, a mysterious Captain Harrison. The captain, later revealed to be South Carolina's Governor Craven, marries Bess Matthews, a girl of the frontier. A central theme in this most popular of Simms's books is the helplessness of the Indians as they lose their lands to the advancing white civilization.

Yerby, Frank [Garvin] (1916–   ) American novelist. Yerby is the author of more than thirty novels, most of which have become best-sellers. Beginning with the popular *The Foxes of Harrow* (1946), a historical melodrama set in the antebellum South, he produced a steady stream of historical, or "costume," novels, among them *An Odor of Sanctity* (1965), set in medieval Spain; *Goat Song* (1968), set in ancient Greece; and *Judas, My Brother* (1968), set at the time of Jesus. *The Dahomean* (1971) is a fictional exploration of Yerby's African ancestry, which was continued in his novel about slavery, *A Darkness at Ingraham's Crest* (1979). *Devilseed* (1984) and *Mackenzie's Hundred* (1985) are among his other novels.

Yerma See GARCÍA LORCA, FEDERICO.

Yesenin, Sergey Aleksandrovich (1895–1925) Russian poet. Born of peasant parents, Yesenin used the theme of the passing of rural Russia in his poetry. One of the finest lyric poets of the early Soviet period, he was for a time connected with a literary group called the Imaginists, which, like the English and American Imagists, stressed the importance of the image in poetry. His growing popularity went hand in hand with an increasingly wild life. For a chaotic year (1922–23), he was married to the dancer Isadora DUNCAN. His drinking bouts grew in length until he finally slashed his wrist, wrote a farewell poem in his own blood, and hanged himself in a hotel room in Leningrad. His suicide was attributed by the Soviet regime to his mental instability, and Yesenin's works have not been suppressed as have those of other disaffected literary figures. His four volumes of lyrics, with their glowing pictures of the Russian countryside, are still popular in Russia.

Yevtushenko, Yevgeny Aleksandrovich (1933–   ) Soviet poet. With Andrey VOZNESENSKY, Yevtushenko stirred new interest in poetry in the Soviet Union during the early 1960s. Much of Yevtushenko's work expresses the impatience of the younger Soviet generation with the cant and smugness that pervaded society throughout Stalin's leadership. A return to the revolutionary fervor of the early Soviet period and a need to regain human values lost during Stalin's fearful rule are demands frequently voiced in Yevtushenko's work. With such poems, he attracted crowds of thousands to his readings, often held in huge outdoor stadiums. His outspokenness has, however, caused him trouble with Soviet authorities. His poem "Babi Yar" (1962), about the notorious Ukrainian ravine where Nazis killed ninety-six thousand Jews during the German occupation, was criticized for implying that the Soviet regime was guilty of anti-Semitism. Shortly after the furor over this work died down, Yevtushenko again got into trouble by publishing his memoirs (tr *A Precocious Autobiography*, 1963) in France without obtaining Soviet permission. The criticisms of the Soviet system implicit in his writings added to his difficulties, although many critics think that since this period Yevtushenko has hidden behind his reputation for brash outspokenness and has taken fewer risks, both politically and stylistically. Yevtushenko is also known for his poems about foreign countries, including "Senegalskaya ballada" (1966; tr "Black and White," 1971), about his visit to Senegal, and "Monolog pesta na alyaskinskoy zveroferme" (1967; tr "Monologue of a Polar Fox on an Alaskan Fur Farm," 1971). *Almost at the End* (1987), a collection of poetry and prose writings, examines the differences between East and West, the effects of censorship, and limitations on personal freedom.

Yggdrasill (ON, "horse of Yggr") In Norse mythology, the great ash tree that supported the universe and sprang from the body of the giant YMIR. It had three roots, which extended to the realms of ASGARD, NIFLHEIM, and Totunnheim. Near it lay the well Urtharbrunn, whose waters the NORNS used to preserve the tree from decay. The squirrel Ratatosk ran up and down the trunk carrying strife. Four stags fed on Yggdrasill's foliage, and an eagle and a hawk sat in its branches.

Yin See SHANG.

yin and yang The Chinese concept of the negative and positive principles of the universe. The words originally meant "shady" and "sunny," and occur very early (8th century BC), but were elaborated into a cosmological system only in the 3rd century BC. *Yin* is female, passive, cold, negative; *yang* is male, active, hot, positive. Unlike Western dualisms, where light is good and darkness bad, yin and yang complement and grow out of each other. Associated with the yin-yang theory is the concept of the five elements or processes (*wu hsing*: wood, metal, fire, water, and earth). Each element is associated with a color, direction, organ of the body, note of the musical scale, and so on, and their sequence was seen to be causal, predictable, and circular. Thus, metal cuts wood, fire melts metal, water puts out fire, earth conquers water, and wood conquers earth. Daily human events as well as great historical movements were explained by associations with the elements. Together with the BOOK OF CHANGES, these concepts were applied to the determination of lucky days for weddings, journeys, and all the other decisions of quotidian activity. These ideas still prevail to a certain extent in East Asia.

Ymir   The primeval giant of Scandinavian mythology from whose body the world was said to be created. Ymir was nourished by the four milky streams which flowed from the cow Audhumla. One legend holds that while Ymir slept, a man and woman grew out of his left arm and sons from his feet, thus generating the race of frost giants. A more popular account is that when ODIN and his two brothers, VILI and VE, slew Ymir and threw his carcass into an abyss, his blood formed the waters, his bones the mountains, his teeth the rocks, his skull the heavens, his brains the clouds, his hair the plants, and his eyebrows the wall of defense against the giants.

Yoga   See DARSHANA.

Yoknapatawpha County   An imaginary county in Mississippi which serves as the setting for many stories by William FAULKNER. Jefferson, the county seat, is modeled in part on Oxford, Mississippi. The novelist gave the county realistic detail, providing a map and population figures.

Yokomitsu Riichi (1889–1947)   Japanese novelist and short-story writer. A restless experimenter, he used Western avant-garde techniques one after another in an attempt to give appropriate literary form to aspects of a complex modern mind. Although he wrote several full-length novels, his best works are short pieces like *Hae* (1923; tr *The Fly*, 1965), *Kikai* (1930; tr *Machine*, 1961), and *Jikan* (1931; tr *Time*, 1956).

Yom Kippur   See DAY OF ATONEMENT.

Yorick   In Shakespeare's HAMLET, the deceased jester of the murdered king of Denmark. Yorick's skull is apostrophized by Hamlet, who remembers him as "a fellow of infinite jest, of most excellent fancy." In Sterne's TRISTRAM SHANDY, Yorick is a humorous parson who claims descent from Shakespeare's Yorick.

Yorktown   The capital of York County, Virginia, site of the surrender of Cornwallis (October 19, 1781), which virtually ended the American Revolution.

Yosano Akiko (1878–1942)   Japanese poet. Yosano's youthful love affair with a married man resulted in her first volume of TANKA, *Midaregami* (1901; tr *Tangled*

Hair, 1935), which startled her contemporaries by its bold affirmation of sensual passion. Although she came to dislike the volume afterwards, it exerted an immense influence on later poets who sought release from semifeudal morality as well as from conventional idioms of *tanka*. In later years she wrote many essays encouraging Japanese women to be more assertive.

Yoshida Kenkō   See ESSAYS IN IDLENESS.

You Can't Go Home Again (1940)   A posthumously published novel by Thomas WOLFE. In this sequel to THE WEB AND THE ROCK, George Webber, having returned from Europe, resumes his affair with Esther Jack and becomes a successful writer. He revisits his hometown and is disillusioned by what he sees, an episode said to parallel Wolfe's own experience in Asheville, North Carolina.

You Can't Take It with You (1936)   A comedy by Moss HART and George S. KAUFMAN. This PULITZER PRIZE winner deals with the bizarre but supremely happy Vanderhof family in New York. They make fireworks in the cellar, write plays, and practice ballet, creating difficulties for the family's one conventional member, who wants to marry the scion of a wealthy but stuffy New York family.

You Know Me, Al: A Busher's Letters (1916)   A collection of short stories by Ring LARDNER, written in the form of letters from a half-literate baseball rookie, Jack Keefe. Perfectly capturing the vernacular speech, tone, and outlook of their protagonist, the stories are excellent examples of Lardner's characteristic combination of humor and misanthropy. They first appeared in the *Saturday Evening Post*.

Youma (1890)   A novel by Lafcadio HEARN. One of Hearn's most distinguished works, it is based on the true story of a black girl's devotion to the daughter of her dead mistress during the slave insurrection in Martinique.

Young, Edward (1683–1765)   English poet and playwright. Young is best known today for NIGHT THOUGHTS ON LIFE, DEATH AND IMMORTALITY, written in defense of Christian orthodoxy against freethinkers and libertines, and *Conjectures on Original Composition, in a Letter to the Author of Sir Charles Grandison* (1759), his last and most brilliant prose essay, a defense of originality in writing. His other works include dramatic tragedies, a series of satires, and *Resignation* (1726), a long poem. In his youth, Young had hoped for a career as a lawyer, but was disappointed, spending most of his life as a country clergyman instead. He also carried on a long correspondence with Samuel RICHARDSON, the closest literary friend of his later years.

Young Goodman Brown (1835)   A story by Nathaniel HAWTHORNE. Brown, a young Puritan, leaves Faith, his wife, for a nighttime journey in the woods. Meeting an older man with a twisted staff, he learns that others have traveled the path before him. Sick at heart, he observes a witches' Sabbath and discovers the presence of his own wife. The next morning Goodman Brown returns to Salem a changed man; stern, sad, and gloomy, he believes that all are blasphemers.

Young Ireland   A militantly anti-English group developed in the 1840s by a dissident faction within the Catholic Association, an organization headed by the great Irish statesman Daniel O'CONNELL. The Catholic Association was opposed to the use of force in redressing its grievances with the English government, and the Young Ireland faction considered this position a fatal weakness. The severe economic privation (and human degradation) which was to reach such calamitous proportions as the result of the potato famine was already in progress in 1846, when the Young Ireland group, under the leadership of William Smith O'Brien (1803–64) and Thomas Meagher (1823–67), broke with the Catholic Association. By 1848 the plight was so great that violence was thought to be the only alternative. The Young Ireland group planned an open rebellion, which, however, was more verbal than actual, with the result that the rebels were arrested before any military action took place. Smith O'Brien and Meagher were sentenced to death and deported, and the Young Ireland group was scattered; many of its members later formed the FENIAN societies in Canada and the U.S.

Young Lions, The (1948)   A novel by Irwin SHAW. The book, Shaw's first novel, begins on New Year's Eve, 1937, and weaves the stories of three men who meet only in the climactic scene: Diestl, a Nazi ski instructor who epitomizes his nation's morality; Michael Whitmore, stage manager of a frivolous Broadway play, who drinks in the New Year, worrying about his wife's infidelity; and Noah Ackerman, a homeless Jew, first seen waiting for his father to die in a cheap California hotel. Ackerman, the book's most sympathetic character, marries a New Englander, with whom he enjoys a brief happiness; he fathers a son before, persecuted and exhausted, he is killed in a German wood. The book is one of the host of World War II novels that attempted to salvage meaning from the wreckage of war.

Young Lonigan   See STUDS LONIGAN.

Young Manhood of Studs Lonigan, The See STUDS LONIGAN.

Young Visitors, The   See ASHFORD, DAISY.

Yourcenar, Marguerite (pen name, anagram, of Marguerite de Crayencour, 1903–   )   Belgian-born French novelist; naturalized American citizen, resident in U.S. since 1940. Yourcenar is known for her historical novels, particularly *Le Coup de grâce* (1939; tr *Coup de Grâce*, 1957), the story of a Prussian officer who murders the woman who loves him because he loves her brother, and *Mémoires d'Hadrien* (1951; tr *Memoirs of Hadrian*, 1954). The memoirs portray the emperor on the eve of his death and describe his reflections as he gazes out upon the city that seemed to him indestructible and that he now fears will fall. As with most of her work, the book is a minutely researched reconstruction of actual events in the distant past through which she develops penetrating and fully credible portraits of the people she describes. Her only novel with a contemporary setting is *Denier du rêve* (1934; tr *A Coin in Nine Hands*, 1982), about an assassination attempt on Mussolini, written while she lived in Italy. Her other novels include *La Nouvelle Eurydice* (1931), *Sous bénéfice d'inventaire* (1962), *L'Oeuvre au noir* (1968; tr *The Abyss*, 1976), *Souvenirs pieux* (1974), and *Alexis* (1965; tr 1984). She has also written the prose poems *Feux* (1935; tr *Fires*, 1981) and *Fleuve profond, sombre rivière* (1974), several plays, and two volumes of her family memoirs, *Le Labyrinthe du monde* (1977) and *Archives du nord* (1977). In January 1981 she became the first woman to be elected to the ACADÉMIE FRANÇAISE.

Youth (1902)   A short story by Joseph CONRAD. Told by MARLOW, it is an account of his first dangerous voyage. From mature memory he looks back on youthful emotion and illusion.

Youth and the Bright Medusa (1920)   A collection of short stories by Willa CATHER. Dealing with the theme of artistic sensibility and talent, the volume includes "Paul's Case," an often anthologized short story of a psychotic boy.

Yuan   Chinese dynasty (1280–1368), following the SUNG dynasty. It was established by GENGHIS KHAN's successors, who integrated the conquered China into the Mongol empire. This period was marked by large-scale contacts among the peoples of China, Central Asia, and Europe. Marco POLO's visit (1275–92) was made during this dynasty. The Mongols despised traditional Chinese thought and institutions and caused serious dislocations for the scholar-official class, with its Confucian ideology of government. The Yuan is noted for developments in drama and literature in colloquial Chinese. It was succeeded by the MING dynasty.

Z

Zabolotsky, Nikolay Alekseyevich (1903–1958) Russian poet. Zabolotsky's first collection of poetry, *Stolbtsy* (1929; tr *Scrolls*, 1971), depicts the time of the NEW ECONOMIC POLICY in Leningrad, using an admixture of various styles of language and literary allusions. This collection was not well received. His publication in 1933 of the narrative poem *Torzhestvo zemledeliya* (*Triumph of Agriculture*), with its fantastic and chaotic elements, only fueled the critics' ire. The appearance of his second narrative poem, *Lodeynikov* (1933), elicited denunciations that ended in the poet's arrest in 1938 and incarceration until 1946.

Zacharias   See JOHN THE BAPTIST.

Zadig, ou la Destinée (1748)   A short novel by VOLTAIRE, first published in 1747 under the title of *Memnon, histoire orientale*. Zadig is a wealthy, honest, well-educated young Babylonian who learns how difficult it is to be happy in this world where almost everything goes wrong in spite of his efforts to do right. Every time he thinks he has achieved contentment, security, or love, something happens to rob him of them; yet he is able to go on by making use of the wisdom he has acquired so painfully from experience. In the end, the angel Jesrad reveals to him that there is no good without evil, or evil without good, and that all is trial or punishment, recompense or foresight. Zadig at last becomes a happy king and a sage. The inevitable Voltairian digs at religion, the clergy, and unjust sovereigns are apparent in this work.

Zadig's characteristic method is to draw inferences from close observation. In one episode, Zadig seemed to know so much about the king's horse, which had been lost, that he was accused of having stolen it. He said he had never seen it, but could describe it perfectly because "I saw the marks of horseshoes, all equal distances apart . . . [therefore] he gallops perfectly. The dust on the trees in this narrow road only seven feet wide brushed off a little right and left three and a half feet from the middle of the road . . . [therefore] he has a tail three and a half feet long. I saw beneath the trees, which made a cradle five feet high, some leaves newly fallen . . . [therefore] he was fifteen hands high. . . ."

Zalambur   See EBLIS.

Zamyatin, Yevgeny Ivanovich (1884–1937) Russian novelist, short-story writer, and playwright. Zamyatin was educated as a naval engineer. His first published tale was *Uyezdnoye* (1913; tr *A Provincial Tale*, 1966). His other early tales include *Na kalichkah* (*Out in the Sticks*, 1914) and two satires on English life, which he had observed while in Britain on naval business: *Ostrovityane* (1918; tr *The Islanders*, 1972) and *Lovets chelovekov* (*The Fisher of Men*, 1922). After the revolution, Zamyatin helped organize the writers' group known as the SERAPION BROTHERS and became a leader and teacher of the circle's young writers. When Zamyatin's major novel, WE, was published abroad in a Russian-language edition in 1929, Zamyatin was castigated by the Soviet authorities, who denounced him as an "internal émigré" and expelled him from the federation of writers, shutting the pages of all journals and newspapers to him. He wrote a letter to Stalin, asking to be allowed to emigrate, and the request was surprisingly granted, supposedly with the help of Maksim GORKY. Zamyatin moved to France in 1931, where he lived until his death.

Zamyatin's plays include *Ogni svyatogo Dominika* (*The Fires of St. Dominic*, 1922), a satire of the Soviet secret police agency, the Cheka; *Obshchestvo pochotnykh zvonarey* (*The Society of Honorary Bellringers*, 1926); and *Blokha* (*The Flea*, 1926), a dramatization of a story by the 19th-century writer Nikolay Leskov.

Zamyatin described himself as a neorealist. He defined his method in the following way: "While neorealism uses a microscope to look at the world, Symbolism used a telescope, a pre-Revolutionary Realism, an ordinary looking glass." Zamyatin's almost surrealistic literary methods had a large influence on such younger writers as Vsevolod Ivanov and Yury Olesha.

Zapata, Emiliano (1877?–1919)   Mexican revolutionary leader. Zapata and the peasant army that he recruited in Morelos and other southern states participated in the revolutionary movement of 1910, devastating plantations and dividing the land among the peons. Although Venustiano Carranza promised agrarian reform upon assuming power in 1915, Zapata was skeptical. He continued to lead his army in ingenious tactical moves against the new government, demanding for the people what the revolution had promised: land and liberty. After accepting an invitation for a parley, he was murdered by an honor guard of *carrancistas*, and quickly became a figure of legend among the Mexican peasants.

Zarathustra   See ZOROASTER.

Zeami Motokiyo (1363–1443)   Japanese actor and playwright. Head of an influential theatrical troupe, Zeami helped to elevate the Nō drama from popular entertainment to a mature art form. Many of the plays in today's Nō repertoire, such as *Atsumori* (tr 1921), *Hagoromo* (tr *The Robe of Feathers*, 1880), and *Utō* (tr *Birds of Sorrow*, 1947), have been attributed to him. He was also a drama critic and established the aesthetic standards under which the plays were performed.

Zechariah   An OLD TESTAMENT book, the eleventh of the Minor PROPHETS. It is in two parts. The first part dates from the restoration of the temple in Jerusalem (c530 BC) and is contemporaneous with HAGGAI, containing the same message. The second part, written after the death of ALEXANDER THE GREAT, in 323 BC, contains visions of Israel's future and Messianic prophecies.

Zeitblom, Serenus   The narrator of Thomas Mann's novel DOKTOR FAUSTUS. Zeitblom is a childhood friend of the hero, Adrian LEVERKÜHN. His very name, Serenus Zeitblom (literally, "serene time-flower"), suggests the complacency of the typical bourgeois and implies that he is simply the passive product of his age. He is, however, too intelligent to be caught up in the fever of Nazism. Thus, he is about halfway between Leverkühn's artistic genius, on the one hand, and his people's political madness, on the other, and is able to comment on both.

Zen Buddhism   A Buddhist sect introduced from China to Japan in the late HEIAN and early KAMAKURA periods by Japanese monks who had visited the mainland and by refugee Chinese priests. Known as CH'AN in Chinese, it emphasizes meditation and physical work as a means to enlightenment, or SATORI, leaving scriptural study to advanced students. The two principal sects are Rinzai (in Chinese, *Lin-chi*), which stems from the Ch'an of the SUNG dynasty and was introduced by Eisai (1141–1215), and Sōtō (in Chinese, *Ts'ao-tung*), first brought to Japan by Dōgen (1200–1253). Rinzai gives particular stress to the study of KŌAN as a means to enlightenment. Sōtō, which contains many purely Japanese elements, concentrates on meditative sitting alone. Zen has had significant influence on many elements of Japanese culture, including Nō drama, martial arts, the tea ceremony, and much literature. Zen was introduced to the West largely through the writings of Daistez Suzuki (1870–1966), whose works include *Essays in Zen Buddhism* (1927) and *The Essence of Buddhism* (1946).

Zenger, John Peter (1697–1746)   German-born American printer and journalist. Zenger came to America in 1710 and established the New York *Weekly Journal* to oppose the policies of the provincial government. Brought to trial for seditious libel (1734–35), he was defended by Andrew Hamilton and acquitted. The decision in this case helped to establish freedom of the press in America.

Zenobia (d after 274)   Queen of Palmyra, joint ruler with her husband, Odenathus. On his death (267), Zenobia assumed complete control of the kingdom. Pretending to be closely allied to Rome, she stationed her armies all over the Near East, in Asia Minor, Syria, Mesopotamia, and Egypt. On the accession of Aurelian (270), she openly defied Rome and attempted to usurp the entire Eastern Empire. Her armies were defeated (271), and she was captured. Aurelian later pardoned her but kept her exiled in Italy. Her name has come to signify a powerful, ambitious woman.

Zeno of Citium   See STOICISM.

Zeno of Elea (fl 460 BC)   Greek philosopher, pupil and associate of Parmenides (fl 485 BC). ARISTOTLE calls him the founder of dialectic. A clever logician, Zeno could draw his own conclusions from tenets his adversary admitted. He defended Parmenides' belief that motion and change are illusory in a series of brilliant paradoxes. In the best known of these, ACHILLES, the fastest runner, cannot catch the tortoise because he must first reach the point where the pursued started. In the meantime, the tortoise has advanced, however little, to a new position.

Zephaniah   A prophet of the OLD TESTAMENT and the book that bears his name. It was written during the reign of King Josiah (c640–609 BC) before the Babylonian captivity. The book contains an apocalyptic vision and warns of "the great day of the Lord" (Zeph. 1:14) when all men and nations shall be called to judgment. After an exhortation to repent, Zephaniah prophesies the restoration of Israel and calls on the Israelites to rejoice in their salvation.

Zephyr   The west wind and god of the west wind in classical mythology. Zephyr was the son of EOS and the father of Xanthus and Balius, the horses of ACHILLES in the TROJAN WAR. It is said that with his brother, BOREAS, Zephyr caused the death of the beautiful HYACINTH out of jealousy of Hyacinth's love for APOLLO.

Zerrissenheit (Ger, "the state of being torn apart")   A German literary term, often translated in English as "disintegration." It refers to the condition of a character, usually an artist, who is unable to reconcile the claims of his subjective experience with the necessities of the "real," objective world. The term was introduced by the poet HEINE, who was himself a victim of this turmoil. Examples are Goethe's Werther in THE SORROWS OF YOUNG

WERTHER, E.T.A. HOFFMANN's Johannes Kreisler, and Harry Haller in Hesse's STEPPENWOLF.

Zeus   The supreme god of the ancient Greeks. Zeus was the Greek version of an almost universally worshiped European god of atmospheric phenomena, especially thunder and lightning, of whom JUPITER is another example. As the god of kingship, he was king of the gods. His principal weapon was the thunderbolt; his famous fringed shield, the AEGIS, he often shared with ATHENE. The most common of many stories of Zeus' origins was that he was a son of CRONOS and RHEA. His mother bore him secretly, to save him from his voracious father, who had swallowed his brothers and sisters. He was brought up in a cave on Mount Dicte in Crete, where he was suckled by the goat Amaltheia, nursed by nymphs, and protected from discovery by the CURETES, sons of Rhea, who drowned his cries by dancing and clashing their shields.

Reaching manhood, Zeus overthrew his father, as his grandmother GE had predicted. The universe was then divided between him and his brothers, whom Cronos had vomited up; Zeus received heaven, POSEIDON the sea, HADES the underworld, with earth and their abode on Mount Olympus as their common property. Before the Olympian gods could establish their supremacy, however, they had to destroy the rebellious TITANS, the GIANTS, and the monster Typhon or Typhoeus, all of whom made war on heaven. Later, when the giants OTUS AND EPHIALTES warred with heaven, Zeus also had to conquer a rebellion in his own family. His sister-wife, HERA, his brother Poseidon, and his daughter Athene managed to bind him, but THETIS saved him by bringing the monster BRIAREUS to his assistance.

In various localities, Zeus was regarded as the consort of the reigning local goddess, often a pre-Hellenic earth goddess. Later, the problem of his many wives was resolved by making him the remarkably unfaithful husband of Hera. Some of his many unions with other goddesses include that with Metis, who conceived Athene; with THEMIS, who bore him the Seasons and the Fates; with Eurynome, who bore him the GRACES (Charites); with DEMETER, who bore him Kore (PERSEPHONE); with LETO, who bore him APOLLO and ARTEMIS. His marriage to Hera, the powerful pre-Hellenic goddess of Argos, brought forth HEBE, ARES, and Eileithyia.

Zeus also had affairs with more or less mortal women, some of which led to famous offspring. Notable among these children were DIONYSUS, son of CADMUS' daughter SEMELE; HERACLES, son of ALCMENA; PERSEUS, son of DANAË; AMPHION and Zethus, sons of Antiope; HELEN, CLYTEMNESTRA, and the Dioscuri (or some combination of them), children of LEDA.

Zhivago, Dr.   See DOCTOR ZHIVAGO.

Zhukovsky, Vasily Andreyevich (1783–1852) Russian poet and translator. Zhukovsky's translations of such works as Schiller's MAID OF ORLEANS, Byron's PRIS-

ONER OF CHILLON, and Gray's ELEGY WRITTEN IN A COUNTRY CHURCHYARD helped introduce Western romanticism into Russia. Zhukovsky also produced a notable translation of Homer's ODYSSEY in 1849. His own poems are among the best written in Russia before PUSHKIN's work appeared. Besides his literary activity, Zhukovsky was also a prominent figure in the Russian court. He was a tutor of the young ALEXANDER II, who became tsar in 1855. His influence is reputed to have helped Pushkin in the younger poet's many scrapes with Tsar NICHOLAS I's government.

Zinovyev, Grigory Yevseyevich (real name Hirsch Apfelbaum, 1883–1936)   Russian Communist leader. Zinovyev shared power with STALIN and KAMENEV after the death of LENIN. He and Kamenev were ousted from power by Stalin in the late 1920s, and in 1936 he was arrested and executed in the first of the notorious purge trials.

Zion   One of the hills on which the city of JERUSALEM is built. On Zion was the fortified acropolis of the Jebusites, which DAVID's soldiers captured by stealth. The word *Zion* was later used to designate the whole city. Allegorically, Zion refers to a house of God, Israel, or the Christian religion.

Zionism   A movement to restore the exiled Jewish people to their homeland. The concept of Zionism first appeared in its modern sense near the end of the 19th century, denoting a movement whose goal it was to return to the land of Israel. Nathan Birnbaum first coined the term as a political organization in his journal *Selbst Emanzipation* (*Self-Emancipation*, 1891). Theodore Herzl (1860–1904) first made the distinction between political zionism and practical zionism. While the former referred to the struggle for creating a politically autonomous Jewish state, the latter called for the philanthropic support of Jewish settlement in the land of Israel.

Ziusudra   The Sumerian NOAH. The single account discovered so far is fragmentary, but it appears to be very similar to the later version in the Babylonian epic of GILGAMESH, where the builder of the ark is named UTNAPISHTIM.

zodiac (Gr, *zodiakos*, "pertaining to animals"; fr *zoon*, "an animal")   An imaginary belt or zone in the heavens. It extends about eight degrees each side of the ecliptic which the sun traverses every year. The zodiac was divided by the ancients into twelve equal parts, proceeding from west to east, each part of thirty degrees, and distinguished by a sign. These originally corresponded to the zodiacal constellations bearing the same names, but now, through the precession of the equinoxes, they coincide with the constellations bearing the names next in order.

Beginning with Aries, there are first six on the north side and six on the south side of the equator. Beginning with Capricornus, there are six *ascending* and six *descending* signs: i.e., six that ascend higher and higher toward the north, and six that descend lower and lower toward the south. The six northern signs are *Aries* (the ram), *Taurus* (the bull), *Gemini* (the twins), spring signs; and *Cancer* (the crab), *Leo* (the lion), *Virgo* (the virgin), summer signs. The six southern are *Libra* (the balance), *Scorpio* (the scorpion), *Sagittarius* (the archer), autumn signs; and *Capricornus* (the goat), *Aquarius* (the waterbearer), and *Pisces* (the fishes), winter signs.

Zoilus (4th century BC)   Greek rhetorician. A literary Thersites, shrewd, witty, and spiteful, Zoilus was nicknamed *Homeromastix* ("Homer's Scourge"), because he mercilessly assailed the epics of HOMER, and called the companions of ODYSSEUS on the island of CIRCE weeping porkers (*Choiridia klaionya*). He also flew at PLATO, Isocrates, and other high game.

Zola, Emile (1840–1902)   French writer and critic, leader of the naturalist school. Raised in the beautiful city of Aix-en-Provence, with his close friend Paul CÉZANNE, Zola went to Paris at the age of eighteen. He worked first as a clerk in a publishing house and later became a journalist. In 1865 his first novel, *La Confession de Claude*, was published. With the publication of *La Fortune des Rougons* (1871), Zola began his twenty-two-year, twenty-volume experiment in the naturalistic novel entitled LES ROUGON-MACQUART. Scientific precision and scrupulous attention to detail mark his lengthy portrait of the Rougon-Macquart family. In 1880 he published *Le Roman expérimental* (*The Experimental Novel*), in which he explained his naturalistic method and set forth his theories of fiction (see NATURALISM). For many years, Zola used his fiction in the service of his passion for social reform, but in his last novels—the two series *Les Trois Villes* (1894–98) and *Quatre Evangiles* (1899–1903)—he speaks directly of his faith in a kind of Christian socialism, which would alleviate the misery and suffering he had long portrayed so faithfully. His zeal for reform and justice was translated into practical action when Zola penned his famous letter J'ACCUSE, in defense of Captain DREYFUS.

Zorba the Greek (Alexis Zorbas, 1946; tr 1952)   A novel by Nikos KAZANTZAKIS. The hero, a still vigorous and passionate old Greek, personifies the Dionysian approach to life that fascinated his creator. He is contrasted with a pallid narrator, who, before meeting the overpowering Zorba, has preferred to contemplate life, rather than to live it. This novel established Kazantzakis's reputation in the English-speaking world.

Zoroaster (or Zarathustra)   The founder (about 1000 BC) of the Perso-Iranian national religion, Zoroastrianism, whose modern version is Parseeism. It was dominant in Western Asia from about 550 BC to AD 650 and is still held by many thousands in Iran and India. The theology is fundamentally dualistic in that the course of the universe is understood as a relentless struggle between Ormuzd (Ahura Mazda), the principle of light and goodness, and Ahriman (Angra Mainyu), the spirit of evil and darkness. Ormuzd will prevail, partly through the help of man,

whom he created to strengthen his forces. All souls will be purified by fire, and a new heaven and earth will be established. Zoroaster, whose name is the Greek form of the Persian Zarathustra, established three commandments: good thoughts, good words, good deeds. See AVESTA; PARSEES.

Zorrilla y Moral, José (1817–1893)   Spanish poet and dramatist. Born in Valladolid, Zorrilla became famous overnight in 1837, when he recited an elegy at the grave of the poet Mariano de Larra, who had committed suicide. He subsequently abandoned his wife, who was many years his senior, and lived in France and Mexico, where he enjoyed the patronage of the emperor Maximilian. After his wife's death, in 1866, he returned to Spain. Though he was usually penniless, he received great popular acclaim and was honored with a golden crown in Granada in 1889.

One of Spain's outstanding romantic poets, Zorrilla was often facile and careless, but he possessed great dramatic and descriptive power, which enabled him to recreate the atmosphere of a past age, as he showed in his many *leyendas*, or legends, of medieval Spain. His best-known verse includes the collection *Cantos del trovador* (1840–41) and the unfinished *Granada* (1852), a richly ornamented account of the intrigues that preceded the city's fall.

Zorrilla's poetry has been largely overshadowed by the fame of his DON JUAN TENORIO, the most successful play of 19th-century Spain. Many of his other plays are based, like his poems, on episodes in Spanish history. Among these are *El zapatero y el rey* (1840–41), *El puñal del Godo* (1842), and *Traidor, inconfeso y mártir* (1849).

Zoshchenko, Mikhail Mikhailovich (1895–1958)   Russian satirist. Zoshchenko is famous for his short, pithy stories of the average Soviet citizen struggling to make his way in a world filled with red tape, regulations, and frustration. He studied law at the University of St. Petersburg, served in the army during World War I, and in the Red Army during the civil war. He began his literary career when he joined the SERAPION BROTHERS in 1921. His first stories were published in the collection entitled *Rasskazy Nazara Ilyicha gospodina Sinebryukhova* (*Stories Told by Nazar Ilyich Mr. Sinebryukhov*, 1922). These and the several volumes of short stories in later years show the influence of the ornamental styles of LESKOV and REMIZOV and Zoshchenko's own mastery of *skaz*—the device of relating a story in the usually semiliterate language of a fictitious narrator, rather than in the less vivid language of conventional narrative prose.

In 1943 Zoshchenko came under attack in the Soviet literary journals for his *Pered voskhodom soltsa* (*Before Sunrise*), of which two parts were published that year. Although Zoshchenko referred to the work as a novel, it appears to be more a personal reminiscence, and this fact seems to be the chief reason for the attacks. Three years later the Central Committee of the Communist Party issued a resolution criticizing various aspects of Soviet literature and singling out Zoshchenko and the poet Anna AKHMATOVA for special condemnation. Zoshchenko's wartime publication of his memoir was recalled and termed a "disgusting" work. Shortly afterward, in a speech, Andrey Zhdanov referred to Zoshchenko as a "vulgarian." After this onslaught, Zoshchenko virtually ceased publishing any new stories, except for a few second-rate efforts in 1947 and 1950.

Zosima In Dostoyevsky's THE BROTHERS KARAMAZOV, Zosima is the elder monk who preaches a message of love and forbearance, which is widely considered to be the religious viewpoint of the author.

Zuckmayer, Carl (1896–1977) German playwright. Although no innovator in dramatic form like the expressionists and BRECHT, Zuckmayer remains one of Germany's most respected playwrights. After a few abortive attempts at EXPRESSIONISM, he began to develop his main quality, the depiction of real and vital individuals, in *Der fröhliche Weinberg* (*The Merry Vineyard*, 1925) and *Schinderhannes* (1927), both dramas dealing with folk characters from his own Rhenish homeland. Also in these plays he began, in the form of satire, to voice his opposition to the militarism and bureaucratic regimentation which were soon to burgeon in HITLER's Germany. This satirical attitude dominates his great comedy *Der Hauptmann von Köpenick* (*The Captain of Köpenick*, 1931). Hitler's rise to power forced him into exile, which began in Austria and Switzerland and continued for seven years in the U.S. There he wrote his passionate protest against Hitler's government, THE DEVIL'S GENERAL. Among Zuckmayer's other significant plays are *Der Gesang im Feuerofen* (*Song in the Fiery Furnace*, 1950), about the Resistance in occupied France, and *Das kalte Licht* (1955; tr *The Cold Light*, 1958), a topical drama about a nuclear scientist turned traitor. His autobiography, *Als wär's ein Stück von mir*, appeared in English in 1970 as *A Part of Myself*.

Zukofsky, Louis (1904–1978) American poet, translator, and editor. Zukofsky, born and educated in New York City, grew up speaking Yiddish; English was his second language. It was language, with its endless sounds, constructions, and flux of meaning, that fascinated and delighted Zukofsky. Committed to the principles of both IMAGISM and OBJECTIVISM, he edited *An "Objectivists" Anthology* in 1932. His own verse was printed only by small presses until the mid-1960s, when *All: The Collected Poems* (2 vols, 1965, 1966) was published. Zukofsky's collections of criticism, *Bottom: On Shakespeare* (1963) and *Prepositions* (1967), both met with critical respect. His major work, however, was unquestionably "A," a poetic sequence begun in 1928 and written over a period of forty-six years (complete edition published in 1978). "A" is a FREE VERSE journal of the poet's meditations, which derives its unity from rich musical metaphors repeated, or recalled in variations, throughout.

Zuleika Dobson (1911) A fantastic, satirical novel by Max BEERBOHM. Zuleika is a beautiful young woman who visits her grandfather, a warden at Oxford University. On the occasion of a boating contest, all the Oxford undergraduates, except one, led by the duke of Dorset, drown themselves in the river for love of her.

Zweig, Arnold (1887–1968) German novelist. Zweig began to write (both fiction and essays) as a Zionist about Judaism and the persecution of the Jews. His service in World War I widened his sphere of concern to include all victims of injustice and inspired a cycle of six war novels called *Der große Krieg der weißen Männer* (*The Great War of the White Man*). By far the best known of these novels is THE CASE OF SERGEANT GRISCHA. Zweig fled Germany when HITLER came to power and lived for fourteen years in Israel. He then went to East Germany, where he spent the rest of his life, highly honored by the Communist Party, whose aesthetic regulations (see SOCIALIST REALISM) he followed loyally.

Zweig, Stefan (1881–1942) Austrian biographer, novelist, essayist, and playwright. Zweig is best known for his humanistic view of European culture, expressed in his numerous essays and biographies of major literary and historical figures, such as *Romain Rolland* (1920); *Drei Meister* (1920; tr *Three Masters*, 1930), on BALZAC, DICKENS, and DOSTOYEVSKY; and *Maria Stuart* (1935; tr *Queen Mary of Scotland and the Isles*, 1935). In his early career he was influenced by the literary impressionism of his friend Hugo von HOFMANNSTHAL, and he developed a psychologically subtle technique of character portrayal that served him well in both his biographical and fictional works. Among the latter are his only novel, *Ungeduld des Herzens* (1939; tr *Beware of Pity*, 1939), three novellas, and *Schachnovelle* (1942; tr *The Royal Game*, 1944). His best-known drama is the biblical play *Jeremias* (1917; tr 1929), one of the many pacifist plays that were written during World War I. In 1938 Zweig left Austria, going first to England and then to Brazil. Homesick for Austria and in despair over the defeat of humanism in the Third Reich, he and his wife committed suicide.

Zwingli, Ulrich (or Huldreich Zwingli, 1484–1531) Swiss religious reformer. Ordained a priest in 1506, Zwingli delivered a series of sermons on the New Testament in Zurich in 1519 that launched the Protestant movement there. Although Zwingli, like other leaders of the Reformation, considered the Bible the sole source of authority and wanted to restore the purity of the early Church, he disagreed with Martin LUTHER's conception of the sacrament of the Eucharist; a conference at Marburg (1529) failed to settle their differences. Zwingli was killed in battle during the armed struggle between Zurich and the Catholic cantons of Switzerland.